INTERNATIONAL LEGAL BOOKS IN PRINT 1990-1991

INTERNATIONAL LEGAL BOOKS IN PRINT

1990-1991

An annotated bibliography

VOLUME 2

SUBJECTS/PUBLISHERS

1990
BOWKER-SAUR

London Melbourne Munich New York

Bowker-Saur is part of the Professional Publishing Division of Reed International Books

British Library Cataloguing in Publication Data
International legal books in print, 1990-1991 : an annotated bibliography.

1. Law - Bibliographies
I. Chapman, Michael D.
016.34
ISBN 0-86291-856-1
ISBN 0-86291-848-0 v. 1
ISBN 0-86291-849-9 v. 2

Library of Congress Cataloguing-in-Publication Data available on request

Cover design by Robin Caira, Typographics, Whitstable

Computer controlled typesetting by Computaprint Ltd., London
Printed and bound by Antony Rowe Ltd., Chippenham

Printed on acid-free paper.

International Legal Books in Print,
1990-1991
is dedicated
to the memory of

Wallace Breem

Librarian and Keeper of Manuscripts
Honourable Society of the Inner Temple
who died on March 12th, 1990

CONTENTS

ABBREVIATIONS

c./ca.	circa
cm.	centimetres
ed.	edition
Hbk	hardback/cased
Llf	looseleaf/spiral bound/ringbound
no.	number
p./pp.	page(s)
Pbk	paperback/softcover
pt.	part(s)
T.p.	title-page
v./vol.	volume(s)

CURRENCY SYMBOLS

£	Pound sterling (UK)
A$	Australian dollar
B$	Bahamaian dollar
BDS$	Bermudan dollar
Bf	Belgian franc
C£	Cyprus pound
Can$	Canadian dollar
Dkr	Danish krona
DM	Deutsche Mark
F	French franc
Fmk	Markka (Finland)
G$	Guyana dollar
G£	Dalasi (Gambia)
Gld	Guilder (Netherlands)
HK$	Hong Kong dollar
Ir£	Irish pounds
J$	Jamaican dollar
K	Kina (Papua New Guinea)
Kr	Krona (Sweden)
KSh	Kenya shilling
L	Lira (Italy)
Le	Leone (Sierra Leone)
Lfr	Luxembourg franc
M$	Malaysian dollar
MK	Malawi kwacha
MR	Mauritius rupee
N	Naira (Nigeria)
NKr	Norwegian krone
NZ$	New Zealand dollar
P	Pula (Botswana)
PP	Philippine peso
Pta	Peseta (Spain)
Rp	Rupiah (Indonesia)
Rs	Indian rupee
S	Schilling (Austria)
Sfr	Swiss fr
S$	Singapore dollar
SL$	Solomon Islands dollar
SLR	Sri Lanka rupee
SR	Seychelles rupee
TSh	Tanzanian shilling
TT$	Trinidad & Tobago dollar
USh	Uganda shilling
WS$	Tala (Samoa)

SUBJECTS

ABBREVIATIONS
—Index to legal citations and abbreviations / by Donald Raistrick. – Abingdon : Professional Books, 1981.
10, 326p. – (Professional Books Law Reference Library).
ISBN 0862050375

ABDUCTION
—Hague Convention on the civil aspects of international child abduction : consultative document / Edinburgh? : Scottish Courts Administration?, 1983.
10 leaves.

—Hague Convention on the Civil Aspects of International Child Abduction : explanatory documentation / prepared for Commonwealth jurisdictions by J.M. Eekelaar in association with the Commonwealth Secretariat. – London : Commonwealth Secretariat, 1981.
v,70p.
ISBN 0850921961

—Measures to be taken in cases of kidnapping followed by a ransom demand : Recommendation No.R(82)14 adopted by the Committee of Ministers of the Council of Europe on 24 September 1982 and Explanatory memorandum / Council of Europe. – Strasbourg : Council of Europe, 1983.
13p; 21cm.
'... prepared by a select committee of experts under the authority of the European Committee on Crime Problems' - verso t.p.. At head of cover title: Legal Affairs.
ISBN 9287102309

—Phenomenology of kidnappings in Sardinia : towards an international perspective of a local crime problem / by I.F. Caramazza, U. Leone. – Rome : Fratelli Palombi, 1984.
211p. – (Publication).
Bibliography: p.182-208.
ISBN 8876218270

ABDUCTION - INDIA
—Law of Kidnapping and Sexual Offences / Singh. – Allahabad : Law Book Company, 1988.
500p.

ABDUCTION - IRELAND
—Report on the Hague Convention on the Civil Aspects of International Child Abduction and some related matters / the Law Reform Commission. – Dublin : The Commission, 1985.
v,76p. – (LRC).
Includes text of Convention.

ABDUCTION - SCOTLAND
—Child abduction / Scottish Law Commission. – Edinburgh : The Commission, 1985.
116p. – (Consultative memorandum).

—Child abduction : report on a reference under section 3(1)(e) of the Law Commissions Act 1965 ... / Scottish Law Commission. – Edinburgh : H.M.S.O., 1987.
vi,50p.
ISBN 010100642X

ABORIGINAL LAW
—Aboriginal Australians / by Keith D. Suter, Kaye Stearman. – New ed. – London : Minority Rights Group, 1982.
20p. – (Report).
Previous ed. published 1978 as: Australia's policy towards Aborigines 1967-1977 / by H.C. Coombs. Bibliography: p.20.

—Aboriginal law bulletin / Kensington : Aboriginal Law Research Unit, 1981.

—International law and aboriginal rights / Oxford : Croom Helm, 1987.
ISBN 0949614351 Hbk £22.50

ABORIGINAL LAW - AFRICA
—Papers on Indigenous Law in Southern Africa / Pretoria : VanSchaik.
ISBN 0627013988 Hbk £17.85

ABORIGINAL LAW - ASIA
—Asian Indigenous Law / Routledge, 1987.
ISBN 0710301138 Hbk £40.00

ABORIGINAL LAW - AUSTRALIA
—Aboriginal customary law : marriage, children and the distribution of property / Australian Law Reform Commission. – Sydney : Australian Law Reform Commission, 1982.
20p. – (Discussion paper).

—Aboriginal customary law : the criminal law, evidence and procedure / Sydney : Australian Law Reform Commission, 1984.
24p. – (Discussion paper).

—Aboriginal land rights : a handbook / edited by Nicolas Peterson. – Canberra City : Australian Institute of Aboriginal Studies, 1981.
vi,297p.
The papers published here were originally prepared as background information for the Aboriginal Land Rights Symposium held as part of the Australian Institute of Aboriginal Studies Biennial Meeting 1981. Bibliography: p269-297.

—Aboriginal legal aid / House of Representatives Standing Committee on Aboriginal Affairs, July 1980. – Canberra : Australian Government Publishing Service, 1980.
xvi,252p.
At head of t.p.: The Parliament of the Commonwealth of Australia.
ISBN 0642051593

—Aborigines and Mining Royalties in the Northern Territory / Canberra City : Australian Institute of Aboriginal Studies, 1983.
182p.
ISBN 0855751495 Hbk £11.95

—Aborigines and the Law / Canberra City : Australian Institute of Aboriginal Studies, 1987.
ISBN 0855751738 Pbk £44.95

—Aborigines, Land and Land Rights / M. Langton. – Canberra City : Australian Institute of Aboriginal Studies, 1983.
476p.
ISBN 0855751436 Hbk £14.90

—Justice for Aboriginal Australians : Report to the World Council of Churches Team Visit to the Aborigines, June 15 to July 3, 1981 / Sydney : Australian Council of Churches.

—Report of the review of the Australian Institute of Aboriginal Studies / by R.J. Walsh. – Canberra : Australian Government Publishing Service, 1982.
89p.
ISBN 0644022698

—Two Laws : Managing Disputes in a Contemporary Aboriginal Community / Canberra City : Australian Institute of Aboriginal Studies, 1986.
176p.
ISBN 0855751746 Hbk £25.95

—Victims of the law / London : Allen & Unwin, 1982.
216p.
ISBN 0868613959 £17.95

ABORIGINAL LAW - CANADA
—Aboriginal Rights Provisions in the Constitution Act, 1982 / Saskatoon : University of Saskatchewan, Native Law Centre, 1987.
276p.
ISBN 0888801920 Hbk £50.00

—Aboriginal Self-Government and Constitutional Reform : Setbacks, Opportunities, and Arctic Experiences / Ottawa : Canadian Arctic Resources Committee, 1988.
168p.
ISBN 0919996353 Pbk £20.00

—Aboriginal Water Rights in Canada : a Study of Aboriginal Title to Water and Indian Water Rights / Calgary : Canadian Institute of Resources Law.
231p.
ISBN 0919269230 Hbk £30.00

—Canadian Native Law Cases / Saskatoon : University of Saskatchewan, Native Law Centre, 1980.
520p.
ISBN 0888800932 Hbk £50.00

Vol. 2 1870-1890 1981.
634p.
ISBN 0888801068 Hbk £65.00

Vol. 3 1891-1910 1985.
663p.
ISBN 0888801467 Hbk £65.00

Vol. 4 1911-1930 1986.
491p.
ISBN 0888801734 Hbk £65.00

Vol. 5 1931-1959 1987.
691p.
ISBN 0888801750 Hbk £70.00

Vol. 6 1960-1970 1988.
781p.
ISBN 0888801947 Hbk £70.00

Vol. 7 1971-1973 1988.
550p.
ISBN 0888802110 Hbk £70.00

ABORTION
—Abortion and protection of the human fetus : legal problems in a cross-cultural perspective / edited by Stanislaw J. Frankowski, George F. Cole. – Dordrecht Netherlands : M. Nijhoff, 1988.
xv, 334 p.; 25 cm.
'Under the auspices of the Institute of International and Comparative Law, the University of Santa Clara.' Includes bibliographies.
ISBN 0898389224 Hbk £175.00

—Abortion and the status of the fetus / edited by William B. Bondeson ... et al. – Dordrecht, Holland : D. Reidel, 1983.
xxxii, 349p.
'This volume grew out of a symposium, 'The Concept of person and its implications for the use of the fetus in biomedicine', held October 29, 30, and 31, 1980, at the Health Science Center of the University of Missouri-Columbia under the sponsorship of the Departments of Medicine and Philosophy, and the Program in Health Care and Human Values'–Editorial pref. Includes bibliographies and index.
ISBN 9027714932

—Abortion Law and Public Policy / Dordrecht : Kluwer, 1985.
104p.
ISBN 9024731070 Pbk £40.00

ABORTION - COMMONWEALTH
—Emerging issues in Commonwealth abortion laws, 1982 / by Rebecca J. Cook and Bernard M. Dickens. – London : Commonwealth Secretariat, 1983.
135p; 30cm.
ISBN 0850922305

ABORTION - INDIA
—Abortion and Termination for Pregnancies in India : Penal Provisions and Punishment, Practice, Procedure and Protection under Law with Rules / Law Publishers, 1980.

ABORTION - NEW ZEALAND
—Ill conceived : law and abortion practice in New Zealand / Jocelyn Brooks et al. – Dunedin : Caveman Press, 1981.
169p.
Bibliography: p.160-166.
ISBN 0908562462

ABORTION - UNITED STATES
—Law and politics of abortion / edited by Carl E. Schneider, Maris A. Vinovskis. – Lexington : Lexington, 1981.
xlvii,268p; 24cm.
Includes index.
ISBN 0669033863 £11.50

ABUSE OF ADMINISTRATIVE POWER - AUSTRALIA
—Review of administrative action / by Mark Aronson and Nicola Franklin : with a chapter on freedom of information legislation by Peter Bayne. – Sydney : Law Book Co., 1987.
lxvii,720p.
Includes bibliographical references and index.
ISBN 0455207216

ABUSE OF ADMINISTRATIVE POWER - CANADA
—Suing Government for Abuse of Power / Vancouver : Continuing Legal Education Society of British Columbia, 1987.
67p.
ISBN 0865043221 Hbk £60.00

ABUSE OF ADMINISTRATIVE POWER – GREAT BRITAIN

—Grievances, remedies and the state / by Patrick Birkinshaw. – London : Sweet & Maxwell, 1985.
xix,192p; 23cm.
Includes index.
ISBN 042132600X Hbk £9.25
ISBN 0421326107 Pbk £8.95

ACADEMIC FREEDOM

—Academic freedom under Israeli military occupation : report of WUS/ICJ mission of enquiry into higher education in the West Bank and Gaza / Adam Roberts, Boel Joergensen, Frank Newman. – London : World University Service (UK), 1984.
87p.
Bibliography: p.84-87.
ISBN 0906405203

ACCIDENT INSURANCE – AUSTRALIA

—Accident compensation in Australia : no-fault schemes / by Mark A. Robinson. – Sydney : Legal Books Pty., 1987.
xiv,94p.
Bibliography: pp.86-89. - Includes index.
ISBN 094955331X

ACCIDENT INSURANCE – AUSTRALIA – NEW SOUTH WALES

—Accident compensation / New South Wales Law Reform Commission. – Sydney : The Commission, 1983.
xix,231p. – (Working paper 22).
Includes bibliographical references.

Interim report : Worker's Compensation (Amendment) Bill 1982 and cognate billsl / New South Wales Law Reform Commission. – 1983.
viii,62p. – (L.R.C. 41).

Final report 1 : Report on a transport accidents scheme for New South Wales / New South Wales Law Reform Commission. – 1984. – (L.R.C. 43).
Includes bibliographies and indexes. Accompanied by: Outline of report on a transport accidents scheme for New South Wales.

ACCIDENT INSURANCE – GREAT BRITAIN

—Personal accident, life and other insurance / 2nd ed. – London : Butterworths, 1980.
ISBN 0406252912 Hbk £52.00

ACCIDENT INSURANCE – NEW ZEALAND

—Accident Compensation in New Zealand / 2nd ed. – Butterworths, 1983.
Takes in new amendments (eg the reorganisation of the statutory body), and discusses the interpretations of the statutory provisions contained in many decisions reported since 1978.
ISBN 0409701602 Pbk £40.70

—Accident compensation scheme : a discussion paper / Law Commission. – Wellington, N.Z. : The Commission, 1987.
v,58p. – (Preliminary paper).

—Accident compensation scheme : interim report on aspects of funding / Law Commission. – Wellington, N.Z. : The Commission, 1987.
vii,39p. – (Report).

ACCIDENT LAW – NEW ZEALAND

—Accident compensation in New Zealand : purpose, progress / Wellington : Accident Compensation Commission, 1980.
29p.
ISBN 0477063632

ACCIDENTS

—Disaster and resolution : two discussion papers dealing with distinct aspects of the aftermath of man-made disasters, the process of litigation, settlement and compensation and the factors affecting the provision of speedy relief and effective rehabiliation / David Wade, Carmel Goldwater : commissioned and published by Centre for Public Affairs Studies. – London : Centre for Public Affairs Studies, 1985.
viii,162p.

ACCIDENTS – AUSTRALIA

—Accident compensation in Australia : no-fault schemes / by Mark A. Robinson. – Sydney : Legal Books Pty., 1987.
xiv,94p.
Bibliography: pp.86-89. - Includes index.
ISBN 094955331X

—Community law reform for the Australian Capital Territory / Law Reform Commission. – Canberra : Australian Government Publishing Service, 1985.
ix,44p. – (Report).
Bibliography: p.41-42 - Includes index.
ISBN 0644013257

ACCIDENTS – AUSTRALIA – VICTORIA

—Accident Compensation Handbook (Vic.) / G. Hughes. – North Ryde : Law Book Co, 1986.
xix, 181p.
ISBN 0455206694 Pbk £25.00

—Accident compensation Victoria / by L.R. Boyes and M. O'Loghlen. – 1. – Sydney : Butterworths, 1987.
looseleaf.
Supersedes: Workers compensation, Victoria, by Anderson and Rendit. Includes: Accident and workers compensation reports.
ISBN 0409492795

ACCIDENTS – CANADA

—Motor Vehicle Accident Claims : 1983 / Vancouver : British Columbia Continuing Legal Education Society.

—Motor vehicle reports : annotated / Toronto : Casrwell, 1988-.

—Study on marine casualty investigations in Canada (for the Minister of Transport) / Bernard M. Desch$enes. – Ottawa : Minister of Supply and Services, 1984.
x,273p.
ISBN 0662134036

ACCIDENTS – ENGLAND

—Accidents, compensation and the law / P.S. Atiyah. – 3rd ed. – London : Weidenfeld and Nicolson, 1980.
xxiv,695p.

ISBN 0297777548

—Atiyah's accidents, compensation and the law / Peter Cane. – 4th ed. – London : Weidenfeld and Nicholson, 1987.
639p.
ISBN 0297790528

—Butterworths Consolidated Legislation Service /. – Professional Publ.
50p.
ISBN 0409014338 £25.00

—Disability and compensation claims / Philip Noble, Bart Hellyer, Elizabeth Fanshawe. – London : Sweet & Maxwell, 1986.
68p; 22cm.
ISBN 042136890X Pbk £6.50 (Sept.)

—Special damages for disability 1988 / by Philip Noble, Elizabeth Fanshawe, Bart Hellyer. – 2nd ed. – London : Sweet & Maxwell, 1988.
x,85p; 22cm.
Catalogues the expenses which a plaintiff in a personal injuries action can claim as part of his award. Each of the expenses, such as accommodation requirements and the cost of future care, are described in the context of the four disabilities of spinal injury, partial and total loss of sight, loss of a limb, and head injury. Each item is given an up-to-date value.
ISBN 0421393807 Pbk £7.50

ACCIDENTS – GREAT BRITAIN

—Accidents, Compensation and The Law (LIC) / 4th ed. – Weidenfeld & Nicolson, 1987.
ISBN 0297790528 Hbk £30.00
ISBN 0297790536 Pbk £14.95

—Disease and the compensation debate / Jane Stapleton. – Oxford : Clarendon, 1986.
224p; 22cm.
Includes index.
ISBN 0198255527 £22.50

—From Accident to Liability / London : Sweet & Maxwell, 1984.
640p. – (Sweet and Maxwell's Law Files Ser.: No. 3).
ISBN 0421321601 Hbk £29.50

—Legalism and Discretion : A Study of Responses to Accidents and Accident Information Systems in the Occupational Health and Safety Administration (OSHA) USA / Oxford : Social Science Research Council, 1988.
ISBN 0948774053 Pbk £2.50

—Manual of Road Accident Investigation / Watts. – Pitman, 1980.
ISBN 0273013254 Hbk £6.50

Vol. 2 1981.
ISBN 0273016008 Hbk £6.50

—Meeting legal needs? : an evaluation of a scheme for personal injury victims / Hazel Genn. – Oxford : SSRC Centre for Socio-Legal Studies, 1982.
ix,69p; 22cm.
A report commissioned by the Greater Manchester Legal Services Committee.
ISBN 0862260442

—Sudden deaths and fatal accident inquiries / Edinburgh : W Green & Son, 1986.
Covers the duties of the procurator fiscal in investigating sudden and unexpected deaths. With a chapter on medical mattres, a summary of the duties of the coroner in England and guidance for the medical professions as to which deaths shuld be reported to the fiscal.
ISBN 0414007751

—Sweet & Maxwell Law / London : Sweet & Maxwell, 1984.
ISBN 0421321601 Pbk £29.50

ACCIDENTS – INDIA

—Dwivedi's Fatal Accidents Act : and Legal Representatives Suits Act / 4th ed. – Allahabad : Law Book Company, 1988.
200p.
With 1986 supplement.

ACCIDENTS – NEW ZEALAND

—Accident Compensation in New Zealand / 2nd ed. – London : Butterworths, 1983.
ISBN 0409701602 Pbk

—Accident Compensation in New Zealand / 2nd ed. – Butterworths, 1983.
Takes in new amendments (eg the reorganisation of the statutory body), and discusses the interpretations of the statutory provisions contained in many decisions reported since 1978.
ISBN 0409701602 Pbk £40.70

—Accident compensation scheme : a discussion paper / Law Commission. – Wellington, N.Z. : The Commission, 1987.
v,58p. – (Preliminary paper).

—Accident compensation scheme : interim report on aspects of funding / Law Commission. – Wellington, N.Z. : The Commission, 1987.
vii,39p. – (Report).

ACCOMPLICES

—Law of criminal complicity / by Peter Gillies. – Sydney : Law Book Co., 1980.
xxi, 319 p.; 24 cm.
Includes bibliographical references and indexes.
ISBN 0455200734

ACCOMPLICES – CANADA

—Parties to an Offence / Agincourt : Carswell, 1982.
226p.
This book deals with issues of complicity and constructive complicity in a wide range of criminal offenses under Canadian law. Aiders and abettors; parties to a common unlawful purpose; inciters; procurers; accessories after the fact; and other crimes involving more than one party are covered in the work.

ACCOMPLICES – NORTHERN IRELAND

—Supergrasses : the use of accomplice evidence in Northern Ireland : a report / by Tony Gifford. – London : Cobden Trust, 1984.
38p.
ISBN 0900137215

ACCOMPLICES – SCOTLAND

—Criminal law : art and part guilt of statutory offences / Scottish Law Commission. – Edinburgh : H.M.S.O., 1985.
v,21p.
ISBN 0101955103

ACCOUNTING

—Basic book-keeping for solicitors / Richard Halberstadt. – 3rd ed. – London : Sweet & Maxwell, 1985.
300p; 23cm.
Previous ed.: 1982. Includes index.
ISBN 042133830X £12.00

—Company accounts / Jenny Bough. – London : Sweet & Maxwell, 1987.
xvii,227p; 26cm.
Includes index.
ISBN 0421360208 £16.50

—Dynamic Management Accountancy / London : Butterworths, 1983.
A theoretical management accounting text which presents new approaches to decision-making and performance measurement. Special attention is paid to questions of inflation accounting, currency realignment, and multinational corporation accounting.
ISBN 0406258104 Pbk

—International accounting and transnational decisions / London : Butterworths, 1983.
ISBN 040810841X Pbk £23.60

—International Accounting and Transnational Decisions / London : Butterworths, 1983.
This book explores the financial and managerial aspects of international accounting. Among the topics covered are: comparative international accounting, international accounting standards, selected transnational financial reporting issues, and transnational financial decision making and control.
ISBN 040810841X Pbk

—International audit in public sector / Simpson. – Cambridge : Woodhead-Faulkner, 1985.
ISBN 0859412725 Pbk £11.95

—International auditing / Davies. – 5th ed. – London : Butterworths, 1980.
ISBN 0372300421 Pbk £8.50

—International bank accounting / Whinney. – 2nd ed. – London : Euromoney, 1987.
ISBN 1870031016 Pbk £75.00

—International group accounting / Coenenberg. – Oxford : Croom Helm, 1988.
ISBN 0709938772 Hbk £35.00

—International Survey of Accounting Principles and Reporting Practices / London : Butterworths, 1980.
ISBN 0406341702 Pbk £13.50

—Interpreting company reports and accounts / Sugden. – 3rd ed. – Cambridge : Woodhead-Faulkner, 1986.
ISBN 085941325X Hbk £25.00
ISBN 0859413268 Pbk £14.95

—Policy for disclosure / L.E. Rockley. – London : Associated Business Press, 1980.
xiii,154p; 23cm.
Includes index.
ISBN 085227226X £10.50

—World accounting / Orsini. – Matthew Bender, 1986.
ISBN 0000999081 Hbk £100.00

ACCOUNTING – AUSTRALIA

—Law and Practice of Company Accounting in Australia / M O Jager, R B Taylor. – 6th ed. – North Ryde : Butterworths (Australia), 1983.
Analysis of the law of company accounting and reporting. Includes aspects of practice as necessary to interpret the law and explain its significance and application. Incorporates developments including the changes effected by the Companies Act 1981 (the National Act), and the latest Accounting Standards.
ISBN 0409493902 Pbk £27.60

—Law and Practice of Company Accounting in Australia / M. Jager. – 6th ed. – Sydney : Butterworths, 1987.
669p.
ISBN 0409491853 Hbk

—Professional negligence : being a discussion of the duties and responsibilities of auditors / by E.F. Mannix and J.E. Mannix. – 3rd ed. – Sydney : Butterworths, 1982.
viii,112p.
Previous ed.: 1976. Includes index.
ISBN 0409309338

—Questions on the Law and Practice of Company Accounting / B. O'Shea. – 4th ed. – Sydney : Butterworths, 1987.
206p.
ISBN 040949206X Pbk

ACCOUNTING – CANADA

—Accounting for Damages : a Framework for Litigation Support / Don Mills : CCH Canadian Ltd, 1987.
240p.
ISBN 0887963986 Hbk £40.00

—Accounting in a Law Office / Toronto : Law Society of Upper Canada.

—Guide to Accounting Pronouncements and Sources / Toronto : Butterworths.
152p.
ISBN 0409805130 Pbk £21.95

—Lawyers' Trust Accounts / Vancouver : Continuing Legal Education Society of British Columbia, 1988.
54p.
ISBN 0865049998 Hbk £40.00

—Rate Regulation : Legislative and Legal Aspects / Hamilton : Society of Management Accountants of Canada.

—Trust Accounting / Vancouver : Continuing Legal Education Society of British Columbia, 1987.
110p.
ISBN 0865043477 Hbk £70.00

ACCOUNTING – EUROPEAN COMMUNITY

—Fourth directive : its effect on the annual accounts of companies in the European Economic Community / Ernst & Whinney. – London : Kluwer, 1980.
440p.
Includes official text of the Fourth Directive. 'This book has been prepared by Ernst & Whinney and its associates under the general editorship of E.G. Bartholomew and A.D. Welchman.'.
ISBN 0903393468

ACCOUNTING – GREAT BRITAIN

—Accountancy / Norkett. – Pitman, 1988.
ISBN 0273029657 Pbk £3.95

—Accountancy In Banking / Cambridge : Woodhead-Faulkner, 1983.
ISBN 0859411923 Hbk £19.95
ISBN 0859411931 Pbk £9.95

—Accountant's professional negligence : developments in legal liability / Jonathan R.H.H. Pockson. – London : Macmillan, 1982.
xxi,212p; 23cm.
Bibliography: p192-208. - Includes index.
ISBN 0333278453 £25.00

—Accountant's Reports on Takeovers, Mergers, Acquisitions and Realisations / Deloitte, Haskins and Sells Staff. – London : Butterworths, 1985.
ISBN 0406500207 Pbk £20.00

—Accountants' Reports for Prospectus Purposes / Deloitte, Haskins and Sells Staff. – London : Butterworths, 1985.
ISBN 0406500215 Pbk £20.00

—Accounting / London : VanNostrand Reinhold, 1988.
ISBN 0278000096 Pbk £13.95

—Accounting and Audit Data / 3rd ed. – Tolley Publishing, 1987.
ISBN 085459308X Pbk £6.95

—Accounting and Financial Management For Charities / Blume. – Turnaround Press, 1985.
ISBN 0907164188 Pbk £5.95

—Accounting For Banks / Matthew Bender, 1982.
ISBN 0000999082 Hbk £55.00

—Accounting for Foreign Exchange / London : Butterworths, 1987.
ISBN 0406503206 Pbk £37.50

—Accounting for goodwill : Accounting Standards Committee exposure draft no. 30 : memorandum / by the Society's Standing Committee on Company law. – London : Law Society, 1983.
4p.

—Accounting For Pensions / Buchanan. – Cambridge : Woodhead-Faulkner, 1981.
ISBN 0859411249 Hbk £25.00

—Accounting For Treasury Products / Conneely. – Cambridge : Woodhead-Faulkner, 1987.
ISBN 0859413896 Hbk £45.00

—Accounting in Business / 5th ed. – London : Butterworths, 1984.
This book sets forth materials and problems in business accounting for accounting students in the United Kingdom. Cost accounting under SSAP 16 and limited company accounting under the 1981 Companies Act are both covered.
ISBN 0408014865 Pbk

—Accounting in Business / 5th ed. – London : Butterworths, 1984.
ISBN 0408014865 Pbk £13.50

—Accounting Requirements of the Companies Acts / R. A. Wyld. – 2nd ed. – London : Butterworths, 1980.
ISBN 0406402035 Pbk £19.65

—Accounting Standards / 2nd ed. – London : Pitman Publishing, 1988.
ISBN 0273027352 Pbk £10.95

—Accounts and Audits of Pension Schemes / Pegler. – London : Butterworths, 1987.
ISBN 040667910X Pbk £18.95

—Accounts' Liability in the 1980's / Nobles. – Oxford : Croom Helm, 1985.
ISBN 0709918305 Hbk £25.00

—Advanced Accounting / 4th ed. – Prentice-Hall, 1988.
ISBN 0130101826 Hbk £46.75

—Audit Guide / Stoy Hayward & Co. – London : Butterworths, 1983.
ISBN 0406270600 Pbk £11.50

—Audit Guide / London : Butterworths, 1983.
A publication for practitioners providing practical explanations of the stages of an audit. The book gives a straightforward discussion of the often confusing topic of the use of statistical sampling methods in the audit. Included are sections on flowcharting, error rate sampling, monetary unit sampling, as well as extracts from standard documentation for an audit.
ISBN 0406270600 Hbk

—Audit Manual / London : Butterworths, 1984.
ISBN 0406258120 Pbk

—Audit Report / London : Butterworths, 1984.
ISBN 040601650X Pbk £15.00

—Audit Report / London : Butterworths, 1984.
A review of the current state of audit reporting which outlines legal and other requirements of the audit. The book surveys a wide range of reporting styles and provides many examples, drawn from published reports, to illustrate problems in modern auditing.
ISBN 040601650X Pbk

—Auditing / Pitman, 8th ed.
– (M & E Handbook Series).
ISBN 0712107932 Pbk £6.95

—Basic Bookkeeping for Solicitors / 2nd ed. – London : Sweet & Maxwell, 1982.
ISBN 0421297603 Pbk £5.95

—Bigger Bang / Waterlow, 1987.
ISBN 0080331009 Pbk £5.50

—Book Keeping and Accounting Examinations Explained / Rizvi. – Croydon : Telles Langdon, 1988.
ISBN 0904467147 Pbk £6.75

—Book-Keeping and Accounts / Pegler. – 19th ed. – London : Butterworths, 1985.
ISBN 0406678103 Pbk £13.50

—Bottom Line / Plymouth : Macdonald & Evans, 1988.
ISBN 0356155382 Hbk £7.95

—Business Accounting / 4th ed. – Pitman, 1984.
ISBN 0582412427 Pbk £7.50

—Butterworths CIMA Student Series : Management Accounting - Decision Making / London : Butterworths, 1987.
ISBN 0406530041 Pbk £16.95

Stage 1-Quantitative Methods 1987.
ISBN 040653005X Pbk £15.95

Stage 2-Financial Accounting 1988.
ISBN 0406530025 Pbk £15.95

Stage 4-Management Accounting-Control and Audit 1988.
ISBN 0406530009 Pbk £15.95

—Charity Accounting / Vincent. – London : Butterworths, 1987.
ISBN 0406261008 Pbk £19.95

—Company Accounting Requirements / Wild. – 2nd ed. – London : Longman Professional, 1985.
ISBN 0851211461 Pbk £19.95

—Company Accounting Requirements : A Practical Guide / R. A. Wyld. – Rev. ed. Repr. of 1983 ed. – London : Oyez Longman.
ISBN 0851207553 Hbk £7.95

—Company Accounts / 3rd ed. – Plymouth : Macdonald & Evans, 1982.
ISBN 0712104704 Pbk £6.95

—Company Law for Accountants / London : Butterworths, 1985.
ISBN 0406009600 Pbk £11.95

—Concise Dictionary of Accounting and Finance / Pitman, 1986.
ISBN 0712106847 Pbk £4.95

—Corporate Cash Management / Cambridge : Woodhead-Faulkner, 1987.
ISBN 085941390X Hbk £40.00

—Corporate Finance / Mosby, 1988.
ISBN 0801642116 Hbk £31.00

—Corporate Finance / London : Butterworths, 1987.
ISBN 0406259569 Hbk £42.00

—Corporate Finance in Multinational Companies / London : Euromoney, 1986.
ISBN 1870031350 Pbk £75.00

—Corporate Finance Law / London : Sweet & Maxwell, 1987.
ISBN 0421311207 Hbk £67.00
ISBN 0421374403 Pbk £12.50

—Cost Accounting / Underdown. – London : Pitman Publishing, 1988.
ISBN 0273025007 Pbk £9.95

—Cost and Management Accounting / Cambridge : Woodhead-Faulkner, 1986.
ISBN 0859413713 Pbk £11.50

—Dictionary of Accounting Terms / London : Financial Training, 1985.
ISBN 0906322677 Pbk £8.95

—Dynamic Management Accountancy / London : Butterworths, 1983.
ISBN 0406258104 Pbk £8.00

—Essential Accounting for Managers / 5th ed. – London : Cassell, 1988.
ISBN 0304314714 Pbk £6.95

—Executorship Law and Accounts / Spicer. – 23rd ed. – London : Butterworths, 1987.
ISBN 0406679010 Hbk £45.00

—Executorship/Trust Law and Accounts / 2nd ed. – London : Pitman Publishing, 1986.
ISBN 0712107517 Pbk £14.95

—Financial Accounting / Maidenhead : McGraw-Hill, 1988.
ISBN 0070590028 Hbk £27.00

—Financial Accounting / Cambridge : Woodhead-Faulkner, 1986.
ISBN 0859413365 Pbk £12.00

—Financial Accounting / London : VanNostrand Reinhold, 1988.
ISBN 0278000150 Pbk £13.00

—Financial services legislation : the auditor's role in the financial services sector : a consultative document / Great Britain. – London : The Division, 1985.
12p.

—Form and Content of Company Accounts / Lybrand. – 3rd ed. – Oxford : Croner Publications, 1986.
ISBN 1851850325 Pbk £9.95

—Governing the Institute : a study, commissioned by the Institute of Chartered Accountants in England and Wales, on the direction, control and regulation of the Institute / R.I. Tricker. – London : The Institute, 1983.
193p; 25cm.
Bibliography: p191-193.
ISBN 0852913427 Pbk Unpriced

—Group Accounting / London : Butterworths, 1987.
ISBN 0406500193 Pbk

—Group Accounting / London : Butterworths, 1988.
ISBN 0406500193 Pbk

—Inquiry and Accounting / Quorum Press, 1988.
ISBN 089930222X Hbk £40.95

—Internal Audit / Ken Impey. – London : Butterworths, 1985.
For students and practitioners, this book uses extensive illustrations and diagrams to present the state of the art in modern internal auditing. Techniques of examination and analysis are discussed.
ISBN 0406013802 Pbk

—Internal audit / Impey. – London : Butterworths, 1985.
ISBN 0406013802 Pbk £18.50

—Introduction to accounting for business studies / Harden. – 4th ed. – London : Butterworths, 1985.
ISBN 040801542 Pbk £11.50

—Investigations manual / Hamlyn. – London : Butterworths, 1985.
ISBN 0406142580 Pbk £13.50

—Law for Accountancy Students / James. – 3rd ed. – London : Butterworths, 1986.
ISBN 0406708835 Pbk £16.95

—Law for Accountancy Students / Jennifer James. – 3rd ed. – London : Butterworths, 1986.
ISBN 0406708835 Pbk

—Legal Liabilities for Practising Accountants / London : Butterworths, 1984.
ISBN 0406259607 Pbk £28.00

—Legal Liabilities of Practising Accountants / London : Butterworths, 1984.
The unprecedented increase in professional liability for accountants and the new legal standards for auditing, accounting and taxation practice are discussed. Oriented to the private practitioner, this book gives practical approaches to minimizing the risk of professional liability.
ISBN 0406259607 Pbk

—Local Government Audit Law / London : HMSO, 1985.
ISBN 0117012599 Hbk £19.50

—Manual of Financial Reporting and Accounting / 2nd ed. – London : Butterworths, 1985.
ISBN 0406500509 Pbk £18.50

—Manual of Financial Reporting and Accounting / Touche Ross and Co. Staff. – 2nd ed. – London : Butterworths, 1985.
This book describes the legal requirements and professional pronouncements relating to audit reports and financial statements. The work gives recommended accounting and consolidating principles, and contains many examples of different types of audit reports.
ISBN 0406500509 Pbk

—On a cloth untrue : Inflation accounting / Cambridge : Woodhead-Faulkner, 1984.
ISBN 0859412504 Hbk £19.95

—PAYE Audits / London : Butterworths, 1988.
ISBN 0406263000 Pbk

—Pension Cost Accounting / London : Butterworths, 1984.
ISBN 0406010544 Pbk

—Practical Auditing / Spice and Pegler Staff. – 17th ed. – London : Butterworths, 1985.
A classic work for students of auditing. The book discusses the impact of the new Auditing Standards and Guidelines on the field. A detailed guide to audit techniques and administration is given.
ISBN 0406678014 Pbk £12.00

—Practical auditing / Pegler. – 17th ed. – London : Butterworths, 1985.
ISBN 0406678014 Pbk £13.50

—Practical guide to creative accounting / London : Kogan Page, 1988.
ISBN 1850913013 Hbk £16.95
ISBN 185091611X Pbk £6.95

—Practice development for accountants / Mountford. – London : Butterworths, 1984.
ISBN 0406260400 Pbk £15.00

—Presenting financial proposals to banks / London : Butterworths, 1986.
ISBN 0406100705 Pbk £15.00

—Property Companies : Accounting, Audit and Tax / Graham Walker. – London : Butterworths, 1986.
A guide to accounting for the property company in an environment of fluctuating interest and inflation rates. This book covers all relevant areas of United Kingdom accounting practice for property companies.
ISBN 0406005249 Pbk

—Property companies : accounting, audit and tax / London : Butterworths, 1988.
ISBN 0406005249 Pbk

—Regulatory Framework of Accounting / Suresh Tanna. – Plymouth : Macdonald & Evans, 1985.
320p. – (M and E Professional Studies Ser.).

—Role of an auditor in detecting fraud and other irregularities : a study / prepared on behalf of The Chartered Association of Certified Accountants. – London : Certified Accountant Publications, 1986.
46p.
'Prepared for publication by Christine Johnston, Technical Officer of the Chartered Association of Certified Accountants in conjunction with the Association's Working Party on Fraud and the Auditor's Responsibility, chaired by the Hon. Sir Irvine Goulding, and the School of Financial Studies, University of Glasgow' - Note.
ISBN 1850110212

—Sage companion / Paradigm, 1988.
ISBN 0948825669 Pbk £5.95

—Solicitors Accounts Rules 1976, The Solicitors Trust Accounts Rules 1986, The Accountants Reports Rules 1986, The Solicitors Accounts (Deposit Interest) Rules 1986 / Law Society. – London : Law Society.

—Solicitors' accounts : student guide / 2nd ed. – London : Financial Training, 1985.
ISBN 0906322944 Pbk £8.95

—Tolley's Accounting Problems of the Companies Acts : Practical Guidance on Recent Legislation / Sells. – Croydon : Tolley, 1984.
136p.
ISBN 0854591478 Hbk £7.95

—Trusts for accountants / London : Butterworths, 1987.
ISBN 0406500908 Pbk £10.95

—Trusts for Accountants / London : Butterworths, 1987.
ISBN 0406500908 Pbk

—UK financial accounting standards / Cambridge : Woodhead-Faulkner, 1983.
ISBN 0859412016 Hbk £25.00
ISBN 0859412024 Pbk £10.95

—Understanding company accounts / 2nd ed. – Pitman, 1983.
ISBN 0273019449 Pbk £4.95

—Understanding company accounts / Newman. – Telegraph Publications, 1988.
ISBN 0863671918 Pbk £6.95

—Understanding company financial statements / 2nd ed. – Pelican, 1982.
ISBN 0140091025 Pbk £4.95

—Work out accounting / Kriefman. – London : Macmillan, 1988.
ISBN 0333451244 Pbk £6.50

—Workbook in accounting / Caldicott. – 3rd ed. – London : Butterworths, 1981.
ISBN 0408106808 Pbk £10.50

ACCOUNTING - INDIA

—Company Law and Auditing / New Delhi : Kalyani Publishers.

—Company Meetings, Accounts, Audit and Investigation / 2nd ed. – Allahabad : Law Book Company, 1987.

ACCOUNTING - IRELAND

—Accounting Law and Practice for Limited Companies : Format and Disclosure Requirements Under the Irish Companies Acts, 1963 to 1986, and Accounting Standards / Dublin : Gill and Macmillan, 1987.
ISBN 0717115186 Hbk £30.00

ACCOUNTING - NEW ZEALAND

—Executorship Law and Accounts / 8th ed. – Wellington : Butterworths, 1980.

—Executorship Law and Accounts / 8th ed. – Butterworths, 1980.
ISBN 0409600733 Pbk £45.65

—Law and Practice of Company Accounting in New Zealand / 6th ed. – Butterworths, 1982.
Treatment of the law relating to company accounting and reporting and of the professional pronouncements and accounting practices which stem from or assist in the application of such law. All SSAPS including the CCA Standard are reproduced in the appendix.
ISBN 040960089X Pbk £82.50

ACCOUNTING - SWEDEN

—Swedish Companies Act 1975 : With Excerpts from the Accounting Act 1976 / Stockholm : Industriforbundet, 1986.
144p.
ISBN 9171761004 Hbk £180.00

ACQUISITIONS (LIBRARIES) - GREAT BRITAIN

—Newsletter / National Acquisitions Group. – s.l. : The Group, 1988.
ISBN 09505326

—Role of subscription agents / by Alan Singleton : with a supplementary report on U.K. libraries, trade with agents by Alan Cooper. – Leicester : Primary Communications Research Centre, University of Leicester, 1981.
68p; 21cm. – (Occasional papers).
ISBN 0906083176 Pbk Unpriced

ACQUITTALS - CANADA - SASKATCHEWAN

—Tentative proposals for compensation of accused on acquittal / Law Reform Commission of Saskatchewan. – Saskatoon : The Commission, 1987.
38p.
Includes bibliographical references. Includes text of proposed Act.

ACQUITTALS - ENGLAND

—Acquittal rates / Sid Butler. – London : Home Office, 1983.
v,32p.
Bibliography: p.10.
ISBN 0862520967

ACTIONS AND DEFENCES

—Commercial litigation : pre-emptive remedies / by Iain S. Goldrein and K.H. P. Wilkinson : with a foreword by Sir John Donaldson. – London : Sweet & Maxwell, 1987.
xlvii,793p; 26cm.
Covers topics in the commercial field where emergency relief may be necessary. Techniques are explained, and relevant reported cases are referred to, including the necessary statutes and court orders. Appendices include forms and precedents, and some Chancery and Queen's Bench Division Practice Directions.
ISBN 0421348003 Hbk £107

—Forms of action at international law : the spirit of English law and international law / H.A. Schwarz-Liebermann von Wahlendorf. – Birmingham : Institute of Judicial Administration, University of Birmingham, 1981.
iii,55p.
ISBN 2903642001

ACTIONS AND DEFENCES - AUSTRALIA - SOUTH AUSTRALIA

—Report...relating to qui tam and penal actions and common informers / Law Reform Committee of South Australia. – Adelaide : Government Printer, 1985.
16p. – (94th report).

ACTIONS AND DEFENCES - CANADA

—Conduct of an Action / R.J. Rolls. – Butterworths, 1982.
216p.
Examination of the legal and practical aspects of non-jury trials. Covers preparation, the brief, the course of the trial, nonsuit, examination in chief, cross-examination, re-examination, argument, and the rights and duties of judge and counsel at trial.
ISBN 0409877107 Hbk £50.00

—Interprovincial product liability litigation / Robert J. Sharpe. – Toronto : Butterworths, 1982.
xxi,145p.
Includes bibliographical references and index.
ISBN 0409866423

—Parties to an action / Scarborough, Ontario : Butterworths (Canada), 1988.
480.
Contains precedents, definitions of key terms, and a table of cases. Demonstrates how various types of 'persons' of groups become parties to a civil action and how they are described in the proceedings. Types of parties covered include infants, mentally incompetent persons, aliens, accused persons and convects, unincorporated associations, foreign sovereigns, states, administrators, and trade unions and employer organizations.
ISBN 0409809560 Hbk

—Parties to an Action / R.A. Meagher. – Butterworths, 1988.
480p.

—Trial of an Action / Butterworths, 1981.
280p.
Examines the legal and practical aspects of a trial from the selection of the tribunal to the final judgement. Looks at rules of practice and procedure, and with tactics and techniques of a trial lawyer. Covers the mode of trial, devices to facilitate or supplant testimony, the role of counsel, the role of the trial judge, the charge to the jury, and the verdict.
ISBN 040986854X Hbk £55.00

—Trial of an Action / Toronto : Butterworths, 1981.
280p.

ACTIONS AND DEFENCES - CANADA - BRITISH COLUMBIA

—Report on the action per quod servitium amisit / Law Reform Commission of British Columbia. – Victoria : Queens Printer, 1986.
20p.
Includes bilbiographical references.
ISBN 0771885490

ACTIONS AND DEFENCES - CANADA - SASKATCHEWAN

—Proposals for a survival of actions act : report to the Minister of Justice / Law Reform Commission of Saskatchewan. – Saskatoon : The Commission, 1985.
19p.
Includes bibliographical references.

ACTIONS AND DEFENCES - ENGLAND

—Civil litigation / John O'Hare, Robert N. Hill. – 2nd ed. – London : Oyez Longman, 1983.
xxii,429p.
ISBN 0851206883

—Litigation : a journal of contentious business / Chichester : Barry Rose, 1981.
With annual index.
ISBN 0859923193

—Small claims in the county court : how to sue and defend actions without a solicitor / by Michael Birks. – Rev. ed. – London : Lord Chancellor's Department, 1984.
73p.

ACTIONS AND DEFENCES - GREAT BRITAIN

—Introduction to criminal and civil litigation / Brian Raymond. – London : Oyez, 1981.
170p; 24cm.
ISBN 0851205569 Pbk Unpriced

—Medical negligence : a plaintiff's guide / Charles J. Lewis. – London, England : F. Cass, 1988.
xxxiv, 379 p.; 24 cm.
'The law is stated as at 1 January 1988'–T.p. verso. Includes index.
ISBN 0714640611 pbk.

—Time-Barred Actions / H. G. Rohreve. – London : LLoyd's of London Press, 1984.

ACTUARIES - CANADA

—Actuarial Evidence / 2nd ed. – Agincourt : Carswell, 1986.
ISBN 045939530 Hbk £18.50

—Actuarial Evidence : Valuing Past and Future Income / 2nd ed. – Agincourt : Carswell, 1986.
116p.
This work is a primer on the role of the actuary in the litigation process in Canada. The text presents numerous examples of the most common actuarial calculations drawn from cases.

ADDRESSES, ESSAYS, LECTURES

—75 years of law at Sheffield, 1909-1984 / edited by David C. Hoath. – Sheffield : University of Sheffield Faculty of Law, 1985.
viii,116p.
Includes bibliographical references.

—Anglo-Sakson gozuyle turk hukuku / An Anglo-Saxon view of Turkish law : Aubrey L. Diamond. – 1981.
2,10 leaves.
Paper presented at the 3rd Turkish Law Conference, Ankara, 1981. English text in typescript, bound with a Turkish translation published as a supplement to the Conference papers.

—Art of arbitration : essays on international arbitration : liber amicorum Pieter Sanders, 12 September 1912-1982 / editors, Jan C. Schultsz, Albert Jan van den Berg. – Deventer, Netherlands : Kluwer Law and Taxation Publishers, 1982.
xxi, 320 p.; 25 cm.
English or French. Includes bibliographical references and index.
ISBN 9065440542

—Commonwealth Caribbean legal essays / edited by Francis Alexis, P.K. Menon, Dorcas White. – Cave Hill, Barbados : Faculty of Law, University of the West Indies, 1982.
iv,303p.
UWI Law Faculty decennial (1970-80) lectures.

—Courts and the Charter / Clare F. Beckton and A. Wayne MacKay, research coordinators. – Toronto : University of Toronto Press in cooperation with the Royal Commission on the Economic Union and Development Prospects for Canada and the Canadian Government Publishing Centre, 1985.
xv,279p. – (Collected research studies).
Includes bibliographies.
ISBN 0802073050

—Criminal law and criminal justice / David Nelken (ed.). – London : University College London, Faculty of Laws, 1986.
70p; 30cm. – (Working papers).

—Current legal problems / edited...on behalf of the Faculty of Laws, University College, London. – London : Stevens, 1948.
Includes cumulative indexes in every 5th volume.

—Essays for Clive Schmitthoff / edited by John Adams. – Abingdon : Professional Books, 1983.
xviii,174p.
ISBN 0862050596

—Essays in European law and integration : to mark the silver jubilee of the Europa Institute, Leiden, 1957-1982 / edited by David O'Keeffe and Henry G. Schermers. – Deventer, Netherlands : Kluwer Law and Taxation Publishers, 1982.
208 p.; 25 cm.
Includes bibliographical references.
ISBN 9065441107 : est.

—Essays in honour of Judge T.O. Elias / edited by J.A. Omotola. – Lagos : Faculty of Law, University of Lagos, 1987.
xxvii,258p.
Includes index.

—Essays in law and society / edited by Zenon Bankowski and Geoff Mungham. – London : Routledge & Kegan Paul, 1980.
vii,207p; 24cm.
Includes bibliographies and index.
ISBN 0710004893 Pbk £6.50

—Essays in legal theory : a collaborated work / edited by D.J. Galligan : editorial advisers Colin Howard and Michael Crommelin. – Melbourne : Melbourne University Press, 1984.
viii,256p; 22cm.
ISBN 0522842836

—Exploitation of science and technology : a world force / by Sir Henry Chilver. – Southampton : University of Southampton, 1985.
At head of title page: The Fawley Foundation.

—Family law in the last two decades of the twentieth century : being a series of articles by a distinguished team of authors, first published in 'Acta juridica' 1983 / editorial board, T.W. Bennett ... et al. – Cape Town : Juta, 1983.
ix,243p.
Includes bibliographical references.
ISBN 0702114650

—Finnish legal system / edited by Jaakko Uotila : translated by Leena Lehto. – 2nd completely rev. ed. – Helsinki : Finnish Lawyers Pub. Co., 1985.
254p; 22cm.
ISBN 9516402445

—Income taxation in eastern Africa : policies and prospects : seven country surveys / edited by Ali Ahmed Suliman and Elizabeth de Brauw-Hay : with a foreword and a concluding chapter by J. van Hoorn, Jr. – Amsterdam, Netherlands : International Bureau of Fiscal Documentation, 1980.
244 p.; 24 cm.
Includes bibliographies.
ISBN 9070125145 pbk.

—Index to legal essays : English language legal essays in festschriften, memorial volumes, conference papers and other collections, 1975-1979 / compiled for the British and Irish Association of Law Librarians under the editorship of Barbara Tearle. – London : Mansell, 1983.
xii,430p; 26cm.
Bibliography: pxii.
ISBN 0720116538 £25.00

—Jurisprudence of orthodoxy : Queen's University essays on H.L.A. Hart / edited by Philip Leith and Peter Ingram. – London : Routledge, 1988.
216p.
Bibliography: pp.201-210. - Includes index.
ISBN 0415003059

—Law in transition : contracts / Don Mills : R. De Boo, 1984.
193p.
Includes bibliographical references and index.
ISBN 0888201826

—Law in transition : evidence / Don Mills : R. De Boo, 1984.
196p.
Includes bibliographical references and index.
ISBN 0888201877

—Legal and economic analyses on multinational enterprises / edited by Klaus J. Hopt. – 2 V. – Berlin : Walter de Gruyter, 1982.
At head of title: European University Institute. Vol. 2, English and French, with summaries for each item in the other language, has also parallel title: Analyses legales et economiques sur les entreprises multinationales. Includes indexes. Contents: v. 1. European merger control – v. 2. Groups of companies in European laws.
ISBN 3110087049 v. 2

—Legal change : essays in honour of Julius Stone / edited by A.R. Blackshield : on behalf of the Committee to honour Professor Julius Stone, OBE : with an introduction by Sir Zelman Cowen. – Sydney : Butterworths, 1983.
xxiv,367p.
Bibliography: p.335-344. - Includes index. Contains contributions from former students and colleagues of Professor Stone, from Australia and around the world. The essays represent broad areas of growth and change in the law, with emphasis on development and prospects for the last quarter of this century.
ISBN 0409491306

—New bearings in the law of the sea : inaugural lecture delivered at the University of Queensland, 29 April 1981 / R.D. Lumb. – St. Lucia, Queensland : University of Queensland Press, 1982.
ISBN 0702216798 pbk.

—Perspectives on the harmonization of law in Canada / Ronald C.C. Cuming research coordinator. – Toronto : University of Toronto Press in cooperation with the Royal Commission on the Economic Union and Development Prospects for Canada and the Canadian Government Publishing Centre, 1985.
xviii,178p. – (Collected research studies).
Bibliography: p.176-177.
ISBN 0802073026

—Public administration in Canada : selected readings / edited by A.M. Willms, W.D.K. Kernaghan. – 4th ed. – Toronto : Methuen, 1982.
viii,354p.
Includes bibliographies.
ISBN 0458952508

—Studies in 13th century justice and administration / C.A.F. Meekings. – London : Hambledon, 1981.
342p; 25cm. – (History series).
ISBN 0950688231

—Torts in the 80s / Don Mills : R. De Boo, 1983.
504p.
Includes bibliographical references and index.
ISBN 0888201508

—Transnational law of international commercial transactions / edited by Norbert Horn and Clive M. Schmitthoff. – Antwerp : Kluwer-Devanter/The Netherlands, 1982.
Includes index and bibliography.
ISBN 9065440925 : est.

ADDRESSES, ESSAYS, LECTURES - AUSTRALIA

—Legislation and society in Australia / edited by Roman Tomasic. – Sydney : The Law Foundation of New South Wales, 1980.
420p.
ISBN 0868610577 Pbk
ISBN 0868610658

ADDRESSES, ESSAYS, LECTURES - INDIA

—Law, men of law and education / H. R. Khanna. – Bombay : Tripathi, 1981.
184p.

ADDRESSES, ESSAYS, LECTURES - SOUTH AFRICA

—Daedalus in the Supreme Court : the common law today / D. P. Visser. – S.l. : University of Cape Town, 1985.
12 p. – (Inaugural lecture).
ISBN 0799209996

—Fiat iustitia : essays in memory of Oliver Deneys Schreiner / edited by Ellison Kahn. – Cape Town : Published for School of Law, University of the Witwatersrand, Johannesburg by Juta, 983.
xxii,405p.
Includes bibliographical references.
ISBN 0702113352

ADMINISTRATION OF JUSTICE

—Causation, prediction and legal analysis / Stuart S. Nagel. – New York : Quarum, 1986.
xxii,276p; 25cm.
Bibliography: p261-268. - Includes index.
ISBN 0899301800 No price

—EDP systems for court adminstration : proceedings of the 3rd Colloquy on the Use of Computers in the Administration of Justice, Strasbourg, 3-5 November / Strasbourg : Council of Europe, 1983.
222,viiip; 30cm.
At head of cover title: Legal Affairs.
ISBN 9287102902

—EDP systems for the administration of courts and related systems : proceedings of the fifth Colloquy on the Use of Computers in the Administration of Justice, Madrid, 14-16 October 1986 / Strasbourg : Council of Europe, 1987.
314p; 29cm.
At head of cover title: Legal affairs.
ISBN 9287110816

—English legal system / by R.J. Walker. – 5th ed. – London : Butterworths, 1980.
xlvi,679p.

ISBN 0406677581

—Faces of justice and state authority : a comparative approach to the legal process / Mirjan R. Damaska. – New Haven : Yale University Press, 1986.
288p; 24cm.
Includes index.
ISBN 0300035675 £26.00 (Oct.)

—Justice and politics in People's China : legal order or continuing revolution? / James P. Brady. – London : Academic Press, 1982.
xiii,268p; 24cm.
Includes index.
ISBN 0121247503 £17.80

—Measures facilitating access to justice : recommendation no. R(81)7 adopted by the Committee of Ministers of the Council of Europe on 14 May 1981 and explanatory memorandum / Council of Europe. – Strasbourg : Council of Europe, 1981.
26p.
Prepared under the authority of the European Committee on Legal Co-operation. At head of cover title: Council of Europe, Legal Affairs.

—Measures to prevent and reduce the excessive workload in the courts : recommendation no. R (86)12 adopted by the Committee of Ministers of the Council of Europe on 16 September 1986 and Explanatory memorandum / Council of Europe. – Strasbourg : Council of Europe, 1987.
17p.
Prepared by a committee of experts on the working of the judicial system set up under the authority of the European Committee on Legal Co-operation. At head of cover title : Council of Europe Legal Affairs.
ISBN 9287110778

—Private justice / Stuart Henry. – London : Routledge & Kegan Paul, 1983.
ix,245p.
Includes index. Bibliography: p229-235.
ISBN 0710097034 pbk.

—Review of the operation of the Northern Ireland (Emergency Provisions) Act 1978 / by Sir George Baker : presented to Parliament by the Secretary of State for Northern Ireland. – London : H.M.S.O., 1984.
171p.
ISBN 0101922205

—Rule of law in the areas administered by Israel / Israel National Section of the International Commission of Jurists. – Tel Aviv : Israel National Section of the International Commission of Jurists, 1981.
xiv,114p.
Includes bibliographical references.

—Windsor yearbook of access to justice / Recueil annuel de Windsor d'acces a la justice. – Windsor, Ontario : University of Windsor, 1981.

ADMINISTRATION OF JUSTICE – AUSTRALIA

—Delays and efficiency in civil litigation / Ross Cranston ... et al. – Melbourne : The Institute of Judicial Administration, 1984.
xviii,230p.
At head of title page: The Australian Institute of Judicial Administration Incorporated.
ISBN 0959002901

—Human Rights Guarantees in the Administration of Criminal Justice / L. T. Wilkins. – Canberra : Australian Institute of Criminology.

—Issues in Criminal Justice Administration / Sandra J. Egger. – North Sydney : Allen & Unwin, 1983.
200p.
ISBN 0868612774 Hbk £29.95
ISBN 0868610542 Pbk £19.95

ADMINISTRATION OF JUSTICE – AUSTRALIA – VICTORIA

—Civil justice project : preliminary study / I. R. Scott, J. R. Pullen, A. J. Robbins. – Melbourne : Government Printer, 1984.
xviii,423p.
Cover title: Preliminary study concerning the administration of civil justice in Victoria.
ISBN 0908417179

—Court surveys and studies 1978-1984, concerning the civil caseloads of the Supreme Court, the County Court and the Magistrates' Courts of Victoria / J.R. Pullen, N.F. Young, S.J. Geddes. – Melbourne : Civil Justice Committee, 1985.
xvi,403p.
At head of title: Civil Justice Committee.

—Report to the Attorney-General concerning the administration of civil justice in Victoria / John Young. – Melbourne : Government Printer, 1984.
xxxiv,382p.
Chairman: Sir John Young.
ISBN 0908417152

Volume 2 : Appendices 1984.
1 vol. (various pagings).
Chairman: Sir John Young.
ISBN 0908417160 Hbk

ADMINISTRATION OF JUSTICE – CANADA

—Civil courts in Canada : Tribunaux civils au Canada / Ottawa : Statistics Canada, Canadian Centre for Justice Statistics, 1985.
183 p.; 29 cm.
English and French. 'July 1985.'.
ISBN 0660522497 pbk. £25.00 (£26.50 other countries)

—Cost of Justice : 1979 Conference of the Canadian Institute for the Administration of Justice / Carswell Legal Publications. – Agincourt : Carswell, 1980.
160p.

—Criminal Justice : 1981 Conference of the Canadian Institute for the Administration of Justice / Carswell Legal Publications. – Agincourt : Carswell, 1982.
300p.

—Judicial administration in Canada / Perry S. Millar and Carl Baar. – Kingston : McGill-Queen's University Press, 1981.
xxiii,452p.
ISBN 0773503676

—Justice beyond Orwell / edited by Rosalie S. Abella and Melvin L. Rothman : Institut canadien dádministration de la justice : Canadian Institute for the Administration of Justice. – Montreal : Yvon Blais, 1985.
516p.
Includes bibliographical references.
ISBN 2890735540

ADMINISTRATION OF JUSTICE – ENGLAND

—Administration of justice / Robin C.A. White. – Oxford : Blackwell, 1985.
400p.
Introduction to the English legal system of justice. Critique of how the system works in reality.
ISBN 0631143068 Hbk £27.50 :
ISBN 0631143076 Pbk £12.50

—Administration of the courts : JUSTICE / a report by John Macdonald, Chairman of committee. – London : JUSTICE, 1986.
46p.
ISBN 0907247083

—Civil justice review / Lord Chancellor's Department. – London : The Department, 1987.
109 leaves.

—Civil justice review : consultation paper no. 6 : general issues / response by JUSTICE. – London : JUSTICE, 1987.
19p.

—Criminology and criminal justice / by J.E. Hall Williams. – London : Butterworths, 1982.
xvii,266p.
Bibliography: p243-254.
ISBN 0406593205

—England's Balme : Proposals By Way of Grievance and Remedy Presented to His Highness and the Parliament Towards the Regulation of the Law and Better Administration of Justice / Repr. of 1657 ed. – Abingdon : Professional Books.
251p.

—English legal system / by Keith J. Eddey. – 4th ed. – London : Sweet & Maxwell, 1987.
xv,196p. – (Concise college texts).
Previous ed.: 1982. Bibliography: p189-190. - Includes index.
ISBN 0421354003 Hbk £13.50
ISBN 0421354100 Pbk £7.50

—English legal system / A.K.R. Kiralfy. – 7th ed. – London : Sweet & Maxwell, 1984.
xli,301p; 22cm.
Previous ed.: 1978. Includes index.
ISBN 0421313706 Pbk £16.50
ISBN 0421313803 Pbk £7.50

—Law machine / Marcel Berlins and Clare Dyer. – 2nd rev ed. – Harmondsworth : Penguin Books, 1986.
185p.
ISBN 0140226958

—Law machine / Marcel Berlins and Clare Dyer. – Harmondsworth : Penguin, 1982.
191p.
Includes index.
ISBN 0140224815

—Modern English legal system / by P.F. Smith and S.H. Bailey. – London : Sweet & Maxwell, 1984.
xxxix,783p; 24cm.
Includes index.
ISBN 0421271809 Hbk £30.00
ISBN 0421271906 Pbk £16.00

—Report of the Review Body on the Chancery Division of the High Court / presented to Parliament by the Lord High Chancellor. – London : H.M.S.O., 1981.
v,115p; 25cm.
Chairman: Lord Justice Oliver.
ISBN 010182050X

—Roll of the Shropshire eyre of 1256 / edited for the Selden Society by Alan Harding. – London : Selden Society, 1981.
lxxiv,403p.

ADMINISTRATION OF JUSTICE – GREAT BRITAIN

—Administration of Justice Act 1982 / with annotations by Michael J. Goodman, J.W.R. Gray. – London : Sweet & Maxwell, 1983.
vii,83p; 24cm.
ISBN 0421312602 Pbk £6.50

—Collection of Statutes Connected With the General Administration of Law, 8 Vols. / Repr. of 1817 ed. – Abingdon : Professional Books.
116p.

—Politics and power / London : Routledge and Kegan Paul, 1981.
328p; 24cm.
ISBN 0710009844

—Records of the general eyre / David Crook. – London : H.M.S.O., 1982.
x, 271p.
ISBN 0114401233

ADMINISTRATION OF JUSTICE – INDIA

—Crisis of the Indian legal system / Upendra Baxi. – New Delhi : Vikas, 1982.
xiii,405p.
Includes index. Bibliography: p393-400.
ISBN 0706913698

—Law and society : lectures and writings of Justice P. Jaganmohan Reddy / edited by M.V.K. Sivamohan. – Delhi : Ajanta Publications, 1986.
xii, 163 p.; 22 cm.
'Continuation of the anthology of lectures and writings of Justice P. Jaganmohan Reddy ... published ... under the title, 'Quest for justice'–Pref. Includes bibliographies and index.
ISBN 8120201566 Rs60.00

ADMINISTRATION OF JUSTICE – IRELAND

—Administration of Justice in Ireland / Lysaght. – repr. 1986. – Dublin : Institute of Public Administration.
105p.

ADMINISTRATION OF JUSTICE – ISRAEL

—Foundations of Law Act, 1980 and its implementation / Jerusalem : The Ministry, 1982.
6p.

ADMINISTRATION OF JUSTICE – NEW ZEALAND

—Practice of the High Court and Court of Appeal of New Zealand / Gordon Cain. – 12th ed. (rev). – Wellington : Butterworths, 1978.
looseleaf.
'Successor to the 11th ed. of the text on the same subject by the late Sir Wilfrid Joseph Sim'.

ADMINISTRATION OF JUSTICE – NIGERIA

—Administration of Justice in the Customary Courts of Yorubaland / Ibadan : University Press, 1982.
128p.

—Administration of justice in the customary courts of Yorubaland / J.O. Ajibola. – Ibadan : University Press, 1982.
ix,89p.
ISBN 019575753X

—Cases and materials on the principles of natural justice in Nigeria / by A. Toriola Oyewo. – Ibadan, Nigeria : Jator Publishing, 1987.
xi,153p.
Includes bibliographical references and index.
ISBN 9782660000

—Crisis of justice / by R. Akinola Aguda. – Akure, Nigeria : Eresu Hills, 1986.
x,73p.

—Quintessence of justice : University of Maiduguri, 6th convocation lecture delivered on Thursday, January 31st, 1985 / by Timothy Akinola Aguda. – Maiduguri, Nigeria : University of Maiduguri, 1985.
34p. – (Convocation lecture).
ISBN 9782323462

—Right to a fair hearing in Nigeria / by Chuks Okpaluba. – Lagos : Shelters International Ltd., 1980.
137p.

ADMINISTRATION OF JUSTICE – NORTHERN IRELAND

—Access to justice and civil litigation in Northern Ireland : report of a conference organised by SLS Legal Publications (NI) and the Northern Ireland Consumer Council held in the Queen's University of Belfast on 29 March 1985 / Belfast : SLS Legal Publications, 1985.
ii,76p.

—Administration of Justice Act 1982 and the Assessment of Damages / Belfast : Queen's University of Belfast, 1983.
28p.

—Ten years on in Northern Ireland : the legal control of political violence / Kevin Boyle, Tom Hadden, Paddy Hillyard. – London : Cobden Trust, 1980.
119p; 21cm.
Includes bibliographies.
ISBN 0900137169 Pbk £2.50

ADMINISTRATION OF JUSTICE - NORWAY
—Administration of justice in Norway : a brief summary / edited by the Royal Ministry of Justice in cooperation with the Royal Ministry of Foreign Affairs. – 2nd ed. – Oslo : Royal Ministry of Justice, 1980.
94p.
ISBN 8200055019

ADMINISTRATION OF JUSTICE - SCOTLAND
—Scottish legal system : an introduction to the study of Scots law / by David M. Walker. – 5th ed., rev. – Edinburgh : Green, 1981.
xlv,543p; 23cm.
Previous ed.: 1976. Includes bibliographies and index.
ISBN 0414006836 Unpriced

—Waiting for justice : an SCC survey of facilities in Scotland's Sheriff Courts : results and recommendations by Sheila Gilmore / Glasgow : Scottish Consumer Council, 1981.
44,A1-A6p,11leaves; 30cm.
ISBN 0907067069 Pbk £1.50

ADMINISTRATION OF JUSTICE - SOUTH AFRICA
—Judges at work : the role and attitudes of the South African appellate judiciary, 1910-50 / by Hugh Corder. – Cape Town : Juta, 1984.
xxxii,252p.
Bibliography: pxxi-xxvi.
ISBN 0702114359

ADMINISTRATION OF JUSTICE - TRINIDAD & TOBAGO
—Report of the proceedings and papers of the second Magistrates' Workshop / compiled and edited by Roland Crawford on behalf of the Magistrates' Association of the Republic of Trinidad and Tobago. – Port-of-Spain : The Association, 1982.
158p.
'Held on the 13th and 14th September, 1980, Chaguaramas Convention Centre'. At head of title: Republic of Trinidad and Tobago, the Magistrates' Association of the Republic of Trinidad and Tobago.

ADMINISTRATION OF JUVENILE JUSTICE
—Implementation of the European Convention on Human Rights in respect of young persons and children placed in care or in institutions following a decision of the administrative or judicial authorities : replies of Governments to the Secretary General's enquiry under Article 57 of the European Convention on Human Rights / Council of Europe. – Strasbourg : Council of Europe, 1986.
196p; 30cm. – (H (86) 1).
At head of cover title: Human rights.

ADMINISTRATION OF JUVENILE JUSTICE - AUSTRALIA
—Juvenile justice in South Australia / by John Seymour. – Sydney : Law Book Company in association with the Australian Institute of Criminology, 1983.
xix,146p.
Includes bibliographical references and index.
ISBN 0455204853

ADMINISTRATION OF JUVENILE JUSTICE - CANADA
—Current Issues in Juvenile Justice / Marc LeBlanc. – Butterworths, 1983.
400p.
ISBN 0409824135 Pbk £26.95

—Innovative approaches to juvenile justice : executive summaries of four juvenile diversion project reports / by Therese Lajeunesse. – Ottawa, Ont. : Consultation Centre, Solicitor General Canada, 1982.
35, 38 p.; 22 cm.
English and French. Title on added t.p.: Approches innovatrices en matiere de justice pour adolescents. .
ISBN 0662518160 pbk.

—Juvenile courts in Canada / by Larry C. Wilson. – Toronto, Canada : Carswell, 1982.
xx, 272 p.; 24 cm.
Includes index. 'Table of cases': p. vii-xx.
ISBN 0459352709

—Young Offenders Act, 1982 : highlights / Canada. – Ottawa : Minister of Supply and Services Canada, 1982.
25,27p.
Added t.p. in French. Text in English and French.
ISBN 0662522206

—Young Offenders Act : highlights / Ottowa : Published under the authority of the Hon. Bob Kaplan, Solicitor General of Canada by Minister of Supply and Services, 1981.
19,21p.
Added t.p. in French. Pages numbered in opposite directions. Text in English and French.
ISBN 066251212X

ADMINISTRATION OF JUVENILE JUSTICE - ENGLAND
—Care and discretion : social workers' decisions with delinquents / Henri Giller, Allison Morris. – London : Burnett in association with Deutsch, 1981.
127p; 21cm.
Bibliography: p120-123. - Includes index.
ISBN 0233972943 HBK £5.95
ISBN 0233973737 Pbk £3.50

—Juvenile sentencing : is there a tariff? / David Moxon, Peter Jones and Roger Tarling. – London : Home Office, 1985.
v,19p.
Bibliography: p.19.
ISBN 0862521874

—Providing criminal justice for children / edited by Allison Morris and Henri Giller. – London : Edward Arnold rc 1983, 1983.
164p; 22cm.
Includes index.
ISBN 0713163976 Pbk £7.95

—Time taken to deal with juveniles under criminal proceedings / Catherine Frankenburg and Roger Tarling. – London : Home Office, 1983.
v,21p.
Bibliography: p.14.
ISBN 0862521025

—Towards a unified family court : court orders concerning children : overlapping jurisdictions / Jean Graham Hall, Douglas F. Martin. – s.l. : s.n., 1986.
88p.

—Understanding juvenile justice / Allison Morris Henri Giller. – London : Croom Helm, 1987.
287p; 23cm.
ISBN 0709938322 Hbk £22.50
ISBN 070993890X Pbk £9.95

ADMINISTRATION OF JUVENILE JUSTICE - GREAT BRITAIN
—Juvenile justice in the United Kingdom : comparisons and suggestions for change / Sarah McCabe and Phyllis Treitel. – London : New Approaches to Juvenile Crime, 1983.
81p.
Includes bibliographical references.
ISBN 0950929905

ADMINISTRATION OF JUVENILE JUSTICE - NETHERLANDS
—Juvenile delinquency in the Netherlands / edited by Josine Junger-Tas and Richard L. Block. – Amstelveen, The Netherlands : Kugler Publications BV, 1988.
xiii, 242 p.; 23 cm.
Includes bibliographies.
ISBN 9062990363 CIP rev.

ADMINISTRATION OF JUVENILE JUSTICE - SCOTLAND
—Children out of court / F.M. Martin et al. – Edinburgh : Scottish Academic Press, 1981.
xi,331p.
Bibliography: p.322-324.
ISBN 0707302870

ADMINISTRATION OF JUVENILE JUSTICE - UNITED STATES
—Juveniles' waiver of rights : legal and psychological competence / Thomas Grisso. – New York : Plenum, 1981.
xiii,295p; 24cm.
Bibliography: p279-286. - Includes index.
ISBN 0306405261 Unpriced

ADMINISTRATIVE AGENCIES - AUSTRALIA
—Commonwealth government directory 1981 / compiled by the Information Services Division, Department of Administrative Services. – Canberra : Australian Government Publishing Service, 1981.
v,457p.
Includes index.

—Commonwealth government directory / Canberra : Australian Government Publishing, 1984.
v,403p.
Previous ed.: 1981. Includes indexes.

—Investigations by Adminstrative Agencies / North Ryde : Law Book Co, 1987.
ca 1,250p.
ISBN 0455205868 Hbk £125.00

—Of manners gentle : enforcement strategies of Australian business regulatory agencies / Peter Grabosky, John Braithwaite. – Melbourne : Oxford University Press, 1986.
viii,260p.
Includes index.
ISBN 0195546911

ADMINISTRATIVE AGENCIES - CANADA
—Index to federal programs and services 1986 / 7th ed. – Ottawa : Supply and Services Canada, 1986.
533p.
ISBN 0660119463

—Parliament and administrative agencies : a study paper prepared for the Law Reform Commission of Canada / by Frans F. Slatter. – Ottawa : Law Reform Commission of Canada, 1982.
6,154p; 25cm. – (Study paper).
ISBN 0662116259

—Report on independent administrative agencies : a framework for decision making / Law Reform Commission of Canada. – Ottawa : Law Reform Commission of Canada, 1985.
101,11p. – (Working paper).
Bibliography: p.87-94. Added t.p. in French: Rapport sur organismes administratifs autonomes. Pages numbered in opposite directions. Text in English and French.
ISBN 0662537483

ADMINISTRATIVE AGENCIES - CANADA - MANITOBA
—Report on administrative law / Manitoba Law Reform Commission. – Winnipeg : Manitoba Law Reform Commission, 1984.
182p.
Includes bibliographical references.

Part 2 : Judicial review of administrative action / Manitoba Law Reform Commission. – 1987.
vi,243p. – (Report).
Includes bibliographical references.
ISBN 0771108338

ADMINISTRATIVE AGENCIES - COMMONWEALTH
—Year book of the Commonwealth 1983 / 15th ed. – London : H.M.S.O., 1983.
vii,535p.
Includes index.
ISBN 0115802320

ADMINISTRATIVE AGENCIES - GREAT BRITAIN
—Report on non-departmental public bodies / presented to Parliament by the Prime Minister .. – London : H.M.S.O., 1980.
iv,186p; 25cm.
ISBN 0101779704 Pbk £5.75

—Whitehall and Westminster : Government informs Parliament : the changing scene / Dermot Englefield. – Harlow : Longman, 1985.
x,218p; 24cm.
Includes index.
ISBN 058290272X Pbk £15.00

ADMINISTRATIVE AGENCIES - NEW ZEALAND
—Statutory functions and responsibilities of New Zealand public service departments 1979 / prepared by C.J. Barton : revised by J. Johnston. – Wellington : Government Printer, 1980.
329p.
Includes index.

ADMINISTRATIVE COURTS - CANADA
—Constitution of Canada : a suggested amendment relating to provincial administrative tribunals : a discussion paper / Department of Justice. – Ottawa : The Department, 1983.
13,14p.
With French t.p.: La Constitution du Canada. English and French texts.

—Handbook of administrative tribunals / Sara Blake. – Scarborough, Ontario : Butterworths (Canada), 1988.
256.
Examination of how tribunals should conduct themselves in order to minimize the risks of judicial review. Cover compliance with prescribed rules, Ontario and Alberta Codes of Procedure, specific procedural rules, parties, notice, disclosure of the case to be met, adjournments, effective participation, the in-camers hearing, evidence, witnesses and the right to make submissions.
ISBN 0409806650 Hbk

ADMINISTRATIVE COURTS - ENGLAND
—Appeals / by David Price. – London : Fourmat, 1982.
xii,439p; 22cm.
Includes index.
ISBN 0906840422 Pbk £12.95

ADMINISTRATIVE COURTS - GREAT BRITAIN
—Tribunals practice and procedure / general editor, John Bowers : with a foreword by Sir Jack Jacob : and an introduction by J.A.G. Griffith. – 1. – London : Legal Studies and Services, 1985.
looseleaf; 26cm.
Includes index.
ISBN 0907822592 £98.00

ADMINISTRATIVE COURTS - NEW ZEALAND

—Appeals on questions of law from administrative tribunals : sixteenth report of the Public and Administrative Law Reform Committee : presented to the Minister of Justice, March 1982 / Wellington : the Committee?, 1982.
17,19p.

ADMINISTRATIVE DISCRETION - GREAT BRITAIN

—Discretion and welfare / edited by Michael Adler and Stewart Asquith. - London : Heinemann Educational, 1981.
vii,296p; 23cm. - (Studies in social policy and welfare).
Conference papers. Bibliography: p273-287. - Index.
ISBN 0435820095 £15.00

—Discretionary powers : a legal study of official discretion / D.J. Galligan. - Oxford : Clarendon, 1986.
xxi,401p; 22cm.
Bibliography: p383-396. - Includes index.
ISBN 0198254989 £30.00

ADMINISTRATIVE LAW

—Administrative Law : a Treatise / Louis Borgeat. - 2nd ed. - Agincourt : Carswell, 1988.
ca 500p.

—Administrative law : ladders and snakes : a public lecture / delivered by Sir Patrick Neill on ... 12th March 1985. - London : Inns of Court School of Law, 1985.
32p.

—Administrative Law, Vol. 1 : a Treatise / Louis Borgeat. - 2nd ed. - Agincourt : Carswell, 1986.
736p.

—Constitutional and Administrative Law / 5th ed. - De Smith, 1985.
ISBN 0140226109 Pbk £11.95

—Lawyers and public administrators : separate and unequal : a public lecture / delivered by Lousi Blom-Cooper on ... 1st March 1984. - London : Inns of Court School of Law, 1984.
20p; 23cm.

—Lectures on Administrative Law / Lucknow : Eastern Book Company, 1980.
xxxviii, 328p.

—Rationalism and the modern state / by Patrick Nerhot. - Florence : European University Institute, 1983.
73p.
At head of title: European University Institute, Florence, Law Department.

ADMINISTRATIVE LAW - AUSTRALIA

—Administrative Law First / Butterworths, 1989.
ca 122p.
ISBN 0409494798 Pbk £10.95

—Administrative Review Council : Annual report 1983-84 / 8th ed. - Canberra : Australian Government Publishing Service, 1984.
101p.

—Administrative Review Council : Seventh Annual Report 1982-1983 / Administrative Review Council. - Canberra : Australian Government Publishing Service.
88p.

—Australian Federal Administrative Law Legislation : with Introductory Commentary / North Ryde : C.C.H. Australia, 1985.
496p.
ISBN 0869037498 Hbk

—Authority and politics in Australia : some key dynamics of Australian politics / Victoria : Oxford University Press, 1988.
320.
Argues that a few basic principles underlie many features of Australian politics and government. It is maintained that in the Australian setting these processes have resulted in continuing restrictive features in Australian law and institutions.
ISBN 0195547446 Pbk £15.00

—Cases and materials on administrative law / Richard R. S. Tracey. - 4th ed. - Sydney : Butterworths, 1982.
lii,547p.
Previous ed.: 1975, by Peter Brett and Peter W. Hogg. First ed.: cases and materials in constitutional and administrative law. Includes index.
ISBN 0409309192 HBK £54
ISBN 0409309206 PBK £42.5

—Commonwealth administrative law / D.C. Pearce. - Sydney : Butterworths, 1986.
xxix,282p.
Includes index.
ISBN 0409490881 Hbk A$45.00
ISBN 0409490881 Pbk A$32.00

—Federal administrative law / by Geoffrey A. Flick : with a foreword by J.D. Davies. - Sydney : Law Book Co., 1983.
xxvii,251p.
Text of several acts and regulations, with commentary. Includes index.
ISBN 0455204489
ISBN 0455204241

—General Principles of Administrative Law / D.J. Lanham. - 3rd ed. - Butterworths, 1989.
ca 450p.
ISBN 0409495395 Pbk £55.00
ISBN 0409495387 Hbk £69.00

—Principles of Australian Administrative Law / 6th ed. - North Ryde : Law Book Co, 1985.
xxxv, 516p.
ISBN 0455205752 Hbk £40.00
ISBN 0455205760 Pbk

—Principles of Australian administrative law / by Harry Whitmore. - 5th ed. - Sydney : Law Book Co., 1980.
xxviii, 289 p.; 25 cm.
ISBN 0455201188 pbk.

—Principles of Australian administrative law / 6th ed. - North Ryde : Law Book Co, 1985.
ISBN 0455205760 Pbk £20.00

ADMINISTRATIVE LAW - AUSTRALIA - NEW SOUTH WALES

—Deregulation : a plan of action to rationalise South Australian legislation : a report to the South Australian Government / by Dianne Gayler. - Adelaide : Government Printer, 1980.
v,85p. - (P.P.).
Includes bibliographical references.

ADMINISTRATIVE LAW - CANADA

—Administrative Law / Borgeat. - 2nd ed. - Agincourt : Carswell, 1986.
ISBN 045938080X Hbk £41.80

—Administrative Law / Vancouver : British Columbia Continuing Legal Education Society, 1985.
297p.
ISBN 0865042411 Hbk £65.00

—Administrative Law : A Treatise / Louis Borgeat. - 2nd ed. - Agincourt : Carswell, 1986.
736p.
This work focuses on the structures, the arts, and the function of 'the Administration' through an examination of the definition of administrative law and its fundamental principles.

—Administrative Law : Cases Text and Materials / Janisch. - 2nd ed. - Aurora : Canada Law Book, 1984.

—Administrative law cases, text, and materials / by J.M. Evans ... et al. - Toronto : Edmond-Montgomery, 1980.
xxv, 1085 p.; 26 cm.
Includes index.
ISBN 0920722024

—Administrative Law : Cases, Text and Materials / H. N. Janisch. - 2nd ed. - Aurora : Canada Law Book Co, 1984.
1100p. - (Case Books).
This text deals with the complex problems that arise in a wide range of governmental and regulatory contexts. Among other topics, the text discusses the impact of the Charter on administrative procedure, the emergence of the 'rational basis' test in jurisdiction cases and its relevance in other contexts, and the Constitutional right to judicial review.

—Administrative law : cases, text, and materials / J.M. Evans ... et al. - 2nd ed. - Toronto : Emond Montgomery, 1984.
xlix,994p.
Previous ed.: 1980. Includes index.
ISBN 0920722156 Hbk £90.00

—Administrative Law Reports / Agincourt : Carswell.

Vols. 1-30 1984-88.
This text contains the administrative law decisions from all the Canadian jurisdictions. Topics include the judicial review of decisions of administrative tribunals, both the availability of and grounds for, delegation of legislative powers, and remedies on judicial review.

—Administrative Law Reports / Agincourt : Carswell.

—Cases and Materials on Administrative Law / Butterworths, 1987.
450p.
Focuses on judicial review of administrative action and includes a discussion of natural justice and fairness, rule-making, bias, standing, grounds for review, and discretionary powers and remedies. Contains excerpts from relevant Acts and materials, a table of cases, a chapter on freedom of information legislation and notes on delegation and privative clauses.
ISBN 0409806277 Pbk £68.00

—Policy implementation, compliance and administrative law / Law Reform Commission of Canada. - Ottawa : Law Reform Commission of Canada, 1986.
105,115p; 25cm. - (Working paper).
Cover title: Administrative law - policy implementation, compliance and administrative law. Added t.p. in French: Droit, objectifs publics et observation des normes. Pages numbered in opposite directions. Text in English and French.
ISBN 0662540832

—Principles of administrative law / by David Philip Jones and Anne S. de Villars. - Toronto : Carswell, 1985.
xlv,489p.
ISBN 0459377604

—Proceedings of the Administrative Law Conference : held at the University of British Columbia Faculty of Law on 18-19 October 1979 / Vancouver : U.B.C. Law Review, 1981.
391p; 23cm.

—Recent developments in administrative law / edited by Neil R. Finkelstein, Brian MacLeod Rogers. - Toronto : Carswell, 1987.
xl,354p.
' ... a collection of essays which were originally presented at programs sponsored by the Law Society of Upper Canada on 'Administrative law: recent developments and emerging trends' in Toronto and Ottawa in November 1986'. - Preface.
ISBN 0459304615

ADMINISTRATIVE LAW - CANADA - ONTARIO

—Charter of Rights and administrative law, 1983-1984 / section head, Garry J. Smith. - Agincourt, Ont. : Carswell Legal Publications, 1983.
xxix, 184 p.; 29 cm. - (Bar admission course materials / Law Society of Upper Canada).
Includes index. Bibliography: p. 173-179.
ISBN 0459360906

ADMINISTRATIVE LAW - COMMONWEALTH

—Commonwealth Administrative Law / London : Butterworths, 1985.
ISBN 0409490881 Pbk £32.40

ADMINISTRATIVE LAW - ENGLAND

—'Without the law' : administrative justice and legal pluralism in nineteenth-century England / H. W. Arthurs. - Toronto : University of Toronto Press, 1985.
xvi,312p; 24cm.
ISBN 0802056547

—Administrative law / by H.W.R. Wade. - 5th ed. - Oxford : Clarendon, 1982.
li,892p; 24cm.
Previous ed.: 1977. Includes index.
ISBN 0198761384 Hbk £25.00
ISBN 0198761392 Pbk £17.50

—Administrative law / David Foulkes. - 6th ed. - London : Butterworths, 1986.
xxxv,477p; 25cm.
This text is a thorough discussion of administrative law in the United Kingdom for students of the subject. Recent developments in caselaw and statutes are described.
ISBN 0406584095 Hbk £28.00
ISBN 0406584109 Pbk £17.95

—Garner's administrative law / B. L. Jones, J. F. Garner. - 6th ed. - London : Butterworths, 1985.
552p; 26cm.
Previous ed.: published as Administrative law. 1979. Includes bibliography and index.
ISBN 0406587981 Hbk
ISBN 040658799X Pbk

—Principles of administrative law / D.C.M. Yardley. - 2nd ed. - London : Butterworths, 1986.
275p; 22cm.
A collection of essays, with particular emphasis on issues of control of power and the maintenance of a fair balance between competing interests of the individual and governmental entities in the United Kingdom, make up this book. Privatization of corporations, rent assessment, and the changing role of the Ombudsman are addressed.
ISBN 040668992X Hbk £14.50
ISBN 0406689938 Pbk £8.95

—Stephen's commentaries on the laws of England / L. Crispin Warmington. - 21st ed. - London : Butterworths, 1950.
xiv,603p.
Index included in Vol. 4.

ADMINISTRATIVE LAW - FRANCE

—French administrative law / J. F. Garner, Jean-Michel Galabert. - 3rd ed. - London : Butterworths, 1983.
xvii,218p.
Previous ed.: 1973. Bibliography: p.205-207.- Includes index.
ISBN 0406561524

—French Administrative Law / Garner. - 3rd ed. - London : Butterworths, 1983.
ISBN 0406561524 Pbk £14.95

ADMINISTRATIVE LAW - GREAT BRITAIN

—Administrative justice : some necessary reforms / (report of the Committee of the JUSTICE-ALL Souls Review of Administrative law in the United Kingdom). – Oxford : Clarendon, 1988.
xxxv,449p; 23cm.
Includes index.
ISBN 019825587X Hbk £25.00
ISBN 0198255861 Pbk £12.50

—Administrative Law / 6th ed. – London : Butterworths, 1985.
ISBN 0406587981 Hbk £28.00
ISBN 040658799X Pbk £21.95

—Administrative law / by P.P. Craig. – London : Sweet & Maxwell, 1983.
xxxiii,636p; 25cm.
Includes index.
ISBN 0421270500 Hbk £21.00
ISBN 0421270608 Pbk £15.50

—Administrative law / by H.W.R. Wade. – 6th ed. – Oxford : Clarendon Press, 1988.
lxxi,1028p.
Includes bibliographical references and index.
ISBN 0198762194 pbk. £30.00
ISBN 0198762208 CASED £60.00

—Administrative Law / 6th ed. – London : Butterworths, 1986.
ISBN 0406584095 Hbk £32.00
ISBN 0406584109 Pbk £19.95

—Administrative Law : Cases and Materials / Matthews. – Oxford : Oxford University Press, 1983.
ISBN 0198253400 Hbk £37.50
ISBN 0198253419 Pbk £19.50

—Administrative law : cases and materials / M H Matthews. – 2nd ed. – Oxford : Clarendon Press, 1988.
700.
A sourcebook for those studying administrative law. The new edition has been revised to include the New Procedural System, Discretionary Powers, and Remedies.
Students in their second or third years
ISBN 0198762062 Hbk £35.00
ISBN 0198762054 Pbk £18.50

—Administrative law : cases and materials / by J. Beatson and M.H. Matthews. – Oxford Oxfordshire : Clarendon Press, 1983.
xxxiv,674p.
Includes index.
ISBN 0198253419 pbk.

—Administrative Law (ILT) / Morgan. – Sweet & Maxwell, 1986.
ISBN 0421330600 Pbk £21.00

—Cases and Materials on Administrative Law / Tracey. – 4th ed. – London : Butterworths, 1982.
ISBN 0409309192 Hbk £41.70
ISBN 0409309206 Pbk £31.60

—Collection of Statutes Connected With the General Administration of Law, 8 Vols. / Repr. of 1817 ed. – Abingdon : Professional Books.
116p.

—Comments on the Justice-All Souls discussion paper on administrative law (April 1981) : memorandum / by the Council's Law Reform Committee. – London : Law Society, 1981.
13,2p.

—Constitutional and Administrative Law / Plymouth : Macdonald & Evans, 1982.
ISBN 0712103988 Pbk £6.50

ELBS edition 1984
ISBN 0421333405 Hbk £3.50

—Constitutional and administrative law / Harry Street and Rodney Brazier; editors. – 5th ed. – Harmondsworth : Penguin, 1985.
748p.
ISBN 0140226109

—Constitutional and administrative law / de Smith. – 4th ed. – Harmondsworth : Penguin, 1981.
728p; 20cm. – (Penguin education).
Previous ed.: 1977. Includes index.
ISBN 0140804552 Pbk £6.95

—Constitutional and administrative law in a nutshell / Greer Hogan. – London : Sweet & Maxwell, 1987.
122p; 22cm.
Includes index.
ISBN 0421368101 Pbk £3.95

—Constitutional and Administrative Law (SWOT) / London : Blackstone Press, 1985.
ISBN 0906322723 Pbk £5.95

—Controlling the state : towards fairer administration / by an SDP working party on citizens' rights and the Social Democratic Lawyers' Association Working Party on Administrative Law : with a foreward by Robert MacLennan. – London : SDP Open Forum Committee, 1983.
26p.

—Discussion paper / J-AS Review of Administrative Law in the United Kingdom. – London : The Review, 1981.
97p.
ISBN 0907247016

—General Principles of Administrative Law / Lanham. – 2nd ed. – London : Butterworths, 1984.
ISBN 0409492515 Hbk £36.10

—Handbook on the Conduct of Administrative Tribunals / Sara Blake. – Toronto : Butterworths.
256p.

—Introduction to Administrative Law / Oxford : ESC Publishing Ltd, 1984.
296p.
ISBN 0906214254 Hbk £19.95
ISBN 0906214246 Pbk £11.95

—Introduction to administrative law / Oxford : Oxford University Press, 1986.
ISBN 0198254849 Hbk £25.00
ISBN 0198254857 Pbk £10.95

—Introduction to administrative law / Oxford : ESC, 1984.
ISBN 0906214246 Pbk £11.95
ISBN 0906214254 Hbk £19.95

—Introduction to administrative law / Peter Cane. – Oxford : Clarendon, 1986.
xxii,325p; 23cm. – (Clarendon law series).
Includes index.
ISBN 0198254849 Hbk £22.50
ISBN 0198254857 Pbk £ 9.50

—Law and administration / Carol Harlow, Richard Rawlings. – London : Weidenfeld and Nicolson, 1984.
xxvi,718p; 22cm.
Bibliography: p686-695. - Includes index.
ISBN 0297782398 Hbk No price
ISBN 0297782401 Pbk £15.95

—O. Hood Phillips' Constitutional and administrative law / Paul Jackson. – 7th ed. – London : Sweet & Maxwell, 1987.
lxxvi,808p; 26cm.
Previous ed.: 1978. Includes index.
ISBN 042135030X Hbk £21.00
ISBN 0421350407 Pbk £16.00

—Principles of administrative law / D.C.M. Yardley. – London : Butterworths, 1981.
xx,238p; 23cm.
Includes index.
ISBN 0406689911 Pbk
ISBN 0406689903

—Principles of administrative law / 2nd ed. – London : Butterworths, 1986.
ISBN 0406689938 Pbk £11.95

—Public Law / A. Bradley. – London : Sweet & Maxwell.

Bound Vol.

Single copy

Back Vols. avail.

—Public Law / 1st ed. – Plymouth : Macdonald & Evans, 1984.
260p.
ISBN 0712117598 Hbk £6.95

—Public law / London : Pitman Publishing, 1984.
ISBN 0712117598 Pbk £7.50

—Public law and politics / edited by Carol Harlow. – London : Sweet & Maxwell, 1986.
250p; 24cm.
Includes index.
ISBN 0421333901 £24.00

—Quasi-legislation : recent developments in secondary legislation / by Gabriele Ganz. – 2nd ed. – London : Sweet & Maxwell, 1987.
xiv,114p; 23cm.
New ed. - Previous ed.: published as Administrative procedures. 1974. Includes index.
ISBN 0421370203 Hbk £18.50
ISBN 0421298502 Pbk £10.95

—Regulation and public law / Robert Baldwin, Christopher McCrudden with contributions by Paul Craig ... et al. – London : Weidenfeld and Nicolson, 1987.
xx,399p; 22cm.
Bibliography: p332-347. - Includes index.
ISBN 0297787802 Hbk No price
ISBN 0297787810 Pbk £14.95

ADMINISTRATIVE LAW - INDIA

—Administrative Law and Tribunal / Calcutta : Eastern Law House, 1987.

—Administrative Law and Tribunals / 2nd ed. – Allahabad : Law Book Company, 1988.
700p.

ADMINISTRATIVE LAW - IRELAND

—Administrative Law / by David Gwynn Morgan and Gerard Hogan. – London : Sweet & Maxwell, 1986.
li,422p; 22cm.
Includes index.
ISBN 0421330600 Pbk £16.00

—Administrative Law in Ireland / Dublin : Institute of Public Administration, 1985.
514p.

—Administrative law in Ireland / Ronald M. Stout. – Dublin : Institute of Public Administration, 1985.
514p.
Includes index.
ISBN 0906980402 £25.00

ADMINISTRATIVE LAW - NEW ZEALAND

—Government directions to statutory bodies : nineteenth report / Public and Administrative Law Reform Committee. – Wellington : The Committee, 1986.
28p.

—Statutory functions and responsibilities of New Zealand public service departments 1979 / prepared by C.J. Barton : revised by J. Johnston. – Wellington : Government Printer, 1980.
329p.
Includes index.

ADMINISTRATIVE LAW - NIGERIA

—Administrative law of Nigeria / by A.R. Tyagi. – Dehra Dun : Afro-Asian Publishers, 1980.
99p.
Bibliography: p.93-99.

—Cases and materials on administrative law in Nigeria / B.O. Iluyomade, B.U. Eka. – Ile-Ife : University of Ife Press, 1980.
xxiii,295p; 26cm.
Includes index.
ISBN 9781360100

—Prerogative writs and orders under Nigerian law and constitution / by S.I.O. Aguolu. – Enugu : Star Printing and Publishing Company, 1981.
xxii,167p.
Includes index.

ADMINISTRATIVE LAW - SOUTH AFRICA

—Administrative Law / Durban : Professional Publisher, 1984.
ISBN 0409067040 Hbk £79.00
ISBN 0409067059 Pbk £69.00

—Administrative law / Lawrence Baxter. – Cape Town : Juta, 1984.
lxi,796p.
Includes bibliographical references and index.
ISBN 0702115118

ADMINISTRATIVE LAW - SRI LANKA

—Essays on Administrative Law / Colombo : Lake House Investments.

ADMINISTRATIVE LAW - WEST GERMANY

—German administrative law in common law perspective / Mahendra P. Singh. – Berlin : Springer-Verlag, 1985.
xxiv,194p.
Bibliography: p.188-191. - Includes index.
ISBN 0387156186

ADMINISTRATIVE PROCEDURE - CANADA - MANITOBA

—Report on administrative law / Manitoba Law Reform Commission. – Winnipeg : The Commission, 1987.
vi,243p. – (Report).
Includes bibliographical references.
ISBN 0771108338

ADMINISTRATIVE REMEDIES - AUSTRALIA

—Workings of the Administrative Appeals Tribunal : a selection of papers from a seminar organised by the Management and Policy Studies Group within the School of Administrative Studies in Canberra, 30 November--1 December 1979 / John Goldring, editor. – Belconnen, A.C.T. : Canberra College of Advanced Education, 1980.
71 p.; 26 cm.
Includes bibliographical references.
ISBN 0858891824 pbk.

ADMINISTRATIVE REMEDIES - AUSTRALIA - WESTERN AUSTRALIA

—Report on judicial review of administrative decisions : procedural aspects and the right to reasons / Law Reform Commission of Western Australia. – Perth : The Commission, 1986.
77p. – (Project).
Includes bibliographical references.

—Report on review of administrative decisions : part 1, appeals / the Law Reform Commission of Western Australia. – Perth : The Commission, 1982.
114p. – (Project).

ADMINISTRATIVE REMEDIES – HONG KONG
—Survey of the complaint-handling institutions in Hong Kong / by Rebecca Wong Kit Lin. – Edmonton : International Ombudsman Institute, 1983.
19 leaves. – (Occasional paper).

ADMINISTRATIVE RESPONSIBILITY – UNITED STATES
—Suing government : citizen remedies for official wrongs / Peter H. Schuck. – New Haven : Yale University Press, 1983.
xxi,262p; 22cm.
Includes index.
ISBN 0300029578 Hbk

ADMISSIONS (LAW) – AUSTRALIA
—Evidence reference / Australian Law Reform Commission. – Sydney : The Commission, 1983.
xxxviii,340p.
Bibliography: p.334-340.

ADMISSIONS (LAW) – AUSTRALIA – NEW SOUTH WALES
—Criminal procedure : unsworn statements of accused persons : report / New South Wales Law Reform Commission. – Sydney : The Commission, 1985.
70p. – (L.R.C. 45).
Bibliography: p.65-66.
ISBN 0730514269 Hbk

ADOLESCENTS
—Laws and policies affecting adolescent health / by John M. Paxman and Ruth Jane Zuckerman. – Geneva : World Health Organization, 1987.
x,300p.
Includes bibliographical references.
ISBN 9241560959

ADOLESCENTS – ENGLAND
—Childright : a bulletin of law and policy affecting children and young people in England and Wales / v. – London : The Children's Legal Centre, 1983.
ISBN 02651459

ADOPTION – CANADA
—Step-Parent Adoptions / North Vancouver : International Self-Counsel Press, 1987.
ISBN 0889086605 Hbk £12.95

ADOPTION – ENGLAND
—Adoption act manual / Richard M. Jones. – London : Sweet & Maxwell, 1988.
vii,263p.
Includes the amended form of the 1976 Act, relevant statutory instruments, and DHSS circulars, and annotated version of the Adoption Rules 1984, the Magistrates Court (Adoption Rules) 1984.
ISBN 0421393505 £15.00

—Adoption practice and procedure / by Nasreen Pearce. – London : Fourmat, 1984.
xii,133p; 22cm.
Includes index.
ISBN 0906840791 Pbk No price

ADOPTION – GREAT BRITAIN
—Adoption / Tavistock, 1984.
ISBN 0422784109 Hbk £19.95

—Adoption Act Manual / London : Sweet & Maxwell, 1988.
ISBN 0421393505 Pbk £18.00

—Adoption Of Children / Levy. – 10th ed. – London : Longman Professional, 1985.
ISBN 0851208665 Pbk £24.00

—Adoption of Children / 9th ed. – London : Oyez Longman, 1980.
– (Oyez Longman Practice Note Ser.: No. 3).
ISBN 0851205410 Hbk £9.95

—Law relating to children and young persons / Clarke Hall and Morrison. – 10th ed. 2. – London : Butterworths, 1985.
looseleaf.
Includes index. Includes the text of the relevant legislation. Spine title: Clarke Hall & Morrison on children. Kept up-to-date by supplements.
ISBN 0406158126

—Mine, Yours Or Ours? A Study of Step-parent Adoption / London : HMSO, 1983.
136p.
Discusses the effect of the changes in law on adoption recommended by the Houghton Committee and enacted in the 1975 Children's Act.
ISBN 0113208359 Pbk £3.95

ADOPTION – MALAYSIA
—Registration of Adoptions Act, 1952 (Act 253) and Adoptions Act, 1952 (Act 257) / Kuala Lumpur : International Law Books Services.

ADOPTION – SCOTLAND
—Adoption of children in Scotland / Peter G.B. McNeill. – Edinburgh : W. Green, 1982.
xx,208p.
Includes index.
ISBN 0414006895

—Adoption of children in Scotland / 2nd. – Edinburgh : W Green & Son, 1986.
Deals with adoptions in the sequence which occurs in practice and the relevant statute and case law. The appendices contain the Adoption (Scot.) Act 1978, the rules of court, and styles of writs, interlocutors and reports.
ISBN 0414007794

ADOPTION – SINGAPORE
—Parent-Child Law in Singapore / Singapore : Butterworths, 1984.
The book provides a discussion of legitimacy, maintenance, guardianship, and adoption under the law of Singapore. The 1980 amendments to the Women's Charter pertaining to maintenance, welfare and custody of children are analyzed in depth.
ISBN 0406181217 Pbk

ADOPTION – UNITED KINGDOM
—Guide to the New Law of Family Proceedings in Magistrates Courts, Including Adoption / Chichester : Barry Rose, 1983.
ii, 49p.
ISBN 0859920631 Hbk £4.60

ADOPTION (HINDU LAW)
—Hindu Adoption and Maintenance Act / 2nd ed. – Allahabad : Law Book Company, 1985.

—Hindu Minority and Guardianship : and Hindu Adoptions and Maintenance Act / 2nd ed. – Allahad : Law Book Company, 1986.
200p.

ADVERSE POSSESSION – INDIA
—Law of Adverse Possession / 2nd ed. – Allahabad : Law Publishers, 1983.

—Law of Adverse Possession / 11th ed. – Allahabad : Law Book Company, 1988.
650p.

ADVERSE POSSESSION – NEW ZEALAND
—Prescriptive title for a co-owner in possession / report of the Property Law and Equity Reform Committee. – Wellington : Government Printer, 1986.
17p.

ADVERTISING
—Advertising and marketing law and practice / London : Frank Cass, 1984-.
Continues: Advertising law and practice.

—Protection of personal data used for the purposes of direct marketing : recommendation no. R(85) 20 adopted by the Committee of Ministers of the Council of Europe on 25 October 1985 and Explanatory memorandum / Council of Europe. – Strasbourg : Council of Europe, 1986.
19p.
Prepared by the committee of experts on data protection set up under the authority of the European Committee on Legal Co-operation. At head of cover title: Council of Europe, Legal Affairs.
ISBN 9287108765

ADVERTISING – AUSTRALIA
—Advertising regulation / by Shenagh Barnes and Michael Blakeney. – Sydney : Law Book Co., 1982.
lii,612p.
Bibliography: p.xlv-lii. - Includes index.
ISBN 0455205450

—Federal deceptive practices and misleading advertising law : judgements, materials and policy / Warren Pengilley and Alan A. Ransom. – Sydney : Legal Books Pty., 1987.
lxiii,1184p.
Bibliography: pp.1021-1022. - Includes index.
ISBN 0949553344

ADVERTISING – AUSTRALIA – NEW SOUTH WALES
—Advertising and specialisation / New South Wales Law Reform Commission. – Sydney : The Commission, 1981.
xxxv,244p; 25cm. – (Discussion paper no 5).
Bibliography: p.228-244.

ADVERTISING – ENGLAND
—Essex County Newspapers Limited : a report by the Director General of Fair Trading on an investigation under Section 3 of the Competition Act 1980 / Office of Fair Trading. – London : Office of Fair Trading, 1983.
41p; 30cm.

—Marketing Legal services / edited by S.C. Silkin. – London : Waterlows, 1984.
86p; 21cm.
Conference papers.
ISBN 0080392156 Pbk £10.50

ADVERTISING – EUROPEAN COMMUNITY
—European regulation of advertising : supranational regulation of advertising in the European economic community / by Rein Rijkens, Gordon E. Miracle. – Amsterdam : North-Holland, 1986.
xxxiv, 375 p.; 25 cm.
Includes index. Bibliography: p. 337-358.
ISBN 0444879722 CIP rev.

ADVERTISING – GREAT BRITAIN
—Advertising and charging rules of the professions serving the construction industry : a report by the Director General of Fair Trading / London : Office of Fair Trading, 1986.
84p.
Bibliography: p.60-63.

—Advertising By Solicitors - A Guide / Stewart (Henry), 1984.
ISBN 0946700109 Pbk £12.50

—Advertising by the professions : a review of the remaining significant restrictions / a report by the Director General of Fair Trading. – London : Office of Fair Trading, 1986.
56p.

—British Broadcasting Corporation and Independent Television Publications Limited : the publication of programme information : a report by the Director General of Fair Trading on investigations under section 3 of the Competition Act 1980 / London : Office of Fair Trading, 1984.
72p; 30cm.

—British Railways Board : Facilities for car hire and advertising of self-drive vehicle hire at railway stations / report by the Director General of Fair Trading on an investigation under section 3 of the Competition Act 1980. – London : Office of Fair Trading, 1983.
47p; 30cm.

—British Telecommunications : (pricing policy for the placing of advertisements in yellow pages directories) : a report / by the Director General of Fair Trading .. – London : Office of Fair Trading, 1984.
54p; 30cm.

—Holmes McDougall Ltd. : restriction of advertisements containing prices : a report by the Director General of Fair Trading on an investigation under section 3 of the Competition Act 1980 / London : Office of Fair Trading, 1985.
39p; 30cm.

—Solicitor's guide to advertising & publicity / Stephen Townley. – 5 pamphlets. – London : Professional Direction and Sweet & Maxwell, 1985.
49p; in folder, 22x31cm.
Authors: Stephen Townley et al.
ISBN 0421342706 £39.50

—Trade Description Act 1970 / London : Wildy & Sons.

—World's Fair Limited and Marcus Publishing PLC : refusal to publish advertisements which contain certain price information : a report by the Director General of Fair Trading on two investigations under section 3 of the Competition Act 1980 / Office of Fair Trading. – London : Office of Fair Trading, 1987.
30p.

ADVERTISING – GREAT BRITAIN – SELF-REGULTAION
—British code of advertising practice / Code of Advertising Prcatice Committee. – 7th ed. – London : Code of Advertising Practice Committee, 1985.
94p.
Includes index. ' ... under the general supervision of the Advertising Standards Authority'. - p.4.

ADVERTISING – LAWYERS – GREAT BRITAIN
—Advertising by solicitors : a guide / Eric Granados. – London : Stewart (Henry), 1984.
107p.
ISBN 0946700109

AFFILIATON – GREAT BRITAIN
—Affiliation Law and Practice / 5th ed. – London : Longman Professional, 1985.
ISBN 0851209912 Pbk £15.95

AGE (LAW)
—Aging world : dilemmas and challenges for law and social policy / edited by John Eekelaar and D. Pearl. – Oxford : OUP, 1989.
900.
Critical examination on an international basis of the problems facing legal and social systems due to an increasing number of elderly within the world's population.*Lawyers, demographers, economists, sociologists and political scientists interested in problems of aging populations*
ISBN 0198254091 Pbk £39.50

AGE (LAW) - HONG KONG
—Report : young persons : effects of age in civil law / the Law Reform Commission of Hong Kong. - Hong Kong : The Commission, 1986. various pagings. - (Topic 11).

AGE (LAW) - IRELAND
—Report on the law relating to the age of majority, the age for marriage and some connected subjects / the Law Reform Commission. - Dublin : The Commission, 1983. v,75p. - (LRC).

AGE (LAW) - SOUTH AFRICA
—Investigation into the advancement of the age of majority / South African Law Commission. - Pretoria : The Commission, 1985.
xviii,63p. - (Report).
Includes bibliographical references.
ISBN 0621102466

AGE OF CONSENT - ENGLAND
—Report on the age of consent in relation to sexual offences / Policy Advisory Committee on Sexual Offences : presented to Parliament by the Secretary of State for the Home Department. - London : H.M.S.O., 1981.
v,32p; 25cm.
ISBN 0101821603 unbound £2.70

AGE OF CONSENT - IRELAND
—Report on the law relating to the age of majority, the age for marriage and some connected subjects / the Law Reform Commission. - Dublin : The Commission, 1983. v,75p. - (LRC).

AGE OF CONSENT - SOUTH AFRICA
—Investigation into the advancement of the age of majority / South African Law Commission. - Pretoria : The Commission, 1985.
xviii,63p. - (Report).
Includes bibliographical references.
ISBN 0621102466

AGENCY
—Agency / Stockholm : Anderson Keenan, 1981. - (Law Unit).
ISBN 0906501237 Pbk £3.00

—International agency, distribution and licensing agreements / London : Longman Professional, 1986.
ISBN 0851211887 Hbk £45.00

—International factoring / by Anthony N. Cox and John A. MacKenzie. - London : Euromoney Publications, 1986.
xv,112p.
ISBN 0903121913

—Law of Agency / Lucknow : Eastern Book Company, 1985.
784p.

—UNIDROIT : Draft Convention on Agency in the International Sale of Goods : memorandum / by a working party of the Council's Law Reform Committee. - London : Law Society, 1983.
2p.

AGENCY - AUSTRALIA - NEW SOUTH WALES
—Sale of Real Property and Law of Agency in New South Wales / R. Sorenson. - 4th ed. - Butterworths, 1983.
176p.
ISBN 0409494119 Pbk £26.00

AGENCY - AUSTRALIA - QUEENSLAND
—Sale of Real Property and Law of Agency in Queensland / W.B. Hutchinson. - Butterworths, 1986.
160p.
This is a working guide for students and those involved with conveyancing transactions. Included are materials on contracts for sale of land, strata titles, registration of titles, agents, commissions, unjust contracts, valuations of land, land subdivisions, and local authority requirements for land development.
ISBN 0409491179 Pbk £26.00

AGENCY - CANADA
—Introduction to business associations in Canada : cases, notes, and materials / by R.L. Simmonds and Peter P. Mercer. - Toronto, Canada : Carswell Legal Publications, 1984.
xxviii, 778 p.; 25 cm.
Spine title: Business associations in Canada.
ISBN 0459365304 pbk.

—Real estate agency law / William F. Foster. - Toronto : Carswell, 1984.
xliii,272p.
Includes bibliographical references and index.
ISBN 0459370502

AGENCY - ENGLAND
—Bowstead on agency / F. M. B. Reynolds. - 15th ed. - London : Sweet & Maxwell, 1985.
cvi,559p; 26cm.
Previous ed.: 1976. Includes index.
ISBN 0421285508 £75

—Casebook on agency / by E.R. Hardy Ivamy. - 2nd ed. - London : Lloyds of London Press, 1980.
xxi,143p.
ISBN 0904093875

—Casebook on agency / E.R. Hardy Ivamy. - 3rd ed. - London : Lloyd's, 1987.
160p; 22cm.
Previous ed.: 1980. Includes index.
ISBN 185044112X Pbk £15.00 (Jan.)

—Law of agency / G.H.L. Fridman. - 5th ed. - London : Butterworths, 1983.
xxxvii, 386p.
This text gives an in-depth exploration of the law of agency. Primary emphasis is put on the evolution of agency law in the United Kingdom through the pure common law system into a coherent set of rules.
ISBN 0406584362 HBK
ISBN 0406584370 PBK

—Law of estate agency and auctions / by J.R. Murdoch. - 2nd ed. - London : Estates Gazette, 1984.
xlii,576p.
Includes bibliographical references and index.

—Outline of the law of agency / by B.S. Markesinis and R.J.C. Munday. - 2nd. - London : Butterworths, 1986.
296p; 22cm.
Previous ed.: 1979. Includes index.
ISBN 040662271X Hbk £12.00 (June)
ISBN 0406622728 Pbk £8.50

AGENCY - EUROPEAN COMMUNITY
—Distributorship, Franchising, Agency : Community and National Laws and Practice in the EEC / Dordrecht : Kluwer, 1987.
274p.
ISBN 9065443290 Hbk £120.00

AGENCY - GREAT BRITAIN
—Incapacitated principal : report on a reference under section 3(1)(e) of the Law Commissions Act 1965 / the Law Commission. - London : H.M.S.O., 1983.
v,104p; 25cm.
ISBN 0101897707

—Law of Agency / 5th ed. - London : Butterworths, 1983.
ISBN 0406584370 Pbk £18.95

—Law of Agricultural Holdings / Densham. - 7th ed. - London : Butterworths, 1988.
ISBN 0406368139 Hbk

—Outline of the law of agency / Munday. - 2nd ed. - London : Butterworths, 1986.
ISBN 040662271X Hbk £15.00
ISBN 0406622728 Pbk £9.95

—Tolley's factoring : a guide to factoring practice and law / by F.R. Salinger. - Croydon : Tolley, 1984.
xvii,253p; 23cm.
Includes index.
ISBN 0854591648 Pbk £17.50

AGENCY - INDIA
—Law of Agency / 2nd ed. - Allahabad : Law Book Company, 1986.
918p.

AGENCY - SCOTLAND
—Scottish cases on agency / Edinburgh : W Green & Son, 1980.
First collection of cases concerning this fundamental branch of Scottish mercantile law.
ISBN 0414006577 SOFTBACK

AGENCY - SOUTH AFRICA
—Law of agency in South Africa / De Villiers and Macintosh. - 3rd ed. - Cape Town : Juta, 1981.
lxviii,684p.
Previous ed.: 1956. Includes index.
ISBN 0702112542

AGGRESSION (INTERNATIONAL LAW)
—Current legal regulation of the use of force / edited by A. Cassese. - Dordrecht : Martinus Nijhoff, 1986.
xiv,536p.
Includes bibliographical references.

AGRICULTURAL HOLDINGS
—Agricultural tenancies : law and practice / by C.P. Rodgers : consulting editor C.V. Margrave-Jones. - London : Butterworth, 1985.
xxxvii,447p; 25cm.
Includes index. Chapter 13 by C.V. Margrave-Jones.
ISBN 0406258406 Pbk £20.00

AGRICULTURAL HOLDINGS - GREAT BRITAIN
—Agricultural Holdings / Oxford : Blackwell Scientific, 1987.
ISBN 0003833364 Hbk £20.00

—Agricultural Holdings Act / Sweet & Maxwell, 1986.
ISBN 0421318007 Hbk £95.00

—Law of Agricultural Holdings / H. A. C. Densham. - 7th ed. - London : Butterworths, 1987.
A thorough treatment of the United Kingdom law of agricultural holdings is included in this text. The work presents a commentary on the law, statutes and statutory instruments, and useful forms and precedents.
ISBN 0406368139 Hbk

AGRICULTURAL HOLDINGS - SCOTLAND
—Law of agricultural holdings in Scotland / Brian Gill. - Edinburgh : Green, 1982.
xxxiv,451p; 25cm.
Includes index. Includes text of 6 acts.
ISBN 0444996656 SET

AGRICULTURAL INSURANCE
—Agricultural insurance legislation / by Beatriz Benilde Galan for Land and Water Legislation Section, Legislation Branch, Legal Office. - Rome : Food and Agriculture Organization of the United Nations, 1981.
vii, 149 p.; 27 cm. - (Legislative study).
ISBN 9251010358 £2.50

AGRICULTURE
—Agricultural census legislation / a joint publication by the Statistics Division and the Legislation Branch, Legal Office. - Rome : Food and Agriculture Organization of the United nations, 1984.
v,117p. - (Legislative study).
ISBN 9251013772

—Food and Agriculture Legislation / Food and Agriculture Organization of the United Nations. - London : HMSO, 1984.
115p.
ISBN 0119410133 Pbk £4.50

—General survey on the application of the conventions on freedom of association, the right to organise and collective bargaining and the convention and recommendation concerning rural workers' organisations : third item on the agenda / International Labour Office. - Geneva : International Labour Office, 1983.
157p.
Cover title: Freedom of association and collective bargaining. Report III (Part 4B).
ISBN 9221031284

—Grain contracts and arbitration for shipments from the United States and Canada / by Albert Slabotzky. - London : Lloyd's, 1984.
x,109p.
Bibliography: p.105-106. - Includes index.
ISBN 0907432883

—Legislation on Productivity in Agriculture : a Comparative Outline / Rome : FAO, Food and Agricultural Organization of the United Nations, 1985.
80p.
ISBN 9251021945 Hbk £6.00

AGRICULTURE - AFRICA
—Agribusiness in Africa : a study of the impact of big business on Africa's food and agricultural production / Barbara Dinham & Colin Hines. - London : Earth Resources Research, 1983.
224p b ill; 21cm.
Includes index. Cover title.
ISBN 0946281009 Pbk £4.95

AGRICULTURE - AUSTRALIA
—Law of Fences and Pastures Protection, NSW / 2nd ed. - North Ryde : Law Book Co, 1984.
xxi, 208p.
ISBN 0455202788 Pbk £37.00

—Rationalising Rustic Regulation / Turramura : Centre for Independent Studies.
96p.
ISBN 0949769029 Hbk £5.50

AGRICULTURE - CANADA
—Agriculture / Agincourt : Carswell, 1983.
240p.
This textbook describes in detail all of the aspects of agricultural law as it is derived from the common law, statutes, and regulatory bodies of the Canadian federal and provincial governments. Extensive references are made to marketing boards, loan associations, and federal and provincial regulating authorities in the work.

—Agriculture : The Legal Framework / Aurora : Canada Law Book Co, 1982.
300p. - (Text Books-Civil).

—Canadian Farm Law / Saskatoon : Western Producer Prairie Books, 1982.
145p.
ISBN 0888330871 Pbk £8.95

AGRICULTURE - ENGLAND

—Green and pleasant land? : social change in rural England / Howard Newby : cartoons by Thelwell. – Updated ed. – London : Wildwood House, 1985.
324 p.
ISBN 0704505053

AGRICULTURE - EUROPEAN COMMUNITY

—Common Agricultural Policy of the European Community : its institutional and administrative organisation / Rosemary Fennell. – 2nd ed. – Oxford : BSP Professional, 1987.
xii,227p; 24cm.
Previous ed.: London : Granada, 1979. Bibliography: p215-220. - Includes index.
ISBN 0632020571 £19.95

—Common Agricultural Policy : past, present and future / Brian E. Hill. – London : Methuen, 1984.
xvi,168p; 23cm. – (The Methuen EEC series).
Bibliography: p160-163. - Includes index.
ISBN 0416321801 Hbk Unpriced
ISBN 0416321909 Pbk Unpriced

—Common agricultural policy, prospects for change / Joan Pearce. – London : Published for Royal Institute of International Affairs by Routledge & K. Paul, 1981.
122p.
Includes bibliographical references.
ISBN 0710090692

—Common ground : how changes in the Common Agricultural Policy affect the Third World / by Adrian Moyes. – Oxford : Oxfam, 1987.
98p; 21cm.
ISBN 0855980788 Pbk £1.50

—Food and farm policies of the European Community / Simon Harris, Alan Swinbank and Guy Wilkinson. – Chichester : Wiley, 1983.
xii,354p; 24cm.
Includes bibliographies and index.
ISBN 047110261X £12.50

—Law of the Common Agricultural Policy / by Francis G. Snyder. – London : Sweet & Maxwell, 1985.
130p; 22cm.
Includes index.
ISBN 0421318805 Hbk £11.50 :
ISBN 0421318902 Pbk £6.50

—Leading Cases and Materials on the Agricultural Policy of the E.E.C. / H.J. Bronkhorst. – Dordrecht : Kluwer, 1984.
ca 250p.
ISBN 9065440704 Hbk £55.00

—Legal aspects of agriculture in the European Community / J.A. Usher. – Oxford : Clarendon Press, 1988.
xxxvi,170p.
Includes index. Examines legal issues arising from the Common Agricultural Policy, and sets out the principles underlying changing legislation. Includes agricultural legislation which is behind European Court case law on the relationship between Community law and national law.
ISBN 0198255659 Hbk £30

—New agricultural structures policy / Luxembourg : Office for Official Publications of the European Communities, 1985.
16p.

—Perspectives for the Common Agricultural Policy / communication of the Commission to the Council and the Parliament. – Luxembourg : Office for Official Publications of the European Communities, 1985.
viii,62p. – (Document).
Includes a statistical annex.
ISBN 9277070285

—Why do we sell butter to Russia? : and other common questions from the Common Market / by Nicholas Bethell. – London : European Democratic Group, 1987.
9 p.

AGRICULTURE - GREAT BRITAIN

—Agricultural Holdings / 13th. 1 volume, supplement. – London : Sweet & Maxwell, 1987.
xxiv,200p.
States the law contained in the Agricultural Holdings Act 1986. Includes the nature and inception of the tenancy of an agricultural holding, termination by notice to quit and otherwise, and the procedure of agricultural land tribunals. Chapter on arbitration revised. Includes annotations, text of statutory instruments, and forms.
ISBN 0421318007 Hbk £95.00

—Agricultural law / C Margrave-Jones. – London : Longman Professional (UK), 1989.
Covers the Agricultural Holdings Act of 1984 and 1986 tenancies, tied accomodation, security of tenure and its removal, and succession to holdings. Sets out cases for possession and compulsory purchase and the relevant compensatory proceedings. Also deals with taxation, public control of land use, resolving agricultural disputes, and European Agricultural law.
ISBN 0851214290 Hbk £27.50

—Agricultural law / McKay. – London : Longman Professional (UK), 1990.
Coverage includes agricultural holdings, milk quotas, product liability, finance and taxation, pollution, employment law, competition law, agrochemicals, recreation and diversification, contracts, housing and share farming.

—Agricultural Valuations / London : Estates Gazette, 1985.
ISBN 0728200872 Pbk £11.00

—Agriculture, the countryside and land use : an economic critique / J.K. Bowers and Paul Cheshire. – London : Methuen, 1983.
x,170p; 20cm.
Includes index.
ISBN 0416318304 Pbk Unpriced

—Countryside law / Garner. – London : Shaw & Sons, 1987.
ISBN 0721910602 Pbk £9.95

—Countryside Law / J. F. Garner. – London : Shaw & Sons, 1987.
ISBN 0721910602 Pbk £9.95

—Farming Futures / Cambridge : Woodhead-Faulkner, 1984.
ISBN 0859412830 Hbk £12.50

—Grain Contracts and Arbitration / London : Lloyd's of London Press, 1984.
ISBN 0907432883 Hbk £24.00

—Law and the countryside / Abingdon : Professional Books, 1987.
ISBN 0862052564 Hbk £37.50

—Taxation of farmers and landowners / 3rd. – London : Butterworths, 1987.
ISBN 040638391X Hbk £20.00

AGRICULTURE - INDIA

—Uttar Pradesh Agricultural Credit Act, 1973 / 4th ed. repr. – Lucknow : Eastern Book Company, 1985.

AGRICULTURE - PHILIPPINES

—Code of Agrarian Reform of the Philippines / Quezon City : University of the Philippines, Law Center, 1981.
338p.

—Philippine Agrarian Reform and The New Taxation / A.O. Yoingco. – Quezon City : Katha Publishing Co., 1983.

AGRICULTURE - SCOTLAND

—Aspects of agricultural law / Edinburgh : Law Society of Scotland, 1981.
93p.
Includes index.
ISBN 0902023055

—Law of agricultural holdings in Scotland / Brian Gill. – Edinburgh : Green, 1982.
xxxiv,451p; 25cm.
Includes index. Includes text of 6 acts.
ISBN 0444996656 SET

AGRICULTURE - SOUTH AFRICA

—Law and Finance for the Farmer / Davis. – Cape Town : Legal and Financial Publishing Co.

AGRICULTURE AND STATE - EUROPEAN ECONOMIC COMMUNITY COUNTRIES

—Agriculture and the European Community / John S. Marsh, Pamela J. Swanney. – London : Allen & Unwin, 1980.
98p; 23cm.
Bibliography: p91-96. - Includes index.
ISBN 0043380921 Hbk £8.95
ISBN 004338093X Pbk No price

AIDS (DISEASE) - AUSTRALIA - NEW SOUTH WALES

—Acquired immune deficiency syndrome (A.I.D.S.) : guidelines for the testing of antibodies to the HTLV - III (A.I.D.S.) virus / Privacy Committee. – Sydney : The Committee, 1986.
5 leaves.

AIDS (DISEASE) - GREAT BRITAIN

—AIDS and Employment Law / Howard. – London : Financial Training, 1988.
ISBN 1851850937 Pbk £14.95

AIDS (DISEASE) - UNITED STATES

—AIDS and the law : a guide for the public / edited by Harlon L. Dalton, Scott Burris and the Yale AIDS Law Project. – New Haven : Yale University Press, 1987.
384p; 24cm.
Includes bibliography and index.
ISBN 0300040776 Hbk £19.95 :
ISBN 0300040784 Pbk £6.95

AIR LAW

—Aeronautical agreements and arrangements : tables of agreements and arrangements registered with the Organization, 1 January 1946 - 31 December 1985 / International Civil Aviation Organization. – 14th ed. – Montreal : International Civil Aviation Orgainization, 1986.
vi,373p. – (Doc 9460-LGB/382).
Kept up to date by supplements and lists. Supplements held: 1st, 1986; 2nd, 1987.

—Aeronautical agreements and arrangements : tables of agreements and arrangements registered with the Organization, 1 January 1946-31 December 1979 / International Civil Aviation Organization. – 13th ed. – Montreal : International Civil Aviation Organization, 1980.
xiv,244p. – (Doc 9307-LGB/347).
Kept up to date by supplements and lists. .

—Air and outer space law / Thessaloniki : Institute of International Public Law and International Relations of Thessaloniki, 1981.
xvi,842p.
Includes bibliographies. Includes chapters in French and German.

—Air cargo : regulation and claims / Jean-Louis Magdelenat. – Toronto : Butterworths, 1983.
xxvi,181p.
Bibliography: p.177-181. Summarizes the rules of liability. governing the carriage of goods by air. Surveys the economic and technical aspects of air cargo, systematically considering all their legal ratifications.
ISBN 0409847836 Hbk £55

—Air law / v. – Deventer : Kluwer, 1975.
Index in each vol.
ISBN 01652079

—Air transport and the consumer : a need for change? : a report on air transport regulation in Europe / National Consumer Council. – London : H.M.S.O., 1986.
xiii,251p.
Includes bibliographical references.
ISBN 0117012688

—Air worthy : liber amicorum, honouring Professor Dr. I.H.Ph. Diederiks-Verschoor / editors J.W.E. Storm van's Gravesande and A. van der Veen Vonk. – Deventer : Kluwer, 1985.
xv,301p.
Bibliography: p.293-301.
ISBN 9065442316

—Annals of Air and Space Law /. – Montreal : Centre for Research of Air and Space Law, 1980.

Vol. 6 1981.

Vol. 7 1982.

Vol. 8 1983.
570p.

Vol. 9 1984.
583p.

Vol. 10 1985.
609p.

Vol. 11 1986.
484p.

Vol. 12 1987.

—Assembly resolutions in force : (as of 10 May 1984) / International Civil Aviation Organization. – 1 v. – Montreal : I.C.A.O., 1984.
various pagings. – (Doc).
Includes index.

—Assembly resolutions in force : (as of 10 October 1986) / International Civil Aviation Organization. – 1. – Montreal : International Civil Aviation Organization, 1986.
various pagings. – (Doc.).
Published by authority of the Secretary General.

—Assembly resolutions in force : (as of 7 October 1980) / International Civil Aviation Organization. – 1. – Montreal : International Civil Aviation Organization, 1981.
various pagings. – (Doc).

—Aviation security : digest of current ICAO policies and actions on the subject of unlawful interference with international civil aviation and its facilities / International Civil Aviation Organization. – 4th ed. – Montreal : International Civil Aviation Organization, 1987.
iii,36p. – (Doc 8849-C/990/4).
Decisions taken and work done by ICAO on the subject of unlawful interference with international civil aviation and its facilities. Includes the texts of three international conventions.

—Competition among international airlines / by Richard Pryke. – Aldershot : Gower for the Trade Policy Research Centre, 1987.
100p; 22cm.
Includes bibliography.
ISBN 0566053330 Pbk £9.00

—Essays in air law / edited by Arnold Kean. – The Hague : Nijhoff, 1982.
xvi, 369 p.; 25 cm.
Includes index.
ISBN 9024725437 Hbk £170.00

—Flying off course : the economics of international airlines / Rigas Doganis. – London : Allen & Unwin, 1985.
ix,271p; 23cm.
Bibliography: p260-264. - Includes index.
ISBN 004387004X £18.00

—IATA review / v. – Geneva : International Air Transport Association, 1985-.
Supersedes: IATA world airline cooperation review.

—International Aviation Law Seminar : the Mount Irvine Bay Hotel, Tobago, West Indies March 16, 17, 18, 19, 1981 / organised by Lloyd's of London Press : sponsored by the Royal Aeronautical Society. – London : Lloyd's of London Press, 1982.
349p; 31cm.
ISBN 0907432271 Unpriced

—International Bibliography of Air Law 1900-1971. Supplements / Dordrecht : Kluwer, 1976.
xxii, 169p.
ISBN 9028605266 Hbk £64.00

1977-1980 1981.
394p.
ISBN 9024725550 Hbk £160.00

1981-1984 1985.
284p.
ISBN 9065442308 Hbk £104.00

—International Conference on Air Law, Montreal, September 1978 : minutes and documents / Montreal : International Civil Aviation Organization, 1982.
viii,383p. – (Doc. 9357-LC/183).
Includes documents in English, French, Russian and Spanish.

—International standards : aircraft nationality and registration marks : annex 7 to the Convention on International Civil Aviation / International Civil Aviation Organization. – 4th ed. - July 1981. 1. – Montreal : International Civil Aviation Organization, 1981.
loose-leaf.
Kept up to date by amendments and supplements.

—International standards and recommended practices : aeronautical charts : annex 4 to the Convention on International Civil Aviation / International Civil Aviation Organization. – 8th ed. 1 v. – Montreal : International Civil Aviation Organization, 1985.
looseleaf.
Kept up to date by amendments and supplements.

—International standards and recommended practices : aeronautical information services : annex 15 to the Convention on International Civil Aviation / International Civil Aviation Organization. – 7th ed. - July 1987. 1. – Montreal : International Civil Aviation Organization, 1987.
looseleaf.
Kept up to date by amendments and supplements.

—International standards and recommended practices : air traffic services ... : annex 11 to the Convention on International Civil Aviation / International Civil Aviation Organization. – 8th ed. - July 1987. 1. – Montreal : International Civil Aviation Organization, 1987.
looseleaf.
Kept up to date by amendments and supplements.

—International standards and recommended practices : aircraft accident investigation : annex 13 to the Convention on International Civil Aviation / International Civil Aviation Organization. – 7th ed. 1. – Montreal : International Civil Aviation Organization, 1988.
looseleaf.
Kept up to date by amendments and supplements.

—International standards and recommended practices : airworthiness of aircraft : annex 8 to the Convention on International Civil Aviation / International Civil Aviation Organization. – 7th ed. - April 1983. 1. – Montreal : International Civil Aviation Organization, 1983.
looseleaf.
Kept up to date by amendments and supplements.

—International standards and recommended practices : environmental protection : annex 16 to the Convention on International Civil Aviation / International Civil Aviation Organization. – 1st ed - 1981. 1. – Montreal : International Civil Aviation Organization, 1981.
loose-leaf; 28cm.
Supersedes: International standards and recommended practices: aircraft noise: annex 16 to the Convention on International Civil Aviation. 3rd ed. - July 1978. Current edition only kept. Kept up to date by amendments and supplements.

—International standards and recommended practices : meteorological service for international air navigation : annex 3 to the Convention on International Civil Aviation / International Civil Aviation Organization. – 10th ed. - July 1986. 1. – Montreal : International Civil Aviation Organisation, 1986.
looseleaf.
Kept up to date by amendments and supplements.

—International standards and recommended practices : operation of aircraft : annex 6 to the Convention on International Civil Aviation / International Civil Aviation Organization. – 4th ed. - July 1983. 1. – Montreal : International Civil Aviation Organization, 1983.
looseleaf.
Kept up to date by amendments and supplements.

Part 2 : International general aviation 1983.
looseleaf.
Kept up to date by amendments and supplements.

Part 3 : International operations - helicopters 1986.
looseleaf.
Kept up to date by amendments and supplements.

—International standards and recommended practices : personnel licensing : annex 1 to the Convention on International Civil Aviation / International Civil Aviation Organization. – 7th ed. - September 1982. 1. – Montreal : International Civil Aviation Organization, 1982.
looseleaf.
Kept up to date by amendments and supplements.

—International standards and recommended practices : security : safeguarding international civil aviation against acts of unlawful interference : annex 17 to the Convention on International Civil Aviation / International Civil Aviation Organization. – 3rd ed. 1. – Montreal : International Civil Aviation Organization, 1986.
looseleaf.
Kept up to date by amendments and supplements.

—International standards and recommended practices : the safe transport of dangerous goods by air : annex 18 to the Convention on International Civil Aviation / International Civil Aviation Organization. – 1st ed. - January 1983. 1 v. – Montreal : International Civil Aviation Organization, 1983.
looseleaf.

—International standards, recommended practices and procedures for air navigation services : aeronautical telecommunications : annex 10 to the Convention on International Civil Aviation / International Civil Aviation Organization. – 4th ed. 1 v. – Montreal : International Civil Aviation Organization, 1985.
looseleaf.
Kept up to date by amendments and supplements.

—International standards : rules of the air : annex 2 to the Convention on International Civil Aviation / International Civil Aviation Organization. – 8th ed. - July 1986. 1. – Montreal : International Civil Aviation Organization, 1986.
looseleaf.
Kept up to date by amendments and supplements.

—International standards : units of measurement to be used in air and ground operations : annex 5 to the Convention on International Civil Aviation / International Civil Aviation Organization. – 4th ed. - July 1979. 1. – Montreal : International Civil Aviation Organization, 1979 -.
loose-leaf.
Kept up to date by amendments and supplements.

—International Transportation : Law of Carriage by Air / New Delhi : Deep and Deep Publications, 1987.
328p.
ISBN 8171000010 Hbk £110.00

—Introduction to air law / by I.H.Ph. Diederiks-Verschoor. – 3rd rev. & enl. ed. – Deventer : Kluwer Law and Taxation, 1988.
xxiv, 197p.
Bibliography: pp.177-189. - Includes index. Translation of: Inleiding tot het luchtrecht.
ISBN 9065443754

—Introduction to air law / by I.H. Ph. Diederiks-Verschoor. – Deventer, Netherlands : Kluwer Law and Taxation Publishers, 1983.
Includes index and bibliography. Translation of: Inleiding tot het luchtrecht.
ISBN 9065440976 : est.

—Liability regime of the international air carrier : a commentary on the present Warsaw system / Rene H. Mankiewicz. – Deventer, The Netherlands : Kluwer, 1981.
xxvii,259p.
Includes index. Bibliography: pxv-xxii.
ISBN 9026811705

—Minutes / Annual General Meeting, International Air Transport Association. – Montreal : IATA, 1981.
Continues: Reports and proceedings.

—Politics of international air transport / Betsy Gidwitz. – Lexington, Mass. : Lexington Books, 1980.
xii,259p; 24cm.
Bibliography: p243-246. - Includes index.
ISBN 0669032344 £16.00

—Principal instruments of the Warsaw system / 2nd ed. – Montreal : I.A.T.A., 1981.
102p.
Prepared by the I.A.T.A. Legal Department.

—Regional differences in fares : rates and costs for international air transport 1978 / Montreal : International Civil Aviation Organization, 1980.
ii,50p.

—Regulatory reform in international air transport : address by H.A. Wassenbergh on the occasion of the introduction of the International Institute of Air and Space Law of the State University at Leyden 17 March 1986 / Deventer : Kluwer Law and Taxation Publishers, 1986.
10p; 25cm.
ISBN 9065442618 Pbk No price

—Report / Second Air Transport Conference, Montreal, 12-28 February 1980. – Montreal : International Civil Aviation Organization, 1980.
iv,82p. – (Doc).

—Report / International Civil Aviation Organization Legal Committee. – Montreal : I.C.A.O., 1983-.
Continues: Report and minutes.

—Report / International Civil Aviation Organization. – s.l. : International Civil Aviation Organaization, 984.
19p. – (LC/SC-ICA-Report 1984 10 03).
'The Sub-Committee met at Montreal and held eleven meetings between 25 September and 3 October 1984' - Introduction.

—Report and minutes / International Civil Aviation Organization Legal Commission. – Montreal : I.C.A.O., 1956.
Continues: Minutes and documents.

—Report and minutes / International Civil Aviation Organization Legal Committee. – Montreal : I.C.A.O., 1983.
v,202p.
Continues: Minutes and documents. - Continued by: Report.

—Review of the economic situation of air transport 1969-1979 / Montreal : International Civil Aviation Organization, 1980.
iv,73p.

—Treatise on air-aeronautical law / Nicolas Mateesco Matte. – Montreal : Institute and Centre of Air and Space Law, McGill University, 1981.
832p; 24cm.
ISBN 0771700407

AIR LAW - CANADA

—Annals of Air and Space Law-Annales de Droit Aerien et Spatial /. – Agincourt : Carswell.

Vol. 5

Vol. 6

Vol. 7

Vol. 8

Vol. 9

Tenth Anniversary Deluxe Edition

Vol. 11

Vol. 12
This work is an annual collection of leading articles examining problems of present and future interest in the air and space law field.

—Treatise on Air-Aeronautical Law / 3rd ed. – Agincourt : Carswell, 1981.
848p.
This work for students of air law in Canada is a comprehensive study of the subject from the first days of flight to the present.

AIR LAW - GREAT BRITAIN

—Air Law / Beaumont. – 4th ed. – London : Butterworths, 1983.
Service to Date.
ISBN 0406373191 Hbk £280.00

—Air Navigation : The Order and the Regulations, 2 ed. / Civil Aviation Authority. – 2nd. ed. Great Britain. – London : Civil Aviation Authority, 1981.
Illus.
ISBN 0860391248 Hbk £17.00

—Aviation Law for Applicants for the Private Pilot's Licence (CAP 85) / Civil Aviation Authority. – 7th ed. Ed. by Great Britain. – London : Civil Aviation Authority, 1985.
v, 62p : Illus.
ISBN 0860391833 Hbk £2.70

—Aviation law for pilots / S.E.T. Taylor, the late H.A. Parmar. – 4th ed. – London : Granada, 1983.
143p; 22cm.
Previous ed.: London : Crosby Lockwood Staples, 1978. Includes index.
ISBN 0246120525 Pbk £6.95

—Aviation Law for Pilots / H. A. Parmar. – 5th ed. – London : Collins, 1986.
172p.
ISBN 0003832732 Pbk £7.95

—Aviation Security / London : Granada Publishing Ltd, 1983.
309p : Illus.
ISBN 0246117400 Hbk £30.00

—British Airways : Civil Aviation Policy and the Privatisation of British Airways / P. J. Forsyth. – London : Institute for Fiscal Studies.
– (Report Ser.).

—Consultation paper : safeguards against monopolistic and anti-competitive behaviour / Civil Aviation Authority. – s.l. : s.n., 1987.
9p.

—Essential Law for Pilots and their Crews London : Oyez Longman, 1980.
ISBN 0851203833 Hbk £10.95

—Registration, Certification and Maintenance of Aircraft-A Guide : Notes on the Legislation Governing Airworthiness of Civil Aircraft Registered in the United Kingdom / Civil Aviation Authority. – 5d ed. Ed. by Great Britain. – London : Civil Aviation Authority, 1981.
vi, 46p : Illus.
ISBN 0860391272 Hbk £1.00

—Regulating the airlines / Oxford : Oxford University Press, 1985.
ISBN 0198275161 Pbk £9.95

—Ship and Aircraft Mortgages / London : LLoyd's of London Press, 1988.
ISBN 1850441049 Hbk

AIR LAW - NEW ZEALAND

—Air Law, 2 Vols. / Beaumont. – 4th ed. – Wellington : Butterworths, 1983.

AIR LAW - UNITED STATES

—Aviation antitrust : the extraterritorial application of the United States antitrust laws and international air transportation / Patricia M. Barlow. – Deventer : Kluwer Law and Taxation, 1987.
xliv,210p.
Bibliography: pp.xxv-xxxv. - Includes index.
ISBN 9065442936

AIR TRANSPORT

—International air transport in the eighties : including the proceedings of the first Netherlands Colloquium on International Air Transport, 'The Changing Scene', Wassenaar, August 25-29, 1980 / edited by H.A. Wassenbergh and H.P. van Fenema : a colloquium organized by the Netherlands Instiute of Transport and the Netherlands Civil Aviation Authority under the auspices of the University of Leyden, Faculty of Law (Air and Space). – Deventer : Kluwer, 1981.
ix,250p; 25cm.
Bibliography: p.248-250.
ISBN 9065440267 Hbk £104.00

—Pricing and capacity determination in international air transport : a legal analysis / by P.P.C. Haanappel. – 2nd ed. – Deventer, Netherlands : Kluwer Law and Taxation Publishers, 1984.
xv, 210 p.; 25 cm.
Rev. ed. of: Ratemaking in international air transport. 1978. Includes index. Bibliography: p. 201-204.
ISBN 9065441549 pbk. CIP rev.

—Regional differences in fares : rates and costs for international air transport 1978 / Montreal : International Civil Aviation Organization, 1980.
ii,50p.

—Regulating the airlines : administrative justice and agency discretion / Robert Baldwin. – Oxford : Clarendon, 1985.
xvi,317p. – (Oxford socio-legal studies).
Includes index.
ISBN 0198275153 Hbk £22.50
ISBN 0198275161 Pbk £9.95

—Report and accounts ... / Air Travel Trust. – London : Published on behalf of the Air Travel Trust by Civil Aviation Authority, 1987.

—Report of the Air Travel Trust Committee ... / Great Britain. – London : Published on behalf of the Air Travel Trust Committee by Civil Aviation Authority, 1987.

AIR TRANSPORT - AUSTRALIA

—Domestic Airline Regulation : Australian Debate / Turramura : Centre for Independent Studies.
120p.
ISBN 0959648593 Hbk £5.50

AIR TRANSPORT - CANADA

—Handbook of Air Transport Legislation / Ottawa : Canadian Government Publishing Centre, 1986.
944p.
ISBN 0660533219 loose £50.00

—International Air Transport : Law, Organization and Policies for the Future / Montreal : Centre for Research of Air and Space Law.
172p.

AIR TRANSPORT - EUROPEAN COMMUNITY

—Toward a Community air transport policy: the legal dimension / P J Slot, P D Dagtoglou. – Kluwer Law and Taxation, 1989.
400.
A selection of essays dealing with the (de)regulation of air transport in the European Community and its member states. Discusses the development of the concept of EC air space law in which all carriers established within the community will be free to compete. Gives views of a European law and the impact on a national level.
ISBN 9065444076 Hbk £41/Dfl 132

AIR TRANSPORT - GREAT BRITAIN

—Airline Marketing and Management / 2nd ed. – Pitman, 1985.
ISBN 0273022407 Hbk £17.95

—Annual report for the year ended 30 September ... / Air Transport Users Committee. – v. – London : The Committee, 1978.
Continues: CIVIL AVIATION AUTHORITY. Airline Users Committee. Annual report.

AIRPORTS

—International standards and recommended practices : aerodromes : annex 14 to the Convention on International Civil Aviation / International Civil Aviation Organization. – 8th ed. - March 1984. 1. – Montreal : International Civil Aviation Organization, 1983.
looseleaf.
Kept up to date by amendments and supplements.

AIRPORTS - ENGLAND

—British Airports Authority : arrangements for the provision of chauffer-driven hire car services at Gatwick Airport : a report / by the Director General of Fair Trading. – London : H.M.S.O., 1984.
50p; 30cm.

—Third London Airport : report / by a Working Group of the Noise Advisory Council i.e. the Working Group on Noise from Air Traffic. – London : H.M.S.O., 1980.
ix,26p; 25cm.
ISBN 0117514748 sd £2.25

AIRPORTS - GREAT BRITAIN

—Airport policy / presented to Parliament by the Secretary of State for Transport. – London : H.M.S.O., 1985.
65p.
ISBN 0101954204

—Fourth report from the Transport Committee, session 1985-86 : airport security : together with the proceedings of the Committee / Great Britain. – London : H.M.S.O., 1986.
xxiii p. – (H.C. 1985-86).
ISBN 0102597863

—Privatising London's Airports / D. Thompson. – London : Institute for Fiscal Studies.
– (Report Ser.).

—Third special report from the Transport Committee, session 1985-86 : government response to the fourth report of the Committee, session 1985-86 : togerther with the proceedings of the Committee / London : H.M.S.O., 1986.
xviii p. – (H.C. 1985-86).
ISBN 0102602867

AIRSPACE (INTERNATIONAL LAW)

—Orbit of space law / Damodar Wadegaonkar : foreword by Y.V. Chandrachud. – London : Stevens, 1984.
xii,172p.
Includes index.
ISBN 0420470107

ALCOHOL - AUSTRALIA

—Alcohol and Crime / Canberra : Australian Institute of Criminology.

—Liquor Laws Guide / Butterworths, 1983.
176p.
ISBN 0409494011 Pbk £27.50

ALCOHOL - AUSTRALIA - NEW SOUTH WALES

—A.B.C of Liquor Law in New South Wales / North Ryde : Law Book Co, 1983.
ix, 197p.
ISBN 0455204209 Pbk £23.50

ALCOHOL - AUSTRALIA - VICTORIA

—Liquor Laws in Victoria / Butterworths, 1982.
ISBN 0409351024 loose £105.00

ALCOHOL - ENGLAND

—Butterworths Consolidated Legislation Service /. – Professional Publ.
249p.
ISBN 0409014230 £55.00

—Drugs and intoxication / by David Farrier. – London : Sweet & Maxwell, 1980.
xix,262p; 19cm.
Includes index.
ISBN 0421271000 Hbk £11.30
ISBN 042127090X Pbk £8.00

ALCOHOL - GREAT BRITAIN

—Underhill's licensing guide / 10th. – London : Longman Professional (UK), 1989.
– (Practitioner series).
Guide to the law and procedure of liquor, gaming, betting and lottery licensing. Details each step in making or opposing a successful licensing application, with key precedents. Revised to take account of the changes introduced by the Licensing Act 1988.
ISBN 0851215378 Hbk £17.95

ALCOHOL - NEW ZEALAND

—Liquor laws : a discussion paper / Wellington : Law Reform Division, Department of Justice, 1985.
22p.
ISBN 0477072100

—Liquor Laws of New Zealand / 4th ed. – Butterworths, 1983.
ISBN 0409600776 Hbk £106.15

—Liquor Laws of New Zealand / Dormer. – 4th ed. – London : Butterworths, 1982.
ISBN 0409600776 Hbk £46.70

ALCOHOLISM

—Law and treatment of drug- and alcohol-dependent persons : a comparative study of existing legislation / by L. Porter, A. E. Arif, W. J. Curran. – Geneva : World Health Organization, 1986.
216p.
Bibliography: p209-216.
ISBN 9241560932

ALCOHOLISM - ENGLAND

—Implementing crime prevention measures / by Tim Hope. – London : H.M.S.O., 1985.
vi,75p; 25cm.
Examines practicality of crime prevention methods. Considers situational measures aimed at dealing with specifically defined offences and community involvement in prevention of crime. Illustrates difficulties by case histories.
ISBN 0113408129

ALCOHOLISM - GREAT BRITAIN

—Alcoholism and social policy / London : H.M.S.O., 1980.
30p; 25cm. – (Home Office research study).
Bibliography: p25-26. A Home Office Research Unit report.
ISBN 011340705X Pbk £2.70

ALCOHOLISM - SOUTH AFRICA

—Offences committed under the influence of liquor or drugs / South African Law Commission. – Pretoria : The Commission, 1984.
vi,118 leaves. – (Project).
Bibliography: p.113-118.

—Offences committed under the influence of liquor or drugs / South African Law Commission. – Pretoria : The Commission, 1986.
vii,132p. – (Report).
Bibliography: p.123-132.
ISBN 0621102075

ALIENS

—Citizenship, aliens and immigration : being Title 27 from Volume 4 of the Canadian encyclopedic digest (Ontario) 3rd ed. / Janet V. Scott, Robert C. Stonehouse. – Agincourt, Ont. : Carswell, 1980.
154p; 24cm.
Includes index. Contents: Immigration / by Janet V. Scott. - Citizenship and aliens / by Robert C. Stonehouse.
ISBN 0459331108

—Civil and Political Rights of the Aliens : a Study in National and International Laws / New Delhi : Deep and Deep Publications, 1982.
224p.

—Expulsion in international law : a study in international aliens law and human rights with special reference to Finland / by Matti Pellonpaa. – Helsinki : Suomalainen Tiedeakatemia, 1984.
xiii, 508 p.; 25 cm.
Includes index. Bibliography: p. 489-506.
ISBN 9514104730

—Human rights of aliens in contemporary international law / Richard Lillich. – Manchester : Manchester University Press, 1984.
xii,177p; 24cm.
Includes index.
ISBN 0719009146 £27.50

—Legal aspects of alien acquisition of real property / edited by Dennis Campbell. – Deventer : Kluwer, 1980.
206p; 25cm.
Includes index.
ISBN 9026811691 Hbk £104.00

—Nationalization of foreign property : a study in North-South dialogue / Subhash C. Jain : foreword by B. Sen. – New Delhi : Deep & Deep, 1983.
298p.
Bibliography: p.268-298 - Includes index.

—Pursuit of nationalized property / M. Sornarajah. – Dordrecht : M. Nijhoff, 1985.
248p.
Bibliography.
ISBN 9024731305 Hbk £120.00

—Rescuing nationals abroad through military coercion and intervention on grounds of humanity / Natalino Ronzitti. – Dordrecht Netherlands : M. Nijhoff Publishers, 1985.
236p.
Includes index. Bibliography.
ISBN 9024731356 Hbk £125.00

—Studies in international labour migration / W.R. Bohning. – London : Macmillan, 1984.
350p.
Bibliography: p293-308. - Includes index.
ISBN 0333369718 £30.00

ALIENS - AUSTRALIA

—Human rights and the deportation of convicted aliens and immigrants / Canberra : Australian Government Publishing Service, 1983.
vii,31p. – (Report).
ISBN 0644026367

ALIENS - EUROPE

—Human rights of aliens in Europe : proceedings of the Colloquy on 'Human Rights of Aliens in Europe' / organised by the Secretariat General of the Council of Europe in co-operation with the Ministries of Justice and for Foreign Affairs of Portugal and with the Regional Government of Madeira, Funchal-Madeira (Portugal) 17-19 October 1983. – Dordrecht : Martinus Nijhoff Publishers, 1985.
x, 474p.
At head of title: Council of Europe, Human Rights Conseil de l'Europe, Droits de l'homme.
ISBN 9024732158 Hbk £225.00

—Immigrant workers in Europe : their legal status : a comparative study / Eric-Jean Thomas, study director. – Paris : Unesco Press, 1982.
245 p.; 25 cm.
Includes bibliographies.
ISBN 9231018671 Hbk £50

ALIENS - SOUTH AFRICA

—Black gold : the Mozambican miner, proletarian and peasant / Ruth First : pictures by Moira Forjaz : work-songs and interviews recorded by Alpheus Manghezi. – Brighton : Harvester, 1983.
xxxi,256p,xvip of plates; 23cm.
Bibliography: p207-211. - Includes index.
ISBN 0710803141 £30.00
ISBN 0312083181

ALUMINIUM INDUSTRY AND TRADE

—Aluminium industry and the Third World : multinational corporations and underdevelopment / Ronald Graham. – London : Zed, 1982.
xii,278p; 22cm.
Bibliography: p263-270. - Includes index.
ISBN 0862320577 Pbk

ANARCHISM

—Community, anarchy and liberty / Michael Taylor. – Cambridge : Cambridge University Press, 1982.
184p; 23cm.
Bibliography: p172-180. - Includes index.
ISBN 0521246210 Hbk £14.00
ISBN 0521270146 Pbk £4.95

—Reading Nozick : essays on Anarchy, state and utopia / edited with an introduction by Jeffrey Paul. – Oxford : Basil Blackwell, 1982.
xi,418p; 22cm.
Originally published: Totowa : Rowman & Littlefield, 1981. Bibliography: p412-416.
ISBN 0631129774 Hbk Unpriced
ISBN 0631129782 Pbk Unpriced

ANECDOTES

—Oxford book of legal anecdotes / edited by Michael Gilbert. – Oxford : Oxford University Press, 1986.
xvi,333p; 23cm.
Includes index.
ISBN 0192141120 £12.50

—Public prosecutor : the memoirs of Sir Norman Skelhorn, Director of Public Prosecutions, 1964-1977 / Sir Norman Skelhorn. – London : Harrap, 1981.
8,207p.
ISBN 0245537635

—Second-best bed : a diversion on wills / Fenton Bresler : illustrations by Michael Heath. – London : Weidenfeld and Nicolson, 1983.
158p; 23cm.
ISBN 0297782134 £7.50

ANIMALS

—Criminal prosecution and capital punishment of animals / E.P. Evans. – London : Faber, 1987.
xxxi,336p; 20cm.
Facsimile of: ed. published London : Heinemann, 1906. Bibliography: p314-323. - Includes index.
ISBN 057114893X Pbk £4.95

—Explanatory report on the European Convention for the Protection of Vertebrate Animals used for Experimental and other Scientific Purposes / Council of Europe. – Strasbourg : Council of Europe, 1986.
75p.
Includes the text of the convention.
ISBN 9287108633

ANIMALS - AUSTRALIA

—Veterinary Law : Ethics, Etiquette and Convention / North Hyde : Law Book Co, 1985.
xvi, 369p.
ISBN 0455205604 Hbk £32.50

ANIMALS - ENGLAND

—Animal law / by Godfrey Sandys-Winsch. – 2nd ed. – London : Shaw & Sons, 1984.
xxxiv,260p.
Includes index.
ISBN 0721908012

—Report to the Secretary of State on the framework of legislation to replace the Cruelty to Animals Act 1876 / Advisory Committee on Animal Experiments. – London : Home Office, 1981.
40p.

ANIMALS - GREAT BRITAIN

—HAC Guide to Taxation of Bloodstock Industry / Stoy Hayward, 1987.
ISBN 0870382005 Hbk £20.00

—Horse and the law / London : David & Charles, 1987.
ISBN 0715388134 Hbk £10.95

—Horse law / Shaw & Sons, 1988.
ISBN 0721911307 Pbk

—Introduction to animal law / London : Academic Press, 1987.
ISBN 0121880303 Hbk

—Your Dog and the Law / London : Shaw & Sons, 1984.
ISBN 0721910106 Pbk £2.25

—Your dog and the law / London : Shaw & Sons, 1984.
ISBN 0721910106 Pbk £2.25

ANIMALS - INDIA

—Cattle Trespass Act along with Prevention of Cruelty of Animals Act / 2nd ed. – Allahabad : Law Publishers, 1983.

—Cattle Trespass Act : as Amended Up-To-Date with Up-To-Date Case Law / 3rd ed. – Allahabad : Law Book Company, 1988.
146p.

ANIMALS - IRELAND

—Report on civil liability for animals / the Law Reform Commission. – Dublin : The Commission, 1982.
v,26p. – (LRC).

ANIMALS, TREATMENT OF - MORAL AND ETHICAL ASPECTS

—Rights, killing, and suffering : moral vegetarianism and applied ethics / R.G. Frey. – Oxford : Blackwell, 1983.
xi,256p; 24cm.
Includes index.
ISBN 0631126848 £17.50

ANONYMOUS LETTERS

—Criminal law : report on poison-pen letters / the Law Commission. – London : H.M.S.O., 1985.
v,39p.
ISBN 0102519854

ANTARCTICA

—Antarctic Law and Politics / London : Dent (J M) & Sons, 1987.
ISBN 0905838394 Hbk £17.50

—Antarctic Treaty regime : law, environment and resources / edited by Gillian D. Triggs under the general editorship of the British Institute of International and Comparative Law. – Cambridge : Cambridge University Press, 1987.
xxi,237p; 23cm.
Conference papers. Bibliography: p234-235.
ISBN 0521327660 £30.00

—Antarctica and international law : a collection of inter-state and national documents / compiled by W.M. Bush. – 4. – London : Oceana Publications, 1982.
Vol. 4 is index.
ISBN 0379203200 V. 1 £45.00
ISBN 0379203219 V. 2 £45.00

—International law and Australian sovereignty in Antarctica / by Gillian D. Triggs. – Sydney : Legal Books, 1986.
xxix,403p.
Bibliography: p.379-391. - Includes index.
ISBN 0949553239

—International Law for Antarctica / Tullio Scovazzi. – Milan : Giuffre, 1988.
xiv, 532p.

ANTINUCLEAR MOVEMENT - GREAT BRITAIN

—Trade union powers and the anti-nuclear campaign / London : Lawyers Versus the Bomb, 1982.
19p; 21cm. – (Pamphlet).

ANTON PILLAR ORDERS - GREAT BRITAIN

—Anton Piller Order and Mareva Injunction : A Practitioner's Guide / London : Butterworths, 1987.

APARTHEID

—Press and Apartheid : Repression and Propaganda in South Africa / C. Anthony Giffard. – London : Macmillan, 1984.
336p.
ISBN 0333384350 Hbk £33.00

—Some aspects of international law considered in relation to apartheid, racism and racial discrimination / by T.O. Elias. – Lagos : Nigerian Institute of Advanced Legal Studies, 1986.
27p. – (Occasional paper).
ISBN 9782353043

APARTHEID - SOUTH AFRICA

—Annual report / Department of Development Planning : Constitutional Development Services. – Pretoria : Government Printer, 1987.
Annual reports of two bodies published together. Text in Afikaans and English.

—Freedom, state security and the rule of law : dilemmas of the apartheid society / Anthony S. Mathews. – Cape Town : Juta, 1986.
xxv,312p.
Bibliography: p.xi-xiv. - Includes index.
ISBN 0702118125

—Mission to South Africa : the Commonwealth report / Malcolm Fraser, Olusegun Obasanjo. – Harmondsworth : Penguin Books for the Commonwealth Secretariat, 1986.
176p.
Co-chairmen: Malcolm Fraser and Olusegun Obasanjo.
ISBN 0140523847

—Race and the law in South Africa : a volume of essays by members of the School of Law, Howard College, University of Natal, Durban, to commemorate the sixtieth anniversary of the Durban School / edited by A. J. Rycroft ... et al. – Cape Town : Juta, 1987.
xx,258p.
Includes bibliographical references and index.
ISBN 0702119105

—Report / Department of Constitutional Development and Planning. – 3. – Pretoria : Government Printer, 1983.
Text in Afrikaans and English.

—South Africa and the consociational option : a constitutional analysis / by L.J. Boulle. – Cape Town : Juta, 1984.
xii, 270 p.; 25 cm.
Includes indexes. Bibliography: p. 227-229.
ISBN 0702114340 pbk.

—South Africa in crisis / edited by Jesmond Blumenfeld. – London : Croom Helm for the Royal Institute of International Affairs, 1987.
x,207p; 23cm.
Includes index.
ISBN 0709942524 £19.95

APPELLATE COURTS

—Stare decisis in Commonwealth appellate courts / David J. Murphy and Robert Rueter. – Toronto : Butterworths, 1981.
xv,117p.
Includes index.
ISBN 0409853739

APPELLATE COURTS - CANADA - BRITISH COLUMBIA

—Advocacy in the Court of Appeal of British Columbia 1982 / Vancouver : Continuing Legal Education Society of British Columbia, 1982.
200p.
ISBN 0865040818 Hbk £55.00

APPELLATE COURTS - GREAT BRITAIN

—Appeals by the Prosecution Against Sentences and Acquittals : A Survey of the Situation in Some Commonwealth Countries / Jill Cottrell. - London : Commonwealth Secretariat, 1984.
ISBN 0850922259 Hbk £2.00

APPELLATE COURTS - NEW ZEALAND

—Practice and Procedure of the High Court and Court of Appeal in New Zealand / 12th ed. - Butterworths.
ISBN 0409667617 loose £264.00

APPELLATE COURTS - NIGERIA

—Manual of brief writing in the Court of Appeal and the Supreme Court of Nigeria / by Philip Nnaemeka-Agu. - Enugu, Nigeria : Fourth Dimension, 1986.
xviii,110p.
Bibliography: p. 109-110. - Includes index.

APPELLATE COURTS - SOUTH AFRICA

—Judges at work : the role and attitudes of the South African appellate judiciary, 1910-50 / by Hugh Corder. - Cape Town : Juta, 1984.
xxxii,252p.
Bibliography: pxxi-xxvi.
ISBN 0702114359

APPELLATE COURTS - UNITED STATES

—Courts of appeals in the federal judicial systems : a study of the Second, Fifth, and District of Columbia Circuits / J. Woodford Howard, Jr. - Princeton : Princeton University Press, 1981.
xxvi,415p; 25cm.
Includes index.
ISBN 0691076235 Hbk £18.10
ISBN 0691101000 Pbk £7.00

APPELLATE PROCEDURE - CANADA

—Factums in Civil Appeals 1985 / Vancouver : Continuing Legal Education Society of British Columbia, 1985.
235p.
ISBN 0865042454 Hbk £55.00

APPELLATE PROCEDURE - ENGLAND

—Appeals / by David Price. - London : Fourmat, 1982.
xii,439p; 22cm.
Includes index.
ISBN 0906840422 Pbk £12.95

—Criminal appeals : a practical guide to appeals to and from the Crown Court / by Ian McLean. - 2nd ed. - London : Barry Rose, 1986.
xxxv,249p.
Previous ed.: 1980. Includes bibliographical references and index. Includes examples of court forms.
ISBN 085992372X

—Criminal appeals : a practical guide to appeals to and from the Crown Court / Ian McLean. - London : Sweet and Maxwell, 1980.
xxxiii,176p; 24cm.
Includes index.
ISBN 0421247606 £8.25

APPELLATE PROCEDURE - GREAT BRITAIN

—Appeals : Practice and Procedure / London : Longman Professional, 1986.
ISBN 0851207626 Pbk £18.95

—Appellate mosaic : being the presidential address of the Rt. Hon. Lord Templeman, president of the Holdsworth Club of the Faculty of Law in the University of Birmingham 1938-84 / Birmingham : The Holdsworth Club of the University of Birmingham, 1984.
18p; 22cm. - (The Holdsworth Club).
ISBN 0704407132

—Problems of a Master of the Rolls : being the presidential address of Sir John Donaldson, president of the Holdsworth Club of a the Faculty of Law in the University of Birmingham, 1985-1986 / Birmingham : University of Birmingham. Holdsworth Club, 1985.
14p. - (The Holdsworth Club).
ISBN 0704407744

APPELLATE PROCEDURE - NIGERIA

—Essays on civil proceedings / by A. Obi-Okoye. - Enugu, Nigeria : Fourth Dimension Publishing, 1980.
155p.
ISBN 9781561203 Hbk

AQUACULTURE - CANADA

—Aquaculture / Vancouver : Continuing Legal Education Society of British Columbia, 1988.
426p.
ISBN 0865049793 Hbk £85.00

—Aquaculture : the Legal Framework / Aurora : Canada Law Book, 1982.

—Aquaculture : the legal framework / Bruce H.Wildsmith. - Toronto : Emond-Montgomery, 1982.
xii,313p.
Bibliography: p.295-305. - Includes index.
ISBN 0920722083 Hbk £45.00

ARAB COUNTRIES

—Arab comparative & commercial law : the international approach : proceedings : International Bar Association first Arab Regional Conference, Cairo 15-19 February 1987 / International Bar Association. - London : Graham & Trotman, 1987.
Contents: v. 1. The Sharia and its relevance to modern transnational transactions. The settlement of disputes through arbitration. Joint ventures. - v. 2. Energy law.
ISBN 086010978X v. 2

—Arab manpower : the crisis of development / J.S. Birks and C.A. Sinclair. - London : Croom Helm, 1980.
17,391p; 23cm.
Bibliography: p.368-383. - Includes index.
ISBN 0856649465 £19.95

—Arab petropolitics / Abdulaziz Al-Sowayegh. - London : Croom Helm, 1984.
207p; 23cm.
Includes index.
ISBN 0709905386 Hbk £15.95
ISBN 0709905408 Pbk £8.95

—Register of laws of the Arabian Gulf / London : Graham & Trotman, 1989.
260.
A database of all laws and regulations originating in each country of the Arabian Gulf from the commencement of legislative promulgation to the present day. Drawn from original Arabic sources.
ISBN 1853331686 Llf £489

ARBITRATION

—Arbitration : an Element of International Law / Stockholm : Almqvist & Wiksell, 1984.
166p.
ISBN 9122007342 Hbk £119.00

—Arbitration and State Enterprises / Paris : International Chamber of Commerce.
115p.

—Arbitration international / v. - London : Chartered Institute of Arbitrators, 1985.

—Conciliation and arbitration procedures in labour disputes : a comparative study / Geneva : International Labour Office, 1980.
x,183p.
Includes bibliographical references.
ISBN 9221023389 Pbk

—Extrajudicial dispute settlement / Clive M. Schmitthoff. - Deventer : Kluwer Law and Taxation, 1985.
18p.
Includes bibliographical references.
ISBN 9065442340

—Guide on Multi-Party Arbitration / Paris : International Chamber of Commerce.
8p.

—Guide to Arbitration / Paris : International Chamber of Commerce.
140p.

—Guide to arbitration : and related services offered by the International Chamber of Commerce / International Chamber of Commerce. - Paris : ICC, 1983.
139p; 25cm. - (ICC publication).
Replaces ICC publication; no.301.
ISBN 9284210186

—International arbitration : 60 years of ICC arbitration : a look at the future / Paris : ICC, 1984.
421p.
Papers given at a conference in Paris, October 1983, to mark the 60th anniversary of the ICC Court of Arbitration. Includes index. Spine title: ICC Court of Arbitration 60th anniversary: a look at the future.
ISBN 9284210208

—International arbitration : three salient problems / by Stephen M. Schwebel. - Cambridge : Grotius Publications, 1987.
xviii,303p.
At head of title: University of Cambridge. Research Centre for International Law.
ISBN 0949009024

—International dispute settlement / by J.G. Merrills. - London : Sweet & Maxwell, 1984.
xvi,211p; 19cm.
Includes index.
ISBN 0421303700 Hbk Unpriced
ISBN 0421303808 Pbk £6.95

—International Maritime Arbitration / Vancouver : Continuing Legal Education Society of British Columbia, 1988.
338p.
ISBN 0865043663 Hbk £100.00

—Journal of international arbitration / v. - Geneva : D. Thompson and J. Werner, 1984-.

—Rules of the ICC Court of Arbitration / Paris : International Chamber of Commerce.
32p.

ARBITRATION - ASIA

—Arbitration Law in Asia / Paris : International Chamber of Commerce, 1986.

ARBITRATION - AUSTRALIA - NEW SOUTH WALES

—Contracts for Work in Industry (NSW) : Section 88F / Butterworths, 1981.
ISBN 0409490474 Pbk £35.00

—New South Wales Industrial Arbitration Act 1940 : including Regulations and Trade Union Legislation / 4th ed. - North Ryde : C.C.H. Australia, 1986.
328p.
ISBN 0869035983 Hbk

ARBITRATION - CANADA

—Arbitration / Victoria : Government of British Columbia, 1982.

—British Columbia Labour Arbitration / Aurora : Canada Law Book Co.
- (Summary Services, Provincial Ser.).

—Canadian labour arbitration / David M. Beatty. - 2nd ed. - Aurora, Ont. : Canada Law Book Ltd., 1984.
clxxiv,723p.
Previous ed.: 1977. Includes index.
ISBN 0888040199

—Collective Agreement Arbitration in Canada / Butterworths.

Supplement-1986
144p.
Covers hearing and grievance procedures, evidentiary problems, the interpretation of collective agreements, discharge and discipline, insubordination, industrial offences, seniority, job benefits, the bargaining unit, and the protection of employment opportunities.
ISBN 0409806358 Pbk £27.95

—Collective agreement arbitration in Canada / Earl Edward Palmer. - 2nd ed. - Toronto : Butterworths, 1983.
cxvi,805p.
Includes bibliographical references and index.
ISBN 0409857726

—Interest arbitration : measuring justice in employment / Joseph M. Weiler, editor. - Toronto : Carswell, 1981.
iv,283p.
Papers presented at a conference sponsored by the Continuing Legal Education Society of British Columbia, in Vancouver B.C., April 1980.
ISBN 0459339206

—Labor Arbitration : 1982 / Vancouver : British Columbia Continuing Legal Education Society, 1982.
194p.
ISBN 0865040567 Hbk £45.00

—Labour Arbitration, 1983 / Vancouver : British Columbia Continuing Legal Education Society, 1983.
130p.
ISBN 0865041121 Hbk £45.00

—Labour Arbitration, 1984 / Vancouver : British Columbia Continuing Legal Education Society, 1984.
ISBN 0865041636 Hbk £50.00

—Labour Arbitration 1988 / Vancouver : Continuing Legal Education Society of British Columbia, 1988.
156p.
ISBN 0865049971 Hbk £70.00

—Labour Arbitration Cases : Consolidated Index / Aurora : Canada Law Book Co, 1985.
- (Law Reports).

—Labour Arbitration Cases : Consolidated Index, List of Awards / Aurora : Canada Law Book Co, 1982.
400p. - (Law Reports).

—Labour Arbitration Cases First Series (1948-1972), 24 Vols. / Aurora : Canada Law Book Co.
- (Law Reports).

Back Vols.

—Labour Arbitration Cases Second Series (1973-1981), 30 Vols. / Aurora : Canada Law Book Co.
- (Law Reports).

Back Vols.

—Labour Arbitration Cases Third Series (1982-Present) / Aurora : Canada Law Book Co.
- (Law Reports).

Back Vols.

—Labour Arbitrations and All That / 2nd ed. - Aurora : Canada Law Book Co, 1985.
146p. - (Text Books-Civil).

—Uncitral Arbitration Model in Canada / Bonita J. Thompson. - Agincourt : Carswell, 1987.
262p.

—Western Labour Arbitration Cases / Vancouver : British Columbia Continuing Legal Education Society, 1981.

Vol. 3 1980.

Vol. I (1979)

Vol. I (1980)

Vol. 2

Vol. II (1979)

Vol. II (1980)

Vol. 3

Vol. 4

ARBITRATION - GREAT BRITAIN

—Arbitration : Principles and Practice / Repr. - London : Collins, 1983.
256p.
ISBN 000383171X Hbk £18.50

—Course in Arbitration, 3 Vols. / College of Estate Management. - Reading : College of Estate Management.

—Dictionary of Arbitration Law and Practice / London : LLoyd's of London Press, 1987.
ISBN 1850441243 Hbk

—London Maritime Arbitration / London : LLoyd's of London Press, 1989.
ISBN 1850442045 Hbk

ARBITRATION - INDIA

—Indian Arbitration Act / 5th ed. - Allahabad : Law Book Company, 1984.
xxxiv, 864p.

—Law of Arbitration / 4th ed. - Lucknow : Eastern Book Company, 1983.
826p.

—Law of Arbitration / 4th ed. - Lucknow : Eastern Book Company, 1983.
826p.

—Law of Arbitration / V.D. Singh. - 8th ed. - Lucknow : Eastern Book Company, 1980.
844p.

ARBITRATION - NETHERLANDS

—Netherlands Arbitration Act : Text and Annotations in English, French and German / A.J. van den Berg. - Dordrecht : Kluwer, 1987.
ISBN 9065442979 Pbk £67.50

ARBITRATION - NEW ZEALAND

—Compulsory arbitration in New Zealand : the first forty years / James Holt. - Auckland : Auckland University Press, 1986.
247p.
Bibliography: p236-242.
ISBN 1869400062

—Judicial Perspective on Industrial Conciliation and Arbitration in New Zealand / Repr. of 1980 ed. - Auckland : Legal Research Foundation, 1982.
49p.
ISBN 0908581076 Pbk £5.50

ARBITRATION - SWEDEN

—Arbitration in Sweden / Second (revised) edition. - Stockholm : The Stockholm Chamber of Commerce, 1984.
xvii,276p.
ISBN 9178100755

ARBITRATION AND AWARD

—Arab comparative & commercial law : the international approach : proceedings : International Bar Association first Arab Regional Conference, Cairo 15-19 February 1987 / International Bar Association. - London : Graham & Trotman, 1987.
Contents: v. 1. The Sharia and its relevance to modern transnational transactions. The settlement of disputes through arbitration. Joint ventures. - v. 2. Energy law.
ISBN 086010978X v. 2

—Arbitration in international trade / Rene David. - Antwerp : Kluwer Law and Taxation Publications, 1985.
xii,482p.
Includes legislation. Includes index. Bibliography: p459-465. Translation of: Arbitrage dans le commerce international.
ISBN 9065441646

—Arbitration in taxation / Gustaf Lindencrona, Nils Mattsson. - Deventer, The Netherlands : Kluwer, 1981.
92 p.; 22 cm.
Includes bibliographical references.
ISBN 9065440003 pbk.

—Arbitration in the Yemen Arab Republic / Isam Ghanem. - Braunton : Merlin, 1988.
22p; 21cm.
ISBN 0863033784 Pbk £2.00

—Arbitration law and practice / Peter M.B. Rowland. - London : Institute of Chartered Accountants, 1988.
xxvii,185p.
ISBN 0852918887

—Arbitration law in Europe / Paris : International Chamber of Commerce, 1981.
368p.
Revision of: Commercial arbitration and the law throughout the world. Publication; no. 353.
ISBN 9284210143

—Art of arbitration : essays on international arbitration : liber amicorum Pieter Sanders, 12 September 1912-1982 / editors, Jan C. Schultsz, Albert Jan van den Berg. - Deventer, Netherlands : Kluwer Law and Taxation Publishers, 1982.
xxi, 320 p.; 25 cm.
English or French. Includes bibliographical references and index.
ISBN 9065440542 CIP rev.

—Commercial arbitration and the law throughout the world : summary of the rules concerning arbitration agreements, procedure, arbitral awards, enforcement of awards, means of recourse / by International Headquarters of the International Chamber of Commerce. - 1. - Basel : Verlag fur Recht und Gesellschaft, 1949.
loose-leaf.
Superseded by the series: Arbitration throughout the world (1981-). Updated to supplement no. 3 (1964). Added t.p. in French. Parallel English and French texts.

—Commercial arbitration institutions : an international directory and guide / Ludwik Kos-Rabcewicz-Zubkowski and Paul J. Davidson. - London : Oceana Publications, 1986.
ix, 186p.
Published under the auspices of the International Federation of Commercial Arbitration Institutions.
ISBN 0379207893

—Comparative arbitration practice and public policy in arbitration / general editor, Pieter Sanders with the cooperation of the T.M.C. Asser Institute for International Law. - Deventer : Kluwer Law and Taxation Publishers, 1987.
x, 402 p.; 25 cm.
At head of title: International Council for Commercial Arbitration. 'VIIIth International Arbitration Congress, New York, 6-9 May 1986'–Series t.p. Includes bibliographical references.
ISBN 9065442960 Pbk £135.00

—Dictionary of arbitration law & practice / Eric Lee. - London : Mansfield Law Publishers, 1986.
185p.

—Encyclopedia of international commercial arbitration / by Eric Lee. - London : Lloyd's of London Press, 1986.
412p; 24cm.
Includes index.
ISBN 185044059X £50.00 (Apr.)

—Hague-Zagreb Essays / edited by C.C.A. Voskuil and J.A. Wade. - Dordrecht : M. Nijhoff, 1985.
193p.
At head of title: TMC Asser Instituut. Reports and discussions of the fifth session of the Hague-Zagreb Colloquium, Isle of Krk, Yugoslavia, 1983. Includes bibliographies.
ISBN 9024731704 Hbk £135.00

—Judges, law, and businessmen / A.H. Hermann. - Deventer, Netherlands : Kluwer Law and Taxation Publishers, 1983.
ISBN 9065440828

—Proceedings of a seminar on commercial arbitration held in Ottawa, 19 June 1985 / edited by Paul J. Davidson. - Ottawa : Canadian Arbitration, Conciliation and Amicable Composition Centre, 1986.
xxi,154p.
At head of t.p.: Canadian Arbitration, Conciliation and Amicable Composition Centre, and Canadian National Section, Inter-American Commercial Arbitration Commission.

—Rules for the ICC court of arbitration / International Chamber of Commerce. - 1980 ed. - Paris : International Chamber of Commerce, 1981.
32p.
Previous ed.: 1975. The Rules of the ICC Court of Arbitration were first published in April 1975 as Publication 291. The text of the Rules remains unchanged in the present edition but a new section called 'the Internal Rules of the Court' has been added to it. 'The schedule of costs' has also been revised..

ARBITRATION AND AWARD - CANADA

—Family Law Awards : In Canada / Toronto : Butterworths, 1987.
328p.
ISBN 0409843938 Hbk £65.00

—Law and practice of commercial arbitration / by Richard H. McLaren and Earl Edward Palmer. - Toronto, Canada : Carswell, 1982.
xlii, 422 p.; 24 cm.
Includes bibliographical references and index.
ISBN 0459349902

—Review of Civil Jury Awards / Victoria : Government of British Columbia, 1984.

—UNCITRAL Arbitration Model in Canada / Thompson. - Agincourt : Carswell, 1987.
262p.
This work outlines the process of adopting and implementing the UNCITRAL Model Law. Canadian legislation and the UNCITRAL Model Law and Rules are provided. Discussions include that of arbitration as a universally accepted method of resolving international commercial disputes and the adoption in British Columbia of the model law on international commercial arbitration.

ARBITRATION AND AWARD - CANADA - ALBERTA

—Proposals for a new Alberta Arbitration Act / Institute of Law Research and Reform, Edmonton, Alberta. - Edmonton : The Institute, 1988.
iv,166p. - (Report).
Includes draft legislation and the text of the Convention on the Recognition and Enforcement of Foreign Arbitral Awards.
ISBN 0888648669

—Towards a new Arbitration Act for Alberta / Institute of Law Research and Reform. - Edmonton, Alberta : Institute of Law Research and Reform, 1987.
xvi,199p.

ARBITRATION AND AWARD - CANADA - BRITISH COLUMBIA

—Report on arbitration / Law Reform Commission of British Columbia. - Vancouver : The Commission, 1982.
149p.
ISBN 0771883110

ARBITRATION AND AWARD - CHINA

—Commercial disputes settlement in China / Eric Lee. - London : Lloyds of London, 1985.
152p; 22cm.
Includes index.
ISBN 1850440638 Pbk No price (Aug.)

ARBITRATION AND AWARD - ENGLAND

—Arbitration / Maurice Kay. - London : Sweet and Maxwell, 1980.
vi,90p; 18cm.
Includes index.
ISBN 0421246901 Pbk £1.25

—Arbitration : principles and practice / John Parris. - London : Granada, 1983.
xi,242p; 25cm.
Includes index.
ISBN 0246118997 Unpriced

—Encyclopedia of arbitration law / Eric Lee. - 1 v. - London : Lloyd's, 1984.
looseleaf.
Includes index.
ISBN 1850440263

—Handbook of arbitration practice / by Ronald Bernstein, contributors John Tackaberry ... et al. : foreword by Sir John Donaldson : introduction by Sir Michael Kerr. - London : Sweet & Maxwell in conjunction with the Chartered Institute of Arbitrators, 1987.
xxv,575p; 26cm.
Examines the constitution of the tribunal, the range of procedures available, conduct of the hearing, the role of advocates and expert witnesses, techniques of enforcement, and remuneration. Advises on arbitration in rent reviews, commodity contracts, maritime and construction disputes, and documents-only disputes.
ISBN 0421317906 £55.00

—Law and practice of commercial arbitration in England / Sir Michael J. Mustill, Stewart C. Boyd. - London : Butterworths, 1985.
lxxiv,727p.
An extensive and detailed treatment of the subject of commercial arbitration is given in this work. The book covers appointment of arbitrators, the arbitration process, the award, and appeals in the United Kingdom.
ISBN 0406311218

—Law of arbitration / Gill. - 3rd ed. - London : Sweet & Maxwell, 1983.
xxv,174p; 22cm.
Previous ed.: 1975. Includes index.
ISBN 0421251107 Pbk £7.50

—Practice and procedure of the commercial court / by Anthony D. Colman. - London : Lloyd's of London Press, 1983.
xxiii,193p.
Includes index.
ISBN 0907432581

—Report of the practitioner members of the Commercial Court Committee approved and adopted by the Commercial Court Committee / London : Lord Chancellor's Department, 1986.
50p.

—Right of appeal : a practical digest of charter-party disputes and the right of appeal under the Arbitration Act 1979 / W.E. Astle. - London : Fairplay, 1983.
153p; 24cm.
ISBN 0905045513 Pbk No price

—Russell on the law of arbitration / Anthony Walton, Mary Vitoria. - 20th ed. - London : Stevens, 1982.
lviii,602p; 26cm.
Previous ed.: 1979. Includes index.
ISBN 0420463801 £57.00

—UNCITRAL model law on international commercial arbitration : a consultative document / Departmental Advisory Committee on Arbitration Law and Scottish Advisory Committee on Arbitration Law. - London : Dept. of Trade and Industry, 1987.
67p.

ARBITRATION AND AWARD – FRANCE

—Arbitration in France : the French law and national and international arbitration / Jean-Louis Delvolve. – Trilangual ed. – Antwerp : Kluwer Law and Taxation Publishers, 1982.
x, 165 p.; 19 cm.
English, French, and German. Bibliography: p. 165.
ISBN 9065440984 CIP rev.

ARBITRATION AND AWARD – GREAT BRITAIN

—Arbitrage / Cambridge : Woodhead-Faulkner, 1986.
ISBN 0859413535 Hbk £55.00

—Arbitration for contractors / Douglas A. Stephenson. – London : Northwood Books, 1982.
ix,150p.
Bibliography: p.145. - Includes index.
ISBN 0719829003

—Arbitration : Principles and Practice / Oxford : Blackwell Scientific, 1983.
ISBN 000383171X Hbk £19.95

—Central Arbitration Committee Awards / London : HMSO, 1984.
ISBN 0118885634 Hbk £7.85

—How to conduct arbitrations / Smith. – London : Architectural Press, 1988.
ISBN 0851392164 Hbk

—Institute of Civil Engineers' arbitration practice / Uff. – Telford (Thomas), 1986.
ISBN 0727702475 Hbk £18.50

—Law of Arbitration / Walton. – 20th ed. – London : Sweet & Maxwell, 1982.
ISBN 0420463801 Hbk £66.00

—Spicer and Pegler's the business of partnerships / by Peter J. Oliver and Nigel T. Davey. – London : Sweet & Maxwell, 1986.
xii,193p; 22cm.
Includes index.
ISBN 0421353309 Pbk £16.75

ARBITRATION AND AWARD – ISLAMIC COUNTRIES

—Commercial arbitration in the Arab Middle East : a study in Shara and statute law / Samir Saleh. – London : Published under the patronage of the International Chamber of Commerce by Graham & Trotman, 1984.
380p.
Bibliography: p445-455. - Includes index.
ISBN 0860104532 £55.00

ARBITRATION AND AWARD – SCOTLAND

—Law of arbitration in Scotland / Robert L.C. Hunter. – Edinburgh : T & T Clark, 1987.
384p; 24cm.
A comprehensive account of the modern law of arbitration in Scotland, the ordinary submission to arbitration clauses, the appointment of arbiters, proceedings, the 'stated case' under the Administration of Justice (Scotland) Act 1972, and the decree-arbitral. The final part contains chapters on quasi-arbitral and equitable procedures, agricultural and industrial arbitrations. There is consideration of the impact of Community law and comparison with the practice of other countries. Includes bibliography and index.
ISBN 0567094804 Hbk £29.95

—UNCITRAL model law on international commercial arbitration : a consultative document / Departmental Advisory Committee on Arbitration Law and Scottish Advisory Committee on Arbitration Law. – London : Dept. of Trade and Industry, 1987.
67p.

ARBITRATION AND AWARD – USSR

—Soviet commercial and maritime arbitration / compiled and edited by William E. Butler. – London : Oceana Publications, 1980.
1 v.; 28 cm. – (A Transnational service).
Includes arbitration awards selected from the English language edition of Arbitrazhnaia praktika, issued by the USSR Foreign Trade Arbitration Commission. Loose-leaf for updating.
ISBN 0379206994 £75.00

ARBITRATION AND AWARD – WEST GERMANY

—Commercial arbitration in the Federal Republic of Germany / by Ottoarndt Glossner. – Deventer : Kluwer Law and Taxation, 1984.
xiv,137p; 25cm.
Bibliography: p113-134. - Includes index.
ISBN 9065441859 Hbk £90.00

ARBITRATION AND AWARD (INTERNATIONAL LAW)

—Arbitration : an Element of International Law / Stockholm : Almqvist & Wiksell, 1984.
166p.
ISBN 9122007342 Hbk £119.00

—Arbitration and conciliation under the UNCITRAL rules : a textual analysis / Issaak I. Dore. – Dordrecht : Nijhoff, 1986.
ISBN 0898389135

—Arbitration and renegotiation of international investment agreements : a study with particular reference to means of conflict avoidance under natural resources investment agreements / Wolfgang Peter. – Dordrecht : M. Nijhoff, 1986.
xxiii, 297p.
Includes index. Bibliography: p.267-284.
ISBN 9024733146

—Arbitration and state enterprises : a survey on the national and international state of law and practice / by Karl-Heinz Bockstiegel. – Deventer : Kluwer Law and Taxation, 1984.
vi,113p; 25cm.
'An international research study of the Institute of International Business Law and Practice of the International Chamber of Commerce'. Bibliography: p75-109.
ISBN 9065441840 Pbk No price

—Arbitration in France : the French law and national and international arbitration / Jean-Louis Delvolve. – Trilangual ed. – Antwerp : Kluwer Law and Taxation Publishers, 1982.
x, 165 p.; 19 cm.
English, French, and German. Bibliography: p. 165.
ISBN 9065440984 CIP rev.

—Arbitration : the IBA rules of evidence : supplementary rules governing the presentation and reception of evidence in international commercial arbitration / International Bar Association, Section on Business Law. – London : The Association, 1986.
8p.
ISBN 0948711043

—Contemporary problems in international arbitration / edited by Julian D. M. Lew. – London : Queen Mary College, Centre for Commercial Law Studies. School of International Arbitration, 1986.
xlv, 380p.
Based on papers presented at a conference organised by the School of International Arbitration, Queen Mary College. Includes bibliographical references and index.
ISBN 0951066412

—Contemporary Problems in International Arbitration / London : Centre for Commercial Law Studies, 1986.
ISBN 0951066412 Hbk £40.00

—Contemporary Problems in International Arbitration / Dordrecht : Kluwer, 1987.
380p.
ISBN 0898389267 Pbk Gld125.00

—International arbitration : a practical study with specific reference to the petroleum industry / a collection of papers presented by the Section of Energy and Natural Resources Law at the International Bar Association's Twentieth Biennial Conference held in Vienna, 2-7 September 1984. – London : International Bar Association, 1984.
Various pagings.

—International commercial and maritime arbitration / edited by F.D. Rose. – London : Sweet & Maxwell, 1988.
118p; 22cm.
Explains aspects of international arbitration, and includes chapters on commercial arbitration, transnational arbitration and English laws, soviet maritime arbitration, arbitral immunity, and salvage arbitration.
ISBN 0421392207 Pbk £15.00

—Iran-United States Claims Tribunal Reports / v. – Cambridge : Grotius Publications, 1983.

—Law and practice of international commercial arbitration / by Alan Redfern, Martin Hunter : foreword by Sir Robert Jennings. – London : Sweet & Maxwell, 1986.
xliii,462p; 24cm.
Reviews the process of international commercial arbitration, from the drafting of the arbitration agreement to the enforcement of the arbitral tribunal's award. Describes the role of the main international arbitral institutions, and comments on institutional and international rules of arbitration.
ISBN 0421324902 £64.00

—Lloyd's arbitration reports / London : Lloyd's of London, 1988-.

—New trends in the development of international commercial arbitration and the role of arbitral and other institutions / general editor Pieter Sanders. – Deventer : Kluwer, 1983.
xii,393p.
Proceedings of a conference organised by the International Council for Commercial Arbitration.
ISBN 9065441204

—New York Arbitration Convention of 1958 : towards a uniform judicial interpretation / door Albert Jan Van Den Berg. – The Hague : T.M.C. Asser Institute, 1981.
xv,480p.
Proefschrift: Erasmus Universiteit, Rotterdam. Bibliography: p440-450. With summary and conclusion in Dutch.
ISBN 9065440356

—New York Convention on the Recognition and Enforcement of Foreign Arbitral Awards : explanatory documentation prepared for Commonwealth jurisdictions / by K.W. Patchett in association with the Commonwealth Secretariat. – London : Commonwealth Secretariat, 1981.
v,62p.
Includes the text of the Convention.
ISBN 0850922038

—Proceedings of a seminar on commercial arbitration held in Ottawa, 19 June 1985 / edited by Paul J. Davidson. – Ottawa : Canadian Arbitration, Conciliation and Amicable Composition Centre, 1986.
xxi,154p.
At head of t.p.: Canadian Arbitration, Conciliation and Amicable Composition Centre, and Canadian National Section, Inter-American Commercial Arbitration Commission.

—Proceedings of Forum London : a seminar organised by the International Bar Association, Section on Business Law, in conjunction with the Solicitors' European Group of the Law Society of England and Wales, 23-26 September 1981, London / London : International Bar Association, 1982.
iv,166p.
ISBN 0950587656

—Proceedings of the First Euro Arab Arbitration Conference / actes de 1er Colloque Euro-Arab sur l'arbitrage : under the high patronage of Habib Bourguiba. – London : Lloyd's of London Press, 1987.
ix,370p; 25cm.
At head of title: Euro-Arab Chambers of Commerce.
ISBN 1850441251 Pbk £60.00 (Apr.)

—Reflections on International Arbitration and Litigation in the International Court of Justice / Dordrecht : Kluwer, 1988.
24p.
ISBN 9065443517 Hbk £30.50

—Reports of International Arbitral Awards / United Nations. – London : HMSO, 1982.
532p.
Reports on awards in three arbitration cases; the delimitation of the continental shelf between UK and France, the air service agreement between USA and France, and the taxation liability of EURATOM.
ISBN 0119074761 Hbk £24.75

—UNCITRAL model law on international commercial arbitration : a consultative document / Departmental Advisory Committee on Arbitration Law and Scottish Advisory Committee on Arbitration Law. – London : Dept. of Trade and Industry, 1987.
67p.

—Uncitral's project for a model law on international commercial arbitration / general editor, Pieter Sanders : with the cooperation of the T.M.C. Asser Institute for International Law. – Deventer, Netherlands : Kluwer Law and Taxation Publishers, 1984.
At head of title: International Council for Commercial Arbitration. Proceedings of the International Council for Commercial Arbitration interim meeting, May 9-12, 1984 in Lausanne, Switzerland.
ISBN 9065441832

ARBITRATION AND AWARD (INTERNATIONAL LAW) – HONG KONG

—Report on the adoption of the UNCITRAL model law of arbitration / the Law Reform Commission of Hong Kong. – Hong Kong : The Commisssion, 1987.
v,121p. – (Topic).
Includes bibliographical references.

ARBITRATION AND AWARD (ISLAMIC LAW) – ISLAMIC COUNTRIES

—Commercial arbitration in the Arab Middle East : a study in Shara and statute law / Samir Saleh. – London : Published under the patronage of the International Chamber of Commerce by Graham & Trotman, 1984.
380p.
Bibliography: p445-455. - Includes index.
ISBN 0860104532 £55.00

ARCHITECTURE

—AJ Legal Handbook / Gregory Stone. – 4th ed. – London : Architectural Press, 1985.
264p : Illus.
ISBN 0851397514 Pbk £19.95

ARCHITECTURE – AUSTRALIA

—Architects and Copyright / Milsons Point : Australian Copyright Council.

ARCHITECTURE – CANADA

—Architects Act, 1983, Bill 122 : An Act to Revise the Architects Act / Ontario : Ontario Government Publications Service, 1983.
55p.

ARCHITECTURE - GREAT BRITAIN

—ACA Architect's Instruction / London : Architectural Press.
- (ACA Contract Documents).
ISBN 0851397425 Pbk £6.32

—ACA Contract Introductory Package / London : Architectural Press, 1985.
- (ACA Contract Documents).
ISBN 0851397301 Hbk £20.00

—ACA Final Certificate / London : Architectural Press.
- (ACA Contract Documents).
ISBN 0851397433 Hbk

—ACA Interim Certificate / London : Architectural Press.
- (ACA Contract Documents).
ISBN 0851397417 Hbk £7.47

—ACA Taking-Over Certificate / London : Architectural Press.
- (ACA Contract Documents).
ISBN 0851397441 Hbk £6.32

—AJ Contracts Guide to ACA Form of Building Agreement 1982 / 2nd ed. - London : Architectural Press, 1984.
- (ACA Contract Documents).
ISBN 0851397565 Hbk £4.95

—AJ Introduction and Complete Index to the 1985 Building Regulations / London : Architectural Press.
60p : Illus.
ISBN 0851398383 Pbk £7.50

—AJ Legal Handbook / Stone. - 4th ed. - London : Architectural Press, 1985.
ISBN 0851397514 Pbk £19.95

—Architect's Guide to Fee Negotiations : An Architecture and Building Practice Guide Book / London : Architectural Press, 1984.
160p.
ISBN 0946228051 Pbk £16.95

—Pre-Contract Practice for Architects and Quantity Surveyors / AQUA Group. - 7th ed. - London : Collins, 1986.
100p : Illus.
ISBN 0003832546 Hbk £8.95

ARCHIVAL RESOURCES - ENGLAND

—Guide to the records of the Lord Chancellor's Department / Patrick Polden. - London : HMSO, 1988.
xxx,376p.
Guide to Lord Chancellor's records on judges, courts and the legal profession and on the making of law on property, divorce, transport and lunacy.
ISBN 0113800150

ARCHIVES

—Disposal and retention of documents / the Institute of Chartered Secretaries and Administrators. - London? : Institute of Chartered Secretaries and Administrators, 1980.
32p.

AREA SPECIALIST LIBRARIANS - GREAT BRITAIN

—Directory of American studies librarians in the UK / Wetherby : British Library Lending Division, 1984.
100p.
ISBN 0712320237 Pbk

ARMAMENTS

—Armaments or disarmament? : SIPRI brochure / Stockholm International Peace Research Institute. - Bergshamra : The Institute, 1983.

—Arms Act, 1959 with Rules, 1962 (Annotated) / 4th ed. - Lucknow : Eastern Book Company, 1984.

ARMAMENTS - INDIA

—Law Relating to Arms, Ammunition and Explosives / K.K. Malik. - 4th rev. ed. - Lucknow : Eastern Book Company, 1985.
920p.

ARMED FORCES

—Handbook on the Law of War for Armed Forces / Geneva : Comite International de la Croix-Rouge, 1987.
254p.

—Law of War and the Armed Forces / 2nd ed. - Geneva : Comite International de la Croix-Rouge, 1981.
44p.

ARMED FORCES - INDIA

—Law Relating to Cantonments / Allahabad : Law Publishers, 1980.

ARMS CONTROL

—Armaments or disarmament? : SIPRI brochure / Stockholm International Peace Research Institute. - Bergshamra : The Institute, 1983.

—Arms Control Agreements : a Handbook / Stockholm : Almqvist & Wiksell, 1983.
328p.
ISBN 0850662486 Hbk £139.00

—Arms Control and Disarmament in Outer Space / Montreal : Centre for Research of Air and Space Law, 1987.
282p.

—Chemical industry and the projected chemical weapons convention : proceedings of a SIPRI/Pugwash conference / 2. - Oxford : Published on behalf of Stockholm International Peace Research Institute by Oxford University Press, 1986.
30cm.
Includes bibliography.
ISBN 0198291094 Pbk £9.95 (Apr.)

—Prohibitions or Restrictions on the Use of Certain Conventional Weapons / Geneva : Comite International de la Croix-Rouge, 1981.
33p.

—Science of peace / by J.G. Starke. - 2nd ed. - Sydney : Law Books, 1986.
xvi,193p.
Previous ed. published by A.W. Sijthoff, 1968. Bibliography: p.180-183. Includes index.
ISBN 0949553298

ARREST - AUSTRALIA - NEW SOUTH WALES

—Criminal procedure : police powers of arrest and detention : discussion paper / Sydney : Law Reform Commission of New South Wales, 1987.
xx,148p. - (D.P.).
Bibliography: p141-144.
ISBN 0730544567

—NSW Police Law Handbook / Sydney : Butterworths, 1988.
176p.
This handbook contains sections devoted to interrogation, arrest, and search and seizure. Included are chapters on detention and questioning, powers of arrest, searches, and search warrants. The intended audience is law enforcement officers.

ARREST - CANADA

—Arrest / Law Reform Commission of Canada. - Ottawa : The Commission, 1985.
143,161p. - (Working paper).
Includes bibliographical references. Added t.p. in French: L'arrestation. Cover title: Criminal law : arrest. Pages numbered in opposite directions. Text in English and French.
ISBN 0662538013

—Police Manual of Arrest, Seizure and Interrogation / 4th ed. - Agincourt : Carswell, 1988.
220p.

—The Police Manual of Arrest, Seizure and Interrogation / 4th ed. - Agincourt : Carswell, 1988.
182p.
This work is an updated handbook relected recent Canadian Criminal Code revisions and recent case law affecting police powers of arrest, seizure, and interrogation.

—Report on arrest / Law Reform Commission of Canada. - Ottawa : Canadian Law Reform Commission, 1986.
65,71p. - (Report).
Pages numbered in opposite directions. Text in English and French.
ISBN 0662544757

ARREST - GREAT BRITAIN

—Calver's Powers of Arrest : Charges / Heavens. - 8th ed. - London : Butterworths, 1987.
ISBN 0406842051 Pbk £5.95

—Constable's Pocket Guide to Powers of Arrest and Charges / Lewis Heavens. - 7th ed. - London : Butterworths, 1982.
This work for practitioner and police officer gives a ready reference to the law on arrest and the formulation of charges. The work includes all new laws and the amendments of the old ones relevant to powers of arrest and charges.*Police officers*
ISBN 0406842043 Pbk

—Notes Taken at the Time / London : Police Review Publishing, 1983.
ISBN 0851640052 Pbk £2.50

—Summonses and Charges / R. Houghton. - 4th rev. ed. - London : Police Review Publishing, 1983.
ISBN 085164001X Pbk £4.25

ARREST - INDIA

—Law of Arrest, Bail, Search and Seizure / 2nd ed. - Lucknow : Eastern Book Company, 1985.

—Law Relating to Wrongful Restraint, Wrongful Confinement, Criminal Force, Assault ... / Allahabad : Law Publishers, 1980.

ARREST - NEW ZEALAND

—Police powers and the rights of suspects / by Tim McBride. - Auckland : Legal Research Foundation, 1982.
23,8,5p.
'Paper presented at Auckland Law Faculty seminar series 1982 at University of Auckland'.
ISBN 0908581246

ARSON - CANADA

—Damage to property : arson / Law Reform Commission of Canada. - Ottawa : The Commission, 1984.
44,52p. - (Working paper).
Includes bibliographical references. Added t.p. in French: Les dommages aux biens : le crime d'incendie. Added t.p. in French: Les dommages aux biens : le crime d'incendie. Pages numbered in opposite directions. Text in English and French.
ISBN 0662532457

ART

—The penal protection of works of art / Siracusa : International Institute of Higher Studies in Criminal Sciences, 1983.
447p.
Includes bibliographical references. English, French or Italian.

ART - GREAT BRITAIN

—Practical Law for Arts Administrators / London : Offord Publications Ltd, 1983.
400p.
ISBN 0903931583 Hbk £8.95

—Sponsorship of sport, arts, and leisure : law, tax and business relationships / by Stephen Townley and Edward Grayson : with forewords by Lord Goodman, Dick Jeeps and Sir William Rees-Mogg. - London : Sweet & Maxwell, 1984.
xliii,333p; 23cm.
Guide to the law and tax considerations involved in the business of sponsorship. The legal status of sponsorship rights and licences is interpreted with reference to statute and case law. Intellectual property law, competition law, copyright and the remedies for its infringement, trade-marks, and passing-off are examined.
ISBN 0421304103 £19.75

ART WORKS

—Existing legislative protection of the cultural and natural heritage of the Pacific region / Patrick O'Keefe, Lyndel V. Prott. - s.l. : UNESCO, 1982.
v,140p.

—Explanatory report on the European Convention on Offences relating to Cultural Property / Strasbourg : Council of Europe, 1985.
35 p.; 21 cm.
'The text of the European Convention on Offences relating to Cultural Property is also reproduced in this publication'–P. 3.
ISBN 9287107955 pbk.

—Law and the cultural heritage / by Lyndel V. Prott and P.J. O'Keefe : foreword by Henry Cleere. - Abingdon : Professional Books, 1983.
xxvii,434p.
Bibliography: p.371-386. - Includes index. Cover title: Law and the cultural heritage/ by P.J. O'Keefe and Lyndel V. Prott.
ISBN 086205060X
ISBN 0862050650

—National legal control of illicit traffic in cultural property / by Lyndel V. Prott, P.J. O'Keefe. - Paris : UNESCO, 1983.
iv,144p.
Bibliography: p.144.

—Protection of movable cultural property : compendium of legislative texts / Hanna Saba, Nabil G Salame. - Paris : Unesco, 1984.
v. 1, 2; 24 cm.
Prepared by Hanna Saba, with assistance of Nabil G. Salame. Translation of: Protection du patrimoine culturel mobilier.
ISBN 9231016385 pbk. : v. 1

ARTICLED CLERKS - CANADA

—Articling Handbook / Butterworths, 1988.
ca 200p.
Guidance on how to deal with the everyday aspects of working in a law office. Advice on how to conduct interviews, handle incorporations, draft pleadings, conduct real estate searches and closings, prepare for examinations for discovery and for trial, and to attend on motions.
ISBN 0409804800 sb

ARTICLED CLERKS - GREAT BRITAIN

—How to survive your articles / London : Waterlow, 1986.
ISBN 0080330681 Pbk £5.95

ARTIFICIAL INSEMINATION

—Artificial family : a consideration of artificial insemination by donor / R. Snowden and G.D. Mitchell. - London : Allen & Unwin, 1981.
138p; 23cm.
Bibliography: p128-136. - Includes index.
ISBN 0041760018 Unpriced

ARTIFICIAL INSEMINATION - AUSTRALIA - NEW SOUTH WALES

—Artificial conception : report 1 : human artificial insemination / New South Wales Law Reform Commission. - Sydney : Government Printer, 1986.
xxxvii,177p. - (L.R.C.).
Bibliography: p.161-172.
ISBN 0730515907

—Human artificial insemination / New South Wales Law Reform Commission. - Sydney : Government Printer, 1984.
xxvi,138p. - (Artificial conception discussion paper).
Includes bibliographical references.

ARTIFICIAL INSEMINATION - CANADA

—Tentative proposals for a human artificial insemination act / Law Reform Commission of Saskatchewan. - 1. - Saskatoon : Law Reform Commission of Saskatchewan, 1981.
various pagings.
Includes bibliographical references.

ARTIFICIAL INSEMINATION - CANADA - SASKATCHEWAN

—Proposals for a Human Artificial Insemination Act / Law Reform Commission of Saskatchewan. - Saskatoon : The Commission, 1987.
12p.

ARTIFICIAL INSEMINATION - GREAT BRITAIN

—New reproductive techniques : a legal perspective / Douglas J. Cusine. - Aldershot, Hants. : Gower, 1988.
x,261p.
Bibliography: pp238-254. - Includes index.
ISBN 0566054108

—Report of the Committee of Inquiry into Human Fertilisation and Embryology / Chairman: Mary Warnock. - London : H.M.S.O., 1984.
At head of title: Department of Health and Social Security.
ISBN 0101931409

ARTIFICIAL INTELLIGENCE

—Automated analysis of legal texts : logic, informatics, law : edited versions of selected papers from the Second International Conference on 'Logic, Informatics, Law,'Florence, Italy, September 1985 / edited by Antonio A. Martino, Fiorenza Socci Natali : editorial assistant, Simona Binazzi. - Amsterdam : North-Holland, 1986.
xxii, 938 p.; 25 cm.
Includes bibliographies and index.
ISBN 0444701117

—Edited versions of selected papers from the international conference on 'Logic, Informatics, Law', Florence, Italy, April 1981 / Constantino Ciampi. - Amsterdam : North Holland Publishing, 1982.
xii,476p.
Bibliographies.

vol.2 : Deontic logic, computational linguistics, and legal information systems : Antonio A. Martino; editor 1982.
xli,518p.
Bibliographies.

ARTISTS - AUSTRALIA

—Visual artist and the law / by Shane Simpson. - Sydney : Law Book Co., 1982.
xiii,182p.
Bibliography: p.169-173. - Includes index.
ISBN 0455204527 Hbk £19

—Visual Artists and Photographers : Copyright and Designs / Milsons Point : Australian Copyright Council.

ARTISTS - CANADA

—Copyright for the Canadian Visual Artist / repr. 1981. - Ottawa : CARFAC.

—Model Agreements for Visual Artists : a Guide to Contracts in the Visual Arts / Ottawa : CARFAC, 1982.

ASIA, SOUTHEASTERN

—Armed separatism in Southeast Asia / edited by Lim Joo-Jock and Vani S. - Singapore : Institute of Southeast Asian Studies, 1984.
270 p.; 23 cm.
ISBN 9971902869

ASSAULT - INDIA

—Law Relating to Wrongful Restraint, Wrongful Confinement, Criminal Force, Assault ... / Allahabad : Law Publishers, 1980.

ASSAULT AND BATTERY - CANADA

—Assault / Law Reform Commission of Canada. - Ottawa : Canadian Law Reform Commission, 1984.
59,68p. - (Working paper).
Includes bibliographical references. Added t.p. in French: Les voies de fait. Pages numbered in opposite directions. Text in English and French.
ISBN 0662534174

ASSIZES - GREAT BRITAIN

—Reports and Pleas of Assizes at York : 1631-50 / Repr. of 1651 ed. - Abingdon : Professional Books.
335p.

ASYLUM

—Harmonisation of National Procedures Relating to Asylum / Strasbourg : Council of Europe, 1982.
ISBN 9287100497

—Protection of persons satisfying the criteria in the Geneva Convention who are not formally recognised as refugees : recommendation no.R (84)1 adopted by the Committee of Ministers of the Council of Europe on 25 January 1984, and Explanatory memorandum / Council of Europe. - Strasbourg : Council of Europe, 1984.
10p; 21cm.
'... prepared by the ad hoc Committee of Experts on Legal Aspects of Territorial Asylum and Refugees' - preface.
ISBN 9287103275

—Territorial asylum / by Atle Grahl-Madsen. - Stockholm : Almqvist & Wiksell International, 1980.
- (Studies in international law).
'Published under the auspices of Svenska institutet for internationell ratt, Uppsala, 1979.'. Includes index.

ASYLUM - GREAT BRITAIN

—Selling for a future : proposals for a British policy on refugees / British Refugee Council. - London : The Council, 1987.
25p.

ATMOSPHERIC POLLUTION

—Acid rain and international law / by Irene H. van Lier. - Halifax : Dalhousie University, 1981.
xxii,278p.
Originally presented as the author's thesis (LL.M.) - Dalhousie University 1980. Bibliography: p.257-266.
ISBN 9028622314 Hbk
ISBN 0770301851 Hbk

—Acid rain and the environment 1980-84 : a select bibliography / compiled and edited by Penny Farmer. - Letchworth : Technical Communications, 1984.
xx,108p; 30cm.
Includes index.
ISBN 0946655049 Pbk No price

—International standards and recommended practices : environmental protection : annex 16 to the Convention on International Civil Aviation / International Civil Aviation Organization. - 1st ed. - 1981. 1. - Montreal : International Civil Aviation Organization, 1981.
loose-leaf; 28cm.
Supersedes: International standards and recommended practices : aircraft noise : annex 16 to the Convention on International Civil Aviation. 3rd ed. - July 1978. Kept up to date by amendments and supplements.

—Transboundary air pollution : international legal aspects of the co-operation of states / editors, K. Flinterman, B. Kwiatkowska, and J. Lammers. - Dordrecht : M. Nijhoff, 1987.
390p.
Includes bibliographies and index.
ISBN 9024732859 Hbk £199.00

ATMOSPHERIC POLLUTION - AUSTRALIA

—National Guidelines for Control of Emission of Air Pollutants from New Stationary Sources / Kingston : Australian Government Publishing Service, 1986.
19p.
ISBN 0644045361 Hbk £2.00

ATMOSPHERIC POLLUTION - GREAT BRITAIN

—Air pollution control : the government response to the Fifth Report of the Royal Commission on Environmental Pollution / London : H.M.S.O., 1982.
At head of title: Department of the Environment, Central Directorate on Environmental Pollution.
ISBN 0117516546

—Industrial air pollution : health and safety 1983 / Health & Safety Executive. - London : H.M.S.O., 1985.
33p.
ISBN 0118837877

—Politics of clean air / Eric Ashby and Mary Anderson. - Oxford : Clarendon, 1981.
viii,178p; 24cm.
Includes index.
ISBN 0198583303 £15.00

AUCTIONS - ENGLAND

—Law of estate agency and auctions / by J.R. Murdoch. - 2nd ed. - London : Estates Gazette, 1984.
xlii,576p.
Includes bibliographical references and index.

AUCTIONS - GREAT BRITAIN

—Auctions : law and practice / Brian W. Harvey, Franklin Meisel. - London : Butterworths, 1985.
300p; 25cm.
Includes index.
ISBN 0406526605 Pbk £17.00

—Auctions Law and Practice / Meisel. - London : Butterworths, 1985.
ISBN 0406526605 Pbk £29.00

—Law of Estate Agency and Auctions / London : Estates Gazette, 1984.
ISBN 0728200724 Pbk £2.00

AUDIT COMMITTEES - GREAT BRITAIN

—Consultative paper by the Bank of England : the role of audit committees in banks / Bank of England. - London : Bank of England, 1987.
12p.

AUDITORS

—International audit in public sector / Simpson. - Cambridge : Woodhead-Faulkner, 1985.
ISBN 0859412725 Pbk £11.95

—International auditing / Davies. - 5th ed. - London : Butterworths, 1980.
ISBN 0372300421 Pbk £8.50

—Regulation of auditors : implementation of the EC Eighth Company Law Directive : a consultative document / Department of Trade and Industry. - London : Department of Trade and Industry, 1987.
77,11 leaves.
Includes the text of the Directive.

AUDITORS - EUROPE

—Court of Auditors : Annual Record Concerning the Financial Year 1983 Accompanied by the Replies of the Institutions-1983 / Kirchberg : Commission of the European Communities, 1984.
253p.

AUDITORS - EUROPEAN COMMUNITY

—Court of Auditors of the European Communities / Kirchberg : Commission of the European Communities, 1984.
24p.

AUDITORS - GREAT BRITAIN

—Accounting and Audit Data / 3rd ed. - Tolley Publishing, 1987.
ISBN 085459308X Pbk £6.95

—Audit Guide / London : Butterworths, 1983.
A publication for practitioners providing practical explanations of the stages of an audit. The book gives a straightforward discussion of the often confusing topic of the use of statistical sampling methods in the audit. Included are sections on flowcharting, error rate sampling, monetary unit sampling, as well as extracts from standard documentation for an audit.
ISBN 0406270600 Hbk

—Audit Guide / Stoy Hayward & Co. - London : Butterworths, 1983.
ISBN 0406270600 Pbk £11.50

—Audit Manual / London : Butterworths, 1984.
ISBN 0406258120 Pbk

—Audit Report / London : Butterworths, 1984.
ISBN 040601650X Pbk £15.00

—Audit Report / London : Butterworths, 1984.
A review of the current state of audit reporting which outlines legal and other requirements of the audit. The book surveys a wide range of reporting styles and provides many examples, drawn from published reports, to illustrate problems in modern auditing.
ISBN 040601650X Pbk

—Auditing / Pitman, 8th ed.
- (M & E Handbook Series).
ISBN 0712107932 Pbk £6.95

—Computer Auditing / London : Butterworths, 1984.
ISBN 0406252629 Pbk

—Internal Audit / Ken Impey. - London : Butterworths, 1985.
For students and practitioners, this book uses extensive illustrations and diagrams to present the state of the art in modern internal auditing. Techniques of examination and analysis are discussed.
ISBN 0406013802 Pbk

—Internal audit / Impey. - London : Butterworths, 1985.
ISBN 0406013802 Pbk £18.50

—Manual of Financial Reporting and Accounting / Touche Ross and Co. Staff. - 2nd ed. - London : Butterworths, 1985.
This book describes the legal requirements and professional pronouncements relating to audit reports and financial statements. The work gives recommended accounting and consolidating principles, and contains many examples of different types of audit reports.
ISBN 0406500509 Pbk

—Practical auditing / Pegler. - 17th ed. - London : Butterworths, 1985.
ISBN 0406678014 Pbk £13.50

—Practical Auditing / Spice and Pegler Staff. – 17th ed. – London : Butterworths, 1985.
A classic work for students of auditing. The book discusses the impact of the new Auditing Standards and Guidelines on the field. A detailed guide to audit techniques and administration is given.
ISBN 0406678014 Pbk £12.00

AUDITORS – SOUTH AFRICA
—Auditor's Manual / Keeton. – Cape Town : Legal & Financial Publishing, 1983.
ISBN 0869940198 Hbk £5.00

AUSTRALIA
—Australian official publications / by Howard Coxon. – Oxford : Pergamon, 1980.
xvi,211p,1 leaf of plates; 26cm. – (Guides to official publications).
Bibliography: p187-199. - Includes index.
ISBN 0080231314 £15.00

—Australian-United States' relations : the extraterritorial application of United States laws / the Parliament of the Commonwealth of Australia Joint Committee on Foreign Affairs and Defence. – Canberra : Australian Government Publishing Service, 1983.
xiii,84p. – (Parliamentary paper).
Includes bibliographical references.

—Bush Capital : How Australia Chose Its Federal City / Neutral Bay : Hale & Iremonger.
ISBN 0868060666 Hbk £24.95, 015

—Cases on the Criminal Code / R.A. Hayes. – North Ryde : Law Book Co, 1984.
xxiii, 739p.
ISBN 0455204276 Hbk £70.50
ISBN 0455204284 Pbk £54.50

—Changing the system : political and constitutional reform, some options and difficulties / by Donald Horne ... et al. – Bedford Park : Australasian Political Studies Association, 1981.
44 p.; 22 cm. – (Monograph / Australasian Political Studies Association).
ISBN 0909266190 pbk.

—Executive power of the Commonwealth of Australia / by H.E. Renfree. – Sydney : Legal books, 1984.
xxxvii,599p.
Includes index.
ISBN 0949553093

—Fractured Federation? / Jennifer Aldred, John Wilkes. – London : Allen and Unwin, 1983.
128p.
ISBN 0868611093 £15.00

AUSTRALIAN ABORIGINES – LEGAL STATUS, LAWS, ETC.
—Aborigines and the law / Peter Hanks. – London : Allen & Unwin, 1984.
400p.
ISBN 0868615447 £20.00

AUTHENTICATION – SCOTLAND
—Constitution and proof of voluntary obligations and the authentication of writings / Scottish Law Commission. – Edinburgh : The Commission, 1985.
v,203p. – (Consultative memorandum).
—Report on requirements of writing / Scottish Law Commission. – Edinburgh : HMSO, 1988.
vii,197p.
Includes bibliographical references. Includes draft legislation.
ISBN 010255188X

AUTHORITY
—Authority and power : studies on medieval law and government presented to Walter Ullmann on his seventieth birthday / edited by Brian Tierney and Peter Linehan. – Cambridge : Cambridge University Press, 1980.
x,274p,1leaf of plates; 24cm.
Bibliography: p255-274.
ISBN 0521222753 £25.00
—Authority of the state / Leslie Green. – Oxford : Clarendon Press, 1988.
x,273p.
: Revision of thesis (D. Phil.)–University of Oxford, 1984. Includes bibliographic references and index.
ISBN 0198249268

AUTHORS – AUSTRALIA
—Writers and the Law / M. McDonald. – North Ryde : Law Book Co, 1986.
xix, 262p.
ISBN 0455207119 Pbk £29.50

AVIATION INSURANCE
—Aviation insurance : the law and practice of aviation insurance including hovercraft and satellite insurance / by R.D. Margo. – London : Butterworths, 1980.
xxxviii,363p.
ISBN 0406288100 Hbk £57.00

AVIATION INSURANCE – GREAT BRITAIN
—Aviation Claims / London : Lloyd's of London Press, 1987.
ISBN 1850440948 Hbk
—Aviation Insurance Abbreviations: Organs and instruments / Witherby, 1983.
ISBN 0900886773 Pbk £4.50

BAIL – AUSTRALIA
—Bail : Issues and Prospects / L. T. Wilkins. – Canberra : Australian Institute of Criminology.

BAIL – AUSTRALIA – NEW SOUTH WALES
—Law of bail : practice, procedure and principles / by Brian Harrie Kevin Donovan : foreword by Mr Justice Roden : introduction by Roger Court. – Sydney : Legal Books, 1981.
xxi,186p.
Includes index.
ISBN 0959656855
—Law of bail : practice, procedure and principles / by Brian Harrie Kevin Donovan : foreword by Mr Justice Roden : introduction by Roger Court. – Sydney : Legal Books, 1981.
xxi,186p.
Includes index.
ISBN 0959656855

BAIL – CANADA
—Judicial interim release (Bail manual) / 1 vol. – Scarborough, Ontario : Butterworths (Canada).
Part one provides a one-paragrah summary of the key cases as they relate to specific sections or sub-sections of the Criminal Code or other relevant statutes. Part two contains a digest of the most cited cases in part one, giving the citation, a review of the facts, and the main issues decided. Part three contains references and excerpts for various Acts.

BAIL – ENGLAND
—Bail : law and practice / Clifford Chatterton. – London : Butterworths, 1986.
xxiii,277p; 25cm.
Includes index.
ISBN 0406101809 Pbk £23.00

BAIL – GREAT BRITAIN
—Bail : County Court Practice Nineteen Eighty-Seven / London : Butterworths, 1986.
ISBN 0406163235 Pbk
—Bail : Law and Practice / London : Butterworths, 1986.
ISBN 0406101809 Pbk £28.00

—The bail lottery / Prison Reform Trust. – London : Prison Reform Trust, 1986.
5 leaves.

BAIL – INDIA
—Law of Arrest, Bail, Search and Seizure / 2nd ed. – Lucknow : Eastern Book Company, 1985.
—Law of Bails / 5th ed. – Allahabad : Law Book Company, 1986.
750p.

—Law of Bails, Forfeiture of Bonds and Habeas Corpus / A.N. Saha. – 2nd ed. – Lucknow : Eastern Book Company, 1985.
391p.

BAIL – NEW ZEALAND
—Report on bail / Criminal Law Reform Committee. – Wellington : Government Printer?, 1982.
113p.

BALANCE OF PAYMENTS
—IMF and the debt crisis : a guide to the Third World's dilemma / Peter Korner ... et al. : translated from the German by Paul Knight. – London : Zed, 1987.
226p; 23cm.
Bibliography: p210-219. - Includes index. Translation of: Im Teufelskreis der Verschuldung.
ISBN 0862324874 Hbk £18.95
ISBN 0862324882 Pbk £6.95

BANK EXAMINATION – GREAT BRITAIN
—Consolidated supervision of institutions authorised under the Banking Act 1979 / Bank of England. – London : Bank of England, 1985.
14,10,9 leaves.
Includes texts of European Communities Consolidated Supervision Directive and the revised Basle Concordat.

BANK LOANS
—Medium-term loan market / J.A. Donaldson and T.H. Donaldson. – London : Macmillan, 1982.
viii,229p.
Includes index.
ISBN 0333326067

BANK LOANS – GREAT BRITAIN
—Bank finance for companies / by R. Pennington. – London : Sweet & Maxwell, 1987.
150p; 22cm.
Discusses bank finance for specific purposes by way of letters of credit, bank guarantees and performance bonds, the issue of settling sterling commercial paper by companies, the legal implications of factoring, the provision of third party guarantees and securities for loans to companies within a group, and legal remedies available to banks to recover advances of all kinds made to them.
ISBN 0421384905 £15.00 (Dec.)
—Law and practice of banking / J. Milnes Holden. – 6th ed. – London : Pitman Publishing, 1980.
xliii,459p.
Previous ed.: 1971. Includes index.
ISBN 0273014226

—Lending in booms and slumps / by L.S. Dyer : delivered under the auspices of King's College London. – London : King's College London, 1981.
35p; 25cm.

BANK MANAGEMENT – GREAT BRITAIN
—Consolidated supervision of institutions authorised under the Banking Act 1979 / Bank of England. – London : Bank of England, 1985.
14,10,9 leaves.
Includes texts of European Communities Consolidated Supervision Directive and the revised Basle Concordat.

BANKING
—Bank accounts : a world guide to confidentiality / Edouard Chambost : translated by Peter Walton and Margaret Thompson. – Chichester : Wiley, 1983.
xii,322p; 24cm.
Includes index. Translation from French.
ISBN 0471900761 Hbk
—Banking Law and Practice, 1985 : Conference Papers / Woolloomooloo : International Business Communications.
ISBN 0582939445 Hbk £49.95

—Banking Law and Practice, 1986 : Conference Papers / Woolloomooloo : International Business Communications.
ISBN 0949072087 Hbk £55.00

—Banking Law and Practice, 1987 : Conference Papers / Woolloomooloo : International Business Communications.
ISBN 0949072125 Hbk £55.00

—Butterworths banking and financial law review / London : Butterworths, 1987.
Index in each vol..

—Current problems of letters of credit and bankers' quarantees / William C. Hillman. – London : International Bar Association, 1985.
iii,404p.
Papers presented at the seminar in Amsterdam, 8-9 May 1984. Seminar Chairman: Judge William C. Hillman.

—Decade of change : banking in Europe : the next ten years / London : Lafferty, 1986.
221p.
A study by Arthur Andersen & Co..
ISBN 094839403X

—Dictionary of banking / F.E. Perry. – 3rd ed. – London : Pitman, 1988.
356p; 19cm.
Previous ed.: Plymouth : Macdonald and Evans, 1983.
ISBN 0712107657 Pbk £9.95
ISBN 0273029614 correct

—Domestic and multinational banking : the effects of monetary policy / Rae Weston. – London : Croom Helm, 1980.
411p.
Bibliographies.
ISBN 0856647101

—Global Investing / Kirzner. – New York : Dow Jones-Irwin, 1988.
ISBN 087094908X Hbk £26.50

—International bank accounting / Whinney. – 2nd ed. – London : Euromoney, 1987.
ISBN 1870031016 Pbk £75.00

—International bank supervision / by Connie M. Friesen. – London : Euromoney, 1986.
xi,124p.
Includes bibliographical references.
ISBN 1870031105

—International Banking Set-Off / London : Sweet & Maxwell.
ISBN 0421324503 Pbk

—Management and regulation of banks / John Cooper. – London : Macmillan, 1984.
xi,395p.
Bibliography: p383-386.
ISBN 0333342348

—Measures against the transfer and the safekeeping of funds of criminal origin : recommendation no. R(80)10 adopted by the Committee of Ministers of the Council of Europe on 27 June 1980 and explanatory memorandum / Council of Europe. – Strasbourg : Council of Europe, 1981.
12p.
'Prepared by a select committee of experts under the authority of the European Committee on Crime Problems' - verso t.p.. At head of cover title: Council of Europe, Legal Affairs.

—New financial instruments / by Ian Cooper ... et al. – London : Chartered Isntitute of Bankers, 1987.
x,89p.
Includes bibliographical references.
ISBN 0852971907

—Prudential supervision in banking / by R. M. Pecchioli. – Paris : Organisation for Economic Co-operation and Development, 1987.
298p.
Bibliography: p279-298.
ISBN 9264129162

—Secondary banking crisis, 1973-75 : its causes and course / Margaret Reid. – London : Macmillan, 1982.
ix,219p.

—Trading with the Enemy Act / London : Butterworths, 1988.
ISBN 0880631880 Hbk

—Wallace and McNeil's banking law / 9th. – Edinburgh : W Green & Son, 1986.
Analyses the banker/customer relationship dealing extensively with special customers. Coverage of bills of exchange and other financial instruments and description of some miscellaneous banking services. Ohter chapters cover securities over heritable and moveable property and personal guarantees. Includes the law of insolvency, sequestration, receivership and liquidation.
ISBN 0414007824

BANKING – AUSTRALIA

—Recent Developments in Banking Series : Off Shore Finance 1984 / Monash University Staff. – Clayton : Monash University Press, 1984.
ISBN 0867463511 Hbk £16.00

—Report of the Committee established by the Premier of New South Wales to report on the steps necessary to establish offshore banking activity in Australia with particular reference to Sydney / Offshore Banking Committee. – Sydney : The Committee, 1984.
28p.

BANKING – CANADA

—Banking and Finance Law Review / Andrew Chant. – Agincourt : Carswell.
This book focuses on issues pertinent to the legal and financial communities. The text is divided into four parts: articles, commentaries on recent developents in banking in Canada and in the world, and casenotes and book reviews.

—Banking Litigation 1986 / Vancouver : British Columbia Continuing Legal Education Society, 1986.
ISBN 0865042527 Hbk £55.00

—Crawford and Falconbridge Banking and Bills of Exchange / 8th ed. – Aurora : Canada Law Book Co, 1986.
2400p.

—Law of banking / by Ian F.G. Baxter. – 3rd ed. – Toronto : Carswell, 1981.
xl,574p.
Previous eds. entitled: The law of banking and the Canadian Bank Act. Includes bibliographical notes and index. Includes text of Banks and Banking Law Revision Act, 1980.
ISBN 0459337408

BANKING – ENGLAND

—Banker's documentary credits : issued in accordance with the Uniform customs and practice (1974 revision) of the International Chamber of Commerce / by F.M. Ventris. – 2nd ed. – London : Lloyd's of London Press, 1983.
xxi,350p.
Previous ed.: 1980. Includes index.
ISBN 0907432379

—Cases in the law of banking 1983-1985 / by P.E. Smart. – 2nd ed. – London : Sweet & Maxwell, 1986.
xxiii,95p; 22cm.
Previous ed.: published as Cases in the law of banking 1977-1980. 1981. Includes index.
ISBN 0421357606 Pbk £6.95

—Chorley and Smart leading cases in the law of banking / P. E. Smart, Robert Samuel Theodore Chorley Chorley. – 5th ed. – London : Sweet & Maxwell, 1983.
xlvi,397p; 23cm.
Previous ed.: 1977. Includes index.
ISBN 0421293403 Hbk £14.50
ISBN 0421293500 Pbk £10.00

—Encyclopaedia of banking law / general editor P.J. Cresswell : editors W.J.L. Blair, G.J.S. Hill, P.R. Wood : consulting editor on consumer credit R.M. Goode. – 2 v. – London : Butterworths, 1982.
loose-leaf; 26cm.
Includes index.
ISBN 0406569835 Unpriced

BANKING – EUROPEAN COMMUNITY

—EEC banking law / by Marc Dassesse and Stuart Isaacs. – London : Lloyd's of London, 1985.
xix,184p; 23cm.
ISBN 0907432808

—European banking law : a guide to Community and member state legislation / Belmont European Community Law Office. – London : Financial Times Business Information Ltd, 1987.
xviii,296p.
ISBN 0902101951

—Regulation of banks in the member states of the EEC / edited by Jane Welch for the British Bankers Association. – 2nd ed. – The Hague : Nijhoff, 1981.
viii,277p; 25cm.
Previous ed.: 1978. Includes index.
ISBN 9024725739 Unpriced

BANKING – GREAT BRITAIN

—Accountancy In Banking / Cambridge : Woodhead-Faulkner, 1983.
ISBN 0859411923 Hbk £19.95
ISBN 0859411931 Pbk £9.95

—Accounting For Banks / Matthew Bender, 1982.
ISBN 0000999082 Hbk £55.00

—Balance Sheets and the Lending Banker / Dyer. – 6th ed. – London : Europa Publications, 1986.
ISBN 0946653291 Pbk £8.95

—Bank Manager's Handbook / Cambridge : Woodhead-Faulkner, 1987.
ISBN 085941342X Hbk £25.00

—Bank Marketing Handbook, The / Cambridge : Woodhead-Faulkner, 1986.
ISBN 0859413330 Hbk £35.00
ISBN 0859413349 Pbk £12.95

—Bank Register / London : Euromoney, 1988.
ISBN 187003161X Hbk £95.00

—Bank security documents / J.R. Lingard. – London : Butterworths, 1985.
xxvi,367p; 26cm.
Includes index.
ISBN 0406258198 £30.00

—Bank Security Documents / London : Butterworths, 1985.
ISBN 0406258198 Hbk £34.00

—Bank security documents / J.R. Lingard. – 2nd ed. – London : Butterworths, 1988.
xxxiii,402p; 26cm.
Previous ed.: 1985. Includes index.
ISBN 0406106258 £45.00

—Banking Law / by G.A. Penn, A.M. Shea and A. Arora. – London : Sweet & Maxwell, 1987.
xlix,537p; 24cm.
In five sections covering bank regulation, the banker-customer relationship, negotiable instruments, guarantees and securities and insolvency. Covers the Insolvency Act 1986, the Financial Services Act 1986, and the Banking Act 1987.
ISBN 042139000X Hbk No price
ISBN 0421360607 Pbk £18.95

—Banking law / by Clive Hamblin. – London : Sweet & Maxwell, 1985.
xxvii,377p; 22cm. – (Concises College Texts).
Includes index.
ISBN 0421327502 Hbk £18.50
ISBN 042132760X Pbk £11.50

—Banking Secrecy and Financial Privacy / Oyez Longman Publishing. – London : Oyez Longman, 1980.
– (Oyez Longman Intelligence Report Ser.).
ISBN 0851204732 Hbk £55.00

—Banking services and the consumer / a report by the National Consumer Council. – London : Methuen, 1983.
x,246p; 24cm.
ISBN 0416357601 Hbk Unpriced
ISBN 0416357709 Pbk Unpriced

—Banking supervision / presented to Parliament by the Chancellor of the Exchequer. – London : H.M.S.O., 1985.
36p.
ISBN 0101969503 PBK £4.30

—Big Bang / Ritchie. – Northcote House, 1988.
ISBN 0746305494 Pbk £4.95

—Big Bank / Weidenfeld & Nicolson, 1986.
ISBN 0297789848 Hbk £9.95

—Bigger Bang / Waterlow, 1987.
ISBN 0080331009 Pbk £5.50

—British Banking 1960-85 / Weale. – London : Macmillan, 1986.
ISBN 0333375084 Hbk £29.50

—Consultative paper by the Bank of England : the role of audit committees in banks / Bank of England. – London : Bank of England, 1987.
12p.

—Correspondent Banking / London : Butterworths, 1988.
ISBN 0880637005 Pbk

—Correspondent Banking / London : Butterworths, 1987.
ISBN 0406007004 Pbk

—Country risk analysis / London : Butterworths, 1985.
ISBN 0406005508 Hbk £38.00

—Dictionary of Banking and Finance / London : Pitman Publishing, 1985.
ISBN 0273018590 Hbk £35.00

—Electronic banking and the law / by Anu Arora. – London : IBC Financial, 1988.
188p.
Includes index.
ISBN 1852710403 £65.00 (June)

—Electronic banking : the legal implications / edited by R.M. Goode. – London : Institute of Bankers, 1985.
xxi,142p; 22cm.
Conference proceedings.
ISBN 0852971303 £9.95

—Electronic treasury management / Cambridge : Woodhead-Faulkner, 1984.
ISBN 0859412733 Hbk £40.00

—Elements of Banking / 3rd ed. – Plymouth : Macdonald & Evans, 1985.
ISBN 071210657X Pbk £4.95

—Elements of Banking / 5th ed. – London : Sweet & Maxwell, 1986.
ISBN 0416383009 Pbk £5.95

—Elements of Banking / 5th ed. – Methuen, 1986.
ISBN 0416383009 Pbk £5.95

—Expert Systems in Banking and Securities / Jeffcoate. – Ovum, 1988.
ISBN 090396936X Hbk £465.00

—Factoring and the Lending Banker / Tolley Publishing, 1986.
ISBN 0854592539 Pbk £4.95

—Financial services legislation : the auditor's role in the financial services sector : a consultative document / Great Britain. – London : The Division, 1985.
12p.

—How to deal with your bank manager / London : Kogan Page, 1988.
ISBN 1850915962 Hbk £12.95
ISBN 1850915970 Pbk £5.95

—Law and practice of banking / J. Milnes Holden. – 4th ed. – London : Pitman, 1986.
lxv,500p; 22cm.
Previous ed.: 1982. Includes index.
ISBN 0273024884 Pbk £12.95

Vol.1 : Banker and customer / J. Milnes Holden. – 1982.
lviii,470p; 23cm.
Previous ed.: 1974. Includes index.
ISBN 0273017616 Unpriced

Vol.2 : Securities for bankers' advances / J. Milnes Holden. – 1986.
512p; 22cm.
Previous ed.: 1980. Includes index.
ISBN 0273022954 Pbk £10.95

—Law and practice relating to banking / F.E. Perry. – 4th ed. – London : Methuen, 1983.
x,566p; 20cm.
Previous ed.: 1981. Includes index.
ISBN 041635680X Pbk Unpriced

—Lloyds Bank Annual Review / Pinter, 1988.
ISBN 0861879740 Hbk £20.00

—Management for Bankers / London : Butterworths, 1988.
ISBN 0406503400 Pbk £13.50

—Mastering Banking / London : Macmillan, 1985.
ISBN 0333369122 Pbk £3.25

—Modern banking law / E.P. Ellinger. – Oxford : Clarendon, 1987.
400p; 24cm.
Includes index.
ISBN 0198761562 Hbk £35.00
ISBN 0198761570 Pbk £12.00

—Modern Merchant Banking / Wheble. – 2nd ed. – Cambridge : Woodhead-Faulkner, 1983.
ISBN 0859412156 Pbk £9.95
ISBN 0859412164 Hbk £17.50

—Money and banking in the United Kingdom / Routledge, 1988.
ISBN 0415004349 Hbk £45.00

—Paget's Law of banking / Maurice Megrah, F. R. Ryder, Antonio Bueno. – 9th ed. – London : Butterworths, 1982.
lxxv,678p; 26cm.
One of the major texts in the field of United Kingdom banking law. The book is fully updated to reflect major changes in legislation affecting banking.
ISBN 0406333521 Hbk £54.00

—Politics of banking / 2nd ed. – London : Macmillan, 1986.
ISBN 0333424123 Pbk £8.95

—Practice of banking/1 / Pitman, 1984.
ISBN 0712116796 Pbk £9.95

—Practice of Banking / E. P. Doyle, J. E. Kelly. – 3rd ed. Repr. of 1981 ed. – Plymouth : Macdonald & Evans, 1984.
400p.
ISBN 0712117555 Pbk £4.95

—Practice of banking / Kelly. – 3rd ed. – Plymouth : Macdonald & Evans, 1981.
ISBN 0712117555 Pbk £5.95

—Presenting financial proposals to banks / London : Butterworths, 1986.
ISBN 0406100705 Pbk £15.00

—Questions and answers on practical banking / Cambridge : Woodhead-Faulkner, 1984.
ISBN 085941258X Pbk £8.95

—Regulation and supervision of financial institutions / by D.T. Llewellyn. – London : Institute of Bankers, 1986.
77p.
Bibliography: p.75-77.
ISBN 0852971745

—Relationships between the supervisors, auditors and managements of banks / consultative paper by the Bank of England. – London : The Bank, 1985.
13,5 leaves.

—Report of the committee set up to consider the system of banking supervision / presented to Parliament by the Chancellor of the Exchequer. – London : H.M.S.O., 1985.
iii,26p.
Chairman: Robert Leigh-Pemberton.
ISBN 0101955006 PBK £3.50

—Sheldon and Fidler's practice and law of banking / P. J. M. Fidler, M. I. Freeman, Herbert Percival Sheldon. – 11th ed. – Plymouth : Macdonald and Evans, 1982.
liv,792p; 22cm.
Previous ed.: published as Sheldon's practice and law of banking. 1972. Bibliography: p769-770. - Includes index.
ISBN 0712119906 Pbk £8.95

—Sterling commercial paper market / Cambridge : Woodhead-Faulkner, 1988.
ISBN 0859414108 Hbk £40.00

—Strategic Planning for Electronic Banking / London : Butterworths, 1987.
ISBN 040610087X Pbk

—Strategic planning for electronic banking / London : Butterworths, 1987.
ISBN 040610087X Pbk £45.00

—Taxation aspects of banking operations / P F Swaine. – London : Butterworths, 1985.
ISBN 0406010692 Hbk £35.00

—Taxation Aspects of Banking Operations / P. F. Swaine. – London : Butterworths, 1985.
This book describes the tax consequences of all significant banking operations and how the effect of various taxes on banks differs from other corporations. An in-depth look at the taxation of banks in the United Kingdom.
ISBN 0406010692 Hbk

BANKING – HONG KONG

—Banking system of Hong Kong / T. K. Ghose. – Singapore : Butterworths, 1987.
viii,282p.
ISBN 0409995320 Hbk £50

—Banking System of Hong Kong / London : Butterworths, 1987.
ISBN 0409995320 Pbk £25.00

BANKING – ISLAMIC COUNTRIES

—Islamic banking and finance : the experience of Iran / by Sayed Hassan Amin. – Glasgow : Royston, 1986.
128p; 22cm.
Includes bibliography and index.
ISBN 0946706301 £27.00 (May)

—Islamic banking : the adaptation of banking practice to conform with Islamic law / S.H. Homoud. – London : Arabian Information, 1985.
300p; 28cm.
Translated from the Arabic.
ISBN 0860105032 Hbk £75.00 :
ISBN 0860105024 Pbk £35.00

BANKING – JAPAN

—Japanese banking, securities and anti-monopoly law / edited by Hiroshi Oda, R. Geoffrey Grice. – London : Butterworths, 1988.
174p.
Includes index. '...a selection of papers delivered at the first Japanese Law Conference held at the Faculty of Law, University College London in September 1987'. - Preface.
ISBN 0406106851 £45.00 (Oct.)

BANKING – MALAYSIA

—Central Banking In Malaysia / London : Butterworths, 1987.
ISBN 0409000000 Pbk

—Central Banking in Malaysia / London : Butterworths, 1987.
ISBN 0409995339 Hbk £78.00

BANKING – NIGERIA

—Law of Banking / Onitsha : Africana-FEP.

BANKING – SOUTH AFRICA

—Banking in South African law / by Nigel Willis. – Cape Town : Juta, 1981.
xxxiii,388p.
Includes bibliographical notes and index.
ISBN 0702112593

—Law of negotiable instruments in South Africa / Denis V. Cowen and Leonard Gering. – Cape Town : Juta, 1985.
xxiv,587.
ISBN 0702115703

BANKING – TURKEY

—Turkey's banks and banking systems / London : Euromoney, 1985.
ISBN 0903121859 Hbk £58.00

BANKING – UNITED STATES

—Banker's Handbook / 3rd ed. – New York : Dow Jones-Irwin, 1988.
ISBN 1556230435 Hbk £69.50

—Banking In The American South From The Age Of Jackson / Louisiana : Louisiana State University Press, 1988.
ISBN 0807114030 Hbk £33.25

BANKING – WEST GERMANY

—German Banking System / H. Hellwig. – 2nd ed. – Plymouth : Macdonald & Evans, 1984.
252p.
ISBN 0712154795 Pbk £22.50

BANKING (INTERNATIONAL LAW)

—Aid : rhetoric and reality / Teresa Hayter, Catharine Watson. – London : Pluto, 1985.
xv,303p; 20cm.
Includes index.
ISBN 0861046269 Pbk £4.95

—Banking law / by G.A. Penn, A.M. Shea and A. Arora. – London : Sweet & Maxwell, 1987.
500p.
Discusses the legal effect of specimen clauses, agreements and other documentation used in international banking transactions. Takes a practical approach to the principles and emerging issues in the area of international financial markets.
ISBN 0421390107 Hbk No price (Oct.)
ISBN 0421390107 Pbk £25.00

—Banks abroad : establishment - operations - supervision / editors Friedrich Schwank & Frank R. Ryder. – London : Kluwer, 1986.
xi,423p.
Includes bibliographies and index.
ISBN 0903393964

—Country risk analysis / John Calverley. – London : Butterworths, 1985.
ix,181p; 23cm.
Includes index.
ISBN 0406005508 No price

—International banking centres / edited by Bowman Brown. – London : Euromoney, 1982.
v,277p.
ISBN 0903121271

—International banking : management and strategies / David B. Zenoff ... et al. – London : Euromoney, 1985.
xv,207p.
ISBN 0903121786

—International financial policy and economic development : a disaggregated approach / Graham Bird. – Basingstoke : Macmillan, 1987.
xvi,348p; 23cm.
Bibliography: p338-343. - Includes index.
ISBN 033340890X £29.50

—International interbank market : a descriptive study / Basle : Bank for International Settlements, 1983.
44p; 21cm.
' ... written by a study group ... under the auspices of the Bank for International Settlements' - inside front cover.

—Internationalisation of banking : the policy issues / by R.M. Pecchioli. – Paris : O.E.C.D., 1983.
221p.
Includes bibliographical references.
ISBN 9264124888

—Journal of international banking law / Oxford : ESC Publishing Ltd., 1986-.

—Law of bankers' commercial credits / Maurice Megrah. – 7th ed. – London : Europa, 1984.
xxxv,343p; 25cm.
Previous ed.: 1979. Bibliography: pxxxiv-xxxv. - Includes index.
ISBN 0905118782 £19.50

—Legal problems of international banking / by F.R. Ryder. – London : Sweet & Maxwell, 1986.
70p; 23cm.
ISBN 0421367806 Pbk £16.00 (Dec.)

—Liability of banks under letters of credit / Matti Kurkela. – Helsinki : Union of the Finnish Lawyers Pub. Co., 1982.
85 p.; 22 cm.
Bibliography: p. 84-85.
ISBN 9516401503 Fmk70.00

—Money lenders : bankers in a dangerous world / Anthony Sampson. – Sevenoaks : Coronet, 1983.
377p; 18cm.
Originally published: London : Hodder and Stoughton, 1981. Includes index.
ISBN 0340287713 Pbk £2.50

—Regulation of international banking / Richard Dale. – Cambridge : Woodhead-Faulkner, 1984.
vii,208p.
ISBN 085941261X

—Supranationals / edited by S. Melvin Rines and Christine A. Bogdanowicz-Bindert. – London : Euromoney, 1986.
200p.
ISBN 0903121840

—UNCITRAL Draft Convention on international bills of exchange and internnational promissory notes, and Draft Convention on international cheques / memorandum by the Joint Working Party of the Law Reform Committees of the Senate of the Inns of Court and the Bar and the Law Society. – London? : the Joint Working Party?, 1983.
7p.

BANKING (ISLAMIC LAW)

—Directory of Islamic Banking and Financial Institutions / Oxford : Croom Helm, 1988.
ISBN 0709913478 Hbk £50.00

—Islamic Banking and Finance / London : Butterworths, 1986.
ISBN 0406100349 Hbk £46.00

—Islamic banking and finance / Butterworths editorial staff. – London : Butterworths, 1986.
xii,149p; 24cm.
Conference papers. Includes index.
ISBN 0406100349 £65.00

BANKING (ISLAMIC LAW) – ISLAMIC COUNTRIES

—Shirazi: Islamic banking / Habib Shirazi. – London : Butterworths, 1990.
170; 248.
Covers the basis of the credit system, regulations and basic criteria, Qardalhasanah grant, Modharabah, civil partnership, equity partnership, direct investment, instalment sales, hire purchase, forward deals, Jo'aalah, Mozara'ah, Mosa'qaat, debt purchase and guarantees.
ISBN 0406100357 Hbk £75.00

BANKING LAW

—Banking Law and Practice / Delhi : Dhanpat Rai and Sons.

—International law of development : comparative perspectives / edited by Francis Snyder and Peter Slinn. – Abingdon : Professional Books, 1987.
ix,322p; 22cm.
ISBN 0862052580

—Objective Type Questions in Banking Law and Practice / 6th rev. ed. – New Delhi : Sultan Chand and Sons, 1985.
iv, 124p.

—Textbook of Banking : Law Practice and Theory of Banking / S.V. Vasudevan. – 3rd ed. – New Delhi : S. Chand and Company, 1984.
xv, 834p.

BANKING LAW – AUSTRALIA

—Banking Law / 2nd ed. – Sydney : Butterworths, 1988.
550p.

—Banking Law and Practice in Australia / F.W. Coops. – 2nd ed. – Butterworths, 1988.
552p.
ISBN 0409494577 Pbk £45.00
ISBN 0409494569 Hbk £65.00

—Law and Practice of Banking / Carleton : Pitman Pty Ltd, 1984.
ISBN 0273315587 Hbk £27.95

BANKING LAW – CANADA

—Acting for Banks and Their Customers / Vancouver : Continuing Legal Education Society of British Columbia, 1984.
445p.
ISBN 0865041504 Hbk £75.00

—Bank Act of Canada / 2nd ed. – Toronto : DeBoo, 1986.
548p.
This text contains the Act, Regulations and Orders as amended to July 31, 1986, as well as Guidelines, Rules, and Interpretation Bulletins issued by the Office of the Inspector General of Banks. Also included are consolidated forms of certain Orders, and reporting and notice requirements.
ISBN 0888202539 Pbk £34.95

—Banking : the Law in Canada / Agincourt : Carswell, 1985.
ISBN 045937290 Pbk £30.80

—Banking : The Law in Canada / Agincourt : Carswell, 1985.
687p.
This book describes the corporate structure of banks in Canada including the role of directors and officers and the rights of shareholders. The Bank Act and the Bills of Exchange Act are set out in the appendices to the work.

—Crawford and Falconbridge Banking and Bills / 8th ed. – Aurora : Canada Law Book, 1986.

—Crawford and Falconbridge banking and bills of exchange / Bradley Crawford. – 8th edition. 2 v. – Aurora : Canada Law Book Co, 1986.
ISBN 0888040369

BANKING LAW – EUROPEAN COMMUNITY

—European Banking Law : An Analysis of Community and Member State Legislation / Margie Lindsay. – London : Financial Times Ltd, 1983.

BANKING LAW – GREAT BRITAIN

—Banking Act 1979 / London : LLoyd's of London Press, 1987.
ISBN 1850441065 Hbk

—Banking Act 1979 / London : Lloyd's of London Press, 1987.
ISBN 1850441065 Pbk £18.50

—Banking Dictionary / Cambridge : Woodhead-Faulkner, 1984.
ISBN 3478512433 Hbk £25.00

—Banking For Students / Pitman, 1986.
ISBN 0273023209 Pbk £7.95

—Banking Law / Howcroft. – Oxford : Blackwell, 1985.
ISBN 0631143025 Pbk £9.50

—Banking Law Review 1987 / London : Butterworths, 1987.
ISBN 0406570582 Hbk £64.00

—Banking Points From Case and Statute Law / F. E. Perry. – London : Waterlow, 1982.
122p.
ISBN 0080390277 Pbk £4.95

—Cases In Banking Law / 3rd ed. – Plymouth : Macdonald & Evans, 1983.
ISBN 0712104771 Pbk £4.95

—Cases in Banking Law / D. Palfreman. – 3rd Rev. ed. – Plymouth : Macdonald & Evans, 1983.
160p. – (M and E Handbook Ser.).
ISBN 0712104771 Hbk £4.50

—Cases in the Law of Banking 1983-1985 / 2nd ed. – London : Sweet & Maxwell, 1986.
ISBN 0421357606 Pbk £7.50

—Encyclopaedia of Banking Law / London : Butterworths, 1982.
Service to Date.
ISBN 0406569835 Hbk £220.00

—Law and Practice of Banking / 4th ed. – London : Pitman Publishing, 1986.
ISBN 027304884 Pbk £12.95

Vol. 2 1988.
ISBN 0273022954 Pbk £13.95

—Law and Practice relating to Banking / 4th ed. – Methuen, 1983.
ISBN 041635680X Pbk £7.50

—Law of Banking / 3rd ed. – Plymouth : Macdonald & Evans, 1986.
ISBN 0712106820 Pbk £6.50

—Law of Banking / 2nd ed. – Plymouth : Macdonald & Evans, 1982.
336p. – (M and E Handbook Ser.).
ISBN 0712112588 Hbk £4.95

—Law of Banking / Megrah. – 10th ed. – London : Butterworths, 1988.
ISBN 040633353X Hbk

—Law Relating to Banking / 5th ed. – London : Butterworths, 1985.
ISBN 0406647682 Hbk £19.50
ISBN 0406647690 Pbk £16.50

—Law Relating to Banking (Q & A) / London : Financial Training, 1984.
ISBN 090632257X Pbk £6.50

—Practice and law of banking / Fidler. – 11th ed. – Pitman, 1982.
ISBN 0712119787 Pbk £11.95

BANKING LAW – HONG KONG

—Hong Kong Banking Ordinance / Anthony Williams. – London : Butterworths, 1988.
350p.
Contains an annotation of the Banking Ordinance of 1986 and the Amendment Ordinance of 1988, annotations that consider the practical implications of the new provisions with reference to extensive legal authorities in Hong Kong and other countries.
ISBN 0409995398 Hbk

—Hong Kong banking ordinance / Williams. – London : Butterworths, 1987.
ISBN 0409995398 Pbk £45.00

BANKING LAW – INDIA

—Banking Law and Practice / S.P. Jain. – New Delhi : Kalyani Publishers.

—Banking Law and Practice / New Delhi : Himalaya Publishing House, 1987.
200p.

—Banking Law and Practice / 5th ed. – New Delhi : Kalyani Publishers, 1988.
ISBN 8170960916 Hbk £60.00

—Banking Regulation Act, 1949 / Allahabad : Law Publishers, 1983.
227p.

—Banking Regulation Act, 1949 : Together with the Banking Companies (Acquisition and Transfer of Undertakings) Act, 1980 and the Public Financial Institutions (Obligations as to Fidelity and Secrecy) Act, 1983 / Lucknow : Eastern Book Company, 1984.
163p.

—Banking Regulation Act along with Rules and Various Allied Laws / 4th ed. – Allahabad : Law Publishers, 1983.

—Elements of Banking Law / New Delhi : Kalyani Publishers, 1987.
ISBN 8170960185 Hbk £25.00

—Manual of Banking and Public Financial Institutions : Laws with Allied Acts, 2 Vols. / Madhya Pradesh : Lawyers Home, 1986.

—Manual of Commercial and Banking Laws, 4 Vols. / Allahabad : Law Publishers, 1983.

BANKING LAW – JAPAN

—Japanese Banking, Securities and Anti-Monopoly Law / Geoffrey Grice. – Butterworths, 1988.
ca 223p.
ISBN 0406106851 Hbk £125.00

BANKING LAW – MALAYSIA

—Central Bank of Malaysia Ordinance 1958 (F.M. No. 61/1958) / Kuala Lumpur : International Law Books Services.

—Central Banking in Malaysia / Singapore : Butterworths (Asia), 1987.
520.
Deals with powers over finance companies, merchant banks, Islamic banks and other deposit takers, issue of currency, monetary policy and regulation of the quantity and direction of credit, and the relationship with the government.
ISBN 0409995339 Hbk

BANKING LAW – NEW ZEALAND

—Banking Law in New Zealand / North Ryde : 43.00, 1986.
xxxiii, 287p.
ISBN 0455206570 Hbk £27.50
ISBN 0455206589 Pbk

—Banking Law in New Zealand / London : Law Book Co, 1986.
ISBN 0455206570 Hbk £21.50
ISBN 0455206589 Pbk £13.75

—Encyclopedia of Banking Law, 2 Vols. / William Blair. – Wellington : Butterworths.
A looseleaf service on banking in the United Kingdom. The material is presented in two sections. First the statutory regulation of banking is presented. Second, materials related to the statutes are set forth.

—Law Relating to Banking / 4th ed. – Wellington : Butterworths, 1980.
ISBN 0406647674 Pbk £29.95

—New Zealand Banking Law / Butterworths.
400p.

BANKING LAW – UNITED STATES

—Banking Law in the USA / London : Butterworths, 1987.
ISBN 040610350X Hbk £80.00

—Pollard : Regulation of US Banking / London : Butterworths, 1987.
ISBN 040610350X Pbk

BANKING LAW – WEST GERMANY

—German Banking Law : A Synoptical Translation of the Banking with an Introduction in English Gesetz Uber das Kreditwesen : Deutsch-Englische Textausgabe Des Gesetzes Uber das Kreditwesen Mit Einer Englischen Einleitung / Martin Peltzer. – 2nd ed. – Cologne : Otto Schmidt, 1986.
x, 85p.
ISBN 3504400048 Hbk

BANKRUPTCY

—Acts and rules relating to insolvency / by George R. Harding and P. MacPherson. – Brisbane : Watson, Ferguson, 1887.
lviii,338p.
Includes index.

—Bankruptcy : Law and practice / Christopher Berry, Edward Bailey : foreword by Sir Nicolas Browne-Wilkinson. – London : Butterworths, 1987.
lx,668p; 26cm.
Includes index.
ISBN 0406526109 £40.00

—Butterworths insolvency law handbook / editor: Michael Crystal. – London : Butterworths, 1987.
vi,1005,29p.
ISBN 0406500061

—Disqualification and personal liability of directors : a guide to the changes made by the Insolvency Act 1985 / L.S. Sealy. – Bicester : CCH, 1986.
iv,27p.
ISBN 0863250920

—Going bust : inside the bankruptcy business / Stephen Aris. – London : Deutsch, 1985.
194p; 23cm.
Includes index.
ISBN 0233976930 £8.95

—Tolley's European insolvency guide / Anthony R. Houghton, Neil H. Cooper. – Croydon : Tolley Publishing Co., 1984.
xv,364p; 23cm. – (An Extel Group publication).
Includes index.
ISBN 0854590978 Pbk £19.95

BANKRUPTCY – AUSTRALIA

—Australian Bankruptcy Act 1966 and Rules / 4th ed. – North Ryde : C.C.H. Australia, 1986.
300p.
ISBN 0869036777 Hbk £24.00

—Australian bankruptcy law / Lewis. – 8th ed. – North Ryde : Law Book Co., 1984.
xxiii,293p.
Includes bibliographical references and index.
ISBN 0455205205

—Australian Bankruptcy Law / Rose. – 8th ed. – London : Law Book Co, 1984.
ISBN 0455205213 Pbk £13.00

—Debt recovery and insolvency / Law Reform Commission. – Canberra : Australian Government Publishing Service, 1987.
xxxii,312p. – (Report).
ISBN 0644013648

—General insolvency inquiry / The Law Reform Commission. – Sydney : The Commission, 1987.
xxv,252p. – (Discussion paper).
Accompanied by Appendix: Draft Legislation (99p.).

—Guidebook to Australian Bankruptcy Law / T.G. Matthews. – North Ryde : C.C.H. Australia, 1982.
255p.

—Guidebook to Australian bankruptcy law / L.G. Priddle and T.G. Matthews. – North Ryde, N.S.W. : CCH Australia, 1982.
vii,255p.
Includes index.
ISBN 0869033727

BANKRUPTCY – CANADA

—Bankruptcy, 1984 / Vancouver : British Columbia Continuing Legal Education Society, 1984.
ISBN 0865041571 Hbk £65.00

—Bankruptcy 1984 / Vancouver : Continuing Legal Education Society of British Columbia, 1984.
321p.
ISBN 0865041571 Hbk £65.00

—Bankruptcy - 1984 / Vancouver : British Columbia Continuing Legal Education Society, 1984.
321p.
ISBN 0865041571 Hbk £65.00

—Bankruptcy law of Canada / by L.W. Houlden and C.H. Morawetz. – New ed. 2 v. – Toronto : Carswell, 1984.
looseleaf.
Previous ed.: 1960. Includes text of Bankruptcy Act.

—Bankruptcy : Present Problems and Future Perspectives / Toronto : DeBoo, 1985.
349p.
ISBN 0888202245 Hbk £75.00

—Canada Bankruptcy Legislation / 2nd ed. - Don Mills : CCH Canadian Ltd, 1984.
360p.
ISBN 0887962505 Pbk £12.95

—Canadian Bankruptcy Reports / David E. Baird. - Agincourt : Carswell.

—Crown priority in insolvency / Anne E. Hardy. - Toronto : Carswell, 1986.
xxxii, 195 p.; 24 cm.
Includes index. Bibliography: p. 179-181.
ISBN 0459391402

—Foreclosures, Debentures, and Bankruptcy for Legal Assistants / Vancouver : British Columbia Continuing Legal Education Society, 1985.
119p.
ISBN 0865042136 Hbk £55.00

—Guide to Commercial Insolvency in Canada / Butterworths, 1988.
ca 388p.
Takes the reader through the relevant proceedings and applicable legislation, covering the commencement of bankruptcy proceedings, receiverships, liquidation of asset; to directors' responsibilities on insolvency and annulment of transactions.
ISBN 0409846740 Hbk

BANKRUPTCY - CANADA - BRITISH COLUMBIA

—Report on fraudulent conveyances and preferences : Law Reform Commission of British Columbia / Law Reform Commission of British Columbia. - Vancouver : The Commission, 1988.
vii,180p.
Includes bibliographical references. Includes draft legislation.
ISBN 0771886314

—Report on the buyer's lien : a new consumer remedy / Law Reform Commission of British Columbia. - Vancouver : The Commission, 1987.
iv,62p.
Includes bibliographical references.
ISBN 0771885954

BANKRUPTCY - CANADA - ONTARIO

—Farm Bankruptcies in Ontario / Ontario : Ontario Government Publications Service, 1983.
5p. - (Research Review: No. 13).

BANKRUPTCY - ENGLAND

—Administrators : part II of the Insolvency Act 1986 / Hamish Anderson. - London : Sweet & Maxwell, 1987.
250p; 26cm.
Guide to the insolvency procedure established by the Insolvency Act 1986, including a commentary on the relevant provisions, and statutory instruments. Examines the status and powers of an administrator, and the effects of an administration order on the members, creditors, and employees of a company.
ISBN 0421348208 £15.00

—Annotated guide to the 1986 insolvency legislation : Insolvency Act 1986, Company Directors Disqualification Act 1986 and Insolvency Rules 1986 / L.S. Sealy, David Milman. - Bicester : CCH Editions, 1987.
viii,994p; 23cm.
Includes index.
ISBN 0863250823 Pbk £12.00

—Butterworths Consolidated Legislation Service /. - Professional Publ.
146p.
ISBN 0409014176 £35.00

—Comments by JUSTICE on the white paper 'A revised framework for insolvency law' (Cmnd. 9175) / JUSTICE. - S.l. : JUSTICE, 1984.
7 leaves; 30cm.

—Corporate insolvency / Peter Totty and Michael Crystal. - London : McGraw-Hill, 1982.
xv,155p; 26cm.
Includes index.
ISBN 0070845824 £12.95

—Guide to the Insolvency Act 1985 / W.F. Ratford ... et al. - London : Financial Training Publications, 1985.
xvi,336p.
Includes index. Includes text of the Act. At head of title: Peat Marwick.
ISBN 0906322847

—Insolvency law & practice / London : F. Cass, 1985-.

—Insolvency law and practice : report of the Review Committee / Chairman Sir Kenneth Cork : presented to Parliament by the Secretary of State for Trade ... - London : H.S.M.O., 1982.
xvi,460p.
ISBN 010185580X

—Muir Hunter on personal insolvency / Muir Hunter and John Briggs. - 1. - London : Stevens, 1987.
looseleaf.
Supersedes 19th ed. of Williams and Muir Hunter on bankruptcy. Includes index.

—Personal insolvency : a practical guide / Ian S. Grier, Richard E. Floyd. - London : Sweet & Maxwell, 1987.
xxiii,224p; 26cm.
Deals with the law and procedure relating to personal insolvency, through the full range of bankruptcy from the pre-petition stage to the closing procedures. Covers changes introduced by the Insolvency Act 1986, and includes forms of available voluntary arrangements, falling short of bankruptcy, and aspects of criminal bankruptcy.
ISBN 0421360100 £19.50

—Revised framework for insolvency law / presented to Parliament by the Secretary of State for Trade and Industry ... - London : H.M.S.O., 1984.
53p.
ISBN 0101917503

—Set-off / S. Rory Derham. - Oxford : Clarendon, 1987.
320p; 22cm.
Includes bibliography and index.
ISBN 019825556X £30.00

—Winding up of insolvent companies in England and France / Christopher Livadas. - Deventer, Netherlands : Kluwer Law and Taxation Publishers, 1983.
xxxvi, 384 p.; 25 cm.
: Originally presented as the author's thesis (Ph.D.–City of London Polytechnic, 1981). Bibliography: p. 383-384.
ISBN 9065440879 CIP rev.

BANKRUPTCY - EUROPE

—Bankruptcy, Winding-Up, Arrangements, Compositions and Similar Proceedings : Draft Convention and Report / Kirchberg : Commission of the European Communities, 1982.
116p.

BANKRUPTCY - EUROPEAN COMMUNITY

—European insolvency practitioners' handbook : the AEPPC compendium of insolvency law and practice / edited by Sir Kenneth Cork and G.A. Weiss. - London : Macmillan, 1984.
xix,291p; 23cm.
Includes index.
ISBN 0333366158 £40.00

BANKRUPTCY - FRANCE

—Winding up of insolvent companies in England and France / Christopher Livadas. - Deventer, Netherlands : Kluwer Law and Taxation Publishers, 1983.
xxxvi, 384 p.; 25 cm.
: Originally presented as the author's thesis (Ph.D.–City of London Polytechnic, 1981). Bibliography: p. 383-384.
ISBN 9065440879 CIP rev.

BANKRUPTCY - GREAT BRITAIN

—Administration procedure / Frank Wooldridge. - Bristol : Jordans, 1987.
xxii,113p; 21cm.
Includes index.
ISBN 0853081247 Pbk £8.50

—Bankruptcy Law / 8th ed. - Plymouth : Macdonald & Evans, 1981.
ISBN 0712102647 Pbk £3.95

—Bankruptcy : Law and Practice / London : Fourmat, 1987.
ISBN 1851900322 Hbk £28.50

—Bankruptcy Manual / Tolley Publishing, 1988.
ISBN 0854592199 Hbk

—Bankruptcy of individuals and partnerships / Bicester : CCH Editions Ltd, 1990.
Describes the procedural and practical processes of the law under the Insolvency Act 1986, the Insolvency Rules 1986, the Insolvency (Amendment) Rules 1987, and the Insolvent Partnerships Order. Also covers jurisdiction in bankruptcy, the trustee in bankruptcy, proof of debts, assets in bankruptcy, the family home, distribution of the estate, and tax consequences of bankruptcy.
ISBN 0863251439 Hbk £48.00
ISBN 086325084X Pbk £36.00

—Bankruptcy of Individuals and Partnerships / London : CCH, 1988.
ISBN 0863251439 Hbk £48.00

—Bankruptcy Procedure / Freize. - 9th ed. - London : Longman Professional, 1987.
ISBN 08512313073 Pbk £13.95

—Bankruptcy: the law and practice / London : Fourmat, 1988.
534.
Discusses new insolvency legislation as it applies to bankruptcy.
ISBN 1851900322 Hbk £32.50

—Corporate rescues and insolvencies / J.R. Lingard. - London : Butterworths, 1986.
xxvi,222p; 26cm.
Includes index.
ISBN 0406100403 No price

—Disqualification and personal liability of directors : a guide to the changes made by the insolvency legislation of 1985 and 1986 / by L.S. Sealy. - 2nd ed. - Bicester : CCH, 1987.
iv,53p.
Explains the rules regarding directors' disqualification, the imposition of personal liability on company directors and others (including wrongful trading), and the rules on the restriction of use of certain company names by directors and shadow directors.
ISBN 0863251307

—Guide to Bankruptcy / P. A. F. De Vos. - revised 1983 ed. - Abingdon : Professional Books, 1984.
ISBN 0903486482 Hbk £19.00
ISBN 090348644X Pbk £12.00

—Handbook Bankruptcy Law and Practice / 4th ed. - London : Longman Professional, 1988.
ISBN 085120726X Hbk

—Handbook of bankruptcy law and practice / Steven A. Frieze. - 4th ed. - London : Longman Professional (UK), 1988.
- (Practitioner Series).
Discusses the new concepts of statutory demands, individual voluntary arrangements and deeds of arrangement, and sets out the procedure leading to a bankruptcy order. Contains a list of courts with bankruptcy jurisdiction.
ISBN 085120726X Hbk £35

—Insolvency / London : Collins, 1986.
200p.
ISBN 0003832937 Hbk £17.50

—Insolvency / Peter Totty and Michael Jordan. - London : Longman Professional (UK).
Covers areas such as the disqualification of directors, wrongful trading, voluntary arrangements, appointment of administrators, and antecedent transactions. Contains statutes, statutory instruments and guidance notes, forms and practice directions, tables of destination, derivations and special definitions. New chapters cover the Government Insolvency Service, the construction industry and insurance companies.
ISBN 0851211429 Llf £205

—Insolvency Act 1985 / with annotations by Ian Fletcher. - London : Sweet & Maxwell, 1986.
various pagings.
Includes index. Includes text of the Act.
ISBN 0421347007

—Insolvency and Company Law : Reform & Renewal / London : Law Society, 1985.
25p. - (Nineteen Eighty-Five Crash Course Transcripts).

—Insolvency law / Steven A. Frieze. - 1st ed. - London : Longman Professional (UK), 1989.
- (Longman Practice Notes).
Covers all forms of insolvency, both corporate and personal. Guidance on voluntary and compulsory winding up, receivership, administration, company voluntary arrangements and deeds of arrangement.
ISBN 0851215114 PBK £9.95

—Insolvency : law and taxation / Timothy J. Lyons. - 1st ed. - London : Longman Professional (UK), 1988.
- (Law and Taxation).
Examines legal aspects and tax implications of both company and partnership insolvency. Chapters deal with the enforcement powers of the Inland Revenue and tax planning opportunities prior to and during an insolvency. Contains worked examples, precedents, forms and non-statutory material.
ISBN 0851214193 Hbk £35

—Insolvency Procedure Notes / Michael Stubbs. - London : Waterlow, 1987.
160p.
ISBN 0080330894 Pbk £17.95

—Law of Bankruptcy / 2nd ed. Repr. of 1895 ed. - Abingdon : Professional Books.

—Personal insolvency / London : Sweet & Maxwell, 1986.
ISBN 0420475605 Hbk £220.00

—Retention of title on the sale of goods / John Parris. - London : Granada, 1982.
186p; 24cm.
Includes index.
ISBN 0246116129 Unpriced

—Winding-up and bankruptcy procedures / Shaws Linton Publications, 1988.
ISBN 0906653142 Hbk £12.95

BANKRUPTCY - INDIA

—Law of Insolvency (In Nutshell) / repr. 1983. - Lucknow : Eastern Book Company.
82p.

—Law Provincial Insolvency Act / 5th ed. - Allahabad : Universal Book Agency, 1988.
212p.

—Provincial Insolvency Act / 5th ed. - Allahabad : Law Book Company, 1988.
xiv, 958p.

BANKRUPTCY - NEW ZEALAND

—Effect of disputed debts, set-offs and counterclaims on winding-up and bankruptcy petitions / by R. J. Calnan. - Auckland : Legal Research Foundation, 1981.
55p.
ISBN 0908581165

—Law of Insolvency / 2nd ed. - Butterworths, 1972-.
ISBN 0409601152 Hbk £90.20

BANKRUPTCY - NORTHERN IRELAND

—Northern Ireland Bankruptcy Law and Practice / Belfast : Queen's University of Belfast, 1984.
350p.
ISBN 0853892334 Hbk £65.00

—Northern Ireland bankruptcy law and practice / by John M. Hunter. - Belfast : SLS Legal Publications, 1984.
lvii,466p.
Includes index.

BANKRUPTCY - SCOTLAND

—Adjudications for debt and related matters / Scottish Law Commission. - 2. - Edinburgh : The Commission, 1988.
- (Discussion paper).

—Bankruptcy / Edinburgh : W Green & Son, 1989.
Commentary on the law and practice of bankruptcy since the Bankruptcy (Scotland) Act 1985. Includes the text of the Act with subsequent amendments.
ISBN 0414008944 Hbk

—Commentaries on the Law of Scotland in Relation to Mercantile and Maritime Laws, Movable and Heritable Rights and Bankruptcy, 2 Vols. / 3rd ed. Repr. of 1819 ed. - Abingdon : Professional Books.

—Equalisation of diligences / Scottish Law Commission. - Edinburgh : The Commission, 1988.
vii,146p. - (Discussion paper).

—Handbook Conveyancing Practice in Scotland / London : Butterworths, 1986.
ISBN 0406206007 Pbk £19.00

—Report on bankruptcy and related aspects of insolvency and liquidation / Scottish Law Commission. - Edinburgh : H.M.S.O., 1982.
xv,597p; 25cm. - (HC).
ISBN 0102176825 Pbk £14.90

—Rights in security over moveables, cautionary obligations and bankruptcy / Edinburgh : W Green & Son, 1983.
Offprint from Scots Mercantile law by the same author, bringing together cahpters relating to the law of insolvency.
ISBN 0414007131 SOFTBACK

BANKRUPTCY - SOUTH AFRICA

—Law of cession / by Susan Scott. - Cape Town : Juta, 1980.
xxiv, 154 p.; 25 cm.
Includes index. Bibliography: p. xi-xvi. Adaptation of author's thesis, University of South Africa, 1977.
ISBN 0702110949

—Law of insolvency / by Catherine Smith. - 2nd ed. - Durban : Butterworths, 1982.
xiii,476p.
Previous ed.: 1973. Includes index.
ISBN 0409056022 HBK R98
ISBN 0409056030 PBK R71

—Law of insolvency in South Africa / by Mars, Harold Edward Hockly. - 7th ed. - Cape Town : Juta & Co., 1980.
lviii, 697 p.; 25 cm.
'Insolvency Act 24 of 1936': p. 526-589. Includes bibliographical references and index.
ISBN 0702111627

—Preferences on insolvency : working paper 1 / South African Law Commission. - Pretoria : Government Printer, 1982.
ix,119p.
On title page: Project 37.
ISBN 0621078387

—Review of preferent claims in insolvency / South African Law Commission. - Pretoria : The Commission, 1984.
viii,75p. - (Report).
Bibliography: p.vii-viii.

BANTU LAW - SOUTH AFRICA

—Seymour's Customary law in Southern Africa / J. C. Bekker, J. J. J. Coertze. - 4th ed. - Cape Town : Juta, 1982.
lxi,446p.
ISBN 070211233X Pbk
ISBN 0702112933

BAR ASSOCIATIONS - CANADA

—Canadian Bar Association : Proceedings of the First, Second and Third Meetings / Agincourt : Carswell, 1984.

BAR ASSOCIATIONS - ENGLAND

—Report of the Committee on the Constitution of the Senate / Chairman: Rt. Hon. Lord Rawlinson of Ewell. - London : Senate of the Inns of Court and the Bar, 1986.
71p.

BARRISTERS - CANADA

—Advocates' Quarterly (1977-Present) / Aurora : Canada Law Book Co.
Back Vols.

BARRISTERS - GREAT BRITAIN

—Barristers' Clerks: The Law's Middlemen / Manchester : Manchester University Press, 1983.
ISBN 0719009286 Hbk £7.50

—Counsel / London : Sweet & Maxwell.

—How to Become a Lay Advocate / 2nd ed. - London : Shelter, 1984.

—Inns of Court and Chancery / Railton. - Southampton : Ashford Press, 1985.
ISBN 090706910X Hbk £24.95

—Inns of Court : Middle Temple Records (1501-1703) / Repr. of 1905 ed. - Abingdon : Professional Books.
214p.

—Rise of the barristers / Oxford : Oxford University Press, 1986.
ISBN 0198217641 Hbk £35.00

BARRISTERS - SOUTH AFRICA

—Second report : Commission of Inquiry into the Appearance of Advocates in the Supreme Court of South Africa / F.S. Smuts. - Pretoria : Printed by and obtainable from the Government Printer, 1985.
70 p.; 30 cm.
Afrikaans and English. Report of F.A. Smuts, the Chairman, and only member of the Commission of Inquiry into the Appearance of Advocates in the Supreme Court of South Africa.
ISBN 0621097195 pbk. R4.00 (R5.00 other countries)

BAUXITE - GUYANA

—Nationalisation of Guyana's bauxite : the case of Alcan / M. Shahabuddeen. - Georgetown : Ministry of Information, 1981.
xvii,306p.
Bibliography: p282-306.

BERLIN

—Legal status of Berlin / by I.D. Hendry and M.C. Wood. - Cambridge : Grotius, 1987.
xxii,388p.
Describes the unique legal position of Berlin as it emerges from the actual practice and positions adopted by the four Occupying Powers. Deals with the original occupation rights of the four Powers, and their agreements and practices. Makes reference to Allied and German legislation, and includes chapters on the institutional framework and law applicable in Berlin, and the special Berlin area.
ISBN 0949009059

BIAS

—Equality and judicial neutrality / Sheilah L. Martin and Kathleen E. Mahoney, editors. - Toronto : Carswell, 1986.
xxvii, 430 p.; 24 cm.
Papers presented at a conference held in Banff, Alta., May 22-24, 1986. Includes bibliographical references.
ISBN 0459308319

—Law of Bias and Malafides / 3rd ed. - Lucknow : Eastern Book Company, 1985.
298p.

BIAS - ENGLAND

—Bias and impartiality in magistrates' courts / R.D.S. Stevens. - Chichester : Rose, 1982.
xvii,105p; 22cm.
Includes index.
ISBN 0859922316 Pbk £6.80

BIBLIOGRAPHY

—Accessions list : India : quinquennial serials cumulation : 1976 / Library of Congress. - 3 v. - New Delhi : Library of Congress Office, 1977.
ISBN 01457608

—Annotated bibliography public opinion and social policy / by Donald J. Bourgeois. - Ottawa : Ministry of the Solicitor General, 1985.
56p. - (Usier report).

—Application of humanitarian law : selective bibliography prepared by the Peace Palace Library / Center for Studies and Research of the Hague Academy of International Law : bibliographie selective preparee par la Bibliotheque du Palais de la Paix : Centre d'Etude et de Recherche de l'Academie du droit Internationale de la Haye. - The Hague : Center for Studies and Research of the Hague Academy of International Law, 1986.
80p.
Preliminary material in English and French.

—Applications of computer technology to law (1969-1978) : a selected bibliography / compiled by Elaine Kozak : edited by M. Anne Foster and Shirley A. Lounder. - Ottawa : Canadian Law Information Council, 1980.
ii,106p. - (Working paper).
Includes index. Cover title: Bibliography computers and law.

—Applications of Computer Technology to Law 1969-78 : a Selected Bibliography / M. Anne Foster. - Ottawa : Canadian Law Information Council, 1980.
110p.

—Applications of computer technology to law (1979-1982) : a selected bibliography / compiled by Judith M. Cameron and edited by Lorna K. Rees-Potter and Allan Kling. - Ottawa : Canadian Law Information Council, 1983.
- (Working paper).
Includes index. Cover title: Bibliography computers and law supplement (1979-1982).

—Basic resourses on Nigerian law / by M.O. Olaitan and Oluremi Jegede. - Lagos : Libriservice, 1983.
iii,64p.
ISBN 9782372048

—Bibliographic control of official publications / edited by John E. Pemberton. - Oxford : Pergamon, 1982.
172p; 22cm. - (Guides to official publications).
Includes bibliographies.
ISBN 0080274196 Unpriced

—Bibliography of Abridgements, Digest, Dictionaries and Indexes of English Law to the Year 1800 / Abingdon : Professional Books, 1984.

—Bibliography of Canadian criminal justice history / Bibliographie sur l'histoire de la justice penale au Canada : Ministry of the Solicitor General, Research division. - Ottawa : Ministry of the Solicitor General, 1984.
426p. - (User report).

—Bibliography of Canadian Law / Ottawa : Canadian Law Information Council, 1982.
271p.
ISBN 0920358012 Hbk £25.00 set

—Bibliography of computers and the law / Melbourne : Victorian Society of Computers and Law, 1984.
22 leaves.

—Bibliography of eighteenth century legal literature : a subject and author catalogue of law treatises and all law related literature held in the main legal collections in England / by J.N. Adams and G. Averley : with historical and technical assistance from F.J.G. Robinson : for the BELL Project at the University of Kent in Canterbury. - Newcastle upon Tyne : Avero, 1982.
xvi,900p; 31cm.
Six microfiche in pocket.
ISBN 0907977014 Unpriced

—Bibliography of Irish Trials / London : Butterworths, 1986.
ISBN 0862050804 Hbk £29.50

—Bibliography of Israeli law in European languages / Renee Sanilevici. - Jerusalem : Harry Sacher Institute for Legislative Research, 1985.
221p.
Supersedes: A bibliography of Israel law in English and other European languages / compiled by Judith Romney Wegner. 1972; and, A bibliography of Israel law ... 1972-1979 / compiled by Judith Deborah Wilkenfeld. 1979. Includes index.

—Bibliography of material on Indonesian law in the English language / by John Ball. - 3rd ed. - Sydney : Faculty of Law, University of Sydney, 1981.
90p.
Includes index.

—Bibliography of materials on legislative and other legal drafting and the interpretation of statutes / 3rd rev. ed. - London : Commonwealth Secretariat, 1985.
62p.
Previous ed.: 1977.

—Bibliography of South African criminal law : general principles / by Andre Rabie. - Cape Town : Juta, 1987.
viii,91p.
ISBN 0702118524

—Bibliography of the International Court / International Court of Justice. - London : HMSO, 1984.
ISBN 0119836971 Hbk £1.90

—Bibliography of the main publications on state and law of Great Britain issued in the USSR in 1946-1983 / Akademiia Nauk SSSR. – Moscow : The Institute, 1984.
14p.
'Prepared by the Group on Foreign Scientific Information of the Institute of State and Law of the Academy of Sciences of the USSR. Translated into English by Yu. D. Kouptsov'.

—Bibliography of Western Australia Royal Commissions : Select Committees of Parliament and Boards of Inquiry 1870-1979 / Helen Stafford. – Blackwood : Zalums & Stafford, 1980.
116p.
ISBN 0959450602 Hbk £20.00

—Bibliography on Ethyl Alcohol for Forensic Science and Medicine and the Law / Edinburgh : Scottish Academic Press Ltd, 1980.
444p.
ISBN 0707302536 Hbk £20.00

—Bibliography on land-locked states / edited by M.I. Glassner. – 2nd rev. and enl. ed. – Dordrecht : M. Nijhoff, 1986.
xiii, 210p.
Includes indexes.
ISBN 9024732611

—Bibliography on the constitutions of Nigeria / compiled by Oluremi Jegede. – London : Oceana, 1981.
vi,72p; 26cm.
Includes index.

—Bibliography on the writings of the Hon. Judge T. O. Elias / by Oluremi Jegede. – 2nd ed. – Lagos : Nigerian Institute of Advanced Legal Studies, 1986.
viii, 51p. – (Occasional paper).
Includes index.
ISBN 9782353027

—Bibliography on transnational law of natural resources / Martin Bartels...et al. – Deventer : Kluwer, 1981.
227p.
Published for the Institut fur Auslandisches und International Wirtschaftsrecht, Frankfurt am Main.
ISBN 9065440410

—Bowker's Law Books and Serial in Print 1985-1986 / London : Butterworths.
ISBN 0835220397 Hbk £840.00

—Bowker's Law Books and Serials in Print Update 1987 / London : Butterworths.
175p.

—British national bibliography 1950-1984 / 430 microfiches. – London : British Library, Bibliographic Services, 1986.
in box.

—British national bibliography 1981-1985 / 125 microfiches. – London : British Library Bibliographic Services, 1987.

—Canadian Telecommunications Regulation Bibliography / Ottawa : Canadian Law Information Council.
ISBN 0921481063 £25.00

—Case Law Reporting : a selected Bibliography and Checklist of Canadian Law Reporting Studies / Ottawa : Canadian Law Information Council, 1980.
86p.
ISBN 0920358055 Pbk £10.00

—Catalogue of the Law Library of Messrs. Hodding and Everett, Solicitors, Salisbury / Repr. of 1834 ed. – Abingdon : Professional Books.

—Checklist of law reports and statutes in Canadian law libraries / National Library of Canada Resources Survey Division, Collections Development Branch : Bibliotheque nationale du Canada, Division de l'inventaire des ressources, Direction du developpement des collections. – Ottawa : The Library, 1981.
xii,249p.
Includes index. Text in English and French.
ISBN 0660504529

—Civil rights with special reference to the Commonwealth Caribbean : a select bibliography / Velma Newton. – Cave Hill, Barbados : Institute of Social and Economic Research (Eastern Caribbean), University of the West Indies, 1981.
110p. – (Occasional bibliography series).
Includes index.

—CLIC Bibliography of Computers and Law 1983-1986 / Ottawa : Canadian Law Information Council.
106p.
ISBN 0921481128 Hbk £20.00

—Commissions of Inquiry under the Inquiries Act, part I, 1967 to date / prepared by Denise Ledoux. – Ottawa : Library of Parliament, Information and Reference Branch, 1980.
p.154-175.
Supplements: Federal Royal Commissions in Canada 1867-1966 : a checklist / George Fletcher Henderson.

—Commonwealth Caribbean legal literature : a bibliography of all primary sources to date and secondary sources for 1971-1985 / Velma Newton. – Cave Hill, Barbados : Faculty of Law Library, University of the West Indies, 1987.
492p.
Includes index.
ISBN 976800116X

—Complete reference guide to United Nations sales publications 1946-1978 / 2. – Berlin : de Gruyter, 1982.
Contents: v.1. The catalogue / compiled and edited by Mary Eva Birchfield - v.2. Indexes : sales number index, title index / compiled by Mary Eva Birchfield; KWIC index / compiled by Jacqueline Coolman.
ISBN 3110087197

—Consumer affairs : a select bibliography / Department of Trade Victoria Street Library : compiled by Linda Wishart. – London : The Library, 1982.
34p.
Includes index.

—Contractual claims : an annotated bibliography / compiled by P.A. Harrow. – 4th ed. – Ascot : Chartered Institute of Building, 1986.
vi,25p; 25cm.
Previous ed.: 1979.
ISBN 0906600847 Pbk No price

—Crime / by Monica A. Walker. – Oxford : Published for the Royal Statistical Society and the Social Science Research Council by Pergamon, 1981.
xii,406p; 26cm.
Bibliography: p281-284. - Includes index. Originally titled: Reviews of United Kingdom statistical sources.
ISBN 0080261043 £18.25

—Criminal investigation : a selective literature review and bibliography / by Duncan Chappell, Robert Gordon, Rhonda Moore. – Ottawa : Ministry of the Solicitor General, Communication Division, 1982.
68p.
ISBN 0662120310

—Documentation sources in human rights / Council of Europe. Directorate of Human Rights. Human Rights Documentation Centre. – Strasbourg : The Council, 1987.
38p. – (H(87)2).

—EC index : an abstracting and indexing guide to publications and documents of the European Communities / Maastricht : Europe Data, 1985-.

—English Legal Manuscripts / Zug : Inter Documentation Company.
ISBN 3857500093 Hbk £50.00

Vol. 2: Catalogue of the Manuscript Year Books, Readings, and Law Reports in Lincoln's Inn, the Bodleian Library and Gray's Inn
ISBN 3857500247 Hbk £118.00

—European integration : select international bibliography of theses and dissertations Europaische Integration : Internationales Auswahlverzeichnis von Dissertationen und Diplomarbeiten Integration europeenne : bibliographie internationale selective de theses et memoires, 1957-1980 / J.P. Siemers, E.H. Siemers-Hidma : preface, Ralf Dahrendorf. – 2nd rev. and enl. ed. – The Hague : Martinus Nijhoff, 1981.
xx, 412 p.; 24 cm.
English, French, German, and Italian. Includes indexes.
ISBN 9024725429

—Function of bibliography / Roy Stokes. – 2nd ed. – Aldershot : Gower, 1982.
xi,201p; 24cm. – (A Grafton book).
Previous ed.: London : Deutsch, 1969. Includes index.
ISBN 0566034409 Unpriced

—Guide to International Law Periodicals / Ibadan : University Press.

—Guide to official industrial property literature : the Netherlands, Belgium, Luxembourg, Benelux / Brenda M. Rimmer. – London : British Library, Science Reference Library, 1981.
28p; 25cm.
Includes index.
ISBN 090291460X Pbk Unpriced

—Guide to purchasing law reports / Doug MacEllven, Guy Tanguay, Lorna K. Rees-Potter : edited by L.K. Rees-Potter. – Ottawa, Ont. : Canadian Law Information Council, 1985.
iv, 115 p.; 23 cm.
Includes index.
ISBN 0920358578

—Guide to United States patent and trademark literature / Brenda M. Rimmer. – London : British Library, Science Reference Library, 1980.
3,24p; 25cm.
Includes index.
ISBN 0902914529 sd £2.50

—How to update a statute for all Canadian jurisdictions : as of April 1980 / edited by Gail S. Dykstra. – Ottawa : Canadian Law Information Council, 1980.
38p.
First published in: CLIC's Legal materials letter, 1979-1980. Later ed. (1985) by Mary Jane T. Sinclair.
ISBN 0920358047

—Human rights reports : an annotated bibliography of fact-finding missions / by Berth Verstappen. – London : Zell, 1987.
400p; 21cm.
Includes index.
ISBN 0905450353 Hbk £45.00

—Index to Canadian Legal Literature : Supplemental Volumes to the Canadian Abridgment, 3 Vols. / Carswell Legal Publications. – Agincourt : Carswell, 1985-1987.
This multi-volume series is a comprehensive index to legal materials published in Canada. The work contains full bibliographic references to Canadian legal monographs, articles, case comments, annotation, and audio-visual materials.

—Index to Legal Books 1988 / New York : Bowker, 1988.
ISBN 0835224368 Hbk £300.00

—Index to legal essays : English language legal essays in festschriften, memorial volumes, conference papers and other collections, 1975-1979 / compiled for the British and Irish Association of Law Librarians under the editorship of Barbara Tearle. – London : Mansell, 1983.
xii,430p; 26cm.
Bibliography: pxii.
ISBN 0720116538 £25.00

—Index to New Zealand legal writing / J.F. Northey. – 2nd ed. – Auckland : Legal Research Foundation, 1982.
ix,260p.
Previous ed.: 1977.
ISBN 090858119X

—Industrial relations : an international and comparative bibliography / compiled by John Bennett and Julian Fawcett for the British Universities Industrial Relations Association. – London : Mansell, 1985.
200p; 23cm.
Includes index.
ISBN 0720117879 £20.00

—Information sources in law / London : Butterworths, 1986.
ISBN 0408114746 Hbk £38.00

—Information sources in law / editor R.G. Logan. – London : Butterworths, 1986.
xiv,370p; 23cm. – (Butterworths guides to information sources).
Commentary on specialist legal literature and electronic data bases. Refers to source materials, textbooks, reference books, journal articles, and visual reports and bibliographies. Covers social law, employment law, United States of America law, European Community law, computer-assisted research, and law books for non-lawyers.
ISBN 0408114746 Hbk £43.00

—International Bibliography of Air Law 1900-1971. Supplements / Dordrecht : Kluwer, 1976.
xxii, 169p.
ISBN 9028605266 Hbk £64.00

1977-1980 1981.
394p.
ISBN 9024725550 Hbk £160.00

1981-1984 1985.
284p.
ISBN 9065442308 Hbk £104.00

—International law of human rights in Africa : basic documents and annotated bibliography / compiled by M. Hamalengwa, C. Flinterman, E.V.O. Dankwa. – Dordrecht : M. Nijhoff, 1988.
xii, 427 p.; 25 cm.
Includes bibliographical references and index.
ISBN 9024735874

—International Law of the Sea : a Bibliography / Dordrecht : Kluwer, 1980.
432p.
ISBN 9028602690 Hbk £196.00

—International law of the sea and marine affairs, a bibliography / edited by Nikos Papadakis, Martin Glassner. – The Hague : M. Nijhoff, 1983.
xxvi,579p.
Supplement to: International law of the sea / N. Papadakis. Includes indexes.
ISBN 9024728150 Hbk £350.00

—Keyguide to information sources on the international protection of human rights / J.A. Andrews and W.D. Hines. – London : Mansell, 1987.
xiii,169p; 24cm.
Includes index.
ISBN 0720118735 £25.00

—Kirsh : Selected Bibliography of Construction Law Writings in Canada / Agincourt : Carswell, 1988.
43p.

—Law : a guide to the collection of Hammersmith & Fulham / Hammersmith & Fulham Libraries. – 2nd ed. – London : Hammersmith & Fulham Libraries, 1987.
40p.
ISBN 0904038068

—Law & science : a selected bibliography / compiled by Morris L. Cohen, Naomi Ronen and Jan Stepan : edited by Vivien B. Shelanski and Marcel C. La Follette. – 2nd ed. reprinted. – Cambridge, Mass. : M.I.T. Press, 1980.
xix,155p; 24cm.
This ed. originally published: 1978. Includes index.
ISBN 026203073X £9.30

—Law books 1876-1981 : books and serials on law and its related subjects / 4. – New York : R R Bowker, 1981.
xviii,5039p; 29cm.
Includes index.
ISBN 0835213978 Hbk £413.00

—Law Books and Serials in Print 1988 / New York : Bowker, 1988.
ISBN 0835224139 Hbk £320.00

—Law journals / Middlesex Polytechnic Library Services. – Hendon : The Polytechnic, 1982.
11p.
'List of law related journals and law reports taken by Middlesex Polytechnic libraries'.

—Law of the Sea : A Select Bibliography / London : HMSO, 1985.
ISBN 9211333350 Hbk £12.00

—Law of the Sea : a Select Bibliography / Geneva : United Nations Publications.
ISBN 9210330633 Hbk £9.50

—Lawyers' Law Books / 2nd ed. – London : Butterworths, 1985.
ISBN 0862050723 Hbk £32.50

—Legal Bibliography, 3 Vols. / Repr. of 1925 ed. – Abingdon : Professional Books.

—List of current legal research topics : being topics forming the subject of research by students for degrees in Universities and Polytechnics in the United Kingdom / Institute of Advanced Legal Studies. – 35th ed. – London : the Institute, 1987.
vii,111p.
Supplements: Legal research in the United Kingdom 1905-1984. Includes indexes.

—Malaysian legal source materials in London, Oxford and Cambridge / by Shaikha Zakaria : with a foreword by M.B. Hooker. – Kuala Lumpur : Perpustakaan Universiti Malaya, 1985.
x,66p.
Includes index.
ISBN 9679430057

—Marine Affairs Bibliography : a Comprehensive Index to Marine Law and Policy Literature / Leslie A. Foster. – Dordrecht : Kluwer, 1987.
702p.
ISBN 902473570X Hbk £375.00

—Maritime boundary delimitation : an annotated bibliography / Ted L. McDorman, Kenneth P. Beauchamp, Douglas M. Johnston. – Lexington, Mass. : Lexington Books, 1983.
xiii,207p; 24cm.
Includes index.
ISBN 0669061468 Unpriced

—Maxwell and Brown's Check List of British and Colonial Reports and Periodicals / 3rd ed. Repr. of 1937 ed. – Agincourt : Carswell.

—Native Law Bibliography / Saskatoon : University of Saskatchewan, Native Law Centre, 1984.
100p.
ISBN 0888801416 Hbk £20.00

—Nigerian elections : a bibliography / by A.T. Agboola. – Lagos : University of Lagos Library, 1983.
ix,45p.
Includes index.

—Official publications of Western Europe / Eve Johansson. – London : Mansell, 1984.
xvi,313p; 24cm.
Includes bibliographies and index.
ISBN 0720116236 £28.00

Vol.2 : Austria, Belgium, Federal Republic of Germany, Greece, Norway, Portugal, Sweden, Switzerland and United Kingdom / edited by Eve Johansson. – 1988.
x,278p.
Includes bibliographies and index.
ISBN 0720116627 Hbk £38.50 (Mar.)

—Overview and annotated bibliography of the needs of crime victims / Colin Meredith. – Ottawa : Ministry of the Solicitor General, 1984.
138p. – (User report).

—Paper Chasing : Resources for Legal Studies / North Ryde : C.C.H. Australia, 1986.
308p.
ISBN 086903670X Hbk

—Police and the community / Eric Edwards. – London : G.L.C., 1983.
20p. – (Research documents guide).
ISBN 0716813688

—Policy formation in the European Communities : a bibliographic guide to Community documentation 1958-1978 / Michael Hopkins. – London : Mansell, 1981.
xx,339p; 24cm.
Includes index.
ISBN 0720115973 £24.50

—Poverty and Policy in the United Kingdom : A Classified Bibliography / London : Policy Studies Institute, 1980.

—Privacy and data protection : an international bibliography / edited with an introduction by David H. Flaherty with the assistance of Terence J. Donohue and Peter J. Harte. – London : Mansell, 1984.
304p.
Includes index.
ISBN 0720117194 £23.50

—Protection du droit a la vie a la lumiere des regles du droit international : bibliographie selective / preparee par la Bibliotheque du Palais de la Paix, La Haye : selective bibliography : prepared by the Library of the Peace Palace, The Hague. – The Hague : Centre for Studies and Research of the Hague Academy of International Law, 1983.
17 leaves.

—Public administration : a select bibliography / 6th rev. ed. – London : Overseas Development Administration, 1986.
iv,25,7p.
Previous ed.: 1985.

—Public administration : a select bibliography / Foreign and Commonwealth Office Overseas Development Administration Library. – 5th ed. – London : The Library, 1985.
64p.
Includes index.

—Public administration : a select bibliography / 4th rev.ed. – London : Overseas Development Administration, 1980.
102p.
Includes index.

—Race and the police / Eric Edwards. – London : G.L.C., 1983.
21p. – (Research documents guide).
ISBN 071681367X

—Rare books for law libraries / by Thomas H. Reynolds. – London : Glanville, 1983.
141p.

—Readability and Legal Writing : a Bibliography / Ottawa : Canadian Law Information Council, 1985.
15p.
ISBN 0920358756 Pbk £2.00

—Real estate law locator 1988 / New York : Bowker, 1988.
ISBN 0835223515 Hbk £30.00

—Reparation and mediation : a bibliography / prepared by Stanley Prashker and Nigel Brearley for Forum for Initiatives in Reparation and Mediation (FIRM). – s.l. : Forum for Initiatives in Reparation and Mediation, 1986.
52p.

—Reports of the European Communities 1952-1977 : an index to authors and chairmen / compiled by June Neilson. – London : Mansell, 1981.
xiv,561p; 23cm.
Includes index.
ISBN 0720115922 £27.50

—Rights of Indigenous Peoples in International Law : an Annotated Bibliography / Ruth Thompson. – Saskatoon : University of Saskatchewan, Native Law Centre, 1986.
33p.
ISBN 0888801769 £9.00

Supplement 1986

—Rights of Indigenous Peoples in International Law : an Annotated Bibliography / Dallas K. Miller. – Saskatoon : University of Saskatchewan, Native Law Centre, 1985.
97p.
ISBN 0888801637 Hbk £35.00

—Statut juridique international des minorites : bibliographie selective / preparee par la Bibliotheque du Palais de la Paix, La Haye : selective biliography : prepared by the Library of the Peace Palace, the Hague. – The Hague : Center for Studies and Research of the Hague Academy of International Law, 1984.
29 leaves.

—Ulrich's international periodicals directory : a classified guide to current periodicals foreign and domestic / 19th ed. – New York : R R Bowker, 1980.
A Bowker serials bibliography.
ISBN 0835212971

—Union list of law periodicals held in libraries within the City of Liverpool / compiled by Susan Frost, Robert Caley. – Liverpool : Liverpool Polytechnic Library Service, 1985.
30p.

—Union list of law reports and statutes held in libraries within the City of Liverpool / compiled by Susan Frost, Robert Caley. – Liverpool : Liverpool Polytechnic Library Service, 1985.
30p.

—Union list of legal bibliographies and digests and other law-related material held in libraries within the City of Liverpool / compiled by Susan Frost, Robert Caley. – Liverpool : Liverpool Polytechnic Library Service, 1985.
15p.

—Urban riots and public order : a select bibliography, 1975-1985 / compiled by: E. Edwards, R. Golland & S. Leach for the GLC Intelligence Unit. – Letchworth : Technical Communications, 1986.
iii,159p; 30cm.
ISBN 0946655103 Hbk

—Vandalism : a bibliography / Jane Pethick and Catherine J. Matthews : prepared for the Task Force on Vandalism (Ontario), chairman L.A. Beaulieu. – Toronto : Centre of Criminology, University of Toronto, 1980.
x,79p; 28cm.
ISBN 0919584462

—W Zealand royal commissions, commissions and committees of inquiry, 1864-1981 : a checklist / compiled by Evelyn Robertson and Peter H. Hughes for the NZLA Professional Division. – Wellington : New Zealand Library Association, 1982.
30p.
ISBN 0908560109

—World oceans : a selected bibliography of social and natural sciences / Des oceans du monde: une selection bibliographique des sciences sociales et naturelles : compiled by Paul Te-Hsien Huang. – Halifax : Huang, 1985.
xii,754p.
ISBN 0969218109

—Worldwide Space Law Bibliography / Montreal : De Daro Publishing.

Yearly Update 1988
ISBN 0969270313 Hbk £20.00

Vol. 1: 1900-1976
ISBN 0969270321 Hbk £65.00

Vol. 2: 1976-1986
ISBN 096927033X Hbk £75.00

BIBLIOGRAPHY - AUSTRALIA

—Law : a Guide to Select Law Sources in the Canberra College of Advanced Education Library / Peter Stone. – 4th ed. – Belconnen : Canberra College of Advanced Education, 1982.
2, 73p.
ISBN 0858892065 Hbk £4.00

BIBLIOGRAPHY - CANADA

—Canadian bibliography of international law / Christian L. Wiktor. – Toronto : University of Toronto Press, 1984.
xxiii, 767 p.; 25 cm.
Includes indexes.
ISBN 0802056156

—Canadian law reports and statutes held by the Faculty of Law Library, University of the West Indies, Cave Hill, Barbados / S.G. Moss : with the assistance of Waveney Webster. – Cave Hill, Barbados : University of the West Indies, Faculty of Law Library, 1986.
42p.

—Canadian legal materials held by the National Library of Australia, February 1980 / compiled by the Australian National Social Sciences Library. – 1 microfiche. – Canberra : National Library of Australia, 1980.

BIBLIOGRAPHY - CANADA - QUEBEC

—Introduction to Quebec legal bibliography : 1980 CALL pre- conference workshop, May 20, 1980 - Montreal, Quebec / 1 (various pagings). – Toronto : Canadian Association of Law Libraries, 1981.

BIBLIOGRAPHY - COMMONWEALTH

—Law reform in the Commonwealth : law reform proposals and their implementation / Commonwealth Secretariat. – London : Commonwealth Secretariat, 1981.
Pilot issue published Oct. 1979.

BIBLIOGRAPHY - ENGLAND

—Current serials available in the University Library and in other libraries connected with the University / Cambridge University Library. – 2. – Cambridge : Published for the Library by Cambridge University Press, 1980.
ISBN 0521238374 £95.00

BIBLIOGRAPHY - EUROPEAN COMMUNITY

—European Community : bibliographical excursions / edited by Juliet Lodge. – London : Pinter, 1983.
259p; 24cm.
Includes bibliographies.
ISBN 0861872444 Hbk £17.00
ISBN 0861872460 Pbk £7.50

BIBLIOGRAPHY - GREAT BRITAIN

—Know how : to find out your rights / Grainne Morby. – London : Pluto, 1982.
188p; 20cm.
Includes index.
ISBN 0861043596 Pbk £3.95

—Lawyers' law books : a practical index to legal literature / by Donald Raistrick. – 2nd ed. – Milton, Oxon. : Professional Books, 1985.
xxxv,604p. – (Professional Books law reference library).
ISBN 0862050723

—Legal research in the United Kingdom 1905-84 : a classified list of legal theses and dissertations successfully completed for postgraduate degrees awarded by universities and polytechnics in the United Kingdom from 1905-1984 / Institute of Advanced Legal Studies. – London : The Institute, 1986.
xxx, ca. 300p.
Supersedes: List of legal research topics completed and approved since about 1935. - 2nd ed. - 1961; and, Supplement 1961-July 1966. Includes indexes. Supplemented by: List of current legal research topics.
ISBN 0901190292

—List of current legal research topics : being topics forming the subject of research by students for degrees in universities and polytechnics in the United Kingdom / University of London, Institute of Advanced Legal Studies. – 33rd ed. – London : The Institute, 1985.
51p.
Includes index. . Supplements: Legal research in the United Kingdom 1905-1984.

—List of current legal research topics : being topics forming the subject of research by students for degrees in universities and polytechnics in the United Kingdom / University of London, Institute of Advanced Legal Studies. – 34th ed. – London : The Institute, 1986.
iv,99p.
Supplements: Legal research in the United Kingdom 1905-1984. Includes indexes.

—Sex discrimination : some recent titles and periodical articles / Department of Employment Library. – London : The Library, 1983.
8p. – (Library checklist).

BIBLIOGRAPHY - IRELAND

—Bibliography of Irish trials and other legal proceedings / Paul OHiggins. – Abingdon, Oxon. : Professional Books, 1986.
xxvii,504p.
Includes indexes.
ISBN 0862050804

BIBLIOGRAPHY - ISLAMIC COUNTRIES

—Introduction to Shii law : a bibliographical study / Hossein Modarressi Tabatabai. – London : Ithaca Press, 1984.
258p; 24cm.
Bibliography: p218-237. - Includes index.
ISBN 0863720153 £18.00

BIBLIOGRAPHY - UNITED STATES

—Affirmative action and preferential admissions in higher education : an annotated bibliography / by Kathryn Swanson. – Metuchen : Scarecrow, 1981.
viii,336p; 23cm.
Includes index.
ISBN 0810814110 £12.25

BIBLIOGRAPHY - USSR

—Bibliography of the Institute of State and Law Scholar's (sic) works (1978 - 1982) / Moscow : The Institute, 1983.
37p.
'Compiled by D. Vassilyev, translated by N. Gheraseva'. At head of title: Academy of Sciences of the USSR, Order of the Red Banner of Labour, Institute of State and Law.

BICYCLE INDUSTRY - GREAT BRITAIN

—TI Raleigh Industries Limited and Raleigh Limited : a report by the Director General of Fair Trading on an investigation under Section 3 of the Competition Act, 1980 / London : Office of Fair Trading, 1981.
40p.

BIG BUSINESS

—Managerial hierarchies : comparative perspectives on the rise of the modern industrial enterprise / edited by Alfred D. Chandler, Jr and Herman Daems. – Cambridge, Mass. : Harvard University Press, 1980.
xi,237p; 24cm. – (Harvard studies in business history).
Includes index.
ISBN 0674547403

BIG BUSINESS - GREAT BRITAIN

—Evolution of giant firms in Britain : a study of the growth of concentration in manufacturing industry in Britain 1909-70 / by S.J. Prais. – 2nd impression. – Cambridge : Cambridge University Press, 1981.
xxii,321p; 23cm. – (NIESR students' edition).
Originally published: 1976. Bibliography: p302-315. - Includes index.
ISBN 052128273X Pbk £7.50

—Rise of the corporate economy / Leslie Hannah. – 2nd ed. – London : Methuen, 1983.
xii,266p; 23cm.
Previous ed.: 1976. Includes index.
ISBN 0416348505 Hbk Unpriced
ISBN 0416348602 Pbk Unpriced

BIG BUSINESS - UNITED STATES

—Corporate control, corporate power / Edward S. Herman. – Cambridge : Cambridge University Press, 1981.
xv,432p; 24cm.
Includes index.
ISBN 0521239966 £25.00

BIGAMY - CANADA

—Bigamy / Law Reform Commission of Canada. – Ottawa : The Commission, 1985.
32,34p. – (Working paper).
Includes bibliographical references. Added t.p. in French: La bigamie. Cover title: Criminal law : bigamy. Pages numbered in opposite directions. Text in English and French.
ISBN 0662538560

BILLS OF EXCHANGE

—UNCITRAL Draft Convention on international bills of exchange and internnational promissory notes, and Draft Convention on international cheques / memorandum by the Joint Working Party of the Law Reform Committees of the Senate of the Inns of Court and the Bar and the Law Society. – London? : the Joint Working Party?, 1983.
7p.

BILLS OF EXCHANGE - CANADA

—Crawford and Falconbridge Banking and Bills of Exchange / 8th ed. – Aurora : Canada Law Book Co, 1986.
2400p.

BILLS OF EXCHANGE - GREAT BRITAIN

—Bills of Exchange / 26th ed. – Sweet & Maxwell, 1988.
ISBN 042138090X Hbk £72.00

—Bills of Exchange Act 1882 / annotated by Anu Arora. – London : Lloyd's of London Press, 1987.
xvi, 100 p.; 22 cm.
Drafted by Sir Mackenzie Chalmers. Includes indexes.
ISBN 1850440956 pbk.

—Bills of Exchange Cheques and Promissory Notes / de Beer. – London : Butterworths, 1983.
ISBN 0409040738 Hbk £47.00
ISBN 0409040746 Pbk £34.70

—Byles on bills of exchange : the law of bills of exchange, promissory notes, bank notes and cheques / Maurice Megrah, F. R. Ryder, Antonio Bueno. – 25th ed. – London : Sweet & Maxwell, 1983.
lxxxv,561p; 26cm.
Previous ed.: 1979. Includes index.
ISBN 0421298308 £50.00

BILLS OF EXCHANGE - SOUTH AFRICA

—Bills of exchange, cheques and promissory notes in South African law / by F.R. Malan ;. assisted by C. R. de Beer. – Durban : Butterworths, 1983.
xii,441p.
Bibliography: p.377-391. - Includes index.
ISBN 0409040738

BILLS OF LADING

—Bills of Lading in International Law and Practice / Lucknow : Eastern Book Company, 1985.

—Cargo key receipt and transport document replacement / Kurt Gronfors. – Goteburg : Akademiforlaget, 1982.
104p. – (Skrifter).
ISBN 9124160555

—Chartering documents / by Per Gram. – London : Lloyd's of London Press, 1981.
xiii,177p.
Includes index.
ISBN 0907432034

—Hamburg Rules : an appreciation of the cause and effect of the amendments to the Hague Rules and the Hague-Visby Rules / W.E. Astle. – London : Fairplay, 1981.
xii,163p; 25cm.
ISBN 0905045319 Pbk No price

—International rules of law relating to bills of lading / compiled by W.E. Astle. – London : Fairplay, 1982.
72p; 25cm.
ISBN 0905045343 Pbk No price

—Law Relating to Bills of Lading and Charterparties / Allahabad : Indian Press.
253p.

—Maritime law in bills of lading : a conference organised by Lloyd's of London Press : the Tower Hotel, London, 23rd June, 1982 / London : Lloyds of London Press, 1982.
96 leaves in various foliations; 31cm.
ISBN 0907432441 Unpriced

—Modern bills of lading / Paul Todd. – London : Collins, 1986.
256p; 24cm.
Includes index.
ISBN 0003833224 £17.50

BILLS OF LADING - GREAT BRITAIN

—Bills of Lading and Practice / London : Sweet & Maxwell, 1982.

—Bills of lading : law and practice / Alan Mitchelhill. – London : Chapman and Hall, 1982.
x,127p; 31cm.
Includes index.
ISBN 0412239604 Hbk Unpriced
ISBN 041223940X Pbk Unpriced

—Cases and Materials on Bills of Lading / Oxford : Blackwell Scientific, 1987.
ISBN 0003833844 Hbk £30.00

—Contracts of Affreightments and Hybrid Conts / Ivre. – London : Lloyd's of London Press, 1985.
ISBN 1850440603 Hbk £25.85

—Guide to the Hague and Hague-Visby Rules / London : Lloyd's of London Press, 1985.
iv,54p. – (An LLP special report).
Includes index. Contains the texts of the Rules.

—Modern Bills of Lading / Oxford : Blackwell Scientific, 1987.
ISBN 0003833224 Hbk £19.95

—Practical guide to contracts of affreightment and hybrid contracts / by Lars Gorton and Rolf Ihre. – London : Lloyd's, 1985.
ix,87p; 25cm.
Includes index.
ISBN 1850440603 £45.00 (Dec.)

—Scrutton on charterparties and bills of lading / Alan Abraham Mocatta, Michael John Mustill, Stewart C. Boyd. – 19th ed. – London : Sweet & Maxwell, 1984.
cv,593p; 25cm.
Section on time charters has been substantially revised and rewritten to take account of developments. Four House of Lords decisions on the problem of withdrawal for non-payment of hire are discussed, and there is an analysis of the related problem of deductions from hire.
ISBN 0421297107 £50.00

BIOGRAPHY

—Albert Venn Dicey : the man and his times / by Trowbridge H. Ford. – Chichester : Barry Rose, 1985.
354p.
Bibliography: p322-335.
ISBN 0859923568

—Andreas Alciates, 2 Vols. / Toronto : University of Toronto Press, 1985.
ISBN 0802024254 Hbk £125.00

—Angelo Branca / Vancouver : Douglas and McIntyre, 1981.
ISBN 0888943237 Hbk £16.95

—Biographical Dictionary of Common Law / London : Butterworths, 1984.
ISBN 040651657X Hbk £32.00

—Biographical dictionary of the common law / edited by A.W.B. Simpson. – London : Butterworths, 1984.
xxv,559p,16p of plates; 23cm.
ISBN 040651657X Unpriced

—Closing Chapter / London : Butterworths, 1983.
ISBN 0406176116 Hbk £12.95
ISBN 0406176124 Pbk £8.95

—Correspondence of Jeremy Bentham / J. R. Dinwiddy. – Oxford : Clarendon, 1984.
xxx,496p; 24cm.
Includes index.
ISBN 0198226136 £40.00

Vol.7 : January 1802 to December 1808 : edited by J.R. Dinwiddy 1988.
500p; 24cm.
Includes index.
ISBN 0198226144 £45.00

Vol. 8 : January 1809 to December 1816 : edited by Stephen Conway 1988.
480p; 24cm.
Includes index.
ISBN 0198226152 No price

—Criminal justice : the story of Edith Thompson / by Rene Weis. – London : Hamish Hamilton, 1988.
xviii,327p,8p of plates; 24cm.
Includes index.
ISBN 0241122635 £14.95

—Diary of Hugh Gaitskell, 1945-1956 / Philip M. Williams. – London : Jonathan Cape, 1983.
ISBN 0224019112 Hbk £25.00

—Dictionary of Business Biography / London : Butterworths, 1984.
ISBN 0406273413 Hbk £72.00

Vol. 2 D-G 1984.
ISBN 0406273421 Hbk £72.00

Vol. 3 H-L 1985.
ISBN 040627343X Hbk £72.00

Vol. 4 M-R 1985.
ISBN 0406273448 Hbk £72.00

Vol. 5 S-Z 1986.
ISBN 0406273456 Hbk £72.00

—Dr. Bhimrao Ramji Ambedkar : a Study in Social Democracy / Kuala Lumpur : Intellectual Book Corner, 1982.
vii, 270p.

—Duff : a Life in the Law / Vancouver : University of British Columbia Press, 1984.
344p.
ISBN 0774802030 Hbk £34.95

—Emily Murphy / Markham : Fitzhenry and Whiteside.
ISBN 0889022348 Pbk £3.75

—Emmett Hall : Establishment Radical / Toronto : Macmillan of Canada, 1985.
256p.
ISBN 0771596898 Hbk £27.95

—F.W. Maitland / G.R. Elton. – London : Weidenfeld and Nicolson, 1986.
viii,118p; 22cm.
Includes index.
ISBN 0297786148 Pbk £12.95
ISBN 029778885X £4.95

—Faces, cases and places / memoirs by Fatayi Williams. – London : Butterworths, 1983.
xv,185p,16p of plates; 23cm.
Includes index.
ISBN 0406514771 Unpriced

—H.B. Higgins / North Sydney : Allen & Unwin, 1984.
248p.
ISBN 0868616818 Hbk £29.95

—He Left Them Laughing When He Said Good-Bye : the Life and Times of Frontier Lawyer Paddy Nolan / Saskatoon : Western Producer Prairie Books, 1987.
ISBN 0888332416 Pbk £12.95

—Hon. Dr. T. Akinola Aguda : the man, his works and society / by I.O. Agbede. – Lagos : Nigerian Institute of Advanced Legal Studies, 1986.
v,30p. – (Occasional paper).
Bibliography: pp.21-30..

—John Austin / London : E. Arnold, 1982.
192p.
ISBN 0713163593 Hbk £11.00
ISBN 0713163607 Pbk £5.50

—Judges I Have Known / Cape Town : Legal & Financial Publishing, 1983.

—Lewis and Lewis / John Juxon. – London : Collins, 1983.
320p,12p of plates; 23cm.
Bibliography: p310-312. - Includes index.
ISBN 0002164760 £10.95

—Lionel Morphy - a Radical Judge : an Appraisal by Eleven Prominent Australians / Carlton : McCulloch Publishing.
276p.
ISBN 0949646172 Hbk £29.95

—List of English law officers, King's counsel and holders of patents of precedence / compiled for the Selden Society by Sir John Sainty. – London : Selden Society, 1987.
xviii, 330p.

—Lives of the Lord Chancellors (1885-1940) / Oxford : Oxford University Press, 1987.
ISBN 0198213123 Hbk £45.00

—Lives of the Lord Chancellors 1940-1970 / by R.F.V. Heuston. – Oxford : Clarendon, 1987.
253p,8p of plates; 24cm.
Includes index.
ISBN 0198200749 £25.00

—Lives of the Lord Chancellors (1940-1970) / Oxford : Oxford University Press, 1987.
ISBN 0198200749 Hbk £25.00

—Lord Atkin / London : Butterworths, 1984.
ISBN 0406272107 Hbk £18.50

—Lord Atkin / by Geoffrey Lewis. – London : Butterworths, 1983.
xi,248p,8p of plates; 25cm.
A biography of Lord Atkin, one of the greatest common lawyers and judges of the twentieth century in England.
ISBN 0406272107 Hbk £14.95

—Lord Cockburn - A Bicentenary Commemoration / Edinburgh : Scottish Academic Press Ltd, 1980.
212p.
ISBN 0707302455 Hbk £8.00

—Lord Wheatley : One Man's Judgment / London : Butterworths, 1987.
ISBN 0406100195 Hbk £17.50

—Man of Influence : Sir Siegmund Warburg / Weidenfeld & Nicolson, 1986.
ISBN 0297789783 Hbk £16.95

—McNee's law / Sir David McNee. – London : Collins, 1983.
256p,8p of plates; 23cm.
Includes index.
ISBN 0002170078 £9.95

—Memoirs of the Life of Sir Samuel Romilly, 3 Vols. / Dublin : Irish Academic Press.
900p.
ISBN 0716517841 Hbk £48.00

—Middleton : the Beloved Judge / Toronto : McClelland & Stewart, 1988.
240p.
ISBN 0771007957 Hbk £37.50

—Neither Roses Nor Thorns : an Autobiography by the Retired Judge of the Supreme Court of India / Lucknow : Eastern Book Company, 1985.
208p.

—On F.R. Scott : Essays on His Contributions to Law, Literature, and Politics / Ronald St. J. MacDonald. – Montreal : McGill-Queen's University Press.
226p.
ISBN 0773503978 Hbk £25.00
ISBN 0773503986 Pbk £8.95

—One man's judgement : an autobiography / Lord Wheatley. – London : Butterworths, 1987.
ix,230p,8p of plates; 24cm.
Includes index.
ISBN 0406100195 £12.95

—Politics of the Imagination : a Life of F.R. Scott / Toronto : McClelland & Stewart.
ISBN 0771028253 Hbk £39.95

—Rankin's Law : Recollections of a Radical / Vancouver : November House.

—Rebel advocate : a biography of Gerald Gardiner / by Muriel Box. – London : Gollancz, 1983.
242p,8p of plates; 24cm.
Bibliography: p236. - Includes index.
ISBN 0575032693 £10.95

—Sir Justice Udo Udoma / by D.S. Udo-Inyang. – Calabar, Nigeria : Wusen Press, 1985.
72p.
ISBN 9782281689

—Sir William Jones, His Mind and Art / New Delhi : S. Chand and Company, 1982.
312p.

—Statesman and the fanatic : Thomas Wolsey and Thomas More / Jasper Ridley. – London : Constable, 1982.
338p,16p of plates; 24cm.
Bibliography: p294-299. - Includes index.
ISBN 009463470X £12.50

—T. O. Elias : citations, honours and awards / edited by M.A. Ajomo. – Lagos : Nigerian Society of International Law, 1983.
viii,38p.
ISBN 9782283037

—Who was who : a cumulated index 1897-1980 / London : Black, 1981.
ISBN 071362177X

BIOGRAPHY - ENGLAND

—And nothing but the truth / Alan King-Hamilton : foreword by Lord Diplock. – London : Weidenfeld and Nicolson, 1982.
xvi,237p,8p of plates; 24cm.
Includes index.
ISBN 0297780530 £12.50

—In my time : an autobiography / Lord Elwyn-Jones. – London : Weidenfeld, 1983.
319p.
Includes bibliography and index.
ISBN 0297781596

—Rule of law : Albert Venn Dicey, Victorian jurist / by Richard A. Cosgrove. – London : Macmillan, 1980.
xv,319p; 24cm.
Bibliography: p301-314. - Includes index.
ISBN 0333307070 £15.00

—Troubled lives : John and Sarah Austin / Lotte and Joseph Hamburger. – Toronto : University of Toronto Press, 1985.
xiii,261p.
Includes index.

BIOGRAPHY - GREAT BRITAIN

—Further particulars / Oxford : OUP, 1987.
240. – (Oxford letters and memoirs).
Second volume of C.H. Rolph's memoirs, taking up the story from 'London Particulars' at the end of the First World War. He describes his 25 years with the City Police, rising to the rank of Chief Inspector, his work as a freelance journalist for the New Statesman and at the BBC.*Legal historians, criminologists*
ISBN 0192117904 Hbk £12.50
ISBN 0192821431 Pbk £4.95

BIOGRAPHY - IRELAND

—George Gavan Duffy 1882-1951 : a legal biography / G.M. Golding. – Blackrock : Irish Academic Press, 1982.
xvi,224p,1leaf of plates; 22cm.
Bibliography: p209-214. - Includes index.
ISBN 0716500787 Hbk £15.00
ISBN 0716502070 Pbk Unpriced

BIOGRAPHY - SCOTLAND

—Scottish jurists / by David M. Walker. – Edinburgh : W. Green, 1985.
xv,492p.
ISBN 0414007573

BIOGRAPHY - SOUTH AFRICA

—Life and works of Hugo Grotius (1583-1645) : address delivered to members of the South African Law Commission and other dignitaries on 26 July 1983 at the University of Pretoria to commemorate the 400th birthday of Hugo Grotius / by Ellison Kahn. – Pretoria : South African Law Commission, 1983.
iii,21p. – (Research series).

BIOGRAPHY - UNITED STATES

—Law practice of Alexander Hamilton : documents and commentary / Julius Goebel, Joseph H. Smith, Winnifred Bowers. – New York : Published under the auspices of the William Nelson Cromwell Foundation by Columbia University Press, 1981.
xiv,754p; 24cm.
Includes index.
ISBN 0231089295 £52.00

—Papers of Daniel Webster / Alfred S. Konefsky, Andrew J. King. – Hanover, N.H. : Published for Dartmouth College by the University Press of New England, 1982.
xxxix,571p; 25cm.
Includes index.
ISBN 0874512328 Unpriced

BIOLOGY

—What's in a name / Denis Owen : illustrated by Andrew Martin. – London : BBC, 1985.
143p; 20cm.
Bibliography: p137-138. - Includes index.
ISBN 0563203358 Pbk £3.95

BIOTECHNOLOGY

—Biotechnology and patent protection : an international review / by F.K. Beier, R.S. Crespi, J. Straus. – Paris : Organisation for Economic Co-operation and Development, 1985.
133p.
ISBN 9264127577

—Committee of Experts on Biotechnological Inventions and Industrial Property : third session, Geneva, June 29 to July 3, 1987 : report prepared by the International Bureau / World Intellectual Property Organization. – Geneva : World Intellectual Property Organization, 1987.
32,11p. – (BioT/CE/III/3).
'Convened ... as part of the 1986/87 program of the International (Paris) Union for the Protection of Industrial Property ...'. - Introduction.

—Committee of Experts on Biotechnological Inventions and Industrial Property : third session, Geneva, June 29 to July 3, 1987 : industrial property protection of biotechnological inventions / revised report prepared by the International Bureau. – Geneva : World Intellectual Property Organization, 1987.
73p. – (BioT/CE/III/2).
At head of cover: International Union for the Protection of Industrial Property (Paris Union).

—Committee of Experts on Biotechological Inventions and Industrial property : first session, Geneva, November 5 to 9, 1984 / report adopted by the Committee of Experts. – Geneva : World Intellectual Property Organizatioan, 1984.
23,7p. – (BioT/CE/I/3).
'Convened ... as part of the 1984/85 program of the International (Paris) Union for the Protection of Industrial Property ... '. - Introduction.

—Intellectual property rights in biotechnology worldwide / Stephen A. Bent ... et al. – London : Macmillan, 1985.
300p.
Includes index.
ISBN 0333392884 Pbk £40.00 (Oct.)
ISBN 094381815X

—Report / adopted by the Committee of Experts. – Geneva : World Intellectual Property Organization, 1986.
10p. – (BIOT/CE/II/3).
'Convened ... as part of the 1986/87 program of the International (Paris) Union for the Protection of Industrial Property' - Introduction.

—Symposium on the Protection of Biotechnological Inventions / Geneva : World Intellectual Property Organization, 1987.
185p.

BIOTECHNOLOGY – GREAT BRITAIN
—Patents in chemistry and biotechnology / 2nd ed. – Oxford : Oxford University Press, 1987.
ISBN 0198552211 Pbk £12.50

BIOTECHNOLOGY – SWEDEN
—Biomedical Research and Research Policy in Sweden / Stockholm : Almqvist & Wiksell, 1980.
16p.

BLACKMAIL
—Extortions under terrorist threats / Council of Europe. – Strasbourg : Council of Europe, 1986.
14p; 21cm. – (Legal affairs).
'... prepared by a select committee of experts under the authority of the European Committee on Crime Problems ... The committee of Ministers of the Council of Europe authorised its publication' - p.3.
ISBN 9287108412

BLAISE (INFORMATION RETRIEVAL SYSTEM)
—BLAISE-LINE user manual / 3. – London : The British Library, Bibliographic Services, 1988.
looseleaf.

BLASPHEMY
—Blasphemer and Reformer : Study of the works of James Leslie Mitchell / Aberdeen : Aberdeen University Press.
224p.
ISBN 0080303730 Hbk £12.50

BLASPHEMY – ENGLAND
—Blasphemy : an ancient wrong or a modern right? / by Louis Blom-Cooper. – London : Essex Hall, 1981.
14p. – (The 1981 Essex Hall lecture).

—Criminal law : offences against religion and public worship / Great Britain. – London : H.M.S.O., 1985.
iv,51p.
ISBN 0102442851

BLASPHEMY – GREAT BRITAIN
—Blasphemy and the battle for faith / London : Hodder & Stoughton, 1990.
208; 18.
ISBN 0340522798 Pbk £2.99

BOOK INDUSTRIES AND TRADE – ENGLAND
—Book trade year book / Publishers Association. – London : Publishhers Association, 1985.

BOOKS
—Preservation, a survival kit / National Preservation Office. – 1 case. – S.l. : The Office, 1987.
various pagings.

BOOKSELLERS AND BOOKSELLING – GREAT BRITAIN
—Mumbys publishing & bookselling in the twentieth century / Ian Norrie, F. A. Mumby. – 6th ed. – London : Bell & Hyman, 1982.
253p; 24cm.
Previous ed.: published as Publishing and bookselling. London : Cape, 1974. Bibliography: p229-232.
ISBN 0713513411 £12.95

BOUNDARIES
—Border and territorial disputes / edited by Alan J. Day : contributors: Judith Bell ... et al. – Harlow : Longman, 1982.
x,406p; 26cm.
Bibliography: p389. - Includes index.
ISBN 0582902517 Unpriced
ISBN 0810320304

—A Guide to Maritime Boundary Delimitation / Adam J. Kerr. – Agincourt : Carswell, 1986.
136p.
This work addresses the technical aspects of maritime boundaries under international law. The book provides commentary on relevant cases which have been refered to the International Court of Justice.

—Maritime boundaries and ocean resources / edited by Gerald Blake : International Geographical Union Study Group on the World Political Map. – London : Croom Helm, 1987.
284p; 23cm.
Bibliography: p257-271. - Includes index.
ISBN 0709939744 £27.50

—Maritime Boundaries and Resource Development / Calgary : Canadian Institute of Resources Law.

—Maritime boundary delimitation : an annotated bibliography / Ted L. McDorman, Kenneth P. Beauchamp, Douglas M. Johnston. – Lexington, Mass. : Lexington Books, 1983.
xiii,207p; 24cm.
Includes index.
ISBN 0669061468 Unpriced

—Maritime political boundaries of the world / J.R.V. Prescott. – London : Methuen, 1985.
xv,377p; 24cm.
Bibliography: 355-360. - Includes index.
ISBN 0416417507 £30.00

—National and international boundaries / Thessaloniki : Institute of Public International Law and International Relations of Thessaloniki, 1985.
xii,905p.
English, French or German.

BOUNDARIES – AUSTRALIA
—Australia's Maritime Boundaries / Deakin : Australian Institute of International Affairs, 1985.

BOUNDARIES – AUSTRALIA – TASMANIA
—Report on private rights of access to neighbouring land / Law Reform Commission of Tasmania. – Hobart : Government Printer, 1985.
23p. – (Report v no 42).

—Report on the Boundary Fences Act 1908 / Law Reform Commission of Tasmania. – Hobart : Government Printer, 1984.
19p. – (Report v no 37).

BOUNDARIES – CANADA
—Boundaries and Surveys / Izaak de Rijcke. – Agincourt : Carswell, 1985.
235p.
This text covers the law of Ontario, Canada relating to boundaries and surveys. Relevant Ontario statutes and digests of cases from other provinces are provided in the appendices.

BOUNDARIES – ENGLAND
—Boundaries, walls and fences / Trevor M. Aldridge. – 6th ed. – London : Longman Professional, 1986.
66p; 22cm.
Previous ed.: London : Oyez Longman, 1982. Includes index.
ISBN 0851212344 Pbk £11.95

—Neighbours and the law / by John Pugh-Smith. – London : Sweet & Maxwell, 1988.
lii,218p.
Discusses the impact of planning permissions, building regulations, and actions in tort, on the way we live as neighbours. Statute case law is cross-referenced, and guidance on litigation procedure and the collection of relevant precedents is also included.
ISBN 0421365706 £20.00 (June)

—Rights of access to neighbouring land / the Law Commission. – London : H.M.S.O., 1985.
v,85p.
ISBN 0101969201

—Rights of access to neighbouring land / the Law Commission. – London : H.M.S.O., 1980.
v,70p; 21cm. – (Working paper).
ISBN 0117301582 Pbk £3.90

—Rights of access to neighbouring land : Law Commission Working paper no. 78 : memorandum / by the Council's Law Reform Committee. – London : Law Society, 1981.
9p; 30cm.

BOUNDARIES (INTERNATIONAL LAW)
—Atlas of the Seabed Boundaries /. – Milan : Giuffre, 1987.
xv, 241p.

—Maritime Boundaries and Resource Development / Calgary : Canadian Institute of Resources Law.

—Theory and History of Ocean Boundary-Making / Montreal : McGill-Queen's University Press, 1988.
ISBN 0773506241 Hbk £39.95

BRAIN STEM
—ABC of brain stem death / Christopher Pallis. – London : British Medical Journal, 1983.
33p; 29cm.
Articles published in the British Medical Journal.
ISBN 0727900994

BRIBERY – PAPUA NEW GUINEA
—What should be done about corruption and bribery? / Law Reform Commission of Papua New Guinea. – Waigani : The Commission, 1982.
24p. – (LRC working paper).
Prepared for the Commission by Ross DeVere.

BRIEFS – NIGERIA
—Manual of brief writing in the Court of Appeal and the Supreme Court of Nigeria / by Philip Nnaemeka-Agu. – Enugu, Nigeria : Fourth Dimension, 1986.
xviii,110p.
Bibliography: p. 109-110. - Includes index.

BRITISH COMMONWEALTH
—Evolution of the modern Commonwealth : 1902-80 / Denis Judd and Peter Slinn. – London : Macmillan, 1982.
xiii,171p.
Bibliography: p153-157.
ISBN 0333308409

—Modern Commonwealth / Sir William Dale. – London : Butterworths, 1983.
xxxi,345p; 26cm.
Bibliography: pxxvii-xxx. - Includes index. Second copy inscribed by the author.
ISBN 0406174040 Unpriced

—Office of Speaker in the Parliaments of the Commonwealth / Philip Laundy. – London : Quiller Press, 1984.
xiii,274p.
Bibliography: p261-269.
ISBN 0907621317

—Recognition of commercial judgments and awards in the Commonwealth / K.W. Patchett. – London : Butterworths, 1984.
xlv,326p; 26cm.
Bibliography: pxxix. - Includes index.
ISBN 0406403201 No price

—Vulnerability : small states in the global society / report of a Commonwealth Consultative Group. – London : Commonwealth Secretariat, 1985.
xii,126p.
Chairman: P. T. Georges.
ISBN 0850922801

—Year book of the Commonwealth 1983 / 15th ed. – London : H.M.S.O., 1983.
vii,535p.
Includes index.
ISBN 0115802320

BRITISH WEST INDIES – GRENADA
—Conquest of Grenada : sovereignty in the periphery / M. Shahabuddeen. – Georgetown : University of Guyana, 1986.
xiv,266p.
Includes bibliographical references. Includes the text of the Treaty Establishing the Orgainisation of Eastern Caribbean States.

BRIXTON, LONDON
—Scarman and after : essays reflecting on Lord Scarman's report, the riots and their aftermath / edited by John Benyon : with an epilogue by Lord Scarman. – Oxford : Pergamon, 1984.
xiv,292p; 24cm.
Conference papers. Bibliography: p263-274. - Includes index.
ISBN 0080302173 Hbk Unpriced
ISBN 0080302181 Pbk £7.50

—Scarman Report : the Brixton disorders, 10-12 April 1981 : report of an inquiry / by Lord Scarman. – Reprint, with preface. – Harmondsworth : Penguin, 1986.
xx,255p. – (Pelican books).
Previous ed.: 1982.
ISBN 014022744X

BROADCASTING
—Cable television : media and copyright law aspects : reports to an ALAI symposium / edited by Herman Cohen Jehoram. – Deventer : Kluwer Law and Taxation, 1983.
xix,236p; 25cm.
ISBN 9065441492 Pbk Unpriced

—Choice by cable : the economics of a new era in television / C.G.Veljanovski and W.D.Bishop. – London : Institute of Economic Affairs, 1983.
120p; 22cm.
ISBN 0255361599

—International Light, Shape and Sound Signals / London : Stanford Maritime Ltd.
ISBN 0540072710 Pbk £6.95

—Satellite and cable television : international protection : a specially commissioned report / by S. Alexander Mosteshar, and Stephen de B. Bate. – London : Longman Professional, 1986.
xiv,134p; 30cm. – (Longman professional intelligence reports).
Originally published: London : Oyez Longman, 1984. Includes index.
ISBN 0851212042 spiral £95.00

—State responsibility and the direct broadcast satellite / Marika Natasha Taishoff. – London : Pinter, 1987.
xii,203p; 24cm.
Bibliography: p183-197. - Includes index. 'A publication of the Graduate Institute of International Studies'.
ISBN 0861877004 Hbk £25

—Television by satellite : legal aspects / edited by Stephen de B. Bate. – Oxford : ESC Publishing, 1987.
vi,146p.
Includes bibliographical references.
ISBN 0906214432

—To see the world / Dordrecht : Martinus Nijhoff, 1989.
600. – (Utrecht studies in air and space law).
Analyses the principles governing the use of artificial earth satellites for international direct television broadcasting, adopted by the United Nations General Assembly in 1982. Proposes revisions to the principles. Includes Appendixes containing United Nations documentation on the subject.
ISBN 9024737443 Hbk £87.50

—Updating of the Radio Regulations / Geneva : International Telecommunications Union, 1984.

—WIPO Worldwide Forum on the Piracy of Broadcasts and of the Printed Word / Geneva : World Intellectual Property Organization, 1983.
ca 240p.

—WIPO Worldwide Forum on the Piracy of Sound and Audiovisual Recordings, Geneva (1981) / Geneva : World Intellectual Property Organization.
240p.

BROADCASTING – AUSTRALIA

—Broadcasting law and policy in Australia / Mark Armstrong. – Sydney : Butterworths, 1982.
xxviii,291p.
Includes index.
ISBN 0409309109

—Broadcasting Law and Practice / D. Catterns. – North Ryde : Law Book Co, 1987.
ca 1,500p.

—Copyright and Cable Television / Milsons Point : Australian Copyright Council.

—New media : law & policy / edited by Mark Armstrong. – Kensington, NSW : Faculty of Law, University of New South Wales, 1981.
vii, 237 p.; 25 cm.
Includes bibliographical references.
ISBN 0858238950 pbk.

—Parliamentary Debates on Establishing the Australian Broadcasting Control Board, 1948 / North Ryde : Australian Film and Television School.
166p.
ISBN 0642924651 Hbk £12.00

BROADCASTING – CANADA

—Broadcasting Law in Canada : Fairness in the Administrative Process / Agincourt : Carswell, 1987.
128p.

—Broadcasting Law in Canada : Fairness in the Administrative Process / Agincourt : Carswell, 1987.
120p.
This book provides a rigorous analysis of the legal problems inherent in the regulation of broadcasting in Canada. The work comprehensively reviews the application of the principles of procedural fairness to the administrative process of the C.T.R.C.

—Cable Television and Defamation / Victoria : Government of British Columbia, 1981.

—Radio Documentary Handbook / North Vancouver : International Self-Counsel Press, 1987.
ISBN 0889086532 Hbk £8.95

BROADCASTING – CANADA – BRITISH COLUMBIA

—Report on cable television and defamation / Victoria : Queen's Printer, 1981.
23p.
ISBN 0771882572

BROADCASTING – ENGLAND

—Media law : the rights of journalists and broadcasters / Geoffrey Robertson, Andrew G.L. Nicol. – 1st ed. – London : Oyez, 1984.
xxxvi,403p.
Includes bibliographical references and index.
ISBN 0851206506

BROADCASTING – EUROPE

—Appendix 26 to the Radio Regulations : Geneva 1959 / Geneva : International Telecommunications Union.

—Appendix 27 Aer2 to the Radio Regulations / 1983 ed. – Geneva : International Telecommunications Union.
ISBN 9261015824 Hbk £18.00

English
ISBN 9261015816 Hbk £18.00

Spanish
ISBN 9261015832 Hbk £18.00

—Copyright Problems of Satellite and Cable Television in Europe / Dordrecht : Kluwer, 1987.
208p.
ISBN 0860109526 Hbk Gld125.00

BROADCASTING – EUROPEAN COMMUNITY

—Television without frontiers : green paper on the establishment of the common market for broadcasting, especially by satellite and cable / communication from the Commission to the Council. – Luxembourg : Office for Official Publications of the European Communities, 1984.
xii,367p. – (Documents).
ISBN 9277010045

BROADCASTING – GREAT BRITAIN

—Bad news / Glasgow University Media Group. – London : Routledge and Kegan Paul, 1980.
450p.
ISBN 0710004141 £8.00

—British Broadcasting Corporation and Independent Television Publications Limited : the publication of programme information : a report by the Director General of Fair Trading on investigations under section 3 of the Competition Act 1980 / London : Office of Fair Trading, 1984.
72p; 30cm.

—Broadcasting in the '90s : competition, choice and quality : the government's plans for broadcasting legislation / presented to Parliament by the Secretary of State for the Home Department by Command of Her Majesty, November 1988. – London : HMSO, 1988.
iv,45p.
ISBN 0101051727

—Cable television : agency franchising and economics / Cento Veljanovski. – London : Faculty of Laws, University College London, 1986.
25p; 30cm. – (Working papers).

—Deregulation of the radio spectrum in the UK / by CSP International. – London : H.M.S.O., 1987.
192p; 30cm.
Bibliography: p185-192. At head of title: Department of Trade and Industry. Text on inside covers.
ISBN 0115139796 Pbk £9.50

—Development of cable systems and services / Home Office, Department of Industry. – London : H.M.S.O., 1983.
90p; 25cm.
ISBN 0101886608 Pbk £6.00

—Media law - the rights of journalists and broadcasters / Geoffrey Robertson and Andrew Nicol. – 2nd ed. – London : Longman Professional (UK), 1989.
An updated second edition which covers recent developments including the Copyright and Patents Act 1988. Also covered are the use of government powers over television, the Video Recordings Act, the Cable Act, recent decisions of the European Court of Human Rights, and European Court, and the right of the media to appeal against 'gag' orders.
ISBN 0851215522 Hbk £55

—Radio : choices and opportunities : a consultative document ... / Great Britain. – London : H.M.S.O., 1987.
iv,44p.
ISBN 0101009224

—Report of the Committee on Financing the BBC / chairman, Alan Peacock. – London : H.M.S.O., 1986.
xx,219p; 30cm.
A report to the Secretary of State for the Home Department.
ISBN 0101982402

—Report of the Inquiry into cable expansion and broadcasting policy / chairman, Lord Hunt of Tanworth : Home Office. – London : H.M.S.O., 1982.
vi,45p; 25cm.
ISBN 0101867905 Pbk £4.40

—Research on the range and quality of broadcasting services : a report for the Committee on Financing the BBC / West Yorkshire Media in Politics Group, Centre for Television Research, The University of Leeds. – London : H.M.S.O., 1986.
180p.
Based on two internal papers, prepared for the Home Office. Provides information on the level of violent crime in England and Wales, the form it takes and the measures being taken to combat it.
ISBN 0113408331

—Subscription television / H.M.S.O., 1987.
213p.
ISBN 0113408552 Pbk £9.50

BROADCASTING – PHILIPPINES

—Philippine International Radio Laws and Regulations / Manila : National Book Store, 1984.
512p.
ISBN 9710804995 Pbk £5.00

BROKERS – GREAT BRITAIN

—Code of conduct for dealers in securities / Council for the Securities Industry. – London : The Council, 1980.
7p. – (CSI no 1).

—Licensed dealers in securities : draft rules & regulations proposed to be made under the Prevention of Fraud (Investments) Act 1958 / London : H.M.S.O., 1982.
iii,60p; 30cm.
At head of title: Department of Trade.
ISBN 0115136509 Pbk £4.25

BUDGET – CANADA

—Expenditure budget process of the Government of Canada : a public choice rent-seeking perspective / Douglas G. Hartle. – Toronto : Canadian Tax Foundation, 1988.
xxvii,316p.
Includes index.
ISBN 0888080301

—Revenue budget process of the Government of Canada : description, appraisal and proposals / Douglas G. Hartle. – Toronto : Canadian Tax Foundation, 1982.
xii,76p.
Includes index.
ISBN 0888080093

BUDGET – GREAT BRITAIN

—Budget and Finance Bill 1985 / London : Law Society, 1985.
28p. – (Nineteen Eighty-Five Crash Course Transcripts).

—Budgetary reform in the U.K : report of a committee chaired by Lord Armstrong of Sanderstead / Oxford : Oxford University Press for the Institute of Fiscal Studies, 1980.
40p.
ISBN 0198290055

BUILDING AND ENGINEERING CONTRACTS

—Basic crucial issues in major construction projects : papers presented at a seminar held jointly with the Institution of Civil Engineers, London, June 1985 / International Bar Association. Section on Business Law. International Construction Contracts Committee. – London : International Bar Association, 1986.
207p.
ISBN 0948711051

—Commercial Claimsmanship : With Special Reference to the FIDIC Form of Contract / King's Ride : Institute of Building, 1983.
9p.
ISBN 0906600642 Hbk £2.00

—Construction contracts : principles and policies in tort and contract / by I.N. Duncan Wallace. – London : Sweet & Maxwell, 1986.
xliii,696p; 26cm.
Contains articles on contractors' claims and owners' damages, certificates and their effect, guarantees and bonds in construction contracts, nominated sub-contractors, choice of contracting agreement, comparative law, the UK JCT standard forms, and the SIA Contract 1980.
ISBN 042134900X Hbk £74

—Contractual claims : an annotated bibliography / compiled by P.A. Harrow. – 4th ed. – Ascot : Chartered Institute of Building, 1986.
vi,25p; 25cm.
Previous ed.: 1979.
ISBN 0906600847 Pbk No price

—Engineer's liability to the contractor : papers presented at the Conference of the International Bar Association's Section on Business Law Conference, Toronto 1983 / International Construction Contracts Committee of the Section on Business Law of the International Bar Assoication. – London : International Bar Association, 1983.
iv,162p.
Includes bibliographical references.

—Guide to the indemnity and insurance aspects of building contracts : based on the JCT Standard Forms of Building Contract / Peter Madge. – London : RIBA, 1985.
285p; 24cm.
ISBN 0900630914

—IBA Construction Law Library / International Bar Association's Construction Contracts Committee. – London : LLoyd's of London Press, 1986.
ISBN 0948711116 Hbk

—International construction contracts / London : Butterworths, 1988.
ISBN 0406009007 Hbk

—Interplay of contracts : papers presented at the International Bar Association's 20th Biennial Conference, Vienna 1984 / International Bar Assoication. Section on Business Law. International Construction Contracts Committee. – London : International Bar Association, 1984.
102p.
Includes bibliographical references.

—Proceedings of the First Euro Arab Arbitration Conference / actes de 1er Colloque Euro-Arab sur l'arbitrage : under the high patronage of Habib Bourguiba. – London : Lloyd's of London Press, 1987.
ix,370p; 25cm.
At head of title: Euro-Arab Chambers of Commerce.
ISBN 1850441251 Pbk £60.00 (Apr.)

BUILDING AND ENGINEERING CONTRACTS - AUSTRALIA

—Building and Construction Contracts in Australia : Law and Practice / John J.A. Sharkey. – North Ryde : Law Book Co, 1981.
lv, 811p.
ISBN 0455200912 Hbk £90.50

—Contract Law in Australia / Carter. – London : Butterworths, 1986.
ISBN 0409491268 Hbk £41.00

BUILDING AND ENGINEERING CONTRACTS - CANADA

—Canadian building contracts / Immanuel Goldsmith. – 3rd ed. – Toronto, Canada : Carswell, 1983.
lxi, 273 p.; 24 cm.
Includes bibliographical references.
ISBN 0459357905

BUILDING AND ENGINEERING CONTRACTS - ENGLAND

—Professional liability and construction / Leo Barros D'Sa. – 1. – Ascot : Chartered Institute of Building, 1987.
30cm. – (Occasional paper).
ISBN 090660088X Pbk No price (Feb.)

BUILDING AND ENGINEERING CONTRACTS - GREAT BRITAIN

—ACA Form of Building Agreement Nineteen Eighty-Two / Association of Consultant Architects. – 1984 ed. – London : Architectural Press, 1984.
28p.
ISBN 0851397530 Pbk £7.50

—ACA Form Of Sub-Contract Nineteen Eighty-Two / Association of Consultant Architects. – London : Architectural Press, 1984.
12p. – (ACA Contract Documents).
ISBN 0851397557 Pbk £7.50

—AJ Contracts Guide / 2nd ed. – London : Architectural Press, 1984.
ISBN 0851397565 Pbk £4.95

—AJ Contracts Guide to ACA Form of Building Agreement 1982 / 2nd ed. – London : Architectural Press, 1984.
– (ACA Contract Documents).
ISBN 0851397565 Hbk £4.95

—Arbitration for contractors / Douglas A. Stephenson. – London : Northwood Books, 1982.
ix,150p.
Bibliography: p.145. - Includes index.
ISBN 0719829003

—BPF-ACA Form of Building Agreement 1984 / London : Architectural Press, 1984.
16p : Illus. – – (ACA Contract Documents).
ISBN 0851397565 Pbk £4.95

—Builder's Claims Under the JCT Form of Contract / King's Ride : Institute of Building, 1983.
46p.

—Builder's Guide to the Agreement for Minor Building Works / King's Ride : Institute of Building, 1983.
ISBN 0906600324 Hbk £2.75

—Building and Civil Engineering Claims / 3rd ed. – London : Estates Gazette, 1985.
ISBN 0728200775 Hbk £26.00

—Building and Civil Engineering Claims In Perspective / 2nd ed. – London : Longman Professional, 1986.
ISBN 0582494702 Hbk £29.00

—Building and Engineering Contracts : Including the Duties and Liabilities of Architects, Engineers and Surveyors / London : Sweet & Maxwell.
ISBN 042125730X Hbk £18.00

—Building contract casebook / Vincent Powell-Smith and Michael Furmston. – Rev ed. – Oxford : BSP Professional Books, 1987.
x,422p.
Previous ed.: 1984. Includes index.
ISBN 0632021098

—Building contract casebook / Vincent Powell-Smith and Michael Furmston. – London : Granada, 1984.
328; 24cm.
Includes index.
ISBN 0246121084 Hbk £27.50

—Building Contract Casebook / Furmston. – 1984 Revised. – Oxford : Blackwell Scientific, 1987.
ISBN 0003833631 Hbk £27.50

—Building contract claims / Vincent Powell-Smith and John Sims. – London : Granada, 1983.
319p; 25cm.
Includes index.
ISBN 0246119683 Unpriced

—Building Contract Claims / John Sims. – London : Collins, 1983.
320p.
ISBN 0003830942 Hbk £20.00

—Building Contract Dictionary / Chappel. – London : Architectural Press, 1985.
ISBN 0851397581 Hbk £35.00

—Building Contract Dictionary : An Architectural Press Legal Guide / David Chappell. – London : Architectural Press, 1985.
464p : Illus.
ISBN 0851397581 Hbk £35.00

—Building contract litigation / Robert Fenwick Elliott. – 2nd ed. – London : Longman, 1985.
xx,206p.
Bibliography: p.200 - Includes index.
ISBN 0851208908

—Building contract litigation / 3rd. – London : Longman Professional (UK), 1989.
– (Prctitioner series).
Reviews the forms of contract and contractual proceedings, and assesses issues involved between litigation and arbitration.
ISBN 0851214274 Hbk £35.00

—Building Contracts and Practice / Bickford-Smith. – 8th ed. – London : Butterworths, 1980.
Service to Date.
ISBN 0406192952 loose £120.00

—Building Contracts Compared and Tabulated / London : Architectural Press, 1987.
ISBN 0851397891 Pbk £39.50

—Building Contracts - Practical Guide / 4th ed. – London : Longman Professional, 1983.
ISBN 0711456569 Hbk £19.95

—Building Contracts Tabulated and Compared : An Architectural Press Legal Guide / David Chappell. – London : Architectural Press, 1987.
320p : Illus.
ISBN 0851397891 Pbk £39.50

—Building Sub-Contract Documentation / Sims. – Oxford : Blackwell Scientific, 1988.
ISBN 0003831558 Hbk £17.00

—Building Sub-contract Documentation / John Sims. – London : Collins, 1987.
300p.
ISBN 0003831558 Hbk £17.00

—Building Sub-Contract Forms / Oxford : Blackwell Scientific, 1985.
ISBN 0003830152 Hbk £22.50

—Building Sub-contract Forms / London : Collins, 1985.
314p.
ISBN 0003830152 Hbk £19.95

—Commentary on the JCT Intermediate Form of Building Contract / Neil F. Jones and David Bergman. – London : Collins, 1985.
viii,351; 25cm.
Includes index.
ISBN 0003830241 Pbk No price

—Competitive Tendering For Engineering Contracts / Spon (E & FN), 1983.
ISBN 0419116303 Hbk £19.95

—Competitive Tendering for Engineering Contracts / London : Sweet & Maxwell, 1983.

—Conditions of contract for minor works / Institute of Civil Engineers. – Telford (Thomas), 1988.
ISBN 0727713299 Pbk £5.00

—Construction Contract Dictionary / Reading : College of Estate Management, 1981.
120p.
ISBN 0902132652 Hbk £12.30
ISBN 0902132636 Pbk £7.50

—Contract Documentation for Contractors / Sims. – Oxford : Blackwell Scientific, 1985.
ISBN 0003830187 Hbk £17.95

—Contract Documentation for Contractors / John Sims. – London : Collins, 1985.
320p.
ISBN 0003830187 Hbk £16.00

—Contract strategies for construction professionals / Oxford : Blackwell Scientific, 1987.
ISBN 0003833259 Hbk £19.95

—Contract Strategies for Construction Projects / London : Collins, 1987.
240p : Illus.
ISBN 0003832716 Hbk £17.50

—Contract Strategies for Construction Projects / Oxford : Blackwell Scientific, 1988.
ISBN 0003832716 Hbk £19.95

—Contractor's Claims Under the GC-Works-1 : Edition 2 Form of Contract / King's Ride : Institute of Building, 1986.
68p.
ISBN 0906600855 Hbk £7.75

—Contracts and Building Law. Vol. 2 / The Chartered Institute of Building, UK. – King's Ride : Institute of Building.

—Contracts Building and Engineering their Planning and Administration / London : Butterworths, 1983.
ISBN 0409701270 Pbk

—Default by sub-contractors and suppliers / John Parris. – London : Collins, 1985.
320p.
Includes index.
ISBN 0003830470 £17.50

—Design and Build Contracts / Stephen J. Pymont. – London : Collins, 1986.
250p.
ISBN 0003830500 Hbk £17.50

—Design and Build Contracts / Pymont. – Oxford : Blackwell Scientific, 1987.
ISBN 0003830500 Hbk £19.95

—Design and Building Contract Practice / London : Longman Professional, 1986.
ISBN 0582494842 Pbk £19.50

—Determination and Suspension of Construction Contracts / John Sims. – London : Collins, 1985.
208p.
ISBN 0003831566 Hbk £17.50

—Determination and Suspension of Construction Contracts / Sims. – Oxford : Blackwell Scientific, 1985.
ISBN 0003831566 Hbk £19.95

—Elements of Engineering Contracts / Roulston. – Spon (E & FN), 1980.
ISBN 0419116109 Pbk £4.75

—Emden's building contracts and practice / E. Freeth. – 8th ed. 5. – London : Butterworths, 1980.
Vols.2-5 looseleaf.
Previous ed. 1969, entitled: Emden and Gill's building contracts and practice.
ISBN 0406192987

—Engineering Contract Casebook / Michael Furmston. – London : Collins, 1987.
350p.
ISBN 0003832627 Hbk £30.00

—Engineering Contract Casebook / Furmston. – Oxford : Blackwell Scientific, 1988.
ISBN 0003832627 Hbk £30.00

—Engineering Tenders, Sales and Contracts / Spon, 1982.
ISBN 0419125302 Hbk £42.00

—Engineering Tenders Sales and Contracts / London : Sweet & Maxwell, 1982.
ISBN 0419125302 Hbk £45.00

—Establishing the validity of contractual claims / King's Ride : Institute of Building, 1983.
28p.
ISBN 0901822191 Hbk £3.85

—Extensions of Time / King's Ride : Institute of Building, 1983.
22p.
ISBN 0906600685 Hbk £6.60

—Guide to the ACA Form of Building Agreement 1982 / 2nd ed. – London : Architectural Press, 1984.
60p. – (ACA Contract Documents).
ISBN 0851397336 Pbk £8.95

—JCT 80 and the Builder : An Introduction / King's Ride : Institute of Building, 1985.
211p.
ISBN 0906600774 Hbk £12.75

—JCT Intermediate Form of Building Contract / Bergman. – Oxford : Blackwell Scientific, 1985.
ISBN 0003830241 Hbk £19.95

—JCT Intermediate Form of Contract / London : Architectural Press, 1985.
ISBN 0851398855 Hbk £19.95

—JCT Intermediate Form of Contract : An Architectural Press Legal Guide / Vincent Powell-Smith. – London : Architectural Press, 1985.
232p : Illus.
ISBN 0851398855 Hbk £19.95

—JCT Minor Works Form of Contract / London : Architectural Press, 1986.
ISBN 0851398863 Pbk £18.00

—JCT Minor Works Form of Contract : An Architectural Press Legal Guide / Vincent Powell-Smith. – London : Architectural Press, 1986.
176p : Illus.
ISBN 0851398863 Hbk £18.00

—Legal and Contract Procedure for Architects / 2nd ed. – London : Architectural Press, 1984.
ISBN 0851393691 Pbk £9.95

—Liability of contractors / edited by Humphrey Lloyd. – London : Centre for Commercial Law Studies, Queen Mary College, 1986.
xxvi,253p; 24cm.
Conference proceedings. Includes index.
ISBN 0582463688 No price

—Managing Construction Conflict / London : Longman Scientific, 1988.
ISBN 0582003504 Pbk £18.00

—New approach to JCT design/building contract / Oxford : Construction Press, 1984.
ISBN 086095904X Hbk £38.00

—Pre-Contract Practice for Architects and Quantity Surveyors / AQUA Group. – 7th ed. – London : Collins, 1986.
100p : Illus.
ISBN 0003832546 Hbk £8.95

—Presentation and settlement of contractors' claims / Geoffrey Trickey. – London : Spon, 1983.
xiv,358p; 24cm.
Includes index.
ISBN 0419114300 Unpriced

—Quantification of building claims / Sims. – Oxford : Blackwell Scientific, 1988.
ISBN 0003832651 Hbk £20.00

—Shorter forms of building contract / 2nd ed. – Oxford : Blackwell Scientific, 1988.
ISBN 0003834123 Pbk £17.95
ISBN 0632018437 Hbk £19.95

—Shorter Forms of Building Contract / London : Collins, 1984.
176p.
ISBN 0246119640 Hbk £17.50

—Small Works Contract Documentation : An Architectural Press Legal Guide / 3rd ed. – London : Architectural Press, 1986.
176p : Illus.
ISBN 0851399762 Hbk £14.95

—Standard contracts for building / London : Longman Professional, 1984.
ISBN 0711457522 Pbk £6.50

—Standard contracts for building / Dennis F. Turner. – London : Godwin, 1984.
x,234p; 22cm. – (Godwin study guides).
Bibliography: p225. - Includes index.
ISBN 0711457522 Pbk £5.95

—Standard form of building contract JCT 1980 / 2nd ed. – Oxford : Blackwell Scientific, 1985.
ISBN 0003830276 Hbk £19.95

—Standard form of building contract : JCT 80 / John Parris. – 2nd ed. – London : Collins, 1985.
xii,256p; 24cm.
Previous ed.: London : Granada, 1982. Includes index.
ISBN 0003830276 £17.50

—Studies in Contractual Claims under the ICE Conditions of Contract / 3rd rev. ed. – King's Ride : Institute of Building, 1987.
34p.
ISBN 0906600170 Hbk £7.75

—Sub-contracts under JCT intermediate form / Oxford : Blackwell Scientific, 1987.
ISBN 0003831752 Hbk £19.95

—Sub-contracts Under the JCT Intermediate Form / London : Collins, 1987.
240p.
ISBN 0003831752 Hbk £19.00

—Variations in construction contracts / Oxford : Blackwell Scientific, 1986.
ISBN 0003831914 Hbk £19.95

—Variations in Construction Contracts / London : Collins, 1986.
240p.
ISBN 0003831914 Hbk £17.95

—Walker-Smith on the Standard Forms of Building Contract / Tonbridge : Ernest Benn.
450p.
ISBN 085314317X Hbk £75.00

BUILDING AND ENGINEERING CONTRACTS - NEW ZEALAND

—Building Contracts and Practice, 4 Vols. / S. Bickford-Smith. – 8th ed. – Wellington : Butterworths, 1980.
This work contains one hard cover volume and three looseleaf binders. The looseleaf binders include the text of JCT documentation, fully annotated, with extensive cross-references and commentary. Forms of contract, conditions and codes of practice, and tables of statutes and cases are provided.

—Contracts Building and Engineering Their Planning and Administration / Butterworths, 1983.
Covers elements of the law of contract, types of engineering and building contract, persons concerned with the contract and its administration, and contract document, calling for tenders, letting the contract, supervision and administration of the contract, trends, and references and a bibliography.
ISBN 0409701270 Pbk £25.85

BUILDING AND ENGINEERING CONTRACTS - NORTHERN IRELAND

—Some Aspects of Building Contracts / Belfast : Queen's University of Belfast, 1982.
31p.

BUILDING AND ENGINEERING CONTRACTS - SOUTH AFRICA

—Engineering and construction law : with illustrations and cases / P.C. Loots. – Cape Town : Juta, 1985.
xxxv, 431 p.; 26 cm.
'Being a commentary on the General conditions of contract for works of civil engineering construction (fifth edition) 1982.'. Includes indexes.
ISBN 0702115630

BUILDING INDUSTRY

—ACA Form Of Sub-Contract Nineteen Eighty-Two / Association of Consultant Architects. – London : Architectural Press, 1984.
12p. – (ACA Contract Documents).
ISBN 0851397557 Pbk £7.50

—Basic crucial issues in major construction projects : papers presented at a seminar held jointly with the Institution of Civil Engineers, London, June 1985 / International Bar Association. Section on Business Law. International Construction Contracts Committee. – London : International Bar Association, 1986.
207p.
ISBN 0948711051

—Construction insurance / Nael G. Bunni. – London : Elsevier Applied Science, 1986.
xviii,336p; 25cm.
Includes index.
ISBN 0853344388 £50.00

—International construction law review / London : Lloyd's of London, 1983-.

—Joint ventures in the construction industry : papers presented at the 7th Conference of the International Bar Association's Section on Business Law, Singapore 1985 / International Construction Contracts Committee of the Section on Business Law of the International Bar Association. – 1. – London : International Bar Association, 1985.
Various pagings.
Includes bibliographical references.

—Selected problems of construction law : international approach / Terence M. Burke ... et al. : published i.e. edited by Peter Gauch and Justin Sweet. – Fribourg : University Press, 1983.
287p.
Includes bibliographical references. 'The papers collected are revised versions of working papers prepared for and presented at the First International Construction Law Conference, Fribourg, 1982'.
ISBN 3727802863
ISBN 0-421-31650-0

BUILDING INDUSTRY - AUSTRALIA

—Law for Architects, Builders and Engineers / 2nd ed. – Butterworths, 1983.
355p.
ISBN 0409493422 Pbk £29.50

BUILDING INDUSTRY - AUSTRALIA - NEW SOUTH WALES

—New South Wales Construction Safety Act 1912 and Regulations / 2nd ed. – North Ryde : C.C.H. Australia, 1985.
300p.
ISBN 0869034855 Hbk £24.00

BUILDING INDUSTRY - ENGLAND

—Construction law : law and practice relating to the construction industry / by John Uff. – 4th ed. – London : Sweet & Maxwell, 1985.
xvii,350p; 22cm.
Deals with the principles of building and civil engineering contracts as well as the standard forms of contract issued by the JCT and the ICE. Enlarged section on the law and practice of arbitration, including an introduction to the ICE Arbitration Procedure 1983. Also covers the Building Act 1984, and the new Building Regulations.
ISBN 0421343605 Hbk £18
ISBN 0421343702 Pbk £16

—Report of the Official Referees' Users' Committee ... / Official Referees' Users' Committee. – London : The Committee, 1983.
1st report covers 1983 to 1986.

BUILDING INDUSTRY - GREAT BRITAIN

—Builders' Claims Under the JCT 1963 Form of Contract / rev. ed. – King's Ride : Institute of Building, 1982.
Illus. – – (Studies in Contractual Claims; 3).
ISBN 0901822531 Hbk £6.75

—Construction law digest / . – s.l. : Construction Law Digest, 1982-.
Parts issued in number order 10 to 1. Part 1 is annual index.
ISBN 02639351 Hbk

—Construction law journal / v. – Andover : Sweet & Maxwell, 1984.
Index in each vol..
ISBN 02672359

—Construction refurbishment and design / London : Estates Gazette, 1986.
ISBN 0728200996 Pbk £15.95

—Delays and Disruptions in Construction : Ascertaining the Cost-A Case Study in Assessing a Contractor's Claim / King's Ride : Institute of Building, 1987.
68p.
ISBN 0906600928 Hbk £7.75

—Design Liability in the Construction Industry / 2nd ed. – Oxford : Blackwell Scientific, 1985.
ISBN 0003830209 Hbk £19.95

—Focus on Construction Industry Tax Deduction Scheme / Croydon : Tolley, 1983.
ISBN 0854591206 Pbk £6.95

—Insurance under the JCT forms / Frank Eaglestone. – London : Collins, 1985.
viii,367p; 24cm.
Includes index. Kept up to date by supplements.
ISBN 0003830225 £20.00

—Public Policy, Bargaining Structure and the Construction Industry / Toronto : Butterworths, 1980.
200p.
ISBN 0409862959 Pbk £29.95

—VAT on construction and development work / Philip S.D. King. – London : Granada, 1984.
194p; 24cm.
Includes index.
ISBN 0246122501 Hbk £17.95

—VAT on construction and development work / Oxford : Blackwell Scientific, 1984.
ISBN 0246122501 Hbk £17.95

BUILDING INDUSTRY - INDIA

—Contract Labour in Construction Industry : a Case Study of Tripura / Calcutta : Firma KLM, 1980.

BUILDING LAW - AUSTRALIA

—Brooking on Building Contracts / R. Brooking. – 2nd ed. – Butterworths, 1980.
272p.
ISBN 0409300209 Hbk £49.00

—Law for Architects, Builders and Engineers / 2nd ed. – Butterworths, 1983.
355p.
ISBN 0409493422 Pbk £29.50

BUILDING LAW - CANADA

—Construction Law Reports / Agincourt : Carswell, 1985.
Vol. 31, 1988
This work contains the key construction law decisions from all Canadian jurisdictions. Topics include building contracts, remedies for their breach, construction liens and bonding issues. Cases on court actions by and against architects, engineers, contractors and subcontractors are also included.

—House Construction and Renovation : a Solicitor's Guide / Vancouver : Continuing Legal Education Society of British Columbia, 1988.
310p.
ISBN 0865049688 Hbk £80.00

—Legislative Changes in the Construction Industry in Nova Scotia 1964 to 1975 : An Exercise in Industrial Democracy / Halifax : Dalhousie University, Institute of Public Affairs.
v, 55p. – (Occasional Papers).
ISBN 088926810X Pbk £5.00

BUILDING LAW - GREAT BRITAIN

—AJ Legal Handbook / Stone. - 4th ed. - London : Architectural Press, 1985.
ISBN 0851397514 Pbk £19.95

—Basic Construction and Surveying Law / London : Collins, 1984.
253p.
ISBN 0246119632 Pbk £9.95

—Basic Construction and Surveying Law / Oxford : Blackwell Scientific, 1984.
ISBN 0246119632 Pbk £10.95

—Building Act 1984 / with annotations by Harold F. Baines. - London : Sweet & Maxwell, 1985.
164p.
Includes index.
ISBN 0421345500

—Building Control In Inner London : The London Building Acts and Bylaws and Their Interpretation / J. Dufton. - London : Architectural Press, 1983.
224p.
ISBN 0851397697 Pbk £16.50

—Building Land and Estates / 2nd ed. - London : Oyez Longman, 1983.
- (Oyez Longman Practice Note Ser.: No. 67).
ISBN 0851206964 Hbk £8.95

—Building Legislation and Historic Buildings / London : Architectural Press, 1987.
176p : Illus.
ISBN 0851397905 Pbk £14.95

—Building Legislation and Historic Buildings / London : Architectural Press, 1987.
ISBN 0851397905 Pbk £14.95

—Building Maintenance Management / 3rd ed. - Oxford : Blackwell Scientific, 1987.
ISBN 0003833755 Pbk £14.95

—Building Project Finance in HK : Law and Practice / London : Butterworths, 1987.
ISBN 0409995363 Hbk £54.00

—Building Subsidence / Apted. - Oxford : Blackwell Scientific, 1988.
ISBN 0003834190 Hbk £22.50

—Construction Law Digest, 3 Vols. / London : Collins.

Vol. 3 1985.
490p.

—Construction Law Reports 10 vols / Vincent Powell-Smith. - London : Architectural Press, 1985.
160p.
ISBN 0851397808 Hbk £18.50

Vol. 2 1985.
ISBN 0851397816 Hbk £18.50

Vol. 3 1985.
ISBN 0851397824 Hbk £18.50

—Construction Law Reports / Powell-Smith. - Vol. 11. - London : Architectural Press, 1988.
ISBN 0851392024 Hbk £25.00

—Contracts and Building Law. Vol. 2 / The Chartered Institute of Building, UK. - King's Ride : Institute of Building.

—Emden's building contracts and practice / E. Freeth. - 8th ed. 5. - London : Butterworths, 1980.
Vols.2-5 looseleaf.
Previous ed. 1969, entitled: Emden and Gill's building contracts and practice.
ISBN 0406192987

—Guide to Building Control by Local Acts 1987 / London : Architectural Press, 1987.
128p : Illus.
ISBN 0851398413 Pbk £19.50

—Guide to Building Control by Local Acts / London : Architectural Press, 1987.
ISBN 0851398413 Pbk £39.50

—Guide to Building Control in Inner London 1986 / London : Architectural Press, 1987.
ISBN 0851398421 Pbk £19.50

—Law of Defective Premises / Stone. - London : Pitman Publishing, 1982.
ISBN 0273017705 Hbk £15.95

—Maintenance of commercial tenanted proerty / a consultative document by a working party of the Building Surveyors Division of the Royal Institution of Chartered Surveyors, January 1987. - London : The Institution, 1987.
9,12p.

—Quantification of Building Claims / John Sims. - London : Collins, 1987.
260p.
ISBN 0003832651 Hbk £20.00

—Selected problems of construction law / Gauch. - London : Sweet & Maxwell, 1983.
ISBN 0421316500 Pbk £28.00

BUILDING LAW - HONG KONG

—Building Project Finance in Hong Kong : Law and Practice / Butterworths, 1987.
265p.
Describes the law and practice of building project finance in Hong Kong. Examines the 'financing', 'project', and 'security' aspects of a project loan in a comprehensive manner. Explains the typical transactions involved, the roles of various documents, and the problems which have to be dealt with.
ISBN 0409995363 Hbk £110.00

BUILDING LAW - MALAYSIA

—Construction law in Singapore and Malaysia / Anthony P Lavers. - Singapore : Butterworths (Asia), 1988.
350.
Explains the main principles governing the law of construction and refers to and treats in detail the local forms of building contracts and statutory provisions in Singapore and Malaysia. The digest section contains summaries and extracts of cases referred to in the text.

—Construction Law in Singapore and Malaysia / Lavers. - London : Butterworths, 1988.
ISBN 0409995614 Hbk

—Street, Drainage and Building Act, 1974 (Act 133) / Kuala Lumpur : International Law Books Services.

—Uniform Building By-Laws, 1964 (G.N. 5178/85) / Kuala Lumpur : International Law Books Services.

BUILDING LAW - SINGAPORE

—Construction Joint Ventures in Singapore / Kok. - London : Butterworths, 1985.
ISBN 0409995029 Hbk £34.00

—Construction Law in Singapore and Malaysia / Lavers. - London : Butterworths, 1988.
ISBN 0409995614 Hbk

—Construction law in Singapore and Malaysia / Anthony P Lavers. - Singapore : Butterworths (Asia), 1988.
350.
Explains the main principles governing the law of construction and refers to and treats in detail the local forms of building contracts and statutory provisions in Singapore and Malaysia. The digest section contains summaries and extracts of cases referred to in the text.

BUILDING LAWSCDEPARTMENT OF THE ENVIRONMENT

—Telecommunications development : draft development control policy note / Department of the Environment. - London : Department of the Environment, 1986.
24p.

BUILDING REGULATIONS - AUSTRALIA - QUEENSLAND

—Regulation of Building Standards Queensland / D.K. Woodhead. - Butterworths, 1988.
ISBN 0409300942 loose

BUILDING REGULATIONS - GREAT BRITAIN

—AJ Index to 1985 Building Regulations / London : Architectural Press, 1986.
ISBN 0851398383 Pbk £7.50

—AJ Introduction and Complete Index to the 1985 Building Regulations / London : Architectural Press.
60p : Illus.
ISBN 0851398383 Pbk £7.50

—Alteration/Conversion Of Houses / Edmunds. - 6th ed. - London : Longman Professional, 1985.
ISBN 0851209971 Pbk £16.95

—Building Regulations 1981 : Second Amendment / London : HMSO.
ISBN 0110173384 Hbk £4.50

—Building Regulations 1983 : Third Amendment / London : HMSO.
ISBN 0110361954 Hbk £1.30

—Building Regulations 1985 Explained / Northwood, 1986.
ISBN 1850320195 Hbk £24.95

—Building Regulations : Explained and Illustrated / Vincent Powell Smith. - 7th ed. - London : Collins, 1986.
310p : Illus.
ISBN 0003832813 Hbk £18.50
ISBN 0003832260 Pbk £10.95

—Building Regulations Explained and Illustrated / Billington. - 7th ed. - Oxford : Blackwell Scientific, 1986.
ISBN 0003832260 Pbk £14.00

—Guide to Building Regulations 1985 / London : Architectural Press, 1986.
ISBN 0851398448 Pbk £16.95

—Guide to the Building Regulations 1985 / 8th ed. - London : Architectural Press, 1986.
256p : Illus.
ISBN 0851398448 Pbk £19.95

—Guide to the Building Regulations Nineteen Seventy-Six / 7th ed. - London : Architectural Press, 1981.
224p : Illus.
ISBN 0851398502 Pbk £11.95

—Guide To The Second Amendment Nineteen Eighty-One : Supplement to Guide to the Building Regulations 1976 / 7th ed. - London : Architectural Press, 1982.
32p : Illus.
ISBN 0851398499 Pbk £4.50

—Specification 87 / London : Architectural Press, 1987.
1400p : Illus.
ISBN 0851396232 Pbk £65.00

BUILDING REGULATIONS - INDIA

—Uttar Pradesh Regulation of Building Operations Act, 1958 : with Rules and Regulations and Urban Planning and Development Act, 1973 / 3rd ed. repr. - Lucknow : Eastern Book Company, 1986.
396p.

BUILDING REGULATIONS - SCOTLAND

—Building Standards (Scotland) Amendment Regulations 1982 / London : HMSO.
ISBN 011027878X Hbk £3.15

—Building Standards (Scotland) Amendment Regulations 1984 / London : HMSO.
ISBN 0110476603 Hbk £1.30

—Building Standards (Scotland) Regulations 1981 / London : HMSO.
ISBN 0110175964 Hbk £13.10

BUILDING REGULATIONS - TANZANIA

—Township : Building, Single Storey Houses, Rules; the Legal Version / Tanzania Building Research Unit. - Dar es Salaaam : Ministry of Lands, Housing and Urban Development, 1980.

BUILDING SOCIETIES - AUSTRALIA - NEW SOUTH WALES

—Community law reform program / New South Wales Law Reform Commission. - Sydney : The Commission, 1985.
xiii,123p. - (L.R.C. 46).
Includes bibliographical references.
ISBN 0730514714 Hbk

BUILDING SOCIETIES - GREAT BRITAIN

—Building societies : a new framework / Treasury : foreword by Nigel Lawson. - London : H.M.S.O., 1984.
iii,44p.
ISBN 0101931603

—Building Societies Act 1986 / with annotations by Elizabeth Ovey and Malcolm Waters. - London : Sweet & Maxwell, 1987.
322,8p; 24cm.
Includes index.
ISBN 0421367008 Pbk No price

—Building societies : the myth of mutuality / Paul Barnes : with a foreword by Ken Weetch. - London : Pluto, 1984.
xv,171p; 20cm.
ISBN 0861047591 Pbk £4.95

—Building Society Law / Mills. - 15th ed. - Sweet & Maxwell, 1988.
ISBN 0420473009 Hbk

—Building Society Law and Practice / Oxford : BPP, 1988.
ISBN 0862772249 Pbk £15.95

—Building society law : cases and materials / C.E.I. Thornton and J.P. McBrien. - 3rd ed. - London : Sweet & Maxwell, 1988.
xxi,202p; 22cm.
Previous ed.: 1975. Includes index.
ISBN 0421383704 Pbk £9.95

—Conversion of building societies to company status : a consultative paper / Great Britain. - London : Treasury, 1985.
9p.
At head of title: Building Societies Bill.

—Financial services legislation : the auditor's role in the financial services sector : a consultative document / Great Britain. - London : The Division, 1985.
12p.

—Model of the building society sector / J. B. Wilcox. - London : Bank of England, 1985.
29p. - (Discussion papers).
Bibliography: p29.
ISBN 090331276X

BULK SALES - CANADA - BRITISH COLUMBIA

—Bulk sales legislation / Law Reform Commission of British Columbia. - Vancouver : The Commission, 1983.
v,115p. - (Working paper).
Includes bibliographical references.

—Report on bulk sales legislation / Law Reform Commission of British Columbia. - Victoria : Queen's Printer, 1983.
45p.
Includes bibliographical references.
ISBN 0771883943

BURDEN OF PROOF – AUSTRALIA

—Evidence reference / Australian Law Reform Commission. – Sydney : The Commission, 1983.
xxi,119p.
Includes bibliographical references.

BURDEN OF PROOF – AUSTRALIA – TASMANIA

—Report on the burden of proof in criminal proceedings and statutory offences / Law Reform Commission of Tasmania. – Hobart : Government Printer, 1987.
26p. – (Report v no 49).

BURDEN OF PROOF – GREAT BRITAIN

—Burden of Proof / London : Butterworths, 1987.
ISBN 0862052157 Hbk £26.50

—Burden of proof / general editor Albert Kiralfy. – Abingdon : Professional, 1987.
xxix,251p; 22cm.
Includes index.
ISBN 0862052157 No price

BURIALS AND CREMATION – GREAT BRITAIN

—Law of Burial, Cremation and Exhumation / 6th ed. – London : Shaw & Sons, 1988.
ISBN 072190064X Pbk

BUS TERMINALS – ENGLAND

—Southern Vectis Omnibus Company Limited : refusal to allow access to Newport bus station, Isle of Wight / a report by the Director General of Fair Trading on an investigation under section 3 of the Competition Act 1980. – London : Office of Fair Trading, 1988.
34p.

BUSINESS

—Basic Law for Business / Palmerston North : Dunmore Press Ltd., 1984.
117p.
ISBN 0864690258 Pbk £9.95

—Concepts and Problems in Mercantile Law / New Delhi : Allied Publishers, 1984.
viii, 372p.

—Dictionary of Business Biography / London : Butterworths, 1984.
ISBN 0406273413 Hbk £72.00

Vol. 2 D-G 1984.
ISBN 0406273421 Hbk £72.00

Vol. 3 H-L 1985.
ISBN 040627343X Hbk £72.00

Vol. 4 M-R 1985.
ISBN 0406273448 Hbk £72.00

Vol. 5 S-Z 1986.
ISBN 0406273456 Hbk £72.00

—Doing Business in Mexico / Matthew Bender, 1980.
ISBN 0000999044 Hbk £135.00

—Doing business in the European Community / John Drew. – 2nd ed. – London : Butterworths, 1983.
vii,293p; 25cm.
Previous ed.: 1979. Includes bibliographies and index.
ISBN 0408108363 Unpriced

—Financing of small business / Desmond L. Hally. – 3rd ed. – London : Sweet and Maxwell, 1982.
xviii,243p; 23cm.
Previous ed.: 1971. Bibliography: p235-238. - Includes index.
ISBN 0421292008 £17.75

—Interference or Internationalism : The Extraterritorial Application of National Laws Regulating Business Activities / Enstone : Ditchley Foundation.
1982p.

—Legal Aspects of Doing Business in... / Dordrecht : Kluwer.

—Lending in booms and slumps / by L.S. Dyer : delivered under the auspices of King's College London. – London : King's College London, 1981.
35p; 25cm.

—Multiparty Business Disputes / Paris : International Chamber of Commerce.
76p.

—Role of local authorities in promoting the creation or operation of small or medium-sized firms within a general policy of endogenous development / report prepared under the guidance of the Committee of Experts on Social and Economic Activities of the Steering Committee for Regional and Municipal Matters by T. Nuttal. – Strasbourg : Council of Europe, 1986.
31p.
Bibliography: p.28-29.

—Secondary banking crisis, 1973-75 : its causes and course / Margaret Reid. – London : Macmillan, 1982.
ix,219p.

—Spanish business law / Bernardo M. Cremades, general editor. – Deventer, The Netherlands : Kluwer Law and Taxation Publishers, 1985.
Includes index.
ISBN 9065442200 Hbk £315.00

—Troubleshooting International Business Problems / Ian Blackshaw. – London : Oyez Longman, 1980.

BUSINESS – AUSTRALIA

—Business Law of Australia / K.E. Lindgren. – 5th ed. – Butterworths, 1987.
1,100p.
ISBN 0409492086 Hbk £39.50

Cumulative Supplement-1985
95p.
ISBN 0409491349

—Business Law of Australia / Lindgren. – 5th ed. – North Ryde : Butterworths (Australia), 1983.
ISBN 0409492086 Hbk £29.00

—Doing Business In Australia / Matthew Bender, 1988.
ISBN 0000999043 Hbk £50.00

—Essentials of Business Law in Australia / Carleton : Pitman Pty Ltd, 1983.
ISBN 0858966697 Hbk £22.95

—Introduction to Business Law / K.E. Lindgren. – 4th ed. – North Ryde : Law Book Co, 1984.
xv, 285p.
ISBN 0455202117 Pbk £7.50

BUSINESS – CANADA

—BAC Business Law / Woods. – Agincourt : Carswell, 1986.
ISBN 045939520 Hbk £36.50

—Business and the Law / Toronto : DeBoo, 1984.
ISBN 0888201699 Hbk £165.00

—Business Associations / Simmonds and Mercer. – Agincourt : Carswell, 1984.
806p.

—Business Law / Judith M. Woods. – Agincourt : Carswell, 1986.
616p. – (Bar Admission Course Materials Ser.).

—Business Legal Advisor / Toronto : DeBoo, 1985.
ISBN 088820194X Hbk £135.00

Supplements
This guide to business transactions contains commentary, materials, and precedents covering buying and selling a business, family trusts, shareholders' buy-sell agreements, Investment Canada, incorporation, and references to pertinent sections of the Income Tax Act and Interpretation bulletins. Numerous sample forms are also included.

—Buying and Selling a Business 1985 / Vancouver : Continuing Legal Education Society of British Columbia, 1985.
311p.
ISBN 0865041970 Hbk £65.00

—Canada Business Corporations Act : An Accountant's Review of the Highlights / 2nd ed. – Toronto : Butterworths, 1981.
128p.
ISBN 0409859737 Pbk £14.95

—Canada Business Corporations Act : an Accountant's View of the Highlights / 3rd ed. – Butterworths, 1987.
136p.
Includes a revised study of the law introduced (in 1975) by the new Act. Covers detailed disclosure requirements for financial statements, information not contained in the body of the Act, but substantially prescribed by regulations.
ISBN 0409806560 Pbk £18.95

—Canada From Abroad : Legal, Business and Tax Aspects / North Ryde : C.C.H. Australia.
210p.
ISBN 0887963129 Pbk £16.95

—Canadian Business Law Journal (1976-Present) / Aurora : Canada Law Book Co.
– (Law Journals).

Back Vols.

—Canadian Business Law Journal (C.B.L.J.) 1976-Present / Aurora : Canada Law Book Co.

Current subscription-Outside Canada

Back Vols.

—Current developments in measuring business income for tax purposes / Corporate Management Tax Conference, 1981. – Toronto, Canada : Canadian Tax Foundation, 1982.
xi, 326 p.; 23 cm.
Includes bibliographical references.
ISBN 0888080085 pbk. £25.00

—Current Issues in Canadian Business Law / Agincourt : Carswell, 1985.
600p.
This work is a collection of essays on a variety of business law topics written by Canadian practitioners. The essays cover topics ranging from corporate and commercial law to secured transactions and instruments of payment.

—Doing Business in Canada / Vancouver : British Columbia Continuing Legal Education Society, 1983.
330p.
ISBN 0865041296 Hbk £60.00

—Doing Business in Canada and B.C. / Vancouver : British Columbia Continuing Legal Education Society, 1986.
234p.
ISBN 0865042195 Hbk £60.00

—Foreign affiliate system : Canadian taxation after 1982 : a structured overview / by Nathan Boidman. – Don Mills, Ont. : CCH Canadian Ltd., 1983.
ix,218p.
Includes index.
ISBN 0887962092

—Government Assistance for Canadian Business / Toronto : DeBoo.
This reference work, intended for business owners and financial advisors seeking financial assistance from the Federal and Provincial governments, sets out the eligibility requirements for all Canadian jurisdictions. Subscribers receive a complimentary newsletter and six updates annually.
ISBN 0888201451 loose £245.00

—Introduction to business associations in Canada : cases, notes, and materials / by R.L. Simmonds and Peter P. Mercer. – Toronto, Canada : Carswell Legal Publications, 1984.
xxviii, 778 p.; 25 cm.
Spine title: Business associations in Canada.
ISBN 0459365304 pbk.

—Ontario Business Corporations Act annotated / Margot Lettner. – Scarborough, Ontario : Butterworths (Canada), 1990.
352.
ISBN 1234124312 Pbk £36

—Recent Developments in Business and Litigation / Vancouver : Continuing Legal Education Society of British Columbia, 1987.
278p.
ISBN 0865043493 Hbk £80.00

U.S./Canada Litigation

—Selected Topics in Canada-Japan Legal and Business Relations / Vancouver : British Columbia Continuing Legal Education Society, 1980.
419p.
ISBN 0865040133 Hbk £65.00

BUSINESS – CANADA – BRITISH COLUMBIA

—Doing Business in Canada and B.C. / Vancouver : British Columbia Continuing Legal Education Society, 1986.
234p.
ISBN 0865042195 Hbk £60.00

BUSINESS – CANADA – QUEBEC

—Legal Aspects of Starting a Business in Quebec / Montreal : McGill Campus Legal Aid Clinic, 1984.
139p.

BUSINESS – CHINA

—Business and Tax Laws of the People's Republic of China / Fred Blaser. – North Ryde : C.C.H. Australia, 1986.
96p.
ISBN 0887963978 Pbk £14.95

—China Business Guide / London : Longman Professional, 1986.
ISBN 0582998026 Pbk £14.95

—Law and Business Practice in Shanghai / London : Longman Professional, 1988.
ISBN 0582997550 Hbk £25.00

—Legal aspects of business transactions and investment in the Far East / D Campbell, A Wolff. – Kluwer Law and Taxation, 1989.
400.
Describes the legal framework for trading with, licensing to, and investing in China, Hong Kong, Indonesia, Japan, Korea, Malaysia, Singapore, Taiwan and Thailand. Includes legal aspects of entering the Japanese market, parallel imports in Japan and legal aspects of trade and investment in Singapore, and forms of foreign investment in the People's Republic of China.
ISBN 9065443150 Pbk £63/Dfl 195

BUSINESS – ENGLAND

—English Business Law Q & A / London : Financial Training, 1986.
ISBN 1851850104 Pbk £7.95

—Tax consequences of receivership and liquidation / David Bertram. – London : Butterworths, 1982.
xxxii,423p; 22cm.
Includes index.
ISBN 0406220603 Pbk £20.00

BUSINESS – EUROPEAN COMMUNITY

—Business law in Europe : legal, tax and labour aspects of business operations in the ten European Community countries and Switzerland / edited by Maarten J. Ellis and Paul M. Storm : Prepared under the auspices of the Association europeenne d'etudes juridiques et fiscales. – Deventer : Kluwer, 1982.
xvi,606p.
Includes bibliographies.
ISBN 9065440402

—Doing Business in the European Community / 2nd ed. – London : Butterworths, 1982.
ISBN 0408108363 Hbk £20.00

—European Community : The Practical Guide for Business and Government / London : Macmillan, 1983.
ISBN 0333262050 Hbk £18.50

BUSINESS – FRANCE

—Doing Business in France / Simeon Moquet Borde & Associes. – Matthew Bender, 1983.
ISBN 0000999039 Hbk £105.00

—French Business Enterprise : Basic Legislative Texts (As Amended to January 1, 1979) / Dordrecht : Kluwer, 1980.
363p.
ISBN 9027116407 Hbk £148.00

BUSINESS – GREAT BRITAIN

—Accounting in Business / 5th ed. – London : Butterworths, 1984.
ISBN 0408014865 Pbk £13.50

—Bennett and Cheesley : Let's Go Into Business / Roger G. Cheesley. – London : Butterworths, 1982.

—Building Your Business : Know Your Law / London : Business Books, 1984.
ISBN 0091518113 Pbk £6.95

—Business Expansion Scheme / VANN, 1984.
ISBN 0852913826 Pbk £8.95

—Business Finance / London : Butterworths, 1986.
ISBN 0406501408 Pbk £13.95

—Business in Society / Chapman. – London : Butterworths, 1981.
ISBN 0408106948 Pbk £7.50

—Business in Society Concensus and Conflict / London : Butterworths.
ISBN 0408106948 Pbk

—Business Law / Riches. – Pitman, 1987.
ISBN 0273024159 Pbk £7.95

—Business Law / Pendlebury. – 3rd ed. – London : DP Publications, 1986.
ISBN 0905435672 Pbk £4.95

—Business Law / London : Pitman Publishing, 1982.
ISBN 0855050624 Pbk £3.95

—Business Law / 1st ed. Repr. of 1982 ed. – Plymouth : Macdonald & Evans, 1983.
288p. – (M and E Handbook Ser.).
ISBN 0712102612 Hbk £5.50

—Business Law / Bradgate. – London : Butterworths, 1987.
ISBN 040601843X Pbk £16.95

—Business Law / London : Butterworths, 1987.
ISBN 040601843X Pbk

—Business Law / Soulsby. – 3rd ed. – Maidenhead : McGraw-Hill, 1985.
ISBN 0070848769 Pbk £7.95

—Business Law / 2nd ed. – London : Pitman Publishing, 1985.
ISBN 0712124055 Pbk £6.95

—Business Law : A Workbook / Pitman, 1984.
ISBN 0712124047 Pbk £2.95

—Business Law (ILT) / London : Sweet & Maxwell, 1982.
ISBN 0421285001 Pbk £14.50

—Business Law : Instructional Manual / N. Pendlebury. – 3rd ed. – Winchester : DP Publications, 1982.
608p.
ISBN 0905435672 Pbk £5.25

—Business Law Review / Butterworth and Co. (Publishers) Ltd. – London : Butterworths.

—Businessman's Guide to Microcomputers / Deloitte Staff. – London : Butterworths, 1984.
This book is designed to give business and legal practitioners a thorough introduction to microcomputers. The book provides in depth information on software packages with business applications.
ISBN 0406016003 Pbk

—Butterworths CIMA Student Series : Management Accounting - Decision Making / London : Butterworths, 1988.
ISBN 0406530033 Pbk £14.95

—Company Director and the Law / 4th ed. – London : Oyez Longman, 1983.
– (It's Your Law Ser.).
ISBN 085120709X Hbk £8.25

—Dictionary of Business Biography / London : Butterworths.
This work contains over 1000 biographies of British businessmen from 1860 to 1980. Each subject is treated in terms of his major successes and failures, innovations, and management style and policies.

—Doing Business in the United Kingdom / Matthew Bender, 1987.
ISBN 0000999036 Hbk £147.00

—Establishing a business in the United Kingdom / by R. M. Cooke and D. C. Borer. – 2nd ed. – London : Institute of Chartered Accountants, 1983.
viii,215p.
ISBN 0852913370

—Exploiting the Business Expansion Scheme / London : Longman Professional, 1987.
ISBN 0851212484 Pbk £17.50

—General Principles of Business Law (Q & A) / De Freitas. – 2nd ed. – London : Castlevale Publishers, 1984.
ISBN 0907235069 Pbk £6.00

—Government Assistance for Businesses / Croydon : Tolley, 1987.
ISBN 0854593209 Hbk £13.95

—Husband and wife business partnership: what the law says / Margo Owles. – London : Graham & Trotman, 1989.
116; 215mm.
Deals with the legal aspects of a business partnership between husband and wife, and examines the nature and formation of a partnership, the partners, liabilities, how to avoid major pitfalls, the present income tax procedure with reference to the separate taxation of spouses due to be implemented in 1990, and how to provide for the future in retirement.
ISBN 1853330574 Hbk £14.95
ISBN 1853333131 Pbk £7.50

—Journal of Business Law / London : Sweet & Maxwell.
Bound Vol.
Back Vols. avail.
Single copy

—Law and Tax for the Family Company / London : Oyez Longman, 1982.
– (Law and Tax Ser.).
ISBN 085120614X Hbk £15.00

—Legal environment : business law / 2nd. – London : Cassell plc.
Introductory text-book on business law.
ISBN 0039106020

—Legal Environment of Business / Reed. – 7th ed. – Maidenhead : McGraw-Hill, 1987.
ISBN 0070132569 Hbk £29.95

—Let's go into business / Cheesley. – London : Butterworths, 1982.
ISBN 0372300235 Pbk £5.50

—Longman Exam Guide : Business Law / Bailey. – London : Longman Professional, 1986.
ISBN 0582296781 Pbk £6.95

—Mastering business law / London : Macmillan, 1988.
ISBN 0333487982 Hbk £13.50
ISBN 0333487990 Pbk £4.50

—N.V. Slavenburg's Bank v. Intercontinental Natural Resources Ltd. : (1980) 1 All E.R. 955 : memorandum / by the Society's Standing Committee on Company Law. – London : Law Society, 1981.
12p; 30cm.

—New form of incorporation for small firms : a consultative document / London : H.M.S.O., 1981.
iii,44p; 25cm.
ISBN 010181710X Pbk £3.20

—Passing Down the Family Business : Solving the Tax Problems / Robert Venables. – 2nd ed. – London : Oyez Longman, 1982.
– (Oyez Longman Intelligence Report Ser.).
ISBN 0851207405 Hbk £45.00

—Practical Business Law / 1st ed. – Plymouth : Macdonald & Evans, 1983.
416p.
ISBN 0712104631 Pbk £7.95

—Practical Business Law / London : Pan Books Ltd, 1984.
ISBN 033026835X Hbk £2.95

—Practical business law / London : Pitman Publishing, 1983.
ISBN 0712104631 Pbk £8.50

—Small businesses / by Michael Chesterman. – 2nd ed. – London : Sweet & Maxwell, 1982.
xxi,288p; 19cm.
Previous ed.: 1977. Includes index.
ISBN 0421286008 Hbk £13.00
ISBN 0421286105 Pbk £7.95

—Starting in business / Cambridge : Woodhead-Faulkner, 1985.
ISBN 0959412954 Pbk £6.95

—Tax Planning for Family Business / London : Butterworths, 1984.
ISBN 0406556806 Pbk

—Tax planning for new businesses / 2nd ed. – Croydon : Tolley, 1987.
ISBN 0854592032 Pbk £9.95

—Terminology of business and company law / Bailey. – London : Kogan Page, 1987.
ISBN 0850914133 Pbk £8.95

—Your Business and the Law / 2nd ed. – London : Oyez Longman, 1983.
– (It's Your Law Ser.).
ISBN 0851207251 Hbk £8.50

BUSINESS – HONG KONG

—Commercial, Business and Trade Laws : Hong Kong 2 volumes / Dobbs Ferry : Oceana, 1982.
ISBN 0379231050 loose £190.00

—Legal aspects of business transactions and investment in the Far East / D Campbell, A Wolff. – Kluwer Law and Taxation, 1989.
400.
Describes the legal framework for trading with, licensing to, and investing in China, Hong Kong, Indonesia, Japan, Korea, Malaysia, Singapore, Taiwan and Thailand. Includes legal aspects of entering the Japanese market, parallel imports in Japan and legal aspects of trade and investment in Singapore, and forms of foreign investment in the People's Republic of China.
ISBN 9065443150 Pbk £63/Dfl 195

BUSINESS – IRELAND

—Doing Business in Ireland / Matthew Bender, 1987.
ISBN 0000999034 Hbk £50.00

BUSINESS – JAPAN

—Doing Business in Japan / Matthew Bender, 1980.
ISBN 0000999041 Hbk £352.00

—Legal aspects of business transactions and investment in the Far East / D Campbell, A Wolff. – Kluwer Law and Taxation, 1989.
400.
Describes the legal framework for trading with, licensing to, and investing in China, Hong Kong, Indonesia, Japan, Korea, Malaysia, Singapore, Taiwan and Thailand. Includes legal aspects of entering the Japanese market, parallel imports in Japan and legal aspects of trade and investment in Singapore, and forms of foreign investment in the People's Republic of China.
ISBN 9065443150 Pbk £63/Dfl 195

—Selected Topics in Canada-Japan Legal and Business Relations / Vancouver : British Columbia Continuing Legal Education Society, 1980.
419p.
ISBN 0865040133 Hbk £65.00

BUSINESS – MALAYSIA

—Legal aspects of business transactions and investment in the Far East / D Campbell, A Wolff. – Kluwer Law and Taxation, 1989.
400.
Describes the legal framework for trading with, licensing to, and investing in China, Hong Kong, Indonesia, Japan, Korea, Malaysia, Singapore, Taiwan and Thailand. Includes legal aspects of entering the Japanese market, parallel imports in Japan and legal aspects of trade and investment in Singapore, and forms of foreign investment in the People's Republic of China.
ISBN 9065443150 Pbk £63/Dfl 195

—Registration of Businesses Act, 1956 (Act 197) / Kuala Lumpur : International Law Books Services.

BUSINESS – NETHERLANDS

—Dutch business law : legal, accounting, and tax aspects of business in the Netherlands / by Steven R. Schuit and Jan M. van der Beek and Bonne K. Raap, and Michael W. den Boogert ... et al. – 2nd ed. – Deventer, Netherlands : Kluwer Law and Taxation Publishers, 1983.
xl, 552 p.; 25 cm.
Includes index.
ISBN 9065441220

BUSINESS – NEW ZEALAND

—Business Law Today / Palmerston North : Dunmore Press Ltd..
368p.
ISBN 0864690398 Pbk £38.45

BUSINESS – SINGAPORE

—Legal aspects of business transactions and investment in the Far East / D Campbell, A Wolff. – Kluwer Law and Taxation, 1989.
400.
Describes the legal framework for trading with, licensing to, and investing in China, Hong Kong, Indonesia, Japan, Korea, Malaysia, Singapore, Taiwan and Thailand. Includes legal aspects of entering the Japanese market, parallel imports in Japan and legal aspects of trade and investment in Singapore, and forms of foreign investment in the People's Republic of China.
ISBN 9065443150 Pbk £63/Dfl 195

BUSINESS – SOUTH AFRICA

—Businessman's Law. Vol. 16 / P. Q. Boberg. – Kenwyn : Juta & Co, 1986.

—Modern Business Law / P. E. J. Brooks. – Durban : Butterworths.

BUSINESS – SPAIN

—Doing Business in Spain / London : Oyez Longman, 1980.
ISBN 085120449X Hbk £19.50

—Doing Business in Spain / Matthew Bender, 1987.
ISBN 0000999037 Hbk £50.00

—Litigating in Spain: considerations for foreign practitioners including international judicial assistance, enforcement of foreign judgements, bankruptcy, arbitration and other civil proceedings in Spain / Kluwer Law and Taxation, 1989.
579.
Informs investors, and potential investors how to protect their investments under Spanish law. Provides footnotes and other information relevant to precedents in Spanish courts. Contains a table of the Spanish Judicial Structure, and an appendix of all the International conventions ratified by Spain.
ISBN 9065443770 Hbk £52.75/Dfl 163

BUSINESS – UNITED STATES

—Arbitration in U.S.-German Business Relations : Schiedsgerichtsbarkeit im deutsch-amerikanischen / K.H. Bockstiegel. – Cologne : Carl Heymanns Verlag, 1985.
vi, 287p.
ISBN 3452202577 Pbk £230.00

—Business and Investment Almanac 1988 / New York : Dow Jones-Irwin, 1988.
ISBN 1556230478 Hbk £31.95

—Doing business in the United States / Frank G. Opton, Herbert Feiler. – Deventer, Netherlands : Kluwer Law and Taxation Publishers, 1984.
Includes index and bibliography.
ISBN 9065441700

—Recent Developments in Business and Litigation /. – Vancouver : Continuing Legal Education Society of British Columbia.

—U.S. Business Law : A Bilingual Guide for the German Businessman and Investor U.S. - Amerikanisches Wirtschaftsrecht : E. Zweisprach. / Martin Peltzer. – Cologne : Otto Schmidt, 1986.
ISBN 3504400048 Hbk £120.00

BUSINESS – WEST GERMANY

—Arbitration in U.S.-German Business Relations : Schiedsgerichtsbarkeit im deutsch-amerikanischen / K.H. Bockstiegel. – Cologne : Carl Heymanns Verlag, 1985.
vi, 287p.
ISBN 3452202577 Pbk £230.00

—Business Law Guide to Germany / London : CCH, 1986.
ISBN 0863250637 Pbk £22.00

BUSINESS ENTERPRISES – CANADA

—Canadian business organizations law / by Tom Hadden, Robert E. Forbes, Ralph L. Simmonds. – Toronto : Butterworths, 1984.
xlix,680p.
Relates common-law rules and statutory provisions to current commercial and industrial practice, distinguishing between the problems of small private businesses and larger public companies. Provides information on current corporate issues; practices and problems in designed instruments of corporate finance, securities law, corporate acquisitions, corporate groups, foreign acquisitions, and lease financing.
ISBN 0409834815 Hbk £95

BUSINESS INSURANCE

—Construction insurance / Nael G. Bunni. – London : Elsevier Applied Science, 1986.
xviii,336p; 25cm.
Includes index.
ISBN 0853344388 £50.00

—Riley on business interruption and consequential loss insurances and claims / by David Cloughton. – 6th ed. – London : Sweet & Maxwell, 1985.
480p.
Examination of business interruption consequential loss insurances and claims with emphasis on practice and procedure. Covers loss of profits, wages, and book debts, and perils and contingencies such as labour disturbances, strikes, riots, and the special conditions applicable in Northern Ireland and South Africa.
ISBN 0421319208 £46.00

BUSINESS INSURANCE – CANADA

—Stock purchase agreements / by Alain John Gaucher. – Toronto, Canada : Carswell, 1984.
xxvii, 286 p.; 24 cm.
Includes index. Bibliography: p. 275-280.
ISBN 045935910X

BUSINESS INSURANCE – GREAT BRITAIN

—Business Interruption and Consequent Loss Insurance / Cloughton. – 6th ed. – London : Sweet & Maxwell, 1985.
ISBN 0421319208 Hbk £50.00

—Consequential loss and business interruption insurances and claims / by Denis Riley. – 5th ed. – London : Sweet & Maxwell, 1981.
x,499columns,15p; 26cm.
Previous ed.: 1977. Includes index.
ISBN 0421287802 £27.50

—Insurance of commercial risks : law and practice / Digby C. Jess. – London : Butterworths, 1986.
445p; 26cm.
Includes index.
ISBN 0406257116 £30.00

—Insurance under the JCT forms / Frank Eaglestone. – London : Collins, 1985.
viii,367p; 24cm.
Includes index. Kept up to date by supplements.
ISBN 0003830225 £20.00

BUSINESS RECORDS – NEW ZEALAND

—Business records and computer output / Evidence Law Reform Committee. – s.l. : Evidence Law Reform Committee, 1985.
43 leaves, 2 leaves. – (Working paper).
Inlcudes bibliographical references.

—Report on business records and computer output / Evidence Law Reform Committee. – Wellington, N.Z. : The Committee, 1987.
58p.
Includes bibliographical references. Includes extract from Evidence Amendment Act (No. 2) 1980.

BUSINESS TENANCIES – AUSTRALIA

—Commercial Rent Reviews / North Ryde : Law Book Co, 1986.
ISBN 0455206414 Pbk £15.00

BUSINESS TENANCIES – CANADA

—Commercial Real Estate Leasing / Vancouver : Continuing Legal Education Society of British Columbia, 1986.
562p.
ISBN 0865042934 Hbk £85.00

—Leasing in Canada : A Business Guide / Toronto : Butterworths, 1986.
ISBN 0409805041 Pbk £35.00

—Shopping Centre Leases, 2 Vols. / Aurora : Canada Law Book Co.
1438p.

Vol. 1

Vol. 2
This is the first Canadian book written specifically for lawyers and their clients interested in Shopping Centres, with particular emphasis on landlord/tenant problems. The text contains 38 separate articles on the subject written by 34 acknowledged experts in the field.

BUSINESS TENANCIES – ENGLAND

—Commercial leases / Stephen Tromans. – London : Sweet & Maxwell, 1987.
250p; 23cm.
Examines the impact of recent case law, rating, and planning development. Covers licences, agreements for lease, rent reviews, 'clear leases', dilapidations, user and covenants, and the practicalities of leaseholding conveyancing in its own right.
ISBN 0421354607 £19.50

—Commercial leases / Malcolm Brahams with Norman Harker. – London : Collins Professional and Technical, 1985.
viii,198p.
Includes index.
ISBN 0003830446 £16.00

—Drafting and negotiating commercial leases / by Murray J. Ross : foreword by John Stuart Colyer. – London : Butterworths, 1980.
xxxv,316p; 23cm.
Includes index.
ISBN 0406359059 £12.95

—Handbook of business tenancies / D.W. Williams : assisted by C.M. Brand : consultant on valuation and practice C.C. Hubbard. – 1. – London : Sweet & Maxwell, 1985.
looseleaf.
Includes index.
ISBN 0421327901 £75.00

—Letting business premises / Trevor M. Aldridge. – 4th ed. – London : Oyez, 1981.
xxxi,178p; 22cm.
Previous ed.: 1978. Includes index.
ISBN 0851205615 Pbk Unpriced

BUSINESS TENANCIES – GREAT BRITAIN

—Business tenancies / London : Longman Professional (UK), 1989.
– (Longman practice notes).
Examines the law pertaining to assigning, subletting, parting with possession and repairs, with specimen letters. Contains details of time limits, costs and fees, and precedent forms for termination of a tenancy under s.25 and a request for a new tenancy under s.26 of the Landlord and Tenant Act 1954.
ISBN 0851215319 Pbk £9.95

—Commentary on a Commercial Lease / Centre for Advanced Land Use Studies. – Reading : College of Estate Management, 1983.
ISBN 0902132725 Pbk £9.50

—Commercial Leases / Oxford : Blackwell Scientific, 1985.
ISBN 0003830446 Hbk £17.50

—Drafting and Negotiating Commercial Leases / 2nd ed. – London : Butterworths, 1984.
ISBN 0406359075 Hbk £29.00

—Drafting Business Leases / 2nd ed. – London : Longman Professional, 1986.
ISBN 0851210244 Hbk £28.95

—Letting business premises / 6th. – London : Longman Professional (UK), 1989.
– (Practitioner series).
Coverage includes the statutory renewal procedure; compensation for tenants' improvements; and the law governing the major lease. Covenants relating to rent, user, alterations and improvements, and assignments and subletting, lettings to partnerships, and special types of business premises.

—Letting Business Premises / 5th ed. – London : Longman Professional, 1985.
ISBN 0851209858 Hbk £28.00

—Negotiation and Drafting of Business Leases / London : Law Society, 1984.
70p.

BUSINESS TENANCIES – SCOTLAND

—Drafting and Negotiating Commercial Leases in Scotland / A. H. Primrose. – London : Butterworths, 1985.
This work deals with the drafting, negotiating, and settling of commercial leases in Scotland. The book provides extensive references to English cases that may have a persuasive influence on judgements made in Scottish courts.
ISBN 0406359067 Hbk £27.00

BUSINESS TENANCIES – WEST GERMANY

—Law Relating to Business Tenancies in Germany / Plymouth : Macdonald & Evans, 1985.
72p.
ISBN 0712154701 Hbk £10.75

BYZANTINE LAW

—Legal links between Cyprus and the Balkans especially Macedonia during the Byzantine era / Criton G. Tornaritis. – Nicosia : s.n., 1982.
24 leaves.

CAMBODIA

—Kampuchea : politics, economics and society / Michael Vickery. – London : Pinter, 1986.
xviii,211p; 23cm.
Bibliography: p199-205. - Includes index.
ISBN 0861874226 Hbk £17.50
ISBN 0931477743 : Pbk £5.95

CAMPAIGN FUNDS – AUSTRALIA

—Report of the Inquiry into Disclosure of Electoral Expenditure / Clarrie W. Harders. – Canberra : Australian Government Publishing Service, 1981.
101p.
Sole member of the Inquiry: Sir Clarrie W. Harders.
ISBN 0642066396

CAMPAIGN FUNDS – GREAT BRITAIN

—Company donations to political parties : a suggested code of practice / Edmund Dell. – London : Constitutional Reform Centre, 1985.
34p.
'The report of the Working Party on Company Political Donations established jointly by the Constitutional Reform Centre and the Hansard Society for Parliamentary Government'. - Back Cover. Chairman: Edmund Dell.
ISBN 0948419008

CANADA

—Canada and the constitution, 1979-1982 : patriation and the charter of rights / Edward McWhinney. – Toronto : University of Toronto Press, 1982.
xii,227p.
Includes bibliographical references and index.
ISBN 0802065015 pbk.

—Canada and the new international law of the sea / Douglas M. Johnston. – Toronto : University of Toronto Press in cooperation with the Royal Commission on the Economic Union and Development Prospects for Canada and the Canadian Government Publishing Centre, 1985.
xviii,124p. – (Collected research studies).
Includes bibliographical references.
ISBN 0802073018

—Canadian official publications / Olga B. Bishop. – Oxford : Pergamon, 1981.
ix,297p.
ISBN 0080246974

—Criminal Code : 1893 / Repr. of 1980 ed. – Agincourt : Carswell.
1200p. – (Carswell's Classic Reprints).
This book is a reproduction of the 1893 treatise on the first Criminal Code of Canada.

—Criminal Code : 1988 / Agincourt : Carswell, 1987.
780p.

—Criminal Code Annotations : 1971-1986 / Agincourt : Carswell, 1984.

Vol. 2

—North American social report : a comparative study of the quality of life in Canada and the USA from 1964 to 1974 / by Alex C. Michalos. – Dordrecht : Reidel, 1980.
xv,252p; 23cm.
ISBN 9027710856

—Snow's Annotated Criminal Code, 1 Vol. / Bound Edition. – Agincourt : Carswell, 1988.
This looseleaf service contains the annotated text of the Criminal Code of Canada and its amendments. Extensive case law citations are provided in the work.

CANADA - CANADA

—Index to federal programs and services 1986 / 7th ed. – Ottawa : Supply and Services Canada, 1986.
533p.
ISBN 0660119463

CANALS - GREAT BRITAIN

—Railway and Canal Traffic Cases : 1835-1950, 36 Vols. / Abingdon : Professional Books.

CANON LAW

—Code of Canon Law / Canon Law Society. – Oxford : Collins, 1983.

—History of Ideas and Doctrines of Canon Law in the Middle Ages / Northampton : Variorum. 394p. – (Collected Ser.: CS 113).
ISBN 0860780589 Hbk £22.00

—Why the history of canon law is not written / Selden Society lecture delivered in the Old Hall of Lincoln's Inn, July 3rd 1984 by Charles Donahue. – London : Selden Society, 1986.
31p. – (Selden Society lecture).
Includes bibliographical references.

CANON LAW - ENGLAND

—Canon law and English common law / by R. H. Helmholz. – London : Selden Society, 1983.
24 p.
'Selden Society lecture delivered in the Old Hall of Lincoln's Inn, July 5th, 1982'.

—Introduction to English Canon Law / Briden. – 2nd ed. – London : Dent (J M) & Sons, 1985.
ISBN 0264668545 Pbk £11.95

—Introduction to English Canon Law / Repr. of 1967 ed. – Aalen Wuertt : Scientia.
xii, 176p.

CAPACITY AND DISABILITY - GREAT BRITAIN

—Incapacitated principal : report on a reference under section 3(1)(e) of the Law Commissions Act 1965 / the Law Commission. – London : H.M.S.O., 1983.
v,104p; 25cm.
ISBN 0101897707

CAPACITY AND DISABILITY - HONG KONG

—Report : young persons : effects of age in civil law / the Law Reform Commission of Hong Kong. – Hong Kong : The Commission, 1986.
various pagings. – (Topic 11).

CAPITAL

—International capital markets 1982 / prepared by Orion Royal Bank Limited. – London : Euromoney, 1982.
viii,187p.
ISBN 0903121263

—International capital markets 1984 / prepared by Orion Royal Bank Limited. – London : Euromoney, 1984.
vi,207p.
ISBN 0903121638

—Sovereign borrowers : guidelines on legal negotiations with commercial lenders / edited by Lars Kalderen, Qamar S. Siddiqi : in co-operation with Francis Chronnell and Patricia Watson. – Uppsala : Dag Hammarskjold Foundation, 1984.
264p.
ISBN 9185214124

CAPITAL - ASIA

—Kemp and Message : Asian Capital and Money Markets / London : Butterworths, 1987.
ISBN 0406103607 Hbk

CAPITAL - CANADA

—Competition and solvency : a framework for financial regulation / Economic Council of Canada. – Ottawa : Minister of Supply and Services, 1986.
x,46p.
ISBN 0660121921

—Small Business Venture Capital Act / Vancouver : Continuing Legal Education Society of British Columbia, 1986.
347p.
ISBN 086504290X Hbk £75.00

CAPITAL - GREAT BRITAIN

—Capital Allowances / London : Oyez Longman, 1980. Includes December 1982 supplement.
ISBN 0851204864 Hbk £25.00

—City code on take-overs and the rules governing substantial acquisitions of shares / April 1985 ed. 1. – London : The Panel on Take-overs and Mergers, 1985.
loose-leaf.
Previous ed.: 1981.
ISBN 0950046663

—Deloitte, Haskins and Sells : Raising Finance in Capital Markets / London : Butterworths, 1987.

—Ferrier and Ferrier : UK Money Markets / London : Butterworths, 1987.
This book describes the operations of the United Kingdom financial sector, concentrating on the principal methods of raising capital. Included in the work is coverage of the key elements in each market together with explanations of the significance of various instruments and forms of finance.
ISBN 0406100306 Hbk

—Ormerod and Burns : Raising Venture Capital in the UK / London : Butterworths, 1987.
ISBN 0406103100 Hbk

—Raising centure capital in the UK / Burns. – London : Butterworths, 1988.
ISBN 0406103100 Hbk £27.50

—UK money markets / David G Ferrier. – London : Butterworths, 1988.
ISBN 0406100306 Hbk

—Venture capital today / Cambridge : Woodhead-Faulkner, 1985.
ISBN 085941275X Hbk £30.00

CAPITAL - INDIA

—Capital Issues (Law and Procedure) / New Delhi : Bharat Law House, 1987.

CAPITAL - SWITZERLAND

—Swiss capital markets / by Henri B. Meier. – 2nd ed. – London : Euromoney, 1985.
xi,128p.
Bibliography: p.125-126 - Includes index.
ISBN 0903121816

CAPITAL FLIGHT TAX

—Taxation aspects of currency fluctuations / Jill C. Pagan. – London : Butterworths, 1983.
xi,162p.
Describes the United Kingdom tax law and the attitude of the Inland Revenue on the subject of currency fluctuations. Foreign exchange management, accounting treatment, and taxation are analyzed in the book.
ISBN 0406406308 Hbk £22.00

CAPITAL GAINS TAX - AUSTRALIA

—Australian Capital Gains Tax / Michael W. Inglis. – Sydney : Butterworths, 1986.
298p.

—Australian Capital Gains Tax / Michael Inglis. – Butterworths, 1986.
298p.
ISBN 0409491578 Pbk £42.00

—Introduction to Capital Gains Tax / Butterworths.
ISBN 0409493066 Pbk £7.95

CAPITAL GAINS TAX - CANADA

—Taxation of capital gains / by Vern Krishna. – Toronto : Butterworths, 1983.
xxiii,251p.
Includes index.
ISBN 0409843776 Hbk £51.95

CAPITAL GAINS TAX - GREAT BRITAIN

—Capital Gains Tax / Wheatcroft. – 3rd ed. – Sweet & Maxwell, 1980.
ISBN 0421380004 Hbk £85.00

1985.
ISBN 0582083397 Pbk £7.95

—Capital Gains Tax / 5th ed. – Plymouth : Macdonald & Evans, 1981.
224p. – (M and E Handbook Ser.).
This looseleaf service for United Kingdom practitioners includes all the relevant Acts and regulations, extra-statutory concessions, statements of practice, case digests, and many worked examples. Specific provisions of capital gains tax relating to corporate bodies, trustees, and others are covered.
ISBN 0712104607 Hbk £4.95

—Capital Gains Tax / London : Butterworths, 1981.
Service to Date.
ISBN 0406538824 loose £80.00

—Capital gains tax / by Anthony Sumption. – London : Butterworths, 1981.
ISBN 0406538824

—Capital Gains Tax / Giles Clarke. – London : Butterworths, 1981.

—Capital Gains Tax / 5th ed. – Plymouth : Macdonald & Evans, 1981.
ISBN 0712104607 Pbk £4.95

—Capital Gains Tax on Business / London : Sweet & Maxwell.
ISBN 0421310405 Hbk £3.50

—Capital gains tax on businesses / by Christopher Cox and Harry J. Ross. – 2nd ed. – London : Sweet & Maxwell, 1986.
xix,231p; 22cm.
Previous ed.: 1982. Includes index.
ISBN 0421339608 Pbk £14.00

—Capital Gains Tax On Businesses / Ross. – 2nd ed. – Sweet & Maxwell, 1986.
ISBN 0421339608 Hbk £21.00

—Capital gains tax on businesses / by Christopher Cox and Harry J. Ross. – London : Sweet & Maxwell, 1982.
xviii,221p,1folded leaf of plates; 23cm.
Includes index.
ISBN 0421282304 £18.00

—CGT Base Date Prices 31st March 1982 / Tolley Publishing, 1986.
ISBN 085459244X Pbk £15.00

—Income Tax, Corporation Tax and Capital Gains Tax 1978-1983, 5 Vols. / London : HMSO, 1984.
– (Taxes Act. Ser.).
ISBN 0116413557 Hbk £42.50

—Indexation of Capital Gains : Computations and Examples / Paul Elliott. – London : Butterworths, 1983.
This work is designed to assist United Kingdom tax practitioners with the new rules for indexing of capital gains. Worked examples are provided throughout the work to explain the subject matter.
ISBN 0406256101 Pbk

—Practical CTT planning / John E. Redman, Nigel Eastaway, Ralph P. Ray. – 2nd ed. – London : Butterworths, 1982.
xix,347p; 22cm. – (Butterworths tax management series).
Previous ed.: published as Practical capital transfer tax planning, 1977. Includes index.
ISBN 0406536155 Pbk Unpriced

—Retirement relief - New CGT Rules / London : CCH, 1986.
ISBN 0863250815 Pbk £7.50

—Roll-over relief for business assets : the Capital Gains Tax Rules explained / Kevin S. Slevin. – Bicester : CCH Editions, 1987.
v,66p; 23cm.
Includes index.
ISBN 0863251196 No price

—Roll over relief - New CGT tax rules explained / London : CCH, 1987.
ISBN 0863251196 Pbk £7.00

—Tax Practitioner's Diary 1986-87 / Butterworth Editorial Staff. – London : Butterworths, 1986.
This book is a diary for tax practitioners in the United Kingdom. Income tax, corporation tax, capital gains tax, capital transfer tax, value added tax, and stamp duties are all covered in the work. A complete list of tax district addresses is included.
ISBN 0406539669 Pbk

—Tolley's capital gains tax 1981-82 / David Harrington and Glyn Saunders. – Croydon : Tolley, 1981.
viii,245p.
Includes index. Up to date to 1 August 1981.
ISBN 0854590315

—Tolley's capital gains tax 1986-87 / Patrick Noakes and John Boulding. – 9th ed. – Croydon : Tolley Publishing, 1986.
viii,349p.
Includes index.
ISBN 0854592407

—Tolley's capital gains tax 1987-88 / Patrick Noakes and John Boulding. – 10th ed. – Croydon : Tolley, 1987.
viii,356p.
ISBN 0854592903

—Tolley's captial gains tax 1988-89 / Patrick Noakes and John Boulding. – Croydon : Tolley, 1988.
viii,376p.
Includes index.
ISBN 0854593489

CAPITAL GAINS TAX - MALAYSIA

—Introduction to real property gains taxation in Malaysia / by Arjunan Subramaniam. – Kuala Lumpur : Malayan Law Journal, 1982.
x,121p.
Bibliography: p.x. - Includes index.

CAPITAL TRANSFER TAX - ENGLAND

—Will precedents and capital transfer tax / D.T. Davies. – 2nd ed. – London : Butterworths, 1983.
xxi,231p; 26cm.
ISBN 040617511X

CAPITAL TRANSFER TAX - GREAT BRITAIN

—Capital Taxes Encyclopaedia, 3 Vols. / Ian A. Marsh. – London : Butterworths.
This looseleaf service provides detailed coverage of capital transfer tax issues and legislation in the United Kingdom. Legislative developments, court decisions, and changes in practice are updated with six service issues per year.

—Capital Transfer Tax / 2nd ed. – Plymouth : Macdonald & Evans, 1981.
336p. – (M and E Handbook Ser.).
ISBN 0712103929 Hbk £4.95

—Capital transfer tax / A.L. Chapman. – 6th ed. – London : Longman, 1985.
xlv,656p; 24cm.
ISBN 0851209335

—Handbook on CTT Act 1984 / Butterworths. - London : Butterworths, 1984.
ISBN 0406505349 Pbk £6.00

—Personal Financial Planning Manual 1986-87 / John Rayer. - London : Butterworths, 1986.
This manual is a guide to the compilation of personal financial packages for United Kingdom investors. Investments, family finances, life insurance, pensions, and capital transfer tax are covered in the book.
ISBN 040600563X Hbk

—Will precedents and Capital Transfer Tax / 2nd ed. - London : Butterworths, 1983.
ISBN 040617511X Hbk £21.00

CAPITAL TRANSFER TAX - NORTHERN IRELAND
—Some Aspects of Capital Transfer Tax for Businesses and Farms / Belfast : Queen's University of Belfast, 1986.
30p.

CAPITALISM
—Capitalist state : Marxist theories and methods / Bob Jessop. - Oxford : Robertson, 1982.
xvi,296p; 24cm.
Bibliography: p260-281. - Includes index.
ISBN 0855202696 Hbk £17.00
ISBN 0855202688 Pbk £5.95

—Law, society and political action : towards a strategy under late capitalism / Thomas Mathiesen. - London : Academic Press, 1980.
ix,323p; 24cm.
Includes index.
ISBN 012479940X Hbk £17.80
ISBN 0124799426 Pbk Unpriced

CAREER DEVELOPMENT - GREAT BRITAIN
—Careers in Local Government / London : Kogan Page, 1981.
96p.
ISBN 0850384370 Hbk £6.95
ISBN 0850384389 Pbk £2.95

—Careers in Politics / London : Kogan Page, 1984.
96p.
ISBN 0850388325 Hbk £6.95
ISBN 0850388333 Pbk £2.95

—Careers In The Law / 2nd ed. - London : Kogan Page, 1986.
ISBN 1850911002 Pbk £3.25

—Careers in the Law in England and Wales / London : Kogan Page, 1982.
125p.
ISBN 0850385180 Hbk £6.95
ISBN 0850385199 Pbk £2.95

—Careers in the Police Force / 2nd ed. - London : Kogan Page, 1986.
96p.
ISBN 18500911703 Hbk £2.95

—Careers Service : Guidance to Local Education Authorities in England and Wales / Dept. of Employment. - rev. ed. Great Britain. - London : Department of the Environment, 1980.
ISBN 090331424X Hbk

—Jobs in Local Authorities / London : Kogan Page, 1985.
95p. - (Jobs In...Ser.).
ISBN 085038978X Pbk £2.95

CARGO HANDLING
—Carriage of Crude Oil by Sea / London : LLoyd's of London Press, 1986.
ISBN 1850440735 Hbk

—Code of Safe Practice for Ships Carrying Timber Deck Cargoes /. - London : International Maritime Organization.

Spanish Edition

Supplement-1978 Amendments, French Edition

Supplement-1978 Amendments, Spanish Edition

—IMO Grain Rules / International Maritime Organization. - London : International Maritime Organization, 1982.

French Edition

—Inert Gas Systems for Ships Carrying Petroleum Products in Bulk / International Maritime Organization. - London : International Maritime Organization, 1982.

French Edition

—International cargo carriers' liabilities : the determination of some current contractual problems arising from the international carriage of goods / W.E. Astle. - London : Fairplay, 1983.
viii,140p; 25cm.
ISBN 0905045416 Pbk No price

—Tonnage Measurement : Treatment of Shelter-Deck and Other 'Open' Spaces /. - London : International Maritime Organization.

CARGO HANDLING - CANADA
—Motor Carrier Cargo Claims / Agincourt : Carswell, 1986.
222p.

CARGO HANDLING - GREAT BRITAIN
—Elements of Cargo Insurance / Whitehead. - Cambridge : Woodhead-Faulkner, 1983.
ISBN 085941227X Pbk £5.25

CARIBBEAN AREA
—Changing Caribbean constitutions / Francis Alexis. - St. Michael, Barbados : Antilles, 1983.
xxviii,281p.
Bibliography: p.270-274. - Includes index.

CARRIAGE OF GOODS
—Air cargo : regulation and claims / Jean-Louis Magdelenat. - Toronto : Butterworths, 1983.
xxvi,181p.
Bibliography: p.177-181. Summarizes the rules of liability. governing the carriage of goods by air. Surveys the economic and technical aspects of air cargo, systematically considering all their legal ratifications.
ISBN 0409847836 Hbk £55

—Carriage of Crude Oil by Sea / London : LLoyd's of London Press, 1986.
ISBN 1850440735 Hbk

—CMR : contracts for the international carriage of goods by road / by D.J. Hill and A.D. Messent. - London : Lloyd's of London Press, 1984.
xliii,288p; 26cm.
Contains the text of the Carriage of Goods by Road Act 1965 and the French (i.e., definitive) text of the CMR.
ISBN 0907432557

—Hague-Zagreb Essays /. - Dordrecht : Kluwer, 1980.
xi, 329p.
ISBN 9028607498 Pbk £72.00

—International cargo carriers' liabilities : the determination of some current contractual problems arising from the international carriage of goods / W.E. Astle. - London : Fairplay, 1983.
viii,140p; 25cm.
ISBN 0905045416 Pbk No price

—International carriage of goods by road : CMR / by Malcolm A. Clarke. - London : Stevens, 1982.
xxvi,212p; 26cm.
Includes index. Appendix in French.
ISBN 0420464905 £19.50

—International carriage of goods by road - CMR / Sweet & Maxwell, 1982.
ISBN 0420464905 Hbk £38.00

—International carriage of goods by road (CMR) / general editor Jan Theunis. - London : Published under the auspices of the International Road Transport Union by Lloyd's of London, 1987.
353p; 24cm.
Conference proceedings.
ISBN 1850441456 £48.00 (Nov.)

—International carriage of goods : some legal problems and possible solutions / edited by C.M. Schmitthoff, R.M. Goode. - London : Centre for Commercial Law Studies, 1988.
xxvii,135p.
Includes index. Includes the text of the Uniform Rules of Conduct for Interchange of Trade Data by Teletransmission (UNCID) and of the United Nations Convention on International Multimodal Transport of Goods.
ISBN 0951066455

—International Transportation : Law of Carriage by Air / New Delhi : Deep and Deep Publications, 1987.
328p.
ISBN 8171000010 Hbk £110.00

—Second International Maritime Law Seminar : Carriage of Goods by Sea, Maritime Liens, Marine Insurance / Vancouver : Continuing Legal Education Society of British Columbia, 1981.
395p.
ISBN 0865040273 Hbk £100.00

CARRIAGE OF GOODS - CANADA
—Motor Carrier Cargo Claims / Agincourt : Carswell, 1986.
222p.

CARRIAGE OF GOODS - GREAT BRITAIN
—Carriage by Sea (BSL) 2 vols. / Colinvaux. - 13th ed. - Sweet & Maxwell, 1982.
ISBN 0420451102 Hbk £180.00

—Carriage of Goods / Professional Books, 1987.
ISBN 0862052394 Pbk £24.50
ISBN 0862052599 Hbk £50.00

—Carriage of Goods by Sea / London : Butterworths, 1986.
ISBN 0409995150 Hbk £38.00

—Carriage of Goods by Sea / Ivamy. - 12th ed. - London : Butterworths, 1985.
ISBN 0406640602 Hbk £18.00
ISBN 0406640610 Pbk £15.95

—Carver's carriage by sea / Raoul Colinvaux. - 13th ed. - London : Stevens, 1982.
2v.
Previous ed.:1971.
ISBN 0420451102 £12.00

—Casebook on carriage by sea / by E.R. Hardy Ivamy. - 5th ed. - London : Lloyd's of London Press, 1982.
xxvii,203p.
Previous ed.: 1979. Includes index.
ISBN 0907432360

—Cases and materials on the carriage of goods by sea / Martin Dockray. - Abingdon : Professional Books, 1987.
xxvi,804p.
ISBN 0862052599

—Encyclopedia of Carriage Law Sources / London : LLoyd's of London Press, 1987.
ISBN 1850441081 Hbk

—Goods in Transit / London : Matthew Bender, 1985.
ISBN 0000999058 Hbk £53.00

—Institute Cargo Clauses (Air) / Witherby, 1986.
ISBN 0900886277 Pbk £9.00

—Introduction to the law of carriage of goods / C Cashmore. - London : Sweet & Maxwell, 1989.
Guide to the law of carriage of goods by land, sea and air, with a brief ssummary of the law relating to passengers and their luggage. Explores the principles of UK law, supplemented by Commonwealth, US and European authorities. Provides an examination of international conventions and the standard conditions of carriage in use in the industry.
ISBN 0420397004 Pbk c.14.00

—Law for the Haulier / London : Kogan Page, 1987.
ISBN 1850911479 Hbk £11.95

—Law for the Haulier / London : Kogan Page, 1987.
250p.
ISBN 1850911479 Hbk £11.95

—Law of Carriage by Inland Transport / 5th ed. - London : Sweet & Maxwell.
ISBN 042046820X Hbk

—Payne and Ivamy's Carriage of goods by sea / E. R. Hardy Ivamy. - 12th ed. - London : Butterworths, 1985.
xlix,366p; 22cm.
This textbook is a straightforward discussion of the field of carriage of goods by sea under the laws of the United Kingdom for students of the subject.
ISBN 0406640602 HBK £18.00
ISBN 0406640610 Pbk £14.95

—Review of Road Freight Regulation in Britain / Bureau of Transport Economics. - Canberra : Australian Government Publishing Service, 1981.
78p. - (BTE Occasional Paper: No. 43).
ISBN 0642067953 Hbk £3.80

CARRIAGE OF GOODS - SOUTH AFRICA
—Law of shipping and carriage in South Africa / by B.R. Bamford. - 3rd ed. - Cape Town : Juta, 1983.
xlvi,389p.
Previous ed.: 1973. Includes index.
ISBN 070211376X

CASES
—Bilingual Editions of Cases / European Court of Human Rights. - Cologne : Carl Heymanns Verlag.

1962: DeBecker

1965-67: Case 'Relating to Certain Aspects of the Laws on the Use of Languages in Belgium' (Vol. 1)

1968: Case 'Relating to Certain Aspects of the Laws on the Use of Languages in Belgium' (Vol. 2)

1968: Wemhoff

1969, 1975: Neumeister

1970: Delcourt

1970: Klass and others

1970: Matznetter

1970: Stogmuller

1971, 1972, 1973: DeWilde, Ooms and Versyp

1972, 1973, 1974: Ringeisen

1975, 1976: 'National Union of Belgian Police' Case

1975: Golder

1976, 1977: Schmidt and Dahlstrom

1976, 1977: 'Swedish Engine Drivers' Union' Case

1976, 1979, 1981: Handyside

1976, 1979: Kjeldsen, Busk, Madsen and Petersen

1977, 1978: Engel and others

1978, 1981: Ireland against United Kingdom

1978: Tyrer

1979, 1980, 1981: Luedicke, Belkacem and Koc

1979: Konig

1980, 1981: Airey

1980: Deweer

1980: Schiesser

1980: Winterwerp

1981: Artico

1981: Buchholz

1981: Guzzardi

1981: Sunday Times

1981: VanOosterwijck

—Canadian Criminal Cases : New Series (1963-1970), 30 Vols. / North Ryde : Law Book Co.

—Canadian Criminal Cases : Old Series (1898-1962), 133 Vols. / North Ryde : Law Book Co.

—Canadian Criminal Cases : Second Series (1971-1983), 70 Vols. / North Ryde : Law Book Co.

Vols. 1-70 Index, Annotations, Table of Cases 1983.
1,184p.

—Canadian Criminal Cases : Third Series (March, 1983-Present) / North Ryde : Law Book Co.

Vols. 1-27, index, Annotations, Table of Cases 1987.

Vols. 1-34, Index, Annotations, Table of Cases 1988.

—Case-Law of the European Commission of Human Rights / Strasbourg : Council of Europe.

Summaries and Indexes Nos. 1-20

—Cases on Irish company law / Michael Forde. – Cork : Mercier, 1986.
461p; 23cm.
Includes index.
ISBN 0853427968 £40.00 (Irish)

—European Patent Office reports / Oxford : ESC Publishing Ltd., 1986-.

—European Social Charter /. – Strasbourg : Council of Europe, 1982.

—List of constitutional and Privy Council judgments affecting the Isle of Man from 1523 to 1986 and a complete year by year list of written Reasons for Judgment of Her Majesty's High Court of Justice of the Isle of Man and other Manx courts from 1884 to 1986 / compiled and with an introduction by Judy Thornley on the directions of H.M. Attorney General for the Isle of Man. – Douglas : Government Printer, 1987.
94p.
Cover title: A book of precedents.

—Selected texts and cases on the Roman law of things : with an excursus on the Roman law of slavery / J.E. Schiller. – Cape Town : Juta, 1982.
xiii,127p; 25cm.
ISBN 0702112941

—Social security reporter / Clayton, Vic. : Legal Service Bulletin Co-operative, 1981.
Indexes: Nos 1-22 in no 22 (Dec 1984); annually in Dec. issue except for 1983.
ISBN 08173524

—Summaries of the judgements delivered in ... / document prepared by the registry of the Court. – v. – Strasbourg : Council of Europe, 1983.
Contains summary judgements not binding on the Court.

CASES - AUSTRALIA

—Legal process : commentary and materials / Maher, Waller, Derham. – 5th ed. – Sydney : Law Book Co, 1988.
xxx, 593 p.; 26 cm.
First to 4th eds. published under title: Cases and materials on the legal process.
ISBN 0455207836 (pbk.)

CASES - CANADA

—Administrative law cases, text, and materials / by J.M. Evans ... et al. – Toronto : Edmond-Montgomery, 1980.
xxv, 1085 p.; 26 cm.
Includes index.
ISBN 0920722024

—Canadian Abridgment, 41 Vols. / Professional Books Staff. – Abingdon : Professional Books, 1984.

—Chitty's Abridgment of Canadian Cases: 1892-1970, 5 Vols. / Canada Law Book Publisher. – Aurora : Canada Law Book Co.

—Rules Review : Summaries of Cases Decided Under the Rules of Civic Procedure / Butterworths, 1987.
288p.
Compendium of relevant cases decided under Ontario's new rules of practice (between January 1985 and December 1986). Follows the order of the rules, and consists of concise case digests. Cases are annotated, with commentary by the author.
ISBN 0409805912 Pbk £29.95

—Select Cases of Newfoundland 1817-1828 / repr. of 1933 ed. – Agincourt : Carswell, 1980.
300p.

CASES - EUROPEAN COMMUNITY

—Gazetteer of European law : case search : European Community law 1953-1983 / by Neville March Hunnings. – Leeds : European Law Centre, 1983.
xiii,234p; 25cm.
ISBN 0907451098

Vol.2 : Case search and indexes / by Neville March Hunnings. – 1983.
viii,p.237-584; 25cm.
ISBN 0907451101 Hbk

—Leading cases on the law of the European Communities / edited by D.J. Gijlstra ... et al. – 4th ed. – Deventer, Netherlands : Kluwer Law and Taxation Publishers, 1982.
xxi, 599 p.
At head of title: Europa Institute, University of Amsterdam. Includes bibliographies and indexes.
ISBN 9065440682 pbk. £28.00

CASES - GREAT BRITAIN

—Copyright / edited by W.R. Cornish. – Oxford : ESC Publishing, 1985.
168p.
ISBN 0906214343

—Test cases for the poor : legal techniques in the politics of social welfare / Tony Prosser. – London : Child Poverty Action Group, 1983.
v,102p.
ISBN 090396371X

CASES - HONG KONG

—Hong Kong tax cases / Hong Kong : Government Printer, 1983.
looseleaf.
Kept up to date by supplements.

CASES - INDIA

—Comparative Tables of Supreme Court Cases, 1950-85 / Lucknow : Eastern Book Company.

CASES - IRELAND

—Notes of Irish Legal Cases, 1969-1978, Vol. 3 / Cork : Cork University Press, 1982.
ISBN 0902561219 Hbk £12.50

CASES - NEW ZEALAND

—Abridgement of New Zealand Case Law / Butterworths.
ISBN 0409701831

Permanent Supplement 1962-1973
ISBN 0409600229

Permanent Supplement 1974-1978
ISBN 0409600563

CASES - NIGERIA

—Cases and materials on the principles of natural justice in Nigeria / by A. Toriola Oyewo. – Ibadan, Nigeria : Jator Publishing, 1987.
xi,153p.
Includes bibliographical references and index.
ISBN 9782660000

—Nigerian weekly law reports / v. – Lagos : Nigerian Law Publications Ltd, 1985-.

CASES - SCOTLAND

—Casebook on Scottish criminal law / by Christopher H.W. Gane and Charles N. Stoddart. – Edinburgh : W. Green, 1980.
xxii,495p; 22cm.
Includes index.
ISBN 041400664X Pbk £10.00

—Scottish criminal case reports / Edinburgh : Law Society of Scotland, 1981-.

CASES - ZAMBIA

—Case book on criminal law / by John Hatchard and Muna Ndulo. – Lusaka : Government Printer, 1983.
viii,425p.
Includes index.
ISBN 0903826585

CATALOGUES

—Checklist of law reports and statutes in Canadian law libraries / National Library of Canada Resources Survey Division, Collections Development Branch : Bibliotheque nationale du Canada, Division de l'inventaire des ressources, Direction du developpement des collections. – Ottawa : The Library, 1981.
xii,249p.
Includes index. Text in English and French.
ISBN 0660504529

—Law : a guide to the collection of Hammersmith & Fulham / Hammersmith & Fulham Libraries. – 2nd ed. – London : Hammersmith & Fulham Libraries, 1987.
40p.
ISBN 0904038068

—Online public access to library files : conference proceedings / edited by Janet Kinsella. – Oxford : Elsevier International Bulletins, 1985.
200p; ?cm.
Includes bibliographies and index.
ISBN 0946395187 Pbk £14.50 (June)

CATALOGUING

—Automated cataloguing in the UK : a guide to services / A.W. Seal. – Bath : Centre for Catalogue Research, Bath University Library, 1980.
114p; 30cm. – (Research and development reports).
Bibliography: p.95-99.
ISBN 0861970233 sp

—ISBD (NBM) : International Standard Bibliographic Description for Non-Book Materials / International Federation of Library Associations and Institutions. – Rev. ed. – London : IFLA Universal Bibliographic Control and International MARC Programme, 1987.
vii,74p; 30cm.
Previous ed.: 1977. Includes index.
ISBN 0903043467 Pbk No price

—ISBD(S) : International Standard Bibliographic Description for Serials / International Federation of Library Associations and Institutions. – Rev ed. – London : IFLA Universat Bibliographic Control and International MARC Programme, 1987.
viii,76p; 30cm.
Previous ed.: i.e., 1st standard ed., 1977. Includes index.
ISBN 0903043491 Pbk No price

—Proceedings of the International Cataloguing-in-Publication Meeting, Ottawa, 16-19 August 1982 / organized by IFLA in association with Unesco : edited by the IFLA International Office for UBC. – London : The Office, 1983.
xxii,91p; 30cm.
Five microfiche containing 13 background papers in pocket.
ISBN 0903043394 Pbk £18.00

—Software for producing library keyword catalogues : a description of selected packages / Steven Prowse. – Oxford : Elsevier International Bulletins, 1984.
viii,48p; 30cm. – (EIB report series).
Bibliography: p48.
ISBN 0946395012 Pbk No price

CATERERS AND CATERING - GREAT BRITAIN

—Hotel and catering law in Britain / by David Field. – 5th ed. – London : Sweet & Maxwell, 1988.
xvii,236p; 23cm.
Discusses the legal framework in England, Scotland and Wales. Covers changes in the law effected by the Wages Act 1986, and the Licensing (Restaurant Meals) Act 1987, and also examines the impact of the new Companies legislation on the catering industry.
ISBN 0421392509 Pbk £8.50

—W. M. Still & Sons Limited, W. M. Still Service Limited : a report by the Director General of Fair Trading on an investigation under section 3 of the Competition Act 1980 / Office of Fair Trading. – London : Office of Fair Trading, 1982.
39p; 30cm.

CENSORSHIP

—Censorship and Political Communication / London : Pinter Publishers Ltd.
180p.
ISBN 0861872614 Hbk £19.00

—Censorship and public morality / P. R. MacMillan. – Aldershot : Gower, 1983.
xxiii,547p; 24cm.
Bibliography: p521-530. - Includes index.
ISBN 0566003767 £22.95

CENSORSHIP - GREAT BRITAIN

—Offensive literature : decensorship in Britain, 1960-1982 / John Sutherland. – London : Junction Books, 1982.
207p; 22cm.
ISBN 0862450640

CENSORSHIP – NEW ZEALAND
—Indecent publications : control in New Zealand / by Stuart Perry. – Wellington : Government Printer, 1980.
101p.

CENSORSHIP – SOUTH AFRICA
—Censorship in South Africa : being a commentary on the application of the Publications Act / J.C.W. van Rooyen. – Cape Town : Juta, 1987.
xxiv,152p.
Includes bibliograpical references and index.
ISBN 0702119059

—Press and Apartheid : Repression and Propaganda in South Africa / C. Anthony Giffard. – London : Macmillan, 1984.
336p.
ISBN 0333384350 Hbk £33.00

CENSORSHIP – WEST GERMANY
—Censorship, Legal Defence and Domestic Intelligence Service in W. Germany / Russell Tribunal, III. – London : Spokesman Books, 1983.
50p.

CHANCERY – GREAT BRITAIN
—Chancery Practice / London : Butterworths, 1983.
ISBN 040622451X Hbk £28.00

—Chancery Practice Handbook / Jaque. – London : Longman Professional, 1983.
ISBN 0851207456 Hbk £25.50

—Christopher St. German on chancery and statute / by J.A. Guy. – London : Selden Society, 1985.
x,149p.

—Daniells Practice in the High Court of Chancery, 2 Vols. / London : Sweet & Maxwell, 1985. – (Sweet and Maxwell Library Reprints).
ISBN 0421351802 Hbk £140.00

—Practice in the High Court of Chancery, 2 Vols. / 8th ed. Repr. of 1914 ed. – Abingdon : Professional Books.

CHARITABLE TRUSTS
—Charitable status : a practical handbook / Andrew Phillips with Keith Smith. – London : Inter-Action Inprint, 1980.
xiii,83p; 22cm. – ().
Bibliography : p.74-76. - Includes index.
ISBN 0904571203 £5.50
ISBN 0904571211

—International tax problems of charities and other private institutions with similar tax treatment : proceedings of a seminar held in 1985 during the 39th Congress of the International Fiscal Association / International Fiscal Association. – Deventer Netherlands : Kluwer Law and Taxation Publishers, 1986.
Conference held in London, England.
ISBN 9065442707

—Law relating to charities / D.G. Cracknell. – 2nd ed. – London : Oyez Longman, 1983.
xxxviii,270p; 24cm.
Previous ed.: 1973. Includes index.
ISBN 0851207014 £17.50

CHARITABLE TRUSTS – AUSTRALIA
—Law of Charitable Trusts / Butterworths, 1983.
212p.
ISBN 0409490709 Hbk £52.00

—Outline of Equity and Trust / Sydney : Butterworths, 1988.
352p.
This introductory text covers such areas as the nature of eqity, equity assignments, fiduciary obligations, marshalling, contribution, subrogation, discretionary trusts, charitable trusts, and the rights of beneficiaries.

CHARITABLE TRUSTS – AUSTRALIA – TASMANIA
—Report on variations of charitable trusts / Law Reform Commission of Tasmania. – Hobart? : Government Printer?, 1984.
23p. – (Report).

CHARITABLE TRUSTS – CANADA
—Canadian Taxation of Charities and Donations / Toronto : DeBoo, 1987.
ISBN 088820258X Hbk £135.00

Supplements
This book deals with registered charities and their income tax obligations, fund raisers and donations, and non-profit organizations. Among the materials included are regulations, bulletins, circulars, and an appendix of statutes.

CHARITABLE TRUSTS – ENGLAND
—Property law : rights of reverter : report on a reference under section 3 (1) (e) of the Law Commissions Act 1965 / the Law Commission. – London : H.M.S.O., 1981.
vi,52p; 25cm.
ISBN 0101841000

CHARITABLE TRUSTS – GREAT BRITAIN
—Bradford disaster appeal : the administration of an appeal fund / by Roger W. Suddards : with contributions by Leolin Price and Hubert Picarda. – London : Sweet & Maxwell, 1986.
169p.
ISBN 0421379901

—Charitable status : a practical handbook / Andrew Phillips with Keith Smith. – 2nd ed. – London : Inter-Action, 1982.
83p; 22cm. – (Inter-action guides).
Previous ed.: 1980. Bibliography: p74-76. - Includes index.
ISBN 0904571394 Pbk £3.95

—Guide to the benefits of charitable status / TUAR, 1982.
ISBN 0907164099 Pbk £4.95

—Law of Charitable Trust / London : Butterworths, 1982.
ISBN 0409490709 Hbk £24.00

—Leaving Money to Charity / TUAR, 1983.
ISBN 0907164129 Pbk £1.95

—Legacies - Practical Guide for Charities / Turnaround Press, 1983.
ISBN 0907164110 Pbk £3.95

—Modern law of charities / George W. Keeton. – 3rd ed. – Cardiff : University College Cardiff Press, 1983.
lxxix,502p; 22cm.
Previous ed.: / by George W. Keeton and L.A. Sheridan. Belfast : Northern Ireland Legal Quarterly. 1971. Includes index.
ISBN 0906449545 £45.00

CHARITABLE TRUSTS – SCOTLAND
—Handbook of Charity Law and Practice / London : Sweet & Maxwell, 1988.
ISBN 0421358106 Pbk £27.50

CHARITABLE TRUSTS (HINDU LAW)
—Law of Hindi Religious and Charitable Endowments / 3rd ed. – Lucknow : Eastern Book Company, 1985.

—Mukherjea's Hindu Law of Religious and Charitable Trusts / 5th ed. – Calcutta : Eastern Law House, 1983.

CHARITIES
—Handbook of charities, 1987-1988 ... / edited by Erroll Christie and Anne Frazer Simpson. – London : Charities Data Services, 1987.
128 p.
'... a guide for those involved in the educational field, community service and the selection and search for organisations in need of support'.
ISBN 1870914007

CHARITIES – CANADA
—Canadian Taxation of Charities and Donations / Toronto : DeBoo, 1987.
ISBN 088820258X Hbk £135.00

Supplements
This book deals with registered charities and their income tax obligations, fund raisers and donations, and non-profit organizations. Among the materials included are regulations, bulletins, circulars, and an appendix of statutes.

—Endowments and Deferred Giving sound recording : a Detailed Explanation of Legalities and Procedures / Toronto : Association of Canadian Orchestras/Ontario Federation of Symphony Orchestras.

CHARITIES – ENGLAND
—Charities law and practice / Elizabeth Cairns. – London : Sweet & Maxwell, 1988.
xxi,258p; 26cm.
Includes the procedure for establishing a new charity and the relative advantages of trusts, companies, and unincorporated associations for different types of charity; how to draft the government instrument, and to what extent charities may engage in political activity. Taxation and administrative matters are also covered.
ISBN 0421358106 £19.50

—Charity, law and social justice / Francis Gladstone. – London : Bedford Square Press, 1982.
v,211p.
ISBN 0719910846

—Sixteenth report from the Committee of Public Accounts, session 1987-88 : monitoring and control of charities in England and Wales / London : H.M.S.O., 1988.
ix,14p; 30cm. – (H.C.).
ISBN 0102116881

—Tudor on charities / Spencer G. Maurice, David B. Parker. – 7th ed. – London : Sweet & Maxwell, 1984.
lxxiii,737p; 26cm.
Previous ed.: 1967. Includes index.
ISBN 0421249102 £75.00

CHARITIES – GREAT BRITAIN
—Accounting and Financial Management For Charities / Blume. – Turnaround Press, 1985.
ISBN 0907164188 Pbk £5.95

—Charitable Status - A Practical Handbook / Smith. – 2nd ed. – TUAR, 1982.
ISBN 0904571394 Pbk £4.50

—Charities Administration / ICSA. – Cambridge : Woodhead-Faulkner, 1986.
ISBN 0902197274 updat £55.00

—Charities in Britain : conservatism or change? / David Gerard. – London : Bedford Square Press/NCVO, 1983.
187p; 22cm.
Bibliography: p171-179. - Includes index.
ISBN 0719910927 Pbk £5.95

—Charities Law and Practice / 3rd ed. – London : Longman Professional, 1987.
ISBN 0851213006 Hbk £29.50

—Charities Manual / 2nd ed. – Tolley Publishing, 1988.
ISBN 085459325X Hbk £25.00

—Charities payroll giving schemes : proposals for tax relief / Inland Revenue. – London : Board of Inland Revenue, 1986.
12p.

—Charity Accounting / Vincent. – London : Butterworths, 1987.
ISBN 0406261008 Pbk £19.95

—Covenants : A Practical Guide to the Tax Advantages of Giving / 4th ed. – Turnaround Press.
ISBN 0907164390 Pbk

—Guide to the benefits of charitable status / TUAR, 1982.
ISBN 0907164099 Pbk £4.95

—Leaving Money to Charity / TUAR, 1983.
ISBN 0907164129 Pbk £1.95

—Legacies - Practical Guide for Charities / Turnaround Press, 1983.
ISBN 0907164110 Pbk £3.95

—Rating Relief for Charitable Organisations : Shaway Guide No. 8 / London : Shaw & Sons, 1982.
ISBN 0721908764 Pbk £2.50

CHARITIES – MALAYSIA
—Law of charities - cases & materials : Singapore & Malaysia / Ter Kah Leng. – Singapore : Butterworths, 1985.
xxvii,353p; 23cm.
Covers trusts for the relief of property, trusts for the advancement of education, religion, and other purposes beneficial to the community, 'Sin Chew' (ancestor worship) and ceremonies in memory of souls, and trusts for graves, memorials, and burial grounds.
ISBN 0409995037 Hbk

—Law of Charities - Cases & Materials - Singapore and Malaysia / London : Butterworths, 1985.
ISBN 0409995037 Hbk £55.00

CHARITIES – NORTHERN IRELAND
—Report : the modernisation of charity law in Northern Ireland / Belfast : H.M.S.O., 1985.
39,ca. 200p.
ISBN 0337203415

CHARITIES – SCOTLAND
—Handbook of Charity Law and Practice / London : Sweet & Maxwell, 1988.
ISBN 0421358106 Pbk £27.50

CHARITIES – SINGAPORE
—Law of Charities - Cases & Materials - Singapore and Malaysia / London : Butterworths, 1985.
ISBN 0409995037 Hbk £55.00

—Law of charities - cases & materials : Singapore & Malaysia / Ter Kah Leng. – Singapore : Butterworths, 1985.
xxvii,353p; 23cm.
Covers trusts for the relief of property, trusts for the advancement of education, religion, and other purposes beneficial to the community, 'Sin Chew' (ancestor worship) and ceremonies in memory of souls, and trusts for graves, memorials, and burial grounds.
ISBN 0409995037 Hbk

CHARTERPARTIES
—Charter-parties conference : a two-day conference / organised by Lloyd's of London Press. – 1. – London : Lloyd's of London Press, 1982.
various pagings.
ISBN 0907432476

—Charterers' liability insurance / by Dieter Schwampe : translated from the German by Burravoe Ltd. – London : Lloyd's of London Press, 1988.
xx,156p; 24cm.
Bibliography: pp.145-151. - Includes index. Translated from the German.
ISBN 1850441847 £45.00 (July)

—Chartering documents / by Per Gram. – London : Lloyd's of London Press, 1981
xiii,177p.
Includes index.
ISBN 0907432034

—Charterparties : a comparative study of South African, English and American law / Anne Waring. – Cape Town : Juta, 1983.
lx,417p.
Based on a thesis submitted for PhD, University of the Witwatersrand, Johannesburg. Bibliography: p.xix-xxvi. - Includes index.
ISBN 0702113441

—Law Relating to Bills of Lading and Charterparties / Allahabad : Indian Press.
253p.

—Safe port of berth reachable on arrival : charterers' and shipowners' responsibilities and liabilities / W.E. Astle. – London : Fairplay, 1986.
x,109p.
Cover title: The safe port.
ISBN 0905045912

—Shipbroking and chartering practice / by Lars Gorton, Rolf Ihre, Arne Sandevarn. – 2nd ed. – London : Lloyd's of London Press, 1984.
xv,298p; 26cm.
Bibliography: p.247. - Includes index.
ISBN 0907432638

—Shipping and contracting / Lars Gorton. – Lund : Juridiska Foreningen i Lund, 1983.
85p.
Includes bibliographical references and index.
ISBN 9154415012

—Time Charters / 3rd ed. – London : LLoyd's of London Press, 1989.
Several standard charter-party documents containing terms and conditions of time charter agreements are reproduced. Decisions, including the formation of the charter, speed and consumption warranties, safe ports, and the scope of the owners' indemnity obligations in regard to bills of lading, are reported.
ISBN 1850441855 Hbk

CHARTERPARTIES - ENGLAND

—Right of appeal : a practical digest of charter-party disputes and the right of appeal under the Arbitration Act 1979 / W.E. Astle. – London : Fairplay, 1983.
153p; 24cm.
ISBN 0905045513 Pbk No price

—Time charter withdrawals : an examination of shipowners' rights to withdraw vessels from the service of time charterers / W.E. Astle. – London : Fairplay, 1984.
xxiii,136p; 25cm.
ISBN 0905045637 Pbk No price

—Time charters / 2nd ed. – London : Lloyd's of London Press, 1982.
lxix,505p; 25cm.
Previous ed.: 1978. Includes index.
ISBN 0907432131

CHARTERPARTIES - GREAT BRITAIN

—Charter Parties / Oxford : Blackwell Scientific, 1988.
ISBN 063202061X Hbk

—Commencement of laytime / by Donald Davies. – London : LLP, 1987.
164p; 22cm.
Includes index.
ISBN 1850441472 £30.00

—Contracts of Affreightments and Hybrid Conts / Ivre. – London : Lloyd's of London Press, 1985.
ISBN 1850440603 Hbk £25.85

—Gram on Chartering Documents / London : LLoyd's of London Press, 1988.
ISBN 1850442037 Hbk

—Laytime / by Michael Brynm$or Summerskill. – 3rd ed. – London : Stevens, 1982.
xxxiii,317p; 26cm.
Previous ed.: 1973. Includes index.
ISBN 0420462104 £38.00

—Laytime / 4th ed. – London : Sweet & Maxwell, 1988.
ISBN 042079708 Hbk

—Laytime and demurrage / by John Schofield. – London : Lloyds of London, 1985.
393p; 24cm.
Include index.
ISBN 1850440573 No price

—Practical guide to contracts of affreightment and hybrid contracts / by Lars Gorton and Rolf Ihre. – London : Lloyd's, 1985.
ix,87p; 25cm.
Includes index.
ISBN 1850440603 £45.00

—Scrutton on charterparties and bills of lading / Alan Abraham Mocatta, Michael John Mustill, Stewart C. Boyd. – 19th ed. – London : Sweet & Maxwell, 1984.
cv,593p; 25cm.
Section on time charters has been substantially revised and rewritten to take account of developments. Four House of Lords decisions on the problem of withdrawal for non-payment of hire are discussed, and there is an analysis of the related problem of deductions from hire.
ISBN 0421297107 £50.00

—Shipbroking and chartering practice / Gordon. – 2nd ed. – London : Lloyd's of London Press, 1984.
ISBN 0907432638 Hbk £39.00

—Tanker voyage charter parties / by F. M. Ventris. – S.l. : Kluwer Law Publishers, 1986.
xvi,411p.
ISBN 0903393972

CHARTERPARTIES - UNITED STATES

—Time charters / 2nd ed. – London : Lloyd's of London Press, 1982.
lxix,505p; 25cm.
Previous ed.: 1978. Includes index.
ISBN 0907432131

CHECKS - SOUTH AFRICA

—Bills of exchange, cheques and promissory notes in South African law / by F.R. Malan : assisted by C. R. de Beer. – Durban : Butterworths, 1983.
xii,441p.
Bibliography: p.377-391. - Includes index.
ISBN 0409040738

CHEMICAL WARFARE

—Chemical industry and the projected chemical weapons convention : proceedings of a SIPRI/Pugwash conference / 2. – Oxford : Published on behalf of Stockholm International Peace Research Institute by Oxford University Press, 1986.
30cm.
Includes bibliography.
ISBN 0198291094 Pbk £9.95

CHEMICALS

—Environmental Law and Chemical Substance / Berlin : Erich Schmidt, 1982.
ISBN 3503021280 Hbk £48.00

—International Register of Potentially Toxic Chemicals, 2 Vols. / United Nations. – London : HMSO, 1984.
Provides information on the danger to humans and the environment of chemicals and details of individual nations' controlling legislation.
ISBN 0119079860 Hbk £58.50

—IRPTC Legal File, 2 Vols. / Geneva : United Nations Publications, 1987.
1,345p.
ISBN 9280711636 Pbk £98.00

CHEMICALS - SWEDEN

—Labelling of chemical products : Swedish regulations and general advice with regard to the classification and labelling of chemical products hazardous to health, flammables and explosives / National Chemicals Inspectorate, National Inspectorate of Explosives and Flammables. – Solna : National Chemicals Inspectorate, 1987.
224p.
ISBN 9138098873

CHILD ABUSE

—Child abuse : a community concern / edited by Kim Oates. – London : Butterworths, 1982.
xiv,321p.
Bibliographies.

—Criminological aspects of the ill-treatment of children in the family : 4th Criminological Colloquium, Strasbourg, 26-28 Nov. 1979 / Council of Europe. – Strasbourg : The Council, 1980.
194p.
Bibliography: p.169-194. 'Secretariat memorandum prepared by the Directorate of Legal Affairs'.

—Politics of child abuse / Nigel Parton. – Basingstoke : Macmillan, 1985.
xii,245p; 22cm.
ISBN 0333363167 Pbk
ISBN 0333363175

—Thou shalt not be aware : society's betrayal of the child / by Alice Miller : translated from the German by Hildegard and Hunter Hannum. – London : Pluto, 1985.
viii, 331p.
Originally published: Frankfurt am Main: Surkamp Verlag, 1981. Bibliography: p.327-331. Translation of: Du sollst nicht merken.
ISBN 0745300499

CHILD ABUSE - AUSTRALIA

—Child abuse: a community concern / North Ryde : Butterworths (Australia).
Gives an overview of the problem of child abuse with particular emphasis on the needs and future development of the battered child. Discusses the various types of children and families who suffer from abuse, considers the emotional stresses that face the professional working with child abuse, and describes research studies which have practical implications for predicting and preventing child abuse.
ISBN 0409303305 Hbk

CHILD ABUSE - AUSTRALIA - TASMANIA

—Child witnesses in sexual assault / Kate Warner. – Hobart : Law Reform Commission of Tasmania, 1987.
123p. – (Discussion paper).
Includes bibliographical references.

CHILD ABUSE - AUSTRALIA - VICTORIA

—Sexual offences against children / Law Reform Commission of Victoria. – Melbourne : The Commission, 1988.
iv,80p. – (Discussion paper).
Includes bibliographical references.
ISBN 0724167218

CHILD ABUSE - CANADA

—Sexual offences against children in Canada : summary of the report of the Committee on Sexual Offences Against Children and Youths appointed by the Minister of Justice and Attorney General of Canada, the Minister of National Health and Welfare, Government of Canada 1984 / Canada. – Ottawa : Supply and Services Canada, 1984.
viii,80p.
ISBN 0660116987

—Sexual offences against children : report of the committee on Sexual Offences Against Children and Youths appointed by the Minister of Justice and Attorney General of Canada, the Minister of National Health and Welfare / Canada. – 2. – Ottawa : Supply and Services Canada, 1984.
Includes bibliographical references.
ISBN 0660116391

—Sexual offences against the person and the protection of young persons : information paper / Infractions sexuelles contre la personne et protection des jeunes : Jean Chretien, Minister of Justice. – Rev. ed. – Ottawa : Minister of Justice, 1980.
43p.
Parallel English and French text.

CHILD ABUSE - ENGLAND

—Child abuse inquiries : a consultative paper from the Department of Health and Social Security / Great Britain. – London : The Department, 1985.
15p.

—Child in trust : the report of the Panel of Inquiry into the Circumstances Surrounding the Death of Jasmine Beckford / presented to Brent Borough Council and to Brent Health Authority by the Members of the Panel of Inquiry ... Louis Blom-Cooper (in the chair). – London : London Borough of Brent, 1985.
304,cxlp; 21cm.
Bibliography: pcxxxix-cxl.
ISBN 0951106805

—Report of the inquiry into child abuse in Cleveland 1987 / presented to Parliament by the Secretary of State for Social Services by Command of Her Majesty, July 1988. – London : HMSO, 1988.
320p.
'Presented to the Secretary of State for Social Services by the Right Honourable Lord Justice Butler-Sloss DBE'. - p.i.
ISBN 0101041225

—Report of the inquiry into child abuse in Cleveland 1987 : short version extracted from the complete text / presented to Parliament by the Secretary of State for Social Services by Command of Her Majesty, July 1988. – London : HMSO, 1988.
21p.
Chairman: ELizabeth Butler-Sloss.
ISBN 0101041322

—Use of video technology at trials of alleged child abusers / Home Office. – London : Home Office, 1987.
14p.
ISBN 0862522749

CHILD ABUSE - GREAT BRITAIN

—Child abuse : a study of inquiry reports, 1973-1981 / Department of Health and Social Security. – London : H.M.S.O., 1982.
vi,93p; 21cm.
ISBN 0113207883

—Child abuse : procedure and evidence in juvenile courts / by Jean Graham Hall and Douglas F. Martin. – 2nd ed. – London : Barry Rose, 1987.
xv,117p.
ISBN 187008070X

—Child in mind : protection of children in a responsible society : the report of the Commission of Inquiry into the Circumstances Surrounding the Death of Kimberley Carlile / presented to the London Borough of Greenwich and the Greenwich Health Authority .. – London : The Borough, 1987.
xii,292p; 24cm.
Chairman: Louis Blom-Cooper.
ISBN 0904399060

—Child sexual abuse : joint investigative project : final report / Metropolitan Police and Bexley London Borough. – London : H.M.S.O., 1987.
93p.
Bibliographical references: p93.
ISBN 0113408862

—Protection of children : state intervention and family life / Robert Dingwall, John Eekelaar, Topsy Murray. - Oxford : Basil Blackwell, 1983.
x,286p; 24cm.
Bibliography: p267-282. - Includes index.
ISBN 0631131051 £22.50

—Social work and child abuse / Ball. - London : Macmillan, 1987.
ISBN 033363973 Hbk £15.00
ISBN 0333363981 Pbk £5.95

—Trends in child abuse, 1977-82 : the fourth report on the children placed on N.S.P.C.C. Special Unit registers / by Susan J. Creighton. - London : N.S.P.C.C., 1984.
57p.
Bibliography: p.35.
ISBN 0902498126

—Understanding child abuse / 2nd ed. - London : Macmillan, 1987.
ISBN 0333428935 Pbk £7.95

CHILD ABUSE - UNITED STATES

—Maltreatment of the school-aged child / edited by Richard Volpe and Margot Breton, Judith Mitton. - Lexington : Lexington, 1980.
xiii,210p; 24cm.
Includes bibliographies and index.
ISBN 0669034630 Pbk £12.00
ISBN 0669041513 Unpriced

CHILD BENEFIT - GREAT BRITAIN

—Commissioners' Decisions : Social Security and Child Benefit Acts / London : HMSO, 1985.
ISBN 0117609218 Hbk

Vol. IX, 1983-84
ISBN 0117607851 Hbk £25.00

—Law Relating to Social Security and Child Benefit, 4 Vols. / London : HMSO.
Sets out the current legislation, both statutes and regulations with footnotes and sidenotes giving the origin of amendments.
ISBN 0117609102 Pbk £95.00

CHILD CARE - AUSTRALIA

—Children in institutional and other forms of care : a national perspective : report of the Senate Standing Committee on Social Welfare / Canberra : Australian Govt. Pub. Service, 1985.
xii, 121 p.; 25 cm.
At head of title: The Parliament of the Commonwealth of Australia. 'June 1985.'. Includes bibliographies.
ISBN 0644040955 pbk.

CHILD PRISONERS

—Children in adult prisons : an international picture / Defence For Children International : compiled by Katarina Tomasevski. - London : Pinter, 1985.
280p; 33cm.
Includes index.
ISBN 0861876172 £18.50

CHILD PSYCHOLOGY

—Maternal deprivation reassessed / Michael Rutter. - 2nd ed. - Harmondsworth : Penguin, 1981.
285p; 18cm. - (Penguin education).
Previous ed.: 1972. Bibliography: p219-272. - Includes index.
ISBN 0180805613 Pbk £1.95

CHILD SUPPORT - AUSTRALIA

—Child Support / Kingston : Australian Government Publishing Service.

CHILD SUPPORT - GREAT BRITAIN

—Child Support : From Debt Collection To Social Policy / Kamerman. - Sage Publications, 1988.
ISBN 080392979X Hbk £29.95

—Reported decisions of the Commissioner under the Social Security and Child Benefit Acts / Department of Health and Social Security. - v. - London : H.M.S.O., 1980-.
Continues: Reported decisions of the Commissioner under the Social Security, National Insurance and Family Allowances Acts.

CHILD SUPPORT - SCOTLAND

—Family law, report on aliment and financial provision / Scottish Law Commission. - Edinburgh : H.M.S.O., 1981.
x,239p; 25cm. - (H.C.).
ISBN 0102002827 Pbk £8.40

CHILD WELFARE

—Beyond the best interests of the child / Joseph Goldstein, Anna Freud, Albert J. Solnit. - New ed. with epilogue. - London : Burnett Books, 1980.
xiv,203p; 21cm.
This ed. originally published: New York : Free Press, 1979. Includes index.
ISBN 0233972420 HBK £7.50
ISBN 0233972684 PBK £5.50

—Family law : an interdisciplinary perspective / Howard H. Irving, editor. - Toronto : Carswell, 1981.
xi,215p.
Includes bibliographical references. Subtitle on cover: Law for the helping professions.
ISBN 0459333801

—Payment by the State of advances on child maintenance : Recommendation No.R (82) 2 adopted by the Committee of Ministers of the Council of Europe on 4 February 1982 and explanatory memorandum / Council of Europe. - Strasbourg : Council of Europe, 1982.
15p; 21cm.
'Prepared by a committee of experts set up under the authority of the European Committee on Legal Co-operation'. At head of cover title : Council of Europe, Legal Affairs.
ISBN 9287101736

CHILD WELFARE - CANADA

—Advocacy in Child Welfare Cases / Agincourt : Carswell, 1985.
258p.
This book discusses the representation of the parties to child welfare cases under the Child Welfare Act and the Child and Family Services Act of Canada.

—Annotated Child Welfare Act / Hartrick and Lazor. - Agincourt : Carswell, 1983.
460p.

CHILD WELFARE - CANADA - ONTARIO

—Child Welfare Act annotated / by Michael D. Hartrick and Yan Arthur M. Lazor. - Toronto : Carswell, 1983.
xxix,431p.
Includes index. Includes text of the Ontario Child Welfare Act 1980 and related Regulations.
ISBN 0459357107

CHILD WELFARE - ENGLAND

—Care proceedings : a practical guide for social workers, health visitors and others / Robert Dingwall and John Eekelaar. - Oxford : Basil Blackwell, 1982.
viii,140p; 23cm.
Bibliography: p135-136. - Includes index.
ISBN 0631127569 Hbk Unpriced
ISBN 0631127577 Pbk Unpriced

—Child in trust : the report of the Panel of Inquiry into the Circumstances Surrounding the Death of Jasmine Beckford / presented to Brent Borough Council and to Brent Health Authority by the Members of the Panel of Inquiry ... Louis Blom-Cooper (in the chair). - London : London Borough of Brent, 1985.
304,cxlp; 21cm.
Bibliography: pcxxxix-cxl.
ISBN 0951106805

—Children in care : Government response to the second report from the Social Services Committee, session 1983-84 / presented to Parliament by the Secretary of State for Social Services. - London : H.M.S.O., 1984.
34p.
ISBN 0101929803

—Childright : a bulletin of law and policy affecting children and young people in England and Wales / v. - London : The Children's Legal Centre, 1983.
ISBN 02651459

—Law of child care / B.I. Slomnicka. - Plymouth : Macdonald & Evans, 1982.
xlvi,415p.
Includes index.
ISBN 0712112529

—Social workers and solicitors in child care cases / by Linden Hilgendorf with the assistance of Deborah Holland, Barrie Irving, Diana Schlaefli. - London : H.M.S.O., 1981.
ix,150p.
ISBN 0113207697

CHILD WELFARE - FINLAND

—Dealing with child offenders in Finland : the Scandinavian child welfare system in operation / Matti Joutsen. - Helsinki : Research Institute of Legal Policy, 1980.
121p.
Bibliography: p.95-100.
ISBN 9517040652

CHILD WELFARE - GREAT BRITAIN

—Child in mind : protection of children in a responsible society : the report of the Commission of Inquiry into the Circumstances Surrounding the Death of Kimberley Carlile / presented to the London Borough of Greenwich and the Greenwich Health Authority .. - London : The Borough, 1987.
xii,292p; 24cm.
Chairman: Louis Blom-Cooper.
ISBN 0904399060

—Encountering diversity : observations on the social work assessment of black children / Richard Pinder. - Leeds : Centre for Social Work and Applied Social Studies, 1982.
32p. - (Occasional paper).
Bibliography: p.31-32.

—Law of Child Care / London : Pitman Publishing, 1982.
ISBN 0712112529 Hbk £12.95

—Law on child care and family services / Department of Health and Social Security...et al. : presented to Parliament by the Secretary of State for Social Services... - London : H.M.S.O., 1987.
iv,22p.
ISBN 0101006225

—Second report from the Social Services Committee, session 1983- 84 : children in care / London : H.M.S.O., 1984.
clxxii p.; 25cm. - (H.C.).
ISBN 0102880840

Vol.2 : Minutes of evidence (24 November 1982-9 February 1983) 1984.
ix,1-410p; 25cm. - (H.C.).
ISBN 0102881847 Hbk

Vol.3 : Minutes of evidence (16 February-4 May 1983 and an appendix 1984.
ix,411-740p; 25cm. - (H.C.).
ISBN 0102882843 Hbk

CHILD WELFARE - NORWAY

—Child welfare and social defence / Tove Stang Dahl : translated by Gunvor Nyquist. - Oslo : Norwegian University Press, 1985.
185p; 23cm.
Bibliography: p175-185. Translation and revision of: Barneven og samfunnsvern.
ISBN 8200071146 £19.45

CHILDREN

—Beyond the best interests of the child / Joseph Goldstein, Anna Freud, Albert J. Solnit. - New ed. with epilogue. - London : Burnett Books, 1980.
xiv,203p; 21cm.
This ed. originally published: New York : Free Press, 1979. Includes index.
ISBN 0233972420 HBK £7.50
ISBN 0233972684 PBK £5.50

—Child Witness : Do the Courts Abuse Children / Drinkwater. - New York : British Psychological Society, 1988.
ISBN 0901715891 Pbk £5.00

—Child's voice in the court of law : an account of the representation of minors in civil proceedings in Canada and some other (mostly common law) jurisdictions / Olive M. Stone. - Toronto : Butterworth & Co. (Canada), 1982.
x, 248p; 24cm.
Examination of the representation of minors in civil litigation, looking primarily at Canadian and English practices. Gives a historical discussion of women's legal position in the past and how the issue of guardianship was affected by it. Description of the relevant Canadian federal and provincial legislation in which each province is treated separately.
ISBN 0409870544

—Children : rights and responsibilities / Jo Boyden and Andy Hudson. - London : Minority Rights Group, 1985.
15p. - (Report).
Bibliography: p14-15.
ISBN 0946690340

—Childright : a bulletin of law and policy affecting children and young people in England and Wales / v. - London : The Children's Legal Centre, 1983.
ISBN 02651459

—Custodianship : the law and practice / by Nasreen Pearce. - London : Fourmat, 1986.
xi,77p.
ISBN 1851900152

—European Convention on Recognition and Enforcement of Decisions concerning Custody of Children and on Restoration of Custody of Children / Strasbourg : Council of Europe, 1980.
ISBN 9287101485 Hbk £1.00

—Explanatory Report on the European Convention on Recognition and Enforcement of Decisions Concerning Custody of Children and on Restoration of Custody of Children / Strasbourg : Council of Europe, 1980.

—Family and child law statutes / compiled by Oyez Longman Editorial Staff. - London : Oyez Longman, 1984.
x,711p; 23cm.
ISBN 0851208894

—A guide to the children's hearings / Edinburgh : W Green & Son, 1989.
Explains the complex legal and administrative provisions and procedures of those involved: panel members, parents, reporters, social workers and the children themselves.
ISBN 0414009045

—Implementation of the European Convention on Human Rights in respect of young persons and children placed in care or in institutions following a decision of the administrative or judicial authorities : replies of Governments to the Secretary General's enquiry under Article 57 of the European Convention on Human Rights / Council of Europe. – Strasbourg : Council of Europe, 1986.
196p; 30cm. – (H (86) 1).
At head of cover title: Human rights.

—International Protection of Minorities / Delhi : Mittal Publications, 1986.

—Justice for children / Allison Morris ... et al. – London : Macmillan, 1980.
vii,146p; 22cm.
Bibliography: p.141-146.
ISBN 0333274865 Unpriced
ISBN 0333274873

—Law of contract : minors' contracts / Law Commission. – London : H.M.S.O., 1984.
v,42p.
ISBN 0102494843

—Medical treatment for minors / the Law Reform Commission of Western Australia. – Perth : the Commission, 1988.
111p. – (Discussion paper).

—Meeting of Experts on the Exploitation of the Child, November 12-13, 1984, Singapore and the Conference on Child Labour and Child Prostitution, February 21-23, 1986, Kuala Lumpur / convened by the LAWASIA Human Rights Standing Committee : editor, Patricia Hyndman. – Sydney : LAWASIA, 1986.
513p.
Includes bibliographical references.

—Parental responsibilities : recommendation no.R (84)4 adopted by the Committee of Ministers of the Council of Europe on 28 February 1984, and Explanatory memorandum / Council of Europe. – Strasbourg : Council of Europe, 1984.
19p; 21cm.
'... prepared by the Committee of Experts on Family Law set up under the authority of the European Committee on Legal Co-operation' - preface..
ISBN 9287103291

—Payment by the State of advances on child maintenance : Recommendation No.R (82) 2 adopted by the Committee of Ministers of the Council of Europe on 4 February 1982 and explanatory memorandum / Council of Europe. – Strasbourg : Council of Europe, 1982.
15p; 21cm.
'Prepared by a committee of experts set up under the authority of the European Committee on Legal Co-operation'. At head of cover title : Council of Europe, Legal Affairs.
ISBN 9287101736

—Report of the Royal Commission on Family and Children's Law / Thomas R. Berger. – 20 v. – Vancouver : Queen's Printer, 1974.
Includes bibliographies. Chairman: Thomas R. Berger.

—Review of child care law : report to ministers of an interdepartmental working party : published by the government as a consultative document / Rupert Hughes. – London : H.M.S.O., 1985.
v,179p.
Chairman: Rupert Hughes. At head of title-page: Department of Health and Social Security.
ISBN 0113210426

—Taking juvenile justice seriously / Ruth M. Adler. – Edinburgh : Scottish Academic Press, 1985.
viii,172p.
Bibliography: p157-167.
ISBN 0707304660

CHILDREN - AUSTRALIA

—Changing laws for changing families / Patricia Harper. – Melbourne : Institute of Family Studies, 1982.
24p. – (Discussion paper).
Paper prepared for the 3rd Australian Conference on adoption, 'Changing Families', Adelaide, 14-19 May 1982.
ISBN 0642884552

—Children in stepfamilies : their legal and family status / Patricia Harper. – Melbourne : Institute of Family Studies, 1984.
– (Policy background paper).
Bibliography: p.28-29.
ISBN 0642876665

—Implications of marital separation for young children / compiled by the Australian Institute of Family Studies from a report of a survey conducted in 1982-83 by G.W. Smiley, E.R. Chamberlain and L.I. Dalgleish. – Melbourne : Australian Institute of Family Studies, 1987.
ix,45p. – (Working paper).
Bibliography: p.33-45.

—Law for parents and children / by Helen Gamble. – 2nd ed. – North Ryde, N.S.W. : Law Book Company, 1986.
vii,392p.
Includes bibliographical references and index.
ISBN 0455206937

—Law relating to parents and children / by Helen Gamble. – Sydney : Law Book Co., 1981.
vii, 341 p.; 19 cm.
'Table of cases': p. 301-308. 'Table of statutes': p. 309-325. Includes bibliographical references and index.
ISBN 0455202540 pbk.

—Rights of the child / Austin Asche. – Melbourne : Institute of Family Studies, 1982.
18p. – (Discussion paper).
Includes bibliographical references. Paper delivered as the first Vernon Collins Memorial Lecture in Melbourne, 14 October, 1981.
ISBN 0642888000

—Youth and the law / Department of Employment and Industrial Relations, Australia. – Canberra : Australian Government Publishing Service, 1982.
vii,77p.
'A study commissioned by the Office of Youth Affairs, October 1981'.
ISBN 0644019298

CHILDREN - AUSTRALIA - TASMANIA

—Working paper on the law relating to contracts and the disposition of property by minors / by D.R.C. Chalmers. – Hobart? : Government Printer?, 1985.
49,iip.
Cover title.

CHILDREN - CANADA

—Canadian children's law : cases, notes and materials / by Nicholas Bala, Heino Lilles and George Thomson. – Toronto : Butterworths, 1982.
xxxi,754p.
Includes index.
ISBN 0409872237

—Child and Family Services Act : a Guide to Part 3 / Douglas J. Manning. – Butterworths, 1986.
208p.
Contains commentary following each section of the act, analysing both similarities and differences in the Child Welfare Act, major changes and modifications and intent in the new Act, selections of summaries of major cases decided under the old Act, and analyses key terms and categories, with reference to other relevant sections.
ISBN 0409805246 Hbk £55.00

—Children and the Law / 2nd ed. – Butterworths, 1986.
860p.
ISBN 040997762X Hbk £85.00

—Children's rights in the practice of family law / edited by Barbara Landau. – Toronto : Carswell, 1986.
xxxviii,378p.
Includes bibliogrpahical references.
ISBN 0459390406

—Nanny for Your Child / North Vancouver : International Self-Counsel Press, 1987.

—Proposals on custody, parental guardianship, and the civil rights of minors : report to the Attorney General / from the Law Reform Commission of Saskatchewan. – Saskatoon : Law Reform Commission of Saskatchewan, 1981.
iv,40p.

—Sentenced to separation : an exploration of the needs and problems of mothers who are offenders and their children / Linda MacLeod. – Ottawa : Ministry of the Solicitor General, 1986.
ii,66p,14p,8p. – (User report).

—So, You Have to Go to Court : a Child's Guide to Testifying as a Witness in Child Abuse Cases / Anne Watson-Russell. – Butterworths, 1986.
48p.
ISBN 040980519X Pbk £7.95

—Up Against It : Children and the Law in Canada / Toronto : House of Ananansi Press, 1980.
166p.
ISBN 0887840760 Hbk £8.95

—Up Against It : Children and the Law in Canada / Toronto : Anansi Press, 1980.
166p.
ISBN 0887840760 Pbk £8.95

—Vicarious liablilty of parents for actions of their children who are found to be delinquent / Elizabeth Beckett. – Ottawa : Ministry of the Solicitor General, 1985.
ii,79 leaves. – (User report).
Includes bibliographical references.

—Wilson: children and the law / Mary Tomlinson. – A completely rev. and re-written 2nd ed. – Toronto : Butterworths, 1986.
liii,505p.
Includes bibliographies and index.
ISBN 040987762X

—Young Offenders Act annotated / by Nicholas Bala and Heino Lilles. – Don Mills : R. De Boo, 1984.
xxxi,453p.
Includes index.
ISBN 0888201842

—Young Offenders Act Manual / Aurora : Canada Law Book Co.
– (Text Books-Criminal).

Binder and Contents
The principles and procedures of The Young Offender's Act, the replacement Act to the Juvenile Delinquents Act, are discussed in this comprehensive reference manual. The Manual includes case annotations, insightful commentary, extensive indexing and accurate cross referencing.

—Young Offenders and the State / Toronto : Butterworths, 1984.
288p.

—Young offenders and the state: Canadian perspective on delinquency / Scarborough, Ontario : Butterworths (Canada), 1984.
288.
Argues that the institutions that the Canadian state has created to del with young offenders - schools, courts, reformatories, group homes and jails, are not politically neutral. Analyses methodological problems in dealing with official statistics and social experiments, and draws upon Canadian, American and British sources.
ISBN 0409875830 Pbk

—Young Offenders Service, 2 vols / Heino Lilles. – Toronto : Butterworths.

—Youth and the Law / Vancouver : Vancouver People's Law School.
30p.

CHILDREN - CANADA - ALBERTA

—Status of children : revised report, 1985 / Institute of Law Research and Reform. – Edmonton : The Institute, 1985.
137p. – (Report).

CHILDREN - CANADA - ONTARIO

—Child Welfare Act annotated / by Michael D. Hartrick and Yan Arthur M. Lazor. – Toronto : Carswell, 1983.
xxix,431p.
Includes index. Includes text of the Ontario Child Welfare Act 1980 and related Regulations.
ISBN 0459357107

CHILDREN - CANADA - SASKATCHEWAN

—Proposals relating to the change of name of children of divorced parents : report to the Minister of Justice / Law Reform Commission of Saskatchewan. – Saskatoon : The Commission, 1985.
8p.

CHILDREN - ENGLAND

—Child Care and Foster Children Acts 1980 / with annotations by M.D.A. Freeman. – London : Sweet and Maxwell, 1980.
vii,108p; 25cm.
ISBN 0421276908 Pbk £5.00

—Child care manual for social workers / by A.E. Leeding. – 4th ed. – London : Butterworth, 1980.
xiii,295p; 22cm.
Previous ed. : 1976. Includes index. Supplements.
ISBN 0406270031 Pbk £7.95

—Child custody and divorce : the law in social context / Susan Maidment. – London : Croom Helm, 1984.
324p; 23cm.
Bibliography: p293-306. - Includes index.
ISBN 0709917376 £16.95

—Child custody : what chance for fathers? / Susan Maidment. – London : National Council for One Parent Families, 1981.
23p.
Bibliography: p.21-23.

—Children Act 1975 : custodianship orders / Department of Health and Social Security. – London : The Department, 1985.
15,xi,3,iip.

—Childright : a bulletin of law and policy affecting children and young people in England and Wales / v. – London : The Children's Legal Centre, 1983.
ISBN 02651459

—Family law : review of child law : guardianship and custody / The Law Commission. – London : HMSO, 1988.
iv,112p. – (1987-88 HC).
Includes text of a proposed children bill.
ISBN 0102594880

—Law of child care / B.I. Slomnicka. – Plymouth : Macdonald & Evans, 1982.
xlvi,415p.
Includes index.
ISBN 0712112529

—Law of contract : minors' contracts / the Law Commission. – London : H.M.S.O., 1982.
vi,179p. – (Working paper).
ISBN 0117301612

—Minors : the law and practice : the juvenile courts, the offences, the role of the local authorities / Kenneth W. Pain. – London : Fourmat Publishing, 1987.
xvii,293p.
Concerns practice and procedure of juvenile courts, offences which can be committed by and against minors and the part played by local authorities in care proceedings.
ISBN 1851900306

—Review of child care law : publication of interim discussion papers by the inter-Departmental working party / Department of Health and Social Security. – 1. – London : The Department, 1986.
various pagings.
ISBN 1851970401

—Surviving the breakup : how children and parents cope with divorce / Judith S. Wallerstein and Joan Berlin Kelly. – London : Grant McIntyre, 1980.
x,341p; 22cm.
Also published: New York : Basic Books, 1980. Includes index.
ISBN 0862160251 £10.95
ISBN 086216026X

CHILDREN – GREAT BRITAIN

—Child Care and Adult Crime / Ashcraft. – Manchester : Manchester University Press, 1988.
ISBN 0719024692 Hbk £29.50

—Child care law : proposals for reform / the Law Society. – London : Law Society, 1983.
14 leaves.
'Prepared by the Law Society's Standing Committee on Criminal Law' - Introduction.

—Child's Voice in Court of Law / London : Butterworths, 1982.
ISBN 0409870544 Hbk £30.00

—Children and divorce : economic factors / by Mavis Maclean and John Eekelaar. – Oxford : SSRC Centre for Socio-Legal Studies, 1983.
vii,39p; 22cm.
ISBN 0862260698

—Children, parents and the state / by Andrew Bainham. – London : Sweet & Maxwell, 1988.
200p; 23cm.
Examines the relationship between children, their parents, and the state, and how their respective powers, duties, and responsibilities interact within the legal system. Also discusses the extent to which the state, through local authorities and the courts, can legitimately intervene in family life.
ISBN 042136310X Hbk £14.00
ISBN 0421363207 Pbk £11.95

—Clarke Hall and Morrison on Children, 2 Vols. / A.C.L. Morrison. – 10th ed. – London : Butterworths, 1986.
ISBN 040615807X loose

Supplement
This looseleaf service in two volumes contains all the relevant statutory material on practice of law relating to children in the United Kingdom. Five main subjects make up the work.
ISBN 040615810X Pbk

—Custodianship : the law and practice / London : Fourmat, 1986.
ISBN 185900152 Pbk £7.95

—Custody and Access to Children / London : Oyez Longman, 1983.
– (Oyez Longman Practice Note Ser.: No. 75).
ISBN 0851207480 Hbk £7.95

—Family and child law statutes / 3rd. – London : Longman Professional (UK), 1990.
Updated with 1988 and 1989 legislative changes including the Children Act 1989, plus the Adoption Act 1976.
ISBN 0851215750 Pbk £24.50

—First rights : a guide to legal rights for young people / Maggie Rae, Patricia Hewitt and Barry Hugill : illustrated by Corinne Pearlman. – 3rd ed. – London : National Council for Civil Liberties, 1985.
128p; 20cm.
Previous ed.: 1981. Includes bibliography and index.
ISBN 0946088152 Pbk £1.95

—In the child's best interest? / Vincent. – London : Sweet & Maxwell, 1987.
ISBN 042261260X Hbk £22.00
ISBN 0422612707 Pbk £10.95

—Law in Relation to Children / Morrison. – 10th ed. – London : Butterworths, 1985.
Service to 31.3.89.
ISBN 0406158126 loose £145.00

—Law Relating to Children / 2nd ed. – London : Butterworths, 1982.
ISBN 0406117039 Hbk

—Law relating to children and young persons / Clarke Hall and Morrison. – 10th ed. 2. – London : Butterworths, 1985.
looseleaf.
Includes index. Includes the text of the relevant legislation. Spine title: Clarke Hall & Morrison on children. Kept up-to-date by supplements.
ISBN 0406158126

—Opportunity lost : a response to the Green Paper on the Reform of Personal Taxation from the Child Poverty Action Group / Ruth Lister and Fran Bennett. – London : Child Poverty Action Group, 1986.
34p.

—Parental supervision and juvenile delinquency / by David Riley and Margaret Shaw. – London : H.M.S.O., 1985.
v,85p; 25cm.
Bibliography: p81-85. A Home Office Research and Planning Unit report. A Home Office Research and Planning Unit report.
ISBN 0113407998

—Practitioner's Guide to Child Care Law / Vaughan Bevan. – Bristol : Jordan & Sons Ltd, 1986.
– (Family Law Practitioner's Ser.).
ISBN 085308100X Pbk

—Prevention of crime among young people / Parliamentary All-Party Penal Affairs Group. – Chichester : Rose, 1983.
112p; 21cm.
ISBN 0859923533 Pbk £7.00

—Providing civil justice for children / Hugh Geach and Elizabeth Szwed. – London : Edward Arnold, 1983.
250p; 22cm.
Includes bibliographies and index.
ISBN 071316400X Pbk £9.95

—Review of the Children Act ten years on : its effect on foster care policy and practice / David Owen ... et al. : with an introduction by Alan Holden. – London : National Foster Care Association, 1986.
44p; 21cm.
ISBN 0946015252 Pbk £2.95

—Rights and wrongs of children / Pinter, 1983.
ISBN 0861872266 Pbk £6.95

—Wardship : the law and practice / by Nasreen Pearce. – London : Fourmat, 1986.
xvii,126p.
ISBN 090684097X

—Wardship : the law and practice / London : Fourmat, 1986.
ISBN 090684097X Pbk £12.95

—White, Carr and Lowe: a guide to the Children Act 1989 / A Carr, N Lowe, Brenda Hoggett. – London : Butterworths, 1990.
255; 248.
This Act is reproduced in full, with annotations. A commentary explains the new law and hows how it will affect, in practical terms, the actions of all who deal with child cases.
ISBN 0406502099 Pbk £12.95

CHILDREN – HONG KONG

—Report : young persons : effects of age in civil law / the Law Reform Commission of Hong Kong. – Hong Kong : The Commission, 1986.
various pagings. – (Topic 11).

CHILDREN – IRELAND

—Report on minors' contracts / the Law Reform Commission. – Dublin : The Commission, 1985.
v,167p. – (LRC).
Bibliography: p.163.

—Report on the liability in tort of minors and the liability of parents for damage caused by minors / the Law Reform Commission. – Dublin : The Commission, 1985.
iv,123p. – (LRC).
Bibliography: pp.118-120.

CHILDREN – LEGAL STATUS, LAWS, ETC. – AUSTRALIA – TASMANIA

—Report on contracts and the disposition of property by minors / Law Reform Commission of Tasmania. – Hobart : Acting Government Printer, 1987.
14p. – (Report).
Includes text of the Infants' Relief Act 1875.

CHILDREN – LEGAL STATUS, LAWS, ETC. – GREAT BRITAIN

—Children act 1975 / by Hugh K. Bevan and Martin L. Parry. – London : Butterworths, 1978.
xviii, 307 p; 26 cm.
Includes index.

CHILDREN – NORTHERN IRELAND

—Consulatative papers related to the revision of the Children and Young Persons Act (Northern Ireland) 1968 / Department of Helath and Social Services. – Belfast : The Department, 1987.
17,11 leaves.
Contents: Consultative paper on regulation of child minding, group day care and care and maintenance of children - Consultative paper on employment of children.

—Family breakdown, children and the law / by Gilliam Kerr. – Belfast : SLS Legal Publications, 1985.
xii,68p.
Includes index.
ISBN 0853892555

CHILDREN – NORWAY

—Child welfare and social defence / Tove Stang Dahl : translated by Gunvor Nyquist. – Oslo : Norwegian University Press, 1985.
185p; 23cm.
Bibliography: p175-185. Translation and revision of: Barneven og samfunnsvern.
ISBN 8200071146 £19.45

CHILDREN – PAPUA NEW GUINEA

—Custody jurisdiction in Papua New Guinea / by Owen Jessep. – Waigani : Law Reform Commission of Papua New Guinea, 1987.
37p. – (LRC working paper).
Includes text of the Infants Act.

CHILDREN – SCOTLAND

—Children's Hearings and the Sheriff Court / London : Butterworths, 1987.
ISBN 0406105650 Hbk £41.00

—Legal capacity and responsibility of minors and pupils / Scottish Law Commission. – Edinburgh : The Commission, 1985.
280p. – (Consultative memorandum).
Includes bibliographical references.

—Report on the legal capacity and responsibility of minors and pupils / Scottish Law Commission. – Edinburgh : HMSO, 1987.
vi,93p.
Includes draft legislation.
ISBN 0102151881

—Social work and criminal law in Scotland / by George Moore and Chris Wood. – Aberdeen : Aberdeen University Press, 1981.
xii,208p; 26cm.
Provides information and guidance about those aspects of the judicial and penal systems and measures relating to child offenders which affect social workers. Chapters cover prosecution, social worker at court, social enquiry reports, non-custodial measures, probation, community service and unpaid work, and custodial measures. Includes bibliography and index.
ISBN 0080257313 Hbk No price

CHILDREN – SINGAPORE

—Parent-Child Law in Singapore / Singapore : Butterworths, 1984.
The book provides a discussion of legitimacy, maintenance, guardianship, and adoption under the law of Singapore. The 1980 amendments to the Women's Charter pertaining to maintenance, welfare and custody of children are analyzed in depth.
ISBN 0406181217 Pbk

—Parent-Child Law in Singapore / Butterworths, 1984.
251p.
Examines legitimacy, illegitimacy, legitimation, maintenance of children, guardianship of infants, adoption of children and the Women's Charter (Amendment) Act 1980.
ISBN 0406181217 Pbk £55.00

CHILDREN – SOUTH AFRICA

—Investigation into the advancement of the age of majority / South African Law Commission. – Pretoria : The Commission, 1984.
iv,36p. – (Project).
Bibliography: p.30-34.

—Law of parent and child / by Erwin Spiro. – 4th ed. – Cape Town : Juta, 1985.
lxv, 661 p.; 26 cm.
Includes bibliographical references and indexes.
ISBN 0702115746

—Recent extra-marital child legislation annotated : being also a cumulative supplement to the fourth edition of Spiro's Law of parent and child / Erwin Spiro. – Cape Town : Juta, 1988.
ix,20p.
Includes index.
ISBN 0702120510

CHILDREN (HINDU LAW)

—Hindu Minority and Guardianship : and Hindu Adoptions and Maintenance Act / 2nd ed. – Allahad : Law Book Company, 1986.
200p.

CHILE

—Chile : evidence of torture / Amnesty International. – London : Amnesty International Publications, 1983.
75p.
ISBN 0862100534

CHINA
—Justice and politics in People's China : legal order or continuing revolution? / James P. Brady. -- London : Academic Press, 1982.
xiii,268p; 24cm.
Includes index.
ISBN 0121247503 £17.80

CHURCH OF ENGLAND
—Canons of the Church of England : Canons Ecclesiastical promulgated by the Convocations of Canterbury and York in 1964 and 1969 and by the General Synod of the Church of England from 1970 / Church of England. – 4th ed. 1 v. – London : Church House Publishing, 1986.
looseleaf.
ISBN 0715137115

—Church of England Faculty Jurisdiction / Sweet & Maxwell, 1988.
ISBN 0421387602 Pbk £13.75

—English church and its laws 12th-14th centuries / C.R. Cheney. – London : Variorum Reprints, 1982.
348p in various pagings; 23cm. – (Collected studies series).
Includes index. Text in English and Latin.
ISBN 0860781089 Unpriced

—Select cases from the ecclesiastical courts of the Province of Canterbury, c.1200-1301 / edited for the Selden Society by Norma Adams and Charles Donahue Jr. – London : Selden Society, 1981.
xxx,119,756p.
Text in Latin and English.

CHURCH OF ENGLAND - ENGLAND
—Church and the English crown, 1305-1334 : a study based on the register of Archbishop Walter Reynolds / by J. Robert Wright. – Toronto, Ont. : Pontifical Institute of Mediaeval Studies, 1980.
xix, 472 p.; 26 cm. – (Studies and texts - Pontifical Institute of Mediaeval Studies).
Includes index. Bibliography: p. 415-440.
ISBN 0888440480

—Church courts, sex and marriage in England 1570-1640 / Cambridge : Cambridge University Press.
Examines the role of Elizabethan Church courts, their jurisdiction and the attitude of the people towards them. Based on records from courts in Wiltshire, Cambridgeshire, Leicestershire and West Sussex.
ISBN 0521232856

CHURCH RESTORATION - ENGLAND
—Property law : liability for chancel repairs / the Law Commission. – London : HMSO, 1985.
v,48p.
ISBN 0102039860

—Transfer of land : liability for chancel repairs / The Law Commission. – London : H.M.S.O., 1983.
vi,62p; 21cm. – (Working paper).
ISBN 0117301663

CITATION OF LEGAL AUTHORITY
—Ontario statute citator / R.S.O. 1970 ed. 2. – Agincourt, Ont. : Canada Law Book, 1975.
loose-leaf.

CITATION OF LEGAL AUTHORITY - AUSTRALIA
—Australian case citator / 1. – North Ryde, N.S.W. : The Law Book Co., 1983.
loose-leaf.
Kept up to date by quarterly cumulative supplements.
ISBN 0455204349

CITATION OF LEGAL AUTHORITY - CANADA
—Guide to Legal Citation : A Canadian Perspective in Common Law Provinces / Toronto : DeBoo, 1984.
190p.
This guide, designed to provide a basis for developing an accurate and consistent citation style in legal writing, features 'citation-style-at-a-glance' diagrams for quick reference.
ISBN 0888201591 Pbk £10.95

—Patterns of authority : an analysis of Canadian citation patterns / by Lorna K. Rees-Potter. – Ontario : Canadian Law Information Council, 1982.
vii,61p. – (Working paper).
ISBN 092035825X

—Tremeear's 1971-1986 criminal annotations / by Leonard J. Ryan : 1985 and 1986 annotations by F. Dwight Richardson. – 2. – Toronto : Carswell, 1986.
Includes index. Kept up to date by annual supplement. Companion volumes to Tremeear's criminal code. Supplement to: Tremeear's annotated criminal code. 6th ed..

—Tremeear's criminal annotations 1964-1970 / being the permanent supplement to the sixth edition of Tremeear's annotated criminal code by Leonard J. Ryan. – Toronto : Carswell, 1981.
xxvi,361p.
Includes index.
ISBN 0459344803

CITATION OF LEGAL AUTHORITY - CANADA - ALBERTA
—Statutes of Alberta judicially considered / R.S.A. 1980 ed. 1 v. – Calgary : Carswell, 1985.
looseleaf.
Previous ed.: 1977-1980.

CITATION OF LEGAL AUTHORITY - CANADA - BRITISH COLUMBIA
—British Columbia statute citator : a complete annotating service for R.S.B.C. / 1. – Agincourt, Ontario : Canada Law Book Co., 1960.
looseleaf.

CITATION OF LEGAL AUTHORITY - CANADA - ONTARIO
—Ontario statute citator / R.S.O. 1980 ed. 2. – Agincourt, Ont. : Canada Law Book, 1981.
loose-leaf.

CITATION OF LEGAL AUTHORITY - GREAT BRITAIN
—Current law / . – London : Sweet & Maxwell, 1947.

—Current law case citator / . – London : Sweet & Maxwell, 1977.
Kept up to date by annual Current law citator.

—Current law citator / . – London : Sweet & Maxwell, 1947.
Updates Current law statute citator and Current law case citator.

—Current law statute citator / . – London : Sweet & Maxwell, 1972.
Kept up to date by annual Current law citator.

—Current law year book : being a complete statement of all the law... from every source / – London : Sweet & Maxwell, 1948.
Cumulation of monthly Current law. 1947-1951 superseded by Current law consolidation. Master volumes for 1956, 1961, 1966 and 1971.

—Scottish current law / . – Edinburgh : W. Green, 1948.
Contains both Scottish and English law.
ISBN 02656159

—Scottish current law case citator / . – Edinburgh : W. Green, 1977.
Kept up to date by annual Scottish current law citator. Contains both Scottish and English law.

—Scottish current law citator / . – Edinburgh : W. Green, 1948.
Updates Scottish current law statute citator and Scottish current law case citator. Contains both Scottish and English law.

—Scottish current law statute citator / . – Edinburgh : W. Green, 1972.
Kept up to date by annual Scottish current law citator. Contains both Scottish and English law.

—Scottish current law year book : being a complete statement of all the law.. from every source / – Edinburgh : W. Green, 1948.
Cumulation of monthly Scottish current law. Master volumes for 1956, 1961, 1966 and 1971. Contains both Scottish and English law.
ISBN 03087166

CITATION OF LEGAL AUTHORITY - HONG KONG
—Hong Kong current law / London : Sweet & Maxwell, 1986.

—Hong Kong law yearbook / London : Sweet & Maxwell, 1985-.

CITATION OF LEGAL AUTHORITY - SCOTLAND
—Scottish current law / . – Edinburgh : W. Green, 1948.
Contains both Scottish and English law.
ISBN 02656159

—Scottish current law case citator / . – Edinburgh : W. Green, 1977.
Kept up to date by annual Scottish current law citator. Contains both Scottish and English law.

—Scottish current law citator / . – Edinburgh : W. Green, 1948.
Updates Scottish current law statute citator and Scottish current law case citator. Contains both Scottish and English law.

—Scottish current law statute citator / . – Edinburgh : W. Green, 1972.
Kept up to date by annual Scottish current law citator. Contains both Scottish and English law.

—Scottish current law year book : being a complete statement of all the law.. from every source / – Edinburgh : W. Green, 1948.
Cumulation of monthly Scottish current law. Master volumes for 1956, 1961, 1966 and 1971. Contains both Scottish and English law.
ISBN 03087166

CITATIONS
—Index to legal citations and abbreviations / by Donald Raistrick. – Abingdon : Professional Books, 1981.
10, 326p. – (Professional Books Law Reference Library).
ISBN 0862050375

—Index to Legal Citations and Abbreviations / London : Butterworths, 1981.
ISBN 0862050375 Hbk £30.25

—Law Reports Citator / London : LLoyd's of London Press, 1988.

CITATIONS - AUSTRALIA
—Australian and New Zealand Citator to UK Reports 1588-1972 / Wellington : Butterworths.
ISBN 0409303100 Pbk

CITATIONS - CANADA
—Canada Statute Annotations (1941-1971) R.S.C. / 1970 Ed. – Aurora : Canada Law Book Co.
523p. – (Statute Services).

—Canada Tax Cases Index and Citator : Consolidated from 1972 / Toronto : DeBoo, 1983.
ISBN 0888201486 Hbk £95.00

—Canadian Abridgment / Agincourt : Carswell.

—Canadian Criminal Cases : Index, Annotations, Table of Cases / Aurora : Canada Law Book Co, 1985.
– (Law Reports).

Vols. 1-70 of Second Series 1983.
1184p. – (Law Reports).

—Canadian Criminal Cases New Series (1963-1970), 30 Vols. / Aurora : Canada Law Book Co.
– (Law Reports).

Back Vols.

—Canadian Criminal Cases Old Series (1898-1962), 133 Vols. / Aurora : Canada Law Book Co.
– (Law Reports).

Back vols.

—Canadian Criminal Cases Second Series (1971-1983), 70 Vols. / Aurora : Canada Law Book Co.
– (Law Reports).

Back Vols.

—Canadian Criminal Cases Third Series (March 1983-Present) / Aurora : Canada Law Book Co.
– (Law Reports).

Bound Vol.

—Canadian Guide to Uniform Legal Citation / McGill Law Journal. – 2nd ed. – Agincourt : Carswell, 1988.
288p.

—Criminal Code Annotations : 1964-1970. / Agincourt : Carswell, 1981.
388p.

—Manitoba Decisions Citator (1981-Present) / Aurora : Canada Law Book Co.
– (Statute Services).

CITATIONS - CANADA - ALBERTA
—Alberta Decisions Citator (1981-Present) / Aurora : Canada Law Book Co.
– (Statute Services).

CITATIONS - CANADA - BRITISH COLUMBIA
—British Columbia Rules Citator (1977-Present) / Aurora : Canada Law Book Co.
– (Statute Services).

—British Columbia Statute Citator (1979-Present) / Aurora : Canada Law Book Co.
– (Statute Services).

CITATIONS - CANADA - NEW BRUNSWICK
—New Brunswick Statute Citator / Agincourt : Carswell, 1987.
1250p.
This single volume looseleaf text contains the legislative history of all the Acts in the Revised Statutes of New Brunswick, 1973 and all of the Public General Statutes enacted subsequently. This is a helpful research tool. Cases interpreting portions of the statutes are digested.

—New Brunswick Statute Citator / Agincourt : Carswell, 1987.
ca 1,250p.

CITATIONS - CANADA - NOVA SCOTIA
—Nova Scotia Statute Citator / Agincourt : Carswell, 1985.
610p.
This work focuses on the Revised Statutes of Nova Scotia 1967. It contains the amendments, repeals and consolidation of all public statutes of Nova Scotia since 1967. The statutes are annotated. Brief digests of the interpreting caselaw are included.

CITATIONS - CANADA - ONTARIO

—Ontario Statute Annotations (R.S.O. 1980 Edition) 1930-80 / Aurora : Canada Law Book Co.
1000p.

—Ontario Statute Annotations, R.S.O. 1980 Edition / North Ryde : Law Book Co.
ca 1,000p.

—Ontario Statute Citator Current Bills Service / Canada Law Book Publisher. – Aurora : Canada Law Book Co.

—Ontario Statute Citator (O.S.C.) R.S.O. 1980 Edition : 1980-Present / Aurora : Canada Law Book Co.

Binders and Contents

CITATIONS - CANADA - SASKATCHEWAN

—Saskatchewan Decisions Citator / Aurora : Canada Law Book Co.

CITATIONS - GREAT BRITAIN

—Lloyd's Law Reporter : Citator and Subject Index 1987-1988 / London : LLoyd's of London Press, 1989.
ISBN 1850442134 Pbk

—Lloyd's Law Reports : Citator 1919-1986 / London : LLoyd's of London Press, 1988.
ISBN 1850441707 Hbk

—New Abridgment of the Law : 1736-1766, 5 Vols. / Abingdon : Professional Books.

CITATIONS - NEW ZEALAND

—Australian and New Zealand Citator to UK Reports 1588-1972 / Wellington : Butterworths.
ISBN 0409303100 Pbk

—Butterworth's Cases Annotations to the New Zealand Statutes Reprint : 1908-1964 / Professional Books Staff. – Abingdon : Professional Books, 1984.

CITIES AND TOWNS

—Cities in the developing world : policies for their equitable and efficient growth / Johannes F. Linn. – Oxford : Published for the World Bank by Oxford University Press, 1983.
xxi,230p; 24cm.
Bibliography: p213-223. - Includes index.
ISBN 0195203828 Hbk Unpriced
ISBN 0195203836 Pbk Unpriced

CITIES AND TOWNS - CANADA

—City of North York Act, 1983, Bill Pr051 : An Act Respecting the City of North York / Ontario : Ontario Government Publications Service, 1983.
6p.

—City of Owen Sound Act, 1983, Bill Pr053 : An Act Respecting the City of Owen Sound / Ontario : Ontario Government Publications Service, 1983.
2p.

—City of Sault Ste. Marie Act, 1983, Bill Pr048 : An Act Respecting the City of Sault Ste. Marie / Ontario : Ontario Government Publications Service, 1983.
2p.

—City of Toronto Act, 1983, Bill Pr036 : An Act Respecting the City of Toronto / Ontario : Ontario Government Publications Service, 1983.
1p.

CITIES AND TOWNS - SOUTH AFRICA

—Commission of Inquiry into Township Establishment and Related Matters / Pretoria : Government Printer, 1984.
2 v.; 30 cm.
Title on added t.p.: Kommissie van Ondersoek na Dorpstigting en Verwante Aangeleenthede. First and second reports of the commission.
ISBN 0621084395 pbk. : v. 2 R3.50 (R4.00 other countries)

CITIZEN SUITS (CIVIL PROCEDURE) - AUSTRALIA

—Standing in public interest litigation / Law Reform Commission. – Canberra : Australian Government Publishing Service, 1985.
xxx,273p. – (Report).
Bibliography: p.259-263 - Includes index.
ISBN 0644013109

CITIZENS' ASSOCIATIONS - ENGLAND

—Case for advice centres / N. Ralph. – Sheffield : Sheffield Advice Centres Group, 1985.
34p.

CITIZENS' ASSOCIATIONS - GREAT BRITAIN

—Review of the National Association of Citizens Advice Bureaux / chairman, Sir Douglas Lovelock : presented to Parliament by the Secretary of State for Trade and Industry ... February 1984. – London : H.M.S.O., 1984.
iii,91p; 25cm.
ISBN 0101913907

CITIZENSHIP

—British nationality law : AGIN full briefing on the white paper, Cmnd. 7987 ... / the Action Group on Immigration and Nationality. – London : the Group, 1980.
12p; 30cm.
Supplement (2p.): New points in the British Nationality Bill 1981.

—Citizenship, aliens and immigration : being Title 27 from Volume 4 of the Canadian encyclopedic digest (Ontario) 3rd ed. / Janet V. Scott, Robert C. Stonehouse. – Agincourt, Ont. : Carswell, 1980.
154p; 24cm.
Includes index. Contents: Immigration / by Janet V. Scott. - Citizenship and aliens / by Robert C. Stonehouse.
ISBN 0459331108

CITIZENSHIP - AUSTRALIA

—Australian Citizenship Act, 1948 / Human Rights Commission. – Canberra : Australian Government Publishing Service, 1982.
27p.
ISBN 0644021373 Hbk £1.80

—Australian citizenship law / by Michael Pryles. – Sydney : Law Book Co., 1981.
xxv,271p.
Includes index.
ISBN 0455203598

—Citizenship, Review and Appeals System : Report, 13 June 1980 / Administrative Review Tribunal. – Canberra : Australian Government Publishing Service, 1981.
8p.
ISBN 0642066981 Hbk £0.40

CITIZENSHIP - GREAT BRITAIN

—British Nationality / Martin. – 2nd ed. – London : CENT, 1984.
ISBN 0946088101 Pbk £2.95

—British nationality and the right of abode 1945-1983 / by K.J. Gray : by C.C. Turpin. – Deventer : Kluwer, 1986.
vii,269p.
Includes bibliographical references.
ISBN 9065442510

—British Nationality Law / London : Fourmat, 1988.
ISBN 1851900381 Pbk

—British Nationality Law / Repr. of 1956 ed. – Aalen Wuertt : Scientia.
xxviii, 306p.

—British Nationality Law / 2nd ed. – London : Fourmat, 1986.
ISBN 1851900020 Pbk £12.95

—British Nationality Law : outline of proposed legislation / Home Office .. – London : H.M.S.O., 1980.
2,ii,33p; 25cm.
ISBN 0101798709 sd £2.25

—British nationality : the new law / by Ivor Stanbrook. – London : Clement, 1982.
xxiii,213p; 23cm.
Includes text of the act.
ISBN 0907027024 £9.50

—British nationality : the report of a working party : a report / by JUSTICE : chairman, Sir Amar Maini. – London : JUSTICE, 1980.
vii, 54p; 22cm.
ISBN 0950524778

—Delinquency and Citizenship / Oxford : Oxford University Press, 1987.
ISBN 0198226640 Hbk £30.00

—Immigration and Nationality : Statutes and Rules / Beg. – London : Shaw & Sons, 1988.
ISBN 072191120X Pbk

—Ins and outs of immigration and nationality law / Lowe. – London : CENT, 1983.
ISBN 0906072050 Pbk £4.95

—New nationality law / Blake. – London : Butterworths, 1982.
ISBN 0406282803 Hbk £21.50

—New nationality law / Ian A. Macdonald and Nicholas Blake. – London : Butterworths, 1982.
208p; 26cm.
This book provides a thorough discussion of the British Nationality Act of 1981. The three new categories of citizenship: British Citizenship, Citizenship of the British Dependent Territories, and British Overseas Citizenship are analyzed in detail.
ISBN 0406282803 Hbk £21.50

—Property, divorce and retirement pension rights / by K.J. Gray : by C.C. Turpin. – Deventer : Kluwer, 1986.
vii,269p.
Includes bibliographical references.
ISBN 9065442510

—Proposed British nationality law : summary of White Paper / Great Britain. – London : The Commission, 1980.
6p.

—Proposed nationality law : Commission for Racial Equality's comments on the government's White Paper on British nationality law : submitted to the Home Office in October 1980 / Great Britain. – London : The Commission, 1980.
4p.
Bound with: Proposed British nationality law: summary of White Paper.

—Tables of persons acquiring citizenship of the United Kingdom and Colonies 1980 / Home Office. – London : H.M.S.O., 1981.
12p.
ISBN 0101832508

CITIZENSHIP - HONG KONG

—Nationality provisions of the Hong Kong Act 1985 : a draft Order-in-Council / presented to Parliament by the Secretary of State for the Home Department. – London : H.M.S.O., 1985.
19p.
ISBN 010196370X

CITIZENSHIP - INDIA

—Law of Citizenship and Passports : with All Allied Laws / 5th ed. – Allahabad : Law Book Company, 1987.
400p.

—Law of Foreigners and Citizenship ... / 3rd ed. – Allahabad : Law Publishers, 1983.

—Law Relating to Foreigners, Passports and Citizenship in India / 6th ed. – Lucknow : Eastern Book Company, 1985.

CITIZENSHIP - USSR

—Citizenship law of the USSR / by George Ginsburgs. – The Hague : M. Nijhoff Publishers, 1984.
xii,394p.
Includes index. Bibliography: p379-390.
ISBN 9024728630 Hbk

CITIZENSHIP (INTERNATIONAL LAW)

—Regulation of nationality in international law / Ruth Donner. – Helsinki : The Finnish Society of Sciences and Letters, 1983.
287p.
Bibliography: p273-284.
ISBN 9516531172

CIVIL DEFENCE (INTERNATIONAL LAW)

—New international status of civil defence : as an instrument for strengthening the protection of human rights / Bosko Jakovljevic. – The Hague : M. Nijhoff Publishers, 1982.
142p.
Includes bibliographical references and index.
ISBN 9024725674

CIVIL ENGINEERING - GREAT BRITAIN

—Building and Civil Engineering Claims / 3rd ed. – London : Estates Gazette, 1985.
ISBN 0728200775 Hbk £26.00

—Building and Civil Engineering Claims In Perspective / 2nd ed. – London : Longman Professional, 1986.
ISBN 0582494702 Hbk £29.00

—Civil Engineering Claims / Stephenson. – Oxford : Blackwell Scientific, 1987.
ISBN 0003830594 Hbk £25.00

—Civil Engineering Contracts : Practice and Procedure / D. S. de Silva. – London : Butterworths, 1982.
ISBN 0408005262 Hbk

—Law for Civil Engineers / London : Collins, 1987.
280p.
ISBN 0003832570 Hbk £19.50

CIVIL LAW

—Commentaries on some detached branches of the law of Scotland / By George Joseph Bell. – Edinburgh : Blackwood, 1828.
217p.
Originally published: in the 5th ed. of the author's Commentaries on the laws of Scotland, and on the principles of mercantile jurisprudence (1826).

—History and principles of Roman Private law / London : Butterworths, 1984.
ISBN 0409060631 Pbk £28.50

—Legal Cooperation in Europe in the Fields of Civil, Commercial and International Law (1957-82) / Strasbourg : Council of Europe, 1983.
ISBN 9287101698

—Principles of Scottish private law / by David M. Walker. – 3rd ed. – Oxford : Clarendon Press, 1983.
cii,698p; 24cm.
Previous ed.: 1975. Bibliography: pxcviii-cii. - Includes index.
ISBN 0198761333 Unpriced

Bk.5 : Law of property / by David M. Walker. – 1983.
lxxvii,608p; 24cm.
Previous ed. published in 2v.: 1975. Bibliography: plxxiii-lxxvii. - Includes index.
ISBN 0198761341 £30.00

Vol.1 / by David M. Walker. - 1982.
lxxvii,482p; 24cm.
Previous ed.: 1975. Includes index.
ISBN 0198761325 £25.00

CIVIL LAW - AUSTRALIA

—Australian civil procedure / Bernard C. Cairns. - 2nd ed. - Sydney : Law Book Company, 1985.
lxvi,584p.
ISBN 0455206260

CIVIL LAW - CANADA

—Canadian Civil Procedure / G. D. Watson. - 3rd ed. - Aurora : Canada Law Book Co, 1988.
950p.
The new third edition of Canadian Civil Procedure is a comprehensive collection of materials on civil procedure with extensive notes, comments and citations. The authors are four leading academics, who examine the full range of procedural topics from pleadings and discovery to res judicata, issue estoppel, legal ethics and legal theory.

—Canadian Civil Procedure / Watson. - 3rd ed. - Aurora : Canada Law Book, 1988.

—Charter Issues in Civil Cases / Brian MacLeod Rogers. - Agincourt : Carswell, 1988.
327p.

—Civil Litigation / 2nd ed. - Agincourt : Carswell, 1986.
ISBN 045938600 Hbk £21.00

—Civil Litigation : A Practical Handbook / 2nd ed. - Agincourt : Carswell, 1986.
286p.
This book presents a guide to modern civil litigation in Canada for the practitioner. Each step in the preparation of a case is accompanied by checklist and sample forms.

—Civil Litigation for Legal Assistants 1986 / Vancouver : Continuing Legal Education Society of British Columbia, 1986.
538p.
ISBN 0865042713 Hbk £65.00

Supplement-1987
162p.
ISBN 0865043272 £60.00

—Civil Litigation in the Public Interest / Victoria : Government of British Columbia, 1980.

—Domaine et L'Interpretation du Code Civil du Bas-Canada / Toronto : Butterworths, 1980.
141p.
ISBN 0409871729 Hbk £22.95

—Preparing and Presenting a Civil Case / Vancouver : British Columbia Continuing Legal Education Society, 1984.
103p.
ISBN 0865041687 Hbk £55.00

—Rules of Civil Procedure : A Guide for Legal Secretaries and Law Clerks / Toronto : Butterworths, 1985.
196p.
Summarizes and explains the various sections of the Courts of Justice Act and the new Rules. Contains special chapters on divorce, family law, and mortgage action proceedings.
ISBN 0409810304 Pbk £24.95

—Scope and Interpretation of the Civil Code of Lower Canada / Butterworths, 1980.
138p.
ISBN 0409871710 Pbk £21.95

—Weekly Digest of Civil Procedure / Agincourt : Carswell, 1987.

CIVIL LAW - CANADA - ONTARIO

—Ontario Annual Practice / Aurora : Canada Law Book Co.
- (Text Books-Civil).

CIVIL LAW - CANADA - QUEBEC

—Codes civils - The Civil Codes / by Lise Saintonge-Poitevin. - Reedition a jour au 1er dec. 1982. 1. - Montreal : Wilson & Lafleur, 1982-.
Previous ed.: 1978. Includes indexes.
ISBN 2891270177 LLF

CIVIL LAW - CHINA

—China's civil and commercial law / Henry R. Zheng. - Singapore : Butterworths, 1988.
lii,490p; 26cm.
Presents an overview of chinese laws and legislative structure, a review of the major principles of the Civil Code, and an examination of the different facets of Chinese business law. Covers principles of civil law, contract law, banking law, insurance law, and foreign investment law.
ISBN 040999555X Hbk £142.50

—China's Civil and Commercial Law / London : Butterworths, 1988.
ISBN 040999555X Hbk £65.00

CIVIL LAW - CZECHOSLOVAKIA

—Commentary on the Czechoslovak civil code / by Th. J. Vondracek. - Dordrecht : Nijhoff, 1988.
504p.
Includes index.
ISBN 9024736692 Hbk £235.00

CIVIL LAW - ENGLAND

—Bar finals guide / Catherine Newman. - 3rd ed. - London : Sweet & Maxwell, 1987.
300p; 23cm.
Previous ed.: 1984. Includes index.
ISBN 0421359102 Pbk £14.50

—Civil jurisdiction and judgments : the application in England of the convention on jurisdiction and the enforcement of judgments in civil and commercial matters under the Civil Jurisdiction and Judgments Act 1982 / by T.C. Hartley. - London : Sweet & Maxwell, 1984.
xxi,233p; 25cm.
Includes index.
ISBN 0421311800 Pbk £18.00

—Fabric of English Civil Justice (Hamlyn 38) / London : Sweet & Maxwell, 1987.
ISBN 0420475303 Hbk £18.50
ISBN 0420475400 Pbk £9.95

—Sources of English legal history : private law to 1750 / (compiled by) J.H. Baker, S.F.C. Milsom. - London : Butterworths, 1986.
xl,698p; 22cm.
Includes index.
ISBN 0406016402 Hbk £35.00
ISBN 0406016410 Pbk £20.00

CIVIL LAW - EUROPE

—Legal Co-operation in Europe in the Fields of Civil, Commercial and International Law 1957-82 / Council of Europe. - London : HMSO, 1983.
112p.
ISBN 9287101698 Pbk £3.90

CIVIL LAW - EUROPEAN COMMUNITY

—Quest for security : employees, tenants, wives / by Tony Honore. - London : Stevens, 1982.
xiv,128p; 19cm.
Includes index.
ISBN 0420464107 Hbk £12.00
ISBN 0420464204 Pbk £5.80

CIVIL LAW - GREAT BRITAIN

—Citizen 16 : The Civil Law and You / London : Macmillan, 1986.
ISBN 0333367944 Pbk £6.95

—Civil Court in Action / 2nd ed. - London : Butterworths, 1985.
ISBN 0406556229 Hbk £21.00
ISBN 0406556237 Pbk £14.95

—Civil Jurisdiction and Judgments Act 1982 / London : Butterworths, 1983.
ISBN 0406005303 Hbk £32.50

—Civil Litigation - a Practice Guide for Advocates / London : Butterworths, 1985.
ISBN 0409492345 Hbk £28.00

—Institutions of Private Law and Their Social Functions / London : Sweet & Maxwell.
ISBN 0710083025 Hbk £16.95

—Recent and Prospective Developments in Civil and Criminal Litigation / London : Law Society, 1985.
32p. - (Nineteen Eighty-Five Crash Course Transcripts).

CIVIL LAW - HONG KONG

—Report : young persons : effects of age in civil law / the Law Reform Commission of Hong Kong. - Hong Kong : The Commission, 1986.
various pagings. - (Topic 11).

CIVIL LAW - INDIA

—Civil Litigation / Calcutta : Eastern Law House.

—Manual of Civil Laws, 4 Vols. / Allahabad : Law Publishers, 1983.

—Mitra's Civil Reference / 2nd ed. - Calcutta : Eastern Law House.

CIVIL LAW - JAPAN

—Civil Code of Japan / translated by Fukio Nakane. - Tokyo : Eibun Horei Sha, 1981.
iv,179,16p.
'Under authorization of the Ministry of Justice & the Codes Translation Committee'.

CIVIL LAW - MALAYSIA

—Civil Law Act, 1956 (Act 67) / Kuala Lumpur : International Law Books Services.

CIVIL LAW - NIGERIA

—Essays on Civil Proceedings, 4 Vols. / Enugu : Fourth Dimension Publishing, 1981.
ISBN 9781561637 Hbk

Vol. 1
240p.
ISBN 9781562277 Hbk £25.00

Vol. 2
168p.
ISBN 9781562447 Hbk £15.00

CIVIL LAW - NORTHERN IRELAND

—Access to Justice and Civil Litigation in Northern Ireland / Desmond S. Greer. - Belfast : Queen's University of Belfast.
76p.

CIVIL LAW - PHILIPPINES

—Answers to Bar Examination Questions / Quezon City : University of the Philippines, Law Center, 1982.
148p.

—Civil Code of the Phillippines / National Book Store. - Manila : National Book Store, 1980.
615p.
ISBN 9710816446 Pbk £3.50

CIVIL LAW - SCOTLAND

—The Civil Evidence (Scotland) Act 1988 / Edinburgh : W Green & Son, 1989.
Annotated text of the Act from Scottish Current Law Statutes, which introduced far-reaching changes to the law of evidence in civil proceedings, including the abolition of the requirement of cooroboration, the admission of hearsay, and authenticated business records.
ISBN 0414008650

—Civil jurisdiction in Scotland / by A.E. Anton. - Edinburgh : W. Green, 1984.
xxiii,306p; 24cm.
Kept up to date by supplements.
ISBN 0414007360

—Principles of Scottish private law / Oxford : Oxford University Press, 1983.
ISBN 019876735X Hbk £30.00

Vol. 1: Introductory international private law, law of persons / by David M. Walker. - 1988.
584; 24cm.
Previous ed.: 1982. Includes index.
ISBN 0198762151 £40.00

Bk.5 : Law of property / by David M. Walker. - 1988.
cxi,595p.
Previous ed: 1983. Includes index.
ISBN 0198762178 £40.00

Vol. 2 1983.
ISBN 0198761333 Hbk £32.50

Vol. 2: Obligations / by David M. Walker. - 1988.
816; 24cm.
Previous ed.: 1982. Includes index. Volume 1 contains an outline of the sources, scope and literature of Scottish private law and discusses fundamental legal concepts and basic doctrines. Volume 2 gives a statement of the principles and rules of the private law of Scotland and specifically examines the law of obligations.
ISBN 019876216X Hbk £40.00

Vol.4 / by David M. Walker. - 1983.
lxix,421p; 24cm.
Previous ed.: 1975. Includes index. Contents: bk.VI. Law of trusts - bk.VII. Law of succession - bk.VIII. Law of civil remedies - bk.IX. Law of diligence - bk.X. Law of insolvency.
ISBN 019876135X Hbk £25.00.

Vol. 4 1983.
ISBN 0198761341 Hbk £32.50

—Report of the Scottish Committee on Jurisdiction and Enforcement / chairman : Lord Maxwell. - Edinburgh : H.M.S.O., 1980.
xii,371p; 21cm.
ISBN 0114916667 Pbk £7.50

—Scottish civil law reports / Edinburgh : Law Society of Scotland, 1987-.
Includes index.

CIVIL LAW - UNITED STATES

—Readings in Ohio Civil Procedure / Agincourt : Carswell, 1987.
1216p.
This text analyzes and discusses common problems often not focused on in texts on this subject. The information is presented in a series of articles of varying length.

CIVIL LAW - USSR

—Soviet civil law / by Olimpiad S. Ioffe. - Dordrecht : M. Nijhoff, 1988.
392p.
Includes index.
ISBN 9024736765 Hbk £205.00

CIVIL LAW - WEST GERMANY

—German private and commercial law : an introduction / by Norbert Horn, Hein Kotz and Hans G. Leser : translated by Tony Weir. - Oxford : Clarendon, 1982.
xvi,355p; 22cm.
Bibliography: p332-334. - Includes index. Translation from the German.
ISBN 0198253826 Hbk £16.50
ISBN 0198253834 Pbk Unpriced

—German Private and Commercial Law-Introduction / Kote. - Oxford : Oxford University Press, 1982.
ISBN 0198253826 Hbk £27.00
ISBN 0198253834 Pbk £15.00

CIVIL PROCEDURE - ENGLAND

—Stephen's commentaries on the laws of England / L. Crispin Warmington. - 21st ed. - London : Butterworths, 1950.
xiv,603p.
Index included in Vol. 4. .

CIVIL SERVICE

—Employer-employee relations in the public service of Canada : proposals for legislative change / J. Finkelman. – 4 v. – Ottawa : Information Canada, 1974.
Includes bibliographical references. Contents: Parts 1-3 - Supplementary observations and recommendations. Parallel English and French texts, Part 3 and Supplementary observations and recommendations.

—Freedom of Association and Procedures for Determining Conditions of Employment in the Public Service : Report 7. Sixty-Third Session of the International Labour Conference, 1977 / Geneva : International Labour Office.
iv, 111p.
ISBN 9221015750 Hbk £17.50

Part 1: Proposed Texts Referred to Governments
45p.

Part 2: Replies of Governments
41p.
ISBN 9221017559 Hbk £12.50

Part 2: Replies of Governments
84p.
ISBN 9221015769 Hbk £17.50

CIVIL SERVICE - EUROPE

—Britons in Brussels : Officials in the European Commission and Council Secretariat / London : Policy Studies Institute, 1983.
ISBN 0853742170 Pbk £3.00

CIVIL SERVICE - GREAT BRITAIN

—Ninth report on top salaries / Review Body on Top Salaries : Chairman, Lord Plowden. – London : H.M.S.O., 1986.
v,31p. – (Report).
ISBN 0101978502

—Purging of the Civil Service / National Council for Civil Liberties. – London : National Council for Civil Liberties, 1985.
20p.
ISBN 0946088179

CIVIL SERVICE - INDIA

—Bombay Civil Services Rules Explained / 7th rev. ed. 1980 rep,. – Nagpur : Wadhura & Co, 1984.

—Civil Service Rules : With Classified Extracts from Judgements and Decisions of the Supreme Court and High Courts in India, Govt of India's Orders, Instructions and Interpretations with Index / Bombay : N.M. Khosla & Co., 1988.

—Commentaries on U.P. Government Servants' Conduct Rules, 1956 / 3rd ed. – Lucknow : Eastern Book Company, 1983.
163p.

—Disciplinary Action Against Government Servants and its Remedies / 5th ed. – Lucknow : Eastern Book Company, 1985.
1,239p.

CIVIL SERVICE PENSIONS - LAW AND LEGISLATION - AUSTRALIA

—Review of the Commonwealth Superannuation Scheme : a report to the Minister for Finance / by E.S. Knight & Co. – Canberra : Australian Government Publishing Service, 1983.
28p.
ISBN 0644027363

CIVILIZATION, MODERN

—Standard of 'civilization' in international society / Gerrit W. Gong. – Oxford : Clarendon, 1984.
xvi,267p; 23cm.
Bibliography: p251-261. - Includes index.
ISBN 0198219482 £19.50

CLAIMS

—United States law of sovereign immunity relating to international financial transactions / John R. Stevenson, Jeffrey F. Browne and Lori Fisler Damrosch. – London : Euromoney Pubns, 1983.
158p.
Includes bibliographical references.
ISBN 090312145X

CLAIMS - AUSTRALIA - NEW SOUTH WALES

—Guidebook to Civil Claims in New South Wales / North Ryde : C.C.H. Australia, 1986.
470p.
ISBN 0869039865 Hbk £38.00

CLAIMS - CANADA

—Motor Carrier Cargo Claims / Agincourt : Carswell, 1986.
222p.

—Motor Vehicle Accident Claims : 1983 / Vancouver : British Columbia Continuing Legal Education Society.

CLAIMS - INDIA

—Law of Claims / Allahabad : Law Book Company, 1981.
Includes 1986 supplement.

CLAIMS - IRAN

—Iran-United States Claims Tribunal Reports / . – Cambridge : Grotius Publications, 1983.

CLAIMS - UNITED STATES

—Iran-United States Claims Tribunal Reports / . – Cambridge : Grotius Publications, 1983.

CLASS ACTIONS - CANADA - ONTARIO

—Report on class actions / Ontario Law Reform Commission. – 3. – Toronto : Ministry of the Attorney General, 1982.
880p.
ISBN 0774370890

CLASSIFICATION

—Card catalog of the Peace Palace at the Hague; classification scheme of the systematic catalog / Peace Palace. – 1. – New York : Clearwater, 1980.
various pagings.
With introduction by Warren F. Kuehl. With second copy of classification scheme.

CLASSIFICATION OF CRIMES - CANADA

—Classification of offences / Law Reform Commission of Canada. – Ottawa : The Commission, 1986.
92,98p. – (Working paper).
Includes bibliographical references. Pages numbered in opposite directions. Text in English and French.
ISBN 0662545699

CLASSIFICATION OF CRIMES - NIGERIA

—Law of Crimes / Zaria : Ahmadu Bello University Press.

CLAUSES (LAW) - AUSTRALIA - TASMANIA

—Report and recommendations relating to exclusion clauses and implied obligations in contracts for the supply of goods and services / Law Reform Commission of Tasmania. – Hobart : Government Printer, 1983.
23p. – (Report).

CLIMATIC CHANGES

—World environment 1972-1982 : a report / by the United Nations Environment Programme : edited by Martin W. Holdgate, Mohammed Kassas, Gilbert F. White with the assistance of David Spurgeon : study co-ordinator Essam El-Hinnawi. – Dublin : Published for the United Nations Environment Programme by Tycooly International, 1982.
xxxii,637p; 25cm.
Includes bibliographies and index.
ISBN 0907567134 Hbk Unpriced
ISBN 0907567142 Pbk Unpriced

CLOSED SHOP - GREAT BRITAIN

—Closed shop agreements and arrangements : code of practice / Great Britain. – London : The Department, 1983.
24p.

—Employers' Guide to the Closed Shop / London : Engineering Employers Federation, 1983.
20p.

—Legal immunities of trade unions and other related matters : draft codes of practice on picketing and the closed shop : record report from the Employment Committee, Session 1979-80 / London : H.M.S.O., 1980.
viiip; 25cm.
ISBN 0100282296 unbound £1.10

CLUBS - AUSTRALIA

—Law of domestic or private tribunals / by J.R.S. Forbes. – Sydney : Law Book, 1982.
xxviii, 247 p.; 22 cm.
Includes index.
ISBN 0455204551 pbk.

CLUBS - ENGLAND

—Law of clubs : with a note on unincorporated associations / J.F. Josling, Lionel Alexander. – 6th ed. – London : Longman, 1987.
242p; 24cm. – (Longman practitioner series).
Previous ed.: London : Oyez Longman, 1984. Includes index.
ISBN 0851212972 Pbk £26.50

—Law of clubs : with a note on unincorporated associations / J.F. Josling, Lionel Alexander. – 4th ed. – London : Oyez, 1981.
xl,235p; 24cm. – (Oyez practitioner series).
Previous ed.: 1975. Includes index.
ISBN 0851205828 Pbk Unpriced

CLUBS - GREAT BRITAIN

—Accounts, Audit and Taxation of Clubs / London : Butterworths, 1983.

—Taxation of clubs and voluntary associations / Croydon : Tolley, 1988.
ISBN 0854593179 Hbk £11.95

COAL

—Coal utilisation : technology, economics and policy / L. Grainger and J. Gibson. – London : Graham & Trotman, 1981.
xxii,503p; 25cm.
Bibliography: p489-496. - Includes index.
ISBN 0860102661 £18.00

COASTAL ZONE MANAGEMENT

—Coastal area management and development / United Nations Department of International Economic and Social Affairs, Ocean Economics and Technology Branch. – Oxford : Pergamon, 1982.
xii,188p; 24cm.
ISBN 0080233937 Pbk £20.00

—International journal of estuarine and coastal law / London : Graham & Trotman, 1986-.

COASTAL ZONE MANAGEMENT - ASIA

—Environmental protection and coastal zone management in Asia and the Pacific / edited by Ichiro Kato ... et al. – Tokyo : University of Tokyo Press, 1985.
xi,244p.
Includes bibliographies and index.
ISBN 0860083926

COASTAL ZONE MANAGEMENT - GREAT BRITAIN

—Waters around the British Isles : their conflicting uses : report of a study group of the David Davies Memorial Institute of International Studies / R.B. Clark. – Oxford : Clarendon, 1987.
xvi,386p; 24cm.
Includes index.
ISBN 0198284926 £32.50

COFFEE

—International Coffee Agreement 1983 : New York, 1 January-30 June 1983 / London : H.M.S.O., 1986.
49p; 25cm.
ISBN 0101977506 unbound £4.90

COHABITATION

—Marriage and cohabitation in contemporary societies : areas of legal, social and ethical change : an international and interdisciplinary study / edited by John M. Eekelaar, Sanford Katz : with an introduction by William J. Goode. – Toronto : Butterworths, 1980.
xviii,454p; 24cm.
Includes bibliographical references. Papers presented at the Third World Conference of the International Society on Family Law, held June 5-9, 1979 at Uppsala, Sweden.
ISBN 0409828602

COHABITATION - AUSTRALIA

—Informal marriages / by Margaret Harrison. – Rev. ed. – Melbourne : Institute of Family Studies, 1982.
12 p.; 23 cm. – (Working paper).
Bibliography: p. 10.
ISBN 0642887780 pbk.

COHABITATION - AUSTRALIA - NEW SOUTH WALES

—De facto relationships / New South Wales Law Reform Commission. – Sydney : The Commission, 1981.
x,120p. – (Issues paper).
Bibliography: p.115-120. Accompanied by: Summary of issues paper (14p).

—Guide to the De Facto Relationships Act-New South Wales / Stephen O'Ryan. – Butterworths, 1985.
127p.
ISBN 040949075X Pbk £22.00

—Report on de facto relationships / New South Wales Law Reform Commission. – Sydney : The Commission, 1983.
xx,423p. – (L.R.C. 36).
Bibliography: p.391-396. Includes index. Accompanied by: Outline of report on de facto relationships (19p).

COHABITATION - CANADA

—Domestic Contracts / Agincourt : Carswell, 1987.
450p.
This looseleaf work is a practitioners guide to the drafting of cohabitation, marriage and separation agreements under the law of Ontario and British Columbia. Checklist, sample agreements, income tax considerations and related materials are included in the volume.

—Unmarried couples : legal aspects of cohabitation / by Winifred H. Holland : Tax aspects, D. Keith McNair. – Toronto : Carswell, 1982.
xxxii,249p.
Includes bibliographical references and index.
ISBN 0459348701

COHABITATION - CANADA - ALBERTA

—Survey of adult living arrangements : a technical report / Institute of Law Research and Reform. – Edmonton : The Institute, 1984.
v,93,19p. – (Research paper).

COHABITATION - ENGLAND

—Cohabitation / by Martin L. Parry : with a foreword by H.K. Bevan. – London : Sweet and Maxwell, 1981.
xxv,162p; 22cm.
Includes bibliographies and index.
ISBN 0421267305 Pbk £5.75

—Cohabitation contracts : extra-marital partnerships and law reform / Chris Barton. – Aldershot : Gower, 1985.
xxi,115p; 23cm.
Bibliography: p97-99. - Includes index.
ISBN 0566007118 £17.95

—Cohabitation : the legal implications / Dawn Oliver. – Bicester : CCH Editions, 1987.
xvi,140p; 23cm.
Includes index.
ISBN 0863251080 Pbk No price

—Cohabitation without marriage : an essay in law and social policy / Michael D.A. Freeman and Christina M. Lyon. – Aldershot : Gower, 1983.
vii,228p; 23cm.
Includes index.
ISBN 0566004550 Unpriced

—Law relating to cohabitation / by Martin L. Parry. – 2nd ed. – London : Sweet & Maxwell, 1988.
xxxiii,263p.
Changes effected by the Family Law Reform Act 1987 and the Social Security Act 1986 are included. Discusses home ownership, home occupation, money, tax, children, violence, death, and contracts, and contains an appendix of precedents.
ISBN 0421371102 £20.00

COHABITATION - EUROPEAN COMMUNITY

—Legal Problems Concerning Unmarried Couples : Proceedings of the 11th Collquy on European Law, Messina 1981 / Strasbourg : Council of Europe, 1982.
ISBN 9287101574 Hbk £6.00

COHABITATION - GREAT BRITAIN

—Cohabitation handbook : a women's guide to the law / Anne Bottomley ... et al. – 2nd ed. – London : Pluto, 1984.
240p; 20cm.
Previous ed.: 1981. Includes index.
ISBN 0861047931 Pbk £5.50

COHABITATION - SCOTLAND

—Living Together : A Guide to the Law on Marriage and Cohabitation in Scotland / Frances Wason. – Edinburgh : Scottish Association of Citizens Advice Bureau, 1984.
96p : Illus.
ISBN 0905831047 Hbk £1.95

—Matrimonial Homes (Family Protection) (Scotland) Act 1981 / by D.I. Nichols and M.C. Meston. – Edinburgh : Green, 1982.
vii,68p.
Includes index.
ISBN 0414006879 PBK £15.75

COHABITATION - SWEDEN

—New Swedish family legislation : the Marriage Code : the Cohabitees (Joint Homes) Act : the Homosexual Cohabitees Act : the Inheritance Code, chapters 1-3 and 7 / Stockholm : Ministry of Justice, 1988.
37p.
'... translations of ... Swedish legislation published in the Swedish Code of Statutes (SFS)'. - p.1.

COLLECTIVE BARGAINING

—Collective bargaining in industrialised market economies : a reappraisal / J. P. Windmuller, W. Albeda. – Geneva : International Labour Office, 1987.
xii,333p; 24cm.
Contents: Part 1.: A comparative study, by John P. Windmuller - Part 2.: Country studies, by W. Albeda ... et al..
ISBN 9221056074

—Freedom of Association, Industrial Relations and Collective Bargaining Practices in Mines Other than Coal Mines / Geneva : International Labour Office, 1984.
iv, 79p.
ISBN 9221034577 Hbk £15.00

—General survey on the application of the conventions on freedom of association, the right to organise and collective bargaining and the convention and recommendation concerning rural workers' organisations : third item on the agenda / International Labour Office. – Geneva : International Labour Office, 1983.
157p.
Cover title: Freedom of association and collective bargaining. Report III (Part 4B).
ISBN 9221031284

—Management of collective bargaining : an international comparison / Keith Sisson. – Oxford : Basil Blackwell, 1987.
280p; 23cm.
Includes bibliography and index.
ISBN 0631134395 £25.00

—OECD guidelines for multinational enterprises and labour relations, 1982-1984 : experience and review / by R. Blanpain : foreword by M. Eyskens. – Deventer : Kluwer Law and Taxation Publishers, 1985.
Includes index.
ISBN 9065442073

COLLECTIVE BARGAINING - CANADA

—Collective Agreement Arbitration in Canada / Butterworths.

Supplement-1986
144p.
Covers hearing and grievance procedures, evidentiary problems, the interpretation of collective agreements, discharge and discipline, insubordination, industrial offences, seniority, job benefits, the bargaining unit, and the protection of employment opportunities.
ISBN 0409806358 Pbk £27.95

—Collective Bargaining / Vancouver : British Columbia Continuing Legal Education Society, 1985.
134p.
ISBN 0865041997 Hbk £55.00

—Interest arbitration : measuring justice in employment / Joseph M. Weiler, editor. – Toronto : Carswell, 1981.
iv,283p.
Papers presented at a conference sponsored by the Continuing Legal Education Society of British Columbia, in Vancouver B.C., April 1980.
ISBN 0459339206

—Labour relations and the collective bargaining cycle / Gerald E. Phillips. – 2nd ed. – Toronto : Butterworths, 1981.
xiii,333p.
Previous ed.: published as 'The practice of labour relations and collective bargaining in Canada', 1977. Includes bibliographies and index.

—Labour Relations and the Collective Bargaining Cycle : Second Edition / Toronto : Butterworths, 1981.
352p.

—Tort Liability in a Collective Bargaining Regime / Butterworths, 1980.
176p.
ISBN 0409871540 Hbk £45.00

COLLECTIVE BARGAINING - EUROPEAN COMMUNITY

—Vredeling proposal : information and consultation of employees in multinational enterprises / R. Blanpain ... et al. : foreword by H. Vredeling. – Deventer : Kluwer, 1983.
219 p.; 25 cm.
Includes bibliographical references.
ISBN 9031202088 CIP rev.

COLLECTIVE BARGAINING - GREAT BRITAIN

—Striking a Bargain? / London : Sweet & Maxwell, 1985.
– (Sweet and Maxwell's Law Files Ser.: No. 7).
ISBN 0421340401 loose £29.50

COLLECTIVE LABOUR AGREEEMENTS - CANADA

—Collective agreement arbitration in Canada / Earl Edward Palmer. – 2nd ed. – Toronto : Butterworths, 1983.
cxvi,805p.
Includes bibliographical references and index.
ISBN 0409857726

COLLECTIVE LABOUR AGREEMENTS - EUROPEAN COMMUNITY

—Law of collective agreements in the countries of the European Community / report submitted by Gian Carlo Perone : with the assistance of Antonio Vallebona. – Luxembourg : Office for Official Publications of the European Communities, 1985.
47p.
Describes the tasks given to the Commission of the European Communities in the social sector, particularly under Articles 117 and 118 of the Treaty of Rome.
ISBN 9282550125 Pbk £3.30

COLLISIONS AT SEA

—Amendments to the Convention on the International Regulations for Preventing Collisions at Sea: 1972 / International Maritime Organization. – London : International Maritime Organization, 1983.

French
ISBN 9280121278 Hbk £1.50

Spanish
ISBN 9280130897 Hbk £1.50

—Collision cases : judgments and diagrams / by H.M.C. Holdert and F.J. Buzek. – London : Lloyd's, 1984.
xvii,190p.
ISBN 0907432964

—Collision regulations : the application and enforcement of the Merchant Shipping (Distress Signals and Prevention of Collisions) Regulations 1983 / by R.H.B. Sturt : illustrations by Ann L. Sturt. – 2nd ed. – London : Lloyd's of London Press, 1984.
xlvi,177p, 5p of plates.
Previous ed.: 1977. Includes index.
ISBN 0907432670

—Collisions at Sea / 12th ed. – London : Sweet & Maxwell, 1987.
– (British Shipping Law Ser.).

—Guide to the Collision Avoidance Rules / J. Lameijer. – London : Stanford Maritime Ltd.
224p.

—Law of Collision at Sea / Amsterdam : Elsevier Science Publishers, 1987.
xxxviii, 608p.
ISBN 0444703071 Hbk £250.00

COLLISIONS AT SEA - GREAT BRITAIN

—Collisions at sea (BSL) / 12th ed. – London : Sweet & Maxwell, 1988.
ISBN 0420448608 hb

COLONIES

—Legal pluralism : proceedings of the Canberra Law Workshop VII / edited by Peter Sack and Elizabeth Minchin. – Canberra : Law Department, Research School of Social Sciences, Australian National University, 1986.
iii,280p.
Includes bibliographical references.
ISBN 0867848375

COLONIES - GREAT BRITAIN

—From dependence to statehood in Commonwealth Africa : selected documents, World War I to independence / by H.H. Marshall. – London : Oceana Publications, 1980.
27cm.
Contents: v.1 Southern Africa - v.2 Central Africa.

—Imperial appeal : the debate on the appeal to the Privy Council, 1833-1986 / David B. Swinfen. – Manchester : Manchester University Press, 1987.
viii,268p; 23cm.
Bibliography: p255-260. - Includes index.
ISBN 0719018951 £35.00

—Year book of the Commonwealth 1983 / 15th ed. – London : H.M.S.O., 1983.
vii,535p.
Includes index.
ISBN 0115802320

COMMERCE

—Cases and materials on international business transactions / T.C. Hartley. – 9 v. – London : London School of Economics, 1984.

—Cases and materials on international business transactions / T.C. Hartley. – London : London School of Economics, 1987.
8.
A collection of course material.

—CMEA uniform law for international sales / by Ivan Szasz. – 2nd rev. ed. – Dordrecht : Nijhoff, 1985.
viii,291p; 25cm.
Previous ed.: published as : A uniform law on international sales of goods, 1976. Includes index. Translation of: A KGST altalanos szalltasi feltelek.
ISBN 9024727855 Hbk £125.00

—Current problems of international trade financing / edited by C.M. Chinkin, P.J. Davidson, W.J.M. Ricquier. – Singapore : Malaya Law Review, 1983.
xxiii,507p.
Includes index. At head of title: Singapore Conferences on International Business Law.
ISBN 0406181144

—Guide to Incoterms / 2nd ed. – Paris : International Chamber of Commerce, 1980.
90p. – (ICC publication).

—Incoterms : international rules for the interpretation of trade terms / Incoterms. – 1980 ed. – Paris : International Chamber of Commerce, 1980.
136p. – (ICC publication).
Parallel text in English and French.

—International Chamber of Commerce Arbitration / Paris : International Chamber of Commerce.
704p.

—Trade financing / edited by Charles J. Gmur. – 2nd ed. – London : Euromoney, 1986.
xxi,234p.
ISBN 0903121999

COMMERCE - CHINA

—Almanac of China's foreign economic relations and trade / the editorial board of the Almanac of China's foreign economic relations and trade. – Hong Kong : China Resources Trade Consultancy, 1986.
Title page also in Chinese.

COMMERCE – EUROPEAN COMMUNITY

—Generalised scheme of preferences : a brief summary of the European Community's scheme for 1985 / Department of Trade and Industry. – London : The Department, 1984.
17p.

—International trade law and practice of the European Community : EEC anti-dumping and other trade protection laws / Ivo van Bael, Jean-Francois Bellis. – Bicester : CCH, 1985.
viii,438p.
Discusses the Community's four main methods of trade protection; anti-dumping rules, anti-subsidy rules, safe-guard measures, and the 'New Commercial Policy Instrument', and comments on the EEC and ECSC Anti-dumping Regulations. Contains tables and annexes.
ISBN 0863250602

COMMERCIAL AGENCY

—Guide for Commercial Agencies / Paris : International Chamber of Commerce.
38p.

—Survey of commercial agency / edited by Hans Henrik Lidgard, Claude D. Rohwer, Dennis Campbell. – Deventer : Kluwer Law and Taxation, 1984.
xxv,718p; 25cm.
Conference papers. Bibliography: p394-395. - Includes index.
ISBN 9065441816 Hbk

COMMERCIAL ARBITRATION

—Arbitration and renegotiation of international investment agreements : a study with particular reference to means of conflict avoidance under natural resources investment agreements / Wolfgang Peter. – Dordrecht : M. Nijhoff, 1986.
xxiii, 297p.
Includes index. Bibliography: p.267-284.
ISBN 9024733146

—Arbitration in settlement of international commercial disputes involving the Far East: arbitration in combined transportation / P Sanders. – Kluwer Law and Taxation, 1989.
428. – (ICCA Congress Series).
Overview of the arbitration situation in the Far East concerning the settlement ofinternational commercial disputes. Also covers Latin America, the CMEA countries, the common law and civil law countries. Discusses ways to overcome regional differences. Examines arbitration in combined transportation.
ISBN 9065444068 Pbk £47/Dfl 150

—Art of arbitration : essays on international arbitration : liber amicorum Pieter Sanders, 12 September 1912-1982 / editors, Jan C. Schultsz, Albert Jan van den Berg. – Deventer, Netherlands : Kluwer Law and Taxation Publishers, 1982.
xxi, 320 p.; 25 cm.
English or French. Includes bibliographical references and index.
ISBN 9065440542

—Commercial Arbitration Worldwide Guide / London : LLoyd's of London Press, 1985.
ISBN 1850440530 Hbk

—Effective dispute resolution for the international commercial lawyer / Dennis Campbell, Peter Summerfield. – Kluwer Law and Taxation, 1989.
240.
Covers practical remedies under German law, arbitration and the enforcement of arbitration awards, mediation-arbitration and other alternatives for resolving international commercial disputes, and government litigation.
ISBN 9065444157 Pbk £31/Dfl 98

—Essays on international commercial arbitration / London : Graham & Trotman, 1989.
256.
Focuses on Model Law as prepared by the United Nations Commission on International Trade Law, accepted by the General Assembly in 1985. Also discusses ICSID arbitration and the New York Convention of 1958.
ISBN 0860107051 Hbk £46.50

—Grain contracts and arbitration for shipments from the United States and Canada / by Albert Slabotzky. – London : Lloyd's, 1984.
x,109p.
Bibliography: p.105-106. - Includes index.
ISBN 0907432883

—Guide to the UNCITRAL model on international commercial arbitration: legislation, history and commentary / J E Neuhaus. – Kluwer Law and Taxation, 1989.
1320.
Gives the legislative history of the new UNCITRAL model arbitration law. Each chapter starts with a commentary on the legislative history of the Article, highlighting the principle issues considered, followed by the legislative history of the article. Text contains documents, including drafts, reports, summary records of debates, government comments and conference room papers.
ISBN 9065443053 Hbk £139/Dfl 450

—Hague-Zagreb Essays /. – Dordrecht : Kluwer, 1980.
xi, 329p.
ISBN 9028607498 Pbk £72.00

—International commercial and maritime arbitration / Sweet & Maxwell, 1988.
ISBN 0421392207 Pbk £18.00

—International Commercial Arbitration / Vancouver : British Columbia Continuing Legal Education Society, 1983.
216p.
ISBN 0865041415 Hbk £50.00

—International handbook on commercial arbitration / general editor Pieter Sanders : with the cooperation of the T.M.C. Asser Institute for International Law, The Hague. – 2. – Deventer : Kluwer Law and Taxation Publishers, 1984.
At head of title page: International Council for Commercial Arbitration.
ISBN 906544999X Llf

—Yearbook Commercial Arbitration /. – Dordrecht : Kluwer, 1980.
344p.
ISBN 9026811527 Hbk Gld62.00

1981 1981.
352p.
ISBN 9065440038 Hbk Gld62.00

1982 1982.
465p.
ISBN 9065440461 Hbk Gld75.00

1983
482p.
ISBN 9065441182 Pbk Gld82.50

1984
ISBN 9065441719 Hbk Gld95.00

1985 1985.
640p.
ISBN 9065442138 Pbk Gld110.00

1986 1986.
716p.
ISBN 9065442472 Pbk Gld150.00

1987 1987.
ISBN 9065443045 Pbk Gld180.00 (Including key index for all volumes 1-12)
ISBN 9065443037 Pbk Gld50.00 (key index only)

1989 1989.
872.
In co-operation with the T M C Asser Institute for International and European law. Covers the national reports and updates, court decisions and updates, commercial and maritime arbitral awards and rules, Iran-US claims tribunal, and court decisions in the New York Convention, the European Convention, and the Washington (ICSID) Convention.
ISBN 9065444084 Pbk Gld59/Dfl 185

—Yearbook Commercial Arbitration, Volumes 1-12 (including Key) / Dordrecht : Kluwer.
ISBN 9065441352 Pbk Gld840.00

—Yearbook Maritime Law / Dordrecht : Kluwer, 1987.
528p.
ISBN 9065442545 Hbk Gld275.00

COMMERCIAL ARBITRATION – AUSTRALIA

—Commercial Arbitration / Dorter. – North Ryde : Law Book Co, 1986.
ISBN 0455205841 Hbk £29.75

COMMERCIAL ARBITRATION – CANADA

—Commercial Arbitration / Vancouver : Continuing Legal Education Society of British Columbia, 1986.
240p.
ISBN 0865042977 Hbk £85.00

—UNCITRAL Arbitration Model in Canada / Thompson. – Agincourt : Carswell, 1987.
262p.
This work outlines the process of adopting and implementing the UNCITRAL Model Law. Canadian legislation and the UNCITRAL Model Law and Rules are provided. Discussions include that of arbitration as a universally accepted method of resolving international commercial disputes and the adoption in British Columbia of the model law on international commercial arbitration.

COMMERCIAL ARBITRATION – ENGLAND

—Law and practice of commercial arbitration in England / Sir Michael J. Mustill, Stewart C. Boyd. – London : Butterworths, 1985.
lxxiv,727p.
An extensive and detailed treatment of the subject of commercial arbitration is given in this work. The book covers appointment of arbitrators, the arbitration process, the award, and appeals in the United Kingdom.
ISBN 0406311218

COMMERCIAL ARBITRATION – HONG KONG

—Report on the adoption of the UNCITRAL model law of arbitration / the Law Reform Commission of Hong Kong. – Hong Kong : The Commisssion, 1987.
v,121p. – (Topic).
Includes bibliographical references.

COMMERCIAL ARBITRATION – WEST GERMANY

—Commercial arbitration in the Federal Republic of Germany / by Ottoarndt Glossner. – Deventer : Kluwer Law and Taxation, 1984.
xiv,137p; 25cm.
Bibliography: p113-134. - Includes index.
ISBN 9065441859 Hbk £90.00

COMMERCIAL COURTS

—Practice and procedure of the Commercial Court / by Anthony D. Colman. – 2nd ed. – London : Lloyd's of London, 1986.
230p; 24cm.
Previous ed.: 1983. Includes index.
ISBN 1850440611 No price

COMMERCIAL COURTS – ENGLAND

—Civil justice review / Lord Chancellor's Department. – London : The Department, 1986.
38 leaves.

Study of the Commercial Court : final report : Coopers & Lybrand Associates Limited / Lord Chancellor's Department. – 1986.
98,25 leaves.

—Comments on the consultation paper no. 3 from the civil justice review relating to the commercial court / JUSTICE. – London : JUSTICE, 1987.
5p.

—Practice and procedure of the commercial court / by Anthony D. Colman. – London : Lloyd's of London Press, 1983.
xxiii,193p.
Includes index.
ISBN 0907432581

—Report of the practitioner members of the Commercial Court Committee approved and adopted by the Commercial Court Committee / London : Lord Chancellor's Department, 1986.
50p.

COMMERCIAL CRIMES

—Combating international commercial crime / by B. Rider. – Barking : International Maritime Bureau, 1984.
36p.

—Economic crime / European Committee on Crime Problems. – Strasbourg : Council of Europe, 1981.
75p.
Recommendation No. R(81)12, adopted by the Committee of Ministers on 25 June 1981. At head of cover title: Council of Europe, Legal Affairs.

—International Commercial Crime Conference / Vancouver : British Columbia Continuing Legal Education Society, 1981.
275p.
ISBN 0865040362 Hbk £25.00

—International commercial crime : second international commercial crime symposium / organised under the auspices of the Commonwealth Secretariat's Commercial Crime Unit, the ICC-International Maritime Bureau and the Centre for Commercial Law Studies, Queen Mary College ... : documentation edited by Susan G. Lie. – London : Queen Mary College. Faculty of Laws, Centre for Commercial Law Studies, 1984.
502p.

—Symposium on Commercial Crime, 15-19 December 1982, Jesus College, Cambridge / organised by the Commonwealth Secretariat and the Centre for Commercial Law Studies : documentation edited by Susan Grace Lie. – S.l. : s.n., 1983.
ii,382p.
Includes bibliographical references.

COMMERCIAL CRIMES – ENGLAND

—Phantom capitalists : the organisation and control of long-firm fraud / by Michael Levi. – London : Heinemann, 1981.
346p; 23cm.
Bibliography: p335-341. - Includes index.
ISBN 0435825208 £16.50

COMMERCIAL CRIMES – HONG KONG

—Problem of the trial of complex commercial crimes : a proposal for reform / Hong Kong : Attorney General's Chambers, 1984.
93p.

COMMERCIAL DOCUMENTS

—Disposal and retention of documents / the Institute of Chartered Secretaries and Administrators. – London? : Institute of Chartered Secretaries and Administrators, 1980.
32p.

COMMERCIAL DOCUMENTS - AUSTRALIA

—Drafting: its applications to conveyancing and commercial documents / North Ryde : Butterworths (Australia), 1973.
Guide to the drafting of legal and commercial documents. Explains the underlying princples of drafting and demonstrates the link between those principles and the rule of law. Discusses the language of law, and generality of expression, and sets out the most salient features of parliamentary drafting practice relevant to document drafting.
ISBN 0409438251 Hbk

COMMERCIAL DOCUMENTS - CANADA

—Drafting Commercial Documents / Vancouver : British Columbia Continuing Legal Education Society, 1981.
278p.
ISBN 0865040206 Hbk £50.00

COMMERCIAL DOCUMENTS - INDIA

—Report on documents of title to goods 1978 / Banking Laws Committee (Government of India). – New Delhi : Controller of Publications, 1980.
xx,294p.
Includes index. Chairman: P.V. Rajamannar.

COMMERCIAL LAW

—Basic documents on international trade law / edited by Chia-Jui Cheng. – The Hague : Martinus Nijhoff, 1985.
Includes index.
ISBN 9024731690 pbk.

—Business law guide to Germany / Strobl, Killius & Vorbrugg. – Bicester, Oxon : CCH Editions, 1986.
xv,387p.
Includes index.
ISBN 0863250637

—Business law in Egypt / by Michael H. Davies. – Deventer, Netherlands : Boston, 1984.
ISBN 9065440860

—Business laws of the United Arab Emirates / translated from Arabic into English by Marjorie J. Hall. – London : Graham & Trotman, 1984.
94p.
ISBN 0860105512

—C. E. R. : the business and law essentials : papers presented at seminar, University of Auckland, 22-23 July 1983 / 3. – Auckland : Legal Research Foundation Inc., 1983.
ISBN 0908581270

—Cases and materials on international business transactions / T.C. Hartley. – London : London School of Economics, 1987.
8.
A collection of course material.

—Challenges to the legal profession : law and investment in developing countries : addresses, committee papers and reports of the 19th biennial conference of the International Bar Association at New Delhi / International Bar Association. – Lucknow : Eastern Book Co. in co-ordination with the International Bar Association and the Bar Association of India, 1984.
xx,787p.

—CMEA uniform law for international sales / by Ivan Szasz. – 2nd rev. ed. – Dordrecht : Nijhoff, 1985.
viii,291p; 25cm.
Previous ed.: published as : A uniform law on international sales of goods, 1976. Includes index. Translation of: A KGST altalanos szalltasi feltelek.
ISBN 9024727855 Hbk £125.00

—Commercial and Consumer Transactions / 2nd ed. – Toronto : Edmond-Montgomery, 1987.
ca 1,400p.
ISBN 0920722202 Hbk £96.00

—Commercial law / by Gordon J. Borrie. – 5th ed. – London : Butterworths, 1980.
xxviii,344p.

ISBN 0406558442

—Commercial Law Digest / Agincourt : Carswell.

—Commercial law in New Zealand / Leys and Northey. – 7th ed. – Wellington : Butterworths, 1982.
xlviii,852p.
Previous ed.: 1978. Includes index.
ISBN 0409600881

—Common Market law review / . – London : Stevens, 1963.
Index in each vol.
ISBN 00103292

—Concepts and Problems in Mercantile Law / New Delhi : Allied Publishers, 1984.
viii, 372p.

—Courts and the Development of Commercial Law / Berlin : Duncker and Humblot, 1987.
203p.
ISBN 3428061764 Pbk £78.00

—Current issues in international business law / edited by David L. Perrott, Istvan Pogany. – Aldershot : Avebury, 1988.
xxvii,239p.
Includes bibliographical references and index.
ISBN 0566054736

—Elements of Mercantile Law : Including Company and Industrial Law / 15th ed. – New Delhi : Sultan Chand and Sons, 1984.
xxviii, 880p.

—Encyclopedia of international commercial arbitration / by Eric Lee. – London : Lloyd's of London Press, 1986.
412p; 24cm.
Includes index.
ISBN 185044059X £50.00 (Apr.)

—Essays for Clive Schmitthoff / edited by John Adams. – Abingdon : Professional Books, 1983.
xviii,174p.
ISBN 0862050596

—Guide to Mercantile Law / New Delhi : S. Chand and Company.

—Hague-Zagreb Essays / edited by C.C.A. Voskuil and C.C.A. Voskuil and J.A. Wade. – Hague : Martinus Nijhoff, 1983.
410p.
ISBN 9024728401 Hbk £135.00

—International business lawyer : journal of the Section on Business Law of the International Bar Association / . – London : International Bar Association, 1973.
Index in each vol., 1979-.
ISBN 03097676

—International business transactions in a nutshell / by Donald T. Wilson. – St. Paul, Minn. : West Publishing Co., 1980.
lvii,393p; 19cm. – (Nutshell series).

—International commercial litigation / Stephen Cromie; consulting editor: William Park. – London : Butterworths, 1990.
600; 24cm.
Focuses on national commercial litigation in its international context. Covers procedural and substantive law of England and Wales, USA, Canada, Frane, Germany, Switzerland, Japan and Australia. The conduct of simultaneous proceedings in the various countries and how decisions may be enforced are also treated.
ISBN 0406290024 Hbk £120

—International trade in a nutshell / D.M. Day. – London : Sweet and Maxwell, 1980.
vii,87p; 18cm.
Includes index.
ISBN 0421265604 Pbk £1.50

—International trade : law and practice / edited by Julian D.M. Lew and Clive Stanbrook. – London : Euromoney Publications, 1983.
xxiii,213p.
Includes bibliographical references and index.
ISBN 0903121468

—International trade regulation : GATT, the United States and the European Community / Edmond McGovern. – 2nd ed. – Exeter : Globefield, 1986.
xliv,629p; 25cm.
Previous ed. 1982. Bibliography: p599-619. - Includes index.
ISBN 0950846341 £36.00

—Journal of business law / – London : Stevens, 1957.
Index in each vol. - Index, 1957-1976. 1977.
ISBN 00219460

—Journal of world trade law / London : Vincent Press, 1967-.
Index in each vol.

—Judges, law, and businessmen / A.H. Hermann. – Deventer, Netherlands : Kluwer Law and Taxation Publishers, 1983.
ISBN 9065440828

—Law and policy of producers' associations / D.E. Pollard. – Oxford : Clarendon, 1984.
xii,372p; 23cm.
Includes index.
ISBN 0198254806 £30.00

—Law of international trade / by D.M. Day. – London : Butterworths, 1981.
xxii,254p,2p of plates; 22cm.
This book is an introduction to the law of international trade. Carriage of goods, insurance of goods in transit, government controls, EEC law, and statutory material are discussed in the work.
ISBN 040657202X
ISBN 0406572011 Pbk

—Law of the economy in the European Communities / by D. Lasok with a chapter on agriculture by J.W. Bridge. – London : Butterworths, 1980.
xxxviii,455p; 23cm.
Bibliography: p431-442. - Includes index.
ISBN 0406268967 Hbk £18.95
ISBN 0406268975 Pbk £11.95

—Lectures on English Commercial Law / Dordrecht : Kluwer.
64p.
ISBN 9065441506 Pbk £30.00

—Legal aspects of doing business in the Middle East / edited by Dennis Campbell. – Deventer, Netherlands : Kluwer Law and Taxation Publishers, 1986.
– (International business series).
Includes index.
ISBN 9065442642

—Legal aspects of international business transactions : the Edinburgh Institute on International Business Transactions 1983 : a project of University of the Pacific McGeorge School of Law international programs / edited by D. Campbell and C. Rohwer. – Amsterdam : North-Holland, 1984.
x,463p; 24cm.
ISBN 0444875069 £34.88

—Legal Cooperation in Europe in the Fields of Civil, Commercial and International Law (1957-82) / Strasbourg : Council of Europe, 1983.
ISBN 9287101698

—Legal opinions in international transactions : foreign lawyers' response to US opinion requests / report of the Subcommittee on Legal Opinions of Committee E of the Section on Business Law of the International Bar Association : Michael Gruson, Michael Kutschera. – London : Graham & Trotman and The Association, 1987.
120p; 23cm.
ISBN 1853330213 £35.00

—Lex mercatoria / Berthold Goldman. – Deventer : Kluwer Law and Taxation Publishers, 1983.
24p.
Includes bibliographical references.
ISBN 9065441948

—Mercantile Law / 4th ed. – Lucknow : Eastern Book Company, 1985.
1,172p.

—Papers and Comments Delivered at the Eighth Annual Workshop on Commercial and Consumer Law / Vancouver : University of British Columbia, Faculty of Commerce & Business Administration, 1980.
– (Toronto Butterworths and Co. Ser.).

—Principles of English Law Including Mercantile Law / Nairobi : Heinemann Educational Books (East Africa), 1982.
276p.

—Principles of Mercantile Law / New Delhi : S. Chand and Company, 1983.

—Problems in Mercantile Law / 7th rev. ed. – New Delhi : Sultan Chand and Sons, 1984.
iv, 238p.

—Recognition of commercial judgments and awards in the Commonwealth / K.W. Patchett. – London : Butterworths, 1984.
xlv,326p; 26cm.
Bibliography: pxxix. - Includes index.
ISBN 0406403201 No price

—Studies in Commercial Law and Judicial Activism / New Delhi : Deep and Deep Publications, 1988.
220p.

—Suggested Answers in Mercantile Law (Q.A.) / 2nd ed. – New Delhi : Sultan Chand and Sons, 1985.
v, 317p.

—Transnational law of international commercial transactions / edited by Norbert Horn and Clive M. Schmitthoff. – Antwerp : Kluwer-Devanter/The Netherlands, 1982.
Includes index and bibliography.
ISBN 9065440925

COMMERCIAL LAW - AUSTRALIA

—Australian mercantile law / Yorston & Fortescue. – 16th ed. – Sydney : Law Book Co., 1981.
xxxi,784p.
Previous ed.: 1978. Includes index.
ISBN 0455203636

—Austrian business law : legal, accounting and tax aspects of business in Austria / by Dr. Kurt Heller ... et al. – Deventer : Klumer Law and Taxation Publishing, 1984.
xxxviii,528p; 25cm.
Includes index.
ISBN 9065441883
ISBN 3214046012

—Bulletin : trade practices developments / Trade Practices Commission. – Belconnen, A.C.T. : Australian Trade Practices Commission, 1981.

—Cases for Students of Commercial Law / North Ryde : C.C.H. Australia, 1987.
114p.
ISBN 0869039288 Hbk

—Cases on Commercial Law / 2nd ed. - North Ryde : Law Book Co, 1984.
ixi, 428p.
ISBN 0455204365 Pbk £29.50

—Commercial Law / A. Freilich. - Butterworths, 1986.
94p. - (Butterworth's Student Companion Ser.).
ISBN 0409490873 Pbk £9.95

—Commercial Law / N. A. Gunningham. - 3rd ed. - Sydney : Butterworths, 1988.
568p.

—Commercial Law / N.A. Cunningham. - 3rd ed. - Butterworths, 1988.
582p.
ISBN 0409492485 Pbk £49.50
ISBN 0409492477 Hbk £65.00

—Commercial Law II /. - Butterworths, 1986.
90p. - (Butterworth's Student Companion Ser.).
ISBN 0409490954 Pbk £9.95

—Contract Chart from Australian Mercantile Law / North Ryde : Law Book Co.
ISBN 045520652X Hbk £3.00

—Dispute Resolution in Commercial Matters : Papers-Colloquium, Australian Academy of Science, Canberra, 6 June 1986 / Kingston : Australian Government Publishing Service, 1986.
175p.
ISBN 0644054344 Hbk £9.95

—Helmore's personal property and mercantile law in New South Wales / by W. J. Chappenden and J. W. Carter. - 9th ed. - Sydney : Law Book Company, 1985.
xlvi,485p.
ISBN 045520294X

—Index to the Companies (South Australia) Code / Adelaide : Government Printer, 1982.
97p.
' ... prepared by the Law Book Company'. - t.p..

—Introduction to Mercantile Law / Swanepoel, Makins, Lapping and Reynecke. - Durban : Professional Publisher, 1984.
ISBN 0409057800 Pbk £39.00

—Law of Commercial Companies / 3rd ed. - North Ryde : Law Book Co, 1987.
xlix, 379p.
ISBN 0455207291 Hbk £59.50
ISBN 0455207305 Pbk £35.00

—Law of international business in Australia / by P.J. O'Keefe and Mark A.G. Tedeschi. - Sydney : Butterworths, 1980.
xix, 220 p.; 25 cm.
'Table of cases': p. xiii-xvii. 'Table of legislation': p. xviii-xix. Includes bibliographical references and index.
ISBN 0409437107 Hbk £49

—Questions in Commercial Law / 2nd ed. - North Ryde : C.C.H. Australia, 1986.
147p.
ISBN 0869037587 Hbk

—Teaching Materials and Cases on Commercial Transactions / 2nd ed. - Butterworths, 1983.
559p.
ISBN 0409493643 Hbk £51.00

COMMERCIAL LAW - AUSTRIA

—Austrian Commercial Code : as of January 1, 1983 / translation into English by Markus Andreewitch. - Wien : Manz, 1987.
xii,180p.
Include indexes. German title on added t.p.: Das osterreichische Handelsgesetzbuch. Text in English and German.
ISBN 3214028987

COMMERCIAL LAW - CANADA

—Business law reports / Agincourt, Ont. : Carswell, 1977-.
24cm.
Cumulative indexes published at intervals.

—Canadian business organizations law / by Tom Hadden, Robert E. Forbes, Ralph L. Simmonds. - Toronto : Butterworths, 1984.
xlix,680p.
Relates common-law rules and statutory provisions to current commercial and industrial practice, distinguishing between the problems of small private businesses and larger public companies. Provides information on current corporate issues; practices and problems in designed instruments of corporate finance, securities law, corporate acquisitions, corporate groups, foreign acquisitions, and lease financing.
ISBN 0409834815 Hbk £95

—Commercial and consumer transactions : cases, text and materials / by Jacob S. Ziegel, Benjamin Geva. - Toronto : Emond-Montgomery, 1981.
xlv,1230p.
Bibliography: p.xliii-xliv. - Includes index.
ISBN 0920722040

—Commercial Case / Vancouver : Continuing Legal Education Society of British Columbia, 1987.
198p.
ISBN 0865043345 Hbk £70.00

—Commercial Law / Hamilton : Society of Management Accountants of Canada.

—Commercial law : recent developments and emerging trends / Don Mills : De Boo, 1985.
294p.
Includes bibliographical references and index.
ISBN 0888202164 Hbk £75.00

—Dangers and Pitfalls in Advising on Commercial Transactions / Vancouver : British Columbia Continuing Legal Education Society, 1983.
283p.
ISBN 086504130X Hbk £55.00

—Drafting Commercial Documents / Vancouver : Continuing Legal Education Society of British Columbia, 1981.
278p.
ISBN 0865040206 Hbk £65.00

—Harmonization of business law in Canada / Ronald C.C. Cuming, research coordinator. - Toronto : University of Toronto Press, 1986.
xx, 245 p.; 23 cm.
Includes bibliographies. Contents: Harmonization of provincial laws, with particular reference to commercial, consumer, and corporate law / Jacob S. Ziegel - The regulation of the securities market and the harmonization of provincial laws / Philip Anisman - Harmonization of Canadian personal property security law / Ronald C.C. Cuming - Harmonization of Canadian insurance law / Marvin G. Baer.
ISBN 0802073034 pbk.

—O'Brien's Encyclopedia of Forms : Division One-Commercial & General / Aurora : Canada Law Book Co.
- (Abridgments and Encyclopedias).

Supplement-1983

—Papers and comments delivered at the eighth annual Workshop on Commercial and Consumer Law, Toronto, October 20-21, 1978 / edited by Jacob S. Ziegel, with the assistance of Owen Johnson. - Toronto : Butterworths, 1980.
vi, 231 p.; 24 cm.
At head of title: Canadian Association of Law Teachers, Faculty of Law, University of Toronto, and the Osgoode Hall Law School of York University. Includes bibliographical references.
ISBN 0409879606

—Papers and comments delivered at the ninth annual Workshop on Commercial and Consumer Law, Toronto, November 2-3, 1979 / edited by Jacob S. Ziegel. - Toronto : Butterworths, 1981.
xi,279p.
Includes bibliographical references. At head of cover title: Canadian Association of Law Teachers, Faculty of Law, University of Toronto and the Osgoode Hall Law School of York University.
ISBN 0409879614

—Papers and comments delivered at the tenth annual Workshop on Commercial and Consumer Law, Toronto, October 17-18, 1980 / edited by Jacob S. Ziegel. - Toronto : Butterworths, 1982.
x,218p.
Includes bibliographical references. At head of title: Canadian Association of Law Teachers, Faculty of Law, University of Toronto, and the Osgoode Hall Law School of York University..
ISBN 0409879622

—Sales and sales financing in Canada : cases and materials / by M.G. Bridge, F.H. Buckley, with the assistance of L.R. Ganong. - Toronto : Carswell, 1981.
xlix,694p.
Includes bibliographical references.
ISBN 0459337505

—Selected income tax aspects of the purchase and sale of a business : Corporate Management Tax Confetence 1984 / Toronto : Canadian Tax Foundation, 1984.
xii,347p.
Bibliography: p.75-82.
ISBN 0888080220

—Sixteenth Annual Workshop on Commercial and Consumer Law, October 17-18, 1986 : papers and other materials / Toronto : Faculty of Law, University of Toronto, 1986.
vi,372p.
Includes bibliographical references.

—Tenth Annual Workshop on Commercial and Consumer Law / Toronto : Butterworths, 1982.
232p.

COMMERCIAL LAW - CAYMAN ISLANDS

—Paget-Brown's commercial law of the Cayman Islands / Grand Cayman : distributed by Graffix, 1982.
235p.

COMMERCIAL LAW - CHINA

—China trade law : code of the foreign trade law of the People's Republic of China / by Francois De Bauw and Bernard Dewit : preface by Michel Verwilghen. - Bruxelles : Emile Bruylant, 1982.
572p.
Includes bibliographical references and index. At head of title: Universite Catholique de Louvain, Faculte de Droit, Centre de Droit des Obligations. Text in English. Preface, introduction, headings and index in French and English..
ISBN 2802702963

—China's Civil and Commercial Law / London : Butterworths, 1988.
ISBN 040999555X Hbk £65.00

—China's civil and commercial law / Henry R. Zheng. - Singapore : Butterworths, 1988.
lii,490p; 26cm.
Presents an overview of chinese laws and legislative structure, a review of the major principles of the Civil Code, and an examination of the different facets of Chinese business law. Covers principles of civil law, contract law, banking law, insurance law, and foreign investment law.
ISBN 040999555X Hbk £142.50

—Commercial disputes settlement in China / Eric Lee. - London : Lloyds of London, 1985.
152p; 22cm.
Includes index.
ISBN 1850440638 Pbk

—Commercial laws & business regulations of the People's Republic of China 1949-1983 / Victor F.S. Sit, editor. - London : Macmillan, 1983.
xix,600p; 27cm.
ISBN 0333361172 £42.50

—Foreign trade, investment, and the law in the People's Republic of China / editor Michael J. Moser : contributors Jesse T.H. Chang ... et al. - 2nd ed. - Hong Kong : Oxford University Press, 1987.
x,603p; 26cm.
An extensively revised and updated second edition. Gives an introduction to the legal framework currently being developed in China with respect to foreign commercial and investment activity.
ISBN 0195840585 £25.00

COMMERCIAL LAW - CYPRUS

—Note on the law of Cyprus relating to offshore operations, shipping operations and shipping companies, foreign investments in Cyprus and transit trade / by Criton G. Tornaritis. - Nicosia : s.n., 1984.
52 leaves.

COMMERCIAL LAW - ENGLAND

—Commercial Law / Sir Gordon Borrie. - 6th ed. - London : Butterworths, 1988.
xxxi,354p; 22cm.
Previous ed.: 1980. Includes index.
ISBN 0406558450 Hbk £19.50
ISBN 0406558469 Pbk £13.95

—Commercial law / R.M. Goode. - Harmondsworth : Penguin Books/Allen Lane, 1982.
1119p. - (Penguin education).
ISBN 0140804595 Allen Lane
ISBN 0713915285

—Commercial law / by Robert Lowe. - 6th ed. - London : Sweet & Maxwell, 1983.
xlvi,578p; 23cm.
Previous ed.: 1976. Includes index.
ISBN 0421298707 Hbk £21.50
ISBN 0421298804 Pbk £14.50

—Commercial law / R.M. Goode. - Harmondsworth : Penguin, 1986.
1119p. - (Pelican books).
Includes bibliographical references and index.
ISBN 0140226346

—Consuetudo Vel Lex Mercatoria, 2 Vols. / Abingdon : Professional Books.
- (Classical English Law Texts Ser.).

—Dictionary of commercial law / by A.H. Hudson. - London : Butterworths, 1983.
289p; 23cm. - (Butterworths professional dictionaries series).
A reference source on commercial law of the United Kingdom. Entries are arranged in alphabetical order, and all terms are fully described, rather than merely defined.
ISBN 0406681597 HBK £17.00
ISBN 0406681600 PBK £10.95

—Half-a-century of commercial law, 1930-1980 / being the presidential address of Lord Roskill ... - Birmingham : Holdsworth Club of the University of Birmingham, 1981.
17p; 21cm. - (Presidential addresses/Holdsworth Club).
ISBN 0704406187

—Introduction to commercial law / F. B. Wright. - 2nd ed. - London : Sweet & Maxwell, 1982.
240p. - (Concise College Texts).
Previous ed. published as: ONC-OND commercial law. 1976.
ISBN 0421285109 Pbk £10.00

—Mercantile law / Kenneth Smith, Denis Keenan. - 5th ed. - London : Pitman, 1982.
xiii,753p; 22cm.
Previous ed.: 1977. Includes index. 3rd ed. and earlier entitled: Essentials of mercantile law.
ISBN 0273017691 Pbk Unpriced

—Smith and Keenan's mercantile law / Denis Keenan. - 7th ed. - London : Pitman, 1988.
688p; 22cm.
Previous ed.: 1985. Includes index.
ISBN 027302843X Pbk £12.95

COMMERCIAL LAW - EUROPE

—Legal aspects of doing business in Western Europe / edited by Dennis Campbell. - Deventer, Netherlands : Kluwer Law and Taxation Publishers, 1983.
viii, 451 p.; 25 cm. - (International business series).
Includes index.
ISBN 0314792899

—Legal Co-operation in Europe in the Fields of Civil, Commercial and International Law 1957-82 / Council of Europe. - London : HMSO, 1983.
112p.
ISBN 9287101698 Pbk £3.90

COMMERCIAL LAW - EUROPEAN COMMUNITY

—Common Market law reports / Edinburgh : Nelson, 1962-.
Decisions of the European Court of Justice.

COMMERCIAL LAW - EUROPEAN ECONOMIC COMMUNITY COUNTRIES

—Trading law / Chichester : Barry Rose, 1981-.
From v.2 Trading law reports published as pullout insert in each issue.

COMMERCIAL LAW - EUROPEAN ECONOMIC COMMUNITY COUNTRIES - CASES

—Trading law reports / - Chichester : Barry Rose, 1983.
Published as pullout insert in Trading law.

COMMERCIAL LAW - GIBRALTAR

—Tolley's taxation in Gibraltar 1981-82 / by James Levy and Simon Caplan : with an introduction by Sir Joshua Hassan. - 2nd ed. - Croydon : Tolley, 1982.
vii,152p.
Includes index.
ISBN 0854590447

COMMERCIAL LAW - GREAT BRITAIN

—Cases and materials on the law of international trade / edited by Mark S. W. Hoyle. - 2nd ed. - London : Laureate-Thomson, 1983.
xviii,342p; 25cm.
Previous ed.: 1980. Includes index.
ISBN 0907392105 Pbk £18.50

—Cases & materials on the law of international trade / edited by Mark S.W. Hoyle. - London : Laureate, 1980.
viii,282p; 31cm.
ISBN 0907392008 Hbk Unpriced
ISBN 0907392016 Pbk Unpriced

—Cases and statutes on commercial law / A. P. Dobson. - 2nd ed. - London : Sweet and Maxwell, 1980.
xviii,206p; 22cm.
Previous ed. by Paul L. Bradbury. 1973. Includes index.
ISBN 0421236809 £8.75
ISBN 0421236906

—Charlesworth's Mercantile law / Clive M. Schmitthoff, David A. G. Sarre. - 14th ed. - London : Stevens, 1984.
ix,733p; 22cm.
Previous ed.: 1977. Includes index.
ISBN 0420465707 Pbk Unpriced
ISBN 0420465804 Pbk £6.50

—Commercial and Consumer Law / Stephenson. - London : Financial Training, 1987.
- (SWOT).
ISBN 1851850430 Pbk £7.50

—Commercial and Industrial Law / Plymouth : Macdonald & Evans, 1981.
336p. - (M and E Handbook Ser.).
ISBN 071210464X Hbk £4.95

—Commercial and Industrial Law / 3rd ed. - Plymouth : Macdonald & Evans, 1984.
ISBN 0712101950 Pbk £6.50

—Commercial Cases : Reports of 1895-1941, 46 Vols. / Abingdon : Professional Books, 1895-1941.

—Commercial Contracts / London : Collins, 1987.
208p.
ISBN 0003832341 Hbk £17.50

—Commercial Law / Rev ed. - Pelican, 1985.
ISBN 0140226346 Pbk £18.95

—Commercial law in a changing economic climate / Clive M. Schmitthoff. - 2nd ed. - London : Sweet & Maxwell, 1981.
xii,78p; 22cm.
Previous ed.: 1977. Includes index. .
ISBN 0421268301 Pbk £5.25

—Company law in Great Britain / Peter Meinhardt with the assistance of Nigel Davis. - Aldershot : Gower, 1982.
178p in various pagings; 24cm.
Bibliography: 2p. - Includes index.
ISBN 056602389X Unpriced

—Consuetodo Vel Lex Mercat / 3rd ed. - Abingdon : Professional Books, 1986 Reprint.
ISBN 0862053250 Hbk £48.50

—Consumer and commercial statutes / London : Longman Professional (UK), 1989.
Covers the Bill of Lading 1855 through to the Consumer Protection Act of 1987, including the EEC Directive on Product Liability. Set out in chronological order including amendments to date.
ISBN 0851215173 Hbk £22.50

—Dictionary of Commercial Law / London : Butterworths, 1983.
ISBN 0406681597 Hbk £15.00
ISBN 0406681600 Pbk £10.95

—Dictionary of Commercial Law / 2nd ed. - Plymouth : Macdonald & Evans, 1980.
992p.
ISBN 0712154892 Hbk £42.75

—Effective retention of title clauses / John Parris. - London : Collins, Profession & Technical, 1986.
256p; 24cm.
Includes index.
ISBN 0003830748 £17.50

—Elements of export law / Geoffrey Whitehead. - Cambridge : Woodhead-Faulkner, 1983.
xiv,255p; 22cm.
Bibliography: p246. - Includes index.
ISBN 0859412288 Hbk

—Establishing a business in the United Kingdom / by R. M. Cooke and D. C. Borer. - 2nd ed. - London : Institute of Chartered Accountants, 1983.
viii,215p.
ISBN 0852913370

—General duty to trade fairly : a discussion paper / Office of Fair Trading. - London : The Office, 1986.
73p.
Bibliography: p.72-73.

—Knight's Industrial and Commercial Reports : 1966-75, 17 Vols. / Professional Books Staff. - Abingdon : Professional Books, 1984.

—Law and Commercial Dictionary - 5 Languages 2 vols. / West, 1985.
ISBN 0314805028 Hbk £170.00

—Law and policy of producer's associations / Oxford : Oxford University Press, 1984.
ISBN 0198254806 Hbk £40.00

—Legal environment of the business world / R.B. Buchanan. - Cheltenham : Stanley Thornes, 1982.
xix,230p; 22cm.
Includes index.
ISBN 0859503054 Pbk £3.75

—Lloyd's law reports / v. - London : Lloyd's, 1919-.
First published as Lloyd's list law reports. Index in each vol. - Consolidated index (1919-1975), v.1. 1981.

—Lloyd's maritime and commercial law quarterly / - London : Lloyd's of London Press, 1974-.
Index in each vol. - Cumulative indexes, 1974-78, 1979-83.

—Making Commercial Contracts / Oxford : Blackwell Scientific, 1988.
ISBN 0632018623 Hbk £19.95

—Mercantile Law / Keenan. - 7th ed. - Pitman, 1988.
ISBN 027302843X Pbk £12.95

—Modern Commercial Knowledge / 4th ed. Repr. of 1977 ed. - Plymouth : Macdonald & Evans, 1982.
320p. - (M and E Handbook Ser.).
ISBN 0712113991 Hbk £3.95

—Nigerian Commercial Law Reports : 1966 to date / London : Sweet & Maxwell.

—Practical commercial precedents / Jeffrey Green. - 4 vols. - London : Longman Professional, 1986.
Contains precedent documents to cover organization of a business, sale of shares and businesses, pensions, computer contracts, sale of goods, leasing and hire, and merchandising and sponsprship. Each precedent has introduction and commentary, which examines tax and stamp duty implications, and offers alternative clauses.
ISBN 0851209386 Llf £395

—Producers, importers and own-branders / Product Liability Briefing, 1988.
ISBN 1870317254 Pbk £6.50

—Ranking, Spicer and Pegler's Mercantile Law / Ernest E. Spicer. - 15th ed. - London : Butterworths.
ISBN 0406361401 Hbk

—Retention of title on the sale of goods / John Parris. - London : Granada, 1982.
186p; 24cm.
Includes index.
ISBN 0246116129 Unpriced

—Schmitthoff's Export trade : the law and practice of international trade / John Adams, Clive M Schmitthoff. - 8th ed. - London : Stevens, 1986.
lix,689p; 26cm.
Includes new chapters on GATT, and product liability, which covers the EEC Directive on Product Liability, and Part I of the Consumer Protection Act 1987. Discusses the Vienna Convention, and the effects on export trade law of the establishment of the Single Market in 1992.
ISBN 0420466401 Hbk £32.00
ISBN 0420466509 Pbk £25.00

—Ship sale and purchase : law and technique / by Iain S. Goldrein. - London : Lloyd's of London, 1985.
345p; 25cm.
Includes index.
ISBN 1850440522 No price

—Textbook of Commerce / 3rd ed. - London : Butterworths, 1981.
A textbook covering many aspects of commerce–distribution, retailing, consumer protection, credit, finance, and marketing. Includes numerous diagrams and illustrations.
ISBN 0408709286 Pbk

—Textbook of commerce / J W Loveridge. - 3rd ed. - London : Butterworths, 1981.
Students
ISBN 0408709286 Pbk £6.95

—Trading law / Chichester : Barry Rose, 1981-.
From v.2 Trading law reports published as pullout insert in each issue.

—Trading law reports / . - Chichester : Barry Rose, 1983.
Published as pullout insert in Trading law.

COMMERCIAL LAW - HONG KONG

—Commercial, Business and Trade Laws : Hong Kong 2 volumes / Dobbs Ferry : Oceana, 1982.
ISBN 0379231050 loose £190.00

COMMERCIAL LAW - INDIA

—Commercial Law / K.C. Garg. - rev. ed. - New Delhi : Kalyani Publishers, 1987.

—Commercial Law : Including Company Law / K.C. Garg. - 5th ed. - New Delhi : Kalyani Publishers, 1984.

—Commercial Reference / Calcutta : Eastern Law House, 1980.

—Fundamentals of Mercantile Law / New Delhi : Vikas Publishing House, 1980.
xxiii, 435p.

—Indian Mercantile Law and Industrial Law / K.C. Garg. - New Delhi : Kalyani Publishers, 1984.

—Industrial and Commercial Law / K.C. Garg. - 7th ed. 1986 repr. - New Delhi : Kalyani Publishers, 1987.
ISBN 8170960932 Hbk £60.00

—Justice Hidayatullah on Commercial Laws / New Delhi : Deep and Deep Publications, 1982.
130p.

—Manual of Commercial and Banking Laws, 4 Vols. / Allahabad : Law Publishers, 1983.

—Manual of Mercantile Law / 12th ed. - New Delhi : S. Chand and Company, 1983.
vii, 906p.

—Mercantile Law / K.C. Garg. - 4th ed. 1987 repr. - New Delhi : Kalyani Publishers.
ISBN 8170960517 Hbk £60.00

—Objective Type Questions and Answers in Mercantile Law / New Delhi : Kalyani Publishers.

—Problems in Mercantile Law / New Delhi : Kalyani Publishers.

COMMERCIAL LAW - IRAN

—Commercial law of Iran : by Sayed Hassan Amin / Tehran : Vahid Publications, 1986.
vii,144p.
Bibliography: p137-140.
ISBN 0946706298

COMMERCIAL LAW - IRELAND

—Business law / by Liam O'Malley. - London : Sweet & Maxwell, 1982.
xxxii,222p.
ISBN 0421285001

—Cases on Irish company law / Michael Forde. - Cork : Mercier, 1986.
461p; 23cm.
Includes index.
ISBN 0853427968 £40.00 (Irish)

—Company law in Ireland / Michael Forde. – Cork : Mercier, 1985.
xlix,552p; 23cm.
Includes index.
ISBN 0853427313 £45.00

COMMERCIAL LAW - JAPAN

—Commercial Code & the Audit Special Exceptions Law of Japan / Japan. – Tokyo : Eibun Horei Sha, 1982.
iii,249,16p.
'Originally translated by the Codes Translation Committee & the Ministry of Justice, revised by Fukio Nakane & Ikue Nishimura'.

COMMERCIAL LAW - MALAYSIA

—Commercial Law of Malaysia and Singapore / Beatrix Vohrah. – Hong Kong : Heinemann Educational Books (Asia), 1980.
286p.

COMMERCIAL LAW - NETHERLANDS

—Dutch business law : legal, accounting, and tax aspects of business in the Netherlands / by Steven R. Schuit and Jan M. van der Beek and Bonne K. Raap, and Michael W. den Boogert ... et al. – 2nd ed. – Deventer, Netherlands : Kluwer Law and Taxation Publishers, 1983.
xl, 552 p.; 25 cm.
Includes index.
ISBN 9065441220

COMMERCIAL LAW - NEW ZEALAND

—Butterworth's Commercial Brief / Wellington : Butterworths.

—Butterworth's Commercial Law / Wellington : Butterworths, 1985.

—Butterworths Commercial Law in New Zealand / London : Butterworths, 1986.
ISBN 0409702145 Pbk £49.00

—Butterworths Commercial Law in New Zealand / Butterworths, 1986.
Contains 48 chapters covering general principles of contract and quasi-contract, specific contracts, secured transactions and hire purchase, competition law, insolvency and dispute resolution. The law is as stated at January 1 1986. Appendices cover interests in land, New Zealand Courts, the present court structure in England and Wales, and a glossary of latin terms.
ISBN 0409702145 Pbk £86.90
ISBN 0409787574 Hbk £107.80

—Butterworths Commercial Service / Butterworths.
ISBN 0409681008 loose

—Mercantile Law in New Zealand / H.R.C. Wild. – 8th ed. – Auckland : Whitcoulls, 1983.
347p.
ISBN 0723307059 Hbk £14.95

—New Zealand Contract and Commercial Legislation / North Ryde : C.C.H. Australia, 1987.
900p.
ISBN 0864750722 Hbk

—Understanding Commercial Law / Lawrence. – Butterworths, 1988.
476p.
ISBN 0409787876 Pbk £65.00

COMMERCIAL LAW - NIGERIA

—Commercial law in Nigeria / by Okay Achike. – Enugu : Fourth Dimension, 1985.
xxii,496p.
Includes bibliographical references.
ISBN 9781561939

—Fundamentals of Nigerian business law / by Lateef Adegbite. – Lagos : Chamber of Commerce and Industry, 1980.
22p. – (Business education series).

—Nigerian business law / by Gaius Ezejiofor and C.O. Okonkwo and C.U. Ilegbune. – London : Sweet & Maxwell, 1982.
lxvii,531p; 22cm.
Includes index.
ISBN 0421301201 Hbk £32.00
ISBN 042129230X Pbk £16.00

—Nigerian business law / Cyprian Okonkwo, Peter Shears. – Ibadan : Spectrum, 1983.
207p; 24cm.
ISBN 0717511855 Pbk £4.85

—Nigerian business law : a guide for students, managers and foreign investors / Efiong J. Etuk, E.K. Quansah. – Basingstoke : Macmillan, 1986.
208p; 22cm.
Includes index.
ISBN 0333435079 Pbk £5.95

—Nigerian Commercial Law / Onitsha : Africana-FEP.

—Nigerian commercial law / by Kingsley Ikem Igweike. – Lahore : St. Hanbal, 1980.
xl,360p.
Includes index.

—Nigerian commercial law and practice / by J. Olakunle Orojo. – 2. – London : Sweet & Maxwell, 1983.
22cm.
Includes index.
ISBN 0421291702 £85.00

—Nigerian Commercial Law Reports : 1966 to date / London : Sweet & Maxwell.

Index 1966-1974

—Nigerian commercial laws : problems and perspectives / I.A. Ayua general editor. – Zaria : Department of Commercial Law, Ahmadu Bello University, 1984.
235p.
Includes bibliographical references.

—Principles of business law / Andrew Emefiene. – Akoka, Lagos : Management Science Centre, 1985.
i,194p.
ISBN 9782404098

COMMERCIAL LAW - NORTHERN IRELAND

—Company law : recent legislative changes : the text of a lecture delivered to the Belfast Solicitors' Association on 10 November 1983 / by Dennis Boyd. – Belfast : SLS Legal Publications, 1983.
i,32p.
Includes bibliographical references.

COMMERCIAL LAW - PAKISTAN

—Comments on Finance Act, 1985 and Amendments in Mercantile Laws / Karachi : Flecbon Corporation, 1987.

—Comments on the Finance Ordinance 1980 and Amendments in Mercantile Laws / Karachi : Flecbon Corporation, 1980.
ca 200p.

COMMERCIAL LAW - PHILIPPINES

—Answers to Bar Examination Questions /. – Quezon City : University of the Philippines, Law Center, 1982.
110p.

—Pandect of Commercial Law and Jurisprudence / Manila : National Book Store, 1984.
515p.
ISBN 9710805185 Hbk £34.00

COMMERCIAL LAW - SAUDI ARABIA

—Saudi business and labor law : its interpretation and application / A. Lerrick and Q.J. Mian. – London : Graham & Trotman, 1982.
xx,289p; 25cm.
Includes index.
ISBN 0860103919 £70.00

—Saudi business and labor law : its interpretation and application / Alison Lerrick, Q. Javed Mian. – 2nd ed. – London : Grahamn & Trotman, 1987.
xlv,589p.
Previous edition: 1982. Includes bibliographical references and index.
ISBN 0860105733

COMMERCIAL LAW - SCOTLAND

—Commentaries on the Law of Scotland in Relation to Mercantile and Maritime Laws, Movable and Heritable Rights and Bankruptcy, 2 Vols. / 3rd ed. Repr. of 1819 ed. – Abingdon : Professional Books.

—Commercial law of Scotland / by Campbell B. Burns and John N. Quar. – 3rd ed. – Glasgow : William Hodge, 1980.
xviii,279p.
Written primarily for students whose study of law is ancillary to their main interests. Covers the law of contracts, sale of goods, agency, partnership, bankruptcy, bills of exchange and other areas of commercial law. Includes a short chapter on merchant shipping. Index.
ISBN 0852791003

—Scots mercantile law / Edinburgh : W Green & Son, 1983.
Covers the major areas of the commercial law of Scotland, with full references to statutory provisions and case law. Notes differences between English and Scottish mercantile law. Student textbook assuming no previous legal knowledge.
ISBN 0414007123

—Scots mercantile law / Enid A. Marshall. – Edinburgh : W. Green, 1983.
xxxviii,665p.
Includes bibliographies and index.
ISBN 0414007204

—Scots Mercantile Law Statutes 1984 / Edinburgh : W Green.
ISBN 0414007441 Hbk £29.25

—Scots Mercantile Law Statutes 1984 / Edinburgh : W Green.
– (Reprint from Parliament House Book).
ISBN 0414007689 Hbk £18.00

—Scottish Cases and Materials in Commercial Law / A. Forte. – London : Butterworths, 1987.
ISBN 0406108706 Pbk

—Scottish cases and materials in commercial law / A Forte. – London : Butterworths, 1987.
ISBN 0406108706 Pbk £25.00

COMMERCIAL LAW - SINGAPORE

—Commercial Law of Malaysia and Singapore / Beatrix Vohrah. – Hong Kong : Heinemann Educational Books (Asia), 1980.
286p.

—Commercial law of Singapore : an introduction / Walter C.M. Woon. – Cambridge : Woodhead-Faulkner, 1986.
256p; 23cm.
Includes bibliography and index.
ISBN 0859412814 £45.00

COMMERCIAL LAW - SOUTH AFRICA

—Contract and mercantile law : a source book / by Ellison Kahn. – 2nd ed. – Cape Town : Juta, 1988.
lix,926p.
Includes index.
ISBN 0702119962

—Contract and mercantile law through the cases / by Ellison Kahn. – 2nd ed. – Cape Town : Juta, 1985.
lix,970p.
Bibliography: p.xxv-xxxviii. - Includes index.
ISBN 0702116548

—Mercantile Law and Mercantile Practice / Rondebosch : University of Cape Town, 1985.
14p.
ISBN 0799210005 Pbk £0.30

—South African mercantile and company law / by J.T.R. Gibson assisted by R. G. Comrie. – 5th ed. – Cape Town : Juta, 1983.
xl,668p.
Previous ed.: 1977. Includes index.
ISBN 070211359X

—Students' Casebook on Mercantile Law / Durban : Professional Publisher, 1975 repr. 1980.
ISBN 0409020303 Pbk £45.00

—Wille and Millin's Mercantile law of South Africa / by Philip Millin and George Wille. – 18th ed. – Johannesburg : Hortors Stationery, 1984.
civ, 952 p.; 26 cm.
Includes indexes. Bibliography: p. ciii-civ.
ISBN 0620073470 R58.00

COMMERCIAL LAW - SOUTH KOREA

—Business laws in Korea : investment, taxation, and industrial property / Chan-jin Kim, editor. – Seoul, Korea : Panmun Book Co., 1982.
xii, 799 p.; 24 cm.
Includes bibliographical references.

COMMERCIAL LAW - SPAIN

—Spanish business law / Bernardo M. Cremades, general editor. – Deventer, The Netherlands : Kluwer Law and Taxation Publishers, 1985.
Includes index.
ISBN 9065442200 Hbk £315.00

COMMERCIAL LAW - SWEDEN

—Swedish intellectual property and market legislation : collection of statutory texts / edited by Ulf Bernitz. – Stockholm : Institute for Intellectual Property and Market Law, Stockholm University, 1984.
ii,181p. – (Publications).
ISBN 9138081717

COMMERCIAL LAW - UNITED ARAB EMIRATES

—Business opportunites in United Arab Emirates : agency law : U.A.E. Federal Law no. 18 of 1981 Concerning the Organisation of Commercial Agencies / British Overseas Trade Board and the Department of Trade. – London : British Overseas Trade Board, 1986.
9 leaves.

COMMERCIAL LAW - UNITED KINGDOM

—Mercantile Law / 5th ed. Repr. of 1979 ed. – Plymouth : Macdonald & Evans, 1982.
320p. – (M and E Handbook Ser.).
ISBN 071211288X Hbk £3.50

COMMERCIAL LAW - UNITED STATES

—Doing business in the United States / Frank G. Opton, Herbert Feiler. – Deventer, Netherlands : Kluwer Law and Taxation Publishers, 1984.
Includes index and bibliography.
ISBN 9065441700

COMMERCIAL LAW - USSR

—Legal aspects of doing business in Eastern Europe and the Soviet Union / edited by Dennis Campbell. – Deventer, The Netherlands : Kluwer Law and Taxation Publishers, 1986.
– (International business series).
Includes index and bibliography.
ISBN 9065442634

COMMERCIAL LAW - WEST GERMANY

—Business law guide to Germany / Strobl, Killius & Vorbrugg. – 2nd ed. – Bicester : CCH Editions, 1988.
450p; 23cm.
Updates the law concerning product liability, taxation, joint ventures, distribution, licensing, franchising and industrial property rights, and includes new material on anti-dumping, mergers and acquisitions, social insurances, leasing and hiring of personnel, real estate and construction and bankruptcy.
ISBN 0863251579 £35.00

—German Private and Commercial Law-Introduction / Kote. – Oxford : Oxford University Press, 1982.
ISBN 0198253826 Hbk £27.00
ISBN 0198253834 Pbk £15.00

—Starting business operations in Germany : a practical guide with emphasis on sales agency agreements, limited liability companies, branch operations / by Harald Jung and Joachim Gres. – Deventer : Kluwer, 1984.
79p.
Bibliography: p.73-74. - Includes index.
ISBN 9065441794
ISBN 3787540229

COMMERCIAL LAW - ZIMBABWE

—Business law in Zimbabwe / R.H. Christie. – Cape Town : Juta, 1985.
lvii, 575 p.; 26 cm.
Includes index.
ISBN 0702115738

COMMERCIAL LAW (ISLAMIC LAW)

—Arab comparative & commercial law : the international approach : proceedings : International Bar Association first Arab Regional Conference, Cairo 15-19 February 1987 / International Bar Association. – London : Graham & Trotman, 1987.
Contents: v. 1. The Sharia and its relevance to modern transnational transactions. The settlement of disputes through arbitration. Joint ventures. – v. 2. Energy law.
ISBN 086010978X v. 2

COMMERCIAL POLICY

—Role of tariff quotas in commercial policy / by Michael Rom : with an introduction by Gerard Curzon. – London : Macmillan for the Trade Policy Research Centre, 1978.
272p.
ISBN 0333176383 £12.00

COMMERCIAL TREATIES

—Regulation of international economic relations through law / by Palitha Tikiri Bandara Kohona. – Dodrecht : M. Nijhoff Publishers, 1985.
Based on author's thesis (Ph. D.)–Cambridge University.
ISBN 9024731046

COMMERCIAL TREATIES - CANADA

—Legal framework for Canada-United States trade / edited by Maureen Irish and Emily F. Carasco. – Toronto : Carswell, 1987.
xxxviii,275p.

COMMERCIAL TREATIES - UNITED STATES

—Legal framework for Canada-United States trade / edited by Maureen Irish and Emily F. Carasco. – Toronto : Carswell, 1987.
xxxviii,275p.

COMMITTEES - GREAT BRITAIN

—Committee Reports Published by HMSO : Indexed By Chairman / London : HMSO.

—Committees of the House of Commons and Northern Ireland Affairs / Belfast : Queen's University of Belfast, 1984.
32p.

COMMODITIES - CANADA

—DeBoo Commodity Tax Reports / Toronto : DeBoo.
These monthly reports, dealing with developments in the reform of Canadian commodity tax law, identify actual and potential areas of concern, with emphasis on tax planning and compliance. Also included are relevant discussion papers, draft legislation, and government policy statements.
ISBN 0888202768 loose £150.00

COMMODITIES - INDIA

—Commentaries on Essential Commodities Act / 4th ed. – Allahabad : Law Publishers, 1982.

—Essential Commodities Act ... / 7th ed. – Allahabad : Law Book Company, 1988.
1,000p.

COMMODITY CONTROL

—Law and organisation of international commodity agreements / Kabir-ur-Rahman Khan. – The Hague : M. Nijhoff, 1982.
xxv,416p.
Includes index. Bibliography: p394-400.
ISBN 9024725542 Hbk £170.00

COMMODITY CONTROL - EUROPEAN COMMUNITY

—Anti-Dumping and Anti-Subsidy Law : the European Communities / A.N. Williams. – Paris : International Chamber of Commerce.
438p.

COMMODITY CONTROL - MALAYSIA

—Commodities Trading Act, 1985 (Act 324) and Subsidiary Legislation Made Thereunder / Kuala Lumpur : International Law Books Services.

COMMODITY EXCHANGES

—Financial futures / by M. Desmond Fitzgerald. – London : Euromoney, 1983.
ix,202p.
Bibliography: p.195-197. - Includes index.
ISBN 0903121433

—Futures markets : modelling, managing and monitoring futures trading / edited by Manfred E. Streit. – Oxford : Blackwell, in cooperation with the European University Institute, Florence, 1983.
viii,324p; 24cm.
Includes bibliographies and index.
ISBN 0631132945 Unpriced

COMMODITY EXCHANGES - UNITED STATES

—Securities and commodities enforcement : criminal prosecutions and civil injunctions / Howard M. Friedman. – Lexington, Mass. : Lexington Books, 1981.
xiii,238p; 24cm.
Includes index.
ISBN 066903617X £21.50

COMMODITY FUTURES

—Current developments in international securities commodities and financial futures markets / edited by Koh Kheng Lian ... et al. – Singapore : Butterworths on behalf of the Faculty of Law, National University of Singapore, 1987.
xxxvi,380p.
ISBN 0409995452

COMMODITY FUTURES - GREAT BRITAIN

—Commodities futures trading / London : Mansell, 1985.
ISBN 0720117038 Pbk £18.00

—Investors' Guide to the Commodities Futures Markets / London : Butterworths, 1986.

—Trading in commodities / 4th ed. – Cambridge : Woodhead-Faulkner, 1983.
ISBN 0859411788 Pbk £10.95
ISBN 0859411796 Hbk £19.95

—Trading in soft commodity futures / Cambridge : Woodhead-Faulkner, 1985.
ISBN 0859412393 Hbk £25.00

COMMON AGRICULTURAL POLICY - EUROPEAN COMMUNITY

—Common Agricultural Policy of EEC / 2nd ed. – Oxford : Blackwell Scientific, 1987.
ISBN 0003833747 Pbk £15.00

COMMON LAW

—Background of the common law : a historical sketch / Derek Roebuck. – Waigani : University of Papua New Guinea Press, 1983.
135p.
Includes index.

—Bentham and the common law tradition / Gerald J. Postema. – Oxford : Clarendon, 1986.
xvi,490p; 23cm. – (Clarendon law series).
Bibliography: p465-476. - Includes indexes.
ISBN 0198255055 £40.00

—Common law / by O.W. Holmes. – London : Macmillan, 1911.
xvi,422p.
Includes bibliographical references and index.

—English-Speaking Justice / Toronto : Anansi Press, 1985.
64p.
ISBN 0887841414 Pbk £5.95

—Historical Foundations of the Common Law / 2nd ed. – Butterworths, 1981.
496p.
ISBN 0409850055 Pbk £29.95

—Keys to English Law / Paris : Cujas, 1980.
208p.

—Legal theory and common law / edited by William Twining. – Oxford : Blackwell, 1986.
300p.
ISBN 0631144773 £22.50

—Precedent and law : dynamics of common law growth / Julius Stone. – Sydney : Butterworths, 1985.
xx,289p.
Account of the sources from which categories of illusory reference in precedent law spring, of the refinements and elaborations of the operations and of the social and political problems which the operation creates. The author's concepts and arguments are applied to the realities of contemporary judicial process.
ISBN 040949304X A$59

COMMON LAW - CANADA

—Chief Justice Samuel Freedman : a great Canadian judge : a collection of the reasons for judgment of the Honourable Samuel Freedman, Justice of the Court of Queen's Bench of Manitobe (1952-60), Justice of the Court of Appeal of Manitoba (1960-83), and Chief Justice of Manitoba (1971-83) / selected and edited by Cameron Harvey : with a bibliographical note by Vivian Rachlis. – Winnipeg : Law Society of Manitoba, 1983.
xi,195p.
ISBN 0969130708

COMMON LAW - ENGLAND

—Canon law and English common law / by R. H. Helmholz. – London : Selden Society, 1983.
24 p.
'Selden Society lecture delivered in the Old Hall of Lincoln's Inn, July 5th, 1982'.

—Common Law of Kent / 3rd ed. Repr. of 1822 ed. – Abingdon : Professional Books.
303p.

—Historical foundations of the common law / S.F.C. Milsom. – 2nd ed. – London : Butterworths, 1981.
xiii,475p; 22cm.
Previous ed.: 1969. Includes index. .
ISBN 0406625026 Hbk Unpriced
ISBN 0406625034 Pbk Unpriced

—History of the Common Law of England, 2 Vols. / 5th ed. – Abingdon : Professional Books.
239p.

—Studies in 13th century justice and administration / C.A.F. Meekings. – London : Hambledon, 1981.
342p; 25cm. – (History series).
ISBN 0950688231

COMMON LAW - GREAT BRITAIN

—Complete Guide for Justices of the Peace : Containing the Common and Statute Laws and Most Authentic Precedents Which Concern the Same / Repr. of 1687 ed. – Abingdon : Professional Books.

—English Law-'O' Level / 4th ed. – London : Butterworths, 1981.
This textbook covers the background and growth of English law, the administration and functions of the courts and their officers, and the basic principles of criminal law, tort, contract, and family law.
ISBN 0406653062 Hbk
ISBN 0406653054 Pbk

—Historical foundations of Common Law / 2nd ed. – London : Butterworths, 1981.
ISBN 0406625025 Hbk £22.50
ISBN 0406625034 Pbk £16.95

—Noy Maxime Common Law / 9th ed. – Abingdon : Professional Books, 1986 Reprint.
ISBN 0862053269 Hbk £35.25

—Status in the Common Law 1953 / London : Wildy & Sons.

COMMON LAW - HONG KONG

—Future of the law in Hong Kong / edited by R.I. Wacks. – Hong Kong : Oxford University Press (Hong Kong), 1989.
320.
Examines the theoretical and procedural aspects of the common law of Hong Kong and evaluates its development up to and beyond 1997 when sovereignty returns to China.
ISBN 0195849183 Hbk £19.50

COMMON LAW - INDIA

—Cases Illustrative of Oriental Life and the Application of English Law to India-Decided in H.M. Supreme Court at Bombay / 1853 repr. – New Delhi : Asian Educational Services, 1988.
620p.

COMMON LAW - MALAYSIA

—Common Law in Singapore and Malaysia / Butterworths, 1985.
401p.
Series of essays which, by presenting a number of case studies of different aspects of local law, explore the problems raised by the application of the common law in Singapore and Malaysia. Includes discussion of the Privy Council as court of last resort in Singapore and Malaysia 1957-1983, and the abuse of discretion. Also looks at Chinese marriage custom.
ISBN 0409995096 Hbk £110.00

—Common Law in Singapore and Malaysia / si : Malaya Law Review.

—Common Law in Singapore and Malaysia / London : Butterworths, 1985.

—Common Law in Singapore and Malaysia / London : Butterworths, 1985.
ISBN 0409995096 Hbk £70.00

COMMON LAW - SCOTLAND

—Elucidations Respecting the Common and Statute Law of Scotland / Repr. of 1800 ed. – Abingdon : Professional Books.
56p.

COMMON LAW - SINGAPORE

—Common Law in Singapore and Malaysia / si : Malaya Law Review.

—Common Law in Singapore and Malaysia / Butterworths, 1985.
401p.
Series of essays which, by presenting a number of case studies of different aspects of local law, explore the problems raised by the application of the common law in Singapore and Malaysia. Includes discussion of the Privy Council as court of last resort in Singapore and Malaysia 1957-1983, and the abuse of discretion. Also looks at Chinese marriage custom.
ISBN 0409995096 Hbk £110.00

—Common Law in Singapore and Malaysia / London : Butterworths, 1985.
ISBN 0409995096 Hbk £70.00

—Common Law in Singapore and Malaysia / London : Butterworths, 1985.

COMMON LAW - SOUTH AFRICA

—Daedalus in the Supreme Court : the common law today / D. P. Visser. – S.l. : University of Cape Town, 1985.
12 p. – (Inaugural lecture).
ISBN 0799209996

COMMON LAW - UNITED STATES

—Common law for the age of statutes / Guido Calabresi. – Cambridge, Mass. : Harvard University Press, 1982.
319p; 24cm.
Bibliography: p300-309. - Includes index.
ISBN 0674146042 Unpriced

COMMONS - ENGLAND

—Law of commons / by G.D. Gadsden. – London : Sweet & Maxwell, 1987.
xlviii,452p; 25cm.
Brings together many aspects of common land, and covers the history and present state of the law. Various types of common, ranging from village greens and urban amenity areas, to upland pastures are examined in the light of rights and obligations concerned.
ISBN 0421365609 £45.00

—Law of commons and village greens / by Ian Campbell and Paul Clayden. – 3rd ed. – Henley-on-Thames : Commons, Open Spaces and Footpaths Preservation Society, 1980.
80p.
Includes index.

COMMUNICATION AND TRAFFIC - UNITED STATES

—Communications deregulation : the unleashing of America's communications industry / Jeremy Tunstall. – Oxford : Blackwell, 1986.
425p; 23cm.
Includes bibliography and index.
ISBN 0631148191 £17.50

COMMUNICATION IN MANAGEMENT

—Policy for disclosure / L.E. Rockley. – London : Associated Business Press, 1980.
xiii,154p; 23cm.
Includes index.
ISBN 085227226X £10.50

COMMUNICATIONS

—Canadian Council on International Law : Conference Proceedings /. – Ottawa : Canadian Council on International Law, 1982.

—Information, freedom and censorship : the Article 19 world report 1988 / prepared by the staff of Article 19. – Harlow : Longman, 1988.
xii,340p; 24cm.
Bibliography: p324-326. - Includes index.
ISBN 0582026245 Pbk £12.95

—International law governing communications and information : a collection of basic documents / prepared by Edward W. Ploman. – London : Pinter, 1982.
xvi,367p; 25cm.
Includes index.
ISBN 0861872045 £25.00

COMMUNICATIONS - GREAT BRITAIN

—Corporate Communications / Churchill. – London : Fitzwilliam, 1988.
ISBN 1870555066 Hbk £25.00

COMMUNISM

—Communist Ideology Law and Crime / London : Macmillan, 1988.
ISBN 0333421078 Hbk £35.00

—Soviet law / London : Butterworths, 1983.
ISBN 0406562601 Hbk £19.50

COMMUNIST PARTIES

—Party statutes of the Communist world / edited by William B. Simons and Stephen White. – The Hague : M. Nijhoff, 1984.
viii,545p.
Prepared for the International Conference on Ruling Parties and their Status under Law, Kiel, Germany, June 1984. Bibliographies.
ISBN 9024729750

—Ruling Communist parties and their status under law / edited by D.A. Loeber (editor in chief) ... et al. – The Hague : M. Nijhoff, 1986.
Includes bibliographies and index.
ISBN 9024732093

COMMUNIST STATE

—Constitutions of the communist world / edited by William B. Simons. – Alphen aan den Rijn : Sijthoff & Noordhoff, 1980.
xvii,644p.

COMMUNITY CENTRES - ENGLAND

—Case for advice centres / N. Ralph. – Sheffield : Sheffield Advice Centres Group, 1985.
34p.

COMMUNITY DEVELOPMENT - ENGLAND

—Power, property and corporatism : the political sociology of planning / James Simmie. – London : Macmillan Press, 1981.
ix,351p.
Bibliography: p.321-345.
ISBN 0333243455

—Unlocking community resources : four experimental government small grants schemes / Hilary Jackson. – London : Home Office, 1986.
iv,61p; 30cm.
Bibliography: p61.
ISBN 0862522617 Pbk No price

COMMUNITY-BASED CORRECTIONS - ENGLAND

—Community service order : a first decade of promise / a review undertaken by Ken Pease on behalf of the Howard League for Penal Reform. – London : Howard League for Penal Reform, 1981.
ix,76p; 21cm.
Bibliography: p66-70.

—Manchester and Wiltshire multifacility schemes : a research report / Iain Crow, Ken Pease, Margy Hillary. – London? : NACRO, 1980.
iii,40p.
Includes bibliographical references.
ISBN 0850690188

COMMUNITY-BASED CORRECTIONS - GREAT BRITAIN

—Decarceration : community treatment and the deviant : a radical view / Andrew Scull. – 2nd ed. – Cambridge : Polity Press, 1984.
202p.
1st ed.: Englewood Cliffs, N.J.: Prentice-Hall, 1977. Bibliography: p191-198.

COMMUNITY-BASED CORRECTIONS - UNITED STATES

—Decarceration : community treatment and the deviant : a radical view / Andrew Scull. – 2nd ed. – Cambridge : Polity Press, 1984.
202p.
1st ed.: Englewood Cliffs, N.J.: Prentice-Hall, 1977. Bibliography: p191-198.

COMPANY LAW

—Australian national companies and securites legislation with state variations ... / Australia. – 5th ed. 2. – North Ryde, N.S.W. : CCH Australia, 1986.
ISBN 0869037013

—Australian national companies and securities legislation / Australia. – 3rd ed. 1. – North Ryde, N.S.W. : CCH Australia, 1982.
various pagings.
Includes index.
ISBN 0869033700

—British companies legislation / Bicester, Oxon. : CCH Editions, 1983.
looseleaf.
Includes indexes. Accompanied by transfer binder: The Companies (Winding Up) Rules 1949.
ISBN 0863250106

—British companies legislation / Bicester : CCH Editions, 1985.
23cm.

—Buying A Company : Checklist Guide / BIM. – VANN, 1982.
ISBN 0859461211 Pbk £4.00

—Cases and materials on corporations and associations / Allen Afterman and Robert Baxt. – 3rd ed . – Sydney : Butterworths, 1980.
lvi,824p.
Includes bibliographical references and index.
ISBN 0409439177

—Company law in Europe / P. Meinhardt. – 3rd ed. 1. – Farnborough, Hants. : Gower, 1981.
loose-leaf; 26cm.
Previous ed.: 1978. Includes bibliographies and index.
ISBN 0566022451 £40.00

—Comparative survey of corporate investments / Gunther H. W. Stratmann. – London : International Bar Association, 1983.
iv,198p.
Based on papers 'presented during the New Delhi Conference of the International Bar Assoiciation ...'. - Introduction.

Vol. 2 parts 1-2 : in Canada, Belgium, France, Federal Republic of Germany ... : written by members of Committee G/Business Organisations of the Section on Business Law of the International Bar Association
A 'set of papers ... presented during the Toronto Conference of the International Bar Association ...'. - Introduction.

—Corporate governance and directors' liabilities : legal, economic, and sociological analyses on corporate social responsibility / edited by Klaus J. Hopt, Gunther Teubner. – Berlin : W. de Gruyter, 1984.
462p. – (Series A, Law).
Includes index.
ISBN 3110100274 £75.00

—Corporate responsibility as a problem of company constitution / by Gunther Teubner. – Florence : European University Institute, 1983.
47p.
At head of title page: European University Institute, Florence, Law Department.

—Corporations : Principles and Policies / Mark Q. Connelly. – 2nd ed. – Toronto : Edmond-Montgomery, 1988.
ca 1,050p.
ISBN 0920722253 Hbk £100.00

—Cross-border transactions between related companies : a summary of tax rules / edited by William R. Lawlor. – Deventer, The Netherlands : Kluwer Law and Taxation Publishers, 1985.
Derived from an international tax planning symposium in New York sponsored by Ernst & Whinney. 'Current to January 1985'–Foreword.
ISBN 9065442324 pbk.

—Elements of Mercantile Law : Including Company and Industrial Law / 15th ed. – New Delhi : Sultan Chand and Sons, 1984.
xxviii, 880p.

—Guide to Company Law / New Delhi : S. Chand and Company.

—Handbook of Corporate Laws / G.K. Kapur. – New Delhi : S. Chand and Company.

—Imputation systems : objectives and consequences : proceedings of a seminar held in Montreal 1982 during the 36th Congress of the International Fiscal Association / organized by the International Fiscal Association. – Deventer : Kluwer, 1983.
129p. – (IFA congress seminar series).
ISBN 9065441212

—Juridification of social spheres : a comparative analysis in the areas of labor, corporate, antitrust, and social welfare law / edited by Gunther Teubner. – Berlin : De Gruyter, 1987.
viii, 446 p.; 24 cm.
Includes bibliographies and index.
ISBN 0899252729

—Minutes of evidence taken before the Company Law Committee / David Llewelyn Jenkins Jenkins. – London : H.M.S.O., 1960.
1607p.
Committee Chairman: Lord Jenkins. Bound with Report and Index.

—Principles of company law / by H.A.J. Ford. – 3rd ed. – Sydney : Butterworths, 1982.
lxix,650p.
Previous ed.: 1978. Includes index.
ISBN 040930932X

—Principles of Company Law / S.S. Gulshan. – 7th ed. – New Delhi : S. Chand and Company.
608p.

—Principles of Law : for Company Secretaries Exam / 4th ed. – New Delhi : Sultan Chand and Sons, 1986.
xiii, 776p.

—Role of Parliament in relation to the national companies scheme / report by Senate Standing Committee on Constitutional and Legal Affairs. – Canberra : Australian Government Publishing Service, 1987.
vii,106p. – (Parliamentary paper).
ISBN 0644051175

—Structure of Public Limited Companies / Kirchberg : Commission of the European Communities.
68p. – (Bulletin of the European Communities Ser.).

—Taxation of corporations and shareholders / Martin Norr. – Deventer, Netherlands : Kluwer Law and Taxation Publishers, 1982.
xii, 214 p.; 25 cm.
On page opposite t.p.: International Tax Program, Harvard Law School. Bibliography: p. 199-214.
ISBN 9065440151

—Tolley's European insolvency guide / Anthony R. Houghton, Neil H. Cooper. – Croydon : Tolley Publishing Co., 1984.
xv,364p; 23cm. – (An Extel Group publication).
Includes index.
ISBN 0854590978 Pbk £19.95

—Towards a 21st century company philosophy : oration delivered in the Assembly Hall at the University of Malta Graduation Ceremony, 26th April 1984 / by J.A. Micallef. – Valletta : Malta University Press, 1984.
9p.

—Trends in corporate governance and investor protection / by Louis Loss. – Lagos : Lagos University Press, 1981.
64p.
Includes bibliographies.
ISBN 9782264261

COMPANY LAW - AUSTRALIA

—Afterman and Baxt's Cases and materials on close coporations and associations / John Latham, R Sappideen. – 4th. – North Ryde : Butterworths (Australia).
Covers unincorporated associations, partnership, the company as a separate legal entity, the memorandum of association, powers of companies and ultra vires, articles of association and contacts within the company, relations between the company and outsiders, control and management of the company, oppression of minority shareholders, and takeovers and reconstructions.
ISBN 0409493120 Pbk

—Afterman and Baxt's Cases and Materials on Corporations and Associations / Sappideen. – Sydney : Butterworths, 1984.
732p.
ISBN 0409493023 Hbk
ISBN 0409493120 Pbk

Supplement - 1986
ISBN 0409491098

—Afterman and Baxt's Cases and Materials on Corporations and Associations / 5th ed. – Sydney : Butterworths, 1988.
900p.

—Annual report and financial statements / National Companies and Securities Commission. – v. – Canberra : Australian Government Publishing Service, 1981.
Second and subsequent report years run 1st July to 30th June.

—Australian Company Law, 4 Vols. / H. H. Ednie. – Wellington : Butterworths, 1982.

—Australian Company Law / Butterworths, 1982.
ISBN 0409441600 loose

—Australian company law / John O'Hair, John (Sean) Kearns. – 4th ed. – Sydney : McGraw-Hill Book Co., 1985.
xvii, 469 p.; 25 cm.
Rev. ed. of: Australian company law / Harvey Mason. 3rd ed. 1981. Includes bibliographical references and indexes.
ISBN 0074520334 pbk.

—Australian company law / H. H. Ednie, H. A. J. Ford. – 3rd ed. – Sydney : Butterworths, 1981.
loose-leaf.
Previous ed.: 1971. Includes: Butterworths company law bulletin.
ISBN 0409441708

—Australian company law / by W.E. Patterson and H.H. Ednie : consultant editors P.R. Adams, M.O. Jager. F.J.O. Ryan. – 2nd ed. 9. – Sydney : Butterworths, 1971-1982.
looseleaf.
Includes index.

—Australian Company Law Casebook / North Ryde : C.C.H. Australia, 1986.
486p.
ISBN 0869038265 Hbk

—Australian Company Law Reports (ACLR) / H. H. Ednie. – Wellington : Butterworths.

—Australian Company Practice / J.C. Cooke. – Butterworths, 1978.
ISBN 0409474703 loose £15.00

—Australian Company Practice / J. C. Cooke. – 2nd ed. – Wellington : Butterworths, 1982.

—Australian Corporate Law Reference / Ken W. Hale. – Woolloomooloo : International Business Communications, 1986.
ca 600p.
ISBN 0949553263 Hbk £49.50

—Australian Corporate Law Reference / Jackson. – London : Legal Books, 1986.
ISBN 0949553263 Hbk £27.50

—Australian National Companies Act with Regulations / 6th ed. – North Ryde : C.C.H. Australia, 1986.
2,000p.
ISBN 0869039792 Hbk

—Australian national companies and securities legislation : up to date to 1 October 1987 / Australia. – 7th ed. 2. – North Ryde, N.S.W. : CCH Australia, 1987.
Index to legislation in vol. 1.
ISBN 1862640068

—Australian Proprietary Company Articles : a Practical Guide with Precedents / North Ryde : C.C.H. Australia, 1982.
320p.

—Bound Australian Company Law Cases 1971-1981, 3 Vols. / North Ryde : C.C.H. Australia.

—Bound Company Law, 3 Vols. / North Ryde : C.C.H. Australia.

—Butterworth's Companies and Securities Codes / 1987 ed. – Sydney : Butterworths.
ISBN 040949237X Pbk £32.00

Vol. I
ISBN 0409492353 Pbk £24.00

Vol. II
ISBN 0409492361 pap £16.50

—Butterworths Companies and Securities Code, 2 Vols. / Butterworths, 1988.
ca 1090p 710p.
ISBN 0409493384 Pbk

Vol. 1
ISBN 0409493368 £29.00

Vol. 2
ISBN 0409493376 £9.50

—Butterworths Company and Securities Codes, 1988 : And Related Legislation / Combined ed. – Sydney : Butterworths, 1988.
1600p.

—Butterworths' Companies Act 1981 : regulations and related legislation / 1982 ed. 1. – Sydney : Butterworths, 1982.
various pagings.
Includes index.
ISBN 0409492302

—Casebook on Australian Company Law / 4th ed. – Butterworths, 1983.
365p.
ISBN 0409491810 Pbk £31.50

—Cases and Materials on Corporations and Associations / R. Baxt. – 5th ed. – Butterworths, 1988.
823p.
ISBN 0409493058 Pbk £62.00 (incl. suppl.)

—CCH Australian companies and securities legislation / by the CCH company law editors. – 3. – North Ryde, N.S.W. : CCH Australia, 1987.
looseleaf.
'Publication originally issued in one volume in July 1982 (vol. 2 in November 1983) titled Australian companies legislation' - t.p. verso. Spine title: Australian companies and securities legislation.
ISBN 1862640270

—Co-operative companies and securities scheme / explanatory paper on exposure draft of Companies and Securities Legislation (Miscellaneous Amendments) Bill 1983 : prepared by the Business Affairs Division of the Commonwealth Attorney-General's Department for and on behalf of the Ministerial Council for Companies and Securities. – Parkes : The Department, 1982.
177p.

—Companies and securities law journal / . – Sydney : Law Book Co., 1982-.

—Company Charges Plus Australian Supplement / Wellington : Butterworths.
ISBN 040949061X Pbk

—Company Law / Sydney : Butterworths, 1986.
117p. – (Butterworth's Student Companion Ser.).
ISBN 0409490962 Pbk £9.95

—Company Law / North Ryde : Law Book Co, 1985.
xi, 116. – (Nutshells).
ISBN 0455205957

—Company Law for Legal Assistants - 1985 / Vancouver : British Columbia Continuing Legal Education Society, 1985.
410p.
ISBN 0865042446 Hbk £65.00

—Company Law in Australia / J. P. Hambrook. – Sydney : Butterworths, 1988.
544p.

—Company Law Lunchtime Series / Monash University Staff. – Clayton : Monash University Press, 1984.
ISBN 086746318X Hbk £15.00

—Contract of Employment : Principles of Australian Employment Law / 3rd ed. – North Ryde : C.C.H. Australia, 1986.
328p.
ISBN 0869036297 Hbk £38.00

—Financial reporting requirements of the Companies Act and Codes / Canberra : Australian Government Publishing Service, 1983.
vi,163p.
ISBN 0644005173

—Guide to Company Law / 2nd ed. – North Ryde : Law Book Co, 1982.
xi, 270p.
ISBN 0455203709 Pbk £15.00

—Guide to Company Law / 2nd ed. – Sydney : Butterworths, 1987.
366p.

—Guide to Company Law : Including 1986 Supplement / 2nd ed. – Butterworths, 1986.
335p.
ISBN 0409491667 Pbk £31.50

—Guide to the national companies and securities scheme / by H.A.J. Ford ... et al. – Sydney : Butterworths, 1982.
xxv,406p.
Includes index.
ISBN 040949335X

—Guide to the national scheme and revised Companies Bill 1980 / by W.E.Paterson, H.H. Ednie and H.A.J. Ford. – 1. – Sydney : Butterworths, 1980.
various pagings; 24cm.
Includes index.
ISBN 0409300462

—Guidebook to Australian Company Law / 9th ed. – North Ryde : C.C.H. Australia, 1986.
320p.
ISBN 0869039962 Hbk £32.00

—Guidebook to Australian company law : an explanation of the National Companies Act / 6th ed. – North Ryde, N.S.W. : CCH Australia, 1982.
vii,320p.
Includes index.
ISBN 0869033603

—Introduction to Company Law / 3rd ed. – North Ryde : Law Book Co, 1985.
xx, 271p.
ISBN 0455204663 Pbk £25.00
ISBN 0455205655 Hbk £38.00

1986 Supplement
35p.
ISBN 0455207240 Pbk £5.00

—Introduction to company law / North Ryde : Law Book Co, 1987.
ISBN 0455207720 Hbk
ISBN 0455207739 Pbk

—Law and Practice of Company Accounting in Australia / M O Jager, R B Taylor. – 6th ed. – North Ryde : Butterworths (Australia), 1983.
Analysis of the law of company accounting and reporting. Includes aspects of practice as necessary to interpret the law and explain its significance and application. Incorporates developments including the changes effected by the Companies Act 1981 (the National Act), and the latest Accounting Standards.
ISBN 0409493902 Pbk £27.60

—Law and Practice of Company Accounting in Australia / M. Jager. – 6th ed. – Sydney : Butterworths, 1987.
669p.
ISBN 0409491853 Hbk

—Law of Companies in Australia / 2nd ed. – North Ryde : C.C.H. Australia, 1986.
670p.
ISBN 0869039814 Hbk £54.00
ISBN 086903930X Pbk £42.00

—Law of Public Company Finance / R. Vann. – North Ryde : Law Book Co, 1986.
xxix, 593p.
ISBN 0455206856 Hbk £89.50

—Mason's Casebook on Australian Company Law / 4th ed. – London : Butterworths, 1983.
ISBN 0409491810 Pbk £19.20

—New Zealand business : entering the Australian market : Legal Research Foundation Inc. Seminar, 19 November 1985 / Barry J. McWilliams. – Auckland : Legal Research Foundation, 1985.
122p.
Papers presented by Barry J. McWilliams and others.
ISBN 0908581408

—Outline of Companies and Securities Law / Sydney : Butterworths, 1988.
222p.

—Outline of Companies and Securities Law / Butterworths, 1987.
221p.
ISBN 040949285X Pbk £19.95

—Powers of Investigation in Revenue, Companies and Trade Practices Law / R.H. Woellner. – Butterworths, 1983.
486p.
ISBN 0409493813 Pbk £65.00

—Principles of company law / H.A.J. Ford. – 4th ed. – Sydney : Butterworths, 1986.
lxxix,774p.
Includes bibliographical references and index.
ISBN 0409490679 Hbk A$59.00
ISBN 0409490687 Pbk A$42.50

—Proprietary Company Practice Manual / 2nd ed. – North Ryde : Law Book Co, 1983.
vii, 162p.
ISBN 0455204128 £21.00

—Understanding Company Law / A. Herzberg. – 2nd ed. 1986. – North Ryde : Law Book Co.
xxxvi, 453p.
ISBN 0455206392 Hbk £42.00
ISBN 0455206406 Pbk £29.50

—Valuation of company shares and businesses / by A. V. Adamson and M. S. Adamson. – 6th ed. – Sydney : Law Book Co., 1980.
xiv,217p.
Bibliography: p.212. - Includes index.
ISBN 0455200750

COMPANY LAW - AUSTRIA

—Austrian law on companies with limited liability : as of January 1, 1984 with excerpted provisions of other relevant laws and annotations / editor Julie Goldberg. – Deventer : Kluwer Law and Taxation Publishers, 1985.
124p; 23 cm.
English and German. Includes index. Bibliography: p. 122.
ISBN 9065442294 Hbk £75.00

COMPANY LAW - CANADA

—Advanced Company Law and Corporate Income Tax / Vancouver : Continuing Legal Education Society of British Columbia, 1985.
355p.
ISBN 0865042357 Hbk £70.00

—Associated corporations / by Richard B. Miner. – Toronto : Carswell, 1983.
xvii,134p.
Includes index.
ISBN 0459354507

—Canada Business Corporations Act : An Accountant's Review of the Highlights / 2nd ed. – Toronto : Butterworths, 1981.
128p.
ISBN 0409859737 Pbk £14.95

—Canada Business Corporations Act and Regs. / 9th ed. – Toronto : DeBoo, 1987.

—Canada Business Corporations Act and Regulations / Toronto : DeBoo, 1987.
256p.
ISBN 0888202717 Pbk £11.50

—Canada Business Corporations Act : with Regulations / 6th ed. – Don Mills : CCH Canadian Ltd, 1985.
224p.
ISBN 0887962955 Pbk £8.95

—Canada Corporation Manual, 3 Vols. / Toronto : DeBoo, 1984.
ISBN 0888201346 Hbk £325.00

—Canadian business organizations law / by Tom Hadden, Robert E. Forbes, Ralph L. Simmonds. – Toronto : Butterworths, 1984.
xlix,680p.
Relates common-law rules and statutory provisions to current commercial and industrial practice, distinguishing between the problems of small private businesses and larger public companies. Provides information on current corporate issues; practices and problems in designed instruments of corporate finance, securities law, corporate acquisitions, corporate groups, foreign acquisitions, and lease financing.
ISBN 0409834815 Hbk £95

—Canadian Company Law : Cases, Notes and Materials / B. Welling. – 3rd ed. – Butterworths, 1986.
640p.
Examines and discusses the main areas of company law in a sequential manner, making use of Canadian, American and Australian authorities. Covers new statutory developments, the corporate constitution, corporate entity, company liability, management, capital structure, and distributions.
ISBN 0409805106 Pbk £70.00

—Canadian Corporation Precedents, 3rd Edition / Agincourt : Carswell, 1987.
440p.

—Canadian Corporation Precedents / 3rd ed. – Agincourt : Carswell.
440p.
This third edition text provides corporation and securities law precedents. Sample forms utilized from incorporation to dissolution are included. Information pertaining to both private and public corporations are included. Additionally, selected forms and precedents have commentaries analyzing the legal history.

—Cases and Materials on Partnerships and Canadian Business Corporations / F. Iacobucci. – Agincourt : Carswell, 1983.
958p.
This work examines the principles of Canadian corporate and partnership law in depth. The book covers the fundamentals of corporate finance and distribution, duties of management, the rights and remedies of shareholders, and more.

—Central Trust Company Act, 1983, Bill 097 : An Act Respecting Central Trust Company and Crown Trust Company / Ontario : Ontario Government Publications Service, 1983.
5p.

—Company Law / Vancouver : Continuing Legal Education Society of British Columbia, 1987.
491p.
ISBN 0865043423 Hbk £90.00

—Company Law for Legal Assistants 1987 / Vancouver : Continuing Legal Education Society of British Columbia, 1987.
299p.
ISBN 0865043507 Hbk £80.00

—Consumer protection, environmental law, and corporate power / Ivan Bernier and Andree Lajoie, research coordinators. – Toronto : University of Toronto Press, 1985.
xv, 220 p.; 23 cm.
'Published ... in cooperation with the Royal Commission on the Economic Union and Development Prospects for Canada and the Canadian Government Publishing Centre, Supply and Services Canada.'. Includes bibliographies.
ISBN 0802072968 pbk.

—Corporate Finance for Legal Assistants / Vancouver : Continuing Legal Education Society of British Columbia, 1988.
299p.
ISBN 0865041644 Hbk £75.00

—Corporate Law in Canada : the Governing Principles / Butterworths, 1984.
784p.
Shows where old law may be safely discarded and demonstrates how current governing principles may be balanced in potential conflict situations. Also looks at the distinction between company statutes in each province, the role of the Charter of Rights in the regulation of corporate activity, corporate crime and tort capital structure, and the legal duties of corporate managers.
ISBN 0409857645 Hbk £100.00

—Corporate law in the 80s / Don Mills : Richard De Boo, 1982.
716 p.; 24 cm.
Includes index.
ISBN 0888201109

—Corporate Procedures for Legal Assistants / Agincourt : Carswell, 1985.
450p.
This book provides a step-by-step analysis of the incorporation procedure under Ontario and Canadian federal corporate law for legal assistants. Forms and precedents are provided in this 'how to' incorporation guide.

—Corporate structure, finance and operations : essays on the law and business practice / edited by Lazar Sarna with the assistance of Warren M. Goodman. – Toronto : Carswell, 1980.
viii,496p.
Includes bibliographical references.
ISBN 0459332007

—Corporate taxation / Kathleen A. Lahey. – Toronto : Emond Montgomery Publications, 1984.
lx,540p.
Includes bibliographical references and index.
ISBN 0920722113

—Corporation Law for Canadian Business / Butterworths, 1981.
448p.
ISBN 0409988340 Hbk £21.95

—Corporations : Cases, Notes and Materials / Mark Connelly. – Toronto : Emond-Montgomery, 1984.
1000p.
ISBN 0920722148 Hbk £90.00

—Corporations : Cases Test and Materials / Connelly. – Aurora : Canada Law Book, 1984.

—Corporations : Cases, Text and Materials / Mark Q. Connelly. – 2nd ed. – Toronto : Edmond-Montgomery, 1988.
1,000p.

—Current developments in measuring business income for tax purposes / Corporate Management Tax Conference, 1987. – 1. – Toronto : Canadian Tax Foundation, 1987.
various pagings.
ISBN 088808031X

—Extra-Provincial Corporations Act, 1983, Bill 103 : An Act in Respect of Extra-Provincial Corporations / Ontario : Ontario Government Publications Service, 1983.
12p.

—Federal Incorporation and Business Guide : How to Form Your Own Federal Corporation Under the Canada Business Corporations Act / 5th ed. – North Vancouver : International Self-Counsel Press, 1986.
122p.
ISBN 088908632X Hbk £14.95

—Golden Handshake : Hiring and Firing / Vancouver : British Columbia Continuing Legal Education Society, 1983.
137p.
ISBN 0865041253 Hbk £45.00

—Guidebook to Canada Business Corporations Act / M.I. Wainberg. – 2nd ed. – Don Mills : CCH Canadian Ltd, 1981.
104p.
ISBN 0887961533 Pbk £9.50

—Harmonization of business law in Canada / Ronald C.C. Cuming, research coordinator. – Toronto : University of Toronto Press, 1986.
xx, 245 p.; 23 cm.
Includes bibliographies. Contents: Harmonization of provincial laws, with particular reference to commercial, consumer, and corporate law / Jacob S. Ziegel – The regulation of the securities market and the harmonization of provincial laws / Philip Anisman – Harmonization of Canadian personal property security law / Ronald C.C. Cuming – Harmonization of Canadian insurance law / Marvin G. Baer.
ISBN 0802073034 pbk.

—Income tax aspects of corporate financing / Toronto : Canadian Tax Foundation, 1980.
xiv,399p.

—Income tax considerations in corporate financing / Corporate Management Tax Conference 1986. – Toronto : Canadian Tax Foundation, 1986.
xv,475p.
Includes bibliographical references.
ISBN 0888080271

—Income tax enforcement, compliance, and administration : Corporate Management Tax Conference 1982 / edited by Christine Purden Nelson. – Toronto : Canadian Tax Foundation, 1983.
x,297p.
ISBN 0888080115

—Introduction to business associations in Canada : cases, notes, and materials / by R.L. Simmonds and Peter P. Mercer. – Toronto, Canada : Carswell Legal Publications, 1984.
xxviii, 778 p.; 25 cm.
Spine title: Business associations in Canada.
ISBN 0459365304 pbk.

—Law of Canadian Companies : 1931 / Repr. of 1980 ed. – Agincourt : Carswell.
1226p.
This book is a reprint of the 1931 text on the Companies Act of Canada and the case law applicable to companies incorporated under the Act.

—Milner's Cases and Materials on Contracts / 4th ed. – Aurora : Canada Law Book, 1985.

—O'Brien's Encyclopedia of Forms : Division Two-Corporations / Aurora : Canada Law Book Co.
– (Abridgments and Encyclopedias).

—Ontario Business Corporations Act annotated / Margot Lettner. – Scarborough, Ontario : Butterworths (Canada), 1990.
352.
ISBN 1234124312 Pbk £36

—Studies in Canadian company law / Etudes sur le droit canadien des compagnies : edited by Jacob S. Ziegel. – 2. – Toronto : Butterworths, 1967.
Includes bibliographical references and index. Vol. 2 signed by the editor. Vol. 2 has subtitle: Corporation and securities law in the seventies. English or French.

COMPANY LAW - CANADA - ALBERTA

—Alberta Corporation Manual / Toronto : DeBoo.
Looseleaf service.
ISBN 0888201303 loose £295.00

—Annotated Business Corporations Act of Alberta / 3rd ed. – Agincourt : Carswell, 1988.
384p.

—Annotated Business Corporations Act of Alberta / 3rd ed. – Agincourt : Carswell, 1988.
384p.
This volume includes a full annotated text of the Act, all regulations under the Act, and annotations on reported and unreported cases dealing with issues arising under the statute.

—Guidebook to Alberta Business Corporations Act / James S. Smeltzer. – North Ryde : C.C.H. Australia, 1984.
134p.
ISBN 0887962556 Hbk £12.00

COMPANY LAW - CANADA - BRITISH COLUMBIA

—Annotated British Columbia Company Act / Agincourt : Carswell, 1986.
268p.
This annotated edition of the British Columbia Company Act presents an analytical interweaving of case and statute law through the annotations in the work. The text of the Act, the regulations, and forms are included in the book.

—British Columbia Company Act / 4th ed. – Toronto : DeBoo, 1985.
168p.
ISBN 0888202113 Pbk £19.95

—British Columbia Company Act with Regulations / Don Mills : CCH Canadian Ltd, 1986.
172p.
ISBN 0887963528 Pbk £8.95

—British Columbia Corporation Manual / Toronto : DeBoo.
Looseleaf service.
ISBN 0888201311 loose £295.00

—Incorporation and Business Guide for British Columbia : How to Form Your Own Corporation / 13th ed. – North Vancouver : International Self-Counsel Press, 1988.
ISBN 0889084319

COMPANY LAW - CANADA - ONTARIO

—Corporate Procedures for Legal Assistants / Agincourt : Carswell, 1985.
450p.
This book provides a step-by-step analysis of the incorporation procedure under Ontario and Canadian federal corporate law for legal assistants. Forms and precedents are provided in this 'how to' incorporation guide.

—Guidebook to Ontario Business Corporations Act / M.I. Wainberg. – 1st ed. – North Ryde : C.C.H. Australia, 1985.
122p.
ISBN 088796267X Pbk £12.00

—Ontario Business Corporations Act, 1982 and Regulation / 14th ed. – Toronto : DeBoo, 1987.

—Ontario Business Corporations Act and Regs. / 10th ed. – Toronto : DeBoo, 1983.
ISBN 0316649X Hbk £13.50

—Ontario Business Corporations Act with Regulations / 10th ed. – Don Mills : CCH Canadian Ltd, 1987.
244p.
ISBN 0887964117 Pbk £10.95

—Ontario Corporation Manual / Toronto : DeBoo.
ISBN 088820132X loose £325.00

COMPANY LAW - CANADA - QUEBEC

—Loi Sur les Compagnies et Reglements du Quebec Companies Act and Regulations 1983 / Toronto : DeBoo, 1983.
382p.

—Manuel des Corporations du Quebec / Toronto : DeBoo, 1983.
ISBN 0888201478 Hbk £365.00

—Quebec Corporation Manual / Toronto : DeBoo.
ISBN 0888201338 loose £140.00

COMPANY LAW - ENGLAND

—Annotated guide to the 1986 insolvency legislation : Insolvency Act 1986, Company Directors Disqualification Act 1986 and Insolvency Rules 1986 / L.S. Sealy, David Milman. – Bicester : CCH Editions, 1987.
viii,994p; 23cm.
Includes index.
ISBN 0863250823 Pbk £12.00

—Commercial litigation : pre-emptive remedies / by Iain S. Goldrein and K.H. P. Wilkinson : with a foreword by Sir John Donaldson. – London : Sweet & Maxwell, 1987.
xlvii,793p; 26cm.
Covers topics in the commercial field where emergency relief may be necessary. Techniques are explained, and relevant reported cases are referred to, including the necessary statutes and court orders. Appendices include forms and precedents, and some Chancery and Queen's Bench Division Practice Directions.
ISBN 0421348003 Hbk £107

—Company law in a nutshell / Francis Roundell. – 3rd ed. – London : Sweet & Maxwell, 1985.
vii,88p. – (New nutshells).
Includes index.
ISBN 0421348402

—Corporate insolvency / Peter Totty and Michael Crystal. – London : McGraw-Hill, 1982.
xv,155p; 26cm.
Includes index.
ISBN 0070845824 £12.95

—Set-off / S. Rory Derham. – Oxford : Clarendon, 1987.
320p; 22cm.
Includes bibliography and index.
ISBN 019825556X £30.00

COMPANY LAW - EUROPE

—Forum Internationale / Marcus Lutter. – Deventer : Kluwer Law and Taxation Publishers, 1983.

COMPANY LAW - EUROPEAN COMMUNITY

—Basic information, classification of companies, share capital and distributions / Peat, Marwick, Mitchell and Co. – London : Peat, Marwick, Mitchell & Co., 1980.
Cover title: Legislation of member States. Loose leaf binder.

—Basic information, share capital and mergers : directives 1,2 and 3 / London : Peat, Marwick, Mitchell & Co., 1980.
152p.
Loose leaf binder. Cover title: EEC company Law. Part 1..

—Company law in the European Communities / Wooldridge. – 3rd ed. – London : Longman Professional, 1982.
ISBN 0851206387 Hbk £25.00

—Company law in the European Communities / Frank Wooldridge. – 3rd ed. – London : Oyez Longman, 1982.
viii,200p.
Previous ed., 1970, entitled: Companies in the Common Market.
ISBN 0851206387

—Draft E.C. regulation on the European economic interest grouping (EEIG) : a consultative document / Great Britain. – London : Department of Trade and Industry, 1983.
15,109p.

—Draft European Communities directive on procedures for informing and consulting employees / Draft European Communities fifth directive on the harmonisation of comapny law : Department of Employment, Department of Trade and Industry. – London : The Departments, 1983.
90p.

—European company law : a guide to Community and member state legislation / Belmont European Community Law Office. – London : Financial Times Business Information Ltd., 1986.
xviii,215p.
ISBN 090319998X

—European tax law for companies / Charles Ferrier. – London : Financial Times Business Information, 1985.
xii,130p; 30cm.
ISBN 0903199890 spiral No price

—Fourth Company Law Directive : Implementation by Member States / J.G. Demas. – Luxembourg : Office for Official Publications of the European Communities, 1987.
100p.
ISBN 9282571211 Pbk £400.00

—Fourth directive : its effect on the annual accounts of companies in the European Economic Community / Ernst & Whinney. – London : Kluwer, 1980.
440p.
Includes official text of the Fourth Directive. 'This book has been prepared by Ernst & Whinney and its associates under the general editorship of E.G. Bartholomew and A.D. Welchman.'.
ISBN 0903393468

—Harmonisation of company and related law in Europe : timetable and progress of draft directives and other proposals / Companies Legislation Division, Department of Trade. – London : The Division, 1983.
15p.
Previous ed.: 1982.

—Harmonisation of company and related law in Europe : timetable and progress of draft directives and other proposals / Companies Division, Department of Trade. – London : Companies Division, Department of Trade, 1982.
13p.

—Harmonisation of company and related law in the European Community : progress on draft directives and other proposals / Department of Trade and Industry, Companies Division. – London : The Division, 1987.
13p.

—Harmonisation of company and related law in the European Community : progress on draft directives and other proposals / Companies Division, Department of Trade and Industry. – Sept. 1987. – London : The Division, 1987.
27p.

—Harmonisation of company and related law in the European Community : timetable and progress of draft directives and other proposals / Companies Legislation Division, Department of Trade and Industry. – London : Companies Legislation Division, Department of Trade and Industry, 1983.
13p.
Previous ed.: published as 'Harmonisation of company and related law in Europe', 1982.

—Implementation of the sixth EC directive on company law : an explanatory and consultative note / Department of Trade and Industry. – 1. – London : The Department, 1984.
various pagings.

—Implementation of the third EC directive on company law : an explanatory and consultative note / Department of Trade. – 1. – London : The Department, 1982.
various pagings.
Includes the text of the directive.

—Legal harmonization and the business enterprise : corporate and capital market law, harmonization policy in Europe and the U.S.A. / by Richard M. Buxbaum and Klaus J. Hopt. – Berlin : De Gruyter, 1988.
– (Series A–Law).
Includes index. Bibliography.
ISBN 0899251277 Hbk £96.00

—Limited liability and the corporation / edited by Tony Orhnial. – London : Croom Helm, 1982.
223p; 23cm.
Conference papers. Includes bibliographies.
ISBN 0709905157 £12.95

—Proposal for a Council regulation on the European Co-operation Grouping (COM (78) 139 Final) : memorandum / by the Society's Standing Committee on Company Law. – London : Law Society, 1981.
4p; 30cm.

—Seventh Directive : consolidated accounts in the EEC / Sharon M. McKinnon : edited by Alan D.H. Newham. – Brentford : Kluwer, 1984.
392p.
Includes the official texts of Fourth and Seventh Directives.
ISBN 0903393700

COMPANY LAW - GREAT BRITAIN

—Accounting Requirements of the Companies Acts / R. A. Wyld. – 2nd ed. – London : Butterworths, 1980.
ISBN 0406402035 Pbk £19.65

—Administration of Corporate Security / Cambridge : Woodhead-Faulkner, 1987.
ISBN 0902197258 Hbk £25.00

—Administration procedure / Frank Wooldridge. – Bristol : Jordans, 1987.
xxii,113p; 21cm.
Includes index.
ISBN 0853081247 Pbk £8.50

—Amendment of the Companies Acts 1948-1983 : report under section 116 of the Companies Act 1981 / The Law Commission and the Scottish Law Commission. – London : H.M.S.O., 1983.
iv,42p; 25cm.
ISBN 0101911408

—Arthur Andersen: management buy-outs / London : Butterworths, 1990.
ix,240; 248.
Sets out some of the main considerations investors and bankers take into account when deciding whether to back buy-outs. Contributions by legal, tax, and pension experts. Contains an executive guide, financing the deal, structuring the finance, buying the company, tax aspects of buy-outs, and legal aspects of buy-outs.
ISBN 0406518904 Hbk £65.00

—Bank finance for companies / by R. Pennington. – London : Sweet & Maxwell, 1987.
150p; 22cm.
Discusses bank finance for specific purposes by way of letters of credit, bank guarantees and performance bonds, the issue of settling sterling commercial paper by companies, the legal implications of factoring, the provision of third party guarantees and securities for loans to companies within a group, and legal remedies available to banks to recover advances of all kinds made to them.
ISBN 0421384905 £15.00 (Dec.)

—Basic Company Law / London : Butterworths, 1984.
ISBN 0409012548 Pbk £14.00

—Boyle & Birds' Company law / editors, A.J. Boyle, John Birds, Graham Penn. – 2nd ed. – Bristol : Jordan, 1987.
lxxxviii,853p.
Previous ed.: 1983. Includes index.
ISBN 0853080909

—Bramwell : Taxation of Companies and Company Reconstructions / Guy Brannan. – 3rd ed. – London : Sweet & Maxwell, 1985.
ISBN 1421325003 Hbk £42.00

—British companies legislation / 4th. 2 vols. – Bicester : CCH Editions Ltd.
Includes tables of derivations and destinations for both the 1985 companies consolidation and the 1986 insolvency consolidation, the Companies Securities (Insider Dealing) Act 1985, the Companies Consolidation (Consequential Provisions) Act 1985, the Insolvency Act 1986, the Company Directors Disqualification Act 1986 and the Financial Services Act 1986.
ISBN 0863251544 Hbk £19.00

—British companies legislation : Companies Act 1985 and related legislation / Great Britain. – 1985 ed. 1 v. – Bicester : CCH Editions Ltd, 1985.
Includes index.
ISBN 0863250572

—British company law & practice / 2. – Bicester, Oxon. : CCH Editions, 1983.
looseleaf.
Includes index. Includes current year of British company law cases.
ISBN 0863250289

—British company law cases / Bicester, Oxon. : CCH Editions, 1986-.

—Buckley on the Companies Acts / by the late Lord Wrenbury. – 14th ed. – London : Butterworths, 1981.
Previous ed.: 1957. Includes index. Post-consolidation materials are set out in a loose-leaf volume.
ISBN 0406141045 v.2 Unpriced
ISBN 0406141053

—Butterworth's Company Law Service / S. J. Barton. – London : Butterworths.

—Butterworth's Dictionary of Company Law / 2nd ed. – Wellington : Butterworths, 1985.
A practical guide to company law of the United Kingdom, this book gives brief details of the Companies Act provisions relating to the terms defined within. Technical phrases from business and finance are listed along with legal terms.
ISBN 0406681635 Hbk
ISBN 0406681643 Pbk

—Butterworths company law cases / v. – London : Butterworths, 1984.
Cumulative tables and index published annually.

—Butterworths company law guide / general editor Michael Renshall : consultant editor Keith Walmsley. – London : Butterworths, 1985.
xxxix,452p.
ISBN 0406197008

—Butterworths company law handbook / consultant editor Keith Walmsley. – 6th ed. – London : Butterworths, 1987.
1358,37p.
ISBN 0406143153

—Cases and Materials in Company Law / 3rd ed. – London : Butterworths, 1985.
ISBN 0406370125 Hbk £29.00
ISBN 0406370133 Pbk £18.95

—Cases and materials in company law / L.S. Sealy. – 3rd ed. – London : Butterworths, 1985.
xxvii,609p.
Previous ed.: 1978. Includes index.
ISBN 0406370125 Pbk £24.00 :
ISBN 0406370133 £15.95

—Cases in Company Law / 3rd ed. – Plymouth : Macdonald & Evans, 1982.
416p. – (M and E Handbook Ser.).
ISBN 0712104666 Hbk £4.95

—Cases in Company Law / 4th ed. – Plymouth : Macdonald & Evans, 1984.
ISBN 0712104844 Pbk £7.50

—Charlesworth's company law / Geoffrey Morse, Enid A. Marshall, Richard- Morris, J. Charlesworth. – 13th ed. – London : Stevens & Sons, 1987.
xciv, 850p.
Previous ed.: published as Company law. 1983. Includes index.
ISBN 0420477209 Pbk £15.00
ISBN 0420477306 £9.50

—Companies Act 1948 : Investigations / Department of Trade. – London : HMSO, 1983.
ISBN 0115136738 Hbk £20.00

—Companies Act 1980 / with annotations by John Tinnion : and, The text of the EEC Second Directive on Company Law. – London : Sweet and Maxwell, 1980.
184p; 25cm.
ISBN 0421278404 Pbk £5.00

—Companies Act 1980 / by Daniel D. Prentice. – London : Butterworths, 1980.
xvii,337p.
ISBN 0406341605

—Companies act 1980 / by Clive M. Schmitthoff. – London : London Chamber of Commerce and Industry, 1981.
x,191p; 30cm.
Includes index.
ISBN 0901902535

—Companies Act 1980 : a new business code / Nigel Savage. – London : McGraw-Hill, 1980.
xi,192p; 23cm.
Includes index.
ISBN 0070845514 Pbk £5.95

—Companies Act 1980 : a practical guide / Victor Joffe, assisted by Andrew Hochhauser. – London : Oyez, 1980.
329p; 22cm.
Includes index.
ISBN 0851204678 Pbk Unpriced

—Companies Act 1980, sections 54 and 55 : transactions or arrangements in which a director has a material interest : memorandum / by the Society's Standing Committee on Company Law. – London : Law Society, 1981.
6p; 30cm.

—Companies Act 1981 : text and commentary / L.H. Leigh, H.C. Edey. – London : Butterworths, 1981.
v,329p.
ISBN 0406845301

—Companies Act 1985 / London : HMSO.
600p.
ISBN 0105406856 Hbk £21.00

—Companies Acts 1980 and 1981 : a practitioners' manual / by Robert R. Pennington. – London : Lloyds of London Press, 1983.
lxii,313p; 25cm.
Includes index.
ISBN 0907432573

—Companies Acts / Parker. – 14th ed. – London : Butterworths, 1981.
Service to Date.
ISBN 0406141037 Hbk £150.00

—Companies Acts : table A 1856-1981 / edited by R.W. Ramage. – London : Butterworths, 1982.
xviii,160p; 23cm.
'Contains the full text of each version of Table A preceded by all relevant extracts from the Act or instrument containing or ... amending it' - Introd..
ISBN 0406351236

—Companies Acts : Table A 1856-1985 / 2nd ed. – London : Butterworths, 1985.
ISBN 0406351244 Hbk £25.00

—Companies consolidatiion legislation 1985 / with annotations by Geoffrey Morse : in collaboration with Ann Arora ... et al. – 1. – London : Sweet & Maxwell, 1985.
various pagings.
Includes index. Contents: Companies Act 1985 - Business Names Act 1985 - Company Securities (Insider Dealing) Act 1985 - Companies Consolidation (Consequential Provisions) Act 1985.
ISBN 0421344407

—Companies Consolidation (Consequential Provisions) Act, 1985 / London : HMSO.
56p.
ISBN 0105409855 Hbk £4.50

—Companies consolidation legislation 1987 / with annotations by Geoffrey Morse in collaboration with Anu Arora ... et al. – London : Sweet & Maxwell, 1987.
xiv,1015,11p; 24cm.
Includes index.
ISBN 0421383607 Pbk £27.00

—Companies Operating Overseas / Dixon. – London : Longman Professional, 1986.
ISBN 0851208770 Hbk £35.00

—Companies purchasing their own shares : memorandum / by the Society's Standing Committee on Revenue Law. – London : Law Society, 1981.
9p; 30cm.
Submitted in reply to the Inland Revenue's consultative document: Companies purchasing their own shares.

—Companies Statutes / Sweet & Maxwell. – 2nd ed. – London : Sweet & Maxwell, 1987.
ISBN 0421383402 Pbk £16.00

—Company accounts / Jenny Bough. – London : Sweet & Maxwell, 1987.
xvii,227p; 26cm.
Includes index.
ISBN 0421360208 £16.50

—Company administration orders and voluntary arrangements / Richard Floyd. – London : Longman Professional (UK), 1988.
– (Practitioner series).
Guide to the law and procedure relating to administration orders, and voluntary arrangements (resulting from the Insolvency Act 1986). Examines corporate administration orders from beginning to end, comparing them to other insolvency proceedings. Includes specimen proposals.
ISBN 0851214800 Hbk £18.95

—Company director and the Law / John A. Franks. – 5th ed. – London : Longman, 1986.
xii,258p; 23cm.
Previous ed.: London : Oyez Longman, 1983. Includes index.
ISBN 085121231X £14.50

—Company director and the law / 5th. – London : Longman Professional (UK), 1986.
Explains the legal responsibilities and obligations of the company director. Covers the changes made by the Companies Act 1985, and the Insolvency Act 1986.
ISBN 085121231X Pbk £17.95

—Company Director and the Law / 4th ed. – London : Oyez Longman, 1983.
– (It's Your Law Ser.).
ISBN 085120709X Hbk £8.25

—Company donations to political parties : a suggested code of practice / Edmund Dell. – London : Constitutional Reform Centre, 1985.
34p.
'The report of the Working Party on Company Political Donations established jointly by the Constitutional Reform Centre and the Hansard Society for Parliamentary Government'. - Back Cover. Chairman: Edmund Dell.
ISBN 0948419008

—Company Forms Manual / London : Butterworths, 1988.
ISBN 0406016305 Hbk £38.00

—Company Law, 3 Vols. / London : Sweet & Maxwell.

—Company law / John H. Farrar assisted by Nigel Furey, Brenda Hannigan with a chapter on company taxation by O.P. Wylie. – London : Butterworths, 1985.
xlvii,636p; 25cm.
Includes index.
ISBN 0406581606 Hbk £18.50
ISBN 0406581614 Pbk £12.50

—Company Law / Benade. – 4th ed. – London : Butterworths, 1982.
ISBN 0409019356 Hbk £82.00
ISBN 0409019364 Pbk £62.00

—Company Law / 5th ed. – London : Butterworths, 1985.
ISBN 0406336830 Hbk £39.00
ISBN 0406336857 Pbk £26.00

—Company Law / 2nd ed. – London : DP Publications, 1986.
ISBN 0905435605 Pbk £4.95

—Company Law / 13th ed. – London : Sweet & Maxwell, 1987.
ISBN 0420477209 Hbk £16.00
ISBN 0420477306 Pbk £9.95

—Company law / John H. Farrar, Nigel E. Furey, Brenda M. Hannigan : with a chapter on taxation by Philip Wylie. – 2nd ed. – London : Butterworths, 1988.
lxiii,680p.
Previous ed.: 1985. Includes index.
ISBN 0406581622 Pbk No price
ISBN 0406581630 No price

—Company law / Thomas Ewan Cain, Geoffrey Morse, Enid A. Marshall. – 12th ed. – London : Stevens, 1983.
700p.
Previous ed.: 1977.
ISBN 0420460306 Hbk £12.00
ISBN 0420460403 Pbk £5.50

—Company Law / London : Castlevale Publishers, 1982.
ISBN 0907235018 Pbk £5.00

—Company law / Kenneth Smith, Denis Keenan. – 5th ed. – London : Pitman, 1984.
xxxix,502p; 22cm.
Previous ed.: 1981. Includes index. .
ISBN 0273019538 Pbk £8.95

—Company law / Robert R. Pennington. – 5th ed. – London : Butterworths, 1985.
cvi,1077p; 26cm.
Previous ed.: 1979. Includes index.
ISBN 0406336830 Hbk £26.00
ISBN 0406336857 Pbk £20.00

—Company Law / 9th ed. Repr. of 1982 ed. – Plymouth : Macdonald & Evans, 1983.
464p. – (M and E Handbook Ser.).
ISBN 0712104755 Hbk £5.50

—Company Law / Spicer. – 13th ed. – London : Butterworths, 1987.
ISBN 0406678901 Pbk £14.95

—Company Law / 2nd ed. – Croydon : Tolley, 1987.
ISBN 0854592598 Pbk £33.95
ISBN 0854592687 Hbk £39.95

—Company Law / Suresh Tanna. – Plymouth : Macdonald & Evans, 1985.
300p. – (M and E Professional Studies Ser.).
ISBN 0712104550 Hbk £12.95

—Company Law / 10th ed. – Plymouth : Macdonald & Evans, 1987.
ISBN 0712106987 Hbk £6.50

—Company Law / Keenan. – 7th ed. – London : Pitman Publishing, 1987.
ISBN 0273027921 Pbk £12.95

—Company Law / 2nd ed. – London : Butterworths, 1988.
ISBN 0406581622 Hbk £38.00
ISBN 0406581630 Pbk £22.50

—Company law and commercial reality / by L.S. Sealy. – London : Sweet & Maxwell, 1984.
xii,91p; 22cm.
Includes index.
ISBN 0421333502 Pbk £12.00

—Company Law for Accountants / London : Butterworths, 1985.
This text is a straightforward presentation of the company law of the United Kingdom for students of accounting.

—Company Law for Accountants / London : Butterworths, 1985.
ISBN 0406009600 Pbk £11.95

—Company Law Guide / 2nd ed. – London : Butterworths, 1988.
ISBN 0406197024 Pbk

—Company Law Handbook / 6th ed. – London : Butterworths, 1987.
ISBN 0406143153 Pbk £16.95

—Company Law : ICSA Study Text / Revised edition. – London : BPP, 1988.
ISBN 0862772109 Pbk £13.95

—Company law in change / edited by B.G. Pettet. – London : Stevens, 1987.
144p; 22cm.
Includes index.
ISBN 0420477500 Pbk £15.00

—Company law in change / London : Sweet & Maxwell, 1987.
ISBN 0420477500 Pbk £17.00

—Company law in Great Britain / Peter Meinhardt with the assistance of Nigel Davis. – Aldershot : Gower, 1982.
178p in various pagings; 24cm.
Bibliography: 2p. - Includes index.
ISBN 056602389X Unpriced

—Company Law : Instructional Manual / 2nd ed. – Winchester : DP Publications, 1983.
400p.
ISBN 0905435605 Pbk £4.95

—Company Law Materials / 10th ed. – Bristol : Jordan & Sons Ltd, 1986.
ISBN 0853080879 Pbk £9.05

—Company liquidations : the substantive law / Robert Pennington. – Bristol : Jordans, 1987.
xxvi,150p; 21cm.
Includes index.
ISBN 0853081220 Pbk £8.50

—Company procedures manual / London : Longman Professional (UK).
Selection of over 300 precedent documents, covering administration, shares and shareholders, officers and loan capital, and includes minutes, resolutions, notices, letters, agreements. Also available on disk.
ISBN 0851212263 Llf £85.00

—Company Reorganisations : Tax and Tax Planning / Noble. – London : Butterworths, 1986.
ISBN 0406501904 Hbk £35.00

—Company's purchase of own shares : Section 53 and Schedule 9 Finance Act 1982 / Inland Revenue. – London : Inland Revenue, 1982.
2,vp. – (Statement of practice).

—Consolidated Gold Fields Limited : investigation under section 172 of the Companies Act 1948 : report / by Bryan James Welch and Michael Charles Anthony Osborne for the Department of Trade. – London : H.M.S.O., 1980.
1v.(various pagings).
ISBN 0115129987

—Control of corporate groups / by Tom Hadden. – London : Institute of Advanced Legal Studies (University of London), 1983.
75p.,4 charts.
ISBN 0901190284

—Controlling Subsidiary Companies / Cambridge : Woodhead-Faulkner, 1986.
ISBN 0859413284 Hbk £40.00

—Corporate failure / Maidenhead : McGraw-Hill, 1986.
ISBN 0070847940 Hbk £17.50

—Corporate finance law / by Robert Burgess. – London : Sweet & Maxwell, 1985.
xxxix,542p; 22cm.
Deals with the processes through which companies and nationalised industries raise funds to meet their perceived capital needs. Discusses financing corporate enterprises, borrowing, leasing, credit factoring and asset realisations, mergers and takeovers, and has a chapter dealing with the role of government and government agencies.
ISBN 0421311207 Hbk £67

—Corporate Law Locator 1988 / New York : Bowker, 1988.
ISBN 0835223523 Hbk £30.00

—Corporate rescues and insolvencies / J.R. Lingard. – London : Butterworths, 1986.
xxvi,222p; 26cm.
Includes index.
ISBN 0406100403 No price

—Corporated donor's handbook / Turnaround Press, 1987.
ISBN 0907164226 Pbk £12.50

—Corporation tax / Great Britain. – London : H.M.S.O., 1982.
viii,153p; 25cm.
'Presented to Parliament by the Chancellor of the Exchequer'.
ISBN 010184560X Pbk £7.10

—Corporation tax : the impact of the 1984 budget / M.P. Devereaux and C.P. Mayer. – London : Institute for Fiscal Studies, 1984.
47p.
Includes bibliographical references.
ISBN 0902992384

—Dictionary of company law / by E.R. Hardy Ivamy. – London : Butterworths, 1983.
265p; 23cm. – (Butterworths professional dictionary series).
ISBN 0406681619 Hbk No price
ISBN 0406681627 Pbk No price

—Directing Corporate Growth / Benson. – London : Fitzwilliam, 1988.
ISBN 1870555074 Hbk £25.00

—EC seventh company law directive on consolidated accounts : a consultative document on implementation / Department of Trade and Industry. – London : The Department, 1985.
39,17p.
Includes the text of the directive.

—Further amendments of the Companies Acts 1948-1983 : report under section 116 of the Companies Act 1981 / The Law Commission and The Scottish Law Commission. – London : H.M.S.O., 1984.
iii,7p; 25cm.
ISBN 0101927207

—Gilgate Holdings Limited, Raybourne Group Limited, Calomefern Limited, Desadean Properties Limited : investigation under Section 165(b) of the Companies Act 1948 / report by R.A. Morritt and P.L. Ainger. – London : Her Majesty's Stationery Office, 1981.
ca.780p; 30cm.
At head of title: Department of Trade.
ISBN 0115134859 Pbk £23.00

—Gore-Browne on companies / general editor A. J. Boyle : consultant editor Richard Sykes. – 44th edition. 2. – Bristol : Jordans, 1986.
looseleaf.
ISBN 0853080828

—Gower's Principles of Modern Company Law / London : Sweet & Maxwell.
ISBN 0420460608 Hbk £2.00

—Guide to Company Flotation / London : Fitzwilliam, 1988.
ISBN 1870555058 Hbk £40.00

—Guide to company law / 2nd ed. – Bicester : CCH Editions, 1987.
307p; 23cm.
Explains the basic principles, alerts the leader to potential pitfalls, and provides solutions to frequently encountered problems. Case examples help to illustrate the commentary, appendices include the new Table A, and relevant schedules showing the prescribed format for company accounts, case table, legislation finding list, and comprehensive index.
ISBN 0863250955 Pbk

—Guide to the 1985 Companies Act / London : Longman Professional, 1985.
ISBN 0851210279 Pbk £8.95

—Guidebook to British company law / Bicester : CCH Editions, 1983.
v,197p; 23cm.
Includes index.
ISBN 0863250084 Pbk

—Hahlo's cases and materials on company law / John H. Farrar, H. R. Hahlo. – 3rd ed. – London : Sweet & Maxwell, 1987.
xxxvi,674p; 24cm.
Previous ed: published as Hahlo's casebook on company law, 1977. Includes index.
ISBN 0421317302 Hbk
ISBN 042131740X Pbk

—Handbook of the Companies Inspection System : Inspections and Departmental Enquiries Under the Companies Act 1985 / London : HMSO, 1986.
ISBN 0115138439 Hbk £4.00

—Handbook of UK Corporate Finance / London : Butterworths, 1987.

—Henochberg on Companies Act / Blackman. – 4th ed. – London : Butterworths, 1985.
ISBN 0409032964 Hbk £117.00

—How to turn round a company / London : Fitzwilliam, 1988.
ISBN 1870555023 Hbk £35.00

—Implementation of the third E.C. directive : Department of Trade explanatory and consultative note : memorandum / by the Society's Standing Committee on Company Law. – London : Law Society, 1982.
10p.

—Insolvency / Peter Totty and Michael Jordan. – London : Longman Professional (UK).
Covers areas such as the disqualification of directors, wrongful trading, voluntary arrangements, appointment of administrators, and antecedent transactions. Contains statutes, statutory instruments and guidance notes, forms and practice directions, tables of destination, derivations and special definitions. New chapters cover the Government Insolvency Service, the construction industry and insurance companies.
ISBN 0851211429 Llf £205

—Insolvency and Company Law : Reform & Renewal / London : Law Society, 1985.
25p. – (Nineteen Eighty-Five Crash Course Transcripts).

—Insolvency law / Steven A. Frieze. – 1st ed. – London : Longman Professional (UK), 1989.
– (Longman Practice Notes).
Covers all forms of insolvency, both corporate and personal. Guidance on voluntary and compulsory winding up, receivership, administration, company voluntary arrangements and deeds of arrangement.
ISBN 0851215114 £9.95

—Insolvency : law and taxation / Timothy J. Lyons. – 1st ed. – London : Longman Professional (UK), 1988.
– (Law and Taxation).
Examines legal aspects and tax implications of both company and partnership insolvency. Chapters deal with the enforcement powers of the Inland Revenue and tax planning opportunities prior to and during an insolvency. Contains worked examples, precedents, forms and non-statutory material.
ISBN 0851214193 Hbk £35

—Introduction to company law / Leigh. – 4th ed. – London : Butterworths, 1987.
ISBN 0406631069 Hbk £27.50
ISBN 0406631077 Pbk £17.95

—Jordan's Guide to Companies Legislation : 1985 / Bristol : Jordan & Sons Ltd, 1985.
ISBN 0853080798 Pbk £10.00

—Law and Tax for the Family Company / London : Oyez Longman, 1982.
– (Law and Tax Ser.).
ISBN 085120614X Hbk £15.00

—N.V. Slavenburg's Bank v. Intercontinental Natural Resources Ltd. : (1980) 1 All E.R. 955 : memorandum / by the Society's Standing Committee on Company Law. – London : Law Society, 1981.
12p; 30cm.

—Nelson's Tables : Company Procedure / 8th ed. – London : Oyez Longman, 1983.
ISBN 0851207154 Hbk £6.95

—Nelson's tables: company procedure / A M Peck, A Robertson. – 10th ed. – London : Longman Professional, 1987.
Contains explanatory notes regarding insolvency and references to relevant statutes and forms. Incorporates the new practice and procedure following on from the Insolvency Act 1986.
ISBN 0851202964 Pbk £14.50

—New form of incorporation for small firms : a consultative document / London : H.M.S.O., 1981.
iii,44p; 25cm.
ISBN 010181710X Pbk £3.20

—Northey & Leigh's introduction to company law / L. H. Leigh, V. H. Joffe, D. Goldberg. – 4th ed. – London : Butterworths, 1987.
546p; 23cm.
Previous ed.: 1983. Includes index.
ISBN 0406631069 Hbk £22.00
ISBN 0406631077 Pbk £15.00

—Norwest Holst Limited : investigation under section 165(b) of the Companies Act 1948 / report by John Davies and Thomas Garrard Harding. – London : H.M.S.O., 1981.
185p; 30cm.
At head of title: Department of Trade.
ISBN 0115134891 Pbk £12.50

—Palmer's company cases / . – London : Stevens, 1985.
Cumulative index.

—Palmer's company law / Clive M. Schmitthoff. – 23rd ed. 1. – London : Stevens, 1982.
various pagings; 26cm.
Previous ed.: 1976. Includes index. Kept up to date by 'Reporter and Supplement' binder.
ISBN 0420457607 set Unpriced
ISBN 0420446605

Vol. 1 : The treatise / under the general editorship of Clive M. Schmitthoff. – 1987.
cci,1857p.
Previous ed.: 1982. Includes index. Kept up to date by 'Reporter and Supplement' binder.
ISBN 0420479104

—Passing Down the Family Business : Solving the Tax Problems / Robert Venables. – 2nd ed. – London : Oyez Longman, 1982.
– (Oyez Longman Intelligence Report Ser.).
ISBN 0851207405 Hbk £45.00

—Practical approach to company law / Stephen W. Mayson and Derek French. – London : Financial Training, 1982.
lxii,421p; 23cm.
ISBN 0906322154

—Practical approach to company law / Stephen W. Mayson, Derek French and Christopher L. Ryan. – 4th ed. – London : Financial Training, 1987.
lxvii,618p.
ISBN 1851850686

—Practical Company Law / London : Pan Books Ltd, 1984.
ISBN 0330282034 Hbk £2.95

—Principles of Company Law / 4th ed. – London : Butterworths, 1986.
ISBN 0409490679 Hbk £42.00
ISBN 0409490687 Pbk £26.00

—Private company law / 1st ed. – London : Longman Professional (UK), 1990.
– (Longman Practice Notes).
Overview of company law, covering the problems faced in the formation of a company, fees, the duties and responsibilities of those involved, and details of practice in relation to termination of a company. Contains checklists, addresses, a table of fees, and a table of company forms.
ISBN 0851215289 £9.95

—Private company share sale manual / 1st ed. – London : Longman Professional (UK), 1988.
– (Longman Commercial Series).
Transaction-based manual, providing a guide through the various stages of a company sale in chronological order. Gives practical suggestions to the vendor and purchaser on procedure. Examines taxation aspects, and contains checklists, case and statute references.
ISBN 0851213146 Hbk £42.00

—Purchase by a company of its own shares : a consultative document / presented to Parliament by the Secretary of State for Trade .. – London : H.M.S.O., 1980.
iii,42p; 25cm.
ISBN 0101794401 sd £2.25

—Recent and Prospective Changes in Company Law / Charles M. Allen-Jones. – London : Law Society, 1982.
– (Oxford Weekend Courses).

—Reconstructions, Hive-Downs and Management Buyouts / London : Law Society, 1984.
28p.

—Reform of the ultra vires rule : a consultative document / Department of Trade and Industry. – London : H.M.S.O., 1986.
4,81p.
'Report by Dr. D.D. Prentice' - Introduction.

—Report of the Working Party on Company Residence, Tax Havens, and Upstream Loans / Edmund Dell. – London : Institute for Fiscal Studies, 1982.
35p; 22cm.
ISBN 0902992309 Pbk Unpriced

—Rights and duties of directors / Touche Ross. – London : Butterworths, 1987.
ISBN 0406504709 Pbk £18.50

—Rise of the corporate economy / Leslie Hannah. – 2nd ed. – London : Methuen, 1983.
xii,266p; 23cm.
Previous ed.: 1976. Includes index.
ISBN 0416348505 Hbk Unpriced
ISBN 0416348602 Pbk Unpriced

—Saint Piran Limited : investigation under Section 165(b) and Section 172 of the Companies Act 1948 : final report / by G.M. Godfrey and A.J. Hardcastle. – London : H.M.S.O., 1981.
228p; 30cm.
At head of title: Department of Trade.
ISBN 0115134735 Pbk £14.00

—Share Capital : Company Law and Taxation / David Bellringer. – London : Butterworths, 1984.
ISBN 0406258163 Hbk

—Share capital : company law and taxation / David Bellringer. – London : Butterworths, 1984.
ISBN 0406258163 Hbk £19.50

—Shareholders' agreements / Graham Stedman and Janet Jones. – London : Longman Professional (UK).
– (Commericial Series).
Examines the nature and effect of shareholders' agreements within the context of minority protection venture capital, joint ventures and partnership companies, covering both company and tax law. Focuses on the difficult interrelationship between the articles of association and shareholders' agreements. Contains precedent agreements.
ISBN 0851210252 Hbk £45

—Smith and Keenan's company law / Denis Keenan, Kenneth Smith. – 7th ed. – London : Pitman, 1987.
xl,596p; 22cm.
Includes index.
ISBN 0273027921 Pbk £11.95

—Smith and Keenan's Company law / Denis Keenan, Kenneth Smith. – 6th ed. – London : Pitman, 1986.
xl,596p; 22cm.
Previous ed.: published as Company law. 1983. Includes index.
ISBN 0273024876 Pbk £10.95

—Specific Performance of Contracts : Including Those of Public Companies / 5th ed. Repr. of 1911 ed. – Abingdon : Professional Books.
131p.

—Spicer and Pegler's management buy-outs / Coyne. – Cambridge : Woodhead-Faulkner, 1987.
ISBN 0859413411 Hbk £30.00

—Statute law revision, eleventh report : obsolete provisions in the Companies Act 1948 / the Law Commission. – London : H.M.S.O., 1984.
ii,14p; 25cm.
ISBN 0101923600

—Sweet & Maxwell's companies statutes for students / edited by Harry Rajak. – 2nd ed. – London : Sweet & Maxwell, 1987.
350p; 26cm.
Previous ed.: 1985. Includes index.
ISBN 0421383402 Pbk £12.95

—Tax havens and the corporate sector : a consultative document / London : Board ofInland Revenue, 1981.
3 leaves.

—Tax strategy for companies / 4th ed. – London : Longman Professional, 1986.
xxviii,511p; 22cm.
Previous ed.: 1983. Includes index.
ISBN 0851209211 Pbk £30.00

—Tax warranties and indemnities / John Clark. – London : Butterworths, 1983.
ISBN 0406395403 Hbk £18.00

—Taxation of companies and company reconstruction / T. P. G. Ivory, Guy Brannan, Richard Bramwell. – 3rd ed. – London : Sweet & Maxwell, 1985.
xliv,504p; 26cm.
Previous ed.: published as Taxation of companies. 1979. Includes index.
ISBN 0421325003 £35.00

—Taxation of Companies and Corporate Investors / London : Butterworths, 1983.
ISBN 0409701424 Pbk £10.50

—Taxation of international business : memorandum / by the Society's Standing Committee on Revenue Law. – London : Law Society, 1983.
21p.

—Terminology of business and company law / Bailey. – London : Kogan Page, 1987.
ISBN 0850914133 Pbk £8.95

—'The free two pence' Section 137 of the Local Government Act 1972 and Section 83 of the Local Governement (Scotland) Act 1973 / by Colin Crawford and Victor Moore. – London : The Chartered Institute of Public Finance and Accountancy, 1983.
x,218p.
ISBN 0852992556

—Tolley's Accounting Problems of the Companies Acts : Practical Guidance on Recent Legislation / Sells. – Croydon : Tolley, 1984.
136p.
ISBN 0854591478 Hbk £7.95

—Tolley's Companies Act : 1980 / George Eccles. – Croydon : Tolley.
324p.
ISBN 0854590595 Hbk £11.95
ISBN 0510494153 Pbk £7.95

—Tolley's Companies Act : 1981 / Jenny Cox. – Croydon : Tolley.
520p.
ISBN 0854590587 Hbk £11.95
ISBN 0854590390 Pbk £8.95

—Tolley's company law / edited by Stephen Barc and Nicholas Bowen. – 2nd ed. 2. – Croydon : Tolley, 1988.
Previous ed.: 1983. Includes indexes.
ISBN 0854592687

—Tolley's company law / edited by A. L. Chapman and R. M. Ballard. – Croydon : Tolley, 1983.
lxxii,959p.
Includes index.
ISBN 0854590692

—Tolley's corporation tax 1981-82 / by Glyn Saunders and David Harrington. – Croydon : Tolley, 1981.
viii,292p.
Includes index. Up to date to 1 August 1981.
ISBN 0854590358

—Tolley's corporation tax 1986-87 / by Glyn Saunders and John Boulding. – 22nd ed. – Croydon : Tolley, 1986.
ix,356p.
ISBN 0854592393

—Tolley's corporation tax 1987-88 / by Glynn Saunders and John Boulding. – Croydon : Tolley Publishing, 1987.
ix,357p.
ISBN 085459289X

—Tolley's corporation tax 1988-89 / by Glyn Saunders and John Boulding. – Croydon : Tolley, 1988.
x,345p.
Includes index.
ISBN 0854593470

—Tolley's focus on the purchase or redemption by a company of its own shares : a review of the tax and company law provisions / by Peter Wolstenholme, Robert Willott. – Croydon : Tolley, 1982.
x,93p.
Includes index.
ISBN 0854590935

—Unquoted companies / London : Macmillan, 1988.
ISBN 03334371995 Hbk £105.00

—Utilising company tax losses and reliefs / by Nigel A. Eastaway and Edward P. Magrin. – 2nd ed. – London : Institute of Chartered Accountants in England and Wales, 1982.
xxxiv,321p; 21cm.
Previous ed.: 1979. Includes index.
ISBN 0852913133 Pbk Unpriced

COMPANY LAW – GREAT BRITAIN – GREAT BRITAIN

—Dunlop Holdings Limited : investigation under Section 172 of the Companies Act 1948 : interim report / by Collingwood William Malcolm Ingram and Francis Herbert Pulling for the Department of Trade. – London : H.M.S.O., 1981.
50p; 30cm.
ISBN 0115131817 Pbk £6.00

COMPANY LAW – HONG KONG

—Companies (Amendment) Ordinance 1984 in perspective / by Christopher Bates. – Hong Kong : Hong Kong Law Journal, 1985.
xv,116p.
Reprinted from the Hong Kong Law Journal vol. 15 (1985). Includes index.

—Company Law in Hong Kong / Butterworths, 1986.
393p.
Deals with Hong Kong company law, in light of the changes introduced by the Companies (Amendments) Ordinance 1984. Gives an account of Company law in Hong Kong, from the incorporation of a company, to its liquidation. Discussion of the registration requirements which companies incorporated overseas must comply if they wish to operate in Hong Kong.
ISBN 0409995223 Pbk £40.00

—Company Law in Hong Kong / London : Butterworths, 1986.
ISBN 0409995223 Pbk £23.00

—Hong Kong Company Law Handbook / London : Butterworths, 1982.
ISBN 0406595607 Pbk

—Hong Kong company legislation / London : Butterworths, 1988.
ISBN 0409995525 loose

—Hong Kong private company : a manual of practice / Singapore : Butterworths (Asia), 1989.
300.
A practical guide to Company Secetarial practice in Hong Kong. Includes forms and precedents, extensive cross-references, and coverage of topics such as future legal developments.
ISBN 0409995703 Hbk

COMPANY LAW – INDIA

—Commentaries on State Financial Corporations Act, 1951 / Kumar Avadhesh Srivastava. – Allahabad : Law Book Company, 1988.
ca 300p.

—Commercial Law : Including Company Law / K.C. Garg. – 5th ed. – New Delhi : Kalyani Publishers, 1984.

—Companies Act / 2nd ed. – Allahabad : Law Book Company, 1986.
2,500p.

—Companies Act / Allahabad : Law Publishers, 1982.

—Companies Act With Exhaustive Referencer / Nagpur : Wadhura & Co, 1988.

—Companies Winding-up / 2nd ed. – Allahabad : Law Book Company, 1988.
700p.

—Company Formations (Private and Public) / New Delhi : Bharat Law House, 1984.

—Company Law / Sexena. – Allahabad : Kitab Mahal, 1980.
430 6p.

—Company Law / 3rd ed. – New Delhi : Vikas Publishing House, 1980.
456p.
ISBN 0706912551 Hbk £60.00

—Company Law / 7th ed. – Lucknow : Eastern Book Company, 1982.
493p.

—Company Law / 3rd ed. – New Delhi : Kalyani Publishers, 1987.
ISBN 817096010X Hbk £42.00

—Company Law / New Delhi : Kalyani Publishers.

—Company Law : an Immediate Approach / Allahabad : Modern Law Publications, 1987.

—Company Law and Auditing / New Delhi : Kalyani Publishers.

—Company Law and Secretarial Practice / New Delhi : S. Chand and Company.

—Company Law Procedures / 3rd ed. – New Delhi : Bharat Law House, 1984.

—Company Meetings, Accounts, Audit and Investigation / 2nd ed. – Allahabad : Law Book Company, 1987.

—Company Resolutions / 3rd ed. repr. 1986. – New Delhi : Bharat Law House.

—Elements of Company Law / K.C. Garg. – New Delhi : Kalyani Publishers.

—Guide to Company Borrowings / New Delhi : Bharat Law House, 1987.

—Guide to company formation / by Nandlal H. Bhatter and Christopher N. Fernandes : foreword by V.B. Haribhakti. – Bombay : Tripathi, 1984.
viii,121p.

—Guide to Company Law Procedures, Vol. 1 / 11th ed. – Nagpur : Wadhura & Co, 1988.

—Guide to Company Management / New Delhi : Bharat Law House, 1985.

—Guide to the Companies Act / 10th ed. – Nagpur : Wadhura & Co, 1984.

—Guide to the Companies Act / 11th rev. ed. – Nagpur : Wadhura & Co, 1988.

—Income Tax Law / New Delhi : Kalyani Publishers.

—Indian Company Law, 2 Vols. / 10th ed. – Nagpur : Wadjura & Co, 1987.
1,360p.

—Law of companies and meetings / B.A. Masodkar. – Bombay : Tripathi, 1984.
xxxii,263p.

—Law Relating to Companies Administration : With several Useful Appendices / 2nd ed. – Allahabad : Law Book Company, 1987.
443p.
ISBN 8185029245 Hbk £150.00

—Law Relating to Private Companies / Avtar Singh. – 4th ed. – Lucknow : Eastern Book Company, 1983.
651p.

—Law Relating to Private Limited Companies / Allahabad : Law Book Company, 1986.
1,422p.

—On the law of ultra vires / Satya Ranjan Das. – 2nd ed. – Calcutta : Cambray, 1981.
xvi,340p.
Previous ed.: published as 'The law of ultra vires in British India', 1923. Includes index.

—Taxation of Companies : a Handbook / Calcutta : Eastern Law House, 1969.
260p.

—Textbook of Company Law / S.B. Saxena. – Delhi : Kitab Mahal, 1980.
462p.

—Twin Acts Simplified : Company and M.R.T.P. Law / P.C. Jain. – New Delhi : S. Chand and Company.

COMPANY LAW - IRELAND

—Casebook on Irish Company Law / Dublin : Gill and Macmillan, 1987.
ISBN 0717114376 Pbk £19.95

—Cases on Irish company law / Michael Forde. – Cork : Mercier, 1986.
461p; 23cm.
Includes index.
ISBN 0853427968 £40.00 (Irish)

—Company law in Ireland / Cork : Mercier Press, 1985.
ISBN 0853427666 Pbk £22.50

—Company law in Ireland / by Patrick Ussher. – London : Sweet & Maxwell, 1986.
xlvii,577p; 22cm.
Includes index.
ISBN 0421297506 Pbk £18.95

—Company Law in the Republic of Ireland / London : Butterworths, 1985.
This book provides practitioners and students a guide to the essential features of Irish company law. The work concentrates on those areas where Irish company law diverges from the English law.
ISBN 0406272905 Hbk

—Company Law in the Republic of Ireland / London : Butterworths, 1985.
ISBN 0406272905 Hbk £22.00

—Principles of corporation tax in the Republic of Ireland / by A. Graham Williams. – 1. – Dublin : Incorporated Law Society of Ireland, 1981.
loose-leaf; 27cm.
Includes index.
ISBN 0902027166

COMPANY LAW - JAPAN

—Audit system for corporate enterprises in Japan : as compared with English company law / Yoshiki Nishiyama. – s.l. : s.n., 1987.
28p.
Offprint from: Kanazawa Law Review, vol. 30, no. 1 (1987).

COMPANY LAW - KENYA

—Questions and Answers Company Law / Nairobi : Heinemann Educational Books (East Africa).
196p.

—Textbook of company law in Kenya / Ashiq Hussain. – Nairobi : Heinemann Educational, 1980.
xii,187p.
Includes index.

—Textbook of Company Law in Kenya / Nairobi : Heinemann Educational Books (East Africa), 1980.
187p.

COMPANY LAW - LIECHTENSTEIN

—Companies and Taxes in Liechtenstein / Goup. – Vaduz, 1983.
99p.

COMPANY LAW - MALAYSIA

—Companies Act, 1965 (Act 125) / Kuala Lumpur : International Law Books Services.

—Companies and Securities H/B Singapore and Malaysia / London : Butterworths, 1984.
ISBN 040999507X Pbk £19.00

—Companies and Securities Handbook Singapore and Malaysia / Butterworths.
ISBN 0409181209 Pbk £195.00

1985 Supplement alone
ISBN 040999507X Pbk £35.00

—Companies and securities handbook : Singapore and Malaysia / by Philip N. Pillai. – Singapore : Butterworths, 1984.
xxv,1401p.
Provides company and securities legislation in Singapore and Malaysia. Coverage includes the text of the Companies Acts and Companies Regulations for Singapore and Malaysia, as well as the Securities Industry legislation for the two legislations. Also contains the Practice Notes and Guidelines issues by the Registrars of Companies in both jurisdictions.
ISBN 0406181209

—Companies and Securities Handbook : Singapore and Malaysia / London : Butterworths, 1984.

—Company Law and Securities Regulation in Malaysia / London : Butterworths, 1987.
ISBN 0409995517 Pbk £28.00

—Director's Liabilities in Singapore and Malaysia after Tarling's Case / Singapore, 1980.

—Law of Company Purchase and Compensation-Singapore and Malaysia / London : Butterworths, 1984.
ISBN 0406181225 Pbk £22.50

—Registration of Businesses Act, 1956 (Act 197) / Kuala Lumpur : International Law Books Services.

—Sourcebook of Singapore and Malaysian company law / Philip N. Pillai. – 2nd ed. – Singapore : Butterworths, 1986.
xlviii,1338p.
Brings together the principle legislative provisions, legislative history and background, all Singapore and Malaysia case law and selected case law from the UK, Australia, and other common law jurisdictions. The cases are set out with brief summaries of the points of law discussed or decided.
ISBN 0409995118

—Sourcebook of Singapore and Malaysian company law / 2nd ed. – London : Butterworths, 1986.
ISBN 0409995118 Hbk £115.00

COMPANY LAW - NEW ZEALAND

—Buckley on the Companies Acts / Martin Buckley. – 14th ed. – Wellington : Butterworths, 1981.

—Butterworth's Company Law Brief / Wellington : Butterworths.

—Butterworth's Company Reports / Wellington : Butterworths.

—Company law : a discussion paper / Law Commission. – Wellington, N.Z. : The Commission, 1987.
xi,104p. – (Preliminary paper).

—Company Law and Securities Regulation in New Zealand / Russell. – London : Butterworths, 1984.
ISBN 0409701688 Pbk £38.00

—Company Law and Securities Regulation in New Zealand / Mark W. Russell. – Butterworths, 1985.
Treatment of the law using economic history to explain the development of law, and using economic theories and empirical data about companies to explain law and practice. Introductory chapters in various sections identify underlying issues.
ISBN 0409701688 Pbk £71.50

—Company takeovers : a review of the law and practice / Wellington : the Commission, 1983.
130p.

—Company takeovers : a review of the law and practice in New Zealand / Wellington : the Commission, 1983.
119p.

Volume 3 : Legislation in New Zealand and selected overseas jurisdictions 1983.
343p.

—Corporate Debt Securities : Priority Rules / Auckland : Legal Research Foundation, 1986.

—Introduction to company law in New Zealand / by J.F. Northey. – 9th ed. – Wellington : Butterworths, 1981.
xxxvi,452p.
Previous ed.: 1976. Includes index.
ISBN 0409600911

—Law and Administration of Incorporated Societies / 2nd ed. – Butterworths, 1986.
276p.
Covers the nature of societies, the procedure of incorporation, branches, the registrar and assistant registrar, rules, members and membership, the secretary and other officers, secretarial and administrative duties, accounts taxation, dissolution and winding up, conduct of meetings, conventions and conferences, public relations, and the law of defamation.
ISBN 0409787442 Pbk £49.50

—Morison's Company Law in New Zealand / London : Butterworths, 1981.
ISBN 040979824X loose £227.00

—Morison's Company law in New Zealand / R. F. Pethig, I. R. Millard. – 4th ed. 2 vols. – Wellington N.Z. : Butterworths, 1981.
Volume 1 contains the Companies Act 1955 and other associated legislation, together with rules and regulations amended up to date. Volume 2 is a treatise on company law and the cases are discussed and cross-referenced to the statutes and regulations discussed in volume 1.
ISBN 0409646962
ISBN 0409646954

—New Zealand Companies and Securities Legislation / C.C.H., 1987.
1,000p.
ISBN 086475082X Hbk £34.00

—New Zealand company law casebook / Wellington : Butterworths (New Zealand), 1984.
ISBN 0409701777 Pbk £22.00

—New Zealand Company Law Casebook / Butterworths, 1984.
Collation of cases that deal with the law relating to companies, in particular the provisions of the Companies Act 1955. Takes into account the Companies Amendment Act 1983 (No 2). Includes leading cases.
ISBN 0409701777 Pbk £41.25

—New Zealand company law cases / Auckland : CCH (New Zealand), 1984-.
Originally published: in the publisher's loose-leaf reporting service, New Zealand company secretary's and company law service. Index in each vol.

COMPANY LAW - NIGERIA

—Company law and practice in Nigeria / by J. Olakunle Orojo. – 2nd ed. 2. – London : Sweet & Maxwell, 1984.
23cm.
Previous ed.: published in 1v. 1976. Includes index.
ISBN 0421312106 £85.00

—Income tax law for corporate and unincorporated bodies in Nigeria / C.S. Ola. – 2nd ed. – Ibadan : Heinemann Educational Books (Nigeria) Ltd, 1981.
xx,556p.
Previous ed. published 1974 under title: Income-tax law and practice in Nigeria.
ISBN 9781292911

—Introduction to Nigerian Company Law / London : Sweet & Maxwell.
ISBN 0421312203 Hbk
ISBN 0421312300 Pbk

—Precedents on objects of incorporation / by Philip Begho. – s.l. : s.n., 1986.
92p.

COMPANY LAW - NORTHERN IRELAND

—Company Law : Recent Legislative Changes / Belfast : Queen's University of Belfast, 1983.
32p.

COMPANY LAW - PAKISTAN

—Comments on Company Law / Karachi : Flecbon Corporation, 1987.

COMPANY LAW - PAPUA NEW GUINEA

—Corporate social responsibility in Papua New Guinea / Law Reform Commission of Papua New Guinea. – Waigani : The Commission, 1981.
ii,17p. – (Occasional paper).
'This paper was researched and written for the Commission by Edward F. Graziono'.

COMPANY LAW – PHILIPPINES

—Corporation Code of the Phillipines with the Omnibus Investment Code / Quezon City : University of the Philippines, Law Center, 1981.
207p.

—Seminar on the Corporation Code of the Philippines / Quezon City : University of the Philippines, Law Center, 1980.
278p.

COMPANY LAW – PORTUGAL

—Public enterprise in Portugal and Spain : analysis from the point of view of competition policy / Luxembourg : Office for Official Publications of the European Communities, 1988.
213p.
At head of title: Commission of the European Communities.
ISBN 9282579107

COMPANY LAW – SCOTLAND

—Guide to liquidation in Scotland / David Flint. – Bristol : Jordan & Sons, 1987.
viii,265p; 25cm.
Provides a brief introduction to the Act and rules. With the text of relevant legislation other than the 1986 Insolvency Act.
ISBN 0853080925 Pbk £12.50

—Scottish cases on partnership and companies / Edinburgh : W Green & Son, 1980.
Source book for those studying business law.
ISBN 0414006585 Pbk

COMPANY LAW – SINGAPORE

—Annotation of the Singapore Companies Act / Walter Woon. – Singapore : Butterworths (Asia).
700.
Covers the relevant case law with cross-references to rules and other relevant legislation, along with the cross-references to parliamentary reports.
ISBN 0409995681 Hbk

—Annotation of the Singapore Companies (Amendment) Act 1987 / Dorothy Chan. – Singapore : Butterworths (Asia), 1987.
212.
Summarizes the changes effected by the Amendment Act and reproduces those provisions in the Companies Act which are affected by the Companies (Amendment) Act 1987. Covers shares, debentures and charges, judicial management, audit, winding-up, and various types of companies.
ISBN 0409995509 Pbk

—Companies and Securities H/B Singapore and Malaysia / London : Butterworths, 1984.
ISBN 040999507X Pbk £19.00

—Companies and Securities Handbook Singapore and Malaysia / Butterworths.
ISBN 0409181209 Pbk £195.00

1985 Supplement alone
ISBN 040999507X Pbk £35.00

—Companies and securities handbook : Singapore and Malaysia / by Philip N. Pillai. – Singapore : Butterworths, 1984.
xxv,1401p.
Provides company and securities legislation in Singapore and Malaysia. Coverage includes the text of the Companies Acts and Companies Regulations for Singapore and Malaysia, as well as the Securities Industry legislation for the two legislations. Also contains the Practice Notes and Guidelines issues by the Registrars of Companies in both jurisdictions.
ISBN 0406181209

—Companies and Securities Handbook : Singapore and Malaysia / London : Butterworths, 1984.

—Company Law and Securities Regulation in Singapore / Butterworths, 1987.
ca 170p.
Examines corporate and securities regulation, with reference to Singapore legislation, regulations, non-statutory guidelines, case law and administrative practice.
ISBN 0409995495 Pbk £55.00

—Director's Liabilities in Singapore and Malaysia after Tarling's Case / Singapore, 1980.

—Law of Company Purchase and Compensation-Singapore and Malaysia / London : Butterworths, 1984.
ISBN 0406181225 Pbk £22.50

—Sourcebook of Singapore and Malaysian company law / Philip N. Pillai. – 2nd ed. – Singapore : Butterworths, 1986.
xlviii,1338p.
Brings together the principle legislative provisions, legislative history and background, all Singapore and Malaysia case law and selected case law from the UK, Australia, and other common law jurisdictions. The cases are set out with brief summaries of the points of law discussed or decided.
ISBN 0409995118

—Sourcebook of Singapore and Malaysian company law / 2nd ed. – London : Butterworths, 1986.
ISBN 0409995118 Hbk £115.00

COMPANY LAW – SOUTH AFRICA

—Close Corporations Act 1984 : a basic introduction / by A. Allan...et al. – Cape Town : Juta for the Bureau of Mercantile Law, University of Port Elizabeth, 1984.
xiv,70p.
ISBN 070211507X

—Company Forms Chart / Cape Town : Legal & Financial Publishing, 1983.
– (Merlen P.A.Y.E. Registers Ser.).

—Company law / M. L. Benade. – 4th ed. – Durban : Butterworths, 1982.
xiv,816p.
Previous ed.: 1977. Includes bibliographical references and index.
ISBN 0409019356

—Company Law and Company Taxation in South Africa / Keeton. – Cape Town : Legal & Financial Publishing, 1983.
ISBN 0869940171 Hbk £32.50

—Company Share Register / Cape Town : Legal & Financial Publishing, 1983.
– (Merlen Ser. of Registers).

—Henochsberg on the Companies Act / Philip M. Meskin. – 4th ed. 2 v. – Durban : Butterworths, 1985.
Previous ed.: 1975. Includes index. Kept up to date by supplements.

—Law and Practice of Close Corporations including Income Tax Aspects / Cape Town : Legal and Financial Publishing Co.

—Modern Business Law / P. E. J. Brooks. – Durban : Butterworths.

—Register of Fixed Assets / Cape Town : Legal & Financial Publishing, 1983.
– (Merlen Ser. of Registers).

—South African company law through the cases : a collection of leading South African and English cases on company law, with explanatory notes and comments / H. R. Hahlo. – 4th ed. – Cape Town : Juta, 1984.
xli,673p.
ISBN 0702114316

—South African mercantile and company law / by J.T.R. Gibson assisted by R. G. Comrie. – 5th ed. – Cape Town : Juta, 1983.
xl,668p.
Previous ed.: 1977. Includes index.
ISBN 070211359X

COMPANY LAW – SPAIN

—Public enterprise in Portugal and Spain : analysis from the point of view of competition policy / Luxembourg : Office for Official Publications of the European Communities, 1988.
213p.
At head of title: Commission of the European Communities.
ISBN 9282579107

COMPANY LAW – SRI LANKA

—Guide to the Companies Act of 1982 / D.C. Jayasuriya. – 1st ed. – Nawala, Sri Lanka : Asian Pathfinder, 1983.
194p.

COMPANY LAW – SWEDEN

—Swedish Companies Act 1975 : With Excerpts from the Accounting Act 1976 / Stockholm : Industriforbundet, 1986.
144p.
ISBN 9171761004 Hbk £180.00

COMPANY LAW – SWITZERLAND

—Swiss company law / translation of the official text with an introduction, synoptic tables, annotations and appendices by Bruno Becchio, Allan D.M. Phillips, Urs Wehinger. – Chichester : Barry Rose, 1984.
184p.
Bibliography: p.12-13.
ISBN 3905203014

COMPANY LAW – UNITED STATES

—Legal harmonization and the business enterprise : corporate and capital market law, harmonization policy in Europe and the U.S.A. / by Richard M. Buxbaum and Klaus J. Hopt. – Berlin : De Gruyter, 1988.
– (Series A–Law).
Includes index. Bibliography.
ISBN 0899251277 Hbk £96.00

—US business tax : law and practice after the Tax Reform Act / Derrick & Margot Owles. – London : Financial Times Business Information, 1987.
xviii,146p; 30cm.
Includes index.
ISBN 0902101994 spiral No price

COMPANY LAW – WEST GERMANY

—Business law guide to Germany / Strobl, Killius & Vorbrugg. – 2nd ed. – Bicester : CCH Editions, 1988.
450p; 23cm.
Updates the law concerning product liability, taxation, joint ventures, distribution, licensing, franchising and industrial property rights, and includes new material on anti-dumping, mergers and acquisitions, social insurances, leasing and hiring of personnel, real estate and construction and bankruptcy.
ISBN 0863251579 £35.00

—German corporation tax law with 1980 amendments / Korperschaftsteurreformgesetz 1977 mit Anderungen von 1980 : comments and translation by Hugh J. Ault, Albert J. Radler. – 2nd rev. ed. – Deventer : Kluwer, 1980.
146p; 25cm. – (Series on international taxation ; no. 2).
Text of the law and amendments in English and German. Includes bibliographical references.
ISBN 9020006428

—German Law Pertaining to Companies with Limited Liability : A Synoptic Translation Including Comprehensive Introductory Comments on the Laws Affecting the German GmbH / Jermyn Brooks. – Cologne : Otto Schmidt, 1986.
ISBN 3504325321 Hbk

—GmbH-German Law Concerning Companies with Limited Liabilities / 4th ed. – Plymouth : Macdonald & Evans, 1981.
176p.
ISBN 0712154809 Casebound £16.00

—Groups of companies : the law and practice in Britain, France and Germany / by Frank Wooldridge. – London : Institute of Advanced Legal Studies, 1981.
xxvi,159p; 21cm.
Includes bibliographical references.
ISBN 0901190268

—Private company in Germany : a translation and commentary / M.C. Oliver, M.A. Barrister. – 2nd ed. – Deventer, Netherlands : Kluwer Law and Taxation Publishers, 1986.
92p.
Includes English and German text of Gesetz betreffend die Gesellschaften mit beschrankter Haftung.
ISBN 9065442448 Pbk £72.00

COMPANY LAW, FOREIGN

—Overseas business activities : proceedings of the Fuji Conference / the International Conference on Business History 9 : edited by Akio Okochi, Tadakatsu Inoue. – Tokyo : University of Tokyo Press, 1984.
xiii, 296 p.; 24 cm.
Includes bibliographies and index.
ISBN 4130470191 Y5000

—Taxation of domestic shareholders on undistributed income of foreign corporate affiliates : objectives, techniques, and consequences : proceedings of a seminar held in New York in 1986 during the 40th Congress of the International Fiscal Association / edited by Brian J. Arnold. – Deventer, Netherlands : Kluwer Law and Taxation Publishers, 1987.
Includes bibliography.
ISBN 9065443347

—Taxation of international business : dual resident companies : consultative document / London : Inland Revenue, 1984.
7p.

COMPANY LAW, FOREIGN – CANADA

—Taxation of controlled foreign corporations : an international comparison / Brian J. Arnold. – Toronto, Ont. : Canadian Tax Foundation, 1986.
xxiii, 816; 23 cm. – (Canadian tax paper).
Includes index. Bibliography: p. 797-811.
ISBN 0888080239 pbk. £75.00

COMPANY LAW, FOREIGN – EUROPEAN COMMUNITY

—Proposal for an eleventh Council directive : based on article 54(3)(g) of the treaty concerning disclosure requirements in respect of branches opened in a member state by certain types of companies governed by the law of another state / Council of the European Communities. – London : Department of Trade and Industry, 1987.
17,7p.
Includes a 'Background note' from the Deparment of Trade and Industry.

COMPANY LAW, FOREIGN – GREAT BRITAIN

—Proposal for an eleventh Council directive : based on article 54(3)(g) of the treaty concerning disclosure requirements in respect of branches opened in a member state by certain types of companies governed by the law of another state / Council of the European Communities. – London : Department of Trade and Industry, 1987.
17,7p.
Includes a 'Background note' from the Deparment of Trade and Industry.

COMPANY LAW, FOREIGN - UNITED STATES

—Introduction to United States international taxation / by Paul R. McDaniel, Hugh J. Ault. - 2nd rev. ed. - Deventer : Kluwer, 1981.
209p; 25cm.
Previous ed.: 1977. Includes index.
ISBN 9065440046 Unpriced

COMPANY LAWYERS

—Lawyers in business : and the law business / Karl J. Mackie. - Basingstoke : Macmillan, 1988.
viii,289p.
Includes bibliography and index.
ISBN 0333419081 £29.50 (July)

COMPANY REPORTS - AUSTRALIA

—Butterworths Company Reports / Butterworths. - (Report Series).

COMPANY REPORTS - GREAT BRITAIN

—Delivery of annual accounts and returns to the Registrar of Companies : a consultative document / Department of Trade and Industry. - London : Department of Trade and Industry, 1986.
35,7p,9 leaves.

COMPANY SECRETARIES - AUSTRALIA

—Duties and Responsibilities of Company Secretaries and Directors in Australia / North Ryde : C.C.H. Australia, 1987.
240p.
ISBN 0869030353 Hbk £27.00

COMPANY SECRETARIES - GREAT BRITAIN

—Company Secretarial Handbook / 9th ed. - London : Longman Professional, 1986.
ISBN 0851210686 Pbk £20.95

—Company Secretarial Practice / Thom. - 6th ed. - Plymouth : Macdonald & Evans, 1984.
ISBN 071210478X Pbk £6.50

—Handbook of company administration / Keith Walmsley, John Birds, A. Harding Boulton. - 4th ed. - Bristol : Published under the authority of the Institute of Chartered Secretaries and Administrators by Jordon & Sons, 1981.
xvi,318p; 21cm.
Previous ed.: / by A. Harding Boulton in collaboration with J.E. Neill. 1977. Includes index.
ISBN 0853080658 Pbk £6.00

COMPARATIVE ECONOMICS

—Political economy of law : a third world reader / edited by Yash Ghai, Robin Luckham, Francis Snyder. - Delhi : Oxford University Press, 1987.
xvi,821p.
A view of Indian legal systems as they operate nationally and internationally. Law is analysed in terms of its relationships to economy, the state, political conflict, class, and international relations.
ISBN 0195619919

COMPARATIVE GOVERNMENT

—Monarchy to republic : Australian republican government / George Winterton. - Melbourne : Oxford University Press, 1986.
xi, 211 p.; 23 cm.
Includes index. Bibliography: p. 192-194.
ISBN 019554563X

COMPARATIVE LAW

—Anglo-Sakson gozuyle turk hukuku / An Anglo-Saxon view of Turkish law : Aubrey L. Diamond. - 1981.
2,10 leaves.
Paper presented at the 3rd Turkish Law Conference, Ankara, 1981. English text in typescript, bound with a Turkish translation published as a supplement to the Conference papers.

—Comparative judicial systems : challenging frontiers in conceptual and empirical analysis / John R. Schmidhauser, editor. - London : Butterworths, 1987.
243p; 22cm.
Conference proceedings. Includes bibliographies.
ISBN 0408031654 £25.00

—Comparative Law Yearbook / Dordrecht : Kluwer, 1978.
352p.
ISBN 9028606785 Hbk £105.00

Vol. 3 1980.
294p.
ISBN 9028603409 Hbk £95.00

Vol. 4 1981.
vi, 371p.
ISBN 9024725631 Hbk £150.00

Vol. 5 1982.
332p.
ISBN 9024726972 Hbk £180.00

Vol. 6 1983.
256p.
ISBN 9024728398 Hbk £145.00

Vol. 7 1984.
200p.
ISBN 9024729661 Hbk £145.00

Vol. 8 1985.
250p.
ISBN 902473178X Hbk £165.00

Vol. 9 1986.
232p.
ISBN 9024733502 Hbk £165.00

—English law and French law : a comparison in substance / Calcutta : Eastern Law House, 1980.
13,223p.
ISBN 042045750X

—Essays on International and Comparative Law : In Honour of Judge Erades / Institute T.M.C. Asser. - Dordrecht : Kluwer, 1983.
285p.
ISBN 902472838X Hbk £95.00

—Fine in Comparative Law : A Survey of 21 Countries / Cambridge : Institute of Criminology, 1982.
- (Occasional Papers Ser.: No. 9).

—Form and substance in Anglo-American law : a comparative study of legal reasoning, legal theory, and legal institutions / P.S. Atiyah and Robert S. Summers. - Oxford : Clarendon, 1987.
444p; 24cm.
Includes bibliography and index.
ISBN 0198255772 £35.00

—General reports to the 10th International Congress of Comparative Law / edited by Zoltan Peteri, Vanda Lamm : publie par Zoltan Peteri, Vanda Lamm. - Budapest : Akademiai Kiado, 1981.
1049p.
ISBN 9630523698

—International encyclopedia of comparative law / under the auspices of the International Association of Legal Science. - Tubingen : Mohr, 1971.

—International law in comparative perspective / edited by William E. Butler. - Alphen aan den Rijn : Sijthoff&Noordhoff, 1980.
vii,315p; 24cm.
Bibliography p.293-305. - Includes index.
ISBN 9028600892

—Introduction to comparative law / Konrad Zweigert and Hein Kotz : translated from the German by Tony Weir. - 2nd rev ed. 2. - Oxford : Clarendon Press, 1987.
Previous edition: 1977. Includes indexes. Contents: v.1 The framework. - v.2 The institutions of private law. German title: Einfuhrung in die Rechtsvergleichung auf dem Gebiete des Privatsrechts.

—Israeli reports to the XI International Congress of Comparative Law / edited by Stephen Goldstein. - Jerusalem : Harry Sacher Institute for Legislative Research and Comparative Law, 1982.
363p.
Cover titles in English and Hebrew.

—Jubilee lectures celebrating the foundation of the Faculty of Law, University of Birmingham / edited by I.R. Scott. - London : Wildy & Sons Ltd, 1981.
viii,215p. - (Wildy's texts in law and jurisprudence).
Contents include: Restraining the misuse of power/by Lord Denning.
ISBN 0854900039

—Judges, legislators and professors : chapters in European legal history / R.C. van Caenegem. - Cambridge : Cambridge University Press, 1987.
x,205p; 23cm.
Examines how continental and common law have come to differ substantially. Describes how European law developed through power struggles between various groups representing certain political and social ambitions.
ISBN 0521340772 £19.50

—Legal Development and Comparative Law 1986 : Selected Essays for the 12th Congres International de Droit Compare / Lamm. - Budapest : Akademiai Kiado, 1986.
330p.
ISBN 9630544342 Hbk £29.00

—Legal institutions : the development of dispute settlement / Peter Stein. - London : Butterworths, 1984.
ix,236p; 23cm.
Includes index.
ISBN 0406400253 Hbk
ISBN 0406400261 Pbk

—Major legal systems in the world today : an introduction to the comparative study of law / Rene David : translated and adapted by John E.C. Brierley. - 3rd ed. - London : Stevens, 1985.
xvi,624p; 22cm.
Previous ed.: 1978. Bibliography: p577-613. - Includes index. Translation of: Les grands systemes de droit contemporains.
ISBN 0420473408 Hbk £21.00
ISBN 0420473505 Pbk £18.75

—People's law and state law : the Bellagio papers / Antony Allott and Gordon R. Woodman (eds.). - Dordrecht : Foris Publications, 1985.
354p.
Papers presented at the first conference of the Commission on Folk Law and Legal Pluralism at Bellagio, Como, Italy from 21st to 25th September 1981.
ISBN 9067651001

—Studies in Comparative Law / Dordrecht : Kluwer, 1974.
320p.
ISBN 9028600744 Hbk £92.00

—Tradition and progress in modern legal cultures / edited by Stig Jrgensen, Juha Poyhonen, Csaba Varga : preface by Jose Llompart Tradition und Fortschritt in den modernen Rechtskulturen / herausgegeben von Stig Jrgensen, Juha Poyhonen, Csaba Varga ; vorwort von Jose Llompart. - Stuttgart : F. Steiner Verlag Wiesbaden, 1985.
263 p.; 24 cm. - (Archives for philosophy of law and social philosophy).
English, French, and German. Includes bibliographies and index. .
ISBN 3515044582 pbk. DM35.00

COMPENSATION - AUSTRALIA - VICTORIA

—Accident Compensation Handbook (Vic.) / G. Hughes. - North Ryde : Law Book Co, 1986.
xix, 181p.
ISBN 0455206694 Pbk £25.00

COMPENSATION - CANADA

—Compensation for Non-Pecuniary Loss / Victoria : Government of British Columbia, 1984.

—Criminal injuries compensation : social remedy or political palliative for victims of crime? / by Peter Burns. - Vancouver : Butterworths, 1980.
xiv, 401 p.; 24 cm.
Includes bibliographical references.
ISBN 0409988286 £65.00

—Sensenbrenner Hospital Employees Compensation Act, 1983, Bill 110 : An Act Respecting the Compensation of Certain Employees at Sensenbrenner Hospital in Kapuskasing / Ontario : Ontario Government Publications Service, 1983.
2p.

COMPENSATION - ENGLAND

—Reparation : a discussion document / London : Home Office, 1986.
7 leaves.
Photocopy.

—Reparation, conciliation and mediation : current projects and plans in England and Wales / Tony F. Marshall : incorporating a survey by the National Association of Victims Support Schemes. - London : Home Office, 1984.
vii,73p.
Bibliography: p.50-73.
ISBN 0862521734

COMPENSATION - GREAT BRITAIN

—Accidents, Compensation and The Law (LIC) / 4th ed. - Weidenfeld & Nicolson, 1987.
ISBN 0297790528 Hbk £30.00
ISBN 0297790536 Pbk £14.95

—Bringing people together : mediation and reparation projects in Great Britain / Tony F. Marshall and Martin E. Walpole. - London : Home Office, 1985.
iv,89p.
ISBN 0862522196

—Compensation and Support For Illness and Injury / Maclean. - Oxford : Oxford University Press, 1984.
ISBN 0198275080 Hbk £20.00
ISBN 0198275137 Pbk £9.50

—Criminal injuries compensation : a statutory scheme / report of an interdepartmental working party. - London : H.M.S.O., 1986.
90p.
Review of Criminal Injuries Compensation Scheme from 1979 to 1984. 68 recommendations for change, including legal right to compensation, allowing compensation in cases of family violence to cover all persons living together and fixed awards for victims of rape who bear children as a result.
ISBN 0113406258

—Key to Personal Injury Practice and Compensation / Margaret R. de Haas. - London : Oyez Longman, 1981.
ISBN 0851206158 Hbk £3.75

—Planning and Compensation Reports : 1950-1981, 42 Vols. / Abingdon : Professional Books.

—Property, Planning and Compensation Reports / London : Sweet & Maxwell.

Bound Vol.

Single copy

Back Vols. avail.

COMPENSATION - HONG KONG
—Land compensation and valuation law in Hong Kong / Gordon N. Cruden. - Singapore : Butterworths, 1986.
xxxii,476p.
Collation and analysis of relevant statutory and case law. References are made to Hong Kong cases, as well as English, Scottish, Australian, Canadian, and New Zealand cases.
ISBN 0409995258 Hbk £137

COMPENSATION - INDIA
—Law of Damages and Compensation, 3 Vols. / 5th ed. - Allahabad : Law Publishers, 1983.

COMPENSATION - NEW ZEALAND
—Accident Compensation in New Zealand / 2nd ed. - Butterworths, 1983.
Takes in new amendments (eg the reorganisation of the statutory body), and discusses the interpretations of the statutory provisions contained in many decisions reported since 1978.
ISBN 0409701602 Pbk £40.70

—Accident Compensation in New Zealand / 2nd ed. - London : Butterworths, 1983.
ISBN 0409701602 Pbk

COMPENSATION - PAPUA NEW GUINEA
—Homicide compensation in Papua New Guinea : problems and prospects / edited by Richard Scaglion. - Papua New Guinea : Published by the Office of Information, Papua New Guinea for the Law Reform Commission of Papua New Guinea, 1981.
102p; 23cm. - (Monograph).
Includes bibliographical references.
ISBN 0724707301

COMPENSATION FOR JUDICIAL ERROR - GREAT BRITAIN
—Compensation for wrongful imprisonment : a report / by JUSTICE : Chairman of Committee : Charles Wegg-Prosser. - London : JUSTICE, 1982.
35p; 22cm.
ISBN 0907247024

COMPENSATION (LAW) - AUSTRALIA
—Accident compensation in Australia : no-fault schemes / by Mark A. Robinson. - Sydney : Legal Books Pty., 1987.
xiv,94p.
Bibliography: pp.86-89. - Includes index.
ISBN 094955331X

—Community law reform for the Australian capital territory : second report : Loss of consortium : compensation for loss of capacity to do housework / the Law Reform Commission. - Canberra : Australian Government Publishing Service, 1986.
viii,28p. - (Report).
Bibliography: p.27. - Includes index.
ISBN 0644013516

COMPENSATION (LAW) - AUSTRALIA - NEW SOUTH WALES
—Traffic accident case studies / New South Wales, Law Reform Commission. - Sydney : New South Wales. Law Reform Commission, 1984.
77p.

COMPENSATION (LAW) - AUSTRALIA - TASMANIA
—Compensation for victims of motor vehicle accidents / Law Reform Commission of Tasmania. - Hobart : Acting Government Printer, 1987.
76p. - (Report).

COMPENSATION (LAW) - AUSTRALIA - VICTORIA
—Accident compensation Victoria / by L.R. Boyes and M. O'Loghlen. - 1. - Sydney : Butterworths, 1987.
looseleaf.
Supersedes: Workers compensation, Victoria, by Anderson and Rendit. Includes: Accident and workers compensation reports.
ISBN 0409492795

COMPENSATION (LAW) - AUSTRALIA - WESTERN AUSTRALIA
—Report on pre-judgment interest / Law Reform Commission of Western Australia. - Perth : Law Reform Commission of Western Australia, 1981.
38p. - (Project v no 70 part 1).

COMPENSATION (LAW) - CANADA - BRITISH COLUMBIA
—Compensation for non-pecuniary loss / Law Reform Commission of British Columbia. - Vancouver : The Commission, 1983.
iii,53p. - (Working paper).
Includes bibliographical references.

COMPENSATION (LAW) - CANADA - ONTARIO
—Report of Inquiry into Motor Vehicle Accident Compensation in Ontario / Coulter A. Osborne, commissioner. - Toronto : Ontario Ministry of the Attorney General, 1988.
2 v.; 25 cm.
Title from cover. Co-published by: Ministry of Financial Institutions. Bibliography: p. 667-712 (v. 2.). Contents: v. 1. Report - v. 2. Research studies and v. 1 appendices.
ISBN 0772938466 (v.2)

—Report of Inquiry into Motor Vehicle Accident Compensation in Ontario : summary of findings and recommendations / Coulter A. Osborne, Commissioner. - Toronto : Ontario Ministry of the Attorney General, 1988.
68, 79 p.; 25 cm.
Title from cover. Co-published by: Ministry of Financial Institutions. Text in English and French with French text on inverted pages. Title on added t.p.: Rapport de l'enquete sur l'indemnisation des victimes d'accidents d'automobiles en Ontario.
ISBN 0772938474

COMPENSATION (LAW) - CANADA - SASKATCHEWAN
—Tentative proposals for compensation of accused on acquittal / Law Reform Commission of Saskatchewan. - Saskatoon : The Commission, 1987.
38p.
Includes bibliographical references. Includes text of proposed Act.

COMPENSATION (LAW) - ENGLAND
—Accidents, compensation and the law / P.S. Atiyah. - 3rd ed. - London : Weidenfeld and Nicolson, 1980.
xxiv,695p.

ISBN 0297777548

—Atiyah's accidents, compensation and the law / Peter Cane. - 4th ed. - London : Weidenfeld and Nicholson, 1987.
639p.
ISBN 0297790528

—Compensation and support for illness and injury / Donald Harris ... et al. - Oxford : Clarendon, 1984.
xix,412p; 22cm. - (Oxford socio-legal studies).
Includes bibliographies and index.
ISBN 0198275080 Hbk £20.00
ISBN 0198275137 Pbk £9.50

—Land compensation : a study of compensation determination / Barry P.D. Denyer-Green. - Cambridge : Granta Editions, 1986.
xi,124p. - (Occasional paper).
Includes bibliographical references.
ISBN 0906782228

COMPENSATION (LAW) - GREAT BRITAIN
—Disease and the compensation debate / Jane Stapleton. - Oxford : Clarendon, 1986.
224p; 22cm.
Includes index.
ISBN 0198255527 £22.50

—Effect of ill-health and subsequent compensation and support on household income : a logistic regression approach / by Yvonne Brittan and Ioannis G. Vlachonikolis. - Oxford : Centre for Socio-Legal Studies, Wolfson College Oxford, 1980.
23p; 21cm. - (Working paper).

—Meeting legal needs? : an evaluation of a scheme for personal injury victims / Hazel Genn. - Oxford : SSRC Centre for Socio-Legal Studies, 1982.
ix,69p; 22cm.
A report commissioned by the Greater Manchester Legal Services Committee.
ISBN 0862260442

COMPENSATION (LAW) - MANITOBA
—Report on prejudgment compensation on money awards : alternatives to interest / Law Reform Commission. - Winnipeg : Queen's Printer, 1982.
iv,108p. - (Report).

COMPENSATION (LAW) - NEW ZEALAND
—Accident compensation : a commentary on the New Zealand scheme / Terence G. Ison. - London : Croom Helm, 1980.
201p; 23cm.
Includes index.
ISBN 0709902492 £14.95

—Accident compensation in New Zealand : purpose, progress / Wellington : Accident Compensation Commission, 1980.
29p.
ISBN 0477063632

—Accident compensation scheme : a discussion paper / Law Commission. - Wellington, N.Z. : The Commission, 1987.
v,58p. - (Preliminary paper).

—Accident compensation scheme : interim report on aspects of funding / Law Commission. - Wellington, N.Z. : The Commission, 1987.
vii,39p. - (Report).

COMPENSATION (LAW) - NORTHERN IRELAND
—Compensation for criminal damage to property / by D.S. Greer and V.A. Mitchell. - Belfast : SLS Legal Publications (N.I.), 1982.
xxxviii,345p.
Includes index.

COMPETENCY TO STAND TRIAL - CANADA - SASKATCHEWAN
—Tentative proposals for a Lieutenant Governor's Review Board in Saskatchewan / Law Reform Commission of Saskatchewan. - Saskatoon : The Commission, 1984.
28p.
Includes text of proposed Act.

COMPETENCY TO STAND TRIAL - UNITED STATES
—Evaluating competencies : forensic assessments and instruments / Thomas Grisso. - New York : Plenum, 1986.
x,404p; 24cm.
Bibliography: p365-383. - Includes index.
ISBN 0306421267 No price

COMPETITION, INTERNATIONAL
—Copyright in free and competitive markets / edited by W.R. Cornish. - Oxford : Published by ESC Publishing for l'Association Litteraire et Artistique Internationale and the British Literary and Artistic Copyright Association, 1986.
vii,138p.
Includes bibliographical references.
ISBN 0906214467

—Swiss review of international competition law / Geneva : Werner & Sieber, 1984.
Continues: Revue suisse du droit international de la concurrence.
ISBN 02558246

COMPETITION LAW
—Competition among international airlines / by Richard Pryke. - Aldershot : Gower for the Trade Policy Research Centre, 1987.
100p; 22cm.
Includes bibliography.
ISBN 0566053330 Pbk £9.00

—Competition policy and joint ventures / Organisation for Economic Co-operation and Development. - Paris : Organisation for Economic Co-operation and Development, 1986.
111p.
ISBN 9264128980

—Extraterritorial control of competition under international law, with special regard to US antitrust law / Erik Nerep. - 2. - Stockholm : Norstedt, 1983.
xxvii,xvii,733p.
Thesis (doctoral) - University of Stockholm 1982?.
Bibliography: p.665-716. - Includes index.
ISBN 9118373127

—Pinner's World unfair competition law : an encyclopedia / Heinz David. - 2d ed. - Alphen aan de Rijn, Netherlands : Sijthoff & Noordhoff, 1978.
v.; 26 cm.
Loose-leaf for updating. Includes bibliographical references.
ISBN 9028605576 v. 1

—Protection of personal and commercial reputation : a study of the law in Western Europe and the United States / Robert M. Kunstadt. - Weinheim : Verlag Chemie for Max Planck Institute for Foreign and International Patent, Copyright, and Competition Law, Munich, 1980.
vii,98p; 24cm.
Bibliography: p.97-98.
ISBN 3527256970
ISBN 0895730286

COMPETITION LAW - AUSTRALIA
—Passing off trade deception trade marks / Charles Joseph Bannon. - Sydney : Butterworths, 1985.
xxv,172p.
ISBN 0409492442 A$59

—Trade associations, fairness and competition / by Warren Pengilley. - Sydney : Law Book Company, 1981.
xxvii,247p.
Includes index. Includes text of Trade Practices Act 1974.
ISBN 0455200866

COMPETITION LAW - CANADA

—Amendments to the Combines Investigation Act : background information and explanatory notes / Department of Consumer and Corporate Affairs. - Ottawa : The Department, 1984.
32p,37p.
With French t.p.: Modifications de la loi relative aux enquetes sur les coalitions. English and French text.

—Annotated Competition Act / commentary prepared by Robert S. Nozick : annotations and index prepared by Charlotte Neff. - Toronto : Carswell, 1987.
xviii,290p.
ISBN 0459396609

—Canadian Competition Law / Vancouver : British Columbia Continuing Legal Education Society, 1984.
341p.
ISBN 0865041555 Hbk £70.00

—Canadian Competition Policy : A Legal and Economic Analysis / David McQueen. - Aurora : Canada Law Book Co, 1987.
300p.

—Competition Act / Vancouver : Continuing Legal Education Society of British Columbia, 1986.
461p.
ISBN 0865042802 Hbk £85.00

—Competition law amendments : a schematic presentation of Bill C-91 and the present act / Ottawa : Consumer and Corporate Affairs Canada, 1986.
98, 99 p.; 28 cm.
English and French. Title on added t.p.: Reforme de la legislation sur la concurrence. Includes complete text of the Competition Tribunal Act and the Competition Act, including the provisions of the current act that are replaced or changed by Bill C-91.
ISBN 0662542282 pbk.

—New Competition Law : Text and Commentary / Don Mills : CCH Canadian Ltd, 1986.
136p.
ISBN 088796396X Pbk £14.95

—Recent Developments in Business and Litigation / Vancouver : Continuing Legal Education Society of British Columbia.

—Trademarks and Unfair Competition / Vancouver : British Columbia Continuing Legal Education Society, 1982.
352p.
ISBN 0865040591 Hbk £55.00

COMPETITION LAW - EUROPE

—Competition Law in Western Europe and the USA / Dordrecht : Kluwer, 1984.

Supplement 59 1985.

Supplement 60 1985.
192p.

Supplement 61 1985.
192p.

Supplement 62 1985.
144p.

—European Competition Law Review / Oxford : ESC Publishing Ltd, 1988.

COMPETITION LAW - EUROPEAN COMMUNITY

—Application of the Competition Rules (Antitrust Law) of the European Economic Community to Enterprises and Arrangements External to the Common Market / Dordrecht : Kluwer, 1981.
474p.

—Competition Law in the E.E.C. and in the E.C.S.C. / Luxembourg : Office for Official Publications of the European Communities, 1986.
220p.
ISBN 9282558320 Pbk

—Competition law in the EEC and in the ECSC : situation at 30 June 1981 / Luxembourg : Office for Official Publications of the European Communities, 1981.
134p.
At head of title: Commission of the European Communities.
ISBN 9282523896

—Competition law of Britain and the Common Market / by Valentine Korah. - 3rd ed. - The Hague : Martinus Nijhoff, 1982.
xxvii,352p.
Bibliography: p321-326. Includes index.
ISBN 9024726158 Hbk £140.00

—EC competition law : a practitioner's textbook / Alan Campbell : foreword by Lord Mackenzie Stuart. - Amsterdam : North-Holland, 1980.
xii,345p; 23cm.
Includes index.
ISBN 0444854967 £24.34

—EEC law and Nordic commercial relations with the Communities / edited by Zacharias Sundstrom ... et al. - Helsinki : Finnish Asssociation for European Law, 1985.
358p.
Proceedings of a seminar held at Hanasaari, Helsinki, 2-4 May 1984. Includes bibliographical references.
ISBN 9519960309

—European Commission's Powers of Investigation in the Enforcement of Competition Law / Luxembourg : Office for Official Publications of the European Communities, 1985.
81p.
ISBN 9282553612 Pbk

—Exclusive dealing agreements in the E.E.C. : Regulation 67/67 replaced / by Valentine Korah. - London : European Law Centre, 1984.
xv,101p; 25cm.
ISBN 090745111X Pbk No price

—Fourteenth Report on Competition Policy / Kirchberg : Commission of the European Communities, 1985.
248p.

—Introductory guide to EEC Competition law and practice / Valentine Korah. - 3rd ed. - Oxford : ESC Publishing, 1986.
xxi,177p; 21cm.
Includes bibliographies and index. Cover title: EEC competition law and practice.
ISBN 0906214394

—Introductory guide to EEC competition law and practice / Valentine Korah. - 2nd ed. - Oxford : ESC, 1981.
xxii,160p; 22cm.
ISBN 0906214084 Pbk Unpriced

—Notices and Group Exemptions in EEC Competition Law / Oxford : ESC Publishing Ltd.
ISBN 0906214041 loose £45.00

—Patent licensing and EEC competition rules : Regulation 2349/84 / Valentine Korah. - Oxford : ESC Publishing, 1985.
xiv,126p. - (European competition law monographs).
Includes bibliographies.
ISBN 090621436X

—R & D and the EEC competition rules : Regulation 418/85 / Valentine Korah. - Oxford : ESC Publishing, 1986.
xxi,114p. - (European competition law monographs).
Bibliography: p.xxi.
ISBN 0906214459

—State aids under the EEC treaty articles 92 to 94 / Despina Schina. - Oxford : ESC Publishing, 1987.
xviii, 221p.
Bibliography: p.179-185. - Includes index.
ISBN 0906214440

—Submission by the Joint Working Party on Competition Law to the House of Lords Select Committee on the European Communities on procedures for administering EEC competition policy / Joint Working Party on Competition Law. - London : Senate of the Inns of Court and the Bar, 1981.
10p; 30cm.
At head of title: The Senate of the Inns of Court and Bar, The Law Society.

—Suitability of concentration measures for EEC competition policy / Walter Piesch, Ingo Schmidt. - Luxembourg : Office for Official Publications of the European Communities, 1983.
101 p.; 25 cm.
ISBN 9282531783 pbk. £5.50

COMPETITION LAW - GREAT BRITAIN

—Anti-competitive practices : a guide to the provisions of the Competition Act 1980 / London : Office of Fair Trading, 1986.
39p.

—Antitrust Economics / Oxford : Blackwell Scientific, 1987.
ISBN 0631153632 Hbk £32.50

—Becton Dickinson UK Limited : the supply of hypodermic syringes and hypodermic needles / a report by the Director General of Fair Trading on an investigation under section 3 of the Competition Act 1980. - London : Office of Fair Trading, 1988.
39p.

—Competition Law / London : Allen & Unwin, 1985.
ISBN 0043430023 Hbk £18.00
ISBN 0043430031 Pbk £7.95

—Competition Law / London : Butterworths, 1985.
ISBN 0406012784 Hbk £33.00
ISBN 0406012792 Pbk £21.95

—Competition Law Handbook / London : Butterworths, 1987.
ISBN 040610400X Pbk £25.00

—Competition law of Britain and the Common Market / by Valentine Korah. - 3rd ed. - The Hague : Martinus Nijhoff, 1982.
xxvii,352p.
Bibliography: p321-326. Includes index.
ISBN 9024726158 Hbk £140.00

—Competition Law of the UK and the Republic of Ireland / Allan. - Matthew Bender, 1988.
ISBN 0000999068 Hbk £59.00

—Competition policy in Britain : the silent revolution / D.P. O'Brien. - Durham : Department of Economics, University of Durham, 1981.
20 leaves. - (Working paper).
Includes bibliographical references.

—Encyclopaedia of Competition Law / London : Sweet & Maxwell, 1988.
ISBN 0421368705 updat £195.00

—Passing off : the law and practice relating to the imitation of goods, businesses and professions / David Young. - 1st ed. - London : Oyez Longman, 1985.
xxviii,152p. - (Oyez Longman practitioner series).
Includes index.
ISBN 0851209866

—Review of legislation on false and misleading price information : report of the inter-departmental working party / Department of Trade and Industry. - London : The Department, 1984.
67p.

—Sheffield Newspapers Limited : a report by the Director General of Fair Trading on an investigation under section 3 of the Competition Act 1980 / London : Office of Fair Trading, 1981.
72p; 30cm.

—TI Raleigh Industries Limited and Raleigh Limited : a report by the Director General of Fair Trading on an investigation under Section 3 of the Competition Act, 1980 / London : Office of Fair Trading, 1981.
40p.

—Unichem Limited : allocation of shares by co-operative upon reconverting to a public limited company / a report by the Director General of Fair Trading on an investigation under section 3 of the Competition Act 1980. - London : Office of Fair Trading, 1988.
49p.

—United Kingdom Competition Law / London : Sweet & Maxwell.
ISBN 0421314907 Hbk

—W. M. Still & Sons Limited, W. M. Still Service Limited : a report by the Director General of Fair Trading on an investigation under section 3 of the Competition Act 1980 / Office of Fair Trading. - London : Office of Fair Trading, 1982.
39p; 30cm.

—World's Fair Limited and Marcus Publishing PLC : refusal to publish advertisements which contain certain price information : a report by the Director General of Fair Trading on two investigations under section 3 of the Competition Act 1980 / Office of Fair Trading. - London : Office of Fair Trading, 1987.
30p.

COMPETITION LAW - IRELAND

—Competition Law of the UK and the Republic of Ireland / Allan. - Matthew Bender, 1988.
ISBN 0000999068 Hbk £59.00

COMPETITION LAW - NEW ZEALAND

—Guidebook to New Zealand's Competition Laws / North Ryde : C.C.H. Australia, 1987.
250p.
ISBN 0864750676 Hbk

—Law of Restrictive Trade Practices in New Zealand / 2nd. ed. - Butterworths, 1982.
ISBN 040960125X Hbk £33.10

COMPETITION LAW - PORTUGAL

—Public enterprise in Portugal and Spain : analysis from the point of view of competition policy / Luxembourg : Office for Official Publications of the European Communities, 1988.
213p.
At head of title: Commission of the European Communities.
ISBN 9282579107

COMPETITION LAW - SPAIN

—Public enterprise in Portugal and Spain : analysis from the point of view of competition policy / Luxembourg : Office for Official Publications of the European Communities, 1988.
213p.
At head of title: Commission of the European Communities.
ISBN 9282579107

COMPETITION LAW - UNITED STATES
—Competition Law in Western Europe and the USA / Dordrecht : Kluwer, 1984.

Supplement 59 1985.

Supplement 60 1985.
192p.

Supplement 61 1985.
192p.

Supplement 62 1985.
144p.

COMPETITION LAW - WEST GERMANY
—German competition law : (legislation and commentary) / by Dietrich Hoffmann in cooperation with Stefan Schaub. - Deventer : Kluwer Law and Taxation Publishers, 1983.
xi,194.
Offprint from Competition law in Western Europe and the USA.
ISBN 9065441425

COMPETITION, UNFAIR - EUROPEAN ECONOMIC COMMUNITY COUNTRIES
—Butterworths competition law handbook / edited by Garth Lindrup. - London : Butterworths, 1987.
vii,419p.
Includes index.
ISBN 040610400X

COMPETITION, UNFAIR - GREAT BRITAIN
—Butterworths competition law handbook / edited by Garth Lindrup. - London : Butterworths, 1987.
vii,419p.
Includes index.
ISBN 040610400X

COMPLAINTS AGAINST POLICE
—Proceedings of the Round Table with European Ombudsmen : Madrid, 5-6 June 1985 / organised by the Secretariat General of the Council of Europe in co-operation with the Spanish Defensor del Pueblo. - Strasbourg : Directorate of Human Rights, Council of Europe, 1987.
141p.
ISBN 928711000X

COMPLAINTS AGAINST POLICE - ENGLAND
—Complaints against the police : a sociological view / Ken Russell. - 3rd rev ed. - Glenfield, Leicester : Milltak, 1985.
iv,132p.
Bibliography: p.125-130. - Includes index.
ISBN 0950490660

—No way in Wapping : the effect of the policing of the News International dispute on Wapping residents / a report by the National Council for Civil Liberties. - London : National Council for Civil Liberties, 1986.
41p.
ISBN 0946088276

—Police Acts 1964 and 1976 : complaints against the police which are withdrawn / Ken Russell. - Leicester : Leicester Polytechnic, 1986.
33p. - (Leicester Polytechnic School of Law Monographs).
Includes bibliographical references.
ISBN 0900937408

—Police complaints and discipline procedures / presented to Parliament by the Secretary of State for the Home Department... - London : H.M.S.O., 1983.
ii,23p.
ISBN 0101907206

COMPLAINTS AGAINST POLICE - GREAT BRITAIN
—Called to account : the case for police accountability in England and Wales / Sarah Spencer. - London : National Council for Civil Liberties, 1985.
146p; 20cm.
Includes bibliography.
ISBN 0946088128 Pbk £3.95

—Fair cop : reforming the police complaints procedure / Patricia Hewitt. - London : National Council for Civil Liberties, 1982.
48p; 20cm.
ISBN 0946088012

—Fourth report from the Home Affairs Committee, session 1981-82 : police complaints procedures / Great Britain. - London : H.M.S.O., 1982.
xlii; 25cm. - (HC98-I).
ISBN 0100080820 Pbk £3.95

Vol.2 : Evidence and appendices 1982.
vii,326p; 25cm. - (HC 98-II).
ISBN 0100080928 Pbk £12.40

—Observations on the triennial review report of the Police Complaints Board / Justice. - London : Justice, 1980.
8p.

—Police Complaints Board Final Report 1977-1985 / London : HMSO.
ISBN 0101958404 Hbk £3.50

—Police Complaints Board Triennial Review Report 1983 / Police Complaints Board. - London : HMSO.
ISBN 010188530X Hbk £3.35

—Police misconduct : legal remedies / John Harrison. - London : Legal Action Group, 1987.
xxix,218p.
Guide to the remedies and procedures available in this area. Covers police complaints, civil actions against the police, the European Convention on Human Rights, police discipline, judicial review, wrongful convictions, criminal proceedings, and legal aid. Appendices include levels of damages and useful names and addresses.
ISBN 0905099168

—Report of Police Complaints Board 1984 / London : HMSO.
ISBN 0102359857 Hbk £7.50

—Suing the police / Hugh Tomlinson. - London : Longman Professional (UK), 1989.
Identifies the clauses of the damages claim and explains the types of damages that can be included. Offers advice on every stage of the procedure from taking instructions and financing the case to the trial itself. Includes costs, fees, and precedents.
ISBN 0851215297 Pbk £14.95

COMPLAINTS (RETAIL TRADE)
—No access to law : alternatives to the American judicial system / Laura Nader editor. - New York : Academic Press, 1980.
xxiii,540p; 24cm.
Includes bibliographies and index.
ISBN 0125135602 Hbk £15.40
ISBN 015135629 Pbk £8.40

COMPLIANCE - CANADA
—Policy implementation, compliance and administrative law / Law Reform Commission of Canada. - Ottawa : Law Reform Commission of Canada, 1986.
105,115p; 25cm. - (Working paper).
Cover title: Administrative law - policy implementation, compliance and administrative law. Added t.p. in French: Droit, objectifs publics et observation des normes. Pages numbered in opposite directions. Text in English and French.
ISBN 0662540832

COMPREHENSION - ENGLAND
—Improving the presentation of information to juries in fraud trials : a report of four research studies / by the MRC Applied Psychology Unit, Cambridge. - London : H.M.S.O., 1986.
vii,63p; 25cm.
Presents the results of research by the Roskill Fraud Trials Committee on the presentation of evidence to juries.
ISBN 0113800096

COMPROMISE (LAW)
—Law of Compromises / S.K. Agrawal. - 4th ed. - Allahabad : Law Book Company, 1986.
600p.
ISBN Hbk £140.00

COMPROMISE (LAW) - BRITISH COLUMBIA
—Report on settlement offers / Law Reform Commission of British Columbia. - Vancouver : Law Reform Commission of British Columbia, 1984.
47p.
ISBN 0771884494

COMPROMISE (LAW) - ENGLAND
—Law and practice of compromise / by David Foskett. - 2nd ed. - London : Sweet & Maxwell, 1985.
xlvii,388p.
Covers the significance of an agreement reached, and its consequence, and also the means by which a concluded agreement can, may or should be implemented. Also discusses the role which lawyers play in the negotiating process.
ISBN 0421324708

COMPULSORY PURCHASE - AUSTRALIA
—Compulsory acquisiton of land in Australia / editor, Graham L. Fricke. - 2nd ed. - Sydney : Law Book Co., 1982.
xxxix,393p.
Previous ed.: 1975. Includes bibliographical references and index.
ISBN 0455204667

COMPULSORY PURCHASE - CANADA
—Compensation for security interests in expropriated land : memorandum for discussion / Institute of Law Research and Reform. - Edmonton, Alta. : The Institute, 1982.
48p.

—Expropriation Act / Vancouver : Continuing Legal Education Society of British Columbia, 1988.
173p.
ISBN 0865043639 Hbk £75.00

—Expropriation in Canada : A Practitioner's Guide / Aurora : Canada Law Book Co, 1988.
200p.
This new monograph provides a practical approach to the principles and practice of expropriation law and property valuation in Canada. The author discusses specific and persistent problems in the subject area, and provides practical approaches for dealing with them.

—Property Rights and Compensation : Compulsory Acquisition and Other Losses / Butterworths, 1983.
192p.
Includes alternative bases for assessing economic losses, compulsory acquisition of business, compensation for goodwill and licences, economic value and property, reservation values and compulsory acquisitions, compensation claims and the taking of public property.
ISBN 0409843059 Hbk £45.00

COMPULSORY PURCHASE - CANADA - ALBERTA
—Compensation for security interests in expropriated land / Institute of Law Research and Reform. - Edmonton : The Institute, 1984.
iii,30p. - (Report).

COMPULSORY PURCHASE - ENGLAND
—Law of compulsory purchase and compensation / Keith Davies. - 4th ed. - London : Butterworths, 1984.
xxxv,364p; 23cm.
Previous ed.: 1978. Includes index.
ISBN 0406571872 Hbk Unpriced
ISBN 0406571880 Pbk Unpriced

COMPULSORY PURCHASE - GREAT BRITAIN
—Boynton's Guide to Compulsory Purchase and Compensation / David J. Hawkins. - 5th ed. - London : Oyez Longman, 1983.
- (Oyez Longman Practitioner Ser.).
ISBN 0851207138 Hbk £17.25

—Casebook on Compulsory Purchase and Compensation / Oxford : Blackwell Scientific, 1988.
ISBN 0003834085 Hbk £35.00

—Compulsory Purchase and Compensation / 4th ed. - London : Butterworths, 1984.
ISBN 0406571872 Hbk £21.00
ISBN 0406571880 Pbk £17.95

—Compulsory Purchase and Compensation / Hawkins. - 5th ed. - London : Longman Professional, 1983.
ISBN 0851207138 Pbk £27.50

—Compulsory Purchase and Compensation / 2nd ed. - London : Estates Gazette, 1985.
ISBN 0728200899 Pbk £14.00

—Encyclopaedia of Compulsory Purchase / London : Sweet & Maxwell, 1988.
ISBN 0421007508 Hbk £195.00

—Encyclopedia of the Law of Compulsory Purchase and Compensation, 2 Vols. / London : Sweet & Maxwell, 1985.
- (Local Government Library).
Includes tables of statutes and cases covered by the encyclopaedia, and a guide to the general principles of compulsory purchase law and practice. Covers rates of interest after entry regulations, and includes the Local Government Act 1988. Also contains a new section with details of major cases.
ISBN 0421007508 Hbk £125.00

Service only

—Land Compensation Reports Consolidated Index, Table of Cases / Aurora : Canada Law Book Co.

—Land Compensation Reports (L.C.R.) 1971-Present / Aurora : Canada Law Book Co.

—Planning and Compensation Reports : 1950-1981, 42 Vols. / Abingdon : Professional Books.

COMPULSORY PURCHASE - HONG KONG
—Land Compensation and Valuation Law in Hong Kong / London : Butterworths, 1986.
ISBN 0409995258 Hbk £78.00

COMPULSORY PURCHASE - INDIA
—Compulsory Acquisition of Land in India, 2 Vols. / Allahabad : Universal Book Agency, 1984.

COMPULSORY PURCHASE - MALAYSIA
—Law of compulsory purchase and compensation - Singapore and Malaysia / N. Khublall. - Singapore : Butterworths, 1984.
xxviii,310p.
Account of the main provisions relating to powers, procedures and appeals, and discusses the concept of market value as the basis for compensation. Cases and statutory provisions are drawn from both Singapore and Malaysia, as well as from England and India.
ISBN 0406181225 £55.00

COMPULSORY PURCHASE - NEW ZEALAND

—Compulsory Acquisition of Land in New Zealand / Butterworths, 1982.
An analysis of the Public Works Act 1981 concerning the taking of land for public purposes and the compensation provided for the acquisition. Includes citation of related cases.
ISBN 0409601225 Hbk £58.30

—Compulsory Acquisition of Land in New Zealand / London : Butterworths, 1984.
ISBN 0409601225 Hbk £25.40

COMPULSORY PURCHASE - SINGAPORE

—Law of compulsory purchase and compensation - Singapore and Malaysia / N. Khublall. – Singapore : Butterworths, 1984.
xxviii,310p.
Account of the main provisions relating to powers, procedures and appeals, and discusses the concept of market value as the basis for compensation. Cases and statutory provisions are drawn from both Singapore and Malaysia, as well as from England and India.
ISBN 0406181225 £55.00

COMPULSORY PURCHASE - SOUTH AFRICA

—Law of expropriation in South Africa / Marcus Jacobs. – Cape Town : Juta, 1982.
xxxiv,700p.
Bibliography: p.xv-xvi. - Includes index.
ISBN 0702112550

COMPULSORY PURCHASE (INTERNATIONAL LAW)

—Nationalization of foreign property : a study in North-South dialogue / Subhash C. Jain : foreword by B. Sen. – New Delhi : Deep & Deep, 1983.
298p.
Bibliography: p.268-298 - Includes index.

—Pursuit of nationalized property / M. Sornarajah. – Dordrecht : M. Nijhoff, 1985.
248p.
Bibliography.
ISBN 9024731305 Hbk £120.00

COMPUTER CONTRACTS

—Computer Contracts / Dordrecht : Kluwer, 1984.
ISBN 9065441980 Pbk £125.00

—Computer contracts / Richard Morgan, Graham Stedman. – 2nd ed. – London : Oyez Longman, 1984.
x,324p.
Previous ed.: 1979. Includes index.
ISBN 0851208568

COMPUTER CONTRACTS - AUSTRALIA

—Computer Contracts : Principles and Practice / A. Sharpe. – North Ryde : Law Book Co, 1987.
xxxi, 605p.

—Negotiating a Database Contract / Hawthorn : Australian Database Development Agency, 1987.
ISBN 0959096736 Hbk £5.00

COMPUTER CONTRACTS - GREAT BRITAIN

—Computer contracts / Graham Stedman. – 3rd ed. – London : Longman, 1987.
x,434p; 24cm. – (Longman commercial series).
Previous ed.: 1984. Includes index.
ISBN 085121259X £40.00

—Computer Contracts / Matthew Bender, 1987.
ISBN 0000999060 Hbk £150.00

—Computer Contracts / 2nd ed. – London : Longman Professional, 1987.
ISBN 085208568 Hbk £40.00

—Computer contracts : the deeper issues : conference organised by the Society for Computers and Law on Monday 19th November 1984 at the Royal Garden Hotel, London, W.8 / speakers Martin Edwards ... et al. : conference organising committee Colin Ellis (Chairman) ... et al. – Didcot : Society for Computers and Law, 1984.
ii,72p.
ISBN 0906122163

—Further computer contracts / London : Sweet & Maxwell, 1989.
Includes precedents for shrink-wrap software license, software development agreements, agreements for the supply of a customised computer system, escrow agreement, agreements for provisions of On-Line service and data protection, and software authors agreements.
ISBN 0421403306 Pbk £25.00

—Understanding computer contracts / London : Waterlow, 1983.
ISBN 0803091346 Pbk £7.95

COMPUTER CRIME

—Computer-related crime : analysis of legal policy / Paris : OECD, 1986.
71p.
'... prepared for the Committee for Information, Computer and Communications Policy ...'. - p.3.

COMPUTER CRIME - AUSTRALIA - TASMANIA

—Report on computer misuse / Law Reform Commission of Tasmania. – Hobart : Government Printer, 1986.
37p. – (Report v no 47).

—Research paper on computer misuse / by W.G. Briscoe. – Hobart? : Government Printer?, . 167p. – (Research paper).

COMPUTER CRIME - ENGLAND

—Computer misuse / the Law Commission. – London : HMSO, 1988.
viii,130p. – (Working paper).
Law Commission Working Paper, examines activities which might constitute computer misuse. Concludes present criminal law is sufficient to deal with computer misuse excepting unauthorised access which might require the creation of a new computer crime.
ISBN 0117301922

COMPUTER CRIME - GREAT BRITAIN

—Computer fraud survey / Audit Commission for Local Authorities in England and Wales. – London : H.M.S.O., 1985.
55p.
ISBN 0117012815 Pbk £3.30

—Computer Fraud Survey / London : HMSO, 1985.
60p.
ISBN 0117012815 Hbk £3.30

—Computer Related Crime / London : HMSO, 1986.
72p.
ISBN 9264128522 Pbk £4.00

—Prevention and prosecution of computer and high-tech crime / Kaplan. – Matthew Bender, 1988.
ISBN 0000999061 Hbk £50.00

—Survey of computer fraud and abuse / Audit Commission for Local Authorities in England and Wales. – London : H.M.S.O., 1987.
88p.
Report finds lack of basic control mechanisms. Suggests that the opportunity for fraud is widespread and a large numnber remain undiscovered.
ISBN 0117010650

COMPUTER CRIME - SCOTLAND

—Computer crime / Scottish Law Commission. – Edinburgh : The Commission, 1986.
146p. – (Consultative memorandum).
Includes bibliographical references.

—Report on computer crime / Scottish Law Commission. – Edinburgh : H.M.S.O., 1987.
v,38p.
Includes bibliographical references. Includes Draft Computer Crime (Scotland) Bill.
ISBN 0101017421

COMPUTER NETWORKS

—Transborder data flows : proceedings of an OECD conference held December 1983 / edited for the OECD by Hans-Peter Gassmann. – Amsterdam : North-Holland, 1985.
Bibliography: p.
ISBN 0444877002

COMPUTER PROGRAMS

—Computer contracts handbook : precedents of contracts for the sale, purchase, support, distribution and licence of computers and computer software / by M.-T. Michele Rennie : consultant editor, Elizabeth Jarvie. – London : Sweet & Maxwell, 1985.
xi,136p; 30cm.
Includes precedents for software licence, software and support agreements, software distributions agreements, escrow agreements, sales agreements, and distribution agreement. Where appropriate, includes two agreements for each subject, one drafted when acting for the supplier, and one when acting for the purchaser.
ISBN 0421332301 Pbk £17.50

—Legal protection of computer programs / Bryan Niblett. – London : Oyez, 1980.
xii,155p; 22cm.
Includes index.
ISBN 0851205097 £10.00

—Legal protection of computer programs and data / by Christopher J. Millard. – London : Sweet & Maxwell, 1985.
xxvi,239p; 23cm.
Includes index.
ISBN 0421334800 Pbk £24.00
ISBN 0459372300 Canada

—Legal protection of computer software / edited by Lawrence Perry and Hugh Brett. – Oxford : ESC, 1981.
xiv,197p; 22cm.
Includes bibliographical references.
ISBN 0906214068 Pbk Unpriced

—Patentability of computer software : an international guide to the protection of computer-related inventions / by H.W.A.M. Hanneman. – Deventer : Kluwer Law and Taxation Publishers, 1985.
257p; 23cm.
ISBN 9065442251

—Software for producing library keyword catalogues : a description of selected packages / Steven Prowse. – Oxford : Elsevier International Bulletins, 1984.
viii,48p; 30cm. – (EIB report series).
Bibliography: p48.
ISBN 0946395012 Pbk

COMPUTER PROGRAMS - CANADA

—Legal Protection of Computer Programs and Data / Agincourt : Carswell, 1985.
250p.
This work provides a systematic investigation of general software copyright issues under American, United Kingdom, and Canadian law. The legal protection of software and data under copyright, trade secrets, confidentiality, contractual arrangements, and criminal law is analyzed in the book.

—Legal Protection of Computer Programs and Data / Agincourt : Carswell, 1985.
250p.

COMPUTER PROGRAMS - GREAT BRITAIN

—Copyright & computers / Cliff Dilloway. – London : Gower in association with Institute of Purchasing and Supply, 1985.
xii,126p; 23cm.
Bibliography: p123-126. Includes: Copyright & computers / R.J. Hart. Originally published: London : British Computer Society, 1983.
ISBN 0566025205 £21.45

COMPUTER SOFTWARE

—Legal Software Directory / London : Longman Professional, 1985.
ISBN 0851210422 Pbk £16.50

—Model Provisions on the Protection of Computer Software : Text of the English Translation of the Stockholm Act (1967) / Geneva : World Intellectual Property Organization.
27p.

COMPUTER SOFTWARE - CANADA

—Legal Protection of Computer Programs and Data / Agincourt : Carswell, 1985.
250p.
This work provides a systematic investigation of general software copyright issues under American, United Kingdom, and Canadian law. The legal protection of software and data under copyright, trade secrets, confidentiality, contractual arrangements, and criminal law is analyzed in the book.

COMPUTER SOFTWARE - GREAT BRITAIN

—Auditing Development of Computer Systems / London : Butterworths, 1987.
ISBN 0406500932 Pbk £26.50

—Businessman's Guide to Microcomputers / Deloitte Staff. – London : Butterworths, 1984.
This book is designed to give business and legal practitioners a thorough introduction to microcomputers. The book provides in depth information on software packages with business applications.
ISBN 0406016003 Pbk

—Butterworth's Income Tax Computer Software / London : Butterworths.

—Computer software : legal protection in the United Kingdom / by Henry Carr. – Oxford : ESC Publishing Ltd., 1987.
xxii, 228p.
ISBN 0906214327

—How to make money from your software / Oxford : ESC, 1984.
ISBN 0906214319 Pbk £9.50

—How to Make Money from Your Software : Legal and Business Aspects / Oxford : ESC Publishing Ltd, 1985.
108p.
ISBN 0906214319 Pbk £9.50

—Lawyer's Guide to Software / Pinter, 1985.
ISBN 0861874978 Hbk £15.00

—Legal Protection of Computer Software / Perry. – Oxford : ESC, 1981.
ISBN 0906214068 Pbk £16.25

COMPUTER-ASSISTED INSTRUCTION - GREAT BRITAIN

—CTISS file / Bath : Computers in Teaching Initiative Support Service, 1986-.

—Learning to live with IT : an overview of the potential of information technology for education and training / Information Technology Advisory Panel. – London : H.M.S.O., 1986.
44p.
ISBN 0116308311

—Report of a working party on computer facilities for teaching in universities / Computer Board for Universities and Research Councils. – London : The Board, 1983.
25,3,11p.
Includes bibliography.

COMPUTERS

—Bibliography of computers and the law / Melbourne : Victorian Society of Computers and Law, 1984.
22 leaves.

—Computer contracts : an international guide to agreements and software protection / Hilary E. Pearson. – London : Financial Training, 1984.
ISBN 0906322480

—Computer law & practice : the journal of computer and communications law / London : F. Cass, 1984-.

—Computers and Penal Legislation / Oslo : Norwegian University Press, 1983.
166p.
ISBN 8200065707 Hbk £84.00

—Data processing and the law : UK National Committee on Comparative Law Annual Colloquium, Leicester, 15-16 September 1982 / Colloquium Chairman Colin Campbell. – 1. – Coventry : UKNCCL, 1982.
various pagings.
Includes bibliographies.

—Harmonisation of laws relating to the requirement of written proof and to the admissibility of reproductions of documents and recordings on computers : Recommendation No.R (81) 20 adopted by the Committee of Ministers of the Council of Europe on 11 December 1981 and Explanatory memorandum / Council of Europe. – Strabourg : Council of Europe, 1982.
21p; 21cm. – (Legal Affairs).
ISBN 9287100446

—International computer law issues / Keustermans. – Matthew Bender, 1988.
ISBN 0000999059 Hbk £53.00

—Issues in Computing, Telecommunications and Information Policy / Paris : International Chamber of Commerce.
24p.

—Patentability of computer software : an international guide to the protection of computer-related inventions / by H.W.A.M. Hanneman. – Deventer : Kluwer Law and Taxation Publishers, 1985.
257p; 23cm.
ISBN 9065442251 No price

—Proceedings of the Conference of Institutions Responsible for Teaching the Subject 'Computers and Law', Rome, 9-11 October 1985 : reports presented at the Conference / Strasbourg : Council of Europe, 1987.
357p; 29cm.
At head of cover title: Legal affairs.
ISBN 9287110603

—Teaching, Research and Training in the Field of Computers and Law / Strasbourg : Council of Europe, 1981.

—Teaching, research and training in the field of 'computers and the law' : recommendation no. R (80)3 adopted by the Committee of Ministers of the Council of Europe on 30 April 1980 and explanatory memorandum / Council of Europe. – Strasbourg : Council of Europe, 1981.
12p.
'Prepared by the Committee of Experts on Legal Data Processing' - verso t.p.. At head of cover title: Council of Europe, Legal Affairs.

—Third party protection of software and firmware : direct protection of zeros and ones / John J. Borking. – Amsterdam : North-Holland, 1985.
xx,521p; 24cm.
Bibliography: p491-510. - Includes index.
ISBN 0444876774 £48.78

COMPUTERS – AUSTRALIA

—Computer law in Australia / London : Legal Books, 1986.
ISBN 0949553271 Pbk £12.00

—Computer law in Australia : a collection of essays / edited by W. John Taggart. – Sydney : Legal Books Pty., 1987.
xii,75p.
Bibliography: pp.61-64. - Includes index.
ISBN 0949553271

—Use of Computers in the Criminal Justice System / Canberra : Australian Institute of Criminology.

COMPUTERS – CANADA

—Applications of Computer Technology to Law 1969-78 : a Selected Bibliography / M. Anne Foster. – Ottawa : Canadian Law Information Council, 1980.
110p.

—CLIC Bibliography of Computers and Law 1983-1986 / Ottawa : Canadian Law Information Council.
106p.
ISBN 0921481128 Hbk £20.00

—Computer-Assisted Legal Research : a Guide for Canadian Law Students / Ottawa : Canadian Law Information Council, 1984.
103p.
ISBN 0920358551 Pbk £15.00

—Computer technology and the law in Canada / J. Frazer Mann. – Toronto : Carswell, 1987.
xxviii,455p.
ISBN 0459398504

—Computers and Legal Assistants / Vancouver : Continuing Legal Education Society of British Columbia, 1988.
83p.
ISBN 0865049955 Hbk £65.00

—Lawyer's Guide to the Computer : Master or Servant / Aurora : Canada Law Book Co, 1986.
283p.

—Lawyer's Guide to the Computer : Master or Servant / Aurora : Canada Law Book, 1986.

—Lawyers : Meet the Computer! / Vancouver : British Columbia Continuing Legal Education Society, 1983.
200p.
ISBN 0865041091 Hbk £55.00

—Nineteen Eighty-Three Computers and Law Institute / Vancouver : British Columbia Continuing Legal Education Society, 1983.
322p.
ISBN 0865041148 Hbk £50.00

—Practical Guide to Law Office Automation : 1988 / Kenneth A. Grant. – Agincourt : Carswell, 1988.
274p.
This 1988 edition provides information towards the selection and implementation of a law office automation system. Guidelines also include a comprehensive directory of software in Canada for lawyers and a glossary of common terms and definitions. The book also outlines the benefits of automation and the process of selecting and implementing a computer system.

COMPUTERS – ENGLAND

—Computer contracts handbook : precedents of contracts for the sale, purchase, support, distribution and licence of computers and computer software / by M.-T. Michele Rennie : consultant editor, Elizabeth Jarvie. – London : Sweet & Maxwell, 1985.
xi,136p; 30cm.
Includes precedents for software licence, software and support agreements, software distributions agreements, escrow agreements, sales agreements, and distribution agreement. Where appropriate, includes two agreements for each subject, one drafted when acting for the supplier, and one when acting for the purchaser.
ISBN 0421332301 Pbk £17.50

—Computer generated output as admissible evidence in civil and criminal cases : a report / by the Professional Advisory Committee of the British Computer Society : edited by T.R.H. Sizer and A. Kelman. – London : Heyden on behalf of the British Computer Society, 1982.
x,41p.
ISBN 0855017414

—Computer in court : a guide to computer evidence for lawyers and computing professionals / Alistair Kelman, Richard Sizer. – Aldershot : Gower, 1982.
viii,104p; 22cm.
Bibliography: p99. - Includes index.
ISBN 0566034190 Unpriced

COMPUTERS – EUROPEAN COMMUNITY

—Freedom of data flows and EEC law / G P V Vandenberghe, Y Poullet. – Kluwer Law and Taxation, 1988.
142. – (Computer/Law Series).
Deals with the legal problems caused by transfrontier flows of information. Includes chapters on the need to speak a common language between partners, data and information in common law, information and data in continental law, and restriction on transborder transmissions of commercial data under EEC law.
ISBN 9065443665 Pbk £32/Dfl 99

COMPUTERS – GREAT BRITAIN

—Businessman's Guide to Microcomputers / Deloitte Staff. – London : Butterworths, 1984.
This book is designed to give business and legal practitioners a thorough introduction to microcomputers. The book provides in depth information on software packages with business applications.
ISBN 0406016003 Pbk

—Computer Appreciation / 3rd ed. – London : Butterworths, 1981.
ISBN 0408004924 Pbk £7.95

—Computer law / Colin Tapper. – 3rd ed. – London : Longman, 1983.
xxvii,242p. – (Business data processing).
Includes index. Bibliography: p231-234.
ISBN 0582497175

—Computer law and security report / v. – Portsmouth : Solent Legal Exchange, 1985.

—Computer Science and Law - An Advanced Course / Cambridge : Cambridge University Press, 1980.
ISBN 0521234514 Hbk £17.50

—Computers and the Law / Salmon. – Oxford : Blackwell Scientific, 1987.
ISBN 0632018496 Hbk

—Computers for lawyers / London : Longman Professional, 1985.
ISBN 0851210406 Pbk £10.50

—Handbook of Computer Security / London : Kogan Page, 1987.
ISBN 185091348X Hbk £14.95

—Information technology & the law / edited by Chris Edwards and Nigel Savage. – Basingstoke : Macmillan, 1986.
viii,283p; 24cm.
Includes index.
ISBN 0333413938 £35.00

—Year Book of law, computers and technology / London : Butterworths, 1990.
25.
ISBN 0406187037 Hbk £24.95

COMPUTERS – NORWAY

—Decade of computers and law / edited by Jon Bing, Knut S. Selmer. – Oslo : Universitetsforlaget, 1980.
475 p.; 22 cm.
Includes bibliographical references.
ISBN 8200053768

COMPUTERS – UNITED STATES

—Computer law / Colin Tapper. – 3rd ed. – London : Longman, 1983.
xxvii,242p. – (Business data processing).
Includes index. Bibliography: p231-234.
ISBN 0582497175

CONCESSIONS

—Collection of international concessions and related instruments : contemporary series / edited and annotated by Peter Fischer : with the collaboration of Thomas W. Waelde. – London : Oceana, 1981.
Contains documents dated from 1975 onwards.

CONCILIATION – ENGLAND

—Fair to the family : a conciliation approach to divorce and separation / by Clare Dyer : illustrated by Claudia Aaron. – East Twickenham : Mediation in Divorce, 1988.
40p.
ISBN 0951313606

—Reparation : a discussion document / London : Home Office, 1986.
7 leaves.
Photocopy.

—Reparation, conciliation and mediation : current projects and plans in England and Wales / Tony F. Marshall : incorporating a survey by the National Association of Victims Support Schemes. – London : Home Office, 1984.
vii,73p.
Bibliography: p.50-73.
ISBN 0862521734

CONCILIATION – GREAT BRITAIN

—Bringing people together : mediation and reparation projects in Great Britain / Tony F. Marshall and Martin E. Walpole. – London : Home Office, 1985.
iv,89p.
ISBN 0862522196

—Conciliation and Divorce / Chichester : Barry Rose, 1981.
248p.
ISBN 0859923061 Hbk £3.85

CONCILIATION – NEW ZEALAND

—Mediation in New Zealand : the Attitudes of the Mediated / Susan Cathro. – Palmerston North : Dunmore Press Ltd..
126p.
ISBN 0864690541 Pbk £28.55

CONCILIATION (INDUSTRIAL)

—Conciliation and arbitration procedures in labour disputes : a comparative study / Geneva : International Labour Office, 1980.
x,183p.
Includes bibliographical references.
ISBN 9221023389 Pbk

—Conciliation by ACAS in complaints by individuals to Industrial Tribunals / Advisory, Conciliation and Arbitration Service. – London : ACAS, 1982.

CONCILIATION (INDUSTRIAL) – AUSTRALIA

—Conciliation and Arbitration Act 1904 : including Regulations and Sections 45D and 45E of the Trade Practice Act / 9th ed. – North Ryde : C.C.H. Australia, 1984.
400p.
ISBN 0869038206 Hbk £24.00

CONCILIATION (INDUSTRIAL) - EUROPEAN COMMUNITY
—Prevention and settlement of industrial conflict in the Community member states / Luxembourg : Office for Official Publications of the European Communities, 1984.
162,16p.
At head of title page: Commission of the European Communities.
ISBN 9282550095

CONCILIATION (INDUSTRIAL) - NEW ZEALAND
—Judicial Perspective on Industrial Conciliation and Arbitration in New Zealand / Repr. of 1980 ed. - Auckland : Legal Research Foundation, 1982.
49p.
ISBN 0908581076 Pbk £5.50

CONDITIONAL SALES
—Commercial and consumer credit : an introduction / by Aubrey L. Diamond. - London : Butterworths, 1982.
xxvii,379p.
Includes index.
ISBN 0406574057

—Hague-Zagreb Essays / edited by C.C.A. Voskuil and J.A. Wade. - Dordrecht : M. Nijhoff, 1985.
193p.
At head of title: TMC Asser Instituut. Reports and discussions of the fifth session of the Hague-Zagreb Colloquium, Isle of Krk, Yugoslavia, 1983. Includes bibliographies.
ISBN 9024731704 Hbk £135.00

CONDITIONAL SALES - AUSTRALIA - VICTORIA
—Deregulation of hire-purchase / Law Reform Commission of Victoria. - Melbourne : The Commission, 1986.
x,22p. - (Report no 4).
Bibliography: p.21-22. Includes text of Hire-purchase (Deregulation) Bill 1986.

CONDITIONAL SALES - NIGERIA
—Hire purchase law and cases / by Olusegun Yerokun. - Jos : Salama Press, 1983.
ix,125p.

CONDITIONAL SALES - SOUTH AFRICA
—Law of credit agreements and hire-purchase in South Africa / P. J. Aronstam. - 5th ed. - Cape Town : Juta, 1982.
lii,505p.
Previous ed., 1978, entitled: The law of hire-purchase in South Africa. Bibliography: p.xxi-xxiii. - Includes index.
ISBN 070211250X

CONDITIONS (LAW) - NEW ZEALAND
—Second rise and fall of fundamental breach / Brian Coote : G.C. Thorpe : D.W. McMorland. - Auckland : Legal Research Foundation, 1980.
127p.
Includes bibliographical references.
ISBN 0908581084

CONDOMINIUMS - CANADA
—Condominiums / Vancouver : Continuing Legal Education Society of British Columbia, 1984.
403p.
ISBN 0865041539 Hbk £70.00

CONDOMINIUMS - CANADA - ALBERTA
—Condominium Law in Alberta / Toronto : Butterworths, 1986.
ISBN 0409980293 Hbk

CONDOMINIUMS - CANADA - BRITISH COLUMBIA
—Condominium Law in British Columbia / Butterworths, 1983.
434p.
Discusses the major participants in a condominium scheme, including the owner, the owner-developer, the lawyer, the Strata counsel, and the Strata corporation.
ISBN 0409988383 Hbk £75.00

CONDOMINIUMS - CANADA - ONTARIO
—Condominium : The Law and Administration in Ontario / Bradley N. McLellan. - Agincourt : Carswell, 1981.
606p.
This book gives a complete description of the law and administration of condominiums in Ontario, Canada. Registration of a condominium, declaration and description, the agreement of purchase and sale, HUDAC, meetings and records for the condominium, and other issues are discussed.

CONDOMINIUMS - ENGLAND
—Commonhold : freehold flats and freehold ownership of other interdependent buildings : report of a working group / chairman: T.M. Aldridge. - London : H.M.S.O., 1987.
v,101p; 30cm.
ISBN 0101017928

CONDOMINIUMS - SOUTH AFRICA
—Sectional titles, share blocks and time-sharing / by C.G. van der Merwe and D.W. Butler. - Durban : Butterworths, 1985.
xiii,573p.
Bibliography: p. xv-xxi. - Includes indexes.
ISBN 0409059293 Hbk R105

CONFESSION (LAW) - NEW ZEALAND
—Report on confessions / Wellington : Evidence Law Reform Committee, 1987.
58p.
Bibliographical references: p.51-55.

CONFESSIONS - AUSTRALIA - NEW SOUTH WALES
—Criminal procedure : unsworn statements of accused persons : report / New South Wales Law Reform Commission. - Sydney : The Commission, 1985.
70p. - (L.R.C. 45).
Bibliography: p.65-66.
ISBN 0730514269 Hbk

CONFESSIONS - ENGLAND
—Confessions / by Peter Mirfield. - London : Sweet & Maxwell, 1985.
165p; 22cm.
Includes index.
ISBN 0421303905 Hbk £12.25
ISBN 0421304006 Pbk £8.25

CONFESSIONS - GREAT BRITAIN
—Confessions in crown court trials / John Baldwin and Michael McConville. - London : H.M.S.O., 1980.
vii,39p. - (Research studies).
Bibliography - p.37-39.
ISBN 0117301248

CONFESSIONS - INDIA
—Law of Confessions Approvers and Accomplices / 7th ed. - Allahabad : Law Book Company, 1988.
ca 600p.

—Statements, Proofs and Confession / 2nd ed. - Allahabad : Law Publishers, 1982.

CONFESSIONS - NEW ZEALAND
—Confessions / Evidence Law Refrom Committee. - s.l. : Evidence Law Reform Committee, 1985.
18, 2 leaves. - (Working paper).
Includes bibliographical references.

CONFIDENTIAL COMMUNICATIONS - SCOTLAND
—Breach of confidence : report on a reference under section 3(1)(e) of the Law Commissions Act 1965 / Scottish Law Commission. - Edinburgh : Scottish Law Commission, 1984.
vi,73p.
ISBN 0101938500

CONFIDENTIAL INFORMATION
—Bank accounts : a world guide to confidentiality / Edouard Chambost : translated by Peter Walton and Margaret Thompson. - Chichester : Wiley, 1983.
xii,322p; 24cm.
Includes index. Translation from French.
ISBN 0471900761 Hbk

—Protection of trade secrets : a general guide / W.R. McComas, Mark R. Davison, David M. Gonski. - Sydney : Butterworths, 1981.
xiv,98p.
ISBN 0409300284 Hbk £48

CONFIDENTIAL INFORMATION - AUSTRALIA
—Action for breach of confidence in Australia / by James Kearney. - Sydney : Legal Books, 1985.
xiv,97p.
Bibliography: p.91-93. - Includes index.
ISBN 0949553204

CONFIDENTIAL INFORMATION - AUSTRALIA - NEW SOUTH WALES
—Acquired immune deficiency syndrome (A.I.D.S.) : guidelines for the testing of antibodies to the HTLV - III (A.I.D.S.) virus / Privacy Committee. - Sydney : The Committee, 1986.
5 leaves.

CONFIDENTIAL INFORMATION - CANADA - MANITOBA
—Report on medical privilege / Manitoba Law Reform Commission. - Winnipeg : The Commission, 1983.
52p. - (Report).
Includes bibliographical references.

CONFIDENTIAL INFORMATION - CANADA - ONTARIO
—Report of the Commission of Inquiry into the Confidentiality of Health Information / Horace Krever. - 3 v. - Toronto : Queen's Printer, 1980.
Commissioner: Horace Krever.
ISBN 0774355670

—Report on political activity, public comment and disclosure by crown employees / Ontario Law Reform Commission. - Toronto : Ministry of the Attorney General, 1986.
xi,381p.
Includes bibliographical references.
ISBN 0772917728

CONFIDENTIAL INFORMATION - ENGLAND
—Breach of confidence / Francis Gurry. - Oxford : Clarendon, 1984.
xxvii,487p; 22cm.
Includes index.
ISBN 0198253788 £40.00

—Breach of confidence : comments on Law Commission report on breach of confidence (Law Com. no. 110) : memorandum / by the Council's Law Reform Committee. - London : Law Society, 1982.
5p.

—Breach of confidence : report on a reference under section 3 (1) (e) of the Law Commissions Act 1965 / the Law Commission. - London : H.M.S.O., 1981.
ix,239p; 25cm.
ISBN 0101838808

—Confidentiality and the law / Brian C. Reid. - London : Waterlow, 1986.
xvi,208p; 24cm.
Includes index.
ISBN 0080392369 £20.00

CONFIDENTIAL INFORMATION - GREAT BRITAIN
—Breach Of Confidence / Oxford : Oxford University Press, 1984.
ISBN 0198253788 Hbk £42.50

—Law of Breach of Confidence / Hoolahan. - London : Butterworths, 1984.
ISBN 0406120102 Hbk

—Purging of the Civil Service / National Council for Civil Liberties. - London : National Council for Civil Liberties, 1985.
20p.
ISBN 0946088179

—Secrecy in Britain / Oxford : Basil Blackwell, 1990.
96; 20.
ISBN 0631169121 Pbk £3.75

CONFIDENTIAL INFORMATION - MALAYSIA
—Breaches of Trust in Singapore and Malaysia / Heong. - London : Butterworths, 1984.
ISBN 0406181152 Pbk £13.00

CONFIDENTIAL INFORMATION - SINGAPORE
—Breaches of Trust in Singapore and Malaysia / Heong. - London : Butterworths, 1984.
ISBN 0406181152 Pbk £13.00

CONFIDENTIAL INFORMATION - SOUTH AFRICA
—Professional secrecy in South Africa : a symposium / edited by G. C. Oosthuizen, H. A. Shapiro, S. A. Strauss. - Cape Town : Oxford University Press, 1983.
178p.
ISBN 0195703200

CONFISCATION
—Measures Against the Transfer and the Safekeeping of Funds of Criminal Origin : Recommendation No. R 80/10 / Strasbourg : Council of Europe, 1981.

CONFLICT MANAGEMENT
—Disputes and settlements : law and human relations in the West / edited by John Bossy. - Cambridge : Cambridge University Press, 1983.
ix,296p; 23cm.
Essays by British, American and French scholars to outline a social history of the West using records of the law in Western Europe from the fall of Rome to the Nineteenth Century.
ISBN 0521252830 £25.00

—Industrial conflict resolution in market economics : a study of Australia, the Federal Republic of Germany, Italy, Japan and the USA / T. Hanami editor : R. Blanpain associate editor. - Deventer : Kluwer Law and Taxation, 1984.
xiv,321p; 25cm.
Includes bibliographies and index.
ISBN 9065441808 Pbk No price

—Settlement of disputes in early medieval Europe / edited by Wendy Davies and Paul Fouracre. - Cambridge : Cambridge University Press, 1986.
549p.
Collection of original essays on settlement of disputes in early middle ages. Case material from the evidence of charters used. Discusses examples from fifth century Gaul, later Merovingian Francia, ninth century Brittany and Anglo Saxon England.
ISBN 0521307880 £30.00

CONFLICT OF INTERESTS - AUSTRALIA - VICTORIA
—Report on pecuniary interests of municipal councillors / Statute Law Revision Committee. - Melbourne : Government Printer, 1981.
ii,27p. - (D v no 14/1980-81.).

CONFLICT OF LAWS

—C. E. R. : the business and law essentials : papers presented at seminar, University of Auckland, 22-23 July 1983 / 3. – Auckland : Legal Research Foundation Inc., 1983.
ISBN 0908581270

—Canadian conflict of laws / J.-G. Castel. – 2nd ed. – Toronto : Butterworths, 1986.
clxvi,652p.
Includes bibliographical references and index.
ISBN 0409821284 Hbk £125

—Cases and Materials Private International Law / North. – London : Butterworths, 1984.
ISBN 0406252645 Hbk £36.00
ISBN 0406252653 Pbk £25.95

—Conflict of Laws / Agincourt : Carswell, 1983.
967p.

—Conflict of laws and contract / by P.R.H. Webb. – Auckland : Legal Research Foundation, 1985.
63p.
Includes bibliographical references.
ISBN 090858136X

—Conflicts of national laws with international business activity : issues of extraterritoriality / by A.H. Hermann. – London : British North American Research Organisation, 1982.
xii,96p.
ISBN 0902594419

—Contemporary Problems in the Conflict of Laws : Essays in Honour of John Humphrey Carlile Morris / British Institute of International Comparative Law. – Dordrecht : Kluwer.
ISBN 9028609687 Hbk Gld60.00

—Dicey and Morris' Conflict of Laws, 2 Vols. / London : Sweet & Maxwell.
ISBN 0420464808 Hbk £7.50

Supplement-1983

—General Problems of Private International Law / 1976 repr. – Dordrecht : Kluwer, 1980.
ISBN 9028606467 Pbk £55.00

—Hague Conference on Private International Law : Collection of Conventions (1951-1980) / Butterworth Staff. – London : Butterworths, 1981.
ISBN 0406658404 Pbk £27.50

—International anti-trust law / edited by Julian Maitland-Walker. – Oxford : ESC Publishing, 1984.
viii,178p.
Includes bibliographical references.
ISBN 090621419X

—International conventions concerning applications for and awards of maintenance : explanatory documentation / prepared for Commonwealth Jurisdictions by David McClean in association with the Commonwealth Secretariat. – London : Commonwealth Secretariat, 1981.
v,83p.
ISBN 0850922003

—International conventions in the field of succession : explanatory documentation / prepared for Commonwealth jurisdictions by Keith Patchett in association with the Commonwealth Secretariat. – London : Commonwealth Secretariat, 1980.
85p.

—Introduction to the conflict of laws / A.J.E. Jaffey. – London : Butterworths, 1988.
300p; 22cm.
Includes bibliography and index.
ISBN 0406500487 Pbk £13.95

—Law of Conflicts and Foreign Trade / L. Vekas. – Budapest : Akademiai Kiado.
xiv, 379p.
ISBN 9630542749 Hbk £38.00

—Law of international transactions / by Ferenc Madl : translated by J. Decsenyi. – Budapest : Akademiai Kiado, 1982.
206p.
Bibliography: p199-206. Translation of: Osszehasonlito nemzetkozi maganjog.
ISBN 9630529327

—Marriage in comparative conflict of laws : substantive conditions / Lennart Palsson. – The Hague : Martinus Nijhoff, 1981.
lxxvi,388p.
Continues Palsson, L. : Marriage and divorce in comparative conflict of laws, Leyden, 1974. Bibliography: pli-lxv.
ISBN 9024725488 Hbk £200.00

—Origins of the conflict of laws / Ronald Graveson. – Tubingen : Mohr, 1981.
p.93-107; 23cm.
Reprinted from: Festschrift fur Konrad Zweigert zum 70. Geburtstag/herausgegeben von Herbert Bernstein, Ulrich Drobnig, Hein Kotz. - Tubingen: Mohr, 1981.

—Principles of the conflict of laws, national and international / by K. Lipstein. – The Hague : Nijhoff, 1981.
xii,144p.
Revised edition of 'The general principles of private international law' published in vol.135 (1972-1) of the Recueil des Cours, The Hague Academy of International Law.
ISBN 9024725445 Hbk £75.00

—Private international law / North. – 11th ed. – London : Butterworths, 1987.
ISBN 0406565708 Hbk £38.00
ISBN 0406565716 Pbk £26.95

—Private International Law-Cases and Materials / London : Laureate-Thomson Press, 1982.
ISBN 0907392059 Pbk £18.75

—Private international law : cases and materials / edited by Mark S.W. Hoyle. – London : Laureate, 1982.
xx,441p; 25cm.
Includes index.
ISBN 0907392040 Hbk No price
ISBN 0907392059 Pbk £16.95

—Private international law : choice of law in tort and delict / Great Britain. – London : H.M.S.O., 1984.
xiv,293p. – (Consultative memorandum).
Includes bibliographical references. Prepared by a Joint Working Party of the Law Commission and the Scottish Law Commission.
ISBN 011730168X

—Private international law : choice of law rules in marriage / the Law Commission and the Scottish Law Commission. – London : H.M.S.O., 1985.
ix,171p. – (Consultative memorandum).
ISBN 0117301701

—Private international law : choice of law rules in marriage / the Law Commission and the Scottish Law Commission. – London : H.M.S.O., 1987.
37p. – (1987/88 HC3).
ISBN 0102003882

—Private international law : foreign money liabilities / the Law Commission. – London : H.M.S.O., 1981.
ix,195p; 22cm. – (Working paper).
ISBN 0117301604

—Private International Law : Indian and English / New Delhi : Deep and Deep Publications, 1988.
700p.

—Private international law : the law of domicile / the Law Commission and the Scottish Law Commission. – London : H.M.S.O., 1985.
vi,92p. – (Consultative memorandum).
ISBN 0117301698

—Private international litigation / general editor, Sir Jack Jacob : contributors, Michael Carpenter ... et al. – London : Longman, 1988.
lxxvii,494p; 25cm.
Includes index.
ISBN 0851208274 £60.00

—Proceedings of Seminar : Protection of Sellers in Transnational Sales - Beyond Letters of Credit, at the Cafe Royal, London, 2- 3 June 1982 / 1. – London : International Bar Association, Section on Business Law, 1982.
various pagings.

—Protection of human rights in Europe : limits and effects : proceedings of the fifth International Colloquy about the European Convention on Human Rights / edited by Irene Maier. – Heidelberg : C.F. Muller Juristischer Verlag, 1982.
xviii, 378 p.; 24 cm.
Includes bibliographical references and index.
ISBN 3811411829

—Theory and Practice of Private International Law / Repr. of 1892 ed. – Aalen Wuertt : Scientia.
xlvi, 1162p.

CONFLICT OF LAWS – AUSTRALIA

—Australian private international law / by Edward I. Sykes and Michael C. Pryles. – 2nd ed. – North Ryde, N.S.W. : Law Book Co, 1987.
lxxxix, 772 p.; 25 cm.
Includes bibliographical references and indexes.
ISBN 0455207038 pbk.

—Conflict of Laws in Australia / 4th ed. – Butterworths, 1984.
608p.
ISBN 0409491926 Hbk £79.00
ISBN 0409492027 Pbk £59.00

—International and interstate conflict of laws / Edward I. Sykes, Michael C. Pryles. – 2nd ed. – Sydney : Butterworths, 1981.
lv,966p.
Bibliography; p.943-950. - Includes index.
ISBN 0409455342 Pbk
ISBN 0409300438

CONFLICT OF LAWS – CANADA

—Conflict of Law / Agincourt : Carswell, 1983.
ISBN 045936860X Hbk £41.80

—Conflict of Laws / Agincourt : Carswell, 1983.
967p.
This textbook for Canadian law students tracts the historical development of the principles of conflict of laws and critically analyzes the policies underlying the rules. The book explores relevant English, American, and Commonwealth laws, in addition to Canadian law.

—Conflict of Laws : Cases, Notes and Materials / 6th ed. – Butterworths, 1988.
904p.
ISBN 0409805955 Pbk £75.00

—Introduction to Conflict of Laws / 2nd ed. – Butterworths, 1986.
240p.
ISBN 0409805920 Pbk £38.95

—Perspectives on the harmonization of law in Canada / Ronald C.C. Cuming research coordinator. – Toronto : University of Toronto Press in cooperation with the Royal Commission on the Economic Union and Development Prospects for Canada and the Canadian Government Publishing Centre, 1985.
xviii,178p. – (Collected research studies).
Bibliography: p.176-177.
ISBN 0802073026

CONFLICT OF LAWS – CANADA – BRITISH COLUMBIA

—Report on foreign money liabilities / Law Reform Commission of British Columbia. – Vancouver : The Commission, 1983.
64p.
Includes bibliographical references.
ISBN 0771883919

CONFLICT OF LAWS – CANADA – QUEBEC

—Droit International Prive Quebecois / Toronto : Butterworths, 1980.
1008p.
ISBN 0409821233 Hbk £95.00
ISBN 0409821241 Pbk £55.00

CONFLICT OF LAWS – ENGLAND

—Cases and materials on private international law / J.H.C. Morris, P.M. North. – London : Butterworths, 1984.
xxviii,757p; 26cm.
Includes index.
ISBN 0406252645 Hbk Unpriced
ISBN 0406252653 Pbk Unpriced

—Cheshire and North private international law / P. M. North, J. J. Fawcett. – 11th ed. – London : Butterworths, 1987.
xcviii,940p; 25cm.
Previous ed.: 1979. Bibliography: pxv-xvi. - Includes index.
ISBN 0406565708 Hbk £28.00
ISBN 0406565716 Pbk £19.00

—Classification of limitation in private international law / the Law Commission. – London : H.M.S.O., 1980.
v,86p; 21cm. – (Working paper).
ISBN 0117301558 Pbk £3.50

—Conflict of laws / by J.H.C. Morris. – 3rd ed. – London : Stevens, 1984.
xxxvii,544p; 25cm.
Previous ed.: 1980. Bibliography: pxxix. - Includes index.
ISBN 0420468900 Hbk Unpriced
ISBN 0420469001 Pbk Unpriced

—Conflict of laws / J.G. Collier. – Cambridge : Cambridge University Press, 1987.
xlvi,377p; 23cm. – (Cambridge studies in international and comparative law).
Includes index.
ISBN 0521323959 Hbk £40.00
ISBN 052131187X Pbk £12.50

—Conflict of laws / by J.H.C. Morris. – 2nd ed. – London : Stevens, 1980.
540p.
Previous ed.: 1971.
ISBN 0420457801 £16.50
ISBN 0420457909

—Dicey and Morris on the conflict of laws / J. H. C. Morris, Lawrence Collins. – 11th ed. 2. – London : Stevens, 1987.
Previous ed.: 1980. Includes index. Kept up to date by supplements.
ISBN 0420471308 £120.00 (June)

—Dicey and Morris on the conflict of laws / J. H. C. Morris. – 10th ed. 2. – London : Stevens, 1980.
cxl,1351p; 26cm.
Previous ed.: 1973. Bibliography: p cxxxix-cxl. - Includes index. Latest supplement held: 4th, up to date to October 1, 1984.
ISBN 0420456902 Pbk £70.00

—Foreign affairs in English courts / F.A. Mann. – Oxford : Clarendon, 1986.
300p; 22cm.
ISBN 0198255640 £30.00

—From imported doctrine to municipal law : a sketch history of foreign influences on the growth of the English law of conflict / paper presented at the eigth British Legal History Conference, Cardiff, July 1987, by A. G. Bischoff. – London : Law Notes Lending Library, 1987.
52p.
Bibliography: pp.43-47..
ISBN 0900516100

CONFLICT OF LAWS – EUROPEAN COMMUNITY

—Conflict of laws and European Community law : with special reference to the Community Conventions on private international law / Ian F. Fletcher. – Amsterdam : North-Holland, 1982.
xxix,395p.
Bibliography: p.xxvii-xxix. - Includes index.
ISBN 0444863761

—Conflict of laws in the European Community / D. Lasok and P. A. Stone. – Abingdon : Professional Books, 1987.
xx,460p.
Bibliography: p xviii-xx.
ISBN 0862050715

—Private international law in the European Community / Stone. – London : Butterworths, 1987.
ISBN 0862050812 Hbk £28.00

CONFLICT OF LAWS – FINLAND

—Private international law in Finland : an outline / by Hannu Tapani Klami. – Turku : Turun yliopiston offsetpaino, 1986.
67 p.; 21 cm. – (Turun yliopiston oikeustieteellisen tiedekunnan julkaisuja. Yksityisoikeuden sarja A).
Bibliography: p. 64-65. Includes index.
ISBN 9516427871

CONFLICT OF LAWS – GREAT BRITAIN

—Conflict of Laws, 2 Vols. / London : Stevens & Sons.
ISBN 0420470204 Pbk

—Conflict of Laws / 3rd ed. – London : Sweet & Maxwell, 1984.
ISBN 0420468900 Hbk £30.00
ISBN 0420469001 Pbk £25.00

—Conflict of Laws / Morris. – 11th ed. – Sweet & Maxwell, 1987.
ISBN 0420471308 Hbk £140.00

—Foreign Affairs in English Courts / Oxford : Oxford University Press, 1986.
ISBN 0198255640 Hbk £27.50

—Private international law : Council of Europe Conventions on Foreign Money Liabilities(1967) and on the Place of Payment of Money Liabilities (1972) : report on a reference under section 3 (1)(e) of the Law Commissions Act 1965 / the Law Commission and the Scottish Law Commission. – London : H.M.S.O., 1981.
iv,53p; 25cm.
Includes the text of the Conventions.
ISBN 0101831803

—Private international law : recognition of foreign nullity decrees and related matters : presented to Parliament ... September 1984 / the Law Commission and the Scottish Law Commission. – London : H.M.S.O., 1984.
v,134p; 25cm.
ISBN 0101934106

CONFLICT OF LAWS – INDIA

—Interpersonal conflict of laws in India, Pakistan and Bangladesh / David Pearl. – London : Stevens, 1981.
xxviii,176p; 25cm.
Bibliography: p.165-69. Includes index.
ISBN 0420457704

CONFLICT OF LAWS – IRELAND

—Irish conflict of laws / by William Binchy. – Dublin? : Butterworths (Ireland), 1988.
lxxiv,691p.
Bibliography: p.lxxi-lxxiv. - Includes index.
ISBN 0862052203 Pbk £65.00
ISBN 0862052211 £25.00

—Irish Conflicts of Law / London : Butterworths, 1988.
ISBN 0862052203 Hbk £50.00
ISBN 0862052211 Pbk £25.00

—Report on domicile and habitual residence as connecting factors in the conflict of laws / the Law Reform Commission. – Dublin : The Commission, 1983.
v,26p. – (LRC).

—Report on jurisdiction in proceedings for nullity of marriage, recognition of foreign nullity decrees, and the Hague Convention on the Celebration and Recognition of the Validity of Marriage (1978) / the Law Reform Commission. – Dublin : The Commission, 1985.
v,63p. – (LRC).
Bibliography: pp.51-2. Includes text of the Convention.

—Report on private international law aspects of capacity to marry and choice of law in proceedings for nullity of marriage / the Law Reform Commission. – Dublin : The Commission, 1985.
v,161p. – (LRC).
Bibliography: pp.156-8.

—Report on recognition of foreign divorces and legal separations / the Law Reform Commission. – Dublin : The Commission, 1985.
v,38p. – (LRC).

—Report on the Hague Convention on the Taking of Evidence Abroad in Civil or Commercial Matters / the Law Reform Commission. – Dublin : The Commission, 1985.
v,75p. – (LRC).
Includes text of the Convention.

CONFLICT OF LAWS – NETHERLANDS

—Private International Law in the Netherlands / M.V. Polak. – Dordrecht : Kluwer, 1987.
350p.
ISBN 9065442863 Hbk £150.00

CONFLICT OF LAWS – PAKISTAN

—Interpersonal conflict of laws in India, Pakistan and Bangladesh / David Pearl. – London : Stevens, 1981.
xxviii,176p; 25cm.
Bibliography: p.165-69. Includes index.
ISBN 0420457704

CONFLICT OF LAWS – SCOTLAND

—International private law : cases and statutes / G. Maher. – Edinburgh : Green, 1985.
xx,294p; 22cm. – (Concise College Texts).
Bibliography: p.xx. - Includes index.
ISBN 0414007611 Pbk £17.50

CONFLICT OF LAWS – SOUTH AFRICA

—Application of customary law in southern Africa : the conflict of personal laws / T.W. Bennett. – Cape Town : Juta, 1985.
xxxvii,250p.
Bibliography: p.xv-xxi. - Includes index.
ISBN 0702116017

—General principles of the conflict of laws : with the exclusion of the special principles relative to the law of persons, property, succession and obligations / Erwin Spiro. – Cape Town : Juta, 1982.
xxxiii,145p.
Bibliography: p.xi-xvi. - Includes index.
ISBN 0702112895

—Private international law : the modern Roman-Dutch law including the jurisdiction of the Supreme Court / C.F. Forsyth assisted by T.W. Bennett. – Cape Town : Juta, 1981.
xxxviii,384p.
Bibliography: p.xiii-xvi. - Includes index.
ISBN 0702112305

CONFLICT OF LAWS – SWITZERLAND

—Switzerland's private international law statute / Pierre A Karrer, Karl W Arnold. – Kluwer Law and Taxation, 1989.
304.
Examines the approximately two hundred articles of the statutes covering international conflicts of jurisdiction, private international law, and recognition and enforcement. Technical terms used by the statutes are rendered in the original, and explained. References to Swiss substantive law, and translations of texts relevant to international arbitration in Switzerland are included.
ISBN 9065442901 Hbk £48.50/Dfl 150

CONFLICT OF LAWS – USSR

—Private international law : the Soviet approach / by M.M. Boguslavskii : translated by David Winter and William B. Simons. – Dordrecht : Nijhoff, 1988.
272p.
Includes index and bibliography.
ISBN 9024736293 Hbk £165.00

CONGRESSES

—Arab comparative & commercial law : the international approach : proceedings : International Bar Association first Arab Regional Conference, Cairo 15-19 February 1987 / International Bar Association. – London : Graham & Trotman, 1987.
Contents: v. 1. The Sharia and its relevance to modern transnational transactions. The settlement of disputes through arbitration. Joint ventures. – v. 2. Energy law.
ISBN 086010978X v. 2

—Automation and serials : proceedings of the UK Serials Group Conference held at South Glamorgan Institute of Higher Education, Cardiff 31 March-3 April 1980 / edited by Margaret E. Graham. – Newcastle upon Tyne? : UK Serials Group, 1981.
120p; 21cm. – (Serials monograph).
ISBN 0906148022 Pbk Unpriced

—C. E. R. : the business and law essentials : papers presented at seminar, University of Auckland, 22-23 July 1983 / 3. – Auckland : Legal Research Foundation Inc., 1983.
ISBN 0908581270

—Cambridge lectures 1981 : selected papers based upon lectures delivered at the Conference of the Canadian Institute for Advanced Legal Studies, 1981, held at Cambridge University, England ... / edited by Nancy E. Eastham and Boris Krivy. – Toronto : Butterworths, 1982.
xix,433p.
Includes bibliographical references.
ISBN 040984392X

—Cambridge lectures 1983 : selected papers based upon lectures at the Conference of the Canadian Institute for Advanced Legal Studies, 1983, held at Cambridge University, England / edited by Elizabeth G. Baldwin. – Toronto : Butterworths, 1985.
xvi,341p.
Includes bibliographical references.
ISBN 0409810320

—Changing policing : a conference based on the Scarman Report, 1 May 1982 : proceedings / edited by David Armstrong. – London : University of London Department of Extra-Mural Studies, 1982.
70p.
'Proceedings of a conference held at the University of London, 1 May 1982'.

—Community policing in the 1980's : recent advances in police programs / edited by Donald J. Loree and Chris Murphy. – Ottawa : Ministry of the Solicitor General, 1986.
v,154p.
'This conference was jointly sponsored by the Canadian Police College ... and by the Secretariat of the Ministry of the Solicitor General of Canada'. - T.p.. Held in Ottawa, March 17-19, 1986.
ISBN 0662158075

—Criteria for energy pricing policy : a collection of papers commissioned for the Energy Pricing Policy Workshop organized under the Regional Energy Development Programme (RAS/84/001), Bangkok, 8-11 May 1984 / edited by Corazon Morales Siddayao. – London : Graham & Trotman, 1985.
247p; 24cm.

—Current issues of international financial law / edited by David G. Pierce ... et al. – Singapore : Malaya Law Review, 1985.
xv,507p.
A collection of papers from the Singapore Conference of International Financial Law. The material covers primarily international banking, bond issues, syndicated loans, South East Asian perspectives on international financial law, and the role of international development banks.
ISBN 0409995088

—Current problems of international trade financing / edited by C.M. Chinkin, P.J. Davidson, W.J.M. Ricquier. – Singapore : Malaya Law Review, 1983.
xxiii,507p.
Includes index. At head of title: Singapore Conferences on International Business Law.
ISBN 0406181144

—Data processing and the law : UK National Committee on Comparative Law Annual Colloquium, Leicester, 15-16 September 1982 / Colloquium Chairman Colin Campbell. – 1. – Coventry : UKNCCL, 1982.
various pagings.
Includes bibliographies.

—Development, human rights and the rule of law : report of a conference held in The Hague on 27 April-1 May 1981 / convened by the International Commission of Jurists. – Oxford : Pergamon, 1981.
vi,237p; 23cm.
ISBN 0080289215 Hbk Unpriced
ISBN 0080289517 Pbk £3.75

—Disarmament : the human factor : proceedings of a colloquium on the societal context for disarmament / sponsored by UNITAR and the Planetary Citizens and held at the United Nations, New York : edited by Ervin Laszlo and Donald Keys. – Oxford : Pergamon, 1981.
x,164p; 24cm.
Includes index.
ISBN 0080247032 Hbk £10.50
ISBN 008028129X Pbk Unpriced

—Economic crime in Europe / edited by L.H. Leigh. – London : Macmillan for the London School of Economics and Political Science, 1980.
xii,211p; 23cm.
Conference papers. Includes bibliographies and index.
ISBN 0333248406 £20.00

—Effect of international consumer protection laws in Europe : third European Seminar on Product Liability, October 15th and 16th 1980 at the Mount Royal Hotel, Marble Arch, London / organised by the Institute of Quality Assurance. – London : European Organisation for Quality Control, 1980.
253p.
'Sponsored by the National Council for Quality & Reliability'. At head of title: European Organisation for Quality Control.

—Engineer's liability to the contractor : papers presented at the Conference of the International Bar Association's Section on Business Law Conference, Toronto 1983 / International Construction Contracts Committee of the Section on Business Law of the International Bar Assoication. – London : International Bar Association, 1983.
iv,162p.
Includes bibliographical references.

—Fiscal policy and tax legislation and administration : technical papers and reports of the 15th General Assembly of the Inter-American Center of Tax Administrators (CIAT), Caracas, Venezuela, 25-27 February 1981 / Inter-American Center of Tax Administrators. – Amsterdam : International Bureau of Fiscal Documentation, 1983.
200p.
'Sponsored by the Government of Venezuela, the German Society for Technical Cooperation (GTZ) and the Inter-American Center of Tax Administrators (CIAT)
ISBN 9070125226

—Fundamental tax audit considerations : technical papers and reports of the 14th General Assembly of the Inter-American Center of Tax Administrators (CIAT) / Inter-American Center of Tax Administrators. – Amsterdam : International Bureau of Fiscal Documentation, 1981.
198p.
ISBN 9070125188

—IMF and the World Bank in Africa : conditionality, impact, and alternatives / edited by Kjell J. Havnevik. – Uppsala : Scandinavian Institute of African Studies, 1987.
177 p.; 23 cm.
Includes bibliographies.
ISBN 9171062645

—Information chain : proceedings of the UK Serials Group conference, held at Christ Church College Canterbury, 29 March - 1 April 1982 / edited by John A. Urquhart. – London : UK Serials Group, 1983.

—Intellectual property in New Zealand and Australia / papers presented by M.P. Crew ... et al. – Auckland : Legal Research Foundation, 1985.
227p.
ISBN 0908581378

—International anti-trust law / edited by Julian Maitland-Walker. – Oxford : ESC Publishing, 1984.
viii,178p.
Includes bibliographical references.
ISBN 090621419X

—International Bar Association, Section on Energy & Natural Resources Law : seminar topics index 1975-84 : Stavanger, 1975; Cambridge 1, 1978; Cambridge II, 1979; Banff, 1981; Singapore, 1982; Houston, 1984; Oslo, 1984 / S.l. : International Bar Association, Section on Energy & Natural Resources Law, 1986.
24p.
ISBN 0948711027

—Interplay of contracts : papers presented at the International Bar Association's 20th Biennial Conference, Vienna 1984 / International Bar Assoication. Section on Business Law. International Construction Contracts Committee. – London : International Bar Association, 1984.
102p.
Includes bibliographical references.

—Joint ventures in the construction industry : papers presented at the 7th Conference of the International Bar Association's Section on Business Law, Singapore 1985 / International Construction Contracts Committee of the Section on Business Law of the International Bar Association. – 1. – London : International Bar Association, 1985.
Various pagings.
Includes bibliographical references.

—Land Use Act : report of a National Workshop held at the University of Lagos, May 25 - May 28, 1981 / edited by J.A. Omotola. – Lagos : Lagos University Press, 1982.
178p.

—Law and economics and the economics of legal regulation / edited by J.-Matthias Graf v.d. Schulenburg, Goran Skogh. – Dordrecht : M. Nijhoff, 1986.
248p. – (International studies in economics and econometrics).
'Selected papers of a conference of the International Institute of Management Wissenschaftszentum Berlin.'. Includes index. Contents: Law and economics and the economics of legal regulation / Goran Skogh – Efficiency, equity, and inalienability / Susan Rose-Ackerman – Negotiated settlement / Gordon Tullock – Economic efficiency and the common law / Peter H. Aranson – Default risk and the optimal pricing of court enforcement services / Hugh Gravelle – Transaction cost and communincation / Michael Hutter – Regulatory measures to enforce quality production of self-employed professinals / J.-Matthias Graf v.d. Schulenburg – Controlling insider trading in Europe and America / David D. Haddock, Jonathan R. Macey – The regulatin of shop opening hours in the United Kingdom / Susan M. Jaffer, John A. Kay Belgian public policy towards the retailing trade / Roger Van den Bergh – Assessing the effectiveness of economic efficiency of an E.E.C. pollution control directive / John Ashworth, Ivy Papps, David J. Storey.
ISBN 9024733774 Hbk £135.00

—Law and history in Australia : selected papers from the fourth and fifth Law in History Conferences held at La Trobe University, 1985 and 1986 / edited by Diane Kirkby. – Melbourne : Legal Studies Department, La Trobe University, 1987.
136p.
Includes bibliographical references.

Vol. 4 / edited by Diane Kirkby. – 1987.
133p.
Includes bibliographical references.

—Law and the citizen : looking to the '80s : a Colloquium on Public Legal Education held on April 29 and 30, 1977 / edited, updated and with present conclusions and recommendations by Frederick B. Sussmann and Bradford W. Morse. – Ottawa, Ont. : University of Ottawa Press, 1981.
ix, 135 p.; 23 cm.
Includes index.
ISBN 2760322297 pbk.

—Law as an instrument of economic policy : comparative and critical approaches / edited by Terence Daintith. – Berlin : W. de Gruyter, 1987.
– (Series A–Law).
Includes index. Bibliography. Based on papers presented at a colloquium held in Florence, Mar. 1985.
ISBN 0899254179

—Law, morality, and rights / edited by M.A. Stewart. – Dordrecht, Holland : Reidel, 1983.
xii,452p. – (Synthese library).
Includes index.
ISBN 902771519X

—Law, politics, and the labor movement / edited by Gareth Evans. – Clayton, Vic. : Legal Service Bulletin in association with Australian Society of Labor Lawyers, 1980.
x, 205 p.; 21 cm.
Papers presented at the First National Conference of Labor Lawyers, held in Adelaide on 20 June-1 July, 1979. Includes bibliographical references and indexes.
ISBN 0959472703 pbk.

—Lawyers and laymen / edited by T.M. Charles-Edwards, Morfydd E. Owen and D. B. Walters. – Cardiff : University of Wales Press, 1986.
394,1p of plates; 23cm.
Bibliography: p355-368. - Includes index. Festschrift in honour of Professor Dafydd Jenkins. Includes two papers in Welsh.
ISBN 0708309259 £25.00

—Legal aid and law clinics in South Africa : proceedings of a conference held at the Howard College School of Law, University of Natal, Durban, from 11-13 July 1983 / Durban : School of Law, Howard College, University of Natal, 1985.
ix,163p.
ISBN 0869804251

—Legal and institutional arrangements in minerals developments : a study based on an international workshop organised in Berlin (West) in August 1980 by the Department of Technical Co-operation for Development, United Nations, and the Development Policy Forum of the German Foundation for International Development / London : Mining Journal Books, 1982.
xi,224p; 23cm.
ISBN 090011729X Pbk Unpriced

—Legal and practical effects of the Transport Licensing Act (No. 2) 1983 : papers presented by R.J. Craddock ... et al., University of Auckland, 23 February 1984 / R. J. Craddock. – Auckland : Legal Research Foundation, 1984.
46p.
At head of title: Legal Research Foundation Inc. seminar.
ISBN 0908581335

—Legal education and lawyer competency : curricula for change / Fernand N. Dutile, editor. – Notre Dame : University of Notre Dame Press, 1981.
viii,155p; 21cm.
Conference proceedings.
ISBN 0268012644 £10.50

—Legal literature in small jurisdictions : a report of a conference held at Osgoode Hall Law School, York University, Downsview, Ontario on 3-5 November 1978 / edited by William Twining and Jenny Uglow for the Canadian Law Information Council, Canada and the Commonwealth Legal Education Association, London. – London : Commonwealth Secretariat, 1981.
188p; 30cm.
Bibliography: p.171-172. - Includes index.
ISBN 085092197X

—Legislating for human rights : seminar papers / Kensington, N.S.W. : University of New South Wales Faculty of Law, 1980.
ii,183p.
Organised by the University of New South Wales's Faculty of Law and the International Commission of Jurists (Australian Section).
ISBN 0858232529

—Mining and environmental law : proceedings of the seminar held at Washington D.C., 4-8 April 1982, ... organised by the Committee on Environmental Law, Section on Business Law, of the International Bar Association, in conjunction with the American Law Institute-American Bar Association Committee on Continuing Professional Education / 2. – London : International Bar Association, 1982.
ISBN 0950587648

—Online public access to library files : conference proceedings / edited by Janet Kinsella. – Oxford : Elsevier International Bulletins, 1985.
200p; ?cm.
Includes bibliographies and index.
ISBN 0946395187 Pbk £14.50 (June)

—Papers presented at the 22nd Australian Legal Convention, Brisbane, 1983 / Brisbane : Queensland Law Society for the Law Council of Australia, 1984.
444p.
Includes bibliographical references.
ISBN 0949677353

—Proceedings of Forum London : a seminar organised by the International Bar Association, Section on Business Law, in conjunction with the Solicitors' European Group of the Law Society of England and Wales, 23-26 September 1981, London / London : International Bar Association, 1982.
iv,166p.
ISBN 0950587656

—Proceedings of Seminar : Protection of Sellers in Transnational Sales - Beyond Letters of Credit, at the Cafe Royal, London, 2- 3 June 1982 / 1. – London : International Bar Association, Section on Business Law, 1982.
various pagings.

—Proceedings of the Conference of Institutions Responsible for Teaching the Subject 'Computers and Law', Rome, 9-11 October 1985 : reports presented at the Conference / Strasbourg : Council of Europe, 1987.
357p; 29cm.
At head of cover title: Legal affairs.
ISBN 9287110603

—Proceedings of the Seminar on Middle East Law, with reference to Bahrein, Egypt, Iran, Kuwait, Oman, Qatar, Saudi Arabia, U.A.E., 1-4 July 1981, Hamburg, Germany / London : International Bar Association, 1981.
170p.
ISBN 0950587664

—Proceedings of the seminar on planning law for industry : March 29th-April 2nd 1981, Churchill College, Cambridge, England / organised by the Committee on Environmental Law (Committee F), Section on Business Law, International Bar Association : edited with discussion summaries by John Salter and Patricia Thomas. – 2. – London : International Bar Association in cooperation with Sweet and Maxwell, 1981.
21cm.
ISBN 0950587621 Pbk Unpriced

—Professional responsibility / Paul Finn. – Auckland : Legal Research Foundation, 1987.
254p.
Includes bibliographical references. At head of t.p.: Legal Research Foundation Inc. seminar. 'University of Auckland, 28/29 May, 1987'. - Cover.

Part 2 : paper presented by Mr. Justice Rogers : and commentaries on papers published in part one presented by John C. Hagen .... et al 1987.
p.255-382.
At head of t.p.: Legal Research Foundation Inc. seminar. 'University of Auckland, 28/29 May, 1987'. - Cover.

—Recent developments in EEC competition law : seminar documentation : Monday 8th December 1986, Cavendish Conference Centre, London W1 / Valentine Korah. - 1. - London : Legal Studies & Services, 1986.
various pagings.
Includes bibliographical references. Chairman: Valentine Korah.

—Reforms of local and regional authorities in Europe : theory, practice and critical appraisal : colloquy organised by the Council of Europe, Linz, 5-6 November 1981 / Strasbourg : Council of Europe, 1983.
220p.
Bibliography: p.181-182.
ISBN 9287101914

—Role of patent information in the transfer of technology : proceedings of the International Conference held at Varna, Bulgaria, May 27-30, 1980 / organised by the World International i.e. Intellectual Property Organization : edited by F.A. Sviridov. - McLean, Va. : Pergamon International Information, 1981.
viii,265p; 23cm.
ISBN 0080275559 Pbk £6.00

—Serials '85 : proceedings ... of the UK Serials Group Conference held at the Jesse Boot Centre, University of Nottingham, 25-28 March 1985 / Brian Cox. - S.l. : UK Serials Group, 1985.
208 p. - (Serials monograph).
ISBN 0906148073

—Serials '86 : proceedings of the UK Serials Group Conference held at the University of Exeter 24-27 March 1986 / edited by Rodney M. Burton. - S.l. : UK Serials Group, 1986.
vii,188p; 21cm. - (Serials monograph).
ISBN 0906148081

—Shagari opens conference of Nigeria judges : spotlight on Mr. President's one day visit to Kwara State / Ilorin : Department of Information, 1982.
38p.

—Spirit of Uppsala : proceedings of the Joint UNITAR-Uppsala University Seminar on International Law and Organization for a New World Order (JUS 81), Uppsala 9-18 June 1981 / edited by Atle Grahl-Madsen and Jiri Toman. - Berlin : W. de Gruyter, 1983.
English and French. Includes index and bibliography.
ISBN 3110088223

—Symposium on Commercial Crime, 15-19 December 1982, Jesus College, Cambridge / organised by the Commonwealth Secretariat and the Centre for Commercial Law Studies : documentation edited by Susan Grace Lie. - S.l. : s.n., 1983.
ii,382p.
Includes bibliographical references.

—Tax policy towards the national heritage : proceedings of a seminar held in Venice, 1983, during the 37th Congress of the International Fiscal Association / organised by the International Fiscal Association. - Deventer, Netherlands : Kluwer Law and Taxation Publishers, 1984.
ISBN 9065441786

—Taxation and human rights : proceedings of a seminar held in Brussels in 1987 during the 41st Congress of the International Fiscal Association / Marc Baltus, chairman of the seminar. - Deventer, Netherlands : Kluwer Law and Taxation, 1988.
vii,83p.
ISBN 9065443843

—Taxation of domestic shareholders on undistributed income of foreign corporate affiliates : objectives, techniques, and consequences : proceedings of a seminar held in New York in 1986 during the 40th Congress of the International Fiscal Association / edited by Brian J. Arnold. - Deventer, Netherlands : Kluwer Law and Taxation Publishers, 1987.
Includes bibliography.
ISBN 9065443347

—Theory of legal science : proceedings of the Conference on Legal Theory and Philosophy of Science, Lund, Sweden, December 11-14, 1983 / edited by Aleksander Peczenik, Lars Lindahl, and Bert van Roermund. - Dordrecht : Reidel, 1984.
xv, 666 p.; 23 cm.
Includes bibliographies and index.
ISBN 9027718342 CIP rev.

—Three international conventions on hijacking and offences on board aircraft : (i) Convention on Offences and Certain Other Acts Committed on Board Aircraft ... 1963. (ii) Convention for Suppression of Unlawful Seizure of Aircraft ... 1970. (iii) Convention for the Suppression of Unlawful Acts Against the Safety of Civil Aviation ... 1971 : explanation documentation prepared for Commonwealth jurisdictions by David Lloyd Jones in association with the Commonwealth Secretariat / David Lloyd Jones. - London : Commonwealth Secretariat, 1982.
vi,146p; 30cm.
ISBN 0850922151

—Uncitral's project for a model law on international commercial arbitration / general editor, Pieter Sanders : with the cooperation of the T.M.C. Asser Institute for International Law. - Deventer, Netherlands : Kluwer Law and Taxation Publishers, 1984.
At head of title: International Council for Commercial Arbitration. Proceedings of the International Council for Commercial Arbitration interim meeting, May 9-12, 1984 in Lausanne, Switzerland.
ISBN 9065441832

CONGRESSES - AFRICA
—Individual under African law : proceedings of the first All-Africa Law Conference, October 11-16, 1981, Royal Swazi Spa, Swaziland / edited by Peter Nanyenya Takirambudde. - Kwaluseni (Sq) : University of Swaziland Department of Law, 1982.
iv,209p.

CONGRESSES - AUSTRALIA
—Law, politics, and the labor movement / edited by Gareth Evans. - Clayton, Vic. : Legal Service Bulletin in association with Australian Society of Labor Lawyers, 1980.
x, 205 p.; 21 cm.
Papers presented at the First National Conference of Labor Lawyers, held in Adelaide on 20 June-1 July, 1979. Includes bibliographical references and indexes.
ISBN 0959472703 pbk.

CONGRESSES - COMMONWEALTH
—Meeting of Commonwealth Law Ministers and Senior Officials : Harare, Zimbabwe, 26 July-1 August 1986 : memoranda / London : Commonwealth Secretariat, 1986.
xxvi,592p.
Includes bibliographical references.
ISBN 0850923093

—Proceedings and papers of the 7th Commonwealth Law Conference, Hong Kong, 18-23 September 1983 / Hong Kong : The Conference, 1984.
xvii,539p.

—Report on the Expert Group Meeting of Law Teachers to Develop Curriculum Materials on Violence against Women : London, 11-15 May 1987 / London : Commonwealth Secretariat, 1987.
19p.

CONSCIENTIOUS OBJECTION
—Conscientious objection to compulsory military service : recommendation no. R(87)8 adopted by the Committee of Ministers on 9 April 1987 and explanatory report / Council of Europe. - Strasbourg : Council of Europe, 1987.
10p. - (H (87) 3).

CONSENT (LAW)
—Law of consent / by Peter W. Young. - Sydney : Law Book Company, 1986.
xxxvi,228p.
ISBN 0455206791

CONSENT (LAW) - GREAT BRITAIN
—Law of Consent / London : Sweet & Maxwell, 1987.
ISBN 045506791 Hbk £19.50

CONSERVATION
—Existing legislative protection of the cultural and natural heritage of the Pacific region / Patrick O'Keefe, Lyndel V. Prott. - s.l. : UNESCO, 1982.
v,140p.

—Introduction to the World conservation strategy / prepared for the International Union for Conservation of Nature and Natural Resources by its Commission on Education : text and selection of photographs, Stan Croner. - Gland, Switzerland : IUCN, 1984.
28 p.; 30 cm.
ISBN 2880327024 pbk. £7.95

—IUCN bulletin : a quarterly journal of the International Union for Conservation of Nature and Natural Resources / International Union for Conservation of Nature and Natural Resources. - Gland, Switzerland : The Union, 1953 -.
ISBN 00209058

CONSERVATION - GREAT BRITAIN
—Creation and Preservation : Law and the Cultural Heritage / L. V. Prott. - Abingdon : Professional Books, 1985.
- (Volume II).
ISBN 0862050774 Hbk £33.50
ISBN 0862050820 Pbk £22.00

—Listed buildings and conservation areas / London : Longman Professional (UK), 1989.
- (Practitioner series).
Explains how a building is listed, how far that listing extends, and considers the designation of conservation areas. Sets out the provisions relating to alteration and repair of listed buildings and the planning cotrols that apply, and sets out the financial considerations. Takes account of the General Development Order 1988.
ISBN 0851214088 Hbk £25.95

CONSTITUTIONAL CONVENTIONS - AUSTRALIA
—Report to Parliament on the Australian Constitutional Convention / Legal and Constitutional Committee. - Melbourne : Government Printer, 1985.
xix,187p.
Bibliography: p.185-187. First report on the Australian Constitutional Convention.

CONSTITUTIONAL CONVENTIONS - AUSTRALIA - VICTORIA
—Report to Parliament on the Australian Constitutional Convention : an assessment of the 1985 Brisbane plenary session; the Convention generally and its future / Legal and Constitutional Committee. - Melbourne : Parliament of Victoria, 1986.
ix,49p.
Cover title: Second report on the Australian Constitutional Convention.

CONSTITUTIONAL CONVENTIONS - GREAT BRITAIN
—Constitutional conventions : the rules and forms of political accountability / Geoffrey Marshall. - Oxford : Clarendon, 1984.
xvi,247p; 23cm.
Bibliography: p233-239. - Includes index.
ISBN 019876183X £16.50

CONSTITUTIONAL COURTS
—Supreme courts and judicial law-making : constitutional tribunals and constitutional review / by Edward McWhinney. - Dordrecht : M. Nijhoff, 1985.
320p.
Includes index.
ISBN 9024732034 Hbk £165.00

CONSTITUTIONAL HISTORY
—Constitution-making : principles, process, practice / Edward McWhinney. - Toronto : University of Toronto Press, 1981.
xiii,231p; 24cm.
Bibliography: p219-225. - Includes index.
ISBN 0802055532 £12.00

—Constitutional development in the USSR : a guide to the soviet constitutions / Aryeh L. Unger. - London : Methuen, 1981.
viii,310p; 22cm.
Bibliography: p297-298. - Includes index. Includes English text of the RSFSR constitution of 1918, and the USSR constitutions of 1924, 1936 and 1977.
ISBN 0416716806 Pbk £13.50
ISBN 0416716903 £7.50

—Religion, law, and the growth of constitutional thought 1150-1650 / Brian Tierney. - Cambridge : Cambridge University Press, 1982.
xi,114p; 23cm.
Bibliography: p109-114.
ISBN 0521234956 £12.50

CONSTITUTIONAL HISTORY - CANADA
—Historical Introduction to Legal Studies / Agincourt : Carswell, 1982.
411p.
This textbook for Canadian law students examines the historical development of the Canadian Constitution and the legal institution of Canada from their Anglo-Saxon origins to the present.

CONSTITUTIONAL HISTORY - ENGLAND
—Constitutional History of England : 1485-1760 / 7th ed. Repr. of 1850 ed. - Abingdon : Professional Books.

—Sources of English Legal and Constitutional History / R. Ian Jack. - Sydney : Butterworths.
This book gives a collection of prominent sources of the legal and constitutional history of England for students of the subject. The work includes materials ranging from the Dooms of the Anglo-Saxon Kings to the Equal Franchise Act of 1928.
ISBN 0409493821 Hbk

—Sources of English Legal and Constitutional History / R. Ian Jack. - Butterworths, 1984.
432p.
ISBN 0409493821 Hbk £49.00

CONSTITUTIONAL HISTORY - GREAT BRITAIN

—British Constitution and British Constitutional History / Bombay : Universal Book Corporation.

—Constitutional history of Jersey / F. de L. Bois. - Rev. repr. 1981. - Jersey : States' Greffe, Jersey, 1981.
311p.
Revision of: 1972 ed.. Includes index.

CONSTITUTIONAL HISTORY - INDIA

—Constitutional and National Development in India : Montagu-Chelmsford Report / Great Britain, India Office. - New Delhi : Ess Ess Publications, 1981.
xix, viii, 243p.

—Constitutional History of India 1765-1984 / New Delhi : S. Chand and Company.

—Constitutional History of India / New Delhi : S. Chand and Company.

—Constitutional History of India, Vol. 1 : 1600-1858 / Calcutta : Mukherjee & Co, 1987.
586p.

—Evolution of the Constitutional History of India (1773-1947) : With Special Reference to the Role of the Indian Congress and the Minorities / Delhi : Mittal Publications, 1987.
272p.
ISBN 8170990106 Hbk £160.00

—Landmarks in Indian Legal Constitutional History / 5th ed. - Lucknow : Eastern Book Company, 1981.
546p.

CONSTITUTIONAL HISTORY - NAMIBIA

—Constitutional Options for Namibia : a Historical Perspective / C. Ushewkunze. - Lusaka : United Nations Institute for Namibia.
72p.

CONSTITUTIONAL HISTORY - NIGERIA

—Constitutional history of Nigeria / by B.O. Nwabueze. - London : C. Hurst, 1982.
xiii,272p; 23cm.
Includes index.
ISBN 0905838793 Hbk £12.50

—Constitutional History of Nigeria / London : Dent (J M) & Sons, 1982.
ISBN 0905838793 Hbk £15.00

CONSTITUTIONAL HISTORY - SPAIN

—Cortes and the King : Constitutional Monarchy in the Iberian World / Glasgow : University of Glasgow, Institute of Latin American Studies, 1981.
- (Occasional Paper: No. 32).

CONSTITUTIONAL LAW

—Cases on the Law of the Constitution / Repr. of 1926 ed. - Aalen Wuertt : Scientia.
xxxvi, 387p.

—Constitution Making in New Island States / Auckland : Legal Research Foundation, 1982.

—Constitutional and Administrative Law / 5th ed. - De Smith, 1985.
ISBN 0140226109 Pbk £11.95

—Constitutional code / F. Rosen, J. H. Burns. - Oxford : Clarendon Press, 1983.
xlv,612p,2folded leaves of plates; 24cm. - (The Collected works of Jeremy Bentham).
Includes index. Author: Jeremy Bentham.
ISBN 019822608X Unpriced

—Constitutional law / 2nd. - Edinburgh : W Green & Son, 1968.
Deals with the relationships of the contral institutions of government, politics, ideas, and their relationships. Copious references to a wide range of legal and non-legal material related to constitutional law. Published under the auspices of the Scottish Universities Law Institute.
ISBN 041400504X

—Constitutional Miscellany / Lucknow : Eastern Book Company, 1986.
256p.

—Constitutions of Nations, 4 Vols. / Dordrecht : Kluwer.

—Constitutions of nations / by Amos J. Peaslee. - Rev. 4th ed. - Dordrecht : M. Nijhoff, 1985.
1824p.
ISBN 902472905X Hbk £60.00

—Essays on Constitutional Law : Alladi Krishnaswami Aiyer Memorial Volume / New Delhi : Concept Publishing Company, 1986.
xvi, 285p.

—Modern Constitution - Constitution Moderne / Fribourg : Universitatsverlag.
256p.
ISBN 2827103923 Pbk £40.00

—Papua New Guinea, in the Supreme Court of Justice ... In the matter of a reference under section 18 of the Constitution, and in the matter of Ralph Rakhinand Premdas against the Independent State of Papua New Guinea, and others. Re Rooney: being a transcript of the proceedings 27th August - 5th and 11th September 1979 / Port Moresby : Council of Law Reporting for Papua New Guinea, 1981.
vi,390p; 34cm.
Cover title: The Rooney case.

—Roman Constitutional History / Rotterdam : A.A. Balkema, 1948.
195p.

—Select Constitutions / New Delhi : S. Chand and Company, 1983.

—Studies in constitutional law / London : Butterworths, 1987.
ISBN 040626144X Hbk £16.50
ISBN 0406261458 Pbk £9.95

—World Constitution / New Delhi : Varma Brothers.

CONSTITUTIONAL LAW - AFGHANISTAN

—Law in Afghanistan : a study of the Constitutions, matrimonial law and judiciary / by Mohammad Hashim Kamali. - Leiden : E. J. Brill, 1985.
viii,265p.
Bibliography: p254-259.
ISBN 9004071288

CONSTITUTIONAL LAW - AFRICA

—Constitutions of Nations, 4 Vols. / 4th rev. ed. - Dordrecht : Kluwer, 1974.
xi, 1141p.
ISBN 9024716810

—From dependence to statehood in Commonwealth Africa : selected documents, World War I to independence / by H.H. Marshall. - London : Oceana Publications, 1980.
27cm.
Contents: v.1 Southern Africa - v.2 Central Africa.

CONSTITUTIONAL LAW - ANTIGUA AND BARBUDA

—Acts : Antigua and Barbuda / v. - Antigua and Barbuda : Government Printer, 1985.
Extracted from the Government gazette.

—Statutory instruments : Antigua and Barbuda / v. - Antigua and Barbuda : Government Printer, 1985-.
Extracted from the Government gazette.

CONSTITUTIONAL LAW - ARGENTINA

—Argentine Supreme Court : the court of constitutional guarantees / German J. Bidart Campos : translated by William J. Brisk, based on the book by German J. Bidart Campos, 'La Corte Suprema, tribunal de las garantias constitucionales'. - Argentine ed. - Buenos Aires : Allende & Brea, 1982.
viii, 143 p.; 26 cm.
Includes bibliographical references.
ISBN 9500621142

CONSTITUTIONAL LAW - ASIA

—Constitutions of nations / by Amos J. Peaslee. - Rev. 4th ed. - Dordrecht : M. Nijhoff, 1985.
1824p.
ISBN 902472905X Hbk £60.00

CONSTITUTIONAL LAW - AUSTRALIA

—Australia Constitutional Law / 3rd ed. - London : Butterworths, 1985.
ISBN 0409494836 Hbk £53.00

—Australia's Constitution : Time for Change? / North Sydney : Allen & Unwin, 1983.
432p.
ISBN 0868610399 Pbk £17.95

—Australian Commonwealth : a fundamental analysis of its constitution / M. J. Detmold. - Sydney : Law Book Company, 1985.
266p.
ISBN 0455205787

—Australian Constitution Annotated : 1976-1979 Cumulative Supplement / Attorney-General's Department. - Canberra : Australian Government Publishing Service, 1980.
94p.
ISBN 0642056609 Hbk £3.20

—Australian constitution annotated : the Commonwealth of Australia Constitution Act, as altered to 31 December 1975, and the acts altering the constitution with case annotations, notes, tables, appendixes and index / compiled and annotated by the Attorney-General's Department. - Canberra : Australian Government Publishing Service, 1980.
li,544p.
ISBN 064202796X

—Australian Constitution : Australia's Most Important Document / Kingston : Australian Government Publishing Service, 1988.

—Australian Constitutional Cases / 4th ed. - North Ryde : Law Book Co, 1982.
xxxv, 774p.
ISBN 0455204608 Pbk £52.50
ISBN 0455204594 Hbk £73.00

—Australian Constitutional Law / 3rd ed. - Butterworths, 1985.
821p.
ISBN 0409494933 Pbk £67.50

—Australian constitutional law / by P.J. Hanks. - 3rd ed. - Sydney : Butterworths, 1985.
xxix,792p.
Previous ed.: 1980, published as Fajgenbaum and Hanks' Australian constitutional law. Includes bibliographical references and index.
ISBN 0409494836

—Australian Constitutionalism / London : Butterworths, 1983.
ISBN 0409493104 Pbk £20.00

—Australian Constitutionalism / Butterworths, 1983.
176p.
ISBN 0409493104 Pbk £29.50

—Australian federal constitutional law / by Colin Howard. - 3rd ed. - Sydney : Law Book Company, 1985.
lxxviii,611p.
Bibliography: pxliii-li.
ISBN 0455205736

—Authority and politics in Australia : some key dynamics of Australian politics / Victoria : Oxford University Press, 1988.
320.
Argues that a few basic principles underlie many features of Australian politics and government. It is maintained that in the Australian setting these processes have resulted in continuing restrictive features in Australian law and institutions.
ISBN 0195547446 Pbk £15.00

—Bill of rights for Australia? : an exposure report for the consideration of senators / Senate Standing Committee on Constitutional and Legal Affairs. - Canberra : Australian Government Publishing Service, 1985.
xi,128p.
Includes the text of the International Covenant on Civil and Political Rights. Lists treaties relating to human rights to which Australia is a party.
ISBN 0644044748

—Constitution : As Altered to 31 October 1986 / Kingston : Australian Government Publishing Service, 1986.
88p.

—Constitution of the Commonwealth of Australia / K.W. Ryan. - 4th ed. - Butterworths, 1986.
441p.
ISBN 0409491284 Hbk £59.00
ISBN 0409491292 Pbk £48.00

—Constitution of the Commonwealth of Australia : Abridged Edition / Kingston : Australian Government Publishing Service, 1987.

—Constitution of the Commonwealth of Australia annotated / by R.D. Lumb and K.W. Ryan. - 3rd ed. - Sydney : Butterworths, 1981.
xxiv, 426 p.; 25 cm.
Includes index. Bibliography: p. 405-410.
ISBN 0409300225 pbk. £42.00

—Constitutional Challenge : Essays on the Australian Constitution, Constitutionalism and Parliamentary Practice / G. S. Reid. - Turramura : Centre for Independent Studies, 1982.
viii, 166p. - (CIS Readings Ser.).
ISBN 0949769010 Hbk £7.95

—Constitutional Commission : First Report, Volumes 1 and 2, 2 Vols. / Kingston : Australian Government Publishing Service.
824p.

—Constitutions of nations / by Amos J. Peaslee. - Rev. 4th ed. - Dordrecht : M. Nijhoff, 1985.
1824p.
ISBN 902472905X Hbk £60.00

—Distribution of Powers : Report of the Advisory Committee to the Constitutional Commission / Kingston : Australian Government Publishing Service, 1987.

—Executive power of the Commonwealth of Australia / by H.E. Renfree. - Sydney : Legal books, 1984.
xxxvii,599p.
Includes index.
ISBN 0949553093

—Fajgenbaum and Hanks' Australian constitutional law / edited by Peter Hanks. - 2nd ed. - Sydney : Butterworths, 1980.
xxxv,724p.
ISBN 0409415707

—Federal constitutional law /. - North Ryde : Law Book Co, 1984.
x, 86p. - (Nutshells).
ISBN 0455203482

—High Court and the Constitution / 2nd ed. – Butterworths, 1987.
423p.
ISBN 0409491780 Hbk £69.00
ISBN 0409491799 Pbk £49.00

—Individual and Democratic Rights : Report of the Advisory Committee to the Constitutional Commission / Kingston : Australian Government Publishing Service, 1987.
xx, 148p.

—Introduction to the Australian constitution / 3rd ed. – London : Law Book Co, 1983.
ISBN 0455202109 Pbk £10.00

—Introduction to the Australian Constitution / 4th ed. – North Ryde : Law Book Co, 1987.
x, 264p.

—Lane's Commentary on the Australian Constitution / North Ryde : Law Book Co, 1986.
xxxvii, 766p.
ISBN 0455207011 Hbk £111.00

—Manual of Australian Constitutional Law / 3rd ed. – North Ryde : Law Book Co, 1984.
xx, 554p.
ISBN 0455202893 Hbk £67.50
ISBN 0455202907 Pbk £48.00

—Manual of Australian Constitutional Law / 3rd ed. – North Ryde : Law Book Co, 1984.
ISBN 0455202893 Hbk £33.00

—Monarchy to republic : Australian republican government / George Winterton. – Melbourne : Oxford University Press, 1986.
xi, 211 p.; 23 cm.
Includes index. Bibliography: p. 192-194.
ISBN 019554563X

—Official record of debates of the Australian Constitutional Convention at Parliament House, Adelaide, 26 to 29 April 1983 / Adelaide : Government Printer, 1983.
299p.
Includes index. Cover title: Proceedings of the Australian Constitutional Convention.

—Parliament, the executive, and the governor-general : a constitutional analysis / George Winterton. – Carlton, Vic. : Melbourne University Press, 1983.
viii, 376 p.; 23 cm.
Includes index. Bibliography: p. 329-346.
ISBN 0522842429

—Report to Parliament on the Australian Constitutional Convention : issues before the 1985 plenary session / Legal and Constitutional Committee. – Melbourne : Parliament of Victoria, 1985.
xix,187p.
Bibliography: p.185-187. Cover title: First report on the Australian Constitutional Convention.

—Statement of preliminary views / Constitutional Commission. Australian Judicial System Advisory Committee. – Canberra : The Commission, 1986.
40p.

CONSTITUTIONAL LAW - AUSTRALIA - SOUTH AUSTRALIA

—Report ... dealing with disparate subjects in the inherited imperial law / Law Reform Committee of South Australia. – Adelaide : Government Printer, 1984.
56p. – (68th report).

—Report ... dealing with the inherited imperial law / Law Reform Committee of South Australia. – Adelaide : Government Printer, 1984.
28p. – (79th report).

—Report ... dealing with the inherited imperial law between 1751 and 1780 / Law Reform Committee of South Australia. – Adelaide : Government Printer, 1984.
46p. – (85th report).

—Report ... dealing with the inherited imperial law between 1781 and 1800 / Law Reform Committee of South Australia. – Adelaide : Government Printer, 1984.
41p. – (86th report).

—Report ... dealing with the inherited imperial law between 1801 and 1820 / Law Reform Committee of South Australia. – Adelaide : Government Printer, 1984.
41p. – (89th report).

—Report ... dealing with the inherited imperial law between 1821 and 1836 / Law Reform Committee of South Australia. – Adelaide : Government Printer, 1985.
32p. – (91st report).

—Report ... relating to the demise of the Crown / Law Reform Committee of South Australia. – Adelaide : Government Printer, 1984.
13p. – (81st report).

—Report ... relating to the inherited imperial law / Law Reform Committee of South Australia. – Adelaide : Government Printer, 1984.
38p. – (80th report).

—Report ... relating to the inherited imperial law and to statutes previously covered by the Colonial Laws Validity Act 1865 / Law Reform Committee of South Australia. – Adelaide : Government Printer, 1986.
22p. – (102nd report).

CONSTITUTIONAL LAW - AUSTRIA

—Austrian Federal Constitution : as revised in 1929 together with subsequent additions and amendments and other important constitutional provisions including the Constitutional Law on the Neutrality of Austria / translated on behalf of the Austrian Federal Ministry for Foreign Affairs by Charles Kessler. – 2nd rev. and amplified ed. – Wien : Manzsche Verlags- und Universitatsbuchhandlung, 1983.
154 p.; 18 cm.
ISBN 3214060015 pbk. S190.00

—Outline of Austrian constitutional law / Kluwer Law and Taxation, 1989.
72.
A brief introduction to the law of Austria. Covers leading statutesand commentaries, basic principles of the constitution, neutrality, and legislation of the Federation.
ISBN 9065444041 Pbk £16.25/Dfl 50

CONSTITUTIONAL LAW - BELGIUM

—Constitutional and legislative provisions concerning the organisation of regional government / Council of Europe. – Strasbourg : Council of Europe, 1982.
i,47p; 30cm.

CONSTITUTIONAL LAW - BELIZE

—Ordinances and acts : Belize / v. – Belmopan : Government Printer, 1973-.
Supplement to the Government gazette. Continues: Ordinances of British Honduras.

—Report of the Belize Constitutional Conference, London, April 1981 / London : H.M.S.O., 1981.
29p; 25cm.
ISBN 0101824505 unbound £2.40

CONSTITUTIONAL LAW - BOPHUTHATSWANA

—Constitutions of Transkei, Bophuthatswana, Venda and Ciskei / editors M.P. Vorster, M. Wiechers, D.J. van Vuuren. – Durban : Butterworths, 1985.
269p.
Includes the texts of the constitutions.
ISBN 040901964X

CONSTITUTIONAL LAW - BOTSWANA

—Statutory instruments : Botswana / v. – Gaborone : Government Printer, 1966-.
Published as supplements to the Republic of Botswana government gazette.

CONSTITUTIONAL LAW - BULGARIA

—Statutes on constitutional law / Sofia : Sofia Press, .
172,1p.
At head of t.p.: National Assembly of the People's Republic of Bulgaria.

CONSTITUTIONAL LAW - CANADA

—Aboriginal Peoples and Section 25 of the Canadian Charter of Rights and Freedoms / Saskatoon : University of Saskatchewan, Native Law Centre, 1988.
52p.
ISBN 0888801939 Hbk £15.00

—Aboriginal Rights Provisions in the Constitution Act, 1982 / Saskatoon : University of Saskatchewan, Native Law Centre, 1987.
276p.
ISBN 0888801920 Hbk £50.00

—Aboriginal Self-Government and Constitutional Reform : Setbacks, Opportunities, and Arctic Experiences / Ottawa : Canadian Arctic Resources Committee, 1988.
168p.
ISBN 0919996353 Pbk £20.00

—Canada Act 1982 annotated / by Peter W. Hogg. – Toronto : Carswell, 1982.
155p.
Includes the Constitution Act, 1982 - the Canadian Bill of Rights - the American Bill of Rights - the International Covenant on Civil and Political Rights. Includes index.
ISBN 0459351303

—Canada and the constitution, 1979-1982 : patriation and the charter of rights / Edward McWhinney. – Toronto : University of Toronto Press, 1982.
xii,227p.
Includes bibliographical references and index.
ISBN 0802065015 pbk.

—Canada and the New Constitution : the Unfinished Agenda, 2 Vols. / Ivan Bernier. – Ottawa : Institute for Research on Public Policy, 1983.
xii, 399p.
ISBN 0920380735 Hbk £10.95

—Canada Notwithstanding : The Making of a Constitution 1976-1982 / John Whyte. – Agincourt : Carswell, 1984.
300p.

—Canada...Notwithstanding : the Marking of the Constitution 1976-1982 / Agincourt : Carswell, 1984.
300p.

—Canadian Charter of Rights and Freedoms / Agincourt : Carswell, 1982.
ISBN 045934920 Hbk £33.00

—Canadian Charter of Rights Annotated / Edward L. Greenspan. – Aurora : Canada Law Book Co. – (Text Books-Civil).

—Canadian Charter of Rights Annotated (C.C.R.) / Aurora : Canada Law Book Co.

Two Binders & Contents

—Canadian Constitution 1981 : a resolution adopted by the Parliament of Canada, December 1981 / Canada. – Ottawa : Government of Canada, 1981.
vi,28,28,vip.
Accompanied by summary 'Highlights' pamphlet. Added t.p. in French: La constitution canadienne 1981: resolution adoptee par le Parlement du Canada en decembre 1981. Pages numbered in opposite directions. Text in English and French.
ISBN 0662516923

—Canadian Constitution and the Courts / 2nd ed. – Toronto : Butterworths, 1983.
352p.
ISBN 0409870765 Hbk £70.00

—Canadian Constitution and the Courts : the Function and Scope of Judicial Review / 3rd ed. – Butterworths, 1988.
400p.
New edition includes coverage of the major increase in the number of cases involving constitutional issues, the dominance of Charter questions in constitutional litigation, and the greatly heightened profile of the Supreme Court of Canada as innovating leader in the interpretation of the new constitutional provisions. Also notes early trends in judicial activism, or restraint, in Charter interpretation.
ISBN 0409806315 Hbk £80.00

—Canadian Constitutional Law / William R. Lederman. – 3rd ed. – Toronto : Butterworths, 1987.
ISBN 0409876046 Hbk
ISBN 0409876054 Pbk

—Canadian Constitutional Law Handbook : Leading Statements, Principles and Precedents / Aurora : Canada Law Book Co, 1985.
1182p. – (Text Books-Civil).

—Charter Issues in Civil Cases / Brian MacLeod Rogers. – Agincourt : Carswell, 1988.
327p.

—Charter of Rights Decisions / Aurora : Canada Law Book Co.
– (Summary Services, National Series).

Back Vols.

—Charterwatch : Reflections on Equality / A. Wayne MacKay. – Agincourt : Carswell, 1986.
320p.
This work presents eight essays on the political and legal implications of the guarantee of equality in the Canadian Charter of Rights and Freedom. The role of the judiciary in shaping the concept of equality in Canadian law is emphasized in the essays.

—Competing Constitutional Visions : the Meech Lake Accord / Carol J. Rogerson. – Agincourt : Carswell, 1988.
338p.

—Consolidation of the Constitution Acts of 1867 to 1982 / Agincourt : Carswell, 1983.
86p.
This work is published by the Department of Justice of Canada and is bilingual. It features the British North America Act 1867 with amendments made to it since its enactment and the Constitution Act 1982. The Constitution Act 1982 contains the Canadian Charter of Rights and Freedoms and the procedure for amending the Constitution of Canada.
ISBN 0660421016 Pbk £4.25

—Constitution 1982 / Ottawa : Canadian Government Publishing Centre, 1983.
120p.
ISBN 0660522934 Pbk £19.95
ISBN 0660522942 Hbk £29.95

—Constitution Act, 1982 / La loi constitutionelle de 1982. – Ottawa : Canadian Government Publishing Centre, 1982.
23i.e.27p.
Parallel English and French text.
ISBN 0660516020

—Constitution and the People of Canada / Ottawa : Canadian Government Publishing Centre, 1982.
87p.

—Constitution and you / Ottawa : Government of Canada, 1982.
32,35p.
Added t.p. in French: Notes sur la constitution. Pages numbered in opposite directions. Text in English and French.
ISBN 0662517547

—Constitution : Getting Our Act Together / Montreal : McGill Campus Legal Aid Clinic, 1982.
232p.

—Constitution of Canada / Toronto : IPI Publishing, 1984.
120p. – (Orig.).

—Constitution of Canada : a suggested amendment relating to provincial administrative tribunals : a discussion paper / Department of Justice. – Ottawa : The Department, 1983.
13,14p.
With French t.p.: La Constitution du Canada. English and French texts.

—Constitution of the Five Nations : or the Iroquois Book of the Great Law / 1916 repr. – Oshweken : Iroqrafts.
158p.
ISBN 0919645003 Hbk £6.95

—Constitutional Change in Canada : Lessons and Analogies From Across the Pacific / North Ryde : Association for Canadian Studies in Australia and New Zealand, 1984.

—Constitutional Law of Canada, 2 Vols. / 3rd ed. – Agincourt : Carswell, 1987.
ISBN 045930961 Hbk £61.60
ISBN 045930951X Pbk £36.00

—Constitutional Law of Canada, 2nd Edition / Agincourt : Carswell, 1982.
130p.

—Constitutional law of Canada : Cases, notes and materials / by Joseph Eliot Magnet. – Toronto : Carswell, 1983.
xxii,1229p.
ISBN 0459356704

—Continuing Canadian constitutional dilemmas : essays on the constitutional history, public law and federal system of Canada / W.R. Lederman. – Toronto : Butterworths, 1981.
xx,442p.
Includes bibliographical references.
ISBN 0409844616 Hbk 55.00
ISBN 0409844608 Pbk 35.00

—Courts and the Charter / Clare F. Beckton and A. Wayne MacKay, research coordinators. – Toronto : University of Toronto Press in cooperation with the Royal Commission on the Economic Union and Development Prospects for Canada and the Canadian Government Publishing Centre, 1985.
xv,279p. – (Collected research studies).
Includes bibliographies.
ISBN 0802073050

—Equality Rights and Canadian Charter Rights and Freedoms / Eberts. – Agincourt : Carswell, 1985.
ISBN 045932210 Hbk £38.50

—Equality Rights and the Canadian Charter of Rights and Freedom : Carswell's Canadian Legal Classic Series / Mary Eberts. – Agincourt : Carswell, 1985.
600p.
This work is a collection of essays examining section 15 of the Canadian Charter of Rights concerning equality rights. Decisions under the Canadian Bill of Rights, federal and provincial human rights statutes are discussed in the book.

—Laskin's Canadian constitutional law / Neil Finkelstein. – 5th ed. – Toronto : Carswell, 1986.
2 v. (1501 p.); 26 cm.
'Canadian Bill of Rights': p. 1495-1497. 'American Bill of Rights': p. 1500-1501.
ISBN 0459384406 v. 2

—Law of the Charter : General Principles / Agincourt : Carswell, 1986.
ISBN 0459389009 Hbk £21.50
ISBN 0459390104 Pbk £14.50

—Law of the Charter : general principles / Dale Gibson. – Toronto : Carswell, 1986.
xxxiii,302p.
ISBN 0459389009

—Law of Your Land : a Practical Guide to the New Canadian Constitution / Toronto : Canadian Broadcasting Corporation Enterprises, 1984.
ISBN 0887941079 Pbk £5.95

—Leading constitutional decisions : cases on the British North America Act / edited and with an introduction by Peter H. Russell. – 3rd ed. – Ottawa : Carleton University Press, 1982.
vii,578p. – (The Carleton Library series).
Bibliography: p575-578.
ISBN 0886290058

—Litigating the Values of a Nation : The Canadian Charter of Rights and Freedoms / Robin M. Elliot. – Agincourt : Carswell, 1986.
448p.
This work is a collection of essays by leading Canadian Charter and American constitutional authorities on legal history, political science, legal philosophy, legal theory, and practical advice to litigators.

—Meech Lake Constitutional Accord Annotated / Agincourt : Carswell, 1988.
93p.

—Meech Lake Constitutional Accord Annotated / Agincourt : Carswell, 1988.
100p.

—Multiculturalism and the Charter : A Legal Perspective / Agincourt : Carswell, 1987.
200p.
This book consists of essays pertaining to s.27 of the Charter of Rights and Freedoms. Discussions include the possible impact of s.27 on other Charter provisions and the resulting effect on Canada's pluralistic society.

—New Canadian Constitution / Toronto : James Lorimer & Co.
240p.
ISBN 0888625448 Pbk £7.95
ISBN 0888625456 Hbk £19.95

—New Constitution and the Charter of Rights : Fundamental Issues and Strategies / Eric Gertner. – Butterworths, 1983.
384p.
ISBN 0409832642 Hbk £55.00

—Newfoundland and Dominion Status / Agincourt : Carswell, 1987.
304p.
This work focuses on the pre-Confederation status of Newfoundland from a legal point of view. It is a comprehensive text providing archival sources in documenting the evolution of Newfoundland's external affairs competence between 1855 and 1934. It also provides a review in terms of Imperial constitutional law and international law. Up-to-date decisions of the Supreme Court of Canada and Newfoundland Court of Appeal are reviewed.

—Origins and Meaning of Section 92A : the 1982 Constitutional Amendment on Resources / Ottawa : Institute for Research on Public Policy, 1985.
xxii, 77p.
ISBN 0886450136 Hbk £10.00

—Politics and the Constitution, The Charter, Federalism and the Supreme Court of Canada / Agincourt : Carswell, 1987.
253p.
This work focuses on the constitutional issues presented to the Supreme Court of Canada over the last ten years. Discussions include a summary of the significance and implications of the initial Charter decisions. Charts and graphs are presented to illustrate the success rate of the Charter arguments.

—Putting the Charter to Work : Designing a Constitutional Labour Code / Montreal : McGill-Queen's University Press, 1987.
ca 240p.
ISBN 0773506004 Hbk £30.00
ISBN 0773506012 Pbk £14.95

—Recent developments in administrative law / edited by Neil R. Finkelstein, Brian MacLeod Rogers. – Toronto : Carswell, 1987.
xl,354p.
' ... a collection of essays which were originally presented at programs sponsored by the Law Society of Upper Canada on 'Administrative law: recent developments and emerging trends' in Toronto and Ottawa in November 1986'. - Preface.
ISBN 0459304615

—Rights, freedoms and the courts : a practical analysis of the Constitution Act, 1982 / Morris Manning. – Toronto : Emond-Montgomery, 1983.
lxiv,760p.
Includes the text of the Act.
ISBN 0920722105

—Role of the United Kingdom in the amendment of the Canadian Constitution : background paper / Jean Chretien, Minister of Justice of Canada. – Ottawa : Government of Canada, 1981.
54p; 23cm.

—Supreme Court decisions on the Canadian Constitution / Canada. – Toronto : J. Lorimer, 1981.
xxi,141p.
ISBN 0888625383

—Taking of 28 : Women Challenge the Constitution / Toronto.
124p.
ISBN 0889610835 Pbk £6.95

—Towards a Constitutional Charter for Canada / Toronto : University of Toronto Press, 1980.
ISBN 0802063993 Pbk £8.50

—Vision and the Game : the Canadian Constitution / Calgary : Detselig Enterprises Ltd., 1987.
197p.
ISBN 0920490670 Pbk £14.95

CONSTITUTIONAL LAW - CANADA - BRITISH COLUMBIA

—British Columbia Act and Regulations / 3rd ed. – Toronto : DeBoo, 1982.
ISBN 0888201079 Hbk £19.95

CONSTITUTIONAL LAW - CARIBBEAN

—Changing Caribbean constitutions / Francis Alexis. – St. Michael, Barbados : Antilles, 1983.
xxviii,281p.
Bibliography: p.270-274. - Includes index.

CONSTITUTIONAL LAW - CHANNEL ISLANDS

—Isle of Man and the Channel Islands : a study of their status under constitutional, international and European law / by Simon A. Horner. – Florence : European University Institute, 1984.
142p.
At head of title: European University Institute, Florence, Law Department.

—Minutes of evidence / Commission on the Constitution. – 6. – London : HMSO, 1970.
1: Wales - 2: Scotland - 3: Northern Ireland - 4: Scotland - 5: Wales - 6: The Channel Islands and the Isle of Man. Bound in one vol..

CONSTITUTIONAL LAW - CHINA

—Constitution of the People's Republic of China / China. – Oxford : Pergamon, 1983.
100p.
Translated from the Chinese.
ISBN 008030818X Hbk £9.95
ISBN 0080308171 Pbk £4.95

—Constitution of the People's Republic of China : adopted on December 4, 1982 by the fifth National People's Congress of the People's Republic of China at its fifth session / China. – Beijing : Foreign Languages Press, 1983.
93p.
ISBN 0835110818

CONSTITUTIONAL LAW - CISKEI

—Constitutions of Transkei, Bophuthatswana, Venda and Ciskei / editors M.P. Vorster, M. Wiechers, D.J. van Vuuren. – Durban : Butterworths, 1985.
269p.
Includes the texts of the constitutions.
ISBN 040901964X

CONSTITUTIONAL LAW - CISKEI - INDIA

—Commentaries on Prevention of Corruption Act, 1947 / 3rd ed. – Lucknow : Eastern Book Company, 1981.
699p.

CONSTITUTIONAL LAW - CYPRUS

—Cyprus and Its Constitutional and Other Legal Problems / Nicosia : MAM, 1980.
ii, 246p.

CONSTITUTIONAL LAW - DENMARK

—Draft Treaty establishing the European Union : constitutional and political implications in Denmark / by Per Lachmann. – Badia Fiesolana : European University Institute, 1985.
39p.
Paper presented at a conference organised by the European Policy Unit of the European University Institute, in collaboration with the University of Strasbourg and TEPSA, October 1984.

CONSTITUTIONAL LAW - ENGLAND

—Ancient constitution and the feudal law : a study of English historical thought in the seventeenth century / J.G.A. Pocock. – Reissue with a retrospect i.e. 2nd ed. – Cambridge : Cambridge University Press, 1987.
xv,402p; 24cm.
Second edition to a work examining seventeenth-century English ideas of constitutionalism as a set of beliefs based on the common law. The Retrospect considers how arguments in the original book may be improved in the light of recent work.
ISBN 0521303524 Hbk £27.50
ISBN 052131643X Pbk £8.95

—English Constitution / Reprint. – London : Fontana, 1983.
ISBN 0006327583 Pbk £2.50

—Freedom, the individual and the law / H. Street. – 5th ed. – Harmondsworth, Eng. : Penguin Books, 1982.
352p. – (Pelican Books).
ISBN 0140206469

—Short constitutional history of England / by H. St. Clair Feilden. – 2nd ed., rev. and enl. – Oxford : Blackwell, 1887.
xii,338p.
Includes bibliographical references and index.

CONSTITUTIONAL LAW - EUROPE

—Constitutions of Nations, 4 Vols. /. – Dordrecht : Kluwer, 1968.
1315p.
ISBN 9024704472

CONSTITUTIONAL LAW - FRANCE

—Decentralisation in France : the distribution of powers / France. – Strasbourg : Council of Europe, 1984.
i,54p; 30cm.
Contents: Act no.83-8 of 7 January 1983 concerning the distribution of powers among the municipalities, departements, regions and central government (1); Act no.83-663 of 22 July 1983 supplementing Act no.83-8; Act no.82-659 of 30 July 1982 conferring special status on the region of Corsica (powers).

—French Constitution / London : Ambassade de France, 1986.
20 p.

CONSTITUTIONAL LAW - GERMANY

—Constitutional history of Germany : in the nineteenth and twentieth centuries / H.W. Koch. – London : Longman, 1984.
xiv,400p; 22cm.
Includes index.
ISBN 0582491827 Pbk £7.95

CONSTITUTIONAL LAW - GREAT BRITAIN

—British Constitution / by Sir Ivor Jennings. – 5th ed. – Cambridge : Cambridge University Press, 1966.
xi, 218p, 4 leaves of plates.
ISBN 0521091365 Hbk

—British Constitution / Rome : Bulzoni Editore.

—British Constitution and British Constitutional History / Bombay : Universal Book Corporation.

—British Constitution : Its Structure and Working / New Delhi : S. Chand and Company, 1977.
386p.

—British Government and Constitution (LIC) / Weidenfeld & Nicolson, 1985.
ISBN 0297786512 Hbk £25.00
ISBN 0297786530 Pbk £15.95

—British government and the constitution : text, cases and materials / Colin Turpin. – London : Weidenfeld & Nicolson, 1985.
xxviii,476p; 25cm.
Includes index.
ISBN 0297786512 Hbk £25.00
ISBN 0297786520 Pbk £15.00

—Changing Constitution / Oliver. – Oxford : Oxford University Press, 1985.
ISBN 0198761759 Pbk £13.95
ISBN 0198761767 Hbk £27.50

—Changing constitution / Jeffrey Jowell, Dawn Oliver. – 2nd. – Oxford : Clarendon Press, 1989.
416; 23.5.
Collections of essays on the nature and evolutin of the British consitution. Essays on local government and on nationalised industries have been rewritten, and there is a new essay on Northern Ireland and the British Constitution.*Students and teachers of consitutional law and administrative law, and British government and politics*
ISBN 0198252765 Hbk £40.00
ISBN 0198252773 Pbk £15.00

—Changing constitution / edited by Jeffrey Jowell and Dawn Oliver. – Oxford : Clarendon, 1985.
xix,377p; 24cm.
Includes index.
ISBN 0198761767 Hbk £25.00
ISBN 0198761759 Pbk £12.95

—Constitution in Flux / Oxford : Blackwell, 1982.
ISBN 0855205229 Pbk £8.50

—Constitution in flux / Philip Norton. – Oxford : Martin Robertson, 1982.
vii,312p; 22cm.
Bibliography: p295-300. - Includes index.
ISBN 0855205210 Hbk Unpriced
ISBN 0855205229 Pbk Unpriced

—Constitutional and Administrative Law / Plymouth : Macdonald & Evans, 1982.
ISBN 0712103988 Pbk £6.50

ELBS edition 1984
ISBN 0421333405 Hbk £3.50

—Constitutional and administrative law / E.C.S. Wade and A.W. Bradley. – 10th ed. – London : Longman, 1985.
xlv,758p; 24cm.
Previous ed.: 1977. Bibliography: p741-748. - Includes index.
ISBN 058249124X Hbk £17.00
ISBN 0582491258 Pbk £14.95

—Constitutional and administrative law / de Smith. – 4th ed. – Harmondsworth : Penguin, 1981.
728p; 20cm. – (Penguin education).
Previous ed.: 1977. Includes index.
ISBN 0140804552 Pbk £6.95

—Constitutional and administrative law / Harry Street and Rodney Brazier; editors. – 5th ed. – Harmondsworth : Penguin, 1985.
748p.
ISBN 0140226109

—Constitutional and Administrative Law (SWOT) / London : Blackstone Press, 1985.
ISBN 0906322723 Pbk £5.95

—Constitutional Convention / Reprint. – Oxford : Oxford University Press, 1986.
ISBN 019876202X Pbk £8.95

—Constitutional conventions : the rules and forms of political accountability / Geoffrey Marshall. – Oxford : Clarendon, 1984.
xvi,247p; 23cm.
Bibliography: p233-239. - Includes index.
ISBN 019876183X £16.50

—Constitutional Fundamentals (Hamlyn 32) / London : Sweet & Maxwell, 1980.
ISBN 0420459103 Pbk £8.00

—Constitutional law in a nutshell / Lynda Banks. – London : Sweet and Maxwell, 1980.
vii,84p; 18cm.
Includes index.
ISBN 0421265205 Pbk £1.50

—Constitutional law viewed in realation to common law, and exemplified by cases / by Herbert Broom. – 2nd ed. – London : W. Maxwell, 1885.
xxv,1026p.
Previous ed.: 1866. Includes index.

—Constitutional law viewed in relation to common law, and exemplified by cases / by Herbert Broom. – London : W. Maxwell, 1866.
xxviii,1012p.
Includes index.

—Constitutional practice / Rodney Brazier. – Oxford : Clarendon Press, 1988.
xix,285p.
Includes index.
ISBN 0198255969

—Constitutional reform : the quarterly review / London : Constitutional Reform Centre, 1986-.
Annual index with Winter issue.

—Draft Treaty establishing the European Union : report on the United Kingdom / by David Edward, Richard McAllister, Robert Lane. – Florence : European University Institute, 1985.
40p.

—Effect on English domestic law of membership of the European Communities and of ratification of the European Convention on Human Rights / edited by M.P. Furmston, Roger Kerridge, B.E. Sufrin. – The Hague : M. Nijhoff, 1983.
viii, 428p.
Papers by members of the University of Bristol Faculty of Law in celebration of the fiftieth anniversary of the Faculty.
ISBN 9024728118 Hbk £130.00

—Enacting a Bill of Rights / Oxford : Oxford University Press, 1980.
ISBN 0198253516 Hbk £30.00

—Enacting a bill of rights : the legal problems / Joseph Jaconelli. – Oxford : Clarendon Press, 1980.
xi,328p; 23cm.
Includes index.
ISBN 0198253516 £14.00

—Government and law : an introduction to the working of the constitution in Britain / by T.C. Hartley and J.A.G. Griffith. – 2nd ed. – London : Weidenfeld and Nicolson, 1981.
xxxii,472p. – (Law in context).
Bibliography: 464-468p.
ISBN 0297779745

—High Court and the Constitution / 2nd ed. – London : Butterworths, 1981.
ISBN 0409491780 Hbk £50.00

—Introduction to British constitutional law / 6th ed. – London : Butterworths, 1984.
ISBN 0406690073 Hbk £12.00
ISBN 0406690081 Pbk £10.50

—Introduction to British constitutional law / D.C.M. Yardley. – 6th ed. – London : Butterworths, 1984.
xviii, 180p; 23cm.
Previous ed.: 1978. Includes index.
ISBN 0406690073 Hbk Unpriced
ISBN 0406690081 Pbk Unpriced

—Introduction to British constitutional law / London : Blackstone Press, 1985.
ISBN 0906322685 Pbk £9.95

—Landmarks in the law / by Lord Denning. – London : Butterworths, 1984.
xvii,394p; 23cm.
Includes index.
ISBN 0406176035 Hbk £12.50
ISBN 0406176140 Pbk No price

—Law, legitimacy and the constitution : essays marking the centenary of Dicey's Law of the Constitution / edited by Patrick McAuslan and John F. McEldowney. – London : Sweet & Maxwell, 1985.
xiv,219p; 22cm.
Includes index.
ISBN 0421331208 Hbk £15.00
ISBN 0421331305 Pbk £8.50

—Law, Legitimacy and the Constitution (MLS) / McEldowney. – London : Sweet & Maxwell, 1985.
ISBN 0421331208 Hbk £19.50
ISBN 0421331305 Pbk £13.50

—Minutes of evidence / Commission on the Constitution. – 6. – London : HMSO, 1970.
1: Wales - 2: Scotland - 3: Northern Ireland - 4: Scotland - 5: Wales - 6: The Channel Islands and the Isle of Man. Bound in one vol..

—Noble lie : the British constitution and the rule of law / Ian Harden and Norman Lewis : foreword by Sir Douglas Wass. – London : Hutchinson, 1986.
xiii,334p; 23cm.
Bibliography: p313-317. - Includes index.
ISBN 0091641306 £25.00

—O. Hood Phillips' Constitutional and administrative law / Paul Jackson. – 7th ed. – London : Sweet & Maxwell, 1987.
lxxvi,808p; 26cm.
Previous ed.: 1978. Includes index.
ISBN 042135030X Hbk £21.00
ISBN 0421350407 Pbk £16.00

—Preserving freedom under the law : being the presidential address of the Rt. Hon. Lord Bridge of Harwich, President of the Holdsworth Club of the Faculty of Law in the University of Birmingham, 1981-82 / Birmingham : Holdsworth Club, 1982.
14p. – (Holdsworth Club Presidential Address 1982).
ISBN 0704406179

—Studies in constitutional law / Colin R. Munro. – London : Butterworths, 1987.
xviii,220p; 22cm.
Includes index.
ISBN 040626144X Hbk £11.00
ISBN 0406261458 Pbk £7.50

—Workable government? : Constitution after 200 years / Norton (WH), 1988.
ISBN 0393024806 Hbk £14.95
ISBN 0393304310 Pbk £7.50

—Constitutional fundamentals / by H.W.R. Wade. – London : Stevens for The Hamlyn Trust, 1980.
xi,83p; 19cm.
Includes index.
ISBN 0420459006 £6.35
ISBN 0420459103

CONSTITUTIONAL LAW - HONG KONG

—Draft agreement between the Government of the United Kingdom of Great Britain and Northern Ireland and the Government of the People's Republic of China on the future of Hong Kong / presented to Parliament by the Secretary of State for Foreign and Commonwealth Affairs. – London : H.M.S.O., 1984.
39p. – (Miscellaneous).
ISBN 010193520X

CONSTITUTIONAL LAW - INDIA

—Caste Reservation in India : Law and the Constitution / Allahabad : Chugh Publications, 1980.
160p.

—Constitution of India / D.K. Singh. – 7th ed. – Lucknow : Eastern Book Company, 1982.
871p.

—Constitution of India / Dordrecht : Law Book Co., 1984.

—Constitution of India / Allahabad : Law Publishers, 1982.

—Constitution of India / 3rd ed. – Delhi : Metropolitan Book Co.
850p.

—Constitution of India / 3rd ed. – Dordrecht : Law Book Co., 1989.
850p.

—Constitution of India / New Delhi : S. Chand and Company, 1984.

—Constitution of India / 7th ed. – New Delhi : Macmillan India.
422p.
ISBN 0333900588 Pbk £25.00

—Constitution of India : as Amended Up to the Constitution 52nd Amendment Act, 1986 with Text of Recent Amending Acts, Subject-Index and Extensive Notes on Recent Supreme Court Case-Law / 7th ed. – Lucknow : Eastern Book Company, 1986.

—Constitutional Government of India / New Delhi : S. Chand and Company.

—Constitutional Law of India / 3rd ed. – London : Sweet & Maxwell, 1983.
ISBN 0421316608 Hbk £54.00

—Constitutional Law of India / Lucknow : Eastern Book Company, 1982.
816p.

—Constitutional Law of India / 6th ed. – Lucknow : Eastern Book Company, 1984.
600p.

—Constitutional Law of India. Vol 1 / London : Lucas Publications, 1986.
ISBN 1851800123 Hbk £50.00

—Democratic Constitution of India / New Delhi : S. Chand and Company, 1983.

—Directive Principles of State Policy in Indian Constitution / New Delhi : Deep and Deep Publications, 1988.
200p.

—Framing of India's Constitution, 5 Vols. / New Delhi : Indian Institute of Public Administration.

—Governor in the Indian Constitution / New Delhi : Heritage Publishers, 1980.
viii, 181p.

—Hindu Law and the Constitution / Calcutta : Eastern Law House, 1983.

—India's choice : president or prime minister? / Cochin : Cochin University, 1980.
p.179-192. – (Notes and comments).
Reprinted from: Cochin University law review, 1980.

—Making of India's Constitution / Lucknow : Eastern Book Company, 1982.
vii, 121p.

—Muslim Law and the Constitution / Calcutta : Eastern Law House, 1985.

—National Integration and Indian Constitution / New Delhi : Deep and Deep Publications, 1986.
198p.

—Power of Taxation Under the Constitution / Lucknow : Eastern Book Company, 1987.

—Present Constitutional Issues and Views / Delhi : Metropolitan Book Co, 1987.
378p.
ISBN 8120002598 Hbk £200.00

—Re-promulgation of ordinances : a fraud on the constitution of India / D. C. Wadhwa. – Pune : Gokhale Institute of Politics and Economics, 1983.
xxxi,259p.
ISBN 0861314328

—Role of Supreme Court in Indian Constitution / New Delhi : Deep and Deep Publications, 1987.
208p.

—Socio-Economic Justice under Indian Constitution / New Delhi : Deep and Deep Publications, 1984.
460p.

—Constitutional law of India : a critical commentary / by H.M. Seervai. – 3rd ed. – Bombay : Tripathi, 1983.
xlvii,1071,262p; 26cm.
Previous ed.: 1975. Includes index. Includes text of the Constitution of India.
ISBN 0421316608 £45.00

Vol.2 / by H.M. Seervai. – 1984.
various pagings; 25cm.
Previous ed.: in 3v. 1975-1979. Includes index.
ISBN 0421339705 £70.00

CONSTITUTIONAL LAW - IRELAND

—Cases and Materials on the Irish Constitution / M. Redmond. – Dublin : Incorporated Law Society of Ireland, 1980.
ISBN 0902027158 Hbk £27.20

—Constitution, fifty years on / Round Hall, 1988.
16p.
ISBN 094768641X Pbk No price (Mar.)

—Constitutional Law and Constitutional Rights in Ireland / 2nd ed. – Dublin : Gill and Macmillan, 1987.
ISBN 0717115550 Pbk £17.95

—Constitutional law and constitutional rights in Ireland / Brian Doolan. – Dublin : Gill and Macmillan, 1984.
xvii,194p; 22cm.
Includes index.
ISBN 0717113310 Pbk £9.95

—Constitutional law in Ireland / by James Casey. – London : Sweet & Maxwell, 1987.
250p; 22cm.
Includes index.
ISBN 042131270X Pbk £19.00

—Constitutional Law of Ireland / Cork : Mercier Press, 1987.
801p.
ISBN 0853428174 Hbk £60.00

—DeValera's Constitution and Ours / Dublin : Gill and Macmillan, 1988.
ISBN 0717116123 Pbk £9.95

—Draft Treaty establishing the European Union and the member states : Ireland / by John Temple-Lang. – Florence : European University Institute, 1985.
38,5p.

—Irish constitution / J.M. Kelly. – 2nd ed. – Dublin : Jurist Publishing, 1984.
xxxi,741p.
Previous ed.: 1980. Includes index. Kept up to date by supplements.

CONSTITUTIONAL LAW - ISLE OF MAN

—Isle of Man and the Channel Islands : a study of their status under constitutional, international and European law / by Simon A. Horner. – Florence : European University Institute, 1984.
142p.
At head of title: European University Institute, Florence, Law Department.

—List of constitutional and Privy Council judgments affecting the Isle of Man from 1523 to 1986 and a complete year by year list of written Reasons for Judgment of Her Majesty's High Court of Justice of the Isle of Man and other Manx courts from 1884 to 1986 / compiled and with an introduction by Judy Thornley on the directions of H.M. Attorney General for the Isle of Man. – Douglas : Government Printer, 1987.
94p.
Cover title: A book of precedents.

—Minutes of evidence / Commission on the Constitution. – 6. – London : HMSO, 1970.
1: Wales - 2: Scotland - 3: Northern Ireland - 4: Scotland - 5: Wales - 6: The Channel Islands and the Isle of Man. Bound in one vol..

CONSTITUTIONAL LAW - JAPAN

—Freedom, peace and their guarantees, from the viewpoint of the Constitution of Japan / Kenji Urata. – s.l. : s.n., 1982.
p.22-45.
'Originally presented as a draft to the Waseda University Centennial International Symposium at Waseda University on August 22 and 23, 1982'. Reprinted from: Waseda bulletin of comparative law, v.2 (1982).

CONSTITUTIONAL LAW - LESOTHO

—Acts : Lesotho / v. – Maseru : Government Printer, 1966-.
Supplements to the Government gazette.

—Legal notices / v. – Maseru : Government Printer, 1966-.
Supplements to the Government gazette.

CONSTITUTIONAL LAW - MALAYSIA

—Constitution of Malaysia / Harry Groves. – 4th. – Singapore : Malayan Law Journal, 1987.
649.
Discusses citizenship, relations between the federation and the states, financial provisions, elections, the judiciary, public services, special and emergency powers, additional protection for Sabah and Sarawak, and temporary and transitional provisions.
ISBN 9971700557 Hbk

—Constitution of Malaysia : further perspectives and developments : essays in honour of Tun Mohamed Suffian / edited by F.A. Trindade and H.P. Lee. – Singapore : Oxford University Press, 1986.
xix,275p.
Includes bibliographical references and index.
ISBN 0195826442 Hbk £60.00

—Federal Constitution / Kuala Lumpur : International Law Books Services.

—Federal Constitution (Handbook) / Kuala Lumpur : International Law Books Services.

—Federal Constitution of Malaysia : a commentary / by K.V. Padmanabha Rau : assisted by Hamid Ibrahim. – Kuala Lumpur : Malaysian Current Law Journal Sdn. Bhd., 1986.
xlvi,605p.
Includes bibliographical references and index.

CONSTITUTIONAL LAW - NIGERIA

—Bibliography on the constitutions of Nigeria / compiled by Oluremi Jegede. – London : Oceana, 1981.
vi,72p; 26cm.
Includes index.

—Constitution and constitutionalism : a analysis of the basic principles of the federal constitution of Nigeria (1979) / by Moses E. Akpan. – Lagos : Paico, 1984.
xiii,133p.
Bibliography: p.128-129. - Includes index.

—Constitution of the Federal Republic of Nigeria 1979 / with annotations by Jadesola O. Akande. – London : Sweet & Maxwell, 1982.
ca.300p.
Cover title: Introduction to the Nigerian constitution.
ISBN 0421289406

—Constitutional law and military rule in Nigeria / Abiola Ojo. – Ibadan, Nigeria : Evans Brothers, 1987.
vii,316p.
ISBN 9781675691

—Doctrine of covering the field (and other constitutional matters) / by Richard O. Akinjide. – Lagos : Department of Information, 1980.
19p.

—Essays in constitutional law of Nigeria / by R.S. Bhalla. – s.l. : s.n., 1984.
v,112p.
Includes bibliographical references and index.
ISBN 9781660139

—Impeachment under the Nigerian Constitution / Igbinewedo Albert Igbinedion. – Benin City : Benfranco Printers, 1983.
76p.

—Judiciary in the second republic of Nigeria, 1979-1983 / by F. Olisa Awogu. – Onitsha : Pacific Colege Press, 1984.
x,176p.
Bibliography: p.163-164. - Includes index.
ISBN 9782347108

—Justiciability of constitutional adjudication / a paper presented by Owolabi Kolawole at the Seminar on the Constitutional Adjudication in a Presidential System of Government, a comparative American and Nigerian experience, held at the Nigerian Institute of Advanced Legal Studies, University of Lagos, on Wednesday September 2, 1981. – Lagos : Nigerian Institute of Advanced Legal Studies, 1981.
20p.

—Legal impact of the Constitution (Suspension and Modification) Decree, 1984 : on the constitution of the Federal Republic of Nigeria, 1979 / Niki Tobi. – Calabar, Nigeria : Centaur Press, 1985.
xi,110p.
Includes the text of the Constitution (Suspension and Modification) Decree 1984.

—Legal implications of the creation of more states in Nigeria : being a paper presented at the National Conference on Creation of States in Nigeria / by T. Akinola Aguda. – Ile Ife : Nigerian Institute of Advanced Legal Studies, 1981.
20p; 25cm.

—Nigeria's presidential constitution : the second experiment in constitution democracy / Ben O. Nwabueze. – London : Longman, 1985.
xiv,488p; 21cm.
ISBN 0582644836 Hbk £15.00
ISBN 0582644747 Pbk £7.50

—Nigerian constitution today / by P.U. Umoh. – Uyo, Nigeria : Modern Business Press, 1985.
x,182p.
Includes bibliographical references and index.

—Nigerian constitutional law / by Hari Chand. – 2nd ed. – Modinagar : Santosh Publishing House, 1982.
296p.
Includes index.

—Nigerian Constitutional Law Reports / Lagos : Nigerian Law Publications, 1981.
ISBN 9782325000 Hbk £60.00
ISBN 9782325007 Hbk £20.00

Vol. 2 1981.
ISBN 9782325008 Hbk £20.00

Vol. 3 1982.
ISBN 9782325009 Hbk £70.00

Vol. 4 1983.
ISBN 9782325333 Hbk £60.00

Vol. 5 1984.
ISBN 9782325147 Hbk £60.00

Vol. 6 1985.
ISBN 9782325155 Hbk £60.00

—Nigerian constitutional law reports / Suru-Lere, Lagos : Nigerian Law Publications, 1981-.

—Nigerian Grundnorm / delivered by Hon. Justice Kayode Eso on Thursday, 31st January 1985 at the University of Benin, Nigeria. – Lagos : Nigerian Law Publications, 1986.
92p.
Bibliography: p.89-90. - Includes index. Published under the auspices of Idigbe Memorial Lectures.

—Presidential Constitution of Nigeria / London : Dent (J M) & Sons, 1982.
ISBN 0905838602 Hbk £25.00

—Presidential constitution of Nigeria / B.O. Nwabueze. – London : Hurst in association with Nwamife, 1982.
xvii,558p; 23cm.
Includes index.
ISBN 0905838602 Pbk : Nigeria £19.50
ISBN 9781240458

—Selected essays on Nigerian constitutional laws / D.O. Aihe. – Benin City : Idodo Umeh Publishers Ltd., 1985.
xxviii,264p.
Bibliography: p.255-257. - Includes index.
ISBN 9782340448

CONSTITUTIONAL LAW - NORTHERN IRELAND

—Constitution of Northern Ireland : Problems and Prospects / London : Policy Studies Institute, 1981.
227p. – (Joint Studies in Public Policy).

—Constitution of Northern Ireland : problems and prospects / edited by David Watt. – London : Heinemann, 1981.
227p; 23cm.
Includes index.
ISBN 0435838075 corrected : Hbk £15.00
ISBN 0435838083 Pbk Unpriced

—Government of Northern Ireland : proposals for further discussion / London : H.M.S.O., 1980.
16p.

—Northern Ireland Act 1982 : Do-It-Yourself Devolution / Belfast : Queen's University of Belfast.
25p.

CONSTITUTIONAL LAW - PACIFIC AREA

—Pacific constitutions : proceedings of the Canberra Law Workshop VI / edited by Peter Sack. – Canberra : Law Department, Research School of Social Sciences, Australian National University, 1982.
xi,374p.
Bibliography: p.361-374.
ISBN 0867841648

CONSTITUTIONAL LAW - PACIFIC ISLANDS

—Constitutional Case Studies of Pacific Island States / Peter Bayne. – Suva : University of the South Pacific, Institute of Pacific Studies.

—Constitutions of the Independent States of Melanesia and Micronesia / Suva : University of the South Pacific, Institute of Pacific Studies, 1986.
432p.

CONSTITUTIONAL LAW - PAPUA NEW GUINEA

—Constitutional review jurisdiction in Papua New Guinea / researched and written by Peter Bayne. – Waigani : Law Reform Commission of Papua New Guinea, 1981.
iii,64p. – (Occasional paper).

—Papua New Guinea, in the Supreme Court of Justice ... In the matter of a reference under section 18 of the Constitution, and in the matter of Ralph Rakhinand Premdas against the Independent State of Papua New Guinea, and others. Re Rooney: being a transcript of the proceedings 27th August - 5th and 11th September 1979 / Port Moresby : Council of Law Reporting for Papua New Guinea, 1981.
vi,390p; 34cm.
Cover title: The Rooney case.

CONSTITUTIONAL LAW - PHILIPPINES

—New Constitution of the Philippines Explained (English and Pilipino) / National Book Store. – Manila : National Book Store, 1983.
92p.
ISBN 9710816780 Pbk £1.00

CONSTITUTIONAL LAW - PORTUGAL

—Constitution of the Portuguese Republic / 1st revision, 1982. – Paris : Association of Secretaries General of Parliaments, 1983.
166p.
Published under the auspices of the Inter-Parliamentary Union.

CONSTITUTIONAL LAW - SCOTLAND

—Of presbyters and kings : Church and State in the law of Scotland / Francis Lyall. – Aberdeen : Aberdeen University Press, 1980.
xii,208p; 22cm.
Includes index.
ISBN 0080257151 £10.00

CONSTITUTIONAL LAW - SINGAPORE

—Introduction to the Singapore legal system / by Helena H.M. Chan. – Singapore : Malayan Law Journal Pte., 1986.
vi,140p.
Covers the legal history of Singapore, sources of law, structure of government, legal institutions, civil and criminal procedure, and a chapter devoted to legal culture and the future development of the law.
ISBN 9971700549

—Statutes of the Republic of Singapore / prepared and published by the Law Revision Commission under the authority of the Revised Edition of the Laws Act (Chapter 275). – Rev. ed. 1985. 12. – Singapore : Government Printer, 1986.
looseleaf.
Includes index.

CONSTITUTIONAL LAW - SOUTH AFRICA

—Annual report / Department of Development Planning : Constitutional Development Services. – Pretoria : Government Printer, 1987.
Annual reports of two bodies published together. Text in Afikaans and English.

—Constitutional change in South Africa : the next five years / (edited by) W. H. B. Dean and Dirk Van Zyl Smit. – Cape Town : Juta, 1983.
8,125p.
ISBN 0702113719

—Report / Department of Constitutional Development and Planning. – 3. – Pretoria : Government Printer, 1983.
Text in Afrikaans and English.

—South Africa and the consociational option : a constitutional analysis / by L.J. Boulle. – Cape Town : Juta, 1984.
xii, 270 p.; 25 cm.
Includes indexes. Bibliography: p. 227-229.
ISBN 0702114340 pbk.

—South African Constitution : Euphoria and Rejection / Johannesburg : Witwatersrand University Press, 1982.
vi, 20p.
ISBN 0854947434 Pbk £3.00

CONSTITUTIONAL LAW - SOUTH AUSTRALIA

—Report ... relating to the inherited imperial law and constitutional statutes / Law Reform Committee of South Australia. – Adelaide : Government Printer, 1985.
9p. – (96th report).

CONSTITUTIONAL LAW - SRI LANKA

—Judicial Role Under Constitutions of Ceylon (Sri Lanka) / Colombo : 16.00.

—Mechanics of constitutional change : the Sri Lankan style / by D.C. Jayasuriya. – Nawala, Sri Lanka : Asian Pathfinder Publishers, 1982.
130p.
Bibliography: p.103-125. - Includes index.

CONSTITUTIONAL LAW - ST. CHRISTOPHER AND NEVIS

—Report of the Saint Christopher and Nevis Constitutional Conference : London, December 1982 / London : H.M.S.O., 1983.
31p; 25cm.
ISBN 0101879601 unbound £2.95

CONSTITUTIONAL LAW - TANZANIA

—Subsidiary legislation to the Gazette of the United Republic of Tanzania / Tanzania. – v. – Dar es Salaam : Government Printer, 1964-.

CONSTITUTIONAL LAW - TRANSKEI

—Constitutions of Transkei, Bophuthatswana, Venda and Ciskei / editors M.P. Vorster, M. Wiechers, D.J. van Vuuren. – Durban : Butterworths, 1985.
269p.
Includes the texts of the constitutions.
ISBN 040901964X

CONSTITUTIONAL LAW - TURKS AND CAICOS ISLANDS

—Report of the constitutional commission 1986 / presented to parliament by the Secretary of State for Foreign and Commonwealth Affairs by Command of Her Majesty April 1987. – London : H.M.S.O., 1987.
iv,43p.
Chairman: Roy Marshall. At head of t.p.: Turks and Caicos Islands.
ISBN 0101011121

CONSTITUTIONAL LAW - UNITED STATES

—Arizona : Its Constitution and Government / 2nd ed. – University Press of America, 1988.
ISBN 0819161446 Pbk £9.25

—Constitutional construction / Chester James Antieau. – London : Oceana Publications, 1982.
xxiv, 255 p.; 25 cm.
Includes bibliographical references and index.
ISBN 037920682X

—Federalism : the founders' design / by Raoul Berger. – Norman : University of Oklahoma Press, 1987.
224p; 24cm.
Includes bibliography and index.
ISBN 0806120592 £16.50

—Fundamental liberties and rights : a 50-State index / by Barbara Faith Sachs : Legislative Drafting Research Fund of Columbia University. – London : Oceana Publications, 1980.
1 v.; 27 cm.
Index to Constitutions of the United States, national and State. 'First in a series of subject matter indices designed to replace the Index digest of State constitutions.'. Loose-leaf for updating.
ISBN 0379204134 £35.00

—Legal English 2 : an Introduction to the American Constitution / Paris : Cujas, 1986.
184p.

—Power and policy in quest of the law : essays in honor of Eugene Victor Rostow / edited by Myres S. McDougal, W. Michael Reisman. – The Hague : M. Nijhoff Publishers, 1984.
640p.
Bibliography: p441-447. Includes index.
ISBN 9024729114 Hbk £235.00

—United States Constitution : Its Birth, Growth and Influence in Asia / Hong Kong : Hong Kong University Press, 1988.
ISBN 9622092102 Pbk £19.00

CONSTITUTIONAL LAW - VENDA

—Constitutions of Transkei, Bophuthatswana, Venda and Ciskei / editors M.P. Vorster, M. Wiechers, D.J. van Vuuren. – Durban : Butterworths, 1985.
269p.
Includes the texts of the constitutions.
ISBN 040901964X

CONSTITUTIONAL LAW - WEST GERMANY

—Constitutional and legislative provisions concerning the organisation of regional government / Council of Europe. – Strasbourg : Council of Europe, 1981.
31p; 30cm.

—Draft Treaty establishing the European Union : report on the Federal Republic of Germany / by Carl Otto Lenz. – Florence : European University Institute, 1985.
21p.

—Law on the Federal Constitutional Court : documents on politics and society in the Federal Republic of Germany / Oguz Akalin. – Bonn : Inter Nationes, 1982.
69p.
Bibliography: p.69. Prepared by Oguz Akalin.

—Rights, institutions and impact of international law according to the German Basic Law : the contribution of the Federal Republic of Germany to the Second World Congress of the International Association of Constitutional law / edited by Christian Starck. – Baden-Baden : Nomos, 1987.
264p.
Includes bibliographical references and index.
ISBN 3789013749

CONSTITUTIONAL LAW - ZAMBIA

—Statutory instruments : Zambia / v. – Lusaka : Government Printer, 1964-.
Published as separate supplements to the Republic of Zambia government gazette.

CONSTITUTIONAL LAW - ZIMBABWE

—Constitution of Zimbabwe / Paris : Association of Secretaries General of Parliaments, 1980.
99p.

—Southern Rhodesia, report of the Constitutional Conference, Lancaster House, London, September-December 1979 .. / London : H.M.S.O., 1980.
vi,57p; 25cm.
ISBN 0101780206 £2.75

—Statutory instruments : Zimbabwe / Salisbury : Government Printer, 1980.
21cm.
Continues the numbering of the Southern Rhodesia statutory instruments issued 1st January - 17th April 1980. Supplement to: Zimbabwe government gazette.

CONSTITUTIONAL LAW (COMMUNIST)

—Constitutions of the communist world / edited by William B. Simons. – Alphen aan den Rijn : Sijthoff & Noordhoff, 1980.
xvii,644p.

CONSUMER CREDIT

—Commercial and consumer credit : an introduction / by Aubrey L. Diamond. – London : Butterworths, 1982.
xxvii,379p.
Includes index.
ISBN 0406574057

—Law of borrowing / London : Sweet & Maxwell, 1989.
Account of the institutional framework within which borrowing takes place, and consideration of the regulation and supervision of banks, building societies, the securities market, the wholesale money market, and consumer credit transactions. Chapter dealing with the characteristics of a loan, and types of loan.
ISBN 0421000000 Llf

CONSUMER CREDIT - AUSTRALIA

—Consumer Credit Law in Australia / S. Barnes. – Sydney : Butterworths, 1988.
592p.

—Consumer Credit Law in Australia : a Commentary on the New Credit Legislation / Sheenagh Barnes. – Butterworths, 1988.
746p.
ISBN 0409494496 Hbk £89.00

CONSUMER CREDIT – AUSTRALIA – NEW SOUTH WALES

—Credit revolution : papers from the seminar on the N.S.W. Credit Bill 1981, organised by the Faculty of Law, University of N.S.W., the N.S.W. Department of Consumer Affairs & the Australian Finance Conference, 13 July 1981 / 1. – Kensington, N.S.W. : Faculty of Law, University of New South Wales, 1981.
various pagings.
At head of title: The University of New South Wales, Faculty of Law.

—New South Wales consumer credit legislation / with annotations by Jane R. Levine. – North Ryde, N.S.W. : CCH Australia, 1985.
xl,449p.
Includes index.
ISBN 0869038354

CONSUMER CREDIT – AUSTRALIA – VICTORIA

—Victorian consumer credit legislation / with annotations by Jane R. Levine. – North Ryde, N.S.W. : CCH Australia, 1984.
xl,353p.
Includes index.
ISBN 086903779X

CONSUMER CREDIT – ENGLAND

—Sale of goods and consumer credit / A.P. Dobson. – 3rd ed. – London : Sweet & Maxwell, 1984.
xxvii,369p; 22cm.
Previous ed.: 1979. Includes index.
ISBN 0421292105 Hbk £14.50
ISBN 0421292202 Pbk £9.50

—Sale of goods and consumer credit in a nutshell / Alan Bond. – London : Sweet and Maxwell, 1980.
vii,88p; 18cm.
Includes index.
ISBN 0421265809 Pbk £1.50

CONSUMER CREDIT – GREAT BRITAIN

—Commercial and Consumer Credit - An Introduction / London : Butterworths, 1982.
ISBN 0406574057 Pbk £14.95

—Consumer Credit / Oxford : Blackwell Scientific, 1987.
ISBN 0003833038 Hbk £19.95

—Consumer Credit / London : Collins, 1987.
256p.
ISBN 0003833038 Hbk £20.00

—Consumer Credit / 1st ed. – Plymouth : Macdonald & Evans, 1981.
176p. – (M and E Handbook Ser.).
ISBN 0712103996 Hbk £4.50

—Consumer Credit / Plymouth : Macdonald & Evans, 1981.
ISBN 0712103996 Pbk £4.95

—Consumer Credit Act 1974 : credit charges : how to calculate the total charge for credit and the annual percentage rate of charge / Office of Fair Trading. – London : The Office, 1980.
20p.

—Consumer Credit Act Manual / 3rd ed. – London : Longman Professional, 1986.
ISBN 0851211003 Pbk £21.00

—Consumer credit act manual / Francis Bennion. – 2nd ed. – London : Oyez, 1981.
ix,208p; 24cm.
Previous ed. : 1978. Includes index.
ISBN 0851205658 Pbk Unpriced

—Consumer Credit Agreements / Fielding. – London : Waterlow, 1985.
ISBN 0080392008 Pbk £18.50

—Consumer Credit Agreements Act / Nettlebed Publications, 1985.
ISBN 0946628025 £45.00

—Consumer credit : law and practice / by Alexander G.L. Hill-Smith. – London : Sweet & Maxwell, 1985.
xxxi,330p; 25cm.
Examines the terminology of the 1974 Consumer Credit Act, the agreements to which the regulations apply, withdrawal and cancellation, debtors' and creditors' rights, the provision of security, and the powers of the court as well as enforcement provisions. Appendix contains a model Cancellable Hire-Purchase Agreement.
ISBN 0421342900 Pbk £29

—Consumer Credit : Points For the Practitioner / London : Law Society, 1985.
19p. – (Nineteen Eighty-Five Crash Course Transcripts).

—Consumers and credit / National Consumer Council. – London : The Council, 1980.
viii,324p; 21cm.
ISBN 0905653297 Pbk £14.50

—Encyclopaedia of Consumer Credit Law / London : Sweet & Maxwell, 1988.
ISBN 0421208104 £175.00

CONSUMER CREDIT – LAW AND LEGISLATION – AUSTRALIA

—Australian consumer sales and credit law reporter / North Ryde, N.S.W. : CCH Australia, 1977.
looseleaf.
Looseleaf issues accompanied by a summary report. - Uniform credit law proposals 1978; Trade Practices Commission guidelines 1974-1982; and 1980- cases filed in transfer binders. 'Uniform credit law proposals 1978' filed in transfer binder.
ISBN 0869030760 v.3
ISBN 0869033077

CONSUMER CREDIT – NEW ZEALAND

—Credit Contracts Act 1981 : an annotated edition of the Statute / by D. F. Dugdale. – Wellington : Butterworths, 1981.
vii,99p.
Includes index.
ISBN 0409601322

CONSUMER CREDIT – SCOTLAND

—Consumer Debt Problems of Scottish Families / Scottish Association of Citizens Advice Bureau, 1988.
ISBN 0905831063 Pbk £2.00

—Debt counselling : an assessment of the services and facilities available to consumer debtors in Scotland / by Ann R. Millar. – Edinburgh : Central Research Unit, 1980.
vii,83p; 30cm.

CONSUMER CREDIT – SOUTH AFRICA

—Law of credit agreements and hire-purchase in South Africa / P. J. Aronstam. – 5th ed. – Cape Town : Juta, 1982.
lii,505p.
Previous ed., 1978, entitled: The law of hire-purchase in South Africa. Bibliography: p.xxi-xxiii. - Includes index.
ISBN 070211250X

CONSUMER LAW

—Commercial and Consumer Law / Stephenson. – London : Financial Training, 1987.
– (SWOT).
ISBN 1851850430 Pbk £7.50

—Commercial and Consumer Transactions / 2nd ed. – Toronto : Edmond-Montgomery, 1987.
ca 1,400p.
ISBN 0920722202 Hbk £96.00

—Consumers or Victims? / North Sydney : Allen & Unwin, 1982.
172p.
ISBN 0868610208 Pbk £15.95

—Effect of international consumer protection laws in Europe : third European Seminar on Product Liability, October 15th and 16th 1980 at the Mount Royal Hotel, Marble Arch, London / organised by the Institute of Quality Assurance. – London : European Organisation for Quality Control, 1980.
253p.
'Sponsored by the National Council for Quality & Reliability'. At head of title: European Organisation for Quality Control.

—European consumer law : prospects for integration of consumer law and policy within the European Community : proceedings of the seminar held in Louvain-la-Neuve on May 14 and 15, 1981 / Th. Bourgoignie, ed. – Louvain-la-Neuve : Cabay, 1982.
x,425p. – (Collection droit et consommation).
Includes bibliographical references. At head of title: Centre de Droit de la Consommation.
ISBN 2870770901

—Laws on the defense of the consumer / German Cavelier. – Bogota : Cavelier Abogados, 1985.
41 leaves.
Contains the text of relevant laws, decrees and resolutions in English.

—Legal protection of the collective interests of consumers by consumer agencies : Recommendation no. R(81)2 adopted by the Committee of Ministers of the Council of Europe on 23 January 1981 and explanatory memorandum / Council of Europe. – Strasbourg : Council of Europe, 1981.
19p; 21cm.
'Prepared by a committee of experts set up under the authority of the European Committee on Legal Cooperation' - verso t.p.. At head of cover title: Council of Europe, Legal Affairs.

—No access to law : alternatives to the American judicial system / Laura Nader editor. – New York : Academic Press, 1980.
xxiii,540p; 24cm.
Includes bibliographies and index.
ISBN 0125135602 Hbk £15.40
ISBN 015135629 Pbk £8.40

—Papers and Comments Delivered at the Eighth Annual Workshop on Commercial and Consumer Law / Vancouver : University of British Columbia, Faculty of Commerce & Business Administration, 1980.
– (Toronto Butterworths and Co. Ser.).

—Role of criminal law in consumer protection / European Committee on Crime Problems. – Strasbourg : Council of Europe, 1983.
24p; 21cm.
Report and recommendations of the European Committee on Crime Problems on the role of criminal law in protecting consumers from exploitation by suppliers.
ISBN 928710218X £1.25

—Role of Industrial Property in the Protection of Consumers / Geneva : World Intellectual Property Organization, 1983.
69p.

CONSUMER LAW – AUSTRALIA

—Consumer protection law and theory / edited by A.J. Duggan and L.W. Darvall. – Sydney : Law Book Co., 1980.
x,269p; 24cm.
ISBN 0455201331

—Consumer Protection Law in Australia / L.W. Maher. – 3rd ed. – Butterworths, 1987.
441p.
ISBN 0409491675 Hbk £69.00
ISBN 0409491683 Pbk £56.00

—Consumer protection law in Australia / John Goldring, Laurence W. Maher. – 2nd ed. – Sydney : Butterworths, 1983.
xxx,413p.
Includes index.
ISBN 0409490903

—Federal deceptive practices and misleading advertising law : judgements, materials and policy / Warren Pengilley and Alan A. Ransom. – Sydney : Legal Books Pty., 1987.
lxiii,1184p.
Bibliography: pp.1021-1022. - Includes index.
ISBN 0949553344

—Guide to amendments to the Trade Practices Act / Trade Practices Commission. – Canberra : Trade Practices Commission, 1986.
13 leaves.

—Sale of Goods and Consumer Law /. – North Ryde : Law Book Co, 1986.
x, 102p. – (Nutshells).
ISBN 0455206783

—Sales and consumer law in Australia and New Zealand / by K.C.T. Sutton. – Being 3rd ed. of The law of sale of goods in Australia and New Zealand. – Sydney : Law Book Co., 1983.
lxx,658p.
Includes bibliographical references and index.
ISBN 0455204675

—Trade practices and consumer protection : a commentary on the Trade Practices Act 1974 / by G.Q. Taperell, R.B. Vermeesch, D.J. Harland. – 3rd ed. – Sydney : Butterworths, 1983.
liii,922p.
Previous ed.: 1978. Includes bibliographies and index. Legislation set against the economic and commercial background in which it operates.
ISBN 0409491217 Pbk

CONSUMER LAW – BELGIUM

—Consumer legislation in Belgium and Luxemburg : a study prepared for the EC Commission / M. Fontaine, Th. Bourgoignie : translated from French by Michael Corkery. – Wokingham, Berkshire : Van Nostrand Reinhold (UK), 1982.
xvi, 229 p.; 24 cm.
Includes bibliographical references and indexes. Translation of: Droit de la consommation en Belgique et Luxembourg.
ISBN 0442304188

CONSUMER LAW – CANADA

—Canadian Market Place : a Consumer Rights Handbook / Patricia McNeill. – Toronto : Canadian Broadcasting Corporation Enterprises.
160p.
ISBN 0887941192 Pbk £5.95

—Commercial and consumer transactions : cases, text and materials / by Jacob S. Ziegel, Benjamin Geva. – Toronto : Emond-Montgomery, 1981.
xlv,1230p.
Bibliography: p.xliii-xliv. - Includes index.
ISBN 0920722040

—Consumer Law / Daniel J. Baum. – Toronto : IPI Publishing, 1983.
84p. – (You and the Law Ser.).
ISBN 0458961302 Pbk £7.95

—Consumer protection, environmental law, and corporate power / Ivan Bernier and Andree Lajoie, research coordinators. – Toronto : University of Toronto Press, 1985.
xv, 220 p.; 23 cm.
'Published ... in cooperation with the Royal Commission on the Economic Union and Development Prospects for Canada and the Canadian Government Publishing Centre, Supply and Services Canada.'. Includes bibliographies.
ISBN 0802072968 pbk.

—Financing Consumer Sales and Product Defences in Canada and the United States / Agincourt : Carswell, 1984.
382p.
This book is a collection of papers and discussion at a Legal Research Institute conference on the question of how well lawyers, police, courts, and lawmakers are perceived to deliver justice and the rule of law to Canadian society.

—Help : Marketplace Handbook of Consumer Rights in Canada / Toronto : Canadian Broadcasting Corporation Enterprises.
84p.

—Papers and comments delivered at the eighth annual Workshop on Commercial and Consumer Law, Toronto, October 20-21, 1978 / edited by Jacob S. Ziegel, with the assistance of Owen Johnson. - Toronto : Butterworths, 1980.
vi, 231 p.; 24 cm.
At head of title: Canadian Association of Law Teachers, Faculty of Law, University of Toronto, and the Osgoode Hall Law School of York University. Includes bibliographical references.
ISBN 0409879606

—Papers and comments delivered at the ninth annual Workshop on Commercial and Consumer Law, Toronto, November 2-3, 1979 / edited by Jacob S. Ziegel. - Toronto : Butterworths, 1981.
xi,279p.
Includes bibliographical references. At head of cover title: Canadian Association of Law Teachers, Faculty of Law, University of Toronto and the Osgoode Hall Law School of York University.
ISBN 0409879614

—Papers and comments delivered at the tenth annual Workshop on Commercial and Consumer Law, Toronto, October 17-18, 1980 / edited by Jacob S. Ziegel. - Toronto : Butterworths, 1982.
x,218p.
Includes bibliographical references. At head of title: Canadian Association of Law Teachers, Faculty of Law, University of Toronto, and the Osgoode Hall Law School of York University..
ISBN 0409879622

—Perspectives on the harmonization of law in Canada / Ronald C.C. Cuming research coordinator. - Toronto : University of Toronto Press in cooperation with the Royal Commission on the Economic Union and Development Prospects for Canada and the Canadian Government Publishing Centre, 1985.
xviii,178p. - (Collected research studies).
Bibliography: p.176-177.
ISBN 0802073026

—Tax Facts 4 : The Canadian Consumer Tax Index and You, No. 4 / Vancouver : Fraser Institute.
ISBN 0889750726 Hbk £4.95

—Tenth Annual Workshop on Commercial and Consumer Law / Toronto : Butterworths, 1982.
232p.

—Used Car Buyers Protection Act, 1983, Bill 131 : An Act to Protect the Purchasers of Used Motor Vehicles / Ontario : Ontario Government Publications Service, 1983.
4p.

CONSUMER LAW - CANADA - BRITISH COLUMBIA

—Buyer's lien : a new consumer remedy / Law Reform Commission of British Columbia. - Vancouver : The Commission, 1986.
iii,52p. - (Working paper).
Includes bibliographical references.

CONSUMER LAW - ENGLAND

—Law of consumer protection and fair trading / by Brian W. Harvey and Deborah L. Parry. - 3rd ed. - London : Butterworths, 1987.
xxxii,435p; 22cm.
Includes parts 1-4 of the Consumer Protection Act 1987.
ISBN 0406222630

CONSUMER LAW - EUROPEAN COMMUNITY

—Consumer Law in the EEC / London : Sweet & Maxwell, 1984.
ISBN 0421326409 Pbk £10.00

—Consumer Law Statutes / 5th ed. - London : Monitor Press, 1986.
ISBN 0906533457 Pbk £14.95

—Consumer Redress : Supplement to the EC Bulletin / Kirchberg : Commission of the European Communities.
43p.

—E.E.C. Consumer Law / Dordrecht : Kluwer, 1986.
488p.
ISBN 9064394067 Pbk £155.00

—EEC consumer law / Bruxelles : Story-Scientia, 1986.
xviii, 432p.
Bibliography: p.391-424. - Includes index.
ISBN 9065442820

—European regulation of advertising : supranational regulation of advertising in the European economic community / by Rein Rijkens, Gordon E. Miracle. - Amsterdam : North-Holland, 1986.
xxxiv, 375 p.; 25 cm.
Includes index. Bibliography: p. 337-358.
ISBN 0444879722

—Legal Protection of the Collective Interests of Consumers by Governments by Consumer Agencies : Recommendation No. R 812/2 and Explanatory Memorandum / Strasbourg : Council of Europe, 1981.

—New Impetus for Consumer Protection Policy / Luxembourg : Office for Official Publications of the European Communities.
17p.
ISBN 9282566498 Pbk £100.00

—New impetus for consumer protection policy / (communication from the Commission to the Council). - Luxembourg : Office for Official Publications of the European Communities, 1985.
23p.
At head of title: Commission of the European Communities.
ISBN 9282556689

—Product differentiation in terms of packaging presentation, advertising, trade marks, etc. : an assessment of the legal situation regarding pharmaceuticals and certain other consumer goods / Jules Stuyck. - Antwerp : Kluwer, 1983.
xv,118p.
Bibliography: p.111-118.
ISBN 9065440844

—Propeosed EC unfair contract terms directive / Department of Trade and Industry. Consumer Affairs Division 3A. - London : The Department, 1987.
45p.
Contents include: Futher draft articles for discussion on unfair terms of contract / European Commission. Also includes examples of relevant European national legislation.

CONSUMER LAW - GREAT BRITAIN

—4 what it's worth / Harriet Wilson. - London : Thames, 1988.
192p; 20cm.
Includes index.
ISBN 0356148629 Pbk £5.95

—Consumer and commercial statutes / London : Longman Professional (UK), 1989.
Covers the Bill of Lading 1855 through to the Consumer Protection Act of 1987, including the EEC Directive on Product Liability. Set out in chronological order including amendments to date.
ISBN 0851215173 Hbk £22.50

—Consumer and trading law : cases and materials / C.J. Miller, Brian W. Harvey. - London : Butterworths, 1985.
xiv,550p.
Includes index.
ISBN 0406012601 Hbk
ISBN 040601261X Pbk

—Consumer and Trading Law - Cases and Materials / Harvey. - London : Butterworths, 1985.
ISBN 0406012601 Hbk £36.00
ISBN 040601261X Pbk £23.95

—Consumer Law / 2nd ed. - Plymouth : Macdonald & Evans, 1986.
ISBN 0712106774 Pbk £4.95

—Consumer law / Peter Walker. - 1st ed. - London : Longman Professional (UK), 1988.
- (Longman Practice Notes).
Covers consumer safety, unsolicited goods, resale prices, sale of goods and services, and consumer credit. Contains precedents and checklists.
ISBN 0851214495 Hbk £9.95

—Consumer law / M.J. Leder. - 2nd ed. - London : Pitman, 1986.
xxxiii,220p; 22cm. - (M & E handbook series).
Previous ed.: Plymouth : Macdonald & Evans, 1980.
Includes index.
ISBN 0712106774 Pbk £4.95

—Consumer Law / Plymouth : Macdonald & Evans, 1980.
232p. - (M and E Handbook Ser.).
ISBN 0712103937 Hbk £3.75

—Consumer law and practice / by Robert Lowe and Geoffrey F. Woodroffe. - 2nd ed. - London : Sweet and Maxwell, 1985.
400p.
Includes the Supply of Goods and Services Act 1982, and explains the Consumer Credit Act 1974 regulations. Deals with the consumer and civil law, the consumer and the criminal law, fair trading, consumer credit, the EEC dimension, and selected codes of practice.
ISBN 0421334002 Hbk £17.75
ISBN 042133410X Pbk £14.00

—Consumer Law for the Motor Trade / 2nd ed. - London : Butterworths, 1987.
ISBN 0406425914 Pbk £13.95

—Consumer Law for the Motor Trade / London : Butterworths, 1981.
This work is a practical non-technical introduction to the law of automobile sales and repairs. The book provides references to leading cases and relevant statutes are included in the text.
ISBN 0406425906 Pbk

—Consumer Law for the Small Business / London : Kogan Page, 1983.
160p.
ISBN 0850386187 Hbk £11.95
ISBN 0850386489 Pbk £5.95

—Consumer law statutes / 3rd. ed. - Sudbury : Monitor, 1982.
359p; 21cm.
Previous ed.: London : Monitor, 1980. 'Proposed alterations' (1 sheet) as insert.
ISBN 0906533031 Pbk Unpriced

—Consumer, Society and the Law / Diamond. - 4th ed. - Pelican, 1981.
ISBN 0140206477 Pbk £4.50

—Consumer, society and the law / Gordon Borrie and Aubrey L. Diamond. - 4th ed. - Harmondsworth : Penguin, 1981.
360p; 20cm. - (Pelican books).
Previous ed.: 1973. Bibliography: p340-343. - Includes index. .
ISBN 0140206477 Pbk £2.95

—Consumers and the law / Ross Cranston. - 2nd ed. - London : Weidenfeld and Nicolson, 1984.
xli, 503p.
ISBN 029778272X

—Consumers : Know Your Rights / 3rd ed. - London : Oyez Longman, 1983.
- (It's Your Law Ser.).
ISBN 0851207286 Hbk £8.50
ISBN 0851207278 Pbk £4.95

—Consumers Know Your Rights (It's Your Law) / 3rd ed. - London : Longman Professional, 1983.
ISBN 0851207804 Pbk £6.25

—Consuming secrets : how official secrecy affects everyday life in Britain / edited by Rosemary Delbridge and Martin Smith : foreword by Harold Evans. - London : Burnett, 1982.
x,249p; 22cm.
Bibliography: p239-241. - Includes index. At head of title: The National Consumer Council.
ISBN 0091475902 Hbk Unpriced
ISBN 0091475910 Pbk £4.95

—Criminal law and consumer protection / by Graham Stephenson. - Chichester : Rose, 1983.
xxxv,151p; 22cm.
Includes index.
ISBN 0859923096 Pbk £12.00

—Development of consumer law and policy - bold spirits and timorous souls / by Sir Gordon Borrie. - London : Published under the auspices of the Hamlyn Trust by Stevens, 1984.
xii,138p; 18cm.
Includes index.
ISBN 0420467904 Pbk Unpriced
ISBN 0420468005 Pbk £5.85

—Development of Consumer Law and Policy (Hamlyn 36) / London : Sweet & Maxwell, 1984.
ISBN 0420467904 Hbk £14.50
ISBN 0420468005 Pbk £6.25

—Encyclopedia of consumer law / general editor : W.H. Thomas ; Scottish editor : Matthew G. Clarke. - London : Sweet & Maxwell, 1980.
1v.(loose-leaf).
ISBN 0421253207

—General duty to trade fairly : a discussion paper / Office of Fair Trading. - London : The Office, 1986.
73p.
Bibliography: p.72-73.

—Guide to Consumer Protection Act / Oxford : Croner Publications, 1987.
ISBN 1851850783 Pbk £11.95

—Guide to the Consumer Protection Act 1987 / Bicester : CCH Editions Ltd, 1988.
Covers what products are covered by the Act, who is liable, and what a defect is, the type of damages recoverable, commencement and limitation, the general safety duty, safety regulations, notices and forfeiture, defences to criminal prosecutions, and civil liability for unsafe goods.
ISBN 0863251358 Pbk £16.00

—Guide to the Consumer Protection Act 1987 / London : CCH, 1988.
ISBN 0863251358 Pbk

—Hiring and Leasing : Practice and Precedents / K. V. Prichard Jones. - London : Butterworths, 1986.
A practical guide to the issues of leasing for the business attorney in the United Kingdom. An extensive appendix of caselaw and commentary is provided.
ISBN 0406101140 Pbk

—Law of Consumer Protection and Fair Trading / 3rd ed. – London : Butterworths, 1987.
ISBN 0406222622 Hbk £25.00
ISBN 0406222630 Pbk £17.95

—Law of consumer protection and fair trading / Brian W. Harvey. – 2nd ed. – London : Butterworths, 1982.
xxviii,424p.
Previous ed.: 1978. Bibliography: p.391-397. - Includes index.
ISBN 0406222606 Pbk
ISBN 0406222614

—Memorandum and articles of association of Consumers' Association : incorporated 18 March 1957 / Consumers' Association. – London : Consumers' Association, 1981.
32p.
At foot of cover: The Companies Act 1948: company limited by guarantee and not having a share capital no. 580128.

—Outline of the law of product liability and consumer protection / by Ronald Irving. – Chichester : Barry Rose, 1980.
312p.
Includes index. Includes texts of the Sale of Goods Act 1979 and the Unfair Contract Terms Act 1977.
ISBN 0859921662

—Practical approach to contract and consumer law / Sewell. – London : Financial Training, 1984.
ISBN 0906322456 Pbk £12.95

—Product liability : the new law under the Consumer Protection Act 1987 / by Rodney Nelson-Jones and Peter Stewart. – London : Fourmat, 1987.
207p.
Contains the text of the Act.
ISBN 1851900349

—Protecting consumers and the public at large / Product Liability Briefing, 1988.
ISBN 1870317157 Pbk £6.50

—Safety of goods / presented to Parliament by the Secretary of State for Trade and Industry. – London : H.M.S.O., 1985.
10p.
ISBN 0101930208

—Service please : services and the law : a consumer view / prepared for the National Consumer Council by Barbara Lantin and Geoffrey Woodroffe. – London : National Consumer Council, 1981.
35p; 30cm.
ISBN 0905653386 Pbk Unpriced

—Small print : the language and layout of consumer contracts : Report to the National Consumer Council / Martin Cutts and Chrissie Maher : Plain English Campaign. – London : National Consumer Council, 1983.
39p.
ISBN 0905653661

—Supply of Goods and Services Act 1982 / London : Longman Professional, 1982.
ISBN 0851206727 Pbk £16.50

—Trade Description Act 1970 / London : Wildy & Sons.

CONSUMER LAW - GREAT BRITAIN

—Sale of goods, consumer credit and bills of exchange, cheques and promissory notes / Edinburgh : W Green & Son, 1983.
Offprint from the author's Scots Mercantile law of chapters covering sale of goods and consumer law.
ISBN 041400714X

CONSUMER LAW - INDIA

—Consumer Protection and Legal Control : Essays and Papers of the U.G.C. National Seminar at University of Cochin / Lucknow : Eastern Book Company, 1984.
346p.

—Consumers, Crimes and the Law / New Delhi : Ashish Publishing House, 1987.
370p.
ISBN 8170240794 Hbk £250.00

CONSUMER LAW - LUXEMBOURG

—Consumer legislation in Belgium and Luxemburg : a study prepared for the EC Commission / M. Fontaine, Th. Bourgoignie : translated from French by Michael Corkery. – Wokingham, Berkshire : Van Nostrand Reinhold (UK), 1982.
xvi, 229 p.; 24 cm.
Includes bibliographical references and indexes. Translation of: Droit de la consommation en Belgique et Luxembourg.
ISBN 0442304188

CONSUMER LAW - NEW ZEALAND

—Consumer law in New Zealand / R.D. Mulholland. – Palmerston North N.Z. : Dunmore Press, 1982.
163p.
Includes index.
ISBN 0908564821

—Sales and consumer law in Australia and New Zealand / by K.C.T. Sutton. – Being 3rd ed. of The law of sale of goods in Australia and New Zealand. – Sydney : Law Book Co., 1983.
lxx,658p.
Includes bibliographical references and index.
ISBN 0455204675

—Trade Practices and Consumer Protection / R. B. Vermeesch. – 3rd ed. – Wellington : Butterworths.

CONSUMER LAW - PAPUA NEW GUINEA

—Consumer protection / Law Reform Commission of Papua New Guinea. – Waigani : The Commission, 1981.
18p. – (LRC working paper).
Includes summary in Papuan.

CONSUMER LAW - SCOTLAND

—Class actions in the Scottish courts : a new way for consumers to obtain redress? / Glasgow : Scottish Consumer Council, 1982.
v,53p; 30cm.
ISBN 0907067123 Pbk Unpriced

—Debt counselling : an assessment of the services and facilities available to consumer debtors in Scotland / by Ann R. Millar. – Edinburgh : Central Research Unit, 1980.
vii,83p; 30cm.

CONSUMER LAW - SOUTH AFRICA

—South African law conference 1981 : consumer protection / Suid-Afrikaanse Regskonferensie 1981 : Verbruikersbeskerming : papers delivered at the SA Law Conference, Durban, 13-16 April 1981. – Pretoria : Association of Law Societies of the Republic of South Africa, 1981.
63p.
Includes bibliographies. Includes six articles in English and two in Afrikaans.
ISBN 0620057319

CONSUMER LAW - SWEDEN

—Consumer protection by public control and legal regulation : report from a symposium in Bastad, Sweden, 21-24 September 1981 / Lund : Juridiska Foreningen i Lund, 1984.
46p.
ISBN 9154416310

—Law and the weaker party : an Anglo-Swedish comparative study / general editors: Steve Anderman...et al. – Abingdon : Professional Books, 1981.

Vol. 2 : The English experience, edited by Steve Anderman / general editors: Steve Anderman...et al.. – 1981.

Vol. 3 : Swedish statutory material : edited by Alan C. Neal and Anders Victorin / general editors: Steve Anderman...et al.. – 1981.

CONSUMER LAW - UNITED KINGDOM

—Guide to Consumer Protection Law / Chichester : Barry Rose.
173p.
ISBN 0859921247 Hbk £5.25

CONSUMER LAW - UNITED STATES

—Economics of consumer protection : a critique of the Chicago School case against intervention / A.J. Duggan. – Adelaide : Adelaide Law Review Association, 1982.
xii,151p.
Includes index.
ISBN 0908448015 Hbk

—Financing Consumer Sales and Product Defences in Canada and the United States / Agincourt : Carswell, 1984.
382p.
This book is a collection of papers and discussion at a Legal Research Institute conference on the question of how well lawyers, police, courts, and lawmakers are perceived to deliver justice and the rule of law to Canadian society.

CONSUMER PROTECTION - LAW AND LEGISLATION - AUSTRALIA

—Australian consumer sales and credit law reporter / North Ryde, N.S.W. : CCH Australia, 1977.
looseleaf.
Looseleaf issues accompanied by a summary report. - Uniform credit law proposals 1978; Trade Practices Commission guidelines 1974-1982; and 1980- cases filed in transfer binders. 'Uniform credit law proposals 1978' filed in transfer binder.
ISBN 0869030760 v.3
ISBN 0869033077

—Australian trade practices reporter / by CCH editorial staff : consultant editors R. Baxt, R.G. Blunt, A.I. Tonking. – 2. – North Ryde, N.S.W. : CCH Australia, 1972-.
loose-leaf; 26cm.
Includes current issues of: Australian trade practices reports. Loose-leaf issues accompanied by a summary report. Pre-current 'Commission decisions : authorizations and notifications' filed in transfer binders.
ISBN 0869030264 v.2
ISBN 0869030280 Hbk

CONTAINER INDUSTRY

—Container lines : the strategy game / by R.F. Gibney. – Colchester : Lloyd's of London Press, 1984.
87p.
ISBN 0907432840

CONTEMPT OF COURT

—History of Contempt of Court / Abingdon : Professional Books.

—Papua New Guinea, in the Supreme Court of Justice ... In the matter of a reference under section 18 of the Constitution, and in the matter of Ralph Rakhinand Premdas against the Independent State of Papua New Guinea, and others. Re Rooney: being a transcript of the proceedings 27th August - 5th and 11th September 1979 / Port Moresby : Council of Law Reporting for Papua New Guinea, 1981.
vi,390p; 34cm.
Cover title: The Rooney case.

CONTEMPT OF COURT - AUSTRALIA

—Australian Supplement to Borrie and Lowe's Law of Contempt / Athol Moffitt. – Butterworths, 1988.
ca 128p.
ISBN 0409494593 Pbk £29.00

—Contempt / Law Reform Commission. – Canberra : Australian Government Publishing Service, 1987.
xcii,643p. – (Report).
Includes index.
ISBN 0644013656

—Contempt and family law / The Law Reform Commission. – Sydney : The Commission, 1985.
76p. – (Discussion paper).

—Contempt and the media / Australian Law Reform Commission. – Sydney : The Commission, 1986.
182p. – (Discussion paper).
Cover title. Bibliography: p.178-182.

—Contempt : disruption, disobedience and deliberate interference / The Law Reform Commission. – Sydney : The Commission, 1986.
130p. – (Discussion paper).
Includes bibliographical references.

—Reference on contempt of court / Australian Law Reform Commission. – Sydney : The Commission, 1984.
viii,119p.
Includes bibliographical references.

—Reference on contempt of court, tribunals and commissions / Australian Law Reform Commission. – Sydney : The Commission, 1986.
v,134p.
Bibliography: p.130-134.

—Reference on contempt of courts, tribunals and commissions / Australian Law Reform Commission. – Sydney : The Commission, 1986.
iv,49p.
Includes bibliographical references.

Research paper no.1 : Contempt in relation to commissions and tribunals / Australian Law Reform Commission. – 1986.
vii,114p.
Bibliography: p.112-114.

Research paper no. 6A : Contempt and family law / Australian Law Reform Commission. – 1985.

CONTEMPT OF COURT - CANADA

—Contempt of Court / Law Reform Commission of Canada. - Ontario : Law Reform Commission of Canada, 1982.
67,69p; 25cm. - (Report).
English and French texts bound in reverse.
ISBN 0662512995

—Libel and Contempt : The Law and the Media / Vancouver : British Columbia Continuing Legal Education Society, 1982.
414p.
ISBN 0865040834 Hbk £65.00

CONTEMPT OF COURT - ENGLAND

—Borrie and Lowe's Law of contempt / N. V. Lowe. - 2nd ed. - London : Butterworths, 1983.
xlv,479p; 26cm.
This book is a comprehensive statement of the law relating to civil and criminal contempt of court in the United Kingdom. The work deals in-depth with the changes brought about by the Contempt of Court Act of 1981.
ISBN 0406129517 Hbk

—Changing contempt of court / by Andrew Nicol and Heather Rogers. - London : National Council for Civil Liberties, 1981.
40p.
ISBN 0901108928

—Sunday Times case / 1 videocassette. - London : Sweet & Maxwell, 1984.
- (Sweet & Maxwell's lawfilms).

CONTEMPT OF COURT - GREAT BRITAIN

—Contempt of court / C.J. Miller. - 2nd ed. - Oxford : Clarendon Press, 1989.
lix,492p.
Previous ed.: 1976. Includes index. This new edition covers developments in the law of contempt and includes the Contempt of Court Act 1981.
ISBN 0198254784 Hbk £75

—Law of Contempt / Lowe. - 2nd ed. - London : Butterworths, 1983.
ISBN 0406129517 Hbk £66.00

—Law of contempt / by Anthony Arlidge and David Eady : consulting editor - (Scotland) Herbert Kerrigan : with a foreword by Lord Justice Lawton. - London : Sweet & Maxwell, 1982.
xxxvi,479p; 26cm.
Intends to reduce the law to basic principles, consonant with the common law and modern statutes. Chapter on the impact of the 1981 Contempt of Court Act on the law of Scotland and Northern Ireland. Considers the effect of the European Convention on Human Rights on the development of the contempt jurisdiction.
ISBN 0421259205 £30.00

—McNae's Essential Law for Journalists / 9th ed. - London : Butterworths, 1985.
This book for working journalists offers information on the ways in which the law effects their professional activities. The work discusses the changes brought about by the Contempt of Court Act of 1981 and recent case in defamation.
ISBN 0406772819 Pbk £17.75

CONTEMPT OF COURT - HONG KONG

—Report on contempt of court / the Law Reform Commission of Hong Kong. - Hong Kong : The Commission, 1986.
v,102p. - (Topic).
Includes bibliographical references.

CONTEMPT OF COURT - INDIA

—Contempt of Court / V.R. Gopalan. - 5th ed. - Lucknow : Eastern Book Company, 1983.
1,146p.

—Law of Contempt of Court / Allahabad : Universal Book Agency.

—Law of Contempt of Courts, Legislatures and Public Servants / 8th ed. - Allahabad : Law Book Company, 1989.
1,000p.

CONTEMPT OF COURT - NIGERIA

—Judicial attitudes to freedom of speech and the press with particular reference to contempt of court / by Isabella E. Adi. - Lagos : Nigerian Institute of Advanced Legal Studies, 1983.
23p.
Seminar paper presented at the Institute on Wednesday, April 20, 1983.

CONTINENTAL SHELF

—International and legal problems of the gulf / S.H. Amin. - London : Middle East and North African Studies Press, 1981.
235p.
Bibls..
ISBN 0906559057

CONTRACEPTION

—Law and planned parenthood : a handbook / compiled and edited for the IPPF Panel on Law & Planned Parenthood by John M. Paxman. - London : I.P.P.F., 1980.
116p; 30cm.
Bibliography: p107-116.
ISBN 0860890325 Pbk £3.00

CONTRACEPTION - COMMONWEALTH

—Issues in reproductice health law in the Commonwealth / by Rebecca J. Cook and Bernard M. Dickens. - London : Commonwealth Secretariat, 1986.
109p.
ISBN 085092295X

CONTRACEPTION - EUROPE

—Family Planning Legislation : Euro Reports and Studies No. 85 / London : HMSO, 1984.
86p.
Report on a survey of family planning legislation in Greece, Italy, Morocco, Portugal, Spain, Tunisia and Turkey.
ISBN 928901251X Hbk £3.20

CONTRACT

—Adaptation and renegotiation of contracts in international trade and finance / edited by Norbert Horn. - Deventer, The Netherlands : Kluwer Law and Taxation Publishers, 1984.
452p.
Includes index.
ISBN 9065441824 Hbk £228.00

—Adaptation of Contracts / Paris : International Chamber of Commerce.
22p.

—Cases and material on contract / by S.S. Ujjannavar. - Hubli India : G. S. Ujjannavar, 1983.
xiv,543p.

—Computer contracts / Richard Morgan, Graham Stedman. - 2nd ed. - London : Oyez Longman, 1984.
x,324p.
Previous ed.: 1979. Includes index.
ISBN 0851208568

—Conflict of laws and contract / by P.R.H. Webb. - Auckland : Legal Research Foundation, 1985.
63p.
Includes bibliographical references.
ISBN 090858136X

—Contract and organization : legal analysis in the light of economic and social theory / edited by Terence Daintith and Gunther Teubner. - Berlin : W. de Gruyter, 1986.
- (Series A-Law).
Includes index. Bibliography.
ISBN 0899251722 Hbk £52.25

—Contract as promise : a theory of contractual obligation / Charles Fried. - Cambridge, Mass. : Harvard University Press, 1981.
162p; 25cm.
Includes index.
ISBN 0674169255 £8.40

—Contract : cases and materials / H.G. Beale, W.D. Bishop, M.P. Furmston. - London : Butterworths, 1985.
xxxvi,737p; 26cm.
ISBN 0406005265 Hbk No price
ISBN 0406005281 Pbk No price

—Contract law in perspective / by John Tillotson. - London : Butterworths, 1981.
xvii,179p; 23cm.
Includes bibliographies and index.
ISBN 0406666202 Unpriced

—Contracts : Cases, Notes and Materials / Barry J. Reiter. - 3rd ed. - Aurora : Canada Law Book Co, 1985.
734p. - (Case Books).
This new edition provides a complete review of contract law including: Remedies for Breach of Contract, The Kinds of Promises that the Law Will Enforce, The Formation of Contracts, The Statute of Frauds, Contractual Undertakings - Their Determination and Range, and Remedies for Breach; Control of Contract Power, and Illegality.

—Contracts with Eastern Europe / 2nd ed. - London : East European Trade Council, 1980.
57p; 30cm.
Previous ed.: 1969.

—Damage measures for breach of contract / Steven Shavell. - s.l. : s.n., 1980.
25p.
Photocopy of an article in Bell Journal of Economics, vol. 11 (1980), p.466-490. Includes bibliographical references.

—Force Majeure and Hardship / Paris : International Chamber of Commerce.

—From the Waidring Conferences, 4 Vols. / Dordrecht : Kluwer, 1987.
292p.
ISBN 9065442790 Pbk £85.00

—Fundamental duties : a volume of essays by present and former members of the Law Faculty of the University of Exeter to commemorate the Silver Jubilee of the University / edited by D. Lasok : with a foreword by Lord Denning of Whitchurch. - Oxford : Pergamon, 1980.
269p; 26cm. - (Pergamon international library).
ISBN 0080240488 Hbk £12.50
ISBN 0080240496 Pbk £4.95

—Guide on Drawing up International Contracts for Services Relating to Maintenance, Repair and Operation of Industrial and Other Works / Geneva : United Nations Publications.
ISBN 9211163846 Hbk £12.00

—History of the common law of contract / Oxford : Oxford University Press, 1987.
ISBN 019825573X Pbk £19.50

—Law of contract : implied terms in contracts for the supply of services Report on a reference under Section 3(1)(e) of the Law Commissions Act 1965 / by the Law Commission. - London : H.M.S.O., 1986.
v, 49p.
ISBN 0101977301

—Law of contract : minors' contracts / Law Commission. - London : H.M.S.O., 1984.
v,42p.
ISBN 0102494843

—Law Relating to C.I.F. Contracts / New Delhi : Deep and Deep Publications, 1982.
142p.

—Letters of intent / London : Butterworths, 1990.
310; 24cm.
Deals with the legal aspects of letters of intent and other pre-contractual documents. It addresses the problem of enforceability of such contracts to contract from the point of view of both common law and civil law jurisdictions as well as their effective use and drafting. Includes specimen documentation and forms.*Lawyers, businessmen and women*
ISBN 0880632305 HBK £50

—Modern liner contracts : an in depth study of current contracts of carriage in liner shipping / London : Lloyd's of London Press, 1984.
90 leaves.
ISBN 1850440328

—On International Construction and Project Export Contracts / Helsinki : Lakimiesliiton kustannus, 1982.
168p.

—Remedies for breach of contract : a comparative account / G.H. Treitel. - Oxford : Clarendon Press, 1988.
xliii,422p.
Includes index. Discusses remedies for a breach of contract from a comparative perspective. Contrasts civil and common law solutions, and differences between English and American common law, and French and German civil law. The aim is to identify types of solutions and consider how far differences in theoretical approaches are reflected in practical results.
ISBN 0198255004 Hbk £45/$60

—Shipbuilding contracts / edited by Malcolm A. Clarke. - London : Lloyd's, 1982.
xx,228p.
Includes index. At head of title: Comite Maritime International.
ISBN 0907432255

—Standard business contracts / A.J Hawkins. - London : Sweet & Maxwell, 1986.
Examines the law with particular reference to exclusion and limitation clauses, and related devices operating as indirect or implied exclusions. Includes clauses of indemnity, insurance, invoicing back, certification and inspection, warning notices, and instructions. Includes the Unfair Contract Terms Act 1977, the Supply of Goods and Services Act 1982, the Hague-Visby Rules, and the Warsaw Convention on Carriage by Air.
ISBN 0421307609 Hbk £72

CONTRACT - AUSTRALIA

—Breach of contract / by J. W. Carter. - Sydney : Law Book Company, 1984.
xlxi,551p.
ISBN 0455205051 Hbk £49

—Butterworths Student Companions /. - 2nd ed. - Butterworths, 1988.
144p.
ISBN 0409493252

—Cases and materials on contract / by P.J. Hocker, Ann Dufty and Peter G. Heffey. - 5th ed. - Sydney : Law Book Co., 1985.
xli,983p.
4th ed., 1979 by C.L. Pannam and P.J. Hocker. Includes bibliographical references and index.
ISBN 0455204039

—Cases and Materials on Contract Law in Australia / D. J. Harland. - Sydney : Butterworths, 1988.
1000p.
Commentary on each of the decisions contained in this casebook includes its status, difficulties associated with it, and, when possible, an in-depth analysis. Among the topics covered are agreement, misrepresentation, duress, damages, and restitution.

—Cases and Materials on Contract Law in Australia / Butterworths, 1988.
979p.
ISBN 040949366X Pbk £58.00

—Cheshire and Fifoot's Law of Contract : Fifth Australian Edition / N. C. Seddon. - Sydney : Butterworths, 1988.
880p.
This new edition has been revised to take into account the legislative and judicial developments in Australian contract law since 1981.

—Contract /. – North Ryde : Law Book Co, 1984.
x, 133p. – (Nutshells).
ISBN 0455203466

—Contract law in Australia / K.E. Lindgren, J.W. Carter, D.J. Harland. – Sydney : Butterworths, 1986.
lxxvii,817p.
Bibliography: p.791-793. - Includes index.
ISBN 0409490970 Hbk A$76.00
ISBN 0409491268 PBK A$59

—Exemption Clauses and Implied Obligations in Contracts / North Ryde : Law Book Co, 1986.
xxxviii, 290p.
ISBN 0455206813 Pbk £45.00

—Guidebook to Contract Law in Australia / 3rd ed. – North Ryde : C.C.H. Australia, 1987.
350p.
ISBN 0869034715 Pbk £35.00

—High Court of Australia on contract, 1950-1980 : cases / edited by M. P. Ellinghaus. – Sydney : Law Book Co., 1983.
xviii,487p.
Includes index.
ISBN 0455205310
ISBN 0455205329

—Law of contract / by D.W.Greig and J.L.R.Davis. – Sydney : The Law Book Company Ltd, 1987.
xc,1542p.
Kept up to date by supplements.
ISBN 0455206198

—Law of Contract / Fifoot. – 5th ed. – Butterworths, 1988.
759p.
ISBN 0409492957 Pbk £65.00
ISBN 0409492973 Hbk £89.00

—Law of Contract / Davis. – North Ryde : Law Book Co, 1986.
ISBN 0455206198 Hbk £47.50
ISBN 0455206201 Pbk £34.50

—Law of Contract : Australian Edition / Fifoot. – 4th ed. – Wellington : Butterworths, 1981.
ISBN 0409490377 Hbk
ISBN 0409490369 Pbk

—Tutorials in Contract / 4th ed. – North Ryde : Law Book Co, 1986.
xxii, 377p.
ISBN 0455206430 Hbk £35.00
ISBN 0455206449 Pbk £25.00

—Understanding Contract Law / Y. Yamouni. – Sydney : Butterworths, 1985.
312p.
The narrative of this book is accompanied by case examples chosen to illustrate the main issues. Among the topics discussed are agreement, consideration, contents of the contract, rights and liabilities under a contract, and remedies for breach.
ISBN 0409490555 Hbk

—Understanding Contract Law / Yvonne Yamouni. – 2nd ed. – Butterworths, 1988.
312p.
ISBN 0409302538 Pbk £32.00

—Unfair Contracts and Copyright / Milsons Point : Australian Copyright Council.

CONTRACT - AUSTRALIA - NEW SOUTH WALES

—Law of unjust contracts : including the Contracts Review Act 1980 (NSW) with detailed annotations, procedure, and pleadings / by John R. Peden. – Sydney : Butterworths, 1981.
xix, 187 p.; 22 cm.
Includes bibliographical references and index.
ISBN 0409309311 Hbk £28.00

CONTRACT - AUSTRALIA - SOUTH AUSTRALIA

—Report ... on the further consideration of the Contracts Review Bill 1978 / Law Reform Committee of South Australia. – Adelaide : Government Printer, 1986.
73p. – (74th report).
Bibliography: p.51-52.

—Report ... relating to the effect of mistake upon contracts / Law Reform Committee of South Australia. – Adelaide : Government Printer, 1987.
112p. – (106th report).
Bibliography: p.109-112.

—Report ... relating to the reform of the law regarding entire contracts and the rule usually known as the rule in Cutter v. Powell / Law Reform Committee of South Australia. – Adelaide : Government Printer, 1986.
29p. – (90th report).

CONTRACT - AUSTRALIA - TASMANIA

—Report and recommendations relating to exclusion clauses and implied obligations in contracts for the supply of goods and services / Law Reform Commission of Tasmania. – Hobart : Government Printer, 1983.
23p. – (Report).

—Working paper on the law relating to contracts and the disposition of property by minors / by D.R.C. Chalmers. – Hobart? : Government Printer?, 1985.
49,iip.
Cover title.

CONTRACT - CANADA

—Contracts : Cases and Commentaries / Percy. – 3rd ed. – Agincourt : Carswell, 1985.
ISBN 0459375105 Hbk £39.60

—Contracts : Cases Notes and Materials / Reiter. – 3rd ed. – Aurora : Canada Law Book, 1985.

—Contracts : Cases, Text, and Materials / Barry J. Reiter. – 4th ed. – Toronto : Edmond-Montgomery, 1985.
732p.
ISBN 0920722164 Hbk £84.00

—Damages for Breach of Contract / Elizabeth Carmen. – Agincourt : Carswell, 1985.
260p.
This book reviews the principles underlying the law of contracts relating to damages for the Canadian Practitioner. The trends of Canadian cases and how the courts are treating breach of contract issues are discussed in depth.

—Domestic Contracts / Kirstie J. MacLise. – Agincourt : Carswell, 1987.
ca 420p.

—Domestic Contracts / Agincourt : Carswell, 1987.
450p.
This looseleaf work is a practitioners guide to the drafting of cohabitation, marriage and separation agreements under the law of Ontario and British Columbia. Checklist, sample agreements, income tax considerations and related materials are included in the volume.

—Inequality of bargaining power : judicial intervention in improvident and unconscionable bargains / Robert W. Clark. – Toronto : Carswell, 1987.
xxxvii,255p.
ISBN 0459388401

—Law in transition : contracts / Don Mills : R. De Boo, 1984.
193p.
Includes bibliographical references and index.
ISBN 0888201826

—Law of contract in Canada / by G.H.L. Fridman. – 2nd ed. – Toronto : Carswell, 1986.
clii,764p.
Previous ed.: 1976. Includes bibliographical references and index.
ISBN 0459382101

—Law of Contracts / 2nd ed. – Agincourt : Carswell, 1986.
916p.

—Law of contracts / S.M.Waddams. – 2nd edition. – Toronto : Canada Law Book Co.Inc, 1984.
cxli,614p.
ISBN 0888040237

—Milner's Cases and Materials on Contracts / 4th ed. – Aurora : Canada Law Book Co, 1985.
884p. – (Case Books).
This casebook examines the present common law of contracts with reference to the leading Canadian and English cases. Chapters include, among others: Remedies for Breach of Promise, The Kind of Promises Legally Enforced, Third Party Beneficiaries, Assignment and Agency, Third Parties and Mistakes in Dealings Between Others, and Written Documents.

—Milner's Cases and Materials on Contracts / 4th ed. – Toronto : Edmond-Montgomery, 1985.
855p.
ISBN 0920722172 Hbk £84.00

—Negotiating, Writing and Administering Contracts / Ottawa : Canadian Library Association, 1981.
28p.

—Studies in contract law / edited by Barry J. Reiter, John Swan. – Toronto : Butterworths, 1980.
xx, 467 p.; 24 cm. – (Canadian legal studies series).
This book gives an in-depth analysis of contemporary contract law issues. Leading Canadian law experts have contributed essays on remedies, consideration, mistake, unconscionability, and the relationship between contracts and torts.
ISBN 040986210X £50.00

—Studies in Contract Law / John Swan. – Butterworths, 1980.
487p.

CONTRACT - CANADA - BRITISH COLUMBIA

—Report on performance under protest / Law Reform Commission of British Columbia. – Vancouver : The Commission, 1985.
21p.
Includes bibliographical references.
ISBN 077188477X

CONTRACT - CANADA - MANITOBA

—Report on small projects / Manitoba Law Reform Commission. – Winnipeg : The Commission, 1985.
iv,48p. – (Report).
Includes bibliographical references.
ISBN 0771101074

CONTRACT - CANADA - ONTARIO

—Ontario Limitation Periods : A Handbook of Limitation Periods and Other Statutory Time Limits / Toronto : Butterworths.

—Report on amendment of the law of contract / Ontario Law Reform Commission. – Toronto : Ministry of the Attorney General, 1987.
xiii,305p.

CONTRACT - CARIBBEAN

—West Indian cases on the law of contract / Roop L. Chaudhary and Andrew Burgess. – 2nd ed. – Barbados : Coles Printery, 1984.
xvii,316p.

CONTRACT - ENGLAND

—Arbitration / Maurice Kay. – London : Sweet and Maxwell, 1980.
vi,90p; 18cm.
Includes index.
ISBN 0421246901 Pbk £1.25

—Casebook on contract / by J.C. Smith and the late J.A.C. Thomas. – 7th ed. – London : Sweet & Maxwell, 1987.
xxxi,604p; 24cm.
Previous ed.: 1977. Includes index.
ISBN 0421283203 Hbk Unpriced
ISBN 0421283300 Pbk £12.95

—Cheshire and Fifoot's law of contract / C. H. S. Fifoot, M. P. Furmston. – 10th ed. – London : Butterworths, 1981.
xliv,636p; 26cm.
Previous ed.: 1976. Includes index.
ISBN 0406565317 Hbk Unpriced
ISBN 0406565325 Pbk Unpriced

—Cheshire, Fifoot and Furmston's Law of contract / C. H. S. Fifoot, M. P. Furmston, G. C. Cheshire. – 11th ed. – London : Butterworth, 1986.
620p; 25cm.
Previous ed.: published as Cheshire and Fifoot's law of contract. 1981. Includes index.
ISBN 040656535X Hbk £28.00
ISBN 0406565368 Pbk £18.95

—Chitty on contracts / A. G. Guest. – 25th ed. 2. – London : Sweet & Maxwell, 1983.
various pagings; 26cm.
Previous ed.: 1977. Includes index.
ISBN 0421285605 Unpriced

—Contract / Ruth Annand, Richard Whish. – London : Sweet & Maxwell, 1987.
xxii,175p; 26cm.
Includes index.
ISBN 0421362405 £16.50

—Contract / by F.R. Davies. – 5th ed. – London : Sweet & Maxwell, 1986.
xxii,290p; 23cm.
Previous ed.: 1981. Includes index.
ISBN 0421350903 Hbk £9.50
ISBN 0421351004 Pbk £5.95

—Contract and conveyance / J.T. Farrand. – 3rd ed. – London : Oyez, 1980.
lxiii,340p.
ISBN 0851204392

—Contract: death or change of life? / 1 v. – London : Institute of Advanced Legal Studies, University of London, 1981.
various pagings. – (W.G. Hart Legal Workshop).
Includes bibliographical references.

—Contract in a nutshell / Robert Duxbury. – London : Sweet & Maxwell, 1987.
117p; 22cm.
Includes index.
ISBN 0421368004 Pbk £3.95

—Contract law in perspective / John Tillotson. – 2nd ed. – London : Butterworths, 1985.
ix,240p; 22cm.
Previous ed.: 1981. Includes bibliographies and index.
ISBN 0406666210 Pbk No price

—Control of Exclusion Clauses England and India / Ravenswood, 1985.
ISBN 0901812595 Hbk £31.00

—Doctrine and discretion in the law of contract : an inaugural lecture delivered before the University of Oxford on 7 March 1980 / by G.H. Treitel. – Oxford : Clarenden, 1981.
31p; 22cm.
ISBN 0199515271 Pbk £1.95

—Essays on contract / P.S. Atiyah. – Oxford : Clarendon, 1986.
vi,363p; 23cm.
Includes index.
ISBN 0198255551 £30.00

—Exclusion clauses in contracts / by David Yates. – 2nd ed. – London : Sweet & Maxwell, 1982.
xxvi,338p; 18cm.
Previous ed.: 1978. Includes index.
ISBN 0421286806 Hbk £9.75
ISBN 0421286903 Pbk £4.85

—Implied terms in the law of contract in England and South Africa / submitted for the degree of PhD by Jacob Petrus Vorster. – S.l. : s.n., 1987.
xii,240p.
Thesis (PhD): St. John's College, Cambridge, 1987.
Bibliography: pp.204-212. - Includes index.
ISBN 0620113057

—Introduction to the law of contract / by P.S. Atiyah. – 3rd ed. – Oxford : Clarendon, 1981.
x,335p; 23cm. – (Clarendon law series).
Previous ed.: 1971. Includes index.
ISBN 0198761406 Hbk Unpriced
ISBN 0198761414 Pbk £5.95

—Law of contract / by G.H. Treitel. – 6th ed. – London : Stevens, 1983.
lxxvi,810p; 24cm.
Previous ed.: 1979. Includes index.
ISBN 0420463607 Hbk Unpriced
ISBN 0420463704 Pbk Unpriced

—Law of contract / Hugh Collins. – London : Weidenfeld and Nicolson, 1986.
xi,236p; 23cm.
Bibliography: p210-224. - Includes index.
ISBN 0297787845 Hbk £14.95
ISBN 0297787853 Pbk £7.50

—Law of contract / by G.H. Treitel. – 7th ed. – London : Stevens, 1987.
850p; 25cm.
Previous ed.: 1983. Includes index.
ISBN 0420474900 Hbk £30.00
ISBN 0420475001 Pbk £22.00

—Law of contract : minors' contracts / the Law Commission. – London : H.M.S.O., 1982.
vi,179p. – (Working paper).
ISBN 0117301612

—Law of contract : pecuniary restitution on breach of contract / The Law Commission. – London : H.M.S.O., 1983.
iv,56p; 25cm.
ISBN 0102034842

—Law of contract : the parol evidence rule / the Law Commission. – London : H.M.S.O., 1986.
iv,31p.
ISBN 0101970005

—Memorandum on Law Commission working paper no. 92: Formalities for contracts for sale of land and Law Commission working paper no. 93: Formalities for deeds and esrows / Justice. – London : Justice .
9 leaves.

—Proprietary rights and insolvency in sales transactions / by R.M. Goode. – London : Sweet & Maxwell, 1985.
xv,137p; 22cm.
Includes index.
ISBN 0421351403 Pbk £13.00

—Remedies for breach of contract / by Hugh Beale. – London : Sweet and Maxwell, 1980.
xxiv,248p; 19cm.
Includes index.
ISBN 0421251409 £10.85
ISBN 0421251506

—Remedies for torts and breach of contract / A.S. Burrows. – London : Butterworths, 1987.
lviii,435p; 22cm.
Includes index.
ISBN 0406501505 Hbk £18.00
ISBN 0406501513 Pbk £12.95

—Remedies in contract and tort / Donald Harris. – London : Weidenfeld & Nicolson, 1988.
xxxvii,411p.
Includes index.
ISBN 0297793551

—Reservation of title : draft Council of Europe Convention (CDCJ(82)15) / memorandum by a Working Party of the Senate of the Inns of Court and the Bar and the Law Society. – London? : the Working Party?, 1983.
4p.
Bound with 'Draft proposal for a Council Directive on the legal consequences of agreements creating simple reservation of title (III/872/79-EN)'.

—Smith and Thomas : a casebook on contract / J. A. C. Thomas, J. C. Smith. – 8th ed. – London : Sweet & Maxwell, 1987.
600p; 24cm.
Previous ed.: published as A casebook on contract. 1982. Includes index.
ISBN 0421346108 Hbk £26.00
ISBN 0421346205 Pbk £18.50

—Transfer of land : the rule in Bain v. Fothergill / The Law Commission. – London : H.M.S.O., 1986.
iv,49p; 21cm. – (Working paper).
Includes bibliographical references.
ISBN 0117301795

—Understanding contract law / John N. Adams and Roger Brownsword. – London : Fontana, 1987.
229p.
Bibliography: p213-216.
ISBN 0006860702

CONTRACT – EUROPEAN COMMUNITY

—Colloquium on choice of law in contract and the E.E.C. Contractual Obligations Convention / Peter North. – 2. – s.l. : s.n., 1981.
Held from 15-16th Sept. 1981. Includes bibliographical references. Chairman: Peter North.

—Contract conflicts : the EEC Convention on the Law Applicable to Contractual Obligations : a comparative study / edited by P.M. North. – Amsterdam : North-Holland, 1982.
xviii,401p; 23cm.
ISBN 0444864466 £24.26

CONTRACT – FRANCE

—Contract law today: Anglo-French comparisons / Denis Tallon. – Oxford : Clarendon Press, 1989.
400.
The result of a joint research project by two research institutes, one in the UK and one in France. It examines the evolution of contract in England and France.
Contract lawyers, comparative lawyers
ISBN 0198355934 Hbk £40

—French Law of Contract / London : Butterworths, 1982.
ISBN 040663095X Pbk £16.95
ISBN 0406630968 Hbk £23.00

—French law of contract / Barry Nicholas. – London : Butterworths, 1982.
xxxviii,253p.
ISBN 0406630968

CONTRACT – GREAT BRITAIN

—ACA Contract Introductory Package / London : Architectural Press, 1985.
– (ACA Contract Documents).
ISBN 0851397301 Hbk £20.00

—Anson's Law of contract / A. G. Guest. – 26th ed. – Oxford : Clarendon, 1984.
lvi,641p; 24cm.
Previous ed.: 1979. Includes index.
ISBN 0198761481 Hbk No price
ISBN 019876149X Pbk £15.95

—Breach of Contract / Sweet & Maxwell, 1985.
ISBN 0455205051 Hbk £52.00

—Breach of contract / by J. W. Carter. – Sydney : Law Book Company, 1984.
xlxi,551p.
ISBN 0455205051 Hbk £49

—Builders' Claims Under the JCT 1963 Form of Contract / rev. ed. – King's Ride : Institute of Building, 1982.
Illus. – – (Studies in Contractual Claims; 3).
ISBN 0901822531 Hbk £6.75

—C.I.F. and F.O.B. contracts / H. Orren Merren. – 3rd ed. – London : Stevens, 1984.
xlv,528p; 26cm.
Previous ed.: 1975. Includes index.
ISBN 0420465308 £60.00

—C.I.F. and F.O.B. contracts / H. Orren Merren. – 3rd ed. – London : Stevens, 1984.
xlv,528p; 26cm.
Previous ed.: 1975. Includes index.
ISBN 0420465308 £60.00

—Cases In Contract Law / 3rd ed. – Plymouth : Macdonald & Evans, 1983.
ISBN 0712104801 Pbk £4.95

—Cases in Contract Law / 3rd ed. Repr. of 1977 ed. – Plymouth : Macdonald & Evans, 1983.
256p. – (M and E Handbook Ser.).
ISBN 0712104801 Hbk £4.50

—CIF and FOB Contracts (BSL) / Merren. – 3rd ed. – London : Sweet & Maxwell, 1984.
ISBN 0420465308 Hbk £80.00

—Commercial Contracts / London : Collins, 1987.
208p.
ISBN 0003832341 Hbk £17.50

—Contract and Conveyance / 4th ed. – London : Oyez Longman, 1983.
ISBN 0851207715 Hbk £15.95

—Contract Documentation for Contractors / Sims. – Oxford : Blackwell Scientific, 1985.
ISBN 0003830187 Hbk £17.95

—Contract law / Inner London Education Authority, Learning Resources Branch. – 1 videocassette. – London : Sweet & Maxwell, 1986.
– (Sweet & Maxwell's lawfilms).

—Contract Law in Perspective / 2nd ed. – London : Butterworths, 1985.
ISBN 0406666210 Pbk £9.95

—Contract law today: Anglo-French comparisons / Denis Tallon. – Oxford : Clarendon Press, 1989.
400.
The result of a joint research project by two research institutes, one in the UK and one in France. It examines the evolution of contract in England and France.
Contract lawyers, comparative lawyers
ISBN 0198355934 Hbk £40

—Contracts and Building Law. Vol. 2 / The Chartered Institute of Building, UK. – King's Ride : Institute of Building.

—Contracts : Cases and Commentaries / David Percy. – 3rd ed. – Agincourt : Carswell, 1985.
932p.
This third edition text updates the previous edition with comprehensive coverage of contracts induced by negligent misrepresentation, current key cases, and a review of statutory references.

—Cracknell LSC : Contract / 6th ed. – London : Butterworths, 1982.
ISBN 0406567034 Pbk £9.95

—Cracknell's Law Students' Companion : Contract / 6th ed. – London : Butterworths, 1982.
This book is an aid to study of English contract law. The work is especially suited to students who have limited access to law libraries. The full text of the Unfair Contract Terms Act is included.
ISBN 0406567034 Pbk £20.00

—Default by Sub-Contractors and Suppliers / Oxford : Blackwell Scientific, 1985.
ISBN 0003830470 Hbk £19.95

—Entertainment Industry Contracts / Matthew Bender, 1987.
ISBN 0000999069 Hbk £197.00

—Essays on Contract / Oxford : Oxford University Press, 1986.
ISBN 0198255551 Hbk £30.00

—Essays on contract / Oxford : Clarendon Press, 1988.
364.
A collection of essays concerned with the theory and foundations of contractual liability, which have been published over the last twenty years. The author has tken the opportunity to revise, and rewrite some of them, and to answer previously made criticisms of his work.
ISBN 0198256418 Pbk £11.95

—Excluding Liability in Contracts / London : Butterworths, 1985.
ISBN 0407995002 Hbk £48.00

—Exclusion Clauses / 2nd ed. – London : Longman Professional, 1983.
ISBN 0851207294 Pbk £21.00

—Exclusion clauses / Richard Lawson. – 2nd ed. – London : Oyez Longman, 1983.
xx,180p; 22cm.
Previous ed.: 1978. Includes index.
ISBN 0851207294 Pbk Unpriced

—Exclusion clauses / Richard Lawson. – 3rd ed. – London : Longman Professional (UK), 1990.
– (Practitioner Series).
Guide to the use of exclusion clauses (as limited by the Unfair Contract Terms Act). Discusses ways in which an exclusion clause can become a contractual term, what loss or damage it covers, and how likely it is to be interpreted by the courts.

—FIDIC Conditions of Contract - Commercial Manual / Waterlow, 1986.
ISBN 0080392342 Hbk £30.00

—Fry : A Treatise on the Specific Performance of Contracts / Repr. of 1921 ed. – London : Sweet & Maxwell.
ISBN 042135190X Hbk £75.00

—GC/Works/1 Conditions of Contract / London : Waterlow, 1985.
ISBN 0080392334 Hbk £20.00

—Grain Contracts and Arbitration / London : Lloyd's of London Press, 1984.
ISBN 0907432883 Hbk £24.00

—Guide to contracting, negotiation and the law / R.I. Akroyd. – London : Routledge & Kegan Paul, 1987.
256p; 22cm.
Includes bibliography and index.
ISBN 0710204868 £22.50

—ICE Conditions of Contract : A Commercial Manual / London : Waterlow, 1985.
304p.
ISBN 0080392326 Hbk £28.00

—Inequality of bargaining power : judicial intervention in improvident and unconscionable bargains / Robert W. Clark. – Toronto : Carswell, 1987.
xxxvii,255p.
ISBN 0459388401

—Interpretation of contracts / London : Sweet & Maxwell, 1989.
Covers the object of integration, implied terms, the canons of construction, ambiguity and uncertainty, mistakes and inconsistencies, preliminary parts of the deed, parcels and subject matter of the contract, exemption clauses, certificates, consents and similar clauses, stipulations as to time, penalties, terminations and forfeiture clauses.
ISBN 042136940X Hbk £45.00

—Introduction to the Law of Contract / 3rd ed. – Oxford : Oxford University Press, 1981.
ISBN 0198761406 Hbk £18.50
ISBN 0198761414 Pbk £9.50

—Introduction to the Law of Obligations / London : Butterworths, 1984.
ISBN 0406260672 Hbk £19.50
ISBN 0406260680 Pbk £13.95

—Landlord and tenant : privity of contract and estate : duration of liability of parties to leases / the Law Commission. – London : HMSO, 1986.
iv,101p. – (Working paper).
Includes bibliographical references.
ISBN 0117301760

—Law of Contract / Fifoot. – 11th ed. – London : Butterworths, 1986.
ISBN 040656535X Hbk £33.00
ISBN 0406565368 Pbk £19.95

—Law of Contract / Guest. – 26th ed. – Oxford : Oxford University Press, 1984.
ISBN 0198761481 Hbk £32.50
ISBN 019876149X Pbk £16.95

—Law of Contract / 7th ed. – London : Sweet & Maxwell, 1987.
ISBN 0420474900 Hbk £34.00
ISBN 042047500X Pbk £19.50

—Law of guarentees / Thomas Putnam and Julienne Walker. – 2nd ed. – London : Longman Professional (UK), 1989.
– (Commercial Series).
Discusses the law relating to contracts where one party agrees to be answerable for the debts or obligations of another to a third party. Deals with guarentees in loans, consumer credit, hire purchase, landlord and tenant (to guarentee payment of rent), building contracts, and commercial contracts. Contains specimen pleadings.
ISBN 0851215395 Hbk £40

—Law of Unjust Contracts / London : Butterworths, 1982.
ISBN 0409309311 Hbk £22.40

—Limitation of Actions / London : Butterworths, 1988.
ISBN 0406102309 Hbk

—Making Commercial Contracts / Oxford : Blackwell Scientific, 1988.
ISBN 0632018623 Hbk £19.95

—Outline of the law of contract / G.H. Treitel. – 3rd ed. – London : Butterworths, 1984.
xxxiii,366p; 22cm.
Previous ed.: 1979. Includes index.
ISBN 0406668485 Pbk Unpriced

—Package holiday law and contracts / Stewart. – 2nd ed. – London : Fourmat, 1988.
ISBN 1851900411 Pbk £14.95

—Practical approach to contract and consumer law / Sewell. – London : Financial Training, 1984.
ISBN 0906322456 Pbk £12.95

—Principles of the law of contract / 3rd ed. – London : Butterworths, 1980.
ISBN 0409037451 Pbk £27.40

—Publishing agreements : a book of precedents / edited by Charles Clark. – 2nd ed. – London : Allen & Unwin, 1984.
xvi,230p; 23cm.
Previous ed.: 1980. Includes index.
ISBN 004655016X £15.00

—Remedies for torts and breach of contract / London : Butterworths, 1987.
ISBN 0406501505 Hbk £24.00

—Remedies under the contract, CS No 3 / Cain. – London : Sweet & Maxwell, 1988.
ISBN 0421381108 Hbk £22.00

—Sanctity of contracts in English law / by Sir David Hughes Parry. – London : Sweet & Maxwell, 1986.
viii,77p. – (Legal reprint series).
Reprint originally published: London, Stevens, 1959. Includes bibliographical references. 'Published under the auspices of the Hamlyn Trust'.
ISBN 0421376007

—Small print : the language and layout of consumer contracts : Report to the National Consumer Council / Martin Cutts and Chrissie Maher : Plain English Campaign. – London : National Consumer Council, 1983.
39p.
ISBN 0905653661

—Specific performance / William Goodhart. – London : Butterworths, 1986.
ISBN 0406258090 Hbk £40.00

—Specific performance / Gareth Jones, William Goodhart. – London : Butterworths, 1986.
lxvi,274p; 25cm.
Bibliography: plxv-lxvi. - Includes index.
ISBN 0406258090 £35.00

—Specific Performance of Contracts : Including Those of Public Companies / 5th ed. Repr. of 1911 ed. – Abingdon : Professional Books.
131p.

—Sweet & Maxwell Law / London : Sweet & Maxwell, 1985.
ISBN 0421340401 Pbk £29.50

—Time barred actions / Rohreke. – London : Lloyd's of London Press, 1984.
ISBN 0907432425 Hbk £34.00

—Time for a change? : deposits on exchange of contracts in residential conveyancing / a consultation paper from the Conveyancing Standing Committee of the Law Commission and the Law Society. – London : Conveyancing Standing Committee, 1988.
14p.

—Ultra Vires : Being an Investigation of the Principles Which Limit the Powers and Liabilities of Corporations, Quasi-Corporate Bodies and Non-Sovereign Legislature / Repr. of 1930 ed. – Abingdon : Professional Books.
344p.

—Understanding contract law / London : Fontana, 1987.
ISBN 0006860702 Pbk £4.95

—Warren's forms of agreement / Markuson. – Matthew Bender, 1987.
ISBN 0000999062 Hbk £223.50

—Introduction to the Scots law of contract / Edinburgh : W Green & Son, 1987.
An introduction to the basic principles at student level.
ISBN 0414008197 SOFTBACK

—Law of contract in Scotland / Edinburgh : W Green & Son, 1987.
The most comprehensive analysis of the practical and theoretical aspects of contract law since Gloag on Contract in 1929. Practical guidance is also provided on drafting some of the commonly found contract clauses.
ISBN 041400793X Hbk

CONTRACT – HONG KONG

—Report on the control of exemption clauses / the Law Reform Commission of Hong Kong. – Hong Kong : The Commission, 1986.
vi,98p. – (Topic).
Includes bibliographical references.

CONTRACT – HUNGARY

—Landmarks in the Development of the Contractual System / Budapest : Akademiai Kiado.
192p.
ISBN 9630536668 Hbk £19.00

CONTRACT – INDIA

—Contract Act and Law Relating to Tenders etc., 3 Vols. / 9th ed. – Allahabad : Law Publishers, 1983.

—Control of Exclusion Clauses England and India / Ravenswood, 1985.
ISBN 0901812595 Hbk £31.00

—Indian Contract Act, 3 Vols. / E.S. Subrahmanyam. – 3rd ed. – Allahabad : Law Book Company, 1989.

—Introduction to the Law of Contract / 2nd ed. – Lucknow : Eastern Book Company, 1983.
419p.

—Law of Contract / 4th ed. – Lucknow : Eastern Book Company, 1985.
526p.

—Law of Contract in India, 3 Vols. / 2nd ed. – Lucknow : Eastern Book Company, 1983-1985.

—Law of Contract in India / New Delhi : Deep and Deep Publications, 1985.
326p.

—Law of Contracts / New Delhi : Association of Indian Universities.
229p.

—Law of Specific Relief / 8th ed. – Allahabad : Law Publishers, 1982.

—Retrenchment, Lay-Off and Closure Based on Latest Amendments and Up-to-date Case-Laws / Allahabad : Law Publishing House, 1982.
ca 400p.

—Specific Relief Act : Based on Tagore Law Lectures / 8th ed. – Allahabad : Law Book Company, 1988.
1,100p.

CONTRACT – IRAN

—Remedies for breach of contract in Islamic and Iranian law / Glasgow : Royston, 1984.
250p.
ISBN 0946706212 £45.95

CONTRACT – IRELAND

—Contract / by Robert Clark. – 2nd ed. 1. – London : Sweet & Maxwell, 1986.
22cm.
Previous ed.: 1982. Includes index.
ISBN 0421344806 Pbk £15.00

—Report on minors' contracts / the Law Reform Commission. – Dublin : The Commission, 1985.
v,167p. – (LRC).
Bibliography: p.163.

CONTRACT – JAPAN

—Law and justice in Tokugawa Japan : materials for the history of Japanese law and justice under the Tokugawa Shogunate 1603-1867 / edited by John Henry Wigmore. – Tokyo : University of Tokyo Press, 1986.
xxix,443p.
Translated and published under the auspices of the Japan Foundation.

CONTRACT – MALAYSIA

—Contracts Act, 1950 (Act 136) and Government Contracts Act, 1949 (Act 120) / Kuala Lumpur : International Law Books Services.

—Law of Contract in Malaysia and Singapore : Cases and Commentaries / 2nd ed. – London : Butterworths, 1987.
ISBN 0409995290 Hbk £78.00

—Law of Contract in Malaysia and Singapore : Cases and Commentary / 2nd ed. – Butterworths, 1987.
900p.
Chapters cover interpretation of contracts, conditional contracts, collateral contracts, economic duress, contracting out of a statute, the application of the doctrine of frustration to contracts for the sale of land, rescission under the Contract Act, equitable relief against forfeiture of deposits and part payments, and Foreign Investment Committee regulations.
ISBN 0409995290 Hbk £160.00

CONTRACT – NEW ZEALAND

—Cheshire and Fifoot's Law of Contract / 7th ed. – Butterworths, 1988.
669p.
ISBN 0409788716 Hbk £120.00
ISBN 0409787973 Pbk £85.00

—Cheshire and Fifoot's Law of Contract / 6th ed. – Butterworths, 1984.
ISBN 0409701645 Hbk £58.30
ISBN 0409701564 Pbk

—Commentary on Standard Conditions of Contract : NZSS 623:1964 / M.C. Barker. – Butterworths, 1983.
ISBN 0409600806 Pbk £52.80

—Contractual Remedies Act 1979 / by Francis Dawson and David W. McLauchlan. – Auckland : Sweet & Maxwell, 1981.
xxii,217p.
Includes bibliographical references and index. Includes the text of the Act.
ISBN 0457017201 Pbk
ISBN 0457016906

—Executory Contracts : a New Area or Study / Palmerston North : Massey University, 1980.

—Law of Contract : New Zealand Edition / Fifoot. – 6th ed. – Wellington : Butterworths, 1984.
ISBN 0409701645 Hbk
ISBN 0409701564 Pbk

—New Zealand Contract and Commercial Legislation / North Ryde : C.C.H. Australia, 1987.
900p.
ISBN 0864750722 Hbk

—Privity of contract / a report by the Contracts and Commercial Law Reform Committee. – New Zealand : The Committee, 1981.
iii,79p.

—Rule in White and Carter (Councils) Limited v. McGregor / a report by the Contracts and Commercial Law Reform Committee. – Wellington : Government Printer, 1983.
15p.

—Second rise and fall of fundamental breach / Brian Coote : G.C. Thorpe : D.W. McMorland. – Auckland : Legal Research Foundation, 1980.
127p.
Includes bibliographical references.
ISBN 0908581084

CONTRACT – NIGERIA

—Broadsheet on the law of contract / by Y.C. Onwuchekwa. – Lagos : s.n., 1984.
42p.

—Casebook on Nigerian Law of Contract / Professional Books, 1983.
ISBN 0862050472 Hbk £37.50
ISBN 0862050533 Pbk £22.00

—Casebook on the Nigerian law of contract / by I.E. Sagay. – Abingdon, Oxon. : Professional Books, 1983.
xxvi,518p.
Includes index.
ISBN 0862050472

—Nigerian law of contract / by I.E. Sagay. – London : Sweet & Maxwell, 1985.
450p.
Includes index.
ISBN 0421304200 Pbk £20.00

—Nigerian Law of Contract (Nigerian Nutshells) / London : Sweet & Maxwell, 1987.
ISBN 0421361409 Pbk £3.95

CONTRACT - NORTHERN IRELAND

—Reservation of title clauses / Brice Dickson. – Belfast : SLS Legal Publications, 1987.
ii,96p.
Bibliography: pp.93-94..

CONTRACT - PAPUA NEW GUINEA

—Context of contract in Papua New Guinea / Derek Roebuck, Dhirendra K. Srivastava, John Nonggorr. – Waigani : University of Papua New Guinea Press, 1984.
268p.
Bibliography: p.256-262. - Includes index.
ISBN 9980840005

CONTRACT - SCOTLAND

—Commercial contracts in Scots law / by William W. McBryde. – Dundee : University of Dundee Centre for Petroleum and Mineral Law Studies, 1980.
29p; 30cm. – (Occasional paper).
An expanded version of a paper given at a conference organised by the Centre on Scots law and the oil industry at Hamilton Hall, St. Andrews, 4-7 April 1979.
ISBN 0906343038 Pbk Unpriced

—Constitution and proof of voluntary obligations and the authentication of writings / Scottish Law Commission. – Edinburgh : The Commission, 1985.
v,203p. – (Consultative memorandum).

—Contract law : exchange of standard term forms in contract formation : law reform proposals / Scottish Law Commission. – 2 v. – Edinburgh : The Commission, 1982.
– (Consultation paper).

—Law of Contract / Edinburgh : W Green, 1985.

—Law of Contract and related obligations in Scotland / 2nd ed. – London : Butterworths, 1985.
ISBN 0406677875 Hbk £44.50

—Obligations : report on rectification of contractual and other documents / Scottish Law Commission. – Edinburgh : H.M.S.O., 1983.
vi,35p.
Includes bibliographical references. Includes Draft Rectification of Documents (Scotland) Bill.
ISBN 0102036845

CONTRACT - SINGAPORE

—Excluding Liability in Contracts / Butterworths, 1985.
227p.
Examines the English and Australian models, and discusses the popular common law concepts of reasonableness and unconscionability. Includes a review of the major cases and legislation aimed at evolving acceptable solutions to the dilemma of exception clauses.
ISBN 0409995002 Hbk £80.00

—Law of Contract in Malaysia and Singapore : Cases and Commentaries / 2nd ed. – London : Butterworths, 1987.
ISBN 0409995290 Hbk £78.00

—Law of Contract in Malaysia and Singapore : Cases and Commentary / 2nd ed. – Butterworths, 1987.
900p.
Chapters cover interpretation of contracts, conditional contracts, collateral contracts, economic duress, contracting out of a statute, the application of the doctrine of frustration to contracts for the sale of land, rescission under the Contract Act, equitable relief against forfeiture of deposits and part payments, and Foreign Investment Committee regulations.
ISBN 0409995290 Hbk £160.00

CONTRACT - SOUTH AFRICA

—Business transactions law / Robert Sharrock Andrew Borrowdale. – Cape Twon : Juta, 1986.
xiv,385p.
Includes index.
ISBN 070211684X

—Contract and mercantile law : a source book / by Ellison Kahn. – 2nd ed. – Cape Town : Juta, 1988.
lix,926p.
Includes index.
ISBN 0702119962

—Contract and mercantile law through the cases / by Ellison Kahn. – 2nd ed. – Cape Town : Juta, 1985.
lix,970p.
Bibliography: p.xxv-xxxviii. - Includes index.
ISBN 0702116548

—General prinicples of the law of contract / D.J. Joubert. – Cape Town : Juta, 1987.
lxvii,344p.
Includes bibliogrpahical references and index.
ISBN 0702118079

—Implied terms in the law of contract in England and South Africa / submitted for the degree of PhD by Jacob Petrus Vorster. – S.l. : s.n., 1987.
xii,240p.
Thesis (PhD): St. John's College, Cambridge, 1987. Bibliography: pp.204-212. - Includes index.
ISBN 0620113057

—Investigation into the legal consequences of suspensive conditions in contracts of sales / South African Law Commission. – Pretoria : The Commission, 1986.
vi,32p. – (Report).
Includes text of draft legislation.
ISBN 0621113506

—Law of contract in South Africa / by R.H. Christie. – Durban : Butterworths, 1981.
lxxiv,575p.
ISBN 0409018317

—Parol evidence with particular reference to contract / by D. T. Zeffertt and A. Paizes. – Johannesburg : Centre for Banking Law, Rand Afrikaans University, 1986.
108p.
Includes bibliographical references.

—Principles of the law of contract / by A.J. Kerr. – 3rd ed. – Durban : Butterworths, 1980.
xiii, 531 p.; 24 cm.
Includes index. Bibliography: p. 489-493.
ISBN 0409037451 pbk.

—Sanctity of contract : wisdom or folly? : an inaugural lecture given in the University of Fort Hare on the 24th May 1984 / by Peter L. Volpe. – Alice, South Africa : Fort Hare University Press, 1984.
14p.
ISBN 094997465X

CONTRACT - SWITZERLAND

—Swiss Federal Code of Obligations : as of January 1, 1984 / Dordrecht : Kluwer, 1987.
318p.
ISBN 9065443231 Hbk £155.00

CONTRACT - USSR

—U.S.S.R. Contract Law / Helsinki : Lakimiesliiton Kustannus, 1982.
219p.

CONTRACT - ZIMBABWE

—Business law in Zimbabwe / R.H. Christie. – Cape Town : Juta, 1985.
lvii, 575 p.; 26 cm.
Includes index.
ISBN 0702115738

—Contract / by Peter L. Volpe. – Salisbury : Zimbabwe Law Journal, 1980.
xxix,221p.
Bibliography: p.xxix. Cover title: The commercial law of Zimbabwe contract.

CONTRACT (INTERNATIONAL LAW)

—Commentary on the international sales law : the 1980 Vienna Sales Convention / by C.M. Bianca, M.J. Bonell. – Milan : Giuffre, 1987.
xvii,886p.
Bibliography: pp.843-873. - Includes index. Includes texts of the Convention in English, Arabic, Chinese, French, Russian, Spanish, German and Italian.
ISBN 8814012768

—Guide on Drawing up International Contracts for Services Relating to Maintenance, Repair and Operation of Industrial and Other Works / Geneva : United Nations Publications.
ISBN 9211163846 Hbk £12.00

—Hague-Zagreb Essays / edited by C.C.A. Voskuil and C.C.A. Voskuil and J.A. Wade. – Hague : Martinus Nijhoff, 1983.
410p.
ISBN 9024728401 Hbk £135.00

—International contract law & finance review yearbook / 1981. 2 v. – London : Euromoney, 1981.
ISBN 0903121360

—Introduction to ICC rules on international contracts / International Chamber of Commerce. – Paris : ICC Services S.A.R.L., 1981.
49p.

—Transnational law of international commercial transactions / edited by Norbert Horn and Clive M. Schmitthoff. – Antwerp : Kluwer-Devanter/The Netherlands, 1982.
Includes index and bibliography.
ISBN 9065440925 : est.

CONTRACT (ISLAMIC LAW)

—Remedies for breach of contract in Islamic and Iranian law / Glasgow : Royston, 1984.
250p.
ISBN 0946706212 £45.95

CONTRACT, JOINT AND SEVERAL - CANADA - SASKATCHEWAN

—Proposals relating to joint obligations : report to the Minister of Justice / Law Reform Commission of Saskatchewan. – Saskatoon : The Commission, 1985.
13p.

CONTRACT, MARITIME

—Asbatankvoy charter : a special report / by D. Thomas McCune. – London : Lloyd's of London Press, 1984.
ii,95 leaves.
Includes indexes.
ISBN 1850440336

—Cargo key receipt and transport document replacement / Kurt Gronfors. – Goteburg : Akademiforlaget, 1982.
104p. – (Skrifter).
ISBN 9124160555

—Shipbroker's manual / compiled by the Institute of Chartered Shipbrokers. – London : Lloyd's of London Press, 1983.
xix,167p.
Includes index.
ISBN 090743259X

—Shipping and contracting / Lars Gorton. – Lund : Juridiska Foreningen i Lund, 1983.
85p.
Includes bibliographical references and index.
ISBN 9154415012

CONTRACT, MARITIME - GREAT BRITAIN

—Bills of lading : law and practice / Alan Mitchelhill. – London : Chapman and Hall, 1982.
x,127p; 31cm.
Includes index.
ISBN 0412239604 Hbk Unpriced
ISBN 041223940X Pbk Unpriced

—C.I.F. and F.O.B. contracts / H. Orren Merren. – 3rd ed. – London : Stevens, 1984.
xlv,528p; 26cm.
Previous ed.: 1975. Includes index.
ISBN 0420465308 £60.00

—Scrutton on charterparties and bills of lading / Alan Abraham Mocatta, Michael John Mustill, Stewart C. Boyd. – 19th ed. – London : Sweet & Maxwell, 1984.
cv,593p; 25cm.
Section on time charters has been substantially revised and rewritten to take account of developments. Four House of Lords decisions on the problem of withdrawal for non-payment of hire are discussed, and there is an analysis of the related problem of deductions from hire.
ISBN 0421297107 £50.00

—Tanker voyage charter parties / by F. M. Ventris. – S.l. : Kluwer Law Publishers, 1986.
xvi,411p.
ISBN 0903393972

CONTRACT, PRELIMINARY

—Pre-contract deposits : a practice recommendation by the Conveyancing Standing Committee / London : Conveyancing Standing Committee, 1987.
ii,5,3p.

CONTRACT (ROMAN LAW)

—Contract in Roman law : from the Twelve Tables to the Glossators / Gy. Diosdi : translated by J. Szabo : translation edited by B. Nemenyi. – Budapest : Akademiai Kiado, 1981.
ISBN 9630524562

CONTRACT (ROMAN-DUTCH) LAW

—Treatise on the quasi-contract called promutuum and on the condictio indebiti / by Robert-Joseph Pothier : translated by W.J. Hosten and C. van Soelen : and editied by W.J. Hosten. – Pretoria : Government Printer on behalf of the South African Law Commission, 1987.
v,40p. – (Research series).
ISBN 0621107220

CONTRACTS - AUSTRALIA - TASMANIA

—Report on contracts and the disposition of property by minors / Law Reform Commission of Tasmania. – Hobart : Acting Government Printer, 1987.
14p. – (Report).
Includes text of the Infants' Relief Act 1875.

CONTRACTS - AUSTRALIA - WESTERN AUSTRALIA

—Report on minors' contracts / the Law Reform Commission of Western Australia. – Perth : Law Reform Commission of Western Australia, 1988.
117p. – (Project).

CONTRACTS - ENGLAND

—Stephen's commentaries on the laws of England / L. Crispin Warmington. – 21st ed. – London : Butterworths, 1950.
xiv,604p.
Index included in Vol. 4. .

—Towards a theory of contract / by A. G. Bischoff. – Reading : Bischoff, 1984.
v,13p.
ISBN 0950971405

CONTRACTUAL PENALTIES - AUSTRALIA - VICTORIA

—Liquidated damages and penalties / Law Reform Commission of Victoria. - Melbourne : The Commission, 1988.
i.20p. - (Discussion paper).
Includes bibliographical references.
ISBN 0724167293

CONVEYANCING

—Barnsley's conveyancing law and practice / P. W. Smith. - 2nd ed. - London : Butterworths, 1982.
lvi,715p; 26cm.
Previous ed.: 1973. Includes index.
ISBN 0406556326 Hbk Unpriced
ISBN 0406556334 Pbk Unpriced

—Scots conveyancing miscellany: essays in honour of Professor J.M. Halliday / Edinburgh : W Green & Son, 1987.
Collection of essays in the fields of conveyancing and related subjects - enforcement of title conditions, floating charges, fair rents, completion of title, land obligations, securities, etc.
ISBN 0414008030 Hbk

CONVEYANCING - AUSTRALIA

—Bound Australian and New Zealand Conveyancing Reports / North Ryde : C.C.H. Australia, 1979/80.

—Drafting: its applications to conveyancing and commercial documents / North Ryde : Butterworths (Australia), 1973.
Guide to the drafting of legal and commercial documents. Explains the underlying princples of drafting and demonstrates the link between those principles and the rule of law. Discusses the language of law, and generality of expression, and sets out the most salient features of parliamentary drafting practice relevant to document drafting.
ISBN 0409438251 Hbk

—Land Transfer Conveyancing Kit / Nunawading : Harrison-Ede Book Publishing.

—Sale of Real Property and Law of Agency in NSW / 4th ed. - Sydney : Butterworths, 1983.
176p.
This book is a working guide for those involved in conveyancing transactions. The fourth edition has been revised and updated to include new materials on the contract of sale of land, strata titles, agents' commissions, registration of titles, valuation of land, and other topics.

—Strata Titles / R. Tzannes. - North Ryde : Law Book Co, 1978.
v, 353p.
ISBN 0455194994 Hbk £64.00

1980 Supplement
ISBN 045520246X £12.00

CONVEYANCING - AUSTRALIA - NEW SOUTH WALES

—Community law reform program / New South Wales Law Reform Commission. - Sydney : The Commission, 1984.
84p. - (L.R.C. 40).
Bibliography: p.83-84.

—Conveyancing Costs Tables, NSW / 2nd ed. - North Ryde : Law Book Co, 1986.
xxi, 112p.
ISBN 045520683X Pbk £12.50

—Conveyancing Manual for New South Wales / Woolloomooloo : International Business Communications, 1987.
ISBN 0949553328 Hbk £25.00

—N.S.W. Strata Titles Act 1973 / North Ryde : C.C.H. Australia, 1987.
200p.
ISBN 0869038648 Hbk

—Strata Title Management Practice in New South Wales / 4th ed. - North Ryde : C.C.H. Australia, 1985.
480p.
ISBN 0869036378 Hbk £35.00

—Strata Title Units in New South Wales - A Guide to the Strata Titles Act / 3rd ed. - Sydney : Butterworths, 1985.
200p.
ISBN 0409493147 Hbk

—Victorian Conveyancing Costs / Butterworths.

CONVEYANCING - AUSTRALIA - TASMANIA

—Report and recommendations for reform on fifteen conveyancing matters / Law Refrom Commission of Tasmania. - Hobart : Government Printer, 1984.
20p. - (Report).

—Report and recommendations on the law and procedure relating to the sale of land by instalments / Law Reform Commission of Tasmania. - Hobart : Government Printer, 1983.
25p. - (Report).

CONVEYANCING - AUSTRALIA - VICTORIA

—Victorian Conveyancing Costs Annotated / 3rd ed. - Sydney : Butterworths, 1983.
80p.
ISBN 0409493112 Pbk

CONVEYANCING - CANADA

—Conveyancing : Current Issues / Vancouver : Continuing Legal Education Society of British Columbia, 1988.
162p.
ISBN 0865043809 Hbk £70.00

—Conveyancing for Legal Assistants 1986 / Vancouver : Continuing Legal Education Society of British Columbia, 1986.
292p.
ISBN 0865042640 Hbk £65.00

Supplement-1987
119p.
ISBN 0865043213 Hbk £55.00

—Conveyancing Made Easy : a Teaching Text for Lawyers and Their Secretaries / Vancouver : Fountain Books, 1982.
254p.
ISBN 0969000901 Hbk £30.00

—Conveyancing requisitions / Scarborough, Ontario : Butterworths (Canada).
232.
Aspects of a real estate transaction are covered, from drafting an agreement of purchase and sale to reviewing the abstract of title, to submission of and response to requisitions and all the requirements of closing.
ISBN 0409866270 Hbk

—Conveyancing Requisitions / Toronto : Butterworths, 1983.
232p.

—O'Brien's Encyclopedia of Forms : Division Three-Conveyancing and Mortgages / Aurora : Canada Law Book Co.
- (Abridgments and Encyclopedias).

Supplement

—Registration of title of Land / Agincourt : Carswell, 1987.
ISBN 045935440 Hbk £48.40

CONVEYANCING - CANADA - ALBERTA

—Alberta conveyancing law and practice / by John Sterk. - Toronto : Carswell, 1981.
xvi,279p.
ISBN 0459337106

—Sterk's Alberta Conveyancing Law and Practice / 2nd ed. - Agincourt : Carswell, 1987.
300p.

—Sterk's Alberta Conveyancing Law and Practice / 2nd ed. - Agincourt : Carswell, 1987.
325p.

—Sterk's Alberta Conveyancing Law and Practice / 2nd ed. - Agincourt : Carswell, 1987.
300p.
This practitioner's quick reference text provides materials on real estate transactions practice in Alberta, Canada. Forms, checklist, precedents, and other items needed to conduct the typical real estate transaction are included.

CONVEYANCING - CANADA - NEW BRUNSWICK

—Professional Liability in Conveyancing in New Brunswick / Agincourt : Carswell, 1986.
127p.
This book addresses the lawyer's liability in conveyancing in New Brunswick, Canada. The role of the real estate practitioner is reviewed and the legal grounds for liability are analyzed in the work.

CONVEYANCING - ENGLAND

—Barnsley's conveyancing law and practice / 3rd ed. - London : Butterworth, 1988.
lxxviii,677p.
Previous ed.: 1982. Includes index.
ISBN 0406556342 Pbk £32.00 (May)
ISBN 0406556350 £19.95

—Concise land registration practice / Christopher West. - 3rd ed. - London : Sweet & Maxwell, 1982.
xvii,313p; 23cm.
Previous ed.: / by Theodore B.F. Ruoff. 1967. Includes index.
ISBN 0421287705 £19.50

—Contract / Ruth Annand, Richard Whish. - London : Sweet & Maxwell, 1987.
xxii,175p; 26cm.
Includes index.
ISBN 0421362405 £16.50

—Contract and conveyance / J.T. Farrand. - 3rd ed. - London : Oyez, 1980.
lxiii,340p.
ISBN 0851204392

—Conveyancing after the Act / Peter H.M. Soar. - London : Butterworth, 1986.
viii,179p; 22cm.
Includes index.
ISBN 0406504105 Pbk £12.50

—Conveyancing in a nutshell / Angela Tannett. - London : Sweet & Maxwell, 1980.
84p; 18cm. - (New nutshells).
Includes index.
ISBN 0421278102 Pbk £1.50

—Enquiries before contract / Ruth Annand, Brian Cain. - London : Sweet & Maxwell, 1986.
xvii,207p; 26cm.
Includes index.
ISBN 0421348100 £16.50

—Gibson's conveyancing / general editor R.A. Donell : assisted by P.R. Dean... et al. - 21st ed. - London : Law Notes Lending Library, 1980.
lxxviii,647p.

—Handbook of conveyancing searches / E.O. Bourne. - 2nd ed. - London : Sweet & Maxwell, 1986.
ix,87p.
ISBN 042136680X

—Lawyers and the courts : time for some changes / a discussion paper issued by the Law Society's Contentious Business Committee : an appraisal published by the Council of the Law Society of the effect of the Building Societies Bill on the solicitors' profession. - London : Law Society, 1986.
10 leaves.
Supplement to the Law Society's 'Gazette', 22 January (1986). Includes bibliographical references.

—Leasehold conveyancing : laid before Parliament by the Lord High Chancellor pursuant to section 3(2) of the Law Commissions Act 1965 / the Law Commission. - London : H.M.S.O., 1987.
iii,37p. - (H.C.).
ISBN 0102360871

—Licensed conveyancing : the new legislation / with annotations by Phillip H. Kenny. - London : Sweet & Maxwell, 1986.
vi,52p.
Text of the Administration of Justice Act 1985, Part II, with Appendix and notes.
ISBN 0421350504

—Making a move? : the guide to your conveyancing / London : Sweet & Maxwell, 1988.
14p.
ISBN 0421399600

—Memorandum of evidence to Farrand Committee on Conveyancing Procedure and Practice / Justice. - London : Justice, 1984.
17p.

—Modern conveyancing / by Ruth Annand and Brian Cain. - London : Sweet & Maxwell, 1984.
xlii,514p; 24cm.
Includes index.
ISBN 0421320907 Hbk No price
ISBN 0421321008 Pbk £15.95

—Preliminary enquiries : house purchase : a practice recommendation / the Conveyancing Standing Committee of the Law Commission. - London : Longman, 1987.
16p; 26x11cm.
ISBN 0851213219 Pbk £4.95

—Prideaux's Forms and precedents in conveyancing / T. K. Wigan, I. M. Phillips. - 25th ed. 3. - London : Sweet & Maxwell in co-operation with Ashford Press, 1985.
24cm.
Previous ed.: London : Stevens & Sons : Solicitors' Law Stationery Society, 1948. Includes index. Editors: T.K. Wigan et al.
ISBN 042134590X £170.00

—Property law : fourth report on land registration / the Law Commission. - London : HMSO, 1988.
iii,147p. - (H.C. 1987-88).
ISBN 0102680884

—Property law : second report on land registration : inspection of the register / the Law Commission. - London : H.M.S.O., 1985.
iii,43p.
ISBN 0102551855

—Property law : third report on land registration, A. overriding interests, B. rectification and indemnity, C. minor interests / the Law Commission. - London : H.M.S.O., 1987.
v,107p.
ISBN 0102269874

—Residential estate conveyancing : practice and precedents / John Cawthorn. - London : Butterworths, 1983.
xviii,501p; 26cm.
Includes index.
ISBN 0406148201 Unpriced

—Transfer of land : implied covenants for title / the Law Commission. - London : HMSO, 1988.
v,57,11p. - (Working paper).
Includes excerpts from relevant acts.
ISBN 0117301892

—Transfer of land : passing of risk from vendor to purchaser / the Law Commission. - London : HMSO, 1988.
v,87p. - (Working paper).
ISBN 0117301914

—Transfer of land : the rule in Bain v. Fothergill / The Law Commission. – London : H.M.S.O., 1986.
iv,49p; 21cm. – (Working paper).
Includes bibliographical references.
ISBN 0117301795

CONVEYANCING - GREAT BRITAIN

—Buying Your Own House / London : Longman Professional, 1988.
ISBN 0851213790 Pbk £4.95

—Concise Precedents in Modern Conveyancing, 2 Vols. / Repr. of 1853 ed. – Abingdon : Professional Books.
175p.

—Contract and Conveyance / 4th ed. – London : Oyez Longman, 1983.
ISBN 0851207715 Hbk £15.95

—Conveyancer and Property Lawyer / London : Sweet & Maxwell.
Bound volume
Cordex binder
Back vols. available

—Conveyancer's Guide To Local and Public Authorities / London : Waterlow, 1988.
ISBN 0080331025 Hbk £12.95

—Conveyancing 1985 / London : Law Society, 1985.
15p. – (Nineteen Eighty-Five Crash Course Transcripts).

—Conveyancing / Donell. – 21st ed. – London : Law Notes Lending Library, 1980.
ISBN 0900516089 Hbk £20.00

—Conveyancing / London : Butterworths, 1983.
This text for students of conveyancing is an introduction to the theory and practice of conveyancing of land in the United Kingdom. A comprehensive work including materials on landlord and tenant, housing, and land law.
ISBN 0406010625 Pbk

—Conveyancing / 2nd ed. – London : Butterworths, 1987.
ISBN 0406010641 Pbk £15.95

—Conveyancing / 2nd ed. – London : Butterworths, 1987.
ISBN 0406010641 Hbk

—Conveyancing After the Act / London : Butterworths, 1986.
ISBN 0406504105 Pbk £9.75

—Conveyancing and Other Non-Contentious Costs / 7th ed. – London : Oyez Longman, 1980. – (Oyez Longman Practice Note Ser.: No. 20).
ISBN 0851204724 Hbk £7.95

—Conveyancing and Residential Tenancies : Conditions of Sale and Other Recent Developments to March 1982 / London : Law Society, 1982.

—Conveyancing Fees and Charges / 11th ed. – London : Longman Professional, 1986.
ISBN 0851212328 Pbk £6.95

—Conveyancing Fees and Charges / Oyez Longman Publishing. – 6th ed. – London : Oyez Longman, 1981.
ISBN 0851205704 Hbk £3.95

—Conveyancing Fees and Duties / Fourmat Publishing. – 6th ed. – London : Fourmat, 1986. – (LCFS 5).
ISBN 1851900209 Pbk £4.50

—Conveyancing Law / C. Bevan. – 2nd ed. – Plymouth : Macdonald & Evans, 1984.
320p. – (M and E Handbook Ser.).
ISBN 0712104828 Pbk £4.50

—Conveyancing Law / Bevan. – 3rd ed. – Plymouth : Macdonald & Evans, 1986.
ISBN 071210755X Pbk £6.50

—Conveyancing Law and Practice / 3rd ed. – London : Butterworths, 1982.
ISBN 040655553424 Hbk

—Conveyancing Practice and Procedure / Gittings. – 2nd ed. – London : Fourmat, 1985.
ISBN 0906840910 Pbk £9.95

—Conveyancing Searches and Enquiries / London : Butterworths, 1985.
ISBN 040625513X Pbk £26.95

—Conveyancing Solutions No. 2 : The Contract / R. Whish. – London : Sweet & Maxwell, 1987.

—Do-It-Yourself Conveyancing / 3rd ed. – London : David & Charles, 1984.
ISBN 0715386697 Hbk £6.95

—Estate Conveyancing / London : Waterlow, 1984.
ISBN 0080391370 Hbk £19.50

—Evidence of the Society for Computers and Law and Technology and Law Limited to The Farrand Conveyancing Committee / Society for Computers and Law. – S.l. : The authors?, 1984.
10p; 30cm.

—Guide to DIY House Buying, Selling and Conveyancing / 2nd ed. – London : Castle Books, 1983.
ISBN 0950717053 Pbk £4.95

—Guide to DIY House Buying : Supp. Leasehold Flats and Houses / London : Castle Books, 1985.
ISBN 0950717096 Pbk £3.50

—House selling the Scottish way for England and Wales / an explanatory guide by the Conveyancing Standing Committee. – London : The Law Commission, Conveyancing Standing Committee, 1985.
20 leaves.

—Introduction to Conveyancing / 2nd ed. – London : Oyez Longman, 1983.
ISBN 0851203663 Hbk £6.50

—Introduction to conveyancing / 2nd ed. – London : Longman Professional, 1983.
ISBN 0851207383 Pbk £14.95

—Law for Licensed Conveyancers / London : Financial Training, 1988.
ISBN 1851850724 Pbk £7.95

—Making a move? Your guide to conveyancing / London : Sweet & Maxwell, 1988.
ISBN 0421399708 Pbk £18.75

—Modern Conveyancing Precedents / 2nd ed. – London : Butterworths, 1988.
ISBN 040633451X Hbk

—Newman's Conveyancing Practice and Procedure / Phyllis E. Newman. – 2nd ed. – London : Fourmat, 1985.
135p.
ISBN 0906840910 Pbk £9.95

—Non-solicitor conveyancers : competence and consumer protection : (the first report of the Conveyancing Committee) / chairman: J. T. Farrand : presented to the Lord Chancellor September 1984. – London : H.M.S.O., 1984.
v,118p.
ISBN 0113906374 PBK £6.30

—Planning Law for Conveyancers / D. W. Williams. – London : Oyez Longman, 1983. – (Oyez Longman Practice Note Ser.: No. 76).
ISBN 0851207731 Hbk £9.95

—Planning law for conveyancers (LPPN 76) / Williams. – 2nd ed. – London : Longman Professional, 1987.
ISBN 0851209963 Pbk £15.95

—Practical conveyancing / 10th ed. – London : Longman Professional, 1986.
ISBN 0851212239 Pbk £16.95

—Practical Conveyancing / 8th ed. – London : Oyez Longman, 1981. – (Oyez Longman Practice Note Ser.: No. 44).
ISBN 0851205917 Hbk £10.95

—Practical conveyancing precedents / London : Longman Professional, 1985.
ISBN 0851207707 updat £95.00

—Precedents for the Conveyancer, 2 Vols. / London : Sweet & Maxwell, 1983.
ISBN 042125520X Hbk £120.00
Service only

—Registered land / by David J. Hayton. – 3rd ed. – London : Sweet & Maxwell, 1981.
xxiii,222p; 20cm.
Previous ed.: 1977. Includes index.
ISBN 042128160X Hbk £10.00
ISBN 0421281707 Pbk £6.50

—Registered land practice notes / Law Society. – 2nd ed. – London : Longman Professional, 1986.
ISBN 0851212573 Pbk £5.95

—Ruoff & Roper on the law and practice of registered conveyancing / Robert B. Roper. – 5th ed. – London : Sweet & Maxwell, 1986.
lxxiv,1233p; 26cm.
Previous ed.: 1979. Includes index.
ISBN 0420469109 £82.00

—Sale and Management of Flats : Practice and Precedents / London : Butterworths, 1985.
This book provides a practical guide to the subject of leasehold conveyancing in the United Kingdom. Particular attention is given to the establishment and maijntenance of subsequent management of the property from the tenant's and developer's point of view.
ISBN 0406526702 Hbk

—Searches and Enquiries : A Conveyancer's Guide / London : Butterworths, 1985.
This book gives a step by step guide to the process of searches and enquiries made by conveyancers in the United Kingdom. The work includes an analysis of common searches and a reference guide to unusual searches.
ISBN 040625513X Pbk

—Second Report : Conveyancing Simplifications / Conveyancing Committee. – London : HMSO, 1985.
ISBN 0113800029 Hbk £8.60

—Stamp duties for conveyancers / Farrand. – 4th ed. – London : Longman Professional, 1986. – (Longman Practice Note. No.48).
ISBN 0851211739 Pbk £15.95

—Stamp Duty for Conveyancers / Roger Gregory. – 3rd ed. – London : Oyez Longman, 1983. – (Oyez Longman Practice Note Ser.: No. 48).
ISBN 0851206352 Hbk £7.95

—Standard conditions of sale / 2nd ed. – London : Butterworths, 1987.
ISBN 0406255113 Pbk £25.95

—Standard Conditions of Sale : A Conveyancer's Guide / London : Butterworths, 1986.
This work comparees the National Conditions of Sale and the Law Society's General Conditions of Sale and analyzes the ways in which they diverge. The discussion of conditions in the book follows that of events in a normal conveyancing transaction in the United Kingdom.
ISBN 0406255113 Pbk

—Subject-to-Contract Procedures in House Purchase / Reading : College of Estate Management, 1984.
28p.
ISBN 0902132989 Hbk £7.50

—Tax Strategy for Conveyancing and Land Transactions / London : Oyez Longman, 1984.
ISBN 0851208797 Hbk

—Touch-Stone of Common Assurances : Treatise Opening the Learning of Common Assurances or Conveyances of the Kingdome / 2nd ed. Repr. of 1648 ed. – Abingdon : Professional Books.
487p.

—Transfer of land : formalities for contracts for sale etc of land / London : H.M.S.O., 1985.
iv,79p. – (Working paper).
ISBN 0117301736

—Transfer of land : formalities for contracts for sale etc. of land / the Law Commission. – London : H.M.S.O., 1987.
37p. – (1987/88 HC2).
ISBN 0102002886

—Transfer of land : formalities for deeds and escrows / London : H.M.S.O., 1985.
iv,44p. – (Working paper).
ISBN 0117301744

CONVEYANCING - HONG KONG

—Annotation of the Hong Kong Conveyancing and Property Ordinance / Butterworths, 1987.
ca 300p.
Deals with the 1984 Conveyancing and Property Ordinance, and annotates the 1988 Conveyancing and Property (Amendment) Ordinance. Discusses the background and the intended effects of the Ordinance, and gives a detailed analysis of each section. Sets out case authorities for the common law position.
ISBN 0409995401 Hbk £50.00

—Conveyancing in Hong Kong / Hartley Bramwell. – London : Butterworths, 1981.
xxvii,403p; 23cm.
Includes index.
ISBN 040666210X

—Hong Kong conveyancing and property ordinance / London : Butterworths, 1988.
ISBN 0409995401 Hbk £42.00

CONVEYANCING - INDIA

—Art of Conveyancing and Pleading / 1974 2nd repr. – Lucknow : Eastern Book Company, 1983.
290p.

—Conveyancing, Draftsman and Legal Interpretation of Deeds, as Interpreted under Income-Tax Law, 5 Vols. / 6th ed. 5v. – Allahabad : Law Publishers, 1982.

—Conveyancing, Precedents and Forms / G.C. Mathur. – 5th ed. – Lucknow : Eastern Book Company, 1983.
704p.

—Law and Practice of Conveyancing / Allahabad : Universal Book Agency.

CONVEYANCING - IRELAND

—Irish conveyancing law / London : Butterworths, 1982.
ISBN 0903486458 Hbk £41.00

CONVEYANCING - MALAYSIA

—Strata Titles Act, 1985 (Act 318) / Kuala Lumpur : International Law Books Services.

—Strata titles in Malaysia : law and practice / L T Khaw. – London : Butterworths, 1987.
ISBN 040999538X Hbk £32.00

CONVEYANCING - NEW ZEALAND

—Bound Australian and New Zealand Conveyancing Reports / North Ryde : C.C.H. Australia, 1979/80.

—Butterworths Conveyancing Bulletin / Butterworths.
ISBN 0409701815 Hbk

—Law and Practice of Conveyancing in New Zealand / Brookfield. – 4th ed. – London : Butterworths, 1981.
ISBN 0409600296 Hbk £41.00

—Law and Practice of Conveyancing Precedents in New Zealand / 4th ed. – Butterworths, 1980.
ISBN 0409600296 Hbk £119.90 (includes supplement)

Supplement-1986
ISBN 040970167X

—New Zealand Conveyancing and Property Reports / Butterworths, 1983.
ISBN 0409701416 Hbk £71.50

—New Zealand Conveyancing and Property Reports / Wellington : Butterworths, 1983.
ISBN 0409701416 Hbk

—New Zealand Conveyancing Bulletin / Wellington : Butterworths.
ISBN 0409781428 Pbk

CONVEYANCING - NORTHERN IRELAND

—Conveyancing and miscellaneous matters / Great Britain. – Belfast : H.M.S.O., 1983.
vii,153p. – (Discussion document).
At head of title-page: Department of Finance and Personnel for Northern Ireland, Office of Law Reform.
ISBN 033723406X

—Occupiers' rights and constructive notice : the text of a lecture delivered to the Belfast Solicitors' Association on 2 December 1982 / by Hebert Wallace. – Belfast : SLS Legal Publications, 1982.
35p.
Includes bibliographical references.

CONVEYANCING - SCOTLAND

—Conveyancing law and practice in Scotland / by John M. Halliday. – Edinburgh : W. Green under the auspices of the Scottish Universities Law Institute, 1985.
xxxviii,491p; 25cm.
Includes index.
ISBN 0414007603 No price

Vol.2 : Feus and dispositions / by John M. Halliday. – 1986.
xxxvii,518p; 25cm.
Includes index.
ISBN 0414007891 Hbk £30.00

Vol.3 : Leases and heritable securities / by John M. Halliday. – 1987.
xxix,550p; 25cm.
Includes index.
ISBN 0414008154 No price

Vol.4. Wills and succession 1990.
Deals with testate and intestate succession both before and after the Succession (Scotland) Act 1964, including statutory prior rights and legal rights, completion of title to both heritable and moveable estate, preparation of wills, administration of executries, destination, entails, judicial transmissons, compulsory acuisition, trusts, taxation, and pension schemes. Includes index for Vols. 1 to 4. Published under the auspices of the Scottish Universities law Institute.
ISBN 0414008936 Hbk

—Conveyancing manual / 4th. – Edinburgh : T & T Clark.
Primarily a student manual written by a former Professor of Conveyancing at Dundee University. Covers, in six parts, preliminary matters, feus, resulting rights of superior and vassal, subordinate rites in the feu - securities and leases, transmission of the feu, and reform.
ISBN 0567291715 Pbk

—Formulary of old Scots legal documents / compiled by Peter Gouldesbrough : with a supplementary essay on Early Scottish conveyancing by Gordon Donaldson. – Edinburgh : Stair Society, 1985.
viii,196p.
Includes index.
ISBN 0902292110

—Response by the Law Society of Scotland to Consultative Paper on Conveyancing by Employed Solicitors in Scotland / Law Society of Scotland. – Edinburgh : The Society, 1984.
20p.

—Scots Conveyancing Statutes 1983 : Reprinted from the Parliament House Book / Edinburgh : W Green, 1983.
ISBN 0414007247 Hbk £5.50

—Scots Conveyancing Statutes 1984 / Edinburgh : W Green.
ISBN 0414007484 Hbk £9.75

CONVEYANCING - SOUTH AFRICA

—Conveyancing in South Africa / R.J.M. Jones. – 3rd ed. – Cape Town : Juta, 1985.
xix, 540 p.; 26 cm.
Rev. ed. of: The law and practice of conveyancing in South Africa. 2nd ed. 1976. Includes indexes.
ISBN 0702115967

CONVEYANCING - WEST GERMANY

—Law of Copyright / Repr. of 1912 ed. – Aalen Wuertt : Scientia.
xxxii, 351p.

COOPERATIVE SOCIETIES - CANADA

—Law of Canadian co-operatives / by Daniel Ish. – Toronto : Burroughs, 1981.
xxvi, 294 p.; 24 cm.
This book reviews co-operative corporation legislation of provincial and federal jurisdictions in Canada. The work analyzes the principles of corporate common law in the context of co-operative corporations, in addition to corporate statutory materials.
ISBN 0459336800 Hbk £46.25

COOPERATIVE SOCIETIES - GREAT BRITAIN

—Co-ops that Work : Constitutions, Conversions and Tax / London : Spokesman Books, 1988.
160p.
ISBN 0851244521 Pbk £25.00
ISBN 0851244629 Pbk £8.95

—Law of co-operatives / Ian Snaith. – London : Waterlow, 1984.
xxviii,218p; 22cm.
Bibliography: p210-213. - Includes index.
ISBN 0080391591 Hbk £31.00

—Law of Co-Operatives / London : Waterlow, 1984.
ISBN 0080391591 Hbk £18.00

COOPERATIVE SOCIETIES - INDIA

—Commentaries on Uttar Pradesh Cooperative Societies Act, 1965 / Sushma Malik. – 4th ed. – Lucknow : Eastern Book Company, 1984.
756p.

—Cooperative Societies Act, 1948 and Rules and Regulations / Allahabad : Law Book Company.

—Maharashtra Cooperative Societies : Acts and Rules; as Amended by Acts no 10 and 20 of 1986, 2 Vols. / Indore : United Law Publishers, 1987.

—Multi-State Cooperative Societies Act, 1984 : With Rules / Indore : United Law Publishers, 1987.

COOPERATIVE SOCIETIES - SOUTH AFRICA

—Taxation of Co-operative Societies in South Africa / Cape Town : Legal & Financial Publishing, 1983.
ISBN 0869940317 Hbk £13.50

COPYING PROCESSES - CANADA

—Impact of reprography on the copyright system / S.J. Liebowitz. – Ottawa : Research and International Affairs Branch, Bureau of Corporate Affairs, Consumer and Corporate Affairs Canada, 1981.
82 p.; 28 cm.
Bibliography: p. 81-82.
ISBN 0662113969 pbk.

COPYRIGHT

—ABC of copyright / Unesco. – Paris : Unesco, 1981.
88p.
Includes discussion of the moral and economic rights of authors, limits to copyright protection, copyright infringement and its remedies and international copyright.
ISBN 9231018892 Hbk

—Copies in copyright / by J.H. Spoor, W.R. Cornish, P.F. Nolan. – Alphen aan den Rijn : Sitthoff & Noordhoff, 1980.
vii, 187p.

—Copies in Copyright / W.R. Cornish. – Dordrecht : Kluwer, 1980.
200p.
ISBN 9028603506 Hbk Gld82.00

—Copyright and Treaties of the World, 3 Vols. and 23 supplements / Paris : UNESCO.
ISBN 9231019465 Hbk £5,590.00

Supplement 22 1979-80.
ISBN 9231019457 Hbk £900.00

—Copyright Bulletin / UNESCO. – London : HMSO.

Single Issues

—Copyright Laws and Treaties of the World / Paris : UNESCO, 1979-1980.
ISBN 9231019457 Hbk

—Copyright Laws and Treaties of the World : Supplement 1981-1983 / London : HMSO.
Review of the national and international laws of copyright and intellectual property protection.
ISBN 0119110636 Hbk £210.00

—Copyright Protection : Conference Papers / Woolloomooloo : International Business Communications, 1986.
ISBN 0949072060 Hbk £55.00

—Copyright system : practice and problems in developing countries / by Denis de Freitas. – London : Commonwealth Secretariat, 1983.
v,87p.
ISBN 085092233X

—Copyright : the development and exercise of the performing right / Eastbourne : Offord, 1980.
205 p. – (City Arts Series).
ISBN 0903931273

—Copyright through the cases / Gavin McFarlane. – London : Waterlow, 1986.
288p; 23cm. – (Waterlow's practitioner's library).
Includes index.
ISBN 0080392083 Pbk £15.00

—Information technology : the challenge to copyright / by James Lahore, Gerald Dworkin, Yvonne M. Smyth. – London : Sweet & Maxwell, 1984.
vii,116p; 22cm.
Includes index.
ISBN 0421322608 Pbk £11.00

—International copyright and neighbouring rights / London : Butterworths, 1983.
ISBN 0406662207 Hbk £73.50

—International copyright and neighbouring rights / Stephen M. Stewart. – London : Butterworths, 1983.
xii,740p; 26cm.
This book covers the underlying general principles of both international and national copyright laws with particular reference to neighbouring rights including coverage of corporate ownership rights. This work is directed at the international law student and practitioner.
ISBN 0406662207 Hbk

—International copyright law and practice / Matthew Bender, 1988.
ISBN 0000999074 Hbk £53.00

—Legal protection of computer programs / Bryan Niblett. – London : Oyez, 1980.
xii,155p; 22cm.
Includes index.
ISBN 0851205097 £10.00

—Legal protection of computer programs and data / by Christopher J. Millard. – London : Sweet & Maxwell, 1985.
xxvi,239p; 23cm.
Includes index.
ISBN 0421334800 Pbk £24.00
ISBN 0459372300 Canada

—Legal protection of computer software / edited by Lawrence Perry and Hugh Brett. – Oxford : ESC, 1981.
xiv,197p; 22cm.
Includes bibliographical references.
ISBN 0906214068 Pbk Unpriced

—Model Provisions on the Protection of Computer Software : Text of the English Translation of the Stockholm Act (1967) / Geneva : World Intellectual Property Organization.
27p.

—Multilateral Convention for the Avoidance of Double Taxation of Copyright Royalties : Original Text of the Convention Adopted by the Madrid Conference (1979) / rep. 1987. – Geneva : World Intellectual Property Organization.
41p.

—Nairobi Treaty on the Protection of the Olympic Symbol (September 26, 1981), Nairobi Conference (1981) / Geneva : World Intellectual Property Organization.
31p.

—The penal protection of works of art / Siracusa : International Institute of Higher Studies in Criminal Sciences, 1983.
447p.
Includes bibliographical references. English, French or Italian.

—Piracy and counterfeiting of industrial property and copyright : papers given at the inaugural conference of the Common Law Institute of Intellectual Property Ltd in London on 28th and 29th January 1983 / edited by W.R. Cornish. – London : Common Law Institute of Intellectual Property, 1983.
143p.
ISBN 0903067277

—Third party protection of software and firmware : direct protection of zeros and ones / John J. Borking. – Amsterdam : North-Holland, 1985.
xx,521p; 24cm.
Bibliography: p491-510. - Includes index.
ISBN 0444876774 £48.78

—Video Piracy and the Law / New Delhi : Deep and Deep Publications, 1986.
160p.

—Vienna Agreement for the Protection of Type Faces and Their International Deposit : Original Text of the Agreement, Regulations and Protocol Adopted by the Vienna Conference / Geneva : World Intellectual Property Organization.
63p.

—WIPO Glossary of Terms of the Law of Copyright and Neighboring Rights / Geneva : World Intellectual Property Organization, 1981.
281p.

Terms and Definitions in English, in Alphabetical Order, with Equivalencies in French and Japanese 1986.
283p.

Terms and Definitions in English, in Alphabetical Order, with Equivalencies in French and Portuguese 1983.
281p.

Terms and Definitions in English, in Alphabetical Order with Equivalencies in French and Russian 1981.
281p.

Terms and Definitions in English, in Alphabetical Order, with Equivalencies in French and Spanish 1980.
281p.

—WIPO International Forum on the Collective Administration of Copyrights and Neighboring Rights / Geneva : World Intellectual Property Organization, 1986.
122p.

COPYRIGHT - AUSTRALIA

—Architects and Copyright / Milsons Point : Australian Copyright Council.

—Computer law in Australia : a collection of essays / edited by W. John Taggart. - Sydney : Legal Books Pty., 1987.
xii,75p.
Bibliography: pp.61-64. - Includes index.
ISBN 0949553271

—Copyright Act / 5th ed. - Allahabad : Law Book Company, 1985.
435p.

—Copyright Amendment Act 1980 / Milsons Point : Australian Copyright Council.

—Copyright and Cable Television / Milsons Point : Australian Copyright Council.

—Copyright and Film / Milsons Point : Australian Copyright Council.

—Copyright and Music / Milsons Point : Australian Copyright Council.

—Copyright and Writers / Milsons Point : Australian Copyright Council.

—Copyright law in Australia and the rights of performers, authors and composers in the Pacific region / by J.A.L. Sterling and Geoffrey E. Hart. - Sydney : Legal Books, 1981.
xli,278p; 23cm.
Bibliography: p.263-265. - Includes index.
ISBN 0959656871

—Copyright protection for artistic works industrially applied / Attorney-General's Department. - Canberra : Australian Government Publishing Service, 1987.
v,62p. - (Discussion paper).
Includes excerpts from the Copyright Act 1968.
ISBN 0644061391

—Intellectual Property in Australia : Patents, Designs, Trade Marks, Confidential Information and Unfair Competition / James W. Dwyer. - Wellington : Butterworths.
This looseleaf service provides exhaustive coverage of the law in Australia relating to copyright in literary and artistic works, sound recordings, film, television and radio broadcasts, and published editions of books and other works. The full text of relevant statutes is provided.

—Performers' Protection / Milsons Point : Australian Copyright Council.

—Performers' Protection / Milsons Point : Australian Copyright Council.

—Photocopying : a guide to the 1980 amendments to the Copyright Act / by James Lahore. - Sydney : Butterworths, 1980.
74 p.; 22 cm.
ISBN 0409490342 £4.95

—Reform Issues : Audiovisual Copying / Milsons Point : Australian Copyright Council.

—Short Note on Anti-Copyright / Wollstone Craft : Leksand Press.
82p.
ISBN 095897800X Hbk £8.00

—Unfair Contracts and Copyright / Milsons Point : Australian Copyright Council.

—User's guide to copyright / Michael F. Flint. - 2nd ed. - North Ryde : Butterworths (Australia), 1985.
xvii,289p; 22cm.
Explains the operation and scope of the law and provides answers to problems. Deals with the copyright problems of particular professions, making use of charts and tables. Includes new chapters dealing with cable and satellite television, video games, teletext and electronic publishing, and piracy and counterfeiting.
ISBN 0406200742 Pbk

—Visual Artists and Photographers : Copyright and Designs / Milsons Point : Australian Copyright Council.

COPYRIGHT - CANADA

—Copyright and Trade Mark Litigation 1988 / Vancouver : Continuing Legal Education Society of British Columbia, 1988.
372p.
ISBN 0865049807 Hbk £85.00

—Copyright, competition and Canadian culture : the impact of alternative Copyright Act import provisions on the book publishing and sound recording industries / Ake G. Blomqvist and Chin Lim. - 2 microfiches. - Ottawa : Minister of Supply and Services, 1981.
159 fr.; 10x15cm.
Bibliography: p.145-147.

—Copyright for the Canadian Visual Artist / repr. 1981. - Ottawa : CARFAC.

—Copyright : Proceedings of the Workshop Held at the Annual Conference of the Canadian Library Association June 7, 1984, Toronto, Ontario / Ottawa : Canadian Library Association, 1985.
72p.
ISBN 0888021925 Hbk £10.00

—Crown copyright in Canada : a legacy of confusion / Barry Torno. - 1 microfiche. - Ottawa : Minister of Supply and Services, 1981.
78 fr.; 10x15cm.
Bibliography: p.65-67.
ISBN 0662113942

—Economic analysis of a performers' right / Steven Globerman and Mitchell P. Rothman. - Ottawa, Ont. : Consumer and Corporate Affairs Canada, 1981.
111 p.; 28 cm.
Bibliography: p. 109-111.

—Hughes on Copyright and Industrial Design, 1 Vol. / Butterworths.

—Hughes on copyright and industrial design / 1 vol. - Scarborough, Ontario : Butterworths (Canada).
Covers registration procedures, assignment and licensing, infringement, and remedies.

—Hughes on Copyright and Industrial Design / Toronto : Butterworths.

—Impact of reprography on the copyright system / S.J. Liebowitz. - Ottawa : Research and International Affairs Branch, Bureau of Corporate Affairs, Consumer and Corporate Affairs Canada, 1981.
82 p.; 28 cm.
Bibliography: p. 81-82.
ISBN 0662113969 pbk.

—Musicians and the law in Canada / by Paul Sanderson. - Toronto : Carswell, 1985.
xxxi, 258 p.; 24 cm.
Includes index.
ISBN 0459372203

—Recent Developments in Business and Litigation /. - Vancouver : Continuing Legal Education Society of British Columbia.

—Term of copyright protection in Canada : present and proposed / Barry Torno. - 1 microfiche. - Ottawa : Minister of Supply and Services Canada, 1980.
52 fr.; 10x15cm.
Bibliography: p.41-42.
ISBN 0662909372

COPYRIGHT - CHINA

—Copyright and China / Milsons Point : Australian Copyright Council.

COPYRIGHT - EUROPE

—Copyright Problems of Satellite and Cable Television in Europe / Dordrecht : Kluwer, 1987.
208p.
ISBN 0860109526 Hbk Gld125.00

COPYRIGHT - EUROPEAN COMMUNITY

—Challenges to copyright and related rights in the European Community / Gillian Davies and Hans Hugo von Rauscher auf Weeg. - Oxford : ESC, 983.
xvii,271p.
Bibliography: p.253-258. - Includes index.
ISBN 0906214149

—Green paper on copyright and the challenge of technology : copyright issues requiring immediate action / communication from the Commission. - Luxembourg : Office for Official Publication of the European Communities, 1988.
vi,237p. - (Document).
ISBN 9277367822

—Piracy of phonograms : a study prepared for the Commission of the European Communities, Directorate-General for Research, Science and Education / Gillian Davies. - Oxford : Published for the Commission of the European Communities, Cultural Sector by ESC Publishing, 1981.
xii,150p; 22cm.
ISBN 0906214076 Pbk Unpriced

—Piracy of phonograms : a study requested by the Commission of the European Communities / Gillian Davies. - 2nd ed. - Oxford : ESC Publishing for the Commission of the European Communities Cultural Sector, 1986.
ix,151p.
ISBN 0906214424

—Private copying of sound and audio-visual recordings / Oxford : ESC, 1984.
180p.
ISBN 0906214262 £22.00

COPYRIGHT - GREAT BRITAIN

—Comments to Her Majesty's Government on the consultative document Cmnd. 8302 : reform of the law relating to copyright, designs and performers' protection / the Publishers Association. - London : The Association, 1982.
69p.

—Copinger and Skone James on copyright / John F. Mummery. - 12th ed. - London : Sweet & Maxwell, 1980.
lxxii, 1196p.
Contains chapters on EEC law with discussion of repercussions on domestic law, passing off, breach of confidence and industrial design, civil remedies, revenue and tax provisions, and the recommendations of the 1977 Whitford Committee on Copyright and Design Law.
ISBN 0421258802

—Copyright / edited by W.R. Cornish. - Oxford : ESC Publishing, 1985.
168p.
ISBN 0906214343

—Copyright / Oxford : ESC, 1985.
- (Casebook).
ISBN 0906214343 Pbk £9.00

—Copyright Cases 1901-1949, 8 Vols. / London : Wildy & Sons.

—Copyright, Designs and Patents Bill H.L. / Great Britain. - London : H.M.S.O., 1987.
xxviii,190p. - (H.L. Bill 1987 (12)).
ISBN 010870128X

—Copyright, Designs and Patents Bill H.L. : as amended by Standing Committee E / House of Lords. - London : HMSO, 1988.
xiii,217p. - (H.L. Bill 1987-88 (176)).
ISBN 0103176888

—Copyright, Designs and Patents Bill H.L. : as amended in committee / London : HMSO, 1988.
xii,191p. - (H.L. Bill 1987-1988 (37)).
ISBN 0108703789

—Copyright : Intellectual Property in the Information Age / Hamilton. - Routledge, 1980.
ISBN 0710005393 Hbk £18.95

—Copyright law in the U.K. / Carpenter. - London : Legal Books, 1986.
ISBN 0947926003 Hbk £47.00

—Copyright law in the United Kingdom and the rights of performers, authors and composers in Europe / by J.A.L. Sterling and M.C.L. Carpenter. - London : Legal Books, 1986.
cxi,749p; 26cm.
Kept up to date by supplements.
ISBN 0947926003 Australia £35.00
ISBN 0949553190

—Copyright through the cases / London : Waterlow, 1986.
ISBN 0080392083 Pbk £15.00

—Economic importance of copyright / Jennifer Phillips. - London : Common Law Institute of Intellectual Property, 1985.
38p.

—Intellectual property law and taxation / by Richard J. Gallafent, Nigel A. Eastaway and Victor A.F. Dauppe. - London : Oyez, 1981.
xxvi,321p; 24cm. - (Law and tax series).
ISBN 0851205925

—Intellectual property law and taxation / by Richard J. Gallafent, Nigel A. Eastaway, and Victor A. F. Dauppe. - 2nd ed. - London : Oyez Longman, 1984.
xxvi,338p.
ISBN 0851208746

—Joynson-Hicks on copyright / Paul Mitchell. - London : Sweet & Maxwell, 1989.
Covers works protected by Copyright Protection, qualifying for protection, first ownership, duration of copyright protection, restricted acts, secondary infringement, permitted acts, subsequent ownership, licensing and exploitation, remedies, moral rights, design rights, performance in rights, and Peter Pan.
ISBN 0421409606 Hbk

—Manager's Guide to Patents, Trade Marks and Copyright / London : Kogan Page, 1986.
ISBN 0850389704 Hbk £12.95

—Manager's Guide to Patents, Trade Marks and Copyright / London : Kogan Page, 1986.
150p.
ISBN 1850912033 Hbk £13.95
ISBN 1850912041 Pbk £6.95

—Media law - the rights of journalists and broadcasters / Geoffrey Robertson and Andrew Nicol. – 2nd ed. – London : Longman Professional (UK), 1989.
An updated second edition which covers recent developments including the Copyright and Patents Act 1988. Also covered are the use of government powers over television, the Video Recordings Act, the Cable Act, recent decisions of the European Court of Human Rights, and European Court, and the right of the media to appeal against 'gag' orders.
ISBN 0851215522 Hbk £55

—Modern law of copyright / Prescott. – 2nd ed. – London : Butterworths, 1988.
ISBN 0406616973 Hbk

—Practical introduction to copyright / Gavin McFarlane. – London : McGraw-Hill, 1982.
xiv,235p; 26cm.
Includes index.
ISBN 0070845697 £14.00

—Problems for the Business Client in the Marketing of Goods : Licensing and the Infringement of Rights / London : Law Society, 1986.
17p.

—Recording and rental of audio and video copyright material : a consultative document / presented to Parliament by the Secretary of State for Trade and Industry. – London : H.M.S.O., 1985.
iii,14p.
ISBN 0101944500

—Reform of the law relating to copyright, designs and performers' protection : a consultative document / presented to Parliament by the Secretary of State for Trade... – London : H.M.S.O., 1981.
25cm.
ISBN 0101830203

—Reprographic copying of books and journals : a guide for librarians, teachers and all users of copyright works / British Copyright Council. – London : British Copyright Council, 1985.
10p.
ISBN 0901737046

—User's guide to copyright / 2nd ed. – London : Butterworths, 1985.
ISBN 0406200742 Pbk £18.50

—User's guide to copyright / Michael F. Flint. – 2nd ed. – North Ryde : Butterworths (Australia), 1985.
xvii,289p; 22cm.
Explains the operation and scope of the law and provides answers to problems. Deals with the copyright problems of particular professions, making use of charts and tables. Includes new chapters dealing with cable and satellite television, video games, teletext and electronic publishing, and piracy and counterfeiting.
ISBN 0406200742 Pbk

—Video law : a specially commissioned report / by Stephen de B. Bate and Richard McD. Bridge. – London : Longman Professional, 1985.
x,119p.
Includes index.
ISBN 0851210287

—Whale on copyright / Jeremy J. Phillips, R. F. Whale. – 3rd ed. – Oxford : ESC Publishing, 1983.
xv,291p; 23cm.
ISBN 0906214181 Hbk £16.50
ISBN 0906214173 Pbk £9.95

COPYRIGHT – NEW ZEALAND

—Copyright in the Performing Arts / Wellington : Queen Elizabeth II Arts Council of New Zealand.

COPYRIGHT – PACIFIC ISLANDS

—Copyright law in Australia and the rights of performers, authors and composers in the Pacific region / by J.A.L. Sterling and Geoffrey E. Hart. – Sydney : Legal Books, 1981.
xli,278p; 23cm.
Bibliography: p.263-265. - Includes index.
ISBN 0959656871

COPYRIGHT – SWEDEN

—Copyright and jurisprudence : selected papers / melanges : Stig Stromholm. – Stockholm : Norstedt, 1983.
291p.
Bibliography: p.271-291. 'Edited by the Faculty of Law, Uppsala University and P.A. Norstedt & Soners forlag, Stockholm' - Cover. Papers in English, French and German.
ISBN 9118276210

COPYRIGHT – UNITED STATES

—Protection for semiconductor chip masks in the United States : analysis of the Semiconductor Chip Protection Act of 1984 / David Ladd, David E. Leibowitz and Bruce G. Joseph. – Weinheim : VCH, 1986.
vi,99p.
ISBN 0895734842

—United States Copyright Act of 1976 / Milsons Point : Australian Copyright Council.

COPYRIGHT, INTERNATIONAL

—Copyright and neighboring rights laws and treaties / compiled and published by the World Intellectual Property Organization Geneva. – Geneva : World Intellectual Property Organization, 1987.

—Copyright in free and competitive markets / edited by W.R. Cornish. – Oxford : Published by ESC Publishing for l'Association Litteraire et Artistique Internationale and the British Literary and Artistic Copyright Association, 1986.
vii,138p.
Includes bibliographical references.
ISBN 0906214467

CORONERS – AUSTRALIA – NEW SOUTH WALES

—Coronial law and practice in New South Wales / by K.M. Waller. – 2nd ed. – Sydney : Law Book Co., 1982.
xvi,215p.
Previous ed.: 1973. Includes bibliographical references and index. Includes the text of the Coroners Act, 1980, No. 27.
ISBN 0455203652 Hbk £39.50

CORONERS – CANADA

—Canadian coroner law : a legal study of coroner and medical examiner systems in Canada / by Christopher Granger. – Toronto, Canada : Carswell, 1984.
xxi, 418 p.; 24 cm.
Includes bibliographical references and indexes.
ISBN 045936460X

—Canadian law of inquests : a handbook for coroners, medical examiners, counsel and the police / by T. David Marshall. – Toronto : Carswell, 1980.
xxvii,147p; 24cm.
Includes index.
ISBN 045933350X

—Inquests and Inquiries / Vancouver : Continuing Legal Education Society of British Columbia, 1988.
89p.
ISBN 0865049858 Hbk £65.00

CORONERS – CANADA – SASKATCHEWAN

—Proposals for a new coroners act : report to the Minister of Justice / Law Reform Commission of Saskatchewan. – Saskatoon : The Commission, 1984.
62p.
Includes bibliographical references.

CORONERS – ENGLAND

—Coroners bill : report on the consolidation of the Coroners Acts 1887 to 1980 and certain related enactments / the Law Commission. – London : H.M.S.O., 1987.
3p.
ISBN 0101017820

—Coroners courts in England and Wales : a report / by JUSTICE : Chairman of Committee Evan Stone. – London : JUSTICE, 1986.
28p.
ISBN 0907247075

—Coroners' rules and statutes / by Giles Kavanagh. – London : Sweet & Maxwell, 1985.
xviii,135p; 25cm.
Includes index.
ISBN 0421338806 Pbk £6.50

—Coronership / Gavin Thurston. – 2nd ed. – Chichester : Rose, 1980.
xviii,242p; 23cm.
Previous ed.: 1976.
ISBN 0859921840 £24.00

—Jervis on the office and duties of coroners : with forms and precedents / Paul- Matthews, J. C. Foreman, John Jervis. – 10th ed. – London : Sweet & Maxwell, 1986.
xl,539p.
Examines the field of the coroner's work; the classification, appointment, office, jurisdiction and powers of the coroner; matters pertaining to the inquest from prehearing to verdict and review of the inquisition and coronial decision, medical matters such as special cases including notifiable accidents and prescribed diseases with reference to the Social Security (Industrial Injuries) Regulations 1985.
ISBN 0421329602 £55.00

—Thurston's coronership : the law and practice on coroners / Paul Knapman, Michael J. Powers. – 3rd ed. – Chichester : Barry Rose, 1985.
xxiv,544p.
Includes index. Includes legislation.
ISBN 085992355X Hbk £85

CORONERS – GREAT BRITAIN

—Sudden deaths and fatal accident inquiries / Edinburgh : W Green & Son, 1986.
Covers the duties of the procurator fiscal in investigating sudden and unexpected deaths. With a chapter on medical mattres, a summary of the duties of the coroner in England and guidance for the medical professions as to which deaths shuld be reported to the fiscal.
ISBN 0414007751

CORONERS – HONG KONG

—Report on coroners / the Law Reform Commission of Hong Kong. – Hong Kong : The Commission, 1987.
viii,176p. – (Topic).
Includes bibliographical references.

CORPORAL PUNISHMENT

—Just and painful : a case for corporal punishment of criminals / Graeme Newman. – New York : Macmillan, 1983.
163p; 23cm.
Includes index.
ISBN 0029231302 £11.95

CORPORATE HEADINGS (CATALOGUING)

—Form and structure of corporate headings : recommendations of the IFLA Working Group on Corporate Headings.. / International Federation of Library Associations and Institutions. – London : IFLA International Office for UBC, 1980.
iii-x,15p; 30cm.
ISBN 0903043289 sd £4.00

—Names of states : an authority list of language forms for catalogue entries / compiled by the IFLA International Office of UBC. – London : The Office, 1981.
viii,49p; 30cm.
At head of title: International Federation of Library Associations and Institutions.
ISBN 0903043327 Pbk Unpriced

CORPORATE LEGAL DEPARTMENTS

—Lawyers in business : and the law business / Karl J. Mackie. – Basingstoke : Macmillan, 1988.
viii,289p.
Includes bibliography and index.
ISBN 0333419081 £29.50 (July)

CORPORATE REORGANIZATIONS

—Default and rescheduling : corporate and sovereign borrowers / edited by David Suratgar. – London : Euromoney, in association with International Law Institute, Washington D.C., 1984.
viii,163p.
'Two international conferences, one in London in late 1981 and the other in New York in 1982, provided the basis for this book' - Editor's preface.
ISBN 0903121530

CORPORATE REORGANIZATIONS – GREAT BRITAIN

—Corporate Rescues and Insolvencies / London : Butterworths, 1986.
ISBN 0406100403 Pbk £27.00

—Tax on company reorganizations / Malcolm Gammie with Susan Ball. – 2nd ed. – London : Taxation Publishing, 1982.
xxvii,518p; 22cm.
Previous ed.: 1980. Includes index.

—Tax on company reorganizations / Malcolm Gammie and Susan Ball. – London : Taxation Publishing, 1980.
xxiv,397p; 22cm.
Includes index.

CORPORATE STATE

—Order and conflict in contemporary capitalism / edited by John H. Goldthorpe : sponsored by the Joint Committee on Western Europe of the American Council of Learned Societies and the Social Science Research Council. – Oxford : Clarendon, 1984.
352p.
Conference papers.
ISBN 0198780087 Hbk £22.50
ISBN 0198780079 Pbk £8.50

CORPORATION TAX

—Corporate Tax Procedures : International Bureau of Fiscal Documentation / KPMG International Tax Centre Staff. – Amsterdam : International Bureau of Fiscal Documentation, 1988.
137p.
ISBN 9070125331 Hbk £65.00

CORPORATION TAX – CANADA

—Corporate Taxation / Aurora : Canada Law Book, 1984.

—Corporate Taxation / Aurora : Canada Law Book Co, 1984.
585p. – (Text Books-Civil).

—Taxation of Corporations and Shareholders : Cases and Materials / D. Keith McNair. – Agincourt : Carswell, 1986.
616p.
This text contains both cases and materials pertaining to corporate tax. The bulk of the text is explanatory in nature. These explanations are supplemented with short cases extracts to further illustrate a point.

CORPORATION TAX – GREAT BRITAIN

—Butterworth's Corporation Tax Program / London : Butterworths.

—Corporation Tax / 9th ed. – London : Pitman Publishing, 1986.
ISBN 0712106944 Pbk £7.95

—Corporation Tax / 5th ed. – Plymouth : Macdonald & Evans, 1981.
240p.
ISBN 0712104674 Hbk £4.95

—Corporation Tax / 5th ed. – Plymouth : Macdonald & Evans, 1981.
ISBN 0712104674 Pbk £4.95

—Corporation Tax / Telegraph Publications, 1988.
ISBN 0863672280 Pbk £6.95

—Corporation Tax Manual / London : Butterworths, 1988.
ISBN 0406502167 Pbk

—Croner's Guide to Corporation Tax / New Malden : Croner Publications.

—Income and Corporation Act 1988 / London : Butterworths, 1988.
ISBN 0406008000 Pbk £18.00

—Income and Corporation Taxes Act 1988 / London : CCH, 1988.
ISBN 086325148X Hbk £32.00

—Income Tax, Corporation Tax and Capital Gains Tax 1978-1983, 5 Vols. / London : HMSO, 1984.
– (Taxes Act. Ser.).
ISBN 0116413557 Hbk £42.50

—Tax planning for groups of companies / London : Butterworths, 1985.
ISBN 0406075808 Hbk £29.95

—Taxation of land transactions / 4th ed. – London : Butterworths, 1988.
ISBN 0406624100 Pbk

CORPORATION TAX – NEW ZEALAND
—Taxation of Companies and Corporate Investors / Wellington : Butterworths, 1984.
ISBN 0409701424 Pbk

CORPORATIONS, GOVERNMENT – CANADA – ONTARIO
—Information access and crown corporations / by Isaiah A. Litrak. – Toronto : Commission on Freedom of Information and Individual Privacy, 1980.
viii,78p. – (Research publication).

CORPORATIONS, GOVERNMENT – FRANCE
—French multinationals / Julien Savary : foreword by Francois Morin. – London : Pinter, 1984.
220p.
Translation of: Les multinationales francaises.
ISBN 0861873637 £16.50

CORPORATIONS, GOVERNMENT – GREAT BRITAIN
—Accountabilities : five public services / Patricia Day, Rudolf Klein. – London : Tavistock, 1987.
259p; 22cm. – (Social science paperbacks).
Includes index.
ISBN 042279340X Hbk £18.00
ISBN 0422793507 Pbk £6.95

—Report on non-departmental public bodies / presented to Parliament by the Prime Minister .. – London : H.M.S.O., 1980.
iv,186p; 25cm.
ISBN 0101779704 Pbk £5.75

CORPORATIONS, GOVERNMENT – INDIA
—Controls over public corporations in India / Ramesh Chandra : foreword by V. R. Krishna Iyer. – Delhi : Delhi University, 1981.
xx,487p.
Bibliography: p.447-482. - Includes index.

CORPORATIONS, GOVERNMENT – PAPUA NEW GUINEA
—Corporate social responsibility in Papua New Guinea / Law Reform Commission of Papua New Guinea. – Waigani : The Commission, 1981.
ii,17p. – (Occasional paper).
'This paper was researched and written for the Commission by Edward F. Graziono'.

CORRECTIONAL INSTITUTIONS
—Implementation of the European Convention on Human Rights in respect of young persons and children placed in care or in institutions following a decision of the administrative or judicial authorities : replies of Governments to the Secretary General's enquiry under Article 57 of the European Convention on Human Rights / Council of Europe. – Strasbourg : Council of Europe, 1986.
196p; 30cm. – (H (86) 1).
At head of cover title: Human rights.

CORRECTIONAL LAW – CANADA
—Behaviour alteration and the criminal law / Law Reform Commission of Canada. – Ottawa : The Commission, 1985.
48,56p. – (Working paper).
Bibliography: p.44-48. Added t.p. in French: Les techniques de modification du comportement et de droit penal. Cover title: Protection of life : behaviour alteration and the criminal law. Pages numbered in opposite directions. Text in English and French.
ISBN 0662538579

CORRECTIONAL LAW – ENGLAND
—Young offenders / Home Office, Welsh Office, Department of Health and Social Security. – London : H.M.S.O., 1980.
17p; 25cm.
ISBN 0101804504 unbound £1.70

CORRECTIONS
—Prisons and the process of justice / Andrew Rutherford. – Oxford : Oxford University Press, 1986.
xii,217p; 20cm. – (Oxford paperbacks).
Originally published: London : Heinemann, 1984.
Bibliography: p193-205. - Includes index.
ISBN 0192819321 Pbk £3.95

CORRECTIONS – ASIA
—Corrections in Asia and the Pacific : Proceedings of the First Asian and Pacific Conference of Correctional Administrators / Canberra : Australian Institute of Criminology.

—Management of Corrections in Asia and the Pacific / Canberra : Australian Institute of Criminology.

CORRECTIONS – AUSTRALIA
—Regional Developments in Corrections / Canberra : Australian Institute of Criminology.

CORRECTIONS – CANADA
—Corrections in Canada : Policy and Practice / Griffiths. – Toronto : Butterworths, 1984.
432p.
ISBN 0409834548 Pbk £23.95

—Corrections in Canada : Policy and Practice / Curt Taylor Griffiths. – 2nd ed. – Toronto : Butterworths, 1988.
456p.
ISBN 0409801593 Hbk £28.95

—Management of Correctional Institutions / Jayewardene. – Toronto : Butterworths, 1981.
208p.
Analyses the aims and objectives of a correctional institution, the context in which it must operate, and the material and human resources available for it to operate, using the framework of extant sociological and physiological theory. Illustrates how from this analysis an efficient program of activity could be derived, using the framework of managerial theory.
ISBN 0409840513 Pbk £21.95

CORRECTIONS – ENGLAND
—Alternatives to prison : an examination of non-custodial sentencing of offenders / Stephen Stanley and Mary Baginsky. – London : Peter Owen, 1984.
183p; 23cm.
Bibliography: p171-175. - Includes index.
ISBN 0720605229 Hbk £12.50
ISBN 0720606268 Pbk £6.95

—Panel services for offenders : comparative studies of England and Poland 1984/85 / edited by Thelma Wilson. – Aldershot : Avebury, 1987.
ix,103p; 22cm.
Bibliography: p96-103.
ISBN 0566054205 £19.50

—Suspended sentence after ten years : a review and reassessment / A.E. Bottoms. – Leeds : University of Leeds Centre for Social Work and Applied Social Studies, 1980.
i,56p. – (Occasional paper).
Includes bibliographical references.

CORRECTIONS – GREAT BRITAIN
—Contrasts in tolerance : post-war penal policy in the Netherlands and England and Wales / David Downes. – Oxford : Clarendon Press, 1988.
226p.
Bibliography: pp.207-218. - Includes index.
ISBN 0198256086

—NACRO news digest / London : NACRO, 1979-.

—Punishment and welfare : a history of penal strategies / David Garland. – Aldershot : Gower, 1985.
x,297p; 23cm.
Bibliography: p280-290. - Includes index. Previous control number ISBN 0-435-82327-2.
ISBN 0566008556 £21.45

—Society against crime : penal practise sic in modern Britain / edited by Howard Jones. – Harmondsworth : Penguin Books, 1981.
284p. – (Penguin education).
Bibliographies.
ISBN 0140804374

CORRECTIONS – NETHERLANDS
—Contrasts in tolerance : post-war penal policy in the Netherlands and England and Wales / David Downes. – Oxford : Clarendon Press, 1988.
226p.
Bibliography: pp.207-218. - Includes index.
ISBN 0198256086

—Studies on the Dutch prison system / edited by M.J.M. Brand-Koolen. – Amstelveen Netherlands : Kugler Publications BV, 1987.
viii, 189 p.; 23 cm.
Includes bibliographies.
ISBN 9062990355 pbk.

CORRECTIONS – POLAND
—Panel services for offenders : comparative studies of England and Poland 1984/85 / edited by Thelma Wilson. – Aldershot : Avebury, 1987.
ix,103p; 22cm.
Bibliography: p96-103.
ISBN 0566054205 £19.50

CORRUPTION
—Report of Commission of Inquiry into the North Creek Development Project 1986-87 / submitted to the Governor, Turks and Caicos Islands, by the Commissioner, Mr. Louis Blom-Cooper : presented to parliament by the Secretary of State for Foreign and Commonwealth Affairs by command of Her Majesty, July 1987. – London : H.M.S.O., 1987.
x,148p.
ISBN 0101019521

CORRUPTION – GREAT BRITAIN
—Corruption : Causes, Consequences and Control / London : Pinter Publishers Ltd, 1983.
319p.
ISBN 0861873408 Hbk £29.50

—Corruption in British Politics 1895-1930 / Oxford : Oxford University Press, 1987.
ISBN 0198229151 Hbk £19.50

CORRUPTION – HONG KONG
—Hard graft in Hong Kong : scandal; corruption; the ICAC / H. J. Lethbridge. – Hong Kong : Oxford University Press, 1985.
viii,247p.
Bibliography: p232-243.
ISBN 0195838963

CORRUPTION – INDIA
—Commentaries on Prevention of Corruption Act / Allahabad : Law Publishers, 1983.

CORRUPTION – MALAYSIA
—Prevention of Corruption Act, 1961 (Act 57) and Emergency (Essential Powers Ordinance 22/1970) / Kuala Lumpur : International Law Books Services.

CORRUPTION – PAPUA NEW GUINEA
—What should be done about corruption and bribery? / Law Reform Commission of Papua New Guinea. – Waigani : The Commission, 1982.
24p. – (LRC working paper).
Prepared for the Commission by Ross DeVere.

CORRUPTION – UNITED STATES
—Allegations Concerning a Judge : Report to the Senate / Senate Select Committee. – Canberra : Australian Government Publishing Service, 1984.

COST CONTROL
—Cost management for library and information services / Stephen A. Roberts. – London : Butterworths, 1985.
181 p.
ISBN 0408013761

COSTS – AUSTRALIA – NEW SOUTH WALES
—Legal Costs, New South Wales / Kingsley Siebel. – Butterworths.

COSTS – CANADA
—Costs and Fees in Family Law Cases / Vancouver : British Columbia Continuing Legal Education Society, 1982.
118p.
ISBN 0865040842 Hbk £50.00

—Costs, Party and Party : Updated / Law Society of Upper Canada. – Toronto : Law Society of Upper Canada.
ISBN 0887590608 Hbk

—Law of Costs / 2nd ed. – Aurora : Canada Law Book, 1987.

—Meaning of cost in Canadian Income Tax / D. Keith McNair. – Toronto : Canadian Tax Foundation, 1982.
vi,277p.
Includes index.
ISBN 0888080123

—Tariff of Costs / Vancouver : British Columbia Continuing Legal Education Society, 1985.

COSTS – ENGLAND
—Price of justice : costs and defendants / Howard Levenson. – London : Cobden Trust, 1981.
88p.
ISBN 0900137177

COSTS – GREAT BRITAIN
—Butterworth's Costs, 2 Vols. / Butterworth Staff. – 5th ed. – London : Butterworths, 1984.
ISBN 0406142475 loose

—Butterworth's Costs Service, 2 Vols. / London : Butterworths, 1986.

Updates avail.

—Contentious Costs : The Discretionary Items / London : Oyez Longman, 1980.
– (Oyez Longman Practice Note Ser.: No. 69).
ISBN 0851204880 Hbk £5.95

—Conveyancing and Other Non-Contentious Costs / 7th ed. – London : Oyez Longman, 1980. – (Oyez Longman Practice Note Ser.: No. 20).
ISBN 0851204724 Hbk £7.95

—Cost Service / Butterworths. – London : Butterworths, 1987.
Service to Date.
ISBN 0406107491 loose £145.00

—Costs in Matrimonial Causes / London : Butterworths, 1984.
This book gives practitioners a practical discussion of the control of costs in matrimonial causes in the United Kingdom. This work provides guidance to the lawyer seeking to avoid costs out of proportion to the settlement in the case.
ISBN 0406255202 Pbk

—County Court Costs / 7th ed. – London : Longman Professional, 1985. – (LPPN24).
ISBN 0851209599 Pbk £11.95

—Fair Charges? Review of Controls of Costs / London : Waterlow, 1982.
ISBN 0900791802 Pbk £4.50

—On costs / Service to Lawyers, 1986.
ISBN 0950417661 updat £69.50

—Reminders on County Court Costs 1983 / London : Oyez Longman, 1983.
ISBN 0851207502 Hbk £3.75

—Robinson's County Court Costs / 6th ed. – London : Oyez Longman, 1982. – (Oyez Longman Practice Note Ser.: No. 24).
ISBN 0851206409 Hbk £7.95

—Supreme Court Taxing Office : Practice Notes on Taxation of Costs / London : HMSO.
40p.
ISBN 0113906269 Hbk

—Taxation of legal costs / London : LEST, 1986.
ISBN 0907822657 Pbk £19.50

COSTS - INDIA

—Law of Court Fees and Suits Valuation in Uttar Pradesh / Surendra Malik. – 5th ed. – Lucknow : Eastern Book Company, 1980.
202p.

COSTS - NORTHERN IRELAND

—Cost of Going to Law / Belfast : Queen's University of Belfast, 1984.
70p.
ISBN 0853892148 Pbk £2.95

COSTS - SCOTLAND

—Expenses in the Supreme and Sheriff Coourts of Scotland / Edinburgh : W Green & Son, 1989.
A follow on as opposed to a revision of Maclaren except where the position has changed since 1912. Unlike Maclaren, it includes all relative material regarding expenses relating to non-contentious business. With chapters on legal aid and additional discretionary fees. Also examines difference between a client or fund paying expenses and an unsuccessful party paying, as well as the extent to which Scottish solicitors 'subsidise' legal aid.
ISBN 0414008928 Hbk

COSTS (LAW) - AUSTRALIA

—Circumstances surrounding the various court actions relating to the film 'The return of Captain Invincible' / Senate Standing Committee on Finance and Government Operations. – Canberra : Government Printer, 1987.
iv,66p. – (Parliamentary paper).
ISBN 064406546X

COSTS (LAW) - ENGLAND

—Fair charges? : a review of controls over solicitors' costs / by M.R. Ludlow. – London : Waterlow Publishers, 1982.
x,64p.
ISBN 0900791802

—Guide to allowances under the Costs in Criminal Cases (Allowances) Regulations 1977 / Lord Chancellor's Department. – London : Lord Chancellor's Department, 1984.
12,vp.

—Improving access to civil justice : the report of the Law Society's Working Party on the Funding of Litigation / Law Society. – London : Law Society, 1987.
11p.
Supplement to the Law Society's Gazette. Includes bibliographical references.

COSTS (LAW) - SOUTH AFRICA

—Law of costs / A.C. Cilliers. – 2nd ed. – Durban : Butterworths, 1984.
lvii, 330 p.; 25 cm.
Includes indexes. Bibliography: p. lvi-lvii.
ISBN 0409019097 R52.50

COUNCIL OF EUROPE

—Council of Europe / pictures, Kurt Wyss : text, Norbert Paul Engel. – Strasbourg : Council of Europe, 1980.
16p.

—Council of Europe : a concise guide / Strasbourg : Directorate of Press and Information, Council of Europe, 1982.
85p.
Includes bibliographical refrences.

—European Council and Agreements /. – Strasbourg : Council of Europe, 1983.
Collection of international treaties concluded within the Council of Europe. Includes conventions on the legal status of children born out of wedlock, extradition, the suppression of terrorism and conservation of European wildlife.
ISBN 9287102031 Hbk £12.00

—Parental responsibilities : recommendation no.R (84)4 adopted by the Committee of Ministers of the Council of Europe on 28 February 1984, and Explanatory memorandum / Council of Europe. – Strasbourg : Council of Europe, 1984.
19p; 21cm.
'... prepared by the Committee of Experts on Family Law set up under the authority of the European Committee on Legal Co-operation' - preface..
ISBN 9287103291

—Payment by the State of advances on child maintenance : Recommendation No.R (82) 2 adopted by the Committee of Ministers of the Council of Europe on 4 February 1982 and explanatory memorandum / Council of Europe. – Strasbourg : Council of Europe, 1982.
15p; 21cm.
'Prepared by a committee of experts set up under the authority of the European Committee on Legal Co-operation'. At head of cover title : Council of Europe, Legal Affairs.
ISBN 9287101736

—Problems raised by certain aspects of the present situation of refugees from the standpoint of the European Convention on Human Rights / by Richard Plender. – Strasbourg : Council of Europe, Directorate of Human Rights, 1984.
38p.
ISBN 9287103550

—Proceedings of the Conference of Institutions Responsible for Teaching the Subject 'Computers and Law', Rome, 9-11 October 1985 : reports presented at the Conference / Strasbourg : Council of Europe, 1987.
357p; 29cm.
At head of cover title: Legal affairs.
ISBN 9287110603

—Protection of personal data used for scientific research and statistics : recommendation no.R (83)10 adopted by the Committee of Ministers of the Council of Europe on 23 September 1983, and Explanatory memorandum / Council of Europe. – Strasbourg : Council of Europe, 1984.
23p; 21cm.
'Prepared by the Committee of Experts on Data Protection set up under the authority of the European Committee on Legal Co-operation'. At head of cover title: Legal Affairs.
ISBN 9287103178

—Protection of personal data used for the purposes of direct marketing : recommendation no. R(85) 20 adopted by the Committee of Ministers of the Council of Europe on 25 October 1985 and Explanatory memorandum / Council of Europe. – Strasbourg : Council of Europe, 1986.
19p.
Prepared by the committee of experts on data protection set up under the authority of the European Committee on Legal Co-operation. At head of cover title: Council of Europe, Legal Affairs.
ISBN 9287108765

—Protection of persons satisfying the criteria in the Geneva Convention who are not formally recognised as refugees : recommendation no.R (84)1 adopted by the Committee of Ministers of the Council of Europe on 25 January 1984, and Explanatory memorandum / Council of Europe. – Strasbourg : Council of Europe, 1984.
10p; 21cm.
'... prepared by the ad hoc Committee of Experts on Legal Aspects of Territorial Asylum and Refugees' - preface.
ISBN 9287103275

—Protection of users of computerised legal information services : Recommendation no.R (83) 3 adopted by the Committee of Ministers of the Council of Europe on 22 February 1983 and Explanatory memorandum / Council of Europe. – Strasbourg : Council of Europe, 1983.
23p; 21cm.
'... prepared by the Committee of Experts on Legal Data Processing un der the authority of the European Committee on Legal Co- operation'. At head of cover: Council of Europe, Legal Affairs.
ISBN 9287102791

—Public liability : Recommendation no.R(84) 15 adopted by the Committee of Ministers of the Council of Europe on 18 September 1984, and explanatory memorandum / Council of Europe. – Strasbourg : Council of Europe, 1985.
19p; 21cm.
'... prepared by the committee of experts on administrative law set up under the authority of the European Committee on Legal Co-operation. On cover: Council of Europe, Legal Affairs.
ISBN 9287103798

—Response of local authorities to central government incitement to reduce expenditure / by W. J. Meadows. – Strasbourg : Council of Europe, 1986.
33p.
Prepared under the guidance of the Committee of Experts on Local and Regional Finance of the Steering Committee for Regional and Municipal Matters.

—Studies on criminal responsibility and psychiatric treatment of mentally ill offenders : reports presented to the seventh Criminological Colloquium (1985) / Council of Europe. – Strasbourg : Council of Europe, 1986.
103p; 21cm. – (Legal affairs).
On cover: European Committee on Crime Problems.
ISBN 9287108994

COUNTERTRADE

—Countertrade / by Leo G.B. Welt. – London : Euromoney, 1985.
xv,185p.
Added cover title: Special Euromoney report.
ISBN 090312176X

COUNTERTRADE - GREAT BRITAIN

—Countertrade Handbook / Cambridge : Woodhead-Faulkner, 1987.
ISBN 0859413519 Hbk £40.00

—Financing of Countertrade / London : Butterworths, 1986.
ISBN 0406102007 Pbk £32.00

COUNTY COURTS - ENGLAND

—ABC guide to the practice of the county court / by Emlyn Williams. – 3rd ed. – London : Sweet & Maxwell, 1987.
200p; 22cm.
Includes amendments embodied in the County Courts Act 1984, and within other acts such as the Administration of Justice Act 1985, the Companies Act 1985 and the Insolvency Act 1986. Updated to cover amended Costs rules, the privatisation of registration of judgements, and the change of procedure in appeals to the Court of Appeal.
ISBN 0421346906 £14.50

—County court litigation / by Eric Owen. – London : Sweet and Maxwell, 1988.
lv,405p; 26cm.
An exposition of practice and procedure in county courts, cross-referenced with the Green and White Books. Suggests ways of handling procedure, and includes a section on preparation for trial and giving evidence. Looks at circumstances such as the financial position of a client on legal aid, and at changes resulting from the Civil Jurisdiction and Judgements Acts.
ISBN 0421354704 £38.00

—County court : practice and procedure, general / by Nicholas Yell and W.T. West. – Chichester : Barry Rose, 1982.
184p; 22cm.
ISBN 0859923347 corrected £27.50

—County court practice handbook / David Price, Robert Blackford. – 7th ed. – London : Oyez Longman, 1984.
xxii,242p; 22cm. – (Oyez Longman practitioner series).
Previous ed.: published as Notes on county court practice and procedure. 1983. Includes index.
ISBN 0851209513 Pbk £14.50

—County Courts Districts (England and Wales) Index of Place Names / 12th ed. – London : HMSO, 1983.
ISBN 0113906315 Hbk £20.00

—Family jurisdiction of the High Court and County Courts : consultation paper / London : Lord Chancellor's Department, 1983.
12p.

—Model code of procedure for small claims divisions of county courts / London : National Consumer Council, 1980.
72p.

—Small claims in the county court : how to sue and defend actions without a solicitor / by Michael Birks. – Rev. ed. – London : Lord Chancellor's Department, 1984.
73p.

COUNTY COURTS - GREAT BRITAIN

—Butterworth's County Court Precedents and Pleadings / A. V. B. Bartlett. – London : Butterworths.

—County Court Practice : 1984 / London : Butterworths, 1984.

—County Court Practice 1986 / D. E. Peck. – London : Butterworths, 1986.
ISBN 0406163227 Hbk

—County Court Practice / Butterworths. – London : Butterworths, 1988.
ISBN 0406163243 Hbk £80.00

—County Court Practice / Butterworth Staff. – London : Butterworths, 1983.
ISBN 0406163162 Hbk £172.50

—County Court Practice and Procedure / 3rd ed. – London : Fourmat, 1984.
160p.
ISBN 0906840805 Pbk £10.95

—County Court Practice and Procedure / 3rd ed. - London : Fourmat, 1984.
ISBN 0906840805 Pbk £10.95

—County Court Practice Handbook / Price. - 8th ed. - London : Longman Professional, 1987.
ISBN 085121147X Pbk £17.95

—County Court Precedents / J. W. Pryke. - 4th ed. - London : Butterworths, 1982.

Supplement only-1982
ISBN 0406292094 Pbk

—London County Courts Directory / 11th ed. - London : HMSO, 1982.
ISBN 0113906323 Hbk £20.00

—Notes on County Court Practice and Procedure / David Price. - 6th ed. - London : Oyez Longman, 1982.
- (Oyez Longman Practitioner Ser.).
ISBN 0851206301 Hbk £9.95

—Reminders on County Court Costs 1983 / London : Oyez Longman, 1983.
ISBN 0851207502 Hbk £3.75

—Robinson's County Court Costs / 6th ed. - London : Oyez Longman, 1982.
- (Oyez Longman Practice Note Ser.: No. 24).
ISBN 0851206409 Hbk £7.95

COUNTY COURTS - MANITOBA
—Report on the structure of the courts / Law Reform Commission. - Winnipeg : Queen's Printer, 1982.
iii,38,6p. - (Report).

COUNTY COURTS - NEW ZEALAND
—County Court Practice 1983 / D. E. Peck. - Wellington : Butterworths, 1983.
ISBN 0406163162 Hbk

COUNTY COURTS - NORTHERN IRELAND
—County court procedure in Northern Ireland including a supplement for the Republic of Ireland / B. J. A. C. Valentine and T. F. Grass. - Belfast : SLS Publications, 1985.
lviii,350p.
Kept up to date by supplements.
ISBN 0853892342

—County Court Rules (Northern Ireland) / Consolidated ed. - Belfast : HMSO, 1987-.
looseleaf.
First published 1981.

COUNTY COURTS - WALES
—County Courts Districts (England and Wales) Index of Place Names / 12th ed. - London : HMSO, 1983.
ISBN 0113906315 Hbk £20.00

COURT CONGESTION AND DELAY
—Report to Parliament on overseas court delays and remedies / Legal and Constitutional Committee. - Melbourne : Parliament of Victoria, 1984.
xxiii,310p.
Bibliography: p.299-310.

COURT CONGESTION AND DELAY - AUSTRALIA
—Delays and efficiency in civil litigation / Ross Cranston ... et al. - Melbourne : The Institute of Judicial Administration, 1984.
xviii,230p.
At head of title page: The Australian Institute of Judicial Administration Incorporated.
ISBN 0959002901

—Preliminary report to Parliament on delays in courts / Legal and Constitutional Committee. - Melbourne : Parliament of Victoria, 1984.
xxvii,395p.
Bibliography: p.391-395.

COURT CONGESTION AND DELAY - COMMONWEALTH
—Delay in the administration of criminal justice : Commonwealth developments and experience / prepared for the Commonwealth Secretariat by Judith A. Osborne. - London : Commonwealth Secretariat, 1980.
226p.
Bibliography: p.217-226.
ISBN 0850921937

COURT CONGESTION AND DELAY - ENGLAND
—Time taken to deal with juveniles under criminal proceedings / Catherine Frankenburg and Roger Tarling. - London : Home Office, 1983.
v,21p.
Bibliography: p.14.
ISBN 0862521025

COURT CONGESTION AND DELAY - SRI LANKA
—Report of the Sri Lanka Law's Delays and Legal Culture Committee / appointed by Hon. Dr. Nissanka Wijeyeratne, Minister of Justice. - Colombo : Ministry of Justice, 1985.
v,69p.
Chairman: R.S. Wanasundera.

COURT INTERPRETERS
—Role of the court interpreter / by Omkar Nath Channan : with a foreword by the Lord Hailsham of St Marylebone. - London : Shaw, 1982.
44p; 22cm.
ISBN 0721909205 Pbk Unpriced

COURT OFFICIALS - ENGLAND
—Management scrutiny : listing officers in the Crown Court / Lord Chancellor's Department. - London : The Department, 1984.
108p.
Includes bibliographical references.

—Order of Serjeants at Law : a chronicle of creations, with related texts and a historical introduction / by J.H. Baker. - London : Selden Society, 1984.
xxvi,610p,xvip of plates.
Includes index.

COURT PROTECTION - GREAT BRITAIN
—Court of Protection Handbook / 7th ed. - London : Longman Professional, 1986.
- (LPPN 39).
ISBN 0851209920 Pbk £13.95

—Court of Protection Practice / Massey. - 11th ed. - London : Sweet & Maxwell, 1985.
ISBN 0420469206 Hbk £80.00

Supplement-1986
ISBN 0420476407 Pbk £9.00

—Court of Protection practice / Heywood & Massey. - 11th ed. - London : Stevens, 1985.
xxix,540p; 26cm.
Previous ed.: 1978. Includes index.
ISBN 0420469206 £58.00

COURT RECORDS
—Eyre of Northamptonshire : 3-4 Edward III, A.D. 1329-1330 / edited for the Selden Society by Donald W. Sutherland. - London : Selden Society, 1983.
lxxv,498,498p; 26cm.
Opposite pages of main sequence bear duplicate numbering. French text with parallel English translation.

Vol.2 / edited for the Selden Society by Donald W. Sutherland. - 1983.
vi,499-770,499-770,771-922p; 26cm.
Opposite pages of main sequence bear duplicate numbering. French text with parallel English translation.

COURT RECORDS - ENGLAND
—Court of Star Chamber and its records to the reign of Elizabeth I / by J. A. Guy. - London : H.M.S.O., 1985.
112 p.
ISBN 0114401918

—Ecclesiastical cause papers at York : Dean and Chapter's court 1350-1843 / Katharine M. Longley. - York : University of York, 1980.
xx,204p.
Includes bibliographical references and index. At head of t.p.: University of York. Borthwick Institute of Historical Research.

—Roll of the Shropshire eyre of 1256 / edited for the Selden Society by Alan Harding. - London : Selden Society, 1981.
1xxiv,403p.

—Select cases from the ecclesiastical courts of the Province of Canterbury, c.1200-1301 / edited for the Selden Society by Norma Adams and Charles Donahue Jr. - London : Selden Society, 1981.
xxx,119,756p.
Text in Latin and English.

COURT RULES
—Procedure in the International Court : a commentary on the 1978 Rules of the International Court of Justice / Shabtai Rosenne. - The Hague : M. Nijhoff, 1983.
xvii, 305p.
Includes bibliographical references and index.
ISBN 9024730457 Hbk £130.00

COURT RULES - AUSTRALIA
—High Court and the Constitution / Leslie Zines. - Sydney : Butterworths, 1981.
xvii, 358 p.; 25 cm.
Includes bibliographical references and index.
ISBN 0409300195

—Rules of Court : a Study of Rule-Making Powers and Procedures / North Ryde : Law Book Co, 1985.
xxix, 271p.
ISBN 0455206309 Hbk £49.50

COURT RULES - AUSTRALIA - NEW SOUTH WALES
—Community law reform program / New South Wales Law Reform Commission. - Sydney : The Commission, 1984.
115p. - (L.R.C. 39).
Bibliography: p.113-115.

COURT RULES - AUSTRALIA - VICTORIA
—New Victorian Supreme Court Rules / Butterworths, 1986.
184p.
ISBN 0409491551 Pbk £18.00

—Supreme court rules : guide to time limits, civil proceedings / Melbourne : Law Institute of Victoria, 1983.
31p.
'Supplement to August 1983 Law Institute journal'.

COURT RULES - AUSTRALIA - WESTERN AUSTRALIA
—Review of the Justices Act 1902-1982 : constitution, powers and procedure of Courts of Petty Sessions / the Law Reform Commission of Western Australia. - Perth : Law Reform Commission of Western Australia, 1984.
ii,253p. - (Discussion paper).
Cover title: Courts of Petty Sessions: constitution, powers and procedure.

—Working paper on Local Courts Act 1904-1982, and rules / the Law Reform Commission of Western Australia. - Perth : Law Reform Commission of Western Australia, 1983.
307p. - (Project).
Bibliography: p.276-279.

COURT RULES - CANADA
—Federal Court Practice : 1988 / Agincourt : Carswell, 1987.
800p.
This is a comprehensive guide to the Federal Court Act, Federal Court Rules, Forms, Tariffs and related statutes. Also included is a guide to difficult jurisdictional issues such as the choice between Federal and provincial courts for commencing proceedings and locus standi.

—Rules of Court / Vancouver : British Columbia Continuing Legal Education Society, 1983.
93p.
ISBN 0865041075 Hbk £45.00

COURT RULES - CANADA - ALBERTA
—Alberta Rules of Court Judicially Considered : 1970-January 1987 / Agincourt : Carswell, 1987.
50p.

COURT RULES - CANADA - BRITISH COLUMBIA
—British Columbia Supreme Court Rules / Toronto : Butterworths.

COURT RULES - CANADA - ONTARIO
—Ontario Provincial Court Civil Division Practice : 1987 / Agincourt : Carswell, 1987.
309p.
This work sets out the complete text of the rules of the civil Division courts, previously known as the 'Small Claims Court'. The book includes commentary and annotations to the rules of practice, along with relevant forms and fee schedules.

COURT RULES - ENGLAND
—Humphrey's Notes on district registry practice and procedure / Steven A. Frieze. - 23rd ed. - London : Oyez Longman, 1983.
x,200p.
Includes index..
ISBN 0851207316

COURT RULES - GREAT BRITAIN
—The Sheriff court rules / 3rd. - Edinburgh : W Green & Son, 1989.
Reprinted from the Parliament House Book, providing updated and amended Ordinary and Summary Cause Rules. Includes Small Claims Rules.
ISBN 0414008839

—Supreme Court Rules : Supplements from January 1978 to March 1981 / London : HMSO.

COURT RULES - INDIA
—Supreme Court Rules, 1950 : as Intepreted by Supreme Court / Allahabad : Law Publishers, 1982.
vi, 199p.

—Supreme Court Rules, 1966 / Lucknow : Eastern Book Company, 1984.
119p.

COURT RULES - MALAYSIA
—Rules of the Federal Court 1980 / Kuala Lumpur : Government Printer, 1980.
46p. - (P.U. (A)).

—Rules of the High Court, 1980 / Kuala Lumpur : International Law Books Services.

—Rules of the High Court 1980 / Kuala Lumpur : Government Printer, 1980.
453p. - (P.U. (A)).

—Rules of the Supreme Court 1980 (P.U.(A) 33/80) / Kuala Lumpur : International Law Books Services.

—Subordinate courts practice 1981 / by K.S. Dass and Abdul Hamid Bin Haji Mohamed : with a foreword by Tun Mohamed Suffian Bin Hashim : and an introduction by Raja Tan Sri Dr. Azlan Shah. - Johor : Asian Book, 1981.
lix,945p.
Includes index.

—Subordinate Courts Rules 1980 (P.U.(A) 328/80) / Kuala Lumpur : International Law Books Services.

COURT RULES - NIGERIA

—Hand book of the Federal Court of Appeal / Nigeria. – Lagos : The Court, 1983.
232p.
At head of title: Federal Republic of Nigeria.

—Supreme Court Rules 1985 / Nigeria. – Lagos : Federal Government Press, 1985.
98p.

COURT RULES - SCOTLAND

—Sheriff Court Rules 1984 / Edinburgh : W Green.
– (Reprint from the Parliament House Book).
ISBN 0414007352 Hbk £2.50

COURT RULES - SOUTH AFRICA

—Civil practice of all courts for blacks in Southern Africa / J.A.M. Khumalo. – 3rd ed. – Cape Town : Juta, 1984.
xli,300p.
Previous ed. (1975) has title: Civil practice and procedure in all Bantu courts in Southern Africa. Bibliography: p.xix. - Includes index.
ISBN 0702114677

—Eenvormige hofreels / deur C.J.M. Nathan, M. Barnett, A. Brink. – 3e uitg. / deur C.J.M. Nathan en M. Barnett. – Kaapstad : Juta, 1984.
lxii, 794 p.; 26 cm.
Title on added t.p.: Uniform rules of court. Afrikaans and English. Includes indexes.
ISBN 0702114154 R84.00

COURT-HOUSES - SCOTLAND

—Waiting for justice : an SCC survey of facilities in Scotland's Sheriff Courts : results and recommendations by Sheila Gilmore / Glasgow : Scottish Consumer Council, 1981.
44,A1-A6p,11leaves; 30cm.
ISBN 0907067069 Pbk £1.50

COURTS

—Courts and Tribunals : a Comparative Study / Budapest : Akademiai Kiado, 1980.
246p.
ISBN 963051799X Hbk £19.00

—Crown Court pattern of sentencing : offenders aged 14 and over : being extracts from the Criminal statisties for England and Wales 1971-1978 / by Ian McLean. – Chichester : Barry Rose, 1981.
254p.
ISBN 085992209X

—European Court of Human Rights : its organisation and working / European Court of Human Rights. – 1. – Strasbourg : Council of Europe, 1984.
various pagings. – (Press release).
'Information document issued by the Registrar of the Court'.

—Fundamental Rights and the Supreme Court : Reasonableness of Restrictions / New Delhi : Deep and Deep Publications, 1984.
232p.

—Judges, law, and businessmen / A.H. Hermann. – Deventer, Netherlands : Kluwer Law and Taxation Publishers, 1983.
ISBN 9065440828

—Marlborough Street : the story of a London court / by Joan Lock. – London : Hale, 1980.
200p,16p of plates; 23cm.
Bibliography: p196-197.
ISBN 0709185812 £7.50

—Order of the Coif / By Alexander Pulling. – London : W. Clowes and sons, 1884.
xxvi, 288 p; 27 cm.
'The subject of this work has been foreshadowed in the article under the same title in the Edinburgh review' for October, 1878.'–Pref.

—Pacific Courts and Legal Systems / rev. ed. – Suva : University of the South Pacific, Institute of Pacific Studies, 1987.
270p.

—Political role of law courts in modern democracies / edited by Jerold L. Waltman and Kenneth M. Holland. – Basingstoke : Macmillan, 1988.
viii,237p; 23cm.
Includes index.
ISBN 0333394054 £25.00

—Revised rules of court (adopted on 24 November 1982) / European Court of Human Rights : Cour Europeenne des Droits de l'Homme. – Strasbourg : Council of Europe, 1983.
90p.

—Supreme Court : Fundamental Rights and Directive Principles / New Delhi : Deep and Deep Publications, 1984.
120p.

COURTS - AUSTRALIA

—A.B.C. Guide to the Federal Court of Australia / North Ryde : Law Book Co, 1986.
xvii, 230p.
ISBN 0455206864 Pbk £29.50

—ABC Guide To The Federal Court / London : Law Book Co, 1986.
ISBN 0455206864 Pbk £15.00

—Australian courts of law / James Crawford. – Melbourne : Oxford University Press, 1982.
297 p.; 21 cm.
Includes bibliographical references and index.
ISBN 0195543076 pbk.

—Federal judicial system of Australia / by Harold Edward Renfree. – Sydney : Legal Books Pty Ltd., 1984.
xxxiii,802p.
Includes bibliographical references and index.
ISBN 0949553085

—High Court and the Constitution / 2nd ed. – Butterworths, 1987.
423p.
ISBN 0409491780 Hbk £69.00
ISBN 0409491799 Pbk £49.00

—High Court of Australia : 1982-1983 Annual Report / Canberra : Australian Government Publishing Service, 1983.
13p.

—Keystone of the federal arch : a historical memoir of the High Court of Australia to 1980 / J.M. Bennett. – Canberra : Australian Government Publishing Service, 1980.
xiv,145p.
ISBN 0642048673 £9.25

—Manual for the Simulation of the Family Court of Australia / Canberra : Australian Government Publishing Service, 1981.
58p.
ISBN 064206749X Hbk £2.60

—Statement of preliminary views / Constitutional Commission. Australian Judicial System Advisory Committee. – Canberra : The Commission, 1986.
40p.

COURTS - AUSTRALIA - NEW SOUTH WALES

—System of Law and Courts Governing New South Wales / 2nd ed. – Butterworths, 1985.
461p.
This book for the beginning law student contains a general examination of the NSW legal system. An institutional as opposed to a rule-oriented approach to law is adopted.
ISBN 0409492531 Hbk £65.00
ISBN 0409492639 Pbk £49.00

COURTS - AUSTRALIA - QUEENSLAND

—Law and Practice of the District Courts of Queensland / 2nd ed. – Butterworths, 1983.
608p.
ISBN 040949240X Hbk £102.00

—Working paper on a bill to alter the civil jurisdiction of the District Court of Queensland / Queensland Law Reform Commission. – Brisbane? : the Commission?, 1984.
41,6p. – (Q.L.R.C.W.P.).

COURTS - AUSTRALIA - TASMANIA

—Report on local courts / Law Reform Commission of Tasmania. – Hobart : Government Printer, 1985.
29p. – (Report v no 45).

COURTS - AUSTRALIA - VICTORIA

—Court surveys and studies 1978-1984, concerning the civil caseloads of the Supreme Court, the County Court and the Magistrates' Courts of Victoria / J.R. Pullen, N.F. Young, S.J. Geddes. – Melbourne : Civil Justice Committee, 1985.
xvi,403p.
At head of title: Civil Justice Committee.

COURTS - AUSTRALIA - WESTERN AUSTRALIA

—Report on the jurisdiction, procedures and administration of local courts / Law Reform Commission of Western Australia. – Perth : Law Reform Commission of Western Australia, 1988.
262p. – (Project).
Cover title: Report on local courts.

—Working paper on Local Courts Act 1904-1982, and rules / the Law Reform Commission of Western Australia. – Perth : Law Reform Commission of Western Australia, 1983.
307p. – (Project).
Bibliography: p.276-279.

—Review of the Justices Act 1902-1982 : constitution, powers and procedure of Courts of Petty Sessions / the Law Reform Commission of Western Australia. – Perth : Law Reform Commission of Western Australia, 1984.
ii,253p. – (Discussion paper).
Cover title: Courts of Petty Sessions: constitution, powers and procedure.

COURTS - CANADA

—Canadian Constitution and the Courts : the Function and Scope of Judicial Review / 3rd ed. – Butterworths, 1988.
400p.
New edition includes coverage of the major increase in the number of cases involving constitutional issues, the dominance of Charter questions in constitutional litigation, and the greatly heightened profile of the Supreme Court of Canada as innovating leader in the interpretation of the new constitutional provisions. Also notes early trends in judicial activism, or restraint, in Charter interpretation.
ISBN 0409806315 Hbk £80.00

—Civil courts in Canada : Tribunaux civils au Canada / Ottawa : Statistics Canada, Canadian Centre for Justice Statistics, 1985.
183 p.; 29 cm.
English and French. 'July 1985.'.
ISBN 0660522497 pbk. £25.00 (£26.50 other countries)

—Courts and the Charter / Clare F. Beckton and A. Wayne MacKay, research coordinators. – Toronto : University of Toronto Press in cooperation with the Royal Commission on the Economic Union and Development Prospects for Canada and the Canadian Government Publishing Centre, 1985.
xv,279p. – (Collected research studies).
Includes bibliographies.
ISBN 0802073050

—Courts of Justice Act, Bill 100, 1983 : An Act to Revise and Consolidate the Law Respecting the Organization, Operation and Proceedings of Courts of Justice in Ontario / Ministry of the Attorney-General. – Ontario : Ontario Government Publications Service, 1983.
91p.

—Supreme Court Chambers Orders / Vancouver : British Columbia Continuing Legal Education Society, 1981.
700p.
ISBN 0865040281 Hbk £70.00

—Supreme Court of Canada : History of the Institution / Frederick Vaughan. – Toronto : University of Toronto Press, 1985.
ISBN 0802034179 Hbk £40.00
ISBN 0802034187 Pbk £17.50

—Supreme Court of Canada Practice and Advocacy / Vancouver : Continuing Legal Education Society of British Columbia, 1987.
297p.
ISBN 0865043310 Hbk £85.00

COURTS - CANADA - BRITISH COLUMBIA

—Practice and Procedure in the Supreme Court of British Columbia / Vancouver : British Columbia Continuing Legal Education Society, 1982.
167p.
ISBN 0865040559 Hbk £17.50

—Progression of Judges : a History of the Supreme Court of British Columbia / Vancouver : University of British Columbia Press, 1988.
197p.
ISBN 0774802936 Hbk £31.95

COURTS - CANADA - MANITOBA

—Report on the structure of the courts / Law Reform Commission. – Winnipeg : Queen's Printer Office, 1983.
iii,56p. – (Report).

COURTS - CANADA - ONTARIO

—Ontario Supreme and District Court Practice 1989 / Michael McGowan. – Agincourt : Carswell, 1988.
1,188p.

—Ontario Supreme and District Court Practice 1989 / Michael M. McGowan. – Agincourt : Carswell, 1988.
1,192p.

COURTS - COMMONWEALTH

—Civil procedure including courts and evidence / J. M. Jacob. – 1. – London : Butterworths, 1966.
various pagings.
Photocopies of articles from Annual survey of Commonwealth Law 1965-1977 bound together in one volume. Includes bibliographical references. 1972 article onwards by I.H. Jacob and J.M. Jacob. 1976 and 1977 articles entitled: Civil procedure including courts.

COURTS - ENGLAND

—ABC guide to the practice of the magistrates' courts / by Emlyn Williams. – London : Sweet & Maxwell, 1986.
viii,187p; 22cm.
ISBN 0421344903 Pbk £14.50

—Administration of the courts : JUSTICE / a report by John Macdonald, Chairman of committee. – London : JUSTICE, 1986.
46p.
ISBN 0907247083

—Appeals / by David Price. – London : Fourmat, 1982.
xii,439p; 22cm.
Includes index.
ISBN 0906840422 Pbk £12.95

—Civil justice review / Lord Chancellor's Department. – London : The Department, 1987.
109 leaves.

—Civil justice review : consultation paper no. 6 : general issues / response by JUSTICE. – London : JUSTICE, 1987.
19p.

—Court of Session Bill : report on the consolidation of certain enactments, and the repeal of other enactments, relating to the Court of Session / presented to Parliament by the Lord Advocate by Command of Her Majesty : Scottish Law Commission. – Edinburgh : HMSO, 1988.
36p.
ISBN 0101031521

—Family jurisdiction of the High Court and County Courts : consultation paper / London : Lord Chancellor's Department, 1983.
12p.

—Magistrates' courts bill : report on the consolidation of certain enactments relating to the jurisdiction of, and the practice and procedure before, magistrates' courts... / the Law Commission. – London : H.M.S.O., 1980.
7p.
ISBN 0101788703

—Power of the Court of Appeal Criminal Division to order a retrial / prepared by the Criminal Law Team of the Law Commission ... – London : The Commission, 1986.
23,4p.
Includes bibliographical references.

—Stephen's commentaries on the laws of England / L. Crispin Warmington. – 21st ed. – London : Butterworths, 1950.
xviii,663p.
Index included in Vol. 4.

—Triable-either-way cases : Crown Court or Magistrates' Court? / by David Riley and Julie Vennard. – London : H.M.S.O., 1988.
52 p.
Discusses whether the balance of either-way business could be redistributed in favour of the Magistrates' Court by encouraging them to accept jurisdiction more often in such cases.
ISBN 0113408900

COURTS – EUROPE

—Court of Auditors : Annual Record Concerning the Financial Year 1983 Accompanied by the Replies of the Institutions-1983 / Kirchberg : Commission of the European Communities, 1984.
253p.

COURTS – EUROPEAN COMMUNITY

—Court of Auditors of the European Communities / Kirchberg : Commission of the European Communities, 1984.
24p.

—Court of Justice of the European Communities / by L. Neville Brown and Francis G. Jacobs. – 2nd ed. – London : Sweet & Maxwell, 1983.
xxxi,305p; 19cm. – (Modern legal studies).
Previous ed.: 1977. Includes index.
ISBN 0421314001 Hbk Unpriced
ISBN 0421314109 Pbk £7.95

—European court practice / by John A. Usher. – London : Sweet & Maxwell, 1983.
xli,357p; 26cm.
Discusses industrial and intellectual property rights, external relations with the UN, the OECD, and North America, Euratom, ECSC, the financing of Community activities including a discussion of the background to Britain's budget rebate. Bibliography annexed to each chapter.
ISBN 0421267801 £32.00

—Judicial protection in the European Communities / Henry G. Schermers. – 3rd ed. – Deventer, 1983.
xvi,495p.
ISBN 9065440518

COURTS – GREAT BRITAIN

—Abolishing the Diplock Courts / White. – London : CENT, 1986.
ISBN 0900137274 Pbk £5.95

—Cases Argued and Decreed in the High Court of Chancery : 1660-80 / 2nd ed. Repr. of 1707 ed. – Abingdon : Professional Books.
345p.

—Court of Protection Procedure / London : Oyez Longman, 1983.
– (Oyez Longman Practice Note Ser.: No. 39).

—Crime and Courts In England 1660-1800 / Oxford : Oxford University Press, 1986.
ISBN 0198200579 Pbk £15.00

—Criminal Statistics, England and Wales : Supplementary Tables 1980, 4 Vols. /. – London : Home Office.
ISBN 0862520142 Hbk £12.75

—Directory of Courts in the UK / London : Shaw & Sons, 1987-1988.
ISBN 0721909841 Pbk £10.95

—Directory of Courts in the United Kingdom : 1988/1989 / London : Shaw & Sons, 1988.
320p.
ISBN 072190985X Pbk £14.95

—English legal process / Terence Ingman. – London : Financial Training, 1983.
xxxiv,267p.
ISBN 0906322243

—Family Court in Action / London : Butterworths, 1983.
ISBN 0406556504 Hbk £20.00
ISBN 0406556512 Pbk £14.95

—High Court and the Constitution / 2nd ed. – London : Butterworths, 1981.
ISBN 0409491780 Hbk £50.00

—Law Courts / London : MIT Press, 1984.
ISBN 0262021994 Hbk £37.50

—New Court Guide / London : Blackstone Press, 1988.
ISBN 185185049X Pbk £5.95

—Practice and procedure in Magistrates' Courts / 2nd ed. – London : Fourmat, 1986.
ISBN 1851900136 Pbk £12.95

—Practice and Procedure of the Supreme Court, Court of Appeal and High Courts of Nigeria / London : Sweet & Maxwell, 1980.
– (Nigerian Practice Library).
ISBN 0421255706 Hbk £95.00

—Practice of the Superior Courts of Common Law / Repr. of 1850 ed. – Abingdon : Professional Books.

—Records of the general eyre / David Crook. – London : H.M.S.O., 1982.
x, 271p.
ISBN 0114401233

—Royal Courts of Justice, 1983 / London : Wildy & Sons.
Illus.

—Sheriff Court practice / Edinburgh : W Green & Son, 1988.
Explains modern statutory rules of proceedure and the principles and practices which regulate the conduct of civil litigation in the Sheriff Court. Covers drafting and amendment of written pleadings, interim orders, debates, proofs and appeals. Covers the practice and procedure in summary causes and the legislation conferring powers and duties on the Sheriff Court.
ISBN 0414008251 Hbk

COURTS – INDIA

—Our Courts on Trial / Delhi : B.R. Publishing Corporation, 1987.
174p.
ISBN 8170184487 Hbk £75.00

—Role of Supreme Court in Indian Constitution / New Delhi : Deep and Deep Publications, 1987.
208p.

—Supreme Court Criminal Digest 1950-80, 2 Vols. / Allahabad : Law Book Company.

—Supreme Court Quinquennial Digest, 1981 to 1985 / Allahabad : Law Book Company.
1,000p.

—Supreme Court Quinquennial Digest / Allahabad : Law Book Company, 1981-85.

COURTS – IRAN

—Law and human rights in the Islamic Republic of Iran : a report covering events within the seven month period following the Revolution of February 1979 / Amnesty International. – London : Amnesty International, 1980.
216p.

COURTS – MANITOBA

—Report on the structure of the courts / Law Reform Commission. – Winnipeg : Queen's Printer, 1982.
iii,38,6p. – (Report).

COURTS – NETHERLANDS

—Interim Measures in the Hague Court : an Attempt at a Scrutiny / Dordrecht : Kluwer, 1983.
350p.
ISBN 9065440933 Hbk £104.00

—Quaestiones juris privati / by Cornelius van Bijnkershoek : translated by R.A. Whitaker. – 2. – Pretoria : Government Printer on behalf of the South African Law Commission, 1987.
– (Research series).
Includes bibliographical references.

COURTS – NEW ZEALAND

—District Court Practice / J. S. Crutchley. – 8th ed. – Wellington : Butterworths, 1981.
ISBN 0409600466 Hbk

—Maori land courts : report of the Royal Commission of Inquiry 1980 / Thaddeus Pearcey McCarthy. – Wellington,N.Z. : Government Printer, 1980.
xiii,149p; 24cm.
Includes bibliographical references and index. Chairman: Sir Thaddeus Pearcey McCarthy.

—Practice and Procedure of the High Court and Court of Appeal in New Zealand / 12th ed. – Butterworths.
ISBN 0409667617 loose £264.00

—Practice and procedure of the High Court in New Zealand / Cain. – London : Butterworths, 1981.
ISBN 0409667617 loose £125.00

—Practice of the High Court and Court of Appeal of New Zealand / Gordon Cain. – 12th ed. (rev). – Wellington : Butterworths, 1978.
looseleaf.
'Successor to the 11th ed. of the text on the same subject by the late Sir Wilfrid Joseph Sim'.

—Structure of the courts : a discussion paper / Law Commission. – Wellington, N.Z. : The Commission, 1987.
x,93p. – (Preliminary paper).
Bibliography: pp.50-54.

COURTS – NIGERIA

—All Nigeria Judges Conference papers : Ilorin, Kwana State, 8-16th March 1982 / London : Sweet & Maxwell, 1984.
xx,391p; 23cm.
Includes index.
ISBN 0421309008 No price

—Federal High Court : law and practice / by A.G. Karibi-Whyte. – Enugu, Nigeria : Fourth Dimension, 1986.
xlvii,344p.
Includes bibliographical references and index.
ISBN 9781562412

—Government views on the report of the Advisory Committee on the Implementation of the Federal Government White Paper of Area Courts Reform / Borno State of Nigeria. – Maiduguri : Government Printer, 1987.
21p.

—Outline of customary court procedure / by R.A.I. Ogbobine. – Benin City, Nigeria : Ruf-Bine, 1985.
vi,46p.
ISBN 9783004514

—Practice and procedure of the High Courts, Nigeria / Sweet & Maxwell, 1980.
ISBN 0421255706 Hbk £99.00

—Role of customary courts in Nigeria / by Martin C. Okany. – Enugu : Fourth Dimension Publishing Co., 1984.
264p.
Includes bibliographical references and index.
ISBN 9781562145

COURTS – NORTHERN IRELAND

—Abolishing the Diplock courts : the case for restoring jury trial to scheduled offences in Northern Ireland / S.C. Greer, A. White. – London : Cobden Trust, 1986.
x,133p; 20cm.
Includes index.
ISBN 0900137274 Pbk £5.95

—County court procedure in Northern Ireland including a supplement for the Republic of Ireland / B. J. A. C. Valentine and T. F. Grass. – Belfast : SLS Publications, 1985.
lviii,350p.
Kept up to date by supplements.
ISBN 0853892342

—Diplock courts in Northern Ireland : a fair trial? : an analysis of the law, based on a study commissioned by Amnesty International / by Douwe Korff. – Utrecht : Studie-en Informatiecentrum Mensenrechten, 1984.
115p.

—Use and abuse of emergency legislation in Northern Ireland / Dermot P. J. Walsh. – London? : Cobden Trust, 1983.
138p.
ISBN 0900137207

COURTS – PACIFIC ISLANDS

—Pacific Courts and Justice. 20 Pacific Writers / 4th ed. – Suva : University of the South Pacific, Institute of Pacific Studies, 1984.
150p.

COURTS – PAPUA NEW GUINEA

—Reorganisation of the lower courts / Law Reform Commission of Papua New Guinea. – Papua New Guinea : The Commission, 1980.
34p. – (LRC working paper).

COURTS – PHILIPPINES

—Supreme Court Rulings / Manila : National Book Store.

COURTS - SCOTLAND

—Index to Sheriff Court districts of Scotland / Edinburgh : W Green & Son, 1981.
Lists alphabetically each Scottish city, town, village and hamlet giving the appropriate sheriffdom and sheriff court for the place.
ISBN 0414006666

—Introduction to ordinary civil procedure in the sheriff court / Brian Kearney. – Edinburgh : Law Society of Scotland, 1982.
xvi,233,1p.
Bibliography: p.233-234.
ISBN 0902023071

—Petition procedure in the Court of Session / by William W. McBryde and Norman J. Dowie. – Edinburgh : W. Green, 1980.
xvii,94p; 22cm.
Includes index.
ISBN 0414006631 Pbk £7.00

—Practice and procedure in Sheriff Court / London : Fourmat, 1988.
ISBN 1851900373 Pbk £12.95

—Report of the Review Body on Use of Judicial Time in the Superior Courts in Scotland / Chairman: The Honourable Lord Maxwell. – Edinburgh : Scottish Courts Administration, 1986.
vi,164p.

COURTS - SOUTH AFRICA

—Second interim report of the Commission of Inquiry into the Structure and Functioning of the Courts / South Africa. – Pretoria : Govt. Printer, 1981.
5, 5 p.; 30 cm.
Title on added t.p.: Tweede tussentydse verslag van die Kommissie van Ondersoek na die Struktuur en Funksionering van die Howe. English and Dutch.
ISBN 0621065781 Hbk R3.60

COURTS - SWEDEN

—Swedish code of judicial procedure : the translation is that of the wording of the code of judicial procedure as at January 1, 1985 / National Council for Crime Prevention Sweden. – Stockholm : The Council, 1985.
230 p.; 25 cm. – (Report).
ISBN 9138088452 pbk.

COURTS - UNITED KINGDOM

—Magistrates' Court : An Index of Common Penalties and Formalities in Cases Before Justices / Peter Morrish. – 7th ed. – Chichester : Barry Rose.
262p.

COURTS - WEST GERMANY

—Law on the Federal Constitutional Court : documents on politics and society in the Federal Republic of Germany / Oguz Akalin. – Bonn : Inter Nationes, 1982.
69p.
Bibliography: p.69. Prepared by Oguz Akalin.

—Supreme Labor Court in Nazi Germany : a jurisprudential analysis / Marc Linder. – Frankfurt a. M. : Klostermann, 1987.
xix,290p.
Includes bibliographical references.
ISBN 3465017579

COURTS, ISLAMIC

—Law in Afghanistan : a study of the Constitutions, matrimonial law and judiciary / by Mohammad Hashim Kamali. – Leiden : E. J. Brill, 1985.
viii,265p.
Bibliography: p254-259.
ISBN 9004071288

COURTS OF LAST RESORT

—Supreme courts and judicial law-making : constitutional tribunals and constitutional review / by Edward McWhinney. – Dordrecht : M. Nijhoff, 1985.
320p.
Includes index.
ISBN 9024732034 Hbk £165.00

COURTS OF LAST RESORT - NEW ZEALAND

—Practice of the High Court and Court of Appeal of New Zealand / Gordon Cain. – 12th ed. (rev). – Wellington : Butterworths, 1978.
looseleaf.
'Successor to the 11th ed. of the text on the same subject by the late Sir Wilfrid Joseph Sim'.

COURTS-MARTIAL - GREAT BRITAIN

—Naval court-martial manual / Ministry of Defence. – 1. – London : H.M.S.O., 1969 - 1984.
looseleaf. – (B.R.11).
Supersedes: Admiralty memorandum on naval court-martial procedure, 1958. Superseded by: Manual of naval law, 1981. Includes index.
ISBN 011770220X

COVENANTS - CANADA - BRITISH COLUMBIA

—Report on covenants in restraint of trade / Law Reform Commission of British Columbia. – Victoria : Queen's Printer, 1984.
76p.
Includes bibliographical references.
ISBN 077188429X

COVENANTS - GREAT BRITAIN

—Covenants : A Practical Guide to the Tax Advantages of Giving / 4th ed. – Turnaround Press.
ISBN 0907164390 Pbk

—Covenants : Practical Guide To Tax Advantages / TUAR, 1982.
ISBN 0907164080 Pbk £3.95

—Deeds of Covenant / 3rd ed. – London : Longman Professional, 1987.
ISBN 0851212182 Pbk £9.50

—Deeds of Covenant / Derek Robinson. – London : Oyez Longman, 1983.
– (Oyez Longman Practical Tax Ser.).

CREDIT

—Commercial and consumer credit : an introduction / by Aubrey L. Diamond. – London : Butterworths, 1982.
xxvii,379p.
Includes index.
ISBN 0406574057

—Legal aspects of syndicated loans / Peter Gabriel. – London : Butterworths, 1986.
xxxvi,276p; 26cm.
Bibliography: p265-267. - Includes index.
ISBN 0406102104 £45.00 (Sept.)

—Sovereign Borrowers : Guidelines on Legal Negotiations with Commercial Lenders / Qamar S. Siddiqi. – Uppsala : Dag Hammarskjold Foundation, 1984.
264p.

CREDIT - CANADA

—Canadian Credit Union Law : a Detailed Survey / Canadian Cooperative Credit Society Ltd. – Don Mills : CCH Canadian Ltd, 1987.
316p.
ISBN 0887964362 Pbk £29.95

—Creditors' Remedies : 1985 Supplement / Vancouver : Continuing Legal Education Society of British Columbia, 1986.
19p.
ISBN 0865043779 Hbk £15.00

CREDIT - ENGLAND

—Butterworths Consolidated Legislation Service / Professional Publ.
32p.
ISBN 0409014141 £25.00

CREDIT - GREAT BRITAIN

—Cash Flow and Credit Management / Slater. – Telegraph Publications, 1988.
ISBN 0863672264 Pbk £6.95

—Commercial and Consumer Credit - An Introduction / London : Butterworths, 1982.
ISBN 0406574057 Pbk £14.95

—Credit Debt and Poverty / London : Policy Studies Institute, 1988.
ISBN 0853743479 Pbk £8.95

—Credit Insurance / Briggs. – Cambridge : Woodhead-Faulkner, 1987.
ISBN 0859411761 Hbk £40.00

—Factoring / Croydon : Tolley, 1984.
ISBN 0854591648 Pbk £17.50

—Syndicated credits market / by I.D.Bond. – London : Economics Division, Bank of England, 1985.
67,28p. – (Bank of England discussion papers).
Bibliography: pi-iii.
ISBN 0903312735

—Understanding factoring and trade credit / Ferrier. – London : Waterlow, 1986.
ISBN 0080392040 Pbk £13.50

CREDIT - NEW ZEALAND

—Credit Contracts Act 1981 / Wellington : Butterworths, 1981.
ISBN 0409601322 Hbk

—Financier's guide to the Credit Contracts Act 1981 / New Zealand. – Wellington : Department of Justice, 1982.
17p.

CREDIT CARDS - GREAT BRITAIN

—Credit cards / Tony Drury, Charles W. Ferrier. – London : Butterworths, 1984.
xiv,177p; 22cm.
Includes index.
ISBN 0406259402 Pbk £6.95

—Credit Cards / Ferrier. – London : Butterworths, 1984.
ISBN 0406259402 Pbk £10.95

—Credit Cards and the Law / London : Fourmat, 1988.
ISBN 1851900462 Hbk £14.95

—Drury and Ferrier : Credit Cards / London : Butterworths, 1984.

CREDIT CONTROL - GREAT BRITAIN

—Credit scoring : A paper / by the Office of Fair Trading. – London : Office of Fair Trading, 1982.
11p.
Cover title: Credit scoring : a consultative document.

CRIME AND CRIMINALS

—Abolitionism : towards a non-repressive approach to crime : proceedings of the Second International Conference on Prison Abolition, Amsterdam, 1985 / edited by Herman Bianchi, Rene van Swaaningen. – Amsterdam : Free University Press, 1986.
247p.
ISBN 9062561799

—Consumerist criminology / Leslie T. Wilkins. – London : Heinemann, 1984.
viii,184p; 23cm.
Includes index.
ISBN 0435825283 Pbk £16.00
ISBN 0389204102

—Crime and criminology : a critical introduction / Nigel Walker. – Oxford : Oxford University Press, 1987.
xv,219p; 23cm.
Bibliography: p210-212. - Includes index.
ISBN 0192192124 Hbk £12.95
ISBN 0192891936 Pbk £4.95

—Crime and public housing : proceedings of a workshop held in September 1980 / edited by Mike Hough and Pat Mayhew. – London : Home Office, 1982.
v,77p. – (Research and Planning Unit paper).
Includes bibliographies.
ISBN 0862520347

—Crime and the law : the social history of crime in Western Europe since 1500 / edited by V.A.C. Gatrell, Bruce Lenman and Geoffrey Parker. – London : Europa, 1980.
xii,381p; 25cm. – (The Europa social history of human experience).
Includes index.
ISBN 0905118545 Unpriced

—Crime, justice and underdevelopment / edited by Colin Sumner. – London : Heinemann, 1982.
xvi,345p; 23cm.
Bibliography: p312-331. - Includes index.
ISBN 0435828886 £19.50

—Criminology / Karl O. Christiansen. – 2nd ed. – London : Allen & Unwin, 1983.
xvi,454p; 24cm.
Previous ed.: 1952. Bibliography: p417-443. - Includes index.
ISBN 0043640125 Unpriced.

—Development of ethnography in Britain : paper prepared for presentation at the BSA Annual Conference, Lancaster, 1980 / Robert Dingwall, Geoff Payne, Judy Payne. – Oxford : Centre for Socio-Legal Studies, 1980.
19,2p.
Bibliography: p.20-21.

—Developments in the study of criminal behaviour / edited by Philip Feldman. – Chichester : Wiley, 1982.
x,238p; 24cm.
Includes bibliographies and index.
ISBN 0471101761 Hbk

Vol.2 : Violence / edited by Philip Feldman. – 1982.
x,254p; 24cm.
Includes bibliographies and index.
ISBN 047110373X Hbk £22.00

—Economic crisis and crime / European Committee on Crime Problems. – Strasbourg : Council of Europe, 1985.
157p; 21cm.
At head of cover-title: Council of Europe, Legal affairs.
ISBN 9287107807

—Eyewitness identification : a system handbook / Gary L. Wells. – Toronto : Carswell, 1988.
xiv,142p. – (The Carswell law enforcement series).
Bibliography: pp.105-115. - Includes index.
ISBN 0459311611

—Guide to United Nations criminal policy / Manuel Lopez-Rey. – Aldershot : Gower, 1985.
xi,142p; 23cm.
Includes index.
ISBN 0566050706 £15.00

—Historical research on crime and criminal justice : sixth Criminological Colloquim (PC-CC), Strasbourg 21-23 November 1983 / Council of Europe. – Strasbourg : Council of Europe, 1984.
ii,153p.
Includes bibliographies. 'Secretariat memorandum prepared by the Directorate of Legal Affairs'.

—Howard journal : a review of modern methods for the prevention and treatment of crime and juvenile delinquency / London : Howard League for Penal Reform, 1921.
Continued by: The Howard journal of penology and crime prevention. Subtitle varies.

—Identification evidence : a psychological evaluation / John W. Shepherd, Hadyn D. Ellis and Graham M. Davies : foreword by Lord Devlin. – Aberdeen : Aberdeen University Press, 1982.
xii,155p; 26cm.
Bibliography: p140-149. - Includes index.
ISBN 0080284418 £12.50

—Illusions about crime & justice / Leon Radzinowicz. – London : Encounter, 1981.
p.31-39.
Extracted from: Encounter, Feb./March 1981.

—Islington crime survey : crime, victimization and policing in inner-city London / Trevor Jones, Brian MacLean and Jock Young. – Aldershot : Gower, 1986.
xiv, 265p; 23cm.
ISBN 0566052644

—Measures against the transfer and the safekeeping of funds of criminal origin : recommendation no. R(80)10 adopted by the Committee of Ministers of the Council of Europe on 27 June 1980 and explanatory memorandum / Council of Europe. – Strasbourg : Council of Europe, 1981.
12p.
'Prepared by a select committee of experts under the authority of the European Committee on Crime Problems' - verso t.p.. At head of cover title: Council of Europe, Legal Affairs.

—Prison information bulletin / Strasbourg : Council of Europe, 1983.

—Radical issues in criminology / edited by Pat Carlen and Mike Collison. – Oxford : Robertson, 1980.
vii,212p.
Includes bibliographies.
ISBN 0855203269

—Reactions to crime : the public, the police, courts, and prisons / edited by David P. Farrington and John Gunn. – Chichester : Wiley, 1985.
ix,189p; 24cm.
Includes bibliographies and index.
ISBN 047190497X £23.00

—Recession, crime and punishment / Steven Box. – London : Macmillan Education, 1987.
240p; 25cm.
Includes index.
ISBN 0333438523 Hbk £20.00 :
ISBN 0333438531 Pbk £6.95

—Understanding deviance : a guide to the sociology of crime and rule-breaking / David Downes and Paul Rock. – 2nd ed. – Oxford : Clarendon Press, 1988.
viii,369p.
Bibliography: pp.335-360. - Includes index.
ISBN 0198762135 pbk.

—Women, crime and criminal justice / Allison Morris. – Oxford : Basil Blackwell, 1987.
256p; 23cm.
Considers all aspects of women and crime including women as defendants and prisoners, as victims and as criminal justice professionals.
ISBN 0631154442 Hbk £25.00 :
ISBN 0631154450 Pbk £7.95

—World directory of criminological institutes / compiled and edited by Carla Masotti Santoro. – 4th ed. – Rome : UNSDRI, 1986.
xxvi,582p. – (Publication).
ISBN 9290780029

CRIME AND CRIMINALS - AUSTRALIA

—Age and Crime / Canberra : Australian Institute of Criminology.

—Alcohol and Crime / Canberra : Australian Institute of Criminology.

—Crime trends in twentieth-century Australia / Satyanshu Kumar Mukherjee, assisted by Evelyn N. Jacobsen, John R. Walker, R. W. Fitzgerald. – Wooden : Australian Institute of Criminology, 1981.
xviii,199p.
Includes bibliographical references and index.
ISBN 086861386X

—National Crimes Commission? / M.J. Young, Special Minister of State, Gareth Evans, Attorney-General. – Canberra : Australian Government Publishing Service, 1983.
iv,41p.
Includes bibliographical references. Cover subtitle: a policy discussion paper.
ISBN 0644026928

—Plotting and Planning / Canberra : Australian Institute of Criminology.

CRIME AND CRIMINALS - AUSTRALIA - NEW SOUTH WALES

—Prison struggle : changing Australia's penal system / George Zdenkowski and David Brown. – Ringwood, Vic., Australia : Penguin Books, 1982.
xxi, 440 p., 8 p. of plates; 21 cm.
Includes bibliographical references and index.
ISBN 014022324X pbk. £14.95

CRIME AND CRIMINALS - CANADA

—Behaviour alteration and the criminal law / Law Reform Commission of Canada. – Ottawa : The Commission, 1985.
48,56p. – (Working paper).
Bibliography: p.44-48. Added t.p. in French: Les techniques de modification du comportement et de droit penal. Cover title: Protection of life : behaviour alteration and the criminal law. Pages numbered in opposite directions. Text in English and French.
ISBN 0662538579

—Crime in Canadian society / James T Teevan. – 3rd. – Scarborough, Ontario : Butterworths (Canada).
440.
Opens with a discussion of the controversy surrounding the definition of crime, and then moves into a discussion and critique of the ways of measuring crime in Canada. Gives various explanations of crime from functional analysis to liberal criminology, labelling theory and critical theory. Concludes with a selection of contemporary Canadian criminological research.
ISBN 040986580X 1986

—From Crime to Punishment / David C. Perrier. – Agincourt : Carswell, 1988.
ca 330p.

—Impact / Ottawa : Ministry of the Solicitor General, 1982-.
Contents: 'a periodical which presents research and statistics about crime and criminal justice'.

—Investigative tests / Law Reform Commission of Canada. – Ottawa : Law Reform Commission of Canada, 1984.
166,186p; 25cm. – (Working paper).
At head of cover title: Criminal law. English and French texts bound back to back.
ISBN 066253039X

—New criminologies in Canada : crime, state and control / edited by Thomas Fleming. – Toronto : Oxford University Press, 1985.
xii,343p.
ISBN 0195404890

—Ordering of justice : a study of accused persons as dependants in the criminal process / Richard V. Ericson, Patricia M. Baranek. – Toronto : Published in association with the Centre of Criminology, University of Toronto by University of Toronto Press, 1982.
xvi, 268 p.; 25 cm.
Includes index. Bibliography: p. 253-261.
ISBN 0802064639 pbk.

—Police guidelines - pretrial eyewitness identification procedures : a study paper / prepared for the Law Reform Commission of Canada by Neil Brooks. – Ottawa : Canadian Law Reform Commission, 1983.
260p; 25cm. – (Criminal law series).
ISBN 0662127315

—Technical report / Solicitor General Canada. Programs Branch. – Ottawa : Solicitor General Canada, 1983.

CRIME AND CRIMINALS - ENGLAND

—Brought to justice / Roy Lewis. – Durham : Casdec, 1983.
83p.
ISBN 0907595111

—City-centre crime : the scope for situational prevention / Malcolm Ramsay. – London : Home Office, 1982.
v,50p.
Bibliography: p.42.
ISBN 0862520665

—Crime and the criminal law : reflections of a magistrate and social scientist / by Barbara Wootton. – 2nd ed. – London : Stevens, 1981.
xii,119p; 19cm.
Previous ed.: 1963.
ISBN 0420461701 Hbk Unpriced
ISBN 0420461809 Pbk £5.00

—Crime on the London Underground / report of a study by the Department of Transport in conjunction with London Underground ... et al. – London : H.M.S.O., 1986.
118p.
Describes a study by the Department of Transport – suggests crime on the Underground is relatively rare – 15300 offences (1600 violent) in 725 million journeys during 1985. Recognises that cost of crime to the system could be 10 million per year and shows that the public are afraid of violence and theft.
ISBN 0115508058

—Criminal and victim : crime and society in early nineteenth-century England / George Rude. – Oxford : Clarendon, 1985.
ix,160p; 22cm.
Includes bibliography and index.
ISBN 0198226462 £17.50

—Criminology and criminal justice / by J.E. Hall Williams. – London : Butterworths, 1982.
xvii,266p.
Bibliography: p243-254.
ISBN 0406593205

—Draft codes of practice for the detention, treatment, questioning and identification of persons by the police; for the searching of premises and seizure of property; and for the exercise of powers of stop and search / London : Home Office, 1985.
iii,80p.
Previous ed.: 1984.

—Draft codes of practice for the detention, treatment, questioning and identification of persons by the police and for the searching of premises and seizure of property / London : Home Office, 1983.
66p.
Revised edition of: Draft codes of practice for the treatment, questioning and identification of persons suspected of crime.
ISBN 086252122X

—Draft codes of practice for the detention, treatment, questioning and identification of persons by the police and for the searching of premises and seizure of property / Rev. ed. – London : Home Office, 1984.
iii,66p.
Previous ed.: 1983.
ISBN 0862521424

—Draft codes of practice for the treatment, questioning and identification of persons suspected of crime / Home Office. – London : Home Office, 1982.
44p.

—Draft codes of practice for the treatment, questioning and identification of persons suspected of crime / Home Office. – Revised draft. – London : Home Office, 1983.
51p.
ISBN 0862520975

—Ethnic minorities, crime and policing : a survey of the experiences of West Indians and whites / by Mary Tuck and Peter Southgate. – London : H.M.S.O., 1981.
iv,50p.
Bibliography: p50. A Home Office Research and Planning Unit report.
ISBN 0113407653

—Persistent petty offenders / by Suzan Fairhead. – London : H.M.S.O., 1981.
vi,74p.
Bibliography: p74. A Home Office Research Unit report.
ISBN 0113407068

CRIME AND CRIMINALS - GREAT BRITAIN

—British crime survey : first report / by Mike Hough and Pat Mayhew. – London : H.M.S.O., 1983.
v,57p; 25cm.
'A Home Office Research and Planning Unit report'.
ISBN 0113407866 PBK £4.35

—Cambridge Institute of Criminology : its background and scope : a report / by Sir Leon Radzinowicz : for the Home Office. – London : H.M.S.O., 1988.
viii,190p.
Describes the formation of the Institute, early problems, the scope and content of courses offered and how the work of the Institute has evolved over the years.
ISBN 0113408846

—Catching Criminals : Some More Basic Skills / London : Police Review Publishing, 1983.
ISBN 0851640044 Pbk £2.50

—Causes of Crime / Cambridge : Cambridge University Press, 1987.
ISBN 0521304024 Hbk £35.00

—Child Care and Adult Crime / Ashcraft. – Manchester : Manchester University Press, 1988.
ISBN 0719024692 Hbk £29.50

—Clearing up crime / by John Burrows and Roger Tarling. – London : H.M.S.O., 1982.
31p; 25cm.
Bibliography: p24-26. A Home Office Research and Planning Unit report.
ISBN 0113407688

—Concerning crime / by John Croft. – London : H.M.S.O., 1982.
iv,16p; 25cm. – (A Home Office Research and Planning Unit report).
ISBN 011340770X £2.45

—Confronting crime / edited by Roger Matthews and Jock Young. – London : Sage, 1986.
264p; 22cm.
Includes bibliography and index.
ISBN 0803997310 Hbk £27.50 :
ISBN 0803997329 Pbk £10.50

—Cox and Crime / Cambridge : Institute of Criminology, 1985.

—Crime / by Monica A. Walker. – Oxford : Published for the Royal Statistical Society and the Social Science Research Council by Pergamon, 1981.
xii,406p; 26cm.
Bibliography: p281-284. - Includes index. Originally titled: Reviews of United Kingdom statistical sources.
ISBN 0080261043 £18.25

—Crime / 1964 Reprint. – London : Sweet & Maxwell, 1986.
ISBN 0421355603 Hbk £100.00

—Crime and Courts In England 1660-1800 / Oxford : Oxford University Press, 1986.
ISBN 0198200579 Pbk £15.00

—Crime and punishment : interpreting the data / A. Keith Bottomley, Ken Pease. – Milton Keynes : Open University Press, 1986.
xviii,185p; 24cm.
Bibliography: p171-180. - Includes index.
ISBN 0335153909 Hbk £25.00
ISBN 0335153895 Pbk £8.95

—Crime and Social Justice / Paul Takagi. – London : Macmillan, 1981.
232p. – (Critical Criminology Ser.).
ISBN 0333282604 Hbk £18.00
ISBN 0333282612 Pbk £6.95

—Crime and society : readings in history and theory / compiled by Mike Fitzgerald, Gregor McLennan and Jennie Pawson. – London : Routledge & Kegan Paul in association with Open University Press, 1981.
vii,504p; 22cm. – (An Open University set book).
Includes bibliographies and index.
ISBN 0710009445 Pbk £8.95

—Crime Guilt and Punishment / Oxford : Oxford University Press, 1987.
ISBN 0198750811 Pbk £8.95
ISBN 019875082X Hbk £19.50

—Crime, justice and the mass media : papers presented to the 14th Cropwood Round-Table Conference, December 1981 / edited by Colin Sumner. – Cambridge : University of Cambridge Institute of Criminology, 1982.
ii,123p.
Includes bibliographical references.

—Crime, Proof and Punishment / London : Butterworths, 1981.
ISBN 0406569991 Hbk £21.50

—Crime, protest, community and police in nineteenth-century Britain / David Jones. – London : Routledge & Kegan Paul, 1982.
xi, 247p.
Includes index. Includes bibliography.
ISBN 0710090080

—Criminal behaviour : an introduction to criminology and the penal system / Herschel Prins. – 2nd ed. – London : Tavistock, 1982.
x,309p; 21cm.
Previous ed.: London : Pitman, 1973. Includes bibliographies and index.
ISBN 0422776807 Hbk Unpriced
ISBN 0422776904 Pbk Unpriced

—Economics of Crime and Law Enforcement / London : Macmillan, 1983.
228p.
ISBN 0333282000 Hbk £33.00

—Fear of crime in England and Wales / by Michael J. Maxfield. – London : H.M.S.O., 1984.
v,46p; 25cm.
'A Home Office Research and Planning Unit report'.
ISBN 0113407726

—Gender Crime and Justice / Open University Press, 1988.
ISBN 0335155057 Hbk £25.00

—History of British criminology / edited by Paul Rock. – Oxford : Clarendon, 1988.
192.
'First appeared as a special issue of the British journal of criminology.' Includes bibliographical references. Focuses on the past and present condition of criminology. Contains a series of essays, some on the history of criminological ideas, some on the formation of particular emphases, methods and problems. Others are personal accounts of major phases in the growth of the discipline.
ISBN 0198256353 Pbk £9.95

—Knots and Crime / London : Police Review, 1985.
ISBN 0851640176 Pbk £3.95

—Law and order : arguments for socialism / Ian Taylor. – London : Macmillan, 1981.
xxii,234p.
Bibliography: p224-234.

—Managing criminological research / by John Croft. – London : H.M.S.O., 1981.
iv,13p.
A Home Office Research Unit report.
ISBN 0113407092

—People's justice : a major poll of public attitudes on crime and punishment / Stephen Shaw. – London : Prison Reform Trust, 1982.
29p; 30cm.
Cover title.
ISBN 0946209006 Pbk £1.00

—Power, crime, and mystification / Steven Box. – London : Tavistock, 1983.
xi,257p; 23cm. – (Tavistock studies in sociology).
Bibliography: p224-246. - Includes index.
ISBN 0422764000 Hbk Unpriced
ISBN 0422764108 Pbk Unpriced

—Research and criminal policy / by John Croft. – London : H.M.S.O., 1980.
iv,10p.
ISBN 0113406991

—Responses to crime / Lord Windlesham. – Oxford : Clarendon, 1987.
xviii,357p; 24cm.
Includes index.
ISBN 0198255837 £17.95

—Russell on Crime / 12th ed. – London : Sweet & Maxwell, 1986.
– (Sweet and Maxwell Library Reprints).
ISBN 0421355603 Hbk £100.00

—Taking account of crime : key findings from the second British crime survey / Mike Hough and Pat Mayhew. – London : H.M.S.O., 1985.
vi,110p.
Reports on extent, risks and nature of selected crime, including incidents neither reported to nor recorded by police. Examines changing trends in crime between 1981 and 1983. Discusses differences between reported and unreported crime, the impact of crime on victims and public attitudes to crime.
ISBN 0113408102

—What is to be done about law and order? / John Lea and Jock Young. – Harmondsworth : Penguin Books in association with the Socialist Society, 1984.
284p.
Includes index. Bibliography: p275-284.
ISBN 0140065938

CRIME AND CRIMINALS - GUYANA

—Crime, race and culture : a study in a developing country / Howard Jones. – Chichester : Wiley, 1981.
xv,184p; 24cm.
Bibliography: p175-179. - Index.
ISBN 047127996X £12.75

CRIME AND CRIMINALS - INDIA

—Identification of Prisoners Act, 1920 / Law Commission of India. – Delhi : Controller of Publications Govt. of India, 1980.
35p. – (87th report).
Includes bibliographical references.

CRIME AND CRIMINALS - PAPUA NEW GUINEA

—Crime In Papua New Guinea / Canberra : Australian Institute of Criminology.

CRIME AND CRIMINALS - SCOTLAND

—British crime survey Scotland / edited by Gerry Chambers and Jacqueline Tombs. – Edinburgh : H.M.S.O., 1984.
vii,62p.
Survey on why crimes not reported to police; identifies groups with high risk of being victims, and describes public attitudes to the criminal justice system.
ISBN 0114923795

CRIME AND CRIMINALS - SOUTH AFRICA

—South African criminal law and procedure / P. M. A. Hunt, J. R. L. Milton. – 2nd ed. – Cape Town : Juta, 1982.
xcv,870p.
Includes bibliographical references and index.
ISBN 0702112569

CRIME AND CRIMINALS - SWITZERLAND

—Snow-white image : the hidden reality of crime in Switzerland / Flemming Balvig. – Oslo : Norwegian University Press, 1988.
123p.
Bibliography: p.119-123.. Translation of: Hvid som sne.
ISBN 8200074722 £17.50

CRIME AND CRIMINALS - UNITED STATES

—Class, state & crime / Richard Quinney. – 2nd ed. – New York : Longman, 1980.
x,213p; 21cm.
Previous ed.: published as 'Class, state and crime : on the theory and practice of criminal justice'. New York : D. McKay, 1977 ; New York ; London : Longman, 1978. Includes index.
ISBN 0582281563 Pbk £4.95

—East side-west side : organizing crime in New York 1930-1950 / Alan Block. – Cardiff : University College Cardiff Press, 1980.
265p.
Bibliographies.
ISBN 0901426997

—Major forms of crime / edited by Robert F. Meier. – Beverly Hills : Sage, 1984.
274p; 22cm. – (Sage criminal justice system annuals 21).
Includes bibliographies.
ISBN 0803920946 Hbk No price
ISBN 0803920954 Pbk £14.00

CRIME AND THE PRESS - GREAT BRITAIN

—Crime, justice and the mass media : papers presented to the 14th Cropwood Round-Table Conference, December 1981 / edited by Colin Sumner. – Cambridge : University of Cambridge Institute of Criminology, 1982.
ii,123p.
Includes bibliographical references.

—Crime, punishment and the press / Marjorie Jones. – London : NACRO, 1980.
30p.
Bibliography: p.29-30.
ISBN 085069020X

CRIME LABORATORIES - ENGLAND

—Effectiveness of the Forensic Science Service / by Malcolm Ramsay. – London : H.M.S.O., 1987.
v,93p; 25cm.
Examines the extent to which the work of the FSS assists the police and courts in solving crimes.
ISBN 0113408420

CRIME PREVENTION

—Crime control strategies : an introduction to the study of crime / Harold E. Pepinsky. – New York : Oxford University Press, 1980.
xvii,352p; 24cm.
Includes bibliographies and index.
ISBN 0195026071 Pbk £6.50

—From Punishment To Prevention / Repr. of 1932 ed. – Aalen Wuertt : Scientia.
xv, 152p.

—Howard journal : a review of modern methods for the prevention and treatment of crime and juvenile delinquency / London : Howard League for Penal Reform, 1921.
Continued by: The Howard journal of penology and crime prevention. Subtitle varies.

—Review of the operation of the Northern Ireland (Emergency Provisions) Act 1978 / by Sir George Baker : presented to Parliament by the Secretary of State for Northern Ireland. – London : H.M.S.O., 1984.
171p.
ISBN 0101922205

—Situational crime prevention : from theory into practice / edited by Kevin Heal and Gloria Laycock. – London : H.M.S.O., 1986.
vii,159p; 25cm.
Research shows doubts as to the ability of traditional responses to control rising crime rates. Discusses the reduction of opportunity for crime as the most promising method of prevention. Examines the theory of crime prevention and its implementation.
ISBN 0113408269

—Understanding crime prevention / National Crime Prevention Institute. – Boston : Butterworths, 1986.
xiv,207p; 24cm.
Includes index.
ISBN 0409900753 No price

—Visions of social control : crime, punishment and classification / Stanley Cohen. – Cambridge : Polity, 1984.
300p.
ISBN 0745600204 Hbk £19.50
ISBN 0745600212 Pbk £7.95

CRIME PREVENTION - AUSTRALIA

—Crime Prevention in Developing Areas / Canberra : Australian Institute of Criminology.

—Crime Prevention : Planning and Participation in Geelong / Canberra : Australian Institute of Criminology.

—Crime Prevention Planning : Proceedings of the United National Interregional Course / Canberra : Australian Institute of Criminology.

—Planning Crime Prevention / Canberra : Australian Institute of Criminology.

CRIME PREVENTION - CANADA

—Cognitive Model of Crime and Delinquency Preventiion and Rehabilitation : Assessment Procedures, 2 Vols. / Elizabeth A. Fabiano. – Ontario : Ontario Government Publications Service, 1983.
89p.
ISBN 0774386681 Hbk free

—Cognitive Model of Crime and Delinquency Prevention and Rehabilitation : Intervention Techniques, 2 Vols. / Elizabeth A. Fabiano. – Ontario : Ontario Government Publications Service, 1983.
89p.
ISBN 0774386673 Hbk free

CRIME PREVENTION - ENGLAND

—Implementing crime prevention measures / by Tim Hope. – London : H.M.S.O., 1985.
vi,75p; 25cm.
Examines practicality of crime prevention methods. Considers situational measures aimed at dealing with specifically defined offences and community involvement in prevention of crime. Illustrates difficulties by case histories.
ISBN 0113408129

CRIME PREVENTION - GREAT BRITAIN

—Co-ordinating crime prevention efforts : a Home Office Crime Policy Planning Unit report / by F.J. Gladstone. – London : H.M.S.O., 1980.
v,73p; 25cm. – (Home Office research study).
Bibliography: p69-70. A Home Office Crime Policy Planning Unit report.
ISBN 0113407025 Pbk £3.95

—Crime and police effectiveness / by Ronald V. Clarke and Mike Hough. – London : H.M.S.O., 1984.
iv,28p; 28cm. – (A Home Office Research and Planning Unit report).
ISBN 0113407734

—Crime control and the police : a review of research / by Pauline Morris and Kevin Heal. – London : H.M.S.O., 1981.
v,67p.
Bibliography: p56-67. A Home Office Research Unit report.
ISBN 0113407076

—Crime prevention publicity : an assessment / by D. Riley and P. Mayhew. – London : H.M.S.O., 1980.
v,43p.
Bibliography: p40-43. A Home Office Research Unit report.
ISBN 0113407033

—Designing out crime / edited by R.V.G. Clarke and P. Mayhew, Home Office Research Unit. – London : H.M.S.O., 1980.
viii,182p.
Studies first published in the Home Office Research Studies series. Bibliography: p163-171. Includes index.
ISBN 0113407327

—Howard journal of penology and crime prevention / Howard League for Penal Reform. – London: Scottish Academic Press, 1965-1983, 1965-.
Continues: The Howard journal; continued by: The Howard journal of criminal justice.

—Law and order : theft of an issue / David Downes. – London : Fabian Society in association with Labour Campaign for Criminal Justice, 1983.
33p.
Bibliography: p32-33.
ISBN 0716304902

—Losing the fight against crime / Richard Kinsey, John Leo, Jock Young. – Oxford : Basil Blackwell, 1986.
viii,221p; 23cm.
Bibliography: p216-218. - Includes index.
ISBN 063113719X Hbk £22.50
ISBN 0631137211 Pbk £6.95

—Prevention and prosecution of computer and high-tech crime / Kaplan. – Matthew Bender, 1988.
ISBN 0000999061 Hbk £50.00

—Prevention of crime among young people / Parliamentary All-Party Penal Affairs Group. – Chichester : Rose, 1983.
112p; 21cm.
ISBN 0859923533 Pbk £7.00

—Prevention of terrorism in British Law / Manchester : Manchester University Press, 1986-1988.
ISBN 0719022037 Pbk £9.95

—Research and criminal policy / by John Croft. – London : H.M.S.O., 1980.
iv,10p.
ISBN 0113406991

—Taking offenders out of circulation / by Stephen Brody and Roger Tarling. – London : H.M.S.O., 1980.
v,42p.
Bibliography: p 38-42. A Home Office Research Unit report.
ISBN 0113407041

CRIME PREVENTION - ISLAMIC COUNTRIES

—The effect of Islamic legislation on crime prevention in Saudi Arabia : proceedings of the symposium held in Riyadh, 16-21 Shawal 1396 A.H. (9-13 October 1976) / Saudi Arabia : Ministry of Interior Crime Prevention Research Centre, 1980.
x,606p.
'Translated, edited and printed in collaboration with the United Nations Social Defence Research Institute (UNSDRI). Translated from the Arabic.

—First Joint International Conference on Research in Crime Prevention, Riyad, 23-25 January 1984 / Rome : United Nations Social Defence Research Institute, 1985.
235 p.; 21 cm.
Bibliography: p. 173-174.
ISBN 8876218262 pbk.

CRIME PREVENTION - JAPAN

—Crime Control in Japan / Canberra : Australian Institute of Criminology.

CRIME PREVENTION - PAPUA NEW GUINEA

—Progress in Crime Prevention In Papua New Guinea / Canberra : Australian Institute of Criminology.

CRIMES AGAINST WOMEN

—Women against violence against women / edited by dusty rhodes and Sandra McNeill. – London : Onlywomen Press, 1985.
280p.
ISBN 0906500168

CRIMES AGAINST YOUTHS - CANADA

—Sexual offences against the person and the protection of young persons : information paper / Infractions sexuelles contre la personne et protection des jeunes : Jean Chretien, Minister of Justice. – Rev. ed. – Ottawa : Minister of Justice, 1980.
43p.
Parallel English and French text.

CRIMES ON BOARD AIRCRAFT

—Aviation security : digest of current ICAO policies and actions on the subject of unlawful interference with international civil aviation and its facilities / International Civil Aviation Organization. – 4th ed. – Montreal : International Civil Aviation Organization, 1987.
iii,36p. – (Doc 8849-C/990/4).
Decisions taken and work done by ICAO on the subject of unlawful interference with international civil aviation and its facilities. Includes the texts of three international conventions.

—International standards and recommended practices : security : safeguarding international civil aviation against acts of unlawful interference : annex 17 to the Convention on International Civil Aviation / International Civil Aviation Organization. – 3rd ed. 1. – Montreal : International Civil Aviation Organization, 1986.
looseleaf.
Kept up to date by amendments and supplements.

—Three international conventions on hijacking and offences on board aircraft : (i) Convention on Offences and Certain Other Acts Committed on Board Aircraft ... 1963. (ii) Convention for Suppression of Unlawful Seizure of Aircraft ... 1970. (iii) Convention for the Suppression of Unlawful Acts Against the Safety of Civil Aviation ... 1971 : explanation documentation prepared for Commonwealth jurisdictions by David Lloyd Jones in association with the Commonwealth Secretariat / David Lloyd Jones. – London : Commonwealth Secretariat, 1982.
vi,146p; 30cm.
ISBN 0850922151

CRIMINAL BEHAVIOUR - CANADA

—Parole decision-making in Canada : research towards decision guidelines / by Joan Nuffield. – Ottawa, Ont. : Communication Division, Solicitor General of Canada, 1982.
iv, 96 p.; 28 cm.
Bibliography: p. 91-96.
ISBN 0662121147 pbk.

CRIMINAL COURTS

—Draft international criminal code and draft statute for an international criminal tribunal / M. Cherif Bassiouni. – 2nd rev. & updated ed. – Dordrecht : M. Nijhoff, 1987.
xxii, 492p.
Rev. ed. of: International criminal law / M. Cherif Bassiouni, 1980. Bibliography: p.267-353.
ISBN 0898389186

CRIMINAL COURTS - ENGLAND

—Case for summary trial : proposals for a redistribution of criminal business / the Justices' Clerks' Society. – Bristol : The Society, 1982.
26p.

—Confessions / by Peter Mirfield. – London : Sweet & Maxwell, 1985.
165p; 22cm.
Includes index.
ISBN 0421303905 Hbk £12.25
ISBN 0421304006 Pbk £8.25

—Distribution of business between the Crown Court and magistrates' courts / London : Home Office, 1986.
17p.

CRIMINAL COURTS - GAMBIA

—Role of district tribunals in the administration of criminal justice in the Gambia : a critical appraisal / by K. Gyeke-Dako. – Banjul : Government Printer, 1984.
20 leaves.

CRIMINAL COURTS - GREAT BRITAIN

—Contested trials in magistrates' courts / by Julie Vennard. – London : H.M.S.O., 1982.
v,32p; 25cm.
Bibliography: p.26-27. 'A Home Office Research and Planning Unit report.'.
ISBN 0113407661

—Criminal Court in Action / 3rd ed. – London : Butterworths, 1983.
ISBN 0406556156 Pbk £17.95

—Criminal Statistics, England and Wales : Supplementary Tables 1980, 4 Vols. / London : Home Office.
ISBN 0862520134 Hbk £18.75

CRIMINAL COURTS - INDIA

—Criminal Court Handbook, Criminal Manual Major Acts / Allahabad : Law Publisher, 1983.

—Criminal Court Practice : with Model Forms / 2nd ed. – North Ryde : Law Book Co, 1987.

CRIMINAL EVIDENCE

—Burden of proof in criminal proceedings : report / by the Senate Standing Committee on Constitutional and Legal Affairs. – Canberra : Australian Government Publishing Service, 1982.
xiii,93p. – (Parliamentary paper).
Includes text of the 11th report of the Criminal Law Revision Committee (Great Britain), 1972 (Cmnd. 4991), on evidence.
ISBN 0644022345

—Evaluating witness evidence : recent psychological research and new perspectives / edited by Sally M.A. Lloyd-Bostock and Brian R. Clifford. – Chichester : Wiley, 1983.
x,305p; 24cm.
Includes bibliographies and index.
ISBN 0471104639 Hbk

—Identification evidence : a psychological evaluation / John W. Shepherd, Hadyn D. Ellis and Graham M. Davies : foreword by Lord Devlin. – Aberdeen : Aberdeen University Press, 1982.
xii,155p; 26cm.
Bibliography: p140-149. - Includes index.
ISBN 0080284418 £12.50

—Proof of fact in criminal trials / Marcus Stone. – Edinburgh : W. Green, 1984.
xxiii,390p; 22cm.
ISBN 0414007379

—Proof of fact in criminal trials / Edinburgh : W Green & Son, 1984.
Based on extensive court experience and psychological study, it is a systematic and comprehensive analysis of the fact-finding process in criminal trials examining lying and its detection, examination of witnesses, how real issues of fact emerge and the principles on which evidence is assessed and verdicts reached.
ISBN 0414007399

CRIMINAL EVIDENCE - AUSTRALIA

—Aboriginal customary law : the criminal law, evidence and procedure / Sydney : Australian Law Reform Commission, 1984.
24p. – (Discussion paper).

—Evidence reference / Australian Law Reform Commission. – Sydney : The Commission, 1982.
xi,269p.
Bibliography: p.267-269.

CRIMINAL EVIDENCE - AUSTRALIA - NEW SOUTH WALES

—Crawford's Proof in criminal cases / Reg Bartley. – 4th ed. – Sydney : Law Book Co., 1982.
xxii, 279 p.; 23 cm.
'Table of cases': p. ix, xxii. Includes index.
ISBN 045520537X £22.50

—Criminal procedure : unsworn statements of accused persons : report / New South Wales Law Reform Commission. – Sydney : The Commission, 1985.
70p. – (L.R.C. 45).
Bibliography: p.65-66.
ISBN 0730514269 Hbk

CRIMINAL EVIDENCE - AUSTRALIA - VICTORIA

—Report to Parliament on the burden of proof in criminal cases / Legal and Constitutional Committee. – Melbourne : Government Printer, 1985.
xvi,101p.
Bibliography: p.100-101.

—Unsworn statements in criminal trials / Law Reform Commissioner, Victoria. – Melbourne : The Commission, 1981.
43p. – (Report no 11).
Includes bibliographical references.

—Unsworn statements in criminal trials / Law Reform Commission of Victoria. – Melbourne : The Commission, 1985.
x,43p. – (Report no 2).
Includes bibliographical references.

CRIMINAL EVIDENCE - CANADA

—Canadian criminal evidence / by Peter K. McWilliams. – 2nd ed. – Aurora : Canada Law Book, 1984.
cxlii,1131p.
Previous ed.: 1974. Includes index.
ISBN 0888040180

—Charter principles and proof in criminal cases / David M. Paciocco. – Toronto : Carswell, 1987.
xlviii,616p.
Includes index.
ISBN 0459308114

—Criminal Evidence / Vancouver : Continuing Legal Education Society of British Columbia, 1985.
81p.
ISBN 0865042381 Hbk £55.00

—Criminal Evidence Handbook / Aurora : Canada Law Book Co, 1988.
400p.
The Criminal Evidence Handbook codifies the rules of criminal evidence into a single easy-to-use reference volume. With the emphasis on principles of evidence, this text can be used to quickly find all the essential points of criminal evidence. To this end, the laws are summarized as precepts, each precept is numbered and locatable in the keyword index.

—Criminal Evidence Handbook / Aurora : Canada Law Book, 1988.

—Criminal Law Evidence : Practice and Procedure / Agincourt : Carswell, 1988.
606p.
This looseleaf volume is a practical guide for researching evidentiary, procedural and practice questions arising in criminal law practice. Topics are varied and contain the relevant sections of the Criminal Code, Canada Evidence Act and the Charter of Rights and Freedoms.

—Investigative tests / Law Reform Commission of Canada. – Ottawa : Law Reform Commission of Canada, 1984.
166,186p; 25cm. – (Working paper).
At head of cover title: Criminal law. English and French texts bound back to back.
ISBN 066253039X

—Similar fact evidence : probative value and prejudice / by Donald K. Piragoff. – Toronto : Carswell, 1981.
xxiii,309p.
Includes bibliographical references and index.
ISBN 0459337807

CRIMINAL EVIDENCE - ENGLAND

—Briefing memorandum on the Police and Criminal Evidence Bill / the Law Society. – London : Law Society, 1982.
5 leaves.

—Cases and statutes on evidence : being based upon Cockle's cases and statutes on evidence / by P.B. Carter. – London : Sweet & Maxwell, 1981.
lviii,864p; 26cm.
Includes index.
ISBN 042120320X Hbk £28.00
ISBN 0421203307 Pbk £15.00

—Criminal evidence / by Richard May. – London : Sweet & Maxwell, 1986.
xlii,368p.
Covers aspects of the law of criminal evidence with emphasis on their practical application. Includes sections on burden and standard of proof, exclusionary rules and exceptions, and rules of evidence connected with the trial. Includes the Police and Criminal Evidence Act 1984.
ISBN 0421302909 Pbk £24

—Exclusion of improperly obtained evidence : with special reference to the Police and Criminal Evidence Act / by David Wolchover. – Chichester : Barry Rose, 1986.
v,260p.
Includes bibliographical references and index.
ISBN 0859923800

—Observations on the Police and Criminal Evidence Bill / the Justices' Clerks' Society. – Bristol : The Society, 1983.
34p.

—Police and Criminal Evidence Act 1984 / by Michael Zander : foreword by Leon Brittan. – London : Sweet & Maxwell, 1985.
xxi,315p; 25cm.
Includes index.
ISBN 0421326905 Pbk £12.50

—Police and Criminal Evidence Act 1984 / with annotations by M.D.A. Freeman. – London : Sweet & Maxwell, 1985.
x,185,44,8p; 24cm.
ISBN 0421329009

—Police and Criminal Evidence Bill 1982 : briefings / National Council for Civil Liberties. – 1. – London : The Council, 1983.
various pagings.
Contents: Clause 1: Stop and search of persons and vehicles - Clauses 9 and 10: Police powers to search private premises for evidence - Clauses 9 and 10: Opinion / by Ben Hytner - Part 3. Police powers of arrest - Part 4. Detention of suspects - Part 5. Questioning and treatment of persons by police - Part 6. Codes of practice - Clause 60: 'Confession' statements and the right to silence.

—Police and criminal evidence bill : briefing guide / London : Home Office, 1983.
67p.
ISBN 0862521211

—Police and Criminal Evidence Bill : draft code of practice for the exercise of powers of stop and search / London : Home Office, 1984.
9p.
ISBN 0862521556

CRIMINAL EVIDENCE - GREAT BRITAIN

—Contested trials in magistrates' courts / by Julie Vennard. – London : H.M.S.O., 1982.
v,32p; 25cm.
Bibliography: p.26-27. 'A Home Office Research and Planning Unit report.'.
ISBN 0113407661

—Contested trials in magistrates' courts : the case for the prosecution / Julie Vennard with the assistance of Karen Williams. – London : H.M.S.O., 1980.
vi,26p. – (Research studies).
Bibliography: p 26.
ISBN 0117301256

—Criminal Evidence and P.P.H. 2 / Wilkie. – 7th ed. – London : Butterworths, 1981.
ISBN 040684131 Pbk £4.95

—Criminal Litigation / M. S. Iller. – London : Butterworths, 1985.
This work is a factual account of all stages in the practice and procedure of criminal litigation in the United Kingdom from investigation to conclusion of the criminal process. The book is directed at students of criminal evidence and procedure*Students*
ISBN 0406258139 Pbk

—Guide to the Police and Criminal Evidence Act 1984 / Vaughan T. Bevan and Ken W. Lidstone. – London : Butterworths, 1985.
xv,554.
This text gives a comprehensive dissertation on every aspect of the Act. The book includes a full text of the United Kingdom's Police and Criminal Evidence Act of 1984.
ISBN 0406014302 Pbk

—Police and Criminal Evidence Act 1984 : Guide / Pickover. – Police Review, 1986.
ISBN 0851640214 Pbk £4.95

—Police and the Criminal Evidence Act 1984 / Magrath. – London : Longman Professional, 1985.
ISBN 0851207669 Pbk £19.95

—Principles of criminal evidence / Oxford : Clarendon Press, 1878.
352; 21.5. – (Clarendon Law Series).
Examines the role played by the lay judgements of jurors. Discusses judicial practices which have evolved to satisfy the desire to discover the truth, the need to protect the innocent from conviction, and the need to maintain standards in the criminal process. A central feature of the law of criminal evidence is the attempt to balance these three principles*Students and teachers of criminal law, evidence and legal philosophy*
ISBN 0198761031 Hbk £30
ISBN 0198762348 Pbk £11.95

CRIMINAL EVIDENCE - HONG KONG

—Criminal Evidence in Hong Kong / McCoy. – London : Butterworths, 1987.
ISBN 0409995479 Hbk £54.00

CRIMINAL EVIDENCE - INDIA

—Criminal Major Acts : Containing I.P.C., Cr.P.C. and Evidence Act / 2nd ed. – Allahabad : Law Publishers, 1983.

CRIMINAL EVIDENCE - NEW ZEALAND

—Proof in Criminal Cases in New Zealand / North Ryde : Law Book Co, 1984.
xxxii, 407p.
ISBN 0455205221 Hbk £49.00
ISBN 0455205930 Pbk £32.00

CRIMINAL EVIDENCE - NORTHERN IRELAND

—Supergrasses : the use of accomplice evidence in Northern Ireland : a report / by Tony Gifford. – London : Cobden Trust, 1984.
38p.
ISBN 0900137215

CRIMINAL EVIDENCE - SCOTLAND

—Criminal evidence : affidavit evidence, hearsay and related matters in criminal proceedings / Scottish Law Commission. – Edinburgh : The Commission, 1988.
iv,145p. – (Discussion paper).
Includes excerpts from the Criminal Justice Act 1967 and the Police and Criminal Evidence Act 1984.

—Evidence : report on evidence in cases of rape and other sexual offences / Scottish Law Commission. – Edinburgh : H.M.S.O., 1983.
vi,33p.
Includes bibliographical references. Includes Draft Evidence in Sexual Offences (Scotland) Bill.
ISBN 0102028842

CRIMINAL INJURIES COMPENSATION - GREAT BRITAIN

—Compensation for criminal injuries / Mitchell. – Sweet & Maxwell, 1988.
ISBN 0421385804 Pbk

—Criminal Injuries Compensation / 2nd ed. – London : Waterlow, 1986.
ISBN 008039244X Pbk £9.95

—Twentieth Report / Criminal Injuries Compensation Board. – London : HMSO, 1984.
ISBN 0101939906 Hbk £4.50

CRIMINAL INVESTIGATION

—Forensic science and the expert witness / by J.H. Phillips, J.K. Bowen : with a foreword by Sir Daryl Dawson. – North Ryde, N.S.W. : Law Book Company, 1985.
ix,114p; 22cm.
Introductory guide to forensic science. Contains chapters on forensic science and crime; crime scene examiners; continuity of exhibits; photographic evidence; forensic chemistry; forensic biology; firearms and toolmarks; fingerprints; and document examination.
ISBN 0455205914 Pbk

—National Crime Authority Bill 1983 : report / by the Senate Standing Committee on Constitutional and Legal Affairs. – Canberra : Australian Government Publishing Service, 1984.
xxv,154p. – (Parliamentary paper).
ISBN 0644033290

—Powers of investigation / Woellner. – London : Butterworths, 1983.
ISBN 0409493813 Hbk £39.00

—World directory of criminological institutes / compiled and edited by Carla Masotti Santoro. – 4th ed. – Rome : UNSDRI, 1986.
xxvi,582p. – (Publication).
ISBN 9290780029

CRIMINAL INVESTIGATION - AUSTRALIA

—Criminal Investigation : Interim Report / Land Reform Commission. – Repr. of 1977 ed. – Canberra : Australian Government Publishing Service, 1983.
224p. – (ALRC Report: No. 2).
ISBN 0642017921 Hbk £13.00

CRIMINAL INVESTIGATION - CANADA

—Commissions of Inquiry under the Inquiries Act, part I, 1967 to date / prepared by Denise Ledoux. – Ottawa : Library of Parliament, Information and Reference Branch, 1980.
p.154-175.
Supplements: Federal Royal Commissions in Canada 1867-1966 : a checklist / George Fletcher Henderson.

—Criminal investigation : a selective literature review and bibliography / by Duncan Chappell, Robert Gordon, Rhonda Moore. – Ottawa : Ministry of the Solicitor General, Communication Division, 1982.
68p.
ISBN 0662120310

—Investigative tests / Law Reform Commission of Canada. – Ottawa : Law Reform Commission of Canada, 1984.
166,186p; 25cm. – (Working paper).
At head of cover title: Criminal law. English and French texts bound back to back.
ISBN 066253039X

—Making crime a study of detective work / Richard V. Ericson. – Toronto : Butterworths, 1981.
xiii,257p.
Bibliography: p243-254.

—Report of the Commission of Inquiry Relating to the Security and Investigation Services Branch Within the Post Office Department / Rene Marin. – Hull, Quebec : Canadian Government Publishing Centre, 1981.
iv,338p.
Commissioner: Rene J. Marin.
ISBN 0660108585

CRIMINAL INVESTIGATION - ENGLAND

—Error of judgment : the Birmingham bombings / by Chris Mullin. – London : Chatto & Windus, 1986.
224p; 23cm.
ISBN 0701129786 £10.95

—Investigating robbery / Michael Banton. – Aldershot : Gower, 1985.
vii,126p; 22cm.
Bibliography: p109-110. - Includes index.
ISBN 0566051141 £16.50

—Investigation and prosecution of criminal offences in England and Wales : the law and procedure / the Royal Commission on Criminal Procedure : Chairman: Sir Cyril Philips. – London : H.M.S.O., 1981.
vii,229p; 25cm.
ISBN 0101809212 Pbk £7.50

—Report / the Royal Commission on Criminal Procedure : chairman: Sir Cyril Philips. – London : H.M.S.O., 1981.
xiii,240p; 25cm.
Includes index.
ISBN 0101809204 Pbk £10.00

—Uncovering crime : the police role / David Steer. – London : H.M.S.O., 1980.
vii,136p; 25cm. – (Research studies).
Bibliography: p127-129. At head of title: Royal Commission on Criminal Procedure.
ISBN 0117301264 Pbk £5.00

CRIMINAL INVESTIGATION - GREAT BRITAIN

—Investigations Manual / Binder Hamlyn Staff. – London : Butterworths, 1985.
Based on an in-house manual for investigation work, this book provides a reference for the preparation and conduct of an investigation. It is intended for use in the opening stages of an investigation to develop the quickest and most productive approach to the work.
ISBN 0406142580 Pbk

—Undercover investigation / London : Butterworths, 1983.
ISBN 0409950769 Hbk £25.00

CRIMINAL INVESTIGATION - INDIA

—Police Investigations and Prosecutions / 5th ed. 1986 repr. 1987. – Allahabad : Law Book Company, 1987.
900p.

CRIMINAL INVESTIGATION - NEW ZEALAND

—Report of the Royal Commission to Inquire into the Circumstances of the Convictions of Arthur Allan Thomas for the Murders of David Harvey Crewe and Jeanette Lenore Crewe / R. L. Taylor. – Wellington : Government Printer, 1980.
124p. – (H.).
Chairman: R.L. Taylor.

CRIMINAL INVESTIGATION - SCOTLAND

—Crime Investigation : Art or Science? / Edinburgh : Scottish Academic Press Ltd, 1984.
102p.
ISBN 0707304377 Hbk £10.00
ISBN 0707304385 Pbk

CRIMINAL JUDGMENTS - GREAT BRITAIN

—Sentence of the court : a handbook for courts on the treatment of offenders / Home Office. – 4th ed. – London : H.M.S.O., 1986.
109p; 21cm.
ISBN 0113408072

CRIMINAL JUSTICE

—Cost of Criminal Justice : A Preliminary International Survey / J. Marjoram. – Canberra : Australian Institute of Criminology.

CRIMINAL JUSTICE - AUSTRALIA

—Australian Criminal Justice System : The Mid 1980's / Paul Wilson. – Butterworths, 1987.
348p.
ISBN 0409491497 Hbk £46.00

—Australian Criminal Justice System : The Mid 1980's / P. Wilson. – Sydney : Butterworths, 1987.
344p.
The authors of this book, who include criminologists, sociologists, lawyers, and academics, cover such matters as sexual assault, corporate crime, terrorism, sentencing, organized crime, and juvenile offenses.

—Cost of Criminal Justice : An Analysis / Canberra : Australian Institute of Criminology.

—Criminal Justice in Australia / Peter Sallmann. – Melbourne : Oxford University Press, 1984.
240p.
ISBN 0195544587 Pbk £11.99

—Criminal Justice Research Methodology / Canberra : Australian Institute of Criminology.

—Evaluation in the Criminal Justice Services / Canberra : Australian Institute of Criminology.

—Human Rights Guarantees in the Administration of Criminal Justice / L. T. Wilkins. – Canberra : Australian Institute of Criminology.

—Issues in Criminal Justice Administration / Sandra J. Egger. – North Sydney : Allen & Unwin, 1983.
200p.
ISBN 0868612774 Hbk £29.95
ISBN 0868610542 Pbk £19.95

—Judicial discretion and criminal litigation / 2nd. – Oxford : Clarendon Press, 1989.
350; 23.5.
Examines the discretions exercised by criminal trial courts both at Crown Court and Magistrates level, and discretion in the criminal appellate process. Intends to provide a theoretical framework within which to discuss and assess the discretions. Concentrates on the law and practice in England and Wales, but also refers to statutes and decision in Australia, New Zealand and Canada.
ISBN 0198255675 Pbk £14.95

—Psychologist in Criminal Justice : An Australian Perspective / Canberra : Australian Institute of Criminology.

—Role of Psychologists in the Criminal Justice System / Canberra : Australian Institute of Criminology.

—Use of Computers in the Criminal Justice System / Canberra : Australian Institute of Criminology.

—Women as Participants In the Criminal Justice System / Canberra : Australian Institute of Criminology.

CRIMINAL JUSTICE - CANADA

—Canadian Criminal Justice History / University of Toronto, 1988.
ISBN 0802057209 Hbk £45.00

—Criminal Jury Trials / Vancouver : Continuing Legal Education Society of British Columbia, 1988.
165p.
ISBN 0865049742 Hbk £70.00

—Criminal Justice : 1981 Conference of the Canadian Institute for the Administration of Justice / Carswell Legal Publications. – Agincourt : Carswell, 1982.
300p.

—Criminal Justice in Canada / John F. Klein. – Butterworths, 1980.
376p.

—Criminal Justice in Canada / Toronto : Butterworths, 1980.
359p.

—Criminal justice in Canada: an introductory text / John F Klein, Simon B Verdun-Jones. – Scarborough, Ontario : Butterworths (Canada).
359.
Overview of the Canadian criminal justice system. Coverage includes corectional institutions, policing in Canada, police powers and discretion, the criminal court system, sentencing, the public and criminal justice system, community-based corrections, juvenile justice system, special categories of offenders, and trends in Canadian criminal justice.
ISBN 0409998022 Pbk

—Criminal Justice Policy : From Research to Reform / Butterworths, 1983.
152p.
Asks whether a particular problem is actually as serious as it is assumed to be, and whether it deserves a prominent place in the agenda of the policy makers. Concludes that neither ple-bargaining nor court delay is as threatening as commonly supposed, and that the processing of minor crimes in court imposes unjustifiably heavy costs.
ISBN 0409868426 Hbk £40.00

—Judicial discretion and criminal litigation / 2nd. – Oxford : Clarendon Press, 1989.
350; 23.5.
Examines the discretions exercised by criminal trial courts both at Crown Court and Magistrates level, and discretion in the criminal appellate process. Intends to provide a theoretical framework within which to discuss and assess the discretions. Concentrates on the law and practice in England and Wales, but also refers to statutes and decision in Australia, New Zealand and Canada.
ISBN 0198255675 Pbk £14.95

—Native criminal justice : research issues and data sources / Wanda Jamieson and Carol Laprairie. – Ottawa : Solicitor General Canada, 1987.
iii,84p. – (User report).
Bibliography: p.78-84. On cover: Programs Branch.

—Open justice: the constitutional right to attend and spek about criminal proceedings / Scarborough, Ontario : Butterworths (Canada), 1985.
416.
Examines the extent to which Canadians are free to attend, criticize and report criminal court proceedings. Considers the impact of the Canadian Charter of Rights and Freedoms on the issues of public access to criminal courts, and assesses the practical aspects of the legal dilemma inherent in the free press/fair trial debate, against the background of the American experience.
ISBN 0409844730 Hbk

CRIMINAL JUSTICE - GREAT BRITAIN

—Criminal Justice Act 1982 : A Guide to Fines / Butterworths Editorial Staff. – London : Butterworths, 1983.
This text for magistrates in the United Kingdom provides a condensation of the changes in the fine schedules for Criminal Acts brought about by the Criminal Justice Act of 1982.
ISBN 0406008604 Pbk

—Criminal Justice Act, 1988 / London : Shaw & Sons.
ISBN 0721910726 Pbk £24.95

—The Criminal Justice Acts 1987 and 1988 : A Commentary / London : Waterlow, 1988.
304p.
ISBN 0080330886 Pbk £26.95

—Criminal Justice History : An International Annual / London : Meckler, 1987.
ISBN 0887361714 Hbk £37.50

—Criminology and Criminal Justice / London : Butterworths, 1982.
ISBN 0406593213 Pbk £9.95

—Guide to the Criminal Justice Act 1982 / Christopher J. Emmins. – London : Financial Training, 1982.
iv, 98p.
ISBN 0906322227

—Judicial discretion and criminal litigation / 2nd. – Oxford : Clarendon Press, 1989.
350; 23.5.
Examines the discretions exercised by criminal trial courts both at Crown Court and Magistrates level, and discretion in the criminal appellate process. Intends to provide a theoretical framework within which to discuss and assess the discretions. Concentrates on the law and practice in England and Wales, but also refers to statutes and decision in Australia, New Zealand and Canada.
ISBN 0198255675 Pbk £14.95

CRIMINAL JUSTICE - INDIA

—Crime and Criminal Justice System in India / New Delhi : Deep and Deep Publications, 1984.
338p.

CRIMINAL JUSTICE - NEW ZEALAND

—Judicial discretion and criminal litigation / 2nd. – Oxford : Clarendon Press, 1989.
350; 23.5.
Examines the discretions exercised by criminal trial courts both at Crown Court and Magistrates level, and discretion in the criminal appellate process. Intends to provide a theoretical framework within which to discuss and assess the discretions. Concentrates on the law and practice in England and Wales, but also refers to statutes and decision in Australia, New Zealand and Canada.
ISBN 0198255675 Pbk £14.95

CRIMINAL JUSTICE, ADMINISTRATION OF - ITALY

—Carlotto affair : a terrible injustice / International Committee 'Justice for Massimo Carlotto'. – London : the Committee, 1987.
40p.

CRIMINAL JUSTICE, ADMINISTRATION OF - UNITED STATES

—Proposal for a commission of inquiry into the effect of domestic intelligence activities on criminal trials in the United States of America / Amnesty International. – London : Amnesty International, 1981.
iii,141p; 30cm.
Cover title.
ISBN 0862100380 Pbk Unpriced

CRIMINAL JUSTICE PERSONNEL - ENGLAND

—Management scrutiny : listing officers in the Crown Court / Lord Chancellor's Department. – London : The Department, 1984.
108p.
Includes bibliographical references.

CRIMINAL LAW

—Causation in the law / by H.L.A. Hart and Tony Honore. – 2nd ed. – Oxford : Clarendon, 1985.
lxxxi,516p; 23cm.
Previous ed.: 1959. Bibliography: p498-507. - Includes index.
ISBN 019825475X Hbk £25.00
ISBN 0198254741 Pbk £14.50

—Codification of the criminal law : a public lecture / delivered by J.C. Smith on ... 17th March 1986. – London : Inns of Court School of Law, 1986.
16p.

—Crime, guilt, and punishment : a philosophical introduction / C.L. Ten. – Oxford : Clarendon, 1987.
176p; 22cm.
Includes bibliography and index.
ISBN 019875082X Hbk £19.50 :
ISBN 0198750811 Pbk £8.95

—Crime, Justice, and Codification : Essays in Commemoration of Jacques Fortin / Agincourt : Carswell, 1986.
196p.
This book contains eleven essays dealing with the theory, philosophy, reform and codification of criminal law. Rationality and legitimacy of criminal law the goals of reform are addressed in the essays.

—Crime, proof and punishment : essays in memory of Sir Rupert Cross / Rupert Cross, Colin Tapper. – London : Butterworths, 1981.
xxvi,336p; 26cm.
Bibliography of works by Sir Rupert Cross: p.323-327. - Includes index. Edited by Colin Tapper.
ISBN 0406569991

—Criminal law and psychiatry / by D.J. Power : co-author D.H.D. Selwood. – S.l. : Barry Rose, 1987.
xviii,265p.
ISBN 1870080254

—Criminal law : cases and materials / J.C. Smith, Brian Hogan. – 3rd ed. – London : Butterworths, 1986.
700p; 25cm.
Previous ed.: 1980. Includes index.
ISBN 0406658242 Pbk
ISBN 0406658250

—Criminal Law : cases and materials / J.C. Smith, Brian Hogan. – 2nd ed. – London : Butterworth, 1980.
xxx,701p; 26cm.
Previous ed.: 1975. Includes index.
ISBN 0406658226 £22.50
ISBN 0406658234

—Criminal Law in Action / Dordrecht : Kluwer, 1986.
440p.
ISBN 9065442782 Hbk Gld100.00

—Criminal law in New South Wales / Howard Purnell, H. M. Hamilton. – 1. – Sydney : Law Book Co., 1972.
loose-leaf.
Supersedes: Hamilton and Addison's Criminal law and procedure.
ISBN 0455167206

Vol. 2 : by Ray Watson and Reg Bartley 1978.
Loose-leaf.
Supersedes: Hamilton and Addison's Criminal law and procedure. Includes index. Contents: Summary offences.

—Essays in Criminal Law / Stockholm : Almqvist & Wiksell, 1988.
152p.
ISBN 9176781186 Hbk £170.00

—Historical research on crime and criminal justice : sixth Criminological Colloquim (PC-CC), Strasbourg 21-23 November 1983 / Council of Europe. – Strasbourg : Council of Europe, 1984.
ii,153p.
Includes bibliographies. 'Secretariat memorandum prepared by the Directorate of Legal Affairs'.

—International Criminal Law : a Draft International Criminal Code / Dordrecht : Kluwer, 1980.
xxxv, 250p.
ISBN 9028601309 Hbk £114.00

—Law of criminal conspiracy / by Peter Gillies. – Sydney : Law Book Co., 1981.
Includes bibliographical references and index.
ISBN 0455200793

—Martin's annual criminal code / with annotations by Edward L. Greenspan. – 1985. – Ontario : Canada Law Book, 1985.
cxx,1117p.
Includes index.

—Martin's annual criminal code / with annotations by Edward L. Greenspan. – 1983. – Aurora, Ont. : Canada Law Book, 1983.
cxii,1054p.
Includes index.

—Martin's annual criminal code / with annotations by Edward L. Greenspan. – 1981. – Aurora, Ont. : Canada Law Book, 1981.
xcix, 948p.
Includes index.

—Martin's annual criminal code / with annotations by Edward L. Greenspan. – 1984. – Ontario : Canada Law Book, 1984.
cxv,1067p.
Includes index.

—Martin's annual criminal code / with annotations by Edward L. Greenspan. – 1980. – Aurora, Ont. : Canada Law Book, 1980.
xci,897p.

—Martin's related criminal statutes 1980 : a selection of important statutes and regulations related to the practice of criminal law / with annotations by Edward L. Greenspan. – Aurora, Ont. : Canada Law Book, 1980.
xxvii,342p.

—Martin's related criminal statutes 1985 : a selection of important statutes and regulations related to the practice of criminal law / with annotations by Edward L. Greenspan. – Aurora, Ont. : Canada Law Book, 1985.
xlii,414p.

—Martin's related statutes 1983 : a selection of important statutes and regulations related to the practice of criminal law / with annotations by Edward L. Greenspan. – 1983. – Aurora, Ont. : Canada Law Book, 1983.
xxxv,379p.

—Moral limits of the criminal law / Joel Feinberg. – New York : Oxford University Press, 1984.
xiii,269p; 25cm.
Includes index.
ISBN 0195034090 No price

Vol.2 : Offense to others / Joel Feinberg. – 1985.
xix,328p.
Includes bibliographical references and index.
ISBN 019503449X Hbk

Volume 3 : Harm to self 1989.
444.
Looks at the problems associated with the commonly proposed principle of 'legal paternalism'. Evaluates and rejects the principle that it can be right to impose coercion on a person for her own good, regardless of her wishes in the matter.
ISBN 0195059239 Pbk £9.95

—Philosophy and the criminal law : Association for Legal and Social Philosophy Tenth Annual Conference at the University of Manchester, 8-10th April 1983 / edited by Antony Duff and Nigel Simmonds. – Wiesbaden West Germany : Franz Steiner, 1984.
120p.
Bibliography: p.117-120.
ISBN 3515041699

—Role of criminal law in consumer protection / European Committee on Crime Problems. – Strasbourg : Council of Europe, 1983.
24p; 21cm.
Report and recommendations of the European Committee on Crime Problems on the role of criminal law in protecting consumers from exploitation by suppliers.
ISBN 928710218X £1.25

—Tremeear's 1981 criminal code and miscellaneous statutes : as amended to January 1, 1981 / William James Tremeear. – Toronto : Carswell, 1981.
xiv,526p.
'The companion volume to Tremeear's Criminal annotations'. Includes index. Earler eds. held.
ISBN 0459335405

—Tremeear's 1982 criminal code and miscellaneous statutes : as amended to January 1, 1982 / William James Tremeear. – Toronto : Carswell, 1982.
xiv,676p.
'The companion volume to Tremeear's Criminal annotations'. Includes index.
ISBN 0459347101

—Tremeear's 1983 criminal code and miscellaneous statutes : as amended to January 1, 1983 / William James Tremeear. – Toronto : Carswell, 1983.
xvi,715p.
Previous ed.: 1982. Includes index. 'The companion volume to Tremeear's Criminal Annotations'.
ISBN 0459355503

—Tremeear's 1984 criminal code and miscellaneous statutes : as amended to January 1, 1984 / William James Tremeear. – Toronto : Carswell, 1984.
xvi,712p.
'The companion volume to Tremeear's Criminal Annotations'. Previous ed.: 1983. Includes index.
ISBN 0459367609

—Tremeear's 1985-86 criminal code and miscellaneous statutes : as amended to January 1, 1986 / William James Tremeear. – Toronto : Carswell, 1985.
xvi,732p.
Previous ed.: 1984. 'The companion volume to the Tremeear's criminal annotations'. Includes index.
ISBN 0459377108

CRIMINAL LAW - AUSTRALIA

—Aboriginal customary law : the criminal law, evidence and procedure / Sydney : Australian Law Reform Commission, 1984.
24p. – (Discussion paper).

—Brett and Waller's Criminal Law : Text and Cases / 5th ed. – Butterworths, 1984.
784p.
This introductory work, containing cases, statutory materials, and commentary, is intended to be equally useful in the common law states of New South Wales, South Australia, and Victoria. Variations in the law from one state to another are discussed.
ISBN 0409492116 Hbk £74.00

—Brett, Waller and Williams Criminal Law Text and Cases / C.R. Williams. – Butterworths, 1989.
ca 960p.
ISBN 0409495336 Hbk £84.00
ISBN 0409495344 Pbk £66.00

—Cases on the Criminal Code / R.A. Hayes. – North Ryde : Law Book Co, 1984.
xxiii, 739p.
ISBN 0455204276 Hbk £70.50
ISBN 0455204284 Pbk £54.50

—Criminal law / by Peter Gillies. – Sydney : Law Book Co., 1985.
lvii,668p.
Includes bibliographical references and index.
ISBN 0455205981

—Criminal law /. – North Ryde : Law Book Co, 1984.
xiv, 98p. – (Nutshells).
ISBN 0455203458 Hbk

—Review of Crimes Act 1914 and other crimes legislation of the Commonwealth / Human Rights Commission. – Canberra : Australian Government Publishing Service, 1983.
viii,44p. – (Report).
Includes extracts from legislation.
ISBN 0644027207

CRIMINAL LAW - AUSTRALIA - NEW SOUTH WALES

—Criminal law in New South Wales / Howard Purnell. – 2nd ed. – Sydney : Law Book Co., 1981-.
Loose-leaf.
Includes index. Contents: Indictable offences.

—Introduction to Criminal Law in New South Wales / 2nd ed. – Butterworths, 1980.
248p.
ISBN 0409436291 Pbk £39.50

—Introduction to criminal law in NSW / Oxley-Oxland. – 2nd ed. – North Ryde : Butterworths (Australia), 1980.
ISBN 0409436291 Pbk £15.20

—Principles of Criminal Law in New South Wales / Butterworths, 1984.
219p.
The cases contained in this introductory text are analyzed by their history, facts, problems, and the basic principles of law involved. Diagrams and tables are included in some chapters.
ISBN 0409491357 Pbk £38.00

CRIMINAL LAW - AUSTRALIA - QUEENSLAND

—Carter's Criminal Law of Queensland / 7th ed. – Sydney : Butterworths, 1988.
1300p.

—Criminal law of Queensland / by Reginald Francis Carter. – 6th ed. – Brisbane : Butterworths, 1982.
lxxvi,1199p.
Includes index.
ISBN 0409303607

—Criminal Law of Queensland / 6th ed. – London : Butterworths, 1982.
ISBN 040930350X Pbk £47.30
ISBN 0409303607 Hbk £65.70

—Criminal Law of Queensland / 7th ed. – Butterworths, 1988.
1,406p.
ISBN 0409493090 Hbk £98.00

—Introduction to the Criminal Law of Queensland and Western Australia / R.G. Kenny. – 2nd ed. – Butterworths, 1984.
259p.
The new edition of this introductory text covers the changes in the law since July 1977. Contained are materials on the extraterritorial competence of the respective State Parliaments and a table of comparative sections, including provisions of the Tasmanian Criminal Code.
ISBN 040949433X Pbk £38.50

—Introduction to the Criminal Law of Queensland and WQ / Kenny. – 2nd ed. – London : Butterworths, 1984.
ISBN 040949433X Pbk £23.20

CRIMINAL LAW - AUSTRALIA - VICTORIA

—Criminal Law, Victoria / Butterworths, 1981.
ISBN 0409352039 loose £220.00

CRIMINAL LAW - AUSTRALIA - WESTERN AUSTRALIA

—Introduction to the Criminal Law of Queensland and Western Australia / R.G. Kenny. – 2nd ed. – Butterworths, 1984.
259p.
The new edition of this introductory text covers the changes in the law since July 1977. Contained are materials on the extraterritorial competence of the respective State Parliaments and a table of comparative sections, including provisions of the Tasmanian Criminal Code.
ISBN 040949433X Pbk £38.50

CRIMINAL LAW - CANADA

—Annual Review of Criminal Law : 1987 / Agincourt : Carswell, Annual, 1986.
304p.
This text, the sixth volume in an annual series, provides a summary and a synopsis of the major issues in Canadian criminal law, practice and evidence. It contains an outline of the trends in judicial interpretations of the Charter. Also included is an index to pertinent periodical literature.

—Annual review of criminal law / v. – Toronto : Carswell, 1982-.

—Canadian Criminal Cases (C.C.C.) 1898-1962, 133 Vols. / Aurora : Canada Law Book Co. – (Old Ser.).
Back Vols.

—Canadian Criminal Cases (C.C.C.) 1963-70, 30 Vols. / Aurora : Canada Law Book Co. – (New Ser.).
Back Vols.

—Canadian Criminal Cases (C.C.C.) 1971-83, 70 Vols. / Aurora : Canada Law Book Co. – (Second Ser.).
Back Vols.

—Canadian Criminal Cases (C.C.C.) March 1983-Present / Aurora : Canada Law Book Co. – (Third Ser.).

—Canadian Criminal Cases : Index, Annotations, Table of Cases / Aurora : Canada Law Book Co, 1985. – (Law Reports).
Vols. 1-70 of Second Series 1983.
1184p. – (Law Reports).

—Canadian Criminal Cases New Series (1963-1970), 30 Vols. / Aurora : Canada Law Book Co. – (Law Reports).
Back Vols.

—Canadian Criminal Cases Old Series (1898-1962), 133 Vols. / Aurora : Canada Law Book Co. – (Law Reports).
Back vols.

—Canadian Criminal Cases Second Series (1971-1983), 70 Vols. / Aurora : Canada Law Book Co. – (Law Reports).
Back Vols.

—Canadian Criminal Cases (Second Series) Index, Annotations, Table of Cases : Covering Vols. 1 through 70 of the Canadian Criminal Cases (Second Series) / Aurora : Canada Law Book Co, 1983.
1184p.

—Canadian Criminal Cases Third Series (March 1983-Present) / Aurora : Canada Law Book Co. – (Law Reports).
Bound Vol.

—Canadian Criminal Code Offences, 1 vol. / Agincourt : Carswell.
This handbook for the Canadian practitioner presents the fifty most commonly charged Criminal Code offenses in forty-seven chapters. A checklist of all facts that must be proved by the prosecution and a summary of the key features of the offense is included in each chapter.

—Canadian Criminal Code Offences / Agincourt : Carswell, 1986.
ca 350p.

—Canadian criminal law : a treatise / by Don Stuart. – Toronto : Carswell, 1982.
liii,602p.
Bibliography: p.xv. - Includes index.
ISBN 0459348000

—Canadian criminal law : cases and comments / by Douglas A. Schmeiser. – 5th ed. – Toronto : Butterworths, 1985.
848.
Previous ed.: published as 'Criminal law', 1977. Incorporates recent Supreme Court decisions on such topics as criminal and transferres intent, mistake of law, necessity, insanity, drunkeness, autrfois convict and autrefois acquit, issue estoppel, Crown liability, police powers, excessive force and attempt. Contains a detailed index.
ISBN 0409865389

—Canadian criminal law, international and transnational aspects / Sharon A. Williams, J.-G. Castel. – Toronto : Butterworths, 1981.
xxx, 513 p.; 24 cm.
Includes bibliographical references and indexes. Part one is devoted to jurisdiction and the criminal law under international law and Canadian law. Part two deals with Canadian law applicable to specific offences of an international and transnational nature. Part three covers international cooperation in the field of criminal law and criminal procedure.
ISBN 0409876348 £80.00

—Century of criminal justice : perspectives on the development of Canadian law / by Martin L. Friedland. – Toronto : Carswell Legal Publications, 1984.
xxii,245p.
ISBN 0459365800

—Conducting a Criminal Case / Vancouver : British Columbia Continuing Legal Education Society, 1983.
331p.
ISBN 0865041369 Hbk £60.00

—Criminal Code : 1893 / Repr. of 1980 ed. – Agincourt : Carswell.
1200p. – (Carswell's Classic Reprints).
This book is a reproduction of the 1893 treatise on the first Criminal Code of Canada.

—Criminal Code : 1988 / Agincourt : Carswell, 1987.
780p.

—Criminal Code Annotations : 1971-1986 / Agincourt : Carswell, 1984.
Vol. 2

—Criminal Law / Daniel J. Baum. – Toronto : IPI Publishing, 1983.
84p. – (You and the Law Ser.).
ISBN 045896140X Pbk £7.95

—Criminal Law / Morris Manning. – 2nd ed. – Butterworths, 1985.
816p.
Revised and expanded to take account of new developments in criminal law. Covers offences and defences, fundamental principles and problems in their application.
ISBN 0409849227 Hbk £95.00

—Criminal Law / Community Legal Education Ontario. – Toronto : Community Legal Education Ontario, 1981.
49p.
ISBN 0889030553 Pbk £6.50

—Criminal Law and the Charter / Vancouver : Continuing Legal Education Society of British Columbia, 1988.
224p.
ISBN 0865049785 Hbk £70.00

—Criminal Law : Current Issues / Vancouver : Continuing Legal Education Society of British Columbia, 1986.
91p.
ISBN 0865042535 Hbk £55.00

—Criminal Law Digest, 9 Vols. / Rev. ed. – Agincourt : Carswell.
This work contains digests of all the reported Canadian criminal cases from 1800. It is a nine volume set that is supplemented every six months.

—Criminal law in Canadian society / Canada. – Ottawa : Govt. of Canada, 1982.
123 p.; 23 cm.
'Sets out the policy of the Government of Canada with respect to the purpose and principles of the criminal law'–Pref.
ISBN 0662120833 pbk.

—Criminal Law Quarterly (1958-Present) / Aurora : Canada Law Book Co. – (Law Journals).
Back Vols.

—Criminal Law Quarterly (C.L.Q.) 1958-Present / Aurora : Canada Law Book Co.
Current subscription-Outside Canada
Back Vols.
C.L.Q. Index (Vols. 1-26)

—Criminal law : the general part : liability and defences / Law Reform Commission of Canada. – Ottawa : Law Reform Commission of Canada, 1982.
12,204,239,10p; 25cm. – (Working paper).
Parallel text in French and English bound in reverse.
ISBN 0662514297

—Criminal Law Update / Vancouver : Continuing Legal Education Society of British Columbia, 1987.
149p.
ISBN 0865043612 Hbk £60.00

—Criminal Lawyers Commonplace Book, 1 vol / Toronto : Butterworths.

—Criminal Lawyers Commonplace Book, 1 Vol. / Butterworths.

—CRIMJI : Canadian Criminal Jury Instructions / Vancouver : Continuing Legal Education Society of British Columbia, 1987.
1,500p.
ISBN 0865043337 Hbk £300.00 (publication and disks)

—Defences to provincial charges / Institute of Law Research and Reform. – Edmonton : The Institute, 1984.
ii,123p. – (Report).

—Entrapment in Canadian Criminal Law / Agincourt : Carswell, 1985.
ISBN 045937060X Hbk £19.80

—Extraterritorial jurisdiction / Law Reform Commission of Canada. – Ottawa : Canadian Law Reform Commission, 1984.
210p. – (Working paper).
Bibliography: p.209-210.
ISBN 0662136039

—Highlights of federal initiatives in criminal justice, 1966- 1980 / prepared by Gerald Woods and Heather Sim. – Ottawa : Research Division, Ministry of the Solicitor General of Canada, 1981.
vii,78p.
Bibliography: p.71-78.
ISBN 0662118294

—Jurisdiction in Criminal Law / Agincourt : Carswell, 1985.
275p.
This work for the practitioner examines all aspects of the exercise of jurisdiction by Canadian criminal courts and discusses the remedies available in cases of error. The book provides a theoretical approach to analyzing the validity of the exercise of jurisdiction.

—Learning Canadian criminal law / by Don Stuart and Ronald Joseph Delisle. – Toronto : Carswell, 1982.
xix,913p.
ISBN 0459348205

—Martin's annual criminal code / with annotations by Edward L. Greenspan. – 1982. – Aurora, Ont. : Canada Law Book, 1982.
cvii,986p.
Includes index.

—Martin's annual criminal code / with annotations by Edward L. Greenspan. – 1988. – Aurora, Ont. : Canada Law Book, 1988.
cxxiv,1089p.
Includes index. Kept up to date by supplements.

—Martin's related criminal statutes 1987 : a selection of important statutes and regulations related to the practice of criminal law / with annotations by Edward L. Greenspan. – Aurora, Ont. : Canada Law Book, 1987.
xlv,499p.

—Nature of Jurisdiction in Canadian Criminal Law / Agincourt : Carswell, 1985.
280p.

—Perspectives in Criminal Law : Essays in Honour of John LL. J. Edwards / Edward L. Greenspan. – North Ryde : Law Book Co, 1984.
384p.

—Perspectives in Criminal Law : Essays in Honour of John LL.J. Edwards / Edward L. Greenspan. – Aurora : Canada Law Book Co, 1984.
384p. – (Text Books-Criminal).
This collection of fifteen essays brings together some of the best legal minds in Canada and elsewhere to explore the key and perplexing issues in the fields of criminal law and criminology. This book also commemorates the founding of the University of Toronto's Centre of Criminology 21 years ago.

—Pocket Criminal Code 1988 / Agincourt : Carswell, 1988.
770p.

—Pocket Criminal Code of Canada / Agincourt : Carswell, 1988.
760p.
This work contains the Criminal Code of Canada including the Young Offenders Act as amended, Canada Evidence Act, Canadian Bill of Rights ss.1 5, Competition Act, Criminal Records Act, Extradition Act, Food and Drugs Act, Interpretation Act, Identification of Criminals Act ss.1 3, Narcotic Control Act and Constitution Act.

—Principles of Criminal Law / Agincourt : Carswell, 1986.
380p.
This work for law students in Canada discusses the fundamental criminal law concepts of mens rea and acutus rea, strict and absolute liability, justification and excuse, diminished metal capacity, and secondary liability under Canadian law.

—Psychiatric Issues in Criminal Law / Vancouver : British Columbia Continuing Legal Education Society, 1982.
ISBN 0865040826 Hbk £45.00

—Reform of the Criminal Law / Agincourt : Carswell.
130p.
This work contains papers that had been delivered at the July 1987 conference on criminal law reform held in London, England. Discussions include white collar crime, sentencing reform and the defenses.

—Report on recodifying criminal law / Law Reform Commission of Canada. – Rev. and enl. ed. – Ottawa : The Commission, 1987.
213,233p; 25cm. – (Report).
Includes text of draft legislation. 'Revised and enlarged edition of Report 30' - t.p.. Added t.p. in French: Rapport pour une nouvelle codification du droit penal. Cover title: Recodifying criminal law. Pages numbered in opposite directions. Pages numbered in opposite directions. In English and French.
ISBN 0662547578

—Snow's Annotated Criminal Code : Bound Edition 1988 / Agincourt : Carswell, 1988.
1,152p.

—Toward a New Criminal Law for Canada / Ottawa : Canadian Criminal Justice Association, 1982.
32p.

—Tremeear's 1971-1986 criminal annotations / by Leonard J. Ryan : 1985 and 1986 annotations by F. Dwight Richardson. – 2. – Toronto : Carswell, 1986.
Includes index. Kept up to date by annual supplement. Companion volumes to Tremeear's criminal code. Supplement to: Tremeear's annotated criminal code. 6th ed..

—Tremeear's 1988 criminal code ... : as amended to Jan. 1, 1988 / Canada. – Toronto : Carswell, 1988.
xviii,751p.
'The companion volume to the Tremeear's criminal annotations' - t.p.. Includes index.
ISBN 045931341X

—Tremeear's criminal annotations 1964-1970 / being the permanent supplement to the sixth edition of Tremeear's annotated criminal code by Leonard J. Ryan. – Toronto : Carswell, 1981.
xxvi,361p.
Includes index.
ISBN 0459344803

—Tremeear's Criminal Code 1988 / Agincourt : Carswell, 1988p.
751.
This volume presents the Criminal Code of Canada in its entirety.

—Tremeears 1987 criminal code and miscellaneous statutes : as amended to January 1, 1987 / William James Tremeear. – Toronto : Carswell, 1987.
xvi,731p.
Previous ed.: 1985-86. Includes index. 'The companion volume to the Tremeears criminal annotations'.
ISBN 0459399209

—Understanding Criminal Offenses / Barrie J. Saxton. – Agincourt : Carswell, 1987.
383p.
This textbook for students of Canadian criminal law discusses the main criminal offenses under the Canadian criminal justice system. Each offense is broken down to the component elements specific to that offense.

—Weekly Criminal Bulletin Current Series (1987), 17 Vols. / Chris N. Buhr. – Aurora : Canada Law Book Co.
– (Summary Services, National Ser.).

—Working Manual of Criminal Law, 1 Vol. / Agincourt : Carswell.
This work for Canadian practitioners in the field of criminal law covers defences, evidence, offenses, procedure, and sentencing. The book is designed to facilitate the preparation of a case for trial as prosecutor or defense counsel.

CRIMINAL LAW - CANADA - ALBERTA

—Alberta-Saskatchewan-Manitoba Criminal Conviction Cases / Aurora : Canada Law Book Co.
– (Summary Services, Provincial Ser.).

CRIMINAL LAW - CANADA - CODIFICATION

—Report on recodifying criminal law / Law Reform Commission of Canada. – v. – Ottawa : Canadian Law Reform Commission, 1986.
– (Report).
Pages numbered in opposite directions. Text in English and French.
ISBN 0662547322

CRIMINAL LAW - CANADA - SASKATCHEWAN

—Alberta-Saskatchewan-Manitoba Criminal Conviction Cases / Aurora : Canada Law Book Co.
– (Summary Services, Provincial Ser.).

—Proposals for defences to provincial offences : report to the Minister of Justice / Law Reform Commission of Saskatchewan. – Saskatoon : The Commission, 1986.
18p.
Includes bibliographical references.

CRIMINAL LAW - ENGLAND

—Bar finals guide / Catherine Newman. – 3rd ed. – London : Sweet & Maxwell, 1987.
300p; 23cm.
Previous ed.: 1984. Includes index.
ISBN 0421359102 Pbk £14.50

—Breaking the rules : the problem of crimes and contraventions : a report / by Justice... – London : JUSTICE, 1980.
v,54p; 22cm.
ISBN 0907247008 sd £2.00 (1.50 to members)

—Casebook on criminal law / by D.W. Elliott and J.C. Wood. – 2nd ed. – London : Sweet & Maxwell, 1982.
xxvii,418p.
Bibliography: p. xxix. - Includes index.
ISBN 0421134100

—Cases and statutes on criminal law / John C. N. Slater. – 2nd ed. – London : Sweet & Maxwell, 1981.
xix,146p; 22cm.
Previous ed.: / by John C.N. Slater. 1973. Includes index.
ISBN 0421248106 Pbk £6.50

—Codification of the criminal law : memorandum on the Law Commission report / Justice. – London : Justice, 1986.
3 leaves.
A commentary on a Law Commission report entitled: Criminal law: codification of the criminal law: a report to the Law Commission.

—Criminal law / L.B. Curzon. – 3rd ed. – Plymouth : Macdonald & Evans, 1980.
xxxvi,316p; 18cm. – (The M.& E. handbook series).
Previous ed.: 1977. Includes index.
ISBN 0712104623 Pbk £3.25

—Criminal law / by Peter Seago. – 2nd ed. – London : Sweet & Maxwell, 1985.
xx,326p; 22cm.
Previous ed.: 1981. Bibliography: p317-318. - Includes index.
ISBN 0421338903 Pbk £9.50

—Criminal law / by J.C. Smith and Brian Hogan. – 6th ed. – London : Butterworths, 1988.
900p; 25cm.
Previous ed.: 1983. Includes index.
ISBN 0406658110 Hbk £35.00 :
ISBN 0406658129 Pbk £19.00

—Criminal law and justice : essays from the W.G. Hart workshop 1986 / edited by Ian H. Dennis. – London : Sweet & Maxwell, 1987.
215p; 22cm.
Includes index.
ISBN 0421377704 No price (June)

—Criminal law : attempt, and impossibility in relation to attempt, conspiracy and incitement / chairman: Michael Kerr. – London : H.M.S.O., 1980.
v,107p.

—Criminal law : essays in honour of J.C. Smith / edited by Peter Smith : with a foreword by the Rt. Hon. Lord Edmund-Davies. – London : Butterworths, 1987.
xxvii,234p; 26cm.
A text for the student of criminal law in the United Kingdom, this work provides detailed explanations of the provisions of all current criminal legislation.
ISBN 0406501106 £19.00

—Criminal law in a nutshell / Marianne Giles. – London : Sweet & Maxwell, 1987.
121p; 23cm.
Includes index.
ISBN 0421368209 Pbk £4.95

—Criminal law : offences relating to public order / the Law Commission. – London : H.M.S.O., 1983.
vii,135p.
ISBN 0102085846

—Criminal law : text and materials / by C.M.V. Clarkson, H.M. Keating. – London : Sweet & Maxwell, 1984.
xxxiv,590p; 25cm.
Includes index.
ISBN 0421309202 Hbk £26.00
ISBN 042130930X Pbk £16.95

—Criminal trials : the search for truth / Tom Sargant, Peter Hill. – London : Fabian Society, 1986.
33p.
ISBN 0716313480

—Cross and Jones' Introduction to criminal law / Richard Card. – 9th ed. – London : Butterworths, 1980.
xxxi,486p.
ISBN 0406570485

—Cross examination in criminal trials / Marcus Stone. – London : Butterworths, 1988.
xix,224p.
Includes index.
ISBN 0406105057 No price

—Elliott and Wood's casebook on criminal law / John C. Wood, Celia Wells. – 4th ed. – London : Sweet & Maxwell, 1982.
xlii,666p; 24cm.
Previous ed.: 1974. Bibliography: pxli-xlii. - Includes index.
ISBN 0421277408 Hbk £24.50
ISBN 0421277505 Pbk £14.50

—Introduction to criminal law / Philip Asterley Jones, Richard Card. – 11th ed. 1 (various pagings). – London : Butterworths, 1988.
22cm.
Previous ed.: 1984. Includes index.
ISBN 0406570523 Hbk £20.00
ISBN 0406570531 Pbk £13.95

—Modern cases and statutes on Crown Court crime / by Richard Bingham. – Chichester : Rose, 1980.
xlix,532p; 26cm.
Includes index.
ISBN 0859921867 £34.75

—Report / Criminal Law Revision Committee. – London : H.M.S.O, 1980.
viii,150p; 25cm.
ISBN 0101784406 Pbk £4.50

—Stephen's commentaries on the laws of England / L. Crispin Warmington. – 21st ed. – London : Butterworths, 1950.
xii,460p.
Includes index. .

—Sweet & Maxwell's criminal law statutes / edited by Sweet & Maxwell's Legal Editorial Staff : advisory editor, I.H. Dennis. – London : Sweet & Maxwell, 1982.
ix,144p; 26cm.
Includes index.
ISBN 042130300X Hbk Unpriced
ISBN 0421303107 Pbk £4.85

—Textbook of criminal law / by Glanville Williams. – 2nd ed. – London : Stevens, 1983.
xlvii,1007p; 24cm.
Previous ed.: 1978. Includes index.
ISBN 0420468501 Hbk Unpriced
ISBN 0420468609 Pbk £16.50

—Towards a rational criminal law : being the Presidential Address of Professor J. C. Smith, President of the Holdsworth Club of the faculty of Law in the University of Birmingham, 1982-83 / Birmingham : Holdsworth Club, 1983.
15p. – (Holdsworth Club Presidential Addresses, 1983).
ISBN 0704406624

CRIMINAL LAW - EUROPE

—European inter-state co-operation in criminal matters/la cooperation inter-etatique europeenne en matiere penale / M.Cherif Bassiouni. – London : Graham & Trotman, 1988.
1500.
Contains the texts of the 18 European penal Conventions and Explanatory Reports, the lists of signatory states and status of ratifications, reservations and declarations by states, and resolutions and recommendations adopted by the Committee of Ministers of the Council of Europe on the application of these conventions.
ISBN 9024734657 £345

CRIMINAL LAW - FINLAND

—Papers : Hungarian-Finnish Penal Law Seminary on Petty Offences / editor, Lenke Feher. – Budapest : Geza Kilenyi, 1984.
199 leaves.

CRIMINAL LAW - GHANA

—Criminal Law in Ghana / Accra : Ghana Publishing Corporation, 1985.
619p.

—Criminal law in Ghana / P.K. Twumasi. – Tema : Ghana Pub. Corp., 1985.
xlviii, 634 p.; 24 cm.
Includes bibliographical references and index.
ISBN 9964102933

CRIMINAL LAW - GREAT BRITAIN

—Behind Closed Doors / Thorsons, 1988.
ISBN 0722515677 Hbk £5.99

—Casebook On Criminal Law / Wood. – 4th ed. – Sweet & Maxwell, 1982.
ISBN 0421277408 Hbk £30.00
ISBN 0421277505 Pbk £18.50

—Cases and Statutes Criminal Law (CCT) / Dobson. – 2nd ed. – London : Sweet & Maxwell, 1981.
ISBN 0421248106 Pbk £8.25

—Cases in Criminal Law / 2nd ed. Repr. of 1978 ed. – Plymouth : Macdonald & Evans, 1981.
400p. – (M and E Handbook Ser.).
ISBN 0712103767 Hbk £4.95

—Concise Criminal Law / D. Pickover. – London : Police Review Publishing, 1984.
ISBN 0851640095 Pbk

—Cox's Criminal Law Cases : 1843-1941, 31 Vols. / Cox. – Repr. of 1978 ed. – London : Butterworths.
This 31 volume work is a comprehensive record of English criminal law cases. The cases reported are those heard in the Courts of Criminal Appeal, the Superior Courts, the Central Criminal Court, the Assizes, and in Ireland.
ISBN 0406015007 Hbk

—Crime and The Criminal Law (Hamlyn 15) / 2nd ed. – London : Sweet & Maxwell, 1981.
ISBN 0420461809 Pbk £6.95

—Criminal Evidence and Procedure, No. 2 / Wilkie. – 7th ed. – London : Butterworths, 1981.
– (Police Promotion Handbooks Ser.).
This work for United Kingdom police officers covers the basic rules of criminal evidence and procedure from the perspective of the officer working in the field.*Police officers*
ISBN 0406841314 Pbk

—Criminal justice : plans for legislation : presented to Parliament by the Secretary of State for the Home Department ... / Home Office. – London : HMSO, 1986.
23p; 25cm.
ISBN 010196580X Hbk £2.80

—Criminal Law / Caldwell. – 6th ed. – London : Butterworths, 1981.
ISBN 040960058X Hbk £46.70

—Criminal Law / Ryan. – London : Financial Training, 1986.
– (SWOT).
ISBN 0906322987 Pbk £6.95

—Criminal Law / Hogan. – 5th ed. – London : Butterworths, 1983.
ISBN 0406658080 Hbk £27.00

—Criminal Law / London : Butterworths, 1983.
ISBN 0409056170 Hbk £46.20
ISBN 0409056189 Pbk £34.70

—Criminal Law and Justice / London : Sweet & Maxwell, 1987.
ISBN 0421377704 Hbk £28.00

—Criminal Law Book Four / D. Pickover. – London : Police Review Publishing, 1980.
ISBN 0851649904 Pbk £4.95

—Criminal law : codification of the criminal law : a report to the Law Commission / Great Britain. – London : H.M.S.O., 1985.
vi,245p.
ISBN 0102270856

—Criminal Law : Essays in Honour of J.C. Smith / London : Butterworths, 1987.
ISBN 0406501106 Hbk £26.00

—Criminal Law, No. 1 / Wilkie. – 6th ed. – London : Butterworths, 1980.
– (Police Promotion Handbooks Ser.).
This work for United Kingdom police officers presents the changes in criminal law brought about by the Theft Act of 1978 and the Criminal Evidence Act of 1979.
Police officers
ISBN 0406841217 Pbk

—Criminal Law P.P.H. 1 / Wilkie. – 7th ed. – London : Butterworths, 1981.
ISBN 0406841217 Pbk £5.95

—Criminal Law Review / Andrew Ashworth. – London : Sweet & Maxwell.

—Criminal Law : The Protection of Property / A. J. Smith. – London : Sweet & Maxwell, 1986.
ISBN 0420470409 Hbk

—Criminal Litigation / Goodwin. – London : Butterworths, 1985.
ISBN 0406258139 Hbk £33.00
ISBN 0406500002 Pbk £18.95

—Criminal Litigation / M. S. Iller. – London : Butterworths, 1985.
This work is a factual account of all stages in the practice and procedure of criminal litigation in the United Kingdom from investigation to conclusion of the criminal process. The book is directed at students of criminal evidence and procedure *Students*
ISBN 0406258139 Pbk

—Crown Law / Abingdon : Professional Books.
– (Classical English Law Texts Ser.).

—Fingertip Guide to Criminal Law / Hamilton. – London : Butterworths, 1986.
ISBN 0406103801 Pbk £17.50

—General View of the Criminal Law of England / Repr. of 1863 ed. – Abingdon : Professional Books.
339p.

—Handling Criminal Cases / London : Waterlow, 1986.
ISBN 0080391583 Pbk £9.95

—History of English criminal law and its administration from 1750 / Roger Hood. – London : Stevens, 1986.
xv,1101p; 26cm.
Bibliography: p781-1039. - Includes index.
ISBN 0420462805 £75.00

—Introduction to criminal law / Jones. – 10th ed. – London : Butterworths, 1984.
ISBN 0406570507 Hbk £20.00
ISBN 0406570515 Pbk £15.95

—Justice and comparative law : Anglo-Soviet perspectives on criminal law, evidence, procedure, and sentencing policy / edited by W.E. Butler. – Dordrecht : M. Nijhoff, 1986.
246p.
Includes index.
ISBN 9024733758 Hbk £125.00

—Recent and Prospective Developments in Civil and Criminal Litigation / London : Law Society, 1985.
32p. – (Nineteen Eighty-Five Crash Course Transcripts).

—Textbook of criminal law / 2nd ed. – London : Sweet & Maxwell, 1983.
ISBN 0420468609 Pbk £19.00

—Ultimate penalties / London : Eurospan, 1988.
ISBN 0814204368 Hbk £23.25

—Understanding public law / London : Fontana, 1987.
ISBN 0006861180 Pbk £4.95

CRIMINAL LAW - HUNGARY

—Papers : Hungarian-Finnish Penal Law Seminary on Petty Offences / editor, Lenke Feher. – Budapest : Geza Kilenyi, 1984.
199 leaves.

CRIMINAL LAW - INDIA

—Central Criminal Minor Acts : With state Amendments / Rakesh Bagga. – 3rd ed. – Allahabad : Law Book Company, 1988.
1,500p.

—Commentaries on Criminal Minor Acts, 6 Vols. / 2nd ed. – Allahabad : Law Publishers, 1982.

—Criminal Major Acts / Calcutta : Eastern Law House, 1985.

—Criminal Major Acts (Pocket Ed.) / Surya Rao,. – Allahabad : Law Book Company, 1987.

—Criminal Manual / Lucknow : Eastern Book Company, 1983.
550p.

—Criminal Practice, 16 Vols. / Allahabad : Ashoka Law House, 1987.

—Criminal Practice (1864-1986), Vol. 6 : P-R / Allahabad : Ashoka Law House, 1987.
836p.

—Criminal Reference / 3rd ed. – Calcutta : Eastern Law House, 1986.

—Ezaj on Law of Crimes, 2 Vols. / 3rd ed. – Allahabad : Ashoka Law House, 1987.

—Law of Crimes, 2 Vols. / Dhirajlal. – 23rd ed. – New Delhi : Bharat Law House, 1987.

—Law of Criminal Appeals and Revisions / 4th ed. – Allahabad : Law Book Company, 1986.
ca 1000p.

—Manual of Criminal Laws, 4 Vols. / Allahabad : Law Publishers, 1983.

—Principles of Criminal Law : With Model Questions and Suggested Readings / 1979 repr. – Lucknow : Eastern Book Company, 1985.
186p.

—Release of Manual of Central Acts and Important Rules : Criminal, Taxation and Labour, 15 Vols. / Allahabad : Law Publishers, 1986.

CRIMINAL LAW - IRELAND

—Cox's Criminal Law Cases : 1843-1941, 31 Vols. / Cox. – Repr. of 1978 ed. – London : Butterworths.
This 31 volume work is a comprehensive record of English criminal law cases. The cases reported are those heard in the Courts of Criminal Appeal, the Superior Courts, the Central Criminal Court, the Assizes, and in Ireland.
ISBN 0406015007 Hbk

—Criminal law in Ireland / Sean E. Quinn. – Bray, Co. Wicklow : Magh Itha, 1988.
xxvii,227p.
Includes index.
ISBN 1871509009 Pbk £20.00
ISBN 1871509017 £10.00

—Judgments of the Court of Criminal Appeal 1924-1978 / edited by Gerard L. Frewen. – Dublin : Law Library, Incorporated Council of Law Reporting for Ireland, 1983.
xxxi,619p.
Includes indexes.
ISBN 0946738009

CRIMINAL LAW - LIBERIA

—Cases and materials on the criminal law of Liberia / by Johnnie N. Lewis. – 3. – S.l. : s.n., 1981.

CRIMINAL LAW - NEW ZEALAND

—Criminal Law : Text and Cases With Supplement 1980 / Wellington : Butterworths.
ISBN 0409433632

—Garrow and Caldwell's criminal law in New Zealand / the original text by J.M.E. Garrow. – 6th ed. – Wellington : Butterworths, 1981.
xxxiii,631p; 26cm.
Previous edition: 1968, entitled Garrow and Willis's criminal law. Includes index.
ISBN 040960058X Hbk £106.15

—Movements and Markers in Criminal Law / Auckland : Legal Research Foundation, 1984.

CRIMINAL LAW - NIGERIA

—Criminal law and procedure of the southern states of Nigeria / C. O. Madarikan. – 3rd ed. – London : Sweet & Maxwell, 1982.
lxxxiv,1061p; 23cm.
Previous ed.: published as Brett and McLean's The criminal law and procedure of the six southern states of Nigeria / by C.O. Madarikan and T. Akinola Aguda. 1974. Includes index.
ISBN 042124920X £58.00

—Criminal Law in Nigeria / M. E. Naish. – 2nd ed. – London : Sweet & Maxwell, 1980.
– (Nigerian Practice Library).
ISBN 0421266007 Hbk £35.00
ISBN 0421266104 Pbk £17.00

—Criminal Law in Nigeria / Naish. – 2nd ed. – London : Sweet & Maxwell, 1980.
ISBN 0421266007 Hbk £35.00

—Criminal law in the northern states of Nigeria / by E.H. Ofori-Amankwah. – Zaria, Nigeria : Gaskiya Coroporation, 1986.
xix,505p.
Includes bibliographical references.
ISBN 9781940808

—History and Sources of Nigerian Criminal Law / Enugu : Fourth Dimension Publishing, 1985.
400p.

—Law of Crimes / Zaria : Ahmadu Bello University Press.

—Law of crimes in Nigeria : skeletal notes and important references / Kharisu Sufiyan Chukkol. – Zaria : Ahmadu Bello University Press, 1981.
iv, 51 leaves.

—Nigerian criminal cases index, 1880-1975 / by M.O. Olaitan. – Lagos : Libriservice Ltd., 1983.
vi,295p.
Includes index.
ISBN 978237203X

—Nigerian Criminal Reports / London : Sweet & Maxwell, 1981.
ISBN 090382647X Hbk £201.00

Vol. 1 1980
ISBN 0903826488 Hbk £36.00

Vol. 2 1980
ISBN 090382650X Hbk £36.00

Vol. 1 1981
ISBN 0903826542 Hbk £36.00

Vol. 2 1981
ISBN 0903826526 Hbk £29.00

CRIMINAL LAW - NORTHERN IRELAND

—Northern Ireland supplement to Smith and Hogan, Criminal law, fifth edition / by John E. Stannard. – Belfast : SLS Legal, 1984.
xxxiv,207p; 25cm.
Includes index.

—Northern Ireland Supplement to Smith and Hogan on Criminal Law / 5th ed. – Belfast : Queen's University of Belfast, 1984.
xxxiv, 207p.
ISBN 0853892350 Pbk £12.95

CRIMINAL LAW - PAPUA NEW GUINEA

—Criminal jurisdiction of magistrates in Papua New Guinea / by N.K.F. O'Neill and R.N. Desailly : with a foreword by Buri Kidu. – 1. – Sydney : New South Wales Institute of Technology, 1982.
loose-leaf.
Includes index.
ISBN 0909684375

—Criminal law and practice of Papua New Guinea / by Donald R. C. Chalmers, David Weisbrot, Warwick John Andrew. – 2nd ed. – Sydney : Law Book Co., 1985.
xxxiv,807p.
Previous ed.: 1979. Includes index.
ISBN 0455203989 Hbk £49.50

CRIMINAL LAW - PHILIPPINES

—Answers to Bar Examination Questions /. – Quezon City : University of the Philippines, Law Center, 1982.
96p.

—Criminal Law / Quezon City : University of the Philippines, Law Center, 1980.
250p.

CRIMINAL LAW - SCOTLAND

—Casebook on Scottish criminal law / by Christopher H.W. Gane and Charles N. Stoddart. – Edinburgh : W. Green, 1980.
xxii,495p; 22cm.
Includes index.
ISBN 041400664X Pbk £10.00

—Casebook on Scottish criminal law / by Christopher H.W. Gane, and Charles N. Stoddart. – 2nd ed. – Edinburgh : Green, 1988.
xxxiv,740p; 22cm.
Previous ed.: 1980. Includes index.
ISBN 041400843X Pbk £25.00

—Criminal justice (Scotland) Act 1980 / Edinburgh : W Green & Son, 1981.
Annotated copy of this Act which introduced important changes relating to Scotttish criminal law and procedure. With the text of the Act of Adjournal providing for some of the procedures under the Act.
ISBN 0414006747

—Laws and Customs of Scotland in Matters Criminal : Wherein is to be Seen How the Civil Law and Laws and Customs of Other Nations Do Not Agree With and Supply Ours / Repr. of 1678 ed. – Abingdon : Professional Books.
74p.

—Prosecution in the public interest / Susan R. Moody and Jacqueline Tombs. – Edinburgh : Scottish Academic Press, 1982.
xii, 167p.
Examines the decision-making process of the Procurator Fiscal as to whether to prosecute, on what, and by what procedure to prosecute. Bibliography: p.160-163.
ISBN 0707303214 Hbk

—Scots criminal law / A J MacLean. – 1st. – London : Butterworths, 1988.
ISBN 0406252696 Hbk

—Scots Criminal Law / A. J. Maclean. – London : Butterworths, 1986.
This student text presents the basic principles of Scottish criminal law. The work discusses the general principles of criminal responsibility and examines the principal substantive offenses.
ISBN 0406252696 Hbk

—Scottish criminal case reports / Edinburgh : Law Society of Scotland, 1981-.

—Scottish Criminal Law : Police Duties and Procedure / Grampian Police. – Aberdeen : Aberdeen University Press.
1590p.
ISBN 0900015454 Hbk

—Social work and criminal law in Scotland / by George Moore and Chris Wood. – Aberdeen : Aberdeen University Press, 1981.
xii,208p; 26cm.
Provides information and guidance about those aspects of the judicial and penal systems and measures relating to child offenders which affect social workers. Chapters cover prosecution, social worker at court, social enquiry reports, non-custodial measures, probation, community service and unpaid work, and custodial measures. Includes bibliography and index.
ISBN 0080257313 Hbk No price

CRIMINAL LAW - SOUTH AFRICA

—Bibliography of South African criminal law : general principles / by Andre Rabie. – Cape Town : Juta, 1987.
viii,91p.
ISBN 0702118524

—Criminal justice in South Africa : selected aspects of discretion / M.C.J. Olmesdahl, N.C. Steytler. – Cape Town : Juta, 1983.
viii,303p.
Includes bibliographical references.
ISBN 0702113379

—Criminal law / by C.R. Snyman : translation by the author, assisted by Lesbury van Zyl. – Durban : Butterworths, 1984.
545; 25 cm.
Includes indexes. Bibliography: p. 486-492. Translation of: Strafreg.
ISBN 0409056189 R64.00

—General principles of criminal law through the cases / by P.J. Visser and J.P. Vorster. – Durban : Butterworths, 1982.
xxv,523p.
Bibliography: p. 487-501. - Includes index.
ISBN 0409061182

—South African criminal law and procedure / E. M. Burchell, P. M. A. Hunt, J. R. L. Milton, J. M. Burchell. – 2nd ed. – Cape Town : Juta, 1983.
lxii,512p.
In 6 vols. Includes bibliographical references and index.
ISBN 070211345X

Vol. 2 : Common-law crimes : by P.M.A. Hunt 1982.
xcv,870p.
Includes bibliographical references and index.
ISBN 0702112569

Vol.5 : Criminal procedure : by Alfred V. Lansdown : Evidence : Jean Campbell 1982.
cxxvi,966p; 26cm.
Previous ed: 1957 by Gardiner and Lansdown.
ISBN 0702112577

CRIMINAL LAW - SWEDEN

—Swedish penal code 1986 / Stockholm : National Council for Crime Prevention, 1986.
110p. – (Report 1986:2).
'The translation is that of the wording of the Penal Code as at April 1, 1986'.
ISBN 9138093049

CRIMINAL LAW - UNITED STATES

—National strategy for containing white-collar crime / edited by Herbert Edelhertz, Charles Rogovin. – Lexington : Lexington, 1980.
xii,138p; 24cm.
Conference papers.
ISBN 0669031666 £10.50

CRIMINAL LAW - USSR

—Justice and comparative law : Anglo-Soviet perspectives on criminal law, evidence, procedure, and sentencing policy / edited by W.E. Butler. – Dordrecht : M. Nijhoff, 1986.
246p.
Includes index.
ISBN 9024733758 Hbk £125.00

CRIMINAL LAW - ZAMBIA

—Case book on criminal law / by John Hatchard and Muna Ndulo. – Lusaka : Government Printer, 1983.
viii,425p.
Includes index.
ISBN 0903826585

CRIMINAL LAW (ISLAMIC LAW)

—Islamic criminal justice system / M. Cherif Bassiouni, editor. – London : Oceana Publications, 1981.
Primarily selected papers from the 1st International Conference on the Protection of Human Rights in the Islamic Criminal Justice System held May 1979 at the International Institute of Higher Studies in Criminal Sciences, Syracuse, Sicily, and sponsored by the International Association of Penal Law and the Arab Organization for Social Defense against Crime. Appendices : A. Summary report of the first International Conference on the Protection of Human Rights in the Islamic Criminal Justice System, May 1979, International Institute of Higher Studies in Criminal Sciences, Siracusa, Italy – B. List of conference participants – C. Final resolution adopted by conference.
ISBN 0379207451 Hbk £30.00

CRIMINAL LIABILITY

—Law of criminal conspiracy / by Peter Gillies. – Sydney : Law Book Co., 1981.
Includes bibliographical references and index.
ISBN 0455200793

—Mental disorder and criminal responsibility / Stephen J. Hucker, Christopher D. Webster, Mark H. Ben-Aron. – Toronto : Butterworths, 1981.
xv,195p.
Examines Anglo-American concepts of criminal responsibility, mental disorder and criminal responsibility in Canadian law, the sense of justice and criminal responsibility, modern neurology and psychiatry and the problem of criminal responsibility, psychiatrists, lawyers and the adversial system, and the long term management of the mentally disordered offender.
ISBN 0409837342

—Studies on criminal responsibility and psychiatric treatment of mentally ill offenders : reports presented to the seventh Criminological Colloquium (1985) / Council of Europe. – Strasbourg : Council of Europe, 1986.
103p; 21cm. – (Legal affairs).
On cover: European Committee on Crime Problems.
ISBN 9287108994

CRIMINAL LIABILITY - AUSTRALIA

—Law of Criminal Complicity / North Ryde : Law Book Co, 1980.
ISBN 0455200734 Hbk £23.00

CRIMINAL LIABILITY - AUSTRALIA - VICTORIA

—Mental malfunction and criminal responsibility / Law Reform Commission of Victoria. – Melbourne : The Commission, 1988.
95p. – (Discussion paper).
Includes bibliographical references.
ISBN 0724167307

CRIMINAL LIABILITY - CANADA

—Law of Criminal Attempt / Agincourt : Carswell, 1984.
330p.
This text examines the law of criminal attempt as set out in legislation and interpreted by the courts around the world, with an emphasis on Canadian law. The book includes numerous comparisons of differing legal responses to similar fact situations in attempt cases.

—Parties to an Offence / Agincourt : Carswell, 1982.
226p.
This book deals with issues of complicity and constructive complicity in a wide range of criminal offenses under Canadian law. Aiders and abettors; parties to a common unlawful purpose; inciters; procurers; accessories after the fact; and other crimes involving more than one party are covered in the work.

—Secondary liability : participation in crime and inchoate offences / Law Reform Commission of Canada. – Ottawa : The Commission, 1985.
53,61p. – (Working paper).
Includes bibliographical references. Added t.p. in French: La responsabilite secondaire: complicite et infractions inchoatives. Cover title: Criminal law - secondary liability. Pages numbered in opposite directions. English and French text.
ISBN 0662537491

CRIMINAL LIABILITY - ENGLAND

—Conspiracy : law, class and society / Robert Spicer. – London : Lawrence and Wishart, 1981.
190p; 23cm.
Bibliography: p178-184. - Includes index.
ISBN 0853155488 £7.50

—Criminal law : conspiracy to defraud : an invitation for views / Law Commission. – London : The Commission, 1987.
14 leaves.

—Towards a middle system of law / David Tench. – London : Consumers' Association, 1981.
73p.
ISBN 085202214X

CRIMINAL LIABILITY - GREAT BRITAIN

—Criminal law: conspiracy to defraud / Great Britain. – London : H.M.S.O., 1987.
x,238p. – (Working paper).
ISBN 0117301868

—Reasonable arm of the law? : the law enforcement procedures of environmental health officers / Bridget M. Hutter. – Oxford : Clarendon Press, 1988.
Includes index. Bibliography.
ISBN 0198255942

—Treaty on Pleading and Parties to Actions with Precedents, 2 Vols. / Repr. of 1809 ed. – Abingdon : Professional Books.
64p.

—Trial by medicine : insanity and responsibility in Victorian trials / by Roger Smith. – Edinburgh : Edinburgh University Press, 1981.
ix,238p.
ISBN 085224407X

CRIMINAL LIABILITY - INDIA

—Forgeries, Cheating and Criminal Liability / Allahabad : Law Publishers, 1980.

CRIMINAL LIABILITY - NIGERIA

—Defences to criminal liability in Nigerian law : a critical appraisal / by Kharisu Sufiyan Chukkol. – s.l. : s.n., 1987.
xiii,135p.
Bibliography: pp.133-135.
ISBN 9781250429

—Defences to Criminal Liability in the Nigerian Law / Zaria : Ahmadu Bello University Press.

CRIMINAL LIABILITY - SCOTLAND

—Criminal law : art and part guilt of statutory offences / Scottish Law Commission. – Edinburgh : H.M.S.O., 1985.
v,21p.
ISBN 0101955103

—Mental element in crime : report on a reference under section 3(1)(e) of the Law Commissions Act 1965 / Scottish Law Commission. – Edinburgh : H.M.S.O., 1983.
v,48p.
Includes bibliographical references.
ISBN 0101904703

CRIMINAL LIABILITY - SRI LANKA

—Fundamental Rights, Vol. 1 : General Principles of Criminal Liability in Ceylon / Colombo : Lake House Investments.

CRIMINAL OMISSION - AUSTRALIA - WESTERN AUSTRALIA

—Report on the liability of highway authorities for non-feasance / Law Reform Commission of Western Australia. – Perth : Law Reform Commission of Western Australia, 1981.
116p. – (Project v no 62).

CRIMINAL OMISSION - CANADA

—Omissions, negligence and endangering / Law Reform Commission of Canada. – Ottawa : The Commission, 1985.
42,48p. – (Working paper).
Includes bibliographical references. Added t.p. in French: L'omission, la negligence et la mise en danger. Pages numbered in opposite directions. Text in English and French.
ISBN 0662540824

CRIMINAL PROCEDURE

—Crime, guilt, and punishment : a philosophical introduction / C.L. Ten. – Oxford : Clarendon, 1987.
176p; 22cm.
Includes bibliography and index.
ISBN 019875082X Hbk £19.50
ISBN 0198750811 Pbk £8.95

—Criminal justice comparisons : the case of Scotland and England and Wales / Lorna J.F. Smith. – London : Home Office, 1983.
v,57p.
Bibliography: p.50.
ISBN 0862521009

—Criminal Trial and Judgement / D.P. Varshni. – 3rd rev. ed. 1981 repr. – Lucknow : Eastern Book Company, 1985.
477p.

—Criminological diagnosis : an international perspective / edited by Franco Ferracuti, Marvin E. Wolfgang. – Lexington, Mass. : Lexington Books, 1983.
xi,297p; 24cm.
ISBN 0669016241 Unpriced

Vol.2 / edited by Franco Ferracuti, Marvin E. Wolfgang. – 1983.
299-619; 24cm.
Bibliography: p543-613.
ISBN 0669059714 set Unpriced
ISBN 0669064343 Hbk Unpriced

—Human rights in criminal procedure : a comparative study / edited by J.A. Andrews. – The Hague : M. Nijhoff, 1981.
451p.
Revisions of papers presented at a conference organized by the United Kingdom National Committee of Comparative Law held at Manchester in Sept., 1978. Includes index.
ISBN 9024725526 Hbk £195.00

—Institutional function and evolution in the criminal process / Richard P. Adelstein. – Oxford : Centre for Socio-Legal Studies, 1980.
126,43p; 21cm. – (Research study).
ISBN 0862260205

—Just and painful : a case for corporal punishment of criminals / Graeme Newman. – New York : Macmillan, 1983.
163p; 23cm.
Includes index.
ISBN 0029231302 £11.95

—Justice and predictability / Antony Cutler and David Nye. – London : Macmillan, 1983.
xi,169p.
Includes index. Bibliography.
ISBN 0333315154

—Martin's related criminal statutes 1980 : a selection of important statutes and regulations related to the practice of criminal law / with annotations by Edward L. Greenspan. – Aurora, Ont. : Canada Law Book, 1980.
xxvii,342p.

—Martin's related criminal statutes 1985 : a selection of important statutes and regulations related to the practice of criminal law / with annotations by Edward L. Greenspan. – Aurora, Ont. : Canada Law Book, 1985.
xlii,414p.

—Martin's related statutes 1983 : a selection of important statutes and regulations related to the practice of criminal law / with annotations by Edward L. Greenspan. – 1983. – Aurora, Ont. : Canada Law Book, 1983.
xxxv,379p.

—Research in criminal justice : stock-taking of criminological research at the Max-Planck-Institute for Foreign and International Penal Law after a decade / edited by the Criminological Research Unit. – Freiburg : Max-Planck-Institute for Foreign and International Penal Law, 1982.
xiii, 508 p.; 21 cm. – (Kriminologische Forschungsberichte aus dem Max-Planck-Institut fur Auslandisches und Internationales Strafrecht, Freiburg).
Includes bibliographies and index.
ISBN 3922498019 pbk.

—Women, crime and criminal justice / Allison Morris. – Oxford : Basil Blackwell, 1987.
256p; 23cm.
Considers all aspects of women and crime including women as defendants and prisoners, as victims and as criminal justice professionals.
ISBN 0631154442 Hbk £25.00 :
ISBN 0631154450 Pbk £7.95

CRIMINAL PROCEDURE - AUSTRALIA

—Criminal justice in Australia / Peter Sallmann and John Willis. – Melbourne : Oxford University Press, 1984.
240p.
Bibliography: p227-235.
ISBN 0195544595

—Criminal procedure / by John Bishop : with a foreword by N.A. Brown. – Sydney : Butterworths, 1983.
lxxix,350p.
Includes bibliographical references and index.
ISBN 0409494607 Pbk
ISBN 0409492019

—Criminal Procedure / 2nd ed. – Sydney : Butterworths, 1988.
512p.

CRIMINAL PROCEDURE - AUSTRALIA - NEW SOUTH WALES

—Criminal procedure : police powers of arrest and detention : discussion paper / Sydney : Law Reform Commission of New South Wales, 1987.
xx,148p. – (D.P.).
Bibliography: p141-144.
ISBN 0730544567

—Criminal procedure : procedure from charge to trial : a general proposal for reform : discussion paper / New South Wales Reform Commission. – Sydney : Government Printer, 1986.
iii,44p,20 leaves. – (D.P.).
ISBN 0730530868

—Criminal procedure : procedure from charge to trial : specific problems and proposals : discussion paper / New South Wales Law Reform Commission. – Sydney : Government Printer, 1987.
xxii,644p. – (D.P.).
Bibliography: p.621-635.
ISBN 0730531333

—Criminal procedure report : the jury in a criminal trial / New South Wales Law Reform Commission. – Sydney : The Commission, 1986.
xxxi,203p. – (L.R.C. 48).
Includes bibliographical references.
ISBN 073051546X Hbk

—Criminal procedure : the jury in a criminal trial : discussion paper / New South Wales Law Reform Commission. – Sydney : Government Printer, 1985.
xxx,285p. – (D.P.).
ISBN 0730514323

CRIMINAL PROCEDURE - AUSTRALIA - QUEENSLAND

—Working paper on legislation to review the role of juries in criminal trials / Queensland Law Reform Commission. – Brisbane : The Commission, 1984.
viii,146p. – (Q.L.R.C.W.P. 28).

CRIMINAL PROCEDURE - AUSTRALIA - VICTORIA

—Rape and allied offences : procedure and evidence / Law Reform Commission of Victoria. – Melbourne : The Commission, 1987.
iii,31p. – (Discussion paper).
Calatogued from cover. Includes bibliographical references.
ISBN 072414319X

—Report on criminal trials / Peter A. Sallmann. – Canberra : Australian Institute of Judicial Administration, 1985.
xiii,217p.
Report of a joint committee of the Victorian Bar Council and the Australian Institute of Judicial Administration. Includes bibliographical references. At head of cover: Shorter Trials Committee. Chairman: Hon. Mr. Justice McGarvie.
ISBN 095900291X

CRIMINAL PROCEDURE - AUSTRALIA - WESTERN AUSTRALIA

—Problem of old convictions / the Law Reform Commission of Western Australia. – Perth : Law Reform Commission of Western Australia, 1984.
97,vip. – (Discussion paper).

—Report on the problem of old convictions / the Law Reform Commission of Western Australia. – Perth : Law Reform Commission of Western Australia, 1986.
267p. – (Project).

—Review of the Justices Act 1902-1982 : constitution, powers and procedure of Courts of Petty Sessions / the Law Reform Commission of Western Australia. – Perth : Law Reform Commission of Western Australia, 1984.
ii,253p. – (Discussion paper).
Cover title: Courts of Petty Sessions: constitution, powers and procedure.

CRIMINAL PROCEDURE - CANADA

—Bibliography of Canadian criminal justice history / Bibliographie sur l'histoire de la justice penale au Canada : Ministry of the Solicitor General, Research division. – Ottawa : Ministry of the Solicitor General, 1984.
426p. – (User report).

—Canadian charter of rights : prosecution and defence of criminal and other statutory offences / by Roderick M. McLeod ... et al. – Toronto, Canada : Carswell, 1983.
1 v. (loose-leaf); 25 cm.
ISBN 0459357409

—Canadian criminal justice system / Craig L. Boydell, Ingrid Arnet Connidis. – Canada : Holt, Rinehart and Winston, 1982.
311p.
Includes bibliographies.
ISBN 003920278X

—Canadian criminal procedure / 4th ed. – Aurora, Ont. : Canada Law Book, 1984.
cv,610p.
Includes index. Latest supplement held: 2nd, 1986.
ISBN 0888040202

—Canadian criminal procedure : cases, notes and materials / Vincent M. Del Buono. – Toronto : Butterworths, 1981.
xxx,929p.
Includes index.
ISBN 0409824801

—Canadian Criminal Procedure : Cases, Notes and Materials / Butterworths, 1981.
960p.
ISBN 040982481X Hbk £90.00

—Century of criminal justice : perspectives on the development of Canadian law / by Martin L. Friedland. – Toronto : Carswell Legal Publications, 1984.
xxii,245p.
ISBN 0459365800

—Charge document in criminal cases / Law Reform Commission of Canada. – Ottawa : The Commission, 1987.
57,63p. – (Working paper).
Includes bibliographical references. Added t.p. in French: Le document d'inculpation. Pages numbered in opposite directions. Text in English and French.
ISBN 0662549635

—Criminal law in Canadian society / Canada. – Ottawa : Govt. of Canada, 1982.
123 p.; 23 cm.
'Sets out the policy of the Government of Canada with respect to the purpose and principles of the criminal law'–Pref.
ISBN 0662120833 pbk.

—Criminal lawyers commonplace book / 1 vol. – Scarborough, Ontario : Butterworths (Canada).
Deals with aspects of a criminal trial, such as cross-examination on criminal records, witnesses using notes, objectionable cross-examination techniques and evidence. Consists of legislation covering a range of issues and a series of digests of leading cases. Makes use of Western Canadian precedents, and those of the Supreme Court.

—Criminal Procedure / Marc Rosenberg. – 2nd ed. – Agincourt : Carswell, 1986.
403p. – (Bar Admission Course Materials Ser.).
This book for law students provides an overview of basic Canadian criminal procedure from police investigation and searches, through arrest, preliminary inquiry, interim release, trial, sentencing, and appeal. Proceedings under the Young Offenders Act is covered in the work.

—Criminal Procedure : Canadian Law and Practice, 3 vol / Toronto : Butterworths.

—Criminal Procedure : Canadian Law and Practice, 3 Vols. / Butterworths.

—Criminal procedure : cases, text and materials / by Louise Arbour and Larry T. Taman. – Toronto : Emond-Montgomery, 1980.
xxiv, 567 p.; 27 cm.
Includes bibliographical references and index.
ISBN 0920722032 £50.00

—Criminal Procedure : Cases, Text and Materials / Larry T. Taman. – Aurora : Canada Law Book Co, 1980.
600p. – (Case Books).

—Criminal Procedure in Canada / 7th ed. – North Vancouver : International Self-Counsel Press, 1986.
168p.
ISBN 0889086354 Hbk £16.95

—Criminal procedure in Canada : studies / edited by Vincent M. Del Buono. – Toronto : Butterworths, 1982.
xc,497p.
ISBN 0409824828

—Criminal Procedure in Practice : a Manual for the Defence of Cases in Provincial Court / N.A. Peel. – 2nd ed. – Butterworths, 1983.
328p.
Outlines what a lawyer ought to do at each stage of the trial process. Covers preparation, tactics, 'case-flow management' and sound law-office administration, and speculation as to the effect of the Canadian Charter of Rights and Freedoms upon criminal procedure.
ISBN 0409812927 Hbk £60.00

—Examination of witnesses in criminal cases / Earl J. Levy. – Toronto : Carswell, 1987.
xxxv,263p.
Includes index.
ISBN 0459308211

—Highlights of federal initiatives in criminal justice, 1966- 1980 / prepared by Gerald Woods and Heather Sim. – Ottawa : Research Division, Ministry of the Solicitor General of Canada, 1981.
vii,78p.
Bibliography: p.71-78.
ISBN 0662118294

—Impact / Ottawa : Ministry of the Solicitor General, 1982-.
Contents: 'a periodical which presents research and statistics about crime and criminal justice'.

—Introduction to the Criminal Process in Canada / Agincourt : Carswell, 1988.
246p.
This is a comprehensive guide to Canadian criminal procedure. The various stages of the criminal process are outlined.

—Introduction to the Criminal Process in Canada / Agincourt : Carswell, 1988.
240p.

—Law and order for Canada's indigenous people / Paul Havemann, Keith Couse, Lori Foster, Rae Matonovich : Prairie Justice Research Consortium, School of Human Justice, University of Regina. – Ottawa : Ministry of the Solicitor General, 1984.
xxxi,187p. – (User report).
Bibliography: p.178-187.

—Learning Canadian Criminal Procedure / Ronald J. Delisle. – Agincourt : Carswell, 1986.
798p.
This work for law students in Canada discusses the principles and policies underlying criminal procedure. Full coverage is given to the Canadian Charter of Rights and Freedoms and its impact on criminal procedure in the text.

—Martin's related criminal statutes 1987 : a selection of important statutes and regulations related to the practice of criminal law / with annotations by Edward L. Greenspan. – Aurora, Ont. : Canada Law Book, 1987.
xlv,499p.

—New criminologies in Canada : crime, state and control / edited by Thomas Fleming. – Toronto : Oxford University Press, 1985.
xii,343p.
ISBN 0195404890

—On Criminal Procedure / Jean-Pierre Lussier. – Agincourt : Carswell, 1982.
481p.

—Open Justice : the Constitutional Right to Attend and Speak About Criminal Proceedings / Butterworths, 1985.
416p.

—Ordering of justice : a study of accused persons as dependants in the criminal process / Richard V. Ericson, Patricia M. Baranek. – Toronto : Published in association with the Centre of Criminology, University of Toronto by University of Toronto Press, 1982.
xvi, 268 p.; 25 cm.
Includes index. Bibliography: p. 253-261.
ISBN 0802064639 pbk.

—Private prosecutions / Law Reform Commission of Canada. – Ottawa : Law Reform Commission of Canada, 1986.
51,59p; 25cm. – (Working paper).
Cover title: Criminal law - private prosecutions. Added t.p. in French: Les poursuites privees. Pages numbered in opposite directions. Text in English and French.
ISBN 0662544595

—Profiles of progress : contributions to criminal justice in Canada / Canada. – OTTAWA : Minister of Supply and Services, 1984.
32p.
ISBN 0662134133

—Provincial Court Criminal Hearings 1985 / Vancouver : Continuing Legal Education Society of British Columbia, 1985.
112p.
ISBN 0865042349 Hbk £55.00

—Report on our criminal procedure / Law Reform Commission of Canada. – Ottawa : Law Reform Commission of Canada, 1988.
56,60p. – (Report).
Includes t.p. in French. Pages numbered in opposite directions. Text in English and French.
ISBN 0662557360

CRIMINAL PROCEDURE – CANADA – ONTARIO

—Ontario provincial offences procedure / by W. Douglas Drinkwalter, J. Douglas Ewart. – Toronto : Carswell, 1980.
lxiii, 701 p.; 24 cm.
Includes texts of the Provincial offences act, 1979 and the Provincial courts amendment act, 1979. Includes bibliographical references and indexes.
ISBN 0459330306

CRIMINAL PROCEDURE – CANADA – SASKATCHEWAN

—Tentative proposals for a Lieutenant Governor's Review Board in Saskatchewan / Law Reform Commission of Saskatchewan. – Saskatoon : The Commission, 1984.
28p.
Includes text of proposed Act.

CRIMINAL PROCEDURE – CHINA

—Criminal Procedure Code of the People's Republic of China / London : Sweet & Maxwell, 1982.
– (American Series of Foreign Penal Codes: No. 25).
ISBN 0421300108 Hbk £33.00

CRIMINAL PROCEDURE – COMMONWEALTH

—Delay in the administration of criminal justice : Commonwealth developments and experience / prepared for the Commonwealth Secretariat by Judith A. Osborne. – London : Commonwealth Secretariat, 1980.
226p.
Bibliography: p.217-226.
ISBN 0850921937

CRIMINAL PROCEDURE – ENGLAND

—Briefing memorandum on the Police and Criminal Evidence Bill / the Law Society. – London : Law Society, 1982.
5 leaves.

—Butterworths Consolidated Legislation Service /. – Professional Publ.
294p.
ISBN 0409014087 £45.00

—Crime and the courts in England, 1660-1800 / J.M. Beattie. – Oxford : Clarendon, 1986.
xxiv, 663p; 25cm.
Bibliography: p645-651. - Includes index.
ISBN 0198200587 Hbk £48.00
ISBN 0198200579 Pbk £15.00

—Criminal appeals : a practical guide to appeals to and from the Crown Court / Ian McLean. – London : Sweet and Maxwell, 1980.
xxxiii,176p; 24cm.
Includes index.
ISBN 0421247606 £8.25

—Criminal court in action / David Barnard : assisted by Peter L. Gray, Paul S. Bogan. – 3rd ed. – London : Butterworth, 1988.
xviii,365p; 25cm.
Previous ed.: 1979. Includes index.
ISBN 0406556148 Hbk £16.50
ISBN 0406556156 Pbk £10.95

—Criminal justice : a working paper / London : Home Office, 1984.
36p.
'Prepared for the Home Office by the Central Office of Information'.
ISBN 0862521483

—Criminal justice : a working paper / Great Britain. – Rev. ed. – London : H.M.S.O., 1986.
51p.
'Designed and produced for the Home Office by the Central Office of Information'.
ISBN 086252265X

—Criminal justice revolution : the third Sir Gwilym Morris memorial lecture delivered on 24th October 1986 / by Graham Zellick. – Cardiff? : University of Wales Institute of Science and Technology, 1986.
24p.
Includes bibliographical references.

—Criminal justice system model : magistrates' courts sub-model / Susan Rice. – London : Home Office, 1984.
vi,66p.
Bibliography: p.59.
ISBN 0862521254

—Criminal justice system model : the flow model / Hugh Pullinger. – London : Home Office, 1985.
vi,56p.
Bibliography: p.56.
ISBN 0862522234

—Criminal law and criminal justice / David Nelken (ed.). – London : University College London, Faculty of Laws, 1986.
70p; 30cm. – (Working papers).

—Criminal procedure / Celia Hampton. – 3rd ed. – London : Sweet & Maxwell, 1982.
lxi,472p; 22cm.
Previous ed.: 1977. Includes index.
ISBN 0421286601 Hbk Unpriced
ISBN 0421286709 Pbk £8.95

—Criminology and criminal justice / by J.E. Hall Williams. – London : Butterworths, 1982.
xvii,266p.
Bibliography: p243-254.
ISBN 0406593205

—Dictionary of criminology / edited by Dermot Walsh and Adrian Poole. – London : Routledge & Kegan Paul, 1983.
xi,242p.
ISBN 0710095562 pbk.

—Framework of criminal justice / Michael King. – London : Croom Helm, 1981.
159p; 23cm.
Bibliography: p153-156. - Includes index.
ISBN 0709904304 Hbk £10.95
ISBN 0709915004 Pbk £6.50

—Judge, discretion, and the criminal trial / by Rosemary Pattenden. – Oxford : Clarendon, 1982.
xv,299p; 23cm.
Includes index.
ISBN 0198253737 £20.00

—Memorandum on the White Paper on Criminal Justice / Justice. – London : Justice, 1986.
7 leaves.

—Modelling the criminal justice system / Patricia M. Morgan. – London : Home Office, 1985.
v,64p.
Bibliography: p.64.
ISBN 0862522161

—Police and criminal evidence bill : briefing guide / London : Home Office, 1983.
67p.
ISBN 0862521211

—Power of the Court of Appeal Criminal Division to order a retrial / prepared by the Criminal Law Team of the Law Commission ... – London : The Commission, 1986.
23,4p.
Includes bibliographical references.

—Practical approach to criminal procedure / Christopher J. Emmins. – 3rd ed. – London : Financial Training, 1985.
xxxiii,473p.
Includes index.
ISBN 0906322774

—Practice and procedure in juvenile courts / by Kenneth W. Pain. – London : Fourmat, 1982.
xiii,149p; 22cm.
Includes index.
ISBN 090684049X Pbk £7.95

—Profits of crime and their recovery / report of a committee chaired by Sir Derek Hodgson. – London : Heinemann, 1984.
viii,165p; 23cm.
Includes index.
ISBN 0435826506 No price

—Public prosecutor : the memoirs of Sir Norman Skelhorn, Director of Public Prosecutions, 1964-1977 / Sir Norman Skelhorn. – London : Harrap, 1981.
8,207p.
ISBN 0245537635

—Public relations and criminal justice policy / Peter Nokes. – Leeds : Centre for Social Work and Applied Social Studies, 1982.
43p. – (Occasional paper).
'Occasioned by the seminar on Alternatives to Imprisonment ... held October 1980 - October 1981 under the auspices of the Centre for Applied Social Studies'. Bibliography: p.42-43.

—Report / Lord Justice Watkins's Working Party on the Criminal Trial. – London : Lord Chancellor's Department, 1982.
23p.

—Review of criminal procedure / the Law Society. – London : Law Society, 1981.
24p.

—Royal Commission on Criminal Procedure : memorandum by the Council of the Law Society on the Royal Commission's Report / Law Society. – London : Law Society, 1981.
38p; 30cm.

—Statistics of the criminal justice system England and Wales / Home Office. – London : H.M.S.O., 1980.
x,104p.
ISBN 0113407351 £5.80

—Truth and the Courts : a report / by JUSTICE : written evidence to the Royal Commission on Criminal Procedure (Part II). – London : JUSTICE, 1980.
4,32p; 22cm.
ISBN 0950524786 sd £1.50

CRIMINAL PROCEDURE – GAMBIA

—Role of district tribunals in the administration of criminal justice in the Gambia : a critical appraisal / by K. Gyeke-Dako. – Banjul : Government Printer, 1984.
20 leaves.

CRIMINAL PROCEDURE – GHANA

—Criminal Procedure in Ghana / London : Pitman Publishing, 1985.
ISBN 09964720092 Pbk £15.95

—Criminal procedure in Ghana / A.N.E. Amissah. – Accra : Sedco, 1982.
xiv, 388 p.; 24 cm.
Includes index.
ISBN 9964720084

CRIMINAL PROCEDURE – GREAT BRITAIN

—Archbold : Pleading, Evidence, and Practice in Criminal Cases / 41st ed. – London : Sweet & Maxwell, 1983.
Fourth cumulative supplement
ISBN 0421273909 Pbk

—Arrest, charge and summons : current practice and resource implications / R. Gemmill and R.F. Morgan-Giles. – London : H.M.S.O., 1980.
ix,70p. – (Research studies).
ISBN 0117301280

—Balance of criminal justice : summary of the report / London : H.M.S.O., 1981.
17p.
Report itself published as Cmnd. 8092, Parliamentary Papers 1980-81.
ISBN 0117301310 PBK £1.95

—Black people and the criminal justice system : report of the NACRO Race Issues Advisory Committee / Clement Richards. – London : NACRO, 1986.
48p.
Includes bibliographical references. Chairman: Clement Richards. Accompanied by 'Summary of the report of the NACRO Race Issues Advisory Committee'.
ISBN 0850690404

—Contrasts in tolerance : post-war penal policy in the Netherlands and England and Wales / David Downes. – Oxford : Clarendon Press, 1988.
226p.
Bibliography: pp.207-218. - Includes index.
ISBN 0198256086

—Conviction : law, the State and the construction of justice / by Doreen J. McBarnet. – London : Macmillan, 1981.
vii,182p.
ISBN 0333255364

—Criminal Evidence and Procedure, No. 2 / Wilkie. – 7th ed. – London : Butterworths, 1981. – (Police Promotion Handbooks Ser.).
This work for United Kingdom police officers covers the basic rules of criminal evidence and procedure from the perspective of the officer working in the field.*Police officers*
ISBN 0406841314 Pbk

—Criminal justice : plans for legislation : presented to Parliament by the Secretary of State for the Home Department ... / Home Office. – London : HMSO, 1986.
23p; 25cm.
ISBN 010196580X Hbk £2.80

—Criminal Litigation / M. S. Iller. – London : Butterworths, 1985.
This work is a factual account of all stages in the practice and procedure of criminal litigation in the United Kingdom from investigation to conclusion of the criminal process. The book is directed at students of criminal evidence and procedure.*Students*
ISBN 0406258139 Pbk

—Criminal Procedure / London : Butterworths, 1983.
ISBN 0409494607 Hbk £39.30

—Criminal Procedure in Magistrates' Courts / London : Butterworths, 1984.
ISBN 0406101676 Pbk £21.95

—Criminal Procedure in Magistrates' Courts / London : Butterworths, 1984.
This work presents a narrative description of procedure in magistrates' courts when dealing with criminal cases in the United Kingdom. Extensive footnotes are included to provide authority for the material described in the text.
ISBN 0406010676 Pbk

—Criminal Proceedings Against Juveniles / London : Longman Professional, 1984.
ISBN 0851208460 Pbk £21.00

—English criminal process : a review of empirical research / Andrew Ashworth. – Oxford : Centre for Criminological Research, University of Oxford, 1984.
135p. – (Occasional paper).
Bibliography: p131-135.
ISBN 094781101X

—Institutional Function and Evolution in the Criminal Process / Oxford : Social Science Research Council, 1980.

—Judge, Discretion and the Criminal Trial / Oxford : Oxford University Press, 1982.
ISBN 0198253737 Hbk £22.50

—Justice and comparative law : Anglo-Soviet perspectives on criminal law, evidence, procedure, and sentencing policy / edited by W.E. Butler. – Dordrecht : M. Nijhoff, 1986.
246p.
Includes index.
ISBN 9024733758 Hbk £125.00

—Law and order : theft of an issue / David Downes. – London : Fabian Society in association with Labour Campaign for Criminal Justice, 1983.
33p.
Bibliography: p32-33.
ISBN 0716304902

—Managing criminal justice : a collection of papers / edited by David Moxon, Home Office Research and Planning Unit. – London : H.M.S.O., 1985.
vi,216p.
Examines the individual's progress through the justice system from arrest to final disposal. Discusses current research on the subject.
ISBN 0113408110

—Written evidence given to the Royal Commission on Criminal Procedure, EV1-EV412 / Great Britain. – London : The Commission, 1978.
16v.
Report of the Royal Commission published as Cmnd. 8092 in Parliamentary Papers, session 1980/81. - Includes index. Gaps occur in numerical sequence of evidence numbers.

CRIMINAL PROCEDURE - HONG KONG

—Law of Evidence in Criminal Trials in Hong Kong / Gerard McCoy. – Butterworths, 1987.
ca 350p.
Examines the principles which govern in Hong Kong the reception of evidence in criminal proceedings: trial, sentence, and appeal. Covers facts which need not be proved, burden and standard of proof, the rule against hearsay and its exceptions, similar fact evidence and other evidence of criminal conduct probative of the guilt of the accused.
ISBN 0409995479 Hbk £97.50

—Problem of the trial of complex commercial crimes : a proposal for reform / Hong Kong : Attorney General's Chambers, 1984.
93p.

CRIMINAL PROCEDURE - INDIA

—Code of Criminal Procedure / Dhirajlal. – 13th ed. – Nagpur : Wadhura & Co, 1987.

—Code of Criminal Procedure / 2nd ed. – Allahabad : Law Publishers, 1983.

—Code of Criminal Procedure / 3rd ed. – Allahabad : Law Book Company, 1988.
1,900p.

—Code of Criminal Procedure in 5 Vols / 18th ed. – Allahabad : Law Book Company, 1984.

—Commentaries on Code of Criminal Procedure, 1973, 3 Vols. / 2nd ed. – Allahabad : Law Publishers, 1980.

—Comments on Civil Procedure Code, 4 Vols. / 2nd ed. – Allahabad : Law Publishers, 1983.

—Criminal Court Handbook (Minor Acts), 4 Vols. / Lucknow : Eastern Book Company, 1985.

—Criminal Court Handbook (Three Major Acts) / 17th ed. 1982 repr. – Lucknow : Eastern Book Company, 1985.
808p.

—Criminal Court Practice : with Model Forms / 2nd ed. – North Ryde : Law Book Co, 1987.

—Ganguly's Criminal Court Practice and Procedure / 8th ed. – Calcutta : Eastern Law House, 1984.

—Outlines of Criminal Procedure / 2nd ed. – Lucknow : Eastern Book Company, 1984.
692p.

—Principles of Law of Conviction / Allahabad : Law Book Company, 1988.

CRIMINAL PROCEDURE - IRELAND

—Irish criminal process / Edward F. Ryan and Philip P. Magee. – Dublin : Mercier Press, 1983.
lxxi,595p.
Includes index.
ISBN 0853427003

CRIMINAL PROCEDURE - KENYA

—Criminal Procedure in Uganda and Kenya / Nairobi : East African Publishing House.
150p.

CRIMINAL PROCEDURE - MALAYSIA

—Criminal Procedure Code (F.M.S. Cap. 6) / Kuala Lumpur : International Law Books Services.

CRIMINAL PROCEDURE - NETHERLANDS

—Contrasts in tolerance : post-war penal policy in the Netherlands and England and Wales / David Downes. – Oxford : Clarendon Press, 1988.
226p.
Bibliography: pp.207-218. - Includes index.
ISBN 0198256086

CRIMINAL PROCEDURE - NEW ZEALAND

—Criminal Procedure in New Zealand / Hodge. – 2nd ed. – London : Law Book Co, 1984.
ISBN 0455203547 Pbk £9.75

—Criminal Procedure in New Zealand / 2nd ed. – North Ryde : Law Book Co, 1984.
xxi, 198p.
ISBN 0455203547 Pbk £21.00

—History of custodial and related penalties in New Zealand / Patricia M. Webb. – Wellington : Government Printer, 1982.
197p.
ISBN 0477011969

—Report of the Penal Policy Review Committee, 1981 / M. E. Casey. – Wellington : Government Printer, 1982.
232p.
Chairman: M. E. Casey.

—Report on discovery in criminal cases / Criminal Law Reform Committee. – Wellington : Government Printer?, 1986.
59p.

CRIMINAL PROCEDURE - NIGERIA

—Criminal procedure in the Northern states of Nigeria / by B.M. Shani. – 2nd ed. – s.l. : s.n., 1985.
xxviii,536p.
Includes bibliographical references.

CRIMINAL PROCEDURE - NORTHERN IRELAND

—Diplock courts in Northern Ireland : a fair trial? : an analysis of the law, based on a study commissioned by Amnesty International / by Douwe Korff. – Utrecht : Studie-en Informatiecentrum Mensenrechten, 1984.
115p.

—Supergrasses : the use of accomplice evidence in Northern Ireland : a report / by Tony Gifford. – London : Cobden Trust, 1984.
38p.
ISBN 0900137215

CRIMINAL PROCEDURE - PAPUA NEW GUINEA

—Criminal jurisdiction of magistrates in Papua New Guinea / by N.K.F. O'Neill and R.N. Desailly : with a foreword by Buri Kidu. – 1. – Sydney : New South Wales Institute of Technology, 1982.
loose-leaf.
Includes index.
ISBN 0909684375

CRIMINAL PROCEDURE - SCOTLAND

—Criminal Procedure According to the Law of Scotland / R. H. Brown. – 5th ed. – Edinburgh : W Green, 1983.
ISBN 0414007158 Hbk £110.00

—Criminal procedure in Scotland : cases & materials / C.H.W. Gane & C.N. Stoddart. – Edinburgh : W. Green, 1983.
xxviii,612p.
Includes index.
ISBN 0414007115

—Criminal Procedure in Scotland : Cases and Materials / C. N. Stoddart. – Edinburgh : W Green, 1983.
ISBN 0414007190 Hbk £18.50

—Criminal Procedure (Scotland) Act 1975, 2 Vols. / London : HMSO.
ISBN 0114920044 loose £47.00

—Operation of the judicial examination procedure : a study in two Scottish cities / Susan R. Moody. – Edinburgh : Scottish Office, 1986.
iv,87p.

CRIMINAL PROCEDURE - UGANDA

—Criminal Procedure in Uganda and Kenya / Nairobi : East African Publishing House.
150p.

CRIMINAL PROCEDURE - UNITED STATES

—Beyond the courtroom : programs in community justice and conflict resolution / Benedict S. Alper, Lawrence T. Nichols. – Lexington, Mass. : Lexington Books, 1981.
xx,299p; 24cm.
Bibliography: p273-288. - Includes index.
ISBN 0669027243 £14.50

—Police community relations and the administration of justice / Pamela D. Mayhall. – 3rd ed. – New York : Wiley, 1984.
ix,438p; 25cm.
Previous ed.: published as: Community relations and the administration of justice. 1979. Includes bibliographies and index.
ISBN 0471060445 £27.95

—Psychology and psychiatry in courts and corrections : controversy and change / Ellsworth A. Fersch, Jr. – New York : Wiley, 1980.
xiii,370p; 24cm.
'A Wiley-Interscience publication'. Text on lining papers. Bibliography: p.323-353. - Includes index.
ISBN 0471056049 £13.00

—Reconstructing reality in the courtroom / W. Lance Bennett and Martha S. Feldman. – London : Tavistock Publications, 1981.
x, 203p.

CRIMINAL PROCEDURE - USSR

—Justice and comparative law : Anglo-Soviet perspectives on criminal law, evidence, procedure, and sentencing policy / edited by W.E. Butler. – Dordrecht : M. Nijhoff, 1986.
246p.
Includes index.
ISBN 9024733758 Hbk £125.00

CRIMINAL PROCEDURE - WEST INDIES

—Trial by jury : social and psychological dynamics / Ramesh Deosaran. – St. Augustine, Trinidad, West Indies : Institute of Social and Economic Research, University of the West Indies, 1985.
324 p.; 23 cm.
Includes indexes. Bibliography: p. 283-297.
ISBN 9766180008 pbk.

CRIMINAL PROCEDURE (ISLAMIC LAW)

—Islamic criminal justice system / M. Cherif Bassiouni, editor. – London : Oceana Publications, 1981.
Primarily selected papers from the 1st International Conference on the Protection of Human Rights in the Islamic Criminal Justice System held May 1979 at the International Institute of Higher Studies in Criminal Sciences, Syracuse, Sicily, and sponsored by the International Association of Penal Law and the Arab Organization for Social Defense against Crime. Appendices : A. Summary report of the first International Conference on the Protection of Human Rights in the Islamic Criminal Justice System, May 1979, International Institute of Higher Studies in Criminal Sciences, Siracusa, Italy – B. List of conference participants – C. Final resolution adopted by conference.
ISBN 0379207451 Hbk £30.00

CRIMINOLOGY

—Criminological diagnosis : an international perspective / edited by Franco Ferracuti, Marvin E. Wolfgang. – Lexington, Mass. : Lexington Books, 1983.
xi,297p; 24cm.
ISBN 0669016241 Unpriced

Vol.2 / edited by Franco Ferracuti, Marvin E. Wolfgang. – 1983.
299-619; 24cm.
Bibliography: p543-613.
ISBN 0669059714 set Unpriced
ISBN 0669064343 Hbk Unpriced

—Criminology : Problems and Perspectives / 2nd ed. – Lucknow : Eastern Book Company, 1983.
483p.

—Dangerousness : problems of assessment and prediction / edited by John W. Hinton. – London : Allen & Unwin, 1983.
x,177p; 25cm.
Bibliography: p158-171. - Includes index.
ISBN 0043640214

—Reactions to crime : the public, the police, courts, and prisons / edited by David P. Farrington and John Gunn. – Chichester : Wiley, 1985.
ix,189p; 24cm.
Includes bibliographies and index.
ISBN 047190497X £23.00

—Women and Crime / L. Gelsthorpe. – Cambridge : Institute of Criminology.
1981p.

CRIMINOLOGY – AUSTRALIA

—Aboriginal Criminological Research / Canberra : Australian Institute of Criminology.

—Australian and New Zealand Journal of Criminology / John Willis. – Wellington : Butterworths.
Back Vols. avail.

—Crime in a New Community : The Case of Tuggeranong / Canberra : Australian Institute of Criminology.

—Criminal records / The Law Reform Commission. – Sydney : The Commission, 1985.
117p. – (Discussion paper).
Bibliography: p.114-117.

—Physical Planning and Crime in Canberra / Canberra : Australian Institute of Criminology.

—Research Guide to Criminology Material / Canberra : Australian Institute of Criminology.

—Review of Australian Criminological Research, 1983 / Canberra : Australian Institute of Criminology.

—Size of the Crime Problem in Australia / 2nd ed. – Canberra : Australian Institute of Criminology.

CRIMINOLOGY – CANADA

—Crime, Capitalism and Community / Toronto : Butterworths, 1983.
168p.
ISBN 0409871923 Pbk £15.95

—Crime in Canadian society / James T Teevan. – 3rd. – Scarborough, Ontario : Butterworths (Canada).
440.
Opens with a discussion of the controversy surrounding the definition of crime, and then moves into a discussion and critique of the ways of measuring crime in Canada. Gives various explanations of crime from functional analysis to liberal criminology, labelling theory and critical theory. Concludes with a selection of contemporary Canadian criminological research.
ISBN 040986580X 1986

CRIMINOLOGY – ENGLAND

—Criminal and Victim : 19th Century England / Oxford : Oxford University Press, 1985.
ISBN 0198226462 Hbk £17.50

CRIMINOLOGY – GREAT BRITAIN

—British Journal of Criminology / London : Sweet & Maxwell.

—Crime and punishment : interpreting the data / Pease. – Open University Press, 1986.
ISBN 0335153895 Pbk £7.95

—Criminology and Criminal Justice / London : Butterworths, 1982.
ISBN 0406593213 Pbk £9.95

—Gender Crime and Justice / Open University Press, 1988.
ISBN 0335155057 Hbk £25.00

—History of British criminology / edited by Paul Rock. – Oxford : Clarendon, 1988.
192.
'First appeared as a special issue of the British journal of criminology.' Includes bibliographical references. Focuses on the past and present condition of criminology. Contains a series of essays, some on the history of criminological ideas, some on the formation of particular emphases, methods and problems. Others are personal accounts of major phases in the growth of the discipline.
ISBN 0198256353 Pbk £9.95

—Licensed to live / Martin. – Oxford : Blackwell, 1985.
ISBN 0631141650 Pbk £17.50

—Response to SNOP / Cambridge : Institute of Criminology, 1986.

—Responses to crime / Oxford : Oxford University Press, 1987.
ISBN 0198255837 Pbk £14.95

—Theoretical criminology / Bernard. – 3rd ed. – Oxford : Oxford University Press, 1986.
ISBN 0195036166 Hbk £17.50

CRIMINOLOGY – UNITED STATES

—Juveniles' waiver of rights : legal and psychological competence / Thomas Grisso. – New York : Plenum, 1981.
xiii,295p; 24cm.
Bibliography: p279-286. - Includes index.
ISBN 0306405261 Unpriced

CROSS-EXAMINATION – AUSTRALIA

—Cross Examination Practice and Procedure : an Australian Perspective / Woolloomooloo : International Business Communications.
281p.
ISBN 0949553166 Hbk £32.50

CROSS-EXAMINATION – CANADA

—Cross-Examination : the Art of the Advocate / Butterworths, 1988.
152p.
Shows how to conduct an effective cross-examination of a witness in criminal and civil trials. Sets out how to properly examine various types of witness, attacking the method used by the expert witness, contradicting the witness by prior testimony, attacking identification evidence, and how to cross-examine on criminal record.
ISBN 0409809691 Hbk £39.95

CROSS-EXAMINATION – ENGLAND

—Cross examination in criminal trials / Marcus Stone. – London : Butterworths, 1988.
xix,224p.
Includes index.
ISBN 0406105057 No price

CROSS-EXAMINATION – GREAT BRITAIN

—Cross Examination Practice and Procedure / London : Legal Books, 1985.
ISBN 0949553166 Hbk £20.00

—Cross Examinations in Criminal Trials / London : Butterworths, 1988.
ISBN 04061050507 Pbk

—Technique of advocacy / by John H. Munkman. – London : Sweet & Maxwell, 1986.
xiv,173p.
Originally published: London: Stevens, 1951. Includes bibliographical references.
ISBN 0421361700

CROSS-EXAMINATION – INDIA

—Art of Lawyer Advocacy : Cross Examination with Classes of Witnesses and Illustrative Cases / Allahabad : Universal Book Agency, 1987.

—Practical Hints on Cross-Examination / 2nd ed. – Allahabad : Law Publishers, 1982.

CROWN – AUSTRALIA

—Royal prerogative / by H.V. Evatt : commentary by Leslie Zines : foreword by Sir Ninian Stephen. – Sydney : Law Book Co. Ltd, 1987.
xviii, 34, 282 p.; 25 cm.
Includes bibliographical references and index.
ISBN 0455207569

CROWN – AUSTRALIA – SOUTH AUSTRALIA

—Report ... relating to the demise of the Crown / Law Reform Committee of South Australia. – Adelaide : Government Printer, 1984.
13p. – (81st report).

—Report ... relating to the inherited imperial law regarding the Crown / Law Reform Committee of South Australia. – Adelaide : Government Printer, 1981.
15p. – (65th report).

CROWN – CANADA

—Crown as Creditor : Priorities and Priveleges / Victoria : Government of British Columbia, 1982.

CROWN – GREAT BRITAIN

—Case for the Crown / Toronto : Equation Press, 1987.
ISBN 1853350112 Hbk £12.95

—Crown Law / Reprint. – Abingdon : Professional Books, 1986.
ISBN 0862053196 Hbk £33.50

—Crown Laws / Repr. of 1762 ed. – Abingdon : Professional Books.
367p.

—Crown Office Proceedings / London : Sweet & Maxwell, 1988.
ISBN 042137960X Hbk

—Law of the Prerogatives of the Crown / Repr. of 1820 ed. – Abingdon : Professional Books.
64p.

—Royal prerogative / by H.V. Evatt : commentary by Leslie Zines : foreword by Sir Ninian Stephen. – Sydney : Law Book Co. Ltd, 1987.
xviii, 34, 282 p.; 25 cm.
Includes bibliographical references and index.
ISBN 0455207569

CROWN COURTS – ENGLAND

—Magistrate in the Crown Court / Robin David. – Chichester : Rose, 1982.
viii,48p; 21cm.
ISBN 0859922294 Pbk £4.25

CROWN COURTS – GREAT BRITAIN

—Criminal Statistics, England and Wales : Supplementary Tables 1980, 4 Vols. /. – London : Home Office.
ISBN 0862520142 Hbk £12.75

CROWN PROSECUTION SERVICE

—Case for the crown : the inside story of the Director of Public Prosecutions / Joshua Rozenberg : foreword by Sir Michael Havers. – Wellingborough : Equation, 1987.
206p,24p of plates; 24cm.
Bibliography: p201-202. - Includes index.
ISBN 0722515332 £12.95
ISBN 1853360112

—Director of Public Prosecutions : principles and practices for the Crown Prosecutor : an inquiry carried out at the Centre for Criminological Research, University of Oxford / Graham Mansfield and Jill Peay : foreword by Sir Thomas Hetherington. – London : Tavistock, 1986.
viii,246p; 23cm.
Bibliography: p237-241. - Includes index.
ISBN 0422600008 £16.00

—Proposed Crown Prosecution Service : The Distribution of Functions Between the Headquarters and Local Offices of the Service / London : HMSO, 1984.
ISBN 0101941102 Hbk £1.30

CULTURE

—Justice, law, and culture / James K. Feibleman. – Dordrecht : Nijhoff, 1985.
xiii, 208p.
ISBN 9024731054

CURRENCY QUESTION

—Price and Henderson currency and interest rate swaps / Schuyler K. Henderson, John A. M. Price. – London : Butterworths, 1984.
xiii,144p; 26cm.
Includes index. At head of title: Price and Henderson.
ISBN 0406073600 No price

—Taxation aspects of currency fluctuations / Jill C. Pagan. – London : Butterworths, 1983.
xi,162p.
Describes the United Kingdom tax law and the attitude of the Inland Revenue on the subject of currency fluctuations. Foreign exchange management, accounting treatment, and taxation are analyzed in the book.
ISBN 0406406308 Hbk £22.00

CUSTODY

—Child's voice in the court of law : an account of the representation of minors in civil proceedings in Canada and some other (mostly common law) jurisdictions / Olive M. Stone. – Toronto : Butterworth & Co. (Canada), 1982.
x, 248p; 24cm.
Examination of the representation of minors in civil litigation, looking primarily at Canadian and English practices. Gives a historical discussion of women's legal position in the past and how the issue of guardianship was affected by it. Description of the relevant Canadian federal and provincial legislation in which each province is treated separately.
ISBN 0409870544

—European Convention on Recognition and Enforcement of Decisions concerning Custody of Children and on Restoration of Custody of Children / Strasbourg : Council of Europe, 1980.
ISBN 9287101485 Hbk £1.00

—Explanatory report on the European Convention on Recognition and Enforcement of Decisions concerning Custody of Children and on Restoration of Custody of Children / Strasbourg : Council of Europe, 1980.
36p; 21cm.
Includes the text of the convention.

—Explanatory Report on the European Convention on Recognition and Enforcement of Decisions Concerning Custody of Children and on Restoration of Custody of Children / Strasbourg : Council of Europe, 1980.

—Hague Convention on the civil aspects of international child abduction : consultative document / Edinburgh? : Scottish Courts Administration?, 1983.
10 leaves.

—Hague Convention on the Civil Aspects of International Child Abduction : explanatory documentation / prepared for Commonwealth jurisdictions by J.M. Eekelaar in association with the Commonwealth Secretariat. - London : Commonwealth Secretariat, 1981.
v,70p.
ISBN 0850921961

—Review of child care law : report to ministers of an interdepartmental working party : published by the government as a consultative document / Rupert Hughes. - London : H.M.S.O., 1985.
v,179p.
Chairman: Rupert Hughes. At head of title-page: Department of Health and Social Security.
ISBN 0113210426

CUSTODY - CANADA

—Family law : dimensions of justice : selected papers presented at the Judicial Conference on Family Law, 1981 / edited by Rosalie S. Abella and Claire L'Heureux-Dube. - Toronto : Butterworths, 1983.
xxxi,330p.
The Canadian Institute for the Administration of Justice brought together judges to consider developments in family law and its social milieu. Includes essays by judges, psychiatrists, an economist and a tax specialist.
ISBN 0409819700

—Family Practice in Provincial Court : Custody, Access, and Maintenance / Vancouver : Continuing Legal Education Society of British Columbia, 1987.
306p.
ISBN 0865043450 Hbk £80.00

—Proposals on custody, parental guardianship, and the civil rights of minors : report to the Attorney General / from the Law Reform Commission of Saskatchewan. - Saskatoon : Law Reform Commission of Saskatchewan, 1981.
iv,40p.

CUSTODY - CANADA - ALBERTA

—Protection of children's interests in custody disputes / Institute of Law Research and Reform. - Edmonton : The Institute, 1984.
ii,42p. - (Report no 43).

CUSTODY - ENGLAND

—Child custody and divorce : the law in social context / Susan Maidment. - London : Croom Helm, 1984.
324p; 23cm.
Bibliography: p293-306. - Includes index.
ISBN 0709917376 £16.95

—Child custody : what chance for fathers? / Susan Maidment. - London : National Council for One Parent Families, 1981.
23p.
Bibliography: p.21-23.

—Children Act 1975 : custodianship orders / Department of Health and Social Security. - London : The Department, 1985.
15,xi,3,iip.

—Custody law in practice in the divorce and domestic courts / by J.A. Priest and J.C. Whybrow. - London : H.M.S.O., 1986.
113p; 21cm.
Supplement to Law Commission working paper no.96 (Family law : review of child law : custody).

—Family law : review of child law : custody / The Law Commission. - London : H.M.S.O., 1986.
viii,233p; 21cm. - (Working paper).
Includes bibliographical references.
ISBN 0117301779

CUSTODY - GREAT BRITAIN

—Accountability in child care - which way forward? / London : Family Rights Group, 1982.
49p; 21cm.
Subtitle: Background papers to a seminar organised on 19 February 1982 to discuss the issues raised by the House of Lords' judgement in A. v Liverpool City Council and to offer and invite suggestions for improving local authority practice and accountability in child care cases.

—Child Custody and Divorce / Oxford : Croom Helm, 1984.
ISBN 0709917988 Pbk £8.95

—Custodianship : the law and practice / by Nasreen Pearce. - London : Fourmat, 1986.
xi,77p.
ISBN 1851900152

—Custody law in practice in the divorce and domestic courts / by J.A. Priest and J.C. Whybrow. - London : H.M.S.O., 1986.
vii,113p.
Supplement to: Working paper no. 96, entitled Family law: review of child law: custody.
ISBN 0117301817

—Family law, custody of children - jurisdiction and enforcement within the United Kingdom : report on a reference under section 3(1)(e) of the Law Commissions Act 1965 / The Law Commission and the Scottish Law Commission. - London : H.M.S.O., 1985.
x,277p; 25cm.
'Report on a reference under section 3(1)(e) of the Law Commissions Act 1985'.
ISBN 0101941900

—Family law : review of child law : Care, supervision and interim orders in custody proceedings / The Law Commission. - London : H.M.S.O., 1987.
v,80p; 21cm. - (Working paper).
Examines the power of the courts to commit a child to local authority care. Makes proposals to reconcile existing inconsistency, simplify and improve the system.
ISBN 0117301825

—Law and practice of custodianship / by Michael D.A. Freeman. - London : Sweet & Maxwell, 1986.
xviii,156p.
Chapters on the origins of the concept of custodianship, the local authority and custodianship, effects of custodianship orders, adoption of custodianship, custodianship and care, disputes between joint custodians, and on the procedure for application for custodianship.
ISBN 042135500X Pbk £12.00

CUSTODY - NORTHERN IRELAND

—Custody of children on breakdown of marriage in Northern Ireland : report of the proceedings of a seminar held in the Queen's University, Belfst, on 12 June 1981 / chairman, the Hon. Mr. Justice MacDermott : editor, Gillian kerr. - Belfast : SLS Publications, 1982.
37,viiip.
Bibliography: p.36. Includes the text of the Matrimonial Causes (N.I.) Order 1978.

CUSTODY - PAPUA NEW GUINEA

—Custody jurisdiction in Papua New Guinea / by Owen Jessep. - Waigani : Law Reform Commission of Papua New Guinea, 1987.
37p. - (LRC working paper).
Includes text of the Infants Act.

CUSTODY - SCOTLAND

—Control Without Custody / A. Swift. - Edinburgh : Scottish Academic Press Ltd, 1987.
256p : Illus.
ISBN 0707304571 Hbk £15.00

CUSTOMARY LAW

—Legal pluralism : proceedings of the Canberra Law Workshop VII / edited by Peter Sack and Elizabeth Minchin. - Canberra : Law Department, Research School of Social Sciences, Australian National University, 1986.
iii,280p.
Includes bibliographical references.
ISBN 0867848375

—Lex Custumaria / 2nd ed. Repr. of 1701 ed. - Abingdon : Professional Books.

CUSTOMARY LAW - AFRICA

—Customary Land Law in Africa : With Reference to Legislation Aimed at Adjusting Customary Tenures to the Needs of Development / 2nd print 1985. - Rome : FAO, Food and Agricultural Organization of the United Nations, 1967.
96p.
ISBN 9251022267 Hbk £7.50

CUSTOMARY LAW - AUSTRALIA

—Aboriginal customary law : the criminal law, evidence and procedure / Sydney : Australian Law Reform Commission, 1984.
24p. - (Discussion paper).

CUSTOMARY LAW - CANADA

—Subject Guide to Native Law Cases and Annotated Text of the Indian Act of Canada / Zandra MacEachern. - Saskatoon : University of Saskatchewan, Native Law Centre, 1985.
267p.
ISBN 0888801599 Hbk £45.00

CUSTOMARY LAW - GHANA

—Ollennu's principles of customary land law in Ghana / Gordon R. Woodman. - 2nd ed. - Birmingham : CAL Press, 1985.
xxviii,184p.
Includes bibliographical references and index.
ISBN 0951053000

CUSTOMARY LAW - INDIA

—Customs and Customary Law in British India / Delhi : Mittal Publications, 1986.

—Digest of Customary Law in the Punjab / 15th ed. - Allahabad : Universal Book Agency, 1980.

—Meos of India : Their Customs and Laws / New Delhi : Deep and Deep Publications, 1983.
211p.

CUSTOMARY LAW - KENYA

—Casebook on Kenya Customary Law / Abingdon : Professional Books, 1985.
350p.
ISBN 0862051118 Hbk £34.00

—Casebook on Kenyan Customary Law / Nairobi : Nairobi University Press.
348p.

—Kamba Customary Law / 3rd ed. - Nairobi : Kenya Literature Bureau, 1983.

—Nandi Customary Law / 4th ed. - Nairobi : Kenya Literature Bureau, 1981.

CUSTOMARY LAW - MALAWI

—Law, custom and social order : the colonial experience in Malawi and Zambia / Martin Chanock. - Cambridge : Cambridge University Press, 1985.
xi,286p; 24cm. - (African studies series).
Examines development of customary law in African law during the colonial period. Studies how customary law developed alongside criminal law in Malawi and Zambia.
ISBN 0521301378 £25.00

CUSTOMARY LAW - MALAYSIA

—Malaysian Customary Laws and Usage / Singapore : Federal Publications.

—Native law in Sabah and Sarawak / by M.B. Hooker. - Singapore : Malayan Law Journal, 1980.
xii,91p.
Summary of the administration of Native law in the states of Sabah and Sarawak in Malaysia. Gives the history of native law administration in Sabah and Sarawak, native law in administrative codes, the structure of the native courts, native law in the High Courts, and legislative and judicial sources of native law in Sabah and Sarawak.
ISBN 9971700085

CUSTOMARY LAW - NETHERLANDS

—Anthropology of law in the Netherlands : essays on legal pluralism / edited by Keebet von Benda-Beckmann and Fons Strijbosch. - Dordrecht : Foris Publications, 1986.
311p.
Includes bibliographical references.
ISBN 9067652032

CUSTOMARY LAW - NIGERIA

—Administration of justice in the customary courts of Yorubaland / J.O. Ajibola. - Ibadan : University Press, 1982.
ix,89p.
ISBN 019575753X

—Customary law : the war without arms / by A.P. Anyebe. - Enugu : Fourth Dimension, 1985.
159p.
Includes bibliographical references.
ISBN 978156184X

—Outline of customary court procedure / by R.A.I. Ogbobine. - Benin City, Nigeria : Ruf-Bine, 1985.
vi,46p.
ISBN 9783004514

—Role of customary courts in Nigeria / by Martin C. Okany. - Enugu : Fourth Dimension Publishing Co., 1984.
264p.
Includes bibliographical references and index.
ISBN 9781562145

CUSTOMARY LAW - PAPUA NEW GUINEA

—Customary law in Papua New Guinea : a Melanesian view / edited by Richard Scaglion. - Port Moresby : Law Reform Commission of Papua New Guinea, 1983.
x,198p. - (Monograph).
Bibliographies.
ISBN 0724707468

—Homicide compensation in Papua New Guinea : problems and prospects / edited by Richard Scaglion. - Papua New Guinea : Published by the Office of Information, Papua New Guinea for the Law Reform Commission of Papua New Guinea, 1981.
102p; 23cm. - (Monograph).
Includes bibliographical references.
ISBN 0724707301

—Marriage in Papua New Guinea / results of a research project conducted by the Law Reform Commission and Administrative College of Papua New Guinea. - Waigani : The Commission, 1986.
xi,223p. - (Monograph).
ISBN 9980550031

CUSTOMARY LAW - SOUTH AFRICA

—Application of customary law in southern Africa : the conflict of personal laws / T.W. Bennett. – Cape Town : Juta, 1985.
xxxvii,250p.
Bibliography: p.xv-xxi. - Includes index.
ISBN 0702116017

—Civil practice of all courts for blacks in Southern Africa / J.A.M. Khumalo. – 3rd ed. – Cape Town : Juta, 1984.
xli,300p.
Previous ed. (1975) has title: Civil practice and procedure in all Bantu courts in Southern Africa. Bibliography: p.xix. - Includes index.
ISBN 0702114677

—Customary law in a changing society / Digby Sqhelo Koyana. – Cape Town : Juta, 1980.
xxii,183p.
Bibliography: p.xi-xii.
ISBN 0702111627

—Marriages and customary unions of black persons / South African Law Commission. – Pretoria : The Commission, 1985.
xix,222p. – (Project).
Bibliography: p.vii-xi.
ISBN 062110180X

—Seymour's Customary law in Southern Africa / J. C. Bekker, J. J. J. Coertze. – 4th ed. – Cape Town : Juta, 1982.
lxi,446p.
ISBN 070211233X Pbk
ISBN 0702112933

CUSTOMARY LAW - SUDAN

—Customary law of the Dinka people of Sudan : in comparison with aspects of western and Islamic laws / by John Wuol Makec. – London : Afroworld, 1988.
287p.
Includes bibliographical references and index.
ISBN 0948583037

CUSTOMARY LAW - ZAMBIA

—Law, custom and social order : the colonial experience in Malawi and Zambia / Martin Chanock. – Cambridge : Cambridge University Press, 1985.
xi,286p; 24cm. – (African studies series).
Examines development of customary law in African law during the colonial period. Studies how customary law developed alongside criminal law in Malawi and Zambia.
ISBN 0521301378 £25.00

CUSTOMARY LAW (INTERNATIONAL LAW)

—Customary international law and treaties : a study of their interactions and interrelations, with special consideration of the 1969 Vienna Convention on the Law of Treaties / Mark E. Villiger. – Dordrecht : Nijhoff, 1985.
xxxiii, 432p. – (Developments in international law).
Originally presented as the author's Habilitationsschrift (University of Zurich). Includes index. Bibliography: p.409-420.
ISBN 9024729807 Hbk £225.00

—Human rights and humanitarian norms as customary law / Oxford : OUP, 1989.
320.
Looks at the relationship between human rights/humanitarian norms and customary law, also between human rights/humanitarian norms and the law of state responsibility. Examines how contemporary human rights mesh with the general principles of international law and particularly with the principles governing the international responsibility of states.
International lawyers, international organizations, scholars and students of international law
ISBN 0198252390 Hbk £30.00

CUSTOMS AND EXCISE - AUSTRALIA

—Customs and excise law / by E.J. Cooper. – Sydney : Legal Books, 1984.
xli, 598 p.; 25 cm.
Includes bibliographies and index.
ISBN 0949553107

CUSTOMS AND EXCISE - CANADA

—Annotated Customs Act / Carswell, 1988.
192p.

—Canadian Customs and Excise Reports / Toronto : Butterworths.
ISBN 0409858129 £110.00

Most recent vol.

Looseleaf Vol.
ISBN 0409858110 Pbk £55.00

Back Vol. of Case Reports, Vol. 8
ISBN 0409857599 Hbk £40.00

Editorial Commentary Binder to Vols. 1-6
ISBN 0409811823 Hbk £15.00

Bound Vol. 1
ISBN 0409858137 Hbk £40.00

Bound Vol. 2
ISBN 0409858188 Hbk £40.00

Bound Vol. 3
ISBN 0409858234 Hbk £40.00

Bound Vol. 4
ISBN 0409858285 Hbk £40.00

Bound Vol. 5
ISBN 0409859079 Hbk £40.00

Bound Vol. 6
ISBN 0409859036 Hbk £40.00

Bound Vo7. 7
ISBN 0409857572 Hbk £40.00

Cumulative Index Vols. 1-7
ISBN 0409810444 Hbk £27.95

—Canadian Customs and Excise Reports / Grant A. Jameson. – Butterworths.

—Customs and Excise / Agincourt : Carswell, 1983.
182p.
This textbook provides a thorough examination of the law with respect to Canadian customs and excise. The work covers the Customs Act, the Anti-Dumping Act, Customs Tariff, the Excise Tax Act, and the Excise Act.

—Customs Valuation in Canada / Don Mills : CCH Canadian Ltd, 1985.
292p.
ISBN 088796284X Hbk £45.00

—Extension of customs jurisdiction over the Canadian Continental Shelf : a background paper / issued by the Honourable Paul Cosgrove, Minister of State (Finance). – Ottawa : Minister of Supply and Services Canada, 1982.
14,16p.
Added t.p. in French. English and French text.
ISBN 066252229X

CUSTOMS AND EXCISE - CHINA

—Official Chinese Customs Guide 1985/86 / London : Longman Professional, 1985.
ISBN 08512010848 Hbk £35.00

CUSTOMS AND EXCISE - EUROPEAN COMMUNITY

—Customs union of the European Economic Community / by Nikolaus Vaulont : translated from the French. – Luxembourg : Office for Official Publications of the European Community, 1981.
87 p.; 25 cm.
Includes bibliographical references.
ISBN 9282519112 pbk. £5.00 (U.S.)

—EEC Customs Law / Onkelinx. – Oxford : ESC, 1986.
ISBN 0906214297 loose £90.00

—EEC Customs Law / Ivo Onkelinx. – Oxford : ESC Publishing Ltd, 1986.
ISBN 0906214297 loose £90.00

—European Community Customs Valuation / 8th ed. – Kirchberg : Commission of the European Communities, 1984.

—Making Customs Procedures Work for You in a Single European Market / London : LLoyd's of London Press, 1989.

—Prohibiting restrictions on trade within the EEC : the theory and application of Articles 30-36 of the EEC Treaty / by Laurence W. Gormley. – Amsterdam : North-Holland, 1985.
xxv,458p.
Bibliography: p.429-443. - Includes index. At head of title: T.M.C. Asser Instituut - The Hague.
ISBN 0444868488

—Structure of tobacco taxes in the European Community / J.A. Kay, M.J. Keen. – London : Institute for Fiscal Studies, 1982.
44p; 22cm.
Bibliography: p44.
ISBN 0902992295 Pbk Unpriced

CUSTOMS AND EXCISE - GREAT BRITAIN

—Customs 88 / London : Kogan Page, 1988.
ISBN 1850915997 Pbk

—Customs & Excise Casebook / London : Waterlow, 1987.
ISBN 0080392458 Hbk £50.00

—HM Customs and Excise Official VAT Guides / Oyez Longman Editorial Staff. – London : Oyez Longman, 1983.
ISBN 0851206832 loose £50.00

CUSTOMS AND EXCISE - INDIA

—Central Excise : Law, Practice and Procedure, 2 Vols. / Allahabad : Modern Law Publications, 1987.

—Commentaries on Central Excise Act / 3rd ed. – Allahabad : Law Publishers, 1982.

—Commentary on the Customs Act with Rule and Notifications / 3rd ed. – Allahabad : Law Publishers, 1982.

—Commentary on the Working of the Customs Act 1962 / New Delhi : S. Chand and Company.

—Customs Act, 1962 / Subodh Markandeya. – Bombay : Jaico Publishing House.

—Customs Act : with Various Useful Appendices 1987 / 5th ed. – Allahabad : Law Book Company, 1988.
1,750p.
ISBN Hbk £375.00

—Digest of Central Excise and Customs Cases / Nagpur : Wadhura & Co, 1987.
1,425p.

—Exhaustive and Critical Commentary on the Customs Act, 1962, Vol. 1 : With Notifications / Delhi : Vinod Prakashan, 1987.
1,121p.

—Uttar Pradesh Excise Act, 1910 : Together with Rules and Notifications / 3rd ed. – Lucknow : Eastern Book Company.

CUSTOMS AND EXCISE - MALAYSIA

—Customs Act, 1967 (Act 235) and Regulations 1977 / Kuala Lumpur : International Law Books Services.

CUSTOMS DUTIES

—Customs Valuation : a Commentary on GATT Customs Valuation Code / H. Glashoff. – Dordrecht : Kluwer, 1988.
400p.
ISBN 9065443215 Hbk £153.00

—Developing countries in the GATT legal system / by Robert E. Hudec. – Aldershot : Gower for the Trade Policy Research Centre, 1987.
xix,259p.
Bibliography: p.236-250..
ISBN 0566056976

—Law and its limitations in the GATT multilateral trade system / Olivier Long. – Dordrecht : M. Nijhoff, 1985.
158p.
'An adaptation in English, brought up to date to the end of 1984, of a series of lectures delivered at the Hague Academy of International Law and published in French in its 'Collected courses' 1983, IV, volume 182'–Pref. Includes index. Bibliography.
ISBN 9024731895 Hbk £100.00

—Role of tariff quotas in commercial policy / by Michael Rom : with an introduction by Gerard Curzon. – London : Macmillan for the Trade Policy Research Centre, 1978.
272p.
ISBN 0333176383 £12.00

—Selective safeguard measures in multilateral trade relations : issues of protectionism in GATT, European Community, and United States law / M.C.E.J. Bronckers. – Deventer, Netherlands : Kluwer Law and Taxation Publishers, 1985.
306p.
Includes index and bibliography.
ISBN 9065442227 Hbk £150.00

CUSTOMS DUTIES - AUSTRALIA

—Customs and excise law / by E.J. Cooper. – Sydney : Legal Books, 1984.
xli, 598 p.; 25 cm.
Includes bibliographies and index.
ISBN 0949553107

—Review of Import Control and Customs Bylaw Decision / Administrative Review Council. – Canberra : Australian Government Publishing Service, 1982.
22p.
ISBN 0642070679 Hbk £1.20

CUSTOMS DUTIES - CANADA

—Extension of customs jurisdiction over the Canadian Continental Shelf : a background paper / issued by the Honourable Paul Cosgrove, Minister of State (Finance). – Ottawa : Minister of Supply and Services Canada, 1982.
14,16p.
Added t.p. in French. English and French text.
ISBN 066252229X

—Legal framework for Canada-United States trade / edited by Maureen Irish and Emily F. Carasco. – Toronto : Carswell, 1987.
xxxviii,275p.

CUSTOMS DUTIES - CHINA

—Foreign trade, investment, and the law in the People's Republic of China / editor Michael J. Moser : contributors Jesse T.H. Chang ... et al. – 2nd ed. – Hong Kong : Oxford University Press, 1987.
x,603p; 26cm.
An extensively revised and updated second edition. Gives an introduction to the legal framework currently being developed in China with respect to foreign commercial and investment activity.
ISBN 0195840585 £25.00

CUSTOMS DUTIES - EUROPEAN COMMUNITY

—Customs law of the European Economic Community / by D. Lasok and W. Cairns. - Deventer : Kluwer, 1983.
xxiii,292p.
Includes bibliography: p.287-289. - Includes index.
ISBN 9065440771

—Customs union of the European Economic Community / by Nikolaus Vaulont : translated from the French. - Luxembourg : Office for Official Publications of the European Community, 1981.
87 p.; 25 cm.
Includes bibliographical references.
ISBN 9282519112 pbk. £5.00

—European Community and GATT / edited by Meinhard Hilf, Francis G. Jacobs, and Ernst-Ulrich Petersmann. - Deventer, the Netherlands : Kluwer, 1986.
xvii, 398 p.; 25 cm.
Includes bibliographical references and index.
ISBN 9065442332

—Explanatory Notes to the Customs Tariff of the European Communities : 23rd Amending Supplement / Kirchberg : Commission of the European Communities, 1984.
44p.

—Protectionism and the European Community : import relief measures taken by the European Economic Community and the member states, and the legal remedies available to private parties / J.H.J. Bourgeois ... et al. - Antwerp : Kluwer, 1983.
xii,199p.
By members of a working group on the law of international relations established by the Europa Institute of the University of Amsterdam. - Edited by E.L.M. Volker.
ISBN 9065441271

—Tariff Classifications : 7th Amending Supplement / Kirchberg : Commission of the European Communities, 1984.
116p.

CUSTOMS DUTIES - UNITED STATES

—Legal framework for Canada-United States trade / edited by Maureen Irish and Emily F. Carasco. - Toronto : Carswell, 1987.
xxxviii,275p.

CUSTOMS UNIONS - EUROPE

—Legal Aspects of the ECU / Dierciex. - London : Butterworths, 1988.
ISBN 0406112002 Hbk

CUSTOMS UNIONS - EUROPEAN COMMUNITY

—Customs Union of the European Economic Community / Kirchberg : Commission of the European Communities, 1980.
89p. - (European Perspectives Series).

—Customs union of the European Economic Community / by Nikolaus Vaulont : translated from the French. - Luxembourg : Office for Official Publications of the European Community, 1981.
87 p.; 25 cm.
Includes bibliographical references.
ISBN 9282519112 pbk. £5.00

—Making Customs Procedures Work for You in a Single European Market / London : LLoyd's of London Press, 1989.

—Practical Guide to the Use of the European Communities' Scheme of Generalized Tariff Preferences / Kirchberg : Commission of the European Communities, 1984.
353p.

CYPRUS

—Cyprus conflict : a lawyer's view / by Zaim M. Nedjatigil. - 2nd ed. - Nicosia : A-Z Publications, 1982.
xii,248p.
Previous ed.: 1981. Includes bibliographical references and index.

DAMAGES

—Damage measures for breach of contract / Steven Shavell. - s.l. : s.n., 1980.
25p.
Photocopy of an article in Bell Journal of Economics, vol. 11 (1980), p.466-490. Includes bibliographical references.

—Damages for personal injuries and death / by John Munkman. - 6th ed. - London : Butterworths, 1980.
xxviii,211p.

ISBN 0406311129

—Damages for personal injury and death in Canada / edited and with introductory notes by Immanuel Goldsmith : case abridgements prepared by Alan Burnside Harvey and by David Carruthers. - Toronto : Carswell, 1959.
xxiii,374p.
Includes index.

DAMAGES - AUSTRALIA

—Assessment of damages for personal injury and death / by Harold Luntz. - 2nd ed. - Sydney : Butterworths, 1983.
lxvii,570p.
Includes index.
ISBN 0409491322

—Community law reform for the Australian Capital Territory / Law Reform Commission. - Canberra : Australian Government Publishing Service, 1985.
ix,44p. - (Report).
Bibliography: p.41-42 - Includes index.
ISBN 0644013257

DAMAGES - AUSTRALIA - SOUTH AUSTRALIA

—Report ... relating to claims for injuries from toxic substances and radiation effects / Law Reform Committee of South Australia. - Adelaide : Government Printer, 1985.
96p. - (87th report).

—Report ... relating to the fatal accidents provisions of the Wrongs Act 1936 / Law Reform Committee of South Australia. - Adelaide : Government Printer, 1981.
9p. - (56th report).

DAMAGES - AUSTRALIA - TASMANIA

—Report on interest on pre- and post-judgment debts / Law Reform Commission of Tasmania. - Hobart : Government Printer, 1985.
17p. - (Report v no 44).

DAMAGES - AUSTRALIA - WESTERN AUSTRALIA

—Report on pre-judgment interest / Law Reform Commission of Western Australia. - Perth : Law Reform Commission of Western Australia, 1981.
38p. - (Project v no 70 part 1).

DAMAGES - BRITISH COLUMBIA

—Report on compensation for non-pecuniary loss / Law Reform Commission of British Columbia. - Vancouver : Law Reform Commission of British Columbia, 1984.
40p.
ISBN 0771884567

DAMAGES - CANADA

—Accounting for Damages : a Framework for Litigation Support / Don Mills : CCH Canadian Ltd, 1987.
240p.
ISBN 0887963986 Hbk £40.00

—Damages 1986 / Vancouver : Continuing Legal Education Society of British Columbia, 1986.
179p.
ISBN 0865042551 Hbk £55.00

—Damages for Breach of Contract / Agincourt : Carswell, 1985.
ISBN 0459373307 Hbk £24.20

—Goldsmith's damages for personal injury and death in Canada : a complete digest service derived from reported and unreported cases / 1. - Toronto : Carswell, 1980.
looseleaf.
Spine title: Damages for personal injury and death.
ISBN 0459316206

—Law of damages / by S.M. Waddams. - Toronto : Canada Law Book Ltd., 1983.
cx,755p.
ISBN 0888040164

—Litigation Accounting : The Quantification of Economic Damages / Toronto : DeBoo, 1986.
ISBN 0888202458 Hbk £135.00

Supplements
This book is intended for those dealing with cases in the areas of personal injury, medical malpractice, wrongful dismissal, matrimonial disputes, and business loss. Included are overviews, cases, and a glossary. Annual supplements are planned.

—Supreme Court of Canada handbook on assessment of damages in personal injury cases / by W.H.R. Charles. - Ontario : Carswell Co., 1982.
129p.
'Reprint of an article in Volume 18 Part 1 of Canadian cases on the law of torts'.
ISBN 0459346709

DAMAGES - CANADA - BRITISH COLUMBIA

—Compensation for non-pecuniary loss / Law Reform Commission of British Columbia. - Vancouver : The Commission, 1983.
iii,53p. - (Working paper).
Includes bibliographical references.

—Court Order Interest Act / Law Reform Commission of British Columbia. - Vancouver : The Commission, 1985.
xi,409p. - (Working paper).

—Report on review of civil jury awards / Law Reform Commission of British Columbia. - Vancouver : The Commission, 1984.
60p.
Includes bibliographical references.
ISBN 0771884478

—Report on the action per quod servitium amisit / Law Reform Commission of British Columbia. - Victoria : Queens Printer, 1986.
20p.
Includes bilbiographical references.
ISBN 0771885490

—Report on the Court Order Interest Act / Law Reform Commission of British Columbia. - Vancouver : The Commission, 1987.
139p.
Includes bibliographical references.
ISBN 077188561X

DAMAGES - CANADA - MANITOBA

—Report on periodic payment of damages for personal injury and death / Manitoba Law Reform Commission. - Winnipeg : The Commission, 1987.
iv,128p. - (Report).
Includes bibliographical references.
ISBN 0771108346

DAMAGES - ENGLAND

—Compensation and support for illness and injury / Donald Harris ... et al. - Oxford : Clarendon, 1984.
xix,412p; 22cm. - (Oxford socio-legal studies).
Includes bibliographies and index.
ISBN 0198275080 Hbk £20.00
ISBN 0198275137 Pbk £9.50

—Damages for personal injuries and death / John Munkman. - 7th ed. - London : Butterworths, 1985.
xxxiii,250p; 23cm.
Previous ed: 1980. Includes index.
ISBN 0406311137 £18.50

—Disability and compensation claims / Philip Noble, Bart Hellyer, Elizabeth Fanshawe. - London : Sweet & Maxwell, 1986.
68p; 22cm.
ISBN 042136890X Pbk £6.50

—Limitation periods in personal injury claims / by Stephen Todd. - London : Sweet & Maxwell, 1982.
xxii,131p; 23cm.
Includes index.
ISBN 0421285907 £13.00

—McGregor on damages / by Harvey McGregor. - 15th ed. - London : Sweet & Maxwell, 1988.
xciii,1232p; 25cm.
Divided into three major sections; General Principles, Particular Contracts, and Torts and Procedures. In each section, the relevant points of law and practice are considered.
ISBN 0421370807 £100.00

—Quantum of damages in personal injury and fatal accident claims / Kemp & Kemp. - Special ed. by David A. McI. Kemp assissted by Derrick Turriff ... et al. 1. - London : Sweet & Maxwell, 1986.
various pagings.
Includes index.
ISBN 0421366001

Vol.2 : law and practice - personal injury reports / Kemp & Kemp. - 1975-.
Volume 1 collects the law and practice applicable to personal injury and to fatal injury claims. Appendices set out the Fatal Accident Acts and other texts. Volume 2 deals with case reports classified according to injury, and the damages awarded.
ISBN 0421216808

—Richards Butler on latent damage / by Robert Merkin. - London : Lloyd's of London Press, 1987.
192p; 22cm.
ISBN 1850441286 £30.00

—Special damages for disability 1988 / by Philip Noble, Elizabeth Fanshawe, Bart Hellyer. - 2nd ed. - London : Sweet & Maxwell, 1988.
x,85p; 22cm.
Catalogues the expenses which a plaintiff in a personal injuries action can claim as part of his award. Each of the expenses, such as accommodation requirements and the cost of future care, are described in the context of the four disabilities of spinal injury, partial and total loss of sight, loss of a limb, and head injury. Each item is given an up-to-date value.
ISBN 0421393807 Pbk £7.50

DAMAGES - GREAT BRITAIN

—Assessment of Damages for Personal Injury and Death / 2nd ed. - London : Butterworths, 1983.
ISBN 0409491322 Hbk £48.00

—Damages for Personal Injuries and Death / 7th ed. - London : Butterworths, 1985.
ISBN 0406311137 Hbk £24.00

—Damages For Personal Injury and Death / 3rd ed. - London : Longman Professional, 1986.
ISBN 0851211178 Pbk £18.95

—Damages for Personal Injury and Death / 2nd ed. - London : Oyez Longman, 1983.
ISBN 0851207308 Hbk £11.50

—Hard bargaining / Oxford : Oxford University Press, 1988.
ISBN 0198255926 Hbk £22.50

—Provisional damages / London : LEST, 1986.
ISBN 0907822835 Pbk £17.50

—Recent Developments in the Law Relating to Damages With Particular Reference to Professional Claims / Alexander Layton. – London : Law Society, 1981.
– (Oxford Weekend Courses).

—Twenty-fourth report (latent damage) / Law Reform Committee. – London : H.M.S.O., 1984.
iv,34p; 25cm. – (Report).
ISBN 0101939000

DAMAGES – HONG KONG

—Damages for personal injuries and fatal accidents in Hong Kong : a review of the law and a digest of the cases / Robyn Martin, Peter Rhodes. – London : Butterworths, 1982.
xxv,563p; 23cm.
Gives general principles of the assessment of damages in personal injuries, and in fatal accident cases, and how these have been applied in Hong Kong. Included in the appendices are multiplier tables, actuarial tables, a glossary of medical terms, and illustrations.
ISBN 0406357102 £45.00

—Damages for Personal Injury and Fatal Accidents in Hong Kong / Rhodes. – London : Butterworths, 1982.
ISBN 0406357102 Hbk £45.00

DAMAGES – INDIA

—Law of Damages and Compensation, 3 Vols. / 5th ed. – Allahabad : Law Publishers, 1983.

DAMAGES – JAMAICA

—Recent personal injury awards made in the Supreme Court of Judicature of Jamaica / compiled by Ursula Khan. – s.l. : s.n., 1981.
xxvii,200p.

DAMAGES – MALAYSIA

—Damages for Personal Injuries and Death in Singapore and Malaysia / Singapore : Butterworths, 1988.
1000p.

—Damages for Personal Injuries and Death in Singapore and Malaysia / Singapore : Malayan Law Journal, 1988.
ca 1,000p.
Presents the main principles governing the assessment of damages for personal injury and death in Singapore and Malaysia, with reference to pertinent cases and statutory provisions.
ISBN 9971700603 Hbk £265.00

DAMAGES – MANITOBA

—Report on prejudgment compensation on money awards : alternatives to interest / Law Reform Commission. – Winnipeg : Queen's Printer, 1982.
iv,108p. – (Report).

DAMAGES – NORTHERN IRELAND

—Administration of Justice Act 1982 and the Assessment of Damages / Belfast : Queen's University of Belfast, 1983.
28p.

—Administration of Justice Act 1982 and the assessment of damages for personal injuries in Northern Ireland : the text of a lecture delivered to the Belfast Solicitors' Association on 24 February 1983 / by D.S. Greer. – Belfast : SLS Legal Publications, 1983.
ii,28p.
Includes bibliographical references.

DAMAGES – SCOTLAND

—Casebook on damages in Scotland / by Robin Gilmour McEwan and Ann Paton. – Edinburgh : Green, 1983.
xxiii,272p; 22cm.
Includes index.
ISBN 0414006984 Pbk Unpriced

—McEwan and Paton on damages in Scotland / Ann Paton. – 2nd. – Edinburgh : W Green & Son, 1989.
Chapters cover damages, provisional damages, interest, loss of earnings and employability, nervous shock, the unaware pursuer, nursing care, special aids, fatal cases, contributory negligence etc. and a review of awards. There is a full collection of recent Scottish decisions (including unreported) on solatium and loss of society, tables of multipliers, an inflation table, diagram of the skeleton. With relevant legislation and rules of court.
ISBN 0414008820

—Report on civil liability : contribution / Scottish Law Commission. – Edinburgh : The Commission, 1988.
vi,75p.
Includes draft of a Bill.
ISBN 0102007896

—Report on section 5 of the Damages (Scotland) Act 1976 / Scottish Law Commission. – Edinburgh : H.M.S.O., 1981.
iii,8p; 25cm. – (HC).
ISBN 0102272816 Pbk £1.80

DAMAGES – SINGAPORE

—Damages for Personal Injuries and Death in Singapore and Malaysia / Singapore : Butterworths, 1988.
1000p.

—Damages for Personal Injuries and Death in Singapore and Malaysia / Singapore : Malayan Law Journal, 1988.
ca 1,000p.
Presents the main principles governing the assessment of damages for personal injury and death in Singapore and Malaysia, with reference to pertinent cases and statutory provisions.
ISBN 9971700603 Hbk £265.00

—Damages-Loss of Expectation of Life : Survival and Deductibility / Singapore : Malayan Law Journal, 1984.
xiii, 82p.
Explores the survival of the claim for loss of expectation of life and the methods employed by courts for its quantification. Intends to determine the justification, if any, for deducting the compensation awarded to the estate under the Fatal Accidents Act 1846-1908. Comparison of the law in England, Canada (Manitoba), Australia and Malaysia.
ISBN 9971700379 Hbk £25.00

DAMAGES – SOUTH AFRICA

—Damages for lost income / Robert J. Koch. – Cape Town : Juta, 1984.
xxxii,367p.
Bibliography: pxvii-xix.
ISBN 0702115126

DAMAGES – UNITED STATES

—Law Suit : A Study in Damages (U.S.A.) 1980 / London : Wildy & Sons.

DANGER (LAW) – CANADA

—Omissions, negligence and endangering / Law Reform Commission of Canada. – Ottawa : The Commission, 1985.
42,48p. – (Working paper).
Includes bibliographical references. Added t.p. in French: L'omission, la negligence et la mise en danger. Pages numbered in opposite directions. Text in English and French.
ISBN 0662540824

DATA PROCESSING

—Computer science and law / edited by Bryan Niblett. – Cambridge : Cambridge University Press, 1980.
viii,238p; 24cm.
' ... proceedings of ... an Advanced Workshop on Computer Science and Law held at Clyne Castle, University College of Swansea, from the 17th to 27th September, 1979' - Preface. Includes bibliographies and index.
ISBN 0521234514 £12.50

—Expert systems in law : a jurisprudential inquiry / Richard E. Susskind. – Oxford : Clarendon, 1987.
xvi,300p; 23cm.
Bibliography: p271-292. - Includes index.
ISBN 0198255829 £30.00

—Explanatory Report on the European Convention for the Protection of Individuals with Regard to Automatic Processing of Personal Data / Strasbourg : Council of Europe, 1981.

—Final report on the operation of national organisations concerned with the co-ordination of computer use in local government / by Serge Duriaud under the guidance of the Committee of Experts on Local and Regional Management. – Strasbourg : Council of Europe, 1980.
iii,39p.

—Lawyers in the eighties : proceedings of the conference held by Society for Computers and Law in York from 3rd to 6th July 1980 / Conference Organising Committee, Richard Morgan ... et al. – Abingdon : The Society, 1980.
70p; 30cm.
Cover title.
ISBN 090612204X spiral £15.00 (10.00 to members of the Society for Computers and Law)

—Protection of users of computerised legal information services : Recommendation no.R (83) 3 adopted by the Committee of Ministers of the Council of Europe on 22 February 1983 and Explanatory memorandum / Council of Europe. – Strasbourg : Council of Europe, 1983.
23p; 21cm.
'... prepared by the Committee of Experts on Legal Data Processing un der the authority of the European Committee on Legal Co- operation'. At head of cover: Council of Europe, Legal Affairs.
ISBN 9287102791

—Software for producing library keyword catalogues : a description of selected packages / Steven Prowse. – Oxford : Elsevier International Bulletins, 1984.
viii,48p; 30cm. – (EIB report series).
Bibliography: p48.
ISBN 0946395012 Pbk No price

—Survey of computing in European local and regional authorities / ... prepared under the guidelines of the Committee of Experts on Management in Local and Regional Government by G.Gaits. – Strasbourg : Council of Europe, 1981.
iii,61p.

DATA PROCESSING – ENGLAND

—Computer in court : a guide to computer evidence for lawyers and computing professionals / Alistair Kelman, Richard Sizer. – Aldershot : Gower, 1982.
viii,104p; 22cm.
Bibliography: p99. - Includes index.
ISBN 0566034190 Unpriced

DATA PROCESSING – EUROPEAN COMMUNITY

—Harmonisation Measures in the Field of Legal Data Processing in the Member States of the Council of Europe / Strasbourg : Council of Europe, 1982.
ISBN 9287100365

—Protection of Privacy, Automatic Data Processing and Progress in Statistical Documentation / Luxembourg : Office for Official Publications of the European Communities, 1986.
348p.

DATA PROCESSING – GREAT BRITAIN

—Data Processing / London : Butterworths, 1984.
ISBN 0408011718 Pbk £8.50

—Newsletter / Law Technology Centre & BILETA. – Warwick : LTC, School of Law, University of Warwick, 1987-.

—Tomorrow's lawyers : computers and legal training : a paper prepared by the Society's Legal Education Committee to discuss the teaching of computer applications to intending lawyers and to qualified practitioners / Society for Computers and Law. – Milton, Oxon : Society for Computers and Law, 1981.
7p; 22cm.
ISBN 0906122082 Pbk Unpriced

DATA PROTECTION

—Business Guide to Privacy and Data 1970 : Protection Legislation / Paris : International Chamber of Commerce.
310p.

—Convention for the Protection of Individuals with Regard to Automatic Processing of Personal Data / Strasbourg : Council of Europe, 1981.
ISBN 9287100225 Hbk £1.00

—Convention for the Protection of Individuals with regard to Automatic Processing of Personal Data (with explanatory report), Strasbourg, 28 January 1981 / London : H.M.S.O., 1981.
33p; 25cm. – (Miscellaneous).
ISBN 0101834101 Pbk £3.05

—Data Protection Act 1984 : an introduction to the Act and guide for data users and computer bureaux / Wilmslow, Cheshire : Data Protection Registrar, 1985.
36p.

—Data Protection Act : subject access to personal health data : a consultation paper / s.l. : s.n., .
9,3,2p.

—Explanatory report on the Convention for the Protection of Individuals with regard to Automatic Processing of Personal Data / Strasbourg : Council of Europe, 1981.
41p; 22cm.
Includes the text of the convention.

—International regulation of data services: the debate over the trade and development issues / London : Pinter, 1990.
250.
Bibliography and index included.
ISBN 0861878531 Hbk £30

—Privacy and data protection : an international bibliography / edited with an introduction by David H. Flaherty with the assistance of Terence J. Donohue and Peter J. Harte. – London : Mansell, 1984.
304p.
Includes index.
ISBN 0720117194 £23.50

—Protection of personal data used for scientific research and statistics : recommendation no.R (83)10 adopted by the Committee of Ministers of the Council of Europe on 23 September 1983, and Explanatory memorandum / Council of Europe. – Strasbourg : Council of Europe, 1984.
23p; 21cm.
'Prepared by the Committee of Experts on Data Protection set up under the authority of the European Committee on Legal Co-operation'. At head of cover title: Legal Affairs.
ISBN 9287103178

—Protection of personal data used for the purposes of direct marketing : recommendation no. R(85) 20 adopted by the Committee of Ministers of the Council of Europe on 25 October 1985 and Explanatory memorandum / Council of Europe. – Strasbourg : Council of Europe, 1986.
19p.
Prepared by the committee of experts on data protection set up under the authority of the European Committee on Legal Co-operation. At head of cover title: Council of Europe, Legal Affairs.
ISBN 9287108765

—Transborder data flows : proceedings of an OECD conference held December 1983 / edited for the OECD by Hans-Peter Gassmann. – Amsterdam : North-Holland, 1985.
Bibliography: p.
ISBN 0444877002

DATA PROTECTION – AUSTRALIA – NEW SOUTH WALES

—Guidelines for the operation of personal data systems : exposure draft / Privacy Committee. – Sydney : The Committee, 1986.
29p.

DATA PROTECTION – CANADA

—Access and privacy : the steps ahead / Canada. – Ottawa : Government of Canada, 1987.
x,57,63,xip.
French title on added t.p.: Acces et renseignements personnels. Pages numbered in opposite directions. Text in English and French.
ISBN 0662554728

—Practice and Procedure Under the Access to Information and Privacy Acts / Toronto : Butterworths, 1986.
128p.
ISBN 0409811645 Hbk

—Workshop on information technologies and personal privacy in Canada / Science Council of Canada. – Ottawa : The Council, 1985.
62p.
Includes bibliographical references.
ISBN 0662140354

DATA PROTECTION – CANADA – ONTARIO

—Privacy and personal data protection : a report on personal record-keeping by the ministries and agencies of the Ontario government / by Michael Brown, Brenda Billingsley and Rebecca Shamai. – Toronto : Commission on Freedom of Information and Individual Privacy, 1980.
xviii,645p. – (Research publication).

DATA PROTECTION – EUROPEAN COMMUNITY

—Protection of Privacy, Automatic Data Processing and Progress in Statistical Documentation / Luxembourg : Office for Official Publications of the European Communities, 1986.
348p.

—Protection of privacy, automatic data processing and progress in statistical documentation / Luxembourg : Office for Official Publications of the European Communities, 1986.
348p. – (Series C).
Eurostat News special edition. 'The papers reproduced in this volume were first presented at an international seminar held under the auspices of the Statistical Office of the European Communities (EUROSTAT) at Luxembourg in December 1984'. - Preface.

DATA PROTECTION – GREAT BRITAIN

—Data processing and the law / edited by Colin Campbell. – London : Sweet & Maxwell, 1984.
viii,264p; 22cm.
Includes index.
ISBN 0421320001 Pbk £20.00

—Data protection : a guide for library and information management / J. Eric Davies. – Oxford : Elsevier International Bulletins, 1985.
220p. – (EIB report series).
Includes bibliography.
ISBN 0946395179 Pbk £20.00 (Jan.)

—Data Protection Act, 1984 / The Data Protection Registrar. – Wilmslow : The Registrar, 1987.
24 p.
ISBN 1870466063

Individual rights / The Data Protection Registrar. – 1987.
28 p.
ISBN 1870466047

Introduction to the Act / The Data Protection Registrar. – 1987.
20 p.
ISBN 1870466004

Summary for computer bureaux / The Data Protection Registrar. – 1987.
8 p.
ISBN 1870466071

The data protection principles / The Data Protection Registrar. – 1987.
28 p.
ISBN 1870466039

The definitions / The Data Protection Registrar. – 1987.
40 p.
ISBN 1870466012

The exemptions / The Data Protection Registrar. – 1987.
36 p.
ISBN 1870466055

The register and registration / The Data Protection Registrar. – 1987.
32 p.
ISBN 1870466020

—Data Protection Act 1984 / with commentary and annotations by Bryan Niblett. – London : Oyez Longman, 1984.
x,155p; 24cm.
ISBN 0851207766 Pbk £16.50

—Data Protection Act 1984 : a guide to the new legislation / J.A.L. Sterling. – 2nd ed. – Bicester : CCH, 1985.
v,330p; 23cm.
Previous ed.: 1984?. Bibliography: p313-314. - Includes index.
ISBN 0863250769 Pbk No price

—Data Protection Act 1984 : New Problems For Solicitors and Their Clients / London : Law Society, 1985.
27p. – (Nineteen Eighty-Five Crash Course Transcripts).

—Data Protection Bill : notes on the passage of the Bill from the House of Lords to the House of Commons / by the Council's Law Reform Committee. – London : The Committee, 1983.
8p.

—Data protection in practice / Kenneth Gulleford. – London : Butterworths, 1986.
xi,306p; 25cm.
Includes index.
ISBN 0406177007 Pbk £20.00

—Data Protection in Practice / London : Butterworths, 1986.
ISBN 0406177007 Pbk £23.00

—Data Protection Kit / Croydon : Tolley, 1985.
ISBN 085459146X Hbk £16.50

—Data protection law / commentary by Simon Chalton, Shelagh Gaskill. – London : Sweet & Maxwell, 1988.
268p in various paging; 24cm.
Includes index.
ISBN 0421398205 Pbk £10.00

—Data protection : the Government's proposals for legislation / Great Britain. – London : H.M.S.O., 1982.
23p; 25cm.
At head of title: Home Office.
ISBN 0101853904 unbound £2.30

—Encyclopaedia of Data Protection / Gaskill. – London : Sweet & Maxwell, 1988.
ISBN 0421369000 loose £185.00

—Encyclopedia of data protection / edited by Simon Chalton, Shelagh Gaskill. – 1. – London : Sweet & Maxwell, 1988.
looseleaf.
Includes index.
ISBN 0421369000

—How to comply with the Data Protection Act : policies, practice and procedures / Alastair Evans and Anthony Korn in association with Percom Limited. – Aldershot : Gower, 1986.
vii,211p; 31cm.
Includes index.
ISBN 0566026325 £22.50

—Implications of the Data Protection Act / R.A. Elbra. – Manchester : NCC Publications, 1985.
75p.
Includes bibliography.
ISBN 085012476X Pbk £5.95

—Public access to Government held information / London : Sweet & Maxwell, 1987.
ISBN 0420476105 Pbk £35.00

—Report of the Data Protection Registrar ... / London : HMSO, 1985-.

DATA PROTECTION – NORTHERN IRELAND

—Access to personal social services records : Data Protection Act 1984, Section 29(2) Order : social work records, Northern Ireland / Northern Ireland. – Belfast : Department of Health and Social Services, 1985.
8 leaves.

DATA TRANSMISSION SYSTEMS

—International regulation of data services: the debate over the trade and development issues / London : Pinter, 1990.
250.
Bibliography and index included.
ISBN 0861878531 Hbk £30

DATA TRANSMISSION SYSTEMS – EUROPEAN COMMUNITY

—Freedom of data flows and EEC law / G P V Vandenberghe, Y Poullet. – Kluwer Law and Taxation, 1988.
142. – (Computer/Law Series).
Deals with the legal problems caused by transfrontier flows of information. Includes chapters on the need to speak a common language between partners, data and information in common law, information and data in continental law, and restriction on transborder transmissions of commercial data under EEC law.
ISBN 9065443665 Pbk £32/Dfl 99

DEAD BODIES (LAW)

—Law of burial, cremation and exhumation / by M.R. Russell Davies. – 5th ed. – London : Shaw, 1982.
lii,244p; 22cm.
Previous ed.: 1974. Includes index.
ISBN 0721900631 Pbk Unpriced

DEATH

—ABC of brain stem death / Christopher Pallis. – London : British Medical Journal, 1983.
33p; 29cm.
Articles published in the British Medical Journal.
ISBN 0727900994

—Damages for personal injury and death in Canada / edited and with introductory notes by Immanuel Goldsmith : case abridgements prepared by Alan Burnside Harvey and by David Carruthers. – Toronto : Carswell, 1959.
xxiii,374p.
Includes index.

DEATH – AUSTRALIA

—Assessment of damages for personal injury and death / by Harold Luntz. – 2nd ed. – Sydney : Butterworths, 1983.
lxvii,570p.
Includes index.
ISBN 0409491322

DEATH – CANADA

—Goldsmith's damages for personal injury and death in Canada : a complete digest service derived from reported and unreported cases / 1. – Toronto : Carswell, 1980.
looseleaf.
Spine title: Damages for personal injury and death.
ISBN 0459316206

DEATH – GREAT BRITAIN

—Damages for Personal Injury and Death / 2nd ed. – London : Oyez Longman, 1983.
ISBN 0851207308 Hbk £11.50

—Death and Taxes / Soares. – London : Longman Professional, 1986.
ISBN 0851209309 Pbk £19.95

—Sudden deaths and fatal accident inquiries / Edinburgh : W Green & Son, 1986.
Covers the duties of the procurator fiscal in investigating sudden and unexpected deaths. With a chapter on medical mattres, a summary of the duties of the coroner in England and guidance for the medical professions as to which deaths shuld be reported to the fiscal.
ISBN 0414007751

DEATH – INDIA

—Law of Dying Declaration / Allahabad : Law Book Company, 1988.
60p.

DEATH – MALAYSIA

—Damages for Personal Injuries and Death in Singapore and Malaysia / Singapore : Butterworths, 1988.
1000p.

—Damages for Personal Injuries and Death in Singapore and Malaysia / Singapore : Malayan Law Journal, 1988.
ca 1,000p.
Presents the main principles governing the assessment of damages for personal injury and death in Singapore and Malaysia, with reference to pertinent cases and statutory provisions.
ISBN 9971700603 Hbk £265.00

DEATH – SCOTLAND

—Report on section 5 of the Damages (Scotland) Act 1976 / Scottish Law Commission. – Edinburgh : H.M.S.O., 1981.
iii,8p; 25cm. – (HC).
ISBN 0102272816 Pbk £1.80

DEATH – SINGAPORE

—Damages for Personal Injuries and Death in Singapore and Malaysia / Singapore : Butterworths, 1988.
1000p.

—Damages for Personal Injuries and Death in Singapore and Malaysia / Singapore : Malayan Law Journal, 1988.
ca 1,000p.
Presents the main principles governing the assessment of damages for personal injury and death in Singapore and Malaysia, with reference to pertinent cases and statutory provisions.
ISBN 9971700603 Hbk £265.00

DEATH - SOUTH AFRICA

—Reform of the South African law of divorce : The dissolution of marriages on presumption of death act 23 of 1979, The divorce act 70 of 1979 / by H. R. Hahlo and June D. Sinclair. – Cape Town : Juta, 1980.
vi, 66 p.; 25 cm.
'Supplement to Hahlo, The South African law of husband and wife, 4 ed. (1975).'. Includes texts of laws. Includes bibliographical references and index.
ISBN 0702110582 pbk.

DEATH PENALTY

—Death penalty: a worldwide perspective / Oxford : Clarendon Press, 1989.
200; 21.5.
Survey of practice literature covering the death penalty, by analysis of the law and practice of all states where the death penalty is, or has been, used in recent years. Discusses whether or not the claimed deterrent effect of the death penalty has any basis in known fact.
ISBN 0198252722 Hbk £20.00

—Explanatory Report on Protocol No. 6 to the Convention for the Protection of Human Rights and Fundamental Freedoms Concerning the Abolition of the Death Penalty / Strasbourg : Council of Europe, 1983.
ISBN 9287102163

—Judicial review of the death penalty / David Pannick. – London : Duckworth, 1982.
245p; 23cm.
Includes index.
ISBN 0715615947 £18.00

—Moral theory and capital punishment / Tom Sorell. – Oxford : Basil Blackwell in association with the Open University, 1987.
240p; 23cm.
Includes index.
ISBN 0631153217 Hbk £25.00
ISBN 0631153225 Pbk £5.95

DEATH PENALTY - CHINA

—China : violations of human rights : prisoners of conscience and the death penalty in the People's Republic of China / Amnesty International. – London : Amnesty International Publications, 1984.
129p.
ISBN 0862100739

DEATH PENALTY - INDIA

—Capital Punishment in India / New Delhi : Deep and Deep Publications, 1986.
240p.

DEATH PENALTY - JAMAICA

—Jamaica : the death penalty : report of an Amnesty International mission to Jamaica / Amnesty International. – London : Amnesty International Publications, 1984.
63p.
ISBN 0862100763

DEATH PENALTY - JAPAN

—Death penalty in Japan : report of an Amnesty International mission to Japan, 21 February - 3 March 1983 / Amnesty International. – s.l. : Amnesty International, 1983.
31p.
ISBN 0862100607

DEATH PENALTY - UNITED STATES

—Capital punishment and the American agenda / Franklin E. Zimring, Gordon Hawkins. – Cambridge : Cambridge University Press, 1987.
xviii,192p; 24cm.
Includes index.
ISBN 0521330335 £20.00

—United States of America - the death penalty / Amnesty International. – London : Amnesty International, 1987.
vi,245p; 22cm.
ISBN 086210114X Pbk No price

DEATH PENALTY - ZIMBABWE

—Aspects of capital punishment / Advisory Committee on Law Reform. – Causeway : The Committee, 1982.
28p. – (Report).
Includes bibliographical references.

DEBT - AUSTRALIA

—Assignments, Arrangements and Compositions by Debtors with Precedents / 2nd ed. – Butterworths, 1986.
176p.
ISBN 0409490652 Hbk £45.00

DEBT - CANADA

—Debt Security Instruments : Creation and Perfection 1988 / Vancouver : Continuing Legal Education Society of British Columbia, 1988.
406p.
ISBN 0865049777 Hbk £85.00

—Debt Security Instruments : Creation and Perfection / Vancouver : British Columbia Continuing Legal Education Society, 1986.
ISBN 0865042543 Hbk £70.00

—Debtor-Creditor Law : Practice and Doctrine / Eric Gertner. – Butterworths, 1985.
768p.
Addresses the practical issues which dominate debtor-creditor law in Canada. Covers execution against negotiable instruments, third party demands, fraudulent conveyances and unjust preferences, PPSA, repossession, corporate receivership, construction liens, the enforcement of foreign judgements, executions against shares in BC and enforcement against life insurance, pensions, and RRSP's.
ISBN 0409868833 Hbk £95.00

—Enforcing Debenture Security / Vancouver : British Columbia Continuing Legal Education Society, 1984.
ISBN 086504144X Hbk £60.00

DEBT - CANADA - BRITISH COLUMBIA

—Debt Security Instruments : Creation and Perfection, Pt. 1 / Vancouver : British Columbia Continuing Legal Education Society, 1981.
430p.
ISBN 0865040168 Hbk £22.00

—Debt Security Instruments : Realization, Pt. 2 / Vancouver : British Columbia Continuing Legal Education Society, 1981.
377p.
ISBN 0865040192 Hbk £11.50

DEBT - ENGLAND

—Preventing rent arrears / Sue Duncan, Keith Kirby. – London : H.M.S.O., 1983.
144p; 21cm.
At head of title: Department of the Environment.
ISBN 0117517100 Pbk £4.00

DEBT - EUROPE

—Debt Problems of Eastern Europe / Cambridge : Cambridge University Press, 1988.
ISBN 0521335426 Hbk £25.00

DEBT - GREAT BRITAIN

—Arrears Proceedings and Related Matters in the Magistrates' Court / Lomax & Reynolds. – Chichester : Barry Rose, 1985.
250p.
ISBN 0859922340 Hbk £19.50

—Credit Debt and Poverty / London : Policy Studies Institute, 1988.
ISBN 0853743479 Pbk £8.95

DEBT - IRELAND

—Report on debt collection : (1) the law relating to sheriffs / the Law Reform Commission. – Dublin : The Commission, 1988.
viii,62p. – (LRC).

DEBT - NEW ZEALAND

—Corporate Debt Securities : Priority Rules / Auckland : Legal Research Foundation, 1986.

DEBT - SCOTLAND

—Law of Scotland relating to debt / W.A. Wilson. – Edinburgh : W Green & Son, 1982.
lxxvii,380p; 22cm.
Deals with ways in which debts arise out of common transactions such as sale and hire purchase, debt recovery and defences such as payment and compensation. Full treatment of relevant sections of the Consumer Credit Act 1974, with discussion of securities, diligence, insolvency and documents on debt. Includes index.
ISBN 0414006828 Pbk Unpriced

—Origins and consequences of default : an examination of the impact of diligence (summary) / by Michael Adler and Edward Wozniak. – Edinburgh : Central Research Unit, 1981.
viii,71p; 30cm.

DEBT - SOUTH AFRICA

—Committal to prison in respect of debt / South African Law Commission. – Pretoria : The Commission, 1986.
viii,37,9p. – (Report).
Includes the text of draft legislation.
ISBN 0621113468

DEBT - ZIMBABWE

—Civil imprisonment / Advisory Committee on Law Reform. – Causeway : The Committee, 1982.
13 leaves. – (Working paper).

DEBT COLLECTION - GREAT BRITAIN

—Debt Management and Collection / London : Butterworths, 1988.
ISBN 040635880X Pbk

—Guide to Successful Debt Collecting / 1st ed. – Bristol : Jordan & Sons Ltd, 1982.

—Recovery of money / 7th. – London : Longman Professional (UK), 1989.
– (Practitioner series).
Guide to the law practice and procedure of debt collection from contract to enforcement. Coverage includes contract drafting and formation, preservation of assets pending proceedings, a consideration of the foreign element, mortgage repossession, computer support and office procedure. Takes account of Consumer Credit Act, Insolvency Act and Rules 1986, and Civil Jurisdiction and Judgements Act.
ISBN 0851215165 Hbk £26.50

—Recovery of money / 6th ed. – London : Longman Professional, 1986.
– (Longman Practitioner Series).
Covers the practice and procedure of debt collection with particular items on contract drafting, mortgage possession and the use of computers for debt collection.
ISBN 0851210031 Pbk £21.00

DEBT RELIEF

—Recent multilateral debt restructurings with official and bank creditors / by a Staff team headed by E. Brau...et al. – Washington, D.C. : International Monetary Fund, 1983.
vii,43p. – (Occasional paper).

DEBTOR AND CREDITOR

—Law of borrowing / London : Sweet & Maxwell, 1989.
Account of the institutional framework within which borrowing takes place, and consideration of the regulation and supervision of banks, building societies, the securities market, the wholesale money market, and consumer credit transactions. Chapter dealing with the characteristics of a loan, and types of loan.
ISBN 0421000000 Llf

—Mareva Injunction and associated orders / by David G. Powles. – Abingdon : Professional Books, 1986.
xxiii,160p.
ISBN 0862050693 Pbk
ISBN 0862052033

—Private international law : Council of Europe Conventions on Foreign Money Liabilities(1967) and on the Place of Payment of Money Liabilities (1972) : report on a reference under section 3 (1)(e) of the Law Commissions Act 1965 / the Law Commission and the Scottish Law Commission. – London : H.M.S.O., 1981.
iv,53p; 25cm.
Includes the text of the Conventions.
ISBN 0101831803

—Private international law : foreign money liabilities / the Law Commission. – London : H.M.S.O., 1981.
ix,195p; 22cm. – (Working paper).
ISBN 0117301604

—Protective measures for recovering commercial debts / London : Euromoney, 1980.
64p.

DEBTOR AND CREDITOR - AUSTRALIA

—Assignments, arrangements and compositions by debtors (with precedents) / 2nd. – North Ryde : Butterworths (Australia).
Practical guide to the workings of administrations under part 10 of the Australian Commonwealth Bankruptcy Act.
ISBN 0409490652 Hbk

—Assignments of Choses in Action in Australia / London : Butterworths, 1982.
ISBN 0409395900 Hbk £28.00

—Debt recovery and insolvency / Law Reform Commission. – Canberra : Australian Government Publishing Service, 1987.
xxxii,312p. – (Report).
ISBN 0644013648

DEBTOR AND CREDITOR - AUSTRALIA - NEW SOUTH WALES

—Community law reform program / New South Wales Law Reform Commission. – Sydney : The Commission, 1983.
46p. – (L.R.C. 35).

DEBTOR AND CREDITOR - AUSTRALIA - TASMANIA

—Report on interest on pre- and post-judgment debts / Law Reform Commission of Tasmania. – Hobart : Government Printer, 1985.
17p. – (Report v no 44).

DEBTOR AND CREDITOR - CANADA

—Creditor-debtor law in Canada / by C.R.B. Dunlop : with chapter 14 / by P.J.M. Lown. – Toronto, Canada : Carswell, 1981.
cxxii, 563 p.; 26 cm.
'Table of cases': p. xiii-lxxxiv. 'Table of statutes, rules and regulations': p. lxxxv-cxvi. Includes index. Bibliography: p. cxvii-cxxii.
ISBN 0459340506 pbk.

—Creditors' and Debtors' Rights 1987-1988 / Agincourt : Carswell, 1988.
563p.

—Creditors' and Debtors' Rights / Agincourt : Carswell, 1988.
500p. – (Bar Admission Course Material Ser.).
This is a guidebook to the rights of creditors and debtors. Topics include types of secured transactions, construction liens, personal property security, receivership and bankruptcy. Also included are sample forms and precedents used in different types of transactions and proceedings.

—Creditors' Remedies - 1985 / Vancouver : British Columbia Continuing Legal Education Society, 1985.
348p.
ISBN 0865042209 Hbk £65.00

—Crown as Creditor : Priorities and Priveleges / Victoria : Government of British Columbia, 1982.

—Debtor and Creditor : Cases and Commentary / 3rd ed. – Agincourt : Carswell, 1987.
1,150p.

—Debtor and Creditor : Cases and Commentary / 3rd ed. – Agincourt : Carswell, 1987.
ISBN 0459304712 Hbk £45.00
ISBN 045930481X Pbk £23.00

—Debtor and Creditor : Cases, Notes and Materials / Eric Gertner. – 2nd ed. – Aurora : Canada Law Book Co, 1982.
1200p. – (Case Books).

—Debtor and Creditor : Cases, Notes and Materials / 2nd ed. – Toronto : Emond-Montgomery, 1982.
1200p.
ISBN 0920722075 Hbk £89.50

DEBTOR AND CREDITOR – CANADA – ALBERTA

—Creditor's Remedies in Alberta / Peter Vaartnou. – Agincourt : Carswell, 1987.
ca 620p.

—Creditors' Remedies in Alberta / Peter Vaartnou. – Agincourt : Carswell, 1987.
620p.
This work focuses on collection practice in Alberta. Discussions are in-depth and include all the issues involved in the collection process, from making the decision to sue to drafting documents, realizing on security and enforcing judgments. Each chapter is arranged so that the procedures and possible problem areas are explained.

—Debt collection practices / Institute of Law Research and Reform. – Edmonton : The Institute.
vi,161p. – (Report no 42).

—Operation of the unsecured creditors' remedies system in Alberta / Institute of Law Research and Reform. – Edmonton : The Institute, 1986.
vii,188p. – (Research paper).
Includes bibliographical references.

—Remedies of unsecured creditors / Institute of Law Research and Reform. – Edmonton : The Institute, 1986.
xiv,370p. – (Report for discussion).
Includes bibliographical references.

DEBTOR AND CREDITOR – CANADA – BRITISH COLUMBIA

—Crown as creditor : priorities and privileges / Law Reform Commission of British Columbia. – Vancouver : Law Reform Commission of British Columbia, 1981.
v,179p. – (Working paper).

—Report on fraudulent conveyances and preferences : Law Reform Commission of British Columbia / Law Reform Commission of British Columbia. – Vancouver : The Commission, 1988.
vii,180p.
Includes bibliographical references. Includes draft legislation.
ISBN 0771886314

—Report on the Crown as creditor : priorities and privileges / Law Reform Commission of British Columbia. – Victoria : Queen's Printer, 1982.
99p.
ISBN 0771883404

DEBTOR AND CREDITOR – CANADA – MANITOBA

—Report on small projects / Manitoba Law Reform Commission. – Winnipeg : The Commission, 1985.
iv,48p. – (Report).
Includes bibliographical references.
ISBN 0771101074

DEBTOR AND CREDITOR – CANADA – ONTARIO

—Report on the enforcement of judgment debts and related matters / Ontario Law Reform Commission. – 5 v. – Toronto : Ministry of the Attorney General, 1981.
Includes bibliographical references.
ISBN 0774360593 v.3

DEBTOR AND CREDITOR – ENGLAND

—Civil justice review / Lord Chancellor's Department. – London : The Department, 1987.
76 leaves.

—Civil justice review : study of debt enforcement procedures / London : Touche Ross, 1986.
iii,90 leaves.
A study carried out as part of the Lord Chancellor's review of civil justice.

—Computerisation of county court procedures in debt cases : the claims registry / Lord Chancellor's Department. – London : The Department, 1987.
27 leaves.
Includes bibliographical references.

—JUSTICE's response to the Lord Chancellor's civil justice review consultation paper no. 4 : enforcement of debt / JUSTICE. – London? : JUSTICE, 1987.
8p.

—Mareva injunction and Anton Piller order : practice and precedents / by Richard N. Ough. – London : Butterworths, 1987.
xxii,175p; 22cm.
Includes index.
ISBN 0406102902 Pbk £25.00

—Mareva injunction and related orders / by Mark S.W. Hoyle. – London : Lloyd's of London Press, 1985.
viii,141p; 22cm.
ISBN 1850440441 No price (June)

—Mareva injunctions / by David Capper. – London : Sweet & Maxwell, 1988.
xxii,135p; 22cm.
Contains the definition and nature of a Mareva injunction, including matters which must be proved, the procedure for application, orders for the discovery of assets, the writ ne exeat regno, Bayer orders, and Anton Piller orders, and Mareva injunctions and the criminal law. Includes an appendix of precedents.
ISBN 0421389605 Pbk No price

—Mareva injunctions : a one-day conference / organised by Lloyds of London Press, the Tower Hotel, London, 22nd June 1982. – 1. – London : Lloyd's of London Press, 1982.
various pagings; 31cm.
ISBN 0907432433 Unpriced

—Mareva injunctions : law and practice / Steven Gee and Geraldine Mary Andrews : foreword by Lord Denning. – London : Longman, 1987.
xxvii,143p; 25cm.
Includes index.
ISBN 0851209394 £30.00

—Payment obligations in commercial and financial transactions / by R.M. Goode. – London : Sweet & Maxwell, 1983.
xxiii,151p; 22cm.
Includes index.
ISBN 0421318104 Pbk £11.00

—Private international law - foreign money liabilities : report on a reference under section 3 (1)(e) of the Law Commissions Act 1965 / The Law Commission. – London : H.M.S.O., 1983.
vii,94p; 25cm.
ISBN 0101906404

DEBTOR AND CREDITOR – GREAT BRITAIN

—Asset Valuation / London : Macmillan, 1988.
ISBN 033336515 Pbk £5.95

—Debtors and Creditors / Abingdon : Professional Books, 1985.
550p.
ISBN 0862051010 Hbk £33.00
ISBN 0862051029 Pbk £19.50

—Debtors and Creditors / London : Butterworths, 1986.
ISBN 0862051010 Hbk £26.95

—Recovery of money / 7th. – London : Longman Professional (UK), 1989.
– (Practitioner series).
Guide to the law practice and procedure of debt collection from contract to enforcement. Coverage includes contract drafting and formation, preservation of assets pending proceedings, a consideration of the foreign element, mortgage repossession, computer support and office procedure. Takes account of Consumer Credit Act, Insolvency Act and Rules 1986, and Civil Jurisdiction and Judgements Act.
ISBN 0851215165 Hbk £26.50

DEBTOR AND CREDITOR – IRELAND

—Report on debt collection : (1) the law relating to sheriffs / the Law Reform Commission. – Dublin : The Commission, 1988.
viii,62p. – (LRC).

DEBTOR AND CREDITOR – MALAYSIA

—Debtors Act, 1957 (Act 256) / Kuala Lumpur : International Law Books Services.

DEBTOR AND CREDITOR – NEW ZEALAND

—Creditor and Debtor Law in Australia and New Zealand / 3rd ed. – North Ryde : C.C.H. Australia, 1986.
333p.
ISBN 0869035908 Hbk £35.00

DEBTOR AND CREDITOR – SCOTLAND

—Adjudications for debt and related matters / Scottish Law Commission. – 2. – Edinburgh : The Commission, 1988.
– (Discussion paper).

—Debt counselling : an assessment of the services and facilities available to consumer debtors in Scotland / by Ann R. Millar. – Edinburgh : Central Research Unit, 1980.
vii,83p; 30cm.

—Debt recovery : a review of creditors' practices and policies / by Barbara Doig and Ann R. Millar. – Edinburgh : Central Research Unit, Scottish Office, 1981.
vii,72p.

—Debtors (Scotland) Act 1987 / Edinburgh : W Green & Son, 1987.
Annotated text of the Act from Scottish Current Law Statutes with two introductory chapters, including a diagram showing the principal effects of the Act on the debt recovery process.
ISBN 0414008227

—Diligence and debtor protection : consultation paper / Scottish Courts Administration. – Edinburgh : Scottish Courts Administration on behalf of the Lord Advocate, 1985.
15 leaves.
Consultation paper on Scottish Law Commission's report on diligence and debtor protection (Scot. Law Com. no. 95.

—Law of Scotland relating to debt / W.A. Wilson. – Edinburgh : W Green & Son, 1982!
lxxvii,380p; 22cm.
Deals with ways in which debts arise out of common transactions such as sale and hire purchase, debt recovery and defences such as payment and compensation. Full treatment of relevant sections of the Consumer Credit Act 1974, with discussion of securities, diligence, insolvency and documents on debt. Includes index.
ISBN 0414006828 Pbk Unpriced

—Report on diligence and debtor protection / Scottish Law Commission. – 2 v. – Edinburgh : H.M.S.O., 1985.
Vol. 2: Appendices.
ISBN 0102005869

—Survey of defenders in debt actions in Scotland / Janet Gregory and Janet Monk. – London : H.M.S.O., 1981.
ix,109p. – (Research report for the Scottish Law Commission).
Includes index.
ISBN 0116907746

DEBTS, EXTERNAL

—The Debt Rescheduling Process / Marko Milivojevic. – London : Pinter, 1985.
200p.
Includes bibliography and index.
ISBN 0861875753 £18.50

—External debt rescheduling / Roland Plan. – Vienna : Manzsche Verlags-und Universitatsbuchhandlung, 1985.
x,276p. – (Law, economics, international trade).
Bibliography: p254-266.
ISBN 3214065572

—International debt game / by Brian Kettell and George Magnus. – London : Graham & Trotman, 1985.
384p; 23cm.
Includes index.
ISBN 0860105717 Pbk £18.75
ISBN 0860108104 £12.50

—Recent multilateral debt restructurings with official and bank creditors / by a Staff team headed by E. Brau...et al. – Washington, D.C. : International Monetary Fund, 1983.
vii,43p. – (Occasional paper).

DECEDENTS' ESTATES – AUSTRALIA – WESTERN AUSTRALIA

—Report on the administration of assets of the solvent estates of deceased persons in the payment of debts and legacies / Law Reform Commission of Western Australia. – Perth : Law Reform Commission of Western Australia, 1988.
50p. – (Project).

DECEDENTS' ESTATES – CANADA – MANITOBA

—Report on intestate succession / Manitoba Law Reform Commission. – Winnipeg : The Commission, 1985.
iii,66p. – (Report).
Includes bibliographical references.

DECEDENTS' ESTATES – CANADA – SASKATCHEWAN

—Tentative proposals relating to testamentary custody and guardianship of children / Law Reform Commission of Saskatchewan. – Saskatoon : The Commission, 1984.
58p.
Includes texts of proposed Acts.

DECEDENTS' ESTATES – UNITED STATES

—Decedents' estates, wills, and trusts in the U.S.A. / by Frank G. Opton. – Deventer, The Netherlands : Kluwer Law and Taxation Publishers, 1986.
Includes index.
ISBN 9065442715 Hbk

DECEDENTS' FAMILY MAINTENANCE – CANADA – MANITOBA

—Report on 'The Testators Family Maintenance Act' / Manitoba Law Reform Commission. – Winnipeg : The Commission, 1985.
iii,125p. – (Report).
Includes bibliographical references.
ISBN 0771101201

DECEDENTS' FAMILY MAINTENANCE - ENGLAND

—Family provision : law and practice / by John G. Ross Martyn. – 2nd ed. – London : Sweet & Maxwell, 1985.
xviii,187p; 22cm.
Previous ed.: published as The modern law of family provision. 1978. Includes index.
ISBN 0421342803 £14.50

DECEDENTS' FAMILY MAINTENANCE - GREAT BRITAIN

—Tyler's family provision / R. D. Oughton. – 2nd ed. – Abingdon : Professional Books, 1984.
xlvi,408p.
Includes index.
ISBN 0862050758

DECEDENTS' FAMILY MAINTENANCE - NORTHERN IRELAND

—Women and children first : the legal obligation to make provision on death for family and dependants / lecture delivered to the Belfast Solicitors' Association by Norma Dawson. – Belfast : SLS Legal Publications, 1984.
45p.
Bibliography: p.46.

DECEDENTS' FAMILY MAINTENANCE - SOUTH AFRICA

—Review of the law of succession : the introduction of a legitimate portion or the granting of a right to maintenance to the surviving spouse / South African Law Commission. – Pretoria : The Commission, 1987.
x,46p. – (Report).
Bibliography: pp.v-ix. Includes draft legislation.
ISBN 0621113603

DECENTRALISATION IN GOVERNMENT

—Decentralisation of local government at neighbourhood level / ... prepared by the Secretariat of the Steering Committee for Regional and Municipal Matters with the assistance of Sven-Runo Bergqvist. – Strasbourg : Council of Europe, 1981.
30p.

DECENTRALISATION IN GOVERNMENT - AFRICA

—Local government in the Third World : the experience of tropical Africa / edited by Philip Mawhood. – Chichester : Wiley, 1983.
xiii,261p; 24cm. – (A Wiley series on public administration in developing countries).
Includes bibliographies and index.
ISBN 0471105104 Unpriced

DECENTRALISATION IN GOVERNMENT - GREAT BRITAIN

—Northern Ireland : a framework for devolution / presented to Parliament by the Secretary of State for Northern Ireland. – London : H.M.S.O., 1982.
17p.
ISBN 0101854102

DECISION-MAKING

—Edited versions of selected papers from the international conference on 'Logic, Informatics, Law', Florence, Italy, April 1981 / Constantino Ciampi. – Amsterdam : North Holland Publishing, 1982.
xii,476p.
Bibliographies.

vol.2 : Deontic logic, computational linguistics, and legal information systems : Antonio A. Martino; editor 1982.
xli,518p.
Bibliographies.

—Reason and reality / Stig Jrgensen. – Aarhus : Aarhus University Press, 1986.
159p.
Includes bibliographical references.
ISBN 8772880023

DECISION-MAKING - CANADA

—Law and Legality : Materials on Legal Decision Making / Butterworths, 1982.
592p.
Describes the institutions of law and identifies the decision makers, and poses questions about the limits of decision making authority. Cases have been selected to increase awareness of the interactions amongst legal decision makers, giving an understanding of the attributes, limits and potential of the legal system.
ISBN 0409824003 Pbk £50.00

—Law and Legality : Materials on Legal Decision Making / Donald J. C. Galloway. – Toronto : Butterworths, 1980.
560p.

DECISION-MAKING - EUROPEAN COMMUNITY

—Policy-making in the European Community / edited by Helen Wallace, William Wallace and Carol Webb. – 2nd ed. – Chichester : Wiley, 1983.
xv,451p; 24cm.
Previous ed.: 1977. Includes index.
ISBN 0471901490
ISBN 0471901504 Pbk

DECISION-MAKING - GREAT BRITAIN

—Decision Making in Magistrates' Courts / Sturges. – London : Fourmat, 1986.
ISBN 1851900179 Pbk £4.95

—Policy arguments in judicial decisions / Oxford : Oxford University Press, 1983.
ISBN 0198255225 Pbk £9.50

DECLARATORY JUDGMENTS - AUSTRALIA

—Declaratory Orders / 2nd ed. – Butterworths, 1984.
276p.
ISBN 0409493538 Hbk £62.00

DECLARATORY JUDGMENTS - CANADA

—Law of Declaratory Judgments / 2nd ed. – Agincourt : Carswell, 1988.
300p.

DECLARATORY JUDGMENTS - ENGLAND

—Family law : declarations in family matters / The Law Commission. – London : H.M.S.O., 1984.
iv,82p; 25cm. – (H.C.).
ISBN 0102263841

DECLARATORY JUDGMENTS - GREAT BRITAIN

—Declaratory Orders / 2nd ed. – London : Butterworths, 1984.
ISBN 0409493538 Hbk £46.00

—Zamir : Declaratory Judgements / Repr. of 1962 ed. – London : Sweet & Maxwell, 1986.
– (Sweet and Maxwell Library Reprints).
ISBN 0421355700 Hbk

DECRIMINALIZATION - GREAT BRITAIN

—Justice annual members' conference held in the Lord Chief Justice's Court on Saturday 27 March 1982 : subject, decriminalisation / Chairman, Sir Derek Hodgson. – London : Justice, 1982.
35 leaves.

DEEDS - BRITISH COLUMBIA

—Deeds and seals / Law Reform Commission of British Columbia. – Victoria : Government of British Columbia, 1987.
ii,39p. – (Working paper).
Includes bibliographical references.
ISBN 0771886020

DEFAULT (FINANCE)

—Default and rescheduling : corporate and sovereign borrowers / edited by David Suratgar. – London : Euromoney, in association with International Law Institute, Washington D.C., 1984.
viii,163p.
'Two international conferences, one in London in late 1981 and the other in New York in 1982, provided the basis for this book' - Editor's preface.
ISBN 0903121530

DEFENCE - EUROPE

—Future of European defence : proceedings of the Second International Round Table Conference of the Netherlands Atlantic Commission on May 24 and 25, 1985 / Frans Bletz and Rio Praaning editors. – Dordrecht : M. Nijhoff, 1986.
ISBN 9024732905 pbk.

DEFENCE (CRIMINAL PROCEDURE) - AUSTRALIA

—Criminal Defences / P. A. Fairall. – 2nd ed. – Sydney : Butterworths, 1988.
288p.

—Criminal Defences / P.A. Fairall. – 2nd ed. – Butterworths, 1988.
250p.
ISBN 0409492760 Hbk £49.00

DEFENCE (CRIMINAL PROCEDURE) - CANADA

—Criminal Law Defences / Agincourt : Carswell, 1987.
200p.

—Criminal Law Defences / Agincourt : Carswell.
200p.
This text contains a comprehensive summary of the 40 defenses used in Canadian criminal law. Principles for application of the defenses and more in-depth information is also included. The main topic headings include exemptions, justifications, excuses, procedural and other defenses.

—Defence Lawyers Trial Book / Fletcher Dawson. – Toronto : Butterworths.

—Defence Lawyers Trial Book / D. Fletcher Dawson. – Toronto : Butterworths.

DEFENCE (CRIMINAL PROCEDURE) - CANADA - SASKATCHEWAN

—Proposals for defences to provincial offences : report to the Minister of Justice / Law Reform Commission of Saskatchewan. – Saskatoon : The Commission, 1986.
18p.
Includes bibliographical references.

DEFENCE (CRIMINAL PROCEDURE) - GREAT BRITAIN

—Defending Lawyer's Practical Guide / 2nd ed. – London : Beattie (Derek), 1984.
ISBN 0907591035 Pbk £8.50

—Guide to Conducting a Criminal Defence / London : Oyez Longman, 1980.

DEFENCE (CRIMINAL PROCEDURE) - NEW ZEALAND

—Defence of Compulsion : an Overview / Auckland : Legal Research Foundation, 1982.

DEFENCE (CRIMINAL PROCEDURE) - SCOTLAND

—Defender / Joseph Beltrami : with a foreword by Nicholas Fairbairn : introduction by William Allsopp. – Edinburgh : W. and R. Chambers, 1980.
8,238p; 23cm.
Includes index.
ISBN 0550203540 £7.95

DEFENCE (CRIMINAL PROCEDURE) - USSR

—Right of the accused to defence in the USSR / Yuri Stetsovsky : translated from the Russian by H. Campell Creighton. – Moscow : Progress Publishers, 1982.
283 p.; 21 cm.
Includes bibliographical references and index.

DELEGATED LEGISLATION

—Commonwealth Conference of Delegated Legislation Committees / Senate Standing Committee on Regulations and Ordinances. – 3 v. – Canberra : Australian Government Publishing Service, 1981.
– (Parliamentary Paper).
Includes bibliography: v.2.p101-102. Contents: v.1.Report of the Conference - v.2.Documents of the Conference - v.3.Transcripts of proceedings.
ISBN 0642057923

—Second Commonwealth Conference on Delegated Legislation / 3 v. – Ottawa? : Queen's Printer, 1983.
Contents: v.1. Report of the conference - v.2. Documents of the conference - v.3. Transcript of proceedings.

DELEGATED LEGISLATION - AUSTRALIA

—Report to Parliament on the Subordinate Legislation (Deregulation) Bill 1983 / Legal and Constitutional Committee. – Melbourne : Parliament of Victoria, 1984.
lxiv,474p.
Bibliography: p.450-474.

DELEGATED LEGISLATION - AUSTRALIA - VICTORIA

—Eighth report to Parliament on subordinate legislation : concerning Metropolitan Fire Brigades Superannuation (Board Scheme) (Further Amendment) Regulations 1986 ... / Legal and Constitutional Committee. – Melbourne : Government Printer, 1987.
v,4p.

—Eleventh report to Parliament on subordinate legislation concerning Freedom of Information (Exemption Offices) Regulations 1987 (SR NO.266/1987 ... / Legal and Constitutional Committee. – Melbourne : Government Printer, 1987.
ix,58p.
Includes text of legislation.

—Fifth report to Parliament on subordinate legislation concerning Film (Amendment) Regulations 1985 ... / Legal and Constitutional Committee. – Melbourne : Government Printer, 1986.
v,4p.

—First report to Parliament on subordinate legislation / Legal and Constitutional Committee. – Melbourne : Government Printer, 1986.
vii,11p.

—Fourth report to Parliament on subordinate legislation concerning Health (Tobacco packages - warnings) Regulations 1986 ... / Legal and Constitutional Committee. – Melbourne : Government Printer, 1986.
vi,48p.

—Ninth report to Parliament on subordinate legislation concerning Fishing (Abalone Licence Fee) Regulations 1987 (Statutory Rule no. 65/1987) / Legal and Constitutional Committee. – Melbourne : Government Printer, 1987.
vi,12p.
Includes Minority report.

—Second report to Parliament on subordinate legislation / Legal and Constitutional Committee. – Melbourne : Government Printer, 1986.
vii,5p.

—Seventh report to Parliament on subordinate legislation concerning Teaching Service ... Regulations 1986 ... / Legal and Constitutional Committee. – Melbourne : Government Printer, 1986.
v,5p.

—Sixth report to Parliament on subordinate legislation concerning County Court (Bailiff's Fees) Order 1986 ... / Legal and Constitutional Committee. – Melbourne : Government Printer, 1986.
v,11p.

—Tenth report to Parliament on subordinate legislation concerning the issues of Premier's certificates / Legal and Constitutional Committee. – Melbourne : Government Printer, 1987.
v,12p.

—Third report to Parliament on subordinate legislation concerning Adoption (Inter County Adoption Fees) Regulations 1986 ... / Legal and Constitutional Committee. – Melbourne : Government Printer, 1986.
v,8p.

—Twelfth report to Parliament on subordinate legislation concerning Melbourne and Metropolitan Board of Works By-law no. 235 : Melbourne and Metropolitan Board of Works Employees' Superannuation Fund Regulations (SR No. 231/1987) / Legal and Constitutional Committee. – Melbourne : Government Printer, 1988.
v,7p.
Includes text of legislation.

DELEGATED LEGISLATION - ENGLAND

—Challenging delegated legislation / Keith Puttick. – London : Waterlow, 1988.
xxxiv,315p; 30cm. – (Waterlow practitioner's library).
Includes index.
ISBN 0080330711 £19.95

DELEGATED LEGISLATION - GREAT BRITAIN

—Challenging Delegated Legislation / Waterlow, 1988.
ISBN 0080330711 Hbk £19.95

—Halsbury's Statutory Instruments, 23 Vols. / London : Butterworths.
This 23 volume work provides a complete reference to every statutory instrument in force and of general application in England and Wales. A separate volume of consolidated index is included in the work.

—Halsbury's Statutory Instruments, 24 Vols. / Abingdon : Professional Books.

DELINQUENCY - GREAT BRITAIN

—Delinquency and Citizenship / Oxford : Oxford University Press, 1987.
ISBN 0198226640 Hbk £30.00

—Good Girls Gone Bad / London : Futura, 1988.
ISBN 0356151603 Pbk £11.95

DELINQUENCY - UNITED STATES

—Girls in the gang : a report from New York City / Anne Campbell. – Oxford : Blackwell, 1984.
vii,277p; 24cm.
Study of girls in New York City gangs.
ISBN 0631133747 Hbk

DELIVERY OF GOODS (LAW) - GREAT BRITAIN

—Goods and services - the new law / by Geoffrey F. Woodroffe. – London : Sweet & Maxwell, 1982.
xviii,164p; 22cm.
Includes index.
ISBN 0421302003 Pbk £9.85

DELIVERY OF GOODS (LAW) - IRELAND

—Sale of goods and supply of services : a guide to the legislation / Vincent Grogan, Thelma King and Edward J. Donelan. – Dublin : Incorporated Law Society of Ireland, 1983.
xxii,133p.
Includes index.
ISBN 0902027239

DEMOCRACY

—Constitutional code / F. Rosen, J. H. Burns. – Oxford : Clarendon Press, 1983.
xlv,612p,2folded leaves of plates; 24cm. – (The Collected works of Jeremy Bentham).
Includes index. Author: Jeremy Bentham.
ISBN 019822608X Unpriced

—Jeremy Bentham and representative democracy : a study of the Constitutional code / Frederick Rosen. – Oxford : Clarendon Press, 1983.
vi,255p; 23cm.
Bibliography: p243-248. - Includes index.
ISBN 019822656X £19.50

—Law, socialism and democracy / Paul Q. Hirst. – London : Allen & Unwin, 1986.
200p; 22cm.
Includes bibliography and index.
ISBN 0043012531 Hbk £15.00 :
ISBN 004301254X Pbk £6.95

—New forms of democracy / edited by David Held and Christopher Pollitt. – London : Sage in association with the Open University, 1987.
256p; 22cm.
Includes bibliography and index.
ISBN 0803980124 Pbk £20.00
ISBN 0803980132 £7.50

DEMOCRACY - AFRICA

—Law and democracy in Africa / by Richard Akinjide. – Lagos : Office of the President, Department of Information, 1981.
22p.

DEMOCRACY - GREAT BRITAIN

—Democracy and Direct Action in Contemporary Europe / Exeter : European Atlantic Movement, 1982.

—Representation, Democracy and Public Law / London : Sweet & Maxwell, 1985.
– (Modern Legal Studies Ser.).

DEPORTATION - AUSTRALIA

—Human rights and the deportation of convicted aliens and immigrants / Canberra : Australian Government Publishing Service, 1983.
vii,31p. – (Report).
ISBN 0644026367

—Rights of review under the Migration Act 1958 and related legislation : interim report on the constitution for the Administrative Appeals Tribunal : report to the Attorney-General / Administrative Review Council. – Canberra : Australian Government Publishing Service, 1983.
v,6p. – (Report).
ISBN 0644028432

DEPRECIATION ALLOWANCES - GREAT BRITAIN

—Capital allowances / by John W. Shock. – 2nd ed. – London : Sweet & Maxwell, 1984.
xxiii,371p; 25cm.
Previous ed.: London : Oyez, 1981. Includes index.
ISBN 0421328207 Pbk £16.95

DEREGULATION - GREAT BRITAIN

—Deregulation for small private companies / Institute of Directors. – London : Institute of Directors, 1986.
13 leaves.

DESCRIPTIVE CATALOGUING

—Concise AACR2 : being a rewritten and simplified version of Anglo-American cataloguing rules, second edition / prepared by Michael Gorman. – Chicago : American Library Association, 1981.
ix,164p; 23cm.
Includes index.
ISBN 0853657335 Pbk Unpriced
ISBN 0838903258

—ISBD(M) : International Standard Bibliographic Description for Monographic Publications / recommended by the ISBD Review Committee : approved by the Standing Committee of the IFLA Section on Cataloguing. – Rev ed. – London : IFLA Universal Bibliographic Control and International MARC Programme, 1987.
viii,62p.
Includes index.

—ISBD (NBM) : International Standard Bibliographic Description for Non-Book Materials / International Federation of Library Associations and Institutions. – Rev. ed. – London : IFLA Universal Bibliographic Control and International MARC Programme, 1987.
vii,74p; 30cm.
Previous ed.: 1977. Includes index.
ISBN 0903043467 Pbk No price

—ISBD(S) : International Standard Bibliographic Description for Serials / International Federation of Library Associations and Institutions. – Rev ed. – London : IFLA Universat Bibliographic Control and International MARC Programme, 1987.
viii,76p; 30cm.
Previous ed.: i.e., 1st standard ed., 1977. Includes index.
ISBN 0903043491 Pbk No price

DETECTIVES - CANADA

—Making crime a study of detective work / Richard V. Ericson. – Toronto : Butterworths, 1981.
xiii,257p.
Bibliography: p243-254.

DETENTION OF PERSONS

—Right to liberty and the rights of persons deprived of their liberty as guaranteed by Article 5 of the European Convention on Human Rights / Strasbourg : Council of Europe, 1981.
22p; 30cm.
'Prepared by the Council of Europe Directorate of Human Rights'.

DETENTION OF PERSONS - CANADA

—Compelling appearance, interim release and pre-trial detention / Law Reform Commission of Canada. – Ottawa : The Commission, 1988.
138,150p. – (Working paper).
Added t.p. in French: Les mesures assurant la comparution, la mise en liberte provisoire et la detention avant le proces. Pages numbered in opposite directions. Text in English and French.
ISBN 0662558960

DETENTION OF PERSONS - CHINA

—China : violations of human rights : prisoners of conscience and the death penalty in the People's Republic of China / Amnesty International. – London : Amnesty International Publications, 1984.
129p.
ISBN 0862100739

DETENTION OF PERSONS - ENGLAND

—Detention at the police station under the Police and Criminal Evidence Act 1984 / by David Brown. – London : HMSO, 1989.
v,88p.
Bibliography: pp.78-80. 'A Home Office Research and Planning Unit Report'. - T.p..
ISBN 0113409087

—First report from the Home Affairs Committee, session 1983-84 : remands in custody / Great Britain. – London : H.M.S.O., 1984.
xxxiip. – (HC 252-I).
ISBN 0102939845

Vol. 2 : Minutes of evidence and appendices 1984.
vii,200p. – (HC252-II).

—Government reply to the first report from the Home Affairs Committee, session 1983-84 HC 252, Remands in custody / presented to Parliament by the Secretary of State for the Home Department. – London : H.M.S.O., 1984.
5p.
ISBN 0101932200

—Intermittent custody / presented to Parliament by the Secretary of State for the Home Department. – London : H.M.S.O., 1984.
17p.
ISBN 0101928106

—Remands in custody : evidence on House of Commons Home Affairs Committee / Justice. – London : Justice, 1984.
3 leaves.

DETENTION OF PERSONS - EUROPEAN COMMUNITY

—Case-law on Article 5 of the Convention for the Protection of Human Rights and Fundamental Freedoms / by Marc-Andre Eissen. – Strasbourg : European Court of Human Rights, 1986.
40p.
ISBN 9287107769

DETENTION OF PERSONS - GREAT BRITAIN

—Prevention of Terrorism Act : the case for repeal / Catherine Scorer and Patricia Hewitt. – London : National Council for Civil Liberties, 1981.
68p; 20cm.
ISBN 0901108944 Pbk £1.75

DETENTION OF PERSONS - INDIA

—Preventive Detention under Indian Constitution / New Delhi : Deep and Deep Publications, 1986.
324p.

—Supreme Court on Preventive Detention, 1950 to Date / Lucknow : Eastern Book Company, 1985.
478p.

DETENTION OF PERSONS - SOUTH AFRICA

—Detention and Torture in South Africa / DENT, 1987.
ISBN 0852553188 Pbk £7.95

—Detention Without Trial in South Africa 1976-1977 / South Africa Institute of Race Relations. – Johannesburg : South African Institute of Race Relations.

—Security, terrorism, and torture : detainees' rights in South Africa and Israel : a comparative study / by Harold Rudolph. – Cape Town : Juta, 1984.
xviii, 270 p.; 22 cm.
Includes indexes. Bibliography: p. 253-259.
ISBN 0702115088 pbk. R38.00

DETERRENCE (STRATEGY)

—Deterrence in the 1980s : crisis and dilemma / edited by R.B. Byers. – London : Croom Helm, 1985.
235p; 22cm.
Includes index.
ISBN 070993288X £18.95

—Nuclear deterrence, morality and realism / John Finnis, Joseph M. Boyle, Jr., Germain Grisez. – Oxford : Clarendon, 1987.
xv,429p; 22cm.
Bibliography: p391-411. - Includes index.
ISBN 0198247923 Hbk £30.00
ISBN 0198247915 Pbk no price

DETINUE - AUSTRALIA - SOUTH AUSTRALIA

—Report ... relating to the law of detinue, conversion and trespass to goods / Law Reform Committee of South Australia. – Adelaide : Government Printer, 1987.
100p. – (95th report).
Bibliography: p.99-100.

DEVELOPING COUNTRIES

—Application of new legal techniques to mining agreements in developing countries / by Carl W. Dundas. – London : Commonwealth Secretariat, 1981.
46p.
Includes bibliographical references.

—Challenges to the Legal Profession : Law and Investment in Developing Countries / International Bar Association. – Lucknow : Eastern Book Company, 1985.
807p.

—Copyright system : practice and problems in developing countries / by Denis de Freitas. – London : Commonwealth Secretariat, 1983.
v,87p.
ISBN 085092233X

—Creation of world poverty / Teresa Hayter. – London : Pluto Press, 1981.
128p.
Bibliography: p.124-127.
ISBN 0861043391

—Criteria for energy pricing policy : a collection of papers commissioned for the Energy Pricing Policy Workshop organized under the Regional Energy Development Programme (RAS/84/001), Bangkok, 8-11 May 1984 / edited by Corazon Morales Siddayao. – London : Graham & Trotman, 1985.
247p; 24cm.

—Developing countries in the GATT legal system / by Robert E. Hudec. – Aldershot : Gower for the Trade Policy Research Centre, 1987.
xix,259p.
Bibliography: p.236-250..
ISBN 0566056976

—Developing Countries Western Interests and Actions / Exeter : European Atlantic Movement, 1982.

—Eritrea : 25 Years of Struggle for Independence / Basil Davidson. – London : Spokesman Books, 1988.
150p. – (A Eutical Appraisal).
ISBN 085124453X Pbk £19.95
ISBN 0851244637 Pbk £5.95

—IMF and stabilisation : developing country experiences / directed and edited by Tony Killick : contributors : Graham Bird ... et al. – London : Gower in association with the Overseas Development Institute, 1985.
viii,216p; 22cm.
Originally published: London : Heinemann Educational in association with the Overseas Development Institute, 1984. Includes bibliographies.
ISBN 0566050412 £13.45

—International law and the developing countries : confrontation or cooperation? / R.P. Anand. – Dordrecht : Martinus Nijhoff, 1987.
xii, 274p.
Includes index and bibliographies.
ISBN 902473438X Hbk £125.00

—Land for housing the poor / edited by Shlomo Angel ... et al. – Singapore : Select Books, 1983.
ix,556p; 22cm.
Papers from a seminar, 'Land for Housing the Poor: Towards Positive Action in Asian Cities' held in Bangkok, 18th and 31st Jan. 1982.
ISBN 9971835517

—Lawyers in the Third World : comparative and developmental perspectives / edited by C.J. Dias ... et al. – Uppsala : Scandinavian Institute of African Studies, 1981.
400p; 22cm.
Bibliography: p.382-399. Sponsored by the Scandinavian Institute of African Studies and the International Center for Law in Development.
ISBN 9171061797 Hbk £25.00 (20.00 in Third World Countries)
ISBN 9171061762 Pbk £16.00 (8.00 in Third World countries)

—Policies in the Developed Countries / London : British-North American Research Association, 1983.

—Political economy of underdevelopment / S.B.D. de Silva. – London : Routledge & Kegan Paul in association with the Institute of Southeast Asian Studies, Singapore, 1983.
viii,645p; 22cm.
Includes index.
ISBN 0710202733 Pbk £12.50

—Principles of international development law : progressive development of the principles of international law relating to the new international economic order / Milan Bulajic. – Dordrecht, Netherlands : Martinus Nijhoff Publishers, 1986.
403p.
Bibliography: p.359-366.
ISBN 9024733049

—Public finance in developing countries / A. R. Prest. – 3rd ed. – London : Weidenfeld and Nicolson, 1985.
xiii,236p.
Bibliography: p226-228.
ISBN 0297785788

—Regulation of international economic relations through law / by Palitha Tikiri Bandara Kohona. – Dodrecht : M. Nijhoff Publishers, 1985.
Based on author's thesis (Ph. D.)–Cambridge University.
ISBN 9024731046

—Roles of Labour Law in Developing Countries : Record of Proceedings of, and Documents Submitted to, a Round Table (Geneva, 10-14 September and Selva di Fasano, Italy, 17-19 September 1974) / Geneva : International Labour Office, 1975.
iii, 266p.
ISBN 9221012875 Hbk £27.50

—Sustainable development : exploring the contradictions / Michael Redclift. – London : Methuen, 1987.
viii,200p; 22cm.
Includes index.
ISBN 0416902405 Hbk £20.00 :
ISBN 0416902502 Pbk £7.95

—Third World Attitudes Toward International Law : an Introduction / S. Sathirathai. – Dordrecht : Kluwer, 1987.
852p.
ISBN 0898389143 Hbk £375.00

—Third World city / David Drakakis-Smith. – London : Methuen, 1987.
vi,116p; 21cm. – (Methuen introductions to development).
Includes bibliography and index.
ISBN 041691960X Pbk No price
ISBN 0416919707

—Trade Policy Issues of Interest to the Third World / London : Trade Policy Research Centre, 1981.
76p.

—Woman's role in economic development / Ester Boserup. – Aldershot : Gower, 1986.
283p.
Originally published: George Allen & Unwin, 1970. Bibliography: pp.263-275. - Includes index. Published in association with the London School of Economics and Political Science.
ISBN 0566051397

DEVELOPMENT LAND TAXES – GREAT BRITAIN

—Development Land Tax 1976-1980 / London : HMSO, 1980.
– (Taxes Act Ser.).
ISBN 0116412313 Pbk £9.95

Supplement 1982
ISBN 0116413670 Hbk £0.95

Supplement 1983
ISBN 0116413697 Hbk £0.40

—Development Land Tax Guide / Tony Johnson. – London : Butterworths, 1984.
ISBN 040626287X Pbk

—Taxation of Land Development / Sheila Parrington. – London : Butterworths.

DEVELOPMENT LAND TAXES – SINGAPORE

—Development Land and Development Charge in Singapore / Butterworths, 1987.
215p.
ISBN 0409995371 Hbk £75.00

DEVIANT BEHAVIOUR

—Deviance, reality and society / Steven Box. – 2nd ed. – London : Holt, Rinehart and Winston, 1981.
vii,248p; 22cm.
Previous ed.: 1971. Includes bibliographies and index.
ISBN 0039102947 Pbk £4.95

—Transcarceration : essays in the sociology of social control / edited by John Lowman, Robert J. Menzies, T.S. Palys. – Aldershot : Gower, 1987.
x,370p; 22cm.
Includes bibliography and index.
ISBN 0566051060 £19.50

—Understanding deviance : a guide to the sociology of crime and rule-breaking / David Downes and Paul Rock. – 2nd ed. – Oxford : Clarendon Press, 1988.
viii,369p.
Bibliography: pp.335-360. - Includes index.
ISBN 0198762135 pbk.

—Visions of social control : crime, punishment and classification / Stanley Cohen. – Cambridge : Polity, 1984.
300p.
ISBN 0745600204 Hbk £19.50
ISBN 0745600212 Pbk £7.95

DEVIANT BEHAVIOUR – CANADA

—Deviant Designations : Crime Law and Deviance in Canada / Visano. – Toronto : Butterworths, 1983.
512p.
Examines the reaction of communities to crime; issues involved in creating deviant designations and controlling the careers of those deemed deviant or criminal; the response of formal agents and agencies of social control (courts, police, and prisons) to be discredited, and emerging theoretical concerns.
ISBN 0409829846 Pbk £25.95

DEVOLUTION – NORTHERN IRELAND

—Northern Ireland Act 1982 : Do-It-Yourself Devolution / Belfast : Queen's University of Belfast.
25p.

DICTIONARIES

—Banking Dictionary / Cambridge : Woodhead-Faulkner, 1984.
ISBN 3478512433 Hbk £25.00

—Biographical Dictionary of Common Law / London : Butterworths, 1984.
ISBN 040651657X Hbk £32.00

—Building Contract Dictionary / Chappel. – London : Architectural Press, 1985.
ISBN 0851397581 Hbk £35.00

—Building Contract Dictionary : An Architectural Press Legal Guide / David Chappell. – London : Architectural Press, 1985.
464p : Illus.
ISBN 0851397581 Hbk £35.00

—Butterworth's Dictionary of Company Law / 2nd ed. – Wellington : Butterworths, 1985.
A practical guide to company law of the United Kingdom, this book gives brief details of the Companies Act provisions relating to the terms defined within. Technical phrases from business and finance are listed along with legal terms.
ISBN 0406681635 Hbk
ISBN 0406681643 Pbk

—Canada Tax Words, Phrases and Rules / Toronto : DeBoo, 1986.
ISBN 0888202504 Hbk £160.00

Supplements
This work identifies words, phrases, and rules judicially considered in income tax cases from 1917 to the present. The alphabetical arrangement allows the reader to compare all definitions of a particular word or phrase. Cross-references and annotations are also included. Annual supplements are planned.

—Concise Dictionary of Accounting and Finance / Pitman, 1986.
ISBN 0712106847 Pbk £4.95

—Concise dictionary of law / Oxford : Oxford University Press, 1983.
ISBN 019253990 Hbk £13.95
ISBN 0192851357 Pbk £4.95

—Concise dictionary of law / editor Elizabeth A. Martin. – Oxford : Oxford University Press, 1983.
394p; 21cm.
ISBN 0198253990 £9.95

—Construction Contract Dictionary / Reading : College of Estate Management, 1981.
120p.
ISBN 0902132652 Hbk £12.30
ISBN 0902132636 Pbk £7.50

—Decisions of the Court of Session : Abridged in Form of a Dictionary / Woodhouselee. – Repr. of 1741 ed. – Abingdon : Professional Books.
57p.

—Dictionary Legal/Commercial Terms : German/English, 2 Vols. / Rutter. – London : Butterworths, 1984.
ISBN 0406038104 Hbk £98.00

—Dictionary of Accounting Terms / London : Financial Training, 1985.
ISBN 0906322677 Pbk £8.95

—Dictionary of arbitration law & practice / Eric Lee. – London : Mansfield Law Publishers, 1986.
185p.

—Dictionary of Arbitration Law and Practice / London : LLoyd's of London Press, 1987.
ISBN 1850441243 Hbk

—Dictionary of banking / F.E. Perry. – 3rd ed. – London : Pitman, 1988.
356p; 19cm.
Previous ed.: Plymouth : Macdonald and Evans, 1983.
ISBN 0712107657 Pbk £9.95
ISBN 0273029614

—Dictionary of banking / F.E. Perry. – 2nd ed. – Plymouth : Macdonald and Evans, 1983.
385p; 23cm. – (M & E professional dictionaries).
Previous ed: 1979.
ISBN 0712104321 Hbk £12.50
ISBN 0712104372 Pbk No price

—Dictionary of Banking and Finance / London : Pitman Publishing, 1985.
ISBN 0273018590 Hbk £35.00

—Dictionary of Business Biography / London : Butterworths, 1984.
ISBN 0406273413 Hbk £72.00

Vol. 2 D-G 1984.
ISBN 0406273421 Hbk £72.00

Vol. 3 H-L 1985.
ISBN 040627343X Hbk £72.00

Vol. 4 M-R 1985.
ISBN 0406273448 Hbk £72.00

Vol. 5 S-Z 1986.
ISBN 0406273456 Hbk £72.00

—Dictionary of Business Biography / London : Butterworths.
This work contains over 1000 biographies of British businessmen from 1860 to 1980. Each subject is treated in terms of his major successes and failures, innovations, and management style and policies.

—Dictionary of Commercial Law / London : Butterworths, 1983.
ISBN 0406681597 Hbk £15.00
ISBN 0406681600 Pbk £10.95

—Dictionary of commercial law / by A.H. Hudson. – London : Butterworths, 1983.
289p; 23cm. – (Butterworths professional dictionaries series).
A reference source on commercial law of the United Kingdom. Entries are arranged in alphabetical order, and all terms are fully described, rather than merely defined.
ISBN 0406681597 £17.00
ISBN 0406681600 £10.95

—Dictionary of Commercial Law / 2nd ed. – Plymouth : Macdonald & Evans, 1980.
992p.
ISBN 0712154892 Hbk £42.75

—Dictionary of Commercial Terms and Abbreviations / Witherby, 1984.
ISBN 0900886900 Pbk £9.50

—Dictionary of company law / by E.R. Hardy Ivamy. – London : Butterworths, 1983.
265p; 23cm. – (Butterworths professional dictionary series).
ISBN 0406681619 Hbk No price
ISBN 0406681627 Pbk No price

—Dictionary of criminology / edited by Dermot Walsh and Adrian Poole. – London : Routledge & Kegan Paul, 1983.
xi,242p.
ISBN 0710095562 pbk.

—Dictionary of Economics and Financial Markets / 5th ed. – London : Butterworths, 1986.
ISBN 0408015705 Hbk £19.95

—Dictionary of Economics and Financial Markets / 5th ed. – London : Butterworths, 1986.
This work contains definitions of economic terminology and concepts and topics related to contemporary applied economics and financial institutions. A bibliography is included in the text.
ISBN 0408015705 Pbk

—Dictionary of employment law / by Norman Selwyn. – London : Butterworths, 1985.
165p; 22cm. – (Butterworths professional dictionary series).
ISBN 0406207909 Hbk No price
ISBN 0406207917 Pbk No price

—Dictionary of Employment Law / London : Butterworths, 1985.
ISBN 0406207909 Hbk £17.00
ISBN 0406207917 Pbk £10.95

—Dictionary of insurance law / by E.R. Hardy Ivamy. – London : Butterworths, 1981.
– (Butterworths professional dictionary series).
This work contains terms in general use in marine as well as in non-marine insurance which have been legally defined in statute or case law. Many entries are accompanied by extracts from cited cases and statutes.
ISBN 0406603014 Pbk £14.95

—Dictionary of Insurance Law / London : Butterworths, 1981.
ISBN 0406603014 Pbk £10.95

—Dictionary of Insurance Terms English-Arabic / Witherby, 1985.
ISBN 090088696X Hbk £34.00

—Dictionary of International Commerce / London : Chapman & Hall, 1985.
ISBN 0412280108 Hbk £37.50

—Dictionary of Law / 2nd ed. Repr. of 1979 ed. – Plymouth : Macdonald & Evans, 1983.
viii, 416p. – (M and E Professional Dictionaries Series).
ISBN 0712104402 Hbk £10.95
ISBN 0712104399 Pbk £4.95

—Dictionary of Law / 3rd ed. – London : Pitman Publishing, 1988.
ISBN 0712107916 Pbk

—Dictionary of legal and commercial terms / Worterbuch der Rechts- und Wirtschaftssprache : by Alfred Romain. – 3rd rev. ed. – London : Butterworths, 1983.
x,841p.
Previous ed.: 1979.
ISBN 0406038112

Part 2 : German-English / Worterbuch der Rechts- und Wirtschaftssprache : by Alfred Romain in collaboration with Derek Rutter. – 1980.
848p.
ISBN 0406038120

—Dictionary of Legal Words and Phrases, 4 vols. /. – Durban : Butterworths.
ISBN 0409018929

Biennial cumulative suppls. avail. Third Cumulative Suppl. 1983.
ISBN 040901897X

—Dictionary of medical ethics / edited by A.S. Duncan, G.R. Dunstan and R.B. Welbourn. – Rev. and enl. ed. – London : Darton, Longman & Todd, 1981.
xxxi,459p; 23cm.
Previous ed.: 1977. Includes bibliographies.
ISBN 0232514925 £12.50

—Dictionary of Modern Legal Usage / Oxford : Oxford University Press, 1988.
ISBN 0195043774 Hbk £25.00

—Dictionary of Political Thought / London : Macmillan, 1982.
512p.
ISBN 0333334396 Hbk £12.00

—Dictionary of Shipping and International Trade Terms / 2nd ed. – Witherby, 1983.
ISBN 0900886706 Pbk £7.50

—Dictionary of shipping and shipbroking terms : French-English and English-French / Dictionnaire du transport et de l'affretement maritime : by Peter R. Brodie. – London : Lloyd's of London Press, 1980.
xvii,195p.
ISBN 0904093824

—Dictionary of Shipping Law / London : Butterworths, 1984.
ISBN 0406623996 Hbk £15.00
ISBN 0406624003 Pbk £10.95

—Dictionary of shipping law / by E.R. Hardy Ivamy. – London : Butterworths, 1984.
179p; 23cm. – (Butterworths professional dictionaries series).
ISBN 0406623996 Hbk No price
ISBN 0406624003 Pbk No price

—Dictionary of Shipping Spanish/English / London : Lloyd's of London Press, 1988.
ISBN 1850444537 Pbk

—Dictionary of shipping terms / by Peter R. Brodie. – London : Lloyd's of London, 1985.
155p; 22cm.
ISBN 1850440697 Pbk £15.00

—Dictionary of taxation / by Gerry Hart : consultant B.E.V. Sabine. – London : Butterworths, 1981.
v,236p; 23cm. – (Butterworths professional dictionaries series).
ISBN 040652159X Hbk £14.00
ISBN 0406521603 Pbk

—Dictionary of the European Communities / John Paxton. – 2nd ed. – London : Macmillan, 1984.
282p; 23cm.
Previous ed.: published as A dictionary of the European Economic Community. 1977. Bibliography: p279-282.
ISBN 0333334388 Hbk £25.00
ISBN 0333370376 Pbk Unpriced

—Dictionnaire Juridique Fr/Eng Eng/Fr / 2nd ed. – London : Edition de Navarre, 1984.
ISBN 2713300045 Pbk £31.00

—Elsevier's Fiscal and Customs Dictionary / Bauduin. – Amsterdam : Elsevier, 1988.
ISBN 0444428917 Hbk

—Encyclopedia of public international law / published under the auspices of the Max Planck Institute for Comparative Public Law and International Law : under the direction of Rudolf Bernhardt. – Amsterdam : North-Holland Pub. Co., 1981.
Issued in parts. Includes index.
ISBN 0444861408

—English-Italian Law Dictionary / London : Sweet & Maxwell, 1985.
ISBN 0421357401 Hbk £50.00

—European Communities glossary : French-English / Council of the European Communities, General Secretariat : Francais-Anglais : Conseil des Communautes europeennes, Secretariat general. – 7th ed. – Luxembourg : Office for Official Publications of the European Communities, 1980.
1182p; 25cm.
ISBN 9282400565

—International encyclopaedia for labour law and industrial relations / editor in chief: R. Blanpain. – n. – Deventer : Kluwer, 1977.
25cm.
Updated periodically by loose leaf supplement.

—International tax glossary / W. G Kuiper. – Amsterdam : International Bureau of Fiscal Documentation, 1988.
xii, 322 p.; 19 cm.
'Prepared by a working group ... headed by Mr. W.G. Kuiper'–P. iv. 'The first volume of a new series of books, entitled 'International tax manuals''–P. vi.
ISBN 9070125366

—Jane's aerospace dictionary / Bill Gunston. – London : Jane's, 1980.
ISBN 0531037029

—Jowitt's dictionary of English law / by the late Earl Jowitt and Clifford Walsh. – 2nd ed. – London : Sweet and Maxwell, 1977.
2v.(11,1935p); 26cm.
Gives a definition and explanation of old and new legal terms in English law. Covers arbitration, trade descriptions, latin maxims and the writings of Glanvil, Bracton, Fitzherbert, Coke, Hale and Blackstone. Also examines the organisation of relevant Ministries, and all new law and statutes of recent years.
ISBN 0421230908 £45.00

—Judicial Dictionary, 6 Vols. / London : Sweet & Maxwell.
ISBN 042137120X Pbk £5.00

—Latin Words and Phrases for Lawyers / London : LEBO, 1980.
ISBN 0889290040 Hbk £19.25

—Latin words & phrases for lawyers / editor-in-chief R.S. Vasan. – Don Mills, Ont : Datinder S. Sodhi for Law and Business Publications (Canada), 1980.
335p.
ISBN 0889290040

—Law and Commercial Dictionary - 5 Languages 2 vols. / West, 1985.
ISBN 0314805028 Hbk £170.00

—Law and commercial dictionary in five languages : definitions of the legal and commercial terms and phrases in American, English and civil law jurisdictions : English to German, Spanish, French, Italian / 2 v. – Munchen : Beck, 1985.
ISBN 031495502X

—Law Dictionary / Whiteley. – 10th ed. – London : Butterworths, 1988.
ISBN 0406625255 Hbk £6.50
ISBN 0406625263 Pbk

—Law Dictionary : Explaining the Rise, Progress, and Present State of the British Law, 2 Vols. / 3rd ed. Repr. of 1820 ed. – Abingdon : Professional Books.
259p.

—Law Dictionary : Interpreting Difficult and Obscure Words and Terms in Common or Statute, Ancient or Modern Laws / 2nd ed. Repr. of 1691 ed. – Abingdon : Professional Books.

—Law dictionary : technical dictionary of the Anglo-Americal legal terminology including commercial and political terms : English-German / von Beseler/Jacobs-Wustefeld. – 4th rev. and enl. ed. – Berlin : W. de Gruyter, 1986.
ISBN 0899251773

—Law Lexicon / rep. 1987. – Nagpur : Wadhura & Co.

—The Layman's Dictionary of English Law / London : Waterlow, 1984.
328p.
ISBN 0080391613 Hbk £8.00

—Layman's Dictionary of English Law / London : Waterlow, 1984.
ISBN 0080391613 Hbk £12.95

—Legal and Commercial Dictionary : English-Italian / Sydney : Butterworths, 1980.
182p.
ISBN 0409300217 Hbk

—Legal dictionary in four languages / 3rd. – London : Sweet & Maxwell, 1987.
Over 13,000 legal expressions are translated, or given corresponding meanings, in the four European languages of English, French, German, and Spanish.
ISBN 0421378204 Hbk £77

—Legal Thesaurus / London : Macmillan, 1980.
ISBN 0026910004 Hbk £38.50

—Macmillan Dictionary of International Finance / 2nd ed. – London : Macmillan, 1986.
ISBN 0333398343 Pbk £8.95

—Marine Encyclopaedic Dictionary / 2nd ed. – London : Lloyd's of London Press, 1988.
ISBN 1850441278 Hbk £37.50

—Mongolian-English-Russian dictionary of legal terms and concepts / compiled and edited by W.E. Butler and A.J. Nathanson. – The Hague : M. Nijhoff, 1982.
ISBN 9024726778

—Motor insurance : German and English / Berlin : Langenscheidt, 1980.
152p; 21cm.
Bibliography: p.10-13. - Includes index. Compiled by a commission of the International Institute for Legal and Administrative Terminology. Added t.p. in German: Kraftfahrtversicherung: Deutsch und Englisch.

—Mozley and Whiteley : Law Dictionary / 10th ed. – Toronto : Butterworths, 1988.
500p.

—Mozley and Whiteley's Law Dictionary / 10th ed. – Butterworths, 1988.
520p.
ISBN 0409308021 Pbk £17.00

—Multilingual Glossary of Tax, Financial and Commercial Terms / London : Oyez Longman, 1983.
ISBN 0851207618 Hbk £9.95

—New Zealand Law Dictionary / M.S. Hinde. – 3rd rev. ed. – Butterworths, 1986.
ISBN 0409787620 Pbk £60.50

—Ontario Health and Safety Guide : A Dictionary of Legal Compliance / Toronto : DeBoo, 1984.
This guidebook provides comprehensive discussion of the legal provisions affecting workplace health and safety in Ontario, Canada. The book is organized to provide quick reference in the design and review of workplace policies and procedures.
ISBN 0888201834 Hbk £85.00

—Osborn's Concise law dictionary / Roger Bird. – 7th ed. – London : Sweet & Maxwell, 1983.
vii,390p; 23cm.
Includes definitions of legal words and phrases, Roman law terms, and a list of Law Reports with their abbreviations. Many developments in the law since the sixth edition are included.
ISBN 0421296704 Hbk £7.50
ISBN 0421296801 Pbk £4.50

—Oxford companion to law / by David M. Walker. – Oxford : Clarendon Press, 1980.
1000p.
Includes bibliographies.
ISBN 019866110X £20.00

—Oxford companion to law / Oxford : Oxford University Press, 1980.
ISBN 019866110X Hbk £20.00

—Sownik prawniczy polsko-angielski [Polish-English law dictionary] / opracowanie redakcyjne Danuta Rydlewska-Szewczykowa, Jolanta Zaczkiewiczowa. – Wrocaw : Zakad Narodowy im. Ossolinskich, 1986.
211 p.; 21 cm.
English and Polish. Title on added t.p.: Polish-English dictionary of legal terms. At head of title: Polska Akademia Nauk. Instytut Panstwa i Prawa.
ISBN 8304018977 z500.00

—Strouds judicial dictionary of words and phrases / John S. James, Frederick Stroud. – 5th ed. 6 v. – London : Sweet & Maxwell, 1986.
Kept up to date by supplements.
ISBN 0421366303

—Supreme Court Guide to Words and Phrases / Calcutta : Eastern Law House, 1986.

—Terminology of business and company law / Bailey. – London : Kogan Page, 1987.
ISBN 0850914133 Pbk £8.95

—Vocabulary of Community Primary Law / Bernard de Mello. – Luxembourg : Office for Official Publications of the European Communities, 1985.
427p.
ISBN 9282554392 Pbk £1,200.00

1985 Provisional Version 1985.
365p.
ISBN 9282556522 Pbk £1,200.00

1986 Provisional Version 1986.
370p.
ISBN 928256486X Pbk £1,200.00

—Witherby dictionary of insurance / 2nd ed. – London : Witherby & Co, 1987.
ISBN 0948691212 Hbk £14.50

—Words and Phrases, 4 Vols. / Toronto : DeBoo.

—Words and Phrases, Legal Maxims, 3 Vols. / 4th ed. – Toronto : DeBoo, 1986.
ISBN 0888202482 Hbk £260.00

Supplements
This text provides meanings of words and phrases as interpreted by the Privy Council and the Federal and Provincial Courts of Canada. Semi-annual updates are planned.

—Words and Phrases Legally Defined / 3rd ed. – Butterworths, 1988-89.

Supplement-1988
ISBN 0409888486

Vol. 1
450p.
The definitions comprise direct quotations from statutes, judicial statements and Halsbury's Laws of England. Also includes materials from Canadian sources. Approximately 700 Canadian entries, with 385 recently decided cases. Also contains extracts from American sources in commercial law areas.
ISBN 0409888443 Hbk £75.00

Vol. 2
ISBN 0409888451

Vol. 3
ISBN 040988846X

Vol. 4
ISBN 0409888478

DICTIONARIES - AUSTRALIA

—Australian legal dictionary / by S. E. Marantelli. – West Melbourne, Vic. : Hargreen Publishing, 1980.
243p.
ISBN 0959669671

—Australian legal dictionary / by S.E. Marantelli. – 6th reprint. – Caulfield East, Victoria : Edward Arnold Australia, 1985.
242p.
ISBN 0713181184

DICTIONARIES - CANADA

—Mozley and Whiteley : Law Dictionary / 10th ed. – Butterworths, 1988.
ca 500p.
Explains the precise meaning of words and phrases, giving where relevant an historical account of the term, and if further information is required, a reference to either statutory case law or other authority.
ISBN 0406625255 Hbk £0406625263

DICTIONARIES - GREAT BRITAIN

—Legal lexicon of taxation / Charles H. Thomas. – Abingdon, Oxon : Professional Books, 1987.
139p; 23cm.
ISBN 0862050367

DICTIONARIES - SCOTLAND

—Laws of Scotland : Stair memorial encyclopaedia / James Dalrymple Stair. – v. – Edinburgh : The Law Society of Scotland, 1987.
Includes indexes.
ISBN 040623700X

DIFFAMATION - CANADA

—Law of libel and slander in Canada / Jeremy S. Williams. – 2nd ed. – Toronto : Butterworths, 1988.
xxxi, 145 p.; 24 cm.
Analysis of the law of defamation as it applies in each common law province of Canada, covering both jurisdictions which retain libel and slander as distinct torts, and jurisdictions which have adopted the Uniform Defamation Act. Covers the publication requirements, credit reporting and other commercial representations, limitation periods, damages and injunctions.
ISBN 0409876410 Hbk £57

DIGESTS

—Abridgment of New Zealand Case Law : 1861-1967, 16 Vols. / Wellington : Butterworths.
ISBN 0409600008 Hbk

Supplement-1962-1973

Supplement-1974-1978

Supplement 1980-to date

—Alberta Weekly Law Digest / Agincourt : Carswell, 1988.

—All England Law Reports Annual Review 1985 / London : Butterworths, 1986.
This work contains detailed analyses of decisions handed down in the Law Courts and the House of Lords during the previous year. The book is written for practitioners and students to provide synopses of current trends in English law.
ISBN 0406879621 Hbk £33.00

—All-India Criminal Digest, 1971-80, 3 Vols. / Allahabad : Law Book Company.

—All-India Quinquennial Criminal Digest, 3 Vols. / Allahabad : Law Book Company.

Vol. 1 : 1941-45

Vol 2 : 1946-50

Vol. 3 in preparation

—Anger's Digest of Canadian Law / 20th ed. – Aurora : Canada Law Book Co, 1987.
1032p.

—Anger's Digest of Canadian Law / 20th ed. – Aurora : Canada Law Book, 1987.

—Annual Digest of Income Tax Reports, 1986 / Madras : Company Law Institute of India, 1986.

—Australian and New Zealand commentary on Halsbury's Laws of England (Fourth Edition) / editor in chief, Garfield Barwick. – v. – Sydney : Butterworths, 1974-.
loose-leaf.
In 2 series: Australian commentary (vols. A-), and New Zealand commentary (vols. A-). Spine title: Commentary on Halsbury's laws of England. - Vol. A of New Zealand commentary has spine sub-title: Australia and New Zealand.

—Australian Sentencing Digest / North Ryde : Law Book Co, 1985.
li, 929p.

Supplement 1985
xvii, 194p.
ISBN 0455206112

—Bisset and Smith's Digest of South African Case Law /. – Abingdon : Professional Books.

Incl. First Consolidated Edition, 1904-21, 6 Vols.

Second Consolidated Edition, 1922-33, 2 Vols.

Third Consolidated Edition, 1934-45, 2 Vols.

Fourth Consolidated Edition, 1946-49, 1 Vol.

—British Columbia Decisions Civil Cases (1979-Present) / Aurora : Canada Law Book Co. – (Summary Services, Provincial Ser.).

—British Columbia Weekly Law Digest / Agincourt : Carswell, 1987.

—Butterworth's Ontario Digest, 14 vols / Toronto : Butterworths.

—Butterworths Law Digest : Malaysia / 2nd ed. – London : Butterworths, 1988.
ISBN 09515720 Hbk

—Canadian Encyclopedic Digest : Ontario, 38 Vols. / Carswell Legal Publications. – 3rd ed. – Agincourt : Carswell.
This set of volumes provides the provincial laws of Ontario and federal laws of Canada as derived from statutes and case law. The 150 subject titles contains an in-depth table of classifications and an index and tables of cases and statutes. A Research Guide and Key and The Legal Deskbook are also included.

—Canadian Parliamentary Digest / Agincourt : Carswell, 1987.

—Canadian Sentencing Digest : Quantam Service, 2 Vols. / Clarey B. Sproule. – Agincourt : Carswell, 1981.
This looseleaf service digest all Canadian cases an quantum of sentence from 1970 to the present. The work is organized by statute and section.

—Carswell's Family Law Digests, 9 Vols. / Agincourt : Carswell.
This text digests all the reported Canadian family law cases arranged according to the Canadian Abridgment classification system. This multi-volume set of books is supplemented by-annually. Special features include a Table of Cases, Index, and Cases and Statutes Judicially Considered.

—Chitty's Abridgment of Canadian Cases (1892-1970), 5 Vols. / Aurora : Canada Law Book Co.
– (Abridgments and Encyclopedias).

—Commercial Law Digest / Agincourt : Carswell.

—Complete Digest of Supreme Court Cases 1950 to Date, 16 Vols. / Lucknow : Eastern Book Company.

—Complete Supreme Court Criminal Digest 1950 to Date, 6 Vols. in 7 / Lucknow : Eastern Book Company, 1983.

—Construction Law Digest, 3 Vols. / London : Collins.

Vol. 3 1985.
490p.

—Criminal Law Digest, 9 Vols. / Rev. ed. – Agincourt : Carswell.
This work contains digests of all the reported Canadian criminal cases from 1800. It is a nine volume set that is supplemented every six months.

—Current Law Back Volumes : Year Book 1982 / London : Sweet & Maxwell.
ISBN 0421320605 Hbk £14.00

—Digest, 73 Vols. / Wellington : Butterworths.

—Digest : annotated British, Commonwealth and European cases : formerly the English and Empire Digest : a user's guide / London : Butterworths, 1983.
26p; 25cm.

—Digest of All India Control of Rent and Eviction Cases, 1970-1976 / Lucknow : Eastern Book Company, 1977.
136p.

—Digest of Australian Constitutional Cases / 2nd ed. – North Ryde : Law Book Co, 1982.
xvi, 359p.
ISBN 0455204748 Hbk £49.00
ISBN 0455204756 Pbk £37.50

—Digest of Case-Law Relating to the European Communities / Kirchberg : Commission of the European Communities, 1983.
1400p. – (A Ser.: Judgements of the Court of Justice of the European Communities).

—Digest of Case-Law Relating to the European Communities / Kirchberg : Commission of the European Communities, 1984.
– (D Ser.: Case-Law on the Convention of 27 September 1968).

—Digest of Cases Decided in the Supreme Courts of Scotland From 1800-1852 / Repr. of 1867 ed. – Abingdon : Professional Books.
104p.

—Digest of Central Excise and Customs Cases / Nagpur : Wadhura & Co, 1987.
1,425p.

—Digest of Customary Law in the Punjab / 15th ed. – Allahabad : Universal Book Agency, 1980.

—Digest of Industrial and Labour Law Cases / Woolloomooloo : International Business Communications, 1983.
430p.

—Digest of Industrial Labour Law Cases / 1st ed. – London : Legal Books, 1983.
ISBN 0949553013 Hbk £20.00
ISBN 0949553018 Pbk £15.00

—Digest of Northern Ireland Law / Valerie Mitchell. – Belfast : Queen's University of Belfast, 1986.

—Digest of Supreme Court Sales Tax Cases 1950-1987 / Allahabad : Modern Law Publications, 1987.

—Digest of the Law of Evidence on the Trial of Civil Actions (Nisi Prius) 5th ed. / Repr. of 1839 ed. – Abingdon : Professional Books.
306p.

—Digest of Wealth Tax Cases 1957 to 1986 / Allahabad : Modern Law Publications, 1986.

—Digests of Irish Reports and Irish Law Times Reports / Abingdon : Professional Books.

1867-93

—Employment Digest / New Malden : Croner Publications.

—Estates Gazette Digest of Cases : 1902-1980 / Abingdon : Professional Books.

—Imo State law reports / v. – Ibadan : Evans Brothers (Nigeria Publishers) for Law Reporting Committee, Ministry of Justice, Imo State of Nigeria, 1977.

—Insurance Case Law Digest : Property and Casualty, 2 vols / Toronto : Butterworths.

—International Digest of Health Legislation / World Health Organization. – London : HMSO.

—Irish Reports Digests : 1894-1970, 6 Vols. / Abingdon : Professional Books.

Vol. 1, 1894-1918

Vol. 2, 1919-1928

Vol. 2. Irish Reports Digests : 1919-1928

Vol. 3, 1929-1938

Vol. 3. Irish Reports Digests : 1929-1938

Vol. 4, 1939-1948

Vol. 5, 1949-1958

Vol. 6, 1959-1970

Repr.

—Justinian's Digest / Repr. of 1971 ed. – Aalen Wuertt : Scientia, 1983.
35p.
ISBN 3511091284 Hbk £15.00

—Juta's index and annotations to the South African law reports 1980-86 / compiled by David S. Fisher and Alan James : assisted by Owen J. Barrow ... et al. – Cape Town : Juta, 1987.
1100p.
Kept up-to-date by supplements.
ISBN 0702118508

—Labour Law Digest, 6 Vols. / Agincourt : Carswell, 1985.
This multi-volume set digests over fifteen thousand reported Canadian labor law cases under federal and provincial law. A cumulative supplement is supplied every six months to keep the work up-to-date.

—Labour Law Journal Digest 1949-1982, 9 Vols. / Nagpur : Wadhura & Co.

—Law Reform Digest / Professional Books Staff. – Abingdon : Professional Books, 1984.

—Law Reports Digest : 1951-1980, 3 Vols. / Professional Books Staff. – Abingdon : Professional Books, 1984.

—Law Reports Digests : 1865-1950, 12 Vols. / Abingdon : Professional Books.

Individual vols.

—Lawyers Weekly : Consolidated Digest / Butterworths.
ISBN 0409806048 Pbk £39.75

Vol. 6
ISBN 0409809411 Pbk £59.95

Vols. 1 and 2 combined
ISBN 0409856657 Pbk £37.95

Vols. 3 and 4 combined
ISBN 0409811653 Pbk £37.95

—Lloyd's Law Reports : Digest / London : LLoyd's of London Press.

—Lloyd's Law Reports : Digests, 1919-1985, 16 Vols. / London : LLoyd's of London Press.

—Modern cases and statutes on Crown Court crime / by Richard Bingham. – Chichester : Rose, 1980.
xlix,532p; 26cm.
Includes index.
ISBN 0859921867 £34.75

—Nigerian Law Reports, Index-Digest 1881-1981, 2 Vols. / Aba : Law & Educational Publishers, 1984.

1982-83 Supplement
ISBN 9782436038

—Nova Scotia Statute Citator / Agincourt : Carswell, 1985.
610p.
This work focuses on the Revised Statutes of Nova Scotia 1967. It contains the amendments, repeals and consolidation of all public statutes of Nova Scotia since 1967. The statutes are annotated. Brief digests of the interpreting caselaw are included.

—Ontario Legislative Digest Service : Carswell / Agincourt : Carswell, 1988.

—Ontario Reports (2d) Consolidated Index, 2 vols / Toronto : Butterworths, 1984.
1296p.

—Payne's Digest on Divorce in Canada (1968-1980) / Toronto : DeBoo, 1982.
ISBN 0888201176 Hbk £100.00

—Payne's Digest on Divorce in Canada / Toronto : DeBoo.
Looseleaf service.
ISBN 0888201206 loose £265.00

—Principles and Digest of the Law of Evidence, 2 Vols. / 6th ed. – Allahabad : Universal Book Agency, 1986.

—Privy Council, Federal Court and Supreme Court : Hindu Law Digest 1837-1986 / 4th ed. – Allahabad : Law Book Company, 1987.
535p.
ISBN 8185029385 Hbk £120.00

—Protection of Movable Cultural Property : Compendium of Legislative Texts /. – Paris : UNESCO.

Vol. 2
ISBN 9231018914 Hbk £80.00

—Saskatchewan Decisions Citator (1979-1983) / Aurora : Canada Law Book Co, 1983.
– (Statute Services).

—Saskatchewan Decisions : Civil and Criminal Cases (1980-Present) / Aurora : Canada Law Book Co.
– (Summary Services, Provincial Ser.).

—Summaries of the judgements delivered in ... / document prepared by the registry of the Court. – v. – Strasbourg : Council of Europe, 1983.
Contains summary judgements not binding on the Court.

—Supreme Court Civil Digest 1950-80, 5 Vols. / 2nd ed. – Allahabad : Law Book Company, 1950-80.

—Supreme Court Criminal Digest 1950-80, 2 Vols. / Allahabad : Law Book Company.

—Supreme Court Industrial, Services and Labour Law Digest, 1977-87 : Central and States / Allahabad : Law Book Company.
500p.

—Supreme Court Labour and Services Digest, 1983-1986, 4 Vols. / Lucknow : Eastern Book Company, 1987.

—Supreme Court Labour Digest, 1950-82. 2 Vols. / V.K. Kharbanda. – 2nd ed. – Allahabad : Law Publishing House, 1984.

—Supreme Court Quinquennial Digest, 1981 to 1985 / Allahabad : Law Book Company.
1,000p.

—Supreme Court Quinquennial Digest / Allahabad : Law Book Company, 1981-85.

—Supreme Court Services and Labour Digest 1950-1979 / Allahabad : Law Book Company, 1976-1979.
851p.

—Supreme Court Yearly Digest /. – Lucknow : Eastern Book Company, 1980.
407p.

1980 1981.
443p.

1981 1982.
391p.

1982 1983.
305p.

1983 1984.
286p.

1984 1985.
467p.

1985 1986.

—U.P. Revenue Digest (1960-1963), 2 Vols. / Allahabad : Law Publishing House, 1984.

—Weekly Digest of Civil Procedure / Agincourt : Carswell, 1987.

—Weekly Digest of Family Law / Agincourt : Carswell, 1986.

—West Bengal Laws, 5 Vols. / Calcutta : Hindustan Law Book Co., 1987.

—West Bengal Laws / Calcutta : Hindustan Law Book Co., 1987.
467p.

—Western Charter Digest : 1983 / Agincourt : Carswell, 1983.
190p.
ISBN 0459364103 Pbk £29.50

—Western Charter Digest : 1984 / Agincourt : Carswell, 1985.
188p.

—Yearly All India Civil Digest, 1986 : Excluding Labour and Taxation / Allahabad : Law Book Company.
750p.

—Yearly All India Civil Digest / Allahabad : Law Book Company, 1987.

—Yearly All-India Criminal Digest, 1986 / Allahabad : Law Book Company, 1987.
400p.

—Yearly Digest of Supreme Court Criminal Cases / Lucknow : Eastern Book Company, 1980.
203p.

1980 1981.
250p.

1982 1983.
174p.

1983 1984.
147p.

—Yearly Supreme Court Digest, 1987 / Allahabad : Law Book Company, 1988.
550p.

DIGESTS – CANADA

—Insurance Case Law Digest : Property and Casualty, 2 Vols. / Butterworths.

—Insurance case law digest: property and casualty / 2 vols. – Scarborough, Ontario : Butterworths (Canada).
Coverage of automobile and property insurance cases in Canada. Each part has a table of cases, and the case digests are arranged to reflect the organizational categories of the standard automobile and home insurance policies.

DIGESTS – NIGERIA

—Federation of Nigeria law reports / v. – Ibadan : Evans Brothers, 1981.
Volume numbering begins anew each year.

—Shari'a law reports / Zaria, Nigeria : Centre for Islamic Studies, Ahmadu Bello University, 1980.
Variant title: Shari'ah law reports. Numbering irregular. In English and Hausa.

DINKA (AFRICAN PEOPLE)

—Customary law of the Dinka people of Sudan : in comparison with aspects of western and Islamic laws / by John Wuol Makec. – London : Afroworld, 1988.
287p.
Includes bibliographical references and index.
ISBN 0948583037

DIPLOMATIC AND CONSULAR LAW

—Diplomacy : the dialogue between states / Adam Watson. – London : Eyre Methuen, 1982.
239p; 24cm.
Bibliography: p227-228. - Includes index.
ISBN 0413481905 £10.50

—International law of diplomacy / Dordrecht : Martinus Nijhoff, 1989.
672. – (New Haven studies in international law and world public order 5).
A legal study from a policy-orientated perspective, which examines new patterns of diplomacy and their influence on the traditional ones. Looks at what world policies have so far regulated the use of the diplomatic process, and whether those policies are needlessly restrictive. Suggests what policies should guide the regulation in future.
ISBN 0792300831 Hbk £95

—Model agreement to enable members of the family forming part of the household of a member of a diplomatic mission or consular post to engage in a gainful occupation : recommendation no. R(87)2 adopted by the Committee of Ministers of the Council of Europe on 12 February 1987 and Explanatory memorandum / Council of Europe. – Strasbourg : Council of Europe, 1987.
13p.
Prepared by the Committee of experts on public international law (CJ-DI) set up under the authority of the European Committee on Legal Co-operation. At head of cover title : Council of Europe, Legal Affairs.
ISBN 9287110859

—Modern Law of Diplomacy : External Missions of States and International Organizations / Dordrecht : Kluwer, 1988.
300p.

—Outrage : the abuse of diplomatic immunity / Chuck Ashman and Pamela Trescott. – London : W.H. Allen, 1986.
224p; 24cm.
ISBN 0491037139 £10.95 (July)

—Protection of officials of foreign states according to international law / Franciszek Przetacznik. – The Hague : Nijhoff, 1983.
xix,390p; 25cm.
Bibliography: p313-344. - Includes index.
ISBN 9024727219 Hbk £160.00

—State and diplomatic immunity / by Charles Lewis. – London : Lloyd's of London Press Ltd., 1980.
135p.
ISBN 0904093816

DIPLOMATIC AND CONSULAR LAW – GREAT BRITAIN

—Diplomatic and consular yearbook 1988 / London : Diplomatic and Consular Yearbook, 1988.
344p.

—Diplomatic immunities and privileges : government report on review of the Vienna Convention on Diplomatic Relations and reply to 'The abuse of diplomatic immunities and privileges' : the first report from the Foreign Affairs Committee in the Session 1984-85 / Great Britain. – London : H.M.S.O., 1985.
29p. – (Miscellaneous).
ISBN 0101949707

—First report from the Foreign Affairs Committee, session 1984-85 : the abuse of diplomatic immunities and privileges : report with an annex; together with the proceedings of the Committee; minutes of evidence taken ... in the last session of Parliament; and appendices / Great Britain. – London : H.M.S.O., 1984.
li,94p; 25cm. – (H.C.).
ISBN 0102127859

—State and diplomatic immunity / 3rd. – London : Lloyds of London Press, 1989.
approx 240.
Explains the law affecting the immunity from judicial action of foreign governments, their embassies, staff, and their property. Includes a new chapter on the International Tin Council Litigation, and a discussion of the effects of the Diplomatic and Consular Premises Act 1987.
ISBN 1850442541 Hbk

—State and diplomatic immunity / by Charles J. Lewis. – 2nd ed. – London : Lloyd's of London, 1985.
xxvi,250p; 22cm.
Previous ed.: 1980. Includes index.
ISBN 1850440476 No price

DIRECTORIES

—1987 annual on terrorism / edited by Yonah Alexander, with contributing editors Abraham H. Foxman and Eugene Mastrangelo. – Dordrecht : Martinus Nijhoff, 1989.
528. – (Annual on Terrorism).
Focuses on national, regional and global developments in the field of terrorism. This volume includes the analysis of domestic and international terrorism, selected papers written during 1987, a statistical synopsis and selected documents, reports and addresses.
ISBN 9024738016 Hbk Gld250.00

—A.A.A. Yearbook /. – Dordrecht : Kluwer, 1981.
vi, 196p.
ISBN 902472323X Hbk £65.00

Vol. 47/48 (1977/78): Foreign Investments Today and Tomorrow 1986.
160p.
ISBN 9024725704 Pbk £75.00

Vol. 49/50 (1979-1980): Functions and Status of the Consul 1982.
200p.
ISBN 9024725712 Pbk £70.00

Vol. 51/52/53 (1981/82/83): International Scientific and Technical Co-operation 1985.
171p.
ISBN 9024731100 Pbk £75.00

Vol. 54/55/56: Natural Resources in International Law 1987.
320p.
ISBN 902473469X Pbk £150.00

—A.M.P.L.A. Yearbook / Melbourne : Australian Mining and Petroleum Law Association.
600p.

—Alberta Legal Telephone Directory : 1986 / Aurora : Canada Law Book Co.
This telephone directory is arranged by name, listing every lawyer and law firm in Alberta. Each listing includes address, telephone number and firm association. Additional entries include, among others, listings for: Courts, Judges, and Court Officials; Land Registration Districts; Legal Services; Law Libraries and Universities; and Provincial Government Departments.

—Annual Catalogue of E.S.C. Opinions. Year 1984 / Luxembourg : Office for Official Publications of the European Communities, 1985.
38p.
ISBN 9283000757 Pbk

—Annual Survey of Australian Law /. – North Ryde : Law Book Co.
xxi, 467p.
ISBN 0455201226 £32.50

1980: 1981
576p.

1985: 1986
xxii, 428p.
ISBN 0455206902 Hbk £65.00

1986: 1987

—Atlantic Legal Directory : 1985-1986 / Aurora : Canada Law Book Co, 1985.

—Atlantic Legal Telephone Directory / Aurora : Canada Law Book Co.
– (Directories).
The Atlantic Legal Telephone Directory unifies law-related offices of the four Atlantic Provinces into a single means of access. Included are listings for lawyers, law firms, law societies, courts, legal aid offices, provincial government departments and other key departments and offices.

—Australian legal directory / Law Council of Australia : in association with the Victoria Law Foundation. – Melbourne : Law Council of Australia, 1977-.

—Australian Legal Directory / Australian Document Exchange Pty Limited. – Sydney : Butterworths.

—Bar List of the United Kingdom / London : Sweet & Maxwell, 1982.
ISBN 0420465200 Pbk £48.25

—British Columbia Legal Telephone Directory : 1985 / Aurora : Canada Law Book Co.
This volume, arranged by name, lists every lawyer and law firm in British Columbia. Each listing includes name, firm association, address and telephone. Listings are also provided for, among others: Courts, Judges and Court Officials; Land Registration Districts; Legal Services; and Law Libraries and Universities.

—British Year Book Of International Law 1985 / Oxford : Oxford University Press, 1986.
ISBN 0198255470 Hbk £55.00

—Butterworth's Law Directory and Diary 1987 / 3rd ed. – London : Butterworths.

—Butterworths Law Directory 1988 / New York : British Media Publications, 1988.
ISBN 0611007169 Hbk £30.00

—Butterworths Legal Services Directory 1988 / New York : British Media Publications, 1988.
ISBN 0611007215 Pbk £18.00

—C.A.L.T. Directory 1987-88 / Canadian Association of Law Teachers. – Agincourt : Carswell, 1987.
186p.

—Canada Legal Directory : 1988 Edition / Toronto : DeBoo, 1988.
This listing of Canadian law firms and the lawyers who practice within them includes an alphabetical listing of law firms by city, with addresses and phone numbers, a separate finding list of the individual lawyers, a listing of corporate in-house counsel, and a comprehensive listing within each province of courts, officials, judicial districts, law societies, etc.
ISBN 0888202407 Hbk £75.00

—Canadian Almanac and Directory / Toronto : DeBoo, 1984.
ISBN 0773040536 Hbk £69.95

—Canadian Directory of Public Legal Education and Information / Ottawa : Canadian Law Information Council.
ISBN 0662104544 Hbk £5.00

National
ISBN 0662104536 Hbk £5.00

Ontario
ISBN 0662104587 Hbk £5.00

P.E.I.
ISBN 0662104609 Hbk £3.00

Quebec
ISBN 0662902726 Hbk £5.00

—Canadian Human Rights Yearbook / Daniel Proulx. – Agincourt : Carswell, 1987.
308p.

Back edition 1986

Back edition 1984-1985

Back edition 1983
This fourth annual volume of the series features current issues in the Canadian and international law of human rights. This text has been prepared under the direction of the Human Rights Research and Education Centre and the University of Ottawa.

—Canadian Yearbook of International Law : 1963-1973, 11 Vols. / Professional Books Staff. – Abingdon : Professional Books, 1984.

—Canadian Yearbook of International Law - Annuaire Canadien de Droit International /. – Vancouver : University of British Columbia Press.
ISBN 0774801123 Hbk £35.00

Vol. 17
ISBN 0774801271 Hbk £44.00

Vol. 18 1980.
437p.
ISBN 0774801379 Hbk £44.00

Vol. 19 1983.
478p.
ISBN 077480162X Hbk £44.00

Vol. 20 1984.
350p.
ISBN 0774801824 Hbk

Vol. 21 1984.
562p.
ISBN 0774802065 Hbk £45.00

Vol. 22 1985.
471p.
ISBN 0774802251 Hbk £45.00

Vol. 23 1986.
560p.
ISBN 0774802596 Hbk £48.00

Vol. 24 1987.
488p.
ISBN 0774802812 Hbk £48.00

Vol. 25 1987.
580p.
ISBN 0774803037 Hbk £60.00

—Checklist of Royal Commissions : Select Committees of Parliament and Boards of Inquiry, Commonwealth, New South Wales, Queensland, Tasmania and Victoria, 1960-1980 and South Australia 1970-1980 / Bundoora : La Trobe University, Borchardt Library, 1986.
ISBN 0858166429 Hbk £45.00

—Checklists For Solicitors / 5th ed. – London : Longman Professional, 1987.
ISBN 0851211720 Pbk £15.95

—Commercial arbitration institutions : an international directory and guide / Ludwik Kos-Rabcewicz-Zubkowski and Paul J. Davidson. – London : Oceana Publications, 1986.
ix, 186p.
Published under the auspices of the International Federation of Commercial Arbitration Institutions.
ISBN 0379207893

—Comparative Law Yearbook / Dordrecht : Kluwer, 1978.
352p.
ISBN 9028606785 Hbk £105.00

Vol. 3 1980.
294p.
ISBN 9028603409 Hbk £95.00

Vol. 4 1981.
vi, 371p.
ISBN 9024725631 Hbk £150.00

Vol. 5 1982.
332p.
ISBN 9024726972 Hbk £180.00

Vol. 6 1983.
256p.
ISBN 9024728398 Hbk £145.00

Vol. 7 1984.
200p.
ISBN 9024729661 Hbk £145.00

Vol. 8 1985.
250p.
ISBN 902473178X Hbk £165.00

Vol. 9 1986.
232p.
ISBN 9024733502 Hbk £165.00

—Consolidated text to the Checklists of Royal Commissions / Tina Montanelli. – Bundoora : La Trobe University, Borchardt Library, 1980.
ISBN 0858162326 Hbk £45.00

—Data base management packages / by Kathy Lang. – Southampton : Ashford Press, 1987
350p.
ISBN 1852530235 unbound £80.00

—Directory of Canadian graduate programmes in law / editor: William H. Angus : redacteur: William H. Angus. – S.l : Association of Canadian Law Teachers, 1980.
ii,125p.
'Sponsored by the Section on Graduate Legal Studies of the Association of Canadian Law Teachers'.

—Directory of Courts in the UK / London : Shaw & Sons, 1987-1988.
ISBN 0721909841 Pbk £10.95

—Directory of Courts in the United Kingdom : 1988/1989 / London : Shaw & Sons, 1988.
320p.
ISBN 072190985X Pbk £14.95

—Directory of Islamic Banking and Financial Institutions / Oxford : Croom Helm, 1988.
ISBN 0709913478 Hbk £50.00

—Directory of law libraries in the British Isles / C. Miskin. – 2nd ed. 1 v. – Yeovil : Legal Library Publishing & Distribution Service for the British and Irish Association of Law Librarians, 1984.
Includes index.

—Directory of Law Teachers / Agincourt : Carswell, 1987-1988.
180p.

—Directory of projects (England & Wales) ... for adult offenders, alcoholics, drug takers, homeless single people and people with histories of mental illness / co-produced by FARE ... et al. – Chichester : Rose, 1980.
xiii,257p.
ISBN 0859921883 Unpriced

—Directory of Schools of Law in the Commonwealth 1985 / London : Commonwealth Secretariat.

—Directory of Specialists in Official Publications / 2nd ed. – Scoop Publications, 1988.
ISBN 0951201115 Pbk £6.00

—European Yearbook in the Sociology of Law 1988 see under 306 / Luxembourg : Office for Official Publications of the European Communities.

—EUSIDIC database guide / Oxford : Learned Information, 1983.
ISBN 0904933377

—Guide to government department and other libraries 1988 / edited by R.T. Adkins. – 28th ed. – London : Science Reference and Information Service, 1988.
100p.
Previous ed.: 1986. Includes indexes.
ISBN 071230746X £20.00

—Hague yearbook of international law : Annuaire de la Haye de droit international / J.G. Lammers. – Dordrecht : Martinus Nijhoff, 1988.
471. – (A.A.A. Yearbook).
In-depth articles on some of the developments taking place in international law institutions such as the International Court of Justice and the Hague Conference on Private International Law. The articles, and summaries, in both English and French, deal with decisions rendered by these institutions.
ISBN 9024737494 Hbk £80

—Head's Legal Guide / New Malden : Croner Publications.

—Index of A.M.P.L.A. Yearbooks 1977-1987 / Melbourne : Australian Mining and Petroleum Law Association.
ISBN 0958991839 Hbk £35.00

—The Institute Clauses Handbook / London : LLoyd's of London Press, 1986.
ISBN 185044093X Hbk

—Inter-American Yearbook on Human Rights / Organization of American States. – Dordrecht : Kluwer, 1987.
1,276p.
ISBN 0898389232 Hbk £450.00

—International directory of legal aid / edited by Judy Lane and Simon Hillyard. – London : International Bar Association, 1985.
244p; 21cm.
ISBN 0421325607 Hbk £30

—International handbook of universities and other institutions of higher education / editor, D.J. Aitken : assistant editor, Ann C.M. Taylor. – 9th ed. – London : Macmillan for the International Association of Universities, 1983.
ix, 1131p.
ISBN 0333274466

—International Organizations and the Law of the Sea : Documentary Yearbook 1985 / Netherlands Institute for the Law of the Sea. – Dordrecht : Kluwer, 1987.
650p.
ISBN 9024734886 Hbk £275.00

—Israel yearbook on human rights / Mala Tabory. – Dordrecht : Martinus Nijhoff, 1989.
312. – (Israel yearbook on human rights 18).
Published under the auspices of the Faculty of Law of Tel Aviv University. Contains studies on human rights in peace and war, . with particular emphasis on problems relevant to the State of Israel, and the Jewish people. Summaries of judicial decisions, and military proclamations are included.
ISBN 0792300173 Hbk £42

—Italian yearbook of international law / v. – Napoli : Editoriale Scientifica, 1975.
Index in each vol..
ISBN 0379008254

—Italian Yearbook of International Law / Milan : Giuffre, 1986.
xii, 467p.

—Juridical Yearbook 1981 / London : HMSO, 1985.
Contains legal documents concerning the United Nations including legislative texts, treaty provisions and a review of the United Nations' legal activities.
ISBN 0119086506 Hbk £25.00

—Kime's international law handbook : brief facts about legal practice in most of the countries of the world / editor : James M. Matthews ; research and compilation : Roderick N. Matthews. – London : Kime's International Law Directory Limited, 1981.
266p.
ISBN 0900503149

—Lawasia directory / Sydney : Lawasia, 1979-.

—Lawyer's Phone Book (Ontario) / North Ryde : Law Book Co.

—Lawyer's Phone Book (Ontario) / Aurora : Canada Law Book Co.
– (Directories).
This directory, published each year in the early spring, lists every individual lawyer and law office in Ontario, complete with telephone number, street address and postal code. Also included are the addresses and telephone numbers of all Provincial, County, and District judicial offices, Legal Aid Offices, Ontario Government Officials and others.

—Lawyer's Pocketbook / Durban : Butterworths, 1985.
ISBN 0409034568 Hbk

—Lawyer's Remembrancer 1986 / London : Butterworths, 1984.
This book is a concise encyclopedia of United Kingdom practice and legislation, together with a diary section running from November, 1985 to January, 1987. Each week in the diary is given two full pages. The references section includes names, addresses, phone numbers, and relevant abbreviations.
ISBN 0406269181 Hbk

—Lawyer's Remembrancer 1987 / London : Butterworths, 1986.

—Lawyers' Law Directory, 1984-85 / Abingdon : Professional Books, 1985.
ISBN 0862050995 Hbk £45.00

—Legal 500 : the major law firms in England, Wales and Scotland / John Pritchard. – London : Legalease, 1988.
352p.

—Legal Desk Book, 1988 / Agincourt : Carswell, 1988.
This book is a compilation of resources and reference materials for the Canadian practitioner. Directories of courts, judges, law associations, government bodies, sources of legal information, and other listings are provided. Substantive law summaries for business law, criminal law, family law, litigation, and real estate are included in the work.

—Legal Deskbook : 1988 / Agincourt : Carswell.
530p.
This softcover text provides a summary of resources and factual information pertinent to legal and non-legal researchers. It includes directories of courts, judges, law associations, government bodies, sources of legal information, etc. Special features include a legal information directory for business law, criminal law, family law and social services, litigation and real estate.

—Legal Software Directory / London : Longman Professional, 1985.
ISBN 0851210422 Pbk £16.50

—Legislative Draftsmen : Short List of Legislative Draftsmen Available for Short Ad Hoc Assignments / London : Commonwealth Secretariat, 1982.

—Lloyd's Survey Handbook / 4th ed. – London : LLoyd's of London Press.
ISBN 185044031X Hbk £27.50

—London County Courts Directory / 11th ed. – London : HMSO, 1982.
ISBN 0113906323 Hbk £20.00

—Magistrate's Court Guide 1988 / London : Butterworths, 1988.
ISBN 0406108412 Pbk £15.95

—Netherlands Yearbook of International Law /. – Dordrecht : Kluwer, 1981.
400p.
ISBN 9028627111 Hbk £80.00/$40.00

Vol. 12 1981.
ix, 438p.
ISBN 9028629610 Hbk Gld80.00/$40.00

Vol. 13 1982.
ca 515p.
ISBN 9024727766 Hbk Gld110.00/$40.00

Vol. 14 1984.
490p.
ISBN 9024729165 Hbk £110.00

Vol. 15 (1984) 1985.
585p.
ISBN 9024731151 Hbk Gld110.00

Vol. 18 (1987) 1988.
510p.
ISBN 9024736382 Hbk Gld135.00

—Netherlands yearbook of international law / T.M.C. Asser Institute. – Dordrecht : Martinus Nijhoff, 1989.
600.
Articles on the practice of the Iran-United States Claims Tribunal. The documentation section surveys Dutch state practice for the parliamentary year 1987-1988; international agreements to which the Netherlands is a party, and Netherlands judicial decisions and municipal legislation involving questions of public international law, and Dutch literature in this field, and related matters.
ISBN 0792301048 Hbk £45

—Netherlands Yearbook of International Law : Index to Vols. 1-10 (1970-1979) / Dordrecht : Kluwer, 1983.
380p.
ISBN 902472774X Hbk Gld150.00/$65.00

—New Court Guide / London : Blackstone Press, 1988.
ISBN 185185049X Pbk £5.95

—Nineteen Eighty-Eight Canadian Almanac and Directory / Agincourt : Carswell, 1987.
1200p.
This is a reference book containing information on Canada. Lists include a directory of names, addresses, telephone numbers; contacts for all libraries, media, associations, foundations, clubs, business and government offices, agencies, and commissions; a directory of lawyers and law firms. Also included is information on the weather, climate, geographical data, population, transportation, astronomical data and forms of address.

—Official Handbook of the European Parliament-1984 / Kirchberg : Commission of the European Communities, 1985.
333p.

—Oyez Longman Directory of Local Authorities 1983 / Oyez Longman Publishing. – London : Oyez Longman, 1983.

—Parliamentary yearbook 1988 / London : Blake's, 1988.
448p.
ISBN 0905846605

—PLEI Directory 1985 / Ottawa : Canadian Law Information Council, 1985.
75p.
ISBN 0920358802 Pbk £4.50

—Scottish law directory / Edinburgh : T & T Clark.
Known as the 'White Book', the directory contains official lists of certified practitioners and professional lists of the Faculty of Advocates, Chartered Accountants and Chartered Surveyors as well as branches of Building Societies, Insurance Companies, Banks, Property and Estate Agents, Messengers-at-Arms, Sheriff Officers, and licensing boards. Other sections deal with Scottish courts, central and local government, fees, Stamp Duties, Scottish Legal Societies, the Rutland Exchange and Fax Users.

—Solicitors and barristers directory and diary / London : Waterlow, 1987.
ISBN 0080330940 Hbk £35.00

—Solicitors Checklists / Stephen A. Karas. – Butterworths, 1988.
ca 232p.
ISBN 0409494690 loose £29.00

—Solicitors' and barristers' directory and diary : an almanac and directory incorporating the Law Society list of practising solicitors and the Senate of the Inns of Court and the Bar list of members / v. – London : Waterlow, 1984.
Merger of: The Bar list of the United Kingdom; and, The Solicitors' diary ... almanac and legal directory.
ISBN 0080391710

—Solicitors' Compendium 1985 / Edinburgh : W Green.
– (Reprint from Parliament House Book).
ISBN 0414007700 Hbk £4.00

—Solicitors' Compendium Nineteen Eighty-Two : Extracted from the Parliament House Book / Edinburgh : W Green, 1983.
ISBN 0414007077 Hbk £3.75

—Solicitors' regional directory 1984 / London : Law Society, 1984.
viii,184p.
Supersedes: The legal aid solicitors list. Includes index.

—Stones Justices Manual / John Richman, A T Draycott. – 3 vols. – London : Butterworths, 1988.
ISBN 0406386803 Hbk £102.00

—Tax Practitioner's Diary, 1984-1985 / London : Butterworths, 1984.
ISBN 0406539642 Pbk

—Tax practitioner's diary 1986-1987 / Butterworths. – London : Butterworths, 1986.
ISBN 0406539669 Pbk £8.50

—Tax Practitioner's Diary 1986-87 / Butterworth Editorial Staff. – London : Butterworths, 1986.
This book is a diary for tax practitioners in the United Kingdom. Income tax, corporation tax, capital gains tax, capital transfer tax, value added tax, and stamp duties are all covered in the work. A complete list of tax district addresses is included.
ISBN 0406539669 Pbk

—Toronto Legal Directory (Metropolitan List) and Tariff Guide / Toronto : University of Toronto Press, 1985.

—World directory of criminological institutes / compiled and edited by Carla Masotti Santoro. – 4th ed. – Rome : UNSDRI, 1986.
xxvi,582p. – (Publication).
ISBN 9290780029

—World Directory of Sources of Patent Information / Geneva : World Intellectual Property Organization, 1985.
ca 300p.

—Year Book of law, computers and technology / London : Butterworths, 1990.
25.
ISBN 0406187037 Hbk £24.95

—Yearbook 1982, 2 Vols. / International Law Commission. – London : HMSO.
ISBN 0119080702 Hbk £18.05

Vol. 2, Part 2

—Yearbook 1982-83 / International Court of Justice. – London : HMSO, 1984.
ISBN 0119080028 Hbk £9.00

—Yearbook Commercial Arbitration /. – Dordrecht : Kluwer, 1980.
344p.
ISBN 9026811527 Hbk Gld62.00

1981 1981.
352p.
ISBN 9065440038 Hbk Gld62.00

1982 1982.
465p.
ISBN 9065440461 Hbk Gld75.00

1983
482p.
ISBN 9065441182 Pbk Gld82.50

1984
ISBN 9065441719 Hbk Gld95.00

1985 1985.
640p.
ISBN 9065442138 Pbk Gld110.00

1986 1986.
716p.
ISBN 9065442472 Pbk Gld150.00

1987 1987.
ISBN 9065443045 Pbk Gld180.00 (Including key index for all volumes 1-12)
ISBN 9065443037 Pbk Gld50.00 (key index only)

1989 1989.
872.
In co-operation with the T M C Asser Institute for International and European law. Covers the national reports and updates, court decisions and updates, commercial and maritime arbitral awards and rules, Iran-US claims tribunal, and court decisions in the New York Convention, the European Convention, and the Washington (ICSID) Convention.
ISBN 9065444084 Pbk Gld59/Dfl 185

—Yearbook Commercial Arbitration, Volumes 1-12 (including Key) / Dordrecht : Kluwer.
ISBN 9065441352 Pbk Gld840.00

—Yearbook Maritime Law / Dordrecht : Kluwer, 1987.
528p.
ISBN 9065442545 Hbk Gld275.00

—Yearbook Nineteen Eighty and Case Citator 1977-80 and Statute Citator 1972-80 / London : Sweet & Maxwell.
ISBN 0421284102 Hbk £14.00

—Yearbook of European law / Oxford : Oxford University Press, 1981.
ISBN 0198253842 Hbk £50.00

Vol. 2 1982.
ISBN 0198254903 Hbk £50.00

Vol. 3 1983.
ISBN 0198255047 Hbk £50.00

Vol. 4 1984.
ISBN 0198255217 Hbk £50.00

Vol. 5 1985.
ISBN 0198255462 Hbk £50.00

Vol. 6 1986.
ISBN 0198256051 Hbk £45.00

Vol. 7 1988.
490.
As well as practical and theoretical articles, contains Annual Surveys of the Council of Europe, the European Convention on Human Rights, and the European Parliament. There is a book review section andlist of Commission Decision Competitors. Fully indexed with a table of cases.
ISBN 0198256256 Hbk £55

—Yearbook of European law / Oxford : Clarendon Press, 1981.

—Yearbook of the European Convention on Human Rights /. – Dordrecht : Kluwer, 1980.
xvii, 688p.
ISBN 9024723833 Hbk Gld275.00

Vol. 23 (1980) 1982.
766p.
ISBN 9024727170 Hbk Gld320.00

Vol. 24 (1981) 1983.
602p.
ISBN 9024727227 Hbk Gld255.00

Vol. 25 (1982) 1986.
896p.
ISBN 902473262X Hbk Gld395.00

Vol. 26 (1983) 1987.
860p.
ISBN 9024732638 Hbk Gld425.00

—Yearbook of the European Institute for Social Security / 1978-1980 /. – Dordrecht : Kluwer, 1980.
ISBN 9031201332 Hbk Gld114.00

Part 1: Retirement Age in Europe 1980.
224p.
ISBN 9031201340 Hbk Gld52.00

Part 2: Social Security Reforms in Europe 1980.
288p.
ISBN 9031201359 Hbk Gld65.00

—Yearbook of the European Institute for Social Security / 1980-1981 /. – Dordrecht : Kluwer, 1982.
ISBN 9031201685 Hbk Gld123.00

Part 1: Social Security Reforms in Europe 2 1982.
285p.
ISBN 9031201669 Hbk Gld72.00

Part 2: Social Security and the Economic Crisis 1982.
146p.
ISBN 9031201677 Hbk Gld60.00

—Yearbook of the European Institute for Social Security / 1982-1983 /. – Dordrecht : Kluwer.

—Yearbook of the International Commission, 1985, Vol. 2, Part 2 : Report of the Commission to the General Assembly on the Work of its 37th Session / Geneva : United Nations Publications.
ISBN 9211332818 Hbk £9.50

—Yearbook of the International Law Commission, 1985, Vol. 2, Part 1 : Documents of the 37th Session / Geneva : United Nations Publications.
ISBN 9211332796 Hbk £25.00

DIRECTORIES - CHINA

—China Law Yearbook 1987 / Butterworths, 1989.
645p.
ISBN 0409995630 Hbk £325.00

DIRECTORIES - COMMONWEALTH

—Admission of Commonwealth lawyers : a technical survey for Commonwealth Law Ministers and the Commonwealth Lawyers' Association / Campbell Alan McLachlan. – London : Commonwealth Secretariat, 1985.
x, 168p.

DIRECTORIES - SCOTLAND

—Edinburgh for lawyers / 2nd. – Edinburgh : W Green & Son.
Includes a map of legal Edinburgh, historical background, the courts with diagrams of the court system, solicitors, and other related matters.
ISBN 0414008561

DIRECTORS

—Aspects of the common-law powers and duties of company directors with special reference to (a) their authority to act on behalf of a company and (b) the scope and effect of certain legislative provisions / by John Stopford McLennan. – 1. – S.l. : s.n., 1984.
various pagings.
Offprints of 4 articles. Thesis (L.L.M.) - University of Witwatersrand 1984. Bibliography: p.i-ii. - Includes index.

—Corporate governance and directors' liabilities : legal, economic, and sociological analyses on corporate social responsibility / edited by Klaus J. Hopt, Gunther Teubner. – Berlin : W. de Gruyter, 1984.
462p. – (Series A, Law).
Includes index.
ISBN 3110100274 £75.00

—Disqualification and personal liability of directors : a guide to the changes made by the Insolvency Act 1985 / L.S. Sealy. – Bicester : CCH, 1986.
iv,27p.
ISBN 0863250920

DIRECTORS - AUSTRALIA

—Australian Legal Director / Butterworths, 1988.
968p.
ISBN 0000126527 Hbk £55.00

—Duties and responsibilities of company directors in Australia / 4th ed. – North Ryde, N.S.W. : CCH Australia, 1982.
vii,143p.
Includes index.
ISBN 0869033328

—Duties and Responsibilities of Company Secretaries and Directors in Australia / North Ryde : C.C.H. Australia, 1987.
240p.
ISBN 0869030353 Hbk £27.00

—Modern Director-Duties and Liabilities 1985 : Centre for Commercial Law and Applied Legal Research / Monash University, Faculty of Law. – Clayton : Monash University Press.
ISBN 0867463848 Hbk £17.00

DIRECTORS - GREAT BRITAIN

—Companies Act 1980, sections 54 and 55 : transactions or arrangements in which a director has a material interest : memorandum / by the Society's Standing Committee on Company Law. – London : Law Society, 1981.
6p; 30cm.

—Company Director and the Law / 5th ed. – London : Longman Professional, 1986.
ISBN 085121231X Hbk £16.95

—Company Director and the Law / 4th ed. – London : Oyez Longman, 1983.
– (It's Your Law Ser.).
ISBN 085120709X Hbk £8.25

—Company director and the law / 5th. – London : Longman Professional (UK), 1986.
Explains the legal responsibilities and obligations of the company director. Covers the changes made by the Companies Act 1985, and the Insolvency Act 1986.
ISBN 085121231X Pbk £17.95

—Company Directors / London : CCH, 1987.
ISBN 0863250947 Pbk £25.00

—Company directors : liabilities, rights and duties / Christopher L. Ryan. – 2nd ed. – Bicester : CCH Editions, 1986.
xvi,407p; 23cm.
Covers the relevant provisions of the Business Names Act 1985, the Companies Act 1985, the Company Securities (Insider Dealing) Act 1985, the Insolvency Act 1986, the Company Directors Disqualification Act 1986, the Financial Services Act 1986, and other relevant statutes.
ISBN 0863250947 Pbk

—Conceptual and policy basis of directors' fiduciary duties under English company law / by David Sugarman. – 2 v. – London : Middlesex Polytechnic Faculty of Business Studies and Management, 1982.
– (Working paper).
Includes bibliographies. Parts 1 and 2.
ISBN 0904804135 pt. 2

—Corporate governance : practices, procedures and powers in British companies and their boards of directors / R.I. Tricker. – Aldershot : Gower, 1984.
vii,319p; 22cm.
Includes index.
ISBN 0566007495 £18.95

—Director's duties and insider dealing / Philip L.R. Mitchell. – London : Butterworths, 1982.
xxiv,268p; 22cm.
Includes index.
ISBN 0406295808 Pbk Unpriced

—Directors' Duties and Insider dealing / London : Butterworths, 1982.
ISBN 0406295808 Pbk £14.50

—Directors' Personal Liability / Oxford : Blackwell Scientific, 1987.
ISBN 0003832945 Hbk £20.00

—Directors' personal liability / 1st. – Oxford : Blackwell Scientific.
270. – (Blackwell Law Library).
Examines the erosion by recent legislation of the principle that neither directors nor shareholders of limited companies are personally liable for their company debts and torts. Advice on potential liabilities is offered in the light of the Companies Act 1985 and the Insolvency Act 1986.*Company directors, Accountants, Solicitors*
ISBN 0632026197 Pbk £19.50

—Directors' personal liability / Robert R. Pennington. – London : Collins Professional and Technical, 1987.
256p; 24cm.
Includes index.
ISBN 0003832945 £20.00

—Disqualification and personal liability of directors : a guide to the changes made by the insolvency legislation of 1985 and 1986 / by L.S. Sealy. – 2nd ed. – Bicester : CCH, 1987.
iv,53p.
Explains the rules regarding directors' disqualification, the imposition of personal liability on company directors and others (including wrongful trading), and the rules on the restriction of use of certain company names by directors and shadow directors.
ISBN 0863251307

—Insolvency : Disqualification and personal liability of directors / London : CCH, 1986.
ISBN 0863250920 Pbk £6.00

—Rights and duties of directors / Desmond Wright. – London : Butterworths, 1987.
140p; 22cm.
Includes index.
ISBN 0406504709 £33.50

—Rights and duties of directors / Touche Ross. – London : Butterworths, 1987.
ISBN 0406504709 Pbk £18.50

—Self-administered pensions for directors / London : Fitzwilliam, 1988.
ISBN 1870555031 Hbk £25.00

—Share options and incentives for directors and employees / Tolley Publishing, 1986.
ISBN 085459180X Pbk £7.95

—Share schemes for directors and employees / London : Butterworths, 1985.
ISBN 0406501203 Pbk £29.95

—Tax strategy for directors, executives and employers / 2nd ed. – London : Longman Professional, 1985.
– (Tax Strategy Series).
ISBN 0851210767 Pbk £30.00

—Taxation of directors / Sargent. – London : CCH, 1986.
ISBN 0863251129 Pbk £5.00

—Tolley's Guide to Directors' Transactions / John Aldis. – Croydon : Tolley.
120p.
ISBN 0854591184 Hbk £5.95

—Worker-directors in private manufacturing industry in Great Britain / Brian Towers, Derek Cox, Elizabeth Chell. – London : Department of Employment, 1987.
34p. – (Research paper).
Bibliography: p33-34.

DIRECTORS – INDIA
—Companies' Directors / 2nd ed. – Allahabad : Law Book Company, 1988.
800p.

DIRECTORS – MALAYSIA
—Director's Liabilities in Singapore and Malaysia after Tarling's Case / Singapore, 1980.

DIRECTORS – SINGAPORE
—Director's Liabilities in Singapore and Malaysia after Tarling's Case / Singapore, 1980.

DISARMAMENT
—Disarmament : the human factor : proceedings of a colloquium on the societal context for disarmament / sponsored by UNITAR and the Planetary Citizens and held at the United Nations, New York : edited by Ervin Laszlo and Donald Keys. – Oxford : Pergamon, 1981.
x,164p; 24cm.
Includes index.
ISBN 0080247032 Hbk £10.50
ISBN 008028129X Pbk Unpriced

—Forgotten treaties : a practical plan for world disarmament / Allan McKnight : with an introduction by Keith Suter. – Melbourne : Law Council of Australia, 1983.
xi,136p.
Includes bibliographical references and index. Part II is text of McKnight's Draft Disarmament Treaty.
ISBN 0959660879

—Human Rights and Disarmament / Vaclav Racek. – London : Spokesman Books, 1983.
60p.

DISASTER RELIEF
—Disaster and resolution : two discussion papers dealing with distinct aspects of the aftermath of man-made disasters, the process of litigation, settlement and compensation and the factors affecting the provision of speedy relief and effective rehabiliation / David Wade, Carmel Goldwater : commissioned and published by Centre for Public Affairs Studies. – London : Centre for Public Affairs Studies, 1985.
viii,162p.

—International humanitarian assistance : disaster relief actions in international law and organization / Peter Macalister-Smith. – Hague : M. Nijhoff Publishers, 1985.
260p.
ISBN 9024729939 Hbk £130.00

DISASTER RELIEF – GREAT BRITAIN
—Bradford disaster appeal : the administration of an appeal fund / by Roger W. Suddards : with contributions by Leolin Price and Hubert Picarda. – London : Sweet & Maxwell, 1986.
169p.
ISBN 0421379901

DISCOVERY (LAW)
—Principles and practice of discovery : with an appendix of forms including suggested forms for stating objections to discovery / by Edward Bray. – London : Reeves and Turner, 1885.
xlix, 704 p.; 22 cm.
Slips inserted containing new material. Includes index.

DISCOVERY (LAW) – AUSTRALIA
—Discovery and Interrogatories / Butterworths, 1984.
325p.
ISBN 0409492728 Hbk £56.00

—Law of Discovery 1885 / Woolloomooloo : International Business Communications, 1985.
872p.
ISBN 0949553212 Hbk £85.00

—Law of discovery in Australia : documents, interrogatories and property / by Bernard C. Cairns. – Sydney : Law Book Co., 1984.
xxv,199p.
Bibliography: p.xxv. - Includes index.
ISBN 0455202842

DISCOVERY (LAW) – ENGLAND
—Discovery : a comparison between English and American civil discovery law with reform proposals / Julius Byron Levine. – Oxford : Clarendon, 1982.
xl,208p; 23cm.
Bibliography: p154-160. - Includes index.
ISBN 0198253680 £16.00

—Discovery of documents and disclosure : Order 24 / London : Lord Chancellor's Department, 1987.
4 leaves.
Memorandum outlining amendments to Order 24 of the Rules of the Supreme Court.

DISCOVERY (LAW) – GREAT BRITAIN
—Discovery and Interrogatories / Bailey. – London : Butterworths, 1984.
ISBN 0409492728 Hbk £33.50

—Discovery Comparison Between England and U.S. Law / Oxford : Oxford University Press, 1982.
ISBN 0198253680 Hbk £20.00

DISCOVERY (LAW) – INDIA
—Law of Identification and Discovery / 6th ed. – Allahabad : Law Book Company, 1988.
500p.

DISCOVERY (LAW) – NEW ZEALAND
—Report on discovery in criminal cases / Criminal Law Reform Committee. – Wellington : Government Printer?, 1986.
59p.

DISCOVERY (LAW) – UNITED STATES
—Discovery : a comparison between English and American civil discovery law with reform proposals / Julius Byron Levine. – Oxford : Clarendon, 1982.
xl,208p; 23cm.
Bibliography: p154-160. - Includes index.
ISBN 0198253680 £16.00

—Discovery Comparison Between England and U.S. Law / Oxford : Oxford University Press, 1982.
ISBN 0198253680 Hbk £20.00

DISCRIMINATION
—Case studies on human rights and fundamental freedoms : a world survey / ed.-in-chief, Willem A. Veenhoven, assistant to the ed.-in-chief, Winifred Crum Ewing, associate editors, Clemens Amelunxen ... et al. – The Hague : Nijhoff, 1975.
5 v; 25 cm.
2 v. Includes bibliographical references.

—Equality and Discrimination under International Law / Oxford : Oxford University Press, 1983.
ISBN 0198255195 Pbk £12.50

—Equality and judicial neutrality / Sheilah L. Martin and Kathleen E. Mahoney, editors. – Toronto : Carswell, 1986.
xxvii, 430 p.; 24 cm.
Papers presented at a conference held in Banff, Alta., May 22-24, 1986. Includes bibliographical references.
ISBN 0459308319

DISCRIMINATION – CANADA
—Discrimination and the Law / Toronto : DeBoo, 1985.
ISBN 0888202148 Hbk £135.00

Supplements
The latest edition of this work has been revised to reflect the impact of the Charter of Rights and Freedoms on discrimination law. Included are extensive case law materials, tables of cases, and a complete listing of board inquiry decisions.

—Discrimination and the law in Canada / by Walter Surma Tarnopolsky. – Toronto : De Boo, 1982.
vii,595p.
Bibliography: p. 493-510. - Includes index.
ISBN 0888201052 Hbk

—On Discrimination / Vancouver : Fraser Institute, 1985.
– (Focus Ser.).
ISBN 0889750807 Hbk £5.00

—Proving Discrimination in Canada / Agincourt : Carswell, 1987.
281p.
This book deals with the factual requirements of the three theories of proving discrimination in Canada and available defenses. Canadian law is analyzed in comparison to the American and British experience.

—Women and Work : Inequality in the Labour Market / Erin Phillips. – Toronto : Lorimer & Co, 1983.
– (Canadian Issues Ser.).
ISBN 0888626088 Hbk £15.95
ISBN 088862607X Pbk £6.95

DISCRIMINATION – GREAT BRITAIN
—Equal Opportunities / Oxford : Blackwell Scientific, 1988.
ISBN 0631159754 Pbk £8.95

—Equality and discrimination : essays in freedom and justice : papers presented at the United Kingdom Association for Legal and Social Philosophy eleventh annual conference at University College London, 6th-8th April 1984 / edited by Stephen Guest and Alan Milne. – Stuttgart : Steiner, 1985.
102p; 24cm.
Bound with Beihefte nos. 22 and 23..

—Positive discrimination, social justice and social policy : moral scrutiny of a policy practice / John Edwards : foreword by Lord Scarman. – London : Tavistock, 1986.
x,243p; 22cm.
Bibliography: p222-235. - Includes index.
ISBN 0422614009 Hbk £19.95
ISBN 0422789909 Pbk £8.95

—Sex and ethnic monitoring, discrimination and equal pay : new codes and regulations / by Greville Janner. – New Malden : Croner Publications, 1984.
vi,120p.
Includes index.
ISBN 0900319321

DISMISSAL
—Law and Practice in the Termination of Employment in ASEAN : a Collection of Papers and the Laws from Six Member States / Geneva : International Labour Office, 1986.
147p.
ISBN 9221054357 Hbk £10.00

—Unfair dismissal : a guide to relevant case law / by Michael Rubenstein and Yvonne Frost – S.l. : s.n., 1983.
63p; 30cm.

DISMISSAL - AUSTRALIA
—Termination of Employment / 2nd ed. – North Ryde : C.C.H. Australia, 1984.
192p.
ISBN 0869037390 Hbk £23.00

DISMISSAL - CANADA
—Butterworths Wrongful Dismissal Practice Manual, 2 Vols. / Butterworths.

—Law of Dismissal in Canada / Aurora : Canada Law Book Co, 1985.
403p. – (Text Books-Civil).

DISMISSAL - EUROPEAN COMMUNITY
—Quest for security : employees, tenants, wives / by Tony Honore. – London : Stevens, 1982.
xiv,128p; 19cm.
Includes index.
ISBN 0420464107 Hbk £12.00
ISBN 0420464204 Pbk £5.80

DISMISSAL - FRANCE
—Comparative dismissal law / B.W. Napier, J.-C. Javillier and P. Verge. – London : Croom Helm, 1982.
175p; 23cm.
ISBN 0709918089 £12.50

DISMISSAL - GREAT BRITAIN
—Comparative dismissal law / B.W. Napier, J.-C. Javillier and P. Verge. – London : Croom Helm, 1982.
175p; 23cm.
ISBN 0709918089 £12.50

—Dismissal and taxation of employees / Barry Titman, Peter Camp. – London : Butterworths, 1982.
xxvi,233p.
ISBN 0406129010

—Dismissed : a study of unfair dismissal and the industrial tribunal system / Linda Dickens ... et al. – Oxford : Blackwell, 1985.
xvi,379p; 23cm.
A Study of Unfair Dismissal and the Industrial Tribunal System.
ISBN 0631139257 £25.00

—Job security / Colin Bourn. – London : Sweet & Maxwell, 1980.
90p; 18cm.
Includes index.
ISBN 0421272805 Pbk £1.95

—Law on unfair dismissal : guidance for small firms / Joan Henderson. – London : H.M.S.O., 1982.
13p.

—Redundancy law and practice / Colin Bourn. – London : Butterworths, 1983.
xxv,320p; 22cm.
Includes index.
ISBN 0406258147 Pbk Unpriced

—Right to dismiss / Michael Whincup. – London : Collins, 1986.
200p; 24cm.
Includes index.
ISBN 0003832449 £17.50

—Right to dismiss / Oxford : Blackwell Scientific, 1987.
ISBN 0632018933 Hbk £17.95

—Termination of employment / Robert Upex. – 2nd ed. – London : Sweet & Maxwell, 1986.
xlii,148p; 26cm.
Examines entitlement to the various remedies, defines the status of employment and 'marginal employment', and looks at statutory rights with regard to redundancy and unfair dismissal. Contains examples of the calculation of compensation for redundancy and unfair dismissal, and looks at taxation of damages, and mitigation.
ISBN 0421347708 £16.50

—Tolley's employees' rights in receiverships and liquidations / Guy T.E. Parsons, William F. Ratford. – 2nd ed. – Croyden : Tolley, 1984.
xiv,210p; 30cm.
Previous ed.: 1979. Bibliography: p201. - Includes index.
ISBN 0854591443 £25.00

—Understanding dismissal law / Martin Edwards. – London : Waterlow, 1984.
xiv,188p; 21cm. – (Waterlow's business library).
Includes index.
ISBN 0080391745 Pbk £7.95

—Unfair dismissal / Malcolm Mead. – London : Oyez, 1981.
xxxv,287p; 24cm.
Includes index.

—Unfair dismissal handbook / Malcolm Mead. – 2nd ed. – London : Oyez Longman, 1983.
xxxvii,368p.
Previous ed.: published as 'Unfair dismissal', 1981.
Includes index.
ISBN 0851206913

DISMISSAL - INDIA
—Law of Dismissals / 7th ed. – Allahabad : Law Book Company, 1985.
1,000p.

—Law of Simple Discharge (In Private and Public Sectors) / Harminder Singh. – Lucknow : Eastern Book Company, 1984.
1,037p.

DISMISSAL - IRELAND
—Dismissal law in the Republic of Ireland / by Mary Redmond. – Dublin : Incorporated Law Society of Ireland, 1982.
xliii, 296 p.; 22 cm.
Includes indexes. Bibliography: p. 274-284.
ISBN 0902027220 pbk.

DISMISSAL - NEW ZEALAND
—Dismissal and Redundancy Procedures / Margaret A. Mulgan. – Butterworths, 1985.
Outline of the different procedures which may be taken by the dismissed employee after the termination of the employment contract. Unjustified and 'victimisation' dismissals are examined in detail with the appropriate remedial procedures. Analyses judicial decisions, and deals with the problems of redundancy dismissals and payment of compensation.
ISBN 040970136X Hbk £57.20

DISPUTE RESOLUTION
—Canadian Council on International Law : Conference Proceedings /. – Ottawa : Canadian Council on International Law, 1984.

—Effective dispute resolution for the international commercial lawyer / Dennis Campbell, Peter Summerfield. – Kluwer Law and Taxation, 1989.
240.
Covers practical remedies under German law, arbitration and the enforcement of arbitration awards, mediation-arbitration and other alternatives for resolving international commercial disputes, and government litigation.
ISBN 9065444157 Pbk £31/Dfl 98

—Extrajudicial dispute settlement / Clive M. Schmitthoff. – Deventer : Kluwer Law and Taxation, 1985.
18p.
Includes bibliographical references.
ISBN 9065442340

—Reparation and mediation : a bibliography / prepared by Stanley Prashker and Nigel Brearley for Forum for Initiatives in Reparation and Mediation (FIRM). – s.l. : Forum for Initiatives in Reparation and Mediation, 1986.
52p.

DISPUTE RESOLUTION - AUSTRALIA
—Dispute Resolution in Commercial Matters : Papers-Colloquium, Australian Academy of Science, Canberra, 6 June 1986 / Kingston : Australian Government Publishing Service, 1986.
175p.
ISBN 0644054344 Hbk £9.95

—Dispute Resolutions in Australia-Japan Transactions / K. Iwasaki. – North Ryde : Law Book Co, 1983.
xxix, 185p.
ISBN 0455202648 Hbk £91.00

—Two Laws : Managing Disputes in a Contemporary Aboriginal Community / Canberra City : Australian Institute of Aboriginal Studies, 1986.
176p.
ISBN 0855751746 Hbk £25.95

DISPUTE RESOLUTION - CANADA
—Family Mediation Handbook / Toronto : Butterworths.

—Family Mediation Handbook / Toronto : Butterworths, 1987.
300p.
Explains what makes mediation different from other forms of dispute resolution, addresses issues such as the establishment of the mediator's impartiality and clarifying the roles of mediator or solicitor, and discusses effects of mediation procedure on children of separation and divorce.
ISBN 0409811610 Pbk £35.95

—Family Mediation : Theory and Practice of Dispute Resolutions / Michael Benjamin. – Agincourt : Carswell, 1987.
320p.
This work is a comprehensive guide to family mediation, the process of resolving property support and custody issues with the aid of a third party in Canada. The effectiveness of various mediation efforts based on empirical studies is presented in the work.

DISPUTE RESOLUTION - JAPAN
—Dispute Resolutions in Australia-Japan Transactions / K. Iwasaki. – North Ryde : Law Book Co, 1983.
xxix, 185p.
ISBN 0455202648 Hbk £91.00

DISSENTING OPINIONS
—Dissenting and separate opinions at the World Court / Ijaz Hussain. – The Hague : M. Nijhoff Publishers, 1984.
xv,335p.
Revision of thesis (doctorate)–University of Nice, 1974 under title: Le r$ole dialectique des opinions dissidentes et individuelles dans le developpement du droit international a la CIJ. Bibliography: p309-321. Includes index.
ISBN 9024729203 Hbk £145.00

DISSERTATIONS, ACADEMIC - GREAT BRITAIN
—Dissertation handbook : a guide to research and writing / by Peter Willis. – London : RIBA, 1983.
55p; 30cm.
ISBN 0900630868

DISTRESS - AUSTRALIA - SOUTH AUSTRALIA
—Report ... relating to the reform of the law of distress / Law Reform Committee of South Australia. – Adelaide : Government Printer, 1983.
8p. – (66th report).

DISTRESS - CANADA
—Distress for Rent / Victoria : Government of British Columbia, 1981.

DISTRESS - CANADA - BRITISH COLUMBIA
—Report on distress for rent / Victoria : Queen's Printer, 1982.
72p.
ISBN 0771882947

DISTRESS - ENGLAND
—Consultation paper on the Distress for Rent Rules 1983 / Lord Chancellor's Department. – London : The Department, 1987.
13,12 leaves. – (HH/290).
Includes the text of draft revised Distress for Rent Rules 1987.

—Distress for rent / the Law Commission. – London : H.M.S.O., 1986.
vi,146p. – (Working paper).
Includes bibliographical references.
ISBN 0117301787

DISTRESS - GREAT BRITAIN
—Law of Distresses and Replevins : With Appendix of English Precedents in Replevins / 3rd ed. Repr. of 1794 ed. – Abingdon : Professional Books.
460p.

DISTRIBUTIVE JUSTICE
—Giving desert its due : social justice and legal theory / Wojciech Sadurski. – Dordrecht : D. Reidel, 1985.
xii, 329p.
Includes index. Bibliography: p 309-318.
ISBN 9027719411 Hbk £47.00

DIVISION OF LABOUR
—Division of labour in society / Emile Durkheim : translated by W.D. Halls : with an introduction by Lewis Coser. – 2nd ed. – Basingstoke : Macmillan, 1984.
lix,352p; 22cm.
Includes index.
ISBN 0333339800 Pbk £18.00
ISBN 0333339819 No price

DIVORCE
—Conciliation in separation and divorce : finding common ground / Lisa Parkinson. – London : Croom-Helm, 1986.
192p; 23cm.
Includes bibliography and index.
ISBN 0709940475 Hbk £17.95
ISBN 070994053X Pbk £8.95

—Divorce mediation and the legal process / edited by Robert Dingwall and John Eekelaar. – Oxford : Clarendon Press, 1988.
197p.
Includes index. Bibliography: p.183-193.
ISBN 0198255764

—Divorce : The Financial Consequences / Belfast : Queen's University of Belfast, 1986.
30p.

—Family law : an interdisciplinary perspective / Howard H. Irving, editor. – Toronto : Carswell, 1981.
xi,215p.
Includes bibliographical references. Subtitle on cover: Law for the helping professions.
ISBN 0459333801

—Marriage and cohabitation in contemporary societies : areas of legal, social and ethical change : an international and interdisciplinary study / edited by John M. Eekelaar, Sanford Katz : with an introduction by William J. Goode. – Toronto : Butterworths, 1980.
xviii,454p; 24cm.
Includes bibliographical references. Papers presented at the Third World Conference of the International Society on Family Law, held June 5-9, 1979 at Uppsala, Sweden.
ISBN 0409828602

—Marriage or Divorce : the Real Issue / Dublin : Four Courts Press.
128p.

—Rights of Spouses Relating to the Occupation of the Family Home and the Use of the Household Contents / Strasbourg : Council of Europe, 1982.
ISBN 928710042X

—A short guide to divorce in the Sheriff Court / 2nd. – Edinburgh : W Green & Son, 1987.
A practical handbook detailing the more important rules and procedure with specimen craves, style divorce writs and the relevant Ordinary Cause forms.
ISBN 0414007816 SOFTBACK

DIVORCE – AUSTRALIA

—Divorce : an Australian Women's Guide / Richmond : Heinemann.
144p.
ISBN 0858593114 Pbk £12.95

—Divorce in Australia / by Donald E. Stewart and Margaret Harrison. – Melbourne, Vic. : Institute of Family Studies, 1982.
9 p.; 23 cm. – (Working paper).
Cover title. 'October 1982.'. Bibliography: p. 9.
ISBN 0642886504 pbk.

—Family law regulations : inquiry into costs : report / by Mr. Justice L.H. Williams. – Canberra : Australian Government Publishing Service, 1980.
58p; 25cm. – (Parliamentary papers).
ISBN 064205827X

—Implications of marital separation for young children / compiled by the Australian Institute of Family Studies from a report of a survey conducted in 1982-83 by G.W. Smiley, E.R. Chamberlain and L.I. Dalgleish. – Melbourne : Australian Institute of Family Studies, 1987.
ix,45p. – (Working paper).
Bibliography: p.33-45.

—Superannuation and family law / Family Law Council. – Canberra : Australian Government Publishing Service, 1980.
xiii,49p. – (Working paper).
ISBN 064205052X

DIVORCE – CANADA

—Canadian divorce law and practice / by James C. MacDonald and Lee K. Ferrier. – 2. – Toronto : Carswell, 1969.
English and/or French. Includes text of Divorce Act 1985.
ISBN 045930450X unpriced

—Canadian divorce law and practice / Lee K. Ferrier. – 2nd ed. – Toronto : Carswell, 1986.
looseleaf.
Includes text of Divorce Act 1985.
ISBN 0459389505

—Divorce Act Update / Vancouver : Continuing Legal Education Society of British Columbia, 1987.
669p.
ISBN 0865043043 Hbk £75.00

—Divorce law in Canada : proposals for change / Canada. – Ottawa : Department of Justice, 1984.
32,32p.
French title: Propositions de reforme du droit du divorce au Canada. Pages numbered in opposite directions. English and French text.
ISBN 0662523504

—Divorce Mediation : The Rational Alternative / Agincourt : Carswell, 1980.
216p.

—Family law in Canada / by Christine Davies. – 4th ed. – Toronto : Carswell Legal Publications, 1984.
cl, 681 p.; 26 cm.
Rev. ed. of: Power on divorce and other matrimonial causes / W. Kent Power. 'Table of cases': p. xvii-cxxv. 'Table of statutes': p. cxxviii-cl. Includes bibliographical references, legislation, and index.
ISBN 045936300X pbk.

—Marriage and Divorce / Community Legal Education Ontario. – 3rd rev. ed. – Toronto : Community Legal Education Ontario, 1982.
47p.
ISBN 088903057X Pbk £6.50

—New divorce law : a commentary on the Divorce Act, 1985 / Alastair Bissett-Johnson and David C. Day. – Toronto : Carswell, 1986.
xxiii, 291 p.; 24 cm.
Includes legislation. Includes bibliographical references and index.
ISBN 0459387405 pbk.

—Payne's Digest on Divorce in Canada (1968-1980) / Toronto : DeBoo, 1982.
ISBN 0888201176 Hbk £100.00

—Payne's Digest on Divorce in Canada / Toronto : DeBoo.
Looseleaf service.
ISBN 0888201206 loose £265.00

—Payne's Divorce and Family Law Digest, 2 Vols. / Toronto : DeBoo.
This looseleaf service contains the information required to negotiate settlements and the materials needed to prepare for litigation involving such issues as support, custody, & property division. The case digests provided cover such areas as Ontario's Family Law Act, 1986, enforcement, costs, evidence, procedure, and tax considerations. Six updates per year are planned.
ISBN 0888202423 loose £265.00

—Reville's Divorce Act Annotated / Aurora : Canada Law Book Co.
The third edition of Reville's Divorce Act Annotated is an immediate guide to the interpretation of any section of the new Divorce Act. Over 1500 cases from the previous Act, with ongoing relevance, are considered in terms of the new Act. The new edition is provided in looseleaf format permitting quarterly updates.

DIVORCE – CANADA – ALBERTA

—Divorce Guide for Alberta : Step-by-Step Guide to Obtaining Your Own Divorce / 5th ed. – North Vancouver : International Self-Counsel Press, 1986.
87p.
ISBN 088908243X Hbk £9.95

—Matrimonial property : division of pension benefits upon marriage breakdown / Institute of Law Research and Reform. – Edmonton : The Institute, 1985.
ii,127,25,13p. – (Report for discussion).

DIVORCE – CANADA – BRITISH COLUMBIA

—Divorce Guide for British Columbia : Step-by-Step Guide to Obtaining Your Own Divorce / 10th ed. – North Vancouver : International Self-Counsel Press, 1986.
88p.
ISBN 0889081816 Hbk £10.95

—Report on spousal agreements / Law Reform Commission of British Columbia. – Victoria : Queens Printer, 1986.
37p.
Includes bibliographical references.
ISBN 0771885326

—Spousal agreements / Law Reform Commission of British Columbia. – Vancouver : The Commission, 1985.
iii,74p. – (Working paper).
Includes bibliographical references.

DIVORCE – CANADA – MANITOBA

—Divorce Guide for Manitoba / North Vancouver : International Self-Counsel Press, 1987.
ISBN 0889085110 Hbk £11.95

DIVORCE – CANADA – ONTARIO

—Divorce Guide for Ontario : Step-by-Step Guide to Obtaining Your Own Divorce / 6th ed. – North Vancouver : International Self-Counsel Press, 1986.
105p.
ISBN 0889083525 Hbk £12.95

—Divorce Guide for Ontario : Step-By-Step Guide to Obtaining Your Own Divorce / 7th ed. – North Vancouver : International Self-Counsel Press, 1988.

DIVORCE – CANADA – SASKATCHEWAN

—Divorce Guide for Saskatchewan / North Vancouver : International Self-Counsel Press, 1987.
ISBN 0889085129 Hbk £12.95

—Proposals relating to the change of name of children of divorced parents : report to the Minister of Justice / Law Reform Commission of Saskatchewan. – Saskatoon : The Commission, 1985.
8p.

DIVORCE – DOMINICAN REPUBLIC

—Dominican Republic : divorce law / Armando E. Gonzales. – Washington, D.C. : Law Library, Library of Congress, 1986.
v,43p.

DIVORCE – ENGLAND

—'Better way out' reviewed : memorandum / by the Society's Standing Committee on Family Law. – London : Law Society, 1982.
41p.

—Distribution of matrimonial assets on divorce / Michael L. Rakusen, D. Peter Hunt. – 2nd ed. – London : Butterworths, 1982.
xxii,375p.
Latest supplement held: 1986.
ISBN 0406351015

—Divorce conciliation : a study of services in England and abroad, with implications for Scotland / Edinburgh : Scottish Council for Single Parents, 1982.
v,99p.
Includes bibliographies.

—Facing the future : a discussion paper on the ground for divorce / the Law Commission. – London : H.M.S.O., 1988.
51p. – (HC).
ISBN 0102479887

—Fair to the family : a conciliation approach to divorce and separation / by Clare Dyer : illustrated by Claudia Aaron. – East Twickenham : Mediation in Divorce, 1988.
40p.
ISBN 0951313606

—Family law : the financial consequences of divorce : the basic policy : a discussion paper / the Law Commission. – London : H.M.S.O., 1980.
57p; 25cm.
ISBN 0101804105 Pbk £3.70

—Family law : the financial consequences of divorce : the response to the Law Commission's Discussion paper, and recommendations on the policy of the law / the Law Commission. – London : H.M.S.O., 1981.
iii,23p; 25cm.
ISBN 0102068828

—Justice and welfare in divorce / Mervyn Murch. – London : Sweet & Maxwell, 1980.
viii,307p; 22cm.
Includes index.
ISBN 0421264004 Pbk £10.75

—Maintenance after divorce / John Eekelaar and Mavis Maclean. – Oxford : Clarendon, 1985.
x,171p; 22cm.
Bibliography: p161-168. - Includes index.
ISBN 0198255306 Pbk £19.50
ISBN 0198255292 £8.95

—Matrimonial and Family Proceedings Act 1984 : a practical guide / Richard M. Smith. – London : Oyez, 1984.
xviii,125p.
Includes index.
ISBN 0851208789

—Rayden and Jackson's law and practice in divorce and family matters / Joseph Jackson, Margaret Booth, G. J. Maple, A. K. Biggs. – 15th ed. 2 v. – London : Butterworths, 1988.
26cm.
Kept up to date by a looseleaf service.
ISBN 0406351317

—Reconciliation and conciliation in the context of divorce / by a committee of the Order of Christian Unity. – 2nd ed. – London : Order of Christian Unity, 1983.
48p.
Includes bibliographies.

—Report of the Matrimonial Causes Procedure Committee : presented to the Lord Chancellor July 1985 / Margaret Booth. – London : H.M.S.O., 1985.
ix,134p.
Chairman: the Hon. Mrs Justice Booth.
ISBN 0113800045

—Surviving the breakup : how children and parents cope with divorce / Judith S. Wallerstein and Joan Berlin Kelly. – London : Grant McIntyre, 1980.
x,341p; 22cm.
Also published: New York : Basic Books, 1980. Includes index.
ISBN 0862160251 £10.95
ISBN 086216026X

—Time restrictions on presentation of divorce and nullity petitions / the Law Commission. – London : H.M.S.O., 1980.
v,83p; 21cm. – (Working paper).
ISBN 0117301566 Pbk £3.50

—Towards a unified Family Court : the collection of maintenance and the enforcement of court orders for maintenance / research by Jean Graham Hall and Douglas F. Martin. – s.l. : s. n., 1984.
ca.200 leaves.
Includes some French text.

DIVORCE – EUROPEAN COMMUNITY

—Quest for security : employees, tenants, wives / by Tony Honore. – London : Stevens, 1982.
xiv,128p; 19cm.
Includes index.
ISBN 0420464107 Hbk £12.00
ISBN 0420464204 Pbk £5.80

DIVORCE – FRANCE

—Towards a unified Family Court : the collection of maintenance and the enforcement of court orders for maintenance / research by Jean Graham Hall and Douglas F. Martin. – s.l. : s. n., 1984.
ca.200 leaves.
Includes some French text.

DIVORCE – GREAT BRITAIN

—British nationality and the right of abode 1945-1983 / by K.J. Gray : by C.C. Turpin. – Deventer : Kluwer, 1986.
vii,269p.
Includes bibliographical references.
ISBN 9065442510

—Brown on Divorce / 2nd ed. – London : Shaw & Sons, 1986.
ISBN 0721910505 loose £75.00

—Brown on Separation / London : Shaw & Sons, 1981.
ISBN 0721908403 Pbk £16.00

—Child Custody and Divorce / Oxford : Croom Helm, 1984.
ISBN 0709917988 Pbk £8.95

—Children and divorce : economic factors / by Mavis Maclean and John Eekelaar. - Oxford : SSRC Centre for Socio-Legal Studies, 1983.
vii,39p; 22cm.
ISBN 0862260698

—Conciliation and Divorce / Chichester : Barry Rose, 1981.
248p.
ISBN 0859923061 Hbk £3.85

—Costs in Matrimonial Causes / London : Butterworths, 1984.
This book gives practitioners a practical discussion of the control of costs in matrimonial causes in the United Kingdom. This work provides guidance to the lawyer seeking to avoid costs out of proportion to the settlement in the case.
ISBN 0406255202 Pbk

—Divorce Handbook / London : Allison & Busby, 1986.
ISBN 185031724X Pbk £4.95

—Divorce Matters / Pelican, 1987.
ISBN 0140226133 Pbk £3.95

—Divorce matters / Jacqueline Burgoyne, Roger Ormrod and Martin Richards. - Harmondsworth : Penguin, 1987.
216p0; 20cm. - (A Pelican book).
ISBN 0140226133

—Divorce Mediation and the Legal Process / Eekelaar. - Oxford : Oxford University Press, 1987.
ISBN 0198255756 Pbk £9.95
ISBN 0198255764 Hbk £20.00

—Family law : financial relief after foreign divorce / Great Britain. - London : H.M.S.O., 1980.
v,83p. - (Working paper).
ISBN 0117301574

—Family law : time restrictions on presentation of divorce and nullity petitions : laid before Parliament ... pursuant to section 3(2) of the Law Commissions Act 1965 / The Law Commission. - London : H.M.S.O., 1982.
iv,77p. - (HC).
ISBN 0102513821

—Grounds for divorce / Gwynn Davis and Mervyn Murch. - Oxford : Clarendon Press, 1988.
x,177p.
Bibliography: pp.169-171. - Includes index. Examines, through social research, the legal ending of marriage. Reviews the present law and suggests future reforms. The focus is on the relationship between the personal experience of parties and legal foms of divorce. The 'process over time' reform proposal has been adopted by the Law Commission.
ISBN 019825220X Hbk £20

—Guide to the Matrimonial and Family Proceedings Act 1984 / M.D.A. Freeman. - Bicester, Oxfordshire : CCH Editions, 1984.
165p; 23cm.
Contains examination of divorce, the new one year ban, extending time limits of nullity proceedings, financial relief in divorce proceedings, and financial relief after overseas divorces, financial provision in Scotland after overseas divorce, family business, and distribution and transfer.
ISBN 0863250319

—Maintenance after Divorce / Maclean. - Oxford : Oxford University Press, 1986.
ISBN 0198255292 Pbk £9.95
ISBN 0198255306 Hbk £22.50

—Matrimonial Causes / Salter. - 17th ed. - London : Longman Professional, 1988.
ISBN 0851211445 Pbk

—Matrimonial Causes (Amend No 2) Rules 1985 / London : Longman Professional, 1986.
ISBN 0851212069 Pbk £6.50

—Matrimonial Proceedings / Marilyn Mornington. - London : Longman Professional, 1988.
ISBN 0851244126 Pbk £9.95

—Matrimonial proceedings before Magistrates / Horsman. - 4th ed. - London : Butterworths, 1981.
ISBN 040634602X Hbk £46.00

—Occupational pension rights on divorce : a consultation paper / Lord Chancellor's Department. - London : The Department, 1985.
30p.
Includes bibliographical references.

—On divorce / 2nd ed. - London : Shaw & Sons, 1986.
ISBN 0721910505 Hbk £75.00

—On divorce and family matters / Jackson. - 15th ed. - London : Butterworths, 1988.
ISBN 0406351317 Hbk £285.00

—On separation / London : Shaw & Sons, 1981.
ISBN 0721908403 Pbk £11.00

—Partisans and mediators : the resolution of divorce disputes / Gwynn Davis. - Oxford : Clarendon Press, 1988.
x,219p.
Bibliography: pp.211-215. - Includes index. Concerns divorcing couples who seek help in negotiating over money or children, and the partisans or mediators who assist. Concludes that the prospect of a genuine non-coercive agreement is being undermined by such considerations as cost, and the limitations of the 'due process'.
ISBN 0198256124 Hbk £25

—Precedents in matrimonial causes and ancillary matters / Turner. - 2nd ed. - London : Sweet & Maxwell, 1988.
ISBN 0421385200 Hbk £95.00

—Property, divorce and retirement pension rights / by K.J. Gray : by C.C. Turpin. - Deventer : Kluwer, 1986.
vii,269p.
Includes bibliographical references.
ISBN 9065442510

—Rayden on Divorce, 2 Vols. / London : Butterworths.
This work in two volumes offers a complete encyclopedia for practitioners in the field of divorce in the United Kingdom. Relevant statutes, statutory instruments, Practice Directions, and material relating to tax and legal aid are included. Cumulative supplements are provided.
ISBN 0406351759 Pbk

—Report / P. D. Robinson. - London : H.M.S.O., 1983.
lv. (various pagings).
Chairman: P. D. Robinson.
ISBN 011390634X

—Services for Conciliation in Divorce / Lisa Parkinson. - Aberdeen : Aberdeen University Press, 1984.
ISBN 008030379X Hbk

—Tax Planning on Marriage Breakdown / 2nd ed. - London : Oyez Longman, 1981.
- (Oyez Longman Practical Tax Ser.).
ISBN 0851206182 Hbk £11.50

—Tax planning on marriage breakdown / 4th ed. - London : Longman Professional, 1986.
ISBN 0851210740 Pbk £26.50

—Taxation of marriage and marriage breakdown / Croydon : Tolley, 1988.
ISBN 0854593233 Hbk

—Taxation on divorce and separation / J. Gray. - Bicester : CCH Editions, 1987.
xi,103p; 23cm.
Includes index.
ISBN 0863251072 Pbk No price

—Victorian divorce / Oxford : Croom Helm, 1985.
ISBN 0709937652 Hbk £17.95

DIVORCE - INDIA

—Family law : law of marriage and divorce in India / by Paras Diwan. - New Delhi : Sterling Publishers, 1983.
xxviii,470p.
Authors name on spine: Paras Diwan.

—Law of Marriage and Divorce in India / Lucknow : Eastern Book Company, 1982.
xxxii, 718p.

DIVORCE - IRELAND

—Case for divorce in the Irish Republic : a report commissioned by the Irish Council for Civil Liberties / William Duncan. - Rev. ed. with postscript. - Dublin : The Council, 1982.
107p.
Includes bibliographical references.

—Is divorce the answer? : an examination of no-fault divorce against the background of the Irish debate / William Binchy. - Blackrock, C. Dublin : Irish Academic, 1984.
115p; 22cm.
Bibliography: p111-115.
ISBN 071650314X Pbk £2.95

—Report on divorce a mensa et thoro and related matters / the Law Reform Commission. - Dublin : The Commission, 1983.
vii,90p. - (LRC).
Includes bibliographical references.

—Report on recognition of foreign divorces and legal separations / the Law Reform Commission. - Dublin : The Commission, 1985.
v,38p. - (LRC).

DIVORCE - NEW ZEALAND

—Divorce in New Zealand : a social history / Roderick Phillips. - Auckland : Oxford University Press, 1981.
154p.
Bibliography: p.149-152. - Includes index.
ISBN 019558077X

DIVORCE - NORTHERN IRELAND

—Family breakdown, children and the law / by Gilliam Kerr. - Belfast : SLS Legal Publications, 1985.
xii,68p.
Includes index.
ISBN 0853892555

—Separation and Divorce in Northern Ireland / Belfast : Queen's University of Belfast, 1986.
125p.

DIVORCE - SCOTLAND

—Divorce conciliation : a study of services in England and abroad, with implications for Scotland / Edinburgh : Scottish Council for Single Parents, 1982.
v,99p.
Includes bibliographies.

—Family law, report on aliment and financial provision / Scottish Law Commission. - Edinburgh : H.M.S.O., 1981.
x,239p; 25cm. - (H.C.).
ISBN 0102002827 Pbk £8.40

—Ground for divorce : should the law be changed? / Scottish Law Commission. - Edinburgh : The Commission, 1988.
23p. - (Discussion paper).

—Scottish Family Conciliation Service (Lothian) : report of an assessment of the first two years of the service, March 1984 - February 1986 / Susan M.G. Matheson, Hugh Gentleman. - Edinburgh : Scottish Office Central Research Unit, 1986.
6,53p.

—Short guide to divorce in the Sheriff Court / S.A. Bennett. - Edinburgh : W. Green, 1984.
xix, 142p; 22cm.
Includes index.
ISBN 041400728X Pbk Unpriced

DIVORCE - SOUTH AFRICA

—Investigation into the possibility of making provision for a divorced woman to share in the pension benefits of her former husband / South African Law Commission. - Pretoria : The Commission, 1984.
v,67leaves. - (Project).
Bibliography: p.66-67.

—Investigation into the possiblity of making provision for a divorced woman to share in the pension benefits of her former husband / South African Law Commission. - Pretoria : The Commission, 1986.
x,77p. - (Report).
Bibliography: pp.vi-x. Includes draft legislation.
ISBN 0621113573

—Reform of the South African law of divorce : The dissolution of marriages on presumption of death act 23 of 1979, The divorce act 70 of 1979 / by H. R. Hahlo and June D. Sinclair. - Cape Town : Juta, 1980.
vi, 66 p.; 25 cm.
'Supplement to Hahlo, The South African law of husband and wife, 4 ed. (1975).'. Includes texts of laws. Includes bibliographical references and index.
ISBN 0702110582 pbk.

DIVORCE - UNITED STATES

—Divorce Guide for Oregon / 4th ed. - North Vancouver : International Self-Counsel Press, 1988.
ISBN 088908825X Hbk

—Divorce Guide for Washington : Step-By-Step Guide for Obtaining Your Own Divorce / 5th ed. - North Vancouver : International Self-Counsel Press, 1988.
ISBN 0889087385 Hbk

DIVORCE (ISLAMIC LAW)

—Law of Muslim Marriage, Dissolution and Maintenance / 2nd ed. - Allahabad : Law Book Company, 1988.
600p.

DNA - SCOTLAND

—Evidence : blood group tests, DNA tests and related matters / Scottish Law Commission. - Edinburgh : The Commission, 1988.
i,45p. - (Discussion paper).

DOCUMENT DELIVERY

—Services of Process Abroad : Hague Convention / London : Butterworths.

DOCUMENT DELIVERY - GREAT BRITAIN

—Service of documents / London : Longman Professional, 1982.
- (LPPN73).
ISBN 0851206867 Pbk £13.95

—Service of documents / 2nd. - London : Longman Professional (UK), 1989.
- (Practitioner series).
Contains a section dealing with service out of the jurisdiction. Second edition revised to take account of new rules governing county court summonses. Includes assessment of the impact of the Judgement Act 1982 (in force 1987), and all new forms and tables are covered.
ISBN 0851216099 Hbk £24.95

DOCUMENT DRAFTING - AUSTRALIA

—Laying Down the Law : The Foundations of Legal Reasoning Research and Writing in Australia and New Zealand / C. Cook. - Sydney : Butterworths, 1988.
304p.
This workbook contains exercises which require students to find cases and statutes, analyze legal problems, interpret judicial decisions and legislation, and use basic research tools such as digests and encyclopedias. Additional material has been included to cover New Zealand.

DOCUMENT DRAFTING - CANADA

—Drafting Commercial Documents / Vancouver : Continuing Legal Education Society of British Columbia, 1981.
278p.
ISBN 0865040206 Hbk £65.00

—Legal Writing for Understanding, Clarity and Precision / Vancouver : British Columbia Continuing Legal Education Society, 1982.
84p.
ISBN 0865040672 Hbk £35.00

DOCUMENT DRAFTING - GREAT BRITAIN

—Drafting / London : Butterworths, 1980.
ISBN 0406358907 Hbk £44.00

—Drafting and Negotiating Commercial Leases / 2nd ed. - London : Butterworths, 1984.
ISBN 0406359075 Hbk £29.00

—Drafting Business Leases / 2nd ed. - London : Longman Professional, 1986.
ISBN 0851210244 Hbk £28.95

—Draftsman's Handbook / London : Longman Professional, 1985.
ISBN 0851209505 Pbk £19.50

—Kelly's Draftsman / Ramage. - 15th ed. - London : Butterworths, 1986.
ISBN 0406263159 Hbk £69.00

—Legislative Draftsmen : Short List of Legislative Draftsmen Available for Short Ad Hoc Assignments / London : Commonwealth Secretariat, 1982.

—Patent claim : drafting and interpretation / London : Longman Professional, 1983.
ISBN 0851206859 Hbk £58.00

—Residential leases : draftsman's handbook / London : Longman Professional, 1985.
ISBN 085120774X Pbk £19.95

—Will draftsman's handbook / 5th ed. - London : Longman Professional, 1987.
ISBN 0851212743 Pbk £18.95

DOCUMENT DRAFTING - NEW ZEALAND

—Kelly's Draftsman / R. W. Ramage. - 15th ed. - Wellington : Butterworths, 1986.
This book is a guide to drafting documents in a variety of commercial law settings. Carefully annotated model contracts are provided in a well organized manner. For the United Kingdom practitioner.
ISBN 0406263159 Hbk

DOCUMENT DRAFTING - SCOTLAND

—Drafting and Negotiating Common Leases Scotland / McKichan. - London : Butterworths, 1985.
ISBN 0406359067 Hbk £41.50

DOCUMENTARY CREDIT

—Current problems of letters of credit and bankers' quarantees / William C. Hillman. - London : International Bar Association, 1985.
iii,404p.
Papers presented at the seminar in Amsterdam, 8-9 May 1984. Seminar Chairman: Judge William C. Hillman.

—Documentary Credits / Dordrecht : Kluwer, 1984.
ISBN 9065440755 Pbk £125.00

—Law of bankers' commercial credits / Maurice Megrah. - 7th ed. - London : Europa, 1984.
xxxv,343p; 25cm.
Previous ed.: 1979. Bibliography: pxxxiv-xxxv. - Includes index.
ISBN 0905118782 £19.50

DOCUMENTARY CREDIT - ENGLAND

—Banker's documentary credits : issued in accordance with the Uniform customs and practice (1974 revision) of the International Chamber of Commerce / by F.M. Ventris. - 2nd ed. - London : Lloyd's of London Press, 1983.
xxi,350p.
Previous ed.: 1980. Includes index.
ISBN 0907432379

DOCUMENTARY CREDIT - GREAT BRITAIN

—Documentary Credits Handbook / Cambridge : Woodhead-Faulkner, 1988.
ISBN 0859413721 Hbk £45.00

DOCUMENTARY EVIDENCE

—Discovery : a comparison between English and American civil discovery law with reform proposals / Julius Byron Levine. - Oxford : Clarendon, 1982.
xl,208p; 23cm.
Bibliography: p154-160. - Includes index.
ISBN 0198253680 £16.00

—Harmonisation of laws relating to the requirement of written proof and to the admissibility of reproductions of documents and recordings on computers : Recommendation No.R (81) 20 adopted by the Committee of Ministers of the Council of Europe on 11 December 1981 and Explanatory memorandum / Council of Europe. - Strabourg : Council of Europe, 1982.
21p; 21cm. - (Legal Affairs).
ISBN 9287100446

DOCUMENTARY EVIDENCE - AUSTRALIA

—Evidence reference / Australian Law Reform Commission. - Sydney : The Commission, 1982.
v,87p.
Includes bibliographical references.

DOCUMENTARY EVIDENCE - CANADA

—Documentary evidence in Canada / by J. Douglas Ewart in association with Michael Lomer and Jeff Casey. - Canada : Carswell Legal Publications, 1984.
xxxvii, 389 p.; 24 cm.
Includes bibliographical references and indexes.
ISBN 0459359509

DOCUMENTARY EVIDENCE - ENGLAND

—Computer generated output as admissible evidence in civil and criminal cases : a report / by the Professional Advisory Committee of the British Computer Society : edited by T.R.H. Sizer and A. Kelman. - London : Heyden on behalf of the British Computer Society, 1982.
x,41p.
ISBN 0855017414

—Discovery of documents and disclosure : Order 24 / London : Lord Chancellor's Department, 1987.
4 leaves.
Memorandum outlining amendments to Order 24 of the Rules of the Supreme Court.

—Documentary evidence / Christopher Style, Charles Hollander : consulting editor: W.D. Park : with a foreword by Robert Alexander. - London : Oyez Longman, 1984.
xxi, 280p.
ISBN 085120970X

DOCUMENTARY EVIDENCE - GREAT BRITAIN

—Documentary Evidence / Hollander. - 2nd ed. - London : Longman Professional, 1981.
ISBN 0851212999 Hbk £35.00

DOCUMENTARY EVIDENCE - NEW ZEALAND

—Business records and computer output / Evidence Law Reform Committee. - s.l. : Evidence Law Reform Committee, 1985.
43 leaves, 2 leaves. - (Working paper).
Inlcudes bibliographical references.

—Report on business records and computer output / Evidence Law Reform Committee. - Wellington, N.Z. : The Committee, 1987.
58p.
Includes bibliographical references. Includes extract from Evidence Amendment Act (No. 2) 1980.

DOCUMENTATION

—Expert systems and scholarly publications / Jean-Claude Gardin. - London : British Library, 1987.
30pin various pagings; 30cm. - (The Fifth British Library Annual Research Lecture).
Includes the text in French, printed t$ete-b$eche, under the title Systemes experts et publications savantes.
ISBN 071233114X Pbk Free

DOMESTIC PROCEEDINGS - CANADA

—Family law in Canada / by Christine Davies. - 4th ed. - Toronto : Carswell Legal Publications, 1984.
cl, 681 p.; 26 cm.
Rev. ed. of: Power on divorce and other matrimonial causes / W. Kent Power. 'Table of cases': p. xvii-cxxv. 'Table of statutes': p. cxxviii-cl. Includes bibliographical references, legislation, and index.
ISBN 045936300X pbk.

DOMESTIC PROCEEDINGS - ENGLAND

—ABC guide to the practice of matrimonial causes / by Roger Bird. - London : Sweet & Maxwell, 1983.
vii,123p; 19cm.
ISBN 0421314206 Pbk £7.50

—ABC guide to the practice of matrimonial causes / by Roger Bird. - 2nd ed. - London : Sweet and Maxwell, 1987.
150p; 22cm.
Now covers the increasing role of conciliation, the principles applicable to ancillary relief applications and the 'clean break' under the Matrimonial and Family Proceedings Act 1984, ouster injunctions, foreign divorce, and the forthcoming changes following the Matrimonial Causes (Costs) Rules 1986.
ISBN 0421370904 Pbk No price

—Family court in action / David Barnard. - London : Butterworths, 1983.
xiv,281p; 26cm.
Includes index.
ISBN 0406556504 Hbk Unpriced
ISBN 0406556512 Pbk Unpriced

—Family law : financial relief after foreign divorce / the Law Commission. - London : H.M.S.O., 1982.
iii,115p. - (HC).
ISBN 0102514828

—Humphreys' matrimonial causes / Thomas S. Humphreys, D. A. Salter. - 16th ed. - London : Oyez Longman, 1984.
xxx,327p; 22cm. - (Oyez Longman practitioner series).
Previous ed.: Published as Humphreys' notes on matrimonial causes proceeding in county courts and district registries. 1981. Includes index.
ISBN 0851208428 £14.50

—Jackson's matrimonial finance and taxation / D. T. A. Davies. - 4th ed. 1. - London : Butterworths, 1986.
Previous ed.: 1980. Includes index.
ISBN 0406254478 £45.00

—Matrimonial jurisdiction of magistrates' courts / by M.D.A. Freeman and Christina M. Lyon. - Chichester : Rose, 1980.
xxv,222p; 21cm.
Includes index.
ISBN 0859921999 Pbk £10.80

—Matrimonial proceedings in magistrates courts / by Billy Strachan. - 2nd ed. - London : Sweet & Maxwell, 1987.
250p; 22cm.
Includes new material dealing with conciliation, and the effect of conduct on the amount of an order. Discusses grounds of an order for periodical payments, calculation and the amount of the order, orders for the custody of children, and for access to children, and the enforcement of orders.
ISBN 0421385006 Pbk £20.00

—Precedents in matrimonial causes and ancillary matters / by Roger Bird and C.F. Turner. - 2nd ed. - London : Sweet & Maxwell, 1988.
looseleaf.
Previous ed.: 1985. Includes index.
ISBN 0421385200 £50.00

—Pugh's matrimonial proceedings before magistrates / J. Basil Horsman. - 4th ed. - London : Butterworths, 1981.
xli, 820p.
ISBN 040634602X

—Report of the Matrimonial Causes Procedure Committee : presented to the Lord Chancellor July 1985 / Margaret Booth. - London : H.M.S.O., 1985.
ix,134p.
Chairman: the Hon. Mrs Justice Booth.
ISBN 0113800045

DOMESTIC PROCEEDINGS - GREAT BRITAIN

—Domestic Proceedings in Magistrates' Courts / Belfast : Queen's University of Belfast, 1984.
26p.

—Domestic Proceedings in the Magistrates' Court / 6th ed. - London : Oyez Longman, 1982.
- (Oyez Longman Practice Note Ser.: No. 30).
ISBN 0851206514 Hbk £12.50

—Matrimonial and Domestic Injunctions / Purdie. - 2nd ed. - London : Butterworths, 1987.
ISBN 0406334412 Pbk £32.00

—Matrimonial Consent Orders and Agreements / London : Longman Professional, 1986.
ISBN 0851211127 Pbk £12.95

—Report / P. D. Robinson. - London : H.M.S.O., 1983.
lv. (various pagings).
Chairman: P. D. Robinson.
ISBN 011390634X

DOMESTIC PROCEEDINGS - IRELAND

—Report on jurisdiction in proceedings for nullity of marriage, recognition of foreign nullity decrees, and the Hague Convention on the Celebration and Recognition of the Validity of Marriage (1978) / the Law Reform Commission. - Dublin : The Commission, 1985.
v,63p. - (LRC).
Bibliography: pp.51-2. Includes text of the Convention.

—Report on private international law aspects of capacity to marry and choice of law in proceedings for nullity of marriage / the Law Reform Commission. - Dublin : The Commission, 1985.
v,161p. - (LRC).
Bibliography: pp.156-8.

DOMESTIC PROCEEDINGS - SCOTLAND

—Family law : report on financial provision after foreign divorce / Scottish Law Commission. - Edinburgh : H.M.S.O., 1982.
47p.
ISBN 0102515824

DOMESTIC RELATIONS

—Intentional Interference with Domestic Relations / Victoria : Government of British Columbia, 1983.

—International conventions concerning applications for and awards of maintenance : explanatory documentation / prepared for Commonwealth Jurisdictions by David McClean in association with the Commonwealth Secretariat. - London : Commonwealth Secretariat, 1981.
v,83p.
ISBN 0850922003

—International economic law / Dordrecht : Martinus Nijhoff, 1989.
274.
Updated and extended version of the General Course held by the author at the Hague Academy of International Law in 1986. References to literature have been increased, and a detailed keyword index and an index of cases cited are included. Contains chapters on various aspects on international law.
ISBN 9024737990 Hbk £47

—Resolution of family conflicts / Sanford N Katz. - Scarborough, Ontario : Butterworths (Canada), 1984.
ISBN 0409839841 Hbk £32.00

DOMESTIC RELATIONS - AUSTRALIA

—Australian family law & practice reporter / by Malcolm D. Broun and Stuart G. Fowler with CCH editorial staff and contributions by Anthony F. Dickey. - North Ryde, N.S.W. : CCH Australia, 1975-.
loose-leaf; 26cm.
Includes current issues of: Australian family law cases. Loose-leaf issues accompanied by a summary report.

—Cinderella Revisited : Rights and Responsibilities in Step-families / Kingston : Australian Government Publishing Service, 1986.
40p.
ISBN 0644054360 Hbk £3.95

—Family law reports : incorporating Family law notes / Sydney : Butterworths, 1976-.
Contains reports and digests of judgments of the High Court of Australia, the Family Court of Australia, the Family Court of Western Australia, the Supreme Courts of the States and Territories.

DOMESTIC RELATIONS - CANADA

—Domestic Contracts / Agincourt : Carswell, 1987.
450p.
This looseleaf work is a practitioners guide to the drafting of cohabitation, marriage and separation agreements under the law of Ontario and British Columbia. Checklist, sample agreements, income tax considerations and related materials are included in the volume.

—Family Dispute Resolution : Litigation and Its Alternatives / Agincourt : Carswell, 1987.
118p.

DOMESTIC RELATIONS - COMMONWEALTH

—Family law : the Commonwealth experience / by Gloria Cumper. - London : Commonwealth Secretariat, 1984.
v,109p.
Includes bibliographies.
ISBN 0850922569

DOMESTIC RELATIONS - ENGLAND

—Family law / P.M. Bromley, N.V. Lowe. - 7th ed. - London : Butterworths, 1987.
lvi,793p; 25cm.
Previous ed. 1981. Includes index. Cover title: Bromley's family law.
ISBN 0406560145 Hbk £30.00
ISBN 0406560153 Pbk £17.95

DOMESTIC RELATIONS - HONG KONG

—Family law in Hong Kong / Leonard Pegg. - London : Butterworths, 1981.
xxii,183p; 23cm.
Includes index.
ISBN 0406667608

DOMESTIC RELATIONS - SCOTLAND

—Family law in Scotland / J.M. Thomson. - London : Butterworths, 1987.
xxiv,232p; 22cm.
Includes index.
ISBN 0406261903 Pbk £20.00

DOMESTIC RELATIONS - SOUTH AFRICA

—Family, things and succession / Lee and Honore. - 2nd ed. - Durban : Butterworths, 1983.
xvii,615p.
Bibliography: p.vii-xiv. - Includes index.
ISBN 0409040533

DOMESTIC VIOLENCE

—Violence against wives : a case against patriarchy / R. Emerson Dobash, Russell Dobash. - London : Open Books, 1980.
xii, 339p.
First published by Free Press, New York, 1979.
ISBN 0729101533

—Violence in the family : Recommendation no.R (85) 4 adopted by the Committee of Ministers of the Council of Europe on 26 March 1985 and Explanatory memorandum / Council of Europe. - Strasbourg : Council of Europe, 1986.
15p; 21cm. - (Legal affairs).
' ... prepared by a select committee of experts under the authority of the European Committee on Crime Problems' - p.3.

DOMESTIC VIOLENCE - AUSTRALIA

—Domestic violence / Law Reform Commission. - Canberra : Australian Government Publishing Service, 1986.
xxvi,98p. - (Report).
Bibliography: p.94-96 - Includes index.
ISBN 0644013397

—Domestic violence and the law : a study of S.99 of the Justices Act (S.A.) / by Ngaire Naffin. - 1. - Adelaide : Women's Adviser's Office, Department of the Premier and Cabinet, 1985.
various pagings.

—National Conference on Domestic Violence : proceedings, 11-15 November 1985 / edited by Suzanne E. Hatty. - Canberra, ACT : Australian Institute of Criminology, 1986.
2 v. (xix, 671 p.); 30 cm.
Includes bibliographies.
ISBN 0642102538 pbk. : v. 2

—Violence in the Family / Canberra : Australian Institute of Criminology.

DOMESTIC VIOLENCE - CANADA

—Federal/provincial/territorial report on wife battering to the meeting of ministers responsible for the status of women, Niagara-on-the Lake, May 28-30, 1984 / Ottawa : Minister of Supply and Services, 1984.
460p.
ISBN 0662133250

DOMESTIC VIOLENCE - ENGLAND

—Dealing with domestic violence / M.D.A. Freeman. - Bicester : CCH Editions, 1987.
xii,150p; 23cm.
Examines the problem, legal resources, divorce and judicial separation, the criminal law, injunctive relief, Matrimonial Homes Act 1983, Domestic Violence Act 1976, Supreme Court Act 1981/County Court Act 1984, Injunctions ancillary to other proceedings, protection in the Magistrates Court, criminal injuries compensation scheme, and the housing law implications of domestic violence.
ISBN 0863251102 Pbk

—Family violence : law & practice / Joanne Foakes. - London : Hemstal Press, 1984.
xvi,176p.
Includes index.

—Matrimonial and domestic injunctions : practice and precedents / Mark Pelling, Robert Purdie : consulting editor Augustus Ullstein : foreword by Dame Margaret Booth. - London : Butterworths, 1982.
xxi,190p; 22cm.
Includes index.
ISBN 0406334404 Pbk Unpriced

DOMESTIC VIOLENCE - GREAT BRITAIN

—Domestic Assault of Women / London : Allyn & Bacon, 1988.
ISBN 0205113230 Hbk £28.90

—Marital violence : the community response / Margaret Borkowski, Mervyn Murch, Val Walker. - London : Tavistock, 1983.
x,230p; 23cm.
Bibliography: p216-222. - Includes index.
ISBN 0422781207 Hbk Unpriced
ISBN 0422781304 Pbk Unpriced

—Private violence and public policy : the needs of battered women and the response of the public services / edited by Jan Pahl. - London : Routledge & Kegan Paul, 1985.
vi,214p; 22cm.
Bibliography: p196-207. - Includes index.
ISBN 0710099924 Pbk £6.95

—Violence against women : report of an ad-hoc working group / Women's National Commission. - London : Cabinet Office, .
59, 28p.
Includes bibliographical references.

—Violence in the Family : Theory and Practice in Social Work / London : HMSO, 1982.
71p.
ISBN 0114919917 Pbk £3.75

DOMESTIC VIOLENCE - PAPUA NEW GUINEA

—Domestic violence in Papua New Guinea / edited by Susan Toft. - Port Moresby : Law Reform Commission, 1985.
160p. - (Monograph).
ISBN 9980550015

—Domestic violence in urban Papua New Guinea / edited by Susan Toft. - Waigani : Law Reform Commission of Papua New Guinea, 1986.
vi,155p. - (Occasional paper).
Includes bibliographical references.
ISBN 9980550023

—Marriage and domestic violence in rural Papua New Guinea / results of a research project conducted by the Law Reform Commission of Papua New Guinea : by Susan Toft and Susanne Bonnell. - Waigani : Law Reform Commission of Papua New Guinea, 1985.
v,116p. - (Occasional paper).
Bibliography: p.111.
ISBN 9980550007

DOMICILE

—Commentary on the European Convention on Establishment / adopted by the Standing Committee : Convention opened for signature on 13 December 1955. - Strasbourg : Council of Europe, 1980.
45p; 21cm.
Includes the text of the European Convention on Establishment. At head of cover title : Council of Europe, Legal Affairs.

DOMICILE - AUSTRALIA

—Practical Guide to Obtaining Permanent Residence in Australia / 3rd ed. - Woolloomooloo : International Business Communications, 1987.
ISBN 0949553387 Hbk £14.50

DOMICILE - CANADA - MANITOBA

—Report on the law of domicile / Law Reform Commission. - Winnipeg : Queen's Printer, 1982.
i,46p. - (Report).

DOMICILE - ENGLAND

—Family law : financial relief after foreign divorce / the Law Commission. - London : H.M.S.O., 1982.
iii,115p. - (HC).
ISBN 0102514828

DOMICILE - GREAT BRITAIN

—Family law, custody of children - jurisdiction and enforcement within the United Kingdom : report on a reference under section 3(1)(e) of the Law Commissions Act 1965 / The Law Commission and the Scottish Law Commission. - London : H.M.S.O., 1985.
x,277p; 25cm.
'Report on a reference under section 3(1)(e) of the Law Commissions Act 1985'.
ISBN 0101941900

—Private international law - the law of domicile / The Law Commission and the Scottish Law Commission. - London : H.M.S.O., 1987.
vi,57p; 30cm.
ISBN 0101020023

—Private international law : the law of domicile / the Law Commission and the Scottish Law Commission. - London : H.M.S.O., 1985.
vi,92p. - (Consultative memorandum).
ISBN 0117301698

—Residence, domicile and UK taxation / London : Butterworths, 1986.
ISBN 0406580103 Pbk £32.00

—Taxation of international business / London : Board of Inland Revenue, 1982.
125 leaves.
Revised draft proposals on international tax avoidance.

DOMICILE - IRELAND

—Report on domicile and habitual residence as connecting factors in the conflict of laws / the Law Reform Commission. - Dublin : The Commission, 1983.
v,26p. - (LRC).

DOMICILE - SCOTLAND

—Matrimonial Homes (Family Protection) (Scotland) Act 1981 / by D.I. Nichols and M.C. Meston. – 2nd ed. – Edinburgh : W. Green, 1986.
x,94p; 25cm.
Previous ed.: 1982. Includes index. Includes the text of the Matrimonial Homes (Family Protection) (Scotland) Act 1981.
ISBN 0414007786 Pbk £10.50

—Report on occupancy rights in the matrimonial home and domestic violence / Scottish Law Commission. – Edinburgh : H.M.S.O, 1980.
vii,148p; 25cm. – (1979-80 H.C. 676).
ISBN 0102676801 Pbk £4.50

DOMICILE - SOUTH AFRICA

—Domicile / South African Law Commission. – Pretoria : The Commission, 1987.
xiii,109p. – (Project).
Bibliography: pp.vi-x.. Includes the text of draft legislation.
ISBN 0797014365

DOMICILE - UNITED STATES

—New U.S. Residency Rules for Canadians : Tax Considerations / North Ryde : C.C.H. Australia, 1986.
98p.
ISBN 0887963250 Pbk £12.00

DOMICILE OF CORPORATIONS - GREAT BRITAIN

—International tax avoidance / Board of Inland Revenue. – London : Board of Inland Revenue, 1981.
66 leaves.

DOUBLE TAXATION

—Arbitration in taxation / Gustaf Lindencrona, Nils Mattsson. – Deventer, The Netherlands : Kluwer, 1981.
92 p.; 22 cm.
Includes bibliographical references.
ISBN 9065440003 pbk.

—British international tax agreements / 2. – Bicester : CCH Editions, 1984.
ISBN 0863250203 unbound Unpriced

—Cross-border transactions between related companies : a summary of tax rules / edited by William R. Lawlor. – Deventer, The Netherlands : Kluwer Law and Taxation Publishers, 1985.
Derived from an international tax planning symposium in New York sponsored by Ernst & Whinney. 'Current to January 1985'–Foreword.
ISBN 9065442324 pbk.

—Handbook on the United States-German Tax Convention / authors Helmut Debatin, Otto L. Walter : in cooperation with Ernst Weber and Eric Osterweil : general editors Piroska Soos and Eugen Jehle. – 4. – Amsterdam : International Bureau of Fiscal Documentation, 1966.
loose-leaf.
Includes texts of Convention and Protocol. With added title-page in German. Final loose-leaf supplement no. 50 (Dec. 1983). Parallel German and English texts.

—International tax planning / Barry Spitz. – 2nd ed. – London : Butterworths, 1983.
xxiii,178p.
This book for the tax planner dealing with international tax issues analyzes the methods of international tax planning and explains the basic techniques. Statutes and treaties in conjunction with case law are used to illustrate the analysis.
ISBN 0406382379 Hbk £18.00

—International tax problems of charities and other private institutions with similar tax treatment : proceedings of a seminar held in 1985 during the 39th Congress of the International Fiscal Association / International Fiscal Association. – Deventer Netherlands : Kluwer Law and Taxation Publishers, 1986.
Conference held in London, England.
ISBN 9065442707

—Model double taxation convention on estates and inheritances and on gifts / report of the OECD Committee on Fiscal Affairs. – Paris : Organisation for Economic Co-operation and Development, 1983.
147p.
ISBN 9264124039

—Principles of international double taxation relief / by David R. Davies. – London : Sweet & Maxwell, 1985.
xix,321p; 26cm.
Includes index.
ISBN 0421317507 £40.00

—United Nations Model Convention for Tax Treaties Between Developed and Developing Countries : a description and analysis / Stanley S. Surrey : with a preface by Helmut F. Debatin. – Amsterdam : International Bureau of Fiscal Documentation, 1980.
x,113p.
Includes bibliographical references.
ISBN 907012517X

DOUBLE TAXATION - GREAT BRITAIN

—UK/US double tax treaties guide / Jerrold Cohen, Roy R. Greenfield. – London : Oyez Publishing, 1980.
xii,217p; 21cm.
Includes index. Contains text of the 1975 Income Convention with notes by Jerrold Cohen and the text of the 1979 Estates Convention, with notes by Roy R. Greenfield.
ISBN 0851204759 Pbk £10.00

—US / UK double tax treaty on income and capital gains / by John Newman. – London : Butterworths, 1980.
viii,128p.
ISBN 040631411X £8.50

DOUBLE TAXATION - UNITED STATES

—UK/US double tax treaties guide / Jerrold Cohen, Roy R. Greenfield. – London : Oyez Publishing, 1980.
xii,217p; 21cm.
Includes index. Contains text of the 1975 Income Convention with notes by Jerrold Cohen and the text of the 1979 Estates Convention, with notes by Roy R. Greenfield.
ISBN 0851204759 Pbk £10.00

—US / UK double tax treaty on income and capital gains / by John Newman. – London : Butterworths, 1980.
viii,128p.
ISBN 040631411X £8.50

DOWRY

—Meaning of marriage payments / edited by J.L. Comaroff. – London : Academic Press, 1980.
xii,264p; 24cm.
Conference papers. Includes bibliographies and index.
ISBN 0121834506 £12.60

DRILLING PLATFORMS

—Safety and health in the construction of fixed offshore installations in the petroleum industry / International Labour Office. – Geneva : International Labour Office, 1981.
135 p.; 18 cm.
Includes index.
ISBN 922102900X pbk. £20.00

DRUG ABUSE AND CRIME - CANADA

—Cannabis criminals : the social effects of punishment on drug users / by Patricia G. Erickson. – Toronto : Addiction Research Foundation of Ontario, 1980.
179p; 23cm. – (ARF books).
Bibliography: p.159-170. - Includes index.
ISBN 0888680465

DRUG OFFENCES

—Law on the misuse of drugs / London : Sweet & Maxwell, 1988.
Refers to the Intoxicating Substances (Supply) Act 1985, and the Drug Trafficking Offences Act 1986 in the context of solvent abuse, drug-kits, and drug-trafficking profits. Lists sentencing examples. Combines an historic perspective of drug misuse with an examination of the legal implications involved.
ISBN 0421396202 Hbk £19

—Misuse of drugs / London : Butterworths, 1986.
Summarises both English and Scots case law arranged in accordance with the sections of the 1971 Misuse of Drugs Act. With a glossary of controlled drugs and words and phrases likely to be encountered in practice. Published by Butterworths on behalf of the Law Society of Scotland.
ISBN 0406103909

DRUG OFFENCES - GREAT BRITAIN

—Misuse of Drugs / Ghodse. – London : Waterlow, 1986.
ISBN 0080330819 Pbk £5.00

—Misuse of Drugs / London : Butterworths, 1986.
ISBN 0406103909 Pbk £27.50

DRUGS

—American Disease : Origins Of Narcotic Control / 2nd ed. – Oxford : Oxford University Press, 1988.
ISBN 0195052110 Hbk £8.95

—Combatting drug abuse and related crime : comparative research on the effectiveness of socio-legal preventive and control measures in different countries on the interaction between criminal behaviour and drug abuse / by Francesco Bruno. – Rome : Fratelli Palombi, 1984.
251p. – (Publication).
Bibliography: p.212-244. 'Funded by the United Nations Fund for Drug Abuse'.
ISBN 8876218262

—Corporate Crime in the Pharmaceutical Industry / London : Sweet & Maxwell, 1984.
ISBN 0710200498 Hbk £30.00

—Law and treatment of drug- and alcohol-dependent persons : a comparative study of existing legislation / by L. Porter, A. E. Arif, W. J. Curran. – Geneva : World Health Organization, 1986.
216p.
Bibliography: p209-216.
ISBN 9241560932

—Legal aspects of international drug control / S.K. Chatterjee. – The Hague : Nijhoff, 1981.
xxiv,587p.
Includes index. Bibliography: p547-555. Based on the author's thesis (doctoral–University of London).
ISBN 9024725569 Hbk £285.00

—Regulation of pharmaceuticals in developing countries : legal issues and approaches / by D.C. Jayasuriya. – Geneva : World Health Organization, 1985.
118p.
Includes bibliographical references.
ISBN 9241560894

—Roche versus Adams / Stanley Adams. – London : Cape, 1984.
xii,236p,8p of plates; 23cm.
Includes index.
ISBN 022402180X £8.95

DRUGS - AUSTRALIA

—Drug offences in Australia / by Fiori Rinaldi. – Sydney : Law Book Co., 1986.
xxv,247p.
Includes index.
ISBN 045520649X

—Operation of the Drug Treaties : Australia 1978-1980 / Department of Health. – Canberra : Australian Government Publishing Service, 1981.
19p.
ISBN 0642068070 Hbk £1.60

—Report / Australian Royal Commission of Inquiry into Drugs. – Canberra : Govt. Pr., 1980.
6 v.; 25 cm.
'The government of the Commonwealth of Australia, and the governments of the states of Victoria, Queensland, Western Australia and Tasmania.'. 'Commissioner: The Hon. Mr. Justice E.S. Williams.'. Includes index.
ISBN 0642047782 pbk. : set

—Sentencing the Federal Drug Offender / John Walker. – Canberra : Australian Institute of Criminology.

DRUGS - AUSTRALIA - NEW SOUTH WALES

—Sentencing Drug Offenders in New South Wales / Canberra : Australian Institute of Criminology.

DRUGS - AUSTRALIA - TASMANIA

—Report and recommendations on the use of tranquillizer guns / Law Reform Commission of Tasmania. – Hobart : Government Printer, 1982.
16p. – (Report).

DRUGS - CANADA

—Drug Industry : A Case Study in Foreign Control / David John Fowler. – Toronto : Lorimer & Co, 1981.
ISBN 0888625367 Hbk £16.95
ISBN 0888625359 Pbk £8.95

—Drug Offences in Canada / 2nd ed. – Aurora : Canada Law Book Co, 1986.
800p. – (Text Books-Criminal).
This monograph is an important research tool for counsel involved in the prosecution or defense of substantive drug charges or drug conspiracies in Canada. The second edition is revised and reorganized to reflect the many judicial decisions delivered since the publication of the first edition, including a full review of the impact of the Canadian Charter of Rights and Freedoms.

—Health protection and drug laws / Educational Services, Health Protection Branch, Department of National Health and Welfare. – Ottawa : The Department, 1982.
45p.
Includes bibliographies.
ISBN 0660112329

DRUGS - ENGLAND

—Drugs and intoxication / by David Farrier. – London : Sweet & Maxwell, 1980.
xix,262p; 19cm.
Includes index.
ISBN 0421271000 Hbk £11.30
ISBN 042127090X Pbk £8.00

DRUGS - EUROPEAN COMMUNITY

—Rules Governing Medicaments in the European Community / Luxembourg : Office for Official Publications of the European Communities, 1985.
115p.
ISBN 9282545318 Pbk £300.00

DRUGS - GREAT BRITAIN

—Becton Dickinson UK Limited : the supply of hypodermic syringes and hypodermic needles / a report by the Director General of Fair Trading on an investigation under section 3 of the Competition Act 1980. – London : Office of Fair Trading, 1988.
39p.

—Butterworths law of food and drugs / editor A.A. Painter : co-ordinating editor Brian Harvey. – 1. – London : Butterworths, 1981.
loose-leaf; 25cm.
Supersedes Bell and O'Keefe's Sale of food and drugs, 14th ed., 1968. 548 pages in various pagings on publication.
ISBN 0406116105 Unpriced

—Controlled Drugs Law and Practice / London : Butterworths, 1984.
ISBN 0406016100 Pbk £20.95

—Drugs law / W.T. West. – Chichester : Rose, 1982.
xiii,93p; 22cm.
Includes index.
ISBN 0859922286 Pbk £12.00

—Drugs Law / Chichester : Barry Rose, 1982.
ISBN 0859922286 Pbk £12.00

—Extradition for Drug-Related Offences : A Study / London : HMSO, 1986.
ISBN 9211480698 Hbk £9.00

—Law and Misuse of Drugs / London : Sweet & Maxwell, 1988.
ISBN 0421396202 Hbk £27.00

—Law on poisons, medicines and related substances / P.F.C. Bayliss. – Beckenham : Ravenswood Publications, 1980.
xviii,103p; 22cm.
Bibliography: p.93. - Includes index.
ISBN 0901812358 £12.25
ISBN 090181234X

—Misuse of Drugs / Ghodse. – London : Waterlow, 1986.
ISBN 0080330819 Pbk £5.00

—Misuse of Drugs / London : Butterworths, 1986.
ISBN 0406103909 Pbk £27.50

—Misuse of drugs / Patrick Bucknell and Hamid Ghodse. – London : Waterlow, 1986.
512p; 23cm.
ISBN 0080392032 £30.00

—Multi-facility induction : the first six months : a report by the Lifeline Project, Manchester, on its induction programme for drug users who wish to reconstruct their lives without recourse to drugs / Lifeline Project. – Manchester : The Project, 1980.
10p.

—Report by Expert Group on Effects of Cannabis Use / London : Home Office, 1982.
ISBN 0862520312 Pbk £3.10

—Tackling drug misuse : a summary of the governments strategy / Home Office. – 2nd ed. – London : Home Office, 1986.
39p.
Includes bibliographical references.
ISBN 086252234X

—Treatment and Rehabilitation : Report of the Advisory Council on the Misuse of Drugs / London : HMSO, 1982.
ISBN 0113208219 Hbk £3.95

DRUGS – HONG KONG

—Drug addiction research programme 1983 / Correctional Services Department, Hong Kong. – Hong Kong : The Department, 1983.
40p.

DRUGS – INDIA

—Commentaries on the Opium Act, 1878 / Lucknow : Eastern Book Company, 1984.
175p.

—Crimes : Commentary on the Narcotic Drugs and Psychotrophic Substances Act, 1985, and the Narcotic Drugs and Psychotrophic Substances Rules, 1985 with State Rules and Notifications / Delhi : Vinod Prakashan, 1987.
615p.

—Drugs and Cosmetics Act, 1940 : Together with Drugs and Cosmetics Rules, 1945 and Drugs (Price control) Order, 1979 / 2nd ed. – Lucknow : Eastern Book Company, 1984.
447p.

—Handbook of Drug Laws : With Appropriate Technology for Drugs and Pharmaceuticals / Allahabad : Universal Book Agency, 1985.

—Handbook on Drug Laws / Allahabad : Law Publishers, 1983.

—Law Relating to Drugs and Cosmetics in India / P.L. Malik. – 3rd ed. – Lucknow : Eastern Book Company, 1984.
1,248p.

DRUGS – MALAYSIA

—Dangerous Drugs Act 1952 (Act 234) and Drug Dependants (Treatment and Rehabilitation) Act, 1983 (Act 283) and Regulations and Rules / Kuala Lumpur : International Law Books Services.

DRUGS – NEW ZEALAND

—Misuse of Drugs / Butterworths, 1989.
251p.
ISBN 0409788163 Pbk £54.00

—Report of the Royal Commission to inquire into certain matters related to drug trafficking / D. G. Stewart. – Wellington : Government Printer, 1983.
110p.
Commissioner: the Hon. Mr. Justice D.G. Stewart.

DRUGS – SOUTH AFRICA

—Offences committed under the influence of liquor or drugs / South African Law Commission. – Pretoria : The Commission, 1986.
vii,132p. – (Report).
Bibliography: p.123-132.
ISBN 0621102075

DRUGS – SWEDEN

—Drug criminality and drug abuse in Sweden, 1969-1981 / Jan Andersson, Artur Solarz. – Stockholm : Research Division, National Swedish Council for Crime Prevention, 1982.
53p. – (Report).
Includes bibliographies.
ISBN 9138072572

DRUGS – UNITED STATES

—Drug Abuse Briefing / New York : Drugs Dependence, 1988.
ISBN 0948830352 Pbk £1.50

DUMPING

—Anti-dumping law in a liberal trade order / Richard Dale. – London : Macmillan for the Trade Policy Research Centre, 1980.
xv,237p; 23cm.
Bibliography: p225-231. - Includes index.
ISBN 0333276507 £20.00

DUMPING – EUROPE

—Dumping and Subsidies / Stanbrook. – London : European Business, 1983.
ISBN 0946262002 Hbk £35.00

DUMPING – EUROPEAN COMMUNITY

—Antidumping law and practice in the United States and the European Communities : a comparative analysis / Edwin A. Vermulst. – Amsterdam : North-Holland, 1987.
xx, 750 p.; 24 cm.
Includes bibliographical references and index.
ISBN 0444702229 Hbk

—Dumping and subsidies : the law and procedures governing the imposition of anti-dumping and countervailing duties in the European Community / Joseph Cunnane and Clive Stanbrook. – London : European Business Publications, 1983.
xvi,227p.
Includes index.
ISBN 0907027040

—EEC Anti-Dumping and other Trade Protection laws / Bellis. – London : CCH, 1985.
ISBN 0863250602 Pbk £16.50

DUMPING – UNITED STATES

—Antidumping law and practice in the United States and the European Communities : a comparative analysis / Edwin A. Vermulst. – Amsterdam : North-Holland, 1987.
xx, 750 p.; 24 cm.
Includes bibliographical references and index.
ISBN 0444702229 Hbk

—Taxing unfair international trade practices : a study of U.S. antidumping and countervailing duty laws / Greyson Bryan. – Lexington : Lexington Books, 1981.
xxii,370p; 24cm.
Includes index.
ISBN 0669037524 £20.00

DURESS (LAW)

—Ethics of Legal Coercion / Dordrecht : Kluwer, 1985.
192p.
ISBN 9027718431 Pbk £52.00

DURESS (LAW) – AUSTRALIA

—Duress and undue influence / North Ryde : Law Book Co, 1985.
ISBN 0455205728 Hbk £19.00

—Duress, Undue Influence and Unconscientious Bargains / North Ryde : Law Book Co, 1985.
xviii, 249p.
ISBN 0455205728 Hbk £40.00

—Unconscionable Contracts and Economic Duress / North Ryde : C.C.H. Australia, 1985.
260p.
ISBN 0869035495

DURESS (LAW) – CANADA

—Inequality of bargaining power : judicial intervention in improvident and unconscionable bargains / Robert W. Clark. – Toronto : Carswell, 1987.
xxxvii,255p.
ISBN 0459388401

DURESS (LAW) – GREAT BRITAIN

—Inequality of bargaining power : judicial intervention in improvident and unconscionable bargains / Robert W. Clark. – Toronto : Carswell, 1987.
xxxvii,255p.
ISBN 0459388401

DUTY

—Fundamental duties : a volume of essays by present and former members of the Law Faculty of the University of Exeter to commemorate the Silver Jubilee of the University / edited by D. Lasok : with a foreword by Lord Denning of Whitchurch. – Oxford : Pergamon, 1980.
269p; 26cm. – (Pergamon international library).
ISBN 0080240488 Hbk £12.50
ISBN 0080240496 Pbk £4.95

DUTY – INDIA

—Law and Practice of Estate Duty : with Rules and Forms / 4th ed. 1982 repr. 1983. – New Delhi : Bharat Law House.

EASEMENTS

—Law of Easements / Sastri. – 5th rev. ed. – Lucknow : Eastern Book Company, 1986.

—Law of Easements / Sastri. – 5th rev. ed. – Lucknow : Eastern Book Company, 1984.
846p.

EASEMENTS – AUSTRALIA

—Easements and Restrictive Covenants in Australia / Neave. – London : Butterworths, 1981.
ISBN 0409300489 Hbk £34.00

EASEMENTS – INDIA

—Commentaries on the Law of Easements and Licences with Model Forms / 2nd ed. – Allahabad : Law Publishers, 1982.

—Law of Easements and Licences / 10th ed. – Allahabad : Law Book Company, 1984.
1,200p.

EAST-WEST TRADE (1945-)

—Contracts with Eastern Europe / 2nd ed. – London : East European Trade Council, 1980.
57p; 30cm.
Previous ed.: 1969.

EAVESDROPPING – CANADA

—Electronic surveillance / Law Reform Commission of Canada. – Ottawa : The Commission, 1986.
109,121p; 25cm. – (Working paper).
Added t.p. in French: La surveillance electronique. Cover title: Criminal law - electronic surveillance. Pages numbered in opposite directions. English and French.
ISBN 0662538862

ECCLESIASTICAL COURTS

—Practice of the Ecclesiastical Courts / Repr. of 1847 ed. – Abingdon : Professional Books.
77p.

ECCLESIASTICAL COURTS – ENGLAND

—Aculty jurisdiction of the Church of England / Sweet & Maxwell, 1988.
xxix,262p.
Deals with the structure and workings of the court, and discusses reported case law since 1950. Analyses the problems faced by those who are entrusted with the care and development of historic buildings. Changes introduced by the Faculty Jurisdiction (Amendment) Rules 1987 are examined.
ISBN 0421387602 Pbk £12.20

—Courts of the County Palatine of Durham from earliest times to 1971 / by Kenneth Emsley and C.M. Fraser. – Durham City : Durham County Local History Society, 1984.
ix,112p; 21cm.
ISBN 0902958070

—Ecclesiastical cause papers at York : Dean and Chapter's court 1350-1843 / Katharine M. Longley. – York : University of York, 1980.
xx,204p.
Includes bibliographical references and index. At head of t.p.: University of York. Borthwick Institute of Historical Research.

—Ecclesiastical Cause papers at York : files transmitted on appeal 1500-1883 / W.J. Sheils. – York : University of York, Borthwick Institute of Historical Research, 1983.
xiv,135p; 25cm.
Includes index.

—Select cases from the ecclesiastical courts of the Province of Canterbury, c.1200-1301 / edited for the Selden Society by Norma Adams and Charles Donahue Jr. – London : Selden Society, 1981.
xxx,119,756p.
Text in Latin and English.

ECCLESIASTICAL COURTS – SCOTLAND

—Court of the official in pre-Reformation Scotland : based on the surviving records of the officials of St. Andrews and Edinburgh / by Simon Ollivant. – Edinburgh : The Stair Society, 1982.
x,224p. – (Publications).
Bibliography: p201-206.
ISBN 0902292099

ECCLESIASTICAL LAW

—Church and the English crown, 1305-1334 : a study based on the register of Archbishop Walter Reynolds / by J. Robert Wright. – Toronto, Ont. : Pontifical Institute of Mediaeval Studies, 1980. xix, 472 p.; 26 cm. – (Studies and texts - Pontifical Institute of Mediaeval Studies).
Includes index. Bibliography: p. 415-440.
ISBN 0888440480

—Clergyman's handbook, and churchwarden's guide : being a manual of the laws affecting the relative rights, position, and duties of the clergy and their parishioners ..., with appendices containing important statutes, including the Benefices Act, 1898 / by James Murray Dale. – 7th ed. – London : Seeley, 1898.
xx,507p.
Includes index. .

—Ecclesiastical Law, 4 Vols. / 8th ed. Repr. of 1824 ed. – Abingdon : Professional Books.

—Heraldry in the Catholic Church : its origin, customs and laws / 2nd enl. and rev. ed. – Gerrards Cross : Van Duren, 1982.
200p.
ISBN 0905715128 Hbk £25.00

—Jurisprudence of the living oracles / Tunji Braithwaite. – Benin City, Nigeria : Ethiope, 1987.
xviii,308p.
Bibliography: p.296-297 . - Includes index. Includes the texts of the Charter of the United Nations and Statute of the International Court of Justice, and the Universal Declaration of Human Rights.
ISBN 9781233176

—Orders of Knighthood, Awards and the Holy See : The Authoritative, Juridical and Practical Compendium / 3rd ed. – Gerrards Cross : Van Duren, 1985.
336p : Illus.
ISBN 0905715268 Hbk £29.50

ECCLESIASTICAL LAW - ENGLAND

—Aculty jurisdiction of the Church of England / Sweet & Maxwell, 1988.
xxix,262p.
Deals with the structure and workings of the court, and discusses reported case law since 1950. Analyses the problems faced by those who are entrusted with the care and development of historic buildings. Changes introduced by the Faculty Jurisdiction (Amendment) Rules 1987 are examined.
ISBN 0421387602 Pbk £12.20

—Defamation and Sexual Slander in Early Modern England : The Church Courts at York / York : St. Anthony's Press, 1980.
– (Borthwick Papers Ser.).

—English church and its laws 12th-14th centuries / C.R. Cheney. – London : Variorum Reprints, 1982.
348p in various pagings; 23cm. – (Collected studies series).
Includes index. Text in English and Latin.
ISBN 0860781089 Unpriced

—Statesman and the fanatic : Thomas Wolsey and Thomas More / Jasper Ridley. – London : Constable, 1982.
338p,16p of plates; 24cm.
Bibliography: p294-299. - Includes index.
ISBN 009463470X £12.50

ECCLESIASTICAL LAW - GREAT BRITAIN

—Codex Ecclesiastici Anglicani : Statutes, Constitutions, Canons, Rubriks, and Articles of the Church of England Digested with a Commentary Historical and Judicial, and Introductory Discourse, and Appendix of Instruments, 2 Vols. / 2nd ed. Repr. of 1761 ed. – Abingdon : Professional Books.
168p.

ECCLESIASTICAL LAW - SPAIN

—Register Notule Communium 14 of the Diocese of Barcelona (1345-1348) A Calendar with Selected Documents / Julio Silano. – Toronto : Pontifical Institute of Mediaeval Studies, 1983.
x, 365p. – (Subsidia Mediaevalia: No. 13).
ISBN 0888443625 Hbk £30.00

ECONOMIC ASSISTANCE

—Adjustment and financing in the developing world : the role of the International Monetary Fund / edited by Tony Killick. – London : Published by the International Monetary Fund in association with the Overseas Development Institute, 1982.
xviii,232p; 24cm.
Conference papers. Includes bibliographies.
ISBN 0939934183 Hbk £6.75
ISBN 0939934191 Pbk £4.50

—Aid : rhetoric and reality / Teresa Hayter, Catharine Watson. – London : Pluto, 1985.
xv,303p; 20cm.
Includes index.
ISBN 0861046269 Pbk £4.95

—International financial policy and economic development : a disaggregated approach / Graham Bird. – Basingstoke : Macmillan, 1987.
xvi,348p; 23cm.
Bibliography: p338-343. - Includes index.
ISBN 033340890X £29.50

—International law of development : comparative perspectives / edited by Francis Snyder and Peter Slinn. – Abingdon : Professional Books, 1987.
ix,322p; 22cm.
ISBN 0862052580

—Second Convention of Lome : EEC aid to the ACP countries (1981-1985) / by Catherine Goybet : with the collaboration of Jane Morrison. – Brussels : Bureau d'Informations Europeennes, 1982.
317 leaves.

ECONOMIC ASSISTANCE - EUROPEAN COMMUNITY

—State aids under the EEC treaty articles 92 to 94 / Despina Schina. – Oxford : ESC Publishing, 1987.
xviii, 221p.
Bibliography: p.179-185. - Includes index.
ISBN 0906214440

ECONOMIC CONDITIONS - AFRICA, SUB-SAHARAN

—IMF and the World Bank in Africa : conditionality, impact, and alternatives / edited by Kjell J. Havnevik. – Uppsala : Scandinavian Institute of African Studies, 1987.
177 p.; 23 cm.
Includes bibliographies.
ISBN 9171062645

ECONOMIC DEVELOPMENT

—Common crisis : North-South : cooperation for world recovery / the Brandt Commission. – London : Pan, 1983.
174p; 18cm. – (Pan world affairs).
Bibliography: p172-174.
ISBN 0330281305 Pbk £1.95

—Development technology / H.J. Duller. – London : Routledge & K. Paul, 1982.
192p.
Includes index. Bibliography: p173-190.
ISBN 0710009909

—International Law and Economic Development and Cooperation / Dordrecht : Kluwer.
ISBN 9065441921

—North-South, a programme for survival : report of the Independent Commission on International Development Issues / Willy Brandt. – London : Pan Books, 1980.
304p; 18cm. – (Pan world affairs).
Chairman: Willy Brandt.
ISBN 0330261401 Pbk £1.95

—Our common future / World Commission on Environment and Development. – Oxford : Oxford University Press, 1987.
320p; 21cm.
ISBN 019282080X Pbk £5.95

ECONOMIC POLICY

—Common crisis : North-South : cooperation for world recovery / the Brandt Commission. – London : Pan, 1983.
174p; 18cm. – (Pan world affairs).
Bibliography: p172-174.
ISBN 0330281305 Pbk £1.95

—Community Order and National Economic Policies : Disciplines Communautaires et Politiques Economiques Nationales / Dordrecht : Kluwer.
538p.
ISBN 9065442014 Pbk £125.00

—Exclusive Economic Zone Claims : an Analysis and Primary Documents / Dordrecht : Kluwer, 1986.
600p.
ISBN 9024732506 Hbk £350.00

—International institutions in trade and finance / A.I. MacBean and P.N. Snowden. – London : Allen & Unwin, 1981.
xiv,255p; 23cm.
Bibliography: p249-252. - Includes index.
ISBN 0043820328 Hbk Unpriced
ISBN 0043820336 Pbk Unpriced

—Law as an instrument of economic policy : comparative and critical approaches / edited by Terence Daintith. – Berlin : W. de Gruyter, 1987.
– (Series A–Law).
Includes index. Bibliography. Based on papers presented at a colloquium held in Florence, Mar. 1985.
ISBN 0899254179

ECONOMIC POLICY - GREAT BRITAIN

—Legal analysis of economic policy / by Terence C. Daintith. – Florence : European University Institute, 1982.
13p.

—Shape of Britain's Tariff / London : Institute of Economic Affairs.

ECONOMIC POLICY - SOUTH AFRICA

—Annual report / Department of Development Planning : Constitutional Development Services. – Pretoria : Government Printer, 1987.
Annual reports of two bodies published together. Text in Afikaans and English.

ECONOMIC STABILIZATION

—IMF and stabilisation : developing country experiences / directed and edited by Tony Killick : contributors : Graham Bird ... et al. – London : Gower in association with the Overseas Development Institute, 1985.
viii,216p; 22cm.
Originally published: London : Heinemann Educational in association with the Overseas Development Institute, 1984. Includes bibliographies.
ISBN 0566050412 £13.45

—Quest for economic stabilisation : the IMF and the Third World / directed and edited by Tony Killick : contributors Graham Bird ... et al. – London : Heinemann Educational in association with the Overseas Development Institute, 1984.
ix,340p; 23cm.
Bibliography: p321-331. - Includes index.
ISBN 043584427X Hbk £16.50
ISBN 0435844288 Pbk Unpriced

ECONOMICS

—Dictionary of Economics and Financial Markets / 5th ed. – London : Butterworths, 1986.
ISBN 0408015705 Hbk £19.95

—Fragmented world : competing perspectives on trade, money and crisis / Chris Edwards. – London : Methuen, 1985.
xvi,350p; 23cm.
Bibliography: p310-333. - Includes index.
ISBN 0416733905 Hbk £14.95
ISBN 0416734006 Pbk £6.95

—International review of law and economics / Sevenoaks : Butterworths, 1981.

—Law and economics / edited by Ross Cranston and Anne Schick. – Canberra : Department of Law, Research School of Social Sciences, Australian National University, 1982.
v,220p.
ISBN 0909596727 Pbk £9

—Law and economics and the economics of legal regulation / edited by J.-Matthias Graf v.d. Schulenburg, Goran Skogh. – Dordrecht : M. Nijhoff, 1986.
248p. – (International studies in economics and econometrics).
'Selected papers of a conference of the International Institute of Management Wissenschaftszentum Berlin.'. Includes index. Contents: Law and economics and the economics of legal regulation / Goran Skogh – Efficiency, equity, and inalienability / Susan Rose-Ackerman – Negotiated settlement / Gordon Tullock – Economic efficiency and the common law / Peter H. Aranson – Default risk and the optimal pricing of court enforcement services / Hugh Gravelle – Transaction cost and communincation / Michael Hutter – Regulatory measures to enforce quality production of self-employed professinals / J.-Matthias Graf v.d. Schulenburg – Controlling insider trading in Europe and America / David D. Haddock, Jonathan R. Macey – The regulatin of shop opening hours in the United Kingdom / Susan M. Jaffer, John A. Kay Belgian public policy towards the retailing trade / Roger Van den Bergh – Assessing the effectiveness of economic efficiency of an E.E.C. pollution control directive / John Ashworth, Ivy Papps, David J. Storey.
ISBN 9024733774 Hbk £135.00

—Law and the economy / Roger Bowles. – Oxford : Martin Robertson, 1982.
xvi,239p; 22cm.
Introduction to law and economics, relating the two subjects to each other.
ISBN 0855204656 Hbk Unpriced
ISBN 0855204745 Pbk £6.95

—Lexeconics : the Interaction of Law and Economics / Dordrecht : Kluwer, 1981.
272p.
ISBN 0898380537 Hbk £75.00

—New law-and-economics : a research review / C.G. Veljanovski. – Oxford : Centre for Socio-Legal Studies, 1982.
xi,169p.
Bibliography: p.144-169.
ISBN 0862260531

—Readings in the economics of law and regulation / edited by A.I. Ogus and C.G. Veljanovski. – Oxford : Clarendon, 1984.
x,361p; 24cm.
Includes index.
ISBN 0198761422 Hbk £17.50
ISBN 0198761430 Pbk £10.95

—Restructuring the International Economic Order : the Role of Law and Lawyers / Dordrecht : Kluwer, 1987.
280p.
ISBN 9065442758 Hbk £125.00

—Tripartism and the International Labour Organisation : a study of the legal concept : its origins, function and evolution in the law of nations / Abdul-Karim Tikriti. – Stockholm : Distributed by Almqvist & Wiksell, 1982.
xxviii,417p. – (Studies in international law).
Thesis (Doctoral) - Uppsala University 1982. Bibliography: p.400-410. - Includes index. Published under the auspices of the Swedish Institute of International Law.
ISBN 9122005609

ECONOMICS - CHINA
—Almanac of China's foreign economic relations and trade / the editorial board of the Almanac of China's foreign economic relations and trade. – Hong Kong : China Resources Trade Consultancy, 1986.
Title page also in Chinese.

ECONOMICS - EUROPEAN COMMUNITY
—Economic Offences in EEC Law : With Special Reference to English and German Law / Kehl am Rhein : Norbert Paul Engel, 1983.
228p.
ISBN 3883570273 Hbk £48.00

—Law of the Economy in the EEC / London : Butterworths, 1980.
ISBN 0406268967 Hbk £21.00
ISBN 0406268975 Pbk £16.50

ECONOMICS - GREAT BRITAIN
—Butterworths CIMA Student Series : Management Accounting - Decision Making /. – London : Butterworths, 1987.
ISBN 0406530068 Pbk £13.95

—Dictionary of Economics and Financial Markets / 5th ed. – London : Butterworths, 1986.
This work contains definitions of economic terminology and concepts and topics related to contemporary applied economics and financial institutions. A bibliography is included in the text.
ISBN 0408015705 Pbk

—Economic negligence / London : Sweet & Maxwell, 1985.
ISBN 0459364707 Hbk £40.00

—Economics of Crime and Law Enforcement / London : Macmillan, 1983.
228p.
ISBN 0333282000 Hbk £33.00

—Housing Economics and Public Policy / London : Macmillan.
176p. – (Studies in Planning Ser.).
ISBN 0333211073 Pbk £4.95

—Keynes's Impact on Monetary Economics / London : Butterworths, 1982.
This book provides a carefully documented survey of the impact of Keynes on monetary economics. The fundamental concepts of Keynes's theories are considered and related to the work of important critics and followers of Keynes.
ISBN 0408107189 Hbk

—Lifting the burden / presented to Parliament by the Minister without Portfolio : supported by the Secretary of State for the Home Department ... et al. – London : H.M.S.O., 1985.
40p.
ISBN 0101957106

—Modern Economic Analysis 2 / London : Butterworths, 1982.
The objective of this book is to provide an analysis of the economic policy of monetarism. The economics of industrial relations, health, housing, as well as, theories of the firm and central government intervention are discussed.
ISBN 0408107715 Pbk

EDUCATION
—Essays on Law, Equality and Education / London : Sweet & Maxwell, 1984.
ISBN 0710098804 Hbk £49.00

—Law and equality in education / edited by Stephen Goldstein. – Jerusalem : The Van Leer Jerusalem Foundation, 1980.
219p.
Adaptations of papers presented at a workshop on Education, Equality and the Law, held under the auspices of the Van Leer Jerusalem Foundation, July 31 to August 2, 1977.

EDUCATION - AUSTRALIA
—Getting a fair go : case studies of occupational socialization and perceptions of discrimination in a sample of seven Melbourne high schools / Brian M. Bullivant. – Canberra : Australian Government Publishing Service, 1986.
xi,296p. – (Occasional paper).
Bibliographical references: p259-296.
ISBN 0644055243

—Law of Education / V.B. Gleeson. – Butterworths, 1982.
211p.
ISBN 0409309230 Pbk £39.00

EDUCATION - CANADA
—Education Act : Elementary and Secondary Schools and Schools for Trainable Retarded Pupils / Office of the Legislative Assembly (Ontario). – Ontario : Ontario Government Publications Service, 1983.
15p.

—Education Act : Supervised Alternative Learning for Excused Pupils / Office of the Legislative Assembly (Ontario). – Ontario : Ontario Government Publications Service, 1983.
3p.

—Education Act : Supervisory Officers / Office of the Legislative Assembly (Ontario). – Ontario : Ontario Government Publications Service, 1983.
6p.

—Education law in Canada / A. Wayne MacKay. – Toronto : Emond-Montgomery, 1984.
xxiv,416p.
Bibliography: p.397-407. - Includes index.
ISBN 0920722121 Hbk £45.00

—Education Law in Canada / Aurora : Canada Law Book, 1984.

—Educational Law in Canada / Aurora : Canada Law Book Co, 1984.
250p. – (Text Books-Civil).

—Educational Rights of Exceptional Children in Canada / Agincourt : Carswell, 1988.
144p.

—Municipal and School Tax Credit Assistance Lien Discharge Act, 1983, Bill 121 : An Act to Provide for the Discharge of Liens Registered Under the Municipal and School Tax Credit Assistance Act / Ontario : Ontario Government Publications Service, 1983.
2p.

—Perspectives on the harmonization of law in Canada / Ronald C.C. Cuming research coordinator. – Toronto : University of Toronto Press in cooperation with the Royal Commission on the Economic Union and Development Prospects for Canada and the Canadian Government Publishing Centre, 1985.
xviii,178p. – (Collected research studies).
Bibliography: p.176-177.
ISBN 0802073026

—Rights freedoms and the education system in Canada / MacKay. – Aurora : Canada Law Book, 1988.

—Rights, Freedoms and the Education System in Canada : Cases and Materials / A. W. MacKay. – Aurora : Canada Law Book Co, 1988.
750p.

—Rights, Freedoms and the Education System in Canada : Cases and Materials / A. Wayne McKay. – Toronto : Edmond-Montgomery, 1988.
ca 750p.
ISBN 0920722237 Hbk £68.00

—Teachers' Superannuation Act, 1983, Bill 148 : An Act to Revise the Teachers' Superannuation Act / Ontario : Ontario Government Publications Service, 1983.
49p.

EDUCATION - ENGLAND
—Education law : an outline of the law relating to the public system of education in England and Wales / K.P. Poole. – London : Sweet & Maxwell, 1988.
lviii,355p; 26cm.
Sets out the framework of the education system, and gives an account of the law on central and local administration. Deals with schools from nursery onwards, up to further education establishments. Considers issues such as awards, and grants, the Manpower Services Commission, adult education and freedom of speech. Includes the Education (no 2) Act 1986, and the Teachers Pay and Conditions Act 1987.
ISBN 0421328304 £30.00

EDUCATION - GREAT BRITAIN
—Education and Poverty in the United Kingdom : A Background Paper / London : Policy Studies Institute, 1981.

—Education and the law / London : Longman Professional, 1986.
ISBN 090031320X Pbk £10.95

—Educational conflict and the law / David Milman. – London : Croom Helm, 1986.
160p; 23cm.
Includes index.
ISBN 0709935218 £16.95

—Essential Law for Teachers / Duncan Bloy. – London : Oyez Longman, 1980.
ISBN 0851204937 Hbk £9.95

—Essential Law for Teachers / Bloy. – London : Longman Professional, 1980.
ISBN 0851204937 Pbk £12.50

—Law of Education / John B. Saunders. – 9th ed. – London : Butterworths.

—Law of Education / Saunders. – 9th ed. – London : Butterworths, 1984.
Service to Date.
ISBN 0406396434 loose £85.00

—Law of Special Educational Needs / Oxford : Croom Helm, 1985.
ISBN 070993498X Pbk £7.95

—Report on secondary education / by an ad-hoc working group of the Women's National Commission. – London : Women's National Commission, 1983.

—Teachers and the Law / J. Partington. – 6th ed. – London : Sweet & Maxwell, 1985.
ISBN 0416421709 Hbk £22.50
ISBN 0416395309 Pbk £12.95

—Teachers and the law / Partington. – 6th ed. – Methuen, 1985.
ISBN 0416395309 Pbk £10.95
ISBN 0416421709 Hbk £18.95

EDUCATION - INDIA
—Intermediate Education Act, 1921 : Together with Amending Acts, Regulations and Notifications / Lucknow : Eastern Book Company, 1982.
173p.

—Law of Education and Educational Institutions in India, 3 Vols. / Allahabad : Law Book Company, 1982-83.
With 1988 supplement.

—Misconduct of students : a legal and disciplinary study / Arun Bhattacharjee. – New Delhi : Deep & Deep, 1981.
440p.
Bibliography: p.425-427. - Includes index.

EDUCATION - PAKISTAN
—Law of Workers' Children Education / Karachi : Bureau of Labour Publications, 1986.
54p.

EDUCATION - SCOTLAND
—Education (Scotland) Bill, report on the consolidation of certain enactments relating to education in Scotland / Scottish Law Commission .. – Edinburgh : H.M.S.O., 1980.
7p; 25cm.
ISBN 010176880X sd £1.00

—Fourteen to Eighteen : The Changing Pattern of Schooling in Scotland / Aberdeen : Aberdeen University Press, 1983.
192p.
ISBN 0080303749 Pbk £8.75

EDUCATION - UNITED STATES
—Beyond the ivory tower : social responsibilities of the modern university / Derek Bok. – Cambridge, Mass. : Harvard University Press, 1982.
318p; 25cm.
Includes index.
ISBN 0674068998 £11.20

EFFECTIVENESS AND VALIDITY OF LAW
—Conditions of validity and cognition in modern legal thought / edited by Neil MacCormick, Stavros Panou, Luigi Lombardi Vallauri : preface by Ralf Dreier Geltungs- und Erkenntnisbedingungen im modernen Rechtsdenken / herausgegeben von Neil MacCormick, Stavros Panou, Luigi Lombardi Vallauri ; vorwort von Ralf Dreier. – Stuttgart : F. Steiner Verlag Wiesbaden, 1985.
214 p.; 24 cm. – (Archives for philosophy of law and social philosophy).
Papers presented at the IVR 11th World Congress, Helsinki, 1983. English, French, and German. Includes bibliographical references and index.
ISBN 3515044604 pbk. DM35.00

ELDERLY PERSONS
—Law and vulnerable elderly people / Mitcham : Age Concern, 1986.
144p.
Bibliography: p.141-143.
ISBN 0862420504

ELDERLY PERSONS - AUSTRALIA
—Know Your Rights When You Retire / Kensington : Bay Books.

—Retirement Villages : Conference Papers / Woolloomooloo : International Business Communications, 1986.
ISBN 0949072095 Hbk £75.00

ELDERLY PERSONS - CANADA
—Senior Citizens and the Law : Towards a Greater Quality of Life / Montreal : McGill Campus Legal Aid Clinic, 1985.
92p.

ELDERLY PERSONS - GREAT BRITAIN
—Housing alternatives for the elderly / Alan Butler and Anthea Tinker. – Leeds : Centre for Applied Social Studies, 1983.
28p. – (Occasional paper).
Includes bibliographical references.

—Housing law for the elderly (LPPN72) / London : Longman Professional, 1982.
ISBN 0851206875 Pbk £12.95

—Law and the Elderly / Oxford : Croom Helm, 1988.
ISBN 0709911629 Hbk

—Legal Aspects of the Care of the Aged / Godrey Gypps. - London : Law Society, 1985. - (Oxford Weekend Courses).

—Population, pension costs and pensioners' incomes : a background paper for the Inquiry into Provision for Retirement / London : H.M.S.O., 1984.
29p.
At head of title page: Department of Health and Social Security.
ISBN 0113210035

ELDERLY PERSONS - SCOTLAND
—Age Concern in Scotland / Edinburgh : Age Concern Scotland, 1988.
ISBN 0946505489 Pbk £1.00

ELECTIONS - AFRICA
—Southern Rhodesia elections February, 1980 : the report of the Commonwealth Observer Group on elections leading to independent Zimbabwe / Commonwealth Observer Group. - London : Commonwealth Secretariat, 1980.
xi,351p; 30cm.
ISBN 0850921775 Pbk Unpriced

ELECTIONS - AUSTRALIA
—Report / Joint Select Committee on Electoral Reform. - Canberra : Australian Government Publishing Service, 1983.
vii,322p.
ISBN 0644028777 Hbk

ELECTIONS - CANADA
—Election Law in Canada : the Law and Procedure of Federal, Provincial and Territorial Elections, 2 Vols. / Butterworths, 1987.
1,632p.
Examines legal status and registration of political parties and candidates, electoral boundaries and representation, the calling of elections, election officials, compiling and revising the lists of voters, general conduct of elections, voting procedures, election results and recounts, election offences and corrupt practices, and controverted elections.
ISBN 0409816000 Hbk £170.00

—Liberation Deferred? : the ideas of the English-Canadian Suffragists / Toronto : University of Toronto Press, 1983.
ISBN 0802024556 Hbk £25.00
ISBN 0802064663 Pbk £9.95

—Money and Message : The Law Governing Election Financing, Advertising, Broadcasting and Campaigning in Canada / Toronto : Butterworths, 1983.
672p.
ISBN 0409816035 Hbk £95.00

—Money and Message : the Law Governing Election Financing, Advertising, Broadcasting and Election Campaigning in Canada / Butterworths, 1983.
672p.
ISBN 0409816305 Hbk £95.00

ELECTIONS - ENGLAND
—Oxfordshire Election of 1754 / Oxfordshire County Record Office. - Oxford : Oxfordshire County Record Office. - (Archive Teaching Unit).

ELECTIONS - EUROPEAN COMMUNITY
—European Parliament : towards a uniform procedure for direct elections / Sasse ... et al. : with contributions by Roland Bieber and Howard C. Yourow. - Luxembourg : Office for Official Publications of the European Communities, 1981.
viii, 449p.
At head of title page: European University Institute.
ISBN 9282525279

—Legislation of direct elections to the European Parliament / edited by Valentine Herman and Mark Hagger. - Farnborough, Hants : Gower, 1980.
ix,320p; 23cm.
Bibliography: p303-311. - Includes index.
ISBN 0566002477 £12.50

—Political rights for European citizens / Guido van den Berghe. - Aldershot : Gower, 1982.
xii,245p; 23cm.
Bibliography: p218-235. - Includes index.
ISBN 0566005247 Unpriced

ELECTIONS - GREAT BRITAIN
—Election Law / Little. - London : Shaw & Sons, 1984.
ISBN 0721903444 Hbk £85.00

—Law and the electoral process / by H.F. Rawlings. - London : Sweet & Maxwell, 1988.
xix,252p; 23cm.
Bibliography: p243-248. - Includes index.
ISBN 0421376406 Pbk £13.50

—O'Malley and Hardcastle's Election Cases : 1869-1929, 7 Vols. / Abingdon : Professional Books.

—Parker's Conduct of Parliamentary Elections / Tonbridge : Ernest Benn, 1983.
610p. - (Knight's Looseleaf Library).
ISBN 0853143137 loose £47.50

ELECTIONS - MALAYSIA
—Elections Laws of Malaysia / Kuala Lumpur : International Law Books Services.

ELECTIONS - NIGERIA
—Judiciary and the 1983 elections / by T. Akinola Aguda. - Lagos : Nigerian Institute of Advanced Legal Studies, 1983.
19p.
Notes of a seminar presented at the Institute on Wednesday, February 23, 1983.

—Nigerian 1979 elections / edited by Oyeleye Oyediran. - London : Macmillan, 1981.
xi,182p.
ISBN 0333317858

—Nigerian elections : a bibliography / by A.T. Agboola. - Lagos : University of Lagos Library, 1983.
ix,45p.
Includes index.

—Nigerian electoral law / by D.I.O. Ewelukwa. - Lagos : Shelters International, 1983.
xii,252p.

ELECTIONS - ZIMBABWE
—Southern Rhodesia elections February, 1980 : the report of the Commonwealth Observer Group on elections leading to independent Zimbabwe / Commonwealth Observer Group. - London : Commonwealth Secretariat, 1980.
xi,351p; 30cm.
ISBN 0850921775 Pbk Unpriced

ELECTRICAL ENGINEERING - GREAT BRITAIN
—I.Mech.E/I.E.E. conditions of contract : a commentary on five I.Mech.E./I.E.E. model forms of general conditions of contract and on the BEAMA contract price adjustment clauses and formulae / by Andrew Pike. - London : Sweet & maxwell, 1984.
xix,333p; 26cm.
Includes index.
ISBN 0421299908 £38.00

ELECTRICITY - CANADA
—Canadian Electricity Exports : Legal and Regulatory Issues / J. Owen Saunders. - Calgary : Canadian Institute of Resources Law.
40p.

ELECTRICITY - GREAT BRITAIN
—London Electricity Board : a report by the Director General of Fair Trading on an investigation under Section 3 of the Competition Act 1980 / Office of Fair Trading. - London : Office of Fair Trading, 1982.
78p; 30cm.

ELECTRICITY - INDIA
—Electricity Laws and Rules / 2nd ed. - Allahabad : Law Publishers, 1983.

—Law of Electricity in Uttar Pradesh / 2nd ed. - Lucknow : Eastern Book Company, 1985.

—Law Relating to Electricity in India / Surendra Malik. - 5th rev. ed. - Lucknow : Eastern Book Company, 1986.
1,088p.

ELECTRICITY - MALAYSIA
—Electrical Inspectorate Act, 1983 (Act 277) and Electrical Inspectorate Regulations, 1984 (P.U.(A) 313/1984) / Kuala Lumpur : International Law Books Services.

—Electricity Act, 1949 (Act 116) / Kuala Lumpur : International Law Books Services.

ELECTRONIC DATA PROCESSING
—Computer insecurity / Adrian R.D. Norman. - London : Chapman and Hall, 1983.
xiv,351p; 24cm.
Bibliography: p337-342. - Includes index.
ISBN 0412223104 Unpriced

—Data processing and the law : UK National Committee on Comparative Law Annual Colloquium, Leicester, 15-16 September 1982 / Colloquium Chairman Colin Campbell. - 1. - Coventry : UKNCCL, 1982.
various pagings.
Includes bibliographies.

—Transborder data flows : proceedings of an OECD conference held December 1983 / edited for the OECD by Hans-Peter Gassmann. - Amsterdam : North-Holland, 1985.
Bibliography: p.
ISBN 0444877002

ELECTRONIC DATA PROCESSING - GREAT BRITAIN
—Data Protection Act 1984 / with commentary and annotations by Bryan Niblett. - London : Oyez Longman, 1984.
x,155p; 24cm.
ISBN 0851207766 Pbk £16.50

—Data protection : perspectives on information privacy : contributions made to a conference on 11 May 1983 at the University of Leicester / edited by Colin Bourn and John Benyon. - Leicester : University of Leicester, Continuing Education Unit, 1983.
101p; 21cm.
ISBN 090150727X Pbk £5.00

—External auditor as privacy inspector : a study / by Deloitte Haskins & Sells and the National Computing Centre. - Manchester : The Centre, 1982.
38,7,5leaves; 30cm.
ISBN 085012381X Pbk £6.50

—Guide to the Data Protection Act : its implications for business / Nigel Savage & Chris Edwards. - London : Financial Training, 1984.
ISBN 0906322537

ELECTRONIC FUNDS TRANSFERS
—Electronic funds transfer / Dimitris N. Chorafas. - London : Butterworths, 1988.
xi,361p; 24cm.
Includes index.
ISBN 0406101000 £38.00

—Electronic trade payments / by Michael Rowe. - London : International Business Communications, 1987.
256p; 25cm. - (The IBC financial technology series).
Includes bibliography and index.
ISBN 1852710152 Pbk £65.00

—Towards a cashless society? : a report to the Prime Minister / by the Australian Science and Technology Council (ASTEC) prepared by the Technological Change Committee. - Canberra : Australian Government Publishing Service, 1986.
xi,175p.
Includes bibliographies.
ISBN 0644049995

ELECTRONIC FUNDS TRANSFERS - AUSTRALIA
—Report / Canberra : Australian Government Publishing Service, 1986.
88p.
ISBN 0644046961

ELECTRONIC FUNDS TRANSFERS - CANADA
—Crawford and Falconbridge banking and bills of exchange / Bradley Crawford. - 8th edition. 2 v. - Aurora : Canada Law Book Co, 1986.
ISBN 0888040369

ELECTRONIC FUNDS TRANSFERS - GREAT BRITAIN
—Electronic banking and the law / by Anu Arora. - London : IBC Financial, 1988.
188p.
Includes index.
ISBN 1852710403 £65.00

—Electronic Funds Transfer / London : Butterworths, 1988.
ISBN 0406101000 Pbk £48.00

ELECTRONIC OFFICE MACHINES
—Information handling and the office of the future : report of a seminar / M. Grieves, editor. - London : British Library Research and Development Department, 1984.
ii,84p.

ELECTRONIC OFFICE MACHINES - GREAT BRITAIN
—Communications : a guide to the electronic office for practising lawyers / compiled by the Communications Committee of the Society for Computers and Law. - 2nd fully rev ed. - Didcot : The Society, 1985.
iii,67 leaves.
ISBN 0906122198

—Communications : a guide to the electronic office for practising lawyers / compiled by the Communications Committee of the Society for Computers and Law. - Milton, Oxon. : The Society, 1983.
39 leaves.
Bibliography: p.39.

ELECTRONIC SURVEILLANCE - GREAT BRITAIN
—Interception of Communications Act 1985 : chapter 56 : report of the Commissioner for ... / London : HMSO, 1987-.

EMERGENCY POWERS

—States of emergency : their impact on human rights / a study prepared by the International Commission of Jurists. – Geneva : International Commission of Jurists, 1983.
iii,477p.
Includes bibliographical references.
ISBN 929037019X

EMERGENCY POWERS – INDIA

—Defence and Emergency Laws / 2nd ed. – Allahabad : Law Publishers, 1980.

EMERGENCY POWERS – NORTHERN IRELAND

—Northern Ireland emergency legislation / London : Butterworths, 1987.
ISBN 0406105774 Pbk £15.00

EMIGRATION AND IMMIGRATION

—Basic documents on international migration law / edited by Richard Plender. – Dordrecht : M. Nijhoff, 1988.
viii,411p.
Companion to: International migration law / Richard Plender. Rev. 2nd ed. 1988.
ISBN 9024736676 pbk.

—Citizenship, aliens and immigration : being Title 27 from Volume 4 of the Canadian encyclopedic digest (Ontario) 3rd ed. / Janet V. Scott, Robert C. Stonehouse. – Agincourt, Ont. : Carswell, 1980.
154p; 24cm.
Includes index. Contents: Immigration / by Janet V. Scott. - Citizenship and aliens / by Robert C. Stonehouse.
ISBN 0459331108

—European immigration policy : a comparative study / edited by Tomas Hammar. – 1. – Cambridge : Cambridge University Press, 1985.
Includes bibliography and index.
ISBN 0521263263 £30.00

—Immigration : the law and practice / Michael Supperstone assisted by Elisabeth Laing. – London : Oyez Longman, 1983.
xxii,251p.
ISBN 0851207472

—International migration law / Richard Plender. – Rev. 2nd ed. – Dordrecht, Netherlands : M. Nijhoff, 1987.
xxvii,587p.
Includes index.
ISBN 9024736048

—Right to leave and return in international law and practice / by Hurst Hannum. – Dordrecht : Nijhoff, 1987.
xiii, 189p. – (International studies in human rights).
Includes index.
ISBN 9024734452

EMIGRATION AND IMMIGRATION – AUSTRALIA

—Getting a fair go : case studies of occupational socialization and perceptions of discrimination in a sample of seven Melbourne high schools / Brian M. Bullivant. – Canberra : Australian Government Publishing Service, 1986.
xi,296p. – (Occasional paper).
Bibliographical references: p259-296.
ISBN 0644055243

—Observance of human rights at the Villawood Immigration Detention Centre / Human Rights Commission. – Canberra : Government Publishing Service, 1983.
viii,37p. – (Report).
ISBN 0644027193 £2.30

EMIGRATION AND IMMIGRATION – CANADA

—Annotated Immigration Act of Canada / edited and annotated by Frank N. Marrocco and Henry M. Goslett. – Toronto, Canada : Carswell Co., 1984.
xxv, 246 p.; 23 cm.
Includes indexes.
ISBN 0459360507 pbk.

—Canada's immigration law : an overview / Employment and Immigration Canada. – Hull, Quebec : Department of Supply and Services, 1983.
31,32p.
With French t.p.: Vue d'ensemble sur la legislation canadienne en matiere d'immigration. English and French texts.
ISBN 0662527798

—Canadian immigration law and procedure / Christopher J. Wydrzynski. – Aurora, Ont. : Canada Law Book, 1983.
xli,511p.
Includes index.
ISBN 0888040156

—Obtaining reasons before applying for judicial scrutiny : Immigration Appeal Board / Law Reform Commission of Canada. – Ottawa : Law Reform Commission of Canada, 1982.
21,25p; 25cm. – (Report).
English and French text, in reverse.
ISBN 0662521064

EMIGRATION AND IMMIGRATION – GREAT BRITAIN

—British Nationality Act 1981 / with annotations by M. D. A. Freeman. – London : Sweet and Maxwell, 1982.
various pagings; 25cm.
ISBN 0421300604

—Comments on the Home Office discussion document : Review of appeals under the Immigration Act, 1971 / Justice. – London : Justice, 1981.
5p; 33cm.

—Development of British immigration law / Vaughan Bevan. – London : Croom Helm, 1986.
512p.
Includes bibliography and index.
ISBN 0709906633 £29.95

—Government reply to the sixth report from the Home Affairs Committee, session 1984-85 HC277 : Immigration and Nationality Department of the Home Office / presented to Parliament by the Secretary of State for the Home Department. – London : H.M.S.O., 1985.
7p.
ISBN 0101963203

—Immigration and Nationality Department report, July 1985 / London, 1985.
30p. – (A Home Office publication).
'Second published report on the work of the Immigration and Nationality Department of the Home Office' -Foreword.

—Immigration and nationality law and practice / London : Frank Cass, 1986-.

—Immigration and the judiciary : law and politics in Britain and America / Stephen H. Legomsky. – Oxford : Clarendon, 1987.
xxxix,345p; 24cm.
Bibliography: p327-345.
ISBN 0198255616 £35.00

—Immigration control procedures : report of a formal investigation / London : Commission for Racial Equality, 1985.
xiv,188p.
ISBN 0907920543

—Immigration law / by J.M. Evans. – 2nd ed. – London : Sweet & Maxwell, 1983.
xxx,452p; 19cm.
Previous ed.: 1976. Includes index.
ISBN 0421299509 Hbk Unpriced
ISBN 0421299606 Pbk £7.50

—Immigration law and practice / Lawrence Grant, Ian Martin. – London : The Cobden Trust, 1982.
xxxii,410p; 22cm.
Includes index.
ISBN 0900137193 Pbk
ISBN 0900137815

—Immigration : the law and practice / Michael Supperstone assisted by Elisabeth Laing. – London : Oyez Longman, 1983.
xxii,251p.
ISBN 0851207472

—Pivot of the system : a briefing paper on immigration appeals / London : The Runnymede Trust, 1981.
32fol.

—Proposals for revision of the Immigration Rules / Home Office. – London : H.M.S.O., 1982.
vii,40p.
ISBN 0101868308

—Proposed new immigration rules and the European Convention on Human Rights : first report from the Home Affairs Committee, 1979-80, together with the proceedings of the Committee, and the minutes of evidence and appendices / Great Britain. – London : H.M.S.O., 1980.
xxi,62p; 25cm. – (1979-80 H.C. 434).
ISBN 0102434808 sd £3.00

—Review of appeals under the Immigration Act 1971 : a discussion document / Home Office. – Croydon : Home Office, 1981.
16p.

—Sixth report form the Home Affairs Committee, session 1984-85 : Immigration and Nationality Department of the Home Office, together with the proceedings of the Committee, minutes of evidence and appendices / London : H.M.S.O., 1985.
xxviii,119p. – (H.C.).
ISBN 0102277850

—Statement of change in immigration rules : laid before Parliament on 21 October 1986 under section 3(2) of the Immigration Act 1971 / London : H.M.S.O., 1986.
1p. – (H.C. 1985-86).
ISBN 0102584869

—Statement of change in immigration rules : laid before Parliament on 29 January 1987 under section 3(2) of the Immigration Act 1971 / London : H.M.S.O., 1987.
1 leaf. – (1986-87 HC).
ISBN 0102154872

—Statement of change in immigration rules : presented to Parliament by the Secretary of State for the Home Department by Command of Her Majesty October 1986 / London : H.M.S.O., 1986.
1 leaf.
ISBN 0101991401

—Statement of changes in immigration rules / presented to Parliament by the Secrtary of State for the Home Department. – London : H.M.S.O., 1985.
2p.
ISBN 0101953909

—Statement of changes in immigration rules / London : H.M.S.O., 1983.
iv,41p; 25cm. – (1982-83 H.C.).
Rules laid down by the Home Secretary.
ISBN 0102169837 unbound £3.80

—Statement of changes in immigration rules : laid before Parliament on 14 December 1987 under section 3(2) of the Immigration Act 1971 / London : HMSO, 1987.
3p. – (1987-88 H.C.).
ISBN 0102208883

—Statement of changes in immigration rules : laid before Parliament on 15 July 1985 under section 3(2) of the Immigration Act 1971 / London : H.M.S.O., 1985.
8p. – (H.C.).
ISBN 0102503850

—Statement of changes in immigration rules : laid before Parliament on 20 February 1980 under Section 3(2) of the Immigration Act 1971 / Home Office. – London : H.M.S.O., 1980.
iii,37p.

—Statement of changes in immigration rules : laid before Parliament on 26 March 1985 under section 3(2) of the Immigration Act 1971 / London : H.M.S.O., 1985.
3p. – (H.C.).
ISBN 0102293856

—Statement of changes in immigration rules : Laid before Parliament on 6 December 1982 under section 3(2) of the Immigration Act 1971 / London : H.M.S.O., 1982.
ii,40p. – (1982-83 H.C. 66).
ISBN 0102066833

—Statement of changes in immigration rules : laid before Parliament on 7 July 1988 under section 3(2) of the Immigration Act 1971 / London : HMSO, 1988.
5p.
ISBN 0102555885

—Towards a just immigration policy / edited by Ann Dummett. – London : Cobden Trust, 1986.
240p; 20cm.
ISBN 0900137266 Pbk £6.95

EMIGRATION AND IMMIGRATION – SOUTH AFRICA – SOUTH AFRICA

—Black migration to South Africa : a selection of policy-oriented research / edited by W. R. Bohning. – Geneva : International Labour Office, 1981.
viii,184p.
Bibliography: p179-184.
ISBN 9221027589

EMIGRATION AND IMMIGRATION – UNITED KINGDOM

—Immigration law and practice in the United Kingdom / Ian A. Macdonald. – 2nd ed. – London : Butterworths, 1987.
560p; 25cm.
Previous ed.: 1983. Includes index.
ISBN 0406283141 £50.55

EMIGRATION AND IMMIGRATION – UNITED STATES

—Immigration and the judiciary : law and politics in Britain and America / Stephen H. Legomsky. – Oxford : Clarendon, 1987.
xxxix,345p; 24cm.
Bibliography: p327-345.
ISBN 0198255616 £35.00

EMPLOYEES' LIABILITY – GREAT BRITAIN

—Wounded soldiers of industry : industrial compensation policy 1833-1897 / P.W.J. Bartrip and S.B. Burman. – Oxford : Clarendon, 1983.
xi,253p; 23cm. – (Oxford socio-legal studies).
Includes index.
ISBN 0198275099 £15.00

EMPLOYERS' LIABILITY – AUSTRALIA

—Industrial Accidents : Employer Liability for Monetary Damages / Audrey Balla. – North Ryde : C.C.H. Australia, 1987.
180p.
ISBN 0869038664 Hbk

EMPLOYERS' LIABILITY - GREAT BRITAIN

—Employer's liability at common law / by John Munkman. – 10th ed. – London : Butterworths, 1985.
lxxi,699p; 22cm.
Previous ed.: 1979. Includes index.
ISBN 0406311072 No price

—Employer's Liability at Common Law / 10th ed. – London : Butterworths, 1985.
ISBN 0406311072 Hbk £48.00

—Forensic audiology / Chuang Wei Ping : foreword by Ronald Hinchcliffe. – Middlesbrough : Chuang Wei Ping, 1985.
108p in various pagings; 22cm.
ISBN 0951080008 Pbk £6.00

EMPLOYMENT

—Australian industrial law review / North Ryde, N.S.W. : CCH Australia, 1959-.
30cm.
'Digests of cases (in which reasons for decision have been published) from Federal and State Courts and Tribunals'.

—Comparative labour law and industrial relations / editor, R. Blanpain : associate editor, F. Millard. – Deventer, The Netherlands : Kluwer, 1982.
411 p.; 25 cm.
Includes indexes.
ISBN 9031201790

—Comparative labour law and industrial relations / editor, Blanpain, R. : contributors Aaron, B. ... et al. – 3rd ed. – Deventer, The Netherlands : Kluwer Law and Taxation Publishers, 1987.
xiii, 527p.
Includes indexes.
ISBN 9065443169

—Constitutional law and practice in the International Labour Organisation / by E. Osieke. – The Hague : M. Hijhoff, 1984.
xxi, 266p.
Bibliography: p.243-258.
ISBN 9024729858 Hbk £160.00

—Contract Labour in the Clothing Industry : Report 2. Second Tripartite Technical Meeting for the Clothing Industry, Geneva, 1980 / Geneva : International Labour Office, 1980.
ii, 75p.
ISBN 9221024326 Hbk £12.50

—Employer-employee relations in the public service of Canada : proposals for legislative change / J. Finkelman. – 4 v. – Ottawa : Information Canada, 1974.
Includes bibliographical references. Contents: Parts 1-3 - Supplementary observations and recommendations. Parallel English and French texts, Part 3 and Supplementary observations and recommendations.

—Encyclopaedia of labour relations law / Sweet & Maxwell, 1988.
ISBN 0421169605 Hbk £265.00

—Equality and prohibition of discrimination in employment / editor R. Blanpain. – Deventer, The Netherlands : Klwver, 1985.
244p.
ISBN 9065442154

—Future of labour law : two views / Graham Mather, W. E. J. McCarthy. – Coventry : Industrial Relations Research Unit, University of Warwick, 1987.
Contents: The future shape of labour legislation/Graham Mather. - The case for a more balanced framework of labour law/W.E.J. McCarthy.

—ILO and the world of work / International Labour Organisation. – Geneva : International Labour Organisation, 1984.
74p.
ISBN 9221031500

—International conflicts of labour law : a survey of the law applicable to the international employment relation / Felice Morgenstern. – Geneva : International Labour Office, 1986.
ix,129p; 25cm.
ISBN 922103593X

—International employment tax handbook / Reading. – Cambridge : Woodhead-Faulkner, 1982.
ISBN 0859411915 Hbk £115.00

—International Encyclopaedia for Labour Law and Industrial Relations. Supplements / Dordrecht : Kluwer.

46

47

48

49 1985.

50 1985.
96p.

51 1985.
208p.

52 1985.
264p.

53 1985.
224p.

54 1985.
168p.

55 1985.
120p.

—International handbook on pensions law and similar employee benefits / London : Graham & Trotman, 1989.
352.
On behalf of the International Association for Insurance Law, examines pension laws in over 17 countries. Topics include surplus reversion and the recapture of assets, predator proofing, the national and international nomad, human rights and sex equality in retirement pensions, share incentive, and stock option plans.
ISBN 0860109941 Hbk £85

—International journal of comparative labour law and industrial relations / v. – Leicester : University of Leicester, 1985.

—International labour conventions and national law : the effectiveness of the automatic incorporation of treaties in national legal systems / Virginia A. Leary. – The Hague : M. Nijhoff, 1982.
xiv,191p.
Revision of thesis (doctoral)–Graduate Institute of International Studies at Geneva. Bibliography: p171-179.
ISBN 9024725518

—International labour conventions and recommendations, 1919-1981 : arranged by subject-matter / Geneva : International Labour Office, 1982.
xxxiv, 1167 p.; 25 cm.
'Conventions and recommendations adopted by the International Labour Conference'–Pref. At head of title: International Labour Organisation.
ISBN 9221029344

—International Labour Law : a Comparative Survey of the Conflict Rules Affecting Labour Legislation and Regulations / A.W. Sijthoff. – Budapest : Akademiai Kiado, 1968.
465p.

—International labour law reports / Benjamin Aaron, Thilo Ramm, Tore Sigeman, Jean-Maurice Verdier, Felice Morgenstern, Lord Wedderburn of Charlton. – Dordrecht : Martinus Nijhoff, 1989.
688. – (International labour law reports).
A volume in the series of annual publications of labour law judgements by the highest courts in a number of jurisdictions. Each judgement reprinted has Headnotes and usually an Annotation setting out the legal issues involved, and basic facts of the case if not included in the judgement. Judgements are normally printed in extenso.
ISBN 0792300998 Hbk £105

—International labour standards : their nature, their working, their value / Geneva : International Labour Office, 1981.
49p.

—Juridification of social spheres : a comparative analysis in the areas of labor, corporate, antitrust, and social welfare law / edited by Gunther Teubner. – Berlin : De Gruyter, 1987.
viii, 446 p.; 24 cm.
Includes bibliographies and index.
ISBN 0899252729

—Knight's industrial and commercial reports / general editor H. Samuels. – 9. – London : Knight, 1966.
Continued by: Knight's industrial reports. Spine title: Knight's industrial reports.

—Knight's industrial reports / general editor H. Samuels. – 8 in 7. – London : Knight, 1971.
Continues: Knight's industrial and commercial reports. - Superseded by: Knight's industrial law reports (1 vol. only). Numbering continued by: Managerial law.

—Labor relations in 17 countries / Christian Bratt : translated by David Jenkins. – Stockholm : Swedish Employers' Confederation, 1982.
134p.
Translated from 'Arbetsmarknaden i 16 lander' by David Jenkins.
ISBN 9171522514

—Labour, law and crime : an historical perspective / edited by Francis Snyder and Douglas Hay. – London : Tavistock, 1987.
x,309p; 23cm.
Bibliography: p292-297. - Includes index.
ISBN 0422608408 £30.00

—Labour law and industrial relations : building on Kahn-Freund / edited by Lord Wedderburn of Charlton, Roy Lewis, Jon Clark. – Oxford : Clarendon Press, 1983.
vii,250p; 23cm.
Includes index.
ISBN 0198253931 Hbk Unpriced
ISBN 0198254822 Pbk £8.95

—Labour law research in twelve countries / editor: Sten Edlund. – Stockholm : Arbetarskyddsfonden & Arbetslivscentrum, 1986.
296p; 25cm.
ISBN 9122008004

—Labour Protection Laws in ASEAN / Geneva : International Labour Office, 1987.
vii, 481p.
ISBN 9221058913 Hbk £30.00

—Labour Relations Laws in ASEAN : a Collection of Current Labour Laws in Six Asean States / Geneva : International Labour Office, 1986.
vii, 365p.
ISBN 9221054349 Hbk £17.50

—Law as an instrument of state intervention in industrial relations / Yiannis Gabriel. – London : Thames Polytechnic School of Business Administration, 1984.

—Law of industrial relations / by J.G. Riddall. – London : Butterworths, 1981.
xxiv,319p; 25cm.
Includes index. Latest supplement held: 1982, covering the Employment Act 1982.
ISBN 0406648107 Pbk Unpriced

—Law of the International Civil Service: as applied by internatinal administrative tribunals / Oxford : Clarendon Press.
686.
ISBN 0198255608 Hbk £60

—Law of the International Civil Service: as applied by internatinal administrative tribunals / Oxford : Clarendon Press.
1350.
On the law as applied by international administrative tribunals in the area of employment relations between international organisations and their staff. Analyses the way in which obligations and rights are enforced and recognised.
ISBN 0198256108 Hbk £60

—Making of labour law in Europe : a comparative study of nine countries up to 1945 / edited by Bob Hepple. – London : Mansell, 1986.
xiv,412p; 24cm.
Bibliography: p387-401. - Includes index.
ISBN 072011697X £39.95

—Maritime Labour Conventions and Recommendations / Geneva : International Labour Office, 1983.
viii, 224p.
ISBN 9221030962 Hbk £17.50

—New family and the new property / Mary Ann Glendon. – Toronto : Butterworths, 1981.
xvii,269p; 23cm.
ISBN 0409834106

—Restructuring labour in the enterprise : law and practice in France, F.R. of Germany, Italy, Sweden and the United Kingdom / edited by R. Blanpain. – Deventer, The Netherlands : Kluwer, .
v,145p.
Includes bibliographical references. At head of cover: Institute for Labour Relations, Catholic University of Leuven.
ISBN 9065442839

—Unfair dismissal : a guide to relevant case law / by Michael Rubenstein and Yvonne Frost. – 4th edition. – London : Industrial Relations Service, 1986.
iv, 84p.

—Unfair dismissal : a guide to relevant case law / by Michael Rubenstein and Yvonne Frost. – S.l. : s.n., 1983.
63p; 30cm.

EMPLOYMENT - AUSTRALIA

—Australian employment legislation / Australia. – 3. – Sydney : CCH Austalia, 1984.
loose-leaf.
Originally published: as part of Australian labour law reporter, 1977-. Includes index. Loose-leaf issues accompanied by a summary report.
ISBN 0869036513

—Australian industrial laws : the constitutional basis / by James Joseph Macken. – 2nd ed. – Sydney : Law Book Co., 1980.
xiii,284p; 25cm.
Previous ed.: 1974. Includes index.
ISBN 045520120X Pbk
ISBN 0455201218

—Employer, the Employee and the Law / 4th ed. – North Ryde : Law Book Co, 1980.
ISBN 0455200718 Pbk £9.50

—Employer, the Employees and the Law / North Ryde : Law Book Co, 1980.
xxi, 198p.
ISBN 0455200718 Pbk £19.00

—Keeping employees informed / Roger Hussey. – Sydney : Butterworths, 1982.
175p.
Discusses various forms of employee communication, including noticeboards, mass meetings and discussion groups. Aims at assisting the manager to assess and improve the standard of his own employee communications by presenting a detailed picture of the current practice in Australia.
ISBN 0409309435 Pbk

—Labour law : materials and commentary / by W. B. Creighton, W. J. Ford, R. J. Mitchell. – North Ryde, N.S.W. : Law Book Co., 1983.
liii,944p; 25cm.
ISBN 0455204136

—Law of Employment / 2nd ed. – North Ryde : Law Book Co, 1984.
xix, 351p.
ISBN 0455205108 Pbk £30.00
ISBN 0455205094 Hbk £42.00

—Law, politics, and the labor movement / edited by Gareth Evans. – Clayton, Vic. : Legal Service Bulletin in association with Australian Society of Labor Lawyers, 1980.
x, 205 p.; 21 cm.
Papers presented at the First National Conference of Labor Lawyers, held in Adelaide on 20 June-1 July, 1979. Includes bibliographical references and indexes.
ISBN 0959472703 pbk.

—Long service leave / by Hugh Selby : with a foreword by F.V. Watson. – Sydney : Law Book Co., 1983.
xxviii,150p.
Includes index.
ISBN 0455204519

—Occupational Regulation and the Public Interest / Turramura : Centre for Independent Studies.
ISBN 0949769134 Hbk £8.95

—Public Employment Law : the Role of the Contract of Employment In / Butterworths, 1987.
207p.
ISBN 0409492566 Pbk £29.00

—Public Employment Law : The Role of the Contract of Employment in Australia and Britain / Sydney : Butterworths, 1987.
208p.
This book describes the statutory and institutional framework of public employment law in Australia and Britain. Also discussed are the distinctions between Crown servants and other public employees, discipline, dismissal, tenure of employment, and remedies.

—Retired, unemployed or at risk : changes in the Australian labour market for older workers / Canberra : Australian Government Publishing Service, 1983.
ix,150p. – (Research report).
Bibliography: p144-150.
ISBN 0644028580 £6.50

—Review of Australian Law and Practice Relating to the Conventions Adopted by the International Labour Conference / Department of Industrial Relations. – Canberra : Australian Government Publishing Service, 1981.
ISBN 0642052166 loose £14.20

—Statutory Conditions of Employment / C. Sappideen. – Butterworths, 1980.
284p.
ISBN 0409328618 Pbk £45.00

—Workers with family responsibilities : implications for employers / Ilene Wolcott. – Melbourne : Australian Institute of Family Studies, 1987.
vii,62p. – (Discussion paper).
Includes bibliographical references.
ISBN 0642110212

EMPLOYMENT - AUSTRALIA - NEW SOUTH WALES

—Contracts for Work in Industry (NSW) : Section 88F / Butterworths, 1981.
ISBN 0409490474 Pbk £35.00

EMPLOYMENT - AUSTRALIA - VICTORIA

—Principles for occupational regulation / Law Reform Commission of Victoria. – Melbourne : The Commission, 1988.
iv,35p. – (Report no 17).
At head of cover title: Regulation Review Unit.
ISBN 0724167234 Hbk

EMPLOYMENT - CANADA

—Anti-discrimination staffing policies : implications of human ruights legislation for employers and trade unions / by Harrish C. Jain. – Ottawa : Department of the Secretary of State of Canada, 1985.
iv,100p.
Includes bibliographical references.
ISBN 0662141474

—Bi-monthly bulletin : summary of cases decided by the Canada Labour Relations Board and court updates ... / Bulletin bimestriel. – Ottawa : The Board, 1987.
Continues: Summary of decisions of the Canada Labour Relations Board and court updates. Parallel text in English and French.

—Brief to the Legislative Committee considering Bill C-62 : an Act respecting employment equity / Canadian Human Rights Commission. – Ottawa : Minister of Supply and Services, 1986.
12,14p.
Added t.p. in French. Cover title: Employment equity. Text in English and French.
ISBN 0662541804

—British Columbia Labour Arbitration / Aurora : Canada Law Book Co.
– (Summary Services, Provincial Ser.).

—Canada Labour Service / Toronto : DeBoo.
This looseleaf volume provides a Consolidation of all Federal and Provincial Canadian Labor Legislation.
ISBN 0888201435 loose £285.00

—Canadian Cases on Employment Law / Agincourt : Carswell, 1987.
Back Vols. 1984-1986.
This reference book contains key decisions in employment law outside the collective bargaining process. Cases on wrongful dismissal, dismissal for cause, constructive dismissal, demotion, employment contracts, employment standards, mandatory retirement policies, wage and remuneration, pensions and profit sharing are included.

—Canadian Cases on Employment Law / Agincourt : Carswell.

—Canadian labour law : a comprehensive text / George W. Adams. – Aurora, Ont. : Canada Law Book Inc., 1985.
cii,983p.
Includes index.
ISBN 088804030X

—Canadian Master Labour Guide / 3rd ed. – Don Mills : CCH Canadian Ltd, 1988.
780p.
ISBN 088796429X Pbk £18.95
ISBN 0887964303 Hbk £21.50

—Employment Equity Act and reporting requirements / Employment and Immigration Canada. – Ottawa : Ministry of Supplies and Services Canada, 1986.
Various pagings.
' ... provided to assist employers to meet their obligations under the Act'. - p.1.
ISBN 0662149777

—Employment law in Canada / Innis Christie : chapter 8 by Brent Cotter. – Toronto : Butterworths, 1980.
lxxvii, 518 p.; 24 cm.
Includes bibliographical references and index.
ISBN 0409823953

—Employment Law in Western Canada / Agincourt : Carswell.
This work provides an in-depth analysis of the common and statutory law of employment in Western Canada. Also included is a comprehensive review of federal and Western Canadian collective bargaining law.

—Employment Law : the New Basics / North Ryde : C.C.H. Australia.
384p.
ISBN 0887964648 Pbk £19.95

—Employment Standards Handbook / Aurora : Canada Law Book Co, 1986.
– (Text Book-Civil).

—Labour Arbitration 1984 / Vancouver : Continuing Legal Education Society of British Columbia, 1987.
161p.
ISBN 0865043302 Hbk £65.00

—Labour Arbitration - 1985 / Vancouver : British Columbia Continuing Legal Education Society, 1985.
116p.
ISBN 0865042063 Hbk £55.00

—Labour Arbitration 1988 / Vancouver : Continuing Legal Education Society of British Columbia, 1988.
156p.
ISBN 0865049971 Hbk £70.00

—Labour Arbitration : Boon or Bane for Unions? / Toronto : Butterworths.
70p.
ISBN 0409988618 Pbk £29.95

—Labour Arbitration Cases : Consolidated Index / Aurora : Canada Law Book Co, 1985.
– (Law Reports).

—Labour Arbitration Cases : Consolidated Index, List of Awards / Aurora : Canada Law Book Co, 1982.
400p. – (Law Reports).

—Labour Arbitration Cases First Series (1948-1972), 24 Vols. / Aurora : Canada Law Book Co.
– (Law Reports).
Back Vols.

—Labour Arbitration Cases Second Series (1973-1981), 30 Vols. / Aurora : Canada Law Book Co.
– (Law Reports).
Back Vols.

—Labour Arbitration Cases Third Series (1982-Present) / Aurora : Canada Law Book Co.
– (Law Reports).
Back Vols.

—Labour Arbitrations and All That / 2nd ed. – Aurora : Canada Law Book Co, 1985.
146p. – (Text Books-Civil).

—Labour law and industrial relations in Canada / by H.W. Arthurs, D.D. Carter, H.J. Glasbeek. – 2nd ed. – Deventer : Kluwer Law and Taxation, 1984.
316p; 25cm.
Deals with Canadian labour movement, the individual employment relationship, legal status and democratic rule in trade unions, the collective bargaining process, industrial conflict and collective agreements. Presents policy themes and typical legal solutions as well as recording significant departures.
ISBN 9065441905
ISBN 0409811858 Hbk

—Labour law and industrial relations in Canada / by H. W. Arthurs, D. D. Carter, H. J. Glasbeek. – Deventer, The Netherlands : Kluwer, 1981.
291p.
Originally published as a monograph in the International encyclopedia of labour law and industrial relations.
ISBN 9031201391 Kluwer

—Labour Law and Practice : Materials Prepared for a Continuing Legal Education Seminar Held in Vancouver, B. C., April 14-15, 1983 / Allan E. Black. – Vancouver : British Columbia Continuing Legal Education Society, 1983.
ISBN 086504094X loose

—Labour Law and Urban Law in Canada / Andree Lajoie. – Toronto : University of Toronto Press, 1986.
232p.
ISBN 0802072976 Hbk £16.95

—Labour Law Digest, 6 Vols. / Agincourt : Carswell, 1985.
This multi-volume set digests over fifteen thousand reported Canadian labor law cases under federal and provincial law. A cumulative supplement is supplied every six months to keep the work up-to-date.

—Labour Relations Act : Rules of Procedure, Regulations and Practice Notes / Office of the Legislative Assembly (Ontario). – Ontario : Ontario Government Publications Service, 1983.
177p.

—Law of Dismissal in Canada / Aurora : Canada Law Book, 1985.

—New Development in Federal and Provincial Labour Law / McGill University. – Toronto : DeBoo, 1980.
– (Meredith Memorial Lecture Ser.).
ISBN 0888200994 Hbk £42.50

—Non-Unionized Workers Protection Act, 1983, Bill 115 : An Act Respecting the Rights of Non-Unionized Workers / Ontario : Ontario Government Publications Service, 1983.
3p.

—Owner-Manager's Employment Manual /. – Toronto : DeBoo.
These manuals, available for the provinces of British Columbia, Ontario, and Quebec, examine the areas of hiring procedures, employment standards, statutory deductions, taxable earnings and benefits, workers compensation, and termination requirements. Also included are regular updates and a complimentary newsletter.
ISBN 0888202687 loose £105.00

—Reconcilable Differences : New Directions in Canadian Labour Law / Agincourt : Carswell, 1980.
348p.
This book describes the evolution and present state of key issues of Canadian labor law and policy. The text illustrates policy dilemmas in labor law with descriptions of real life labor disputes.

—Reconcilable differences : new directions in Canadian labour law / Paul Weiler. – Toronto : Carswell, 1980.
xi,335p.
Includes bibliographical references and index.
ISBN 0459330802

—Studies in labour law / edited by Kenneth P. Swan, Katherine E. Swinton. – Toronto : Butterworths, 1983.
xxiii,349p. – (Canadian legal studies series).
Includes index.
ISBN 040987129X

—Studies in Labour Law / Katherine E. Swinton. – Toronto : Butterworths, 1983.
384p.

—Studies in Labour Law / Katherine E. Swinton. – Butterworths, 1983.
384p.

—Summary of decisions of the Canada Labour Relations Board and court updates ... / Resume des decisions du Conseil Canadien des Relations du Travail et mise a jour des dossiers a la cour ... – Ottawa : The Board, 1987.
Parallel text in English and French.

—Termination and Dismissal / Vancouver : British Columbia Continuing Legal Education Society, 1985.
65p.
ISBN 0865042098 Hbk £50.00

EMPLOYMENT - CANADA - ALBERTA

—Employee-Employer Rights in Alberta : a Guide to Alberta Labour Law / Tim Christian. – 2nd ed. – North Vancouver : International Self-Counsel Press, 1984.
95p.
ISBN 0889082324 Hbk £6.95

—Employment in Alberta : a Guide to Conditions of Work and Employee Benefits, 1 Vol. / Butterworths.

—Employment in Alberta : A Guide to Conditions of Work and Employment Benefits / Toronto : Butterworths.

EMPLOYMENT - CANADA - BRITISH COLUMBIA

—British Columbia Labour Code, 2 vols / Toronto : Butterworths.
– (British Columbia Annotated Legislation).

—British Columbia Labour Code : B.C. Annotated Legislation Series, 2 Vols. / Butterworths.

—British Columbia Labour Relations Board Decisions / Aurora : Canada Law Book Co.

—Employee-Employer Rights : a Guide for the British Columbia Work Force / 7th ed. – North Vancouver : International Self-Counsel Press, 1984.
137p.
ISBN 0889081522 Hbk £7.95

—Employment in British Columbia : a Guide to Conditions of Work and Employee Benefits, 1 Vol. / Butterworths.

—Employment in British Columbia : A Guide to Conditions of Work and Employee Benefits / Toronto : Butterworths.

—Owner-Manager's Employment Manual / Toronto : DeBoo.
ISBN 0888202679 loose £105.00

—Report on the action per quod servitium amisit / Law Reform Commission of British Columbia. – Victoria : Queens Printer, 1986.
20p.
Includes bilbiographical references.
ISBN 0771885490

EMPLOYMENT - CANADA - ONTARIO

—Annotated Employment Law Statutes of Ontario / Carswell, 1987.
308p.

—Annotated Employment Law Statutes of Ontario / John H. McNair. – Agincourt : Carswell, 1987.
308p.
This text annotates the following: the Occupational Health and Safety Act, Employment Standards Act, Industrial Standards Act, Human Rights Code, Pension Benefits Act, of the Ontario employment legislation.

—Annual report / Ontario Labour Relations Board / Ontario Labour Relations Board. – v. – Toronto : The Board, 1981.
Report year ends 31 Mar..
ISBN 0711849X

—Employee-Employer Rights : a Complete Guide for the Ontario Work Force / 6th ed. – North Vancouver : International Self-Counsel Press, 1988.
113p.
ISBN 0889083681 Hbk

—Employment in Ontario : a Guide to Conditions of Work and Employee Benefits, 1 Vol. / Butterworths.

—Employment in Ontario : A Guide to Conditions of Work and Employee Benefits / Toronto : Butterworths.

—Ontario Employment Law Handbook : an Employer's Guide / rev. ed. – Butterworths, 1986.
96p.

—Ontario employment law handbook: an employer's guide / Scarborough, Ontario : Butterworths (Canada), 1986.
96.
Examines the changes in Ontario's employment law since the fist edition in 1982. Covers the hours of work and minimum wages, overtime pay and public holidays, health and safety regulations, unemployment insurance, lockouts and strikes, and negotiations and arbitration.
ISBN 0409804860 Pbk

—Ontario Employment Law Handbook : An Employer's Guide Revised Edition / Toronto : Butterworths, 1986.
96p.

—Ontario Labour Relations Board Law and Practice : Citation Updater / Toronto : Butterworths.

—Owner-Manager's Employment Manual /. – Toronto : DeBoo.
ISBN 0888202660 loose £105.00

EMPLOYMENT - CARIBBEAN

—Studies in Caribbean labour relations / Roop L. Chaudhary. – 2nd ed. – Barbados : Coles Printery, 1984.
xi,234p.
Includes index.

EMPLOYMENT - CHINA

—Chinese Labour Under British Rule / Rear. – Oxford : Oxford University Press, 1981.
ISBN 0195802829 Hbk £12.50

EMPLOYMENT - DENMARK

—Perspective on labour law / Ole Hasselbalch, Alan C. Neal, Anders Victorin. – Stockholm : Almqvist & Wiksell, 1982.
128p.
ISBN 0421307102

EMPLOYMENT - ENGLAND

—Labour law / M. Wright and C.J. Carr. – 4th ed. – Plymouth : MacDonald and Evans, 1984.
xx,211p. – (The M & E handbook series).
Bibliography: p.195. - Includes index.
ISBN 0712101918

—Labour law : cases and materials / Patrick Elias, Brian Napier, Peter Wallington. – London : Butterworths, 1980.
xl,819p.
Includes index.
ISBN 0406577587 Hbk £26.00
ISBN 0406577595 Pbk £15.95

EMPLOYMENT - EUROPE

—European Employment Handbook / 3rd ed. – London : Engineering Employers Federation, 1985.

—European trade unions in figures / Kluwer Law and Taxation, 1989.
Presents a comparative set of data and sources on union membership in ten European countries - Austria, Denmark, France, West Germany, Italy, the Netherlands, Norway, Sweden, Switzerland and the UK. Gives emphasis to comparative definitions of union membership and union density, that is, the ratio of actual to potential memberships.
ISBN 9065444092 Pbk £24.50/Dfl 79

—Handbook on European employee co-maangement / W Kolvenbach, P Hanau. – Kluwer Law and Taxation, 1989.
818.
ISBN 90T2802003 Llf £102/Dfl 325

Supplement 1989.
308.
Covers the co-determination laws, contractual agreements, and other regulations of European countries, and existing regulations of the OECD and ILO. A comparison with the US is made. Includes participative institutions at shop floor level, employee participation at board level, and selected documentation in each chapter.
ISBN 90T2800019 Llf £73/Dfl 231

—Immigrant workers in Europe : their legal status : a comparative study / Eric-Jean Thomas, study director. – Paris : Unesco Press, 1982.
245 p.; 25 cm.
Includes bibliographies.
ISBN 9231018671 Hbk £50

—Long Suffering British Workers : Working Time in Europe / London : Labour Research Department.
24p.
ISBN 0900508434 Hbk £0.60

—Women employment and European law / Oxford : Eclipse, 1988.
ISBN 1870771001 Hbk £25.00

EMPLOYMENT - EUROPEAN COMMUNITY

—Business law in Europe : legal, tax and labour aspects of business operations in the ten European Community countries and Switzerland / edited by Maarten J. Ellis and Paul M. Storm : Prepared under the auspices of the Association europeenne d'etudes juridiques et fiscales. – Deventer : Kluwer, 1982.
xvi,606p.
Includes bibliographies.
ISBN 9065440402

—Rights of working women in the European Community / by Eve C. Landau. – Luxembourg : Office for Official Publications of the European Communities, 1985.
244p.
At head of title: Commission of the European Communities.
ISBN 9282553418 Hbk £3.00

EMPLOYMENT - FINLAND

—Labour law and industrial relations in Finland / by A.J. Suviranta. – Helsinki : Finnish Lawyers, 1987.
187p; 25cm.
Bibliography: p57-61. - Includes index.
ISBN 9065443444 Pbk No price
ISBN 9516403573 Finland

EMPLOYMENT - FRANCE

—French Labour Code, Part 1: Laws / Geneva : International Labour Office, 1982.
204p.
ISBN 9221030830 Hbk £20.00

—Labour law and industrial relations in France / by Michel Despax and Jacques Rojot. – Deventer : Kluwer Law and Taxation, 1987.
314p.
Includes index.
ISBN 9065443436

EMPLOYMENT - GREAT BRITAIN

—A-Z of Employment and Safety Law / London : Kogan Page, 1981.
516p.
ISBN 085038446X Hbk £16.95

—AIDS and Employment Law / Howard. – London : Financial Training, 1988.
ISBN 1851850937 Pbk £14.95

—Alternatives to unemployment : special employment measures in Britain / David Metcalf. – London : Policy Studies Institute, 1982.
66p. – (Policy Studies Institute).

—Business transfers and employee rights / John McMullen. – London : Butterworths, 1987.
xxix,253p; 22cm.
Bibliography: p239-241. - Includes index.
ISBN 0406658544 Pbk £15.00

—Business Transfers and Employees Rights / London : Butterworths, 1987.
ISBN 0406658544 Pbk £21.95

—Business transfers and employment law: a practical guide / London : Sweet & Maxwell, 1989.
Outlines the development of the Transfer of Undertakings Regulations, including the loopholes and starting blocks facing the employer involved in a business transfer. Practical consideration of aspects of the law such as 'living down', the effect of regulations on both individual and collective employment law. Appendix of statutory instruments.
ISBN 0421405309 Hbk £27.50

—Butterworths employment law handbook / edited by Peter Wallington. – 4th ed. – London : Butterworths, 1987.
xxx,892,14p.
ISBN 0406142637

—Case through the courts : Ford v. Warwickshire / Philip Britton and Ian Thompson. – 1 videocassette. – London : Sweet & Maxwell in association with the University of Warwick, 1985.
– (Sweet & Maxwell's lawfilms).
Accompanied by Teaching materials. - 64p. (in folder).

—Cases in Labour Law / Bercusson. – London : Sweet & Maxwell, 1987.
ISBN 0421278706 Pbk £25.00

—Clearing banks and the trade unions / by L. D. Cowan. – London : Institute of Bankers, 1984.
64p.
'Delivered under the auspices of King's College, London'.
ISBN 0852971168

—Comparative labour law : Anglo-Soviet perspectives / edited by W.E. Butler, B.A. Hepple, Alan C. Neal. – Aldershot : Gower in conjunction with the International journal of comparative labour law and industrial relations, 1987.
xii,219p; 23cm.
Conference proceedings. Bibliography: p217-219.
ISBN 056605387X £18.50

—Compensation for dismissal / Croydon : Tolley, 1987.
ISBN 0854592733 Pbk £13.95

—Contracts at work / Erich Suter. – London : Institute of Personnel Management, 1982.
x,276p; 22cm.
Includes index.
ISBN 0852922973 Pbk £13.95

—Contracts of Employment / Crump. – 6th ed. – London : Butterworths, 1980.
ISBN 0406178216 Hbk £62.00

Nineteen Eighty-Three supplement only
This work is a practical handbook for employment law in the United Kingdom. The book includes checklists and sample contracts of employment in its appendices.
ISBN 0406178224 Pbk

—Croner's Employment Law / Croner Publications. – New Malden : Croner Publications, 1986.

Annual renewal updates

—Croner's Reference Book for Employers / Croner Publications. – New Malden : Croner Publications, 1986.

Annual renewal updates

—Daily Mail Guide to Employment Law / Southampton : Associated Magazines, 1988.
ISBN 0851444261 Pbk £5.95

—Dictionary of Employment Law / London : Butterworths, 1985.
ISBN 0406207909 Hbk £17.00
ISBN 0406207917 Pbk £10.95

—Dismissal and Redundancy Procedures / Mulgan. - London : Butterworths, 1984.
ISBN 040970136X Pbk £30.00

—Dix and Crump on contracts of employment / D. W. Crump. - 6th ed. - London : Butterworth, 1980.
liv,497p; 26cm.
Previous ed.: 1976. Includes index.
ISBN 0406178216 £26.50

—EEF Employment Guide / London : Engineering Employers Federation, 1986.
203p.

—Effect of ex post compensation on absence from work / by Paul Fenn. - Oxford : Centre for Socio-Legal Studies, 1980.
23p. - (Working paper).
Bibliography: p.23.

—Employee ownership / Nuttall. - London : Fourmat, 1987.
ISBN 1851900330 Pbk £14.95

—Employer and employee : a complete and practical guide to the modern law of employment / by G. Barrie Marsh. - 2nd ed. - London : Shaw, 1981.
lix, 616p.
ISBN 0721907415

—Employers Guide to the Employment Act 1982 / London : Engineering Employers Federation, 1982.
16p.

—Employers' use of outwork : a study using the 1980 Workplace industrial relations survey and the 1981 National survey of homeworking / by Catherine Hakim. - London : Department of Employment, 1985.
107p. - (Research paper).
Bibliography: p.104-107.

—Employing People in Voluntary Organisations : An NCVO Practical Guide / London : Bedford Square Press, 1984.
ISBN 0719911095 Hbk £2.95

—Employing Union Members / Income Data Services Staff. - London : Incomes Data Services, 1980.
191p. - (IDS Handbook Ser.: No. 18).

—Employment / London : HMSO.
ISBN 0118102710 Hbk £105.00

—Employment Act 1980 : an analysis / Karl Mackie. - Nottingham : The University of Leeds and the University of Nottingham in association with the Institute of Personnel Management, 1980.
iii,37p; 22cm.
ISBN 0852922981

—Employment Act 1982 / Croydon : Tolley, 1983.
ISBN 085459082X Pbk £7.95

—Employment Act Nineteen-Eighty : A Practical Guide / London : Oyez Longman, 1980.
ISBN 0851205062 Hbk £10.95

—Employment Acts 1974-1980, with commentary / by Charles D. Drake and Brian Bercusson. - London : Sweet & Maxwell, 1981.
ca.500p.
ISBN 0421282509

—Employment bill / London : HMSO, 1987.
vi,45p. - (H.C. Bill 1987-88 17).
ISBN 0103017887

—Employment Claims in the County Court / Lloyd-Jones. - London : Low Pay Unit, 1988.
ISBN 0905211413 Pbk £1.00

—Employment Digest / New Malden : Croner Publications.

—Employment Handbook / 4th ed. - Croydon : Tolley, 1987.
ISBN 0854592091 Pbk £15.95

—Employment Law / Holmes. - London : Financial Training, 1988.
- (SWOT).
ISBN 1851850848 Pbk £7.50

—Employment law / Hepple & O'Higgins. - 4th ed. - London : Sweet & Maxwell, 1981.
lvii,430p; 25cm.
Previous ed.: 1979. Bibliography: p401-402. - Includes index.
ISBN 0421288302 Pbk £13.25

—Employment Law Handbook / 4th ed. - London : Butterworths, 1987.
ISBN 0406142637 Pbk £23.00

—Employment Law (ILT) / 2nd ed. - London : Sweet & Maxwell, 1988.
ISBN 0421380705 Pbk

—Employment law in a nutshell / Philip Marshall. - London : Sweet and Maxwell, 1980.
vii,83p; 18cm.
Includes index.
ISBN 0421265507 Pbk £1.50

—Employment Law Manual / Parsons. - London : Sweet & Maxwell, 1988.
ISBN 0421370505 updat £85.00

—Employment legislation : statutes (as amended to 16 August 1983) / compiled by Sir Arnold de Montmorency, Bart. - 1. - S.l. : s.n., 1983.
loose-leaf.
Contents on publication: Trade Union and Labour Relations Act 1974 - Employment Protection Act 1975 - Employment Proection (Consolidation) Act 1975 - Employment Act 1980. Spine title: Integration of employment legislation. Kept up to date by loose-leaf supplements.

—Equal Opportunities / Oxford : Blackwell Scientific, 1988.
ISBN 0631159754 Pbk £8.95

—Fair and efficient selection : guidance on equal opportunities policies in recruitment and selection procedures / Great Britain. - London : H.M.S.O., 1986.
50p.
ISBN 0117013013

—Guide to Employment Practices / London : Industrial Society.
- (Managers Ser.).

—Guide to Redundancy Law / London : Macmillan, 1985.
ISBN 0333388526 Hbk £25.00

—Haldane Society employment law bulletin / v. - London : Haldane Society of Socialist Lawyers, 1983.

—Industrial law journal / London : Sweet & Maxwell for the Industrial Law Society, 1972-.
Supersedes: Bulletin of the Industrial Law Society. Index in each vol..

—Industrial relations and employment law / editor in chief R. J. Harvey. - 2 vols. - London : Butterworths, 1984.
Cover title: Harvey on Industrial relations and employment law. Loose leaf.
ISBN 0406221731

—Industrial relations and the law in the 1980's : issues and future trends / edited by Patricia Fosh and Craig R. Littler. - Aldershot : Gower, 1985.
xv,199p; 23cm.
Includes bibliographies and index.
ISBN 0566009781 Hbk £20.45
ISBN 0566009811 Pbk £9.50

—Industrial tribunal / Mclean. - Chichester : Barry Rose, 1982.
ISBN 0859922243 Hbk £20.00

—Industrial tribunal practice / London : Longman Professional (UK), 1988.
- (Practitioner series).
Analysis of the expanding case law on procedure with practical hints. Takes account of the procedures ofr equal value claims, with worked examples, precedents and statutory materials.
ISBN 0851213766 Pbk £16.95

—Industrial tribunal practice / Walker. - 2nd ed. - Stewart (Henry), 1985.
ISBN 0946700184 Pbk £24.00

—Industrial tribunals / Tolley Publishing, 1984.
ISBN 0854591540 Pbk £14.95

—Industrial tribunals / Pluto Press, 1983.
ISBN 0861043685 Pbk £6.95

—Introduction to the Law of Employment / 3rd ed. - London : Butterworths, 1982.
ISBN 0409601063 Pbk £17.60

—Job security / Colin Bourn. - London : Sweet & Maxwell, 1980.
90p; 18cm.
Includes index.
ISBN 0421272805 Pbk £1.95

—Kahn-Freund's Labour and the law / P. L. Davies, M. R. Freedland. - 3rd ed. - London : Stevens, 1983.
xxvii,375p; 23cm. - (Hamlyn lecture series).
Previous ed.: published as Labour and the law. 1977.
ISBN 0420462201 Hbk Unpriced
ISBN 0420462309 Pbk £10.50

—Labour injunctions / Chichester : Wiley, 1990.
104; 25.
ISBN 0471515868 Pbk £44.35

—Labour law / by Charles D. Drake. - 3rd ed. - London : Sweet & Maxwell, 1981.
278p; 23cm. - (Concise college texts).
Previous ed.: 1973. Includes index.
ISBN 0421281006 Hbk Unpriced
ISBN 0421281103 Pbk £7.50

—Labour Law and Industrial Relations / Oxford : Oxford University Press, 1983.
ISBN 0198254822 Pbk £9.50

—Labour law and industrial relations in Great Britain / by B.A. Hepple, S. Fredman. - Deventer : Kluwer Law and Taxation, 1986.
295p.
: 'Originally published as a monograph in the International encyclopaedia for labour law and industrial relations.'. Includes index. Bibliography: p.257-259.
ISBN 9065442626

—Labour law and the community : perspectives for the 1980's / Editors, Lord Wedderburn of Charlton and W.T. Murphy. - London : Institute of Advanced Legal Studies, University of London, 1982.
viii,189p.
Includes bibliographical references. Papers presented at a workshop for law teachers held in 1982 at the Institute of Advanced Legal Studies.
ISBN 0901190276

—Labour law cases and materials / by Roger Benedictus & Brian Bercusson. - London : Sweet & Maxwell, 1987.
700p; 25cm.
Includes index.
ISBN 0421278609 Hbk No price
ISBN 0421278706 Pbk No price

—Labour Law - Cases and Materials / 2nd ed. - London : Butterworths, 1988.
ISBN 0406577501 Hbk £19.95
ISBN 0406577593 Pbk

—Labour law in Britain / edited by Roy Lewis. - Oxford : Blackwell, 1986.
700p; 23cm.
Examines legal aspects of industrial relations in Britain today.
ISBN 0631137548 Hbk £37.50
ISBN 0631137556 Pbk £10.00

—Labour law in Great Britain and Ireland to 1978 : a companion volume to A bibliography of the literature on British and Irish labour law / B.A. Hepple ... et al. - London : Sweet & Maxwell, 1981.
xxii,131p; 25cm.
Includes index.
ISBN 0421288000 Unpriced

—Labour law : text and materials / Paul Davies, Mark Freedland. - 2nd ed. - London : Weidenfeld and Nicolson, 1984.
xlii,964p; 24cm.
Previous ed.: 1979. Includes index.
ISBN 0297780891 Hbk £30.00
ISBN 0297780905 Pbk £17.95

—Labour law with a Labour government : a workers' charter / Haldane Society. Employment Law Committee. - London : The Society, 1987.
9p.

—Law of employment / N.M. Selwyn. - 6th ed. - London : Butterworths, 1988.
xlv,582p.
Previous ed.: 1985. Includes index. Cover title: Selwyn's law of employment.
ISBN 0406653461 £14.95 (Apr.)

—Law of Employment / 5th ed. - London : Butterworths, 1985.
ISBN 0406653445 Pbk £15.95

—Law of Unfair Dismissal / 2nd ed. - London : Butterworths, 1985.
ISBN 0406107076 Pbk £21.95

—Long Suffering British Workers : Working Time in Europe / London : Labour Research Department.
24p.
ISBN 0900508434 Hbk £0.60

—Managerial law / Hull : Barmarick Publications, 1966-.
'Knight's Industrial Law Reports in their revised edition'. Supersedes: Knight's industrial law reports (1 vol. only). - Continues: Knight's industrial reports.

—Modern employment law : a guide to job security and safety at work / Michael Whincup. - 3rd ed. - London : Heinemann, 1980.
xli,318p; 22cm.
Previous ed.: 1978. Includes index.
ISBN 0434922447 Pbk £8.50

—Negotiating shorter working hours / Palmer. - London : Macmillan, 1985.
ISBN 0333388585 Hbk £29.50

—New Employment Law Legislation : A Guide to the Employment Acts 1980 and 1982 / London : Kogan Page, 1983.
192p.
ISBN 0850386144 Hbk £12.50

—New politics of labour law / Lord Wedderburn of Charlton. - Durham : The University of Durham, Industrial Relations Group, 1983.
- (Occasional paper).

—Part-time employment and sex discrimination legislation in Great Britain : a study of the demand for part-time labour and of sex discrimination in selected organizations and establishments / by Olive Robinson and John Wallace. - London : H.M.S.O., 1984.
53p. - (Research paper).

—PAYE Audits / London : Butterworths, 1988.
ISBN 0406263000 Pbk

—Payments on termination of employment / 2nd ed. - London : Longman Professional, 1984.
ISBN 0851206662 Pbk £9.95

—Payments on Termination of Employment / London : Oyez Longman, 1981.

—People and employment / Baruch. - London : Butterworths, 1981.
ISBN 0408106921 Pbk £8.50

—Perspective on labour law / Ole Hasselbalch, Alan C. Neal, Anders Victorin. - Stockholm : Almqvist & Wiksell, 1982.
128p.
ISBN 0421307102

—Picketing : industrial disputes, tactics and the law / by Peggy Kahn...et al. - London : Routledge & Kegan Paul, 1983.
xv,223p.
Bibliography: p219-220.
ISBN 0710095341

—Practical approach to employment law / John Bowers. - 2nd ed. - London : Financial Training, 1986.
liv,385p.
ISBN 1851850279

—Practice and procedure in industrial tribunals / London : Legal Action Group, 1986.
ISBN 0905099141 Pbk £7.50

—Public Employment Law : The Role of the Contract of Employment in Australia and Britain / Sydney : Butterworths, 1987.
208p.
This book describes the statutory and institutional framework of public employment law in Australia and Britain. Also discussed are the distinctions between Crown servants and other public employees, discipline, dismissal, tenure of employment, and remedies.

—Redundancy law and practice / London : Butterworths, 1983.
ISBN 0406258147 Pbk £26.00

—Rideout's Principles of labour law / Jacqueline C. Dyson. - 4th ed. - London : Sweet & Maxwell, 1983.
lxxvi,658p; 25cm.
Previous ed.: 1979. Includes index.
ISBN 0421296100 Hbk £20.00
ISBN 0421296208 Pbk Unpriced

—Rights at work / 2nd ed. - Pluto Press, 1983.
ISBN 0861047303 Pbk £7.95

—Service Agreements / 5th ed. - London : Longman Professional (UK), 1986.
- (Practitioner Series).
Guidance on drafting service agreements. Looks at different types of agreement showing benefits designed to protect compant interests and to offer security to the employee.
ISBN 0851212212 Pbk £22.50

—Sex and ethnic monitoring, discrimination and equal pay : new codes and regulations / by Greville Janner. - New Malden : Croner Publications, 1984.
vi,120p.
Includes index.
ISBN 0900319321

—Sex and race discrimination in employment / Poulton. - London : Sweet & Maxwell, 1987.
ISBN 0905099176 Pbk £14.00

—Sex and race discrimination in employment / Camilla Palmer and Kate Poulton. - London? : Legal Action Group, 1987.
xli,189p.
Bibliography: pp.183-184. - Includes index.
ISBN 0905099176

—Shorter working time through national industry agreements / by Michael White. - London : Department of Employment, 1982.
- (Research paper).

—Social welfare law / David Pearl and Kevin Gray. - London : Croom Helm, 1981.
308p; 23cm.
Bibliography: p265. - Includes index.
ISBN 085664644X Hbk £14.95
ISBN 0709920040 Pbk £8.95

—Striking a balance? : employment law after the 1980 Act / Roy Lewis and Bob Simpson. - Oxford : Martin Robertson, 1981.
ix,269p; 22cm.
Includes index.
ISBN 0855204427 Hbk Unpriced
ISBN 0855204435 Pbk £4.95

—Sweet and Maxwell's Employment Law Manual / London : Sweet & Maxwell, 1987.
ISBN 0421352205 Hbk

—Sweet and Maxwell's labour relations statutes and materials / edited by Sweet & Maxwell's legal editorial staff : advisory editors B.A. Hepple, Paul O'Higgins, Lord Wedderburn of Charlton. - 2nd ed. - London : Sweet & Maxwell, 1983.
x,693p; 25cm.
Previous ed.: 1979. Includes index.
ISBN 0421320109 Pbk £15.00

—Termination of Employment / London : Sweet & Maxwell, 1983.
ISBN 0421293608 Hbk £19.50

—Termination of employment / Robert Upex. - 2nd ed. - London : Sweet & Maxwell, 1986.
xlii,148p; 26cm.
Examines entitlement to the various remedies, defines the status of employment and 'marginal employment', and looks at statutory rights with regard to redundancy and unfair dismissal. Contains examples of the calculation of compensation for redundancy and unfair dismissal, and looks at taxation of damages, and mitigation.
ISBN 0421347708 £16.50

—Time, Rates of Wages and Hours of Work 1982 / London : HMSO, 1982.
276p.
ISBN 0113612281 Hbk £17.00

—Titman & Camp, individual employment law / Barry Titman, Peter Camp. - 2nd ed. - London : Sweet & Maxwell, 1986.
xxv,240p; 22cm.
Includes the contract of employment, termination; wrongful and unfair dismissal, remedies for unfair dismissal, redundancy, problems arising on the change of employer, overlapping claims, and procedure before industrial tribunals. Contains forms and codes of practice.
ISBN 0421353201 Pbk £9.95

—Tolley's employees' rights in receiverships and liquidations / Guy T.E. Parsons, William F. Ratford. - 2nd ed. - Croyden : Tolley, 1984.
xiv,210p; 30cm.
Previous ed.: 1979. Bibliography: p201. - Includes index.
ISBN 0854591443 £25.00

—Tolley's Employment Act 1982 / Croydon : Tolley.
256p.
ISBN 085459082X Hbk £7.95

—Tolley's Employment Handbook / 5th ed. - Croydon : Tolley.
456p.
Includes Employment Act 1988. Gives information on: ACAS, Disabled Employees, Equal Pay, Maternity Rights, Racial Discrimination, Trade Unions and Unfair Dismissal.
ISBN 0854593276 Hbk £17.95

—Trade union law / Richard Kidner. - 2nd ed. - London : Stevens, 1983.
xl,290p; 25cm.
Previous ed.: London : Sweet & Maxwell, 1979. Includes index.
ISBN 0420465502 £25.00

—Trade union law and the pursuit of prosperity - the next step : submission to the Secretary of State for Employment in response to the green paper on trade union immunities / prepared by Roderick Thomas. - London : Director Publications, 1981.
66p; 30cm.
At head of title: Institute of Directors.

—Trade unions and the individual / by Alan Campbell and John Bowyer with assistance from Michael Soole : foreword by Lord Wilberforce. - Oxford : ESC Publishing, 1980.
xliv,491p; 23cm.
Includes index.
ISBN 090621405X Unpriced

—Wages and the law / London : Shaw & Sons, 1988.
ISBN 0721911102 Pbk

—Women and harassment at work / Pluto Press, 1983.
ISBN 086104729X Pbk £3.95

—Worker and the law / Lord Wedderburn. - 3rd ed. - London : Sweet & Maxwell, 1986.
xiv,1026p.
Traces the developing relationship between the worker and the law, by analysis of the employment relationship, job security and dismissal, industrial conflict and the law, and trade unions and their members. Seeks to show the patterns which run through labour law.
ISBN 0421370602

—Worker-controlled businesses and the law / Spokesman Books, 1988.
ISBN 0851244521 Hbk £25.00
ISBN 0851244629 Pbk £8.95

—Your rights at work / Bill Birtles and Patricia Hewitt. - London : National Council for Civil Liberties, 1980.
95p.
ISBN 090110888X

EMPLOYMENT - INDIA

—Commentaries on Contract Labour Act, 1970 : Regulation and Abolition / G. Saran. - 3rd rev. ed. - Lucknow : Eastern Book Company, 1982.
520p.

—Commentaries on Employees' Provident Funds and Miscellaneous Provisions Act, 1952 : Together with Schemes and Notifications / 5th ed. - Lucknow : Eastern Book Company, 1985.

—Commentaries on Industrial Employment Standing Orders Act, 1946 : Including Model Standing Orders, Recognition of Unions and Unfair Labour Practices / 2nd ed. - Lucknow : Eastern Book Company, 1982.
844p.

—Commentaries on Payment of Bonus Act with Rules / 2nd ed. - Allahabad : Law Publishers, 1982.

—Contract Labour in Construction Industry : a Case Study of Tripura / Calcutta : Firma KLM, 1980.

—Contract Labour : Regulation and Abolition Act, 1970 / G. Saran. - 4th ed. - Lucknow : Eastern Book Company, 1987.
602p.

—Employees' Misconduct : As Cause for Discipline and Dismissal in India and the Commonwealth / Allahabad : Law Book Company, 1987.
900p.

—Employment : Its Terms and Conditions in Public and Private Sectors / Lucknow : Eastern Book Company, 1981.
1,322p.

—Handbook of Labour and Industrial Law / 2nd ed. - Lucknow : Eastern Book Company, 1986.

—Handbook of Labour and Industrial Law / 3rd ed. - Lucknow : Eastern Book Company, 1986.

—Industrial and Labour Law / Calcutta : Eastern Law House.
1,298p.

—Labour Law Journal Digest 1949-1982, 9 Vols. / Nagpur : Wadhura & Co.

—Labour Laws in Uttar Pradesh / Kamlesh Chopra. - 3rd ed. - Lucknow : Eastern Book Company, 1985.
2,131p.

—Labour Manual, 2 Vols. / Allahabad : Law Publishers, 1983.

—Labour Welfare Laws and Employment Conditions in India / New Delhi : Deep and Deep Publications, 1985.
235p.

—Law Relating to Appointment : Enquiry and Disciplinary Action of Workmen, with Model Forms / 2nd ed. - Allahabad : Law Publishers, 1982.

—Motor Transport Workers Act : with States Rules / Venkanna. - 3rd ed. - Allahabad : Law Book Company.

—Outline of Labour Legislation and Practices in India / New Delhi : Indian Investment Centre.
48p.

—Release of Manual of Central Acts and Important Rules : Criminal, Taxation and Labour, 15 Vols. / Allahabad : Law Publishers, 1986.

—Supreme Court on Constitutional Aspects of Labour Laws / Allahabad : Law Publishing House, 1987.
1,400p.

—Textbook of Labour and Industrial Laws / Lucknow : Eastern Book Company, 1980.
416p.

EMPLOYMENT - IRELAND

—Employment law / by Ferdinand von Prondzynski and Charles McCarthy : foreword by John Horgan. - London : Sweet & Maxwell, 1984.
xxxii,211p; 22cm.
Includes index.
ISBN 0421312408 Pbk £13.95

—Employment legislation in Ireland : a practical guide and handbook / the Institute of Chartered Secretaries and Administrators. - 3rd ed. - Dublin : Institute of Chartered Secretaries and Administrators, Republic of Ireland Region, 1980.
117p.
Previous ed.: 1978. Includes index.

—Irish trade union law / Tony Kerr and Gerry Whyte. - Abingdon : Professional Books, 1985.
lxiv,383p.
ISBN 0862050510

—Journal of the Irish Society for Labour Law / v. - Dublin : The Society, 1982.

—Labour law and industrial relations in Ireland / Mary Redmond. - Dublin : Bridgefoot Press, 1984.
188p.
Includes index. Cover title: Redmonds guide to Irish labour law.

—Labour law in Great Britain and Ireland to 1978 : a companion volume to A bibliography of the literature on British and Irish labour law / B.A. Hepple ... et al. - London : Sweet & Maxwell, 1981.
xxii,131p; 25cm.
Includes index.
ISBN 0421288000 Unpriced

EMPLOYMENT - JAPAN

—Labour law and industrial relations in Japan / by T.A. Hanami. - 2nd ed. - Deventer, Netherlands : Kluwer Law and Taxation, 1985.
171p.
Bibliography: p78-80. Includes index.
ISBN 9065442146

EMPLOYMENT - LESOTHO

—General Survey of Employment Protection Laws in Lesotho / Maseru : National University of Lesotho, Institute of Labour Studies, 1983.
32p.

EMPLOYMENT - MALAYSIA

—Employees Provident Fund Act, 1951 (Act 272) and Employees Provident Fund Regulations 1969 and Rules / Kuala Lumpur : International Law Books Services.

—Employer, the Employee and the Law in Malaysia / London : Butterworths, 1985.
ISBN 0409995045 Hbk £32.00

—Employer, the employee and the law in Malaysia / Dunston Ayadurai. - Singapore : Butterworths, 1985.
xxiv,335p.
Discusses the Malaysian industrial relations system in the context of the laws in force. Deals with employer-employee relationships, covering both the collective and the individual relationship between employers and workers. Also covers trade unions, and other similar organisations.
ISBN 0409995045

—Employment Act, 1955 (Act 265) and Regulations and Orders / Kuala Lumpur : International Law Books Services.

EMPLOYMENT - NEW ZEALAND

—Framework of industrial law in New Zealand : resource material / L.G. Campbell. - Wellington : Industrial Relations Centre, Victoria University of Wellington, 1980.
ii,88p.

—Introduction to the Law of Employment / 3rd ed. - Butterworths, 1988.
435p.
ISBN 0409787922 Pbk £90.00

—Introduction to the law of employment / by Alexander Szakats. - 2nd ed., completely revised. - Wellington : Butterworths, 1981.
li,522p.
Previous ed.: 1975. Includes bibliographical references and index.
ISBN 0409601063

EMPLOYMENT - NIGERIA

—National Industrial Court law reports / Nigeria. - v. - Lagos : Federal Government Press, 1980.
Published by the authority of the National Industrial Court.

—Nigerian labour law / by Akintunde Emiola. - 2nd ed. - Ibadan : Ibadan University Press, 1982.
xxxviii,599p.
Previous ed.: 1979. Bibliography: p.599. - Includes index.
ISBN 9781211377

EMPLOYMENT - NORTHERN IRELAND

—Consulatative papers related to the revision of the Children and Young Persons Act (Northern Ireland) 1968 / Department of Helath and Social Services. - Belfast : The Department, 1987.
17,11 leaves.
Contents: Consultative paper on regulation of child minding, group day care and care and maintenance of children - Consultative paper on employment of children.

—Encyclopedia of Northern Ireland labour law and practice / editor, Sir John Wood. - v. - Belfast : Labour Relations Agency, 1983.
Looseleaf.
Includes bibliographical references and index.

—Recent Developments in Individual Employment Law / Belfast : Queen's University of Belfast, 1982.
31p.

—Some recent developments in individual employment law and practice : the text of a lecture delivered to the Belfast Solicitors' Association on 11th March 1982 / by Richard Steele. - Belfast : SLS, 1982.
31p.
Includes bibliographical references.

EMPLOYMENT - PAKISTAN

—Complete Set of Labour Laws / 12th ed. - Karachi : Bureau of Labour Publications, 1986.
407p.

—Encyclopedia of Labour Law / Karachi : Bureau of Labour Publications, 1988.
ca 800p.

—Hours of Work and Over Time / 3rd ed. - Karachi : Bureau of Labour Publications, 1987.

—Labour Law Cases LLC (Pakistan) : Decisions of Supreme Court, High Courts and Labour Courts on Labour Laws, 21 Vols. / Karachi : Bureau of Labour Publications, 1947-1980.

—Law of industrial relations in Pakistan : commentary on the Industrial Relations Ordinance 1969 / Obaidur Rahman. - Karachi : Asia Law House, 1984.
v,43p.
Bibliography: p.44.

—Leave and Holidays / 3rd ed. - Karachi : Bureau of Labour Publications, 1987.

—Mining Labour Code / 6th ed. - Karachi : Bureau of Labour Publications, 1987.
315p.

—Pakistan Labour Statutes PLS : Acts, Ordinances, Rules, Regulations, 21 Vols. / Karachi : Bureau of Labour Publications, 1983-87.

EMPLOYMENT - PHILIPPINES

—Answers to Bar Examination Questions /. - Quezon City : University of the Philippines, Law Center, 1982.
104p.

—First Asian Congress of Labour Law and Social Security / Quezon City : University of the Philippines, Law Center, 1982.
608p.

EMPLOYMENT - SAUDI ARABIA

—Saudi business and labor law : its interpretation and application / Alison Lerrick, Q. Javed Mian. - 2nd ed. - London : Grahamn & Trotman, 1987.
xlv,589p.
Previous edition: 1982. Includes bibliographical references and index.
ISBN 0860105733

EMPLOYMENT - SINGAPORE

—Butterworths Handbook of Singapore Employment Law / Butterworths Editorial Staff. - 2nd ed. - Butterworths, 1986.
787p.
Contains coverage of employment law, the central provident fund, skills development levy, payroll tax, redundancy payments fund, factories, workmen's compensations fund, industrial relations, trade disputes, and trade unions.
ISBN 0409995142 Pbk £99.00

—Handbook of Singapore Employment Law / 2nd ed. - London : Butterworths, 1986.
ISBN 0409995142 Pbk £65.00

EMPLOYMENT - SOUTH AFRICA

—Basic employment law / Julian Riekert. - Cape Town : Juta, 1987.
xvii,120p.
ISBN 0702118427

—Complete Wiehahn report / with notes by N.E. Wiehahn. - Johannesburg : Lex Patria, 1982.
xxxvii,761p.
Contents: Report of the Commission of Inquiry into Labour Legislation, parts 1-6 and the White Paper on each part.
ISBN 0628021690

—Incorporation and Exclusion : Recent Developments in Labour Law and Inflex Control / Johannesburg : South African Institute of Race Relations, 1984.

—Law and practice of employment / by H.G. Ringrose. - 2nd ed. - Cape Town : Juta, 1983.
xi,275p.
Previous ed.: 1976. Includes index.
ISBN 0702114057

—New labour law : strikes, dismissals and the unfair labour practice in South African law / by M.S.M. Brassey ... et al. - Cape Town : Juta, 1987.
xxix,478p.
Includes bibliographical references.
ISBN 0702118281

EMPLOYMENT - SOUTHEAST ASIA

—Labour protection and labour relations in ASEAN : the impact of protective labour laws on labour relations / Geneva : International Labour Office, 1986.
v,204p.
Papers presented at ' ... the ASEAN Tripartite Symposium on Labour Protection and Labour Relations held in Kuala Lumpur, Malaysia on 16-19 September 1986 ... '. - p.v. 'Published ... under the auspices of the joint ILO/UNDP/ASEAN Programme on Industrial Relations for Development.' - T.p..
ISBN 922105893X

EMPLOYMENT - SRI LANKA

—Some Concepts of Labour Law / Colombo : Lake House Investments.

EMPLOYMENT - SWEDEN

—Labour law in Sweden : a brief outline / Reinhold Fahlbeck. - Lund : Juridiska Foreningen i Lund, 1980.
66p.
Bibliography: p.64-66.
ISBN 915441251X

—Law and the weaker party : an Anglo-Swedish comparative study / general editors: Steve Anderman...et al. - Abingdon : Professional Books, 1981.

Vol. 2 : The English experience, edited by Steve Anderman / general editors: Steve Anderman...et al.. - 1981.

Vol. 3 : Swedish statutory material : edited by Alan C. Neal and Anders Victorin / general editors: Steve Anderman...et al.. - 1981.

—Perspective on labour law / Ole Hasselbalch, Alan C. Neal, Anders Victorin. - Stockholm : Almqvist & Wiksell, 1982.
128p.
ISBN 0421307102

EMPLOYMENT - UNITED KINGDOM

—Foreman's Guide to National Agreements (Manual Workers) / Engineering Employers' Federation. - revised ed. - London : Engineering Employers Federation, 1980.
ISBN 0901700134 Hbk £2.00

EMPLOYMENT - UNITED STATES

—Labour Law and Industrial Relations in the United States of America / 2nd ed. - Dordrecht : Kluwer, 1984.
374p.
ISBN 9065441689 Pbk £95.00

EMPLOYMENT - USSR

—Comparative labour law : Anglo-Soviet perspectives / edited by W.E. Butler, B.A. Hepple, Alan C. Neal. - Aldershot : Gower in conjunction with the International journal of comparative labour law and industrial relations, 1987.
xii,219p; 23cm.
Conference proceedings. Bibliography: p217-219.
ISBN 056605387X £18.50

EMPLOYMENT - WEST GERMANY

—Handbook of German employment law : a practical guide to the legal aspects of employment - from hiring through termination : with a bi-lingual selection of relevant German statutes and sample forms / by Joachim Gres and Harald Jung. - Deventer, The Netherlands : Kluwer, 1983.
305p; 26cm.
ISBN 9065441441 Hbk £90.00

—Labour law and industrial relations in the Federal Republic of Germany / Manfred Weiss. - Deventer : Kluwer, 1987.
190p; 25cm.
Bibliography: p37. - Includes index.
ISBN 9065443002 Pbk No price

—Supreme Labor Court in Nazi Germany : a jurisprudential analysis / Marc Linder. - Frankfurt a. M. : Klostermann, 1987.
xix,290p.
Includes bibliographical references.
ISBN 3465017579

EMPLOYMENT - ZAMBIA

—Zambia industrial cases reports / compiled by K.C. Muwang'u. - v. - Lusaka : Ministry of Labour and Social Services, 1983.

EMPLOYMENT AND WOMEN

—Woman's role in economic development / Ester Boserup. - Aldershot : Gower, 1986.
283p.
Originally published: George Allen & Unwin, 1970. Bibliography: pp.263-275. - Includes index. Published in association with the London School of Economics and Political Science.
ISBN 0566051397

—Women's work, men's work : the ambivalence of equality / Virginia Novarra. - London : Marion Boyars, 1980.
8,152p; 21cm.
Bibliography : p.146-152.
ISBN 0714526800 £5.95
ISBN 0714526819

EMPLOYMENT AND WOMEN - GREAT BRITAIN

—Equal pay and the industrial tribunals / London : Sweet & Maxwell, 1984.
80p.
ISBN 0421328002 Pbk £7.15

—Equal treatment for men and women / Great Britain. - Equal Opportunities Commission, 1988.
26p.
ISBN 1870358015 Pbk No price

—Men's jobs? women's jobs? : practical guidance on why many jobs are done only by men or only by women, and how this pattern 'job segregation' can and should be changed / London : HMSO, 1986.
vii,34p; 21cm.
At head of title: Equal Opportunities Commission.
ISBN 0117012998 Pbk £2.20

—Women's rights at work : campaigns and policy in Britain and the United States / Elizabeth M. Meehan. – Basingstoke : Macmillan, 1985.
xvii,253p; 22cm.
Bibliography: p227-241. - Includes index.
ISBN 0333361253 Hbk No price
ISBN 0333361261 Pbk £5.95

EMPLOYMENT AND WOMEN – UNITED STATES

—Women's rights at work : campaigns and policy in Britain and the United States / Elizabeth M. Meehan. – Basingstoke : Macmillan, 1985.
xvii,253p; 22cm.
Bibliography: p227-241. - Includes index.
ISBN 0333361253 Hbk No price
ISBN 0333361261 Pbk £5.95

ENCYCLOPEDIAS

—Atkin's Encyclopaedia of Court Forms, 41 Vols. / 2nd. ed. – Abingdon : Professional Books, 1984.

—Atkin's Encyclopaedia of Court Forms in Civil Proceedings, 42 Vols. / J. M. Dyson. – 2nd ed. – Wellington : Butterworths.

—Australian Encyclopedia of Forms and Precedents 1984 Cumulative Supplement / C. Croft. – Wellington : Butterworths.
ISBN 0409787140 Hbk

—Australian Encyclopedia of Forms and Precedents / Wellington : Butterworths.

—Blackwells Encyclopedia of Political Instructions / Oxford : Blackwell Scientific, 1987.
ISBN 0631138412 Hbk £45.00

—Capital Taxes Encyclopaedia, 3 Vols. / Ian A. Marsh. – London : Butterworths.
This looseleaf service provides detailed coverage of capital transfer tax issues and legislation in the United Kingdom. Legislative developments, court decisions, and changes in practice are updated with six service issues per year.

—Encyclopaedia Financial Services / Sweet & Maxwell, 1988.
ISBN 0421368802 Hbk £265.00

—Encyclopaedia of Banking Law / London : Butterworths, 1982.
Service to Date.
ISBN 0406569835 Hbk £220.00

—Encyclopaedia of Competition Law / London : Sweet & Maxwell, 1988.
ISBN 0421368705 updat £195.00

—Encyclopaedia of Compulsory Purchase / London : Sweet & Maxwell, 1988.
ISBN 0421007508 Hbk £195.00

—Encyclopaedia of Consumer Credit Law / London : Sweet & Maxwell, 1988.
ISBN 0421208104 £175.00

—Encyclopaedia of Crimes and Justice / 4 vols. – London : Macmillan, 1983.
ISBN 0029181100 Hbk £300.00

—Encyclopaedia of Data Protection / Gaskill. – London : Sweet & Maxwell, 1988.
ISBN 0421369000 loose £185.00

—Encyclopaedia of environmental health law and practice / Sweet & Maxwell, 1988.
ISBN 0421133600 £190.00

—Encyclopaedia of Forms and Precedents, 42 Vols. / M. J. R. Wear. – 5th ed. – London : Butterworths.

4th ed. also partly available
A 42 volume set of forms for property, local government, company, and commercial law matters in the United Kingdom. A looseleaf service keeps this work continually up to date.

—Encyclopaedia of Health and Safety at Work / London : Sweet & Maxwell, 1988.
ISBN 0421007109 Hbk £220.00

—Encyclopaedia of Health Services/Medical Law / London : Sweet & Maxwell, 1988.
ISBN 0421315008 Hbk £180.00

—Encyclopaedia of highway law and practice / Sweet & Maxwell, 1988.
ISBN 0421044500 Hbk £195.00

—Encyclopaedia of housing law and practice / Sweet & Maxwell, 1988.
ISBN 0421007303 Hbk £210.00

—Encyclopaedia of Information Technology Law / London : Sweet & Maxwell, 1988.
ISBN 0421372109 Hbk

—Encyclopaedia of Insurance Law / London : Sweet & Maxwell, 1988.
ISBN 0421281502 Hbk £165.00

—Encyclopaedia of International Telecommunications Law / London : Butterworths, 1987.

—Encyclopaedia of Investor Protection / London : Butterworths, 1987.

—Encyclopaedia of labour relations law / Sweet & Maxwell, 1988.
ISBN 0421169605 Hbk £265.00

—Encyclopaedia of Local Government Law / London : Sweet & Maxwell, 1988.
ISBN 0421260505 Hbk £195.00

—Encyclopaedia Of Planning Law and Practice / Sweet & Maxwell, 1988.
ISBN 0421007400 Hbk £265.00

—Encyclopaedia of Professional Partnerships / London : Sweet & Maxwell, 1988.
ISBN 0421332905 Hbk £195.00

—Encyclopaedia of Road Traffic Law and Practice / London : Sweet & Maxwell, 1988.
ISBN 0421007605 Hbk £210.00

—Encyclopaedia of Social Services Law / London : Sweet & Maxwell, 1988.
ISBN 0421254505 Hbk £195.00

—Encyclopaedia of Value Added Tax / London : Sweet & Maxwell, 1988.
ISBN 0421178604 loose £190.00

—Encyclopaedia Rating Law and Practice / Sweet & Maxwell, 1988.
ISBN 0421263105 Hbk £95.00

—Encyclopedia of Banking Law, 2 Vols. / William Blair. – Wellington : Butterworths.
A looseleaf service on banking in the United Kingdom. The material is presented in two sections. First the statutory regulation of banking is presented. Second, materials related to the statutes are set forth.

—Encyclopedia of Carriage Law Sources / London : LLoyd's of London Press, 1987.
ISBN 1850441081 Hbk

—Encyclopedia of European Community Law : Volume B : European Community Treaties / Edinburgh : W Green.

Service

—Encyclopedia of Health and Safety at Work : Law and Practice, 3 Vols. / M. C. Walker. – London : Sweet & Maxwell, 1985.
ISBN 0421007109 loose £162.00

Service only

—Encyclopedia of Insurance Law, 1 Vol. / London : Sweet & Maxwell.

—Encyclopedia of Labour Law / Karachi : Bureau of Labour Publications, 1988.
ca 800p.

—Encyclopedia of Petroleum Laws / Allahabad : Universal Book Agency, 1982/83.

—Encyclopedia of Public International Law / 1st repr. 1985 (nos. 1-6). – Amsterdam : Elsevier Science Publishers, 1981.

2: Decisions of International Courts and Tribunals 1981.
ISBN 0444862129 Hbk

3: Use of Force, A.-M. 1982.
xvi, 300p.
ISBN 044486234X Hbk

4: Use of Force, N-Z 1982.
xvi, 370p.
ISBN 0444862358 Hbk

5: International Organizations 1983.
xvi, 428p.
ISBN 0444862366 Hbk

6: Regional Cooperation, Organizations and Problems 1983.
xvi, 382p.

7: History of International Law. Foundations and Principles of International Law. Sources of International Law. Law of Treaties 1985.
x, 556p.
ISBN 0444862382 Hbk

8: Human Rights and the Individual in International Law. International Economic Relations 1985.
xvi, 55p.
ISBN 0444879110

9: International Relations and Legal Cooperation in General Diplomacy and Consular Relations 1986.
xvi, 426p.
ISBN 0444862404

10. States - Responsibility of States - International Law and Municipal Law - 10
xvi, 544p.
ISBN 0444862412 Hbk

—Encyclopedia of road traffic law and practice / R Hosking, M Brealey. – 4 looseleaf volumes. – London : Sweet & Maxwell, 1989.
Contains annotated versions of the relevant statutes and statutory instruments, a revised EEC section and a section on general procedure in Britain. Includes tables of Statutes, SLs and cases, and an index. Three updating issues per year and 'stop press' bulletins.
ISBN 0421007605 Llf £210.00

—Encyclopedia of Shipping Law Sources UK / London : LLoyd's of London Press, 1988.
ISBN 1850440115 Hbk £175.00

—Encyclopedia of Soviet law / edited by F.J.M. Feldbrugge, Ger P. van den Berg, William B. Simons. – 2nd rev. ed. – Dordrecht : M. Nijhoff Publishers, 1984.
1,012p.
Bibliography.
ISBN 9024730759 Hbk £450.00

—Encyclopedia of the Law of Compulsory Purchase and Compensation, 2 Vols. / London : Sweet & Maxwell, 1985.
– (Local Government Library).
Includes tables of statutes and cases covered by the encyclopaedia, and a guide to the general principles of compulsory purchase law and practice. Covers rates of interest after entry regulations, and includes the Local Government Act 1988. Also contains a new section with details of major cases.
ISBN 0421007508 Hbk £125.00

Service only

—Encyclopedia of United Kingdom and European Patent Law, 1 Vol. / London : Sweet & Maxwell.

—English Encyclopedia of Forms and Precedents / R. B. Roper. – 5th ed. – Wellington : Butterworths.

Updating suppls. avail.

—European Community Law : Encyclopedia of, 3 Vols. / Abingdon : Professional Books.

Vol. B. European Community Treaties

Vol. C. Community Secondary Legislation

—International Encyclopaedia for Labour Law and Industrial Relations. Supplements / Dordrecht : Kluwer.

46

47

48

49 1985.

50 1985.
96p.

51 1985.
208p.

52 1985.
264p.

53 1985.
224p.

54 1985.
168p.

55 1985.
120p.

—International taxation encyclopaedia / London : Butterworths, 1988.
Service.

—Lawyer's Remembrancer 1986 / London : Butterworths, 1984.
This book is a concise encyclopedia of United Kingdom practice and legislation, together with a diary section running from November, 1985 to January, 1987. Each week in the diary is given two full pages. The references section includes names, addresses, phone numbers, and relevant abbreviations.
ISBN 0406269181 Hbk

—Marine encyclopaedic dictionary / 2nd. – London : Lloyds of London Press, 1988.
Updated from the first edition, it contains definitions of technical shipping expressions, Latin usage in law and business. Abbreviations included carry varying meanings according to usage in different countries.
ISBN 1850441278 Hbk

—Marine Encyclopaedic Dictionary / 2nd ed. – London : Lloyd's of London Press, 1988.
ISBN 1850441278 Hbk £37.50

—O'Brien's Encyclopedia of Forms: 1893-Present, 1 Vol. / Aurora : Canada Law Book Co.
– (Division 3-Conveyancing and Mortgages Ser.).

Supplement

Vol. 8
– (Division 4-Leases Ser.).

Vol. 9
– (Division 5-Wills and Trusts Ser.).

Supplement

—O'Brien's Encyclopedia of Forms: 1893-Present, 3 Vols. / Aurora : Canada Law Book Co.
– (Division 1-Commercial and General Ser.).

Supplement

—O'Brien's Encyclopedia of Forms : 1893-Present, 9 Vols. / Aurora : Canada Law Book Co. – (Divisions 1-5 Covering All Ser.).

Binder

—O'Brien's Encyclopedia of Forms, 9 Vols. / Aurora : Canada Law Book Co. – (Abridgements and Encyclopedias).

Ontario Residents

Binder for Supplements

—O'Brien's Encyclopedia of Forms : Division Five-Wills and Trusts / Aurora : Canada Law Book Co. – (Abridgments and Encyclopedias).

Supplement

—O'Brien's Encyclopedia of Forms : Division Four-Leases / Aurora : Canada Law Book Co. – (Abridgments and Encyclopedias).

—O'Brien's Encyclopedia of Forms : Division One-Commercial & General / Aurora : Canada Law Book Co. – (Abridgments and Encyclopedias).

Supplement-1983

—O'Brien's Encyclopedia of Forms : Division Three-Conveyancing and Mortgages / Aurora : Canada Law Book Co. – (Abridgments and Encyclopedias).

Supplement

—O'Brien's Encyclopedia of Forms : Division Two-Corporations / Aurora : Canada Law Book Co. – (Abridgments and Encyclopedias).

—South African Encyclopedia of Forms and Precedents, 16 vols. / Durban : Butterworths. – (Eng. and Afrikaans).

Suppl. 1984
ISBN 0409006033 Pbk

—United Kingdom Sources / Edinburgh : W Green.

ENCYCLOPEDIAS – CANADA – ONTARIO

—Ontario employment law handbook: an employer's guide / Scarborough, Ontario : Butterworths (Canada), 1986.
96.
Examines the changes in Ontario's employment law since the fist edition in 1982. Covers the hours of work and minimum wages, overtime pay and public holidays, health and safety regulations, unemployment insurance, lockouts and strikes, and negotiations and arbitration.
ISBN 0409804860 Pbk

ENCYCLOPEDIAS – GREAT BRITAIN

—Medico-Legal Encyclopaedia / London : Butterworths, 1987.
ISBN 0407003746 Hbk £55.00

ENERGY

—Criteria for energy pricing policy : a collection of papers commissioned for the Energy Pricing Policy Workshop organized under the Regional Energy Development Programme (RAS/84/001), Bangkok, 8-11 May 1984 / edited by Corazon Morales Siddayao. – London : Graham & Trotman, 1985.
247p; 24cm.

—Energy law 1981 : 26 April-2 May 1981 at the Banff Centre, Banff, Alberta, Canada : seminar organised by the Committee on Energy and Natural Resources, Section on Business Law, International Bar Association : proceedings / 2. – London : IBA in cooperation with Sweet and Maxwell, 1981.
'The fourth in the International Bar Association series of residential seminars on energy law'.
ISBN 095058763X

—Energy law '88 : proceedings of the advanced seminar on petroleum, minerals and energy resources law organised by the IBA's Section on Energy and Natural Resources Law in Sydney, Australia, March 1988 / London : Graham & Trotman and International Bar Association, 1988.
xii,865p.
ISBN 1853330973

—Integration through law : Europe and the American Federal experience : a series / under the general editorship of Mauro Cappelletti, Monica Seccombe, Joseph Weiler. – Berlin : W. de Gruyter, 1987.
xxvii,176p. – (Series A, Law).
Includes bibliographical references and index.
ISBN 3110107430 Hbk

—International Bar Association, Section on Energy & Natural Resources Law : seminar topics index 1975-84 : Stavanger, 1975; Cambridge 1, 1978; Cambridge II, 1979; Banff, 1981; Singapore, 1982; Houston, 1984; Oslo, 1984 / S.l. : International Bar Association, Section on Energy & Natural Resources Law, 1986.
24p.
ISBN 0948711027

—International energy markets / edited by Paul Tempest. – Cambridge Mass. : Oelgeschlager, Gunn & Main, 1983.
xxi,353p; 24cm.
Conference proceedings - papers and abstracts. Includes bibliographies and index.
ISBN 0860104028 £18.00
ISBN 0899462014

—International energy options : an agenda for the 1980s : selected papers from leading contributors to the 1980 Annual Conference of the International Association of Energy Economists in Cambridge, UK / edited by Paul Tempest. – Cambridge, Mass. : Oelgeschlager, Gunn & Hain, 1981.
xv,304p.
Includes bibliographical references and index.
ISBN 086010303X Oelschlager, Gunn & Hain
ISBN 0899460895

—Journal of energy & natural resources law / v. – London : Sweet & Maxwell, 1983-.
Co-sponsored by the Section on Energy and Natural Resources Law (S.E.R.L) of the International Bar Association and the Centre for Petroleum and Mineral Law Studies, University of Dundee, Scotland.

—Property rights and sovereign rights : the case of North Sea oil / Peter D. Cameron. – London : Academic Press, 1983.
x,210p; 24cm.
Bibliography: p194-202. - Includes index.
ISBN 0121570606 No price

—Shipping, energy, and environment : Southeast Asian perspectives for the eighties : proceedings of a Workshop held in Honolulu, Hawaii, 10-12 December 1980 / edited by Mark J. Valencia ... et al. – Halifax, N.S. : Dalhousie Ocean Studies Programme, 1982.
xi,333p.
Held at the Environment and Policy Institute of the East-West Center at the University of Hawaii.
ISBN 0770302769

—Solar energy and the law / North Ryde : Law Book Co, 1984.
ISBN 0455203407 Pbk £25.00

ENERGY – AUSTRALIA

—Solar Energy and the Law / North Ryde : Law Book Co, 1984.
xxxiii, 324p.
ISBN 0455203407 Pbk £54.50

ENERGY – CANADA

—Canada Energy Law Service, 3 Vols. / Canadian Institute of Resource Law. – Toronto : DeBoo, 1984.
This looseleaf service monitors the decisions of those tribunals which regulate Canada's energy resources. Included are commentaries, case digests, and legislation. Six updates per year are planned.
ISBN 0888201087 Hbk £650.00

—Fuels and the national policy / John N. McDougall. – Toronto : Butterworths, 1982.
vi,199p.
Bibliography: p188-194.

ENERGY – EUROPE

—Europe and world energy / Hanns Maull. – London : Butterworth for Sussex European Research Centre, University of Sussex, 1980.
vii,342p; 24cm. – (Butterworths European studies).
Includes index.
ISBN 0408106298 £16.50

ENERGY – EUROPEAN COMMUNITY

—Energy strategy in Europe : the legal framework / by Terence Daintith and Leigh Hancher. – Berlin : W. de Gruyter, 1986.
ix,190p. – (Series A, Law).
Includes bibliographical references and index.
ISBN 0899251730

ENERGY – GREAT BRITAIN

—Energy Finance / London : Euromoney, 1983.
ISBN 0903121476 Pbk £75.00

—Fifth report from the Energy Committee : session 1984-85 : government oil price policy and the spring supplementary estimate for 20 million in respect of the British National Oil Corporation including Government repsonse to Committee's fourth report of session 1984-85 ... together with minutes of proceedings relating to the report and minutes of evidence and appendices / ordered by the House of Commons to be printed 8 March 1985. – London : H.M.S.O., 1985.
xxiv,72p. – (1984-85 HC).
Includes bibliographical references. Chairman: Ian Lloyd.
ISBN 010223485X

—Fourth report from the Energy Committee : session 1984-85 : the winter supplementary estimate for 45 million in respect of the British National Oil Corporation together with minutes of proceedings relating to the report and minutes of evidence and appendices / ordered by the House of Commons to be printed 12 December 1984. – London : H.M.S.O., 1984.
xiv,34p. – (1984-85 HC).
Includes bibliographical references. Chairman: Ian Lloyd.
ISBN 0102126852

ENERGY – IRELAND

—Energy and mineral resources law in Ireland / Edward J. Donelan : with a foreword by A.J.F. O'Reilly. – Blackrock : Round Hall in association with Irish Academic, 1985.
214p; 25cm.
Includes index.
ISBN 0950872547 No price

ENGAGEMENT – CANADA

—Breach of Promise of Marriage / Victoria : Government of British Columbia, 1983.

ENGAGEMENT – CANADA – BRITISH COLUMBIA

—Report on breach of promise of marriage / Law Reform Commission of British Columbia. – Victoria : Queen's Printer, 1983.
36p.
ISBN 0771883811

ENGAGEMENT – CANADA – MANITOBA

—Report on breach of promise to marry / Manitoba Law Reform Commission. – Winnipeg : The Commission, 1984.
33p. – (Report).
Includes bibliographical references. Breach of promise; Manitoba.

ENGAGEMENT – IRELAND

—First report on family law : criminal coversation, enticement and harbouring of a spouse or child, loss of consortium, personal injury to a child, seduction of a child, matrimonial property and breach of promise of marriage / the Law Reform Commission. – Dublin : The Commission, 1981.
iii,32p. – (LRC).

ENGINEERING – CANADA

—Canadian Law of Architecture and Engineering / Wilfred J. Wallace. – Butterworths, 1987.
544p.
Coverage includes contract and tort, claims avoidance, liability insurance, copyright and patents, and remuneration. Collection of form contracts, municipal forms, and explanatory notes. Canadian statutes and cases provide the focus of the study, but the laws of other jurisdictions, notably England are included. Analyses the civil law of Quebec.
ISBN 0409804819 Hbk £100.00

ENGINEERING – GREAT BRITAIN

—Competitive Tendering for Engineering Contracts / London : Sweet & Maxwell, 1983.

—Elements of Engineering Contracts / Roulston. – Spon (E & FN), 1980.
ISBN 0419116109 Pbk £4.75

—Handbook of National Agreements / London : Engineering Employers Federation, 1985.

—Lift and Escalator Erection Repair and Maintenance Consolidated Agreement / London : Engineering Employers Federation, 1985.

ENGINEERS

—Engineer's liability to the contractor : papers presented at the Conference of the International Bar Association's Section on Business Law Conference, Toronto 1983 / International Construction Contracts Committee of the Section on Business Law of the International Bar Assoication. – London : International Bar Association, 1983.
iv,162p.
Includes bibliographical references.

ENGINEERS – AUSTRALIA

—Law for Architects, Builders and Engineers / 2nd ed. – Butterworths, 1983.
355p.
ISBN 0409493422 Pbk £29.50

ENGINEERS – CANADA

—Professional Engineers Act, 1983, Bill 123 : An Act to Revise the Professional Engineers Act / Ontario : Ontario Government Publications Service, 1983.
49p.

ENGINEERS – MALAYSIA

—Registration of Engineers Act, 1967 (Act 138) and Rules, 1972 / Kuala Lumpur : International Law Books Services.

ENGLAND

—Family, sex and marriage in England 1500-1800 / Lawrence Stone. – Abridged ed. – Harmondsworth : Penguin, 1982.
446p,16p of plates; 20cm. – (A Peregrine book).
Previous ed.: London : Weidenfeld & Nicolson, 1977.
Includes index.
ISBN 0140551670 Pbk £3.50

ENGLAND – ENGLAND

—Law, economy and society, 1750-1914 : essays in the history of English law / edited by G.R. Rubin, David Sugarman. – Abingdon : Professional Books, 1984.
iv,503,xxviii p; 24cm.
ISBN 0862050855

ENTAIL
—Queensberry leases : petitions, answers, speeches and other documents of the Court of Session regarding leases on the entailed estates of the late William, Duke of Queensberry / 6 v. – Edinburgh : s.n., 1813.
Various printers. Ms. contents lists and marginalia. Spine title. Includes Latin text.

ENTRAPMENT - CANADA
—Entrapment in Canadian Criminal Law / Agincourt : Carswell, 1985.
250p.
This book focuses on the problems inherent in the investigations of victimless crimes and sets out the theoretical bases for the defense of entrapment in criminal cases under Canadian law.

—Entrapment in Canadian Criminal Law / Agincourt : Carswell, 1985.
250p.

—Entrapment in Canadian Criminal Law / Agincourt : Carswell, 1985.
ISBN 045937060X Hbk £19.80

ENVIRONMENTAL HEALTH
—Encyclopaedia of environmental health law and practice / Sweet & Maxwell, 1988.
ISBN 0421133600 £190.00

ENVIRONMENTAL HEALTH - ENGLAND
—Environmental health law / by Charles A.R. Webster. – London : Sweet & Maxwell, 1981.
xxiii,177p; 22cm.
Includes index.
ISBN 0421266201 Hbk £11.50
ISBN 0421266309 Pbk £1.50

—Environmental health procedures / W.H. Bassett. – London : H.K. Lewis, 1983.
xiv,266p; 25cm.
ISBN 0718604709 £13.00

—Public Health (Control of Disease) Bill : report on the consolidation of certain enactments relating to the control of disease / The Law Commission. – London : H.M.S.O., 1984.
6p; 25cm.
ISBN 0101912803

ENVIRONMENTAL HEALTH - GREAT BRITAIN
—Knight's Environmental and Public Health Acts / Tonbridge : Ernest Benn.
5000p.
ISBN 0853140235 loose £495.00

ENVIRONMENTAL IMPACT ANALYSIS
—Environmental assessment procedures : a study which focuses on certain oil and gas developments in Scotland in light of the proposed EEC directive : final report August 1984 / prepared by Centre for Environmental Management and Planning, University of Aberdeen. – Aberdeen : Centre for Environmental Management and Planning, 1984.
x, 68p, 6p.

ENVIRONMENTAL IMPACT ANALYSIS - CANADA
—Issues in Environmental Impact Assessment / Downsview : York University, Faculty of Environmental Studies, 1983.
128p.
ISBN 0919762220 pb

ENVIRONMENTAL LAW
—Environment Protection : Problems, Policy Administration Law / New Delhi : Deep and Deep Publications, 1987.
568p.
ISBN 8171000037 Hbk £350.00

—Environmental Law / North Vancouver : International Self-Counsel Press.

—Environmental Law and Chemical Substance / Berlin : Erich Schmidt, 1982.
ISBN 3503021280 Hbk £48.00

—Environmental law and policy in the Pacific basin area / edited by Ichiro Kato, Nobuo Kumamoto, and William H. Matthews. – Tokyo : University of Tokyo Press, 1981.
ix, 229 p.; 24 cm.
Includes bibliographical references and index.
ISBN 0860082857 Y5400

—Environmental law in New Zealand / by D.A.R. Williams. – Wellington : Butterworth, 1980.
xxx,330p; 25cm.
Exposition of the fundamental principles governing the areas of the new environmental law, which lie outside the subject of town planning strictly considered.
ISBN 0409600458

—Environmental Law in the 1980s : a New Beginning / Alastair R. Lucas. – Calgary : Canadian Institute of Resources Law.
233p.

—Environmental Law of the Sea / Gland : International Union for Conservation of Nature and Natural Resources, 1981.
419p.

—Environmental Regulation : Its Impact on Major Oil and Gas Projects / Alastair R. Lucas. – Calgary : Canadian Institute of Resources Law.
167p.

—Future of the International Law of the Environment : Workshop 1984 / Dordrecht : Kluwer, 1985.
536p.
ISBN 9024732395 Hbk £155.00

—Industry and the regulatory agencies : a collection of the papers given at the fourth seminar organised by Committee F of the International Bar Association's Section on Business Law in April 1985 at Stratford-upon-Avon / edited by John H. Bates. – 4. – London : International Bar Association, 1985.
Includes bibliographical references.

—International Environmental Law Information System / Berlin : Erich Schmidt.
354p. – (BZU Ser.: Vol. B3).
ISBN 3503010181 Pbk £39.00

—Journal of Planning and Environment Law / London : Sweet & Maxwell.

Single copies

Back Vols.

—Law and the Environment : an Essay / Hobart : University of Tasmania, Centre for Environmental Studies, 1980.
33p.

—Maritime Safety and Environment Conventions / London : Sweet & Maxwell, 1983.
– (British Shipping Laws).

—Mining and environmental law : proceedings of the seminar held at Washington D.C., 4-8 April 1982, ... organised by the Committee on Environmental Law, Section on Business Law, of the International Bar Association, in conjunction with the American Law Institute-American Bar Association Committee on Continuing Professional Education / 2. – London : International Bar Association, 1982.
ISBN 0950587648

—More Favourable Law Principle in Transfrontier Environmental Protection : A Means of Strengthening the Protection of the Individual / Berlin : Erich Schmidt, 1980.
87p. – (BZU Ser.: Vol. A68).
ISBN 3503018522 Pbk £24.00

—Problems encountered by local and regional authorites as a result of their new tasks in respect of environmental protection / report prepared under the guidance of the Committee of Experts on Social and Economic Activities of the Steering Committee for Regional and Municpal Matters by G. Tendron. – Strasbourg : Council of Europe, 1986.
29p.
Bibliography: p.28-29.

—Selected Multilateral Treaties in the Field of the Environment / Geneva : United Nations Publications.
525p.

—Setting environmental standards : guidelines for decision-making / edited by H.W. de Koning. – Geneva : World Health Organization, 1987.
vii,98p; 24cm.
Bibliography: p71-76.
ISBN 9241542144 Pbk No price

—Trends in Environmental Policy and Law / Gland : International Union for Conservation of Nature and Natural Resources, 1980.
404p.

—UNEP Environmental Law In-Depth Review 1981 / Berlin : Erich Schmidt, 1982.
ISBN 3503021213 Hbk £24.00

ENVIRONMENTAL LAW - ASIA
—Environmental protection and coastal zone management in Asia and the Pacific / edited by Ichiro Kato ... et al. – Tokyo : University of Tokyo Press, 1985.
xi,244p.
Includes bibliographies and index.
ISBN 0860083926

—Water management and environmental protection in Asia and the Pacific / edited by Ichiro Kato ... et al. – Tokyo : University of Tokyo Press, 1983.
x, 202 p.; 24 cm.
Includes bibliographies and index.
ISBN 0860083357 Y5000

ENVIRONMENTAL LAW - AUSTRALIA
—Environmental law in Australia / by G.M. Bates. – Sydney : Butterworths, 1983.
xxvi,236p.
Bibliography: p.224-231. - Includes index.
ISBN 0409495182

—Environmental Noise Control Legislation in Australia / Australian Environment Council-Environmental Noise Control Committee. – Canberra : Australian Government Publishing Service, 1982.
27p.
ISBN 064401914X Hbk £2.50

—Green Bans : The Birth of Australian Environmental Politics / Neutral Bay : Hale & Iremonger.
ISBN 090809423X Hbk £17.95

—Guide to Environmental Legislation and Administrative Arrangements in Australia / 2nd ed. – Kingston : Australian Government Publishing Service, 1987.
363p.

ENVIRONMENTAL LAW - AUSTRALIA - NEW SOUTH WALES
—Environmental planning and development law (NSW) / by A.J. Nott. – Sydney : Penman, 1982.
xlix,417p.
Includes index.
ISBN 0959431608

ENVIRONMENTAL LAW - AUSTRALIA - SOUTH AUSTRALIA
—Report ... relating to a general rule of standing in environmental matters / Law Reform Committee of South Australia. – Adelaide : Government Printer, 1987.
141,5,4p. – (97th report).
Bibliography: p.1-2. Includes text of draft bill..

ENVIRONMENTAL LAW - CANADA
—Canadian Environmental Law, 7 vols / Alastair Lucas. – Toronto : Butterworths.

—Canadian Environmental Law, 7 Vols. / Alastair R. Lucas. – Butterworths.

—Canadian Environmental Law Reports / Agincourt : Carswell.

—Consumer protection, environmental law, and corporate power / Ivan Bernier and Andree Lajoie, research coordinators. – Toronto : University of Toronto Press, 1985.
xv, 220 p.; 23 cm.
'Published ... in cooperation with the Royal Commission on the Economic Union and Development Prospects for Canada and the Canadian Government Publishing Centre, Supply and Services Canada.'. Includes bibliographies.
ISBN 0802072968 pbk.

—Crimes against the environment / Law Reform Commission of Canada. – Ottawa : The Commission, 1985.
75,85p. – (Working paper).
Bibliography: p.71-72. Cover title: Protection of life: crimes against the environment. Added t.p. in French: Les crimes contre l'environment. Pages numbered in opposite directions. Text in English and French.
ISBN 0662539907

—Cross-Border Litigation : Environmental Rights in the Great Lakes Ecosystem / Agincourt : Carswell, 1986.
445p.
This book analyzes the pollution control legislation of the American states and Canadian provinces bordering the Great Lakes and discusses the procedural difficulties confronting potential individual litigants.

—Cross-Border Litigation : Environmental Rights in the Great Lakes Ecosystem / Agincourt : Carswell, 1986.
445p.

—Environmental Law / Agincourt : Carswell, 1984.
460p.
This text is structured around the various aspects of the environment to be controlled by Canadian regulations. Sections on air, water, waste management, pits and quarries, noise, and other environmental hazards are included in the book. A large appendix of relevant statutes and regulations is provided.

—Environmental Law and Practice / Vancouver : British Columbia Continuing Legal Education Society, 1983.
309p.
ISBN 0865041245 Hbk £60.00

—Environmental Regulation in Canada : an Assessment of the Regulatory Process / Vancouver : University of British Columbia, Westwater Research Center, 1981.
134p.
ISBN 0920146090 Pbk £6.95

—Environmental rights in Canada / Canadian Environmental Law Research Foundation : edited by John Swaigen. – Toronto : Butterworths, 1981.
vii,447p.
ISBN 0409818801

—Sentencing in environmental cases : a study paper / prepared for the Law Reform Commission of Canada by John Swaigan and Gail Bunt. – Ottawa : The Commission, 1985.
81p. – (Study paper).
ISBN 0662138295

ENVIRONMENTAL LAW - CANADA - BRITISH COLUMBIA

—Environmental Law, British Columbia Handbook, 1984 / Gwen M. Edwards. – Toronto : Butterworths.
285p.

—Environmental Law, British Columbia Handbook, 1984 / Gwen M. Edwards. – Butterworths, 1984.
285p.
ISBN 0409988642 Pbk £40.00

ENVIRONMENTAL LAW - ENGLAND

—Policing pollution : a study of regulation and enforcement / Genevra Richardson with Anthony Ogus and Paul Burrows. – Oxford : Clarendon Press, 1982.
ix,204p; 23cm.
Includes index.
ISBN 0198275102 Hbk £15.00
ISBN 0198275129 Pbk Unpriced

ENVIRONMENTAL LAW - EUROPEAN COMMUNITY

—EEC environmental policy and Britain / Nigel Haigh. – 2nd ed. – Harlow : Longman, 1987.
250p; 24cm.
Previous ed.: 1984.
ISBN 0582016096 Pbk £25.00

—EEC environmental policy and Britain : an essay and a handbook / Nigel Haigh. – London : Environmental Data Services, 1984.
ii,324p; 23cm.
ISBN 0905347501

—Environmental law of the European communities : Droit de l'environnement des communautes Europeennes Umweltrecht der Europaischen Gemeinschaften / edited by Wolfgang E. Burhenne. – Berlin : E. Schmidt, 1976-.
22 cm.
English and/or French and/or German. Loose-leaf for updating. 'FUST-Project Nr. 75.'.
ISBN 3503014802 LLF

—European Community environmental policy in practice / Nigel Haigh, Graham Bennett. – London : Graham & Trotman, 1986.
106p.
ISBN 0860105490

Vol. 2 : Netherlands : water and waste : a study of the implementation of the EEC directives : by Graham Bennett 1986.
96p.
ISBN 0860105571 Hbk

Vol. 3 : France : water and waste : a study of the implementation of the EEC directives : by Thierry Lavoux 1986.
vi,104p.
ISBN 0860106322 Hbk

Vol. 4 : Federal Republic of Germany : water and waste : a study of the implementation of the EEC directives : by Pascale Kromarek 1986.
x,133p.
A series of studies by the Institute for European Environmental Policy.
ISBN 0860106330 Hbk

—European environment review : the journal of European Community and international environmental policy and law / English ed. – Brussels : Environmental Law Forum, 1986-.
Also published in French and German.

ENVIRONMENTAL LAW - FRANCE

—European Community environmental policy in practice / Thierry Lavoux. – London : Graham & Trotman, 1986.
vi,104p.
ISBN 0860106322 Hbk

ENVIRONMENTAL LAW - GHANA

—Ghana, water supply and control : a record and analysis of legislation / by A.J. Adamson ... et al. – London : Commonwealth Secretariat, 1985.
xv, 133 p.; 30 cm.
Bibliography: p. 113-122. Includes indexes.
ISBN 085092278X pbk. £10.00

ENVIRONMENTAL LAW - GREAT BRITAIN

—Coastal Law / London : LLoyd's of London Press, 1989.
ISBN 1850441642 Hbk

—EEC environmental policy and Britain / Nigel Haigh. – 2nd ed. – Harlow : Longman, 1987.
250p; 24cm.
Previous ed.: 1984.
ISBN 0582016096 Pbk £25.00

—EEC environmental policy and Britain : an essay and a handbook / Nigel Haigh. – London : Environmental Data Services, 1984.
ii,324p; 23cm.
ISBN 0905347501

—Environment and enforcement / Oxford : Oxford University Press, 1984.
ISBN 0198275145 Pbk £7.50

—Environmental law / David Hughes. – London : Butterworths, 1986.
400p; 22cm.
Includes bibliographies and index.
ISBN 0406016909 Hbk No price :
ISBN 0406016917 Pbk £9.95

—Journal of Planning and Environmental Law : 1948-1981, 34 Vols. / Abingdon : Professional Books.

—Knight's Environmental and Public Health Acts / Tonbridge : Ernest Benn.
5000p.
ISBN 0853140235 loose £495.00

—Planning and pollution : an examination of the role of land use planning in the protection of environmental quality / Christopher Miller and Christopher Wood. – Oxford : Clarendon, 1983.
xi,232p; 23cm.
Includes index.
ISBN 0198232454 Unpriced

—Public access to environmental information : report of an interdepartmental Working Party on public access to information held by pollution control authorities / Great Britain. – London : H.M.S.O., 1986.
ISBN 0117518654

—Reasonable arm of the law? : the law enforcement procedures of environmental health officers / Bridget M. Hutter. – Oxford : Clarendon Press, 1988.
Includes index. Bibliography.
ISBN 0198255942

—Transport and the environment / Department of Transport. – London : The Department, 1987.
32p.

—United Kingdom marine pollution law / by John H. Bates. – London : Lloyds of London Press, 1985.
xxxii,461p.
ISBN 185044028X

ENVIRONMENTAL LAW - INDIA

—Environmental Laws in India / Madhya Pradesh : Lawyers Home, 1986.
663p.

ENVIRONMENTAL LAW - INDONESIA

—Environmental Legislation in Indonesia / Yogyakarta : Gadjah Mada University Press, 1985.
41p.
ISBN 9794200468 Pbk £4.00

ENVIRONMENTAL LAW - ISLAMIC COUNTRIES

—Islamic Environmental Systems Engineering : A Systems Study of Environmental Engineering Planning and the Law, Politics, Education, Economics and Sociology of Science and Culture of Islam / London : Macmillan, 1980.
ISBN 0333261399 Pbk £5.95

ENVIRONMENTAL LAW - JAPAN

—Water management and environmental protection in Asia and the Pacific / edited by Ichiro Kato ... et al. – Tokyo : University of Tokyo Press, 1983.
x, 202 p.; 24 cm.
Includes bibliographies and index.
ISBN 0860083357 Y5000

ENVIRONMENTAL LAW - NETHERLANDS

—European Community environmental policy in practice / Graham Bennett. – London : Graham & Trotman, 1986.
96p.
ISBN 0860105571 Hbk

ENVIRONMENTAL LAW - NEW ZEALAND

—Planning and development law in New Zealand / by Kenneth A. Palmer : with a foreword by Sir Robin Cooke. – 2nd ed. 2. – Sydney : Law Book Co., 1984.
lviii,1023p.
ISBN 0455203725

ENVIRONMENTAL LAW - UNITED STATES

—Cross-Border Litigation : Environmental Rights in the Great Lakes Ecosystem / Agincourt : Carswell, 1986.
445p.

—Water management and environmental protection in Asia and the Pacific / edited by Ichiro Kato ... et al. – Tokyo : University of Tokyo Press, 1983.
x, 202 p.; 24 cm.
Includes bibliographies and index.
ISBN 0860083357 Y5000

ENVIRONMENTAL LAW - USSR

—Ecology : political institutions and legislation : environmental law in the USSR / Oleg Kolbasov. – Moscow : Progress, 1983.
215p; 21cm.
Translation of: Ekologia.
ISBN 0714719277 £3.95

ENVIRONMENTAL LAW - WEST GERMANY

—European Community environmental policy in practice / Pascale Kromarek. – London : Graham and Trotman, 1986.
x,133p.
A series of studies by the Institute for European Environmental Policy.
ISBN 0860106330 Hbk

ENVIRONMENTAL LAW (INTERNATIONAL LAW)

—Acid rain and international law / by Irene H. van Lier. – Halifax : Dalhousie University, 1981.
xxii,278p.
Originally presented as the author's thesis (LL.M.) - Dalhousie University 1980. Bibliography: p.257-266.
ISBN 9028622314 Hbk
ISBN 0770301851 Hbk

—Convention on Early Notification of a Nuclear Accident and Convention on Assistance in the Case of a Nuclear Accident or Radiological Emergency / Vienna : International Atomic Energy Agency, 1987.
126p. – (Legal series).
ISBN 9201760876

—Environmental protection and sustainable development : legal principles and recommendations / R.D. Munro, J.G. Lammers : adopted by the Experts Group on Environmental Law of the World Commission on Environment and Development, June 1986 ; with a foreword by Nagendra Singh. – London : Graham & Trotman, 1987.
xxi, 196 p.; 25 cm.
Bibliography: p. 133-143.
ISBN 0860109100 Hbk

—International environment law : multilateral treaties Droit international de l'environnement : traites multilateraux Internationales Umweltrecht : multilaterale Vertrage / editor, W. E. Burhenne : compiled by Robert Muecke. – Berlin : E. Schmidt, 1974-.
1 v.; 32 cm.
Cover title: Internationales Umweltrecht. Loose-leaf for updating. Parallel text in English and/or French and/or German. 'FUST-Projekt nr. 51.'.
ISBN 3503011048 Hbk

—International protection of the environment on a regional level / Thessaloniki : Institute of Public International Law and International Relations, 1982.
xii,768p.
Includes bibliographies. English or French text.

—International wildlife law : an analysis of international treaties concerned with the conservation of wildlife / by Simon Lyster. – Cambridge : Grotius Publications, 1985.
xxiii,470p.
Covers the international conventions on whaling, wetlands, protection of cultural and natural heritage, international trade in endangered species, and Antarctic marine living resources.
ISBN 0906496225

—Marine environment law in the United Nations Environment Programme : an emergent eco-regime / compiled by Peter H. Sand. – London : Tycooly, 1988.
xxvi,265p.
Contains the text of international treaties adopted under the United Nations Environment Programme.
ISBN 1851480242

—Marine pollution in international law : material obligations and jurisdiction with special reference to the Third United Nations Conference on the Law of the Sea / by Kari Hakapaa. – Helsinki : Suomalainen Tiedeakatemia, 1981.
341 p.; 25 cm.
Errata slip and notice of public dissertation discussion inserted. Thesis (doctoral)–University of Helsinki, 1981. Includes indexes. Bibliography: p. 299-336.
ISBN 9514104021

ENVIRONMENTAL POLICY

—Development and the environmental crisis : red or green alternatives? / Michael Redclift. – London : Methuen, 1984.
149p; 23cm.
Bibliography: p131-146. - Includes index.
ISBN 0416321305 Hbk Unpriced
ISBN 0416321402 Pbk Unpriced

—Environment ideology and policy / Francis Sandbach. – Oxford : Blackwell, 1980.
xvi,254p; 24cm.
Bibliography : p.225-248. - Includes index.
ISBN 0631104917 £12.50
ISBN 0631128115

—Environment Protection : Problems, Policy Administration Law / New Delhi : Deep and Deep Publications, 1987.
568p.
ISBN 8171000037 Hbk £350.00

—Environmental groups in politics / Philip Lowe & Jane Goyder with additional contributions from Richard Bate, Sarah Buchanan and John McBride. – London : Allen & Unwin, 1983.
xii,208p; 24cm.
Bibliography: p186-197. - Includes index.
ISBN 0043290434 Hbk Unpriced
ISBN 0043290442 Pbk

—Environmental law and policy in the Pacific basin area / edited by Ichiro Kato, Nobuo Kumamoto, and William H. Matthews. – Tokyo : University of Tokyo Press, 1981.
ix, 229 p.; 24 cm.
Includes bibliographical references and index.
ISBN 0860082857 Y5400

—Integration through law : Europe and the American federal experience : a series / under the general editorship of Mauro Cappelletti, Monica Seccombe, Joseph Weiler. – Berlin : W. de Gruyter, 1985.
xxiv,350p. – (Series A, Law).
Includes bibliographical references and indexes.

—Introduction to the World conservation strategy / prepared for the International Union for Conservation of Nature and Natural Resources by its Commission on Education : text and selection of photographs, Stan Croner. – Gland, Switzerland : IUCN, 1984.
28 p.; 30 cm.
ISBN 2880327024 pbk. £7.95

—Trends in Environmental Policy and Law / Gland : International Union for Conservation of Nature and Natural Resources, 1980.
404p.

ENVIRONMENTAL POLICY - AUSTRALIA - NEW SOUTH WALES

—Loval Government and Environmental Planning Law in New South Wales / North Ryde : Law Book Co, 1981.
xvi, 174p.
ISBN 045520361X Pbk £28.50

ENVIRONMENTAL POLICY - CANADA

—Environmental rights in Canada / Canadian Environmental Law Research Foundation : edited by John Swaigen. – Toronto : Butterworths, 1981.
vii,447p.
ISBN 0409818801

ENVIRONMENTAL POLICY - EUROPE

—Competence of the European Parliament for Environmental Policy / Berlin : Erich Schmidt.
101p. – (BZU Ser.: Vol. A63).
ISBN 3503015698 Pbk £22.50

ENVIRONMENTAL POLICY - EUROPEAN COMMUNITY

—Environmental policy of the European Communities / Guy Corcelle. – London : Graham & Trotman, 1989.
336. – (International environmental law and policy).
Survey of the legislation on environmental policy introduced by the European Community in recent years. Covers pollution control, environmental impact assessment, and nature conservation. Gives the full text of the Declaration on the Environment adopted by the European Council meeting at Rhodes in 1988.
ISBN 1853332259 Hbk £45

—European environment policy : air, water, waste management / Brussels : Economic and Social Committee, 1987.
48 p.; 30 cm.
'Document prepared by the Studies and Research Division of the General Secretariat of the Economic and Social Committee.'. Includes bibliographies.
ISBN 9283001087

—State of the environment in the European Community, 1986 / Commission of the European Communities, Directorate-General Environment, Consumer Protection and Nuclear Safety. – Luxembourg : Commission of the European Communities, 1987.
xvi,370p.
ISBN 928256973X

ENVIRONMENTAL POLICY - GREAT BRITAIN

—Controlling pollution : principles and prospects : the government's response to the tenth report of the Royal Commission on Environmental Pollution / Great Britain. – London : H.M.S.O., 1984.
vii,35p.
ISBN 0117517585

—Environment and enforcement / Oxford : Oxford University Press, 1984.
ISBN 0198275145 Pbk £7.50

—Environmental planning, 1939-1969 / J. B. Cullingworth. – London : HMSO, 1980.
xv,582p,1p. of plates (folded).

—First Report from the Environment Committee 1983-84 : Green Belt and Land for Housing, 3 Vols. / London : HMSO, 1984.
ISBN 0102962847 Hbk £3.75

Vol. 2: Minutes of evidence appendices
ISBN 0102946841 Hbk £17.20

Vol. 3: Appendices pages 540-664
ISBN 0102893845 Hbk £7.65

—Land policy in planning / Nathaniel Lichfield and Haim Darin-Drabkin. – London : Allen & Unwin, 1980.
viii,321p; 24cm.
Bibliography: p304-313. - Includes index.
ISBN 0043330177 £18.00

ENVIRONMENTAL POLICY - USSR

—Environmental policy in the USSR / Charles E. Ziegler. – London : Pinter, 1987.
195p; 24cm.
Includes index.
ISBN 0861879015 £18.50

EPILEPTICS - AUSTRALIA

—Epilepsy and human rights / Canberra : Australian Government Publishing Service, 1985.
144p. – (Occasional paper).
ISBN 0644038462

EPILEPTICS - ENGLAND

—Epilepsy and the law : a medical symposium on the current law / proceedings of a symposium sponsored by Labaz Sanofi UK Ltd., held at the Royal College of Physicians, London on 18 June 1984 : edited by Peter Fenwick and Elizabeth Fenwick. – London : Royal Society of Medicine, 1985.
viii,88p; 24cm. – (International congress and symposium series).
Bibliography: p79-80.
ISBN 0199220220 Pbk £9.00

EQUAL PAY FOR EQUAL WORK - CANADA

—Women and Work : Inequality in the Labour Market / Erin Phillips. – Toronto : Lorimer & Co, 1983.
– (Canadian Issues Ser.).
ISBN 0888626088 Hbk £15.95
ISBN 088862607X Pbk £6.95

EQUAL PAY FOR EQUAL WORK - GREAT BRITAIN

—Discrimination equal pay / John Whitmore. – London : Sweet & Maxwell, 1989.
Presents the law of discrimination and institutions through which it functions. Looks at discrimination in employment, education, and the provision of goods and services. Also examines the practical aspects of the powers embodied in the Commission for Racial Equality, and the Equal Opportunities Commission, and tribunal procedures and remedies.
ISBN 0421389907 Hbk

—Employers Guide to Equal Pay Legislation in Great Britain / London : Engineering Employers Federation, 1984.
32p.

—Equal pay and opportunities : a study of the implementation and effects of the Equal Pay and Sex Discrimination Acts in 26 organizations / by M.W. Snell, P. Glucklich and M. Povall. – London : Department of Employment, 1981.
7,110p. – (Research paper).
Bibliography: p108-110.

—Equal pay for work of equal value / London : Macmillan, 1984.
ISBN 0333375572 Hbk £22.50

—Sex and ethnic monitoring, discrimination and equal pay : new codes and regulations / by Greville Janner. – New Malden : Croner Publications, 1984.
vi,120p.
Includes index.
ISBN 0900319321

EQUAL PAY FOR EQUAL WORK - NORTHERN IRELAND

—Equal Pay In Northern Ireland / Belfast : Queen's University of Belfast, 1986.
60p.

EQUALITY

—Equality and Discrimination under International Law / Oxford : Oxford University Press, 1983.
ISBN 0198255195 Pbk £12.50

—Equality, markets and the state / Raymond Plant. – London : Fabian Society, 1984.
28p.
ISBN 0716304945

—Essays on Law, Equality and Education / London : Sweet & Maxwell, 1984.
ISBN 0710098804 Hbk £49.00

—Inequalities and the Law / Lucknow : Eastern Book Company, 1984.
192p.

—Morality of freedom / Joseph Raz. – Oxford : Clarendon, 1986.
432p; 22cm.
ISBN 0198247729 £30.00

—Spheres of justice : a defence of pluralism and equality / Michael Walzer. – Oxford : Robertson, 1983.
xviii,345p; 24cm.
Introduction for students to abstract discussions of justice. Includes case studies.
ISBN 0855206837 £15.00

EQUALITY - CANADA

—Charterwatch : Reflections on Equality / A. Wayne MacKay. – Agincourt : Carswell, 1986.
320p.
This work presents eight essays on the political and legal implications of the guarantee of equality in the Canadian Charter of Rights and Freedom. The role of the judiciary in shaping the concept of equality in Canadian law is emphasized in the essays.

—Equality Rights / Vancouver : Continuing Legal Education Society of British Columbia, 1985.
248p.
ISBN 0865042217 Hbk £60.00

—Equality Rights and the Canadian Charter of Rights and Freedoms / Mary Eberts. – Agincourt : Carswell, 1985.
600p.

—Equality Rights and their Limitations / Agincourt : Carswell, 1987.
ISBN 0459398407 Hbk £36.00

—Equality Rights and Their Limitations in the Charter / Agincourt : Carswell, 1987.
450p.
This book is a practitioner's sourcebook to Section 15 of the Canadian Charter. The history of the equality rights section of the Charter and Key Canadian decisions touching on equality issues are presented and criticized in the work.

—Righting the Balance : Canada's New Equality Rights / Agincourt : Carswell, 1986.
450p.

—Women's Economic Equality Act, 1983, Bill 108 : An Act to Provide for Affirmative Action and Equal Pay for Work of Equal Value / Ontario : Ontario Government Publications Service, 1983.
11p.

EQUALITY - SWEDEN

—Step by Step : National Plan of Action for Equality, Stockholm, 1979 / Sweden. Jamstalldhetskommitten. – Vaellinby : Liberfoerlag, 1980.
197p : Illus.

EQUALITY BEFORE THE LAW

—Equality and judicial neutrality / Sheilah L. Martin and Kathleen E. Mahoney, editors. – Toronto : Carswell, 1986.
xxvii, 430 p.; 24 cm.
Papers presented at a conference held in Banff, Alta., May 22-24, 1986. Includes bibliographical references.
ISBN 0459308319

EQUALITY BEFORE THE LAW - CANADA

—Equality issues in federal law : a discussion paper / Canada. – Ottawa : Minister of Supply and Services Canada, 1985.
65,79p.
With French title-page: Les droits et l'egalite et la legislation federale. Pages numbered in opposite directions. English and French text.
ISBN 0662534956

—Toward equality : the response to the report of the Parliamentary Committee on Equality Rights / Ottawa, Ont. : Communications and Public Affairs, Dept. of Justice Canada, 1986.
65, 69 p.; 28 cm.
English and French. Title on added t.p.: Cap sur l'egalite.
ISBN 0662543181 pbk.

EQUALITY BEFORE THE LAW - GREAT BRITAIN

—Equality and discrimination : essays in freedom and justice : papers presented at the United Kingdom Association for Legal and Social Philosophy eleventh annual conference at University College London, 6th-8th April 1984 / edited by Stephen Guest and Alan Milne. – Stuttgart : Steiner, 1985.
102p; 24cm.
Bound with Beihefte nos. 22 and 23..

EQUALITY OF STATES

—Common crisis : North-South : cooperation for world recovery / the Brandt Commission. – London : Pan, 1983.
174p; 18cm. – (Pan world affairs).
Bibliography: p172-174.
ISBN 0330281305 Pbk £1.95

—North-South, a programme for survival : report of the Independent Commission on International Development Issues / Willy Brandt. – London : Pan Books, 1980.
304p; 18cm. – (Pan world affairs).
Chairman: Willy Brandt.
ISBN 0330261401 Pbk £1.95

EQUITABLE REMEDIES

—Equity, trusts, specific relief / Durga Das Basu. – 5th ed. – New Delhi : Prentice-Hall, 1983.
xxiv,336p.
Includes index.
ISBN 0876922329

EQUITABLE REMEDIES - AUSTRALIA

—Assignments of Choses in Action in Australia / London : Butterworths, 1982.
ISBN 0409395900 Hbk £28.00

—Equity, doctrines, and remedies / R.P. Meagher, W.M.C. Gummow, J.R.F. Lehane : with a foreword from the first edition by Sir Frank Kitto. – 2nd ed. – Sydney : Butterworths, 1984.
xciii, 912 p.; 25 cm.
Includes bibliographical references and index.
ISBN 0409491527 pbk. A$62

—Principles of Equitable Remedies / 3rd ed. – North Ryde : Law Book Co, 1984.
lix, 668p.
ISBN 0455203997 Hbk £73.00

EQUITABLE REMEDIES - CANADA

—Inequality of bargaining power : judicial intervention in improvident and unconscionable bargains / Robert W. Clark. – Toronto : Carswell, 1987.
xxxvii,255p.
ISBN 0459388401

EQUITABLE REMEDIES - ENGLAND

—Principles of equitable remedies : specific performance, injunctions, rectification and equitable damages / by I.C.F. Spry. – 3rd ed. – London : Sweet & Maxwell, 1984.
lix,668p; 25cm.
Sets out the principles by reference to which injunctions and orders for specific performance are granted and analyses equitable doctrines such as laches and part performance. Covers the changes in the law relating to Mareva injunctions and Anton Piller orders. Also includes a new chapter on rectification.
ISBN 0421332409 Canada No price
ISBN 0459368001

EQUITABLE REMEDIES - GREAT BRITAIN

—Inequality of bargaining power : judicial intervention in improvident and unconscionable bargains / Robert W. Clark. – Toronto : Carswell, 1987.
xxxvii,255p.
ISBN 0459388401

EQUITY

—Ashburner's Principles of Equity (1933) / 2nd ed. – Woolloomooloo : International Business Communications, 1983.
ISBN 0949553077 Hbk £60.00

—Equity, Trusts and Specific Relief / Lucknow : Eastern Book Company, 1983.
624p.

—Equity, trusts, specific relief / Durga Das Basu. – 5th ed. – New Delhi : Prentice-Hall, 1983.
xxiv,336p.
Includes index.
ISBN 0876922329

—Modern equity / by Harold Greville Hanbury. – 11th ed. – London : Stevens, 1981.
cvi,796p; 25cm.
Previous ed.: 1976. Includes index.
ISBN 0420461302 Hbk £27.50
ISBN 042046140X Pbk £16.50

—Principles and practice of discovery : with an appendix of forms including suggested forms for stating objections to discovery / by Edward Bray. – London : Reeves and Turner, 1885.
xlix, 704 p.; 22 cm.
Slips inserted containing new material. Includes index.

EQUITY - AUSTRALIA

—Cases and Materials on Equity and Trusts / R.P. Austin. – 3rd ed. – Butterworths, 1989.
1024p.
ISBN 0409495239 Hbk £89.00
ISBN 0409495247 Pbk £69.00

—Cases and materials on equity and trusts / by J.D. Heydon, W.M.C. Gummow, R.P. Austin. – 2nd ed. – Sydney : Butterworths, 1982.
xxxvi,934p.
This book introduces the main principles and remedies of Anglo-Australasian equity. A range of questions have been provided for undergraduate law students.
ISBN 0409309389

—Equity / Butterworths, 1989.
116p.

—Equity and Commercial Relationships / North Ryde : Law Book Co, 1987.
ca 288p.
ISBN 0455207259 Hbk

—Equity, doctrines, and remedies / R.P. Meagher, W.M.C. Gummow, J.R.F. Lehane : with a foreword from the first edition by Sir Frank Kitto. – 2nd ed. – Sydney : Butterworths, 1984.
xciii, 912 p.; 25 cm.
Includes bibliographical references and index.
ISBN 0409491527 pbk. A$62

—Essays in equity / edited by P.D. Finn. – Sydney : Law Book Company, 1985.
xxv,256p; 25cm.
ISBN 045520585X

—Outline of Equity and Trust / Sydney : Butterworths, 1988.
352p.
This introductory text covers such areas as the nature of eqity, equity assignments, fiduciary obligations, marshalling, contribution, subrogation, discretionary trusts, charitable trusts, and the rights of beneficiaries.

—Outline of Equity and Trusts / Butterworths, 1988.
xlii, 365p.
ISBN 0409493767 Hbk £45.00
ISBN 0409493546 Pbk £35.00

EQUITY - AUSTRALIA - NEW SOUTH WALES

—Equity - Practice and Procedure in New South Wales / Woolloomooloo : International Business Communications, 1987.

—Equity Practice and Procedure in New South Wales / London : Legal Books, 1987.
ISBN 0949533352 Pbk £65.00
ISBN 0949553352 Hbk £100.00

—Equity proceedings with precedents (New South Wales) / by A.G. Nevill and A.W. Ashe : consultant A.V. Ritchie : with a foreword by M.M. Helsham. – Sydney : Butterworths, 1981.
lii,379p.
Includes index.
ISBN 0409490393 Hbk A$77

EQUITY - AUSTRALIA - SOUTH AUSTRALIA

—Report ... on the inherited imperial statute law in this state relating to the topics of property, trusts, uses, equity and wills / Law Reform Committee of South Australia. – Adelaide : Government Printer, 1980.
16p. – (54th report).

EQUITY - ENGLAND

—Chancery practice / Edmund Heward. – London : Butterworths, 1983.
xx,198p.
Includes index.
ISBN 040622451X

—Equity / by George W. Keeton and L.A. Sheridan. – 3rd ed. – Chichester : Barry Rose, 1987.
cxxvi,576p.
Previous ed.: 1976. Includes index.
ISBN 1870080300

—Equity and the law of trusts / Philip H. Pettit. – 5th ed. – London : Butterworths, 1984.
lvii,649p; 26cm.
Previous ed.: 1979. Includes index.
ISBN 0406641676 Hbk No price
ISBN 0406641684 Pbk No price

—Modern equity / by Harold Greville Hanbury and Ronald Harling Maudsley. – 12th ed. – London : Stevens, 1985.
cxiv,920p; 26cm.
Previous ed.: 1981. Includes index.
ISBN 0420470506 Hbk £30.00
ISBN 0420470603 Pbk £19.75

—Snell's Principles of equity / P. V. Baker, P. St. J. Langan. – 28th ed. – London : Sweet & Maxwell, 1982.
clv,703p; 25cm.
Previous ed.: 1973. Includes index.
ISBN 0421250208 £22.00

EQUITY - GREAT BRITAIN

—Ashburner's Principles of Equity 1933 / 2nd ed. – London : Legal Books, 1983.
ISBN 0949553077 Hbk £35.00

—Cases in Equity : During the Time of Chancellor Talbot (1730-37) From Notes of Alexander Forrester / Repr. of 1741 ed. – Abingdon : Professional Books.
345p.

—Collection of Acts and Records of Parliament : With Reports of Cases in Courts of Law and Equity (1224-1800) Respecting Tithes, 4 Vols. / Repr. of 1801 ed. – Abingdon : Professional Books.
192p.

—Equity and the Law of Trusts / 5th ed. – London : Butterworths, 1984.
ISBN 0406641676 Hbk £25.00
ISBN 0406641684 Pbk £21.95

—Equity and Trusts / London : Financial Training, 1986.
– (SWOT).
ISBN 1851850457 Pbk £7.95

—Equity and Trusts / Plymouth : Macdonald & Evans, 1985.
ISBN 0712106685 Pbk £7.95

—Equity and Trusts / Plymouth : Macdonald & Evans, 1985.
304p. – (M and E Handbook Ser.).
ISBN 0712106685 Hbk £5.50

—Equity Doctrines and Remedies / Gummow. – 2nd ed. – London : Butterworths, 1984.
ISBN 040949142X Hbk £52.10
ISBN 0409491527 Pbk £39.30

—Essays in Equity / London : Sweet & Maxwell, 1985.
ISBN 045520585X Hbk £23.00

—Modern Cases / Repr. of 1730 ed. – Abingdon : Professional Books.
305p.
Orig. Title : Modern Cases in Law and Equity.

—Modern Equity / Maudsley. – 12th ed. – London : Sweet & Maxwell, 1985.
ISBN 0420470506 Hbk £32.00
ISBN 0420470603 Pbk £24.00

EQUITY - IRELAND

—Casebook on Equity and Trusts in Ireland / London : Butterworths, 1985.
ISBN 0862051126 Hbk £32.50
ISBN 0862051142 Pbk £25.00

—Casebook on Equity and Trusts in Ireland / Abingdon : Professional Books, 1985.
700p.
ISBN 0862051126 Hbk £44.00
ISBN 0862051142 Pbk £34.00

—Equity and the law of trusts in the Republic of Ireland / Ronan Keane. – London : Butterworths, 1988.
liii,387p.
Includes index.
ISBN 0406102708 Hbk £27.50

—Law of Equity in Republic of Ireland / London : Butterworths, 1988.
ISBN 0406102708 Hbk £29.50

EQUITY - NIGERIA

—Equity and trusts in Nigeria / by J.O. Fabunmi. – Ile-Ife : University of Ife Press, 1986.
lii,301p.
Includes bibliographical references and index.
ISBN 9781360453

—Principles of equity / by M. I. Jegede. – Benin City, Nigeria : Ethiope Publishing Corporation, 1981.
xxv,262p. – (Ethiope law series).
Includes bibiographical references and index.

ERITREA

—Nationalism and self determination in the Horn of Africa / edited by I. M. Lewis. – London : Ithaca Press, 1983.
ix,226p.
ISBN 0903729938

ESCHEAT - AUSTRALIA - SOUTH AUSTRALIA

—Report ... relating to the amendment of the law of escheat / Law Reform Committee of South Australia. – Adelaide : Government Printer, 1983.
7p. – (64th report).

ESCROWS - ENGLAND

—Deeds and escrows / the Law Commission. – London : H.M.S.O., 1987.
29p. – (1987/88 HC1).
ISBN 010200188X

ESCROWS - GREAT BRITAIN

—Transfer of land : formalities for deeds and escrows / London : H.M.S.O., 1985.
iv,44p. – (Working paper).
ISBN 0117301744

ESKIMOS - CANADA

—Inuit (Eskimo) of Canada / by Ian Creery. – London : Minority Rights Group, 1983.
16p. – (Report).
Bibliography: p.16.

ESTATE AGENCY - AUSTRALIA

—Sale of Real Property and Law of Agency in NSW / 4th ed. – Sydney : Butterworths, 1983.
176p.
This book is a working guide for those involved in conveyancing transactions. The fourth edition has been revised and updated to include new materials on the contract of sale of land, strata titles, agents' commissions, registration of titles, valuation of land, and other topics.

ESTATE AGENCY - AUSTRALIA - NEW SOUTH WALES

—Estate Agency Law and Practice in New South Wales / 2nd ed. – North Ryde : Law Book Co, 1985.
xxix, 481p.
ISBN 0455205817 Pbk £33.00

—Estate Agency Practise in New South Wales / North Ryde : Law Book Co, 1985.
xxix, 363p.
ISBN 0455202931 Pbk £33.00

ESTATE AGENCY - AUSTRALIA - QUEENSLAND

—Real Estate Agency Law in Queensland / North Ryde : Law Book Co, 1985.
xxiv, 273p.
ISBN 0455202915 Pbk £32.50

ESTATE AGENCY - GREAT BRITAIN
—Estate Agents Act 1979 / 2nd ed. - London : Estates Gazette, 1982.
ISBN 0728200430 Pbk £7.60

—Law of Estate Agency and Auctions / London : Estates Gazette, 1984.
ISBN 0728200724 Pbk £2.00

ESTATES (LAW) - CANADA
—Estate Litigation / Agincourt : Carswell, 1987.
400p.
This is an in-depth guide to various types of proceedings which can arise when dealing with an estate. Discussions include committeeship proceedings, proceedings related to mental incapability, and the role of the Official Guardian in estate matters related to children. Also included is a comprehensive discussion of the entire process of estate litigation.

—Estates and Trusts Quarterly / Aurora : Canada Law Book Co.
- (Law Journals).

Back Vols.

Binder and Contents

—Estates & trusts reports / Agincourt, Ont. : Carswell, 1978-.
24cm.
Cumulative indexes published at intervals.

—Workbook on Estates and Future Interests / Agincourt : Carswell, 1987.
130p.
Discussions include a review of the common law in its present form as it relates to property law, a survey of the rules set in textual format, and a quick review of the subject matter from the advanced reader. This text has been written from use with a first year property text.

ESTATES (LAW) - CANADA - BRITISH COLUMBIA
—Land (Settled Estate) Act / Law Reform Commission of British Columbia. - Vancouver : The Commission, 1988.
iii,38p. - (Working paper).
ISBN 077188625X

—Report on obsolete remedies against estate property : Estate Administration Act, Part 9 / Law Reform Commission of British Columbia. - Vancouver : The Commission, 1987.
22p.
Includes bibliographical references.
ISBN 0771885695

ESTATES (LAW) - CANADA - ONTARIO
—Estate Administration : A Solicitor's Reference Manual, 1 Vol. / Agincourt : Carswell, 1984.
700p.
This book is a guide for the solicitor dealing with all aspects of estate administration in Ontario, Canada. The text includes all relevant statutes and regulations. Numerous forms, letters, and checklists are provided.

—Ontario Estate Administration : A Guide for Legal Secretaries and Law Clerks / Toronto : Butterworths, 1987.
162p.

ESTATES (LAW) - ENGLAND
—Essay on the learning of contingent remainders and executory devises / by Charles Fearne. - 9th ed. - London : Saunders and Benning, 1831.
lvi,730p.
Includes index.

ESTATES (LAW) - GREAT BRITAIN
—Law for Estate Management Students / Murdoch. - 2nd ed. - London : Butterworths, 1986.
ISBN 0406562911 Pbk £18.95

—Taxation - A Handbook for Insurance and Estate Planners / 1986 Edition. - Don Mills : Life Underwriters Association of Canada.
ISBN 0921219032 Hbk £22.50

ESTATES (LAW) - INDIA
—Law and Practice of Estate Duty : with Rules and Forms / 4th ed. 1982 repr. 1983. - New Delhi : Bharat Law House.

ETHICS
—Ethics and mental retardation / edited by Loretta Kopelman and John C. Moskop. - Dordrecht : D. Reidel, 1984.
xvi, 258p.
Includes index.
ISBN 9027716307

—Ethics of Legal Coercion / Dordrecht : Kluwer, 1985.
192p.
ISBN 9027718431 Pbk £52.00

—Expanding circle : ethics and sociobiology / Peter Singer. - Oxford : Clarendon Press, 1981.
xii,190p; 22cm.
Includes index.
ISBN 0198246463 £6.95

—Fundamentals of ethics / by John Finnis. - Oxford : Clarendon, 1983.
x,163p; 23cm.
Includes index.
ISBN 0198246838 Hbk £14.00
ISBN 0198246846 Pbk £4.95

—John Locke's moral philosophy / John Colman. - Edinburgh : Edinburgh University Press, 1983.
viii,282p; 22cm.
Bibliography: p270-276. - Includes index.
ISBN 0852244452 £20.00

—Journal of applied philosophy : journal of the Society for Applied Philosophy / Abingdon : Carfax, 1984.

—Law and the moral order / W.D. Lamont. - Aberdeen : Aberdeen University Press, 1981.
xxviii,115p.
Includes bibliography.
ISBN 0080257429
ISBN 0080257461

—Moral foundation of rights / L.W. Sumner. - Oxford : Clarendon Press, 1987.
228p; 22cm.
Includes bibliography and index.
ISBN 0198247516 £22.50

—Morality, religious and secular : the dilemma of the traditional conscience / by Basil Mitchell. - Oxford : Clarendon Press, 1980.
ix,168p; 23cm.
'... revised version of the Gifford Lectures delivered at the University of Glasgow in 1974 and 1975' - Preface. Includes index.
ISBN 0198245378 £7.50

—Plato on punishment / Mary Margaret Mackenzie. - Berkeley Calif. : University of California Press, 1981.
vii,278p; 25cm.
Bibliography: p251-259. - Includes index.
ISBN 0520041690 £17.25

—Utilitarianism / On liberty : John Stuart Mill : edited with an introduction by Mary Warnock. - 17th impression. - Glasgow : Fontana, 1985.
352p.
This selection originally published: 1962. Bibliography: p.343-4. - Includes index.

—Utility and rights / R.G. Frey, editor. - Oxford : Blackwell, 1985.
ix,245p; 24cm.
Includes index.
ISBN 0631137130 £19.50

—Whose justice? Which rationality? / Alasdair MacIntyre. - London : Duckworth, 1988.
422p; 24cm.
Includes index.
ISBN 071562198X Hbk £35.00 :
ISBN 0715621998 Pbk £12.95

ETHIOPIA
—Nationalism and self determination in the Horn of Africa / edited by I. M. Lewis. - London : Ithaca Press, 1983.
ix,226p.
ISBN 0903729938

ETHNIC MINORITIES
—Amerindians of South America / by Andrew Gray. - London : Minority Rights Group, 1987.
26p. - (Report).
Includes bibliographical references.
ISBN 0946690529

—Armenians / by David Marshall Lang and Christopher J. Walker. - New rev ed. - London : Minority Rights Group, 1987.
20p. - (Report).
Previous ed.: 1981. Bibliography: p.20.
ISBN 094669043X

—Central America's Indians / by David Stephen and Phillip Wearne : with a summary by Rodolfo Stavenhagen. - London : Minority Rights Group, 1984.
23p. - (Report).

—Minorities and human rights law / Patrick Thornberry. - London : Minority Rights Group, 1987.
19p. - (Report).
Bibliography: p19.
ISBN 0946690480

—Minorities : community and identity : report of the Dahlem Workshop on Minorities - Community and Identity, Berlin 1982, Nov. 28 - Dec. 3 / C. Fried, editor : rapporteurs A.M.A. Dummett ... et al. - Berlin : Springer-Verlag, 1983.
x,417p.
Includes bibliographies and indexes.
ISBN 354012747X

—Minorities in National and International Laws / New Delhi : Deep and Deep Publications, 1985.
376p.

—Roma : Europe's gypsies / by Grattan Puxon. - Rev updated ed. - London : Minority Rights Group, 1987.
15p. - (Report).
Bibliography: p.13.
ISBN 0946690456

—Statut juridique international des minorites : bibliographie selective / preparee par la Bibliotheque du Palais de la Paix, La Haye : selective biliography : prepared by the Library of the Peace Palace, the Hague. - The Hague : Center for Studies and Research of the Hague Academy of International Law, 1984.
29 leaves.

—Western Saharans / by Tony Hodges. - London : Minority Rights Group, 1984.
20p. - (Report).
Bibliography: p.19-20.
ISBN 0946690219

—World minorities / edited by Georgina Ashworth. - Sunbury : Quartermaine House, 1980.
xvii,174p.
Includes bibliography.
ISBN 0905898117

ETHNIC MINORITIES - AFRICA
—Jehovah's Witnesses in Africa / by Tony Hodges. - New rev. ed. - London : Minority Rights Group, 1985.
16p. - (Report).
Previous ed. published as: Jehovah's Witnesses in Central Africa. Bibliography: p.14.
ISBN 0946690227

—New position of East Africa's Asians : problems of a displaced minority / by Yash Tandon and Arnold Raphael. - 2nd rev. ed. - London : Minority Rights Group, 1984.
20p. - (Report).
Previous ed.: 1978. Bibliography: p.20.
ISBN 0946690200

ETHNIC MINORITIES - AUSTRALIA
—Aboriginal Australians / by Keith D. Suter, Kaye Stearman. - New ed. - London : Minority Rights Group, 1982.
20p. - (Report).
Previous ed. published 1978 as: Australia's policy towards Aborigines 1967-1977 / by H.C. Coombs. Bibliography: p.20.

ETHNIC MINORITIES - BANGLADESH
—Bharis in Bangladesh / 4th rev. ed. - London : Minority Rights Group, 1982.
31p. - (Report).
Previous ed.: 1977.

ETHNIC MINORITIES - BOTSWANA
—San of the Kalahari / by David Stephen. - London : Minority Rights Group, 1982.
16p. - (Report).
Includes bibliographical references.

ETHNIC MINORITIES - CANADA
—Canada's Indians / by James Wilson. - Rev. ed. - London : Minority Rights Group, 1982.
20p. - (Report).
Previous ed.: 1977. Bibliography: p.20.

—Inuit (Eskimo) of Canada / by Ian Creery. - London : Minority Rights Group, 1983.
16p. - (Report).
Bibliography: p.16.

—Law and order for Canada's indigenous people / Paul Havemann, Keith Couse, Lori Foster, Rae Matonovich : Prairie Justice Research Consortium, School of Human Justice, University of Regina. - Ottawa : Ministry of the Solicitor General, 1984.
xxxi,187p. - (User report).
Bibliography: p.178-187.

—Law and the Chinese in Canada : a Case Study in Ethnic Perceptions of the Law / John Hagan. - Toronto : University of Toronto, Centre of Criminology, 1982.
viii, 103p.
ISBN 0919584551 Pbk £6.00

—Quest for Justice : Aboriginal Peoples and Aboriginal Rights / Toronto : University of Toronto Press, 1985.
ISBN 0802025722 Hbk £45.00
ISBN 0802065899 Pbk £17.50

ETHNIC MINORITIES - CANADA - QUEBEC
—French Canada in crisis : a new society in the making? / Camille Legendre. - Rev. ed. - London : Minority Rights Group, 1982.
20p. - (Report).
Previous ed.: 1980. Bibliography: p.17-18.

ETHNIC MINORITIES - CHINA
—Tibetans : two perspectives on Tibetan-Chinese relations / by Chris Mullin and Phuntsog Wangyal. - New ed. - London : Minority Rights Group, 1983.
27p. - (Report).
Previous ed.: 1981. Includes bibliographical references.
ISBN 0946690014

ETHNIC MINORITIES - CYPRUS
—Cyprus / by Keith Kyle. - New 1984 ed. - London : Minority Rights Group, 1984.
23p. - (Report).
Bibliography: p.23.
ISBN 0946690103

ETHNIC MINORITIES - ENGLAND

—Ethnic minorities and complaints against the police / Philip Stevens and Carole Willis with the assistance of Clare Oxby. - London : Home Office, 1981.
v,40p. - (Research and Planning Unit paper).
Bibliography: p.33-34.
ISBN 0862520266

—Ethnic minorities, crime and policing : a survey of the experiences of West Indians and whites / by Mary Tuck and Peter Southgate. - London : H.M.S.O., 1981.
iv,50p.
Bibliography: p50. A Home Office Research and Planning Unit report.
ISBN 0113407653

—Police and people in London / Stephen Small. - London : Policy Studies Institute, 1983.
169p. - (PSI).
ISBN 0853742243

ETHNIC MINORITIES - EUROPE

—Co-existence in some plural European societies / London : Minority Rights Group, 1986.
17p. - (Report).
ISBN 0946690448

—Policing Minorities in Europe : Proceedings foom the Cranfield-Wolfson Colloquium / London : Police Review Publishing, 1984.
ISBN 0851640087 Pbk

ETHNIC MINORITIES - GREAT BRITAIN

—Abstracts of race relations research / edited by George Mair and Philip Stevens. - London : Home Office, 1982.
vii,86p.
Includes index.
ISBN 0862520436

—Attitudes of ethnic minorities / Simon Field. - London : HMSO, 1984.
49p; 25cm.
Review of currently available research literature on the subject. Indicates the need for caution about accepting commonly expressed judgements on black and Asian attitudes.
ISBN 0113407742

—Black people and the criminal justice system : report of the NACRO Race Issues Advisory Committee / Clement Richards. - London : NACRO, 1986.
48p.
Includes bibliographical references. Chairman: Clement Richards. Accompanied by 'Summary of the report of the NACRO Race Issues Advisory Committee'.
ISBN 0850690404

—Encountering diversity : observations on the social work assessment of black children / Richard Pinder. - Leeds : Centre for Social Work and Applied Social Studies, 1982.
32p. - (Occasional paper).
Bibliography: p.31-32.

—English Law and Ethnic Minority Customs / London : Butterworths, 1986.
ISBN 040618008 Pbk £27.95

—Ethnic minorities in Britain : a study of trends in their position since 1961 / by Simon Field ... et al. - London : H.M.S.O., 1981.
v,44p.
Bibliography: p42-44. A Home Office Research Unit report.
ISBN 0113407084

—Family law and the immigrant communities / David Pearl. - Bristol : Family law, 1986.
xxi,104p; 21cm. - (Guide and practice series).
ISBN 0853081026

—Outsider : newsletter of the Minority Rights Group / London : The Group, 1984.
Continues: Newsletter.

—Policing immigration : Britain's internal controls / Paul Gordon. - London : Pluto, 1985.
v,160p.
Includes index.
ISBN 0861046234 Pbk £4.95

ETHNIC MINORITIES - GUYANA

—East Indians of Guyana and Trinidad / by Malcolm Cross. - New ed. - London : Minority Rights Group, 1980.
18p. - (Report).
Previous ed.: 1972. Bibliography: p.18.

ETHNIC MINORITIES - INDIA

—Competing equalities : law and the backward classes in India / Marc Galanter. - Berkeley : University of California Press, 1984.
xxii,625p; 24cm.
Bibliography: p575-611. - Includes index.
ISBN 0520042891 Pbk £38.25

—Cultural and Educational Rights of the Minorities under Indian Constitution / New Delhi : Deep and Deep Publications, 1985.
286p.

—Meos of India : Their Customs and Laws / New Delhi : Deep and Deep Publications, 1983.
211p.

—Sikhs / by Christopher Shackle. - Rev. ed. - London : Minority Rights Group, 1986.
19p. - (Report).
Bibliography: p.18.
ISBN 0946690413

—Untouchability in India : Implementation of the Law and Abolition / New Delhi : Deep and Deep Publications, 1986.
368p.

—Untouchables of India / by Dilip Hiro. - New 1982 ed. - London : Minority Rights Group, 1982.
19p. - (Report).
Previous ed.: 1975. Bibliography: p.19.

ETHNIC MINORITIES - INDONESIA

—Chinese in Indonesia, the Philippines and Malaysia / by Charles A. Coppel and Hugh and Ping-ching Mabbett. - Rev. ed. - London : Minority Rights Group, 1982.
16p. - (Report).
Previous ed. 1972. Bibliography: p.16.

—East Timor and West Irian / by Keith Suter. - Rev. ed. - London : Minority Rights Group, 1982.
24p. - (Reports).
Previous ed. published 1979, as: West Irian, East Timor and Indonesia. Bibliography: p.24.

ETHNIC MINORITIES - IRAN

—Baha'is of Iran / by Roger Cooper. - Rev. and updated ed. - London : Minority Rights Group, 1985.
16p. - (Report).
Bibliography: p.16.
ISBN 0946690316

—Baluchis and Pathans / by Robert G. Wirsing. - Rev & updated ed. - London : Minority Rights Group, 1987.
23p. - (Report).
Previous ed.: 1981. Bibliography: p.20.
ISBN 0946690510

—Kurds / by David McDowall. - New ed. - London : Minority Rights Group, 1985.
32p. - (Report).
Previous ed.: by Martin Short and Anthony McDermott. 1981. Bibliography: p.24.
ISBN 094669026X

ETHNIC MINORITIES - IRELAND

—Two Irelands : the problem of the double minority / by Harold Jackson and Anne McHardy. - 3rd rev. ed. - London : Minority Rights Group, 1984.
16p. - (Report).
Bibliography: p.16.

ETHNIC MINORITIES - JAPAN

—Japan's minorities : Burakumin, Koreans, Ainu and Okinawans / by George A. De Vos and William O. Wetherall. - New ed. - London : Minority Rights Group, 1983.
18p. - (Report).
Previous ed.: 1974. Bibliography: p. 17-18.
ISBN 0946690022

ETHNIC MINORITIES - MALAYSIA

—Chinese in Indonesia, the Philippines and Malaysia / by Charles A. Coppel and Hugh and Ping-ching Mabbett. - Rev. ed. - London : Minority Rights Group, 1982.
16p. - (Report).
Previous ed. 1972. Bibliography: p.16.

ETHNIC MINORITIES - NAMIBIA

—Namibians / by Peter Fraenkel and Roger Murray : with additional material by Kaye Stearman. - New ed. - London : Minority Rights Group, 1985.
31p. - (Report).
Bibliography: p.31.
ISBN 0946690278

—San of the Kalahari / by David Stephen. - London : Minority Rights Group, 1982.
16p. - (Report).
Includes bibliographical references.

ETHNIC MINORITIES - NEW CALEDONIA

—Kanaks of New Caledonia / by Ingrid A. Kircher. - London : Minority Rights Group, 1986.
20p. - (Report).
Bibliography: p.20.
ISBN 0946690405

ETHNIC MINORITIES - NEW ZEALAND

—Maori of New Zealand / by Robert Macdonald. - London : Minority Rights Group, 1985.
16p. - (Report).
Bibliography: p.16.
ISBN 0946690367

ETHNIC MINORITIES - NORTHERN IRELAND

—Two Irelands : the problem of the double minority / by Harold Jackson and Anne McHardy. - 3rd rev. ed. - London : Minority Rights Group, 1984.
16p. - (Report).
Bibliography: p.16.

ETHNIC MINORITIES - PAKISTAN

—Baluchis and Pathans / by Robert G. Wirsing. - Rev & updated ed. - London : Minority Rights Group, 1987.
23p. - (Report).
Previous ed.: 1981. Bibliography: p.20.
ISBN 0946690510

ETHNIC MINORITIES - PHILIPPINES

—Chinese in Indonesia, the Philippines and Malaysia / by Charles A. Coppel and Hugh and Ping-ching Mabbett. - Rev. ed. - London : Minority Rights Group, 1982.
16p. - (Report).
Previous ed. 1972. Bibliography: p.16.

ETHNIC MINORITIES - SCANDINAVIA

—Sami of Lapland / by Mervyn Jones. - London : Minority Rights Group, 1981.
15p. - (Report).
Bibliography: p.15.

ETHNIC MINORITIES - SINGAPORE

—The legal status of the Muslims in Singapore / Singapore : Malayan Law Journal, 1965.
95.
Intends to set out the legal position of the Muslims, including the Malays, in Singapore. Contains a historical introduction, a summary of the existing statute and the case law relating to the family law, the law of property and the law relating to the construction of wills and trust instruments as they affect the Muslims in Singapore, and the history of Muslim endowments.

ETHNIC MINORITIES - SOUTH AFRICA

—Black migration to South Africa : a selection of policy-oriented research / edited by W. R. Bohning. - Geneva : International Labour Office, 1981.
viii,184p.
Bibliography: p179-184.
ISBN 9221027589

—Indian South Africans / by Frene Ginwala. - New ed. - London : Minority Rights Group, 1985.
20p. - (Report).
Includes bibliographical references.
ISBN 0946690294

—Race and the law in South Africa : a volume of essays by members of the School of Law, Howard College, University of Natal, Durban, to commemorate the sixtieth anniversary of the Durban School / edited by A. J. Rycroft ... et al. - Cape Town : Juta, 1987.
xx,258p.
Includes bibliographical references and index.
ISBN 0702119105

ETHNIC MINORITIES - SPAIN

—Basques and Catalans / by Professor Kenneth Medhurst. - Rev 3rd ed. - London : Minority Rights Group, 1987.
12p. - (Report).
Includes bibliographical references.
ISBN 0946690537

ETHNIC MINORITIES - SRI LANKA

—Democracy in peril : Sri Lanka : a country in crisis : report to the LAWASIA Human Rights Standing Committee / by Patricia Hyndman. - Sydney : LAWASIA, 1985.
xi,483p.

—Tamils of Sri Lanka / by Walter Schwarz. - 3rd rev ed. - London : Minority Rights Group, 1986.
15p. - (Report).
Previous edition: 1983.
ISBN 0946690375

ETHNIC MINORITIES - TIBET

—Tibetans : two perspectives on Tibetan-Chinese relations / by Chris Mullin and Phuntsog Wangyal. - New ed. - London : Minority Rights Group, 1983.
27p. - (Report).
Previous ed.: 1981. Includes bibliographical references.
ISBN 0946690014

ETHNIC MINORITIES - TRINIDAD & TOBAGO

—East Indians of Guyana and Trinidad / by Malcolm Cross. - New ed. - London : Minority Rights Group, 1980.
18p. - (Report).
Previous ed.: 1972. Bibliography: p.18.

ETHNIC MINORITIES - UGANDA

—Uganda and Sudan - North and South / London : Minority Rights Group, 1982.
27p. - (Report).
Bibliographies.
ISBN 0946690243

ETHNIC MINORITIES - UNITED STATES

—Haitian refugees in the U.S. / by Alex Stepick : with the assistance of Dale Frederick Swartz. - Updated ed. - London : Minority Rights Group, 1986.
20p. - (Report).
Bibliography: p.18-19.
ISBN 0946690464

—Original Americans : U.S. Indians / by James Wilson. - New ed. - London : Minority Rights Group, 1986.
24p. - (Report).
Previous edition: 1980. Bibliography: p.24.
ISBN 0946690391

ETHNIC MINORITIES - USSR

—Crimean Tatars, Volga Germans and Meskhetians : Soviet treatment of some national minorities / Bohdan Nahaylo. - 2nd rev. ed. - London : Minority Rights Group, 1980.
28p. - (Report).
Previous ed.: 1973. Bibliography: p.28.

—Religious minorities in the Soviet Union : a report / prepared for the Minority Rights Group by Michael Bourdeaux and two associates, Kathleen Matchett and Cornelia Gerstenmaier. - Rev. 4th ed. - London : Minority Rights Group, 1984.
24p. - (Report).
Bibliography: p.23.
ISBN 0946690154

—Ukrainians and Georgians / by Bohdan Nahaylo and C.J. Peters. - London : Minority Rights Group, 1981.
20p. - (Report).
Bibliography: p.20.

ETHNOLOGICAL JURISPRUDENCE

—Sociology of law and legal anthropology in the Dutch speaking countries / J. van Houtte, editor. - Dordrecht : M. Nijhoff Publishers, 1985.
Bibliography of 'The sociology of law in Dutch-speaking countries': p67-102. Bibliography of 'Current legal anthropology in the Netherlands': p149-162.
ISBN 9024731755

ETHNOLOGY

—Development of ethnography in Britain : paper prepared for presentation at the BSA Annual Conference, Lancaster, 1980 / Robert Dingwall, Geoff Payne, Judy Payne. - Oxford : Centre for Socio-Legal Studies, 1980.
19,2p.
Bibliography: p.20-21.

EURO-DOLLAR MARKET

—Economics of the Euro-market : history, theory and policy / R. B. Johnston. - London : Macmillan, 1983.
x,321p.
Bibliography: p308-316.
ISBN 0333334183

—Euronotes and euro-commercial paper / Gareth Bullock. - London : Butterworths, 1987.
vii,136p; 23cm.
Includes index.
ISBN 0406104107 £32.00

EUROPE

—Change in Eastern Europe / Exeter : European Atlantic Movement, 1982.

—Decade of change : banking in Europe : the next ten years / London : Lafferty, 1986.
221p.
A study by Arthur Andersen & Co..
ISBN 094839403X

—Development of maritime islands as extreme examples of peripheral regions / report prepared by the Committee of Experts on Social and Economic Activities of the Steering Committee for Regional and Municipal Matters, with the assistance of Italo Ferrari. - Strasbourg : Council of Europe, 1986.
26p.

—Economic crime in Europe / edited by L.H. Leigh. - London : Macmillan for the London School of Economics and Political Science, 1980.
xii,211p; 23cm.
Conference papers. Includes bibliographies and index.
ISBN 0333248406 £20.00

—Economic crisis, trade unions and the state / edited by Otto Jacobi ... et al. - London : Croom Helm, 1986.
295p; 23cm.
Includes bibliographies and index. Includes papers translated from German and Italian.
ISBN 0709914474 £19.95

—Economics and sociology of rural communities : East-West perspectives / edited by Daniel Thorniley. - Aldershot : Gower, 1987.
229p; 23cm.
Includes bibliographies.
ISBN 0566054299 £19.50

—Economics of the Common Market / Dennis Swann. - 6th ed. - Harmondsworth : Penguin, 1988.
Previous ed.: 1984.
ISBN 0140227814

—Economics of the Euro-market : history, theory and policy / R. B. Johnston. - London : Macmillan, 1983.
x,321p.
Bibliography: p308-316.
ISBN 0333334183

—Encyclopedia of U.K. and European patent law / edited by T.A. Blanco White and others. - London : Sweet & Maxwell, 1977.
Loose-leaf with up-dating service.
ISBN 0421233508

—European challenge, 1992 : the benefits of a single market / Paolo Cecchini : with Michel Catinat and Alexis Jacquemin. - English ed. - Aldershot : Gower, 1988.
xxi, 127 p.; 23 cm.
Spine title: 1992, the European challenge. Bibliography: p. 110-111.
ISBN 0704506130 pbk.

—Impact of European Community law on the implementation of the European Convention on Human Rights / by Maurice Mendelson. - Strasbourg : Council of Europe, 1984.
43p.
ISBN 928710350X

—International law of take-overs and mergers : the EEC, Northern Europe and Scandinavia / H. Leigh Ffrench. - New York : Quorum, 1987.
416p; 22cm.
Includes bibliography and index.
ISBN 0899300774 £51.75

—International tax avoidance and evasion : colloquy of 5-7 March 1980 (Strasbourg), compendium of documents / Amsterdam : International Bureau of Fiscal Documentation, 1981.
184p.
ISBN 9070125196

—Legal and economic analyses on multinational enterprises / edited by Klaus J. Hopt. - 2 V. - Berlin : Walter de Gruyter, 1982.
At head of title: European University Institute. Vol. 2, English and French, with summaries for each item in the other language, has also parallel title: Analyses legales et economiques sur les entreprises multinationales. Includes indexes. Contents: v. 1. European merger control - v. 2. Groups of companies in European laws.
ISBN 3110087049 v. 2

—Legal protection of the collective interests of consumers by consumer agencies : Recommendation no. R(81)2 adopted by the Committee of Ministers of the Council of Europe on 23 January 1981 and explanatory memorandum / Council of Europe. - Strasbourg : Council of Europe, 1981.
19p; 21cm.
'Prepared by a committee of experts set up under the authority of the European Committee on Legal Cooperation' - verso t.p.. At head of cover title: Council of Europe, Legal Affairs.

—Order and conflict in contemporary capitalism / edited by John H. Goldthorpe : sponsored by the Joint Committee on Western Europe of the American Council of Learned Societies and the Social Science Research Council. - Oxford : Clarendon, 1984.
352p.
Conference papers.
ISBN 0198780087 Hbk £22.50
ISBN 0198780079 Pbk £8.50

—Papers from the European Conference on Football Violence : held at the Tickled Trout Hotel, Salmesbury, Preston, Lancashire, 10-13 April 1987 / edited by Tim O'Brien. - Preston? : Lancashire Polytechnic, 1987.
81p.
Bibliographies.
ISBN 090669406X

—Patent claim drafting and interpretation / general editor John A. Kemp. - London : Oyez Longman, 1983.
xi,251p; 23cm.
Includes index.
ISBN 0851206859 Unpriced

—Policies with regard to grants to local authorities / report prepared by the Committee of Experts on Local and Regional Finance of the Steering Committee for Regional and Municipal Matters and drafted by J. Lotz, Chairman. - Strasbourg : Council of Europe, 1986.
35p.

—Prison information bulletin / Strasbourg : Council of Europe, 1983.

—Prison regimes / study prepared by the Select Committee of Experts on Prison Regimes and Prison Leave. - Strasbourg : Council of Europe, 1986.
33p. - (CDPC (84) 8 rev. addendum VI).

—Private international law : Council of Europe Conventions on Foreign Money Liabilities(1967) and on the Place of Payment of Money Liabilities (1972) : report on a reference under section 3 (1)(e) of the Law Commissions Act 1965 / the Law Commission and the Scottish Law Commission. - London : H.M.S.O., 1981.
iv,53p; 25cm.
Includes the text of the Conventions.
ISBN 0101831803

—Private international law : foreign money liabilities / the Law Commission. - London : H.M.S.O., 1981.
ix,195p; 22cm. - (Working paper).
ISBN 0117301604

—Private international law - foreign money liabilities : report on a reference under section 3 (1)(e) of the Law Commissions Act 1965 / The Law Commission. - London : H.M.S.O., 1983.
vii,94p; 25cm.
ISBN 0101906404

—Problems encountered by local and regional authorites as a result of their new tasks in respect of environmental protection / report prepared under the guidance of the Committee of Experts on Social and Economic Activities of the Steering Committee for Regional and Municpal Matters by G. Tendron. - Strasbourg : Council of Europe, 1986.
29p.
Bibliography: p.28-29.

—Problems of regional and local authorities involved in planning policies : report / prepared under the guidance of the Committee of Experts on Social and Economic Activities of the Steering Committee for Regional and Municipal Matters by Jacques Robert. - Strasbourg : Council of Europe, 1985.
36p.

—Protection of human rights in Europe / Council of Europe. - New ed. - Strasbourg : Council of Europe, 1983.
16p.

—Protection of human rights in Europe / Council of Europe. - Strasbourg : Council of Europe, 1981.
16p.

—Protection of the individual with reagard sic to the acts of the tax and customs administrations : proceedings of the colloquy organised by the Council of Europe in co-operation with the International Centre of Sociological and Penitentiary Research and Studies in Messina 25-27 March 1986 / Strasbourg : Council of Europe, 1986.
39p.
ISBN 9287108749

—Reforms of local and regional authorities in Europe : theory, practice and critical appraisal : colloquy organised by the Council of Europe, Linz, 5-6 November 1981 / Strasbourg : Council of Europe, 1983.
220p.
Bibliography: p.181-182.
ISBN 9287101914

—Regional and local affairs : news / Strasbourg : Council of Europe, 1982-.
Supersedes: Information bulletin: municipal and regional matters.

—Regional development agencies and peripheral regions : report / prepared under the guidance of the Committee of Experts on Social and Economic Activities of the Steering Committee for Regional and Municipal Matters by Jacques Robert. - Strasbourg : Council of Europe, 1985.
23p.

—Reservation of title : draft Council of Europe Convention (CDCJ(82)15) / memorandum by a Working Party of the Senate of the Inns of Court and the Bar and the Law Society. - London? : the Working Party?, 1983.
4p.
Bound with 'Draft proposal for a Council Directive on the legal consequences of agreements creating simple reservation of title (III/872/79-EN)'.

—Right to liberty and the rights of persons deprived of their liberty as guaranteed by Article 5 of the European Convention on Human Rights / Strasbourg : Council of Europe, 1981.
22p; 30cm.
'Prepared by the Council of Europe Directorate of Human Rights'.

—Right to respect for private and family life, home and correspondence as guaranteed by Article 8 of the European Convention on Human Rights / by Andrew Drzemczewski. - Strasbourg : Council of Europe, Directorate of Human Rights, 1984.
29p.
ISBN 9287103526

—Role of local authorities in promoting the creation or operation of small or medium-sized firms within a general policy of endogenous development / report prepared under the guidance of the Committee of Experts on Social and Economic Activities of the Steering Committee for Regional and Municipal Matters by T. Nuttal. – Strasbourg : Council of Europe, 1986.
31p.
Bibliography: p.28-29.

—Study on common standards for query languages in computerised legal retrieval systems / prepared for the Council of Europe by Werner Robert Svoboda. – Strasbourg : Council of Europe, 1981.
52p.
'Based on a proposal put forward by Working Party No. II of the Committee of Experts on Legal Data Processing' - p.4. At head of cover title: Council of Europe, Legal Affairs.

—Summaries of the judgements delivered in ... / document prepared by the registry of the Court. – v. – Strasbourg : Council of Europe, 1983.
Contains summary judgements not binding on the Court.

—Survey of computing in European local and regional authorities / ... prepared under the guidelines of the Committee of Experts on Management in Local and Regional Government by G.Gaits. – Strasbourg : Council of Europe, 1981.
iii,61p.

—Teaching, research and training in the field of 'computers and the law' : recommendation no. R (80)3 adopted by the Committee of Ministers of the Council of Europe on 30 April 1980 and explanatory memorandum / Council of Europe. – Strasbourg : Council of Europe, 1981.
12p.
'Prepared by the Committee of Experts on Legal Data Processing' - verso t.p.. At head of cover title: Council of Europe, Legal Affairs.

—Texts adopted / Standing Conference of Local and Regional Authorities of Europe : Conference Permanente des Pouvoirs Locaux et Regionaux de l'Europe. – v. – Strasbourg : Council of Europe, 1984.
Continues: Texts adopted / Conference of Local and Regional Authorities of Europe. Parallel English and French texts.

—Use of management techniques in regional and local government : report / prepared under the guidance of the Committee of Experts on Management in Local and Regional Government of the Steering Committee for Regional and Municipal Matters by F. Boersma. – Strasbourg : Council of Europe, 1985.
38p.
Bibliography: p.33.

EUROPE – NORWAY

—Norway and Europe in the 1970's / Oslo : University of Forlag.
289p.

EUROPE, EASTERN

—Legal aspects of doing business in Eastern Europe and the Soviet Union / edited by Dennis Campbell. – Deventer, The Netherlands : Kluwer Law and Taxation Publishers, 1986.
– (International business series).
Includes index and bibliography.
ISBN 9065442634

EUROPEAN COMMUNITIES

—Basic Community cases / Bernard Rudden. – Oxford : Clarendon, 1987.
360p; 24cm.
Includes index.
ISBN 0198762127 Hbk £28.00
ISBN 0198762119 Pbk £11.50

—Basic Community laws / edited by Bernard Rudden and Derrick Wyatt. – 2nd ed. – Oxford : Clarendon, 1986.
xvi,407p.
Previous ed.: 1980.
ISBN 0198761996 Pbk £25.00
ISBN 0198761988 £9.95

—Basic community laws / edited by Bernard Rudden and Derrick Wyatt. – Oxford : Clarendon, 1980.
xv,301p; 24cm.
ISBN 0198761198 Hbk £14.00
ISBN 0198761201 Pbk Unpriced

—European Community law and national law : the irreversible transfer? / John Usher. – London : University Association for Contemporary European Studies, 1981.
96p; 23cm.
Bibliography: p85-91. - Includes index.
ISBN 0043410170 Pbk £6.95
ISBN 0043410189 Unpriced

—European Community Treaties / Edinburgh : W Green, 1983.
– (Encyclopedia of European Community Law Ser.: Vol. 2).

—European Union Treaty / Oxford : Oxford University Press, 1987.
ISBN 0198255489 Hbk £35.00

—European Union treaty : commentary on the draft adopted by the European Parliament on 14 February 1984 / by Francesco Capotorti ... et al. – Oxford : Clarendon, 1986.
xii,327p; 23cm.
Bibliography: p325-327. Translation of: Le Traite d'union europeenne.
ISBN 0198255489 £35.00

—Free movement in European Community law / F. Burrows. – Oxford : Clarendon, 1987.
xxxvii,346p; 24cm.
Bibliography: xxxvii - Includes index.
ISBN 019825492X £35.00

—Future of Europe in a world of change / by Willy Brandt. – Southampton : University of Southampton, 1980.
15p; 21cm. – (Fawley Foundation lectures).
ISBN 0854322108 Pbk Unpriced

—Guide to European Community law / by P.S.R.F. Mathijsen : preface by J.D.B. Mitchell. – 3rd ed. – London : Sweet & Maxwell, 1980.
xxxiii,256p; 23cm.
Previous ed.: 1975. Includes index.
ISBN 0421259000 Hbk £12.95
ISBN 0421259108 Pbk £9.75

—Law of the economy in the European Communities / by D. Lasok with a chapter on agriculture by J.W. Bridge. – London : Butterworths, 1980.
xxxviii,455p; 23cm.
Bibliography: p431-442. - Includes index.
ISBN 0406268967 Hbk £18.95
ISBN 0406268975 Pbk £11.95

—Official Journal of the European Communities / London : HMSO.
– (Ser. L: Legislation, Ser. C: Information and Notices, and Series S: Supplement).

Ser. S: Supplement

—Policy formation in the European Communities : a bibliographic guide to Community documentation 1958-1978 / Michael Hopkins. – London : Mansell, 1981.
xx,339p; 24cm.
Includes index.
ISBN 0720115973 £24.50

—Proceedings of the Court of Justice of the European Communities / Court of Justice of the European Communities. – Luxembourg : Information Office of the Court of Justice of the European Communities, 1975.

—Publications, documentation and means for their dissemination in the Commission of the European Communities / M. Hopkins. – London : British Library, 1981.
iv,28p; 30cm.
ISBN 0905984692 Pbk Unpriced

—Reports of the European Communities 1952-1977 : an index to authors and chairmen / compiled by June Neilson. – London : Mansell, 1981.
xiv,561p; 23cm.
Includes index.
ISBN 0720115922 £27.50

—Select Committee on the European Communities / London : HMSO.
ISBN 0104204826 Hbk £10.00

Report No. 18, 1984

—Select Committee on the European Communities / London : HMSO.
ISBN 0104239867 Hbk £6.50

—Working for Europe : January 1981 - January 1985 / The European Commission. – Luxembourg : Office for Official Publications of the European Communities, 1984.
79p; 25cm.
Preface by Gaston E. Thorn.
ISBN 928254740X

—Prospects for the European Community in 1982 : the Exeter Lecture in European Community law, delivered in the University on 19 February 1982 / by Douglas Hurd. – Exeter : University of Exeter, Centre for European Legal Studies, 1982.
12p.

EUROPEAN COMMUNITY

—Catalogue of Community Legal Acts and Other Texts Relating to the Elimination of Technical Barriers to Trade for Industrial Products and Nomenclature for Iron and Steel Products : December 1983 / Kirchberg : Commission of the European Communities, 1984.
174p.

—Collection of Agreements Concluded By the European Communities / European Communities. – London : HMSO, 1984.
1557p.
ISBN 9282532321 Hbk £37.20

—Collection of the Agreements Concluded by the European Communities / Luxembourg : Office for Official Publications of the European Communities, 1985.
1,136p.
ISBN 9277002034 Hbk

Vol. 11 (1981) Part 2 1985.
xliv, 2,738p.
ISBN 9277002107 Hbk £3,700.00

Vol. 12 (1982) 1986.
xxxvi, 1,482p.
ISBN 9277041137 Hbk £3,800.00

—Collection of the Agreements Concluded by the European Communities : Index and Alphabetical List of Countries and International Organizations, Vol. 1-11 / Luxembourg : Office for Official Publications of the European Communities, 1986.
136p.
ISBN 9282403041 Pbk £200.00

—Common Market law / Alan Campbell. – 4 v. – London : Longmans, 1969.
25cm.
Supplement, published in 1975, assimilated the contents of previous loose-leaf binders. Earlier ed. by Campbell and D.C. Thompson.

—Common Market law review / v. – London : Stevens, 1963.
Index in each vol.
ISBN 00103292

—Draft Treaty Establishing the European Union / Kirchberg : Commission of the European Communities, 1984.
46p.

—European Challenge : 1992 / Wildwood House, 1988.
ISBN 0704506130 Pbk £6.95

—European challenge, 1992 : the benefits of a single market / Paolo Cecchini : with Michel Catinat and Alexis Jacquemin. – English ed. – Aldershot : Gower, 1988.
xxi, 127 p.; 23 cm.
Spine title: 1992, the European challenge. Bibliography: p. 110-111.
ISBN 0704506130 pbk.

—European Community, International Organizations and Multilateral Agreements / European Communities. – 3rd ed. – London : HMSO, 1983.
285p.
Describes relationships established between the European Community and world and regional intergovernmental organisations.
ISBN 9282537757 Pbk £3.90

—European Community Treaties, 3 Vols. / Edinburgh : W Green, 1985.
– (Encyclopedia of European Community Law Ser.).
ISBN 0421193603 loose £170.00

Service for 1985 only (post-free)

—European Community Treaties / Edinburgh : W Green.

—Exclusive Dealing Agreements in the EEC / London : European Law Centre, 1984.
ISBN 090745111X Pbk £17.50

—From nine to twelve : Europe's destiny? / edited by J.W. Schneider. – Alphen aan den Rijn : Sijthoff and Noordhoff, 1980.
xvi,242p.
Publication of the John F. Kennedy Institute, Center for International Studies, Tilburg, The Netherlands..

—Fundamental rights and the EEC / by David Sugarman. – London : Middlesex Polytechnic Faculty of Business Studies and Management, 1981.
34p. – (Working paper).
ISBN 0904804119

—Future of Europe in a world of change / by Willy Brandt. – Southampton : University of Southampton, 1980.
15p; 21cm. – (Fawley Foundation lectures).
ISBN 0854322108 Pbk Unpriced

—Generalised scheme of preferences : a brief summary of the European Community's scheme for 1985 / Department of Trade and Industry. – London : The Department, 1984.
17p.

—Industrial policies in the European Community / Victoria Curzon Price. – London : Macmillan for the Trade Policy Research Centre, 1981.
xvi,141p.
Bibliography: p132-135.
ISBN 0333319117

—Intra-Group Arrangements under Articles 85 and 86 of the Treaty Establishing the European Economic Community : with a Comparative Survey / Bern : Peter Lang, 1984.
xii, 173p.
ISBN 3820451668 Pbk £41.00

—Investing in Europe's future / edited by Arnold Heertje : contributors Michel Albert ... et al. : preface by Yves Le Portz. – Oxford : Blackwell, for the European Investment Bank, 1983.
x,218p; 24cm.
ISBN 0631134050 Unpriced

—Ireland and the European Communities : Ten Years of Membership / Dublin : Gill & MacMillan, 1983.
ISBN 0717113264 Hbk £20.00

—One Europe: one world : a first exploration of Europe's potential contribution to world order / a report by Christopher Layton in conjunction with a gorup sponsored by the Federal Trust for Education and Research, the Wyndham Place Trust and the One World Trust. – London : Journal of World Trade Law, 1986.
70p.
Special supplement no. 4 to the Journal of World Trade Law, vol. 20 (1986).

—Progress of scrutiny / House of Lords Select Committee on the European Communities. – London : H.M.S.O., 1981.
First three reports entitled: Report on the progress of scrutiny.

—Second enlargement of the EEC : the integration of unequal partners / edited by Dudley Seers and Constantine Vaitsos : with the assistance of Marja-Liisa Kiljunen. – London : Macmillan, 1982.
xx,275p; 23cm.
ISBN 0333291891

—Summary of proceedings... / ACP-EEC Joint Assembly. – Luxembourg : Directorate-General for Information and Public Relations, 1985-.
This single new body replaces the two institutions set up under the first two Lome Conventions, i.e. the Consultative Assembly and the Joint Committee. Title varies.

EUROPEAN COMMUNITY – CONSTITUTIONAL LAW

—Duties of national courts under the constitutional law of the European Community / John Temple Lang. – Exeter : University of Exeter, 1987.
40p; 21cm.
The Dominik Lasok lecture in European Community law delivered in the University on 23rd January 1987.

EUROPEAN COMMUNITY – ECONOMIC POLICY

—Economics of the Common Market / Dennis Swann. – 6th ed. – Harmondsworth : Penguin, 1988.
Previous ed.: 1984.
ISBN 0140227814

EUROPEAN COMMUNITY

—Tolley's trading within the European Community : a United Kingdom executive guide / Dennis Evans. – Croydon : Tolley, 1983.
xviii,212p; 30cm.
Bibliography: p206-208. - Includes index. Cover title: Trading within the European Community.
ISBN 085459132X Pbk Unpriced

EUROPEAN COMMUNITY COUNTRIES

—Social policy harmonisation in the European Community / John Holloway. – Farnborough, Hants. : Gower, 1981.
vi,318p; 23cm.
Bibliography: p305-318.
ISBN 0566001969 £10.50

EUROPEAN COMMUNITY LAW

—Basic Community Cases / Oxford : Oxford University Press, 1987.
ISBN 0198762127 Hbk £30.00

—Basic Community Laws / Wyatt. – 2nd ed. – Oxford : Oxford University Press, 1986.
ISBN 0198761988 Pbk £9.95
ISBN 0198761996 Hbk £25.00

—Community Law / Luxembourg : Office for Official Publications of the European Communities, 1985.
29p.
Covers the general principles of Community Law, its structures and powers and its relationship with national law.
ISBN 9282552438 Pbk £140.00

—Community Law / Luxembourg : Office for Official Publications of the European Communities, 1987.
33p.
ISBN 9282569489 Pbk £150.00

—Community Law / Luxembourg : Office for Official Publications of the European Communities, 1986.
39p.
ISBN 9282562247 Pbk £150.00

—Community Law : Offprint from the Sixteenth General Report on the Activities of the European Communities / European Communities. – London : HMSO, 1983.
ISBN 9282534812 Hbk £1.40

—Community Secondary Legislation / Edinburgh : W Green, 1983.
– (Encyclopedia of European Community Law Ser.: Vol. 3).

Service only

—Digest of Case-Law Relating to the European Communities / Kirchberg : Commission of the European Communities, 1984.
– (D Ser.: Case-Law on the Convention of 27 September 1968).

—Digest of Case-Law Relating to the European Communities / Kirchberg : Commission of the European Communities, 1983.
1400p. – (A Ser.: Judgements of the Court of Justice of the European Communities).

—Directory of Community Legislation in Force / 1985 / Luxembourg : Office for Official Publications of the European Communities, 1985.
758p.
ISBN 9282548171 Pbk £2,500.00 (Vols. 1 and 2 together)

Vol. 1: Analytical Register 1985.
ISBN 9282548031

Vol. 2: Chronological and Alphabetical Indexes 1985.
ISBN 9282548104

Vol. 3: Addendum 1985.
ISBN 9282549313 free to purchasers of Vols. 1 and 2

—Directory of Community Legislation in Force / 1986 /. – Luxembourg : Office for Official Publications of the European Communities, 1986.
859p.
ISBN 9282552136 Pbk £2,700.00 (Vols. 1 and 2 together)

Vol. 1: Analytical Register 1986.
ISBN 9282551997

Vol. 2: Chronological and Alphabetical Indexes 1986.
ISBN 9282552063

—Directory of Community Legislation in Force / 1987 /. – Luxembourg : Office for Official Publications of the European Communities, 1987.
746p.
ISBN 9282570967 Pbk £2,800.00 (Vols. 1 and 2 together)

Vol. 1: Analytical Register 1987.
ISBN 9282570789

Vol. 2: Chronological and Alphabetical Indexes 1987.
ISBN 9282570878

—Encyclopedia of European Community Law : Volume B : European Community Treaties / Edinburgh : W Green.

Service

—European Community Law : Encyclopedia of, 3 Vols. / Abingdon : Professional Books.

Vol. B. European Community Treaties

Vol. C. Community Secondary Legislation

—European Community law in the United Kingdom / Lawrence Collins. – 3rd ed. – London : Butterworths, 1984.
xxxvi,233p; 22cm.
Previous ed.: 1980. Includes index.
ISBN 040626922X Hbk No price
ISBN 0406269238 Pbk No price

—Foundations of European community law : an introduction to the constitutional and administrative law of the European Community / by T.C. Hartley. – 2nd ed. – Oxford : Clarendon Press, 1988.
li,496p.
Includes bibliographies and index. Revised from the 1981 edition. Discusses the basic principles of European Community law and examines aspects of interes to lawyers. The new edition takes into account changes in treaty, statute and case law since 1981.
ISBN 0198762070 Pbk £17.95
ISBN 0198762089 Hbk £40

—General principles of EEC law and the individual / Leicester : Leicester University Press, 1989.
320.
Examines the tendency for the European Court to go beyond the application of the written law to regulate the trading of corporations within member states and to apply general principles of law to individual's grievances.
ISBN 0718513193 Hbk £45

—Guide to European Community law / by P.S.R.F. Mathijsen. – 4th ed. – London : Sweet & Maxwell, 1985.
xl,284p; 22cm.
Previous ed.: 1980. Includes bibliographies and index. Includes index.
ISBN 0421339306 Pbk £16.50
ISBN 0421339209 Hbk £22

—Introduction to the law and institutions of the European Communities / by D. Lasok and J.W. Bridge. – 3rd ed. – London : Butterworths, 1982.
lvi, 453p.
Includes index. Bibliography: p422-436.
ISBN 0406268940

—Introduction to the law and instsitutions of the European Communities / Bridge. – 4th ed. – London : Butterworths, 1987.
ISBN 0406268800 Hbk £28.00
ISBN 0406268819 Pbk £21.95

—Law and institutions of the European Communities / D. Lasok, J.W. Bridge. – 4th ed. – London : Butterworths, 1987.
570p; 22cm.
Previous ed.: published as An introduction to the law and institutions of the European communities. 1982. Includes index.
ISBN 0406268800 Hbk £23.00 :
ISBN 0406268819 Pbk £16.00

—Law of Collective Agreements in the Countries of the European Community / Kirchberg : Commission of the European Communities.
47p.

—Law of the European Communities, 2 Vols. / London : Butterworths, 1986.
ISBN 0406003009 Hbk £140.00

—Parallel imports / Oxford : Blackwell Scientific, 1987.
ISBN 0003833666 Hbk £20.00

—Practical approach to EEC Law / London : Financial Training, 1988.
ISBN 1851850988 Pbk £14.95

—Register of Current Community Legal Instruments, 2 Vols. / European Communities. – London : HMSO.
ISBN 9282536580 Hbk £30.50

—Thirty Years of Community Law : European Perspectives / Kirchberg : Commission of the European Communities.
498p.

—Treaties Establishing the European Communities Amending Treaties : Other Basic Instruments / abr. ed. – Kirchberg : Commission of the European Communities, 1983.
542p.

—United Kingdom Sources / Edinburgh : W Green.

—Vocabulary of Community Primary Law / Kirchberg : Commission of the European Communities.
427p.

EUROPEAN COMMUNITY LAW – GREAT BRITAIN

—European Community Law in the UK / 3rd ed. – London : Butterworths, 1984.
ISBN 040626922X Hbk £17.50
ISBN 0406269238 Pbk £13.95

EUROPEAN COMMUNITY LAW – IRELAND

—EEC Law in Ireland / London : Butterworths, 1988.
ISBN 0862052378 Hbk £35.00

EUROPEAN CONVENTION ON HUMAN RIGHTS

—Collected Edition of the 'Travaux Preparatoires' of the European Convention on Human Rights /. – Dordrecht : Kluwer, 1985.
318p.
ISBN 9024722306 Hbk Gld175.00

Vol. 7 1985.
347p.
ISBN 9024728924 Hbk Gld225.00

Vol. 8 1985.
221p.
ISBN 9024728932 Hbk Gld175.00

—Dynamics of Development in the European Human Rights Convention System / Dordrecht : Kluwer, 1981.
192p.
ISBN 9024725461 Hbk £100.00

—European Convention of Human Rights / 2nd ed. – Oxford : Oxford University Press, 1987.
ISBN 00198255098 Pbk £15.00
ISBN 00198255101 Hbk £35.00

—European Convention on Human Rights : Cases and Materials / 4th ed. – Cologne : Carl Heymanns Verlag, 1981.
440p.

—Sixth International Colloquy About the European Convention of Human Rights / Council of Europe. – Dordrecht : Kluwer, 1987.
1,168p.
ISBN 9024735394 Hbk £550.00

—Yearbook of the European Convention on Human Rights /. – Dordrecht : Kluwer, 1980.
xvii, 688p.
ISBN 9024723833 Hbk Gld275.00

Vol. 23 (1980) 1982.
766p.
ISBN 9024727170 Hbk Gld320.00

Vol. 24 (1981) 1983.
602p.
ISBN 9024727227 Hbk Gld255.00

Vol. 25 (1982) 1986.
896p.
ISBN 902473262X Hbk Gld395.00

Vol. 26 (1983) 1987.
860p.
ISBN 9024732638 Hbk Gld425.00

EUROPEAN COOPERATION

—Belgrade and beyond : the CSCE process in perspective / edited by Nils Andren and Karl E. Birnbaum. – Alphen aan den Rijn : Sijthoff & Noordhoff, 1980.
xi,180p.
ISBN 902860250X

—Making European Policies Work / Ziller. – Sage Publications, 1988.
ISBN 0803981376 Hbk £25.00

—Growing together / European Parliament, Directorate General for Research and Documentation. – Luxembourg : The Directorate, 1982.
56p.

EUROPEAN COURT OF JUSTICE

—Court of Justice of the European Communities / Luxembourg : Office for Official Publications of the European Communities, 1985.

—Court of Justice of the European Communities : References for Preliminary Rulings Under Article 177 of the E.E.C. Treaty and Cooperation between the Court and National Courts / Luxembourg : Office for Official Publications of the European Communities, 1986.
47p.

—Court of Justice of the European Community / 4th ed. – Luxembourg : Office for Official Publications of the European Communities, 1987.
91p.
ISBN 9282566048 Hbk free

—European Court of Justice Practice and Procedure / London : Butterworths, 1984.
ISBN 040626810X Hbk £56.00

—European Court of Justice Reporter / Oxford : ESC Publishing Ltd, 1982.

—Formal Sittings of the Court of Justice of the European Communities 1982 and 1983 / Kirchberg : Commission of the European Communities, 1984.
64p.

—Pleading Before the Court of Justice of the European Communities : The Law Society's European Group / London : Law Society.

—Proceedings of the Court of Justice of the European Communities / Kirchberg : Commission of the European Communities.
10p.

—Synopsis of the Work of the Court of Justice of the European Communities in 1984 and 1985 : and Record of Formal Sittings in 1984 and 1985 / Luxembourg : Office for Official Publications of the European Communities, 1987.
177p.
ISBN 9282901416 Pbk

EUROPEAN FEDERATION

—Belgium and the draft treaty establishing the European Union / by Jan de Meyer. – Florence : European University Institute, 1985.
38p.

—Creation of the European Union and its relation to the EEC treaties / by Joseph Weiler and James Modrall. – Florence : European University Institute, 1985.
44p.

—Draft Treaty establishing the European Union and the member states : Ireland / by John Temple-Lang. – Florence : European University Institute, 1985.
38,5p.

—Draft Treaty establishing the European Union : constitutional and political implications in Denmark / by Per Lachmann. – Badia Fiesolana : European University Institute, 1985.
39p.
Paper presented at a conference organised by the European Policy Unit of the European University Institute, in collaboration with the University of Strasbourg and TEPSA, October 1984.

—Draft Treaty establishing the European Union : report on the Federal Republic of Germany / by Carl Otto Lenz. – Florence : European University Institute, 1985.
21p.

—Draft Treaty establishing the European Union : report on the United Kingdom / by David Edward, Richard McAllister, Robert Lane. – Florence : European University Institute, 1985.
40p.

—Economic and social powers of the European Union and the member states : subordinate or coordinate relationship? / by John Pinder. – Florence : European University Institute, 1985.
47p.

—European Communities and the proposed European Union / by rstrom Mller. – Florence : European University Institute, 1985.
53p.

—European integration : select international bibliography of theses and dissertations Europaische Integration : Internationales Auswahlverzeichnis von Dissertationen und Diplomarbeiten Integration europeenne : bibliographie internationale selective de theses et memoires, 1957-1980 / J.P. Siemers, E.H. Siemers-Hidma : preface, Ralf Dahrendorf. – 2nd rev. and enl. ed. – The Hague : Martinus Nijhoff, 1981.
xx, 412 p.; 24 cm.
English, French, German, and Italian. Includes indexes.
ISBN 9024725429

—European law review / v. – London : Sweet & Maxwell, 1975.
Index in each vol.
ISBN 03075400

—European union : one character in search of an author / by Giulio Andreotti. – Luxembourg : Office for Official Publications of the European Communities, 1985.
24p.

—European union or decline : to be or not to be / by Gaston Thorn. – Luxembourg : Office for Official Publications of the European Communities, 1984.
23p; 23cm.
Seventh Jean Monnet lecture delivered at the European University Institute, Florence, 24 May 1984.

—Ever closer union : a critical analysis of the draft treaty establishing the European Union / Roland Bieber, Jean-Paul Jacque, Joseph H. H. Weiler. – Luxembourg : Office for Official Publications of the European Communities, 1985.
345p.
At head of title page: Commission of the European Communities.
ISBN 9282552209

—Foreign affairs, powers and policy in the draft treaty establishing the European Union / by Peter Bruckner. – Florence : European University Institute, 1985.
30p.

—Institutions and the decision-making process in the draft treaty / by Gianfranco Pasquino and Luciano Bardi. – Florence : European University Institute, 1985.
66p.

—Institutions and the decision-making process in the Draft Treaty establishing the European Union / by Roland Bieber. – Badia Fiesolana : European University Institute, 1985.
26,3p.
Paper presented at a conference organised by the European Policy Unit of the European University Institute, in colloboration with the University of Strasbourg and TEPSA, October 1984. Includes bibliographical references.

—Integration through law : Europe and the American federal experience : a series / under the general editorship of Mauro Cappelletti, Monica Seccombe, Joseph Weiler. – 3 v. – Berlin, : W. de Gruyter, 1986.
– (Series A, Law).
Includes bibliographical references and index. Contents: bk.1. A political, legal and economic overview - bk.2. Political organs, integration techniques and judicial process - bk.3. Forces and potential for a European identity.

Vol. 2 : Environmental protection policy : by Eckard Rehbinder and Richard Stewart : associate editor Patrick del Duca / under the general editorship of Mauro Cappelletti, Monica Seccombe, Joseph Weiler. – 1985.
xxiv,350p. – (Series A, Law).
Includes bibliographical references and indexes.

Vol. 5 : The legal integration of energy markets : by Terence Daintith and Stephen F. Williams / under the general editorship of Mauro Cappelletti, Monica Seccombe, Joseph Weiler. – 1987.
xxvii,176p. – (Series A, Law).
Includes bibliographical references and index.
ISBN 3110107430 Hbk

—Judicial system envisaged in the draft treaty / by Thijmen Koopmans. – Florence : European University Institute, 1985.
57p.

—Legal issues of European integration / v. – Deventer : Kluwer, 1974-.
Law review of the Europa Instituut, University of Amsterdam.

—Single act and Europe : a moment of truth / by Jacques Delors. – Luxembourg : Office for Official Publications of the European Communities, 1986.
37p.

—Single European Act / and, Final Act. – Luxembourg : Office for Official Publications of the European Communities, 1986.
v, 76p.
Title on cover: Single European Act.
ISBN 9282403289

—Texts adopted for transmission to national parliaments / Assembly of Western European Union. – v. – Paris : The Assembly, 1955.
From 22nd session, entitled: Texts adopted and brief account of the session. Some parts in French.

—Towards the European union : Florence, 13 June 1983 / by Altiero Spinelli. – Luxembourg : Office for Official Publications of the European Communities, 1983.
28p.

EUROPEAN PARLIAMENT

—Amendments to the 1978 Edition of the 'Treaties Establishing the European Communities' / Kirchberg : Commission of the European Communities, 1982.
32p.

—Europe Elects Its Parliament / London : Policy Studies Institute, 1980.
ISBN 0853741832 Pbk £2.50

—European Parliament / Kirchberg : Commission of the European Communities, 1984.
24p.

—European Parliament and Article 173 of the EEC Treaty / by John Barnard. – Florence : European University Institute, 1987.
59p.

—European Parliament : Its Powers / Kirchberg : Commission of the European Communities, 1983.
22p.

—Fact Sheets on the European Parliament and the Activities of the European Community / European Parliament-Directorate General for Research. – 2nd ed. – Kirchberg : European Parliament, 1989.
ISBN 9282301265 Hbk

—Forging ahead : thirty years of the European Parliament 1952- 1982 / European Parliament. – S.l. : Directorate-General for Research and Documentation, 1982.
237p.
Bibliography: p.215-220. - Includes index.

—Growing Together : European Parliament Resolutions on Inter-Institutional Relations / European Parliament, Directorate General for Research. – Kirchberg : European Parliament, 1983.

—Official Handbook of the European Parliament-1984 / Kirchberg : Commission of the European Communities, 1985.
333p.

—Rules of procedure / European Parliament. – Strasbourg : European Parliament, 1981.
108p.

EUTHANASIA

—Ending Lives / Collinson. – Oxford : Blackwell Scientific, 1988.
ISBN 0631153314 Pbk £6.95

—Medical treatment for the dying / the Law Reform Commission of Western Australia. – Perth : the Commission, 1988.
66p. – (Discussion paper).

EVICTION

—Quest for security : employees, tenants, wives / by Tony Honore. – London : Stevens, 1982.
xiv,128p; 19cm.
Includes index.
ISBN 0420464107 Hbk £12.00
ISBN 0420464204 Pbk £5.80

EVICTION - ENGLAND

—Quiet enjoyment : remedies for harassment and illegal eviction / by Andrew Arden and Martin Partington. Edited by S. Carrott and C. Hunter. – 3rd. – London : Legal Action Group, 1990.
127.
Includes index.
ISBN 0905099265 Pbk £11

EVICTION - INDIA

—Commentaries on Uttar Pradesh Public Premises (Eviction of Unauthorised Occupants) Act, 1972 / 2nd ed. – Lucknow : Eastern Book Company, 1983.
154p.

EVICTION - NORTHERN IRELAND

—Ejectment for non-payment of rent / by J. A. Dowling : with a supplement for the Republic of Ireland by G. McCormack. - Belfast : Faculty of Law, the Queen's University of Belfast, 1986.
xvii,84p.
ISBN 0853892695

EVICTION - SCOTLAND

—Research paper on actions of ejection and removing / by A.G.M. Duncan. - Edinburgh : Law Commission, 1984.
xv,204p.
'Published by the Scottish Law Commission in connection with Consultative Memorandum No. 59'. Includes bibliographical references.

EVIDENCE

—Crime, proof and punishment : essays in memory of Sir Rupert Cross / Rupert Cross, Colin Tapper. - London : Butterworths, 1981.
xxvi,336p; 26cm.
Bibliography of works by Sir Rupert Cross: p.323-327. - Includes index. Edited by Colin Tapper.
ISBN 0406569991

—Evidence and advocacy / Peter Murphy and David Barnard. - London : Financial Training, 1984.
vii,199p; 22cm. - (Temple lectures).
ISBN 0906322197

—Evidence, proof and probability / Sir Richard Eggleston. - 2nd ed. - London : Weidenfeld and Nicolson, 1983.
xiv,274p; 22cm.
Previous ed.: 1978. Bibliography: p262-266. - Includes index.
ISBN 0297782622 Hbk £16.50
ISBN 0297782630 Pbk £7.95

—Facts in law / Association for legal and social philosophy : ninth annual conference at Hatfield College, University of Durham, 2nd-4th April 1982 : edited by William Twining. - Wiesbaden : Franz Steiner, 1983.
ix,157p.
Bibliography: p156-157.
ISBN 3515038973

—Hague Convention on the Taking of Evidence Abroad : explanatory documentation prepared for Commonwealth jurisdicitons / by David McClean and Campbell McLachlan : in association with the Commonwealth Secretariat. - Revised. - London : Commonwealth Secretariat, 1986.
30,16p.
Includes the text of the Convention.
ISBN 0850922879

—Hearken to the Evidence / Stittsville : Canada's Wings, 1983.
254p.
ISBN 0920002242 Hbk £18.95

—Note on the operation of the Hague Convention of 18 March 1970 on the taking of evidence abroad in civil or commercial matters / drawn up by the Permanent Bureau of the Hague Conference on Private International Law. - 1. - The Hague : The Bureau, 1985.
various pagings. - (Preliminary document).
Added title in French. English and French parallel texts.

—Outline of the law of evidence / by Sir Rupert Cross and Nancy Wilkins. - 5th ed. - London : Butterworths, 1980.
xxv,336p.
Previous ed.: 1975. Northern Ireland supplement 1983, held.
ISBN 0406570671

—Phipson on evidence / Richard May, M.N Howard. - 13th. - London : Sweet & Maxwell, 1982 & 1987.
- (Common Law Library).
Includes changes in the chapters which deal with problems that regularly arise in modern civil and criminal legislation, and new material in the chapters on confessions and the course of the trial. Extra sections have been added to the chapters on public policy and privilege.
ISBN 0421269901 Hbk £108
ISBN 042137070X SUPPLEMENT £9

—Probability Theory and Circumstantial Evidence / Oslo : Norwegian University Press, 1983.
38p.
ISBN 8200067467 Hbk £23.00

—Study in Law of Evidence / Lucknow : Eastern Book Company, 1982.
292p.

—Theories of evidence : Bentham and Wigmore / William Twining. - London : Weidenfeld & Nicolson, 1985.
x,265p.
Includes bibliographical references and index.
ISBN 0297786687

—Well and truly tried : essays on evidence in honour of Sir Richard Eggleston / edited by Enid Campbell and Louis Waller, assisted by Gretchen Kewley. - Sydney : Law Book Company, 1982.
xxxvi,307p.
Bibliography: p8-9.
ISBN 0455204470 Hbk £30

EVIDENCE - AUSTRALIA

—Australian Evidence / Butterworths, 1988.
443p.
ISBN 0409493562 Hbk £65.00
ISBN 0409493287 Pbk £42.50

—Australian Evidence / Sydney : Butterworths, 1988.
488p.

—Australian Evidence Cases and Commentary / Butterworths, 1988.
732p.
ISBN 040949447X Pbk £65.00

—Australian Evidence : Cases and Commentary / Sydney : Butterworths, 1988.
608p.
This casebook contains materials on the burden of proof, circumstantial evidence, witnesses, judicial discretion, hearsay, res gestae, admissions, and other topics.

—Cases and Materials on Evidence / C.R. Williams. - 2nd ed. - North Ryde : Law Book Co, 1985.
iii, 860p.
ISBN 0455205671 Hbk £75.00
ISBN 045520568X Pbk £57.50

—Cases on evidence in Australia / by Eric J. Edwards. - 3rd ed. - Sydney : Law Book Co., 1981.
xxix,795p.
Includes index.
ISBN 0455202443 Pbk
ISBN 0455202435

—Cross on Evidence : with Supplement 1980 / D. Byrne. - 3rd ed. - Butterworths, 1986.
734p.
ISBN 040949139X Hbk £89.00
ISBN 0409491489 Pbk £65.00

—Evidence / Australian Law Reform Commission. - Sydney : The Commission, 1981.
xiii,468p.

Research paper no. 2 : Common law evidence : areas of disagreement and uncertainty / Australian Law Reform Commission. - 1981.
viii,233p.
Bibliography: p.228-233.

—Evidence / Law Reform Commission. - 2 v. - Canberra : Australian Government Publishing Service, 1985.
- (Report).
Interim report.
ISBN 0644013028

—Evidence /. - North Ryde : Law Book Co, 1984.
x, 78p.
ISBN 0455203423

—Evidence / Law Reform Commission. - Canberra : Australian Government Publishing Service, 1987.
xliii,320p. - (Report).
Includes index.
ISBN 0644013710

—Evidence and Advocacy / Butterworths, 1988.
327p.
ISBN 040949349X Hbk £59.00

—Evidence and Advocacy / Sydney : Butterworths, 1988.
360p.

—Evidence law reform stage 2 / Sydney : Law Reform Commission, 1985.
18p. - (Discussion paper).

—Evidence reference / Australian Law Reform Commission. - Sydney : The Commission, 1982.
vii,154p.
Includes bibliographical references.

Research paper no. 13 : Opinion evidence / Australian Law Reform Commission. - 1983.
xiv,340p.
Bibliography: p.328-340.

Research paper no. 14 : Aspects of proof / Australian Law Reform Commission. - 1983.
xxi,119p.
Includes bibliographical references.

Research paper no. 6 : Sworn and unsworn evidence / Australian Law Reform Commission. - 1982.
vii,133p.
Includes bibliographical references.

Research paper no. 7 : Relevance / Australian Law Reform Commission. - 1982.
iv,80p.
Includes bibliographical references.

Research paper no. 8 : Manner of giving evidence / Australian Law Reform Commission. - 1982.
x,255p.
Includes bibliographical references.

—Law of Evidence in Australia / Woolloomooloo : International Business Communications, 1987.
650p.
ISBN 0949553360 Hbk £85.00

—Law of Evidence in Australia / London : Legal Books, 1987.
ISBN 0949553360 Hbk £45.00
ISBN 0959553395 Pbk £30.00

—Litigation : Evidence and Procedure / 4th ed. - Butterworths, 1988.
1,108p.
ISBN 0409495077 Hbk £60.00

—Principles of evidence / 3rd ed. - North Ryde : Law Book Co, 1985.
ISBN 0455206139 Pbk £12.50
ISBN 0455206147 Hbk £19.00

—Principles of Evidence / 3rd ed. - North Ryde : Law Book Co, 1985.
322p.
ISBN 0455206139 Pbk £27.50
ISBN 0455206147 Hbk £41.50

EVIDENCE - AUSTRALIA - NEW SOUTH WALES

—Evidence report / New South Wales Law Reform Commission. - Sydney : Government Printer, 1988.
xv,179p. - (L.R.C.).
Includes text of draft bill.
ISBN 0730555410

EVIDENCE - AUSTRALIA - QUEENSLAND

—Evidence in Queensland : the Statute Law / North Ryde : Law Book Co, 1986.
xxxix, 236p.
ISBN 045520618X Pbk £32.50

EVIDENCE - AUSTRALIA - SOUTH AUSTRALIA

—Report ... relating to civil actions for perjury committed in criminal proceedings and to the tort of malicious prosecution / Law Reform Committee of South Australia. - Adelaide : Government Printer, 1984.
13p. - (83rd report).
Bibliography: p.14.

EVIDENCE - AUSTRALIA - TASMANIA

—Report on the rule in Hollington v. Hewthorn / Law Reform Commission of Tasmania. - Hobart : Government Printer, 1982.
7p. - (Report v no 29).

EVIDENCE - CANADA

—Actuarial Evidence / 2nd ed. - Agincourt : Carswell, 1986.
ISBN 045939530 Hbk £18.50

—Civil Evidence Handbook / Agincourt : Carswell, 1987.
520p.

—Civil Evidence Handbook / Agincourt : Carswell, 1987.
520p.
This text contains the Evidence Acts and the Canada Evidence Acts. Topics include admissibility, relevance, burden of proof, presumption, judicial notice, competence and compellability, pleadings, interpreters, examination in chief, impeaching your own witness, cross examination, re-examination, reply evidence, experts, parole evidence rule, hearsay, exceptions to the hearsay rule, and demonstrative evidence.

—Criminal Law Evidence, Practice and Procedure / Agincourt : Carswell, 1988.
606p.

—Evidence / Vancouver : Continuing Legal Education Society of British Columbia, 1987.
230p.
ISBN 0865043078 Hbk £70.00

—Evidence in the litigation process / by Stanley A. Schiff. - 2nd ed. 2. - Toronto : Carswell, 1983.
xxxiv,1211p.
Previous ed.: 1978. Includes bibliographical references and index.
ISBN 045935650X

—Evidence : Principles and Problems / Agincourt : Carswell, 1984.
416p.
This textbook explores the historical background of existing Canadian Rules of Evidence and analyzes the rules in terms of underlying policy considerations. Numerous concrete examples drawn from hypothetical fact situations illustrate the general principles of the rules of evidence.

—Evidence : Principles and Problems / Agincourt : Carswell, 1984.
ISBN 0459364200 Hbk £34.50

—Law in transition : evidence / Don Mills : R. De Boo, 1984.
196p.
Includes bibliographical references and index.
ISBN 0888201877

—Practical Application of Evidence : Materials Prepared for a Continuing Legal Education Seminar Held in Vancouver, B.C., February 19, 1983 / Thomas J. Chamber. – Vancouver : British Columbia Continuing Legal Education Society, 1983.
ISBN 0865041024 Hbk

—Psycholinguistic Principles Applicable to the Formulation of Jury Instructions : an Annotated Bibliography / Ottawa : Canadian Law Information Council, 1985.
60p.
ISBN 0920358853 Pbk £5.00

—Recent Developments in the Law of Evidence / Taylor. – Toronto : Butterworths, 1980.
116p.
ISBN 0409988324 Pbk £9.95

—Report of the Federal/Provincial Task Force on Uniform Rules of Evidence / prepared for the Uniform Law Conference of Canada. – Toronto, Canada : Carswell, 1982.
xxxiv, 615 p.; 26 cm.
Includes bibliographical references, legislation, and indexes.
ISBN 0459349309

—Statements By An Accused / Vancouver : British Columbia Continuing Legal Education Society, 1981.
252p.
ISBN 0865040214 Hbk £45.00

—Uniform Rules of Evidence : Report of the Federal-Provincial Task Force / Carswell Legal Publications. – Agincourt : Carswell, 1982.
650p.
This report contains a complete statement of the current Canadian law of evidence, with proposals for reform.

EVIDENCE - CANADA - ALBERTA

—Evidence and related subjects : specific proposals for Alberta legislation / Institute of Law Research and Reform. – Edmonton : The Institute, 1982.
iii,177p. – (Report).

—Uniform Evidence Act 1981 : a basis for uniform evidence legislation / Institute of Law Research and Reform. – Edmonton : The Institute, 1982.
ii,109p. – (Report).

EVIDENCE - COMMONWEALTH

—Civil procedure including courts and evidence / J. M. Jacob. – 1. – London : Butterworths, 1966.
various pagings.
Photocopies of articles from Annual survey of Commonwealth Law 1965-1977 bound together in one volume. Includes bibliographical references. 1972 article onwards by I.H. Jacob and J.M. Jacob. 1976 and 1977 articles entitled: Civil procedure including courts.

EVIDENCE - ENGLAND

—Computer generated output as admissible evidence in civil and criminal cases : a report / by the Professional Advisory Committee of the British Computer Society : edited by T.R.H. Sizer and A. Kelman. – London : Heyden on behalf of the British Computer Society, 1982.
x,41p.
ISBN 0855017414

—Computer in court : a guide to computer evidence for lawyers and computing professionals / Alistair Kelman, Richard Sizer. – Aldershot : Gower, 1982.
viii,104p; 22cm.
Bibliography: p99. - Includes index.
ISBN 0566034190 Unpriced

—Elliott and Phipson manual of the law of evidence / D. W. Elliott, Sidney L. Phipson. – 12th ed. – London : Sweet & Maxwell, 1987.
380p; 24cm.
Previous ed.: published as Phipson and Elliott manual of the law of evidence. 1980. Includes index.
ISBN 0421338105 Hbk £20.00 (Apr.)
ISBN 0421338202 Pbk £15.00

—Evidence & advocacy / Peter Murphy and David Barnard. – 2nd ed. – London : Published for Temple Lectures by Financial Training, 1986.
xi,227p; 22cm.
Previous ed.: 1984. Includes index.
ISBN 0906322960 Pbk £7.95

—Evidence and procedure in the Magistrates' Court / P.J. Rowe, S.J. Knapp. – London : Oyez Longman, 1982.
xxx,220p; 22cm.
Includes index.
ISBN 0851206697 Pbk Unpriced

—Evidence : cases and argument / Peter Murphy and John Beaumont. – London : Financial Training, 1982.
xxv,469p; 23cm.
ISBN 0906322103

—Evidence : cases and materials / J.D. Heydon. – 2nd ed. – London : Butterworths, 1984.
510p.
Previous ed: published as Cases and materials on evidence. 1975. Includes index.
ISBN 0406594872 Hbk No price
ISBN 0406594880 Pbk No price

—Evidence in a nutshell / Stephen Seabrooke. – London : Sweet & Maxwell, 1981.
vii,84p; 18cm. – (New nutshells).
Includes index.
ISBN 042127820X Pbk £1.75

—Law of contract : the parol evidence rule / the Law Commission. – London : H.M.S.O., 1986.
iv,31p.
ISBN 0101970005

—Line of the law of evidence / Cross and Wilkins. – 6th ed. – London : Butterworths, 1986.
xxix,307p; 22cm.
Previous ed.: 1980. Includes index.
ISBN 0406570809 Hbk £14.00
ISBN 0406570817 Pbk £10.95

—Modern law of evidence / by Adrian Keane. – Abingdon : Professional Books, 1985.
lxv,544p.
ISBN 0862051037 Pbk
ISBN 0862051045

—Phipson on evidence / John Huxley Buzzard, Richard May, M. N. Howard. – 13th ed. – London : Sweet & Maxwell, 1982.
ccvi,1166p; 26cm.
ISBN 0421269901 £65.00

—Practical approach to evidence / Peter Murphy. – 2nd ed. – London : Financial Training, 1985.
xliv,477p; 24cm.
Previous ed.: 1980. Includes index.
ISBN 0906322693 Pbk £11.95

—Role of psychiatric reports in the Crown Court trial processes / Leicester : Leicester Polytechnic Law School, 1986.
21p. – (Leicester Polytechnic Law School monographs).
Includes bibliographical references.
ISBN 0948997303

—Use of video technology at trials of alleged child abusers / Home Office. – London : Home Office, 1987.
14p.
ISBN 0862522749

EVIDENCE - GREAT BRITAIN

—Archbold : Pleading, Evidence, and Practice in Criminal Cases / 41st ed. – London : Sweet & Maxwell, 1983.
Fourth cumulative supplement
ISBN 0421273909 Pbk

—Cases and Materials On Evidence / Williams. – 2nd ed. – London : Law Book Co, 1985.
ISBN 0455205671 Hbk £37.50
ISBN 045520568X Pbk £27.50

—Criminal Evidence and Procedure, No. 2 / Wilkie. – 7th ed. – London : Butterworths, 1981. – (Police Promotion Handbooks Ser.).
This work for United Kingdom police officers covers the basic rules of criminal evidence and procedure from the perspective of the officer working in the field.*Police officers*
ISBN 0406841314 Pbk

—Criminal Law, No. 1 / Wilkie. – 6th ed. – London : Butterworths, 1980.
– (Police Promotion Handbooks Ser.).
This work for United Kingdom police officers presents the changes in criminal law brought about by the Theft Act of 1978 and the Criminal Evidence Act of 1979.
Police officers
ISBN 0406841217 Pbk

—Digest of the Law of Evidence on the Trial of Civil Actions (Nisi Prius) 5th ed. / Repr. of 1839 ed. – Abingdon : Professional Books.
306p.

—Evidence / 6th ed. – London : Butterworths, 1985.
ISBN 0406570078 Pbk £21.95

—Evidence and Advocacy / Barnard. – 2nd ed. – London : Blackstone Press, 1986.
ISBN 0906322960 Pbk £8.95

—Evidence and Procedure in Magistrates Courts / Knapp. – 2nd ed. – London : Longman Professional, 1985.
ISBN 0851208681 Pbk £19.95

—Evidence and Procedure in Magistrates' Courts / Stephen Knapp. – London : Oyez Longman, 1982.
– (Oyez Longman Practitioner Ser.).
ISBN 0851202926 Hbk £12.95

—Evidence : Cases and Materials / 2nd ed. – London : Butterworths, 1984.
ISBN 0406594880 Pbk £18.95

—Evidence Law and Practice / Clegg. – 2nd ed. – London : Longman Professional, 1985.
ISBN 0851213502 Pbk £15.95

—Evidence : Material for Discussion / Beaumont. – 2nd ed. – London : Blackstone Press, 1987.
ISBN 0906322979 Pbk £18.95

—Law of Evidence / 13th ed. – London : Sweet & Maxwell, 1982.
– (Common Law Library : No. 10).
Supplement only

—Law of Evidence / Plymouth : Macdonald & Evans, 1985.
288p.
ISBN 0712106758 Hbk £5.95

—Law of Evidence / McGechan. – 7th ed. – London : Butterworths, 1984.
ISBN 0409601314 Hbk £34.60
ISBN 0409701742 Pbk £29.10

—Law of Evidence / 2nd ed. – Plymouth : Macdonald & Evans, 1986.
ISBN 0712106758 Pbk £6.50

—Law of Evidence / Beaumont. – London : Financial Training, 1985.
– (SWOT).
ISBN 090632274X Pbk £7.50

—Litigation - Evidence and Procedure / Reaburn. – 3rd ed. – London : Butterworths, 1982.
ISBN 0409307947 Pbk £40.00

—Modern law of evidence / London : Butterworths, 1985.
ISBN 0862051037 Hbk £22.50
ISBN 0862051045 Pbk £11.95

—Notes taken at the time / London : Police Review, 1983.
ISBN 0851640552 Pbk £2.50

—Notes Taken at the Time / London : Police Review Publishing, 1983.
ISBN 0851640052 Pbk £2.50

—Outline of the law of evidence / Wilkins. – 6th ed. – London : Butterworths, 1986.
ISBN 0406570809 Hbk £19.00
ISBN 0406570817 Pbk £12.95

—Phipson on Evidence / London : Sweet & Maxwell.

—Pleading, Evidence and Practice / 43rd ed. – London : Sweet & Maxwell, 1988.
ISBN 0421363606 Hbk £49.00
ISBN 0421054808 Hbk £60.00

—Police Officer in Court : A Guide to Presenting Evidence / London : Police Review Publishing, 1983.
ISBN 0851640060 Pbk

—Practical approach to evidence / 2nd ed. – London : Blackstone Press, 1985.
ISBN 0906322693 Pbk £11.95

—Rationale of Judicial Evidence Specially Applied to English Practice, 5 Vols. / J. Bentham. – Repr. of 1827 ed. – Abingdon : Professional Books.

—Reconstructing reality in the courtroom / Feldman. – Tavistock, 1981.
ISBN 0422778400 Hbk £2.95

—Theories of evidence : Bentham and Wigmore / Weidenfeld & Nicolson, 1986.
ISBN 0297786687 Hbk £17.95
ISBN 0297786695 Pbk £8.95

—Treatise on Judicial Evidence / J. Bentham. – Repr. of 1825 ed. – Abingdon : Professional Books.

—Well and truly tried / Waller. – London : Sweet & Maxwell, 1983.
ISBN 0455204470 Hbk £30.00

EVIDENCE - HONG KONG

—Law of Evidence in Criminal Trials in Hong Kong / Gerard McCoy. – Butterworths, 1987.
ca 350p.
Examines the principles which govern in Hong Kong the reception of evidence in criminal proceedings: trial, sentence, and appeal. Covers facts which need not be proved, burden and standard of proof, the rule against hearsay and its exceptions, similar fact evidence and other evidence of criminal conduct probative of the guilt of the accused.
ISBN 0409995479 Hbk £97.50

EVIDENCE - INDIA

—Cases and Materials on Law of Evidence / Lucknow : Eastern Book Company, 1983.
578p.

—Cases and Materials on Law of Evidence / Lucknow : Eastern Book Company, 1983.
578p.

—Circumstantial and Presumptive Evidence / Nagpur : Wadhura & Co.
455p.

—Disputed Documents, Handwriting and Thumb-print Identification / Rao Chiyod Seshagiri. – 4th ed. – Allahabad : Law Book Company, 1988.
400p.

—Elements of the Law of Evidence / 3rd ed. – Lucknow : Eastern Book Company, 1984.
411p.

—Expert Evidence, Expert Opinion and Evidence of Third Persons / 2nd ed. – Allahabad : Law Publishers, 1982.

—Field's Law of Evidence in India and Pakistan, 4 Vols. / Allahabad : Law Publishers, 1983.

—Indian Evidence Act, 1872 / 2nd ed. - Lucknow : Eastern Book Company, 1980.
425p.

—Law of Evidence / Dhirajlal. - 17th ed. - Nagpur : Wadhura & Co, 1987.

—Law of Evidence / Calcutta : Eastern Law House, 1987.

—Law of Evidence. Short Edition in One Volume / Allahabad : Universal Book Agency, 1984.

—Principles and Digest of the Law of Evidence, 2 Vols. / 6th ed. - Allahabad : Universal Book Agency, 1986.

—Statements, Proofs and Confession / 2nd ed. - Allahabad : Law Publishers, 1982.

EVIDENCE - IRELAND

—Irish cases on evidence / by J.S.R. Cole. - 2nd ed. - Dublin : Incorporated Law Society of Ireland, 1982.
xxi, 264 p.; 22 cm.
Includes index.
ISBN 0902027190

—Report on the Hague Convention on the Taking of Evidence Abroad in Civil or Commercial Matters / the Law Reform Commission. - Dublin : The Commission, 1985.
v,75p. - (LRC).
Includes text of the Convention.

EVIDENCE - LIBERIA

—Evidence law of Liberia : statutes, cases and materials / by Tuan Wreh. - 2nd ed. - Monrovia, Liberia : Wreh Agency, 1981.
vii,357p.

EVIDENCE - MALAYSIA

—Cases and materials on evidence in Malaysia and Singapore / Singapore : Malayan Law Journal, 1990.
500.
Deals with the cases and statutory provisions on the law of evidence in Malaysia and Singapore, based on the Malaysian Evidence Act 1950 (revised 1971), and the Singapore Evidence Act 1976 (revised 1985). Examines the general position of the law, in each chapter, and then sets out the important judgements of cases in Singapore and Malaysia.

—Evidence Act, 1950 (Act 56) / Kuala Lumpur : International Law Books Services.

EVIDENCE - NEW ZEALAND

—Cross on Evidence : 4th New Zealand Edition 1989 / Butterworths.
700p.
ISBN 0409616540 Hbk £92.95

—Law of evidence / 7th ed. - Wellington : Butterworths (New Zealand), 1984.
ISBN 0409601314 Hbk £71.50
ISBN 0409701742

—Report on corroboration / Evidence Law Reform Committee, New Zealand. - Wellington : The Committee, 1984.
59p.
Includes bibliographical references.

EVIDENCE - NIGERIA

—Law and Practical Evidence in Nigeria / London : Sweet & Maxwell, 1980.
ISBN 0421256206 Hbk £66.00

—Law and Practice Relating to Evidence in Nigeria / London : Sweet & Maxwell, 1980.
- (Nigerian Practice Library).
ISBN 0421256206 Hbk £62.00

—Law of Evidence in Nigeria / 3rd ed. - London : Sweet & Maxwell, 1987.
ISBN 0421378506 Pbk £20.00

—Modern Nigerian law of evidence / by Fidelis Nwadialo. - Benin City : Ethiope Publishing, 1981.
xlix,306p.
Includes bibliographical references and index.
ISBN 9781231068

EVIDENCE - NORTHERN IRELAND

—Northern Ireland Supplement to Cross on Evidence / 5th ed. - Belfast : Queen's University of Belfast, 1984.
xli, 194p.
ISBN 0853892253 Pbk £9.75

EVIDENCE - PAKISTAN

—Field's Law of Evidence in India and Pakistan, 4 Vols. / Allahabad : Law Publishers, 1983.

EVIDENCE - SCOTLAND

—The Civil Evidence (Scotland) Act 1988 / Edinburgh : W Green & Son, 1989.
Annotated text of the Act from Scottish Current Law Statutes, which introduced far-reaching changes to the law of evidence in civil proceedings, including the abolition of the requirement of cooroboration, the admission of hearsay, and authenticated business records.
ISBN 0414008650

—Evidence of children and other potentially vulnerable witnesses / Scottish Law Commission. - Edinburgh : The Commission, 1988.
iv,160p. - (Discussion paper).

—Evidence : report on corroboration, hearsay and related matters in civil proceedings / Scottish Law Commission. - Edinburgh : H.M.S.O., 1986.
vi,63p.
Includes bibliographical references.
ISBN 010237886X

—Law of Evidence in Nigeria / 3rd ed. - London : Sweet & Maxwell, 1987.
ISBN 0421378506 Pbk

—Law of evidence in Scotland / by David Field. - Edinburgh : W. Green, 1988.
xxxv,359p; 22cm.
Includes index.
ISBN 0414008421 Pbk No price

—Law of evidence in Scotland / N M L Walker. - Edinburgh : T & T Clark, 1986.
A practical handbook for practitioners and for situations in which questions of evidence arise. Where the law is undecided, the authors indicate the general principle which should be applied. There is a concluding chapter on international private law.
ISBN 0852791208 Pbk

—Scottish Law of Evidence / London : Butterworths, 1986.
ISBN 0406261105 Pbk £21.50

—Scottish law of evidence / A.B. Wilkinson. - London : Butterworths, 1986.
200p; 22cm.
Includes index.
ISBN 0406261105 Pbk £25.00

EVIDENCE - SINGAPORE

—Cases and materials on evidence in Malaysia and Singapore / Singapore : Malayan Law Journal, 1990.
500.
Deals with the cases and statutory provisions on the law of evidence in Malaysia and Singapore, based on the Malaysian Evidence Act 1950 (revised 1971), and the Singapore Evidence Act 1976 (revised 1985). Examines the general position of the law, in each chapter, and then sets out the important judgements of cases in Singapore and Malaysia.

—Evidence / Butterworths, 1988.
xxiii, 243p.
ISBN 0409995355 Pbk £60.00

—Evidence in Singapore / London : Butterworths, 1988.
- (Singapore Law Series).
ISBN 0409995355 Pbk

EVIDENCE - SOUTH AFRICA

—Evidence / S.E. van der Merwe ... et al. - Cape Town : Juta, 1983.
xxxviii,450p.
Includes index.
ISBN 0702113778

—Parol evidence with particular reference to contract / by D. T. Zeffertt and A. Paizes. - Johannesburg : Centre for Banking Law, Rand Afrikaans University, 1986.
108p.
Includes bibliographical references.

—Review of the law of evidence / South African Law Commission. - Pretoria : The Commission, 1986.
vii,88 leaves. - (Project).
Bibliography: p.81-88.

—Review of the law of evidence / South African Law Commission. - Pretoria : The Commission, 1986.
xi,60p. - (Report).
Bibliography: pp.vi-ix. Includes draft legislation.
ISBN 0621113484

—South African law of evidence / D. T. Zeffertt. - 3rd ed. - Durban : Butterworths, 1981.
lxxii,504p.
Previous ed.: 1970. Includes index.
ISBN 0409033227 Pbk
ISBN 0409033235

EVIDENCE - SRI LANKA

—Law of Evidence in Sri Lanka / Colombo : Lake House Investments.

EVIDENCE - SUDAN

—Law of evidence in the Sudan / by Krishna Vasdev. - London : Butterworths, 1981.
xlviii,486p; 22cm.
Includes index.
ISBN 0406406103 Pbk Unpriced

EVIDENCE - UNITED STATES

—Evidence : common law and federal rules of evidence / Paul R. Rice. - New York : Matthew Bender, 1987.
xlvi,1212p.
Bibliography : pp.LR1-5. - Includes index. With a separate 'Teacher's guide'.

—Linguistic evidence : language, power, and strategy in the courtroom / William M. O'Barr. - New York : Academic Press, 1982.
xv,192p; 24cm.
Bibliography: p182-187. - Includes index.
ISBN 0125235208 £15.60

EVIDENCE (LAW) - ENGLAND

—Cross on evidence / Colin Tapper, Rupert Cross. - 6th ed. - London : Butterworth, 1985.
xcvii,663p; 25cm.
Previous ed.: published as Evidence. 1979. Includes index.
ISBN 040657006X Hbk £27.00
ISBN 0406570078 Pbk £17.95

EXAMINATION OF WITNESSES - AUSTRALIA

—Evidence reference / Australian Law Reform Commission. - Sydney : The Commission, 1982.
x,255p.
Includes bibliographical references.

EXAMINATION OF WITNESSES - CANADA

—Examination of Witnesses 2 / Vancouver : Continuing Legal Education Society of British Columbia, 1986.
202p.
ISBN 0865043000 Hbk £55.00

—Examination of Witnesses / Vancouver : Continuing Legal Education Society of British Columbia, 1985.
241p.
ISBN 0865042438 Hbk £45.00

—Examination of Witnesses in Criminal Cases / Agincourt : Carswell, 1987.
275p.

—Examination of witnesses in criminal cases / Earl J. Levy. - Toronto : Carswell, 1987.
xxxv,263p.
Includes index.
ISBN 0459308211

EXAMINATIONS - GREAT BRITAIN

—Longman Exam Guide : Business Law / Bailey. - London : Longman Professional, 1986.
ISBN 0582296781 Pbk £6.95

—Statutes for the Law Society Finals / London : Sweet & Maxwell, 1985.
ISBN 0421325208 Pbk £16.95

EXAMINATIONS - PHILIPPINES

—Answers to Bar Examination Questions / Quezon City : University of the Philippines, Law Center, 1982.
148p.

Commercial Law (1975-1981) 1982.
110p.

Criminal Law (1975-1981) 1982.
96p.

Labor and Social Legislation (1975-1981) 1982.
104p.

Legal Ethics and Practical Exercises (1975-1981) 1982.
104p.

Taxation (1964-1981) 1982.
312p.

EXCHANGE CONTROL - AUSTRALIA

—Foreign Investment and Exchange Control / Woolloomooloo : International Business Communications, 1985.
ISBN 0949072001 loose £185.00

EXCHANGE CONTROL - MALAYSIA

—Exchange Control Act, 1953 (Act 17) / Kuala Lumpur : International Law Books Services.

EXECUTION (ADMINISTRATIVE LAW) - GREAT BRITAIN

—Planning controls and their enforcement / by A.J. Little. - 5th ed. - London : Shaw, 1983.
xlix,345p.
Previous ed. published as 'The enforcement of planning control' 1977. Includes index.
ISBN 0721904920

EXECUTIONS AND EXECUTIONERS - GUATEMALA

—Guatemala : a government program of political murder / Amnesty International. - London : Amnesty International, 1981.
32p; 30cm.
Cover title.
ISBN 0862100267 Pbk Unpriced

EXECUTIONS (LAW) - ALBERTA - CANADA - ALBERTA

—Operation of the unsecured creditors' remedies system in Alberta / Institute of Law Research and Reform. - Edmonton : The Institute, 1986.
vii,188p. - (Research paper).
Includes bibliographical references.

EXECUTIONS (LAW) - AUSTRALIA

—Reference on service and execution of process / Australian Law Reform Commission. - Sydney : The Commission, 1984.
vii,87p.
Bibliography: p.86-87.

Research paper no. 4 : Enforcement of judgments / Australian Law Reform Commission. - 1984.
iv,89p.
Bibliography: p.89.

Reserach paper no. 7 : Discussion of reference : Draft Interstate Procedure Bill and regulations / Australian Law Reform Commission. – 1986. iii,80p.
Includes text of draft bill.

—Reference on service and execution of warrants and writs of attachment / Australian Law Reform Commission. – Sydney : The Commission, 1984. v,109,6p.
Bibliography: p.109.

—Service and execution of process / Law Reform Commission. – Canberra : Australian Government Publishing Service, 1987. lix,539p. – (Report).
Bibliography: pp.527-531. - Includes index. Includes draft legislation.
ISBN 0644013796

EXECUTIONS (LAW) - AUSTRALIA - QUEENSLAND

—Working paper on a bill to amend the real property acts with respect to those provisions relating to writs of execution, bills of encumbrance and bills of mortgage, and caveats / Brisbane : The Commission, 1982. 28p. – (Q.L.R.C.W.P.).

EXECUTIONS (LAW) - CANADA - BRITISH COLUMBIA

—Execution against shares / Law Reform Commission of British Columbia. – Vancouver : The Commission, 1987. iii,88p. – (Working paper).

EXECUTIONS (LAW) - CANADA - ONTARIO

—Report on the enforcement of judgment debts and related matters / Ontario Law Reform Commission. – 5 v. – Toronto : Ministry of the Attorney General, 1981.
Includes bibliographical references.
ISBN 0774360593 v.3

EXECUTIONS (LAW) - SCOTLAND

—Diligence and debtor protection : consultation paper / Scottish Courts Administration. – Edinburgh : Scottish Courts Administration on behalf of the Lord Advocate, 1985. 15 leaves.
Consultation paper on Scottish Law Commission's report on diligence and debtor protection (Scot. Law Com. no. 95.

—Law of inhibition and adjudication / George Lidderdale Gretton. – London : Butterworths, 1987. 200p; 22cm.
Includes index.
ISBN 0406104336 Pbk £16.95

—Report on diligence and debtor protection / Scottish Law Commission. – 2 v. – Edinburgh : H.M.S.O., 1985.
Vol. 2: Appendices.
ISBN 0102005869

EXECUTIVE ORDERS - INDIA

—Re-promulgation of ordinances : a fraud on the constitution of India / D. C. Wadhwa. – Pune : Gokhale Institute of Politics and Economics, 1983. xxxi,259p.
ISBN 0861314328

EXECUTIVE POWER - AUSTRALIA

—Executive power of the Commonwealth of Australia / by H.E. Renfree. – Sydney : Legal books, 1984. xxxvii,599p.
Includes index.
ISBN 0949553093

—Parliament, the executive, and the governor-general : a constitutional analysis / George Winterton. – Carlton, Vic. : Melbourne University Press, 1983. viii, 376 p.; 23 cm.
Includes index. Bibliography: p. 329-346.
ISBN 0522842429

EXECUTIVE POWER - GREAT BRITAIN

—Parliament and the executive / London : Royal Institute of Public Administration, 1982. 66p; 21cm.
ISBN 0900628278 Pbk £3.50

EXECUTIVE PRIVILEGE (GOVERNMENT INFORMATION) - GREAT BRITAIN

—Politics of secrecy / James Michael. – Harmondsworth : Penguin, 1982. 240p; 20cm.
Bibliography: p225-229. - Includes index.
ISBN 0140220607 Pbk £2.50

EXECUTORS AND ADMINISTRATORS

—Administration of Foreign Estates / Sweet & Maxwell, 1988.
ISBN 0421346507 Hbk £34.00

—Adminstration of foreign estates / edited by John Pugh : contributors L. Ruiz Barrero ... et al. – London : Sweet & Maxwell, 1988. 300p; 25cm.
Guide to the probate procedures pertaining to eight countries, namely, Spain, Portugal, Italy, France, Guernsey, Jersey, the Isle of Man and also Florida. Covers areas such as registration of death, making a will, and the administration of realty and personalty, death duties, and the distribution of the estate. Each chapter has an appendix of forms.
ISBN 0421346507 £35.00

EXECUTORS AND ADMINISTRATORS - AUSTRALIA

—Administration of the Estates of Deceased Persons in Victoria / 2nd ed. – Sydney : Butterworths, 1988. 288p.

—Will Making and the Administration of Estates : a Short Guide / Butterworths, 1984. 223p.
This book aims at assisting the practitioner in the drafting of a will which accurately effects and carries out the wishes of the testator and then the efficient administration of the estate after death.
ISBN 0409492329 Hbk £36.00

—Wills, Probate and the Administration of the Estates of Deceased Persons in Victoria / 2nd ed. – Butterworths, 1988. 272p.
ISBN 0409494747 Hbk £54.00
ISBN 0409338613 Pbk £35.00

EXECUTORS AND ADMINISTRATORS - AUSTRALIA - NEW SOUTH WALES

—Wills Probate and Administration Service, New South Wales / L.G. Handler. – Butterworths, 1985.
ISBN 0409491314 Hbk

EXECUTORS AND ADMINISTRATORS - CANADA

—Annual Report 1979 : Limitation Periods in Actions Against Estates / Victoria : Government of British Columbia, 1980.

—Estate and Trusts Reports / Agincourt : Carswell.
These volumes contain the key decisions in estates and trust law from Canadian jurisdictions. Topics include wills, estate administration, devolution of estate, dependents relief, and tax matters relating to trusts. Wills are covered in depth.

—Estate Planning and Administration / Agincourt : Carswell, 1985-1986. 406p. – (Bar Admission Course Material Ser.).
This text discusses will planning and drafting, administration of an estate and how to advise the executor on applications for probate or distribution of the estate.

—Ontario estate administration: a guide for legal secretaries and law clerks / Scarborough, Ontario : Butterworths (Canada), 1987. 162.
Contains details on opening the file, application for probate, application for Letters of Administration, estate administration, estate accounting, executors fees, passing of accounts and income tax compliance.
ISBN 0409806510 Pbk

—Ontario Estate Administration : a Guide for Legal Secretaries and Law Clerks / Butterworths, 1987. 162p.

EXECUTORS AND ADMINISTRATORS - CANADA - ONTARIO

—Ontario estate administration: a guide for legal secretaries and law clerks / Scarborough, Ontario : Butterworths (Canada), 1987. 162.
Contains details on opening the file, application for probate, application for Letters of Administration, estate administration, estate accounting, executors fees, passing of accounts and income tax compliance.
ISBN 0409806510 Pbk

EXECUTORS AND ADMINISTRATORS - ENGLAND

—Vickery's law and accounts of executors administrators and trustees / 21st. – London : Cassell plc.
Textbook for people taking examinations for the Institute of Chartered Accountants in England and Wales. Relates developments in the subject, including inheritance tax, since 1980.
ISBN 0304313890

EXECUTORS AND ADMINISTRATORS - GREAT BRITAIN

—Executors, Administration and Probate / Mortimer. – 16th ed. – London : Sweet & Maxwell, 1982.
ISBN 0420455000 Hbk £120.00

—Executorship and Administration / London : Fourmat, 1986.
ISBN 1851900039 Pbk £12.95

—Executorship and Trust Law and Accounts / Suresh Tanna. – Plymouth : Macdonald & Evans, 1985. 360p. – (M and E Professional Studies Ser.).
ISBN 0712104585 Hbk £13.95

—Executorship Law and Accounts / Spicer. – 23rd ed. – London : Butterworths, 1987.
ISBN 0406679010 Hbk £45.00

—Executorship/Trust Law and Accounts / 2nd ed. – London : Pitman Publishing, 1986.
ISBN 0712107517 Pbk £14.95

—Law of Wills and Administration / Alston. – London : Butterworths, 1984.
ISBN 0409601306 Hbk £40.00

—Nelson's Tables : Administration of Estates / 7th ed. – London : Oyez Longman, 1983.
ISBN 0851207219 Hbk £2.95

—Office and Duty of Executors : Treatise of Wills and Executors Directed to Testators in the Choice of Their Executors and Contrivance of Their Wills / Repr. of 1774 ed. – Abingdon : Professional Books. 494p.

—Spicer's and Pegler's Executorship Law and Accounts / 21st ed. – London : HFL, 1983.

—Tax Aspects of the Administration of Estates / Elizabeth Stuart-Buttle. – London : Butterworths, 1984.
This work discusses the numerous tax considerations associated with the administration of an estate in the United Kingdom. The book details the appropriate procedures which are a pre-condition to a grant of probate.
ISBN 0406259003 Pbk

—Taxation for Executors and Trustees / 6th ed. – London : Butterworths, 1984.
ISBN 0406623961 Hbk
ISBN 040662397X Pbk

—Williams, Mortimer and Sunnucks on executors, administrators and probate / by J.H.G. Sunnucks, J.G. Ross Martyn, K.M. Garnett. – London : Stevens & Sons, 1982. clxxxviii,1157p; 26cm.
Concerned with probate practice and the work of executors and administrators, discussions of changes in the law of family provision, capital transfer tax and social security. Includes appendices which set out the relevant statutes, rules of court and statutory instruments.
ISBN 0420455000 £75.00

—Wills, administration and taxation : a practical guide / King. – London : Sweet & Maxwell, 1988.
ISBN 0421382708 Pbk £17.50

EXECUTORS AND ADMINISTRATORS - MALAYSIA

—Probate and Administration Act, 1959 (Act 97) / Kuala Lumpur : International Law Books Services.

EXECUTORS AND ADMINISTRATORS - NEW ZEALAND

—Brief Outline of the Law Relating to Trusts, Wills, Executors, and Administrators / 2nd ed. – Butterworths, 1982.
ISBN 04094267127 Pbk £25.85

—Brief Outline of the Law Relating to Trusts, Wills, Executors, and Administrators / 2nd ed. – Wellington : Butterworths, 1982.
ISBN 0409627127 Hbk

—Executorship Law and Accounts / 8th ed. – Butterworths, 1980.
ISBN 0409600733 Pbk £45.65

—Executorship Law and Accounts / 8th ed. – Wellington : Butterworths, 1980.

—Law of Wills and Administration / 5th ed. – Butterworths, 1984.
Takes into account the significant developments made by the Wills Amendment Act 1977, and amendments to the Administration Act 1969, and the Status of Children Act 1969.
ISBN 0409601306 Hbk £90.75

—Nevill's Law of Trusts, Wills and Administration in New Zealand / 8th ed. – Butterworths, 1985.
Guide to the law of trusts, wills and administration in New Zealand. Includes new chapters on unincorporated associations and construction of wills.
ISBN 040970170X Hbk £76.45
ISBN 0409701858 Pbk £50.05

—Nevill's Law of Trusts, Wills and Administrators in New Zealand / 8th ed. – London : Butterworths, 1985.
ISBN 0409701858 Pbk £26.00

—Probate and Administration Practice in New Zealand / J.B.K. Curran. – 4th ed. – Butterworths, 1986.
Includes material from various statutes, regulations, the new High Court Rules, Court decisions, and textbooks. Covers the developments in probate and administration law in New Zealand. Cross-referenced to Garrow and Alston's Law of Wills and Administration 5th edition 1984.
ISBN 0409621412 Hbk £91.30

EXECUTORS AND ADMINISTRATORS – NORTHERN IRELAND
—Women and children first : the legal obligation to make provision on death for family and dependants / lecture delivered to the Belfast Solicitors' Association by Norma Dawson. – Belfast : SLS Legal Publications, 1984.
45p.
Bibliography: p.46.

EXECUTORS AND ADMINISTRATORS – SCOTLAND
—Report on powers of judicial factors / Scottish Law Commission. – Edinburgh : H.M.S.O., 1980.
iv,17p; 25cm. – (Comnd. 7904).
ISBN 0101790406 sd £1.75

EXECUTORS AND ADMINISTRATORS – SOUTH AFRICA
—Administration of Deceased Estates / Kenwyn : Juta & Co.
31p.
ISBN 0702114898 Hbk £600.00

—Supplement to the Administration of Deceased Estates in South Africa, Trusts in South Africa, The Making of a Will Plus The Matrimonial Property Act Including Estate Duty Aspects / Cape Town : Legal & Financial Publishing, 1985.

EXECUTORY INTERESTS – ENGLAND
—Essay on the learning of contingent remainders and executory devises / by Charles Fearne. – 9th ed. – London : Saunders and Benning, 1831.
lvi,730p.
Includes index.

EXHAUSTION OF LOCAL REMEDIES
—Application of the rule of exhaustion of local remedies in international law : its rationale in the international protection of individual rights / A.A. Cancado Trindade. – Cambridge Cambridgeshire : Cambridge University Press, 1983.
xiii,443p.
Includes index. Bibliography: p422-440.
ISBN 0521229472

EXPERT EVIDENCE
—Court appointed experts in maritime cases : a comparative law study / by Arthur M. Boal and David R. Owen. – Antwerp : International Maritime Committee, 1981.
ii,83p.
Contents: questionnaire answers, compiled by Arthur M. Boal and David R. Owen.

—Facts / by G.H. Kendal. – Toronto : Butterworths, 1980.
x, 106 p.; 24 cm.
Includes bibliographical references and index.
ISBN 0409842451 £13.50

—Reconstructing the past : the role of psychologists in criminal trials / edited by Arne Trankell. – Deventer, The Netherlands : Kluwer, 1982.
398p.
'This book contains papers and panels from the first international conference on Witness Psychology...Stockholm...September 1981'.
ISBN 9065441123

—Trial of the expert : a study of expert evidence and forensic experts / Ian R. Freckelton. – Melbourne : Oxford University Press, 1987.
xxxii,289p.
A textbook of the rules of expert evidence, and an analysis of the difficulties experienced when experts from non-legal disciplines are called as witnesses. Examines the impact of new scientific disciplines, and looks at how the forensic expert's duties to maintain confidentiality may conflict with the court's need for all the relevant evidence.
ISBN 0195545664 Hbk £30

EXPERT EVIDENCE – AUSTRALIA
—Evidence reference / Australian Law Reform Commission. – Sydney : The Commission, 1983.
xiv,340p.
Bibliography: p.328-340.

EXPERT EVIDENCE – CANADA – MANITOBA
—Report on medical privilege / Manitoba Law Reform Commission. – Winnipeg : The Commission, 1983.
52p. – (Report).
Includes bibliographical references.

EXPERT EVIDENCE – ENGLAND
—Expert evidence in actions for personal injuries / Supreme Court Rule Committee. – London : Supreme Court Rule Committee, 1987.
4,1 leaves.

—Expert witness and his evidence / Michael P. Reynolds and Philip S.D. King. – London : BSP Professional, 1988.
x,160p; 24cm.
Includes index.
ISBN 0632018542 £17.95

—Medical evidence : the report of a Joint Committee of the British Medical Association, the Senate of the Inns of the Court and the Bar and the Law Society / British Medical Association. – London : British Medical Association, 1981.
iiileaves,37p; 30cm.

EXPERT EVIDENCE – GREAT BRITAIN
—Expert witness / R. H. Mildred : with a foreword by the Right Honourable Lord Diplock. – London : Godwin, 1982.
x,131p; 24cm.
ISBN 0711456801

EXPERT EVIDENCE – INDIA
—Expert Evidence, Expert Opinion and Evidence of Third Persons / 2nd ed. – Allahabad : Law Publishers, 1982.

EXPERT SYSTEMS (COMPUTER SCIENCE)
—Expert systems and scholarly publications / Jean-Claude Gardin. – London : British Library, 1987.
30pin various pagings; 30cm. – (The Fifth British Library Annual Research Lecture).
Includes the text in French, printed t$ete-b$eche, under the title Systemes experts et publications savantes.
ISBN 071233114X Pbk Free

—Expert systems in law : a jurisprudential inquiry / Richard E. Susskind. – Oxford : Clarendon, 1987.
xvi,300p; 23cm.
Bibliography: p271-292. - Includes index.
ISBN 0198255829 £30.00

—Expert systems : principles and case studies / edited by Richard Forsyth. – London : Chapman and Hall, 1984.
xii,231p; 24cm. – (Chapman and Hall computing).
Bibliography: p227-228. - Includes index.
ISBN 0412262703 Hbk No price
ISBN 0412262800 Pbk No price

EXPERT SYSTEMS (COMPUTER SCIENCE) – GREAT BRITAIN
—Expert Systems in Banking and Securities / Jeffcoate. – Ovum, 1988.
ISBN 090396936X Hbk £465.00

—Expert Systems in Law / Oxford : Oxford University Press, 1987.
ISBN 0198255829 Hbk £25.00

EXPLOSION INVESTIGATION
—Explosion investigation / by H.J. Yallop : with a foreword by S.S. Kind. – Harrogate : Forensic Science Society, 1980.
xiv,276p; 23cm. – (Monographs).
Includes index.
ISBN 0950242551

EXPLOSIVES – INDIA
—Explosives Act, 1884 / 4th ed. – Lucknow : Eastern Book Company.
288p.

—Indian Explosives Act, 1884 and Explosive Rules, 1983 : Together with Explosive Substances Act, 1908, Gas Cylinders Rules, 1981 and Static Mobile Pressure Vessels (Unfired) Rules, 1981 / 3rd ed. – Lucknow : Eastern Book Company, 1984.
255p.

—Law and Practice of Arms and Explosives : With Explosives Rules 1988 / 10th ed. – Allahabad : Law Book Company, 1988.
1,000p.

—Law of Arms and Explosives : Acts and Rules / 3rd ed. – Allahabad : Ashoka Law House, 1987.
657p.

—Law of Arms and Explosives : with Act Rules and Notifications / 4th ed. – Allahabad : Law Publishers, 1982.

EXPLOSIVES – MALAYSIA
—Explosives, Malaysian Legislation On / Kuala Lumpur : International Law Books Services.

EXPLOSIVES – SWEDEN
—Labelling of chemical products : Swedish regulations and general advice with regard to the classification and labelling of chemical products hazardous to health, flammables and explosives / National Chemicals Inspectorate, National Inspectorate of Explosives and Flammables. – Solna : National Chemicals Inspectorate, 1987.
224p.
ISBN 9138098873

EXPORT CREDIT
—Current problems of international trade financing / edited by C.M. Chinkin, P.J. Davidson, W.J.M. Ricquier. – Singapore : Malaya Law Review, 1983.
xxiii,507p.
Includes index. At head of title: Singapore Conferences on International Business Law.
ISBN 0406181144

—Export credit financing systems in OECD member countries / 3rd ed. – Paris : OECD, 1987.
285p.
ISBN 9264129472

—Export finance / by Angus Dunn and Martin Knight. – London : Euromoney Publications, 1982.
vi,154p.
ISBN 0903121328

—Trade financing / edited by Charles J. Gmur. – 2nd ed. – London : Euromoney, 1986.
xxi,234p.
ISBN 0903121999

EXPORT CREDIT INSURANCE
—Export finance / by Angus Dunn and Martin Knight. – London : Euromoney Publications, 1982.
vi,154p.
ISBN 0903121328

—Forfaiting : an alternative approach to export trade finance / Ian Guild and Rhodri Harris. – Cambridge : Woodhead-Faulkner, 1985.
160p.
Includes index.
ISBN 0859413160 £17.50

EXPORT MARKETING
—Euromoney issues : papers presented to the Section on Business Law Committee Q (Issues and Trading in Securities) at the International Bar Association 20th biennial conference, Vienna, September 1984 / London : International Bar Association, 1985.
xvi,112p.

EXPORT MARKETING – GREAT BRITAIN
—Elements of Export Marketing / Cambridge : Woodhead-Faulkner, 1984.
ISBN 0859412334 Pbk £7.95

—Elements of Export Marketing and Management / London : Sweet & Maxwell, 1984.

—Elements of Export Marketing and Management / London : Chapman & Hall, 1984.
ISBN 0412163500 Pbk £9.95

EXPORT SALES
—Hague-Zagreb Essays / edited by C.C.A. Voskuil and C.C.A. Voskuil and J.A. Wade. – Hague : Martinus Nijhoff, 1983.
410p.
ISBN 9024728401 Hbk £135.00

—UNIDROIT : Draft Convention on Agency in the International Sale of Goods : memorandum / by a working party of the Council's Law Reform Committee. – London : Law Society, 1983.
2p.

—Uniform law for international sales under the 1980 United Nations convention / by John O. Honnold. – Deventer, Netherlands : Kluwer Law and Taxation Publishers, 1982.
586p.
'United Nations Convention on Contracts for the International Sale of Goods': p. 469-503. Includes index. Bibliography: p29-36.
ISBN 9065440453 CIP rev.

EXPORT SALES – CANADA
—New Developments in the Law of Export Sales / Toronto : DeBoo, 1982.
337p.
ISBN 088820146X Hbk £59.95

EXPORT SALES – EUROPE
—From the Waidring Conferences, 4 Vols. / edited by Louis Lafili, Franklin Gevurtz, Dennis Campbell. – Deventer Netherlands : Kluwer Law and Taxation Publishers, 1986.
380p.
Includes bibliographies.
ISBN 9065442413 Pbk £95.00

—Schmitthoff's export trade : the law and practice of international trade / by Clive M. Schmitthoff. – 7th ed. – London : Stevens, 1980.
xxxvii,515p.

ISBN 0420454101

EXPORT SALES CONTRACTS
—Commentary on the international sales law : the 1980 Vienna Sales Convention / by C.M. Bianca, M.J. Bonell. – Milan : Giuffre, 1987.
xvii,886p.
Bibliography: pp.843-873. - Includes index. Includes texts of the Convention in English, Arabic, Chinese, French, Russian, Spanish, German and Italian.
ISBN 8814012768

EXPORT TRADING COMPANIES - GREAT BRITAIN
—Exporting goods from the United Kingdom : export co-operatives and contract warehousing / by Paul Vaughan, with John Sykes and Derek Pool. – London : Thames Polytechnic, School of Business, 1986.
22 p.
ISBN 0948296046

EXPORTS
—Schmitthoff's Export Trade : the Law and Practice of International Trade / 8th ed. – Agincourt : Carswell.
689p.

EXPORTS - GREAT BRITAIN
—Croner's Reference Book for Exporters / New Malden : Croner Publications.

—Elements of export law / Geoffrey Whitehead. – Cambridge : Woodhead-Faulkner, 1983.
xiv,255p; 22cm.
Bibliography: p246. - Includes index.
ISBN 0859412288 Hbk

—Elements of Export Practice / 2nd ed. – London : Chapman & Hall, 1985.
ISBN 0412270005 Pbk £9.95

—Export Finance / London : Sweet & Maxwell.
ISBN 0421333103 Pbk

—Export For The Small Business / London : Kogan Page, 1984.
ISBN 085038771X Pbk £5.95

—Export Trade, Law and Practice / 8th ed. – London : Sweet & Maxwell, 1986.
ISBN 0420466509 Pbk £29.00

—Guide to Export Finance / Mills. – London : Euromoney, 1987.
ISBN 1870031458 Pbk £75.00

—How Protection Taxes Exporters / Larry A. Sjaastad. – London : Trade Policy Research Centre, 1985.
87p.

—Schmitthoff's Export trade : the law and practice of international trade / John Adams, Clive M Schmitthoff. – 8th ed. – London : Stevens, 1986.
lix,689p; 26cm.
Includes new chapters on GATT, and product liability, which covers the EEC Directive on Product Liability, and Part I of the Consumer Protection Act 1987. Discusses the Vienna Convention, and the effects on export trade law of the establishment of the Single Market in 1992.
ISBN 0420466401 Hbk £32.00
ISBN 0420466509 Pbk £25.00

EXPORTS - NIGERIA
—Export (Incentives and Miscellaneous Provisions) Decree 1986 : with explanatory note on its provisions / prepared by International Trade Development Centre (ITDC). – Lagos, Nigeria : The Centre, 1986.
20p.

EXPORTS - UNITED STATES
—Overview of US export controls / B C Murphy. – Kluwer Law and Taxation, 1989.
160.
A general overview of the US laws controlling the export of goods and technology from the US. Covers individual validated licenses, special licenses, technical data, Nuclear Short Supply Controls, restrictive trade practices and boycotts, and common exporting terms and acronyms.
ISBN 9065443967 Pbk £28/Dfl 85

EXTRADITION
—Political offence exception to extradition : the delicate problem of balancing the rights of the individual and the international public order / Christine van den Wijngaert. – Deventer, the Netherlands : Kluwer, 1980.
xxi,263p.
Bibliography: p231-248. Translation from Dutch. Based on the author's thesis, Free University of Brussels, 1979.
ISBN 9026811853

—Territorial asylum / by Atle Grahl-Madsen. – Stockholm : Almqvist & Wiksell International, 1980.
– (Studies in international law).
'Published under the auspices of Svenska institutet for internationell ratt, Uppsala, 1979.'. Includes index.

EXTRADITION - COMMONWEALTH
—Survey of extradition and fugitive offenders legislation as between Commonwealth jurisdictions / prepared for the Commonwealth Secretariat by the Commonwealth Legal Advisory Service of the British Institute of International and Comparative Law. – Rev. – London : Commonwealth Secretariat, 1982.
iii,70p; 30cm.
Previous ed.: 1977.
ISBN 0850922356 Pbk £10.00

EXTRADITION - GREAT BRITAIN
—British extradition law and procedure : including extradition between the United Kingdom and foreign states, The Commonwealth and dependent countries and the Republic of Ireland / by V.E. Hartley Booth : assisted by Peter Sells. – Alphen aan den Rijn : Sijthoff & Noordhoff, 1980.
2vols.

—Extradition / presented to Parliament by the Secretary of State for the Home Department. – London : H.M.S.O., 1985.
23p.
ISBN 0101942109

—Extradition : a review of the law and practice of extradition in the United Kingdom : comments on the report of an interdepartmental working party / Justice. – London : Justice, 1985.
4 leaves.

—Extradition for Drug-Related Offences : A Study / London : HMSO, 1986.
ISBN 9211480698 Hbk £9.00

—Extradition : the Law and Practice / Stanbrook. – Chichester : Barry Rose, 1980.
ISBN 085992162X Hbk £35.00

—Law and practice of extradition / by Ivor Stanbrook and Clive Stanbrook : with a foreword by Lord Hailsham of St. Marylebone. – Chichester : Rose, 1980.
202,xxvp; 26cm.
Includes index.
ISBN 085992162X £30.00

—Review of the law and practice of extradition in the United Kingdom / Report of an interdepartmental working party. – London : Criminal Justice Department, Home Office, 1982.
vii,128p.

—Survey of extradition and fugitive offenders legislation as between Commonwealth jurisdictions / prepared for the Commonwealth Secretariat by the Commonwealth Legal Advisory Service of the British Institute of International and Comparative Law. – Rev. – London : Commonwealth Secretariat, 1982.
iii,70p; 30cm.
Previous ed.: 1977.
ISBN 0850922356 Pbk £10.00

EXTRADITION - IRELAND
—Extradition law in Ireland / Michael Forde : with a foreword by Niall McCarthy. – Dublin : Round Hall Press, 1988.
xviii,260p; 24cm.
Includes index.
ISBN 094768624X £35.00

EXTRATERRITORIAL CRIME
—Computer-related crime : analysis of legal policy / Paris : OECD, 1986.
71p.
' ... prepared for the Committee for Information, Computer and Communications Policy ...'. - p.3.

EXTRATERRITORIALITY
—Australian-United States' relations : the extraterritorial application of United States laws / the Parliament of the Commonwealth of Australia Joint Committee on Foreign Affairs and Defence. – Canberra : Australian Government Publishing Service, 1983.
xiii,84p. – (Parliamentary paper).
Includes bibliographical references.

—Canadian Council on International Law : Conference Proceedings /. – Ottawa : Canadian Council on International Law, 1983.

—Conflicts of national laws with international business activity : issues of extraterritoriality / by A.H. Hermann. – London : British North American Research Organisation, 1982.
xii,96p.
ISBN 0902594419

—Extra-territorial application of laws and responses thereto / edited by Cecil J. Olmstead. – Oxford : International Law Association in association with ESC Publishing Ltd, 1984.
xv,236p.
Proceedings of an International Law Association Conference, 11-12 May 1983.
ISBN 0906214289 £28.00

—Extraterritorial Application of National Laws / G. Born. – Dordrecht : Kluwer, 1987.
72p.
ISBN 9065443061 Pbk £50.00

—Extraterritorial jurisdiction / Law Reform Commission of Canada. – Ottawa : Canadian Law Reform Commission, 1984.
210p. – (Working paper).
Bibliography: p.209-210.
ISBN 0662136039

—Extraterritorial jurisdiction : an annotated collection of legal materials / by A.V. Lowe. – Cambridge : Grotius Publications, 1983.
xxiii,273p.
Bibliography: p.269-270. - Includes index.
ISBN 0906496357

—Interference or Internationalism : The Extraterritorial Application of National Laws Regulating Business Activities / Enstone : Ditchley Foundation.
1982p.

—International business and national jurisdiction / A.D. Neale and M.L. Stephens. – Oxford : Clarendon Press, 1988.
xix,216p.
Examines the relationship between issues in international and municipal law, specifically the relationship between historically exclusive spheres of sovereign interest, and legal and practical requirements of the modern international commercial environment. Concentrates on US antitrust law, but some EEC and English decisions are included.
ISBN 0198255322 Hbk £52.00

—National laws and international commerce : the problem of extraterritoriality / Douglas E. Rosenthal and William M. Knighton. – London : Routledge & Kegan Paul, 1982.
xi,96p.
Bibliography: p94-96.
ISBN 0710093381

EXTRATERRITORIALITY - CANADA
—Extraterritoriality in International Trade : Canada and the United States of America Practices Compared / Butterworths, 1988.
288p.
Study of conflicts of jurisdiction involving international busness transactions. Attempts to define the permissible limits to the assertion of jurisdiction to prescribe, to adjudicate and to enforce a rule of law under traditional principles of public international law and what these limits should be today in the economic field.
ISBN 0409805025 Hbk

EXTRATERRITORIALITY - UNITED STATES
—Extraterritoriality in International Trade : Canada and the United States of America Practices Compared / Butterworths, 1988.
288p.
Study of conflicts of jurisdiction involving international busness transactions. Attempts to define the permissible limits to the assertion of jurisdiction to prescribe, to adjudicate and to enforce a rule of law under traditional principles of public international law and what these limits should be today in the economic field.
ISBN 0409805025 Hbk

FACTORIES - GREAT BRITAIN
—Health and safety in factories / Fife. – 2nd ed. – London : Butterworths, 1982.
ISBN 0406353077 Hbk £52.00

—Industrial air pollution : health and safety 1983 / Health & Safety Executive. – London : H.M.S.O., 1985.
33p.
ISBN 0118837877

—Redgrave's health and safety in factories / Ian Fife, E. Anthony Machin. – 2nd ed. – London : Butterworths, 1982.
lix,1932p; 18cm.
Previous ed.: i.e. new ed. 1976. Includes index. Includes the text of relevant legislation. Kept up to date by supplements.
ISBN 0406353077 Unpriced

FACTORIES - INDIA
—Exhaustive Guide to the Factories Act, 1948 / Delhi : Metropolitan Book Co, 1987.
424p.
ISBN 812000275X Hbk £150.00

—Factories Act, 1948 / 4th ed. – Lucknow : Eastern Book Company, 1984.

—Factories Act / 2nd ed. – Allahabad : Law Book Company, 1967.
500p.
With 1986 supplement.

FACTORIES - MALAYSIA
—Factories and Machinery Act, 1967 (Act 139) and Regulations and Rules / Kuala Lumpur : International Law Books Services.

FACTORIES - PAKISTAN
—Law of Factories / 5th ed. – Karachi : Bureau of Labour Publications, 1987.
60p.

FACTS - INDIA
—Law Relating to Estoppel / Allahabad : Law Publishers, 1980.

FACTS (PHILOSOPHY)
—Facts in law / Association for legal and social philosophy : ninth annual conference at Hatfield College, University of Durham, 2nd-4th April 1982 : edited by William Twining. – Wiesbaden : Franz Steiner, 1983.
ix,157p.
Bibliography: p156-157.
ISBN 3515038973

FALKLAND ISLANDS

—Annotated legal chronology of the Malvinas (Falkland) Islands controversy / Cronologia legal anotada sobre la cuestion Malvinas (resumen) : Enrique Ferrer Vieyra. – Cordoba : Marcos Lerner, 1985.
173p.
Bibliography: p13-15. Inscribed by the author. Spanish summary.

—Falkland Islands dispute in international law and politics : a documentary sourcebook / edited by Raphael Perl : with an historic chronology and bibilography by Everette E. Larson. – London : Oceana Publications, 1983.
xiii,722p.
Bibliography: p. 691-722.
ISBN 0379112515

—Falkland Islands gazette / v. – Stanley : Goverment Printing Office, 1891.
Contains proclamations and regulations. Vol. 1, no. 1 published as: Falkland gazette.

—Falklands/Malvinas conflict : a spur to arms build-ups / Jozef Goldblat and Victor Millan. – Stockholm : SIPRI, 1983.
vii,63p; 23cm.
Originally published as: World armaments and disarmament in SIPRI Yearbook : London and New York, 1983.
ISBN 9185114308

—Security Council adopts resolution demanding cessation of hostilities and withdrawal of Argentine forces from the Falkland Islands : Council also calls for diplomatic solution of the situation / London : United Nations Information Centre, 1982.
9 leaves. – (BR/82/10).
'Background information for media only'.

—Struggle for the Falkland Islands : a study in legal and diplomatic history / Julius Goebel : with a preface and an introduction by J.C.J. Metford. – New Haven : Yale University Press, 1982.
xxx,482p; 23cm.
Originally published: 1927. Includes index.
ISBN 0300029438 Hbk £12.00
ISBN 0300029446 Pbk £5.95

FALKLAND ISLANDS - GREAT BRITAIN

—Right to know : the inside story of the Belgrano affair / Clive Ponting. – London : Sphere Books, 1985.
214p.
ISBN 0722169442

FALSE PERSONATION - GREAT BRITAIN

—Passing off : the law and practice relating to the imitation of goods, businesses and professions / David Young. – 1st ed. – London : Oyez Longman, 1985.
xxviii,152p. – (Oyez Longman practitioner series).
Includes index.
ISBN 0851209866

FAMILY

—Family in change / edited by Jan Trost. – Vasteras : International Library, 1980.
165p.
Bibliography: p.164-165.
ISBN 9185898023

—Marriage and cohabitation in contemporary societies : areas of legal, social and ethical change : an international and interdisciplinary study / edited by John M. Eekelaar, Sanford Katz : with an introduction by William J. Goode. – Toronto : Butterworths, 1980.
xviii,454p; 24cm.
Includes bibliographical references. Papers presented at the Third World Conference of the International Society on Family Law, held June 5-9, 1979 at Uppsala, Sweden.
ISBN 0409828602

FAMILY - AUSTRALIA

—Family : Australian family studies database / edited by Deborah Whithear. – Melbourne : Family Information Centre, Insitute of Family Studies, 1985.
xv,246p.
First annual volume published in 1984. Includes indexes.

—FAMILY thesaurus : Australian family studies indexing terms / prepared by the Australian Institute of Family Studies : edited by Deborah Whithear. – 2nd ed. – Melbourne : Australian Institute of Family Studies, 1987.
98p.
ISBN 0642118515

FAMILY - CANADA

—Children's rights in the practice of family law / edited by Barbara Landau. – Toronto : Carswell, 1986.
xxxviii,378p.
Includes bibliogrpahical references.
ISBN 0459390406

FAMILY - ENGLAND

—Family, sex and marriage in England 1500-1800 / Lawrence Stone. – Abridged ed. – Harmondsworth : Penguin, 1982.
446p,16p of plates; 20cm. – (A Peregrine book).
Previous ed.: London : Weidenfeld & Nicolson, 1977.
Includes index.
ISBN 0140551670 Pbk £3.50

—Justice and welfare in divorce / Mervyn Murch. – London : Sweet & Maxwell, 1980.
viii,307p; 22cm.
Includes index.
ISBN 0421264004 Pbk £10.75

FAMILY - FRANCE

—Child and the state : the intervention of the state in family life / Philippe Meyer : translated by Judith Ennew and Janet Lloyd. – Cambridge : Cambridge University Press, 1983.
128p; 23cm.
Translation of: L'enfant et la raison d'etat.
ISBN 052124871X Hbk £18.50
ISBN 2735100626 France : Pbk £5.95

FAMILY - GREAT BRITAIN

—Families in the future / final report of the Study Commission. – London : Study Commission on the Family, 1983.
56p; 21cm.
ISBN 0907051170 Pbk £3.25

—Statutory maternity allowance : a consultation paper / issued by the Department of Health and Social Security. – London : The Department, 1985.
11,12 leaves.
Includes press release.

—Tax planning for the family / 3rd ed. – London : Longman Professional, 1986.
ISBN 0851209203 Pbk £22.00

—Values and the changing family / a final report from the Working Party on Values. – London : Study Commission on the Family, 1982.
52p; 21cm.
Bibliography: p48. Cover title.
ISBN 0907051138 Pbk £2.75

FAMILY CREDIT - GREAT BRITAIN

—National Insurance and Family Allowances Acts, 4 Vols. / London : HMSO.
ISBN 0117600016 Hbk £1.50

Vol. VI
ISBN 0117605166 Hbk £2.00

Vol. VII
ISBN 0117605166 Hbk £7.00

Vol. VIII
ISBN 011760643X Hbk £15.00

FAMILY LAW

—Australian family law cases / North Ryde, N.S.W. : CCH Australia, 1975.
23cm.
Issued annually as bound volumes, with current issues forming part of the service to the loose-leaf publication: Australian family law & practice reporter.

—Family and child law statutes / compiled by Oyez Longman Editorial Staff. – London : Oyez Longman, 1984.
x,711p; 23cm.
ISBN 0851208894

—Family law : an interdisciplinary perspective / Howard H. Irving, editor. – Toronto : Carswell, 1981.
xi,215p.
Includes bibliographical references. Subtitle on cover: Law for the helping professions.
ISBN 0459333801

—Family law in the last two decades of the twentieth century : being a series of articles by a distinguished team of authors, first published in 'Acta juridica' 1983 / editorial board, T.W. Bennett ... et al. – Cape Town : Juta, 1983.
ix,243p.
Includes bibliographical references.
ISBN 0702114650

—Family, Things and Succession / H.J. Erasmus. – 2nd ed. – Durban : Professional Publishers, 1983.
ISBN 0409040525 Pbk £79.00

—International conventions concerning applications for and awards of maintenance : explanatory documentation / prepared for Commonwealth Jurisdictions by David McClean in association with the Commonwealth Secretariat. – London : Commonwealth Secretariat, 1981.
v,83p.
ISBN 0850922003

—International Invitational Conference on Matrimonial and Child Support, May 27-30, 1981, Edmonton, Alberta, Canada : conference materials / Edmonton : Institute of Law Research and Reform, University of Alberta, 1982.
xv,146p. – (Research paper).
Conference convened by the Institute of Law Research and Reform.

—International journal of law and the family / Oxford : Oxford University Press, 1987-.

—New family and the new property / Mary Ann Glendon. – Toronto : Butterworths, 1981.
xvii,269p; 23cm.
ISBN 0409834106

—Parents and children: the law of parental responsibility / 3rd. – London : Sweet & Maxwell, 1987.
Places legal problems in their social context, and discusses the nature of parental rights and duties, the consequences of marriage breakdown, and the legal response to child abuse. Covers the Family Law Reform Act, the legal implications of surrogacy arrangements, the sterilisation of a mentally handicapped ward of court, the custodianship provision of the Children Act 1975, and the Law Commission's review of the private law relating to children.
ISBN 042136050X Pbk £17

—Recognition of family judgments in the Commonwealth / J.D. McClean. – London : Butterworths, 1983.
xxxvii,370p; 26cm.
Includes index.
ISBN 040640321X Unpriced

—Report of the Royal Commission on Family and Children's Law / Thomas R. Berger. – 20 v. – Vancouver : Queen's Printer, 1974.
Includes bibliographies. Chairman: Thomas R. Berger.

—Resolution of family conflict : comparative legal perspectives / edited by John M. Eekelaar, Sanford N. Katz. – Toronto : Butterworths, 1984.
xviii,610p.
Includes bibliographical references.
ISBN 0409839841 Hbk £41.95

—Resolution of family conflicts / Sanford N Katz. – Scarborough, Ontario : Butterworths (Canada), 1984.
ISBN 0409839841 Hbk £32.00

—State, the law, and the family / critical perspectives : edited by Michael D.A. Freeman. – London : Tavistock, 1984.
318p; 22cm.
Includes bibliographies and index.
ISBN 042279080X Pbk No price

FAMILY LAW - AUSTRALIA

—Administration of Family Law in Australia : Report to the Attorney-General / Family Law Council. – Canberra : Australian Government Publishing Service, 1985.
185p : Illus.
ISBN 0644039892 Hbk £7.50

—Advanced Family Law Seminar / Monash University Staff. – Clayton : Monash University Press, 1984.
ISBN 086746318X Hbk £15.00

—Australian family law / Richard Chisholm, Carol Foreman and Stephen O'Ryan. – Sydney : Butterworths, 1987.
looseleaf.
Includes both Commonwealth and state legislation and practice and procedure of the Family Court.
ISBN 0409491950 LLF A$575

—Australian Family Law Act 1975 Family Law Rules : Family Law Regulations / Butterworths, 1988.
ISBN 0409493686 Hbk £29.00

—Australian Family Law Forms and Precedents / Alexander Duff. – Woolloomooloo : International Business Communications, 1987.
ISBN 0949553247 Hbk £225.00

—Australian family property law / by I. J. Hardingham and M. A. Neave. – Sydney : Law Book Company, 1984.
liii,647p.
ISBN 0455205132

—Australian journal of family law / Sydney : Butterworths, 1986-.

—Bound Family Law Cases / North Ryde : C.C.H. Australia, 1986.
770p.

—Butterworths Student Companions /. – Butterworths, 1986.
ISBN 0409491365

—Changing laws for changing families / Patricia Harper. – Melbourne : Institute of Family Studies, 1982.
24p. – (Discussion paper).
Paper prepared for the 3rd Australian Conference on adoption, 'Changing Families', Adelaide, 14-19 May 1982.
ISBN 0642884552

—Children in stepfamilies : their legal and family status / Patricia Harper. – Melbourne : Institute of Family Studies, 1984.
– (Policy background paper).
Bibliography: p.28-29.
ISBN 0642876665

—Community law reform for the Australian capital territory : second report : Loss of consortium : compensation for loss of capacity to do housework / the Law Reform Commission. – Canberra : Australian Government Publishing Service, 1986.
viii,28p. – (Report).
Bibliography: p.27. - Includes index.
ISBN 0644013516

—Contempt and family law / The Law Reform Commission. – Sydney : The Commission, 1985.
76p. – (Discussion paper).

—Family Law / North Ryde : Law Book Co, 1985.
ISBN 0455203075 Hbk £31.00
ISBN 0455203083 Pbk £22.75

—Family Law / North Ryde : Law Book Co, 1985.
lxxxvi, 685p.
ISBN 0455203075 Hbk £66.00
ISBN 0455203083 Pbk £49.50

—Family Law Act, Rules and Regulations / Sydney : Butterworths, 1988.
470p.

—Family Law Act, Rules and Regulations : Students Edition / Butterworths, 1989.
ca 600p.
ISBN 0409303224 loose £39.00

—Family Law Case Citator and Table of Cases Judicially Considered 1978-1984 / Woolloomooloo : International Business Communications, 1980.
ISBN 0959656863 Hbk £20.00

—Family law casebook / by Frank Bates and J. Neville Turner. – North Ryde, N.S.W. : Law Book Co., 1985.
xxxvii,732p.
Includes bibliographical references and index.
ISBN 0455203946

—Family Law : Cases and Commentary / Butterworths, 1985.
867p.
This book, intended primarily for law students, places its greatest emphasis on matrimonial property, maintenance, and constitutional issues. Coverage is also given to areas which fall outside Commonwealth jurisdiction and differences in the laws of the various Australian states and territories.
ISBN 0409490490 Hbk £77.00
ISBN 0409490598 Pbk £56.00

—Family Law Council; 1982-1983 Annual Report / Canberra : Australian Government Publishing Service, 1983.
70p.

—Family law handbook : containing: Family Law Act 1975 and Family Law Regulations, together with an explanatory summary and an index to the Act and Regulations / prepared by the Attorney-General's Department. – 2nd ed. – Camberra : Australian Government Publishing Service, 1980.
iii,249p.
Includes index.
ISBN 0642035342 loose-leaf
ISBN 0642035334

—Family Law in Australia / 3rd ed. – London : Butterworths, 1984.
ISBN 0409494003 Hbk £36.00

—Family Law in Australia / Family Law Act (Parliamentary Joint Select) Committee. – 2 vols. – Canberra : Australian Government Publishing Service, 1980.
247p.
ISBN 0642051704 Hbk £7.00

—Family Law in Australia / Rebecca Bailey-Harris. – 4th ed. – Butterworths, 1989.
ca 517p.
ISBN 0409495212 Hbk £69.00
ISBN 0409495220 Pbk £49.00

—Family law reports : incorporating Family law notes / Sydney : Butterworths, 1976-.
Contains reports and digests of judgments of the High Court of Australia, the Family Court of Australia, the Family Court of Western Australia, the Supreme Courts of the States and Territories.

—Guide to Family Law / Kensington : Bay Books.

—Guide to the Family Law Act / 4th ed. – Sydney : Butterworths, 1986.
240p.
The fifth edition of this work has been revised to reflect the changes to the Act that have occurred since 1982. It discusses jurisdictional grounds for dissolution and settlement, proceedings relating to children, ancillary property proceedings, preparation for hearings, and other topics.
ISBN 0409491055 Hbk £45.00
ISBN 0409491063 Pbk £32.00

—Guidebook to Australian Family Law / 6th ed. – North Ryde : C.C.H. Australia, 1985.
302p.
ISBN 086903541X Hbk £38.00

—Implications of marital separation for young children / compiled by the Australian Institute of Family Studies from a report of a survey conducted in 1982-83 by G.W. Smiley, E.R. Chamberlain and L.I. Dalgleish. – Melbourne : Australian Institute of Family Studies, 1987.
ix,45p. – (Working paper).
Bibliography: p.33-45.

—Law for parents and children / by Helen Gamble. – 2nd ed. – North Ryde, N.S.W. : Law Book Company, 1986.
vii,392p.
Includes bibliographical references and index.
ISBN 0455206937

—Manual for the Simulation of the Family Court of Australia / Canberra : Australian Government Publishing Service, 1981.
58p.
ISBN 064206749X Hbk £2.60

—Property and Finance in Family Law / R. Bailey. – Canberra : Australian National University, Research School of Social Sciences, 1981.
ISBN 0909596662 Pbk £9.00

—Reference on contempt of courts, tribunals and commissions / Australian Law Reform Commission. – Sydney : The Commission, 1985.
various pagings.

—Select Cases on the Family Law Act 1976-1985 / North Ryde : C.C.H. Australia, 1986.
1,006p.

Supplement-1987
48p.
ISBN 0869039652

FAMILY LAW - CANADA

—Canadian Family Law Cases : 1959-1977 / Butterworth & Co. (Canada) Ltd. – Toronto : Butterworths.
420p.
ISBN 0409989916 Pbk £60.00

Suppl. 1980
ISBN 0409989940 Pbk £40.00

—Canadian Family Law Cases 1983 Supplement / Toronto : Butterworths, 1983.
ISBN 0409989967 Hbk £40.00

—Carswell's Family Law Digest : 3rd Permanent Supplement / Agincourt : Carswell.

—Carswell's Family Law Digests, 9 Vols. / Agincourt : Carswell.
This text digests all the reported Canadian family law cases arranged according to the Canadian Abridgment classification system. This multi-volume set of books is supplemented by-annually. Special features include a Table of Cases, Index, and Cases and Statutes Judicially Considered.

—Child and Family Services Act : a Guide to Part 3 / Douglas J. Manning. – Butterworths, 1986.
208p.
Contains commentary following each section of the act, analysing both similarities and differences in the Child Welfare Act, major changes and modifications and intent in the new Act, selections of summaries of major cases decided under the old Act, and analyses key terms and categories, with reference to other relevant sections.
ISBN 0409805246 Hbk £55.00

—Contemporary Trends in Family Law : A National Perspective / Bartha Maria Knoppers. – Agincourt : Carswell, 1984.
334p.
This work is a collection of papers on Canadian family law presented at the Family Law Section of the Canadian Association of Law Teachers.

—Costs and Fees in Family Law Cases / Vancouver : British Columbia Continuing Legal Education Society, 1982.
118p.
ISBN 0865040842 Hbk £50.00

—Crisis intervention training for police / Don Dutton and Bruce Levens under the auspices of United Way of the Lower Mainland. – Ottawa : Ministry of the Solicitor General, 1985.
66p. – (User report).
Bibliography: p.51.

—Domestic Contracts / Agincourt : Carswell, 1987.
450p.
This looseleaf work is a practitioners guide to the drafting of cohabitation, marriage and separation agreements under the law of Ontario and British Columbia. Checklist, sample agreements, income tax considerations and related materials are included in the volume.

—Family Day Care Services Act, 1983, Bill Pr019 : An Act Respecting Family Day Care Services / Ontario : Ontario Government Publications Service, 1983.
1p.

—Family Dispute Resolution : Litigation and Its Alternatives / Agincourt : Carswell, 1987.
112p.

—Family Law : 1981 / Adams. – 2nd ed. – Auckland : Legal Research Foundation, 1982. – (Seminar Papers Ser.).

—Family Law / Daniel J. Baum. – Toronto : IPI Publishing, 1982.
84p. – (You and the Law Ser.).

—Family Law Agreements Manual / Vancouver : Continuing Legal Education Society of British Columbia, 1986.
418p.
ISBN 0865042780 Hbk £135.00

—Family Law and Practice for Legal Assistants / Vancouver : British Columbia Continuing Legal Education Society, 1983.
208p.
ISBN 0865041040 Hbk £50.00

—Family law and social welfare legislation in Canada / Ivan Bernier and Andree Lajoie, research coordinators. – Toronto : University of Toronto Press, 1986.
xv, 133 p.; 23 cm.
'Published by the University of Toronto Press in cooperation with the Royal Commission on the Economic Union and Development Prospects for Canada and the Canadian Government Publishing Centre, Supply and Services Canada.'. Includes bibliographies. Contents: Family law in Canada and the financial consequences of marriage breakdown and divorce / Julien D. Payne – Family law and social welfare in Canada / Mary Jane Mossman – Development and trends in Canadian social law, 1940-1984 / Robert D. Bureau, Katherine Lippel, and Lucie Lamarche.
ISBN 0802072941 pbk.

—Family Law Appeals and Injunctions / Vancouver : British Columbia Continuing Legal Education Society, 1984.
152p.
ISBN 0865041679 Hbk £55.00

—Family Law Awards : In Canada / Toronto : Butterworths, 1987.
328p.
ISBN 0409843938 Hbk £65.00

—Family Law Awards in Canada / Butterworths, 1987.
304p.
ISBN 0409409843938 Hbk £70.00

—Family law : cases, notes and materials / by Berend Hovius. – Toronto : Carswell, 1982.
xxix,885p.
ISBN 0459347802

—Family Law : Cases Notes Materials / 2nd ed. – Agincourt : Carswell, 1987.
ISBN 045930261 Hbk £33.00

—Family Law Cumulative Index 1971-1982 / Bristol : Jordan & Sons Ltd, 1985.

—Family law : dimensions of justice : selected papers presented at the Judicial Conference on Family Law, 1981 / edited by Rosalie S. Abella and Claire L'Heureux-Dube. – Toronto : Butterworths, 1983.
xxxi,330p.
The Canadian Institute for the Administration of Justice brought together judges to consider developments in family law and its social milieu. Includes essays by judges, psychiatrists, an economist and a tax specialist.
ISBN 0409819700

—Family Law in Canada / Agincourt : Carswell, 1984.
831p.

—Family Law in Canada : Carswell's Canadian Legal Classic Series / Agincourt : Carswell, 1984.
831p.

—Family Law Litigation / Vancouver : British Columbia Continuing Legal Education Society, 1980.
614p.

—Family Law Review : 1981 / Vancouver : British Columbia Continuing Legal Education Society, 1981.
277p.
ISBN 0865040249 Hbk £50.00

—Family Law : Solicitors' Considerations / Vancouver : Continuing Legal Education Society of British Columbia, 1986.
165p.

—Family Law Update / Vancouver : British Columbia Continuing Legal Education Society, 1982.
226p.
ISBN 0865040869 Hbk £55.00

—Family Mediation Handbook / Toronto : Butterworths, 1987.
300p.
Explains what makes mediation different from other forms of dispute resolution, addresses issues such as the establishment of the mediator's impartiality and clarifying the roles of mediator or solicitor, and discusses effects of mediation procedure on children of separation and divorce.
ISBN 0409811610 Pbk £35.95

—Family Mediation Handbook / Toronto : Butterworths.

—Family Mediation : Theory and Practice of Dispute Resolutions / Michael Benjamin. – Agincourt : Carswell, 1987.
320p.
This work is a comprehensive guide to family mediation, the process of resolving property support and custody issues with the aid of a third party in Canada. The effectiveness of various mediation efforts based on empirical studies is presented in the work.

—Family Practice in Provincial Court : Custody, Access, and Maintenance / Vancouver : Continuing Legal Education Society of British Columbia, 1987.
306p.
ISBN 0865043450 Hbk £80.00

—Income Tax and Family Law Handbook, 1 Vol. / Mary Lou Benotto. – Butterworths.
ISBN 0409806471 loose £100.00

—Income tax and family law handbook / Mary Lou Benotto. – 1 vol. – Scarborough, Ontario : Butterworths (Canada).
Includes coverage of alimony and maintenance, attribution, child care expenses, child tax credit, common law spouses, dependants, family allowances, legal costs, pension benefits, principle residence, property division, registered retirement savings plan, and tax liability.
ISBN 0409806471 Loose leaf

—Introduction to Family Law / Butterworths, 1983.
180p.
Outlines how the law operates in each common law province. Coverage includes marriage, rights and duties, marriage and property, termination of marriage, children, and reform in children's law.
ISBN 040984828X Pbk £21.95

—Introduction to Family Law / Toronto : Butterworths, 1983.
180p.

—National Themes in Family Law / Diane Pask. – Agincourt : Carswell, 1988.
320p.

—Ontario annotated family law service / Student edition. – Scarborough, Ontario : Butterworths (Canada), 1988.
Covers leading cases relating to a particular section, annotated, all Ontario and Federal statutes pertaining to federal law, together with regulations made under the statutes, and a legislative history following each amended section, giving the citation of the amendment.
ISBN 0409887021 Llf

—Payne's Divorce and Family Law Digest, 2 Vols. / Toronto : DeBoo.
This looseleaf service contains the information required to negotiate settlements and the materials needed to prepare for litigation involving such issues as support, custody, & property division. The case digests provided cover such areas as Ontario's Family Law Act, 1986, enforcement, costs, evidence, procedure, and tax considerations. Six updates per year are planned.
ISBN 0888202423 loose £265.00

—Practical Guide to the Family Law Act 1986 / Agincourt : Carswell, 1988.
230p.

—Practical Guide to the Family Law Act / Agincourt : Carswell, 1988.
238p.
This is an in-depth guide to the law pursuant to the Family Law Act, 1986. Discussions include jurisdiction, property, matrimonial home, support obligations and domestic contracts. The complete text of the Act is included. Also included is the relevant caselaw.

—Reports of Family Law : 1824-1970, 5 Vols. / Agincourt : Carswell.
– (Reprint Ser.).

—Reports of Family Law, 50 / Carswell Legal Publications. – Agincourt : Carswell.
– (Second Ser.).
Back Vols.

—Reports of Family Law Consolidated Index, 4 Vols. / Agincourt : Carswell, 1980.
1331p.
Vol. 2 1980.
Vol. 3 1984.
Vol. 4 1986.

—Weekly Digest of Family Law / Agincourt : Carswell, 1986.

—Women and the constitution in Canada / edited by Audrey Doerr and Micheline Carrier. – Ottawa : Canadian Advisory Council on the Status of Women, 1981.
x,223p.
Includes bibliographical notes. Contains papers prepared for Canadian Advisory Council on the Status of Women conference scheduled for September 1980.
ISBN 0660108720

FAMILY LAW - CANADA - ALBERTA

—Alberta Family Law / Student ed. – Toronto : Butterworths, 1983.
ISBN 0409996823 Hbk £26.95

—Alberta Family Law / Toronto : Butterworths.
– (Alberta Annotated Legislation Ser).

—Alberta Family Law : Alberta Annotated Legislation Series, 1 Vol. / Butterworths.

—Marriage and Family Law in Alberta : the Rights of Husbands, Wives, Children, and Common-Law / 3rd ed. – North Vancouver : International Self-Counsel Press, 1987.
203p.
ISBN 0889082456 Hbk £8.95

FAMILY LAW - CANADA - BRITISH COLUMBIA

—British Columbia Family Law, 2 vols / Toronto : Butterworths.
Illus.

—British Columbia Family Law, 2 Vols. / rev. ed. – Butterworths.

—Butterworth's British Columbia Family Law Quantum Service, 2 vol / Anisa Dhanja. – Toronto : Butterworths.

—Butterworths British Columbia Family Law Quantum Service, 2 Vols. / Anisa Dhanji. – Butterworths.

—Butterworths British Columbia Family Law Quantum Service / Anisa Dhanji. – Toronto : Butterworths.

—Intentional interference with domestic relations / Law Reform Commission of British Columbia. – Vancouver : The Commission, 1983.
iii,55p. – (Working paper).
Includes bibliographical references.

—Marriage and Family Law in British Columbia : the Rights of Husbands, Wives, Children, and Common-Law / 6th ed. – North Vancouver : International Self-Counsel Press, 1985.
160p.
ISBN 0889081697 Hbk £7.95

—Report on international interference with domestic relations / Law Reform Commission of British Columbia. – Victoria : Queen's Printer, 1983.
27p.
Includes bibliographical references.
ISBN 0771883986

—Reports of family law / Toronto : Carswell, 1971.
Consolidated indexes published for first and second series.

FAMILY LAW - CANADA - ONTARIO

—Butterworth's Ontario Family Law Quantum Service, 2 vols / Ellen E. Mole. – Toronto : Butterworths.

—Butterworths Ontario Family Law Quantum Service, 2 Vols. / Ellen E. Mole. – Butterworths.

—Butterworths Ontario Family Law Quantum Service, 2 vols / Ellen E. Mole. – Toronto : Butterworths.

—Family law in the family courts / 2nd ed. v. – Toronto : Carswell, 1981.
Previous ed.: 1973, edited by H.T.G. Andrews. Includes index.
ISBN 0459337300

—Famiy Law Reform Act, 1983, Bill 093 : An Act to Amend the Family Law Reform Act / Ontario : Ontario Government Publications Service, 1983.
1p.

—Law and Practice Under the Family Law Act of Ontario / Revised Edit. – Agincourt : Carswell, 1986.
This looseleaf work provides analysis of the Family Law Act of Ontario for the practitioner, along with summaries of relevant case law. Problems in preparation and drafting of domestic documents are discussed in the work, as well as, income tax implications and the valuation of family property.

—Law and Practice under the Family Law Act of Ontario / rev. ed. – Agincourt : Carswell, 1986.
ca 650p.

—Marriage and Family Law in Ontario : the Rights of Husbands, Wives, Children, and Common-Law Spouses / 4th ed. – North Vancouver : International Self-Counsel Press, 1986.
203p.
ISBN 0889083606 Hbk £6.95

—Ontario Annotated Family Law Service, 1 Vol. / Butterworths.

—Ontario Annotated Family Law Service / Toronto : Butterworths.

—Ontario annotated family law service / Student edition. – Scarborough, Ontario : Butterworths (Canada), 1988.
Covers leading cases relating to a particular section, annotated, all Ontario and Federal statutes pertaining to federal law, together with regulations made under the statutes, and a legislative history following each amended section, giving the citation of the amendment.
ISBN 0409887021 Llf

—Ontario Family Law Act / Aurora : Canada Law Book Co.
– (Text Books-Civil).
This manual is a working guide to the Ontario Family Law Act of 1986. Divided into four main parts, this manual includes the full text of each section of the Act, insightful author commentary, convenient cross-referencing and case law with unreported decisions.

—Ontario Family Law Reform Act Manual (O.F.L.R.) 1979-Present / Aurora : Canada Law Book Co.
Bdrs. and Contents

—Ontario Family Law Reports / Jeffery Wilson. – Butterworths.
ISBN 0409809136 loose £135.00

FAMILY LAW - CHINA

—Conservatism in Modern Chinese Family Law / Leiden : E.J. Brill, 1956.
ISBN 9004032630 Hbk £28.00

FAMILY LAW - COMMONWEALTH

—Decade of women and the law in the Commonwealth / prepared by Margaret Rogers for the Hubert Humphrey Institute of Public Affairs in association with the Commonwealth Secretariat. – London : Legal Division, Commonwealth Secretariat, 1985.
xvii,342p.
ISBN 0850922720

—Family law : the Commonwealth experience / by Gloria Cumper. – London : Commonwealth Secretariat, 1984.
v,109p.
Includes bibliographies.
ISBN 0850922569

—Recognition of family judgements in the Commonwealth / London : Butterworths, 1983.
ISBN 040640321X Hbk £42.00

FAMILY LAW - ENGLAND

—Butterworths family law service / general editor P.M. Bromley : editors H.K. Bevan et al. – London : Butterworths, 1983.
looseleaf.
Includes bibliographical references and index.
ISBN 040610719X

—Domestic injunctions / Margaret R. de Haas : with a foreword by H.H. Judge Nance. – London : Sweet & Maxwell, 1987.
xxviii,187p; 26cm.
Explains the steps involved in proceeding with an action, from originating application to enforcement, including procedures under the Child Abduction and Custody Act 1985. Includes selected rules of the Supreme and County Courts, precedents and forms, and a precis of decisions.
ISBN 0421365102 £19.50

—Elements of family law / by Stephen M. Cretney. – London : Sweet & Maxwell, 1987.
280p; 24cm.
Includes index.
ISBN 0421352302 Hbk £19.50
ISBN 042135240X Pbk £11.95

—Essays in family law 1985 / edited by M.D.A. Freeman. – London : Stevens, 1986.
xiv,118p; 22cm.
Includes index.
ISBN 0420475109 Pbk £13.50

—Family and child law statutes / Paul H. Niekirk. – 2nd ed. 1. – London : Longman, 1987.
23cm.
Previous ed.: compiled by Oyez Longman editorial staff. 1984.
ISBN 0851213480 Pbk £19.95

—Family Court reporter / Chicester : Justice of the Peace Ltd., 1987-.

—Family home / by W.T. Murphy and Hilary Clark. – London : Sweet & Maxwell, 1983.
229p; 19cm. – (Modern legal studies).
Includes index.
ISBN 0421287403 Hbk Unpriced
ISBN 0421287500 Pbk £6.95

—Family jurisdiction of the High Court and County Courts : consultation paper / London : Lord Chancellor's Department, 1983.
12p.

—Family law / P.M. Bromley, N.V. Lowe. – 7th ed. – London : Butterworths, 1987.
lvi,793p; 25cm.
Previous ed. 1981. Includes index. Cover title: Bromley's family law.
ISBN 0406560145 Hbk £30.00
ISBN 0406560153 Pbk £17.95

—Family law / Grant and Levin. – 4th ed. – London : Sweet & Maxwell, 1982.
xxi,146p; 23cm.
Previous ed.: 1977. Includes index.
ISBN 0421302402 Hbk £9.75
ISBN 0421282800 Pbk £5.50

—Family law and practice / Peter D. Reekie and Richard Tuddenham. – London : Sweet & Maxwell, 1988.
xxxv,415p; 22cm.
Sections cover divorce and other decrees; financial provision (including property adjustment); children; and family violence. Also contains a chapter on legal aid and legal advice and assistance, and discusses the courts and conciliation.
ISBN 0421360003 Pbk £13.50

—Family, law and society : cases and materials / Brenda M. Hoggett, David S. Pearl. – 2nd ed. – London : Butterworths, 1987.
670p; 25cm.
Previous ed.: 1983. Includes bibliography and index.
ISBN 0406595925 Pbk £30.00 :
ISBN 0406595933 £22.50

—Family law : declarations in family matters / The Law Commission. – London : H.M.S.O., 1984.
iv,82p; 25cm. – (H.C.).
ISBN 0102263841

—Family law in a nutshell / Victor Davidson. – London : Sweet and Maxwell, 1980.
vi,90p; 18cm.
Includes index.
ISBN 0421265701 Pbk £1.50

—Family property and financial provision / by J.G. Miller. – 2nd ed. – London : Sweet & Maxwell, 1983.
xlvi,517p; 26cm.
Previous ed.: 1974. Includes index.
ISBN 0421282401 £36.00

—Family violence : law & practice / Joanne Foakes. – London : Hemstal Press, 1984.
xvi,176p.
Includes index.

—Justice annual member's conference held in the Lord Chief Justice's Court on Saturday 26th March, 1983 : subject family law / chairman Lord McGregor. – London : Justice, 1983.
44p.

—Practical family law / John Richman and F.S.T. Dealy. – Chichester : Rose, 1980.
57p; 21cm.
ISBN 0859922081 Pbk £3.50

—Principles of family law / by S.M. Cretney. – 4th ed. – London : Sweet & Maxwell, 1984.
lxxx,1018p; 25cm.
Covers marriage, the termination of marriage, protection, children and family law, family financial obligations and property rights and the courts. Includes changes effected by the Matrimonial and Family Proceedings Act 1984, and the section on the law governing children in care has been expanded.
ISBN 042128840X Hbk No price
ISBN 0421288507 Pbk £19.50

—Rayden and Jackson's law and practice in divorce and family matters / Joseph Jackson, Margaret Booth, G. J. Maple, A. K. Biggs. – 15th ed. 2 v. – London : Butterworths, 1988.
26cm.
Kept up to date by a looseleaf service.
ISBN 0406351317

—Resolving family conflict in the 1980s : a unified family court / Justices' Clerks' Society. – Bristol : The Society, 1982.
88p.

—Sweet & Maxwell's family law statutes / Olive M. Stone, Jenny Bough. – 3rd ed. – London : Sweet & Maxwell, 1981.
xiii,549p; 25cm.
Previous ed.: 1976. Includes index.
ISBN 0421280808 Hbk £15.50
ISBN 0421280905 Pbk £12.65

FAMILY LAW - GAMBIA

—Memoranda and draft : bills re : christian marriage, matrimonial causes, offences relating to property and lands (Banjul and Kombo St. Mary) / Law Reform Commission of the Gambia. – Banjul : The Commission?, 1985.
xv,112p.
Includes the text of draft legislation.

—Women and legal affairs / a paper jointly prepared by Mariam Denton, Amie Bensouda, Fola Mendy Allen. – Banjul, the Gambia? : s.n., 1985.
10p.
At head of cover title: The Gambia National Women's Council and Bureau. Cover title: End of Women's Decade Conference on Women in Development, 24th-26th April 1985.

FAMILY LAW - GREAT BRITAIN

—Butterworth's Family Law Service / H. K. Bevan. – Wellington : Butterworths, 1986.
ISBN 0406107203 loose

—Current Practice Directions : Family and Probate / London : Family Law, 1988.
ISBN 0853081085 loose £35.00

—Custodianship : the law and practice / London : Fourmat, 1986.
ISBN 185900152 Pbk £7.95

—Divided Families / Turnaround Press, 1987.
ISBN 0902397575 Pbk £2.95

—Elements of Family Law / London : Sweet & Maxwell, 1987.
ISBN 0421352302 Hbk £19.50
ISBN 042135240X Pbk £13.50

—Emergency Family Remedies / London : Longman Professional, 1987.
ISBN 0851211143 Pbk £12.50

—Essays in Family Law / London : Sweet & Maxwell, 1986.
ISBN 0420475109 Pbk £18.50

—Family and child law statutes / 3rd. – London : Longman Professional (UK), 1990.
Updated with 1988 and 1989 legislative changes including the Children Act 1989, plus the Adoption Act 1976.
ISBN 0851215750 Pbk £24.50

—Family at Law / Police Review, 1985.
ISBN 085164051X Pbk £2.50

—Family Court in Action / London : Butterworths, 1983.
ISBN 0406556504 Hbk £20.00
ISBN 0406556512 Pbk £14.95

—Family Law / 3rd ed. – Plymouth : Macdonald & Evans, 1986.
ISBN 0712107584 Pbk £6.50

—Family Law / 2nd ed. – Plymouth : Macdonald & Evans, 1984.
288p. – (M and E Handbook Ser.).
ISBN 0712106472 Hbk £5.95

—Family Law / 7th ed. – London : Butterworths, 1987.
ISBN 0406560145 Hbk £38.00
ISBN 0406560153 Pbk £23.95

—Family law and social policy / John Eekelaar. – 2nd ed. – London : Weidenfeld and Nicolson, 1984.
xviii,263p.
Includes index. Bibliography: p241-255.
ISBN 0297782746

—Family, Law and Society : Cases and Materials / 2nd ed. – London : Butterworths, 1987.

—Family Law and Society : Cases and Materials / Pearl. – 2nd ed. – London : Butterworths, 1987.
ISBN 0406595925 Hbk £38.00
ISBN 0406595933 Pbk £23.95

—Family law and the immigrant communities / David Pearl. – Bristol : Family law, 1986.
xxi,104p; 21cm. – (Guide and practice series).
ISBN 0853081026

—Family Law In 1985 : A New Look At Some Old Problems / London : Law Society, 1985.
23p. – (Nineteen Eighty-Five Crash Course Transcripts).

—Family Law Journal / Elizabeth Walsh. – Bristol : Jordan & Sons Ltd, 1986.

—Family Law Reports Cumulative Index 1980-1984 / Bristol : Jordan & Sons Ltd, 1985.

—Family Law Reports. Vol. 6 / I. W. Crompton. – Bristol : Jordan & Sons Ltd, 1986.

—Family Law (SWOT) / London : Blackstone Press, 1985.
ISBN 0906322901 Pbk £7.50

—Family, state and law in Britain today / 1 v. – London : Institute of Advanced Legal Studies, University of London, 1983.
various pagings. – (W.G. Hart Legal Workshop).
Includes bibliographical references.

—Guide to the New Law in Family Proceedings in Magistrates Courts / 2nd ed. – Chichester : Barry Rose, 1981.
ISBN 0859922065 Pbk £6.00

—In Place of a Parent / Bristol : Jordan & Sons Ltd, 1986.
– (Family Law Practitioner's Ser.).
ISBN 0853081018 Pbk

—Law and Practice in Matrimonial Causes / Caroline Harmer. – 4th ed. – London : Butterworths, 1985.
This text is an introduction to matrimonial law and a guide to developments in the area for students of the subject in England. All forms and model pleadings reflect the Matrimonial and Family Proceedings Act of 1984 and the Matrimonial Homes Act of 1983.
ISBN 0406637083 Hbk
ISBN 0406637075 Pbk

—Law in Relation to Children / Morrison. – 10th ed. – London : Butterworths, 1985.
Service to 31.3.89.
ISBN 0406158126 loose £145.00

—Matrimonial and Family Law Up to Date / London : Law Society, 1985.
69p.

—Matrimonial Consent Orders and Agreements / London : Longman Professional, 1986.
ISBN 0851211127 Pbk £12.95

—Parents and Children / London : Sweet & Maxwell, 1987.
ISBN 042136050X Pbk £17.00

—Practical approach to family law / 2nd ed. – London : Blackstone Press, 1988.
ISBN 1854310813 Pbk £14.95

—Reports of Family Law /. – Agincourt : Carswell.

—Social welfare law / David Pearl and Kevin Gray. – London : Croom Helm, 1981.
308p; 23cm.
Bibliography: p265. - Includes index.
ISBN 085664644X Hbk £14.95
ISBN 0709920040 Pbk £8.95

—Standing of a Common Law Spouse to Apply Under the Family Compensation Act / Victoria : Government of British Columbia, 1983.

—State, law and the family / London : Sweet & Maxwell, 1984.
ISBN 042279080X Pbk £9.95

—When salem came to the Boro / Pan Books, 1988.
ISBN 0330305034 Pbk £3.99

—Women and Children First / Belfast : Queen's University of Belfast.
48p.

FAMILY LAW - HONG KONG

—Family law in Hong Kong / Leanard Pegg. – 2nd ed. – Singapore : Butterworths (Asia), 1986.
vii,256.
Explains the current law relating to the family in Hong Kong. Deals with the transition from customary to enacted law, and notes the problems that have arisen, and could arise in the future. Covers marriage and concubinage, matrimonial causes, financial obligations to the family, and adoption.
ISBN 040999524X Hbk £80

—Family Law in Hong Kong / London : Butterworths, 1986.
ISBN 040999524X Pbk £38.00

—Family law in Hong Kong / Leonard Pegg. – London : Butterworths, 1981.
xxii,183p; 23cm.
Includes index.
ISBN 0406667608

FAMILY LAW - INDIA

—Hindu Family Law and Social Change / Bombay : University of Bombay, Publications Department.

FAMILY LAW - IRELAND

—Casebook on Family Law in Ireland / Abingdon : Professional Books, 1984.

—Casebook on Irish Family Law / Abingdon : Professional Books, 1984.
487p.
ISBN 0862050847 Hbk £42.50
ISBN 0862050898 Pbk £34.00

—Casebook on Irish Family Law / London : Butterworths, 1984.
ISBN 0862050898 Pbk £22.50

—First report on family law : criminal coversation, enticement and harbouring of a spouse or child, loss of consortium, personal injury to a child, seduction of a child, matrimonial property and breach of promise of marriage / the Law Reform Commission. – Dublin : The Commission, 1981.
iii,32p. – (LRC).

—Shatter's Family law in the Republic of Ireland / Alan Joseph Shatter. – 3rd ed. – Dublin : Wolfhound, 1986.
608p; 25cm.
Previous ed.: published as Family law in the Republic of Ireland. 1981. Includes index.
ISBN 0863270808 HBK £45.00
ISBN 0863270816 Pbk £30.00

FAMILY LAW - JAMAICA

—Planning and implementing the Family Court project, Jamaica / Gloria Cumper. – Kingston, Jamaica : Institute of Social and Economic Research, University of the West Indies, 1981.
i,75p. – (Working paper).

FAMILY LAW - LESOTHO

—Law and population growth in Lesotho / Sebastian Poulter...et al. – Roma, Lesotho : Law and Population Project, Faculty of Law, National University of Lesotho, 1981.
96p.

FAMILY LAW - MALAYSIA

—Family law in Malaysia and Singapore / by Tan Sri Datuk Professor Ahmad Ibrahim. – 2nd ed. – Singapore : Malayan Law Journal, 1984.
xxvi,359p.
Covers the family law of non-muslims, marriage, and its effects on status and property, divorce and matrimonial proceedings, inheritance rights, the effect of marriage on the legal status of women under Islamic law, the dissolution of Muslim marriage, and inheritance rights.
ISBN 9971700395 Hbk

FAMILY LAW - NEW ZEALAND

—Butterworth's Family Law Bulletin / Hellen Papadopoulas. – Wellington : Butterworths.

—Butterworths Family Law Guide / 3rd ed. - Butterworths, 1989.
ISBN 0409788805 Pbk

—Butterworths Family Law Reports / Butterworths.

—Butterworths Family Law Service / Butterworths.

—Domestic violence : the Domestic Protection Bill 1982 : paper presented at Auckland law Faculty Seminar Series 1982 at University of Auckland / by Pauline Tapp. - Auckland : Legal Research Foundation Inc., 1982.
14,14p.
Includes the text of the Bill.
ISBN 090858122X

—Family Court Code / Butterworths, 1983.
Discusses the Family Courts Act 1980, the Family Proceedings Act 1980, the Guardianship Act 1968 as amended in 1980, the Status of Children Act 1969, the Domestic Protection Act 1969, the Family Proceedings Rules 1981, and the Domestic Protection Rules 1983.
ISBN 0409601276 Hbk

—Family law 1981 / by P.R.H. Webb and J.G. Adams. - New Zealand : Legal Research Foundation Inc., 1981.
128p; 21cm.
Includes bibliographical references. At head of title: Legal Research Foundation Inc. Seminar.
ISBN 0908581122

—Family law 1984 style / by P.R.H. Webb and J.G. Adams. - Auckland : Legal Research Foundation, 1984.
182p.
Includes bibliographical references. At head of title: Legal Research Foundation Inc. Seminar.
ISBN 0908581327

—Family law 1986 style / by Professor P.R.H. Webb and J.G. Adams. - 4th ed. - Auckland : Legal Research Foundation, 1986.
i,207p.
Previous edition: 1984. Includes bibliographical references.
ISBN 0908581416

—Family Law Statutes / Butterworths of New Zealand. - 2nd ed. - Butterworths, 1988.
516p.
ISBN 0409788627 Pbk £54.00

—New Zealand Family Law Legislation / North Ryde : C.C.H. Australia, 1987.
1,600p.
ISBN 086475003X Hbk £30.00

—Practice and procedure in the Family Court : papers presented at the Family Law Seminar, University of Auckland, 26 May, 1984 / by B.D. Inglis. - Auckland : Legal Research Foundation, 1984.
22p.
At head of title: Legal Research Foundation Inc. Family Law Seminar.
ISBN 0908581351

FAMILY LAW - NIGERIA

—Casebook on Nigerian Family Law and Succession / Abingdon : Professional Books, 1986.
800p.
ISBN 0862051150 Hbk £42.00

FAMILY LAW - PACIFIC ISLANDS

—Family Law and Population in the Pacific Islands / Suva : University of the South Pacific, Institute of Pacific Studies.

FAMILY LAW - PAPUA NEW GUINEA

—Principles of family law in Papua New Guinea / by Owen Jessep and John Luluaki. - Waigani : University of Papua New Guinea Press, 1985.
205p.
Bibliography: pp.194-197. - Includes index.
ISBN 9980840137

FAMILY LAW - PHILIPPINES

—Personal and Family Law / Manila : National Book Store, 1984.
602p.
ISBN 9710805282 Hbk £35.00

FAMILY LAW - SCOTLAND

—Family Law in Scotland / London : Butterworths, 1987.
ISBN 0406261903 Pbk £18.00

—Family law in Scotland / J.M. Thomson. - London : Butterworths, 1987.
xxiv,232p; 22cm.
Includes index.
ISBN 0406261903 Pbk £20.00

—The Family Law (Scotland) Act 1985 / Edinburgh : W Green & Son, 1986.
Full text of the Act with annotations reprinted from Scottish Current Law Statutes. The Act provides a new statement of the obligations of aliment and a new code for the settling of property and financial claims on a divorce.
ISBN 0414007840

—Family property in Scotland : an enquiry carried out on behalf of the Scottish Law Commission by the Social Survey Division of the Office of Population Censuses and Surveys in 1979 / A.J. Manners, I. Rauta. - London : H.M.S.O., 1981.
iv,45p.
ISBN 0116907797

—Guide to Family Law (Scotland) Act 1985 / London : CCH, 1986.
ISBN 0863250629 Pbk £9.00

—Guide to the Family Law (Scotland) Act 1985 / Bicester : CCH Editions Ltd.
Includes the full text of the Act and of the new Rules of Court. Contains useful illustrations of how the principles will operate in practice. Covers obligations of aliment, actions for aliment, financial provisions on divorce, orders for financial provisions on divorce, nullity, agreements on aliment and financial provisions, and matrimonial property.
ISBN 0863250629 Pbk £9.00

—Guide to the Family Law (Scotland) Act 1985 / H.R.M. MacDonald. - London : CCH Editions, 1986.
vi,118p.
Includes the text of the Family Law (Scotland) Act 1985.
ISBN 0863250807

—Matrimonial Homes (Family Protection) (Scotland) Act 1981 / by D.I. Nichols and M.C. Meston. - Edinburgh : Green, 1982.
vii,68p.
Includes index.
ISBN 0414006879 PBK £15.75

—Scots Statutes 1983 : Family Law; Succession, Trusts, Liferents and Judicial Factors / Edinburgh : W Green, 1983.
ISBN 0414007255 Hbk £6.50

—Scots Statutes 1984 : Family Law; Succession, Trusts, Liferents and Judicial Factors / Edinburgh : W Green.
ISBN 041400745X Hbk £14.75

—Scots Statutes 1985 : Family Law - Succession, Trusts, Liferent andJudicial Factors / Edinburgh : W Green.
- (Reprint from the Parliament House Book).
ISBN 0414007662 Hbk £10.00

FAMILY LAW - SINGAPORE

—Family law in Malaysia and Singapore / by Tan Sri Datuk Professor Ahmad Ibrahim. - 2nd ed. - Singapore : Malayan Law Journal, 1984.
xxvi,359p.
Covers the family law of non-muslims, marriage, and its effects on status and property, divorce and matrimonial proceedings, inheritance rights, the effect of marriage on the legal status of women under Islamic law, the dissolution of Muslim marriage, and inheritance rights.
ISBN 9971700395 Hbk

—Parent-Child Law in Singapore / London : Butterworths, 1984.
ISBN 0406181217 Pbk £25.00

FAMILY LAW - SOUTH AFRICA

—Family, things and succession / Lee and Honore. - 2nd ed. - Durban : Butterworths, 1983.
xvii,615p.
Bibliography: p.vii-xiv. - Includes index.
ISBN 0409040533

—South African law of husband and wife / H. R. Hahlo. - 5th ed. - Cape Town : Juta, 1985.
lxx,526p.
ISBN 0702115681

—South African law of persons and family law / by P.J.J. Olivier. - 2nd ed. - Durban : Butterworths, 1980.
xxvi,356p; 22cm.
Includes index.
ISBN 0409046167 Pbk
ISBN 0409046175

—Two lectures on law reform : delivered at the workshop on Marriage and Family Life by the Human Sciences Research Council on 26 September 1985 / by J.T. Delport and C.R.M. Dlamini. - Pretoria : Government Printer on behalf of the South African Law Comission, 1987.
iv,38p. - (Research series).
Bibliography: pp.19-21.
ISBN 0621106704

FAMILY LAW - SRI LANKA

—Legal Status of the Female in the Sri Lanka Law on Family Relations / Colombo : Gunasena and Co..

FAMILY LAW - SWEDEN

—New Swedish family legislation : the Marriage Code : the Cohabitees (Joint Homes) Act : the Homosexual Cohabitees Act : the Inheritance Code, chapters 1-3 and 7 / Stockholm : Ministry of Justice, 1988.
37p.
'... translations of ... Swedish legislation published in the Swedish Code of Statutes (SFS)'. - p.1.

FAMILY LAW - UNITED KINGDOM

—Guide to the New Law of Family Proceedings in Magistrates Courts, Including Adoption / Chichester : Barry Rose, 1983.
ii, 49p.
ISBN 0859920631 Hbk £4.60

FAMILY LAW - UNITED STATES

—Marriage and Family Law in Washington : the Rights of Husbands, Wives, Children and Cohabiting Couples / 3rd ed. - North Vancouver : International Self-Counsel Press, 1988.
ISBN 0889087377 Hbk

FAMILY LAW COURTS - AUSTRALIA

—Jurisdiction of magistrates under the Family Law Act 1975 / Family Law Council. - Canberra : Australian Government Publishing Service, 1980.
27p. - (Working paper).
ISBN 0642050384

FAMILY LAW COURTS - CANADA - ONTARIO

—Family law in the family courts / 2nd ed. v. - Toronto : Carswell, 1981.
Previous ed.: 1973, edited by H.T.G. Andrews. Includes index.
ISBN 0459337300

FAMILY LAW COURTS - ENGLAND

—'Better way out' reviewed : memorandum / by the Society's Standing Committee on Family Law. - London : Law Society, 1982.
41p.

—Family jurisdiction of the High Court and County Courts : consultation paper / London : Lord Chancellor's Department, 1983.
12p.

—Interdepartmental review of family and domestic jurisdiction : a consultation paper / London : Lord Chancellors Department, 1986.
96p.

—Magistrates' domestic courts : new perspectives / edited by Tony F. Marshall. - London : Home Office, 1984.
v,49p.
Conference papers.
ISBN 0862521696

—Matrimonial jurisdiction of magistrates' courts / by M.D.A. Freeman and Christina M. Lyon. - Chichester : Rose, 1980.
xxv,222p; 21cm.
Includes index.
ISBN 0859921999 Pbk £10.80

—Reciprocal enforcement : a practical guide to magistrates' courts' jurisdiction & procedure in international domestic proceedings / Desmond A.G. James : with a foreword by Dewi E. Davies. - Chichester : Rose, 1984.
133p; 22cm.
Includes index.
ISBN 0859923320 £17.75

—Towards a unified family court : court orders concerning children : overlapping jurisdictions / Jean Graham Hall, Douglas F. Martin. - s.l. : s.n., 1986.
88p.

FAMILY LAW (ISLAMIC LAW)

—Family Laws of Islam / Lahore : Kazi Publications.

—Islamic family law / Jane Connors. - London : Graham & Trotman, 1989.
350; 240mm.
Covers current research into areas of Islamic family law in the form of articles. Addresses historical issues such as the development of the law of succession in Islamic law, the colonial encounter and its impact on Islamic family law in India, as well as contemporary law of the family in Egypt, the sub-continent, Iran and Europe, and the law of minorities in their relation to the state.
ISBN 1853333018 Hbk £35

—Islamic Family Law (Federal Territory) Act, 1984 (Act 303) / Kuala Lumpur : International Law Books Services.

—Muslim family law : a sourcebook / Keith Hodkinson. - London : Croom Helm, 1984.
401p; 22cm.
Bibliography: p367-377. - Includes index.
ISBN 0709912560 Pbk £14.95

FAMILY LAW (ROMAN-DUTCH LAW)

—Quaestiones juris privati / by Cornelius van Bijnkershoek : translated by R.A. Whitaker. - 2. - Pretoria : Government Printer on behalf of the South African Law Commission, 1987.
- (Research series).
Includes bibliographical references.

FAMILY POLICY - AUSTRALIA

—Annual report/Institute of Family Studies, Australia / Institute of Family Studies. - Melbourne : Australian Institute of Family Studies, 1980-.

FAMILY PROVISION (SUCCESSION) - GREAT BRITAIN

—Family Provision / Oughton. – 2nd ed. – London : Butterworths, 1984.
ISBN 0862050758 Hbk £30.75

—Family Provision on Death (LPPN33) / 6th ed. – London : Longman Professional, 1987.
ISBN 0851210694 Pbk £14.95

—Family Provision Practice / 5th ed. – London : Oyez Longman, 1983.
– (Oyez Longman Practice Note Ser.: No. 33).
ISBN 0851207243 Hbk £8.95

FEDERAL AREAS WITHIN STATES - NIGERIA

—Constitutional relevance of the provision for the seat of government / by Jadesola O. Akande. – Lagos : Nigerian Institute of Advanced Legal Studies, 1983.
15p.
Seminar paper presented at the Institute on Wednesday, March 23, 1983.

FEDERAL GOVERNMENT

—Component units of federal states and international agreements / Luigi Di Marzo. – Aalphen aan den Rijn : Sijthoff & Noordhoff, 1980.
xxvi,242p.
Bibliography: p.229-235.
ISBN 9028603301

—Federal finance in comparative perspective / Richard M. Bird. – Toronto : Canadian Tax Foundation, 1986.
x,250p.
Includes bibliographical references.
ISBN 0888080247

—Integration through law : Europe and the American federal experience : a series / under the general editorship of Mauro Cappelletti, Monica Seccombe, Joseph Weiler. – 3 v. – Berlin, : W. de Gruyter, 1986.
– (Series A, Law).
Includes bibliographical references and index. Contents: bk.1. A political, legal and economic overview - bk.2. Political organs, integration techniques and judicial process - bk.3. Forces and potential for a European identity.

Vol. 2 : Environmental protection policy : by Eckard Rehbinder and Richard Stewart : associate editor Patrick del Duca / under the general editorship of Mauro Cappelletti, Monica Seccombe, Joseph Weiler. – 1985.
xxiv,350p. – (Series A, Law).
Includes bibliographical references and indexes.

Vol. 5 : The legal integration of energy markets : by Terence Daintith and Stephen F. Williams / under the general editorship of Mauro Cappelletti, Monica Seccombe, Joseph Weiler. – 1987.
xxvii,176p. – (Series A, Law).
Includes bibliographical references and index.
ISBN 3110107430 Hbk

FEDERAL GOVERNMENT - AUSTRALIA

—Australian federal constitutional law / by Colin Howard. – 3rd ed. – Sydney : Law Book Company, 1985.
lxxviii,611p.
Bibliography: pxliii-li.
ISBN 0455205736

—Federal Power in Australia's Cities / Neutral Bay : Hale & Iremonger.
ISBN 0908094043 Hbk £19.00, 015

FEDERAL GOVERNMENT - CANADA

—Canada in question : federalism in the eighties / Donald V. Smiley. – 3rd ed. – Toronto : McGraw-Hill Ryerson, 1980.
xii,347p.
Bibliographies.

—Legal status of the federal administration / Law Reform Commission of Canada. – Ottawa : The Commission, 1985.
106,111p. – (Working paper).
Includes bibliographical references. Added t.p. in French: Le statut juridique de l'administration federale. Pages numbered in opposite directions.

—Notes on Canadian federalism / Canada. – Ottawa : Minister of Supply and Services, 1984.
54p.
ISBN 0662130049

FEDERAL GOVERNMENT - EUROPEAN COMMUNITY

—Integration through law : Europe and the American federal experience / under the general editorship of Mauro Cappelletti, Monica Seccombe and Joseph Weiler. – Berlin : Walter de Gruyter, 1987.
xxiii,271p. – (Series A, Law).
Bibliographical references.

FEDERAL GOVERNMENT - NIGERIA

—Constitutional relevance of the provision for the seat of government / by Jadesola O. Akande. – Lagos : Nigerian Institute of Advanced Legal Studies, 1983.
15p.
Seminar paper presented at the Institute on Wednesday, March 23, 1983.

—Federalism in Nigeria under the presidential constitution / by B.O. Nwabueze. – London : Sweet & Maxwell, 1983.
400p.
Includes index.
ISBN 0421316101 Hbk No price
ISBN 0421315806 Pbk £16.00

FEDERAL GOVERNMENT - UNITED STATES

—Integration through law : Europe and the American federal experience / under the general editorship of Mauro Cappelletti, Monica Seccombe and Joseph Weiler. – Berlin : Walter de Gruyter, 1987.
xxiii,271p. – (Series A, Law).
Bibliographical references.

FEDERAL-PROVINCIAL RELATIONS - CANADA

—Perspectives on the harmonization of law in Canada / Ronald C.C. Cuming research coordinator. – Toronto : University of Toronto Press in cooperation with the Royal Commission on the Economic Union and Development Prospects for Canada and the Canadian Government Publishing Centre, 1985.
xviii,178p. – (Collected research studies).
Bibliography: p.176-177.
ISBN 0802073026

FEDERALISM - CANADA

—Recurring Issues in Canadian Federalism / A. Wayne Mackay. – Toronto : University of Toronto Press, 1986.
232p.
ISBN 0802073042 Hbk £14.95

FEES - CANADA

—Lawyers' Fees / Vancouver : Continuing Legal Education Society of British Columbia, 1987.
133p.
ISBN 0865043108 Hbk £65.00

—Lawyers' Fees / Vancouver : British Columbia Continuing Legal Education Society, 1981.
154p.
ISBN 0865040397 Hbk £8.00

FEES - EUROPEAN COMMUNITY

—Regulation of Expert's Fees in the European Community / 3rd rev. exp. ed. – Dusseldorf : VDI-Verlag, 1986.
70p.
ISBN 3184007405 Pbk £28.00

FEES - GREAT BRITAIN

—Advertising and charging rules of the professions serving the construction industry : a report by the Director General of Fair Trading / London : Office of Fair Trading, 1986.
84p.
Bibliography: p.60-63.

—Architect's Guide to Fee Negotiations : An Architecture and Building Practice Guide Book / London : Architectural Press, 1984.
160p.
ISBN 0946228051 Pbk £16.95

FEES - INDIA

—Law of Court Fees and Suits Valuation in India / H.N. Seth. – 6th ed. – Allahabad : Universal Book Agency, 1988.
ca 1,000p.

FEMALE OFFENDERS

—Women and crime / Frances Heidensohn. – Basingstoke : Macmillan, 1985.
xii,216p; 23cm.
Bibliography: p201-213. - Includes index.
ISBN 0333362160 Hbk £20.00
ISBN 0333362179 Pbk £6.95

—Women and crime : papers presented to the 13th Cropwood Round Table Conference, December 1980 / edited by Allison Morris with the assistance of Loraine Gelsthorpe. – Cambridge : University of Cambridge Institute of Criminology, 1981.
iii,141p.
Includes bibliographical references.

—Women, crime and criminal justice / Allison Morris. – Oxford : Basil Blackwell, 1987.
256p; 23cm.
Considers all aspects of women and crime including women as defendants and prisoners, as victims and as criminal justice professionals.
ISBN 0631154442 Hbk £25.00
ISBN 0631154450 Pbk £7.95

—Women, crime and justice / edited by Susan K. Datesman, Frank R. Scarpitti. – New York : Oxford University Press, 1980.
viii,376p; 21cm.
Includes bibliographies.
ISBN 0195026764 Pbk £3.95

FEMALE OFFENDERS - CANADA

—Sentenced to separation : an exploration of the needs and problems of mothers who are offenders and their children / Linda MacLeod. – Ottawa : Ministry of the Solicitor General, 1986.
ii,66p,14p,8p. – (User report).

FEMALE OFFENDERS - ENGLAND

—Trend of offending by women in England and Wales, 1963-77 / by N. Goodman. – Strasbourg : Council of Europe, 1980.
42p.
Bibliography: p.34-42. At head of title: European Committee on Crime Problems, Co- ordinated Criminological Research Fellowship. Bound with other reports.

FEMALE OFFENDERS - GREAT BRITAIN

—Women in the penal system / by Baroness Seear and Elaine Player : report prepared for the Howard League for Penal Reform. – London : Howard League for Penal Reform, 1986.
20p.

—Women on trial : a study of the female suspect, defendant and offender in the criminal law and criminal justice system / Susan S.M. Edwards. – Manchester : Manchester University Press, 1984.
1v.
Bibliography: p227-236. - Includes index.
ISBN 0719009952 £14.50

FEMALE OFFENDERS - ITALY

—Female criminality in Italy / by M. Fontanesi. – Strasbourg : Council of Europe, 1980.
59p.
Bibliography: p.58-59. At head of title: European Committee on Crime Problems, Co- ordinated Criminological Research Fellowship. .

—Female criminality in the Federal Republic of Germany, in Italy and in England and Wales / Council of Europe. – Strasbourg : Council of Europe, 1980.
4p.

Foreword / European Committee on Crime Problems, Co- ordinated Criminological Research Fellowship. – 1980.
4p.

FEMALE OFFENDERS - SWITZERLAND

—Female criminality in the Federal Republic of Germany : development and present situation (including some comments on Switzerland and Austria) / by H. Einsele. – Strasbourg : Council of Europe, 1980.
90,viiip.
Bibliography: p.i-viii. At head of title: European Committee on Crime Problems, Co- ordinated Criminological Research Fellowship. .

FEMALE OFFENDERS - WEST GERMANY

—Female criminality in the Federal Republic of Germany : development and present situation (including some comments on Switzerland and Austria) / by H. Einsele. – Strasbourg : Council of Europe, 1980.
90,viiip.
Bibliography: p.i-viii. At head of title: European Committee on Crime Problems, Co- ordinated Criminological Research Fellowship. .

—Female criminality in the Federal Republic of Germany, in Italy and in England and Wales / Council of Europe. – Strasbourg : Council of Europe, 1980.
4p.

Foreword / European Committee on Crime Problems, Co- ordinated Criminological Research Fellowship. – 1980.
4p.

FIDEICOMMISSUM (ROMAN LAW)

—Roman law of trusts / David Johnston. – Oxford : Clarendon Press, 1988.
xiii,306p.
Discusses the Roman equivalent of a trust, a fideicommissum, which affected the strategies of succession open to testators. Provides an illustration of the emperor's involvement in building private law. Relates Roman law to social history and uses the development of the trust as a case study in legal evolution.
ISBN 0198252161 Hbk £37.50

FIDUCIA

—Conceptual and policy basis of directors' fiduciary duties under English company law / by David Sugarman. – 2 v. – London : Middlesex Polytechnic Faculty of Business Studies and Management, 1982.
– (Working paper).
Includes bibliographies. Parts 1 and 2.
ISBN 0904804135 pt. 2

—Fiduciary duties of directors : a review / John Lowry. – London : Thames Polytechnic School of Business Administration, 1984.

FIDUCIA - GREAT BRITAIN

—Law of Fiduciaries / London : Sweet & Maxwell, 1982.
ISBN 0459343009 Hbk £35.00

FILM

—Film Finance : Conference Papers / Woolloomooloo : International Business Communications, 1987.
ISBN 0949072109 Hbk £34.95

FILM - AUSTRALIA

—Circumstances surrounding the various court actions relating to the film 'The return of Captain Invincible' / Senate Standing Committee on Finance and Government Operations. – Canberra : Government Printer, 1987.
iv,66p. – (Parliamentary paper).
ISBN 064406546X

—Copyright and Film / Milsons Point : Australian Copyright Council.

—Tax and the Australian film industry : being a commentary on division 10BA of the Income Assessment Act 1936 together with text of the legislation / by E.F. Mannix. – Sydney : Butterworths, 1981.
xii,92p.
Includes index.
ISBN 040936018X

FILM - GREAT BRITAIN

—Cinemas Bill : report on the consolidation of the Cinematograph Acts 1909 to 1982 and related enactments... / the Law Commission. – London : H.M.S.O., 1985.
7p.
With errata.
ISBN 0101942508

—Intelligence report : the film business / London : Longman Professional, 1986.
ISBN 0851212387 Hbk £95.00

FILM - INDIA

—Law of Cinematograph (Central and States), 1987 / 3rd ed. – Allahabad : Law Book Company, 1987.

FINANCE

—Dictionary of Economics and Financial Markets / 5th ed. – London : Butterworths, 1986.
ISBN 0408015705 Hbk £19.95

—Existing and new forms of financing, University of Auckland, 27 May 1982 : papers presented at seminar / by David Ross, Rudolf A. de Monchy, Barry J. McWilliams. – Auckland : Legal Research Foundation Inc., 1982.
44p.
ISBN 0908581173

—Guide to the financial markets / Charles R. Geisst. – London : Macmillan, 1982.
xv,144p; 23cm.
Includes bibliographies and index.
ISBN 0333309197 £15.00

—International financial law / edited by Robert S. Rendell. – 2nd ed. 2. – London : Euromoney Publications, 1983.
ISBN 0903121557

—International financial law : lending, capital transfers and institutions / edited by Robert S. Rendell. – London : Euromoney, 1980.
319p; 30cm.
ISBN 0903121131 Pbk Unpriced

—Legal aspect of money : with special reference to comparative private and public international law / by F.A. Mann. – 4th ed. – Oxford : Clarendon, 1982.
lvi,602p; 25cm.
Previous ed.: Oxford : Oxford University Press, 1971.
Bibliography: pliv. - Includes index.
ISBN 0198253672 £35.00

—Secured Financing : Conference Papers / Woolloomooloo : International Business Communications, 1987.
ISBN 0949072133 Hbk £95.00

—Swap agreement documentation / Klein. – London : Euromoney, 1987.
ISBN 1870031717 Pbk £110.00

—Swap Finance / London : Euromoney, 1987.
Service.
ISBN 0903121875 Pbk £75.00

—Trade financing / edited by Charles J. Gmur. – 2nd ed. – London : Euromoney, 1986.
xxi,234p.
ISBN 0903121999

—UK Companies Operating Overseas : Tax and Financial Strategies / M. J. Packman. – London : Oyez Longman, 1981.
– (Oyez Longman Intelligence Report Ser.).
ISBN 0851205321 Hbk £45.00

FINANCE - AUSTRALIA

—Australian financial system : interim report of the Committee of Inquiry / J. K. Campbell. – Canberra : Australian Government Publishing Service, 1980.
xii,572p.
Includes index. Chairman: J.K. Campbell.
ISBN 0642034419

—Concepts for Financial Statements / 2nd ed. – North Ryde : Law Book Co, 1984.
viii, 70p.
ISBN 0455202125 Pbk £8.50

—Financial Reporting Requirements in Australia / Arthur Andersen and Company. – Butterworths.
ISBN 0409492574 Pbk £42.00

—Financial Reporting Requirements in Australia : a Concise Illustrated Accounting Disclosures Manual / Butterworths, 1987.
216p.
ISBN 0409492574 Pbk £42.00

FINANCE - CANADA

—Banking and Finance Law Review / Andrew Chant. – Agincourt : Carswell.
This book focuses on issues pertinent to the legal and financial communities. The text is divided into four parts: articles, commentaries on recent developents in banking in Canada and in the world, and casenotes and book reviews.

—Corporate Cash Management in Canada / Toronto : DeBoo.
This looseleaf service covers the basic principles and practical methods of corporate cash management and treasury management. Six updates per year are planned, each with an accompanying newsletter.
ISBN 0888202733 loose £275.00

—Corporate Finance for Legal Assistants / Vancouver : Continuing Legal Education Society of British Columbia, 1988.
299p.
ISBN 0865041644 Hbk £75.00

—Financial Management for Law Firms / M. W. Zwicker. – Vancouver : British Columbia Continuing Legal Education Society, 1982.
82p.
ISBN 0865040451 Hbk £6.50

—Foreign Money Liabilities / Victoria : Government of British Columbia, 1983.

—National Finances / Toronto : Canadian Tax Foundation, 1985-86.
Issue from 1984-85

—Provincial and Municipal Finances / Toronto : Canadian Tax Foundation, 1985.

FINANCE - ENGLAND

—Financial law reports / London : Sweet & Maxwell, 1985.

FINANCE - EUROPE

—Effective Parliamentary Control of European Finances / European Parliament, Directorate General for Research. – 3rd ed. – Kirchberg : European Parliament, 1989.

—Eurobond Market / Cambridge : Woodhead-Faulkner, 1988.
ISBN 0859413373 Hbk £40.00

—Euronotes and Euro-Commercial Paper / London : Butterworths, 1987.
ISBN 0406104107 Hbk £38.00

FINANCE - EUROPEAN COMMUNITY

—Finances of Europe / by Daniel Strasser. – Revised and enlarged edition. – Luxembourg : Office for Official Publications of the European Communities, 1981.
xix,422p.
At head of title: Commission of the European Communities.
ISBN 9282520722

FINANCE - GREAT BRITAIN

—Banking Secrecy and Financial Privacy / Oyez Longman Publishing. – London : Oyez Longman, 1980.
– (Oyez Longman Intelligence Report Ser.).
ISBN 0851204732 Hbk £55.00

—Budget and Finance Bill 1985 / London : Law Society, 1985.
28p. – (Nineteen Eighty-Five Crash Course Transcripts).

—Business Finance / London : Butterworths, 1986.
ISBN 0406501408 Pbk £13.95

—Consumer Credit Act 1974 : credit charges : how to calculate the total charge for credit and the annual percentage rate of charge / Office of Fair Trading. – London : The Office, 1980.
20p.

—Corporate Finance / Mosby, 1988.
ISBN 0801642116 Hbk £31.00

—Corporate Finance / London : Butterworths, 1987.
ISBN 0406259569 Hbk £42.00

—Corporate Finance in Multinational Companies / London : Euromoney, 1986.
ISBN 1870031350 Pbk £75.00

—Corporate Finance Law / London : Sweet & Maxwell, 1987.
ISBN 0421311207 Hbk £67.00
ISBN 0421374403 Pbk £12.50

—Currency and Interest Rate Swaps / Henderson. – 2nd ed. – London : Butterworths, 1988.
ISBN 0406073619 Hbk £40.00

—Deloitte, Haskins and Sells : Raising Finance in Capital Markets / London : Butterworths, 1987.

—Dictionary of Banking and Finance / London : Pitman Publishing, 1985.
ISBN 0273018590 Hbk £35.00

—Energy Finance / London : Euromoney, 1983.
ISBN 0903121476 Pbk £75.00

—Evolution of the British financial system / by D.T. Llewellyn. – London : Institute of Bankers, 1985.
59p.
Bibliography: p.59.
ISBN 0852971362

—Export Finance / London : Sweet & Maxwell.
ISBN 0421333103 Pbk

—Family Finance / Cambridge : Woodhead-Faulkner, 1987.
ISBN 0859414205 Pbk £4.95

—Ferrier and Ferrier : UK Money Markets / London : Butterworths, 1987.
This book describes the operations of the United Kingdom financial sector, concentrating on the principal methods of raising capital. Included in the work is coverage of the key elements in each market together with explanations of the significance of various instruments and forms of finance.
ISBN 0406100306 Hbk

—Finance / Townsley. – London : Pitman Publishing, 1986.
ISBN 0273025872 Pbk £6.95

—Finance Act 1984 / Butterworth Staff. – London : Butterworths, 1984.
ISBN 0406548234 Hbk £60.00

—Finance Act Nineteen Eighty-One / Butterworth and Co. (Publishers) Ltd. – London : Butterworths, 1981.
ISBN 0406548080 Hbk £38.95

—Finance of Foreign Trade / 6th ed. – Plymouth : Macdonald & Evans, 1986.
ISBN 0712106618 Pbk £4.95

—Finance of International Trade / 5th ed. – London : Pitman Publishing, 1987.
ISBN 0273027344 Pbk £8.95

—Financial Deregulation / Cambridge : Woodhead-Faulkner, 1986.
ISBN 0859413667 Hbk £30.00

—Financial Engineering / London : Fourmat, 1986.
ISBN 1851900187 Pbk £12.95

—Financial Instruments for Corporate Treasurer / London : Butterworths, 1988.
ISBN 0406103550 Pbk

—Financial Law Reports / London : Sweet & Maxwell, 1986.
ISBN 0421345004 Hbk £28.00

—Financial Management / London : Butterworths, 1984.
ISBN 0406181160 Pbk £10.00

—Financial Management for Contractors / Oxford : Blackwell Scientific, 1987.
ISBN 0003830616 Hbk £19.95

—Financial Management For Solicitors / 3rd ed. – London : Longman Professional, 1985.
ISBN 0851209998 Pbk £15.95

—Financing International Trade / London : Butterworths, 1988.
ISBN 0880631503 Hbk

—Fiscal studies : the journal of the Institute for Fiscal Studies / Institute for Fiscal Studies. – London : Institute for Fiscal Studies, 1979-.

—Guide to the Financial Services Act 1986 / A.J. Wedgwood ... et al. – London : Financial Training, 1986.
xi,371p.
Includes index. Includes the text of the Act.
ISBN 1851850503

—Handbook of UK Corporate Finance / London : Butterworths, 1987.

—Managing your finances / London : Longman Professional, 1988.
ISBN 0851213723 Pbk £4.95

—Parkinson : Financial Instruments for the Corporate Treasurer / London : Butterworths, 1987.
ISBN 0406103550 Pbk

—Paying for politics / the report of the Commission upon the financing of political parties. – London : Hansard Society, 1981.
49 p.

—Personal financial planning manual / 3rd ed. – London : Butterworths, 1986.
ISBN 040600563X Pbk £16.95

—Principles of corporate finance / Myers. – 2nd ed. – Maidenhead : McGraw-Hill, 1986.
ISBN 007007383X Pbk £14.50

—Project financing / by Peter K. Nevitt. – 4th ed. – London : Euromoney, 1983.
xiii,273p.
Includes index.
ISBN 0903121395

—Raising centure capital in the UK / Burns. – London : Butterworths, 1988.
ISBN 0406103100 Hbk £27.50

—Regulating the city / Open University Press, 1986.
ISBN 0335153828 Pbk £7.95

—Role of the Comptroller and Auditor General / presented to Parliament by the Chancellor of the Exchequer. – London : H.M.S.O., 1980.
44 p.
ISBN 0101784503

—Smith : Trading Financial Options / London : Butterworths, 1986.
ISBN 0406100470 Pbk £57.75

—Sterling commercial paper market / Cambridge : Woodhead-Faulkner, 1988.
ISBN 0859414108 Hbk £40.00

—Tax Benefits and Family Finance / T. Lyon. – London : Sweet & Maxwell, 1985.
ISBN 0421324600 Hbk

—Understanding personal and business finance / 2nd ed. – Cambridge : Woodhead-Faulkner, 1986.
ISBN 0859413624 Pbk £5.25

—Valuation and selection of convertible bonds / Praeger, 1988.
ISBN 0275924661 Hbk £27.50

—Venture capital today / Cambridge : Woodhead-Faulkner, 1985.
ISBN 085941275X Hbk £30.00

—What goes on in the City? / 4th ed. – Cambridge : Woodhead-Faulkner, 1986.
ISBN 0859413217 Hbk £7.95
ISBN 0859413225 Pbk £4.25

FINANCE – HONG KONG

—Building Project Finance in Hong Kong : Law and Practice / Butterworths, 1987.
265p.
Describes the law and practice of building project finance in Hong Kong. Examines the 'financing', 'project', and 'security' aspects of a project loan in a comprehensive manner. Explains the typical transactions involved, the roles of various documents, and the problems which have to be dealt with.
ISBN 0409995363 Hbk £110.00

FINANCE – JAPAN

—Japanese finance : Deregulation / London : Euromoney, 1986.
ISBN 1870031253 Hbk £110.00

FINANCE – MALAYSIA

—Financial Procedure Act, 1957 (Act 61) / Kuala Lumpur : International Law Books Services.

—Handbook of Singapore and Malaysian Corporate Finance / Tan. – London : Butterworths, 1988.
ISBN 0409995487 Pbk £120.00

FINANCE – SINGAPORE

—Financial Management / Butterworths, 1984.
387p.
ISBN 0406181160 Pbk £30.00

—Handbook of Singapore and Malaysian Corporate Finance / Tan. – London : Butterworths, 1988.
ISBN 0409995487 Pbk £120.00

—Real property financing in Singapore / Singapore : Malayan Law Journal, 1988.
390.
Examines the law and practice of the security and documentation involved in real property financial transactions in Singapore. Covers the security and financing devices adopted by financiers to protect their interest, a list of financing institutions, both public and private, and the various financing schemes available. Provides a number of forms and precedents of loans documents.
ISBN 997170062X Hbk

—Ship financing in Singapore / Singapore : Malayan Law Journal, 1983.
xxi,305.
An examination of ship financing in Singapore on two levels; the individual in the commercial world, and the national on the international scene.
ISBN 9971700301 Hbk

FINANCE – SOUTH AFRICA

—Law and Finance for the Farmer / Davis. – Cape Town : Legal and Financial Publishing Co.

FINANCE (ISLAMIC LAW)

—Islamic law and finance / edited by Chibli Mallat. – London : Graham & Trotman, 1988.
xiv,196p.
Includes bibliographical references and index.
ISBN 185333121X

FINANCIAL INSTITUTIONS

—Financial services legislation : the auditor's role in the financial services sector : a consultative document / Great Britain. – London : The Division, 1985.
12p.

—International institutions in trade and finance / A.I. MacBean and P.N. Snowden. – London : Allen & Unwin, 1981.
xiv,255p; 23cm.
Bibliography: p249-252. - Includes index.
ISBN 0043820328 Hbk Unpriced
ISBN 0043820336 Pbk Unpriced

FINANCIAL INSTITUTIONS – AUSTRALIA

—Australian financial system : interim report of the Committee of Inquiry / J. K. Campbell. – Canberra : Australian Government Publishing Service, 1980.
xii,572p.
Includes index. Chairman: J.K. Campbell.
ISBN 0642034419

FINANCIAL INSTITUTIONS – CANADA

—Canadian financial institutions : changing the regulatory environment / edited by Jacob Ziegel, Leonard Waverman, David W. Conklin. – Toronto : Ontario Economic Council, 1985.
viii,474p. – (Special research report).
Based on ' ... a conference entitled the Changing Regulatory Environment for Canadian Financial Institutions held 22-23 May 1985 at the Sutton Place Hotel, Toronto, Ontario'. - Foreword. Includes bibliographical references.
ISBN 0772909563

—Competition and solvency : a framework for financial regulation / Economic Council of Canada. – Ottawa : Minister of Supply and Services, 1986.
x,46p.
ISBN 0660121921

FINANCIAL INSTITUTIONS – ENGLAND

—Capital city : London as a financial centre / Hamish McRae and Frances Cairncross. – New and fully rev. ed. – London : Methuen, 1984.
264p; 23cm.
Previous ed.: 1973. Includes index.
ISBN 0413511200 Hbk £8.95
ISBN 041357900X PBK £3.95

—London money market / E.R. Shaw. – 3rd ed. – London : Heinemann, 1981.
xiv,267p; 22cm.
Previous ed.: 1975. Bibliography: p259-261. - Includes index.
ISBN 0434918334 Pbk £7.50

FINANCIAL INSTITUTIONS – ENGLAND – LONDON

—Inside the city : a guide to London as a financial centre / William M. Clarke. – Rev. ed. – London : Allen & Unwin, 1983.
xii,283p; 22cm.
Previous ed.: 1979. Includes index.
ISBN 0043320910 Pbk £6.95

FINANCIAL INSTITUTIONS – GREAT BRITAIN

—Encyclopedia of financial services law / editors Eva Z. Lomnicka, John L. Powell. – 2. – London : Sweet & Maxwell, 1987.
loose-leaf; 26cm.
Includes index.
ISBN 0421368802 £100.00

—Financial Services Act 1986 / with annotations by Alan Page and Robert Ferguson. – London : Sweet & Maxwell, 1987.
298,14p; 24cm.
Includes index.
ISBN 0421366907 Pbk £12.00

—Financial Services Act 1986 : a guide to the new law / Andrew Whittaker, Geoffrey Morse. – London : Butterworths, 1987.
vii,475p; 26cm.
Includes index.
ISBN 0406551014 £25.00

—Financial Services Bill : as amended in Committee / Great Britain. – London : H.M.S.O., 1986.
ix,254p.
ISBN 0104238860

—Financial services in the United Kingdom : a new framework for investor protection / presented to Parliament by the Secretary of State for Trade and Industry... – London : H.M.S.O., 1985.
iii,43p.
ISBN 0101943202

—Financial services legislation : treatment of members od certain professions : a consultative document / Great Britain. – London : The Division, 1985.
16p.

—Guide to the Financial Services Act 1986 / Barry A.K. Rider, David A. Chaikin, Charles Abrams. – Bicester : CCH Editions, 1987.
xxii,472p; 23cm.
Examines Investor protection, the Act and the City revolution, the regulatory structure, the need for authorisation, obtaining authorisation, the conduct of investment business, insider dealing, public issues, marketing of investments, and collective investment schemes.
ISBN 0863250785 Pbk £15.00

—London markets after the Financial Services Act / David F. Lomax. – London : Butterworths, 1987.
225p; 24cm.
Includes bibliography and index.
ISBN 0406100748 £15.00

—Pension funds and British capitalism : the ownership and control of shareholdings / Richard Minns. – London : Heinemann, 1980.
viii,176p; 23cm.
Includes index.
ISBN 0435845101 £13.00

—Regulation and supervision of financial institutions / by D.T. Llewellyn. – London : Institute of Bankers, 1986.
77p.
Bibliography: p.75-77.
ISBN 0852971745

—Securities and Investments Board / a report by the Director General of Fair Trading to the Secretary of State for Trade and Industry. – London : Office of Fair Trading, 1987.
77p.

FINANCIAL INSTITUTIONS – INDIA

—Manual of Banking and Public Financial Institutions : Laws with Allied Acts, 2 Vols. / Madhya Pradesh : Lawyers Home, 1986.

FINANCIAL INSTITUTIONS – MALAYSIA

—Finance Companies Act, 1969 (Act 6) / Kuala Lumpur : International Law Books Services.

FINANCIAL SERVICES – GREAT BRITAIN

—Encyclopaedia Financial Services / Sweet & Maxwell, 1988.
ISBN 0421368802 Hbk £265.00

—Financial Services Act 1986 / Morse. – London : Butterworths, 1987.
ISBN 0406551014 Hbk £25.00

—Financial Services Act 1986 / Ferguson. – London : Sweet & Maxwell, 1987.
ISBN 0421366907 Pbk £13.50

—Financial Services Act: Index / Faulkner. – Cambridge : Woodhead-Faulkner, 1986.
ISBN 0859413888 Hbk £16.50

—Financial Services Law / Potts. – London : Sweet & Maxwell, 1988.
ISBN 0421386002 Pbk

—Financial services : regulating investment business / Simon Morris. – 1st ed. – London : Longman Professional (UK), 1989.
Examines the Financial Services Act 1986, and details its impact on areas of investment business, including the international aspect and the run up to 1992, and civil and criminal liability for operations outside the FSA.
ISBN 0851215572 Hbk £37.50

—London Markets after Financial Services Act / London : Butterworths, 1987.
ISBN 0406100748 Pbk £28.00

—Marketing Financial Services / Watkins. – London : Butterworths, 1986.
ISBN 0402502706 Hbk £18.95

—Marketing Financial Services / London : Butterworths, 1986.

—Money advice services / Berthoud. – Policy Studies Institute, 1988.
ISBN 0853743789 Pbk £8.95

—Regulation after the Financial Services Act / London : Butterworths, 1987.
ISBN 0406100748 Pbk

—Retail financial services : development and future / London : Butterworths, 1988.
ISBN 0406259437 Pbk

—Scottish Mutual guide to the Financial Services Act / Rosters Ltd, 1988.
ISBN 0948032162 Hbk £12.95

FINANCIAL STATEMENTS

—Information disclosure and the multinational corporation / S.J. Gray with L.B. McSweeney, J.C. Shaw. – Chichester : Wiley, 1984.
xi,236p; 24cm. – (Wiley/IRM series on multinationals).
Includes index.
ISBN 0471904244 Hbk

—Interpreting company reports and accounts / Sugden. – 3rd ed. – Cambridge : Woodhead-Faulkner, 1986.
ISBN 085941325X Hbk £25.00
ISBN 0859413268 Pbk £14.95

FINANCIAL STATEMENTS - AUSTRALIA

—Financial Reporting Requirements in Australia / Sydney : Butterworths, 1987.
216p.

—Law and Practice of Company Accounting in Australia / M O Jager, R B Taylor. – 6th ed. – North Ryde : Butterworths (Australia), 1983.
Analysis of the law of company accounting and reporting. Includes aspects of practice as necessary to interpret the law and explain its significance and application. Incorporates developments including the changes effected by the Companies Act 1981 (the National Act), and the latest Accounting Standards.
ISBN 0409493902 Pbk £27.60

FINANCIAL STATEMENTS - CANADA

—Financial Statements : a Lawyer's Guide / Vancouver : Continuing Legal Education Society of British Columbia, 1988.
131p.
ISBN 0865049696 Hbk £70.00

—Lawyer's Guide to Financial Statements - 1985 / Vancouver : British Columbia Continuing Legal Education Society, 1985.
125p.
ISBN 0865041938 Hbk £65.00

—Lawyer's Guide to Financial Statements / Vancouver : British Columbia Continuing Legal Education Society, 1984.
ISBN 0865041490 Hbk £45.00

—Lawyer's Use of Financial Statements : 1982 / Vancouver : British Columbia Continuing Legal Education Society, 1983.
464p.
ISBN 0865040508 Hbk £14.50

FINANCIAL STATEMENTS - GREAT BRITAIN

—Accountants' Reports for Prospectus Purposes / Deloitte, Haskins and Sells Staff. – London : Butterworths, 1985.
ISBN 0406500215 Pbk £20.00

—Cases In Company Financial Reporting / Wearing. – Paul Chapman, 1988.
ISBN 1853960047 Pbk £5.95

—Financial Reporting in the Public Sector / London : Butterworths, 1983.
ISBN 0406361401 Pbk

—Financial Reporting in the Public Sector / London : Butterworths, 1983.
ISBN 0406361401 Pbk £13.50

—Form and Content of Company Accounts / Lybrand. – 3rd ed. – Oxford : Croner Publications, 1986.
ISBN 1851850325 Pbk £9.95

—Manual of Financial Reporting and Accounting / 2nd ed. – London : Butterworths, 1985.
ISBN 0406500509 Pbk £18.50

—Manual of Financial Reporting and Accounting / Touche Ross and Co. Staff. – 2nd ed. – London : Butterworths, 1985.
This book describes the legal requirements and professional pronouncements relating to audit reports and financial statements. The work gives recommended accounting and consolidating principles, and contains many examples of different types of audit reports.
ISBN 0406500509 Pbk

—Model financial statements / Stoy Hayward & Co. – London : Butterworths, 1986.
ISBN 0406503907 Pbk £16.50

—Understanding company accounts / 2nd ed. – Pitman, 1983.
ISBN 0273019449 Pbk £4.95

—Understanding company accounts / Newman. – Telegraph Publications, 1988.
ISBN 0863671918 Pbk £6.95

—Understanding company financial statements / 2nd ed. – Pelican, 1982.
ISBN 0140091025 Pbk £4.95

FINES

—Fine in comparative law / by Gerhardt Grebing. – Cambridge : University of Cambridge, Institute of Criminology, 1982.
xvi,279p. – (Institute of Criminology occasional papers).
Includes bibliographical references. Translation of: 'Die Geldstrafe im deutschen und auslandischen Recht', Part II 'Die Geldstrafe in rechtsvergleichender Darstellung' / edited by Hans-Heinrich Jescheck and Gerhardt Grebing.

FINES - AUSTRALIA - TASMANIA

—Report on fines / Law Reform Commission of Tasmania. – Hobart : Government Printer, 1985.
12p. – (Report v no 41).

—Research paper on fines / by C.A. Warner. – Hobart? : Government Printer?, 1984.
vi,115,6p. – (Research paper).
Includes bibliographical references.

FINES - ENGLAND

—Fine enforcement : an evaluation of the practices of individual courts / Paul Softley and David Moxon. – London : Home Office, 1982.
iv,23p; 30cm.
Bibliography: p16.
ISBN 0862520711 Pbk Unpriced

FINES - GREAT BRITAIN

—Criminal Justice Act 1982 : A Guide to Fines / Butterworths Editorial Staff. – London : Butterworths, 1983.
This text for magistrates in the United Kingdom provides a condensation of the changes in the fine schedules for Criminal Acts brought about by the Criminal Justice Act of 1982.
ISBN 0406008604 Pbk

—Suggestions for traffic offence penalties / Magistrates' Association. – 8th ed. – London : The Association, 1983.
4p.

FINES - NEW ZEALAND

—Evaluation of fines enforcement / written and researched by Robert Brown ... et al. – Wellington : Department of Justice, 1985.
xiv,316,98p. – (Study series).
Bibliography: p.313-316. - Includes index.

FINES - SCOTLAND

—Civil liability : contribution / Scottish Law Commission. – Edinburgh : Scottish Law Commission, 1986.
iv,230p. – (Consultative memorandum).

FIRE INSURANCE - GREAT BRITAIN

—Fire and motor insurance / E.R. Hardy Ivamy. – 4th ed. – London : Butterworths, 1984.
xxxviii,518p; 26cm. – (Butterworths insurance library).
Previous ed.: 1978. Includes index.
ISBN 040625253X Unpriced

—Fire and Motor Insurance / 4th ed. – London : Butterworths, 1984.
ISBN 040625253X Hbk £49.00

FIREARMS - AUSTRALIA

—Firearms Laws in Australia / North Ryde : C.C.H. Australia, 1985.
175p.
ISBN 0869034936 Hbk

FIREARMS - CANADA

—Canadian Firearms Law / Butterworths, 1988.
152p.
Guidance on all aspects of the criminal and civil law relating to gun use and misuse in Canada. Provides an outline of history and purpose of current legislation, and analysis of current legislation and all relevant case law, a discussion of various types of certificates and permits required, contains a step by step procedure to be followed upon, and discussion of the law governing, refusal or revocation of certificates and permits.
ISBN 0409806455 Hbk £42.50

—Evaluation of the Canadian gun control legislation : final report / by Elisabeth Scarff. – Ottawa : Ministry of the Solicitor General, 1983.
xxiv,217p.
Includes English and French parallel texts of the Criminal Law Amendment Act 1977. 'A research report prepared under contract with the Research Division of the Programs Branch, Ministry of the Solicitor General of Canada' - t.p. verso.
ISBN 0660114046 Hbk

Executive summary / by Elisabeth Scarff. – 1983.
14,17p.
With French t.p.: L'Evaluation des mesures legislatives canadiennes relatives au controle des armes a feu: rapport final: resume. English and French text.
ISBN 0662526015 Hbk

—Evaluation of the Canadian gun control legislation : first progress report / project team: Elisabeth Scarff ... et al. – Ottawa : Communication Division, Ministry of the Solicitor General, 1981.
ixx,166,74p.
A research report prepared under contract with the Research Division, Ministry of the Solicitor General of Canada.
ISBN 0662115236

FIREARMS - GREAT BRITAIN

—Firearms Act 1968 : proposals for reform / presented to Parliament by the Secretary of State for the Home Department and the Secretary of State for Scotland by command of Her Majesty, December 1987. – London : HMSO, 1987.
9p.
ISBN 0101026129

—Gun Law / 5th ed. – Shaw & Sons, 1988.
ISBN 0721903630 Pbk £6.00

—Law relating to firearms / by P. J. Clarke and John W. Ellis. – London : Butterworths, 1981.
xxvi,272p.
ISBN 0406158207

—Legitimate pursuit / Southampton : Ashford Press, 1988.
ISBN 1852531045 Hbk £12.95

—Weapons Law / London : Waterlow, 1988.
144p.
ISBN 0080331041 Pbk £17.95

FIREARMS - INDIA

—Law and Practice of Arms and Explosives : With Explosives Rules 1988 / 10th ed. – Allahabad : Law Book Company, 1988.
1,000p.

—Law of Arms and Explosives : Acts and Rules / 3rd ed. – Allahabad : Ashoka Law House, 1987.
657p.

—Law of Arms and Explosives : with Act Rules and Notifications / 4th ed. – Allahabad : Law Publishers, 1982.

—Law Relating to Arms, Ammunition and Explosives / K.K. Malik. – 4th rev. ed. – Lucknow : Eastern Book Company, 1985.
920p.

FIREARMS - MALAYSIA

—Arms Act, 1960 (Act 206) and Regulations 1961 and Firearms (Increased Penalties) Act 1971 (Act 37) / Kuala Lumpur : International Law Books Services.

FISCAL POLICY

—Effects of Monetary and Fiscal Policy : A Contribution to Pure Theory / Stockholm : Almqvist & Wiksell.
74p.

FISCAL POLICY - CANADA

—Fiscal dimensions of Canadian federalism / edited by Richard M. Bird. – Toronto : Canadian Tax Foundation, 1980.
v,151p.
ISBN 0888080050

FISCAL POLICY - UNITED STATES

—Fiscal policy and tax legislation and administration : technical papers and reports of the 15th General Assembly of the Inter-American Center of Tax Administrators (CIAT), Caracas, Venezuela, 25-27 February 1981 / Inter-American Center of Tax Administrators. – Amsterdam : International Bureau of Fiscal Documentation, 1983.
200p.
'Sponsored by the Government of Venezuela, the German Society for Technical Cooperation (GTZ) and the Inter-American Center of Tax Administrators (CIAT)'
ISBN 9070125226

FISHING

—Coastal state requirements for foreign fishing / by Gerald K. Moore. – Rev. ed. – Rome : Food and Agriculture Organization of the United Nations, 1983.
iv,242p. – (Legislative study).
Previous ed. published as: Legislation on coastal state requirements for foreign fishing.
ISBN 9251015031

—Coastal State Requirements for Foreign Fishing / Rome : FAO, Food and Agricultural Organization of the United Nations, 1985.
302p.
ISBN 925102359X Hbk £19.50

—Fisheries Regime of the Exclusive Economic Zone / Dordrecht : Kluwer, 1987.
200p.
ISBN 902473374X Hbk £145.00

—Impacts of the UN Convention on the Law of the Sea on tuna regulation / by W.T. Burke. – Rome : Food and Agriculture Organization of the United Nations, 1982.
v,19p. – (Norway funds-in-trust).
Discusses impact of the Third United Nations Convention on the Law of the Sea on tuna management, especially Article 64 concerning conservation.
ISBN 925101292X

—International Law of Fisheries : a Framework for Policy-Oriented Inquiries / Dordrecht : Kluwer, 1987.
632p.
ISBN 089838902X Hbk £225.00

—Legal measures for the conservation of marine mammals / Gland, Switzerland : International Union for Conservation of Nature and Natural Resources, 1982.
1 v. (loose-leaf); 23 cm.
Includes bibliographical references.
ISBN 2880320879

—Legislation on coastal state requirements for foreign fishing / by Gerald Moore. – Rome : Food and Agriculture Organization of the United Nations, 1981.
viii, 411 p.; 28 cm. – (Legislative study / Food and Agriculture Organization of the United Nations).
ISBN 9251010382 pbk.

—Politics of international fisheries management : the case of the Northeast Atlantic / Arild Underdal. – Oslo : Universitetsforl., 1980.
Oslo; 1980.
Bibliography: p. 232-239.
ISBN 8200054144 pbk. kr99.00

—Regional compendium of fisheries legislation (Indian Ocean Region) / prepared by Legislation Branch, FAO Legal Office, with the assistance of the International Centre for Ocean Development. – Provisional ed. 2. – Rome : Food and Agriculture Organization of the United Nations, 1986.
– (Legislative study).

—Regional compendium of fisheries legislation (Western Pacific region) / prepared by Legislation Branch, Legal office, FAO, in cooperation with the South Pacific Forum Fisheries Agency. – 2 v. – Rome : F.A.O., 1984.
– (Legislative study).
ISBN 925102202X

FISHING - AFRICA

—Regional compendium of fisheries legislation West Africa (CECAF region) / prepared under the direction of the Legislation Branch, Legal Office Compendium regional de la legislation sur la peche l'Afrique occidentale (region du COPACE) / prepare sous la direction du Service de legislation, Bureau juridique. – Rome : Food and Agriculture Organization of the United Nations, 1983.
v, 525 p.; 30 cm. – (Legislative study).
At head of title: Norway Funds-in-trust, FI: GCP/INT/400/NOR. English and French. Includes bibliographical references.
ISBN 9250013078 pbk.

FISHING - AUSTRALIA - VICTORIA

—Ninth report to Parliament on subordinate legislation concerning Fishing (Abalone Licence Fee) Regulations 1987 (Statutory Rule no. 65/1987) / Legal and Constitutional Committee. – Melbourne : Government Printer, 1987.
vi,12p.
Includes Minority report.

FISHING - CANADA

—Fisheries Law / Vancouver : Continuing Legal Education Society of British Columbia, 1985.
384p.
ISBN 0865042039 Hbk £75.00

FISHING - CANADA - ONTARIO

—Game and Fish Act : Revised Statutes of Ontario, 1980 / Office of the Legislative Assembly (Ontario). – Ontario : Ontario Government Publications Service, 1983.
38p.

FISHING - ENGLAND

—Freshwater fishery law / William Howarth. – London : Financial Training, 1987.
xxiv,311p; 23cm.
Bibliography: p302-304. - Includes index. Includes text of the Salmon and Freshwater Fisheries Act 1975. Originally published: London : H.M.S.O., 1975.
ISBN 1851850309 £17.95

—Salmon and Freshwater Fisheries Act 1975 / William Howarth. – London : Financial Training, 1987.
xxiv,311p; 23cm.
Bibliography: p302-304. - Includes index. Includes text of the Salmon and Freshwater Fisheries Act 1975. Originally published: London : H.M.S.O., 1975.
ISBN 1851850309 £17.95

FISHING - EUROPEAN COMMUNITY

—EEC fisheries law / R.R. Churchill. – Dordrecht : M. Nijhoff, 1987.
xxviii, 299 p.; 25 cm.
Includes index. Bibliography: p. 285-289.
ISBN 9024735459 Hbk £165.00

FISHING - GREAT BRITAIN

—Friends in conflict : the Anglo-Icelandic cod wars and the law of the sea / Hannes Jonsson. – London : C.Hurst, 1982.
xi,240p.
Bibliography: p225-233.

FISHING - ICELAND

—Friends in conflict : the Anglo-Icelandic cod wars and the law of the sea / Hannes Jonsson. – London : C.Hurst, 1982.
xi,240p.
Bibliography: p225-233.

FISHING - MALAYSIA

—Some Aspects of the Malaysian Fisheries Law with Regards to Fisheries Management and Conservation / Malaysia Ministry of Agriculture. – Kuala Lumpur : Ministry of Agriculture, 1980.

FISHING - NEW ZEALAND

—Maori Fishing Rights in New Zealand : an Economic Perspective / Canterbury : Agricultural Economics Research Unit, 1986.
9p.

FISHING - SCOTLAND

—Fishing in Scotland : law for the angler / by Lord Jauncey. – 2nd ed. – Edinburgh : W. Green, 1984.
vi,17p; 21cm.
Previous ed.: 1952.
ISBN 0414007344 Pbk Unpriced

FISHING - SOUTHEAST ASIA

—Law of the Sea : Problems of Conflict and Management of Fisheries in Southeast Asia / Metro Manila : International Center for Living Aquatic Resources Management.
68p.

FLATS - GREAT BRITAIN

—Law of Flats / London : Longman Professional, 1982.
ISBN 085101388X Pbk £25.50

—Law of flats / 2nd. – London : Longman Professional (UK), 1989.
– (Practitioner series).
New edition takes account of the Landlord and Tenant Acts of 1985 and 1987 and changes resulting from the Housing Act 1988, including assured tenancies. Includes new chapters on disposition, the landlord's identity and the right of first refusal.
ISBN 085121388X Hbk £27.50

—Sale and management of flats : practice and precedents / London : Butterworths, 1985.
ISBN 0406526702 Hbk £38.00

—Sale and Management of Flats : Practice and Precedents / London : Butterworths, 1985.
This book provides a practical guide to the subject of leasehold conveyancing in the United Kingdom. Particular attention is given to the establishment and maijntenance of subsequent management of the property from the tenant's and developer's point of view.
ISBN 0406526702 Hbk

FLIGHT CREWS

—International standards and recommended practices : personnel licensing : annex 1 to the Convention on International Civil Aviation / International Civil Aviation Organization. – 7th ed. - September 1982. 1. – Montreal : International Civil Aviation Organization, 1982.
looseleaf.
Kept up to date by amendments and supplements.

FLOATING CHARGES - NEW ZEALAND

—Floating charges, crystallisation and after-acquired property / by G.C. Thorpe. – Auckland : Legal Research Foundation, 1981.
49p.
ISBN 0908581130

FLOATING CHARGES - SCOTLAND

—Floating charges and receivers / Scottish Law Commission. – Edinburgh : The Commission, 1986.
iv,151p. – (Consultative memorandum).
Includes bibliographical references. Catalogued from cover.

FLOATING RATE NOTES

—Floating rate notes / by Georges Ugeux : preface by Michael von Clemm. – 2nd ed. – London : Euromoney, 1985.
xix,171p.
Bibliography: p.171.
ISBN 0903121808

FOOD

—Food policy / Paris : Organisation for Economic Co- operation and Development, 1981.
75 p.; 24 cm.
'This report and five Country Notes were discussed and adopted by the OECD Working Party on Agricultural Policies and by the Committee for Agriculture 28th April 1981.'. Includes bibliographical references.
ISBN 0702216283 pbk.

—Right to Food : Guide through Applicable International Law / Dordrecht : Kluwer, 1986.
388p.
ISBN 9024733650 Hbk £165.00

FOOD - EUROPEAN COMMUNITY

—Why do we sell butter to Russia? : and other common questions from the Common Market / by Nicholas Bethell. – London : European Democratic Group, 1987.
9 p.

FOOD - INDIA

—Prevention of Food Adulteration and the Law / New Delhi : Deep and Deep Publications, 1985.
278p.

FOOD - SRI LANKA

—Food Famine and the Legal Order / Julio Menezes. – Colombo : Lake House Investments.

FOOD LAW AND LEGISLATION

—Food and Agriculture Legislation / Food and Agriculture Organization of the United Nations. – London : HMSO, 1984.
115p.
ISBN 0119410133 Pbk £4.50

—Labelling and Advertising Regulations on Food Products / European Food Law Association. – Brussels : Editions de l'Universite de Bruxelles, 1980.
490p.
ISBN 2800407344 Hbk £780.00

—Legislation on foods for infants and small children / Rome : Food and Agriculture Organization of the United Nations, 1983.
v,104p. – (Legislative study).
Includes bibliographical references.
ISBN 9251014876

—Model food legislation / National Health and Medical Research Council. – Canberra : Australian Govt. Pub. Service, 1983.
1 v. (loose-leaf); 28 cm.
Includes index.
ISBN 0644027282

FOOD LAW AND LEGISLATION - AUSTRALIA

—Food Law in Australia / Gerkens. – North Ryde : Law Book Co, 1985.
ISBN 0455203016 Pbk £16.00

FOOD LAW AND LEGISLATION - CANADA

—Health protection and food laws / 4th rev ed. – Ottawa : Minister of National Health and Welfare, 1987.
95p.
Includes bibliographical references.
ISBN 0660121808

FOOD LAW AND LEGISLATION - GREAT BRITAIN

—Butterworths law of food and drugs / editor A.A. Painter : co-ordinating editor Brian Harvey. – 1. – London : Butterworths, 1981.
loose-leaf; 25cm.
Supersedes Bell and O'Keefe's Sale of food and drugs, 14th ed., 1968. 548 pages in various pagings on publication.
ISBN 0406116105 Unpriced

—Farm Gate Sales to the Public / London : Shaw & Sons.
1987p.
ISBN 0721910807 Pbk £7.95

—Food Hygiene I: Market Stalls and Delivery Vehicles / London : Shaw & Sons, 1981.
– (Shaway Guide : No. 5).
ISBN 072190873X Pbk £2.50

—Food Hygiene II: Food Premises / London : Shaw & Sons, 1981.
– (Shaway Guide: No. 6).
ISBN 0721908748 Pbk £2.50

—Food legislation in the UK : a concise guide / D.J. Jukes. – London : Butterworths, 1984.
128p; 22cm.
Includes index.
ISBN 0407003576 Pbk Unpriced

—Food Legislation of the UK / 2nd ed. – London : Butterworths, 1987.
ISBN 0407015507 Pbk £12.50

—Practical food law / Gresty. – London : Sweet & Maxwell, 1988.
ISBN 0421251608 loose £95.00

—Practical food law manual / 1. – London : Sweet & Maxwell, 1988-.
Includes index.
ISBN 0421351608 LLF

—Product Safety in the Food and Drink Industry / London : LLoyd's of London Press, 1986.
ISBN 1850440247 Hbk

FOOD LAW AND LEGISLATION - INDIA

—Comments on Prevention of Food Adulteration Act with Central and All State Rules / Seth. – Allahabad : Law Publishers, 1982.

—Prevention of Food Adulteration Act / H.D. Trivedi. – 8th ed. – Lucknow : Eastern Book Company, 1983.
838p.

—Prevention of Food Adulteration Act / H.D. Trivedi. – 8th ed. – Lucknow : Eastern Book Company, 1983.
838p.

—Prevention of Food Adulteration Act with Central and State Rules and Foreign Law on the Subject / 1983. – Allahabad : Law Book Company.
xxii, 548p.

FOOD LAW AND LEGISLATION - MALAYSIA

—Food Act, 1983 (Act 281) and Regulations, 1985 (P.U.(A) 437/85) / Kuala Lumpur : International Law Books Services.

FORECLOSURE - AUSTRALIA - VICTORIA

—Mortgagee sales and judgment debts / Law Reform Commission of Victoria. – Melbourne : The Commission, 1986.
iii,10p. – (Discussion paper of Victoria).
Includes bibliographical references.

—Mortgagee sales and judgment debts / Law Reform Commission of Victoria. – Melbourne : The Commission, 1987.
iv,17p. – (Report no 8).
Includes bibliographical references.

FORECLOSURE - CANADA

—Calculation of Interest on Foreclosure / Victoria : Government of British Columbia, 1980.

—Foreclosure Update 1988 / Vancouver : Continuing Legal Education Society of British Columbia, 1988.
111p.
ISBN 0865043655 Hbk £70.00

—Foreclosures : 1987 / Vancouver : Continuing Legal Education Society of British Columbia, 1987.
586p.
ISBN 0865043051 Hbk £85.00

—Foreclosures, Debentures, and Bankruptcy for Legal Assistants / Vancouver : British Columbia Continuing Legal Education Society, 1985.
119p.
ISBN 0865042136 Hbk £55.00

—Foreclosures for Legal Assistants / Vancouver : British Columbia Continuing Legal Education Society, 1983.
177p.
ISBN 0865041350 Hbk £50.00

—Mortgages and Foreclosure : Know Your Rights / 4th ed. – North Vancouver : International Self-Counsel Press, 1987.
105p.
ISBN 0889086567 Hbk £7.95

FOREIGN AID

—Development aid / London : Butterworths, 1988.
ISBN 0408009918 Hbk £55.00

FOREIGN BONDS

—International bonds / by Frederick G. Fisher, III. – London : Euromoney Publications, 1981.
199p; 30cm.
Bibliography: p195. - Includes index.
ISBN 0903121220 Pbk Unpriced

FOREIGN EXCHANGE

—Foreign Currency Exposure Management / London : Butterworths, 1987.
ISBN 0406570906 Pbk

—How to account for foreign currencies / Jeff Pearcy. – London : Macmillan, 1984.
x,264p; 22cm.
ISBN 0333365461 £30.00

—International monetary system : efficiency and practical alternatives / Herbert G. Grubel. – 4th ed. – Harmondsworth : Penguin, 1984.
214p.
Bibliography: p201-206.
ISBN 0140808183

—Price and Henderson currency and interest rate swaps / Schuyler K. Henderson, John A. M. Price. – London : Butterworths, 1984.
xiii,144p; 26cm.
Includes index. At head of title: Price and Henderson.
ISBN 0406073600 No price

—Private international law : Council of Europe Conventions on Foreign Money Liabilities(1967) and on the Place of Payment of Money Liabilities (1972) : report on a reference under section 3 (1)(e) of the Law Commissions Act 1965 / the Law Commission and the Scottish Law Commission. – London : H.M.S.O., 1981.
iv,53p; 25cm.
Includes the text of the Conventions.
ISBN 0101831803

—Private international law : foreign money liabilities / the Law Commission. – London : H.M.S.O., 1981.
ix,195p; 22cm. – (Working paper).
ISBN 0117301604

—Taxation aspects of currency fluctuations / Jill C. Pagan. – London : Butterworths, 1983.
xi,162p.
Describes the United Kingdom tax law and the attitude of the Inland Revenue on the subject of currency fluctuations. Foreign exchange management, accounting treatment, and taxation are analyzed in the book.
ISBN 0406406308 Hbk £22.00

FOREIGN EXCHANGE – CANADA – BRITISH COLUMBIA

—Foreign money liabilities / Law Reform Commission of British Columbia. – Vancouver : Law Reform Commission of British Columbia, 1982.
iv,121p. – (Working paper).

—Report on foreign money liabilities / Law Reform Commission of British Columbia. – Vancouver : The Commission, 1983.
64p.
Includes bibliographical references.
ISBN 0771883919

FOREIGN EXCHANGE – GREAT BRITAIN

—Accounting for Foreign Exchange / London : Butterworths, 1987.
ISBN 0406503206 Pbk £37.50

—Currency Fluctuation / 2nd ed. – Cambridge : Woodhead-Faulkner, 1984.
ISBN 0859412652 Hbk £30.00

—Economics of Foreign Exchange / Sanderson. – Cambridge : Woodhead-Faulkner, 1988.
ISBN 0859413640 Hbk £40.00

—Foreign Currency Exposure Management / London : Butterworths, 1987.
ISBN 0406507906 Pbk £22.00

—Foreign Exchange Dealer's Handbook / 2nd ed. – Cambridge : Woodhead-Faulkner, 1986.
ISBN 0859413438 Hbk £35.00

—Foreign Exchange Manual / Cambridge : Woodhead-Faulkner, 1988.
ISBN 0859414396 Hbk £150.00

—Foreign Exchange Risk : A Tax and Financial Analysis / London : Oyez Longman, 1983. – (Oyez Longman Intelligence Report Ser.).
ISBN 0851205313 Hbk £45.00

—Foreign Investment and Exchange Control / London : Legal Books, 1985.
ISBN 0949072001 Hbk £100.00

—Introduction to Foreign Exchange / 2nd ed. – Cambridge : Woodhead-Faulkner, 1984.
ISBN 0859412865 Pbk £9.95

—Managing a foreign exchange department / Cambridge : Woodhead-Faulkner, 1985.
ISBN 0859412768 Hbk £45.00

—Trading in currency options / Cambridge : Woodhead-Faulkner, 1987.
ISBN 0859413233 Hbk £45.00

FOREIGN EXCHANGE – INDIA

—Commentaries on Foreign Exchange Regulations Act and Rules Notification with Model Forms and Allied Laws / 2nd ed. – Allahabad : Law Publishers, 1982.

—Conservation of Foreign Exchange and Prevention of Smuggling Act, 1987 / 1987. – Allahabad : Law Book Company.
250p.

—Conservation of Foreign Exchange and Prevention of Smuggling Activities Act / Allahabad : Law Book Company, 1987.
250p.

—Foreign Exchange Regulations Act, 1973 / Subodh Markandeya. – Bombay : Jaico Publishing House.

—Guide to Foreign Exchange Regulation / new ed. – Nagpur : Wadhura & Co, 1988.

—Guide to Foreign Exchange Regulations / Lucknow : Eastern Book Company, 1981.
336p.

FOREIGN INVESTMENTS

—Arbitration and renegotiation of international investment agreements : a study with particular reference to means of conflict avoidance under natural resources investment agreements / Wolfgang Peter. – Dordrecht : M. Nijhoff, 1986.
xxiii, 297p.
Includes index. Bibliography: p.267-284.
ISBN 9024733146

—Canadian Council on International Law : Conference Proceedings /. – Ottawa : Canadian Council on International Law, 1983.

—Comparative survey of corporate investments / Gunther H. W. Stratmann. – London : International Bar Association, 1983.
iv,198p.
Based on papers 'presented during the New Delhi Conference of the International Bar Assoiciation ...'. - Introduction.

Vol. 2 parts 1-2 : in Canada, Belgium, France, Federal Republic of Germany ... : written by members of Committee G/Business Organisations of the Section on Business Law of the International Bar Association
A 'set of papers ... presented during the Toronto Conference of the International Bar Association ...'. - Introduction.

—Contractual adaptation and conflict resolution, based on venture contracts for mining projects in developing countries / Martin Bartels : translation by James E. Silva. – Deventer, Netherlands : Kluwer Law and Taxation, 1985.
187 p.; 25 cm. – (Studies in transnational law of natural resources).
Includes bibliographical references. 'List of cited agreements': p. 177-187.
ISBN 3787540237

—Finance and protection of investments in developing countries / Ingrid Detter De Lupis. – 2nd ed. – Aldershot : Gower, 1987.
xvii,183p; 23cm.
Previous ed.: 1973. Includes index.
ISBN 0566054655 £25.00

—Foreign investment & technology transfer : fiscal and non-fiscal aspects : country profiles on fiscal and non-fiscal regimes affecting two-way flow of investment and technology transfer between the developed countries and the Asian-Pacific region / editor, Ahmad Khan. – Singapore : Asian-Pacific and Investment Research Centre, 1985.
vi,262p.
'A series of contributions ... to the 2nd Asian-Pacific Tax Conference held in Singapore in December 1984 by the Asian-Pacific Tax and Investment Research Centre' - Preface. Includes bibliographical references.

—Foreign investment and the new international economic order / by David Flint. – Sydney : International Law Association, 1981.
89p.
ISBN 0949685003

—Foreign investment in mining projects : case studies of recent experiences / Raymond F. Mikesell : a project sponsored and administered by the FMME. – Cambridge, Mass. : Oelgeschlager, Gunn & Hain, 1983.
xv,297p; 24cm.
Bibliography: p281-285. - Includes index.
ISBN 0899461700 Unpriced

—Joint development of resources projects : a comparison : proceedings of the Regional Energy Law Seminar, Singapore, 30 September 1985 / International Bar Association. Section on Energy and Natural Resources Law. – London : International Bar Assocation, 1985.
Various pagings.

—Legal aspects of doing business in Asia and the Pacific / edited by Dennis Campbell. – Deventer, Netherlands : Kluwer Law and Taxation Publishers, 1984.
– (International business series).
Includes index. Kept up to date by supplements.
ISBN 9065449825

—Legal aspects of doing business in Latin America / edited by Dennis Campbell. – Deventer, The Netherlands : Kluwer Law and Taxation Publishers, 1984.
vii, 351 p.; 25 cm. – (International business series).
Includes index.
ISBN 9065441026

—Mining ventures in developing countries / Erich Schanze. – Deventer : Kluwer, 1981.
281p.
First published: Frankfurt am Main, Metzner; Deventer, Kluwer; 1977- , as 'Rohstofferschliessungsvorhaben in Entwicklungslandern'. Translated from German into English.
ISBN 9065440380

—Overseas business activities : proceedings of the Fuji Conference / the International Conference on Business History 9 : edited by Akio Okochi, Tadakatsu Inoue. – Tokyo : University of Tokyo Press, 1984.
xiii, 296 p.; 24 cm.
Includes bibliographies and index.
ISBN 4130470191 Y5000

—Protection against the expropriation risk in investing abroad / Matthew Bender, 1988.
ISBN 0000999071 Hbk £50.00

—Protection of foreign investments: a private law study of safeguarding devices in international crisis situations / Kluwer Law and Taxation, 1989.
500.
Deals primarily with the situation in the USA, but also summarises the discussions and ideas developed from twenty years of practical studies. Includes chapters on the Canadian Trading with the Enemy Act, the treatment of Private Enemy Property in the USA, proof of ownershihp and documentation.
ISBN 9065443827 Hbk £54/Dfl 165

FOREIGN INVESTMENTS – AFRICA

—Legal aspects of doing business in Africa / edited by Dennis Campbell. – Deventer, The Netherlands : Kluwer Law and Taxation Publishers, 1986.
– (International business series).
Includes index.
ISBN 9065442685

FOREIGN INVESTMENTS – ASIA

—Income taxation and foreign investment in developing countries / M.P. Dominic. – Amsterdam : International Bureau of Fiscal Documentation, 1980.
xviii, 354, 28 p.; 24 cm.
Includes indexes. Bibliography: p. 7-16 (2d group).
ISBN 9070125137 pbk.

FOREIGN INVESTMENTS – AUSTRALIA

—Foreign Investment and Exchange Control / Woolloomooloo : International Business Communications, 1985.
ISBN 0949072001 loose £185.00

—Foreign investment law in Australia / by David Flint. – Sydney : Law Book Company, 1985.
xxxi,519p.
ISBN 0455204624

FOREIGN INVESTMENTS - CANADA

—Foreign Investment Review Law in Canada / W.P. Rosenfeld. - Butterworths, 1984.
432p.
Provides practical information and a commentary for those who must deal with the Foreign Investment Review Act (FIRA). Shows the reader how to proceed with applications under the Act, describes the business and political context in which it operates, and clarifies the meaning of its essential concepts. Chapters deal with FIRA-related problems particular to the petroleum and banking industries.
ISBN 0409863009 Hbk £75.00

—International issues in taxation : the Canadian perspective / Donald J.S. Brean. - Toronto : Canadian Tax Foundation, 1984.
xiii,180p.
Bibliography: p.166-176. - Includes index.
ISBN 0888080190

FOREIGN INVESTMENTS - CHINA

—China's foreign economic legislation Chung-kuo tui wai ching chi fa kuei hui pien / 1st ed. - Bejing, China : Foreign Languages Press, 1982.
v. 1; 19 cm.
ISBN 0835109836 pbk.

—Foreign trade, investment, and the law in the People's Republic of China / editor Michael J. Moser : contributors Jesse T.H. Chang ... et al. - 2nd ed. - Hong Kong : Oxford University Press, 1987.
x,603p; 26cm.
An extensively revised and updated second edition. Gives an introduction to the legal framework currently being developed in China with respect to foreign commercial and investment activity.
ISBN 0195840585 £25.00

—Taxation of foreign investment in the People's Republic of China / A J Easson, L Jinyan. - Kluwer Law and Taxation, 1989.
260.
Describes China's tax laws as they relate to foreign business and investment within the context of current economic reforms and the overall policy towards economic relations, including investment incentives and the impact of China's tax treaties. Reference is made to other Chinese legislation. Covers the situation at February 1988.
ISBN 9065443835 Hbk £56.25/Dfl 174

FOREIGN INVESTMENTS - CYPRUS

—Note on the law of Cyprus relating to offshore operations, shipping operations and shipping companies, foreign investments in Cyprus and transit trade / by Criton G. Tornaritis. - Nicosia : s.n., 1984.
52 leaves.

FOREIGN INVESTMENTS - GREAT BRITAIN

—Foreign Investment and Exchange Control / London : Legal Books, 1985.
ISBN 0949072001 Hbk £100.00

—Foreign Investment Debt and Economy / Salazar-Carillo. - London : Macmillan, 1988.
ISBN 0333402081 Hbk £37.50

—Inward investment : policy options for the United Kingdom / Michael Brech and Margaret Sharp. - London : Routledge and Kegan Paul, 1983.

—Taxation of international business : the charge to tax on investment managers acting for non-residents : consultative paper / London : Inland Revenue, 1984.
5p.

FOREIGN INVESTMENTS - NEW ZEALAND

—New Zealand business : entering the Australian market : Legal Research Foundation Inc. Seminar, 19 November 1985 / Barry J. McWilliams. - Auckland : Legal Research Foundation, 1985.
122p.
Papers presented by Barry J. McWilliams and others.
ISBN 0908581408

FOREIGN INVESTMENTS - SAUDI ARABIA

—Legal regime of foreign private investment in the Sudan and Saudi Arabia : a case study of developing countries / Fath el Rahman Abdalla El Sheikh. - Cambridge : Cambridge University Press in association with Khartoum University Press, 1984.
xxxix,462p; 23cm. - (Cambridge studies in international and comparative law).
Bibliography: p446-458. - Includes index.
ISBN 0521252865 No price

FOREIGN INVESTMENTS - SOUTH KOREA

—Business laws in Korea : investment, taxation, and industrial property / Chan-jin Kim, editor. - Seoul, Korea : Panmun Book Co., 1982.
xii, 799 p.; 24 cm.
Includes bibliographical references.

FOREIGN INVESTMENTS - SUDAN

—Legal regime of foreign private investment in the Sudan and Saudi Arabia : a case study of developing countries / Fath el Rahman Abdalla El Sheikh. - Cambridge : Cambridge University Press in association with Khartoum University Press, 1984.
xxxix,462p; 23cm. - (Cambridge studies in international and comparative law).
Bibliography: p446-458. - Includes index.
ISBN 0521252865 No price

FOREIGN INVESTMENTS - THAILAND

—Technology transfer : a case study / Mingsam Santikam. - Singapore : Singapore University Press, 1981.
xiv,270p.
Bibliography: p257-264.

FOREIGN INVESTMENTS - UNITED STATES

—Structuring Foreign Investment in U.S. Real Estate / Dordrecht : Kluwer.
600p.

FOREIGN INVESTMENTS (INTERNATIONAL LAW)

—Finance and protection of investments in developing countries / Ingrid Detter De Lupis. - 2nd ed. - Aldershot : Gower, 1987.
xvii,183p; 23cm.
Previous ed.: 1973. Includes index.
ISBN 0566054655 £25.00

FOREIGN JUDGMENTS - ASIA

—International jurisdiction and the recognition and enforcement of foreign judgements in the LAWASIA region : a comparative study of the laws of eleven Asian countries inter-se and with the E.E.C. countries / Bradford A. Caffrey. - Sydney : CCH Australia, 1985.
xxxii,407p.
Cover title: Enforcement of foreign judgements.
ISBN 0869037897

FOREIGN JUDGMENTS - CANADA - MANITOBA

—Report on section 83 of 'The Queen's Bench Act' : the conclusiveness of foreign judgments in Manitoba / Manitoba Law Reform Commission. - Winnipeg : The Commission, 1986.
i,22p. - (Report).
Includes bibliographical references.

FOREIGN JUDGMENTS - COMMONWEALTH

—Recognition and enforcement of judgments and orders and the service of process within the Commonwealth : a report of a working meeting held in Nairobi, Kenya, 9-14 January 1980 / London : Commonwealth Secretariat, 1980.
xii,160p.

FOREIGN JUDGMENTS - EEC

—Guide to the civil jurisdiction and judgments convention / by Alan Dashwood, Richard Hacon & Robin White. - Deventer : Kluwer Law and Taxation, 1986.
648p.
Includes index and bibliography.
ISBN 9065442693 Hbk £265.00

FOREIGN JUDGMENTS - ENGLAND

—Civil jurisdiction and enforcement of foreign judgments : the application in England and Wales of the Brussels Convention of 1968 on Jurisdiction and Enforcement of Judgments in Civil and Commercial Matters under the Civil Jurisdiction and Judgments Act 1982 / by Peter Kaye. - Abingdon : Professional Books, 1987.
cxvi, 1949p; 24cm.
Includes the text of the Civil Jurisdiction and Judgments Act 1982.
ISBN 0862050812

—Family law : financial relief after foreign divorce / the Law Commission. - London : H.M.S.O., 1982.
iii,115p. - (HC).
ISBN 0102514828

—Private international law - foreign money liabilities : report on a reference under section 3 (1)(e) of the Law Commissions Act 1965 / The Law Commission. - London : H.M.S.O., 1983.
vii,94p; 25cm.
ISBN 0101906404

FOREIGN JUDGMENTS - GREAT BRITAIN

—Civil Jurisdictions and Judgment Acts 1982 / London : Butterworths, 1983.
This work provides a procedural guide to the Act. The 1982 Act incorporates into United Kingdom law the 1968 EEC Convention on jurisdiction and the enforcement of judgements in civil matters.
ISBN 0406005303 Hbk

—Family law : financial relief after foreign divorce / Great Britain. - London : H.M.S.O., 1980.
v,83p. - (Working paper).
ISBN 0117301574

FOREIGN JUDGMENTS - SCOTLAND

—Family law : report on financial provision after foreign divorce / Scottish Law Commission. - Edinburgh : H.M.S.O., 1982.
47p.
ISBN 0102515824

FOREIGN LICENSING AGREEMENTS

—International business agreements : a practical guide to the negotiation and formulation of agency distribution and intellectual property licensing agreements / Patrick Hearn. - Aldershot : Gower, 1987.
viii,222p; 24cm.
Includes index.
ISBN 0566025973 £27.50

—International technology licensing : compensation, costs, and negotiation / Farok J. Contractor. - Lexington : Lexington Books, 1981.
xiv,193p; 24cm.
Bibliography: p185-189. - Includes index.
ISBN 0669043591 £22.50

—Know-how contract in Germany, Japan, and the United States / edited by Herbert Stumpf. - Deventer, The Netherlands : Kluwer Law and Taxation, 1984.
309 p.; 25 cm.
Includes bibliographies.
ISBN 9065441379 pbk.

FOREIGN LOANS

—Country risk analysis / John Calverley. - London : Butterworths, 1985.
ix,181p; 23cm.
Includes index.
ISBN 0406005508 No price

—Default and rescheduling : corporate and sovereign borrowers / edited by David Suratgar. - London : Euromoney, in association with International Law Institute, Washington D.C., 1984.
viii,163p.
'Two international conferences, one in London in late 1981 and the other in New York in 1982, provided the basis for this book' - Editor's preface.
ISBN 0903121530

—Recent multilateral debt restructurings with official and bank creditors / by a Staff team headed by E. Brau...et al. - Washington, D.C. : International Monetary Fund, 1983.
vii,43p. - (Occasional paper).

—Sovereign lending : managing legal risk / edited by Michael Gruson and Ralph Reisner. - London : Euromoney Publications, 1985.
xii,257p; 30cm.
Includes bibliographical references.
ISBN 0903121611

FOREIGN RELATIONS

—Great debate : New Zealand, Britain and the EEC : the shaping of attitudes / Robert ,McLuskie. - Wellington : Decision Research Centre, Victoria University of Wellington, 1986.
iv,175p.
Includes bibliographical references and index.
ISBN 0908772009

FOREIGN RELATIONS - AFRICA, SOUTHERN

—Beggar your neighbours : apartheid power in Southern Africa / Joseph Hanlon. - London : Catholic Institute for International Relations in collaboration with Currey, 1986.
xi,352p; 24cm.
Includes index.
ISBN 0852553072 Hbk £25.00
ISBN 0946848270 CIIR (pbk) £8.95

FOREIGN RELATIONS - EUROPEAN ECONOMIC COMMUNITY

—Leading cases and materials on the external relations law of the European Community, with emphasis on the common commercial policy / by E.L.M. Volker and J. Steenbergen. - Deventer, The Netherlands : Kluwer Law and Taxation Publishers, 1985.
At head of title: Europa Institute, University of Amsterdam.
ISBN 9065442219

FOREIGN RELATIONS - UNITED STATES

—United States foreign relations law : documents and sources / edited by Michael J. Glennon, Thomas M. Franck. - London : Oceana Publications, 1980.
v. 1-2; 25 cm.
Includes bibliographical references. Contents: v. 1. Executive agreements.–v. 2. Treaties.
ISBN 0379203553 v. 1 £40.00

FOREIGN TRADE

—Current problems of international trade financing / edited by C.M. Chinkin, P.J. Davidson, W.J.M. Ricquier. - Singapore : Malaya Law Review, 1983.
xxiii,507p.
Includes index. At head of title: Singapore Conferences on International Business Law.
ISBN 0406181144

—Employment, trade, and north-south co-operation / edited by Geoffrey Renshaw. - Geneva : International Labour Office, 1981.
xiv, 263 p.; 25 cm. - (A WEP study / ILO).
Working documents in revised and condensed form which formed the basis for discussions at a Tripartite Symposium on Employment, International Trade, and North-South Co-operation, convened in Geneva in May 1980 by the International Labour Organisation. Includes bibliographical references and index.
ISBN 9221025306 pbk. £27.50F

—Law of Conflicts and Foreign Trade / L. Vekas. - Budapest : Akademiai Kiado.
xiv, 379p.
ISBN 9630542749 Hbk £38.00

FOREIGN TRADE - CHINA

—Almanac of China's foreign economic relations and trade / the editorial board of the Almanac of China's foreign economic relations and trade. - Hong Kong : China Resources Trade Consultancy, 1986.
Title page also in Chinese.

—Compendium of China's Laws and Regulations on External Economic Relations and Trade / Hong Kong : Economic Information and Agency.

—Foreign Trade, Investment and the Law in the PRC / Oxford : Oxford University Press, 1987.
ISBN 0195840585 Hbk £27.50

FOREIGN TRADE - GREAT BRITAIN

—Finance of Foreign Trade / 6th ed. - Plymouth : Macdonald & Evans, 1986.
ISBN 0712106618 Pbk £4.95

FOREIGN TRADE REGULATION

—Basic documents on international trade law / edited by Chia-Jui Cheng. - The Hague : Martinus Nijhoff, 1985.
Includes index.
ISBN 9024731690 pbk.

—Conflicts of national laws with international business activity : issues of extraterritoriality / by A.H. Hermann. - London : British North American Research Organisation, 1982.
xii,96p.
ISBN 0902594419

—Developing countries in the GATT legal system / by Robert E. Hudec. - Aldershot : Gower for the Trade Policy Research Centre, 1987.
xix,259p.
Bibliography: p.236-250..
ISBN 0566056976

—International business and national jurisdiction / A.D. Neale and M.L. Stephens. - Oxford : Clarendon Press, 1988.
xix,216p.
Examines the relationship between issues in international and municipal law, specifically the relationship between historically exclusive spheres of sovereign interest, and legal and practical requirements of the modern international commercial environment. Concentrates on US antitrust law, but some EEC and English decisions are included.
ISBN 0198255322 Hbk £52.00

—International business transactions and economic relations : cases, notes and materials on the law as it applies to Canada / J.G.Castel, A.L.C. deMestral, W.C.Graham. - Toronto(Ont.) : Edmond Montgomery Publications Ltd, 1986.
xxii,925p.
ISBN 0920722067 Hbk £119.50

—International business transactions in a nutshell / by Donald T. Wilson. - St. Paul, Minn. : West Publishing Co., 1980.
lvii,393p; 19cm. - (Nutshell series).

—Law and its limitations in the GATT multilateral trade system / Olivier Long. - Dordrecht : M. Nijhoff, 1985.
158p.
'An adaptation in English, brought up to date to the end of 1984, of a series of lectures delivered at the Hague Academy of International Law and published in French in its 'Collected courses' 1983, IV, volume 182'–Pref. Includes index. Bibliography.
ISBN 9024731895 Hbk £100.00

—National laws and international commerce : the problem of extraterritoriality / Douglas E. Rosenthal and William M. Knighton. - London : Routledge & Kegan Paul, 1982.
xi,96p.
Bibliography: p94-96.
ISBN 0710093381

—Protectionism and the European Community : Import Relief Measures Taken by the European Economic Community and the Member States, and the Legal Remedies Available to Private Parties / 1983 2nd rev. update ed. - Dordrecht : Kluwer, 1987.
252p.
ISBN 9065443134 Pbk £94.00

—Selective safeguard measures in multilateral trade relations : issues of protectionism in GATT, European Community, and United States law / M.C.E.J. Bronckers. - Deventer, Netherlands : Kluwer Law and Taxation Publishers, 1985.
306p.
Includes index and bibliography.
ISBN 9065442227 Hbk £150.00

—Transnational law of international commercial transactions / edited by Norbert Horn and Clive M. Schmitthoff. - Antwerp : Kluwer-Devanter/The Netherlands, 1982.
Includes index and bibliography.
ISBN 9065440925

FOREIGN TRADE REGULATION - AUSTRALIA

—Review of Import Control and Customs Bylaw Decision / Administrative Review Council. - Canberra : Australian Government Publishing Service, 1982.
22p.
ISBN 0642070679 Hbk £1.20

FOREIGN TRADE REGULATION - CHINA

—China trade law : code of the foreign trade law of the People's Republic of China / by Francois De Bauw and Bernard Dewit : preface by Michel Verwilghen. - Bruxelles : Emile Bruylant, 1982.
572p.
Includes bibliographical references and index. At head of title: Universite Catholique de Louvain, Faculte de Droit, Centre de Droit des Obligations. Text in English. Preface, introduction, headings and index in French and English..
ISBN 2802702963

FOREIGN TRADE REGULATION - EUROPE

—Catalogue of Community Legal Acts and Other Texts Relating to the Elimination of Technical Barriers to Trade for Industrial Products and Nomenclature for Iron and Steel Products : December 1983 / Kirchberg : Commission of the European Communities, 1984.
174p.

—Legal aspects of doing business in Western Europe / edited by Dennis Campbell. - Deventer, Netherlands : Kluwer Law and Taxation Publishers, 1983.
viii, 451 p.; 25 cm. - (International business series).
Includes index.
ISBN 0314792899 West Pub. Co.

FOREIGN TRADE REGULATION - EUROPEAN COMMUNITY

—Anti-dumping and anti-subsidy law : the European Communities / by J. i.e. H. F. Beseler and A.N. Williams. - London : Sweet & Maxwell, 1986.
xx,438p; 26cm.
Examines the interpretation and application of the anti-dumping and anti-subsidy laws in the EEC in the light of the relevant GATT codes. Compares practices with those of the USA and Canada. Deals with the current attempts within GATT to obtain an international consensus on the way anti-subsidy law should be applied in specific circumstances.
ISBN 0421358009 £58.00

—Dumping and subsidies : the law and procedures governing the imposition of anti-dumping and countervailing duties in the European Community / Joseph Cunnane and Clive Stanbrook. - London : European Business Publications, 1983.
xvi,227p.
Includes index.
ISBN 0907027040

—European Community and GATT / edited by Meinhard Hilf, Francis G. Jacobs, and Ernst-Ulrich Petersmann. - Deventer, the Netherlands : Kluwer, 1986.
xvii, 398 p.; 25 cm.
Includes bibliographical references and index.
ISBN 9065442332

—International trade law and practice of the European Community : EEC anti-dumping and other trade protection laws / Ivo van Bael, Jean-Francois Bellis. - Bicester : CCH, 1985.
viii,438p.
Discusses the Community's four main methods of trade protection; anti-dumping rules, anti-subsidy rules, safe-guard measures, and the 'New Commercial Policy Instrument', and comments on the EEC and ECSC Anti-dumping Regulations. Contains tables and annexes.
ISBN 0863250602

FOREIGN TRADE REGULATION - GREAT BRITAIN

—Case Against General Import Restrictions / W. M. Corden. - London : Trade Policy Research Centre, 1980.
107p.
ISBN 0900842504 Hbk £5.00

—Cases & materials on the law of international trade / edited by Mark S.W. Hoyle. - London : Laureate, 1980.
viii,282p; 31cm.
ISBN 0907392008 Hbk Unpriced
ISBN 0907392016 Pbk Unpriced

—Croner's Reference Book for Importers / Croner Publications. - New Malden : Croner Publications, 1986.

Annual renewal updates

—Guide to Importing / Cambridge : Woodhead-Faulkner, 1987.
ISBN 0859413101 Pbk £14.95

—Importing for the Small Business / London : Kogan Page, 1985.
128p.
ISBN 0850388694 Pbk £6.95

—Schmitthoff's export trade : the law and practice of international trade / by Clive M. Schmitthoff. - 7th ed. - London : Stevens, 1980.
xxxvii,515p.

ISBN 0420454101

FOREIGN TRADE REGULATION - USSR

—Handbook on foreign trade arbitration in the CMEA countries / S. N. Lebedev, A. G. Dmitriev, V. A. Kabatov. - Moscow : s.n., 1983.
112p.
Editors: A.G. Dmitriev, V.A. Kabatov; General Editor, S.N. Lebedev. Translated from the Russian.

—Soviet commercial and maritime arbitration / compiled and edited by William E. Butler. - London : Oceana Publications, 1980.
1 v.; 28 cm. - (A Transnational service).
Includes arbitration awards selected from the English language edition of Arbitrazhnaia praktika, issued by the USSR Foreign Trade Arbitration Commission. Loose-leaf for updating.
ISBN 0379206994 £75.00

FORENSIC PSYCHIATRY

—Psychiatry, law, and ethics / edited by A. Carmi : with contributions by G. Ammon ... et al. - Berlin : Springer-Verlag, 1984.
ISBN 0387157425

FORENSIC PSYCHOLOGY

—Criminological diagnosis : an international perspective / edited by Franco Ferracuti, Marvin E. Wolfgang. - Lexington, Mass. : Lexington Books, 1983.
xi,297p; 24cm.
ISBN 0669016241 Unpriced

Vol.2 / edited by Franco Ferracuti, Marvin E. Wolfgang. - 1983.
299-619; 24cm.
Bibliography: p543-613.
ISBN 0669059714 set Unpriced
ISBN 0669064343 Hbk Unpriced

—Evaluating witness evidence : recent psychological research and new perspectives / edited by Sally M.A. Lloyd-Bostock and Brian R. Clifford. - Chichester : Wiley, 1983.
x,305p; 24cm.
Includes bibliographies and index.
ISBN 0471104639 Hbk

—Law and psychology : papers presented at SSRC Law and Psychology Conferences 1979-1980 / edited by Sally LLoyd-Bostock. - Oxford : SSRC Centre for Socio-Legal Studies, 1981.
x,165p; 21cm. - (Conference papers).
Includes bibliographical references. 'The papers in this collection were originally presented at two meetings of the SSRC Law and Psychology Seminar Group, held in Oxford during 1979-1980'.
ISBN 0862260752

—Reconstructing the past : the role of psychologists in criminal trials / edited by Arne Trankell. - Deventer, The Netherlands : Kluwer, 1982.
398p.
'This book contains papers and panels from the first international conference on Witness Psychology...Stockholm...September 1981'.
ISBN 9065441123

—Trial by jury : social and psychological dynamics / Ramesh Deosaran. - St. Augustine, Trinidad, West Indies : Institute of Social and Economic Research, University of the West Indies, 1985.
324 p.; 23 cm.
Includes indexes. Bibliography: p. 283-297.
ISBN 9766180008 pbk.

FORENSIC PSYCHOLOGY - AUSTRALIA

—Forensic Psychologists / Canberra : Australian Institute of Criminology.

FORENSIC PSYCHOLOGY – GREAT BRITAIN

—Forensic Psychology / London : Batsford, 1981.
ISBN 0713424753 Hbk £15.00

FORENSIC PSYCHOLOGY – UNITED STATES

—Psychology and psychiatry in courts and corrections : controversy and change / Ellsworth A. Fersch, Jr. – New York : Wiley, 1980.
xiii,370p; 24cm.
'A Wiley-Interscience publication'. Text on lining papers. Bibliography: p.323-353. - Includes index.
ISBN 0471056049 £13.00

FORENSIC SCIENCE

—Bibliography on Ethyl Alcohol for Forensic Science and Medicine and the Law / Edinburgh : Scottish Academic Press Ltd, 1980.
444p.
ISBN 0707302536 Hbk £20.00

—Eight Peak Index of Mass Spectra of Compounds of Forensic Interest / C. Brown. – Edinburgh : Scottish Academic Press Ltd, 1983.
296p.
ISBN 0707303419 Hbk £50.00

—Equal Justice and Forensic Process : Truth and Myth / Lucknow : Eastern Book Company, 1986.
146p.

—Guide to pathological evidence for lawyers and police officers / Frederick A. Jaffe. – 2nd ed. – Toronto : Carswell, 1983.
xv,204p.
Bibliography: p.189-197. - Includes index.
ISBN 0459355406

—Law and psychiatry : rethinking the relationship / Michael S. Moore. – Cambridge : Cambridge University Press, 1984.
xiv,527p; 24cm.
Bibliography: p495-513. - Includes index.
ISBN 0521255988 £35.00

—Psychiatry and the criminal process / edited by Ronnie Mackay and Ken Russell. – Leicester : Leicester Polytechnic Law School, 1986.
48p. – (Leicester Polytechnic Law School monographs).
Includes bibliographical references.
ISBN 0948997281

—Scientific Identification of Disputed Documents, Fingerprints and Ballistics / 3rd ed. 1980 repr. – Lucknow : Eastern Book Company, 1984.
155p.

FORENSIC SCIENCE – CANADA

—Clinical assessment before trial : legal issues and mental disorder / Christopher D. Webster, Robert J. Menzies, Margaret A. Jackson : with the collaboration of Brian T. Butler...et al. – Toronto : Butterworths, 1982.
xxvii,319p.
Discusses fitness to stand trial, psychiatric recommendations for treatment, evaluation of mental status and the clinical prediction of dangerous behaviour. Chapter deals with the effect of psychiatric opinion on judicial decision-making.
ISBN 0409875775

FORENSIC SCIENCE – ENGLAND

—Effectiveness of the Forensic Science Service / by Malcolm Ramsay. – London : H.M.S.O., 1987.
v,93p; 25cm.
Examines the extent to which the work of the FSS assists the police and courts in solving crimes.
ISBN 0113408420

FORENSIC SCIENCE – GREAT BRITAIN

—Forensic Medicine / Shapiro. – 3rd ed. – Edinburgh : Churchill Livingstone, 1988.
ISBN 0443034400 Hbk £29.50

—Forensic Medicine / Johnson. – London : Waterlow, 1987.
ISBN 0080392199 Hbk £30.00

—Forensic Medicine / Knight. – 9th ed. – London : Edward Arnold, 1985.
ISBN 073144521 Pbk £17.50

—Forensic Medicine for Lawyers / 2nd ed. – London : Butterworths, 1983.
ISBN 0407013709 Pbk £19.00

FORENSIC SCIENCE – NEW ZEALAND

—Report of the Royal Commission to Inquire into the Circumstances of the Convictions of Arthur Allan Thomas for the Murders of David Harvey Crewe and Jeanette Lenore Crewe / R. L. Taylor. – Wellington : Government Printer, 1980.
124p. – (H.).
Chairman: R.L. Taylor.

FORENSIC SCIENCE – UNITED STATES

—Reconstructing reality in the courtroom / W. Lance Bennett and Martha S. Feldman. – London : Tavistock Publications, 1981.
x, 203p.

FORESTS – AFRICA

—Forest Legislation in Selected African Countries / Rome : FAO, Food and Agricultural Organization of the United Nations, 1986.
462p.
ISBN 9251023220 Hbk £28.50

FORESTS – AUSTRALIA – TASMANIA

—Content and Historical Development of Forestry Legislation in Tasmania / Hobart : University of Tasmania, Centre for Environmental Studies, 1981.
38p.

FORESTS – INDIA

—Forest Law : Containing Commentaries on Indian Forest Act with State Amendments and Rules as Amended... / 6th ed. – Allahabad : Hind Publishing House, 1986.

—Law of Forests : Central and States / 5th ed. – Allahabad : Law Book Company.

—Law Relating to Forests in Uttar Pradesh / 1981 repr. ed. – Lucknow : Eastern Book Company, 1984.
206p.

FORMS AND PRECEDENTS

—Encyclopaedia of Forms and Precedents, 42 Vols. / M. J. R. Wear. – 5th ed. – London : Butterworths.

4th ed. also partly available
A 42 volume set of forms for property, local government, company, and commercial law matters in the United Kingdom. A looseleaf service keeps this work continually up to date.

FORMS AND PRECEDENTS – AUSTRALIA

—Australian Encyclopaedia of Forms and Precedents : 1987 Cumulative Supplement / Butterworths, 1987.
905p.

—Australian Encyclopedia of Forms and Precedents 1984 Cumulative Supplement / C. Croft. – Wellington : Butterworths.
ISBN 0409787140 Hbk

—Australian Encyclopedia of Forms and Precedents / Wellington : Butterworths.

FORMS AND PRECEDENTS – CANADA

—Guide to Surrogate Court Forms and Procedures / 2nd ed. – Butterworths, 1980.
224p.
ISBN 0409843326 Hbk

—O'Brien's Encyclopedia of Forms: 1893-Present, 1 Vol. / Aurora : Canada Law Book Co.
– (Division 3-Conveyancing and Mortgages Ser.).

Supplement

Vol. 8
– (Division 4-Leases Ser.).

Vol. 9
– (Division 5-Wills and Trusts Ser.).

Supplement

—O'Brien's Encyclopedia of Forms: 1893-Present, 3 Vols. / Aurora : Canada Law Book Co.
– (Division 1-Commercial and General Ser.).

Supplement

—O'Brien's Encyclopedia of Forms : 1893-Present, 9 Vols. / Aurora : Canada Law Book Co.
– (Divisions 1-5 Covering All Ser.).

Binder

—O'Brien's Encyclopedia of Forms, 9 Vols. / Aurora : Canada Law Book Co.
– (Abridgements and Encyclopedias).

Binder for Supplements

—O'Brien's Encyclopedia of Forms : Division Five-Wills and Trusts / Aurora : Canada Law Book Co.
– (Abridgments and Encyclopedias).

Supplement

—O'Brien's Encyclopedia of Forms : Division Four-Leases / Aurora : Canada Law Book Co.
– (Abridgments and Encyclopedias).

—O'Brien's Encyclopedia of Forms : Division One-Commercial & General / Aurora : Canada Law Book Co.
– (Abridgments and Encyclopedias).

Supplement-1983

—O'Brien's Encyclopedia of Forms : Division Three-Conveyancing and Mortgages / Aurora : Canada Law Book Co.
– (Abridgments and Encyclopedias).

Supplement

—O'Brien's Encyclopedia of Forms : Division Two-Corporations / Aurora : Canada Law Book Co.
– (Abridgments and Encyclopedias).

—Williston and Rolls : Court Forms, 2 Vols. / 2nd ed. – Butterworths.
ISBN 0409801836 loose £150.00

FORMS AND PRECEDENTS – CANADA – BRITISH COLUMBIA

—British Columbia Court Forms, 3 Vols. / James P. Taylor. – Butterworths.

—British Columbia Court Forms, 3 vols / James Taylor. – Toronto : Butterworths.

FORMS AND PRECEDENTS – CANADA – NEW BRUNSWICK

—New Brunswick Court Forms : Formulaire de procedure du Nouveau-Brunswick / Douglas G. Rouse. – Agincourt : Carswell, 1985.
800p.
This looseleaf volume presents in both French and English over two hundred eighty separate forms which document the steps of a civil action in the courts of New Brunswick, Canada.

FORMS AND PRECEDENTS – CANADA – ONTARIO

—O'Brien's Encyclopedia of Forms, 9 Vols. / Aurora : Canada Law Book Co.

FORMS AND PRECEDENTS – ENGLAND

—Forms of Practical Proceedings in the Courts of King's Bench / 6th ed. Repr. of 1824 ed. – Abingdon : Professional Books.
357p.

—Practice and procedure of the Admiralty Court : forms and precedents / Nigel Meeson. – London : Lloyd's, 1986.
296p; 24cm.
Includes index.
ISBN 1850440875 £35.00 (Nov.)

FORMS AND PRECEDENTS – GREAT BRITAIN

—Atkin's Encyclopaedia of Court Forms, 41 Vols. / 2nd. ed. – Abingdon : Professional Books, 1984.

—Atkin's Encyclopaedia of Court Forms in Civil Proceedings, 42 Vols. / J. M. Dyson. – 2nd ed. – Wellington : Butterworths.

—Butterworth's County Court Precedents and Pleadings / A. V. B. Bartlett. – London : Butterworths.

—County Court Precs. / London : Butterworths, 1985.
Service to Date.
ISBN 040629240X Hbk £110.00

—English Encyclopedia of Forms and Precedents / R. B. Roper. – 5th ed. – Wellington : Butterworths.

Updating suppls. avail.

—Formulae Bene Placitandi : A Book of Entries Containing Precedents, 2 Vols. / Repr. of 1671 ed. – Abingdon : Professional Books.
264p.

—Local Government Forms and Precedents : 1953-1956, 5 Vols. / Abingdon : Professional Books.

—Oke's Magisterial Formulist, 2 Vols. / Stuart Baker. – 20th ed. – London : Butterworths, 1986.
This looseleaf service provides immediate access to all the prescribed forms relating to proceeding in British magistrates' courts. A comprehensive range of precedents for all statutory offenses and many regulatory offenses within the jurisdiction of the courts is included.

—Oke's Magisterial Formulist / Pearson. – 20th ed. – London : Butterworths, 1985.
Service.
ISBN 040632400X Hbk £125.00

—Oke's Magisterial Formulist / London : Shaw & Sons.
This looseleaf service provides immediate access to all prescribed forms rel of completed forms and draft leare included.
ISBN 0406326118 Hbk

—Seton : Forms of Judgements and Orders in the High Court of Appeal, 3 Vols. / London : Sweet & Maxwell, 1985.
– (Sweet and Maxwell Library Reprints).

FORMS AND PRECEDENTS – NEW ZEALAND

—High Court Forms / A.A.P Willy. – Butterworths, 1985.
Contains 167 forms for use with the new High Court Rules. Of those, 114 are completely new. All the forms, including the Schedule forms, are annotated. The book is cross-referenced with Sim and Cain's Practice and Procedure.
ISBN 0409600792 Hbk £89.10

—High Court Forms / E. H. J. Wily. – Wellington : Butterworths.

FORMS AND PRECEDENTS – SOUTH AFRICA

—South African Encyclopedia of Forms and Precedents, 16 vols. / Durban : Butterworths.
– (Eng. and Afrikaans).

Suppl. 1984
ISBN 0409006033 Pbk

FORMS (LAW)
—O'Brien's encyclopedia of forms / Editor-in chief-: John D. Honsberger. – 10th ed. 9. – Toronto : Canada Law Book Co., 1966.
First edition by A.H. O'Brien entitled: The new conveyancer. Title of subsequent editions varies.

FORMS (LAW) – AUSTRALIA
—Precedents in practice / by Tony Graham : illustrated by George Haddon : with a foreword by H. G. Ogden. – Sydney : Law Book Co., 1983.
xiii,263p.
Includes index.
ISBN 0455204926

FORMS (LAW) – AUSTRALIA – VICTORIA
—Victorian pleading precedents / by Tony Graham : with a foreword by Norman M. O'Bryan. – Sydney : Law Book Co., 1982.
xii,333p.
Includes index.
ISBN 0455203628

FORMS (LAW) – CANADA
—O'Briens encyclopedia of forms / Editor-in-chief: John D. Honsberger. – 11th ed. – Aurora, Ont. : Canada Law Book Inc., 1987.
looseleaf.
First edition by A.H. O'Brien entitled: The new conveyancer. Title of subsequent editions varies.
ISBN 088804044X Hbk

FORMS (LAW) – GREAT BRITAIN
—Atkin's encyclopaedia of court forms in civil proceedings : a user's guide / James Richard Atkin Atkin. – 2nd ed. – London : Butterworths, 1983.
24p; 25cm.

—Encyclopaedia of court forms in civil proceedings / 2nd edition. v. – London : Butterworths, 1961.

—Encyclopaedia of forms and precedents / Raymond Walton. – 5th ed. v. – London : Butterworths, 1985.
Includes bibliographical references. - Index included in each volume. Partially supersedes 4th ed., entitled: The encyclopaedia of forms and precedents other than court forms. Kept up to date by looseleaf service volume.
ISBN 0406023603

—Encyclopaedia of forms and precedents other than court forms / L. G. Jory. – 4th ed. 28 v. – London : Butterworths, 1964-.
Includes bibliographical references and index. Managing editor L.G. Jory. Partially superseded by 5th ed., entitled: The encyclopaedia of forms and precedents.

FORMS (LAW) – NEW ZEALAND
—New Zealand encyclopaedia of forms and precedents other than court forms / editor, E.C. Adams. – 15. – Wellington : Butterworths, 1963.
Superseded by: New Zealand forms and precedents, 1986.

—New Zealnd forms and precedents / editor in chief, the Hon. Mr. Justice Barker. – Wellington : Butterworths, 1986.
Supersedes: New Zealand encyclopaedia of forms and precedents, 1963-70. With index volume.
ISBN 0409702080

FORMS (LAW) – SCOTLAND
—Formulary of old Scots legal documents / compiled by Peter Gouldesbrough : with a supplementary essay on Early Scottish conveyancing by Gordon Donaldson. – Edinburgh : Stair Society, 1985.
viii,196p.
Includes index.
ISBN 0902292110

FORMS OF ADDRESS
—Titles and forms of address : a guide to correct use / 18th ed. – London : Black, 1985.
224p.
Previous ed.: 1980. Includes index.
ISBN 0713626941 Pbk £5.95

FOSSIL FUELS – CANADA
—Fuels and the national policy / John N. McDougall. – Toronto : Butterworths, 1982.
vi,199p.
Bibliography: p188-194.

FRANCE
—Essays in Medieval diplomacy and administration / Pierre Chaplais. – London : Hambledon, 1981.
496p in various pagings,16p of plates; 25cm.
Includes index. English and French text.
ISBN 0950688223 No price

—French official publications / by Gloria Westfall. – Oxford : Pergamon, 1980.
xv,209p; 26cm.
Includes bibliographies and index.
ISBN 0080218385 £13.00

FRANCHISING
—International franchising - an overview / papers presented to the International Franchising Committee at the SBL Conferences, held in Toronto, October, 1983 : organized by SBL Section on Business Law of the International Bar Association : edited by Martin Mendelsohn. – Amsterdam : North-Holland, 1984.
xxvii,407p; 23cm.
ISBN 0444875484 No price

—International franchising : overview / North-Holland, 1985.
ISBN 0444875484 Hbk £49.95

—Journal of international franchising & distribution law / London : Frank Cass, 1986-.

FRANCHISING – AUSTRALIA
—Franchising in Australia : a legal guide / by David Shannon. – Sydney : Law Book Co., 1982.
xxii,275p.
Includes index.
ISBN 045520456X

FRANCHISING – CANADA
—Canadian Franchise Guide / Zaid. – Toronto : DeBoo.
Designed for franchisees, franchisors, and their professional advisors, this all-Canadian service discusses legal and tax considerations, current and future trends, marketing and financial planning strategies, and contains a selection of forms and agreements. Monthly updates are also provided.
ISBN 0888201397 loose £275.00

—Franchising 2 / Vancouver : Continuing Legal Education Society of British Columbia, 1985.
699p.
ISBN 0865042071 Hbk £90.00

—Franchising / Vancouver : British Columbia Continuing Legal Education Society, 1981.
703p.
ISBN 0865040303 Hbk £85.00

FRANCHISING – EUROPEAN COMMUNITY
—Distributorship, Franchising, Agency : Community and National Laws and Practice in the EEC / Dordrecht : Kluwer, 1987.
274p.
ISBN 9065443290 Hbk £120.00

FRANCHISING – GREAT BRITAIN
—Franchising : Practice and Precedents / Prichard-Jones. – 2nd ed. – London : Butterworths, 1987.
ISBN 0406101043 Hbk £50.00

—Franchising : practice and precedents in business format franchising / John Adams, K.V. Prichard Jones. – 2nd ed. – London : Butterworths, 1987.
xxxvii,409p; 25cm.
Previous ed.: 1981. Includes index.
ISBN 0406101043 £35.00

—Guide to franchising / by Martin Mendelsohn. – 4th ed. – Oxford : Pergamon, 1985.
xvii,319p; 24cm.
Previous ed.: 1982. Includes index.
ISBN 0080312829 £25.00

—Law and Practice of Franchising / Drysdale. – Pergamon, 1989.
ISBN 0080240356 Hbk

—Taking Up a Franchise / Colin Barrow. – 3rd ed. – London : Kogan Page, 1986.
264p.
ISBN 1850910758 Hbk £12.95

FRAUD
—Avoidance of fraudulent transfers and related bankruptcy crimes : papers delivered at the meetings of Committee J - Creditor's Rights, Insolvency, Liquidation and Reorganizations, Vienna, 2-7 September 1984 / Barrett. – London : International Bar Association, 1984.
166p.
Chairman: John A. Barrett.

—Corporate fraud / Michael J. Comer. – 2nd ed. – London : McGraw-Hill, 1985.
xvi,453p; 23cm.
Previous ed.: 1977. Includes bibliography and index.
ISBN 0070847916 £16.50

—International maritime fraud / by Eric Ellen, and Donald Campbell. – London : Sweet & Maxwell, 1981.
viii,174p; 22cm.
Bibliography: p160. - Includes index.
ISBN 0421271507 Pbk £8.00

FRAUD – AUSTRALIA
—Passing off trade deception trade marks / Charles Joseph Bannon. – Sydney : Butterworths, 1985.
xxv,172p.
ISBN 0409492442 A$59

FRAUD – AUSTRALIA – NEW SOUTH WALES
—Community law reform program / New South Wales Law Reform Commission. – Sydney : The Commission, 1983.
61p. – (L.R.C. 34).

FRAUD – CANADA
—Criminal fraud / J. Douglas Ewart. – Toronto : Carswell, 1986.
xv, 182 p.; 24 cm.
Includes bibliographical references and index.
ISBN 045938550X

—Fraud in Commercial Transactions / Vancouver : British Columbia Continuing Legal Education Society, 1982.
192p.
ISBN 086504080X Hbk £17.50

FRAUD – CANADA – BRITISH COLUMBIA
—Fraudulent conveyances and preferences / Law Reform Commission of British Columbia. – Vancouver : The Commission, 1986.
viii,216p. – (Working paper).
Includes bibliographical references.

—Report on fraudulent conveyances and preferences : Law Reform Commission of British Columbia / Law Reform Commission of British Columbia. – Vancouver : The Commission, 1988.
vii,180p.
Includes bibliographical references. Includes draft legislation.
ISBN 0771886314

FRAUD – ENGLAND
—Control of commercial fraud / L.H. Leigh. – London : Heinemann, 1982.
xii,339p; 23cm. – (Cambridge studies in criminology).
Bibliography: p315-326p. - Includes index.
ISBN 0435825194 £16.50

—Counterfeiting and forgery : a practical guide to the law / Roland Rowell. – London : Butterworths, 1986.
220p; 22cm.
Includes index.
ISBN 0406101108 Pbk £25.00

—Criminal law : conspiracy to defraud : an invitation for views / Law Commission. – London : The Commission, 1987.
14 leaves.

—Fraud / Anthony J. Arlidge and Jacques Parry. – London : Waterlow, 1985.
xlii,368p; 24cm.
Includes index.
ISBN 008039163X £30.00

—Misrepresentation / by David K. Allen. – London : Sweet & Maxwell, 1988.
xxii,178p; 22cm.
Includes index.
ISBN 0421347201 Hbk £16.00
ISBN 0421347309 Pbk £10.00

—Phantom capitalists : the organisation and control of long-firm fraud / by Michael Levi. – London : Heinemann, 1981.
346p; 23cm.
Bibliography: p335-341. - Includes index.
ISBN 0435825208 £16.50

FRAUD – GREAT BRITAIN
—Counterfeiting and Forgery : Practical Guide / London : Butterworths, 1986.
ISBN 0406101108 Pbk £32.00

—Criminal law: conspiracy to defraud / Great Britain. – London : H.M.S.O., 1987.
x,238p. – (Working paper).
ISBN 0117301868

—Fraud / London : Sweet & Maxwell, 1988.
ISBN 0421365307 Hbk

—Kerr on the Law of Fraud and Mistake / London : Sweet & Maxwell, 1986.
– (Sweet and Maxwell Library Reprints).
ISBN 0421355409 Hbk £50.00

—Licensed dealers in securities : draft rules & regulations proposed to be made under the Prevention of Fraud (Investments) Act 1958 / London : H.M.S.O., 1982.
iii,60p; 30cm.
At head of title: Department of Trade.
ISBN 0115136509 Pbk £4.25

—Role of an auditor in detecting fraud and other irregularities : a study / prepared on behalf of The Chartered Association of Certified Accountants. – London : Certified Accountant Publications, 1986.
46p.
'Prepared for publication by Christine Johnston, Technical Officer of the Chartered Association of Certified Accountants in conjunction with the Association's Working Party on Fraud and the Auditor's Responsibility, chaired by the Hon. Sir Irvine Goulding, and the School of Financial Studies, University of Glasgow' - Note.
ISBN 1850110212

FRAUD – INDIA
—Forgeries, Cheating and Criminal Liability / Allahabad : Law Publishers, 1980.

—Law of Forgeries, Counterfeiting and Cheating / 3rd ed. – Allahabad : Law Book Company, 1982.

FRAUD - SCOTLAND

—Obligations : report on negligent misrepresentation / Scottish Law Commission. - Edinburgh : H.M.S.O., 1985.
v,13p.
Includes bibliographical references.
ISBN 0102143854

FREE TRADE

—Courts and free markets (US and Europe) / Stein. - Oxford : Oxford University Press, 1982.
ISBN 0198253664 Hbk £22.50

Vol. 2 1982.
ISBN 0198253923 Hbk £30.00

—Myth of free trade : patterns of protectionism since 1945 / Harry Shutt. - Oxford : Blackwell, 1985.
193p.
Includes index.
ISBN 0631139974 £17.50

FREE TRADE - CANADA

—Concise Guide to the Canada-United States Free Trade Agreement / Colin H. McNairn. - Agincourt : Carswell, 1988.
100p.

—Legal framework for Canada-United States trade / edited by Maureen Irish and Emily F. Carasco. - Toronto : Carswell, 1987.
xxxviii,275p.

—Understanding the Canada-U.S. Free Trade Agreement / Debra P. Steger. - Ottawa : Institute for Research on Public Policy, 1988.
ISBN 0886450799 Hbk

FREE TRADE - EUROPEAN COMMUNITY

—Convention establishing the European Free Trade Association / New ed., incorporating all amendments up to 1st February 1982. 1. - Geneva : European Free Trade Association, 1982.
various pagings.
Previous ed.: 1979. Added t.-p. in French. Parallel English and French texts.

—Free movement of goods in the EEC / London : European Law Centre, 1982.
285p.
Supplement 1984.
ISBN 0907451055 £34.00

FREE TRADE - UNITED STATES

—Concise Guide to the Canada-United States Free Trade Agreement / Colin H. McNairn. - Agincourt : Carswell, 1988.
100p.

—Legal framework for Canada-United States trade / edited by Maureen Irish and Emily F. Carasco. - Toronto : Carswell, 1987.
xxxviii,275p.

—Understanding the Canada-U.S. Free Trade Agreement / Debra P. Steger. - Ottawa : Institute for Research on Public Policy, 1988.
ISBN 0886450799 Hbk

FREEDOM OF ASSOCIATION

—Freedom of Association : a Workers' Education Manual / Geneva : International Labour Office, 1987.
xi, 149p.
ISBN 9221057828 Hbk £15.00

—Freedom of association and industrial relations : a comparative study / Ferdinand von Prondzynski. - London : Mansell, 1987.
250p; 24cm.
Includes bibliography and index.
ISBN 0720117755 Pbk £30.00
ISBN 0720118700 £15.00

—Freedom of Association and Procedures for Determining Conditions of Employment in the Public Service : Report 7. Sixty-Third Session of the International Labour Conference, 1977 / Geneva : International Labour Office.
iv, 111p.
ISBN 9221015750 Hbk £17.50

Part 1: Proposed Texts Referred to Governments
45p.

Part 2: Replies of Governments
84p.
ISBN 9221015769 Hbk £17.50

Part 2: Replies of Governments
41p.
ISBN 9221017559 Hbk £12.50

—Freedom of association : digest of decisions and principles of the Freedom of Association Committee of the governing body of the ILO / International Labour Office. - 3rd ed. - Geneva : International Labour Office, 1985.
xii, 140 i.e. 262 p.; 24 cm.
ISBN 9221050734 pbk. £30.00F

—Freedom of Association, Industrial Relations and Collective Bargaining Practices in Mines Other than Coal Mines / Geneva : International Labour Office, 1984.
iv, 79p.
ISBN 9221034577 Hbk £15.00

—General survey on the application of the conventions on freedom of association, the right to organise and collective bargaining and the convention and recommendation concerning rural workers' organisations : third item on the agenda / International Labour Office. - Geneva : International Labour Office, 1983.
157p.
Cover title: Freedom of association and collective bargaining. Report III (Part 4B).
ISBN 9221031284

—Right of peaceful assembly in the A.C.T. / Canberra : Australian Government Publishing Service, 1985.
233p. - (Occasional paper).
Bibliography: p194-205.
ISBN 0644038934

—The right of peaceful assembly : its evolution and limits in a democratic society : a conference jointly organised by the British Institute of Human Rights and the United Kingdom Association for European Law in the Old Hall, Lincoln's Inn, on 30th April, 1982 / report prepared by Anthony McNulty. - London : British Institute of Human Rights, 1982.
ii,94p.
ISBN 0950835706

FREEDOM OF ASSOCIATION - AUSTRALIA

—Public order and the law / by Andrew Hiller : with a foreword by Judge Gibney. - Sydney : Law Book Co., 1983.
xx,230p.
Bibliography: p.xix-xx. - Includes index.
ISBN 0455202761
ISBN 0455204101 £26.00

FREEDOM OF ASSOCIATION - ENGLAND

—Criminal law : offences relating to public order / the Law Commission. - London : H.M.S.O., 1983.
vii,135p.
ISBN 0102085846

—Offences against public order / the Law Commission. - London : H.M.S.O., 1982.
viii,194p. - (Working paper).
ISBN 0117301620

FREEDOM OF ASSOCIATION - INDIA

—Fundamental right to freedom of association in Indo-Pak-Bangladesh sub-continent / Hamiduddin Khan : foreword by Ahsanuddin Chowdhury. - Dacca : University of Dacca, 1980.
xii,552p.
Bibliography: p.490-503. - Includes index.

FREEDOM OF ASSOCIATION - PAKISTAN

—Fundamental right to freedom of association in Indo-Pak-Bangladesh sub-continent / Hamiduddin Khan : foreword by Ahsanuddin Chowdhury. - Dacca : University of Dacca, 1980.
xii,552p.
Bibliography: p.490-503. - Includes index.

FREEDOM OF EXPRESSION

—Free speech : a philosophical enquiry / Frederick Schauer. - Cambridge : Cambridge University Press, 1982.
xiv,.237p; 24cm.
Bibliography: p222-229. - Includes index.
ISBN 0521243408 Hbk £20.00
ISBN 0521286174 Pbk £6.50

—Freedom of speech / Eric Barendt. - Oxford : Clarendon, 1985.
xxii,314p; 22cm.
Includes index.
ISBN 0198253818 £35.00

FREEDOM OF EXPRESSION - CANADA

—Open justice: the constitutional right to attend and spek about criminal proceedings / Scarborough, Ontario : Butterworths (Canada), 1985.
416.
Examines the extent to which Canadians are free to attend, criticize and report criminal court proceedings. Considers the impact of the Canadian Charter of Rights and Freedoms on the issues of public access to criminal courts, and assesses the practical aspects of the legal dilemma inherent in the free press/fair trial debate, against the background of the American experience.
ISBN 0409844730 Hbk

FREEDOM OF EXPRESSION - GREAT BRITAIN

—Freedom of Speech / Oxford : Oxford University Press, 1985.
ISBN 0198253818 Hbk £35.00

—Freedom, the Individual and the Law / 5th ed. - Pelican, 1982.
ISBN 0140206469 Pbk £6.95

FREEDOM OF EXPRESSION - NIGERIA

—Judicial attitudes to freedom of speech and the press with particular reference to contempt of court / by Isabella E. Adi. - Lagos : Nigerian Institute of Advanced Legal Studies, 1983.
23p.
Seminar paper presented at the Institute on Wednesday, April 20, 1983.

FREEDOM OF INFORMATION

—Freedom of information trends in the information age / edited by Tom Riley and Harold C. Relyea. - London : Frank Cass, 1983.
172p; 23cm.
Papers originally presented in the Journal of media law and practice, vol.3, no.1. Bibliography: p169-172.
ISBN 071463221X £15.00

—Information, freedom and censorship : the Article 19 world report 1988 / prepared by the staff of Article 19. - Harlow : Longman, 1988.
xii,340p; 24cm.
Bibliography: p324-326. - Includes index.
ISBN 0582026245 Pbk £12.95

—Public access to government-held information : a comparative symposium / general editor, Norman S. Marsh ... et al. - London : Stevens, 1987.
xxi, 342 p.; 22 cm.
Includes bibliographical references and index.
ISBN 0420476105 pbk.

FREEDOM OF INFORMATION - AUSTRALIA

—Access to information and policy making : a comparative study / by Heather Mitchell. - Toronto : Commission on Freedom of Information and Individual Privacy, 1980.
ix,223p. - (Research publication).

—Freedom of Information / North Ryde : Law Book Co, 1984.
ISBN 0455203563 Hbk £16.50

—Freedom of Information / North Ryde : Law Book Co, 1984.
xxix, 347p.
ISBN 0455203563 Hbk £36.00

—Freedom of Information Act 1982 : Annual Report 1984-85 / Kingston : Australian Government Publishing Service, 1985.
481p.

—Guideline to Freedom of Information Act / Attorney-General's Department. - Canberra : Australian Government Publishing Service, 1982.
398p.
ISBN 0644022752 Hbk £14.00

—Operation and Administration of the Freedom of Information Legislation / Kingston : Australian Government Publishing Service.
340p.

—Review of administrative action / by Mark Aronson and Nicola Franklin : with a chapter on freedom of information legislation by Peter Bayne. - Sydney : Law Book Co., 1987.
lxvii,720p.
Includes bibliographical references and index.
ISBN 0455207216

FREEDOM OF INFORMATION - AUSTRALIA - VICTORIA

—Eleventh report to Parliament on subordinate legislation concerning Freedom of Information (Exemption Offices) Regulations 1987 (SR NO.266/1987 ... / Legal and Constitutional Committee. - Melbourne : Government Printer, 1987.
ix,58p.
Includes text of legislation.

FREEDOM OF INFORMATION - CANADA

—Access and privacy : the steps ahead / Canada. - Ottawa : Government of Canada, 1987.
x,57,63,xip.
French title on added t.p.: Acces et renseignements personnels. Pages numbered in opposite directions. Text in English and French.
ISBN 0662554728

—Freedom of Information : Canadian Perspectives / Butterworths, 1981.
344p.
ISBN 0409857130 Hbk £75.00

—Freedom of Information Legislation in Nova Scotia, New Brunswick, Newfoundland, and Quebec / Ontario : Ontario Government Publications Service, 1983.
16p. - (Current Issue Paper: No. 21).

—How to Fight for What's Right : the Citizen's Guide to Public Interest Law / Toronto : James Lorimer & Co.
ISBN 0888624220 Pbk £12.95
ISBN 0888624239 Hbk £24.95

—Interim policy guide : Access to Information Act and the Privacy Act / Treasury Board of Canada Secretariat. - 1. - Ottawa : Minister of Supply and Services, 1983.
loose-leaf.
English and French text.
ISBN 0660522551

—Open and Shut : Enhancing the Right to Know and the Right to Privacy / Ottawa : Canadian Government Publishing Centre, 1987.
130p.

—Public and media access to the criminal process / Law Reform Commission of Canada. – Ottawa : The Commission, 1987.
106,120p. – (Working paper).
Includes bibliographical references. Added t.p. in French: L'acces du public et des medias au processus penal. Pages numbered in opposite directions. Text in English and French.
ISBN 0662551168

FREEDOM OF INFORMATION - CANADA - NEW BRUNSWICK

—Freedom of Information Legislation in Nova Scotia, New Brunswick, Newfoundland, and Quebec / Ontario : Ontario Government Publications Service, 1983.
16p. – (Current Issue Paper: No. 21).

FREEDOM OF INFORMATION - CANADA - NOVA SCOTIA

—Freedom of Information Legislation in Nova Scotia, New Brunswick, Newfoundland, and Quebec / Ontario : Ontario Government Publications Service, 1983.
16p. – (Current Issue Paper: No. 21).

FREEDOM OF INFORMATION - CANADA - ONTARIO

—Freedom of information and the policy-making process in Ontario / by John Eichmanis. – Toronto : Commission on Freedom of Information and Individual Privacy, 1980.
viii,169p. – (Research publication).

—Information access and crown corporations / by Isaiah A. Litrak. – Toronto : Commission on Freedom of Information and Individual Privacy, 1980.
viii,78p. – (Research publication).

—Public access to commercial information in government files / by Susan Soloway. – Toronto : Commission on Freedom of Information and Individual Privacy, 1980.
viii,145p. – (Research publication).

—Public government for private people : the report of the Commission on Freedom of Information and Individual Privacy / D. C. Williams. – Toronto : Commission on Freedom of Information and Individual Privacy, 1980.
3v.. Chairman: D.C. Williams.
ISBN 0774354321

FREEDOM OF INFORMATION - CANADA - QUEBEC

—Freedom of Information Legislation in Nova Scotia, New Brunswick, Newfoundland, and Quebec / Ontario : Ontario Government Publications Service, 1983.
16p. – (Current Issue Paper: No. 21).

FREEDOM OF INFORMATION - ENGLAND

—Right to know / Floyd Abrams, Michael Kirby, Lord Scarman. – London : Granada, 1985.
79p.
Includes bibliographical references.
ISBN 0586066810

FREEDOM OF INFORMATION - EUROPEAN COMMUNITY

—Freedom of data flows and EEC law / G P V Vandenberghe, Y Poullet. – Kluwer Law and Taxation, 1988.
142. – (Computer/Law Series).
Deals with the legal problems caused by transfrontier flows of information. Includes chapters on the need to speak a common language between partners, data and information in common law, information and data in continental law, and restriction on transborder transmissions of commercial data under EEC law.
ISBN 9065443665 Pbk £32/Dfl 99

FREEDOM OF INFORMATION - GREAT BRITAIN

—Access to information in local government / by Tim Harrison. – London : Sweet & Maxwell, 1988.
110p.
Covers the Local Government (Access to Information) Act 1985, including a chapter on access by elected members of councils. Also contains the Data Protection Act 1984 as it relates to councils, the Access to Personal Files Act 1987, and the common law.
ISBN 0421384107 £10.00

—Open government : freedom of information and local government : a study conducted for the Local Government Legal Society Trust and the Society of Town Clerks' Education and Research Trust / Patrick Birkinshaw. – London : Local Government Legal Society Trust in association with the Society of Town Clerks' Education and Research Trust, 1985.
84p.
ISBN 0951110101

—Public access to environmental information : report of an interdepartmental Working Party on public access to information held by pollution control authorities / Great Britain. – London : H.M.S.O., 1986.
ISBN 0117518654

—Right to know : the inside story of the Belgrano affair / Clive Ponting. – London : Sphere Books, 1985.
214p.
ISBN 0722169442

—Secrecy, or the right to know? : a study of the feasibility of freedom of information for the United Kingdom / Freedom of Information Campaign. – London : Library Association, 1980.
110p; 21cm.
ISBN 0853659435 Pbk Unpriced

—Secrets file : the case for freedom of information in Britain today / Des Wilson. – London : Heinemann Educational Books, 1984.
viii,(2),166p.
Bibliography: p59.
ISBN 0435839403

FREEDOM OF INFORMATION - NEW ZEALAND

—Towards open government / Alan Danks. – Wellington : Government Printer, 1981.
54p.

2 : Supplementary report 1981.
138p.
Chairman: Sir Alan Danks.

FREEDOM OF INFORMATION - POLAND

—Freedom of information and expression in Poland / Article 19. – London : Article 19, 1987.
28p.

FREEDOM OF INFORMATION - SWEDEN

—Access to information and policy making : a comparative study / by Heather Mitchell. – Toronto : Commission on Freedom of Information and Individual Privacy, 1980.
ix,223p. – (Research publication).

FREEDOM OF INFORMATION - TUNISIA

—Freedom of information and expression in Tunisia / Article 19. – London : Article 19, 1987.
29p.

FREEDOM OF INFORMATION - UNITED STATES

—Access to information and policy making : a comparative study / by Heather Mitchell. – Toronto : Commission on Freedom of Information and Individual Privacy, 1980.
ix,223p. – (Research publication).

FREEDOM OF INFORMATION (INTERNATIONAL LAW)

—Communications : (includes telecommunications) / Thessaloniki, Greece : Institute of International Public Law and International Relations of Thessaloniki, 1987.
530p.
Includes bibliographical references. Text in English and French.

FREEDOM OF MOVEMENT

—Commentary on the European Convention on Establishment / adopted by the Standing Committee : Convention opened for signature on 13 December 1955. – Strasbourg : Council of Europe, 1980.
45p; 21cm.
Includes the text of the European Convention on Establishment. At head of cover title : Council of Europe, Legal Affairs.

—Right to leave and return in international law and practice / by Hurst Hannum. – Dordrecht : Nijhoff, 1987.
xiii, 189p. – (International studies in human rights).
Includes index.
ISBN 9024734452

FREEDOM OF MOVEMENT - EUROPEAN COMMUNITY

—Professions and services in the European Economic Community / by D. Lasok. – Deventer, The Netherlands : Kluwer Law and Taxation Publishers, 1986.
ISBN 9065442537 Hbk

FREEDOM OF MOVEMENT - INDIA

—Right to Freedom of Movement (1968, Bangalore) / Geneva : International Commission of Jurists.

—Right to Travel Under the Constitution / Lucknow : Eastern Book Company, 1986.
272p.

FREEDOM OF RELIGION - ENGLAND

—Religion and the law : religious liberty in Modern English law / St John A. Robilliard. – Manchester : Manchester University Press, 1984.
xii,223p; 23cm.
Includes index.
ISBN 0719009561 £22.50

FREEDOM OF RELIGION - NIGERIA

—Religion and religious liberty in Nigerian law (from the colonial days to 1983) / Ikem Bu Chukwu B. Ngwoke. – Roma : Pontificia Universita Lateranense, 1984.
xvi,531p.
Bibliography: p.520-531.

FREIGHT

—International cargo carriers' liabilities : the determination of some current contractual problems arising from the international carriage of goods / W.E. Astle. – London : Fairplay, 1983.
viii,140p; 25cm.
ISBN 0905045416 Pbk No price

—International carriage of goods by road : CMR / by Malcolm A. Clarke. – London : Stevens, 1982.
xxvi,212p; 26cm.
Includes index. Appendix in French.
ISBN 0420464905 £19.50

FREIGHT - ENGLAND

—Law of the carriage of goods by land, sea and air / by Jasper Ridley. – 6th ed. – London : Shaw, 1982.
xlviii,328p; 22cm.
Previous ed.: 1978. Includes index.
ISBN 0721906222 Pbk £9.50

FREIGHT - GREAT BRITAIN

—Review of Road Freight Regulation in Britain / Bureau of Transport Economics. – Canberra : Australian Government Publishing Service, 1981.
78p. – (BTE Occasional Paper: No. 43).
ISBN 0642067953 Hbk £3.80

FRONTIERS

—European Outline Convention on Transfrontier Co-operation between Territorial Communities or Authorities / Strasbourg : Council of Europe, 1980.

FUND IN COURT - GREAT BRITAIN

—Funds in Court in England and Wales : Account 1981-1982 / London : HMSO, 1983.

FUND RAISING - ENGLAND

—Gaming, lotteries, fundraising and the law / by Jarlath Finney : foreword by Sir David Napley. – London : Sweet & Maxwell, 1982.
xxiv,218p; 25cm.
Includes index.
ISBN 0421299800 Pbk £18.50

FUTURES MARKET

—Futures markets : modelling, managing and monitoring futures trading / edited by Manfred E. Streit. – Oxford : Blackwell, in cooperation with the European University Institute, Florence, 1983.
viii,324p; 24cm.
Includes bibliographies and index.
ISBN 0631132945 Unpriced

FUTURES MARKET - GREAT BRITAIN

—Futures Game / Jones. – 2nd ed. – Maidenhead : McGraw-Hill, 1986.
ISBN 0070637288 Hbk £39.95

—Guide to Financial Futures / London : Butterworths, 1988.
ISBN 0406200106 Hbk £35.00

—Handbook of Financial Futures and Options / Krikic. – Cambridge : Woodhead-Faulkner, 1986.
ISBN 0859414116 Hbk £25.00

—Investors' Guide to Commodities Futures Markets / Bettelheim. – London : Butterworths, 1986.
ISBN 0406101906 Hbk £17.95

—Law and Practice of Futures and Options / Cregan. – London : Sweet & Maxwell, 1988.
ISBN 04213914006 Hbk

GAMBLING - AUSTRALIA

—Legal Control of Casinos / Canberra : Australian Institute of Criminology.

GAMBLING - AUSTRALIA - SOUTH AUSTRALIA

—Report ... relating to the inherited imperial law on gaming and wagering in South Australia / Law Reform Committee of South Australia. – Adelaide : Government Printer, 1982.
9p. – (68th report).

GAMBLING - ENGLAND

—Gaming, lotteries, fundraising and the law / by Jarlath Finney : foreword by Sir David Napley. – London : Sweet & Maxwell, 1982.
xxiv,218p; 25cm.
Includes index.
ISBN 0421299800 Pbk £18.50

—Law of betting, gaming and lotteries / by Colin M. Smith & Stephen P. Monkcom. – London : Butterworth, 1987.
600p.
Includes index.
ISBN 0406296596 £50.00

GAMBLING - GREAT BRITAIN

—Law of Betting, Gaming and Lotteries / Monkcom. – London : Butterworths, 1987.
ISBN 0406296596 Hbk £85.00

—Lotteries and Gaming - Voluntary Organisations and the Law / NCVO. – London : Bedford Square Press, 1981.
ISBN 0719910706 Pbk £1.95

—Underhill's licensing guide / 10th. – London : Longman Professional (UK), 1989.
– (Practitioner series).
Guide to the law and procedure of liquor, gaming, betting and lottery licensing. Details each step in making or opposing a successful licensing application, with key precedents. Revised to take account of the changes introduced by the Licensing Act 1988.
ISBN 0851215378 Hbk £17.95

GAMBLING - MALAYSIA
—Common Gaming Houses Act, 1953 (Act 289) / Kuala Lumpur : International Law Books Services.

GAMBLING - UNITED KINGDOM
—Guide to Licensing Law : For Betting Shops, Bookmakers, Clubs and Licensed Premises / Charles Joseph Acred. – 3rd ed. – Chichester : Barry Rose, 1980.
vii, 212p : Illus.
ISBN 0859920631 Hbk £9.00

GAME LAWS
—Legislation on wildlife, hunting, and protected areas in some European countries / by Christian du Saussay for the Legislation Branch, Legal Office. – Rome : Food and Agriculture Organization of the United Nations, 1980.
vi, 49 p.; 28 cm. – (Legislative study).
Includes bibliographies references.
ISBN 9251008787 pbk.

GAME LAWS - AFRICA
—Legislation on wildlife and protected areas in Africa / by Christian du Saussay for Legislation Branch, Legal Office, FAO. – Rome : Food and Agriculture Organization of the United Nations, 1984.
vii,158p. – (Legislative study).
Includes bibliographical references.
ISBN 9251011710

GAME LAWS - CANADA - ONTARIO
—Game and Fish Act : Revised Statutes of Ontario, 1980 / Office of the Legislative Assembly (Ontario). – Ontario : Ontario Government Publications Service, 1983.
38p.

GAME LAWS - GREAT BRITAIN
—Hunting law / London : Shaw & Sons, 1988.
ISBN 0721911404 Pbk

GAME LAWS - UNITED STATES
—American wildlife law / Thomas A. Lund. – Berkeley : University of California Press, 1980.
ix,177p; 24cm.
Includes index.
ISBN 0520038835 £7.75

GARDENS - ENGLAND
—Garden law / by Godfrey Sandys-Winsch. – London : Shaw & Sons, 1982.
xiii,245p; 22cm.
Includes index.
ISBN 0721909302 Pbk Unpriced

GAZETTEERS
—Countries and islands of the world : a guide to nomenclature / Julie Wilcocks. – London : Bingley, 1981.
133p; 23cm.
ISBN 085157338X Unpriced

GENERAL AVERAGE
—General average : the practical problems / Kaj Pineus. – Stockholm, Sweden : Almqvist & Wiksell International, 1985.
58 p.; 21 cm.
Includes bibliographical references.
ISBN 9122007326 pbk. kr150

—Guide to the Hague and Hague-Visby rules / 2nd. – London : Lloyds of London Press, 1989.
Revised and updated since the 1985 edition. Includes the York-Antwerp Rules related to General Average, and details of the Hague-Visby SDR Convention and the Limitation Convention. Also includes the latest position in the 'Gold Clause Agreement', and a list of signatories to both sets of rules.
ISBN 1850442436 Pbk

GENERAL AVERAGE - GREAT BRITAIN
—Arnould's law of marine insurance and average / Michael J. Mustill, Jonathan C. B. Gilman. – 16th ed. 2. – London : Stevens, 1981.
lxxv,1242p; 26cm.
Previous ed.: 1961. Includes index.
ISBN 0420445005 £95.00

GENETIC ENGINEERING
—Legal protection for microbiological and genetic engineering inventions / Roman Saliwanchik. – London : Addison-Wesley, 1982.
xiii,256p; 25cm.
Includes index.
ISBN 0201109387 £33.30

GENETIC ENGINEERING - AUSTRALIA - VICTORIA
—Genetic manipulation / Law Reform Commission of Victoria. – Melbourne : The Commission, 1987.
ii,41p. – (Discussion paper).
Includes bibliographical references.
ISBN 0724167285

GENETIC ENGINEERING - UNITED STATES
—Genetics and the law II / edited by Aubrey Milunsky and George J. Annas. – New York : Plenum Press, 1980.
xix,480p; 26cm.
'...a second national conference ... held in Boston in May, 1979...' - Preface. Bibliography: p.441-474. - Includes index.
ISBN 0306403889 Unpriced

—Genetics and the law III / proceedings of the Third National Symposium on Genetics and the Law, held April 2-4, 1984, in Boston, Massachusetts : cosponsored by the American Society of Law and Medicine ... et al. : edited by Aubrey Milunsky and George J. Annas. – New York : Plenum, 1985.
xix,514p; 26cm.
Bibliography: p491-504. - Includes index.
ISBN 0306419831 No price

GENOCIDE
—International action against genocide / by Leo Kuper. – Rev. 1984 ed. – London : Minority Rights Group, 1984.
19p. – (Report).
Bibliography: p.18.

GENOCIDE - BURUNDI
—Burundi since the genocide / by Reginald Kay. – London : Minority Rights Group, 1987.
12p. – (Report).
'This report was first published under the title Selective genocide in Burundi by Professor Rene Lemarchand and David Martin in July 1974'. - Front cover verso.
ISBN 0946690472

GEOLOGY - NIGERIA
—Nigeria : its petroleum geology, resources and potential / by Arthur Whiteman. – 2 v. – London : Graham & Trotman, 1982.
394p,5leaves of plates(folded).
In 2 vols. Bibliography: p.376-381.
ISBN 0860102645

GIFTS
—Gifts and promises : Continental and American law compared / John P. Dawson. – New Haven : Yale University Press, 1980.
ix,240p; 22cm.
Bibliography: p.ix. - Includes index.
ISBN 0300024460 £10.70

GIFTS - AUSTRALIA
—Stamp Duty Aspects of Trusts, Settlements and Gifts in Australia / F.P. Zipfinger. – Butterworths, 1984.
367p.
ISBN 0409494216 Hbk £56.00

GIFTS - CANADA
—Taxation and estate planning / by Maurice C. Cullity and Catherine A. Brown. – 2nd ed. – Toronto, Canada : Carswell Co., 1984.
xxvi, 764 p.; 24 cm.
At head of title: Cullity, Forbes, Brown. Includes bibliographical references and index.
ISBN 0459362305 pbk.

GIFTS - IRELAND
—Capital acquisitions tax / by Norman Bale & John Condon. – Dublin : Institute of Taxation in Ireland, 1982.
244p.
Includes index.

GIFTS - NEW ZEALAND
—New Zealand duties guide / Auckland : Commerce Clearing House (New Zealand), 1985-.
Title history; New Zealand duties and sales tax guide (1983-1985). Includes index. Loose-leaf issues accompanied by a summary report.

GIPSIES
—Roma : Europe's gypsies / by Grattan Puxon. – Rev updated ed. – London : Minority Rights Group, 1987.
15p. – (Report).
Bibliography: p.13.
ISBN 0946690456

GIPSIES - GREAT BRITAIN
—Travellers' handbook - guide to law affecting gypsies / TUAR, 1985.
ISBN 0948309008 Pbk £5.95

GOLD
—International monetary system : efficiency and practical alternatives / Herbert G. Grubel. – 4th ed. – Harmondsworth : Penguin, 1984.
214p.
Bibliography: p201-206.
ISBN 0140808183

GOLD - GREAT BRITAIN
—Trading in gold futures / Cambridge : Woodhead-Faulkner, 1985.
ISBN 0859412687 Hbk £25.00

GOLD - INDIA
—Handbook on Gold Control Act, Rules and Notifications / 3rd ed. – Allahabad : Law Publishers, 1982.

GOLD MINERS - SOUTH AFRICA
—Black gold : the Mozambican miner, proletarian and peasant / Ruth First : pictures by Moira Forjaz : work-songs and interviews recorded by Alpheus Manghezi. – Brighton : Harvester, 1983.
xxxi,256p,xvip of plates; 23cm.
Bibliography: p207-211. - Includes index.
ISBN 0710803141 £30.00
ISBN 0312083181

GOOD-WILL (BUSINESS) - GREAT BRITAIN
—Passing off : the law and practice relating to the imitation of goods, businesses and professions / David Young. – 1st ed. – London : Oyez Longman, 1985.
xxviii,152p. – (Oyez Longman practitioner series).
Includes index.
ISBN 0851209866

GOVERNMENT
—Administrative politics in British government / Andrew Gray and William I. Jenkins. – Brighton : Wheatsheaf, 1985.
x,259p; 23cm.
Bibliography: p235-250. - Includes index.
ISBN 0710801432 Hbk £18.95
ISBN 0312004613 £6.95

—Natal and KwaZulu : constitutional and political options; proceedings of the workshop... / edited by Laurence Boulle and Lawrence Baxter. – Cape Town : Juta, 1981.
viii,211p.
Includes chapter in Afrikaans.

—Policy process in the modern capitalist state / Christopher Ham and Michael Hill. – Brighton : Wheatsheaf Books Ltd, 1984.
xiii,210p.
Bibliography: p190-204.
ISBN 0710801904

GOVERNMENT - AUSTRALIA
—Australia's Government and Parliament / 7th ed. – Melbourne : Nelson, 1987.
194p : Illus.
ISBN 0170071944 Hbk £16.95

GOVERNMENT - CANADA
—Government Regulation : Scope, Growth, Process / Vancouver : University of British Columbia, Faculty of Commerce & Business Administration, 1980.
xxvi, 267p. – (Montreal Institute for Research on Public Policy Ser.).

—Public administration in Canada : selected readings / edited by A.M. Willms, W.D.K. Kernaghan. – 4th ed. – Toronto : Methuen, 1982.
viii,354p.
Includes bibliographies.
ISBN 0458952508

GOVERNMENT - ENGLAND
—English administrative system 1780-1870 / Sir Norman Chester. – Oxford : Clarendon Press, 1981.
398p; 23cm.
Bibliography: p385-389. - Includes index.
ISBN 0198226438 £22.50

—Government of England / Repr. of 1904 ed. – Abingdon : Professional Books.
220p.

GOVERNMENT - GREAT BRITAIN
—British Government and Constitution (LIC) / Weidenfeld & Nicolson, 1985.
ISBN 0297786512 Hbk £25.00
ISBN 0297786530 Pbk £15.95

—British Government and Politics / 3rd ed. – Plymouth : Macdonald & Evans, 1984.
ISBN 0712124071 Pbk £3.95

—British Government and Politics / 3rd ed. – Plymouth : Macdonald & Evans, 1984.
xi, 288p. – (M and E Handbook Ser.).
ISBN 0712102922 Hbk £3.95

—Government & Pressure Groups in Britain / Richardson. – Oxford : Oxford University Press, 1987.
ISBN 0198761678 Hbk £30.00

—Home Office 1848-1914 : from clerks to bureaucrats / Jill Pellew. – London : Heinemann, 1982.
xi,271p; 22cm.
Bibliography: p225-233. - Includes index.
ISBN 0435326856 £12.50

—Home Office : perspectives on policy and administration : bicentenary lectures 1982 / London : Royal Institute of Public Administration, 1983.
98p; 21cm.
ISBN 0900628308 Pbk £6.00

—Local and Central Government / 4th ed. – London : Hutchinson, 1984.
128p.
ISBN 0091588715 Pbk £3.95

—Parliament Government in Britain / Carleton : Pitman Pty Ltd, 1984.
ISBN 0273016156 Hbk £38.95, 015

—Purposes of Government Expenditure / London : Policy Studies Institute, 1984.
38p.

—Reports / London : H.M.S.O., 1985.
8 p.
ISBN 0101956304

—Table of Governmental Orders / London : HMSO, 1983.
ISBN 0118402382 Hbk £65.00

GOVERNMENT - IRAN

—Islamic government and the revolution in Iran / by Ayatollah Allama Yahya Noori. – 2nd ed. – Glasgow : Royston, 1985.
74,xip; 23cm.
New ed. - Previous ed.: 1984. Includes index.
ISBN 0946706255 £18.95

GOVERNMENT - JAPAN

—Public administration in Japan / edited by IIAS Tokyo Round Table organizing committee. – Tokyo : Institute of Administrative Management, 1982.
299p.
Proceedings of a conference.

GOVERNMENT - PHILIPPINES

—Government in Transition / Quezon City : University of the Philippines, Law Center, 1980.
263p.

GOVERNMENT - ZAMBIA

—Dynamics of the one-party state in Zambia / Cherry Gertzel ..., Carolyn Baylies, Morris Szeftel. – Manchester : Manchester University Press, 1984.
xi,262p; 23cm.
Bibliography: p247-258. - Includes index.
ISBN 0719010691 £28.50

GOVERNMENT ADVERTISING - GREAT BRITAIN

—Crime prevention publicity : an assessment / by D. Riley and P. Mayhew. – London : H.M.S.O., 1980.
v,43p.
Bibliography: p40-43. A Home Office Research Unit report.
ISBN 0113407033

GOVERNMENT AND THE PRESS - GREAT BRITAIN

—Handling of press and public information during the Falklands conflict : observations presented by the Secretary of State for Defence on the First Report from the Defence Committee / presented to Parliament by the Secretary of State for Defence. – London : H.M.S.O., 1983.
5p.
ISBN 0101882009

GOVERNMENT ATTORNEYS - GREAT BRITAIN

—Review of government legal services / report by Sir Robert Andrew. – London : HMSO, 1989.
102p.
At head of title: Cabinet Office.
ISBN 0114300348

GOVERNMENT BUSINESS ENTERPRISES

—Arbitration and State Enterprises / Paris : International Chamber of Commerce.
115p.

—Arbitration and state enterprises : a survey on the national and international state of law and practice / by Karl-Heinz Bockstiegel. – Deventer : Kluwer Law and Taxation, 1984.
vi,113p; 25cm.
'An international research study of the Institute of International Business Law and Practice of the International Chamber of Commerce'. Bibliography: p75-109.
ISBN 9065441840 Pbk No price

—Nationalised industries and public control : legal, constitutional and political issues / Tony Prosser. – Oxford : Blackwell, 1986.
220p; 23cm.
Examines constitutional form of nationalised industries and their relationship with government. Studies the role of public law in defining and limiting state activity as applied to nationalised industries.
ISBN 0631139982 £17.50

GOVERNMENT BUSINESS ENTERPRISES - INDIA

—Law and Practice Relating to Government Companies / New Delhi : Bharat Law House, 1987.

GOVERNMENT BUSINESS ENTERPRISES - SINGAPORE

—State enterprise in Singapore : legal importation and development / Philip Nalliah Pillai. – Singapore : Singapore University Press, National University of Singapore, 1983.
xxiv, 223 p.; 23 cm.
Originally presented as the author's thesis (doctoral–Harvard). Includes bibliographical references and index.
ISBN 9971690764 pbk.

GOVERNMENT CONTRACTS - INDIA

—Government Contracts : Law and Procedure / Delhi : Eastern Book Corporation, 1984.
xxxv, 532p.
ISBN 8185077010 Hbk £70.00

GOVERNMENT CONTRACTS - MALAYSIA

—Contracts Act, 1950 (Act 136) and Government Contracts Act, 1949 (Act 120) / Kuala Lumpur : International Law Books Services.

GOVERNMENT INFORMATION

—Public access to government-held information : a comparative symposium / general editor, Norman S. Marsh ... et al. – London : Stevens, 1987.
xxi, 342 p.; 22 cm.
Includes bibliographical references and index.
ISBN 0420476105 pbk.

GOVERNMENT INFORMATION - CANADA

—Interim policy guide : Access to Information Act and the Privacy Act / Treasury Board of Canada Secretariat. – 1. – Ottawa : Minister of Supply and Services, 1983.
loose-leaf.
English and French text.
ISBN 0660522551

GOVERNMENT INFORMATION - CANADA - ONTARIO

—Public access to commercial information in government files / by Susan Soloway. – Toronto : Commission on Freedom of Information and Individual Privacy, 1980.
viii,145p. – (Research publication).

GOVERNMENT INFORMATION - GREAT BRITAIN

—Public access to environmental information : report of an interdepartmental Working Party on public access to information held by pollution control authorities / Great Britain. – London : H.M.S.O., 1986.
ISBN 0117518654

—Third report from the Defence Committee, session 1979-80 : the D Notice system : together with the minutes of proceedings of the Committee ... / London : H.M.S.O., 1980.
xxiii,150p; 25cm. – (HC).
Bound with: Observations presented by the Secretary of State for Defence (Cmnd. 8129).
ISBN 010027739X

—Third report from the Defence Committee : the D notice system : House of Commons paper 773 session 1979-80 : observations presented by the Secretary of State for Defence / London : H.M.S.O., 1981.
2p; 25cm.
Bound with: Third report from the Defence Committee.
ISBN 0101812906

—Whitehall and Westminster : Government informs Parliament : the changing scene / Dermot Englefield. – Harlow : Longman, 1985.
x,218p; 24cm.
Includes index.
ISBN 058290272X Pbk £15.00

GOVERNMENT INFORMATION - NEW ZEALAND

—Official Information Bill / by Ian Eagles. – Auckland : Legal Research Foundation Inc., 1982.
31p.
'Paper presented at Auckland Law Faculty Seminar Series 1982 at University of Auckland'.

—Resolution of disputes under the Official Information Act 1982 / by K. J. Keith. – Wellington : Information Authority, 1984.
12p. – (Occasional paper).

—Towards open government / Alan Danks. – Wellington : Government Printer, 1981.
54p.

2 : Supplementary report 1981.
138p.
Chairman: Sir Alan Danks.

GOVERNMENT LIABILITY

—Public liability : Recommendation no.R(84) 15 adopted by the Committee of Ministers of the Council of Europe on 18 September 1984, and explanatory memorandum / Council of Europe. – Strasbourg : Council of Europe, 1985.
19p; 21cm.
'... prepared by the committee of experts on administrative law set up under the authority of the European Committee on Legal Co-operation. On cover: Council of Europe, Legal Affairs.
ISBN 9287103798

GOVERNMENT LIABILITY - AUSTRALIA

—Public torts and contracts / by Mark Aronson and Harry Whitmore. – Sydney : Law Book Co., 1982.
xviii, 296 p.; 25 cm.
Includes bibliographical references and indexes.
ISBN 0455204411 pbk.

GOVERNMENT LIABILITY - AUSTRALIA - SOUTH AUSTRALIA

—Report ... relating to proceedings by and against the crown / Law Reform Committee of South Australia. – 1. – Adelaide : Government Printer, 1987.
Various pagings. – (104th report).

GOVERNMENT LIABILITY - AUSTRALIA - WESTERN AUSTRALIA

—Report on the liability of highway authorities for non-feasance / Law Reform Commission of Western Australia. – Perth : Law Reform Commission of Western Australia, 1981.
116p. – (Project v no 62).

GOVERNMENT LIABILITY - GREAT BRITAIN

—Compensation and government torts / by Carol Harlow. – London : Sweet & Maxwell, 1982.
xvii,173p; 19cm.
Bibliography: p163-167. - Includes index.
ISBN 0421292504 Hbk £12.50
ISBN 0421292601 Pbk No price

GOVERNMENT LIABILITY - UNITED STATES

—Suing government : citizen remedies for official wrongs / Peter H. Schuck. – New Haven : Yale University Press, 1983.
xxi,262p; 22cm.
Includes index.
ISBN 0300029578 Hbk

GOVERNMENT LIABILITY (INTERNATIONAL LAW)

—State responsibility / by Ian Brownlie. – Oxford : Clarendon, 1983.
xvi,302p; 24cm.
Includes index.
ISBN 0198254520 £25.00

GOVERNMENT LITIGATION - NIGERIA

—Civil proceedings by and against the State in Nigeria / by F. Olisa Awogu. – Onitsha : Pacific College Press, 1981.
x,167p.
Includes index.

GOVERNMENT OWNERSHIP

—Nationalization of foreign property : a study in North-South dialogue / Subhash C. Jain : foreword by B. Sen. – New Delhi : Deep & Deep, 1983.
298p.
Bibliography: p.268-298 - Includes index.

GOVERNMENT OWNERSHIP - GREAT BRITAIN

—Selling the state : privatisation in Britain / Cento Veljanovski. – London : Weidenfeld and Nicolson, 1987.
xiv, 239p.
Bibliography: p.213-217.
ISBN 0297790803

GOVERNMENT OWNERSHIP - GUYANA

—Nationalisation of Guyana's bauxite : the case of Alcan / M. Shahabuddeen. – Georgetown : Ministry of Information, 1981.
xvii,306p.
Bibliography: p282-306.

GOVERNMENT OWNERSHIP - INDIA

—Controls over public corporations in India / Ramesh Chandra : foreword by V. R. Krishna Iyer. – Delhi : Delhi University, 1981.
xx,487p.
Bibliography: p.447-482. - Includes index.

GOVERNMENT PUBLICATIONS

—Official publications of Western Europe / Eve Johansson. – London : Mansell, 1984.
xvi,313p; 24cm.
Includes bibliographies and index.
ISBN 0720116236 £28.00

Vol.2 : Austria, Belgium, Federal Republic of Germany, Greece, Norway, Portugal, Sweden, Switzerland and United Kingdom / edited by Eve Johansson. – 1988.
x,278p.
Includes bibliographies and index.
ISBN 0720116627 Hbk £38.50 (Mar.)

GOVERNMENT PUBLICATIONS - GREAT BRITAIN

—Catalogue of British official publications not published by HMSO / Cambridge : Chadwyck-Healey, 1981-.
30cm.

—Official publications in Britain / David Butcher. – London : Bingley, 1983.
161p; 23cm.
Includes index.
ISBN 0851573517 Unpriced

—Whitehall and Westminster : Government informs Parliament : the changing scene / Dermot Englefield. – Harlow : Longman, 1985.
x,218p; 24cm.
Includes index.
ISBN 058290272X Pbk £15.00

GOVERNMENT TRADING

—Legal aspects of doing business in Eastern Europe and the Soviet Union / edited by Dennis Campbell. – Deventer, The Netherlands : Kluwer Law and Taxation Publishers, 1986. – (International business series).
Includes index and bibliography.
ISBN 9065442634

GOVERNMENTAL INVESTIGATIONS

—Law reform digests : a digest of the reports of law reform agencies in Australia, New Zealand and Papua New Guinea, 1910-1980 / Canberra : Australian Government Publishing, 1983.
xviii,754p.
Includes index.
ISBN 0644016280

GOVERNMENTAL INVESTIGATIONS – AUSTRALIA

—Royal commissions and boards of inquiry : some legal and procedural aspects / by Leonard Arthur Hallett. – Sydney : Law Book Company, 1982.
xxxvi,368p.
Bibliography: pxxxi-xxxvi.
ISBN 0455204721

GOVERNMENTAL INVESTIGATIONS – AUSTRALIA – NEW SOUTH WALES

—Community law reform program / New South Wales Law Reform Commission. – Sydney : The Commission, 1984.
115p. – (L.R.C. 39).
Bibliography: p.113-115.

GOVERNMENTAL INVESTIGATIONS – GREAT BRITAIN

—Fifth report from the Environment Committee, session 1985-86 : planning: appeals, call-in and major public inquiries / Great Britain. – London : H.M.S.O., 1986.
xcvi p. – (H.C. 1985-86).
ISBN 0100110657

Vol. 2 : Minutes of evidence and appendices 1986.
viii,466p. – (H.C. 1985-86).
ISBN 0100110754

—Social research and Royal Commissions / edited by Martin Bulmer. – London : Allen & Unwin, 1980.
xv,198p; 23cm.
Bibliography: p189-192. - Includes index.
ISBN 0043510558 No price

GOVERNMENTAL INVESTIGATIONS – INDIA

—Commissions of Inquiry Act 1952 : fully annotated with exhaustive commentaries / by K.A. Ramasubramaniam. – Bombay : Tripathi, 1980.
xxviii,131p; 23cm.
Includes index.

GOVERNMENTAL INVESTIGATIONS – NEW ZEALAND

—W Zealand royal commissions, commissions and committees of inquiry, 1864-1981 : a checklist / compiled by Evelyn Robertson and Peter H. Hughes for the NZLA Professional Division. – Wellington : New Zealand Library Association, 1982.
30p.
ISBN 0908560109

GRANTS-IN-AID

—Policies with regard to grants to local authorities / report prepared by the Committee of Experts on Local and Regional Finance of the Steering Committee for Regional and Municipal Matters and drafted by J. Lotz, Chairman. – Strasbourg : Council of Europe, 1986.
35p.

—Response of local authorities to central government incitement to reduce expenditure / by W. J. Meadows. – Strasbourg : Council of Europe, 1986.
33p.
Prepared under the guidance of the Committee of Experts on Local and Regional Finance of the Steering Committee for Regional and Municipal Matters.

GRANTS-IN-AID – CANADA

—Need for and the feasibility of an appeals process in regard to municipal grants-in-lieu of taxes : a report prepared for the Minister of Public Works Canada / I.C. Pollack, R. Gaulin, G. Simpson. – Ottawa : Minister of Supply and Services Canada, 1983.
324 p. in various pagings; 28 cm.
English and French. Added t.p.: La necessite et la faisabilite d'une procedure d'appel dans le regime de subventions aux municipalites en compensation d'imp$ots.
ISBN 0662524039

GRANTS-IN-AID – GREAT BRITAIN

—Government Grants : An NCVO Practical Guide / 4th ed. – London : Bedford Square Press, 1987.
ISBN 0719912008 Hbk £3.50

GREAT BRITAIN

—England and its rulers 1066-1272 : foreign lordship and national identity / M.T. Clanchy. – Oxford : Basil Blackwell in association with Fontana, 1983.
317p; 23cm.
First published by Fontana Paperbacks in the 'Fontana history of England', 1983. Bibliography: p299-308. - Includes index.
ISBN 0631133720 £15.00

—Essays in Medieval diplomacy and administration / Pierre Chaplais. – London : Hambledon, 1981.
496p in various pagings,16p of plates; 25cm.
Includes index. English and French text.
ISBN 0950688223 No price

—Evolution of the British welfare state : a history of social policy since the Industrial Revolution / Derek Fraser. – 2nd ed. – London : Macmillan, 1984.
xxxii,326p; 22cm.
Previous ed.: 1973. Bibliography: p303-322.
ISBN 0333359992

—Family law and social policy / John Eekelaar. – 2nd ed. – London : Weidenfeld and Nicolson, 1984.
xviii,263p.
Includes index. Bibliography: p241-255.
ISBN 0297782746

—Fooled again? : the Anglo-Irish Agreement and after / Anthony Coughlan. – Cork : Mercier, 1986.
88p; 21cm.
ISBN 0853427747 Pbk £4.95

—Government and law : an introduction to the working of the constitution in Britain / by T.C. Hartley and J.A.G. Griffith. – 2nd ed. – London : Weidenfeld and Nicolson, 1981.
xxxii,472p. – (Law in context).
Bibliography: 464-468p.
ISBN 0297779745

—Investing in Britain : jobs and industry / Labour Party. – London : Labour Party, 1985.
23p.

—Law : a guide to the collection of Hammersmith & Fulham / Hammersmith & Fulham Libraries. – 2nd ed. – London : Hammersmith & Fulham Libraries, 1987.
40p.
ISBN 0904038068

—Law and order / by Ralf Dahrendorf. – London : Stevens, 1985.
160p. – (Hamlyn lectures).
Includes index.
ISBN 0420472401 Hbk £14.00
ISBN 0420472509 Pbk £7.00

—Law Officers' opinions to the Foreign Office 1793-1860 : a reproduction of the manuscript series with index and commentaries / prepared and edited by Clive Parry. – 97. – Farnborough, Hants. : Gregg International, 1970.
25cm.
Later printed reports published in microfilm under the title: Great Britain Law Officers' opinions. - Dobbs Ferry, N.Y.: Trans-Media, 1976.
ISBN 0576012009

—Lord Reading : Rufus Isaacs, First Marquess of Reading, Lord Chief Justice and Viceroy of India, 1860-1935 / Denis Judd. – London : Weidenfeld and Nicolson, 1982.
x,316p.
Bibliography: p303-307.
ISBN 029778014X

—Progress of scrutiny / House of Lords Select Committee on the European Communities. – London : H.M.S.O., 1981.
First three reports entitled: Report on the progress of scrutiny.

—Scripta diversa / G.O. Sayles. – London : Hambledon, 1982.
xi,371p; 24cm.
Includes index. Includes text in Latin.
ISBN 0907628125 £22.00

—Secondary banking crisis, 1973-75 : its causes and course / Margaret Reid. – London : Macmillan, 1982.
ix,219p.

—Whitehall and Westminster : Government informs Parliament : the changing scene / Dermot Englefield. – Harlow : Longman, 1985.
x,218p; 24cm.
Includes index.
ISBN 058290272X Pbk £15.00

—Women and men in Britain : a research profile / Equal Opportunities Commission. – London : HMSO, 1988.
79p.
Bibliography: pp.74-76. - Includes index.
ISBN 0117013897

GREAT BRITAIN – GREAT BRITAIN

—English Parliament in the Middle Ages / H.G. Richardson and G.O. Sayles. – London : The Hambledon Press, 1981.
560p in various pagings; 25cm.
Includes bibliographical references and index.
ISBN 0950688215

—Positive discrimination, social justice and social policy : moral scrutiny of a policy practice / John Edwards : foreword by Lord Scarman. – London : Tavistock, 1986.
x,243p; 22cm.
Bibliography: p222-235. - Includes index.
ISBN 0422614009 Hbk £19.95
ISBN 0422789909 Pbk £8.95

GRENADA

—Grenada : a study in politics and the limits of international law / Scott Davidson. – Aldershot : Avebury, 1987.
xii,196p; 22cm.
Bibliography: p184-190. - Includes index.
ISBN 0566050528 £18.50

GRENADA – GRENADA

—Conquest of Grenada : sovereignty in the periphery / M. Shahabuddeen. – Georgetown : University of Guyana, 1986.
xiv,266p.
Includes bibliographical references. Includes the text of the Treaty Establishing the Orgainisation of Eastern Caribbean States.

GUARDIANSHIP

—Testamentary guardianship in the Australian Capital Territory / Human Rights Commission. – Canberra : Australian Government Publishing Service, 1983.
vii,10p. – (Report).
ISBN 0644024593

GUARDIANSHIP – AUSTRALIA

—Ethical and Legal Issues in Guardianship Options for Intellectually Disadvantaged People / Peter Singer. – Kingston : Australian Government Publishing Service, 1986.
124p.
ISBN 0644034335 Hbk £14.95

GUARDIANSHIP – CANADA

—Authority of a Guardian / Victoria : Government of British Columbia, 1985.

—Proposals for a guardianship act : Report to the Attorney General / Law Reform Commission of Saskatchewan. – Saskatoon : Law Reform Commission of Saskatchewan, 1983.
19p.

GUARDIANSHIP – CANADA – BRITISH COLUMBIA

—Authority of a guardian / Law Reform Commission of British Columbia. – Vancouver : Law Reform Commission of British Columbia, 1985.
13p.
ISBN 0771884664

GUARDIANSHIP – CANADA – SASKATCHEWAN

—Tentative proposals relating to testamentary custody and guardianship of children / Law Reform Commission of Saskatchewan. – Saskatoon : The Commission, 1984.
58p.
Includes texts of proposed Acts.

GUARDIANSHIP – ENGLAND

—Family law : review of child law : guardianship / The Law Commission. – London : H.M.S.O., 1985.
viii,205p; 21cm. – (Working paper).
Includes bibliographical references.
ISBN 0117301728

—Family law : review of child law : guardianship and custody / The Law Commission. – London : HMSO, 1988.
iv,112p. – (1987-88 HC).
Includes text of a proposed children bill.
ISBN 0102594880

—Family law : review of child law : wards of court / the Law Commission. – London : H.M.S.O., 1987.
v,86p. – (Working paper).
ISBN 0117301833

—Guide for guardians ad litem in the juvenile court / London : Department of Health and Social Security, 1984.
61p.

—Memorandum on guardianship : Law Commission working paper no. 91 / Justice. – London : Justice, 1986.
6 leaves.
A commentary on the Law Commission's working paper no. 91 entitled Family law: review of child law: guardianship.

—Wards of court : Law Commission working paper no. 101 / JUSTICE. – London : JUSTICE, 1987.
3 leaves.

GUARDIANSHIP - GREAT BRITAIN

—Law relating to children and young persons / Clarke Hall and Morrison. – 10th ed. 2. – London : Butterworths, 1985.
looseleaf.
Includes index. Includes the text of the relevant legislation. Spine title: Clarke Hall & Morrison on children. Kept up-to-date by supplements.
ISBN 0406158126

—Wards of court / N. V. Lowe and R. A. H. White. – 2nd ed. – London : Barry Rose, part of Kluwer Law Publishers, 1986.
xxviii,388p; 23cm.

GUARDIANSHIP - INDIA

—Guardians and Wards Act, 1890 and certain provisions of the Hindu Minority and Guardianship Act, 1956 / Law Commission of India. – Delhi : Controller of Publications Govt. of India, 1980.
iii,93p. – (83rd report).
Includes bibliographical references.

GUARDIANSHIP - SINGAPORE

—Parent-Child Law in Singapore / Singapore : Butterworths, 1984.
The book provides a discussion of legitimacy, maintenance, guardianship, and adoption under the law of Singapore. The 1980 amendments to the Women's Charter pertaining to maintenance, welfare and custody of children are analyzed in depth.
ISBN 0406181217 Pbk

GUARDIANSHIP (HINDU LAW)

—Hindu Minority and Guardianship : and Hindu Adoptions and Maintenance Act / 2nd ed. – Allahad : Law Book Company, 1986.
200p.

GUILDFORD (SURREY)

—Trial and error : the Maguires, the Guildford pub bombings and British justice / Robert Kee. – London : Hamish Hamilton, 1986.
284p; 22cm.
Includes index.
ISBN 0241119588 £10.95

GUILT (LAW) - SCOTLAND

—Criminal law : art and part guilt of statutory offences / Scottish Law Commission. – Edinburgh : H.M.S.O., 1985.
v,21p.
ISBN 0101955103

GUYANA - GUYANA

—From plantocracy to nationalisation : a profile of sugar in Guyana / M. Shahabuddeen. – Georgetown? : University of Guyana, 1983.
xiii,440p.
Bibliography: p411-440.

HABEAS CORPUS

—Law of habeas corpus / Oxford : Clarendon Press, 1989.
300; 21.5.
Updated to include references to current developments in the law of habeas corpus. Examines the nature of the judicial reivew exercised on habeas corpus, and explores the past, present, and potential uses of the writ. Also contains discussions on the law in Commonwealth countries.
ISBN 0198254040 Hbk £30.00

HABEAS CORPUS - INDIA

—Law of Bails, Forfeiture of Bonds and Habeas Corpus / A.N. Saha. – 2nd ed. – Lucknow : Eastern Book Company, 1985.
391p.

HABEAS CORPUS - NIGERIA

—Nigerian law of habeas corpus / Lagos : Nigerian Law Publications, 1986.
lxvi,457p.
Contains cases on habeas corpus.
ISBN 9782325163

HANDICAPPED

—Treatment of disabled persons in social security and taxation law / Canberra : Australian Government Publishing Service, 1986.
viii,149p. – (Occasional paper).
Bibliography: p134-149.
ISBN 0644048123

—Vocational Rehabilitation Services for Disabled Persons : Legislative Provisions / Geneva : International Labour Office, 1982.
ii, 120p.
ISBN 9221030156 Hbk £17.50

HANDICAPPED - CANADA

—Persons with Special Needs : Law and the Handicapped / Montreal : McGill Campus Legal Aid Clinic, 1981.
100p.

HANDICAPPED - COMMONWEALTH

—Survey of legal measures in the Commonwealth designed to assist the disabled / a survey prepared by the Commonwealth Secretariat for the International Year of Disabled Persons. – London : Commonwealth Secretariat, 1981.
60p.

HANDICAPPED - GREAT BRITAIN

—Disability : Legislation and Practice / London : Macmillan, 1981.
264p.
ISBN 0333315758 Pbk £8.95

—Disabled people on supplementary benefit : interim report / Richard Stowell. – Oxford : Centre for Socio-Legal Studies, 1980.
145p; 21cm. – (Research study).
ISBN 0862260655

HANDICAPPED - INDIA

—Assessment of Medical Impairment and Disability / Madhya Pradesh : Lawyers Home, 1987.

HANDICAPPED CHILDREN - AUSTRALIA

—Legal and ethical aspects of the management of newborns with severe disabilities / Canberra : Australian Government Publishing Service, 1985.
71p. – (Occasional paper).
Includes bibliographical references.
ISBN 0644043849

HARBOURS

—Safe port of berth reachable on arrival : charterers' and shipowners' responsibilities and liabilities / W.E. Astle. – London : Fairplay, 1986.
x,109p.
Cover title: The safe port.
ISBN 0905045912

—Safety Recommendations on the Use of Ports by Nuclear Merchant Ships / International Maritime Organization. – London : International Maritime Organization, 1980.

French Edition

HARBOURS - GREAT BRITAIN

—Harbour Law / 3rd ed. – London : LLoyd's of London Press, 1989.
ISBN 1850441685 Hbk

—Harbour Law / 2nd ed. – London : Lloyd's of London Press, 1983.
ISBN 0907432646 Hbk £22.50

—Outline of the law relating to harbours in Great Britain managed under statutory powers / by R.P.A. Douglas. – 2nd ed. – London : Lloyd's of London, 1983.
xxiv,234p.
Previous ed.: 1979. Includes index. Cover title: Harbour law.
ISBN 0907432646

HATE MAIL

—Criminal law : report on poison-pen letters / the Law Commission. – London : H.M.S.O., 1985.
v,39p.
ISBN 0102519854

HAZARDOUS GEOGRAPHIC ENVIRONMENTS - CANADA

—Political economy of environmental hazards : a study paper prepared for the Law Reform Commission of Canada / by T.F. Schrecker. – Ottawa : Law Reform Commission of Canada, 1984.
vi,112p.
ISBN 066213236X

HAZARDOUS SUBSTANCES

—Carriage of dangerous goods by sea : the role of the International Maritime Organisation in international legislation / by Cleopatra Henry. – London : Pinter, 1985.
iii,184; 23cm.
Includes index. Clarifies the work of the IMO revealing its methods and mandate for enacting maritime controls on the transportation of controversial toxins.
ISBN 0861875699 Hbk £25

—Emergency Procedures for Ships Carrying Dangerous Goods : Group Emergency Schedules / International Maritime Organization. – London : International Maritime Organization, 1981.

French Edition

—International Maritime Dangerous Goods Code : Amendment 19-80 / International Maritime Organization. – London : International Maritime Organization, 1981.
ISBN 9280111264 loose £11.00

French
ISBN 9280121073 loose £11.00

—International Maritime Dangerous Goods Code : Amendment 20-82 / International Maritime Organization. – London : International Maritime Organization.
ISBN 9280111507 Hbk £12.50

French
ISBN 9280121200 Hbk £12.50

—International Maritime Dangerous Goods Code : Amendment 22-84 / International Maritime Organization. – London : International Maritime Organization.

French
ISBN 9280121553 Hbk £18.00

—International Maritime Dangerous Goods Code : Amendment 22-86 / International Maritime Organization. – London : International Maritime Organization.
ISBN 9280112031 Hbk £2.50

French
ISBN 9280121618 Hbk £2.50

—International Maritime Dangerous Goods Code : Amendments 21-83 and 21-84 / International Maritime Organization. – London : International Maritime Organization.
ISBN 9280111698 Hbk £8.00

French
ISBN 9280121340 Hbk £8.00

—International Maritime Dangerous Goods Code (IMDG, 5 Vols.) / International Maritime Organization. – London : International Maritime Organization, 1981.
ISBN 9280111256 loose £60.00

French
ISBN 9280121057 loose £55.00

—International Maritime Dangerous Goods Code : Indexes to Amendment 22-84 / International Maritime Organization. – London : International Maritime Organization.
ISBN 9280111957 Hbk £4.00

French
ISBN 9280121561 Hbk £4.00

—International Register of Potentially Toxic Chemicals, 2 Vols. / United Nations. – London : HMSO, 1984.
Provides information on the danger to humans and the environment of chemicals and details of individual nations' controlling legislation.
ISBN 0119079860 Hbk £58.50

—International standards and recommended practices : the safe transport of dangerous goods by air : annex 18 to the Convention on International Civil Aviation / International Civil Aviation Organization. – 1st ed. - January 1983. 1 v. – Montreal : International Civil Aviation Organization, 1983.
looseleaf.

—Regulations governing the transport of radioactive materials / Paris : Organisation for Economic Co-operation and Development, Nuclear Energy Agency, 1980.
201p.
ISBN 9264121587

HAZARDOUS SUBSTANCES - CANADA

—Handle with Caution : Liability in the Production, Transportation and Disposal of Dangerous Substances / Agincourt : Carswell, 1986.
280p.

—Handle with Caution : Liability in the Production, Transportation and Disposal of Dangerous Substances / Agincourt : Carswell, 1986.
280p.
This book explains the responsibilities and liabilities, under new Canadian federal and Ontario provincial laws, of generating, transporting, hauling, and disposing of waste and dangerous goods. The new governmental powers, enforcement provisions, and compensation schemes are described in the work.

—Hazardous Products : Canada's Right-to-Know Laws / Don Mills : CCH Canadian Ltd.
310p.
ISBN 0887964524 Pbk £18.95

—Political economy of environmental hazards : a study paper prepared for the Law Reform Commission of Canada / by T.F. Schrecker. – Ottawa : Law Reform Commission of Canada, 1984.
vi,112p.
ISBN 066213236X

HAZARDOUS SUBSTANCES - CANADA - ONTARIO

—Handle with Caution : Liability in the Production, Transportation and Disposal of Dangerous Substances / Agincourt : Carswell, 1986.
280p.
This book explains the responsibilities and liabilities, under new Canadian federal and Ontario provincial laws, of generating, transporting, hauling, and disposing of waste and dangerous goods. The new governmental powers, enforcement provisions, and compensation schemes are described in the work.

HAZARDOUS SUBSTANCES - EUROPEAN COMMUNITY

—Legislation on Dangerous Substances : Classification and Labelling in the European Communities / Luxembourg : Office for Official Publications of the European Communities, 1987.
xvi, 288p.
ISBN 928257279X Pbk £1,250.00

HAZARDOUS SUBSTANCES - GREAT BRITAIN

—Dangerous Substances / New Malden : Croner Publications.

HEADS OF STATE - INDIA

—Indian Presidency / New Delhi : Deep and Deep Publications, 1988.
124p.

—President in the Indian Constitution / New Delhi : Deep and Deep Publications, 1985.
180p.

HEADS OF STATE - NIGERIA

—Presidential Constitution of Nigeria / London : Dent (J M) & Sons, 1982.
ISBN 0905838602 Hbk £25.00

HEALTH

—International Digest of Health Legislation / World Health Organization. – London : HMSO.

—International Health Regulations (1969) / World Health Organization. – 3rd ed. – London : HMSO, 1983.
ISBN 9241580070 Hbk £4.40

—Well-being : its meaning, measurement, and moral importance / James Griffin. – Oxford : Clarendon Press, 1988.
xii,412p.
Bibliography: pp.391- 402. - Includes index.
ISBN 0198249039

HEALTH - AUSTRALIA

—Health Act-Victoria / North Ryde : Law Book Co, 1983.
xxxi, 493p.
ISBN 0455204985 Hbk £65.50

HEALTH - CANADA

—Canadian Dental Law / Butterworths, 1987.
152p.
ISBN 0409863351 Hbk £40.00

—Canadian Law of Consent to Treatment / Fay A. Rozovsky. – Butterworths, 1988.
ca 288p.
Deals with specific medico-legal consent problems such as consent relating to the treatment of children, prisoners and the mentally handicapped. Details circumstances in which consent may be waived, examines the essential elements of consent litigation, discusses how to prevent consent litigation and includes a special section on documenting consent.
ISBN 0409806307 Hbk £70.00

—Canadian Law of Patient Records / Fay A. Rozovsky. – Butterworths, 1984.
168p.
Examines the legal problems arising from patient records and how to avoid such problems. Contains incident reports as a tool for preventing possible serious injury to patients, the identification, evaluation elimination, reduction and prevention of risks, and practical advice on drafting administrative rules and guidelines on minimizing legal risks.
ISBN 0409862886 Hbk £40.00

—Law of Health Care Facility Administration / Butterworths, 1988.
ca 224p.
Deals with issues such as quality assurance – payment for services, physicians privileges, liability issues and employment relations.
ISBN 0409801747 Hbk

—Law of Health Care Facility Administration / Toronto : Butterworths, 1988.
224p.
ISBN 0409801747 Hbk

HEALTH - COMMONWEALTH

—Commonwealth Developments in Health Law / Legal Division, Commonwealth Secretariat. – London : Commonwealth Secretariat, 1984.
324p.
ISBN 0850922283 Hbk £6.00
ISBN 0850922070 Pbk £6.00

HEALTH - ENGLAND

—Compensation and support for illness and injury / Donald Harris ... et al. – Oxford : Clarendon, 1984.
xix,412p; 22cm. – (Oxford socio-legal studies).
Includes bibliographies and index.
ISBN 0198275080 Hbk £20.00
ISBN 0198275137 Pbk £9.50

HEALTH - GREAT BRITAIN

—Disease and the Compensation Debate / Oxford : Oxford University Press, 1986.
ISBN 0198255527 Hbk £25.00

—Disease and the compensation debate / Jane Stapleton. – Oxford : Clarendon, 1986.
224p; 22cm.
Includes index.
ISBN 0198255527 £22.50

—Encyclopaedia of Health Services/Medical Law / London : Sweet & Maxwell, 1988.
ISBN 0421315008 Hbk £180.00

—Environmental health standards in housing / David Ormandy & Roger Burridge. – London : Sweet & Maxwell, 1988.
xlv,373p.
Covers the initial inspection of a house, the assessment of conditions (including particular problems of dampness), the application of the various standards, the drafting of the notices and the steps involved in the enforcement of statutory standards.
ISBN 0421365501 £25.00

—Forensic audiology / Chuang Wei Ping : foreword by Ronald Hinchcliffe. – Middlesbrough : Chuang Wei Ping, 1985.
108p in various pagings; 22cm.
ISBN 0951080008 Pbk £6.00

—Health Law in Canada / Toronto : Butterworths.

—Health Policy in Britain : The Organisation and Politics of the NHS / 2nd ed. – London : Macmillan, 1985.
192p. – (Studies in Social Policy, General Ser.).
ISBN 0333394925 Hbk £20.00
ISBN 0333394933 Pbk £6.95

—On industrial relations : interprofessional relationships in health care and the role of criminal law in industrial relations / R. Dyson and A.N. Khan. – Leeds : Centre for Social Work and Applied Social Studies, University of Leeds, 1982.
27p. – (Occasional papers).

—Patients' Rights : A guide for NHS Patients and Doctors / London : HMSO, 1983.
60p.
ISBN 0117010448 Pbk £1.50

—Vaccination Certificate Requirements for International Travel and Health Advice to Travellers 1985 / World Health Organization. – London : HMSO, 1985.
81p.
ISBN 9241580100 Hbk £4.80

HEALTH AND SAFETY AT WORK - AUSTRALIA

—Guidebook to Occupational Health and Safety Laws in Australia / 2nd ed. – North Ryde : C.C.H. Australia, 1986.
600p.
ISBN 0869036939 Hbk £38.00

—Legislation at Work : Safety and Health / Department of Science and Technology. – 2nd ed. – Canberra : Australian Government Publishing Service, 1981.
41p. – (Occupational Safety & Health Working Environment: No. 4).
ISBN 0642052212 Hbk £1.90

—Occupational Health and Safety Committees Manual / North Ryde : C.C.H. Australia, 1987.
60p.
ISBN 086903460X Hbk

—Safeguarding the worker / North Ryde : Law Book Co, 1984.
ISBN 0455205043 Pbk £25.00

—Safeguarding the Worker : Job Hazards and the Role of the Law / North Ryde : Law Book Co, 1984.
xxiv, 426p.
ISBN 0455205043 Pbk £51.50

—Understanding Occupational Health and Safety Law in Victoria / North Ryde : C.C.H. Australia, 1986.
236p.
ISBN 0869038389

—Understanding the Occupational Health and Safety Act 1983 / 2nd ed. – North Ryde : C.C.H. Australia, 1985.
90p.
ISBN 086903605X £25.00

HEALTH AND SAFETY AT WORK - AUSTRALIA - NEW SOUTH WALES

—Guide to Safety and Industry Laws, New South Wales / Sydney : Butterworths, 1981.
320p.
ISBN 0409690385 Pbk

—New South Wales Construction Safety Act 1912 and Regulations / 2nd ed. – North Ryde : C.C.H. Australia, 1985.
300p.
ISBN 0869034855 Hbk £24.00

HEALTH AND SAFETY AT WORK - CANADA

—Ontario Health and Safety Guide : A Dictionary of Legal Compliance / Toronto : DeBoo, 1984.
This guidebook provides comprehensive discussion of the legal provisions affecting workplace health and safety in Ontario, Canada. The book is organized to provide quick reference in the design and review of workplace policies and procedures.
ISBN 0888201834 Hbk £85.00

HEALTH AND SAFETY AT WORK - GREAT BRITAIN

—A-Z of Employment and Safety Law / London : Kogan Page, 1981.
516p.
ISBN 085038446X Hbk £16.95

—Croner's Health and Safety at Work / Croner Publications. – New Malden : Croner Publications, 1986.

Annual renewal updates

—Disease and the Compensation Debate / Oxford : Oxford University Press, 1986.
ISBN 0198255527 Hbk £25.00

—Encyclopaedia of Health and Safety at Work / London : Sweet & Maxwell, 1988.
ISBN 0421007109 Hbk £220.00

—Encyclopedia of Health and Safety at Work : Law and Practice, 3 Vols. / M. C. Walker. – London : Sweet & Maxwell, 1985.
ISBN 0421007109 loose £162.00

Service only

—Fighting Asbestos at Work and at Home / London : Labour Research Department, 1984.
ISBN 0900508639 Pbk £0.85

—Health and Safery at Work Handbook / 2nd ed. – Croydon : Tolley.
752p.
Examines safety duties of employers and others and provides officially recommended practices and procedures. The law is stated as at 30 April 1988 and later proposals for change are included.
ISBN 0854593098 Pbk £29.95
ISBN 0854593829 Hbk £39.95

—Health and safety at work / London : Sweet & Maxwell, 1988.
ISBN 0421376708 Pbk £18.00

—Health and safety at work: law and practice / London : Sweet & Maxwell, 1988.
Examines claims in industrial tribunals relating to dismissal and constructive dismissal for health and safety reasons, and the rights of safety representatives to times off. Analysis of sickness and invalidity benefits, practice and procedure in social security appeal tribunals, and the grounds for action by the Health and Safety Executive.
ISBN 0421376708 Hbk £18.00

—Health and Safety Enforcement / London : Shaw & Sons, 1980.
– (Shaway Guide: No. 3).
ISBN 0721908721 Pbk £2.50

—Health and safety in factories / Fife. – 2nd ed. – London : Butterworths, 1982.
ISBN 0406353077 Hbk £52.00

—Health and safety practice / Dewis. – London : Pitman Publishing, 1986.
ISBN 0273025996 Pbk £22.50

—Law of Health and Safety at Work / London : Butterworths, 1982.
ISBN 0406667500 Pbk £10.95

—Legalism and Discretion : A Study of Responses to Accidents and Accident Information Systems in the Occupational Health and Safety Administration (OSHA) USA / Oxford : Social Science Research Council, 1988.
ISBN 0948774053 Pbk £2.50

—Protection of people at work / Product Liability Briefing, 1988.
ISBN 1870317203 Pbk £6.50

—Safe place of work / London : Butterworths, 1983.
ISBN 0406013044 Hbk £9.50

—Safety at Work / 2nd ed. – London : Butterworths, 1986.
This textbook provides a comprehensive discussion of safety management, law, occupational health and hygiene, and other issues of work safety. Recent changes in safety legislation in the United Kingdom are reflected in the text.
ISBN 0408008407 Pbk

HEARSAY EVIDENCE - AUSTRALIA

—Evidence reference / Australian Law Reform Commission. – Sydney : The Commission, 1981.
v,174p.
Includes bibliographical references.

Research paper no. 9 : Hearsay evidence : which approach? / Australian Law Reform Commission. – 1982.
33p.
Includes bibliographical references.

HEARSAY EVIDENCE - IRELAND

—Report on the rule against hearsay in civil cases / the Law Reform Commission. – Dublin : The Commission, 1988.
vii,34p. – (LRC).

HEARSAY EVIDENCE - SCOTLAND

—Evidence : report on corroboration, hearsay and related matters in civil proceedings / Scottish Law Commission. – Edinburgh : H.M.S.O., 1986.
vi,63p.
Includes bibliographical references.
ISBN 010237886X

HEDGING (FINANCE)

—Financial futures / by M. Desmond Fitzgerald. – London : Euromoney, 1983.
ix,202p.
Bibliography: p.195-197. - Includes index.
ISBN 0903121433

HELICOPTERS
—International standards and recommended practices : operation of aircraft : annex 6 to the Convention on International Civil Aviation / International Civil Aviation Organization. – 1st ed. - November 1986. – Montreal : International Civil Aviation Organisation, 1986.
looseleaf.
Kept up to date by amendments and supplements.

HIGHER EDUCATION – AUSTRALIA
—Compendium of human rights courses in Australian tertiary institutions / compiled by Alex Castles and Leonie Farrell. – Canberra : Australian Government Publishing Service, 1983.
xiv,39p. – (Occasional paper).
Includes index.
ISBN 0644027649

HIGHER EDUCATION – GREAT BRITAIN
—Excellence in diversity : towards a new strategy for higher education : the Leverhulme report / Guildford : Society for Research into Higher Education, 1983.
79p; 21cm.
ISBN 0900868996 Pbk £3.75

HIGHER EDUCATION – UNITED STATES
—Some of the selective institutions of higher learning in USA / Hong Kong : Hang Seng Bank, 1981.
423 p.

HIJACKING
—Aerial piracy and international terrorism : the illegal diversion of aircraft and international law / Edward McWhinney. – 2nd rev. ed. – Dordrecht, the Netherlands : M. Nijhoff, 1987.
Rev. ed. of: Aerial piracy and international law / by Edward McWhinney and others. 1971. Includes index. Bibliography..
ISBN 0898389194

—Aircraft Hijacking and the Developing Law / New Delhi : Ashish Publishing House, 1985.
160p.

—International standards and recommended practices : security : safeguarding international civil aviation against acts of unlawful interference : annex 17 to the Convention on International Civil Aviation / International Civil Aviation Organization. – 3rd ed. 1. – Montreal : International Civil Aviation Organization, 1986.
looseleaf.
Kept up to date by amendments and supplements.

—Three international conventions on hijacking and offences on board aircraft : (i) Convention on Offences and Certain Other Acts Committed on Board Aircraft ... 1963. (ii) Convention for Suppression of Unlawful Seizure of Aircraft ... 1970. (iii) Convention for the Suppression of Unlawful Acts Against the Safety of Civil Aviation ... 1971 : explanation documentation prepared for Commonwealth jurisdictions by David Lloyd Jones in association with the Commonwealth Secretariat / David Lloyd Jones. – London : Commonwealth Secretariat, 1982.
vi,146p; 30cm.
ISBN 0850922151

HIJACKING – AUSTRALIA
—How to Combat Hijacking / Canberra : Australian Institute of Criminology.

HINDU LAW
—Dvystattva of Raghunandana Bhattacharya : Ordeals in Classical Hindu Law / New Delhi : Manohar Publications, 1981.
280p.

—Hindu Family Law and Social Change / Bombay : University of Bombay, Publications Department.

—Hindu Law / 2nd ed. – Allahabad : Law Book Company, 1986.
1,000p.

—Hindu law / 8th ed. – Nagpur : Wadhura & Co, 1987.

—Hindu Law and the Constitution / Calcutta : Eastern Law House, 1983.

—Hindu Law and Usage / 12th ed. repr. 1986. – New Delhi : Bharat Law House.

—Hindu Law (Students Ed.) / 6th ed. – Lucknow : Eastern Book Company, 1982.
354p.

—Hindu Undivided Family : Law, Judiciary and Bankers / Delhi : UDH Publishers, 1986.

—Kautilyan jurisprudence / by V.K. Gupta. – Delhi : B.D. Gupta, 1987.
xii,356p.
Includes excerpts from Kautilya's Arthasastra in Sanskrit.

—Modern Hindu Law / Lucknow : Eastern Book Company, 1983.
992p.

—Position of Women in Hindu Law / 1913 repr. – New Delhi : Inter-India Publications, 1984.
vi, ii, xxxii, xix, 707p.
ISBN 8121001641 Hbk £380.00

—Principles of Hindu law, with a general introduction to Hindu law and with commentaries on the Hindu Marriage Act, 1955, the Hindu Succession Act, 1956, the Hindu Minority & Guardianship Act, 1956, the Hindu Adoptions & Maintenance Act, 1956 / Sunderlal Trikamlal Desai. – 15th ed. – Bombay : N.M. Tripathi Private, 1982.
lxxix, 1233 p.; 25 cm.
Title on spine: Hindu law. Includes index.

—Statutory Changes in Hindu Law / Allahabad : Law Publishers, 1982.

HIRE PURCHASE – GREAT BRITAIN
—Hiring and Leasing : Practice and Precedents / Prichard-Jones. – London : Butterworths, 1988.
ISBN 0406101140 Pbk

HIRE PURCHASE – INDIA
—Commentaries on Hire-Purchase Act, 1972 with Model Forms / 2nd ed. – Allahabad : Law Publishers, 1983.

—Sale of Goods and Hire-Purchase / 3rd ed. – Lucknow : Eastern Book Company, 1985.
189p.

HIRE PURCHASE – MALAYSIA
—Hire Purchase Act, 1967 (Act 212) and Regulations, Orders and Guide Lines / Kuala Lumpur : International Law Books Services.

HIRE PURCHASE – NEW ZEALAND
—New Zealand Hire Purchase Law / 3rd ed. – Butterworths, 1977.
ISBN 0409621811 Hbk £64.35

HISTORIC BUILDINGS – GREAT BRITAIN
—Building Legislation and Historic Buildings / London : Architectural Press, 1987.
ISBN 0851397905 Pbk £14.95

—Building Legislation and Historic Buildings / London : Architectural Press, 1987.
176p : Illus.
ISBN 0851397905 Pbk £14.95

—Historic buildings : the law and practice / 2nd ed. – London : Sweet & Maxwell, 1988.
ISBN 0421381302 Hbk £40.00

—Listed buildings : the law and practice of historic buildings, ancient monuments and conservation areas / by Roger W. Suddards. – 2nd ed. – London : Sweet & Maxwell, 1988.
xxxi,307p.
Sets out and discusses the statutory basis for the protection and preservation of our 'built heritage'. Deals with listed buildings, conservation area control and the law relating to ancient monuments. Describes the effect of fixing canopies to listed buildings, and problems arising from cladding, rendering and cleaning of such buildings.
ISBN 0421381302 £40.00

HISTORIC SITES
—Tax policy towards the national heritage : proceedings of a seminar held in Venice, 1983, during the 37th Congress of the International Fiscal Association / organised by the International Fiscal Association. – Deventer, Netherlands : Kluwer Law and Taxation Publishers, 1984.
ISBN 9065441786

HISTORIC SITES – GREAT BRITAIN
—Modern legislation for the protection of history : the ancient monuments and archaeological areas act 1979 / by Clive M. Brand : with an introduction by Ronald G. Cant. – Glasgow : The Planning Exchange, 1980.
30p; 30cm.

HISTORIOGRAPHY
—Lessons of history : an inaugural lecture delivered before the vice-chancellor and Fellows of the University of Oxford on Friday 6 March 1981 / by Michael Howard. – Oxford : Clarendon, 1981.
21p; 22cm.
ISBN 0199515328 Pbk £1.95

HISTORY
—'Nonsense upon stilts' : Bentham, Burke and Marx on the rights of man / edited with introductory and concluding essays by Jeremy Waldron. – London : Methuen, 1987.
256p; 22cm.
Includes bibliography and index.
ISBN 0416918905 Pbk £6.95

—Agriculture, the countryside and land use : an economic critique / J.K. Bowers and Paul Cheshire. – London : Methuen, 1983.
x,170p; 20cm.
Includes index.
ISBN 0416318304 Pbk Unpriced

—Bibliography of Canadian criminal justice history / Bibliographie sur l'histoire de la justice penale au Canada : Ministry of the Solicitor General, Research division. – Ottawa : Ministry of the Solicitor General, 1984.
426p. – (User report).

—Chart of Privy Council decisions with reference to the British North America Act / 4 folded charts. – Ottawa : Canadian Law Information Council, .

—Conspiracy : law, class and society / Robert Spicer. – London : Lawrence and Wishart, 1981.
190p; 23cm.
Bibliography: p178-184. - Includes index.
ISBN 0853155488 £7.50

—Development of ethnography in Britain : paper prepared for presentation at the BSA Annual Conference, Lancaster, 1980 / Robert Dingwall, Geoff Payne, Judy Payne. – Oxford : Centre for Socio-Legal Studies, 1980.
19,2p.
Bibliography: p.20-21.

—Essays in Medieval diplomacy and administration / Pierre Chaplais. – London : Hambledon, 1981.
496p in various pagings,16p of plates; 25cm.
Includes index. English and French text.
ISBN 0950688223 No price

—Family, sex and marriage in England 1500-1800 / Lawrence Stone. – Abridged ed. – Harmondsworth : Penguin, 1982.
446p,16p of plates; 20cm. – (A Peregrine book).
Previous ed.: London : Weidenfeld & Nicolson, 1977. Includes index.
ISBN 0140551670 Pbk £3.50

—Historical Foundations of the Common Law / 2nd ed. – Butterworths, 1981.
496p.
ISBN 0409850055 Pbk £29.95

—History, Law and the Human Sciences : Medieval and Renaissance Perspectives / Northampton : Variorum.
334p.
ISBN 0860781534 Hbk £28.00

—History of Contempt of Court / Abingdon : Professional Books.

—History of Ideas and Doctrines of Canon Law in the Middle Ages / Northampton : Variorum.
394p. – (Collected Ser.: CS 113).
ISBN 0860780589 Hbk £22.00

—Humanity in warfare : the modern history of the international law of armed conflicts / Geoffrey Best. – London : Weidenfeld and Nicolson, 1980.
xi,400p; 23cm.
Bibliography: p.376-387. - Includes index.
ISBN 0297777378

—Max Weber / Anthony T. Kronman. – London : Edward Arnold, 1983.
214p; 22cm.
Includes bibliographies and index.
ISBN 0713163615 Pbk £9.95
ISBN 0713163623 Pbk £4.95

—Medieval Diplomacy and the Fourth Crusade / Northampton : Variorum, 1980.
322p. – (Collected Studies: No. 114).
ISBN 0860780597 Hbk £22.00

—Natural Law, Conciliarism and Consent in the Middle Ages / Northampton : Variorum, 1984.
350p. – (Collected Studies Ser.: No. 189).
ISBN 0860781372 Hbk £26.00

—Oxford book of legal anecdotes / edited by Michael Gilbert. – Oxford : Oxford University Press, 1986.
xvi,333p; 23cm.
Includes index.
ISBN 0192141120 £12.50

—Reminiscences and Reflections of a Chief Justice / Delhi : B.R. Publishing Corporation, 1985.
ix, 234p.
ISBN 8170182530 Hbk £150.00

—Rise of the corporate economy / Leslie Hannah. – 2nd ed. – London : Methuen, 1983.
xii,266p; 23cm.
Previous ed.: 1976. Includes index.
ISBN 0416348505 Hbk Unpriced
ISBN 0416348602 Pbk Unpriced

—Roman Constitutional History / Rotterdam : A.A. Balkema, 1948.
195p.

—Scripta diversa / G.O. Sayles. – London : Hambledon, 1982.
xi,371p; 24cm.
Includes index. Includes text in Latin.
ISBN 0907628125 £22.00

—Trial and error : the Maguires, the Guildford pub bombings and British justice / Robert Kee. – London : Hamish Hamilton, 1986.
284p; 22cm.
Includes index.
ISBN 0241119588 £10.95

—Unequal struggle? : British socialism and the capitalist enterprise / Jim Tomlinson. – London : Methuen, 1982.
160p; 23cm.
Bibliography: p149-157. - Includes index.
ISBN 0416331505 Hbk Unpriced
ISBN 0416331602 Pbk Unpriced

—War crimes and laws of war / Donald A. Wells. – Lanham : University Press of America, 1984.
x,137p; 24cm.
Bibliography: p123-132. - Includes index.
ISBN 081913841X Hbk No price
ISBN 0819138428 Pbk £8.25

—Western idea of law / by J. C. Smith and David N. Weisstub. – London : Butterworths, 1983.
xxii,685p.
Highlights the unique aspects of Western law by comparing it to other legal traditions, past and present. More than 170 great thinkers are excerpted, and a feminist perspective is incorporated, raising questions about women and power. Covers issues such as state sovereignty egalitarianism, and constitutional guarantees of human rights.
ISBN 0409868191

—Witness of war crimes in Lebanon / testimony given to the Nordic Commission, Oslo, October 1982. – London : EAFORD, 1983.
xviii,146p; 22cm.
ISBN 0863720056 Pbk £4.50

—Women's rights at work : campaigns and policy in Britain and the United States / Elizabeth M. Meehan. – Basingstoke : Macmillan, 1985.
xvii,253p; 22cm.
Bibliography: p227-241. - Includes index.
ISBN 0333361253 Hbk No price
ISBN 0333361261 Pbk £5.95

HISTORY - AUSTRALIA

—Chronological Account of Crime, Public Order and Police in Sydney 1788-1810 / Canberra : Australian Institute of Criminology.

HISTORY - CANADA - BRITISH COLUMBIA

—Progression of Judges : a History of the Supreme Court of British Columbia / Vancouver : University of British Columbia Press, 1988.
197p.
ISBN 0774802936 Hbk £31.95

HISTORY - ENGLAND

—'Without the law' : administrative justice and legal pluralism in nineteenth-century England / H. W. Arthurs. – Toronto : University of Toronto Press, 1985.
xvi,312p; 24cm.
ISBN 0802056547

—Acts and Ordinances of the Interregnum : 1642-1660, 3 Vols. / R. S. Rait. – Abingdon : Professional Books.

—Confiscation and Restoration : The Archbishopric Estates and the Civil War / W. J. Sheils. – York : St. Anthony's Press, 1981.
– (Borthwick Papers Ser.).

—Criminal and Victim : 19th Century England / Oxford : Oxford University Press, 1985.
ISBN 0198226462 Hbk £17.50

—Crown Pleas of the Devon Eyre of 1238 / Exeter : Devon & Cornwall Record Society, 1985.
ISBN 0901853283 Hbk £8.00

—Ecclesiastical cause papers at York : Dean and Chapter's court 1350-1843 / Katharine M. Longley. – York : University of York, 1980.
xx,204p.
Includes bibliographical references and index. At head of t.p.: University of York. Borthwick Institute of Historical Research.

—Ecclesiastical Cause papers at York : files transmitted on appeal 1500-1883 / W.J. Sheils. – York : University of York, Borthwick Institute of Historical Research, 1983.
xiv,135p; 25cm.
Includes index.

—English church and its laws 12th-14th centuries / C.R. Cheney. – London : Variorum Reprints, 1982.
348p in various pagings; 23cm. – (Collected studies series).
Includes index. Text in English and Latin.
ISBN 0860781089 Unpriced

—English Village Constable 1580-1642 / Oxford : Oxford University Press, 1986.
ISBN 0198229135 Hbk £27.50

—Foundations of the modern Bar / by Raymond Cocks. – London : Sweet & Maxwell, 1983.
vii,257p; 22cm.
Bibliography: p235-249. - Includes index.
ISBN 0421303603 Pbk £9.50

—Imprisonment in England and Wales : a concise history / Christopher Harding ... et al. – London : Croom Helm, 1985.
xiii,308p,8p of plates; 23cm.
Includes index.
ISBN 0709912943 £25.00

—Old Poor Law, 1795-1834 / prepared for the Economic History Society by J.D. Marshall. – 2nd ed. – Basingstoke : Macmillan, 1985.
57p; 22cm.
Previous ed.: 1968. Bibliography: p51-54. - Includes index.
ISBN 0333398807 Pbk £3.95

—Oxfordshire Election of 1754 / Oxfordshire County Record Office. – Oxford : Oxfordshire County Record Office.
– (Archive Teaching Unit).

—Papacy and England : 12th-14th Centuries / Northampton : Variorum, 1982.
346p : Illus.. – – (Collected Studies Ser.: CS 154).
ISBN 0860780996 Hbk £24.00

—Papal government and England during the pontificate of Honorius III / Cambridge : Cambridge University Press.
Studies thirteenth-century administrative revolution of the papacy. Gives details of registers and the registrative system. Discusses development of canon law in relation to England.
ISBN 0521259118 Hbk £32.50

—Pastoral Discipline and the Church Courts : The Hexham Court, 1680-1730 / York : St. Anthony's Press, 1982.
– (Borthwick Papers Ser.).

—Poverty and the Poor Law in the North Riding of Yorkshire : Circa 1780-1837 / York : St. Anthony's Press, 1982.
– (Borthwick Papers Ser.).

—Relief of poverty, 1834-1914 / prepared for the Economic History Society by Michael E. Rose. – 2nd ed. – Basingstoke : Macmillan, 1986.
92p; 22cm.
Previous ed.: 1972. Includes bibliography and index.
ISBN 0333424158 Pbk £3.95

—Studies in 13th century justice and administration / C.A.F. Meekings. – London : Hambledon, 1981.
342p; 25cm. – (History series).
ISBN 0950688231

—Ungovernable people : the English and their law in the seventeenth and eighteenth centuries / edited by John Brewer and John Styles. – London : Hutchinson, 1983.
400p,4p of plates; 22cm.
Includes index.
ISBN 0091382017 Pbk £6.95

—Wives and Property : Reform of the Married Women's Property Law in Nineteenth-Century England / Toronto : University of Toronto Press, 1982.
ISBN 0802055737 Hbk £35.00
ISBN 0802064760 Pbk £12.50

HISTORY - EUROPE

—Culture and Censorship in Late Renaissance Italy and France / Northampton : Variorum, 1981.
318p : Illus.. – – (Collected Studies Ser.: No. 138).
ISBN 0860780848 Hbk £24.00

—Law and Society in Medieval Europe / London : Variorum, 1988.
ISBN 0860782190 Hbk £32.00

HISTORY - GREAT BRITAIN

—Acts of David II 1329-71 / Edinburgh : Edinburgh University Press.
550p. – (Regesta Regum Scottorum Ser.: Vol. 6).
ISBN 0852243952 Hbk £35.00

—Acts of Malcolm IV 1153-1165 / Edinburgh : Edinburgh University Press.
358p. – (Regesta Regum Scottorum Vol. 1).
ISBN 0852241410 Hbk £20.00

—Acts of William I, 1165-1214 / Edinburgh : Edinburgh University Press.
570p. – (Regesta Regum Scottorum Vol. 2).
ISBN 0852241429 Hbk £20.00

—History of English criminal law and its administration from 1750 / Roger Hood. – London : Stevens, 1986.
xv,1101p; 26cm.
Bibliography: p781-1039. - Includes index.
ISBN 0420462805 £75.00

—Law and disorder / John Alderson. – London : Hamilton, 1984.
vii,247p; 23cm.
Includes index.
ISBN 0241112591 £8.95

—Legislation and public policy : public bills in the 1970-74 Parliament / by Ivor Burton and Gavin Drewry. – London : Macmillan, 1981.
xii,322p; 23cm.
Bibliography: p280-283. - Includes index.
ISBN 0333152042 £25.00

—Modern Legislation for the Protection of History / Glasgow : Planning Exchange, 1980.
80p. – (Scottish Planning Law and Practice Occasional Paper Ser.: No. 2).

—Survey of Documentary Sources for Property-Holding in London Before the Great Fire / V. A. Harding. – London : London Record Society, 1985.
ISBN 0900952229 Hbk £12.00

—Workmen's compensation in twentieth century Britain : law, history and social policy / P.W.J. Bartrip. – Aldershot : Gower, 1987.
262p; 22cm.
Includes index.
ISBN 056605485X £17.50

HISTORY - GREECE

—Economic Rights of Women in Ancient Greece / Edinburgh : Edinburgh University Press.
180p.
ISBN 0852244231 Pbk £7.50

HISTORY - INDIA

—Naradiya Dharmasastra : Judicial System in Ancient India / Delhi : Ajanta Books International, 1981.
180p.
ISBN 8120200578 Hbk £70.00

HISTORY - IRAN

—Labour unions, law and conditions in Iran (1900-1941) / by Willem Floor. – Durham City : Centre for Middle Eastern and Islamic Studies, University of Durham, 1985.
124p; 21cm. – (Occasional paper series).
Bibliography: p119-124.

HISTORY - IRELAND

—Irish at law : a selection of famous and unusual cases / James Comyn. – London : Sphere, 1983.
ix,261p; 18cm.
Originally published: London : Secker & Warburg, 1981.
ISBN 0722125615 Pbk £1.95

HISTORY - NEW ZEALAND

—History of custodial and related penalties in New Zealand / Patricia M. Webb. – Wellington : Government Printer, 1982.
197p.
ISBN 0477011969

HISTORY - SCOTLAND

—Scottish Poor Law 1745-1845 / Edinburgh : Scottish Academic Press Ltd, 1981.
186p.
ISBN 0707302897 Hbk £8.75

HISTORY - SOUTH AFRICA

—Our legal heritage / co-editors, H.F. Mellet, Susan Scott, Paul van Warmelo. – Durban : Butterworths, 1982.
12,204p.
'A project of De rebus–the South African attorneys' journal, under the auspices of the Association of Law Societies of the Republic of South Africa.'. Includes index. Bibliography: p194.
ISBN 0409040843 PBK R29

HISTORY - SWEDEN

—Novgorod Kabala Books of 1614-1616 / Stockholm : Almqvist & Wiksell, 1982.
x, 200p.
ISBN 9122005528 Hbk £84.00

HISTORY - UNITED STATES

—East side-west side : organizing crime in New York 1930-1950 / Alan Block. – Cardiff : University College Cardiff Press, 1980.
265p.
Bibliographies.
ISBN 0901426997

HISTORY AND CRITICISM

—Challenge of the Nigerian nation : an examination of its legal development, 1960-1985 / edited by T. Akinola Aguda. – Lagos : Nigerian Institute of Advanced Legal Studies, 1985.
xxxi,260p.
Includes bibliographical references and index.
ISBN 978129292X

—Closing chapter / by Lord Denning. – London : Butterworths, 1983.
xvii,293p; 23cm.
Includes index.
ISBN 0406176116 Hbk £10.50
ISBN 0406176124 Pbk £6.50

—Dwelling on the threshold : critical essays on modern legal thought / Allan C. Hutchinson. – Toronto : Carswell, 1988.
ix,326p.
Bibliography: pp.324-325..
ISBN 0421400501

—Evolution of law / Alan Watson. – Oxford : Blackwell, 1985.
xi,155p; 23cm.
Discusses theory that legal tradition is the most important factor in legal development.
ISBN 0631142983 £17.50

—History of English law before the time of Edward I / by Sir Frederick Pollock and Frederic William Maitland. – 2nd edition. – Cambridge : Cambridge University Press, 1988.
xxxviii,688p.
ISBN 0521095166 Hbk

Vol. 2 / by Sir Frederick Pollock and Frederic William Maitland. – 1988.
xiv,691p.

—Indonesian legal history 1602-1848 / Sydney : Oughtershaw Press, 1982.
viii,300p.
Bibliography: p.275-293. - Includes index.
ISBN 0959342001

—Indonesian legal history : British West Sumatra, 1685-1825 / John Ball. – Sydney : Oughtershaw Press, 1984.
viii, 307 p.; 21 cm.
Includes index. Bibliography: 296-299.
ISBN 095934201X pbk.

—International law in the Netherlands / edited by H.F. van Panhuys...et al. – Alphen aan den Rijn : Sijthoff & Noordhoff, 1978.
v; 25 cm.
Organised by the T.M.C. Asser Institute. Includes bibliographical references and index.

—Introduction to European legal history / by O.F. Robinson, T.D. Fergus and W.M. Gordon. – Abingdon, Oxon. : Professional Books, 1985.
x,570p; 24cm.
ISBN 086205107X

—Invitation to law / by A.W.B. Simpson. – Oxford : Blackwell, 1988.
227p.
Includes index.
ISBN 0631145389 pbk.

—Law and government in colonial Australia / Paul Finn. – Melbourne : Oxford University Press, 1987.
xix,216p.
Bibliography: p.207-212. - Includes index.
ISBN 0195547462

—Law, litigants and the legal profession / papers presented to the Fourth British Legal History Conference at the University of Birmingham, 10-13 July, 1979 : edited by E.W. Ives and A.H. Manchester. – London : Royal Historical Society, 1983.
xii,233p; 26cm.
Includes index.
ISBN 0901050911 £11.25
ISBN 0391029258

—Law-making and law-makers in British history : papers presented to the Edinburgh Legal History Conference, 1977 / edited by Alan Harding. – London : Royal Historical Society, 1980.
viii,223p; 23cm.
Includes index.
ISBN 0901050776 £15.25

—Law of Hywel Dda : law texts of medieval Wales / translated and edited by Dafydd Jenkins. – Llandysul : Gomer, 1986.
xlvii,425p; 22cm.
Bibliography: pxliii-xlvii. - Includes index.
ISBN 0863832776 £14.95

—Legal evolution : the story of an idea / Peter Stein. – Cambridge : Cambridge University Press, 1980.
xi,131p; 23cm.
ISBN 0521227836 £9.50

—Modern legal history of England and Wales 1750-1950 / by A.H. Manchester. – London : Butterworths, 1980.
xxv,419p.
ISBN 0406622639

—Reeves' history of the English law, from the time of the Romans to the end of the reign of Elizabeth / W. F. Finlason. – New ed. 3 v. – London : Reeves & Turner, 1869.
Includes index. .

—Sources of law, legal change, and ambiguity / Alan Watson. – Edinburgh : T. & T. Clark, 1985.
xviii,164p; 23cm.
Previously published: Philadelphia : University of Pennsylvania Press, 1984.
ISBN 0567093603

—Ulrich Zasius : a jurist in the German Renaissance, 1461-1535 / Steven Rowan. – Frankfurt a. M. : Klostermann, 1987.
xiii,286p.
Includes bibliographies and index.
ISBN 3465017722

HISTORY AND CRITICISM - AUSTRALIA

—Law and history in Australia : selected papers from the fourth and fifth Law in History Conferences held at La Trobe University, 1985 and 1986 / edited by Diane Kirkby. – Melbourne : Legal Studies Department, La Trobe University, 1987.
136p.
Includes bibliographical references.

Vol. 4 / edited by Diane Kirkby. – 1987.
133p.
Includes bibliographical references.

HISTORY AND CRITICISM - CANADA

—Essays in the history of Canadian law / David H. Flaherty. – Toronto : Published for the Osgoode Society by University of Toronto Press, 1981.
xvi,428p; 23cm.
Includes index.
ISBN 0802033822 Unpriced

HISTORY AND CRITICISM - ENGLAND

—Background of the common law : a historical sketch / Derek Roebuck. – Waigani : University of Papua New Guinea Press, 1983.
135p.
Includes index.

—Law, economy and society, 1750-1914 : essays in the history of English law / edited by G.R. Rubin, David Sugarman. – Abingdon : Professional Books, 1984.
iv,503,xxviii p; 24cm.
ISBN 0862050855

—Lawyers and laymen / edited by T.M. Charles-Edwards, Morfydd E. Owen and D. B. Walters. – Cardiff : University of Wales Press, 1986.
394,1p of plates; 23cm.
Bibliography: p355-368. - Includes index. Festschrift in honour of Professor Dafydd Jenkins. Includes two papers in Welsh.
ISBN 0708309259 £25.00

—Order of Serjeants at Law : a chronicle of creations, with related texts and a historical introduction / by J.H. Baker. – London : Selden Society, 1984.
xxvi,610p,xvip of plates.
Includes index.

—Roll of the Shropshire eyre of 1256 / edited for the Selden Society by Alan Harding. – London : Selden Society, 1981.
1xxiv,403p.

—Studies in English legal history / T.F.T. Plucknett. – London : Hambledon, 1983.
352p in various pagings; 24cm.
Includes index. Includes text in Latin.
ISBN 0907628117 £24.00

HISTORY AND CRITICISM - FINLAND

—Legalists : Finnish legal science in the period of autonomy, 1809-1917 / by Hannu Tapani Klami. – Helsinki : Societas Scientiarum Fennica, 1981.
153 p., 4 leaves of plates; 24 cm.
Includes index. Bibliography: p. 141-150. Translation with revisions of: Oikeustaistelijat.
ISBN 9516531008 pbk.

HISTORY AND CRITICISM - GREAT BRITAIN

—Judge, jurist and legislature : a public lecture / delivered by the Right Honourable The Lord Goff of Chieveley. – London : Child & Co., 1986.
17p.

—Nature of Blackstones achievement : Selden Society lecture delivered at Oxford on May 31st, 1980 in association with Pembroke College to commemorate Blackstones bicentenary / by S.F.C. Milsom. – London : Selden Society, 1981.
12p; 25cm.
The text of this lecture was set as part of the first issue of the Oxford Journal of Legal studies and is simultaneously published in the journal and in the Societys lecture series.

HISTORY AND CRITICISM - MEXICO

—Introduction to the history of Mexican law / Guillermo Floris Margadant S. – 1st English ed. – London : Oceana Publications, 1981.
Includes bibliographical references and index. Translation of: Introduccion a la historia del derecho mexicano, 4th ed.
ISBN 0379207443

HISTORY AND CRITICISM - SCOTLAND

—Legal history of Scotland / by David M. Walker. – Edinburgh : W Green & Son, 1988.
xxi,435p; 24cm.
A systematic examination of the development of public, criminal and private law up to the death of Alexander III, with attention to the emerging lawmaking institutions, the deciding of cases and the procedure and principles of substantive law. Bibliography: p408-420. - Includes index.
ISBN 0414008162 No price

—Miscellany two / by various authors : edited by David Sellar : with a preface by Lord Avonside. – Edinburgh : The Stair Society, 1984.
ix,339p.
Includes indexes.
ISBN 0902292102

HISTORY AND CRITICISM - USSR

—Growth of the law in medieval Russia / Daniel H. Kaiser. – Princeton : Princeton University Press, 1980.
xii,308p; 24cm.
Bibliography: p275-308. - Includes index.
ISBN 0691053111 £14.00

HOMELESSNESS - GREAT BRITAIN

—Act of Compromise : An Appraisal of the Effects of the Housing (Homeless Persons) Act 1977 / London : Shelter.

—Developments in homelessness and the law 1983-1985 / by Paul Q. Watchman and Peter Robson. – Glasgow : Planning Exchange, 1986.
ii, 118p.
Supplements the authors' Homelessness and the law (1983). Bilbiography: p.98-103 - Includes index.
ISBN 090501121X

—Homeless person's handbook / London : Allison & Busby, 1988.
ISBN 085031769 Pbk £4.95

—Homeless Persons Act / Andrew Arden. – London : Legal Action Group, 1982.
x,190p.
Includes index. Includes text of the Housing (Homeless Persons) Act 1977.

—Homeless persons - Housing Act 1985 Pt 3 / London : Legal Action Group, 1986.
ISBN 0905099125 Pbk £10.50

—Homeless persons : the Housing Act 1985 Part III / Andrew Arden. – 2nd ed. – London : Legal Action Group, 1986.
xxiii,200p.
Previous ed.: published as 'The Homeless Persons Act' 1982. Includes index. Includes text of act.

—Homeless young offenders : an action programme : the Report of a NACRO Group / NACRO. – London : NACRO, 1981.
69p.
Bibliography: p.67-69.
ISBN 0850690242

—Homelessness / by David C. Hoath. – London : Sweet & Maxwell, 1983.
xxi,217p; 18cm.
Bibliography: p215-217.
ISBN 0421281804 Hbk £11.50
ISBN 0421281901 Pbk £6.75

—Homelessness among women : report of an Ad Hoc Working Group, Women's National Commission / Norma Nelson. – London : Cabinet Office, 1983.
56p; 30cm.
Report prepared under the chairmanship of Norma Nelson.

—Homelessness and the law / by Paul Q. Watchman and Peter Robson. – Glasgow : The Planning Exchange, 1983.
xvi,182p; 21cm.
Bibliography: p148-158. - Includes index.
ISBN 0905011201 Pbk £6.95

—Housing (Homeless Persons) Act 1977 : code of guidance (England and Wales) / Great Britain. – 2nd ed. – London : H.M.S.O., 1983.
42p.
First published 1977. Includes index.
ISBN 0117516945

—Ordinary People : Homeless in the Housing Crisis / Shelter. – London : Shelter, 1982.
ISBN 0901242659 Pbk £2.50

HOMICIDE - AUSTRALIA

—Homicide : the law and the Proofs / G.K. Jaisimaha Rao. – North Ryde : Law Book 6, 1986.
ca xvi, 210p.
ISBN 0455206740 jb £45.00

—Homicide, the law and the proofs / North Ryde : Law Book Co, 1986.
ISBN 0455206740 Hbk £22.75

HOMICIDE - AUSTRALIA - VICTORIA

—Homicide / Law Reform Commission of Victoria. – Melbourne : The Commission, 1988.
72p. – (Discussion paper).
Includes bibliographical references.
ISBN 0724167137

—Law of homicide in Victoria : the sentence for murder / Law Reform Commission of Victoria. – Melbourne : The Commission, 1985.
viii,27p. – (Report v no 1).
Bibliography: p.25-27.

HOMICIDE - CANADA

—Homicide / Law Reform Commission of Canada. – Ottawa : Law Reform Commission of Canada, 1984.
117,128p; 25cm. – (Working paper).
At head of cover title: Criminal law. English and French texts bound back to back.
ISBN 0662529871

HOMICIDE - GREAT BRITAIN

—Massacre of the innocents - Infanticide / Routledge, 1986.
ISBN 071020339X Hbk £16.95

—Murder into manslaughter / Oxford : Oxford University Press, 1984.
ISBN 0197121519 Hbk £10.00

HOMICIDE - INDIA
—Law of Culpable Homicide, Murder and Punishment in India / New Delhi : Deep and Deep Publications, 1988.
464p.

HOMICIDE - SCOTLAND
—Attempted homicide / Scottish Law Commission. - Edinburgh : Scottish Law Commission, 1984.
52p. - (Consultative memorandum).

HOMICIDE (GREEK LAW)
—Drakon and early Athenian homicide law / Michael Gagarin. - New Haven : Yale University Press, 1981.
xvii,175p; 22cm. - (Yale classical monographs).
Includes index. Includes the Greek text and English translation of Drakon's law.
ISBN 0300026277 Hbk

HOMOSEXUALITY
—Homosexuality : power & politics / edited by Gay Left Collective. - London : Allison & Busby, 1980.
223p; 22cm.
Includes index.
ISBN 0850313740 Hbk £9.95
ISBN 0850313759 Pbk £3.95

HOMOSEXUALITY - GREAT BRITAIN
—Gays and the law / Paul Crane. - London : Pluto, 1982.
x,244p; 20cm.
Includes index.
ISBN 0861043863 Pbk £4.95

HONG KONG
—Basic Law and Hong Kong's Future / Albert H.Y. Chen. - Butterworths, 1988.
ca 400p.
Covers the present constitution of Hong Kong, the political values of the Hong Kong Chinese, the Hong Kong model of 'one country, two systems', the relationship between central government and the SAR, the protection of civil liberties, economic, cultural and social aspects, and foreign, external and defence affairs.
ISBN 0409995673 Pbk £145.00
ISBN 040999569X Hbk £230.00

—Draft agreement between the government of the United Kingdom of Great Britain and Northern Ireland and the government of the People's Republic of China on the future of Hong Kong / China. - Hong Kong : Government Printer, 1984.
46p.
'This White Paper reproduces the text of the White Paper published by Her Majesty's Government in London on 26 September 1984.'.

—Treaty, grant, usage or sufferance? : some legal aspects of the status of Hong Kong / by Anthony Dicks. - London : Contemporary China Institute, School of Oriental and African Studies, 1983.
p.427-455.
Offprint from: The China quarterly (September 1983).

HORSE RACING - GREAT BRITAIN
—Filmed horse racing / Christopher C. Hallsworth and Barry O. Johnson. - Chichester : Barry Rose, 1983.
26p.

HORSES - GREAT BRITAIN
—Essential Law for Horseowners / Oxford : Blackwell Scientific, 1987.
ISBN 0003832864 Pbk £9.95

—Horse and the law / London : David & Charles, 1987.
ISBN 0715388134 Hbk £10.95

—Horse law / Shaw & Sons, 1988.
ISBN 0721911307 Pbk

HOSPITALS - CANADA
—Canadian Law of Consent to Treatment / Fay A. Rozovsky. - Butterworths, 1988.
ca 288p.
Deals with specific medico-legal consent problems such as consent relating to the treatment of children, prisoners and the mentally handicapped. Details circumstances in which consent may be waived, examines the essential elements of consent litigation, discusses how to prevent consent litigation and includes a special section on documenting consent.
ISBN 0409806307 Hbk £70.00

—Canadian Law of Patient Records / Fay A. Rozovsky. - Butterworths, 1984.
168p.
Examines the legal problems arising from patient records and how to avoid such problems. Contains incident reports as a tool for preventing possible serious injury to patients, the identification, evaluation elimination, reduction and prevention of risks, and practical advice on drafting administrative rules and guidelines on minimizing legal risks.
ISBN 0409862886 Hbk £40.00

—Legal Liability of Doctors and Hospitals / 2nd ed. - Agincourt : Carswell, 1984.
ISBN 0459358200 Hbk £38.75

—Ottawa Civic Hospital Act, 1983, Bill Pr043 : An Act Respecting the Ottawa Civic Hospital / Ontario : Ontario Government Publications Service, 1983.
7p.

HOSPITALS - GREAT BRITAIN
—Medicine, Patients and the Law / Pelican, 1987.
ISBN 0140225579 Pbk £5.95

HOTELS - ENGLAND
—Liquor licensing law / by David Field and Matthew Pink. - London : Sweet & Maxwell, 1983.
xxi,206p; 25cm.
Looks at how to obtain a justices licence, including the stages of deciding the relevant licence, the permitted hours in licensed premises, how to renew an existing licence, and its removal and transfer through to the conduct of licensed premises. Also contains a chapter on the nature of a registered club.
ISBN 0421299703 Pbk £11.50

HOTELS - GREAT BRITAIN
—Hotel and catering law in Britain / by David Field. - 5th ed. - London : Sweet & Maxwell, 1988.
xvii,236p; 23cm.
Discusses the legal framework in England, Scotland and Wales. Covers changes in the law effected by the Wages Act 1986, and the Licensing (Restaurant Meals) Act 1987, and also examines the impact of the new Companies legislation on the catering industry.
ISBN 0421392509 Pbk £8.50

HOUSE OF COMMONS
—House of Commons Weekly Information Bulletin / London : HMSO.
Single Issue

—Sessional information digest / House of Commons. - London : H.M.S.O., 1983.
Compiled in the Public Information Office, Department of the Library, House of Commons.

HOUSE OF COMMONS - GREAT BRITAIN
—Committees of the House of Commons and Northern Ireland Affairs / Belfast : Queen's University of Belfast, 1984.
32p.

HOUSE OF LORDS (APPEAL COURT) - GREAT BRITAIN
—Law lords / Alan Paterson. - London : Macmillan, 1982.
x,288p; 23cm.
ISBN 0333238869

HOUSE OF LORDS (PARLIAMENT) - GREAT BRITAIN
—House of Lords / Allan (Philip), 1988.
ISBN 086003402X Hbk £34.50
ISBN 0860037029 Pbk £14.95

HOUSES - GREAT BRITAIN
—Guarantees For New Homes / Rolfe. - 3rd ed. - London : Longman Professional, 1981.
ISBN 0851295437 Pbk £23.00

—Guarantees for the New Homes : A Guide to the NHBC Scheme / R. Rolfe. - 2nd ed. - London : Oyez Longman, 1981.
ISBN 0851205437 Hbk £14.50

—Right to buy in rural areas : an investigation of section 19 of the Housing Act 1980 / Neil Hawke. - Leicester : Leicester Polytechnic. School of Law, 1985.
33p. - (Research monographs).

—Right to buy : legislative proposals / Great Britain. - London : Department of the Environment, 1987.
3p.

HOUSING
—Encyclopaedia of housing law and practice / Sweet & Maxwell, 1988.
ISBN 0421007303 Hbk £210.00

—Land for housing the poor / edited by Shlomo Angel ... et al. - Singapore : Select Books, 1983.
ix,556p; 22cm.
Papers from a seminar, 'Land for Housing the Poor: Towards Positive Action in Asian Cities' held in Bangkok, 18th and 31st Jan. 1982.
ISBN 9971835517

—Land, the central human settlement issue / H. Peter Oberlander. - Vancouver : University of British Columbia Press, 1985.
x, 103 p., 4 p. of plates; 24 cm.
Bibliography: p. 93-101.
ISBN 0774802359

—Low-income housing in the developing world : the role of sites and services and settlement upgrading / Geoffrey K. Payne. - Chichester : Wiley, 1984.
xii,271p; 25cm. - (A Wiley series on public administration in developing countries).
Includes bibliographies and index.
ISBN 0471902128 £29.95

HOUSING - CANADA
—Canadian Housing Policies / Toronto : Butterworths, 1980.
224p.
ISBN 0409863157 Pbk £29.95

—Family Home and Income Tax / Agincourt : Carswell, 1986.
245p.
This work is a guide to the tax consequences of home ownership in Canada for tax practitioners. The book treats the subject of capital gains exemptions, home improvements, mixed use properties, recreational dwellings, and other tax issues.

HOUSING - ENGLAND
—Civil justice review / Lord Chancellor's Department. - London : The Department, 1987.
52 leaves.

—Civil justice review : study of housing cases b final report to Lord Chancellor's Department / Bristol : University of Bristol, School for Advanced Urban Studies, 1987.
129p.

—Comments on civil justice review of housing cases / JUSTICE. - London : JUSTICE, 1987.
7 leaves.

—Housing Act 1980, as amended by the Housing and Building Control Act 1984 / Trevor M. Aldridge. - London : Oyez, 1984.
xxxix,334p.
Previous ed.: 1980, titled The Housing Act 1980: a practical guide. Includes index.
ISBN 0851207650

—Housing Act 1985 / with annotations by Andrew Arden. - 1. - London : Sweet & Maxwell, 1986.
various pagings.
Includes index.
ISBN 0421353708

—Housing Associations Act 1985 / with annotations by Andrew Arden and James Ramage. - London : Sweet & Maxwell, 1986.
141p.
Includes index.
ISBN 0421359005

—Housing disrepair / Nicholas C. Martyn and Edward Lloyd-Jones. - London : Longman Professional, 1985.
xxv,187p; 22cm. - (Longman professional practitioner series).
Includes index.
ISBN 0851209904 Pbk £13.50

—Housing law / by Andrew Arden, Martin Partington. - 1. - London : Sweet & Maxwell, 1983.
various pagings; 26cm.
Defines legal statutes likely to affect all classes of occupiers of residential accommodation, deals with the law relating to housing finance, the private and public law relating to housing conditions, the rights of occupation in housing, and special categories of occupier such as agricultural workers, and occupiers of mobile homes.
ISBN 0421242108 £58.00

—Housing law reports / edited by Andrew Arden. - Harlow : G. Godwin, 1982-.
Annual indexes.

—Land law & landscape / Philip Britton and Ian Thompson. - 1 videocassette. - London : Sweet & Maxwell in association with the University of Warwick, 1986.
- (Sweet & Maxwell's lawfilms).

—Law of flats / Trevor M. Aldridge. - London : Oyez Longman, 1982.
xxii,208p; 24cm. - (Oyez Longman practitioner series).
Includes index.
ISBN 0851206255 Pbk Unpriced

—Race and council housing in Hackney / report of a formal investigation conducted by the Commission for Racial Equality into the allocation of housing in the London Borough of Hackney. - London : The Commission, 1984.
145p; 30cm.
ISBN 0907920411 Pbk Unpriced

—Report of the Committee of Inquiry on the Management of Privately Owned Blocks of Flats / E. G. Nugee. - 2 v. - London : The Committee, 1985.
Chairman: E.G. Nugee.

—Sale of flats / by Edward F. George and Arthur George. - 5th ed. - London : Sweet & Maxwell, 1984.
xxvii,447p; 23cm.
Expanded section on the treatment of remedies. Covers the 1980 Housing Act, and schedule 19 to the 1980 Act on services and service charges is examined in detail. New chapter on leases demanded by secure tenants from local authorities. Contains precedents, including articles of association of a management company.
ISBN 0421305509 £25.00

HOUSING - GREAT BRITAIN

—Act of Compromise : An Appraisal of the Effects of the Housing (Homeless Persons) Act 1977 / London : Shelter.

—Alteration/Conversion Of Houses / Edmunds. – 6th ed. – London : Longman Professional, 1985.
ISBN 0851209971 Pbk £16.95

—Build Homes, Build Hope : 1981 Campaign Report / Shelter UK Publisher. – London : Shelter, 1981.
ISBN 0901242608 Pbk Individuals 2.25

—Casebook on repairs / London : Estates Gazette, 1987.
ISBN 0728201038 Pbk £16.00

—Environmental health standards in housing / David Ormandy & Roger Burridge. – London : Sweet & Maxwell, 1988.
xlv,373p.
Covers the initial inspection of a house, the assessment of conditions (including particular problems of dampness), the application of the various standards, the drafting of the notices and the steps involved in the enforcement of statutory standards.
ISBN 0421365501 £25.00

—Ferndale : A Caring Repair Service for Elderly Home Owners / Shelter. – London : Shelter, 1982.
ISBN 0901242632 Pbk £2.50

—Forgotten Problem / Shelter. – London : Shelter, 1980.
ISBN 0901242519 Pbk £2.25

—Future for rented housing? : responses to the Government's proposals / National Housing Forum. – London : National Federation of Housing Associations, 1988.
iv,47p; 30cm.
ISBN 0862971306 Pbk No price

—Home-owner's guide / Cambridge : Woodhead-Faulkner, 1987.
ISBN 085941423X Pbk £4.95

—Homelessness / by David C. Hoath. – London : Sweet & Maxwell, 1983.
xxi,217p; 18cm.
Bibliography: p215-217.
ISBN 0421281804 Hbk £11.50
ISBN 0421281901 Pbk £6.75

—Homes Wasted / Shelter Publications Staff. – London : Shelter, 1982.
ISBN 0901242640 Hbk £2.50

—Houses in Multiple Occupation / London : Shaw & Sons, 1980.
– (Shaway Guide: No. 2).
ISBN 0721908713 Pbk £2.50

—Housing alternatives for the elderly / Alan Butler and Anthea Tinker. – Leeds : Centre for Applied Social Studies, 1983.
28p. – (Occasional paper).
Includes bibliographical references.

—Housing and Building Control Act 1984 / with annotations by Andrew Arden and Charles Cross. – London : Sweet & Maxwell, 1984.
127p; 24cm.
ISBN 0421330805 Pbk £7.50

—Housing and Campaigning / Shelter. – London : Shelter, 1983.
ISBN 0901242667 Pbk £3.00/Members 1.25

—Housing and the Whitehall Bulldozer / London : Institute of Economic Affairs.

—Housing Economics and Public Policy / London : Macmillan.
176p. – (Studies in Planning Ser.).
ISBN 0333211073 Pbk £4.95

—Housing finance / 2nd ed. – Turnaround Press, 1986.
ISBN 090120273X Pbk £3.95

—Housing Finance : Who Gains? / London : Policy Studies Institute, 1984.
83p.

—Housing grants / 2nd ed. – London : Kogan Page, 1983.
ISBN 0850387116 Pbk £4.50

—Housing inequality and deprivation / Alan Murie. – London : Heinemann Educational, 1983.
250p; 23cm.
Bibliography: p237-246. - Includes index.
ISBN 0435826263 £13.50

—Housing Law for the Elderly / London : Oyez Longman, 1982.
– (Oyez Longman Practice Note Ser.: No. 72).
ISBN 0851206875 Hbk £7.95

—Housing management / Baker. – 4th ed. – London : Estates Gazette, 1982.
ISBN 0728200368 Pbk £18.00

—Housing Policy and Housing Needs / London : Macmillan.
160p. – (Building and Survey Ser.).
ISBN 0333307011 Hbk £14.00
ISBN 0333236955 Pbk £6.95

—Housing Policy and Practice / Alan Murie. – London : Macmillan, 1982.
216p. – (Public Policy and Politics, General Ser.).
ISBN 0333328426 Hbk £15.00
ISBN 0333328434 Pbk £5.95

—Housing Requirements : A Guide to Information and Techniques / London : HMSO, 1980.
152p.
Guide to housing requirements. Explains the use of the terms connected with the subject.
ISBN 0117514772 Hbk £4.75

—Housing rights guide / 2nd ed. – Turnaround Press, 1987.
ISBN 0948854145 Pbk £4.95

—Housing : the government's proposals / presented to parliament by the Secretaries of State for the Environment and Wales by command of Her Majesty, September 1987. – London : HMSO, 1987.
iii,18p.
ISBN 0101021429

—Keeping pace with change / papers from a conference held at Oxford, September 1987, organised by the Bar Council, the Law Society and the Royal Institution of Chartered Surveyors. – London : Sweet & Maxwell, 1988.
85p.
ISBN 042140390X £25.00

—Landlord and tenant in urban Britain 1838-1918 / David Englander. – Oxford : Clarendon Press, 1983.
xviii,342p; 23cm.
Bibliography: p318-335. - Includes index.
ISBN 0198226802 £22.50

—Overcrowding : Part IV Housing Act 1957 / Shelter National Housing Aid Trust. – London : Shelter, 1984.
ISBN 0862650097 Hbk £1.75

—Problems of public housing / Policy Studies Institute, 1988.
ISBN 0853743509 Pbk £6.95

—Report on the consolidation of the Housing Acts : Housing Bill, Housing Associations Bill, Landlord and Tenant Bill / the Law Commission and the Scottish Law Commission. – London : H.M.S.O., 1985.
49p.
ISBN 0101951507

—Restrictive Practices / Shelter Publications Staff. – London : Shelter, 1984.
ISBN 0901242691 Hbk £1.50

—Right to a Home / Labour Housing Group. – London : Spokesman Books, 1984.
165p.
ISBN 0851243991 Hbk £15.00
ISBN 0851244009 Pbk £4.95

HOUSING - NORTHERN IRELAND

—Northern Ireland housing law : the public and private rented sectors / by T.B. Hadden and W.D. Trimble. – Belfast : SLS Legal Publications, 1986.
xxxvi,323p.
Includes bibliographical references and index.
ISBN 0853892806

HOUSING - SCOTLAND

—Housing (Scotland) Bill : report on the consolidation of certain enactments relating to housing in Scotland ... / Scottish Law Commission. – Edinburgh : H.M.S.O., 1987.
11p.
ISBN 0101010427

—Public sector housing law in Scotland / by Chris Himsworth. – 2nd ed. – Glasgow : Planning Exchange, 1986.
vii, 150p.
Previous ed.: 1982. Includes bibliographical references and indexes.
ISBN 0905011228

HOUSING - SOUTH AFRICA

—Sectional titles, share blocks and time-sharing / by C.G. van der Merwe and D.W. Butler. – Durban : Butterworths, 1985.
xiii,573p.
Bibliography: p. xv-xxi. - Includes indexes.
ISBN 0409059293 Hbk R105

HOUSING - SWEDEN

—Law and the weaker party : an Anglo-Swedish comparative study / general editors: Steve Anderman...et al. – Abingdon : Professional Books, 1981.

Vol. 2 : The English experience, edited by Steve Anderman / general editors: Steve Anderman...et al.. – 1981.

Vol. 3 : Swedish statutory material : edited by Alan C. Neal and Anders Victorin / general editors: Steve Anderman...et al.. – 1981.

HOUSING ASSOCIATIONS - GREAT BRITAIN

—Housing Associations Act 1985 / Ramage. – London : Sweet & Maxwell, 1986.
ISBN 0421359005 Pbk £7.50

HOUSING BENEFIT - GREAT BRITAIN

—Guide to Housing Benefit / Raynsford. – Rev. – London : CENT, 1986.
ISBN 0948857056 Pbk £4.95

HOUSING CO-OPERATIVES - ENGLAND

—Housing association law / by John Alder and Christopher R. Handy. – London : Sweet & Maxwell, 1987.
xlii,330p; 21cm.
Text examines the partnership between public and private sector in providing low-cost housing, 'new' forms of tenure as a means of extending owner-occupation and tenant self-management, and tenants' rights and accountability to the Housing Corporation.
ISBN 042134430X Pbk £15.00

HOUSING LAW

—Manual of housing law / 4th. – London : Sweet & Maxwell, 1989.
Taking into account changes due to the Housing Act 1988, covers occupation status, security of tenure by Rent and Housing Acts, restricted security, lack of security, harassment and illegal eviction, break-up of relationships, homelessness and disrepair, multiple occupation and common lodging houses, and overcrowding.
ISBN 042140650X Pbk £14.95

HOUSING LAW - CANADA

—House Construction and Renovation : a Solicitor's Guide / Vancouver : Continuing Legal Education Society of British Columbia, 1988.
310p.
ISBN 0865049688 Hbk £80.00

—Residential Complex Sales Representation Act, 1983, Bill 113 : An Act to Regulate Conveyances of Dwelling Units in Residential Complexes / Ontario : Ontario Government Publications Service, 1983.
3p.

HOUSING LAW - ENGLAND

—Housing association allocations : Achieving racial equality : a West Midlands case study : summary of a report by Pat Niner in association with Valerie Karn / Anne Grosskurth. – London : Runnymede Trust, 1985.
20p.
ISBN 0902397540

—Race and council housing in Hackney / report of a formal investigation conducted by the Commission for Racial Equality into the allocation of housing in the London Borough of Hackney. – London : The Commission, 1984.
145p; 30cm.
ISBN 0907920411 Pbk Unpriced

HOUSING LAW - GREAT BRITAIN

—Compulsory Improvement of Dwellings / London : Shaw & Sons, 1980.
– (Shaway Guide: No. 1).
ISBN 0721908705 Pbk £2.50

—Homeless persons - Housing Act 1985 Pt 3 / London : Legal Action Group, 1986.
ISBN 0905099125 Pbk £10.50

—Homeowner's guide to the law / London : Fourmat, 1987.
ISBN 1851900233 Pbk £6.95

—Housing Act 1980 : amended 1984 / 2nd ed. – London : Longman Professional, 1984.
ISBN 0851207650 Pbk £27.00

—Housing Act 1985 / London : Sweet & Maxwell, 1986.
ISBN 0421353708 Pbk £17.50

—Housing Act Nineteen-Eighty / London : Butterworths, 1981.
This book gives an extensive narrative exposition of the Act followed by the text of the Act with extensive annotations. The work is a thorough guide to the provisions of the United Kingdom's Housing Act of 1980.
ISBN 0406657904 Hbk

—Housing Act Nineteen Eighty : The Tenant's Charter / Shleter. – London : Shelter, 1981.
ISBN 0901242578 Pbk £1.75

—Housing Consolidation 1985 / London : Sweet & Maxwell, 1986.
ISBN 0421360801 Pbk £25.00

—Housing law / Partington. – London : Sweet & Maxwell, 1983.
ISBN 0421242108 Hbk £110.00

—Housing law for the elderly (LPPN72) / London : Longman Professional, 1982.
ISBN 0851206875 Pbk £12.95

—Housing Law Reports / London : Sweet & Maxwell.

Bound Vol.

Back Vols.

Single copies

—Law for Housing Managers / 2nd ed. – London : Business Education, 1986.
ISBN 0907679145 Pbk £13.95

—'Right to Buy' Handbook / Butterworths Editorial Staff. – London : Butterworths, 1984.
This book sets out the text of the Housing and Building Control Act of 1984 concerning the 'right to buy' provisions of the United Kingdom Housing Act of 1980. Detailed annotations to the Act are provided.
ISBN 0406548250 Hbk

—You and your home / London : Shaw & Sons, 1984.
ISBN 0721909906 Pbk £4.50

HOUSING LAW - MALAYSIA

—Housing Developers (Control and Licensing) Act, 1966 (Act 118) and Regulations 1982 / Kuala Lumpur : International Law Books Services.

HOUSING LAW - NORTHERN IRELAND

—Housing Law in Northern Ireland / W. David Trimble. – Belfast : Queen's University of Belfast, 1986.
350p.

HOUSING LAW - SCOTLAND

—Housing (Scotland) Act 1988 / Edinburgh : W Green & Son, 1988.
The annotated Act reprinted from Scottish Current Law Statutes with an introduction and the text of the regulations made under the Act which introduced new categories of tenancies in the private sector with corresponding effects on security of tenure. Rights of succession were also curtailed.
ISBN 0414008960

HOUSING POLICY - SOUTH AFRICA

—Commission of Inquiry into Township Establishment and Related Matters / Pretoria : Government Printer, 1984.
2 v.; 30 cm.
Title on added t.p.: Kommissie van Ondersoek na Dorpstigting en Verwante Aangeleenthede. First and second reports of the commission.
ISBN 0621084395 pbk. : v. 2 R3.50 (R4.00 other countries)

HOUSING SUBSIDIES - GREAT BRITAIN

—Cost of chaos : a survey of the housing benefits scheme / Peter Kemp. – London : SHAC, 1984.
85p; 22cm. – (SHAC research report).
ISBN 0903113759

—Guide to housing benefit / by Nick Raynsford, Peter McGurk. – Rev. ed. – London : SHAC, 1987.
xvi,137p.
Includes index.
ISBN 0948857161

—Housing Grants / 2nd ed. – London : Kogan Page, 1983.
172p.
ISBN 0850387108 Hbk £9.95
ISBN 0850387116 Pbk £4.50

HUMAN ECOLOGY

—Environment ideology and policy / Francis Sandbach. – Oxford : Blackwell, 1980.
xvi,254p; 24cm.
Bibliography : p.225-248. - Includes index.
ISBN 0631104917 £12.50
ISBN 0631128115

HUMAN EXPERIMENTATION IN MEDICINE

—Experience at a clinical research ethical review committee / Ethical Committee, University College Hospital. – London : British Medical Association, 1981.
7p.
Reprinted from: British medical journal, 14 Nov. 1981, 283, 1312-1314.

HUMAN REPRODUCTION

—Industrialisation and reproductive rights / by Paulin sic Jackson. – Florence : European University Institute, 1986.
ii,24p.
Bibliography: p.22-24.

—Legal issues in human reproduction / edited by Sheila McLean. – Aldershot, Hants. : Gower, 1989.
vii,238p.
Includes bibliographical references and index.
ISBN 0566053934

—Legislation on human infertility services and embryo research : a consultation paper / Department of Health and Social Security. – London : H.M.S.O., 1987.
15p.
ISBN 0101004621

—Question of life : the Warnock report on human fertilisation and embryology / chairwoman Mary Warnock. – Oxford : Blackwell, 1985.
xvii,110p; 20cm.
The Warnock Report on Human Fertilization and Embryology. Discusses medical, legal and moral aspects of the subject.
ISBN 0631142576 Pbk £4.95

HUMAN REPRODUCTION - CANADA - ONTARIO

—Report on human artificial reproduction and related matters / Ontario Law Reform Commission. – 2 v. – Toronto : Ministry of the Attorney General, 1985.
ISBN 0772900019

HUMAN REPRODUCTION - GREAT BRITAIN

—Human fertilisation and embryology : a framework for legislation / presented to Parliament by the Secretary of State for Social Services ...et al. by Command of Her Majesty November 1987. – London : H.M.S.O., 1987.
20p.
ISBN 0101025920

HUMAN RIGHTS

—'Nonsense upon stilts' : Bentham, Burke and Marx on the rights of man / edited with introductory and concluding essays by Jeremy Waldron. – London : Methuen, 1987.
256p; 22cm.
Includes bibliography and index.
ISBN 0416918905 Pbk £6.95

—Against oblivion : Amnesty International's fight for human rights / Jonathan Power. – London : Fontana, 1981.
254p; 18cm.
Includes index.
ISBN 0006364268 Pbk £1.95

—... and now for the next sketch ... cartoons for Amnesty / London : Amnesty International, 1986.
70p.
A collection of original cartoons exhibited at The Barbican Centre in May/June 1986 in commemoration of the 25th. anniversary of the foundation of Amnesty International..

—Application of Humanitarian Law / Centre d'Etude et de Recherche de Droit International et de Relations Internationales. – Dordrecht : Kluwer, 1987.
106p.
ISBN 9024735084 Pbk £50.00

—Application of humanitarian law : selective bibliography prepared by the Peace Palace Library / Center for Studies and Research of the Hague Academy of International Law : bibliographie selective preparee par la Bibliotheque du Palais de la Paix : Centre d'Etude et de Recherche de l'Academie du droit Internationale de la Haye. – The Hague : Center for Studies and Research of the Hague Academy of International Law, 1986.
80p.
Preliminary material in English and French.

—Argentine Supreme Court : the court of constitutional guarantees / German J. Bidart Campos : translated by William J. Brisk, based on the book by German J. Bidart Campos, 'La Corte Suprema, tribunal de las garantias constitucionales'. – Argentine ed. – Buenos Aires : Allende & Brea, 1982.
viii, 143 p.; 26 cm.
Includes bibliographical references.
ISBN 9500621142

—Armenians / by David Marshall Lang and Christopher J. Walker. – New rev ed. – London : Minority Rights Group, 1987.
20p. – (Report).
Previous ed.: 1981. Bibliography: p.20.
ISBN 094669043X

—Basic Human Rights / Dhaka : Islamic Foundation Bangladesh.

—Battle of Human Rights : Gross, Systematic Violations and the Inter-American System / Dordrecht : Kluwer, 1988.
390p.
ISBN 9024736870 Hbk £170.00

—Bibliography of International Humanitarian Law / Geneva : Comite International de la Croix-Rouge, 1987.
605p.

—Brief Outline of International Humanitarian Law / Geneva : Comite International de la Croix-Rouge, 1984.
48p.

—Brownlie's Law of public order and national security / edited by Michael Supperstone. – 2nd ed. – London : Butterworths, 1981.
lvii,415p.
Previous ed. entitled: The law relating to public order. Includes index.
ISBN 0406137013

—Case-Law of the European Commission of Human Rights / Strasbourg : Council of Europe.

Summaries and Indexes Nos. 1-20

—Case studies on human rights and fundamental freedoms : a world survey / ed.-in-chief, Willem A. Veenhoven, assistant to the ed.-in-chief, Winifred Crum Ewing, associate editors, Clemens Amelunxen ... et al. – The Hague : Nijhoff, 1975.
5 v; 25 cm.
2 v. Includes bibliographical references.

—Central America's Indians / by David Stephen and Phillip Wearne : with a summary by Rodolfo Stavenhagen. – London : Minority Rights Group, 1984.
23p. – (Report).

—Children : rights and responsibilities / Jo Boyden and Andy Hudson. – London : Minority Rights Group, 1985.
15p. – (Report).
Bibliography: p14-15.
ISBN 0946690340

—Childright : a bulletin of law and policy affecting children and young people in England and Wales / v. – London : The Children's Legal Centre, 1983.
ISBN 02651459

—Collection of resolutions adopted by the Committee of Ministers in application of Article 32 of the European Convention for the Protection of Human Rights and Fundamental Freedoms, 1959-1981 / Council of Europe. – Strasbourg : Council of Europe, 1981.
various pagings; 30cm.
At head of title: Human Rights.

—Collection of resolutions adopted by the Committee of Ministers in application of article 54 of the European Convention for the Protection of Human Rights and Fundamental Freedoms / Recueil des resolutions du Comite des Ministres adoptees en application de l'article 54 de la Convention Europeenne de Sauvegarde des Droits de l'Homme et des Libertes Fondamentales. – Strasbourg : Council of Europe, 1981.
various pagings; 30cm.
Preface by Peter Leuprecht, Director of Human Rights. At head of title: Human Rights.

—Collection of resolutions adopted by the Committee of Ministers in application of articles 32 and 54 of the European Convention for the Protection of Human Rights and Fundamental Freedoms, 1959-1983 / Council of Europe. – Strasbourg : Council of Europe, 1984.
148p; 30cm.
'Publication prepared by the Human Rights Documentation Centre...'. Kept up to date by supplements.

—Colloquy: Democracy and Human Rights / organised by the Government of Greece and the Secretariat General of the Council of Europe in co-operation with the Centre of International and European Economic Law of Thessaloniki, Thessaloniki (Greece), 24-26 September 1987. – Strasbourg : Council of Europe, 1987.
17p. – (H/Coll (87) 6).
Includes bibliographical references.

—Concept and present status of the international protection of human rights : forty years after the universal declaration / Dordrecht : Martinus Nijhoff, 1989.
624. – (International Studies in Human Rights 13).
In commemoration of the fortieth anniversary of the Universal Declaration of Human Rights. Explores how the United Nations has been able to establish and operate instruments and procedures of protection, to place a shield around groups in jeopardy. Deals with the concept of protection in existing law and practice, and practice notes from the author's files are appended to the chapters.
ISBN 9024737591 Hbk Gld295.00

—Conference on prospects for the establishment of an inter-governmental human rights commission in the South Pacific / convened by the LAWASIA Human Rights Standing Committee in Fiji 12-14 April, 1985. – Sydney : Law Association for Asia and the Pacific, 1985.
iv,528p.

—Conference on the application of international humanitarian law : March 12th, 1986, London SW1 / report on the proceedings by Michael A. Meyer. – s.l. : s.n., 1986.
23,vp.
'Organised by the British Red Cross Society'. - Front cover.

—Development and Principles of International Humanitarian Law / Geneva : Comite International de la Croix-Rouge, 1983.
99p.

—Development and the Rule of Law, Prevention Versus Cure as a Human Rights Strategy / Geneva : International Commission of Jurists, 1981.
125p.

—Development, Human Rights and the Rule of Law : 1981 Hague Conference / Geneva : International Commission of Jurists, 1981.
237p.

—Development, human rights and the rule of law : report of a conference held in The Hague on 27 April-1 May 1981 / convened by the International Commission of Jurists. – Oxford : Pergamon, 1981.
vi,237p; 23cm.
ISBN 0080289215 Hbk Unpriced
ISBN 0080289517 Pbk £3.75

—Digest of Strasbourg case-law relating to the European Convention on Human Rights / Council of Europe. – Koln : Heymanns-Verlag, 1984.
xvii,669p.
ISBN 3452194035 Hbk

v.6 : General index to volumes 1-5 1985.
xxxix,662p.
ISBN 3452194116

v.2 : (Article 6) / Council of Europe. – 1984.
xviii,922p.
ISBN 3452194043 Hbk

v.3 : (Articles 7-12) / Council of Europe. – 1984.
xvii,601p.
ISBN 3452194051 Hbk

v.4 : (Articles 13-25) / Council of Europe. – 1985.
xviii,453p.
ISBN 345219406X Hbk

v.5 : (Articles 26-66, protocols to the Convention) 1985.
xxvi,899p.
At head of title: Council of Europe.
ISBN 3452195260 Hbk

—Documentation sources in human rights / Council of Europe. Directorate of Human Rights. Human Rights Documentation Centre. – Strasbourg : The Council, 1987.
38p. – (H(87)2).

—Drifting into a law and order society / Stuart Hall. – London : Cobden Trust, 1980.
17p. – (Human Rights Day Lectures).
ISBN 0900137150

—Dynamics of development in the European human rights convention system / Clovis C. Morrisson. – The Hague : Martinus Nijhoff, 1981.
xii,176p.

—Education and information in the field of human rights : activities of the Council of Europe / Secretariat memorandum prepared by the Directorate of Human Rights. – Strasbourg : Council of Europe, 1987.
11p. – (H (87) 5).
At head of cover title: Committee of Experts for the Promotion of Education and Information in the Field of Human Rights (DH-ED).

—Education and information in the field of human rights : activities of the Council of Europe : Secretariat memorandum / prepared by the Directorate of Human Rights. – Strasbourg : Council of Europe, 1984.
9p.

—Effect on English domestic law of membership of the European Communities and of ratification of the European Convention on Human Rights / edited by M.P. Furmston, Roger Kerridge, B.E. Sufrin. – The Hague : M. Nijhoff, 1983.
viii, 428p.
Papers by members of the University of Bristol Faculty of Law in celebration of the fiftieth anniversary of the Faculty.
ISBN 9024728118 Hbk £130.00

—Enforcement of human rights in peace and war and the future of humanity / Nagendra Singh. – Dordrecht : Nijhoff, 1986.
ISBN 9024733022 Hbk

—Essays on human rights in the Helsinki process / edited by A. Bloed and P. van Dijk. – Dordrecht : M. Nijhoff, 1985.
285p.
At head of title: TMC Asser Instituut. Contents: Detente and the concluding document of Madrid / by Arie Bloed – The Madrid Meeting, 1980-1983 / by Harm J. Hazewinkel – Some aspects of the socialist view of human rights / by Arie Bloed & Fried van Hoof – Human rights and non-intervention / by Arie Bloed & Pieter van Dijk – Trade union freedom in socialist states and the Madrid Meeting, with special reference to the Soviet Union / by Ger P. van den Berg – The right to work in East and West / by Ger P. van den Berg & Rene M.A. Guldenmund – Helsinki, Madrid, and the working conditions for western journalists in Eastern Europe / by Andre Gerrits & Joanka Prakken – Jamming of foreign radio broadcasts / by Arie Bloed & Pascale C.A.E. de Wouters d'Oplinter – The boycott of the 1980 Moscow Olympic Games and detente / by Rob C.R. Siekmann.
ISBN 9024732115 Hbk £145.00

—Ethics and mental retardation / edited by Loretta Kopelman and John C. Moskop. – Dordrecht : D. Reidel, 1984.
xvi, 258p.
Includes index.
ISBN 9027716307

—European Commission of Human Rights. Decisions and Reports, 26 Vols. / Strasbourg : Council of Europe.

—European Convention for the Prevention of Torture and Inhuman or Degrading Treatment or Punishment : the text of the Convention and explanatory report / Strasbourg : Council of Europe, 1987.
30p. – (H(87)4).
At head of front cover: Council of Europe, Human Rights.

—European Convention on Human Rights : collected texts / Convention Europeenne des Droits de l'Homme. – Dordrecht : Nijhoff, 1986.
xi,228p; 25cm.
Previous ed.: 1981. Published for the Council of Europe. Parallel English and French texts.
ISBN 9024732662 Hbk No price
ISBN 9024734010 Pbk No price

—European Convention on Human Rights : collected texts / Council of Europe : recueil de textes : Conseil de l'Europe. – 1. – Strasbourg : Council of Europe, 1981.
various pagings.
Parallel English and French texts.

—European Court of Human Rights : its organisation and working / European Court of Human Rights. – 1. – Strasbourg : Council of Europe, 1984.
various pagings. – (Press release).
'Information document issued by the Registrar of the Court'.

—European human rights reports / London : European Law Centre, 1979-.
Irregular.

—European Social Charter / Strasbourg : Council of Europe, 1961.
ISBN 9287100888 Hbk £1.00

Addendum to Conclusions 6: Iceland's First Report 1983.
ISBN 9287102287

Case-Law on the European Social Charater 1982.

Conclusions of the Committee of Independent Experts on the European Social Charter, 7 Vols.

—European Social Charter / Council of Europe. – Strasbourg : Directorate of Press and Information, 1981.
36p.

—Explanatory Report on Protocol No. 6 to the Convention for the Protection of Human Rights and Fundamental Freedoms Concerning the Abolition of the Death Penalty / Strasbourg : Council of Europe, 1983.
ISBN 9287102163

—Fire Under the Carpet / London : CENT, 1986.
ISBN 0853156549 Pbk £4.95

—Four Studies of International Humanitarian Law / Geneva : Comite International de la Croix-Rouge, 1985.
58p.

—Frontiers of Human Rights Education / Marek Thee. – Oslo : Norwegian University Press, 1985.
148p.
ISBN 8200067769 Pbk £95.00

—Human rights / Miller. – Oxford : Blackwell, 1984.
ISBN 0631136991 Pbk £6.95

—Human rights / Pike. – Bradford : Mary Glasgow, 1988.
ISBN 01852341688 Hbk £16.95

—Human Rights : A Compilation of International Instruments / United Nations. – London : HMSO, 1983.
ISBN 0119078589 Hbk £13.50

—Human rights and conditions of the people of East Timor / Senate Standing Committee on Foreign Affairs and Defence, the Parliament of the Commonwealth of Australia. – Canberra : Australian Government Publishing Service, 1983.
xvii,106p.
Includes bibliographical references.
ISBN 0644027800

—Human Rights and Disarmament / Vaclav Racek. – London : Spokesman Books, 1983.
60p.

—Human rights and human diversity : an essay in the philosophy of human rights / A.J.M. Milne. – London : Macmillan, 1986.
240p; 22cm.
Includes index.
ISBN 0333406184 £25.00

—Human rights and international relations / Cambridge : Cambridge University Press, 1987.
ISBN 0521327989 Hbk £20.00
ISBN 0521339952 Pbk £7.95

—Human Rights and Obligations / Lahore, 1980.
160p.

—Human Rights and the Law / Hilarie McMurray. – Toronto : IPI Publishing, 1980.
127p. – (In the Public Interest Ser.).
ISBN 0920702163 Pbk £6.95

—Human Rights and the Law : Teacher's Manual / Hilarie McMurray. – Toronto : IPI Publishing, 1980.
44p. – (In the Public Interest Ser.).
ISBN 0920702171 Hbk £6.25

—Human rights and the police / by J. Alderson. – Strasbourg : Council of Europe, Directorate of Human Rights, 1984.
207p.
Illustrates how awareness of concepts of human rights defined by the European Convention should affect the way police carry out duties. Training guidelines and case law examples are considered.
ISBN 9287103666 PBK £10.90

—Human Rights and U.S. Foreign Policy Under President Carter / Lagos : Nigerian Institute of International Affairs, 1980.
120p.

—Human Rights and World Peace / Enstone : Ditchley Foundation, 1981.
– (Ditchley Conference Reports).

—Human Rights First : the Child / Dandenong : Society of Those Who Have Less, 1982.

—Human rights in a state of emergency / London : Pinter, 1989.
288.
Illustrates the International Law Association's attempt to develop minimum standards for a rule of law during a state of emergency.
ISBN 0861877373 Hbk £35

—Human rights in criminal procedure : a comparative study / edited by J.A. Andrews. – The Hague : M. Nijhoff, 1981.
451p.
Revisions of papers presented at a conference organized by the United Kingdom National Committee of Comparative Law held at Manchester in Sept., 1978. Includes index.
ISBN 9024725526 Hbk £195.00

—Human Rights in Europe : Being an Account of the European Convention for the Protection of Human Rights and Fundamental Freedoms Signed in Rome on 4 November 1950 of the Protocol Thereto and of the Machinery Created Thereby : The European Commission of Human Rights and the European Court of Human Rights / Amsterdam : University Press.

—Human rights in International law / rep 1986. – Oxford : Oxford University Press, 1984.
ISBN 0198255403 Pbk £17.50

—Human Rights in International Law / New Delhi : Deep and Deep Publications, 1986.
212p.

—Human rights in prisons / by A. Reynaud. – Strasbourg : Council of Europe, Directorate of Human Rights, 1986.
218p.
Describes human rights problems prison establishments may encounter. Outlines the relevant international human rights law, in particular the European Convention on Human Rights and its case law.
ISBN 9287108811

—Human rights in the Israeli-occupied territories, 1967-1982 / Esther Rosalind Cohen. – Manchester : Manchester University Press, 1985.
xxii,500p.
Bibliography: p470-498. - Includes index.
ISBN 0719017262 £30.00

—Human Rights in the U.N. Declaration / Stockholm : Almqvist & Wiksell, 1984.
209p.
ISBN 9155415482 Pbk £110.00

—Human Rights in Urban Areas / Paris : UNESCO, 1983.
169p.
ISBN 923101983X Hbk £35.00

—Human rights : information sheet / Strasbourg : Council of Europe, 1982-.

—Human rights law-making in the United Nations / Oxford : Oxford University Press, 1986.
ISBN 0198255497 Hbk £35.00

—Human rights missions : a study of the fact-finding practice of non-governmental organizations / Hans Thoolen and Berth Verstappen. – Dordrecht : M. Nijhoff, 1986.
ISBN 9024733642 pbk.

—Human Rights : Myth and Reality / Kuala Lumpur : Intellectual Book Corner, 1987.
xxviii, 188p.

—Human rights of aliens in Europe : proceedings of the Colloquy on 'Human Rights of Aliens in Europe' / organised by the Secretariat General of the Council of Europe in co-operation with the Ministries of Justice and for Foreign Affairs of Portugal and with the Regional Government of Madeira, Funchal-Madeira (Portugal) 17-19 October 1983. – Dordrecht : Martinus Nijhoff Publishers, 1985.
x, 474p.
At head of title: Council of Europe, Human Rights Conseil de l'Europe, Droits de l'homme.
ISBN 9024732158 Hbk £225.00

—Human rights or a way of life in a democracy / by Jean-Bernard Marie. – Strasbourg : Council of Europe, 1985.
114p.
Studies the extent to which respect for human rights depends on the public and the impact of those rights on daily life.
ISBN 9287103852 PBK £3.80

—Human rights : our country in Europe : a public lecture / delivered by J.E.S. Fawcett. – London : Inns of Court School of Law, 1983.
11p; 23cm.

—Human rights reports : an annotated bibliography of fact-finding missions / by Berth Verstappen. – London : Zell, 1987.
400p; 21cm.
Includes index.
ISBN 0905450353 Hbk £45.00

—HURIDOCS standard formats for the recording and exchange of information on human rights / by Bjrn Stormorken : with the assistance of Annie McMorris. – Dordrecht : M. Nijhoff, 1985.
112p.
ISBN 9024731879 Hbk £80.00

—Image of Man in Human Rights Legislation / Rome : Herder, 1985.
243p.

—Impact of European Community law on the implementation of the European Convention on Human Rights / by Maurice Mendelson. – Strasbourg : Council of Europe, 1984.
43p.
ISBN 928710350X

—Index of International Humanitarian Law / J. Ashley Roach. – Geneva : Comite International de la Croix-Rouge, 1987.
283p.

—Indoctrination, curriculum and the law / Southampton : Association for Curriculum Development, 1988.
ISBN 185401066 Pbk £4.00

—Inter-American Yearbook on Human Rights / Organization of American States. – Dordrecht : Kluwer, 1987.
1,276p.
ISBN 0898389232 Hbk £450.00

—International enforcement of human rights : reports submitted to the Colloquium of the International Association of Legal Science, Heidelberg, 28-30 August 1985 / edited by Rudolf Bernhardt, John-Anthony Jolowicz. – Berlin : Springer-Verlag, 1987.
Includes index.
ISBN 0387175741

—International law of human rights / Oxford : Oxford University Press, 1984.
ISBN 0198760973 Pbk £21.00

—International protection of human rights / Hines. – Sweet & Maxwell, 1987.
ISBN 00720118735 Hbk £28.00

—Israel yearbook on human rights / v. – Tel Aviv : Published under the auspices of the Faculty of Law, Tel Aviv University, 1971.
ISBN 03335925

—Israel yearbook on human rights / Mala Tabory. – Dordrecht : Martinus Nijhoff, 1989.
312. – (Israel yearbook on human rights 18).
Published under the auspices of the Faculty of Law of Tel Aviv University. Contains studies on human rights in peace and war, . with particular emphasis on problems relevant to the State of Israel, and the Jewish people. Summaries of judicial decisions, and military proclamations are included.
ISBN 0792300173 Hbk £42

—Law, Legislation and Liberty / Revised edition. – Routledge, 1982.
ISBN 0710092113 Pbk £7.95

—Law, rights and the welfare state / edited by C.J.G. Sampford and D.J. Galligan. – London : Croom Helm, 1986.
xv,215p; 23cm.
Bibliography: p200-207. - Includes index.
ISBN 0709938381 £25.00

—Left and rights : a conceptual analysis of the Socialist rights / Tom Campbell. – London : Routledge & Kegan Paul, 1982.
253p.
Includes bibliographical references and index. Bibliography: p216-249.
ISBN 0710090854 pbk.

—Migrant workers and civil liberties / by Alexis Pauly and Rene Diederich. – Florence : European University Institute, 1983.
102p.

—Migrant workers in the Gulf / by Roger Owen. – London : Minority Rights Group, 1985.
23p. – (Report).
Bibliography: p.23.
ISBN 0946690332

—Moral foundation of rights / Oxford : Oxford University Press, 1987.
ISBN 0198247516 Hbk £22.50

—Moral foundation of rights / L.W. Sumner. – Oxford : Clarendon Press, 1987.
228p; 22cm.
Includes bibliography and index.
ISBN 0198247516 £22.50

—Origin and Development of International Humanitarian Law / Geneva : Comite International de la Croix-Rouge, 1982.
40p.

—Palestinians / by David McDowall. – New ed. – London : Minority Rights Group, 1987.
35p. – (Report).
Previous ed.: 1984. Includes bibliographical references.
ISBN 0946690421

—Proceedings of the Round Table with European Ombudsmen : Madrid, 5-6 June 1985 / organised by the Secretariat General of the Council of Europe in co-operation with the Spanish Defensor del Pueblo. – Strasbourg : Directorate of Human Rights, Council of Europe, 1987.
141p.
ISBN 928711000X

—Protecting Human Rights in the Americas : Selected Problems / Robert Norris. – Kehl am Rhein : Norbert Paul Engel, 1982.
xviii, 338p.
ISBN 388357015X Pbk £19.00

—Protection of human rights in Europe / Council of Europe. – New ed. – Strasbourg : Council of Europe, 1983.
16p.

—Protection of human rights in Europe / Council of Europe. – Strasbourg : Council of Europe, 1981.
16p.

—Protection of human rights in Europe : limits and effects : proceedings of the fifth International Colloquy about the European Convention on Human Rights / edited by Irene Maier. – Heidelberg : C.F. Muller Juristischer Verlag, 1982.
xviii, 378 p.; 24 cm.
Includes bibliographical references and index.
ISBN 3811411829

—Protocol No. 6 to the Convention for the Protection of Human Rights and Fundamental Freedoms Concerning the Abolition of the Death Penalty / Strasbourg : Council of Europe, 1983.
ISBN 928710235X

—Psychiatry, Human Rights and the Law / Bluglass. – Cambridge : Cambridge University Press, 1985.
ISBN 0521261945 Hbk £30.00

—Reading Nozick : essays on Anarchy, state and utopia / edited with an introduction by Jeffrey Paul. – Oxford : Basil Blackwell, 1982.
xi,418p; 22cm.
Originally published: Totowa : Rowman & Littlefield, 1981. Bibliography: p412-416.
ISBN 0631129774 Hbk Unpriced
ISBN 0631129782 Pbk Unpriced

—Republic of Korea : violations of human rights : an Amnesty International report / London : Amnesty International Publications, 1981.
43p; 30cm.
ISBN 0862100313 unbound Unpriced

—Revised rules of court (adopted on 24 November 1982) / European Court of Human Rights : Cour Europeenne des Droits de l'Homme. – Strasbourg : Council of Europe, 1983.
90p.

—Right to Communicate : a New Human Right / L.S. Harms. – Dublin : Boole Press Ltd., 1983.
xxvi, 229p.
ISBN 0906783186 Hbk £45.00
ISBN 0906783194 Pbk £30.00

—Right to Liberty and the Rights of Persons Deprived of Their Liberty as Guaranteed by Article 5 of the European Convention of Human Rights / Strasbourg : Council of Europe, 1981.

—Right to respect for private and family life, home and correspondence as guaranteed by Article 8 of the European Convention on Human Rights / by Andrew Drzemczewski. – Strasbourg : Council of Europe, Directorate of Human Rights, 1984.
29p.
ISBN 9287103526

—Rights and Statutes of the Individual in International Law / New Delhi : Deep and Deep Publications, 1984.
200p.

—Rights of Indigenous Peoples in International Law : Selected Essays on Self-Determination / Saskatoon : University of Saskatchewan, Native Law Centre, 1987.
68p.
ISBN 0888801858 Hbk £15.00

—Rights of Indigenous Peoples in International Law : Workshop Report / Saskatoon : University of Saskatchewan, Native Law Centre, 1986.
66p.
ISBN 0888801696 Hbk £15.00

—Rights of mentally ill people / Chris Heginbotham. – London : Minority Rights Group, 1987.
12p. – (Report).
ISBN 0946690499

—Rights of peoples / edited by James Crawford. – Oxford : Clarendon Press, 1988.
x,236p.
Bibliography: pp.213-232. - Includes index. Includes the texts of selected treaties, resolutions and other documents. The essays in this volume discuss the claims made for a third generation of peoples rights, including the rights of communities under colonial rule, the claims of the Aborigines in Australia, and economic rights such as the right to development, and the right to permanent sovereignty over natural resources.
ISBN 0198256248 Hbk £25

—State as defendant : governmental accountability and the redress of individual grievances / Leon Hurwitz. – London : Aldwych Press, 1981.
xv,211p.
Bibliography: p.197-203.
ISBN 0861720172

—States of emergency : their impact on human rights / a study prepared by the International Commission of Jurists. – Geneva : International Commission of Jurists, 1983.
iii,477p.
Includes bibliographical references.
ISBN 929037019X

—Structures of Injustice : a Report of a Consultation on Violations of Human Rights, held in Khartoum, Sudan from 16-22 February, 1975 / All Africa Conference of Churches. – Nairobi Westlands : All Africa Conference of Churches.
47p.

—Studies and Essays on International Humanitarian Law and Red Cross Principles, in Honour of Jean Pictet / Geneva : Comite International de la Croix-Rouge, 1984.
1,143p.

—Summaries of the judgements delivered in ... / document prepared by the registry of the Court. – v. – Strasbourg : Council of Europe, 1983.
Contains summary judgements not binding on the Court.

—Summary : 1A : the Human Rights Committee / Amnesty International. – 1. – London : Amnesty International, 1987.
various pagings.
'This is a summary of a paper with the same title'. - Cover. Includes the text of the International Covenant on Civil and Political Rights.

—Summary : 1B : the Human Rights Committee : examination of individual complaints under the optional protocol / Amnesty International. – London : Amnesty International, 1987.
71p in various pagings.
'This is a summary of a paper by the same title' - Cover. Includes the text of the International Covenant on Civil and Political Rights.

—Summary : 1C : general comments of the Human Rights Committee / Amnesty International. – London : Amnesty International, 1987.
3,7,22,8p.
'This is a summary of a paper by the same title'. - Cover. Includes the text of the International Covenant on Civil and Political Rights.

—Taxation and human rights : proceedings of a seminar held in Brussels in 1987 during the 41st Congress of the International Fiscal Association / Marc Baltus, chairman of the seminar. – Deventer, Netherlands : Kluwer Law and Taxation, 1988.
vii,83p.
ISBN 9065443843

—Teaching human rights / edited by Alice Ehr-Soon Tay in collaboration with Graeme Connelly and Roger Wilkins. – Canberra : Australian Government Publishing Service, 1981.
vi,216p.
Bibliography: p.207-208. - Includes index. Papers presented at a seminar held in the University of Sydney Law School, 20-22 June 1980. At head of title: Australian National Commission for UNESCO.
ISBN 0642067627

—Teaching of human rights : proceedings of the conference held by the Human Rights Commission and UNESCO in Adelaide, 25-27 August 1983 / Canberra : Australian Government Publishing Service, 1984.
167p. – (Occasional paper).
Bibliography: p.150-167.
ISBN 0644035714

—Theories of rights / Oxford : Oxford University Press, 1984.
ISBN 0198750633 Pbk £4.95

—Theory and practice of human rights / Smith (Maurice Temple), 1985.
ISBN 0851172563 Hbk £12.95

—Theory and practice of human rights / Leslie J. Macfarlane. – London : Temple Smith, 1985.
193p; 23cm.
Includes index.
ISBN 0851172563 £12.95

—Voices for freedom / Amnesty International. – London : Amnesty International, 1986.
208p; 27cm.
Includes index.
ISBN 086210095X Pbk No price

—Western Saharans / by Tony Hodges. – London : Minority Rights Group, 1984.
20p. – (Report).
Bibliography: p.19-20.
ISBN 0946690219

HUMAN RIGHTS – AFRICA

—Human and peoples' rights in Africa and the African Charter : report of a conference held in Nairobi from 2 to 4 December 1985 convened by the International Commission of Jurists / International Commission of Jurists. – Geneva : International Commission of Jurists, 1986.
101p.
Includes the text of the African charter on Human and Peoples' Rights.
ISBN 9290370289

—Human Rights in Africa / Apapa : Heritage Books.

—Individual under African law : proceedings of the first All-Africa Law Conference, October 11-16, 1981, Royal Swazi Spa, Swaziland / edited by Peter Nanyenya Takirambudde. – Kwaluseni (Sq) : University of Swaziland Department of Law, 1982.
iv,209p.

—International law and struggle for the freedom and welfare of man in Africa / by Itsejuwa E. Sagay. – Ile-Ife : University of Ife Press, 1983.
41p. – (Inaugural lecture series).
'An inaugural lecture delivered at the University of Ife on 3rd June, 1982'.

—International law of human rights in Africa : basic documents and annotated bibliography / compiled by M. Hamalengwa, C. Flinterman, E.V.O. Dankwa. – Dordrecht : M. Nijhoff, 1988.
xii, 427 p.; 25 cm.
Includes bibliographical references and index.
ISBN 9024735874

—Jehovah's Witnesses in Africa / by Tony Hodges. – New rev. ed. – London : Minority Rights Group, 1985.
16p. – (Report).
Previous ed. published as: Jehovah's Witnesses in Central Africa. Bibliography: p.14.
ISBN 0946690227

—New position of East Africa's Asians : problems of a displaced minority / by Yash Tandon and Arnold Raphael. – 2nd rev. ed. – London : Minority Rights Group, 1984.
20p. – (Report).
Previous ed.: 1978. Bibliography: p.20.
ISBN 0946690200

—Summary : 2 : the Organization of African Unity and human rights / Amnesty International. – London : Amnesty International, 1987.
21,10,1p.
'This is a summary of a paper by the same title'. - Cover. Bibliography: pp.17-21. Includes the text of the African Charter on Human and Peoples' Rights.

HUMAN RIGHTS – ALBANIA

—Albania : political imprisonment and the law / Amnesty International. – London : Amnesty International Publications, 1984.
58p.
ISBN 086210078X

HUMAN RIGHTS – ASIA

—Lawasia human rights bulletin / v. – Sydney : Lawasia, 1982-.

—Recent trends in human rights / Lawasia Human Rights Standing Committee. – Sydney : Law Association for Asia and the Western Pacific, 1982.
viii,112p.

HUMAN RIGHTS – AUSTRALIA

—Aboriginal reserves by-laws and human rights / Canberra : Australian Government Publishing Service, 1983.
93p. – (Occasional paper).
ISBN 0644028939

—Bill of rights for Australia? : an exposure report for the consideration of senators / Senate Standing Committee on Constitutional and Legal Affairs. – Canberra : Australian Government Publishing Service, 1985.
xi,128p.
Includes the text of the International Covenant on Civil and Political Rights. Lists treaties relating to human rights to which Australia is a party.
ISBN 0644044748

—Civil liberties in Australia / by Geoffrey A. Flick. – Sydney : Law Book Company Limited, 1981.
xxxviii,249p.
ISBN 045520084X

—Compendium of human rights courses in Australian tertiary institutions / compiled by Alex Castles and Leonie Farrell. – Canberra : Australian Government Publishing Service, 1983.
xiv,39p. – (Occasional paper).
Includes index.
ISBN 0644027649

—Epilepsy and human rights / Canberra : Australian Government Publishing Service, 1985.
144p. – (Occasional paper).
ISBN 0644038462

—Human rights and the deportation of convicted aliens and immigrants / Canberra : Australian Government Publishing Service, 1983.
vii,31p. – (Report).
ISBN 0644026367

—Human Rights and the Migrant Act / Kingston : Australian Government Publishing Service.
209p.

—Human Rights for Australia : Survey of Literature and Developments, and a Select and Annotated Bibliography of Recent Literatue in Australia and Abroad / Kingston : Australian Government Publishing Service, 1986.
360p.
ISBN 0644034327 Hbk £6.00

—Human Rights Guarantees in the Administration of Criminal Justice / L. T. Wilkins. – Canberra : Australian Institute of Criminology.

—Human Rights in the Administration of Criminal Justice : Report on the United Nations Course / Canberra : Australian Institute of Criminology.

—Individual and Democratic Rights : Report of the Advisory Committee to the Constitutional Commission / Kingston : Australian Government Publishing Service, 1987.
xx, 148p.

—Law and justice / Australian Labor Party. – s.l. : The Party, 1983.
iii,24p.
'Policy launched by Senator Gareth Evans, ... Melbourne, 23 February, 1983'.

—Lawasia human rights bulletin / v. – Sydney : Lawasia, 1982-.

—Legislating for human rights : seminar papers / Kensington, N.S.W. : University of New South Wales Faculty of Law, 1980.
ii,183p.
Organised by the University of New South Wales's Faculty of Law and the International Commission of Jurists (Australian Section).
ISBN 0858232529

—Review of Crimes Act 1914 and other crimes legislation of the Commonwealth / Human Rights Commission. – Canberra : Australian Government Publishing Service, 1983.
viii,44p. – (Report).
Includes extracts from legislation.
ISBN 0644027207

—Rights of the child / Austin Asche. – Melbourne : Institute of Family Studies, 1982.
18p. – (Discussion paper).
Includes bibliographical references. Paper delivered as the first Vernon Collins Memorial Lecture in Melbourne, 14 October, 1981.
ISBN 0642888000

—Teaching, enacting and sticking up for human rights : an evaluation report on the Human Rights Commission's 'Teaching for Human Rights: Activities for Schools'. / Colin Henry, David Hitchcock, Michelle Michie. – Canberra : Australian Government Publishing Service, 1985.
viii,83p. – (Occasional paper).
Includes bibliographical references.
ISBN 0644039639

HUMAN RIGHTS – AUSTRALIA – VICTORIA

—Report to Parliament on the desirability or otherwise of legislation defining and protecting Human rights / Legal and Constitutional Committee. – Melbourne : Government Printer, 1987.
xxiii,225p.

HUMAN RIGHTS – BANGLADESH

—Bangladesh : unlawful killings and torture in the Chittagong hill tracts / Amnesty International. – London : Amnesty International, 1986.
38p.
ISBN 0862101107

—Fundamental Rights and Personal Liberty in India, Pakistan and Bangladesh / New Delhi : Deep and Deep Publications, 1988.
480p.

HUMAN RIGHTS – BOTSWANA

—San of the Kalahari / by David Stephen. – London : Minority Rights Group, 1982.
16p. – (Report).
Includes bibliographical references.

HUMAN RIGHTS – BULGARIA

—Bulgaria : imprisonment of ethnic Turks : human rights abuses during the forced assimilation of the ethnic Turkish minority / Amnesty International. – London : Amnesty International, 1986.
40p.
ISBN 0862100976

HUMAN RIGHTS – CANADA

—Canadian Charter of Rights and Freedoms / Vancouver : University of British Columbia Law Review, 1982.
236p.
Special edition of: University of British Columbia Law Review (1982).

—Canadian charter of rights and freedoms : commentary / edited by Walter S. Tarnopolsky and Gerald-A. Beaudoin. – Toronto, Canada : Carswell, 1982.
liii, 590 p.; 26 cm.
Includes index. Bibliography: p. 563-579.
ISBN 045935230X pbk.

—Canadian Charter of Rights : law practice revolutionized / editor A. Wayne MacKay : associate editors Clare F. Beckton and Bruce H. Wildsmith. – Halifax, N.S. : Faculty of Law, Dalhousie University, 1982.
xv,391p. – (Dalhousie Continuing Legal Education Ser.: No. 22).
Jointly sponsored by Dalhousie Law School and University of Maine Law School.
ISBN 0770303226 Hbk £20.00

—Canadian charter of rights : prosecution and defence of criminal and other statutory offences / by Roderick M. McLeod ... et al. – Toronto, Canada : Carswell, 1983.
1 v. (loose-leaf); 25 cm.
ISBN 0459357409

—Canadian human rights reporter / Saskatoon : s.n., 1980.
loose-leaf; 29cm.
Supplement: Legislation and regulations.
ISBN 02262177

—Canadian Human Rights Yearbook 1986 / Agincourt : Carswell, 1986.
308p.

—Canadian Human Rights Yearbook / Daniel Proulx. – Agincourt : Carswell, 1987.
308p.

Back edition 1986

Back edition 1984-1985

Back edition 1983
This fourth annual volume of the series features current issues in the Canadian and international law of human rights. This text has been prepared under the direction of the Human Rights Research and Education Centre and the University of Ottawa.

—Canadian Human Rights Yearbook / David Proulx. – Agincourt : Carswell, 1987.
308p.

—Charter of Rights, 1987 / Vancouver : Continuing Legal Education Society of British Columbia, 1987.
299p.
ISBN 0865043116 Hbk £70.00

—Civil liberties in Canada : entering the 1980s / edited by Gerald L. Gall. – Toronto : Butterworths, 1982.
xv,259p.
Examines the changing relationship between the individual and government bureaucracy, the law relating to women and children, international aspects of civil liberties, and the codification of rights in the Charter. Contains a historical perspective, a modern appraisal, current issues, and speculations for the future.
ISBN 0409832146

—Civil Rights : the Law, the Police, and You / 8th ed. – North Vancouver : International Self-Counsel Press, 1985.
228p.
ISBN 0889086222 Hbk £8.95

—Courts and the Charter / Clare F. Beckton and A. Wayne MacKay, research coordinators. – Toronto : University of Toronto Press in cooperation with the Royal Commission on the Economic Union and Development Prospects for Canada and the Canadian Government Publishing Centre, 1985.
xv,279p. – (Collected research studies).
Includes bibliographies.
ISBN 0802073050

—Equality Rights and the Canadian Charter of Rights and Freedoms / Mary Eberts. – Agincourt : Carswell, 1985.
600p.

—Fragile Freedoms : Human Rights and Dissent in Canada / Richmond Hill : Irwin Publishing Inc..
298p.
ISBN 0772013586 Hbk £17.95
ISBN 0772013772 Pbk £9.95

—Human Rights and Freedoms in Canada : Cases, Notes and Materials / William Pentney. – Butterworths, 1987.
672p.
ISBN 0409813087 Pbk £80.00

—Human Rights and Social Policy in Newfoundland 1832-1982 : Search for a Just Society / St. John's : Harry Cuff Publications Ltd., 1985.
256p.
ISBN 0919095798 Pbk £14.95

—Justice beyond Orwell / edited by Rosalie S. Abella and Melvin L. Rothman : Institut canadien dadministration de la justice : Canadian Institute for the Administration of Justice. – Montreal : Yvon Blais, 1985.
516p.
Includes bibliographical references.
ISBN 2890735540

—Law of the Charter : general principles / Dale Gibson. – Toronto : Carswell, 1986.
xxxiii,302p.
ISBN 0459389009

—Legal rights in the Canadian Charter of Rights and Freedoms : a manual of issues and sources / David C. McDonald. – Toronto : Carswell, 1982.
xxv,275p.
Includes index.

—Origin of rights / by Roger E. Salhany. – Toronto : Carswell, 1986.
viii, 175 p.; 24 cm.
Includes index. Bibliography: p. 163-171.
ISBN 045938760X pbk.

—The Origins of Rights / Agincourt : Carswell, 1986.
186p.
This work traces the historical and legal development of such fundamental freedoms as freedom of religion; freedom of the press; freedom from arbitrary detention and search and seizure; freedom from self incrimination; and the right to counsel.

—Proposals on custody, parental guardianship, and the civil rights of minors : report to the Attorney General / from the Law Reform Commission of Saskatchewan. – Saskatoon : Law Reform Commission of Saskatchewan, 1981.
iv,40p.

—Quest for Justice : Aboriginal Peoples and Aboriginal Rights / Toronto : University of Toronto Press, 1985.
ISBN 0802025722 Hbk £45.00
ISBN 0802065899 Pbk £17.50

—Righting the Balance : Canada's New Equality Rights / Agincourt : Carswell, 1986.
450p.

—Rights, freedoms and the courts : a practical analysis of the Constitution Act, 1982 / Morris Manning. – Toronto : Emond-Montgomery, 1983.
lxiv,760p.
Includes the text of the Act.
ISBN 0920722105

—Toward equality : the response to the report of the Parliamentary Committee on Equality Rights / Ottawa, Ont. : Communications and Public Affairs, Dept. of Justice Canada, 1986.
65, 69 p.; 28 cm.
English and French. Title on added t.p.: Cap sur l'egalite.
ISBN 0662543181 pbk.

—When Freedoms Collide : the Case for Our Civil Liberties / Toronto : Lester & Orpen Dennys, 1988.
384p.
ISBN 0886191890 Hbk £27.95

HUMAN RIGHTS - CANADA - BRITISH COLUMBIA

—Human Rights in B.C. / Vancouver : Continuing Legal Education Society of British Columbia, 1985.
132p.
ISBN 086504239X Hbk £55.00

—Recommendations for changes to the Human Rights Code of British Columbia / Human Rights Commission of British Columbia. – Victoria, B.C. : The Commission, 1981.
22p.

HUMAN RIGHTS - CANADA - ONTARIO

—Charter of Rights and administrative law, 1983-1984 / section head, Garry J. Smith. – Agincourt, Ont. : Carswell Legal Publications, 1983.
xxix, 184 p.; 29 cm. – (Bar admission course materials / Law Society of Upper Canada).
Includes index. Bibliography: p. 173-179.
ISBN 0459360906

—Handbook to the Ontario Human Rights Code / Connie Nakatsu. – Agincourt : Carswell, 1988.
250p.
This book focuses on issues pertinent to the Ontario Human Rights Code. Topics include policy of the code, prohibited grounds and areas of discrimination, processing a human rights complaint, jurisdiction of the commission, evidence required in human rights cases, findings and awards by Board of Inquiry, review and enforcement of board decisions and alternate remedies.

—Human rights in Ontario / by Judith Keene. – Toronto : Carswell, 1983.
xxxv,367p.
Includes bibliographical references and index. Includes text of the Human Rights Code, 1981.
ISBN 0459354604

HUMAN RIGHTS - CARIBBEAN

—Civil rights with special reference to the Commonwealth Caribbean : a select bibliography / Velma Newton. – Cave Hill, Barbados : Institute of Social and Economic Research (Eastern Caribbean), University of the West Indies, 1981.
110p. – (Occasional bibliography series).
Includes index.

—International human rights law in the Commonwealth Caribbean / edited for the International Center for the Legal Protection of Human Rights (Interights) by Angela D. Byre. – Dordrecht : Martinus Nijhoff, 1989.
408. – (International Studies in Human Rights).
Collection of papers concerning the protection of human rights under Bills of Rights in Commonwealth Carribean countries and under regional and international human rights treaties. Demonstrates the relevance of international human rights law in domestic cases and considers practical ways of strengthening human rights protection.
ISBN 9024737850 Hbk Gld150.00

HUMAN RIGHTS - CHILE

—Chile : Amnesty International briefing / Amnesty International. – London : Amnesty International, 1986.
22p.

—Chile : evidence of torture / Amnesty International. – London : Amnesty International Publications, 1983.
75p.
ISBN 0862100534

HUMAN RIGHTS - CHINA

—China : violations of human rights : prisoners of conscience and the death penalty in the People's Republic of China / Amnesty International. – London : Amnesty International Publications, 1984.
129p.
ISBN 0862100739

—Human rights in the People's Republic of China / Westview Press, 1988.
ISBN 0813374391 Hbk £29.95

HUMAN RIGHTS - CZECHOSLOVAKIA

—Charter 77 and human rights in Czechoslovakia / H. Gordon Skilling. – London : Allen & Unwin, 1981.
xv,363p; 24cm.
Bibliography: p345-351. - Includes index.
ISBN 0043210260 Unpriced

—Czechoslovakia / Amnesty International. – 2nd ed. – London : Amnesty International, 1981.
17p. – (Amnesty International Briefing).

HUMAN RIGHTS - EGYPT

—Egypt : violations of human rights / an Amnesty International report. – London : Amnesty International Publications, 1983.
38p.
ISBN 0862100526

HUMAN RIGHTS - ENGLAND

—Civil liberties : cases and materials / S.H. Bailey, D.J. Harris, B.L. Jones. – 2nd ed. – London : Butterworths, 1985.
xxxvii, 612p.
ISBN 040655482X

—Freedom, the individual and the law / H. Street. – 5th ed. – Harmondsworth, Eng. : Penguin Books, 1982.
352p. – (Pelican Books).
ISBN 0140206469

—Public order : a guide to the 1986 Public Order Act / by John Marston. – London : Fourmat Publishing, 1987.
189p.
ISBN 1851900241

—Public rights and private interests / J. A. G. Griffith. – Trivandrum : Academy of Legal Publications, 1981.
12196,iv.

HUMAN RIGHTS - EUROPE

—European Commission of Human Rights : Decisions and Reports / European Commission of Human Rights. – London : HMSO.

—European Human Rights Convention on Domestic Law / Oxford : Oxford University Press, 1983.
ISBN 019825525X Pbk £12.50

—Europeans, You Have Rights / Luxembourg : Office for Official Publications of the European Communities, 1987.
48p.
ISBN 9282566854 Pbk

—Lights on human rights / by Sir James Fawcett. – Strasbourg : Council of Europe, 1987.
13p. – (H(87)1).
'Prepared at the request of the Committee of Experts for the Promotion of Education and Information in the Field of Human Rights of the Council of Europe'. - t.p..

HUMAN RIGHTS - EUROPEAN COMMUNITY

—European Convention on Human Rights and Fundamental Freedoms : cases and materials : a reader for students of the international law of human rights / edited by Herbert Petzold. – 3rd ed. – Strasbourg : International Institute of Human Rights, 1980.
ix,404p.

—European protection of human rights : the practice and procedure of the European Commission of Human Rights on the admissibility of applications from individuals and states / Laurids Mikaelsen. – Alphen aan den Rijn. : Sijthoff & Noordhoff, 1980.
xiii, 273 p.; 25 cm.
Bibliography: p. 247-250.
ISBN 902860409X fl 85.00

—Fundamental rights and the EEC / by David Sugarman. – London : Middlesex Polytechnic Faculty of Business Studies and Management, 1981.
34p. – (Working paper).
ISBN 0904804119

—Right to strike in Community law : the incorporation of fundamental rights in the legal order of the European Communities / by Lammy Betten. – Amsterdam : North-Holland, 1985.
xviii, 319p.
At head of title: T.M.C. Asser Instituut, The Hague. Includes index. Bibliography: p.291-306.
ISBN 0444878459

HUMAN RIGHTS - FIJI

—Fiji / Professor Hugh Tinker et al. – London : Minority Rights Group, 1987.
15p. – (Report).
ISBN 0946690545

HUMAN RIGHTS - FINLAND

—Finland and the international norms of human rights / K. Tornudd. – Dordrecht : M. Nijhoff, 1986.
Bibliography.
ISBN 9024732573

HUMAN RIGHTS - GHANA

—Human rights in Ghana : report of a mission / by Cees Flinterman for the International Commission of Jurists and Netherlands Committee for Human Rights. – Utrecht : SIM, 1984.
47 p.; 21 cm.
ISBN 9290370254 pbk.

HUMAN RIGHTS - GREAT BRITAIN

—Abuse of power : civil liberties in the United Kingdom / Patricia Hewitt. - Oxford : Robertson, 1982.
xiv,295p; 24cm.
Bibliography: p267-279. - Includes index.
ISBN 085520379X Hbk £15.00
ISBN 0855203803 Pbk £4.95

—Basic Documents On Human Rights / 2nd ed. - Oxford : Oxford University Press, 1981.
ISBN 0198761252 Pbk £14.95

—Bill of Rights? / Michael Zander. - 3rd ed. - London : Sweet & Maxwell, 1985.
viii,105p; 22cm.
Previous ed.: Chichester : Rose for the British Institute of Human Rights, 1979. Bibliography: p92-93.
ISBN 0421345101 Pbk £3.50

—Cases and materials on civil liberties / by Paul O'Higgins. - London : Sweet & Maxwell, 1980.
xxxv,482p; 26cm.
Bibliography: pxxxi-xxxiii. - Includes index.
ISBN 042125050X Hbk £17.25
ISBN 0421250607 Pbk £14.25

—Civil Liberties 1984 / Oxford : Blackwell, 1984.
ISBN 0855207027 Pbk £7.50

—Civil Liberties / London : Butterworths, 1988.
ISBN 0406555109 Hbk
ISBN 0406555117 Pbk

—Civil Liberties - Cases and Materials / Harris. - 2nd ed. - London : Butterworths, 1985.
ISBN 040655482X Hbk £33.00
ISBN 0406554838 Pbk £19.95

—Civil liberties in conflict / edited by Larry Gostin. - London : Routledge, 1988.
xix,215p.
Includes bibliographical references and index.
ISBN 0415006805 pbk.

—Civil Liberties in Conflict / London : Tavistock Publications, 1988.
ISBN 042260450X Pbk £8.95
ISBN 0422624209 Hbk £25.00

—Enacting a bill of rights : the legal problems / Joseph Jaconelli. - Oxford : Clarendon Press, 1980.
xi,328p; 23cm.
Includes index.
ISBN 0198253516 £14.00

—Foreign Policy and Human Rights / Cambridge : Cambridge University Press, 1986.
ISBN 0521323967 Hbk £25.00

—Human rights : from rhetoric to reality / edited by Tom Campbell ... et al. - Oxford : Blackwell, 1986.
vi,280p; 23cm.
Discusses issues involved in the argument for a British bill of rights.
ISBN 0631143610 Hbk £25.00 :
ISBN 0631143629 Pbk £9,50

—Human rights in the United Kingdom / prepared by Reference Division, Central Office of Information. - London : H.M.S.O., 1984.
3,50p; 24cm.
Bibliography: p.49-50.
ISBN 0117009857 sd £1.25

—Independent schools and the European Convention on Human Rights : a joint opinion / by Anthony Lester and David Pannick. - London : ISIS, 1982.
16p.
Published on behalf of The Association of Governing Bodies of Public Schools and The Association of Governing Bodies of Girls' Public Schools.

—Judicial protection of fundamental rights under English law / by J. A. Jolowicz. The infiltration of equity into English commercial law / by G. Jones. - Deventer, The Netherlands : Kluwer, 1980.
- (The Cambridge-Tilburg law lectures ; 2d ser., 1979).
ISBN 9026811667

—Know how : to find out your rights / Grainne Morby. - London : Pluto, 1982.
188p; 20cm.
Includes index.
ISBN 0861043596 Pbk £3.95

—Outsider : newsletter of the Minority Rights Group / London : The Group, 1984.
Continues: Newsletter.

—Preserving freedom under the law : being the presidential address of the Rt. Hon. Lord Bridge of Harwich, President of the Holdsworth Club of the Faculty of Law in the University of Birmingham, 1981-82 / Birmingham : Holdsworth Club, 1982.
14p. - (Holdsworth Club Presidential Address 1982).
ISBN 0704406179

—Prevention of Terrorism Act : the case for repeal / Catherine Scorer and Patricia Hewitt. - London : National Council for Civil Liberties, 1981.
68p; 20cm.
ISBN 0901108944 Pbk £1.75

—Protection of liberty / I.N. Stevens & D.C.M. Yardley. - Oxford : Basil Blackwell, 1982.
x,188p; 24cm.
Examines the extent to which incursions are made on our civil liberties.
ISBN 0631129448 Hbk £15.00
ISBN 0631131760 Pbk £5.95

—Providing civil justice for children / Hugh Geach and Elizabeth Szwed. - London : Edward Arnold, 1983.
250p; 22cm.
Includes bibliographies and index.
ISBN 071316400X Pbk £9.95

—Public interest law / edited by Jeremy Cooper and Rajeev Dhavan. - Oxford : Basil Blackwell, 1986.
xviii,482p.
Discusses the conflict between rights and duties of individuals and public interest in the legal system.
ISBN 0631142991 £25.00

—Right to strike in Britain/ the English floating charge / K D Ewing, R M Goode. - Kluwer Law and Taxation, 1989.
72. - (Lectures on the common law).
Covers the position under the common law, protection of the trade unions from the common law, legislation and the individual striker, the foundation of security, the priority of security interests, and the second creditors rights over the assets given in security.
ISBN 9065444114 Pbk £15/Dfl 48

—Rights / Oxford : Oxford University Press, 1984.
ISBN 0198249233 Pbk £6.95

—Rights and wrongs of children / M.D.A. Freeman. - London : Pinter, 1983.
295p; 24cm.
Includes index.
ISBN 0903804204 Hbk Unpriced
ISBN 0861872266 Pbk Unpriced

—Rights of children / edited by Bob Franklin. - Oxford : Blackwell, 1986.
x,237p; 24cm.
Includes index.
ISBN 063114711X Hbk £22.50
ISBN 0631147128 Pbk £7.95

—Social control and the state : historical and comparative essays / edited by Stanley Cohen and Andrew Scull. - Oxford : Basil Blackwell, 1985.
vii,341p; 23cm.
Survey of the way society maintains conformity and responds to deviance. Discusses state, class and individual power, legal repression and civil rights and role of reform movements in producing social change.
ISBN 0631142614

—Stonehenge : a report into the civil liberties implications of the events relating to the convoys of summer 1985 and 1986 / National Council for Civil Liberties. - London : National Council for Civil Liberties, 1986.
43p.
ISBN 0946088284

HUMAN RIGHTS - GREAT BRITAIN - SCOTLAND

—Civil liberties in Scotland: cases and materials / W Finnie. - 2nd. - Edinburgh : W Green & Son, 1988.
Covers law on liberty and police powers, freedom from discrimination, freedom of religion, of expression and of assembly. There are special chapters on the European Convention on Human Rights and Privacy.
ISBN 0414008448

HUMAN RIGHTS - GREECE

—Greek case before the Commission of Human Rights of the Council of Europe / Greece. - Athens : R. Ministry of Foreign Affairs, 1970.
v.; 27 cm.
Contents: v. 1. The report of the Commission of Human Rights: unfounded conclusions based on an illegal procedure.

HUMAN RIGHTS - HAITI

—Haiti : Amnesty International briefing / Amnesty International. - London : Amnesty International, 1985.
14p; ill.
ISBN 086210081X

HUMAN RIGHTS - HONG KONG

—Civil liberties in Hong Kong / editor, Raymond Wacks : contributors, Johannes Chan ... et al. - Hong Kong : Oxford University Press, 1988.
Includes index and bibliography.
ISBN 0195827244 £35.00

HUMAN RIGHTS - INDIA

—Competing equalities : law and the backward classes in India / Marc Galanter. - Berkeley : University of California Press, 1984.
xxii,625p; 24cm.
Bibliography: p575-611. - Includes index.
ISBN 0520042891 Pbk £38.25

—Fundamental Rights and Personal Liberty in India, Pakistan and Bangladesh / New Delhi : Deep and Deep Publications, 1988.
480p.

—Human rights in India / R.C. Hingorani. - New Delhi : Oxford & IBH, 1985.
vii, 181 p.; 22 cm.
Includes bibliographical references and index.
ISBN 8120400208 Rs95.00

—Implementation of human rights covenants : with special reference to India / H.O. Agarwal. - Allahabad : Kitab Mahal, 1983.
x,210p.
Includes index. Includes the text of the International Covenant on Economic, Social and Cultural Rights and the International Covenant on Civil and Political Rights.

—Nagaland File : A Question of Human Rights / Nandita Haksar. - New Delhi : Lancer International, 1984.
277p.

—Protection of Civil Rights Act / 2nd ed. - Allahabad : Law Book Company, 1986.

HUMAN RIGHTS - INDONESIA

—East Timor and West Irian / by Keith Suter. - Rev. ed. - London : Minority Rights Group, 1982.
24p. - (Reports).
Previous ed. published 1979, as: West Irian, East Timor and Indonesia. Bibliography: p.24.

—Indonesia and the rule of law: twenty years of 'New Order' government / Hans Thoolen. - Pinter, 1987.
224.
Sets out the constitutional provisions and legislation relating to human rights and assesses their practical application.
ISBN 0861879198 Hbk £29.50

HUMAN RIGHTS - IRAN

—Kurds / by David McDowall. - New ed. - London : Minority Rights Group, 1985.
32p. - (Report).
Previous ed.: by Martin Short and Anthony McDermott. 1981. Bibliography: p.24.
ISBN 094669026X

—Law and human rights in the Islamic Republic of Iran : a report covering events within the seven month period following the Revolution of February 1979 / Amnesty International. - London : Amnesty International, 1980.
216p.

HUMAN RIGHTS - IRAQ

—Report and recommendations of an Amnesty International mission to the government of the Republic of Iraq, 22-28 January 1983, including the government's response and Amnesty International comments / Amnesty International. - s.l. : Amnesty International, 1983.
74p.
ISBN 0862100615

HUMAN RIGHTS - JAPAN

—Freedom, peace and their guarantees, from the viewpoint of the Constitution of Japan / Kenji Urata. - s.l. : s.n., 1982.
p.22-45.
'Originally presented as a draft to the Waseda University Centennial International Symposium at Waseda University on August 22 and 23, 1982'. Reprinted from: Waseda bulletin of comparative law, v.2 (1982).

—Human rights and mental patients in Japan : report of a mission by Dr. T. W. Harding, Judge J. Schneider, Dr. H. M. Visotsky and Dr. C. L. Graves on behalf of the International Commission of Jurists and the International Commission of Health Professionals / T.W. Harding. - Geneva : International Commission of Jurists, 1985.
94p.
Bibliography: p.87-93.
ISBN 9290370327

HUMAN RIGHTS - KOREA (SOUTH)

—South Korea : violations of human rights / Amnesty International. - London : Amnesty International Publications, 1986.
109p,18p. of plates.
ISBN 086210100X

HUMAN RIGHTS - NAMIBIA
—Namibians / by Peter Fraenkel and Roger Murray : with additional material by Kaye Stearman. – New ed. – London : Minority Rights Group, 1985.
31p. – (Report).
Bibliography: p.31.
ISBN 0946690278

—San of the Kalahari / by David Stephen. – London : Minority Rights Group, 1982.
16p. – (Report).
Includes bibliographical references.

HUMAN RIGHTS - NEW ZEALAND
—Bill of Rights for New Zealand : a white paper / presented to the House of Representatives by leave by the Hon. Geoffrey Palmer, Minister of Justice. – Wellington : Goverment Printer, 1985.
157p.
Bibliography: p.119-123.

—Bill of Rights for New Zealand : papers precsented by A. Sharp ... et al. / A. Sharp. – Auckland : Legal Research Foundation, 1985.
216p.
At head of title: Legal Research Foundation Inc. Seminar, 16 August, 1985.
ISBN 0908581386

—Maori of New Zealand / by Robert Macdonald. – London : Minority Rights Group, 1985.
16p. – (Report).
Bibliography: p.16.
ISBN 0946690367

—New Zealand Civil Rights Handbook / Wellington : Butterworths, 1980.
624p.
ISBN 0409600970 Pbk

—Standard for justice : a critical commentary on the proposed Bill of Rights for New Zealand / Jerome Elkind and Antony Shaw : with a foreword by P.T. Mahon. – Auckland : Oxford University Press, 1986.
xvi,238p.
Includes index.
ISBN 019558144X

HUMAN RIGHTS - NICARAGUA
—Nicaragua : the human rights record / Amnesty International. – London : Amnesty International, 1986.
36p; 27cm.
ISBN 0862100941 Pbk No price

HUMAN RIGHTS - NIGERIA
—Fundamental rights in Nigeria / Hari Chand : foreword by A. Obi Okoye. – Jos : Unico Press, 1980.
96p; 25cm.
Includes index. On verso of title page: 'The author himself is the publisher of this book'.

HUMAN RIGHTS - PACIFIC ISLANDS
—Recent trends in human rights / Lawasia Human Rights Standing Committee. – Sydney : Law Association for Asia and the Western Pacific, 1982.
viii,112p.

HUMAN RIGHTS - PAKISTAN
—Fundamental Rights and Personal Liberty in India, Pakistan and Bangladesh / New Delhi : Deep and Deep Publications, 1988.
480p.

—Pakistan : human rights violations and the decline of the rule of law / an Amnesty International report. – London : Amnesty International, 1982.
57p; 30cm.
ISBN 0862100410

HUMAN RIGHTS - PERU
—Peru : 'disappearances', torture and summary executions by government forces after the prison revolts of June 1986 / Amnesty International. – London : Amnesty International, 1987.
ii,71p.
ISBN 0862101166

HUMAN RIGHTS - PHILIPPINE ISLANDS
—Report of an Amnesty International mission to the Republic of the Philippines 11-28 November 1981 / Amnesty International. – London : Amnesty International Publications, 1982.
ii,127p.
Includes bibliographical references.
ISBN 086210050X

HUMAN RIGHTS - PHILIPPINES
—Philippines: human rights after martial law / report of a mission by Virginia Leary, A.A. Ellis, Kurt Madlener. – Geneva : International Commission of Jurist, 1984.
123p.
Includes bibliographical references.
ISBN 9290370238

HUMAN RIGHTS - ROMANIA
—Romania / Amnesty International. – London : Amnesty International, 1980.
19p.

HUMAN RIGHTS - SCANDINAVIA
—Sami of Lapland / by Mervyn Jones. – London : Minority Rights Group, 1981.
15p. – (Report).
Bibliography: p.15.

HUMAN RIGHTS - SCOTLAND
—Civil liberties in Scotland : cases & materials / K.D. Ewing & W. Finnie. – Edinburgh : Green, 1982.
xiv,285p.
Includes index.
ISBN 0414007069

—Your rights : a guide to civil liberties in Scotland / Contributors: Lynda Clark and others. Editor: Paul Gordon. – Edinburgh : EUSPB; Polygon Books, 1980.
xii,210p.
ISBN 0904919420

HUMAN RIGHTS - SENEGAL
—Freedom of information and expression in Senegal / a commentary by Article 19 on the report submitted to the United Nations Human Rights Committee by the government of the Republic of Senegal. – London : Article 19, 1987.
30p.
Bibliography: p.30.

HUMAN RIGHTS - SOUTH AFRICA
—Freedom, state security and the rule of law : dilemmas of the apartheid society / Anthony S. Mathews. – Cape Town : Juta, 1986.
xxv,312p.
Bibliography: p.xi-xiv. - Includes index.
ISBN 0702118125

—Human rights and the rule of law / Geoffrey Brindman. – Pinter, 1988.
164.
Report of a mission sent to South Africa by the Internaitonal Commission of Jurists. Gives a detailed account of the legislation used to frustrate human rights.
ISBN 0861879791 Hbk £30
ISBN 0861877799 Pbk £9.95

—Indian South Africans / by Frene Ginwala. – New ed. – London : Minority Rights Group, 1985.
20p. – (Report).
Includes bibliographical references.
ISBN 0946690294

—Legislation and civil liberties in South Africa / A.S. Mathews. – S.l. : s.n., 1984.
p.10-15.

—Security, terrorism, and torture : detainees' rights in South Africa and Israel : a comparative study / by Harold Rudolph. – Cape Town : Juta, 1984.
xviii, 270 p.; 22 cm.
Includes indexes. Bibliography: p. 253-259.
ISBN 0702115088 pbk. R38.00

—South African journal on human rights / Braamfontein : Ravan Press, 1985.

HUMAN RIGHTS - SOUTHEAST ASIA
—Rural development and human rights in South East Asia : report of a seminar in Penang, December 1981 / organized by the International Commission of Jurists and Consumers' Association of Penang. – Geneva : International Commission of Jurists, 1982.
254p.
ISBN 9290370173

HUMAN RIGHTS - SRI LANKA
—'Disappearances' in Sri Lanka / Amnesty International. – London : Amnesty International, 1986.
89p.
ISBN 0862101085

—Tamils of Sri Lanka / by Walter Schwarz. – 3rd rev ed. – London : Minority Rights Group, 1986.
15p. – (Report).
Previous edition: 1983.
ISBN 0946690375

HUMAN RIGHTS - SWEDEN
—Human rights in Sweden : the annual reports 1982-1984 from the national correspondent for Sweden to the Documentation Center for Human Rights at the Directorate for Human Rights, Council of Europe / Jacob W.F. Sundberg. – Stockholm : Institutet for offentlig och internationell ratt, 1985.
ix,118p. – (Publications).
Includes bibliographical references and index.
ISBN 9103487806

—Implementing the European Convention on Human Rights in Sweden : the Boll discussion / by Jacob W. F. Sundberg. – Stockholm : s.n., 1983.
14,9 leaves.
Includes bibliographical references.

HUMAN RIGHTS - SYRIA
—Report from Amnesty International to the government of the Syrian Arab Republic / Amnesty International. – s.l. : Amnesty International, 1983.
ii,65p.
ISBN 0862100585

HUMAN RIGHTS - UNITED STATES
—Civil liberties in conflict / edited by Larry Gostin. – London : Routledge, 1988.
xix,215p.
Includes bibliographical references and index.
ISBN 0415006805 pbk.

—Fundamental liberties and rights : a 50-State index / by Barbara Faith Sachs : Legislative Drafting Research Fund of Columbia University. – London : Oceana Publications, 1980.
1 v.; 27 cm.
Index to Constitutions of the United States, national and State. 'First in a series of subject matter indices designed to replace the Index digest of State constitutions.'. Loose-leaf for updating.
ISBN 0379204134 £35.00

—Natural rights and natural law : the legacy of George Mason / edited by Robert P. Davidow. – 1. – Fairfax, Va. : George Mason University Press, 1987.
23cm.
Includes index.
ISBN 080260000X Hbk £17.95 (Mar.)
ISBN 0802600018 Pbk £11.95

—Origin of rights / by Roger E. Salhany. – Toronto : Carswell, 1986.
viii, 175 p.; 24 cm.
Includes index. Bibliography: p. 163-171.
ISBN 045938760X pbk.

—Original Americans : U.S. Indians / by James Wilson. – New ed. – London : Minority Rights Group, 1986.
24p. – (Report).
Previous edition: 1980. Bibliography: p.24.
ISBN 0946690391

—Protecting human rights in the Americas : selected problems / Thomas Buergenthal, Robert Norris, Dinah Shelton. – 2nd rev ed. – Kehl, W. Germany : Engel, 1986.
xviii,389p.
Previous ed.: 1982. Bibliography: pp.315-322. - Includes index. Includes the texts of the Charter of the Organization of American States, the American Convention on Human Rights and other basic documents.
ISBN 3883570559

—Values in conflict : life, liberty, and the rule of law / compiled by Burton M. Leiser. – London : Collier Macmillan, 1981.
xii,478p; 24cm.
ISBN 002369520X Pbk £7.50

HUMAN RIGHTS - USSR
—Crimean Tatars, Volga Germans and Meskhetians : Soviet treatment of some national minorities / Bohdan Nahaylo. – 2nd rev. ed. – London : Minority Rights Group, 1980.
28p. – (Report).
Previous ed.: 1973. Bibliography: p.28.

—Ukrainians and Georgians / by Bohdan Nahaylo and C.J. Peters. – London : Minority Rights Group, 1981.
20p. – (Report).
Bibliography: p.20.

HUMAN RIGHTS - VIETNAM
—Report of an Amnesty International mission to the Socialist Republic of Viet Nam, 10-21 December 1979 : including memoranda exchanged between the government and Amnesty International / Amnesty International. – London : Amnesty International, 1981.
ii,42p.
ISBN 086210033X

HUMAN RIGHTS - WEST GERMANY
—Rights, institutions and impact of international law according to the German Basic Law : the contribution of the Federal Republic of Germany to the Second World Congress of the International Association of Constitutional law / edited by Christian Starck. – Baden-Baden : Nomos, 1987.
264p.
Includes bibliographical references and index.
ISBN 3789013749

HUMAN RIGHTS - YUGOSLAVIA
—Yugoslavia : prisoners of conscience : an Amnesty International report / Amnesty International. – London : Amnesty International, 1982.
50p.
ISBN 0862100437

HUMAN RIGHTS - ZAIRE
—Zaire : reports of torture and killings committed by the armed forces in Shaba region / Amnesty International. – London : Amnesty International, 1986.
24p.
ISBN 0862100968

HUMAN RIGHTS - ZAMBIA

—Civil liberties cases in Zambia / compiled by Muna Ndulo and Kaye Turner. – Oxford : African Law Reports, 1984.
xxii,579p; 24cm.
Includes index.
ISBN 0903826704 Hbk No price
ISBN 0903826712 Pbk No price

HUMAN RIGHTS - ZIMBABWE

—Inequalities in Zimbabwe / by Christopher Hitchens and David Stephen : with a foreword by Garfield Todd. – Rev. ed. – London : Minority Rights Group, 1981.
20p. – (Report).
Previous ed.: 1979. Bibliography: p.20.

HUMAN RIGHTS (INTERNATIONAL LAW)

—Application of the European Convention on Human Rights / by J.E.S. Fawcett. – 2nd ed. – Oxford : Clarendon, 1987.
xiii,444p; 22cm.
Previous ed.: 1969. Includes index.
ISBN 0198255101 Hbk £25.00
ISBN 0198255098 Pbk £15.00

—Application of the rule of exhaustion of local remedies in international law : its rationale in the international protection of individual rights / A.A. Cancado Trindade. – Cambridge Cambridgeshire : Cambridge University Press, 1983.
xiii,443p.
Includes index. Bibliography: p422-440.
ISBN 0521229472

—Basic documents on human rights / edited by Ian Brownlie. – 2nd ed. – Oxford : Clarendon Press, 1981.
x,505p; 24cm.
Previous ed.: 1971. Includes index.
ISBN 0198761244 Hbk £22.50
ISBN 0198761252 Pbk Unpriced

—The Bulletin : a report on developments ... relative to Third Basket issues of the Final Act of the Conference on Security and Cooperation in Europe / North Atlantic Assembly, Committtee on education, cultural affairs and information, Sub-committee on the free flow of information. – v. – Brussels : International Secretariat of the North Atlantic Assembly, 1976.
English edition.

—Conceptual thinking about the individual in international law / Rosalyn Higgins. – S.l. : s.n., 1981.
19p; 25cm.
Photocopy from: British Journal of International Studies 4 (1978).

—Development of international humanitarian law / by Geza Herczegh. – Budapest : Akademiai Kiado, 1984.
239p.
Bibliography: p231-235.
ISBN 9630534487

—Directory of human rights information and documentation facilities in the field of human rights in western Europe / 1. – London : Human Rights International Documentation System, 1982.
various pagings.
Includes index.

—Effects of the various international human rights instruments providing a mechanism for individual communications on the machinery of protection established under the European Convention on Human Rights : Secretariat memorandum / prepared by the Directorate of Human Rights of the Council of Europe. – Strasburg : Council of Europe, 1985.
25p. – (H(85)3).

—Equality and discrimination under international law / Warwick McKean. – Oxford : Clarendon, 1983.
ix,333p; 23cm.
Includes index.
ISBN 0198253117 £30.00

—Etudes et essais sur le droit international humanitaire et sur les principes de la Croix-Rouge en l'honneur de Jean Pictet : Studies and essays on international humanitarian law and Red Cross principles in honour of Jean Pictet / Christophe Swinarski, redacteur. – The Hague : Martinus Nijhoff, 1984.
English and French. Bibliography.
ISBN 9024730791 Pbk £150.00

—European human rights convention in domestic law : a comparative study / Andrew Z. Drzemczewski. – Oxford : Clarendon, 1983.
xiv,372p; 23cm.
Bibliography: p348-360. - Includes index.
ISBN 0198253966 Unpriced

—Finland and the international norms of human rights / K. Tornudd. – Dordrecht : M. Nijhoff, 1986.
Bibliography.
ISBN 9024732573

—Greek case before the Commission of Human Rights of the Council of Europe / Greece. – Athens : R. Ministry of Foreign Affairs, 1970.
v.; 27 cm.
Contents: v. 1. The report of the Commission of Human Rights: unfounded conclusions based on an illegal procedure.

—Guide to international human rights practice / edited for the International Human Rights Law Group by Hurst Hannum. – London : Macmillan, 1984.
xvi,310p; 24cm.
ISBN 0333370767

—Guide to the 'travaux preparatoires' of the International Covenant on Civil and Political Rights / Marc J. Bossuyt. – Dordrecht : M. Nijhoff, 1987.
Includes text of the covenant. Includes index. Bibliography.
ISBN 9024734673

—Human rights and Europe : a study of the machinery of human rights protection of the Council of Europe / by Ralph Beddard. – 2nd ed. – London : Sweet & Maxwell, 1980.
vii,217p; 20cm.
Previous ed.: 1973. Bibliography: p212. - Includes index.
ISBN 0421264403 Hbk £12.00
ISBN 0421264500 Pbk £8.25

—Human rights and foreign policy / Evan Luard. – S.l. : s.n., 1986.
p.579-606.
Photocopy from: International affairs, vol. 56, no. 4 (Autumn 1980).

—Human rights and humanitarian norms as customary law / Oxford : OUP, 1989.
320.
Looks at the relationship between human rights/humanitarian norms and customary law, also between human rights/humanitarian norms and the law of state responsibility. Examines how contemporary human rights mesh with the general principles of international law and particularly with the principles governing the international responsibility of states.
International lawyers, international organizations, scholars and students of international law
ISBN 0198252390 Hbk £30.00

—Human rights in internal strife : their international protection / by Theodor Meron. – Cambridge : Grotius, 1987.
xiii,172p.
An examination of the problem of protecting human rights in internal strife and of developing adequate safeguards in areas beyond the scope of the Geneva Conventions.
ISBN 0949009040

—Human rights in international law : basic texts / Strasbourg : Council of Europe, 1985.
261p.
ISBN 9287103992

—Human rights in international law : legal and policy issues / edited by Theodor Meron. – 2 vols. – Oxford : Clarendon Press, 1983.
Includes bibliographies and index.
ISBN 0198254881 v. 2

—Human rights in the world : an introduction to the study of the international protection of human rights / by A.H. Robertson. – 2nd ed. – Manchester : Manchester University Press, 1982.
viii,243p; 23cm.
Previous ed.: 1972. Includes index.
ISBN 0719008638 £17.50

—Human rights law journal / Kehl am Rhein : Engel, 1980-.
Absorbed: Human rights review, 1982.

—Human rights law-making in the United Nations : a critique of instruments and process / Theodor Meron. – Oxford : Clarendon, 1986.
350p; 22cm.
Includes index.
ISBN 0198255497 £35.00

—Human rights of aliens in contemporary international law / Richard Lillich. – Manchester : Manchester University Press, 1984.
xii,177p; 24cm.
Includes index.
ISBN 0719009146 £27.50

—Humanitarian good offices in international law : the good offices of the United Nations Secretary General in the field of human rights : the 1981 Reid Lectures delivered at Acadia University, Wolfville, Nova Scotia, Canada / B.G. Ramcharan. – The Hague : Nijhoff, 1983.
xii,220p; 25cm.
Bibliography: p217-218. - Includes index.
ISBN 9024728053 Hbk £95.00

—Interights / v. – London : International Human Rights Law Centre, 1983.
Continued by: Interights bulletin. Only one issue published.

—Interights bulletin / London : International Centre for the Protection of Human Rights, 1985.
Continues: Interights.
ISBN 02683709

—International human rights instruments of the United Nations 1948-1982 / collected and arranged by the UNIFO editorial staff. – London : Mansell, 1984.
ix,175p; 29cm.
Originally published: Pleasantville, N.Y. : UNIFO Publishers, 1983. Includes index.
ISBN 0720116988 £25.00

—International law and fact - finding in the field of human rights / edited by B.G. Ramcharan. – The Hague : Nijhoff, 1982.
x,259p; 25cm.
Bibliography: p255-256. - Includes index.
ISBN 9024730422 Hbk £110.00

—Keyguide to information sources on the international protection of human rights / J.A. Andrews and W.D. Hines. – London : Mansell, 1987.
xiii,169p; 24cm.
Includes index.
ISBN 0720118735 £25.00

—Lawful rights of mankind : an introduction to the international legal code of human rights / Paul Sieghart. – Oxford : Oxford University Press, 1985.
xiii,252p; 23cm.
Bibliography: p247-248. - Includes index.
ISBN 019219190X £9.95

—Nuremberg and after : the continuing history of war crimes and crimes against humanity / by Geoffrey Best. – Reading : University of Reading, 1984.
29p.
ISBN 0704902141

—Petitioning the United Nations : a study in human rights / Ton J.M. Zuijdwijk. – Aldershot : Gower, 1982.
xv,397p; 23cm.
Bibliography: p383-389. - Includes index.
ISBN 0566004631 Unpriced
ISBN 0312603819

—Rescuing nationals abroad through military coercion and intervention on grounds of humanity / Natalino Ronzitti. – Dordrecht Netherlands : M. Nijhoff Publishers, 1985.
236p.
Includes index. Bibliography.
ISBN 9024731356 Hbk £125.00

—Rights without remedies : the European Convention of Human Rights and UK immigration law / Camilla Palmer. – London : Runnymede Trust, 1981.
29,5p.
Bibliography p.5. - Includes index.

—Teaching human rights / edited by Alice Ehr-Soon Tay in collaboration with Graeme Connelly and Roger Wilkins. – Canberra : Australian Government Publishing Service, 1981.
vi,216p.
Bibliography: p.207-208. - Includes index. Papers presented at a seminar held in the University of Sydney Law School, 20-22 June 1980. At head of title: Australian National Commission for UNESCO.
ISBN 0642067627

—Theory and practice of the European convention on human rights / P. van Dijk, G.J.H. van Hoof. – Deventer : Kluwer Law and Taxation, 1984.
xiii,512p; 25cm.
Bibliography: p489-493. - Includes index. Translated from Dutch.
ISBN 9065440798 Pbk No price

—Treatment of prisoners under international law / Nigel S. Rodley. – Paris : Unesco, 1987.
xxii,374; 25cm.
Includes index.
ISBN 0198255519 Hbk £40.00
ISBN 0198255632 Pbk £15.00

—United Nations norms and guidelines in criminal justice : from standard setting to implementation / P.R. Loof. – Canberra : Australian Government Publishing Service, 1980.
v,38p. – (Australian discussion paper).
Includes bibliographical references.
ISBN 0642048185

HUMAN RIGHTS (INTERNATIONAL LAW) - AFRICA

—International law and struggle for the freedom and welfare of man in Africa / by Itsejuwa E. Sagay. – Ile-Ife : University of Ife Press, 1983.
41p. – (Inaugural lecture series).
'An inaugural lecture delivered at the University of Ife on 3rd June, 1982'.

HUMAN RIGHTS (ISLAMIC LAW) - ISLAMIC COUNTRIES

—Human rights in Islam : report of a seminar held in Kuwait, December 1980 / organised by the International Commission of Jurists, University of Kuwait and Union of Arab Lawyers. – Geneva : International Commission of Jurists, 1982.
ii,95p.

HUMAN SETTLEMENTS
—Land, the central human settlement issue / H. Peter Oberlander. – Vancouver : University of British Columbia Press, 1985.
x, 103 p., 4 p. of plates; 24 cm.
Bibliography: p. 93-101.
ISBN 0774802359

HUMAN SETTLEMENTS - ENGLAND
—Strict settlement : a guide for historians / Barbara English and John Saville. – Hull : University of Hull Press, 1983.
144p. – (Occasional papers in economic and social history).
Bibliography: p.132-137. - Includes index.
ISBN 0859584399

HUMANISM
—Ulrich Zasius : a jurist in the German Renaissance, 1461-1535 / Steven Rowan. – Frankfurt a. M. : Klostermann, 1987.
xiii,286p.
Includes bibliographies and index.
ISBN 3465017722

HUMOUR
—Great legal fiascos / Stephen Tumim. – London : Arthur Barker, 1985.
126p.
ISBN 0213169274

—Legal Wit and Whimsy : an Anthology of Legal Humour / Agincourt : Carswell, 1988.
168p.

HUMOUR - CANADA
—Legal Wit and Whimsy : An Anthology of Legal Humor / Agincourt : Carswell, 1988.
156p.

HUMOUR - CANADA - ALBERTA
—Talk to My Lawyer : Great Stories of Southern Alberta's Bar and Bench / Edmonton : Hurtig.
224p.
ISBN 0888303254 Hbk £24.95

IDENTIFICATION
—Identification evidence : a psychological evaluation / John W. Shepherd, Hadyn D. Ellis and Graham M. Davies : foreword by Lord Devlin. – Aberdeen : Aberdeen University Press, 1982.
xii,155p; 26cm.
Bibliography: p140-149. - Includes index.
ISBN 0080284418 £12.50

—International recognition of national identity cards : recommendation no.R(83)11 adopted by the Committee of Ministers of the Council of Europe on 23 September 1983 and Explanatory memorandum / Council of Europe. – Strasbourg : Council of Europe, 1984.
10p; 21cm.
'... prepared by the ad hoc Committee of experts for identity documents and movement of persons (CAHID)'. At head of cover title: Legal Affairs.
ISBN 9287103186

—Law Relating to Identification and Expert Opinion / H.D. Trivedi. – 3rd ed. – Lucknow : Eastern Book Company, 1983.
236p.

IDENTIFICATION - AUSTRALIA
—Evidence reference / Australian Law Reform Commission. – Sydney : The Commission, 1982.
viii,96p.
Includes bibliographical references.

IDENTIFICATION - INDIA
—Law of Identification and Discovery / 6th ed. – Allahabad : Law Book Company, 1988.
500p.

IDENTIFICATION - SCOTLAND
—Evidence : blood group tests, DNA tests and related matters / Scottish Law Commission. – Edinburgh : The Commission, 1988.
i,45p. – (Discussion paper).

IDENTIFICATION (PSYCHOLOGY)
—Identification evidence : a psychological evaluation / John W. Shepherd, Hadyn D. Ellis and Graham M. Davies : foreword by Lord Devlin. – Aberdeen : Aberdeen University Press, 1982.
xii,155p; 26cm.
Bibliography: p140-149. - Includes index.
ISBN 0080284418 £12.50

IDEOLOGY
—Legality, ideology and the state / edited by David Sugarman. – London : Academic Press, 1983.
xiv,304p; 24cm.
Includes bibliographies and index.
ISBN 0126760802 Unpriced

ILLEGAL CONTRACTS - CANADA - BRITISH COLUMBIA
—Illegal contracts / Law Reform Commission of British Columbia. – Vancouver : The Commission, 1982.
vi,179p. – (Working paper).
Includes bibliographical references.

—Report on illegal transactions / Law Reform Commission of British Columbia. – Victoria : Queen's Printer, 1983.
115p.
ISBN 077188401X

ILLEGAL CONTRACTS - EUROPEAN COMMUNITY
—Propeosed EC unfair contract terms directive / Department of Trade and Industry. Consumer Affairs Division 3A. – London : The Department, 1987.
45p.
Contents include: Futher draft articles for discussion on unfair terms of contract / European Commission. Also includes examples of relevant European national legislation.

ILLEGITIMACY - ENGLAND
—Family law - illegitimacy / the Law Commission. – London : H.M.S.O., 1982.
x,379p.
ISBN 0102098832

—Family law - illegitimacy (second report) / the Law Commission. – London : H.M.S.O., 1986.
iii,82p.
ISBN 0101991304

—Illegitimacy : R.O.W. evidence to the Law Commission / Rights of Women. – London : Rights of Women, 1980.
28p; 30cm.
Evidence presented in response to the Law Commission's Working paper no. 74, 'Family law : illegitimacy'.

ILLEGITIMACY - GREAT BRITAIN
—Accident of birth : a response to the Law Commission's Working Paper on illegitimacy / National Council for One Parent Families. – London : National Council for One-Parent Families, 1980.
20p.

ILLEGITIMACY - IRELAND
—Report on illegitimacy / the Law Reform Commission. – Dublin : The Commission, 1982.
vii,182p. – (LRC).

ILLEGITIMACY - SCOTLAND
—Family law : illegitimacy / Scottish Law Commission. – Edinburgh : The Commission, 1982.
170p. – (Consultative memorandum).

—Family law : report on illegitimacy / Scottish Law Commission. – Edinburgh : H.M.S.O., 1984.
vii,134p.
Includes bibliographical references.
ISBN 0102186847

ILLEGITIMACY - SOUTH AFRICA
—Investigating into the legal position of illegitimate children / South African Law Commission. – Pretoria : The Commission, 1984.
viii,167 leaves. – (Project).
Bibliography: p.161-167.

—Investigation into the legal position of illegitimate children / South African Law Commission. – Pretoria : The Commission, 1985.
xx,157p. – (Report).
Includes bibliographical references.
ISBN 0621102059

IMMIGRANTS - GREAT BRITAIN
—Immigrants and the Welfare State / NACAB. – London : CENT, 1983.
ISBN 0906072069 Pbk £4.80

IMMIGRATION - CANADA
—Annotated Immigration Act of Canada 1988 / Henry M. Goslett. – Carswell, 1988.
482p.

—Cumulative Index to the Decisions of the Immigration Appeal Board / Agincourt : Carswell, 1987.
180p.

—How to Become an Immigrant to Canada and the United States of America / Lucknow : Eastern Book Company, 1985.

—Immigrant's Handbook : a Critical Guide / Law Union of Ontario. – Montreal : Black Rose Books, 1981.
263p.

—Immigrating to Canada : Who is Allowed? What is Required? How to Do It / 6th ed. – North Vancouver : International Self-Counsel Press, 1986.
179p.
ISBN 0889086133 Hbk £14.95

—Immigration / Vancouver : British Columbia Continuing Legal Education Society, 1985.
302p.
ISBN 0865042322 Hbk £70.00

—Immigration Law : 1987 / Vancouver : Continuing Legal Education Society of British Columbia, 1987.
386p.
ISBN 0865043582 Hbk £85.00

—Immigration Law in Canada / Butterworths, 1984.
264p.
Analysis of immigration law at the Federal Court level, covering relevant sections of the Immigration Act, 1976, an assessment of all relevant cases and other statutory provisions. Defines key terms, and a whole chapter is devoted to the relationship between human rights and immigrations law, covering refugee status, ministerial permits, and the reunion of families in Canada.
ISBN 0409834505 Hbk £60.00

—Immigration Practice and Procedure / Vancouver : British Columbia Continuing Legal Education Society, 1982.
436p.
ISBN 0865040516 Hbk £75.00

—Index to the Decisions Rendered by the Immigration Appeal Board / Agincourt : Carswell, 1988.
174p.

—Index to the Decisions Rendered By the Immigration Appeal Board / Agincourt : Carswell, 1987.
168p.
This is a comprehensive index to the decisions of the Immigration Appeal Board from 1976 through to 1987. Special legal research features include a key word index, and alphabetical listing by style of case, and a case citator.

—Rules to Keep the Rascals Out / Vancouver : November House.
ISBN 0920156045 Hbk £1.95

IMMIGRATION - CANADA - QUEBEC
—Quebec Guide to Immigration / Montreal : McGill Campus Legal Aid Clinic, 1981.
77p.

IMMIGRATION - GREAT BRITAIN
—Immigration and Nationality : Statutes and Rules / Beg. – London : Shaw & Sons, 1988.
ISBN 072191120X Pbk

—Immigration Appeal Reports / London : HMSO, 1984.
ISBN 0113407939 Hbk £9.95

—Immigration Emergency Procedures / Webb. – London : Legal Action Group, 1986.
ISBN 0905099117 Pbk £11.00

—Immigration Into Britain / 2nd ed. – London : HMSO.
ISBN 0117012548 Hbk £3.00

—Immigration into Britain : Notes on the Regulations and Procedures / Great Britain Central Office of Information, Reference Division. – rev. ed. – London : Central Office of Information, 1980.
19p.

—Immigration law and practice / Martin. – London : CENT, 1982.
ISBN 0900137185 Pbk £28.25

—Immigration law and practice in the UK / 2nd ed. – London : Butterworths, 1987.
ISBN 04062983141 Hbk £54.00

—Immigration law handbook / Handsworth Law Centre. – 3rd ed. – TUAR, 1985.
ISBN 0951074504 Pbk £2.50

—Ins and outs of immigration and nationality law / Lowe. – London : CENT, 1983.
ISBN 0906072050 Pbk £4.95

—Towards a just immigration policy / London : CENT, 1986.
ISBN 0900137266 Pbk £7.95

IMMIGRATION - MALAYSIA
—Immigration Act, 1959/1963, (Act 155) Regulations and Orders / Kuala Lumpur : International Law Books Services.

IMMIGRATION - NIGERIA
—Illegal aliens under Nigerian law / R.C. Chhangani. – Jodhpur : Associated Law Publications, 1983.
91p.
Includes index.

IMMIGRATION - UNITED STATES
—How to Become an Immigrant to Canada and the United States of America / Lucknow : Eastern Book Company, 1985.

—Immigrating to the U.S.A. / 4th ed. – North Vancouver : International Self-Counsel Press, 1983.
208p.
ISBN 0889089124 Hbk £14.95

IMMUNITIES OF FOREIGN STATES

—Sovereign lending : managing legal risk / edited by Michael Gruson and Ralph Reisner. - London : Euromoney Publications, 1985.
xii,257p; 30cm.
Includes bibliographical references.
ISBN 0903121611

—State and diplomatic immunity / by Charles Lewis. - London : Lloyd's of London Press Ltd., 1980.
135p.
ISBN 0904093816

—State immunity : an analytical and prognostic view / Gamal Moursi Badr. - The Hague : M. Nijhoff, 1984.
248p.
Includes bibliographical references and index.
ISBN 9024728800 Hbk £120.00

—State immunity : some recent developments / by Christoph H. Schreuer. - Cambridge : Grotius, 1988.
xxiii,200p.
Examines the principle international and national aspects of suits against States and State-owned corporations in foreign courts.
ISBN 0949009148

—United States law of sovereign immunity relating to international financial transactions / John R. Stevenson, Jeffrey F. Browne and Lori Fisler Damrosch. - London : Euromoney Pubns, 1983.
158p.
Includes bibliographical references.
ISBN 090312145X

IMMUNITIES OF FOREIGN STATES - AUSTRALIA

—Foreign state immunity / The Law Reform Commission. - Sydney : The Commission, 1983.
8p. - (Discussion paper).
Summary dicussion paper.

—Foreign state immunity / the Law Reform Commission. - Canberra : Australian Government Publishing Service, 1984.
xxiv,168p. - (Report).
Bibliography: p.162-5. Includes index.
ISBN 0644012811

IMMUNITIES OF FOREIGN STATES - GREAT BRITAIN

—State and diplomatic immunity / by Charles J. Lewis. - 2nd ed. - London : Lloyd's of London, 1985.
xxvi,250p; 22cm.
Previous ed.: 1980. Includes index.
ISBN 1850440476 No price

IMPORTS - GREAT BRITAIN

—Importing for the small business / London : Kogan Page, 1985.
ISBN 0850388694 Pbk £6.95

IMPRINTS - NEW ZEALAND

—New Zealand national bibliography to the year 1960 / editor and principal compiler A.G. Bagnall. - Wellington : P.D. Hasselberg, 1969.
5v.
Prepared in the National Library Centre, National Library Service and National Library of New Zealand.

INCAPACITY - CANADA

—Incapacity / Vancouver : Continuing Legal Education Society of British Columbia, 1988.
205p.
ISBN 0865049750 Hbk £70.00

INCOME

—Impact of residual disability from illness and injury on the distribution of household income : a lognormal approach / by Yvonne Brittan and Ioannis G. Vlachonikolis. - Oxford : SSRC-Social Science Research Council, 1981.
23p. - (Working paper).

INCOME - CANADA

—Economics of Poverty and Income Distribution / Toronto : Butterworths.
192p.
ISBN 0409834750 Hbk

INCOME - GREAT BRITAIN

—Impact of Residual Disability from Illness and Injury on the Distribution of Household Income / I. Vlachonikolis. - Oxford : Social Science Research Council, 1981.

—National welfare benefits handbook / London : Child Poverty Action Group, 1987.
288p; 21cm.
Includes index.
ISBN 0946744009 Pbk £4.50

—Penguin guide to supplementary benefits : supplementary benefits, the new regulations, the family income supplement and the appeals tribunal / Tony Lynes. - 4th ed. - Harmondsworth : Penguin, 1981.
319p; 18cm.
Previous ed.: 1975. Includes index. .
ISBN 0140464239 Pbk £2.50

—Reform of social security / London : H.M.S.O., 1985.
51p.
Technical annex to White Paper Cmnd 9691. Contents: 1. Illustrations of individuals' future pensions expectations. 2. Illustrative effects of reforming the structure of income-related benefits.
ISBN 0113210183 Hbk

INCOME SUPPORT - GREAT BRITAIN

—Family Income Support Part 4 : Widow Benefits / London : Policy Studies Institute, 1984.
119p.

INCOME TAX

—Annual Digest of Income Tax Reports, 1986 / Madras : Company Law Institute of India, 1986.

—Empirical analysis of changes in personal income taxes / a report by the Committee on Fiscal Affairs. - Paris : Organisation for Economic Co-operation and Development, 1986.
38p.
ISBN 926412778X

—Irish income tax and corporation profits tax by F.N. Kelly and K.S. Carmichael / K. S. Carmichael. - 8th ed. 1 v. - London : HFL, 1975.
looseleaf.
Includes index.
ISBN 0372016529

—Model Income Tax Treaties / Dordrecht : Kluwer.
ISBN 9065441484 Pbk £30.00

—New Zealand income tax law and practice / by Donald H. Simcock and John F.S. Rooke with CCH editorial staff. - 3. - Auckland : Commerce Clearing House (New Zealand), 1973.
looseleaf.
Loose-leaf issues accompanied by a summary report and a supplement.
ISBN 0869032003 v.3
ISBN 0869031966

—New Zealand tax cases / Auckland : Commerce Clearing House (New Zealand), 1975.
23cm.
Issued as bound volumes every two years, with the current issues forming part of the service to the loose-leaf publication: New Zealand income tax law and practice / by Donald H. Simcock and John F.S. Rooke. Looseleaf issues accompanied by a summary report.

—Personal income tax systems under changing economic conditions / report by the Committee on Fiscal Affairs of OECD. - Paris : Organisation for Economic Co-operation and Development, 1986.
381p.
ISBN 9264127895

—Rating and income tax / 53 v. - London : Solicitors' Law Stationery Society, 1924.
Continued by: Rating and valuation reporter.

—Schedular, Global and Dualistic Patterns of Income Taxation / International Bureau of Fiscal Documentation. - Amsterdam : International Bureau of Fiscal Documentation, 1988.
188p.
ISBN 9070125358 Hbk £85.00

—Taxation of domestic shareholders on undistributed income of foreign corporate affiliates : objectives, techniques, and consequences : proceedings of a seminar held in New York in 1986 during the 40th Congress of the International Fiscal Association / edited by Brian J. Arnold. - Deventer, Netherlands : Kluwer Law and Taxation Publishers, 1987.
Includes bibliography.
ISBN 9065443347

—Taxation of Private Investment Income / International Bureau of Fiscal Documentation. - Amsterdam : International Bureau of Fiscal Documentation, 1988.
- (Guides to European Taxation Ser.: Vol. 3).

Supplements-1989 renewal

INCOME TAX - AFRICA

—Income taxation in eastern Africa : policies and prospects : seven country surveys / edited by Ali Ahmed Suliman and Elizabeth de Brauw-Hay : with a foreword and a concluding chapter by J. van Hoorn, Jr. - Amsterdam, Netherlands : International Bureau of Fiscal Documentation, 1980.
244 p.; 24 cm.
Includes bibliographies.
ISBN 9070125145 pbk.

INCOME TAX - ASIA

—Income taxation and foreign investment in developing countries / M.P. Dominic. - Amsterdam : International Bureau of Fiscal Documentation, 1980.
xviii, 354, 28 p.; 24 cm.
Includes indexes. Bibliography: p. 7-16 (2d group).
ISBN 9070125137 pbk.

INCOME TAX - AUSTRALIA

—1987 Australian Income Tax Legislation, 3v / North Ryde : C.C.H. Australia, 1987.
2,300p.
ISBN 0869038990 Hbk

—Australian and New Zealand Income Tax Reports (AITR) / Wellington : Butterworths.

—Australian income tax guide 1988 / E.F. Mannix ... et al. - 33rd ed. - Sydney : Butterworths, 1988.
xxiv,1304p.
' ... the 33rd edition of Gunn's Guide to Commonwealth income tax'. - t.p.. Includes index.
ISBN 0409494267 Hbk

—Australian income tax legislation / 1985 ed. 3 v. - North Ryde, N.S.W. : CCH Australia, 1985.
'Incorporating all amendments to 31 December 1984'.
ISBN 086903684X

—Australian Income Tax Questions / B. T. Colditz. - 4th ed. - Sydney : Butterworths, 1988.
244p.

—Butterworths Australian Income Tax Guide : 1988 / Sydney : Butterworths, 1988.

—Butterworths Income Tax Assessment Act, 3 vols. / Sydney : Butterworths, 1988.

—Butterworths Income Tax Assessment Act and Related Legislation / Butterworths, 1988.
1468p.

—Canada Income Tax Regulation Service / Toronto : DeBoo.
This multi-volume looseleaf reference work includes Canadian Income Tax Regulations, Interpretation Bulletins, Information Circulars, tax rulings, current forms, and indices.
ISBN 0888201354 loose £255.00

—Entertainment Expenses and Substantiation : the New Tax Rules / North Ryde : C.C.H. Australia, 1986.
94p.
ISBN 0869038656 Hbk

—International transactions and Australian income tax : being a commentary on Division 13 of the Income Tax Assessment Act 1936 together with the text of the Legislation / by E. F. Mannix. - Sydney : Butterworths, 1982.
x,46p.
Includes index.
ISBN 0409493554

—Leading Cases on Australian Income Tax / J.E. Mannix. - 5th ed. - Butterworths, 1985.
720p.
ISBN 0409493929 Hbk £61.00

1984.
ISBN 0409493929 Pbk £31.30

—Manual of the Law of Income Tax in Australia / 6th ed. - North Ryde : Law Book Co, 1987.
xxvi, 360p.
ISBN 0455202974 Hbk £38.50
ISBN 0455202982 Pbk £26.50

Supplement 1987
ISBN 0455207313 Hbk £2.50

—Materials on Canadian Income Tax / 7th ed. - Toronto : DeBoo, 1987.
908p.
This text, intended primarily for student use, includes an appendix that reviews the amendments contained in Bill C-64 and the White Paper on tax reform issued on June 18, 1987. Also contained is a table of cases, a table of statutory references, and a topical index.
ISBN 0888202741 Pbk £79.00

—New Cases Companion to Ryans Income Tax Manual / 2nd ed. - North Ryde : Law Book Co, 1983.
xiii, 314p.
ISBN 0455204098 29.00

—Principles of Income Tax / P. C. Green. - 3rd ed. - Sydney : Butterworths, 1986.
288p.

—Principles of Income Taxation / Green. - Sydney : Butterworths, 1985.
256p.
ISBN 040949058X Hbk

—Tax and the Australian film industry : being a commentary on division 10BA of the Income Assessment Act 1936 together with text of the legislation / by E.F. Mannix. - Sydney : Butterworths, 1981.
xii,92p.
Includes index.
ISBN 040936018X

—Understanding Income Tax Law the Flowchart Way / 3rd ed. - Butterworths, 1985.
436p.
ISBN 0409491748 Pbk £39.00

Supplement-1983 1983.
45p.
ISBN 0409491519 Pbk £5.00

INCOME TAX - CANADA

—Advanced Company Law and Corporate Income Tax / Vancouver : Continuing Legal Education Society of British Columbia, 1985.
355p.
ISBN 0865042357 Hbk £70.00

—Canada income tax guide / 3. – Don Mills : CCH Canadian, 1982.
looseleaf.
Includes index.

—Canadian Income Taxation / 4th ed. – Butterworths, 1986.

Supplement-1988

—Canadian income taxation / 4th ed. – Toronto : Butterworths, 1986.
xxv,776p.
Previous ed.: 1983. Includes index.
ISBN 0409805149

—Canadian mining taxation / Robert B. Parsons. – Toronto : Butterworths, 1982.
x,253p.
ISBN 0409859745

—Family Home and Income Tax / Agincourt : Carswell, 1986.
250p.

—Farano's Income Tax Cases / Aurora : Canada Law Book Co, 1981.
506p.

—Foreign affiliate system : Canadian taxation after 1982 : a structured overview / by Nathan Boidman. – Don Mills, Ont. : CCH Canadian Ltd., 1983.
ix,218p.
Includes index.
ISBN 0887962092

—Fundamentals of Canadian Income Tax / 2nd ed. – Agincourt : Carswell, 1986.
1288p.
This textbook for students of Canadian income tax law deals with the fundamental structure of the income tax system and the underlying principles and concepts of taxation. Numerous computational examples are provided in the work to illustrate the operation of tax principles.

—Fundamentals of Canadian Income Tax : an Introduction / Agincourt : Carswell.
946p.

—Income tax and family law handbook / Mary Lou Benotto. – 1 vol. – Scarborough, Ontario : Butterworths (Canada).
Includes coverage of alimony and maintenance, attribution, child care expenses, child tax credit, common law spouses, dependants, family allowances, legal costs, pension benefits, principle residence, property division, registered retirement savings plan, and tax liability.
ISBN 0409806471 Loose leaf

—Income Tax Appeals : Law and Practice / Toronto : Butterworths, 1981.
136p. – (Butterworths Tax Practice Ser.).
ISBN 0409827614 Hbk £31.95

—Income tax aspects of corporate financing / Toronto : Canadian Tax Foundation, 1980.
xiv,399p.

—Income tax aspects of executive and employee compensation / Toronto : Canadian Tax Foundation, 1980.
xii,294p.
ISBN 0888080026

—Income tax aspects of real estate transactions / Corporate Management Tax Conference 1983. – Toronto : Canadian Tax Foundation, 1983.
xv,450p.

—Income tax considerations in corporate financing / Corporate Management Tax Conference 1986. – Toronto : Canadian Tax Foundation, 1986.
xv,475p.
Includes bibliographical references.
ISBN 0888080271

—Income tax enforcement, compliance, and administration : Corporate Management Tax Conference 1982 / edited by Christine Purden Nelson. – Toronto : Canadian Tax Foundation, 1983.
x,297p.
ISBN 0888080115

—Income Tax for the Corporate and Commercial Lawyer / Vancouver : Continuing Legal Education Society of British Columbia, 1986.
267p.
ISBN 0865042500 Hbk £65.00

—Income Tax for the General Practitioner, 1983 / Vancouver : British Columbia Continuing Legal Education Society, 1983.
236p.
ISBN 0865040966 Hbk £50.00

—Income tax for the general practitioner / Toronto : Deboo, 1986.
449p.
Includes bibliographical references and index.
ISBN 0888202490 £75.00

—Income Tax Law in Canada / Douglas S. Ewens. – Agincourt : Carswell, 1983.
640p. – (Bar Admission Course Materials Ser.).
This treatise for law students follows the same general structure as the Income Tax Act of Canada to review the Canadian tax system. Personal and corporate taxation, tax deferral plans, assessment, appeals, and administration are covered in the work.

—Income Tax References / Toronto : DeBoo.
This service contains primary and secondary tax references from English and French language sources. Included are articles, treatises, case summaries, Income Tax Regulations, and government bulletins going back to 1972. Six updates per year are planned, in addition to annual consolidations.
ISBN 0888201214 loose £175.00

—Income taxation of partnerships and their partners / by Brian J. Arnold, D. Keith McNair. – Toronto : Carswell, 1981.
v,212p.
Contents: Ch. 8 and part of ch. 19 of: Current tax planning / by Ward, Smith and Arnold.
ISBN 0459339109

—Meaning of cost in Canadian Income Tax / D. Keith McNair. – Toronto : Canadian Tax Foundation, 1982.
vi,277p.
Includes index.
ISBN 0888080123

—Selected income tax aspects of the purchase and sale of a business : Corporate Management Tax Confetence 1984 / Toronto : Canadian Tax Foundation, 1984.
xii,347p.
Bibliography: p.75-82.
ISBN 0888080220

—Stikeman Income Tax Act / 13th ed. – Toronto : DeBoo, 1984.
ISBN 0888201621 Hbk £39.95
ISBN 088820163X Pbk £31.50

—Stikeman Income Tax Act, Annotated / 17th ed. – Toronto : DeBoo, 1988.
1536p.
This book contains the full text of the Canadian Income Tax Act as amended to the date of publication, along with annotations which discuss Interpretation Bulletins, Information Circulars, prescribed forms, Income Tax Regulations, Income Tax Application Rules, and related provisions and definitions. Also included are U.S. and U.K. tax conventions.
ISBN 0888202563 Hbk £39.95
ISBN 0888202571 Pbk £31.50

—Taxation and estate planning / by Maurice C. Cullity and Catherine A. Brown. – 2nd ed. – Toronto, Canada : Carswell Co., 1984.
xxvi, 764 p.; 24 cm.
At head of title: Cullity, Forbes, Brown. Includes bibliographical references and index.
ISBN 0459362305 pbk.

—Taxation of controlled foreign corporations : an international comparison / Brian J. Arnold. – Toronto, Ont. : Canadian Tax Foundation, 1986.
xxiii, 816; 23 cm. – (Canadian tax paper).
Includes index. Bibliography: p. 797-811.
ISBN 0888080239 pbk. £75.00

—Taxation of income of foreign affiliates / by David A. Ward. – Toronto : Carswell, 1983.
vi,237p.
Includes index. 'Being Chapter 20 of Ward's Tax Law and Planning by The Partners of Davies, Ward & Beck and Brian J. Arnold' - t.p.
ISBN 0459358707

—Taxation of Resource Industries / Agincourt : Carswell, 1987.
392p.
This text discusses the relevant sections of the Income Tax Act. Also included are discussions on depletion, successor corporation rules and resource allowances. Special coverage includes sample calculations and tables listing the order of deductions for different types of enterprises.

—Taxes on capital income in Canada : analysis and policy / Robin W. Boadway, Neil Bruce, Jack M. Mintz. – Toronto : Canadian Tax Foundation, 1987.
xi,176p.
Includes index.
ISBN 088808028X Hbk

—Timing and income taxation : the principles of income measurement for tax purposes / B. J. Arnold. – Toronto : Canadian Tax Foundation, 1983.
xiv,388p.
Includes index.
ISBN 088808014X

—Ward's Tax Law and Planning, 6 Vols. / Beck. – Agincourt : Carswell, 1983.
This multi-volume looseleaf service is a comprehensive treatise on Canadian tax law. Analysis of the statutory language of the Canadian Income Tax Act is the main focus of the work.

INCOME TAX - CANADA - ALBERTA

—Alberta Corporate Income Tax / Toronto : Butterworths.
– (Alberta Annotated Legislation).

—Alberta Corporate Income Tax : Alberta Annotated Legislation Series, 1 Vol. / Butterworths.

INCOME TAX - CANADA - ONTARIO

—Law and Practice Under the Family Law Act of Ontario / Revised Edit. – Agincourt : Carswell, 1986.
This looseleaf work provides analysis of the Family Law Act of Ontario for the practitioner, along with summaries of relevant case law. Problems in preparation and drafting of domestic documents are discussed in the work, as well as, income tax implications and the valuation of family property.

—Ontario Corporation and Income Tax Legislation : with Related Taxes / 25th ed. – North Ryde : C.C.H. Australia, 1988.
254p.
ISBN 0887964745 Pbk £13.95

INCOME TAX - GHANA

—Ghana income tax law and practice / P.O. Andah. – Accra : Sedco, 1987.
xii,252p.
ISBN 9964720718

—Ghana's Income Tax Law and the Investor / Accra : Ghana Universities Press.
25p.

INCOME TAX - GREAT BRITAIN

—Butterworth's Income Tax Assessment Act 1987 / Sydney : Butterworths, 1987.

—Butterworth's Income Tax Computer Software / London : Butterworths.

—Butterworth's Income Tax Service / Butterworths Editorial Staff. – London : Butterworths.
This looseleaf service for United Kingdom practitioners covers extra-statutory concessions, statements of practice, and tables of rates and relief. The work is updated with monthly bulletins and quarterly service issues.

—Butterworth's Income Tax System / London : Butterworths.

—Capital allowances in law and practice / R. J. Pickerill. – 2nd ed. – London : Institute of Chartered Accountants, 1981.
xix,307p. – (Chartac taxation guides).
ISBN 0852913079

—Cases in Income Tax Law / 1st ed. – Plymouth : Macdonald & Evans, 1981.
276p. – (M and E Handbook Ser.).
ISBN 0712103783 Hbk £4.95

—Charities payroll giving schemes : proposals for tax relief / Inland Revenue. – London : Board of Inland Revenue, 1986.
12p.

—Dismissal and taxation of employees / Barry Titman, Peter Camp. – London : Butterworths, 1982.
xxvi,233p.
ISBN 0406129010

—How to pay less income tax / London : Pitman Publishing, 1986.
ISBN 0712108254 Pbk £2.95

—Income and Corporation Act 1988 / London : Butterworths, 1988.
ISBN 0406008000 Pbk £18.00

—Income and Corporation Taxes Act 1988 / London : CCH, 1988.
ISBN 086325148X Hbk £32.00

—Income tax 1980 / Wheatcroft. – 2nd ed. – London : Sweet & Maxwell, 1980.
ISBN 0421204303 Hbk £85.00

—Income Tax / G. S. A. Wheatcroft. – 2nd ed. – London : Sweet & Maxwell, 1976.
Previous ed.: published as 'Whiteman and Wheatcroft on income tax and surtax' / by Peter G. Whiteman and G.S.A. Wheatcroft. 1971. Includes index.
ISBN 0421204303 Hbk £76.00

Nineteen Eighty-Six Supplement
ISBN 0421369108 Pbk

—Income Tax, Corporation Tax and Capital Gains Tax 1978-1983, 5 Vols. / London : HMSO, 1984.
– (Taxes Act. Ser.).
ISBN 0116413557 Hbk £42.50

—Income tax guide / London : Daily Mail, 1988/89.
ISBN 0851444369 Pbk £1.95

—Income tax (Jersey) Law, 1961 (as amended up to 30th July, 1982) / Jersey. – 1. – Jersey : States Greffe, 1983.
loose-leaf.
Subsequently amended up to 18th November 1983. Cover title.

—Income Tax (Jersey) Law, 1961 (as amended up to 30th November, 1987) / Jersey. – 1. – Jersey : States Greffe, 1988.
looseleaf.

—Practical share valuation / Booth. – 2nd ed. – London : Butterworths, 1987.
ISBN 0406190143 Hbk £26.00

—Remuneration planning manual / London : Butterworths, 1986.
ISBN 040650430X Pbk £19.95

—Residence, domicile and UK taxation / London : Butterworths, 1986.
ISBN 0406580103 Pbk £32.00

—Retirement relief; the capital gains tax rules explained / 2nd. – Bicester : CCH Editions Ltd, 1988.
Examines the changes introduced by the 1987 and 1988 Finance Acts. Includes two new chapters on two-tier relief and the Inland Revenue concession on date of disposal. Also covers how retirement relief works, the date of disposal, unincorporated businesses, partners, directors, trustees, full-time employees, furnished holiday lettings, husband and wife, interactions with tax, and a legislation finding list.
ISBN 0863251668 Hbk £15.50

—Revenue investigations manual / Sabine. – London : Butterworths, 1987.
ISBN 0406500703 Pbk £19.50

—Revenue law / London : Financial Training, 1987.
– (SWOT).
ISBN 090632291X Pbk £8.95

—Revenue law / Stuart-Buttle. – 4th ed. – London : Butterworths, 1986.
ISBN 040600532X Pbk £20.95

—Share valuation cases / Harry Booth. – London : Butterworths, 1985.
ISBN 0406009805 Hbk £67.50

—Share valuation handbook / London : Fourmat, 1986.
ISBN 0906840988 Pbk £12.95

—Simon's taxes : income tax, corporation tax, capital gains tax / John Allsebrook Simon Simon. – Rev. 3rd ed. 1. – London : Butterworths, 1985.
looseleaf.
Previous ed.: 3rd ed. 1970. 'Originally published under the editorship of the Right Hon. Viscount Simon'.
ISBN 0406072426

E : Individuals 1985.
looseleaf.
Previous ed.: 3rd ed. 1970. 'Originally published under the editorship of the Right Hon. Viscount Simon'.
ISBN 0406072442

I : Tables of statutes and cases, master index 1985.
looseleaf.
Previous ed.: 3rd ed. 1976. 'Originally published under the editorship of the Right Hon. Viscount Simon'.

—Taxation of land transactions / 4th ed. – London : Butterworths, 1988.
ISBN 0406624100 Pbk

—Taxation of non-resident entertainers and sportsmen / Croydon : Tolley, 1987.
ISBN 0854593128 Hbk £35.00

—Taxation of overseas income and gains / Anthony Sumption. – 4th ed. – London : Butterworths, 1982.
xix,207p.
Previous ed.: 1979.
ISBN 0406538735

—Tolley's income tax 1986-87 / by Eric L. Harvey and Glyn Saunders with Patrick Noakes. – 71st ed. – Croydon : Tolley Publishing, 1986.
xi,596p.
Includes index.
ISBN 0854592385

—Tolley's income tax 1988-89 / by Eric L. Harvey and Glyn Saunders : with David Smailes. – 73rd ed. – Croydon, Surrey : Tolley, 1988.
xii,623p.
Includes index.
ISBN 0854593462

—Tolley's taxation in the Channel Islands and Isle of Man 1987 / John Boulding. – Croydon : Tolley, 1987.
vi,207p.
ISBN 0854592954

—Tolley's taxation in the Channel Islands and Isle of Man / Croydon : Tolley Pub. Co., 1981.
vi,163p.
ISBN 0854590269 £6.25

INCOME TAX - HONG KONG

—Asian income tax laws / by D.S. Chopra. – Singapore : Malayan Law Journal Pte., 1986.
lx,992p.
Compendium of the substantive provisions of the tax laws of the three major Asian countries. Gives a brief introduction to the income-tax laws of each of the countries, covers all tax concessions, incentives, rebates and reliefs in the income-tax laws of each country, the current income-tax rates prevailing, and important judicial decisions in respect of the provisions of the income-tax laws of each country.
ISBN 9971700468

—Hong Kong revenue law / Matthew Bender, 1981.
ISBN 0000999046 Hbk £140.00

INCOME TAX - INDIA

—Asian income tax laws / by D.S. Chopra. – Singapore : Malayan Law Journal Pte., 1986.
lx,992p.
Compendium of the substantive provisions of the tax laws of the three major Asian countries. Gives a brief introduction to the income-tax laws of each of the countries, covers all tax concessions, incentives, rebates and reliefs in the income-tax laws of each country, the current income-tax rates prevailing, and important judicial decisions in respect of the provisions of the income-tax laws of each country.
ISBN 9971700468

—Corporate Income Tax and Profit Rates / New Delhi : Deep and Deep Publications, 1984.
268p.

—Elements of Income Tax Law / Allahabad : Law Book Company.

—Income Tax Law / S.M. Pithisaria. – 3rd ed. – Calcutta : Eastern Law House.

Vol. 2: 1982

Vol. 3: 1983

Vol. 4: 1984

Vol. 5: 1986

Vol. 6: in prep.

—Income Tax Law and Practice / 7th ed. – New Delhi : Allied Publishers, 1984.

—Income Tax Law and Practice / D.B. Narang. – 15th ed. – New Delhi : Kalyani Publishers.

—Income Tax Law and Practice : Jabalpur Edition / New Delhi : Kalyani Publishers.

—Income Tax Ready Reckoner, 1987-88 / New Delhi : Konark, 1987.

—Indian Income Tax Law and Practice / 14th ed. – Nagpur : Wadhura & Co, 1982.
ca 1,050p.

—Law of Income Tax / 3rd ed. – Lucknow : Eastern Book Company, 1982.
350p.

—Personal Income Taxation in India / Allahabad : Chugh Publications, 1987.
296p.
ISBN 8185076197 Hbk £175.00

—Reports of Income Tax Cases (1886-1937), Vols. / Allahabad : Law Publishers.

—Sampath Iyengar's Law of Income Tax, 4 Vols. / 7th ed. – New Delhi : Bharat Law House, 1981-83.

—Taxation of Income and Tax Laws / New Delhi : Deep and Deep Publications.
240p.

INCOME TAX - IRELAND

—Income tax / by Willie McAteer & George Reddin. – Dublin : Institute of Taxation in Ireland, 1981.
331p; 25cm.
Includes index.

—Taxation of capital gains / by Tony Appleby & John Roche. – Dublin : Institute of Taxation in Ireland, 1980.
255p; 24cm.
Includes index.

INCOME TAX - MALAYSIA

—Asian income tax laws / by D.S. Chopra. – Singapore : Malayan Law Journal Pte., 1986.
lx,992p.
Compendium of the substantive provisions of the tax laws of the three major Asian countries. Gives a brief introduction to the income-tax laws of each of the countries, covers all tax concessions, incentives, rebates and reliefs in the income-tax laws of each country, the current income-tax rates prevailing, and important judicial decisions in respect of the provisions of the income-tax laws of each country.
ISBN 9971700468

—How to Pay Less Malaysian Income Tax / Singapore, 1982.

—Income Tax Act, 1967 (Act 53) / Kuala Lumpur : International Law Books Services.
With case notes.

—Income tax case law of Malaysia and Singapore / Singapore : Malayan Law Journal, 1984.
xix,1031.
Collection of cases containing decisions on the relevant legislation since the introduction of income tax law in Malaysia and Singapore. Decisions include those of the old Boards of Review of Singapore and in the Federation of Malaya.
ISBN 9971700425 Hbk £230.00

—Introduction to tax appeals in Malaysia : notes on practice and procedure in appeals to the Special Commissioners of Income Tax / by Sim Ewe Eong : with a foreword by Tun Dr. Mohamed Suffian. – Kuala Lumpur : Malayan Law Journal, 1981.
xii,88p.
ISBN 9971700182

—Revenue law in Singapore and Malaysia / cases and commentary : Leo D. Pointon. – Singapore : Butterworths, 1986.
xxvii,281p.
Includes the interpretation of statutes and cases, administration, income, exempt income, deductions, capital allowances, personal reliefs, partnerships, and estate duty.
ISBN 0409995266 Hbk £78

—Revenue law in Singapore and Malaysia / London : Butterworths, 1986.
ISBN 0409995266 Pbk £38.00

INCOME TAX - NEW ZEALAND

—Australian and New Zealand Income Tax Reports (AITR) / Wellington : Butterworths.

—Income tax practice notes / 2. – Wellington : Butterworths, 1976.
looseleaf.
Includes index.

—Taxation of International Income / Butterworths, 1987.
ISBN 0409788015 Pbk

INCOME TAX - NIGERIA

—Guidance notes on Finance (Miscellaneous) Taxation Provisions Decree 1985 / by Zubair Alhaji Abdullahi. – Zaria, Nigeria? : the Author, 1986.
i,92p.
Includes index.

—Income tax and administration in Nigeria / by S.M. Adesola. – Ife-Ife, Nigeria : University of Ife Press, 1986.
viii,264p.
Includes index.
ISBN 9781360585

—Income tax law for corporate and unincorporated bodies in Nigeria / C.S. Ola. – 2nd ed. – Ibadan : Heinemann Educational Books (Nigeria) Ltd, 1981.
xx,556p.
Previous ed. published 1974 under title: Income-tax law and practice in Nigeria.
ISBN 9781292911

—Nigerian income tax law and practice : incorporating income tax laws relating to personal income tax law, partnership tax law, companies income tax law, petroleum profits tax law, capital gains tax law, capital transfer tax law and guidelines to a tax system under the presidential system of government with accountancy and decided cases illustrations and a supplement (1985) / C.S. Ola. – London : Macmillan, 1985.
xxvi,566p; 22cm.
Includes index.
ISBN 0333400070 Pbk £8.95

—Nigerian personal taxation : Law and practice with selected tax cases / S.A. Rabiu. – Ikeja, Nigeria : John West, 1986.
xiv,431p.
ISBN 978163040X

INCOME TAX - SCOTLAND

—Revenue Law in Scotland / London : Butterworths, 1984.
ISBN 0406258201 Pbk

—Revenue law in Scotland / Mackintosh. – London : Butterworths, 1986.
ISBN 040650170X Pbk £18.50

INCOME TAX - SINGAPORE

—Income tax case law of Malaysia and Singapore / Singapore : Malayan Law Journal, 1984.
xix,1031.
Collection of cases containing decisions on the relevant legislation since the introduction of income tax law in Malaysia and Singapore. Decisions include those of the old Boards of Review of Singapore and in the Federation of Malaya.
ISBN 9971700425 Hbk £230.00

—Revenue law in Singapore and Malaysia / cases and commentary : Leo D. Pointon. – Singapore : Butterworths, 1986.
xxvii,281p.
Includes the interpretation of statutes and cases, administration, income, exempt income, deductions, capital allowances, personal reliefs, partnerships, and estate duty.
ISBN 0409995266 Hbk £78

—Revenue law in Singapore and Malaysia / London : Butterworths, 1986.
ISBN 0409995266 Pbk £38.00

INCOME TAX - SOUTH AFRICA

—1985/86 Income Tax Statutory Amendments and Recent Amendments to the Estate Duty Act Including Estate Planning Aspects / Cape Town : Legal and Financial Publishing Co.

—1986-87 Income Tax Legislation and Recent Estate Duty Amendments : Together with Income Tax and Estate Duty Tables / Cape Town : Legal and Financial Publishing Co, 1987.

—Butterworths Income Tax Service / Professional Publ.
ISBN 0409013706 Hbk £65.00 with binder
ISBN 0409013870 £25.00 binder only

—Every Man His Own Income Tax Consultant / Cape Town : Legal & Financial Publishing.

—Fifty-Six Schedule / Cape Town : Legal & Financial Publishing, 1983.
- (Merlen P.A.Y.E. Registers Ser.).

—Income Tax Statutory Amendments and Recent Amendments to the Estate Duty Act Including Estate Planning Aspects, 1985-1986 / Cape Town : Legal & Financial Publishing.

—Income Tax Statutory Amendments and Supplement to the Taxation of Fringe Benefits, 1984-1985 / Cape Town : Legal & Financial Publishing, 1985.
ISBN 0869940368 Hbk £5.75

—Law and Practice of Close Corporations including Income Tax Aspects / Cape Town : Legal and Financial Publishing Co.

—Outline of Income Tax Statutory Amendments : 1971-1985 / Cape Town : Legal & Financial Publishing, 1983.

—Outline of the Income Tax Statutory Amendments 1971/1985 / Cape Town.

—Silke on South African income tax : being an exposition of the law, practice and incidence of income tax in South Africa / Costa Divaris, Michael L. Stein. - 10th ed. - Cape Town : Juta, 1982.
xlvii,1696p.
Includes index.
ISBN 0702113360

—Studies in Income Tax / 2nd ed. - Cape Town : Legal and Financial Publishing Co.

—Twelve Schedule / Cape Town : Legal & Financial Publishing, 1983.
- (Merlen P.A.Y.E. Registers).

—Twenty-four Schedule / Cape Town : Legal & Financial Publishing, 1983.
- (Merlen P.A.Y.E. Registers Ser.).

—What Every Attorney Should Know About Income Tax / Cape Town : Legal & Financial Publishing, 1983.
- (Merlen Ser. of Income Tax Publications).

—What Every Company Secretary Should Know About Income Tax / Cape Town : Legal & Financial Publishing, 1983.
- (Merlen Ser. of Income Tax Publications).

—What Every Dental Surgeon Should Know About Income Tax / Cape Town : Legal & Financial Publishing, 1983.
- (Merlen Ser. of Income Tax Publications).
ISBN 0869940341 Hbk £12.64

—What Every Executor-Trustee Should Know About Income Tax / Cape Town : Legal & Financial Publishing, 1983.
- (Merlen Ser. of Income Tax Publications).
ISBN 0869940201 Hbk £12.64

—What Every Farmer Should Know About Income Tax / Cape Town : Legal & Financial Publishing, 1983.
- (Merlen Ser. of Income Tax Publications).

—What Every Hotelier Should Know About Income Tax / Cape Town : Legal & Financial Publishing, 1983.
- (Merlen Ser. of Income Tax Publications).
ISBN 0869940074 Hbk £12.64

—What Every Insurance Company or Broker Should Know About Income Tax / Cape Town : Legal & Financial Publishing, 1983.
- (Merlen Series of Income Tax Publications).
ISBN 0869940228 Hbk £12.64

—What Every Medical Practitioner Should Know About Income Tax / Cape Town : Legal & Financial Publishing, 1983.
- (Merlen Ser. of Income Tax Publications).

—What Every Merchant-Trader Should Know About Income Tax / Cape Town : Legal & Financial Publishing, 1983.
- (Merlen Ser. of Income Tax Publications).
ISBN 0869940112 Hbk £12.64

—What Every Ophthalmic Surgeon Should Know About Income Tax / Cape Town : Legal & Financial Publishing, 1983.
- (Merlen Ser. of Income Tax Publications).
ISBN 086994021X Hbk £12.64

—What Every Pharmacist Should Know About Income Tax / Cape Town : Legal & Financial Publishing, 1983.
- (Merlen Ser. of Income Tax Publications).
ISBN 086994035X Hbk £12.64

—What Every Professional Person Should Know About Income Tax / Cape Town : Legal & Financial Publishing, 1983.
- (Merlen Ser. of Income Tax Publications).
ISBN 0869940082 Hbk £12.64

—What Every Property Owner Should Know About Income Tax / Cape Town : Legal & Financial Publishing, 1983.
- (Merlen Ser. of Income Tax Publications).

—What Every Real Estate Agent Should Know About Income Tax / Cape Town : Legal & Financial Publishing, 1983.
- (Merlen Ser. of Income Tax Publications).
ISBN 0869940066 Hbk £12.64

—What Every Salaried Person Should Know About Income Tax / Cape Town : Legal & Financial Publishing, 1983.
- (Merlen Ser. of Income Tax Publications).
ISBN 0869940104 Hbk £12.64

—What Every Taxpayer Should Know About Income Tax / 9th ed. - Cape Town : Legal & Financial Publishing, 1983.
- (Merlen Ser. of Income Tax Publications).

INCOME TAX - UNITED KINGDOM

—Income Tax, 1983-84 / 13th ed. Repr. of 1981 ed. - Plymouth : Macdonald & Evans, 1984.
xi, 192p. - (M and E Handbook Ser.).
ISBN 0712109706 Hbk £3.95

INCOME TAX - ZIMBABWE

—Judgments / Income Tax Appeals Special Court of Zimbabwe. - Zimbabwe : The Court, 1980-.
Continues: Income tax appeal: judgment / Income Tax Appeals Special Court, Southern Rhodesia.

INCOME TAX (HINDU LAW)

—Hindu Law of Partition under Income-Tax Law / 2nd ed. repr. - Allahabad : Law Book Company, 1983.

INCORPOREAL HEREDITAMENTS - AUSTRALIA - QUEENSLAND

—Working paper on a bill to amend the real property acts with respect to those provisions relating to writs of execution, bills of encumbrance and bills of mortgage, and caveats / Brisbane : The Commission, 1982.
28p. - (Q.L.R.C.W.P.).

INDEMNITY AGAINST LIABILITY - CANADA

—Law of guarantee : a treatise on guarantee, indemnity and the standby letter of credit / by Kevin Patrick McGuinness. - Toronto : Carswell, 1986.
lxv,456p.
Bibliography: p.lxii-lxv. - Includes index.
ISBN 0459383906

INDEMNITY AGAINST LIABILITY - ENGLAND

—Warranties and indemnities on share sales / Neil Sinclair. - London : Oyez Longman, 1984.
xxiv,331p.
Includes index.
ISBN 0851208703

INDEMNITY AGAINST LIABILITY - GREAT BRITAIN

—Indemnity and Insurance / RIBA Publications, 1985.
ISBN 0900630914 Hbk £12.50

INDEPENDENT REGULATORY COMMISSIONS - CANADA

—Report on independent administrative agencies : a framework for decision making / Law Reform Commission of Canada. - Ottawa : Law Reform Commission of Canada, 1985.
101,11p. - (Working paper).
Bibliography: p.87-94. Added t.p. in French: Rapport sur organismes administratifs autonomes. Pages numbered in opposite directions. Text in English and French.
ISBN 0662537483

INDEXES

—Anguilla consolidated index of statutes and subsidiary legislation to 1st January 1983 / compiled at the Faculty of Law Library, University of the West Indies, Barbados. - Rev. ed. - Barbados : s.n., 1983.
v,73p.
Previous ed.: 1st January 1980. One of a series in the West Indian Legislation Indexing Project (WILIP) compiled in cooperation with the British Development Division.

—Antigua and Barbuda consolidated index of statutes and subsidiary legislation to !st January 1984 / compiled at the Faculty of Law Library, University of the West Indies, Barbados. - Barbados? : s.n., 1984.
iii,87p.
Previous ed.: 1st January 1981. One of a series in the West Indian Legislation Indexing Project (WILIP) compiled in cooperation with the British Development Division.

—Bahamas consolidated index of statutes and subsidiary legislation to 1st January 1982 / compiled at the Faculty of Law Library, University of the West Indies, Barbados. - Barbados : s.n., 1982.
iv,93p.
One of a series in the West Indian Legislation Indexing Project (WILIP) compiled in cooperation with the British Development Division.

—Barbados consolidated index of statutes and subsidiary legislation to 1st January 1986 / compiled at the Faculty of Law Library, University of the West Indies, Barbados. - Bridgetown : Faculty of Law Library, University of the West Indies, 1986.
xi,122p.
Previous ed.: 1st January 1985. 'One of a series in the West Indian Legislation Indexing Project (WILIP) compiled in co-operation with the British Development Division'.

—British Virgin Islands consolidated index of statutes and subsidiary legislation to 1st January 1983 / compiled at the Faculty of Law Library, University of the West Indies, Barbados. - Rev. ed. - Barbados : s.n., 1983.
ii,56p.
Previous ed.: 1st January 1981. One of a series in the West Indian Legislation Indexing Project (WILIP) compiled in cooperation with the British Development Division.

—British Virgin Islands consolidated index of statutes and subsidiary legislation to 1st January 1985 / compiled at the Faculty of Law Library, University of the West Indies, Barbados. - Barbados : s.n., 1985.
iv,67p.
Previous ed.: 1st January 1984. 'One of a series in the West Indian Legislation Indexing Project (WILIP) compiled in coorporation with the British Development Division'.

—Canada Regulations Index, 2 Vols. / Agincourt : Carswell, 1987.

—Canadian Criminal Cases : Index, Annotations, Table of Cases / Aurora : Canada Law Book Co, 1985.
- (Law Reports).

Vols. 1-70 of Second Series 1983.
1184p. - (Law Reports).

—Canadian Criminal Cases New Series (1963-1970), 30 Vols. / Aurora : Canada Law Book Co.
- (Law Reports).

Back Vols.

—Canadian Criminal Cases Old Series (1898-1962), 133 Vols. / Aurora : Canada Law Book Co.
- (Law Reports).

Back vols.

—Canadian Criminal Cases Second Series (1971-1983), 70 Vols. / Aurora : Canada Law Book Co.
- (Law Reports).

Back Vols.

—Canadian Criminal Cases Third Series (March 1983-Present) / Aurora : Canada Law Book Co.
- (Law Reports).

Bound Vol.

—Case-Law of the European Commission of Human Rights /. - Strasbourg : Council of Europe.

—Cayman Islands consolidated index of statutes and subsidiary legislation to 1st January 1980 / compiled at the Faculty of Law and Law Library, University of the West Indies, Barbados. - Bridgetown, Barbados? : Faculty of Law Library, University of the West Indies?, 1980.
iv,64 leaves.
One of a series in the West Indian Legislation Indexing Project (WILIP) compiled in cooperation with the British Development Division.

—Consolidated Index and Noter-up to the South African Law Reports 1973-1979 / Durban : Professional Publishers, 1980.
ISBN 0409016543 Hbk £95.00

—Dominica consolidated index of statutes and subsidiary legislation to 1st January 1984 / compiled at the Faculty of Law Library, University of the West Indies, Barbados. – Bridgetown? : Faculty of Law Library, University of the West Indies, 1984.
iv,97p.
One of a series in the West Indian Legislation Indexing Project (WILIP) compiled in cooperation with the British Development Division.

—Family Law Cumulative Index 1971-1982 / Bristol : Jordan & Sons Ltd, 1985.

—Family Law Reports Cumulative Index 1980-1984 / Bristol : Jordan & Sons Ltd, 1985.

—Fundamental liberties and rights : a 50-State index / by Barbara Faith Sachs : Legislative Drafting Research Fund of Columbia University. - London : Oceana Publications, 1980.
1 v.; 27 cm.
Index to Constitutions of the United States, national and State. 'First in a series of subject matter indices designed to replace the Index digest of State constitutions.'. Loose-leaf for updating.
ISBN 0379204134 £35.00

—Index and Noter-up to the South African Law Reports : 1980-1984 / Durban : Butterworths, 1985.
ISBN 0409016675

—Index of Arab Laws / London : LLoyd's of London Press, 1985.

—Index of International Humanitarian Law / J. Ashley Roach. – Geneva : Comite International de la Croix-Rouge, 1987.
283p.

—Index to Canadian Legal Literature : Supplemental Volumes to the Canadian Abridgment, 3 Vols. / Carswell Legal Publications. – Agincourt : Carswell, 1985-1987.
This multi-volume series is a comprehensive index to legal materials published in Canada. The work contains full bibliographic references to Canadian legal monographs, articles, case comments, annotation, and audio-visual materials.

—Index to Commonwealth Legal Periodicals : 1978-1981, 1 Bound Vol. / Agincourt : Carswell, 1982.

—Index to Governmental Orders in Force on 31-12-83, 2 Vols. / London : HMSO.
ISBN 0118402366 Hbk £105.00

—Index to Irish Superior Court Written Judgments, 1976-1982 / Maeve Doyle. – Galway : Irish Association of Law Teachers.
ISBN 095093240X Hbk

—Index to Legal Citations and Abbreviations / London : Butterworths, 1981.
ISBN 0862050375 Hbk £30.25

—Index to Reports of Tax Cases : 1875-1981, 52 Vols. / Abingdon : Professional Books, 1984.
ISBN 0862050707 Hbk £63.00

—Index to Singapore/Malaysia legal periodicals 1932-1984 / Compiled by the staff of the Law Library, National University of Singapore Library : edited by Molly Cheang, Sng Yok Fong, Carolyn Wee. – Singapore : Malayan Law Journal Pte., 1986.
xvi,431p.
ISBN 9971700506 Hbk £160.00

—Index to Singapore/Malaysia Legal Periodicals / Kent Ridge : Malaya Law Review.

—Index to statutes in force / London : Sweet & Maxwell, 1988.
ISBN 0421317809 Hbk

—Index to the Decisions Rendered By the Immigration Appeal Board / Agincourt : Carswell, 1987.
168p.
This is a comprehensive index to the decisions of the Immigration Appeal Board from 1976 through to 1987. Special legal research features include a key word index, and alphabetical listing by style of case, and a case citator.

—Index to the South African Law Reports : 1828-1946, 2 vols. / F. R. Malan. – Durban : Butterworths.
ISBN 0409040770 Hbk

—Index to the statutes of Alberta, including Spring sitting 1983 / prepared for the Province of Alberta by Canadian Law Information Council. – Edmonton : Queen's Printer, 1983.
vii,876p.

—Index to the Subsidiary Legislation of the Republic of Cyprus / Nicosia : MAM, 1980.
xi, 573p.

1978 and 1979 1980.
v, 43p.

—Index to the Treaty Series / London : HMSO.
ISBN 0101920903 Hbk £3.15

No. 63, 1982
ISBN 0101899203 Hbk £2.70

No. 96, 1981
ISBN 0101856601 Hbk £2.95

No. 97, 1980
ISBN 0101817606 Hbk £2.40

—Indexes to the legislation of Tasmania / Hobart : Office of the Parliamentary Counsel, 1984.
104,124,79p.
Originally published in 3 parts. Contents: Alphabetical table of Tasmanian Acts 1826-1983 - Subject index to statute law - Subject index to subordinate legislation.

—International Bar Association, Section on Energy & Natural Resources Law : seminar topics index 1975-84 : Stavanger, 1975; Cambridge 1, 1978; Cambridge II, 1979; Banff, 1981; Singapore, 1982; Houston, 1984; Oslo, 1984 / S.l. : International Bar Association, Section on Energy & Natural Resources Law, 1986.
24p.
ISBN 0948711027

—Juta's index and annotations to the South African law reports 1980-86 / compiled by David S. Fisher and Alan James : assisted by Owen J. Barrow ... et al. – Cape Town : Juta, 1987.
1100p.
Kept up-to-date by supplements.
ISBN 0702118508

—Labour Arbitration Cases (Second Series) Consolidated Index, List of Awards Vols. 1-30 / Aurora : Canada Law Book Co, 1982.
400p.

—Legal journals index / v. – Hebden Bridge, Yorkshire : Legal Information Resources, 1986.
ISBN 09504206

—Lloyd's Law Reporter : Citator and Subject Index 1987-1988 / London : LLoyd's of London Press, 1989.
ISBN 1850442134 Pbk

—Lloyd's Law Reports : Subject Index 1919-1986, 2 Vols. / London : LLoyd's of London Press, 1988.
ISBN 1850441715 Hbk

—Montserrat consolidated index of statutes and subsidiary legislation to 1st January 1983 / compiled at the Faculty of Law Library, University of the West Indies, Barbados. – Rev. ed. – Barbados : s.n., 1983.
iv,74p.
Previous ed.: 1st January 1980. One of a series in the West Indian Legislation Indexing Project (WILIP) compiled in cooperation with the British Development Division.

—Official Catchword Index to the Fourth Edition (1984) of the International Patent Classification / World Intellectual Property Organization. – Cologne : Carl Heymanns Verlag.
335p.
ISBN 3452200299 Pbk £125.00

—Ontario Revised Statutes : Sectional Tables of Concordance 1980-1970, 1970-1980 / Agincourt : Carswell, 1983.
576p.

—Reports of Family Law Consolidated Index, 4 Vols. / Agincourt : Carswell, 1980.
1331p.

Vol. 2 1980.

Vol. 3 1984.

Vol. 4 1986.

—Saint Christopher and Nevis consolidated index of statutes and subsidiary legislation to 1st January 1984 / compiled at the Faculty of Law Library, University of the West Indies, Barbados. – Barbados? : s.n., 1984.
iv,78p.
Previous ed.: 1st January 1980. One of a series in the West Indian Legislation Indexing Project (WILIP) compiled in cooperation with the British Development Division.

—Saint Christopher, Nevis & Anguilla consolidated index of statutes and subsidiary legislation to 1st January 1980 / compiled at the Faculty of Law and Law Library, University of the West Indies, Barbados. – Cave Hill : Faculty of Law Library, University of the West Indies, 1980.
iv,74p.
One of a series in the West Indies Legislation Indexing Project (WILIP) compiled in cooperation with the British Development Division.

—Saint Lucia consolidated index and subsidiary legislation to 1st January 1984 / compiled at the Faculty of Law Library, University of the West Indies, Barbados. – Barbados? : s.n., 1984.
v,108p.
Previous ed.: 1st January 1983. One of a series in the West Indian Legislation Indexing Project (WILIP) compiled in cooperation with the British Development Division.

—Saint Vincent and the Grenadines consolidated index of statutes and subsidiary legislation to 1st January 1986 / compiled at the Faculty of Law Library, University of the West Indies, Barbados in co-operation with the Ministry of Legal affairs, Kingston, St. Vincent. – Holmes Beach, Fla. : Gaunt, 1986.
ix,103p.
Previous ed.: 1st January 1985. 'One of a series in the West Indian Legislation Indexing Project (WILIP) compiled in co-operation with the British Development Division'.

—Saskatchewan Decisions Citator / Aurora : Canada Law Book Co.

—Subject guide and chronological tables to the subordinate legislation of the Isle of Man / prepared on the directions of H.M. Attorney General for the Isle of Man. – v. – Douglas : Isle of Man Government Printer, 1983-.
looseleaf.

—Subject Index to the Acts and Regulations of the Commonwealth of Australia, 1986 Edition / North Ryde : Law Book Co, 1987.

—Subject index to the acts and regulations of the Commonwealth of Australia / B. M. Wicks. – 1982 ed. – Sydney : Law Book Co., 1983.
146p.
Previous ed. published as: Subject index to the acts of the Parliament of the Commonwealth of Australia (1979). Includes index.

—Subject index to the Acts of New South Wales / compiled by B.M. Wicks. – 1983 ed. – Sydney : Law Book Co., 1984.
141p.

—Tables to the statutes of Saskatchewan and Saskatchewan regulations / Saskatchewan : Queen's Printer, 1980-.
26cm.

—Trinidad and Tobago consolidated index of statutes and subsidiary legislation to 1st January 1983 / compiled at the Faculty of Law Library, University of the West Indies, Barbados. – Rev. ed. – Port-of-Spain : Government Printer, 1983.
ix,105p.
Previous ed.: 1st January 1979. One of a series in the West Indian Legislation Indexing Project (WILIP) compiled in cooperation with the British Development Division.

—Turks and Caicos Islands consolidated index of statutes and subsidiary legislation to 1st January 1983 / compiled at the Faculty of Law Library, University of the West Indies, Barbados. – Rev. ed. – Barbados : s.n., 1983.
iv,46p.
Previous ed.: 1st January 1981. One of a series in the West Indian Legislation Indexing Project (WILIP) compiled in cooperation with the British Development Division.

—Turks and Caicos Islands consolidated index of statutes and subsidiary legislation to 1st January 1981 / compiled at the Faculty of Law Library, University of the West Indies, Barbados. – Bridgetown, Barbados? : Faculty of Law Library, University of the West Indies?, 1981.
iv,43 leaves.
One of a series in the West Indian Legislation Indexing Project (WILIP) compiled in cooperation with the British Development Division.

INDEXES - AUSTRALIA - TASMANIA

—Alphabetical table of Tasmanian acts 1826-1980 / Tasmania : Government Printer, 1980.
75p; 25cm.

INDEXES - CANADA

—Cumulative Index to the Decisions of the Immigration Appeal Board / Agincourt : Carswell, 1987.
180p.

—Index to the Decisions Rendered by the Immigration Appeal Board / Agincourt : Carswell, 1988.
174p.

INDEXES - CANADA - ALBERTA

—Statutes of Alberta judicially considered / R.S.A. 1980 ed. 1 v. – Calgary : Carswell, 1985.
looseleaf.
Previous ed.: 1977-1980.

INDEXES - GREAT BRITAIN

—Subject guide to the Acts of Tynwald / Rev. to 31 Oct. 1984. – Douglas : Isle of Man Government, 1984.
84p.

INDEXES - GRENADA

—Grenada consolidated index of statutes and subsidiary legislation to 29th July 1983 / compiled at the Faculty of Law Library, University of the West Indies, Barbados. – Barbados : s.n., 1983.
vi,104p.
One of a series in the West Indian Legislation Indexing Project (WILIP) compiled in cooperation with the British Development Division.

INDEXES - GUYANA

—Guyana consolidated index of statutes and subsidiary legislation to 1st January 1982 / compiled at the Faculty of Law Library, University of the West Indies, Barbados. – Barbados : s.n., 1983.
x,89p.
One of a series in the West Indian Legislation Indexing Project (WILIP) compiled in cooperation with the British Development Division.

INDEXES - IRELAND

—Index to Irish statutory instruments / Richard F. Humphreys. – 3. – Dublin : Butterworths, 1988.
Contents: v. 1 Statutory instruments - v.2 Enabling Acts - v.3 Subject index.
ISBN 0862052327

INDEXES - JAMAICA

—Jamaica consolidated index of statutes and subsidiary legislation to 1st January 1982 / compiled at the Faculty of Law Library, University of the West Indies, Barbados. – Barbados : s.n., 1983.
v,104p.
One of a series in the West Indian Legislation Indexing Project (WILIP) compiled in cooperation with the British Development Division.

—Jamaica consolidated index of statutes and subsidiary legislation to 1st January 1983 / compiled at the Faculty of Law Library, University of the West Indies, Barbados. – Barbados? : s.n., 1984.
v,146p.
Previous ed.: 1st January 1982. One of a series in the West Indian Legislation Indexing Project (WILIP) compiled in cooperation with the British Development Division.

INDEXES - NIGERIA

—Nigeria-Federal Statutes in Force 1982 : An Index of the Laws of Nigeria Which Are Still in Force As At the 31st December 1984 / Abingdon : Professional Books, 1984.
ISBN 0862050731 Hbk £24.00

INDEXES - SOUTH AFRICA

—Government gazette index : an index to the Government gazette of the Republic of South Africa / Pretoria : State Library, 1979 -.
Indexes Gazette no. 6263 onwards.
ISBN 03796078

INDIA

—Indian Penal Code / Dhirajlal. – 26th ed. – Nagpur : Wadhura & Co, 1987.

—Partition in Ireland, India and Palestine : theory and practice / T.G. Fraser. – London : Macmillan, 1984.
xiii,225p; 23cm.
Bibliography: p210-213. - Includes index.
ISBN 0333322800 £22.50

INDIA - INDIA

—Competing equalities : law and the backward classes in India / Marc Galanter. – Berkeley : University of California Press, 1984.
xxii,625p; 24cm.
Bibliography: p575-611. - Includes index.
ISBN 0520042891 Pbk £38.25

INDIANS OF NORTH AMERICA

—Canada's Indians / by James Wilson. – Rev. ed. – London : Minority Rights Group, 1982.
20p. – (Report).
Previous ed.: 1977. Bibliography: p.20.

—Indian Act Annotated / 2nd ed. – Agincourt : Carswell, 1986.
124p.
This work is a section-by-section analysis of the recently amended Canadian Indian Act. Significant treaties are presented in the appendices to the book. The extent of provincial legislative control of Indians in the areas of matrimonial property division, child welfare, and other topics is addressed in the book.

—Indian Title in Canada / Agincourt : Carswell, 1987.
154p.

—Indian Title in Canada / Agincourt : Carswell, 1987.
154p.
This work focuses on the basis of Indian land claims in Canada and provides a thorough discussion of the court's responses to these claims. The author integrates history and law in explaining the issues.

—Indians and Taxation in Canada, Second Edition / 2nd ed. – Saskatoon : University of Saskatchewan, Native Law Centre, 1987.
88p.
ISBN 0888801823 Hbk £25.00

—Indians and the Law / Vancouver : British Columbia Continuing Legal Education Society, 1982.
420p.
ISBN 0865040524 Hbk £65.00

—Indians and the Law III / Vancouver : British Columbia Continuing Legal Education Society, 1986.
ISBN 0865042675 Hbk £60.00

—Original Americans : U.S. Indians / by James Wilson. – New ed. – London : Minority Rights Group, 1986.
24p. – (Report).
Previous edition: 1980. Bibliography: p.24.
ISBN 0946690391

INDIANS OF NORTH AMERICA - CANADA

—Aboriginal peoples and the law : Indian, Metis and Inuit rights in Canada / edited by Bradford W. Morse. – Ottawa : Carleton University Press, 1985.
xlv,794p. – (Carleton Library Series).
ISBN 0886290198

—Children or Brethren : Aboriginal Rights in Colonial Iroquoia / Saskatoon : University of Saskatchewan, Native Law Centre, 1985.
338p.
ISBN 0888801718 Hbk £75.00

—Indian Act of Canada, Second Edition / 2nd ed. – Saskatoon : University of Saskatchewan, Native Law Centre, 1988.
48p.
ISBN 0888802048 Hbk £10.00

—Indian acts and amendments 1868-1975 : an indexed collection / Sharon Helen Venne. – Saskatchewan : University of Saskatchewan Native Law Centre, 1981.
lxvii,460p.
Includes index. Includes: Consolidation of Indian legislation / prepared by Gail Hinge for the Office of Native Claims, Dept. of Indian and Northern Affairs. Vol.2: Indian acts and amendments, 1868-1975.
ISBN 0888801041

—Indians and the Law 2 / Vancouver : Continuing Legal Education Society of British Columbia, 1985.
181p.
ISBN 0865041334 Hbk £60.00

—Indians and the Law 3 / Vancouver : Continuing Legal Education Society of British Columbia, 1986.
243p.
ISBN 0865042675 Hbk £60.00

—Indians and the Law / Vancouver : Continuing Legal Education Society of British Columbia, 1982.
420p.
ISBN 0865040524 Hbk £70.00

INDIANS OF SOUTH AMERICA

—Amerindians of South America / by Andrew Gray. – London : Minority Rights Group, 1987.
26p. – (Report).
Includes bibliographical references.
ISBN 0946690529

INDICTMENTS - CANADA

—Charge document in criminal cases / Law Reform Commission of Canada. – Ottawa : The Commission, 1987.
57,63p. – (Working paper).
Includes bibliographical references. Added t.p. in French: Le document d'inculpation. Pages numbered in opposite directions. Text in English and French.
ISBN 0662549635

INDICTMENTS - ENGLAND

—Triable-either-way cases : Crown Court or Magistrates' Court? / by David Riley and Julie Vennard. – London : H.M.S.O., 1988.
52 p.
Discusses whether the balance of either-way business could be redistributed in favour of the Magistrates' Court by encouraging them to accept jurisdiction more often in such cases.
ISBN 0113408900

INDIVIDUALISM

—Public and private in social life / edited by S.I. Benn and G.F. Gaus. – London : Croom Helm, 1983.
viii,412p; 23cm.
Includes indexes.
ISBN 0709906684 £19.95
ISBN 0312653573

INDUSTRIAL ACCIDENTS - AUSTRALIA

—Industrial Accidents : Employer Liability for Monetary Damages / Audrey Balla. – North Ryde : C.C.H. Australia, 1987.
180p.
ISBN 0869038664 Hbk

INDUSTRIAL ACCIDENTS - GREAT BRITAIN

—Forensic audiology / Chuang Wei Ping : foreword by Ronald Hinchcliffe. – Middlesbrough : Chuang Wei Ping, 1985.
108p in various pagings; 22cm.
ISBN 0951080008 Pbk £6.00

INDUSTRIAL CONCENTRATION - EUROPEAN COMMUNITY

—Suitability of concentration measures for EEC competition policy / Walter Piesch, Ingo Schmidt. – Luxembourg : Office for Official Publications of the European Communities, 1983.
101 p.; 25 cm.
ISBN 9282531783 pbk. £5.50

INDUSTRIAL CONCENTRATION - GREAT BRITAIN

—Concentration in British industry 1935-75 : a study of the growth, causes and effects of concentration in British manufacturing industries / P.E. Hart and R. Clarke. – Cambridge : Cambridge University Press, 1980.
xiv,164p; 24cm. – (Occasional papers).
Includes index.
ISBN 0521233933 £10.00

INDUSTRIAL EQUIPMENT LEASES

—Leasing finance / edited by Tom Clark. – London : Euromoney Publications, 1985.
ix,147p.
ISBN 0903121778

INDUSTRIAL HYGIENE

—Deterrence and compensation : legal liability in occupational safety and health / Felice Morgenstern. – Geneva : International Labour Office, 1982.
iii,76p.
Bibliography: p73-74.
ISBN 9221030105

INDUSTRIAL HYGIENE - EUROPEAN COMMUNITY

—Law and practice concerning occupational health in the member states of the European Community / Environmental Resources Limited for the Commission of the European Communities. – London : Graham & Trotman for The Commission, 1985.
22cm. – (EUR).
Includes index.
ISBN 0860106268 Hbk £55

Vol. 2 / Environmental Resources Limited for the Commission of the European Communities. – 1985.
22cm. – (EUR).
Includes index.
ISBN 0860106276 Hbk £55

Vol. 3 / Environmental Resources Limited for the Commission of the European Communities. – 1985.
22cm. – (EUR).
Includes index.
ISBN 0860106284 Hbk £45

Vol. 4 / Environmental Resources Limited for the Commission of the European Communities. – 1985.
22cm. – (EUR).
Includes index.
ISBN 0860107949 Hbk £45

Vol. 5 / Environmental Resources Limited for the Commission of the European Communities. – 1985.
22cm. – (EUR).
Includes index.
ISBN 0860107957 Hbk £50

INDUSTRIAL HYGIENE - GREAT BRITAIN

—Health and safety at work : excluding factories and mines / by Ian Fife and E. Anthony Machin. – London : Butterworth, 1980.
lvii,980p; 18cm.
Includes index. Includes the text of relevant legislation.
ISBN 0406200548 £33.00

—Law of health and safety at work / Norman Selwyn. – London : Butterworths, 1982.
xxviii,354p; 22cm.
Includes index.
ISBN 0406667500 Pbk Unpriced

—Law of health and safety at work : the new approach / by Charles D. Drake and Frank B. Wright : with a foreword by John H. Locke. – London : Sweet & Maxwell, 1983.
xii; 25cm.
Includes index.
ISBN 0421286202 Hbk £22.00
ISBN 042128630X Pbk £13.85

INDUSTRIAL HYGIENE - NEW ZEALAND

—Occupational safety : an inquiry into the coordination of legislation on industrial safety, health, and welfare / by I.K. Walker. – Wellington, N.Z. : State Services Commission, 1981.
vi, 142 p.; 30 cm.
Bibliography: p. 140-142.
ISBN 0477015085 pbk.

INDUSTRIAL INJURIES

—Industrial Employment Injuries : an Overview of the Legal Protection System / New Delhi : Deep and Deep Publications, 1986.
388p.

INDUSTRIAL INJURIES - GREAT BRITAIN

—Compensation for Industrial Disablement / London : Butterworths, 1987.
ISBN 0862052149 Hbk £26.50

—National Insurance (Industrial Injuries) Acts, 3 Vols. / London : HMSO.

Vol. II

Vol. VI
ISBN 0117603821 Hbk £2.20

INDUSTRIAL LAW

—Aluminium industry and the Third World : multinational corporations and underdevelopment / Ronald Graham. – London : Zed, 1982.
xii,278p; 22cm.
Bibliography: p263-270. - Includes index.
ISBN 0862320577 Pbk

—Disciplinary Proceedings in Industries and Adjudication / 2nd ed. – Calcutta : Eastern Law House, 1984.

—Elements of Mercantile Law : Including Company and Industrial Law / 15th ed. – New Delhi : Sultan Chand and Sons, 1984.
xxviii, 880p.

—Industrial Law / 14th ed. – Lucknow : Eastern Book Company, 1985.
1,774p.

—Industrial Law / Narang. – Delhi : Dhanpat Rai and Sons.

—Labour Arbitration Cases (L.A.C.) 1948-72, 24 Vols. / Aurora : Canada Law Book Co.

—Law and economics and the economics of legal regulation / edited by J.-Matthias Graf v.d. Schulenburg, Goran Skogh. – Dordrecht : M. Nijhoff, 1986.
248p. – (International studies in economics and econometrics).
'Selected papers of a conference of the International Institute of Management Wissenschaftszentum Berlin.'. Includes index. Contents: Law and economics and the economics of legal regulation / Goran Skogh – Efficiency, equity, and inalienability / Susan Rose-Ackerman – Negotiated settlement / Gordon Tullock – Economic efficiency and the common law / Peter H. Aranson – Default risk and the optimal pricing of court enforcement services / Hugh Gravelle – Transaction cost and communincation / Michael Hutter – Regulatory measures to enforce quality production of self-employed professinals / J.-Matthias Graf v.d. Schulenburg – Controlling insider trading in Europe and America / David D. Haddock, Jonathan R. Macey – The regulatin of shop opening hours in the United Kingdom / Susan M. Jaffer, John A. Kay Belgian public policy towards the retailing trade / Roger Van den Bergh – Assessing the effectiveness of economic efficiency of an E.E.C. pollution control directive / John Ashworth, Ivy Papps, David J. Storey.
ISBN 9024733774 Hbk £135.00

—Law as an instrument of economic policy : comparative and critical approaches / edited by Terence Daintith. – Berlin : W. de Gruyter, 1987.
– (Series A–Law).
Includes index. Bibliography. Based on papers presented at a colloquium held in Florence, Mar. 1985.
ISBN 0899254179

—Legal aspects of doing business in Asia and the Pacific / edited by Dennis Campbell. – Deventer, Netherlands : Kluwer Law and Taxation Publishers, 1984.
– (International business series).
Includes index. Kept up to date by supplements.
ISBN 9065449825

—Legal aspects of doing business in Latin America / edited by Dennis Campbell. – Deventer, The Netherlands : Kluwer Law and Taxation Publishers, 1984.
vii, 351 p.; 25 cm. – (International business series).
Includes index.
ISBN 9065441026

—Legal aspects of doing business in the Middle East / edited by Dennis Campbell. – Deventer, Netherlands : Kluwer Law and Taxation Publishers, 1986.
– (International business series).
Includes index.
ISBN 9065442642

INDUSTRIAL LAW – AFRICA

—Legal aspects of doing business in Africa / edited by Dennis Campbell. – Deventer, The Netherlands : Kluwer Law and Taxation Publishers, 1986.
– (International business series).
Includes index.
ISBN 9065442685

INDUSTRIAL LAW – AUSTRALIA

—Cases and materials on industrial law in Australia / R. Tracey. – Butterworths, 1980.
680p.
This volume, which blends cases and text, has been necessitated by changes in the industrial legislation sphere. Practical problems are presented and references are made to leading articles and books.
ISBN 0409322512 Pbk £57.50

—Current Issues in Industrial Law / Sydney : Butterworths, 1980.
189p.
ISBN 0409412902 Pbk

—Guidebook to Australian Industrial Law / 4th ed. – North Ryde : C.C.H. Australia, 1984.
620P.
ISBN 0869036742 Hbk £40.00

INDUSTRIAL LAW – AUSTRALIA – VICTORIA

—Industrial Law, Victoria / Butterworths, 1981.
ISBN 0409490415 loose

INDUSTRIAL LAW – CANADA

—Canadian Industrial Incentives Legislation, 2 Vols. / Janice A. Lacke. – Butterworths.

—Canadian Industrial Incentives Legislation, 2 vols / Toronto : Butterworths.

—Labour Arbitration Cases (L.A.C.) 1973-81, 30 Vols. / Aurora : Canada Law Book Co.
– (Second Ser.).
Back Vols.

—Labour Arbitration Cases (L.A.C.) 1982-Present / Aurora : Canada Law Book Co.
– (Third Ser.).
Back Vols.
Current subscription-Outside Canada

—Labour Arbitration Cases (Second Series) Consolidated Index, List of Awards Vols. 1-30 / Aurora : Canada Law Book Co, 1982.
400p.

—Law, society, and the economy / Ivan Bernier and Andree Lajoie, research coordinators. – Toronto : University of Toronto Press, 1986.
xv, 230 p.; 23 cm.
Includes bibliographies.
ISBN 0802072917 pbk.

INDUSTRIAL LAW – EUROPEAN COMMUNITY

—Courts and free markets : perspectives from the United States and Europe / edited by Terrance Sandalow and Eric Stein. – Oxford : Clarendon, 1982.
xxxix,271p; 24cm.
ISBN 0198253664 £20.00
Vol.2 / edited by Terrance Sandalow and Eric Stein. – 1982.
vip,p273-600; 24cm.
ISBN 0198253923 Pbk Unpriced

INDUSTRIAL LAW – GREAT BRITAIN

—Burdens on business : report of a scrutiny of administrative and legislative requirements / for the Department of Trade and Industry. – London : H.M.S.O., 1985.
vi,71p.
Team leader: N. P. Brecknell.
ISBN 011513820X

—Commercial and Industrial Law / 3rd ed. – Plymouth : Macdonald & Evans, 1984.
ISBN 0712101950 Pbk £6.50

—Commercial and Industrial Law / Plymouth : Macdonald & Evans, 1981.
336p. – (M and E Handbook Ser.).
ISBN 071210464X Hbk £4.95

—Industrial Development Act 1982 / London : HMSO, 1983.
ISBN 0102072841 Hbk £8.60

—Industrial law / I.T. Smith, Sir John C. Wood. – 3rd ed. – London : Butterworths, 1986.
516p; 25cm.
Previous ed.: 1983. Includes index.
ISBN 0406381445 Hbk No price
ISBN 0406381453 Pbk No price

—Industrial law / Wood. – 3rd ed. – London : Butterworths, 1986.
ISBN 0406381453 Pbk £17.95

—Knight's Industrial and Commercial Reports : 1966-75, 17 Vols. / Professional Books Staff. – Abingdon : Professional Books, 1984.

—Liability of an Industrialist / London : Sweet & Maxwell, 1985.
– (Sweet and Maxwell's Law Files Ser.: No. 6).
ISBN 0421340304 loose £29.50

—Practice and procedure in industrial tribunals / London : Legal Action Group, 1986.
ISBN 0905099141 Pbk £7.50

—Procedure in Industrial Tribunals / London : Engineering Employers Federation, 1985.

INDUSTRIAL LAW – INDIA

—Commentaries on Industrial Employment Standing Orders Act, 1946 : Including Model Standing Orders, Recognition of Unions and Unfair Labour Practices / 2nd ed. – Lucknow : Eastern Book Company, 1982.
844p.

—Commentaries on the Industrial Disputes Act 1947 / 3rd ed. – Allahabad : Law Publishing House, 1983.
ca 1,000p.

—Handbook of Labour and Industrial Law / 2nd ed. – Lucknow : Eastern Book Company, 1986.

—Handbook of Labour and Industrial Law / 3rd ed. – Lucknow : Eastern Book Company, 1986.

—Idra and Industrial Licensing : With Rules Forms Notifications, Press Notes, Guidelines, Policies / New Delhi : Bharat Law House, 1987.

—Indian Mercantile Law and Industrial Law / K.C. Garg. – New Delhi : Kalyani Publishers, 1984.

—Industrial and Commercial Law / K.C. Garg. – 7th ed. 1986 repr. – New Delhi : Kalyani Publishers, 1987.
ISBN 8170960932 Hbk £60.00

—Industrial and Labour Law / Calcutta : Eastern Law House.
1,298p.

—Law of Industrial Disputes : as Amended by Amendment Act No. 46 of 1982, 2 Vols. / 2nd ed. – New Delhi : Bharat Law House, 1986.

—Textbook of Industrial Law / K.C. Garg. – 5th ed. – New Delhi : Kalyani Publishers, 1986.

—Textbook of Labour and Industrial Laws / Lucknow : Eastern Book Company, 1980.
416p.

INDUSTRIAL LAW – NETHERLANDS

—Dutch business law : legal, accounting, and tax aspects of business in the Netherlands / by Steven R. Schuit and Jan M. van der Beek and Bonne K. Raap, and Michael W. den Boogert ... et al. – 2nd ed. – Deventer, Netherlands : Kluwer Law and Taxation Publishers, 1983.
xl, 552 p.; 25 cm.
Includes index.
ISBN 9065441220

INDUSTRIAL LAW – NEW ZEALAND

—Industrial Law / Stepensons. – 7th ed. – Wellington : Butterworths.
ISBN 0409667706 Hbk

—Industrial Law Bulletin / Alexander Szakats. – Wellington : Butterworths.
ISBN 040978107X Pbk

—Mazengarb's Industrial Law / Angus McLeod. – Butterworths.

INDUSTRIAL LAW – UNITED STATES

—Courts and free markets : perspectives from the United States and Europe / edited by Terrance Sandalow and Eric Stein. – Oxford : Clarendon, 1982.
xxxix,271p; 24cm.
ISBN 0198253664 £20.00
Vol.2 / edited by Terrance Sandalow and Eric Stein. – 1982.
vip,p273-600; 24cm.
ISBN 0198253923 Pbk Unpriced

INDUSTRIAL LAW – USSR

—Legal aspects of doing business in Eastern Europe and the Soviet Union / edited by Dennis Campbell. – Deventer, The Netherlands : Kluwer Law and Taxation Publishers, 1986.
– (International business series).
Includes index and bibliography.
ISBN 9065442634

INDUSTRIAL LAW – ZAMBIA

—Zambia industrial cases reports / compiled by K.C. Muwang'u. – v. – Lusaka : Ministry of Labour and Social Services, 1983.

INDUSTRIAL MANAGEMENT – GREAT BRITAIN

—Man mismanagement / Alan Fox. – 2nd ed. – London : Business Books, 1985.
224p.
Previous ed.: London : Hutchinson, 1974. Includes bibliography and index.
ISBN 0091593808 Pbk £7.95

INDUSTRIAL MARKETING

—Collective bargaining in industrialised market economies : a reappraisal / J. P. Windmuller, W. Albeda. – Geneva : International Labour Office, 1987.
xii,333p; 24cm.
Contents: Part 1.: A comparative study, by John P. Windmuller - Part 2.: Country studies, by W. Albeda ... et al..
ISBN 9221056074

INDUSTRIAL ORGANIZATION

—Collective bargaining in industrialised market economies : a reappraisal / J. P. Windmuller, W. Albeda. – Geneva : International Labour Office, 1987.
xii,333p; 24cm.
Contents: Part 1.: A comparative study, by John P. Windmuller - Part 2.: Country studies, by W. Albeda ... et al..
ISBN 9221056074

—Managerial hierarchies : comparative perspectives on the rise of the modern industrial enterprise / edited by Alfred D. Chandler, Jr and Herman Daems. – Cambridge, Mass. : Harvard University Press, 1980.
xi,237p; 24cm. – (Harvard studies in business history).
Includes index.
ISBN 0674547403

INDUSTRIAL PROMOTION

—Role of local authorities in promoting the creation or operation of small or medium-sized firms within a general policy of endogenous development / report prepared under the guidance of the Committee of Experts on Social and Economic Activities of the Steering Committee for Regional and Municipal Matters by T. Nuttal. – Strasbourg : Council of Europe, 1986.
31p.
Bibliography: p.28-29.

INDUSTRIAL PROMOTION - EUROPEAN COMMUNITY

—State and community aids for European industry : their control and grant / Philip Bentley. – 1 v. – London : European Business Publications, 1983. looseleaf.
ISBN 0946262012

INDUSTRIAL PROMOTION - GREAT BRITAIN

—Building businesses - not barriers / presented to Parliament by the Secretary of State for Employment : supported by the Secretary of State for Foreign and Commonwealth Affairs ... et al. – London : H.M.S.O., 1986.
80p; 25cm.
ISBN 0101979401

INDUSTRIAL PROPERTY

—Committee of Experts on Biotechnological Inventions and Industrial Property : third session, Geneva, June 29 to July 3, 1987 : industrial property protection of biotechnological inventions / revised report prepared by the International Bureau. – Geneva : World Intellectual Property Organization, 1987.
73p. – (BioT/CE/III/2).
At head of cover: International Union for the Protection of Industrial Property (Paris Union).

—Committee of Experts on Biotechnological Inventions and Industrial Property : third session, Geneva, June 29 to July 3, 1987 : report prepared by the International Bureau / World Intellectual Property Organization. – Geneva : World Intellectual Property Organization, 1987.
32,11p. – (BioT/CE/III/3).
'Convened ... as part of the 1986/87 program of the International (Paris) Union for the Protection of Industrial Property ...'. - Introduction.

—Committee of Experts on Biotechological Inventions and Industrial property : first session, Geneva, November 5 to 9, 1984 / report adopted by the Committee of Experts. – Geneva : World Intellectual Property Organizatioan, 1984.
23,7p. – (BioT/CE/I/3).
'Convened ... as part of the 1984/85 program of the International (Paris) Union for the Protection of Industrial Property ... '. - Introduction.

—Guide on the Industrial Property Activities of Enterprises in Developing Countries / Geneva : World Intellectual Property Organization, 1983.
31p.

—Licensing Guide for Developing Countries : the Legal Aspects of the Negotiation and Preparation of Industrial Property Licenses and Technology Transfer Agreements Appropriate to the Needs of Developing Countries (1977) / Geneva : World Intellectual Property Organization, 1987.
184p.

—Paris Convention for the Protection of Industrial Property from 1883 to 1983 / Geneva : World Intellectual Property Organization, 1983.
229p.

—Paris Convention for the Protection of Industrial Property : Official English Text of the Stockholm Act (1967) / rep. 1987. – Geneva : World Intellectual Property Organization.
43p.

—Piracy and counterfeiting of industrial property and copyright : papers given at the inaugural conference of the Common Law Institute of Intellectual Property Ltd in London on 28th and 29th January 1983 / edited by W.R. Cornish. – London : Common Law Institute of Intellectual Property, 1983.
143p.
ISBN 0903067277

—Report / adopted by the Committee of Experts. – Geneva : World Intellectual Property Organization, 1986.
10p. – (BIOT/CE/II/3).
'Convened ... as part of the 1986/87 program of the International (Paris) Union for the Protection of Industrial Property' - Introduction.

—Role of Government Industrial Property Authorities and the Legal Profession in Administering Industrial Property Rights in Asia and the Pacific / Geneva : World Intellectual Property Organization, 1983.
314p.

—Role of Industrial Property in the Protection of Consumers / Geneva : World Intellectual Property Organization, 1983.
69p.

—Seminar on Computerization in Industrial Property Administration for Asian Countries / Geneva : World Intellectual Property Organization, 1987.
222p.

—Symposium on Industrial Property and Economic and Technological Development / Geneva : World Intellectual Property Organization, 1988.
ca 150p.

—Symposium on the Effective Protection of Industrial Property Rights / Geneva : World Intellectual Property Organization, 1987.
299p.

INDUSTRIAL PROPERTY - AFRICA

—Situation of Industrial Property in the Countries of Africa / Geneva : World Intellectual Property Organization, 1987.
715p.

INDUSTRIAL PROPERTY - ASIA

—Situation of Industrial Property in the Countries of Asia and the Pacific / Geneva : World Intellectual Property Organization, 1984.
420p.

INDUSTRIAL PROPERTY - GREAT BRITAIN

—Industrial property citator / by Michael Fysh and Robert Wilson Thomas. – London : European Law Centre, 1982.
321p; 26cm.
Includes index.
ISBN 0907451047 Unpriced

—Intellectual property rights and innovation : presented to Parliament by the Prime Minister ... December 1983 / Great Britain. – London : H.M.S.O., 1983.
45p; 25cm.
ISBN 010191170X Pbk £4.65

—International business agreements : a practical guide to the negotiation and formulation of agency distribution and intellectual property licensing agreements / Patrick Hearn. – Aldershot : Gower, 1987.
viii,222p; 24cm.
Includes index.
ISBN 0566025973 £27.50

—Passing off : law and practice / John Drysdale, Michael Silverleaf. – London : Butterworths, 1986.
xxxiv,224p; 26cm.
Includes index.
ISBN 0406253404 £25.00

INDUSTRIAL PROPERTY - HONG KONG

—Law of Intellectual and Industrial Property in Hong Kong / London : Butterworths, 1984.
ISBN 0406181179 Pbk £50.00

—Law of intellectual and industrial property in Hong Kong : a guide to trade marks, copyright, patents, registered designs and other protected commercial information / Michael D. Pendleton. – London : Butterworth, 1984.
xxxix,556p.
Deals with Hong Kong's intellectual property law, including both civil and criminal remedies. Discusses passing off, registered trademarks, trade descriptions, legislation, copyright, patents, registered designs, and trade secrets.
ISBN 0406181179

INDUSTRIAL PROPERTY - OCEANIA

—Situation of Industrial Property in the Countries of Asia and the Pacific / Geneva : World Intellectual Property Organization, 1984.
420p.

INDUSTRIAL PROPERTY - SOUTH KOREA

—Business laws in Korea : investment, taxation, and industrial property / Chan-jin Kim, editor. – Seoul, Korea : Panmun Book Co., 1982.
xii, 799 p.; 24 cm.
Includes bibliographical references.

INDUSTRIAL PROPERTY - WEST GERMANY

—Industrial property laws of the Federal Republic of Germany : patent, utility model, trademark, design : texts of the laws, orders, regulations, guidelines and index / translated and edited by Volker Vossius and Ulrich C. Hallmann. – 2nd ed. – Munchen : Wila Verlag fur Wirtschaftswerbung Wilhelm Lampl, 1985.
278p.
Includes index.
ISBN 3879101477

INDUSTRIAL PROPERTY (INTERNATIONAL LAW)

—Committee of Experts on Biotechological Inventions and Industrial property : first session, Geneva, November 5 to 9, 1984 / report adopted by the Committee of Experts. – Geneva : World Intellectual Property Organizatioan, 1984.
23,7p. – (BioT/CE/I/3).
'Convened ... as part of the 1984/85 program of the International (Paris) Union for the Protection of Industrial Property ... '. - Introduction.

—Industrial property laws and treaties / compiled and published by the World Intellectual Property Organization. – Geneva : WIPO, 1976-.

INDUSTRIAL RELATIONS

—Comparative industrial relations : an introduction to cross-national perspectives / R. Bean. – London : Croom Helm, 1985.
iv,288p.
Includes bibliography and index.
ISBN 0709932510 Hbk £19.95
ISBN 0709932812 Pbk £9.95

—Comparative labour law and industrial relations / editor, Blanpain, R. : contributors Aaron, B. ... et al. – 3rd ed. – Deventer, The Netherlands : Kluwer Law and Taxation Publishers, 1987.
xiii, 527p.
Includes indexes.
ISBN 9065443169

—Comparative labour law and industrial relations / editor, R. Blanpain : associate editor, F. Millard. – Deventer, The Netherlands : Kluwer, 1982.
411 p.; 25 cm.
Includes indexes.
ISBN 9031201790

—Cooperation between management and labor : a survey of co-determination mechanisms in European corporations / Walter Kolvenbach. – Deventer, Netherlands : Kluwer Law and Taxation Publishers, 1982.
89 p.; 25 cm.
ISBN 9065440666 pbk.

—Economic crisis, trade unions and the state / edited by Otto Jacobi ... et al. – London : Croom Helm, 1986.
295p; 23cm.
Includes bibliographies and index. Includes papers translated from German and Italian.
ISBN 0709914474 £19.95

—Employee participation / Terence P. Kenny. – 1 sound cassette. – London : Instructional Dynamics, 1974.

—Employer-employee relations in the public service of Canada : proposals for legislative change / J. Finkelman. – 4 v. – Ottawa : Information Canada, 1974.
Includes bibliographical references. Contents: Parts 1-3 - Supplementary observations and recommendations. Parallel English and French texts, Part 3 and Supplementary observations and recommendations.

—Equality and prohibition of discrimination in employment / editor R. Blanpain. – Deventer, The Netherlands : Klwver, 1985.
244p.
ISBN 9065442154

—Freedom of Association, Industrial Relations and Collective Bargaining Practices in Mines Other than Coal Mines / Geneva : International Labour Office, 1984.
iv, 79p.
ISBN 9221034577 Hbk £15.00

—Industrial conflict resolution in market economics : a study of Australia, the Federal Republic of Germany, Italy, Japan and the USA / T. Hanami editor : R. Blanpain associate editor. – Deventer : Kluwer Law and Taxation, 1984.
xiv,321p; 25cm.
Includes bibliographies and index.
ISBN 9065441808 Pbk No price

—Industrial relations : an international and comparative bibliography / compiled by John Bennett and Julian Fawcett for the British Universities Industrial Relations Association. – London : Mansell, 1985.
200p; 23cm.
Includes index.
ISBN 0720117879 £20.00

—Industrial relations and multinational corporations in Europe / Bruno Liebhaberg. – Farnborough, Hants. : Gower in association with the European Centre for Study and Information on Multinational Corporations (ECSM), 1980.
xiv,107p; 23cm.
ISBN 0566003635 £9.50

—Industrial relations : challenges and prospects : a report on the Warwick conference of March 1986 / P.K.Edwards. – Coventry : Industrial Relations Research Unit, School of Industrial and Business Studies, University of Warwick, 1986.

—International Encyclopaedia for Labour Law and Industrial Relations. Supplements / Dordrecht : Kluwer.

46
47
48
49 1985.
50 1985.
96p.
51 1985.
208p.
52 1985.
264p.
53 1985.
224p.
54 1985.
168p.
55 1985.
120p.

—International issues in industrial relations / Industrial Relations Society of Australia. – Gordon, N.S.W. : The Society, 1983.
vi,125p.
Convention proceedings. Includes bibliographical references.

—International journal of comparative labour law and industrial relations / v. – Leicester : University of Leicester, 1985.

—Labor relations in 17 countries / Christian Bratt : translated by David Jenkins. – Stockholm : Swedish Employers' Confederation, 1982.
134p.
Translated from 'Arbetsmarknaden i 16 lander' by David Jenkins.
ISBN 9171522514

—Law as an instrument of state intervention in industrial relations / Yiannis Gabriel. – London : Thames Polytechnic School of Business Administration, 1984.

—Legal implications of disclosure in the public interest : an analysis of prohibitions and protections with particular reference to employers and employees / Yvonne Cripps. – Oxford : ESC, 1986.
xx,299p; 24cm.
Bibliography: p289-296. - Includes index.
ISBN 0906214408 Pbk £32.50

—OECD guidelines for multinational enterprises and labour relations, 1982-1984 : experience and review / by R. Blanpain : foreword by M. Eyskens. – Deventer : Kluwer Law and Taxation Publishers, 1985.
Includes index.
ISBN 9065442073

—Order and conflict in contemporary capitalism / edited by John H. Goldthorpe : sponsored by the Joint Committee on Western Europe of the American Council of Learned Societies and the Social Science Research Council. – Oxford : Clarendon, 1984.
352p.
Conference papers.
ISBN 0198780087 Hbk £22.50
ISBN 0198780079 Pbk £8.50

—Restructuring labour in the enterprise : law and practice in France, F.R. of Germany, Italy, Sweden and the United Kingdom / edited by R. Blanpain. – Deventer, The Netherlands : Kluwer, .
v,145p.
Includes bibliographical references. At head of cover: Institute for Labour Relations, Catholic University of Leuven.
ISBN 9065442839

—Selected Basic Agreements and Joint Declarations on Labour-Management Relations / Geneva : International Labour Office, 1983.
iv, 299p.
ISBN 9221034607 Hbk £25.00

—Technological change, rationalisation and industrial relations / edited by Otto Jacobi ... et al. – London : Croom Helm, 1986.
283p; 23cm.
Includes bibliography and index.
ISBN 0709914482 £19.95

—Workplace communications / Advisory Conciliation and Arbitration Service. – rev. – London : ACAS, 1983.
– (Advisory booklet).
ISBN 0906073057 Hbk

INDUSTRIAL RELATIONS - AUSTRALIA

—Australian industrial relations system / Department of Industrial Relations. – Rev. ed. – Canberra : Australian Government Publishing Service, 1980.
23p.
ISBN 0642016771

—Industrial Relations Legislation : Interim Report, September, 1982 / Industrial Relations Legislation (Senate Select) Committee. – Canberra : Australian Government Publishing Service, 1982.

—Unions and Arbitration '81 - Papers and Discussion of the Armidale Industrial Law and Relations Seminar / D. Smith. – Sydney : Butterworths, 1981.
152p.
ISBN 040930929X Pbk

INDUSTRIAL RELATIONS - CANADA

—Canada Labour Relations Board : Federal Law and Practice / Agincourt : Carswell, 1983.
450p.

—Canada Labour Relations Board : Federal Law and Practice / Agincourt : Carswell, 1983.
450p.
This book provides a description and discussion of the character, activity, practice, and role of the Canadian Labour Relations Board in its historical, constitutional, and institutional setting.

—Canada Labour Relations Board Policies and Procedure / Toronto : Butterworths, 1986.
640p.

—Canada Labour Relations Board Policies and Procedures / Butterworths, 1986.
640p.
Describes the rules and practices of the Canada Labour Relations Board in the administration of Parts IV and V of the Canada Labour Code. Makes reference to all numbered decisions of the CLRB since 1973, decisions of the Federal Court and the Supreme Court of Canada, reviewing CLRB decisions. Also includes decisions of the Canadian common law courts which have interpreted the code.
ISBN 0409819751 Hbk £95.00

—Canadian Labour Relations Board Report / Toronto : Butterworths.

—Canadian Labour Relations Board Reports / Labour Relations Board of British Columbia. – Butterworths.

—Essays in Labour Relations Law / Don Mills : CCH Canadian Ltd.
290p.
ISBN 0887963153 Pbk £16.00

—Industrial Relations Reform Act / Vancouver : Continuing Legal Education Society of British Columbia, 1987.
157p.
ISBN 0865043329 Hbk £70.00

—Labour Arbitration - 1985 / Vancouver : British Columbia Continuing Legal Education Society, 1985.
116p.
ISBN 0865042063 Hbk £55.00

—Labour Arbitration : Boon or Bane for Unions? / Toronto : Butterworths.
70p.
ISBN 0409988618 Pbk £29.95

—Labour Arbitration Cases : Consolidated Index / Aurora : Canada Law Book Co, 1985.
– (Law Reports).

—Labour Arbitration Cases : Consolidated Index, List of Awards / Aurora : Canada Law Book Co, 1982.
400p. – (Law Reports).

—Labour Arbitration Cases First Series (1948-1972), 24 Vols. / Aurora : Canada Law Book Co.
– (Law Reports).

Back Vols.

—Labour Arbitration Cases Second Series (1973-1981), 30 Vols. / Aurora : Canada Law Book Co.
– (Law Reports).

Back Vols.

—Labour Arbitration Cases Third Series (1982-Present) / Aurora : Canada Law Book Co.
– (Law Reports).

Back Vols.

—Labour Arbitrations and All That / 2nd ed. – Aurora : Canada Law Book Co, 1985.
146p. – (Text Books-Civil).

—Labour law and industrial relations in Canada / by H. W. Arthurs, D. D. Carter, H. J. Glasbeek. – Deventer, The Netherlands : Kluwer, 1981.
291p.
Originally published as a monograph in the International encyclopedia of labour law and industrial relations.
ISBN 9031201391 Kluwer

—Labour Relations Act : Rules of Procedure, Regulations and Practice Notes / Office of the Legislative Assembly (Ontario). – Ontario : Ontario Government Publications Service, 1983.
177p.

—Labour relations and the collective bargaining cycle / Gerald E. Phillips. – 2nd ed. – Toronto : Butterworths, 1981.
xiii,333p.
Previous ed.: published as 'The practice of labour relations and collective bargaining in Canada', 1977. Includes bibliographies and index.

—Labour Relations and the Collective Bargaining Cycle : Second Edition / Toronto : Butterworths, 1981.
352p.

—Labour Relations Board Practice / Vancouver : British Columbia Continuing Legal Education Society, 1985.
193p.
ISBN 0865042144 Hbk £55.00

—Practical guide to labour arbitration procedure / Aurora : Canada Law Book, 1987.

INDUSTRIAL RELATIONS - CANADA - BRITISH COLUMBIA

—British Columbia Annotated Industrial Relations Act, 2 vols. / Toronto : Butterworths.

—British Columbia annotated Industrial Relations Act / Russell, DuMoulin. – 2 vols. – Scarborough, Ontario : Butterworths (Canada).
Provides a section by section annotation of the Act. Contains digests of key British Columbia Labour Relations Board and Curt decisions, with commentary, tables of concordance, and an index.

—British Columbia Labour Relations Board Decisions (1979-Present) / Aurora : Canada Law Book Co.
– (Summary Services, Provincial Ser.).

INDUSTRIAL RELATIONS - CANADA - ONTARIO

—Annual report / Ontario Labour Relations Board / Ontario Labour Relations Board. – v. – Toronto : The Board, 1981.
Report year ends 31 Mar..
ISBN 0711849X

—Ontario Labour Relations Board Law and Practice / C. Michael Mitchell. – Butterworths, 1985.
ca 736p.
Deals with labour relations issues dealt with by the Ontario Labour Relations Board. Issues and proceedings covered include certification and termination of bargaining rights, unfair labour practices, sale of a business and related employer provisions, jurisdictional disputes, occupational health and safety, all construction matters and judicial review.
ISBN 0409865400 Hbk £115.00

—Ontario Labour Relations Board Law and Practice : Citation Updater, 1 Vol. / Butterworths.
ISBN 0409847887 loose £40.00

—Ontario Labour Relations Board Law and Practice : Citation Updater / Toronto : Butterworths.

—Ontario Labour Relations Board Reports : A Monthly Series of Decisions from the Ontario Labour Relations Board / Ontario Labour Relations Board. – Ontario : Ontario Government Publications Service, 1983.
215p.

INDUSTRIAL RELATIONS - EUROPE

—European trade unions in figures / Kluwer Law and Taxation, 1989.
Presents a comparative set of data and sources on union membership in ten European countries - Austria, Denmark, France, West Germany, Italy, the Netherlands, Norway, Sweden, Switzerland and the UK. Gives emphasis to comparative definitions of union membership and union density, that is, the ratio of actual to potential memberships.
ISBN 9065444092 Pbk £24.50/Dfl 79

INDUSTRIAL RELATIONS - EUROPEAN COMMUNITY

—Draft European Communities directive on procedures for informing and consulting employees / Draft European Communities fifth directive on the harmonisation of comapny law : Department of Employment, Department of Trade and Industry. – London : The Departments, 1983.
90p.

—EEC Vth Directive - a Trojan bullock? / prepared by Andrew Hutchinson. – London : Institute of Directors, 1980.
48p; 30cm.

—Prevention and settlement of industrial conflict in the Community member states / Luxembourg : Office for Official Publications of the European Communities, 1984.
162,16p.
At head of title page: Commission of the European Communities.
ISBN 9282550095

—Workers' participation in the European Community : the fifth directive / R. Blanpain, J. L. Janssen van Raay, A. Mouty. – Deventer : Kluwer, 1984.
ix,294p.
ISBN 9065441875

INDUSTRIAL RELATIONS – FINLAND

—Labour law and industrial relations in Finland / by A.J. Suviranta. – Helsinki : Finnish Lawyers, 1987.
187p; 25cm.
Bibliography: p57-61. - Includes index.
ISBN 9065443444 Pbk No price
ISBN 9516403573 Finland

INDUSTRIAL RELATIONS – FRANCE

—Labour law and industrial relations in France / by Michel Despax and Jacques Rojot. – Deventer : Kluwer Law and Taxation, 1987.
314p.
Includes index.
ISBN 9065443436

INDUSTRIAL RELATIONS – GREAT BRITAIN

—Authority and participation in industry / Peter Brannen. – London : Batsford Academic and Educational, 1983.
173p; 22cm.
Bibliography: p157-168. - Includes index.
ISBN 0713443987 Pbk £6.95

—British workplace industrial relations 1980-1984 : the DE/PSI/ESRC/ACAS surveys / Neil Millward and Mark Stevens. – Aldershot : Gower, 1986.
xxi,341p; 22cm.
Includes index.
ISBN 0566053918 Hbk £22.50
ISBN 0566053969 Pbk £9.95

—Case Studies in Industrial Relations / London : Kogan Page, 1982.
226p.
ISBN 0850384184 Hbk £13.50

—Changing contours of British industrial relations : a survey of manufacturing industry / edited by William Brown : with contributions by Eric Batstone ... et al. – Oxford : Basil Blackwell, 1981.
xi,160p; 23cm.
Bibliography: p149-153. - Includes index.
ISBN 0631127755 Hbk £10.00
ISBN 0631128255 Pbk £4.50

—Conflict or cooperation? : the growth of industrial democracy / 2nd ed. – London : Kogan Page, 1983.
350p.
Previous ed.: 1978.
ISBN 0850387477 Hbk £12.00
ISBN 0850387582 Pbk £6.95

—Employee participation : practice and attitudes in north-west manufacturing industry / by M.J. Dowling...et al. – London : Department of Employment, 1981.
44p. – (Research paper).

—History of British industrial relations 1875-1914 / edited by Chris Wrigley. – Brighton : Harvester, 1982.
xv,269p; 23cm.
Includes index.
ISBN 0710803168 £25.00

—Industrial relations / Routledge, 1986.
ISBN 0710097964 Hbk £16.95

—Industrial relations / 3rd ed. – Oxford : Croom Helm, 1985.
ISBN 0709914741 Pbk £9.95

—Industrial relations in Britain / edited by George Sayers Bain. – Oxford : Blackwell, 1983.
xii,516p; 24cm.
Bibliography: p457-487. - Includes index.
ISBN 0631131388 Hbk Unpriced
ISBN 0631132953 Pbk £9.95

—Industrial relations law reports / London : Eclipse Publications, 1972-.
Annual cumulative indexes.

—Industrial Tribunal Reports : 1966-1978, 13 Vols. / Professional Books Staff. – Abingdon : Professional Books, 1984.

—Labour Law and Industrial Relations / Oxford : Oxford University Press, 1983.
ISBN 0198254822 Pbk £9.50

—Labour Relations and the Law / London : Butterworths, 1988.
ISBN 0406015503 Hbk

—Labour Relations Statutes and Materials / 2nd ed. – London : Sweet & Maxwell, 1983.
ISBN 0421320109 Pbk £17.50

—Law of Industrial Conflict / London : Macmillan, 1987.
ISBN 0333419138 Hbk £35.00

—Law of Industrial Relations / London : Butterworths, 1981.
ISBN 0406648107 Pbk £12.95

—Man mismanagement / Alan Fox. – 2nd ed. – London : Business Books, 1985.
224p.
Previous ed.: London : Hutchinson, 1974. Includes bibliography and index.
ISBN 0091593808 Pbk £7.95

—On industrial relations : interprofessional relationships in health care and the role of criminal law in industrial relations / R. Dyson and A.N. Khan. – Leeds : Centre for Social Work and Applied Social Studies, University of Leeds, 1982.
27p. – (Occasional papers).

—Politics in industrial society : the experience of the British system since 1911 : by Keith Middlemas / London : Deutsch, 1980.
512p; 24m.
Originally published: 1979. Includes index.
ISBN 0233973028 Pbk £5.95

—Politics of industrial relations / Colin Crouch. – 2nd ed. – London : Fontana, 1982.
255p.
Bibliography: p223-239.

—War, law and labour : the Munitions Acts, state regulation and the unions, 1915-1921 / Gerry R. Rubin. – Oxford : Clarendon Press, 1987.
288p; 22cm.
Includes index.
ISBN 0198255381 £25.00

—Worker-directors in private manufacturing industry in Great Britain / Brian Towers, Derek Cox, Elizabeth Chell. – London : Department of Employment, 1987.
34p. – (Research paper).
Bibliography: p33-34.

—Working order : workplace industrial relations over two decades / Eric Batstone. – Oxford : Basil Blackwell, 1984.
viii,363p; 24cm.
Bibliography: p344-357. - Includes index.
ISBN 0631137513 £19.50

—Workplace industrial relations and technical change / W.W. Daniel. – London : F. Pinter in association with Policy Studies Institute, 1987.
312 p.; 23 cm.
Includes bibliographical references and index.
ISBN 0861879171

—Workplace industrial relations in Britain : the DE/PSI/SSRC survey / W.W. Daniel and Neil Millward. – London : Heinemann Educational, 1983.
xiii,338p; 23cm.
Includes index.
ISBN 0435831909

INDUSTRIAL RELATIONS – INDIA

—Commentaries on Industrial Disputes Act, 1947 / 6th ed. – Lucknow : Eastern Book Company, 1985.
1,590p.

—Commentaries on the Uttar Pradesh Industrial Disputes Act, 1947 / 4th ed. – Lucknow : Eastern Book Company.

INDUSTRIAL RELATIONS – MALAYSIA

—Industrial Disputes Law in Malaysia / Singapore : Malayan Law Journal, 1984.
393p.
Reproduces the Industrial Relations Act with annotations from the decisions of the Industrial Court and the superior courts of Malaysia. Covers protection of rights of workmen and employers and their trade unions, collective bargaining and collective agreement, representation on dismissals, Industrial Relations Regulations 1967, and 1980.
ISBN 967962000X Hbk £90.00

INDUSTRIAL RELATIONS – NEW ZEALAND

—System of Industrial Relations in New Zealand / 2nd rev. ed. – Butterworths, 1988.
496p.
ISBN 0409788546 Pbk £70.00

—System of Industrial Relations in New Zealand / Wellington : Butterworths, 1983.
Gives a definition of industrial relations and a description of the New Zealand system, covers the parties involved in industrial relations, government, workers and unions, managers and employers, deals with the making and interpretation of rules and regulations, and discusses strikes, industrial conflict, dismissal and redundancy.
ISBN 0409621609 Pbk

INDUSTRIAL RELATIONS – NORTHERN IRELAND

—Industrial Tribunals in Northern Ireland / John McKee. – 2nd ed. – Belfast : Queen's University of Belfast, 1986.
125p.

INDUSTRIAL RELATIONS – PAKISTAN

—Law of industrial relations in Pakistan : commentary on the Industrial Relations Ordinance 1969 / Obaidur Rahman. – Karachi : Asia Law House, 1984.
v,43p.
Bibliography: p.44.

INDUSTRIAL RELATIONS – SCOTLAND

—Industrial democracy and participation : a Scottish survey / by Peter Cressey...et al. – London : Department of Employment, 1981.
62p. – (Research paper).

INDUSTRIAL RELATIONS – UNITED STATES

—Labour Law and Industrial Relations in the United States of America / 2nd ed. – Dordrecht : Kluwer, 1984.
374p.
ISBN 9065441689 Pbk £95.00

INDUSTRIAL RELATIONS – WEST GERMANY

—German Labour Management Relations Act / Rolf Boer. – 3rd ed. Repr. of 1976 ed. – Plymouth : Macdonald & Evans, 1983.
384p.
ISBN 0712154736 Hbk £32.50

—Industrial relations in West Germany : a case study of the car industry / Wolfgang Streeck. – London : Heinemann, 1984.
178p; 23cm.
Bibliography: p170-172. - Includes index. At head of title: Policy Studies Institute.
ISBN 0435838393 £16.50

—Labour law and industrial relations in the Federal Republic of Germany / Manfred Weiss. – Deventer : Kluwer, 1987.
190p; 25cm.
Bibliography: p37. - Includes index.
ISBN 9065443002 Pbk No price

INDUSTRIAL RELATIONS – YUGOSLAVIA

—Workers' management in Yugoslavia : recent developments and trends / edited by Najdan Pasic, Stanislav Grozdanic, Milorad Radevic. – Geneva : International Labour Office, 1982.
viii, 198 p.; 24 cm.
ISBN 9221030342 hard £25.00

INDUSTRIAL RESEARCH – CANADA

—Canadian R & D incentives : their adequacy and impact / Donald G. McFetridge, Jacek P. Warda. – Toronto, Canada : Canadian Tax Foundation, 1983.
vii, 100 p.; 23 cm.
Includes index. Bibliography: p. 93-97.
ISBN 0888080131 pbk. £10.00

INDUSTRIAL RESEARCH – EUROPEAN COMMUNITY

—R & D and the EEC competition rules : Regulation 418/85 / Valentine Korah. – Oxford : ESC Publishing, 1986.
xxi,114p. – (European competition law monographs).
Bibliography: p.xxi.
ISBN 0906214459

INDUSTRIAL SAFETY

—Deterrence and compensation : legal liability in occupational safety and health / Felice Morgenstern. – Geneva : International Labour Office, 1982.
iii,76p.
Bibliography: p73-74.
ISBN 9221030105

INDUSTRIAL SAFETY – AUSTRALIA – NEW SOUTH WALES

—Guide to Safety and Industry Laws New South Wales / Butterworths, 1981.
320p.
ISBN 0409490385 Pbk £49.00

—Safety and Industry Laws, New South Wales / G.A. Miller. – Butterworths.
ISBN 0409412503 Hbk

Vol. 2
ISBN 0409412511 Hbk

INDUSTRIAL SAFETY – CANADA

—Occupational safety and health : guide to regulations / Canada. – Ottawa : Minister of Supply and Services, 1984.
14,14p.
With French t.-p: Securite et hygiene au travail: guide des reglements. English and French text.
ISBN 0662529553

—Political economy of environmental hazards : a study paper prepared for the Law Reform Commission of Canada / by T.F. Schrecker. – Ottawa : Law Reform Commission of Canada, 1984.
vi,112p.
ISBN 066213236X

INDUSTRIAL SAFETY – EUROPEAN COMMUNITY

—Law and practice concerning occupational health in the member states of the European Community / Environmental Resources Limited for the Commission of the European Communities. – London : Graham & Trotman for The Commission, 1985.
22cm. – (EUR).
Includes index.
ISBN 0860106268 Hbk £55

Vol. 2 / Environmental Resources Limited for the Commission of the European Communities. – 1985.
22cm. – (EUR).
Includes index.
ISBN 0860106276 Hbk £55

Vol. 3 / Environmental Resources Limited for the Commission of the European Communities. - 1985.
22cm. - (EUR).
Includes index.
ISBN 0860106284 Hbk £45

Vol. 4 / Environmental Resources Limited for the Commission of the European Communities. - 1985.
22cm. - (EUR).
Includes index.
ISBN 0860107949 Hbk £45

Vol. 5 / Environmental Resources Limited for the Commission of the European Communities. - 1985.
22cm. - (EUR).
Includes index.
ISBN 0860107957 Hbk £50

INDUSTRIAL SAFETY - GREAT BRITAIN

—Health and safety at work : excluding factories and mines / by Ian Fife and E. Anthony Machin. - London : Butterworth, 1980.
lvii,980p; 18cm.
Includes index. Includes the text of relevant legislation.
ISBN 0406200548 £33.00

—Law of health and safety at work / Norman Selwyn. - London : Butterworths, 1982.
xxviii,354p; 22cm.
Includes index.
ISBN 0406667500 Pbk Unpriced

—Law of health and safety at work : the new approach / by Charles D. Drake and Frank B. Wright : with a foreword by John H. Locke. - London : Sweet & Maxwell, 1983.
xii; 25cm.
Includes index.
ISBN 0421286202 Hbk £22.00
ISBN 042128630X Pbk £13.85

INDUSTRIAL SAFETY - NEW ZEALAND

—Occupational safety : an inquiry into the coordination of legislation on industrial safety, health, and welfare / by I.K. Walker. - Wellington, N.Z. : State Services Commission, 1981.
vi, 142 p.; 30 cm.
Bibliography: p. 140-142.
ISBN 0477015085 pbk.

INDUSTRY

—Corporate governance and directors' liabilities : legal, economic, and sociological analyses on corporate social responsibility / edited by Klaus J. Hopt, Gunther Teubner. - Berlin : W. de Gruyter, 1984.
462p. - (Series A, Law).
Includes index.
ISBN 3110100274 £75.00

—Industry and the regulatory agencies : a collection of the papers given at the fourth seminar organised by Committee F of the International Bar Association's Section on Business Law in April 1985 at Stratford-upon-Avon / edited by John H. Bates. - 4. - London : International Bar Association, 1985.
Includes bibliographical references.

INDUSTRY - CANADA

—Taxation of Resource Industries / Agincourt : Carswell, 1987.
ca 370p.

INDUSTRY - EUROPEAN COMMUNITY

—Change and Adjustment : External Relations and Industrial Policy of the European Communities / Dordrecht : Kluwer, 1983.
240p.
ISBN 9065440887 Pbk £120.00

INDUSTRY - GREAT BRITAIN

—Emergency Protection in the Footwear Industry / London : Trade Policy Research Centre, 1983.
99p. - (Thames Essays Ser.: No. 36).
ISBN 0900842652 Hbk £3.00

—Fighting Closures / Hugo Levie. - London : Spokesman Books, 1984.
ISBN 0851243614 Hbk £15.00
ISBN 0851243622 Pbk £5.95

—Industrial Innovation and Public Policy : Preparing for the 1980's and the 1990's / Walter Zegveld. - London : Pinter Publishers Ltd, 1981.
251p.
ISBN 0903804921 Hbk £17.50
ISBN 0861872509 Pbk £7.75

—Planning for industry : papers from a conference held at Cambridge September 1979 / organised by the Bar Council, the Law Society and the Royal Institution of Chartered Surveyors. - London : Sweet & Maxwell, 1980.
v,78p; 25cm.
ISBN 042127140X Pbk £10.00

—Unequal struggle? : British socialism and the capitalist enterprise / Jim Tomlinson. - London : Methuen, 1982.
160p; 23cm.
Bibliography: p149-157. - Includes index.
ISBN 0416331505 Hbk Unpriced
ISBN 0416331602 Pbk Unpriced

INDUSTRY - INDIA

—Industries Development and Regulation / 3rd ed. - Lucknow : Eastern Book Company, 1985.
337p.

INDUSTRY AND STATE - AUSTRALIA

—Framework of consensus : government, business and trade unions / W. J. Byrt. - Melbourne : Law Book Company Ltd., 1985.
ix,220p.
Bibliography: p211-218.
ISBN 0455205779

—Of manners gentle : enforcement strategies of Australian business regulatory agencies / Peter Grabosky, John Braithwaite. - Melbourne : Oxford University Press, 1986.
viii,260p.
Includes index.
ISBN 0195546911

INDUSTRY AND STATE - CANADA

—Canadian R & D incentives : their adequacy and impact / Donald G. McFetridge, Jacek P. Warda. - Toronto, Canada : Canadian Tax Foundation, 1983.
vii, 100 p.; 23 cm.
Includes index. Bibliography: p. 93-97.
ISBN 0888080131 pbk. £10.00

INDUSTRY AND STATE - GREAT BRITAIN

—Building businesses - not barriers / presented to Parliament by the Secretary of State for Employment : supported by the Secretary of State for Foreign and Commonwealth Affairs ... et al. - London : H.M.S.O., 1986.
80p; 25cm.
ISBN 0101979401

—DTI : the department for enterprise / presented to Parliament by the Secretary of State for Trade and Industry and the Chancellor of the Duchy of Lancaster by command of Her Majesty, January 1988. - London : HMSO, 1988.
vii,41p.
ISBN 0101027826

INFANT FORMULAS

—Legislation on foods for infants and small children / Rome : Food and Agriculture Organization of the United Nations, 1983.
v,104p. - (Legislative study).
Includes bibliographical references.
ISBN 9251014876

INFERTILITY - COMMONWEALTH

—Issues in reproductice health law in the Commonwealth / by Rebecca J. Cook and Bernard M. Dickens. - London : Commonwealth Secretariat, 1986.
109p.
ISBN 085092295X

INFORMATION - AUSTRALIA

—Australasian Computerised Legal Information Handbook / Butterworths, 1988.
446p.
ISBN 0409494453 Pbk £39.00

INFORMATION - CANADA

—Charge document in criminal cases / Law Reform Commission of Canada. - Ottawa : The Commission, 1987.
57,63p. - (Working paper).
Includes bibliographical references. Added t.p. in French: Le document d'inculpation. Pages numbered in opposite directions. Text in English and French.
ISBN 0662549635

INFORMATION - GREAT BRITAIN

—Information sources in law / London : Butterworths, 1986.
ISBN 0408114746 Hbk £38.00

INFORMATION NETWORKS

—I'M : information market, marche d'information, Informationsmarkt / Luxembourg : Commission of the European Communities, 1985.
Continues: Euronet Diane news. Multilingual text.

—Information system dynamics : the impact of interactive information networks on the UK library and information system : final report for the period August 1979 - July 1982 : report to the British Library Research and Development Dept., on project SI/G/327 / Brian C. Vickery, Richard G. Heseltine, Carolyn S. Brown. - London : School of Library, Archive and Information Studies, University College London, 1982.
392p; 30cm.

INFORMATION RETRIEVAL

—Study on Common Standards for Query Languages in Computerised Legal Systems / Strasbourg : Council of Europe, 1981.

INFORMATION RETRIEVAL - GREAT BRITAIN

—Reports / London : H.M.S.O., 1980.
158 p.

INFORMATION RETRIEVAL - ITALY

—Italian Legal Information Retrieval / London : Sweet & Maxwell, 1984.
173p.
ISBN 0421329106 Pbk £8.50

—Italian legal information retrieval / London : Sweet & Maxwell, 1984.
ISBN 0421239106 Pbk £8.50

INFORMATION SERVICES

—Can knowledge survive? / Sir Harry Hookway. - London : British Library, 1986.
8p; 30cm. - (The Fourth British Library Annual Research Lecture).
ISBN 0712330747 Pbk Free

—Cost management for library and information services / Stephen A. Roberts. - London : Butterworths, 1985.
181 p.
ISBN 0408013761

—Creating an information service / Sylvia P. Webb : illustrated by Patricia Calderhead. - London : Aslib, 1983.
v,101p; 24cm.
ISBN 0851421865

—EUSIDIC database guide / Oxford : Learned Information, 1983.
ISBN 0904933377

—Information sources in law / editor R.G. Logan. - London : Butterworths, 1986.
xiv,370p; 23cm. - (Butterworths guides to information sources).
Commentary on specialist legal literature and electronic data bases. Refers to source materials, textbooks, reference books, journal articles, and visual reports and bibliographies. Covers social law, employment law, United States of America law, European Community law, computer-assisted research, and law books for non-lawyers.
ISBN 0408114746 Hbk £43.00

—Information system dynamics : the impact of interactive information networks on the UK library and information system : final report for the period August 1979 - July 1982 : report to the British Library Research and Development Dept., on project SI/G/327 / Brian C. Vickery, Richard G. Heseltine, Carolyn S. Brown. - London : School of Library, Archive and Information Studies, University College London, 1982.
392p; 30cm.

—International Environmental Law Information System / Berlin : Erich Schmidt.
354p. - (BZU Ser.: Vol. B3).
ISBN 3503010181 Pbk £39.00

—Libraries in support of scholarly communications in the humanities / by Alexander Wilson. - London : University of London Library Resources Co-ordinating Committee, 1987.
18 p. - (Occasional publication).
ISBN 0718708040

—Library and information services for the legal profession / C. Miskin. - London : British Library, 1981.
iv,60p; 30cm.
ISBN 0905984730 Pbk Unpriced

—Study on Common Standards for Query Languages in Computerised Legal Systems / Strasbourg : Council of Europe, 1981.

INFORMATION SERVICES - AFRICA

—SCOLMA directory of libraries and special collections on Africa in the United Kingdom and Western Europe / edited by Harry Hannam. - 4th rev. and expanded ed. - Munchen : Saur, 1983.
183p.
Previous ed: London: Crosby Lockwood Staples, 1973.

INFORMATION SERVICES - AUSTRALIA

—Legal and Commercial Looseleaf Services Available in Australia and New Zealand / Melbourne : , 1987.

INFORMATION SERVICES - CANADA

—CLIC Abstracts on PLEI Research / Ottawa : Canadian Law Information Council, 1983.
670p.
ISBN 0920358403 loose £50.00

1985 Supplement

—Telephone Legal Information Services : Review and Current Issues / Ottawa : Canadian Law Information Council, 1982.
37p.
ISBN 0920358993 Pbk £5.00

INFORMATION SERVICES - GREAT BRITAIN

—Joint enterprise : roles and relationships of the public and private sectors in the provision of library and information services / report of Library and Information Services Council and British Library Research and Development Department Working Party. – London : H.M.S.O., 1987.
vii, 49p.
On cover: Office of Arts and Libraries.
ISBN 011430016X

—Making a business of information : a survey of new opportunities / London : H.M.S.O., 1983.
53p; 21cm.
Bibliography: p48. At head of title: Cabinet Office, Information Technology Advisory Panel.
ISBN 0116308249 Pbk £4.20

INFORMATION SERVICES - NEW ZEALAND

—Legal and Commercial Looseleaf Services Available in Australia and New Zealand / Melbourne : , 1987.

INFORMATION SERVICES AND STATE - GREAT BRITAIN

—Joint enterprise : roles and relationships of the public and private sectors in the provision of library and information services / report of Library and Information Services Council and British Library Research and Development Department Working Party. – London : H.M.S.O., 1987.
vii, 49p.
On cover: Office of Arts and Libraries.
ISBN 011430016X

—Report by the Minister for the Arts on library and information matters during ... / presented to Parliament by the Secretary of State for Education and Science. – London : H.M.S.O., 1981-.
v.

INFORMATION STORAGE AND RETRIEVAL SYSTEMS

—Applications of computer technology to law (1969-1978) : a selected bibliography / compiled by Elaine Kozak : edited by M. Anne Foster and Shirley A. Lounder. – Ottawa : Canadian Law Information Council, 1980.
ii,106p. – (Working paper).
Includes index. Cover title: Bibliography computers and law.

—Applications of computer technology to law (1979-1982) : a selected bibliography / compiled by Judith M. Cameron and edited by Lorna K. Rees-Potter and Allan Kling. – Ottawa : Canadian Law Information Council, 1983.
– (Working paper).
Includes index. Cover title: Bibliography computers and law supplement (1979-1982).

—Automated analysis of legal texts : logic, informatics, law : edited versions of selected papers from the Second International Conference on 'Logic, Informatics, Law,'Florence, Italy, September 1985 / edited by Antonio A. Martino, Fiorenza Socci Natali : editorial assistant, Simona Binazzi. – Amsterdam : North-Holland, 1986.
xxii, 938 p.; 25 cm.
Includes bibliographies and index.
ISBN 0444701117

—Automation in the law school, including law libraries / by Betty W. Taylor and Dan F. Henke. – London : Glanville, 1986.
iv,124p.
Includes bibliographical references and appendices.
ISBN 0878020829

—BLAISE-LINE mini manual / London : British Library, Automated Services Dept., 1984.
66p.
ISBN 0712310150 spiral £10.00 (1 copy free to subscribers)

—Bulletin / LEXIS Educational User's Group. – 4. – London : The Group, 1984.

—Coming information society / London : British Library, 1984.
1v.
ISBN 0712330364 Pbk

—Common standards for legal retrieval systems : proposals for a model retrieval language for legal users / Important features of a common command language within a network of legal information systems : studies prepared for the Council of Europe and the Commission of the European Communities by Werner Robert Svoboda. – Strasbourg : Council of Europe, 1983.
104p; 21cm.
At head of title: Legal Affairs.
ISBN 9287102732

—Counsel's guide to computers for the Bar : an introduction for barristers, their clerks and instructing solicitors / London : Senate of Inns of Court and the Bar, 1986.
32p.
Published with Counsel: The Journal of the Bar of England and Wales, Easter term issue (1986)..

—Edited versions of selected papers from the international conference on 'Logic, Informatics, Law', Florence, Italy, April 1981 / Constantino Ciampi. – Amsterdam : North Holland Publishing, 1982.
xii,476p.
Bibliographies.

vol.2 : Deontic logic, computational linguistics, and legal information systems : Antonio A. Martino; editor 1982.
xli,518p.
Bibliographies.

—EDP systems for the administration of courts and related systems : proceedings of the fifth Colloquy on the Use of Computers in the Administration of Justice, Madrid, 14-16 October 1986 / Strasbourg : Council of Europe, 1987.
314p; 29cm.
At head of cover title: Legal affairs.
ISBN 9287110816

—Handbook of legal information retrieval / edited by Jon Bing in cooperation with Tove Fjeldvig, Trygve Harvold and Robert Svoboda. – Amsterdam : North-Holland, 1984.
xviii,580p; 23cm.
Bibliography: p505-532. - Includes index.
ISBN 044487576X £58.82

—Information computer communication policy / Organisation for Economic Co-operation and Development. – Paris : O.E.C.D., 1983.
136p; 24cm.
Discusses the development of computer and communications technologies with relation to the existing legal regulations.
ISBN 9264125272 Pbk £7.00

—Information handling and the office of the future : report of a seminar / M. Grieves, editor. – London : British Library Research and Development Department, 1984.
ii,84p.

—Information service 1986 : technology for solicitors / the Law Society. – 1. – London : Law Society, 1986.
various pagings.

—Information system dynamics : the impact of interactive information networks on the UK library and information system : final report for the period August 1979 - July 1982 : report to the British Library Research and Development Dept., on project SI/G/327 / Brian C. Vickery, Richard G. Heseltine, Carolyn S. Brown. – London : School of Library, Archive and Information Studies, University College London, 1982.
392p; 30cm.

—Italian legal information retrieval : a handbook / by Ettore Giannantonio. – Milano : Giuffre, 1984.
xii,181p; 25cm. – (Informatica e ordinamento giuridico).
ISBN 881400143X

—Legal databases in Europe : user attitudes and supplier strategies / Michael Lloyd. – Amsterdam : North-Holland, 1986.
xiii, 218 p.; 24 cm.
At head of title: Commission of the European Communities. 'Report no. EUR 10439 of the Commission of the European Communities'–T.p. verso. Bibliography: p.205.
ISBN 044470048X

—Libraries in support of scholarly communications in the humanities / by Alexander Wilson. – London : University of London Library Resources Co-ordinating Committee, 1987.
18 p. – (Occasional publication).
ISBN 0718708040

—Online bibliographic databases : a directory and sourcebook / Marjorie J. Brown. – 3rd ed. – London : Aslib, 1983.
xiv,383p; 24cm.
Previous ed.: 1981. Bibliography: p315-331. - Includes index.
ISBN 0851421679 North America Unpriced
ISBN 0810305305

—Online bibliographic databases : an international directory / Marjorie J. Brown. – 2nd ed. – London : Aslib, 1981.
xxx,213p; 25cm.
Previous ed.: published as On line bibliographic data bases directory / J.L. Hall. Includes index.
ISBN 0851421385 North America Unpriced
ISBN 081030528o

—Organising Knowledge : an introduction to information retrieval / Jennifer E. Rowley. – Aldershot : Gower, 1987.
xviii,454p; 23cm.
Includes bibliographies and index. Previous control number ISBN 0566034867.
ISBN 056603574X Hbk £25.00
ISBN 0566034867 Pbk £12.95

—Papers : communication's changing face - the challenge to libraries : Blackpool 1982 / the Library Association Conference. – London : The Association, 1983.
viii,91p; 21cm.
Includes index.
ISBN 0853658455 Pbk Unpriced

—Protection of users of computerised legal information services : Recommendation no.R (83) 3 adopted by the Committee of Ministers of the Council of Europe on 22 February 1983 and Explanatory memorandum / Council of Europe. – Strasbourg : Council of Europe, 1983.
23p; 21cm.
'... prepared by the Committee of Experts on Legal Data Processing un der the authority of the European Committee on Legal Co- operation'. At head of cover: Council of Europe, Legal Affairs.
ISBN 9287102791

—Security computer based information systems / London : Macmillan, 1985.
ISBN 0333364376 Pbk £7.95

—Study on common standards for query languages in computerised legal retrieval systems / prepared for the Council of Europe by Werner Robert Svoboda. – Strasbourg : Council of Europe, 1981.
52p.
'Based on a proposal put forward by Working Party No. II of the Committee of Experts on Legal Data Processing' - p.4. At head of cover title: Council of Europe, Legal Affairs.

—Teaching, research and training in the field of 'computers and the law' : recommendation no. R (80)3 adopted by the Committee of Ministers of the Council of Europe on 30 April 1980 and explanatory memorandum / Council of Europe. – Strasbourg : Council of Europe, 1981.
12p.
'Prepared by the Committee of Experts on Legal Data Processing' - verso t.p.. At head of cover title: Council of Europe, Legal Affairs.

INFORMATION STORAGE AND RETRIEVAL SYSTEMS - AUSTRALIA

—Australasian Legal Information Retrieval Handbook / A. Mowbray. – Sydney : Butterworths, 1988.
208p.
This guide to legal databases includes descriptions of CLIRS, SCALE, LEXIS, MAYNELAW, AUSINET, ESTOPEL, and others. Also contained is an introduction of the principles of computerized legal information retrieval, a set of tutorials for the main retrieval systems, and a directory of all databases containing Australian, New Zealand, and common law.

INFORMATION STORAGE AND RETRIEVAL SYSTEMS - CANADA

—CLIC service centres : ready to meet practitioners / by M. Anne Foster. – Ottawa : Canadian Law Information Council, 1980.
10 leaves.

—CLIC : service centres : the first year and a half, 1979- 1980 / Canadian Law Information Council. – Ottawa : The Council, 1980.
36 leaves.
Photocopy.

INFORMATION STORAGE AND RETRIEVAL SYSTEMS - ENGLAND

—Computerisation of county court procedures in debt cases : the claims registry / Lord Chancellor's Department. – London : The Department, 1987.
27 leaves.
Includes bibliographical references.

—Information technology and polytechnic libraries : discussion papers / Council of Polytechnic Librarians. – S.l. : COPOL, 1984.
28p.
ISBN 0907130062

INFORMATION STORAGE AND RETRIEVAL SYSTEMS - LAW - BIBLIOGRAPHY

—Applications of computer technology to law : a selected bibliography (1969-1981) for British lawyers / Society for Computers and Law. – Didcot : Society for Computers and Law, 1982.
60p.
ISBN 0906122112

INFORMATION STORAGE AND RETRIEVAL SYSTEMS - LAW - GREAT BRITAIN

—Applications of computer technology to law : a selected bibliography (1969-1981) for British lawyers / Society for Computers and Law. – Didcot : Society for Computers and Law, 1982.
60p.
ISBN 0906122112

INFORMATION STORAGE AND RETRIEVAL SYSTEMS – NORWAY

—Decade of computers and law / edited by Jon Bing, Knut S. Selmer. – Oslo : Universitetsforlaget, 1980.
475 p.; 22 cm.
Includes bibliographical references.
ISBN 8200053768

INFORMATION TECHNOLOGY

—Advanced topics of law and information technology / G P V Vandenberghe, Y Poullet. – Kluwer Law and Taxation, 1989.
210. – (Computer/Law Series).
Covers the law with regard to information technology, the challenge of computer law, privacy protection and transborder data flow, standards for computer crime, and expert systems and copyright.
ISBN 9065443916 Pbk £43.75/Dfl 135

—Information technology : the challenge to copyright / by James Lahore, Gerald Dworkin, Yvonne M. Smyth. – London : Sweet & Maxwell, 1984.
vii,116p; 22cm.
Includes index.
ISBN 0421322608 Pbk £11.00

INFORMATION TECHNOLOGY – CANADA

—Handbook of Information Technology / Donald A. Brown. – Toronto : DeBoo, 1987.
ISBN 0888202830 Hbk £150.00
Supplements
This reference contains consumer comparisons, checklists, tables, and evaluations. Semi-annual supplements are planned.

—Research and Development in Canada : A Practical Guide to Financing, Protecting and Exploiting New Technology / Daniel R. Bereskin. – Toronto : Butterworths, 1987.
288p.

INFORMATION TECHNOLOGY – EUROPEAN COMMUNITY

—Freedom of data flows and EEC law / G P V Vandenberghe, Y Poullet. – Kluwer Law and Taxation, 1988.
142. – (Computer/Law Series).
Deals with the legal problems caused by transfrontier flows of information. Includes chapters on the need to speak a common language between partners, data and information in common law, information and data in continental law, and restriction on transborder transmissions of commercial data under EEC law.
ISBN 9065443665 Pbk £32/Dfl 99

INFORMATION TECHNOLOGY – GREAT BRITAIN

—Encyclopaedia of Information Technology Law / London : Sweet & Maxwell, 1988.
ISBN 0421372109 Hbk

—WArwick 1984 communications conference held at the University of Warwick in Coventry from Thursday 5 July to Sunday 8 July 1984 / Society for Computer and Law. – Didcot, Oxon. : Society for Computers and Law, 1984.
93p.
ISBN 0906122155

INFORMED CONSENT – CANADA

—Behaviour alteration and the criminal law / Law Reform Commission of Canada. – Ottawa : The Commission, 1985.
48,56p. – (Working paper).
Bibliography: p.44-48. Added t.p. in French: Les techniques de modification du comportement et de droit penal. Cover title: Protection of life : behaviour alteration and the criminal law. Pages numbered in opposite directions. Text in English and French.
ISBN 0662538579

INFORMED CONSENT (MEDICAL LAW) – AUSTRALIA – VICTORIA

—Informed consent to medical treatment / Law Reform Commission of Victoria. – Melbourne : The Commission, 1987.
iv,45p. – (Discussion paper).
Includes bibliographical references. 'Issued in conjunction with Australian Law Reform Commission and New South Wales Law Reform Commission' - cover.
ISBN 0724166467

INHERITANCE AND TRANSFER TAX – CANADA

—Taxation and estate planning / by Maurice C. Cullity and Catherine A. Brown. – 2nd ed. – Toronto, Canada : Carswell Co., 1984.
xxvi, 764 p.; 24 cm.
At head of title: Cullity, Forbes, Brown. Includes bibliographical references and index.
ISBN 0459362305 pbk.

INHERITANCE AND TRANSFER TAX – ENGLAND

—Tolley's inheritance tax 1987-88 / by Robert Wareham and John Newth. – Croydon : Tolley Publishing, 1987.
viii,246p.
ISBN 0854592911

—Will precedents and inheritance tax / D.T. Davies. – 3rd ed. – London : Butterworth, 1988.
xxiii,283p.
Previous ed.: published as Will precedents and capital transfer tax. 1983. Includes index.
ISBN 0406175128 £25.00 (Jan.)

INHERITANCE AND TRANSFER TAX – GREAT BRITAIN

—Butterworth's Inheritance Tax Guide / London : Butterworths, 1986.
ISBN 0406500347 Pbk £31.50

—Capital transfer tax / by Barry D. McCutcheon. – 2nd ed. 2. – London : Sweet & Maxwell, 1984.
26cm.
Previous ed.: published as Understanding and planning for capital transfer tax. Maidenhead : McGraw-Hill, 1980.
ISBN 042131950X £80.00

—Capital transfer tax / by A.L. Chapman. – 4th ed. – Oxford : Tax Lawyer, 1980.
xxxi, 510p.
ISBN 0854590072

—Capital transfer tax : a practical guide / J. Philip Hardman, Russ Stanfield, Geoffrey A. Wignall. – 4th ed. – Bristol : Jordan & Sons, 1980.
64p; 30cm.
Previous ed.: London : Thorton Baker, 1978. Includes index.
ISBN 0853080623 Pbk £5.00

—Capital Transfer Tax Act 1984 / with annotations by Ian Ferrier. – London : Sweet & Maxwell, 1984.
237p.
ISBN 0421339500

—Capital transfer tax : discretionary trusts : memorandum by the Society's Standing Committee on Revenue Law commenting on draft clauses published by the Inland Revenue / Law Society. – London : Law Society, 1982.
9p; 30cm.

—Dymond's capital transfer tax / Roy R. Greenfield, Reginald K. Johns. – 2nd ed. – London : Oyez Longman, 1983.
cii,1328p; 24cm.
Previous ed.: 1977. Includes index.
ISBN 0851206425 set Unpriced

Vol.2 : Statutes, etc. 1983.
vii,535p; 24cm.
Previous ed.: London : Oyez, 1977.
ISBN 0851206425 Hbk Unpriced

—Guide to the new Inheritance Tax / Tolley Publishing, 1986.
ISBN 0854592563 Pbk £4.95

—Inheritance tax / by John Coombes and Gordon Channon. – London : Sweet & Maxwell, 1987.
xxxiv,305p; 22cm.
Includes index.
ISBN 0421370300 Pbk £18.00

—Inheritance tax / London : Pitman Publishing, 1986.
ISBN 0712106928 Pbk £7.95

—Inheritance tax / London : Longman Professional, 1988.
ISBN 0851213812 Hbk

—Inheritance tax / 7th ed. – London : Longman Professional, 1987.
ISBN 085121326X Hbk £48.00
ISBN 0851214673 Pbk

—Inheritance tax / 3rd ed. – London : Sweet & Maxwell, 1988.
ISBN 042139790X Pbk £110.00

—Inheritance tax guide / Butterworths. – London : Butterworths, 1986.
ISBN 0406500347 Pbk £16.50

—Inheritance tax on lifetime gifts / by Thomas Ivory ... et al. – London : Sweet & Maxwell, 1987.
xix,181p; 26cm.
Includes index.
ISBN 0421379103 £25.00

—Inheritance tax on lifetime gifts / Ivory. – London : Sweet & Maxwell, 1987.
ISBN 04212379103 Hbk £24.50

—Inheritance tax planning / Thornhill. – 2nd ed. – London : Longman Professional, 1988.
ISBN 0851213669 Hbk £85.00

—Intelligence report : inheritance tax / London : Longman Professional, 1986.
ISBN 085121245X Hbk £75.00

—Practical inheritance tax / London : Butterworths, 1988.
ISBN 040600710 Pbk

—Taxation of land transactions / 4th ed. – London : Butterworths, 1988.
ISBN 0406624100 Pbk

—Tolley's capital transfer tax 1981-82 / by Eric L. Harvey. – Croydon : Tolley, 1981.
vii,63p.
Includes index. Up to date to 1 August 1981.
ISBN 0854590366

—Tolley's inheritance tax 1986-87 / by Robert Wareham. – Croydon : Tolley Publishing, 1986.
viii,223,iv,236p.
Includes indexes. Contents: Tolley's inheritance tax 1986-1987 - Tolley's capital transfer tax final edition.
ISBN 0854592415

—Tolley's inheritance tax 1988-89 / by Patrtick Noakes and John Newth. – Croydon : Tolley, 1988.
viii,245p.
Includes index.
ISBN 0854593497

INHERITANCE AND TRANSFER TAX – IRELAND

—Capital acquisitions tax / by Norman Bale & John Condon. – Dublin : Institute of Taxation in Ireland, 1982.
244p.
Includes index.

INHERITANCE AND TRANSFER TAX – NEW ZEALAND

—New Zealand duties guide / Auckland : Commerce Clearing House (New Zealand), 1985-.
Title history; New Zealand duties and sales tax guide (1983-1985). Includes index. Loose-leaf issues accompanied by a summary report.

INHERITANCE AND TRANSFER TAX – NORTHERN IRELAND

—Some aspects of inheritance tax for businesses and farms / David Moore. – Belfast : SLS Legal Publications, 1986.
40p.
Includes bibliographical references.

INHERITANCE AND TRANSFER TAX – SOUTH AFRICA

—Estate duty : principles and planning / by Aubrey S. Silke and Michael L. Stein. – Kenwyn : Juta in association with Divaris Stein, 1984.
369 p.; 23 cm.
Includes indexes.
ISBN 0702115347

INJUNCTIONS

—Injunctions and specific performance / by Robert J. Sharpe. – Toronto : Canada Law Book Ltd., 1983.
lxxiv,450p.
ISBN 0888040172

—Mareva Injunction and associated orders / by David G. Powles. – Abingdon : Professional Books, 1986.
xxiii,160p.
ISBN 0862050693 Pbk
ISBN 0862052033

INJUNCTIONS – CANADA

—Injunctions / Vancouver : British Columbia Continuing Legal Education Society, 1985.
155p.
ISBN 0865041989 Hbk £55.00

—Injunctions / Agincourt : Carswell, 1985.
ISBN 0459376500 Hbk £19.80

—Injunctions : A Practical Handbook / Agincourt : Carswell, 1985.
725p.
This manual is a practitioners' guide to the preparation and presentation of injunction motions in Canadian courts. Sample forms and model motions are provided in the book.

—Injunctions and specific performance / Phil. – Aurora : Canada Law Book, 1983.

—Mareva Injunctions / 2nd ed. – Agincourt : Carswell, 1987.
ISBN 045939780 Hbk £16.75

INJUNCTIONS – ENGLAND

—Injunctions / David Bean. – 3rd ed. – London : Oyez Longman, 1984.
xxvi,149p; 22cm. – (Oyez Longman practice notes).
Previous ed.: 1982. Includes index.
ISBN 0851208576 Pbk £9.95

—Mareva injunction and Anton Piller order : practice and precedents / by Richard N. Ough. – London : Butterworths, 1987.
xxii,175p; 22cm.
Includes index.
ISBN 0406102902 Pbk £25.00

—Mareva injunction and related orders / by Mark S.W. Hoyle. – London : Lloyd's of London Press, 1985.
viii,141p; 22cm.
ISBN 1850440441 No price

—Mareva injunctions / by David Capper. - London : Sweet & Maxwell, 1988.
xxii,135p; 22cm.
Contains the definition and nature of a Mareva injunction, including matters which must be proved, the procedure for application, orders for the discovery of assets, the writ ne exeat regno, Bayer orders, and Anton Piller orders, and Mareva injunctions and the criminal law. Includes an appendix of precedents.
ISBN 0421389605 Pbk No price

—Mareva injunctions : a one-day conference / organised by Lloyds of London Press, the Tower Hotel, London, 22nd June 1982. - 1. - London : Lloyd's of London Press, 1982.
various pagings; 31cm.
ISBN 0907432433 Unpriced

—Mareva injunctions : law and practice / Steven Gee and Geraldine Mary Andrews : foreword by Lord Denning. - London : Longman, 1987.
xxvii,143p; 25cm.
Includes index.
ISBN 0851209394 £30.00

—Matrimonial and domestic injunctions : practice and precedents / Mark Pelling, Robert Purdie : consulting editor Augustus Ullstein : foreword by Dame Margaret Booth. - London : Butterworths, 1982.
xxi,190p; 22cm.
Includes index.
ISBN 0406334404 Pbk Unpriced

INJUNCTIONS - GREAT BRITAIN

—Anton Piller Orders and Mareva Injunctions: a Practitioner's Guide / London : Butterworths, 1987.
ISBN 0406102902 Pbk £28.95

—Injunctions (LPPN66) / 4th ed. - London : Longman Professional, 1984.
ISBN 0851212980 Pbk £14.95

—Mareva injunction and related orders / 2nd. - London : Lloyds of London Press, 1989.
Sets out the framework for applications in court for Mareva injunctions, Anton Pillar orders and similar and ancillary relief. The position in EEC countries is given, including the implications of the Civil Jurisdiction and Judgements Act 1982. The international section covers developments in Commonwealth and other jurisdictions.
ISBN 1850441618 Hbk

—Mareva Injunctions and Associated Orders / London : Butterworths, 1985.
ISBN 0862050693 Hbk £35.00
ISBN 0862052033 Pbk £17.95

INJUNCTIONS - INDIA

—Law of Injunctions, 2 Vols. / 6th ed. - Allahabad : Law Book Company, 1985.
2,200p.

INSANITY

—Criminal Jurisprudence and Law of Insanity / New Delhi : Deep and Deep Publications, 1988.
172p.

—Legal protection of persons suffering from mental disorder placed as involuntary patients : Recommendation No.R(83)2 adopted by the Committee of Ministers of the Council of Europe on 22 February 1983, and Explanatory memorandum / Council of Europe. - Strasbourg : Council of Europe, 1983.
22p; 21cm.
'... prepared by a committee of experts on Legal Problems in the Medical Field set up under the authority of the European Committee on Legal Co-operation'. At head of title: Legal Affairs.
ISBN 9287102996

—Mental disorder and criminal responsibility / Stephen J. Hucker, Christopher D. Webster, Mark H. Ben-Aron. - Toronto : Butterworths, 1981.
xv,195p.
Examines Anglo-American concepts of criminal responsibility, mental disorder and criminal responsibility in Canadian law, the sense of justice and criminal responsibility, modern neurology and psychiatry and the problem of criminal responsibility, psychiatrists, lawyers and the adversial system, and the long term management of the mentally disordered offender.
ISBN 0409837342

—Mental illness : law and public policy / edited by Baruch A. Brody and H. Tristram Engelhardt, Jr. - Dordrecht : Reidel, 1980.
xvii,254p; 23cm. - (Philosophy and medicine).
Includes index.
ISBN 9027710570 Unpriced

—Psychiatry and the criminal process / edited by Ronnie Mackay and Ken Russell. - Leicester : Leicester Polytechnic Law School, 1986.
48p. - (Leicester Polytechnic Law School monographs).
Includes bibliographical references.
ISBN 0948997281

—Psychiatry, law, and ethics / edited by A. Carmi : with contributions by G. Ammon ... et al. - Berlin : Springer-Verlag, 1984.
ISBN 0387157425

—Studies on criminal responsibility and psychiatric treatment of mentally ill offenders : reports presented to the seventh Criminological Colloquium (1985) / Council of Europe. - Strasbourg : Council of Europe, 1986.
103p; 21cm. - (Legal affairs).
On cover: European Committee on Crime Problems.
ISBN 9287108994

INSANITY - AUSTRALIA - VICTORIA

—Mental malfunction and criminal responsibility / Law Reform Commission of Victoria. - Melbourne : The Commission, 1988.
95p. - (Discussion paper).
Includes bibliographical references.
ISBN 0724167307

INSANITY - AUSTRALIA - WESTERN AUSTRALIA

—Criminal process and persons suffering from mental disorder / Law Reform Commission of Western Australia. - Perth : Law Reform Commission of Western Australia, 1987.
i,146p. - (Discussion paper).

INSANITY - ENGLAND

—Compulsory admissions to mental hospitals / Philip Bean. - Chichester : Wiley, 1980.
xii,278p; 24cm.
Bibliography: p267-273. - Includes index.
ISBN 0471277584 £16.70

—Mental disorder and legal control / Philip Bean. - Cambridge : Cambridge University Press, 1986.
304p.
Includes bibliographical references and index.
ISBN 0521302099 £27.50

—Observations on the Mental Health (Amendment) Bill / the Justices' Clerks' Society. - Bristol : The Society, 1982.
8p.

—Offenders suffering from psychopathic disorder / joint DHSS-Home Office consultation document. - London : Department of Health and Social Security, 1986.
13p.

—Role of psychiatric reports in the Crown Court trial processes / Leicester : Leicester Polytechnic Law School, 1986.
21p. - (Leicester Polytechnic Law School monographs).
Includes bibliographical references.
ISBN 0948997303

INSANITY - GREAT BRITAIN

—Court of protection : a legal and policy analysis of the guardianship of the estate / Larry Gostin : foreword by Peter Jefferys. - London : Mind, National Association for Mental Health, 1983.
60p.
Bibliography: p.48.
ISBN 0900557567

—Dangerous behaviour, the law, and mental disorder / Herschel Prins. - London : Tavistock, 1986.
xiii,258p; 20cm. - (Social science paperback).
Includes bibliographies and index.
ISBN 0422792209 Pbk £6.95

—Health service development : Mental Health Act 1983 : draft code of practice / Department of Health and Social Security. - London : The Department, 1987.
45p. - (Local authority circular).
Cover title: Mental Health Act 1983.

—Offenders, deviants, or patients? : an introduction to the study of socio-forensic problems / Herschel Prins. - London : Tavistock Publications, 1980.
viii,369p.
Bibliographies.
ISBN 0422768006

—Report by the Committee for Privileges on parliamentary privilege and the mental health legislation, together with the minutes of evidence / London : H.M.S.O., 1984.
xi,26p. - (254).
ISBN 010425484X

—Sentenced to hospital : offenders in Broadmoor / by Susanne Dell, Graham Robertson. - Oxford : Oxford University Press, 1988.
x, 170 p.; 25 cm.
Based on interviews with staff and patients at Broadmoor, it describes how men come to be sent to Broadmoor, and their subsequent treatment, including procedures and decision-making related to discharge. Recommends controversial changes in the law and in detention policy.
ISBN 019712156X Hbk £22.50

—Trial by medicine : insanity and responsibility in Victorian trials / by Roger Smith. - Edinburgh : Edinburgh University Press, 1981.
ix,238p.
ISBN 085224407X

INSANITY - NEW ZEALAND

—Mental health : a case for reform / papers presented by John Dawson ... et al. - Auckland : Legal Research Foundation, 1986.
161p.
Includes bibliographical references. At head of t.p.: Legal Research Foundation Inc., Seminar, 5 September 1986.
ISBN 0908581432
ISBN 0908581432

INSPECTORATES IN GOVERNMENT - GREAT BRITAIN

—Inspectorates in British government : law enforcement and standards of efficiency / Gerald Rhodes. - London : Allen & Unwin for the Royal Institute of Public Administration, 1981.
xiii,281p; 23cm.
Includes index.
ISBN 0043510566 £15.00

INSTITUTIONAL CARE - ENGLAND

—Law of residential homes and day-care establishments / M.D.A. Freeman and Christina M. Lyon. - London : Sweet & Maxwell, 1984.
xxvi,239p; 22cm.
Deals with children, the elderly, and the physically handicapped. Includes the Mental Health Act 1983 and the Health and Social Services and Social Security Adjudications Act 1983.
ISBN 0421258608 Pbk No price

INSTITUTIONAL CARE - GREAT BRITAIN

—Registered Homes Act 1984 / with annotations by Richard M. Jones. - London : Sweet & Maxwell, 1984.
58p; 24cm.
ISBN 0421333707 Pbk £4.00

—Registered Homes Bill : report on the consolidation of certain enactments relating to residential care homes and nursing homes and registered homes tribunals / The Law Commission. - London : H.M.S.O., 1983.
3p; 25cm.
ISBN 0101911505

INSURANCE

—Dictionary of Insurance Terms English-Arabic / Witherby, 1985.
ISBN 090088696X Hbk £34.00

—Golding: The law and practice of reinsurance / by C.E. Golding. - 5th ed. - London : Witherby, 1987.
x,285p; 23cm. - (Monument series).
Previous ed.: 1965. Includes index.
ISBN 094869114X No price

—Insurance development in the Arab world : retention relationship capacity and the demand for international reinsurance / by Abdul Zahra Abdullah Ali. - London : Graham & Trotman, 1985.
369p; 25cm.
Bibliography: p352-362. - Includes index.
ISBN 0860107078 £73.00

—Insurance in Rabbinic Law / Edinburgh : Edinburgh University Press.
230p.
ISBN 0852242581 Hbk £10.00

—International insurance industry guide / 3rd ed. - London : Lloyd's of London Press, 1985.
ISBN 1850440468 Pbk £10.50

—International reinsurance : the law and market practice : an RRG seminar / 1. - Colchester : Lloyd's of London Press, 1982.
various pagings.

—Marine reinsurance / by Robert H. Brown and Peter B. Reed. - London : Witherby, 1981.
xi,343p; 23cm.
Includes index.
ISBN 0900886617 £21.00

—Medical responsibility in Western Europe : research study of the European Science Foundation / edited by E. Deutsch and H.-L. Schreiber : with contributions by J. Blackie ... et al. - Berlin : Springer-Verlag, 1985.
ISBN 0387153659

—Practical Guide to Accepting Insurance Risks / Woolloomooloo : International Business Communications, 1986.
ISBN 0949553255 Hbk £13.50

—Reinsurance / R.L. Carter. - 2nd ed. - Brentford : Kluwer in association with the Mercantile and General Reinsurance Company plc, 1983.
xv,630p; 24cm.
Previous ed.: 1979. Bibliography: p613-622. - Includes index.
ISBN 0903393654 £65.00

—Reinsurance in the Third World / London : Witherby & Co, 1980.
ISBN 0900886714 Hbk £13.50

—Reinsurance law / John S. Butler and Robert M. Merkin. - 2. - London : Kluwer, 1986.
looseleaf.
ISBN 1870080076

—Subrogation in insurance law / by S.R. Derham. – North Ryde, N.S.W. : Law Book Co. Ltd., 1985.
xxxiii,164p.
Bibliography: p.xxix-xxxiii. - Includes index.
ISBN 0455205922

INSURANCE - AFRICA

—Insurance law in Africa / Witherby, 1987.
ISBN 0948691255 Hbk £35.00

INSURANCE - AUSTRALIA

—Australian Insurance Law / North Ryde : Law Book Co, 1987.
xlv, 368p.
ISBN 0455207232 Pbk £49.50

—Cases and text on insurance law: Australia and New Zealand / North Ryde : Butterworths (Australia).
Explains the insurance law of Australia and New Zealand, and illustrates how the law is interpeted with a selection of modern cases as well as relevant statutory material.
ISBN 0409308706 Pbk

—Guidebook to Insurance Law in Australia and New Zealand / North Ryde : C.C.H. Australia, 1987.
341p.
ISBN 0869036378 Pbk £35.00

—Insurance Agents and Brokers / Law Reform Commission. – Canberra : Australian Government Publishing Service, 1980.
142p. – (ALRC Report: No. 16).
ISBN 0642034435 Hbk £5.50

—Insurance contracts / Law Reform Commission. – Canberra : Australian Government Publishing Service, 1982.
xxxx,372p. – (Report).
Bibliography: p.352-357. - Includes index.
ISBN 064401217X

—Insurance law in Australia and New Zealand / by K.C.T. Sutton. – Sydney : Law Book Co., 1980.
lvii, 684 p.; 25 cm.
Includes bibliographical references and indexes.
ISBN 0455200742

—Insurance Legislation Manual / Minhael Ball. – Butterworths, 1986.
131p.
ISBN 0409491195 Pbk £33.00

INSURANCE - AUSTRALIA - NEW SOUTH WALES

—Community law reform program / New South Wales Law Reform Commission. – Sydney : The Commission, 1983.
61p. – (L.R.C. 34).

INSURANCE - CANADA

—Canadian Insurance Law Review / Agincourt : Carswell, 1988.
360p.

—Cases of the Canadian Law of Insurance / James A. Rendall. – 4th ed. – Agincourt : Carswell, 1988.
854p.

—Cases on the Canadian law of insurance / edited by Marvin G. Baer, James A. Rendall. – 3rd ed. – Calgary, Alta. : Carswell, 1983.
xl,760p.

—Effective Insurance : A Guide For Buyer and Seller / Paul Braithwaite. – Toronto : Butterworths, 1984.
352p.
Topics covered include insurers, agents, brokers, reinsurers, various types of coverage, policies, riders, endorsements (with appropriate illustrations) and specific advice on minimizing corporate insurance costs.
ISBN 0409872857 Hbk £39.95

—Insurance Case Law Digest : Property and Casualty, 2 vols / Toronto : Butterworths.

—Insurance case law digest: property and casualty / 2 vols. – Scarborough, Ontario : Butterworths (Canada).
Coverage of automobile and property insurance cases in Canada. Each part has a table of cases, and the case digests are arranged to reflect the organizational categories of the standard automobile and home insurance policies.

—Insurance Law : 1982 / Vancouver : British Columbia Continuing Legal Education Society, 1982.
115p.
ISBN 0865040745 Hbk £45.00

—Insurance Law 1988 / Vancouver : Continuing Legal Education Society of British Columbia, 1988.
150p.
ISBN 0865049823 Hbk £70.00

—Insurance Law for General Practitioners / Vancouver : British Columbia Continuing Legal Education Society, 1980.
147p.

—Insurance Law for the General Practitioner / Toronto : DeBoo, 1987.
288p.
This book contains seventeen lectures by attorneys and insurance industry specialists. Among the main topics discussed are the insurance crisis and new directions in insurance law.
ISBN 0888202849 Hbk £79.95

INSURANCE - CANADA - ONTARIO

—Annotated Insurance Act of Ontario, 2 Vols. / Agincourt : Carswell, 1986.
This two volume looseleaf work contains the Insurance Act of Ontario, with amendments, extensive case annotations, schedules, and regulations. Each section of the Act is cross-referenced to equivalent sections in the law of all Canadian common law provinces.

—Annotated Insurance Act of Ontario / Harry B. Radomski. – Butterworths, 1987.
704p.
Contains summary and analysis of the law under each section of the Act, traces the legislative history of each section to the present, defines problem wording and terms, directing the reader to all possible interpretations, and covers several thousand relevant cases from all Canadian jurisdictions.
ISBN 0409811440 Hbk £120.00

INSURANCE - CARIBBEAN

—Life Insurance in the Commonwealth Caribbean / London : Butterworths, 1984.
ISBN 0406076308 Hbk £17.00

INSURANCE - ENGLAND

—Butterworths Consolidated Legislation Service /. – Professional Publ.
201p.
ISBN 0409014206 £55.00

—Butterworths insurance law handbook / Richard-Hudson, E. R. Hardy Ivamy. – 2nd ed. – London : Butterworths, 1986.
591,10p; 25cm.
Previous ed.: 1983. Includes index.
ISBN 040617637X Pbk £22.00

—Encyclopedia of insurance law / general editor Anthony O'Dowd : assistant general editor John Birds. – 1. – London : Sweet & Maxwell, 1983.
loose-leaf; 25cm.
Includes index.
ISBN 0421281502 £85.00

—General principles of insurance law / E.R. Hardy Ivamy. – 5th ed. – London : Butterworths, 1986.
1050p; 26cm.
This text provides an account of insurance law procedure from contract drafting to the final settlement of claims in the United Kingdom. The impact of the Insurance Companies Act of 1982 is fully discussed.
ISBN 0406252807 Hbk £70.00

—Insurance intermediaries and the law / by R.W. Hodgin. – 1. – London : Lloyd's of London Press, 1987.
22cm.
Includes bibliography and index.
ISBN 1850441073 Pbk £14.50

—Insurance law reports / edited by F.N. Eaglestone and K.S. Cannar. – Harlow : G. Goodwin, 1982-.
Annual index.

—Law of insurance / by Raoul Colinvaux. – 5th ed. – London : Sweet & Maxwell, 1984.
xci,553p; 26cm.
Deals with policies of insurance, parties to insurance contracts, and special types of insurance. New chapter on marine insurance. Covers the Insurance Companies Act 1982, and the Insurance Companies Regulations. Implications of EEC membership, New York law, Lloyd's standard policy terms and the Marine Insurance Act are also included.
ISBN 042131110X £42.00

—MacGillivray and Parkington on insurance law : relating to all risks other than marine / Michael Parkington. – 8th ed. – London : Sweet & Maxwell, 1988.
cxli,1014p.
Discusses legal aspects of the insurance contract and the insurance business. Includes a new chapter on Reinsurance, and looks at certain types of policy including those covering indemnity, personal accident, fire, motor vehicle and aviation, pecuniary loss and contractors' risk. Refers to North American decisions and to Scots law.
ISBN 0421354801 £90.00

—Transfer of land : passing of risk from vendor to purchaser / the Law Commission. – London : HMSO, 1988.
v,87p. – (Working paper).
ISBN 0117301914

INSURANCE - EUROPEAN COMMUNITY

—European insurance law : a guide to Community and member state legislation / Belmont European Community Law Office. – London : Financial Times Business Information, 1987.
ix,147p.
'The first edition of this report was published in 1982 and revised in 1983'. - T.p. verso.
ISBN 090210196X

—European Insurance Law : An Analysis of Community and Member State Legislation / Margie Lindsay. – Rev. ed. – London : Financial Times Ltd, 1983.

INSURANCE - FIJI

—Report of the Select Committee on Insurance Laws and Practices / Fiji. – Suva : Parliament of Fiji, 1984.
115p. – (Parliamentary paper).

INSURANCE - GREAT BRITAIN

—Administration of Insurance / ICSA. – Cambridge : Woodhead-Faulkner, 1987.
ISBN 0902197428 Hbk £25.00

—Captive Insurance : A Tax and Financial Analysis / 2nd ed. – London : Oyez Longman, 1984. – (Oyez Longman Intelligence Report Ser.).
ISBN 085120872X Hbk £65.00

—Casebook on Insurance Law / 4th ed. – London : Butterworths, 1984.
ISBN 0406602638 Pbk £14.95

—Construction Insurance Claims and Management / Spon (E & FN), 1987.
ISBN 0419138404 Hbk £22.50

—Credit Insurance / Briggs. – Cambridge : Woodhead-Faulkner, 1987.
ISBN 0859411761 Hbk £40.00

—Dictionary of insurance law / by E.R. Hardy Ivamy. – London : Butterworths, 1981. – (Butterworths professional dictionary series).
This work contains terms in general use in marine as well as in non-marine insurance which have been legally defined in statute or case law. Many entries are accompanied by extracts from cited cases and statutes.
ISBN 0406603014 Pbk £14.95

—Dictionary of Insurance Law / London : Butterworths, 1981.
ISBN 0406603014 Pbk £10.95

—Elements of Cargo Insurance / Whitehead. – Cambridge : Woodhead-Faulkner, 1983.
ISBN 085941227X Pbk £5.25

—Elements of Insurance / 3rd ed. Repr. of 1979 ed. – Plymouth : Macdonald & Evans, 1984.
320p. – (M & E Handbook).
ISBN 0712105638 Pbk £3.25

—Elements of Insurance / McMurdie. – 5th ed. – Pitman, 1980.
ISBN 0273014145 Pbk £6.95

—Elements of Insurance / J. T. Steele. – 1st ed. – Plymouth : Macdonald & Evans, 1981.
224p : Illus.. – – (M and E Belbook Ser.).
ISBN 0712105840 Hbk £4.95

—Elements of Insurance / 4th ed. – Plymouth : Macdonald & Evans, 1985.
ISBN 0712106723 Pbk £5.95

—Encyclopaedia of Insurance Law / London : Sweet & Maxwell, 1988.
ISBN 0421281502 Hbk £165.00

—Encyclopedia of Insurance Law, 1 Vol. / London : Sweet & Maxwell.

—Essential cases in insurance law / Kenneth Cannar. – Cambridge : Woodhead-Faulkner, 1985.
240p.
ISBN 0859412849 £25.00

—Foreign Currency Claims / London : LLoyd's of London Press, 1989.
ISBN 1850441677 Hbk

—General Principles of Insurance Law / 5th ed. – London : Butterworths, 1986.
ISBN 0406252807 Hbk £80.00

—Guide to Insurance Professional Negligence Risks / London : Butterworths, 1982.
ISBN 0406257108 Pbk £21.95

—Guide to the Insurance of Professional Negligence Risks / Wellington : Butterworths, 1982.
This book discusses in detail the coverage provided by the 'basic' United Kingdom professional indemnity policy and some of the more popular extensions in common practice. The work provides a general explanation of the law of professional negligence and insurance law.
ISBN 0406257108 Pbk £35.00

—Hazard unlimited / 3rd ed. – London, 1987.
ISBN 1850441316 Pbk £5.95
ISBN 1850441375 Hbk £14.50

—Household insurance / a report by the Director General of Fair Trading. – London : Office of Fair Trading, 1985.
58p.

—Houseman and Davies law of life assurance / B. P. A. Davies. – 10th ed. – London : Butterworths, 1984.
xxiv,378p; 26cm.
This work for practitioners covers general United Kingdom contract law, law relating to insurance policies, legislation on insurance supervision, and relevant EEC developments in insurance law. Model contracts and trust agreements are included in the appendix.
ISBN 0406597073 Hbk £68.75

—Indemnity and Insurance / RIBA Publications, 1985.
ISBN 0900630914 Hbk £12.50

—Insurance: competition or regulation? : a comparative study of the insurance markets in the United Kingdom and the Federal Republic of Germany / Jorg Finsinger, Elizabeth Hammond and Julian Tapp. – London : Institute for Fiscal Studies, 1985.
197p.
Bibliography: p191-197.
ISBN 090299249X

—Insurance contract law / Robert M. Merkin and Andrew McGee : editorial advisors, John S. Butler, Alison A. Green. – 2. – London : Kluwer, 1988.
looseleaf.
Includes index.
ISBN 1870080475

—Insurance Contracts / London : LLoyd's of London Press, 1989.
ISBN 1850442061 Hbk

—Insurance handbook / 1st ed. – London : Legal Books, 1985.
ISBN 0949553182 Pbk £12.00

—Insurance law handbook / 2nd ed. – London : Butterworths, 1985.
ISBN 040617637X Pbk £23.00

—Insurance law : non disclosure and breach of warranty : report on a reference under Section 3 (1)(e) of the Law Commissions Act 1965 / chairman: Michael Kerr. – London : H.M.S.O., 1980.
vii,165p.

—The Insurance of Average Disbursements / London : LLoyd's of London Press, 1987.
ISBN 1850441693 Hbk

—Insurance of average disbursements / London : Lloyd's of London Press, 1988.
ISBN 1850441693 Pbk £8.95

—Insurance of commercial risks / London : Butterworths, 1986.
ISBN 0406257116 Hbk £36.00

—Insurance under the JCT Forms / Oxford : Blackwell Scientific, 1985.
ISBN 0003830225 Hbk £25.00

—Introduction to insurance / G.C.A. Dickson, J.T. Steele. – 2nd ed. – London : Pitman, 1984.
xii,212p.
Includes index.
ISBN 0273027905

—Introduction to risk management / 2nd ed. – Cambridge : Woodhead-Faulkner, 1986.
ISBN 0859413322 Hbk £19.95

—Introduction to working in the Lloyds Market / Wormell. – Witherby, 1987.
ISBN 0948691387 Pbk £10.00

—Liability Insurance Claims / Witherby, 1983.
ISBN 0900886803 Hbk £28.00

—Lloyd's of London : a reputation at risk / Godfrey Hodgson. – London : Allen Lane, 1984.
378p.
ISBN 0713913673

—Modern insurance law / by John Birds. – 2nd ed. – London : Sweet & Maxwell, 1988.
xxxviii,335p.
Explanation of the fundamental principles of insurance law, including the meaning of insurance, the basic elements of the contract – parties, the insurable interest, formation, void and voidable contracts and premiums, agency and asigment and mechanisms for claiming under the policy. Discusses the Insurance Companies Act 1982, and the Financial Services Act 1986.
ISBN 0421371404 Pbk
ISBN 0421371501

—New foundations for insurance law / edited by F.D. Rose. – London : Stevens, 1987.
xvii,106p.
Collection of papers discussing the industry's revised scheme for self-regulation, the theory and practice of the fundamental obligation of utmost good faith, and the implication of that obligation for insurers, and the claims process with reference to the problems of causation and proof of loss in the context of marine insurance.
ISBN 0420477802

—New foundations for insurance law / London : Sweet & Maxwell, 1987.
ISBN 0420477802 Pbk £18.50

—Personal accident, life and other insurance / 2nd ed. – London : Butterworths, 1980.
ISBN 0406252912 Hbk £52.00

—Personal accident, life and other insurances / by E.R. Hardy Ivamy. – 2nd ed. – London : Butterworths, 1980.
xlii, 439p. – (Butterworths insurance library).
This volume for the United Kingdom insurance practitioner is divided into seven sections: Personal Accident Insurance; Life Insurance; Industrial Assurance; Property Insurance; Liability Insurance; Guarantee Insurance; and Reinsurance.
ISBN 0406252912 Hbk £100.00

—Principles and practice of interruption insurance / London : Witherby & Co, 1982.
ISBN 0900886560 Hbk £35.00

—Protection of the Insured / London : LLoyd's of London Press, 1989.
ISBN 1850442053 Hbk

—Regulation of insurance in the United Kingdom and Ireland / editor: T. Henry Ellis : associate editor: James A. Wiltshire : life assurance contributor: Peter G. Ward. – v. – London : Kluwer, 1983.
looseleaf.
Includes index.
ISBN 0903393638

—Reinsurance for the beginner / 2nd ed. – London : Witherby & Co, 1980.
ISBN 090088648X Pbk £4.00

—Reinsurance in practice / 2nd ed. – London : Witherby & Co, 1986.
ISBN 0900886986 Hbk £30.00

—Subrogation in insurance law / London : Sweet & Maxwell, 1986.
ISBN 0455205922 Hbk £19.50

—Taxation - A Handbook for Insurance and Estate Planners / 1986 Edition. – Don Mills : Life Underwriters Association of Canada.
ISBN 0921219032 Hbk £22.50

—Taxation of insurance business / A R Levitt. – London : Butterworths, 1985.
ISBN 0406501009 Hbk £30.00

—Taxation of Lloyds Underwriters / 2nd ed. – Croydon : Tolley.
300p.
ISBN 0854593063 Hbk £29.95

—Textbook of insurance broking / 2nd ed. – Cambridge : Woodhead-Faulkner, 1987.
ISBN 0859413861 Hbk £25.00

—Third Party Rights Against Insurers / London : LLoyd's of London Press, 1989.
ISBN 1850441669 Hbk

—Understanding Insurance / London : Waterlow, 1983.
112p.
ISBN 0080391389 Pbk £15.75

—The Underwriter's Bedside Book / London : LLoyd's of London Press, 1987.

—Underwriters bedside book / London : Lloyd's of London Press, 1987.
ISBN 1850441332 Hbk £16.50

—What goes on in insurance? / Cambridge : Woodhead-Faulkner, 1982.
ISBN 0859411613 Pbk £3.95

—Witherby dictionary of insurance / 2nd ed. – London : Witherby & Co, 1987.
ISBN 0948691212 Hbk £14.50

INSURANCE - HONG KONG

—Report on laws on insurance / the Law Reform Commission of Hong Kong. – Hong Kong : The Commission, 1986.
vi,172p. – (Topic 9).
Bibliography: p.97-102. Summary in Chinese.

INSURANCE - INDIA

—Handbook on Insurance Laws / 2nd ed. – Allahabad : Law Publishers, 1983.

INSURANCE - IRELAND

—Regulation of insurance in the United Kingdom and Ireland / editor: T. Henry Ellis : associate editor: James A. Wiltshire : life assurance contributor: Peter G. Ward. – v. – London : Kluwer, 1983.
looseleaf.
Includes index.
ISBN 0903393638

INSURANCE - MALAYSIA

—Insurance Act, 1963 (Act 89) and Insurance Regulations and Orders / Kuala Lumpur : International Law Books Services.

—Law of insurance / by Poh Chu Chai. – Singapore : Malayan Law Journal Pte., 1986.
xxv,289p.
Covers the principles of insurance law with regard to insurable interest, duty of disclosure, formation of the contract of insurance, insurance agents, construction of policies, proximate cause of loss, subrogation and contribution, and assignment of policies. Three chapters cover motor insurance and the Motor Insurers' Bureau.
ISBN 9971700484

INSURANCE - MALPRACTICE

—Legal profession / New South Wales Law Reform Commission. – Sydney : The Commission, 1980.
106p; 24cm. – (Discussion paper 2).

INSURANCE - MALPRACTICE - ENGLAND

—Guide to the insurance of professional negligence risks / Digby Charles Jess. – London : Butterworths, 1982.
xxiv,239p; 21cm.
Includes index.
ISBN 0406257108 Pbk Unpriced

INSURANCE - MALPRACTICE - GREAT BRITAIN

—Insurance law : non disclosure and breach of warranty : report on a reference under Section 3 (1)(e) of the Law Commissions Act 1965 / chairman: Michael Kerr. – London : H.M.S.O., 1980.
vii,165p.

INSURANCE - NEW ZEALAND

—Aspects of insurance law (2) / a report by the Contracts and Commercial Law Reform Committee. – Wellington : Government Printer, 1983.
53p.
Contains text of a Draft Insurance Law Reform Bill.

—Cases and text on insurance law: Australia and New Zealand / North Ryde : Butterworths (Australia).
Explains the insurance law of Australia and New Zealand, and illustrates how the law is interpeted with a selection of modern cases as well as relevant statutory material.
ISBN 0409308706 Pbk

—Guidebook to Insurance Law in Australia and New Zealand / North Ryde : C.C.H. Australia, 1987.
341p.
ISBN 0869036378 Pbk £35.00

—Insurance law in Australia and New Zealand / by K.C.T. Sutton. – Sydney : Law Book Co., 1980.
lvii, 684 p.; 25 cm.
Includes bibliographical references and indexes.
ISBN 0455200742

—Insurance law in New Zealand / by A.A. Tarr. – Sydney : Law Book Co., 1985.
xxxv,257p.
Includes bibliographical references and index.
ISBN 0455205698

INSURANCE - SINGAPORE

—Insurance Law in Singapore / Singapore : Butterworths, 1988.
600p.

—Law of insurance / by Poh Chu Chai. – Singapore : Malayan Law Journal Pte., 1986.
xxv,289p.
Covers the principles of insurance law with regard to insurable interest, duty of disclosure, formation of the contract of insurance, insurance agents, construction of policies, proximate cause of loss, subrogation and contribution, and assignment of policies. Three chapters cover motor insurance and the Motor Insurers' Bureau.
ISBN 9971700484

INSURANCE - SOUTH AFRICA

—Decline, revival and future of the Roman-Dutch law of insurance in South Africa / by J.P. van Niekerk. – s.l. : Department of Mercantile Law, University of South Africa, 1986.
78p. – (Monograph series).
Includes bibliographical references.
ISBN 0869814001

—Gordon and Getz on the South African law of insurance / W. S. Getz, D. M. Davis. – 3rd ed. – Cape Town : Juta, 1983.
xl,624p.
Bibliography: p.ix-xii. - Includes index. Cover title: The South African law of insurance.
ISBN 0702113751

INSURANCE - WEST GERMANY

—Allianz Handbook of Loss Prevention / Dusseldorf : VDI-Verlag, 1987.
xvi, 928p.
ISBN 3184191036 Hbk £198.00

—German Insurance Laws : Statutes and Regulations Concerning Insurance Supervision and Insurance Contracts / 2nd ed. – Wiesbaden : Versicherungswirtschaft, 1986.
viii, 252p.

INSURANCE, ACCIDENT - NEW ZEALAND

—Accident compensation coverage : the administration of the Accident compensation act 1972 / J.L. Fahy. – 4th ed. – Wellington : Accident Compensation Commission, 1980.
55 p.; 21 cm.
ISBN 0477063705 Hbk

INSURANCE, AUTOMOBILE - LAW AND LEGISLATION - PAPUA NEW GUINEA

—Motor Vehicles (Third Party Insurance) (Basic Protection Compensation) Act, (revised laws of Papua New Guinea, chapter no. 296) : a fourth review / Law Reform Commission of Papua New Guinea. - Waigani : Law Reform Commission of Papua New Guinea, 1983.
12p. - (LRC working paper).
Includes bibliographical references.

INSURANCE COMPANIES - GREAT BRITAIN

—Captive Insurance Companies / 2nd ed. - Cambridge : Woodhead-Faulkner, 1987.
ISBN 0859413829 Hbk £45.00

—Regulatory arrangements at Lloyd's : report of the Committee of Inquiry / chairman: Sir Patrick Neill : presented to Parliament by the Secretary of State for Trade and Industry... - London : H.M.S.O., 1987.
ix,117p.
ISBN 010100592X

INSURANCE LAW - AUSTRALIA

—Insurance law in Australia and New Zealand / by P. E. Joske and Robert Brooking. - Sydney : Butterworths, 1975.
xxxix, 302 p.; 25 cm.
Includes index. Sets out insurance law both in terms of general principles and explains how these principles have been applied to particular aspects of insurance in the courts of Australia and New Zealand. Refers to decisions of the UK.
ISBN 0409436305 £20.00

INSURANCE LAW - GREAT BRITAIN

—Casebook on insurance law / 4th ed. - London : Butterworths, 1984.
372p.
Previous ed.: 1977.
ISBN 0406602638 Pbk

INSURANCE LAW - NEW ZEALAND

—Insurance law in Australia and New Zealand / by P. E. Joske and Robert Brooking. - Sydney : Butterworths, 1975.
xxxix, 302 p.; 25 cm.
Includes index. Sets out insurance law both in terms of general principles and explains how these principles have been applied to particular aspects of insurance in the courts of Australia and New Zealand. Refers to decisions of the UK.
ISBN 0409436305 £20.00

—Preliminary to the preparation of a third report on aspects of insurance law / Wellington : Contracts and Commercial Law Reform Committee, 1984.
i,9 leaves. - (Discussion paper).

INTANGIBLE PROPERTY - GREAT BRITAIN

—Passing off : the law and practice relating to the imitation of goods, businesses and professions / David Young. - 1st ed. - London : Oyez Longman, 1985.
xxviii,152p. - (Oyez Longman practitioner series).
Includes index.
ISBN 0851209866

INTEGRATED CIRCUITS

—Draft Treaty : Memorandum of the Director General / World Intellectual Property Organization. - Geneva : World Intellectual Property Organization, 1985.
29p. - (IPIC/CE/I/2).
The Committee met in Geneva from November 26 to 29, 1985. 'Draft treaty on the protection of intellectual property in respect of integrated circuits'.

—Report : adopted by the Committee of Experts / World Intellectual Property Organization. - Geneva : World Intellectual Property Organization, 1985.
22,10p. - (IPIC/CE/I/7).
The Committee met in Geneva from November 26 to 29, 1985. Draft treaty entitled: Draft Treaty on the Protection of Intellectual Property in Respect of Integrated Circuits.

INTELLECTUAL PROPERTY

—Agreement between the United Nations and the World Intellectual Property Organization / Geneva : World Intellectual Property Organization.
55p.

—Background Reading Material on Intellectual Property / Geneva : World Intellectual Property Organization, 1988.
400p.

—Berne Convention for the Protection of Literary and Artistic Works / rep. 1987. - Geneva : World Intellectual Property Organization.
101p.

—Berne Convention for the Protection of Literary and Artistic Works from 1886 to 1986 / Geneva : World Intellectual Property Organization, 1986.
241p.

—Berne Convwention for the Protection of Literary and Artistic Works, Guide / rep. 1987. - Geneva : World Intellectual Property Organization.
190p.

—Butterworths intellectual property law handbook / London : Butterworths, 1989.
624; 248.
Includes patents, copyright, semiconductor typographies, registered designs, unregistered design right, trademarks, plant varieties protection, intellectual property and competition, professional status, and practice.
ISBN 0406504717 Pbk £19.95

—Model Provisions on the Protection of Computer Software : Text of the English Translation of the Stockholm Act (1967) / Geneva : World Intellectual Property Organization.
27p.

—Regional Forum on the Judiciary and the Intellectual Property system / organized jointly by the World Intellectual Property Organization (WIPO) and the judges of the Superior Courts of Pakistan in association with the Law Association for Asia and the Western Pacific (LAWASIA) and with the assistance of the United Nations Development Programme, Islamabad, Pakistan, October 5 to 9, 1986. - Geneva : WIPO, 1987.
303p.
At head of t.p.: World Intellectual Property Organization; Supreme Court of Pakistan.

—Regional Symposium on Intellectual Property Law Teaching and Research in Asia and the Pacific / Geneva : World Intellectual Property Organization, 1987.
ca 300p.

INTELLECTUAL PROPERTY - ASIA

—Intellectual Property Colloquium of Judges in Asia and the Pacific / Geneva : World Intellectual Property Organization, 1984.
260p.

—Protecting intellectual property in Asia - Pacific : a specially commissioned report / edited by John A. Connors. - London : Oyez Longman, 1984.
108 leaves; 30cm. - (Oyez Longman intelligence reports).
Bibliography: leaf 108.
ISBN 0851208851 Pbk No price

INTELLECTUAL PROPERTY - AUSTRALIA

—Butterworths Student Companions /. - Butterworths, 1988.
111p.
ISBN 0409492892

—Intellectual Property / Sydney : Butterworths, 1988.
144p. - (Student Companion Ser.).
This guide contains over 200 summaries of cases in the area of intellectual property. It is intended for use in conjunction with lecture notes, textbooks, and other working documents.

—Intellectual Property : Commentary and Materials / J. McKeough. - North Ryde : Law Book Co, 1986.
xlviii, 741p.
ISBN 0455206945 Hbk £80.00
ISBN 0455206953 Pbk £59.50

—Intellectual property in Australia / editor, James Lahore. - 2. - Sydney : Butterworths, 1981.
looseleaf.
ISBN 0409300373

—Intellectual Property in Australia : Patents, Designs, Trade Marks, Confidential Information and Unfair Competition / James W. Dwyer. - Wellington : Butterworths.
This looseleaf service provides exhaustive coverage of the law in Australia relating to copyright in literary and artistic works, sound recordings, film, television and radio broadcasts, and published editions of books and other works. The full text of relevant statutes is provided.

—Intellectual property in New Zealand and Australia / papers presented by M.P. Crew ... et al. - Auckland : Legal Research Foundation, 1985.
227p.
ISBN 0908581378

—Intellectual Property Law in New Zealand and Australia / Auckland : Legal Research Foundation, 1985.

—Intellectual Property Reports / John J. Garsney. - Wellington : Butterworths.
These comprehensive reports are complete with headnotes, catchwords, holdings, court hearings, and final judgement dates for all major decisions in field of intellectual property in Australia.

—Intellectual property reports : being reports of judgments of the High Court of Australia, the Federal Court of Australia, the Supreme Courts of the states and territories of Australia, the Patent, Trade Marks and Designs Office, the Copyright Tribunal and incorporating reports of signficant cases decided by the courts in the United Kingdom, the United States of America and other international jurisdictions / editor, James Lahore. - Vol. 1, pt.1 (Oct. 1983)-. - Sydney : Butterworths, 1983-.

—Law of intellectual property / by Staniforth Ricketson. - North Ryde : Law Book Co., 1985.
clxxv,1201p.
Bibliography: p.cxxxix-clxxv. - Includes index.
ISBN 0455204179

INTELLECTUAL PROPERTY - CANADA

—Canadian Intellectual Property Reports / Agincourt : Carswell, 1987.
This reference text contains the key decisions in the intellectual property law area. Topics include copyrights, industrial designs, patents of invention, and trademarks.

—Intellectual Property Journal / Agincourt : Carswell, 1985.

INTELLECTUAL PROPERTY - CHINA

—Chinese intellectual property and technology transfer Law / by Zheng Chengsi with Michael D. Pendleton. - London : Sweet & Maxwell, 1987.
xli,331p; 26cm.
Presents a summary and analysis of Chinese intellectual property and technology transfer law covering the Chinese system, patents, trademarks, copyright, transfer of technology and software protection, taxation in the field of intellectual property, and containing appendices of original source material.
ISBN 0421383801 £50.00

—Intellectual Property and Technology Transfer in the People's Republic of China / Hong Kong : Hong Kong University Press, 1988.
ISBN 9622092020 Hbk

—Intellectual property law in People's Republic of China / London : Butterworths, 1986.
ISBN 0409995193 Pbk £17.00

—Intellectual property law in the People's Republic of China : a guide to patents, trade marks and technology transfer / Michael D.Pendleton. - Singapore : Butterworths, 1986.
xvii,138p.
ISBN 0409995193

INTELLECTUAL PROPERTY - EUROPEAN COMMUNITY

—EEC and intellectual property / Diana Guy and Guy I.F. Leigh. - London : Sweet & Maxwell, 1981.
xxiv,375p; 25cm.
Includes index.
ISBN 0421234202 £30.00

INTELLECTUAL PROPERTY - GREAT BRITAIN

—Commercial exploitation of personality / London : Sweet & Maxwell, 1987.
ISBN 0455206929 Hbk £19.50

—Copyright : Intellectual Property in the Information Age / Hamilton. - Routledge, 1980.
ISBN 0710005393 Hbk £18.95

—Draft clauses of a bill to reform the law of copyright and other intellectual property / Department of Trade and Industry. - London : The Department, 1987.
viii,74p.

—Forms/Agreements Intellectual Property 2 vols. / London : Sweet & Maxwell, 1988.
ISBN 0421253002 Hbk

—Intellectual property and innovation / presented to Parliament by the Secretary of State for Trade and Industry. - London : H.M.S.O., 1986.
iv,78p.
Bibliography: p.77-78.
ISBN 0101971206

—Intellectual Property Law / London : Butterworths, 1982.
ISBN 0406593590 Hbk

—Intellectual property law and taxation / Eastaway. - 3rd ed. - London : Longman Professional, 1988.
ISBN 0851213227 Pbk

—Intellectual property law and taxation / by Richard J. Gallafent, Nigel A. Eastaway and Victor A.F. Dauppe. - London : Oyez, 1981.
xxvi,321p; 24cm. - (Law and tax series).
ISBN 0851205925

—Intellectual property law and taxation / by Richard J. Gallafent, Nigel A. Eastaway, and Victor A. F. Dauppe. - 2nd ed. - London : Oyez Longman, 1984.
xxvi,338p.
ISBN 0851208746

—Intellectual property : patents, copyright, trade marks and allied rights / by W.R. Cornish. – London : Sweet & Maxwell, 1981.
lxi,630p; 23cm.
Includes index.
ISBN 0421243104 Hbk £26.50
ISBN 0421243309 Pbk £16.50

—Intellectual property rights and innovation : presented to Parliament by the Prime Minister ... December 1983 / Great Britain. – London : H.M.S.O., 1983.
45p; 25cm.
ISBN 010191170X Pbk £4.65

—Introduction to intellectual property law / Jeremy Phillips. – London : Butterworths, 1986.
230p; 22cm.
Includes index.
ISBN 0406258325 Hbk £18.00
ISBN 0406258333 Pbk £12.50

—Introduction to Intellectual Property law / London : Butterworths, 1986.
ISBN 0406258333 Pbk £14.95

—Merchandising intellectual property / John Adams : with an introduction by Iain C Baillie : and a chapter on taxation by K.V. Prichard Jones. – London : Butterworths, 1987.
xxxi,345p,2p of plates; 26cm.
Includes index.
ISBN 0406103402 £30.00

—Passing off : law and practice / John Drysdale, Michael Silverleaf. – London : Butterworths, 1986.
xxxiv,224p; 26cm.
Includes index.
ISBN 0406253404 £25.00

—Patents, trade marks, copyright and industrial designs / Robin Jacob. – 3rd ed. – London : Sweet & Maxwell, 1986.
xiv,182p; 22cm.
Previous ed.: 1978. Includes index.
ISBN 0421349603 Hbk £13.50
ISBN 0421349700 Pbk £8.95

—Practical guide to intellectual property / London : Butterworths, 1988.
ISBN 040610140X Pbk

—Practical Guide to Intellectual Property / London : Butterworths, 1987.
ISBN 040610140X Pbk

—Taxation of Transactions in Intellectual Property / W. G. S. Massey. – London : Sweet & Maxwell, 1982.

—Taxation of Transactions in Intellectual Property / W. G. Massey. – London : Sweet & Maxwell.
ISBN 042129390X Hbk

INTELLECTUAL PROPERTY - HONG KONG

—Law of Intellectual and Industrial Property in Hong Kong / London : Butterworths, 1984.
ISBN 0406181179 Pbk £50.00

—Law of intellectual and industrial property in Hong Kong : a guide to trade marks, copyright, patents, registered designs and other protected commercial information / Michael D. Pendleton. – London : Butterworth, 1984.
xxxix,556p.
Deals with Hong Kong's intellectual property law, including both civil and criminal remedies. Discusses passing off, registered trademarks, trade descriptions, legislation, copyright, patents, registered designs, and trade secrets.
ISBN 0406181179

INTELLECTUAL PROPERTY - JAPAN

—Intellectual Property Law of Japan / Dordrecht : Kluwer, 1980.
352p.
ISBN 9028606491 Hbk £149.00

INTELLECTUAL PROPERTY - NEW ZEALAND

—Intellectual property in New Zealand and Australia / papers presented by M.P. Crew ... et al. – Auckland : Legal Research Foundation, 1985.
227p.
ISBN 0908581378

—Intellectual Property Law in New Zealand and Australia / Auckland : Legal Research Foundation, 1985.

—Intellectual Property Reports, Vol. 1, 1989 / edited by Brown. – Wellington : Butterworths (New Zealand).
435p.
ISBN 0409787361 Hbk £190.00

—Law of Intellectual Property in New Zealand / Grant. – Butterworths, 1989.
715p.
ISBN 0409787981 Hbk £130.00

INTELLECTUAL PROPERTY - OCEANIA

—Intellectual Property Colloquium of Judges in Asia and the Pacific / Geneva : World Intellectual Property Organization, 1984.
260p.

INTELLECTUAL PROPERTY - SOUTH KOREA

—Intellectual property laws of Korea / by Kyung Jae Park. – Seoul : Lee & Ko, 1986.
xx,372p.

INTELLECTUAL PROPERTY - SWEDEN

—Swedish intellectual property and market legislation : collection of statutory texts / edited by Ulf Bernitz. – Stockholm : Institute for Intellectual Property and Market Law, Stockholm University, 1984.
ii,181p. – (Publications).
ISBN 9138081717

INTELLECTUAL PROPERTY (INTERNATIONAL LAW)

—Berne Convention for the Protection of Literary and Artistic Works : 1886-1986 / Sam Ricketson. – London : Centre for Commercial Law Studies, Queen Mary College, 1987.
lxii,1030p.
Bibliography: pp.981-1006. - Includes index. Includes the text of the Convention with revisions.

—Draft Treaty : Memorandum of the Director General / World Intellectual Property Organization. – Geneva : World Intellectual Property Organization, 1985.
29p. – (IPIC/CE/I/2).
The Committee met in Geneva from November 26 to 29, 1985. 'Draft treaty on the protection of intellectual property in respect of integrated circuits'.

—Draft treaty with explanatory notes / memorandum of the Director General. – Geneva : World Intellectual Property Organization, 1986.
45,3p. – (IPIC/CE/II/2).
'Submitted by the Director General of W.I.P.O. for what will be the second session of the W.I.P.O. Committee of Experts on Intellectual Property in Respect of Integrated Circuits ... to take place from June 23 to 27, 1986, at Geneva' - Background. Draft treaty entitled: Draft Treaty on the Protection of Intellectual Property in Respect of Semiconductor Integrated Circuits.

—Report : adopted by the Committee of Experts / World Intellectual Property Organization. – Geneva : World Intellectual Property Organization, 1985.
22,10p. – (IPIC/CE/I/7).
The Committee met in Geneva from November 26 to 29, 1985. Draft treaty entitled: Draft Treaty on the Protection of Intellectual Property in Respect of Integrated Circuits.

INTELLIGENCE SERVICE - AUSTRALIA

—Big Brother or Democracy : The Case for the Abolition of the Australian Security Intelligence Organisation / London : Spokesman Books, 1983.
161p.
ISBN 085124307X Pbk £2.95

INTELLIGENCE SERVICE - CANADA

—Certain R.C.M.P. activities and the question of governmental knowledge : third report / Commission of Inquiry Concerning Certain Activities of the Royal Canadian Mounted Police. – Ottawa : Canadian Government Publishing Centre, 1981.
xv,527p; 25cm.
Chairman: D.C. McDonald.
ISBN 0660109530

—Freedom and security under the law : second report / Commission of Inquiry Concerning Certain Activities of the Royal Canadian Mounted Police. – 2. – Ottawa : Canadian Government Publishing Centre, 1981.
xxii,1257p; 25cm.
Bibliography: p.1117-1144. Chairman: D.C. McDonald.
ISBN 0660109506 v.2
ISBN 0660109522

INTELLIGENCE SERVICE - GREAT BRITAIN

—British Intelligence Services in Action / 2nd ed. – Newtownabbey : Dunrod Press, 1981.
312p.
ISBN 0862021111 Hbk £19.75

—Interception of communications in Great Britain / Home Office. – London : H.M.S.O., 1980.
8p.

—Who's watching you? / Crispin Aubrey. – Harmondsworth : Penguin, 1981.
204p,8p of plates; 18cm. – (Pelican books).
Bibliography: p197-199. - Includes index.
ISBN 0140222839 Pbk £1.50

INTELLIGENCE SERVICE - UNITED STATES

—ITT-CIA Subversion in Chile : A Case Study of U.S. Corporate Intrigue in the Third World / Spokesman University. – London : Spokesman Books, 1983.
114p.
ISBN 0851240402 Pbk £2.50

INTELLIGENCE SERVICE - WEST GERMANY

—Censorship, Legal Defence and Domestic Intelligence Service in W. Germany / Russell Tribunal, III. – London : Spokesman Books, 1983.
50p.

INTER-LIBRARY LOANS

—Model handbook for interlending and copying / Graham P. Cornish. – Wetherby : Published jointly by IFLA Office for International Lending and Unesco, 1988.
79p; 30cm.
Bibliography: p72.
ISBN 0712320458 Pbk £5.00

INTEREST AND USURY - MALAYSIA

—Law of interest / by K.S. Dass : with a foreword by Raja Tan Sri Azlan Shah. – Batu Pahat, Malaysia : New Law Publishers, 1980.
xiv,79p.
Includes index.

INTEREST (LAW) - AUSTRALIA - TASMANIA

—Report on interest on pre- and post-judgment debts / Law Reform Commission of Tasmania. – Hobart : Government Printer, 1985.
17p. – (Report v no 44).

INTEREST (LAW) - CANADA - BRITISH COLUMBIA

—Report on the Court Order Interest Act / Law Reform Commission of British Columbia. – Vancouver : The Commission, 1987.
139p.
Includes bibliographical references.
ISBN 077188561X

INTEREST RATES

—Price and Henderson currency and interest rate swaps / Schuyler K. Henderson, John A. M. Price. – London : Butterworths, 1984.
xiii,144p; 26cm.
Includes index. At head of title: Price and Henderson.
ISBN 0406073600 No price

INTERGOVERNMENTAL FISCAL RELATIONS

—Federal finance in comparative perspective / Richard M. Bird. – Toronto : Canadian Tax Foundation, 1986.
x,250p.
Includes bibliographical references.
ISBN 0888080247

INTERGOVERNMENTAL FISCAL RELATIONS - CANADA

—Acceptable mean : the tax rental agreements, 1941-1962 / R.M. Burns. – Toronto : Canadian Tax Foundation, 1980.
viii,285p.
ISBN 0888080018

—Fiscal dimensions of Canadian federalism / edited by Richard M. Bird. – Toronto : Canadian Tax Foundation, 1980.
v,151p.
ISBN 0888080050

—Intergovernmental transfers in Canada / by Robin W. Boadway. – Toronto : Canadian Tax Foundation, 1980.
ix,93p.
ISBN 0888080034

—Need for and the feasibility of an appeals process in regard to municipal grants-in-lieu of taxes : a report prepared for the Minister of Public Works Canada / I.C. Pollack, R. Gaulin, G. Simpson. – Ottawa : Minister of Supply and Services Canada, 1983.
324 p. in various pagings; 28 cm.
English and French. Added t.p.: La necessite et la faisabilite d'une procedure d'appel dans le regime de subventions aux municipalites en compensation d'imp$ots.
ISBN 0662524039

—Need for and the feasibility of an appeals process in regard to municipal grants-in-lieu of taxes : a report prepared for the Minister of Public Works Canada / I.C. Pollack, R. Gaulin, G. Simpson. – Ottawa : Minister of Supply and Services Canada, 1983.
324 p. in various pagings; 28 cm.
English and French. Added t.p.: La necessite et la faisabilite d'une procedure d'appel dans le regime de subventions aux municipalites en compensation d'imp$ots.
ISBN 0662524039

INTERGOVERNMENTAL TAX RELATIONS - CANADA

—Acceptable mean : the tax rental agreements, 1941-1962 / R.M. Burns. – Toronto : Canadian Tax Foundation, 1980.
viii,285p.
ISBN 0888080018

INTERNAL REVENUE LAW - AUSTRALIA

—Powers of Investigation in Revenue, Companies and Trade Practices Law / R.H. Woellner. – Butterworths, 1983.
486p.
ISBN 0409493813 Pbk £65.00

INTERNAL REVENUE LAW - GREAT BRITAIN

—Report / Committee on Enforcement Powers of the Revenue Departments : chairman, Lord Keith of Kinkel. – London : H.M.S.O., 1983.
xiv,334p; 25cm.

Vol.2 : Chapters 16-28 and notes / Committee on Enforcement Powers of the Revenue Departments : chairman, Lord Keith of Kinkel. - 1983.
336-804p; 25cm.

Vol.3 : Chapters 29-33 and notes : Development land tax, petroleum revenue tax, capital transfer tax and stamp duties / Committee on Enforcement Powers of the Revenue Departments : chairman, Lord Keith of Kinkel. - 1984.
iv,251p; 25cm.

—Revenue law / John Tiley. – 3rd ed. – London : Butterworths, 1981.
lvi,873,28p; 26cm.
Bibliography: p.xv-xvi. - Includes index. Kept up to date by supplements.
ISBN 0406665958 Pbk
ISBN 0406665966

INTERNAL SECURITY - GREAT BRITAIN

—Interception of communications in Great Britain / Home Office. – London : H.M.S.O., 1980.
8p.

INTERNATIONAL ADMINISTRATIVE COURTS

—Documents on international administrative tribunals / Oxford : Clarendon Press, 1989.
274.
A volume of documents, each of which sets out the interests, purposes, structureand powers of the tribunal to which it relates. Gives an account of the role and responsibility of each tribunal.
ISBN 0198256361 Hbk £27.50

INTERNATIONAL AGENCIES

—Concept of international organization / edited by Georges Abi-Saab. – Paris : UNESCO, 1981.
245 p.; 25 cm.
Includes bibliographical references.
ISBN 923101742X

—Explanatory report on the European Convention on the Recognition of the Legal Personality of International Non-Governmental Organisations / Strasbourg : Council of Europe, 1986.
17p.
Includes text of the Convention. Drawn up within the Council of Europe by a select committee of experts under the authority of the European Committee on Legal Co-operation.
ISBN 9287108978

—Handbook of international economic institutions / M. A. G. van Meerhaeghe. – Extensively rev. and enl. ed. – The Hague : Martinus Nijhoff Publishers, 1980.
xxii,441p.
Published in 1971 under title: International economic institutions. Includes bibliographies.
ISBN 9024723574

—International Committee of the Red Cross / Dordrecht : Kluwer, 1984.
300p.
ISBN 9024730643 Hbk £120.00

—International institutional law / Henry G. Schermers. – 3. – Leiden : Sijthoff, 1972.
Volumes 1 and 2 superseded by later edition in one volume. Includes bibliography and index.
ISBN 9028603948 v.3

—International institutional law / Henry G. Schermers. – 2nd ed. – Alphen aan den Rijn : Sijthoff & Noordhoff, 1980.
xxxiii,1054p.
Supersedes volumes 1 and 2 of first edition. Bibliography: p.948-978. - Includes index.
ISBN 9028603204

—International organizations / Clive Archer. – London : Allen & Unwin, 1983.
xii,193p; 23cm.
Bibliography: p180-188. - Includes index.
ISBN 0043201563 Hbk Unpriced
ISBN 0043201571 Pbk Unpriced

—Law of international institutions / D.W. Bowett. – 4th ed. – London : Sweet & Maxwell, 1982.
xv,431p; 23cm.
Published under the auspices of the London Institute for World Affairs by Stevens & Sons Previous ed.: 1975. Includes index.
ISBN 0420460101 Hbk £19.00
ISBN 0420460209 Pbk £12.50

—Legal problems of international organizations / by Felice Morgenstern. – Cambridge : Grotius Publications, 1986.
xiv,147p.
Includes bibliographical references and index. At head of title: University of Cambridge Research Centre for International Law.
ISBN 0906496241

—Politics and process in the specialised agencies of the United Nations / Houshang Ameri. – Aldershot : Gower, 1982.
xiii,284p; 23cm.
Bibliography: p265-273. - Includes index.
ISBN 0566005387 Unpriced

—Specialized agencies and the United Nations : the system in crisis / Douglas Williams : with a foreword by Sir Anthony Parsons. – London : Hurst in association with the David Davies Memorial Institute of International Studies, London, 1987.
xvi,279p; 23cm.
Bibliography: p271-274. - Includes index.
ISBN 185065025X £17.50

INTERNATIONAL AND MUNICIPAL LAW

—Decisions of international institutions before domestic courts / Christoph Schreuer. – London : Oceana, 1981.
xiii,407p; 25cm.
Revised and updated version of 1977 German original.
ISBN 0379207095

—Effect on English domestic law of membership of the European Communities and of ratification of the European Convention on Human Rights / edited by M.P. Furmston, Roger Kerridge, B.E. Sufrin. – The Hague : M. Nijhoff, 1983.
viii, 428p.
Papers by members of the University of Bristol Faculty of Law in celebration of the fiftieth anniversary of the Faculty.
ISBN 9024728118 Hbk £130.00

—Guide to EEC law in Northern Ireland / by Sylvia E. Paisley. – Belfast : SLS Legal Publications (NI), Queen's University, Belfast, 1986.
xxii,247p; 21cm.
Bibliography: p237. - Includes index.
ISBN 0853892628 Pbk No price

—International labour conventions and national law : the effectiveness of the automatic incorporation of treaties in national legal systems / Virginia A. Leary. – The Hague : M. Nijhoff, 1982.
xiv,191p.
Revision of thesis (doctoral)–Graduate Institute of International Studies at Geneva. Bibliography: p171-179.
ISBN 9024725518 CIP rev.

INTERNATIONAL AND MUNICIPAL LAW - AUSTRALIA

—International law in Australia / K. W Ryan. – 2nd ed. – North Ryde, N.S.W. : Published for the Australian Institute of International Affairs by the Law Book Co., 1984.
xliii, 523 p.; 25 cm.
Includes bibliographical references.
ISBN 0455202699 pbk.

INTERNATIONAL AND MUNICIPAL LAW - EUROPEAN COMMUNITY

—Supervision in European Community law : observance by the member states of their treaty obligations : a treatise on international and supra-national supervision / H.A.H. Audretsch. – 2nd rev. ed. – Amsterdam : North-Holland, 1986.
xix,782p.
Previous ed.: 1978. Bibliography: p.591-613. - Includes index.
ISBN 0444700277

INTERNATIONAL BUSINESS

—Agribusiness in Africa : a study of the impact of big business on Africa's food and agricultural production / Barbara Dinham & Colin Hines. – London : Earth Resources Research, 1983.
224p b ill; 21cm.
Includes index. Cover title.
ISBN 0946281009 Pbk £4.95

—Aluminium industry and the Third World : multinational corporations and underdevelopment / Ronald Graham. – London : Zed, 1982.
xii,278p; 22cm.
Bibliography: p263-270. - Includes index.
ISBN 0862320577 Pbk

—Application of new legal techniques to mining agreements in developing countries / by Carl W. Dundas. – London : Commonwealth Secretariat, 1981.
46p.
Includes bibliographical references.

—Britain and the multinationals / John Stopford and Louis Turner. – Chichester : Wiley, 1985.
xiv,282p; 24cm. – (Wiley/IRM series on multinationals).
Includes index.
ISBN 0471908398 £12.75

—Codes of conduct for transnational corporations : signals of public expectation? : a discussion arranged by the International Bar Association's Section on Business Law, etc. / Berlin : International Bar Association, 1980.
4,146p.
ISBN 0950587613

—Conflicts of national laws with international business activity : issues of extraterritoriality / by A.H. Hermann. – London : British North American Research Organisation, 1982.
xii,96p.
ISBN 0902594419

—Corporations in and under international law / by Ignaz Seidl-Hohenveldern. – Cambridge : Grotius, 1987.
xviii,138p.
Covers the nationality of corporations and the effect upon them of nationalisation measures, as well as the special responsibilities of state-owned corporations. The second part of the book examines problems connected with the legal personality of international organizations.
ISBN 0949009091

—Cross-border transactions between related companies : a summary of tax rules / edited by William R. Lawlor. – Deventer, The Netherlands : Kluwer Law and Taxation Publishers, 1985.
Derived from an international tax planning symposium in New York sponsored by Ernst & Whinney. 'Current to January 1985'–Foreword.
ISBN 9065442324 pbk.

—Economics of multinational enterprise / Neil Hood, Stephen Young. – 5th impression. – London : Longman, 1984.
xv,412p.
This ed. originally published: 1979. Bibliography: p.393-407. - Includes index.

—Foreign investment in mining projects : case studies of recent experiences / Raymond F. Mikesell : a project sponsored and administered by the FMME. – Cambridge, Mass. : Oelgeschlager, Gunn & Hain, 1983.
xv,297p; 24cm.
Bibliography: p281-285. - Includes index.
ISBN 0899461700 Unpriced

—French multinationals / Julien Savary : foreword by Francois Morin. – London : Pinter, 1984.
220p.
Translation of: Les multinationales francaises.
ISBN 0861873637 £16.50

—Governments and multinationals : policies in the developed countries / A. E. Safarian. – London : British North American Research Organisation, 1983.
x,118p.
Bibliography: p105-110.
ISBN 089068071X

—Growth of international business / edited by Mark Casson : contributors; authors Peter J. Buckley ... et al. : reviewers and discussants: Charles E. Harvey ... et al. – London : Allen & Unwin, 1983.
xii,276p; 23cm.
Bibliography: p258-272. - Includes index.
ISBN 0043303331 £15.00

—Handbook of international joint ventures / John Walmsley. – London : Graham & Trotman, 1983.
viii,161p; 24cm.
Includes index.
ISBN 0860103692 £22.00

—ILO research on multinational enterprises and social policy : an overview / 2nd (revised) ed. – Geneva : International Labour Office, 1982.
ii,33p.
Bibliography: p27-33.
ISBN 9221029182

—Industrial relations and multinational corporations in Europe / Bruno Liebhaberg. – Farnborough, Hants. : Gower in association with the European Centre for Study and Information on Multinational Corporations (ECSM), 1980.
xiv,107p; 23cm.
ISBN 0566003635 £9.50

—Information disclosure and the multinational corporation / S.J. Gray with L.B. McSweeney, J.C. Shaw. – Chichester : Wiley, 1984.
xi,236p; 24cm. – (Wiley/IRM series on multinationals).
Includes index.
ISBN 0471904244 Hbk

—International business and national jurisdiction / A.D. Neale and M.L. Stephens. – Oxford : Clarendon Press, 1988.
xix,216p.
Examines the relationship between issues in international and municipal law, specifically the relationship between historically exclusive spheres of sovereign interest, and legal and practical requirements of the modern international commercial environment. Concentrates on US antitrust law, but some EEC and English decisions are included.
ISBN 0198255322 Hbk £52.00

—International business transactions in a nutshell / by Donald T. Wilson. – St. Paul, Minn. : West Publishing Co., 1980.
lvii,393p; 19cm. – (Nutshell series).

—International contract law & finance review yearbook / 1981. 2 v. – London : Euromoney, 1981.
ISBN 0903121360

—International financial law review / London : Euromoney, 1983-.
Supersedes: The international contract law & finance review.

—International production and the multinational enterprise / John H. Dunning. – London : Allen & Unwin, 1981.
viii,439p; 23cm.
Includes bibliographies and index.
ISBN 0043303196 Hbk Unpriced
ISBN 004330320X Pbk Unpriced

—International transactions and Australian income tax : being a commentary on Division 13 of the Income Tax Assessment Act 1936 together with the text of the Legislation / by E. F. Mannix. – Sydney : Butterworths, 1982.
x,46p.
Includes index.
ISBN 0409493554

—Legal and economic analyses on multinational enterprises / edited by Klaus J. Hopt. – 2 V. – Berlin : Walter de Gruyter, 1982.
At head of title: European University Institute. Vol. 2, English and French, with summaries for each item in the other language, has also parallel title: Analyses legales et economiques sur les entreprises multinationales. Includes indexes. Contents: v. 1. European merger control – v. 2. Groups of companies in European laws.
ISBN 3110087049 v. 2

—Legal control of the multinational enterprise : national regulatory techniques and the prospects for international controls / Cynthia D. Wallace. – The Hague : Martinus Nijhoff, 1983.
354p.
Originally presented as the author's thesis (Ph.D.)–Cambridge University. Includes index. Bibliography: p331-355.
ISBN 9024726689 Hbk £135.00

—Legal problems of codes of conduct for multinational enterprises / edited by Norbert Horn. – Antwerp : Kluwer, 1980.
xiv,509p.
Consists of papers presented at an international conference of experts held July 16-18, 1979, at the Center for Interdisciplinary Research, University of Bielefeld, Germany. Includes index. Bibliography: p443-450.
ISBN 9026811276

—Multinational corporation / Sanjaya Lall. – London : Macmillan, 1980.
xii,264p.
ISBN 0333277465 £20.00
ISBN 0333281705

—Multinational enterprise and economic analysis / Richard E. Caves. – Cambridge : Cambridge University Press, 1982.
xi,346p; 22cm. – (Cambridge surveys of economic literature).
Bibliography: p306-335. - Includes index.
ISBN 0521249902 Hbk £20.00
ISBN 0521271150 Pbk £7.50

—Multinational enterprise between hammer and anvil / Georges van Hecke. – Deventer : Kluwer Law and Taxation Publishers, 1984.
16p.
Includes bibliographical references.
ISBN 9065441956

—Multinational enterprise in historical perspective / edited by Alice Teichova, Maurice Levy-Leboyer and Helga Nussbaum. – Cambridge : Cambridge University Press, 1986.
viii,396p; 24cm.
Conference proceedings. Includes index.
ISBN 0521320402 France £30.00
ISBN 2735101517

—Multinationals and political control / John Robinson. – Aldershot : Gower, 1983.
xxi,507p; 23cm.
Includes index.
ISBN 0566003945 Unpriced

—Multinationals beyond the market : intra-firm trade and the control of transfer pricing / edited by Robin Murray. – Brighton : Harvester, 1981.
335p; 24cm. – (Harvester studies in development).
Includes bibliographies and index.
ISBN 0855272031 £22.50

—Multinationals : company performance and global trends / John M. Stopford and John H. Dunning...et al. – London : Macmillan, 1983.
ix,147p.
Bibliographies.
ISBN 0333340930

—Multinationals : theory and history / edited by Peter Hertner and Geoffrey Jones. – Aldershot : Gower, 1986.
vii,200p; 22cm.
Conference proceedings. Includes index.
ISBN 0566050781 £18.50

—National laws and international commerce : the problem of extraterritoriality / Douglas E. Rosenthal and William M. Knighton. – London : Routledge & Kegan Paul, 1982.
xi,96p.
Bibliography: p94-96.
ISBN 0710093381

—Oil companies and the Arab world / Giacomo Luciani. – London : Croom Helm, 1984.
197p; 23cm.
Includes index. Rev. translation of: Compagnie petrolifere e paesi arabi.
ISBN 0709916191 £15.95
ISBN 0312582765

—Oil companies in the international system / Louis Turner. – 3rd ed. – London : Allen & Unwin for the Royal Institute of International Affairs, 1983.
279p; 22cm.
Previous ed.: 1980. Bibliography: p253-268. - Includes index.
ISBN 0043820409 Pbk Unpriced

—Overseas business activities : proceedings of the Fuji Conference / the International Conference on Business History 9 : edited by Akio Okochi, Tadakatsu Inoue. – Tokyo : University of Tokyo Press, 1984.
xiii, 296 p.; 24 cm.
Includes bibliographies and index.
ISBN 4130470191 Y5000

—Review of International Business Law / Agincourt : Carswell, 1987.
This work focuses on international trade, securities and banking law, international commercial arbitration and dispute settlement, foreign investment, transactional resource issues, and international taxation issues. There are articles, updates on current issues, case comments and book reviews.

—Strategic management in multinational companies / by Yves Doz. – Oxford : Pergamon, 1985.
250p; 25cm.
ISBN 0080318088 Hbk £19.25
ISBN 008031807X Pbk £10.75

—Transfer pricing and multinational enterprises : three taxation issues : reports of the OECD Committee on Fiscal Affairs, 1984 / Paris : O.E.C.D., 1984.
91p.
ISBN 9264126260

—Transnational corporations in world development / United Nations. – London : Published in co-operation with the United Nations by Graham & Trotman, 1984.
256p.
ISBN 0860105083 £37.00

—Tripartite Declaration of Principles concerning Multinational Enterprises and Social Policy : history, contents, follow-up and relationship with relevant instruments of other organisations / Hans Gunter. – Geneva : Interntional Labour Office, 1981.
iii,29p.
ISBN 9221029093

INTERNATIONAL BUSINESS – EUROPEAN COMMUNITY

—Opinion on the proposal for a tenth Council directive based on Article 54(3)(g) of the Treaty concerning cross-border mergers of public limited companies / (COM(84)727 final) : European Communities. Economic and Social Committee. – Luxembourg : Office for Official Publications of the European Communities, 1985.
9 leaves. – (CES(85) 780).
ISBN 9277085061

—Proposal for an eleventh Council directive : based on article 54(3)(g) of the treaty concerning disclosure requirements in respect of branches opened in a member state by certain types of companies governed by the law of another state / Council of the European Communities. – London : Department of Trade and Industry, 1987.
17,7p.
Includes a 'Background note' from the Deparment of Trade and Industry.

INTERNATIONAL BUSINESS – GREAT BRITAIN

—Proposal for an eleventh Council directive : based on article 54(3)(g) of the treaty concerning disclosure requirements in respect of branches opened in a member state by certain types of companies governed by the law of another state / Council of the European Communities. – London : Department of Trade and Industry, 1987.
17,7p.
Includes a 'Background note' from the Deparment of Trade and Industry.

—Taxation of international business : memorandum / by the Society's Standing Committee on Revenue Law. – London : Law Society, 1983.
21p.

INTERNATIONAL BUSINESS – PAPUA NEW GUINEA

—Corporate social responsibility in Papua New Guinea / Law Reform Commission of Papua New Guinea. – Waigani : The Commission, 1981.
ii,17p. – (Occasional paper).
'This paper was researched and written for the Commission by Edward F. Graziono'.

INTERNATIONAL BUSINESS – SCOTLAND

—Multinationals in retreat : the Scottish experience / by Neil Hood and Stephen Young. – Edinburgh : Edinburgh University Press, 1982.
xi,193p; 24cm.
Includes index.
ISBN 0852244282 Pbk £10.00

INTERNATIONAL BUSINESS – UNITED STATES

—Employment effects of multinational enterprises : the case of the United States / by D.Kujawa. – Geneva : International Labour Office, 1980.
ISBN 9221022765

INTERNATIONAL COMMUNICATION

—International Law Governing Communications and Information / London : Pinter Publishers Ltd, 1982.
367p.
ISBN 0861872045 Hbk £25.00

—International media law : a monthly bulletin on rights, clearances and legal practice / v. – London : Oyez Longman, 1982.
ISBN 02636395

INTERNATIONAL COOPERATION

—Cooperation and Conflict : Nordic Journal of International Politics / Oslo : University of Forlag.

—European Outline Convention on Transfrontier Co-operation between Territorial Communities or Authorities / Strasbourg : Council of Europe, 1980.

—Explanatory Report on the European Outline Convention on Transfrontier Co-operation between Territorial Communities or Authorities / Strasbourg : Council of Europe, 1980.
ISBN 9287100616 Hbk £1.75

—Legal co-operation in Europe in the fields of civil, commercial, public and international law, 1957-1982 / Strasbourg : Council of Europe, 1983.
112p; 21cm.
Preface by Erik Harremoes, Director of Legal Affairs. - 'This brochure was produced according to a classification plan devised by the Secretariat' - pref.. At head of cover title: Legal Affairs.
ISBN 9287101698 Pbk £3.90

—Legal Cooperation in Europe in the Fields of Civil, Commercial and International Law (1957-82) / Strasbourg : Council of Europe, 1983.
ISBN 9287101698

—One Europe: one world : a first exploration of Europe's potential contribution to world order / a report by Christopher Layton in conjunction with a gorup sponsored by the Federal Trust for Education and Research, the Wyndham Place Trust and the One World Trust. – London : Journal of World Trade Law, 1986.
70p.
Special supplement no. 4 to the Journal of World Trade Law, vol. 20 (1986).

—Summary of proceedings... / ACP-EEC Joint Assembly. – Luxembourg : Directorate-General for Information and Public Relations, 1985-.
This single new body replaces the two institutions set up under the first two Lome Conventions, i.e. the Consultative Assembly and the Joint Committee. Title varies.

INTERNATIONAL COOPERATION – COMMONWEALTH

—Memoranda / London : Commonwealth Secretariat, 1980.
xi,375p.
ISBN 0850921872

—Ocean management : a regional perspective : the prospects for Commonwealth maritime co-operation in Asia and the Pacific / report by a Commonwealth Group of Experts. – London : Commonwealth Secretariat, 1984.
Chairman: Satya N. Nandan.
ISBN 0850922615

INTERNATIONAL COURT OF JUSTICE

—International Court of Justice and some contemporary problems : essays on international law / Taslim O. Elias. – The Hague : Nijhoff, 1983.
ix,374p; 25cm.
Bibliography: p361-364. - Includes index.
ISBN 902472791X Hbk £150.00

—International Court of Justice and the Western Tradition of International Law / Dordrecht : Kluwer, 1987.
172p.
ISBN 9024735246 Hbk £125.00

—Law and procedure of the International Court of Justice / by the late Sir Gerald Fitzmaurice. – Cambridge : Grotius, 1986.
xli,427p; 26cm.
An analysis of the decisions of the International Court of Justice given in its formative years. A series of articles, with a consolidated index.
ISBN 0906496330 £95.00

Vol.2 / by the late Sir Gerald Fitzmaurice. – 1986.
pi-xiv,429-860; 26cm.
Includes index.
ISBN 0906496381 Hbk £95.00

—Litigation strategy at the International Court / Dordrecht : Martinus Nijhoff, 1989.
375. – (Legal aspects of international organization 9).
Examines the reasons States have for utilizing or resisting the utilization of the International Court as a means of pursuing and achieving foreign policy goals, and the methods they employ within the scope of the possibilities offered by the Courts Statute and Rule of procedure. This model is applied to the Nicaragua case.
ISBN 0792303326 Hbk £56

—Non-appearance before the International Court Justice / Cambridge : Cambridge University Press, 1985.
ISBN 0521265940 Hbk £27.50

—Reflections on International Arbitration and Litigation in the International Court of Justice / Dordrecht : Kluwer, 1988.
24p.
ISBN 9065443517 Hbk £30.50

—Reports of Judgments, Advisory Opinions and Orders / International Court of Justice. – Geneva : United Nations Publications.

ICJ No 523: Case Concerning Border and Transborder Armed Actions (Nicaragua/Costa Rica), Order of 21 October 1986

ICJ No 524: Case Concerning Border and Transborder Armed Actions (Nicaragua/Honduras), Order of 22 October 1986

ICJ No 525: Case Concerning the Frontier Dispute (Burkina Faso/Republic of Mali), Judgment of 22 December 1986

ICJ No 526: Case Concerning Elettronica Sicula S.p.A. (ELSI) (U.S.A./Italy), Order of 2 March 1987, Constitution of Chamber

ICJ No 527: Case Concerning the Frontier Dispute (Burkina Faso/Republic of Mali), Order of 9 April 1987, Nominations of Experts

ICJ No 528: Bibliography No 39, 1985

ICJ No 529: Case Concerning the Land, Island and Maritime Frontier Dispute (El Salvador/Honduras), Order of 8 May 1987, Constitution of Chamber

ICJ No 530: Index 1986

ICJ No 531: Case Concerning the Land, Island and Maritime Frontier Dispute (El Salvador/Honduras), Order of 27 May 1987

ICJ No 532: Application for Review of Judgment No 333 of the United Nations Administrative Tribunal, Advisory Opinion of 27 May 1987

ICJ No 533: Case Concerning the Land, Island and Maritime Frontier Dispute (El Salvador/Honduras), Order of 29 May 1987

ICJ No 534: Case Concerning Border and Transborder Armed Actions (Nicaragua/Costa Rica), Order of 21 July 1987

ICJ No 535: Case Concerning Border and Transborder Armed Actions (Nicaragua/Costa Rica), Order of 19 August 1987

Reports of Judgments, Advisory Opinions and Orders 1986.

Reports of Judgments Advisory Opinions and Orders 1986.

INTERNATIONAL COURTS

—Bibliography of the International Court / International Court of Justice. – London : HMSO, 1984.
ISBN 0119836971 Hbk £1.90

—Interim protection : a functional approach / Jerome B. Elkind. – The Hague : Martinus Nijhoff, 1981.
xxiv,287p.
Bibliography: p263-266.
ISBN 9024725399

—International adjudication : procedural aspects / V.S. Mani. – The Hague : Martinus Nijhoff, 1980.
xx,456p.
Bibliography: p421-448.
ISBN 9024723671

—International courts and international politics / Robert Yewdall Jennings. – Hull : Hull University Press, 1986.
17p.
Josephine Onoh Memorial Lecture.
ISBN 0859584550

—Iran-United States Claims Tribunal Reports / v. – Cambridge : Grotius Publications, 1983.

—Law and practice of the International Court / Shabtai Rosenne. – Dordrecht : Martinus Nijhoff, 1985.
xxv, 811p.
Reprint. Originally published: Leyden : A.W. Sijthoff, 1965. Includes index.
ISBN 9024729866 Hbk £350.00

—Rules for the ICC court of arbitration / International Chamber of Commerce. – 1980 ed. – Paris : International Chamber of Commerce, 1981.
32p.
Previous ed.: 1975. The Rules of the ICC Court of Arbitration were first published in April 1975 as Publication 291. The text of the Rules remains unchanged in the present edition but a new section called 'the Internal Rules of the Court' has been added to it. 'The schedule of costs' has also been revised..

INTERNATIONAL ECONOMIC INTEGRATION

—Handbook of international economic institutions / M. A. G. van Meerhaeghe. – Extensively rev. and enl. ed. – The Hague : Martinus Nijhoff Publishers, 1980.
xxii,441p.
Published in 1971 under title: International economic institutions. Includes bibliographies.
ISBN 9024723574

—Legal problems arising from supranational institutions : the Andean Pact : a case study / by Jorge Uribe-Rolden. – London : The author, 1984.
55 leaves.
Includes bibliographical references.

INTERNATIONAL ECONOMIC RELATIONS

—Changing structure of international economic law : a contribution of legal history, of comparative law and of general legal theory to the debate on a new international economic order / by Pieter VerLoren van Themaat. – The Hague : Martinus Nijhoff, 1981.
xxv,395p.
English edition of VerLoren van Themaat, P. : Rechtsgrondslagen van een nieuwe internationale economische orde.
ISBN 9024725402 Hbk £165.00

—Common crisis : North-South : cooperation for world recovery / the Brandt Commission. – London : Pan, 1983.
174p; 18cm. – (Pan world affairs).
Bibliography: p172-174.
ISBN 0330281305 Pbk £1.95

—Conflicts of national laws with international business activity : issues of extraterritoriality / by A.H. Hermann. – London : British North American Research Organisation, 1982.
xii,96p.
ISBN 0902594419

—Do we know where we're going? / Sir Jeremy Morse. – s.l. : Per Jacobsson Foundation, 1985.
v,31p.
Given at the Sejong Cultural Center, Seoul, Korea, Sunday, October 6, 1985.

—Economic relationships among states : a further study in international sociology / Evan Luard. – London : Macmillan, 1984.
xiii,328p.
ISBN 0333294777

—Exclusive Economic Zone in International Law / Oxford : Oxford University Press, 1987.
ISBN 01987255411 Hbk £27.50

—From Lome 1 towards Lome 2 : texts of the report and resolution adopted on 26 September 1980 by the APC-EEC Consultative Assembly / Katharina Focke. – Luxembourg : Office for Official Publications of the European Communities, 1980.
88p.

—Handbook of international economic institutions / M. A. G. van Meerhaeghe. – Extensively rev. and enl. ed. – The Hague : Martinus Nijhoff Publishers, 1980.
xxii,441p.
Published in 1971 under title: International economic institutions. Includes bibliographies.
ISBN 9024723574

—International Business Transactions and Economic Relations : Cases, Notes and Materials on the Law as it Applies to Canada / W. C. Graham. – Aurora : Canada Law Book Co, 1986.
935p.

—International economic law and developing states : some aspects / Gillian M. White ... et al. : edited by Hazel Fox. – London : British Institute of International & Comparative Law, 1988.
x,148p.
'Based on revised papers originally given at the Commonwealth Law Students' Conference held by the British Institute of International and Comparative Law at Manchester University in April 1987'. - T.p.. Includes index.
ISBN 0903067293 £15.00

—International economics / Sidney J. Wells. – 3rd ed. – London : Allen & Unwin, 1985.
xxiii,369p; 25cm.
Previous ed.: by Sidney J. Wells. 1973. Bibliography: p343-362. - Includes index.
ISBN 0043303498 Hbk £20.00
ISBN 0043303501 Pbk £9.95

—Law of international transactions / by Ferenc Madl : translated by J. Decsenyi. – Budapest : Akademiai Kiado, 1982.
206p.
Bibliography: p199-206. Translation of: Osszehasonlito nemzetkozi maganjog.
ISBN 9630529327

—Legal Aspects of the New International Economic Order / London : Pinter Publishers Ltd, 1980.
285p.
ISBN 0903804506 Hbk £17.50

—National laws and international commerce : the problem of extraterritoriality / Douglas E. Rosenthal and William M. Knighton. – London : Routledge & Kegan Paul, 1982.
xi,96p.
Bibliography: p94-96.
ISBN 0710093381

—New economic order and international development law / by Oswaldo de Rivero B. – Oxford : Pergamon, 1980.
xvi,141p; 22cm.
Bibliography: p137-138. - Includes index.
ISBN 0080247067 £8.00

—New international economic order legal debate : background, status, and alternatives / Gabe Shawn Varges. – Frankfurt am Main : Peter Lang, 1983.
vi,138p.
Bibliography: p. 121-128.
ISBN 382047613X

—Oil and world power / Peter R. Odell. – 7th ed. – Harmondsworth : Penguin, 1983.
287p; 20cm.
Previous ed.: 1981. Includes index.
ISBN 0140222847 Pbk £2.95

—One Europe: one world : a first exploration of Europe's potential contribution to world order / a report by Christopher Layton in conjunction with a gorup sponsored by the Federal Trust for Education and Research, the Wyndham Place Trust and the One World Trust. – London : Journal of World Trade Law, 1986.
70p.
Special supplement no. 4 to the Journal of World Trade Law, vol. 20 (1986).

—Political economy of law : a third world reader / edited by Yash Ghai, Robin Luckham, Francis Snyder. – Delhi : Oxford University Press, 1987.
xvi,821p.
A view of Indian legal systems as they operate nationally and internationally. Law is analysed in terms of its relationships to economy, the state, political conflict, class, and international relations.
ISBN 0195619919

—Politics of international economic relations / Joan Edelman Spero. – 3rd. ed. – London : Allen & Unwin, 1985.
viii,447p.
Bibliography: p405-431.
ISBN 0043820441

—Principles of international development law : progressive development of the principles of international law relating to the new international economic order / Milan Bulajic. – Dordrecht, Netherlands : Martinus Nijhoff Publishers, 1986.
403p.
Bibliography: p.359-366.
ISBN 9024733049

—Reforming the International Economic Order : German Legal Comments / Ernst-Ulrich Petersmann. – Berlin : Duncker and Humblot, 1987.
264p.
ISBN 3428062191 Hbk £98.00

—Regulation of international economic relations through law / by Palitha Tikiri Bandara Kohona. – Dodrecht : M. Nijhoff Publishers, 1985.
Based on author's thesis (Ph. D.)–Cambridge University.
ISBN 9024731046

—Second ACP-EEC Convention : signed at Lome on 31 October 1979 and related documents / ACP-EEC Council of Ministers, Brussels. – 1981 ed. – Luxembourg : Office for Official Publications of the European Communities, 1981.
549p; 21cm.
ISBN 9282400719

—Some key issues for the world periphery : selected essays / by Miguel S. Wionczek. – Oxford : Pergamon, 1982.
xiv,432p; 24cm.
Includes bibliographies and index.
ISBN 0080257836 £37.50

—Summary of proceedings... / ACP-EEC Joint Assembly. – Luxembourg : Directorate-General for Information and Public Relations, 1985-.
This single new body replaces the two institutions set up under the first two Lome Conventions, i.e. the Consultative Assembly and the Joint Committee. Title varies.

—Transnational law of international commercial transactions / edited by Norbert Horn and Clive M. Schmitthoff. – Antwerp : Kluwer-Devanter/The Netherlands, 1982.
Includes index and bibliography.
ISBN 9065440925 : est.

INTERNATIONAL FINANCE

—Country risk analysis / London : Butterworths, 1985.
ISBN 0406005508 Hbk £38.00

—Credit and Guarantee Financing, Transfer of Technology / edited by C.C.A. Voskuil, Z. Parac. J.A. Wade. – Dordrecht : M. Nijhoff, 1987.
xvii,372p.
Includes bibliographical references.
ISBN 9024735297 Hbk £165.00

—Current Issues in International Financial Law / Kent Ridge : Malaya Law Review.

—Current issues of international financial law / edited by David G. Pierce ... et al. – Singapore : Malaya Law Review, 1985.
xv,507p.
A collection of papers from the Singapore Conference of International Financial Law. The material covers primarily international banking, bond issues, syndicated loans, South East Asian perspectives on international financial law, and the role of international development banks.
ISBN 0409995088

—Euromoney issues : papers presented to the Section on Business Law Committee Q (Issues and Trading in Securities) at the International Bar Association 20th biennial conference, Vienna, September 1984 / London : International Bar Association, 1985.
xvi,112p.

—Euronotes and euro-commercial paper / Gareth Bullock. – London : Butterworths, 1987.
vii,136p; 23cm.
Includes index.
ISBN 0406104107 £32.00

—Euronotes : RUFs, TRUFs, NIFs, SNIFs and BONUSes / edited by Lloyd Bankson and Michael Lee. – London : Euromoney, 1985.
viii,183p.
ISBN 0903121743

—Evolution of the international monetary system, 1945-85 / Brian Tew. – 3rd ed. – London : Hutchinson, 1985.
256p; 22cm.
Previous ed.: 1982. Includes bibliography and index.
ISBN 0091615615 Pbk £7.95

—Foreign investment and the new international economic order / by David Flint. – Sydney : International Law Association, 1981.
89p.
ISBN 0949685003

—IMF and the World Bank in Africa : conditionality, impact, and alternatives / edited by Kjell J. Havnevik. – Uppsala : Scandinavian Institute of African Studies, 1987.
177 p.; 23 cm.
Includes bibliographies.
ISBN 9171062645

—International contract law & finance review / 3 v. – Lausanne : Seminar Services, 1980.
Superseded by: International financial law review.

—International financial law review / London : Euromoney, 1983-.
Supersedes: The international contract law & finance review.

—International interbank market : a descriptive study / Basle : Bank for International Settlements, 1983.
44p; 21cm.
' ... written by a study group ... under the auspices of the Bank for International Settlements' - inside front cover.

—International monetary system / 2nd ed. – Matthew Bender, 1984.
ISBN 0000999050 Hbk £26.50

—International monetary system and the less developed countries / Graham Bird. – 2nd ed. – London : Macmillan, 1982.
xi,352p.
Bibliography: p331-350.
ISBN 0333330021

—International monetary system : efficiency and practical alternatives / Herbert G. Grubel. – 4th ed. – Harmondsworth : Penguin, 1984.
214p.
Bibliography: p201-206.
ISBN 0140808183

—International money and finance / Michael Melvin. – New York : Harper & Row, 1985.
xiii,200p; 25cm.
Includes bibliographies and index.
ISBN 0060444177 £12.95

—International money and the real world / Paul Davidson. – London : Macmillan, 1982.
XI,312p.

—International money game / 5th ed. – London : Macmillan, 1988.
ISBN 0333467817 Hbk £29.50
ISBN 0333467825 Pbk £9.95

—International money : theory, evidence and institutions / Paul Hallwood and Ronald MacDonald with contributions from Robert Shaw. – Oxford : Basil Blackwell, 1986.
272p; 23cm.
Includes bibliography and index.
ISBN 0631144455 Hbk £25.00 :
ISBN 0631144463 Pbk £8.95

—International syndicated loans / by Robert P. McDonald. – London : Euromoney, 1982.
ix,264p.
Bibliography: p.261-262. - Includes index.
ISBN 0903121441

—International trade finance / Weston. – North Ryde : Law Book Co, 1986.
ISBN 0455203504 Pbk £11.25

—International trade in service : securities / Paris : OECD, 1987.
125p.

—International treasury management / Cambridge : Woodhead-Faulkner, 1987.
ISBN 0859413632 Hbk £45.00

—Law and practice of international finance / by Philip Wood. – London : Sweet & Maxwell, 1980.
xiii,462p; 26cm.
Discusses matters relating to conflicts of law, bond issues, taxation, project finance, ship finance, exchange controls. Contains a project eurocurrency term loan agreement outline.
ISBN 0421264101 £35.00

—Macmillan Dictionary of International Finance / 2nd ed. – London : Macmillan, 1986.
ISBN 0333398343 Pbk £8.95

—New Developments in International Finance / Chew. – Oxford : Blackwell, 1988.
ISBN 063115115X Hbk £40.00
ISBN 0631152040 Pbk £15.00

—New financial instruments / by Ian Cooper ... et al. – London : Chartered Isntitute of Bankers, 1987.
x,89p.
Includes bibliographical references.
ISBN 0852971907

—Political economy of international money : in search of a new order / edited by Loukas Tsoukalis. – London : Royal Institute of International Affairs, 1985.
313p; 22cm.
Includes index.
ISBN 0803997108 Hbk No price
ISBN 0803997116 Pbk £9.50

—Reflections on the international monetary system / Guillaume Guindey and Charles A. Coombs. – Basle : Auditorium Bank for International Settlements, 1980.
v,28p. – (1980 Per Jacobsson Lecture).

—Securitisation in International Finance / London : Butterworths, 1987.
ISBN 0406100616 Pbk

—Securitisation in international finance / London : Butterworths, 1988.
ISBN 0406100616 Pbk

—Sovereign borrowers : guidelines on legal negotiations with commercial lenders / edited by Lars Kalderen, Qamar S. Siddiqi : in co-operation with Francis Chronnell and Patricia Watson. – Uppsala : Dag Hammarskjold Foundation, 1984.
264p.
ISBN 9185214124

—Tax havens and offshore finance : a study of transnational economic development / Richard Anthony Johns. – London : Frances Pinter, 1983.
xiv,259p.
Bibliography: p248-255.

—United States law of sovereign immunity relating to international financial transactions / John R. Stevenson, Jeffrey F. Browne and Lori Fisler Damrosch. – London : Euromoney Pubns, 1983.
158p.
Includes bibliographical references.
ISBN 090312145X

—World finance and adjustment : an agenda for reform / Graham Bird. – London : Macmillan, 1985.
288p.
Includes bibliography and index.
ISBN 0333314778 Hbk £25.00
ISBN 0333388771 Pbk £8.95

INTERNATIONAL LAKES

—Law of international water resources : some general conventions, declarations, and resolutions adopted by governments, international legal institutions, and international organizations, on the management of international water resources / compiled by Dante A. Caponera. – Rome : Food and Agriculture Organization of the United Nations, 1980.
xi, 324 p.; 28 cm.
Includes bibliographical references.
ISBN 9251010366 pbk.

INTERNATIONAL LAW

—Anatomy of international law : a study of the role of international law in the contemporary world / by J.G. Merrills. – 2nd ed. – London : Sweet and Maxwell, 1981.
xv,146p; 19cm.
Previous ed.: 1976. Bibliography: p137-141. - Includes index.
ISBN 0421280107 Hbk £9.85
ISBN 0421280204 Pbk £6.00

—Antarctica and international law : a collection of inter-state and national documents / compiled by W.M. Bush. – 4. – London : Oceana Publications, 1982.
Vol. 4 is index.
ISBN 0379203200 V. 1 £45.00
ISBN 0379203219 V. 2 £45.00

—Application of humanitarian law : selective bibliography prepared by the Peace Palace Library / Center for Studies and Research of the Hague Academy of International Law : bibliographie selective preparee par la Bibliotheque du Palais de la Paix : Centre d'Etude et de Recherche de l'Academie du droit Internationale de la Haye. – The Hague : Center for Studies and Research of the Hague Academy of International Law, 1986.
80p.
Preliminary material in English and French.

—Arbitration : an Element of International Law / Stockholm : Almqvist & Wiksell, 1984.
166p.
ISBN 9122007342 Hbk £119.00

—Basic documents in international law / edited by Ian Brownlie. – 3rd ed. – Oxford : Clarendon, 1983.
xi,406p; 21cm.
Previous ed.: 1972. Includes index.
ISBN 0198761589 Hbk £15.00
ISBN 0198761597 Pbk £8.95

—British Year Book Of International Law 1985 / Oxford : Oxford University Press, 1986.
ISBN 0198255470 Hbk £55.00

—British year book of international law / Derek Bownett. – Oxford : Clarendon Press, 1989.
650; 23.5.
Contains major articles and reviews of books on international law, as well as surveys of decisions of British courts involving questions of international law. Also surveys decisions of the European Convention on Human Rights, and the Court of Justice of the European Communities.
ISBN 0198254083 Hbk £65.00

—Canadian Council on International Law : Conference Proceedings /. – Ottawa : Canadian Council on International Law, 1981.

15: International Law and Development 1986.

9: International Law and Canadian Foreign Policy in the 1980's 1980.

200-350p ea.

—Cases and materials on international law / by D.J. Harris. – 3rd ed. – London : Sweet & Maxwell, 1983.
li,810p; 24cm.
Previous ed.: 1979. Includes index.
ISBN 0421292709 Hbk £26.00
ISBN 0421292806 Pbk £19.50

—Change and stability in international law-making / edited by Antonio Cassese and Joseph H.H. Weiler. – Berlin : De Gruyter, 1988.
– (Series A–Law).
Includes indexes. Based on the proceedings of two international colloquia held at the European University Institute, Florence.
ISBN 0899254209 Hbk £55.00

—Change and Stability in International Law-Making / Joseph H.H. Weiler. – Berlin : De Gruyter, 1988.
x, 214p.
ISBN 3110114941 Hbk £90.00

—Chinese yearbook of international law and affairs / v. – Baltimore : Occasional Papers/Reprints Series in Contemporary Asian Studies, Inc. for the Chinese Society of International Law - Chinese (Taiwan) Branch of International Law Association, 1983-.
Continues: The annals of the Chinese Society of International Law.

—Concept of international law / by Ingrid Detter De Lupis. – Stockholm : Norstedts Forlag, 1987.
145p.
Bibliography: p137-145.
ISBN 911867562X

—Conflict and compromise : international law and world order in a revolutionary age / Edward McWhinney. – Alphen aan den Rijn : Sijthoff and Noordhoff, 1981.
160p.
Bibliography: p156-158.
ISBN 0887940900

—Conflicts and compromise : International law and world order in a revolutionary age / Dordrecht : Kluwer, 1981.
160p.
ISBN 9028626719 Hbk Gld40 /$17.50

—Construction contracts : principles and policies in tort and contract / by I.N. Duncan Wallace. – London : Sweet & Maxwell, 1986.
xliii,696p; 26cm.
Contains articles on contractors' claims and owners' damages, certificates and their effect, guarantees and bonds in construction contracts, nominated sub-contractors, choice of contracting agreement, comparative law, the UK JCT standard forms, and the SIA Contract 1980.
ISBN 042134900X Hbk £74

—Contemporary issues in international law : essays in honor of Louis B. Sohn / edited by T. Buergenthal. – 1st ed. – Kehl : N.P. Engel, 1984.
viii, 571 p., 1 leaf of plates; 24 cm.
English, French, German, and Spanish. 'Louis B. Sohn bibliography': p. 561-570.
ISBN 3883570400

—Contemporary problems of international law : essays in honour of Georg Schwarzenberger on his eightieth birthday / edited by Bin Cheng and Eddie Brown. – London : Stevens & Sons, 1988.
360p; 24cm.
Collection of essays written in honour of Professor Georg Schwarzenberger, in the field of international law and relations. Includes an appraisal of international arbitration and negotiation techniques, and the mechanism and functions of the United Nations. Also contains discussion of international terrorism, human rights, and the law of treaties.
ISBN 0420479201 £18.00 (May)

—Conventional International Law : Public, Economic and Trade / Foreign Service Institute (Manila). – Metro Manila : Foreign Service Institute, 1980.
308p.

—Decay of international law? : a reappraisal of the limits of legal imagination in international affairs / Anthony Carty. – Manchester : Manchester University Press, 1986.
x,138p; 24cm. – (The Melland Schill monographs in international law).
Includes index.
ISBN 0719018501 £25.00

—Defence - the legal implications / Pergamon, 1987.
ISBN 0080335969 Hbk £29.95

—Development of International Law by the International Court / Cambridge : Grotius.
408p.
ISBN 0906496306 Hbk £30.00

—Dissenting and separate opinions at the World Court / Ijaz Hussain. – The Hague : M. Nijhoff Publishers, 1984.
xv,335p.
Revision of thesis (doctorate)–University of Nice, 1974 under title: Le r$ole dialectique des opinions dissidentes et individuelles dans le developpement du droit international a la CIJ. Bibliography: p309-321. Includes index.
ISBN 9024729203 Hbk £145.00

—Encyclopedia of Public International Law / 1st repr. 1985 (nos. 1-6). – Amsterdam : Elsevier Science Publishers, 1981.

2: Decisions of International Courts and Tribunals 1981.
ISBN 0444862129 Hbk

3: Use of Force, A.-M. 1982.
xvi, 300p.
ISBN 044486234X Hbk

4: Use of Force, N-Z 1982.
xvi, 370p.
ISBN 0444862358 Hbk

5: International Organizations 1983.
xvi, 428p.
ISBN 0444862366 Hbk

6: Regional Cooperation, Organizations and Problems 1983.
xvi, 382p.

7: History of International Law. Foundations and Principles of International Law. Sources of International Law. Law of Treaties 1985.
x, 556p.
ISBN 0444862382 Hbk

8: Human Rights and the Individual in International Law. International Economic Relations 1985.
xvi, 55p.
ISBN 0444879110

9: International Relations and Legal Cooperation in General Diplomacy and Consular Relations 1986.
xvi, 426p.
ISBN 0444862404

10. States - Responsibility of States - International Law and Municipal Law - 10
xvi, 544p.
ISBN 0444862412 Hbk

—Encyclopedia of public international law / published under the auspices of the Max Planck Institute for Comparative Public Law and International Law : under the direction of Rudolf Bernhardt. – Amsterdam : North-Holland Pub. Co., 1981.
Issued in parts. Includes index.
ISBN 0444861408

—Enforcing international law : a way to world peace : a documentary history and analysis / by Benjamin B. Ferencz. – 2 v. – London : Oceana, 1983.
xix,890p.
Includes bibliographies and index.
ISBN 0379121476

—Essays in international law in honour of Judge Manfred Lachs / Etudes de droit international en l'honneur du Juge Manfred Lachs : edited by Jerzy Makarczyk. – The Hague : M. Nijhoff, 1984.
760p.
Bibliography: p.18-23. At head of title: Institute of State and Law of the Polish Academy of Sciences Institut de l'Etat et de Droit de l'Academie Polonaise des Sciences. English or French text.
ISBN 9024730716 Hbk £295.00

—Essays on International and Comparative Law : In Honour of Judge Erades / Institute T.M.C. Asser. – Dordrecht : Kluwer, 1983.
285p.
ISBN 902472838X Hbk £95.00

—Essays on International Law and Organization, 2 Vols. / Dordrecht : Kluwer.
1,230p.
ISBN 9024729106 Hbk £450.00

—Essays on the development of the international legal order : in memory of Haro F. Van Panhuys / edited by Frits Kalshoven, Pieter Jan Kuyper and Johan G. Lammers. – Alphen aan den Rijn : Sijthoff & Noordhoff, 1980.
xi,226p.
Bibliography: p221-226.

—Evolution of the law of the sea : a study of resources and strategy with special regard to the polar regions / Bo Johnson Theutenberg. – Dublin : Tycooly International, 1984.
viii,261p; 25cm.
Bibliography: p97-111. Includes full text of United Nations Convention on the Law of the Sea. Spine title : The law of the sea.
ISBN 0863460410 Hbk Unpriced
ISBN 0863460429 Pbk Unpriced

—Explanatory report on the European Convention on the Recognition of the Legal Personality of International Non-Governmental Organisations / Strasbourg : Council of Europe, 1986.
17p.
Includes text of the Convention. Drawn up within the Council of Europe by a select committee of experts under the authority of the European Committee on Legal Co-operation.
ISBN 9287108978

—Falklands war : lessons for strategy, diplomacy, and international law / edited by Alberto R. Coll and Anthony C. Arend. – Boston : Allen & Unwin, 1985.
xiv,252p; 22cm.
Includes index.
ISBN 0043270751 Hbk £18.00
ISBN 004327076X Pbk £7.95

—Forms of action at international law : the spirit of English law and international law / H.A. Schwarz-Liebermann von Wahlendorf. – Birmingham : Institute of Judicial Administration, University of Birmingham, 1981.
iii,55p.
ISBN 2903642001

—Future of International Law in a Multicultural World : Workshop 1983 / Dordrecht : Kluwer, 1984.
510p.
ISBN 9024730708 Hbk £135.00

—General Principles of Law : As Applied by International Courts and Tribunals / Cambridge : Grotius, 1987.
541p.
A presentation of general principles of law as used by international tribunals in relation to such subjects as self-preservation, good faith, State responsibility and judicial proceedings. First published in 1953.
ISBN 0949009067 Hbk £78.00

—German Yearbook of International Law /. – Berlin : Duncker and Humblot, 1980.
585p.
ISBN 3428046331 Hbk £168.00

Vol. 23 (1980) 1981.
567p.

Vol. 24 (1981) 1982.
566p.
ISBN 3428051521 Hbk £178.00

Vol. 25 (1982) 1983.
722p.

—A Guide to Maritime Boundary Delimitation / Adam J. Kerr. – Agincourt : Carswell, 1986.
136p.
This work addresses the technical aspects of maritime boundaries under international law. The book provides commentary on relevant cases which have been refered to the International Court of Justice.

—Hague yearbook of international law : Annuaire de la Haye de droit international / J.G. Lammers. – Dordrecht : Martinus Nijhoff, 1988.
471. – (A.A.A. Yearbook).
In-depth articles on some of the developments taking place in international law institutions such as the International Court of Justice and the Hague Conference on Private International Law. The articles, and summaries, in both English and French, deal with decisions rendered by these institutions.
ISBN 9024737494 Hbk £80

—Human rights and humanitarian norms as customary law / Oxford : OUP, 1989.
320.
Looks at the relationship between human rights/humanitarian norms and customary law, also between human rights/humanitarian norms and the law of state responsibility. Examines how contemporary human rights mesh with the general principles of international law and particularly with the principles governing the international responsibility of states.
International lawyers, international organizations, scholars and students of international law
ISBN 0198252390 Hbk £30.00

—Human Rights in International Law / New Delhi : Deep and Deep Publications, 1986.
212p.

—Human rights in International law / rep 1986. – Oxford : Oxford University Press, 1984.
ISBN 0198255403 Pbk £17.50

—Implementation of international humanitarian law / Y Sandoz. – Dordrecht : Martinus Nijhoff, 1989.
488.
A collection of articles resulting from the 1986 session of the Centre for Studies and Research in International Law and International Relations of the Hague Academy. Explores humanitarian law from the viewpoint of implementation and enforcement, and offers suggestions for improvement.
ISBN 9024737842 Hbk £85

—Individual's Petition in International Law / New Delhi : Deep and Deep Publications, 1985.
287p.

—Intellectual property rights in biotechnology worldwide / Stephen A. Bent ... et al. – London : Macmillan, 1985.
300p.
Includes index.
ISBN 0333392884 Pbk £40.00 (Oct.)
ISBN 094381815X

—International business lawyer : journal of the Section on Business Law of the International Bar Association / v. – London : International Bar Association, 1973.
Index in each vol., 1979-.
ISBN 03097676

—International carriage of goods : some legal problems and possible solutions / edited by C.M. Schmitthoff, R.M. Goode. – London : Centre for Commercial Law Studies, 1988.
xxvii,135p.
Includes index. Includes the text of the Uniform Rules of Conduct for Interchange of Trade Data by Teletransmission (UNCID) and of the United Nations Convention on International Multimodal Transport of Goods.
ISBN 0951066455

—International Court of Justice and some contemporary problems : essays on international law / Taslim O. Elias. – The Hague : Nijhoff, 1983.
ix,374p; 25cm.
Bibliography: p361-364. - Includes index.
ISBN 902472791X Hbk £150.00

—International economic law / Dordrecht : Martinus Nijhoff, 1989.
274.
Updated and extended version of the General Course held by the author at the Hague Academy of International Law in 1986. References to literature have been increased, and a detailed keyword index and an index of cases cited are included. Contains chapters on various aspects on international law.
ISBN 9024737990 Hbk £47

—International economic law and developing states : some aspects / Gillian M. White ... et al. : edited by Hazel Fox. – London : British Institute of International & Comparative Law, 1988.
x,148p.
'Based on revised papers originally given at the Commonwealth Law Students' Conference held by the British Institute of International and Comparative Law at Manchester University in April 1987'. - T.p.. Includes index.
ISBN 0903067293 £15.00

—International Labour Law : a Comparative Survey of the Conflict Rules Affecting Labour Legislation and Regulations / A.W. Sijthoff. – Budapest : Akademiai Kiado, 1968.
465p.

—International Law, 2 Vols. / Calcutta : Mukherjee & Co.

—International Law / by Malcolm N. Shaw. – 2nd ed. – Cambridge : Grotius, 1986.
39,627p; 23cm.
A revised and updated edition. An introduction to international law, setting the subject in the context of world political events. Also examines the importance of the political, cultural and economic influences that affect international law. Student text, also for private practitioners, governmental and civil servants.
ISBN 0906496373 Pbk £10.95

—International law / N.A. Maryan Green. – 3rd ed. – London : Pitman, 1987.
384p; 22cm.
Previous ed.: Plymouth : Macdonald and Evans, 1982. Includes bibliography and index.
ISBN 0273027328 £25.00

—International law / by Rebecca M.M. Wallace. – London : Sweet and Maxwell, 1986.
275p; 18cm.
Includes index.
ISBN 0421335009 Hbk £15.00
ISBN 0421335106 Pbk £10.00

—International Law / 3rd ed. – London : Butterworths, 1987.
ISBN 0406591857 Hbk

—International law and aboriginal rights / Oxford : Croom Helm, 1987.
ISBN 0949614351 Hbk £22.50

—International Law and Economic Development and Cooperation / Dordrecht : Kluwer.
ISBN 9065441921

—International Law and Municipal Law : Deutsch-Argentinisches Verfassungsrechtskolloquium, Buenos Aires, April 1979 / Berlin : Duncker and Humblot.
322p.
ISBN 3428050738 Pbk £116.00

—International Law and Municipal Law : Proceedings of the German-Soviet Colloquy on International Law at the Institut fur Internationales Recht an der Universitat Kiel 4 to 8 May 1987 / Rudiger Wolfrum. – Berlin : Duncker and Humblot, 1988.
210p.
ISBN 3428064267 Hbk £96.00

—International law and the developing countries : confrontation or cooperation? / R.P. Anand. – Dordrecht : Martinus Nijhoff, 1987.
xii, 274p.
Includes index and bibliographies.
ISBN 902473438X Hbk £125.00

—International Law and the International System / Dordrecht : Kluwer, 1987.
208p.
ISBN 9024735343 Hbk £125.00

—International Law and World Revolution / Toronto : Canadian Broadcasting Corporation Enterprises.
116p.

—International Law as Applied by International Courts and Tribunals / London : Sweet & Maxwell, 1985.
ISBN 0420446109 Hbk £85.00

Vol.4 : International judicial law / by Georg Schwarzenberger. – 1986.
lxx,899p.
Bibliography: p823-888. - Includes index.
ISBN 0420446109 £90.00

—International law at a time of perplexity / Mala Tabory. – Dordrecht : Martinus Nijhoff, 1989.
1040.
A collection of essays in honour of the seventieth birthday of Professor Rosenne. The contributions from friends and colleagues deal with humanitarian law, human rights, the law of treaties, and dispute settlement.
ISBN 9024736544 Hbk £142.50

—International law : chiefly as interpreted and applied in Canada / Hugh M. Kindred ... et al. – 4th ed. – Toronto : Emond Montgomerry Publications, 1987.
xlix,958p.
Includes bibliographical references and index, as well as the texts of the Charter of the United Nations and the Statute of the International Court of Justice.
ISBN 0920722210 Hbk £96.00

—International Law Commission / by Sir Ian Sinclair. – Cambridge : Grotius, 1987.
viii,177p.
Examines the constitution and working methods of the International Law Commission, and reviews the activity of the Commission since 1949 in the codification process. Analyses the contribution it has made to the development of general international law.
ISBN 0949009105

—International Law for Antarctica / Tullio Scovazzi. – Milan : Giuffre, 1988.
xiv, 532p.

—International law governing communications and information : a collection of basic documents / prepared by Edward W. Ploman. – London : Pinter, 1982.
xvi,367p; 25cm.
Includes index.
ISBN 0861872045 £25.00

—International law in a divided world / Antonio Cassese. – Oxford : Clarendon, 1986.
xiii,420p; 24cm.
Includes bibliography and index.
ISBN 0198761945 £40.00

—International law in comparative perspective / edited by William E. Butler. – Alphen aan den Rijn : Sijthoff&Noordhoff, 1980.
vii,315p; 24cm.
Bibliography p.293-305. - Includes index.
ISBN 9028600892

—International law in historical perspective / By J. H. W. Verzijl. – Rockville : Sijthoff & Noordhoff, 1968-.
v.; 24 cm. – (Nova et vetera iuris gentium. Series A, Modern international law, no. 4, 6-9, 12-14).
Contents: v. 1. General subjects.–v. 2. International persons.–v. 3. State territory.–v. 4. Stateless domain.–v. 5. Nationality and other matters relating to individuals.–v. 6. Juridical facts as sources of international rights and obligations.–v. 7. State succession.–v. 8. Inter-state disputes and their settlements.–pt. 9a. The laws of war.–pt. 9b. The law of neutrality.

—International law in the Netherlands / edited by H.F. van Panhuys...et al. – Alphen aan den Rijn : Sijthoff & Noordhoff, 1978.
v; 25 cm.
Organised by the T.M.C. Asser Institute. Includes bibliographical references and index.

—International law : law of peace / 3rd ed. – London : Pitman Publishing, 1987.
ISBN 0273027328 Pbk £25.00

—International law : law of peace / N. A. Maryan Green. – 2nd ed. – Plymouth : Macdonald & Evans, 1982.
xxxiv,254p.
ISBN 0712109560

—International law of human rights / Oxford : Oxford University Press, 1984.
ISBN 0198760973 Pbk £21.00

—International Law of International Welfare : The Politics of Law-Making / London : Pinter Publishers Ltd, 1984.
200p.
ISBN 0861872894 Hbk £21.00

—International law quarterly / 4 v. – London : Stevens, 1947.
Merged with Journal of the Society of Comparative Legislation to form International and comparative law quarterly. Index in each vol..

—International Law Reports, 77 Vols. / Cambridge : Grotius.

Vols. 1-50

Vols. 51-74

Vols. 75-77

Index to Vols. 1-35

Index to Vols. 36-45

—International law teaching and practice / edited by Bin Cheng. – London : Stevens, 1982.
xxix,287p; 25cm.
Conference papers. Includes index.
ISBN 042046350X £23.00

—International Law : the Essential Treaties / Berlin : De Gruyter, 1985.
ca 832p.
ISBN 3110101122 Hbk £158.00

—International Legal Environment / Toronto : University of Toronto Press, 1986.
288p.
ISBN 0802072984 Hbk £18.95

—International legal structures / David Kennedy. – Baden-Baden : Nomos, 1987.
294p.
Includes bibliographical references.
ISBN 3789013676

—International maritime law conventions / compiled by Maharaj Nagendra Singh. – Updated ed. 4. – London : Stevens, 1983.
xxvii,,3305p; 26cm.
Previous ed.: published in 1v. as International conventions of maritime shipping. 1973. Includes index.
ISBN 0420466002 £24.00

—International Maritime Organisation / Samir Mankabady. – 2nd ed. – London : Croom Helm, 1987.
xxvii,452p; 23cm.
Previous ed.: published in 1 vol. 1984. Includes index.
ISBN 0709946406 Hbk £50.00

—International Maritime Organization / Samir Mankkabady. – 2nd ed. – London : Croom Helm, 1986.
xxi,450p; 23cm.
Previous ed.: published in 1 vol. 1984. Includes index.
ISBN 0709935919 £45.00

—International organization and integration : annotated basic documents and descriptive directory of international organizations and arrangements / board of editors, P.J.G. Kapteyn ... et al. : with a foreword by Louis B. Sohn. – 2nd, completely rev. ed. n v. – The Hague : Martinus Nijhoff Publishers, 1981.
25cm.
Tables inserted in each volume. Includes indexes. Contents: v.1A: The United Nations Organization - v.2A: European Communities - v.2B-2K.
ISBN 9024725798

—International organization and integration : annotated basic doucments of international organizations and arrangements / selected by Louis B. Sohn. – Student ed. – Dordrecht Netherlands : Martinus Nijhoff, 1986.
xxviii, 1082 p.; 24 cm.
Includes index. Based on the five-volume set International organization and integration.
ISBN 0898389151 pbk. CIP rev.

—International review of contemporary law / Brussels : International Association of Democratic Lawyers, 1982-.
Continues: Review of contemporary law.

—International society as a legal community / by Hermann Mosler. – Alphen aan den Rijn : Sijthoff & Noordhoff, 1980.
xix,327p.
A revised version of lectures originally published in vol.140 of the Collected Courses of the Hague Academy of International Law.
ISBN 9028600809

—International trade in a nutshell / D.M. Day. – London : Sweet and Maxwell, 1980.
vii,87p; 18cm.
Includes index.
ISBN 0421265604 Pbk £1.50

—International trade regulation : GATT, the United States and the European Community / Edmond McGovern. – 2nd ed. – Exeter : Globefield, 1986.
xliv,629p; 25cm.
Previous ed. 1982. Bibliography: p599-619. - Includes index.
ISBN 0950846341 £36.00

—Internationial law in a divided world / Oxford : Oxford University Press, 1988.
ISBN 019876233X Pbk £16.95

—Introduction to International Law / Armand L.C. de Mestral. – 2nd ed. – Butterworths, 1987.
472p.
Contains new material on the treaty-implementation power in Canada, recognition of foreign states and governments, sovereign immunity, the international protection of human rights, the international protection of the environment, the law of the sea, fisheries, international crimes, and extraterritoriality.
ISBN 0409875597 Pbk £70.00

—Introduction to International Law / 9th ed. – London : Butterworths, 1984.
ISBN 0406659575 Hbk £25.00
ISBN 0406659583 Pbk £18.95

—Introduction to international law / J.G. Starke. – 9th ed. – London : Butterworths, 1984.
xxviii,664p; 23cm.
Previous ed.: 1977. Includes index.
ISBN 0406659575 Hbk Unpriced
ISBN 0406659583 Pbk Unpriced

—Italian yearbook of international law / v. – Napoli : Editoriale Scientifica
Index in each vol..
ISBN 0379008254

—Italian Yearbook of International Law / Milan : Giuffre, 1986.
xii, 467p.

—Judicial remedies in international law / Christine D. Gray. – Oxford : Clarendon Press, 1987.
300p; 24cm. – (Oxford monographs in international law).
Includes bibliography and index.
ISBN 0198255713 £30.00

—Judicial remedies in International Law / Oxford : Oxford University Press, 1987.
ISBN 0198255713 Hbk £27.50

—Jurisdiction to tax in international law: theory and practice of legislative fiscal jurisdiction / Kluwer Law and Taxation, 1989.
238. – (Series on International Taxation 9).
Deals with the bases and the limits of the right of states under international lw to create tax obligations on persons within and outside their territory. Describes the practice of states on matters of taxation in terms of the doctrine of jurisdiction in international law. Examines topics such as the taxation of mining activities on the continental shelf.
ISBN 9065444165 Hbk £51/Dfl 160

—Law among nations : an introduction to public international law / Gerhard von Glahn. – 4th ed. – New York : Macmillan, 1981.
xv,810p; 25cm.
Previous ed.: 1976. Includes bibliographies and index.
ISBN 0024231606 £15.95

—Law and power in international relations / James Fawcett. – London : Faber and Faber, 1982.
140p; 23cm.
ISBN 0571105378 £9.50

—Law of Deep Sea-Bed Mining : a Study of the Progressive Development of International Law Concerning the Management of the Polymetallic Nodules of the Deep Sea-Bed / Stockholm : Almqvist & Wiksell, 1987.
356p.
ISBN 9122011560 Hbk £525.00

—Law of international institutions / 4th ed. – London : Sweet & Maxwell, 1982.
ISBN 0420460101 Hbk £30.00
ISBN 0420460209 Pbk £21.00

—Law of international institutions / D.W. Bowett. – 4th ed. – London : Sweet & Maxwell, 1982.
xv,431p; 23cm.
Published under the auspices of the London Institute for World Affairs by Stevens & Sons Previous ed.: 1975. Includes index.
ISBN 0420460101 Hbk £19.00
ISBN 0420460209 Pbk £12.50

—Law of international trade / by D.M. Day. – London : Butterworths, 1981.
xxii,254p,2p of plates; 22cm.
This book is an introduction to the law of international trade. Carriage of goods, insurance of goods in transit, government controls, EEC law, and statutory material are discussed in the work.
ISBN 040657202X
ISBN 0406572011 Pbk

—Legal aspects of international business transactions : the Edinburgh Institute on International Business Transactions 1983 : a project of University of the Pacific McGeorge School of Law international programs / edited by D. Campbell and C. Rohwer. – Amsterdam : North-Holland, 1984.
x,463p; 24cm.
ISBN 0444875069 £34.88

—Legal Cooperation in Europe in the Fields of Civil, Commercial and International Law (1957-82) / Strasbourg : Council of Europe, 1983.
ISBN 9287101698

—Legal developments in maritime commerce : matters of general interest and importance arising out of selected legal issues / W.E. Astle. – London : Fairplay, 1983.
viii,125p; 25cm.
ISBN 0905045432 Pbk No price

—Legal opinions in international transactions : foreign lawyers' response to US opinion requests / report of the Subcommittee on Legal Opinions of Committee E of the Section on Business Law of the International Bar Association : Michael Gruson, Michael Kutschera. – London : Graham & Trotman and The Association, 1987.
120p; 23cm.
ISBN 1853330213 £35.00

—Liber amicorum for the Rt. Hon. Lord Wilberforce / edited by Maarten Bos and Ian Brownlie. – Oxford : Clarendon, 1987.
vi,251p; 24cm.
Includes index.
ISBN 0198255950 £30.00

—Methodology of international law / by Maarten Bos. – Amsterdam : North-Holland, 1984.
xxi,357p; 23cm.
'Published in collaboration with Interuniversitair Instituut voor Internationaal Recht T.M.C. Asser Instituut' - T.p. verso. Includes index.
ISBN 044486847X No price

—Military intervention in democratic societies / Whelan. – Oxford : Croom Helm, 1985.
ISBN 0709922418 Hbk £18.95

—Mixed agreements / edited by David O'Keeffe and Henry G. Schermers. – Deventer : Kluwer, 1983.
x,248p.
At head of title: Europa Institute Leiden.
ISBN 9065441530

—Multilingualism in international law and institutions / Mala Tabory. – Alphen aan den Rijn : Sijthoff & Noordhoff, 1980.
xx,283p.
Bibliography: p260-268.
ISBN 9028602100

—Netherlands Yearbook of International Law /. – Dordrecht : Kluwer, 1981.
400p.
ISBN 9028627111 Hbk £80.00/$40.00

Vol. 12 1981.
ix, 438p.
ISBN 9028629610 Hbk Gld80.00/$40.00

Vol. 13 1982.
ca 515p.
ISBN 9024727766 Hbk Gld110.00/$40.00

Vol. 14 1984.
490p.
ISBN 9024729165 Hbk £110.00

Vol. 15 (1984) 1985.
585p.
ISBN 9024731151 Hbk Gld110.00

Vol. 18 (1987) 1988.
510p.
ISBN 9024736382 Hbk Gld135.00

—Netherlands yearbook of international law / T.M.C. Asser Institute. – Dordrecht : Martinus Nijhoff, 1989.
600.
Articles on the practice of the Iran-United States Claims Tribunal. The documentation section surveys Dutch state practice for the parliamentary year 1987-1988; international agreements to which the Netherlands is a party, and Netherlands judicial decisions and municipal legislation involving questions of public international law, and Dutch literature in this field, and related matters.
ISBN 0792301048 Hbk £45

—Netherlands Yearbook of International Law : Index to Vols. 1-10 (1970-1979) / Dordrecht : Kluwer, 1983.
380p.
ISBN 902472774X Hbk Gld150.00/$65.00

—New Directions in International Law : Essays in Honour of Wolfgang Abendroth / Frankfurt : Campus Verlag, 1982.
592p.
ISBN 3593330229 Hbk £178.00

—New economic order and international development law / by Oswaldo de Rivero B. – Oxford : Pergamon, 1980.
xvi,141p; 22cm.
Bibliography: p137-138. - Includes index.
ISBN 0080247067 £8.00

—New horizons in international law / by T. O. Elias. – Alphen aan den Rijn : Sijthoff & Noordhoff, .
xxii,260p.
ISBN 9028600396

—New perspectives and conceptions of international law : an Afro-European dialogue / edited by K. Ginther, W. Benedek. – Wien : Springer-Verlag, 1983.
ix,261p.
ISBN 3211817808

—New trends in contemporary international law / T.O. Elias. – Hull : Hull University Press, 1985.
14p; 21cm. – (Josephine Onoh memorial lecture).
ISBN 0859584496

—Non forcible counter measures in international law / Oxford : Oxford University Press, 1988.
ISBN 019825590X Hbk

—Nordic journal of international law / Acta scandinavica juris gentium. – v. – Kbenhavn : Nordisk Tidsskrift for International Ret, 1986-.
Continues: Nordisk tidsskrift for international ret Acta scandinavica juris gentium.

—Of order and disorder : the relevance of international law : an inaugural lecture delivered at the University of Lagos on Wednesday, 15th February, 1984 / by M.A. Ajomo. – Lagos : Lagos University Press, 1984.
35p. – (Inaugural lecture series).
Includes bibliographical references.
ISBN 9782264490

—Peremptory Norma (Jus Cogens) in International Law : Historical Development, Criteria, Present Status / Helsinki : Lakimiesliiton Kustannus, 1988.
781p.
ISBN 9516403948 Hbk £519.00

—Power and policy in quest of the law : essays in honor of Eugene Victor Rostow / edited by Myres S. McDougal, W. Michael Reisman. – The Hague : M. Nijhoff Publishers, 1984.
640p.
Bibliography: p441-447. Includes index.
ISBN 9024729114 Hbk £235.00

—Proceedings of the seventh, eighth and ninth annual conferences of the Nigerian Society of International Law, 1975-1978 / M. A. Ajomo. – Lagos : Nigerian Institute of International Affairs, 1982.
x,221p.
Includes bibliographical references. Edited by M.A. Ajomo.
ISBN 9782276111

—Public international law / London : Pitman Publishing, 1987.
ISBN 0712107568 Pbk £13.95

—Public international law in the modern world / David H. Ott. – London : Pitman, 1987.
480p; 18cm.
Includes bibliography and index.
ISBN 0712107568 Pbk £12.00
ISBN 0273028154

—Questions of international law / Gyorgy Haraszti. – Alphen a/d Rijn : Sijthoff and Noordhoff, 1981.
244p.
ISBN 9028608303

—Readings in international law from the Naval War College review, 1947-1977 / edited by Richard B. Lillich and John Norton Moore. – Newport, R.I. : Naval War CollegePress, 1980.
2 v.; 24 cm. – (U.S. Naval War College international law studies).
Includes bibliographical references and index. Contents: v. 1. Role of international law and an evolving ocean law.–v. 2. The use of force, human rights, and general international legal issues.

—Realism in Law-Making : Essays on International Law in Honour of Willem Riphagen / Hugo Siblesz. – Dordrecht : Kluwer, 1986.
316p.
ISBN 9024733995 Hbk £165.00

—Recognition of commercial judgments and awards in the Commonwealth / K.W. Patchett. – London : Butterworths, 1984.
xlv,326p; 26cm.
Bibliography: pxxix. - Includes index.
ISBN 0406403201 No price

—Rethinking the sources of international law / by G. J. H. van Hoof. – Deventer : Kluwer, 1983.
xiv,322p; 25cm.
Dutch summary, p.313-321.
ISBN 9065440852 Pbk £121.00

—Rights and Statutes of the Individual in International Law / New Delhi : Deep and Deep Publications, 1984.
200p.

—Role of law in society : East and West, national and international / by Bin Cheng. – S.l. : s.n., 1981.
p.15-18.
Reprinted from: Chinese University bulletin, Winter 1978. Cover title with subtitle: 'Address on behalf of the honorary graduates at the twentieth Congregation of the Chinese University of Hong Kong on Thursday, 30th November 1978'.

—Selected articles from Chinese yearbook of international law / edited by Chinese Society of International Law. – Beijing : China Translation & Publishing Corporation, 1983.
vi,308p.

—Spirit of Uppsala : proceedings of the Joint UNITAR-Uppsala University Seminar on International Law and Organization for a New World Order (JUS 81), Uppsala 9-18 June 1981 / edited by Atle Grahl-Madsen and Jiri Toman. – Berlin : W. de Gruyter, 1983.
English and French. Includes index and bibliography.
ISBN 3110088223

—State responsibility / by Ian Brownlie. – Oxford : Clarendon, 1983.
xvi,302p; 24cm.
Includes index.
ISBN 0198254520 £25.00

—Statut juridique international des minorites : bibliographie selective / preparee par la Bibliotheque du Palais de la Paix, La Haye : selective biliography : prepared by the Library of the Peace Palace, the Hague. – The Hague : Center for Studies and Research of the Hague Academy of International Law, 1984.
29 leaves.

—Structure and Process of International Law : Essays in Legal Philosophy, Doctrine and Theory / Douglas M. Johnston. – Dordrecht : Kluwer, 1986.
1,234p.
ISBN 9024732735 Pbk £175.00

—Studies in International Law / Colombo : Lake House Investments.

—Teacher in international law : (teachings and teachers) / Manfred Lachs. – The Hague : Nijhoff, 1982.
236p; 25cm.
Bibliography: p211-225. - Includes index.
ISBN 9024725666 Unpriced

—Teacher in international law : teachings and teaching / Manfred Lachs. – Rev. 2nd ed. – Dordrecht : M. Nijhoff, 1986.
Includes index. Bibliography.
ISBN 9024733138 pbk.

—Teaching and research in international law in Asia and the Pacific : report of a regional consultation meeting including nine country status surveys Seoul, Republic of Korea 10-13 October 1984 / Unesco. – Bangkok : Unesco Regional Office for Education in Asia and the Pacific, 1985.
264p.
Includes bibliographcial references.

—Third World Attitudes Toward International Law : an Introduction / S. Sathirathai. – Dordrecht : Kluwer, 1987.
852p.
ISBN 0898389143 Hbk £375.00

—UN international law and Rhodesian industrial crisis / Oxford : Oxford University Press, 1985.
ISBN 019825394X Hbk £30.00

—UNCITRAL : the United Nations Commission on International Law / Geneva : United Nations Publications.
ISBN 9211332842 Hbk £15.00

—Unification : and comparative law in theory and practice : et le droit compare dans la theorie et la pratique / contributions in honour of Jean Georges Sauveplanne. – Deventer : Kluwer Law & Taxation, 1984.
vi,307p; 25cm.
Text in English and French.
ISBN 9065441735 No price

—United Nations and international law / Cambridge : Cambridge University Press, 1986.
ISBN 0521338743 Pbk £2.95

—United Nations Convention on the Law of the Sea / Bo Johnson Theutenberg. – Dublin : Tycooly International, 1984.
viii,261p; 25cm.
Bibliography: p97-111. Includes full text of United Nations Convention on the Law of the Sea. Spine title : The law of the sea.
ISBN 0863460410 Hbk Unpriced
ISBN 0863460429 Pbk Unpriced

—Weekly news summary / United Nations Information Centre for the United Kingdom and Ireland. – v. – London : The Centre, 1982.
Continues: London weekly summary.

—What is International Law and How Do We Tell it When We See It? / J.R. Spencer. – Dordrecht : Kluwer.
66p.

INTERNATIONAL LAW - AFRICA

—International Law and Colonialism in Africa / Enugu : Nwamife, 1980.
173p.
ISBN 9781240342 Hbk £11.20

—International law and the new states of Africa : a study of the international legal problems of state succession in the newly independent states of Eastern Africa / by Yilma Makonnen : with a foreword by T.O. Elias. – Addis Ababa : Ethiopian National Agency for UNESCO, 1983.
xxvi, 575 p.; 23 cm.
'Published with the assistance of UNESCO under the Regional Participation Programme for Africa.'. Includes index. Bibliography: p. 541-564.
ISBN 0961193409 pbk.

INTERNATIONAL LAW - ANTARCTIC REGIONS

—Antarctic law and politics / F.M. Auburn. – London : Hurst, 1982.
xx,361p; 23cm.
Bibliography: p337-356. - Includes index.
ISBN 0905838394 £17.50

INTERNATIONAL LAW - AUSTRALIA

—International law in Australia / 2nd ed. – North Ryde : Law Book Co, 1984.
ISBN 0455202699 Pbk £25.00
ISBN 0455205183 Hbk £35.00

—International Law in Australia / 2nd ed. – Deakin : Australian Institute of International Affairs, 1985.

—International law in Australia / K. W Ryan. – 2nd ed. – North Ryde, N.S.W. : Published for the Australian Institute of International Affairs by the Law Book Co., 1984.
xliii, 523 p.; 25 cm.
Includes bibliographical references.
ISBN 0455202699 pbk.

INTERNATIONAL LAW - CANADA

—Canadian bibliography of international law / Christian L. Wiktor. – Toronto : University of Toronto Press, 1984.
xxiii, 767 p.; 25 cm.
Includes indexes.
ISBN 0802056156

—Canadian Yearbook of International Law : 1963-1973, 11 Vols. / Professional Books Staff. – Abingdon : Professional Books, 1984.

—Canadian Yearbook of International Law - Annuaire Canadien de Droit International /. – Vancouver : University of British Columbia Press.
ISBN 0774801123 Hbk £35.00

Vol. 17
ISBN 0774801271 Hbk £44.00

Vol. 18 1980.
437p.
ISBN 0774801379 Hbk £44.00

Vol. 19 1983.
478p.
ISBN 077480162X Hbk £44.00

Vol. 20 1984.
350p.
ISBN 0774801824 Hbk Can$45.00

Vol. 21 1984.
562p.
ISBN 0774802065 Hbk £45.00

Vol. 22 1985.
471p.
ISBN 0774802251 Hbk £45.00

Vol. 23 1986.
560p.
ISBN 0774802596 Hbk £48.00

Vol. 24 1987.
488p.
ISBN 0774802812 Hbk £48.00

Vol. 25 1987.
580p.
ISBN 0774803037 Hbk £60.00

—International law : a Canadian perspective / by L.C. Green. – Toronto : Carswell, 1984.
vii,352p.
Includes index.
ISBN 0459366904

—International Law : Chiefly as Interpreted and Applied in Canada / J. G. Castel. – 4th ed. – Aurora : Canada Law Book Co.

—International law : chiefly as interpreted and applied in Canada / Castel. – 4th ed. – Aurora : Canada Law Book, 1986.

—Introduction to International Law /. – Toronto : Butterworths.
ISBN 0409824852 Pbk £31.95

—Proceedings of the Conference on International Law : critical choices for Canada, 1985-2000 / Droit international. – Kingston Ont. : Queens Law Journal, 1986.
xxxiv,563p.
Includes bibliographical references. Cover title: International law: critical choices for Canada, 1985-2000.
ISBN 0889114706

INTERNATIONAL LAW - CANADA - ONTARIO

—International law : a Canadian perspective / by L.C. Green. – 2nd ed. – Toronto : Carswell Company, 1988.
vii,409p.
'Textbook edition of Title 81 of The Canadian Encyclopedic Digest (Ontario) third edition' - t.p.. Includes index.
ISBN 0459319817

INTERNATIONAL LAW - CYPRUS

—Cyprus question and the Turkish position in international law / Oxford : OUP, 1989.
275.
Recounts the recent history o Cyprus and deals with the international law aspects of the developments since 1963. The 'doctrine of necessity', the Treaty of Guarantee and Turkish intervention of 1974, human rights and the constitutional proposals of the respective sides of future federation for Cyprus are discussed.
ISBN 0198252250 Hbk £27.50

INTERNATIONAL LAW - EUROPE

—Legal Co-operation in Europe in the Fields of Civil, Commercial and International Law 1957-82 / Council of Europe. – London : HMSO, 1983.
112p.
ISBN 9287101698 Pbk £3.90

INTERNATIONAL LAW - HUNGARY

—Hungarian perspectives on questions of international law / edited by Hanna Bokor-Szego. – Dordrecht : M. Nijhoff, 1986.
276p.
ISBN 902473293X Hbk £125.00

INTERNATIONAL LAW - JAPAN

—Practice of Japan in international law, 1961-1970 / edited by Shigeru Oda and Hisashi Owada, with the assistance of Kazuya Hirobe. – Tokyo : University of Tokyo Press, 1982.
xxxii, 471 p.; 24 cm.
Includes bibliographical references and index.
ISBN 0860083012 Y10000

INTERNATIONAL LAW - NIGERIA

—Proceedings of the 7th, 8th and 9th Annual Conferences of the Nigerian Society of International Law / Lagos : Nigerian Institute of International Affairs, 1983.
227p.

—Theory and practice of international law in Nigeria / by C. Nwachukwu Okeke. – Enugu, Nigeria : Fourth Dimension Publishers, 1986.
xx, 316p.
Bibliography: p.293-309. - Includes index.
ISBN 9781562420

INTERNATIONAL LAW - PALESTINE

—Palestine yearbook of international law / Al-Shaybani Society of International Law. – Nicosia : Al Shaybani Society of International Law, 1984-.

INTERNATIONAL LAW - UNITED STATES

—International civil litigation in United States courts: commentary and materials / David Westin. – Kluwer Law and Taxation, 1989.
720.
A treatment of international civil litigation in US courts. Covers personal jurisdiction over foreign defendants, services outside the US, discovery of materials outside the US including the Hague Evidence Convention and the Aerospatiale decision.
ISBN 9065443800 Hbk £54/Dfl 168

INTERNATIONAL LAW - USSR

—History of international law in Russia 1647-1917 / Translated by W. E. Butler. – Oxford : Clarendon Press, 1988.
600.
An account of the develoment of the study of international law and the revolution of 1917. A guide to the Russian literature on the law of nations in a contemporary context. The translator's introduction and bibliography are new, and place the work in its historical context.
ISBN 0198254954 Hbk £40

—Soviet Views on the Use of Force in International Law / Hong Kong : Asian Research Service.
ca 200p.

INTERNATIONAL OFFENCES

—Canadian criminal law, international and transnational aspects / Sharon A. Williams, J.-G. Castel. – Toronto : Butterworths, 1981.
xxx, 513 p.; 24 cm.
Includes bibliographical references and indexes. Part one is devoted to jurisdiction and the criminal law under international law and Canadian law. Part two deals with Canadian law applicable to specific offences of an international and transnational nature. Part three covers international cooperation in the field of criminal law and criminal procedure.
ISBN 0409876348 £80.00

—Draft international criminal code and draft statute for an international criminal tribunal / M. Cherif Bassiouni. – 2nd rev. & updated ed. – Dordrecht : M. Nijhoff, 1987.
xxii, 492p.
Rev. ed. of: International criminal law / M. Cherif Bassiouni, 1980. Bibliography: p.267-353.
ISBN 0898389186

—International criminal responsibility of states : a study on the evolution of state responsibility with particular emphasis on the concept of crime and criminal responsibility / by Farhad Malekian. – Stockholm : s.n., 1985.
xviii,234p.
Thesis (Doctor of Laws) - University of Stockholm, 1985. Bibliography: p.198-209. - Includes index.
ISBN 9171465022

INTERNATIONAL OFFICIALS AND EMPLOYEES

—Law of the International Civil Service: as applied by internatinal administrative tribunals / Oxford : Clarendon Press.
686.
ISBN 0198255608 Hbk £60

—Law of the International Civil Service: as applied by internatinal administrative tribunals / Oxford : Clarendon Press.
1350.
On the law as applied by international administrative tribunals in the area of employment relations between international organisations and their staff. Analyses the way in which obligations and rights are enforced and recognised.
ISBN 0198256108 Hbk £60

INTERNATIONAL ORGANISATION

—All-in-One Guide to European-Atlantic Organisations : Intergovernmental and Supporting Voluntary Bodies : What They Are, What They Do, and Where to Get Further Information / European-Atlantic Movement. – 9th ed., revised ed. – Exeter : European Atlantic Movement, 1985.
ISBN 0854500057 Hbk £0.25

—Concept of international organization / edited by Georges Abi-Saab. – Paris : UNESCO, 1981.
245 p.; 25 cm.
Includes bibliographical references.
ISBN 923101742X

—International Monetary Fund 1972-1978 : Cooperation on trial / edited by Margaret Garritsen de Vries. – 3 v. – Washington, D.C. : International Monetary Fund, 1985.
Vols.I and II: Narrative and analysis. Vol.III: Documents.
ISBN 0939934434

—Search for world order : a study of thought and action / by Cornelius F. Murphy, Jr. – Dordrecht : M. Nijhoff, 1985.
xiii, 192 p.; 25 cm. – (Developments in international law).
Includes bibliographical references and index.
ISBN 9024731887 CIP rev.

—Spirit of Uppsala : proceedings of the Joint UNITAR-Uppsala University Seminar on International Law and Organization for a New World Order (JUS 81), Uppsala 9-18 June 1981 / edited by Atle Grahl-Madsen and Jiri Toman. – Berlin : W. de Gruyter, 1983.
English and French. Includes index and bibliography.
ISBN 3110088223

INTERNATIONAL RELATIONS

—Arbitration in U.S.-German Business Relations : Schiedsgerichtsbarkeit im deutsch-amerikanischen / K.H. Bockstiegel. – Cologne : Carl Heymanns Verlag, 1985.
vi, 287p.
ISBN 3452202577 Pbk £230.00

—Australian-United States' relations : the extraterritorial application of United States laws / the Parliament of the Commonwealth of Australia Joint Committee on Foreign Affairs and Defence. – Canberra : Australian Government Publishing Service, 1983.
xiii,84p. – (Parliamentary paper).
Includes bibliographical references.

—Canadian Council on International Law : Conference Proceedings /. – Ottawa : Canadian Council on International Law, 1987.

—Cooperation and Conflict : Nordic Journal of International Politics / Oslo : University of Forlag.

—Cultural Relations in the Global Community : Problems and Prospects / J. Philip Puthenparampil. – New Delhi : Abhinav Publications, 1981.
xii, 255p.
ISBN 8170171369 Hbk £75.00

—Defining status: a comprehensive analysis of United States/territorial relations / Dordrecht : Martinus Nijhoff, 1989.
752.
Analyses the possibility of Statehood for Guam and the Virgin Islands, and explores the bounds of the Commonwealth and Freely Associated States. These status alternatives are discussed against a backdrop of the political, economic, geographic, and cultural uniqueness of each territory.
ISBN 0792300696 Hbk £115

—East-West Tensions World Wide / Exeter : European Atlantic Movement, 1982.

—European Community, International Organizations and Multilateral Agreements / European Communities. – 3rd ed. – London : HMSO, 1983.
285p.
Describes relationships established between the European Community and world and regional intergovernmental organisations.
ISBN 9282537757 Pbk £3.90

—Expansion of international society / edited by Hedly Bull and Adam Watson. – Oxford : Clarendon, 1984.
xi,479p; 24cm.
Bibliography: p453. - Includes index.
ISBN 0198219423 £25.00

—Focus on Beirut / by Georg Schwarzenberger. – Leeds : University of Leeds, 1983.
11p.
Bibliography: p.10-11.

—Human rights and international relations / Cambridge : Cambridge University Press, 1987.
ISBN 0521327989 Hbk £20.00
ISBN 0521339952 Pbk £7.95

—Implementation of international humanitarian law / Y Sandoz. – Dordrecht : Martinus Nijhoff, 1989.
488.
A collection of articles resulting from the 1986 session of the Centre for Studies and Research in International Law and International Relations of the Hague Academy. Explores humanitarian law from the viewpoint of implementation and enforcement, and offers suggestions for improvement.
ISBN 9024737842 Hbk £85

—International Arbitration : a Look at the Future / Paris : International Chamber of Commerce.
421p.

—International Chamber of Commerce Arbitration / Paris : International Chamber of Commerce.
704p.

—International Maritime Arbitration Organization / Paris : International Chamber of Commerce.
64p.

—Law and power in international relations / James Fawcett. – London : Faber and Faber, 1982.
140p; 23cm.
ISBN 0571105378 £9.50

—Maritime dimension / edited by R.P. Barston and Patricia Birnie. – London : Allen & Unwin, 1980.
194p; 23cm.
Includes index.
ISBN 0043410154 Hbk £11.95
ISBN 0043410162 Pbk £5.50

—Mercenarism and international law / Chief R. O. A. Akinjide. – s.l. : s.n., 1986.
13p.
Lecture delivered at the International Law Seminar, Palais des nations, Geneva, on 27.5.1986.

—Multilateral Conventions and Agreements : Signatures and/or Conclusions by the European Communities / Luxembourg : Office for Official Publications of the European Communities, 1987.
cxiv, 361p.
ISBN 9282567966 Pbk £1,200.00

—Multilateral mediation : practical experiences and lessons / Dordrecht : Martinus Nijhoff, 1989.
384.
Analyses the successful mediation; the resolution of the dispute amongst members of the East African Community after its termination in 1977. By narrating his own involvement in a mediation exercise, the author intends to provide governments, practitioners and scholars of international law with a guide to the settlement process.
ISBN 9024737796 Hbk Gld175.00

—Parliamentary control over foreign policy : legal essays / edited by Antonio Cassese. – Alphen aan den Rijn : Sijthoff & Noordhoff, 1980.
206 p.
ISBN 9028600191

—Peace and security : the United Nations and national interests : report of the nineteenth United Nations of the Next Decade Conference convened June 17-22 1984 in Cape Cod, Mass., USA / sponsored by the Stanley Foundation. – Muscatine, Iowa : Stanley Foundation, 1984.
40p; 22cm.

—Small is dangerous : micro states in a macro world: report of a Study Group of the David Davies Memorial Institute of International Studies / edited by Sheila Harden. – London : Frances Pinter, 1985.
ix,212p.

—System for Settlement of Disputes under the United Nations Convention on the Law of the Sea : a Drafting History and a Commentary / Dordrecht : Kluwer, 1987.
302p.
ISBN 9024733243 Hbk £165.00

—United Nations and international law: : the Rede Lecture / Brian Urquhart. – Cambridge : Cambridge University Press, 1985.
20p.

—United Nations, divided world : the UN's roles in international relations / edited by Adam Roberts and Benedict Kingsbury. – Oxford : Clarendon Press, 1988.
xii, 287 p.; 23 cm.
Bibliography: p. 274-278. Includes index.
ISBN 0198275447

—Vulnerability : small states in the global society / report of a Commonwealth Consultative Group. – London : Commonwealth Secretariat, 1985.
xii,126p.
Chairman: P. T. Georges.
ISBN 0850922801

INTERNATIONAL RELATIONS - CANADA

—Canada and the Reagan Challenge : Crisis in the Canadian-American Relationship / Toronto : Lorimer & Co, 1985.
ISBN 0888627912 Hbk £26.95
ISBN 0888627904 Pbk £16.95

—Guide to Canadian Diplomatic Relations 1925-1983 / Ottawa : Canadian Library Association, 1985.

INTERNATIONAL RELATIONS - CHINA

—China and the European Economic Community : the new connection / Harish Kapur. – Dordrecht : Nijhoff, 1986.
xv, 351p.
Includes index. Bibliography: p.99-110.
ISBN 9024732301

INTERNATIONAL RELATIONS - CYPRUS

—Present position of the association of Cyprus with the European Economic Community / Criton G. Tornaritis. – Thessaloniki : Institute of Public International Law and International Relations, 1980.
p.297-305.
Reprinted from: Hellenic review of international relations, v. 1, no. 2 (1980).

INTERNATIONAL RELATIONS - EUROPEAN COMMUNITY

—China and the European Economic Community : the new connection / Harish Kapur. – Dordrecht : Nijhoff, 1986.
xv, 351p.
Includes index. Bibliography: p.99-110.
ISBN 9024732301

—Present position of the association of Cyprus with the European Economic Community / Criton G. Tornaritis. – Thessaloniki : Institute of Public International Law and International Relations, 1980.
p.297-305.
Reprinted from: Hellenic review of international relations, v. 1, no. 2 (1980).

INTERNATIONAL RELATIONS - UNITED STATES

—Canada and the Reagan Challenge : Crisis in the Canadian-American Relationship / Toronto : Lorimer & Co, 1985.
ISBN 0888627912 Hbk £26.95
ISBN 0888627904 Pbk £16.95

—Human Rights and U.S. Foreign Policy Under President Carter / Lagos : Nigerian Institute of International Affairs, 1980.
120p.

INTERNATIONAL RELIEF

—International humanitarian assistance : disaster relief actions in international law and organization / Peter Macalister-Smith. – Hague : M. Nijhoff Publishers, 1985.
260p.
ISBN 9024729939 Hbk £130.00

INTERNATIONAL RIVERS

—Law of international water resources : some general conventions, declarations, and resolutions adopted by governments, international legal institutions, and international organizations, on the management of international water resources / compiled by Dante A. Caponera. – Rome : Food and Agriculture Organization of the United Nations, 1980.
xi, 324 p.; 28 cm.
Includes bibliographical references.
ISBN 9251010366 pbk.

—Pollution of international watercourses : search for substantive rules and principles of law / by J.G. Lammers. – The Hague : M. Nijhoff, 1984.
xxvi, 724 p.; 25 cm.
Includes indexes. Bibliography: p. 663-703.
ISBN 9024729556 Hbk £275.00

INTERNATIONAL SECURITY

—Belgrade and beyond : the CSCE process in perspective / edited by Nils Andren and Karl E. Birnbaum. – Alphen aan den Rijn : Sijthoff & Noordhoff, 1980.
xi,180p.
ISBN 902860250X

—Peace and security : the United Nations and national interests : report of the nineteenth United Nations of the Next Decade Conference convened June 17-22 1984 in Cape Cod, Mass., USA / sponsored by the Stanley Foundation. – Muscatine, Iowa : Stanley Foundation, 1984.
40p; 22cm.

—Science of peace / by J.G. Starke. – 2nd ed. – Sydney : Law Books, 1986.
xvi,193p.
Previous ed. published by A.W. Sijthoff, 1968.
Bibliography: p.180-183. Includes index.
ISBN 0949553298

INTERNATIONAL SERIALS DATA SYSTEM

—News from ISDS / v. – Paris : ISDS International Centre, 1984.
ISBN 02570009

INTERNATIONAL TRADE

—Adaptation and renegotiation of contracts in international trade and finance / edited by Norbert Horn. – Deventer, The Netherlands : Kluwer Law and Taxation Publishers, 1984.
452p.
Includes index.
ISBN 9065441824 Hbk £228.00

—Basic Documents on International Trade Law / Dordrecht : Kluwer, 1986.
766p.
ISBN 9024731682 Hbk £350.00

—Canadian Regulation of International Trade and Investment / Agincourt : Carswell, 1986.
470p.

—Cases and Materials On International Trade / 2nd ed. – London : Laureate-Thomson Press, 1983.
ISBN 0907392105 Pbk £17.00

—Catalogue of Community Legal Acts and Other Texts Relating to the Elimination of Technical Barriers to Trade for Industrial Products and Nomenclature for Iron and Steel Products : December 1983 / Kirchberg : Commission of the European Communities, 1984.
174p.

—Commentary on the international sales law : the 1980 Vienna Sales Convention / by C.M. Bianca, M.J. Bonell. – Milan : Giuffre, 1987.
xvii,886p.
Bibliography: pp.843-873. - Includes index. Includes texts of the Convention in English, Arabic, Chinese, French, Russian, Spanish, German and Italian.
ISBN 8814012768

—Current issues in international business law / edited by David L. Perrott, Istvan Pogany. – Aldershot : Avebury, 1988.
xxvii,239p.
Includes bibliographical references and index.
ISBN 0566054736

—Current Problems of International Trade Financing / London : Butterworths, 1983.
ISBN 0406181144 Hbk £49.30

—Dictionary of International Commerce / London : Chapman & Hall, 1985.
ISBN 0412280108 Hbk £37.50

—Dictionary of Shipping and International Trade Terms / 2nd ed. – Witherby, 1983.
ISBN 0900886706 Pbk £7.50

—Documentary history of the 1980 uniform law for international sales / Kluwer Law and Taxation, 1989.
896.
Covers the United Nations Commission on International Trade Law (1969-1977) and the Vienna Diplomatic Conference (1980). Compiled from documents in the nine volumes of the UNCITRAL yaerbook and the Official Records on the 1980 Conference.
ISBN 9065443738 Hbk £105/Dfl 350

—Elements of International Trade and Payments / Cambridge : Woodhead-Faulkner, 1983.
ISBN 0859412261 Pbk £6.25

—Export Trade : Law and Practice of International Trade / 7th ed. – London : Sweet & Maxwell, 1980.
ISBN 0420457402 Pbk £19.95

—Extraterritoriality in International Trade : Canada and the United States of America Practices Compared / Butterworths, 1988.
288p.
Study of conflicts of jurisdiction involving international busness transactions. Attempts to define the permissible limits to the assertion of jurisdiction to prescribe, to adjudicate and to enforce a rule of law under traditional principles of public international law and what these limits should be today in the economic field.
ISBN 0409805025 Hbk

—Guidelines for National Implementation of the Convention on International Trade in Endangered Species of Wild Fauna and Flora-Cities / Gland : International Union for Conservation of Nature and Natural Resources, 1981.
148p.

—Hague-Zagreb Essays / edited by C.C.A. Voskuil and C.C.A. Voskuil and J.A. Wade. – Hague : Martinus Nijhoff, 1983.
410p.
ISBN 9024728401 Hbk £135.00

5: On the Law of International Trade / edited by C.C.A. Voskuil and J.A. Wade. – 1985.
193p.
At head of title: TMC Asser Instituut. Reports and discussions of the fifth session of the Hague-Zagreb Colloquium, Isle of Krk, Yugoslavia, 1983. Includes bibliographies.
ISBN 9024731704 Hbk £135.00

—International Industrial Purchasing / Stockholm : Almqvist & Wiksell, 1982.
74p.
ISBN 9155412661 Hbk £51.00

—International private trade / 2nd ed. – Matthew Bender, 1981.
ISBN 0000999048 Hbk £26.50

—International trade finance / Weston. – North Ryde : Law Book Co, 1986.
ISBN 0455203504 Pbk £11.25

—International trade in endangered species / Dordrecht : Martinus Nijhoff, 1989.
424.
Discusses each article of the Convention on International Trade in Endangered Species, each with a separate chapter. Gives background information on the drafting of the treaty, problems of implementation and economic consequences of world trade in wildlife and plants.
ISBN 0792301145 Hbk £75

—Introduction to ICC Rules on International Contracts / Paris : International Chamber of Commerce.
50p.

—Law of international trade / Mark S.W. Hoyle. – 2nd ed. – Bicester : CCH Editions, 1985.
vii,518p; 23cm.
Previous ed.: 1981?. Bibliography: p471-472. - Includes index.
ISBN 0863250726 Pbk No price

—Legal Acceptance of International Trade Data Transmitted by Electronic Means : CompLex 10/83 / Oslo : Norwegian University Press, 1983.
90p.

—New GATT round of multilateral trade negotiations: legal and economic problems / E -U Petersman, M Hilf. – Kluwer Law and Taxation, 1989.
– (Studies in Transitional Economic Law).
Reproduces contributions to an international conference in 1987 on the current 'Uruguay Round' of multilateral negotiations. Part 1 examines proposals for the strengthening of the internatinal framework of GATT systems, and for the implementation of GATT rules within the major trading countries.
ISBN 9065443657 Hbk £81/Dfl 250

—New Protectionism : Non-Tariff Barriers and Their Effects for Canada / Toronto : Lorimer & Co, 1981.
ISBN 0888624425 Hbk £16.95
ISBN 0888624417 Pbk £7.95

—Schmitthoff's Export Trade : the Law and Practice of International Trade / 8th ed. – Agincourt : Carswell.
689p.

—Selective safeguard measures in multilateral trade relations : issues of protectionism in GATT, European Community, and United States law / M.C.E.J. Bronckers. – Deventer, Netherlands : Kluwer Law and Taxation Publishers, 1985.
306p.
Includes index and bibliography.
ISBN 9065442227 Hbk £150.00

—Uniform sales law : the UN Convention on Contracts for the International Sale of Goods / Peter Schlectriem. – Wien : Manz, 1986.
120p.
Bibliography: pp.11-16. - Includes index. Translation of: Einheitliches UN-Kaufrecht. - Tubingen: Mohr, 1981.
ISBN 3214065580

—United Nations Commission of International Trade Law Yearbook / United Nations. – London : HMSO, 1984.
Includes reports on international trade contracts, international payments, commercial arbitration and conciliation and transport law.
ISBN 0119082985 Hbk £36.10

INTERNATIONAL TRADE – CANADA

—Canadian Regulation of International Trade and Investment / Agincourt : Carswell, 1986.
470p.
This work describes and analyzes international conventions and domestic legislation that regulate Canadian world trade. International barriers to foreign investment and the new domestic laws that embody the flexible Canadian approach to the issues are discussed in the book.

—Legal Counselling in Canada-Japan Business Transactions - II / Vancouver : British Columbia Continuing Legal Education Society, 1983.
425p.
ISBN 0865041016 Hbk £65.00

—New dimensions in international trade law : a Canadian perspective / edited by Jacob S. Ziegel and William C. Graham for the Faculty of Law, University of Toronto and The Canadian Bar Association - Ontario. – Toronto : Butterworths, 1982.
ix,211p.
Papers presented at a Conference held in Toronto, November 14, 1980. Includes bibliographical references.
ISBN 0409818828

—U.S. Trade Expansion Act of 1962 : How Will It Affect Canadian-U.S. Trade? / Toronto : C.D. Howe Institute, 1963.
ISBN 0888060998 Hbk £5.00

INTERNATIONAL TRADE – EUROPE

—Political and legal framework of trade relations between the european community and eastern europe / Dordrecht : Martinus Nijhoff, 1989.
352.
Historical reflection on relations between the EEC and COMECON, and on analysis of the position of Western European countries in their relations with Eastern Europe, European enterprises in the EEC, export controls, financial cooperation and countertrade, and the position of Eastern European countries in the GATT.
ISBN 0792300467 Hbk £42

INTERNATIONAL TRADE – EUROPEAN COMMUNITY

—Completing the internal market : white paper from the Commission to the European Council / Commission of the European Communities. – Luxembourg : Office for Official Publications of the European Communities, 1985.
55,35p. – (Document).
ISBN 9282554368

—European Economic Community : Trade and Investment / Matthew Bender, 1986.
ISBN 0000999064 Hbk £50.00

INTERNATIONAL TRADE – GREAT BRITAIN

—Cases & materials on the law of international trade / edited by Mark S.W. Hoyle. – London : Laureate, 1980.
viii,282p; 31cm.
ISBN 0907392008 Hbk Unpriced
ISBN 0907392016 Pbk Unpriced

—Finance of International Trade / 5th ed. – London : Pitman Publishing, 1987.
ISBN 0273027344 Pbk £8.95

—Financing International Trade / London : Butterworths, 1988.
ISBN 0880631503 Hbk

INTERNATIONAL TRADE – JAPAN

—Legal Counselling in Canada-Japan Business Transactions - II / Vancouver : British Columbia Continuing Legal Education Society, 1983.
425p.
ISBN 0865041016 Hbk £65.00

INTERNATIONAL TRADE – UNITED STATES

—U.S. Trade Expansion Act of 1962 : How Will It Affect Canadian-U.S. Trade? / Toronto : C.D. Howe Institute, 1963.
ISBN 0888060998 Hbk £5.00

INTERNATIONAL UNIFICATION

—Judicial review, transnational and federal : its impact on integration / by Mauro Cappelletti and David Golay. – Florence : European University Institute, 1981.
143p.

—Social policy harmonisation in the European Community / John Holloway. – Farnborough, Hants. : Gower, 1981.
vi,318p; 23cm.
Bibliography: p305-318.
ISBN 0566001969 £10.50

INTERPRETATION AND CONSTRUCTION

—Bibliography of materials on legislative and other legal drafting and the interpretation of statutes / 3rd rev. ed. – London : Commonwealth Secretariat, 1985.
62p.
Previous ed.: 1977.

—How to do things with rules : a primer of interpretation / William Twining, David Miers. – 2nd ed. – London : Weidenfeld and Nicholson, 1982.
xx,387p; 23cm.
Previous ed. 1976.
ISBN 0297780832

—Interpretation of Statutes / 2nd ed. – Calcutta : Eastern Law House, 1983.

—Rational as reasonable : a treatise on legal justification / Aulis Aarnio. – Dordrecht : D. Reidel, 1986.
xix, 276p.
Includes index. Bibliography: p 261-271.
ISBN 9027722765 Hbk

—Selected Problems of Construction Law : International Approach / London : Sweet & Maxwell, 1983.
ISBN 0421316500 Hbk £25.00

—Statutory interpretation : codified, with a critical commentary / F.A.R. Bennion. – London : Butterworths, 1984.
cii,904p; 26cm.
Includes index.
ISBN 0406259208 No price

INTERPRETATION AND CONSTRUCTION - AUSTRALIA

—Construction Law in Australia / North Ryde : Law Book Co, 1981.
xviii, 318p.
ISBN 0455202605 Pbk £31.00

—Extrinsic aids to statutory interpretation / Attorney-General's Department. – 2nd impression. – Canberra : Australian Government Publishing Service, 1982.
v,25p. – (Policy discussion paper).
Includes bibliographical references.
ISBN 0644020083

—Law-making in Australia / edited by Alice Erh-Soon Tay and Eugene Kamenka. – London : Edward Arnold, 1980.
vii,328p; 22cm.
Includes index.
ISBN 0713180021 £18.50

—Report to Parliament on the proposals contained in the Interpretation Bill 1982 / Legal and Constitutional Committee. – Melbourne : Parliament of Victoria, 1983.
xxvii,235p.
Bibliography: p.228-235.

—Statutory interpretation in Australia / by D.C. Pearce. – 2nd ed. – Sydney : Butterworths, 1981.
xxxv, 208 p.; 24 cm.
Includes index.
ISBN 0409490458

—Symposium on statutory interpretaion, Canberra, 5 February 1983 / Canberra : Australian Government Publishing Service, 1983.
iii,136p.
At head of title: Attorney-General's Department.
ISBN 0644025859

INTERPRETATION AND CONSTRUCTION - AUSTRALIA - VICTORIA

—First report to Parliament on the operation of section 32 of the Interpretation of Legislation Act 1984 / Legal and Constitutional Committee. – Melbourne : Government Printer, 1986.
vii,10p.

—Second report to Parliament on the operation of section 32 of the Interpretation of Legislation Act 1984 ... / Legal and Constitutional Committee. – Melbourne : Government Printer, 1986.
v,3p.

—Third report to Parliament on the operation of section 32 of the Interpretation of Legislation Act 1984 concerning Dental Technicians (Members Fees) (Amendment) Regulations 1986 (S.R. No. 180/1986) / Legal and Constitutional Committee. – Melbourne : Government Printer, 1987.
v,6p.

INTERPRETATION AND CONSTRUCTION - CANADA

—Construction Disputes / Vancouver : Continuing Legal Education Society of British Columbia, 1988.
177p.
ISBN 0865043728 Hbk £70.00

—Construction of statutes / Elmer A. Driedger. – 2nd ed. – Toronto : Butterworths, 1983.
xvi,385p. – (Canadian legal manual series).
Contains a new chapter on bilingual statutes, and expanded discussion of departure from the ordinary meaning for the professed reason of 'absurdity', and a refinement of the author's commentary on the presumption against retrospective operation.
ISBN 0409828033

—Construing bilingual legislation in Canada / Remi Michael Beaupre. – Toronto : Butterworths, 1981.
xxi,161p.
Bibliography: p.149-151. - Includes index.
ISBN 0409813400

—Drafting and Interpreting Legislation / 3rd ed. – Agincourt : Carswell, 1988.
110p.

—Interpreting Bilingual Legislation, 2nd Edition / Agincourt : Carswell, 1986.
236p.

—Interpreting bilingual legislation / Michael Beaupre. – 2nd ed. – Toronto : Carswell, 1986.
xvi, 236 p.; 24 cm.
Rev. ed. of: Construing bilingual legislation in Canada. Includes index. Bibliography: p. 223-227.
ISBN 0459390600

INTERPRETATION AND CONSTRUCTION - ENGLAND

—Law-making process... / Michael Zander. – 2nd. ed. – London : Weidenfeld, 1985.
xxiv, 416p.
ISBN 0297786628 Pbk
ISBN 0297786636

—Statutory interpretation / by the late Sir Rupert Cross. – 2nd ed. – London : Butterworths, 1987.
xviii,206p; 22cm.
Previous ed.: 1976. Includes index.
ISBN 0406570175 Pbk £12.95

INTERPRETATION AND CONSTRUCTION - GREAT BRITAIN

—Statute law / F. A. R. Bennion. – 2nd ed. – London : Oyez Longman, 1983.
xxvi,339p; 21cm.
Previous ed.: 1980.
ISBN 0851208029

INTERPRETATION AND CONSTRUCTION - INDIA

—Intepretation of Statutes / 7th ed. – Allahabad : Law Book Company, 1984.
400p.

—Interpretation of Statues / 3rd ed. – Lucknow : Eastern Book Company, 1986.
704p.

—Interpretation of Taxing Statutes / Allahabad : Law Publishing House, 1984.

INTERPRETATION AND CONSTRUCTION - MALAYSIA

—Construction Law in Singapore and Malaysia / Anthony P. Lavers. – Butterworths, 1988.
ISBN 0409995614 Hbk £90.00

—Interpretation Act, 1967 (Act 23 of 1967) / Kuala Lumpur : International Law Books Services.

INTERPRETATION AND CONSTRUCTION - NEW ZEALAND

—Legislation and its interpretation : the Acts Interpretation Act 1924 and related legislation : a discussion paper and questionnaire / Law Commission. – Wellington, N.Z. : The Commission, 1987.
xii,83p. – (Preliminary paper).

INTERPRETATION AND CONSTRUCTION - SINGAPORE

—Construction Law in Singapore and Malaysia / Anthony P. Lavers. – Butterworths, 1988.
ISBN 0409995614 Hbk £90.00

INTERPRETATION AND CONSTRUCTION - SOUTH AFRICA

—Interpretation of statutes / Gail-Maryse Cockram. – 3rd ed. – Cape Town : Juta, 1987.
xvi,181p.
Previous ed.: 1983. Includes index.
ISBN 0702118346

—Interpretation of Statutes / Durban : Butterworths.

INTERPROFESSIONAL RELATIONS

—Responsibility in health care / edited by George J. Agich. – Dordrecht, Holland : D. Reidel, 1982.
xxiii, 285p.
Outgrowth of the Eleventh Trans-disciplinary Symposium on Philosophy and Medicine held in Springfield, Ill., on March 16-18, 1981. Includes bibliographies and index.
ISBN 9027714177

INTERSTATE COMMERCE - AUSTRALIA

—Freedom of interstate trade under the Australian constitution / by Michael Coper. – Sydney : Butterworths, 1983.
xiii,394p.
Bibliography: p.371-380. - Includes index.
ISBN 0409491802

INTERVENTION (CIVIL PROCEDURE) - AUSTRALIA - SOUTH AUSTRALIA

—Report ... relating to the law governing locus standi : non-party interventions and amici curiae in relation to proceedings in civil jurisdiction / Law Reform Committee of South Australia. – Adelaide : Government Printer, 1982.
9p. – (67th report).

INTERVENTION (INTERNATIONAL LAW)

—Grenada : a study in politics and the limits of international law / Scott Davidson. – Aldershot : Avebury, 1987.
xii,196p; 22cm.
Bibliography: p184-190. - Includes index.
ISBN 0566050528 £18.50

—Grenada intervention : analysis and documentation / William C. Gilmore. – London : Mansell, 1984.
116p; 22cm.
Includes index.
ISBN 0720117232 Pbk £5.95

—Intervention in world politics / edited by Hedley Bull. – Oxford : Clarendon, 1984.
198p; 23cm.
Includes index.
ISBN 019827467X £12.50

—Rescuing nationals abroad through military coercion and intervention on grounds of humanity / Natalino Ronzitti. – Dordrecht Netherlands : M. Nijhoff Publishers, 1985.
236p.
Includes index. Bibliography.
ISBN 9024731356 Hbk £125.00

INTERVIEWING IN LAW ENFORCEMENT - CANADA

—Police Manual of Arrest, Seizure and Interrogation / 4th ed. – Agincourt : Carswell, 1988.
220p.

INTERVIEWING IN LAW ENFORCEMENT - GREAT BRITAIN

—Tape-recording of police interviews with suspects : an interim report / Carole F. Willis. – London : H.M.S.O., 1984.
v,39p.
Outlines background to field trials of tape recording police interviews. Reviews literature describing research methodologies used in trials. Discusses preliminary results of the research.
ISBN 0113407769

INTERVIEWING IN LAW PRACTICE

—Client interviewing for lawyers : an analysis and guide / by Avrom Sherr. – London : Sweet & Maxwell, 1986.
190p; 22cm.
Includes bibliography and index.
ISBN 0421361603 Pbk £7.95

INTERVIEWING IN LAW PRACTICE - CANADA

—Interviewing and Counselling : Skills for Legal Practitioners / Toronto : Butterworths, 1987.
168p.
ISBN 0409873454 Hbk

INTOXICATION - AUSTRALIA - VICTORIA

—Criminal responsibility : intention and gross intoxication / Law Reform Commission of Victoria. – Melbourne : The Commission, 1986.
v,31p. – (Report no 6).
Includes bibliographical references.

INTOXICATION - NEW ZEALAND

—Report on intoxication as a defence to a criminal charge / Criminal Law Reform Committee. – Sydney : Law Reform Commission of New South Wales, 1984.
55p.
Includes bibliographical references.

INTOXICATION - SOUTH AFRICA

—Offences committed under the influence of liquor or drugs / South African Law Commission. – Pretoria : The Commission, 1984.
vi,118 leaves. – (Project).
Bibliography: p.113-118.

—Offences committed under the influence of liquor or drugs / South African Law Commission. – Pretoria : The Commission, 1986.
vii,132p. – (Report).
Bibliography: p.123-132.
ISBN 0621102075

INUIT - CANADA

—Aboriginal peoples and the law : Indian, Metis and Inuit rights in Canada / edited by Bradford W. Morse. – Ottawa : Carleton University Press, 1985.
xlv,794p. – (Carleton Library Series).
ISBN 0886290198

INVENTIONS

—Employees' inventions : a comparative study / edited by Jeremy Phillips. – Sunderland : Fernsway, 1981.
212p; 21cm.
ISBN 0950762601 Pbk Unpriced

—WIPO Model Law for Developing Countries on Inventions, Vol. 2 (Know-How) : Examination and Registration of Contracts; Inventor's Certicates; Technovations; Transfer of Technology Patents / Geneva : World Intellectual Property Organization, 1980.
102p.

INVENTIONS - CANADA

—Patents of Inventions / 3rd ed. – Agincourt : Carswell, 1981.
ISBN 045934500 Hbk £25.30

INVENTIONS - GREAT BRITAIN

—Employees' inventions in the United Kingdom : law and practice / by Jeremy Phillips and Michael J. Hoolahan. – Oxford : ESC, 1982.
xviii,164p; 22cm.
ISBN 0906214114 Pbk £9.50
ISBN 0906214106

—Inventors' information guide / by Tamara S. Eisenschitz and Jeremy Phillips. – 2nd edition. – London : The Intellectual Property Law Unit Centre for Commercial Law Studies, 1985.
viii, 100p.
ISBN 0951066404

—Inventors' Information Guide / Phillips. – 2nd ed. – London : Centre for Commercial Law Studies, 1985.
ISBN 0951066404 Pbk £6.50

—Patent system and inventive activity / Manchester : Manchester University Press, 1984.
ISBN 0719009979 Hbk £21.00

—Patents for inventions / 5th ed. – London : Sweet & Maxwell, 1983.
ISBN 0420463100 Hbk £44.00

INVESTMENT

—Financial services : regulating investment business / Simon Morris. – 1st ed. – London : Longman Professional (UK), 1989.
Examines the Financial Services Act 1986, and details its impact on areas of investment business, including the international aspect and the run up to 1992, and civil and criminal liability for operations outside the FSA.
ISBN 0851215572 Hbk £37.50

—Investing in Europe's future / edited by Arnold Heertje : contributors Michel Albert ... et al. : preface by Yves Le Portz. – Oxford : Blackwell, for the European Investment Bank, 1983.
x,218p; 24cm.
ISBN 0631134050 Unpriced

—Investment incentives worldwide / London : Butterworths, 1988.
ISBN 040800900X Hbk £55.00

INVESTMENT - CANADA

—Guide to the Investment Canada Act / Gabor S.G. Takach. – Butterworths, 1986.
176p.
ISBN 0409805203 Hbk £50.00

INVESTMENT - CHINA

—China Investment Guide / London : Longman Professional, 1987.
ISBN 0582997747 Hbk £75.00

—China's Investment Laws : New Directions / London : Butterworths, 1988.
ISBN 0409995606 Hbk £60.00

INVESTMENT - EUROPEAN COMMUNITY

—European Economic Community : Trade and Investment / Matthew Bender, 1986.
ISBN 0000999064 Hbk £50.00

INVESTMENT - GREAT BRITAIN

—BASIC Investment Appraisal / London : Butterworths, 1985.
ISBN 0408015675 Pbk

—Investment / London : Pitman Publishing, 1988.
ISBN 0273028944 Pbk £9.95

—Law of the investment markets / Oxford : Blackwell Scientific, 1990.
672. – (Blackwell Law Library).
A detailed guide to the complex rules and procedures prescribed by the Financial Services Act 1986; covers the history, structure, and regulation of investment markets. Further chapters cover finacial, accounting and reporting rules, the marketing of unlisted securities, unit trusts, investment schemes and overseas aspects of investments.
Investment practitioners, Lawyers, Investors, Financial advisors
ISBN 0632023724 Hbk £85

—Modern Investment Management / Oxford : Oxford University Press, 1986.
ISBN 0195041968 Hbk £29.50

—Pension fund investment / Cambridge : Woodhead-Faulkner, 1987.
ISBN 0859414000 Hbk £35.00

—Successful investment strategy / 2nd ed. – Cambridge : Woodhead-Faulkner, 1988.
ISBN 0859413837 Hbk £25.00

—Sunday Telegraph 101 ways of investing / Telegraph Publications, 1988.
ISBN 0863672027 Pbk £2.95

INVESTMENT - NEW ZEALAND

—Property Investment / 2nd ed. – Butterworths, 1980.
ISBN 0409600814 Pbk £33.00

—Taxation of Companies and Corporate Investors / Butterworths, 1984.
ISBN 0409701424 Pbk £33.55

INVESTMENT - SPAIN

—Litigating in Spain: considerations for foreign practitioners including international judicial assistance, enforcement of foreign judgements, bankruptcy, arbitration and other civil proceedings in Spain / Kluwer Law and Taxation, 1989.
579.
Informs investors, and potential investors how to protect their investments under Spanish law. Provides footnotes and other information relevant to precedents in Spanish courts. Contains a table of the Spanish Judicial Structure, and an appendix of all the International conventions ratified by Spain.
ISBN 9065443770 Hbk £52.75/Dfl 163

INVESTMENT - UNITED STATES

—Business and Investment Almanac 1988 / New York : Dow Jones-Irwin, 1988.
ISBN 1556230478 Hbk £31.95

—Structuring foreign investment in US real estate / W D Knight, R L Doernberg. – Kluwer Law and Taxation, 1989.
780.
Explores the considerations of concern to foreign individuals and organisations making US real property investments. Covers US income, estate, and gift tax aspects of foreign investment. Also techniques that may be employed to reduce or eliminate US tax liability. Includes the Foreign Investment in Real Property Act 1980.
ISBN 9065449752 Llf £112/Dfl 350

Supplement 1989.
ISBN 90T275002X Llf £80.75/Dfl 250

INVESTMENT TAX CREDITS - ASIA

—Income taxation and foreign investment in developing countries / M.P. Dominic. – Amsterdam : International Bureau of Fiscal Documentation, 1980.
xviii, 354, 28 p.; 24 cm.
Includes indexes. Bibliography: p. 7-16 (2d group).
ISBN 9070125137 pbk.

INVESTMENT TAX CREDITS - CANADA

—Tax incentives for investment : the state of the art / Richard M. Bird. – Toronto : Canadian Tax Foundation, 1980.
ix, 68 p.; 23 cm.
Includes index. Bibliography: p. 61-66.
ISBN 0888080042 pbk. £4.50

INVESTMENT TRUSTS - GREAT BRITAIN

—Investment trusts explained / A.A. Arnaud. – 2nd ed. – Cambridge : Woodhead-Faulkner in co-operation with the Association of Investment Trust Companies, 1983.
xiii,.145p; 24cm.
Previous ed.: 1977. Includes index.
ISBN 0859412431 Hbk Unpriced
ISBN 0859412490 Pbk £6.95

—Regulation of authorised unit trust schemes : a consultative document on the proposed regulations for unit trust schemes authorised under the Financial Services Bill / Department of Trade and Industry. – London : HMSO, 1986.
viii.74p.
ISBN 0115138498

INVESTMENTS

—Bilateral Treaties for International Private Investment / Paris : International Chamber of Commerce.
31p.

—Canadian Regulation of International Trade and Investment / Agincourt : Carswell, 1986.
470p.

—Comparative survey of corporate investments / Gunther H. W. Stratmann. – London : International Bar Association, 1983.
iv,198p.
Based on papers 'presented during the New Delhi Conference of the International Bar Assoiciation ...'. - Introduction.

Vol. 2 parts 1-2 : in Canada, Belgium, France, Federal Republic of Germany ... : written by members of Committee G/Business Organisations of the Section on Business Law of the International Bar Association
A 'set of papers ... presented during the Toronto Conference of the International Bar Association ...'. - Introduction.

—Review of investor protection : report / L. C. B. Gower. – London : H.M.S.O., 1985.
vii,64p.
Part 1 published as Command Paper 9125 in Parliamentary Papers 1983-84.
ISBN 0115138234

INVESTMENTS - AFRICA

—Investment codes of North Africa : Tunisia / compiled and translated by Elizabeth de Brauw. – Amsterdam : International Bureau of Fiscal Documentation, 1980.
92p; 25cm. – (Publications of the International Bureau of Fiscal Documentation).
ISBN 9070125153

—Investment Laws and Opportunities in Africa / Apapa : Heritage Books.

INVESTMENTS - AUSTRALIA

—Tax and the Australian film industry : being a commentary on division 10BA of the Income Assessment Act 1936 together with text of the legislation / by E.F. Mannix. – Sydney : Butterworths, 1981.
xii,92p.
Includes index.
ISBN 040936018X

INVESTMENTS - CANADA

—Foreign affiliate system : Canadian taxation after 1982 : a structured overview / by Nathan Boidman. – Don Mills, Ont. : CCH Canadian Ltd., 1983.
ix,218p.
Includes index.
ISBN 0887962092

—Investing in the Oil and Gas Industry in Canada / Vancouver : British Columbia Continuing Legal Education Society, 1981.
222p.
ISBN 0865040354 Hbk £40.00

—Roitman Investments Limited Act, 1983, Bill Pr009 : An Act to Revive Roitman Investments Limited / Ontario : Ontario Government Publications Service, 1983.
2p.

—Tax incentives for investment : the state of the art / Richard M. Bird. – Toronto : Canadian Tax Foundation, 1980.
ix, 68 p.; 23 cm.
Includes index. Bibliography: p. 61-66.
ISBN 0888080042 pbk. £4.50

—Taxation of income of foreign affiliates / by David A. Ward. – Toronto : Carswell, 1983.
vi,237p.
Includes index. 'Being Chapter 20 of Ward's Tax Law and Planning by The Partners of Davies, Ward & Beck and Brian J. Arnold' - t.p.
ISBN 0459358707

INVESTMENTS - CHINA

—China's investment laws : new directions / Guiguo Wang. – Singapore : Butterworths, 1988.
ix,272p.
Covers China's investment environment, foreign investment, new revisions promulgated by the central government, the relaxed rules of the SEZ, the corporate law of the SEZ, SEZ regulations on foreign banks, comparative analysis of the new laws, and the practical significance of the new law. An appendix gives practical guidance to investing in China. With an index.
ISBN 0409995606 Hbk £119

INVESTMENTS - ENGLAND

—Regulation of investment business / The Securities and Investments Board. – 2 (loose-leaf). – London : The Board, 1986.
34cm.
Accompanied by: Further ammendments proposed to the February drafts of rules ... xix,125p.

—Rules and regulations / The Securities and Investments Board. – 3. – London : The Board, 1987.
looseleaf.
Accompanied by: Overview, consultative papers and documents, etc..

INVESTMENTS - EUROPEAN COMMUNITY

—Reports of the ninth Congress, 25-27 September 1980 / Federation Internationale pour le Droit Eruopeen. – 3. – S.l. : FIDE, 1980.
21cm.
Includes papers in French and German.
ISBN 0421278501 Pbk £25.00

INVESTMENTS - GREAT BRITAIN

—Allied Hambro Expatriate Tax and Investment Guide / London : Oyez Longman, 1984.
ISBN 0851208355 Hbk £9.95

—Allied Hambro Investment Guide 1984 / London : Oyez Longman, 1984.
ISBN 085120838X Hbk £10.95

—Basic Investment Appraisal / London : Butterworths, 1985.
ISBN 0408015675 Pbk £10.95

—Bulletin / the Securities Association. – London : The Association, 1988.
Alternative title: TSA bulletin.

—Capital allowances in law and practice / R. J. Pickerill. – 2nd ed. – London : Institute of Chartered Accountants, 1981.
xix,307p. – (Chartac taxation guides).
ISBN 0852913079

—Conduct of business rules : a new approach / Securities and Investments Board. – 1. – London : The Board, 1988.
various pagings.

—Encyclopaedia of Investor Protection / London : Butterworths, 1987.

—Guide to the Financial Services Act 1986 / A.J. Wedgwood ... et al. – London : Financial Training, 1986.
xi,371p.
Includes index. Includes the text of the Act.
ISBN 1851850503

—Investing in Britain : jobs and industry / Labour Party. – London : Labour Party, 1985.
23p.

—Investment in Shares and Securities / London : Butterworths, 1988.
ISBN 0406504504 Pbk £40.00

—Investment Institutions / 4th ed. – Plymouth : Macdonald & Evans, 1984.
180p.
ISBN 0712155074 Pbk £4.75

—Investments / 3rd ed. – Prentice-Hall, 1985.
ISBN 0135047137 Pbk £18.50

—Inward investment : policy options for the United Kingdom / Michael Brech and Margaret Sharp. – London : Routledge and Kegan Paul, 1983.

—Personal Financial Planning Manual 1986-87 / John Rayer. – London : Butterworths, 1986.
This manual is a guide to the compilation of personal financial packages for United Kingdom investors. Investments, family finances, life insurance, pensions, and capital transfer tax are covered in the book.
ISBN 040600563X Hbk

—Project financing / by Peter K. Nevitt. – 4th ed. – London : Euromoney, 1983.
xiii,273p.
Includes index.
ISBN 0903121395

—The Regulation of Unit Trusts / London : LLoyd's of London Press, 1989.
ISBN 1850441626 Hbk

—Rules / The Securities Association. – 3rd ed. 1. – London : The Association, 1988.
looseleaf.
Popular title: TSA rule book.

—Securities and Investments Board / a report by the Director General of Fair Trading to the Secretary of State for Trade and Industry. – London : Office of Fair Trading, 1987.
77p.

INVESTMENTS - HONG KONG

—Guidebook to Taxation and Investment Law in Hong Kong / 2nd ed. – North Ryde : C.C.H. Australia, 1985.
276p.
ISBN 0869037811

—Investor Prot., Corp. Disclosure and Insider Dealing in HK / London : Butterworths, 1988.
ISBN 0409995460 Hbk

INVESTMENTS - INDIA

—Non-Residents : Taxation and Investment in India / G.S. Pikale. – Bombay : Jaico Publishing House.

INVESTMENTS - PHILIPPINES

—Corporation Code of the Phillipines with the Omnibus Investment Code / Quezon City : University of the Philippines, Law Center, 1981.
207p.

INVESTMENTS - SWEDEN

—Studies in Swedish Post-War Industrial Investments / Stockholm : Almqvist & Wiksell, 1982.
122p.
ISBN 9155413587 Hbk £62.00

INVESTMENTS - UNITED STATES

—Investment in US Real Estate / London : Oyez Longman, 1984.
– (Oyez Longman Intelligence Report Ser.).
ISBN 0851208495 Hbk

IRAN

—International and legal problems of the gulf / S.H. Amin. – London : Middle East and North African Studies Press, 1981.
235p.
Bibls..
ISBN 0906559057

—Iran-Iraq war : legal implications / S.H. Amin. – Glasgow : Royston, 1982.
26p.
Reprinted from Marine Policy, vol. 6, no. 3 (July 1982).

IRAQ

—International and legal problems of the gulf / S.H. Amin. – London : Middle East and North African Studies Press, 1981.
235p.
Bibls..
ISBN 0906559057

—Iran-Iraq war : legal implications / S.H. Amin. – Glasgow : Royston, 1982.
26p.
Reprinted from Marine Policy, vol. 6, no. 3 (July 1982).

IRAQI-IRANIAN CONFLICT, 1980–

—Iran-Iraq war : legal implications / S.H. Amin. – Glasgow : Royston, 1982.
26p.
Reprinted from Marine Policy, vol. 6, no. 3 (July 1982).

IRELAND

—Fooled again? : the Anglo-Irish Agreement and after / Anthony Coughlan. – Cork : Mercier, 1986.
88p; 21cm.
ISBN 0853427747 Pbk £4.95

—Irish offical publications : a guide to Republic of Ireland papers, with a breviate fo reports 1922-1972 / by Arthur Maltby and Brian McKenna. – Oxford : Pergamon, 1980.
xi,377p; 26cm. – (Guides to official publications).
Includes index.
ISBN 0080237037 £22.50

—Partition in Ireland, India and Palestine : theory and practice / T.G. Fraser. – London : Macmillan, 1984.
xiii,225p; 23cm.
Bibliography: p210-213. - Includes index.
ISBN 0333322800 £22.50

IRRIGATION

—Irrigation users' organizations in the legislation and administration of certain Latin American countries / by Miguel Solanes. – Rome : Food and Agriculture Organization of the United Nations, 1983.
vii,87p. – (Legislative study).
Includes bibliographical references.
ISBN 9251011702

ISLAM - INDONESIA

—Struggle of Islam in modern Indonesia / B. J. Boland. – The Hague : Martinus Nijhoff, 1982.
viii,283p.
'Slightly revised reprint' of 1971 edition. Bibliography: p267-274.
ISBN 9024761816 Hbk

ISLAM - SINGAPORE

—The legal status of the Muslims in Singapore / Singapore : Malayan Law Journal, 1965.
95.
Intends to set out the legal position of the Muslims, including the Malays, in Singapore. Contains a historical introduction, a summary of the existing statute and the case law relating to the family law, the law of property and the law relating to the construction of wills and trust instruments as they affect the Muslims in Singapore, and the history of Muslim endowments.

ISLAM AND JUSTICE

—Islamic conception of justice / Majid Khadduri. – Baltimore : Johns Hopkins University Press, 1984.
xvi,256p; 24cm.
Bibliography: p243-249. - Includes index.
ISBN 0801832454 £22.20

ISLAMIC COUNTRIES

—Charter of the Islamic Conference and legal framework of economic co-operation among its member states : a study of the charter, the General Agreement for Economic, Technical and Commercial Co-operation and the Agreement for Promotion, Protection and Guarantee of Investments among Member States of the OIC / Hasan Moinuddin. – Oxford : Clarendon, 1986.
xx,322p; 22cm.
Bibliography: p297-313. - Includes index.
ISBN 0198255241 £30.00

ISLAMIC LAW

—Analogical Reasoning in Islamic Jurisprudence / Islamabad : Islamic Research Institute, 1986.
viii, 489p.
ISBN 9694080649 Hbk £20.00

—Charter of the Islamic Conference and legal framework of economic co-operation among its member states : a study of the charter, the General Agreement for Economic, Technical and Commercial Co-operation and the Agreement for Promotion, Protection and Guarantee of Investments among Member States of the OIC / Hasan Moinuddin. – Oxford : Clarendon, 1986.
xx,322p; 22cm.
Bibliography: p297-313. - Includes index.
ISBN 0198255241 £30.00

—Code of Muslim personal law / by Tanzil-ur-Rahman. – 2. – Karachi : Hamdard Academy, 1978.
Bibliography: vol.1, p.v-viii. - Includes index. Vol. 2 published: Karachi: Islamic Publishers.
ISBN 0195772857 v.2

—The effect of Islamic legislation on crime prevention in Saudi Arabia : proceedings of the symposium held in Riyadh, 16-21 Shawal 1396 A.H. (9-13 October 1976) / Saudi Arabia : Ministry of Interior Crime Prevention Research Centre, 1980.
x,606p.
'Translated, edited and printed in collaboration with the United Nations Social Defence Research Institute (UNSDRI). Translated from the Arabic.

—First Step in Islamic Law in West Africa / Alexander David Russel. – Lagos : Islamic Publications Bureau, 1986.
ISBN 9782470120 Hbk £7.50

—Humanism and the law : the case of the shari'ah / by Isma'il R. Al Faruqi. – Lagos : Nigerian Institute of Advanced Legal Studies, 1983.
17p. – (Occasional paper).

—Islamic criminal justice system / M. Cherif Bassiouni, editor. – London : Oceana Publications, 1981.
Primarily selected papers from the 1st International Conference on the Protection of Human Rights in the Islamic Criminal Justice System held May 1979 at the International Institute of Higher Studies in Criminal Sciences, Syracuse, Sicily, and sponsored by the International Association of Penal Law and the Arab Organization for Social Defense against Crime. Appendices : A. Summary report of the first International Conference on the Protection of Human Rights in the Islamic Criminal Justice System, May 1979, International Institute of Higher Studies in Criminal Sciences, Siracusa, Italy – B. List of conference participants – C. Final resolution adopted by conference.
ISBN 0379207451 Hbk £30.00

—Islamic Jurisprudence / Islamabad : Islamic Research Institute.
ca 500p.

—Islamic Jurisprudence / New Delhi : Deep and Deep Publications, 1988.
338p.

—Islamic jurisprudence : an international perspective / C.G. Weeramantry : foreword by M. Hidayatullah : message from His Eminence the Grand Sheikh of Al-Azhar University, Cairo. – Basingstoke : Macmillan, 1988.
xix,207p; 23cm.
Bibliography: p189-200. - Includes index.
ISBN 0333446682 £29.50

—Islamic Jurisprudence and the Rule of Necessity and Need / Islamabad : Islamic Research Institute, 1980.
72p.
ISBN 9694080355 Hbk £3.00

—Islamic law in South-East Asia / M.B. Hooker. – Singapore : O.U.P., 1984.
xxx,330p.
Bibliography: p.281-296. - Includes index.
ISBN 0195825039

—Islamic law in the contemporary world : introduction, glossary and bibliography / by Sayed Hassan Amin. – Glasgow : Royston, 1985.
ix,190p; 22cm.
Bibliography: p153-172. - Includes index.
ISBN 0946706247 Pbk £15.00

—Juristic Differences and How to Solve Them in an Islamic State / Lagos : Islamic Publications Bureau.

—Lawful and the Prohibited in Islam / London : Shorouk International, 1985.
ISBN 1850240027 Pbk £6.50

—Legal and political structure of an Islamic state : implications for Iran and Pakistan / by Y. Noori and S.H. Amin. – Glasgow : Royston, 1986.
144p; 22cm.
Includes bibliography and index.
ISBN 094670631X £30.00

—Muslim Law / 2nd ed. 1980 repr. – Lucknow : Eastern Book Company, 1985.
376p.

—Muslim Law and the Constitution / Calcutta : Eastern Law House, 1985.

—Non-Muslims under Shari'ah : (Islamic Law) / Lahore : Kazi Publications.

—Penal Law of Islam / Lahore : Kazi Publications.

—Roman, provincial and Islamic law : the origins of the Islamic patronate / Patricia Crone. – Cambridge : Cambridge University Press, 1987.
178p; 23cm. – (Cambridge studies in Islamic civilization).
Examines cultural origins of Islamic Law. Studies hypothesis that a substantial source was Roman law with reference to patronate. Concludes Roman law contributed only through being part of the law of Near Eastern provinces.
ISBN 0521322537 £25.00

—Shariahi : Islamic Law / Ta-Ha Publishers, 1984.
ISBN 0907461387 Pbk £6.50

—Sources and development of Mulim law / Singapore : Malayan Law Journal, 1965.
142.
Studies the sources of Muslim law, and attempts to bring together the views of the 'Orientalists' and the Muslim authorities. Traces the development of Muslim law from the year 13 before Hijrah to the present day, and also looks to the future of Muslim law. Looks at the writing of Muslim jurists.

—Unlawful gain and legitimate profit in Islamic law : riba, gharar and Islamic banking / Nabil A. Saleh. – Cambridge : Cambridge University Press, 1986.
xii,130p; 24cm. – (Cambridge studies in Islamic civilization).
Examines ban on taking interest and rejection of aleatory contracts in Islamic law. Considers consequent conflict with world banking system. Studies these rules in the four Sunni schools of law and the Ibadi.
ISBN 0521322987 £19.50

—Woman in Shari'ah (Islamic law) / Abdur Rahman I. Doi. – s.l. : s.n., 1983.
286p.
Bibliography: pp.267-281. - Includes index.

ISLAMIC LAW - ISLAMIC COUNTRIES
—Commercial arbitration in the Arab Middle East : a study in Shara and statute law / Samir Saleh. – London : Published under the patronage of the International Chamber of Commerce by Graham & Trotman, 1984.
380p.
Bibliography: p445-455. - Includes index.
ISBN 0860104532 £55.00

ISLAMIC LAW - NIGERIA
—Islamic Law in Nigeria / Lagos : Islamic Publications Bureau, 1988.
ISBN 9782470376 Hbk £25.00

—Shari'a law reports / Zaria, Nigeria : Centre for Islamic Studies, Ahmadu Bello University, 1980.
Variant title: Shari'ah law reports. Numbering irregular. In English and Hausa.

ISLAMIC LAW - PERIODICALS
—Journal of Islamic and comparative law : journal of the Centre of Islamic Legal Studies, Faculty of Law, Ahmadu Bello University, Zaria, Nigeria / Zaria : The Centre, 1968.
Continues: Journal of the Centre of Islamic Legal Studies.

ISLANDS
—Development of maritime islands as extreme examples of peripheral regions / report prepared by the Committee of Experts on Social and Economic Activities of the Steering Committee for Regional and Municipal Matters, with the assistance of Italo Ferrari. – Strasbourg : Council of Europe, 1986.
26p.

ISLE OF MAN - GREAT BRITAIN
—Isle of Man : a low-tax area / by Mark Solly. – Croydon : Tolley, 1984.
ix,458p.
Includes index.
ISBN 0854591397

ISRAEL
—Israel and Palestine / Preparatory Committee for the Russell Hearings on Lebanon and the Occupied Territories. – London : Spokesman Books, 1984.
– (End Papers: No. 9).
ISBN 0851244041 Hbk £3.95

ISRAEL-ARAB BORDER CONFLICTS, 1949-
—Arab-Israeli conflict : a politico-legal analysis / J.R. Gainsborough. – Aldershot : Gower, 1987.
xxxv,345p; 23cm.
Bibliography: p319-334. - Includes index.
ISBN 0566008181 £25.00

ISRAEL-ARAB WAR, 1948-1949
—Arab-Israeli conflict : a politico-legal analysis / J.R. Gainsborough. – Aldershot : Gower, 1987.
xxxv,345p; 23cm.
Bibliography: p319-334. - Includes index.
ISBN 0566008181 £25.00

ISRAEL-ARAB WAR, 1967
—Civilian administration in the occupied West Bank : analysis of Israeli Military Government Order no. 947 / by Jonathan Kuttab and Raja Shehadeh. – Ramallah : Law in the Service of Man, 1982.
44p.
ISBN 9290370181

—Human rights in the Israeli-occupied territories, 1967-1982 / Esther Rosalind Cohen. – Manchester : Manchester University Press, 1985.
xxii,500p.
Bibliography: p470-498. - Includes index.
ISBN 0719017262 £30.00

—Rule of law in the areas administered by Israel / Israel National Section of the International Commission of Jurists. – Tel Aviv : Israel National Section of the International Commission of Jurists, 1981.
xiv,114p.
Includes bibliographical references.

JERSEY - GREAT BRITAIN
—Constitutional history of Jersey / F. de L. Bois. – Rev. repr. 1981. – Jersey : States' Greffe, Jersey, 1981.
311p.
Revision of: 1972 ed.. Includes index.

JEWISH LAW
—Jewish law annual / Leiden : Brill, 1978-.

—Law and religion : the Jewish experience / Ze'ev W. Falk. – Jerusalem : Mesharim, 1981.
238p.
Bibliography: p.237-238.

—Modern research in Jewish law / edited by Bernard S. Jackson. – Leiden : E.J. Brill, 1980.
vii157p; 24cm.
ISBN 9004061290

—Tree of life : diversity, flexibility, and creativity in Jewish law / Louis Jacobs. – Oxford : Published for the Littman Library by Oxford University Press, 1984.
310p; 25cm.
Bibliography: p278-293. - Includes index.
ISBN 0197100392 £18.00

JEWISH-ARAB RELATIONS
—Palestinians / by David McDowall. – New ed. – London : Minority Rights Group, 1987.
35p. – (Report).
Previous ed.: 1984. Includes bibliographical references.
ISBN 0946690421

JEWS
—Israel yearbook on human rights / v. – Tel Aviv : Published under the auspices of the Faculty of Law, Tel Aviv University, 1971.
ISBN 03335925

—Jews of Africa and Asia : contemporary anti-semitism and other pressures / Tudor Parfitt. – London : Minority Rights Group, 1987.
15p. – (Report).
Bibliography: p.15.
ISBN 0946690561

JOB EVALUATION - ENGLAND
—Job evaluation schemes free of sex bias / Equal Opportunities Commission. – Manchester : The Commission, 1981.
ISBN 0905829395

JOINT VENTURES
—Approach to the analysis of joint ventures / by Neil Kay, Jean-Philippe Robe and Patrizia Zagnoli. – Florence : European University Institute, 1987.
39p.

—Arab comparative & commercial law : the international approach : proceedings : International Bar Association first Arab Regional Conference, Cairo 15-19 February 1987 / International Bar Association. – London : Graham & Trotman, 1987.
Contents: v. 1. The Sharia and its relevance to modern transnational transactions. The settlement of disputes through arbitration. Joint ventures. – v. 2. Energy law.
ISBN 086010978X v. 2

—Competition policy and joint ventures / Organisation for Economic Co-operation and Development. – Paris : Organisation for Economic Co-operation and Development, 1986.
111p.
ISBN 9264128980

—Contractual adaptation and conflict resolution, based on venture contracts for mining projects in developing countries / Martin Bartels : translation by James E. Silva. – Deventer, Netherlands : Kluwer Law and Taxation, 1985.
187 p.; 25 cm. – (Studies in transnational law of natural resources).
Includes bibliographical references. 'List of cited agreements': p. 177-187.
ISBN 3787540237

—Energy law '88 : proceedings of the advanced seminar on petroleum, minerals and energy resources law organised by the IBA's Section on Energy and Natural Resources Law in Sydney, Australia, March 1988 / London : Graham & Trotman and International Bar Association, 1988.
xii,865p.
ISBN 1853330973

—Handbook of international joint ventures / John Walmsley. – London : Graham & Trotman, 1983.
viii,161p; 24cm.
Includes index.
ISBN 0860103692 £22.00

—Joint development of resources projects : a comparison : proceedings of the Regional Energy Law Seminar, Singapore, 30 September 1985 / International Bar Association. Section on Energy and Natural Resources Law. – London : International Bar Assocation, 1985.
Various pagings.

—Joint ventures / Edgar Herzfeld. – Bristol : Jordan, 1983.
vii,105p.
Bibliography: p.99-102. - Includes index.
ISBN 0853080704

—Joint ventures in the construction industry : papers presented at the 7th Conference of the International Bar Association's Section on Business Law, Singapore 1985 / International Construction Contracts Committee of the Section on Business Law of the International Bar Association. – 1. – London : International Bar Association, 1985.
Various pagings.
Includes bibliographical references.

—Legal aspects of joint ventures in Eastern Europe / edited Dennis Campbell. – Deventer : Kluwer, 1981.
133p; 25cm.
Includes index.
ISBN 9065440348 Unpriced

—Mining ventures in developing countries / Erich Schanze. – Deventer : Kluwer, 1981.
281p.
First published: Frankfurt am Main, Metzner; Deventer, Kluwer; 1977- , as 'Rohstofferschliessungsvorhaben in Entwicklungslandern'. Translated from German into English.
ISBN 9065440380

JOINT VENTURES - CHINA
—Guide to joint equity ventures / 2nd ed. – Beijing : External Services Department of Economic Daily, 1986.
243p.
Includes text of legislation. Includes title in Chinese. Text in English and Chinese.

JOINT VENTURES - EUROPE
—Mergers and joint ventures in Europe: the law and policy of the EEC / London : Graham & Trotman, 1989.
220; 240mm.
Explores how articles 85 and 86 of the Treaty of Rome would operate in the context of mergers and production joint ventures, and to non EEC firms seeking to acquire firms in the EEC. Analyses the Draft Regulation for the Control of Mergers, and includes its text in the Annexes.
ISBN 185333314X Hbk £50

JOINT VENTURES - EUROPEAN COMMUNITY
—Joint ventures and Article 85 / Jonathan Faull. – London : Law Society Solicitors' European Group, 1985.
26p.
'Transcript of a talk given to the Solicitor's European Group on March 19th 1984'.

JOINT VENTURES - GREAT BRITAIN
—Joint ventures / London : Longman Professional, 1988.
ISBN 0851213189 Hbk

—Joint ventures in the Kingdom of Saudi Arabia / John Walmsley. – 2nd ed. – London : Graham & Trotman, 1985.
388p; 25cm.
Previous ed.: 1979. Bibliography: p381. - Includes index.
ISBN 0860106799 £43.00

JOINT VENTURES - SAUDI ARABIA
—Joint ventures in the Kingdom of Saudi Arabia / John Walmsley. – 2nd ed. – London : Graham & Trotman, 1985.
388p; 25cm.
Previous ed.: 1979. Bibliography: p381. - Includes index.
ISBN 0860106799 £43.00

JOINT VENTURES - SINGAPORE
—Construction Joint Ventures in Singapore / Butterworths, 1985.
332p.
Covers legal form and operational structure, the sponsor, selection of the joint venture partners, constituting the joint venture, the management board, implications arising from the construction contract, legal implications of a joint venture partnership, legal issues affecting the corporate joint venture, governing law, and minority protection.
ISBN 0409995029 Hbk £75.00

JOINT VENTURES - UNITED STATES
—Joint ventures in the United States / edited by John I. Forry, Mark R. Joelson. – London : Butterworths, 1988.
200p; 24cm.
Includes index.
ISBN 0406499616 £40.00

JUDAISM AND STATE
—Law, religion and the Jewish community / by Graham Zellick. – London : Jews' College, 1987.
Delivered at Jews' College on April 2 1986. Revised February 1987.

JUDGMENTS
—Enforcement of Money Judgments Abroad / Matthew Bender, 1988.
ISBN 0000999070 Hbk £53.00

—Judgements and How to Write Them / 3rd ed. – Lucknow : Eastern Book Company, 1974.
216p.

JUDGMENTS - CANADA
—Reasons for Judgment / Toronto : Butterworths, 1980.
112p.
ISBN 0409843644 Hbk £40.00

JUDGMENTS - CANADA - BRITISH COLUMBIA
—Report on the Court Order Interest Act / Law Reform Commission of British Columbia. – Vancouver : The Commission, 1987.
139p.
Includes bibliographical references.
ISBN 077188561X

JUDGMENTS - ENGLAND

—Justice, Lord Denning and the constitution / edited by Peter Robson and Paul Watchman. – Farnborough, Hants. : Gower, 1981.
xvi,253p; 23cm.
Bibliography: px-xi. - Includes index.
ISBN 0566003996 Hbk £10.50
ISBN 0566004542 Pbk £5.95

—Lord Denning : the judge and the law / edited by J.L. Jowell, J.P.W.B. McAuslan. – London : Sweet & Maxwell, 1984.
xxxv,486p; 26cm.
Bibliography: p477-478. - Includes index.
ISBN 0421281200 £25.00

JUDGMENTS - GREAT BRITAIN

—Civil Jurisdictions and Judgment Acts 1982 / London : Butterworths, 1983.
This work provides a procedural guide to the Act. The 1982 Act incorporates into United Kingdom law the 1968 EEC Convention on jurisdiction and the enforcement of judgements in civil matters.
ISBN 0406005303 Hbk

—Enforcement of a Judgement (LPPN4) / 7th ed. – London : Longman Professional, 1986.
ISBN 0851210236 Pbk £15.50

JUDGMENTS - INDIA

—Supreme Court Labour Judgments 1950-1983. 15 Vols. / Allahabad : Law Publishing House, 1984.

JUDGMENTS - NIGERIA

—Selected Judgments of the Federal Supreme Court of Nigeria : 1956-60, 3 Vols. / Professional Books Staff. – Abingdon : Professional Books, 1984.
ISBN 0862050480 Hbk £104.00

—Selected Judgments of the High Court of Oyo State : 1976-1980 / Professional Books Staff. – Abingdon : Professional Books, 1984.

JUDGMENTS AND ORDERS - AUSTRALIA

—Reference on service and execution of warrants and writs of attachment / Australian Law Reform Commission. – Sydney : The Commission, 1984.
v,109,6p.
Bibliography: p.109.

JUDGMENTS AND ORDERS - AUSTRALIA - NEW SOUTH WALES

—Community law reform program / New South Wales Law Reform Commission. – Sydney : The Commission, 1985.
xiii,123p. – (L.R.C. 46).
Includes bibliographical references.
ISBN 0730514714 Hbk

JUDGMENTS AND ORDERS - CANADA - ONTARIO

—Report on the enforcement of judgment debts and related matters / Ontario Law Reform Commission. – 5 v. – Toronto : Ministry of the Attorney General, 1981.
Includes bibliographical references.
ISBN 0774360593 v.3

JUDGMENTS AND ORDERS - COMMONWEALTH

—Recognition of family judgements in the Commonwealth / London : Butterworths, 1983.
ISBN 040640321X Hbk £42.00

JUDGMENTS AND ORDERS - GREAT BRITAIN

—Forms of Judgement and Orders in the High Court of Justice and Court of Appeal, 3 Vols. / London : Sweet & Maxwell, 1985.
ISBN 0421346000 Hbk £150.00

—Judgments and Orders / 3 vols. – London : Sweet & Maxwell, 1981 Reprint.
ISBN 0421346000 Hbk £150.00

—Law of Inhibition and Adjudication / London : Butterworths, 1987.
ISBN 0406104336 Pbk £18.00

JUDGMENTS, CRIMINAL - ITALY

—Carlotto affair : a terrible injustice / International Committee 'Justice for Massimo Carlotto'. – London : the Committee, 1987.
40p.

JUDICIAL ASSISTANCE

—Canadian criminal law, international and transnational aspects / Sharon A. Williams, J.-G. Castel. – Toronto : Butterworths, 1981.
xxx, 513 p.; 24 cm.
Includes bibliographical references and indexes. Part one is devoted to jurisdiction and the criminal law under international law and Canadian law. Part two deals with Canadian law applicable to specific offences of an international and transnational nature. Part three covers international cooperation in the field of criminal law and criminal procedure.
ISBN 0409876348 £80.00

—Explanatory report on the European Convention on Recognition and Enforcement of Decisions concerning Custody of Children and on Restoration of Custody of Children / Strasbourg : Council of Europe, 1980.
36p; 21cm.
Includes the text of the convention.

JUDICIAL ASSISTANCE - COMMONWEALTH

—Recognition and enforcement of judgments and orders and the service of process within the Commonwealth : a report of a working meeting held in Nairobi, Kenya, 9-14 January 1980 / London : Commonwealth Secretariat, 1980.
xii,160p.

JUDICIAL ASSISTANCE - ENGLAND

—Civil jurisdiction and enforcement of foreign judgments : the application in England and Wales of the Brussels Convention of 1968 on Jurisdiction and Enforcement of Judgments in Civil and Commercial Matters under the Civil Jurisdiction and Judgments Act 1982 / by Peter Kaye. – Abingdon : Professional Books, 1987.
cxvi, 1949p; 24cm.
Includes the text of the Civil Jurisdiction and Judgments Act 1982.
ISBN 0862050812

JUDICIAL ASSISTANCE - EUROPEAN COMMUNITY

—Guide to the civil jurisdiction and judgments convention / by Alan Dashwood, Richard Hacon & Robin White. – Deventer : Kluwer Law and Taxation, 1986.
648p.
Includes index and bibliography.
ISBN 9065442693 Hbk £265.00

JUDICIAL ASSISTANCE - GREAT BRITAIN

—International mutual asssistance in criminal matters : a discussion paper / Great Britain. – London : Criminal Department, Home Office, 1988.
6,24p.
Includes the text of the European Convention on Mutual Assitance in Criminal Matters.
ISBN 0862523362

JUDICIAL ASSISTANCE - IRELAND

—Hague Convention on the Service Abroad of Judicial and Extrajudicial Documents in Civil or Commercial Matters (1965) / the Law Reform Commission. – Dublin : The Commission, 1987.
vii,36p. – (LRC).
Includes the text of the convention. Cover title: Service of documents abroad re civil proceedings.

JUDICIAL DISCRETION - ENGLAND

—Judge, discretion, and the criminal trial / by Rosemary Pattenden. – Oxford : Clarendon, 1982.
xv,299p; 23cm.
Includes index.
ISBN 0198253737 £20.00

—Judicial discretion in sentencing by judges and magistrates / by Vivian Gerald Hines. – 1. – Chichester : Rose, 1982.
27cm.
Includes index.
ISBN 0859923169 £42.50

JUDICIAL DISCRETION - GREAT BRITAIN

—Judge, Discretion and the Criminal Trial / Oxford : Oxford University Press, 1982.
ISBN 0198253737 Hbk £22.50

JUDICIAL NOTICE - AUSTRALIA

—Evidence reference / Australian Law Reform Commission. – Sydney : The Commission, 1982.
vii,154p.
Includes bibliographical references.

JUDICIAL NOTICE - INDIA

—Law of Notices : Civil and Criminal, with Model Forms / 4th ed. – Allahabad : Law Book Co, 1984.

JUDICIAL OPINIONS

—Dissenting and separate opinions at the World Court / Ijaz Hussain. – The Hague : M. Nijhoff Publishers, 1984.
xv,335p.
Revision of thesis (doctorate)–University of Nice, 1974 under title: Le r$ole dialectique des opinions dissidentes et individuelles dans le developpement du droit international a la CIJ. Bibliography: p309-321. Includes index.
ISBN 9024729203 Hbk £145.00

JUDICIAL POWER

—Argentine Supreme Court : the court of constitutional guarantees / German J. Bidart Campos : translated by William J. Brisk, based on the book by German J. Bidart Campos, 'La Corte Suprema, tribunal de las garantias constitucionales'. – Argentine ed. – Buenos Aires : Allende & Brea, 1982.
viii, 143 p.; 26 cm.
Includes bibliographical references.
ISBN 9500621142

—Challenges to the legal profession : law and investment in developing countries : addresses, committee papers and reports of the 19th biennial conference of the International Bar Association at New Delhi / International Bar Association. – Lucknow : Eastern Book Co. in co-ordination with the International Bar Association and the Bar Association of India, 1984.
xx,787p.

—Judges and the judicial power : essays in honour of Justice V.R. Krishna Iyer / edited by Rajeev Dhavan, R. Sudarshan and Salman Khurshid. – London : Sweet & Maxwell, 1985.
xii,340p; 25cm.
Includes index.
ISBN 0421288604 No price

—Judicial independence : the contemporary debate / edited by Shimon Shetreet and Jules Desch $enes. – Dordrecht, the Netherlands : M. Nijhoff, 1985.
720p.
Includes index.
ISBN 9024731828 Hbk £245.00

—Judicial system envisaged in the draft treaty / by Thijmen Koopmans. – Florence : European University Institute, 1985.
57p.

—Role of the judge in contemporary society / Rome : Fratelli Palombi for UNSDRI and the International Association of Judges, 1984.
80p. – (Publication).

JUDICIAL POWER - AFRICA

—Contribution of the courts to government : a West African view / A.N.E. Amissah. – Oxford : Clarendon, 1981.
x,382p; 22cm.
Includes index.
ISBN 0198253567 £25.00

JUDICIAL POWER - AUSTRALIA

—Federal judicial system of Australia / by Harold Edward Renfree. – Sydney : Legal Books Pty Ltd., 1984.
xxxiii,802p.
Includes bibliographical references and index.
ISBN 0949553085

JUDICIAL POWER - EUROPEAN COMMUNITY

—Development of judicial control of the European Communities / Gerhard Bebr. – The Hague : Nijhoff, 1981.
xviii,882p; 25cm.
Bibliography: p719-808. - Includes index.
ISBN 9024725410 Hbk £360.00

JUDICIAL POWER - NIGERIA

—All Nigeria Judges Conference papers : Ilorin, Kwana State, 8-16th March 1982 / London : Sweet & Maxwell, 1984.
xx,391p; 23cm.
Includes index.
ISBN 0421309008 No price

—Judiciary in the government of Nigeria / by T. Akinola Aguda. – Ibadan : New Horn Press, 1983.
xii,183p.
Bibliography: p.183.
ISBN 9782266051

—Judiciary in the second republic of Nigeria, 1979-1983 / by F. Olisa Awogu. – Onitsha : Pacific Colege Press, 1984.
x,176p.
Bibliography: p.163-164. - Includes index.
ISBN 9782347108

—Relevance of the judiciary in the polity : in historical perspective / by A.G. Karibi-Whyte. – Lagos : Nigerian Institute of Advanced Legal Studies, 1987.
100p.
ISBN 9782353051

JUDICIAL PRECEDENT

—Stare decisis in Commonwealth appellate courts / David J. Murphy and Robert Rueter. – Toronto : Butterworths, 1981.
xv,117p.
Includes index.
ISBN 0409853739

—Supreme courts and judicial law-making : constitutional tribunals and constitutional review / by Edward McWhinney. – Dordrecht : M. Nijhoff, 1985.
320p.
Includes index.
ISBN 9024732034 Hbk £165.00

JUDICIAL PRECEDENT - ENGLAND

—Law-making process / Michael Zander. – London : Weidenfeld and Nicolson, 1980.
xxvi,309p.
ISBN 0297777505

—Precedent in law / edited by Laurence Goldstein. – Oxford : Clarendon Press, 1987.
xvi,279p; 23cm.
Bibliography: p249-273. - Includes index.
ISBN 0198255268 £27.50

JUDICIAL PRECEDENT - GREAT BRITAIN

—Precedent in law / Oxford : Oxford University Press, 1988.
ISBN 0198255268 Hbk £27.50

JUDICIAL PRECEDENT - IRELAND

—Sir John Davies and the conquest of Ireland / Cambridge : Cambridge University Press.
Examines law reports of Sir John Davies as Solicitor-General and Attorney-General in Ireland in the seventeenth-century. Discusses the use of law in consolidating the conquest of Ireland. Examines the origin of precedent in Anglo-American law.
ISBN 0521253284

JUDICIAL PRECEDENT - NIGERIA

—Precedent in Nigerian courts / by P.U. Umoh. - Enugu : Fourth Dimension Publishers, 1984.
xxviii,334p.
Bibliography: p.xxv-xxvi. Based on University of London Ph.D. thesis no. 526.
ISBN 9781561696

JUDICIAL PROCESS

—Appellate decision making in the common law world / Alan Paterson : Aleksander Peczenik. - Arnhem : Gouda Quint, 1985.
52p.
Papers presented at the first Symposium on Legal Decision Making of the Institute of Legal Decision Making, Erasmus University.
ISBN 9060003772

—Automated analysis of legal texts : logic, informatics, law : edited versions of selected papers from the Second International Conference on 'Logic, Informatics, Law,'Florence, Italy, September 1985 / edited by Antonio A. Martino, Fiorenza Socci Natali : editorial assistant, Simona Binazzi. - Amsterdam : North-Holland, 1986.
xxii, 938 p.; 25 cm.
Includes bibliographies and index.
ISBN 0444701117

—Equality and judicial neutrality / Sheilah L. Martin and Kathleen E. Mahoney, editors. - Toronto : Carswell, 1986.
xxvii, 430 p.; 24 cm.
Papers presented at a conference held in Banff, Alta., May 22-24, 1986. Includes bibliographical references.
ISBN 0459308319

—Judging : towards a rational judicial process / H. J. M. Boukema. - Zwolle, Holland : W.E.J. Tjeenk Willink, 1980.
xvi,181p.
Includes index. Bibliography: p141-148.
ISBN 9027117276

—Reason and reality / Stig Jrgensen. - Aarhus : Aarhus University Press, 1986.
159p.
Includes bibliographical references.
ISBN 8772880023

—Report of the seventh Commonwealth Magistrates' Conference : Nicosia, Cyprus 8th to 14th September 1985 / London : Commonwealth Magistrates' Association, 1985.
294p.

JUDICIAL PROCESS - AFRICA

—Judicial Process in Commonwealth Africa / Accra : Ghana Universities Press.
124p.

JUDICIAL PROCESS - BRITISH COMMONWEALTH

—Report of the sixth Commonwealth Magistrates' Conference, Port of Spain, 12-18 September 1982 / London : Commonwealth Magistrates' Association, 1983.
223p.
Includes bibliographical references. Includes keynote address: 'The judge and justice'.

JUDICIAL PROCESS - COMMONWEALTH

—Expediting Civil Litigation : A Study of Commonwealth Jurisdictions / London : Commonwealth Secretariat, 1983.
ISBN 0850922313 Hbk £5.00

—Judicial Process in Commonwealth Africa / Accra : Ghana Universities Press.
124p.

JUDICIAL PROCESS - ENGLAND

—Judges and the processes of judging / by Sir Roger Ormrod. - s.l. : s.n., 1980.
17p.
Holdsworth Club Presidential Address, 7th March 1980.

JUDICIAL PROCESS - EUROPEAN COMMUNITY

—On law and policy in the European Court of Justice : a comparative study in judicial policymaking / by Hjalte Rasmussen. - Dordrecht : M. Nijhoff, 1986.
xxv, 555 p.; 25 cm.
Summary in Danish. Thesis (doctoral)-University of Copenhagen, 1985. Includes bibliographies and indexes.
ISBN 9024732174 Hbk £295.00

JUDICIAL PROCESS - GREAT BRITAIN

—Policy arguments in judicial decisions / by John Bell. - Oxford : Clarendon, 1983.
xiv,283p; 23cm.
Bibliography: p271-276. - Includes index.
ISBN 0198253974 Unpriced

JUDICIAL PROCESS - INDIA

—Judicial reform : working paper : Conference on the Reform on sic the Indian Legal System / New Delhi : Indian Law Institute, 1983.
53p.
Caption title: Judicial reforms.

—Principles and Practices of Judicial Propriety : With Precedents and Case-Law / Allahabad : Hind Publishing House, 1986.
359p.

JUDICIAL PROCESS - NIGERIA

—Development and Judicial Trial in Nigeria / Onitsha : Africana-FEP.

JUDICIAL PROCESS - SRI LANKA

—Judicial Role Under Constitutions of Ceylon (Sri Lanka) / Colombo : 16.00.

JUDICIAL REVIEW

—Argentine Supreme Court : the court of constitutional guarantees / German J. Bidart Campos : translated by William J. Brisk, based on the book by German J. Bidart Campos, 'La Corte Suprema, tribunal de las garantias constitucionales'. - Argentine ed. - Buenos Aires : Allende & Brea, 1982.
viii, 143 p.; 26 cm.
Includes bibliographical references.
ISBN 9500621142

—Continental systems of judicial review (I) / Hideo Wada. - Tokyo : Institute of Social Sciences, Meiji University, 1981.
30p.
Reprint from: Bulletin of the Institute of Social Sciences Meiji University, Vol. 5, no. 1 (1981).

—Continental systems of judicial review (II) / Hideo Wada. - Tokyo : Institute of Social Sciences, Meiji University, 1981.
16p.
Reprint from: Bulletin of the Institute of Social Sciences Meiji University, Vol. 5, no. 2 (1981).

—European Parliament and Article 173 of the EEC Treaty / by John Barnard. - Florence : European University Institute, 1987.
59p.

—Judicial review in comparative perspective / Oxford : Clarendon Press, 1989.
300.
Applies the comparative method to the analysis of basic features of the judicial process, and their evolution in modern societies, especially Europe and America.
ISBN 0198256345 Hbk £30.00

—Judicial review of administrative action in the 1980's : problems and prospects : papers presented at a Conference held by the Legal Research Foundation Inc. at the University of Auckland on 20 and 21 February 1986 / edited by Michael Taggart : with a foreword by Lord Wilberforce. - Auckland : Oxford University Press, in association with the Legal Research Foundation Inc, 1986.
xx,208p; 24cm.
ISBN 0195581512

—Judicial review of the death penalty / David Pannick. - London : Duckworth, 1982.
245p; 23cm.
Includes index.
ISBN 0715615947 £18.00

—Judicial review, transnational and federal : its impact on integration / by Mauro Cappelletti and David Golay. - Florence : European University Institute, 1981.
143p.

—Supreme courts and judicial law-making : constitutional tribunals and constitutional review / by Edward McWhinney. - Dordrecht : M. Nijhoff, 1985.
320p.
Includes index.
ISBN 9024732034 Hbk £165.00

JUDICIAL REVIEW - CANADA

—Canadian Constitution and the Courts : the Function and Scope of Judicial Review / 3rd ed. - Butterworths, 1988.
400p.
New edition includes coverage of the major increase in the number of cases involving constitutional issues, the dominance of Charter questions in constitutional litigation, and the greatly heightened profile of the Supreme Court of Canada as innovating leader in the interpretation of the new constitutional provisions. Also notes early trends in judicial activism, or restraint, in Charter interpretation.
ISBN 0409806315 Hbk £80.00

—Government Procurement and Judicial Review / Agincourt : Carswell, 1988.
375p.

—Guide to Judicial Review / 2nd ed. - Agincourt : Carswell, 1984.
320p.
This work classifies and categorizes the most important principles of judicial review in Canada. The right to the opportunity to be heard, procedural aspect of judicial review, evidentiary aspect of judicial review, and other topics are discussed in the book.

—Guide to Judicial Review / 2nd ed. - Agincourt : Carswell, 1984.
ISBN 0459366106 Hbk £23.00

—Judicial Review Procedure Act / Vancouver : British Columbia Continuing Legal Education Society, 1980.
269p.

—Judicial Review Update / Vancouver : Continuing Legal Education Society of British Columbia, 1984.
184p.
ISBN 0865041563 Hbk £55.00

JUDICIAL REVIEW - EUROPEAN COMMUNITY

—Control of power within the European Communities : being the presidential address of Lord Mackenzie Stuart, president of the Holdsworth Club of the Faculty of Law in the University of Birmingham, 1985-1986 / Birmingham : Holdsworth Club of the University of Birmingham, 1986.
18p. - (The Holdsworth Club).
ISBN 0704408953

—Judicial protection in the European Communities / Henry G. Schermers. - 3rd ed. - Deventer, 1983.
xvi,495p.
ISBN 9065440518

JUDICIAL REVIEW - GREAT BRITAIN

—Judicial protection of fundamental rights under English law / by J. A. Jolowicz. The infiltration of equity into English commercial law / by G. Jones. - Deventer, The Netherlands : Kluwer, 1980.
- (The Cambridge-Tilburg law lectures ; 2d ser., 1979).
ISBN 9026811667

—Judicial review / Profex, 1985.
ISBN 095102860X Pbk £10.95

—Judicial review / Oliver. - London : Sweet & Maxwell, 1988.
- (Current Legal Problems).
ISBN 0421478000 Pbk

—Judicial review of public duties / Oxford : Clarendon Press, 1989.
300.
Examines the principles and remedies which have been applied in public duty cases such as postal strikes and licence applications. Argues that public duties should be taken more seriously by the courts.
ISBN 0198256078 Hbk £30

JUDICIAL REVIEW - INDIA

—Exclusion of Judicial Review : Administrative Efficiency Confronts Legitimacy of Power / Delhi : Metropolitan Book Co, 1987.
349p.
ISBN 8120002679 Hbk £200.00

JUDICIAL REVIEW - NIGERIA

—Justiciability of constitutional adjudication / a paper presented by Owolabi Kolawole at the Seminar on the Constitutional Adjudication in a Presidential System of Government, a comparative American and Nigerian experience, held at the Nigerian Institute of Advanced Legal Studies, University of Lagos, on Wednesday September 2, 1981. - Lagos : Nigerian Institute of Advanced Legal Studies, 1981.
20p.

JUDICIAL REVIEW - PAPUA NEW GUINEA

—Constitutional review jurisdiction in Papua New Guinea / researched and written by Peter Bayne. - Waigani : Law Reform Commission of Papua New Guinea, 1981.
iii,64p. - (Occasional paper).

JUDICIAL REVIEW - SOUTH AFRICA

—Investigation into the courts' powers of review of administrative acts / South African Law Commission. - Pretoria : The Commission, 1986.
v,110p. - (Project).

JUDICIAL REVIEW - WEST GERMANY

—Federalism and judicial review in West Germany / by Philip M. Blair. - Oxford : Clarendon Press, 1981.
xvii, 332p; 23cm.
Bibliography: p314-322. - Includes index.
ISBN 0198274270 £22.50

JUDICIAL REVIEW OF ADMINISTRATIVE ACTIONS

—Judicial Review of Governmental Action and the Requirement of an Interest to Sue : a Comparative Study on the Requirement of an Interest to Sue in National and International Law / Dordrecht : Kluwer, 1980.
lx, 557p.
ISBN 9028601201 Hbk £220.00

JUDICIAL REVIEW OF ADMINISTRATIVE ACTIONS - AUSTRALIA - WESTERN AUSTRALIA

—Working paper : the judicial review of administrative decisions / Law Reform Commission of Western Australia. – Perth : Law Reform Commission of Western Australia, 1981.
178p. – (Project).
Includes bibliographical references.

JUDICIAL REVIEW OF ADMINISTRATIVE ACTIONS - GREAT BRITAIN

—Judicial review of administrative action / Evans. – 4th ed. – London : Sweet & Maxwell, 1980.
ISBN 0420454004 Hbk £48.00

JUDICIAL REVIEW OF ADMINISTRATIVE ACTIONS - INDIA

—Judicial Control of Adminstrative Action / 2nd ed. – Allahabad : Law Book Company.

JUDICIAL REVIEW OF ADMINISTRATIVE ACTS - AUSTRALIA

—Cases and materials on review of administrative action / by S.D. Hotop. – 2nd ed. – Sydney : Law Book Co., 1983.
xxxiii,1219p.
Previous ed.: 1979. Includes bibliographical references and index.
ISBN 0455203776

—Review of administrative action / by Mark Aronson and Nicola Franklin : with a chapter on freedom of information legislation by Peter Bayne. – Sydney : Law Book Co., 1987.
lxvii,720p.
Includes bibliographical references and index.
ISBN 0455207216

—Review of pensions decisions under repatriation legislation : report to the Attorney-General / Administrative Review Council. – Canberra : Australian Government Publishing Service, 1983.
vi,60p. – (Parliamentary paper).
ISBN 0644028920

—Rights of review under the Migration Act 1958 and related legislation : interim report on the constitution for the Administrative Appeals Tribunal : report to the Attorney-General / Administrative Review Council. – Canberra : Australian Government Publishing Service, 1983.
v,6p. – (Report).
ISBN 0644028432

JUDICIAL REVIEW OF ADMINISTRATIVE ACTS - AUSTRALIA - WESTERN AUSTRALIA

—Report on judicial review of administrative decisions : procedural aspects and the right to reasons / Law Reform Commission of Western Australia. – Perth : The Commission, 1986.
77p. – (Project).
Includes bibliographical references.

JUDICIAL REVIEW OF ADMINISTRATIVE ACTS - CANADA

—Principles of administrative law / by David Philip Jones and Anne S. de Villars. – Toronto : Carswell, 1985.
xlv,489p.
ISBN 0459377604

JUDICIAL REVIEW OF ADMINISTRATIVE ACTS - CANADA - ALBERTA

—Judicial review of administrative action : application for judicial review / Institute of Law Research and Reform. – Edmonton : Institute of Law Research and Reform, 1984.
v,125p. – (Report).

JUDICIAL REVIEW OF ADMINISTRATIVE ACTS - CANADA - MANITOBA

—Report on administrative law / Manitoba Law Reform Commission. – Winnipeg : The Commission, 1987.
vi,243p. – (Report).
Includes bibliographical references.
ISBN 0771108338

JUDICIAL REVIEW OF ADMINISTRATIVE ACTS - CANADA - ONTARIO

—Charter of Rights and administrative law, 1983-1984 / section head, Garry J. Smith. – Agincourt, Ont. : Carswell Legal Publications, 1983.
xxix, 184 p.; 29 cm. – (Bar admission course materials / Law Society of Upper Canada).
Includes index. Bibliography: p. 173-179.
ISBN 0459360906

JUDICIAL REVIEW OF ADMINISTRATIVE ACTS - ENGLAND

—'Without the law' : administrative justice and legal pluralism in nineteenth-century England / H. W. Arthurs. – Toronto : University of Toronto Press, 1985.
xvi,312p; 24cm.
ISBN 0802056547

JUDICIAL REVIEW OF ADMINISTRATIVE ACTS - EUROPEAN COMMUNITY

—Judicial review of Community administrative acts / Sir Gordon Slynn. – Exeter : University of Exeter, 1985.
16p.
Includes bibliographical references.

JUDICIAL REVIEW OF ADMINISTRATIVE ACTS - GREAT BRITAIN

—Applications for judicial review : law and practice / Grahame Aldous, John Alder. – London : Butterworths, 1985.
250p; 26cm.
Includes index.
ISBN 0406273200 Pbk No price

—De Smith's judicial review of administrative action / by the late S.A. De Smith. – 4th ed. – London : Stevens, 1980.
lxviii,626p; 26cm.
Deals with ultra vires doctrine, the concept of jurisdiction, questions of law and questions of fact, natural justice, the review of discretionary powers, and the statutory restriction of judicial review. Section on Judicial Remedies, which includes a chapter on the procedure of application for judicial review.
ISBN 0420454004 Hbk £40.00

—Judicial review : law and procedure / by R.J.F. Gordon : foreword by the Hon. Mr Justice Mann. – London : Sweet & Maxwell, 1985.
xxxviii,207p; 26cm.
Includes index.
ISBN 0421334908 £19.85

—Judicial review : legal limits of official power / by C.T. Emery and B. Smythe : foreword by Sir Gordon Slynn. – London : Sweet & Maxwell, 1986.
xxxi,330p; 23cm.
Includes index.
ISBN 0421345209 Hbk £16.00
ISBN 0421345306 Pbk £11.95

—Justice : annual members conference held in the Lord Chief Justice's Court on Saturday 30th May 1987 : subject: judicial review of administrative action / Chairmen, Lord Scarman, Sir Patrick Neill. – London : Justice, 1987.
39 leaves.

—New directions in judicial review / edited by J.L. Jowell and D. Oliver. – London : Stevens, 1988.
xiii,96p.
Includes index.
ISBN 0420478000 £16.00

JUDICIAL REVIEW OF ADMINISTRATIVE ACTS - NEW ZEALAND

—Basis of judicial review in administrative law / by J.F. Northey. – Auckland : Legal Research Foundation, 1981.
31p.
Bibliography: p.30-31.
ISBN 0908581149

JUDICIAL REVIEW OF ADMINISTRATIVE ACTS - NIGERIA

—Prerogative writs and orders under Nigerian law and constitution / by S.I.O. Aguolu. – Enugu : Star Printing and Publishing Company, 1981.
xxii,167p.
Includes index.

JUDICIAL REVIEW OF ADMINISTRATIVE ACTS - SCOTLAND

—Judicial review in Scotland / John St. Clair, Neil F. Davidson. – Edinburgh : W. Green, 1986.
xxi,94p; 22cm.
Includes index.
ISBN 0414007743 £8.00

JUDICIAL SALES - MALTA

—Legal requirements for arrest and enforced sale of vessels : a comparative study / Malcolm H. Pace. – S.l. : s.n., 1983.
xxvi,144 leaves.
Thesis (LL.D.) - University of Malta 1983. Bibliography: p.142-144.

JUDICIARY

—Judge in developing countries / by Akinola Aguda. – Lagos : Nigerian Institute of Advanced Legal Studies, 1980.
38p. – (Occasional paper).
Includes bibliographical references.

—Judges and the judicial power : essays in honour of Justice V.R. Krishna Iyer / edited by Rajeev Dhavan, R. Sudarshan and Salman Khurshid. – London : Sweet & Maxwell, 1985.
xii,340p; 25cm.
Includes index.
ISBN 0421288604 No price

—Judicial independence : the contemporary debate / edited by Shimon Shetreet and Jules Desch $enes. – Dordrecht, the Netherlands : M. Nijhoff, 1985.
720p.
Includes index.
ISBN 9024731828 Hbk £245.00

—Order of the Coif / By Alexander Pulling. – London : W. Clowes and sons, 1884.
xxvi, 288 p; 27 cm.
'The subject of this work has been foreshadowed in the article under the same title in the Edinburgh review' for October, 1878.'–Pref.

—Report of the seventh Commonwealth Magistrates' Conference : Nicosia, Cyprus 8th to 14th September 1985 / London : Commonwealth Magistrates' Association, 1985.
294p.

—Role of the judge in contemporary society / Rome : Fratelli Palombi for UNSDRI and the International Association of Judges, 1984.
80p. – (Publication).

—Role of the judiciary in plural societies / edited by Neelan Tiruchelvam and Radhika Coomaraswamy. – London : Pinter, 1987.
xxi,193p; 23cm.
Includes index.
ISBN 0861876644 £22.50

JUDICIARY - AUSTRALIA

—Australian Judicial System : Report of the Advisory Committee to the Constitutional Commission / Kingston : Australian Government Publishing Service, 1987.
140p.

JUDICIARY - AUSTRALIA - NEW SOUTH WALES

—Justices Act and Summary Offences, New South Wales / R.N. Howie. – Butterworths, 1980.
ISBN 0409417408 loose £190.00

JUDICIARY - AUSTRALIA - VICTORIA

—Judges Through the Years : Being a Chronology of the Judges of the County Court of Victoria from its Inception (1852) / South Yarra : Hyland House, 1984.
176p.
ISBN 0908090676 Hbk £25.00

JUDICIARY - BRITISH COMMONWEALTH

—Report of the sixth Commonwealth Magistrates' Conference, Port of Spain, 12-18 September 1982 / London : Commonwealth Magistrates' Association, 1983.
223p.
Includes bibliographical references. Includes keynote address: 'The judge and justice'.

JUDICIARY - CANADA

—Book for Judges / Ottawa : Canadian Government Publishing Centre, 1980.
114p.

—Judges / Toronto : Macmillan of Canada.
ISBN 0771597290 Hbk £24.95

—Report and recommendations of Commission on Judges' Salaries and Benefits / Submitted to the Minister of Justice of Canada. – Ottawa : Department of Justice, 1983.
16,16p.
With French t.-p.: Rapport et recommandations de la Commission sur le Traitement et les Avantages des Juges. French and English text.
ISBN 0662527208

JUDICIARY - ENGLAND

—And nothing but the truth / Alan King-Hamilton : foreword by Lord Diplock. – London : Weidenfeld and Nicolson, 1982.
xvi,237p,8p of plates; 24cm.
Includes index.
ISBN 0297780530 £12.50

—English Judiciary in the Age of Glanvill and Bracton / Cambridge : Cambridge University Press, 1985.
ISBN 052126510X Hbk £30.00

—In my time : an autobiography / Lord Elwyn-Jones. – London : Weidenfeld, 1983.
319p.
Includes bibliography and index.
ISBN 0297781596

—Judges / David Pannick. – Oxford : Oxford University Press, 1987.
224p; 22cm.
Includes index.
ISBN 0192159569 £10.95

—Judges and the processes of judging / by Sir Roger Ormrod. – s.l. : s.n., 1980.
17p.
Holdsworth Club Presidential Address, 7th March 1980.

—Judging judges / Simon Lee. – London : Faber, 1988.
350p; 22cm.
Includes bibliography and index.
ISBN 0571148301 £12.95

—Judicial appointments : the Lord Chancellors policies and procedures / Great Britain. – London : Central Office of Information, 1986.
iv,20p.

—Judicial Bench in England, 1727-1875 : The Reshaping of a Professional Elite / London : Royal Historical Society, 1982.
– (Studies in History (London) Ser.: Vol. 29).
ISBN 0901050806 Hbk £19.60

—Law, justice and democracy / Lord McCluskey. – London : Sweet & Maxwell, 1987.
116p; 21cm.
Includes index.
ISBN 0421378905 Hbk £9.95
ISBN 0563205490 Pbk £5.95

—Report / Judicial Studies Board. – London : H.M.S.O., 1983-.

—Solicitors' and barristers' directory and diary : an almanac and directory incorporating the Law Society list of practising solicitors and the Senate of the Inns of Court and the Bar list of members / v. – London : Waterlow, 1984.
Merger of: The Bar list of the United Kingdom; and, The Solicitors' diary ... almanac and legal directory.
ISBN 0080391710

JUDICIARY - GREAT BRITAIN

—Judicial Pensions Bill : report on the consolidation of certain enactments relating to pensions and other benefits payable in respect of service in judicial office / the Law Commission and the Scottish Law Commission : chairmen: Michael Kerr, Law Commission; J.O.M. Hunter, Scottish Law Commission. – London : H.M.S.O., 1980.
11p.

—Law, Justice and the Judiciary : Transitional / Sinnadurai. – Professional Law, 1988.
ISBN 09679958002 Hbk £95.00

—Ninth report on top salaries / Review Body on Top Salaries : Chairman, Lord Plowden. – London : H.M.S.O., 1986.
v,31p. – (Report).
ISBN 0101978502

—Political judges and the rule of law / by Ronald Dworkin. – London : British Academy, 1980.
p.259-287.
From the Proceedings of the British Academy, v. 64 (1978).
ISBN 0856721824

JUDICIARY - GREAT BRITAIN - ENGLAND

—English judiciary in the age of Glanvill and Bracton c.1176-1239 / Cambridge : Cambridge University Press, 1985.
335.
Study of the evolution of the professional judiciary in medieval England. Describes the growth of a professional civil service.
ISBN 052126510X Hbk £30.00

JUDICIARY - INDIA

—Judiciary today : a plea for a collegium / Ramakrishna Hedge. – Bangalore : Governmnet of Karnataka, .
80p.

—Judiuciary today : disturbing trends and suggestion for reforms / Ramakrishna Hedge. – s.l. : Government of Karnataka, 1986.
15p.
'Address by Sir Ramakrishna Hedge, Chief Minister of Karnataka, delivered on 27th June, 1986 at the Bar Association of India Conference 1986 held at Bangalore'. - t.p. verso.

JUDICIARY - NIGERIA

—All Nigeria Judges Conference papers : Ilorin, Kwana State, 8-16th March 1982 / London : Sweet & Maxwell, 1984.
xx,391p; 23cm.
Includes index.
ISBN 0421309008 No price

—Judiciary in the government of Nigeria / by T. Akinola Aguda. – Ibadan : New Horn Press, 1983.
xii,183p.
Bibliography: p.183.
ISBN 9782266051

—Law and the twin pillars of justice / by C.A. Oputa. – Owerri Nigeria : Government Printer, 1981.
146p.
Collection of law lectures and papers presented by the author at various seminars and symposia.

—Shagari opens conference of Nigeria judges : spotlight on Mr. President's one day visit to Kwara State / Ilorin : Department of Information, 1982.
38p.

—Who is who in the judiciary / Rosaline Odeh. – Lagos : Department of Information, 1983.
105p.
Editor, Rosaline Odeh.

JUDICIARY - SCOTLAND

—Report of the Review Body on Use of Judicial Time in the Superior Courts in Scotland / Chairman: The Honourable Lord Maxwell. – Edinburgh : Scottish Courts Administration, 1986.
vi,164p.

JUDICIARY - SOUTH AFRICA

—Judges at work : the role and attitudes of the South African appellate judiciary, 1910-50 / by Hugh Corder. – Cape Town : Juta, 1984.
xxxii,252p.
Bibliography: pxxi-xxvi.
ISBN 0702114359

JUDICIARY - UNITED STATES

—Political judges and the rule of law / by Ronald Dworkin. – London : British Academy, 1980.
p.259-287.
From the Proceedings of the British Academy, v. 64 (1978).
ISBN 0856721824

JURIES - CANADA

—Criminal Jury Trials / Vancouver : Continuing Legal Education Society of British Columbia, 1988.
165p.
ISBN 0865049742 Hbk £70.00

—CRIMJI : Canadian Criminal Jury Instructions / Vancouver : Continuing Legal Education Society of British Columbia, 1987.
1,500p.
ISBN 0865043337 Hbk £300.00 (publication and disks)

—Jury Trials - 1985 / Vancouver : British Columbia Continuing Legal Education Society, 1985.
165p.
ISBN 0865041903 Hbk £60.00

—Peremptory Challenges in Civil Jury Trials / Victoria : Government of British Columbia, 1983.

—Psycholinguistic Principles Applicable to the Formulation of Jury Instructions : an Annotated Bibliography / Ottawa : Canadian Law Information Council, 1985.
60p.
ISBN 0920358853 Pbk £5.00

JURIES - IRELAND

—Judge or Jury? : the Jury Trial for Personal Injury Cases in Ireland / Cork : Cork University Press, 1985.
35p.
ISBN 0902561383 Pbk £1.50

JURISDICTION

—Jurisdiction to tax in international law: theory and practice of legislative fiscal jurisdiction / Kluwer Law and Taxation, 1989.
238. – (Series on International Taxation 9).
Deals with the bases and the limits of the right of states under international lw to create tax obligations on persons within and outside their territory. Describes the practice of states on matters of taxation in terms of the doctrine of jurisdiction in international law. Examines topics such as the taxation of mining activities on the continental shelf.
ISBN 9065444165 Hbk £51/Dfl 160

—Political role of law courts in modern democracies / edited by Jerold L. Waltman and Kenneth M. Holland. – Basingstoke : Macmillan, 1988.
viii,237p; 23cm.
Includes index.
ISBN 0333394054 £25.00

JURISDICTION - AUSTRALIA - QUEENSLAND

—Working paper on a bill to alter the civil jurisdiction of the District Court of Queensland / Queensland Law Reform Commission. – Brisbane? : the Commission?, 1984.
41,6p. – (Q.L.R.C.W.P.).

JURISDICTION - CANADA

—Interest and Jurisdictional Limits in the County and Provincial Courts / Victoria : Government of British Columbia, 1982.

—Minor Report on the Jurisdiction of Local Judges : Stays of Execution and Installment Orders / Victoria : Government of British Columbia, 1984.

—Nature of Jurisdiction in Canadian Criminal Law / Agincourt : Carswell, 1985.
280p.

—Perspectives on the harmonization of law in Canada / Ronald C.C. Cuming research coordinator. – Toronto : University of Toronto Press in cooperation with the Royal Commission on the Economic Union and Development Prospects for Canada and the Canadian Government Publishing Centre, 1985.
xviii,178p. – (Collected research studies).
Bibliography: p.176-177.
ISBN 0802073026

JURISDICTION - ENGLAND

—Civil jurisdiction and judgments : the application in England of the convention on jurisdiction and the enforcement of judgments in civil and commercial matters under the Civil Jurisdiction and Judgments Act 1982 / by T.C. Hartley. – London : Sweet & Maxwell, 1984.
xxi,233p; 25cm.
Includes index.
ISBN 0421311800 Pbk £18.00

JURISDICTION - GREAT BRITAIN

—Civil Jurisdictions and Judgment Acts 1982 / London : Butterworths, 1983.
This work provides a procedural guide to the Act. The 1982 Act incorporates into United Kingdom law the 1968 EEC Convention on jurisdiction and the enforcement of judgements in civil matters.
ISBN 0406005303 Hbk

—Industrial tribunal : a guide to the jurisdiction of industrial tribunals within the provisions of the following Acts : The Employment Act 1975, The Employment Protection (Consolidation) Act 1978, The Employment Act 1980, The Equal Pay Act 1970, The Sex Discrimination Act 1975, The Race Relations Act 1976 / Arthur H. Howell. – Chichester : Barry Rose, 1981.
38p; 26cm.
Cover title.
ISBN 0859922189 spiral £7.75

JURISDICTION - SCOTLAND

—Civil jurisdiction : the new rules : a guide for the perplexed / Robert Black. – Edinburgh : Law Society of Scotland, 1983.
vii,111p.
Includes index.
ISBN 0902023101

—Report of the Scottish Committee on Jurisdiction and Enforcement / chairman : Lord Maxwell. – Edinburgh : H.M.S.O., 1980.
xii,371p; 21cm.
ISBN 0114916667 Pbk £7.50

JURISDICTION (INTERNATIONAL LAW)

—Non-appearance before the International Court of Justice : functional and comparative analysis / Jerome B. Elkind. – Dordrecht : Martinus Nijhoff, 1984.
xiv,233p.
Bibliography: 207-213.
ISBN 9024729211 Hbk £110.00

—State immunity : an analytical and prognostic view / Gamal Moursi Badr. – The Hague : M. Nijhoff, 1984.
248p.
Includes bibliographical references and index.
ISBN 9024728800 Hbk £120.00

JURISDICTION (INTERNATIONAL LAW) - ASIA

—International jurisdiction and the recognition and enforcement of foreign judgements in the LAWASIA region : a comparative study of the laws of eleven Asian countries inter-se and with the E.E.C. countries / Bradford A. Caffrey. – Sydney : CCH Australia, 1985.
xxxii,407p.
Cover title: Enforcement of foreign judgements.
ISBN 0869037897

JURISPRUDENCE

—Analogical Reasoning in Islamic Jurisprudence / Islamabad : Islamic Research Institute, 1986.
viii, 489p.
ISBN 9694080649 Hbk £20.00

—Anthropological jurisprudence? : Leopold Pospisil and the comparative study of legal cultures / by Csaba Varga. – Budapest : Hungarian Academy of Sciences, Institute of Sociology, 1986.
34p. – (Underdevelopment and modernization).
Bibliography: p.30-34.

—Central issues in jurisprudence : justice, law and rights / by N.E. Simmonds. – London : Sweet & Maxwell, 1986.
xi,155p; 22cm.
Includes bibliographies and index.
ISBN 0421351101 Hbk £18.00
ISBN 0421351209 Pbk £8.95

—Concept of a legal system : an introduction to the theory of legal system / Joseph Raz. – 2nd ed. – Oxford : Clarendon Press, 1980.
ix,245p; 23cm.
Previous ed.: 1970. Bibliography: p.239-241. - Includes index. .
ISBN 019825363X Hbk £8.95
ISBN 0198253621

—Critical legal studies movement / Roberto Mangabeira Unger. – Cambridge, Mass. : Harvard University Press, 1986.
128p; 24cm.
Bibliography: p121-122. - Includes index.
ISBN 0674177355 Hbk £15.25
ISBN 0674177363 Pbk No price

—English-Speaking Justice / Toronto : Anansi Press, 1985.
64p.
ISBN 0887841414 Pbk £5.95

—Essays in jurisprudence and philosophy / by H.L.A. Hart. – Oxford : Clarendon, 1983.
viii,396p; 23cm.
Collection of essays first published between 1953 and 1981. Includes index.
ISBN 0198253877 Pbk Unpriced
ISBN 0198253885 £7.50

—Essays in Jurisprudence and Philosophy / Oxford : Oxford University Press, 1983.
ISBN 0198253877 Hbk £19.50
ISBN 0198253885 Pbk £8.95

—Essays in legal theory : a collaborated work / edited by D.J. Galligan : editorial advisers Colin Howard and Michael Crommelin. – Melbourne : Melbourne University Press, 1984.
viii,256p; 22cm.
ISBN 0522842836

—Essays on Bentham : studies on jurisprudence and political theory / by H.L.A. Hart. – Oxford : Clarendon, 1982.
272p; 23cm.
Includes index.
ISBN 0198253486 Hbk £15.00
ISBN 0198254687 Pbk £4.95

—Essays on Kelsen / edited by Richard Tur and William Twining. – Oxford : Clarendon, 1986.
288p; 22cm.
Includes index.
ISBN 0198254709 £30.00

—Essays on Third World Perspectives in Jurisprudence / W.E. Conklin. – Singapore : Malayan Law Journal, 1984.
xvii, 442p.
Collection of jurisprudentially-orientated essays with particular reference to the problems and issues peculiar to the third world. Covers constitutional obligation in the third world, liberal conceptions and their applicability to the third world. and the jurisprudence of indigenous law.
ISBN 9971700352 Pbk £45.00

—Fundamental legal concepts of China and the West : a comparative study / Hyung I. Kim. – Port Washington : National University Publications, 1981.
xiii,175p; 23cm.
Bibliography: p165-175.
ISBN 0804692750 £14.85

—Grounds of liability : an introduction to the philosophy of law / Alan R. White. – Oxford : Clarendon, 1985.
x,128p; 23cm.
Bibliography: p122-126. - Includes index.
ISBN 0198761910 Hbk £15.00
ISBN 019876197X Pbk £6.95

—H.L.A. Hart / Neil MacCormick. – London : Edward Arnold, 1981.
184p; 22cm.
Includes index.
ISBN 071316333X Hbk Unpriced
ISBN 0713163348 Pbk £4.95

—Harm to others / Oxford : Oxford University Press, 1984.
ISBN 0195034090 Hbk £22.50

—Institutional theory of law : new approaches to legal positivism / Neil MacCormick and Ota Weinberger. – DordrechtHolland : Reidel, 1986.
xiv, 229p. – (Law and philosophy library).
ISBN 9027720797

—Invitation to the law / by C.G. Weeramantry. – Sydney : Butterworths, 1982.
xiv,369p.
Includes bibliographies and index.
ISBN 0409309346

—Islamic Jurisprudence / Islamabad : Islamic Research Institute.
ca 500p.

—Islamic Jurisprudence and the Rule of Necessity and Need / Islamabad : Islamic Research Institute, 1980.
72p.
ISBN 9694080355 Hbk £3.00

—Jurisprudence / R.W.M. Dias. – 5th ed. – London : Butterworths, 1985.
505p; cased.
Previous ed.: 1976. Includes index.
ISBN 0406574324 Pbk £24.50
ISBN 0406574316 £16.95

—Jurisprudence : a descriptive and normative analysis of law / Anthony D'Amato. – Dordrecht, The Netherlands : Nijhoff, 1984.
xiv, 334 p.; 25 cm.
Includes bibliographical references and index.
ISBN 902472919X Hbk £140.00

—Jurisprudence and Legal Theory / 3rd ed. – Lucknow : Eastern Book Company, 1986.
358p.

—Jurisprudence and Legal Theory / 9th ed. 1975 repr. – Lucknow : Eastern Book Company, 1985.

—Jurisprudence in a nutshell / Ian Duncanson, Geoffrey Samuel. – London : Sweet & Maxwell, 1980.
vii,84p; 18cm. – (New nutshells).
Includes bibliographies and index.
ISBN 0421273100 Pbk £1.50

—Jurisprudence of orthodoxy : Queen's University essays on H.L.A. Hart / edited by Philip Leith and Peter Ingram. – London : Routledge, 1988.
216p.
Bibliography: pp.201-210. - Includes index.
ISBN 0415003059

—Karl Llewellyn and Realist Movement (LIC) / Weidenfeld & Nicolson, 1985.
ISBN 0297786679 Pbk £12.95
ISBN 0297994828 Hbk £20.00

—Lack of Discretion of Judgment because of Schizophrenia : Doctrine and Recent Rotal Jurisprudence / Rome : Editrice Pontificia Universitana Gregoriana, 1986.
256p.

—Law and philosophy : an international journal for jurisprudence and legal philosophy / Dordrecht : D. Reidel, 1982-.

—Law, morality, and rights / edited by M.A. Stewart. – Dordrecht, Holland : Reidel, 1983.
xii,452p. – (Synthese library).
Includes index.
ISBN 902771519X

—Law, norms and authority / George C. Christie. – London : Duckworth, 1982.
x,181p; 23cm.
Includes index.
ISBN 0715615939 £18.00

—Legal theory : papers presented at the W.G. Hart Legal Workshop, 3rd-6th July 1984 at the Institute of Advanced Legal Studies, University of London / academic director: William Twining. – 1 v. – London : The Institute, 1984.
various pagings. – (W.G. Hart Legal Workshop).

—Lloyd's Introduction to Jurisprudence / M. D. A. Freedman. – 5th ed. – Agincourt : Carswell, 1985.
1257p.
This book is an anthology of selected extracts from the work of one hundred noted jurists throughout history. A discussion of different theories of jurisprudence from Plato to the present day is provided in the work.

—Lloyd's Introduction to jurisprudence / M. D. A. Freeman. – 5th ed. – London : Sweet & Maxwell, 1985.
1300p.
Previous ed.: published as Introduction to jurisprudence. London : Stevens, 1979. Includes index.
ISBN 042047160X Hbk £30.00
ISBN 0420471707 Pbk £22.50

—Making law bind / Oxford : Oxford University Press, 1987.
ISBN 0198254670 Hbk £30.00

—Nature of social laws / Reprint. – Cambridge : Cambridge University Press, 1986.
ISBN 0521338298 Pbk £9.95

—Oxford essays in jurisprudence / Bell. – Oxford : Oxford University Press, 1987.
– (3rd series).
ISBN 0198255071 Pbk £27.50

—Oxford essays in jurisprudence : third series / edited by John Eekelaar and John Bell. – Oxford : Clarendon, 1987.
267p; 22cm.
Includes index.
ISBN 0198255071 £27.50

—Oxford Jurisprudence / Oxford : Croom Helm, 1988.
ISBN 0709941560 Hbk £25.00

—Principles of Jurisprudence and Legal Theory / 4th ed. – Lucknow : Eastern Book Company, 1980.
482p.

—Principles of law : a normative analysis / Michael D. Bayles. – Dordrecht : D. Reidel, 1987.
xxi, 398p.
Includes index. Bibliography: p.372-380.
ISBN 902772413X pbk.

—Promises, morals and law / Oxford : Oxford University Press, 1981.
ISBN 0198254792 Pbk £7.95

—Ratio Juris : an international journal of jurisprudence and philosophy of law / Oxford : Blackwell, 1988-.

—Reason and reality / Stig Jrgensen. – Aarhus : Aarhus University Press, 1986.
159p.
Includes bibliographical references.
ISBN 8772880023

—Ronald Dworkin and contemporary jurisprudence / edited and with a preface by Marshall Cohen. – London : Duckworth, 1984.
xii,304p; 24cm.
Originally published: Totowa, N.J. : Rowman and Allanheld, 1983. Bibliography: p301-302.
ISBN 071561813X Unpriced

—Ronald Dworkin and contemporary jurisprudence / London : Duckworth (Gerald), 1984.
ISBN 0715618172 Pbk £9.95

—Science of a legislator : the natural jurisprudence of David Hume and Adam Smith / Knud Haakonssen. – Cambridge : Cambridge University Press, 1981.
vii,240p; 24cm.
Bibliography: p227-229. - Includes index.
ISBN 0521238919 £17.50

—Sociological theory of law / Routledge, 1985.
ISBN 0710097476 Hbk £32.50

—Studies on criminal responsibility and psychiatric treatment of mentally ill offenders : reports presented to the seventh Criminological Colloquium (1985) / Council of Europe. – Strasbourg : Council of Europe, 1986.
103p; 21cm. – (Legal affairs).
On cover: European Committee on Crime Problems.
ISBN 9287108994

—Theory of legal science : proceedings of the Conference on Legal Theory and Philosophy of Science, Lund, Sweden, December 11-14, 1983 / edited by Aleksander Peczenik, Lars Lindahl, and Bert van Roermund. – Dordrecht : Reidel, 1984.
xv, 666 p.; 23 cm.
Includes bibliographies and index.
ISBN 9027718342

—Thought of John Austin : jurisprudence, colonial reform and the British constitution / Wilfrid E. Rumble. – London : Athlone, 1985.
278p.
Includes bibliography and index.
ISBN 0485112922 £20.00

—Utilitarianism / On liberty : John Stuart Mill : edited with an introduction by Mary Warnock. – 17th impression. – Glasgow : Fontana, 1985.
352p.
This selection originally published: 1962. Bibliography: p.343-4. - Includes index.

—Western idea of law / David N Weisstub. – London : Butterworths, 1983.
ISBN 0409868191 Hbk £28.00

—What next in the law / London : Butterworths, 1982.
ISBN 0406176019 Hbk £13.95
ISBN 0406176027 Pbk £9.50

—Women's law : an introduction to feminist jurisprudence / Oxford : Oxford University Press, 1988.
ISBN 0820084900 Hbk £20.00

JURISPRUDENCE - CANADA

—Canadian journal of law and jurisprudence / London, Ont. : Faculty of Law, University of Western Ontario, 1988-.
Continues: University of Western Ontario law review.

—Lloyd's Introduction to Jurisprudence / 5th ed. – Agincourt : Carswell, 1985.
1,301p.

JURISPRUDENCE - ENGLAND

—Sir Henry Maine : a study in Victorian jurisprudence / Cambridge : Cambridge University Press.
Study of the ideas on jurisprudence of Sir Henry Maine, an important member of the Victorian intellectual establishment.
ISBN 0521353432

JURISPRUDENCE - GREAT BRITAIN

—Court of protection : a legal and policy analysis of the guardianship of the estate / Larry Gostin : foreword by Peter Jefferys. – London : Mind, National Association for Mental Health, 1983.
60p.
Bibliography: p.48.
ISBN 0900557567

—Essays in Jurisprudence 1931 / London : Wildy & Sons.

—Jurisprudence / 5th ed. – London : Butterworths, 1985.
ISBN 0406574316 Pbk £21.95
ISBN 0406574324 Hbk £28.00

—Treat me right : essays in medical law and ethics / Ian Kennedy. – Oxford : Clarendon Press, 1988.
xvii,375p.
Bibliography: pp.365-370. - Includes index.
ISBN 0198255586

JURISPRUDENCE - INDIA

—Guide to Jurisprudence / New Delhi : B. Jain Publishers.

JURISPRUDENCE - PHILIPPINES
—Pandect of Commercial Law and Jurisprudence / Manila : National Book Store, 1984.
515p.
ISBN 9710805185 Hbk £34.00

JURISPRUDENCE - SWEDEN
—Copyright and jurisprudence : selected papers / melanges : Stig Stromholm. - Stockholm : Norstedt, 1983.
291p.
Bibliography: p.271-291. 'Edited by the Faculty of Law, Uppsala University and P.A. Norstedt & Soners forlag, Stockholm' - Cover. Papers in English, French and German.
ISBN 9118276210

JURISPRUDENCE - USSR
—Legal philosophies of Russian liberalism / Andrzej Walicki. - Oxford : Clarendon, 1987.
480p; 22cm.
Includes index.
ISBN 0198249306 £45.00

JURISPRUDENCE (ISLAMIC LAW)
—Islamic Jurisprudence / New Delhi : Deep and Deep Publications, 1988.
338p.

JURISTIC PERSONS
—Enterprise corporatism : new industrial policy and the 'essence' of the legal person / by Gunther Teubner. - Florence : European University Institute, 1987.
47p.

JURISTIC PERSONS - ENGLAND
—Stephen's commentaries on the laws of England / L. Crispin Warmington. - 21st ed. - London : Butterworths, 1950.
xiv,604p.
Index included in Vol. 4.

JURISTS
—Andreas Alciates, 2 Vols. / Toronto : University of Toronto Press, 1985.
ISBN 0802024254 Hbk £125.00

JURY
—Jury Under Attack / Peter Duff. - Butterworths, 1988.
243p.
ISBN 0409493481 Pbk £39.00

—Problems of jury trials in small jurisdictions / John Spry. - London : Commonwealth Secretariat, 1985.
19p.
Includes bibliographical references.

JURY - AUSTRALIA
—Jury Under Attack / P. Duff. - Sydney : Butterworths, 1988.
264p.

—Statement of preliminary views / Constitutional Commission. Australian Judicial System Advisory Committee. - Canberra : The Commission, 1986.
40p.

JURY - AUSTRALIA - NEW SOUTH WALES
—Community law reform program / New South Wales Law Reform Commission. - Sydney : The Commission, 1984.
53p. - (L.R.C. 42).

—Criminal procedure report : the jury in a criminal trial / New South Wales Law Reform Commission. - Sydney : The Commission, 1986.
xxxi,203p. - (L.R.C. 48).
Includes bibliographical references.
ISBN 073051546X Hbk

—Criminal procedure research report : the jury in a criminal trial : empirical studies / Sydney : Law Reform Commission of New South Wales, 1986.
xii,ii,164p. - (RR).
ISBN 0730524477

—Criminal procedure : the jury in a criminal trial : discussion paper / New South Wales Law Reform Commission. - Sydney : Government Printer, 1985.
xxx,285p. - (D.P.).
ISBN 0730514323

JURY - AUSTRALIA - QUEENSLAND
—Working paper on legislation to review the role of juries in criminal trials / Queensland Law Reform Commission. - Brisbane : The Commission, 1984.
viii,146p. - (Q.L.R.C.W.P. 28).

JURY - AUSTRALIA - SOUTH AUSTRALIA
—Report ... relating to maintenance, champerty, embracery and barratry, malicious prosecution and abuse of process / Law Reform Committee of South Australia. - Adelaide : Government Printer, 1987.
86,3p. - (101st report).
Includes text of the Abolition of Obsolete Offences Act (1969).

JURY - AUSTRALIA - VICTORIA
—Role of the jury in criminal trials / Law Reform Commission of Victoria. - Melbourne : The Commission, 1985.
xxvi,220p. - (Background paper).
Bibliography: pp.185-220.. With appendices in separate vol..

JURY - CANADA
—Jury Trials / Vancouver : British Columbia Continuing Legal Education Society, 1981.
202p.
ISBN 0865040419 Hbk £11.50

—Report on the jury / Law Reform Commission of Canada. - Ottowa : Minister of Supply and Services, 982.
86p,91p. - (Report).
Added t.p. in French: Rapport sur le jury. Pages numbered in opposite directions. Text in English and French.
ISBN 0662518667

JURY - CANADA - BRITISH COLUMBIA
—Peremptory challenges in civil jury trials / Law Reform Commission of British Columbia. - Vancouver : The Commission, 1982.
ii,31p. - (Working paper).
Includes bibliographical references.

—Report on peremptory challenges in civil jury trials / Law Reform Commission of British Columbia. - Victoria : Queen's Printer, 1983.
22p.
ISBN 0771883773

—Review of civil jury awards / Law Reform Commission of British Columbia. - Vancouver : The Commission, 1983.
iii,104p. - (Working paper).
Includes bibliographical references.

JURY - ENGLAND
—Improving the presentation of information to juries in fraud trials : a report of four research studies / by the MRC Applied Psychology Unit, Cambridge. - London : H.M.S.O., 1986.
vii,63p; 25cm.
Presents the results of research by the Roskill Fraud Trials Committee on the presentation of evidence to juries.
ISBN 0113800096

JURY - GREAT BRITAIN
—Jury Service / London : Hale, 1983.
142p.
ISBN 0709012845 Hbk £7.95

—Jury under attack / Duff. - London : Butterworths, 1988.
ISBN 0406503109 Pbk £14.95

JURY - HONG KONG
—Problem of the trial of complex commercial crimes : a proposal for reform / Hong Kong : Attorney General's Chambers, 1984.
93p.

JURY - WEST INDIES
—Trial by jury : social and psychological dynamics / Ramesh Deosaran. - St. Augustine, Trinidad, West Indies : Institute of Social and Economic Research, University of the West Indies, 1985.
324 p.; 23 cm.
Includes indexes. Bibliography: p. 283-297.
ISBN 9766180008 pbk.

JUSTICE
—Countrey Justice / Abingdon : Professional Books.
- (Classical English Law Tests Ser.).

—English-Speaking Justice / Toronto : Anansi Press, 1985.
64p.
ISBN 0887841414 Pbk £5.95

—Hague Convention on International Access to Justice : Explanatory Documentation Prepared for Commonwealth Jurisdictions / London : Commonwealth Secretariat, 1982.
ISBN 085092216X Hbk £4.00

—Hume's Theory of Justice / Oxford : Oxford University Press, 1983.
ISBN 0198247249 Pbk £8.95

—Justice and liberty / D.D. Raphael. - London : Athlone, 1980.
192p; 23cm.
Includes index.
ISBN 0485111950 £13.00

—Justice at Home / 3rd ed. - Chichester : Barry Rose, 1983.
21p.
ISBN 0859923592 Hbk £3.50

—Justice in Wartime / London : Spokesman Books, 1983.
232p.
ISBN 0851240895 Hbk £6.00

—Justice, law, and argument : essays on moral and legal reasoning / Ch. Perelman : with an intod. by Harold J. Berman. - Dordrecht, Holland : D. Reidel Pub. Co., 1980.
xiii,181p.
Includes bibliographical references and index.
ISBN 9027710902 pbk.

—Justice, law, and culture / James K. Feibleman. - Dordrecht : Nijhoff, 1985.
xiii, 208p.
ISBN 9024731054

—Liberty and Justice / Oxford : Croom Helm, 1986.
ISBN 070994523X Hbk £25.00

—Matters of Justice / Oxford : Croom Helm, 1986.
ISBN 0709914709 Hbk £22.50

—Procedures Facilitating Access to Justice : Replies by Governments to the Questionnaire of Procedures Facilitating Access to Justice / Strasbourg : Council of Europe, 1980.

—Understanding tuvenile justice / Oxford : Croom Helm, 1987.
ISBN 0709938322 Hbk £22.50

JUSTICE - AUSTRALIA
—Justice for Aboriginal Australians : Report to the World Council of Churches Team Visit to the Aborigines, June 15 to July 3, 1981 / Sydney : Australian Council of Churches.

JUSTICE - CANADA
—Justice Denied / Toronto : Macmillan of Canada.
ISBN 0771596901 Hbk £24.95

—Open Justice / Toronto : Butterworths, 1985.
416p.

JUSTICE - ENGLAND
—Fabric of English Civil Justice (Hamlyn 38) / London : Sweet & Maxwell, 1987.
ISBN 0420475303 Hbk £18.50
ISBN 0420475400 Pbk £9.95

JUSTICE - GREAT BRITAIN
—Beyond Justice / Oxford : Blackwell, 1987.
ISBN 0631152067 Hbk £25.00

—Country Justice / 2nd ed. - Abingdon : Professional Books, 1986 Reprint.
ISBN 0862053137 Hbk £30.00

—Foundations of Justice / Oxford : Oxford University Press, 1986.
ISBN 0195040767 Hbk £22.50

—Justice and the Law in Britain / United Kingdom Central Office of Information. - London : Central Office of Information, 1982.
- (References Services Ser.).
ISBN 0117010340 Hbk £3.15

—Justice at home / 3rd ed. - Chichester : Barry Rose, 1983.
ISBN 0859923592 Pbk £5.00

—Law, Justice and the Judiciary : Transitional / Sinnadurai. - Professional Law, 1988.
ISBN 09679958002 Hbk £95.00

—Machinery of Justice in England / 8th ed. - Cambridge : Cambridge University Press, 1987.
ISBN 052129231X Pbk £19.50

—On justice / Oxford : Oxford University Press, 1980.
ISBN 019824598X Hbk £17.50

—Quest for Justice / Repr. of 1951 ed. - London : Sweet & Maxwell, 1986.
ISBN 0421355107 Hbk £15.00

JUSTICE - INDIA
—Justice on Trial / Allahabad : A.H. Wheeler, 1980.
300p.

JUSTICE - NORTHERN IRELAND
—Access to Justice and Civil Litigation in Northern Ireland / Desmond S. Greer. - Belfast : Queen's University of Belfast.
76p.

JUSTICE - PHILIPPINES
—Tiruray Justice / Metro Manila : Institute of Philippine Culture.

JUSTICE - SOUTH AFRICA
—Justice in South Africa / Ibadan : Heinemann Educational Books (Nigeria).

JUSTICE - USSR
—Soviet system of Justice : figures and policy / by Ger P. van den Berg. - The Hague : M. Nijhoff Publishers, 1984.
Includes bibliographical references and index.
ISBN 9024730864

JUSTICE, ADMINISTRATION OF
—Politics of informal justice / edited by Richard L. Abel. - 2. - 1981.
- (Studies on law and social control).
Includes bibliographies. Contents: v.1. The American experience - v.2. Comparative studies.
ISBN 0120415011 v. 1

JUSTICE, ADMINISTRATION OF - UNITED STATES

—Politics of informal justice / edited by Richard L. Abel. – 2. – 1981.
– (Studies on law and social control).
Includes bibliographies. Contents: v.1. The American experience - v.2. Comparative studies.
ISBN 0120415011 v. 1

JUSTICE (PHILOSOPHY)

—Liberalism and the limits of justice / Michael J. Sandel. – Cambridge : Cambridge University Press, 1982.
ix,191p; 24cm.
Bibliography: p184-186. - Includes index.
ISBN 052124501X Hbk £17.50
ISBN 0521270774 Pbk £5.95

—Marx and justice : the radical critique of liberalism / Allen E. Buchanan. – London : Methuen, 1982.
xiv,206p; 25cm.
Bibliography: p197-199. - Includes index.
ISBN 0416334504 £12.95

—On justice... / by J.R. Lucas. – Oxford : Clarendon Press, 1980.
vii,270p; 23cm.
Includes index.
ISBN 019824598X £10.00

JUTE

—International Agreement on Jute and Jute Products, 1982 : New York, 3 January-30 June 1983 / London : H.M.S.O., 1983.
27p; 25cm.
ISBN 0101882505 unbound £2.95

JUVENILE CORRECTIONS - ENGLAND

—Custodial sentences for young offenders : a discussion paper / Home Office. – London : Home Office, 1986.
12p.

—Delinquency and citizenship : reclaiming the young offender, 1914-1948 / Victor Bailey. – Oxford : Clarendon, 1987.
viii,352p; 22cm.
Bibliography: p331-341. - Includes index.
ISBN 0198226640 £30.00

—Monitoring the Criminal Justice Act : youth custody service / NACRO. – London : NACRO, 1984.
6p.

—Out of care : the community support of juvenile offenders / D.H. Thorpe ... et al. – London : Allen & Unwin for the Centre of Youth, Crime and Community, University of Lancaster, 1980.
vii,183p; 23cm.
Includes index.
ISBN 0043640184 Hbk £10.95
ISBN 0043640192 Pbk £3.95

—Statutory restrictions on the use of custody for young offenders : a consultative paper / Parliamentary All-Party Penal Affairs Group. – London : Parliamentary All-Party Penal Affairs Group, 1985.
8,3 leaves.

—Young offenders / Home Office, Welsh Office, Department of Health and Social Security. – London : H.M.S.O., 1980.
17p; 25cm.
ISBN 0101804504 unbound £1.70

JUVENILE CORRECTIONS - GREAT BRITAIN

—Children in custody / Gill Stewart, Norman Tutt. – Aldershot : Avebury, 1987.
viii,237p; 23cm.
Bibliography: p223-230. - Includes index.
ISBN 0566050757 £17.50

—Junior attendance centres / by Anne B. Dunlop. – London : H.M.S.O., 1980.
v,43p.
Bibliography- p.41.
ISBN 0113407009

—Politics of juvenile crime / John Pitts. – London : Sage, 1988.
192p; 22cm. – (Sage contemporary criminology).
Includes bibliography and index.
ISBN 0803981325 Hbk £22.50
ISBN 0803981333 Pbk £7.95

JUVENILE COURTS - CANADA

—Juvenile courts in Canada / by Larry C. Wilson. – Toronto, Canada : Carswell, 1982.
xx, 272 p.; 24 cm.
Includes index. 'Table of cases': p. vii-xx.
ISBN 0459352709

JUVENILE COURTS - CANADA - ONTARIO

—Family law in the family courts / 2nd ed. v. – Toronto : Carswell, 1981.
Previous ed.: 1973, edited by H.T.G. Andrews. Includes index.
ISBN 0459337300

JUVENILE COURTS - ENGLAND

—Juvenile court : a guide to law and practice / by Terence G. Moore and Tony P. Wilkinson. – Chichester : Barry Rose, 1984.
xiii,231p; 23cm.
Includes index.
ISBN 0859923355 No price

—Minors : the law and practice : the juvenile courts, the offences, the role of the local authorities / Kenneth W. Pain. – London : Fourmat Publishing, 1987.
xvii,293p.
Concerns practice and procedure of juvenile courts, offences which can be committed by and against minors and the part played by local authorities in care proceedings.
ISBN 1851900306

—Practice and procedure in juvenile courts / by Kenneth W. Pain. – London : Fourmat, 1982.
xiii,149p; 22cm.
Includes index.
ISBN 090684049X Pbk £7.95

—Sentencing young people : what went wrong with the Criminal Justice Act 1982 / Elizabeth Burney. – Aldershot : Gower, 1985.
120p; 22cm.
ISBN 0566051273 £14.50

JUVENILE COURTS - GREAT BRITAIN

—Criminal Proceedings Against Juveniles / London : Longman Professional, 1984.
ISBN 0851208460 Pbk £21.00

—Summary of the powers of the juvenile court / by Clifford E.M. Chatterton. – Plymouth : Basset Publications, 1985.
viii,33p.
ISBN 0946873089

—Table of Proceedings in Juvenile Courts / London : Shaw & Sons, 1984.
ISBN 0721901891 Hbk £0.80

JUVENILE COURTS - NEW ZEALAND

—Evaluation of the children's advocate scheme pilot in the Auckland Children and Young Persons Court / by Dr. Terrence Loomis : a study commissioned by the Department of Justice. – Auckland : Social Research and Development Trust, 1985.
88,26p.
'Carried out for the Department of Justice by the Social Research and Development Trust of Auckland'. - Abstract.

JUVENILE COURTS - SCOTLAND

—Children and justice : decision-making in children's hearings and juvenile courts / by Stewart Asquith. – Edinburgh : Edinburgh University Press, 1983.
vii,258p; 22cm.
Bibliography: p238-250. - Includes index.
ISBN 0852244290 Hbk £8.50
ISBN 0852244665 Pbk Unpriced

—Children out of court / F.M. Martin et al. – Edinburgh : Scottish Academic Press, 1981.
xi,331p.
Bibliography: p.322-324.
ISBN 0707302870

—Scottish juvenile justice system / edited by F.M. Martin and Kathleen Murray. – Edinburgh : Scottish Academic Press, 1982.
xii, 200p.
Replaces earlier edition: 'Children's hearings', Edinburgh: Scottish Academic Press, 1976. Bibliography: p.198-200.
ISBN 070730296X

JUVENILE DELINQUENCY

—Action-oriented research on youth crime : an international perspective / edited by Ugljesa Zvekic. – Rome : United Nations Social Defence Research Institute, 1986.
275p. – (Publication).
Bibliography: p235-270. Research workshop on perspectives in action-oriented research: youth, crime and juvenile justice held in the framework of the Seventh United Nations Congress on the Prevention of Crime and the Treatment of Offenders, Milan.
ISBN 9290780010

—History of Juvenile Delinquency, 2 Vols. / Priscilla F. Clement. – Aalen Wuertt : Scientia, 1989.

—In whose best interests? : the unjust treatment of children in courts and institutions / Laurie Taylor, Ron Lacey and Denis Bracken. – London : Cobden Trust, MIND, 1980.
109p.
Includes bibliographies.
ISBN 0900137134

—Justice for children / Allison Morris ... et al. – London : Macmillan, 1980.
vii,146p; 22cm.
Bibliography: p.141-146.
ISBN 0333274865 Unpriced
ISBN 0333274873

—Juvenile delinquency : trends and perspectives / Michael Rutter and Henri Giller. – Harmondsworth : Penguin, 1983.
432p; 20cm. – (Penguin education).
Bibliography: p363-415. - Includes index. Also published: New York, Guilford Press, 1984.
ISBN 0140804625 Pbk £5.95

—Juvenile social maladjustment and human rights in the context of urban development / United Nations Social Defence Research Institute. – Rome : Fratelli Palombi, 1984.
504p. – (Publication).
'Funded by the United Nations Development Programme'. Parallel Spanish and French titles. English, Spanish and French text.
ISBN 8876218289

—Psychology of juvenile crime / Amy Lamson. – New York : Human Sciences, 1983.
123p; 22cm.
Includes index.
ISBN 0898850606 Unpriced

—Western systems of juvenile justice / edited by Malcolm W. Klein. – Beverly Hills : Sage, 1984.
240p; 23cm.
Includes bibliographies and index.
ISBN 080392125X £22.00

JUVENILE DELINQUENCY - CANADA

—Vicarious liablilty of parents for actions of their children who are found to be delinquent / Elizabeth Beckett. – Ottawa : Ministry of the Solicitor General, 1985.
ii,79 leaves. – (User report).
Includes bibliographical references.

—Young Offenders Act annotated / by Nicholas Bala and Heino Lilles. – Don Mills : R. De Boo, 1984.
xxxi,453p.
Includes index.
ISBN 0888201842

—Young Offenders Act : highlights / Ottowa : Published under the authority of the Hon. Bob Kaplan, Solicitor General of Canada by Minister of Supply and Services, 1981.
19,21p.
Added t.p. in French. Pages numbered in opposite directions. Text in English and French.
ISBN 066251212X

JUVENILE DELINQUENCY - ENGLAND

—Delinquency and human nature / D.H. Stott. – 2nd ed. – London : Hodder and Stoughton, 1980.
xvi,432p.
Previous ed: 1950. Includes index.
ISBN 0340245891 £9.95

—NACRO juvenile crime briefing / . – London : NACRO, 1985-.

—Receiving juvenile justice : adolescents and state care and control / Howard Parker, Maggie Casburn, David Turnbull. – Oxford : Basil Blackwell, 1981.
259p; 23cm.
Criticises official discretion, deviation and diversity in the selection and sentencing process.
ISBN 0631127275 Hbk £12.00
ISBN 0631127453 Pbk £5.50

JUVENILE DELINQUENCY - FINLAND

—Dealing with child offenders in Finland : the Scandinavian child welfare system in operation / Matti Joutsen. – Helsinki : Research Institute of Legal Policy, 1980.
121p.
Bibliography: p.95-100.
ISBN 9517040652

JUVENILE DELINQUENCY - GREAT BRITAIN

—Delinquency : its roots, careers and prospects / D.J. West. – London : Heinemann Educational, 1982.
186p; 23cm. – (The Heinemann library of criminology and penal reform).
Bibliography: p172-181. - Includes index.
ISBN 0435829327 Hbk £13.50
ISBN 0435829335 Pbk Unpriced

—Delinquent : directions for social control / Masud Hoghughi. – London : Burnett, 1983.
317p; 24cm.
Bibliography: p295-310. - Includes index.
ISBN 0091506808 Hbk £15.00
ISBN 0091506816 Pbk £6.95

—Good Girls Gone Bad / London : Futura, 1988.
ISBN 0356151603 Pbk £11.95

—Growing out of crime / Andrew Rutherford. – Harmondsworth : Penguin Books, 1986.
188p.
Bibliography: p176-182.
ISBN 0140223835

—Homeless young offenders : an action programme : the Report of a NACRO Group / NACRO. – London : NACRO, 1981.
69p.
Bibliography: p.67-69.
ISBN 0850690242

—Hooligan : a history of respectable fears / Geoffrey Pearson. - London : Macmillan, 1983.
xi,283p.
Bibliography: p244-275.
ISBN 0333233999

—Parental supervision and juvenile delinquency / by David Riley and Margaret Shaw. - London : H.M.S.O., 1985.
v,85p; 25cm.
Bibliography: p81-85. A Home Office Research and Planning Unit report. A Home Office Research and Planning Unit report.
ISBN 0113407998

—Prevention of crime among young people / Parliamentary All-Party Penal Affairs Group. - Chichester : Rose, 1983.
112p; 21cm.
ISBN 0859923533 Pbk £7.00

JUVENILE DELINQUENCY - HONG KONG

—Report of the Working Group on Juvenile Crime / Hong Kong. - 1. - Hong Kong : Government Printer, 1981.
various pagings.

JUVENILE DELINQUENCY - INDIA

—Juvenile Delinquency and Indian Justice System / New Delhi : Deep and Deep Publications, 1988.
516p.

JUVENILE DELINQUENCY - NETHERLANDS

—Juvenile delinquency in the Netherlands / edited by Josine Junger-Tas and Richard L. Block. - Amstelveen, The Netherlands : Kugler Publications BV, 1988.
xiii, 242 p.; 23 cm.
Includes bibliographies.
ISBN 9062990363

JUVENILE DELINQUENCY - NEW ZEALAND

—Report of Advisory Committee on Youth and Law in our Multicultural Society / E. Te R. Tauroa. - Wellington : The Committee, 1983.
284p.

JUVENILE DELINQUENCY - UNITED STATES

—Adolescent subcultures and delinquency / Herman Schwendinger and Julia Siegel Schwendinger. - Research ed. - New York : Praeger, 1985.
xvi,524p; 25cm.
Bibliography: p497-511. - Includes index.
ISBN 0030009391 Hbk £76.95
ISBN 0030009421 Pbk No price

—Juvenile justice policy : analyzing trends and outcomes / edited by Scott H. Decker. - Beverly Hills : Sage in cooperation with the Academy of Criminal Justice Sciences, 1984.
168p; 23cm.
Includes bibliographies.
ISBN 0803921977 Hbk Unpriced
ISBN 0803921985 Pbk £7.95

JUVENILE DETENTION HOMES - ENGLAND

—Locked up in care : a report on the use of secure accommodation for young people in care / Children's Legal Centre. - London : Children's Legal Centre, 1982.
36p; 30cm.
Bibliography: p36. 'Locked up in care - new legislation' (sheet (2p)) as insert.
ISBN 0946109001 Pbk £3.00

—Tougher regimes in detention centres : report of an evaluation by the Young Offender Psychology Unit / by David Thornton ... et al. - London : H.M.S.O., 1984.
v,277p; 25cm.
Reports findings of Young Offenders Psychology Unit investigating the effectiveness of tougher regimes designed to provide a 'short, sharp shock'. Doubt is cast on whether pilot regimes are sufficiently more rigorous. Finds that pilot regimes had the same effect on reconviction rates as ordinary detention centres.
ISBN 0113407963 Pbk £6.50

JUVENILE OFFENDERS - CANADA

—Young Offenders Act / Vancouver : Continuing Legal Education Society of British Columbia, 1984.
551p.
ISBN 0865041547 Hbk £60.00

Update 1988.
169p.
ISBN 0865049912 Hbk £65.00

—Young Offenders Service, 2 Vols. / Heino Lilles. - Butterworths.

KOREA (SOUTH)

—Doing business in Korea / edited by Arthur M. Whitehill. - London : Croom Helm, 1987.
xvi,121p; 23cm. - (The Croom Helm series in international business).
Conference papers.
ISBN 0709952260 £25.00

—Republic of Korea : violations of human rights : an Amnesty International report / London : Amnesty International Publications, 1981.
43p; 30cm.
ISBN 0862100313 unbound Unpriced

KWAZULU

—Natal and KwaZulu : constitutional and political options; proceedings of the workshop... / edited by Laurence Boulle and Lawrence Baxter. - Cape Town : Juta, 1981.
viii,211p.
Includes chapter in Afrikaans.

LABELS

—Labelling and Advertising Regulations on Food Products / European Food Law Association. - Brussels : Editions de l'Universite de Bruxelles, 1980.
490p.
ISBN 2800407344 Hbk £780.00

—Pesticide Labelling Legislation / Rome : FAO, Food and Agricultural Organization of the United Nations, 1988.
159p.
ISBN 925102619X Hbk £10.50

LABELS - EUROPE

—Informative Labelling in Some European Countries : Proceedings of the 1st Symposium of the Committee on Producer-Consumer Relations, 1981 / Bern : European Office for Quality Control.

LABELS - SWEDEN

—Labelling of chemical products : Swedish regulations and general advice with regard to the classification and labelling of chemical products hazardous to health, flammables and explosives / National Chemicals Inspectorate, National Inspectorate of Explosives and Flammables. - Solna : National Chemicals Inspectorate, 1987.
224p.
ISBN 9138098873

LABOR LAWS AND LEGISLATION - GREAT BRITAIN

—Encyclopedia of health and safety at work : Law and practice / 3. - London : Sweet & Maxwell, 1962.
loose-leaf.
Includes indexes.

LABOUR AND LABOURING CLASSES - SOUTH AFRICA

—Code of conduct for companies with interests in South Africa : government guidance to British companies on the code of conduct adopted by the governments of the member states of the European Community on 19 November 1985 / presented to Parliament by the Secretary of State for Trade and Industry. - London : H.M.S.O., 1986.
16p.
Supersedes code published in 1978 as Cmnd. 7233.
ISBN 0101986009

LABOUR AND LABOURING CLASSES - TANZANIA

—Law, state and the working class in Tanzania : c.1920-1964 / Issa G. Shivji. - London : Currey, 1986.
xix,268p; 24cm.
Bibliography: p253-260. - Includes index.
ISBN 0852553021 Hbk £25.00
ISBN 043508013X £9.95

LABOUR CONTRACT - ENGLAND

—Service agreements / Trevor M. Aldridge. - 4th ed. - London : Oyez Longman, 1982.
xxi,196p.
Includes index.
ISBN 0851207006

LABOUR CONTRACT - GREAT BRITAIN

—Contracts at work / Erich Suter. - London : Institute of Personnel Management, 1982.
x,276p; 22cm.
Includes index.
ISBN 0852922973 Pbk £13.95

—Rideout's Principles of labour law / Jacqueline C. Dyson. - 4th ed. - London : Sweet & Maxwell, 1983.
lxxvi,658p; 25cm.
Previous ed.: 1979. Includes index.
ISBN 0421296100 Hbk £20.00
ISBN 0421296208 Pbk Unpriced

—Transfer of undertakings : the legal pitfalls : a specially commissioned report / by Patrick Elias and John Bowers. - London : Longman Professional, 1985.
54 leaves.
ISBN 0851208061

LABOUR CONTRACT - GUYANA

—Contract of service and the worker : with special reference to Guyana / Roop L. Chaudhary, Hubert N. Rodney. - Barbados : Coles Printery, 1980.
98p.
Includes index. Cover title: Contract of service and the worker in a Caribbean jurisdiction.

LABOUR CONTRACT - NIGERIA

—From contract to status in quest for security : an inaugural lecture delivered at the University of Lagos on Wednesday, 9th April, 1986 / by A.A. Adeogun. - Lagos : Lagos University Press, 1986.
60p. - (Inaugural lecture series).
Includes bibliographical references.
ISBN 9782264709

LABOUR COURTS

—Conciliation by ACAS in complaints by individuals to Industrial Tribunals / Advisory, Conciliation and Arbitration Service. - London : ACAS, 1982.

—Industrial tribunal practice in Scotland / by William Leslie. - Edinburgh : Green, 1981.
xxxxi,323p; 21cm.
Includes index.
ISBN 0414006801 Pbk Unpriced

LABOUR COURTS - CANADA - ONTARIO

—Annual report / Ontario Labour Relations Board / Ontario Labour Relations Board. - Toronto : The Board, 1981.
Report year ends 31 Mar..
ISBN 0711849X

LABOUR COURTS - ENGLAND

—Industrial tribunal : a practical guide to employment law and tribunal procedure / by John Mulhern and Ian McLean. - Chichester : Rose, 1982.
280p; 23cm.
Includes index.
ISBN 0859922243 £19.50

—Industrial tribunals : practice and procedure / by Donald B. Williams and D.J. Walker. - London : Butterworth, 1980.
xxii,258p; 25cm.
Includes index. Includes the text of relevant legislation.
ISBN 0406421056 £15.50

LABOUR COURTS - EUROPE

—Labour courts in Europe : proceedings of a meeting organised by the International Institute for Labour Studies / edited by Bert Essenberg. - Geneva : International Institute for Labour Studies, 1986.
68p.
ISBN 9290144076 Hbk £10.00

LABOUR COURTS - GREAT BRITAIN

—Dismissed : a study of unfair dismissal and the industrial tribunal system / Linda Dickens ... et al. - Oxford : Blackwell, 1985.
xvi,379p; 23cm.
A Study of Unfair Dismissal and the Industrial Tribunal System.
ISBN 0631139257 £25.00

—Industrial tribunal : a guide to the jurisdiction of industrial tribunals within the provisions of the following Acts : The Employment Act 1975, The Employment Protection (Consolidation) Act 1978, The Employment Act 1980, The Equal Pay Act 1970, The Sex Discrimination Act 1975, The Race Relations Act 1976 / Arthur H. Howell. - Chichester : Barry Rose, 1981.
38p; 26cm.
Cover title.
ISBN 0859922189 spiral £7.75

—Industrial tribunal law / R. W. Rideout. - London : McGraw-Hill, 1980.
199p.
ISBN 0070845352 £10.95
ISBN 0070845328

—Industrial tribunals : a report / by JUSTICE : chairman of committee Bob Hepple. - London : JUSTICE, 1987.
72p.
ISBN 0907247105

—Industrial tribunals : practice and procedure / by Michael J. Goodman. - 4th ed. - London : Sweet & Maxwell, 1987.
xxv,120p; 22cm.
Overview of the tribunals' principle jurisdictions, and analysis of practice and procedure before industrial tribunals. Covers the changes made by the Wages Act 1986. Contains model forms for application and response to an industrial tribunal, and the text of the Industrial Tribunals (Rules of Procedure) Regulations 1985.
ISBN 0421391200 Pbk No price

—Judging inequality : the effectiveness of the tribunal system in sex discrimination and equal pay cases / Alice M. Leonard. - London : Cobden Trust, 1987.
160p; 20cm.
Includes bibliography.
ISBN 0900137282 Pbk £7.95

—Pyrrhic victories : winning sex discrimination and equal pay cases in the industrial tribunals, 1980-84 / Alice M. Leonard. - London : H.M.S.O., 1987.
55p; 30cm. - (Research series).
ISBN 0117013285

LABOUR COURTS - NORTHERN IRELAND
—Industrial tribunals in Northern Ireland : a practical guide / by Phyllis Bateson and John McKee. - Belfast : SLS Publications, Faculty of Law, Queen's University, Belfast, 1981.
xi,146p; 21cm.
Includes index. Latest supplement held: 1981,up to date to August 1981.
ISBN 0853891915 Pbk Unpriced

LABOUR DISCIPLINE - GREAT BRITAIN
—Disciplinary and other procedures in employment : consultative document on a draft code of practice / Advisory, Conciliation and Arbitration Service. - London : The Service, 1985.
29p.

LABOUR DISPUTES
—Industrial conflict resolution in market economics : a study of Australia, the Federal Republic of Germany, Italy, Japan and the USA / T. Hanami editor : R. Blanpain associate editor. - Deventer : Kluwer Law and Taxation, 1984.
xiv,321p; 25cm.
Includes bibliographies and index.
ISBN 9065441808 Pbk No price

LABOUR DISPUTES - CANADA
—Western Labour Arbitration Cases / Vancouver : British Columbia Continuing Legal Education Society, 1981.

LABOUR DISPUTES - ENGLAND
—Conflict and order : the police and labour disputes in England and Wales, 1900-1939 / Jane Morgan. - Oxford : Clarendon, 1987.
325p,4p of plates; 22cm.
Includes bibliography and index.
ISBN 0198201281 £30.00

LABOUR DISPUTES - EUROPEAN COMMUNITY
—Prevention and settlement of industrial conflict in the Community member states / Luxembourg : Office for Official Publications of the European Communities, 1984.
162,16p.
At head of title page: Commission of the European Communities.
ISBN 9282550095

LABOUR DISPUTES - GREAT BRITAIN
—On industrial relations : interprofessional relationships in health care and the role of criminal law in industrial relations / R. Dyson and A.N. Khan. - Leeds : Centre for Social Work and Applied Social Studies, University of Leeds, 1982.
27p. - (Occasional papers).

—Picketing : industrial disputes, tactics and the law / by Peggy Kahn...et al. - London : Routledge & Kegan Paul, 1983.
xv,223p.
Bibliography: p219-220.
ISBN 0710095341

—Policing industrial disputes: 1893 to 1985 / Roger Geary. - Cambridge : Cambridge University Press, 1985.
vii,171p; 24cm.
Includes index.
ISBN 052130315X £19.50

LABOUR DISPUTES - INDIA
—Law of Industrial Disputes : as Amended by Amendment Act No. 46 of 1982, 2 Vols. / 2nd ed. - New Delhi : Bharat Law House, 1986.

LABOUR ECONOMICS
—Labour law and industrial relations : building on Kahn-Freund / edited by Lord Wedderburn of Charlton, Roy Lewis, Jon Clark. - Oxford : Clarendon Press, 1983.
vii,250p; 23cm.
Includes index.
ISBN 0198253931 Hbk Unpriced
ISBN 0198254822 Pbk £8.95

LABOUR ECONOMICS - GREAT BRITAIN
—Effect of ex post compensation on absence from work / by Paul Fenn. - Oxford : Centre for Socio-Legal Studies, 1980.
23p. - (Working paper).
Bibliography: p.23.

LABOUR LAW - AUSTRALIA
—Australian labour law reporter / 4. - North Ryde, N.S.W. : CCH Australia, 1977-.
loose-leaf.
Contents: 3 vols. of reports and index vol.. Loose-leaf issues accompanied by a summary report.
ISBN 0869031465 Hbk

LABOUR MOBILITY
—Studies in international labour migration / W.R. Bohning. - London : Macmillan, 1984.
350p.
Bibliography: p293-308. - Includes index.
ISBN 0333369718 £30.00

LABOUR MOBILITY - GREAT BRITAIN
—Unemployment and labour market flexibility : the United Kingdom / Guy Standing. - Geneva : International Labour Office, 1986.
xi, 147 p.; 24 cm.
Includes bibliographies.
ISBN 9221052915 pbk. £30.00

LABOUR POLICY
—Roles of Labour Law in Developing Countries : Record of Proceedings of, and Documents Submitted to, a Round Table (Geneva, 10-14 September and Selva di Fasano, Italy, 17-19 September 1974) / Geneva : International Labour Office, 1975.
iii, 266p.
ISBN 9221012875 Hbk £27.50

—Selected International Labour Conventions and Recommendations / Geneva : International Labour Office, 1984.
xv, 216p.
ISBN 9221038386 Pbk £14.00

Vol. 2 1985.
iv, 205p.
ISBN 9221038955 Pbk £14.00

Vol. 2 1985.
iv, 205p.
ISBN 9221038963 Hbk £17.50

LABOUR POLICY - GREAT BRITAIN
—States of emergency : British governments and strikebreaking since 1919 / Keith Jeffery and Peter Hennessy. - London : Routledge & K. Paul, 1983.
312p.
Includes index. Bibliography: p300-304.
ISBN 0710094647

LABOUR POLICY - UNITED STATES
—International Labor Organization : an American view / Walter Galenson. - Madison : University of Wisconsin Press, 1981.
xi,351p; 23cm.
Includes index.
ISBN 0299085406 Hbk £13.95
ISBN 0299085449 Pbk £5.05

LABOUR SUPPLY
—Arab manpower : the crisis of development / J.S. Birks and C.A. Sinclair. - London : Croom Helm, 1980.
17,391p; 23cm.
Bibliography: p.368-383. - Includes index.
ISBN 0856649465 £19.95

LABOUR SUPPLY - GREAT BRITAIN
—Unemployment and labour market flexibility : the United Kingdom / Guy Standing. - Geneva : International Labour Office, 1986.
xi, 147 p.; 24 cm.
Includes bibliographies.
ISBN 9221052915 pbk. £30.00

LAND CHARGES - GREAT BRITAIN
—Local land charges / by J.F. Garner. - 10th ed. - London : Shaw & Sons, 1987.
xxv,173p.
Previous ed.: 1982. Includes index.
ISBN 0721901255

—Local land charges / by J.F. Garner. - 9th ed. - London : Shaw, 1982.
xxvii,171p; 22cm.
Previous ed.: 1977. Includes index.
ISBN 0721901247 Pbk Unpriced

LAND CHARGES - SINGAPORE
—Development Land and Development Charge in Singapore / London : Butterworths, 1987.
ISBN 0409995371 Hbk £36.00

—Development Land and Development Charge in Singapore / Butterworths, 1987.
215p.
ISBN 0409995371 Hbk £75.00

LAND LAW
—Ghosh's Land Acquisition Act / 7th ed. - Calcutta : Eastern Law House, 1984.

—History of the land law / 2nd ed. - Oxford : Oxford University Press, 1986.
ISBN 0198255365 Pbk £12.50
ISBN 0198255373 Hbk £25.00

—Land Law / Stockholm : Anderson Keenan, 1982.
- (Law Unit).
ISBN 0906501288 Pbk £4.30

LAND LAW - AFRICA
—Customary Land Law in Africa : With Reference to Legislation Aimed at Adjusting Customary Tenures to the Needs of Development / 2nd print 1985. - Rome : FAO, Food and Agricultural Organization of the United Nations, 1967.
96p.
ISBN 9251022267 Hbk £7.50

LAND LAW - AUSTRALIA
—Introduction to Land Law / North Ryde : Law Book Co, 1980.
xxxi, 395p.
ISBN 0455201358 Hbk £49.50
ISBN 0455201366 Pbk £32.00

—Land Acquisition / 1983.
209p.
ISBN 0409490911 Hbk £59.00

—Lands Acquisitions and Compensation / Law Reform Commission. - Canberra : Australian Government Publishing Service, 1980.
258p. - (ALRC Report: No. 14).
ISBN 0642034281 Hbk £7.95

—Understanding land law / Stein. - North Ryde : Law Book Co, 1985.
ISBN 0455203032 Hbk £13.00
ISBN 0455203040 Pbk £8.50

—Understanding Land Law / R.T.J. Stein. - North Ryde : Law Book Co, 1985.
xx, 171p.
ISBN 0455203032 Hbk £25.00
ISBN 0455203040 Pbk £14.00

LAND LAW - CANADA
—Ancestral Lands, Alien Laws : Judicial Perspectives on Aboriginal Title / Saskatoon : University of Saskatchewan, Native Law Centre, 1983.
49p.
ISBN 0888801009 Hbk £9.00

—Land Compensation Reports : Consolidated Index, Tables of Cases / Aurora : Canada Law Book Co, 1985.
382p. - (Law Reports).

—Land Compensation Reports Current Series (1971-Present) / Aurora : Canada Law Book Co. - (Law Reports).

Back Vols.

—Minor Report on the Land Act / Victoria : Government of British Columbia, 1984.

—Municipal Tax Sales Act, 1983, Bill 138 : An Act Respecting the Sale of Lands for Arrears of Municipal Taxes / Ontario : Ontario Government Publications Service, 1983.
16p.

—Native Claims in Rupert's Land and the North-Western Territory : Canada's Constitutional Obligations / Saskatoon : University of Saskatchewan, Native Law Centre, 1982.
41p.
ISBN 0888801181 Hbk £8.00

—Smyth Town Plot Land Act, 1983, Bill Pr033 : An Act Respecting Certain Land in the Town of Smyth, in the District of Nipissing / Ontario : Ontario Government Publications Service, 1983.
3p.

LAND LAW - CANADA - ONTARIO
—Provincial Land Tax Act : Revised Statutes of Ontario, 1980 / Office of the Legislative Assembly (Ontario). - Ontario : Ontario Government Publications Service, 1983.
42p.

LAND LAW - COMMONWEALTH
—Common law aboriginal title / Oxford : Clarendon Press.
360.
Addresses the land rights question applied throughout the British Empire. Assesses the impact of English law in a colony acquired by settlememt where no form of aboriginal land ownership had previously existed. Conclusions reached suggest a doctrinal approach which could be used to resolve outstanding aboriginal land claims.*Academics, lawyers representing aboriginal peoples, students of human rights*
ISBN 0198252234 Hbk £35

LAND LAW - GREAT BRITAIN
—Building Land and Estates / 2nd ed. - London : Oyez Longman, 1983.
- (Oyez Longman Practice Note Ser.: No. 67).
ISBN 0851206964 Hbk £8.95

—Cases and Statutes On Land Law (CCC) / 2nd ed. - London : Sweet & Maxwell, 1986.
ISBN 0421343508 Pbk £13.00

—Claims to the Possession of Land : Law and Practice / Harris. - London : Fourmat, 1987.
ISBN 1851900004 Hbk £37.50

—Common Recoveries : Their Nature and Use / 2nd ed. Repr. of 1770 ed. – Abingdon : Professional Books.
490p.

—Compulsory Purchase and Compensation / 4th ed. – London : Butterworths, 1984.
ISBN 0406571872 Hbk £21.00
ISBN 0406571880 Pbk £17.95

—Compulsory Purchase and Compensation / 2nd ed. – London : Estates Gazette, 1985.
ISBN 0728200899 Pbk £14.00

—Compulsory Purchase and Compensation / Hawkins. – 5th ed. – London : Longman Professional, 1983.
ISBN 0851207138 Pbk £27.50

—Elements of Land Law / London : Butterworths, 1987.
ISBN 0406501602 Hbk £38.00
ISBN 0406501610 Pbk £23.95

—Essential Law for Landowners and Farmers / Parrish. – 2nd ed. – Oxford : Blackwell Scientific, 1987.
ISBN 0003832694 Pbk £9.95

—Introduction to Land Law / 4th ed. – London : Butterworths, 1988.
ISBN 0406648395 Pbk £14.95
ISBN 0406648441 Hbk £30.00

—Introduction to Land Law / McMorland. – 2nd ed. – London : Butterworths, 1987.
ISBN 0409636045 Hbk £111.50
ISBN 0409701726 Pbk £51.00

—Land acquisition / 2nd ed. – London : Butterworths, 1983.
ISBN 0409490911 Hbk £31.30

—Land and Tax Planning / London : Oyez Longman, 1982.
300p. – (Oyez Longman Practical Tax Ser.).
ISBN 0851206077 Hbk £15.00

—Land development and the infrastructure Lottery / J. Rowan-Robinson, M.G. Lloyd. – Edinburgh : T. & T. Clark, 1988.
xvi,160p; 22cm.
Includes index. Examines the relationship between local authorities and the private sector in the provision of supporting services and 'infrastructure' for private development. Looks at the discretionary powers of local authorities, at the legislation conferring this discretion and at how this is exercised.
ISBN 0567291499 Pbk £12.50

—Land Law / Henderson. – 5th ed. – London : Sweet & Maxwell, 1988.
ISBN 0421384409 Pbk £9.95

—Land Law / 3rd ed. – London : Pitman Publishing, 1983.
ISBN 0273018582 Pbk £9.95

—Land Law / 4th ed. – Plymouth : Macdonald & Evans, 1982.
ISBN 0712112596 Pbk £6.50

—Land Law / Houghton. – London : Financial Training, 1987.
– (SWOT).
ISBN 1851850465 Pbk £7.50

—Land Law / 4th ed. – Plymouth : Macdonald & Evans, 1982.
320p. – (M and E Handbook Ser.).
ISBN 0712112596 Hbk £5.95

—Land Law - Cases and Materials / Burn. – 5th ed. – London : Butterworths, 1986.
ISBN 0406623082 Hbk £34.50

—Land Law : Cohabitating Owners / London : Sweet & Maxwell, 1984.
640p. – (Sweet and Maxwell's Law Files Ser.: No. 1).
ISBN 0421321407 Hbk £29.50

—Land options / 2nd. – London : Longman Professional (UK), 1990.
– (Practitioner series).
Covers the law relating to the creation, transfer and exercise of options to purchase, rights of pre-emption, options to renew and determine leases and rent review clauses. Comments on relevant precedents, and considers the tax implications.

—Law for Estate Management Students / John Murdoch, Peter Schofield. – London : Butterworths, 1986.
A review of the basics of United Kingdom law for students of estate management. The English legal system, including elements of constitutional law, contracts, torts, and land law, are outlined in this book.
ISBN 0406562911 Pbk

—Local Government Planning and Land Act 1980 / London : Butterworths, 1981.
ISBN 0406584303 Hbk £32.50

—Local Government, Planning and Land Act 1980 / London : Butterworths, 1981.
This book consists of an annotated guide to the complete Act. A table of cases and a guide to the definitions used in the Act is also included.
ISBN 0406584303 Hbk

—National Land Code : a Commentary / London : Sweet & Maxwell, 1982.
ISBN 0421306300 Hbk £95.00

—Practical approach to land law / Phillips. – London : Financial Training, 1986.
ISBN 1851850244 Pbk £14.95

—Stonehenge : a report into the civil liberties implications of the events relating to the convoys of summer 1985 and 1986 / National Council for Civil Liberties. – London : National Council for Civil Liberties, 1986.
43p.
ISBN 0946088284

—Sweet & Maxwell Law / London : Sweet & Maxwell, 1984.
ISBN 0421321407 Pbk £29.50

File 4, Land law (Neighbours) 1985.
ISBN 0421340010 Pbk £29.50

—Tax Strategy for Conveyancing and Land Transactions / London : Oyez Longman, 1984.
ISBN 0851208797 Hbk

—Valuation and development appraisal / London : Estates Gazette, 1982.
ISBN 0728201097 Pbk £16.50

—Valuation and investment appraisal / London : Estates Gazette, 1983.
ISBN 0728200686 Pbk £18.00

LAND LAW - INDIA

—Cases and Material on the Urban Land (Ceiling and Regulation) Act, 1976, Act No 33 of 1976 : Along with Rules and Notifications / Madhya Pradesh : Lawyers Home, 1986.
152p.

—Commentaries on Urban Land (Ceiling and Regulation) Act, 1976 / 2nd ed. – Allahabad : Law Publishers, 1983.

—Commentaries on Uttar Pradesh Imposition of Ceiling on Land Holdings Act, 1960 / Lucknow : Eastern Book Company, 1977.
304p.

—Compulsory Acquisition of Land in India, 2 Vols. / Allahabad : Universal Book Agency, 1984.

—Land Aquisition / Allahabad : Universal Book Agency, 1985.

—Law of Land Acquisition and Compensation, 2 Vols. / 7th ed. – Lucknow : Eastern Book Company, 1986.
2,144p.

—Law of Land Acquisition and Compensation, 2 Vols. / 7th ed. – Allahabad : Law Book Company, 1984.
With 1987 supplement.

—Reforms to Pre-Empt Change : Land Legislation in Karnataka / New Delhi : Concept Publishing Company, 1983.
x, 122p.

—Uttar Pradesh Land Revenue Act, 1901 / P.L. Malik. – 7th ed. – Lucknow : Eastern Book Company, 1983.
243p.

LAND LAW - IRELAND

—Casebook on Irish Land Law / London : Butterworths, 1984.
ISBN 0862050642 Hbk £32.50
ISBN 086205074X Pbk £25.00

—Irish land law / 2nd ed. – London : Butterworths, 1986.
ISBN 0862052173 Hbk £32.50
ISBN 0862052181 Pbk £25.00

LAND LAW - MALAYSIA

—Land Acquisition Act, 1960 (Act No. 34 of 1960) / Kuala Lumpur : International Law Books Services.

—Land Law in Malaysia : Cases and Commentary / Lake Tee Khaw. – 1987. – Butterworths.
539p.
Covers the Malaysian Torrens system, rights and powers of the State authority, the nature and extent of private ownership, the registration of dealings, transfers, leases and tenancies, security transactions, restraints of dealings, planning law use under the national code, and powers of the court.
ISBN 0409995312 Hbk £130.00

—Land Law in Malaysia : Cases and Commentary / London : Butterworths, 1987.
ISBN 0409995312 Hbk £61.00

—National Land Code (Act 56 of 1965) / Kuala Lumpur : International Law Books Services.

—Strata titles in Malaysia : law and practice / L T Khaw. – London : Butterworths, 1987.
ISBN 040999538X Hbk £32.00

LAND LAW - NEW ZEALAND

—Compulsory Acquisition of Land in New Zealand / London : Butterworths, 1984.
ISBN 0409601225 Hbk £25.40

—Introduction to Land Law / D.W. McMorland. – 2nd ed. – Butterworths, 1987.
708p.
Covers title to land, freehold estates, future interests, leasehold estates, easements and profits, licenses, land as security, mortgages and other charges, the holding of interest in land, the transfer of interest in land, covenants affecting freehold land, and the extent of landholder's rights.
ISBN 0409701726 Pbk £82.50

—Land Law, 2 Vols. / Butterworths, 1978.
ISBN 0409636002 Hbk

with Supplement-1981
ISBN 0409636045

—Maori land laws of New Zealand / Saskatoon : University of Saskatchewan, Native Law Centre, 1983.
86p.
ISBN 088880122X Hbk £13.00

LAND LAW - SCOTLAND

—Scottish land law / Edinburgh : W Green & Son, 1989.
A fresh treatment of Scottish land law, filling the gap since the last edition of Rankine's 'Landownership' (1909), with particular attention to the very large body of legislation affecting the use of land in the intervening 80 years. The increasing impact of European law, particularly affecting the enviroment, is also noted. With full cross references to Halliday's 'Conveyancing Law and Practice'. Published under the auspices of the Scottish Universities Law Institute.
ISBN 0414008812 Hbk

LAND LAW - SINGAPORE

—Butterworths Handbook of Singapore Land Law / Butterworths, 1986.
917p.
Examines the sale of property, statutes which affect the transfer of property, registration of property, planning and development control, maintenance and management of property, property tax and land revenue, land acquisition, and the control of rent.
ISBN 0409995169 Pbk £99.00

—Handbook of Singapore Land Law / London : Butterworths, 1986.
ISBN 0409995169 Hbk £69.00

—Land Law / Singapore : University of Singapore, 1985.
– (Singapore Law Series).
The text discusses the structure of Singapore land law and considers the various basic land law concepts. Topics covered include: types of land transfer and registration, consideration of commercial interests in land, and land planning and the planning acts.
ISBN 0409995010 Hbk £25.00

LAND LAW - SOUTH AFRICA

—Practitioner's Guide to the Alienation of Land Act / S. H. Treisman. – 2nd ed. – Durban : Butterworths, 1984.
– (Eng. & Afrikaans).
ISBN 040906078X Hbk
ISBN 0409060798 Pbk

LAND LAW - ZAMBIA

—Land Law and Policy in Zambia / Lusaka : University of Zambia, Publications Office, 1982.
112p.

LAND REFORM - NIGERIA

—Land law and development : an inaugural lecture delivered at the University of Lagos on Thursday, 17th January, 1980 / by M.I. Jegede. – Lagos : University of Lagos Press, 1981.
39p. – (Inaugural lecture series).
Includes bibliographical references.
ISBN 978226413X

LAND REGISTRATION - CANADA

—Land Registration Reform Act, 1983, Bill 156 : An Act Respecting Conveyancing Documents and Procedures and the Recording of Title to Real Property / Ontario : Ontario Government Publications Service, 1983.
33p.

—Real Estate and Landlord and Tenant / 2nd ed. – Agincourt : Carswell, 1986.
853p. – (Bar Admission Course Materials).
This work for the law student is a practical guide to the handling of most real estate transactions under Canadian law. The Planning Act of 1983 and the Land Registration Reform Act of 1984 are reviewed in the text.

—Real Estate Law / R. C. B. Risk. – 3rd ed. – Aurora : Canada Law Book Co, 1986.
1300p. – (Text Books-Civil).
The third edition of this text has undergone significant changes to make it an even more useful and relevant sourcebook for Canadian Real Estate practitioners. This new edition includes up-to-date forms and materials used in routine real estate transactions reflecting the changes brought about by the Land Registration Reform Act.

—Registration of title of Land / Agincourt : Carswell, 1987.
ISBN 045935440 Hbk £48.40

—Registration of Title to Land, 2 Vols. / Agincourt : Carswell, 1987.
950p.

—Registration of Title to Land / Agincourt : Carswell, 1987.
950p.
This work is a comparitive analysis of the Canadian Torrens Acts with the representative body of Australian, New Zealand, and Tasmanian Acts. The book examines the application of the Torrens system in the context of transfer, leases, mortgages, lis pendens, restrictive covenants, and other dealings in all the jurisdictions.

LAND REGISTRATION - CANADA - ONTARIO
—Document User Guide : Ontario Land Registration Reform Act / North Ryde : C.C.H. Australia, 1986.
148p.
ISBN 0887963404 Pbk £8.00

LAND REGISTRATION - GREAT BRITAIN
—Registered Land Practice Notes / Joint Advisory Committee on the Law Society. – London : Oyez Longman, 1982.
ISBN 0851207162 Hbk £2.25

—Registered land practice notes / Law Society. – 2nd ed. – London : Longman Professional, 1986.
ISBN 0851212573 Pbk £5.95

LAND REGISTRATION - SOUTH AFRICA
—Law and Practice of Deeds Registration / W. V. de Beer. – Repr. of 1978 ed. – Durban : Butterworths.
ISBN 0409045500 Hbk

Supplement
ISBN 0409045527 Hbk

LAND REGISTRY - GREAT BRITAIN
—Guide to Land Registry Practice / Timothy. – 16th ed. – London : Longman Professional, 1985.
ISBN 0851212840 Pbk £19.95

LAND REGISTRY - NORTHERN IRELAND
—Land Registry Practice in Northern Ireland / Belfast : Queen's University of Belfast, 1984.
xxiii, 142p.
Main work only
ISBN 085389194X Hbk £10.95

Supplement only

LAND SETTLEMENT - COMMONWEALTH
—Common law aboriginal title / Oxford : Clarendon Press.
360.
Addresses the land rights question applied throughout the British Empire. Assesses the impact of English law in a colony acquired by settlememt where no form of aboriginal land ownership had previously existed. Conclusions reached suggest a doctrinal approach which could be used to resolve outstanding aboriginal land claims.*Academics, lawyers representing aboriginal peoples, students of human rights*
ISBN 0198252234 Hbk £35

LAND SETTLEMENT - ENGLAND
—Strict settlement : a guide for historians / Barbara English and John Saville. – Hull : University of Hull Press, 1983.
144p. – (Occasional papers in economic and social history).
Bibliography: p.132-137. - Includes index.
ISBN 0859584399

LAND TENURE - AFRICA
—Title to territory in Africa / Oxford : Oxford University Press, 1986.
ISBN 0198253796 Hbk £35.00

LAND TENURE - AUSTRALIA
—Aboriginal land rights : a handbook / edited by Nicolas Peterson. – Canberra City : Australian Institute of Aboriginal Studies, 1981.
vi,297p.
The papers published here were originally prepared as background information for the Aboriginal Land Rights Symposium held as part of the Australian Institute of Aboriginal Studies Biennial Meeting 1981. Bibliography: p269-297.

—Aboriginal land rights legislation : an examination of the publications associated with Commonwealth legislation / Gregory P. Jones. – Belconnen, A.C.T., Australia : Canberra College of Advanced Education, Library, 1983.
iii, 196 p.; 25 cm.
Includes bibliographical references.
ISBN 0858892391 pbk. £9.00

—Aboriginal Landrights in New South Wales / Chippendale : Alternative Publishing Cooperative, 1985.
ISBN 090918884X Hbk £22.50
ISBN 0909188858 Pbk £12.95

—Aborigines, Land and Land Rights / M. Langton. – Canberra City : Australian Institute of Aboriginal Studies, 1983.
476p.
ISBN 0855751436 Hbk £14.90

—Aborigines Today : Land and Justice / Burger. – Third World Publications, 1988.
ISBN 0900918225 Pbk £4.95

—Landrights : a Christian Perspective / Chippendale : Alternative Publishing Cooperative, 1980.
159p.
ISBN 0909188408 Hbk £19.95
ISBN 0909188424 Pbk £9.95

LAND TENURE - CANADA
—Indian Reserves in the Atlantic Provinces of Canada / Saskatoon : University of Saskatchewan, Native Law Centre, 1986.
92p.
ISBN 088880167X Hbk £25.00

—Indian Title in Canada / Agincourt : Carswell, 1987.
154p.
This work focuses on the basis of Indian land claims in Canada and provides a thorough discussion of the court's responses to these claims. The author integrates history and law in explaining the issues.

—Native Rights and the Boundaries of Rupert's land and the North-Western Territory / Saskatoon : University of Saskatchewan, Native law Centre, 1982.
72p.
ISBN 0888801114 Hbk £12.00

—Proposed amendments to the Indian Act concerning conditionally surrendered land and band taxation powers / Canada. – Ottawa : Department of Indian Affairs and Northern Development, 1987.
iii,11,12,iiip.
French title on added t.p.: Modifications proposees a la Loi sur les Indiens concernant les terres cedees sous condition et les pouvoirs d'imposition des bandes indiennes. Pages numbered in opposite directions. Text in English and French.
ISBN 0662552555

LAND TENURE - CANADA - BRITISH COLUMBIA
—Co-ownership of land / Law Reform Commission of British Columbia. – Vancover : The Commission, 1987.
ii,75p. – (Working paper).
Caatalogued from cover. Includes bibliographical references. Includes Draft Property Law Amendment Act.
ISBN 0771886071

LAND TENURE - CANADA - QUEBEC
—Indian Reserves in Quebec / Saskatoon : University of Saskatchewan, Native Law Centre, 1984.
44p.
ISBN 0888801408 Hbk £20.00

LAND TENURE - ENGLAND
—Land compensation : a study of compensation determination / Barry P.D. Denyer-Green. – Cambridge : Granta Editions, 1986.
xi,124p. – (Occasional paper).
Includes bibliographical references.
ISBN 0906782228

—Land law / Patrick J. Dalton. – 3rd ed. – London : Pitman, 1983.
xliii,377p; 22cm.
Previous ed.: London : Oyez, 1975. Includes index.
ISBN 0273018582 Pbk £9.95

—Land law & landscape / Philip Britton and Ian Thompson. – 1 videocassette. – London : Sweet & Maxwell in association with the University of Warwick, 1986.
– (Sweet & Maxwell's lawfilms).

—Law of allotments / by J.F. Garner. – 4th ed. – London : Shaw and Sons, 1984.
xxii,113p; 22cm.
Previous ed.: 1977. Includes index.
ISBN 0721901425 Pbk Unpriced

LAND TENURE - GAMBIA
—Memoranda and draft : bills re : christian marriage, matrimonial causes, offences relating to property and lands (Banjul and Kombo St. Mary) / Law Reform Commission of the Gambia. – Banjul : The Commission?, 1985.
xv,112p.
Includes the text of draft legislation.

LAND TENURE - GHANA
—Ollennu's principles of customary land law in Ghana / Gordon R. Woodman. – 2nd ed. – Birmingham : CAL Press, 1985.
xxviii,184p.
Includes bibliographical references and index.
ISBN 0951053000

LAND TENURE - GREAT BRITAIN
—Agricultural Holdings Bill : report on the consolidation of certain enactments relating to agricultural holdings / the Law Commission. – London : H.M.S.O., 1985.
7p.
ISBN 0101966504

—Compleate Copyholder : Wherein is Contained a Learned Discourse of the Antiquity and Nature of Manors and Copy-Holds, with the Forme of Keeping a Copy-Hold Court and Court Baron / Repr. of 1673 ed. – Abingdon : Professional Books.
399p.

—Introduction to the Law of Tenures / Repr. of 1730 ed. – Abingdon : Professional Books.
460p.

LAND TENURE - HONG KONG
—Land compensation and valuation law in Hong Kong / Gordon N. Cruden. – Singapore : Butterworths, 1986.
xxxii,476p.
Collation and analysis of relevant statutory and case law. References are made to Hong Kong cases, as well as English, Scottish, Australian, Canadian, and New Zealand cases.
ISBN 0409995258 Hbk £137.5

LAND TENURE - IRELAND
—Casebook on Irish land law / by J.C.W. Wylie. – Abingdon, Oxon. : Professional Books, 1984.
xxxxii,723p.
Includes index.
ISBN 0862050642

—Irish land law / by J.C.W. Wylie : consultant editor for the Republic of Ireland, The Hon. Mr. Justice Kenny. – 2nd ed. – Abingdon, Oxon. : Professional Books, 1986.
cxxi,1004p.
Previous ed.: 1975. Includes index.
ISBN 0862052173

LAND TENURE - MALAYSIA
—Private caveats : entry, extension, removal and appeals / by Wong Kim Fatt : with a foreword by Mohamed Suffian. – Singapore : Malayan Law Journal, 1980.
xvi,141p.
Contains a table of cases, judicial pronouncements on caveats, applications for entry, extension of private caveats, removal under section 326, 327, appeal under section 418, caveating a portion of land, and taxation of costs.
ISBN 9971700107 Hbk £20.00

LAND TENURE - NEW ZEALAND
—Fragmentation of Maori Land / Auckland : Legal Research Foundation, 1980.
53p.
ISBN 0908581106 Pbk £5.50

LAND TENURE - NIGERIA
—Land law and development : an inaugural lecture delivered at the University of Lagos on Thursday, 17th January, 1980 / by M.I. Jegede. – Lagos : University of Lagos Press, 1981.
39p. – (Inaugural lecture series).
Includes bibliographical references.
ISBN 978226413X

—Land law in Nigeria / M. G. Yakubu. – London : Macmillan, 1985.
xxvi,270p. – (Macmillan international college edition).
Bibliography: p.260-261. - Includes index.
ISBN 0333350901

—Land Use Act : a study / by H. Chand. – S.l. : s.n., 1986.
98p.
Includes bibliographical references.

—Land Use Act : issues and controversies / by Hari C. Chand. – Jos, Nigeria : University of Jos, 1985.
22p. – (Postgraduate open lectures series).
Includes bibliographical references.

—Oshimili and Aniocha : their people and land tenure / by R.A.I. Ogbobine. – S.l. : s.n., 1981.
viii,192p.

LAND TENURE - PAPUA NEW GUINEA
—Land law and policy in Papua New Guinea : by R.W. James / Port Moresby : Papua New Guinea Law Reform Commission, 1985.
xix,204p. – (Monograph).
Includes bibliographical references.
ISBN 998055004X

LAND TENURE - SCOTLAND
—Law of agricultural holdings in Scotland / Brian Gill. – Edinburgh : Green, 1982.
xxxiv,451p; 25cm.
Includes index. Includes text of 6 acts.
ISBN 0444996656 SET

LAND TENURE (MAORI LAW)
—Maori land courts : report of the Royal Commission of Inquiry 1980 / Thaddeus Pearcey McCarthy. – Wellington,N.Z. : Government Printer, 1980.
xiii,149p; 24cm.
Includes bibliographical references and index. Chairman: Sir Thaddeus Pearcey McCarthy.

LAND USE - CANADA
—Canadian Law of Planning and Zoning, 1 Vol. / Agincourt : Carswell.
318p.
This looseleaf service covers every aspect of land use in Canada including: master plans, non-conforming uses, building construction permits, enforcement, appeals, and remedies. The work contains the text of planning legislation from all provinces.

—Land Use Law : B.C. Handbook / Z. Pereboom. – Toronto : Butterworths, 1984.
310p.
ISBN 0409988634 Pbk £40.00

—Land Use Planning : Practice Procedure and Policy / Robert Macaulay. - Toronto : Butterworths.

LAND USE - CANADA - BRITISH COLUMBIA

—Land Use Law : British Columbia Handbook / Butterworths, 1984.
310p.
ISBN 0409988634 Pbk £40.00

LAND USE - CANADA - ONTARIO

—Land use planning / Robert Macaulay. - Scarborough, Ontario : Butterworths (Canada).
Survey of Ontario Municipal Board cases, precedents, pointers on the impact of the Charter of Rights, and relevant legislation, regulations, guidelines and interpretation bulletins. Covers planning authorities, provincial planning, official plans, zoning and development control, development levies and municipal finance, and the conduct of a planning application.

LAND USE - GREAT BRITAIN

—Land policy in planning / Nathaniel Lichfield and Haim Darin-Drabkin. - London : Allen & Unwin, 1980.
viii,321p; 24cm.
Bibliography: p304-313. - Includes index.
ISBN 0043330177 £18.00

—Land Use Control Handbook / Reading : College of Estate Management, 1981.
400p. - (College of Estate Management Handbooks Ser.).

—Landscape, Land use and the Law / Spon (E & FN), 1984.
ISBN 0419125205 Pbk £16.95

LAND USE - HONG KONG

—Land-use planning in Hong Kong : history, policies and procedures / Roger Bristow. - Hong Kong : Oxford University Press, 1984.
xii, 328p, 8 leaves of plates.
Bibliography: p299-317.
ISBN 0195814967

LAND USE - INDIA

—Socio-economic and legal implications of Urban Land (Ceiling and Regulation) Act, 1976 / Gopal Bhargava. - New Delhi : Adhinav, 1983.
xiv,172p.
Bibliography: p.167-170. - Includes index. Includes the text of the Urban Land Ceiling Bill.

LAND USE - NIGERIA

—Cases on the Land Uses Act / J.A. Omotola. - Lagos : Lagos University Press, 1983.
170p.
ISBN 9782264407

—Essays on the Nigerian Land Use Act 1978 / Akoka : University of Lagos Library, 1980.
57p.
ISBN 9782264253 Pbk £4.00

—Land Use Act / Zaria : Ahmadu Bello University Press.

—Land Use Act : a study / by H. Chand. - S.l. : s.n., 1986.
98p.
Includes bibliographical references.

—Land Use Act : issues and controversies / by Hari C. Chand. - Jos, Nigeria : University of Jos, 1985.
22p. - (Postgraduate open lectures series).
Includes bibliographical references.

—Land Use Act : Report of a National Workshop / Akoka : University of Lagos Library.
178p.

—Land Use Act : report of a National Workshop held at the University of Lagos, May 25 - May 28, 1981 / edited by J.A. Omotola. - Lagos : Lagos University Press, 1982.
178p.

—Land Use Act revisited / by Alhaji Isa Alabi. - Kano, Nigeria : Alhaji Isa Alabi, 1984.
v,63p.

—Nigerian Land Use Act : policy and principles / by R.W. James. - Ife-Ife, Nigeria : University of Ife Press, 1987.
xxxi,195p.
Includes bibliographical references and index.
ISBN 9781360690

LAND USE - SCOTLAND

—Onshore oil and gas pipelines : the problems / by Kevan MacDonald. - Dundee : University of Dundee, Centre for Petroleum and Mineral Studies, 1981.
xiii,102p. - (Occasional paper).

LAND USE - SOUTH AFRICA

—Removal of certain restrictions in respect of land / South African Law Commission. - Pretoria : The Commission, 1984.
iv,9p. - (Report).
ISBN 0621102008

LAND VALUE TAXATION

—Rating and income tax / 53 v. - London : Solicitors' Law Stationery Society, 1924.
Continued by: Rating and valuation reporter.

—Rating and valuation reporter / v. - London : Solicitor's Law Stationery Department, 1961-.
Continues: Rating and income tax reporter. Published: London: Rating Publishers, 1965-.
ISBN 00486817

LAND VALUE TAXATION - ENGLAND

—Rates : proposals for rate limitation and reform of the rating system / presented to Parliament by the Secretary of State for the Environment and the Secretary of State for Wales ... - London : H.M.S.O., 1983.
24p.
ISBN 0101900805

LAND VALUE TAXATION - GREAT BRITAIN

—Development land tax / by Robert W. Maas. - 4th ed. - Croydon : Tolley, 1982.
xiii,244p; 23cm.
Previous ed.: 1981. Includes index.
ISBN 0854590560 Pbk £10.50

LAND VALUE TAXATION - SCOTLAND

—Valuation and rating in Scotland: proposals for reform / presented to Parliament by the Secretary of State for Scotland. - London : H.M.S.O., 1983.
10p.
ISBN 0101901801

LANDLORD AND TENANT

—Codification of the law of landlord and tenant : forfeiture of tenancies / The Law Commission. - London : H.M.S.O., 1985.
ix,195p; 25cm. - (H.C. 1984-85).
ISBN 0102279853

—Limits of the legal process : a study of landlords, law and crime / David Nelken. - London : Academic Press, 1983.
xiii,241p; 24cm.
Bibliography: p219-225. - Includes index.
ISBN 0125152809 Unpriced

—Queensberry leases : petitions, answers, speeches and other documents of the Court of Session regarding leases on the entailed estates of the late William, Duke of Queensberry / 6 v. - Edinburgh : s.n., 1813.
Various printers. Ms. contents lists and marginalia. Spine title. Includes Latin text.

—Rent Acts / 10th ed. 3. - London : Stevens, 1967.

LANDLORD AND TENANT - AUSTRALIA

—Australian Tenancy Practice and Precedents / Michael Redfern. - Butterworths, 1987.
ISBN 0409494909 loose £235.00

—Commercial Rent Reviews : Law and Valuation Practice / North Ryde : Law Book Co, 1986.
xxvii, 205p.
ISBN 0455206414 Pbk £27.50

LANDLORD AND TENANT - AUSTRALIA - NEW SOUTH WALES

—Residential Tenancies Handbook - Victoria / Butterworths, 1982.
224p.
ISBN 0409309168 Pbk £39.00

—Tenancy Law and Practice Victoria / A.A. Chernov. - 2nd ed. - Butterworths, 1980.
664p.
ISBN 0409356115 Hbk £85.00

LANDLORD AND TENANT - AUSTRALIA - SOUTH AUSTRALIA

—Residential tenancy law and practice / by Adrian J. Bradbrook, Susan V. MacCallum, Anthony P. Moore : with a foreword by the Honourable Mr. Justice King. - Sydney : Law Book Co., 1983.
lx,940p.
Bibliography: p.891-898. - Includes index. Includes texts of Residential Tenancies Act 1980 of Victorian jurisdiction and Residential Tenancies Act 1978-81 of South Australian jurisdiction.
ISBN 0455204977

LANDLORD AND TENANT - AUSTRALIA - TASMANIA

—Research paper on occupiers' liability law / Max Atkinson. - Hobart : Government Printer?, 1984.
iv,75p.

LANDLORD AND TENANT - AUSTRALIA - VICTORIA

—Consultation and government : report of the inquiry into processes of consultation in Victoria with special reference to the case of tenancy law reform / with papers by Ronald F. Henderson ... et al. - Melbourne : Victorian Council of Social Service, 1981.
xii,273p.
Includes bibliographical notes.
ISBN 0949748072

—Manual of the Victorian Residential Tenancies Act / North Ryde : Law Book Co, 1982.
xx, 299p.
ISBN 045520540X Pbk £37.00

—Residential tenancy law and practice / by Adrian J. Bradbrook, Susan V. MacCallum, Anthony P. Moore : with a foreword by the Honourable Mr. Justice King. - Sydney : Law Book Co., 1983.
lx,940p.
Bibliography: p.891-898. - Includes index. Includes texts of Residential Tenancies Act 1980 of Victorian jurisdiction and Residential Tenancies Act 1978-81 of South Australian jurisdiction.
ISBN 0455204977

LANDLORD AND TENANT - CANADA

—Leasing in Canada : A Business Guide / Toronto : Butterworths, 1986.
ISBN 0409805041 Pbk £35.00

—Real Estate and Landlord and Tenant / 2nd ed. - Agincourt : Carswell, 1986.
853p. - (Bar Admission Course Materials).
This work for the law student is a practical guide to the handling of most real estate transactions under Canadian law. The Planning Act of 1983 and the Land Registration Reform Act of 1984 are reviewed in the text.

—Residential Tenancies / 4th ed. - Agincourt : Carswell, 1983.
366p.
This textbook is a comprehensive treatment of the Canadian law of landlord and tenant in the residential tenancy. Numerous reported and unreported decisions from courts across Canada are summarized in the work.

—Williams and Rhodes on the Canadian Law of Landlord and Tenant / 6th ed. - Agincourt : Carswell, 1988.
432p.

—Williams' and Rhodes' Canadian Law of Landlord and Tenant, 2 Vols. / 5th ed. - Agincourt : Carswell, 1983.
1400p.
This two volume looseleaf text is a comprehensive guide to commercial and residential tenancies in every province of Canada. Topics covered include: rent control, the creation of the landlord and tenant relationship, recovery of rent, and related issues.

LANDLORD AND TENANT - CANADA - ALBERTA

—Landlord-Tenant Rights in Alberta / 5th ed. - North Vancouver : International Self-Counsel Press, 1986.
106p.
ISBN 0889082413 Hbk £6.95

LANDLORD AND TENANT - CANADA - BRITISH COLUMBIA

—Co-ownership of land / Law Reform Commission of British Columbia. - Vancover : The Commission, 1987.
ii,75p. - (Working paper).
Caatalogued from cover. Includes bibliographical references. Includes Draft Property Law Amendment Act.
ISBN 0771886071

—Commercial Tenancy Act / Law Reform Commission of British Columbia. - Vancouver : Law Reform Commission of British Columbia, 1988.
v,185p. - (Working paper).
Includes extracts from legislation.
ISBN 0771886624

—Landlord-Tenant Rights in British Columbia / 4th ed. - North Vancouver : International Self-Counsel Press, 1985.
ISBN 0889081565 Hbk £7.95

—Report on co-ownership of land / Law Reform Commmission of British Columbia. - Vancouver : The Commission, 1988.
Includes bibliographical references. Includes draft legislation and text of the Partition of Property Act.
ISBN 0771887256

—Report on distress for rent / Victoria : Queen's Printer, 1982.
72p.
ISBN 0771882947

LANDLORD AND TENANT - CANADA - ONTARIO

—Annotated Ontario Landlord and Tenant Statutes / John A. McNair. - Agincourt : Carswell, 1986.
300p.
This book fully annotates the Landlord and Tenant Act, the Residential Tenancies Act, and the Residential Complexes Financing Cost Restraint Act of Ontario, Canada. Digests of Residential Tenancy Commission decisions and relevant court decisions are included in the work.

—Landlord-Tenant Rights in Ontario / 6th ed. - North Vancouver : International Self-Counsel Press, 1986.
168p.
ISBN 0889083592 Hbk £7.95

LANDLORD AND TENANT - ENGLAND

—Adkin's landlord and tenant / Raymond Walton, Michael Essayan. - 18th ed. - London : Estates Gazette, 1982.
xxxiii,440p.
Includes index. .

—Butterworths landlord and tenant handbook / edited by Lexis editorial staff : consulting editor David lloyd Evans. - London : Butterworths, 1982.
vii,597,9p.
Includes index. Contains statutes and statutory instruments up to date to 23 April 1982.
ISBN 0406253706

—Co-ownership / M.P. Thompson. - London : Sweet & Maxwell, 1988.
xxv,151p.
Analyses forms of co-ownership of freehold and leasehold interests in real property, and such items of personal property as joint bank accounts. Explores the legal principles involved, and applies them to practical problems. Co-habitation, financial contribution, marriage, divorce, death and insolvency are also discussed.
ISBN 0421375000 £19.50

—Comments on civil justice review of housing cases / JUSTICE. - London : JUSTICE, 1987.
7 leaves.

—Consultation paper on the Distress for Rent Rules 1983 / Lord Chancellor's Department. - London : The Department, 1987.
13,12 leaves. - (HH/290).
Includes the text of draft revised Distress for Rent Rules 1987.

—Hill and Redman's law of landlord and tenant / General editor, Michael Barnes. - 18th ed. 2. - London : Butterworths, 1988.
looseleaf.
Includes index. Previous ed.: 1982.
ISBN 0406227403

—Housing Act 1980, as amended by the Housing and Building Control Act 1984 / Trevor M. Aldridge. - London : Oyez, 1984.
xxxix,334p.
Previous ed.: 1980, titled The Housing Act 1980: a practical guide. Includes index.
ISBN 0851207650

—Housing disrepair / Nicholas C. Martyn and Edward Lloyd-Jones. - London : Longman Professional, 1985.
xxv,187p; 22cm. - (Longman professional practitioner series).
Includes index.
ISBN 0851209904 Pbk £13.50

—Landlord and Tenant Act 1985 / with annotations by Andrew Arden and Siobhan McGrath. - London : Sweet & Maxwell, 1986.
75p.
Includes index.
ISBN 0421358904

—Landlord and tenant : compensation for tenants' improvements / The Law Commission. - London : H.M.S.O., 1987.
iv,104p; 22cm. - (Working paper).
ISBN 0117301841

—Landlord and tenant law / by David Yates and A.J. Hawkins. - 2nd ed. - London : Sweet & Maxwell, 1986.
cviii,839p; 26cm.
Includes legislation enacted between 1980 and 1985. Covers the common law framework of landlord and tenant, the Rent Acts, protected tenants, council tenants, housing associations, the Housing Act 1985, the Landlord and Tenant Act 1985, the Housing Associations Act 1985, and the Housing (Consequential Provisions) Act 1985. The law applying to business tenants, and agricultural tenants is also discussed.
ISBN 0421354208 Hbk £36.50
ISBN 0421354305 Pbk £26.50

—Landlord and tenant law : privity of contract and estate / the Law Commission. - London : HMSO, 1988.
v,67p. - (H.C. 1988-89).
Includes the text of a draft Landlord and Tenant (Covenants) bill.
ISBN 0102008892

—Landlord and tenant - reform of the law / The Law Commission. - London : H.M.S.O., 1987.
iv,35p; 30cm.
ISBN 010101452X

—Landlord and tenant : text and materials on housing and law / Martin Partington. - 2nd ed. - London : Weidenfeld and Nicolson, 1980.
xxxviii,554p; 23cm.
Previous ed.: 1975. Bibliography: p533-544. - Includes index. .
ISBN 0297777904 Hbk £20.00
ISBN 0297777912 Pbk £10.50

—Law of landlord and tenant / Evans. - 2nd ed. - London : Butterworths, 1985.
xlvii,505p.
Previous ed.: 1974. Includes index.
ISBN 0406577323 Hbk £22.00
ISBN 0406577331 Pbk £14.50

—Leasehold conveyancing : laid before Parliament by the Lord High Chancellor pursuant to section 3(2) of the Law Commissions Act 1965 / the Law Commission. - London : H.M.S.O., 1987.
iii,37p. - (H.C.).
ISBN 0102360871

—Leasehold law / Trevor M. Aldridge. - v. - London : Oyez Longman, 1980.
looseleaf.
Includes index.
ISBN 0851204716

—Part II of the Landlord and Tenant Act 1954 / the Law Commission. - London : HMSO, 1988.
viii,144p. - (Working paper).
Includes sections from the Act.
ISBN 0117301930

—Private sector tenancies / Philip H. Pettit. - 2nd ed. - London : Butterworths, 1981.
li,327p; 26cm.
Previous ed.: published as Landlord and tenant under the Rent Act 1979. 1978. Includes index.
ISBN 0406337225 Unpriced

—Quiet enjoyment : remedies for harassment and illegal eviction / by Andrew Arden and Martin Partington. Edited by S. Carrott and C. Hunter. - 3rd. - London : Legal Action Group, 1990.
127.
Includes index.
ISBN 0905099265 Pbk £11

—Rent acts and regulations amended and annotated / Andrew Arden, J. T. Farrand. - 2nd ed. - London : Sweet & Maxwell, 1981.
xl,435p; 26cm.
ISBN 0421282207 £16.50

—Rent control and leasehold enfranchisement / Trevor M. Aldridge. - 8th ed. - London : Oyez, 1980.
205p; 22cm.
Previous ed.: 1977. Includes index.
ISBN 0851205461 Pbk £9.50

—Security of tenure under the Rent Act / by Jill E. Martin. - London : Sweet & Maxwell, 1986.
xxi,163p; 22cm.
Includes index.
ISBN 0421363304 Hbk £14.00
ISBN 0421363401 Pbk £10.50

LANDLORD AND TENANT - GREAT BRITAIN

—Business tenancies / London : Longman Professional (UK), 1989.
- (Longman practice notes).
Examines the law pertaining to assigning, subletting, parting with possession and repairs, with specimen letters. Contains details of time limits, costs and fees, and precedent forms for termination of a tenancy under s.25 and a request for a new tenancy under s.26 of the Landlord and Tenant Act 1954.
ISBN 0851215319 Pbk £9.95

—Casebook on Rent Review and Lease Renewal / Mark Pawlowski. - London : Collins, 1986.
600p.
ISBN 0003831957 Hbk £35.00

—Casebook on Rent Review and Lease Renewal / Pawlowski. - Oxford : Blackwell Scientific, 1986.
ISBN 0003831957 Hbk £40.00

—Casebook on repairs / London : Estates Gazette, 1987.
ISBN 0728201038 Pbk £16.00

—Codification of the law of landlord and tenant : covenants regarding dispositions, alterations and change of user / The Law Commission. - London : H.M.S.O., 1985.
x,139p; 25cm. - (H.C. 1984-85).
ISBN 0102278857

—Conveyancing and Residential Tenancies : Conditions of Sale and Other Recent Developments to March 1982 / London : Law Society, 1982.

—Drafting Business Leases / London : Oyez Longman, 1980.
ISBN 0851204082 Hbk £13.50

—Drafting residential leases / 2nd. - 1193, 1989.
Coverage includes the terms of the lease, premises, easements and ancillary rights, rents and rent increases, service charges anmd insurance. New edition covers changes resulting from the Housing Act 1988.
ISBN 0851214355 Hbk £35.00

—Fair rents : a practical guide to the law relating to the rents of residential tenancies including the work of rent officers, rent assessment committees and rent tribunals / by John Prophet. - 3rd ed. - London : Shaw and Sons, 1985.
xxxi,243p.
ISBN 0721907024

—Future for rented housing? : responses to the Government's proposals / National Housing Forum. - London : National Federation of Housing Associations, 1988.
iv,47p; 30cm.
ISBN 0862971306 Pbk No price

—Landlord and Tenant / Smith. - 2nd ed. - London : Butterworths, 1985.
ISBN 0406577323 Hbk £28.00
ISBN 0406577331 Pbk £17.95

—Landlord and Tenant / 2nd ed. - Plymouth : Macdonald & Evans, 1985.
304p. - (M and E Handbook Ser.).
ISBN 0712128050 Hbk £5.95

—Landlord and Tenant / 1st ed. - Plymouth : Macdonald & Evans, 1982.
304p. - (M and E Handbook Ser.).
ISBN 0712112510 Hbk £3.95

—Landlord and Tenant / 2nd ed. - Plymouth : Macdonald & Evans, 1985.
ISBN 071210500X Pbk £6.50

—Landlord and Tenant Act 1985 / McGrath. - London : Sweet & Maxwell, 1986.
ISBN 0421358904 Pbk £5.75

—Landlord and Tenant Act 1987 / London : Shaw & Sons, 1987.
ISBN 072191070X Pbk £10.95

—Landlord and Tenant Act, 1987 / London : Shaw & Sons, 1987.
ISBN 072191070X Pbk £10.95

—Landlord and Tenant Casebook / London : Estates Gazette, 1985.
ISBN 0728200880 Pbk £12.00

—Landlord and Tenant Handbook / Butterworths. - 2nd ed. - London : Butterworths, 1987.
ISBN 0406253714 Pbk £22.95

—Landlord and Tenant Law / London : Collins, 1986.
256p.
ISBN 0003831183 Pbk £9.95

—Landlord and Tenant Law / Oxford : Blackwell Scientific, 1986.
ISBN 0003831183 Pbk £12.95

—Landlord and tenant : privity of contract and estate : duration of liability of parties to leases / the Law Commission. - London : HMSO, 1986.
iv,101p. - (Working paper).
Includes bibliographical references.
ISBN 0117301760

—Landlord and Tenant Up-to-Date / London : Law Society, 1985.
23p. - (Nineteen Eighty-Five Crash Course Transcripts).

—Landlord and Tenants / Redman. - 18th ed. - London : Butterworths, 1988.
Service to date.
ISBN 040612987X Hbk £200.00

—Law of Dilapidations / 9th ed. - London : Estates Gazette, 1988.
ISBN 0728200449 Pbk £11.00
ISBN 0728201151 Hbk £18.50

—Law of flats / 2nd. - London : Longman Professional (UK), 1989.
- (Practitioner series).
New edition takes account of the Landlord and Tenant Acts of 1985 and 1987 and changes resulting from the Housing Act 1988, including assured tenancies. Includes new chapters on disposition, the landlord's identity and the right of first refusal.
ISBN 085121388X Hbk £27.50

—Law of Sale and Lease / London : Butterworths, 1984.
ISBN 0409037494 Hbk £27.40
ISBN 0409037508 Pbk £19.50

—Lease or Licence / London : Longman Professional, 1985.
ISBN 0851211240 Pbk £10.50

—Made Simple : Housing Tenancy and Planning Law / London : MADE, 1981.
ISBN 0434984876 Pbk £2.95

—New tenancy agreements : a model for landlords and tenants based on the Housing Act 1980 / National Consumer Council. - London : The Council, 1981.
22p.
ISBN 0905653378

—Private rented sector : the government's legislative proposals / Great Britain. - London? : Dept. of the Environment, Welsh Office, 1987.
10p.
At foot of last page: Department of the Environment, Welsh Office.

—Private sector tenancies / 2nd ed. – London : Butterworths, 1981.
ISBN 0406337225 Hbk £20.00

—Private tenants handbook / London : Allison & Busby, 1985.
ISBN 0850316200 Pbk £3.95

—Quiet enjoyment / Partington. – 2nd ed. – London : Legal Action Group, 1985.
ISBN 0905099087 Pbk £7.00

—Real estate and landlord and tenant / Agincourt : Carswell, 1986.
ISBN 045939500 Hbk £39.60

—Rent Act Nineteen Seventy-Seven Revised / London : Oyez Longman, 1981.
ISBN 0851206131 Hbk £7.50

—Rent arrears and the courts : a report by the Lay Advocacy Service / by Les Burrows. – Bristol : Lay Advocacy Service, 1986.
63p.
ISBN 0951115006

—Rent Reviews and Variable Rents / J. E. Adams. – London : Oyez Longman, 1981.
– (Oyez Longman Practitioner Ser.).
ISBN 0851204910 Hbk £16.00

—Repairs : tenants' rights / London : Legal Action Group, 1986.
ISBN 0905099133 Pbk £11.00

—Resident landlords and owner-occupiers / London : Longman Professional, 1987.
ISBN 085121293X Pbk £13.95

—Resident landlords and owner-occupiers: law and practice / London : Longman Professional (UK), 1987.
– (Practitioner series).
Details the issues raised by the relationship between resident landlords, owner-occupiers, and their tenants. Analyses the nature of tenancies, and gives advice on the correct formalities and procedures to be followed, including the right of the landlord to possession.
ISBN 085121293X Hbk £14.50

—Residential leases : draftsman's handbook / London : Longman Professional, 1985.
ISBN 085120774X Pbk £19.95

—Residential possession proceedings / Davidson. – 2nd ed. – London : Longman Professional, 1984.
– (Longman Practitioner Series).
Contains legal and procedural instruction as to how to effect or prevent the recovery of possession of residential premises. Includes over forty specimen forms.
ISBN 0851212751 Pbk £22.00

—Residential tenancies / London : Longman Professional (UK), 1988.
– (Longman practice notes).
Contains information on the law and procedure of private residential tenancies. Covers precedents for use in court proceedings, and procedures such as obtaining possession of premises, applying for a fair rent, granting tenancies or bringing an action for arrears of rent.
ISBN 0851214479 Pbk £9.95

—Residential tenancies / London : Butterworths, 1988.
ISBN 0409787507 Pbk £34.00

—Sale and Management of Flats : Practice and Precedents / London : Butterworths, 1985.
This book provides a practical guide to the subject of leasehold conveyancing in the United Kingdom. Particular attention is given to the establishment and maijntenance of subsequent management of the property from the tenant's and developer's point of view.
ISBN 0406526702 Hbk

—Services charges-Law and practice / Shapiro. – Stewart (Henry), 1986.
ISBN 0946700311 Pbk £17.50

—Short guide to Landlord and Tenant Act 1987 / Whippman. – Temple Lectures, 1987.
ISBN 1870800052 Pbk £8.00

LANDLORD AND TENANT - HONG KONG

—Hong Kong tenancy law / London : Butterworths, 1985.
ISBN 0409995126 Pbk £24.00

—Hong Kong tenancy law : an introduction to the law of landlord and tenant / Malcolm Merry. – Singapore : Butterworths, 1985.
xix,343p.
Includes index. English and Chinese forms.
ISBN 0409995126

—Report of the Committee of Review, Landlord and Tenant (Consolidatioin) Ordinance / Hong Kong. – Hong Kong : Government Printer, 1981.
vii,269p.

LANDLORD AND TENANT - INDIA

—Commentaries on Uttar Pradesh Urban Buildings (Regulation of Letting, Rent and Eviction) Act, 1972 / 4th ed. – Lucknow : Eastern Book Company, 1981.
493p.

—Digest of All India Control of Rent and Eviction Cases, 1970-1976 / Lucknow : Eastern Book Company, 1977.
136p.

—Law of Rent Control, Eviction and Leases in India, 3 Vols. / 2nd ed. 1980-1 repr. – Allahabad : Law Book Company, 1982.

—Rent Act : Including Ownership of Old Buildings / Bombay : Universal Book Corporation.

—Uttar Pradesh Urban Buildings (Regulation of Letting, Rent and Eviction) Act, 1972 / 2nd ed. – Lucknow : Eastern Book Company, 1983.
833p.

—West Bengal Premises Tenancy Act 1956 / Calcutta : B. Chand and Sons.

LANDLORD AND TENANT - IRELAND

—Irish Landlord and Tenant Law / John Farrell. – Abingdon : Professional Books, 1984.
ISBN 0862050626 Hbk £63.00
ISBN 0862050677 Pbk

LANDLORD AND TENANT - ITALY

—Landlords and tenants in Imperial Rome / by Bruce W. Frier. – Princeton : Princeton University Press, 1980.
xxxii,251p,8p of plates; 23cm.
Includes index.
ISBN 0691052999 £9.80

LANDLORD AND TENANT - MALAYSIA

—Occupiers' Liability in Singapore and Malaysia / London : Butterworths, 1986.
ISBN 0409995134 Hbk £43.00

—Rent Control Legislation in Malaysia / Butterworths, 1986.
292p.
Covers tenancy and licence, premises, parties, rent, rent tribunals, recovery of possession of premises, subtenancies, penal provisions, the repeal provisions, redevelopment, decontrol, and notice to quit.
ISBN 0409995231 Hbk £85.00

—Rent control legislation in Malaysia / London : Butterworths, 1986.
ISBN 0409995231 Hbk £41.00

LANDLORD AND TENANT - NEW ZEALAND

—Final report on legislation relating to landlord and tenant / report of the Property Law and Equity Reform Committee. – Wellington : The Committee, 1986.
3,105p.

—Interim report on legislation relating to landlord and tenant / report of the Property Law and Equity Reform Committee. – Wellington : The Committee, 1983.
29p.

—Landlord and Tenant, 2 Vols. / Redman. – 17th ed. – Wellington : Butterworths, 1982.

—Report on residential tenancies / Property Law and Equity Reform Committee. – Wellington : The Committee, 1985.
66p.

LANDLORD AND TENANT - NORTHERN IRELAND

—Ejectment for non-payment of rent / by J. A. Dowling : with a supplement for the Republic of Ireland by G. McCormack. – Belfast : Faculty of Law, the Queen's University of Belfast, 1986.
xvii,84p.
ISBN 0853892695

—Landlord and tenant / Great Britain. – Belfast : H.M.S.O., 1982.
vi,88p. – (Discussion document).
At head of title page: Department of Finance and Personnel for Northern Ireland, Office of Law Reform.
ISBN 0337233853

—Occupiers' Rights and Constructive Notice / Belfast : Queen's University of Belfast, 1982.
35p.

LANDLORD AND TENANT - SCOTLAND

—Introduction to the Scottish Law of Leases / London : Butterworths, 1988.
ISBN 0406105898 Pbk

—Irritancies in leases / Scottish Law Commission. – Edinburgh : Scottish Law Commission, 1981.
42p. – (Memorandum).

—Irritancies in leases : report on a reference under section 3(1)(e) of the Law Commissions Act 1965 / Scottish Law Commission. – Edinburgh : H.M.S.O., 1983.
vi,41p.
ISBN 0101876009

—Recovery of possession of heritable property / Scottish Law Commission. – Edinburgh : The Commission, 1984.
iii,122p. – (Consultative memorandum no 59).
Includes bibliographical references.

—Research paper on actions of ejection and removing / by A.G.M. Duncan. – Edinburgh : Law Commission, 1984.
xv,204p.
'Published by the Scottish Law Commission in connection with Consultative Memorandum No. 59'. Includes bibliographical references.

—Under One Roof : A Guide for Flat Owners in Scotland / London : HMSO, 1984.
95p : Illus.
ISBN 0114923809 Pbk £2.00

LANDLORD AND TENANT - SINGAPORE

—Landlord and Tenant / London : Butterworths, 1988.
– (Singapore Law Series).
ISBN 0409995347 Pbk

—Occupiers' Liability in Singapore and Malaysia / London : Butterworths, 1986.
ISBN 0409995134 Hbk £43.00

—Singapore Law Series /. – Butterworths, 1988.
ca 200p.
Discusses leases, and the relationship between landlords and tenants, and contains chapters on leases of major landlords such as the Jurong Town Corporation and the Urban Renewal Authority, and rent control.
ISBN 0409995347 Pbk

LANDLORD AND TENANT (ROMAN LAW) - ITALY

—Landlords and tenants in Imperial Rome / by Bruce W. Frier. – Princeton : Princeton University Press, 1980.
xxxii,251p,8p of plates; 23cm.
Includes index.
ISBN 0691052999 £9.80

LANGUAGE

—Case for the conversational analysis of courtroom interaction : some interactional dimensions of legal procedures / by Philip Wilkinson. – Oxford : Centre for Socio-Legal Studies, 1981.
24p. – (Working paper).
Includes bibliographical references.

—Legal discourse : studies in linguistics, rhetoric and legal analysis / Peter Goodrich. – London : Macmillan, 1987.
x,266p; 23cm. – (Language, discourse, society series).
Bibliography: p247-258. - Includes index.
ISBN 0333419499 £29.50

—Linguistic evidence : language, power, and strategy in the courtroom / William M. O'Barr. – New York : Academic Press, 1982.
xv,192p; 24cm.
Bibliography: p182-187. - Includes index.
ISBN 0125235208 £15.60

—Plain English and the law : a report / Law Reform Commission of Victoria. – Melbourne : The Commission, 1987.
xvi,109p. – (Report no 9).
Includes bibliographical references and index.
Accompanied by appendices 1-8 (3v.).

LANGUAGE - AUSTRALIA - VICTORIA

—Legislation, legal rights and plain English / Law Reform Commission of Victoria. – Melbourne : The Commission, 1986.
iv,56p. – (Discussion paper).
Includes bibliographical references.

LANGUAGE - CANADA

—Construing bilingual legislation in Canada / Remi Michael Beaupre. – Toronto : Butterworths, 1981.
xxi,161p.
Bibliography: p.149-151. - Includes index.
ISBN 0409813400

—Interpreting bilingual legislation / Michael Beaupre. – 2nd ed. – Toronto : Carswell, 1986.
xvi, 236 p.; 24 cm.
Rev. ed. of: Construing bilingual legislation in Canada. Includes index. Bibliography: p. 223-227.
ISBN 0459390600

—Legal drafting / by Robert C. Dick. – 2nd ed. – Toronto : Carswell, 1985.
xiii,234p.
Includes bibliographical references and index.
ISBN 045937740X

—Plain Language and the Law / Ottawa : Canadian Law Information Council.

LANGUAGE - ENGLAND

—Plain English for lawyers : some guidelines on writing and designing legal documents / London : National Consumer Council, 1984.
26p; 30cm.
ISBN 0905653726

—Plain words for consumers : the language and layout of consumer contracts : the case for a plain language law / Liz Dunbar. – London : National Consumer Council, 1984.
78p.
'Written by Richard Thomas with considerable help from Liz Dunbar'.
ISBN 090565370X

LANGUAGE - INDIA

—Language and Law / Rajul Bhargava. – New Delhi : Macmillan India.
224p.

LANGUAGE – SRI LANKA
—Changing the language of the law : the Sri Lanka experience / L. J. Mark Cooray. – Quebec : Presses de l'Universite Laval, 1985.
183p.
ISBN 2763770800

LANGUAGES
—Multilingualism in international law and institutions / Mala Tabory. – Alphen aan den Rijn : Sijthoff & Noordhoff, 1980.
xx,283p.
Bibliography: p260-268.
ISBN 9028602100

LATENT DAMAGE – GREAT BRITAIN
—Building and Engineering Claims / A. Ranson. – London : Oyez Longman, 1980 Incl. July 1980 supplement.
ISBN 0851204252 Hbk £9.95

—Latent Damage Act 1986 / London : LEST, 1987.
ISBN 1852710080 Pbk £28.50

LATIN AMERICA
—Legal aspects of doing business in Latin America / edited by Dennis Campbell. – Deventer, The Netherlands : Kluwer Law and Taxation Publishers, 1984.
vii, 351 p.; 25 cm. – (International business series).
Includes index.
ISBN 9065441026

—Politics of Latin American development / Gary W. Wynia. – 2nd ed. – Cambridge : Cambridge University Press, 1984.
xv,318p,2p of plates; 24cm.
Previous ed.: 1978. Includes bibliographies and index.
ISBN 0521261201 Hbk £25.00
ISBN 0521278422 Pbk Unpriced

LATIN AMERICA – GREAT BRITAIN
—ACOLAM newsletter / Advisory Committee on Latin American Materials. – v. – London? : Institute of Latin American Studies?, 1980.
ISBN 02636832

LAW
—Annual volumes of the laws of North-Eastern State of Nigeria ... i.e. Gongola State of Nigeria / Gongola State of Nigeria. – Jumeta, Nigeria? : Government Printer, 1977.
Originally published as individual supplements to the Gongola State of Nigeria gazette. Description based on: 1977 vol..

—Causation in the law / by H.L.A. Hart and Tony Honore. – 2nd ed. – Oxford : Clarendon, 1985.
lxxxi,516p; 23cm.
Previous ed.: 1959. Bibliography: p498-507. - Includes index.
ISBN 019825475X Hbk £25.00
ISBN 0198254741 Pbk £14.50

—Common Market law / Alan Campbell. – 4 v. – London : Longmans, 1969.
25cm.
Supplement, published in 1975, assimilated the contents of previous loose-leaf binders. Earlier ed. by Campbell and D.C. Thompson.

—Dwelling on the threshold : critical essays on modern legal thought / Allan C. Hutchinson. – Toronto : Carswell, 1988.
ix,326p.
Bibliography: pp.324-325..
ISBN 0421400501

—Economic approach to law / edited by Paul Burrows, Cento G. Veljanovski. – London : Butterworths, 1981.
xi,343p; 25cm.
This book of essays provides an introduction to economic aspects of legal analysis. The contributors discuss the economic framework underlying the substance and procedures of the legal system.
ISBN 0408106867 HBK £27.50
ISBN 0408106859 Pbk £12.95

—Edicts / South-Eastern State of Nigeria. – 8 v. – Calabar : Min. of Home Affairs and Information, 1968.
Published as supplements to the South-Eastern State of Nigeria gazette. Includes subsidiary legislation. This library lacks 1975. Numbering begins anew each year.

—Essays in memory of Professor F.H. Lawson / edited by Peter Wallington, Robert M. Merkin. – London : Butterworths, 1986.
ix,200p; 26cm.
Includes index.
ISBN 0406500304 £18.00

—Essays on Law, Equality and Education / London : Sweet & Maxwell, 1984.
ISBN 0710098804 Hbk £49.00

—Executive instruments / Ghana. – Accra : Ghana Publishing Corporation
Issued with: Ghana gazette.

—Function of the law and the lawyer in development administration / by Heinrich Scholler. – Lagos : Nigerian Institute of Advanced Legal Studies, University of Lagos, 1980.
14p; 23cm. – (Occasional papers).
Includes bibliographical references.

—Guide to European Community law / by P.S.R.F. Mathijsen : preface by J.D.B. Mitchell. – 3rd ed. – London : Sweet & Maxwell, 1980.
xxxiii,256p; 23cm.
Previous ed.: 1975. Includes index.
ISBN 0421259000 Hbk £12.95
ISBN 0421259108 Pbk £9.75

—Historical Law Tracts, 2 Vols. / Repr. of 1758 ed. – Abingdon : Professional Books.
34p.

—International law of development : comparative perspectives / edited by Francis Snyder and Peter Slinn. – Abingdon : Professional Books, 1987.
ix,322p; 22cm.
ISBN 0862052580

—International Law of International Welfare : The Politics of Law-Making / London : Pinter Publishers Ltd, 1984.
200p.
ISBN 0861872894 Hbk £21.00

—International review of law and economics / Sevenoaks : Butterworths, 1981.

—Introduction to the Singapore legal system / by Helena H.M. Chan. – Singapore : Malayan Law Journal Pte., 1986.
vi,140p.
Covers the legal history of Singapore, sources of law, structure of government, legal institutions, civil and criminal procedure, and a chapter devoted to legal culture and the future development of the law.
ISBN 9971700549

—Invitation to the Law / Butterworths, 1982.
384p.

—Law and economics / edited by Ross Cranston and Anne Schick. – Canberra : Department of Law, Research School of Social Sciences, Australian National University, 1982.
v,220p.
ISBN 0909596727 Pbk £9

—Law and state in Papua New Guinea / Peter Fitzpatrick. – London : Academic Press, 1980.
xi,290p; 24cm.
Bibliography: p256-284. - Includes index.
ISBN 0122578805 £12.60

—Law and the economy / Roger Bowles. – Oxford : Martin Robertson, 1982.
xvi,239p; 22cm.
Introduction to law and economics, relating the two subjects to each other.
ISBN 0855204656 Hbk Unpriced
ISBN 0855204745 Pbk £6.95

—Law, Freedom and Change / New Delhi : Affiliated East-West Press.

—Law of Nature and Nations / B. Kennett. – Repr. of 1703 ed. – Abingdon : Professional Books.
597p.

—Laws of Saint Christopher, Nevis and Anguilla : printed by authority / Saint Christopher, Nevis and Anguilla. – v. – St. Michael, Barbados : Coles Printer, appointed Government Printer, 1982.
Continued in part by: Laws of Anguilla, 1971-. Includes ordinances and statutory rules and orders.

—Laws of the Australian Capital Territory made during the year ... / Australian Capital Territory. – Canberra : Commonwealth Government Printer, 1964.
Contains ordinances and regulations.

—Legal systems, North and South : a study prepared for the New Ireland Forum / by C. K. Boyce. – Dublin : Stationery Office, 1984.
60p.

—Nature of Law / Amsterdam : Elsevier Science Publishers, 1980.
xiv, 246p.
ISBN 0444854223 Hbk £130.00

—Nederlandse wetboeken : zoals zij tot op 1 januari 1984 zijn gewijzigd en aangevuld / uitgegeven door J.A. Fruin : bewerkt door M.P.J.A. Cremers, J.H.F.J. Cremers, P.H.A.J. Cremers. – Zwolle : Tjeenk Willink, 1984.
2107p.
Includes index.
ISBN 9027121346

—New law-and-economics : a research review / C.G. Veljanovski. – Oxford : Centre for Socio-Legal Studies, 1982.
xi,169p.
Bibliography: p.144-169.
ISBN 0862260531

—Ordinance of British Columbia / British Columbia. – 63 leaflets. – Victoria? : s.n., 1864.
Continues British Columbia proclamations, 1858-1863. Continued by ordinances of the combined colonies of British Columbia and Vancouver Island, 1867-1870. This library has 1864 only. Bound with British Columbia proclamations, 1858-1863. Numbering begins anew each year.

—Ordinances / Australian Capital Territory. – Canberra : Commonwealth Government Printer, 1911.
Extracted from: Commonwealth of Australia Gazette. This library has 1939-1959 in this form. Ordinances 1960 onwards are included in the bound volumes of 'Laws of the Australian Capital Territory made during the year ...'.

—Ordinances, laws and proclamations / compiled and edited by Charles Fitzwilliam Cadiz and Robert Lyon. – Pietermaritzburg : Vause, Slatter & Co., 1879.
'By authority'. Includes index. Contents: vol. 1. 1845-70 - vol. 2. 1870-79.

—Principles of Irish law / Brian Doolan. – Dublin : Gill and Macmillan, 1981.
xx,300p; 22cm.
Includes index.
ISBN 0717111245 Pbk £6.30

—Proclamations / by James Douglas, governor and commander-in-chief of Her Majesty's colony of British Columbia and its dependencies. – 72 leaflets. – Victoria : s.n., 1858.
Continued by British Columbia ordinances, 1864-1866. Proclamations nos. 1-3, 1858 issued by James Douglas as governor of Vancouver Island and its dependencies. Bound together with British Columbia ordinances, 1864. Numbering begins anew each year.

—Public General Acts and General Synod Measures / Great Britain. – London : H.M.S.O., 1973.
Continues: The Public General Acts and the Church Assembly Measures.

—Readings in the economics of law and regulation / edited by A.I. Ogus and C.G. Veljanovski. – Oxford : Clarendon, 1984.
x,361p; 24cm.
Includes index.
ISBN 0198761422 Hbk £17.50
ISBN 0198761430 Pbk £10.95

—Revised regulations of Ontario, 1980 : a revision and consolidation of regulations published under the authority of the Regulations Revision Act, 1979 / Ontario. – 8. – Toronto : Queen's Printer, 1981.
Accompanied by: Supplement (2v.).

—Rule of law in the areas administered by Israel / Israel National Section of the International Commission of Jurists. – Tel Aviv : Israel National Section of the International Commission of Jurists, 1981.
xiv,114p.
Includes bibliographical references.

—Statutes of Natal / compiled and edited by R. L. Hitchins : assisted and revised on behalf of the colonial government by G.W. Sweeney. – 3 v. – Pietermaritzburg : P. Davis, 1900.
Includes index. A compilation of the statutes of the colony for the period 1845 to 1899 with an appendix containing the Acts of 1900.

—Statutory instruments / Belize. – Belmopan : Government Printery, 1973
Supplement to the Government gazette. Continues: Statutory instruments of British Honduras.

—Statutory instruments other than those of a local, personal or temporary character / Great Britain. – v. – London : H.M.S.O., 1949.
Continues: Statutory rules and orders other than those of a local, personal, or temporary character.

—Statutory rules and orders and statutory instruments revised to December 31, 1948 / Great Britain. – 3rd ed. 25 v. – London : H.M.S.O., 1949.
Previous ed.: 1903. Prepared under the direction of the Statute Law Committee.

—Statutory rules and orders : other than those of a local, personal, or temporary character : issued prior to 1890, and now in force / Great Britain. – 8 v. – London : H.M.S.O., 1896.
Prepared under the direction of the Statute Law Committee. Title page heading and spine title: The Statutory rules and orders revised.

LAW – AFGHANISTAN
—Journal of African law / London : Butterworth, 1957-.

LAW – AFRICA
—Eastern Africa law review : a journal of law and development / Dar es Salaam : East African Literature Bureau, 1968-.

—Internal conflict of law problems in African legal systems / Fafa E M'Bai. – Banjul : Xam Xam, 198?.

—Law and democracy in Africa / by Richard Akinjide. – Lagos : Office of the President, Department of Information, 1981.
22p.

—Southern Africa in need of law reform : proceedings of the Southern African Law Reform Conference, Sun City, Bophuthatswana, 11-14 August 1980 / edited by A.J.G.M. Sanders. – Durban : Butterworths, 1981.
256p.
Includes bibliographical references.
ISBN 0409051845

—Zulu Law / Shooter. – Pietermaritzburg : Shuter & Shooter, 1984.

LAW - ANGUILLA

—Anguilla consolidated index of statutes and subsidiary legislation to 1st January 1983 / compiled at the Faculty of Law Library, University of the West Indies, Barbados. – Rev. ed. – Barbados : s.n., 1983.
v,73p.
Previous ed.: 1st January 1980. One of a series in the West Indian Legislation Indexing Project (WILIP) compiled in cooperation with the British Development Division.

—Laws of Anguilla : printed by authority / Anguilla. – v. – St. Michael, Barbados : Coles Printery, appointed as Government Printer for Anguilla, 1982.
Continues in part: Laws of Saint Christopher, Nevis and Anguilla, 1961-1970. Half title, 1972 onwards: Anguilla ordinances and statutory rules and orders.

LAW - ANTIGUA AND BARBUDA

—Antigua and Barbuda consolidated index of statutes and subsidiary legislation to !st January 1984 / compiled at the Faculty of Law Library, University of the West Indies, Barbados. – Barbados? : s.n., 1984.
iii,87p.
Previous ed.: 1st January 1981. One of a series in the West Indian Legislation Indexing Project (WILIP) compiled in cooperation with the British Development Division.

LAW - ARABIAN GULF

—Register of laws of the Arabian Gulf / London : Graham & Trotman, 1989.
260.
A database of all laws and regulations originating in each country of the Arabian Gulf from the commencement of legislative promulgation to the present day. Drawn from original Arabic sources.
ISBN 1853331686 Llf £489

LAW - ASIA

—Asian indigenous law in interaction with received law / edited by Masaji Chiba. – London : KPI, 1986.
xiii,416p.
ISBN 0710301138

—Laws of South East Asia : Pre-Modern Texts / London : Butterworths, 1986.
ISBN 0409995061 Hbk £143.00

LAW - AUSTRALIA

—Acts of the Parliament / Canberra : Australian Government Publishing Service, 1979-.
loose-leaf.
Reprints of Acts incorporating amendments, issued as pamphlets.

—Annual survey of Australian law / Sydney : Law Book Co., 1976-.
Continues: An annual survey of law.

—Australian and New Zealand Citator to UK Reports 1588-1972 / Wellington : Butterworths.
ISBN 0409303100 Pbk

—Australian Bar review / Australian Bar Association. – Sydney : Butterworths, 1985-.
'Published under the auspices of the Australian Bar Association'. - T.p..

—Australian Commentary to Halsbury's Laws of England / Wellington : Butterworths.

—Australian Current Law / Jean Maior. – Wellington : Butterworths.

—Australian Law Reports (ALR) / J. D. Heydon. - Wellington : Butterworths.

—Butterworths Video videorecording : How Laws Are Made-VHS / Butterworths.

—Introducing the law / Dennis Easton ... et al. – 2nd ed. – North Ryde : CCH Australia, 1985.
x,374p.
Includes bibliographical references.
ISBN 0869035002

—It's All Quite Legal / Butterworths, 1982.
48p.
ISBN 0409491500 Pbk £21.50

—Law and government in colonial Australia / Paul Finn. – Melbourne : Oxford University Press, 1987.
xix,216p.
Bibliography: p.207-212. - Includes index.
ISBN 0195547462

—Law and justice / Australian Labor Party. – s.l. : The Party, 1983.
iii,24p.
'Policy launched by Senator Gareth Evans, ... Melbourne, 23 February, 1983'.

—Law Has Long Ears / Fitzroy : Wildgrass Books, 1986.
256p.

—Law in Action / 2nd ed. – North Ryde : C.C.H. Australia, 1985.
364p.
ISBN 0869035088 Hbk £22.00

—Legal process : commentary and materials / Maher, Waller, Derham. – 5th ed. – Sydney : Law Book Co, 1988.
xxx, 593 p.; 26 cm.
First to 4th eds. published under title: Cases and materials on the legal process.
ISBN 0455207836 (pbk.)

—Let's Look at Law / Jennifer Bollen. – Butterworths, 1985.
78p.
ISBN 0409492647 Pbk £9.50

—Our Legal System / 2nd ed. 1983. – North Ryde : Law Book Co.
ISBN 0455202680 Pbk £19.00

—Papers presented at the 22nd Australian Legal Convention, Brisbane, 1983 / Brisbane : Queensland Law Society for the Law Council of Australia, 1984.
444p.
Includes bibliographical references.
ISBN 0949677353

—Subject index to the acts and regulations of the Commonwealth of Australia / B. M. Wicks. – 1982 ed. – Sydney : Law Book Co., 1983.
146p.
Previous ed. published as: Subject index to the acts of the Parliament of the Commonwealth of Australia (1979). Includes index.

—Understanding Law / Netthelm. – Sydney : Butterworths, 1984.
147p.
This introductory text for first year law students provides an overview of the Australian legal system. Emphasized are the ways in which laws are made and the function of courts and lawyers. A list of suggested further reading is also included.
ISBN 0409493724

—Understanding law : an introduction to Australian legal system / Nettheim. – 2nd ed. – London : Butterworths, 1984.
ISBN 0409493724 Pbk £6.80

LAW - AUSTRALIA - NEW SOUTH WALES

—Subject index to the Acts of New South Wales / compiled by B.M. Wicks. – 1983 ed. – Sydney : Law Book Co., 1984.
141p.

—System of law and courts governing New South Wales / 2nd ed. – London : Butterworths, 1985.
ISBN 0409492531 Hbk £40.00

LAW - AUSTRALIA - QUEENSLAND

—Queensland statutes (1962) reprint / Queensland. – 20 v. – Brisbane : Butterworths, 1963.
Previous ed.: 1936. 'Containing a classified and annotated reprint of the Public Acts of Queensland 1828-1962'. .

—Queensland statutes reprint : 1982 / Queensland. – Brisbane : Lawyers Bookshop, 1982.
looseleaf.
Previous ed.: 1962. Title from spine.

LAW - AUSTRALIA - SOUTH AUSTRALIA

—Lawmakers and Wayward Whigs : Law and Justice in South Australia / Michael Harris. – Cowandilla : Wakefield Press, 1986.
256p.
ISBN 0949268607 Pbk £50.00

ISBN 0949268623 Hbk

LAW - AUSTRALIA - TASMANIA

—Indexes to the legislation of Tasmania / Hobart : Office of the Parliamentary Counsel, 1984.
104,124,79p.
Originally published in 3 parts. Contents: Alphabetical table of Tasmanian Acts 1826-1983 - Subject index to statute law - Subject index to subordinate legislation.

LAW - AUSTRALIA - WESTERN AUSTRALIA

—Western Australian introduction to law / 2nd ed. – London : Butterworths, 1986.
ISBN 0409490571 Pbk £18.00

—Western Australian Introduction to Law / 2nd ed. – Butterworths, 1986.
255p.
ISBN 0409490571 Pbk £23.50

LAW - BAHAMAS

—Bahamas consolidated index of statutes and subsidiary legislation to 1st January 1982 / compiled at the Faculty of Law Library, University of the West Indies, Barbados. – Barbados : s.n., 1982.
iv,93p.
One of a series in the West Indian Legislation Indexing Project (WILIP) compiled in cooperation with the British Development Division.

LAW - BARBADOS

—Barbados, Laws Of (Subsidiary Legis 78) / Sweet & Maxwell, 1983.
ISBN 0421317604 Hbk £260.00

—Laws of Barbados : subsidiary legislation in force on the 31st day of December, 1978 / prepared under the authority of the Law Revision Act cap. 2 by Wilfred K. Fergusson. – 3. – Bridgetown : Government Printer, 1982.
looseleaf.

—Subsidiary Legislation, 1978 : Laws of Barbados / London : Sweet & Maxwell, 1983.
ISBN 0421317604 loose £260.00

LAW - BOTSWANA

—Acts / Botswana. – Gaborone : Government Printer, 1966.
Published as supplements to the Republic of Botswana government gazette.

LAW - BRITISH VIRGIN ISLANDS

—British Virgin Islands consolidated index of statutes and subsidiary legislation to 1st January 1983 / compiled at the Faculty of Law Library, University of the West Indies, Barbados. – Rev. ed. – Barbados : s.n., 1983.
ii,56p.
Previous ed.: 1st January 1981. One of a series in the West Indian Legislation Indexing Project (WILIP) compiled in cooperation with the British Development Division.

LAW - CANADA

—All-Canada Weekly Summaries First Ser. (1977-1979), 9 Vols. / Aurora : Canada Law Book Co.
– (Summary Services, National Series).

Back Vols.

—Anger's Digest of Canadian Law / 20th ed. – Aurora : Canada Law Book Co, 1987.
1032p.

—Canada From Abroad : Legal, Business and Tax Aspects / North Ryde : C.C.H. Australia.
210p.
ISBN 0887963129 Pbk £16.95

—Canada Regulations Index, 2 Vols. / Agincourt : Carswell, 1987.

—Canadian Abridgment, 110 Vols. / Carswell Legal Publications. – 2nd ed. – Agincourt : Carswell.

—Canadian Council on International Law : Conference Proceedings /. – Ottawa : Canadian Council on International Law, 1981.

—Canadian legal materials in microform / compiled by Meena Nadkarni. – Downsview, Ont. : York University Law Library in co-operation with the Canadian Association of Law Libraries, 1981.

—Canadian legal system / Gerald L. Gall. – 2nd ed. – Toronto : Carswell, 1983.
xxiv, 348 p.; 24 cm.
'With Chapter 8, The Quebec legal system, by Mr. Justice Paul Reeves of the Quebec Superior Court.'. Includes bibliographical references and index.
ISBN 0459358103 pbk.

—Consolidated Regulations of Canada, 1978, 18 Vols. /. – Aurora : Canada Law Book Co.

Regulations and Index
ISBN Hbk £520.00
ISBN Pbk £320.00

Canada Gazette
ISBN Hbk £87.00
ISBN Pbk £69.00

—Everyday Law : a Survival Guide for Canadians / Marjorie Harris. – Toronto : Key Key Porter Books, 1987.
224p.
ISBN 1550130412 Pbk £14.95

—Federal State of Canada Service, 2 vols / Toronto : Butterworths.

—Foundations of Canadian Law / Morse. – Toronto : Butterworths, 1987.
ISBN 0409811513 Hbk

—Halsbury's Laws of England : Canadian Converters, 9 vols / Toronto : Butterworths.
ISBN 0409801453 Hbk

—Law and You / Toronto : Canadian Broadcasting Corporation Enterprises.
64p.

—Law in a Cynical Society? : Opinion and Law in the 1980's / Janet K. Baldwin. – Agincourt : Carswell, 1985.
475p.

—Law, society, and the economy / Ivan Bernier and Andree Lajoie, research coordinators. – Toronto : University of Toronto Press, 1986.
xv, 230 p.; 23 cm.
Includes bibliographies.
ISBN 0802072917 pbk.

—Northwest Territories Ordinances 1975-1986 / Agincourt : Carswell, 1987.

—Northwest Territories Revised Regulations Consolidated to 1980 / Agincourt : Carswell.

—Revised regulations of the Northwest Territories 1980 : a consolidation and revision of the regulations of the Northwest Territories prepared by the Registrar of Regulations and representing the laws as at 31st December, 1980 / Northwest Territories. – Yellowknife : Territorial Printer, Northwest Territories, 1981.
xii,1679p.

—Revised statutes of Canada, 1985 : prepared under the authority of the Statute Revision Act / Lois revisees du Canada, 1985. – 13. – Ottawa : Queen's Printer, 1985.
looseleaf.
. Spine titles: Statutes of Canada Lois du Canada. Updated to 1988 by special supplements and by looseleaf insertions thereafter. Parallel text in English and French.

—Take Notice : An Introduction to Canadian Law / Alenda S. Spetz. – 2nd ed. – Toronto : Copp Clark, 1984.
512p : Illus.
ISBN 0773043144 Hbk £24.94

—Women in Canadian Law / Markham : Fitzhenry and Whiteside.
96p.
ISBN 0889023778 Pbk £4.95

—You and the Law / M.J. McDonald. – Toronto : Maclean-Hunter.
ISBN 0888960875 Hbk £9.95
ISBN 0770516491 Pbk £6.95

LAW - CANADA - ALBERTA

—Alberta Decisions Citator (1981-Present) / Aurora : Canada Law Book Co.
– (Statute Services).

—Alberta Decisions : Civil and Criminal Cases (1980-Present) / Aurora : Canada Law Book Co.
– (Summary Services, Provincial Ser.).

—Alberta Law for the Nineteen Eighties / Legal Education Society of Alberta & Butterworth & Co. (Canada) Ltd. – Toronto : Butterworths, 1981.
250p.
ISBN 0409987034 Pbk £21.00

—Alberta Law Reports / 2nd ed. – Agincourt : Carswell.

—Alberta Regulations Service, 3 vols / Toronto : Butterworths.

—Index to the statutes of Alberta, including Spring sitting 1983 / prepared for the Province of Alberta by Canadian Law Information Council. – Edmonton : Queen's Printer, 1983.
vii,876p.

—Revised statutes of Alberta 1980 / Alberta. – 8. – Edmonton : Queen's Printer, 1981.

—Statutes of Alberta judicially considered / R.S.A. 1970 ed. – Calgary : Burroughs, 1980.
looseleaf.

LAW - CANADA - BRITISH COLUMBIA

—British Columbia Decisions Civil Cases (1979-Present) / Aurora : Canada Law Book Co.
– (Summary Services, Provincial Ser.).

—British Columbia Decisions Criminal Conviction and Sentence Cases (1979-Present) / Aurora : Canada Law Book Co.
– (Summary Services, Provincial Ser.).

—British Columbia Law Reports / Agincourt : Carswell, 1988.
– (Second Ser., 1-18).
This text includes all the cases from the courts of British Columbia and appeals from that court to the Supreme Court of Canada. The cases are all headnoted, there is a topical index, and an index of cases reported.

—British Columbia Practice, 3 vols / James Taylor. – 2nd ed. – Toronto : Butterworths.

—British Columbia Rules Citator / Aurora : Canada Law Book Co.

LAW - CANADA - MANITOBA

—Manitoba statutes / Manitoba. – 30. – Winnipeg : Queen's Printer, 1970.
looseleaf.
'Based on Revised statutes of Manitoba, 1970' - A bibliography of Canadian law/ Reynold Boult (1977). Includes index (3v.).

—Re-enacted statutes of Manitoba 1987 : being a consolidation and revision of certain acts in the Continuing Consolidation of the Statutes of Manitoba ... / Lois readoptees du Manitoba de 1987. – Winnipeg : Queen's Printer for the Province of Manitoba, 1987.
looseleaf.
Parallel text in English and French.

LAW - CANADA - NOVA SCOTIA

—Law in Colonial Society : The Nova Scotia Experience / Agincourt : Carswell, 1984.
300p.
ISBN 0459364200 Hbk £36.50

LAW - CANADA - ONTARIO

—All-Canada Weekly Summaries Ontario Edition Current Series (1981-Present) / Aurora : Canada Law Book Co.
– (Summary Services, Provincial Ser.).
Parts only
Back Vols.

—Butterworth's Ontario Digest, 14 vols / Toronto : Butterworths.

—Ontario Regulations : 1981, 2 Vols. / Agincourt : Carswell.

—Ontario Regulations : 1982, 2 Vols. / Agincourt : Carswell, 1982.

—Ontario Regulations : 1983, 2 Vols. / Agincourt : Carswell, 1983.

—Ontario Regulations, 1984, 3 Vols. / Agincourt : Carswell, 1984.

—Ontario Regulations Service 1987 / Agincourt : Carswell, 1987.

—Ontario Regulations Service 1988, 2 Vols. / Agincourt : Carswell, 1988.

—Ontario Revised Regulations : The Official Government Edition-1980, 8 Vols. / Carswell Legal Publications. – Agincourt : Carswell, 1980.

—Revised statutes of Ontario, 1980 : being a revision and consolidation of the Public General Acts of the legislature of Ontario, published under the authority of the Statutes Revision Act, 1979 / Ontario. – 9. – Toronto : Queen's Printer, 1981.

LAW - CANADA - QUEBEC

—Introduction to Quebec Law / David Franklin. – 3rd ed. – Toronto : Copp Clark, 1983.
352p : Illus.
ISBN 0773042903 Pbk £15.37

LAW - CANADA - SASKATCHEWAN

—Tables to the statutes of Saskatchewan and Saskatchewan regulations / Saskatchewan : Queen's Printer, 1980-.
26cm.

LAW - CAYMAN ISLANDS

—Cayman Islands consolidated index of statutes and subsidiary legislation to 1st January 1980 / compiled at the Faculty of Law and Law Library, University of the West Indies, Barbados. – Bridgetown, Barbados? : Faculty of Law Library, University of the West Indies?, 1980.
iv,64 leaves.
One of a series in the West Indian Legislation Indexing Project (WILIP) compiled in cooperation with the British Development Division.

LAW - CHINA

—China law and practice : documenting and analysing the development of the Chinese legal system / Hong Kong : China Law and Practice, 1987.

—Fundamental legal concepts of China and the West : a comparative study / Hyung I. Kim. – Port Washington : National University Publications, 1981.
xiii,175p; 23cm.
Bibliography: p165-175.
ISBN 0804692750 £14.85

—Law in the People's Republic of China: commentary, readings and materials / Ralph H Folsom, John H Minan. – Dordrecht : Martinus Nijhoff, 1989.
1100.
Reviews the Chinese legal tradition. Each chapter focuses on the emerging law as related to a selected topic, giving an overview, and then edited excerpts selected from a wide range of legal materials.
ISBN 0792300556 Hbk £159/Dfl495

—People's Republic of China : Modernisation and Legal Development / London : Oyez Longman, 1983.
ISBN 0851208045 Hbk £22.50

—Statutes and regulations of the People's Republic of China / China. – 3. – Hong Kong : University of East Asia Press, 1987.
looseleaf.
Cumulative index issued annually as a bound vol..

LAW - COMMONWEALTH

—Meeting of Commonwealth law ministers, Colombo,Sri Lanka, 14-18 February 1983 : memoranda / London : Commonwealth Secretariat, 1983.
xv,597p; 30cm.
ISBN 085092247X

—Meeting of Law Officers of Small Commonwealth Jurisdictions : Port Vila, Vanuatu, 29 July to 2 August 1985 / London : Commonwealth Secretariat, 1985.
156p.
Includes bibliographical references.

—Memoranda / London : Commonwealth Secretariat, 1980.
xi,375p.
ISBN 0850921872

—Proceedings and papers of the Sixth Commonwealth Law Conference, Lagos, Nigeria, 17th-23rd August 1980 / Lagos : Nigerian Bar Association, 1980.
xxxviii,623p; 22cm.

—Meeting of law officers of small Commonwealth jurisdictions, Douglas, Isle of Man, 4th to 8th July 1983 / Douglas : Isle of Man Government, 1984.
iii,235p; 30cm.
ISBN 0904869105

LAW - CYPRUS

—Legal links between Cyprus and the Balkans especially Macedonia during the Byzantine era / Criton G. Tornaritis. – Nicosia : s.n., 1982.
24 leaves.

LAW - DENMARK

—Danish law : a general survey / edited by Hans Gammeltoft- Hansen, Bernhard Gomard, Allan Philip. – Copenhagen : G.E.C. Gad, 1982.
395p.
Previous ed.: published as 'Danish and Norwegian law', 1963. Copyright by the Danish Committee on Comparative Law.
ISBN 8712235253

LAW - ENGLAND

—75 years of law at Sheffield, 1909-1984 / edited by David C. Hoath. – Sheffield : University of Sheffield Faculty of Law, 1985.
viii,116p.
Includes bibliographical references.

—'A' Level law / Brian Hogan, Peter Seago, Geoffrey Bennett. – London : Sweet & Maxwell, 1983.
xxix,521p; 23cm.
Includes index.
ISBN 0421297905 Hbk Unpriced
ISBN 0421298006 Pbk £6.50

—'A' Level Law / 2nd ed. – Plymouth : Macdonald & Evans, 1984.
ISBN 0712101926 Pbk £4.95

—'A' Level Law / London : Butterworths, 1988.
ISBN 0406208506 Pbk £9.95

—'A' Level Law / Pannett. – London : Financial Training, 1988.
– (SWOT).
ISBN 1851850651 Pbk £7.50

—'A' level law : cases and materials / Brian Hogan, Peter Seago, Geoffrey Bennett. – London : Sweet & Maxwell, 1986.
xxvii,507p; 22cm.
Includes index.
ISBN 0421352906 Pbk £8.50

—'A' Level English Law / Scott. – 6th ed. – London : Butterworths, 1984.
ISBN 0406657076 Hbk £14.00
ISBN 0406657084 Pbk £8.95

—'A' Level Law (CCT) / Seago. – 2nd ed. – Sweet & Maxwell, 1988.
ISBN 0421352906 Pbk £8.95
ISBN 042138820X Hbk £9.95

—Administration of justice / Robin C.A. White. – Oxford : Blackwell, 1985.
400p.
Introduction to the English legal system of justice. Critique of how the system works in reality.
ISBN 0631143068 Hbk £27.50 :
ISBN 0631143076 Pbk £12.50

—Analysis of the Laws of England : Introductory Discourse on the Study of the Law / 3rd ed. Repr. of 1757 ed. – Abingdon : Professional Books.

—Australian Commentary to Halsbury's Laws of England / Wellington : Butterworths.

—Bulwark of the law / the Right Honourable Lord Edmund-Davies. – Cardiff : Law Department, UWIST, 1984.
20p.

—Cases and materials on the English legal system / Michael Zander. – 4th ed. – London : Weidenfeld and Nicolson, 1984.
xxx,631p.
Previous ed.: 1980. Bibliography: p.xxviii-xxx. - Includes index. .
ISBN 0297784579 Hbk £19.50
ISBN 0297784587 Pbk £10.95

—Cases and materials on the English legal system / Michael Zander. – 5th ed. – London : Weidenfeld and Nicolson, 1988.
xxix,641p; 23cm.
Previous ed.: 1984. Includes index.
ISBN 0297793535 Hbk No price
ISBN 0297793543 Pbk £14.95

—Cases and materials on the English legal system / Michael Zander. – 3rd ed. – London : Weidenfeld and Nicolson, 1980.
xxvii,476p; 23cm. – (Law in context).
Previous ed.: 1976. Includes index. .
ISBN 0297778226 Hbk £17.50
ISBN 0297778234 Pbk £8.95

—Changing law / Robin White, Patfield. - London : Pinter, 1990.
224.
A survey of the radical and rapid changes to English law in the last 25 years. Covers negligence, land, family, financial regulation, civil liberties, social security, EC law, reform of the legal profession and codification of common law principles.
ISBN 0718513312 Hbk £29.50

—Classical English Law Texts Series, 136 Vols. / Abingdon : Professional Books.

—Closing chapter / by Lord Denning. - London : Butterworths, 1983.
xvii,293p; 23cm.
Includes index.
ISBN 0406176116 Hbk £10.50
ISBN 0406176124 Pbk £6.50

—Commentaries on Laws of England / Abingdon : Professional Books.
- (Classical English Law Texts Ser.).

—Commentaries on the Laws England. 4 vols. / Reprint. - Abingdon : Professional Books, 1986.
ISBN 0862053102 Hbk £142.00

—Due process of law / by... Lord Denning. - London : Butterworths, 1980.
xviii,263p.
Describes the workings of contempt of court, judicial enquiries, and the powers of arrest and search from the personal experiences and anecdotes of the author.
ISBN 0406176078 £8.95
ISBN 0406176086

—England's Balme : Proposals By Way of Grievance and Remedy Presented to His Highness and the Parliament Towards the Regulation of the Law and Better Administration of Justice / Repr. of 1657 ed. - Abingdon : Professional Books.
251p.

—English-Italian Law Dictionary / London : Sweet & Maxwell, 1985.
ISBN 0421357401 Hbk £50.00

—English law / Denis Keenan. - 7th ed. - London : Pitman, 1982.
838p.
Previous ed.: 1979.
ISBN 0273018299 Pbk £8.50

—English Law / Keenan. - 8th ed. - London : Pitman Publishing, 1986.
ISBN 027302342X Pbk £11.95
ISBN 0406677611 Hbk £19.50

—English Law for GCSE / Giles. - 5th ed. - London : Butterworths, 1987.
ISBN 0406653070 Pbk £5.50

—English legal system / Walker & Walker. - 6th ed. - London : Butterworths, 1985.
li,709p; 25cm.
ISBN 0406677603

—English legal system / by Keith J. Eddey. - 4th ed. - London : Sweet & Maxwell, 1987.
xv,196p. - (Concise college texts).
Previous ed.: 1982. Bibliography: p189-190. - Includes index.
ISBN 0421354003 Hbk £13.50
ISBN 0421354100 Pbk £7.50

—English legal system / A.K.R. Kiralfy. - 7th ed. - London : Sweet & Maxwell, 1984.
xli,301p; 22cm.
Previous ed.: 1978. Includes index.
ISBN 0421313706 Pbk £16.50
ISBN 0421313803 Pbk £7.50

—Essays in law and society / edited by Zenon Bankowski and Geoff Mungham. - London : Routledge & Kegan Paul, 1980.
vii,207p; 24cm.
Includes bibliographies and index.
ISBN 0710004893 Pbk £6.50

—First Book of English Law / Hood. - 8th ed. - London : Sweet & Maxwell, 1988.
ISBN 0421393602 Hbk £16.00
ISBN 042139370X Pbk £11.50

—First Part of the Institutes of the Lawes of England : Commentary Upon Littleton / Repr. of 1628 ed. - Abingdon : Professional Books.
449p.

—Form and substance in Anglo-American law : a comparative study of legal reasoning, legal theory, and legal institutions / P.S. Atiyah and Robert S. Summers. - Oxford : Clarendon, 1987.
444p; 24cm.
Includes bibliography and index.
ISBN 0198255772 £35.00

—Form and Substances in Anglo American Law / Summers. - Oxford : Oxford University Press, 1987.
ISBN 0198255772 Hbk £35.00

—Fulbeck's direction, or preparative to the study of the law / by William Fulbeck : introduction by Peter Birks. - Godstone : Gregg International, 1987.
xviii,252p; 21cm.
Facsimile ed., first published by J. and W. T. Clarke, London, 1829.
ISBN 057640005X

—GCSE and 'O' level law / by W.J. Brown. - 3rd ed. - London : Sweet & Maxwell, 1986.
280p; 22cm.
Previous ed.: published as O level law. 1982. Includes index.
ISBN 0421352507 Hbk £9.50
ISBN 0421352604 Pbk £6.95

—GCSE Law / London : Financial Training, 1987.
ISBN 1851850546 Pbk £7.95

—General Principles of English Law / 5th ed. - Plymouth : Macdonald & Evans, 1988.
ISBN 0712107479 Pbk £6.95

—General principles of law / by Clive R. Newton. - 3rd ed. - London : Sweet & Maxwell, 1983.
xix,373p; 22cm.
Previous ed.: 1977. Bibliography: p362-364. - Includes index.
ISBN 042128580X Pbk £7.95

—General principles of law in a nutshell / Josephine Dominic. - London : Sweet & Maxwell, 1981.
vii,82p; 18cm. - (New nutshells).
Includes index.
ISBN 0421278307 Pbk £1.75

—Halsbury's Laws of England : 1907-1917, 31 Vols. / Abingdon : Professional Books.

—Halsbury's Laws of England : 1931-1942, 37 Vols. / 2nd ed. - Abingdon : Professional Books.

—Halsbury's Laws of England : 1952-1964, 43 Vols. / 3rd ed. - Abingdon : Professional Books.

—Halsbury's Laws of England, 56 Vols. / 4th ed. - London : Butterworths.

—Halsbury's Laws of England / Abingdon : Professional Books.

1931-1942, 37 Vols. 2nd ed.

1953-1975, 43 Vols. 3rd ed. Incl. 1975 supplement

1973-date, 56 Vols. 4th ed.

—Halsbury's Laws of England / 4th ed. - Abingdon : Professional Books, 1984.

—Halsbury's statutes of England / Great Britain. - 3rd ed. 53. - London : Butterworths, 1968.
Superseded in part by 4th ed.
ISBN 0406042004

—Introduction to English Law / 11th ed. - London : Butterworths, 1985.
ISBN 0406605017 Hbk £18.00
ISBN 0406605025 Pbk £12.95

—Introduction to English law / William Geldart. - 9th ed. - Oxford : Oxford University Press, 1984.
viii,180p; 20cm.
Previous ed.: published as Elements of English law. 1975. Bibliography: p166-170. - Includes index.
ISBN 0192891715 Pbk £3.95

—Introduction to English law / Philip S. James. - 11th ed. - London : Butterworths, 1985.
xxxv,569p; 22cm.
Previous ed.: 1979. Includes index.
ISBN 0406605017 Hbk No price
ISBN 0406605025 Pbk No price

—Introduction to law / Phil Harris. - London : Weidenfeld and Nicolson, 1980.
xvi,320p; 22cm.
Bibliography: p.303-311. - Includes index.
ISBN 0297778269 £11.50
ISBN 0297778277

—Introduction to law / by L.A. Rutherford, I.A. Todd, M.G. Woodley. - London : Sweet and Maxwell published in association with the Institute of Legal Executives, 1982.
xxiii,379p; 25cm.
Includes index.
ISBN 0421293802 Pbk £14.50

—Introduction to law / by L.A. Rutherford, I.A. Todd and M.G. Woodley. - 2nd ed. - London : Sweet & Maxwell published in association with the Institute of Legal Executives, 1987.
400p; 26cm.
Previous ed.: 1982. Includes index.
ISBN 0421367601 Pbk £17.50

—Introduction to legal method / Anthony M. Dugdale. - 2nd ed. - London : Sweet & Maxwell, 1984.
xxiii,307p; 22cm.
Previous ed.: 1977. Bibliography: p296-298. - Includes index.
ISBN 0421297700 Hbk £10.75
ISBN 0421297808 Pbk £6.50

—Jowitt's dictionary of English law / by the late Earl Jowitt and Clifford Walsh. - 2nd ed. - London : Sweet and Maxwell, 1977.
2v.(11,1935p); 26cm.
Gives a definition and explanation of old and new legal terms in English law. Covers arbitration, trade descriptions, latin maxims and the writings of Glanvil, Bracton, Fitzherbert, Coke, Hale and Blackstone. Also examines the organisation of relevant Ministries, and all new law and statutes of recent years.
ISBN 0421230908 £45.00

—Jubilee lectures celebrating the foundation of the Faculty of Law, University of Birmingham / edited by I.R. Scott. - London : Wildy & Sons Ltd, 1981.
viii,215p. - (Wildy's texts in law and jurisprudence).
Contents include: Restraining the misuse of power/by Lord Denning.
ISBN 0854900039

—Law / Emile Woolf, Suresh Tanna, Karam Singh. - Plymouth : Macdonald & Evans, 1985.
1v.
ISBN 0712104860 Pbk

—Law and modern society / P.S. Atiyah. - Oxford : Oxford University Press, 1983.
viii,158p; 23cm.
Bibliography: p150-155. - Includes index.
ISBN 0192191667 £9.95

—Law and society in England / Bob Roshier and Harvey Teff. - London : Tavistock Publications, 1980.
258p; 23cm.
Bibliography: p226-242. - Includes index.
ISBN 0422767204 Hbk £15.50
ISBN 0422767301 Pbk £7.95

—Law for GCSE / Collins. - London : Pitman Publishing, 1987.
ISBN 0273028367 Pbk £5.95

—Law machine / Marcel Berlins and Clare Dyer. - Harmondsworth : Penguin, 1982.
191p.
Includes index.
ISBN 0140224815

—Law machine / Marcel Berlins and Clare Dyer. - 2nd rev ed. - Harmondsworth : Penguin Books, 1986.
185p.
ISBN 0140226958

—Lawyers and laymen / edited by T.M. Charles-Edwards, Morfydd E. Owen and D. B. Walters. - Cardiff : University of Wales Press, 1986.
394,1p of plates; 23cm.
Bibliography: p355-368. - Includes index. Festschrift in honour of Professor Dafydd Jenkins. Includes two papers in Welsh.
ISBN 0708309259 £25.00

—Mastering basic English Law / London : Macmillan, 1985.
ISBN 0333382897 Pbk £3.95

—Modern English legal system / by P.F. Smith and S.H. Bailey. - London : Sweet & Maxwell, 1984.
xxxix,783p; 24cm.
Includes index.
ISBN 0421271809 Hbk £30.00
ISBN 0421271906 Pbk £16.00

—Moriarty's police law : an arrangement of law and regulations for the use of police officers / James Fryer, Walter Stansfield. - 24th ed. - London : Butterworths, 1981.
xviii,767p; 19cm.
Previous ed.: 1976. Includes index.
ISBN 0406846081 Pbk Unpriced

—'O' level law / Collins. - London : Pitman Publishing, 1984.
ISBN 0273025538 Pbk £4.95

—Osborn's Concise law dictionary / Roger Bird. - 7th ed. - London : Sweet & Maxwell, 1983.
vii,390p; 23cm.
Includes definitions of legal words and phrases, Roman law terms, and a list of Law Reports with their abbreviations. Many developments in the law since the sixth edition are included.
ISBN 0421296704 Hbk £7.50
ISBN 0421296801 Pbk £4.50

—Pragmatism and theory in English law / by P.S. Atiyah. - London : Stevens & Sons under the auspices of the Hamlyn Trust, 1987.
193p; 18cm.
Includes index.
ISBN 0420475907 Hbk £18.50
ISBN 0420476008 Pbk £10.50

—Questions and answers on English law / London : Financial Training, 1983.
ISBN 0906322391 Pbk £5.95

—Scott's English Law for GCSE / 5th ed. - London : Butterworths, 1987.
ISBN 0406653070 Pbk £10.50

—Second Part of the Institutes of the Lawes of England : Containing the Exposition of Many Ancient and Other Statutes / Repr. of 1642 ed. – Abingdon : Professional Books.
546p.

—Selections from the Laws of England, 2 Vols. / Repr. of 1806 ed. – Abingdon : Professional Books.

—Social workers, their clients and the law / Michael Zander. – 3rd ed. – London : Sweet & Maxwell, 1981.
xiv,180p; 22cm.
Previous ed.: 1977. Includes index.
ISBN 0421279303 Pbk £5.75

—Spelmanni Reliquiae : The Posthumous Works of Sir Henry Spelman Relating to the Laws and Antiquity of England / Repr. of 1698 ed. – Abingdon : Professional Books.
37p.

—Strouds judicial dictionary of words and phrases / John S. James, Frederick Stroud. – 5th ed. 6 v. – London : Sweet & Maxwell, 1986.
Kept up to date by supplements.
ISBN 0421366303

—Third and Fourth Parts of the Institutes of the Lawes of England : Concerning High Treason and Other Pleas of the Crown and Criminal Causes / Repr. of 1644 ed. – Abingdon : Professional Books.
360p.

—Treatise of the Principle Grounds and Maximes of the Lawes of This Kingdome by W.N. A Dialogue and Treatise of the Laws of England and on Tenures, Estates, Heriditaments and Chattels / W. N. Bythewood. – 9th ed. Repr. of 1821 ed. – Abingdon : Professional Books.
243p.

—Welfare law and order : a critical introduction to law for social workers / Pete Alcock and Phil Harris. – London : Macmillan, 1982.
xvi,219p. – (Critical texts in social work and the welfare state).
Includes index. Bibliography: p207-213.
ISBN 0333294904

—What next in the law / by Lord Denning. – London : Butterworths, 1982.
xxiii,352p.
Amended version of original ed. which was withdrawn from sale on legal advice shortly after publication. Includes index.

—Where's the justice ? : a manifesto of law reform / Tony Gifford. – Harmondsworth : Penguin, 1986.
126p. – (A Penguin special).
ISBN 0140523588

LAW – EUROPE

—European Law and Institutions / Edinburgh : Edinburgh University Press.
60p.

—Yearbook of European law / Oxford : Oxford University Press, 1981.
ISBN 0198253842 Hbk £50.00

Vol. 2 1982.
ISBN 0198254903 Hbk £50.00

Vol. 3 1983.
ISBN 0198255047 Hbk £50.00

Vol. 4 1984.
ISBN 0198255217 Hbk £50.00

Vol. 5 1985.
ISBN 0198255462 Hbk £50.00

Vol. 6 1986.
ISBN 0198256051 Hbk £45.00

Vol. 7 1988.
490.
As well as practical and theoretical articles, contains Annual Surveys of the Council of Europe, the European Convention on Human Rights, and the European Parliament. There is a book review section andlist of Commission Decision Competitors. Fully indexed with a table of cases.
ISBN 0198256256 Hbk £55

LAW – EUROPEAN COMMUNITY

—Basic Community cases / Bernard Rudden. – Oxford : Clarendon, 1987.
360p; 24cm.
Includes index.
ISBN 0198762127 Hbk £28.00
ISBN 0198762119 Pbk £11.50

—Basic Community laws / edited by Bernard Rudden and Derrick Wyatt. – 2nd ed. – Oxford : Clarendon, 1986.
xvi,407p.
Previous ed.: 1980.
ISBN 0198761996 Pbk £25.00
ISBN 0198761988 £9.95

—Basic community laws / edited by Bernard Rudden and Derrick Wyatt. – Oxford : Clarendon, 1980.
xv,301p; 24cm.
ISBN 0198761198 Hbk £14.00
ISBN 0198761201 Pbk Unpriced

—Cases and materials on the law of the European Communities / compiled by Richard Plender and John Usher : with a foreword by Lord Mackenzie Stuart. – London : Macmillan, 1980.
xxxv,457p; 25cm.
Includes bibliographies and index.
ISBN 0333231449 Hbk £25.00
ISBN 0333231457 Pbk £15.00

—Community legal order / by Jean-Victor Louis. – Luxembourg : Office for Official Publications of the European Communities, 1980.
145p; 25cm.
Bibliography: p.131-136. At head of title: Commission of the European Communities. Translated from the French.
ISBN 9282510530

—Division of powers between the European communities and their member states in the field of external relations : colloquium, 30 and 31 May 1980 / Albert Bleckmann ... et al. : organized by Europa Instituut of the University of Amsterdam and Section for European - and Economic Law of the University of Croningen. – Deventer, Netherlands : Kluwer, 1980.
149p.
ISBN 9026812086

—EEC Law / James Dinnage. – 2nd ed. – London : Sweet & Maxwell, 1981.
lvi,531p; 25cm.
Previous ed.: 1973. Includes index.
ISBN 0421260904 Hbk £25.00
ISBN 0421261005 Pbk £16.00

—Essays in European law and integration : to mark the silver jubilee of the Europa Institute, Leiden, 1957-1982 / edited by David O'Keeffe and Henry G. Schermers. – Deventer, Netherlands : Kluwer Law and Taxation Publishers, 1982.
208 p.; 25 cm.
Includes bibliographical references.
ISBN 9065441107

—European Communities legislation : current status / London : Butterworths, 1988-.
Each annual supersedes preceding year's. Cumulative index wuth each quarterly supplement. Annual index published separately.

—European Community law and national law : the irreversible transfer? / John Usher. – London : University Association for Contemporary European Studies, 1981.
96p; 23cm.
Bibliography: p85-91. - Includes index.
ISBN 0043410170 Pbk £6.95
ISBN 0043410189 Unpriced

—European Community : law in action / Stanley Clinton Davis. – Exeter : University of Exeter, 1986.
11p.

—European Community's legal system / 2nd ed. – Luxembourg : Office for Official Publications of the European Communities, 1984.
43p.
Bibliography: p.43.
ISBN 928254432X

—European law review / . – London : Sweet & Maxwell, 1975.
Index in each vol.
ISBN 03075400

—Free movement in European Community law / F. Burrows. – Oxford : Clarendon, 1987.
xxxvii,346p; 24cm.
Bibliography: xxxvii - Includes index.
ISBN 019825492X £35.00

—Guide to EEC law in Northern Ireland / by Sylvia E. Paisley. – Belfast : SLS Legal Publications (NI), Queen's University, Belfast, 1986.
xxii,247p; 21cm.
Bibliography: p237. - Includes index.
ISBN 0853892628 Pbk No price

—Guide to EEC-legislation / editors, Alfred E. Kellermann...et al. : T.M.C. Asser Institute, The Hague. – 2nd ed. 3 v. – Amsterdam : North-Holland, 1983.
2522p.
Previous ed.: 1979. Includes index. Kept up to date by supplements.
ISBN 0444853200

—In memoriam J.D.B. Mitchell / editors St. John Bates ... et al. : foreword Lord Cameron. – London : Sweet & Maxwell, 1983.
xxxix,247p,1leaf of plates; 23cm.
Includes index.
ISBN 042129700X £19.50

—Institutional framework of the European Communities / D.A.C. Freestone and J.S. Davidson. – London : Croom Helm, 1988.
17,221p; 23cm.
Includes index.
ISBN 0709910487 Hbk £27.50
ISBN 0709949081 Pbk £9.95

—Introduction to the law of the European Communities: after the coming into force of the Single European Act / Edited by L. W. Gormley. – 2nd. – Kluwer Law and Taxation, 1989.
850.
A revised second edition, taking into account the Single European Act. As well as basic sources and material of the law of the European Communities, deals with the increased case law of the Court of Justice.
ISBN 9065444009 Hbk £65/Dfl 230

—Materials on the law of the European Communities / edited by D.J. Gijlstra and E.L.M. Volker. – 1st ed. – Deventer, Netherlands : Kluwer Law and Taxation Publishers, 1983.
xxi, 530 p.; 25 cm.
'Europe Institute, University of Amsterdam.'.
ISBN 9065440690 pbk. fl 78.00

—Parliamentary challenge to the community law making process : the Exeter Lecture in European Community Law, delivered in the University on 4 March 1983 / by Alan R. Tyrrell. – Exeter : University of Exeter, 1983.
11p.

—Practical introduction to European Community law / by Richard Plender. – London : Sweet & Maxwell, 1980.
xxiii,166p; 22cm.
Bibliography: p147-163. - Includes index.
ISBN 0421252707 Pbk £6.25

—Substantive law of the EEC / by Derrick Wyatt and Alan Dashwood. – 2nd ed. – London : Sweet & Maxwell, 1987.
450p; 25cm.
Previous ed.: 1980. Includes index.
ISBN 0421348704 Hbk No price
ISBN 0421348801 Pbk No price

—Sweet & Maxwell's European Community treaties : including the European Communities Act 1972 / edited by Sweet & Maxwell's legal editorial staff : advisory editor K.R. Simmonds. – 4th ed. – London : Sweet & Maxwell, 1980.
xvi,410p; 25cm.
Previous ed.: 1977.
ISBN 0421272104 Hbk £11.50
ISBN 0421272201 Pbk £8.50

—Thirty years of Community law / Commission of the European Communities. – Luxembourg : Office for Official Publications of the European Communities, 1981.
xxiv,498p.
ISBN 9282526526 Pbk £8.50

—Yearbook of European law / A Barav, D Wyatt, Joan Wyatt. – Oxford : Clarendon Press, 1989.
500; 23.5.
Contains articles on prominent aspects of EEC law, including one by O. Due. Covers the European monetary system, the Lugano Convention on Civil Jurisdiction and Judgements, the application of EEC compeition rules to trade associations, and the Strasbourg option for regulating transfrontier television. Contains book reviews and tables of cases.
ISBN 0198252633 Hbk £60.00

LAW – FINLAND

—Finnish legal system / edited by Jaakko Uotila. – Helsinki : Union of Finnish Lawyers Publishing, 1985.
263p.
Includes bibliographies and index.

—Making and Applying Law in Finland / Helsinki : Suomen valtio, 1983.
20p.
ISBN 9514670361 Hbk £15.00

LAW – FRANCE

—Dictionnaire Juridique Fr/Eng Eng/Fr / 2nd ed. – London : Edition de Navarre, 1984.
ISBN 2713300045 Pbk £31.00

—Science du Droit Dans le Midi de la France au Moyen Age / Northampton : Variorum, 1984.
360p : Illus.. – – (Collected Studies Ser.: 196).
ISBN 0860781445 Hbk £28.00

LAW – GHANA

—Constitutional instruments / Ghana. – Accra : Ghana Publishing Corporation, .
Issued with: Ghana gazette.

—Ghana : the people, the laws and the courts / by E.S. Aidoo. – Legon : Institute of Statistical, Social and Economic Research, University of Ghana, 1985.
37p.
'Paper first presented at the Seventh Annual Alumni Lecture of the University of Ghana'.

—Legislative instruments / Ghana. – Accra : Ghana Publishing Corporation, .
Issued with: Ghana gazette.

—Review of Ghana law / Accra : General Legal Council, 1969-.
Index in each vol.

—University of Ghana law journal / v. – London : Sweet & Maxwell, 1964-.

LAW - GREAT BRITAIN

—Annual report / the Law Commission. – London : HMSO, 1986.
v,71p.
ISBN 0102247862

—Australian and New Zealand commentary on Halsbury's Laws of England (Fourth Edition) / editor in chief, Garfield Barwick. – v. – Sydney : Butterworths, 1974-.
loose-leaf.
In 2 series: Australian commentary (vols. A-), and New Zealand commentary (vols. A-). Spine title: Commentary on Halsbury's laws of England. - Vol. A of New Zealand commentary has spine sub-title: Australia and New Zealand.

—Basic Law / Repr. of 1978 ed. – Plymouth : Macdonald & Evans, 1981.
176p. – (M and E Handbook Ser.).
ISBN 0712102450 Hbk £2.25

—Basic Law / 2nd ed. – Plymouth : Macdonald & Evans, 1985.
ISBN 0712106553 Pbk £4.95

—Basic Law : An Introduction for Students / 2nd ed. – Plymouth : Macdonald & Evans, 1985.
176p. – (M and E Handbook Ser.).
Students
ISBN 0712106553 Hbk £3.95

—Baty : Polarised Law / Repr. of 1914 ed. – London : Sweet & Maxwell, 1986.
– (Sweet and Maxwell Library Reprints).
ISBN 0421355204 Hbk

—Bibliography of the main publications on state and law of Great Britain issued in the USSR in 1946-1983 / Akademiia Nauk SSSR. – Moscow : The Institute, 1984.
14p.
'Prepared by the Group on Foreign Scientific Information of the Institute of State and Law of the Academy of Sciences of the USSR. Translated into English by Yu. D. Kouptsov'.

—Butterworth's Annotated Legislation Service : 1939-1981, 280 Vols. / Abingdon : Professional Books.

—Butterworth's Current Law / Phillippa Oldham. – Wellington : Butterworths.

—Butterworth's Emergency Legislation Service, 158 Vols. / Abingdon : Professional Books, 1984.

—Code of conduct for the Bar of England and Wales : effective from 1st January 1981 / The Senate of the Inns of Court and the Bar. – London : The Senate, 1980.
56p.

—Current law statutes annotated / Great Britain. – London : Sweet & Maxwell, 1947.

—Dictionnaire Juridique Fr/Eng Eng/Fr / 2nd ed. – London : Edition de Navarre, 1984.
ISBN 2713300045 Pbk £31.00

—Every Man's Own Lawyer / 71st ed. – London : Macmillan, 1981.
896p.
ISBN 0333218493 Hbk £15.00
ISBN 0333318358 Pbk £7.95

—Halsbury's statutes of England and Wales / managing editor Paul Brown. – 4th ed. 50 v. – London : Butterworths, 1985.
With Users guide and Alphabetical list of statutes. Updating service.
ISBN 0406214093

—Hamlyn revisited : the British legal system today / by Lord Hailsham of St. Marylebone. – London : Published under the auspices of the Hamlyn Trust by Stevens & Sons, 1983.
xii,89p; 18cm.
Includes index.
ISBN 0420467203 Hbk Unpriced
ISBN 0420467300 Pbk £4.95

—Introduction to Law / ILEX. – 2nd ed. – London : Sweet & Maxwell, 1987.
ISBN 0421367601 Pbk £17.00

—Introduction to Law (LIC) / 2nd ed. – Weidenfeld & Nicolson, 1984.
ISBN 0297784595 Hbk £12.95
ISBN 0297784609 Pbk £7.95

—Is it in force? / London : Butterworths, 1988.
ISBN 0406072833 Pbk £15.00

—Is It In Force? 1987 / Butterworths Editorial Staff. – London : Butterworths, 1987.
ISBN 0406072825 Pbk £33.00

—Isle of Man statutes in force / Isle of Man. – Douglas : Isle of Man Government, 1985.
loose-leaf.

—Landmarks in the Law / London : Butterworths, 1984.
ISBN 0406176035 Hbk £14.95
ISBN 0406176140 Pbk £9.95

—Law and Order (Hamlyn 37) / London : Sweet & Maxwell, 1985.
ISBN 0420472509 Pbk £8.25

—Law for the Small Business : 'The Daily Telegraph' Guide / 4th ed. – London : Kogan Page, 1985.
264p.
ISBN 0850388937 Hbk £11.95
ISBN 0850388945 Pbk £6.95

—Law, Justice and the Judiciary : Transitional / Sinnadurai. – Professional Law, 1988.
ISBN 09679958002 Hbk £95.00

—Law, litigants and the legal profession / papers presented to the Fourth British Legal History Conference at the University of Birmingham, 10-13 July, 1979 : edited by E.W. Ives and A.H. Manchester. – London : Royal Historical Society, 1983.
xii,233p; 26cm.
Includes index.
ISBN 0901050911 £11.25
ISBN 0391029258

—Law-making and law-makers in British history : papers presented to the Edinburgh Legal History Conference, 1977 / edited by Alan Harding. – London : Royal Historical Society, 1980.
viii,223p; 23cm.
Includes index.
ISBN 0901050776 £15.25

—Lawyer's Remembrancer 1986 / London : Butterworths, 1984.
This book is a concise encyclopedia of United Kingdom practice and legislation, together with a diary section running from November, 1985 to January, 1987. Each week in the diary is given two full pages. The references section includes names, addresses, phone numbers, and relevant abbreviations.
ISBN 0406269181 Hbk

—Legal action : the bulletin of the Legal Action Group / London : Legal Action Group, 1984.
Continues: LAG bulletin.

—Legally yours - law and the individual / Reed. – 2nd ed. – Maidenhead : McGraw-Hill, 1985.
ISBN 0070848777 Pbk £5.95

—Limits of the Law / London : Butterworths, 1980.
ISBN 0406552436 Pbk £13.95

—Matter of justice : the legal system in ferment / Michael Zander. – London : Tauris, 1987.
250p; 22cm.
Includes bibliography and index.
ISBN 1850430403 £14.95

—McKenna law letter : current developments in the law / London : McKenna & Co., 1980.

—Modern Introduction to Law / London : Edward Arnold, 1984.
544p.
ISBN 0713109041 Pbk £8.95

—Modern Introduction to Law / London : Edward Arnold, 1984.
ISBN 0713109041 Pbk £8.25

—Penguin guide to the law / 2nd ed. – Penguin, 1986.
ISBN 0140511466 Pbk £9.95

—Politics and power / London : Routledge and Kegan Paul, 1981.
328p; 24cm.
ISBN 0710009844

—Prevention of terrorism in British law / Clive Walker. – Manchester : Manchester University Press, 1986.
xi,272p; 25cm.
Bibliography: p236-239. - Includes index.
ISBN 0719017823 £27.50

—Rights of way guide to law and practice / Trevelyan. – Open Spaces Society, 1983.
ISBN 0946574006 Hbk £4.00

—Role of Law in Central-Local Relations / Oxford : Social Science Research Council, 1981.
105p.
ISBN 0862260248 Pbk £2.50

—Scottish current law statutes / Edinburgh : Green, 1961-.
Contains both English and Scottish law. Not published: 1963-1972.

—Stage One Law / Northwick Publishers, 1983.
ISBN 0907135102 Pbk £6.00

—Subject guide to the Acts of Tynwald / Rev. to 31 Oct. 1984. – Douglas : Isle of Man Government, 1984.
84p.

LAW - GREAT BRITAIN - PERIODICALS

—Haldane Society of Socialist Lawyers bulletin / London : The Society, 1970.

LAW - HONG KONG

—Discussion paper on the laws in Chinese / Hong Kong : Attorney General's Chambers, 1986.
99p.

—Future of the law in Hong Kong / edited by R.I. Wacks. – Hong Kong : Oxford University Press (Hong Kong), 1989.
320.
Examines the theoretical and procedural aspects of the common law of Hong Kong and evaluates its development up to and beyond 1997 when sovereignty returns to China.
ISBN 0195849183 Hbk £19.50

—Introduction to the Hong Kong legal system / Peter Wesley-Smith. – Hong Kong : Oxford University Press, 1987.
ix, 118 p.; 22 cm.
An overview of the Hong Kong legal system; the constitution, imported law and law made in Hong Kong, literary sources, structure of the courts, operation of judge-made laws, the process of legislative law-making, and the institutions of the law.
ISBN 0195840577 pbk. £10.00

—Law in Hong Kong / 2nd ed. – London : Federal, 1986.
ISBN 9623020015 Pbk £15.00

LAW - INDIA

—Law and Order in India / New Delhi : Abhinav Publications, 1987.
359p.
ISBN 8170172160 Hbk £190.00

—Law and society in modern India / New Delhi : Oxford University Press India, 1989.
430.
Thirteen articles examine the way that modern Indian law operates. Shows the ways that a complex body of formal law adjusts itself to local conditions. The essays cover equality, hierarchy, panchayat justice, caste and policies of discrimination. The introduction by Rajeev Ddhavan traces the history of law in India.
ISBN 0195622944 £15.00

LAW - INDONESIA

—Indonesian legal history 1602-1848 / Sydney : Oughtershaw Press, 1982.
viii,300p.
Bibliography: p.275-293. - Includes index.
ISBN 0959342001

—Indonesian legal history : British West Sumatra, 1685-1825 / John Ball. – Sydney : Oughtershaw Press, 1984.
viii, 307 p.; 21 cm.
Includes index. Bibliography: 296-299.
ISBN 095934201X pbk.

LAW - IRAN

—Law and human rights in the Islamic Republic of Iran : a report covering events within the seven month period following the Revolution of February 1979 / Amnesty International. – London : Amnesty International, 1980.
216p.

LAW - IRELAND

—Dublin University law journal / Dublin : Law School, Trinity College, Dublin, 1976-.

—Introduction to law in the Republic of Ireland : its history, principles, administration & substance / Richard H. Grimes and Patrick T. Horgan. – Portmarnock : Wolfhound, 1981.
368p; 22cm.
Bibliography: p348-351. - Includes index.
ISBN 0905473558 Pbk £15.00
ISBN 0905473566 unpriced

—Irish current law statutes annotated / editorial board, Jennefer Aston... et al. : general editor, Kevin Boyle : assistant editor, Robert Clark : legal research, Maeve Doyle. – London : Sweet & Maxwell, 1984-.
looseleaf.
ISBN 0421327405 Hbk

—Legal systems, North and South : a study prepared for the New Ireland Forum / by C. K. Boyce. – Dublin : Stationery Office, 1984.
60p.

—New Library of Irish Material Now on LEXIS / London : Butterworths.

—Principles of Irish law / Brian Doolan. – 2nd ed. – Dublin : Gill and Macmillan, 1986.
xix,395p.
Previous ed.: 1981. Includes index.
ISBN 0717114384 £12.50

LAW - ISLE OF MAN

—Isle of Man Orders in Council : consisting of Orders in Council extending or applying Acts of Parliament and Statutory Instruments to the Isle of Man / edited and annotated with an introduction by K.F.W. Gumbley. – Douglas : Government Printer, 1987-.
looseleaf.

—Subject guide and chronological tables to the subordinate legislation of the Isle of Man / prepared on the directions of H.M. Attorney General for the Isle of Man. – v. – Douglas : Isle of Man Government Printer, 1983-.
looseleaf.

LAW - ISRAEL

—Foundations of Law Act, 1980 and its implementation / Jerusalem : The Ministry, 1982.
6p.

LAW - ITALY

—English-Italian Law Dictionary / London : Sweet & Maxwell, 1985.
ISBN 0421357401 Hbk £50.00

—Italian legal system / G. Leroy Certoma. - London : Butterworths, 1985.
xxiv,520p; 23cm. - (Butterworths' legal systems of the world).
Bibliography: p493-500. - Includes index.
ISBN 040639993X Hbk £43.00

LAW - JAPAN

—Modern Japanese Law / London : Butterworths, 1988.
ISBN 040666921X Hbk

—Ritsumeikan law review / International ed. - Kyoto, Japan : Ritsumeikan University, 1986-.
International ed. of: Ritsumeikan law review. Includes articles in German, French and Japanese.

LAW - KENYA

—Law of Kenya : an Introduction / 1st ed. - Nairobi : Kenya Literature Bureau, 1980.

—Law of Kenya : Cases and Statutes / Nairobi : Kenya Literature Bureau, 1986.

LAW - KIRIBATI

—Laws of the Republic of Kiribati : containing the Acts, Ordinances and Subsidiary Legislation thereunder, enacted before the 1st day of January 1980, together with certain Orders in Council and other provisions relating to Kiribati / Michael Jennings, C. J. Lynch. - Rev. ed. 1979. 3. - Bairiki : Office of the Attorney-General, 1980.
loose-leaf; 26cm.

LAW - LESOTHO

—Cumulative index to the statute law of Lesotho 5 March 1960 to 31 December 1982 : including tables of repealed/amended statutes between 5 March 1960 and December 1982, statutes of Lesotho (including Cape statutes) in force on the 31 December 1982 / by Robert J.W. Kukubo. - Roma, Lesotho : University Press of Lesotho, 1983.
xiv,351p.
Includes an appendix for 1983.

—Lesotho law journal : a journal of law and development / Lesotho : Faculty of Law, National University of Lesotho, 1985-.
Includes bibliographical references.

LAW - MALAWI

—Acts / Malawi. - Zomba : Government Printer, 1964.
Supplement to: Malawi gazette.

—Government notices / Malawi. - Zomba : Government Printer, 1964.
Supplement to: Malawi gazette.

LAW - MALAYSIA

—Applicable law in Singapore and Malaysia:a guide to reception, precedent and sources of law in the republic of Singapore and the federation of Malaysia / Singapore : Malayan Law Journal, 1990.
600.
Account of the applicable law in Singapore and Malaysia, and a summary of legislation and case law. Appendices contain a digest of selected cases, politico-legal landmarks reception in other countries, comparative charts of the English and Singapore legal system, and a chart on precedent in Singapore.

—Index to Singapore/Malaysia legal periodicals 1932-1984 / Compiled by the staff of the Law Library, National University of Singapore Library : edited by Molly Cheang, Sng Yok Fong, Carolyn Wee. - Singapore : Malayan Law Journal Pte., 1986.
xvi,431p.
ISBN 9971700506 Hbk £160.00

—Introduction to the Malaysian legal system / Wu Min Aun. - Rev. 3rd ed. - Kuala Lumpur : Heinemann Educational (Asia), 1982.
xii,196p.
Previous ed.: 1978. Bibliography: p.189-196.

—Malaya Law Review / National University of Singapore, Faculty of Law. - Singapore : University of Singapore.
ISBN 0542335X Hbk £45.00

—Malaysian Law / Professional Law, 1988.
ISBN 09679958001 Hbk £35.00

—Malaysian legal essays : a collection of essays in honour of Professor Emeritus Datuk Ahmad Ibrahim / edited by M.B. Hooker. - Kuala Lumpur : Malayan Law Journal, 1986.
xxxii,456p.
Collection of essays in honour of Professor Datuk Ahmad Ibrahim, covering aspects of Malaysian law, including family law, Islamic law, and legal history.
ISBN 9971700476

—Malaysian legal source materials in London, Oxford and Cambridge / by Shaikha Zakaria : with a foreword by M.B. Hooker. - Kuala Lumpur : Perpustakaan Universiti Malaya, 1985.
x,66p.
Includes index.
ISBN 9679430057

—Sesquicentennial Chronological Tables of the Written Laws of the Republic of Singapore 1834-1984 / Srinivasagam. - Kent Ridge : Malaya Law Review.

—Survey of Malaysian Law /. -
ISBN 9971700131 Hbk £46.00

1980 1980.
ISBN 9971700239 £60.00

1981 1983.
xvi, 304p.
ISBN 9971700328 Spiral bound £46

1982 1984.
xvi, 306p.
ISBN 9971700360 Spiral bound £50

1983 1985.
399.

1984 1985.
360.

LAW - MALTA

—Laws / Malta. - Rev. ed. - Valletta : Legal (Publishing) Enterprises, 1978.

—Revised edition of the laws of Malta, in force on 1st January, 1984 / prepared under the authority of the Statute Law Revision Act, 1980 by the Law Commission. - Valletta : Information Division, 1986.
English version of L-edizzjoni riveduta tal-ligijiet ta Malta.

LAW - MANITOBA

—Manitoba regulations / Manitoba. - v. - Winnipeg : Queen's Printer, 1975.

LAW - MEXICO

—Introduction to the history of Mexican law / Guillermo Floris Margadant S. - 1st English ed. - London : Oceana Publications, 1981.
Includes bibliographical references and index. Translation of: Introduccion a la historia del derecho mexicano, 4th ed.
ISBN 0379207443

LAW - MONGOLIA

—Mongolian legal system : contemporary legislation and documentation / edited by W.E. Butler : translations from Mongolian by A.J. Nathanson, translations from Russian by W.E. Butler. - The Hague : Nijhoff, 1982.
xxiii, 995 p.; 25 cm.
ISBN 9024726859 Hbk £450.00

LAW - NEAR EAST

—Middle East legal systems / S.H. Amin. - Glasgow : Royston, 1985.
320p.
ISBN 0946706220 £29.95

LAW - NEW ZEALAND

—Abridgment of New Zealand Case Law : 1861-1967, 16 Vols. / Wellington : Butterworths.
ISBN 0409600008 Hbk

Supplement-1962-1973

Supplement-1974-1978

Supplement 1980-to date

—Auckland Law School centenary lectures / L.C.B. Gower ... et al. - Auckland : Legal Research Foundation, 1983.
103p.
ISBN 0908581297

—Australian and New Zealand Citator to UK Reports 1588-1972 / Wellington : Butterworths.
ISBN 0409303100 Pbk

—Butterworth's District Court Reports / Wellington : Butterworths.

—Butterworths annotations to the New Zealand statutes : 2nd ed. : 1908-1982 / by Martin Fine. - Wellington : Butterworths, 1982.
Previous ed.: Butterworths cases annotations of the New Zealand statutes reprint 1908-1957, published 1960-1961. Looseleaf issues accompanied by monthly Butterworths Automatic Annotations Bulletin.
ISBN 0409701262

—Introduction to New Zealand Law / Farrand. - 4th ed. - London : Butterworths, 1981.
ISBN 0409655376 Pbk £34.00

—Introduction to New Zealand Law / W.L. Farrand. - 4th ed. - Butterworths, 1980.
ISBN 0409655376 Pbk £59.95

—Introduction to the New Zealand legal system / by R.D. Mulholland. - Wellington : Butterworths, 1980.
xvii,350p.
Includes index.
ISBN 0409600865

—New Zealand Commentary to Halsbury's Laws of England / Wellington : Butterworths.

—New Zealand Law Reports / New Zealand Council of Law Reporting. - Wellington : Butterworths.

—New Zealand Recent Law / Auckland : Legal Research Foundation, 1986.

Back Issues

—Tokelau : subdelgated legislation 1877 - 1948 / Union Islands. - Wellington : Tokelau Administration, 1986.
399p.

LAW - NIGERIA

—Annual volume of the laws of Eastern Region of Nigeria ... : containing the ordinances of Eastern Region of Nigeria and subsidiary legislation made thereunder / Eastern Region of Nigeria. - 19 v. - Enugu : Government Printer, 1952.
Originally published as individual supplements to Eastern Nigeria gazette. 1967 volume also contains legislation enacted by the Republic of Biafra. Entitled Laws Eastern Nigeria: 1959-1967.

—Annual volume of the laws of Imo State of the Federal Republic of Nigeria containing edicts and subsidiary legislation / Imo State of Nigeria. - Owerri : Government Printer, 1976.
Consolidated index 1976-1985 published separately, 1986.

—Annual volume of the laws of Kaduna State of Nigeria ... / Kaduna State of Nigeria. - Kaduna, Nigeria : Government Printer, 1976.
Originally published as individual supplements to the Kaduna State of Nigeria gazette. Index in each vol..

—Annual volume of the laws of Ogun State of Nigeria : containing the laws of Ogun state of Nigeria and subsidiary legislation made thereunder / Ogun State of Nigeria. - v. - Abeokuta? : Government Printer?, 1976-.
Previously published as separate supplements to Ogun State of Nigeria Gazette.

—Annual volume of the laws of the Western Region of Nigeria ... : containing the laws of the Western Region of Nigeria and subsidiary legislation made thereunder / Western Region of Nigeria. - 15 v. - Ibadan : Government Printer, 1954-.
Previously published as separate supplements in the Western Regional Gazette, vol. 1 (1952)-v.9(1960) and the Western Nigeria Gazette, vol.10(1961)-v.15(1966).

—Annual volumes of the laws of North-Eastern State of Nigeria ... / North-Eastern State of Nigeria. - Kaduna, Nigeria : Government Printer, 1969-.
Originally published as individual supplements to the Norht-Eastern State of Nigeria gazette. Covers of vols. for 1971-1974 incorrectly headed: Gongola State of Nigeria. Annual except for 1967/1968 and 1969/1970.

—Annual volumes of the laws of the North-Central State of Nigeria ... / North-Central State of Nigeria. - Kaduna, Nigeria : Government Printer, 1971-.
Originally published as individual supplements to the North-Central State of Nigeria gazette.

—Annual volumes of the laws of Western State of Nigeria : containing the laws of Western State of Nigeria and subsidiary legislation made thereunder / Western State of Nigeria. - Ibadan : Government Printer, 1967-.
Previously published as separate supplements to the Western State of Nigeria Gazette, vol. 16(1967)-v.25 (1976).

—Basic resourses on Nigerian law / by M.O. Olaitan and Oluremi Jegede. - Lagos : Libriservice, 1983.
iii,64p.
ISBN 9782372048

—Colonial legal heritage in Nigeria / by Emmanuel Omoh Esiemokhai. - Akure, Nigeria : Fagbamigbe, 1986.
xii,82p.
Bibliography: p.79. - Includes index.
ISBN 9781642483

—Index to Nigerian legal periodicals, 1946-1981 / compiled by the Library, Nigerian Institute of Advanced Legal Studies. - Lagos : NIALS Library, 1983.
v,33p.

—Introduction to Nigerian law / edited by C.O. Okonkwo. - London : Sweet and Maxwell, 1980.
xxxvi,444p; 23cm.
Includes index.
ISBN 0421239409 £21.00
ISBN 0421239506

—Law and development / edited by J.A. Omotola and A.A. Adeogun. – Lagos : Lagos University Press, 1987.
xviii,336p.
Includes index.
ISBN 9782264822

—Law for Everyman / Onitsha : Africana-FEP.

—Law is for all / by Hon. Justice Akin. Apara. – Enugu : Fourth Dimension Publishers, 1982.
x,118p.
Includes index.

—Laws of Federation of Nigeria, 12 Vols. / Professional Books Staff. – Abingdon : Professional Books, 1984.

—Laws of the Federation of Nigeria and Lagos : 1958, 12 Vols. / Abingdon : Professional Books.

—New perspective in law and justice in Nigeria : the distinguished annual lecture delivered at the National Institute on 25th October, 1985 / by Timothy Akinola Aguda. – Kuru, Nigeria : National Institute for Policy and Strategic Studies, 1985.
16p. – (Distinguished lecture series).
Includes bibliographical references.

—Nigeria-Federal Statutes in Force 1982 : An Index of the Laws of Nigeria Which Are Still in Force As At the 31st December 1984 / Abingdon : Professional Books, 1984.
ISBN 0862050731 Hbk £24.00

—Nigeria journal of contemporary law / v. – Lagos : University of Lagos, 1970-.

—Nigerian law journal / Lagos : African Universities Press, 1964-.

—Nigerian legal system : pluralism and conflict of laws in the Northern States / Ahmed Beita Yusuf. – New Delhi : National, 1982.
xiv,274p : 3 maps.
Bibliography: p.243-266. - Includes index.

—Nigerian periodicals index / Jos? : Committee of University Librarians of Nigerian Universities, 1986-.

—Peoples' law : a journal of contemporary Nigerian and African laws, justice and legality / Lagos, Nigeria : Pan-Afrika Peoples' Law Center and Akademy, 1987.

—Philosophy of law / by Z. O. Aje. – s.l. : s.n., 1986.
ix,160p.
Includes bibliographical references.

—Supplement to Ondo State of Nigeria gazette / Ondo State of Nigeria. – Akure : Government Printer, 1976.
Edicts and legal notices.

—Supreme Court of Nigeria Law Reports / Lagos : Nigerian Law Publications, 1983.
ISBN 9782325010 Hbk £40.00

—Transplants and mongrels and the law : the Nigerian experiment : an inaugural lecture delivered at the University of Ife on 17th May, 1983 / by A.A.O. Okunniga. – Ile-Ife, Nigeria : University of Ife Press, 1984.
32p. – (Inaugural lecture series).
Includes bibliographical references.

—University of Jos law journal / Jos, Nigeria : Faculty of Law, University of Jos, 1984-.

—West Nigerian Law Reports / London : Sweet & Maxwell, Rp 1982 (1955-66).
ISBN 0421291605 Hbk £170.00

—You and the law / Enugu : ABC Books, 1982.
vi,57p.

—You and the law : layman's guide to rights and liabilities / by Funke Fagbohun. – Lagos : MIJ Professional Publishers, 1986.
xxii,211p.
ISBN 9782486035

LAW – NIGERIA – CROSS RIVER STATE

—Annual volume of the laws of the Cross River State of Nigeria containing edicts and subsidiary legislation made in the year ... / v. – Kano : Government Printing Press, 1976-.
Originally published as individual supplements to Cross River State of Nigeria gazette.

—Laws of Cross River State of Nigeria : containing the laws of the State in force on 30th September 1979 together with certain subsidiary legislation and Federal acts and decrees / Lionel Brett. – Rev. ed. 7 v. – s.l. : s.n., 1981.
Includes index. Printed by Eyre and Spottiswoode, London, authorised by the Government of Cross River State of Nigeria.

LAW – NORTHERN IRELAND

—Bulletin of Northern Ireland law / Belfast : S.L.S., Faculty of Law, Queen's University, 1981-.

—Digest of Northern Ireland Law / Valerie Mitchell. – Belfast : Queen's University of Belfast, 1986.

—Guide to EEC law in Northern Ireland / by Sylvia E. Paisley. – Belfast : SLS Legal Publications (NI), Queen's University, Belfast, 1986.
xxii,247p; 21cm.
Bibliography: p237. - Includes index.
ISBN 0853892628 Pbk No price

—Public General Acts of ... Northern Ireland ... / Northern Ireland. – Belfast : HMSO, 1921.
Legislation enacted as Orders in Council from 1972. Looseleaf from 1982.

—Statutes revised, Northern Ireland / 2nd ed. – Belfast : H.M.S.O., 1982.
Previous ed.: 1956. Contents: Public general statute law in force in Northern Ireland on 31 March 1981 except for Acts of the United Kingdom Parliament passed after 1920.
ISBN 0337233640 Llf

LAW – NORWAY

—Continuity and development in law and society / Torstein Eckhoff. – Oxford : OUP.
Essays on general questions of law and legal reasoning. Presents the results of the author's research into the development of Norwegian constitutions in the nineteenth and twentieth centuries and the history of the legal profession to the first half of the eighteenth century.
Students of sociology of law, sociology and law
ISBN 8200183661 Hbk £40.00

—Norwegian laws / selected for the Foreign Service. – Oslo : Royal Ministry of Foreign Affairs, 1980.
997p; 24cm.
Includes index.

LAW – PAPUA NEW GUINEA

—Introduction to the law in Papua New Guinea / by D.R.C. Chalmers and A.H. Paliwala. – 2nd ed. – North Ryde, N.S.W. : Law Book Co, 1984.
xxiv,236p.
Includes bibliographies and index.
ISBN 0455203806

—Law and social change in Papua New Guinea / editors David Weisbrot, Abdul Paliwala, Akilagpa Sawyerr. – Sydney : Butterworths, 1982.
xxiv, 319p.
'A successor to Fashion of law in New Guinea, edited for Butterworths by B.J. Brown in 1969' - Pref..
Bibliography: p291-301 - Includes index.
ISBN 0409309184

LAW – PERIODICALS

—Haldane Society of Socialist Lawyers bulletin / London : The Society, 1970.

LAW – SAINT CHRISTOPHER AND NEVIS

—Saint Christopher and Nevis consolidated index of statutes and subsidiary legislation to 1st January 1984 / compiled at the Faculty of Law Library, University of the West Indies, Barbados. – Barbados? : s.n., 1984.
iv,78p.
Previous ed.: 1st January 1980. One of a series in the West Indian Legislation Indexing Project (WILIP) compiled in cooperation with the British Development Division.

LAW – SAINT CHRISTOPHER, NEVIS AND ANGUILLA

—Saint Christopher, Nevis & Anguilla consolidated index of statutes and subsidiary legislation to 1st January 1980 / compiled at the Faculty of Law and Law Library, University of the West Indies, Barbados. – Cave Hill : Faculty of Law Library, University of the West Indies, 1980.
iv,74p.
One of a series in the West Indies Legislation Indexing Project (WILIP) compiled in cooperation with the British Development Division.

LAW – SAINT LUCIA

—Saint Lucia consolidated index and subsidiary legislation to 1st January 1984 / compiled at the Faculty of Law Library, University of the West Indies, Barbados. – Barbados? : s.n., 1984.
v,108p.
Previous ed.: 1st January 1983. One of a series in the West Indian Legislation Indexing Project (WILIP) compiled in cooperation with the British Development Division.

LAW – SAINT LUCIA – INDEXES

—Saint Lucia consolidated index of statutes and subsidiary legislation to 1st January 1983 / compiled at the Faculty of Law Library, University of the West Indies, Barbados. – Cave Hill : Faculty of Law Library, University of the West Indies, 1983.
vi,112p.
One of a series in the West Indian Legislation Indexing Project (WILIP) compiled in cooperation with the British Development Division.

LAW – SAINT VINCENT AND THE GRENADINES – INDEXES

—Saint Vincent and the Grenadines consolidated index of statutes and subsidiary legislation to 1st January 1980 / compiled at the Faculty of Law and Law Library, University of the West Indies, Barbados in co- operation with the Ministry of Legal Affairs, Kingstown, St. Vincent. – Rev. ed. – Cave Hill : Faculty of Law Library, University of the West Indies, 1980.
iii,172 leaves; 30cm.
One of a series in the West Indian Legislation Indexing Project (WILIP) compiled in co-operation with the British Development Division.

LAW – SCANDINAVIA

—Scandinavian Studies in Law, 30 Vols. / Folke Schmidt. – Stockholm : Almqvist & Wiksell.
Vol. 31 (1987) 1988.
238p.
ISBN 9185142417 Hbk £188.00

LAW – SCOTLAND

—Answers to Dirleton's Doubts in the Laws of Scotland / Repr. of 1715 ed. – Abingdon : Professional Books.
117p.

—Commentaries on the Law of Scotland in Relation to Mercantile and Maritime Laws, Movable and Heritable Rights and Bankruptcy, 2 Vols. / 3rd ed. Repr. of 1819 ed. – Abingdon : Professional Books.

—Commentaries on the Law of Scotland Respecting Trial for Crimes / Repr. of 1800 ed. – Abingdon : Professional Books.
52p.

—General principles of Scots law / by Enid A. Marshall. – 4th ed. – Edinburgh : Green, 1982.
xxiv,584p; 22cm. – (Concise college texts).
Previous ed.: 1978. Includes bibliographies and index.
ISBN 041400681X Pbk

—Institute of the Law of Scotland, 2 Vols. / Repr of 1773 ed. – Abingdon : Professional Books.

—Institute of the Laws of Scotland in Civil Rights with Observations upon the Agreement or Diversity Between Them and the Laws of England, 3 Vols. / Repr. of 1753 ed. – Abingdon : Professional Books.

—Institutions of the law of Scotland : deduced from its originals, and collated with the civil, canon and feudal laws, and with the customs of neighbouring nations in iv books / by James, Viscount of Stair : edited by David M. Walker. – Edinburgh : University Presses of Edinburgh and Glasgow, 1981.
xvii,1186p,1leaf of plates; 24cm.
Originally published: Edinburgh : s.n., 1693. Includes index.
ISBN 0852243979 £40.00

—Institutions of the Law of Scotland : Deduced From its Originals and Collated With the Civil, Canon, and Feudal Laws and With the Customs of Neighbouring Nations / Repr. of 1681 ed. – Abingdon : Professional Books.
108p.

—Institutions of the Laws of Scotland / 5th ed. Repr. of 1723 ed. – Abingdon : Professional Books.
73p.

—Introduction to the law of Scotland / by W.M.Gloag and R.Candlish Henderson. – 8th ed. – Edinburgh : W.Green & Son, 1980.
cxxxiii,932p.

ISBN 0414006259

—Introduction to the law of Scotland / by W.M. Gloag and R. Candlish Henderson. – 9th ed. – Edinburgh : W. Green, 1987.
clii,1020p.
Previous ed.: 1980. Includes index.
ISBN 0414008189

—Introductory essays on Scots law / by W.A. Wilson. – 2nd ed. – Edinburgh : Green, 1984.
ix,156p; 21cm.
Previous ed.: 1978. Includes index.
ISBN 0414007298 Pbk No price

—Laws of Scotland : Stair memorial encyclopaedia / James Dalrymple Stair. – v. – Edinburgh : The Law Society of Scotland, 1987.
Includes indexes.
ISBN 040623700X

—Parliament House book / 1st looseleaf ed. 2. – Edinburgh : Green, 1982-.
Previous ed.: 156th, 1981.
ISBN 0414006887 Loose leaf

—Principles of the Law of Scotland, 2 Vols. / Repr. of 1754 ed. – Abingdon : Professional Books.

—Scottish current law statutes / Edinburgh : Green, 1961-.
Contains both English and Scottish law. Not published: 1963-1972.

—Stair Society Publications, 28 Vols. / Professional Books Staff. – Abingdon : Professional Books, 1984.

LAW - SCOTLAND - SCOTLAND

—Stair tercentenary studies / by various scholars : edited by David M. Walker. – Edinburgh : The Stair Society, 1981.
viii,267. – (Publications).
Bibliography: p253-259.
ISBN 0902292080

LAW - SINGAPORE

—Applicable law in Singapore and Malaysia:a guide to reception, precedent and sources of law in the republic of Singapore and the federation of Malaysia / Singapore : Malayan Law Journal, 1990.
600.
Account of the applicable law in Singapore and Malaysia, and a summary of legislation and case law. Appendices contain a digest of selected cases, politico-legal landmarks reception in other countries, comparative charts of the English and Singapore legal system, and a chart on precedent in Singapore.

—Index to Singapore/Malaysia legal periodicals 1932-1984 / Compiled by the staff of the Law Library, National University of Singapore Library : edited by Molly Cheang, Sng Yok Fong, Carolyn Wee. – Singapore : Malayan Law Journal Pte., 1986.
xvi,431p.
ISBN 9971700506 Hbk £160.00

—New Tables of the Written Laws of the Republic of Singapore / Kent Ridge : Malaya Law Review, 1982.
ISBN 9971620332 Hbk £99.00

—Sesquicentennial choronological tables of the written laws of the republic of Singapore 1834-1984 / Elizabeth Srinivasagam, Pascal Netto. – Singapore : Malayan Law Journal, 1987.
cxii,350.
Examines the legislative history of the Straits settlements and Singapore. Lists all the Indian acts from 22 November 1814 to 1 April 1867, and all other local legislation from 1867 to 1984. Each act is indicated as to its applicability to the present. Account of the various legislatures for Singapore over the last 150 years.
ISBN 9971700530 Hbk

LAW - SOLOMON ISLANDS

—Solomon Islands law reports / Solomon Islands : s.n., 1982.
'Published by authority of the High Court of Solomon Islands'. Annual indexes.

LAW - SOUTH AFRICA

—Current Law / Erna Jansen. – Durban : Butterworths.

—Essays on law and social practice in South Africa / edited by Hugh Corder. – Cape Town : Juta, 1988.
xii,368p.
Inlcudes bibliographical references and index.
ISBN 0702120057

—Index and Noter-up to the South African Law Reports : 1980-1984 / Durban : Butterworths, 1985.
ISBN 0409016675

—Index to the South African Law Reports : 1828-1946, 2 vols. / F. R. Malan. – Durban : Butterworths.
ISBN 0409040770 Hbk

—Introduction to South African law and legal theory / W.J. Hosten ... et al. – Rev. reprint. – Durban : Butterworths, 1980.
xv,948p; 25cm.
Bibliography: p.ix-xiv. - Includes index.
ISBN 0409033480

—Law of South Africa, 18 vols. / T. J. Scott. – Durban : Butterworths.

—Ordinances and regulations of the Province of the Orange Free State / compiled by W.E. Verschuur : saamgestel deur W.E. Verschuur. – v. – Johannesburg : Lex-Patria, 1971.
looseleaf.
Previous ed.: Ordinances of the Province of the Orange Free State 1911-1965. Includes index. Contains enactments since 1911 which are still in force. Added t.p. in Afrikaans. Spine title: Consolidated ordinances and regulations Orange Free State. Parallel text in English and Afrikaans.

—Province of Natal consolidated ordinances and regulations / compiled by H.L. Van Graan : saamgestel deur H.L. Van Graan. – v. – Johannesburg : Lex-Patria, 1964.
looseleaf.
Includes index. Contains enactments since 1911 which are still in force. Added t.p. in Afrikaans. Spine title: Consolidated ordinances and regulations Natal. Parallel text in English and Afrikaans.

—Province of Transvaal ordinances and regulations : including pre-union legislation in force in that province together with a reference to decided cases / compiled and anotated by C.W.B. Hart : insluitende voor-unie-wetgewing van krag in daardie provinsie tesame met 'n verwysing na gewysde sake : saamgestel en geannoteer deur C.W.B. Hart. – v. – Johannesburg : Lex Patris, 1961.
looseleaf.
Previous ed.: Consolidated ordinances of the Transvaal 1902 to 1947 / compiled by S.A. Lombard. Includes index. Added t.p. in Afrikaans. Spine title: Consolidated ordinances and regulations Transvaal. Parallel text in English and Afrikaans.

LAW - SOUTH KOREA

—Business laws in Korea : investment, taxation, and industrial property / Chan-jin Kim, editor. – Seoul, Korea : Panmun Book Co., 1982.
xii, 799 p.; 24 cm.
Includes bibliographical references.

LAW - SOUTHEAST ASIA

—Laws of South-East Asia / edited by M.B. Hooker. – Singapore : Butterworth, 1986.
xvi,624p.
Introduction to the pre-modern laws of South-East Asia. Analyses the nature, problems and difficulties of the Burmese Dhammathat, the Thai Thammasat, the epigraphy of Angkorian Cambodia, the law texts of Java and Bali, and the law texts of Muslim South-East Asia.
ISBN 0409995061

LAW - SWEDEN

—Introduction to Swedish law / edited by Stig Stromholm. – 2. – Deventer : Kluwer, 1981.
436p; 23cm.
Includes bibliographies.
ISBN 9065440194 Hbk £212.00

—Introduction to Swedish law / edited by Stig Stromholm. – 2nd ed. – Stockholm, Sweden : Norstedts, 1988.
532 p.; 23 cm.
Includes bibliographies and index.
ISBN 9118771521 Hbk £382.00

LAW - SWITZERLAND

—Introduction to Swiss law / edited by F. Dessemontet and T. Ansay. – Deventer : Kluwer law and taxation, 1981.
x,292p.
Bibliography: p.273-286. - Includes index.
ISBN 9065440208

LAW - TANZANIA

—Acts supplement to the Gazette of the United Republic of Tanzania / Tanzania. – v. – Dar es Salaam : Government Printer, 1964.

—Tanzania law reports / Dar es Salaam : s.n., 1987.
Cover cases decided in the Court of Appeal of Tanzania and the High Court of Tanzania.

LAW - TIBET

—Status of Tibet : history, rights and prospects in international law / Michael C. van Walt van Praag : with a foreword by Franz Michael and an introduction by Rikhi Jaipal. – London : Wisdom, 1987.
400p; 23cm.
Includes bibliography and index.
ISBN 0861710703 Pbk

LAW - TRINIDAD & TOBAGO

—Laws of Trinidad and Tobago / London : Sweet & Maxwell, 1981.
ISBN 0421287306 Hbk £245.00

—Trinidad and Tobago Laws / Sweet & Maxwell, 1981.
ISBN 0421287306 Hbk £245.00

LAW - TURKEY

—Introduction to Turkish law / edited by Tugrul Ansay and Don Wallace, Jr. – 3rd ed. – Deventer : Kluwer, 1987.
xiv,279p; 25cm.
Previous ed.: Ankara: Society of Comparative Law, Turkey and Middle East Technical University, Faculty of Administrative Sciences, 1966. Bibliography: p261-269. - Includes index.
ISBN 9065442987 No price

LAW - TURKS AND CAICOS ISLANDS

—Turks and Caicos Islands consolidated index of statutes and subsidiary legislation to 1st January 1981 / compiled at the Faculty of Law Library, University of the West Indies, Barbados. – Bridgetown, Barbados? : Faculty of Law Library, University of the West Indies?, 1981.
iv,43 leaves.
One of a series in the West Indian Legislation Indexing Project (WILIP) compiled in cooperation with the British Development Division.

—Turks and Caicos Islands consolidated index of statutes and subsidiary legislation to 1st January 1983 / compiled at the Faculty of Law Library, University of the West Indies, Barbados. – Rev. ed. – Barbados : s.n., 1983.
iv,46p.
Previous ed.: 1st January 1981. One of a series in the West Indian Legislation Indexing Project (WILIP) compiled in cooperation with the British Development Division.

LAW - TUVALU

—Laws of Tuvalu / London : Sweet & Maxwell, 1982.
ISBN 0421330503 Hbk £40.00

LAW - UNITED STATES

—Form and substance in Anglo-American law : a comparative study of legal reasoning, legal theory, and legal institutions / P.S. Atiyah and Robert S. Summers. – Oxford : Clarendon, 1987.
444p; 24cm.
Includes bibliography and index.
ISBN 0198255772 £35.00

—Form and Substances in Anglo American Law / Summers. – Oxford : Oxford University Press, 1987.
ISBN 0198255772 Hbk £35.00

—Law & policy / Oxford : Blackwell for the Baldy Center for Law and Social Policy, State University of New York at Buffalo, 1984-.
Continues: Law & policy quarterly. Includes bibliographies.

—U.S. legal system : a practice handbook / edited by Dennis Campbell and Winifred Hepperle. – The Hague : Nijhoff, 1983.
x,319p; 25cm.
Includes bibliography.
ISBN 9024727820 Hbk £130.00

LAW - USSR

—Distinctiveness of Soviet law / edited by F.J.M. Feldbrugge. – Dordrecht : Martinus Nijhoff, 1988.
292p.
'Selected papers from The Third World Congress for Soviet and East European Studies, Washington, D.C., 30 October-4 November 1985, sponsored by the International Committee for Soviet and East European Studies and the American Association for the Advancement of Slavic Studies.'. Includes index.
ISBN 9024735769 Hbk £185.00

—Encyclopedia of Soviet law / edited by F.J.M. Feldbrugge, Ger P. van den Berg, William B. Simons. – 2nd rev. ed. – Dordrecht : M. Nijhoff Publishers, 1984.
1,012p.
Bibliography.
ISBN 9024730759 Hbk £450.00

—Law and the Gorbachev era : essays in honor of Dietrich Andre Loeber / edited by Donald D. Barry ... et al. – Dordrecht : M. Nijhoff, 1988.
xix,426p.
Chiefly English; some German. 'List of publications of Dietrich Andre Loeber' included.
ISBN 9024736781

—Managing change in the USSR : the politico-legal role of the Soviet jurist / John N. Hazard. – Cambridge : Cambridge University Press, 1983.
ix,182p; 23cm.
'The Goodhart lectures 1982'. Bibliography: p175-177. - Includes index.
ISBN 0521253160 £17.50

—Russian serials / ... prepared by Alistair Ricketts ... in cyrillic script, with a transliterated version and an English translation. – Oxford : Bodleian Law Library, 1986.
12 leaves.

—Soviet law / W.E. Butler. – London : Butterworths, 1983.
xxi,374p; 23cm. – (Butterworths' legal systems of the world).
Includes index.
ISBN 0406562601 Hbk £19.50

—Soviet law / W.E. Butler. – 2nd ed. – London : Butterworths, 1988.
xxiii,430p; 22cm. – (Butterworths' legal systems of the world).
Previous ed.: 1983. Bibliography: p403-414. - Includes index.
ISBN 040656261X Hbk £19.00
ISBN 0406562644 Pbk No price

—Soviet law / London : Butterworths, 1983.
ISBN 0406562601 Hbk £19.50

—Soviet law and economy / Olimpiad S. Ioffe and Mark W. Janis, editors. – Dordrecht Holland : M. Nijhoff, 1986.
300p. – (Law in Eastern Europe).
Includes index.
ISBN 9024732654 Hbk £165.00

—Soviet law and Soviet reality / Olimpiad S. Ioffe. – Dordrecht : M. Nijhoff, 1985.
240p. – (Law in Eastern Europe).
Includes bibliographies and index.
ISBN 9024731062 Hbk £135.00

LAW - YEMEN

—Law and justice in contemporary Yemen : the People's Democratic Republic of Yemen and the Yemen Arab Republic by S.H. Amin / Glasgow : Royston, 1987.
v,159p; 23cm.
Bibliography: p129-140. - Includes index.
ISBN 0946706360 £18.75

LAW - ZAMBIA

—Acts / Zambia. – v. – Lusaka : Government Printer, 1964.
Published as separate supplements to the Republic of Zambia government gazette.

LAW - ZIMBABWE

—Acts / Zimbabwe. – Salisbury : Government Printer, 1980.
30cm.
Issued with: Zimbabwe government gazette.

—Introduction to the legal system of Zimbabwe / by John Redgment. – 2nd ed., rev. and enl. – Salisbury Rhodesia : Book Centre, 1981.
107p.
Bibliography: p.106-107.

LAW AND ANTHROPOLOGY

—Discourse of law / edited by Sally Humphreys. – London : Harwood Academic Publishers, 1985.
p.241-465.
Includes bibliographies.

—Man, law, and modern forms of life / edited by Eugenic Bulygin, Jean-Louis Gardies, and Ilkka Niiniluoto : introduction by Michael D. Bayles. – Dordrecht Netherlands : D. Reidel, 1985.
'Proceedings of the 11th IVR World Congress on Philosophy of Law and Social Philosophy ... held on August 14-20, 1983 in Helsinki'–Introd. Includes bibliographies and index.
ISBN 9027718695 Hbk £39.50

—Social justice and individual responsibility in the welfare state / edited by Jan M. Broekman, Kazimierz Opaek, Djangir A.A. Kerimov : preface by Carl Wellman Soziale Gerechtigkeit und individuelle Verantwortlichkeit im Wohlfahrtsstaat / herausgegeben von Jan M. Broekman, Kazimierz Opaek, Djangir A.A. Kerimov ; vorwort von Carl Wellman. – Stuttgart : F. Steiner Verlag Wiesbaden, 1985.
299 p.; 24 cm. – (Archives for philosophy of law and social philosophy).
English, French, and German. 'Eleventh World Congress of the IVR convened in Helsinki 15-20 August 1983'–P. 5. Includes bibliographical references and index.
ISBN 3515044590 pbk. DM35.00

LAW AND ART

—The penal protection of works of art / Siracusa : International Institute of Higher Studies in Criminal Sciences, 1983.
447p.
Includes bibliographical references. English, French or Italian.

—Visual artist and the law / by Shane Simpson. – Sydney : Law Book Co., 1982.
xiii,182p.
Bibliography: p.169-173. - Includes index.
ISBN 0455204527 Hbk £19

LAW AND ECONOMICS

—Political economy of law / Oxford : Oxford University Press, 1988.
ISBN 0195619919 Hbk £32.50

LAW AND ECONOMICS - AUSTRALIA

—Economics of Bureaucracy and Statutory Authorities / Warren Hogan. – Turramura : Centre for Independent Studies.
112p.
ISBN 094976910X Hbk £5.95

LAW AND ECONOMICS - CANADA

—Women, the Law and the Economy / Toronto : Butterworths, 1985.
414p.
ISBN 0409988650 Pbk £31.95

LAW AND ECONOMICS - EUROPE

—Law and Inflation / London : HMSO, 1986.
32p.
Reviews the European provision for inflation in law. Includes details of current legislation in most Western European countries.
ISBN 9287108323 Hbk £3.30

LAW AND ECONOMICS - GREAT BRITAIN

—Economic Approach to Law / Veljanovski. – London : Butterworths, 1981.
ISBN 0408106859 Pbk £13.95
ISBN 0408106867 Hbk £27.50

—Economic negligence / London : Sweet & Maxwell, 1985.
ISBN 0459364707 Hbk £40.00

—Economics of the Common Law / 1984 ed. – Oxford : Social Science Research Council.
ISBN 0862260841 Pbk £2.00

—Law and Economic Organization / Cambridge : Cambridge University Press, 1985.
ISBN 0512128966 Pbk £7.95

—Law, Economy and Society / Sugarman. – London : Butterworths, 1984.
ISBN 0861050855 Hbk 32.40
ISBN 0862050987 Pbk 19.25

—Readings in economics of law and regulation / Veljanovski. – Oxford : Oxford University Press, 1984.
ISBN 0198761430 Pbk £12.95

—Rise and fall of economic justice / Oxford : Oxford University Press, 1987.
ISBN 0192153609 Hbk £12.50
ISBN 0192851861 Pbk £4.95

LAW AND ETHICS

—Contract as promise : a theory of contractual obligation / Charles Fried. – Cambridge, Mass. : Harvard University Press, 1981.
162p; 25cm.
Includes index.
ISBN 0674169255 £8.40

—Ethics and the rule of law / David Lyons. – Cambridge : Cambridge University Press, 1984.
x,229p; 21m.
Bibliography: p220-226. - Includes index.
ISBN 0521257859 Hbk £17.50
ISBN 0521277124 Pbk £4.95

—Ethics of legal coercion / John D. Hodson. – Dordrecht, Holland : D. Reidel Pub. Co., 1983.
xiv, 174 p.; 22 cm.
Includes indexes. Bibliography: p. 163-168.
ISBN 9027714940 Hbk

—Justice, law, and argument : essays on moral and legal reasoning / Ch. Perelman : with an intod. by Harold J. Berman. – Dordrecht, Holland : D. Reidel Pub. Co., 1980.
xiii,181p.
Includes bibliographical references and index.
ISBN 9027710902 pbk.

—Law and morals : Warnock, Gillick and beyond / Simon Lee. – Oxford : Oxford University Press, 1986.
144p; 22cm.
Includes bibliography and index.
ISBN 0192177532 Hbk £12.50
ISBN 019283052X Pbk £4.95

—Law, morality, and rights / edited by M.A. Stewart. – Dordrecht, Holland : Reidel, 1983.
xii,452p. – (Synthese library).
Includes index.
ISBN 902771519X

—Moral and legal reasoning / Samuel Stoljar. – London : Macmillan, 1980.
ix, 172p; 23cm.
Also published: New York : Barnes and Noble, 1980. Includes index.
ISBN 0333277716 £8.95

—Unity of law and morality : a refutation of legal postivisim / M.J. Detmold. – London : Routledge & Kegan Paul, 1984.
xix,271p; 23cm.
Bibliography: p265-268. - Includes index.
ISBN 0710200307 £15.00

LAW AND FACT

—Facts / by G.H. Kendal. – Toronto : Butterworths, 1980.
x, 106 p.; 24 cm.
Includes bibliographical references and index.
ISBN 0409842451 £13.50

LAW AND LITERATURE

—Law and letters in American culture / Robert A. Ferguson. – Cambridge, Mass. : Harvard University Press, 1984.
viii,417p; 25cm.
Includes index.
ISBN 0674514653 £22.50

LAW AND POLITICS

—Colonial legal heritage in Nigeria / by Emmanuel Omoh Esiemokhai. – Akure, Nigeria : Fagbamigbe, 1986.
xii,82p.
Bibliography: p.79. - Includes index.
ISBN 9781642483

—Comparative judicial systems : challenging frontiers in conceptual and empirical analysis / John R. Schmidhauser, editor. – London : Butterworths, 1987.
243p; 22cm.
Conference proceedings. Includes bibliographies.
ISBN 0408031654 £25.00

—Dwelling on the threshold : critical essays on modern legal thought / Allan C. Hutchinson. – Toronto : Carswell, 1988.
ix,326p.
Bibliography: pp.324-325..
ISBN 0421400501

—International Law of International Welfare : The Politics of Law-Making / London : Pinter Publishers Ltd, 1984.
200p.
ISBN 0861872894 Hbk £21.00

—Judging the World : Law and Politics in the World's Leading Courts / Philip Chubb. – Sydney : Butterworths, 1988.
573p.

—Judging the World : Law and Politics in the World's Leading Courts / Philip Chubb. – Butterworths, 1988.
573p.
ISBN 0409301167 Hbk £49.95

—Judicial Politics in Europa : an Impact Analysis / Bern : Peter Lang, 1986.
xii, 325p.
ISBN 0820402893 Hbk £35.05

—Law, society and political action : towards a strategy under late capitalism / Thomas Mathiesen. – London : Academic Press, 1980.
ix,323p; 24cm.
Includes index.
ISBN 012479940X Hbk £17.80
ISBN 0124799426 Pbk Unpriced

—Misuse of power : the Richard Dimbleby lecture, November 1980 / Lord Denning. – London : British Broadcasting Corporation, 1980.
19p; 21cm. – (The Richard Dimbleby lectures).
ISBN 0563178949 Pbk £1.50

—Political aspects of the Westland affair / editor, Dawn Oliver. – London : Faculty of Laws, University College London, 1986.
51p; 30cm. – (Working papers (University College London, Faculty of Laws)).

—Political economy of law / Oxford : Oxford University Press, 1988.
ISBN 0195619919 Hbk £32.50

—Political economy of law : a third world reader / edited by Yash Ghai, Robin Luckham, Francis Snyder. – Delhi : Oxford University Press, 1987.
xvi,821p.
A view of Indian legal systems as they operate nationally and internationally. Law is analysed in terms of its relationships to economy, the state, political conflict, class, and international relations.
ISBN 0195619919

—Public law and politics / edited by Carol Harlow. – London : Sweet & Maxwell, 1986.
250p; 24cm.
Includes index.
ISBN 0421333901 £24.00

LAW AND POLITICS - ANTARCTICA

—Antarctic Law and Politics / London : Dent (J M) & Sons, 1987.
ISBN 0905838394 Hbk £17.50

LAW AND POLITICS - CANADA

—How Ottawa Spends Your Tax Dollars : The Liberals, The Opposition and Federal Priorities 1983 / Toronto : Lorimer & Co, 1983.
264p.
ISBN 0888626428 Pbk £12.95

—Politics and the Constitution : the Charter, Federalism and the Supreme Court of Canada / Agincourt : Carswell, 1987.
250p.

—Supreme Court of Canada as an Instrument of Political Change / Andree Lajoie. – Toronto : University of Toronto Press, 1986.
240p.
ISBN 0802072925 Hbk £16.95

LAW AND POLITICS - ENGLAND

—Conspiracy : law, class and society / Robert Spicer. – London : Lawrence and Wishart, 1981.
190p; 23cm.
Bibliography: p178-184. - Includes index.
ISBN 0853155488 £7.50

LAW AND POLITICS - GREAT BRITAIN

—Blackwells Encyclopedia of Political Instructions / Oxford : Blackwell Scientific, 1987.
ISBN 0631138412 Hbk £45.00

—British Government and Politics / 3rd ed. – Plymouth : Macdonald & Evans, 1984.
xi, 288p. – (M and E Handbook Ser.).
ISBN 0712102922 Hbk £3.95

—British Government and Politics / 3rd ed. – Plymouth : Macdonald & Evans, 1984.
ISBN 0712124071 Pbk £3.95

—Discipline of Politics / London : Butterworths, 1981.
ISBN 0408106855 Pbk £9.95

LAW AND POLITICS - INDIA

—Origin and Development of Legal and Political System in India, 3 Vols. / 2nd ed. – New Delhi : Deep and Deep Publications, 1982.
ca 700p.

LAW AND POLITICS - SWEDEN

—Political Value Patterns and Parties in Sweden / Ulla Bergryd. – Stockholm : Almqvist & Wiksell.
ISBN 9122004130 Hbk £165.00

LAW AND SOCIALISM

—Haldane journal : a journal of law and socialism / v. – London : Haldane Society, 1985-.

—Law and order : arguments for socialism / Ian Taylor. – London : Macmillan, 1981.
xxii,234p.
Bibliography: p224-234.

—Left and rights : a conceptual analysis of the Socialist rights / Tom Campbell. – London : Routledge & Kegan Paul, 1982.
253p.
Includes bibliographical references and index.
Bibliography: p216-249.
ISBN 0710090854 pbk.

—Marx and Engels on law and laws / Paul Phillips. – Oxford : Robertson, 1980.
xiii,238p; 23cm.
Bibliography: p225-238.
ISBN 0855203552 Hbk £15.00
ISBN 0855203560 Pbk £5.25

—Marxism and law / Hugh Collins. – Oxford Oxfordshire : Clarendon Press, 1982.
viii,159p.
Bibliography: p150-155. .
ISBN 0198760930 Oxford University Press

—Max Weber / Anthony T. Kronman. – London : Edward Arnold, 1983.
214p; 22cm.
Includes bibliographies and index.
ISBN 0713163615 Pbk £9.95
ISBN 0713163623 Pbk £4.95

LAW AND SOCIALISM – GREAT BRITAIN
—Socialist lawyer / London : Haldane Society of Socialist Lawyers, 1986.

LAW AND SOCIALISM – USSR
—Perspectives on Soviet law for the 1980s / edited by F.J.M. Feldbrugge and William B. Simons. – The Hague : M. Nijhoff, 1982.
Selected papers from the Second World Congress for Soviet and East European Studies, held in Garmisch-Patenkirchen, Germany, Sept. 30-Oct. 4, 1980, organized by Deutsche Gesellschaft fur Osteuropakunde and the International Committee for Soviet and East European Studies. Includes bibliographical references and index.
ISBN 9024725615 Hbk £75.00

LAW ENFORCEMENT
—Drifting into a law and order society / Stuart Hall. – London : Cobden Trust, 1980.
17p. – (Human Rights Day Lectures).
ISBN 0900137150

—Environment and enforcement : regulation and the social definition of pollution / Keith Hawkins. – Oxford : Clarendon Press, 1983.
xvi,253p.
Includes index. Bibliography: p235-247.
ISBN 0198275145 pbk.

LAW ENFORCEMENT – GREAT BRITAIN
—Clearing up crime / by John Burrows and Roger Tarling. – London : H.M.S.O., 1982.
31p; 25cm.
Bibliography: p24-26. A Home Office Research and Planning Unit report.
ISBN 0113407688

—Law and order : arguments for socialism / Ian Taylor. – London : Macmillan, 1981.
xxii,234p.
Bibliography: p224-234.

—Police and Law Enforcement / London : Eurospan, 1988.
ISBN 0404112080 Hbk £47.25

—Policing liberal society / Steve Uglow. – Oxford : Oxford University Press, 1988.
viii, 165 p.; 23 cm. – (An OPUS book).
Examines the role of the police force in late twentieth-century Britain; how it has changed, and prospects for the future. Questions whether the police are crime-fighters, social workers, guardians of the law, or maintainers of public order. Suggests that the constitutional role of the police should be re-examined.
ISBN 0192192221 Hbk £19.50

LAW ENFORCEMENT – INDIA
—Crisis of the Indian legal system / Upendra Baxi. – New Delhi : Vikas, 1982.
xiii,405p.
Includes index. Bibliography: p393-400.
ISBN 0706913698

LAW FIRMS
—Basic book-keeping for solicitors / Richard Halberstadt. – 3rd ed. – London : Sweet & Maxwell, 1985.
300p; 23cm.
Previous ed.: 1982. Includes index.
ISBN 042133830X £12.00

LAW FIRMS – CANADA
—Building a Successful Law Firm / Vancouver : British Columbia Continuing Legal Education Society, 1985.
103p.
ISBN 0865042284 Hbk £50.00

—Canada Legal Directory : 1988 Edition / Toronto : DeBoo, 1988.
This listing of Canadian law firms and the lawyers who practice within them includes an alphabetical listing of law firms by city, with addresses and phone numbers, a separate finding list of the individual lawyers, a listing of corporate in-house counsel, and a comprehensive listing within each province of courts, officials, judicial districts, law societies, etc.
ISBN 0888202407 Hbk £75.00

—Financial Management for Law Firms / M. W. Zwicker. – Vancouver : British Columbia Continuing Legal Education Society, 1982.
82p.
ISBN 0865040451 Hbk £6.50

—How to Market and Advertise Your Law Practice / Aurora : Canada Law Book Co, 1987.
288p.
This is a focused, practical guidebook intended for any law firm which desires seriously, professionally and successfully to market its services. The reader is guided step-by-step through the key functions of: market research, television advertising, print media advertising, radio advertising, the use of brochures and the implementation of effective public relations programs.

—Law Firm of the Future - Today : Materials Prepared for a Continuing Legal Education Seminar Held February 5, 1983 / Phil Baudin. – Vancouver : British Columbia Continuing Legal Education Society, 1983.
ISBN 0865041008 loose £45.00

—Law office practice management guide / Scarborough, Ontario : Butterworths (Canada), 1988.
350.
Guide to the operation and management of a law office practice. Provides information on starting the practice, human resource planning, interviewing process selection and salary determination, avoiding wrongful dismissal, financing the practice, law firm recruitment, performance appraisal techniques, training and development, and marketing of professional services.
ISBN 0409805610 Hbk

LAW FIRMS – ENGLAND
—Organisation and management of a solicitor's practice / general editors Peter J. Purton, David Andrews, L. Peter K. Brindley. – London : Oyez, 1980.
2 v. (loose-leaf).
Includes index.
ISBN 0851204805

—Practice today / – London : Julian Harris, 1985-.
Supplement to: Solicitors' journal. Added t.p. title: The management magazine for solicitors.

LAW FIRMS – GREAT BRITAIN
—Good Practice : A Management Guide for the Profession / London : Butterworths.
ISBN 0406502803 Pbk

LAW LIBRARIANS – AUSTRALIA
—Seminar for Librarians in the Criminal Justice System / Canberra : Australian Institute of Criminology.

LAW LIBRARIANS – CANADA
—Directory / Canadian Association of Law Libraries : Association Canadienne des Bibliotheques de Droit. – Toronto : The Association, 1982.
Continues: List of members.

LAW LIBRARIES
—Automation in the law school, including law libraries / by Betty W. Taylor and Dan F. Henke. – London : Glanville, 1986.
iv,124p.
Includes bibliographical references and appendices.
ISBN 0878020829

—Caribbean law librarian : bulletin of the Caribbean Assocation of Law Libraries / Jamaica : Caribbean Association of Law Librarians, 1984-.

—Courts, law libraries and legal information in a changing society : 25. IALL Anniversary, Freiburg i. Br., July 15-20, 1984 / S.l. : International Association of Law Libraries, 1984.
184p.
Conference proceedings. Includes bibliographical references.

—Law librarianship / Adrian Blunt. – New York : Saur, 1980.
126p; 23cm.
Bibliography: p.121. - Includes index.
ISBN 0851572995 £4.50
ISBN 0896644340

—Manual of law librarianship : the use and organization of legal literature / edited by Elizabeth M. Moys. – 2nd ed. – Aldershot : Gower, for the British and Irish Association of Law Librarians, 1987.
xxxv,915p; 23cm.
Previous ed.: London : Deutsch, 1976. Bibliography: p802-891. - Includes index.
ISBN 056603512X £39.50

—Rare books for law libraries / by Thomas H. Reynolds. – London : Glanville, 1983.
141p.

LAW LIBRARIES – AUSTRALIA
—National survey of law libraries in Australia / by Beth Wilson : supervised by E.J. Glasson ; prepared for the Australian Law Librarians' Group. – Sydney : Australian Law Librarian's Group, 1984.
xv, 479 p.; 31 cm.
Includes bibliographical references.
ISBN 0959135901 £39.95

LAW LIBRARIES – CANADA
—Law Libraries in Canada / Joan Fraser. – Agincourt : Carswell, 1988.
This work presents a series of articles written about Canadian law library services and delivery of legal information in Canada. Topics include the types of primary legal materials and law libraries found in Canada, development of law collections, library automation and the impact of bilingualism. Information as to Canadian universities, courthouses, legislative law libraries, government publishing agencies, and more, are also included.

—Law Libraries in Canada / Agincourt : Carswell, 1988.
242p.

—Using a law library / 4th ed. – Agincourt : Carswell, 1985.
ISBN 0459376101 Hbk £17.60

LAW LIBRARIES – ENGLAND
—How to use a law library / by Jean Dane and Philip A. Thomas. – 2nd ed. 1. – London : Sweet & Maxwell, 1987.
23cm.
Previous ed.: 1979. Includes bibliography and index.
ISBN 0421360305 Hbk £12.50
ISBN 0421360402 Pbk £8.50

LAW LIBRARIES – GREAT BRITAIN
—Directory of law libraries in the British Isles / edited by Christine Miskin. – 3rd ed. – Hebden Bridge, W. Yorks. : Published for the British & Irish Association of Law Librarians by Legal Information Resources Limited, 1988.
ix,120p.
Previous ed.: 1984. Includes indexes.
ISBN 1870369025

—Directory of law libraries in the British Isles / C. Miskin. – 2nd ed. 1 v. – Yeovil : Legal Library Publishing & Distribution Service for the British and Irish Association of Law Librarians, 1984.
Includes index.

—Newsletter / British and Irish Association of Law Librarians / British and Irish Association of Law Librarians. – London : The Association, 1983.

—Recommended Holdings for Law Libraries : The Law Librarian / London : Sweet & Maxwell, 1983.
ISBN 0421317205 Pbk £2.50

LAW LIBRARIES – INDIA
—Law Library Administration and Reference / Delhi : Metropolitan Book Co.
182p.

LAW LIBRARIES – IRELAND
—Directory of law libraries in the British Isles / edited by Christine Miskin. – 3rd ed. – Hebden Bridge, W. Yorks. : Published for the British & Irish Association of Law Librarians by Legal Information Resources Limited, 1988.
ix,120p.
Previous ed.: 1984. Includes indexes.
ISBN 1870369025

LAW LIBRARIES – NIGERIA
—Communique of the national seminar on effective law library services in Nigeria, June 5-7, 1984, held under the sponsorship of the Nigerian Institute of Advanced Legal Studies / Nigerian Institute of Advanced Legal Studies. – Lagos : The Institute, 1984.
8p.

—Law Library manual / by N.O. Obi. – Lagos : Law Library, Federal Ministry of Justice, 1984.
23p.
Includes a list of commonly used author and title abbreviations.

—Standard Holdings for Law Office Libraries in Nigeria / Abingdon : Professional Books, 1986.
ISBN 0862050782 Hbk £14.00

LAW OF THE SEA
—200 mile exclusive economic zone in the new law of the sea / Dordrecht : Martinus Nijhoff, 1989.
408. – (Publications on ocean development 14).
Examines the rights and duties of states with regard to activities such as fisheries and navigation. Also evaluates the existing and potential impact of the EEZ upon the socioeconomic development of states and the reduction of disparities between the developing and industrialised countries.
ISBN 0792300742 Hbk £60

—Annual review of ocean affairs / United Nations Office for Ocean Affairs and the Law of the Sea. – 2 vol. – London : Lloyds of London Press, 1989.
These two volumes contain protocols, conventions, treaties, decisions, and other matters enacted by governmental organisations concerned with ocean affairs. Includes illicit drug-trafficking, fisheries management, and the marine environment. This first edition contains documentation covering the years 1985-1987.

—Archipelagic Concept in the Law of the Sea : Problems and Perspectives / Metro Manila : Development Academy of the Philippines, 1982.
vii, 26p.
ISBN 9711520028 Pbk £2.80

—Convention on the Law of the Sea / Metro Manila : Development Academy of the Philippines, 1983.
xii, 263p.
ISBN 9711520788 Hbk £9.00

—Deepsea mining and the law of the sea / Alexandra Merle Post. – The Hague : M. Nijhoff Publishers, 1983.
xxiii,358p.
Bibliography: p329-358.
ISBN 902473049X

—Development of the law of the sea with special reference to the exclusive economic zone / S.l. : s.n., 1982.
p.297-307.

—Environmental Law of the Sea / Gland : International Union for Conservation of Nature and Natural Resources, 1981.
419p.

—Frontier of the seas : the problems of delimitation : proceedings of the 5th International Ocean Symposium November 26-27, 1980, the Japan Shipping Club, Tokyo / Tokyo : Ocean Association of Japan, 1981.
80p; 26cm.
Edited by the Ocean Association of Japan. Title also in Japanese.

—IMO Search and Rescue Manual / International Maritime Organization. – London : International Maritime Organization, 1980.

—Index of Multilateral Treaties on the Law of the Sea / Milan : Giuffre, 1985.
viii, 376p.

—International law of the sea / Oxford : Oxford University Press, 1982.
ISBN 019825346X Hbk £45.00
ISBN 0198254695
Vol. 2 1984.

—International Law of the Sea : a Bibliography / Dordrecht : Kluwer, 1980.
432p.
ISBN 9028602690 Hbk £196.00

—International law of the sea and marine affairs, a bibliography / edited by Nikos Papadakis, Martin Glassner. – The Hague : M. Nijhoff, 1983.
xxvi,579p.
Supplement to: International law of the sea / N. Papadakis. Includes indexes.
ISBN 9024728150 Hbk £350.00

—International organizations and the law of the sea / Netherlands Institute for the Law of the Sea (NILOS). – Dordrecht : Martinus Nijhoff, 1989.
712. – (ILOS yearbook 3).
An annual publication. Reproduces the most important documents related to the law of the sea that are issued each year by international organisations.
ISBN 1853331627 Hbk £97

—International Organizations and the Law of the Sea : Documentary Yearbook 1985 / Netherlands Institute for the Law of the Sea. – Dordrecht : Kluwer, 1987.
650p.
ISBN 9024734886 Hbk £275.00

—Law of the sea / R.R. Churchill and A.V. Lowe. – Manchester : Manchester University Press, 1983.
xxxiii,321p; 24cm.
Includes bibliographies and index.
ISBN 0719009367 £19.50

—Law of the Sea : a Select Bibliography / Geneva : United Nations Publications.
ISBN 9210330633 Hbk £9.50

—Law of the Sea : A Select Bibliography / London : HMSO, 1985.
ISBN 9211333350 Hbk £12.00

—Law of the sea and maritime boundary delimitation in South-East Asia / Kriangsak Kittichaisaree. – Singapore : Oxford University Press, 1987.
xv, 209 p.; 23 cm.
Discusses maritime boundary delimination in international law. Concentrates on South-East Asia, but legal analyses are examined in a global context, using South-East Asian practice as concrete instances to elaborate particular legal problems.
ISBN 0195888626 Hbk £20.00

—Law of the Sea : Caracas and Beyond / Dordrecht : Kluwer, 1980.
xii, 399p.
ISBN 9024723663 Hbk £120.00

—Law of the sea : Caracas and beyond / edited by Ram Prakash Anand. – The Hague : Martinus Nijhoff, 1980.
xi,399p.
Contains revised versions of papers presented at the Semimar held in December 1976 in the International Legal Studies Division of the school of International Studies, Jawaharlal Nehru University, New Delhi.

—Law of the Sea Convention 1982 : Text and Commentary / London : Butterworths, 1985.
ISBN 0406252610 Hbk

—Law of the Sea : Current Developments in State Practice / Geneva : United Nations Publications.
ISBN 9211332850 Hbk £23.00

—Law of the Sea : Status of the UN Convention on the Law of the Sea / London : HMSO, 1986.
52p.
Contains declarations explaining the understanding and interpretation of the Law of the Sea by its international signatories.
ISBN 9211332699 Hbk £8.00

—Law of the Sea : Text of U.N. Conventions / Delhi : Mittal Publications, 1985.

—Law of the Sea Zones in the Pacific Ocean / Singapore : Institute of Southeast Asian Studies, 1987.
120p.
ISBN 9971988739 Hbk £26.00

—Legal Regime for Deep Seabed Mining under the Law of the Sea Convention / Dordrecht : Kluwer, 1983.
250p.
ISBN 9065441166 Hbk £107.00

—Legal Regime for Deep Seabed Mining under the Law of the Sea Convention / Frankfurt : Alfred Metzner, 1984.
ISBN 3787540180 Hbk £98.00

—Management of Humanity's Resources : the Law of the Sea. Workshop 1981 / Dordrecht : Kluwer, 1982.
xvi, 434p.
ISBN 9024727626 Hbk £120.00

—Mare Clausum : The Right and Dominion of the Sea / Repr. of 1663 ed. – Abingdon : Professional Books.
515p.

—New directions in the law of the sea : new series / compiled and edited by Kenneth R. Simmonds : with the collaboration of specialist consulting editors. – v. – London : Oceana, 1983.
looseleaf.
ISBN 0379165503

—New law of the sea : selected and edited papers of the Athens colloquium on the law of the sea, September 1982 / edited by Christos L. Rozakis and Constantine A. Stephanou. – Amsterdam : North-Holland, published in collaboration with the Pantios School of Political Science, Athens, 1983.
xiv,354p; 23cm.
Includes index.
ISBN 0444868046 Unpriced

—Origin and development of the law of the sea : history of international law revisited / R.P. Anand. – The Hague : Nijhoff, 1983.
xvi,249p; 25cm.
Includes index.
ISBN 9024726174 Hbk £115.00

—Pollution by Dumping. The Law of the Sea / Geneva : United Nations Publications.
77p.

—Public Order of the Oceans : a Contemporary International Law of the Sea / William T. Burke. – Dordrecht : Kluwer, 1987.
1,300p.
ISBN 0898389011 Hbk £400.00

—Quiet Revolution / United Nations. – London : HMSO, 1984.
61p. – (The United Nations Convention on the Law of the Sea).
Describes the processes by which the negotiation of the Convention on the Law of the Sea took place.
ISBN 0119081733 Pbk £4.75

—Recueil des cours / Academie de Droit International de la Haye. – Dordrecht : Martinus Nijhoff, 1988.
406.
Includes chapters on the concept and claims of geographically disadvantaged states at the third UN Law of the Sea Conference, geographically disadvantaged states of the Exclusive Economic Zone, and these states and the exploitation of the mineral resources of the sea-bed and ocean floor.
ISBN 0792300580 Hbk £57.50

—Relevant circumstances and maritime delimitation / Oxford : OUP, 1988.
288.
Examines delimitation as a process. The conceptual basis of seabed jurisdiction and the historical development of delimitation criteria are discussed. Also contains an extended study of the features and factors considered relevant to continental shelf and EEC delimitation.
ISBN 0198252404 Hbk £27.50

—Right of innocent passage and the evolution of the international law of the sea / London : Pinter, 1990.
250.
Debates the right of innocent passage in the light of the 1982 Law of the Sea Convention. Discusses the right of a coastal state to determine what is and is not innocent and to react accordingly.
ISBN 0861878515 Hbk £30

—Seerecht : Testausgabe Law of the sea / Renate Platzoder, Wolfgang Graf Vitzthum. – 1. Aufl. – Baden-Baden : Nomos, 1984.
500 p.; 18 cm.
Contains conventions adopted by the United Nations conferences on the law of the sea, and related legislation of various countries. English and German.
ISBN 3789009318

—Selected Essays on the Law of the Sea / Metro Manila : Development Academy of the Philippines, 1982.
vii, 26p.
ISBN 9711520028 Pbk £2.50

—Third United Nations Conference on the Law of the Sea / United Nations. – London : HMSO, 1984.
243p.
Official records of the conference and a list of documents issued during the tenth session.
ISBN 0119080710 Pbk £20.70

—Third United Nations Conference on the Law of the Sea : documents / compiled and edited by Renate Platzoder. – London : Oceana Publications, 1982.
v. 1; 27 cm.
ISBN 0379207249 v. 1 £100

—To Settle the Oceans : the Law of the Sea in Practice / Toronto : University of Toronto Press, 1986.
256p.
ISBN 0802057071 Hbk £30.00
ISBN 0802066356 Pbk £14.95

—UN Draft Convention on the Law of the Sea : how it affects the United Kingdom's oil rights / E.D. Brown. – S.l. : s.n., 1981.
56p.
'Paper read at seminar on recent developments in U.K. petroleum law, London, June, 1981'. Includes bibliographical references.

—United Nations Convention on the Law of the Sea, 1982 : a commentary / Myron H. Nordquist. – Dordrecht : Martinus Nijhoff, 1985.
512p.
At head of title: Center for Oceans Law and Policy, University of Virginia.
ISBN 9024731453 Hbk £265.00

—United Nations Convention on the Law of the Sea / Bo Johnson Theutenberg. – Dublin : Tycooly International, 1984.
viii,261p; 25cm.
Bibliography: p97-111. Includes full text of United Nations Convention on the Law of the Sea. Spine title : The law of the sea.
ISBN 0863460410 Hbk Unpriced
ISBN 0863460429 Pbk Unpriced

—United States and the Law of the Sea Treaty / Peter Digester. – John Hopkins University, Foreign Policy Institute, 1990.
52; 23.
ISBN 0941700542 Pbk £12

—USSR, Eastern Europe and the development of the law of the sea / compiled, translated and edited by William E. Butler. – New ed. 2 v. – London : Oceana, 1983.
looseleaf.
Previously published as: The Eastern European states and the development of the law of the sea / by Viktor Sebek. 1979. Bibliography: Vol. 2.
ISBN 0379208512

LAW OF THE SEA – SOUTH AFRICA

—Southern Africa and the Law of the Sea : Problems Common, Uncommon and Unique / Rondebosch : University of Cape Town, 1986.
17p.
ISBN 0799210242 Pbk £0.30

LAW OFFICERS – AUSTRALIA

—Attorney General's Annual Report, 1983-84 / Canberra : Australian Government Publishing Service, 1984.
218p.

—Attorney General's Department; 1980-1981 Annual Report / Canberra : Australian Government Publishing Service, 1981.
73p.

—Attorney General's Department; 1981-1982 Annual Report / Canberra : Australian Government Publishing Service, 1982.
84p.

—Attorney General's Department; 1982-1983 Annual Report / Canberra : Australian Government Publishing Service, 1983.
159p.

—Opinions of Attorneys General of the Commonwealth of Australia / Attorney-General's Department. – Canberra : Australian Government Publishing Service, 1981.
723p.
ISBN 0642066043 Hbk £49.50

—Special Prosecutors Office : Report to the Attorney-General / Canberra : Australian Government Publishing Service, 1983.
15p.
ISBN 0644012528 Hbk £1.70

LAW OFFICERS – CANADA

—Correctional Officer / Toronto : Butterworths, 1981.
342p.
ISBN 0409863203 Pbk £36.95

—Ministerial responsibility for national security as it relates to the Offices of Prime Minister, Attorney General, and Solicitor General of Canada / by J.Ll.J. Edwards. – Ottawa : Commission of Inquiry Concerning Certain Activities of the Royal Canadian Mounted Police, 1980.
x, 146 p.; 25 cm.
Includes bibliographical references.
ISBN 0660105012 pbk. £5.25 (£6.30 other countries)

—Study Paper on the Office of the Sheriff / Victoria : Government of British Columbia, 1983.

LAW OFFICERS – CANADA – BRITISH COLUMBIA

—Office of sheriff / by Gordon Turriff and Elizabeth Edinger. – Victoria : Queen's Printer, 1983.
246p.
'A study prepared for the Law Reform Commission of British Columbia with financial assistance from the Law Foundation of British Columbia' - title page.
ISBN 0771883927

LAW OFFICERS – GREAT BRITAIN

—Officium Clerici Pacis : A Book of Indictments, Information, Appeals, and Inquisitions / 3rd ed. Repr. of 1726 ed. – Abingdon : Professional Books.
232p.

LAW OFFICERS – SOUTH AFRICA

—Report of the Select Committee on the Advocate-General Bill / Pretoria : Government Printer.
Parliament

LAW OFFICES

—Solicitor and the automated office / Theodore Ruoff. – London : Sweet & Maxwell, 1984.
x,136p; 22cm.
Includes index.
ISBN 0421331100 £8.50

LAW OFFICES – AUSTRALIA

—Deputy Crown Solicitors Office Perth : Report of Enquiry Concerning the Office / Attorney-General's Department. – Canberra : Australian Government Publishing Service, 1983.
142p.
ISBN 0644024135 Hbk £5.00

LAW OFFICES – CANADA

—Law Office Practice Management Guide / Toronto : Butterworths, 1987.
350p.

—Law office practice management guide / Scarborough, Ontario : Butterworths (Canada), 1988.
350.
Guide to the operation and management of a law office practice. Provides information on starting the practice, human resource planning, interviewing process selection and salary determination, avoiding wrongful dismissal, financing the practice, law firm recruitment, performance appraisal techniques, training and development, and marketing of professional services.
ISBN 0409805610 Hbk

—Organizing a Law Office : Law Office Management Series / Agincourt : Carswell, 1988.
160p.
This is a guidebook to correct law office management. The author presents flow charts, sample precedents, effective accounting procedures and, in general, a cost efficient operation.

—Practical Guide to Law Office Automation : 1988 / Kenneth A. Grant. – Agincourt : Carswell, 1988.
274p.
This 1988 edition provides information towards the selection and implementation of a law office automation system. Guidelines also include a comprehensive directory of software in Canada for lawyers and a glossary of common terms and definitions. The book also outlines the benefits of automation and the process of selecting and implementing a computer system.

LAW OFFICES – ENGLAND

—Marketing Legal services / edited by S.C. Silkin. – London : Waterlows, 1984.
86p; 21cm.
Conference papers.
ISBN 0080392156 Pbk £10.50

LAW OFFICES – GREAT BRITAIN

—Communications : a guide to the electronic office for practising lawyers / compiled by the Communications Committee of the Society for Computers and Law. – 2nd fully rev ed. – Didcot : The Society, 1985.
iii,67 leaves.
ISBN 0906122198

—Communications : a guide to the electronic office for practising lawyers / compiled by the Communications Committee of the Society for Computers and Law. – Milton, Oxon. : The Society, 1983.
39 leaves.
Bibliography: p.39.

—Solicitor's guide to advertising & publicity / Stephen Townley. – 5 pamphlets. – London : Professional Direction and Sweet & Maxwell, 1985.
49p; in folder, 22x31cm.
Authors: Stephen Townley et al.
ISBN 0421342706 £39.50

LAW OFFICES – NIGERIA

—Standard Holdings for Law Office Libraries in Nigeria / Abingdon : Professional Books, 1986.
ISBN 0862050782 Hbk £14.00

LAW PARTNERSHIPS – GREAT BRITAIN

—Good Practice : A Management Guide for the Profession / London : Butterworths.
ISBN 0406502803 Pbk

LAW PARTNERSHIPS – NEW YORK

—Howe & Hummel / Richard H. Rovere. – London : Arlington, 1986.
xvii,169p; 22cm.
Originally published: New York : Farrar, Straus and Giroux, 1985.
ISBN 0851406890 £9.95

LAW PUBLISHING

—Law publishing and legal information : small jurisdictions of the British Isles / edited by William Twining and Jennifer Uglow. – London : Sweet & Maxwell, 1981.
181p; 22cm.
Bibliography: p150-178. - Includes index.
ISBN 0421289309 Pbk £10.00

LAW REFORM

—Annual report / Great Britain. – London : H.M.S.O., 1985.
v,67p; 25cm. – (HC).
ISBN 0102214859

—Law reform commissions in the United Kingdom, Australia and Canada / by William H. Hurlburt. – Edmonton : Juriliber, 1986.
vii,514p.
Bibliography: p.498-514.
ISBN 0919311032

—Law reform digests : a digest of the reports of law reform agencies in Australia, New Zealand and Papua New Guinea, 1910-1980 / Canberra : Australian Government Publishing, 1983.
xviii,754p.
Includes index.
ISBN 0644016280

—Legal Change : Essays in Honour of Julius Stone / London : Butterworths, 1982.

—Sources of law, legal change, and ambiguity / Alan Watson. – Edinburgh : T. & T. Clark, 1985.
xviii,164p; 23cm.
Previously published: Philadelphia : University of Pennsylvania Press, 1984.
ISBN 0567093603

LAW REFORM – AFRICA

—Southern Africa in need of law reform : proceedings of the Southern African Law Reform Conference, Sun City, Bophuthatswana, 11-14 August 1980 / edited by A.J.G.M. Sanders. – Durban : Butterworths, 1981.
256p.
Includes bibliographical references.
ISBN 0409051845

LAW REFORM – AUSTRALIA

—Australian Law Reform Agencies Conference : Hobart July 1981, Adelaide September 1982, Brisbane July 1983 / Australia : s.n., .
262p.
Includes index. Includes the records and minutes of the 6th, 7th and 8th Conferences.

—Community law reform for the Australian Capital Territory / Law Reform Commission. – Canberra : Australian Government Publishing Service, 1985.
ix,44p. – (Report).
Bibliography: p.41-42 - Includes index.
ISBN 0644013257

—Law Reform Commission, Annual Report, 1980 / Law Reform Commission. – Canberra : Australian Government Publishing Service, 1980.
66p. – (ALRC Report: No. 17).

—Law Reform Commission, Annual Report, 1981 / Law Reform Commission. – Canberra : Australian Government Publishing Service, 1981.
69p. – (ALRC Report: No. 19).

—Law Reform Commission, Annual Report, 1982 / Law Reform Commission. – Canberra : Australian Government Publishing Service, 1982.
73p. – (ALRC Report: No. 21).

—Law Reform Commission, Annual Report, 1983 / Law Reform Commission. – Canberra : Australian Government Publishing Service, 1983.
73p. – (ALRC Report: No. 23).

—Rape Law Reform / Canberra : Australian Institute of Criminology.

—Reform the law : essays on the renewal of the Australian legal system / Michael Kirby. – Melbourne, Oxford : Oxford University Press, 1983.
xii,284p; 21cm.
ISBN 0195543955 Pbk £12.99
ISBN 0195543955 Hbk £27.50

LAW REFORM – AUSTRALIA – NEW SOUTH WALES

—Community law reform program / New South Wales Law Reform Commission. – Sydney : The Commission, 1983.
61p. – (L.R.C. 34).

2nd report : Interest on certain debts / New South Wales Law Reform Commission. – 1983.
46p. – (L.R.C. 35).

3rd report : Service of civil process on Sunday / New South Wales Law Reform Commission. – 1983.
61p. – (L.R.C. 37).

4th report : Sound recording of proceedings of courts and commissions : the media, authors and parties / New South Wales Law Reform Commission. – 1984.
115p. – (L.R.C. 39).
Bibliography: p.113-115.

5th report : Passing of risk between vendor and purchaser of land / New South Wales Law Reform Commission. – 1984.
84p. – (L.R.C. 40).
Bibliography: p.83-84.

6th report : Conscientious objection to jury service / New South Wales Law Reform Commission. – 1984.
53p. – (L.R.C. 42).

7th report : Attachment of moneys deposited with building societies and credit unions / New South Wales Law Reform Commission. – 1985.
xiii,123p. – (L.R.C. 46).
Includes bibliographical references.
ISBN 0730514714 Hbk

8th report : Wills - execution and revocation / New South Wales Law Reform Commission. – 1986.
175p. – (L.R.C. 47).
Includes bibliographical references.
ISBN 0730514943 Hbk

LAW REFORM – AUSTRALIA – VICTORIA

—Annual report / Law Reform Commission of Victoria. – Melbourne : The Commission, 1985.
Published as part of the report series of the Commission.

—Consultation and government : report of the inquiry into processes of consultation in Victoria with special reference to the case of tenancy law reform / with papers by Ronald F. Henderson ... et al. – Melbourne : Victorian Council of Social Service, 1981.
xii,273p.
Includes bibliographical notes.
ISBN 0949748072

LAW REFORM – CANADA

—Reform of the Criminal Law / Agincourt : Carswell.
130p.
This work contains papers that had been delivered at the July 1987 conference on criminal law reform held in London, England. Discussions include white collar crime, sentencing reform and the defenses.

—Regulatory Reform in Canada / Fred Thompson. – Vancouver : University of British Columbia, Faculty of Commerce & Business Administration, 1982.
– (Montreal Institute for Research on Public Policy Ser.).

LAW REFORM – CANADA – SASKATCHEWAN

—Annual report and review / Law Reform Commission of Saskatchewan. – Saskatoon : The Commission, 1988.
Supersedes: Yearly review.

LAW REFORM – COMMONWEALTH

—Law Reform in the Commonwealth : A Report on the 1983 Meeting of Commonwealth Law Reform Agencies / London : Commonwealth Secretariat.

—Law reform in the Commonwealth : law reform proposals and their implementation / Commonwealth Secretariat. – London : Commonwealth Secretariat, 1981.
Pilot issue published Oct. 1979.

LAW REFORM – ENGLAND

—Breaking the rules : the problem of crimes and contraventions : a report / by Justice... – London : JUSTICE, 1980.
v,54p; 22cm.
ISBN 0907247008 sd £2.00 (1.50 to members)

—Changing law / Robin White, Patfield. – London : Pinter, 1990.
224.
A survey of the radical and rapid changes to English law in the last 25 years. Covers negligence, land, family, financial regulation, civil liberties, social security, EC law, reform of the legal profession and codification of common law principles.
ISBN 0718513312 Hbk £29.50

—Law Commission and law reform / edited by Graham Zellick. – London : Sweet & Maxwell, 1988.
xiii,157p.
Includes index. Includes a list of Law Commission publications.
ISBN 0421404604 £32.00

—Law reforms in a democratic society / the Rt. Hon. Lord Scarman. – New Delhi : National Publishing House, 1985.
114p.
Includes index.

—Report / Criminal Law Revision Committee. – London : H.M.S.O, 1980.
viii,150p; 25cm.
ISBN 0101784406 Pbk £4.50

—Sexual offences : fifteenth report / Criminal Law Revision Committee. – London : H.M.S.O., 1984.
ix,105p; 25cm.
ISBN 0101921306 Pbk £6.40

—Unlawful sex : offences, victims and offenders in the criminal justice system of England and Wales / the report of a Howard League working party. – London : Waterlow, 1985.
xvi,264p. – (Waterlow's legal and social policy library).
Includes bibliography and index.
ISBN 0080392202 Pbk £9.95

LAW REFORM – GREAT BRITAIN

—Annual report / London : H.M.S.O., 1965-.

—Law Commission Reports, 13 Vols. / Repr. – Abingdon : Professional Books.

Individual vols.

—Law Reform Digest / Professional Books Staff. – Abingdon : Professional Books, 1984.

—Law under review : a quarterly bulletin of law reform projects / Law Commission. – London : Law Commission, 1987.
Includes index.

—More law reform NOW : a collection of essays on law reform / and edited by Peter Archer and Andrew Martin. – Chichester : Barry Rose, 1983.
ix,304p.
Published in association with the Society of Labour Lawyers.
ISBN 0859923495

—Social history and law reform / by O.R. McGregor. – London : Stevens, 1981.
x,66p; 19cm.
Includes index.
ISBN 0420459200 Hbk £9.50
ISBN 0420459308 Pbk £4.25

—Statute law revision / the Law Commission and Scottish Law Commission. – London : H.M.S.O., 1985.
ii,107p.
ISBN 0101964803

—Statute law revision : tenth report : draft Statute Law (Repeals) Bill / the Law Commission and the Scottish Law Commission. – London : H.M.S.O., 1980.
ii,70p; 25cm.
ISBN 0101808909 Pbk £4.20

—What Next in the Law / Wellington : Butterworths, 1982.
This work deals with proposals for reform in various areas of the law of the United Kingdom, including: trial by jury, legal aid, personal injuries, libel, privacy, and confidence.
ISBN 0406176019 Hbk
ISBN 0406176027 Pbk

—Wives and property : reform of the married women's property law in nineteenth-century England / Lee Holcombe. – Oxford : Martin Robertson, 1983.
viii,311p; 24cm.
Bibliography: p275-292. - Includes index.
ISBN 0855206071 £15.00

LAW REFORM – GUYANA

—Law reform in Guyana / address delivered by Attorney General to Guyana Bar Association on 21st September 1981. – S.l. : s.n., 1981.
43p.
At head of title: 'Extracts printed in the Guyana Bar Association journal'.. Includes bibliographical references.

LAW REFORM – INDIA

—Judicial reform : working paper : Conference on the Reform on sic the Indian Legal System / New Delhi : Indian Law Institute, 1983.
53p.
Caption title: Judicial reforms.

LAW REFORM – JAPAN

—Formation of the early Meiji legal order : the Japanese code of 1871 and its Chinese foundation / by Paul Heng-Chao Ch'en. – Oxford : Oxford University Press, 1981.
xxii,204p; 23cm.
Bibliography: p187-190. - Includes index.
ISBN 019713601X £12.00

LAW REFORM – NEW ZEALAND

—Annual report of the Law Commission ... / New Zealand. – Wellington, N.Z. : The Commission, 1987.
Published as part of the report series of the Commission. 1st report covers years ended 31 March 1986 and 31 March 1987.

—Business records and computer output / Evidence Law Reform Committee. – s.l. : Evidence Law Reform Committee, 1985.
43 leaves, 2 leaves. – (Working paper).
Inlcudes bibliographical references.

—Confessions / Evidence Law Refrom Committee. – s.l. : Evidence Law Reform Committee, 1985.
18, 2 leaves. – (Working paper).
Includes bibliographical references.

LAW REFORM – NIGERIA

—Law reform / Nigerian Law Reform Commission. – Lagos? : The Commission, 1980.

LAW REFORM – NORTHERN IRELAND

—Abolishing the Diplock courts : the case for restoring jury trial to scheduled offences in Northern Ireland / S.C. Greer, A. White. – London : Cobden Trust, 1986.
x,133p; 20cm.
Includes index.
ISBN 0900137274 Pbk £5.95

LAW REFORM – PAPUA NEW GUINEA

—Land law and policy in Papua New Guinea : by R.W. James / Port Moresby : Papua New Guinea Law Reform Commission, 1985.
xix,204p. – (Monograph).
Includes bibliographical references.
ISBN 998055004X

LAW REFORM – SCOTLAND

—Annual report / Scottish Law Commission. – Edinburgh : H.M.S.O., 1966-.
Numbered in series Scot Law Com.

—Fourth programme of consolidation and statute law revision / Scottish Law Commission. – Edinburgh : H.M.S.O., 1982.
10p.
ISBN 0102516820

—Law Reform (Miscellaneous Provisions) (Scotland) Act 1985 / Edinburgh : W Green & Son, 1986.
Annotated text of the Act from Scottish Current Law Statutes.
ISBN 0414007883

LAW REFORM – SOUTH AFRICA

—Southern Africa in need of law reform / London : Butterworths, 1981.
ISBN 0409051845 Pbk £19.20

—Two lectures on law reform : delivered at the workshop on Marriage and Family Life by the Human Sciences Research Council on 26 September 1985 / by J.T. Delport and C.R.M. Dlamini. – Pretoria : Government Printer on behalf of the South African Law Comission, 1987.
iv,38p. – (Research series).
Bibliography: pp.19-21.
ISBN 0621106704

LAW REFORM – ZIMBABWE

—Annual report / Zimbabwe Advisory Committee on Law Reform / Zimbabwe. – v. – Causeway : The Committee, 1982.

LAW REPORTS

—Administrative Law Reports / Agincourt : Carswell.

Vols. 1-30 1984-88.
This text contains the administrative law decisions from all the Canadian jurisdictions. Topics include the judicial review of decisions of administrative tribunals, both the availability of and grounds for, delegation of legislative powers, and remedies on judicial review.

—Alberta Decisions : Civil and Criminal Cases (1980-Present) / Aurora : Canada Law Book Co. – (Summary Services, Provincial Ser.).

—Alberta Decisions Civil and Criminal Cases / Aurora : Canada Law Book Co.

—Alberta Law Reports : 1909-1932 / Carswell Legal Publications. – Agincourt : Carswell.

—Alberta Law Reports / 2nd ed. – Agincourt : Carswell.

—Alberta, Saskatchewan, Manitoba Criminal Conviction Cases / Aurora : Canada Law Book Co.

—Alberta-Saskatchewan-Manitoba Criminal Conviction Cases / Aurora : Canada Law Book Co.
– (Summary Services, Provincial Ser.).

—All-Canada Weekly Summaries First Ser. (1977-1979), 9 Vols. / Aurora : Canada Law Book Co.
– (Summary Services, National Series).

Back Vols.

—All Canada Weekly Summaries-National (A.C.W.S.) 1977-79, 9 Vols. / Canada Law Book Publisher. – Aurora : Canada Law Book Co.
– (First Ser.).

Back Vols.

—All Canada Weekly Summaries-National (A.C.W.S.) 1980-1986, 39 Vols. / Canada Law Book Publisher. – Aurora : Canada Law Book Co.
– (Second Ser.).

—All Canada Weekly Summaries-Ontario Edition (A.C.W.S. ONT) June 1981-1986, 30 Vols. / Canada Law Book Publisher. – Aurora : Canada Law Book Co.

Back Vols.

Binder

—All-Canada Weekly Summaries Ontario Edition Current Series (1981-Present) / Aurora : Canada Law Book Co.
– (Summary Services, Provincial Ser.).

Parts only

Back Vols.

—All-Canada Weekly Summaries Third Ser. (1986-Present) / Aurora : Canada Law Book Co. – (Summary Services, National Series).

Parts only

Back Vols.

—All England Law Reports : 1936-1985, 143 Vols. / P. Hutchesson et al. – Wellington : Butterworths.

Weekly Parts-1986

Bound Vols. Service-1986

Noter-Up Service-1986

Consolidated Index (1936-76) 3 Vols.
ISBN 0406862141 Hbk

Cumulative Table and Index (1977-80)
ISBN 0406866759 Hbk

Back Vols. and Binding Services

Reprint (1558-1935)

—All England Law Reports Annual Review 1985 / London : Butterworths, 1986.
This work contains detailed analyses of decisions handed down in the Law Courts and the House of Lords during the previous year. The book is written for practitioners and students to provide synopses of current trends in English law.
ISBN 0406879621 Hbk £33.00

—All Nigeria Law Reports : 1961-1970, 10 Vols. / Repr. – London : Sweet & Maxwell, 1983.

Includes index 1961-1970
ISBN 0421300701 Hbk £460.00

Index 1983 alone
ISBN 0421313005 Hbk £39.00

—Annotated Tax Cases : 1922-1975, 54 Vols. / Abingdon : Professional Books.

—Antitrust Cases from Common Market Law Reports : Cartels / London : European Law Centre.

—Appellate Division Reports of the Union of South Africa : 1910-1946, 37 Vols. / Kenwyn : Juta & Co, 1985.

—Argument and Decisions in Remarkable Cases Before the High Court of Justiciary : 1670-1773 / Repr. of 1774 ed. – Abingdon : Professional Books.
76p.

—Aspinall's Reports of Maritime Cases : 1870-1940, 20 Vols. / Professional Books Staff. – Abingdon : Professional Books, 1984.

—Australian and New Zealand Citator to UK Reports 1588-1972 / Wellington : Butterworths.
ISBN 0409303100 Pbk

—Australian and New Zealand Income Tax Reports (AITR) / Wellington : Butterworths.

—Australian Company Law Reports (ACLR) / H. H. Ednie. – Wellington : Butterworths.

—Australian current law / Sydney : Butterworths, 1981-.
26cm.

—Australian family law cases / North Ryde, N.S.W. : CCH Australia, 1975.
23cm.
Issued annually as bound volumes, with current issues forming part of the service to the loose-leaf publication: Australian family law & practice reporter.

—Australian Law Reports (ALR) / J. D. Heydon. – Wellington : Butterworths.

—Australian Tax : Tax Reports : 1969 to Present / Wellington : Butterworths.

Back Vols. avail.

—British Columbia Decisions Civil Cases (1979-Present) / Aurora : Canada Law Book Co. – (Summary Services, Provincial Ser.).

—British Columbia Decisions Civil Cases / Aurora : Canada Law Book Co.

—British Columbia Decisions Criminal Conviction and Sentence Cases (1979-Present) / Aurora : Canada Law Book Co.
– (Summary Services, Provincial Ser.).

—British Columbia Labour Relations Board Decisions / Aurora : Canada Law Book Co.

—British Columbia Law Reports / Agincourt : Carswell, 1988.
– (Second Ser., 1-18).
This text includes all the cases from the courts of British Columbia and appeals from that court to the Supreme Court of Canada. The cases are all headnoted, there is a topical index, and an index of cases reported.

—British Columbia Reports : 1867-1945, 63 Vols. / Carswell Legal Publications. – Agincourt : Carswell.

—Buchanan's Appeal Cases, 1880-6 and 1904-11, 4 Vols. / Kenwyn : Juta & Co, 1985.
– (Cape Reports).

—Buchanan's Reports, 1868-1879, 10 Vols. / Kenwyn : Juta & Co, 1985.
– (Cape Reports).

—Butterworth's District Court Reports / Wellington : Butterworths.

—Butterworth's Family Law Reports / Hellen Papadopoulas. – Wellington : Butterworths.

—Butterworths annotations to the New Zealand statutes : 2nd ed. : 1908-1982 / by Martin Fine. – Wellington : Butterworths, 1982.
Previous ed.: Butterworths cases annotations of the New Zealand statutes reprint 1908-1957, published 1960-1961. Looseleaf issues accompanied by monthly Butterworths Automatic Annotations Bulletin.
ISBN 0409701262

—Canada Federal Court Reports : 1971-1983 / Agincourt : Carswell, 1986.

—Canada Law Reports : 1923-1970 / Agincourt : Carswell, 1984.

—Canada Supreme Court Reports : 1876-1922, 64 Vols. / Agincourt : Carswell, 1984.

—Canadian Bankruptcy Reports / David E. Baird. – Agincourt : Carswell.

—Canadian Criminal Cases (C.C.C.) 1898-1962, 133 Vols. / Aurora : Canada Law Book Co.
– (Old Ser.).

Back Vols.

—Canadian Criminal Cases (C.C.C.) 1963-70, 30 Vols. / Aurora : Canada Law Book Co.
– (New Ser.).

Back Vols.

—Canadian Criminal Cases (C.C.C.) 1971-83, 70 Vols. / Aurora : Canada Law Book Co.
– (Second Ser.).

Back Vols.

—Canadian Criminal Cases (C.C.C.) March 1983-Present / Aurora : Canada Law Book Co.
– (Third Ser.).

—Canadian Criminal Cases : Index, Annotations, Table of Cases / Aurora : Canada Law Book Co, 1985.
– (Third Ser.).

—Canadian Criminal Cases (Second Series) Index, Annotations, Table of Cases : Covering Vols. 1 through 70 of the Canadian Criminal Cases (Second Series) / Aurora : Canada Law Book Co, 1983.
1184p.

—Canadian Current Law / Agincourt : Carswell, 1987.

Issues and Index from 1985, 4 Vols.

Issues and Index from 1984, 4 Vols.

Issues and Index from 1983, 3 Vols.

Issues and Index from 1982, Vols.

—Canadian Customs and Excise Reports / Toronto : Butterworths.
ISBN 0409858129 £110.00

Looseleaf Vol.
ISBN 0409858110 Pbk £55.00

Back Vol. of Case Reports, Vol. 8
ISBN 0409857599 Hbk £40.00

Editorial Commentary Binder to Vols. 1-6
ISBN 0409811823 Hbk £15.00

Bound Vol. 1
ISBN 0409858137 Hbk £40.00

Bound Vol. 2
ISBN 0409858188 Hbk £40.00

Bound Vol. 3
ISBN 0409858234 Hbk £40.00

Bound Vol. 4
ISBN 0409858285 Hbk £40.00

Bound Vol. 5
ISBN 0409859079 Hbk £40.00

Bound Vol. 6
ISBN 0409859036 Hbk £40.00

Bound Vo7. 7
ISBN 0409857572 Hbk £40.00

Cumulative Index Vols. 1-7
ISBN 0409810444 Hbk £27.95

—Canadian encyclopedic digest (Western) : being a complete digest on the encyclopedic plan of all reported decisions in Alberta, British Columbia, Manitoba, Saskatchewan and appealed therefrom / 2nd ed. – Calgary : Burroughs, 1956-.
Gradually superseded by 3rd ed. - Those Titles not yet superseded kept up to date by supplements. Set includes: First permanent supplement 1969, Second permanent supplement 1976.

—Canadian Environmental Law Reports / Agincourt : Carswell.

—Canadian Family Law Cases : 1959-1977 / Butterworth & Co. (Canada) Ltd. – Toronto : Butterworths.
420p.
ISBN 0409989916 Pbk £60.00

Suppl. 1980
ISBN 0409989940 Pbk £40.00

—Canadian Intellectual Property Reports / Agincourt : Carswell, 1987.
This reference text contains the key decisions in the intellectual property law area. Topics include copyrights, industrial designs, patents of invention, and trademarks.

—Canadian Labour Relations Board Report / Toronto : Butterworths.

—Canadian Patent Reporter: 1985 / Aurora : Canada Law Book Co, 1985.
– (Third Ser.).

Back Vols.

—Canadian Patent Reporter (C.P.R.) 1942-71, 65 Vols. / Aurora : Canada Law Book Co.
– (First Ser.).

Back Vols.

—Canadian Patent Reporter (C.P.R.) 1971-1984 / Aurora : Canada Law Book Co.
– (Second Ser.).

Back Vols.

—Canadian Patent Reporter First Series (1942-1971) 65 Vols. / Aurora : Canada Law Book Co.
– (Law Reports).

Back Vols.

—Canadian Patent Reporter Second Series (1971-1984), 82 Vols. / Aurora : Canada Law Book Co.
– (Law Reports).

Back Vols.

—Canadian Patent Reporter Second Series : Table of Cases / Aurora : Canada Law Book Co.
– (Law Reports).

—Canadian Patent Reporter Third Series (1985-Present) / Aurora : Canada Law Book Co.
– (Law Reports).

Back Vols.

—Canadian Reports Appeal Cases : 1807-1913, 24 Vols. / Carswell Legal Publications. – Agincourt : Carswell, 1983.

—Canadian Transport Cases (1966-1977), 7 Vols. / Aurora : Canada Law Book Co.
– (Law Reports).

—Canadian Transport Cases : 1966-77, 7 Vols. / Aurora : Canada Law Book Co.
– (Earlier Series Entitled Canadian Railway and Transport Cases).

Index (Vols. 50-85) of the Earlier Series

—Canadian Weekly Law Sheet / Toronto : Butterworths.

—Cases Argued and Decreed in the High Court of Chancery : 1660-80 / 2nd ed. Repr. of 1707 ed. – Abingdon : Professional Books.
345p.

—Cases Determined at Nisi Prius in the Court of King's Bench from Easter Term : 30 Geo 3 to Michaelmas Term, 35 Geo 3 / Repr. of 1795 ed. – Abingdon : Professional Books.
335p.

—Cases in Chancery During the Time of Lord Eldon / Repr. of 1815 ed. – Abingdon : Professional Books.
77p.

—Cases in Equity : During the Time of Chancellor Talbot (1730-37) From Notes of Alexander Forrester / Repr. of 1741 ed. – Abingdon : Professional Books.
345p.

—Cayman Islands law reports / Oxford : Law Reports International, 1986-.

—Collection of Acts and Records of Parliament : With Reports of Cases in Courts of Law and Equity (1224-1800) Respecting Tithes, 4 Vols. / Repr. of 1801 ed. – Abingdon : Professional Books.
192p.

—Commercial Cases : Reports of 1895-1941, 46 Vols. / Abingdon : Professional Books, 1895-1941.

Individual vols.

—Commissioners' Decisions : Social Security and Child Benefit Acts / London : HMSO, 1985.
ISBN 0117609218 Hbk

Vol. IX, 1983-84
ISBN 0117607851 Hbk £25.00

—Consolidated Index and Noter-up to the South African Law Reports 1973-1979 / Durban : Professional Publishers, 1980.
ISBN 0409016543 Hbk £95.00

—Construction Law Reports 10 vols / Vincent Powell-Smith. – London : Architectural Press, 1985.
160p.
ISBN 0851397808 Hbk £18.50

Vol. 2 1985.
ISBN 0851397816 Hbk £18.50

Vol. 3 1985.
ISBN 0851397824 Hbk £18.50

—Construction Law Reports / Agincourt : Carswell, 1985.

Vol. 31, 1988
This work contains the key construction law decisions from all Canadian jurisdictions. Topics include building contracts, remedies for their breach, construction liens and bonding issues. Cases on court actions by and against architects, engineers, contractors and subcontractors are also included.

—Construction Law Reports / Powell-Smith. – Vol. 11. – London : Architectural Press, 1988.
ISBN 0851392024 Hbk £25.00

—Court of Appeal (Civil Division) judgments, 1951-1980 / Victor Tunkel. – Microfiche ed. 222 microfiches. – London : HMSO Books, 1986.
in 12 ring binders.
Includes indexes of judges, plaintiffs and defendants. Accompanied by looseleaf insert in binder 1: The Court of Appeal transcripts 1951-1980: the microfiche edition: an introduction / by Victor Tunkel. - 33p..

—Court of Chancery Reports / Repr. of 1758 ed. – Abingdon : Professional Books.
344p.

—Court of Session Cases : Series 1-5, 1821-1906, 63 Vols. / Abingdon : Professional Books.

2nd Series, 1838-1862, 24 Vols.

3rd Series, 1862-1873, 11 Vols.

4th Series, 1873-1898, 25 Vols.

5th Series, 1898-1906, 8 Vols.

—Cox's Criminal Law Cases : 1843-1941, 31 Vols. / Cox. – Repr. of 1978 ed. – London : Butterworths.
This 31 volume work is a comprehensive record of English criminal law cases. The cases reported are those heard in the Courts of Criminal Appeal, the Superior Courts, the Central Criminal Court, the Assizes, and in Ireland.
ISBN 0406015007 Hbk

—Criminal Appeal Reports / London : Sweet & Maxwell.
Bound Vol.
Back Vols.

—Criminal Appeal Reports (Sentencing) / London : Sweet & Maxwell.
Bound Vol.
Indiv. parts

—Crown Cases Reserved for Consideration and Decided by the Twelve Judges of England : 1824-1844, 2 Vols. / Repr. of 1844 ed. – Abingdon : Professional Books.
247p.

—Daily Telegraph law reports / London : The Daily Telegraph, 1987-.

—Decisions of the Court of Session : 1781-1822 / Repr. of 1839 ed. – Abingdon : Professional Books.
52p.

—Decisions of the Court of Session : Abridged in Form of a Dictionary / Woodhouselee. – Repr. of 1741 ed. – Abingdon : Professional Books.
57p.

—Decisions of the Court of Session from 1681-91 / Repr. of 1757 ed. – Abingdon : Professional Books.
51p.

—Digest of appeal cases ... : Supreme Court and Federal Court of Appeal / Lagos, Nigeria : Olba Publishers, 1985-.

—Digest of case-law relating to the European Communities / Court of Justice of the European Communities. – 1. – Luxembourg : Office for Official Publications of the European Communities, 1984.
loose-leaf; 23cm.
Periodically updated by supplements.
ISBN 9282900614

D series : Judgements of the Court of Justice of the European Communities and selected discussions of courts of Member States on the Convention of 27 September 1969 on jurisdiction and the enforcement of judgements in civil and commercial matters 1981.
Judgements of the Court of Justice of the European Communities and selected decisions of courts of member states on the convention of jurisdiction and the enforcement of judgements in civil and commercial matters.
ISBN 9282900398 Pbk £25.60

—Digest of Cases Decided in the Supreme Courts of Scotland From 1800-1852 / Repr. of 1867 ed. – Abingdon : Professional Books.
104p.

—Digests of Irish Reports and Irish Law Times Reports / Abingdon : Professional Books.
1867-93

—Dominion Law Reports : 1969-1984, 150 Vols. / Aurora : Canada Law Book Co, 1984.
– (Third Ser.).
Back Vols.

—Dominion Law Reports (D.L.R.) 1912-22, 70 vols. / Aurora : Canada Law Book Co.
– (Old Ser.).
Back Vols.

—Dominion Law Reports (D.L.R.) 1923-55, 133 vols. / Aurora : Canada Law Book Co.

– (New Ser.).

—Dominion Law Reports (D.L.R.) 1956-68, 70 vols. / Aurora : Canada Law Book Co.
– (Second Ser.).
Back Vols.
Table of Cases Vol.

—Dominion Law Reports (D.L.R.) 1984-present / Aurora : Canada Law Book Co.
– (Fourth Ser.).
Current subscription-outside Canada
Back Vols. 1-5 copies
More than 6 Back Vols.
Bound Vol. Only in Canada

—Dominion Law Reports Fourth Series (1984-Present) / Aurora : Canada Law Book Co.
– (Law Reports).
Bound Vol. only

—Dominion Law Reports Fourth Series Index and Annotation Service / Aurora : Canada Law Book Co, 1987.
– (Law Reports).

—Dominion Law Reports New Series, 133 Vols. / Aurora : Canada Law Book Co.
– (Law Reports).
Back Vols.

—Dominion Law Reports Old Series (1912-1922), 70 Vols. / Aurora : Canada Law Book Co.
– (Law Reports).
Back Vols.

—Dominion Law Reports (Second & Third Series) Annotation Service : 1984, 1 Vol. / Aurora : Canada Law Book Co.
1084p.

—Dominion Law Reports Second and Third Series Annotation Service / Aurora : Canada Law Book Co, 1984.
1084p. – (Law Reports).

—Dominion Law Reports Second Series (1956-1968), 70 Vols. / Aurora : Canada Law Book Co.
– (Law Reports).
Back Vols.
Table of Cases

—Dominion Law Reports Third Series (1969-1984), 150 Vols. / Aurora : Canada Law Book Co.
– (Law Reports).
Back Vols.

—Dominion Law Reports Third Series Index, 2 Vols. / Aurora : Canada Law Book Co, 1986.
– (Law Reports).

—East African Law Reports : 1957-1975, 20 Vols. / Professional Books Staff. – Abingdon : Professional Books, 1984.

—English and Empire digest, with complete and exhaustive annotations / Green band ed. v. – London : Butterworth, 1971-.
Previous (Blue band) ed.: 1951-71. Includes indexes. From vol.21 (1981) title changes to The digest. Vol.28, Income tax and related taxes (1971), first vol. to be re-issued in new ed.. Kept up to date by continuation vols. and cumulative supplements.
ISBN 0406025002

—English Reports : 1220-1865, 178 Vols. / Abingdon : Professional Books.
Individual vols.
Wall chart
Index Vols. 177 and 178

—European Court of Justice Reporter / Oxford : ESC Publishing Ltd, 1982.

—Faculty Decisions : Three Series, 1752-1841, 37 Vols. / Abingdon : Professional Books.
New Series, 1808-1825, 7 Vols.
Third Series, 1825-1841, 16 Vols.

—Family Law Reports Cumulative Index 1980-1984 / Bristol : Jordan & Sons Ltd, 1985.

—Family law reports : incorporating Family law notes / Sydney : Butterworths, 1976-.
Contains reports and digests of judgments of the High Court of Australia, the Family Court of Australia, the Family Court of Western Australia, the Supreme Courts of the States and Territories.

—Family Law Reports. Vol. 6 / I. W. Crompton. – Bristol : Jordan & Sons Ltd, 1986.

—Federal Court of Appeal Decisions (1981-Present) / Aurora : Canada Law Book Co. – (Summary Services, National Series).

—Federal Court of Appeal Decisions / Aurora : Canada Law Book Co.

—Federal Court of Canada Service, 2 vols / Toronto : Butterworths.

—Federal Court reports : the authorised reports of decisions of the Federal Court of Australia / editor C.A. Sweeney. – Sydney : Law Book Co., 1984-.
Indexes.

—Financial Law Reports / London : Sweet & Maxwell, 1986.
ISBN 0421345004 Hbk £28.00

—Financial Times law reports / Brentford : Kluwer Law, 1986-.

—Gazette Law Reports of New Zealand 1898-1952, 54 Vols. / Wellington : Butterworths.

—Ghana law reports digest : being a digest of cases determined by the High Court and the Court of Appeal of the Republic of Ghana / Accra : Council for Law Reporting, 1980-.
Includes index.

—Gibraltar Law Reports 1812-1979, 3 vols / London : African Law Reports, 1985.

—Gilbert Islands law reports / compiled by J.A. O'Brien Quinn. – 2 v. – Tarawa : High Court, 1977-.
Continued by: The Kiribati law reports. 'Published by authority'.

—Guardian Law reports / Lodnon : The Guardian, 1987-.

—Guide to EC court decisions / editors, Alfred E. Kellermann ... et al. – Amsterdam : North-Holland Pub. Co., 1982.
At head of title: T.M.C. Asser Institute–The Hague. Includes index.
ISBN 0444864571

—High Court of Nigeria Law Reports / Lagos : Nigerian Law Publications, 1985.
ISBN 978232518X Hbk £100.00

—High Courts of Nigeria law reports / Lagos : Nigerian Law Publications, 1987-.

—History of the Law Reports 1884 / London : Wildy & Sons.

—House of Lords Appeals : 1821-1873, 28 Vols. / Abingdon : Professional Books.
1825-1835, 7 Vols.
1835-1838, 3 Vols.
1838-1839, 1 Vol.
1840-1841, 2 Vols.
1842-1850, 7 Vols.
1851-1865, 4 Vols.
1866-1873, 2 Vols.

—Housing Law Reports / London : Sweet & Maxwell.
Bound Vol.
Back Vols.
Single copies

—Housing law reports / edited by Andrew Arden. – Harlow : G. Godwin, 1982-.
Annual indexes.

—Imo State law reports / v. – Ibadan : Evans Brothers (Nigeria Publishers) for Law Reporting Committee, Ministry of Justice, Imo State of Nigeria, 1977.

—Independent law reports / London : The Independent, 1986-.

—Index and Noter-up to the South African Law Reports : 1980-1984 / Durban : Butterworths, 1985.
ISBN 0409016675

—Index to Reports of Tax Cases : 1875-1981, 52 Vols. / Abingdon : Professional Books, 1984.
ISBN 0862050707 Hbk £63.00

—Index to the South African Law Reports : 1828-1946, 2 vols. / F. R. Malan. – Durban : Butterworths.
ISBN 0409040770 Hbk

—Index to the Southern African law reports 1828-1946 / editors, F.R. Malan, J.C. Van der Walt. – Durban : Butterworths, 1981.
729p.
Covers the major law reports published in Southern Africa prior to 1947.
ISBN 0409040789

Vol. 2 : Cape / editors, F.R. Malan, J.C. Van der Walt. – 1983.
1006p.
Covers the major law reports published in Southern Africa prior to 1947.
ISBN 0409040797 Hbk

—Individual Cases Reports : 1972-1981 / Abingdon : Professional Books.

—Industrial relations law reports / London : Eclipse Publications, 1972-.
Annual cumulative indexes.

—Industrial Tribunal Reports : 1966-1978, 13 Vols. / Professional Books Staff. – Abingdon : Professional Books, 1984.

—Insurance law reports / edited by F.N. Eaglestone and K.S. Cannar. – Harlow : G. Goodwin, 1982-.
Annual index.

—Intellectual Property Reports / John J. Garsney. – Wellington : Butterworths.
These comprehensive reports are complete with headnotes, catchwords, holdings, court hearings, and final judgement dates for all major decisions in field of intellectual property in Australia.

—Intellectual Property Reports, Vol. 1, 1989 / edited by Brown. – Wellington : Butterworths (New Zealand).
435p.
ISBN 0409787361 Hbk £190.00

—International Labour Law Reports / Dordrecht : Kluwer.

Volume 7 1989.
688. – (International labour law reports).
A volume in the series of annual publications of labour law judgements by the highest courts in a number of jurisdictions. Each judgement reprinted has Headnotes and usually an Annotation setting out the legal issues involved, and basic facts of the case if not included in the judgement. Judgements are normally printed in extenso.
ISBN 0792300998 Hbk £105

Vol. 1 (1974-1975) 1978.
398p.
ISBN 9028608982

Vol. 3 (1976-1977)
xix, 399p.
ISBN 9028600604 Hbk £200.00

Vol. 4 1986.
462p.
ISBN 9024733073 Hbk £225.00

Vol. 5 1987.
442p.
ISBN 9024734738 Hbk £225.00

Vol. 6 1988.
444p.
ISBN 9024736056 Hbk £225.00

—International Law Reports, 77 Vols. / Cambridge : Grotius.

Vols. 1-50

Vols. 51-74

Vols. 75-77

Index to Vols. 1-35

Index to Vols. 36-45

—Irish law reports monthly / Dublin : Irish Academic Press, 1981.
From vol. 1, - vol. 3, no. 2 (1981-83) incorporates Irish law times.
ISBN 03323293

—Irish Reports : 1838-1979, 233 Vols. / Professional Books Staff. – Abingdon : Professional Books, 1984.

—Irish Reports : 1894-1979, 118 Vols. / Repr. – Abingdon : Professional Books.

1894-1925 (Ser. V)

1926-1979 (Ser. VI)

Individual vols. Ser. V

Individual vols. Ser. VI

—Irish Reports Digests : 1894-1970, 6 Vols. / Abingdon : Professional Books.

Vol. 1, 1894-1918

Vol. 2, 1919-1928

Vol. 2. Irish Reports Digests : 1919-1928

Vol. 3, 1929-1938

Vol. 3. Irish Reports Digests : 1929-1938

1939-1948

Vol. 4, 1939-1948

1949-1958

Vol. 5, 1949-1958

1959-1970

Vol. 6, 1959-1970

Repr.

—Jersey law reports / Oxford : Law Reports International, 1987-.
Continues : Judgments of the Royal Court of Jersey and of the Court of Appeal of Jersey.

—Judgments / Income Tax Appeals Special Court of Zimbabwe. – Zimbabwe : The Court, 1980-.
Continues: Income tax appeal: judgment / Income Tax Appeals Special Court, Southern Rhodesia.

—Judgments of the Court of Criminal Appeal 1924-1978 / edited by Gerard L. Frewen. – Dublin : Law Library, Incorporated Council of Law Reporting for Ireland, 1983.
xxxi,619p.
Includes indexes.
ISBN 0946738009

—Justice of the peace reports / Chichester : Justice of the Peace Ltd., 1983-.
Continues: Justice of the peace and local government reports.

—Kings Bench Decision upon Settlement Cases : From 1732-76 / Repr. of 1776 ed. – Abingdon : Professional Books.
286p.

—Knight's Industrial and Commercial Reports : 1966-75, 17 Vols. / Professional Books Staff. – Abingdon : Professional Books, 1984.

—Knight's industrial and commercial reports / general editor H. Samuels. – 9. – London : Knight, 1966.
Continued by: Knight's industrial reports. Spine title: Knight's industrial reports.

—Knight's industrial reports / general editor H. Samuels. – 8 in 7. – London : Knight, 1971.
Continues: Knight's industrial and commercial reports. - Superseded by: Knight's industrial law reports (1 vol. only). Numbering continued by: Managerial law.

—Labour Arbitration Cases First Series (1948-1972), 24 Vols. / Aurora : Canada Law Book Co.
– (Law Reports).

Back Vols.

—Labour Arbitration Cases (L.A.C.) 1948-72, 24 Vols. / Aurora : Canada Law Book Co.

—Labour Arbitration Cases (L.A.C.) 1973-81, 30 Vols. / Aurora : Canada Law Book Co.
– (Second Ser.).

Back Vols.

—Labour Arbitration Cases (L.A.C.) 1982-Present / Aurora : Canada Law Book Co.
– (Third Ser.).

Back Vols.

Current subscription-Outside Canada

—Labour Arbitration Cases Second Series (1973-1981), 30 Vols. / Aurora : Canada Law Book Co.
– (Law Reports).

Back Vols.

—Labour Arbitration Cases (Second Series) Consolidated Index, List of Awards Vols. 1-30 / Aurora : Canada Law Book Co, 1982.
400p.

—Labour Arbitration Cases Third Series (1982-Present) / Aurora : Canada Law Book Co.
– (Law Reports).

Back Vols.

—Labour Law Cases LLC (Pakistan) : Decisions of Supreme Court, High Courts and Labour Courts on Labour Laws, 21 Vols. / Karachi : Bureau of Labour Publications, 1947-1980.

—Land Compensation Reports : Consolidated Index, Tables of Cases / Aurora : Canada Law Book Co, 1985.
382p. – (Law Reports).

—Land Compensation Reports Current Series (1971-Present) / Aurora : Canada Law Book Co.
– (Law Reports).

Back Vols.

—Land Compensation Reports (L.C.R.) 1971-Present / Aurora : Canada Law Book Co.

—Law England Reports Annual Review Nineteen Eighty-Six / Leading Academic Lawyers. – London : Butterworths, 1987.
ISBN 040687963X Pbk

—Law Journal County Court Reports : 1934-1947, 14 Vols. / Abingdon : Professional Books.

—Law Reporting : Pre-Confederation to the Computer Era / Aurora : Canada Law Book Co.

—Law Reports : 1865-date / Professional Books Staff. – Abingdon : Professional Books, 1984.

—Law Reports Citator / London : LLoyd's of London Press, 1988.

—Law Reports Digest : 1951-1980, 3 Vols. / Professional Books Staff. – Abingdon : Professional Books, 1984.

—Law Reports Digests : 1865-1950, 12 Vols. / Abingdon : Professional Books.

Individual vols.

—Law Reports of Nigeria : 1980-date / Professional Books Staff. – Abingdon : Professional Books, 1984.
This series of law reports provides information and guidance arising from the interpretation of common law principles and customary law by the Nigerian courts. The reports cover all the major Federal courts of Nigeria.

—Law Reports of Nigeria, 3 Vols. / F. A. Ajayi. – London : Butterworths.

—Law reports of the Eastern Region of the Federation of Nigeria : including certain hitherto unreported cases previously decided in the Supreme Court of Nigeria / 2 v. – Enugu? : Government Printer, 1956.
Continued by: Law reports of Eastern Nigeria. Bound with vols. 3-6 of the Law reports of Eastern Nigeria. Popular title: Eastern Region law reports.

—Law reports of the Kwara State of Nigeria ... / compiled by the Law Reporting Committee. – Ilorin : Government Printer, 1979-.

—Law Reports Reprint : 1865-1971, 565 Vols. / Butterworth Staff. – Wellington : Butterworths.

Annual continuation Vols., 1972 to date

—Law Times : 1843-1965, 235 Vols. / Professional Books Staff. – Abingdon : Professional Books, 1984.

—List of constitutional and Privy Council judgments affecting the Isle of Man from 1523 to 1986 and a complete year by year list of written Reasons for Judgment of Her Majesty's High Court of Justice of the Isle of Man and other Manx courts from 1884 to 1986 / compiled and with an introduction by Judy Thornley on the directions of H.M. Attorney General for the Isle of Man. – Douglas : Government Printer, 1987.
94p.
Cover title: A book of precedents.

—Lloyd's Law Reporter : Citator and Subject Index 1987-1988 / London : LLoyd's of London Press, 1989.
ISBN 1850442134 Pbk

—Lloyd's Law Reports : 1919-82, 146 Vols. / Professional Books Staff. – Abingdon : Professional Books, 1984.

—Lloyd's law reports / v. – London : Lloyd's, 1919-.
First published as Lloyd's list law reports. Index in each vol. - Consolidated index (1919-1975), v.1. 1981.

—Lloyd's Law Reports : Bound Volumes, 1919-1987, 158 Vols. / London : LLoyd's of London Press.

—Lloyd's Law Reports : Citator 1919-1986 / London : LLoyd's of London Press, 1988.
ISBN 1850441707 Hbk

—Lloyd's Law Reports : Consolidated Index 1919-1975 / London : LLoyd's of London Press.

—Lloyd's Law Reports : Digest / London : LLoyd's of London Press.

—Lloyd's Law Reports : Digests, 1919-1985, 16 Vols. / London : LLoyd's of London Press.

—Lloyd's Law Reports : Microfiche 1919-1985 / London : LLoyd's of London Press.

—Lloyd's Law Reports : Subject Index 1919-1986, 2 Vols. / London : LLoyd's of London Press, 1988.
ISBN 1850441715 Hbk

—Malayan Cases, Vol 6 / Singapore : Malayan Law Journal, 1980.
ISBN 9971700093 Hbk £135.00

—Managerial law / Hull : Barmarick Publications, 1966-.
'Knight's Industrial Law Reports in their revised edition'. Supersedes: Knight's industrial law reports (1 vol. only). - Continues: Knight's industrial reports.

—Manitoba Decisions (1980-Present) Civil and Criminal Cases / Aurora : Canada Law Book Co.
– (Summary Services, Provincial Ser.).

—Manitoba Decisions Civil and Criminal Cases / Aurora : Canada Law Book Co.

—Manitoba Law Reports : 1884-1962, 67 Vols. / Carswell Legal Publications. – Agincourt : Carswell, 1983.

—Manx law reports / – Oxford : Law Reports International, 1985-.

—Maritime Provinces Reports : 1929-1968, 53 Vols. / Carswell Legal Publications. – Agincourt : Carswell, 1983.

—Modern Cases / Repr. of 1730 ed. – Abingdon : Professional Books.
305p.
Orig. Title : Modern Cases in Law and Equity.

—Modern Reports : From the 21st to the 29th of King Charles II in the King's Bench and Common Pleas, with the Great Case in Chancery, 22. Car 2 Between Fry and Porter / Repr. of 1682 ed. – Abingdon : Professional Books.
304p.

—Motor Vehicle Reports, 50 Vols. / Carswell Legal Publications. – Agincourt : Carswell, 1983.

—Motor Vehicle Reports / Agincourt : Carswell, 1988.
This multi-volume set of books contains the key decisions in motor vehicle law from all Canadian jurisdictions. Discussions include alcoholic related offenses, civil actions relating to motor vehicles, and registration and licensing issues.

—National Industrial Court law reports / Nigeria. – v. – Lagos : Federal Government Press, 1980.
Published by the authority of the National Industrial Court.

—New Brunswick Reports : 1825-1930, 54 Vols. / Carswell Legal Publications. – Agincourt : Carswell, 1983.

—New South Wales Law Reports : 1971-date / Professional Books Staff. – Abingdon : Professional Books, 1984.

—New Zealand Conveyancing and Property Reports / Wellington : Butterworths, 1983.
ISBN 0409701416 Hbk

—New Zealand Law Reports : 1883-date / Professional Books Staff. – Abingdon : Professional Books, 1984.

—New Zealand Law Reports / New Zealand Council of Law Reporting. – Wellington : Butterworths.

—Nigeria Law Reports : 1881-1955, 21 Vols. / London : Sweet & Maxwell.
ISBN 0421121602 Hbk £195.00

—Nigerian bulletin of contemporary law / Benin City : Faculty of Law, University of Benin, 1985-.
Reports of cases in State and Federal courts of superior jurisdiction. Index in each vol..

—Nigerian Commercial Law Reports : 1966 to date / London : Sweet & Maxwell.

Ea. Vol. until 1977

Index 1966-1974

—Nigerian Constitutional Law Reports / Lagos : Nigerian Law Publications, 1981.
ISBN 9782325000 Hbk £60.00
ISBN 9782325007 Hbk £20.00

Vol. 2 1981.
ISBN 9782325008 Hbk £20.00

Vol. 3 1982.
ISBN 9782325009 Hbk £70.00

Vol. 4 1983.
ISBN 9782325333 Hbk £60.00

Vol. 5 1984.
ISBN 9782325147 Hbk £60.00

Vol. 6 1985.
ISBN 9782325155 Hbk £60.00

—Nigerian Criminal Reports / London : Sweet & Maxwell, 1981.
ISBN 090382647X Hbk £201.00

Vol. 1 1980
ISBN 0903826488 Hbk £36.00

Vol. 2 1980
ISBN 090382650X Hbk £36.00

Vol. 1 1981
ISBN 0903826542 Hbk £36.00

Vol. 2 1981
ISBN 0903826526 Hbk £29.00

—Nigerian current law review / – Lagos : Nigerian Institute of Advanced Legal Studies, 1982-.

—Nigerian Current Law Review / London : Sweet & Maxwell, 1982.
ISBN 0421316004 Hbk £35.00

—Nigerian Law Reports, Index-Digest 1881-1981, 2 Vols. / Aba : Law & Educational Publishers, 1984.

1982-83 Supplement
ISBN 9782436038

—Nigerian Supreme Court Law Reports 1956-1983 : Lawyers Edition 1956-1983, 16 Vols. / Aba : Law & Educational Publishers.
ISBN 9782436046 Hbk

—Northern Ireland law reports bulletin of judgements delivered in the High Court of Justice and the Court of Appeal in Northern Ireland / Belfast : Incorporated Council of Law Reporting for Northern Ireland, 1980-.

—Northern Territory Supreme Court judgements : table of cases ... / Northern Territory, Australia. – s.l. : s.n., 1987.
Coverage begins in 1951.

—Northwest Territories Reports / Agincourt : Carswell, 1988.
This text is published under the authority of the Law Society of the Northwest Territories and contains in-depth coverage of cases reported in the Northwest Territories. It includes four parts per year plus a bound volume.

—Northwest Territories Supreme Court Reports : 1887-1898, 2 Vols. / Carswell Legal Publications. – Agincourt : Carswell, 1983.

—Nova Scotia Reports : 1834-1930, 60 Vols. / Carswell Legal Publications. – Agincourt : Carswell, 1983.

—Ontario Decisions Criminal Conviction and Sentence Cases / Aurora : Canada Law Book Co. – (Summary Services, Provincial Ser.).

—Ontario Labour Relations Board Reports : A Monthly Series of Decisions from the Ontario Labour Relations Board / Ontario Labour Relations Board. – Ontario : Ontario Government Publications Service, 1983.
215p.

—Ontario Law Reports (1901-1930), 66 Vols. / Aurora : Canada Law Book Co.
– (Law Reports).

Back Vols.

—Ontario Law Reports (O.L.R.) 1901-1931, 66 Vols. / Law Society of Upper Canada. – Aurora : Canada Law Book Co.
– (Predecessor to the Ontario Reports (O.R.)).

Back Vols.

Table of Cases 1901-1908

—Ontario Law Reports : Tables of Cases (For Vols. 1-66) / Aurora : Canada Law Book Co.
247p. – (Law Reports).

—Ontario Law Reports : Years 1901-1930 / North Ryde : Law Book Co.

—Ontario Municipal Board Reports Current Series (1972-Present) / Aurora : Canada Law Book Co. – (Law Reports).

Back Vols.

—Ontario Municipal Board Reports (O.M.B.R.) 1972-Present / Aurora : Canada Law Book Co.
1000p.

Back Vols.

—Ontario Reports (2d) Consolidated Index, 2 vols / Toronto : Butterworths, 1984.
1296p.

1987 suppl.
ISBN 0409805866 Pbk

—Ontario Reports / Toronto : Butterworths.
ISBN 0409880027 15.00

Bound Vol. 35
ISBN 0409880043 15.00

Bound Vol. 36

Bound Vol. 37
ISBN 0409880086 15.00

Bound Vol. 38
ISBN 0409880116 15.00

Bound Vol. 39
ISBN 0409880159 15.00

Bound Vol. 40
ISBN 0409880183 15.00

Consolidated Index, 2nd series, 2 Vol. set

Supplement 1985 to Index

—Ontario Reports New Series (1963-1973), 26 Vols. / Aurora : Canada Law Book Co.
– (Law Reports).

Back Vols.

—Ontario Reports (O.R.) 1931-62, 32 Vols. / Aurora : Canada Law Book Co.
– (Old Ser.).

Back Vols.

—Ontario Reports (O.R.) 1963-73, 26 Vols. / Aurora : Canada Law Book Co.
– (New Ser.).

Back Vols.

—Ontario Reports (O.R.) 1974-Present / Aurora : Canada Law Book Co.
– (Second Ser.).

Current subscriptions-outside Canada

Current Subscription

—Ontario Reports Old Series (1931-1962), 32 Vols. / Aurora : Canada Law Book Co.
– (Law Reports).

Back Vols.

—Ontario Reports Second Series (1974-Present) / Aurora : Canada Law Book Co.
– (Law Reports).

Back Vols.

—Ontario Weekly Notes, 13 Vols. / Carswell Legal Publications. – Agincourt : Carswell.

Series 1933-1962

—Ontario Weekly Reporter : 1902-1916, 27 Vols. / Agincourt : Carswell.

—Papua New Guinea law reports : cases determined in the Supreme Court of the Territory of Papua and New Guinea, the Supreme Court of Papua New Guinea and in the High Court of Australia / v. – Sydney : Law Book Co., 1963-.

—Planning and Compensation Reports : 1950-1981, 42 Vols. / Abingdon : Professional Books.

—Plateau law reports : containing selected cases decided in the High Court of Plateau State and in the other superior courts in Nigeria including the Supreme Court and the Federal Court of Appeal, and also of certain tribunals / v. – Enugu : Fourth Dimension Publishing, 1981.

—Privy Council judgments : opinions of the Judicial Committee of the Privy Council in appeals from West Africa,1841 to 1973 / by Olisa Chukura. – Ibadan : Gillford, 1981.
xxxii,1063p.
Includes index.

—Proceedings of the Court of Justice of the European Communities / Court of Justice of the European Communities. – Luxembourg : Information Office of the Court of Justice of the European Communities, 1975.

—Property, Planning and Compensation Reports / London : Sweet & Maxwell.

Bound Vol.

Single copy

Back Vols. avail.

—Quebec Law Reports : 1874-1971, 17 Vols. / Agincourt : Carswell, 1983.

—Queensland State Reports : 1860-date / Professional Books Staff. – Abingdon : Professional Books, 1984.

—Real Property Reports : With Consolidated and Cumulative Index / Agincourt : Carswell.

—Remarkable Decisions in the Court of Session : 1716-52, 2 Vols. / 2nd ed. Repr. of 1799 ed. – Abingdon : Professional Books.
57p.

—Reports and Pleas of Assizes at York : 1631-50 / Repr. of 1651 ed. – Abingdon : Professional Books.
335p.

—Reports Court of Chancery : 1737-83 / Repr. of 1790 ed. – Abingdon : Professional Books.
344p.

—Reports King's Bench : 1737-1738 / Repr. of 1754 ed. – Abingdon : Professional Books.
292p.

—Reports of Cases in King's Bench / Repr. of 1766 ed. – Abingdon : Professional Books.
298p.

—Reports of Cases in the Court of King's Bench : With Some Special Cases in the Courts of Chancery, Common Pleas and Exchequer, Alphabetically Digested Under Proper Heads for the 1st of William and Mary to the 10th of Anne (1689-1712, 3 Vols. / Repr. of 1724 ed. – Abingdon : Professional Books.
308p.

—Reports of Family Law : 1824-1970, 5 Vols. / Agincourt : Carswell.
– (Reprint Ser.).

—Reports of Family Law, 50 / Carswell Legal Publications. – Agincourt : Carswell.
– (Second Ser.).

Back Vols.

—Reports of Family Law /. – Agincourt : Carswell.

—Reports of Family Law Consolidated Index, 4 Vols. / Agincourt : Carswell, 1980.
1331p.

Vol. 2 1980.

Vol. 3 1984.

Vol. 4 1986.

—Reports of International Arbitral Awards / United Nations. – London : HMSO, 1982.
532p.
Reports on awards in three arbitration cases; the delimitation of the continental shelf between UK and France, the air service agreement between USA and France, and the taxation liability of EURATOM.
ISBN 0119074761 Hbk £24.75

—Reports of Judgments, Advisory Opinions and Orders / International Court of Justice. – Geneva : United Nations Publications.

ICJ No 523: Case Concerning Border and Transborder Armed Actions (Nicaragua/Costa Rica), Order of 21 October 1986

ICJ No 524: Case Concerning Border and Transborder Armed Actions (Nicaragua/Honduras), Order of 22 October 1986

ICJ No 525: Case Concerning the Frontier Dispute (Burkina Faso/Republic of Mali), Judgment of 22 December 1986

ICJ No 526: Case Concerning Elettronica Sicula S.p.A. (ELSI) (U.S.A./Italy), Order of 2 March 1987, Constitution of Chamber

ICJ No 527: Case Concerning the Frontier Dispute (Burkina Faso/Republic of Mali), Order of 9 April 1987, Nominations of Experts

ICJ No 528: Bibliography No 39, 1985

ICJ No 529: Case Concerning the Land, Island and Maritime Frontier Dispute (El Salvador/Honduras), Order of 8 May 1987, Constitution of Chamber

ICJ No 530: Index 1986

ICJ No 531: Case Concerning the Land, Island and Maritime Frontier Dispute (El Salvador/Honduras), Order of 27 May 1987

ICJ No 532: Application for Review of Judgment No 333 of the United Nations Administrative Tribunal, Advisory Opinion of 27 May 1987

ICJ No 533: Case Concerning the Land, Island and Maritime Frontier Dispute (El Salvador/Honduras), Order of 29 May 1987

ICJ No 534: Case Concerning Border and Transborder Armed Actions (Nicaragua/Costa Rica), Order of 21 July 1987

ICJ No 535: Case Concerning Border and Transborder Armed Actions (Nicaragua/Costa Rica), Order of 19 August 1987

Reports of Judgments, Advisory Opinions and Orders 1986.

Reports of Judgments Advisory Opinions and Orders 1986.

—Reports of Tax Cases : 1875-1982, 53 Vols. / Professional Books Staff. – Abingdon : Professional Books, 1984.

—River State Law Reports Vol. 1 (1980) / River State Law Reporting Committee. – Enugu : Fourth Dimension Publishing, 1982.
304p.
ISBN 9781561866 Hbk £20.00

—Road Traffic Reports : 1986 / N. P. Metcalf. – London : Mason Publications Ltd, 1987.
416p. – (Road Traffic Reports Ser.).
ISBN 0859373398 Hbk £20.00

—Saskatchewan Decisions Citator (1979-1983) / Aurora : Canada Law Book Co, 1983.
– (Statute Services).

—Saskatchewan Decisions : Civil and Criminal Cases (1980-Present) / Aurora : Canada Law Book Co.
– (Summary Services, Provincial Ser.).

—Saskatchewan Decisions Civil and Criminal Cases / Aurora : Canada Law Book Co.

—Saskatchewan Law Reports : 1908-1931, 25 Vols. / Agincourt : Carswell, 1983.
1200p.

—Scots Revised Reports : 1707-1873, 45 Vols. / Abingdon : Professional Books.

Court of Session Cases : 1838-1862, 13 Vols.

Court of Session Cases : 1863-1873, 11 Vols.

House of Lords Cases : 1707-1865, 10 Vols.

Faculty Decisions : 1807-1825, 2 Vols.

Scottish Jurist : 1829-1865, 1 Vol.

Morison's Dictionary : 1806-1816, 2 Vols.

—Scottish Law Reporter : 1865-1924, 61 Vols. / Professional Books Staff. – Abingdon : Professional Books, 1984.

—Select Cases of Newfoundland : 1817-1828 / Repr. of 1938 ed. – Agincourt : Carswell.
600p. – (Carswell's Classic Reprints).
This work is a reprint of a rare 1893 collection of early decisions of the courts of province of Newfoundland, Canada.

—Selected Judgments of the Federal Supreme Court of Nigeria : 1956-60, 3 Vols. / Professional Books Staff. – Abingdon : Professional Books, 1984.
ISBN 0862050480 Hbk £104.00

—Selected Judgments of the High Court of Oyo State : 1976-1980 / Professional Books Staff. – Abingdon : Professional Books, 1984.

—Selected judgments of the Ogun State High Court / Ogun State of Nigeria. – Abeokuta : High Court of Justice, 1978-.

—Session Cases : New Series, 1907-date / Professional Books Staff. – Abingdon : Professional Books, 1984.

—Solomon Islands law reports / Solomon Islands : s.n., 1982.
'Published by authority of the High Court of Solomon Islands'. Annual indexes.

—Solomon Islands Law Reports for 1983, 1984, 1985 / Suva : University of the South Pacific, Institute of Pacific Studies.
296p.

—Some cases heard in the Hooge Raad / reported by Willem Pauw : translated and edited by R. Feenstra, P. van Warmelo, D.T. Zeffertt. – Pretoria : Government Printer on behalf of the South African Law Commission, 1985.
viii,117p. – (Research series).
Includes index. Translation of: Observationes tumultuariae novae.
ISBN 0621097152

—South African Law Reports (1947 to Date) / J. L. Buchanan. – Durban : Butterworths.

—South Australian Reports : 1865-date / Professional Books Staff. – Abingdon : Professional Books, 1984.

—Summaries of the judgements delivered in ... / document prepared by the registry of the Court. – Strasbourg : Council of Europe, 1983.
Contains summary judgements not binding on the Court.

—Supreme Court Decisions / Manila : National Book Store.

Vol. 1 January, 1982 1982.
586p.
ISBN 9710817078 Pbk £6.65

Vol. 2 February, 1982 1982.
388p.
ISBN 9710817086 Pbk £5.00

Vol. 3 March, 1982 1982.
752p.
ISBN 9710800418 Pbk £9.00

Vol. 4 April, 1982 1982.
342p.
ISBN 9710800426 Pbk £5.00

Vol. 5 May, 1982 1982.
352p.
ISBN 9710800434 Pbk £5.50

Vol. 6 June, 1982 1982.
582p.
ISBN 9710800442 Pbk £7.50

Vol. 7 July, 1982 1982.
858p.
ISBN 9710817094 Pbk £12.00

Vol. 8 August, 1982 1982.
510p.
ISBN 9710817108 Hbk £10.00

Vol. 9 September, 1982 1983.
972p.
ISBN 9710800515 Hbk £17.50

Vol. 10 October, 1982 1983.
432p.
ISBN 971080054X £9.50

Vol. 11 November, 1982 1983.
774p.
ISBN 971080085X Hbk £15.00

Vol. 12 December, 1982 1983.
528p.
ISBN 9710801090 Hbk £12.00

Vol. 13 January, 1983 1983.
788p.
ISBN 9710801104 Hbk £12.00

Vol. 14 February, 1983 1983.
479p.
ISBN 9710801767 Hbk £9.50

Vol. 15 March, 1983 1983.
440p.
ISBN 9710802275 Hbk £9.50

Vol. 16 April, 1983 1983.
558p.
ISBN 9710802879 Hbk £12.00

Vol. 17 May, 1983 1983.
720p.
ISBN 9710803557 Hbk £16.00

Vol. 18 June, 1983 1983.
640p.
ISBN 971080393X Hbk £14.00

Vol. 19 July, 1983 1984.
608p.
ISBN 971080412X Hbk £18.00

Vol. 20 August, 1983 1984.
472p.
ISBN 9710805177 Hbk £15.00

—Supreme Court of Canada Decisions (1980-Present) / Aurora : Canada Law Book Co.
– (Summary Services, National Ser.).

—Supreme Court of Canada Decisions / Aurora : Canada Law Book Co.

—Supreme Court of Canada Reports Service, 6 vols / Toronto : Butterworths.

—Supreme Court of Nigeria judgments / Kaduana Nigeria : Liberty Publications, 1987-.

—Supreme Court of Nigeria Law Reports / Lagos : Nigerian Law Publications, 1983.
ISBN 9782325010 Hbk £40.00

—Supreme Court of Nigeria law reports / by Chief Gani Fawehinmi. – Surulere : Nigerian Law Publications, 1984.
Includes indexes.

—Supreme Court on Direct Taxes 1950 to 1986 / Allahabad : Modern Law Publications, 1986.

—Supreme Court Rulings / Manila : National Book Store.

1: January 1984 1984.
147p.
ISBN 9710805223 £7.00

2: February 1984 1984.
152p.
ISBN 9710805460 Hbk £8.00

3: March 1984 1984.
175p.
ISBN 9710806564 Hbk £9.80

4: April 1984 1984.
153p.
ISBN 9710808869 £9.80

5: May 1984 1984.
177p.
ISBN 9710816861 £9.50

6: June 1984 1984.
158p.
ISBN 9710819291 £8.80

7: July 1984 1984.
211p.
ISBN 9710821687 £11.40

8: August 1984 1985.
167p.
ISBN 9710822241 £6.80

—Survey and Analysis of 1979 Supreme Court Decisions and Presidential Decrees / Quezon City : University of the Philippines, Law Center, 1980.

—Sweet and Maxwell's Students' Law Reporter / London : Sweet & Maxwell.
ISBN 0421360909 Hbk £6.50

Summer 1986
ISBN 042136100X Hbk £6.50

Autumn 1986
ISBN 0421361107 Hbk £6.50

—Tanzania law reports / Dar es Salaam : s.n., 1987.
Cover cases decided in the Court of Appeal of Tanzania and the High Court of Tanzania.

—Tasmanian reports / v. – Hobart : Law Book Co. for the Council of Law Reporting of Tasmania, 1897-.
Continues: The Tasmanian state reports.

—Tax Administration Reports, 2 Vols. / Goodman. – Toronto : DeBoo.
This service provides an analysis of every new or revised Interpretation Bulletin and Advance Tax Ruling since November 1985. Analyses contain summaries of bulletin contents, a listing of Income Tax Act and Regulations references, cross-references to other relevant bulletins, and evaluations of Revenue Canada's positions. Semi-monthly updates and a complimentary newsletter are also included.
ISBN 0888202237 loose £275.00

—Tax Reports (New Zealand), 10 Vols. / Wellington : Butterworths, 1986.

Back Vols. avail.

—Times Law Reports : 1884-1952, 71 Vols. / Abingdon : Professional Books.

—Times Law Reports / Professional Books Staff. – Abingdon : Professional Books, 1984.

—Union list of law reports and statutes held in libraries within the City of Liverpool / compiled by Susan Frost, Robert Caley. – Liverpool : Liverpool Polytechnic Library Service, 1985.
30p.

—Value Added Tax Tribunal Reports : 1973-82, 10 Vols. / Professional Books Staff. – Abingdon : Professional Books, 1984.

—Wall Chart of the English Reports Reprint / Agincourt : Carswell.

—West African Court of Appeal Reports : 1930-1960 / London : Sweet & Maxwell, 1960.
ISBN 0421123508 Hbk £260.00

—West Indian Law Reports : 1959-date / Professional Books Staff. – Abingdon : Professional Books, 1984.

—West Indian Reports, 32 Vols. / Butterworth Staff. – London : Butterworths.

Index to Vols. 1-30
This series of law reports covers decisions of The Privy Council and The Courts of Appeal and The Supreme Courts of Jamaica, Trinidad and Tobago, Guyana, and the Eastern Carribean States.

—West Nigerian Law Reports / London : Sweet & Maxwell, Rp 1982 (1955-66).
ISBN 0421291605 Hbk £170.00

—Western Weekly Reports : 1911-1950, 108 Vols. / Carswell Legal Publications. – Agincourt : Carswell, 1983.

Index to Vols. 1-75

—Western Weekly Reports : 1951-1970, 75 Vols. / Carswell Legal Publications. – Agincourt : Carswell, 1983.
– (New Ser. 1951-1970).

Consolidated Index Vols. 1-75

—Western Weekly Reports : 1971-1980, 60 Vols. / Carswell Legal Publications. – Agincourt : Carswell, 1983.

Vol. 1 1987.

—Western Weekly Reports : 1981-1985, 31 Vols. / Agincourt : Carswell, 1981-82.

Individual Vols.

—Zambia industrial cases reports / compiled by K.C. Muwang'u. – v. – Lusaka : Ministry of Labour and Social Services, 1983.

—Zimbabwe law reports / Causeway, Zimbabwe : Ministry of Justice, 1980.
Continues: The Rhodesian law reports. Index in every vol.

LAW REPORTS – AUSTRALIA

—Australian Current Law / Jean Malor. – Butterworths, 1987.
ISBN 0409410543 loose £75.00

—Case notes index 1968-1979 / Monash University Law Library. – 1 microfiche. – Clayton, Vic. : The Law Library, 1980.
Previous ed.: 1968-77, shelved at Depository F1686.

—Intellectual property reports : being reports of judgments of the High Court of Australia, the Federal Court of Australia, the Supreme Courts of the states and territories of Australia, the Patent, Trade Marks and Designs Office, the Copyright Tribunal and incorporating reports of signficant cases decided by the courts in the United Kingdom, the United States of America and other international jurisdictions / editor, James Lahore. – Vol. 1, pt.1 (Oct. 1983)-. – Sydney : Butterworths, 1983-.

—Motor Vehicle Reports / Butterworths.

LAW REPORTS – AUSTRALIA – NORTHERN TERRITORY

—Northern Territory judgments 1951-1976 : a selection of the judgments of the Supreme Court of the Northern Territory of Australia / Canberra : Australian Government Publishing Service, 1982.
xviii,1079p.
Includes indexes which also cover Northern Territory Supreme Court judgments reported in Australian Law Reports, Australian Argus Law Reports and Federal Law Reports. Contains a selection of judgments not reported in Australian Law Reports, Australian Argus Law Reports and Federal Law Reports.
ISBN 0642050309

LAW REPORTS – BARBADOS

—Barbados law reports / Barbados : Ministry of the Attorney General, 1981.
Being published retrospectively. First volume issued: Vol. 11(1976).

LAW REPORTS – BOTSWANA

—Botswana law reports / Gaborone : Government Printer, 1966.
Continues: Bechuanaland law reports,.

LAW REPORTS – CANADA

—Administrative Law Reports / Agincourt : Carswell.

—Canadian Customs and Excise Reports / Grant A. Jameson. – Butterworths.

—Canadian Rights Reporter / Butterworths.

—Case law indexing in Canada / by Mary Burbidge Helleiner. – Ottawa : Canadian Law Information Council, 1980.
v,142p; 28cm. – (Working paper).
Bibliography: p.141-142.

—Case Law Reporting : a selected Bibliography and Checklist of Canadian Law Reporting Studies / Ottawa : Canadian Law Information Council, 1980.
86p.
ISBN 0920358055 Pbk £10.00

—Hughes : Federal Court of Canada Service, 2 Vols. / Butterworths.

—Supreme Court of Canada Reports Service, 6 Vols. / Butterworths.

LAW REPORTS – CANADA – BRITISH COLUMBIA

—British Columbia law reports / Toronto : Carswell, 1977.
Consolidated indexes published for v. 1-10 and v. 31-70.

—Reports of family law / Toronto : Carswell, 1971.
Consolidated indexes published for first and second series.

LAW REPORTS – CANADA – ONTARIO

—Ontario Reports, Second Consolidated Index, 2 Vols. / Butterworths, 1984.
1296p.

Index and Supplement
ISBN 0409844330 Hbk £140.00

Supplement-1988 1988.
544p.
ISBN 0409808970 Pbk £70.00

LAW REPORTS – COMMONWEALTH

—Law reports of the Commonwealth / – Abingdon : Professional Books, 1985.
Includes indexes.

LAW REPORTS – ENGLAND

—Introduction to Fitzherbert's Abridgement / by Frederick Lister Boersma. – Abingdon : Professional Books, 1981.
6,117p; 23cm.
ISBN 0862050413

—Times law reports / v. – Abingdon, Oxon. : Professional Books, 1985.
Index published separately annually and kept up to date by interim issues.

LAW REPORTS – GAMBIA

—Gambia law reports / cyclostyled series. – Banjul : Supreme Court of The Gambia, 1984.
'Cases ... covering the Supreme Court as well as the Court of Appeal' - Preface.

—Judgments and orders in the Gambia court of Appeal / Gambia. – Banjul : The Court, 1982.

LAW REPORTS – GREAT BRITAIN

—Current law / – London : Sweet & Maxwell, 1947.

—Current law year book : being a complete statement of all the law... from every source / v. – London : Sweet & Maxwell, 1948.
Cumulation of monthly Current law. 1947-1951 superseded by Current law consolidation. Master volumes for 1956, 1961, 1966 and 1971.

—Daily law reports index / Hebden Bridge, W. Yorks. : Legal Information Resources, 1988.
v.
ISBN 09550798

—Estates gazette law reports / London : Estates Gazette, 1986-.
Continues : The Estates gazette : digest of land and property cases. Cumulative index published annually as a supplement.

—Financial law reports / London : Sweet & Maxwell, 1985.

—Palmer's company cases / . – London : Stevens, 1985.
Cumulative index.

—Scottish current law / . – Edinburgh : W. Green, 1948.
Contains both Scottish and English law.
ISBN 02656159

—Scottish current law year book : being a complete statement of all the law.. from every source / v. – Edinburgh : W. Green, 1948.
Cumulation of monthly Scottish current law. Master volumes for 1956, 1961, 1966 and 1971. Contains both Scottish and English law.
ISBN 03087166

—Simon's tax cases / . – London : Butterworths, 1974.
Kept up to date by supplement, Simon's weekly tax service. Index in each vol. - Cumulative tables and index, 1973-1985. 1986.

LAW REPORTS – INDIA

—Supreme Court Cases 1987, Vol. 1 / Lucknow : Eastern Book Company, 1987.

LAW REPORTS – IRELAND

—Sir John Davies and the conquest of Ireland / Cambridge : Cambridge University Press.
Examines law reports of Sir John Davies as Solicitor-General and Attorney-General in Ireland in the seventeenth-century. Discusses the use of law in consolidating the conquest of Ireland. Examines the origin of precedent in Anglo-American law.
ISBN 0521253284

LAW REPORTS – ISLE OF MAN

—Manx law bulletin / Douglas : Attorney General's Chambers, 1983-.
Covers legislation 'in a limited manner' and 'all written judgments from the High Courts'.

LAW REPORTS – KENYA

—Kenya Law Reports / Nairobi : East African Publishing House, 1976.

—Kenya law reports / Nairobi : Published under the authority of the Attorney- General of the Republic of Kenya by East African Publishing House, 1981.

Continues in part: East Africa law reports.

LAW REPORTS – NEW ZEALAND

—Butterworths Current Law / Butterworths.

—Butterworths District Court Reports / Butterworths.

—Butterworths Family Law Reports / Butterworths.

—Gazette Law Reports of New Zealand 1898-1952 microform , 54 Vols. / Butterworths.

—New Zealand Conveyancing and Property Reports / Butterworths, 1983.
ISBN 0409701416 Hbk £71.50

—New Zealand Law Reports / Butterworths.

—Tax Reports New Zealand / Butterworths.

LAW REPORTS – NIGERIA

—Federation of Nigeria law reports / . – Ibadan : Evans Brothers, 1981.
Volume numbering begins anew each year.

—Judgments of the Supreme Court of Nigeria / Nigeria. – Lagos : Department of Information Printing Division, 1981-.
Continues: Reserved judgments of the Supreme Court of Nigeria. 'Published by authority of the Supreme Court'.

—Nigeria Court of Appeal reports / Yaba : MIJ Publishers, 1985-.

—Nigerian law times reports / Benin City? : Patrac, 1986.
ISBN 07945892

—Quarterly law reports of Nigeria / Ibadan : University Press, 1986.
Includes practice notes.

—Shari'a law reports / Zaria, Nigeria : Centre for Islamic Studies, Ahmadu Bello University, 1980.
Variant title: Shari'ah law reports. Numbering irregular. In English and Hausa.

—Western Nigeria law reports / Western Region of Nigeria. – 3. – London : Reprinted for the Institute of Advanced Legal Studies, Lagos, Nigeria by Sweet & Maxwell, 1955.
Originally published as: Law reports of cases decided in the Federal Supreme Court (on appeal from the High Court of the Western Region) and the High Court of the Western Region / edited by the Committee for Law Reporting, Western Region, Nigeria. - Ibadan : Government Printer, 1956-1967?. Original title varies.
ISBN 0421291605

LAW REPORTS – NORTHERN IRELAND

—Digest of Northern Ireland law / Belfast : SLS Legal Publications, 1988.
looseleaf.
Includes indexes.

LAW REPORTS – SCOTLAND

—Greens weekly digest : current Scottish case law / Edinburgh : W. Green, 1986.
looseleaf.

—Scottish current law / v. – Edinburgh : W. Green, 1948.
Contains both Scottish and English law.
ISBN 02656159

—Scottish current law year book : being a complete statement of all the law.. from every source / v. – Edinburgh : W. Green, 1948.
Cumulation of monthly Scottish current law. Master volumes for 1956, 1961, 1966 and 1971. Contains both Scottish and English law.
ISBN 03087166

—Session cases / 3-4 parts. – Edinburgh : T & T Clark.
The official law reports in Scotland. Publication commenced in 1821. Prepared and edited by members of the Scottish Bar, the judgements are checked and revised by the judges. Where appropriate, exerpts from the written pleadings and arguments of counsel are included. The reports cover actions in the supreme civil and criminal courts (Justiciary cases) in Scotland, as well as civil cases appealed to the House of Lords. Each annual volume contains an index and case tables.

LAW REPORTS – SEYCHELLES

—Seychelles law reports / . – Seychelles : Government Printer, .

LAW REPORTS – SOUTH AFRICA

—Juta's index and annotations to the South African law reports 1980-86 / compiled by David S. Fisher and Alan James : assisted by Owen J. Barrow ... et al. – Cape Town : Juta, 1987.
1100p.
Kept up-to-date by supplements.
ISBN 0702118508

LAW REPORTS – YUKON TERRITORY

—Yukon reports / . – Fredericton, New Brunswick : Maritime Law Book, 1986-.

LAW REPORTS, DIGESTS, ETC. – SEYCHELLES

—Seychelles digest / by M.J. Gerard Lalouette. – 1. – Oxford : African Law Reports, 1982.
Covers cases from 1936 onwards.

LAW SOCIETIES – CANADA

—Law Society of Upper Canada - Special Lectures Series / Law Society of Upper Canada. – Toronto : DeBoo, 1980-83.
ISBN 0888201729 Hbk Four vol. set 175.00
Thirty-One vol. set incl. index

LAW SOCIETIES – GREAT BRITAIN

—Handbook for Local Law Societies / London : Law Society.

LAW TEACHERS – CANADA

—Canadian law professors : a report to the Consultative Group on Research and Education in Law based on the 1981 survey of full-time law professors in Canada / John S. McKennirey. – Ottawa : Consultative Group on Research and Education in Law, 1982.
viii,133p.

—Canadian law professors : a staff report on the survey of full-time law professors in Canada / submitted to the Consultative Group on Research and Education in Law by John S. McKennirey. – Ottawa : Social Sciences and Humanities Research Council of Canada, 1982.
vi,51,92 leaves.

—Law and learning : report to the Social Science and Humanities Research Council of Canada / by the Consultative Group on Research and Education in Law. – Ottawa : The Council, 1983.
ix, 186, 212, x p.; 23 cm.
English and French. Title on added t.p.: Le droit et le savoir. Includes bibliographies.
ISBN 0662524365 pbk.

LAW TEACHERS - GREAT BRITAIN

—Handbook 1980 / Assocation of Law Teachers. - Coalville : Association of Law Teachers, 1980.
75p.

—Handbook / The Association of Law Teachers. - Sheffield? : Association of Law Teachers, 1986.
80p.

LAW (THEOLOGY)

—Jurisprudence of the living oracles / Tunji Braithwaite. - Benin City, Nigeria : Ethiope, 1987.
xviii,308p.
Bibliography: p.296-297 . - Includes index. Includes the texts of the Charter of the United Nations and Statute of the International Court of Justice, and the Universal Declaration of Human Rights.
ISBN 9781233176

LAWYERS - ENGLAND

—State of knowledge about the English legal profession / by Michael Zander. - Chichester : Barry Rose, 1980.
ix,91p.
ISBN 0859921700

LAWYERS - GREAT BRITAIN

—Legal profession in England and Wales / Richard L. Abel. - Oxford, Oxfordshire, UK : Blackwell, 1988.
xxiii, 548p.
Includes index. Bibliography: p.507-537.
ISBN 0631141111

LAWYERS - PAPUA NEW GUINEA

—Seminar on a legal profession act for Papua New Guinea : Port Moresby, 4th & 5th of May 1982 / Law Reform Commission and Legal Training Institute. - 1. - Waigani : Law Reform Commission of Papua New Guinea, 1982.
various pagings. - (LRC Working Paper).

LAY PROSECUTORS - AUSTRALIA

—Standing in public interest litigation / Law Reform Commission. - Canberra : Australian Government Publishing Service, 1985.
xxx,273p. - (Report).
Bibliography: p.259-263 - Includes index.
ISBN 0644013109

LAYOFF SYSTEMS

—Workforce reductions in undertakings : policies and measures for the protection of redundant workers in seven industrialised market economy countries / edited by Edward Yemin. - Geneva : International Labour Office, 1982.
x, 214 p.; 24 cm.
Includes bibliographical references.
ISBN 9221029107 hard

LAYOFF SYSTEMS - GREAT BRITAIN

—Twenty years of statutory redundancy payments in Great Britain / Paul Lewis. - Nottingham : The Universities of Leeds and Nottingham in association with the Institute of Personnel Management, 1985.
50p; 21cm.
ISBN 0900572639

LEAGUE OF NATIONS

—League of Nations in retrospect : proceedings of the symposium / organized by the United Nations Library and the Graduate Institute of International Studies, Geneva, 6-9 November 1980 La Societe des Nations, retrospective : actes du colloque / organise par la Bibliotheque des Nations Unies et l'Institut universitaire de hautes etudes internationales, Geneve 6-9 novembre 1980. - Berlin : W. de Gruyter, 1983.
xii, 427 p.; 24 cm. - (Serial publications / United Nations Library, Geneva. Series E, Guides and studies).
Includes bibliographical references and index.
ISBN 3110087332 £77.00 DM154.00

—League of Nations : its life and times 1920-1946 / F.S. Northedge. - Leicester : Leicester University Press, 1985.
viii,342p; 22cm.
Bibliography: p311-316. - Includes index.
ISBN 0718511948 £28.00

LEASES - AUSTRALIA

—Sackville and Neave Property Law : Cases and Materials / C. Rossiter. - 4th ed. - Sydney : Butterworths, 1988.
992p.
The fourth edition of this casebook contains revised materials on the Trade Practices Act, leases, and mortgages.

LEASES - CANADA

—Commercial Real Estate Leasing / Vancouver : Continuing Legal Education Society of British Columbia, 1986.
562p.
ISBN 0865042934 Hbk £85.00

—Lease Drafting / Vancouver : Continuing Legal Education Society of British Columbia, 1985.
252p.
ISBN 0865042004 Hbk £55.00

—Leasing, 1984 / Vancouver : British Columbia Continuing Legal Education Society, 1984.
ISBN 0865041598 Hbk £60.00

—Leasing for General Practitioners / Vancouver : Continuing Legal Education Society of British Columbia, 1986.
166p.
ISBN 0865042942 Hbk £65.00

—O'Brien's Encyclopedia of Forms : Division Four-Leases / Aurora : Canada Law Book Co. - (Abridgments and Encyclopedias).

LEASES - ENGLAND

—Handbook of leasehold reform / C.C. Hubbard and Delyth W. Williams. - 21. - London : Sweet & Maxwell, 1988.
loose-leaf; 32cm.
Includes index.
ISBN 0421351306 £80.00

—Landlord and tenant law : privity of contract and estate / the Law Commission. - London : HMSO, 1988.
v,67p. - (H.C. 1988-89).
Includes the text of a draft Landlord and Tenant (Covenants) bill.
ISBN 0102008892

—Leasehold enfranchisement / by N.T. Hague. - 2nd ed. - London : Sweet & Maxwell, 1987.
xxxix,519p; 25cm.
Previous ed.: 1967. Includes index.
ISBN 0421283602 £35.00

—Leasehold law / Trevor M. Aldridge. - London : Oyez Longman, 1980.
looseleaf.
Includes index.
ISBN 0851204716

—Understanding residential leases / by Charles Boston. - 2nd ed. - London : Sweet & Maxwell, 1986.
22p; 21cm.
ISBN 0421366109 Pbk £1.75

LEASES - GREAT BRITAIN

—Drafting and Negotiating Commercial Leases / 2nd ed. - London : Butterworths, 1984.
ISBN 0406359075 Hbk £29.00

—Drafting Business Leases / 2nd ed. - London : Longman Professional, 1986.
ISBN 0851210244 Hbk £28.95

—Drafting residential leases / 2nd. - 1193, 1989.
Coverage includes the terms of the lease, premises, easements and ancillary rights, rents and rent increases, service charges anmd insurance. New edition covers changes resulting from the Housing Act 1988.
ISBN 0851214355 Hbk £35.00

—Landlord and tenant : privity of contract and estate : duration of liability of parties to leases / the Law Commission. - London : HMSO, 1986.
iv,101p. - (Working paper).
Includes bibliographical references.
ISBN 0117301760

—Practical lease precedents / London : Longman Professional, 1988.
ISBN 0851211542 loose £95.00

—Practical lease precedents / London : Longman Professional (UK).
Provides forms of leases, tenancy agreements and licenses for offices, shops, industrial and storage property, other business property, residential property and agricultural property. Forms commence with a summary of the five vital provisions: rent, repairs, decorations, insurance, and dealings.
ISBN 0851211542 Llf £98.00

—Residential leases : draftsman's handbook / London : Longman Professional, 1985.
ISBN 085120774X Pbk £19.95

—Sale and Management of Flats : Practice and Precedents / London : Butterworths, 1985.
This book provides a practical guide to the subject of leasehold conveyancing in the United Kingdom. Particular attention is given to the establishment and maijntenance of subsequent management of the property from the tenant's and developer's point of view.
ISBN 0406526702 Hbk

LEASES - SCOTLAND

—Drafting and Negotiating Common Leases Scotland / McKichan. - London : Butterworths, 1985.
ISBN 0406359067 Hbk £41.50

—Introduction to the Scottish Law of Leases / London : Butterworths, 1988.
ISBN 0406105898 Pbk

—Irritancies in leases / Scottish Law Commission. - Edinburgh : Scottish Law Commission, 1981.
42p. - (Memorandum).

—Irritancies in leases : report on a reference under section 3(1)(e) of the Law Commissions Act 1965 / Scottish Law Commission. - Edinburgh : H.M.S.O., 1983.
vi,41p.
ISBN 0101876009

—Recovery of possession of heritable property / Scottish Law Commission. - Edinburgh : The Commission, 1984.
iii,122p. - (Consultative memorandum no 59).
Includes bibliographical references.

—Report on the Scottish term and quarter days / presented to Parliament by the Lord Advocate by Command of Her Majesty, October 1987. - Edinburgh : HMSO, 1987.
vi,29p.
ISBN 0101020821

—Research paper on actions of ejection and removing / by A.G.M. Duncan. - Edinburgh : Law Commission, 1984.
xv,204p.
'Published by the Scottish Law Commission in connection with Consultative Memorandum No. 59'. Includes bibliographical references.

LEASES - SOUTH AFRICA

—Law of sale and lease / by A.J. Kerr. - Durban, South Africa : Butterworth Publishers, 1984.
xxxii, 352 p.; 25 cm.
Includes indexes.
ISBN 0409037508 pbk.

LEAVE OF ABSENCE - AUSTRALIA

—Long service leave / by Hugh Selby : with a foreword by F.V. Watson. - Sydney : Law Book Co., 1983.
xxviii,150p.
Includes index.
ISBN 0455204519

LEBANON

—Focus on Beirut / by Georg Schwarzenberger. - Leeds : University of Leeds, 1983.
11p.
Bibliography: p.10-11.

—Witness of war crimes in Lebanon / testimony given to the Nordic Commission, Oslo, October 1982. - London : EAFORD, 1983.
xviii,146p; 22cm.
ISBN 0863720056 Pbk £4.50

LEGAL AID

—Access to justice and the welfare state / edited by Mauro Cappelletti : with the assistance of John Weisner and Monica Seccombe. - Alphen aan den Rijn : Sijthoff, 1981.
xiv,365p.
Revised reports considered at the Access to Justice conference, October 15-18, 1979.
ISBN 9028625410 Hbk £76.00

—International directory of legal aid / edited by Judy Lane and Simon Hillyard. - London : International Bar Association, 1985.
244p; 21cm.
ISBN 0421325607 Hbk £30

—Legal Aid and Advice : Replies made by Governments to the Questionnaire on Legal Aid and Advice / Strasbourg : Council of Europe, 1978.

—Legal aid : annual reports of the Law Society and of the Lord Chancellor's Advisory Committee / Law Society of Northern Ireland. - Belfast : H.M.S.O., 1983.
Continues: Report of the Incorporated Law Society of Northern Ireland on the Legal Aid Scheme; and, Report of the Legal Aid Advisory Committee on the Report of the Incorporated Law Society of Northern Ireland. 1981/1982 issue includes 16th (final) Report of the Law Society of Northern Ireland on legal aid in criminal proceedings.

—Neighborhood law firms for the poor: a comparative study of recent developments in legal aid and in the legal profession / Alphen aan den Rijn : Sijthoff and Noordhoff, 1980.
xxi, 259p.

—Windsor yearbook of access to justice / Recueil annuel de Windsor d'acces a la justice. - Windsor, Ontario : University of Windsor, 1981.

LEGAL AID - AUSTRALIA

—Aboriginal legal aid / House of Representatives Standing Committee on Aboriginal Affairs, July 1980. - Canberra : Australian Government Publishing Service, 1980.
xvi,252p.
At head of t.p.: The Parliament of the Commonwealth of Australia.
ISBN 0642051593

—Accountability through self-evaluation : an introduction to self-evaluation for legal aid agencies / Canberra : Commonwelth Legal Aid Commission, 1981.
20p.

—Annual report / Commonwealth Legal Aid Council / 4 v. - Canberra : Australian Government Publishing Service, 1982-.
Continues: Annual report / Commonwealth Legal Aid Commission. Report year runs 1 July to 30 June.

—Annual report / Legal Aid Commission (A.C.T.) / Australian Capital Territory. - Canberra : Australian Government Publishing Service, 1978-.
Report year runs 1 July to 30 June.

—Directory of legal aid services in Australia / Commonwealth Legal Aid Commission. – Canberra : Australian Government Publishing Service, 1980.
iv,114p; 25cm.
'Cat. no. 79 8998 8'.
ISBN 0642047243

—Legal aid cost comparison : salaried and private lawyers / by G.G. Meredith. – Canberra : Australian Government Publishing Service, 1983.
viii,61p.
Bibliography: p.61. At head of title: Commonwealth Legal Aid Council, Attorney-General's Department.
ISBN 0644025441

—Legal service bulletin / assisted by the Fitzroy Legal Service. – Clayton, Vic. : Faculty of Law, Monash University, 1974.
Cumulative index: vols. 1-10 (1974-1985) published separately, 1986.
ISBN 08173516

—Relationship between legal aid agencies and social agencies : research report for the Commonwealth Legal Aid Council / by Peter Hanks, Kate Lavender, Guy Powles. – Canberra : Australian Government Publishing Service, 1983.
51p.
Bibliography: p.48.
ISBN 0644024674

—Report of Providing and Funding Legal Aid Conference / Canberra : Commonwealth Legal Aid Commission, 1981.
46,8p; 25cm.
ISBN 0642895538

LEGAL AID - CANADA - QUEBEC

—Evaluation of legal aid : final report / Quebec. – 1 v. – Montreal? : Ministere de la justice du Quebec, Service de la statistique, 1983.
various pagings.
Includes bibliographical references.

LEGAL AID - ENGLAND

—Improving access to civil justice : the report of the Law Society's Working Party on the Funding of Litigation / Law Society. – London : Law Society, 1987.
11p.
Supplement to the Law Society's Gazette. Includes bibliographical references.

—Law in the balance : legal services in the 1980s / edited by Philip A. Thomas. – Oxford : Robertson, 1982.
x,245p; 23cm.
Includes bibliographies and index.
ISBN 0855204443 Hbk £18.50
ISBN 0855204826 Pbk £6.50

—Legal aid : efficiency scrutiny / Lord Chancellors Department. – 2 v. – London : The Department, 1986.

—Legal aid in England and Wales : a new framework / presented to Parliament by the Lord Chancellor .. – London : H.M.S.O., 1987.
ii,22p; 30cm.
ISBN 0101011822

—Price of justice : costs and defendants / Howard Levenson. – London : Cobden Trust, 1981.
88p.
ISBN 0900137177

LEGAL AID - GREAT BRITAIN

—Assessing Legal Aid Costs / London : Longman Professional, 1984.
ISBN 0851209629 Pbk £8.95

—Criminal Legal Aid 1984 / London : Law Society.

—Law centres news / quarterly bulletin of the Law Centres Federation. – London : The Federation, 1979 -.

—Legal aid handbook 1981 / prepared by the Law Society. – 5th ed. – London : H.M.S.O., 1981.
329p; 25cm.

ISBN 0113906307

—Legal aid handbook 1983 / prepared by the Law Society. – 5th i.e. 6th ed. – London : H.M.S.O., 1983.
v,351p.
Includes index.
ISBN 0113906331

—Legal aid handbook 1984 / prepared by the Law Society. – London : HMSO, 1984.
v,404p; 25cm.
ISBN 0113906358 £6.95

—Legal aid handbook 1986 / prepared by the Law Society. – 7th ed. – London : HMSO, 1986.
v,460p.
Contains eligibility tables, a list of legal aid forms with explanatory notes, all Acts and Regulations covering legal aid, notes for guidance issued by the Council of the Law Society, practice directions and articles on criminal legal aid.
ISBN 0113800010 £7.95

—Legal Aid - How to use it / Levenson. – London : Legal Action Group, 1985.
ISBN 0905099095 Pbk £11.00

—Legal Aid Summary / New ed. – London : Oyez Longman, 1983.
ISBN 0851205879 Hbk

—Meeting legal needs? : an evaluation of a scheme for personal injury victims / Hazel Genn. – Oxford : SSRC Centre for Socio-Legal Studies, 1982.
ix,69p; 22cm.
A report commissioned by the Greater Manchester Legal Services Committee.
ISBN 0862260442

—Memorandum to the Lord Chancellor's Advisory Committee on Legal Aid / JUSTICE. – S.l. : JUSTICE, 1984.
9p; 30cm.

—Perspective on Legal Aid / London : Pinter Publishers Ltd.

—Practical Legal Aid / 3rd ed. – London : Oyez Longman, 1982.
– (Oyez Longman Practice Note Ser.: No. 62).
ISBN 0851205860 Hbk £11.95

—Thirty-Second Legal Aid Annual Report of the Law Society and of the Lord Chancellor's Advisory Committee 1981-82 / London : HMSO, 1983.
ISBN 0102189838 Hbk £9.25

LEGAL AID - NEW ZEALAND

—Access to the law : a research and discussion peper / New Zealand. – Wellington : The Division, 1981.
214p. – (Study series).
Bibliography: p.203-204.

LEGAL AID - SCOTLAND

—Compendium of Legal Aid and Advice Nineteen Eighty-Three : Extracted from the Parliament House Book / W. Green and Son Publishing. – Edinburgh : W Green, 1983.
ISBN 0414007220 Hbk £5.00

—Law and Practice of Legal Aid in Scotland / 2nd ed. – Edinburgh : W Green, 1985.
ISBN 0414007638 loose £18.00

LEGAL AID - SOUTH AFRICA

—Legal aid and law clinics in South Africa : proceedings of a conference held at the Howard College School of Law, University of Natal, Durban, from 11-13 July 1983 / Durban : School of Law, Howard College, University of Natal, 1985.
ix,163p.
ISBN 0869804251

—Outline of legal aid in South Africa / by David J. McQuoid-Mason. – Durban : Butterworths, 1982.
xxvii,310p.
Bibliography: pxiii-xvi.
ISBN 0409040894

LEGAL ASSISTANCE

—Access to justice and the welfare state / edited by Mauro Cappelletti : with the assistance of John Weisner and Monica Seccombe. – Alphen aan den Rijn : Sijthoff, 1981.
xiv,365p.
Revised reports considered at the Access to Justice conference, October 15-18, 1979.
ISBN 9028625410 Hbk £76.00

LEGAL ASSISTANCE - AUSTRALIA

—Community legal education : preventive legal aid : proceedings of the Commonwealth Legal Aid Commission Seminar / edited by Ben Boer. – Canberra : Commonwealth Legal Aid Commission, 1980.
339p; 25cm.
Includes bibliographical references. Includes index.
ISBN 0642897344

LEGAL ASSISTANCE - ENGLAND

—Duty solicitor scheme, HMP Strangeways / North Western Legal Services Committee. – S.l. : The Committee, 1985.
30p.

LEGAL ASSISTANCE - GREAT BRITAIN

—Be Well Advised : A Visual Guide to Legal Pitfalls For the Layman / London : Law Society, 1980.

—Board of visitor adjudications / David Smith, Claire Austin and John Ditchfield. – London : Home Office, 1981.
v,45p. – (Research Unit paper).
Bibliography: p40.
ISBN 0862520045 Unpriced

—Legal advice and assistance / London : Policy Studies Institute, 1989.
160; 21.
A study commissioned by the Law Society to examine social welfare advice. Surveys the nature of the work of solicitors and advice services and their inter-relationship in thre areas - the London Borough of Newham, the Metropolitan Borough of Oldham, and Cornwall.
ISBN 0853744769 Pbk £6.95

—Legal services for low income persons in the United States and Britain : trends for consideration in Australia / Edna R. Chamberlain. – Canberra : Commonwealth Legal Aid Commission, 1981.
30p.
Includes bibliographical references.

—Rent arrears and the courts : a report by the Lay Advocacy Service / by Les Burrows. – Bristol : Lay Advocacy Service, 1986.
63p.
ISBN 0951115006

LEGAL ASSISTANCE - UNITED STATES

—Legal services for low income persons in the United States and Britain : trends for consideration in Australia / Edna R. Chamberlain. – Canberra : Commonwealth Legal Aid Commission, 1981.
30p.
Includes bibliographical references.

LEGAL ASSISTANTS - ENGLAND

—Barristers' clerks : the law's middlemen / John A. Flood. – Manchester : Manchester University Press, 1983.
vii,164p; 23cm.
Bibliography: p157-162. - Includes index.
ISBN 0719009286 £17.50

LEGAL COMPOSITION

—Elements of drafting / by E.L. Piesse. – 6th ed. – Sydney : Law Book Co., 1981.
xv,154p; 19cm.
Bibliography: p.ix-x. - Includes index.
ISBN 0455202559

LEGAL COMPOSITION - CANADA

—Legal drafting / by Robert C. Dick. – 2nd ed. – Toronto : Carswell, 1985.
xiii,234p.
Includes bibliographical references and index.
ISBN 045937740X

—Manual of instructions for legislative and legal writing / Elmer A. Driedger. – Ottawa : Canadian Government Publishing Centre, 1982.
6 v, vi, 568.; 25 cm.
Includes bibliographical references.
ISBN 0660111187 pbk. : set £25.00 (£30.00 other countries)

LEGAL COMPOSITION - GREAT BRITAIN

—Small print : the language and layout of consumer contracts : Report to the National Consumer Council / Martin Cutts and Chrissie Maher : Plain English Campaign. – London : National Consumer Council, 1983.
39p.
ISBN 0905653661

LEGAL CRUELTY - GREAT BRITAIN

—Marital violence : the community response / Margaret Borkowski, Mervyn Murch, Val Walker. – London : Tavistock, 1983.
x,230p; 23cm.
Bibliography: p216-222. - Includes index.
ISBN 0422781207 Hbk Unpriced
ISBN 0422781304 Pbk Unpriced

—Private violence and public policy : the needs of battered women and the response of the public services / edited by Jan Pahl. – London : Routledge & Kegan Paul, 1985.
vi,214p; 22cm.
Bibliography: p196-207. - Includes index.
ISBN 0710099924 Pbk £6.95

LEGAL DOCUMENTS

—Disposal and retention of documents / the Institute of Chartered Secretaries and Administrators. – London? : Institute of Chartered Secretaries and Administrators, 1980.
32p.

LEGAL DOCUMENTS - CANADA

—Legal Secretary's Handbook / Toronto : Butterworths, 1986.
288p.
Contains standard forms (not found in the Rules of Civil Procedure), prescribed Forms and proper usage, examinations for discovery and discovery of documents, pleadings, defences, counterclaims, crossclaims, third and subsequent party claims, amendments of pleadings, briefs, preparation of pleadings, discovery and trial briefs assembly of documents and sample Indexes.
ISBN 0409801720 Hbk £40.00

LEGAL DOCUMENTS - CANADA - QUEBEC

—Quebec Legal Documentation at the Beginning of the 80's : the Results of a Survey / Ottawa : Canadian Law Information Council, 1981.
30p.
ISBN 0920358160 Pbk £10.00

LEGAL DOCUMENTS - GREAT BRITAIN

—Service of Documents / London : Oyez Longman, 1982.
– (Oyez Longman Practice Note Ser.: No. 73).
ISBN 0851206867 Hbk £7.95

LEGAL DOCUMENTS - IRELAND

—Hague Convention on the Service Abroad of Judicial and Extrajudicial Documents in Civil or Commercial Matters (1965) / the Law Reform Commission. - Dublin : The Commission, 1987.
vii,36p. - (LRC).
Includes the text of the convention. Cover title: Service of documents abroad re civil proceedings.

LEGAL DOCUMENTS - SCOTLAND

—Formulary of old Scots legal documents / compiled by Peter Gouldesbrough : with a supplementary essay on Early Scottish conveyancing by Gordon Donaldson. - Edinburgh : Stair Society, 1985.
viii,196p.
Includes index.
ISBN 0902292110

LEGAL EDUCATION

—Journal of the Society of Public Teachers of Law : 1924-date / Abingdon : Professional Books.

—Legal Training Course on Trademarks / Geneva : World Intellectual Property Organization, 1982.
ca 600p.

LEGAL EDUCATION - ASIA

—Teaching and Research in International Law in Asia and the Pacific / Paris : UNESCO.
ISBN 9231023950 Hbk £60.00

—Teaching and Research in International Law in Asia and the Pacific / Paris : UNESCO.
ISBN 9231023950 Hbk £60.00

LEGAL EDUCATION - AUSTRALIA

—Mastering Law Studies and Law Exam Techniques / Sydney : Butterworths, 1986.
184p.
This book is designed to show students how to learn law and organize their study habits using exam-oriented techniques. Sample exam questions and answers are included. Other sections discuss study hints and how to read and brief a case.

—Understanding Law / Netthelm. - Sydney : Butterworths, 1984.
147p.
This introductory text for first year law students provides an overview of the Australian legal system. Emphasized are the ways in which laws are made and the function of courts and lawyers. A list of suggested further reading is also included.
ISBN 0409493724

LEGAL EDUCATION - AUSTRALIA - TASMANIA

—Textbook for Legal Studies - Tasmania / Butterworths, 1983.
322p.
ISBN 0409491209 Hbk £23.00

LEGAL EDUCATION - CANADA

—Approach to Searching for Research and Evaluation Reports in the Field of Public Legal Education and Information (PLEI) / Ottawa : Canadian Law Information Council, 1984.
28p.
ISBN 0920358608 Pbk £7.50

—Cambridge Lectures 1979 / Toronto : Butterworths, 1981.
304p.

—Canadian Directory of Public Legal Education and Information /. - Ottawa : Canadian Law Information Council.
ISBN 0662104536 Hbk £5.00

P.E.I.
ISBN 0662104609 Hbk £3.00

—Canadian law faculties : a report to the Consultative Group on Research and Education in Law based on the 1981 survey of Canadian law faculties and statistics of the Canadian deans of law / John S. McKennirey. - Ottawa : Consultative Group on Research and Education in Law, 1982.
149p.

—Change : a Time for Reflection : a National Invitational Symposium on Public Legal Education / Ottawa : Canadian Law Information Council, 1983.
150p.
ISBN 0920358438 Pbk £15.00

—Directory of Canadian graduate programmes in law / editor: William H. Angus : redacteur: William H. Angus. - S.l : Association of Canadian Law Teachers, 1980.
ii,125p.
'Sponsored by the Section on Graduate Legal Studies of the Association of Canadian Law Teachers'.

—Directory of Law Teachers / Agincourt : Carswell, 1987-1988.
180p.

—Historical Introduction to Legal Studies / Agincourt : Carswell, 1982.
411p.
This textbook for Canadian law students examines the historical development of the Canadian Constitution and the legal institution of Canada from their Anglo-Saxon origins to the present.

—How to Study Law in Canada / Butterworths, 1988.
72p.
Examines how to approach research problems and exam questions. Also includes brief outlines of major subject areas, and tactical tips on how to best structure your time and select the most appropriate courses for career development. Looks at extra-curricular activities, and contains a glossary of legal words and phrases.
ISBN 0409806056 Pbk £5.00

—Introduction to the Study of Law / 3rd ed. - Agincourt : Carswell, 1987.
ISBN 0459302418 Hbk £11.50

—Law School Orientation : Cases and Materials / Agincourt : Carswell, 1986.
341p.
This work for law students provides a series of introductory readings, cases, and materials for students beginning their studies at American law schools.

—Review and Analysis of Canadian PLEI Research / Ottawa : Canadian Law Information Council, 1983.
104p.
ISBN 0920358527 Pbk £7.50

LEGAL EDUCATION - CANADA - BRITISH COLUMBIA

—Canadian Directory of Public Legal Education and Information / Ottawa : Canadian Law Information Council.
ISBN 0662104544 Hbk £5.00

LEGAL EDUCATION - CANADA - ONTARIO

—Canadian Directory of Public Legal Education and Information /. - Ottawa : Canadian Law Information Council.
ISBN 0662104587 Hbk £5.00

—Fiercest Debate : Caesar Wright, the Benchers, and Legal Education in Ontario / Jerome E. Bickenbach. - Toronto : University of Toronto Press, 1987.
ca 374p.
ISBN 0802039863 Hbk £40.00

LEGAL EDUCATION - CANADA - QUEBEC

—Canadian Directory of Public Legal Education and Information /. - Ottawa : Canadian Law Information Council.
ISBN 0662902726 Hbk £5.00

LEGAL EDUCATION - COMMONWEALTH

—Directory of Schools of Law in the Commonwealth 1985 / London : Commonwealth Secretariat.

—Directory of schools of law in the Commonwealth / Commonwealth Legal Education Association. - London : The Association, 1983.
56p.

—Directory of schools of law in the Commonwealth / Commonwealth Legal Education Association. - 1985. - London : The Association, 1985.
60p.

LEGAL EDUCATION - ENGLAND

—'A' Level law / Brian Hogan, Peter Seago, Geoffrey Bennett. - London : Sweet & Maxwell, 1983.
xxix,521p; 23cm.
Includes index.
ISBN 0421297905 Hbk Unpriced
ISBN 0421298006 Pbk £6.50

—A-Level English Law / Scott. - 6th ed. - London : Butterworths, 1984.
This work includes theoretical and empirical material designed to set legal principles in a sociological context for students requiring an introduction to the English legal system.
ISBN 0406657076 Hbk
ISBN 0406657084 Pbk

—'A' Level Law / 2nd ed. - Plymouth : Macdonald & Evans, 1984.
ISBN 0712101926 Pbk £4.95

—'A' Level Law / London : Butterworths, 1988.
ISBN 0406208506 Pbk £9.95

—'A' Level Law / Pannett. - London : Financial Training, 1988.
- (SWOT).
ISBN 1851850651 Pbk £7.50

—'A' level law : cases and materials / Brian Hogan, Peter Seago, Geoffrey Bennett. - London : Sweet & Maxwell, 1986.
xxvii,507p; 22cm.
Includes index.
ISBN 0421352906 Pbk £8.50

—'A' Level English Law / Scott. - 6th ed. - London : Butterworths, 1984.
ISBN 0406657076 Hbk £14.00
ISBN 0406657084 Pbk £8.95

—'A' Level Law (CCT) / Seago. - 2nd ed. - Sweet & Maxwell, 1988.
ISBN 0421352906 Pbk £8.95
ISBN 042138820X Hbk £9.95

—English Law for GCSE / Giles. - 5th ed. - London : Butterworths, 1987.
ISBN 0406653070 Pbk £5.50

—GCSE Law / London : Financial Training, 1987.
ISBN 1851850546 Pbk £7.95

—Law for GCSE / Collins. - London : Pitman Publishing, 1987.
ISBN 0273028367 Pbk £5.95

—Leading Cases in Negligence for 'A' Level / 2nd ed. - London : Butterworths, 1986.
ISBN 0406016828 Pbk £5.50

—Negligence for 'A' Level / 2nd ed. - London : Sweet & Maxwell, 1983.
ISBN 0421321709 Pbk £5.95

—'O' level law / Collins. - London : Pitman Publishing, 1984.
ISBN 0273025538 Pbk £4.95

—Scott's English Law for GCSE / 5th ed. - London : Butterworths, 1987.
ISBN 0406653070 Pbk £10.50

LEGAL EDUCATION - GREAT BRITAIN

—A-Level Law / Plymouth : Macdonald & Evans, 1984.
240p. - (M and E Handbook Ser.).
ISBN 0712101608 Pbk £3.25

—Current Legal Problems : Lectures Delivered in the Faculty of Laws of University College / Roger Rideout. - London : Sweet & Maxwell, 1983.
ISBN 042046770X Hbk £22.00

—Current Legal Problems : Lectures Delivered in the Faculty of Laws of University College London / Roger Rideout. - London : Sweet & Maxwell, 1982.
ISBN 0420465405 Hbk £22.00

—English Law-'O' Level / 4th ed. - London : Butterworths, 1981.
This textbook covers the background and growth of English law, the administration and functions of the courts and their officers, and the basic principles of criminal law, tort, contract, and family law.
ISBN 0406653062 Hbk
ISBN 0406653054 Pbk

—How to study law / London : Sweet & Maxwell, 1986.
ISBN 042134380X Hbk £9.50
ISBN 0421343907 Pbk £7.50

—How to survive your articles / London : Waterlow, 1986.
ISBN 0080330681 Pbk £5.95

—Journal of the Society of Public Teachers of Law : New Series, 1946-1980, 14 Vols. / Professional Books Staff. - Abingdon : Professional Books, 1984.

—Learning the Law / 11th ed. - London : Sweet & Maxwell, 1982.
ISBN 0420463003 Pbk £4.50

—Legal Studies : The Journal of the Society of Public Teachers of Law / London : Butterworths, 1986.

Back issues avail.

—'O' level law / Paulene Collins. - Plymouth : Macdonald & Evans, 1984.
ISBN 0712115420 Pbk £4.75

—Second Survey of Legal Education in the United Kingdom : Supplement No. 2 / S. B. Marsh. - London : Institute of Advanced Legal Studies, 1981.
ISBN 090119025X Hbk £2.00

—Statutes for the Law Society Finals / London : Sweet & Maxwell, 1985.
ISBN 0421325208 Pbk £16.95

—Studying law / London : Butterworths, 1985.
ISBN 0406016089 Hbk £9.50
ISBN 0406016097 Pbk £5.50

LEGAL EDUCATION - UNITED STATES

—Law School Orientation : Cases and Materials / Agincourt : Carswell, 1986.
341p.
This work for law students provides a series of introductory readings, cases, and materials for students beginning their studies at American law schools.

LEGAL ETHICS - AUSTRALIA - NEW SOUTH WALES

—Fourth report on the legal profession : solicitors' trust accounts / New South Wales Law Reform Commission. - Sydney : The Commission, 1984.
viii,228p. - (L.R.C. 44).
Bibliography: p.212-214. Includes indexes.

—Legal profession / New South Wales Law Reform Commission. - Sydney : The Commission, 1980.
168p; 24cm. - (Background paper 3).
Includes index.

—Second report on the legal profession : complaints, discipline and professional standards / New South Wales Law Reform Commission. – Sydney : The Commission, 1982.
121p. – (L.R.C.32).
Includes index.

LEGAL ETHICS – GREAT BRITAIN

—Code of conduct for the Bar of England and Wales : effective from 1st January 1981 / Senate of the Inns of Court and the Bar. – 3rd ed. (incorporating all amendments up to 31st December 1984). – London : The Senate, 1985.
74p.
Includes index.

—Code of conduct for the Bar of England and Wales : effective from 1st January 1981 / Senate of the Inns of Court and the Bar. – 2nd ed. Incorporating all amendments up to 31st December 1982. – London : The Senate, 1983.
76p.
Previous ed.: 1981. Includes index.

LEGAL ETHICS – INDIA

—Professional Ethics of the Bar / 2nd ed. – Allahabad : Law Book Company, 1987.
370p.

LEGAL ETHICS – PHILIPPINES

—Answers to Bar Examination Questions /. – Quezon City : University of the Philippines, Law Center, 1982.
104p.

LEGAL ETHICS – SOUTH AFRICA

—Legal ethics : a guide to professional conduct for South African attorneys / E.A.L. Lewis. – Cape Town : Juta, 1982.
xix,339p.
Bibliography: p.xiii-xiv. - Includes index.
ISBN 0702113026

LEGAL ETIQUETTE – INDIA

—Lawyers' Etiquette / 2nd ed. – Allahabad : Law Book Company, 1988.

LEGAL HISTORY

—Administration of Justice in Ancient India / New Delhi : Harnam Publications, 1988.
296p.

—All jangle and riot / Abingdon : Professional Books, 1986.
ISBN 0862050839 Hbk £14.95

—Boke of Justices of the Peas / Abingdon : Professional Books.
– (Classical English Law Texts Ser.).

—Book Called the Mirror of Justices : With the Book (By Sir Anthony Fitzherbert), Called the Divinity of Courts and Their Jurisdictions / William Hughes. – Repr. of 1646 ed. – Abingdon : Professional Books.
40p.

—Civilian Writers of Doctors' Commons, London : Three Centuries of Juristic Innovation in Comparative, Commercial and International Law / Berlin : Duncker and Humblot, 1988.
303p.
ISBN 3428061772 Hbk £148.00

—De Pace Regis Et Regni / Abingdon : Professional Books.
– (Classical English Law Texts Ser.).

—Delineation of Universal Law / Fettiplace Bellers. – 2nd ed. Repr. of 1750 ed. – Abingdon : Professional Books.
592p.

—Eirenarcha / Abingdon : Professional Books.
– (Classical English Law Texts Ser.).

—Eirenarcha / 1st ed. – Professional Books, 1986 Reprint.
ISBN 0862053242 Hbk £24.75

—Essays upon several subjects concerning British antiquities / Repr. of 1747 ed. – Abingdon : Professional Books.
58p.

—Faithful Councellor or Marrow of the Law in English / 2nd ed. Repr. of 1653 ed. – Abingdon : Professional Books.
278p.

—Gratian and the Schools of Law : 1140-1234 / Northampton : Variorum, 1983.
396p. – (Collected Studies Ser.: CS 185).
ISBN 086078133X Hbk £30.00

—Hear the other side : Audi alteram partem / London : Butterworths, 1985.
ISBN 0406502404 Hbk £14.95

—Henrik Brenkman (1681-1736). Jurist and Classicist : a Chapter from the History of Roman Law as Part of the Classical Tradition / Groningen : Egbert Forsten Publishing, 1981.
viii, 141p.
ISBN 9060880757 Hbk £38.50

—Historia Placitorum Coronae, 2 Vols. / Abingdon : Professional Books.
– (Classical English Law Texts Ser.).

—History and principles of Roman Private law / London : Butterworths, 1984.
ISBN 0409060631 Pbk £28.50

—History of the common law of contract / Oxford : Oxford University Press, 1987.
ISBN 019825573X Pbk £19.50

—History of the land law / 2nd ed. – Oxford : Oxford University Press, 1986.
ISBN 0198255365 Pbk £12.50
ISBN 0198255373 Hbk £25.00

—L'Office Et Aucthoritie de Justices de Peace / Abingdon : Professional Books.
– (Classical English Law Texts Ser.).

—Law and politics in Aztec Texcoco / Cambridge : Cambridge University Press, 1984.
354.
Analyses the Aztec legal system. Discusses land tenure, inheritance, kinship relations, business trade and local and imperial administration.
ISBN 0521234751 Hbk £35.00

—Legal theory and legal history : essays on the common law / A.W.B. Simpson. – London : Hambledon, 1987.
xiii,432p; 24cm.
Includes index.
ISBN 0907628834 £24.00

—New Nature Brevium : With a Table of the Most Material Things Contained Therein, Composed by William Rastal, (also) the Authorities in Law Newly Translated by William Hughes / Repr. of 1652 ed. – Abingdon : Professional Books.
269p.

—Newe Boke of Justice of the Peas / Abingdon : Professional Books.
– (Classical English Law Texts Ser.).

—Office Aucthoritie / 2nd ed. – Professional Books, 1986 Reprint.
ISBN 086205317X Hbk £30.00

—Officium Vicecomitum (1623) / Reprint. – Abingdon : Professional Books, 1986.
ISBN 0862053455 Hbk £35.00

—Old Tenures and Old Natura Brevium / Reprint. – Abingdon : Professional Books, 1986.
ISBN 0862053293 Hbk £27.00

—Old Tenures and Old Natura Brevium / Abingdon : Professional Books.
– (Classical English Law Texts Ser.).

—Posthumous Works : Consisting of a Reading on the Statute of Inrolments, Arguments in the Case of General Stanwix, and Cases and Opinions / T. M. Shadwell. – 2nd ed. Repr. of 1797 ed. – Abingdon : Professional Books.
338p.

—Three law tracts / Reprint. – Abingdon : Professional Books, 1986.
ISBN 0862053129 Hbk £32.75

—Three Law Tracts / Abingdon : Professional Books.
– (Classical English Law Texts Ser.).

—Trial By Fire and Water / Oxford : Oxford University Press, 1986.
ISBN 0198219733 Hbk £19.50

LEGAL HISTORY – AUSTRALIA

—Australian Legal History / London : Law Book Co, 1982.
ISBN 0455196095 Pbk £17.75

—Australian Legal History / North Ryde : Law Book Co, 1982.
xx, 553p.
ISBN 04551956095 £63.00

LEGAL HISTORY – CANADA

—Essays in the History of Canadian Law, Vol. 2 / Toronto : University of Toronto Press, 1983.
ISBN 0802033911 Hbk £45.00

—Law and Justice in a New Land : Essays in Western Canadian Legal History / Agincourt : Carswell, 1986.
300p.

—Law and Justice in a New Land : Essays in Western Canadian Legal History / Agincourt : Carswell, 1986.
300p.
This work is a collection of essays incorporating primary historical research on topics relating to aboriginal and Indian land and resource law; law, politics, and justice in frontier communities; and legal and social problems in urban settings of Western Canada.

—Supreme Court of Canada : History of the Institution / Frederick Vaughan. – Toronto : University of Toronto Press, 1985.
ISBN 0802034179 Hbk £40.00
ISBN 0802034187 Pbk £17.50

LEGAL HISTORY – ENGLAND

—Brought to justice / Roy Lewis. – Durham : Casdec, 1983.
83p.
ISBN 0907595111

—Church courts, sex and marriage in England 1570-1640 / Cambridge : Cambridge University Press.
Examines the role of Elizabethan Church courts, their jurisdiction and the attitude of the people towards them. Based on records from courts in Wiltshire, Cambridgeshire, Leicestershire and West Sussex.
ISBN 0521232856

—Common peace / Cambridge : Cambridge University Press.
Examines attitudes behind the enforcement of criminal law in seventeenth-century England. Based on court records but concerned with popular rather than professional legal culture.
ISBN 052133313X Hbk £25.00

—Course of lectures on the English law : delivered at the University of Oxford, 1767-1773 / by Sir Robert Chambers : and composed in association with Samuel Johnson : edited by Thomas M. Curley. – 2. – Oxford : Clarendon, 1986.
23cm.
Bibliography: p301-335. - Includes index.
ISBN 0198185448 £70.00

—Crime in seventeenth century England / Cambridge : Cambridge University Press.
Studes court records in Essex. Analyses social processes involved in prosecution.
ISBN 0521250749 Hbk £32.50

—Domesday book and beyond / Cambridge : Cambridge University Press.
Uses information in the Domesday book to analyse the society, law, government, economy and culture of early medieval England.
ISBN 0521341124

—English judiciary in the age of Glanvill and Bracton c.1176-1239 / Cambridge : Cambridge University Press, 1985.
335.
Study of the evolution of the professional judiciary in medieval England. Describes the growth of a professional civil service.
ISBN 052126510X Hbk £30.00

—History of the English Bar 1929 / London : Wildy & Sons.

—History of the Law Reports 1884 / London : Wildy & Sons.

—Modern legal history of England and Wales / London : Butterworths, 1980.
ISBN 0406622369 Hbk £26.00
ISBN 0406622647 Hbk £18.95

—New River : a legal history / Bernard Rudden. – Oxford : Clarendon, 1985.
xiii,335p,iileaves of plates; 23cm.
Bibliography: p321-329. - Includes index.
ISBN 0198254970 £20.00

—Parliament of England 1559-1581 / Cambridge : Cambridge University Press, 1986.
411.
Study of functions of parliament, political and legislative. Finds that legislative capacity was far more important. Discusses the interests involved in promoting bills and problems associated with making them law.
ISBN 0521328357 Hbk £32.50

—Sir Henry Maine : a study in Victorian jurisprudence / Cambridge : Cambridge University Press.
Study of the ideas on jurisprudence of Sir Henry Maine, an important member of the Victorian intellectual establishment.
ISBN 0521353432

—Sir William Scott, Lord Stowell / Cambridge : Cambridge University Press.
Analyses Sir William Scott's work as a judge of the admiralty court during the Revolutionary and Napoleonic wars. Illustrates his contribution to the development of the international law of war, especially concerning neutral and belligerant rights at sea.
ISBN 0521340764

—Sources of English Legal and Constitutional History / R. Ian Jack. – Butterworths, 1984.
432p.
ISBN 0409493821 Hbk £49.00

—Sources of English Legal and Constitutional History / R. Ian Jack. – Sydney : Butterworths.
This book gives a collection of prominent sources of the legal and constitutional history of England for students of the subject. The work includes materials ranging from the Dooms of the Anglo-Saxon Kings to the Equal Franchise Act of 1928.
ISBN 0409493821 Hbk

—Sources of English legal history 1750-1950 / London : Butterworths, 1984.
ISBN 0406516596 Hbk £39.00

—Sources on English legal history : private law to 1750 / Milsomm. – London : Butterworths, 1986.
ISBN 0406016410 Pbk £21.95

—Textbook of English Legal History / 2nd ed. – Lucknow : Eastern Book Company, 1983.
296p.

—Trial Jury in England, France, Germany 1700-1900 / Berlin : Duncker and Humblot, 1987.
305p.
ISBN 3428061780 Hbk £124.00

—William Sheppard: Cromwell's law reformer / Cambridge : Cambridge University Press.
Appraisal of William Sheppard's legal works including writings on conveyancing, tithe collection and guides for local law enforcement. Examines the importance of Sheppard's books to his contemporaries and to legal literature in general.
ISBN 0521264839

LEGAL HISTORY – EUROPE

—Introduction to European legal history / London : Butterworths, 1985.
ISBN 086205107X Hbk £35.00
ISBN 0862051088 Pbk £16.95

LEGAL HISTORY – FRANCE

—Science du Droit Dans le Midi de la France au Moyen Age / Northampton : Variorum, 1984.
360p : Illus.. – – (Collected Studies Ser.: 196).
ISBN 0860781445 Hbk £28.00

—Trial Jury in England, France, Germany 1700-1900 / Berlin : Duncker and Humblot, 1987.
305p.
ISBN 3428061780 Hbk £124.00

LEGAL HISTORY – GREAT BRITAIN

—Historical English Law before Edward I / Mateland. – 2nd ed. – Cambridge : Cambridge University Press, 1988.
ISBN 0521095166 Pbk £30.00

—Historical foundations of Common Law / 2nd ed. – London : Butterworths, 1981.
ISBN 0406625025 Hbk £22.50
ISBN 0406625034 Pbk £16.95

LEGAL HISTORY – INDIA

—Law of Procedure and Justice in Ancient India / New Delhi : Deep and Deep Publications, 1986.
320p.

—Naradiya Dharmasastra : Judicial System in Ancient India / Delhi : Ajanta Books International, 1981.
180p.
ISBN 8120200578 Hbk £70.00

LEGAL HISTORY – IRELAND

—Essays in Irish Legal History / P. O'Higgins. – Dublin : Irish Academic Press, 1988.
ca 220p.
ISBN 0716523973 Hbk £27.50

LEGAL HISTORY – SCOTLAND

—Legal history of Scotland / by David M. Walker. – Edinburgh : W Green & Son, 1988.
xxi,435p; 24cm.
A systematic examination of the development of public, criminal and private law up to the death of Alexander III, with attention to the emerging lawmaking institutions, the deciding of cases and the procedure and principles of substantive law. Bibliography: p408-420. - Includes index.
ISBN 0414008162 No price

—New perspectives in Scottish legal history / Albert Kiralfy, Hector L. Macqueen. – London : Cass, 1983.
100p.
ISBN 0714632511 £18.50

LEGAL HISTORY – SOUTH AFRICA

—Catalogue of the Van Zyl Collection of Antiquarian Legal Materials at the University of Cape Town / Rondebosch : University of Cape Town, 1985.
ii, 164p.
ISBN 0799209856 Pbk £5.00

—Legal History : Does it Still Deserve Its Place in the Curriculum? / Rondebosch : University of Cape Town, 1981.
10p.
ISBN 0799204153 Pbk £0.30

LEGAL HISTORY – UNITED STATES

—Cross-examination of law and literature / Cambridge : Cambridge University Press, 1987.
312.
Studies the effect of the American legal system on the formation of American consciousess. Describes the relationship between law and literature in the nineteenth century.
ISBN 0521330815 Hbk £27.50

—State and the unions : labour relations, law and the organized labour movement in America, 1880-1960 / Cambridge : Cambridge University Press, 1985.
364.
Examines the impact of the National Labour Relations Act on American trade unions.
ISBN 0521258405 Hbk £35.00
ISBN 0521314526 Pbk £12.50

LEGAL HISTORY – USSR

—History of international law in Russia 1647-1917 / Translated by W. E. Butler. – Oxford : Clarendon Press, 1988.
600.
An account of the develoment of the study of international law and the revolution of 1917. A guide to the Russian literature on the law of nations in a contemporary context. The translator's introduction and bibliography are new, and place the work in its historical context.
ISBN 0198254954 Hbk £40

LEGAL HISTORY – WALES

—Modern legal history of England and Wales / London : Butterworths, 1980.
ISBN 0406622369 Hbk £26.00
ISBN 0406622647 Hbk £18.95

LEGAL HISTORY – WEST GERMANY

—Trial Jury in England, France, Germany 1700-1900 / Berlin : Duncker and Humblot, 1987.
305p.
ISBN 3428061780 Hbk £124.00

LEGAL INSTITUTIONS

—Lament for the Law Commission / R.T. Oerton. – Chichester : Countrywise Press, 1987.
v,117p.

—On the Legal Institutions of Socialist Democracy / London : Spokesman Books, 1983.
50p.

LEGAL INSTITUTIONS – AFRICA

—Traditional and Modern Legal Institutions in Asia and Africa / Leiden : E.J. Brill, 1967.
ISBN 9004010505 Hbk £48.00

LEGAL INSTITUTIONS – ASIA

—Traditional and Modern Legal Institutions in Asia and Africa / Leiden : E.J. Brill, 1967.
ISBN 9004010505 Hbk £48.00

LEGAL INSTITUTIONS – GREAT BRITAIN

—Fundamental Legal Institutions / London : Butterworths, 1984.

—Legal Institutions / London : Butterworths, 1984.
ISBN 0406400253 Hbk £16.00
ISBN 0406400261 Pbk £12.95

LEGAL INSTRUMENTS

—Drafting : its application to conveyancing and commercial documents / Stanley Robinson. – London : Buttterworths, 1980.
xxxiv,428p; 26cm.
Describes how to draft legal documents in the common law system with certainty and using the minimum amount of legalese. The work examines principles of parliamentary drafting relevant to documents and demonstrates how these principles can be applied to drafting legal documents.
ISBN 0406358907 £30.00

LEGAL INSTRUMENTS – CANADA

—Charge document in criminal cases / Law Reform Commission of Canada. – Ottawa : The Commission, 1987.
57,63p. – (Working paper).
Includes bibliographical references. Added t.p. in French: Le document d'inculpation. Pages numbered in opposite directions. Text in English and French.
ISBN 0662549635

LEGAL INSTRUMENTS – SCOTLAND

—Formulary of old Scots legal documents / compiled by Peter Gouldesbrough : with a supplementary essay on Early Scottish conveyancing by Gordon Donaldson. – Edinburgh : Stair Society, 1985.
viii,196p.
Includes index.
ISBN 0902292110

—Obligations : report on rectification of contractual and other documents / Scottish Law Commission. – Edinburgh : H.M.S.O., 1983.
vi,35p.
Includes bibliographical references. Includes Draft Rectification of Documents (Scotland) Bill.
ISBN 0102036845

—Report on requirements of writing / Scottish Law Commission. – Edinburgh : HMSO, 1988.
vii,197p.
Includes bibliographical references. Includes draft legislation.
ISBN 010255188X

LEGAL INVESTMENTS – AUSTRALIA – WESTERN AUSTRALIA

—Report on trustees' powers of investment / Law Reform Commission of Western Australia. – Perth : Government Printer, 1984.
141p. – (Project v no 34 part 5).
Includes bibliographical references.

LEGAL INVESTMENTS – CANADA – MANITOBA

—Report on investment provisions under 'The Trustee Act' / Law Reform Commission. – Winnipeg : Queen's Printer, 1982.
i,38p. – (Report).

LEGAL LANGUAGE – CANADA

—Legal Terminology : an Historical Guide to the Technical Language of Law / Peterborough : Broadview Press Ltd., 1986.
192p.
ISBN 0921149026 Hbk £18.95

—Trouble with Legal Language / Ottawa : Canadian Law Information Council, 1985.
33p.
ISBN 0920358845 Pbk

LEGAL LITERATURE

—Cannibalism and the common law / University of Chicago Press, 1984.
ISBN 0226759423 Hbk £21.25

—Clinging to the wreckage / Penguin, 1982.
ISBN 0297780107 Pbk £1.95

—Courts, law libraries and legal information in a changing society : 25. IALL Anniversary, Freiburg i. Br., July 15-20, 1984 / S.l. : International Association of Law Libraries, 1984.
184p.
Conference proceedings. Includes bibliographical references.

—Current legal theory : international journal for documentation on legal theory (bibliography - abstracts - reviews) / Centrum voor Grondslagenonderzoek van het Recht. – Leuven : Acco, 1983-.

—Error of judgment / Aurora : Cape, 1986.
ISBN 0701129786 Hbk £10.95

—Essays in Honour of Schwarzenberger / Brown. – London : Sweet & Maxwell, 1988.
ISBN 0420479201 Hbk £36.00

—Essays in Memory of Professor R.H. Lawson / London : Butterworths, 1986.
ISBN 0406500304 Hbk £21.00

—Essays on Kelsen / Twining. – Oxford : Oxford University Press, 1986.
ISBN 0198254709 Hbk £35.00

—Faces Cases and Places / London : Butterworths, 1983.
ISBN 0406514771 Hbk £18.20

—Family Story / London : Butterworths, 1981.
ISBN 0406176094 Hbk £14.50

—Fiercest Debate / Bickenbach. – University of Ontario, 1988.
ISBN 0802039863 Hbk £28.00

—Great Legal Fiascos / Weidenfeld & Nicolson, 1985.
ISBN 0213169274 Hbk £5.95

—Humerus of the long arm of the law / Stockwell, 1988.
ISBN 0722322194 Pbk £6.60

—Leaders and lawyers / Brownstone. – London : Facts On File, 1986.
ISBN 0816013675 Hbk £7.95

—Leaves from My Library / London : Butterworths, 1986.
ISBN 0406176159 Hbk £13.95

—Legal literature in small jurisdictions : a report of a conference held at Osgoode Hall Law School, York University, Downsview, Ontario on 3-5 November 1978 / edited by William Twining and Jenny Uglow for the Canadian Law Information Council, Canada and the Commonwealth Legal Education Association, London. – London : Commonwealth Secretariat, 1981.
188p; 30cm.
Bibliography: p.171-172. - Includes index.
ISBN 085092197X

—Legal Mind - Essays For Tony Honore / Birks. – Oxford : Oxford University Press, 1986.
ISBN 0198761961 Hbk £35.00

—Legal Right and Social Democracy-Essays / Oxford : Oxford University Press, 1984.
ISBN 0198255020 Pbk £9.95

—Liber Amicorum for Lord Wilberforce / Brownie. – Oxford : Oxford University Press, 1987.
ISBN 0198255950 Hbk £30.00

—Lost causes / Secker & Warburg, 1982.
ISBN 0436105810 Hbk £8.50

—Oxford book of lagal anecdotes / Michael Gilbert. – Oxford : OUP, 1989.
352; 19.5.
Anthology of over 350 anecdotes about legal goings-on in Britain, the United States, and Australia.*Anyone practising, or interested in, law*
ISBN 0192821121 Pbk £4.95

—Power, prejudice and pride / Southampton : Ashford Press, 1987.
ISBN 0950764612 Hbk £8.95

—Prospect of Gray's Inn / 2nd ed. – London : GRAY, 1985.
ISBN 0420473300 Hbk £10.00

—Quotable lawyer / Frost. – London : Facts On File, 1986.
ISBN 0816011842 Hbk £17.95

—Using a law library : a guide for students and lawyers in the Common Law provinces of Canada / Margaret A. Banks. – 3rd ed. – Toronto : Carswell, 1980.
ix,212p.
Includes bibliographies.
ISBN 0459330403

LEGAL LITERATURE - CANADA

—Using a law library : a guide for students and lawyers in the common law provinces of Canada / Margaret A. Banks. – 4th ed. – Toronto : Carswell, 1980.
xiii,249p.
Includes bibliographical references and index.
ISBN 0459376101

LEGAL LITERATURE - ENGLAND

—Introduction to Fitzherbert's Abridgement / by Frederick Lister Boersma. – Abingdon : Professional Books, 1981.
6,117p; 23cm.
ISBN 0862050413

LEGAL LITERATURE - GREAT BRITAIN

—Comic Blackstone / Southampton : Ashford Press, 1985.
ISBN 0907069398 Hbk £18.95

—Cross Examination of Law and Literature / Cambridge : Cambridge University Press, 1987.
ISBN 0521330815 Hbk £27.50

—Easing the Passing / London : CAPE, 1985.
ISBN 0370306279 Hbk £12.50
ISBN 0571139930 Pbk £4.95

—End of Law? / Oxford : Blackwell, 1985.
ISBN 0631145354 Pbk £7.50

—Lawyers' law books : a practical index to legal literature / by Donald Raistrick. – 2nd ed. – Milton, Oxon. : Professional Books, 1985.
xxxv,604p. – (Professional Books law reference library).
ISBN 0862050723

—Trollope and the law / London : Macmillan, 1986.
ISBN 0333400135 Hbk £25.00

LEGAL MAXIMS

—Regulae Iuris: From Juristic Rules to Legal Maxims / J. Shand. – Edinburgh : Edinburgh University Press.
216p.
ISBN 0852241437 Hbk £8.50

LEGAL OPINION - CANADA

—Solicitors' Legal Opinions / Vancouver : Continuing Legal Education Society of British Columbia, 1985.
244p.
ISBN 0865042403 Hbk £60.00

LEGAL POSITIVISM

—Institutional theory of law : new approaches to legal positivism / Neil MacCormick and Ota Weinberger. – DordrechtHolland : Reidel, 1986.
xiv, 229p. – (Law and philosophy library).
ISBN 9027720797

—Judging : towards a rational judicial process / H. J. M. Boukema. – Zwolle, Holland : W.E.J. Tjeenk Willink, 1980.
xvi,181p.
Includes index. Bibliography: p141-148.
ISBN 9027117276

LEGAL PROFESSION

—Advising a suspect in the police station : guidelines for solicitors / Law Society's Criminal Law Committee. – London : Law Society.

—Annual report of the Council of the Law Society : intended to be presented to the general meeting of the members on ... / Law Society. – v. – London : Spottiswoode, 1903.
Continues: Annual report of the Council of the Incorporated Law Society. 1975 onwards incorporates the interim report and accounts of the Solicitors Benevolent Association. Cover title, 1966/67 onwards: Annual report of the Council and accounts. Published by the Law Society, 1945 onwards.

—Art of the advocate / Richard Du Cann. – 1st ed. reprinted with revisions. – Harmondsworth : Penguin, 1980.
186p; 18cm. – (A pelican original).
Originally published : 1964. .
ISBN 0140206655 Pbk £1.50

—Challenges to the Legal Profession : Law and Investment in Developing Countries / International Bar Association. – Lucknow : Eastern Book Company, 1985.
807p.

—Divided we stand : a report on the legal profession / Social Democratic Lawyers' Association : chairman William Goodhart. – London : The Association, 1986.
53p.

—Function of the law and the lawyer in development administration / by Heinrich Scholler. – Lagos : Nigerian Institute of Advanced Legal Studies, University of Lagos, 1980.
14p; 23cm. – (Occasional papers).
Includes bibliographical references.

—Independent solicitor : journal of the British Legal Association / British Legal Association. – Tunbridge Wells : British Legal Association, .
From 1983 incorporates BLA solicitor.

—International Legal Practitioner / London : Sweet & Maxwell.

—Invitation to law / by A.W.B. Simpson. – Oxford : Blackwell, 1988.
227p.
Includes index.
ISBN 0631145389 pbk.

—Kime's international law handbook : brief facts about legal practice in most of the countries of the world / editor : James M. Matthews ; research and compilation : Roderick N. Matthews. – London : Kime's International Law Directory Limited, 1981.
266p.
ISBN 0900503149

—Law and the Lawyers / Ahmedabad : Navajivan Publishing House.

—Lawyers in business : and the law business / Karl J. Mackie. – Basingstoke : Macmillan, 1988.
viii,289p.
Includes bibliography and index.
ISBN 0333419081 £29.50

—Lawyers in early modern Europe and America / edited by Wilfrid Prest. – London : Croom Helm, 1981.
216 p.

—Lawyers in the eighties : proceedings of the conference held by Society for Computers and Law in York from 3rd to 6th July 1980 / Conference Organising Committee, Richard Morgan ... et al. – Abingdon : The Society, 1980.
70p; 30cm.
Cover title.
ISBN 090612204X spiral £15.00 (10.00 to members of the Society for Computers and Law)

—Lawyers in the Third World : comparative and developmental perspectives / edited by C.J. Dias ... et al. – Uppsala : Scandinavian Institute of African Studies, 1981.
400p; 22cm.
Bibliography: p.382-399. Sponsored by the Scandinavian Institute of African Studies and the International Center for Law in Development.
ISBN 9171061797 Hbk £25.00 (20.00 in Third World Countries)
ISBN 9171061762 Pbk £16.00 (8.00 in Third World countries)

—Legal profession / New South Wales Law Reform Commission. – Sydney : The Commission, 1981.
229p; 25cm. – (Background paper 4).

—Legal profession / New South Wales Law Reform Commission. – Sydney : The Commission, 1980.
106p; 24cm. – (Discussion paper 2).

—Legal secretary's handbook / Ann Newington and Hilary Willoughby. – 4th ed. – London : Longman Professional (UK), 1989.
Contains descriptions of the work of the various departments of a solicitor's practice and barrister's chambers. It includes an explanation of legal terms and gives examples of completed legal forms. Takes account of latest office technology, updates and useful addresses.
Legal secretaries, secretarial colleges, careers offices, practices, chambers
ISBN 0851215785 Sbd £18.95

—Order of the Coif / By Alexander Pulling. – London : W. Clowes and sons, 1884.
xxvi, 288 p; 27 cm.
'The subject of this work has been foreshadowed in the article under the same title in the Edinburgh review' for October, 1878.'–Pref.

—Present and the future of the profession : (the Elzaburu survey) / compiled by Alberto de Elizaburu. – Special ed. – Edinburgh : F.I.C.P.I., 1982.
266p.
A survey presented to the F.I.C.P.I. (International Federation of Industrial Property Attorneys) World Congress, Edinburgh, October 1981.

—Proceedings and resolutions of the ... provincial meeting of the members of the Society / the Law Society. – 25 v. – London : The Law Society, 1903.
Continues: Proceedings and resolutions / Incorporated Law Society. Continued by: Annual conference of the Law Society, 1st(1948). Bound with the annual reports of the Council of the Law Society. Typewritten index to proceedings for 1887-1928 bound with our 1924-1928 volume.

—Sociology of the professions : lawyers, doctors and others / edited by Robert Dingwall and Philip Lewis. – London : Macmillan, 1983.
ix,314p; 23cm.
Bibliography: p286-306. - Includes index.
ISBN 0333309618 Hbk £15.00

—Technique of persuasion / David Napley : with a foreword by Melford Stevenson. – 3rd ed. – London : Sweet & Maxwell, 1983.
xvi,187p; 18cm.
Follows the same pattern as previous editions, but includes a new section on the strategy and tactics of advocacy. Also considers topics such as preparation for trial, the ethics of advocacy, and presentation in court.
ISBN 0421252804 Hbk £14.00
ISBN 0421252901 Pbk £5.85

—Transnational legal practice : a survey of selected countries / edited by Dennis Campbell. – Deventer, The Netherlands : Kluwer, 1981.
Includes index.
ISBN 9065440186 v. 2

—Victorian Bar / Robert Hale, 1982.
ISBN 0709005334 Hbk £9.95

—Whose interest? : solicitors and their clients' accounts : a discussion paper / London : National Consumer Council, 1984.
74p.
ISBN 0905653556

LEGAL PROFESSION - ASIA

—Lawasia directory / Sydney : Lawasia, 1979-.

—Lawasia newsletter / . – Sydney : Law Association for Asia and the Western Pacific, 1977-.

LEGAL PROFESSION - AUSTRALIA

—Handy Hints on Legal Practice / E.J. Kyrou. – North Ryde : Law Book Co, 1985.
xiv, 196p.
ISBN 0455206058 Pbk £19.50

—Lawyers / North Ryde : Law Book Co, 1986.
ISBN 0455206538 Hbk £37.50
ISBN 0455206546 Pbk £29.50

—Lawyers / North Ryde : Law Book Co, 1986.
xli, 944p.
ISBN 0455206538 Hbk £75.00
ISBN 0455206546 Pbk £59.00

—Organisation and Management of a Solicitor's Practice / Woolloomooloo : International Business Communications, 1984.
ISBN 094907201X loose £175.00

LEGAL PROFESSION - AUSTRALIA - NEW SOUTH WALES

—Advertising and specialisation / New South Wales Law Reform Commission. – Sydney : The Commission, 1981.
xxxv,244p; 25cm. – (Discussion paper no 5).
Bibliography: p.228-244.

—First report on the legal profession : general regulation and structure / New South Wales Law Reform Commission. – Sydney : The Commission, 1982.
242p. – (L.R.C.31).
Bibliography: p.227-229. - Includes index.

—Legal profession / New South Wales Law Reform Commission. – Sydney : The Commission, 1981.
vii,228p.

—Legal profession / New South Wales Law Reform Commission. – Sydney : The Commission, 1980.
168p; 24cm. – (Background paper 3).
Includes index.

—Second report on the legal profession : complaints, discipline and professional standards / New South Wales Law Reform Commission. – Sydney : The Commission, 1982.
121p. – (L.R.C.32).
Includes index.

—Solicitors' trust accounts and the Solicitors' Fidelity Fund / New South Wales Law Reform Commission. – Sydney : The Commission, 1981.
xxix,241p; 25cm. – (Discussion paper no 6).

—Structure of the profession / New South Wales Law Reform Commission. – Sydney : The Commission, 1981.
340p; 25cm. – (Discussion paper no 4 (1)).
Bibliography: p. 324-340.

Part 2 / New South Wales Law Reform Commission. – 1981.
p.344-644; 25cm. – (Discussion paper no 4 (2)).

—Third report on the legal profession : advertising and specialisation / New South Wales Law Reform Commission. – Sydney : The Commission, 1982.
155p. – (L.R.C. 33).

LEGAL PROFESSION - CANADA

—Advocacy : views from the bench / Robert F. Reid and Richard E. Holland. - Aurora, Ont. : Canada Law Book, 1984.
xii,164p.
Includes index.
ISBN 0888040245

—Canada Legal Directory : 1988 Edition / Toronto : DeBoo, 1988.
This listing of Canadian law firms and the lawyers who practice within them includes an alphabetical listing of law firms by city, with addresses and phone numbers, a separate finding list of the individual lawyers, a listing of corporate in-house counsel, and a comprehensive listing within each province of courts, officials, judicial districts, law societies, etc.
ISBN 0888202407 Hbk £75.00

—Canadian Bar Association : Proceedings of the First, Second and Third Meetings / Agincourt : Carswell, 1984.

—Canadian Bar Review : 1923-Date / Professional Books Staff. - Abingdon : Professional Books, 1984.

—Canadian Law List / Aurora : Canada Law Book Co.
1882p.

For 1987 Edition Only
This volume lists all lawyers in Canada by province, municipality and firm. A special section listing lawyers alphabetically with firm association and location is also provided. Listings are also included for all Canadian Courts, judges, cabinets, departments, ministries, boards, crown corporations, legal aid offices and others, on a province by province basis.

—How to Survive Practicing Law in the 80's / Vancouver : British Columbia Continuing Legal Education Society, 1982.
77p.
ISBN 0865040761 Hbk £7.50

—Law and the Legal Profession in Canada / Toronto : Butterworths, 1987.
250p.
ISBN 0409834343 Hbk £55.00

—Law office practice management guide / Scarborough, Ontario : Butterworths (Canada), 1988.
350.
Guide to the operation and management of a law office practice. Provides information on starting the practice, human resource planning, interviewing process selection and salary determination, avoiding wrongful dismissal, financing the practice, law firm recruitment, performance appraisal techniques, training and development, and marketing of professional services.
ISBN 0409805610 Hbk

—Managing Profitability and Lawyer Compensation / Vancouver : British Columbia Continuing Legal Education Society, 1986.
70p.
ISBN 0865042470 Hbk £45.00

—Mobile Homes for Legal Assistants / Vancouver : British Columbia Continuing Legal Education Society, 1981.
142p.
ISBN 0865040400 Hbk £35.00

—Solicitors' Considerations for Family Law Lawyers / Vancouver : British Columbia Continuing Legal Education Society, 1983.
310p.
ISBN 0865040885 Hbk £60.00

—Taxation of Lawyers' Accounts / Vancouver : Continuing Legal Education Society of British Columbia, 1986.
130p.
ISBN 086504256X Hbk £55.00

LEGAL PROFESSION - CANADA - ALBERTA

—Alberta Legal Telephone Directory : 1986 / Aurora : Canada Law Book Co.
This telephone directory is arranged by name, listing every lawyer and law firm in Alberta. Each listing includes address, telephone number and firm association. Additional entries include, among others, listings for: Courts, Judges, and Court Officials; Land Registration Districts; Legal Services; Law Libraries and Universities; and Provincial Government Departments.

LEGAL PROFESSION - CANADA - BRITISH COLUMBIA

—British Columbia Legal Telephone Directory : 1985 / Aurora : Canada Law Book Co.
This volume, arranged by name, lists every lawyer and law firm in British Columbia. Each listing includes name, firm association, address and telephone. Listings are also provided for, among others: Courts, Judges and Court Officials; Land Registration Districts; Legal Services; and Law Libraries and Universities.

LEGAL PROFESSION - CANADA - ONTARIO

—Ontario Legal Practice Manual-Ontario Edition / Toronto : DeBoo.

LEGAL PROFESSION - COMMONWEALTH

—Practice relating to the appointment of Queen's Counsel and senior counsel in some Commonwealth jurisdictions / Rev. ed. - London : Commonwealth Secretariat, 1981.
33p.
Previous ed.: 1973.

LEGAL PROFESSION - ENGLAND

—Annual members' conference held in the Lord Chief Justice's Court on Saturday, 30th March, 1985 : subject, the future of the legal profession / Chairman, Sir Nicholas Browne-Wilkinson. - London : Justice, 1985.
55 leaves.

—Are two legal professions necessary? / Peter Reeves. - London : Waterlow, 1986.
xiii,175p; 21cm.
Bibliography: p145-171. - Includes index.
ISBN 0080392180 Pbk £11.95

—Brief to counsel / by Henry Cecil : illustrated by Edward Ardizzone. - 3rd ed. - Chichester : Rose, 1982.
204p; 21cm.
Previous ed.: i.e. New ed. London : Joseph, 1972. Includes index.

—Common lawyers of pre-Reformation England : Thomas Kebell : a case study / by E.W. Ives. - Cambridge : Cambridge University Press, 1983.
xxx,536p; 23cm. - (Cambridge studies in English legal history).
Includes index.
ISBN 0521240115 £40.00

—Contingency fees / presented to Parliament by the Lord High Chancellor by Command of Her Majesty, January 1989. - London : HMSO, 1989.
13p.
ISBN 0101057121

—Cordery's law relating to solicitors / Frederic T. Horne. - 8th ed. - London : Butterworths, 1988.
540p; 25cm.
Previous ed: 1981. Includes index.
ISBN 0406161712 £60.00

—Cordery's law relating to solicitors / Frederic T. Horne. - 7th ed. - London : Butterworths, 1981.
xci,457p; 26cm.
ISBN 0406161569 Unpriced

—Counsel : the journal of the Bar of England and Wales / London : Senate of the Inns of Court and the Bar, 1985.
ISBN 02683784

—Cross examination in criminal trials / Marcus Stone. - London : Butterworths, 1988.
xix,224p.
Includes index.
ISBN 0406105057 No price

—English and Colonial bars in the nineteenth century / Daniel Duman. - London : Croom Helm, 1983.
228p; 23cm.
Bibliography: p212-221. - Includes index.
ISBN 0856644684 £13.95

—English Lawyer / Abingdon : Professional Books. - (Classical English Law Texts Ser.).

—English Lawyer / 2nd ed. - Abingdon : Professional Books, 1986 Reprint.
ISBN 0862053145 Hbk £27.00

—Fair charges? : a review of controls over solicitors' costs / by M.R. Ludlow. - London : Waterlow Publishers, 1982.
x,64p.
ISBN 0900791802

—Foundations of the modern Bar / by Raymond Cocks. - London : Sweet & Maxwell, 1983.
vii,257p; 22cm.
Bibliography: p235-249. - Includes index.
ISBN 0421303603 Pbk £9.50

—History of the English Bar 1929 / London : Wildy & Sons.

—Huddy: Introduction to legal practice / Grenfell Huddy, Charles Blake. - 2nd ed. - London : Published in association with the Institute of Legal Executive by Sweet & Maxwell, 1985.
xx,323p.
Previous ed.: published as Introduction to legal practice. 1982. Includes index.
ISBN 0421332204 Pbk £14.50

—Introduction to legal practice / Charles Blake, Grenfell Huddy. - London : Published in association with the Institute of Legal Executives by Sweet & Maxwell, 1983.
xii,287p; 25cm.
Includes index.
ISBN 0421293004 Pbk £14.50

Vol.2 : edited by Craig Osborne 1987.
300p; 26cm.
Previous ed.: 1983. Includes index.
ISBN 0421367903 Pbk £16.50

—Law in the balance : legal services in the 1980s / edited by Philip A. Thomas. - Oxford : Robertson, 1982.
x,245p; 23cm.
Includes bibliographies and index.
ISBN 0855204443 Hbk £18.50
ISBN 0855204826 Pbk £6.50

—Lawyers and the courts : time for some changes / a discussion paper issued by the Law Society's Contentious Business Committee : an appraisal published by the Council of the Law Society of the effect of the Building Societies Bill on the solicitors' profession. - London : Law Society, 1986.
10 leaves.
Supplement to the Law Society's 'Gazette', 22 January (1986). Includes bibliographical references.

—List of barristers by chambers, with index / 12th ed. - London : Holborn Law Society, 1983.
xlii,121p.

—List of English law officers, King's counsel and holders of patents of precedence / compiled for the Selden Society by Sir John Sainty. - London : Selden Society, 1987.
xviii, 330p.

—Marketing Legal services / edited by S.C. Silkin. - London : Waterlows, 1984.
86p; 21cm.
Conference papers.
ISBN 0080392156 Pbk £10.50

—Order of Serjeants at Law : a chronicle of creations, with related texts and a historical introduction / by J.H. Baker. - London : Selden Society, 1984.
xxvi,610p,xvip of plates.
Includes index.

—Pettyfoggers and vipers of the Commonwealth : the 'lower branch' of the legal profession in early modern England / C.W. Brooks. - Cambridge : Cambridge University Press, 1986.
410p; 23cm. - (Cambridge studies in English legal history).
Researches professional and social history of attorneys, solicitors, clerical officials and court holders in early modern society. Examines the nature of legal services provided for the public, considers how the legal system responded to the increase in litigation of the late sixteenth century.
ISBN 0521305748 £30.00

—Practice today / . - London : Julian Harris, 1985-.
Supplement to: Solicitors' journal. Added t.p. title: The management magazine for solicitors.

—Reflections on the Royal Commission on Legal Services : a public lecture / delivered by Lord Benson. - London : Inns of Court School of Law, 1981.
10p; 23cm.

—Rise of the barristers : a social history of the English bar, 1590-1640 / Wilfrid R. Prest. - Oxford : Clarendon, 1986.
xii,440p; 22cm.
Includes index.
ISBN 0198217641 £30.00

—Rule of law : Albert Venn Dicey, Victorian jurist / by Richard A. Cosgrove. - London : Macmillan, 1980.
xv,319p; 24cm.
Bibliography: p301-314. - Includes index.
ISBN 0333307070 £15.00

—Solicitor's practice / editor Peter H.M. Soar. - 1. - London : Butterworths, 1981.
loose-leaf; 26cm.
ISBN 0406373531 unbound Unpriced

—Solicitors and the wider community / David Podmore. - London : Heinemann, 1980.
xvii,212p.
Includes bibliographies.
ISBN 0435826964

—Solicitors' and barristers' directory and diary : an almanac and directory incorporating the Law Society list of practising solicitors and the Senate of the Inns of Court and the Bar list of members / v. - London : Waterlow, 1984.
Merger of: The Bar list of the United Kingdom; and, The Solicitors' diary ... almanac and legal directory.
ISBN 0080391710

—Solicitors' regional directory 1984 / London : Law Society, 1984.
viii,184p.
Supersedes: The legal aid solicitors list. Includes index.

—Survey of the structure and finances of the legal profession in private practice 6th January 1986 / Law Society, Special Committee on Remuneration. - 3. - London : Law Society, 1986.
Contents: v.1 Commentary - v.2 Major tables - v.3 Detailed tables.

—Time for change / report of the Committee. - London : General Council of the Bar, 1988.
221p.
At head of t.p.: The Committee on the Future of the Legal Profession (The Marre Committee). Chairman: Lady Marre.

—Troubled lives : John and Sarah Austin / Lotte and Joseph Hamburger. - Toronto : University of Toronto Press, 1985.
xiii,261p.
Includes index.

—Work and organisation of the legal profession / presented to Parliament by the Lord High Chancellor by Command of Her Majesty, January 1989. - London : HMSO, 1989.
iv,72p.
ISBN 0101057024

LEGAL PROFESSION - EUROPEAN COMMUNITY

—Lawyers in the European Community / from the French original by Serge-Pierre Laguette : updated for this Engish language version in collaboration with Patrick Latham. - Luxembourg : Office for Official Publications of the European Communities, 1987.
293p.
At head of title: Commission of the European Communities.
ISBN 9282569780

—Role of the Lawyer in the European Communities / Edinburgh : Edinburgh University Press.
106p.

LEGAL PROFESSION - GREAT BRITAIN

—All Jangle and Riot : A History of the Bar / Abingdon : Professional Books, 1984.
ISBN 0862050839 Hbk £17.00
ISBN 086205088X Pbk

—Are Two Legal Professions Necessary? / London : Waterlow, 1986.
ISBN 0080392180 Pbk £11.95

—Bar List of the United Kingdom / London : Sweet & Maxwell, 1982.
ISBN 0420465200 Pbk £48.25

—Barristers' Clerks: The Law's Middlemen / Manchester : Manchester University Press, 1983.
ISBN 0719009286 Hbk £7.50

—Before You See A Solicitor (It's Your Law) / 2nd ed. - London : Longman Professional, 1983.
ISBN 0851207790 Pbk £6.95

—Black communities and the legal profession / summary of Nottingham Regional Conference, October 1986. - s.l. : Standing Committee on the Black Communities and the Legal Profession, 1986.
11p.
Includes bibliographical references.

—Careers In The Law / 2nd ed. - London : Kogan Page, 1986.
ISBN 1850911002 Pbk £3.25

—Check-Lists for Solicitors / 4th ed. - London : Oyez Longman, 1983.

—Code of conduct for the Bar of England and Wales : effective from 1st January 1981 / Senate of the Inns of Court and the Bar. - 2nd ed. Incorporating all amendments up to 31st December 1982. - London : The Senate, 1983.
76p.
Previous ed.: 1981. Includes index.

—Code of conduct for the Bar of England and Wales : effective from 1st January 1981 / Senate of the Inns of Court and the Bar. - 3rd ed. (incorporating all amendments up to 31st December 1984). - London : The Senate, 1985.
74p.
Includes index.

—Cordery on Solicitors / Wellington : Butterworths.
This book discusses the rights and liabilities of an English solicitor. Materials on a solicitors relationship with his client; his liability in negligence; his entitlement to remuneration; his relations with partners and employees; and The Law Society are included.
ISBN 0406161585 Pbk

—Cordery's Law Relating to Solicitors / 8th ed. - London : Butterworths, 1988.
ISBN 0406161712 Hbk £75.00

—Financial Management For Solicitors / 3rd ed. - London : Longman Professional, 1985.
ISBN 0851209998 Pbk £15.95

—Good Practice : A Management Guide for the Profession / London : Butterworths.
ISBN 0406502803 Pbk

—Guide for Articled Clerks and Trainee Legal Executives / London : Sweet & Maxwell, 1984.
ISBN 0421320508 Pbk £5.50

—History of Freshfields / Judy Slinn. - London : Freshfields, 1984.
208p.
Bibliography: p.181-187. - Includes index.

—International Business Lawyer / London : Sweet & Maxwell.

—Lawyer's Peregrination / 2nd ed. - London : Sweet & Maxwell, 1987.
ISBN 0421391804 Pbk £1.95

—Lawyers and the courts : the response of the Bar to a discussion paper issed bu the Law Society's Contentious Business Committee / Senate of the Inns of Court and the Bar. - London : Senate of the Inns of Court and the Bar, 1986.
14p.
Includes bibliographical references. At head of p.3: Seanate of the Inns of Court and the Bar.

—Lawyers in the United Kingdom / Richard Abel. - 1st draft. - S.l. : s.n., 1983.
xvi,209p.
'Prepared for the meeting of the Working Group for Comparative Study of Legal Professions of the ISA Research Committee on Sociology of Law, to be held at the Villa Serbelloni, Bellagio, Italy, July 16-21, 1984'. Bibliography: p.199-209.

—Legal 500 : the major law firms in England, Wales and Scotland / John Pritchard. - London : Legalease, 1988.
352p.

—Legal Secretary Pitman 2000 / Pitman, 1986.
ISBN 0273022261 Pbk £4.95

—Legal Secretary Today / Holden. - Maidenhead : McGraw-Hill, 1986.
ISBN 0070849749 Pbk £4.95

—Legal Secretary's Handbook / Willoughby. - 3rd ed. - London : Longman Professional, 1986.
ISBN 0851212077 Pbk £15.95

—Legal Secretary's Handbook / H. M. Willoughby. - 2nd ed. - London : Oyez Longman, 1982.
ISBN 085120628X Pbk £10.95

—On solicitors / 8th ed. - London : Butterworths, 1988.
ISBN 04061617120 Hbk

—Organisation and management of a solicitor's practice / London : Legal Books, 1984.
ISBN 094907201X Hbk £95.00

—Planned practice development / London : Longman Professional, 1984.
ISBN 0851208673 Pbk £13.95

—Practical Skills of the Solicitor / London : Oyez Longman, 1981.
ISBN 0851206107 Hbk £6.95

—Practical skills of the solicitor / 2nd ed. - London : Longman Professional, 1985. - (Practice Today Series).
ISBN 0851209947 Pbk £12.50

—Practice of Law / Bowstock. - Methuen, 1988.
ISBN 0901715662 Pbk £6.50
ISBN 0901715670 Hbk £15.00

—Professional conduct of solicitors / Law Society. - 1. - London : The Society, 1986.
loose-leaf; 23cm.

—Rise of the barristers / Oxford : Oxford University Press, 1986.
ISBN 0198217641 Hbk £35.00

—Solicitor and The Silicon Chip / London : Oyez Longman, 1981.
ISBN 0851205690 Hbk £6.95

—Solicitor's Journal : 1855-1981, 125 Vols. / Abingdon : Professional Books.

—Solicitors and barristers directory and diary / London : Waterlow, 1987.
ISBN 0080330940 Hbk £35.00

—Solicitors and their business clients / Barlow. - 3rd ed. - London : Financial Training, 1986.
ISBN 1851850317 Pbk £16.50

—Solicitors and VAT / Gizzi. - London : Butterworths, 1986.
ISBN 0406503605 Pbk £8.75

—Solicitors' practice / London : Butterworths, 1980.
ISBN 0406373531 loose £50.00

—Specimen letters for solicitors / London : Longman Professional, 1987.
ISBN 0851208630 Pbk £15.95

—Starting in practice / London : Sweet & Maxwell, 1984.
ISBN 0421320508 Pbk £6.95

—Studying rural lawyers : research strategy and context / Kim Economides, Charles Watkins and Mark Blacksell. - Exeter : University of Exeter, 1985.
66,9p. - (Working paper).

—Tomorrow's lawyers : computers and legal training : a paper prepared by the Society's Legal Education Committee to discuss the teaching of computer applications to intending lawyers and to qualified practitioners / Society for Computers and Law. - Milton, Oxon : Society for Computers and Law, 1981.
7p; 22cm.
ISBN 0906122082 Pbk Unpriced

—Use of the law list to assess the distribution and characteristics of solicitors in England and Wales / Charles Watkins, Mark Blacksell and Kim Economides. - Exeter : University of Exeter, 1984.
24p. - (Working paper).
Bibliography: p.23-24.

—WArwick 1984 communications conference held at the University of Warwick in Coventry from Thursday 5 July to Sunday 8 July 1984 / Society for Computer and Law. - Didcot, Oxon. : Society for Computers and Law, 1984.
93p.
ISBN 0906122155

—Which firm of solicitors? / 2nd ed. - London : Legalease, 1988.
ISBN 1870854101 Hbk £6.90

LEGAL PROFESSION - INDIA

—Art of Attracting Clients / Allahabad : Law Book Company, 1988.
64p.

—Art of Becoming a Successful Criminal Lawyer / 3rd ed. - Allahabad : Law Book Company, 1988.

—Law Relating to Notaries Act / Bhatnagar. - Allahabad : Ashoka Law House, 1987.
300p.

LEGAL PROFESSION - IRELAND

—Legal profession in Ireland 1789-1922 / Dublin : Incorporated Law Society of Ireland, 1986.
xii,176p.
Bibliography: p.165-169. - Includes index.
ISBN 090202728X

LEGAL PROFESSION - NEW ZEALAND

—Cordery on Solicitors / Wellington : Butterworths.
This book discusses the rights and liabilities of an English solicitor. Materials on a solicitors relationship with his client; his liability in negligence; his entitlement to remuneration; his relations with partners and employees; and The Law Society are included.
ISBN 0406161585 Pbk

LEGAL PROFESSION - NIGERIA

—Law and the twin pillars of justice / by C.A. Oputa. - Owerri Nigeria : Government Printer, 1981.
146p.
Collection of law lectures and papers presented by the author at various seminars and symposia.

LEGAL PROFESSION - PACIFIC ISLANDS

—Lawasia directory / Sydney : Lawasia, 1979-.

LEGAL PROFESSION - PHILIPPINES

—Survey of the Legal Profession in the Philippines : Focus on Region 4 / Merlin M. Magalona. - Quezon City : University of the Philippines, Law Center, 1982.
182p.

LEGAL PROFESSION - SCOTLAND

—Minute book of the Faculty of Advocates / edited by John MacPherson Pinkerton. - Edinburgh : The Stair Society, 1980.
6v,274p. - (Publications).
Cover title: Faculty of Advocates minute book.
ISBN 0902292072

—Practice of the solicitor profession in Scotland : a discussion paper / Scottish Home and Health Department. - Edinburgh : The Department, 1987.
13p.

—Scottish jurists / by David M. Walker. - Edinburgh : W. Green, 1985.
xv,492p.
ISBN 0414007573

—Solicitors' Compendium Nineteen Eighty-Two : Extracted from the Parliament House Book / Edinburgh : W Green, 1983.
ISBN 0414007077 Hbk £3.75

LEGAL PROFESSION - USSR

—Lawyer-economist extraordinary : the Soviet jurisconsult / Jane Giddings. - s.l. : National Association for Soviet and East European Studies, 1981.
29p; 30cm.

—Right of the accused to defence in the USSR / Yuri Stetsovsky : translated from the Russian by H. Campell Creighton. - Moscow : Progress Publishers, 1982.
283 p.; 21 cm.
Includes bibliographical references and index.

LEGAL REASONING

—Laying Down the Law : the Foundations of Legal Reasoning, Research and Writing in Australia / 2nd ed. – Butterworths, 1988.
306p.
ISBN 0409493074 Pbk £26.00

—Legal mind : essays for Tony Honore / edited by Neil MacCormick and Peter Birks. – Oxford : Clarendon, 1986.
304p; 24cm.
Includes bibliography and index.
ISBN 0198761961 £35.00

—Moral and legal reasoning / Samuel Stoljar. – London : Macmillan, 1980.
ix, 172p; 23cm.
Also published: New York : Barnes and Noble, 1980. Includes index.
ISBN 0333277716 £8.95

—Unity of law and morality : a refutation of legal postivisim / M.J. Detmold. – London : Routledge & Kegan Paul, 1984.
xix,271p; 23cm.
Bibliography: p265-268. - Includes index.
ISBN 0710200307 £15.00

LEGAL REASONING - AUSTRALIA

—Laying Down the Law : The Foundations of Legal Reasoning Research and Writing in Australia and New Zealand / C. Cook. – Sydney : Butterworths, 1988.
304p.
This workbook contains exercises which require students to find cases and statutes, analyze legal problems, interpret judicial decisions and legislation, and use basic research tools such as digests and encyclopedias. Additional material has been included to cover New Zealand.

LEGAL RESEARCH

—Italian legal information retrieval : a handbook / by Ettore Giannantonio. – Milano : Giuffre, 1984.
xii,181p; 25cm. – (Informatica e ordinamento giuridico).
ISBN 881400143X

—Law and social enquiry : case studies of research / edited by Robin Luckham. – Uppsala : Scandinavian Institute of African Studies, 1981.
290p.
Includes bibliographical references.
ISBN 9171061819 Pbk
ISBN 9171061789

—Legal databases in Europe : user attitudes and supplier strategies / Michael Lloyd. – Amsterdam : North-Holland, 1986.
xiii, 218 p.; 24 cm.
At head of title: Commission of the European Communities. 'Report no. EUR 10439 of the Commission of the European Communities'–T.p. verso. Bibliography: p.205.
ISBN 044470048X

—List of current legal research topics : being topics forming the subject of research by students for degrees in Universities and Polytechnics in the United Kingdom / Institute of Advanced Legal Studies. – 35th ed. – London : the Institute, 1987.
vii,111p.
Supplements: Legal research in the United Kingdom 1905-1984. Includes indexes.

—Using a law library : a guide for students and lawyers in the Common Law provinces of Canada / Margaret A. Banks. – 3rd ed. – Toronto : Carswell, 1980.
ix,212p.
Includes bibliographies.
ISBN 0459330403

LEGAL RESEARCH - AUSTRALIA

—Laying Down the Law : The Foundations of Legal Reasoning Research and Writing in Australia and New Zealand / C. Cook. – Sydney : Butterworths, 1988.
304p.
This workbook contains exercises which require students to find cases and statutes, analyze legal problems, interpret judicial decisions and legislation, and use basic research tools such as digests and encyclopedias. Additional material has been included to cover New Zealand.

LEGAL RESEARCH - CANADA

—Annual report / Canadian Law Information Council / Canadian Law Information Council. – Ottawa : CLIC, 1982-.
Annual reports for 1978/1979 and 1979/1980 published as one volume entitled: Yesterday, today and tomorrow : 1978-1980 / Canadian Law Information Council. Annual report for 1980/1981 entitled: Progress through partnership : 1980/1981 / Canadian Law Information Council.

—Comparison of automated and manual legal research : a computer study / by Michael Iosipescu and John Yogis. – Ottawa : Canadian Law Information Council, 1981.
ii, 86 p.; 28 cm. – (Canadian Law Information Council working paper).
Cover title: Legal research.
ISBN 092035808X pbk. £13.50

—Computer-Assisted Legal Research : a Guide for Canadian Law Students / Ottawa : Canadian Law Information Council, 1984.
103p.
ISBN 0920358551 Pbk £15.00

—Dossier : an inventory of Current Legal Research in Canada / Ottawa : Canadian Law Information Council.
169p.

—How to update a statute for all Canadian jurisdictions : as of April 1980 / edited by Gail S. Dykstra. – Ottawa : Canadian Law Information Council, 1980.
38p.
First published in: CLIC's Legal materials letter, 1979-1980. Later ed. (1985) by Mary Jane T. Sinclair.
ISBN 0920358047

—Inventory of current legal research in Canada / l'inventaire des activites de recherche juridique courantes au Canada : compilers, Catherine M. Parker, Laurie A. Davidson. – Ottawa : Canadian Law Information Council, 1986.
vi,169p.
Includes index.
ISBN 0920358888

—Legal research handbook / Douglass T. MacEllven. – 2nd ed. – Toronto : Butterworths, 1986.
xxix,411p.
Guide to all current sources of Canadian law. Includes additional chapters on legal writing and government and social science publications. Quebec material has been augmented. Includes a master research checklist, subject area checklists, and examination of management of law firm libraries, computer assisted research, and indices of research centres and legal publishers.
ISBN 0409847798 Hbk £60

—Legal writing and research manual / John A. Yogis and Innis M. Christie. – 3rd ed. – Toronto : Butterworths, 1988.
xx, 199 p.; 23 cm.
Intends to help develop an understanding of, and some facility in, the techniques of legal research and writing. The distinction between primary and secondary materials is explained, Canadian and English sources are emphasised, but an outline of principle American materials is also provided.
ISBN 0409811548

—Profile of published legal research : a report to the Consultative Group on Research and Education in Law based on a survey of Canadian legal publications / Alice Janisch. – Ottawa : Consultative Group on Research and Education in Law, 1982.
39p.

—Progress through partnership : 1980/1981 / Canadian Law Information Council. – Ottawa : CLIC, 1981-.
36p.
Annual reports for 1978/1979 and 1979/1980 published as one volume entitled: Yesterday, today and tomorrow : 1978-1980 / Canadian Law Information Council. Continued by: Annual report / Canadian Law Information Council, 1981/1982 onwards. Includes annual report of CLIC for 1980/1981.

—Sources of support for legal research : a report to the Consultative Group on Research and Education in Law based on a survey of foundations, law reform commissions, departments of justice, and attorneys and solicitors general in Canada / John S. McKennirey. – Ottawa : Consultative Group on Research and Education in Law, 1982.
iii,53p.

—Updating statutes and regulations for all Canadian jurisdictions (as of Dec. 1984) / by Mary Jane T. Sinclair. – New ed. – Ottawa : Canadian Law Information Council, 1985.
44p.
Previous ed.: published as How to update a statute for all Canadian jurisdictions / edited by Gail S. Dykstra.
ISBN 0920358772

—Using a law library : a guide for students and lawyers in the common law provinces of Canada / Margaret A. Banks. – 4th ed. – Toronto : Carswell, 1980.
xiii,249p.
Includes bibliographical references and index.
ISBN 0459376101

—Yesterday, today and tomorrow : 1978-1980 / Canadian Law Information Council. – Ottawa : CLIC, 1980.
32p.
Annual report for 1980/1981 entitled: Progress through Partnership : 1980/1981 / Canadian Law Information Council. Continued by: Annual report / Canadian Law Information Council, 1981/1982 onwards. Includes annual reports of CLIC for 1978/1979 and 1979/1980.

LEGAL RESEARCH - GREAT BRITAIN

—English criminal process : a review of empirical research / Andrew Ashworth. – Oxford : Centre for Criminological Research, University of Oxford, 1984.
135p. – (Occasional paper).
Bibliography: p131-135.
ISBN 094781101X

—Legal Research Handbook / London : Butterworths, 1983.
ISBN 0409848298 Hbk £40.00

—Legal research in the United Kingdom 1905-84 : a classified list of legal theses and dissertations successfully completed for postgraduate degrees awarded by universities and polytechnics in the United Kingdom from 1905-1984 / Institute of Advanced Legal Studies. – London : The Institute, 1986.
xxx, ca. 300p.
Supersedes: List of legal research topics completed and approved since about 1935. - 2nd ed. - 1961; and, Supplement 1961-July 1966. Includes indexes. Supplemented by: List of current legal research topics.
ISBN 0901190292

—Legal research techniques / by Nigel Smith. – Hebden Bridge : Legal Information Resources, 1987.
ii,40p.
ISBN 1870369017

—List of current legal research topics : being topics forming the subject of research by students for degrees in universities and polytechnics in the United Kingdom / University of London, Institute of Advanced Legal Studies. – 33rd ed. – London : The Institute, 1985.
51p.
Includes index. . Supplements: Legal research in the United Kingdom 1905-1984.

—List of current legal research topics : being topics forming the subject of research by students for degrees in universities and polytechnics in the United Kingdom / University of London, Institute of Advanced Legal Studies. – 34th ed. – London : The Institute, 1986.
iv,99p.
Supplements: Legal research in the United Kingdom 1905-1984. Includes indexes.

LEGAL RESEARCH - NEW ZEALAND

—Index to New Zealand legal writing / J.F. Northey. – 2nd ed. – Auckland : Legal Research Foundation, 1982.
ix,260p.
Previous ed.: 1977.
ISBN 090858119X

LEGAL RESEARCH - NORTHERN IRELAND

—Annual report / Servicing the Legal System, Queen's University of Belfast / Servicing the Legal System. – v. – Belfast : Servicing the Legal System, 1981-.
Servicing the Legal System was originally established as a committee of the Faculty of law, Queen's University of Belfast. Report year ends 31 July.

LEGAL RESEARCH - OCEANIA

—Teaching and Research in International Law in Asia and the Pacific / Paris : UNESCO.
ISBN 9231023950 Hbk £60.00

—Teaching and Research in International Law in Asia and the Pacific / Paris : UNESCO.
ISBN 9231023950 Hbk £60.00

LEGAL SERVICES

—Data processing and the law / edited by Colin Campbell. – London : Sweet & Maxwell, 1984.
viii,264p; 22cm.
Includes index.
ISBN 0421320001 Pbk £20.00

—Independent solicitor : journal of the British Legal Association / British Legal Association. – Tunbridge Wells : British Legal Association, .
From 1983 incorporates BLA solicitor.

—Public legal services : a comparative study of policy, politics and practice / by Jeremy Cooper. – London : Sweet & Maxwell, 1983.
ix,320p; 22cm.
Bibliography: p305-313. - Includes index.
ISBN 0421303506 Pbk £9.50

—Public legal services in three countries : a study of the relationship between policy and practice / Jeremy Cooper. – Florence : European University Institute, Department of Law, 1981.
436p.
Thesis (Doctoral) - European University Institute,1981. Includes bibliographical references.

LEGAL SERVICES - AUSTRALIA

—Access to law / the Second Seminar on Australian Lawyers and Social Change, held by the Faculty of Law, Australian National University : editors, John Goldring ... et al. – Canberra : Faculty of Law, Australian National University in association with Australian National University Press, 1980.
336 p.; 25 cm.
Includes bibliographical references and index.
ISBN 0708113052 pbk.

LEGAL SERVICES - CANADA

—Annual report / Canadian Law Information Council / Canadian Law Information Council. – Ottawa : CLIC, 1982-.
Annual reports for 1978/1979 and 1979/1980 published as one volume entitled: Yesterday, today and tomorrow : 1978-1980 / Canadian Law Information Council. Annual report for 1980/1981 entitled: Progress through partnership : 1980/1981 / Canadian Law Information Council.

—Lawyers and the consumer interest : regulating the market for legal services / edited by Robert G. Evans, Michael J. Trebilcock. – Toronto : Butterworths, 1982.
xxiii,459p.
Includes bibliographical references.
ISBN 0409873543

—Legal profession and quality of service : further report and proposals : report and materials of a National Workshop on Quality of Legal Services held in Toronto in October, 1980, as a sequel to the National Conference on Quality of Legal Services held in Ottawa in October, 1978 / editor and commentator, W.H. Hurlburt. – Edmonton, Alberta? : Federation of Law Societies of Canada, 1981.
417p.
Includes two parts in English and French.
ISBN 0969087101

—Progress through partnership : 1980/1981 / Canadian Law Information Council. – Ottawa : CLIC, 1981-.
36p.
Annual reports for 1978/1979 and 1979/1980 published as one volume entitled: Yesterday, today and tomorrow : 1978-1980 / Canadian Law Information Council. Continued by: Annual report / Canadian Law Information Council, 1981/1982 onwards. Includes annual report of CLIC for 1980/1981.

—Yesterday, today and tomorrow : 1978-1980 / Canadian Law Information Council. – Ottawa : CLIC, 1980.
32p.
Annual report for 1980/1981 entitled: Progress through Partnership : 1980/1981 / Canadian Law Information Council. Continued by: Annual report / Canadian Law Information Council, 1981/1982 onwards. Includes annual reports of CLIC for 1978/1979 and 1979/1980.

LEGAL SERVICES - CANADA - ONTARIO

—Legal services in rural areas : an evaluation : report / prepared for the Department of Justice, Ottawa, and the Faculty of Law, Queen's University by D. Laureen Snider. – Rev. ed. – Ottawa : Department of Justice, Evaluation and Statistics Section, 1981.
303p. – (An evaluation report).
Bibliography: p.257-266.

LEGAL SERVICES - ENGLAND

—Government response to the report of the Royal Commission on Legal Services / presented to Parliament by the Lord High Chancellor... – London : H.M.S.O., 1983.
34p.
ISBN 0101907702 PBK £3.75

—Law in the balance : legal services in the 1980s / edited by Philip A. Thomas. – Oxford : Robertson, 1982.
x,245p; 23cm.
Includes bibliographies and index.
ISBN 0855204443 Hbk £18.50
ISBN 0855204826 Pbk £6.50

LEGAL SERVICES - GREAT BRITAIN

—Before You See A Solicitor (It's Your Law) / 2nd ed. – London : Longman Professional, 1983.
ISBN 0851207790 Pbk £6.95

—Equal justice : report of a joint working party / Hebden Bridge, W. Yorks. : Hebden Royd Publications, 1986.
25p.
The report of a joint working party set up by the Social Democratic Lawyers Association and the Association of Liberal Lawyers.
ISBN 1851870296

—Law centre staff research project / Francis Stevens. – London : Law Centres Federation, 1983.
34p.
Summary of a report commissioned by the Law Centres Federation Evaluation Sub-Committee.

—Legal services : - a new start : LAG's response to the report of the Royal Commission on Legal Services / London : Legal Action Group, 1980.
50p.

—Legal services in rural Britain : access, accessibility and need / Mark Blacksell, Kim Economides and Charles Watkins. – Exeter : University of Exeter, 1984.
26p. – (Working paper).
Bibliography: p.22-26.

—Marketing Legal Services / Patrick McKenna. – Toronto : Butterworths, 1988.
180p.
Designed to help lawyers attract targeted clientele and expand their client base. Discusses how to plan to reach goals, whether or not to advertise, and how.
ISBN 0409806366 Hbk

LEGAL SERVICES - NEW ZEALAND

—Access to the law : a research and discussion peper / New Zealand. – Wellington : The Division, 1981.
214p. – (Study series).
Bibliography: p.203-204.

LEGAL SERVICES - NORTHERN IRELAND

—Annual report / Servicing the Legal System, Queen's University of Belfast / Servicing the Legal System. – v. – Belfast : Servicing the Legal System, 1981-.
Servicing the Legal System was originally established as a committee of the Faculty of law, Queen's University of Belfast. Report year ends 31 July.

LEGAL SERVICES - SCOTLAND

—Royal Commission on Legal Services in Scotland 1980, 2 Vols. / Royal Commission on Criminal Procedure. – London : HMSO.
ISBN 0101784600 Hbk £8.50
Vol. 2: Appendices
ISBN 0101784619 Hbk £12.50

—Scottish Consumer Council's response to the Hughes report : the report of the Royal Commission on Legal Services in Scotland (Volume one : Cmnd 7846) / Scottish Consumer Council. – Glasgow : The Council, 1981.
28p; 30cm.
ISBN 0907067026 Pbk £1.00

LEGAL SERVICES - SOUTH AFRICA

—Legal aid and law clinics in South Africa : proceedings of a conference held at the Howard College School of Law, University of Natal, Durban, from 11-13 July 1983 / Durban : School of Law, Howard College, University of Natal, 1985.
ix,163p.
ISBN 0869804251

LEGAL SERVICES - UNITED STATES

—Butterworths Legal Services Directory 1988 / New York : British Media Publications, 1988.
ISBN 0611007215 Pbk £18.00

LEGAL SYSTEM

—Cases and Materials On English Legal Systems / Bailey. – Sweet & Maxwell, 1987.
ISBN 0421359404 Hbk
ISBN 0421359501 Pbk

—Law and politics in Aztec Texcoco / Cambridge : Cambridge University Press, 1984.
354.
Analyses the Aztec legal system. Discusses land tenure, inheritance, kinship relations, business trade and local and imperial administration.
ISBN 0521234751 Hbk £35.00

—Legal System and Social Systems / Etal. – Oxford : Croom Helm, 1985.
ISBN 0709936125 Hbk £18.95

—Major legal systems in the world today / Brierly. – 3rd ed. – London : Sweet & Maxwell, 1985.
ISBN 0420473408 Hbk £28.00
ISBN 0420473505 Pbk £23.00

—Pacific Courts and Legal Systems / rev. ed. – Suva : University of the South Pacific, Institute of Pacific Studies, 1987.
270p.

LEGAL SYSTEM - AUSTRALIA

—Our Legal System / Gifford. – 2nd ed. – North Ryde : Law Book Co, 1983.
ISBN 0455202680 Pbk £10.50

—Understanding law : an introduction to Australian legal system / Nettheim. – 2nd ed. – London : Butterworths, 1984.
ISBN 0409493724 Pbk £6.80

—Understanding Law : Introduction to Australia's Legal System 1978 / Garth Nettheim. – 3rd ed. – Butterworths, 1988.
ca 152p.
ISBN 0409495190 Pbk £14.00

LEGAL SYSTEM - AUSTRALIA - NEW SOUTH WALES

—System of law and courts governing New South Wales / 2nd ed. – London : Butterworths, 1985.
ISBN 0409492531 Hbk £40.00

—System of Law and Courts Governing New South Wales / 2nd ed. – Butterworths, 1985.
461p.
This book for the beginning law student contains a general examination of the NSW legal system. An institutional as opposed to a rule-oriented approach to law is adopted.
ISBN 0409492531 Hbk £65.00
ISBN 0409492639 Pbk £49.00

LEGAL SYSTEM - CHINA

—China Modernisation and Legal Development / 2nd ed. – London : Longman Professional, 1987.
ISBN 0851208045 Hbk £27.50
ISBN 0851208043 Pbk £17.50

LEGAL SYSTEM - ENGLAND

—Changing law / Robin White, Patfield. – London : Pinter, 1990.
224.
A survey of the radical and rapid changes to English law in the last 25 years. Covers negligence, land, family, financial regulation, civil liberties, social security, EC law, reform of the legal profession and codification of common law principles.
ISBN 0718513312 Hbk £29.50

—English Legal System / London : Financial Training, 1988.
– (SWOT).
ISBN 1851850449 Pbk £7.50

LEGAL SYSTEM - FINLAND

—Finnish Legal System / Helsinki : Lakimiesliiton Kustannus, 1985.
ISBN 9516402445 Hbk £25.00

LEGAL SYSTEM - GREAT BRITAIN

—Concept of a legal system / 2nd ed. – Oxford : Oxford University Press, 1980.
ISBN 0198253621 Pbk £8.95

LEGAL SYSTEM - INDIA

—Development of Indian Legal System / New Delhi : Deep and Deep Publications, 1987.
428p.

—Growth of Legal System in Indian Society / Srirama Indradeva. – New Delhi : Allied Publishers, 1980.
vi, 220p.

—Origin and Development of Legal and Political System in India, 3 Vols. / 2nd ed. – New Delhi : Deep and Deep Publications, 1982.
ca 700p.

LEGAL SYSTEM - IRELAND

—Irish Legal System : Cases and Materials / McCutcheon. – London : Butterworths, 1986.
ISBN 086205222X Hbk £22.50
ISBN 0862052238 Pbk £12.50

LEGAL SYSTEM - ITALY

—Italian Legal System / Sydney : Butterworths, 1985.
ISBN 0409490849 Hbk £37.00

—Italian legal system / London : Butterworths, 1985.
ISBN 040639993X Hbk £33.00

LEGAL SYSTEM - NEW ZEALAND

—Introduction to the New Zealand Legal System / 6th ed. – Butterworths, 1985.
ISBN 0409702285 Pbk £52.80

—Introduction to the New Zealand Legal System / 6th ed. – London : Butterworths, 1986.
ISBN 0409702285 Pbk £31.00

—Introduction to the New Zealand legal system / by R.D. Mulholland. – Wellington : Butterworths, 1980.
xvii,350p.
Includes index.
ISBN 0409600865

LEGAL SYSTEM - NORTHERN IRELAND

—Legal system of Northern Ireland / by Brice Dickson. – Belfast : SLS Legal Publications (NI), 1984.
x,225p.
ISBN 0853892369

LEGAL SYSTEM - SCOTLAND

—Legal System of Scotland / London : HMSO, 1982.
54p.
ISBN 0114917477 Pbk £3.50

—Legal system of Scotland : cases and materials / A.A.Paterson and T.St.J.N.Bates. – 2nd ed. – Edinburgh : Green, 1986.
xviii,395p.
ISBN 0414007832

—The legal system of Scotland: cases and materials / J Bates. – 2nd. – Edinburgh : W Green & Son, 1986.
Analyses the use of the principal sources of Scots law, in particular precedent and statutory interpretation. Considers the legal profession, the administration of civil and criminal justice and the operation of tribunals. Also deals with the Court of Justice of the European Communities and the European Commission and Court of Human Rights.
ISBN 0414007382

—Scottish legal system : an introduction to the study of Scots law / by David M. Walker. – 5th ed., rev. – Edinburgh : Green, 1981.
xlv,543p; 23cm.
Previous ed.: 1976. Includes bibliographies and index.
ISBN 0414006836 Unpriced

LEGAL SYSTEM - UNITED STATES

—U.S. legal system : a practice handbook / edited by Dennis Campbell and Winifred Hepperle. – The Hague : Nijhoff, 1983.
x,319p; 25cm.
Includes bibliography.
ISBN 9024727820 Hbk £130.00

LEGAL THEORY

—Bentham and the common law tradition / Oxford : Clarendon Press, 1989.
506. – (Clarendon Law Series).
Offers a philosphical interpretation of the historical debate between Bentham and classical common law theory, which has shaped contemporary conceptions of the nature, tasks and limits of law and adjudication.
ISBN 0198256515 Pbk £15
ISBN 0198255055 Hbk £40

—Crime, Justice, and Codification : Essays in Commemoration of Jacques Fortin / Agincourt : Carswell, 1986.
196p.
This book contains eleven essays dealing with the theory, philosophy, reform and codification of criminal law. Rationality and legitimacy of criminal law the goals of reform are addressed in the essays.

—Definition and rule in legal theory : a reassessment of H.L.A. Hart and the positivist tradition / Robert N. Moles. – Oxford : Basil Blackwell, 1987.
xii,285p; 24cm.
Bibliography: p275-278. - Includes index.
ISBN 063115342X £25.00

—Essays on Bentham / Oxford : Oxford University Press, 1982.
ISBN 0198253486 Hbk £17.50

—Hume's Theory of Justice / Oxford : Oxford University Press, 1983.
ISBN 0198247249 Pbk £8.95

—Idea of law / Rev Ed. – Pelican, 1981.
ISBN 0140206884 Pbk £4.95

—Jurisprudence and Legal Theory / 3rd ed. – Lucknow : Eastern Book Company, 1986.
358p.

—Jurisprudence and Legal Theory / 9th ed. 1975 repr. – Lucknow : Eastern Book Company, 1985.

—Jurists : Profiles in Legal Theory / London : Edward Arnold.

—Law, or a Discourse Thereof / 4th ed. Repr. of 1661 ed. – Abingdon : Professional Books.
238p.

—Legal Philosophies / London : Butterworths, 1980.
ISBN 0406593612 Pbk £10.95

—Legal Philosophies / Wellington : Butterworths, 1980.
This book concentrates on recent legal theorists, such as Rawls and Dworkin, whose work is difficult to grasp for students without a background in philosophy. The text is punctuated by questions, criticisms, and comparisons.
ISBN 0406593612 Pbk

—Legal theory and common law / edited by William Twining. – Oxford : Blackwell, 1986.
300p.
ISBN 0631144773 £22.50

—Legal theory and legal history : essays on the common law / A.W.B. Simpson. – London : Hambledon, 1987.
xiii,432p; 24cm.
Includes index.
ISBN 0907628834 £24.00

—Legal Theory Meets Legal Practice / Montreal : Academic Printing and Publishing, 1988.
400p.
ISBN 0920980228 Hbk £69.95
ISBN 0920980236 Pbk £34.95

—Modern Theories of Law 1933 / London : Wildy & Sons.

—On the Utility of Legal Theory / Mark van Hoecke. – Tampere : A-Tiete Oy.
ISBN 9519464352 Pbk £140.00

—Principles of Jurisprudence and Legal Theory / 4th ed. – Lucknow : Eastern Book Company, 1980.
482p.

—Structure and Process of International Law : Essays in Legal Philosophy, Doctrine and Theory / Douglas M. Johnston. – Dordrecht : Kluwer, 1983.
1,242p.
ISBN 9024728827 Hbk £325.00

LEGAL THEORY - ENGLAND

—Pragmatism and theory in English law / London : Sweet & Maxwell, 1987.
ISBN 0420475907 Hbk £14.50
ISBN 0420476008 Pbk £8.50

LEGAL THEORY - GREAT BRITAIN

—Bentham and The Common Systems / Oxford : Oxford University Press, 1986.
ISBN 0198255055 Hbk £45.00

—Introduction to the Principles of Morals and Legislation / Repr. of 1879 ed. – Abingdon : Professional Books.

—Law and the Individual / London : Pitman Publishing, 1982.
ISBN 071211260X Pbk £4.95

—Theory of Legislation / R. Hildreth. – Repr. of 1864 ed. – Abingdon : Professional Books.

LEGAL THEORY - SOUTH AFRICA

—Introduction to South African law and legal theory / W.J. Hosten ... et al. – Rev. reprint. – Durban : Butterworths, 1980.
xv,948p; 25cm.
Bibliography: p.ix-xiv. - Includes index.
ISBN 0409033480

LEGISLATION

—Butterworths Consolidated Legislation Service / Professional Publ.
ISBN 0409014478 loose £15.00 (additional binder)

—Computers and Penal Legislation / Oslo : Norwegian University Press, 1983.
166p.
ISBN 8200065707 Hbk £84.00

LEGISLATION - AUSTRALIA

—Legislation handbook / Canberra : Australian Government Publishing Service, 1980.
v,61p.
Previous ed.: 1975, compiled by the Australian Public Service Board.
ISBN 0642048487 PBK £2.20

—Report to Parliament on a proposal for a Statute Law (Miscellaneous Provisions) Bill / Legal and Constitutional Committee. – Melbourne : Government Printer, 1985.
xii,189p.

LEGISLATION - AUSTRALIA - NEW SOUTH WALES

—Deregulation : a plan of action to rationalise South Australian legislation : a report to the South Australian Government / by Dianne Gayler. – Adelaide : Government Printer, 1980.
v,85p. – (P.P.).
Includes bibliographical references.

LEGISLATION - AUSTRALIA - VICTORIA

—Report on Statute Law Revision Bill 1984 / Legal and Constitutional Committee. – Melbourne : Government Printer, 1984.
xiii,52p.
Bibliography: p.52.

—Report on the Statute Law Revision Bill / Statute Law Revision Committee. – Melbourne : Government Printer, 1981.
ii,5p.

LEGISLATION - CANADA

—Construction of statutes / Elmer A. Driedger. – 2nd ed. – Toronto : Butterworths, 1983.
xvi,385p. – (Canadian legal manual series).
Contains a new chapter on bilingual statutes, and expanded discussion of departure from the ordinary meaning for the professed reason of 'absurdity', and a refinement of the author's commentary on the presumption against retrospective operation.
ISBN 0409828033

—Updating statutes and regulations for all Canadian jurisdictions (as of Dec. 1984) / by Mary Jane T. Sinclair. – New ed. – Ottawa : Canadian Law Information Council, 1985.
44p.
Previous ed.: published as How to update a statute for all Canadian jurisdictions / edited by Gail S. Dykstra.
ISBN 0920358772

LEGISLATION - CANADA - ALBERTA

—Table of Alberta Legislation / Edmonton : Queen's Printer, 1981.
151p.

LEGISLATION - ENGLAND

—Law-making process... / Michael Zander. – 2nd. ed. – London : Weidenfeld, 1985.
xxiv, 416p.
ISBN 0297786628 Pbk
ISBN 0297786636

LEGISLATION - EUROPEAN COMMUNITY

—Community Secondary Legislation, 3 Vols. / Edinburgh : W Green, 1985.
– (Encyclopedia of European Community Law Ser.).
ISBN 0421207604 loose £480.00

LEGISLATION - GREAT BRITAIN

—Chronological table of local legislation / the Law Commission and the Scottish Law Commission. – 2 v. – London : Law Commission, 1985.
Contents: Part 1. Local and personal acts 1797-1908 - Part 2. Local and personal acts 1909-1973, private acts 1539-1973.

—Factsheet / Public Information Office, House of Commons. – v. – London : The Office, 1985.
No. 1 is revised ed., Nov. 1984.
ISBN 01444689

—Law-making process / Michael Zander. – London : Weidenfeld and Nicolson, 1980.
xxvi,309p.
ISBN 0297777505

—Legislation / by David R. Miers and Alan C. Page. – London : Sweet & Maxwell, 1982.
xviii,266p; 23cm.
Bibliography: p247-255. - Includes index.
ISBN 0421271108 Hbk £13.50
ISBN 0421271205 Pbk Unpriced

—Legislation and public policy : public bills in the 1970-74 Parliament / by Ivor Burton and Gavin Drewry. – London : Macmillan, 1981.
xii,322p; 23cm.
Bibliography: p280-283. - Includes index.
ISBN 0333152042 £25.00

LEGISLATION - INDIA

—Re-promulgation of ordinances : a fraud on the constitution of India / D. C. Wadhwa. – Pune : Gokhale Institute of Politics and Economics, 1983.
xxxi,259p.
ISBN 0861314328

LEGISLATION - SOUTH AFRICA

—Butterworth's Consolidated Legislation Service / Durban : Butterworths, 1986.
ISBN 0409014001 Pbk

LEGISLATION (THEORY)

—Codification of the criminal law : a public lecture / delivered by J.C. Smith on ... 17th March 1986. – London : Inns of Court School of Law, 1986.
16p.

LEGISLATIVE BODIES

—Parliaments of the world : a comparative reference compendium / 2nd ed. 2. – Aldershot : Gower, 1986.
1422p; 25cm.
Previous ed.: published in 1 vol. London : Macmillan, 1976. Includes index.
ISBN 0566052288 v.2 £65.00

LEGISLATIVE BODIES - AUSTRALIA

—Report relating to the use of or reference to the records of proceedings of the House in the courts : together with minutes of proceedings of the Committee / the Parliament of the Commonwealth of Australia, House of Representatives, Committee of Privileges. – Canberra : Commonwealth Government Printer, 1981.
vii,108p. – (Parliamentary paper).
ISBN 0642057206

LEGISLATIVE BODIES - AUSTRALIA - VICTORIA

—Progress report on the Constitution Act 1975 : the role of Upper Houses of Parliament (interim report) / Statute Law Revision Committee. – Melbourne : Government Printer, 1982.
iv,4p. – (D v no 1/1982).

LEGISLATIVE BODIES - CANADA

—Parliamentary privilege in Canada / by Joseph Maingot. – Toronto : Butterworths, 1982.
xxx,290p.
Sets out the law relating to parliamentary procedures, giving an outline of the privilege procedure in the House of Commons. Traces the history, development and scope of parliamentary immunity, rights and privileges, including the privilege of freedom of speech. Also covers proceedings in Parliament, the Offical Secrets Act, and the criminal law.
ISBN 0409847860 Hbk £75

LEGISLATIVE BODIES - CANADA - ONTARIO

—Report on witnesses before legislative committees / Ontario Law Reform Commission. – Toronto : Ministry of the Attorney-General, 1981.
vii,129p.
ISBN 0774367296

LEGISLATIVE BODIES - IRELAND

—Elements of the Law and Practice of Legislative Assemblies in the U.S.A. / Dublin : Irish Academic Press.
560p.
ISBN 0716520206 Hbk £55.00

LEGISLATIVE DRAFTING

—Bibliography of materials on legislative and other legal drafting and the interpretation of statutes / 3rd rev. ed. – London : Commonwealth Secretariat, 1985.
62p.
Previous ed.: 1977.

—Law drafting and sociology : a seminar report / edited by Antti Kivivuori. – Helsinki : Ministry of Justice, Law Drafting Dept., 1985.
122 p.; 25 cm. – (Publication series / Ministry of Justice, Law Drafting Department).
Includes bibliographical references.
ISBN 9514686764 pbk.

—Legislative drafting / G.C. Thornton. – 3rd ed. – London : Butterworth, 1987.
396p; 24cm.
Previous ed.: 1979. Includes index.
ISBN 0406399824 £38.00

LEGISLATIVE DRAFTING - AUSTRALIA

—Making an Act of Parliament : Legislative Process / House of Representatives Practice. – Canberra : Australian Government Publishing Service, 1981.

LEGISLATIVE DRAFTING - AUSTRALIA - VICTORIA

—Plain English and the law : a report / Law Reform Commission of Victoria. – Melbourne : The Commission, 1987.
xvi,109p. – (Report no 9).
Includes bibliographical references and index.
Accompanied by appendices 1-8 (3v.).

—Report on Statute Law Revision Bill 1984 / Legal and Constitutional Committee. – Melbourne : Government Printer, 1984.
xiii,52p.
Bibliography: p.52.

—Report on the Statute Law Revision Bill / Statute Law Revision Committee. – Melbourne : Government Printer, 1981.
ii,5p.

LEGISLATIVE DRAFTING - CANADA

—Drafting and Interpreting Legislation / 3rd ed. – Agincourt : Carswell, 1988.
110p.

—Legal drafting / by Robert C. Dick. – 2nd ed. – Toronto : Carswell, 1985.
xiii,234p.
Includes bibliographical references and index.
ISBN 045937740X

—Manual of instructions for legislative and legal writing / Elmer A. Driedger. – Ottawa : Canadian Government Publishing Centre, 1982.
6 v, vi, 568.; 25 cm.
Includes bibliographical references.
ISBN 0660111187 pbk. : set £25.00 (£30.00 other countries)

LEGISLATIVE DRAFTING - FRANCE

—British and French statutory drafting : the proceedings of the Franco-British conference of 7 and 8 April 1986 / edited by Sir William Dale. – London : Institute of Advanced Legal Studies, 1986.
xix,176p; 21cm.
Conference organized by and held at the Institute of Advanced Legal Studies.

LEGISLATIVE DRAFTING - GREAT BRITAIN

—British and French statutory drafting : the proceedings of the Franco-British conference of 7 and 8 April 1986 / edited by Sir William Dale. – London : Institute of Advanced Legal Studies, 1986.
xix,176p; 21cm.
Conference organized by and held at the Institute of Advanced Legal Studies.

—Manual on Legislative Drafting / London : Commonwealth Secretariat, 1984.

—Plain English for lawyers : some guidelines on writing and designing legal documents / London : National Consumer Council, 1984.
26p; 30cm.
ISBN 0905653726

—Preparation of Legislation / London : Sweet & Maxwell, 1981.
ISBN 0421291907 Pbk £7.25

—Preparation of legislation / London : Sweet & Maxwell, 1981.
ISBN 0421291907 Pbk £8.50

—Statute law / F. A. R. Bennion. – 2nd ed. – London : Oyez Longman, 1983.
xxvi,339p; 21cm.
Previous ed.: 1980.
ISBN 0851208029

LEGISLATIVE HEARINGS - CANADA - ONTARIO

—Report on witnesses before legislative committees / Ontario Law Reform Commission. – Toronto : Ministry of the Attorney-General, 1981.
vii,129p.
ISBN 0774367296

LEGISLATIVE POWER - CANADA

—Laskin's Canadian constitutional law / Neil Finkelstein. – 5th ed. – Toronto : Carswell, 1986.
2 v. (1501 p.); 26 cm.
'Canadian Bill of Rights': p. 1495-1497. 'American Bill of Rights': p. 1500-1501.
ISBN 0459384406 v. 2

LEGISLATORS - ITALY

—Career and recruitment patterns of Italian legislators : a contribution to the understanding of a polarized political system / by Maurizio Cotta. – Florence : European University Institute, 1983.
49p.
At head of title page: European University Institute, Department of Political and Social Sciences.

LEGISLATURES - INDIA

—Central Legislature in India (1909-1935) / Calcutta, 1984.
282p.
ISBN 8185109389 Hbk £90.00

—Comparative Legislative Behaviour / New Delhi : Uppal Publishing House, 1980.

LETTERS - GREAT BRITAIN

—Interception of Communications Act 1985 : chapter 56 : report of the Commissioner for ... / London : HMSO, 1987-.

—Specimen letters for solicitors / London : Longman Professional, 1987.
ISBN 0851208630 Pbk £15.95

LETTERS OF CREDIT

—Law Relating to Bankers Letters of Credit / Allahabad : Indian Press.
290p.

—Letters of credit / London : Euromoney, 1985.
xiv,174p.
ISBN 0903121794

—Liability of banks under letters of credit / Matti Kurkela. – Helsinki : Union of the Finnish Lawyers Pub. Co., 1982.
85 p.; 22 cm.
Bibliography: p. 84-85.
ISBN 9516401503 Fmk70.00

LETTERS OF CREDIT - CANADA

—Law of guarantee : a treatise on guarantee, indemnity and the standby letter of credit / by Kevin Patrick McGuinness. – Toronto : Carswell, 1986.
lxv,456p.
Bibliography: p.lxii-lxv. - Includes index.
ISBN 0459383906

—Letters of credit : the law and current practice / by Lazar Sarna. – 2nd ed. – Toronto : Carswell, 1986.
xxii,254p.
Includes bibliographical references and index.
ISBN 045938810X

—Letters of credit : the law and current practice / by Lazar Sarna. – Toronto : Carswell Legal Publications, 1984.
xv, 204 p.; 24 cm.
Includes bibliographical references and indexes.
ISBN 0459359908 Hbk £27

LETTERS OF CREDIT - GREAT BRITAIN

—Letters of Credit / 2nd ed. – London : Sweet & Maxwell, 1986.
ISBN 045938810X Hbk £33.00

LETTERS ROGATORY

—Letters rogatory for the interception of telecommunications : Recommendation no.R (85) 10 adopted by the Committee of Ministers of the Council of Europe on 28 June 1985 and Explanatory memorandum / Council of Europe. – Strasbourg : Council of Europe, 1986.
15p; 21cm. – (Legal affairs).
' ... prepared by a select committee of experts under the authority of the European Committee on Crime Problems' - p.3.
ISBN 9287108390

LEXIS

—Information on LEXIS Prepared Specifically for Tax Specialist / London : Butterworths.

—New Library of Irish Material Now on LEXIS / London : Butterworths.

LIABILITY

—Liability of banks under letters of credit / Matti Kurkela. – Helsinki : Union of the Finnish Lawyers Pub. Co., 1982.
85 p.; 22 cm.
Bibliography: p. 84-85.
ISBN 9516401503 Fmk70.00

—Liability of the States and Regional and Local Authorities for Damage Caused by their Agents and Administrative Services / Strasbourg : Council of Europe, 1981.

—Limitation of liability for maritime claims / by Patrick Griggs and Richard Williams. – London : Lloyd's, 1986.
122p; 22cm.
ISBN 1850440832 £24.00

—Tortious liability for unintentional harm in the common law and the civil law / by F.H. Lawson, B.S. Markesinis. – 2. – Cambridge : Cambridge University Press, 1982.
Includes index.
ISBN 0521235863 v. 2

LIABILITY - CANADA

—Liability in negligence / by J.C. Smith. – Toronto : Carswell, 1984.
xxxiii, 273 p.; 24 cm.
Includes indexes.
ISBN 0459366009 pbk.

LIABILITY - CANADA - BRITISH COLUMBIA

—Apportionment of Liability in British Columbia, 1 Vol. / Butterworths.

—Apportionment of Liability in British Columbia / Toronto : Butterworths.

—Shared liability / Law Reform Commission of British Columbia. – Vancouver : The Commission, 1985.
iv,62p. – (Working paper).
Includes bibliographical references.

LIABILITY - CANADA - NEW BRUNSWICK

—Professional Liability in Conveyancing in New Brunswick / Agincourt : Carswell, 1986.
127p.
This book addresses the lawyer's liability in conveyancing in New Brunswick, Canada. The role of the real estate practitioner is reviewed and the legal grounds for liability are analyzed in the work.

LIABILITY - ENGLAND

—Landlord and tenant law : privity of contract and estate / the Law Commission. – London : HMSO, 1988.
v,67p. – (H.C. 1988-89).
Includes the text of a draft Landlord and Tenant (Covenants) bill.
ISBN 0102008892

—Liability for defective services / Derrick Owles & Hugh Cockerell. – London : Financial Times Business Information, 1985.
168p; 30cm.
ISBN 0903199858

—Strict and vicarious liability : a study in administrative criminal law / by L.H. Leigh. – London : Sweet & Maxwell, 1982.
xix,121p; 19cm.
Includes index.
ISBN 0421267607 Hbk Unpriced
ISBN 0421267704 Pbk £6.85

—Towards a middle system of law / David Tench. – London : Consumers' Association, 1981.
73p.
ISBN 085202214X

LIABILITY - GREAT BRITAIN

—Accountant's professional negligence : developments in legal liability / Jonathan R.H.H. Pockson. – London : Macmillan, 1982.
xxi,212p; 23cm.
Bibliography: p192-208. - Includes index.
ISBN 0333278453 £25.00

—Causation in the law / Honore. – 2nd ed. – Oxford : Oxford University Press, 1985.
ISBN 0198254741 Pbk £14.50
ISBN 019825475X Hbk £25.00

—Civil Liability for Defective Premises / Allen. – London : Butterworths, 1982.
ISBN 0406233403 Hbk £34.00

—Civil Liability Statutes / London : Blackstone Press, 1987.
ISBN 1815850538 Pbk £8.95

—Directors' personal liability / 1st. – Oxford : Blackwell Scientific.
270. – (Blackwell Law Library).
Examines the erosion by recent legislation of the principle that neither directors nor shareholders of limited companies are personally liable for their company debts and torts. Advice on potential liabilities is offered in the light of the Companies Act 1985 and the Insolvency Act 1986.*Company directors, Accountants, Solicitors*
ISBN 0632026197 Pbk £19.50

—From Accident to Liability / London : Sweet & Maxwell, 1984.
640p. – (Sweet and Maxwell's Law Files Ser.: No. 3).
ISBN 0421321601 Hbk £29.50

—Grounds of Liability / Oxford : Oxford University Press, 1985.
ISBN 0198761910 Hbk £16.00
ISBN 019876197X Pbk £6.50

—Limitation of Liability / London : Fairplay Publication, 1984.
ISBN 0905045637 Pbk £12.00

—Limitation of Shipowners' Liability / London : Sweet & Maxwell, 1986.
ISBN 042134890 Hbk £38.00

—Professional Liability : An Architectural Press Legal Guide / 2nd ed. – London : Architectural Press, 1986.
208p : Illus.
ISBN 0851399525 Hbk £18.00

—Vicarious liability / Witherby, 1986.
ISBN 094869100X Pbk £7.50

LIABILITY - HONG KONG

—Report on the control of exemption clauses / the Law Reform Commission of Hong Kong. – Hong Kong : The Commission, 1986.
vi,98p. – (Topic).
Includes bibliographical references.

LIABILITY - IRELAND

—Report on the liability in tort of mentally disabled persons / the Law Reform Commission. – Dublin : The Commission, 1985.
v,78p. – (LRC).
Bibliography: p.75.

—Report on the liability in tort of minors and the liability of parents for damage caused by minors / the Law Reform Commission. – Dublin : The Commission, 1985.
iv,123p. – (LRC).
Bibliography: pp.118-120.

LIABILITY - MALAYSIA

—Occupiers' Liability in Singapore and Malaysia / Butterworths, 1986.
320p.
Covers the duty of reasonable care arising in particular circumstances, out of a special status, and out of current operations or activities, classes of entrant, duty to invitees, to licensees and to trespassers, defences, public and private premises, multiple defendants, and duties towards children.
ISBN 0409995134 Hbk £90.00

LIABILITY - SCOTLAND

—Civil liability : contribution / Scottish Law Commission. – Edinburgh : Scottish Law Commission, 1986.
iv,230p. – (Consultative memorandum).

—Legal capacity and responsibility of minors and pupils / Scottish Law Commission. – Edinburgh : The Commission, 1985.
280p. – (Consultative memorandum).
Includes bibliographical references.

—Report on civil liability : contribution / Scottish Law Commission. – Edinburgh : The Commission, 1988.
vi,75p.
Includes draft of a Bill.
ISBN 0102007896

LIABILITY - SINGAPORE

—Excluding Liability in Contracts / Butterworths, 1985.
227p.
Examines the English and Australian models, and discusses the popular common law concepts of reasonableness and unconscionability. Includes a review of the major cases and legislation aimed at evolving acceptable solutions to the dilemma of exception clauses.
ISBN 0409995002 Hbk £80.00

—Occupiers' Liability in Singapore and Malaysia / Butterworths, 1986.
320p.
Covers the duty of reasonable care arising in particular circumstances, out of a special status, and out of current operations or activities, classes of entrant, duty to invitees, to licensees and to trespassers, defences, public and private premises, multiple defendants, and duties towards children.
ISBN 0409995134 Hbk £90.00

LIABILITY - SOUTH AFRICA

—Risk as a ground for liability in delict / South African Law Commission. – Pretoria : The Commission, 1986.
x,41p. – (Report).
Includes bibliographical references.
ISBN 0621102024

LIABILITY FOR AIRCRAFT ACCIDENTS

—Aviation liabilities in the 1980s : a non-technical summary for insurers / S.l. : Swiss Reinsurance Company, 1981.
36p.

—Liability regime of the international air carrier : a commentary on the present Warsaw system / Rene H. Mankiewicz. – Deventer, The Netherlands : Kluwer, 1981.
xxvii,259p.
Includes index. Bibliography: pxv-xxii.
ISBN 9026811705

—Monetary limitations of liability in air law : legal, economic and socio-political aspects / Aleksander Tobolewski. – Montreal : De Daro, 1986.
vii,277p.
Bibliography: p.261-277.
ISBN 0969270305

—Monetary Limitations of Liability in Air Law : Legal, Economic and Socio-Political Aspects / Montreal : De Daro Publishing.

LIABILITY FOR ANIMALS - AUSTRALIA - WESTERN AUSTRALIA

—Report on liability for stock straying on to the highway / Law Reform Commission of Western Australia. – Perth : Law Reform Commission of Western Australia, 1981.
51p. – (Project).

LIABILITY FOR ANIMALS - SCOTLAND

—Civil liability in relation to animals / Scottish Law Commission. – Edinburgh : Scottish Law Commission, 1982.
xiii,180p. – (Consultative memorandum).

—Obligations : report on civil liability in relation to animals / Scottish Law Commission. – Edinburgh : The Commission, 1985.
vi,72p.
Includes bibliographical references. Includes Draft Animals (Scotland) Bill.
ISBN 0102004862

LIABILITY FOR BUILDING ACCIDENTS - ENGLAND

—Civil liability for defective premises / J. H. Holyoak, David K. Allen. – London : Butterworths, 1982.
xxvii,278p.
This book provides United Kingdom practitioners with a comprehensive guide to liabilities of occupier, owner, builder, and other parties in cases of defective premises. Measure of damages, claims for economic loss, limitation periods, and misrepresentation are also covered.
ISBN 0406233403 Hbk £27.00

—Design liability in the construction industry / Davids L. Cornes. – 2nd ed. – London : Collins, 1985.
viii,232p; 24cm.
Previous ed.: London : Granada, 1983. Includes index.
ISBN 0003830209 £17.50

—Negligence in surveying and building / Malcolm Ross. – London : Estates Gazette, 1986.
xxii,247p.
Bibliography: p.238-239. - Includes index.
ISBN 0728200953

—Professional liability and construction / Leo Barros D'Sa. – 1. – Ascot : Chartered Institute of Building, 1987.
30cm. – (Occasional paper).
ISBN 090660088X Pbk No price

LIABILITY FOR BUILDING ACCIDENTS - GREAT BRITAIN

—Law of defective premises / Anthony Speight, Gregory Stone : foreword by the Honourable Mr Justice Wood. – London : Pitman, 1982.
xxi,205p; 23cm.
Includes index.
ISBN 0273017705 £15.00

LIABILITY FOR CONDITION AND USE OF LAND - ENGLAND

—Civil liability for defective premises / J. H. Holyoak, David K. Allen. – London : Butterworths, 1982.
xxvii,278p.
This book provides United Kingdom practitioners with a comprehensive guide to liabilities of occupier, owner, builder, and other parties in cases of defective premises. Measure of damages, claims for economic loss, limitation periods, and misrepresentation are also covered.
ISBN 0406233403 Hbk £27.00

LIABILITY FOR ENVIRONMENTAL DAMAGES

—Compensation for pollution damage / Paris : Organisation for Economic Co-operation and Development, 1981.
208 p.; 24 cm.
'Document'–Cover. Includes bibliographical references.
ISBN 9264122141 pbk.

LIABILITY FOR MARINE ACCIDENTS

—Limitation of shipowners' liability : the new law / London : Sweet & Maxwell, 1986.
xxv,378p; 22cm.
Includes index.
ISBN 0421348909 £35.00

—Official records of the International Conference on the Limitation of Liability for Maritime Claims, 1976 / London : International Maritime Organization, 1983.
vii,527p.
ISBN 9280111566

—Time bars in maritime matters : a study / by Kaj Pineus. – London : Lloyd's of London Press, 1982.
168p.
ISBN 0907432425

LIABILITY FOR SPACE VEHICLE ACCIDENTS

—Outer space and legal liability / by Morris D. Forkosch. – The Hague : Nijhoff, 1982.
xvi,290p.
Includes index. Bibliography: p267-270.
ISBN 9024725828 Hbk £100.00/$43.50

—Settlement of space law disputes : the present state of the law and perspectives of further development : proceedings of an internat. colloquium, Munich, September 13 and 14, 1979 / organized by the Inst. of Air and Space Law, Univ. of Cologne : ed. by Karl-Heinz Bockstiegel : in cooperation with the Space Law Committee of the Internat. Law Assoc. ... et al. – Koln : Heymann, 1980.
ix, 415 p.; 23 cm.
Includes legislation in English, French and German. Bibliography: p. 201-205.
ISBN 3452187942 pbk. DM148.00

LIABILITY FOR THE CONDITION AND USE OF LAND - AUSTRALIA

—Occupiers' liability / The Law Reform Commission. – Sydney : The Commission, 1987.
13p. – (Discussion paper).
Bibliography: p.13.

LIABILITY FOR THE CONDITION AND USE OF LAND - AUSTRALIA - WESTERN AUSTRALIA

—Report on alteration of ground levels / the Law Reform Commission of Western Australia. – Perth : The Commission, 1986.
94p. – (Project).
Includes bibliographical references.

LIABILITY FOR THE CONDITION AND USE OF LAND - CANADA

—Occupiers' liability / by J. Victor Di Castri. – Agincourt, Ont. : Burroughs, 1980.
xlii, 284 p.; 24 cm.
Includes indexes. Bibliography: p. xli-xlii.
ISBN 0459335502

LIABILITY FOR THE CONDITION AND USE OF LAND - ENGLAND

—Occupiers' liability and access to the countryside / memorandum by the Council's Law Reform Committee. – London : Law Society, 1982.
7p.

LIABILITY FOR THE CONDITION AND USE OF LAND - GREAT BRITAIN

—Law of defective premises / Anthony Speight, Gregory Stone : foreword by the Honourable Mr Justice Wood. – London : Pitman, 1982.
xxi,205p; 23cm.
Includes index.
ISBN 0273017705 £15.00

LIABILITY FOR THE CONDITION AND USE OF LAND - IRELAND

—Report on defective premises / the Law Reform Commission. – Dublin : The Commission, 1982.
v,49p. – (LRC).

LIABILITY FOR TRAFFIC ACCIDENTS - AUSTRALIA - SOUTH AUSTRALIA

—Report ... relating to the review and reappraisal of the twenty-fifth report of this committe sic on the subject of misfeasance and non-feasance / Law Reform Committee of South Australia. – Adelaide : Government Printer, 1986.
48p. – (51st report).
Bibliography: p.39-40.

LIABILITY FOR TRAFFIC ACCIDENTS - AUSTRALIA - WESTERN AUSTRALIA

—Report on the liability of highway authorities for non-feasance / Law Reform Commission of Western Australia. – Perth : Law Reform Commission of Western Australia, 1981.
116p. – (Project v no 62).

LIABILITY FOR TRAFFIC ACCIDENTS - CANADA - BRITISH COLUMBIA

—Apportionment of liability in British Columbia / Scarborough, Ontario : Butterworths (Canada).
Digest of the British Columbia Cases which address the question of liability in motor vehicle accidents. Each chapter begins with a topical index, and the text includes a table of cases.

—Vicarious liability under the Motor Vehicle Act / Law Reform Commission of British Columbia. – Vancouver : The Commission, 1988.
ii,60p. – (Working paper).
ISBN 0771886241

LIABILITY FOR TRAFFIC ACCIDENTS - CANADA - ONTARIO

—Report of Inquiry into Motor Vehicle Accident Compensation in Ontario / Coulter A. Osborne, commissioner. – Toronto : Ontario Ministry of the Attorney General, 1988.
2 v.; 25 cm.
Title from cover. Co-published by: Ministry of Financial Institutions. Bibliography: p. 667-712 (v. 2.). Contents: v. 1. Report – v. 2. Research studies and v. 1 appendices.
ISBN 0772938466 (v.2)

—Report of Inquiry into Motor Vehicle Accident Compensation in Ontario : summary of findings and recommendations / Coulter A. Osborne, Commissioner. – Toronto : Ontario Ministry of the Attorney General, 1988.
68, 79 p.; 25 cm.
Title from cover. Co-published by: Ministry of Financial Institutions. Text in English and French with French text on inverted pages. Title on added t.p.: Rapport de l'enquete sur l'indemnisation des victimes d'accidents d'automobiles en Ontario.
ISBN 0772938474

LIABILITY FOR TRAFFIC ACCIDENTS - GREAT BRITAIN - CASES

—Bingham's motor claims cases / J. A. Taylor. – 9th ed. – London : Butterworths, 1986.
xlv,1003p; 26cm.
Previous ed.: 1980. Includes index.
ISBN 0406118132 £60.00

LIABILITY FOR TRAFFIC ACCIDENTS - SOUTH AFRICA

—Motor law / by W.E. Cooper. – Cape Town : Juta, 1987.
li,507p.
Replaces: South African motor law / by W.E. Cooper and B.R. Bamford. Bibliography: p.xi-xiii. - Includes index.
ISBN 0702119067 Hbk

LIABILITY FOR WATER POLLUTION DAMAGES

—Pollution of international watercourses : search for substantive rules and principles of law / by J.G. Lammers. – The Hague : M. Nijhoff, 1984.
xxvi, 724 p.; 25 cm.
Includes indexes. Bibliography: p. 663-703.
ISBN 9024729556 Hbk £275.00

LIABILITY (INSURANCE)

—Charterers' liability insurance / by Dieter Schwampe : translated from the German by Burravoe Ltd. – London : Lloyd's of London Press, 1988.
xx,156p; 24cm.
Bibliography: pp.145-151. - Includes index. Translated from the German.
ISBN 1850441847 £45.00

LIABILITY (INSURANCE) - CANADA

—Insurance law in Canada : a treatise on the principles of indemnity insurance as applied in the common law provinces of Canada / by Craig Brown and Julio Menezes. – Toronto, Canada : Carswell, 1982.
lxxix, 518 p.; 26 cm.
Includes bibliographical references and indexes.
ISBN 0459339605

LIABILITY (INSURANCE) - GREAT BRITAIN

—Guide to the indemnity and insurance aspects of building contracts : based on the JCT Standard Forms of Building Contract / Peter Madge. – London : RIBA, 1985.
285p; 24cm.
ISBN 0900630914

LIBEL AND SLANDER

—Carter-Ruck on libel and slander / Richard-Walker. – 3rd ed. – London : Butterworths, 1985.
lvi,553p; 26cm.
Previous ed.: published as Libel & slander. London : Faber, 1972. Includes index.
ISBN 0406009708 £35.00

—Protection of personal and commercial reputation : a study of the law in Western Europe and the United States / Robert M. Kunstadt. – Weinheim : Verlag Chemie for Max Planck Institute for Foreign and International Patent, Copyright, and Competition Law, Munich, 1980.
vii,98p; 24cm.
Bibliography: p.97-98.
ISBN 3527256970
ISBN 0895730286

LIBEL AND SLANDER - AUSTRALIA

—Unfair Publication : Defamation and Privacy / Kingston : Australian Government Publishing Service.
273p.

LIBEL AND SLANDER - AUSTRALIA - SOUTH AUSTRALIA

—Report ... relating to group defamation / Law Reform Committee of South Australia. – Adelaide : Government Printer, 1982.
13p. – (69th report).

LIBEL AND SLANDER - CANADA

—Cable Television and Defamation / Victoria : Government of British Columbia, 1981.

—Canadian Libel Practice / David Potts. – Butterworths, 1986.
336p.
Deals with procedural aspects of the conduct of libel actions. Takes the reader through the mechanics of pleadings and evidentiary questions, examines aspects of a libel jury address, libel legislation in all Canadian jurisdictions, model charge to the jury used by Ontario Supreme Court Justice and gives sample questions to the Jury.
ISBN 0409860891 Hbk £75.00

—Hate propaganda / Law Reform Commission of Canada. – Ottawa : The Commission, 1986.
57,63p. – (Working paper).
Includes bibliographies. Added t.p. in French: La propagande haineuse. Pages numbered in opposite directions. Text in English and French.

—Law of Defamation / Agincourt : Carswell, 1987.
1540p.
This treatise provides a thorough treatment of the Canadian law of defamation. All significant Canadian cases, as well as, major cases from the Commonwealth and U.S. on defamation are included in the work. The practice and procedure for defamation cases is discussed in the book.

—Law of Defamation / Agincourt : Carswell, 1987.
ISBN 045939630 Hbk £55.00

—Law of Defamation in Canada, 2 Vols. / Agincourt : Carswell, 1987.
1,540p.

—Law of libel and slander in Canada / Jeremy S. Williams. – 2nd ed. – Toronto : Butterworths, 1988.
xxxi, 145 p.; 24 cm.
Analysis of the law of defamation as it applies in each common law province of Canada, covering both jurisdictions which retain libel and slander as distinct torts, and jurisdictions which have adopted the Uniform Defamation Act. Covers the publication requirements, credit reporting and other commercial representations, limitation periods, damages and injunctions.
ISBN 0409876410 Hbk £57

—Libel and Contempt : The Law and the Media / Vancouver : British Columbia Continuing Legal Education Society, 1982.
414p.
ISBN 0865040834 Hbk £65.00

LIBEL AND SLANDER - CANADA - BRITISH COLUMBIA

—Report on cable television and defamation / Victoria : Queen's Printer, 1981.
23p.
ISBN 0771882572

LIBEL AND SLANDER - ENGLAND

—Criminal law : report on criminal libel / by the Law Commission. – London : HMSO, 1985.
iv,80p.
ISBN 0101961804

—Criminal libel / the Law Commission. – London : H.M.S.O., 1982.
viii,207p; 21cm. – (Working paper).
ISBN 0117301647

—Duncan and Neill on defamation / foreword to the first edition, Lord Salmon. – 2nd ed. – London : Butterworths, 1983.
xxii,205p; 26cm.
This work incorporates all the statutory material along with a full discussion of relevant United Kingdom cases on defamation. Where the common law is uncertain, the book suggests solutions which accord with the principles presented.
ISBN 0406178305 Unpriced

—Gatley on libel and slander / Philip Lewis, J. E. Previte, R. W. Ground. – 8th ed. – London : Sweet & Maxwell, 1981.
cxxxvii,751p; 26cm.
Fifteen of the chapters are new or substantially rewritten, with emphasis on defences and the stages of pleading and settlement. Contains a new chapter on apology, payment into court, and settlement. The relationship between the law of defamation and the law of contempt has been clarified. Developments in Australia, Canada and New Zealand are discussed.
ISBN 0421243406 £60.00

—Select cases on defamation to 1600 / edited for the Selden Society by R.H. Helmholz. – London : Selden Society, 1985.
cxi,118p.
Includes bibliographical references and index.

LIBEL AND SLANDER - GREAT BRITAIN

—Defamation / Neill. – 2nd ed. – London : Butterworths, 1984.
ISBN 0406178305 Hbk £34.00

—Libel and Slander / 3rd ed. – London : Butterworths, 1985.
ISBN 0406009708 Hbk £55.00

LIBEL AND SLANDER - INDIA

—Law of Defamation and Malicious Prosecution / 9th ed. – Allahabad : Law Publishers, 1987.
500p.

—Law of Defamation and Malicious Prosecution (Civil and Criminal) / 2nd ed. – Allahabad : Law Publishers, 1982.

LIBEL AND SLANDER - IRELAND

—Irish law of defamation / Marc McDonald : with a foreword by Thomas A. Finlay. – Dublin : Round Hall in association with Irish Academic Press, 1987.
xx,304p; 24cm.
Includes index.
ISBN 0947686150 £30.00

LIBEL AND SLANDER - MALAYSIA

—Defamation Act, 1957 (Act 286) / Kuala Lumpur : International Law Books Services.

—Law of Defamation in Singapore and Malaysia / Singapore : Butterworths, 1988.
200p.

—Law of defamation in Singapore and Malaysia / Singapore : Malayan Law Journal, 1988.
ca 200p.
Gives a thorough discussion of the principle aspects of a defamation action, with precedents, and a review of the principles expounded in the local cases and legislation. Appendices cover the relevant statutory provision, cases judicially considered, statutes judicially considered, and a damage digest.
ISBN 9971700611 Hbk £90.00

LIBEL AND SLANDER - SINGAPORE

—Law of Defamation in Singapore and Malaysia / Singapore : Butterworths, 1988.
200p.

—Law of defamation in Singapore and Malaysia / Singapore : Malayan Law Journal, 1988.
ca 200p.
Gives a thorough discussion of the principle aspects of a defamation action, with precedents, and a review of the principles expounded in the local cases and legislation. Appendices cover the relevant statutory provision, cases judicially considered, statutes judicially considered, and a damage digest.
ISBN 9971700611 Hbk £90.00

LIBEL AND SLANDER - SOUTH AFRICA

—Law of defamation in South Africa / Jonathan M. Burchell. – Cape Town : Juta, 1985.
xxxii, 359 p.; 26 cm.
Includes bibliographical references and index.
ISBN 0702115673

LIBEL AND SLANDER (ROMAN-DUTCH LAW)

—Defamation and Other Aspects of the Actio Iniuriarum in Roman-Dutch Law / Colombo : Lake House Investments.

LIBERALISM - USSR

—Legal philosophies of Russian liberalism / Andrzej Walicki. – Oxford : Clarendon, 1987.
480p; 22cm.
Includes index.
ISBN 0198249306 £45.00

LIBERTY

—Freedom, peace and their guarantees, from the viewpoint of the Constitution of Japan / Kenji Urata. – s.l. : s.n., 1982.
p.22-45.
'Originally presented as a draft to the Waseda University Centennial International Symposium at Waseda University on August 22 and 23, 1982'. Reprinted from: Waseda bulletin of comparative law, v.2 (1982).

—Human rights : information sheet / Strasbourg : Council of Europe, 1982-.

—John Stuart Mill's On liberty / John C. Rees : constructed from published and unpublished sources by G.L. Williams. – Oxford : Clarendon, 1985.
xi,210p; 22cm.
Bibliography: p204-207. - Includes index.
ISBN 0198247664 £19.50

—Justice and liberty / D.D. Raphael. – London : Athlone, 1980.
192p; 23cm.
Includes index.
ISBN 0485111950 £13.00

—Liberalism and the limits of justice / Michael J. Sandel. – Cambridge : Cambridge University Press, 1982.
ix,191p; 24cm.
Bibliography: p184-186. - Includes index.
ISBN 052124501X Hbk £17.50
ISBN 0521270774 Pbk £5.95

—Liberty and Justice / Oxford : Croom Helm, 1986.
ISBN 070994523X Hbk £25.00

—Liberty of the citizen / Franklin Thomas, John Mortimer, Lord Hunt of Tanworth. – London : Granada, 1983.
93p.
ISBN 0246121157

—Lives, liberties and the public good : new essays in political theory for Maurice Cranston / edited by George Feaver and Frederick Rosen. – Basingstoke : Macmillan in association with the London School of Economics and Political Science, 1987.
ix,272p; 23cm.
Bibliography: p259-266. - Includes index.
ISBN 0333392868 £27.50

—Mill on Liberty / C.L. Ten. – Oxford : Clarendon Press, 1980.
x, 195p.
ISBN 0198246439

—Morality of freedom / Joseph Raz. – Oxford : Clarendon, 1986.
432p; 22cm.
ISBN 0198247729 £30.00

—Public liberty and the police role / Philip Knights. – S.l. : University of Wales. Institute of Science and Technology, 1985.
23p.
Bibliography: p22-23.

—Utilitarianism / On liberty : John Stuart Mill : edited with an introduction by Mary Warnock. – 17th impression. – Glasgow : Fontana, 1985.
352p.
This selection originally published: 1962. Bibliography: p.343-4. - Includes index.

LIBERTY - BANGLADESH
—Fundamental Rights and Personal Liberty in India, Pakistan and Bangladesh / New Delhi : Deep and Deep Publications, 1988.
480p.

LIBERTY - INDIA
—Fundamental Rights and Personal Liberty in India, Pakistan and Bangladesh / New Delhi : Deep and Deep Publications, 1988.
480p.

—Right to Life and Personal Liberty in India / New Delhi : Deep and Deep Publications, 1987.
296p.

LIBERTY - PAKISTAN
—Fundamental Rights and Personal Liberty in India, Pakistan and Bangladesh / New Delhi : Deep and Deep Publications, 1988.
480p.

LIBRARIES
—Automated cataloguing in the UK : a guide to services / A.W. Seal. – Bath : Centre for Catalogue Research, Bath University Library, 1980.
114p; 30cm. – (Research and development reports).
Bibliography: p.95-99.
ISBN 0861970233 sp

—Cost management for library and information services / Stephen A. Roberts. – London : Butterworths, 1985.
181 p.
ISBN 0408013761

—Do we really need libraries? : an assessment of approaches to the evaluation of the performance of libraries / John Blagden. – New York : Saur, 1980.
162p; 23cm.
Bibliography: p147-157. - Includes index.
ISBN 0851573088 £7.75
ISBN 0896644421

—Electronic library : the international journal for minicomputer, microcomputer and software applications in libraries / . – Oxford : Learned Information, 1983.
ISBN 02640473

—Public relations for librarians / K.C. Harrison. – 2nd rev. ed. – Aldershot : Gower, 1982.
xiii,124p; 23cm. – (A Grafton book).
Previous ed.: London : Deutsch, 1973. Bibliography: p120-121. - Includes index.
ISBN 0566034549 Unpriced

—Use of paperbacks in public libraries in the United Kingdom : a review of research / edited by Marilyn Hart. – Loughborough : Centre for Library and Information Management, Department of Library and Information Studies, Loughborough University, 1983.
iii,103p. – (Report).
Includes bibliographical references.
ISBN 0904924483

LIBRARIES - ENGLAND
—Parliament and information : the Westminster scene / Dermot Englefield. – London : Library Association, 1981.
vii,132p; 24cm.
Includes index.
ISBN 0853655707 Hbk Unpriced
ISBN 0853659931 Pbk Unpriced

LIBRARIES - GREAT BRITAIN
—ACOLAM newsletter / Advisory Committee on Latin American Materials. – v. – London? : Institute of Latin American Studies?, 1980.
ISBN 02636832

—Guide to government department and other libraries 1988 / edited by R.T. Adkins. – 28th ed. – London : Science Reference and Information Service, 1988.
100p.
Previous ed.: 1986. Includes indexes.
ISBN 071230746X £20.00

—Joint enterprise : roles and relationships of the public and private sectors in the provision of library and information services / report of Library and Information Services Council and British Library Research and Development Department Working Party. – London : H.M.S.O., 1987.
vii, 49p.
On cover: Office of Arts and Libraries.
ISBN 011430016X

—Making a business of information : a survey of new opportunities / London : H.M.S.O., 1983.
53p; 21cm.
Bibliography: p48. At head of title: Cabinet Office, Information Technology Advisory Panel.
ISBN 0116308249 Pbk £4.20

—UC & R newsletter / University, College and Research Section of the Library Association. – v. – London : The Section, 1980.
ISBN 0144056X

LIBRARIES AND STATE - GREAT BRITAIN
—Report by the Minister for the Arts on library and information matters during ... / presented to Parliament by the Secretary of State for Education and Science. – London : H.M.S.O., 1981-.

LIBRARY ADMINISTRATION
—Cost management for library and information services / Stephen A. Roberts. – London : Butterworths, 1985.
181 p.
ISBN 0408013761

LIBRARY ADMINISTRATION - GREAT BRITAIN
—Report by the Minister for the Arts on library and information matters during ... / presented to Parliament by the Secretary of State for Education and Science. – London : H.M.S.O., 1981-.

LIBRARY COOPERATION
—BLL review / British Library Lending Division. – London : H.M.S.O., 1973.
Continues: NLL review; continued by: Interlending review. Index: 1971/1975.

LIBRARY EDUCATION
—Junior staff training / edited by David Baker. – Leicester : University, College & Research Section of the Library Association (East Midlands Branch), 1980.
35 p.
ISBN 0853658730

LIBRARY FINANCE
—Cost management for library and information services / Stephen A. Roberts. – London : Butterworths, 1985.
181 p.
ISBN 0408013761

LIBRARY PERSONNEL MANAGEMENT
—Staff management in library and information work / Noragh Jones, Peter Jordan. – Aldershot : Gower, 1982.
vii,215p; 23cm. – (A Grafton book).
Bibliography: p205-212. - Includes index.
ISBN 0566034301 Unpriced

LIBRARY RESOURCES
—SCOLMA directory of libraries and special collections on Africa in the United Kingdom and Western Europe / edited by Harry Hannam. – 4th rev. and expanded ed. – Munchen : Saur, 1983.
183p.
Previous ed: London: Crosby Lockwood Staples, 1973.

LIBRARY RESOURCES - CANADA
—Checklist of law reports and statutes in Canadian law libraries / National Library of Canada Resources Survey Division, Collections Development Branch : Bibliotheque nationale du Canada, Division de l'inventaire des ressources, Direction du developpement des collections. – Ottawa : The Library, 1981.
xii,249p.
Includes index. Text in English and French.
ISBN 0660504529

LIBRARY SCIENCE - GREAT BRITAIN
—Research bulletin : British Library Research and Development Department / British Library Research and Development Department. – London : The Department, 1987.
Continues: Newsletter.
ISBN 09522832

LICENSE SYSTEM - ENGLAND
—Liquor licensing law / by David Field and Matthew Pink. – London : Sweet & Maxwell, 1983.
xxi,206p; 25cm.
Looks at how to obtain a justices licence, including the stages of deciding the relevant licence, the permitted hours in licensed premises, how to renew an existing licence, and its removal and transfer through to the conduct of licensed premises. Also contains a chapter on the nature of a registered club.
ISBN 0421299703 Pbk £11.50

LICENSES - INDIA
—Law of Easements and Licences / 10th ed. – Allahabad : Law Book Company, 1984.
1,200p.

LICENSING
—From the Waidring Conferences, 4 Vols. /. – Dordrecht : Kluwer.
444p.
ISBN 9065443142

—International agency, distribution and licensing agreements / London : Longman Professional, 1986.
ISBN 0851211887 Hbk £45.00

LICENSING - ENGLAND
—Licensing Entertainments in England and Wales / London : Butterworths, 1985.
ISBN 0406200300 Pbk £24.00

LICENSING - GREAT BRITAIN
—Guide to Licensing Law / Berryman. – 3rd ed. – Chichester : Barry Rose, 1980.
ISBN 0859920631 Pbk £10.00

—Licensing Act, 1984 / 92nd ed. – London : Butterworths, 1984.
ISBN 0406335176 Hbk

—Licensing Acts Nineteen Eighty-Seven / 95th ed. – London : Butterworths, 1986.
ISBN 0406335206 Hbk

—Licensing Acts Nineteen Eighty-Two / J. N. Martin. – 90th ed. – London : Butterworths, 1982.
ISBN 0406334528 Hbk £92.50

—Licensing Guide / 9th ed. – London : Longman Professional, 1985.
– (LPPN38).
ISBN 0851209955 Pbk £15.95

—Licensing Guide / 8th ed. – London : Oyez Longman, 1982.
– (Oyez Longman Practice Note Ser.: No. 38).
ISBN 0851205887 Hbk £7.95

—Licensing Practice and Procedure / 2nd ed. – London : Fourmat, 1986.
ISBN 1851900098 Hbk £12.95

—Local Authority Licensing and Registration / Rosson. – London : Longman Professional, 1985.
ISBN 085120886X updat £125.00

—Paterson's Licensing Acts 1986 / 95th ed. – London : Butterworths, 1986.
ISBN 0406335206 Hbk £56.00

—Paterson's Licensing Acts / London : Shaw & Sons.

—Underhill's licensing guide / 10th. – London : Longman Professional (UK), 1989.
– (Practitioner series).
Guide to the law and procedure of liquor, gaming, betting and lottery licensing. Details each step in making or opposing a successful licensing application, with key precedents. Revised to take account of the changes introduced by the Licensing Act 1988.
ISBN 0851215378 Hbk £17.95

LICENSING - SCOTLAND
—Licensing (Scotland) Act 1976 / Heather Baillie. – 2nd. – Edinburgh : W Green & Son, 1989.
Annotated text of the Act, originally produced by J. Allen and C.D. Chapman (1977), as subsequently amended and taking into account case law since the publication of the original edition. Also includes an expanded introduction and details of individual licensing boards.
ISBN 041400826X

LICENSING - WALES
—Licensing Entertainments in England and Wales / London : Butterworths, 1985.
ISBN 0406200300 Pbk £24.00

LIE DETECTORS AND DETECTION
—Polygraph test : lies, truth and science / editor, Anthony Gale. – London : Sage, 1988.
256p; 22cm.
Includes bibliography and index.
ISBN 0803981228 £19.95

LIECHTENSTEIN
—Economy of the Principality of Liechtenstein / edited by Walter Kranz : translated from the German by John Anthony Nicholls. – Liechtenstein : Government Press and Information Office, 1982.
154 p.

LIECHTENSTEIN - LIECHTENSTEIN
—Principality of Liechtenstein : a documentary handbook / edited by Walter Kranz : translated from the German by J.A.Nicholls. – 5th rev ed. – Vaduz : Press and Information Office of the Government of the Principality of Liechtenstein, 1981.

LIENS
—Maritime liens and claims / William Tetley with assistance from Brian G. McDonough. – London : Business Law Communications, 1985.
lxiv,686p.
Includes bibliographical references and index.
ISBN 0948406003

—Second International Maritime Law Seminar : Carriage of Goods by Sea, Maritime Liens, Marine Insurance / Vancouver : Continuing Legal Education Society of British Columbia, 1981.
395p.
ISBN 0865040273 Hbk £100.00

LIENS - CANADA
—Construction and Mechanics' Liens in Canada / David I. Bristow. – 5th ed. – Agincourt : Carswell, 1985.
1,015p.

—Construction and Mechanics' Liens in Canada : Carswell's Canadian Legal Classic Series / David Bristow. – 5th ed. – Agincourt : Carswell, 1985.
1015p.
This work examines the Ontario Construction Lien Act of 1983 in detail and discusses the changes this new Act makes to the law under the former Mechanics' Lien Act. The statute and case law of all Canadian provinces is presented in the text.

—Working paper on the Mechanics' Liens Act : certain substantive issues / Newfoundland Law Reform Commission. – St.John's : The Commission, 1987.
vi,294p.
Includes bibliographical references. Includes text of the Acts.

LIENS - CANADA - BRITISH COLUMBIA
—Buyer's lien : a new consumer remedy / Law Reform Commission of British Columbia. – Vancouver : The Commission, 1986.
iii,52p. – (Working paper).
Includes bibliographical references.

—Report on the buyer's lien : a new consumer remedy / Law Reform Commission of British Columbia. – Vancouver : The Commission, 1987.
iv,62p.
Includes bibliographical references.
ISBN 0771885954

LIENS - CANADA - ONTARIO
—Construction and Mechanics' Liens in Canada : Carswell's Canadian Legal Classic Series / David Bristow. – 5th ed. – Agincourt : Carswell, 1985.
1015p.
This work examines the Ontario Construction Lien Act of 1983 in detail and discusses the changes this new Act makes to the law under the former Mechanics' Lien Act. The statute and case law of all Canadian provinces is presented in the text.

—Construction lien remedies in Ontario / by Kevin Patrick McGuinness. – Toronto, Canada : Carswell Legal Publications, 1983.
xxxiii, 423 p.; 24 cm.
Includes index. Bibliography: p. 415-418.
ISBN 0459359606

—Kirsh : a Guide to Construction Liens in Ontario / Butterworths, 1984.
480p.
Overview of the flow of funds on construction projects. Covers preserving and protecting the lien, practice and procedure in the lien action, the statutory holdbacks, the new trust fund provisions and liability for breach of trust, liens against Crown lands and municipal streets, labour and material bonds, and the appointment of trustee.
ISBN 0409842869 Hbk £80.00

LIENS - ENGLAND
—Maritime liens / by D.R. Thomas. – London : Stevens, 1980.
xlix,397p.

LIENS - GREAT BRITAIN
—Contractors' Liens and Charges / 2nd ed. – London : Butterworths, 1981.
ISBN 0409676004 Hbk £15.80

—Law of lien / Alfred H. Silvertown. – London : Butterworth, 1988.
190p; 25cm.
Includes index.
ISBN 040610395X £25.00

—Law of Liens / London : Butterworths, 1988.
ISBN 040610395X Hbk £29.00

—Law of Maritime Liens / Reprint of 1940 edition. – Abingdon : Professional Books.

—Maritime Liens / London : Sweet & Maxwell, 1980.
– (British Shipping Laws Ser.).
Analysis of the law of maritime liens and the nature of the right enjoyed by a maritime lienee. Examines the principle liens recognised by the English Admiralty Court; damage; salvage; seamen' wages; and Bottomry bonds. Also looks at the rights in rem enjoyed against the Crown and foreign sovereigns.
ISBN 0420460500 Hbk £58.00

—Maritime Liens (BSL) / London : Sweet & Maxwell, 1980.
ISBN 0421460500 Hbk £65.00

LIFE IMPRISONMENT - ENGLAND
—Life-sentence prisoners / Parliamentary All-Party Penal Affairs Group. – Chichester : Barry Rose, 1986.
44p.
ISBN 085992386X

LIFE INSURANCE - CANADA
—Life Insurance Laws of Canada / Genevieve Faribault. – Don Mills : Life Underwriters Association of Canada, 1985.
ISBN 0919361757 Hbk £15.95

LIFE INSURANCE - CARIBBEAN
—Life Insurance in the Commonwealth Caribbean / London : Butterworths, 1984.
ISBN 0406076308 Hbk £17.00

LIFE INSURANCE - GREAT BRITAIN
—Houseman and Davies law of life assurance / B. P. A. Davies. – 10th ed. – London : Butterworths, 1984.
xxiv,378p; 26cm.
This work for practitioners covers general United Kingdom contract law, law relating to insurance policies, legislation on insurance supervision, and relevant EEC developments in insurance law. Model contracts and trust agreements are included in the appendix.
ISBN 0406597073 Hbk £68.75

—How to plan your life insurance / 2nd ed. – Cambridge : Woodhead-Faulkner, 1986.
ISBN 0859413004 Hbk £10.95
ISBN 0859413012 Pbk £4.95

—Law of Life Assurance / Davies. – 10th ed. – London : Butterworths, 1984.
ISBN 0406597073 Hbk £33.95

—Personal accident, life and other insurance / 2nd ed. – London : Butterworths, 1980.
ISBN 0406252912 Hbk £52.00

—Personal Financial Planning Manual 1986-87 / John Rayer. – London : Butterworths, 1986.
This manual is a guide to the compilation of personal financial packages for United Kingdom investors. Investments, family finances, life insurance, pensions, and capital transfer tax are covered in the book.
ISBN 040600563X Hbk

LIFE INSURANCE - INDIA
—Law and Practice of Life Insurance in India / New Delhi : Deep and Deep Publications, 1987.
448p.

LIFE INSURANCE - SINGAPORE
—Damages-Loss of Expectation of Life : Survival and Deductibility / Singapore : Malayan Law Journal, 1984.
xiii, 82p.
Explores the survival of the claim for loss of expectation of life and the methods employed by courts for its quantification. Intends to determine the justification, if any, for deducting the compensation awarded to the estate under the Fatal Accidents Act 1846-1908. Comparison of the law in England, Canada (Manitoba), Australia and Malaysia.
ISBN 9971700379 Hbk £25.00

LIFE INSURANCE - TRINIDAD & TOBAGO
—Life Insurance Law in the Commonwealth Caribbean / London : Butterworths, 1984.
xxiii,226; 23cm.
This book provides a comprehensive study of the English law of life insurance as it applies in Trinidad and Tobago.
ISBN 0406076308 Pbk

LIMITATION - CANADA
—Federal Limitation Periods : A Handbooks of Limitation Periods and Other Statutory Time Limits / Toronto : Butterworths.

LIMITATION - CANADA - ALBERTA
—Alberta Limitations Manual / Toronto : Butterworths.

LIMITATION - INDIA
—Supreme Court on Law of Limitation 1950-79 / Lucknow : Eastern Book Company, 1981.
226p.

LIMITATION - MALAYSIA
—Limitation Act, 1953 (Act 253) / Kuala Lumpur : International Law Books Services.

LIMITATION OF ACTIONS
—Report on the limitation of actions / Newfoundland Law Reform Commission. – St. John's : The Commission, 1986.
vi,29p.

—Time bars in maritime matters : a study / by Kaj Pineus. – London : Lloyd's of London Press, 1982.
168p.
ISBN 0907432425

LIMITATION OF ACTIONS - AUSTRALIA - NEW SOUTH WALES
—Community law reform program / New South Wales Law Reform Commission. – Sydney : Goverment Printer, 1986.
xv,89p. – (L.R.C.).
Includes bibliographical references.
ISBN 073052535X

LIMITATION OF ACTIONS - AUSTRALIA - SOUTH AUSTRALIA
—Report ... relating to prescription and limitation of actions / Law Reform Committee of South Australia. – Adelaide : Government Printer, 1987.
59,14p. – (76th report).

LIMITATION OF ACTIONS - AUSTRALIA - WESTERN AUSTRALIA
—Report on limitation and notice of actions : latent disease and injury / Law Reform Commission of Western Australia. – Perth : The Commission, 1982.
125p. – (Project).

LIMITATION OF ACTIONS - CANADA
—Federal Limitation Periods : a Handbook of Limitation Periods ad Other Statutory Time Limits, 1 Vol. / Butterworths.

—Limitation of Actions / 2nd ed. – Toronto : Butterworths.
344p.

—Limitation of Actions in Canada / 2nd ed. – Butterworths, 1980.
344p.
ISBN 040987616X Hbk £55.00

—Limitations Act, 1983, Bill 160 : An Act to Revise the Limitations Act / Ontario : Ontario Government Publications Service, 1983.
18p.

—Tentative proposals for changes in limitations legislation / Law Reform Commission of Saskatchewan. – Saskatoon : Law Reform Commission of Saskatchewan, 1981.
27p.

—Working paper on limitation of actions / Newfoundland Law Reform Commission. – St. John's : The Commission, 1985.
xi,481p.
Includes bibliographical references. With a supplement.

LIMITATION OF ACTIONS - CANADA - ALBERTA
—Alberta Limitations Manual, 1 Vol. / Butterworths.

—Limitations / Institute of Law Research and Reform. – Edmonton : The Institute, 1986.
vii,370p. – (Report for discussion).

LIMITATION OF ACTIONS - CANADA - ONTARIO
—Ontario Limitation Periods : a Handbook of Limitation Periods and Other Statutory Time Limits, 1 Vol. / Butterworths.

—Ontario Limitation Periods : A Handbook of Limitation Periods and Other Statutory Time Limits / Toronto : Butterworths.

LIMITATION OF ACTIONS - CANADA - SASKATCHEWAN
—Proposals for a survival of actions act : report to the Minister of Justice / Law Reform Commission of Saskatchewan. – Saskatoon : The Commission, 1985.
19p.
Includes bibliographical references.

—Tentative proposals for changes in limitations legislation / Law Reform Commission of Saskatchewan. – Saskatoon : The Commission, 1986.
149p.

LIMITATION OF ACTIONS - ENGLAND
—Classification of limitation in private international law / the Law Commission. – London : H.M.S.O., 1980.
v,86p; 21cm. – (Working paper).
ISBN 0117301558 Pbk £3.50

—Classification of limitation in private international law : report on a reference under section 3(1)(e) of the Law Commissions Act 1965 / the Law Commission. – London : H.M.S.O., 1982.
v,60p.
ISBN 0101857004

—Limitation periods in personal injury claims / by Stephen Todd. – London : Sweet & Maxwell, 1982.
xxii,131p; 23cm.
Includes index.
ISBN 0421285907 £13.00

—Periods of limitation : with practical notes / J.F. Josling. – 6th ed. – London : Longman Professional, 1986.
144p; 22cm. – (Longman professional practice notes).
Previous ed.: London : Oyez, 1981.
ISBN 0851211453 Pbk £12.95

—Richards Butler on latent damage / by Robert Merkin. – London : Lloyd's of London Press, 1987.
192p; 22cm.
ISBN 1850441286 £30.00

LIMITATION OF ACTIONS - GREAT BRITAIN

—Latent damage : consultative document / Law Reform Committee. – 1. – London : Law Reform Committee 1981, 1981.
various pagings.

—Limitation of Actions / London : Butterworths, 1988.
ISBN 0406102309 Hbk

—Periods of Limitation / 5th ed. – London : Oyez Longman, 1981.
– (Oyez Longman Practice Note Ser.: No. 25).
ISBN 0851205895 Hbk £8.95

—Time barred actions / Rohreke. – London : Lloyd's of London Press, 1984.
ISBN 0907432425 Hbk £34.00

—Time-Barred Actions / H. G. Rohreke. – London : LLoyd's of London Press, 1984.
ISBN 1850440271 Hbk

LIMITATION OF ACTIONS - IRELAND

—Report on the statute of limitations : claims in respect of latent personal injuries / c the Law Reform Commission. – Dublin : The Commission, 1987.
65p. – (LRC).
Cover title: Personal injuries.

LIMITATION OF ACTIONS - NEW ZEALAND

—Limitation Act 1950 : a discussion paper / Law Commision. – Wellington, N.Z. : The Commission, 1987.
v,92p. – (Preliminary paper).
Bibliography: pp.66-67. Includes text of the Act.

—Prescriptive title for a co-owner in possession / report of the Property Law and Equity Reform Committee. – Wellington : Government Printer, 1986.
17p.

LIMITATION OF ACTIONS - SCOTLAND

—Law of Prescription and Limitation of Actions in Scotland / 3rd ed. – Edinburgh : W Green, 1981.
ISBN 0414006674 Hbk £12.50

—Prescription and limitation of actions (latent damage) / Scottish Law Commission. – Edinburgh : The Commission, 1987.
v,162p. – (Consultative memorandum).
Includes bibliographical references.

—Prescription and the limitation of actions : report on personal injuries actions and private international law questions / Scottish Law Commission. – Edinburgh : H.M.S.O., 1983.
v,61p.
ISBN 0102153833

LIMITATION OF ACTIONS - SOUTH AFRICA

—Investigation into the limits for the institution of actions against the state / South African Law Commission. – Pretoria : The Commission, 1985.
iv,50p. – (Report).
Includes bibliographical references. Includes draft of Bill.

LIMITED LIABILITY - EUROPEAN COMMUNITY

—Limited liability and the corporation / edited by Tony Orhnial. – London : Croom Helm, 1982.
223p; 23cm.
Conference papers. Includes bibliographies.
ISBN 0709905157 £12.95

LIMITED LIABILITY - GREAT BRITAIN

—Limited Liability in Collision Cases / H. G. Rohreke. – London : LLoyd's of London Press, 1984.

LIMITED PARTNERSHIP - CANADA

—Limited Partnerships and Their Use in Syndications / Vancouver : British Columbia Continuing Legal Education Society, 1983.
205p.
ISBN 0865041318 Hbk £55.00

LIQUIDATED DAMAGES - AUSTRALIA - VICTORIA

—Liquidated damages and penalties / Law Reform Commission of Victoria. – Melbourne : The Commission, 1988.
i.20p. – (Discussion paper).
Includes bibliographical references.
ISBN 0724167293

LIQUIDATION - AUSTRALIA

—Assignments, arrangements and compositions by debtors (with precedents) / 2nd. – North Ryde : Butterworths (Australia).
Practical guide to the workings of administrations under part 10 of the Australian Commonwealth Bankruptcy Act.
ISBN 0409490652 Hbk

—Company receivers and managers / by James O'Donovan. – Sydney : Law Book Copany, 1981.
lxxxiii,545p.
Includes index.
ISBN 0455200823

—Corporate Securities and Creditors Rights on Insolvency 1984 / Monash University Staff. – Clayton : Monash University Press, 1984.
ISBN 0867463414 Hbk £15.00

—Law of company litigation : being the law relating to liquidation of limited liability companies / by B. H. McPherson. – 3rd ed. – Sydney : Law Book Co., 1987.
lxxxii,501p.
Previous ed.: 1980. Bibliography: pp.lxxix-lxxx. - Includes index.
ISBN 0455207410

—Law of Company receiverships in Australia and New Zealand / North Ryde : Butterworths (Australia), 1983.
ISBN 0409491632 Hbk £25.60

—Law of company receiverships in Australia and New Zealand / by Peter Blanchard. – Sydney : Butterworths, 1983.
xxvi,213p.
Includes index.
ISBN 0409491632

—Law of company receiverships in New Zealand and Australia / by Peter Blanchard. – Wellington : Butterworths, 1982.
xxvi,213p.
Covers the law governing receiverships initiated by the holders of charges over corporate assets in New Zealand and Australia.
ISBN 0409601330

—Winding up and receivership under the Companies Act 1981 / by James O'Donovan. – Sydney : Law Book Co., 1982.
xix,48p.
ISBN 0455204438

LIQUIDATION - CANADA

—Commercial Insolvency Reporter / Toronto : Butterworths.
ISBN 0409806218 Hbk

—Guide to Commercial Insolvency in Canada / Butterworths, 1988.
ca 388p.
Takes the reader through the relevant proceedings and applicable legislation, covering the commencement of bankruptcy proceedings, receiverships, liquidation of asset; to directors' responsibilities on insolvency and annulment of transactions.
ISBN 0409846740 Hbk

—Lending and Recovery : Benefits and Pitfalls of Consulting Engagements / Peter W. Aykroyd. – Agincourt : Carswell, 1985.
150p.
This work addresses the problems faced by Canadian corporations, financial institutions, insolvency consultants, and attorneys as they deal with questions of the solvency of a corporation to whom a loan has been made.

—Realization and Insolvency / Vancouver : Continuing Legal Education Society of British Columbia, 1986.
229p.
ISBN 0865042691 Hbk £55.00

—Receivers / Vancouver : Continuing Legal Education Society of British Columbia, 1985.
97p.
ISBN 0865042225 Hbk £55.00

—Receiverships / Agincourt : Carswell, 1985.
ISBN 0459374303 Hbk £38.75

—Receiverships / Agincourt : Carswell, 1985.
588p.

—Receiverships : Carswell's Canadian Legal Classic Series / Agincourt : Carswell, 1985.
588p.
This work explains all aspects of the receivership process in Canada from the use of consultants in the decision to appoint a receiver through to the discharge. A table of cases and extensive precedents are included in the book.

LIQUIDATION - ENGLAND

—Administrative receivers and administrators / Gordon Stewart. – Bicester : CCH Editions, 1987.
xvii,359p; 23cm.
Traces receiverships and administrations from the events leading up to appointment through to termination and discharge of the office holder. Gives details of licensing requirements, and covers for both receivers and administrators, the appointment, nature and capacity, powers and duties. Also looks at payments and duties, termination, tax, and relevant forms.
ISBN 0863251404 Hbk
ISBN 0863250858 Pbk

—Corporate receiverships : a practical approach / by Stanley Samwell. – London : Institute of Chartered Accountants in England and Wales, 1981.
xv,190p; 22cm.
Includes index.
ISBN 0852912870 Unpriced

—Law of receivers of companies / by Gavin Lightman and Gabriel Moss : with a foreword by Sir John Vinelott. – London : Sweet & Maxwell, 1986.
xlix,358p; 24cm.
Guide to the law relating to administrative receiverships, covering all aspects of practice and procedure. Includes sections on administrators, title retention clauses, and the role of the receiver in the winding up of a company.
ISBN 0421300906 £38.00

—Law relating to receivers and managers / Hubert Picarda. – London : Butterworths, 1984.
lxi,493p; 26cm.
Bibliography: p483-484. - Includes index.
ISBN 0406337608 No price

—Liquidation manual / John Powell, Malcolm London. – 2nd ed. – Croydon : Tolley, 1988.
xxii,318p.
Guide to conduct of UK company liquidations including creditors' voluntary liquidations. Explains liquidator's role and responsibilities to creditors, employees and members.
ISBN 0854592229

—Liquidation manual / Paul Shewell, John Powell. – Croydon : Tolley, 1983.
xxi,368p.
Includes index. Cover title: Tolley's liquidation manual.
ISBN 0854590285

—Loose on liquidators : the role of a liquidator in a voluntary winding-up / Michael Crystal, John-Higham. – 2nd ed. – Bristol : Jordan, 1981.
xxviii,219p; 23cm.
Previous ed.: 1972. Includes index.
ISBN 085308064X £10.50

—Receivership manual / Martin Iredale, Christopher Hughes. – 3rd ed. – Croydon : Tolley, 1987.
xiv,178p.
Guide to receivership including recent Insolvency Acts and company law changes.
ISBN 0854592202

—Tax consequences of receivership and liquidation / David Bertram. – London : Butterworths, 1982.
xxxii,423p; 22cm.
Includes index.
ISBN 0406220603 Pbk £20.00

—Voluntary liquidation and receivership : a practical guide / Ian S. Grier and Richard E. Floyd. – London : Oyez Longman, 1985.
xvii,187p.
Includes index.
ISBN 0851209548

—Winding up of insolvent companies in England and France / Christopher Livadas. – Deventer, Netherlands : Kluwer Law and Taxation Publishers, 1983.
xxxvi, 384 p.; 25 cm.
: Originally presented as the author's thesis (Ph.D.–City of London Polytechnic, 1981). Bibliography: p. 383-384.
ISBN 9065440879

LIQUIDATION - EUROPE

—Bankruptcy, Winding-Up, Arrangements, Compositions and Similar Proceedings : Draft Convention and Report / Kirchberg : Commission of the European Communities, 1982.
116p.

LIQUIDATION - FRANCE

—Winding up of insolvent companies in England and France / Christopher Livadas. – Deventer, Netherlands : Kluwer Law and Taxation Publishers, 1983.
xxxvi, 384 p.; 25 cm.
: Originally presented as the author's thesis (Ph.D.–City of London Polytechnic, 1981). Bibliography: p. 383-384.
ISBN 9065440879

LIQUIDATION - GREAT BRITAIN

—Annotated guide to the 1986 insolvency legislation: Insolvency Act 1986, Company Directors Disqualification Act 1986 and Insolvency Rules 1986 (as amended) / David Milman. – 2nd. – Bicester : CCH Editions Ltd, 1988.
Reproduces the Act in full text, together with commentary and notes to each provision, explaining its meaning, effort and implications. Includes lists of statutory definitions, a table of destinations, reference to the rules and regulations, and a comprehensive index.
ISBN 0863251617 Hbk £26.00

—Companies in 1983 Annual Report / Insolvency Service of the Department of Trade and Industry. – London : HMSO, 1984.
ISBN 0115137025 Hbk £4.75

—Companies in 1984 - Annual Report / London : HMSO, 1985.
ISBN 0115138277 Hbk £4.95

—Company administration orders and voluntary arrangements / Richard Floyd. – London : Longman Professional (UK), 1988.
– (Practitioner series).
Guide to the law and procedure relating to administration orders, and voluntary arrangements (resulting from the Insolvency Act 1986). Examines corporate administration orders from beginning to end, comparing them to other insolvency proceedings. Includes specimen proposals.
ISBN 0851214800 Hbk £18.95

—Company director and the law / 5th. – London : Longman Professional (UK), 1986.
Explains the legal responsibilities and obligations of the company director. Covers the changes made by the Companies Act 1985, and the Insolvency Act 1986.
ISBN 085121231X Pbk £17.95

—Company Insolvency and Liquidation / French. – London : Blackstone Press, 1988.
ISBN 1854310143 Hbk

—Company liquidations / Harry Rajak. – Bicester : CCH, 1988.
xxvii,628p.
Discusses the legal principles of corporate insolvency, examines the law of company liquidation, and provides a guide to the increasingly complex practice and procedure governing the life of an insolvent company before and after liquidation. Contains a chapter on the taxation questions, copies of relevant forms, a case table, legislation finding list, and index. Covers the Insolvency (Amendment) Rules 1987.
ISBN 0863251447 Pbk £48.00
ISBN 0863250831 Hbk £36.00

—Company Liquidations / London : CCH, 1988.
ISBN 0863250831 Pbk £36.00
ISBN 0863251447 Hbk £48.00

—Company liquidations : the substantive law / Robert Pennington. – Bristol : Jordans, 1987.
xxvi,150p; 21cm.
Includes index.
ISBN 0853081220 Pbk £8.50

—Compulsory Winding-Up Procedure / London : Oyez Longman, 1983.
– (Oyez Longman Practice Note Ser.: No. 77).
ISBN 0851207758 Hbk £7.95

—Compulsory winding-up procedure / 2nd. – London : Longman Professional (UK), 1987.
Revised following the Insolvency Act 1986. Step by step guide through the process of compulsory winding-up for a limited liability company from the role of the liquidation committee to the proofs of debt and dividend. Appendix contains procedural forms.
ISBN 0851211798 Pbk £14.50

—Corporate Insolvency / Durrant. – London : Sweet & Maxwell, 1987.
ISBN 0421365005 Hbk £24.00

—Corporate Insolvency Practice Manual / London : Butterworths, 1988.
ISBN 0406503508 Pbk

—Corporate Receiverships : A Practical Approach / London : VanNostrand Reinhold, 1981.
ISBN 0852912870 Hbk £11.95

—Corporate Rescues and Insolvencies / London : Butterworths, 1986.
ISBN 0406100403 Pbk £27.00

—Insolvency / London : Collins, 1986.
200p.
ISBN 0003832937 Hbk £17.50

—Insolvency Act 1985 / with annotations by Ian Fletcher. – London : Sweet & Maxwell, 1986.
various pagings.
Includes index. Includes text of the Act.
ISBN 0421347007

—Insolvency and Company Law : Reform & Renewal / London : Law Society, 1985.
25p. – (Nineteen Eighty-Five Crash Course Transcripts).

—Insolvency : Disqualification and personal liability of directors / London : CCH, 1986.
ISBN 0863250920 Pbk £6.00

—Insolvency - Introduction to the 1985 Act / Jordan. – London : Longman Professional, 1986.
ISBN 0851212166 Pbk £7.95

—Insolvency law handbook / London : Butterworths, 1987.
ISBN 0406500061 Pbk £23.50

—Insolvency Procedure Notes / Michael Stubbs. – London : Waterlow, 1987.
160p.
ISBN 0080330894 Pbk £17.95

—Insolvency - Understanding the new law / London : Financial Training, 1987.
ISBN 1851850627 Pbk £9.95

—Law and Practice as to Receivers / Walton. – 17th ed. – London : Sweet & Maxwell, 1988.
ISBN 0421296909 Hbk

—Law of corporate insolvency / London : Waterlow, 1990.
912; 23.
ISBN 0080392059 Hbk £70

—Law of Insolvency / McKenzie. – 2nd ed. – London : Butterworths, 1981.
ISBN 0409667900 Hbk £25.50

—Law of Insolvency / 2nd ed. – London : Butterworths, 1982.
ISBN 0409056022 Hbk £38.30
ISBN 0409056030 Pbk £30.30

—Law Relating to Receivers and Managers / London : Butterworths, 1984.
ISBN 0406337608 Hbk £66.00

—Liquidation Manual / 2nd ed. – Tolley Publishing, 1988.
ISBN 0854592229 Hbk £29.95

—Liquidation of Insolvent Private Companies / London : Butterworths, 1988.
ISBN 0406267006 Pbk

—Nelson's tables: company procedure / A M Peck, A Robertson. – 10th ed. – London : Longman Professional, 1987.
Contains explanatory notes regarding insolvency and references to relevant statutes and forms. Incorporates the new practice and procedure following on from the Insolvency Act 1986.
ISBN 0851202964 Pbk £14.50

—Receivers and receiverships / David Milman and Jonathan Rushworth. – Bristol : Jordans, 1987.
xxi,82p; 21cm.
Includes index.
ISBN 0853081239 Pbk £8.50

—Receivership manual / Donald Chilvers, Paul Shewell. – 2nd ed. – Croydon : Tolley, 1983.
xi,123p.
Includes index.
ISBN 0854590706

—Receivership manual / 3rd ed. – Croydon : Tolley, 1987.
ISBN 0854592202 Hbk £21.95

—Rights and duties of directors / Touche Ross. – London : Butterworths, 1987.
ISBN 0406504709 Pbk £18.50

—Set-off in insolvencies / Oxford : Oxford University Press, 1988.
ISBN 019825556X Hbk £40.00

—Taxation of insolvent companies / Croydon : Tolley, 1986.
ISBN 0854592326 Pbk £9.95

—Tolley's employees' rights in receiverships and liquidations / Guy T.E. Parsons, William F. Ratford. – 2nd ed. – Croyden : Tolley, 1984.
xiv,210p; 30cm.
Previous ed.: 1979. Bibliography: p201. - Includes index.
ISBN 0854591443 £25.00

—Winding-up and bankruptcy procedures / Shaws Linton Publications, 1988.
ISBN 0906653142 Hbk £12.95

LIQUIDATION - INDIA

—Basu's Law of Receivers / 3rd ed. – Calcutta : Eastern Law House, 1984.

—Law of Receivers / P.M.K. Nair. – 3rd ed. – Allahabad : Law Book Company, 1988.
1,000p.

LIQUIDATION - NEW ZEALAND

—Effect of disputed debts, set-offs and counterclaims on winding-up and bankruptcy petitions / by R. J. Calnan. – Auckland : Legal Research Foundation, 1981.
55p.
ISBN 0908581165

—Law of company receiverships in Australia and New Zealand / by Peter Blanchard. – Sydney : Butterworths, 1983.
xxvi,213p.
Includes index.
ISBN 0409491632

—Law of Company receiverships in Australia and New Zealand / North Ryde : Butterworths (Australia), 1983.
ISBN 0409491632 Hbk £25.60

—Law of company receiverships in New Zealand and Australia / by Peter Blanchard. – Wellington : Butterworths, 1982.
xxvi,213p.
Covers the law governing receiverships initiated by the holders of charges over corporate assets in New Zealand and Australia.
ISBN 0409601330

—New Zealand Insolvency Legislation / North Ryde : C.C.H. Australia, 1987.
200p.
ISBN 086475082X Hbk

LIQUIDATION - NORTHERN IRELAND

—Winding up of companies in Northern Ireland : a practitioner's guide / by John M. Hunter. – Belfast : SLS Legal Publications, 1984.
xxxvi,142p.
Bibliography: p.135. - Includes index.
ISBN 0853892482

LIQUIDATION - SCOTLAND

—Floating charges and receivers / Scottish Law Commission. – Edinburgh : The Commission, 1986.
iv,151p. – (Consultative memorandum).
Includes bibliographical references. Catalogued from cover.

—Guide to liquidation in Scotland / David Flint. – Bristol : Jordan & Sons, 1987.
viii,265p; 25cm.
Provides a brief introduction to the Act and rules. With the text of relevant legislation other than the 1986 Insolvency Act.
ISBN 0853080925 Pbk £12.50

—Law and practice of receivership in Scotland / J.H. Greene, I.M. Fletcher. – London : Butterworths, 1987.
xxxviii,355p; 26cm.
Includes index.
ISBN 0406005273 £27.50

—Law of corporate insolvency in Scotland / by John B. St. Clair and J.E. Drummond Young. – Edinburgh : W. Green & Son Ltd., 1988.
xxix,381p; 25cm.
Includes index. A comprehensive guide to the law of corporate insolvency in the light of the reforming legislation of 1986. Deals with winding-up, receivership, administration and related problems such as trust and retention of title.
ISBN 0414008170 Pbk No price

LIS PENDENS - CANADA - MANITOBA

—Report on certificates of lis pendens / Law Reform Commission. – Winnipeg : Queen's Printer, 1983.
28p. – (Report).

LLOYD'S OF LONDON

—Lloyd's of London : a reputation at risk / Godfrey Hodgson. – London : Allen Lane, 1984.
378p.
ISBN 0713913673

—Tax and financial planning for Lloyd's members / London : Longman Professional, 1988.
– (A Longman Intelligence Report).
ISBN 0851213421 Hbk £85.00

—Taxation of Lloyd's Underwriters / Croydon : Tolley, 1984.
ISBN 085459129X Pbk £17.50

—Taxation of Lloyd's Underwriters / P H Wolstenholme. – 2nd ed. – London : Butterworths, 1985.
ISBN 0406678804 Pbk £15.00

—Taxation of Lloyds Underwriters / 2nd ed. – Croydon : Tolley.
300p.
ISBN 0854593063 Hbk £29.95

LLOYD'S OF LONDON - GREAT BRITAIN

—Introduction to working in the Lloyds Market / Wormell. – Witherby, 1987.
ISBN 0948691387 Pbk £10.00

LOANS

—Euronotes : RUFs, TRUFs, NIFs, SNIFs and BONUSes / edited by Lloyd Bankson and Michael Lee. – London : Euromoney, 1985.
viii,183p.
ISBN 0903121743

—International syndicated loans / by Robert P. McDonald. – London : Euromoney, 1982.
ix,264p.
Bibliography: p.261-262. - Includes index.
ISBN 0903121441

—Legal aspects of syndicated loans / Peter Gabriel. – London : Butterworths, 1986.
xxxvi,276p; 26cm.
Bibliography: p265-267. - Includes index.
ISBN 0406102104 £45.00

—Legal problems of credit and security / by R.M. Goode. – London : Sweet & Maxwell, 1982.
xviii,133p; 22cm.
Includes index.
ISBN 0421302704 Pbk £10.00

—Loan agreement documentation : sample annotated loan agreement for a syndicated Eurodollar transaction / by Anthony C. Gooch, Linda B. Klein. – London : Euromoney Publications, 1986.
iii,93p.
ISBN 1870031407

—Medium-term loan market / J.A. Donaldson and T.H. Donaldson. – London : Macmillan, 1982.
viii,229p.
Includes index.
ISBN 0333326067

LOANS - CANADA

—New Developments in Commercial Lending / McGill University. – Toronto : DeBoo, 1981. – (Meredith Memorial Lecture Ser.).
ISBN 0888201095 Hbk £49.50

LOANS - GREAT BRITAIN

—Legal Aspects of Syndicated Loans / London : Butterworths, 1986.
ISBN 0406102104 Hbk £50.00

—Legal problems of credit and security / by R.M. Goode. – 2nd ed. – London : Sweet & Maxwell, 1988.
xxxv,218p; 23cm.
Contains chapters on the nature and forms of consensual security and concepts of attachments and perfection. Section on treatment of negative pledges has been expanded. Analysis of the legal nature of subparticipation in loan assessments, and examination of twelve typical priority conflicts and their resolution, and an enlarged chapter on equitable, statutory and contractual set-off and set-off on insolvency.
ISBN 0421384301 Pbk £14.00

—Lending Packages for Small and Medium-Sized Companies / Oxford : Croom Helm, 1983.
ISBN 070992254X Pbk £8.95

LOANS - SCOTLAND

—Financing and security in Scots law / by Ian B. Inglis. – Dundee : University of Dundee Centre for Petroleum and Mineral Law Studies, 1980.
47p; 30cm. – (Occasional paper).
An expanded version of a paper given at a conference organised by the Centre on Scots law and the oil industry at Hamilton Hall, St. Andrews, 4-7 April 1979.
ISBN 090634302X Pbk Unpriced

LOBBYING - GREAT BRITAIN

—Lobbying government : understanding and influencing the corridors of power / Charles Miller. – Oxford : Basil Blackwell, 1987.
200p; 23cm.
Includes index.
ISBN 0631155252 £25.00

LOCAL AUTHORITY CARE

—Foster families : recommendation no. R(87)6 adopted by the Committee of Ministers of the Council of Europe on 20 March 1987 and Explanatory memorandum / Council of Europe. – Strasbourg : Council of Europe, 1987.
15p.
Prepared by the Committee of experts on family law set up under the authority of the European Committee on Legal Co-operation. At head of cover title : Council of Europe, Legal Affairs.
ISBN 9287110875

—Review of child care law : report to ministers of an interdepartmental working party : published by the government as a consultative document / Rupert Hughes. – London : H.M.S.O., 1985.
v,179p.
Chairman: Rupert Hughes. At head of title-page: Department of Health and Social Security.
ISBN 0113210426

LOCAL AUTHORITY CARE - CANADA

—Report of the Task Force on Child Care / Canada. – Ottawa, Ont. : Status of Women Canada, 1986.
xxvi, 395 p.; 23 cm.
Bibliography: p. 345-365.
ISBN 0660120380 pbk. £9.95 (£11.95 other countries)

LOCAL AUTHORITY CARE - ENGLAND

—Decision making in statutory reviews on children in care / Ruth Sinclair. – Aldershot : Gower, 1984.
vi,171p; 23cm.
Bibliography: p165-171.
ISBN 0566007576 £16.45

—Minors : the law and practice : the juvenile courts, the offences, the role of the local authorities / Kenneth W. Pain. – London : Fourmat Publishing, 1987.
xvii,293p.
Concerns practice and procedure of juvenile courts, offences which can be committed by and against minors and the part played by local authorities in care proceedings.
ISBN 1851900306

—Review of child care law : publication of interim discussion papers by the inter-Departmental working party / Department of Health and Social Security. – 1. – London : The Department, 1986.
various pagings.
ISBN 1851970401

—Social work decisions in child care : recent research findings and their implications / appraisal by the Research on Child Care Working Party of Child Care Practitioners; report written by Jane Rowe. – London : H.M.S.O., 1985.
73p.
Includes summaries of the reports discussed. At head of title-page: Department of Health and Social Security. 7 sheets of charts in end pocket.
ISBN 0113210469

LOCAL AUTHORITY CARE - GREAT BRITAIN

—Accountability in child care - which way forward? / London : Family Rights Group, 1982.
49p; 21cm.
Subtitle: Background papers to a seminar organised on 19 February 1982 to discuss the issues raised by the House of Lords' judgement in A. v Liverpool City Council and to offer and invite suggestions for improving local authority practice and accountability in child care cases.

—Care cases : proposals for legal reform / Family Rights Group. – London : Family Rights Group, 1985.
54p.
Includes bibliographical references.

—Care Proceedings / 2nd ed. – London : Oyez Longman, 1983.
– (Oyez Longman Practitioner Ser.).
ISBN 0851207235 Hbk £8.95

—Children in care : memorandum of evidence / by the Association of County Councils. – London : The Association, 1983.
10p.
At head of title: House of Commons Social Services Committee.

—Family law : review of child law : Care, supervision and interim orders in custody proceedings / The Law Commission. – London : H.M.S.O., 1987.
v,80p; 21cm. – (Working paper).
Examines the power of the courts to commit a child to local authority care. Makes proposals to reconcile existing inconsistency, simplify and improve the system.
ISBN 0117301825

—Law on child care and family services / Department of Health and Social Security...et al. : presented to Parliament by the Secretary of State for Social Services... – London : H.M.S.O., 1987.
iv,22p.
ISBN 0101006225

—Second report from the Social Services Committee, session 1983- 84 : children in care / London : H.M.S.O., 1984.
clxxii p.; 25cm. – (H.C.).
ISBN 0102880840

Vol.2 : Minutes of evidence (24 November 1982-9 February 1983) 1984.
ix,1-410p; 25cm. – (H.C.).
ISBN 0102881847 Hbk

Vol.3 : Minutes of evidence (16 February-4 May 1983 and an appendix 1984.
ix,411-740p; 25cm. – (H.C.).
ISBN 0102882843 Hbk

LOCAL AUTHORITY CARE - NORTHERN IRELAND

—Consulatative papers related to the revision of the Children and Young Persons Act (Northern Ireland) 1968 / Department of Helath and Social Services. – Belfast : The Department, 1987.
17,11 leaves.
Contents: Consultative paper on regulation of child minding, group day care and care and maintenance of children - Consultative paper on employment of children.

LOCAL AUTHORITY HOUSING - SCOTLAND

—Public sector housing law in Scotland / 3rd. – Edinburgh : W Green & Son, 1989.
Describes the functions with regard to housing responsibilities of local authorities, the Scottish Office, Scottish Homes and housing associations. Chapter on public sector secure tenancies, assured tenancies for housing associations, the right to buy, homelessness and the improvement of sub-standard housing.
ISBN 041400891X

LOCAL FINANCE

—Financial apportionment and equalisation / report prepared under the guidance of the members of the Committee of Experts on Local and Regional Finance by Graham Kelly. – Strasbourg : Council of Europe, 1981.
95p.
Up-dated and expanded version of: Financial structures of local and regional authorities in Europe. - Vol. 2. - 1976. - (Study series local and regional authorities in Europe ; no. 13).

—Financial resources for local and regional authorities : report / prepared under the guidance of the Committee of Experts on Local and Regional Finance of the Steering Committee for Regional and Municipal Matters by G. Kelly. – Strasbourg : Council of Europe, 1985.
79p; 30cm.

—Fiscal tiers : the economics of multi-level government / David N. King. – London : Allen & Unwin in association with the Centre for Research on Federal Finance Relations, the Australian National University, 1984.
v,326p; 24cm.
Bibliography: p305-316. - Includes index.
ISBN 0043360815 Hbk Unpriced
ISBN 004336084X Pbk £8.95

—Local authority accounting in Europe : report / prepared by the Committee of Experts on Local and Regional Finance of the Steering Committee for Regional and Municipal Matters. – Strasbourg : Council of Europe, 1985.
120p.

—Policies with regard to grants to local authorities / report prepared by the Committee of Experts on Local and Regional Finance of the Steering Committee for Regional and Municipal Matters and drafted by J. Lotz, Chairman. – Strasbourg : Council of Europe, 1986.
35p.

—Response of local authorities to central government incitement to reduce expenditure / by W. J. Meadows. – Strasbourg : Council of Europe, 1986.
33p.
Prepared under the guidance of the Committee of Experts on Local and Regional Finance of the Steering Committee for Regional and Municipal Matters.

LOCAL FINANCE - CANADA

—Local government finance in Canada / Harry M. Kitchen. – Toronto : Canadian Tax Foundation, 1984.
xvii,495p.
Includes bibliographical references and index.
ISBN 0888080204

LOCAL FINANCE - ENGLAND

—Local Government Finance Act 1982 / with annotations by Reginald Jones. – London : Sweet & Maxwell, 1982.
51p; 24cm.
ISBN 0421310006 Pbk £5.50

LOCAL FINANCE - GREAT BRITAIN

—Finance of local government / by N.P. Hepworth. – 7th ed. – London : Allen & Unwin, 1984.
xvi,349p; 20cm.
Previous ed.: 1980. Bibliography: p335-339. - Includes index.
ISBN 0043521118 Hbk No price
ISBN 0043521150 No price

—Rate capping and the law / by Malcolm Grant. – 2nd ed. – London : Association of Metropolitan Authorities, 1986.
xiii,123p.
Previous ed.: 1984.
ISBN 0902052063

—'The free two pence' Section 137 of the Local Government Act 1972 and Section 83 of the Local Governement (Scotland) Act 1973 / by Colin Crawford and Victor Moore. – London : The Chartered Institute of Public Finance and Accountancy, 1983.
x,218p.
ISBN 0852992556

LOCAL GOVERNMENT

—Decentralisation of local government at neighbourhood level / ... prepared by the Secretariat of the Steering Committee for Regional and Municipal Matters with the assistance of Sven-Runo Bergqvist. – Strasbourg : Council of Europe, 1981.
30p.

—Explanatory report on the European Outline Convention on Transfrontier Co-operation between Territorial Communities or Authorities / Strasbourg : Council of Europe, 1980.
49p; 21cm.
Includes text of the convention.

—Final report on the operation of national organisations concerned with the co-ordination of computer use in local government / by Serge Duriaud under the guidance of the Committee of Experts on Local and Regional Management. – Strasbourg : Council of Europe, 1980.
iii,39p.

—Liability of the States and Regional and Local Authorities for Damage Caused by their Agents and Administrative Services / Strasbourg : Council of Europe, 1981.

—Management structures in local and regional government : report / prepared under the guidance of the Committee of Experts on Management in Local and Regional Government of the Steering Committee for Regional and Municipal Matters, by G. Kelly. – Strasbourg : Council of Europe, 1985.
54p.

—Problems encountered by local and regional authorites as a result of their new tasks in respect of environmental protection / report prepared under the guidance of the Committee of Experts on Social and Economic Activities of the Steering Committee for Regional and Municpal Matters by G. Tendron. – Strasbourg : Council of Europe, 1986.
29p.
Bibliography: p.28-29.

—Problems of regional and local authorities involved in planning policies : report / prepared under the guidance of the Committee of Experts on Social and Economic Activities of the Steering Committee for Regional and Municipal Matters by Jacques Robert. – Strasbourg : Council of Europe, 1985.
36p.

—Reforms of local and regional authorities in Europe : theory, practice and critical appraisal : colloquy organised by the Council of Europe, Linz, 5-6 November 1981 / Strasbourg : Council of Europe, 1983.
220p.
Bibliography: p.181-182.
ISBN 9287101914

—Regional and local affairs : news / Strasbourg : Council of Europe, 1982-.
Supersedes: Information bulletin: municipal and regional matters.

—Role of local authorities in promoting the creation or operation of small or medium-sized firms within a general policy of endogenous development / report prepared under the guidance of the Committee of Experts on Social and Economic Activities of the Steering Committee for Regional and Municipal Matters by T. Nuttal. – Strasbourg : Council of Europe, 1986.
31p.
Bibliography: p.28-29.

—Survey of computing in European local and regional authorities / ... prepared under the guidelines of the Committee of Experts on Management in Local and Regional Government by G.Gaits. – Strasbourg : Council of Europe, 1981.
iii,61p.

—Texts adopted / Standing Conference of Local and Regional Authorities of Europe : Conference Permanente des Pouvoirs Locaux et Regionaux de l'Europe. – v. – Strasbourg : Council of Europe, 1984.
Continues: Texts adopted / Conference of Local and Regional Authorities of Europe. Parallel English and French texts.

—Use of management techniques in regional and local government : report / prepared under the guidance of the Committee of Experts on Management in Local and Regional Government of the Steering Committee for Regional and Municipal Matters by F. Boersma. – Strasbourg : Council of Europe, 1985.
38p.
Bibliography: p.33.

LOCAL GOVERNMENT – AUSTRALIA – SOUTH AUSTRALIA

—Council Meetings Law and Procedures in South Australia / North Ryde : Law Book Co, 1980.
xxvii, 116p.
ISBN 0455201374 Pbk £26.00

LOCAL GOVERNMENT – ENGLAND

—Cross on local government law / S. H. Bailey, C. A. Cross. – 7th ed. – London : Sweet & Maxwell, 1986.
xiii,666p; 24cm.
Previous ed.: published as Principles of local government law. London : Sweet & Maxwell, 1981. Includes index.
ISBN 0421341904 Hbk £32.00
ISBN 0421342005 Pbk £22.00

—Encyclopedia of local government law / Charles Cross, Stephen Bailey, Stephen Campbell, Reginald Jones. – 4 volumes. – London : Sweet & Maxwell, 1980.
25cm : loose-leaf.
Release number fourteen included the relevant sectins of the Local Governments Finance Act 1988, annotated, and cross-referenced to other parts of the work. Also covers the Local Government Act 1988, and the Rate Support Grants Act 1988. Statutory instruments, selected precedents, circulars, and full tables and index are also contained.
ISBN 0421260505 Llf £195.00

—Law for councillors / by Barbara Turner. – London : Sweet & Maxwell, 1986.
xii,146p; 21cm.
ISBN 0421353600 Pbk £5.00

—Local government in the modern states / by Martin Loughlin. – London : Sweet & Maxwell, 1986.
xxv,222p; 23cm.
Bibliography: p202-217. - Includes index.
ISBN 0421338601 Hbk £13.50
ISBN 0421338709 Pbk £12.50

—Local government law / Keith Davies. – London : Butterworths, 1983.
xxxvi,352p; 23cm.
Includes index.
ISBN 0406252661 Hbk Unpriced
ISBN 040625267X Pbk Unpriced

—Local Government, Planning and Land Act 1980 / with annotations by Victor Moore and Louise Catchpole. – London : Sweet & Maxwell, 1981.
294p; 25cm.
ISBN 0421288701 Pbk £10.00

—Local government, the law and the constitution / Martin Loughlin. – s.l. : Local Government Legal Society Trust, 1983.
ii,143p.

—Principles of local government law / by C.A. Cross. – 6th ed. – London : Sweet & Maxwell, 1981.
ISBN 0421248602
ISBN 042124870X

—Solicitors and local authorities / by R.J.B. Morris. – Chichester : Rose, 1983.
ciii,349p; 23cm.
Includes index.
ISBN 0859923304 Unpriced

—Streamlining the cities : an analysis of the Government's case for reorganising local government in the six Metropolitan Counties : first report / Coopers & Lybrand Associates. – London? : Coopers & Lybrand Associates, 1983.
28p.

—Streamlining the cities : government proposals for reorganising local government in Greater London and the metropolitan counties / presented to Parliament by the Secretary of State for the Environment ... – London : H.M.S.O., 1983.
31p.
ISBN 0101906307

LOCAL GOVERNMENT – EUROPE

—Texts adopted / Conference of Local and Regional Authorities of Europe : Conference Permanente des Pouvoirs Locaux et Regionaux de l'Europe. – Strasbourg : Council of Europe, 1976-.
Continues: Texts adopted / European Conference of Local Authorities. - Continued by : Texts adopted / Standing Conference of Local and Regional Authorities of Europe. Parallel English and French texts.

LOCAL GOVERNMENT – FRANCE

—Constitutional and legislative provisions concerning the organisation of regional government / Council of Europe. – Strasbourg : Council of Europe, 1982.
i,37p.

LOCAL GOVERNMENT – GREAT BRITAIN

—Access to information in local government / by Tim Harrison. – London : Sweet & Maxwell, 1988.
110p.
Covers the Local Government (Access to Information) Act 1985, including a chapter on access by elected members of councils. Also contains the Data Protection Act 1984 as it relates to councils, the Access to Personal Files Act 1987, and the common law.
ISBN 0421384107 £10.00

—Careers in Local Government / London : Kogan Page, 1981.
96p.
ISBN 0850384370 Hbk £6.95
ISBN 0850384389 Pbk £2.95

—Councillor / 10th ed. – London : Shaw & Sons, 1987.
ISBN 0721908519 Pbk £4.95

—Encyclopaedia of Local Government Law / London : Sweet & Maxwell, 1988.
ISBN 0421260505 Hbk £195.00

—Essays on the future of local government / edited by Michael Goldsmith. – S.l. : s.n., 1986.
139p.
Includes bibliographies. 'Sponsored by West Yorkshire Metropolitan County Council' - Preface.

—Government by Consent : The Principle and Practice of Accountability in Local Government / London : Bedford Square Press, 1985.
ISBN 0719911400 Hbk £2.95

—Guide to Enquiries of Local Authorities / 2nd ed. – London : Oyez Longman, 1982.
ISBN 085120645X Hbk £3.25

—Guide to Enquiries of Local Authorities / 2nd ed. – London : Longman Professional, 1982.
ISBN 085120645X Pbk £5.95

—Knight's Local Government and Magisterial Reports, Statutes and Orders : 1903-date, 234 Vols. / Abingdon : Professional Books.

—Local and Central Government / 4th ed. – London : Hutchinson, 1984.
128p.
ISBN 0091588715 Pbk £3.95

—Local Authority Licensing and Registration / Rosson. – London : Longman Professional, 1985.
ISBN 085120886X updat £125.00

—Local Government Act 1985 / London : Sweet & Maxwell, 1985.
ISBN 0421353503 Pbk £9.75

—Local Government Acts : 1987-1988 / London : Shaw & Sons, 1988.
ISBN 0721910718 Pbk £10.95

—Local Government Administration / 2nd ed. – London : Shaw & Sons, 1987.
ISBN 0721907121 Pbk £11.95

—Local Government Audit Law / London : HMSO, 1985.
ISBN 0117012599 Hbk £19.50

—Local Government Forms and Precedents : 1953-1956, 5 Vols. / Abingdon : Professional Books.

—Local Government Law / London : Butterworths, 1983.
ISBN 040625267X Pbk £17.95

—Local Government Review : 1909-1914, 7 Vols. / Abingdon : Professional Books.

—Management by Objectives in Local Government / R. E. H. Bullock. – Tonbridge : Ernest Benn.
255p.

—Open government : freedom of information and local government : a study conducted for the Local Government Legal Society Trust and the Society of Town Clerks' Education and Research Trust / Patrick Birkinshaw. – London : Local Government Legal Society Trust in association with the Society of Town Clerks' Education and Research Trust, 1985.
84p.
ISBN 0951110101

—Oyez Longman Directory of Local Authorities 1983 / Oyez Longman Publishing. – London : Oyez Longman, 1983.

—Role of law in central-local relations / by Michael J. Elliott. – London : Social Science Research Council, 1981.
105p; 30cm.
ISBN 0862260248 Pbk £2.50

LOCAL GOVERNMENT – IRELAND

—Law of local government in the Republic of Ireland / by Ronan Keane. – Dublin : Incorporated Law Society of Ireland, 1982.
xliv,423p.
Includes index.
ISBN 0902027212

LOCAL GOVERNMENT – MALAYSIA

—Local Government Act, 1976 (Act 171) / Kuala Lumpur : International Law Books Services.

LOCAL GOVERNMENT – NIGERIA

—Principles of administrative and local government law in Nigeria / by A. Toriola Oyewo. – Ibadan, Nigeria : Jator Publishing, 1987.
xxiii,276p.
Bibliography: p.xix-xxiii. - Includes index.
ISBN 9782660019

LOCAL GOVERNMENT – SCOTLAND

—Local government in Scotland / G Coutts. – 2nd. – Edinburgh : W Green & Son, 1989.
Provides an introduction to the Scottish local government system including its historical context and possible future reforms. Updated to include the community charge and the changing relationship of local and central government.
ISBN 0414008898

LOCAL GOVERNMENT – SOUTH AFRICA

—Butterworths Legislation Service for Black Local Government / Professional Publ, 1984.
ISBN 0409069736 loose £155.00

LOCAL GOVERNMENT – SPAIN

—Constitutional and legislative provisions concerning the organisation of regional government / Council of Europe. – Strasbourg : Council of Europe, 1983.
72p.

LOCAL GOVERNMENT OFFICERS – CANADA

—Municipal Officers / Vancouver : British Columbia Continuing Legal Education Society, 1982.
100p.
ISBN 0865040702 Hbk £35.00

LOCAL GOVERNMENT OFFICERS – GREAT BRITAIN

—Councillor / 10th ed. – London : Shaw & Sons, 1987.
ISBN 0721908519 Pbk £4.95

LOCAL LAWS – GREAT BRITAIN

—Chronological table of local legislation / the Law Commission and the Scottish Law Commission. – 2 v. – London : Law Commission, 1985.
Contents: Part 1. Local and personal acts 1797-1908 - Part 2. Local and personal acts 1909-1973, private acts 1539-1973.

LOCAL LAWS - INDIA
—Maharashtra Local Laws, 14 Vols. / Allahabad : Ashoka Law House, 1987.

LOCAL REMEDY RULE (INTERNATIONAL LAW)
—Exhaustion of Local Remedies in International Law / Cambridge : Cambridge University Press, 1983.
ISBN 0521229472 Hbk £42.50

—Nationalization of foreign property : a study in North-South dialogue / Subhash C. Jain : foreword by B. Sen. – New Delhi : Deep & Deep, 1983.
298p.
Bibliography: p.268-298 - Includes index.

LOCAL TAXATION
—Local taxes in Europe : an analysis of how they function / Amsterdam : International Bureau of Fiscal Documentation, 1985.
72p.
Conference proceedings.
ISBN 9070125269

LOCAL TAXATION - ENGLAND
—Bean and Lockwood's Rating valuation practice / Arthur Lockwood, John C. Bassett, David MacKmin, William Thomas. – 7th ed. – London : Sweet & Maxwell, 1987.
xxxiv,483p; 26cm.
New edition with an enlarged chapter dealing with appeals to the Local Valuation Court and Lands Tribunal, and the role of the valuer appearing before them. The valuation of properties, including retail, office and industrial property, and licensed premises is covered.
ISBN 042047420X £40.00

—Local taxation : national legislation and the problems of enforcement / J.V. Beckett. – London : Bedford Square Press for the Standing Conference for Local History, 1980.
4,49p; 21cm.
Bibliography: p.42-44.
ISBN 0719910307 sd £2.50

LOCAL TAXATION - GREAT BRITAIN
—Encyclopedia of rating and local taxation : law and practice / Harry Sales, Christopher Lewsley, J.H. Emlyn Jones, V.G. Wellings. – 1. – London : Sweet & Maxwell, 1988.
Contains the relevant legislation on rating, primary and subordinate, set out in full and amended where necessary. Also includes court rules, circulars, and a digest of cases. Annotated and cross-referenced. Supersedes the Encyclopedia of Rating Law and Practice.
ISBN 0421236105 Llf £130.00

LOCAL TAXATION - SCOTLAND
—Rating appeals and the 1985 revaluation : proceedings of a Planning Exchange conference / edited by Clive Martlew. – Glasgow : Planning Exchange, 1985.
29 leaves. – (Occasional paper).

LOCUS STANDI - AUSTRALIA
—Standing in public interest litigation / Law Reform Commission. – Canberra : Australian Government Publishing Service, 1985.
xxx,273p. – (Report).
Bibliography: p.259-263 - Includes index.
ISBN 0644013109

LOCUS STANDI - AUSTRALIA - SOUTH AUSTRALIA
—Report ... relating to a general rule of standing in environmental matters / Law Reform Committee of South Australia. – Adelaide : Government Printer, 1987.
141,5,4p. – (97th report).
Bibliography: p.1-2. Includes text of draft bill..

—Report ... relating to locus standi : prisoners' rights / Law Reform Committee of South Australia. – Adelaide : Government Printer, 1982.
6p. – (70th report).

—Report ... relating to the law governing locus standi : non-party interventions and amici curiae in relation to proceedings in civil jurisdiction / Law Reform Committee of South Australia. – Adelaide : Government Printer, 1982.
9p. – (67th report).

LOCUS STANDI - CANADA
—Locus standi : a commentary on the law of standing in Canada / Toronto : Carswell, 1986.
xxiv,221p.
Includes index.
ISBN 0459388207

LONDON (ENGLAND)
—Islington crime survey : crime, victimization and policing in inner-city London / Trevor Jones, Brian MacLean and Jock Young. – Aldershot : Gower, 1986.
xiv, 265p; 23cm.
ISBN 0566052644

LONG-TERM IMPRISONMENT
—Psychological survival : the experience of long-term imprisonment / Stanley Cohen and Laurie Taylor. – 2nd ed. – Harmondsworth : Penguin, 1981.
239p; 19cm. – (Pelican books).
Previous ed.: 1972. Bibliography: p230-239.
ISBN 014021657X Pbk £2.25

LOST ARTICLES (LAW) - SCOTLAND
—Report on lost and abandoned property / Scottish Law Commission. – Edinburgh : H.M.S.O., 1980.
v,94p; 25cm. – (1979-80 H.C. 346).
ISBN 0102346801 sd £2.50

MAGISTRATES
—Magistrate : 1921-1975, 31 Vols. / Professional Books Staff. – Abingdon : Professional Books, 1984.

—Magistrates' Summary Jurisdiction : Guide to Sentencing Powers / 6th ed. – Chichester : Barry Rose, 1983.
ISBN 0859923681 Hbk £4.50

—Report of the seventh Commonwealth Magistrates' Conference : Nicosia, Cyprus 8th to 14th September 1985 / London : Commonwealth Magistrates' Association, 1985.
294p.

MAGISTRATES - AUSTRALIA - NEW SOUTH WALES
—Magistracy : interim report : first appointments as magistrates under the Local Courts Act, 1982 / New South Wales Law Reform Commission. – Sydney : The Commission, 1983.
xiii,87p. – (L.R.C. 38).

MAGISTRATES - AUSTRALIA - SOUTH AUSTRALIA
—Report ... on the inherited imperial statute law with regard to proceedings in summary jurisdiction / Law Reform Committee of South Australia. – Adelaide : Government Printer, 1981.
16p. – (58th report).

MAGISTRATES - CANADA
—Christian Magistrate and State Church / Toronto : University of Toronto Press, 1982.
ISBN 0802055893 Hbk £30.00

—Judges of New Brunswick and Their Times / D.G. Bell. – Fredericton : Acadiensis Press, 1985.
552p.
ISBN 0919107044 Hbk £45.00

MAGISTRATES - COMMONWEALTH
—Layman as a magistrate / prepared for the Commonwealth Secretariat by Jane Kellock. – London : The Secretariat, 1988.
viii,32p.

MAGISTRATES - ENGLAND
—Anthony & Berryman's Magistrates' court guide 1985 / by A.P. Carr. – London : Butterworths, 1985.
vii,457p.
Includes index.
ISBN 0406108382 PBK £12.95

—Bias and impartiality in magistrates' courts / R.D.S. Stevens. – Chichester : Rose, 1982.
xvii,105p; 22cm.
Includes index.
ISBN 0859922316 Pbk £6.80

—Butterworths Consolidated Legislation Service /. – Professional Publ.
264p.
ISBN 0409014265 £40.00

—Lay justice? / Z.K. Bankowski, N.R. Hutton and J.J. McManus. – Edinburgh : T. & T. Clark, 1987.
xi,187p; 22cm.
Includes index. An analysis of the work of lay justice and a comprehensive study of the structure, operation and criteria of the Scottish District Courts.
ISBN 0567291391 Pbk £9.95

—Magistrate in the Crown Court / Robin David. – Chichester : Rose, 1982.
viii,48p; 21cm.
ISBN 0859922294 Pbk £4.25

—Magistrates' courts bill : report on the consolidation of certain enactments relating to the jurisdiction of, and the practice and procedure before, magistrates' courts... / the Law Commission. – London : H.M.S.O., 1980.
7p.
ISBN 0101788703

—Matrimonial jurisdiction of magistrates' courts / by M.D.A. Freeman and Christina M. Lyon. – Chichester : Rose, 1980.
xxv,222p; 21cm.
Includes index.
ISBN 0859921999 Pbk £10.80

MAGISTRATES - GREAT BRITAIN
—Book of the Bench / London : Wildy & Sons.
84p : Illus.

—Changing Image of the Magistracy / 2nd ed. – London : Macmillan, 1984.
272p.
ISBN 0333362799 Hbk £33.00
ISBN 0333362802 Pbk £7.95

—Contested trials in magistrates' courts / by Julie Vennard. – London : H.M.S.O., 1982.
v,32p; 25cm.
Bibliography: p.26-27. 'A Home Office Research and Planning Unit report.'.
ISBN 0113407661

—Criminal law : binding over - the issues / The Law Commission. – London : H.M.S.O., 1987.
vi,113p; 21cm. – (Working paper).
ISBN 011730185X

—Justice of the peace reports / Chichester : Justice of the Peace Ltd., 1983-.
Continues: Justice of the peace and local government reports.

—Magistrate as Chairman / Norman. – London : Butterworths, 1987.
ISBN 0406104697 Pbk £8.95

—Magistrate as Chairman / London : Butterworths, 1987.
ISBN 0406104697 Pbk

—Stone's Justices' Manual, 1984, 3 vols. / A. T. Draycott. – 116th ed. – London : Butterworths, 1984.
ISBN 0406386641 Hbk

—Stone's Justices' Manual 1986, 3 Vols. / John Richman. – 118th ed. – Wellington : Butterworths, 1986.
This three volume text is an amalgamation of all material relevant to the magisterial function in the United Kingdom. The work includes the entire text of the Police and Criminal Evidence Act.
ISBN 0406386722 Hbk

—Stone's Justices' Manual / London : Butterworths, 1983.
ISBN 0406386609 Hbk £181.25

—Stone's Justices' Manual Nineteen Eighty-Seven / 119th ed. – London : Butterworths, 1987.
ISBN 0406386765 Hbk £211.00

—Work of the Magistrate / 4th ed. – London : Shaw & Sons, 1980.
ISBN 0721905617 Pbk £5.75

MAGISTRATES - IRELAND
—Irish Justice of the Peace and Treatise on the Powers and Duties of Justices of the Peace in Ireland, 2 Vols. /. – Abingdon : Professional Books.

MAGISTRATES - SCOTLAND
—Lay justice? / Z.K. Bankowski, N.R. Hutton and J.J. McManus. – Edinburgh : T. & T. Clark, 1987.
xi,187p; 22cm.
Includes index. An analysis of the work of lay justice and a comprehensive study of the structure, operation and criteria of the Scottish District Courts.
ISBN 0567291391 Pbk £9.95

MAGISTRATES - UNITED KINGDOM
—Magistrate's Companion : Guide for Magistrates in Announcing Sentence and Other Orders of the Court / 3rd ed. – Chichester : Barry Rose, 1985.
88p.
ISBN 0859922332 Hbk £3.75

MAGISTRATES' COURTS - GREAT BRITAIN
—Anthony and Berryman's Magistrates' Court Guide / London : Butterworths, 1987.
ISBN 0406108404 Pbk

—Arrears Proceedings and Related Matters in the Magistrates' Court / Lomax & Reynolds. – Chichester : Barry Rose, 1985.
250p.
ISBN 0859922340 Hbk £19.50

—Chairmanship in Magistrates' Courts / Keith Clarke. – Chichester : Barry Rose, 1981.
93p.
ISBN 0859921875 Hbk £4.00

—Criminal Procedure in Magistrates' Courts / London : Butterworths, 1984.
ISBN 0406101676 Pbk £21.95

—Criminal Statistics, England and Wales : Supplementary Tables 1980, 4 Vols. / London : Home Office.
ISBN 0862520134 Hbk £18.75

—Domestic Proceedings in the Magistrates' Court / 6th ed. – London : Oyez Longman, 1982.
– (Oyez Longman Practice Note Ser.: No. 30).
ISBN 0851206514 Hbk £12.50

—Evidence and Procedure in Magistrates' Courts / Stephen Knapp. – London : Oyez Longman, 1982.
– (Oyez Longman Practitioner Ser.).
ISBN 0851202926 Hbk £12.95

—Magistrate's Court Guide 1984 / Berryman. – London : Butterworths, 1984.
ISBN 0406108374 Hbk £29.40

—Magistrate's Court Guide 1988 / London : Butterworths, 1988.
ISBN 0406108412 Pbk £15.95

—Magistrates Court / London : Longman Professional, 1988.
ISBN 0851214118 Pbk £9.95

—Practice and Procedure in Magistrates' Courts / London : Fourmat, 1982.
186p.
ISBN 0906840503 Pbk £8.95

—Practice and procedure in Magistrates' Courts / 2nd ed. – London : Fourmat, 1986.
ISBN 1851900136 Pbk £12.95

—Practice, Procedure and Sentencing in the Magistrates' Courts / Chichester : Barry Rose, 1986.
543p.
ISBN 0859923606 Hbk £65.00

—Sentencing Handbook : A Guide to Sentencing in the Magistrates' Courts / London : Oyez Longman, 1980.
ISBN 0851204554 Hbk £7.95

—Stone's Justices' Manual / A. T. Draycott. – London : Shaw & Sons.

MAGNETIC RECORDERS AND RECORDING

—Police interrogation : tape recording / J.A. Barnes and N. Webster for the Royal Commission on Criminal Procedure. – London : H.M.S.O., 1980.
x,106p; 25cm. – (Research studies).
Bibliography: p49.
ISBN 0117301272 Pbk £4.75

MAINTENANCE

—Family law : financial relief after foreign divorce / the Law Commission. – London : H.M.S.O., 1982.
iii,115p. – (HC).
ISBN 0102514828

—Payment by the State of advances on child maintenance : Recommendation No.R (82) 2 adopted by the Committee of Ministers of the Council of Europe on 4 February 1982 and explanatory memorandum / Council of Europe. – Strasbourg : Council of Europe, 1982.
15p; 21cm.
'Prepared by a committee of experts set up under the authority of the European Committee on Legal Co-operation'. At head of cover title : Council of Europe, Legal Affairs.
ISBN 9287101736

MAINTENANCE - AUSTRALIA

—Maintenance agency for Australia / report of the National Maintenance Inquiry. – Canberra : Government Printer, 1984.
xx,381p. – (Parliamentary paper).
Includes bibliographical references. At head of t.p.: Parliament of the Commonwealth of Australia.
ISBN 0644031433 £13.00

MAINTENANCE - CANADA

—Family law : dimensions of justice : selected papers presented at the Judicial Conference on Family Law, 1981 / edited by Rosalie S. Abella and Claire L'Heureux-Dube. – Toronto : Butterworths, 1983.
xxxi,330p.
The Canadian Institute for the Administration of Justice brought together judges to consider developments in family law and its social milieu. Includes essays by judges, psychiatrists, an economist and a tax specialist.
ISBN 0409819700

—Family Practice in Provincial Court : Custody, Access, and Maintenance / Vancouver : Continuing Legal Education Society of British Columbia, 1987.
306p.
ISBN 0865043450 Hbk £80.00

—Spousal Maintenance / Vancouver : Continuing Legal Education Society of British Columbia, 1988.
164p.
ISBN 086504984X Hbk £70.00

MAINTENANCE - CANADA - ALBERTA

—Matrimonial support failures : reasons, profiles and perceptions of individuals involved / by the Canadian Institute for Research and the Steering Committee : prepared for the Institute of Law Research and Reform. – 2. – Edmonton : Institute of Law Research and Reform, 1981.

MAINTENANCE - CANADA - SASKATCHEWAN

—Tentative proposals for an Enforcement of Maintenance Orders Act / Law Reform Commission of Saskatchewan. – Saskatoon : The Commission, 1982.
100,xiiip.

MAINTENANCE - ENGLAND

—Distribution of matrimonial assets on divorce / Michael L. Rakusen, D. Peter Hunt. – 2nd ed. – London : Butterworths, 1982.
xxii,375p.
Latest supplement held: 1986.
ISBN 0406351015

—Family law : the financial consequences of divorce : the basic policy : a discussion paper / the Law Commission. – London : H.M.S.O., 1980.
57p; 25cm.
ISBN 0101804105 Pbk £3.70

—Family law : the financial consequences of divorce : the response to the Law Commission's Discussion paper, and recommendations on the policy of the law / the Law Commission. – London : H.M.S.O., 1981.
iii,23p; 25cm.
ISBN 0102068828

—Family property and financial provision / by J.G. Miller. – 2nd ed. – London : Sweet & Maxwell, 1983.
xlvi,517p; 26cm.
Previous ed.: 1974. Includes index.
ISBN 0421282401 £36.00

—Towards a unified Family Court : the collection of maintenance and the enforcement of court orders for maintenance / research by Jean Graham Hall and Douglas F. Martin. – s.l. : s. n., 1984.
ca.200 leaves.
Includes some French text.

MAINTENANCE - FRANCE

—Towards a unified Family Court : the collection of maintenance and the enforcement of court orders for maintenance / research by Jean Graham Hall and Douglas F. Martin. – s.l. : s. n., 1984.
ca.200 leaves.
Includes some French text.

MAINTENANCE - GREAT BRITAIN

—Family law : financial relief after foreign divorce / Great Britain. – London : H.M.S.O., 1980.
v,83p. – (Working paper).
ISBN 0117301574

—Maintenance after Divorce / Maclean. – Oxford : Oxford University Press, 1986.
ISBN 0198255292 Pbk £9.95
ISBN 0198255306 Hbk £22.50

—Tax on Maintenance Payments : 1982-1983 / Joel Newman. – London : Oyez Longman, 1982. – (Oyez Longman Practical Tax Ser.).
ISBN 0851206581 Hbk £45.00

MAINTENANCE - NEW ZEALAND

—Further aspects of maintenance law : some post 'Family law 1981' chapters / by P.R.H. Webb. – Auckland : Legal Research Foundation, 1981.
44p.
ISBN 0908581157

MAINTENANCE - SCOTLAND

—Family law : report on financial provision after foreign divorce / Scottish Law Commission. – Edinburgh : H.M.S.O., 1982.
47p.
ISBN 0102515824

MAINTENANCE AND CHAMPERTY - AUSTRALIA - SOUTH AUSTRALIA

—Report ... relating to maintenance, champerty, embracery and barratry, malicious prosecution and abuse of process / Law Reform Committee of South Australia. – Adelaide : Government Printer, 1987.
86,3p. – (101st report).
Includes text of the Abolition of Obsolete Offences Act (1969).

MALICIOUS MISCHIEF - IRELAND

—Report on malicious damage / the Law Reform Commission. – Dublin : The Commission, 1988.
viii,56p. – (LRC).

MALICIOUS PROSECUTION - AUSTRALIA - SOUTH AUSTRALIA

—Report ... relating to civil actions for perjury committed in criminal proceedings and to the tort of malicious prosecution / Law Reform Committee of South Australia. – Adelaide : Government Printer, 1984.
13p. – (83rd report).
Bibliography: p.14.

—Report ... relating to maintenance, champerty, embracery and barratry, malicious prosecution and abuse of process / Law Reform Committee of South Australia. – Adelaide : Government Printer, 1987.
86,3p. – (101st report).
Includes text of the Abolition of Obsolete Offences Act (1969).

MALICIOUS PROSECUTION - INDIA

—Law of Defamation and Malicious Prosecution / 9th ed. – Allahabad : Law Publishers, 1987.
500p.

—Law of Defamation and Malicious Prosecution (Civil and Criminal) / 2nd ed. – Allahabad : Law Publishers, 1982.

MALPRACTICE - AUSTRALIA

—Professional negligence / by David F. Partlett. – Sydney : Law Book Co., 1985.
xxxvii, 425 p.; 25 cm.
Includes bibliographical references and indexes.
ISBN 0455205949

MALPRACTICE - ENGLAND

—Professional negligence / A.M. Dugdale, K.M. Stanton. – London : Butterworths, 1982.
xlii,400p.
Includes index.
ISBN 0406179107

—Professional negligence / by Rupert M. Jackson and John L. Powell. – 2nd ed. – London : Sweet & Maxwell, 1987.
xlvii,472p; 25cm.
Considers the reported cases on professional negligence, with particular emphasis on recent developments. Uses cases reported in established law reports, but also those appearing in individual professional journals. Commonwealth cases are also included.
ISBN 0421341602 £36.00

MALPRACTICE - GREAT BRITAIN

—Professional negligence / by Ashley Underwood and Stephen Holt. – London : Fourmat, 1981.
xv,96p; 23cm.
ISBN 0906840368

—Professional negligence : a journal of liability, ethics and discipline / London : Cass, 1985-.

MALPRACTICE (MEDICINE)

—Facilitations of Proof in Medical Malpractice Cases : a Comparative Analysis of American and German Law / Bern : Peter Lang, 1981.
approx 140p.
ISBN 3820470042 Pbk £31.00

—International medical malpractice law : a comparative law study of civil liability arising from medical care / by Dieter Giesen : with a foreword by Lord Kilbrandon. – Tubingen : Mohr, 1988.
940p; 24cm.
Includes bibliography and index.
ISBN 9024737052 Germany
ISBN 3166453229

—Medical responsibility in Western Europe : research study of the European Science Foundation / edited by E. Deutsch and H.-L. Schreiber : with contributions by J. Blackie ... et al. – Berlin : Springer-Verlag, 1985.
ISBN 0387153659

MALPRACTICE (MEDICINE) - CANADA

—Medical Malpractice / Vancouver : Continuing Legal Education Society of British Columbia, 1987.
181p.
ISBN 0865043035 Hbk £65.00

MALPRACTICE (MEDICINE) - GREAT BRITAIN

—Medical negligence : a plaintiff's guide / Charles J. Lewis. – London, England : F. Cass, 1988.
xxxiv, 379 p.; 24 cm.
'The law is stated as at 1 January 1988'–T.p. verso. Includes index.
ISBN 0714640611 pbk.

MAN - INFLUENCE ON NATURE

—World environment 1972-1982 : a report / by the United Nations Environment Programme : edited by Martin W. Holdgate, Mohammed Kassas, Gilbert F. White with the assistance of David Spurgeon : study co-ordinator Essam El-Hinnawi. – Dublin : Published for the United Nations Environment Programme by Tycooly International, 1982.
xxxii,637p; 25cm.
Includes bibliographies and index.
ISBN 0907567134 Hbk Unpriced
ISBN 0907567142 Pbk Unpriced

MANAGEMENT

—Fiduciary duties of directors : a review / John Lowry. – London : Thames Polytechnic School of Business Administration, 1984.

—Managerial hierarchies : comparative perspectives on the rise of the modern industrial enterprise / edited by Alfred D. Chandler, Jr and Herman Daems. – Cambridge, Mass. : Harvard University Press, 1980.
xi,237p; 24cm. – (Harvard studies in business history).
Includes index.
ISBN 0674547403

MANAGEMENT - CANADA

—Institute of Management Consultants of Ontario Act, 1983, Bill Pr026 : An Act Respecting the Institute of Management Consultants of Ontario / Ontario : Ontario Government Publications Service, 1983.
4p.

MANAGEMENT - EUROPE

—Handbook on European employee co-maangement / W Kolvenbach, P Hanau. – Kluwer Law and Taxation, 1989.
818.
ISBN 90T2802003 Llf £102/Dfl 325

Supplement 1989.
308.
Covers the co-determination laws, contractual agreements, and other regulations of European countries, and existing regulations of the OECD and ILO. A comparison with the US is made. Includes participative institutions at shop floor level, employee participation at board level, and selected documentation in each chapter.
ISBN 90T2800019 Llf £73/Dfl 231

MANAGEMENT - EUROPEAN COMMUNITY

—Workers' participation in the European Community : the fifth directive / R. Blanpain, J. L. Janssen van Raay, A. Mouty. – Deventer : Kluwer, 1984.
ix,294p.
ISBN 9065441875

MANAGEMENT - GREAT BRITAIN

—Administrator : the journal of the Institute of Chartered Secretaries and Administrators / v. – London : Institute of Chartered Secretaries and Administrators, 1982-.
Continues: Professional administration, new series vol. 1, no. 1(Jan. 1981)-v. 1, no. 11(Dec. 1981).

—Computer-Aided Management / Cambridge : Woodhead-Faulkner, 1986.
ISBN 085941308X Hbk £19.95

—Employee participation : practice and attitudes in north-west manufacturing industry / by M.J. Dowling...et al. – London : Department of Employment, 1981.
44p. – (Research paper).

—Good Practice : Management Guide for Professions / London : Butterworths, 1988.
ISBN 0406502803 Pbk

—Legal and Management Guides / London : Architectural Press.

—Management Contracting / A. C. Sidwell. – London : Collins, 1987.
250p.
ISBN 0003833143 Hbk £17.50

—Management for Bankers / London : Butterworths, 1988.
ISBN 0406503400 Pbk £13.50

—Nature of Management / London : Butterworths, 1987.
ISBN 0406503400 Pbk

MANAGEMENT INFORMATION SYSTEMS

—Information for academic library decision making : the case for organizational information management / Charles R. McClure. – London : Aldwych Press, 1980.
xvi,227p; 22cm.
Bibliography: p211-219. - Includes index.
ISBN 0861720113 £19.50

—Uniformed police work and management technology / J.M. Hough. – London : Home Office, 1980.
v,56p. – (Research Unit paper).
Bibliography: p.48-51.

MANAGEMENT INFORMATION SYSTEMS - CANADA

—Study of police management information systems / study team: Ted M. Zaharchuk (project director), Robert M. Atcheson ...et al. – Ottawa : Communication Division, Ministry of the Solicitor General of Canada, 1981.
vii,58p.
Bibliography: p.24-58. 'Prepared by Decision Dynamics Corporation under contract with the Research Division, Ministry of the Solicitor General of Canada' - verso t.p..
ISBN 0662116437

MANDATES - NAMIBIA

—South West Africa and the sacred trust 1919-1972 / T.D. Gill. – The Hague : T.M.C. Asser Instituut, 1984.
ix,107p.
Bibliography: p.106-107.
ISBN 9067040274

MANITOBA

—Manitoba government publications for the month of ... : monthly checklist / compiled in the Legislative Library. – Winnipeg : Queen's Printer, 1975.
Continues: Publications of the Government of Manitoba.
ISBN 03181200

MANPOWER POLICY - GREAT BRITAIN

—Unemployment and labour market flexibility : the United Kingdom / Guy Standing. – Geneva : International Labour Office, 1986.
xi, 147 p.; 24 cm.
Includes bibliographies.
ISBN 9221052915 pbk. £30.00

MANUAL LABOUR - GREAT BRITAIN

—Workers and the new depression / Robert Taylor. – London : Macmillan, 1982.
x,212p; 23cm.
Includes index.
ISBN 0333192958 Hbk Unpriced
ISBN 0333334116 Pbk Unpriced

MARC SYSTEM - GREAT BRITAIN

—MARC : an introduction / Ellen Gredley. – London : Polytechnic of North London, School of Librarianship and Information Studies, 1983.
47p. – (Occasional publication).
Bibliography: p.45. - Includes index.
ISBN 0900639245

MAREVA INJUNCTIONS - CANADA

—Mareva Injunctions / 2nd ed. – Agincourt : Carswell, 1987.
138p.
This work presents the history and current legal status of the Canadian Mareva Injunction. Procedural issues involved in obtaining and enforcing this unique remedy are reviewed in the book.

MAREVA INJUNCTIONS - GREAT BRITAIN

—Anton Piller Order and Mareva Injunction : A Practitioner's Guide / London : Butterworths, 1987.

MARINE ACCIDENTS - CANADA

—Study on marine casualty investigations in Canada (for the Minister of Transport) / Bernard M. Desch$enes. – Ottawa : Minister of Supply and Services, 1984.
x,273p.
ISBN 0662134036

MARINE ECOLOGY

—Maritime Safety and Environment Conventions / London : Sweet & Maxwell, 1983.
– (British Shipping Laws).

—Problems of development and ocean management in the eastern Caribbean : economic, legal, environmental and planning aspects : proceedings of an international seminar held in Kingstown, St. Vincent & the Grenadines, West Indies, May 11-13, 1981 / edited by Edgar Gold, Norman G. Letalik, Carlyle L. Mitchell. – 2nd printing. – Halifax, N.S. : Dalhousie Ocean Studies Programme, 1982.
xviii,184p.
'Held under the auspices of the West Indies (Associated States) Council of Ministers and sponsored by the Dalhousie Ocean Studies Programme in cooperation with the Foundation Reshaping the International Order (RIO)'

MARINE INSURANCE

—Charterers' liability insurance / by Dieter Schwampe : translated from the German by Burravoe Ltd. – London : Lloyd's of London Press, 1988.
xx,156p; 24cm.
Bibliography: pp.145-151. - Includes index. Translated from the German.
ISBN 1850441847 £45.00 (July)

—Institute cargo clauses 1982 / by Robert H. Brown. – 2nd ed. – London : Witherby, 1983.
v,59p; 30cm.
Previous ed.: 1982. Includes index.
ISBN 0900886846 Pbk

—Institute time clauses - Hulls 1983 : full conditions / by Robert H. Brown. – London : Witherby, 1983.
vi,45p; 30cm.
ISBN 0900886897 Pbk

—Institute time clauses : hulls : a comparison between the 1983 clauses and the 1970 clauses with subsequent amendments / by J. Kenneth Goodacre. – London : Witherby, 1983.
vii,67p.
Includes the text of the Marine Insurance Act, 1906. 'In co-operation with the U.K. Society of Average Adjusters'.

—Insurance in the Arab world : a Lloyd's List conference-London / 1. – London : Lloyd's of London Press, 1982.
various pagings.
ISBN 0907432492

—International Conference on Liability and Compensation for Damage in Connection with the Carriage of Certain Substances By Sea : 1984 / International Maritime Organization. – London : International Maritime Organization.
ISBN 9280111922 Hbk £4.50

French
ISBN 9280121537 Hbk £4.50

Russian
ISBN 9280140507 Hbk £4.50

Spanish
ISBN 9280134078 Hbk £4.50

Arabic
ISBN 9280150030 Hbk £4.50

Chinese
ISBN 9280160044 Hbk £4.50

—Law Relating to Marine Insurance / Allahabad : Indian Press.
371p.

—Marine Cargo Claims / 3rd ed. – Montreal : International Shipping Publications, 1988.
1,448p.

—Marine claims handbook / by N.G. Hudson and J.C. Allen. – 4th ed. – London : Lloyds of London Press, 1984.
vi,102p.
ISBN 0907432913

—Marine claims handbook / by N.G. Hudson and J.C. Allen. – 3rd ed. – London : Lloyd's of London Press, 1980.
vi,74p.
Earlier eds. by N.G. Hudson and D.G. Milburn.
ISBN 0904093867

—Marine reinsurance / by Robert H. Brown and Peter B. Reed. – London : Witherby, 1981.
xi,343p; 23cm.
Includes index.
ISBN 0900886617 £21.00

—Operation and management of protection and indemnity clubs / Stuart D. Capewell. – London : Insurance Institute of London, 1983.
81 leaves.
Bibliography: 1.61-64.

—Second International Maritime Law Seminar : Carriage of Goods by Sea, Maritime Liens, Marine Insurance / Vancouver : Continuing Legal Education Society of British Columbia, 1981.
395p.
ISBN 0865040273 Hbk £100.00

—War risks : the Tower Hotel, London, 24th June 1982 / London : Lloyd's of London Press, 1982.
49leaves; 31cm.
Conference papers.
ISBN 090743245X Unpriced

MARINE INSURANCE - CANADA

—Marine Insurance Law of Canada / Butterworths, 1987.
304p.
Examines the Canadian judicial decisions in marine insurance, using as its basis the Marine Insurance Act, RSO 1980. Includes a table of statute concordance.
ISBN 0409805319 Hbk £70.00

MARINE INSURANCE - ENGLAND

—Marine claims (hull) for indemnity : the Eugenides Foundation, Athens, April 29/30, 1982 / London : Lloyd's of London Press, 1982.
139leaves; 31cm.
Conference papers.
ISBN 0907432409 Unpriced

—Marine insurance / by Robert H. Brown. – 4th ed., completely rev. – London : Witherby, 1985.
xiii,442,xxxviip; 23cm.
Previous ed.: 1979. Includes index. Contains text of the clauses.
ISBN 0900886838 No price

—Marine insurance claims / by J. Kenneth Goodacre. – 2nd ed. – London : Witherby, 1981.
liv,1015p,12p of plates; 23cm. – (Monument series).
Previous ed.: 1974. Includes index.
ISBN 0900886536 £35.00

—New Institute clauses : a commentary on the new standard policy forms for marine risks issued by the London insurance market / by N.G. Hudson and J.C. Allen. – London : Lloyd's, 1986.
217p; 24cm.
ISBN 185044093X £47.50

MARINE INSURANCE - GREAT BRITAIN

—Analysis Of Marine Insurance Clauses / Witherby, 1982.
ISBN 0900886765 Pbk £6.00

Book 2 1983.
ISBN 0900886897 Pbk £6.00

—Arnould's law of marine insurance and average / Michael J. Mustill, Jonathan C. B. Gilman. – 16th ed. 2. – London : Stevens, 1981.
lxxv,1242p; 26cm.
Previous ed.: 1961. Includes index.
ISBN 0420445005 £95.00

—Chalmers' Marine Insurance Act 1906 / by the late Sir Mackenzie D. Chalmers. – 9th ed. – London : Butterworths, 1983.
xxxvi,288p; 23cm.
This book gives a detailed examination of the law of marine insurance in the United Kingdom. The new forms of policy used by Lloyd's and other insurance companies are reproduced in the appendices of this work.
ISBN 040656423X Unpriced

—Collected papers on marine claims / Witherby, 1980.
ISBN 0900886471 Pbk £10.00

—Companies' marine policy : attached clauses / Institute of London Underwriters. – London : The Institute, 1982.
26p.
Contents: Insurance cargo clauses (A), (B), and (C) - Institute war clauses (Cargo) - Institute strikes clauses (Cargo) - Institute war clauses (sendings by post) - Institute war clauses (Air cargo) (excluding sendings by post) - Institute cargo clauses (Air) (excluding sendings by post) - Institute strikes clauses (Air cargo) - Institute standard conditons for cargo contracts - Companies' marine policy form.

—Enforcement of maritime claims / by D.C. Jackson. – London : Lloyd's of London Press, 1985.
lxi,483p; 26cm.
ISBN 1850440018

—Hague Rules law digest : a practical digest and comprehensive cross-referenced index to leading British cases governing the interpretation of the Hague Rules : by W.E. Astle / London : Fairplay Publications, 1981.
ix,90p.
ISBN 0905045246

—Law and Practice of Marine Insurance and Average / London : Sweet & Maxwell, 1988.
ISBN 0420476504 Hbk £145.00

—Law of Marine Insurance / Abingdon : Professional Books, 1984.
ISBN 086205091X Hbk £63.00
ISBN 0862050960 Pbk £25.50

—Law of Marine Insurance and Average / London : Sweet & Maxwell, 1988.
ISBN 0420445005 Hbk £150.00

—Law of Marine Insurance and Average (BSL) / 16th ed. 2 vols. – London : Sweet & Maxwell, 1981.
ISBN 0420445005 Hbk £170.00

—Marine Claims Handbook / Allen. – 4th ed. – London : Lloyd's of London Press, 1984.
ISBN 0907432913 Pbk £13.50

—Marine insurance / by Robert H. Brown. – 5th ed. – London : Witherby & Co. Ltd, 1986.
xix,343p; 22cm.
ISBN 0948691190

—Marine insurance / E.R. Hardy Ivamy. – 4th ed. – London : Butterworths, 1985.
lii,613p; 26cm. – (Butterworths insurance library).
Previous ed.: 1979. Includes index.
ISBN 0406253137 No price

—Marine Insurance / Lamberth. – 6th ed. – Pitman, 1986.
ISBN 0273025376 Hbk £50.00

—Marine Insurance / 4th ed. – London : Butterworths, 1985.
ISBN 0406253137 Hbk £68.00

—Marine Insurance Act 1906 / 9th ed. – London : Butterworths, 1983.
ISBN 040656423X Hbk £20.50

—Marine Insurance Clauses / R. Swatton. – London : LLoyd's of London Press, 1985.
ISBN 1850440581 Hbk

—Principles of marine insurance / Alexander. – 7th ed. – Stone & Cox, 1986.
ISBN 0854431128 Pbk £15.00

—Reference book of marine insurance clauses / 58th ed. – London : Witherby & Co, 1986.
ISBN 0948691182 Pbk £18.00

—Shipbroker's manual / compiled by the Institute of Chartered Shipbrokers. – London : Lloyd's of London Press, 1983.
xix,167p.
Includes index.
ISBN 090743259X

—Templeman on marine insurance : its principles and practice / R. J. Lambeth, F. Templeman. – 5th ed. – Plymouth : Macdonald and Evans, 1981.
xxv,574p; 25cm.
Previous ed.: published as Marine insurance / F. Templeman and C.T. Greenacre. 1934. Includes index.
ISBN 0712113959 £18.50

—Templeman on marine insurance : its principles and practice / R. J. Lambeth. – 6th ed. – London : Pitman, 1986.
608p.
Previous ed.: 1981. Includes index. Previous control number ISBN 0-7121-0654-5.
ISBN 0273025376 No price

MARINE INSURANCE – SOUTH AFRICA

—South African Maritime Law and Marine Insurance : Selected Topics / Durban : Professional Publishers, 1983.
ISBN 0409023779 Pbk £55.00

MARINE INSURANCE – UNITED STATES

—Law and practice of marine insurance and average / by Alex L. Parks. – 2 v. – London : Stevens, 1988.
Concentrates on United States marine insurance law, and practice, and includes relevant case citations, extending to those not directly concerned with marine insurance, but of fundamental importance in understanding the liabilities which underwriters insure, such as collision wreck removal, personal injury and cargo damage.
ISBN 0420476504 £140.00

MARINE MAMMALS

—Legal measures for the conservation of marine mammals / Gland, Switzerland : International Union for Conservation of Nature and Natural Resources, 1982.
1 v. (loose-leaf); 23 cm.
Includes bibliographical references.
ISBN 2880320879

MARINE MINERAL RESOURCES

—Sea-bed energy and mineral resources and the law of the sea / London : Graham & Trotman, 1984.
350p in various pagings; 25cm.
Includes index.
ISBN 0860104605 Hbk £39.00
ISBN 0860106152 unbound £35.00

Vol.2 : The areas beyond the limits of national jurisdiction / by E.D. Brown. – 1986.
400p; 24cm.
Includes index.
ISBN 0860106233 Hbk £45.00
ISBN 0860106217 loose-leaf £45.00

Vol.3 : Selected documents, tables, bibliography / by E.D. Brown. – 1986.
520p; 24cm.
Includes bibliography.
ISBN 0860106241 Hbk £55.00
ISBN 0860106225 loose-leaf £55.00

MARINE POLLUTION

—Control of Marine Pollution in International Law / London : LLoyd's of London Press, 1985.
ISBN 1850441154 Hbk

—Control of marine pollution in international law / Ramanlal Soni. – Cape Town : Juta, 1985.
301p.
Bibliography: p277-293.
ISBN 0702116602

—Environmental cooperation between the North Sea states : success or failure? / Sunneva Saetevik. – London : Belhaven Press, 1988.
xiv,173p.
Revision of thesis (cand. polit.): University of Oslo, 1986. Bibliography: p.161-165..
ISBN 1852930489 £22.50 (July)

—Environmental law of the sea / by Douglas M. Johnston. – Berlin : E. Schmidt, 1981.
419 p.; 21 cm.
Includes bibliographical references.
ISBN 3503021116 pbk.

—Hague-Zagreb Essays /. – Dordrecht : Kluwer, 1980.
xi, 329p.
ISBN 9028607498 Pbk £72.00

—Handbook on marine pollution / Arendal : Assuranceforeningen Gard, 1985.
247p.
Bibliography: p.174-179.

—IMO-UNEP Guidelines on Oil Spill Disperant Application and Environmental Considerations : Practical Information On the Use of Disperants for Dealing With Oil Spills at Sea / International Maritime Organization Staff. – London : International Maritime Organization, 1982.

—Inter-Governmental Conference on the Convention on the Dumping of Wastes at Sea /. – London : International Maritime Organization.

Russian Edition

Spanish Edition

—International conference on liability and compensation for damage in connexion with the carriage of certain substances by sea, 1984 : final act of the conference with resolutions : Protocol of 1984 to amend the International Convention on Civil Liability for Oil Pollution Damage, 1969 : Protocol of 1984 to amend the International Convention on the Establishment of an International Fund for Compensation for Oil Pollution Damage, 1971 ... / London : International Maritime Organization, 1985.
iv,90p.
Includes the text of the International Convention on Civil Liability for Oil Pollution Damage, 1984 and of the International Convention on the Establishment of an International Fund for Compensation for Oil Pollution Damage, 1984.

—International Control of Marine Pollution / Dordrecht : Kluwer, 1980.
1,338p.
ISBN 9028605606 Hbk £150.00

—Land-based marine pollution : international law development / by Meng Qing-nan. – London : Graham & Trotman, 1987.
xvi,254p.
Bibliography: p464-476. - Includes index.
ISBN 0860109097

—Legal regime of the protection of the Mediterranean against pollution from land-based sources / Dublin : Tycooly International, 1984.
256p.
ISBN 0907567827 Hbk £19.50
ISBN 0907567835 Pbk £11.50

—Marine environment and the Caracas Convention on the Law of the Sea : a study of the Third United Nations Conference on the Law of the Sea and other Related Marine Environmental Activities / by Ted L. McDorman...et al. – Halifax, Nova Scotia : Dalhousie Ocean Studies Programme, 1981.
ix,127p.
ISBN 0770300790

—Marine environment law in the United Nations Environment Programme : an emergent eco-regime / compiled by Peter H. Sand. – London : Tycooly, 1988.
xxvi,265p.
Contains the text of international treaties adopted under the United Nations Environment Programme.
ISBN 1851480242

—Marine pollution / R.B. Clark. – Oxford : Clarendon, 1986.
xiii,215p; 24cm.
Bibliography: p208-209. - Includes index.
ISBN 019854183X Pbk £19.50
ISBN 0198541821 Pbk £9.50

—Marine pollution in international and Middle Eastern law / by Sayed Hassan Amin : foreword by John P. Grant. – Glasgow : Royston, 1986.
138p; 22cm.
Bibliography: p119-135. - Includes index.
ISBN 0946706263 £30.00

—Marine pollution in international law : material obligations and jurisdiction with special reference to the Third United Nations Conference on the Law of the Sea / by Kari Hakapaa. – Helsinki : Suomalainen Tiedeakatemia, 1981.
341 p.; 25 cm.
Errata slip and notice of public dissertation discussion inserted. Thesis (doctoral)–University of Helsinki, 1981. Includes indexes. Bibliography: p. 299-336.
ISBN 9514104021

—Nineteen Seventy-Eight Protocol Relating to the International Convention for the Prevention of Pollution from Ships, 1973 : Regulations for the Prevention of Pollution by Oil-'86 Consolidated Version / International Maritime Organization. – London : International Maritime Organization.
ISBN 9280111981 Hbk £7.00

—Oily-Water Separating and Monitoring Equipment / International Maritime Organization. – English Edition. – London : International Maritime Organization, 1982.

—Pollution by Dumping. The Law of the Sea / Geneva : United Nations Publications.
77p.

—Prevention, 4 Vols. / International Maritime Organization Staff. – rev. ed. – London : International Maritime Organization, 1983. – (Manual on Oil Pollution Ser.).

—Problems of development and ocean management in the eastern Caribbean : economic, legal, environmental and planning aspects : proceedings of an international seminar held in Kingstown, St. Vincent & the Grenadines, West Indies, May 11-13, 1981 / edited by Edgar Gold, Norman G. Letalik, Carlyle L. Mitchell. – 2nd printing. – Halifax, N.S. : Dalhousie Ocean Studies Programme, 1982.
xviii,184p.
'Held under the auspices of the West Indies (Associated States) Council of Ministers and sponsored by the Dalhousie Ocean Studies Programme in cooperation with the Foundation Reshaping the International Order (RIO) '

—Regulations for the Prevention of Pollution by Oil / International Maritime Organization. – London : International Maritime Organization, 1982.

—Supplement Relating to the International Convention for the Prevention of Pollution of the Sea by Oil : 1954 (As Amended in 1962 and 1969) / International Maritime Organization Staff. – London : International Maritime Organization, 1981.

MARINE POLLUTION – GREAT BRITAIN

—Oil pollution from ships / Jarashow. – 2nd ed. – London : Sweet & Maxwell, 1985.
ISBN 042047000X Hbk £95.00

—UK marine oil pollution legislation / London : Lloyd's of London Press, 1987.
ISBN 185044028 Hbk £45.00
ISBN 185044109X Pbk £16.50

—UK Marine Oil Pollution Legislation / London : LLoyd's of London Press, 1987.
ISBN 185044109X Pbk

—United Kingdom marine pollution law / by John H. Bates. - London : Lloyds of London Press, 1985.
xxxii,461p.
ISBN 185044028X

MARINE RESOURCES

—Development of the law of the sea with special reference to the exclusive economic zone / S.l. : s.n., 1982.
p.297-307.

—Evolution of the law of the sea : a study of resources and strategy with special regard to the polar regions / Bo Johnson Theutenberg. - Dublin : Tycooly International, 1984.
viii,261p; 25cm.
Bibliography: p97-111. Includes full text of United Nations Convention on the Law of the Sea. Spine title : The law of the sea.
ISBN 0863460410 Hbk Unpriced
ISBN 0863460429 Pbk Unpriced

—International law of the ocean development : basic documents / by Shigeru Oda. - 2nd ed. 2. - Leiden : Sijthoff, 1977.
looseleaf.

—Rights to oceanic resources / Louis DeVorsey, Jr. - Dordrecht : Martinus Nijhoff, 1989.
224. - (Publications on ocean development 13).
Collection of presentations from a multi-disciplinary group of experts involved in the resolution of maritime jurisdictional disputes, at state, national, and international levels. Papers discuss equitable resource management, develop an international analytical methodology, and identify the possible impact of dispute resolution on the principles used as state level.
ISBN 079230019X Hbk £39

—United Nations Convention on the Law of the Sea / Bo Johnson Theutenberg. - Dublin : Tycooly International, 1984.
viii,261p; 25cm.
Bibliography: p97-111. Includes full text of United Nations Convention on the Law of the Sea. Spine title : The law of the sea.
ISBN 0863460410 Hbk Unpriced
ISBN 0863460429 Pbk Unpriced

MARINE RESOURCES - CANADA

—Canada and the new international law of the sea / Douglas M. Johnston. - Toronto : University of Toronto Press in cooperation with the Royal Commission on the Economic Union and Development Prospects for Canada and the Canadian Government Publishing Centre, 1985.
xviii,124p. - (Collected research studies).
Includes bibliographical references.
ISBN 0802073018

MARINE RESOURCES - GREAT BRITAIN

—Greenwich Forum IX : Britain and the sea : future dependence - future opportunities : conference papers delivered 14-16 September, 1983 / conference organizers: A.J. Smith, Lady Elizabeth Kennet, M.B.F. Ranken : editor of proceedings Commander M.B.F. Ranken. - Edinburgh : Scottish Academic Press, 1984.
xxiii,364p; 25cm.
Conference papers.
ISBN 0707303532 Hbk No price
ISBN 0707304423 Pbk No price

MARINE RESOURCES - GRENADA

—Integration of marine space in national development strategies of small island states : the case of the Caribbean states of Grenada and St. Lucia / Carlyle L. Mitchell and Edgar Gold. - Halifax, N.S. : Dalhousie Ocean Studies Programme, 1982.
x,346p.
Bibliography: p338-345.

MARINE RESOURCES - ST. LUCIA

—Integration of marine space in national development strategies of small island states : the case of the Caribbean states of Grenada and St. Lucia / Carlyle L. Mitchell and Edgar Gold. - Halifax, N.S. : Dalhousie Ocean Studies Programme, 1982.
x,346p.
Bibliography: p338-345.

MARINE RESOURCES CONSERVATION

—Bibliography on land-locked states / edited by M.I. Glassner. - 2nd rev. and enl. ed. - Dordrecht : M. Nijhoff, 1986.
xiii, 210p.
Includes indexes.
ISBN 9024732611

—Environmental cooperation between the North Sea states : success or failure? / Sunneva Saetevik. - London : Belhaven Press, 1988.
xiv,173p.
Revision of thesis (cand. polit.): University of Oslo, 1986. Bibliography: p.161-165.
ISBN 1852930489 £22.50

—Environmental law of the sea / by Douglas M. Johnston. - Berlin : E. Schmidt, 1981.
419 p.; 21 cm.
Includes bibliographical references.
ISBN 3503021116 pbk.

—Marine environment law in the United Nations Environment Programme : an emergent eco-regime / compiled by Peter H. Sand. - London : Tycooly, 1988.
xxvi,265p.
Contains the text of international treaties adopted under the United Nations Environment Programme.
ISBN 1851480242

MARKETING

—Advertising and marketing law and practice / London : Frank Cass, 1984-.
Continues: Advertising law and practice.

MARKETING - CANADA

—Canadian Cases in Marketing Communications / Butterworths, 1983.
480p.
ISBN 0409840645 Hbk £36.95

MARKETING - GREAT BRITAIN

—Merchandising intellectual property / John Adams : with an introduction by Iain C Baillie : and a chapter on taxation by K.V. Prichard Jones. - London : Butterworths, 1987.
xxxi,345p,2p of plates; 26cm.
Includes index.
ISBN 0406103402 £30.00

MARKS OF ORIGIN

—Protection of geographic denominations of goods and services / edited by Herman Cohen Jehoram. - Alphen aan den Rijn : Sijthoff & Noordhoff, 1980.
vii,207p.

MARKS OF ORIGIN - GREAT BRITAIN

—Trade Descriptions Act 1972 : possible successor regime / Department of Trade and Industry. - London : The Department, 1987.
4,5 leaves.
Includes the text of the proposed Trade Descriptions (Places of Production) (Marking) Order 1988.

MARRIAGE

—Kinship and marriage : an anthropological perspective / Robin Fox. - Cambridge : Cambridge University Press, 1983.
273p; 20cm.
ISBN 0521260736

—Marriage and cohabitation in contemporary societies : areas of legal, social and ethical change : an international and interdisciplinary study / edited by John M. Eekelaar, Sanford Katz : with an introduction by William J. Goode. - Toronto : Butterworths, 1980.
xviii,454p; 24cm.
Includes bibliographical references. Papers presented at the Third World Conference of the International Society on Family Law, held June 5-9, 1979 at Uppsala, Sweden.
ISBN 0409828602

—Marriage in comparative conflict of laws : substantive conditions / Lennart Palsson. - The Hague : Martinus Nijhoff, 1981.
lxxvi,388p.
Continues Palsson, L. : Marriage and divorce in comparative conflict of laws, Leyden, 1974. Bibliography: pli-lxv.
ISBN 9024725488 Hbk £200.00

—Marriage or Divorce : the Real Issue / Dublin : Four Courts Press.
128p.

—Meaning of marriage payments / edited by J.L. Comaroff. - London : Academic Press, 1980.
xii,264p; 24cm.
Conference papers. Includes bibliographies and index.
ISBN 0121834506 £12.60

—Private international law : choice of law rules in marriage / the Law Commission and the Scottish Law Commission. - London : H.M.S.O., 1985.
ix,171p. - (Consultative memorandum).
ISBN 0117301701

—Private international law : recognition of foreign nullity decrees and related matters : presented to Parliament ... September 1984 / the Law Commission and the Scottish Law Commission. - London : H.M.S.O., 1984.
v,134p; 25cm.
ISBN 0101934106

MARRIAGE - AUSTRALIA

—Aboriginal customary law : marriage, children and the distribution of property / Australian Law Reform Commission. - Sydney : Australian Law Reform Commission, 1982.
20p. - (Discussion paper).

—Informal marriages / by Margaret Harrison. - Rev. ed. - Melbourne : Institute of Family Studies, 1982.
12 p.; 23 cm. - (Working paper).
Bibliography: p. 10.
ISBN 0642887780 pbk.

MARRIAGE - CANADA

—Carswell's Matrimonial Quantum and Custody Award Service / Agincourt : Carswell.

—Domestic Contracts / Agincourt : Carswell, 1987.
450p.
This looseleaf work is a practitioners guide to the drafting of cohabitation, marriage and separation agreements under the law of Ontario and British Columbia. Checklist, sample agreements, income tax considerations and related materials are included in the volume.

—Marriage Agreements / Vancouver : British Columbia Continuing Legal Education Society, 1980.
527p.

—Marriage and Divorce / Community Legal Education Ontario. - 3rd rev. ed. - Toronto : Community Legal Education Ontario, 1982.
47p.
ISBN 088903057X Pbk £6.50

—Marriage and Family Law in British Columbia : the Rights of Husbands, Wives, Children, and Common-Law / 6th ed. - North Vancouver : International Self-Counsel Press, 1985.
160p.
ISBN 0889081697 Hbk £7.95

MARRIAGE - CANADA - ALBERTA

—Marriage and Family Law in Alberta : the Rights of Husbands, Wives, Children, and Common-Law / 3rd ed. - North Vancouver : International Self-Counsel Press, 1987.
203p.
ISBN 0889082456 Hbk £8.95

—Matrimonial property : division of pension benefits upon marriage breakdown / Institute of Law Research and Reform. - Edmonton : Institute of Law Research and Reform, 1986.
viii,115p. - (Report).

—Matrimonial property : division of pension benefits upon marriage breakdown / Institute of Law Research and Reform. - Edmonton : The Institute, 1985.
ii,127,25,13p. - (Report for discussion).

MARRIAGE - CANADA - BRITISH COLUMBIA

—Intentional interference with domestic relations / Law Reform Commission of British Columbia. - Vancouver : The Commission, 1983.
iii,55p. - (Working paper).
Includes bibliographical references.

—Interspousal immunity in tort / Law Reform Commission of British Columbia. - Vancouver : The Commission, 1982.
iii,42p. - (Working paper).
Includes bibliographical references.

—Report on international interference with domestic relations / Law Reform Commission of British Columbia. - Victoria : Queen's Printer, 1983.
27p.
Includes bibliographical references.
ISBN 0771883986

—Report on interspousal immunity in tort / Law Reform Commission of British Columbia. - Victoria : Queen's Printer, 983.
21p.

—Report on spousal agreements / Law Reform Commission of British Columbia. - Victoria : Queens Printer, 1986.
37p.
Includes bibliographical references.
ISBN 0771885326

—Spousal agreements / Law Reform Commission of British Columbia. - Vancouver : The Commission, 1985.
iii,74p. - (Working paper).
Includes bibliographical references.

MARRIAGE - CANADA - ONTARIO

—Marriage and Family Law in Ontario : the Rights of Husbands, Wives, Children, and Common-Law Spouses / 4th ed. - North Vancouver : International Self-Counsel Press, 1986.
203p.
ISBN 0889083606 Hbk £6.95

MARRIAGE - CANADA - SASKATCHEWAN

—Proposals for an Equality of Status of Married Persons Act : report to the Attorney General / Law Reform Commission of Saskatchewan. - Saskatoon : The Commission, 1982.
17p.

—Proposals relating to matrimonial property legislation / Law Reform Commission of Saskatchewan. - Saskatoon : The Commission, 1985.
22p.

—Tentative proposals for reform of the Matrimonial Property Act / Law Reform Commission of Saskatchewan. - Saskatoon : The Commission, 1984.
167p.
Includes bibliographical references.

MARRIAGE - ENGLAND

—Church courts, sex and marriage in England 1570-1640 / Cambridge : Cambridge University Press.
Examines the role of Elizabethan Church courts, their jurisdiction and the attitude of the people towards them. Based on records from courts in Wiltshire, Cambridgeshire, Leicestershire and West Sussex.
ISBN 0521232856

—Distribution of matrimonial assets on divorce / Michael L. Rakusen, D. Peter Hunt. - 2nd ed. - London : Butterworths, 1982.
xxii,375p.
Latest supplement held: 1986.
ISBN 0406351015

—Law of marriage / Susan M. Blake. - Chichester : Rose, 1982.
liii,280p; 20cm.
Includes index.
ISBN 0859923142 Hbk £14.00
ISBN 0859923088 Pbk £10.50

—Matrimonial and Family Proceedings Act 1984 : a practical guide / Richard M. Smith. - London : Oyez, 1984.
xviii,125p.
Includes index.
ISBN 0851208789

—Matrimonial proceedings in magistrates courts / by Billy Strachan. - 2nd ed. - London : Sweet & Maxwell, 1987.
250p; 22cm.
Includes new material dealing with conciliation, and the effect of conduct on the amount of an order. Discusses grounds of an order for periodical payments, calculation and the amount of the order, orders for the custody of children, and for access to children, and the enforcement of orders.
ISBN 0421385006 Pbk £20.00

—No just cause : the law of affinity in England and Wales : some suggestions for change / a report by a group appointed by the Archbishop of Canterbury. - London : CIO, 1984.
vi,151p; 21cm.
ISBN 0715136976 Pbk £5.50

—Pugh's matrimonial proceedings before magistrates / J. Basil Horsman. - 4th ed. - London : Butterworths, 1981.
xli, 820p.
ISBN 040634602X

—Ties that bind : law, marriage and the reproduction of patriarchal relations / Carol Smart. - London : Routledge & Kegan Paul, 1984.
xiv,273p; 22cm.
Bibliography: p259-268. - Includes index.
ISBN 0710098324 Pbk £6.95

MARRIAGE - GREAT BRITAIN

—Change in marriage : a collection of papers presented at the National Guidance Council study days / Rugby : National Marriage Guidance Council, 1982.
139p; 21cm.
ISBN 0853510563 Pbk £3.50

—Costs in Matrimonial Causes / Format. - London : Fourmat, 1985.
- (LCFS 2).
ISBN 090684004X Pbk £2.45

—Family law : time restrictions on presentation of divorce and nullity petitions : laid before Parliament ... pursuant to section 3(2) of the Law Commissions Act 1965 / The Law Commission. - London : H.M.S.O., 1982.
iv,77p. - (HC).
ISBN 0102513821

—Family law : transfer of money between spouses : the Married Women's Property Act 1964 / the Law Commission. - London : H.M.S.O., 1985.
iii,29p; 21cm. - (Working paper).
ISBN 011730171X

—Fees in Matrimonial Proceedings / Format. - 4th ed. - London : Fourmat, 1986.
- (LCFS 9).
ISBN 1851900160 Pbk £3.25

—Law and Practice in Matrimonial Causes / Harmer. - 4th ed. - London : Butterworths, 1985.
ISBN 0406637075 Pbk £21.95
ISBN 0406637083 Hbk £38.00

—Matrimonial Advocacy and Litigation / London : Butterworths, 1987.

—Matrimonial Advocacy and Litigation / London : Butterworths, 1988.
ISBN 0406103305 Pbk £19.95

—Matrimonial and Domestic Injunctions / Purdie. - 2nd ed. - London : Butterworths, 1987.
ISBN 0406334412 Pbk £32.00

—Matrimonial and Family Law Up to Date / London : Law Society, 1985.
69p.

—Matrimonial Causes / Salter. - 17th ed. - London : Longman Professional, 1988.
ISBN 0851211445 Pbk

—Matrimonial Causes (Amend No 2) Rules 1985 / London : Longman Professional, 1986.
ISBN 0851212069 Pbk £6.50

—Matrimonial Proceedings / 2nd ed. - London : Fourmat, 1984.
180p.
ISBN 0906840783 Pbk £9.95

—Private international law : choice of law rules in marriage / the Law Commission and the Scottish Law Commission. - London : H.M.S.O., 1987.
37p. - (1987/88 HC3).
ISBN 0102003882

—Some tax implications of marriage breakdown / David Moore. - Belfast : SLS Legal Publications, 1987.
35p.
Includes bibliographical references.

—Some Tax Implications of Marriage Breakdown / Belfast : Queen's University of Belfast, 1981.
26p.

—Taxation of marriage and marriage breakdown / Croydon : Tolley, 1988.
ISBN 0854593233 Hbk

—Tolley's taxation of marriage and marriage breakdown / by David Brodie. - Croydon : Tolley, 1988.
xxiii,184p; 23cm.
Includes index.
ISBN 0854593233 Pbk £14.95

MARRIAGE - INDIA

—Child Marriage Restraint Act / 4th ed. - Allahabad : Law Book Company, 1988.
70p.

—Family law : law of marriage and divorce in India / by Paras Diwan. - New Delhi : Sterling Publishers, 1983.
xxviii,470p.
Authors name on spine: Paras Diwan.

—Law of Marriage and Divorce in India / Lucknow : Eastern Book Company, 1982.
xxxii, 718p.

—Offences Relating to Marriage and Punishments in India / Allahabad : Law Publishers, 1980.

MARRIAGE - IRELAND

—First report on family law : criminal coversation, enticement and harbouring of a spouse or child, loss of consortium, personal injury to a child, seduction of a child, matrimonial property and breach of promise of marriage / the Law Reform Commission. - Dublin : The Commission, 1981.
iii,32p. - (LRC).

—Report on jurisdiction in proceedings for nullity of marriage, recognition of foreign nullity decrees, and the Hague Convention on the Celebration and Recognition of the Validity of Marriage (1978) / the Law Reform Commission. - Dublin : The Commission, 1985.
v,63p. - (LRC).
Bibliography: pp.51-2. Includes text of the Convention.

—Report on nullity of marriage / the Law Reform Commission. - Dublin : The Commission, 1984.
ix,193p. - (LRC).
Bibliography: p.193.

—Report on private international law aspects of capacity to marry and choice of law in proceedings for nullity of marriage / the Law Reform Commission. - Dublin : The Commission, 1985.
v,161p. - (LRC).
Bibliography: pp.156-8.

—Report on restitution of conjugal rights, jactitation of marriage and related matters / the Law Reform Commission. - Dublin : The Commission, 1983.
v,31p. - (LRC).
Includes bibliographical references.

—Report on the law relating to the age of majority, the age for marriage and some connected subjects / the Law Reform Commission. - Dublin : The Commission, 1983.
v,75p. - (LRC).

MARRIAGE - NIGERIA

—Customary law : the war without arms / by A.P. Anyebe. - Enugu : Fourth Dimension, 1985.
159p.
Includes bibliographical references.
ISBN 978156184X

—Marriage laws of Nigeria : papers presented at a national workshop held at the Nigerian Institute of Advanced Legal Studies / edited by T. Akinola Aguda : assisted by Isabella Adi. - Lagos : The Nigerian Institute of Advanced Legal Studies, 1981.
170p.
ISBN 9782353000

MARRIAGE - PAPUA NEW GUINEA

—Marriage in Papua New Guinea / results of a research project conducted by the Law Reform Commission and Administrative College of Papua New Guinea. - Waigani : The Commission, 1986.
xi,223p. - (Monograph).
ISBN 9980550031

MARRIAGE - SCOTLAND

—Family law : report on matrimonial property / Scottish Law Commission. - Edinburgh : H.M.S.O., 1984.
v,35p.
Includes draft Bill.
ISBN 0102467846

—Family law : report on outdated rules in the law of husband and wife / Scottish Law Commission. - Edinburgh : H.M.S.O., 1983.
vi,53p.
ISBN 0102330832

—Law of husband and wife in Scotland / by Eric M. Clive. - 2nd ed. - Edinburgh : W Green & Son, 1982.
lxxiv,756p. - (Scottish Universities' Law Institute Ser.).
Chapters describe the general development of the law from before the Reformation to the present day, the formation and termination of marriage and the legal effects of marriage. Bibliography: plxxi-lxxiv. Published under the auspices of the Scottish Universities Law Institute.
ISBN 0414006682 Hbk £47

—Living Together : A Guide to the Law on Marriage and Cohabitation in Scotland / Frances Wason. - Edinburgh : Scottish Association of Citizens Advice Bureau, 1984.
96p : Illus.
ISBN 0905831047 Hbk £1.95

—Matrimonial Homes (Family Protection) (Scotland) Act 1981 / by D.I. Nichols and M.C. Meston. - Edinburgh : Green, 1982.
vii,68p.
Includes index.
ISBN 0414006879 PBK £15.75

—Some obsolete and discriminatory rules in the law of husband and wife / Scottish Law Commission. - Edinburgh : The Commission, 1982.
61p. - (Consultative memorandum).

MARRIAGE - SOUTH AFRICA

—Introduction to the Matrimonial Property Act 1984 / June D. Sinclair. - Cape Town : Juta, 1984.
ix,102p.
ISBN 0702115096

—Marriage, money, property, and the law : a guide to the legal and financial consequences of a marriage between Africans / by J.C. Bekker. - Durban, South Africa : Butterworths, 1983.
53 p.; 24 cm.
Bibliography: p. 53.
ISBN 0409012106 pbk.

—Marriages and customary unions of black persons / South African Law Commission. - Pretoria : The Commission, 1985.
xix,222p. - (Project).
Bibliography: p.vii-xi.
ISBN 062110180X

—Mixed Marriages Act : a Historical and Theological Study / Rondebosch : University of Cape Town, 1983.
viii, 108p.
ISBN 0799205206 Pbk £5.00

—South African law of husband and wife / H. R. Hahlo. - 5th ed. - Cape Town : Juta, 1985.
lxx,526p.
ISBN 0702115681

MARRIAGE - UNITED STATES

—Marriage and Family Law in Washington : the Rights of Husbands, Wives, Children and Cohabiting Couples / 3rd ed. - North Vancouver : International Self-Counsel Press, 1988.
ISBN 0889087377 Hbk

MARRIAGE (HINDU LAW)

—Hindu Law of Marriage and Stridhana / Delhi : Mittal Publications, 1984.

—Hindu Marriage Act / 2nd ed. - Allahabad : Law Book Company, 1986.

MARRIAGE (ISLAMIC LAW)

—Law in Afghanistan : a study of the Constitutions, matrimonial law and judiciary / by Mohammad Hashim Kamali. - Leiden : E. J. Brill, 1985.
viii,265p.
Bibliography: p254-259.
ISBN 9004071288

—Law of Muslim Marriage, Dissolution and Maintenance / 2nd ed. - Allahabad : Law Book Company, 1988.
600p.

MARRIAGE (ISLAMIC LAW) - GAMBIA

—Muslim marriages : formation and dissolution / Banjul, The Gambia? : s.n., 1987.
17,xixp. - (Law reform project).
Contains a draft Muslim Marriages (Formation and Short Title Dissolution) Bill and a commentary.

MARRIAGE LAW - BRITISH COLUMBIA

—Breach of promise of marriage / Law Reform Commission of British Columbia. - Vancouver : Law Reform Commission of British Columbia, 1983.
iii,67p. - (Working paper).

MARTIAL LAW

—Rule of law in the areas administered by Israel / Israel National Section of the International Commission of Jurists. - Tel Aviv : Israel National Section of the International Commission of Jurists, 1981.
xiv,114p.
Includes bibliographical references.

MARXIAN ECONOMICS

—Capitalist state : Marxist theories and methods / Bob Jessop. - Oxford : Robertson, 1982.
xvi,296p; 24cm.
Bibliography: p260-281. - Includes index.
ISBN 0855202696 Hbk £17.00
ISBN 0855202688 Pbk £5.95

MARXISM

—Marxism and Law / Oxford : Oxford University Press, 1982.
ISBN 0192851446 Pbk £4.50

MASS MEDIA

—International media law : a monthly bulletin on rights, clearances and legal practice / v. - London : Oyez Longman, 1982.
ISBN 02636395

—Manufacture of news : social problems, deviance and the mass media / Stanley Cohen and Jock Young (editors). - rev. ed. - London : Constable, 1981.
506p.
ISBN 0094637806

MASS MEDIA - AUSTRALIA

—Media law in Australia / Mark Armstrong, Michael Blakeney, Ray Watterson. - Melbourne : Oxford University Press, 1983.
x,274p; 21cm.
Bibliography: p242-267. - Includes index.
ISBN 0195544447 Hbk Unpriced
ISBN 0195544439 Pbk £13.00

MASS MEDIA - CANADA

—Law and the media in Canada / Clare F. Beckton. - Toronto, Canada : Carswell, 1982.
xvi, 161 p.; 24 cm.
Includes index. Bibliography: p. xi-xvi.
ISBN 0459344501 pbk.

MASS MEDIA - ENGLAND

—Media law : the rights of journalists and broadcasters / Geoffrey Robertson, Andrew G.L. Nicol. - 1st ed. - London : Oyez, 1984.
xxxvi,403p.
Includes bibliographical references and index.
ISBN 0851206506

MASS MEDIA - GREAT BRITAIN

—Crime, justice and the mass media : papers presented to the 14th Cropwood Round-Table Conference, December 1981 / edited by Colin Sumner. - Cambridge : University of Cambridge Institute of Criminology, 1982.
ii,123p.
Includes bibliographical references.

MATERNAL AND INFANT WELFARE - COMMONWEALTH

—Issues in reproductice health law in the Commonwealth / by Rebecca J. Cook and Bernard M. Dickens. - London : Commonwealth Secretariat, 1986.
109p.
ISBN 085092295X

MATERNAL DEPRIVATION

—Maternal deprivation reassessed / Michael Rutter. - 2nd ed. - Harmondsworth : Penguin, 1981.
285p; 18cm. - (Penguin education).
Previous ed.: 1972. Bibliography: p219-272. - Includes index.
ISBN 0180805613 Pbk £1.95

MATERNITY LEAVE - CANADA

—Report of the Task Force on Child Care / Canada. - Ottawa, Ont. : Status of Women Canada, 1986.
xxvi, 395 p.; 23 cm.
Bibliography: p. 345-365.
ISBN 0660120380 pbk. £9.95 (£11.95 other countries)

MATERNITY LEAVE - GREAT BRITAIN

—Guide to Statutory Maternity Pay / Croydon : Tolley.
104p.
Gives information on conditions of eligibility, dispute settlement procedure, unfair dismissal on grounds of pregnancy and provisions of the Employment Protection (Consolidation) Act 1978.
ISBN 0854593373 Hbk £8.95

—Maternity rights / London : Incomes Data Services, 1983.
44p. - (Handbook series).

—Maternity Rights : The Experience of Employers / London : Policy Studies Institute, 1981.
89p.

—Parenthood in the balance : an assessment of benefits and leave around the time of childbirth / Equal Opportunities Commission. - Manchester : Equal Opportunities Commission, 1982.
28,ivp; 21cm.
ISBN 0905829603 Pbk Unpriced

MATHEMATICAL STATISTICS

—Elementary statistical methods / G. Barrie Wetherill. - 3rd ed. - London : Chapman and Hall, 1982.
356p; 24cm. - (Science paperbacks).
Previous ed.: 1972. Bibliography: p348-351. - Includes index.
ISBN 0412240009 Pbk £7.95

MATRIMONIAL PROPERTY

—Power to Dispose of the Assets of the Universal Matrimonial Community of Property / Pijnacker : Dutch Efficiency Bureau.
ISBN 9062310060 Hbk £43.60

MATRIMONIAL PROPERTY - AUSTRALIA

—Australian family property law / by I. J. Hardingham and M. A. Neave. - Sydney : Law Book Company, 1984.
liii,647p.
ISBN 0455205132

—Matrimonial property / Law Reform Commission. - Canberra : Australian Government Publishing Service, 1987.
xxxiv,382p. - (Report).
Bibliography: p.367-372. - Includes index.

—Matrimonial property law / Australian Law Reform Commission. - Sydney : Australian Law Reform Commission, 1985.
iv,105p. - (Discussion paper).

—Property Division on Marriage Breakdown / North Ryde : C.C.H. Australia, 1984.
660p.
ISBN 0869035797 Hbk £50.00

MATRIMONIAL PROPERTY - CANADA

—Marital Property Agreements / Vancouver : Continuing Legal Education Society of British Columbia, 1988.
369p.
ISBN 086504970X Hbk £70.00

—Matrimonial Property Law in Canada, 1 vol. / Winifred H. Holland. - Agincourt : Carswell, 1980.
This looseleaf volume contains commentary and analysis of the matrimonial property Acts of each province in Canada. The law of each province is discussed in a separate chapter and the complete text of each matrimonial property Act is included in the text.

—Matrimonial property law in Canada / editors: Alastair Bissett-Johnson, Winifred H. Holland. - s.l. : Burroughs, 1980.
Looseleaf binder.
ISBN 0459332708

MATRIMONIAL PROPERTY - CANADA - ALBERTA

—Matrimonial property : division of pension benefits upon marriage breakdown / Institute of Law Research and Reform. - Edmonton : Institute of Law Research and Reform, 1986.
viii,115p. - (Report).

—Matrimonial property : division of pension benefits upon marriage breakdown / Institute of Law Research and Reform. - Edmonton : The Institute, 1985.
ii,127,25,13p. - (Report for discussion).

MATRIMONIAL PROPERTY - CANADA - BRITISH COLUMBIA

—Family property / by Thomas G. Anderson and Michael Karton. - Victoria : Queen's Printer, 1986.
189p.
Date on front cover: 1985. 'A study paper prepared for the Law Reform Commission of British Columbia'. Includes bibliographical references.
ISBN 0771884931

—Report on spousal agreements / Law Reform Commission of British Columbia. - Victoria : Queens Printer, 1986.
37p.
Includes bibliographical references.
ISBN 0771885326

MATRIMONIAL PROPERTY - CANADA - MANITOBA

—Report on 'The Married Women's Property Act' and related matters / Manitoba Law Reform Commission. - Winnipeg : The Commission, 1985.
i,76p. - (Report).
Includes bibliographical references.
ISBN 0771101163

MATRIMONIAL PROPERTY - CANADA - ONTARIO

—Division of Matrimonial Assets in Ontario / Aurora : Canada Law Book Co, 1982.
438p. - (Text Books-Civil).
Supplement-1985

—Spousal Property Rights Under the Ontario Family Law Act / Butterworths, 1987.
80p.
Contains commentary on present and prospective interpretation of the Act, insights into the prospective operation of Parts I, II, and IV of the Act, up-to-date reported and unreported judgements incorporated in the commentary, applicable provincial rules and forms, and an analysis of issues including business valuation, professional licences and pensions.
ISBN 0409809365 Hbk £55.00

MATRIMONIAL PROPERTY - CANADA - SASKATCHEWAN

—Proposals relating to matrimonial property legislation / Law Reform Commission of Saskatchewan. - Saskatoon : The Commission, 1985.
22p.

—Tentative proposals for reform of the Matrimonial Property Act / Law Reform Commission of Saskatchewan. - Saskatoon : The Commission, 1984.
167p.
Includes bibliographical references.

MATRIMONIAL PROPERTY - ENGLAND

—Family law : matrimonial property / the Law Commission. - London : HMSO, 1988.
iii,30p. - (H.C. 1988-89).
ISBN 0102009899

—Wives and Property : Reform of the Married Women's Property Law in Nineteenth-Century England / Toronto : University of Toronto Press, 1982.
ISBN 0802055737 Hbk £35.00
ISBN 0802064760 Pbk £12.50

—Wives and property : reform of the married women's property law in nineteenth-century England / Lee Holcombe. - Oxford : Martin Robertson, 1983.
viii,311p; 24cm.
Bibliography: p275-292. - Includes index.
ISBN 0855206071 £15.00

MATRIMONIAL PROPERTY - GREAT BRITAIN

—Family law : transfer of money between spouses : the Married Women's Property Act 1964 / the Law Commission. - London : H.M.S.O., 1985.
iii,29p; 21cm. - (Working paper).
ISBN 011730171X

—Financial and Property Problems on Marriage Breakdown / Godfrey Gypps. - London : Law Society, 1982.
- (Oxford Weekend Courses).

—Fisher on Matrimonial Property / 2nd ed. - London : Butterworths, 1985.
ISBN 0409600395 Hbk £51.00

—Law and Practice in Matrimonial Causes / Caroline Harmer. - 4th ed. - London : Butterworths, 1985.
This text is an introduction to matrimonial law and a guide to developments in the area for students of the subject in England. All forms and model pleadings reflect the Matrimonial and Family Proceedings Act of 1984 and the Matrimonial Homes Act of 1983.
ISBN 0406637083 Hbk
ISBN 0406637075 Pbk

—Matrimonial Conveyancing / 3rd ed. - London : Longman Professional, 1988.
ISBN 0851212832 Pbk £22.00

—Matrimonial Conveyancing : A Draftsman's Handbook / London : Oyez Longman, 1981.
ISBN 0851206034 Hbk £9.95

—Matrimonial Finance and Taxation / Davies. - 4th ed. - London : Butterworths, 1986.
ISBN 0406254478 Hbk £52.00

—Matrimonial Property and Finance / 3rd ed. - London : Longman Professional, 1987.
ISBN 0851212816 Hbk £47.50

—Matrimonial Property and Finance / 2nd ed. - London : Oyez Longman, 1983.
- (Oyez Longman Practitioner Ser.).
ISBN 0851206670 Hbk £17.95

—Property and marriage : an integrated approach : property, tax, pensions and benefits in the family / Judith Freeman...et al. - London : Institute for Fiscal Studies, 1988.
viii,170p. - (Report series).
Bibliography: p156-161.
ISBN 0902992686

—Property distribution on divorce / De Haas. - 2nd ed. - London : Longman Professional, 1985.
ISBN 0851210015 Pbk £14.95

—Property Distribution on Divorce / Margaret R. De Haas. - London : Oyez Longman, 1982.
ISBN 0851207529 Hbk £5.95

MATRIMONIAL PROPERTY - NEW ZEALAND

—Fisher on Matrimonial Property / 2nd ed. - Butterworths, 1984.
ISBN 0409600393 Hbk £90.75

MATRIMONIAL PROPERTY - SCOTLAND

—Family law : report on matrimonial property / Scottish Law Commission. - Edinburgh : H.M.S.O., 1984.
v,35p.
Includes draft Bill.
ISBN 0102467846

—Matrimonial property / Scottish Law Commission. - Edinburgh : Scottish Law Commission, 1983.
207p. - (Consultative memorandum).

MATRIMONIAL PROPERTY - SOUTH AFRICA

—Introduction to the Matrimonial Property Act 1984 / June D. Sinclair. - Cape Town : Juta, 1984.
ix,102p.
ISBN 0702115096

—Marriage, money, property, and the law : a guide to the legal and financial consequences of a marriage between Africans / by J.C. Bekker. - Durban, South Africa : Butterworths, 1983.
53 p.; 24 cm.
Bibliography: p. 53.
ISBN 0409012106 pbk.

MATRIMONIAL PROPERTY - UNITED KINGDOM

—Matrimonial Suits and Property Proceedings : A Practitioner's Index of Practice and Procedure / Maurice Young. - 2nd ed. - Chichester : Barry Rose, 1986.
xliii, 222p.
ISBN 0859921328 Hbk £30.00

MECHANICAL ENGINEERING CONTRACTS - GREAT BRITAIN

—I.Mech.E/I.E.E. conditions of contract : a commentary on five I.Mech.E./I.E.E. model forms of general conditions of contract and on the BEAMA contract price adjustment clauses and formulae / by Andrew Pike. - London : Sweet & maxwell, 1984.
xix,333p; 26cm.
Includes index.
ISBN 0421299908 £38.00

MEDICAL CARE

—Laws and policies affecting adolescent health / by John M. Paxman and Ruth Jane Zuckerman. - Geneva : World Health Organization, 1987.
x,300p.
Includes bibliographical references.
ISBN 9241560959

MEDICAL CARE - ENGLAND

—Health services law / by John D. Finch. - London : Sweet & Maxwell, 1981.
xix,338p; 23cm.
Includes index.
ISBN 0421264608 Hbk £11.30
ISBN 0421264705 Pbk £7.30

MEDICAL CARE - GREAT BRITAIN

—Medical negligence / edited by Michael J. Powers and Nigel H. Harris; consulting editor: Andrew Lockhart-Miriams. - London : Butterworths, 1990.
900; 24cm.
Deals with all aspects of medical negligence claims. The book explains the relevant rules of law, identifies the practical difficulties in bringing an action for damages in respect of negligent medical treatment, and shows how to prepare the medical evidence on liability, how to complete the medical report on quantum, and how to present the experts evidence at court.
ISBN 0406130019 Hbk £120

MEDICAL ETHICS

—Behaviour alteration and the criminal law / Law Reform Commission of Canada. - Ottawa : The Commission, 1985.
48,56p. - (Working paper).
Bibliography: p.44-48. Added t.p. in French: Les techniques de modification du comportement et de droit penal. Cover title: Protection of life : behaviour alteration and the criminal law. Pages numbered in opposite directions. Text in English and French.
ISBN 0662538579

—Experience at a clinical research ethical review committee / Ethical Committee, University College Hospital. - London : British Medical Association, 1981.
7p.
Reprinted from: British medical journal, 14 Nov. 1981, 283, 1312-1314.

—Human life and medical practice / J.K. Mason. - Edinburgh : Edinburgh University Press, 1988.
192p; 22cm.
Includes bibliography and index.
ISBN 0852245602 Hbk £15.00
ISBN 085224584X Pbk £7.50

—Nursing law and ethics / edited by A. Carmi and S. Schneider : by M.B. Agostino ... et al. - Berlin : Springer-Verlag, 1985.
ISBN 0387152539

—Responsibility in health care / edited by George J. Agich. - Dordrecht, Holland : D. Reidel, 1982.
xxiii, 285p.
Outgrowth of the Eleventh Trans-disciplinary Symposium on Philosophy and Medicine held in Springfield, Ill., on March 16-18, 1981. Includes bibliographies and index.
ISBN 9027714177 CIP rev.

—Unmasking of medicine / Ian Kennedy. - London : Allen & Unwin, 1981.
xiii,189p; 23cm.
Bibliography: p169-182. - Includes index.
ISBN 0046100164 Unpriced

MEDICAL ETHICS - GREAT BRITAIN

—Health, rights and resources / edited by Peter Byrne. - London : King Edward's Hospital Fund for London, 1988.
201p; 23cm.
Includes index.
ISBN 0197246451 £16.95

—Law and Medical Ethics / McCall-Smith. - 2nd ed. - London : Butterworths, 1987.
ISBN 0406501300 Hbk £18.00
ISBN 0406501319 Pbk £14.50

—Medical Law and Ethics / Grubb. - London : Butterworths, 1988.
ISBN 0406500401 Hbk

—Medical Law and Ethics Commentary and Materials / London : Butterworths.
ISBN 0406500401 Hbk

—Medicine, Ethics and the Law / London : Sweet & Maxwell, 1988.
ISBN 042048020X Pbk £18.00

—Medicine in contemporary society / edited by Peter Byrne. - London : King Edward's Hospital Fund for London, 1987.
156p; 23cm.
Includes index.
ISBN 0197246427 £16.95

—Medicine, morals and the law / Sheila McLean and Gerry Maher. - Aldershot : Gower, 1983.
ix,214p; 23cm.
Includes index.
ISBN 0566005336 Unpriced

—Rights and wrongs in medicine : King's College studies 1985-6 / edited by Peter Byrne. - London : King Edward's Hospital Fund for London, 1986.
ISBN 0197246370

—Treat me right : essays in medical law and ethics / Ian Kennedy. - Oxford : Clarendon Press, 1988.
xvii,375p.
Bibliography: pp.365-370. - Includes index.
ISBN 0198255586

—Treat me right : essays on medical law and ethics / Oxford : Oxford University Press, 1988.
Brings together a wide selection of the author's work in the field of medical law and ethics. Many of the articles contained have already been published in journals, but some appear for the first time.*Lawyers, doctors, students of law, ethics and medicine*
ISBN 0198255586 Pbk
ISBN 0198255594 Hbk £35

MEDICAL EXAMINERS (LAW) - CANADA

—Canadian coroner law : a legal study of coroner and medical examiner systems in Canada / by Christopher Granger. - Toronto, Canada : Carswell, 1984.
xxi, 418 p.; 24 cm.
Includes bibliographical references and indexes.
ISBN 045936460X

—Canadian law of inquests : a handbook for coroners, medical examiners, counsel and the police / by T. David Marshall. - Toronto : Carswell, 1980.
xxvii,147p; 24cm.
Includes index.
ISBN 045933350X

MEDICAL EXAMINERS (LAW) - ENGLAND

—Coronership / Gavin Thurston. - 2nd ed. - Chichester : Rose, 1980.
xviii,242p; 23cm.
Previous ed.: 1976.
ISBN 0859921840 £24.00

—Thurston's coronership : the law and practice on coroners / Paul Knapman, Michael J. Powers. - 3rd ed. - Chichester : Barry Rose, 1985.
xxiv,544p.
Includes index. Includes legislation.
ISBN 085992355X Hbk £85

MEDICAL INSURANCE - GREAT BRITAIN

—Income during initial sickness : a new strategy ... / Department of Health and Social Security. - London : H.M.S.O, 1980.
iii,26p; 25cm. - (Cmnd. 7864).
ISBN 0101786409 sd £2.00

MEDICAL JURISPRUDENCE

—Guide to pathological evidence for lawyers and police officers / Frederick A. Jaffe. - 2nd ed. - Toronto : Carswell, 1983.
xv,204p.
Bibliography: p.189-197. - Includes index.
ISBN 0459355406

—Medicine and law : an international journal / Berlin : Springer, 1982.
Supersedes: International journal of medicine and law.
ISBN 07231393

—Principle and Practice of Medical Jurisprudence / Mant. - 13th ed. - Edinburgh : Churchill Livingstone, 1984.
ISBN 0443014817 Hbk £35.00

—Trial of the expert : a study of expert evidence and forensic experts / Ian R. Freckelton. - Melbourne : Oxford University Press, 1987.
xxxii,289p.
A textbook of the rules of expert evidence, and an analysis of the difficulties experienced when experts from non-legal disciplines are called as witnesses. Examines the impact of new scientific disciplines, and looks at how the forensic expert's duties to maintain confidentiality may conflict with the court's need for all the relevant evidence.
ISBN 0195545664 Hbk £30

MEDICAL JURISPRUDENCE - ENGLAND

—Medical evidence : the report of a Joint Committee of the British Medical Association, the Senate of the Inns of the Court and the Bar and the Law Society / British Medical Association. - London : British Medical Association, 1981.
iiileaves,37p; 30cm.

MEDICAL JURISPRUDENCE - GREAT BRITAIN

—Forensic medicine for lawyers / J.K. Mason with chapters by A.K.M. Macrae, J.S. Oliver, A.T. Proudfoot. - 2nd ed. - London : Butterworths, 1983.
xv,418p; 24cm.
Previous ed.: Bristol : J. Wright, 1978. Bibliography: p398-399. - Includes index.
ISBN 0407002448 Unpriced

—Legal issues in medicine / edited by Sheila A.M. McLean. - Aldershot : Gower, 1981.
xiv,219p; 23cm.
ISBN 0566004283 Unpriced

MEDICAL JURISPRUDENCE - INDIA

—Medical Jurisprudence / Raju. - 4th ed. 1981 repr. - Lucknow : Eastern Book Company, 1982.
681p.

—Medical Jurisprudence and Toxicology / 5th ed. - Allahabad : Law Book Company, 1987.
800p.

MEDICAL JURISPRUDENCE - SCOTLAND

—Evidence : blood group tests, DNA tests and related matters / Scottish Law Commission. - Edinburgh : The Commission, 1988.
i,45p. - (Discussion paper).

MEDICAL LAW

—Law-Medicine Relations : a Philosophical Exploration : Proceedings of the 8th Trans-Disciplinary Symposium on Philosophy and Medicine Held at Farmington, Conn., 1978 / J.M. Healey. - Dordrecht : Kluwer, 1981.
319p.
ISBN 9027712174 Hbk £75.00

—Medicine and law : an international journal / Berlin : Springer, 1982.
Supersedes: International journal of medicine and law.
ISBN 07231393

—Medicine and the law / convocation address at the Second Convocation of the National Post-graduate Medical College of Nigeria on March 10, 1983, in Lagos, Nigeria : by R.O.A. Akinjide. - Lagos : s.n., 1983.
16p.

MEDICAL LAW - AUSTRALIA

—Medicine and surgery for lawyers / North Ryde : Law Book Co, 1986.
ISBN 0455206759 Hbk £45.00

—Medicine and Surgery for Lawyers / North Ryde : Law Book Co, 1986.
xxi, 675p.
ISBN 0455206759 Hbk £89.50

MEDICAL LAW - CANADA

—Current Issues in Medical Law / Montreal : McGill Campus Legal Aid Clinic, 1982.
173p.

—Law and Medicine in Canada / Glenn Ivan Sawyer. - 2nd ed. - Butterworths, 1987.
704p.
Analysis of recent case law and a review of statutory developments. Covers consent, the confidentiality of health records, artificial reproduction, biomedical research involving human subjects. Separate chapters discuss in more detail experimentation, organ transplants, determination of death, and a completely new chapter on abortion.
ISBN 0409865907 Hbk £85.00

—Legal Liability of Doctors and Hospitals / 2nd ed. - Agincourt : Carswell, 1984.
ISBN 0459358200 Hbk £38.75

—Medical Law Handbook / North Vancouver : International Self-Counsel Press, 1985.
131p.
ISBN 0889086036 Hbk £6.95

—Medicine for Lawyers : 11 / Vancouver : British Columbia Continuing Legal Education Society, 1984.
ISBN 086504161X Hbk £55.00

—Medicine for Lawyers 3 : the Whiplash Injury / Vancouver : Continuing Legal Education Society of British Columbia, 1985.
83p.
ISBN 0865042128 Hbk £55.00

—Medicine for Lawyers 4 / Vancouver : Continuing Legal Education Society of British Columbia, 1986.
156p.
ISBN 0865042756 Hbk £55.00

—Medicine for Lawyers / Vancouver : British Columbia Continuing Legal Education Society, 1982.
163p.
ISBN 0865040753 Hbk £50.00

—Report on some aspects of medical treatment and criminal law / Law Reform Commission of Canada. - Ottawa : The Commission, 1986.
19,19p. - (Report).
Pages numbered in opposite directions. Text in English and French.
ISBN 0662543793

MEDICAL LAW - ENGLAND

—Law and medical ethics / J.K. Mason, R.A. McCall Smith. - 2nd ed. - London : Butterworths, 1987.
345p; 22cm.
Previous ed.: 1983. Includes index.
ISBN 0406501300 Hbk £18.95
ISBN 0406501319 Pbk £12.95

—Law, ethics and medicine : studies in medical law / by P.D.G. Skegg. - Oxford : Clarendon, 1984.
xii,268p; 23cm.
Includes index.
ISBN 0198253656 £25.00

—Sweet & Maxwell's encyclopedia of health services and medical law / London : Sweet & Maxwell, 1987.
loose-leaf.
Includes index.
ISBN 0421315008 £145.00

MEDICAL LAW - GREAT BRITAIN

—Beginning Lives / Oxford : Blackwell, 1987.
ISBN 0631153284 Pbk £8.95

—Health, rights and resources / edited by Peter Byrne. - London : King Edward's Hospital Fund for London, 1988.
201p; 23cm.
Includes index.
ISBN 0197246451 £16.95

—Human Body and the Law / Edinburgh : Edinburgh University Press.
215p.
ISBN 0852241739 Hbk £10.00

—Law for Doctors and Nurses / Tingle. - London : Financial Training, 1988.
ISBN 1851851011 Pbk £15.00

—Legal aspects of medical practice / Bernard Knight. - 4th ed. - Edinburgh : Churchill Livingstone, 1987.
336p; 22cm.
Previous ed.: 1982. Includes bibliography and index.
ISBN 0443037817 Pbk £4.95

—Legal aspects of medical practice / Bernard Knight. - 3rd ed. - Edinburgh : Churchill Livingstone, 1982.
viii,302p; 22cm. - (Churchill Livingstone medical text).
Previous ed.: 1976.
ISBN 0443025584

—Legal issues in medicine / edited by Sheila A.M. McLean. - Aldershot : Gower, 1981.
xiv,219p; 23cm.
ISBN 0566004283 Unpriced

—Medical Law and Ethics / Grubb. - London : Butterworths, 1988.
ISBN 0406500401 Hbk

—Medical Law and Ethics Commentary and Materials / London : Butterworths.
ISBN 0406500401 Hbk

—Medical-Legal Issues : Report of a Combined Medical-Legal Workshop Held in Malawi, October 1979 / London : Commonwealth Secretariat, 1980.

—Medical Negligence : a Plaintiff's Guide / Agincourt : Cass, 1988.
ISBN 0714633399 Hbk £20.00
ISBN 0714640611 Pbk £12.00

—Medicine, Ethics and the Law / London : Sweet & Maxwell, 1988.
ISBN 042048020X Pbk £18.00

—Medicine in contemporary society / edited by Peter Byrne. - London : King Edward's Hospital Fund for London, 1987.
156p; 23cm.
Includes index.
ISBN 0197246427 £16.95

—Medicine, Patients and the Law / Pelican, 1987.
ISBN 0140225579 Pbk £5.95

—Medico-Legal Encyclopaedia / London : Butterworths, 1987.
ISBN 0407003746 Hbk £55.00

—Rights and wrongs in medicine : King's College studies 1985-6 / edited by Peter Byrne. - London : King Edward's Hospital Fund for London, 1986.
ISBN 0197246370

—Treat me right : essays in medical law and ethics / Ian Kennedy. - Oxford : Clarendon Press, 1988.
xvii,375p.
Bibliography: pp.365-370. - Includes index.
ISBN 0198255586

MEDICAL LEGISLATION

—Medical responsibility in Western Europe : research study of the European Science Foundation / edited by E. Deutsch and H.-L. Schreiber : with contributions by J. Blackie ... et al. - Berlin : Springer-Verlag, 1985.
ISBN 0387153659

MEDICAL POLICY

—Additional Protocol to the European Agreement on the Exchange of Therapeutic Substances of Human Origin / Strasbourg : Council of Europe, 1983.
ISBN 9287101949 Hbk

—Additional Protocol to the European Agreement on the Exchanges of Blood-Grouping Reagents / Strasbourg : Council of Europe, 1983.
ISBN 9287101965

—Laws and policies affecting adolescent health / by John M. Paxman and Ruth Jane Zuckerman. - Geneva : World Health Organization, 1987.
x,300p.
Includes bibliographical references.
ISBN 9241560959

MEDICAL PROFESSION

—Legislation Concerning Nursing/Midwifery Services and Education : Report on a WHO Working Group (Hamburg, 1979) / Geneva : World Health Organization, 1981.
47p.
ISBN 9289012110 Hbk £4.00

—Nursing law and ethics / edited by A. Carmi and S. Schneider : by M.B. Agostino ... et al. - Berlin : Springer-Verlag, 1985.
ISBN 0387152539

—Sociology of the professions : lawyers, doctors and others / edited by Robert Dingwall and Philip Lewis. - London : Macmillan, 1983.
ix,314p; 23cm.
Bibliography: p286-306. - Includes index.
ISBN 0333309618 Hbk £15.00

MEDICAL PROFESSION - AUSTRALIA

—Law for Nurses / 3rd ed. - North Ryde : Law Book Co, 1983.
xi, 282p.
ISBN 0455204950 Pbk £28.50

—Law for the Medical Profession / Butterworths, 1988.
356p.
ISBN 040949318X Hbk £39.00

MEDICAL PROFESSION - CANADA

—Canadian Dental Law / Butterworths, 1987.
152p.
ISBN 0409863351 Hbk £40.00

—Insurance Law for General Practitioners / Vancouver : British Columbia Continuing Legal Education Society, 1980.
147p.

—Leasing for General Practitioners / Vancouver : Continuing Legal Education Society of British Columbia, 1986.
166p.
ISBN 0865042942 Hbk £65.00

—Sensenbrenner Hospital Employees Compensation Act, 1983, Bill 110 : An Act Respecting the Compensation of Certain Employees at Sensenbrenner Hospital in Kapuskasing / Ontario : Ontario Government Publications Service, 1983.
2p.

MEDICAL PROFESSION - ENGLAND

—Theatre nurse and the law / Eileen Dixon. - London : Croom Helm, 1984.
141p; 22cm.
Includes index.
ISBN 0709908180 Pbk £8.95

MEDICAL PROFESSION - GREAT BRITAIN

—Dentists Bill : report on the consolidation of the Dentists Acts 1957 to 1983 / The Law Commission and The Scottish Law Commission. - London : H.M.S.O., 1984.
5p; 25cm.
ISBN 0101911904

—Law and Health Visitors / London : B Edsall, 1982.
72p.
ISBN 0902623354 Pbk £3.00

—Medical Bill : draft report on the consolidation of the Medical Acts 1956 to 1978 and certain related provisions ... / the Law Commission and the Scottish Law Commission. - London : H.M.S.O., 1983.
11p; 25cm.
ISBN 0101883900

—Nurses, Midwives and Health Visitors Act 1979 / Welsh National Board for Nursing. - London : HMSO, 1983.

—Tax planning for medical practitioners / Stephen Burwood. - 2nd ed. - London : Butterworths, 1987.
ISBN 04066190054 Pbk £18.50

MEDICAL RECORDS

—Report of the Commission of Inquiry into the Confidentiality of Health Information / Horace Krever. - 3 v. - Toronto : Queen's Printer, 1980.
Commissioner: Horace Krever.
ISBN 0774355670

MEDICAL RESEARCH - GREAT BRITAIN

—Medical research : civil liability and compensation for personal injury : a discussion paper / chairman: David Evered. - London : Ciba Foundation, 1980.
16p.

—Medical research with children / Oxford : Oxford University Press, 1986.
ISBN 0192615289 Hbk £12.50

MEDICAL RESEARCH - SWEDEN

—Biomedical Research and Research Policy in Sweden / Stockholm : Almqvist & Wiksell, 1980.
16p.

MEDIEVAL LAW
—Authority and power : studies on medieval law and government presented to Walter Ullmann on his seventieth birthday / edited by Brian Tierney and Peter Linehan. – Cambridge : Cambridge University Press, 1980.
x,274p,1leaf of plates; 24cm.
Bibliography: p255-274.
ISBN 0521222753 £25.00

—Select cases of trespass from the King's Courts, 1307-1399 / Morris S. Arnold. – London : Selden Society, 1985.
lxxxv,179,179p; 26cm.
Opposite pages of main sequence bear duplicate numbering. Parallel Latin text and English translation.

MEDIEVAL LAW – ENGLAND
—Lawyers and laymen / edited by T.M. Charles-Edwards, Morfydd E. Owen and D. B. Walters. – Cardiff : University of Wales Press, 1986.
394,1p of plates; 23cm.
Bibliography: p355-368. - Includes index. Festschrift in honour of Professor Dafydd Jenkins. Includes two papers in Welsh.
ISBN 0708309259 £25.00

MEDITERRANEAN REGION
—European Community and the Mediterranean Basin : study on the consequences of the process of enlargement both for the Mediterranean zone and for the Community itself and the conditions necessary for the definition of a global and forward-looking policy of the Community towards the Mediterranean basin / Francois Duch$ene ... et al. – Luxembourg : Office for Official Publications of the European Communities, 1984.
175p.
At head of title page: Commission of the European Communities.
ISBN 9282547582

MEETINGS – AUSTRALIA
—Joske's law and procedure at meetings in Australia / by W.J. Chappenden. – 7th ed. – Sydney : Law Book Co., 1982.
xxiii,211p.
Includes index.
ISBN 0455205388

MEETINGS – AUSTRALIA – SOUTH AUSTRALIA
—Council Meetings Law and Procedures in South Australia / North Ryde : Law Book Co, 1980.
xxvii, 116p.
ISBN 0455201374 Pbk £26.00

MEETINGS – CANADA
—Conduct of Canadian Meetings : Company Law and Common Law / Toronto : Butterworths, 1983.
256p.
Explains the nature and purpose of meetings, the role of the players, and the proper procedures for the most successful progress of a meeting. Covers the chairman and secretary, notice, agenda, quorum, voting adjournment, motions and resolutions, minutes, the annual meeting, special share-holders meetings, directors and committee meetings.
ISBN 0409840653 Hbk £50.00

—Procedures for meetings and organizations / M. Kaye Kerr and Hubert W. King. – Agincourt, Ont. : Carswell Legal Publications, 1984.
xv, 313 p.; 24 cm.
Includes index. Bibliography: p. 276.
ISBN 0459361503

MEETINGS – ENGLAND
—Shackleton on the law and practice of meetings / I. Shearman. – 7th ed. – London : Sweet & Maxwell, 1983.
xxix,368p; 23cm.
Previous ed.: 1977. Includes index.
ISBN 0421296305 £17.00

MEETINGS – GREAT BRITAIN
—Conduct of Meetings / 22nd ed. – Bristol : Jordan & Sons Ltd, 1982.
ISBN 0907313019 Pbk £6.00

—How to make meetings work / London : Kogan Page, 1988.
ISBN 0850915077 Pbk

—How to run committees and meetings / London : Macmillan, 1982.
ISBN 0333207533 Hbk £33.00
ISBN 0333290356 Pbk £4.95

—Law and Procedure of Meetings / London : Sweet & Maxwell, 1983.
– (Concise College Texts Ser.).
ISBN 0421253401 Pbk £7.50

—Meetings / 3rd ed. – Plymouth : Macdonald & Evans, 1984.
ISBN 0712104496 Pbk £5.95

—Meetings : Law and Practice / Rigby. – 4th ed. – Plymouth : Macdonald & Evans, 1987.
ISBN 0712113002 Pbk £6.50

—Points of Order / 4th ed. – London : Shaw & Sons, 1987.
ISBN 0721904025 Pbk £4.95

MEETINGS – INDIA
—Law of companies and meetings / B.A. Masodkar. – Bombay : Tripathi, 1984.
xxxii,263p.

MEETINGS – NEW ZEALAND
—Law of Meetings / Butterworths, 1980.
ISBN 040963560X Pbk £54.45

—Law of Meetings / Paul. – New Zealand ed. – London : Butterworths, 1981.
ISBN 040963560X Pbk £23.50

MENS REA – ENGLAND
—Mens Rea : Imputability Under the Law of England / Repr. of 1914 ed. – Abingdon : Professional Books.
345p.

MENS REA – SCOTLAND
—Mental element in crime : report on a reference under section 3(1)(e) of the Law Commissions Act 1965 / Scottish Law Commission. – Edinburgh : H.M.S.O., 1983.
v,48p.
Includes bibliographical references.
ISBN 0101904703

MENTAL HEALTH
—Ethics and mental retardation / edited by Loretta Kopelman and John C. Moskop. – Dordrecht : D. Reidel, 1984.
xvi, 258p.
Includes index.
ISBN 9027716307

—Mental illness : law and public policy / edited by Baruch A. Brody and H. Tristram Engelhardt, Jr. – Dordrecht : Reidel, 1980.
xvii,254p; 23cm. – (Philosophy and medicine).
Includes index.
ISBN 9027710570 Unpriced

MENTAL HEALTH – AUSTRALIA
—Mental health and the law / by John O'Sullivan. – Sydney : Law Book Co., 1981.
xiv,200p.
Includes index.
ISBN 0455203601

—Mental retardation : law, policy and administration / by Susan C. Hayes and Robert Hayes : with a foreword by M. D. Kirby. – North Ryde : Law Book Co, 1982.
xxviii,428p.
Includes index.
ISBN 0455204691 Pbk
ISBN 0455204705

MENTAL HEALTH – AUSTRALIA – AUSTRALIAN CAPITAL TERRITORY
—Proposed A.C.T. Mental Health Ordinance 1981 / Human Rights Commission. – Canberra : Australian Government Publishing Service, 1982.
vii,44p. – (Report).
ISBN 0644022477

MENTAL HEALTH – CANADA
—Mental Disability and the Law in Canada / Agincourt : Carswell, 1987.
518p.
This work contains a discussion of the common law and legislation of Canada's common law jurisdictions relating to the effect of mental disability on legal rights and liabilities. Topics include committees of estate and personal guardians, contracts, succession, tort liability, family law issues, the right to vote, discrimination and the Charter, litigation, admission to, and rights of patients in, mental health facilities.

—Mental Health Law in Canada / Carla A. McKague. – Butterworths, 1987.
384p.
Assesses legal tools available to combat discrimination in employment, and against former psychiatric patients, analyses Lieutenant Governor Warrants, and offers procedural reforms to have them comply with Charter provisions, and includes recent human rights legislation and compares provincial human rights code provisions to those in the Charter.
ISBN 0409865095 Hbk £60.00

—Tentative proposals for a compulsory mental health care act / Law Reform Commission of Saskatchewan. – Saskatoon : Law Reform Commission of Saskatchewan, 1981.
46,xlixp.

MENTAL HEALTH – CANADA – ONTARIO
—Social Work : Annotated Ontario Mental Health Statutes / Agincourt : Carswell, 1988.
358p.

MENTAL HEALTH – CANADA – SASKATCHEWAN
—Proposals for a compulsory mental health care act : report to the Minister of Justice / Law Reform Commission of Saskatchewan. – Saskatoon : The Commission, 1985.
40p.
Includes bibliographical references.

MENTAL HEALTH – ENGLAND
—Biennial report of the Mental Health Act Commission / laid before Parliament by the Secretary of State for Social Services pursuant to Section 121(10) of the Mental Health Act 1983. – London : H.M.S.O., 1985-.

—Consent to treatment / Mental Health Act Commission. – London : The Commission, 1985.
43p.

—Mental disorder and legal control / Philip Bean. – Cambridge : Cambridge University Press, 1986.
304p.
Includes bibliographical references and index.
ISBN 0521302099 £27.50

—Mental Health Act manual / edited by Richard M. Jones. – 2nd ed. – London : Sweet & Maxwell, 1988.
339p; 25cm.
Includes the Mental Health Act 1983, Mental Health Tribunal Rules 1983, Mental Health (Hospitals, Guardianship and Consent to Treatment) Regulations 1983, Court of Protection Rules 1984, and DHSS and Mental Health Act Commission Circulars.
ISBN 0421393300 Pbk £19.50

—Mental health law / Brenda M. Hoggett. – 2nd ed. – London : Sweet & Maxwell, 1984.
xxiv,370p; 22cm.
Account of the basic legal rights of psychiatric patients before, during and after hospital confinement. Explains Mental Health Tribunals, and the Court of Protection. Also covers the Mental Health Act 1983.
ISBN 0421302208 Pbk £12.95

—Mental illness and the law / Tony Whitehead. – Oxford : Basil Blackwell, 1982.
viii,181p; 23cm.
Includes index.
ISBN 0631127216 Hbk Unpriced
ISBN 0631126155 Pbk Unpriced

—Politics of mental health legislation / Clive Unsworth. – Oxford : Clarendon, 1987.
384p; 22cm.
Includes bibliography and index.
ISBN 0198255128 £30.00

—Practical guide to mental health law : the Mental Health Act 1983 and related legislation / Larry Gostin : foreword by Lady Bingley : edited by Janet Manning. – Rev ed. – London : MIND, 1983.
xvi,102p; 21cm.
Bibliography: p77-78.
ISBN 0900557591 Pbk Unpriced

—Reform of mental health legislation / Department of Health and Social Security ... et al. – London : H.M.S.O., 1981.
26p; 25cm.
ISBN 0101840500 Pbk £2.65

—Representing the mentally ill and handicapped : a guide to Mental Health Review Tribunals / Larry Gostin and Elaine Rassaby : with a foreword by Tom Harper. – Sunbury : Quartermine House Ltd for National Association for Mental Health and the Legal Action Group, 1980.
xix,215p; 21cm.
Bibliography: p.209. - Includes index.

MENTAL HEALTH – GREAT BRITAIN
—Court of protection : a legal and policy analysis of the guardianship of the estate / Larry Gostin : foreword by Peter Jefferys. – London : Mind, National Association for Mental Health, 1983.
60p.
Bibliography: p.48.
ISBN 0900557567

—Draft guidelines for approval of social workers under the proposed Mental Health (Amendment) Act : Working Party draft for consultation / Department of Health and Social Security. – London : The Department, 1981.
11p.

—Law of mental health / London : Fourmat, 1990.
244; 22.
ISBN 1851900837 Pbk

—Mental Health Act 1983 : memorandum on Parts I to VI, VIII and X / Great Britain. – London : D.H.S.S., 1983.
iv,85p.

—Mental Health Act 1983 : section 118 : draft code of practice / Great Britain. – London : Mental Health Division, Department of Health and Social Security, 1985.
236p.
Includes index.

—Mental Health Act, 1983 : Summary of Procedural Requirements in Respect of Compulsory Admission to Hospital and Guardianship, Pt. II / London : Shaw & Sons, 1983.
ISBN 0721901964 Hbk £0.80

—Mental Health Act Manual / 2nd ed. – London : Sweet & Maxwell, 1988.
ISBN 0421393300 Pbk £21.00

—Mental Health Procedural Tables / London : Shaw & Sons, 1983.
ISBN 0721901964 Pbk £0.80

—Mental Health Services - Law and Practice / London : Shaw & Sons, 1986.
912p.
ISBN 0721901972 Hbk £85.00

—Mental Health Services : Law and Practice / London : Shaw & Sons, 1986.
ISBN 0721901972 £85.30

—Mental health, social policy and the law / London : Macmillan, 1985.
ISBN 0333373014 Hbk £25.00

—Mental Health-Tribunal Procedure / London : Longman Professional, 1984.
ISBN 0851208444 Pbk £14.95

—Mental Health : Tribunal Procedure / London : Oyez Longman, 1984.
– (Oyez Longman Practice Note Ser.: No. 78).
ISBN 0851208444 Hbk

—Notes on the Mental Health Act 1983 / London : Shaw & Sons, 1983.
ISBN 0721902049 Pbk £1.95

—Notes on the Mental Health Act Nineteen Eighty-Three / London : Shaw & Sons, 1984.
ISBN 0721902049 Pbk £1.95

—Secure provision / Tavistock, 1985.
ISBN 0422784303 Pbk £7.95

MENTAL HEALTH - IRELAND

—Report on the liability in tort of mentally disabled persons / the Law Reform Commission. – Dublin : The Commission, 1985.
v,78p. – (LRC).
Bibliography: p.75.

MENTAL HEALTH - NEW ZEALAND

—Mental health : a case for reform / papers presented by John Dawson ... et al. – Auckland : Legal Research Foundation, 1986.
161p.
Includes bibliographical references. At head of t.p.: Legal Research Foundation Inc., Seminar, 5 September 1986.
ISBN 0908581432
ISBN 0908581432

MENTAL HEALTH - NORTHERN IRELAND

—Guide to the Mental Health (NI) Order 1986 / Belfast : Queen's University of Belfast, 1986.
150p.

MENTAL HEALTH - SOUTH AFRICA

—Mental Health Law in South Africa / Durban : Butterworths, 1980.
ISBN 0409037540 Hbk

MENTAL HEALTH - UNITED STATES

—Legal rights and mental-health care / Stanley S. Herr, Stephen Arons, Richard E. Wallace. – Lexington, Mass. : Lexington Books, 1983.
xv,180p; 24cm.
Includes index.
ISBN 0669049107 £19.50

—Mental health law : major issues / David B. Wexler. – New York : Plenum, 1981.
x,270p; 24cm.
Includes index.
ISBN 0306405385 Unpriced

MENTAL HEALTH REVIEW TRIBUNALS - GREAT BRITAIN

—Mental Health-Tribunal Procedure / London : Longman Professional, 1984.
ISBN 0851208444 Pbk £14.95

—Tribunals on trial: a study of decision-making under the Mental Health Review Tribunals. Based on empirical enquiry into the operation of the Tribunal system, assesses the process of decision-making from the initial application by a patiTribunals on trial: a study of decision-making under the Mental Health Act 1983 / Oxford : Clarendon Press, 1989.
240; 21.5.
Insight into the decision-making processes of the Mental Health Review Tribunals. Based on empirical enquiry into the operation of the Tribunal system, assesses the process of decision-making from the initial application by a patient, through descriptions of tribunal hearings, to an examination of their deliberations. Examines individual cases in detail.
ISBN 0198252498 Hbk £25.00

MENTAL PATIENTS - GREAT BRITAIN

—Secure Provision for Mental Patients / London : Sweet & Maxwell, 1985.
ISBN 0422784206 Hbk £16.95
ISBN 0422784303 Pbk £7.95

MENTALLY HANDICAPPED

—Advocacy and Mental Handicap / Raquel Schuster-Herr. – Brussels : International League of Societies for Persons with Mental Handicap, 1984.

MENTALLY HANDICAPPED - AUSTRALIA - VICTORIA

—Rape and allied offences : victims with impaired mental functioning / Law Reform Commission of Victoria. – Melbourne : The Commission, 1987.
39p. – (Discussion paper).
Includes bibliographical references.
ISBN 0724167064

—Sexual offences against people with impaired mental functioning / Law Reform Commission of Victoria. – Melbourne : The Commission, 1988.
ii,52p. – (Report no 15).
ISBN 0724167153 Hbk

MENTALLY HANDICAPPED - CANADA

—Mental Disability and the Law in Canada / Agincourt : Carswell, 1987.
450p.

MENTALLY ILL

—Lack of Discretion of Judgment because of Schizophrenia : Doctrine and Recent Rotal Jurisprudence / Rome : Editrice Pontificia Universitana Gregoriana, 1986.
256p.

—Rights of mentally ill people / Chris Heginbotham. – London : Minority Rights Group, 1987.
12p. – (Report).
ISBN 0946690499

MENTALLY ILL - AUSTRALIA - VICTORIA

—Rape and allied offences : victims with impaired mental functioning / Law Reform Commission of Victoria. – Melbourne : The Commission, 1987.
39p. – (Discussion paper).
Includes bibliographical references.
ISBN 0724167064

MENTALLY ILL - CANADA

—Mental Disability and the Law in Canada / Agincourt : Carswell, 1987.
518p.
This work contains a discussion of the common law and legislation of Canada's common law jurisdictions relating to the effect of mental disability on legal rights and liabilities. Topics include committees of estate and personal guardians, contracts, succession, tort liability, family law issues, the right to vote, discrimination and the Charter, litigation, admission to, and rights of patients in, mental health facilities.

—Mental disorder and the criminal trial process / Scarborough, Ontario : Butterworths (Canada), 1978.
368.
Focuses on legal problems and procedures peculiar to the use of psychiatric expertise at the pre-trial and trial stages. Fitness to stand trial, 'psychiatric defences', and the consequences of a determination of abnormality are discussed.
ISBN 0409865605 Hbk

MENTALLY ILL - GREAT BRITAIN

—Dangerous behaviour, the law, and mental disorder / Herschel Prins. – London : Tavistock, 1986.
xiii,258p; 20cm. – (Social science paperback).
Includes bibliographies and index.
ISBN 0422792209 Pbk £6.95

—Offenders, deviants, or patients? : an introduction to the study of socio-forensic problems / Herschel Prins. – London : Tavistock Publications, 1980.
viii,369p.
Bibliographies.
ISBN 0422768006

—Prosecution of the Mentally Disturbed / D. Chiswick. – Aberdeen : Aberdeen University Press, 1984.
192p.
ISBN 0080284817 Hbk £16.50

MENTALLY ILL - JAPAN

—Human rights and mental patients in Japan : report of a mission by Dr. T. W. Harding, Judge J. Schneider, Dr. H. M. Visotsky and Dr. C. L. Graves on behalf of the International Commission of Jurists and the International Commission of Health Professionals / T.W. Harding. – Geneva : International Commission of Jurists, 1985.
94p.
Bibliography: p.87-93.
ISBN 9290370327

MERCENARIES

—Mercenarism and international law / Chief R. O. A. Akinjide. – s.l. : s.n., 1986.
13p.
Lecture delivered at the International Law Seminar, Palais des nations, Geneva, on 27.5.1986.

METHODOLOGY

—Automated analysis of legal texts : logic, informatics, law : edited versions of selected papers from the Second International Conference on 'Logic, Informatics, Law,'Florence, Italy, September 1985 / edited by Antonio A. Martino, Fiorenza Socci Natali : editorial assistant, Simona Binazzi. – Amsterdam : North-Holland, 1986.
xxii, 938 p.; 25 cm.
Includes bibliographies and index.
ISBN 0444701117

—Development of ethnography in Britain : paper prepared for presentation at the BSA Annual Conference, Lancaster, 1980 / Robert Dingwall, Geoff Payne, Judy Payne. – Oxford : Centre for Socio-Legal Studies, 1980.
19,2p.
Bibliography: p.20-21.

—Dilemmas of law in the welfare state / edited by Gunther Teubner. – Berlin : W. de Gruyter, 1986.
viii,341p. – (Series A, Law).
Includes bibliographies and index.
ISBN 0899251080

—Judging : towards a rational judicial process / H. J. M. Boukema. – Zwolle, Holland : W.E.J. Tjeenk Willink, 1980.
xvi,181p.
Includes index. Bibliography: p141-148.
ISBN 9027117276

—Justice, law, and argument : essays on moral and legal reasoning / Ch. Perelman : with an intod. by Harold J. Berman. – Dordrecht, Holland : D. Reidel Pub. Co., 1980.
xiii,181p.
Includes bibliographical references and index.
ISBN 9027710902 pbk.

—Man, law, and modern forms of life / edited by Eugenic Bulygin, Jean-Louis Gardies, and Ilkka Niiniluoto : introduction by Michael D. Bayles. – Dordrecht Netherlands : D. Reidel, 1985.
'Proceedings of the 11th IVR World Congress on Philosophy of Law and Social Philosophy ... held on August 14-20, 1983 in Helsinki'–Introd. Includes bibliographies and index.
ISBN 9027718695 Hbk £39.50

—Rational as reasonable : a treatise on legal justification / Aulis Aarnio. – Dordrecht : D. Reidel, 1986.
xix, 276p.
Includes index. Bibliography: p 261-271.
ISBN 9027722765 Hbk

—Rules of sociological method and selected texts on sociology and its method / Emile Durkheim : edited with an introduction by Steven Lukes : translated by W. D. Halls. – London : Macmillan, 1982.
vi,264p.
ISBN 0333280717

METROPOLITAN GOVERNMENT

—Government and administration of metropolitan areas in Western democracies : a survey of approaches to the administrative problems of major conurbations in Europe and Canade / Alan Norton. – Birmingham : Institute of Local Government Studies, University of Birmingham, 1983.
60 p.
ISBN 070440690X

—Models of organisation for the government of conurbations : report / prepared under the guidance of the Committee of Experts on Local and Regional Structures of the Steering Committee for Regional and Municipal Matters by Finn Bruun. – Strasbourg : Council of Europe, 1986.
24p; 30cm.

METROPOLITAN GOVERNMENT - ENGLAND

—Streamlining the cities : government proposals for reorganising local government in Greater London and the metropolitan counties / presented to Parliament by the Secretary of State for the Environment ... – London : H.M.S.O., 1983.
31p.
ISBN 0101906307

MICROCOMPUTERS - GREAT BRITAIN

—Businessman's Guide to Microcomputers / Haskins. – 2nd ed. – London : Butterworths, 1984.
ISBN 0406016003 Pbk £9.00

MICROELECTRONICS - GREAT BRITAIN

—Learning to live with IT : an overview of the potential of information technology for education and training / Information Technology Advisory Panel. – London : H.M.S.O., 1986.
44p.
ISBN 0116308311

MICROFORM CATALOGUES
—Canadian legal materials in microform / compiled by Meena Nadkarni. – Downsview, Ont. : York University Law Library in co-operation with the Canadian Association of Law Libraries, 1981.

MIGRANT LABOUR
—Migrant workers and civil liberties / by Alexis Pauly and Rene Diederich. – Florence : European University Institute, 1983.
102p.

MIGRANT LABOUR – AUSTRALIA
—Law for Migrant Welfare Workers / North Sydney : Allen & Unwin, 1983.
112p.
ISBN 0868610380 Hbk £19.95
ISBN 0868610461 Pbk £12.95

MIGRANT LABOUR – EUROPE
—Western Europe's migrant workers / by Jonathan Power in collaboration with Anna Hardman. – 2nd rev. ed. – London : Minority Rights Group, 1984.
35p. – (Report).
Bibliography: p.34.
ISBN 0946690197

MILITARY DISCIPLINE – GREAT BRITAIN
—Special report from the Select Committee on the Armed Forces Bill / London : H.M.S.O., 1981.
xix,130p.
ISBN 0102253811 £7.00

MILITARY GOVERNMENT – NIGERIA
—Constitutional law and military rule in Nigeria / Abiola Ojo. – Ibadan, Nigeria : Evans Brothers, 1987.
vii,316p.
ISBN 9781675691

—Legal impact of the Constitution (Suspension and Modification) Decree, 1984 : on the constitution of the Federal Republic of Nigeria, 1979 / Niki Tobi. – Calabar, Nigeria : Centaur Press, 1985.
xi,110p.
Includes the text of the Constitution (Suspension and Modification) Decree 1984.

MILITARY LAW
—Study and Practice of Military Law / New Delhi : Deep and Deep Publications, 1988.
496p.
ISBN 8171000126 Hbk £250.00

MILITARY LAW – AUSTRALIA
—Some aspects of aid to the civil power in Australia / B.D. Beddie and S. Moss. – Canberra : Department of Government, University of New South Wales, 1982.
92p. – (Occasional monograph).
ISBN 0959325409

MILITARY LAW – GREAT BRITAIN
—Special report from the Select Committee on the Armed Forces Bill / London : H.M.S.O., 1981.
xix,130p.
ISBN 0102253811 £7.00

MILITARY LAW – INDIA
—Law Relating to Cantonments / Allahabad : Law Publishers, 1980.

—Military Law in India : a Commentary / C.G. Goel. – New Delhi : Deep and Deep Publications, 1984.
450p.

MINERAL INDUSTRIES
—Application of new legal techniques to mining agreements in developing countries / by Carl W. Dundas. – London : Commonwealth Secretariat, 1981.
46p.
Includes bibliographical references.

—Foreign investment in mining projects : case studies of recent experiences / Raymond F. Mikesell : a project sponsored and administered by the FMME. – Cambridge, Mass. : Oelgeschlager, Gunn & Hain, 1983.
xv,297p; 24cm.
Bibliography: p281-285. - Includes index.
ISBN 0899461700 Unpriced

—Legal and institutional arrangements in minerals developments : a study based on an international workshop organised in Berlin (West) in August 1980 by the Department of Technical Co-operation for Development, United Nations, and the Development Policy Forum of the German Foundation for International Development / London : Mining Journal Books, 1982.
xi,224p; 23cm.
ISBN 090011729X Pbk Unpriced

MINERS' STRIKE, 1984–85 – GREAT BRITAIN
—Some legal issues arising out of the miners' strike 1984/5 / Dawn Oliver. – London : Faculty of Laws, University College London, 1985.
26p. – (Working papers).
Includes bibliographical references. Edited by Dawn Oliver. Caption title.

MINING
—Contractual adaptation and conflict resolution, based on venture contracts for mining projects in developing countries / Martin Bartels : translation by James E. Silva. – Deventer, Netherlands : Kluwer Law and Taxation, 1985.
187 p.; 25 cm. – (Studies in transnational law of natural resources).
Includes bibliographical references. 'List of cited agreements': p. 177-187.
ISBN 3787540237

—Indigenous Resource Rights and Mining Companies in North America and Australia, February 1986 / G.J. Crough. – Kingston : Australian Government Publishing Service, 1986.
132p.
ISBN 0644046392 Hbk £7.60

—Joint development of resources projects : a comparison : proceedings of the Regional Energy Law Seminar, Singapore, 30 September 1985 / International Bar Association. Section on Energy and Natural Resources Law. – London : International Bar Assocation, 1985.
Various pagings.

—Joint Venture Agreement for Seabed Mining / Dordrecht : Kluwer.
127p.
ISBN 9065440135 Hbk £44.00

—Law of Deep Sea-Bed Mining : a Study of the Progressive Development of International Law Concerning the Management of the Polymetallic Nodules of the Deep Sea-Bed / Stockholm : Almqvist & Wiksell, 1987.
356p.
ISBN 9122011560 Hbk £525.00

—Legal Regime for Deep Seabed Mining under the Law of the Sea Convention / Frankfurt : Alfred Metzner, 1984.
ISBN 3787540180 Hbk £98.00

—Legal Regime for Deep Seabed Mining under the Law of the Sea Convention / Dordrecht : Kluwer, 1983.
250p.
ISBN 9065441166 Hbk £107.00

—Mining and environmental law : proceedings of the seminar held at Washington D.C., 4-8 April 1982, ... organised by the Committee on Environmental Law, Section on Business Law, of the International Bar Association, in conjunction with the American Law Institute-American Bar Association Committee on Continuing Professional Education / 2. – London : International Bar Association, 1982.
ISBN 0950587648

—Mining ventures in developing countries / Erich Schanze. – Deventer : Kluwer, 1981.
281p.
First published: Frankfurt am Main, Metzner; Deventer, Kluwer; 1977- , as 'Rohstofferschliessungsvorhaben in Entwicklungslandern'. Translated from German into English.
ISBN 9065440380

—World coal mining law : a comparative survey / edited by Ronald V. Cowles. – 2. – London : International Bar Association, 1984.
At foot of t.p.: Section on Energy and National Resources Law, International Bar Association.

MINING – AFRICA
—Study on the legislative framework, agreements and financial impositions affecting the mining industry in African Commonwealth countries / prepared for the Commonwealth Fund for Technical Co-operation by Macbul Rahim and Juliet Broad under the supervision of Roland Brown and Mike Faber. – 1. – London : Commonwealth Secretariat, 1981.
various pagings.
Cover title: The legislative framework, agreements and financial impositions affecting the mining industry in African Commonwealth countries.

MINING – AUSTRALIA
—A.M.P.L.A. Yearbook / Melbourne : Australian Mining and Petroleum Law Association.
600p.

—Aborigines and Mining Royalties in the Northern Territory / Canberra City : Australian Institute of Aboriginal Studies, 1983.
182p.
ISBN 0855751495 Hbk £11.95

—Australian Mining and Petroleum Law Association yearbook / . – Melbourne : The Association, 1983.
Includes index.
ISBN 0812857X

—Australian Mining and Petroleum Laws / A. J. Lang. – 2nd ed. – Sydney : Butterworths, 1987.
360p.
This reference describes the Petroleum (Submerged Lands) Act 1982, the Mining Act 1983 (NT), the Petroleum Act 1984 (NT), the Mining Act 1978-81 (WA), the Mining Amendment Act 1985 (WA). Also included are materials on environmental law and joint ventures.

—Australian Mining and Petroleum Laws Introduction / J.R.S. Forbes. – 2nd ed. – Butterworths, 1987.
375p.
ISBN 0409492159 Hbk £59.00

—Index of A.M.P.L.A. Yearbooks 1977-1987 / Melbourne : Australian Mining and Petroleum Law Association.
ISBN 0958991839 Hbk £35.00

—Indigenous Resource Rights and Mining Companies in North America and Australia, February 1986 / G.J. Crough. – Kingston : Australian Government Publishing Service, 1986.
132p.
ISBN 0644046392 Hbk £7.60

—Uranium Mining Laws in the Northern Territory / Uranium Advisory Council. – Canberra : Australian Government Publishing Service, 1981.
177p.
ISBN 0642068607 Hbk £6.60

MINING – CANADA
—Aboriginal Title and Mining Legislation in the Northwest Territories / Saskatoon : University of Saskatchewan, Native Law Centre, 1982.
32p.
ISBN 0888801149 Hbk £8.00

—Canadian Mining Law, 6 vols / Toronto : Butterworths.

—Canadian mining taxation / Robert B. Parsons. – Toronto : Butterworths, 1982.
x,253p.
ISBN 0409859745

—Mining Act, 1983, Bill 129 : An Act to Revise the Mining Act / Ontario : Ontario Government Publications Service, 1983.
90p.

—Mining Exploration Agreements / Montreal : Canadian Institute of Mining and Metallurgy.

—Mining Law, 1983 / Vancouver : British Columbia Continuing Legal Education Society, 1983.
760p.
ISBN 0865041377 Hbk £85.00

—Mining Law : 1986 / Vancouver : Continuing Legal Education Society of British Columbia, 1986.
330p.
ISBN 0865042861 Hbk £85.00

—Reference Guide to Mining Legislation in Canada / 2nd ed. – Calgary : Canadian Institute of Resources Law, 1988.
120p.
ISBN 0919269257 Hbk £30.00

—Teco Mines and Oils Limited Act, 1983, Bill Pr052 : An Act to Revive Teco Mines and Oils Limited / Ontario : Ontario Government Publications Service, 1983.
2p.

MINING – GREAT BRITAIN
—History and practice of the law of mines and minerals / Jean Cantlie Stewart. – Banff : Rowan Books, 1987.
ISBN 0950993212

MINING – NEW ZEALAND
—Outline of mining law : paper presented at Auckland Law Faculty Seminar Series 1982 at University of Auckland / by Kenneth Palmer. – Auckland : Legal Research Foundation Inc., 1982.
29p.
ISBN 0908581254

MINING – PACIFIC
—Study on the legislative framework, agreements and financial impositions affecting the mining industry in Pacific Commonwealth countries / by Macbul Rahim and Ruckia Hamisi. – 1. – London : Commonwealth Secretariat, 1981.
various pagings.
Cover title: The legislative framework, agreements and financial impositions affecting the mining industry in Pacific Commonwealth countries.

MINING – PAKISTAN
—Mining Labour Code / 6th ed. – Karachi : Bureau of Labour Publications, 1987.
315p.

MINING – SOUTH AFRICA
—Mining and mineral laws of South Africa / by Blen Lloyd Stuart Franklin and Morris Kaplan. – Durban : Butterworths, 1982.
Bibliography: p.lxxvii-lxxviii. - Includes index.
ISBN 0409028983 Hbk R335

MINING – UNITED STATES
—Legal aspects of geology / Ronald W. Tank. – New York : Plenum, 1983.
xii,583p; 24cm.
Includes bibliographies and index.
ISBN 0306411598 Hbk Unpriced
ISBN 0306412152 Pbk Unpriced

MINING - ZAMBIA
—Mines and Minerals Act, 1969, and the Mineral Tax Act, 1970 / E.J. Langevad. – Lusaka : Geological Survey of Zambia.

MINORITIES - BULGARIA
—Bulgaria : imprisonment of ethnic Turks : human rights abuses during the forced assimilation of the ethnic Turkish minority / Amnesty International. – London : Amnesty International, 1986.
40p.
ISBN 0862100976

MINORS - AUSTRALIA - WESTERN AUSTRALIA
—Report on minors' contracts / the Law Reform Commission of Western Australia. – Perth : Law Reform Commission of Western Australia, 1988.
117p. – (Project).

MISCARRIAGE OF JUSTICE
—Rough justice / Martin Young & Peter Hill. – London : British Broadcasting Corporation, 1983.
176p,4p of plates; 20cm. – (Ariel books).
ISBN 0563201290 Pbk £1.95

MISCARRIAGE OF JUSTICE - ENGLAND
—Government reply to the Sixth report from the Home Affairs Committee, session 1981-82, HC421 : miscarriages of justice / London : H.M.S.O., 1983.
6p; 25cm.
ISBN 0101885601 unbound £1.30

—Miscarriages of justice / Bob Woffinden. – London : Hodder & Stoughton, 1987.
xiii,376p; 24cm.
Bibliography: p367. - Includes index.
ISBN 0340374209 £14.95

—Sixth report from the Home Affairs Committee, session 1981-82 : miscarriages of justice : together with proceedings of the Committee, the minutes of evidence and appendix / London : H.M.S.O., 1982.
xix,69p. – (HC).
ISBN 010242182X

MISCONDUCT IN OFFICE - GREAT BRITAIN
—Conduct unbecoming / London : Tavistock Publications, 1985.
ISBN 0422792101 Pbk £7.95

—Conduct Unbecoming : The Social Construction of Police Deviance and Control / London : Tavistock Publications, 1985.
300p.
ISBN 0422792101 Pbk £7.95

MISSING PERSONS - CHILE
—Where is William Beausire? : disappearance in Chile / Amnesty International. – London : Amnesty International, 1981.
57p.

MISTAKE - CANADA
—Benefits Conferred Under a Mistake of Law / Victoria : Government of British Columbia, 1981.

MISTAKE (LAW) - AUSTRALIA - NEW SOUTH WALES
—Community law reform program / New South Wales Law Reform Commission. – Sydney : Government Printer, 1987.
xiii,95p. – (L.R.C).
Bibliography: pp.79-81. Includes text of draft bill.
ISBN 073054429X

1st report : Insurance contracts : non-disclosure and misrepresentation / New South Wales Law Reform Commission. – 1983.
61p. – (L.R.C. 34).

MISTAKE (LAW) - AUSTRALIA - SOUTH AUSTRALIA
—Report ... relating to the effect of mistake upon contracts / Law Reform Committee of South Australia. – Adelaide : Government Printer, 1987.
112p. – (106th report).
Bibliography: p.109-112.

—Report ... relating to the irrecoverability of benefits obtained by reason of mistake of law / Law Reform Committee of South Australia. – Adelaide : Government Printer, 1984.
40p. – (84th report).

MOBILE HOMES - ENGLAND
—Mobile homes and the law / by C.M. Brand. – London : Sweet & Maxwell, 1986.
xxiv,210p; 26cm.
Includes index.
ISBN 0421334703 £24.00

MOBILE HOMES - GREAT BRITAIN
—Law Relating to Mobile Homes and Caravans / 2nd ed. – London : Shaw & Sons, 1985.
Orig. Title : Caravans and the Law.
ISBN 072190811X Pbk £10.50

—Law Relating to Mobile Homes and Caravans / London : Shaw & Sons, 1985.
ISBN 072190811X Pbk £10.50

—Mobile Homes : An Occupier's Guide / London : Shelter, 1988.

MONETARY POLICY
—International monetary system and the less developed countries / Graham Bird. – 2nd ed. – London : Macmillan, 1982.
xi,352p.
Bibliography: p331-350.
ISBN 0333330021

MONETARY POLICY - CANADA
—Monetary policy : finding a place to stand / Gerald K. Bouey. – Toronto : Per Jacobsson Foundation, 1983.
v,28p.
Lecture delivered at the University of Toronto, 5 September 1982.

MONETARY POLICY - SOUTH AFRICA
—Monetary system and monetary policy in South Africa : final report of the Commission of Inquiry into the Monetary System and Monetary Policy in South Africa / South Africa. – Pretoria : Government Printer, 1985.
1 vol. (various pagings).
Chairman: G. P. C. de Kock. Included in: South Africa. Parliament. House of Assembly. Votes and proceedings; (with printed annexures). Report no. RP70/1984.
ISBN 0621090336

MONETARY UNIONS
—International financial integration : the limits of sovereignty / David T. Llewellyn. – London : Macmillan, 1980.
xii,215p; 24cm.
Includes bibliographies and index.
ISBN 0333167155 Pbk £12.00
ISBN 0333211303 Pbk £4.95

—International Monetary Fund 1972-1978 : Cooperation on trial / edited by Margaret Garritsen de Vries. – 3 v. – Washington, D.C. : International Monetary Fund, 1985.
Vols.I and II: Narrative and analysis. Vol.III: Documents.
ISBN 0939934434

MONEY
—Economics of the Euro-market : history, theory and policy / R. B. Johnston. – London : Macmillan, 1983.
x,321p.
Bibliography: p308-316.
ISBN 0333334183

—International money and the real world / Paul Davidson. – London : Macmillan, 1982.
XI,312p.

—Legal and institutional aspects of the International Monetary System : selected essays / Washington, D.C. : International Monetary Fund, 1984.
xviii,947p.
Includes bibliographies and index.
ISBN 0939934345

—Legal aspect of money : with special reference to comparative private and public international law / by F.A. Mann. – 4th ed. – Oxford : Clarendon, 1982.
lvi,602p; 25cm.
Previous ed.: Oxford : Oxford University Press, 1971. Bibliography: pliv. - Includes index.
ISBN 0198253672 £35.00

—Standard Catalog of World Paper Money / Munich : Ernst Battenberg, 1983.
959p.

—Swap agreement documentation / Klein. – London : Euromoney, 1987.
ISBN 1870031717 Pbk £110.00

—Swap Finance / London : Euromoney, 1987.
Service.
ISBN 0903121875 Pbk £75.00

MONEY - EUROPEAN COMMUNITY
—European monetary system--past, present, and future / by Peter Coffey. – 2nd rev. ed. – Dordrecht : Kluwer, 1987.
x,163p.
Includes bibliographical references and index.
ISBN 9024734460

MONEY - GREAT BRITAIN
—Legal Aspect of Money / 4th ed. – Oxford : Oxford University Press, 1982.
ISBN 0198253672 Hbk £45.00

—Plastic and Electronic Money / Cambridge : Woodhead-Faulkner, 1985.
ISBN 0859412903 Hbk £40.00

—Sterling commercial paper market / Cambridge : Woodhead-Faulkner, 1988.
ISBN 0859414108 Hbk £40.00

MONEY - SOUTH AFRICA
—Monetary system and monetary policy in South Africa : final report of the Commission of Inquiry into the Monetary System and Monetary Policy in South Africa / South Africa. – Pretoria : Government Printer, 1985.
1 vol. (various pagings).
Chairman: G. P. C. de Kock. Included in: South Africa. Parliament. House of Assembly. Votes and proceedings; (with printed annexures). Report no. RP70/1984.
ISBN 0621090336

MONEY MARKET
—International financial markets / Cambridge : Woodhead-Faulkner, 1988.
ISBN 085941440X Hbk £35.00

—Law of borrowing / London : Sweet & Maxwell, 1989.
Account of the institutional framework within which borrowing takes place, and consideration of the regulation and supervision of banks, building societies, the securities market, the wholesale money market, and consumer credit transactions. Chapter dealing with the characteristics of a loan, and types of loan.
ISBN 0421000000 Llf

—Wardley guide to world money and securities markets / by Lynette J. Kemp. – London : Euromoney Publications, 1984.
xvii,472p.
ISBN 0903121662

MONEY MARKET - ASIA
—Asian Capital and Money Markets / Message. – London : Butterworths, 1988.
ISBN 0406103607 Hbk

—Kemp and Message : Asian Capital and Money Markets / London : Butterworths, 1987.
ISBN 0406103607 Hbk

MONEY MARKET - ENGLAND
—London money market / E.R. Shaw. – 3rd ed. – London : Heinemann, 1981.
xiv,267p; 22cm.
Previous ed.: 1975. Bibliography: p259-261. - Includes index.
ISBN 0434918334 Pbk £7.50

MONEY MARKET - GREAT BRITAIN
—Ferrier and Ferrier : UK Money Markets / London : Butterworths, 1987.
This book describes the operations of the United Kingdom financial sector, concentrating on the principal methods of raising capital. Included in the work is coverage of the key elements in each market together with explanations of the significance of various instruments and forms of finance.
ISBN 0406100306 Hbk

—London Markets after Financial Services Act / London : Butterworths, 1987.
ISBN 0406100748 Pbk £28.00

—UK money markets / David G Ferrier. – London : Butterworths, 1988.
ISBN 0406100306 Hbk

MONEYLENDERS - ENGLAND
—Butterworths Consolidated Legislation Service /. – Professional Publ.
468p.
ISBN 0409014427 £65.00

MONEYLENDERS - MALAYSIA
—Moneylenders Ordinance 1951 (F.M. Ord. No. 42 of 1951) / Kuala Lumpur : International Law Books Services.

MONEYLENDERS - NEW ZEALAND
—Credit Contracts Act 1981 : an annotated edition of the Statute / by D. F. Dugdale. – Wellington : Butterworths, 1981.
vii,99p.
Includes index.
ISBN 0409601322

MONGOLIAN LAW
—Mongolian legal system : contemporary legislation and documentation / edited by W.E. Butler : translations from Mongolian by A.J. Nathanson, translations from Russian by W.E. Butler. – The Hague : Nijhoff, 1982.
xxiii, 995 p.; 25 cm.
ISBN 9024726859 Hbk £450.00

MONOPOLIES
—EEC antitrust procedure / by C.S. Kerse. – 2nd ed. – London : European Law Centre, 1988.
xlii,398p; 26cm.
Previous ed.: 1981. Includes index.
ISBN 0907451160 No price

—Enforcing antitrust against foreign enterprises : procedural problems in the extraterritorial application of antitrust laws / general rapporteur, Cornelis Canenbley, with the assistance of Amanda Dalton. – Deventer, Netherlands : Kluwer, 1981.
xiii,125p.
'Report submitted to Committee C–Antitrust Law and Monopolies during the IBA Berlin Conference, August 1980.'.
ISBN 9065440143

—International business and national jurisdiction / A.D. Neale and M.L. Stephens. – Oxford : Clarendon Press, 1988.
xix,216p.
Examines the relationship between issues in international and municipal law, specifically the relationship between historically exclusive spheres of sovereign interest, and legal and practical requirements of the modern international commercial environment. Concentrates on US antitrust law, but some EEC and English decisions are included.
ISBN 0198255322 Hbk £52.00

—Juridification of social spheres : a comparative analysis in the areas of labor, corporate, antitrust, and social welfare law / edited by Gunther Teubner. – Berlin : De Gruyter, 1987.
viii, 446 p.; 24 cm.
Includes bibliographies and index.
ISBN 0899252729

—Law and policy of producers' associations / D.E. Pollard. – Oxford : Clarendon, 1984.
xii,372p; 23cm.
Includes index.
ISBN 0198254806 £30.00

—Law of Monopolies, Restrictive and Unfair Trade Practices / Lucknow : Eastern Book Company, 1984.
134p.

—Legal and economic analyses on multinational enterprises / edited by Klaus J. Hopt. – 2 V. – Berlin : Walter de Gruyter, 1982.
At head of title: European University Institute. Vol. 2, English and French, with summaries for each item in the other language, has also parallel title: Analyses legales et economiques sur les entreprises multinationales. Includes indexes. Contents: v. 1. European merger control – v. 2. Groups of companies in European laws.
ISBN 3110087049 v. 2

MONOPOLIES – AUSTRALIA

—Crime, Law and Business : The Sociological Sources of Australian Monopoly Law / Canberra : Australian Institute of Criminology.

—Mal practice : the administration of the Murphy trade practices act : antitrust as a australian poshlost / V.G. Venturini. – Sydney : Non Mollare, 1980.
ix, 465 p.; 23 cm.
Includes bibliographical references and index.
ISBN 0959462902 pbk.

—Restrictive trade practices : judgments, materials and policy / Alan A. Ransom and Warren Pengilley. – Sydney : Legal Books Pty, 1985.
xlix,1193p.
Includes index.
ISBN 0949553158

MONOPOLIES – CANADA

—Annotated Competition Act / commentary prepared by Robert S. Nozick : annotations and index prepared by Charlotte Neff. – Toronto : Carswell, 1987.
xviii,290p.
ISBN 0459396609

—Anticombines and antitrust : the competition law of Canada and the antitrust law of the United States / R. J. Roberts. – Toronto : Butterworths, 1980.
xxx, 799 p.; 24 cm. – (Canadian legal textbook series).
Includes bibliographies and index. Uses a comparative approach to explain the anticombines laws of Canada. Contains an overview of the history , policy and the constitutional roadblock to enforcement, criminal prohibitions, matters civilly reviewable, exempt activities, services and professions,, and enforcement and remedies.
ISBN 0409862800

—Competition law amendments : a schematic presentation of Bill C-91 and the present act / Ottawa : Consumer and Corporate Affairs Canada, 1986.
98, 99 p.; 28 cm.
English and French. Title on added t.p.: Reforme de la legislation sur la concurrence. Includes complete text of the Competition Tribunal Act and the Competition Act, including the provisions of the current act that are replaced or changed by Bill C-91.
ISBN 0662542282 pbk.

MONOPOLIES – EUROPE

—Comparative law of monopolies / London : Graham & Trotman, 1989.
590.
ISBN 1853332763 Llf £172

Supplement service 1989.

Examines the laws on restrictive agreements, monopolies and mergers in the jurisdictions of the US, the UK, the Federal Republic of Germany and the European Community. Standards applied in each jurisdiction are analysed and the similarities and differences are explored in detail.
ISBN 1853332682 £54

—Law of Groups of Companies in Europe : a Challenge for Jurisprudence / Dordrecht : Kluwer, 1984.
ISBN 9065441654 Pbk £25.00

MONOPOLIES – EUROPEAN COMMUNITY

—Commercial agreements and competition law : practice and procedure in the UK and EEC / Nicholas Green. – London : Graham & Trotman, 1986.
lxxviii,763p.
Bibliography: p.lxix-lxx - Includes index.
ISBN 0860107884

—Common Market law of competition / Graham D. Child. – 3rd ed. – London : Sweet & Maxwell, 1987.
lviii,874p; 25cm.
Outlines the relevant provision of the EEC Treaty and of Community legislation. Examines collaboration in research, development, and production, industrial property rights, mergers and acquisitions, notification and its effects, civil remedies, enforcement and procedure, special sectors, and state aid. States the relationship between Community law and national law, especially British.
ISBN 0421282002 No price

—Comparative law of monopolies / London : Graham & Trotman, 1989.
590.
ISBN 1853332763 Llf £172

Supplement service 1989.
120.
Examines the laws on restrictive agreements, monopolies and mergers in the jurisdictions of the US, the UK, the Federal Republic of Germany and the European Community. Standards applied in each jurisdiction are analysed and the similarities and differences are explored in detail.
ISBN 1853332682 £54

—Competition law / Richard Whish. – London : Butterworths, 1985.
350p; 22cm.
Includes index.
ISBN 0406012792 Pbk No price

—Competition law : antitrust policy in the U.K. and the EEC / by Robert Merkin and Karen Williams. – London : Sweet & Maxwell, 1984.
xliii,492p; 22cm.
Bibliography: p485-486. - Includes index.
ISBN 0421307307 Hbk £30.00
ISBN 0421307404 Pbk £22.50

—Competition law of Britain and the Common Market / by Valentine Korah. – 3rd ed. – The Hague : Martinus Nijhoff, 1982.
xxvii,352p.
Bibliography: p321-326. Includes index.
ISBN 9024726158 Hbk £140.00

—Competition law of the EEC / Ivo van Bael, Jean-Francois Bellis. – Bicester : CCH Editions, 1987.
xii,690p; 23cm.
Analysis of EEC Competition Rules, with a critical commentary on the rules and practical guidance on their application. Covers basic provisions, including Articles 85 and 86, distribution, industrial and commercial property rights, co-operation agreements, mergers and acquisitions, trade associations and trade fairs, price fixing, market-sharing, boycotts and crisis cartels.
ISBN 0863250610 Pbk £30.00

—EC competition law : a practitioner's textbook / Alan Campbell : foreword by Lord Mackenzie Stuart. – Amsterdam : North-Holland, 1980.
xii,345p; 23cm.
Includes index.
ISBN 0444854967 £24.34

—EEC Antitrust Compliance / London : European Business, 1986.
ISBN 094262055 Pbk £36.00

—EEC competition law / D.G. Goyder. – Oxford : Clarendon Press, 1988.
xxxi,447p.
Account of the substantive law, and an assessment of the historical development and overall effectiveness of the competition policy. Suggests ways of improving co-ordination and implementation of competition policy. Examines the foundations of the last thirty years, and how they can be built upon.
ISBN 0198254032 pbk. £18.95
ISBN 0198255357 Hbk £45

—EEC competition law : business issues and legal principles in Common Market antitrust cases / Utz Toepke. – 1. – New York : Wiley, 1982.
27cm.
Bibliography: p907-909. - Includes index.
ISBN 0471093661

—Exclusive dealing agreements in the E.E.C. : Regulation 67/67 replaced / by Valentine Korah. – London : European Law Centre, 1984.
xv,101p; 25cm.
ISBN 090745111X Pbk No price

—International anti-trust law / edited by Julian Maitland-Walker. – Oxford : ESC Publishing, 1984.
10,116p.
Contains contributions to the 1st International Anti-trust Law Conference, Oxford, 1982.
ISBN 0906214203

—Introductory guide to EEC Competition law and practice / Valentine Korah. – 3rd ed. – Oxford : ESC Publishing, 1986.
xxi,177p; 21cm.
Includes bibliographies and index. Cover title: EEC competition law and practice.
ISBN 0906214394

—Introductory guide to EEC competition law and practice / Valentine Korah. – 2nd ed. – Oxford : ESC, 1981.
xxii,160p; 22cm.
ISBN 0906214084 Pbk Unpriced

—Leading cases and materials on the competition law of the E.E.C. / edited by D.G. Gijlstra and D.F. Murphy. – 3rd ed. – Deventer : Kluwer, 1984.
xviii,679p; 25cm.
Previous ed: 1979. At head of title: Europa Institute, University of Amsterdam.
ISBN 9065441115 Pbk No price

—Merger control in the EEC : a survey of European competition laws / prepared by the Brussels offices at Avenue de la Joyeuse Entree 1, Blijde Inkomstlaan 1 of : Advokaterne Bredgade 3 ... et al. – Deventer : Kluwer Law and Taxation Publishers, 1988.
xii,306p.
ISBN 9065443541

—R & D and the EEC competition rules : Regulation 418/85 / Valentine Korah. – Oxford : ESC Publishing, 1986.
xxi,114p. – (European competition law monographs).
Bibliography: p.xxi.
ISBN 0906214459

—Recent developments in EEC competition law : seminar documentation : Monday 8th December 1986, Cavendish Conference Centre, London W1 / Valentine Korah. – 1. – London : Legal Studies & Services, 1986.
various pagings.
Includes bibliographical references. Chairman: Valentine Korah.

—United States and Common Market antitrust policies / Matthew Bender, 1987.
ISBN 0000999063 Hbk £50.00

MONOPOLIES – GREAT BRITAIN

—Antitrust Economics / Oxford : Blackwell Scientific, 1987.
ISBN 0631153632 Hbk £32.50

—Commercial agreements and competition law : practice and procedure in the UK and EEC / Nicholas Green. – London : Graham & Trotman, 1986.
lxxviii,763p.
Bibliography: p.lxix-lxx - Includes index.
ISBN 0860107884

—Competition Act 1980 / introductory commentary by James P. Cunningham : the Act annotated by John Tinnion. – London : Sweet & Maxwell, 1980.
57,43p; 25cm.
ISBN 0421278803 Pbk £8.00

—Competition law / Richard Whish. – London : Butterworths, 1985.
350p; 22cm.
Includes index.
ISBN 0406012792 Pbk No price

—Competition law of Britain and the Common Market / by Valentine Korah. – 3rd ed. – The Hague : Martinus Nijhoff, 1982.
xxvii,352p.
Bibliography: p321-326. Includes index.
ISBN 9024726158 Hbk £140.00

—Encyclopaedia of competition law / editor Robert Merkin : consultant editors Karen Williams, Geoffrey Harding. – 1. – London : Sweet & Maxwell, 1987.
loose-leaf; 24cm.
Includes index.
ISBN 0421368705 £185.00

—Monopolies and Mergers Commission Reports / London : HMSO, 1983.
ISBN 0101904606 Hbk £3.30

—Monopolies and Mergers Commission Reports / London : HMSO, 1986.
ISBN 010198670X Hbk £9.80

—Private antitrust legislation / London : MIT Press, 1988.
ISBN 026223131X Hbk £35.95

MONOPOLIES – INDIA

—Law of monopolies and restrictive trade practices in India / H.M. Jhala. – 2nd ed. – Bombay : N M Tripathi, 1984.
xxxvii,456p.
Includes index.

MONOPOLIES – JAPAN

—Antimonopoly legislation of Japan / edited by Masanao Nakagawa. – Tokyo : Kosei Torihiki Kyokai, 1984.
ix,361p.
Includes index. English-Japanese and Japanese-English indexes.
ISBN 4876220018

—Japanese banking, securities and anti-monopoly law / edited by Hiroshi Oda, R. Geoffrey Grice. – London : Butterworths, 1988.
174p.
Includes index. '...a selection of papers delivered at the first Japanese Law Conference held at the Faculty of Law, University College London in September 1987'. - Preface.
ISBN 0406106851 £45.00

—Japanese Banking, Securities and Anti-Monopoly Law / Geoffrey Grice. – Butterworths, 1988.
ca 223p.
ISBN 0406106851 Hbk £125.00

MONOPOLIES – UNITED STATES

—Anticombines and antitrust : the competition law of Canada and the antiturst law of the United States / R. J. Roberts. – Toronto : Butterworths, 1980.
xxx, 799 p.; 24 cm. – (Canadian legal textbook series).
Includes bibliographies and index. Uses a comparative approach to explain the anticombines laws of Canada. Contains an overview of the history , policy and the constitutional roadblock to enforcement, criminal prohibitions, matters civilly reviewable, exempt activities, services and professions,, and enforcement and remedies.
ISBN 0409862800

—Aviation antitrust : the extraterritorial application of the United States antitrust laws and international air transportation / Patricia M. Barlow. – Deventer : Kluwer Law and Taxation, 1987.
xliv,210p.
Bibliography: pp.xxv-xxxv. - Includes index.
ISBN 9065442936

—Comparative law of monopolies / London : Graham & Trotman, 1989.
590.
ISBN 1853332763 Llf £172

Supplement service 1989.

Examines the laws on restrictive agreements, monopolies and mergers in the jurisdictions of the US, the UK, the Federal Republic of Germany and the European Community. Standards applied in each jurisdiction are analysed and the similarities and differences are explored in detail.
ISBN 1853332682 £54

—International anti-trust law / edited by Julian Maitland-Walker. – Oxford : ESC Publishing, 1984.
10,116p.
Contains contributions to the 1st International Anti-trust Law Conference, Oxford, 1982.
ISBN 0906214203

—Law and economy : the legal regulation of corporate capital / Kelvin Jones. – London : Academic Press, 1982.
xvi,190p; 24cm.
Bibliography: p179-184. - Includes index.
ISBN 0123900409 £16.00

—United States and Common Market antitrust policies / Matthew Bender, 1987.
ISBN 0000999063 Hbk £50.00

MONOPOLIES – WEST GERMANY

—Comparative law of monopolies / London : Graham & Trotman, 1989.
590.
ISBN 1853332763 Llf £172

Supplement service 1989.

Examines the laws on restrictive agreements, monopolies and mergers in the jurisdictions of the US, the UK, the Federal Republic of Germany and the European Community. Standards applied in each jurisdiction are analysed and the similarities and differences are explored in detail.
ISBN 1853332682 £54

—German Antitrust Law / Hannes Schneider. – 2nd ed. – Plymouth : Macdonald & Evans, 1981.
296p.
ISBN 0712154817 Casebound £23.00

—German antitrust law : an introduction to the German antitrust law with German text and synoptic English translation of the Act against Restraints of Competition / Martin H. Heidenhain, Hannes Schneider. – 2nd rev. ed. – Frankfurt am Main : Fritz Knapp, 1981.
291p.
Previous ed., 1973, published as: The German law against restraints of competition. Added t.p. in German: Das Recht gegen Wettbewerbsbeschrankungen.
ISBN 3781928306

—German Monopolies Commission 1973-1983 : summaries of the first five biennial reports / Monopolkommission. – Baden-Baden : Nomos Verlagsgellschaft, 1987.
175p.
ISBN 378901348X

MONOPOLIES (INTERNATIONAL LAW)

—Extraterritorial control of competition under international law, with special regard to US antitrust law / Erik Nerep. – 2. – Stockholm : Norstedt, 1983.
xxvii,xvii,733p.
Thesis (doctoral) - University of Stockholm 1982?. Bibliography: p.665-716. - Includes index.
ISBN 9118373127

—International anti-trust law / edited by Julian Maitland-Walker. – Oxford : ESC Publishing, 1984.
viii,178p.
Includes bibliographical references.
ISBN 090621419X

MORTGAGES

—Law of mortgages / London : Sweet & Maxwell, 1989.
– (Property and conveyancing library).
Guide to types of mortgages of real and personal property. Covers the creation of mortgages and charges, local authority and building society mortgages, debentures and priority of mortgages. Contains forms and precedents and considers the Housing Acts, Matrimonial Homes Acts 1983, and the Building Societies Act 1986.
ISBN 0421344105 Hbk

MORTGAGES – AUSTRALIA

—Morgage Debenture / 3rd ed. – North Ryde : Law Book Co, 1985.
xii, 108p.
ISBN 0455206031 Pbk £21.50

—Mortgagee's Power of Sale / Butterworths, 1980.
207p.
ISBN 0409448508 Hbk £48.00

—Mortgages and Securities / Thomas. – 3rd ed. – Sydney : Butterworths, 1986.

—Sackville and Neave Property Law : Cases and Materials / C. Rossiter. – 4th ed. – Sydney : Butterworths, 1988.
992p.
The fourth edition of this casebook contains revised materials on the Trade Practices Act, leases, and mortgages.

MORTGAGES – AUSTRALIA – QUEENSLAND

—Working paper on a bill to amend the real property acts with respect to those provisions relating to writs of execution, bills of encumbrance and bills of mortgage, and caveats / Brisbane : The Commission, 1982.
28p. – (Q.L.R.C.W.P.).

MORTGAGES – AUSTRALIA – VICTORIA

—Mortgagee sales and judgment debts / Law Reform Commission of Victoria. – Melbourne : The Commission, 1986.
iii,10p. – (Discussion paper of Victoria).
Includes bibliographical references.

—Mortgagee sales and judgment debts / Law Reform Commission of Victoria. – Melbourne : The Commission, 1987.
iv,17p. – (Report no 8).
Includes bibliographical references.

MORTGAGES – CANADA

—Canadian Mortgage Practice Reporter / Gershman. – Toronto : DeBoo.
ISBN 0888200870 loose £375.00

—Mortgages - 1985 / Vancouver : British Columbia Continuing Legal Education Society, 1985.
292p.
ISBN 0865042276 Hbk £60.00

—Mortgages / Vancouver : Continuing Legal Education Society of British Columbia, 1984.
163p.
ISBN 0865041431 Hbk £55.00

—Mortgages : Advanced Topics / Vancouver : Continuing Legal Education Society of British Columbia, 1987.
230p.
ISBN 0865043124 Hbk £70.00

—Mortgages and Foreclosure : Know Your Rights / 4th ed. – North Vancouver : International Self-Counsel Press, 1987.
105p.
ISBN 0889086567 Hbk £7.95

—O'Brien's Encyclopedia of Forms : Division Three-Conveyancing and Mortgages / Aurora : Canada Law Book Co.
– (Abridgments and Encyclopedias).

Supplement

—Practice in Mortgage Actions in Alberta / Marguerite Trussler. – Agincourt : Carswell, 1985.
630p.
This work reviews the law and practice in Alberta including relevant case law from other provinces in Canada relating to mortgage law.

MORTGAGES – CANADA – ALBERTA

—Practice in Mortgage Actions in Alberta / Marguerite Trussler. – Agincourt : Carswell, 1985.
630p.
This work reviews the law and practice in Alberta including relevant case law from other provinces in Canada relating to mortgage law.

MORTGAGES – CANADA – BRITISH COLUMBIA

—Personal liability under a mortgage or agreement for sale / Law Reform Commission of British Columbia. – Vancouver : The Commission, 1985.
ii,52p. – (Working paper).
Includes bibliographical references.

—Report on mortgages of land : the priority of further advances / Law Reform Commission of British Columbia. – Vancouver : The Commission, 1986.
60p.
Includes bibliographical references.
ISBN 0771885067

—Report on personal liability under a mortgage or agreement for sale / Law Reform Commission of British Columbia. – Victoria : Queen's Printer, 1986.
37p.
Date on front cover: 1985. Includes bibliographical references.
ISBN 0771884982

MORTGAGES – CANADA – ONTARIO

—Marriott and Dunn : Practice in Mortgage Actions in Ontario / 4th ed. – Agincourt : Carswell, 1982.
575p.
This fourth edition text is a guide to what you need to know to decide upon and obtain remedies. Topics include the power of sales procedure and an analysis of all other types of remedies in mortgage actions in Ontario.

—Practice in mortgage actions in Ontario : the practice in mortgage actions and in exercising power of sale / Marriott and Dunn. – 4th ed. – Toronto : Carswell, 1982.
xliii,511p.
Includes index.
ISBN 0459348809

—Report on the law of mortgages / Ontario Law Reform Commission. – Toronto : Ministry of the Attorney General, 1987.
xiii,401p.
Includes text of draft bill.
ISBN 0772923205

MORTGAGES – ENGLAND

—Fisher & Lightwood's law of mortgage / J. M. Lightwood, E. L. G. Tyler, R. D. Oughton. – 10th ed. – London : Butterworths, 1988.
940p; 25cm.
Gives detailed practical presentation of United Kingdom mortgage law for practitioners. Regular supplements will be issued to keep pace with the rapid changes in the field. Copious source references and footnotes are provided throughout the book.
ISBN 0406201064 £90.00

—Land mortgages / the Law Commission. – London : HMSO, 1986.
xv,254,48p. – (Working paper).
ISBN 0117301809

—Mortgages / by Paul B. Fairest. – 2nd ed. – London : Sweet & Maxwell, 1980.
xviii,157p; 20cm.
Previous ed.: 1975.
ISBN 0421248408 Hbk £11.25
ISBN 0421248505 Pbk £6.50

MORTGAGES – GREAT BRITAIN

—Law of Mortgage / Lightwood. – 10th ed. – London : Butterworths, 1987.
ISBN 0406201064 Hbk £85.00

—Mortgages and Securities / 3rd ed. – London : Butterworths, 1986.
ISBN 0409491633 Hbk £55.00

—Mortgages of Ships / London : Lloyd's of London Press, 1988.
ISBN 1850441049 Hbk

—Ship and Aircraft Mortgages / London : LLoyd's of London Press, 1988.
ISBN 1850441049 Hbk

—Tax Aspects of Home Ownership / Butterworth Staff. – London : Butterworths, 1983.
ISBN 0406254311 Pbk £20.00

—Your mortgage / Penguin, 1988.
ISBN 0140105611 Pbk £4.95

MORTGAGES – NEW ZEALAND

—Effect of a caveat on a mortgagee's power of sale : report of the Property Law and Equity Reform Committee / New Zealand. – Wellington : Government Printer, 1981.
7,2p.

—Proposals under the Securities Act 1978 for regulations relating to contributory mortgages / Securities Commission. – Wellington : The Commission, 1981.
50,48p.

MORTGAGES – SOUTH AFRICA

—Wille's law of mortgage and pledge in South Africa / T. J. Scott, Susan Scott. – 3rd ed. – Cape Town : Juta, 1987.
lvi,283p.
Previous ed. published in 1961 as: The law of mortgage and pledge in South Africa. Bibliography: pp.xxi-xxii. - Includes index. .
ISBN 0702118966

MOTOR INSURANCE

—Motor insurance : German and English / Berlin : Langenscheidt, 1980.
152p; 21cm.
Bibliography: p.10-13. - Includes index. Compiled by a commission of the International Institute for Legal and Administrative Terminology. Added t.p. in German: Kraftfahrtversicherung: Deutsch und Englisch.

MOTOR INSURANCE – CANADA

—Annotated British Columbia Insurance (Motor Vehicle) Act / Cedric H.L. Hughes. – Agincourt : Carswell, 1987.
ca 220p.

—I.C.B.C. Claims and Impaired Driving / Vancouver : British Columbia Continuing Legal Education Society, 1985.
310p.
ISBN 0865042462 Hbk £65.00

—Insurance case law digest: property and casualty / 2 vols. – Scarborough, Ontario : Butterworths (Canada).
Coverage of automobile and property insurance cases in Canada. Each part has a table of cases, and the case digests are arranged to reflect the organizational categories of the standard automobile and home insurance policies.

—Motor Vehicle Accident Claims - 1983 / Vancouver : British Columbia Continuing Legal Education Society, 1983.
547p.
ISBN 0865040141 Hbk £70.00

—No-Fault Automobile Insurance in Canada / Agincourt : Carswell, 1988.
250p.

—No-Fault Automobile Insurance in Canada / Elizabeth C. Seto. – Agincourt : Carswell, 1988.
200p.

—Standard Automobile Policy Annotated / Toronto : Butterworths, 1986.
296p.

—Standard Automobile Policy Annotated / Butterworths, 1986.
288p.

MOTOR INSURANCE – CANADA – BRITISH COLUMBIA

—Annotated British Columbia Insurance (Motor Vehicle) Act / Agincourt : Carswell.
220p.
This text contains the Insurance (Motor Vehicle) Act and the Revised Regulations with annotations. Topics include a description of the history of the legislation and the policy that governed its development. Current caselaw and pertinent older cases are discussed.

MOTOR INSURANCE – CANADA – ONTARIO

—Report of Inquiry into Motor Vehicle Accident Compensation in Ontario / Coulter A. Osborne, commissioner. – Toronto : Ontario Ministry of the Attorney General, 1988.
2 v.; 25 cm.
Title from cover. Co-published by: Ministry of Financial Institutions. Bibliography: p. 667-712 (v. 2.). Contents: v. 1. Report – v. 2. Research studies and v. 1 appendices.
ISBN 0772938466 (v.2)

—Report of Inquiry into Motor Vehicle Accident Compensation in Ontario : summary of findings and recommendations / Coulter A. Osborne, Commissioner. – Toronto : Ontario Ministry of the Attorney General, 1988.
68, 79 p.; 25 cm.
Title from cover. Co-published by: Ministry of Financial Institutions. Text in English and French with French text on inverted pages. Title on added t.p.: Rapport de l'enquete sur l'indemnisation des victimes d'accidents d'automobiles en Ontario.
ISBN 0772938474

MOTOR INSURANCE – CANADA – SASKATCHEWAN

—Proposals for restoring civil remedies lost upon forfeiture under the Automobile Accident Insurance Act : report to the Minister of Justice / Law Reform Commission of Saskatchewan. – Saskatoon : The Commission, 1984.
11p.
Includes bibliographical references.

MOTOR INSURANCE – GREAT BRITAIN

—Fire and Motor Insurance / 4th ed. – London : Butterworths, 1984.
ISBN 040625253X Hbk £49.00

—Fire and motor insurance / E.R. Hardy Ivamy. – 4th ed. – London : Butterworths, 1984.
xxxviii,518p; 26cm. – (Butterworths insurance library).
Previous ed.: 1978. Includes index.
ISBN 040625253X Unpriced

—Motor Claims Cases / Taylor. – 9th ed. – London : Butterworths, 1986.
ISBN 0406118132 Hbk £68.00

—Motor insurance and the consumer / Dickinson. – Cambridge : Woodhead-Faulkner, 1980.
ISBN 0859411478 Pbk £14.95

MOTOR INSURANCE – INDIA

—Claims for compensation under Chapter 8 of the Motor Vehicles Act, 1939 / Law Commission of India. – Delhi : Controller of Publications Govt. of India, 1980.
86p. – (85th report).
Includes bibliographical references.

MOTOR INSURANCE – NEW ZEALAND

—Motor Claims Cases / Wellington : Butterworths.
ISBN 0406118116 Pbk

MOTOR INSURANCE – SOUTH AFRICA

—Suzman, Gordon and Hodes on the law of compulsory motor vehicle insurance in South Africa / Lionel H. Hodes. – 3rd ed. – Cape Town : Juta, 1982.
xxxvii,538p.
Previous ed.: 1970, entitled: Suzman and Gordon on the law of compulsory motor vehicle insurance in South Africa. Bibliography: p.ix. - Includes index.
ISBN 0702112585

MOTOR TRANSPORT

—International carriage of goods by road : CMR / by Malcolm A. Clarke. – London : Stevens, 1982.
xxvi,212p; 26cm.
Includes index. Appendix in French.
ISBN 0420464905 £19.50

—Motoring Law A-Z / Ibadan : African Universities Press.

MOTOR TRANSPORT – GREAT BRITAIN

—Croner's Road Transport Operation / Croner Publications. – New Malden : Croner Publications, 1986.
Annual renewal updates

—HGV Law Guide / London : Butterworths, 1981.
This work is written for those who operate or are responsible for goods vehicles in the United Kingdom. The Construction and Use Regulations of 1978 and the Special Types Order of 1979 are analyzed in the book. Numerous diagrams illustrate the text.
ISBN 0408005696 Hbk

—Motorist and the Law / 2nd ed. – London : Oyez Longman, 1982.
– (It's Your Law Ser.).
ISBN 0851204775 Hbk £3.95
ISBN 0851204783 Pbk

—Motorist and the law / Penguin, 1987.
ISBN 0140068228 Pbk £4.95

—Motorist's Guide to the Law / London : Fourmat, 1986.
ISBN 0906840953 Pbk £4.95

MOTOR TRANSPORT – INDIA

—Motor Transport Workers Act : with States Rules / Venkanna. – 3rd ed. – Allahabad : Law Book Company.

MOTOR TRANSPORT – NEW ZEALAND

—New Zealand goods and services tax guide / Auckland : Commerce Clearing House (New Zealand), 1985-.
Title history: New Zealand duties and sales tax guide (1983-1985);New Zealand sales, goods and services taxes guide (1983-1987). Includes index.

MOTOR TRANSPORT – WEST GERMANY

—Industrial relations in West Germany : a case study of the car industry / Wolfgang Streeck. – London : Heinemann, 1984.
178p; 23cm.
Bibliography: p170-172. - Includes index. At head of title: Policy Studies Institute.
ISBN 0435838393 £16.50

MOTOR VEHICLES

—Ford Motor Company Limited : licensing for the manufacture or sale of replacement body parts : a report by the Director General of Fair Trading on an investigation under section 3 of the Competition Act 1980 / London : Office of Fair Trading, 1984.
43p.

—Motoring Law A-Z / Ibadan : African Universities Press.

MOTOR VEHICLES – AUSTRALIA

—Car Stealing In Australia : Facts and Figures / Canberra : Australian Institute of Criminology.

—Motor Vehicle Reports / Butterworths.

—Road Vehicle Regulations : Information Paper 1 / Kingston : Australian Government Publishing Service, 1987.
xi, 209p.

MOTOR VEHICLES – CANADA

—Manual of Motor Vehicle Law, 2 Vols. / 3rd ed. – Agincourt : Carswell, 1982.
This looseleaf service is an annotated guide to the text of the Highway Traffic Act of Ontario, Canada. Cases and statutory references to the motor vehicle law of all provinces is included in the work.

—Motor Vehicle Accident Claims : 1983 / Vancouver : British Columbia Continuing Legal Education Society.

—Motor Vehicle Reports, 50 Vols. / Carswell Legal Publications. – Agincourt : Carswell, 1983.

—Motor Vehicle Reports / Agincourt : Carswell, 1988.
This multi-volume set of books contains the key decisions in motor vehicle law from all Canadian jurisdictions. Discussions include alcoholic related offenses, civil actions relating to motor vehicles, and registration and licensing issues.

—Off-Road Vehicles Act, 1983, Bill 061 : An Act to Regulate Off-Road Vehicles / Ontario : Ontario Government Publications Service, 1983.
11p.

—Used Car Buyers Protection Act, 1983, Bill 131 : An Act to Protect the Purchasers of Used Motor Vehicles / Ontario : Ontario Government Publications Service, 1983.
4p.

MOTOR VEHICLES – CANADA – BRITISH COLUMBIA

—Annotated Motor Vehicle Legislation in British Columbia / Agincourt : Carswell, 1987.
ca 200p.

—Annotated Motor Vehicle Legislation in British Columbia / Agincourt : Carswell, 1987.
200p.
This compact volume contains the complete text of the Motor Vehicle Act, Motor Dealer Act, and Motor Vehicle (All Terrain) Act of British Columbia, along with selected regulations under the Acts.

MOTOR VEHICLES – ENGLAND

—British Airports Authority : arrangements for the provision of chauffer-driven hire car services at Gatwick Airport : a report / by the Director General of Fair Trading. – London : H.M.S.O., 1984.
50p; 30cm.

—Butterworths Consolidated Legislation Service /. – Professional Publ.
50p.
ISBN 0409014338 £25.00

MOTOR VEHICLES – GREAT BRITAIN

—British Railways Board : Facilities for car hire and advertising of self-drive vehicle hire at railway stations / report by the Director General of Fair Trading on an investigation under section 3 of the Competition Act 1980. – London : Office of Fair Trading, 1983.
47p; 30cm.

—Consumer Law for the Motor Trade / London : Butterworths, 1981.
This work is a practical non-technical introduction to the law of automobile sales and repairs. The book provides references to leading cases and relevant statutes are included in the text.
ISBN 0406425906 Pbk

—Disposal of Abandoned Vehicles and Other Refuse / London : Shaw & Sons, 1981.
– (Shaway Guide: No. 4).
ISBN 0721908756 Pbk £2.50

—Guide to the Heavy Goods Vehicle Driving Test and Licenses / 5th ed. – London : Kogan Page, 1986.
120p.
ISBN 1850911304 Pbk £5.95

—HGV law guide / London : Butterworths, 1981.
ISBN 0408005696 Pbk £10.00

—HGV Law Guide / London : Butterworths, 1981.
This work is written for those who operate or are responsible for goods vehicles in the United Kingdom. The Construction and Use Regulations of 1978 and the Special Types Order of 1979 are analyzed in the book. Numerous diagrams illustrate the text.
ISBN 0408005696 Hbk

—Law relating to goods vehicles by John Pugh / Chichester : Rose, 1980.
8,xv,384p; 23cm.
Includes index.
ISBN 0859921425 £17.00

—Offences Relating to Motor Vehicles, England and Wales 1980 : Supplementary Tables / London : Home Office, 1981.
ISBN 0862520231 Pbk £4.00

—Road Traffic (Jersey) Law, 1956 (as amended up to 3rd February, 1981) / Jersey. – 1. – Jersey : States Greffe, 1981.
loose-leaf.
Subsequently amended up to 25th October, 1983. Cover title.

MOTOR VEHICLES – INDIA
—Basu's Motor Vehicles Act / 6th ed. – Calcutta : Eastern Law House, 1984.

—Commentaries on Motor Vehicles Act, 2 Vols. / 8th ed. – Lucknow : Eastern Book Company, 1982.
2,000p.

—Law of Motor Vehicles in U.P. / 3rd ed. – Lucknow : Eastern Book Company, 1984.
820p.

—Motor Vehicles Act, 1939 : With All State Amendments, 2 Vols. / Allahabad : Ashoka Law House, 1987.
1,600p.

—Motor Vehicles Act. 1986 supplement / 7th ed. – Allahabad : Law Book Company, 1980.
1,100p.

—Motor Vehicles Act, 2 Vols. / 5th ed. – Allahabad : Law Publishers, 1982.

MOTOR VEHICLES – NORTHERN IRELAND
—Motoring Law in Northern Ireland / Belfast : Queen's University of Belfast, 1986.
350p.

MOTOR VEHICLES – SOUTH AFRICA
—Motor law / by W.E. Cooper : specialist contributor T.G. Schwar. – Cape Town : Juta, 1982.
cxxvi,740p.
Replaces: South African motor law / by W.E. Cooper and B.R. Bamford. Bibliography: p.xv. - Includes index.
ISBN 0702112534

Vol. 2 : Principles of liability for patrimonial loss / by W.E. Cooper. – 1987.
li,507p.
Replaces: South African motor law / by W.E. Cooper and B.R. Bamford. Bibliography: p.xi-xiii. - Includes index.
ISBN 0702119067 Hbk

MOTOR VEHICLES – UNITED STATES
—Motor vehicle safety standards and product liability in the USA / by John Lambert. – London : Economist Intelligence Unit, 1982.
131p.

MULTILINGUALISM
—Multilingualism in international law and institutions / Mala Tabory. – Alphen aan den Rijn : Sijthoff & Noordhoff, 1980.
xx,283p.
Bibliography: p260-268.
ISBN 9028602100

MULTINATIONAL COMPANIES
—Corporate Finance in Multinational Companies / London : Euromoney, 1986.
ISBN 1870031350 Pbk £75.00

—Emp. Consultation and Information in Multinational Corps. / Oxford : Croom Helm, 1986.
ISBN 0709926243 Hbk £19.95

—Legal control of the multinational enterprise : national regulatory techniques and the prospects for international controls / Cynthia D. Wallace. – The Hague : Martinus Nijhoff, 1983.
354p.
Originally presented as the author's thesis (Ph.D.)–Cambridge University. Includes index. Bibliography: p331-355.
ISBN 9024726689 Hbk £135.00

—Question of a Reference to International Obligations in the United Nations Code of Conduct on Transnational Corporations : a Different View / Geneva : United Nations Publications.
ISBN 9211041864 Hbk £4.00

MULTINATIONAL COMPANIES – CANADA
—Canadian Multinationals / Maule. – Toronto : Butterworths, 1981.
192p.
Examines the nature of Canadian direct investment abroad, its impact on Canada, and the policy alternatives which need to be considered. Topics include the extent and nature of Canadian investment abroad, economic impact of outward investment on Canada and the existing Canadian policies.
ISBN 0409845256 Hbk

MULTINATIONAL FORCES
—Basic documents on United Nations and related peace-keeping forces / compiled by Robert C.R. Siekmann. – Dordrecht, Holland : M. Nijhoff, 1985.
At head of title: T.M.C. Asser Instituut.
ISBN 9024731631

MUNICIPAL CORPORATIONS – CANADA
—Law of Canadian municipal corporations / by Ian MacF. Rogers. – 2d ed. – Toronto : Carswell, 1971.
2 v. (loose-leaf); 25 cm.
ISBN 0459307606

—Municipal and planning law reports / Toronto : Carswell, 1976-.
24cm.

MUNICIPAL CORPORATIONS – CANADA – ONTARIO
—Municipal councillors' handbook / Ian MacF. Rogers. – 4th ed. – Toronto : Carswell, 1982.
xi,135p.
Previous ed.: 1977. Bibliography: p.119. - Includes index.
ISBN 0459347306

MUNICIPAL CORPORATIONS – SOUTH AFRICA
—Municipal administration : a handbook / by D.L. Craythorne. – Cape Town : Juta, 1980.
xxi, 309 p.; 25 cm.
Includes indexes. Bibliography: p. xv-xviii.
ISBN 0702111074 pbk.

MUNICIPAL FINANCE – UNITED STATES
—Urban government finance : emerging trends / edited by Roy Bahl. – Beverly Hills : Sage, 1981.
287p; 22cm. – (Urban affairs annual reviews 20).
Includes bibliographies.
ISBN 0803915640 Hbk Unpriced
ISBN 0803915659 Pbk Unpriced

MUNICIPAL GOVERNMENT
—Government and administration of metropolitan areas in Western democracies : a survey of approaches to the administrative problems of major conurbations in Europe and Canade / Alan Norton. – Birmingham : Institute of Local Government Studies, University of Birmingham, 1983.
60 p.
ISBN 070440690X

—Politics, planning and the city / Michael Goldsmith. – London : Hutchinson, 1980.
216p; 23cm.
Bibliography: p198-209. - Includes index.
ISBN 0091413702 Hbk £9.50
ISBN 0091413710 Pbk £4.95

MUNICIPAL GOVERNMENT – CANADA
—1987 Municipal Law Amendments / Vancouver : Continuing Legal Education Society of British Columbia, 1987.
34p.
ISBN 0865043361 Hbk £65.00

—Municipal Act Amendments / Vancouver : British Columbia Continuing Legal Education Society, 1986.
ISBN 0865042586 Hbk £55.00

—Municipal Law : 11 / Vancouver : British Columbia Continuing Legal Education Society, 1983.
388p.
ISBN 0865041229 Hbk £65.00

—Municipal Law / Vancouver : British Columbia Continuing Legal Education Society, 1981.
548p.
ISBN 0865040257 Hbk £21.00

—Regulation by Municipal Licensing / Toronto : University of Toronto Press, 1984.
ISBN 0802033903 Pbk £6.50

MUNICIPAL GOVERNMENT – GREAT BRITAIN
—Modern Development of City Government in the United Kingdom and the United States, 2 Vols. / Repr. of 1927 ed. – Aalen Wuertt : Scientia.
764p : Illus.

MUNICIPAL GOVERNMENT – INDIA
—Law of Municipalities and Municipal Corporations / 3rd ed. – Allahabad : Law Book Company, 1987.
1,800p.

MUNICIPAL GOVERNMENT – SOUTH AFRICA
—Municipal administration : a handbook / by D.L. Craythorne. – Cape Town : Juta, 1980.
xxi, 309 p.; 25 cm.
Includes indexes. Bibliography: p. xv-xviii.
ISBN 0702111074 pbk.

MUNICIPAL GOVERNMENT – UNITED STATES
—Modern Development of City Government in the United Kingdom and the United States, 2 Vols. / Repr. of 1927 ed. – Aalen Wuertt : Scientia.
764p : Illus.

MURDER
—Leonski the Brown-out Strangler / Neutral Bay : Hale & Iremonger.
ISBN 0908094981 Hbk £24.95
ISBN 090809499X Pbk £11.95

—Lust to kill : a feminist investigation of sexual murder / Deborah Cameron and Elizabeth Frazer. – Cambridge : Polity in association with Basil Blackwell, 1987.
xv,207p; 22cm.
Bibliography: p195-203. - Includes index.
ISBN 0745603351 Hbk £25.00
ISBN 074560336X Pbk £7.95

—Political killings by governments / Amnesty International. – London : Amnesty International, 1983.
131p; 22cm.
Includes index.
ISBN 0862100518 Pbk Unpriced

—Serial murder / Deburger. – Sage Publications, 1988.
ISBN 0803928408 Hbk £25.95
ISBN 0803928416 Pbk £12.00

—Unsolved : classic true murder cases / Star Books, 1988.
ISBN 0352321741 Pbk £2.95

—Wallace : the final verdict / Roger Wilkes. – London : Bodley Head, 1984.
269p,16p of plates; 22cm.
Bibliography: p261-263. - Includes index.
ISBN 037030571X £8.95

MURDER – AUSTRALIA
—Royal Commission of Inquiry into Chamberlain Convictions / report of the Commissisoner T.R. Morling. – Canberra : Government Printer, 1987.
379p. – (Parliamentary paper).
At head of cover title: Parliament of the Commonwealth of Australia.
ISBN 0724512985

MURDER – AUSTRALIA – VICTORIA
—Diminshed responsibility as a defence to murder / Law Reform Commissioner, Victoria. – Melbourne : The Commission, 1981.
40p. – (Working paper no 7).
Includes bibliographical references.

—Law of homicide in Victoria : the sentence for murder / Law Reform Commission of Victoria. – Melbourne : The Commission, 1985.
viii,27p. – (Report v no 1).
Bibliography: p.25-27.

—Murder : mental element and punishment / Law Reform Commissioner, Victoria. – Melbourne : The Commission, 1984.
52p. – (Working paper no 8).
Includes bibliographical references.

—Provocation and diminished responsibility as defences to murder / Law Reform Commissioner, Victoria. – Melbourne : The Commission, 1982.
48p. – (Report no 12).
Includes bibliographical references.

MURDER – CANADA
—Clues to Murder / Aurora : Cape, 1986.
ISBN 0370308522 Hbk £12.95

MURDER – EL SALVADOR
—Extrajudicial executions in El Salvador : report of an Amnesty International mission to examine post-mortem and investigative procedures in political killings, 1-6 July 1983 / Amnesty International. – London : Amnesty International, 1984.
48p; 30cm.
ISBN 0862100704 Pbk No price

MURDER – ENGLAND
—Criminal justice : the story of Edith Thompson / by Rene Weis. – London : Hamish Hamilton, 1988.
xviii,327p,8p of plates; 24cm.
Includes index.
ISBN 0241122635 £14.95

—Jack the Ripper : A Casebook 1976 / London : Wildy & Sons.

MURDER – GREAT BRITAIN
—Murder into manslaughter / Oxford : Oxford University Press, 1984.
ISBN 0197121519 Hbk £10.00

MURDER – INDIA
—Law of Culpable Homicide, Murder and Punishment in India / New Delhi : Deep and Deep Publications, 1988.
464p.

MURDER – NEW ZEALAND
—Report of the Royal Commission to Inquire into the Circumstances of the Convictions of Arthur Allan Thomas for the Murders of David Harvey Crewe and Jeanette Lenore Crewe / R. L. Taylor. – Wellington : Government Printer, 1980.
124p. – (H.).
Chairman: R.L. Taylor.

MURDER – UGANDA

—Uganda : six years after Amin : torture, killings, disappearances / Amnesty International. – London : Amnesty International, 1985.
40p.

MUSIC – AUSTRALIA

—Copyright and Music / Milsons Point : Australian Copyright Council.

—Music : the Business and the Law / G. Stevens. – North Ryde : Law Book Co, 1986.
xii, 247p.
ISBN 045520621X Pbk £24.00

MUSIC – CANADA

—Musicians and the Law in Canada / Agincourt : Carswell, 1985.
258p.
This work examines the law of Canada impacting on musicians and their business affairs. Issues discussed include: copyright, music publishing, live performance, management and agency, merchandising, personal service contracts, income taxes, and other relevant topics.

—Musicians and the law in Canada / by Paul Sanderson. – Toronto : Carswell, 1985.
xxxi, 258 p.; 24 cm.
Includes index.
ISBN 0459372203

MUSLIM WOMEN

—Woman in Shari'ah (Islamic law) / Abdur Rahman I. Doi. – s.l. : s.n., 1983.
286p.
Bibliography: pp.267-281. - Includes index.

MUTUAL FUNDS – GREAT BRITAIN

—Authorised unit trust schemes : investment and borrowing powers : draft regulations under section 81(2)(d) of the Financial Services Act 1986 relating to properties unit trusts, futures and options funds and mixed funds / Department of Trade and Industry. – London : The Department, 1987.
3,6,5,4p.

—Authorized unit trust schemes : investment and borrowing powers : draft regulations under section 81(2)(d) of the Financial Services Act 1986 relating to securities unit trusts and money market unit trusts / Department of Trade and Industry. – London : The Department, 1987.
20p.

NAMES

—Protection of geographic denominations of goods and services / edited by Herman Cohen Jehoram. – Alphen aan den Rijn : Sijthoff & Noordhoff, 1980.
vii,207p.

NAMES – AUSTRALIA

—Business Names Guide / 3rd ed. – North Ryde : C.C.H. Australia, 1985.
154p.
ISBN 0869034413 Hbk £28.00

NAMES – GREAT BRITAIN

—Business Names Act 1985 / London : HMSO.
12p.
ISBN 0105407852 Pbk £1.75

—Change of name / 13th ed. – London : Longman Professional, 1985.
ISBN 0851209890 Pbk £11.95

—Change of Name / 12th ed. – London : Oyez Longman, 1980.
– (Oyez Longman Practice Note Ser.: No. 1).
ISBN 0851204104 Hbk £4.95

—Trade marks and names / Oxford : ESC, 1985.
– (Casebook).
ISBN 0906214351 Pbk £9.00

NAMES (GEOGRAPHICAL)

—Names of states : an authority list of language forms for catalogue entries / compiled by the IFLA International Office of UBC. – London : The Office, 1981.
viii,49p; 30cm.
At head of title: International Federation of Library Associations and Institutions.
ISBN 0903043327 Pbk Unpriced

NAMES (PERSONAL) – AUSTRALIA – NEW SOUTH WALES

—Registration and certification of births and deaths : discussion paper / New South Wales Law Reform Commission. – Sydney : Government Printer, 1987.
vii,33p. – (D.P. v 17.).
ISBN 0730546276 Hbk

NAMIBIA – NAMIBIA

—South West Africa and the sacred trust 1919-1972 / T.D. Gill. – The Hague : T.M.C. Asser Instituut, 1984.
ix,107p.
Bibliography: p.106-107.
ISBN 9067040274

NARCOTICS, CONTROL OF – AUSTRALIA

—Report / Royal Commission of Inquiry into Drug Trafficking, the Government of the Commonwealth of Australia and the Governments of the States of New South Wales, Victoria and Queensland. – Canberra : Australian Government Publishing Service, 1983.
xv,908p.
Includes bibliographical references and index.
ISBN 0644024747

NARCOTICS, CONTROL OF – NEW ZEALAND

—Report / Royal Commission of Inquiry into Drug Trafficking, the Government of the Commonwealth of Australia and the Governments of the States of New South Wales, Victoria and Queensland. – Canberra : Australian Government Publishing Service, 1983.
xv,908p.
Includes bibliographical references and index.
ISBN 0644024747

NATAL

—Natal and KwaZulu : constitutional and political options; proceedings of the workshop... / edited by Laurence Boulle and Lawrence Baxter. – Cape Town : Juta, 1981.
viii,211p.
Includes chapter in Afrikaans.

NATIONAL LIBERATION MOVEMENTS

—International law and the use of force by national liberation movements / Heather A. Wilson. – Oxford : Clarendon, 1988.
208p; 24cm.
Includes bibliography and index.
ISBN 0198255705 £22.50

NATIONAL LIBRARIES

—BLL review / British Library Lending Division. – London : H.M.S.O., 1973.
Continues: NLL review; continued by: Interlending review. Index: 1971/1975.

—NLL review / National Lending Library for Science and Technology. – London : H.M.S.O., 1971.
Continued by: BLL review.

NATIONAL LIBRARIES – GREAT BRITAIN

—Reports / London : H.M.S.O., 1980.
158 p.

NATIONAL PARKS

—Legislation on wildlife, hunting, and protected areas in some European countries / by Christian du Saussay for the Legislation Branch, Legal Office. – Rome : Food and Agriculture Organization of the United Nations, 1980.
vi, 49 p.; 28 cm. – (Legislative study).
Includes bibliographies references.
ISBN 9251008787 pbk.

NATIONAL PARKS – AFRICA

—Legislation on wildlife and protected areas in Africa / by Christian du Saussay for Legislation Branch, Legal Office, FAO. – Rome : Food and Agriculture Organization of the United Nations, 1984.
vii,158p. – (Legislative study).
Includes bibliographical references.
ISBN 9251011710

NATIONAL PARKS – ENGLAND

—National parks : conservation or cosmetics? / Ann and Malcolm MacEwen. – London : Allen & Unwin, 1982.
xxii,314p; 24cm.
Bibliography: p287-297. - Includes index.
ISBN 0047190035 Hbk Unpriced
ISBN 0047190043 Pbk £8.50

NATIONAL TERRITORY

—Border and territorial disputes / edited by Alan J. Day : contributors: Judith Bell ... et al. – Harlow : Longman, 1982.
x,406p; 26cm.
Bibliography: p389. - Includes index.
ISBN 0582902517 Unpriced
ISBN 0810320304

NATIONAL TERRITORY – AFRICA

—Title to territory in Africa : international legal issues / Malcolm Shaw. – Oxford : Clarendon, 1985.
xii,428p; 22cm.
Includes bibliography and index.
ISBN 0198253796 £35.00

NATIONALISED INDUSTRIES – AUSTRALIA

—Australian National Companies Act with Regulations / 6th ed. – North Ryde : C.C.H. Australia, 1986.
2,000p.
ISBN 0869039792 Hbk

NATIONALISM

—Political economy of nationalism / Dudley Seers. – Oxford : Oxford University Press, 1983.
218p; 22cm.
Bibliography: p198-203. - Includes index.
ISBN 019828456X Hbk Unpriced
ISBN 019828473X Pbk £6.95

NATURAL JUSTICE

—Hobbes's Science of Natural Justice / P.J. Johnson. – Dordrecht : Kluwer, 1987.
326p.
ISBN 9024732263 Hbk £195.00

—Natural Justice / 2nd ed. – London : Butterworths, 1984.
ISBN 0409491233 Hbk £40.00

—Natural Justice : Principles and Practical Application / 2nd ed. – Butterworths, 1984.
205p.
ISBN 0409491233 Pbk £49.00

NATURAL JUSTICE – INDIA

—Administration of Natural Justice in India / New Delhi : Uppal Publishing House, 1986.
358p.
ISBN 818502409X Hbk £250.00

NATURAL LAW

—Law of Fundamental Rights / Chaudhari. – 2nd ed. – Allahabad : Law Book Company, 1984.

—Moral foundation of rights / L.W. Sumner. – Oxford : Clarendon Press, 1987.
228p; 22cm.
Includes bibliography and index.
ISBN 0198247516 £22.50

—Natural law and natural rights / by John Mitchell Finnis. – Oxford : Clarendon Press, 1980.
350p. – (Clarendon law series).
ISBN 0198760981 £9.00

—Natural law and natural rights / Rev 1986. – Oxford : Oxford University Press, 1980.
ISBN 0198761104 Pbk £9.95

—Natural Law, Conciliarism and Consent in the Middle Ages / Northampton : Variorum, 1984.
350p. – (Collected Studies Ser.: No. 189).
ISBN 0860781372 Hbk £26.00

—Nature of social laws : Machiavelli to Mill / Robert Brown. – Cambridge : Cambridge University Press, 1984.
ix,270p; 24cm.
Includes index.
ISBN 0521257824 £22.50

—Tradition and progress in modern legal cultures / edited by Stig Jrgensen, Juha Poyhonen, Csaba Varga : preface by Jose Llompart Tradition und Fortschritt in den modernen Rechtskulturen / herausgegeben von Stig Jrgensen, Juha Poyhonen, Csaba Varga ; vorwort von Jose Llompart. – Stuttgart : F. Steiner Verlag Wiesbaden, 1985.
263 p.; 24 cm. – (Archives for philosophy of law and social philosophy).
English, French, and German. Includes bibliographies and index. .
ISBN 3515044582 pbk. DM35.00

NATURAL LAW – AUSTRALIA

—Natural Law and Consciousness / West Perth : Gantheaume Press, 1987.
ISBN 0958861013 Hbk £8.95

NATURAL RESOURCES

—Arbitration and renegotiation of international investment agreements : a study with particular reference to means of conflict avoidance under natural resources investment agreements / Wolfgang Peter. – Dordrecht : M. Nijhoff, 1986.
xxiii, 297p.
Includes index. Bibliography: p.267-284.
ISBN 9024733146

—Bibliography on transnational law of natural resources / Martin Bartels...et al. – Deventer : Kluwer, 1981.
227p.
Published for the Institut fur Auslandisches und International Wirtschaftsrecht, Frankfurt am Main.
ISBN 9065440410

—Enforcement of Natural Resources Legislation : A Handbook / Agincourt : Carswell, 1988.

—Global resources and international conflict : environmental factors in strategic policy and action / edited by Arthur H. Westing : Stockholm International Peace Research Institute, United Nations Environment Programme. – Oxford : Oxford University Press, 1986.
xv,250p; 22cm.
Includes bibliography and index.
ISBN 0198291043 £17.50

—Journal of energy & natural resources law / v. – London : Sweet & Maxwell, 1983-.
Co-sponsored by the Section on Energy and Natural Resources Law (S.E.R.L) of the International Bar Association and the Centre for Petroleum and Mineral Law Studies, University of Dundee, Scotland.

—Law and international resource conflicts / by J.E.S. Fawcett and Audrey Parry. – Oxford : Issued under the auspices of the Royal Institute of International Affairs by Clarendon Press, 1981.
xiv, 254p; 23cm.
Bibliography: p244-246. - Includes index.
ISBN 0198253591 £20.00

—Natural resources forum / Dordrecht : Reidel for the United Nations, 1976.
Edited by: United Nations. Centre for Natural Resources, Energy and Transport. Vol. 7 onwards published by Graham & Trotman for the United Nations.
ISBN 01650203

—Permanent sovereignty over natural resources in international law / Kamal Hossain, Subrata Roy Chowdhury. – London : Pinter, 1984.
250p.
ISBN 0861873025 £16.50

—Progress in natural resource economics : essays in resource analysis by members of the Programme in Natural Resource Economics (PNRE) at the University of British Columbia / edited by Anthony Scott with the assistance of John Helliwell, Tracy Lewis and Philip Neher. – Oxford : Clarendon, 1984.
vii,440p; 24cm.
ISBN 0198284608 £20.00

—Settlement of Disputes on the New Natural Resources : Workshop 1982 / Dordrecht : Kluwer, 1983.
502p.
ISBN 9024729017 Hbk £120.00

NATURAL RESOURCES – ANTARCTIC REGIONS

—Antarctic resources policy : scientific, legal and political issues / edited by Francisco Orrego Vicuna. – Cambridge : Cambridge University Press, 1983.
viii,335p.
The contributions published in this book were prepared for the Conference on Antarctic Resources Policy organized by the Institute of International Studies of the University of Chile in the Antarctic Station Teniente Marsh, 6-9 October, 1982.

NATURAL RESOURCES – CANADA

—Managing Natural Resources in a Federal State / Agincourt : Carswell, 1986.
354p.
This work contains a collection of articles on the development and control of northern and offshore oil and gas, development of resources within federal parks and aboriginal lands, revenue sharing, environmental management, and interjurisdictional cooperation.

—Trading Canada's Natural Resources : (Essays from the Third Banff Conference on Natural Law) Canadian Institute of Resources Law / Agincourt : Carswell, 1987.
374p.
This work contains a collection of essays outlining the issues associated with the resource sector trade in Canada. It provides a discussion of Canadian and international trade in natural resources. Other discussions include trade distortions brought about by government protectionism, the impact of domestic regulatory schemes, and the ways in which private sector players can best structure their own legal relations in order to adapt to the changing nature of resources trade.

NAVAL LAW

—Queen's Regulations for the Royal Navy / Consolidated ed., incorporating changes 1-61. 2 v. – London : H.M.S.O., 1984.
looseleaf. – (B.R. 31).
Includes index.
ISBN 011772386X

NAVAL LAW – AUSTRALIA

—Admiralty jurisdiction / Sydney : Law Reform Commission, 1984.
20p. – (Discussion paper).

NAVAL LAW – GREAT BRITAIN

—BR11 Manual of naval law / issued by command of the Defence Council. – 2 v. – London : H.M.S.O., 1981.
loose-leaf; 26cm.
Supersedes BR11 Naval Court Martial Manual dated 1969. Vol.2 contains Appendixes to BR11 Manual of Naval Law.
ISBN 0117723614

NAVAL STRATEGY

—Maritime strategy for medium powers / J.R. Hill. – London : Croom Helm, 1985.
247p; 23cm.
ISBN 0709937199 £19.95

NAVIGATION

—International code of signals / London : IMO, 1985.
vii,175p; 31cm.
Includes index.
ISBN 9280111841 £14.00

NAVIGATION – GREAT BRITAIN

—Law of pilotage / by G.K. Geen and R.P.A. Douglas. – 2nd ed. – London : Lloyd's of London, 1983.
xx,177p.
Previous ed. published as: The law and administration of pilotage. 1977. Bibliography: p.xxi. - Includes index.
ISBN 0907432662

—Law of Tug, Tow and Pilotage / 2nd ed. – London : Chapman & Hall, 1982.
ISBN 0412250209 Hbk £60.00

—Marine pilotage : legislative proposals / presented to Parliament by the Secretary of State for Transport... – London : H.M.S.O., 1986.
iii,12p.
ISBN 0101001525

—Modern law of pilotage / by F.D. Rose. – London : Sweet & Maxwell, 1984.
xxi,138p; 25cm.
Includes index.
ISBN 0421322705 Pbk £12.00

—Pilotage Act 1987 / London : Lloyd's of London Press, 1987.
ISBN 1850441391 Pbk £18.75

—Pilotage Act : 1987 / London : LLoyd's of London Press, 1987.
ISBN 1850441391 Pbk

NEAR EAST

—International and legal problems of the gulf / S.H. Amin. – London : Middle East and North African Studies Press, 1981.
235p.
Bibls..
ISBN 0906559057

—Legal aspects of doing business in the Middle East / edited by Dennis Campbell. – Deventer, Netherlands : Kluwer Law and Taxation Publishers, 1986.
– (International business series).
Includes index.
ISBN 9065442642

—Proceedings of the Seminar on Middle East Law, with reference to Bahrein, Egypt, Iran, Kuwait, Oman, Qatar, Saudi Arabia, U.A.E., 1-4 July 1981, Hamburg, Germany / London : International Bar Association, 1981.
170p.
ISBN 0950587664

NEGLIGENCE – AUSTRALIA

—Community law reform for the Australian Capital Territory / Law Reform Commission. – Canberra : Australian Government Publishing Service, 1985.
ix,44p. – (Report).
Bibliography: p.41-42 - Includes index.
ISBN 0644013257

—Negligence and economic torts : selected aspects : papers presented at seminars conducted by the New South Wales Bar Association / edited by T. Simos. – Sydney : Published by the Law Book Co. for the New South Wales Bar Association, 1980.
vii,159p.
Includes bibliographical references.
ISBN 0455202486

—Occupiers' liability / The Law Reform Commission. – Sydney : The Commission, 1987.
13p. – (Discussion paper).
Bibliography: p.13.

—Professional negligence : being a discussion of the duties and responsibilities of auditors / by E.F. Mannix and J.E. Mannix. – 3rd ed. – Sydney : Butterworths, 1982.
viii,112p.
Previous ed.: 1976. Includes index.
ISBN 0409309338

NEGLIGENCE – AUSTRALIA – QUEENSLAND

—Working paper on a bill to prevent the avoidance of civil liability in cases of death or personal injury caused by negligence / Queensland Law Reform Commission. – Brisbane? : the Commission?, 1984.
8 leaves. – (Q.L.R.C.W.P.).
Includes text of proposed Act.

NEGLIGENCE – CANADA

—Liability in negligence / by J.C. Smith. – Toronto : Carswell, 1984.
xxxiii, 273 p.; 24 cm.
Includes indexes.
ISBN 0459366009 pbk.

—Negligence Law in the 1990's / Vancouver : Continuing Legal Education Society of British Columbia, 1985.
76p.
ISBN 0865041911 Hbk £50.00

—Omissions, negligence and endangering / Law Reform Commission of Canada. – Ottawa : The Commission, 1985.
42,48p. – (Working paper).
Includes bibliographical references. Added t.p. in French: L'omission, la negligence et la mise en danger. Pages numbered in opposite directions. Text in English and French.
ISBN 0662540824

NEGLIGENCE – CANADA -- ONTARIO

—Apportionment of fault in tort / David Cheifetz. – Ontario : Canada Law Book, 1981.
xlii,355p.
ISBN 0888040091

—Economic negligence : the recovery of pure economic loss / by Bruce Feldthusen. – Toronto, Canada : Carswell Legal Publications, 1984.
xxvi, 306 p.; 24 cm.
Includes bibliographical references and indexes.
ISBN 0459364707 Hbk £40

NEGLIGENCE – ENGLAND

—Charlesworth & Percy on negligence / J. Charlesworth, R. A. Percy. – 7th ed. – London : Sweet & Maxwell, 1983.
cxxxviii,1092p; 26cm.
Includes changes and developments in the law of negligence since the 1977 edition, and has been divided into six major sections. Updated to include the Unfair Contract Terms Act 1977, the Limitation Act 1980, the British Telecommunications Act 1981, the Civil Aviation Act 1982, and the Administration of Justice Act 1982.
ISBN 042129020X £70.00

—Leading Cases in Negligence for 'A' Level / 2nd ed. – London : Butterworths, 1986.
ISBN 0406016828 Pbk £5.50

—Liability for defective services / Derrick Owles & Hugh Cockerell. – London : Financial Times Business Information, 1985.
168p; 30cm.
ISBN 0903199858

—Modern law of negligence / R.A. Buckley. – London : Butterworths, 1988.
lvii,402p.
Includes index.
ISBN 0406113009 No price

—Negligence for 'A' Level / 2nd ed. – London : Sweet & Maxwell, 1983.
ISBN 0421321709 Pbk £5.95

—Negligence in surveying and building / Malcolm Ross. – London : Estates Gazette, 1986.
xxii,247p.
Bibliography: p.238-239. - Includes index.
ISBN 0728200953

—Professional negligence / A.M. Dugdale, K.M. Stanton. – London : Butterworths, 1982.
xlii,400p.
Includes index.
ISBN 0406179107

—Professional negligence / by Rupert M. Jackson and John L. Powell. – 2nd ed. – London : Sweet & Maxwell, 1987.
xlvii,472p; 25cm.
Considers the reported cases on professional negligence, with particular emphasis on recent developments. Uses cases reported in established law reports, but also those appearing in individual professional journals. Commonwealth cases are also included.
ISBN 0421341602 £36.00

—Professional negligence / by Ashley Underwood and Stephen Holt. – London : Fourmat, 1981.
xv,96p; 23cm.
ISBN 0906840368

NEGLIGENCE – GREAT BRITAIN

—Accountant's professional negligence : developments in legal liability / Jonathan R.H.H. Pockson. – London : Macmillan, 1982.
xxi,212p; 23cm.
Bibliography: p192-208. - Includes index.
ISBN 0333278453 £25.00

—Latent damage : consultative document / Law Reform Committee. – 1. – London : Law Reform Committee 1981, 1981.
various pagings.

—Leading Cases in the Law of Negligence for 'A' Level / Butterworth Staff. – London : Butterworths, 1981.
This book provides the student in the United Kingdom taking the AEB 'A' level optional paper on negligence with all required cases as originally reported in the All England Law Reports.
ISBN 0406016801 Pbk

—Liability in Negligence / London : Sweet & Maxwell, 1984.
ISBN 0459365908 Hbk £24.00

—Medical research : civil liability and compensation for personal injury : a discussion paper / chairman: David Evered. – London : Ciba Foundation, 1980.
16p.

—Modern Cases of Negligence / 3rd ed. – London : Sweet & Maxwell, 1985.
ISBN 042132810X Hbk £12.50

—Modern law of negligence / London : Butterworths, 1988.
ISBN 0862052505 Hbk

—Negligence and Damages for Personal Injuries : Some Recent Developments / Belfast : Queen's University of Belfast, 1981.
34p.

—Negligence for 'A' Level / 2nd ed. - London : Sweet & Maxwell, 1981.
ISBN 0421289805 Pbk £8.25

—Professional negligence today : the text of two lectures delivered to the Belfast Solicitors' Association on 9 and 23 May 1985 / by D.S. Greer and Ethne E. Harkness. - Belfast : SLS Legal Publications, 1985.
61p.
Includes bibiographical references.

—Twenty-fourth report (latent damage) / Law Reform Committee. - London : H.M.S.O., 1984.
iv,34p; 25cm. - (Report).
ISBN 0101939000

NEGLIGENCE - NEW ZEALAND

—Working paper on contribution in civil cases / Contracts and Commercial Law Reform Committee. - Wellington : Contracts and Commercial Law Reform Committee, 1983.
ii,49 leaves.
Bibliography: 1.37. Includes extracts from the Law Reform Act 1936 and the Contributory Negligence Act 1947 and the text of the Civil Liability (Contribution) Act 1978 (U.K.).

NEGOTIABLE INSTRUMENTS

—Law of Negotiable Instruments / Singapore : Malayan Law Journal, 1984.
139p.
Discusses what constitutes a valid negotiable instrument, problems arising in cases of forgery and material alterations, concepts of holder and holder in due course, and provisions relating to cheques under the Singapore provisions that are in line with the English Cheques Act 1957.
ISBN 9971700417 Pbk £28.00

NEGOTIABLE INSTRUMENTS - AUSTRALIA

—Law of Negotiable Instruments in Australia / 2nd ed. - Butterworths, 1989.
256p.
ISBN 0409495271 Hbk £59.00
ISBN 040949528X Pbk £39.00

—Law Relating to Negotiable Instruments in Australia / London : Butterworths, 1980.
ISBN 0409490407 Pbk £28.00

—Law relating to negotiable instruments in Australia / by M.J.L. Rajanayagam. - Sydney : Butterworths, 1980.
xviii, 231 p.; 25 cm.
Includes index. Bibliography: p. 227-228.
ISBN 0409490407 pbk.

NEGOTIABLE INSTRUMENTS - CANADA

—Crawford and Falconbridge banking and bills of exchange / Bradley Crawford. - 8th edition. 2 v. - Aurora : Canada Law Book Co, 1986.
ISBN 0888040369

NEGOTIABLE INSTRUMENTS - ENGLAND

—Guide to negotiable instruments and the Bills of Exchange Acts / Dudley Richardson. - 7th ed. - London : Butterworths, 1983.
viii,220p; 22cm.
A student and reference introduction to the law of negotiable instruments in the United Kingdom. The impact of cheque cards and credit cards on the negotiable instrument is discussed in detail.
ISBN 0406648247 Pbk £22.40

NEGOTIABLE INSTRUMENTS - GREAT BRITAIN

—Bills of exchange and bankers' documentary credits / by William Hedley. - London : Lloyd's, 1986.
320p; 25cm.
Includes index.
ISBN 1850440840 No price

—Byles on bills of exchange : the law of bills of exchange, promissory notes, bank notes and cheques / Maurice Megrah, F. R. Ryder, Antonio Bueno. - 25th ed. - London : Sweet & Maxwell, 1983.
lxxxv,561p; 26cm.
Previous ed.: 1979. Includes index.
ISBN 0421298308 £50.00

—Guide to Negotiable Instruments / 7th ed. - London : Butterworths, 1983.
ISBN 0406648247 Pbk £9.95

—Negotiable Instruments / Scott. - Stockholm : Anderson Keenan, 1980.
- (Law Unit).
ISBN 0906501156 Pbk £2.75

—Negotiable Instruments / Vanessa Stott. - Winchester : DP Publications.
ISBN 0905435583 Hbk £3.50

NEGOTIABLE INSTRUMENTS - INDIA

—Introduction to Negotiable Instrument Act / Bombay : Universal Book Corporation.

—Negotiable Instruments Act / Adiga. - 14th ed. - New Delhi : Bharat Law House, 1983.

—Negotiable Instruments Act / 9th ed. - Allahabad : Law Book Company, 1988.
950p.

—Negotiable Instruments with Supplement / 1980 repr. - Lucknow : Eastern Book Company, 1984.
329p.

NEGOTIABLE INSTRUMENTS - MALAYSIA

—Law of negotiable instruments in Singapore and Malaysia / Singapore : Malayan Law Journal, 1984.
xxviii,225.
Account of the basic law governing negotiable instruments, covering the curent practice where relevant. Includes status of parties to the bill upon its enforceability. Relevant Asian and English cases are discussed including some of the leading Commonwealth authorities from Australia and Canada.
ISBN 9971700409 Hbk £50.00

NEGOTIABLE INSTRUMENTS - SINGAPORE

—Law of negotiable instruments in Singapore and Malaysia / Singapore : Malayan Law Journal, 1984.
xxviii,225.
Account of the basic law governing negotiable instruments, covering the curent practice where relevant. Includes status of parties to the bill upon its enforceability. Relevant Asian and English cases are discussed including some of the leading Commonwealth authorities from Australia and Canada.
ISBN 9971700409 Hbk £50.00

NEGOTIABLE INSTRUMENTS - SOUTH AFRICA

—Bills of exchange, cheques and promissory notes in South African law / by F.R. Malan : assisted by C. R. de Beer. - Durban : Butterworths, 1983.
xii,441p.
Bibliography: p.377-391. - Includes index.
ISBN 0409040738

—Law of negotiable instruments in South Africa / Denis V. Cowen and Leonard Gering. - Cape Town : Juta, 1985.
xxiv,587.
ISBN 0702115703

—Negotiable Instruments / T. J. Scott. - Durban : Professional Publisher, 1984.
ISBN 0409040215 Pbk £30.00

NEGOTIABLE INSTRUMENTS - UNITED STATES

—Commercial paper / edited by Richard Felix. - London : Euromoney Publications, 1987.
ix,182p.
ISBN 1870031601

NEGOTIATION

—Getting to YES : negotiating agreement without giving in / Roger Fisher and William Ury : with Bruce Patton, editor. - London : Business Books, 1986.
xiii,161p; 23cm.
Originally published: Boston, Mass. : Houghton Mifflin, 1981 ; London : Hutchinson, 1982.
ISBN 0091493706 Hbk No price
ISBN 0091640717 Pbk No price

NEGOTIATION - CANADA

—Negotiation / Vancouver : Continuing Legal Education Society of British Columbia, 1986.
140p.
ISBN 0865042489 Hbk £50.00

NEIGHBOURHOOD JUSTICE CENTRES - AUSTRALIA

—On tap not on top : legal centres in Australia, 1972-1982 / edited by David Neal. - S.l. : Legal Service Bulletin, 1984.
64p.
ISBN 0959472738

NEW BRUNSWICK

—New Brunswick government publications : quarterly list / Publication du government du Nouveau-Brunswick. - Fredericton, N.B. : Legislative Library, 1986.
Annual cumulation entitled : New Brunswick government documents : a checklist of New Brunswick government documents received at the Legislative Library, Fredericton, N.B. during the calendar year ... (ISSN 0548-4006). Text in English and French.
ISBN 08301085

NEW HAMPSHIRE - UNITED STATES

—Papers of Daniel Webster / Alfred S. Konefsky, Andrew J. King. - Hanover, N.H. : Published for Dartmouth College by the University Press of New England, 1982.
xxxix,571p; 25cm.
Includes index.
ISBN 0874512328 Unpriced

NEW TOWNS - GREAT BRITAIN

—New Towns Act 1981 : Report of the Cumbran Development Corporation / London : HMSO, 1983.

NEW YORK (N.Y.)

—East side-west side : organizing crime in New York 1930-1950 / Alan Block. - Cardiff : University College Cardiff Press, 1980.
265p.
Bibliographies.
ISBN 0901426997

NEW YORK (N.Y.) - UNITED STATES

—Two cultures of policing : street cops and management cops / Elizabeth Reuss-Ianni. - New Brunswick, N.J. : Transaction Books, 1983.
145p; 24cm.
Bibliography: p137-142. - Includes index.
ISBN 0878554696 Unpriced

NEWFOUNDLAND

—Newfoundland and Dominion Status / Agincourt : Carswell, 1988.
280p.

—Report on the limitation of actions / Newfoundland Law Reform Commission. - St. John's : The Commission, 1986.
vi,29p.

—Working paper on limitation of actions / Newfoundland Law Reform Commission. - St. John's : The Commission, 1985.
xi,481p.
Includes bibliographical references. With a supplement.

—Working paper on powers of attorney / Newfoundland Law Reform Commission. - St. John's : The Commission, 1987.
iv,64p.
Includes bibliographical references.

—Working paper on the Mechanics' Liens Act : certain substantive issues / Newfoundland Law Reform Commission. - St.John's : The Commission, 1987.
vi,294p.
Includes bibliographical references. Includes text of the Acts.

NEWSPAPER COURT REPORTING - AUSTRALIA

—Contempt and the media / Australian Law Reform Commission. - Sydney : The Commission, 1986.
182p. - (Discussion paper).
Cover title. Bibliography: p.178-182.

NIGERIA

—Federalism in Nigeria under the presidential constitution / by B.O. Nwabueze. - London : Sweet & Maxwell, 1983.
400p.
Includes index.
ISBN 0421316101 Hbk No price
ISBN 0421315806 Pbk £16.00

—Marriage laws of Nigeria : papers presented at a national workshop held at the Nigerian Institute of Advanced Legal Studies / edited by T. Akinola Aguda : assisted by Isabella Adi. - Lagos : The Nigerian Institute of Advanced Legal Studies, 1981.
170p.
ISBN 9782353000

NIGERIA - NIGERIA

—Transplants and mongrels and the law : the Nigerian experiment : an inaugural lecture delivered at the University of Ife on 17th May, 1983 / by A.A.O. Okunniga. - Ile-Ife, Nigeria : University of Ife Press, 1984.
32p. - (Inaugural lecture series).
Includes bibliographical references.

NITRATES

—Nitrate in water : a report of the Nitrate Coordination Group / Central Directorate of Environmental Protection, Department of the Environment. - London : H.M.S.O., 1986.
ISBN 0117518662

NO-STRIKE CLAUSE - GREAT BRITAIN

—Strike-free procedures : are they what they seem? / Roy Lewis. - Coventry : University of Warwick. School of Industrial and Business Studies. Industrial Relations Research Unit, 1988.
14 leaves.
Bibliography: p14.

NOISE

—International standards and recommended practices : environmental protection : annex 16 to the Convention on International Civil Aviation / International Civil Aviation Organization. - 1st ed - 1981. 1. - Montreal : International Civil Aviation Organization, 1981.
loose-leaf; 28cm.
Supersedes: International standards and recommended practices: aircraft noise: annex 16 to the Convention on International Civil Aviation. 3rd ed. - July 1978. Current edition only kept. Kept up to date by amendments and supplements.

—Noise Levels on Board Ships / International Maritime Organization. - London : International Maritime Organization, 1982.

French Edition

Spanish Edition

NOISE - AUSTRALIA

—Environmental Noise Control Legislation in Australia / Australian Environment Council-Environmental Noise Control Committee. - Canberra : Australian Government Publishing Service, 1982.
27p.
ISBN 064401914X Hbk £2.50

NOISE - ENGLAND

—Aircraft noise and sleep disturbance : a selection of tabulations of the responses to the administered surveys for the main phase of the study / prepared by the Civil Aviation Authority London on behalf of the Department of Trade. - Cheltenham : Civil Aviation Authority, 1980.
17,16p,3 leaves of places (2 folded).

—Aircraft noise and sleep disturbance : a selection of tabulations of the responses to the postal surveys for the main phase of the study / prepared by the Civil Aviation Authority on behalf of the Department of Trade. - Cheltenham : Civil Aviation Authority, 1980.
71p in various pagings, 3 leaves of plates (2 folded).

—Aircraft noise and sleep disturbance : final report / prepared by the Civil Aviation Authority, London on behalf of the Department of Trade. - Cheltenham : Civil Aviation Authority, 1980.
166p in various pagings, 3 leaves of plates (2 folded).
Includes bibliographical references.

—Aircraft noise and sleep disturbances : designated night data for sites surveyed in the main phase of the study / prepared by the Civil Aviation Authority London on behalf of the Department of Trade. - Cheltenham : Civil Aviation Authority, 1980.
49p,3 leaves of plates (2 folded).

—Third London Airport : report / by a Working Group of the Noise Advisory Council i.e. the Working Group on Noise from Air Traffic. - London : H.M.S.O., 1980.
ix,26p; 25cm.
ISBN 0117514748 sd £2.25

NOISE - GREAT BRITAIN

—Forensic audiology / Chuang Wei Ping : foreword by Ronald Hinchcliffe. - Middlesbrough : Chuang Wei Ping, 1985.
108p in various pagings; 22cm.
ISBN 0951080008 Pbk £6.00

NON PROFIT ORGANISATIONS

—Non-profit-making associations in some Council of Europe countries / Council of Europe Directorate of Legal Affairs. - Strasbourg : Council of Europe, 1981.
10p; 30cm. - (Legislative dossier).

NON PROFIT ORGANISATIONS - AUSTRALIA

—Law Relating to Non-Profit Associations in Australia and New Zealand / North Ryde : Law Book Co, 1986.
xl, 380p.
ISBN 0455206236 Hbk £48.00

NON PROFIT ORGANISATIONS - CANADA - ALBERTA

—Proposals for a new Alberta Incorporated Associations Act / Institute of Law Research and Reform, Edmonton, Alberta. - Edmonton : The Institute, 1987.
i,223p. - (Report).

NON PROFIT ORGANISATIONS - NEW ZEALAND

—Law Relating to Non-Profit Associations in Australia and New Zealand / North Ryde : Law Book Co, 1986.
xl, 380p.
ISBN 0455206236 Hbk £48.00

NORTHAMPTONSHIRE

—Eyre of Northamptonshire : 3-4 Edward III, A.D. 1329-1330 / edited for the Selden Society by Donald W. Sutherland. - London : Selden Society, 1983.
lxxv,498,498p; 26cm.
Opposite pages of main sequence bear duplicate numbering. French text with parallel English translation.
Vol.2 / edited for the Selden Society by Donald W. Sutherland. - 1983.
vi,499-770,499-770,771-922p; 26cm.
Opposite pages of main sequence bear duplicate numbering. French text with parallel English translation.

NORTHERN IRELAND

—Data Protection Act : subject access to personal health data : a consultation paper / s.l. : s.n., .
9,3,2p.

—Fooled again? : the Anglo-Irish Agreement and after / Anthony Coughlan. - Cork : Mercier, 1986.
88p; 21cm.
ISBN 0853427747 Pbk £4.95

—Northern Ireland : A Problem to Every Solution / London : Quaker Peace & Service, 1982.
147p.
ISBN 0901689173 Pbk £1.30

—Road to Hillsborough : the shaping of the Anglo-Irish agreement / by Anthony Kenny. - Oxford : Pergamon, 1986.
xi,141p; 21cm.
ISBN 0080347754 Pbk £12.95
ISBN 0080342485 £6.50

NORTHERN IRELAND - GREAT BRITAIN

—Northern Ireland : a framework for devolution / presented to Parliament by the Secretary of State for Northern Ireland. - London : H.M.S.O., 1982.
17p.
ISBN 0101854102

NOTARIES - GREAT BRITAIN

—Brooke's Treatise on the Office and Practice of a Notary of England / Repr. of 1939 ed. - London : Sweet & Maxwell, 1985.
- (Sweet and Maxwell Library Reprints).
ISBN 0421351705 Hbk £50.00

NOTARIES - INDIA

—Commentaries on Notaries Act, 1985 : Act No. 53, 1952 / J.P. Bhatnagar. - Allahabad : Ashoka Law House, 1987.
240p.

—Law Relating to Notaries Act / Bhatnagar. - Allahabad : Ashoka Law House, 1987.
300p.

NOTARIES - IRELAND

—Irish Notary / London : Butterworths, 1987.
ISBN 0862052386 Hbk £35.00

NOTTINGHAM (NOTTINGHAMSHIRE)

—Max Weber / Anthony T. Kronman. - London : Edward Arnold, 1983.
214p; 22cm.
Includes bibliographies and index.
ISBN 0713163615 Pbk £9.95
ISBN 0713163623 Pbk £4.95

NUCLEAR ACCIDENTS

—Chernobyl and the safety of nuclear reactors in OECD countries : report / by an NEA group of experts. - Paris : Nuclear Energy Agency, Organisation for Economic Co-operation and Development, 1987.
96 p.; 23 cm.
ISBN 9264129758 pbk.

—Chernobyl : law and communication : transboundary nuclear air pollution : the legal materials / Philippe Sands. - Cambridge : Grotius, 1988.
xxxiii,312p.
Reproduces texts including multilateral and bilateral treaties, non-binding acts of international organisations and private associations of scholars, and national legislation. Covers the development of the law up to and including the 1986 IAEA Conventions on Early Notification and assistance, and the 1987 Resolution of the Institut de Droit International on Transboundary Air Pollution.
ISBN 0949009229 £38.00

—IAEA Notification and Assistance Conventions in Case of a Nuclear Accident : Landmarks in the History of the Multilateral Treaty-Making Process / Dordrecht : Kluwer, 1987.
226p.
ISBN 9024736161 Hbk £125.00

NUCLEAR ACCIDENTS - USSR

—Chernobyl : the real story / by Richard F. Mould. - Oxford : Pergamon, 1988.
90p; 25cm.
Includes index.
ISBN 0080357180 Hbk £12.90
ISBN 0080357199 Pbk £6.90

NUCLEAR ARMS CONTROL

—Arms control and disarmament in outer space : lecture-seminars given at the Centre for Research of Air and Space Law / edited by Nicolas Mateesco Matte. - Montreal, Canada : Centre for Research of Air and Space Law, McGill University, 1985.
viii, 203 p.; 23 cm.
Includes bibliographical references.
ISBN 0771701233 pbk.

—Nuclear war, nuclear proliferation and their consequences : proceedings of the Vth international colloquium organized by the Groupe de Bellerive, Geneva 27-29 June 1985 / edited by Sadruddin Aga Khan. - Oxford : Clarendon, 1986.
xii,483p; 25cm.
Includes index.
ISBN 0198255438 Hbk £25.00
ISBN 019825542X Pbk £12.50

NUCLEAR DISARMAMENT

—Arms control and disarmament in outer space : lecture-seminars given at the Centre for Research of Air and Space Law / edited by Nicolas Mateesco Matte. - Montreal, Canada : Centre for Research of Air and Space Law, McGill University, 1985.
viii, 203 p.; 23 cm.
Includes bibliographical references.
ISBN 0771701233 pbk.

NUCLEAR ENERGY

—Agreements registered with the International Atomic Energy Agency : definitive entries up to 31 December 1980; provisional entries up to 31 December 1982 / International Atomic Energy Agency. - 9th ed. - Vienna : IAEA, 1985.
262p. - (Legal series).
ISBN 920176085X

—Agreements registered with the International Atomic Energy Agency (up to 31 December 1978) / International Atomic Energy Agency. - 8th ed. - Vienna : International Atomic Energy Agency, 1981.
253p; 24cm. - (Legal series).
ISBN 9201760817

NUCLEAR FUELS

—Rationality and ritual : the Windscale inquiry and nuclear decisions in Britain / Brian Wynne. - Faringdon : British Society for the History of Science, 1982.
x,222p. - (Monographs).
Bibliography: p178.
ISBN 0906450020

NUCLEAR NONPROLIFERATION

—Nuclear non-proliferation and global security / edited by David B. Dewitt. - London : Croom Helm, 1987.
x,283p; 23cm.
Conference proceedings. Includes index.
ISBN 0709908962 £25.00

—Nuclear non-proliferation treaty : origin and implementation, 1959-1979 / by Mohamed I. Shaker. - London : Oceana Publications, 1980.
3 v. (xxiv, 1526 p.); 25 cm.
A revision of the author's thesis, Geneva, published in 1976 under title: The treaty on the non-proliferation of nuclear weapons. Includes index. Bibliography: v. 3, p. 1457-1504.
ISBN 0379204703 v. 1 £40.00

NUCLEAR POWER

—Chernobyl and the safety of nuclear reactors in OECD countries : report / by an NEA group of experts. - Paris : Nuclear Energy Agency, Organisation for Economic Co-operation and Development, 1987.
96 p.; 23 cm.
ISBN 9264129758 pbk.

—Code of Safety for Nuclear Merchant Ships / International Maritime Organization. - London : International Maritime Organization, 1982.

French Edition

Spanish Edition

—Convention on the physical protection of nuclear material / Vienna : International Atomic Energy Agency, 1982.
- (Legal series).
ISBN 9201760825

—Future of nuclear power / London : Graham & Trotman, 1988.
ix,213p.
ISBN 0860109879 No price (Oct.)

—Rationality and ritual : the Windscale inquiry and nuclear decisions in Britain / Brian Wynne. - Faringdon : British Society for the History of Science, 1982.
x,222p. - (Monographs).
Bibliography: p178.
ISBN 0906450020

—Safety Recommendations on the Use of Ports by Nuclear Merchant Ships / International Maritime Organization. - London : International Maritime Organization, 1980.

French Edition

—Sizewell Syndrome : Nuclear Power, Nuclear Weapons and Public Policy / London : Spokesman Books, 1984.
128p. - (Endpapers Ser. No. 7).
ISBN 0851244025 Hbk £3.95

—Utilization of nuclear energy and international law / Vanda Lamm. - Budapest : Akademiai Kiado, 1984.
155p.
ISBN 963053892X

NUCLEAR POWER - GREAT BRITAIN
—Commercial nuclear power / legal and constitutional issues : edited by Richard Macrory : with a foreword by the Lord Flowers. – London : Imperial College Centre for Environmental Technology, 1982.
69p; 22cm.
ISBN 0950774405 Pbk Unpriced

—Nuclear Law Bulletin / Organisation for Economic Co-operation and Development. – London : HMSO.

NUCLEAR WARFARE
—Deterrence in the 1980s : crisis and dilemma / edited by R.B. Byers. – London : Croom Helm, 1985.
235p; 22cm.
Includes index.
ISBN 070993288X £18.95

—Nuclear deterrence, morality and realism / John Finnis, Joseph M. Boyle, Jr., Germain Grisez. – Oxford : Clarendon, 1987.
xv,429p; 22cm.
Bibliography: p391-411. - Includes index.
ISBN 0198247923 Hbk £30.00
ISBN 0198247915 Pbk no price

NUCLEAR WASTE
—Rationality and ritual : the Windscale inquiry and nuclear decisions in Britain / Brian Wynne. – Faringdon : British Society for the History of Science, 1982.
x,222p. – (Monographs).
Bibliography: p178.
ISBN 0906450020

NUCLEAR WEAPONS
—Cultural norms, war and the environment / edited by Arthur H. Westing. – Oxford : Oxford University Press, 1988.
xiv,177p.
On t.p.: Sipri, Stockholm International Peace Research Institute; UNEP, United Nations Environment Programme. Includes bibliographical references and index.
ISBN 0198291256 Hbk £42.00

—Forgotten treaties : a practical plan for world disarmament / Allan McKnight : with an introduction by Keith Suter. – Melbourne : Law Council of Australia, 1983.
xi,136p.
Includes bibliographical references and index. Part II is text of McKnight's Draft Disarmament Treaty.
ISBN 0959660879

—Nuclear arms control : with effective international agreements / Julie Dahlitz : foreword by Rikhi Jaipal. – London : Allen & Unwin, 1983.
238p; 24cm.
Bibliography: p217-232. - Includes index.
ISBN 0043410235 Hbk £15.00
ISBN 0043410243 Pbk £4.95

—Sizewell Syndrome : Nuclear Power, Nuclear Weapons and Public Policy / London : Spokesman Books, 1984.
128p. – (Endpapers Ser. No. 7).
ISBN 0851244025 Hbk £3.95

—Trade union powers and the anti-nuclear campaign / London : Lawyers Versus the Bomb, 1982.
19p; 21cm. – (Pamphlet).

NUCLEAR WEAPONS (INTERNATIONAL LAW)
—Illegality of nuclear warfare / Lawyers for Nuclear Disarmament. – London : Lawyers for Nuclear Disarmament, 1983.
26p.
Originally published: 1982. Bibliography: p.19.
ISBN 0946499004

—Nuclear weapons, the peace movement and the law / edited by John Dewar ... et al. – Basingstoke : Macmillan, 1986.
xix,255p; 22cm.
Bibliography: p241-251. - Includes index.
ISBN 0333414101 Hbk £27.50
ISBN 033341411X Pbk £9.95

NUCLEAR-WEAPON-FREE ZONES
—Indian Ocean as a zone of peace : Workshop on the Indian Ocean as a Zone of Peace, Dhaka, People People's Republic of Bangladesh, November 23-25, 1985 / Dordrecht : Martinus Nijhoff, 1986.
Sponsored and organized by the Bangladesh Institute of International and Strategic Studies in association with the International Peace Academy.
ISBN 0898389178 pbk.

NUISANCE - ENGLAND
—Law of nuisance / R. A. Buckley. – London : Butterworths, 1981.
xxxv,181p.
ISBN 040614110X

NUISANCE - GREAT BRITAIN
—Law of Nuisance / London : Butterworths, 1981.
ISBN 040614110X Hbk £22.00

—Law of Nuisance / Wellington : Butterworths, 1981.
This work on torts and the law of nuisance in United Kingdom is directed at practitioners and academics. The book presents a lengthy discussion of recent developments in the law on liability for natural occurrences.
ISBN 040614110X Hbk

—Nuisance / London : Oyez Longman, 1982. – (Oyez Longman Practice Note Ser.: No. 71).
ISBN 0851206247 Hbk £6.95

—Nuisance (LPPN71) / London : Longman Professional, 1982.
ISBN 0851206247 Pbk £14.95

—Odour nuisances and their control / London : Shaw & Sons, 1984.
ISBN 0721910009 Pbk £9.00

—Odour Nuisances and Their Control / London : Shaw & Sons, 1984.
ISBN 0721910009 Pbk £9.00

—Offence to others / Oxford : Oxford University Press, 1985.
ISBN 019503449X Hbk £25.00

NURSING HOMES - GREAT BRITAIN
—Registered Homes Bill : report on the consolidation of certain enactments relating to residential care homes and nursing homes and registered homes tribunals / The Law Commission. – London : H.M.S.O., 1983.
3p; 25cm.
ISBN 0101911505

NUTRITION
—Food policy / Paris : Organisation for Economic Co- operation and Development, 1981.
75 p.; 24 cm.
'This report and five Country Notes were discussed and adopted by the OECD Working Party on Agricultural Policies and by the Committee for Agriculture 28th April 1981.'. Includes bibliographical references.
ISBN 0702216283 pbk.

—Laws and Statutes for Production and Marketing of Nutrition / Oslo : Fabritius og Sonners, 1984.
804p. – (Food).
ISBN 8207009020 Hbk £230.00

OATHS
—Evidence reference / Australian Law Reform Commission. – Sydney : The Commission, 1982.
vii,133p.
Includes bibliographical references.

OATHS - AUSTRALIA - QUEENSLAND
—Working paper of the Law Reform Commission on a bill in respect of an act to replace the Oaths Act 1867-1981 / Brisbane : Queensland. Law Reform Commission?, 1988.
iii,162p. – (Q.L.R.C.W.P.).

OATHS - INDIA
—Oaths Act / Shanglo. – 2nd ed. – Allahabad : Law Book Company, 1988.
60p.

OBLIGATIONS (LAW) - ENGLAND
—Introduction to the law of obligations / A.M. Tettenborn. – London : Butterworths, 1984.
xxv,238p; 23cm.
Includes index.
ISBN 0406260672 Hbk Unpriced
ISBN 0406260680 Pbk Unpriced

OBSCENITY
—Pornography and politics : the Williams Committee in retrospect / A. W. B. Simpson. – London : Waterlow Publishers, 1983.
143p.
ISBN 0080391567

OBSCENITY - CANADA
—Pornography and prostitution in Canada : report of the Special Committee on Pornography and Prostitution / Canada. – 2 v. – Ottawa : Canadian Government Publishing Centre, 1985.
ISBN 0660118092

—Pornography and prostitution in Canada : report of the Special Committee on Pornography and Prostitution : summary / Canada. – Ottawa : Department of Justice, 1985.
65,71p.
With French t.p.: La pornographie et la prostitution au Canada. Pages numbered in opposite directions. English and French text.
ISBN 066253686X

—Pornography and prostitution : issues paper : this is a discussion paper / prepared by the Special Committee on Pornography and Prostitution appointed by the Minister of Justice for Canada. – Ottawa, Canada : Dept. of Justice, Communications and Public Affairs, 1983.
ii, 78, 100 p.; 28 cm.
English and French. Title on added t.p.: Pornographie et prostitution.
ISBN 0662527682 pbk.

OBSCENITY - GREAT BRITAIN
—Offensive literature : decensorship in Britain, 1960-1982 / John Sutherland. – London : Junction Books, 1982.
207p; 22cm.
ISBN 0862450640

OBSCENITY - INDIA
—Law of Obscenity : a Comparative Study / Delhi : Mittal Publications, 1988.

OBSTETRICS
—Savage enquiry : who controls childbirth? / Wendy Savage. – London : Virago, 1986.
xvii,189p,8p of plates; 20cm.
ISBN 0860688593 Pbk £2.95

OCCUPANCY - SCOTLAND
—Report on occupancy rights in the matrimonial home and domestic violence / Scottish Law Commission. – Edinburgh : H.M.S.O, 1980.
vii,148p; 25cm. – (1979-80 H.C. 676).
ISBN 0102676801 Pbk £4.50

OCCUPATIONAL TRAINING - GREAT BRITAIN
—Who controls training? : the rise of the Manpower Services Commission / Caroline St John-Brooks. – London : Fabian Society, 1985.
20p; 22cm.
ISBN 0716305062 unbound £1.50

OCEAN BOTTOM (INTERNATIONAL LAW)
—Taxation of the income arising from the international seabed : proceedings of a seminar held in Berlin in 1981 during the 35th Congress of the International Fiscal Association / organised by the International Fiscal Association. – Deventer : Kluwer, 1982.
159p. – (IFA congress seminar series).
ISBN 9065440593

OCEAN BOTTOM (SHIPPING LAW)
—International Law of Ocean Development, 2 Vols. / Leiden : Sijthoff, 1975-1982.
Bibliography: v.1, p.515-519; v.2, 629-631.
ISBN 9028601228 loose £10.00

—Internationalizing the seabed / Roderick Ogley. – Aldershot : Gower, 1984.
vii,256,9p; 23cm.
Bibliography: p248-256. - Includes index.
ISBN 0566006294 £17.95

—UN Draft Convention on the Law of the Sea : how it affects the United Kingdom's oil rights / E.D. Brown. – S.l. : s.n., 1981.
56p.
'Paper read at seminar on recent developments in U.K. petroleum law, London, June, 1981'. Includes bibliographical references.

OCEAN ENGINEERING
—International cooperation in marine science and technology in the Pacific region : proceedings of the 6th International Ocean Symposium November 5-6, 1981, the Japan Shipping Club, Tokyo, Japan / Tokyo : Ocean Association of Japan, 1982.
69p.
Edited by the Ocean Association of Japan. Title also in Japanese.

—Transfer of marine technology to developing nations in international law / Boleslaw A. Boczek. – Honolulu : Law of the Sea Institute, University of Hawaii, 1982.
vi,79p. – (Occasional paper).
Includes bibliographical references.

OCEAN MINING
—Deepsea mining and the law of the sea / Alexandra Merle Post. – The Hague : M. Nijhoff Publishers, 1983.
xxiii,358p.
Bibliography: p329-358.
ISBN 902473049X

—Taxation of the income arising from the international seabed : proceedings of a seminar held in Berlin in 1981 during the 35th Congress of the International Fiscal Association / organised by the International Fiscal Association. – Deventer : Kluwer, 1982.
159p. – (IFA congress seminar series).
ISBN 9065440593

OCEAN MINING - UNITED STATES
—Common heritage or common burden: the US position on the development of a regime for deep seabed mining in the law of the sea convention / Oxford : Clarendon Press, 1989.
288; 23.5.
Assesses the US role in the negotiations on the UN Convention on the LAW of the Sea, particularly with regard to the ocean floor. Examines the US view of the lawfulness of deep seabed mining under international law. Suggests that despite significant compromises negotiated between the US and developing countries at the Conference up to 1980, the emerging seabed regime was not as widely endorsed by US officials as is assumed.
ISBN 0198252277 Hbk £30.00

OCEANOGRAPHIC RESEARCH

—Marine scientific research and the law of the sea / Alfred H.A. Soons. – Deventer, Netherlands : Kluwer Law and Taxation Publishers, 1982.
xix, 383 p.; 24 cm.
At head of title: T.M.C. Asser Instituut, The Hague. Includes index. Bibliography: p. 370-377.
ISBN 9065440658

OCEANS

—Evolution of Ocean Property Rights / London : Trade Policy Research Centre.

—International Law of Ocean Development, 2 Vols. /. – Dordrecht : Kluwer.
ISBN 9028601775 Hbk £578.00

—Ocean and Coastal Law / Johnson. – Prentice-Hall, 1983.
ISBN 0136292046 Hbk £35.05

—Public Order of the Oceans : a Contemporary International Law of the Sea / William T. Burke. – Dordrecht : Kluwer, 1987.
1,300p.
ISBN 0898389011 Hbk £400.00

—Times atlas of the oceans / edited by Alastair Couper. – London : Times Books, 1983.
272p; 37cm.
Bibliography: p256-257. - Includes index.
ISBN 0723002460 £30.00

OCEANS – COMMONWEALTH

—Ocean management : a regional perspective : the prospects for Commonwealth maritime co-operation in Asia and the Pacific / report by a Commonwealth Group of Experts. – London : Commonwealth Secretariat, 1984.
Chairman: Satya N. Nandan.
ISBN 0850922615

OCEANS – GREAT BRITAIN

—Marginal Seabed and U.K. Legal Practice / Oxford : Oxford University Press, 1981.
ISBN 0198253699 Hbk £22.50

OFFENCES – AUSTRALIA

—Property Offences / M.S. Weinberg. – 2nd ed. – North Ryde : Law Book Co, 1986.
xl, 445p.
ISBN 0455206325 Hbk £65.00
ISBN 0455206333 Pbk £45.00

OFFENCES – AUSTRALIA – WESTERN AUSTRALIA

—Police Offences In Western Australia / Sydney : Butterworths, 1981.
243p.

OFFENCES – CANADA

—Canadian Criminal Code Offences, 1 vol. / Agincourt : Carswell.
This handbook for the Canadian practitioner presents the fifty most commonly charged Criminal Code offenses in forty-seven chapters. A checklist of all facts that must be proved by the prosecution and a summary of the key features of the offense is included in each chapter.

—Secondary liability : participation in crime and inchoate offences / Law Reform Commission of Canada. – Ottawa : The Commission, 1985.
53,61p. – (Working paper).
Includes bibliographical references. Added t.p. in French: La responsabilite secondaire: complicite et infractions inchoatives. Cover title: Criminal law - secondary liability. Pages numbered in opposite directions. English and French text.
ISBN 0662537491

—Understanding Criminal Offenses / Barrie J. Saxton. – Agincourt : Carswell, 1987.
383p.
This textbook for students of Canadian criminal law discusses the main criminal offenses under the Canadian criminal justice system. Each offense is broken down to the component elements specific to that offense.

OFFENCES – EUROPEAN COMMUNITY

—Economic Offences in EEC Law : With Special Reference to English and German Law / Kehl am Rhein : Norbert Paul Engel, 1983.
228p.
ISBN 3883570273 Hbk £48.00

OFFENCES – GREAT BRITAIN

—Points to Prove : How to Deal with Day-to-Day Offences / London : Police Review Publishing, 1981.
ISBN 0851649912 Pbk £3.50

—Protection of Offences / London : Sweet & Maxwell, 1986.
ISBN 0421349107 Pbk

OFFENCES – SRI LANKA

—Offences Under the Penal Code of Ceylon / Colombo : Lake House Investments.

OFFENCES AGAINST PROPERTY

—Explanatory report on the European Convention on Offences relating to Cultural Property / Strasbourg : Council of Europe, 1985.
35 p.; 21 cm.
'The text of the European Convention on Offences relating to Cultural Property is also reproduced in this publication'–P. 3.
ISBN 9287107955 pbk.

OFFENCES AGAINST PROPERTY – NORTHERN IRELAND

—Compensation for criminal damage to property / by D.S. Greer and V.A. Mitchell. – Belfast : SLS Legal Publications (N.I.), 1982.
xxxviii,345p.
Includes index.

OFFENCES AGAINST PROPERTY – SOUTH AFRICA

—Anton Piller-type orders / South African Law Commission. – Pretoria : The Commission, 1986.
iii,23 leaves. – (Poject).

OFFENCES AGAINST PUBLIC SAFETY

—Brownlie's Law of public order and national security / edited by Michael Supperstone. – 2nd ed. – London : Butterworths, 1981.
lvii,415p.
Previous ed. entitled: The law relating to public order. Includes index.
ISBN 0406137013

OFFENCES AGAINST PUBLIC SAFETY – AUSTRALIA

—Public order and the law / by Andrew Hiller : with a foreword by Judge Gibney. – Sydney : Law Book Co., 1983.
xx,230p.
Bibliography: p.xix-xx. - Includes index.
ISBN 0455202761
ISBN 0455204101 PBK £26.00

OFFENCES AGAINST RELIGION – ENGLAND

—Criminal law : offences against religion and public worship / Great Britain. – London : H.M.S.O., 1985.
iv,51p.
ISBN 0102442851

—Offences against religion and public worship / the Law Commission. – London : H.M.S.O., 1981.
vi,166p; 21cm. – (Working paper).
ISBN 0117301590 Pbk £5.70

OFFENCES AGAINST THE PERSON – CANADA

—New Offences Against the Person : the Provisions of Bill C-127 / Butterworths, 1984.
288p.
Contains analysis of all relevant decisions, tables of included offences, assaults, abduction offences, evidentiary and procedural rules, hypothetical examples, sample verdict sheets simplifying the jury's task, sexual assaults and defences and exemptions.
ISBN 0409875759 Hbk £65.00

—Report on some aspects of medical treatment and criminal law / Law Reform Commission of Canada. – Ottawa : The Commission, 1986.
19,19p. – (Report).
Pages numbered in opposite directions. Text in English and French.
ISBN 0662543793

OFFENCES AGAINST THE PERSON – ENGLAND

—Report / Criminal Law Revision Committee. – London : H.M.S.O, 1980.
viii,150p; 25cm.
ISBN 0101784406 Pbk £4.50

OFFENCES AGAINST THE PERSON – GREAT BRITAIN

—Criminal Law-Offences Against Person / Pickover. – London : Police Review, 1987.
ISBN 085164029X Pbk £5.60

—Personal violence / by Roy Walmsley. – London : H.M.S.O., 1986.
vi, 79p; 25cm.
A Home Office Research and Planning Unit report.
ISBN 0113408277

OFFENDERS – CANADA

—Parole decision-making in Canada : research towards decision guidelines / by Joan Nuffield. – Ottawa, Ont. : Communication Division, Solicitor General of Canada, 1982.
iv, 96 p.; 28 cm.
Bibliography: p. 91-96.
ISBN 0662121147 pbk.

—Young Offenders Act Manual / Aurora : Canada Law Book Co.
– (Text Books-Criminal).

Binder and Contents
The principles and procedures of The Young Offender's Act, the replacement Act to the Juvenile Delinquents Act, are discussed in this comprehensive reference manual. The Manual includes case annotations, insightful commentary, extensive indexing and accurate cross referencing.

—Young Offenders and the State / Toronto : Butterworths, 1984.
288p.

—Young offenders and the state: Canadian perspective on delinquency / Scarborough, Ontario : Butterworths (Canada), 1984.
288.
Argues that the institutions that the Canadian state has created to del with young offenders - schools, courts, reformatories, group homes and jails, are not politically neutral. Analyses methodological problems in dealing with official statistics and social experiments, and draws upon Canadian, American and British sources.
ISBN 0409875830 Pbk

—Young Offenders Service, 2 vols / Heino Lilles. – Toronto : Butterworths.

OFFENDERS – COMMONWEALTH

—Survey of extradition and fugitive offenders legislation as between Commonwealth jurisdictions / prepared for the Commonwealth Secretariat by the Commonwealth Legal Advisory Service of the British Institute of International and Comparative Law. – Rev. – London : Commonwealth Secretariat, 1982.
iii,70p; 30cm.
Previous ed.: 1977.
ISBN 0850922356 Pbk £10.00

OFFENDERS – ENGLAND

—Sentencing and penal policy / Andrew Ashworth. – London : Weidenfeld and Nicolson, 1983.
xx,500p; 22cm.
Bibliography: p487-495. - Includes index.
ISBN 0297782363 Hbk Unpriced

—Sentencing law and practice / by C.K. Boyle and M.J. Allen. – London : Sweet & Maxwell, 1985.
xxxvi,338p.
Includes index.
ISBN 0421344008 Pbk £15.00

—Validity of the reconviction prediction score / by Denis Ward. – London : HMSO, 1987.
vi,45p.
Describes the method used to calculate the score, based on data for men discharged in 1965. Compares this with data from 1977-79. Concludes that the RPS should continue in substantially its present form.
ISBN 011340882X

OFFENDERS – GREAT BRITAIN

—Criminal Women / Oxford : Blackwell, 1985.
ISBN 0745600883 Pbk £5.95

—Keeping Offenders Out of Court : Further Alternatives to Prosecution / Committee on Alternatives to Prosecution. – London : HMSO, 1983.
ISBN 0101895801 Hbk £6.00

—Social work with young offenders / Behan. – London : Butterworths, 1981.
ISBN 0406556903 Pbk £7.50

—Survey of extradition and fugitive offenders legislation as between Commonwealth jurisdictions / prepared for the Commonwealth Secretariat by the Commonwealth Legal Advisory Service of the British Institute of International and Comparative Law. – Rev. – London : Commonwealth Secretariat, 1982.
iii,70p; 30cm.
Previous ed.: 1977.
ISBN 0850922356 Pbk £10.00

OFFENDERS – HONG KONG

—Rate of recidivism : a 3-year follow-up study of male prisoners discharged in 1978 / Hong Kong. – Hong Kong : Correctional Services Department, 1980.
9p.

OFFENDERS – INDIA

—Probation of Offenders Act and Rules : Central and States / 6th ed. – Allahabad : Law Book Company, 1988.

OFFENDERS – MALAYSIA

—Registration of Criminals and Undesirable Persons Act, 1969 (Act 7) / Kuala Lumpur : International Law Books Services.

OFFENDERS – ZIMBABWE

—Habitual criminals and the indeterminate sentence / Advisory Committee on Law Reform. – Causeway : The Committee, 1981.
52 leaves. – (Working paper).

—Habitual criminals and the indeterminate sentence / Advisory Committee on Law Reform. – Causeway : The Committee, 1981.
50p. – (Report).

OFFICE PRACTICE

—Information handling and the office of the future : report of a seminar / M. Grieves, editor. – London : British Library Research and Development Department, 1984.
ii,84p.

—Information service 1986 : accounting and time recording systems for solicitors / the Law Society. – 1. – London : Law Society, 1986.
various pagings.

—Information service 1986 : technology for solicitors / the Law Society. – 1. – London : Law Society, 1986.
various pagings.

OFFICE PRACTICE - GREAT BRITAIN

—Handbook of company administration / Keith Walmsley, John Birds, A. Harding Boulton. – 4th ed. – Bristol : Published under the authority of the Institute of Chartered Secretaries and Administrators by Jordon & Sons, 1981.
xvi,318p; 21cm.
Previous ed.: / by A. Harding Boulton in collaboration with J.E. Neill. 1977. Includes index.
ISBN 0853080658 Pbk £6.00

OFFICIAL SECRETS

—Public secrets : a study in the development of government secrecy / K. G. Robertson. – London : Macmillan, 1982.
x,216p.
Bibliography: p198-209.

OFFICIAL SECRETS - CANADA - ONTARIO

—Report on political activity, public comment and disclosure by crown employees / Ontario Law Reform Commission. – Toronto : Ministry of the Attorney General, 1986.
xi,381p.
Includes bibliographical references.
ISBN 0772917728

OFFICIAL SECRETS - GREAT BRITAIN

—Consuming secrets : how official secrecy affects everyday life in Britain / edited by Rosemary Delbridge and Martin Smith : foreword by Harold Evans. – London : Burnett, 1982.
x,249p; 22cm.
Bibliography: p239-241. - Includes index. At head of title: The National Consumer Council.
ISBN 0091475902 Hbk Unpriced
ISBN 0091475910 Pbk £4.95

—Politics of secrecy / James Michael. – Harmondsworth : Penguin, 1982.
240p; 20cm.
Bibliography: p225-229. - Includes index.
ISBN 0140220607 Pbk £2.50

—Protection of military information : government response to the report of the Study Group on Censorship / Ministry of Defence. – London : H.M.S.O., 1985.
10p.
ISBN 0101949901

—Protection of military information : report of the Study Group on Censorship ... : presented to Parliament by the Secretary of State for Defence ... December 1983 / Study Group on Censorship. – London : H.M.S.O., 1983.
vii,91p; 25cm.
Bibliography: p60-63. - Includes index.
ISBN 0101911203 Pbk £6.40

—Public access to Government held information / London : Sweet & Maxwell, 1987.
ISBN 0420476105 Pbk £35.00

—Report of the Security Commission, May 1981 / London : H.M.S.O., 1981.
9p; 25cm.
ISBN 0101823509 unbound £1.40

—Secrets file : the case for freedom of information in Britain today / Des Wilson. – London : Heinemann Educational Books, 1984.
viii,(2),166p.
Bibliography: p59.
ISBN 0435839403

—Third report from the Defence Committee, session 1979-80 : the D Notice system : together with the minutes of proceedings of the Committee ... / London : H.M.S.O., 1980.
xxiii,150p; 25cm. – (HC).
Bound with: Observations presented by the Secretary of State for Defence (Cmnd. 8129).
ISBN 010027739X

—Third report from the Defence Committee : the D notice system : House of Commons paper 773 session 1979-80 : observations presented by the Secretary of State for Defence / London : H.M.S.O., 1981.
2p; 25cm.
Bound with: Third report from the Defence Committee.
ISBN 0101812906

OFFICIAL SECRETS - MALAYSIA

—Official Secrets Act, 1972 (Act 88) / Kuala Lumpur : International Law Books Services.

OFFSHORE COMPANIES - AUSTRALIA

—Recent Developments in Banking Series : Off Shore Finance 1984 / Monash University Staff. – Clayton : Monash University Press, 1984.
ISBN 0867463511 Hbk £16.00

OFFSHORE COMPANIES - GREAT BRITAIN

—Companies operating overseas: UK tax, law and practice / John Dixon. – London : Longman Professional (UK), 1986.
– (Commercial series).
Examination of the UK tax implications for any company which trades abroad and is concerned with reducing the risks involved. Looks at problems such as the treatment of double taxation agreements, legislation on controlled foreign companies, and the international VAT implications.
ISBN 0851218770 Pbk £17.50

—United Kingdom Offshore Legislation Guide / Tonbridge : Ernest Benn.
300p.
ISBN 0854591524 Hbk £110.00

OIL AND GAS

—Arab comparative & commercial law : the international approach : proceedings : International Bar Association first Arab Regional Conference, Cairo 15-19 February 1987 / International Bar Association. – London : Graham & Trotman, 1987.
Contents: v. 1. The Sharia and its relevance to modern transnational transactions. The settlement of disputes through arbitration. Joint ventures. – v. 2. Energy law.
ISBN 086010978X v. 2

—Arab petropolitics / Abdulaziz Al-Sowayegh. – London : Croom Helm, 1984.
207p; 23cm.
Includes index.
ISBN 0709905386 Hbk £15.95
ISBN 0709905408 Pbk £8.95

—Changing structure of the world oil industry / edited by David Hawdon. – London : Croom Helm, 1985.
1v.
Conference papers.
ISBN 0709937172 £14.95

—Code for the Construction and Equipment of Mobile Offshore Drilling Units : MODU Code / International Maritime Organization. – London : International Maritime Organization, 1980.
French Edition
Spanish Edition

—Employment and safety in the offshore oil industry / Brenda Barrett, Brian Hindley and Richard Howells. – London : Kogan Page, 1987.
200p; 24cm.
ISBN 1850910707 £45.00

—Environmental Regulation : Its Impact on Major Oil and Gas Projects / Alastair R. Lucas. – Calgary : Canadian Institute of Resources Law.
167p.

—Inert Gas Systems for Ships Carrying Petroleum Products in Bulk / International Maritime Organization. – London : International Maritime Organization, 1982.
French Edition

—International arbitration : a practical study with specific reference to the petroleum industry / a collection of papers presented by the Section of Energy and Natural Resources Law at the International Bar Association's Twentieth Biennial Conference held in Vienna, 2-7 September 1984. – London : International Bar Association, 1984.
Various pagings.

—International oil industry : an interdisciplinary perspective / edited by Judith Rees and Peter Odell. – Basingstoke : Macmillan, 1987.
xii,181p; 23cm.
Includes bibliographies and index.
ISBN 0333436601 £25.00

—International petroleum exploration and exploitation agreements : legal, economic and policy aspects / by Keith W. Blinn ... et al. : preface by Ibrahim F.I. Shihata. – London : Euromoney Publications, 1986.
431p.
Bibliography: p.322-323.
ISBN 0903121921

—The Joint Operating Agreement : oil and gas law / M.P.G. Taylor, with T.P. Winsor and S.M. Tyne. – 1st ed. – London : Longman Professional (UK), 1989.
Examination of the Joint Operating Agreement, including a full specimen JOA, with key clauses considered in detail. Discusses the legal relationships created by the Agreement, and contains seperate chapters on withdrawal, and abandonment of fields.
ISBN 0851212395 Hbk £50

—Legal character of petroleum licences : a comparative study / edited by Terence Daintith. – Dundee : University of Dundee, Centre for Petroleum and Mineral Law Studies, 1981.
xv,225p; 21cm.
Conference papers.
ISBN 0906343089 Pbk £13.00

—Mobile Offshore Units : Regulations Laid Down by Norwegian Official Control Institutions / New complete. – Oslo : Fabritius og Sonners.
ISBN 8207009225 Hbk £1.452

—Natural Gas Clauses in Petroleum Arrangements / Geneva : United Nations Publications.
ISBN 9211041988 Hbk £8.00

—Oil & gas law and taxation review : a monthly review covering court decisions, legislation and international news / Oxford : ESC, 1982-.

—Oil and world power / Peter R. Odell. – 7th ed. – Harmondsworth : Penguin, 1983.
287p; 20cm.
Previous ed.: 1981. Includes index.
ISBN 0140222847 Pbk £2.95

—Oil companies and the Arab world / Giacomo Luciani. – London : Croom Helm, 1984.
197p; 23cm.
Includes index. Rev. translation of: Compagnie petrolifere e paesi arabi.
ISBN 0709916191 £15.95
ISBN 0312582765

—Oil companies in the international system / Louis Turner. – 3rd ed. – London : Allen & Unwin for the Royal Institute of International Affairs, 1983.
279p; 22cm.
Previous ed.: 1980. Bibliography: p253-268. - Includes index.
ISBN 0043820409 Pbk Unpriced

—Oil supplies industry : a comparative study of legislative restrictions and their impact / Peter Cameron. – London : Financial Times Business Information, 1986.
ix,242p.
Bibliography: p.238-242..
ISBN 0903199920

—OPEC official resolutions and press releases 1960-1983 / Organization of the Petroleum Exporting Countries. – 2nd ed. – Oxford : Published and distributed on behalf of OPEC, Vienna by Pergamon, 1984.
x,216p; 30cm.
Previous ed.: published as OPEC official resolutions and press releases 1960-1980. 1980. Includes index. Latest supplement held: 1984-1985.
ISBN 0080311229 Pbk £31.25

—Petroleum licensing : a comparative study / Peter Cameron. – London : Financial Times Business Information, 1984.
x,195p.
Bibliography: pp.191-194.
ISBN 0903199785

—Proceedings of the Regional Energy Law Seminar, Oslo, Norway, 8-9 May 1984 / the Section on Energy and Natural Resources Law of the International Bar Association in conjunction with the Scandinavian Institute of Maritime Law, University of Oslo. – London : International Bar Association, 1984.
Various pagings.
Includes bibliographical references.

—Property rights and sovereign rights : the case of North Sea oil / Peter D. Cameron. – London : Academic Press, 1983.
x,210p; 24cm.
Bibliography: p194-202. - Includes index.
ISBN 0121570606 No price

—Sea-bed energy and mineral resources and the law of the sea / London : Graham & Trotman, 1984.
350p in various pagings; 25cm.
Includes index.
ISBN 0860104605 Hbk £39.00
ISBN 0860106152 unbound £35.00

Vol.2 : The areas beyond the limits of national jurisdiction / by E.D. Brown. – 1986.
400p; 24cm.
Includes index.
ISBN 0860106233 Hbk £45.00
ISBN 0860106217 loose-leaf £45.00

Vol.3 : Selected documents, tables, bibliography / by E.D. Brown. – 1986.
520p; 24cm.
Includes bibliography.
ISBN 0860106241 Hbk £55.00
ISBN 0860106225 loose-leaf £55.00

—United States and the control of world oil / Ed Shaffer. – London : Croom Helm, 1983.
246p; 23cm.
Bibliography: p232-236. - Includes index.
ISBN 070992366X £15.95

OIL AND GAS - AUSTRALIA

—A.M.P.L.A. Yearbook / Melbourne : Australian Mining and Petroleum Law Association.
600p.

—Australian Mining and Petroleum Law Association yearbook / v. – Melbourne : The Association, 1983.
Includes index.
ISBN 0812857X

—Australian Mining and Petroleum Laws / A. J. Lang. – 2nd ed. – Sydney : Butterworths, 1987.
360p.
This reference describes the Petroleum (Submerged Lands) Act 1982, the Mining Act 1983 (NT), the Petroleum Act 1984 (NT), the Mining Act 1978-81 (WA), the Mining Amendment Act 1985 (WA). Also included are materials on environmental law and joint ventures.

—Australian Mining and Petroleum Laws Introduction / J.R.S. Forbes. – 2nd ed. – Butterworths, 1987.
375p.
ISBN 0409492159 Hbk £59.00

—Index of A.M.P.L.A. Yearbooks 1977-1987 / Melbourne : Australian Mining and Petroleum Law Association.
ISBN 0958991839 Hbk £35.00

—Petroleum Taxation Law / Glenside : Australian Mineral Foundation, 1985.

OIL AND GAS – CANADA

—Canadian Oil and Gas, 9 vols / Andrew Thompson. – Toronto : Butterworths.

—Canadian Oil and Gas, 9 Vols. / Andrew R. Thompson. – Butterworths.

—Classifying Non-Operating Interests in Oil and Gas / Calgary : Canadian Institute of Resources Law.

—International Legal Context of Petroleum Operations in Canadian Arctic Waters / Calgary : Canadian Institute of Resources Law.
76p.

—Investing in the Oil and Gas Industry in Canada / Vancouver : British Columbia Continuing Legal Education Society, 1981.
222p.
ISBN 0865040354 Hbk £40.00

—Liability for Drilling- and Production-Source Oil Pollution in the Canadian Offshore / Calgary : Canadian Institute of Resources Law.
84p.
ISBN 0919269206 Hbk £17.00

—Oil and gas in Canada : a new environment for development / Colin and Pamela Karasek. – London : Financial Times Business Information, 1985.
ix,206p.
Bibliography: p.201-206.
ISBN 0903199939

—Petroleum Operations on the Canadian Continental Margin : the Legal Issues in a Modern Perspective / Calgary : Canadian Institute of Resources Law.
113p.

—Silverstone Oil Company Limited Act, 1983, Bill Pr022 : An Act to Revive Silverstone Oil Company Limited / Ontario : Ontario Government Publications Service, 1983.
2p.

—Surveying offshore Canada lands for mineral resource development / edited by Harold E. Jones. – 3rd ed. – Ottawa : Department of Energy, Mines and Resources, Surveys and Mapping Branch, 1982.
viii,158p.
Bibliography: p.149-154. - Includes index. 'Based on the findings of government/industry workshops convened between 1970 and 1982 to study the technical and legal aspects of surveying for mineral resource development on offshore Canada lands'.
ISBN 0660113430

—Taxation of Canadian Oil and Gas Income / R. H. Bowhay. – Toronto : DeBoo, 1986.
This text discusses non-deductibility of payments to the Crown, investment tax credits, successor corporation rules, joint exploration corporations, and the National Energy Program. Annual consolidated supplements are planned.
ISBN 0888202474 Hbk £135.00

—Teco Mines and Oils Limited Act, 1983, Bill Pr052 : An Act to Revive Teco Mines and Oils Limited / Ontario : Ontario Government Publications Service, 1983.
2p.

OIL AND GAS – CANADA – ALBERTA

—Alberta Petroleum Incentives Program / Toronto : Butterworths.
– (Alberta Annotated Legislation Ser.).

OIL AND GAS – GREAT BRITAIN

—Fifth report from the Energy Committee : session 1984-85 : government oil price policy and the spring supplementary estimate for 20 million in respect of the British National Oil Corporation including Government repsonse to Committee's fourth report of session 1984-85 ... together with minutes of proceedings relating to the report and minutes of evidence and appendices / ordered by the House of Commons to be printed 8 March 1985. – London : H.M.S.O., 1985.
xxiv,72p. – (1984-85 HC).
Includes bibliographical references. Chairman: Ian Lloyd.
ISBN 010223485X

—Fourth report from the Energy Committee : session 1984-85 : the winter supplementary estimate for 45 million in respect of the British National Oil Corporation together with minutes of proceedings relating to the report and minutes of evidence and appendices / ordered by the House of Commons to be printed 12 December 1984. – London : H.M.S.O., 1984.
xiv,34p. – (1984-85 HC).
Includes bibliographical references. Chairman: Ian Lloyd.
ISBN 0102126852

—Governmental powers and project financings in the North Sea : the United Kingdom experience / Rory E.S. Argyle. – Dundee : University of Dundee Centre for Petroleum and Mineral Law Studies, 1980.
iv,65,viiip; 30cm. – (Occasional paper).
ISBN 0906343046 Pbk Unpriced

—North Sea taxation for the 1990s / Stephen Bond, Michael Devereux and Michael Saunders. – London : Institute for Fiscal Studies, 1987.
113p; 22cm.
Bibliography: p112-113.
ISBN 0902992651 Pbk No price

—Offshore safety : report of the committee / chairman J.H. Burgoyne : presented to Parliament by the Secretary of State for Energy .. – London : H.M.S.O., 1980.
vii,300p; 25cm.
ISBN 0101786603 Pbk

—Oil and Gas : Law and Taxation Review / Oxford : ESC Publishing Ltd, 1982.

—Oil Taxation Acts 1975-1983 / London : HMSO, 1984.
– (Taxes Act Ser.).
ISBN 0116413506 Pbk £11.95

—The Oil Taxation Acts / London : HMSO, 1985.
ISBN 0116413514 Pbk £12.50

—Other price of Britain's oil : safety and control in the North Sea / W.G. Carson. – Oxford : Robertson, 1981.
xi,320p; 24cm.
Includes index.
ISBN 0855203927 Hbk £15.00
ISBN 0855203935 Pbk £5.95

—Petroleum Development : Law and Policy, a Comparative Study / London : Commonwealth Secretariat.

—Taxation of North Sea Oil / London : Institute for Fiscal Studies, 1981.
24p.

—U.K. onshore oil and gas law : a practical guide to the legal regime relating to United Kingdom onshore oil and gas operations / by J.R. Salter : preface by Terence Daintith and Geoffrey Willoughby. – London : Sweet & Maxwell, 1986.
xxvi,505p; 25cm.
A compendium of the relevant statute law and all the secondary legislation made pursuant to it. Includes forms and precedents for every stage of legal proceedings and a section on government memoranda, departmental guidance notes, and other policy documents.
ISBN 0421347805 £55.00

—UK oil taxation / 2nd. – London : Longman Professional, 1988.
ISBN 0851214207 Pbk £50

—UN Draft Convention on the Law of the Sea : how it affects the United Kingdom's oil rights / E.D. Brown. – S.l. : s.n., 1981.
56p.
'Paper read at seminar on recent developments in U.K. petroleum law, London, June, 1981'. Includes bibliographical references.

—United Kingdom oil and gas law / edited by Terence Daintith and Geoffrey Willoughby. – 2nd ed. 1. – London : Sweet & Maxwell, 1984.
loose-leaf; 26cm.
Describes the historical development of the industry, and examines the different roles of the government and the oil companies. Looks at offshore licensing operations, and discusses the legal and commercial implications of financing such operations. Also outlines the various forms of UK taxation of the oil industry.
ISBN 0421307005 £130.00 (non-net)

OIL AND GAS – INDIA

—Encyclopedia of Petroleum Laws / Allahabad : Universal Book Agency, 1982/83.

OIL AND GAS – LIBYA

—Principles of petroleum legislation : the case of a developing country / by Anis Al-Qasem. – London : Graham & Trotman, 1985.
xiv,245p.
ISBN 0860105601

OIL AND GAS – MALAYSIA

—Petroleum income tax in Malaysia / Singapore : Malayan Law Journal, 1982.
xv,240.
Covers oil exploration and PETRONAS, taxation of petroleum companies, and administration and appeals. Appendices reproduce the Petroleum (Income Tax) Act 1967 and all subsequent Amendments up to 1977, the Petroleum Mining Act 1966, and a map showing the location of oil and gas fields in Malaysia.

OIL AND GAS – NEW ZEALAND

—Petroleum development and New Zealand law : essays prepared for the Faculty of Law, Victoria University of Wellington / Wellington, N.Z. : Victoria University Press, 1984.
118p.
Reprinted in Victoria University of Wellington Law Review, vol. 14, no.1. Includes bibliographical references.
ISBN 0864730144

OIL AND GAS – NIGERIA

—Nigeria : its petroleum geology, resources and potential / by Arthur Whiteman. – 2 v. – London : Graham & Trotman, 1982.
394p,5leaves of plates(folded).
In 2 vols. Bibliography: p.376-381.
ISBN 0860102645

—Nigerian petroleum law / G. Etikerentse. – London : Macmillan, 1985.
x,356p; 24cm.
Includes index.
ISBN 0333393570 Pbk £7.95

—Nigerian petroleum law and practice / Martin M. Olisa. – Ibadan, Nigeria : Fountain Books, 1987.
x,261p.
Includes bibliographical references.
ISBN 978233118X

OIL AND GAS – NORWAY

—Norwegian petroleum guide / s.l. : Stokkand Forlag, 1984.
258p.
'... a translated edition of the Norwegian Petroleum Guide 1983 with four new articles ...' - Preface.
ISBN 8290496044

OIL AND GAS – SCOTLAND

—Onshore oil and gas pipelines : the problems / by Kevan MacDonald. – Dundee : University of Dundee, Centre for Petroleum and Mineral Studies, 1981.
xiii,102p. – (Occasional paper).

OIL AND GAS – UNITED ARAB EMIRATES

—Petroleum concession agreements of the United Arab Emirates, 1939-1981 (Abu Dhabi) / compiled by Mana Saeed al-Otaiba. – 2. – London : Croom Helm, 1982.
26cm.
In slip-case.
ISBN 0709919158 Unpriced

Vol.2 : 1972-1981 / Mana Saeed Al-Otaiba. – 1982.
385p.

OMBUDSMAN

—Directory of ombudsmen and other complaint-handlers / Edmonton : International Ombudsman Institute, 1983.
29p.

—Judicial teeth for local ombudsmen? : proceedings of a conference held at the University of Edinburgh, 13th December 1984 / edited by Chris Himsworth. – Edinburgh : Department of Constitutional and Administrative Law, University of Edinburgh, 1985.
63p.
Bibliography: p.60.

—Legitimate grievance : a report on the role of the ombudsman in the prison system / Geoffrey Wener. – London : Prison Reform Trust, 1983.
23p.
Bibliography: p20.
ISBN 0946209030

—Ombudsman journal / Edmonton, Alta. : International Ombudsman Institute, Faculty of Law, University of Alberta, 1981-.

—Ombudsman seminar, held at the Oude Libertas Centre, Stellenbosch, South Africa, on 30th and 31st March 1982 / Edmonton : International Ombudsman Institute, 1982.
161p.
Organised by the International Bar Association Ombudsman Forum, in association with the International Ombudsman Institute and the Association of Law Societies of the Republic of South Africa.

—Proceedings of the Round Table with European Ombudsmen : Madrid, 5-6 June 1985 / organised by the Secretariat General of the Council of Europe in co-operation with the Spanish Defensor del Pueblo. – Strasbourg : Directorate of Human Rights, Council of Europe, 1987.
141p.
ISBN 928711000X

OMBUDSMAN - AUSTRALIA

—Annual report/Commonwealth Ombudsman / Canberra : Australian Government Publishing Service, 1977/78-.

—Jurisdiction of Ombudsman : Report of Working Party / Canberra : Australian Government Publishing Service, 1980.
88p.
ISBN 0642058644 Hbk £2.40

OMBUDSMAN - CANADA

—Ombudsmen in the provinces of Canada / by Ulf Lundvik. – Edmonton? : International Ombudsman Institute, 1981.
103p.

—Seventh annual conference of Canadian legislative ombudsmen, Saskatoon, Saskatchewan, August 30 - September 3, 1981 : the ombudsman in the eighties : new challenges / Edmonton : International Ombudsman Institute, 1981.
143p.
Includes appendices in French.

OMBUDSMAN - CANADA - ONTARIO

—Annual report / The Ombudsman, Ontario. – Toronto : The Ombudsman, 1977 -.

OMBUDSMAN - COMMONWEALTH

—Ombudsmen in the Commonwealth : a survey / Rev. – London : Commonwealth Secretariat, 1983.
ii leaves,28p.
Previous edition: 1980. Bibliography: p.24-28.
ISBN 0850922488

—Ombudsmen in the Commonwealth : a survey / prepared for the Commonwealth Secretariat by the International Ombudsman Institute. – London : Commonwealth Secretariat, 1980.
34p.
Bibliography: p.29-34.
ISBN 0850921910

OMBUDSMAN - CYPRUS

—Institution of Ombudsman in the English legal system and especially that of Cyprus / by Criton G. Tornaritis. – Nicosia : s.n., 1983.
27 leaves.

OMBUDSMAN - ENGLAND

—Ombudsman : an autobiography / by Pat Cook. - London : BKT, 1981.
155p; 22cm.
ISBN 0904677192 £6.95

OMBUDSMAN - EUROPEAN COMMUNITY

—Spread of the ombudsman plan in western Europe / by Donald C. Rowat. – Edmonton : International Ombudsman Institute, 1983.
30p. – (Occasional paper).
'An excerpt from the chapter on developed countries in Professor Rowat's book, The Ombudsman Plan (Toronto, McClelland and Stewart, 1973), as revised for publication in Japanese by Waseaa University Press, Tokyo, in 1983'.

OMBUDSMAN - FRANCE

—City of Paris Mediateur : an ombudsman a la francaise / by David Clark. – Edmonton, Alta. : International Ombudsman Institute, 1983.
47p. – (Occasional paper).
Originally published: in Local government studies, vol. 8, no. 5 (Sept.-Oct. 1982).

OMBUDSMAN - GREAT BRITAIN

—Grievances, remedies and the state / by Patrick Birkinshaw. – London : Sweet & Maxwell, 1985.
xix,192p; 23cm.
Includes index.
ISBN 042132600X Hbk £9.25
ISBN 0421326107 Pbk £8.95

—Local ombudsmen : a review of the first five years: a report / chairmen of committee Victor Moore and Harry Sales. – London : Justice, 1980.
160 p.
ISBN 0950524794

—Ombudsmen and the constitution / Allan Blake in association with Lancashire Polytechnic. – 2 videocassettes. – London : Sweet & Maxwell, 1985.
– (Sweet & Maxwell's lawfilms).
Contents: Ombudsmania - The Local Ombudsman investigates.

OMBUDSMAN - INDIA

—Lokapukta (Ombudsman in India) : a Socio-Legal Study / S.S. Singh. – New Delhi : Indian Institute of Public Administration, 1988.

OMBUDSMAN - JAPAN

—Critique of the Japanese study group's report on the ombudsman / by Donald C. Rowat. – Edmonton : International Ombudsman Institute, 1983.
16 leaves. – (Occasional paper).

OMBUDSMAN - NIGERIA

—Public Complaints Commission in a presidential system with particular reference to Nigeria / by P.A. Oluyede. – Lagos : Nigerian Institute of Advanced Legal Studies, 1983.
19p.
Seminar paper presented at the Institute on Thursday May 19th, 1983. Includes bibliographical references.

OMBUDSMAN - SCOTLAND

—Work of the Commissioner for Local Administration in Scotland, 1975-1983 / by Ken Bratton. – Edmonton, Alta. : International Ombudsman Institute, 1984.
78p. – (Occasional paper).

OMBUDSMAN - SWEDEN

—Swedish Parliamentary Ombudsmen / Ulf Lundvik. – Stockholm : JO, 1982.
29p.
Bibliography: p.29.

ON-LINE BIBLIOGRAPHIC SEARCHING

—Computerized literature searching research stratagies and databases / Charles L. Gilreath. – Epping : Bowker, 1984.
xiv,177p; 24cm. – (Westview special studies in information science and management).
Includes index.
ISBN 0865315264 No price

—Online bibliographic databases : a directory and sourcebook / Marjorie J. Brown. – 3rd ed. – London : Aslib, 1983.
xiv,383p; 24cm.
Previous ed.: 1981. Bibliography: p315-331. - Includes index.
ISBN 0851421679 North America Unpriced
ISBN 0810305305

—Online bibliographic databases : an international directory / Marjorie J. Brown. – 2nd ed. – London : Aslib, 1981.
xxx,213p; 25cm.
Previous ed.: published as On line bibliographic data bases directory / J.L. Hall. Includes index.
ISBN 0851421385 North America Unpriced
ISBN 081030528o

—Online searching : an introduction / W.M. Henry ... et al. – London : Butterworths, 1980.
209p; 24cm.
Includes bibliographies and index.
ISBN 0408106964 £10.00

ORDEAL

—Trial by fire and water : the medieval judicial ordeal / Robert Bartlett. – Oxford : Clarendon, 1986.
xiii,200p; 22cm.
Includes bibliography and index.
ISBN 0198219733 £19.50

ORDER (PHILOSOPHY)

—Autopoietic law : a new approach to law and society / edited by Gunther Teubner. – Berlin : W. de Gruyter, 1987.
Includes index and bibliography.

ORGAN TRANSPLANTATION

—Body as property / Russell Scott. – London : Allen Lane, 1981.
x,274p; 24cm.
Includes index.
ISBN 0713913215 £7.95

ORGAN TRANSPLANTATION - CANADA - MANITOBA

—Report on 'The Human Tissue Act' / Manitoba Law Reform Commission. – Winnipeg : The Commission, 1986.
iv,145p. – (Report).
Bibliography: p. 134-145.

ORGANISATION

—Organisation in its environment / I. A. Todd. – 2nd ed. – London : Sweet & Maxwell, 1984.
xiII,624p; 22cm.
'The Organisation in its environment is a new edition, in one volume of ... Organisation series.' - Preface. Includes index.
ISBN 042132290X Pbk £9.50

—Writers on organizations / D. S. Pugh, D. J. Hickson and C. R. Hinings. – 3rd ed. – Harmondsworth : Penguin, 1983.
234p; 20cm. – (Penguin education).
Previous ed.: 1971. Includes bibliographies and indexes.
ISBN 0140802665 Pbk £2.50

ORGANISED CRIME

—Victims Before the Law : the Organizational Domination of Criminal Law / Butterworths, 1983.
304p.

ORGANOTIN COMPOUNDS

—Organotin in antifouling paints : environmental considerations / prepared by the Central Directorate of Environmental Protection, the Department of the Environment. – London : H.M.S.O., 1986.
ISBN 0117519030

OUTDOOR RECREATION - GREAT BRITAIN

—Planning for leisure in the countryside : papers from a conference held at Oxford September 1982 / organised by the Bar Council, the Law Society and the Royal Institution of Chartered Surveyors. – London : Sweet & Maxwell, 1984.
vi,107p; 25cm.
Conference papers.
ISBN 0421326700 Pbk £18.00

PACIFIC AREA

—Environmental law and policy in the Pacific basin area / edited by Ichiro Kato, Nobuo Kumamoto, and William H. Matthews. – Tokyo : University of Tokyo Press, 1981.
ix, 229 p.; 24 cm.
Includes bibliographical references and index.
ISBN 0860082857 Y5400

—Existing legislative protection of the cultural and natural heritage of the Pacific region / Patrick O'Keefe, Lyndel V. Prott. – s.l. : UNESCO, 1982.
v,140p.

PACIFIC OCEAN

—Environmental protection and coastal zone management in Asia and the Pacific / edited by Ichiro Kato ... et al. – Tokyo : University of Tokyo Press, 1985.
xi,244p.
Includes bibliographies and index.
ISBN 0860083926

PACIFIC SETTLEMENT OF INTERNATIONAL DISPUTES

—Cultural norms, war and the environment / edited by Arthur H. Westing. – Oxford : Oxford University Press, 1988.
xiv,177p.
On t.p.: Sipri, Stockholm International Peace Research Institute; UNEP, United Nations Environment Programme. Includes bibliographical references and index.
ISBN 0198291256 Hbk £42.00

—Dispute settlement in public international law : texts and materials / compiled by Karin Oellers-Frahm und Norbert Wuhler. – Berlin : Springer Verlag, 1984.
At head of title: Max-Planck-Institut fur Auslandisches Offentliches Recht und Volkerrecht. English and German text. Includes index. Bibliography: p.
ISBN 0387131906

—International dispute settlement / by J.G. Merrills. – London : Sweet & Maxwell, 1984.
xvi,211p; 19cm.
Includes index.
ISBN 0421303700 Hbk Unpriced
ISBN 0421303808 Pbk £6.95

—Settlement of space law disputes : the present state of the law and perspectives of further development : proceedings of an internat. colloquium, Munich, September 13 and 14, 1979 / organized by the Inst. of Air and Space Law, Univ. of Cologne : ed. by Karl-Heinz Bockstiegel : in cooperation with the Space Law Committee of the Internat. Law Assoc. ... et al. – Koln : Heymann, 1980.
ix, 415 p.; 23 cm.
Includes legislation in English, French and German. Bibliography: p. 201-205.
ISBN 3452187942 pbk. DM148.00

PACKAGING - EUROPEAN COMMUNITY

—Product differentiation in terms of packaging presentation, advertising, trade marks, etc. : an assessment of the legal situation regarding pharmaceuticals and certain other consumer goods / Jules Stuyck. – Antwerp : Kluwer, 1983.
xv,118p.
Bibliography: p.111-118.
ISBN 9065440844

PAINT

—Organotin in antifouling paints : environmental considerations / prepared by the Central Directorate of Environmental Protection, the Department of the Environment. – London : H.M.S.O., 1986.
ISBN 0117519030

PALESTINE

—Israel and Palestine / Preparatory Committee for the Russell Hearings on Lebanon and the Occupied Territories. – London : Spokesman Books, 1984.
– (End Papers: No. 9).
ISBN 0851244041 Hbk £3.95

—Palestine in perspective : politics, human rights and the West Bank / David H. Ott. – London : Quartet Books, 1980.
157p.
Includes bibliographies.
ISBN 0704322633

—Partition in Ireland, India and Palestine : theory and practice / T.G. Fraser. – London : Macmillan, 1984.
xiii,225p; 23cm.
Bibliography: p210-213. - Includes index.
ISBN 0333322800 £22.50

PAN-AMERICAN TREATIES AND CONVENTIONS

—Inter-American system : treaties, conventions & other documents : a compilation / annotated by F.V. Garcia-Amador. – v. – London : Oceana Publications for the Secretariat for Legal Affairs, General Secretariat of the Organization of American States, 1983.
Includes bibliographical references.

PAPACY

—Church and the English crown, 1305-1334 : a study based on the register of Archbishop Walter Reynolds / by J. Robert Wright. – Toronto, Ont. : Pontifical Institute of Mediaeval Studies, 1980.
xix, 472 p.; 26 cm. – (Studies and texts - Pontifical Institute of Mediaeval Studies).
Includes index. Bibliography: p. 415-440.
ISBN 0888440480

PAPUA NEW GUINEA

—Law and state in Papua New Guinea / Peter Fitzpatrick. – London : Academic Press, 1980.
xi,290p; 24cm.
Bibliography: p256-284. - Includes index.
ISBN 0122578805 £12.60

PARENT AND CHILD (LAW) – GREAT BRITAIN

—Children act 1975 / by Hugh K. Bevan and Martin L. Parry. – London : Butterworths, 1978.
xviii, 307 p; 26 cm.
Includes index.

PARENTING – SINGAPORE

—Parent-Child Law in Singapore / Singapore : Butterworths, 1984.
The book provides a discussion of legitimacy, maintenance, guardianship, and adoption under the law of Singapore. The 1980 amendments to the Women's Charter pertaining to maintenance, welfare and custody of children are analyzed in depth.
ISBN 0406181217 Pbk

PARISH COUNCILS (LOCAL GOVERNMENT) – ENGLAND

—Law for councillors / by Barbara Turner. – London : Sweet & Maxwell, 1986.
xii,146p; 21cm.
ISBN 0421353600 Pbk £5.00

PARISH COUNCILS (LOCAL GOVERNMENT) – GREAT BRITAIN

—Parish Councillor's Guide / 15th ed. – London : Shaw & Sons, 1988.
ISBN 0721905137 Pbk

—Parish Councillor's Guide / London : Shaw & Sons, 1988.
246p.
ISBN 0721905137 Pbk £6.50

PARLIAMENT

—Parliament in the 1980s / edited by Philip Norton. – Oxford : Blackwell, 1985.
240p.
Includes bibliography and index.
ISBN 0631140565 Hbk £17.50
ISBN 0631140573 Pbk £5.95

PARLIAMENT – AUSTRALIA

—Australia's Government and Parliament / 7th ed. – Melbourne : Nelson, 1987.
194p : Illus.
ISBN 0170071944 Hbk £16.95

—Parliament and Bureaucracy / Neutral Bay : Hale & Iremonger.
ISBN 0868060143 Hbk £24.95
ISBN 0868060151 Pbk £12.95

—Report to Parliament on a proposal for a Statute Law (Miscellaneous Provisions) Bill / Legal and Constitutional Committee. – Melbourne : Government Printer, 1985.
xii,189p.

PARLIAMENT – CANADA

—Canadian Parliamentary Digest / Agincourt : Carswell, 1987.

—Parliamentary privilege in Canada / by Joseph Maingot. – Toronto : Butterworths, 1982.
xxx,290p.
Sets out the law relating to parliamentary procedures, giving an outline of the privilege procedure in the House of Commons. Traces the history, development and scope of parliamentary immunity, rights and privileges, including the privilege of freedom of speech. Also covers proceedings in Parliament, the Offical Secrets Act, and the criminal law.
ISBN 0409847860 Hbk £75

—Standing Orders of the House of Commons : Feb. 1986 / Ottawa : Canadian Government Publishing Centre, 1986.
182p.
ISBN 0660532751 Pbk £22.50

PARLIAMENT – CANADA – BRITISH COLUMBIA

—Parliamentary Practice in British Columbia / Victoria : Government of British Columbia, 1981.

ISBN 0771882467 Hbk £55.00

PARLIAMENT – ENGLAND

—Parliament of England 1559-1581 / Cambridge : Cambridge University Press, 1986.
411.
Study of functions of parliament, political and legislative. Finds that legislative capacity was far more important. Discusses the interests involved in promoting bills and problems associated with making them law.
ISBN 0521328357 Hbk £32.50

PARLIAMENT – GREAT BRITAIN

—Command Papers / London : HMSO, 1983.
– (Treaty Ser.).
ISBN 0101929404 Hbk £1.30

—Command Papers / London : HMSO, 1985.
– (Treaty Ser.).
ISBN 0101982909 Hbk £2.90

—Command Papers / London : HMSO, 1984.
– (European Communities Ser.).
ISBN 0101927401 Hbk £0.75

—Command Papers / London : HMSO, 1986.
– (Miscellaneous Ser.).
ISBN 0101981708 Hbk £0.80

—Command Papers / London : HMSO, 1985.
– (Country Ser.).
ISBN 0101974906 Hbk £1.35

—Commons today / edited by S.A. Walkland and Michael Ryle for the Study of Parliament Group. – Rev. ed. – London : Fontana, 1981.
333p; 18cm.
Previous ed.: published as The Commons in the seventies. 1977. Includes index.
ISBN 0006361870 Pbk £2.95

—House of Lords / Allan (Philip), 1988.
ISBN 086003402X Hbk £34.50
ISBN 0860037029 Pbk £14.95

—New select committees : a study of the 1979 reforms / edited by Gavin Drewry for the Study of Parliament Group. – Oxford : Clarendon, 1985.
x,340p; 25cm.
Includes bibliography and index.
ISBN 019822785X Hbk £17.50
ISBN 0198227841 Pbk No price

—Parliament Government in Britain / Carleton : Pitman Pty Ltd, 1984.
ISBN 0273016156 Hbk £38.95, 015

—Ruling performance / Seldon. – Oxford : Blackwell Scientific, 1987.
ISBN 0631156453 Hbk £25.00

—Standing Order 5 / London : Home Office, 1981.
ISBN 0862520207 Pbk £1.00

—Workable government? : Constitution after 200 years / Norton (WH), 1988.
ISBN 0393024806 Hbk £14.95
ISBN 0393304310 Pbk £7.50

PARLIAMENT – INDIA

—Constituent Power of the Indian Parliament / Delhi : Anmol Publications, 1987.

—Parliamentary Privileges in India / New Delhi : Deep and Deep Publications, 1986.
268p.

—Sovereignty of Parliament in India / New Delhi : Deep and Deep Publications, 1985.
212p.

PARLIAMENTARY PRACTICE

—Parliamentary Assembly : procedure and practice / Kenneth Bradshaw, John Sweetman. – 8th ed. – Strasbourg : Council of Europe, 1983.
370p.
Includes index.
ISBN 9287102325

PARLIAMENTARY PRACTICE – AUSTRALIA

—Legislation handbook / Canberra : Australian Government Publishing Service, 1980.
v,61p.
Previous ed.: 1975, compiled by the Australian Public Service Board.
ISBN 0642048487 PBK £2.20

PARLIAMENTARY PRACTICE – CANADA

—Procedures for meetings and organizations / M. Kaye Kerr and Hubert W. King. – Agincourt, Ont. : Carswell Legal Publications, 1984.
xv, 313 p.; 24 cm.
Includes index. Bibliography: p. 276.
ISBN 0459361503

PARLIAMENTARY PRACTICE – ENGLAND

—Shackleton on the law and practice of meetings / I. Shearman. – 7th ed. – London : Sweet & Maxwell, 1983.
xxix,368p; 23cm.
Previous ed.: 1977. Includes index.
ISBN 0421296305 £17.00

PARLIAMENTARY PRACTICE – GREAT BRITAIN

—Erskine May's treatise on the law, privileges, proceedings and usage of Parliament / Charles Gordon. – 20th ed. – London : Butterworths, 1983.
xlviii,1200p.
This book is a comprehensive work on the law, privileges, proceedings, and usage of the British Parliament. The book gives accurate and detailed information on the constituent parts of Parliament, its powers and jurisdiction, membership of either House, financial procedure, and the process of debate.
ISBN 0406291039 Hbk £55.00

—Factsheet / Public Information Office, House of Commons. – v. – London : The Office, 1985.
No. 1 is revised ed., Nov. 1984.
ISBN 01444689

—Parliamentary Practice / May. – 20th ed. – London : Butterworths, 1983.
ISBN 0406291039 Hbk £68.00

—Private Members' Bills / Read. – Cambridge : Cambridge University Press, 1988.
ISBN 0521330513 Hbk £22.50

PAROLE – AUSTRALIA

—Probation and Parole : Interstate Supervision and Enforcement / Mary W. Daunton-Fear. – Canberra : Australian Institute of Criminology.

PAROLE – CANADA

—National Parole Board handbook for judges and crown attorneys / Bruce Mann. – Ottawa : Govt. of Canada, National Parole Board, 1983.
70, 72 p.; 23 cm.
English and French. Title on added t.p.: Un Manuel de la Commission nationale des liberations conditionnelles a l'intention des juges et avocats de la couronne. Includes bibliographical references.
ISBN 066252361X pbk.

—Parole decision-making in Canada : research towards decision guidelines / by Joan Nuffield. – Ottawa, Ont. : Communication Division, Solicitor General of Canada, 1982.
iv, 96 p.; 28 cm.
Bibliography: p. 91-96.
ISBN 0662121147 pbk.

—Solicitor General's study of conditional release : report of the Working Group, March 1981 / Ottawa : Minister of Supply and Services Canada, 1981.
vii,155,55,63,192,viip.
Includes bibliography. Pages numbered in opposite directions. Text in English and French.
ISBN 0662514521

PAROLE – ENGLAND

—Freedom on licence : the development of parole and proposals for reform : report of a Howard League Working Party under the chairmanship of Professor the Lord McGregor of Durris .. / Howard League for Penal Reform. – Sunbury : Quartermaine House, 1981.
xxvi,70p; 22cm.
Bibliography: p70.
ISBN 0905898141 Pbk £4.25

—Parole system in England and Wales : report of the Review Committee / presented to Parliament by the Secretary of State for the Home Department by Command of Her Majesty , November 1988. – London : HMSO, 1988.
v,148p.
Chairman: Lord Carlisle of Bucklow.
ISBN 0101053223

—Validity of the reconviction prediction score / by Denis Ward. – London : HMSO, 1987.
vi,45p.
Describes the method used to calculate the score, based on data for men discharged in 1965. Compares this with data from 1977-79. Concludes that the RPS should continue in substantially its present form.
ISBN 011340882X

PAROLE - GREAT BRITAIN

—Prospects for parole : a review of the present system and attitudes towards it / by Stephanie Mackey : Foreword by Lord Hunt. - London : NACRO, 1980.
25p.
Includes bibliographical references.

—Equality and judicial neutrality / Sheilah L. Martin and Kathleen E. Mahoney, editors. - Toronto : Carswell, 1986.
xxvii, 430 p.; 24 cm.
Papers presented at a conference held in Banff, Alta., May 22-24, 1986. Includes bibliographical references.
ISBN 0459308319

PARTITION

—Partition in Ireland, India and Palestine : theory and practice / T.G. Fraser. - London : Macmillan, 1984.
xiii,225p; 23cm.
Bibliography: p210-213. - Includes index.
ISBN 0333322800 £22.50

PARTITION - INDIA

—Partition Act, 1893 / Law Commission of India. - Delhi : Controller of Publications Govt. of India, 1980.
iii,48p. - (86th report).
Includes bibliographical references.

—Partition Act / 4th ed. - Allahabad : Law Publishers, 1983.
178p.

—Vivadaratnakara of Candesvara Thakkura : Law of Partition and Inheritance / Digambar Chattopadhyaya. - Delhi : Gian Publishing House, 1986.
ii, liii, 94, 61, xvp.
ISBN 8121200121 Hbk £140.00

PARTITION - SRI LANKA

—Servitude and Partition / Colombo : Lake House Investments.

PARTITION (HINDU LAW)

—Hindu Law of Partition under Income-Tax Law / 2nd ed. repr. - Allahabad : Law Book Company, 1983.

PARTNERSHIP - AUSTRALIA

—Guidebook to partnership law / R. Baxt, L. Bialkower, R.J. Morgan. - North Ryde, N.S.W. : CCH Australia Ltd., 1980.
vii, 307 p.; 23 cm.
'Case table': p. 293-298. Includes bibliographical references and index.
ISBN 086903250X pbk.

—Guidebook to Partnership Law in Australia / 2nd ed. - North Ryde : C.C.H. Australia, 1984.
350p.
ISBN 086903457X Pbk £38.00

–Higgins and Fletcher the law of partnership in Australia and New Zealand / K. L. Fletcher. - 5th ed. - North Ryde, N.S.W. : Law Book Co.,, 1987.
lxvii,394p.
Previous ed.: 1981. Includes index. Spine title: The law of partnership in Australia and New Zealand.
ISBN 0455207097

—Law of partnership in Australia and New Zealand / K. L. Fletcher. - 4th ed. - Sydney : Law Book Co., 1981.
lxiii,383p.
Previous ed.: 1975. Includes index.
ISBN 0455202370 Pbk
ISBN 0455202389

PARTNERSHIP - CANADA

—Cases and Materials on Partnerships and Canadian Business Corporations / F. Iacobucci. - Agincourt : Carswell, 1983.
958p.
This work examines the principles of Canadian corporate and partnership law in depth. The book covers the fundamentals of corporate finance and distribution, duties of management, the rights and remedies of shareholders, and more.

—Income taxation of partnerships and their partners / by Brian J. Arnold, D. Keith McNair. - Toronto : Carswell, 1981.
v,212p.
Contents: Ch. 8 and part of ch. 19 of: Current tax planning / by Ward, Smith and Arnold.
ISBN 0459339109

—Introduction to business associations in Canada : cases, notes, and materials / by R.L. Simmonds and Peter P. Mercer. - Toronto, Canada : Carswell Legal Publications, 1984.
xxviii, 778 p.; 25 cm.
Spine title: Business associations in Canada.
ISBN 0459365304 pbk.

—Limited Partnerships / Toronto : DeBoo, 1983.
ISBN 0888201192 Hbk £135.00

—Taxation of Partnerships in Canada / Carl F. Steiss. - Butterworths, 1983.
104p.
ISBN 0409859761 Hbk £29.95

PARTNERSHIP - ENGLAND

—Casebook on partnership / by E.R. Hardy Ivamy. - 2nd ed. - Abingdon, Oxfordshire : Professional Books, 1982.
xv,99p; 23cm.

—Law of partnership / by Charles D. Drake. - 3rd ed. - London : Sweet & Maxwell, 1983.
xxx,391p; 22cm.
Previous ed.: 1977. Includes index.
ISBN 0421298405 Pbk £10.50

—Lindley on the law of partnership / Ernest H. Scamell, R. C. I'Anson Banks. - 15th ed. - London : Sweet and Maxwell, 1984.
clxxxiv,1214p; 26cm.
Previous ed.: 1979. Includes index.
ISBN 042129860X £70.00

—Underhill's principles of the law of partnership / D. R. Jones, E. R. Hardy Ivamy. - 12th ed. - London : Butterworths, 1986.
250p; 22cm.
Previous ed.: published as Principles of the law of partnership. 1981. Includes index.
ISBN 0406669074 HBK £23.00
ISBN 0406669082 Pbk £15.00

PARTNERSHIP - GREAT BRITAIN

—Casebook On Partnership / 2nd ed. - Professional Books, 1982.
ISBN 086205043X Hbk £13.20

—Encyclopaedia of Professional Partnerships / London : Sweet & Maxwell, 1988.
ISBN 0421332905 Hbk £195.00

—Encyclopedia of professional partnerships / by R.C. I'Anson Banks. - London : Sweet & Maxwell, 1987.
1000p; 25cm.
Includes index.
ISBN 0421332905 £165.00

—Guide to Partnership Problems and Pitfalls / Young Solicitors Group. - 2nd ed. - London : Law Society, 1983.

—Introduction to partnership law / Geoffrey Morse. - London : Financial Training, 1986.
xiv,176p; 23cm.
Includes index.
ISBN 1851850252 Pbk £6.95

—Law and tax for professional partnerships / Peter White. - London : Oyez, 1984.
xx,182p.
Includes index.
ISBN 0851206948

—Law and Tax for Professional Partnerships / London : Longman Professional, 1984.
ISBN 0851206948 Pbk £24.00

—Law of Partnership / Scammell. - 15th ed. - London : Sweet & Maxwell, 1984.
ISBN 042129860X Hbk £92.00

—Law of Partnership : Including Limited Partnership / 15th ed. - London : Sweet & Maxwell, 1984.
ISBN 042129860X Hbk £82.00

—Modern partnership law / David Milman and Terence Flanagan. - London : Croom Helm, 1983.
xxix,178p; 23cm.
Includes index.
ISBN 0709910142 Hbk £15.95
ISBN 0709910150 Pbk Unpriced

—Partnership law and practice : in England and Scotland / by Robert Burgess and Geoffrey Morse. - London : Sweet & Maxwell in association with the Institute of Chartered Secretaries and Administrators, 1980.
xxv,273p; 22cm.
Includes index.
ISBN 0421264209 Hbk £16.50
ISBN 0421264306 Pbk £12.50

—Partnership taxation / Nigel T. Davey. - 3rd ed. - London : Butterworth, 1987.
372p; 25cm.
Previous ed.: London : HFL, 1978. Includes index.
ISBN 0406678200 Pbk £20.00

—Partnership Taxation / 3rd ed. - London : Butterworths, 1987.
ISBN 0406678200 Pbk £25.00

—Partnership taxation : basis of assessment : a consultative document / London : Inland Revenue, 1984.
19p.

—Partnerships / Stockholm : Anderson Keenan, 1980.
- (Law Unit).
ISBN 0906501148 Pbk £2.40

—Planned practice development / London : Longman Professional, 1984.
ISBN 0851208673 Pbk £13.95

—Practical partnership / Camp. - London : Longman Professional, 1982.
ISBN 0851210392 Pbk £13.95

—Practical Partnership / P. Camp. - London : Oyez Longman, 1982.
ISBN 0851206638 Hbk £6.95

—Practical partnership for solicitors / C. Harmer and P. Camp. - 2nd ed. - London : Longman Professional (UK), 1990.
Examines drafting a partnership agreement, taxation, finance, accounts, and matters of professional conduct. Covers the Practice Rules, Publicity Code 1988 and the Introductions and Referrals Code 1988. Includes material on practising abroad, the Overseas Practice Rules 1987, and the effect of the European element and 1992 on the profession. Also deals with Solicitors Incorporated Practice Rules 1988.
ISBN 0851215513 Hbk £29.50

—Principles of the law of partnership / Webb. - 4th ed. - London : Butterworths, 1988.
ISBN 0409787892 Pbk

—Principles of the law of partnership / Ivamy. - 12th ed. - London : Butterworths, 1986.
ISBN 0406669074 Hbk £14.95
ISBN 0406669082 Pbk £12.95

—Professional partnerships: law and taxation / 2nd. - London : Longman Professional (UK), 1990.
Considers partnerships from the time of creation through changes in the partnerships by admission, retirement and merger, to the ultimate dissolution. Covers the Insolvency Act 1986, and changes brought about by the Finance Act 1989. New chapter on mergers and demergers.
ISBN 0851215734 Pbk £35.00

—Spicer and Pegler's the business of partnerships / by Peter J. Oliver and Nigel T. Davey. - London : Sweet & Maxwell, 1986.
xii,193p; 22cm.
Includes index.
ISBN 0421353309 Pbk £16.75

—Tax and financial planning for professional partnerships / Brian Gilligan. - 2nd ed. - London : Butterworths, 1986.
ISBN 0406501807 Pbk £18.50

—Tax and Financial Planning for Professional Partnerships / Brian Gilligan. - 2nd ed. - London : Butterworths, 1986.
This work explains how the tax liability of United Kingdom professional partnerships can be minimized by effective tax planning. The effects of the Finance Act of 1985 on professional partnerships is discussed in detail.
ISBN 0406501807 Pbk

PARTNERSHIP - INDIA

—Indian Partnership Act : With a Special Reference to Taxation Laws / 5th ed. - Allahabad : Law Book Company, 1986.
1,700p.

—Law of Partnership / 3rd ed. - Lucknow : Eastern Book Company, 1982.
828p.

—Law of Partnership : Principles, Practice, Taxation / Lucknow : Eastern Book Company, 1981.
627p.

—Law of Partnership with Central and All State Rules, 2 Vols. / 2nd ed. - Allahabad : Law Publishers, 1983.

—Law of Partnership : with Tax-Planing at a Glance / Allahabad : Modern Law Publications, 1987.

PARTNERSHIP - MALAYSIA

—Partnership Act, 1961 (Act 135) and Specific Relief Act, 1950 (Act 137) / Kuala Lumpur : International Law Books Services.

PARTNERSHIP - NEW ZEALAND

—Higgins and Fletcher the law of partnership in Australia and New Zealand / K. L. Fletcher. - 5th ed. - North Ryde, N.S.W. : Law Book Co.,, 1987.
lxvii,394p.
Previous ed.: 1981. Includes index. Spine title: The law of partnership in Australia and New Zealand.
ISBN 0455207097

—Law of partnership in Australia and New Zealand / K. L. Fletcher. - 4th ed. - Sydney : Law Book Co., 1981.
lxiii,383p.
Previous ed.: 1975. Includes index.
ISBN 0455202370 Pbk
ISBN 0455202389

—Principles of the Law of Partnership / Anne Webb. - 3rd ed. - Wellington : Butterworths, 1984.

—Principles of the Law of Partnership / Anne Webb. - 4th ed. - Butterworths, 1987.
ISBN 0409787892 Pbk

PARTNERSHIP - SCOTLAND

—Scottish cases on partnership and companies / Edinburgh : W Green & Son, 1980.
Source book for those studying business law.
ISBN 0414006585 Pbk

PARTNERSHIP - SOUTH AFRICA

—Bamford on the law of partnership and voluntary association in South Africa / by Brian Bamford. - 3rd ed. - Cape Town : Juta, 1982.
xlvii,274p.
Previous ed.: 1971. Includes index.
ISBN 0702112526

—Partnership / Henning and Delport. - Durban : Professional Publisher, 1984.
ISBN 0409040223 Hbk £33.00

PARTNERSHIP - UNITED KINGDOM

—Partnership Law / Ernest Miles Taylor. - 11th ed. Repr. of 1977 ed. - Plymouth : Macdonald & Evans, 1981.
160p. - (M and E Handbook Ser.).
ISBN 0712116745 Hbk £3.95

PASSIVE RESISTANCE - AUSTRALIA

—Papers / Canberra : Australian Government Publishing Service, 1986.
xiv,402p. - (Occasional paper).
Includes bibliographical references.
ISBN 0644055901 £19.95

PATENTS

—Biotechnology and patent protection : an international review / by F.K. Beier, R.S. Crespi, J. Straus. - Paris : Organisation for Economic Co-operation and Development, 1985.
133p.
ISBN 9264127577

—Budapest Treaty on the International Recognition of the Deposit of Microorganisms for the Purposes of Patent Procedure : Original Text of the Treaty Adopted by the Budapest Conference (1977) and Regulations (as of Jan 31, 1981) / Geneva : World Intellectual Property Organization.
53p.

—Class and Subclass Titles of the International Patent Classification, 1984 (Fourth Edition) : Synopsis of Classes and Subclasses with Information on the Number of Subdivisions / Geneva : World Intellectual Property Organization, 1984.
129p.

—Committee of Experts on Biotechnological Inventions and Industrial Property : third session, Geneva, June 29 to July 3, 1987 : report prepared by the International Bureau / World Intellectual Property Organization. - Geneva : World Intellectual Property Organization, 1987.
32,11p. - (BioT/CE/III/3).
'Convened ... as part of the 1986/87 program of the International (Paris) Union for the Protection of Industrial Property ...'. - Introduction.

—Committee of Experts on Biotechnological Inventions and Industrial Property : third session, Geneva, June 29 to July 3, 1987 : industrial property protection of biotechnological inventions / revised report prepared by the International Bureau. - Geneva : World Intellectual Property Organization, 1987.
73p. - (BioT/CE/III/2).
At head of cover: International Union for the Protection of Industrial Property (Paris Union).

—Design Law and Treaties of the World : World Rights Outside the U.S.A. / Dordrecht : Kluwer.

—Future of legal protection for industrial design / Christine Fellner. - Oxford : ESC, 1985.
xxxviii,210p.
A report commissioned by the Common Law Institute of Intellectual Property and the Intellectual Property Unit, Queen Mary College.
ISBN 0906214270

—Guide for Developing Countries on the Examination of Patent Applications / Geneva : World Intellectual Property Organization, 1982.
62p.

—Guide to official industrial property literature : the Netherlands, Belgium, Luxembourg, Benelux / Brenda M. Rimmer. - London : British Library, Science Reference Library, 1981.
28p; 25cm.
Includes index.
ISBN 090291460X Pbk Unpriced

—Guide to the International Deposit of Industrial Designs (Hague Union) / Geneva : World Intellectual Property Organization, 1982.
200p.

—How to get a European patent : guide for applicants / European Patent Office. - 6th ed. - Munchen : European Patent Office, 1983.
72p.
Accompanied by Schedule of fees (13p).

—Hughes and Woodley on patents / John M Woodley. - 1 vol. - Scarborough, Ontario : Butterworths (Canada).
Covers the requirements for patentability, infringement actions (the grounds, defences, parties, procedure, remedies and jurisdiction), Patent Office procedure and practice, and conflicting applications.

—Importation of patented products in the Andean group / by German Cavelier. - Bogota, Columbia : Cavelier Abogados, 1985.
11 leaves.

—International Patent Classification : Valid by the 1st January 1985, 9 Vols. / World Intellectual Property Organization. - 4th ed. - Cologne : Carl Heymanns Verlag, 1984.
ISBN 3452185990 Pbk DM618.00

Vol. 1, Section A: Human Necessities
133p.
ISBN 3452194140 Pbk DM69.00

Vol. 2, Section B: Performing Operations, Transporting
314p.
ISBN 3452194159 Pbk £143.00

Vol. 3, Section C: Chemistry; Metallurgy
213p.
ISBN 3452194167 Pbk £98.00

Vol. 4, Section D: Textiles and Paper
57p.
ISBN 3452194175 Pbk £40.00

Vol. 5, Section E: Fixed Constructions
71p.
ISBN 3452194183 Pbk £46.00

Vol. 6, Section F: Mechanical Engineering, Lighting, Heating, Weapons, Blasting
167p.
ISBN 3452194191 Pbk £88.00

Vol. 7, Section G: Physics
145p.
ISBN 3452194205 Pbk £77.00

Vol. 8, Section H: Electricity
137p.
ISBN 3452194213 Pbk £77.00

Vol. 9: Guide, Survey of Classes and Summary of Maingroups
xxx, 279p.
ISBN 3452194221 Pbk £46.00

—Minimum Documentation under Rule 34.1 of the Regulations under the Patent Cooperation Treaty (PCT) : Non-Patent Literature, List of Perodicals / Geneva : World Intellectual Property Organization.

—Official Catchword Index to the Fourth Edition (1984) of the International Patent Classification / World Intellectual Property Organization. - Cologne : Carl Heymanns Verlag.
335p.
ISBN 3452200299 Pbk £125.00

—Official journal of the European Patent Office / Amtsblatt des Europaischen Patentamts. - Munchen : European Patent Office, 1981-.

—P.C.T. Applicant's Guide : General Information for Users of the Patent Cooperation Treaty /. - Geneva : World Intellectual Property Organization.

—Patent claim drafting and interpretation / general editor John A. Kemp. - London : Oyez Longman, 1983.
xi,251p; 23cm.
Includes index.
ISBN 0851206859 Unpriced

—Patent Cooperation Treaty (PCT) : Original Text of the Treaty and Regulations as in Force on Jan 1, 1981 / Geneva : World Intellectual Property Organization.
166p.

—Patent Information and Documentation Handbook / Geneva : World Intellectual Property Organization.
1,600p.

—Patentability of computer software : an international guide to the protection of computer-related inventions / by H.W.A.M. Hanneman. - Deventer : Kluwer Law and Taxation Publishers, 1985.
257p; 23cm.
ISBN 9065442251 No price

—Patents at a Glance : a Survey of Substantive Law and Formalities in 46 Countries / 3rd repr. - Cologne : Carl Heymanns Verlag, 1980.
147p.
ISBN 3452188345 Hbk £92.00

—Patents for inventions : and the protection of industrial designs / by T.A. Blanco White. - 5th ed. - London : Stevens, 1983.
xxxv,304p; 26cm.
Previous ed.: 1974. Includes index.
ISBN 0420463100 £35.00

—Patents in perspective : a collection of essays / edited by Jeremy Phillips. - Oxford : ESC Publishing Ltd, 1985.
xii,121p.
ISBN 0906214378

—Role of patent information in the transfer of technology : proceedings of the International Conference held at Varna, Bulgaria, May 27-30, 1980 / organised by the World International i.e. Intellectual Property Organization : edited by F.A. Sviridov. - McLean, Va. : Pergamon International Information, 1981.
viii,265p; 23cm.
ISBN 0080275559 Pbk £6.00

—Shanghai Advanced Patent Course / Geneva : World Intellectual Property Organization, 1985.
ca 400p.

—Symposium on the Protection of Biotechnological Inventions / Geneva : World Intellectual Property Organization, 1987.
185p.

—Terrell on the law of patents / William Aldous. - 13th ed. - London : Sweet & Maxwell, 1984.
lxi,1157p; 26cm.
The text and rules of the 1977 Patents Act are reproduced, and their effect is examined. Provisions of the 1949 Act which are still in force are also discussed. Contains an appraisal of the European Patent Convention.
ISBN 0421249005 Unpriced

—Training Course on Patent Information / Geneva : World Intellectual Property Organization, 1987.
620p.

—Use of the Patent System by Industrial Enterprises in Developing Countries / Geneva : World Intellectual Property Organization, 1981.
97p.

—World Directory of Sources of Patent Information / Geneva : World Intellectual Property Organization, 1985.
ca 300p.

PATENTS - AUSTRALIA

—Australian Patent Law / Butterworths, 1984.
349p.
ISBN 0409492035 Hbk £65.00

—Australian Patent Law / London : Butterworths, 1984.
ISBN 0409492035 Hbk £48.00

—Computer law in Australia : a collection of essays / edited by W. John Taggart. - Sydney : Legal Books Pty., 1987.
xii,75p.
Bibliography: pp.61-64. - Includes index.
ISBN 0949553271

—Guide for Applicants for Patents / Patent Trade Marks & Designs Office. - Canberra : Australian Government Publishing Service, 1981.
45p.
ISBN 0642060371 Hbk £2.30

—Industrial design law in Australia and New Zealand / Sydney : Butterworths, 1986.
256p.
Chapters include the role of design in modern society, recent changes in design law, design basics, application for registration, the registrar of design, the owner, the scope of legal protection for designs, design duration and fees, specific features of the New Zealand law of industrial designs, and design legislation in Australia and New Zealand.
ISBN 0409490482 Hbk £55.00

PATENTS - CANADA

—Canadian Patent Reporter: 1985 / Aurora : Canada Law Book Co, 1985.
- (Third Ser.).

Back Vols.

—Canadian Patent Reporter (C.P.R.) 1942-71, 65 Vols. / Aurora : Canada Law Book Co.
- (First Ser.).

Back Vols.

—Canadian Patent Reporter (C.P.R.) 1971-1984 / Aurora : Canada Law Book Co.
- (Second Ser.).

Back Vols.

—Canadian Patent Reporter First Series (1942-1971) 65 Vols. / Aurora : Canada Law Book Co.
- (Law Reports).

Back Vols.

—Canadian Patent Reporter Second Series (1971-1984), 82 Vols. / Aurora : Canada Law Book Co.
- (Law Reports).

Back Vols.

—Canadian Patent Reporter Second Series : Table of Cases / Aurora : Canada Law Book Co.
- (Law Reports).

—Canadian Patent Reporter Third Series (1985-Present) / Aurora : Canada Law Book Co.
- (Law Reports).

Back Vols.

—Fox's Patent Cases : Canada, 22 Vols. / Carswell Legal Publications. – Agincourt : Carswell, 1983.
This multi-volume work covers the years 1940 to 1971 and contains all judgements of the Canadian courts on the patent law published in full. All relevant statutes, statutory amendments, Orders-in-Council, Rules of Practice, and other official acts impacting on patent law are included in the work.

—Hughes and Woodley on Patents, 1 Vol. / John M. Woodley. – Butterworths.

—Hughes and Woodley on Patents / John M. Woodley. – Toronto : Butterworths.

—Hughes on Copyright and Industrial Design, 1 Vol. / Butterworths.

—Patenting Manual / 2nd. – Waterloo, 1983.
381p.
ISBN 094341802X Hbk £48.50

—Patents of Invention / Agincourt : Carswell, 1981.
420p.
This textbook includes the text of the Patent Act of Canada and rules, as well as, an exhaustive summation of case law and statutes pertaining to patent law.

—Patents of Inventions / 3rd ed. – Agincourt : Carswell, 1981.
ISBN 045934500 Hbk £25.30

—Trade marks and industrial designs / by Immanuel Goldsmith. – Toronto : Carswell, 1982.
ix,344p.
Reprinted from the Canadian Encyclopedic Digest 3rd ed.
ISBN 0459349805

PATENTS - CHINA

—Guide to the patent law of the People's Republic of China / by Philip Gladwin in conjunction with Ajmal Hameed. – London : Graham & Trotman, 1985.
70p; 22cm.
ISBN 0860106306

—Intellectual property law in the People's Republic of China : a guide to patents, trade marks and technology transfer / Michael D.Pendleton. – Singapore : Butterworths, 1986.
xvii,138p.
ISBN 0409995193

—Patent and Trademark Law of the People's Republic of China (1985) / Geneva : World Intellectual Property Organization, 1984.
66p.

PATENTS - EUROPE

—Decisions of the Boards of Appeal of the European Patent Office : Entscheidungen der Beschwerdekammern des Europaischen Patentamts / Cologne : Carl Heymanns Verlag, 1983.
xii, 432p.
ISBN 3452194817 Hbk £128.00

Vol. 2 1983.
xvi, 392p.
ISBN 3452194825 Hbk £128.00

Vol. 3 1984.
xvi, 352p.
ISBN 3452199592 Hbk £128.00

Vol. 4 1985.
xv, 323p.
ISBN 3452201511 Hbk £128.00

Vol. 5 1985.
ca 340p.
ISBN 3452201511 Hbk £128.00

—Encyclopaedia of UK and European Patent Law / London : Sweet & Maxwell, 1988.
ISBN 0421233508 Hbk £165.00

—Encyclopedia of United Kingdom and European Patent Law, 1 Vol. / London : Sweet & Maxwell.

—European Patent Applications : Q & A / London : Longman Professional, 1984.
ISBN 085120855X Hbk £32.00

—European Patent Applications Questions and Answers / London : Oyez Longman, 1984.
ISBN 085120855X Hbk

—European Patent Convention : Convention of the Grant of European Patents / Cologne : Carl Heymanns Verlag, 1980.
vii, 260p.
ISBN 3452185842 Pbk £52.00

—European Patent Convention : Convention on the Grant of European Patents / Cologne : Carl Heymanns Verlag, 1980.
viii, 268p.
ISBN 3452185842 Pbk £52.00

—European Patents Handbook, 3 Vols. / Chartered Institute of Patent Agents. – London : Oyez Longman, 1983.
ISBN 0851203299 Hbk £145.00

—Patent law of Europe and the United Kingdom / by A.M. Walton and others. – 2. – London : Butterworths, 1981.
looseleaf.
ISBN 040641503X

—Patent Law of Europe and the United Kingdom / H. I. L. Laddie. – Wellington : Butterworths.
This looseleaf work describes the effects of the Patents Act of 1977 and the implementation of various European conventions. All relevant text and commentary on United Kingdom legislation and conventions are included in two volumes that make up the work.

—Patent licensing in Europe / 2nd ed. – London : Butterworths, 1986.
ISBN 0406148414 Hbk £47.00

PATENTS - EUROPEAN COMMUNITY

—Draft protocol on the settlement of litigation concerning the infringement and validity of Community patents / as agreed by the Interim Committee at its 13th session of 11 and 12 July 1985. – Brussels : Community Patent Interim Committee, 1985.
54p. – (CIBC).
This draft is intended to serve as a basis for a possible Interngovernmental Conference. Includes the preliminary draft of a Protocol on Privileges and Immunities of the Community Patent Appeal Court.

—European Patent Office reports / Oxford : ESC Publishing Ltd., 1986-.

—Patent licensing and EEC competition rules : Regulation 2349/84 / Valentine Korah. – Oxford : ESC Publishing, 1985.
xiv,126p. – (European competition law monographs).
Includes bibliographies.
ISBN 090621436X

—Patent licensing in Europe / by B.I. Cawthra. – 2nd ed. – London : Butterworths, 1986.
xxi,249p; 22cm.
Previous ed.: 1978. Bibliography: p236-240. - Includes index.
ISBN 0406148414 £40.00

—Records of the Luxembourg Conference on the Community patent, 1975 / Luxembourg : Office for Official Publications of the European Communities, 1982.
334p.
ISBN 9282400891

—Texts established by the Luxembourg Conference on the Community Patent, 1985 / Luxembourg : Office for Official Publications of the European Communities, 1986.
214p.
ISBN 9282403122

PATENTS - GREAT BRITAIN

—C.I.P.A. guide to The Patents Acts / The Chartered Institute of Patent Agents. – 3rd. – London : Sweet & Maxwell, 1989.
liii,772p; 26cm.
Includes tables of statutes, statutory instruments, EPO, PCT, and CPC references. Sections of the Act are printed in full and followed by the relevant rules, including the 1989 consolidation patent rules. Previous ed.: 1984. Kept up to date by supplements.
ISBN 0421397608 Hbk £95.00

—CIPA guide to the Patent Act 1977 : texts, commentary and notes on practice / the Chartered Institute of Patent Agents. – London : Sweet and Maxwell, 1980.
xvii,471p; 26cm.
Includes index. Includes the text of the Act.
ISBN 0421262605 £31.00

—Comments to Her Majesty's Government on the consultative document Cmnd. 8302 : reform of the law relating to copyright, designs and performers' protection / the Publishers Association. – London : The Association, 1982.
69p.

—Design Protection / 2nd ed. – London : Design Council Books, 1986.
ISBN 0850721652 Hbk £8.95

—Design : the modern law and practice / by A.I. Morris and Barry Quest. – London : Butterworth, 1987.
xxvii,377p,12p of plates; 25cm.
Bibliography: p369-370. - Includes index.
ISBN 0406103216 Hbk £32.00
ISBN 0406103208

—Design : the Modern Law and Practice / Quest. – London : Butterworths, 1987.
ISBN 0406103208 Hbk £52.00

—Encyclopaedia of UK and European Patent Law / London : Sweet & Maxwell, 1988.
ISBN 0421233508 Hbk £165.00

—Encyclopedia of U.K. and European patent law / edited by T.A. Blanco White and others. – London : Sweet & Maxwell, 1977.
Loose-leaf with up-dating service.
ISBN 0421233508

—Encyclopedia of United Kingdom and European Patent Law, 1 Vol. / London : Sweet & Maxwell.

—Hayward's Patent Cases 1600-1883 11 vols. / Abingdon : Professional Books, 1988 & Index.
ISBN 0862052793 Hbk £750.00

—How to patent without a lawyer / Spon (E & FN), 1984.
ISBN 0915586088 Hbk £18.00

—Industrial property citator / by Michael Fysh and Robert Wilson Thomas. – London : European Law Centre, 1982.
321p; 26cm.
Includes index.
ISBN 0907451047 Unpriced

—Intellectual property case books / edited by W.R. Cornish. – Oxford : ESC, 1985.
212p.
ISBN 0906214335

—Inventors' information guide / by Tamara S. Eisenschitz and Jeremy Phillips. – 2nd edition. – London : The Intellectual Property Law Unit Centre for Commercial Law Studies, 1985.
viii, 100p.
ISBN 0951066404

—Manager's Guide to Patents, Trade Marks and Copyright / London : Kogan Page, 1986.
ISBN 0850389704 Hbk £12.95

—Manager's Guide to Patents, Trade Marks and Copyright / London : Kogan Page, 1986.
150p.
ISBN 1850912033 Hbk £13.95
ISBN 1850912041 Pbk £6.95

—Patent Cases : 1600-1883 / Abingdon : Professional Books, 1984.

—Patent claim : drafting and interpretation / London : Longman Professional, 1983.
ISBN 0851206859 Hbk £58.00

—Patent cooperation treaty : a new era : papers prepared for presentation at a seminar held at the Brewery Conference Centre...November 11, 1985 / edited by James Lahore. – London : Centre for Commercial Law Studies, Queen Mary College, University of London, 1986.
vi, 46p.
ISBN 0951066420

—Patent Law of Europe and the United Kingdom / H. I. L. Laddie. – Wellington : Butterworths.
This looseleaf work describes the effects of the Patents Act of 1977 and the implementation of various European conventions. All relevant text and commentary on United Kingdom legislation and conventions are included in two volumes that make up the work.

—Patent law of Europe and the United Kingdom / by A.M. Walton and others. – 2. – London : Butterworths, 1981.
looseleaf.
ISBN 040641503X

—Patent system and inventive activity / Manchester : Manchester University Press, 1984.
ISBN 0719009979 Hbk £21.00

—Patents for inventions / 5th ed. – London : Sweet & Maxwell, 1983.
ISBN 0420463100 Hbk £44.00

—Patents in chemistry and biotechnology / 2nd ed. – Oxford : Oxford University Press, 1987.
ISBN 0198552211 Pbk £12.50

—Practical guide to patent law / Brian C. Reid. – Oxford : ESC Publishing Limited, 1984.
xxii,438p.
ISBN 0906214165

—Problems for the Business Client in the Marketing of Goods : Licensing and the Infringement of Rights / London : Law Society, 1986.
17p.

—Reform of the law relating to copyright, designs and performers' protection : a consultative document / presented to Parliament by the Secretary of State for Trade... – London : H.M.S.O., 1981.
25cm.
ISBN 0101830203

—Reports of Patent Cases : 1884-date, 98 Vols. (subject to contractual arrangements with Patent Office) / Abingdon : Professional Books.

—Service marks : a guide to the new law : Trade Marks Act 1938 as amended by the Trade Marks (Amendment) Act 1984 and the Patents, Designs and Marks Act 1986 / Christopher Morcom. – Oxford : ESC Publishing, 1987.
vi,165p.
Includes texts from the Acts.
ISBN 0906214483

—Trade mark cases and passing off cases / 2 vols. – Sweet & Maxwell, 1986.
ISBN 0421344601 Hbk £110.00

PATENTS - INDIA

—Patent Law / Calcutta : Eastern Law House, 1985.
950p.

PATENTS - ITALY
—Italian patent law / Guido Jacobacci, Giuseppe Sena. - Milano : Giuffre, 1985.
vii, 156p.
ISBN 8814007179

PATENTS - MALAYSIA
—Patents Act, 1983 (Act 291) / Kuala Lumpur : International Law Books Services.

PATENTS - NEW ZEALAND
—Industrial design law in Australia and New Zealand / Sydney : Butterworths, 1986.
256p.
Chapters include the role of design in modern society, recent changes in design law, design basics, application for registration, the registrar of design, the owner, the scope of legal protection for designs, design duration and fees, specific features of the New Zealand law of industrial designs, and design legislation in Australia and New Zealand.
ISBN 0409490482 Hbk £55.00

PATENTS - SOUTH AFRICA
—Burrell's patent law reports / compiled and edited by Timothy D. Burrell. - 8. - Cape Town : Juta, 1981.

—South African patent law and practice / by Timothy Donald Burrell. - 2nd ed. - Durban : Butterworths, 1986.
xxxvii,699p.
ISBN 0409013552

—South African patent law and practice / 2nd ed. - London : Butterworths, 1985.
ISBN 0409013544 Hbk £53.00

PATENTS - UNITED STATES
—Guide to United States patent and trademark literature / Brenda M. Rimmer. - London : British Library, Science Reference Library, 1980.
3,24p; 25cm.
Includes index.
ISBN 0902914529 sd £2.50

—US design patents / Washington Group. - London : Butterworths, 1985.
ISBN 040665865 Hbk £100.00

PATENTS - WEST GERMANY
—German Patent Law, 1981 : With Annotations / Cologne : Carl Heymanns Verlag, 1981.
xiii, 99p.
ISBN 3452190005 Pbk £39.00

—New German Patent Law (1981) in English and German / translated by Hermann Kinkeldey and Wilfried Stockmair. - Weinheim : Verlag Chemie, 1981.
199 p.; 21 cm.
ISBN 3527259368

PATRIARCHY
—Violence against wives : a case against patriarchy / R. Emerson Dobash, Russell Dobash. - London : Open Books, 1980.
xii, 339p.
First published by Free Press, New York, 1979.
ISBN 0729101533

PAWNBROKING - AUSTRALIA - WESTERN AUSTRALIA
—Report on the Pawnbrokers Act 1860-1984 / the Law Reform Commission of Western Australia. - Perth : The Commission, 1985.
82p. - (Project).

—Review of the Pawnbrokers Act, 1860 : proposals paper / the Law Reform Commission of Western Australia. - Perth : The Commission, 1985.
46 leaves. - (Project).

PAYMENT
—The Debt Rescheduling Process / Marko Milivojevic. - London : Pinter, 1985.
200p.
Includes bibliography and index.
ISBN 0861875753 £18.50

—International debt game / by Brian Kettell and George Magnus. - London : Graham & Trotman, 1985.
384p; 23cm.
Includes index.
ISBN 0860105717 Pbk £18.75
ISBN 0860108104 £12.50

PAYMENT - AUSTRALIA
—Australian Law of Cheques and Payment Orders / Butterworths, 1988.
199p.
ISBN 0409495417 Pbk £35.00

PAYMENT - AUSTRALIA - NEW SOUTH WALES
—Community law reform program / New South Wales Law Reform Commission. - Sydney : The Commission, 1983.
46p. - (L.R.C. 35).

PAYMENT - ENGLAND
—Payment obligations in commercial and financial transactions / by R.M. Goode. - London : Sweet & Maxwell, 1983.
xxiii,151p; 22cm.
Includes index.
ISBN 0421318104 Pbk £11.00

—Private international law - foreign money liabilities : report on a reference under section 3 (1)(e) of the Law Commissions Act 1965 / The Law Commission. - London : H.M.S.O., 1983.
vii,94p; 25cm.
ISBN 0101906404

PAYMENT - GREAT BRITAIN
—Private international law : Council of Europe Conventions on Foreign Money Liabilities(1967) and on the Place of Payment of Money Liabilities (1972) : report on a reference under section 3 (1)(e) of the Law Commissions Act 1965 / the Law Commission and the Scottish Law Commission. - London : H.M.S.O., 1981.
iv,53p; 25cm.
Includes the text of the Conventions.
ISBN 0101831803

—Private international law : foreign money liabilities / the Law Commission. - London : H.M.S.O., 1981.
ix,195p; 22cm. - (Working paper).
ISBN 0117301604

—Private international law - foreign money liabilities : report on a reference under section 3 (1)(e) of the Law Commissions Act 1965 / The Law Commission. - London : H.M.S.O., 1983.
vii,94p; 25cm.
ISBN 0101906404

PEACE
—Freedom, peace and their guarantees, from the viewpoint of the Constitution of Japan / Kenji Urata. - s.l. : s.n., 1982.
p.22-45.
'Originally presented as a draft to the Waseda University Centennial International Symposium at Waseda University on August 22 and 23, 1982'. Reprinted from: Waseda bulletin of comparative law, v.2 (1982).

—Science of peace / by J.G. Starke. - 2nd ed. - Sydney : Law Books, 1986.
xvi,193p.
Previous ed. published by A.W. Sijthoff, 1968.
Bibliography: p.180-183. Includes index.
ISBN 0949553298

—Third generation world organization / Dordrecht : Martinus Nijhoff, 1989.
232.
Describes why the search for peace through international organisations has always failed. Proposes a theory of peace and its relationship with the mode of production. Shows that the present United Nations System, including the Bretton Woods organizations, is not equipped for the needs of the modern world.
ISBN 0792303822 Hbk £40

PEERAGE - GREAT BRITAIN
—Barony of Strange / Committee for Privileges. - London : H.M.S.O., 1986.
1 leaf. - (1985-86 H.L. 175).
ISBN 0104175869

—Peerage law / by R.P. Gadd. - Bristol : ISCA Publishing Ltd., 1985.
viii,178p.
Bibliography: p.163-164. - Includes index.
ISBN 0948343001

PEERAGE - IRELAND
—Peerage law / by R.P. Gadd. - Bristol : ISCA Publishing Ltd., 1985.
viii,178p.
Bibliography: p.163-164. - Includes index.
ISBN 0948343001

PEERAGE - SCOTLAND
—Earldom of Annandale and Hartfell : report from the Committee for Privileges together with the proceedings of the Committee and the speeches of Counsel / London : HMSO, 1985.
xliv,150p.
ISBN 0104961856

PENAL CODE
—Penal Law of Islam / Lahore : Kazi Publications.

PENAL CODE - INDIA
—Indian Penal Code, 1860, 2 Vols. / 4th ed. - Lucknow : Eastern Book Company.

—Indian Penal Code / 2nd ed. - Lucknow : Eastern Book Company, 1981.
406p.

—Indian Penal Code in 2 Vols / 7th ed. - Allahabad : Law Book Company, 1981-83.

—Penal Law of India : Being an Analytical, Critical and Expository Commentary on the Indian Penal Code, 4 Vols. / Allahabad : Law Publishers, 1983.

PENAL CODE - MALAYSIA
—Penal Code (F.M.S. Cap. 45) / Kuala Lumpur : International Law Books Services.

PENAL CODE - NIGERIA
—Notes on Penal Code / Zaria : Ahmadu Bello University Press.

—Penal Code of Northern Nigeria / London : Sweet & Maxwell.
ISBN 0421318201 Hbk

PENSIONS
—International handbook on pensions law and similar employee benefits / London : Graham & Trotman, 1989.
352.
On behalf of the International Association for Insurance Law, examines pension laws in over 17 countries. Topics include surplus reversion and the recapture of assets, predator proofing, the national and international nomad, human rights and sex equality in retirement pensions, share incentive, and stock option plans.
ISBN 0860109941 Hbk £85

—International tax problems of charities and other private institutions with similar tax treatment : proceedings of a seminar held in 1985 during the 39th Congress of the International Fiscal Association / International Fiscal Association. - Deventer Netherlands : Kluwer Law and Taxation Publishers, 1986.
Conference held in London, England.
ISBN 9065442707

—Matrimonial property : division of pension benefits upon marriage breakdown / Institute of Law Research and Reform. - Edmonton : The Institute, 1985.
ii,127,25,13p. - (Report for discussion).

PENSIONS - AUSTRALIA
—Final report of the Commonwealth Task Force on Occupational Superannuation / Australia. - Canberra : Australian Government Publishing Service, 1983.
48p.
ISBN 0644026537

—Law of Superannuation in Australia / Woolloomooloo : International Business Communications.
476p.
ISBN 0959029001 Hbk £60.00

—Permanent incapacity : invalid pension in Australia / Alan Jordan. - Canberra : Department of Social Security, 1984.
264p. - (Research paper).
ISBN 0642515565

—Review of pensions decisions under repatriation legislation : report to the Attorney-General / Administrative Review Council. - Canberra : Australian Government Publishing Service, 1983.
vi,60p. - (Parliamentary paper).
ISBN 0644028920

—Superannuation and family law / Family Law Council. - Canberra : Australian Government Publishing Service, 1980.
xiii,49p. - (Working paper).
ISBN 064205052X

—Superannuation and Insurance and the Sex Discrimination Act 1984 / Kingston : Australian Government Publishing Service, 1986.
127p.
ISBN 0644054964 Hbk £7.95

—Superannuation and Retirement Benefits in Australia / John V. Edstein. - Butterworths, 1988.
ca 550p.
ISBN 0409494461 loose £245.00

—Veterans' Entitlements Act 1986 / North Ryde : C.C.H. Australia, 1986.
ISBN 0869035673 Hbk

PENSIONS - CANADA
—Better pensions for Canadians / Canada. - Ottawa, Ont. : Government of Canada, 1982.
vi, 61, 68, vi p.; 28 cm.
English and French. Title on added t.p.: De meilleures pensions pour les Canadiens.
ISBN 0662520513 pbk.

—Issues regarding the reform of Canada's private pensions system / James E. Pesando. - Canada : Policy Research, Analysis and Liaison Directorate, Consumer and Corporate Affairs, 1983.
ISBN 0662121643

—Minutes of proceedings and evidence of the Special Committee on Pension Reform / Proces-verbaux et temoignages du Comite special sur la reforme des pensions. - Ottawa : The Special Committee, 1983.
x,168p. - (House of Commons issue no 38).
'First session of the Thirty-second Parliament, 1980-81-82-83'. Cover title: Report of the Parliamentary Task Force on Pension Reform.

—Pension Plan Financial Statements / Toronto : Butterworths, 1986.
96p.
ISBN 0409801798 Pbk

—Pension Plans 2 / Vancouver : Continuing Legal Education Society of British Columbia, 1987.
223p.
ISBN 0865043132 Hbk £70.00

—Pension Plans / Vancouver : Continuing Legal Education Society of British Columbia, 1986.
492p.
ISBN 0865042519 Hbk £70.00

—Teachers' Superannuation Act, 1983, Bill 148 : An Act to Revise the Teachers' Superannuation Act / Ontario : Ontario Government Publications Service, 1983.
49p.

PENSIONS - CANADA - ALBERTA

—Matrimonial property : division of pension benefits upon marriage breakdown / Institute of Law Research and Reform. - Edmonton : Institute of Law Research and Reform, 1986.
viii,115p. - (Report).

PENSIONS - GREAT BRITAIN

—Accounting For Pensions / Buchanan. - Cambridge : Woodhead-Faulkner, 1981.
ISBN 0859411249 Hbk £25.00

—Accounts and Audits of Pension Schemes / Pegler. - London : Butterworths, 1987.
ISBN 040667910X Pbk £18.95

—British nationality and the right of abode 1945-1983 / by K.J. Gray : by C.C. Turpin. - Deventer : Kluwer, 1986.
vii,269p.
Includes bibliographical references.
ISBN 9065442510

—Butterworth's Retirement Annuity Premiums Planner / London : Butterworths.

—Coopers and Lybrand: tax and financial planning through pensions / Paul G Meins. - London : Butterworths, 1987.
ISBN 0406500800 Pbk £16.00

—Duties and Responsibilities of Pension Plan Trustees / Williams. - London : CCH, 1984.
ISBN 0863250300 Pbk £11.50

—Guide to Personal Pensions / Tolley Publishing, 1988.
ISBN 0854593101 Hbk £9.95

—Hosking's Pension schemes and retirement benefits / K. Muir McKelvey, Tony Round, Michael Fairclough, Gordon A. Hosking. - 5th ed. - London : Sweet & Maxwell, 1985.
272p.
Previous ed: published as Pension schemes and retirement benefits. 1977. Includes index.
ISBN 0421309601 Pbk £16.00

—Local Government Superannuation Scheme : An Explanation / London : Shaw & Sons, 1982.
ISBN 0721903568 Pbk £0.48

—Occupational pension rights on divorce : a consultation paper / Lord Chancellor's Department. - London : The Department, 1985.
30p.
Includes bibliographical references.

—Pension Cost Accounting / London : Butterworths, 1984.
ISBN 0406010544 Pbk

—Pension fund investment / Cambridge : Woodhead-Faulkner, 1987.
ISBN 0859414000 Hbk £35.00

—Pension fund reform / London : Longman Professional, 1986.
ISBN 0851211828 Pbk £10.95

—Pension funds and British capitalism : the ownership and control of shareholdings / Richard Minns. - London : Heinemann, 1980.
viii,176p; 23cm.
Includes index.
ISBN 0435845101 £13.00

—Pension scheme accounts : a discussion paper by the Accounting Standards Committee : memorandum / by the Society's Standing Committee on Company Law. - London : Law Society, 1982.
4p.

—Pension Schemes / London : Butterworths, 1982.
ISBN 0406406502 Hbk

—Pensions : a practical guide / 3rd ed. - London : Longman Professional, 1987.
ISBN 0851211879 Pbk £25.00

—Pensions : A Practical Guide / J. W. Selley. - London : Oyez Longman, 1980.
- (Oyez Longman Practice Note Ser.: No. 68).
ISBN 0851204619 Hbk £8.95

—Pensions : agenda for change / Cambridge : Woodhead-Faulkner, 1987.
ISBN 0859413802 Hbk £32.50

—Pensions guide / Allied Hambro. - London : Longman Professional, 1984.
ISBN 0851209750 Hbk £11.95

—Personal Financial Planning Manual 1986-87 / John Rayer. - London : Butterworths, 1986.
This manual is a guide to the compilation of personal financial packages for United Kingdom investors. Investments, family finances, life insurance, pensions, and capital transfer tax are covered in the book.
ISBN 040600563X Hbk

—Planning your pension / London : Longman Professional, 1988.
ISBN 0851213715 Pbk £4.95

—Population, pension costs and pensioners' incomes : a background paper for the Inquiry into Provision for Retirement / London : H.M.S.O., 1984.
29p.
At head of title page: Department of Health and Social Security.
ISBN 0113210035

—Powers and liabilities of pension fund trustees / Oxford : Blackwell Scientific, 1987.
ISBN 000383302X Hbk £20.00

—Powers and Liabilities of Pension Fund Trustees / London : Collins, 1987.
200p.
ISBN 000383302X Hbk £17.50

—Property, divorce and retirement pension rights / by K.J. Gray : by C.C. Turpin. - Deventer : Kluwer, 1986.
vii,269p.
Includes bibliographical references.
ISBN 9065442510

—Retirement Planning for Solicitors and Other Self-Employed Persons : 1984 Crash Course Lecture / London : Law Society, 1984.
20p.

—Self-administered pensions for directors / London : Fitzwilliam, 1988.
ISBN 1870555031 Hbk £25.00

—Small self-administered pension scheme / Croydon : Tolley, 1988.
ISBN 085459311X Hbk £16.95

—Taxing Pensions : The Taxation of Occupational Pension Schemes in the United Kingdom / E. M. Hammond. - London : Institute for Fiscal Studies.
- (Report Ser.).

—Understanding pension schemes / 3rd ed. - London : Fourmat, 1987.
ISBN 185190025X Pbk £10.95

—Your new pensions choice / Davies. - 2nd ed. - Croydon : Tolley, 1988.
ISBN 0854593330 Hbk £2.95

PENSIONS - SOUTH AFRICA

—Investigation into the possiblity of making provision for a divorced woman to share in the pension benefits of her former husband / South African Law Commission. - Pretoria : The Commission, 1986.
x,77p. - (Report).
Bibliography: pp.vi-x. Includes draft legislation.
ISBN 0621113573

PENSIONS AND WOMEN - AUSTRALIA

—Superannuation and Insurance and the Sex Discrimination Act 1984 / Kingston : Australian Government Publishing Service, 1986.
127p.
ISBN 0644054964 Hbk £7.95

PENSIONS AND WOMEN - CANADA

—Better pensions for Canadians : focus on women / Ottawa : Minister of Supply and Services, 1982.
18,19p.
With French t.p.: De meilleures pensions pour les Canadiens: la part des femmes. English and French text.
ISBN 066252053X

PERFORMANCE - AUSTRALIA - SOUTH AUSTRALIA

—Report relating to the doctrine of frustration in the law of contract / Law Reform Committee of South Australia. - Adelaide : Government Printer, 1983.
40p. - (71st report).

PERFORMANCE - CANADA - SASKATCHEWAN

—Proposals for a Frustrated Contracts Act : report to the Minister of Justice / Law Reform Commission of Saskatchewan. - Saskatoon : The Commission, 1988.
31p.

—Tentative proposals for a Frustrated Contracts Act / Law Reform Commission of Saskatchewan. - Saskatoon : The Commission, 1987.
55p.
Includes text of proposed Act.

PERFORMANCE - GREAT BRITAIN

—Performance / 2nd ed. - London : Offord Publications Ltd, 1985.
600p.
ISBN 0903931362 Hbk £18.00
ISBN 0903931591 Pbk £14.95

PERFORMANCE CONTRACTS

—Performance bonds and contract guarantees : with special reference to the risk of unfair calling and injunction procedures : proceedings of the seminar held in Paris in January, 1982 / International Bar Association Section on Business Law (London), Institute of International Business Law and Practice (Paris). - London : International Bar Association, 1983.
ii,126p.
The papers contained in this volume are reproduced from transcripts of the speeches delivered at the Seminar rather than written articles.

PERFORMANCE (LAW) - AUSTRALIA

—Time in the performance of contracts : especially for the sale of land / K.E. Lindgren. - 2nd ed. - Sydney : Butterworths, 1982.
xxv,201p.
Previous ed.: 1976. Includes bibliographical references and index.
ISBN 0409303909 Hbk £49

PERFORMANCE (LAW) - CANADA - BRITISH COLUMBIA

—Performance under protest / Law Reform Commission of British Columbia. - Vancouver : The Commission, 1984.
ii,35p. - (Working paper).
Includes bibliographical references.

—Report on performance under protest / Law Reform Commission of British Columbia. - Vancouver : The Commission, 1985.
21p.
Includes bibliographical references.
ISBN 077188477X

PERFORMING ARTS SPONSORSHIP - GREAT BRITAIN

—Sponsorship of sport, arts, and leisure : law, tax and business relationships / by Stephen Townley and Edward Grayson : with forewords by Lord Goodman, Dick Jeeps and Sir William Rees-Mogg. - London : Sweet & Maxwell, 1984.
xliii,333p; 23cm.
Guide to the law and tax considerations involved in the business of sponsorship. The legal status of sponsorship rights and licences is interpreted with reference to statute and case law. Intellectual property law, competition law, copyright and the remedies for its infringement, trade-marks, and passing-off are examined.
ISBN 0421304103 £19.75

PERIODICALS

—ACOLAM newsletter / Advisory Committee on Latin American Materials. - London? : Institute of Latin American Studies?, 1980.
ISBN 02636832

—Administrator : the journal of the Institute of Chartered Secretaries and Administrators / v. - London : Institute of Chartered Secretaries and Administrators, 1982-.
Continues: Professional administration, new series vol. 1, no. 1(Jan. 1981)-v. 1, no. 11(Dec. 1981).

—Advertising and marketing law and practice / London : Frank Cass, 1984-.
Continues: Advertising law and practice.

—Adviser : a bi-monthly guide on social security, housing, money advice and employment / London : National Association of Citizens Advice Bureaux and Shelter, 1986-.
Continues: Rights Workers Bulletin, Housing Aid and In the Black. Supplement: Computanews.

—Advocates' Quarterly (1977-Present) / Aurora : Canada Law Book Co.

Back Vols.

—Advocates' Quarterly (A.Q.) / Garry D. Watson. - Aurora : Canada Law Book Co.

—Africa south of the Sahara / London : Europa Publications, 1971-.

—Ahmadu Bello University law journal / Zaria : Faculty of Law, Ahmadu Bello University, 1983-.

—Alberta Weekly Law Digest / Agincourt : Carswell, 1988.

—All-Canada Weekly Summaries Third Ser. (1986-Present) / Aurora : Canada Law Book Co. - (Summary Services, National Series).

Parts only

Back Vols.

—American studies library newsletter / American Studies Library Group. - Manchester : American Studies Library Group, 1984-.
Continues: ASLG newsletter.

—Annual report for the year ended 30 September ... / Air Transport Users Committee. - v. - London : The Committee, 1978.
Continues: CIVIL AVIATION AUTHORITY. Airline Users Committee. Annual report.

—Annual report of the Council of the Law Society : intended to be presented to the general meeting of the members on ... / Law Society. – v. – London : Spottiswoode, 1903.
Continues: Annual report of the Council of the Incorporated Law Society. 1975 onwards incorporates the interim report and accounts of the Solicitors Benevolent Association. Cover title, 1966/67 onwards: Annual report of the Council and accounts. Published by the Law Society, 1945 onwards.

—Annual report / Servicing the Legal System, Queen's University of Belfast / Servicing the Legal System. – v. – Belfast : Servicing the Legal System, 1981-.
Servicing the Legal System was originally established as a committee of the Faculty of law, Queen's University of Belfast. Report year ends 31 July.

—Annual report / Zimbabwe Advisory Committee on Law Reform / Zimbabwe. – v. – Causeway : The Committee, 1982.

—Annual review of ocean affairs / United Nations Office for Ocean Affairs and the Law of the Sea. – 2 vol. – London : Lloyds of London Press, 1989.
These two volumes contain protocols, conventions, treaties, decisions, and other matters enacted by governmental organisations concerned with ocean affairs. Includes illicit drug-trafficking, fisheries management, and the marine environment. This first edition contains documentation covering the years 1985-1987.

—Arab law newsletter / London : Lloyd's of London, 1985-.
Covers Arab Middle East, Gulf States and North Africa.

—Arab law quarterly / London : Lloyd's of London, 1985-.
Issued by: Society of Arab Comparative and International Law.

—ASLG newsletter / American Studies Library Group. – 8 v. – Manchester : ASLG, 1980-.
Continues: Newsletter / American Studies Library Group. - Continued by: American studies library newsletter.

—Australian and New Zealand Journal of Criminology / John Willis. – Wellington : Butterworths.

Back Vols. avail.

—Australian Bar review / Australian Bar Association. – Sydney : Butterworths, 1985-.
'Published under the auspices of the Australian Bar Association'. - T.p..

—Australian Current Law / Jean Maior. – Wellington : Butterworths.

—Australian journal of family law / Sydney : Butterworths, 1986-.

—Australian journal of law and society / – North Ryde : Macquarie University, School of Law, 1982.
ISBN 07293356

—BLAISE-LINE mini manual / London : British Library, Automated Services Dept., 1984.
66p.
ISBN 0712310150 spiral £10.00 (1 copy free to subscribers)

—British Columbia Weekly Law Digest / Agincourt : Carswell, 1987.

—British Journal of Criminology / London : Sweet & Maxwell.

Bound volume

Single copy

Back vols. avail.

—Bulletin of Northern Ireland law / Belfast : S.L.S., Faculty of Law, Queen's University, 1981-.

—Business Law Review / Butterworth and Co. (Publishers) Ltd. – London : Butterworths.

—Butterworth's Current Law / Phillippa Oldham. – Wellington : Butterworths.

—Butterworth's Family Law Bulletin / Hellen Papadopoulas. – Wellington : Butterworths.

—Butterworths banking and financial law review / London : Butterworths, 1987.
Index in each vol..

—Canada Gazette : Statutes, Pt. III / Agincourt : Carswell, 1987.

—Canada Tax Letter / Toronto : DeBoo.
This series of studies, intended for the tax specialist, contains analyses and opinions of important legislation and jurisprudence. Approximately six issues per year are planned.
ISBN 0888201664 Hbk £140.00

—Canadian Bar Review : 1923-Date / Professional Books Staff. – Abingdon : Professional Books, 1984.

—Canadian Business Law Journal (1976-Present) / Aurora : Canada Law Book Co.
– (Law Journals).

Back Vols.

—Canadian Business Law Journal (C.B.L.J.) 1976-Present / Aurora : Canada Law Book Co.

Current subscription-Outside Canada

Back Vols.

—Canadian Current Law / Agincourt : Carswell, 1987.

Issues and Index from 1985, 4 Vols.

Issues and Index from 1984, 4 Vols.

Issues and Index from 1983, 3 Vols.

—Canadian journal of law and jurisprudence / London, Ont. : Faculty of Law, University of Western Ontario, 1988-.
Continues: University of Western Ontario law review.

—Canadian Rights Reporter, 6 vols / Toronto : Butterworths.

—Canadian Weekly Law Sheet / Toronto : Butterworths.

—Capital taxes : a quarterly commentary / v. – London : Sweet & Maxwell, 1984.
Index in each vol.
ISBN 02659514

—Caribbean law librarian : bulletin of the Caribbean Assocation of Law Libraries / Jamaica : Caribbean Association of Law Librarians, 1984-.

—Chinese yearbook of international law and affairs / – Baltimore : Occasional Papers/Reprints Series in Contemporary Asian Studies, Inc. for the Chinese Society of International Law - Chinese (Taiwan) Branch of International Law Association, 1983-.
Continues: The annals of the Chinese Society of International Law.

—Civil justice quarterly / London : Sweet & Maxwell in association with the Institute of Judicial Administration at the University of Birmingham, 1982-.
25cm.

—Commercial Insolvency Reporter / Toronto : Butterworths.
ISBN 0409806218 Hbk

—Commonwealth Law Bulletin / Legal Division, Commonwealth Secretariat. – London : Commonwealth Secretariat, 1983.
– (Quarterly).

—Companies and securities law journal / . – Sydney : Law Book Co., 1982-.

—Computer law & practice : the journal of computer and communications law / London : F. Cass, 1984-.

—Construction law journal / . – Andover : Sweet & Maxwell, 1984.
Index in each vol..
ISBN 02672359

—Counsel : the journal of the Bar of England and Wales / London : Senate of the Inns of Court and the Bar, 1985.
ISBN 02683784

—Criminal Law Quarterly (1958-Present) / Aurora : Canada Law Book Co.
– (Law Journals).

Back Vols.

—Criminal Law Quarterly (C.L.Q.) 1958-Present / Aurora : Canada Law Book Co.

Current subscription-Outside Canada

Back Vols.

C.L.Q. Index (Vols. 1-26)

—Criminal Law Review / Andrew Ashworth. – London : Sweet & Maxwell.

Bound Vol.

Single copy

Vol. 1-32

—CTISS file / Bath : Computers in Teaching Initiative Support Service, 1986-.

—Current Law / Erna Jansen. – Durban : Butterworths.

—Current Law Back Volumes : Current Law Statutes Annotated 1981, 2 Vols. / London : Sweet & Maxwell, 1982.
ISBN 0421301406 Hbk £36.00

—Current Law Back Volumes : Year Book 1979 / London : Sweet & Maxwell, 1980.
ISBN 0421269103 Hbk £14.00

—Current Law Back Volumes : Year Book 1981 / London : Sweet & Maxwell, 1982.
ISBN 0421301309 Hbk £14.00

—Current Law Back Volumes : Year Book 1982 / London : Sweet & Maxwell.
ISBN 0421320605 Hbk £14.00

—Current legal problems / edited...on behalf of the Faculty of Laws, University College, London. – London : Stevens, 1948.
Includes cumulative indexes in every 5th volume.

—Current legal theory : international journal for documentation on legal theory (bibliography - abstracts - reviews) / Centrum voor Grondslagenonderzoek van het Recht. – Leuven : Acco, 1983-.

—Dublin University law journal / Dublin : Law School, Trinity College, Dublin, 1976-.

—Eastern Africa law review : a journal of law and development / Dar es Salaam : East African Literature Bureau, 1968-.

—Electronic library : the international journal for minicomputer, microcomputer and software applications in libraries / . – Oxford : Learned Information, 1983.
ISBN 02640473

—Encyclopedia of local government law / Charles Cross, Stephen Bailey, Stephen Campbell, Reginald Jones. – 4 volumes. – London : Sweet & Maxwell, 1980.
25cm : loose-leaf.
Release number fourteen included the relevant sectins of the Local Governments Finance Act 1988, annotated, and cross-referenced to other parts of the work. Also covers the Local Government Act 1988, and the Rate Support Grants Act 1988. Statutory instruments, selected precedents, circulars, and full tables and index are also contained.
ISBN 0421260505 Llf £195.00

—Equality now! : a magazine of the Equal Opportunities Commission / Manchester : Equal Opportunities Commission, 1983-.
Continues: EOC news.

—ESRC newsletter / . – London : Economic and Social Research Council, 1984-.
Continues SSRC newsletter.

—Estates and Trusts Quarterly / Aurora : Canada Law Book Co.
– (Law Journals).

Back Vols.

Binder and Contents

—Estates and Trusts Quarterly (E. & T.Q.) 1974-Present / Aurora : Canada Law Book Co.

Current subscription-Outside Canada

Back Vols.

—Estates Gazette Journal : 1858-1980 / Abingdon : Professional Books.

—European Communities publications : a guide to British Library resources / British Library. – London : British Library, 1983.
iii,46p.
ISBN 0712320156

—European Competition Law Review / Oxford : ESC Publishing Ltd, 1988.

—European environment review : the journal of European Community and international environmental policy and law / English ed. – Brussels : Environmental Law Forum, 1986-.
Also published in French and German.

—European human rights reports / London : European Law Centre, 1979-.
Irregular.

—European law review / . – London : Sweet & Maxwell, 1975.
Index in each vol.
ISBN 03075400

—Falkland Islands gazette / . – Stanley : Goverment Printing Office, 1891.
Contains proclamations and regulations. Vol. 1, no. 1 published as: Falkland gazette.

—FCO press conference / Great Britain. – London : Foreign and Commonwealth Office, 1987.

—Fiscal studies : the journal of the Institute for Fiscal Studies / Institute for Fiscal Studies. – London : Institute for Fiscal Studies, 1979-.

—Guide to International Law Periodicals / Ibadan : University Press.

—Haldane journal : a journal of law and socialism / v. – London : Haldane Society, 1985-.

—Haldane Society employment law bulletin / – London : Haldane Society of Socialist Lawyers, 1983.

—House of Commons Weekly Information Bulletin / London : HMSO.

Single Issue

—Howard journal of criminal justice / . – Oxford : Basil Blackwell for the Howard League, 1984.
Continues: The Howard journal of penology and crime prevention.

—Howard journal of penology and crime prevention / Howard League for Penal Reform. – London: Scottish Academic Press, 1965-1983, 1965-.
Continues: The Howard journal; continued by: The Howard journal of criminal justice.

—Human rights law journal / Kehl am Rhein : Engel, 1980-.
Absorbed: Human rights review, 1982.

—I'M : information market, marche d'information, Informationsmarkt / Luxembourg : Commission of the European Communities, 1985.
Continues: Euronet Diane news. Multilingual text.

—IATA review / v. – Geneva : International Air Transport Association, 1985-.
Supersedes: IATA world airline cooperation review.

—Immigration and nationality law and practice / London : Frank Cass, 1986-.

—Index to Commonwealth Legal Periodicals : 1978-1981, 1 Bound Vol. / Agincourt : Carswell, 1982.

—Index to Nigerian legal periodicals, 1946-1981 / compiled by the Library, Nigerian Institute of Advanced Legal Studies. – Lagos : NIALS Library, 1983.
v,33p.

—Index to Singapore/Malaysia Legal Periodicals / Kent Ridge : Malaya Law Review.

—Industrial Law Bulletin / Alexander Szakats. – Wellington : Butterworths.
ISBN 040978107X Pbk

—Industrial law journal / London : Sweet & Maxwell for the Industrial Law Society, 1972-.
Supersedes: Bulletin of the Industrial Law Society. Index in each vol..

—Insolvency law & practice / London : F. Cass, 1985-.

—Intellectual Property Journal / Agincourt : Carswell, 1985.

—International business lawyer : journal of the Section on Business Law of the International Bar Association / v. – London : International Bar Association, 1973.
Index in each vol., 1979-.
ISBN 03097676

—International construction law review / London : Lloyd's of London, 1983-.

—International contract law & finance review / 3 v. – Lausanne : Seminar Services, 1980.
Superseded by: International financial law review.

—International financial law review / London : Euromoney, 1983-.
Supersedes: The international contract law & finance review.

—International journal of comparative labour law and industrial relations / v. – Leicester : University of Leicester, 1985.

—International journal of estuarine and coastal law / London : Graham & Trotman, 1986-.

—International journal of law and the family / Oxford : Oxford University Press, 1987-.

—International media law : a monthly bulletin on rights, clearances and legal practice / v. – London : Oyez Longman, 1982.
ISBN 02636395

—International review of contemporary law / Brussels : International Association of Democratic Lawyers, 1982-.
Continues: Review of contemporary law.

—Jewish law annual / Leiden : Brill, 1978-.

—Journal of African law / London : Butterworth, 1957-.

—Journal of Business Law / London : Sweet & Maxwell.

Bound Vol.

Back Vols. avail.

Single copy

—Journal of Contemporary Roman-Dutch law / Durban : Butterworths.
– (Eng. and Afrikaans).

—Journal of energy & natural resources law / v. – London : Sweet & Maxwell, 1983-.
Co-sponsored by the Section on Energy and Natural Resources Law (S.E.R.L) of the International Bar Association and the Centre for Petroleum and Mineral Law Studies, University of Dundee, Scotland.

—Journal of international arbitration / v. – Geneva : D. Thompson and J. Werner, 1984-.

—Journal of international banking law / Oxford : ESC Publishing Ltd., 1986-.

—Journal of international franchising & distribution law / London : Frank Cass, 1986-.

—Journal of law and society / Oxford : Basil Blackwell, 1974-.
Continues: British journal of law and society.

—Journal of Planning and Environmental Law : 1948-1981, 34 Vols. / Abingdon : Professional Books.

—Journal of private & property law / . – Lagos : Department of Private & Property Law, University of Lagos, 1984-.

—Journal of professional legal education / Sydney, 1983-.
Index published every two years.

—Journal of Social Welfare Law / Christina M. Lyon. – London : Sweet & Maxwell.

Bound Vol.

Single copy

Back Vols. avail.

—Journal of the Society of Public Teachers of Law : 1924-date / Abingdon : Professional Books.

—Journal of the Society of Public Teachers of Law : New Series, 1946-1980, 14 Vols. / Professional Books Staff. – Abingdon : Professional Books, 1984.

—Journal of world trade law / London : Vincent Press, 1967-.
Index in each vol.

—Law and philosophy : an international journal for jurisprudence and legal philosophy / Dordrecht : D. Reidel, 1982-.

—Law & policy / Oxford : Blackwell for the Baldy Center for Law and Social Policy, State University of New York at Buffalo, 1984-.
Continues: Law & policy quarterly. Includes bibliographies.

—Law journals / Middlesex Polytechnic Library Services. – Hendon : The Polytechnic, 1982.
11p.
'List of law related journals and law reports taken by Middlesex Polytechnic libraries'.

—Law Librarian : Bulletin of the British and Irish Association of Law Librarians / London : Sweet & Maxwell, 1986.

—Law Quarterly Review / London : Sweet & Maxwell, 1982.

—Law Teacher : Journal of the Association of Law Teachers / John Tilotson. – London : Sweet & Maxwell, 1986.

—Law under review : a quarterly bulletin of law reform projects / Law Commission. – London : Law Commission, 1987.
Includes index.

—Lawasia human rights bulletin / v. – Sydney : Lawasia, 1982-.

—Lawasia newsletter / v. – Sydney : Law Association for Asia and the Western Pacific, 1977-.

—Lawyer : journal of the Law Society, University of Lagos, Lagos, Nigeria / v. – Lagos : Faculty of Law, University of Lagos, 1960-.

—Legal issues of European integration / v. – Deventer : Kluwer, 1974-.
Law review of the Europa Instituut, University of Amsterdam.

—Legal service bulletin / assisted by the Fitzroy Legal Service. – Clayton, Vic. : Faculty of Law, Monash University, 1974.
Cumulative index: vols. 1-10 (1974-1985) published separately, 1986.
ISBN 08173516

—Legal Studies : The Journal of the Society of Public Teachers of Law / London : Butterworths, 1986.

Back issues avail.

—Lesotho law journal : a journal of law and development / Lesotho : Faculty of Law, National University of Lesotho, 1985-.
Includes bibliographical references.

—List of current periodicals currently received in the Legal Advisers Library and the legal section, Cornwall House / Great Britain. – London : Foreign and Commonwealth Office, 1987.
5 leaves.

—Lloyd's maritime and commercial law quarterly / . – London : Lloyd's of London Press, 1974-.
Index in each vol. - Cumulative indexes, 1974-78, 1979-83.

—Malaya Law Review / National University of Singapore, Faculty of Law. – Singapore : University of Singapore.
ISBN 0542335X Hbk £45.00

—Manx law bulletin / Douglas : Attorney General's Chambers, 1983-.
Covers legislation 'in a limited manner' and 'all written judgments from the High Courts'.

—McKenna law letter : current developments in the law / London : McKenna & Co., 1980.

—Middle East and North Africa / London : Europa Publications, 1964-.
Continues: Middle East.

—Modern Law Review : 1937-date / Professional Books Staff. – Abingdon : Professional Books, 1984.

—Modern Law Review / London : Sweet & Maxwell.

Bound Vol.

Single copy

Index Vols. 1-33

Back Vols. avail.

—NACRO briefing / . – London : NACRO, 1982-.

—NACRO juvenile crime briefing / . – London : NACRO, 1985-.

—NACRO news digest / London : NACRO, 1979-.

—Natal University law and society review / Durban : University of Natal, 1985.
Continues: Natal University law review.

—Natural resources forum / Dordrecht : Reidel for the United Nations, 1976.
Edited by: United Nations. Centre for Natural Resources, Energy and Transport. Vol. 7 onwards published by Graham & Trotman for the United Nations.
ISBN 01650203

—New Law Journal : 1965-date / Professional Books Staff. – Abingdon : Professional Books, 1984.

—New Law Journal / Butterworth Staff. – London : Butterworths.

Microfiche (1965-1977)
ISBN 0406886032

—New Zealand Law Journal / Wellington : Butterworths.

—New Zealand University Law Review : 1963-date / Professional Books Staff. – Abingdon : Professional Books, 1984.

—Newsletter / Law Technology Centre & BILETA. – Warwick : LTC, School of Law, University of Warwick, 1987-.

—Nigeria journal of contemporary law / . – Lagos : University of Lagos, 1970-.

—Nigerian Current Law Review / London : Sweet & Maxwell, 1982.
ISBN 0421316004 Hbk £35.00

—Nigerian current law review / . – Lagos : Nigerian Institute of Advanced Legal Studies, 1982-.

—Nigerian current legal problems / . – Lagos : Nigerian Institute of Advanced Legal Studies, 1985-.

—Nigerian law journal / Lagos : African Universities Press, 1964-.

—Nigerian periodicals index / Jos? : Committee of University Librarians of Nigerian Universities, 1986-.

—Nordic journal of international law / Acta scandinavica juris gentium. – . – Kbenhavn : Nordisk Tidsskrift for International Ret, 1986-.
Continues: Nordisk tidsskrift for international ret Acta scandinavica juris gentium.

—Northern Ireland Legal Quarterly : 1936-1982, 33 Vols. / Professional Books Staff. – Abingdon : Professional Books, 1984.

—Northern Ireland Legal Quarterly / Belfast : Queen's University of Belfast, 1986.
100p.

—Nuclear Law Bulletin / Organisation for Economic Co-operation and Development. – London : HMSO.

—Official Journal of the European Communities / London : HMSO.
– (Ser. L: Legislation, Ser. C: Information and Notices, and Series S: Supplement).

Ser. S: Supplement

—Official journal of the European Patent Office / Amtsblatt des Europaischen Patentamts. – Munchen : European Patent Office, 1981-.

—Oil & gas law and taxation review : a monthly review covering court decisions, legislation and international news / Oxford : ESC, 1982-.

—Ombudsman journal / Edmonton, Alta. : International Ombudsman Institute, Faculty of Law, University of Alberta, 1981-.

—Orders in Council / Toronto : DeBoo.
This service, published weekly, contains all Federal Cabinet Orders In Council and ministerial orders, as well as regulations and appointments. A semi-annual cumulative subject index is also provided.

—Peoples' law : a journal of contemporary Nigerian and African laws, justice and legality / Lagos, Nigeria : Pan-Afrika Peoples' Law Center and Akademy, 1987.

—Practice today / . – London : Julian Harris, 1985-.
Supplement to: Solicitors' journal. Added t.p. title: The management magazine for solicitors.

—Probation journal / London : National Association of Probation Officers, 1974-.
Continues: Probation.

—Proceedings and resolutions of the ... provincial meeting of the members of the Society / the Law Society. – 25 v. – London : The Law Society, 1903.
Continues: Proceedings and resolutions / Incorporated Law Society. Continued by: Annual conference of the Law Society, 1st(1948). Bound with the annual reports of the Council of the Law Society. Typewritten index to proceedings for 1887-1928 bound with our 1924-1928 volume.

—Professional negligence : a journal of liability, ethics and discipline / London : Cass, 1985-.

—Ratio Juris : an international journal of jurisprudence and philosophy of law / Oxford : Blackwell, 1988-.

—Regional and local affairs : news / Strasbourg : Council of Europe, 1982-.
Supersedes: Information bulletin: municipal and regional matters.

—Research bulletin : British Library Research and Development Department / British Library Research and Development Department. – London : The Department, 1987.
Continues: Newsletter.
ISBN 09522832

—Review of Ghana law / Accra : General Legal Council, 1969-.
Index in each vol.

—Revista de la Facultad de Ciencias Juridicas y Politicas / Caracas : Universidad Central de Venezuela, 1976.
Continues: Revista de la Facultad de Derecho.

—Ritsumeikan law review / International ed. – Kyoto, Japan : Ritsumeikan University, 1986-.
International ed. of: Ritsumeikan law review. Includes articles in German, French and Japanese.

—Russian serials / ... prepared by Alistair Ricketts ... in cyrillic script, with a transliterated version and an English translation. – Oxford : Bodleian Law Library, 1986.
12 leaves.

—Serials '85 : proceedings ... of the UK Serials Group Conference held at the Jesse Boot Centre, University of Nottingham, 25-28 March 1985 / Brian Cox. – S.l. : UK Serials Group, 1985.
208 p. – (Serials monograph).
ISBN 0906148073

—Serials '86 : proceedings of the UK Serials Group Conference held at the University of Exeter 24-27 March 1986 / edited by Rodney M. Burton. – S.l. : UK Serials Group, 1986.
vii,188p; 21cm. – (Serials monograph).
ISBN 0906148081

—Socialist lawyer / London : Haldane Society of Socialist Lawyers, 1986.

—Solicitor's Journal : 1855-1981, 125 Vols. / Abingdon : Professional Books.

—South African Tax Journal / H. R. Levin. – Durban : Butterworths, 1985.

—South America, Central America and the Caribbean: survey and directory of the countries of the region / London : Europa Publications, 1985-.

—Statistical bulletin / Scottish Home and Health Department : prepared by the Government Statistical Service. – v. – Edinburgh : The Department, 1983.
ISBN 02641178

—Statute Law Review / London : Sweet & Maxwell.

Bound Vol.

Back Vols. avail.

—Supreme Court Law Review / Eric Gertner. – Butterworths.
544p.
ISBN 0409832618 Hbk £75.00

Vol. 2: 1981
496p.
ISBN 0409832626 Hbk £75.00

Vol. 3: 1982
616p.
ISBN 0409832634 Hbk £75.00

Vol. 5: 1983
464p.
ISBN 0409832650 Hbk £95.00

Vol. 8: 1986
580p.
ISBN 0409804843 Hbk £110.00

Vol. 9: 1987
544p.
Analysis of the Supreme Court of Canada's key decision and a critical examination of the Court's performance in reaching them. This volume covers the Court's decisions for 1985 and 1986.
ISBN 0409806412 Hbk £128.00

—Swiss review of international competition law / Geneva : Werner & Sieber, 1984.
Continues: Revue suisse du droit international de la concurrence.
ISBN 02558246

—Trust law & practice : pension funds, commercial trusts and charities / London : Cass, 1986-.

—Union list of law periodicals held in libraries within the City of Liverpool / compiled by Susan Frost, Robert Caley. – Liverpool : Liverpool Polytechnic Library Service, 1985.
30p.

—University of British Columbia Law Review : 1959-date / Professional Books Staff. – Abingdon : Professional Books, 1984.

—University of Ghana law journal / v. – London : Sweet & Maxwell, 1964-.

—University of Jos law journal / Jos, Nigeria : Faculty of Law, University of Jos, 1984-.

—University of Toronto Faculty of Law Review / Agincourt : Carswell.

—University of Toronto Law Journal : 1935-date / Professional Books Staff. – Abingdon : Professional Books, 1984.

—Weekly Criminal Bulletin Current Series (1987), 17 Vols. / Chris N. Buhr. – Aurora : Canada Law Book Co.
– (Summary Services, National Ser.).

—Weekly Criminal Bulletin (W.C.B.) 1987-Present / Chris N. Buhr. – Aurora : Canada Law Book Co.

Back Vols. 31.00 ea.

Binder

Parts Only

—Weekly Digest of Civil Procedure / Agincourt : Carswell, 1987.

—Weekly Digest of Family Law / Agincourt : Carswell, 1986.

—Zimbabwe law journal / Salisbury, Zimbabwe : Department of Law, University of Zimbabwe, 1979-.
Continues: Rhodesian law journal. Includes indexes.

—Zimbabwe law review / v. – Harare : Department of Law, University of Zimbabwe, 1985-.

PERIODICALS - AUSTRALIA

—Union list of legal periodicals held in Australia and New Zealand / compiled by Monash University Law Library 1979. – 1 microfiche. – Clayton, Vic. : The Law Library, 1980.
10 x 15 cm.

PERIODICALS - CANADA

—Canadian Tax News / Agincourt : Carswell, 1987.

PERIODICALS - COMMONWEALTH

—Commonwealth lawyer : the journal of the Commonwealth Lawyers' Association / v. – London : The Association, 1984.
ISBN 02658100

PERIODICALS - EUROPEAN COMMUNITY

—Journal of the Irish Society for European Law / v. – Dublin : Irish Society for European Law, 1977 -.
ISBN 03324753

PERIODICALS - GREAT BRITAIN

—Denning law journal / Buckingham : University of Buckingham, 1986.
ISBN 02691922

—Legal journals index / v. – Hebden Bridge, Yorkshire : Legal Information Resources, 1986.
ISBN 09504206

—Serials '83 : proceedings of the UK Serials Group Conference held at the University of Durham, 21-24 March 1983 / edited by Rodney M. Burton. – S.l. : The Group, 1984.
144 p. – (Serials monograph).
ISBN 0906148057

—Serials '84 : proceedings of the UK Serials Group Conference held at the University of Surrey, Guildford, England 26-29 March 1984 / edited by Brian Cox. – Heddington : The Group, 1985.
vii, 168p.
ISBN 0906148065

PERIODICALS - MALAYSIA

—Index to Singapore/Malaysia legal periodicals 1932-1984 / Compiled by the staff of the Law Library, National University of Singapore Library : edited by Molly Cheang, Sng Yok Fong, Carolyn Wee. – Singapore : Malayan Law Journal Pte., 1986.
xvi,431p.
ISBN 9971700506 Hbk £160.00

—Survey of Malaysian law / Kuala Lumpur : Published for the Faculty of Law, University of Malaya by Malayan Law Journal, 1979 -.
ISBN 02173239

PERIODICALS - MAURITIUS

—Mauritius law review / Revue de droit et de jurisprudence mauricienne. – v. – Port Louis : s.n., 1977.

PERIODICALS - NEW ZEALAND

—Union list of legal periodicals held in Australia and New Zealand / compiled by Monash University Law Library 1979. – 1 microfiche. – Clayton, Vic. : The Law Library, 1980.
10 x 15 cm.

PERIODICALS - NIGERIA

—Attorney : a journal of the Nigerian Association of Law Students / v. – Nigeria : The Association, 1980.

—Ibadan University law review : the journal of the Faculty of Law, University of Ibadan / Ibadan, Nigeria : Evans Brothers, 1986.

—Legal practitioners' review / Ibadan : Spectrum Books, 1986.

—Lord justice : a journal of the Law Students' Society, University of Ibadan / Ibadan, Nigeria : Law Students' Society, University of Ibadan, 1987.

—Nigeria lawyers' quarterly / v. – Lagos : s.n., 1964.
2 issues only held: vol. 5, nos. 1-4, and vol. 7, nos. 1-4.
ISBN 00290025

—Nigerian juridical review / Nsukka, Nigeria : University of Nigeria Press, 1976.

—Solicitor and advocate : journal of the Law Students' Association, University of Maiduguri, Nigeria / v. – Maiduguri : Law Students' Association, 1980.

—University of Ife law journal / Ife, Nigeria : University of Ife Press, 1986.

PERIODICALS - PHILIPPINES

—Bar Review Guide in Political Law / 3rd ed. – Quezon City : University of the Philippines, Law Center, 1981.
190p.

PERIODICALS - SINGAPORE

—Index to Singapore/Malaysia legal periodicals 1932-1984 / Compiled by the staff of the Law Library, National University of Singapore Library : edited by Molly Cheang, Sng Yok Fong, Carolyn Wee. – Singapore : Malayan Law Journal Pte., 1986.
xvi,431p.
ISBN 9971700506 Hbk £160.00

PERIODICALS - SOUTH AFRICA

—Transkei law journal / Umtata, Transkei : University of Transkei, 1986.
ISBN 02591286

PERIODICALS - TRINIDAD & TOBAGO

—Lawyer : a quarterly journal of the Trinidad & Tobago Bar Association / Port of Spain : Trinidad and Tobago Bar Association, 1977.
28cm.
Includes: Digest of cases with editorial notes. Subtitle varies.

PERIODICALS - ZAMBIA

—Zambia law journal / v. – Lusaka : University of Zambia, 1969.

PERJURY - AUSTRALIA - SOUTH AUSTRALIA

—Report ... relating to civil actions for perjury committed in criminal proceedings and to the tort of malicious prosecution / Law Reform Committee of South Australia. – Adelaide : Government Printer, 1984.
13p. – (83rd report).
Bibliography: p.14.

PERPETUITIES - AUSTRALIA

—Perpetuities Act 1984 / P.J. Butt. – North Ryde : Law Book Co, 1986.
xx, 188p.
ISBN 0455206082 Hbk £25.00

PERPETUITIES - AUSTRALIA - TASMANIA

—Report and recommendations upon perpetuities and accumulations / Law Reform Commission of Tasmania. – Hobart : Government Printer, 1983.
25p. – (Report).

PERPETUITIES - CANADA - SASKATCHEWAN

—Proposals relating to the rules against perpetuities and accumulations : report to the Minister if Justice / Law Reform Commission of Saskatchewan. – Saskatoon : The Commission, 1987.
29p.

PERPETUITIES - GREAT BRITAIN

—Rule Against Perpetuities / Leach. – London : Sweet & Maxwell, 1986.
ISBN 0421355506 Hbk £32.00

PERPETUITIES - MANITOBA

—Report on the rules against accumulations and perpetuities / Law Reform Commission. – Winnipeg : Queen's Printer, 1982.
i,105p. – (Report).

PERSECUTION - BURUNDI

—Burundi since the genocide / by Reginald Kay. – London : Minority Rights Group, 1987.
12p. – (Report).
'This report was first published under the title Selective genocide in Burundi by Professor Rene Lemarchand and David Martin in July 1974'. - Front cover verso.
ISBN 0946690472

PERSECUTION - IRAN

—Baha'is of Iran / by Roger Cooper. – Rev. and updated ed. – London : Minority Rights Group, 1985.
16p. – (Report).
Bibliography: p.16.
ISBN 0946690316

PERSIAN GULF

—International and legal problems of the gulf / S.H. Amin. – London : Middle East and North African Studies Press, 1981.
235p.
Bibls..
ISBN 0906559057

PERSONAL INJURIES

—Damages for personal injuries and death / by John Munkman. – 6th ed. – London : Butterworths, 1980.
xxviii,211p.

ISBN 0406311129

—Damages for personal injury and death in Canada / edited and with introductory notes by Immanuel Goldsmith : case abridgements prepared by Alan Burnside Harvey and by David Carruthers. – Toronto : Carswell, 1959.
xxiii,374p.
Includes index.

—Meeting legal needs? : an evaluation of a scheme for personal injury victims / Hazel Genn. – Oxford : SSRC Centre for Socio-Legal Studies, 1982.
ix,69p; 22cm.
A report commissioned by the Greater Manchester Legal Services Committee.
ISBN 0862260442

PERSONAL INJURIES - AUSTRALIA

—Assessment of damages for personal injury and death / by Harold Luntz. – 2nd ed. – Sydney : Butterworths, 1983.
lxvii,570p.
Includes index.
ISBN 0409491322

—Community law reform for the Australian Capital Territory / Law Reform Commission. – Canberra : Australian Government Publishing Service, 1985.
ix,44p. – (Report).
Bibliography: p.41-42 - Includes index.
ISBN 0644013257

—Medical Assessment of Injuries for Legal Purposes / 4th ed. – Sydney : Butterworths, 1985.
372p.
ISBN 0409492981 Hbk

PERSONAL INJURIES - AUSTRALIA - NEW SOUTH WALES

—Community law reform program / New South Wales Law Reform Commission. – Sydney : Goverment Printer, 1986.
xv,89p. – (L.R.C.).
Includes bibliographical references.
ISBN 073052535X

PERSONAL INJURIES - AUSTRALIA - SOUTH AUSTRALIA

—Report ... relating to claims for injuries from toxic substances and radiation effects / Law Reform Committee of South Australia. – Adelaide : Government Printer, 1985.
96p. – (87th report).

PERSONAL INJURIES - CANADA

—Assessment of Personal Injury Damages / Butterworths, 1985.
378p.
ISBN 0409814075 Hbk £75.00

—Goldsmith's damages for personal injury and death in Canada : a complete digest service derived from reported and unreported cases / 1. – Toronto : Carswell, 1980.
looseleaf.
Spine title: Damages for personal injury and death.
ISBN 0459316206

—Personal Injury / Vancouver : Continuing Legal Education Society of British Columbia, 1988.
115p.
ISBN 0865049904 Hbk £70.00

—Personal Injury : A Medico-Legal Guide to the Spine and Limbs / Aurora : Canada Law Book Co, 1986.
350p. – (Text Books-Civil).
This text is written specifically for lawyers and explains the medical aspects of a wide range of personal injuries in lay terms. Throughout, the text focuses on the functional and economic impact of particular injuries and considers the long-term life style effects of various disabilities.

—Personal injury damages in Canada / by Kenneth D. Cooper- Stephenson and Iwan B. Saunders. – Toronto : Carswell, 1981.
lii,762p; 26cm.
Includes index.
ISBN 0459333305

—Personal Injury Practice / Vancouver : Continuing Legal Education Society of British Columbia, 1986.
260p.
ISBN 0865042799 Hbk £65.00

—Supreme Court of Canada handbook on assessment of damages in personal injury cases / by W.H.R. Charles. – Ontario : Carswell Co., 1982.
129p.
'Reprint of an article in Volume 18 Part 1 of Canadian cases on the law of torts'.
ISBN 0459346709

PERSONAL INJURIES - CANADA - ALBERTA

—Personal Injury Damage Assessments in Alberta, 1 Vol. / Butterworths.

—Personal Injury Damage Assessments in Alberta / Toronto : Butterworths.

—Personal injury damage assessments in Alberta / 1 vol. – Scarborough, Ontario : Butterworths (Canada).
Catalogue of Alberta judicial awards in motor vehicle accident cases since 1969 arranged under 14 categories of injury. Group one relates to the damage assessment arising in death, group two to cases of gravest injury and subsequent groups are classified by specific part of the body or other specific nature of the injuries.

PERSONAL INJURIES - CANADA - BRITISH COLUMBIA

—Personal Injury Damage Assessments in British Columbia, 2 Vols. / Butterworths.

—Personal Injury Damage Assessments in British Columbia, 2 vols / Toronto : Butterworths.

—Personal injury damage assessments in British Columbia / 2 vols. – Scarborough, Ontario : Butterworths (Canada).
Catalogue of British Columbia judicial awards in motor vehicle accident cases since 1969 arranged under 15 categories of injury. Group one relates to the damage assessment arising in death, group two to cases of gravest injury and subsequent groups are classified by specific part of the body or other specific nature of the injuries.

PERSONAL INJURIES - CANADA - MANITOBA

—Report on periodic payment of damages for personal injury and death / Manitoba Law Reform Commission. – Winnipeg : The Commission, 1987.
iv,128p. – (Report).
Includes bibliographical references.
ISBN 0771108346

PERSONAL INJURIES - ENGLAND

—Civil justice review / Lord Chancellors Department. – London : The Department, 1986.
50p.

—Comments on consultation paper on personal injuries litigation : civil justice review / JUSTICE. – London : JUSTICE, 1986.
9p.

—Compensation and support for illness and injury / Donald Harris ... et al. – Oxford : Clarendon, 1984.
xix,412p; 22cm. – (Oxford socio-legal studies).
Includes bibliographies and index.
ISBN 0198275080 Hbk £20.00
ISBN 0198275137 Pbk £9.50

—Damages for personal injuries and death / John Munkman. – 7th ed. – London : Butterworths, 1985.
xxxiii,250p; 23cm.
Previous ed: 1980. Includes index.
ISBN 0406311137 £18.50

—Disability and compensation claims / Philip Noble, Bart Hellyer, Elizabeth Fanshawe. – London : Sweet & Maxwell, 1986.
68p; 22cm.
ISBN 042136890X Pbk £6.50

—Expert evidence in actions for personal injuries / Supreme Court Rule Committee. – London : Supreme Court Rule Committee, 1987.
4,1 leaves.

—Limitation periods in personal injury claims / by Stephen Todd. – London : Sweet & Maxwell, 1982.
xxii,131p; 23cm.
Includes index.
ISBN 0421285907 £13.00

—Lord Chancellor's review of civil justice in England and Wales : personal injury litigation : a consumer response / National Consumer Council. – London : National Consumer Council, 1986.
38p.
At head to t.p.: Personal injury litigation.

—Richards Butler on latent damage / by Robert Merkin. – London : Lloyd's of London Press, 1987.
192p; 22cm.
ISBN 1850441286 £30.00 (Aug.)

—Special damages for disability 1988 / by Philip Noble, Elizabeth Fanshawe, Bart Hellyer. – 2nd ed. – London : Sweet & Maxwell, 1988.
x,85p; 22cm.
Catalogues the expenses which a plaintiff in a personal injuries action can claim as part of his award. Each of the expenses, such as accommodation requirements and the cost of future care, are described in the context of the four disabilities of spinal injury, partial and total loss of sight, loss of a limb, and head injury. Each item is given an up-to-date value.
ISBN 0421393807 Pbk £7.50

PERSONAL INJURIES - GREAT BRITAIN

—Assessment of Damages for Personal Injury and Death / 2nd ed. – London : Butterworths, 1983.
ISBN 0409491322 Hbk £48.00

—Compensation and Support For Illness and Injury / Maclean. – Oxford : Oxford University Press, 1984.
ISBN 0198275080 Hbk £20.00
ISBN 0198275137 Pbk £9.50

—Damages for Personal Injuries and Death / 7th ed. – London : Butterworths, 1985.
ISBN 0406311137 Hbk £24.00

—Damages for Personal Injury and Death / 2nd ed. – London : Oyez Longman, 1983.
ISBN 0851207308 Hbk £11.50

—Damages For Personal Injury and Death / 3rd ed. – London : Longman Professional, 1986.
ISBN 0851211178 Pbk £18.95

—Key to Personal Injury Practice and Compensation / Margaret R. de Haas. – London : Oyez Longman, 1981.
ISBN 0851206158 Hbk £3.75

—Key to Personal Injury Practice and Compensation / De Haas. – London : Longman Professional, 1981.
ISBN 0851206158 Pbk £8.95

—Medical research : civil liability and compensation for personal injury : a discussion paper / chairman: David Evered. – London : Ciba Foundation, 1980.
16p.

—Meeting Legal Needs : An Evaluation of a Scheme for Personal Injury Victims / Oxford : Social Science Research Council, 1982.

—Negligence and Damages for Personal Injuries : Some Recent Developments / Belfast : Queen's University of Belfast, 1981.
34p.

—Personal Injury File / London : Butterworths.

—Personal injury litigation / 5th ed. – London : Longman Professional, 1986.
ISBN 0851212034 Pbk £26.00

—Personal Injury Litigation / 3rd ed. – London : Oyez Longman, 1980.
– (Oyez Longman Practitioner Ser.).
ISBN 0851205232 Hbk

—Personal Injury Litigation : Practice and Precedents / Margaret De Haas. – London : Butterworths, 1985.
This work for personal injury practitioners in the United Kingdom covers a wide range of procedural and practical points. The book includes chapters on deduction of collateral benefits, the Motor Insurers' Bureau, medical examination of plaintiffs, and limitation of damages.
ISBN 0406016607 Hbk

PERSONAL INJURIES - HONG KONG

—Damages for personal injuries and fatal accidents in Hong Kong : a review of the law and a digest of the cases / Robyn Martin, Peter Rhodes. – London : Butterworths, 1982.
xxv,563p; 23cm.
Gives general principles of the assessment of damages in personal injuries, and in fatal accident cases, and how these have been applied in Hong Kong. Included in the appendices are multiplier tables, actuarial tables, a glossary of medical terms, and illustrations.
ISBN 0406357102 £45.00

—Damages for Personal Injury and Fatal Accidents in Hong Kong / Rhodes. – London : Butterworths, 1982.
ISBN 0406357102 Hbk £45.00

PERSONAL INJURIES - INDIA
—Socio-Economic Re-evaluation of the Torts Law of Liability for Personal Injuries / Lucknow : Eastern Book Company, 1962.
115p.

PERSONAL INJURIES - IRELAND
—Judge or Jury? : the Jury Trial for Personal Injury Cases in Ireland / Cork : Cork University Press, 1985.
35p.
ISBN 0902561383 Pbk £1.50

—Report on the statute of limitations : claims in respect of latent personal injuries / c the Law Reform Commission. - Dublin : The Commission, 1987.
65p. - (LRC).
Cover title: Personal injuries.

PERSONAL INJURIES - JAMAICA
—Recent personal injury awards made in the Supreme Court of Judicature of Jamaica / compiled by Ursula Khan. - s.l. : s.n., 1981.
xxvii,200p.

PERSONAL INJURIES - MALAYSIA
—Damages for Personal Injuries and Death in Singapore and Malaysia / Singapore : Malayan Law Journal, 1988.
ca 1,000p.
Presents the main principles governing the assessment of damages for personal injury and death in Singapore and Malaysia, with reference to pertinent cases and statutory provisions.
ISBN 9971700603 Hbk £265.00

—Damages for Personal Injuries and Death in Singapore and Malaysia / Singapore : Butterworths, 1988.
1000p.

PERSONAL INJURIES - NEW ZEALAND
—Accident compensation : a commentary on the New Zealand scheme / Terence G. Ison. - London : Croom Helm, 1980.
201p; 23cm.
Includes index.
ISBN 0709902492 £14.95

PERSONAL INJURIES - SCOTLAND
—Casebook on damages in Scotland / by Robin Gilmour McEwan and Ann Paton. - Edinburgh : Green, 1983.
xxiii,272p; 22cm.
Includes index.
ISBN 0414006984 Pbk Unpriced

—Prescription and the limitation of actions : report on personal injuries actions and private international law questions / Scottish Law Commission. - Edinburgh : H.M.S.O., 1983.
v,61p.
ISBN 0102153833

PERSONAL INJURIES - SINGAPORE
—Damages for Personal Injuries and Death in Singapore and Malaysia / Singapore : Malayan Law Journal, 1988.
ca 1,000p.
Presents the main principles governing the assessment of damages for personal injury and death in Singapore and Malaysia, with reference to pertinent cases and statutory provisions.
ISBN 9971700603 Hbk £265.00

—Damages for Personal Injuries and Death in Singapore and Malaysia / Singapore : Butterworths, 1988.
1000p.

PERSONAL PROPERTY - AUSTRALIA
—Helmore's personal property and mercantile law in New South Wales / by W. J. Chappenden and J. W. Carter. - 9th ed. - Sydney : Law Book Company, 1985.
xlvi,485p.
ISBN 045520294X

—Law of securities : an account of the law pertaining to securities over real and personal property under the laws of the Australian States / Edward I.Sykes. - 4th edition. - Sydney : Law Book Company, 1986.
xcv,1043p.
ISBN 0455206287

PERSONAL PROPERTY - CANADA
—Handbook on the Saskatchewan Personal Property Security Act / by Ronald C.C. Cuming and Roderick J. Wood. - Saskatoon? : Law Reform Commission of Saskatchewan, 1987.
xxx,386p.
'Funded by the Law Foundation of Saskatchewan.' - T.p..
ISBN 0921923007

—Personal Property Security Act Cases, Vol. 4 : Supplement to Secured Transactions in Personal Property in Canada / Agincourt : Carswell.

—Personal Property Security : An Introductory Analysis / DeJong. - 4th ed. - Agincourt : Carswell, 1987.
454p.

PERSONAL PROPERTY - CANADA - ONTARIO
—Report on the Minister's Advisory Committee on the Personal Property Security Act / Toronto : Ministry of Consumer and Commercial Relations, 1984.
iii,106p.

PERSONAL PROPERTY - ENGLAND
—Co-ownership / M.P. Thompson. - London : Sweet & Maxwell, 1988.
xxv,151p.
Analyses forms of co-ownership of freehold and leasehold interests in real property, and such items of personal property as joint bank accounts. Explores the legal principles involved, and applies them to practical problems. Co-habitation, financial contribution, marriage, divorce, death and insolvency are also discussed.
ISBN 0421375000 £19.50

PERSONAL PROPERTY - GREAT BRITAIN
—Individual Property Rights and Conceptions of Privacy in the Family / Emmanuel Lazega. - Oxford : Social Science Research Council, 1988.
ISBN 094877410X Pbk £2.50

—Retention of title on the sale of goods / John Parris. - London : Granada, 1982.
186p; 24cm.
Includes index.
ISBN 0246116129 Unpriced

PERSONALITY (LAW) - AUSTRALIA
—Commercial exploitation of personality / by Samuel K. Murumba. - North Ryde : Law Book Co, 1986.
xvii,184p.
Bibliography and index. Includes the text of a Draft Commonwealth Bill for an Unfair Publication Act.
ISBN 0455206929

PERSONS - AUSTRALIA - NEW SOUTH WALES
—Protected Persons and Their Property in N.S.W. / Mark Robinson. - North Ryde : Law Book Co, 1987.
xiv, 176p.
ISBN 0455207194 Pbk £27.50

PERSONS - SOUTH AFRICA
—Application of customary law in southern Africa : the conflict of personal laws / T.W. Bennett. - Cape Town : Juta, 1985.
xxxvii,250p.
Bibliography: p.xv-xxi. - Includes index.
ISBN 0702116017

PERSONS (INTERNATIONAL LAW)
—Conceptual thinking about the individual in international law / Rosalyn Higgins. - S.l. : s.n., 1981.
19p; 25cm.
Photocopy from: British Journal of International Studies 4 (1978).

—Corporations in and under international law / by Ignaz Seidl-Hohenveldern. - Cambridge : Grotius, 1987.
xviii,138p.
Covers the nationality of corporations and the effect upon them of nationalisation measures, as well as the special responsibilities of state-owned corporations. The second part of the book examines problems connected with the legal personality of international organizations.
ISBN 0949009091

PERSONS (ISLAMIC LAW)
—Islamic law of personal status / Jamal J. Nasir. - London : Graham & Trotman, 1986.
xiv,328p; 25cm.
Bibliography: p314-319. - Includes index.
ISBN 0860108252 deluxe £45.00
ISBN 0860108260 £75.00

—Reform of Muslim Personal Law / New Delhi : Deep and Deep Publications, 1988.
172p.

—Textbook on Muslim personal law / David Pearl. - 2nd ed. - London : Croom Helm, 1987.
284p; 23cm.
ISBN 0709940890 Pbk £14.95

PERSONS (LAW) - ENGLAND
—Stephen's commentaries on the laws of England / L. Crispin Warmington. - 21st ed. - London : Butterworths, 1950.
xiv,604p.
Index included in Vol. 4. .

PERSONS (LAW) - SOUTH AFRICA
—South African law of persons and family law / by P.J.J. Olivier. - 2nd ed. - Durban : Butterworths, 1980.
xxvi,356p; 22cm.
Includes index.
ISBN 0409046167 Pbk
ISBN 0409046175

PESTICIDES
—Pesticide Labelling Legislation / Rome : FAO, Food and Agricultural Organization of the United Nations, 1988.
159p.
ISBN 925102619X Hbk £10.50

—Pesticides : Recommendations on the Safe Use of Pesticides in Ships / International Maritime Organization. - Rev. ed. - London : International Maritime Organization, 1981.
French Edition

PESTICIDES - CANADA
—Pesticides in Canada : an examination of federal law and policy / a study paper prepared for the Law Reform Commission of Canada by J.F. Castrilli, Toby Vigod. - Ottawa : The Commission, 1987.
131p. - (Study paper).
Added t.p. in French: Les pesticides au Canada. Pages numbered in opposite directions. Text in English and French.
ISBN 0662554132

PETROLEUM REVENUE TAXATION - CANADA
—Taxation of Canadian Oil and Gas Income / R. H. Bowhay. - Toronto : DeBoo, 1986.
This text discusses non-deductibility of payments to the Crown, investment tax credits, successor corporation rules, joint exploration corporations, and the National Energy Program. Annual consolidated supplements are planned.
ISBN 0888202474 Hbk £135.00

PETROLEUM REVENUE TAXATION - GREAT BRITAIN
—Consultation on valuation and pricing proposals / Inland Revenue. - London : Inland Revenue Press Office, 1987.
3,8p. - (Press release).

—North sea oil taxation : the development of the North Sea tax system / M. P. Devereux and C. N. Morris. - London : Institute for Fiscal Studies, 1983.
93p.
Bibliography: p90-91.

—Oil Taxation Acts 1975-1983 / London : HMSO, 1984.
- (Taxes Act Ser.).
ISBN 0116413506 Pbk £11.95

—The Oil Taxation Acts / London : HMSO, 1985.
ISBN 0116413514 Pbk £12.50

—Petroleum revenue tax : valuation and pricing / Inland Revenue. - London : Inland Revenue Press Office, 1986.
3p. - (Press release).

—Petroleum Tax Analysis : North Sea : A Comparative Study of the Oil Exploitation Taxation System of the United Kingdom, Norway, Denmark and the Netherlands / David Rose. - London : Financial Times Ltd, 1983.

—Taxation of North Sea Oil / London : Institute for Fiscal Studies, 1981.
24p.

—Taxes Acts : the oil taxation enactments in force from 8 May up to and including the Finance (No. 2) Act 1987 : with other legislation and statutory regulations affecting the application of the tax and an index / London : HMSO, 1988.
iv,436p.
On cover: 1987 ed.. At head of title: Inland Revenue. Spine title: The Oil Taxation Acts.
ISBN 0116413751

PETROLEUM REVENUE TAXATION - MALAYSIA
—Petroleum income tax in Malaysia / by Arjunan Subramaniam. - Kuala Lumpur : Malayan Law Jounal, 1982.
xv,240p.
Bibliography: p.xiv-xv. - Includes index.

—Petroleum income tax in Malaysia / Singapore : Malayan Law Journal, 1982.
xv,240.
Covers oil exploration and PETRONAS, taxation of petroleum companies, and administration and appeals. Appendices reproduce the Petroleum (Income Tax) Act 1967 and all subsequent Amendments up to 1977, the Petroleum Mining Act 1966, and a map showing the location of oil and gas fields in Malaysia.

PETROLEUM REVENUE TAXATION - NIGERIA
—Nigerian petroleum law and practice / Martin M. Olisa. - Ibadan, Nigeria : Fountain Books, 1987.
x,261p.
Includes bibliographical references.
ISBN 978233118X

PHILIPPINES
—Civil Code of the Phillippines / National Book Store. - Manila : National Book Store, 1980.
615p.
ISBN 9710816446 Pbk £3.50

—Revised Penal Code / Quezon City, 1983.
366p.

PHILOSOPHERS

—Correspondence of Jeremy Bentham / J. R. Dinwiddy. – Oxford : Clarendon Press, 1988.
500p; 24cm.
Includes index.
ISBN 0198226144 £45.00

Vol. 8 : January 1809 to December 1816 : edited by Stephen Conway 1988.
480p; 24cm.
Includes index.
ISBN 0198226152 No price

PHILOSOPHY

—After legal instrumentalism? : strategic models of post- regulatory law / by Gunther Teubner. – Florence : European University Institute, 1984.
58p.
Bibliography: p.52-58. At head of title: European University Institute, Florence, Law Department.

—Autopoietic law : a new approach to law and society / edited by Gunther Teubner. – Berlin : W. de Gruyter, 1987.
Includes index and bibliography.

—Conditions of validity and cognition in modern legal thought / edited by Neil MacCormick, Stavros Panou, Luigi Lombardi Vallauri : preface by Ralf Dreier Geltungs- und Erkenntnisbedingungen im modernen Rechtsdenken / herausgegeben von Neil MacCormick, Stavros Panou, Luigi Lombardi Vallauri ; vorwort von Ralf Dreier. – Stuttgart : F. Steiner Verlag Wiesbaden, 1985.
214 p.; 24 cm. – (Archives for philosophy of law and social philosophy).
Papers presented at the IVR 11th World Congress, Helsinki, 1983. English, French, and German. Includes bibliographical references and index.
ISBN 3515044604 pbk. DM35.00

—Critical legal studies / edited by Peter Fitzpatrick and Alan Hunt. – Oxford : Basil Blackwell, 1987.
197p.
Originally issued as Journal of Law a philosophy, v.14,no.1.
ISBN 0631157182

—Decline of juridical reason : doctrine and theory in the legal order / N.E. Simmonds. – Manchester : Manchester University Press, 1984.
137p; 23cm.
Includes index.
ISBN 0719010896 £19.50

—Dialectic of nihilism : post-structuralism and law / Gillian Rose. – Oxford : Blackwell, 1984.
232p; 24cm.
Critique of post-structuralist theory related to law.
ISBN 0631131914 Hbk £22.00
ISBN 0631137084 Pbk No price

—End of law? / Timothy O'Hagan. – Oxford : Blackwell, 1984.
vii,183p; 23cm.
ISBN 0855205962

—Essays in jurisprudence and philosophy / by H.L.A. Hart. – Oxford : Clarendon, 1983.
viii,396p; 23cm.
Collection of essays first published between 1953 and 1981. Includes index.
ISBN 0198253877 Pbk Unpriced
ISBN 0198253885 £7.50

—Essays in Jurisprudence and Philosophy / Oxford : Oxford University Press, 1983.
ISBN 0198253877 Hbk £19.50
ISBN 0198253885 Pbk £8.95

—Ethics of legal coercion / John D. Hodson. – Dordrecht, Holland : D. Reidel Pub. Co., 1983.
xiv, 174 p.; 22 cm.
Includes indexes. Bibliography: p. 163-168.
ISBN 9027714940 Hbk

—Giving desert its due : social justice and legal theory / Wojciech Sadurski. – Dordrecht : D. Reidel, 1985.
xii, 329p.
Includes index. Bibliography: p 309-318.
ISBN 9027719411 Hbk £47.00

—Idea of law / Dennis Lloyd. – Repr. with revisions. – Harmondsworth : Penguin, 1981.
365p; 20cm. – (Pelican books).
Originally published: 1964. Bibliography: p360. - Includes index.
ISBN 0140206884 Pbk £2.95

—Institutional theory of law : new approaches to legal positivism / Neil MacCormick and Ota Weinberger. – DordrechtHolland : Reidel, 1986.
xiv, 229p. – (Law and philosophy library).
ISBN 9027720797

—Invitation to law / by A.W.B. Simpson. – Oxford : Blackwell, 1988.
227p.
Includes index.
ISBN 0631145389 pbk.

—Issues in contemporary legal philosophy : the influence of H.L.A. Hart / edited by Ruth Gavison. – Oxford : Clarendon, 1988.
368p; 22cm.
Includes bibliography and index. A collection of essays on legal philosophy themes, influenced by the work of H L A Hart. Pays tribute to Hart as a teacher, rather than being an introduction to his work.
ISBN 0198255179 Hbk £35.00
ISBN 0198256566 Pbk £12.95

—Journal of applied philosophy : journal of the Society for Applied Philosophy / Abingdon : Carfax, 1984.

—Juridical law and physical law : towards a realist foundation for human law / by Thomas F. Torrance. – Edinburgh : Scottish Academic Press, 1982.
xii,70p.
ISBN 0707303141

—Jurisprudence : a descriptive and normative analysis of law / Anthony D'Amato. – Dordrecht, The Netherlands : Nijhoff, 1984.
xiv, 334 p.; 25 cm.
Includes bibliographical references and index.
ISBN 902472919X Hbk £140.00

—Justice, law, and argument : essays on moral and legal reasoning / Ch. Perelman : with an intod. by Harold J. Berman. – Dordrecht, Holland : D. Reidel Pub. Co., 1980.
xiii,181p.
Includes bibliographical references and index.
ISBN 9027710902 pbk.

—Justice, law, and culture / James K. Feibleman. – Dordrecht : Nijhoff, 1985.
xiii, 208p.
ISBN 9024731054

—Law and its presuppositions : actions, agents and rules / S.C. Coval and J.C. Smith. – London : Routledge & Kegan Paul, 1986.
viii, 141p. – (International library of philosophy).
ISBN 0710204469

—Law and philosophy : an international journal for jurisprudence and legal philosophy / Dordrecht : D. Reidel, 1982-.

—Law and society east and west / dharma, li and nomos : by Reinhard May. – Wiesbaden : Franz Steiner, 1985.
251p,9p.
Revised version of the London Doctoral Theses 'An enquiry in comparative jurisprudene. Similarity and disparity between dharma, li, and nomos.'. Bibliography p.227-250. - Includes index.
ISBN 3515045376

—Law as a moral judgment / Deryck Beyleveld, Roger Brownsword. – London : Sweet & Maxwell, 1986.
xxix,483p; 24cm.
Bibliography: p457-462. - Includes index.
ISBN 0421329203 £30.00

—Law from anarchy to Utopia : an exposition of the logical, epistemological and ontological foundations of the idea of law, by an inquiry into the nature of legal propositions and the basis of legal authority / Chhatrapati Singh. – Delhi : Oxford University Press, 1986.
xxi,299p; 22cm.
Bibliography: p278-292. - Includes index.
ISBN 0195617045 £30.00

—Law, morality, and rights / edited by M.A. Stewart. – Dordrecht, Holland : Reidel, 1983.
xii,452p. – (Synthese library).
Includes index.
ISBN 902771519X

—Legal philosophies / by J.W. Harris. – London : Butterworths, 1980.
x,282.
Bibliographies.
ISBN 0406859361

—Legal Philosophy : Western, Eastern and Filipino / Tacloban City : Divine Word University of Tacloban, 1984.
208p.
ISBN 9711060213 Hbk £7.00

—Legal right and social democracy : essays in legal and political philosophy / Neil MacCormick. – Oxford : Clarendon, 1982.
viii,272p; 23cm.
Includes index.
ISBN 0198253850 £17.50

—Limits of law / by Antony Allott. – London : Butterworth, 1980.
xxii,322p; 22cm.
This work presents a critical analysis of the 'effectiveness of law'. The book demonstrates how law functions in coordination with other forces in society, such as morality, religion, custom, and economics.
ISBN 0406552428 £11.50
ISBN 0406552436

—Making law bind : essays legal and philosophical / Tony Honore. – Oxford : Clarendon, 1987.
288p; 22cm.
Includes index.
ISBN 0198254679 £25.00

—Man, law, and modern forms of life / edited by Eugenic Bulygin, Jean-Louis Gardies, and Ilkka Niiniluoto : introduction by Michael D. Bayles. – Dordrecht Netherlands : D. Reidel, 1985.
'Proceedings of the 11th IVR World Congress on Philosophy of Law and Social Philosophy ... held on August 14-20, 1983 in Helsinki'–Introd. Includes bibliographies and index.
ISBN 9027718695 Hbk £39.50

—Meaning and Truth in Juridical Decision / Tampere : A-Tiete Oy.
ISBN 9419464271 Pbk £130.00

—Nature of law / by Thomas Glyn Watkin. – Amsterdam : North-Holland Pub. Co., 1980.
xiv, 246 p; 23 cm. – (European studies in law).
Includes index. Bibliography: p. 237-239.

—Philosophy of law / by Z. O. Aje. – s.l. : s.n., 1986.
ix,160p.
Includes bibliographical references.

—Philosophy of law : an introduction / Thomas Morawetz. – New York : Macmillan, 1980.
x,238p; 21cm.
Includes index.
ISBN 0023833408 Pbk £5.95

—Political justice : outline of a philosophical theory / by Otfried Hoffe. – Florence : European University Institute, 1985.
20p.

—Principles of law : a normative analysis / Michael D. Bayles. – Dordrecht : D. Reidel, 1987.
xxi, 398p.
Includes index. Bibliography: p.372-380.
ISBN 902772413X pbk.

—Private justice / Stuart Henry. – London : Routledge & Kegan Paul, 1983.
ix,245p.
Includes index. Bibliography: p229-235.
ISBN 0710097034 pbk.

—Role of law in society : East and West, national and international / by Bin Cheng. – S.l. : s.n., 1981.
p.15-18.
Reprinted from: Chinese University bulletin, Winter 1978. Cover title with subtitle: 'Address on behalf of the honorary graduates at the twentieth Congregation of the Chinese University of Hong Kong on Thursday, 30th November 1978'.

—Security and society : reflections on law, order and politics / R.N. Berki. – London : Dent, 1986.
256p.
Includes bibliography and index.
ISBN 0460046551 Hbk £15.00
ISBN 0460024698 Pbk £6.95

—Selection from the Proceedings of the Royal Institute of Philosophy Conference on the Philosophy of Law (September 1979) / Dordrecht : Kluwer, 1982.
184p.

—Semiotics and legal theory / Bernard S. Jackson. – London : Routledge and Kegan Paul, 1985.
xii,373p; 22cm.
Bibliography: p.349-373.
ISBN 0710097190

—Semiotics, law and social science / edited by Domenico Carzo and Bernard S. Jackson. – Roma : Gangemi, 1985.
227p.
'Based largely upon papers prepared for a colloquium on legal semiotics organised by Professor Roque Carrion-Wam in March 1985'. Includes bibliographies. At head of title: Congress volume for Aix Colloquium.

—Short history of legal thinking in the West / Stig Stromholm. – Stockholm, Sweden : Norstedts, 1985.
317 p.; 23 cm.
Includes index.
ISBN 9118571425

—Structure and Process of International Law : Essays in Legal Philosophy, Doctrine and Theory / Douglas M. Johnston. – Dordrecht : Kluwer, 1986.
1,234p.
ISBN 9024732735 Pbk £175.00

—Theory of legal science : proceedings of the Conference on Legal Theory and Philosophy of Science, Lund, Sweden, December 11-14, 1983 / edited by Aleksander Peczenik, Lars Lindahl, and Bert van Roermund. – Dordrecht : Reidel, 1984.
xv, 666 p.; 23 cm.
Includes bibliographies and index.
ISBN 9027718342

—Tradition and progress in modern legal cultures / edited by Stig Jrgensen, Juha Poyhonen, Csaba Varga : preface by Jose Llompart Tradition und Fortschritt in den modernen Rechtskulturen / herausgegeben von Stig Jrgensen, Juha Poyhonen, Csaba Varga ; vorwort von Jose Llompart. – Stuttgart : F. Steiner Verlag Wiesbaden, 1985.
263 p.; 24 cm. – (Archives for philosophy of law and social philosophy).
English, French, and German. Includes bibliographies and index. .
ISBN 3515044582 pbk. DM35.00

—Western idea of law / by J. C. Smith and David N. Weisstub. – London : Butterworths, 1983.
xxii,685p.
Highlights the unique aspects of Western law by comparing it to other legal traditions, past and present. More than 170 great thinkers are excerpted, and a feminist perspective is incorporated, raising questions about women and power. Covers issues such as state sovereignty egalitarianism, and constitutional guarantees of human rights.
ISBN 0409868191

PHILOSOPHY – GREAT BRITAIN

—Philosophy and Law / Oxford : Blackwell, 1987.
ISBN 0631125271 Pbk £8.50

—Philosophy of Law / Paul. – Oxford : Blackwell Scientific, 1987.
ISBN 0631152571 Pbk £8.95

PHYSICIAN–PATIENT RELATIONS

—Responsibility in health care / edited by George J. Agich. – Dordrecht, Holland : D. Reidel, 1982.
xxiii, 285p.
Outgrowth of the Eleventh Trans-disciplinary Symposium on Philosophy and Medicine held in Springfield, Ill., on March 16-18, 1981. Includes bibliographies and index.
ISBN 9027714177

PICKETING – GREAT BRITAIN

—Give the picketing code the sanction of law : submission by the Trade Union Reform Committee of the Centre for Policy Studies to the Rt Hon. James Prior MP, Secretary of State for Employment in response to his request for the pulic's views as part of a process of consultation / James Prior. – London : The Centre, 1980.
18,6p; 32cm.
ISBN 0905880315 spiral Unpriced

—Legal immunities of trade unions and other related matters : draft codes of practice on picketing and the closed shop : record report from the Employment Committee, Session 1979-80 / London : H.M.S.O., 1980.
viiip; 25cm.
ISBN 0100282296 unbound £1.10

—Picketing : industrial disputes, tactics and the law / by Peggy Kahn...et al. – London : Routledge & Kegan Paul, 1983.
xv,223p.
Bibliography: p219-220.
ISBN 0710095341

PIPELINES – GREAT BRITAIN

—Pipes, mains, cables and sewers / 5th. – London : Longman Professional (UK), 1989.
– (Practitioner series).
Guide to the basic principles of the law governing the laying of conduits by private agreement and statutory authority for electricity, telecommunicatins, water, gas, oil and effluent. Takes account of the privatisation of British Telecom, British Gas and British Petroleum, the building of the Channel Tunnel, and the abolition of the Metropolitan Councils. Includes about 60 new cases.

PIRACY

—Law of international sea piracy / Barry Hart Dubner. – The Hague : M. Nijhoff, 1980.
xiii,176p.
Bibliography - p167-173.

—WIPO Worldwide Forum on the Piracy of Broadcasts and of the Printed Word / Geneva : World Intellectual Property Organization, 1983.
ca 240p.

—WIPO Worldwide Forum on the Piracy of Sound and Audiovisual Recordings, Geneva (1981) / Geneva : World Intellectual Property Organization.
240p.

PLANNING

—Cities in the developing world : policies for their equitable and efficient growth / Johannes F. Linn. – Oxford : Published for the World Bank by Oxford University Press, 1983.
xxi,230p; 24cm.
Bibliography: p213-223. - Includes index.
ISBN 0195203828 Hbk Unpriced
ISBN 0195203836 Pbk Unpriced

—Encyclopaedia Of Planning Law and Practice / Sweet & Maxwell, 1988.
ISBN 0421007400 Hbk £265.00

—Inside Third World cities / Stella Lowder. – London : Routledge, 1988.
xii,292p.
Originally published: London : Croom Helm, 1986. Bibliography: pp.270-286. - Includes index.
ISBN 0415027756 No price (Aug.)

—Journal of Planning and Environment Law / London : Sweet & Maxwell.

Single copies

Back Vols.

—Land for housing the poor / edited by Shlomo Angel ... et al. – Singapore : Select Books, 1983.
ix,556p; 22cm.
Papers from a seminar, 'Land for Housing the Poor: Towards Positive Action in Asian Cities' held in Bangkok, 18th and 31st Jan. 1982.
ISBN 9971835517

—Land, the central human settlement issue / H. Peter Oberlander. – Vancouver : University of British Columbia Press, 1985.
x, 103 p., 4 p. of plates; 24 cm.
Bibliography: p. 93-101.
ISBN 0774802359

—Outline of planning law / 9th. – London : Sweet & Maxwell, 1987.
Examines the Acts and statutory instruments regulating planning law, including the nine new acts introduced since the 1982 edition. Contains discussion of the impact of the abolition of the Metropolitan County Councils, and planning gain, use and misuse of planning conditions, conservation areas, and National Parks.
ISBN 042125459X Pbk £22.50

—Planning and the environment in the modern world / Gordon E. Cherry. – London : Mansell Publishing, 1980.
xii,259p; 24cm.
In 3 vols. Includes index.
ISBN 0720109035 £14.75

—Planning law in Western Europe / edited by J.F. Garner and N.P. Gravells. – 2nd. rev. ed. – Amsterdam : North-Holland, 1986.
Bibliography.
ISBN 044487996X

—Problems and planning in Third World cities / edited by Michael Pacione. – London : Croom Helm, 1981.
290p; 23cm.
Includes bibliographies and index.
ISBN 0709901925 £12.95

—Problems of regional and local authorities involved in planning policies : report / prepared under the guidance of the Committee of Experts on Social and Economic Activities of the Steering Committee for Regional and Municipal Matters by Jacques Robert. – Strasbourg : Council of Europe, 1985.
36p.

—Proceedings of the seminar on planning law for industry : March 29th-April 2nd 1981, Churchill College, Cambridge, England / organised by the Committee on Environmental Law (Committee F), Section on Business Law, International Bar Association : edited with discussion summaries by John Salter and Patricia Thomas. – 2. – London : International Bar Association in cooperation with Sweet and Maxwell, 1981.
21cm.
ISBN 0950587621 Pbk Unpriced

—Rating and income tax / 53 v. – London : Solicitors' Law Stationery Society, 1924.
Continued by: Rating and valuation reporter.

—Rating and valuation reporter / v. – London : Solicitor's Law Stationery Department, 1961-.
Continues: Rating and income tax reporter. Published: London: Rating Publishers, 1965-.
ISBN 00486817

—Scottish planning law and procedure / by Eric Young and Jeremy Rowan-Robinson : with a contribution by C.M.G. Himsworth. – Glasgow : William Hodge, 1985.
xliv,564p.
Supersedes Eric Youngs The law of planning in Scotland. Includes index. Provides a guide through the legislative and regulatory system of Scottish planning law and procedure and sets the subject matter in the context of administrative law. Considerable attention is given to control of development.
ISBN 0852791224

—Urban land policy : issues and opportunities / Harold B. Dunkerley, cordinating editor : with the assistance of Christine M.E. Whitehead. – New York : Oxford University Press for the World Bank, 1983.
viii,214p; 25cm.
Bibliography: p199-206. - Includes index.
ISBN 0195204034 £15.00

PLANNING – ASIA

—Urban planning practice in developing countries / editors, John L. Taylor and David G. Williams. – Oxford : Pergamon, 1982.
x,357p; 24cm. – (Pergamon international library).
Includes bibliographies.
ISBN 0080222250 £19.50

PLANNING – AUSTRALIA – NEW SOUTH WALES

—Environmental planning and development law (NSW) / by A.J. Nott. – Sydney : Penman, 1982.
xlix,417p.
Includes index.
ISBN 0959431608

—Local Government Planning and Environment Service, New South Wales / Butterworths.

PLANNING – BRAZIL

—Greater Carajas Program : legislation and norms / Presidency of the Republic of Brazil, Secretariat of Planning. – Brailia : The Secretariat, 1984.
55p. – (Publications no 5/84).

PLANNING – CANADA

—Canadian Municipal and Planning Law / Agincourt : Carswell, 1983.
ISBN 045935700 Hbk £23.00

—Canadian Municipal and Planning Law / Agincourt : Carswell, 1983.
358p.
This work examines the structure, organization, and authority of local government in Canada. Municipal finance, zoning, land use control and development control, municipal planning process, and other related issues are discussed in the book.

—Municipal and planning law reports / Toronto : Carswell, 1976-.
24cm.

—Municipal and Planning Law Text / Agincourt : Carswell, 1983.
500p.

PLANNING – CANADA – ONTARIO

—Land use planning / Robert Macaulay. – Scarborough, Ontario : Butterworths (Canada).
Survey of Ontario Municipal Board cases, precedents, pointers on the impact of the Charter of Rights, and relevant legislation, regulations, guidelines and interpretation bulletins. Covers planning authorities, provincial planning, official plans, zoning and development control, development levies and municipal finance, and the conduct of a planning application.

—Law of Subdivision Control in Ontario : a Practical Guide to Section 49 of the Planning Act / Agincourt : Carswell, 1988.
350p.

PLANNING – ENGLAND

—Blundell and Dobry's planning appeals and inquiries / George Dobry, Robert Carnwath. – 3rd ed. – London : Sweet & Maxwell, 1982.
xxi,146p; 25cm.
Reviews planning inquiry and appeals procedure at all levels. Deals with evidence, enforcement notices, refusals, determination of rights, and presentation of appeals before inspectors and the High Court. Includes referrals to the Secretary of State.
ISBN 0421253509 Pbk £9.75

—Enforcement and stop notices : a practical guide / Felix Bourne. – London : Sweet & Maxwell, 1986.
175p; 24cm.
Contains, in chronological order, the relevant information from a variety of statutes, statutory instruments and circulars. Follows procedure from the preliminary points of consideration to the questions arising on appeal, both from the perspective of the local authority, and that of the private developer.
ISBN 0421364106 Pbk £15.00

—Guide to development and planning / by R.N.D. Hamilton. – 7th ed. – London : Oyez, 1981.
lxiv,510p; 23cm.
Previous ed.: 1975. Includes index.
ISBN 0851205496 Unpriced

—Ideologies of planning law / Patrick McAuslan. – Oxford : Pergamon, 1980.
xiii,282p; 26cm. – (Pergamon international library).
Includes index.
ISBN 0080236960 £17.00
ISBN 0080251986

—Outline of planning law / Sir Desmond Heap. – 9th ed. – London : Sweet & Maxwell, 1987.
350p; 22cm.
Previous ed.: 1982. Includes index.
ISBN 0421354402 Hbk £20.00
ISBN 042135450X Pbk £12.50

—Planning appeal decisions / v. – London : Sweet & Maxwell, 1985-.

—Planning decisions digest / Michael Purdue and Vincent Fraser. – London : Sweet & Maxwell, 1986.
300p; 24cm.
Covers judicial decisions back to 1948, and selected ministerial decisions since 1974. Brief summaries of each decision are included, and referenced. Material is arranged under subject headings following the structure of the Town and Country Planning Act 1971.
ISBN 0421325704 Pbk £19.00

—Planning law and procedure / A.E. Telling. – 6th ed. – London : Butterworths, 1982.
xxix,321p.
Previous ed.: 1977. Includes index.
ISBN 0406665095

—Planning law casebook / London : Laureate-Thomson, 1984.
288p.
ISBN 0907392091 Pbk £17.50

—Planning law for conveyancers / Clive Brand and D.W. Williams. – 3rd ed. – London : Longman Professional (UK), 1989.
– (Longman Practitioner Series).
Gives practical advice on how to solve such problems as planning authorities car parking standards, and conversion of roof space. Contains new chapters on planning policy guidance, housing action trust areas, and minerals policy, and covers the Town and Country Planning Regulations of 1988 and 1989, and the General Development Order 1988.*Conveyancing solicitors and licensed conveyancers, chartered surveyors, local authority planning departments, students*
ISBN 0851216226 PBK £22.50

PLANNING - EUROPE

—Planning and Politics in Western Europe / London : Macmillan, 1982.
Illus.
ISBN 0333300815 Hbk £20.00

PLANNING - GREAT BRITAIN

—Britain's inner cities / Paul Lawless. – London : Harper and Row, 1981.
224p.
ISBN 0063181843 Hbk £8.95
ISBN 0063181851 Pbk £4.95

—Butterworths planning law handbook / edited by Keith Davies. – London : Butterworths, 1987.
viii, 734, 11p.
ISBN 0406505802

—Challenging decision : papers from a conference held at Oxford, September 1985 / organised by the Bar Council, the Law Society and the Royal Institution of Chartered Surveyors. – London : Sweet & Maxwell, 1986.
vi,101p; 25cm.
Conference paper.
ISBN 0421361301 Pbk £22.00

—Chief Planning Inspector's report to the Secretary of State for the Environment, the Secretary of State for Transport and the Secretary of State for Wales / the Planning Inspectorate. – v. – London : H.M.S.O., 1982.

—Competency of Interdict in the Enforcement of Planning Control / Glasgow : Planning Exchange, 1983.
41p. – (Scottish Planning Law and Practice Ser.).

—Contemporary planning policies : papers from a conference entitled Making the Planning System Work held at Oxford, September 1983 / organised by the Bar Council, the Law Society, and the Royal Institution of Chartered Surveyors. – London : Sweet & Maxwell, 1984.
vi,72p; 25cm.
Conference papers.
ISBN 0421326603 Pbk £18.00

—Countryside Planning in Practice / Stirling University Press, 1988.
ISBN 0948812028 Hbk £22.50

—Development and Planning Law / 2nd ed. – London : Estates Gazette, 1987.
ISBN 0728201135 Pbk £6.00

—Development and planning law / by Barry Denyer-Green. – 2nd ed. – London : Estates Gazette, 1987.
xxxix,337p.
Includes index.
ISBN 0728201135

—Development and planning law / Barry Denyer-Green. – London : Estates Gazette, 1982.
xxxiv,260p.
Includes index.

—Development Control / Nott. – London : Butterworths, 1988.
ISBN 0406502501 Hbk £24.00
ISBN 040650551X Pbk

—Effective Planning Appeals / Oxford : Blackwell Scientific, 1988.
ISBN 0632021241 Hbk

—Enforcement of planning control / London : Longman Professional (UK), 1988.
– (Practitioner series).
Concentrates on the practical procedures and litigation techniques facing those who wish to appeal against enforcement notices including an explanation of the issues of nullity and invalidity.
ISBN 0851214096 Hbk £15.95

—Enforcement of Planning Control / London : Longman Professional, 1988.
ISBN 0851214096 Pbk £14.95

—Environmental planning, 1939-1969 / J. B. Cullingworth. – London : HMSO, 1980.
xv,582p,1p. of plates (folded).

—Fifth report from the Environment Committee, session 1985-86 : planning: appeals, call-in and major public inquiries / Great Britain. – London : H.M.S.O., 1986.
xcvi p. – (H.C. 1985-86).
ISBN 0100110657

Vol. 2 : Minutes of evidence and appendices 1986.
viii,466p. – (H.C. 1985-86).
ISBN 0100110754

—Fighting Planning Appeals / Oxford : Construction Press, 1985.
ISBN 0860957322 Hbk £14.95

—Guide to Development and Planning / 7th ed. – London : Longman Professional, 1981.
ISBN 0851205496 Hbk £37.00

—Guidelines for the administration and use of part II of the Register of Applications for Planning Permission / prepared by a joint working party of the RICS/RTPI/Law Society. – London : Royal Town Planning Institute, 1987.
3p.
Published as part of The Planner, Jan (1987) p. 21-23.

—Howell James' Notes on the Need for Planning Permission / D. W. Williams. – 3rd ed. – London : Oyez Longman, 1984.
ISBN 0851207146 Hbk

—Inner city in context : the final report of the Social Science Research Council Inner Cities Working Party / edited by Peter Hall. – London : Heinemann, 1981.
viii,175p; 23cm.
Bibliography: p154-163. - Includes index.
ISBN 0435357174 Hbk £12.50
ISBN 0435357182 Pbk Unpriced

—Introduction to town and country planning / John Ratcliffe. – 2nd ed. – London : Hutchinson, 1981.
506p; 22cm.
Previous ed.: 1974. Bibliography: p483-487. - Includes index.
ISBN 0091440203 Hbk £15.00
ISBN 0091440211 Pbk £6.95

—Journal of Planning and Environmental Law : 1948-1981, 34 Vols. / Abingdon : Professional Books.

—JPEL occasional papers : challenging decisions / London : Sweet & Maxwell, 1986.
ISBN 0421361301 Pbk £22.00

—JPEL occasional papers : planning for growth and decline / London : Sweet & Maxwell, 1987.
ISBN 0421382600 Pbk £25.00

—Keeping pace with change / papers from a conference held at Oxford, September 1987, organised by the Bar Council, the Law Society and the Royal Institution of Chartered Surveyors. – London : Sweet & Maxwell, 1988.
85p.
ISBN 042140390X £25.00

—Listed buildings and conservation areas / London : Longman Professional (UK), 1989.
– (Practitioner series).
Explains how a building is listed, how far that listing extends, and considers the designation of conservation areas. Sets out the provisions relating to alteration and repair of listed buildings and the planning cotrols that apply, and sets out the financial considerations. Takes account of the General Development Order 1988.
ISBN 0851214088 Hbk £25.95

—Local Government, Planning and Land Act 1980 / London : Butterworths, 1981.
This book consists of an annotated guide to the complete Act. A table of cases and a guide to the definitions used in the Act is also included.
ISBN 0406584303 Hbk

—Local Government Planning and Land Act 1980 / London : Butterworths, 1981.
ISBN 0406584303 Hbk £32.50

—Local plans in British land use planning / by Patsy Healey. – Oxford : Pergamon, 1983.
xv,324p; 24cm.
Bibliography: p303-318. - Includes index.
ISBN 0080252427 £16.50

—Made Simple : Housing Tenancy and Planning Law / London : MADE, 1981.
ISBN 0434984876 Pbk £2.95

—Metropolitan problem : papers from a conference held at Oxford, September 1984, organised by the Bar Council, the Law Society, and the Royal Institution of Chartered Surveyors / Gordon V. Hyde. – London : Sweet & Maxwell, 1985.
vi,102p; 25cm. – (Journal of planning and environmental law occasional papers).
ISBN 0421341505 Pbk £19.00

—Notes on need for planning permission / 3rd ed. – London : Longman Professional, 1984.
ISBN 0851207146 Pbk £16.95

—Planning and Compensation Reports : 1950-1981, 42 Vols. / Abingdon : Professional Books.

—Planning and pollution : an examination of the role of land use planning in the protection of environmental quality / Christopher Miller and Christopher Wood. – Oxford : Clarendon, 1983.
xi,232p; 23cm.
Includes index.
ISBN 0198232454 Unpriced

—Planning appeals and inquiries / Dobry. – 4th ed. – London : Sweet & Maxwell, 1988.
ISBN 0421390700 Pbk

—Planning : appeals, call-in and major public inquiries : the Government's response to the fifth report from the Environment Committee, session 1985-86 / presented to Parliament by the Secretary of State for the Environment supported by the Secretary of State for Scotland...et al. – London : H.M.S.O., 1986.
44p.
ISBN 010100432X

—Planning Application Fees / London : Oyez Longman, 1981.
ISBN 085120600X Hbk £2.95

—Planning applications / Oxford : Blackwell Scientific, 1987.
ISBN 0632018941 Pbk £19.95

—Planning applications and appeals / London : Architectural Press, 1987.
ISBN 085139504X Pbk £39.50

—Planning control : philosophies, prospects and practice / edited by M.L. Harrison and R. Mordey. – London : Croom Helm, 1986.
234p; 23cm. – (Croom Helm series in geography and environment).
Bibliography: p227-232. - Includes index.
ISBN 0709937903 £25.00

—Planning controls and their enforcement / by A.J. Little. – 5th ed. – London : Shaw, 1983.
xlix,345p.
Previous ed. published as 'The enforcement of planning control' 1977. Includes index.
ISBN 0721904920

—Planning for growth and decline : papers from a conference held at Oxford, September 1986, organised by the Bar Council, the Law Society and the Royal Institution of Chartered Surveyors / London : Sweet & Maxwell, 1987.
vi,70p; 25cm.
Conference proceedings.
ISBN 0421382600 Pbk £20.00

—Planning for industry : papers from a conference held at Cambridge September 1979 / organised by the Bar Council, the Law Society and the Royal Institution of Chartered Surveyors. – London : Sweet & Maxwell, 1980.
v,78p; 25cm.
ISBN 042127140X Pbk £10.00

—Planning for leisure in the countryside : papers from a conference held at Oxford September 1982 / organised by the Bar Council, the Law Society and the Royal Institution of Chartered Surveyors. – London : Sweet & Maxwell, 1984.
vi,107p; 25cm.
Conference papers.
ISBN 0421326700 Pbk £18.00

—Planning inquiries / Gordon Hyde. – London : Sweet & Maxwell, 1983.
75p.
Conference papers.
ISBN 0421318600 Pbk £12.00

—Planning law / London : Longman Professional (UK), 1988.
– (Longman practice notes).
Sets out procedure from initial stages to the final decision of the planning authority. Contains information on how to challenge a planning application, sample forms and precedents, and details time limits and fees.
ISBN 0851214452 Pbk £9.95

—Planning law and practice in dwelling houses / Morgan. – London : Sweet & Maxwell, 1987.
ISBN 0421366206 Hbk

—Planning law and procedure / 7th ed. – London : Butterworths, 1986.
ISBN 0406665214 Hbk £22.00
ISBN 0406665222 Pbk £14.50

—Planning law and procedure / London : Butterworths, 1988.
ISBN 0406103836 Hbk

—Planning law and procedure / A.E. Telling. – 7th ed. – London : Butterworth, 1986.
xxxii,351p; 23cm.
Previous ed.: 1982. Includes index.
ISBN 0406665214 Hbk £18.00
ISBN 0406665222 Pbk £11.95

—Planning law casebook / London : Laureate-Thomson Press, 1984.
ISBN 0907392091 Pbk £19.50

—Planning Law for Conveyancers / D. W. Williams. – London : Oyez Longman, 1983. – (Oyez Longman Practice Note Ser.: No. 76).
ISBN 0851207731 Hbk £9.95

—Planning law for conveyancers (LPPN 76) / Williams. – 2nd ed. – London : Longman Professional, 1987.
ISBN 0851209963 Pbk £15.95

—Planning law handbook / Butterworths. – London : Butterworths, 1987.
ISBN 0406505802 Pbk £22.50

—Planning law handbook / by Malcolm Grant. – London : Sweet & Maxwell, 1981.
xxx,488p; 25cm.
ISBN 0421285702 Pbk £12.50

—Planning Law in Practice / London : Butterworths, 1985.
ISBN 0406260508 Hbk £22.50

—Planning Office's Advice and Undertakings : Estoppel and Personal Bar in Public Law / Colin T. Reid. – Glasgow : Planning Exchange, 1982.
70p. – (Scottish Planning Law and Practice Occasional Paper Ser.: No. 3).

—Planning Procedure Tables / 4th ed. – London : Oyez Longman, 1981.
ISBN 0851205585 Hbk £9.25

—Planning use classes / Oxford : Blackwell Scientific, 1987.
ISBN 063202125X Pbk £14.95

—Property, Planning and Compensation Reports / London : Sweet & Maxwell.

Bound Vol.

Single copy

Back Vols. avail.

—Remaking cities : contradictions of the recent urban environment / Alison Ravetz. – London : Croom Helm, 1980.
375p; 23cm.
Bibliography: p349-370. - Includes index.
ISBN 0856642932 £14.95

—Town and country planning / report of a Committee of Inquiry appointed by the Nuffield Foundation. – London : Nuffield Foundation, 1986.
xiv,204p.
ISBN 0904956253

—Town and country planning in Britain / J.B. Cullingworth. – 9th ed. – London : Allen & Unwin, 1985.
430p; 22cm.
Previous ed.: 1982. Includes bibliography and index.
ISBN 0047110139 Pbk £8.95

—Town and country planning in Britain / J.B. Cullingworth. – 8th ed. – London : Allen & Unwin, 1982.
369p; 23cm.
Previous ed.: 1979. Bibliography: p349-360. - Includes index.
ISBN 0047110104 Hbk Unpriced
ISBN 0047110112 Pbk Unpriced

—Town and country planning law / Plymouth : Macdonald & Evans, 1981.
ISBN 0712120319 Pbk £3.95

—Town and Country Planning Law / 1st ed. – Plymouth : Macdonald & Evans, 1981.
128p. – (M and E Handbook Ser.).
ISBN 0712120319 Hbk £3.95

—Town planning in practice / London : Butterworths, 1988.
ISBN 0406500754 Pbk

—Urban land economics / Paul N. Balchin and Jeffrey L. Kieve. – 3rd ed. – London : Macmillan, 1985.
xvi,302p; 22cm. – (Macmillan building and surveying series).
Previous ed.: 1977. Bibliography: p282-283. - Includes index.
ISBN 0333397843 Pbk £7.95

—Urban planning law / 2nd ed. – London : Sweet & Maxwell, 1986.
ISBN 0421395605 Hbk £18.95

PLANNING - HONG KONG

—Land-use planning in Hong Kong : history, policies and procedures / Roger Bristow. – Hong Kong : Oxford University Press, 1984.
xii, 328p, 8 leaves of plates.
Bibliography: p299-317.
ISBN 0195814967

PLANNING - IRELAND

—Guide to planning legislation in the Republic of Ireland / by Kevin Ingram Nowlan. – Dublin : Incorporated Law Society of Ireland, 1988.
xxiii,375p; 26cm.
Includes index.
ISBN 0902027301 No price

—Planning and development law / by Edward M. Walsh. – 2nd ed. – Dublin : Incorporated Law Society of Ireland, 1984.
xxi,209p.
Previous ed.: 1979. Includes index.
ISBN 0902027247

—Sourcebook on planning law in Ireland / Katherine Shepherd. – Abingdon : Professional Books, 1984.
ISBN 0862050901 Hbk £31

Supplement 1987 1984.
ISBN 0862050901 Hbk £31.00

Supplement 1987.
ISBN 086205219X Hbk £11

—Sourcebook on planning law in Ireland / by Philip O'Sullivan and Katharine Shepherd. – Abingdon : Professional books, 1984.
xxxviii,568p.
Includes index.
ISBN 0862050901

PLANNING - MALAYSIA

—Town and Country Planning Act, 1976 (Act 172) / Kuala Lumpur : International Law Books Services.

PLANNING - NEW ZEALAND

—Law of Town and Country Planning / 3rd ed. – Butterworths, 1981.
ISBN 0409600377 Hbk £103.95

Supplement
ISBN 0409701513 Hbk £35.75

Supplement-1985 to 3rd ed.
ISBN 0409701513

—New Zealand Town Planning Appeals / Wellington : Butterworths.

—Planning and development law in New Zealand / by Kenneth A. Palmer : with a foreword by Sir Robin Cooke. – 2nd ed. 2. – Sydney : Law Book Co., 1984.
lviii,1023p.
ISBN 0455203725

PLANNING - SCOTLAND

—Planning by agreement in Scotland / E Young. – Edinburgh : W Green & Son, 1989.
Provides a guide to the law and practice of planning by agreement with an examination of the complexities that can arrive from section 50 of the Town and Country Planning (Scotland) Act 1972, the mechanics of such agreements and descriptions of the purposes for which they have been employed. Covers other statutory agreements governing land use, particularly the countryside. Concludes with a review of the arguments for and against the pursuit of 'planning gain'.
ISBN 0414008553

—Planning by Agreement in Scotland : The Law and Practice / Eric Young. – Glasgow : Planning Exchange, 1982.
110p. – (Scottish Planning Law and Practice Occasional Paper Ser.: No. 4).

—Scottish Planning Appeal Decisions : Monthly / Planning Exchange. – Glasgow : Planning Exchange.
ISBN 01438972 Pbk £70.00

—Scottish Planning Law Practice / Glasgow : Planning Exchange, 1983.
36p.
ISBN 01448196 Pbk £7.50

Back issues 1-6, June 1982

Back issues 7, October 1982-present

PLANNINGAUSTRALIA - NEW SOUTH WALES

—Planning and Environment Law Service, Victoria / Butterworths, 1984.
ISBN 040949321X Hbk £215.00

PLANT PROTECTION

—Plant protection legislation / by Luis M. Bombin. – Rome : Food and Agriculture Organization of the United Nations, 1984.
165p. – (Legislative study).
ISBN 9251014604

PLEADING

—Advocacy and Mental Handicap / Raquel Schuster-Herr. – Brussels : International League of Societies for Persons with Mental Handicap, 1984.

—Principles and Precedents of Pleadings / 2nd ed. – Lucknow : Eastern Book Company, 1983.
1,174p.

PLEADING - AUSTRALIA

—Advocacy with Honour / Allahabad : Law Book Company, 1985.
xi, 100p.
ISBN 0455206511 Pbk £14.00

—Advocacy With Honour / North Ryde : Law Book Co, 1985.
ISBN 0455206511 Pbk £7.50

—Advocates Act and Legal Practitioners Act / 5th ed. – Allahabad : Law Book Company, 1987.
600p.

—Civil Litigation : a Practice Guide for Advocates / Butterworths, 1985.
296p.
ISBN 0409492345 Hbk £49.00

—Evidence and Advocacy / Sydney : Butterworths, 1988.
360p.

—Pleading Precedents / 3rd ed. – North Ryde : Law Book Co, 1984.
xvii, 285p.
ISBN 0455202923 Hbk £43.00

—Pleading precedents / 3rd ed. – North Ryde : Law Book Co, 1984.
ISBN 0455202923 Hbk £43.00

PLEADING - AUSTRALIA - VICTORIA

—Victorian pleading precedents / by Tony Graham : with a foreword by Norman M. O'Bryan. – Sydney : Law Book Co., 1982.
xii,333p.
Includes index.
ISBN 0455203628

PLEADING - CANADA

—Advocacy / Law Society of Upper Canada. – Toronto : DeBoo, 1982.
ISBN 0888201117 Hbk £100.00

—Advocacy in Child Welfare Cases / Agincourt : Carswell, 1985.
258p.
This book discusses the representation of the parties to child welfare cases under the Child Welfare Act and the Child and Family Services Act of Canada.

—Advocacy in Court : a Tribute to Arthur Maloney, Q.C. / Aurora : Canada Law Book Co, 1987.
192p.

—Advocacy : Views from the Bench / R. E. Holland. – Aurora : Canada Law Book Co, 1984.
176p. – (Text Books-Civil).

—Manes Organized Advocacy : a Manual for the Litigation Practitioner / Valerie Edwards. – rev. ed. – Agincourt : Carswell, 1988.
ca 550p.

—Practice and Advocacy in the Supreme Court of Canada / Vancouver : British Columbia Continuing Legal Education Society, 1983.
463p.
ISBN 0865041180 Hbk £65.00

—Public Advocate Act, 1983, Bill 125 : An Act to Provide for a Public Advocate in Ontario / Ontario : Ontario Government Publications Service, 1983.
3p.

PLEADING - CANADA - BRITISH COLUMBIA

—Advocacy in the Court of Appeal of British Columbia 1982 / Vancouver : Continuing Legal Education Society of British Columbia, 1982.
200p.
ISBN 0865040818 Hbk £55.00

PLEADING - EUROPEAN COMMUNITY

—Pleading Before the Court of Justice of the European Communities : The Law Society's European Group / London : Law Society.

PLEADING - GREAT BRITAIN

—Evidence and Advocacy / Barnard. – 2nd ed. – London : Blackstone Press, 1986.
ISBN 0906322960 Pbk £8.95

—Liber Placitandi : A Book of Special Pleadings Containing Precedents of Pleas in Abatement, Declaration, Barrs, etc., in the Now Most Common and Ordinary Actions, Also the Forms of Entries in Writs of Error etc. / 2nd ed. Repr. of 1674 ed. – Abingdon : Professional Books.
273p.

—Matrimonial Advocacy and Litigation / London : Butterworths, 1987.

—Matrimonial Advocacy and Litigation / London : Butterworths, 1988.
ISBN 0406103305 Pbk £19.95

—Pleader's Guide / 5th ed. Repr. of 1808 ed. – Abingdon : Professional Books.
262p.

—Pleading, Evidence and Practice / 43rd ed. – London : Sweet & Maxwell, 1988.
ISBN 0421363606 Hbk £49.00
ISBN 0421054808 Hbk £60.00

—Practical Precedents in Pleading / Repr. of 1835 ed. – Abingdon : Professional Books.
278p.

—Principles of pleading and practice in civil actions / Casson. – 22nd ed. – London : Sweet & Maxwell, 1981.
ISBN 0420457100 Pbk £17.50

—Treaty on Pleading and Parties to Actions with Precedents, 2 Vols. / Repr. of 1809 ed. – Abingdon : Professional Books.
64p.

PLEADING - INDIA

—Art of Conveyancing and Pleading / 1974 2nd repr. – Lucknow : Eastern Book Company, 1983.
290p.

—Ghosh on Principles and Forms of Pleading / H.K. Saharay. – 4th ed. – Calcutta : Eastern Law House, 1984.

—Mogha's Law of Pleadings / 14th ed. – Calcutta : Eastern Law House, 1987.

—Pleading and Precedents in India / 2nd ed. – Allahabad : Law Publishers, 1983.

—Pleadings and Practice. 2 Vols / 7th ed. – Allahabad : Law Book Company, 1984.

PLEADING - SCOTLAND

—Pleading in court / by Robin Gilmour McEwan. – Edinburgh : Green, 1980.
xxi,46p.
Includes index.
ISBN 0414006569

PLEADING - SOUTH AFRICA

—Beck's theory and principles of pleading in civil actions / I. Isaacs. – 5th ed. – Pretoria : Butterworths, 1982.
lxxiii,358p.
Includes index.
ISBN 0409012351
ISBN 040901236X

PLEADING (CRIMINAL PROCEDURE) - CANADA

—Criminal Pleadings and Practice in Canada / 2nd ed. – Aurora : Canada Law Book, 1987.

—Report on disclosure by the prosecution / Law Reform Commission of Canada. – Ottawa : Canadian Law Reform Commission, 1984.
38,36p. – (Report).
Pages numbered in opposite directions. Text in English and French.
ISBN 0662530942

PLEADING (CRIMINAL PROCEDURE) - GREAT BRITAIN

—Archbold : Pleading, Evidence, and Practice in Criminal Cases / 41st ed. – London : Sweet & Maxwell, 1983.

Fourth cumulative supplement
ISBN 0421273909 Pbk

PLEADING (CRIMINAL PROCEDURE) - INDIA

—Criminal Pleadings / 3rd ed. – Allahabad : Law Book Company, 1986.
1,000.

PLEADING (CRIMINAL PROCEDURE) - SOUTH AFRICA

—VanDerMerwe, Kemp and Barton : Plea Procedures in Summary Criminal Trials / VanDerMerwe, Kemp and Barton. – Durban : Professional Publisher, 1983.
ISBN 0409059285 Pbk £49.00

PLEAS (CRIMINAL PROCEDURE) - AUSTRALIA

—Criminal Law Advocacy / Nicholas Pengelley. – Cowandilla : Wakefield Press, 1986.
192p.
ISBN 0949268445 Pbk £17.50

PLEAS (CRIMINAL PROCEDURE) - CANADA

—Ordering of justice : a study of accused persons as dependants in the criminal process / Richard V. Ericson, Patricia M. Baranek. – Toronto : Published in association with the Centre of Criminology, University of Toronto by University of Toronto Press, 1982.
xvi, 268 p.; 25 cm.
Includes index. Bibliography: p. 253-261.
ISBN 0802064639 pbk.

PLEAS OF THE CROWN

—Eyre of Northamptonshire : 3-4 Edward III, A.D. 1329-1330 / edited for the Selden Society by Donald W. Sutherland. – London : Selden Society, 1983.
lxxv,498,498p; 26cm.
Opposite pages of main sequence bear duplicate numbering. French text with parallel English translation.

Vol.2 / edited for the Selden Society by Donald W. Sutherland. – 1983.
vi,499-770,499-770,771-922p; 26cm.
Opposite pages of main sequence bear duplicate numbering. French text with parallel English translation.

—Historia Placitorum Coronae, 2 Vols. / Abingdon : Professional Books.
– (Classical English Law Texts Ser.).

—Placita Coronae : Pleas of the Crown in Matters Criminal and Civil / Repr. of 1723 ed. – Abingdon : Professional Books.
366p.

—Pleas of the Crown 1678 / Reprint. – Abingdon : Professional Books, 1986.
ISBN 0862053218 Hbk £24.75

—Pleas of the Crown, 2 Vols. / Abingdon : Professional Books.
– (Classical English Law Texts Ser.).

—Pleas of the Crown, 2 Vols. / Abingdon : Professional Books.
– (Classical English Law Texts Ser.).

—Pleas of the crown / 1st ed. – Abingdon : Professional Books, 1986 Reprint.
ISBN 0862053234 Hbk £48.50

—Pleas of the Crown : Summary / Abingdon : Professional Books.
– (Classical English Law Texts Ser.).

—Plees del Coron / 1st ed. – Abingdon : Professional Books, 1986 Reprint.
ISBN 0862053285 Hbk £24.75

—Plees del Coron / Abingdon : Professional Books.
– (Classical English Law Texts Ser.).

—Crown Pleas of the Devon Eyre of 1238 / Exeter : Devon & Cornwall Record Society, 1985.
ISBN 0901853283 Hbk £8.00

—Historia Placitorum Coronae / Reprint. – Abingdon : Professional Books, 1986.
ISBN 086205320X Hbk £53.75

—Summary of the Pleas of the Crown : A Brief But Full Account of Whatsoever Can Be Found Relating to That Subject / Repr. of 1716 ed. – Abingdon : Professional Books.
362p.

PLEBISCITE - CANADA

—Lawmaking by the people : referendums and plebiscites in Canada / J. Patrick Boyer. – Toronto : Butterworths, 1982.
xxxii,304p.
Outlines the laws which make possible the existence of political rights in Canada by exploring constitutional conventions such as responsible government, parliamentary democracy, and the role of political parties. It examines municipal and provincial laws regarding signs, posters and parades, as well as federal broadcasting laws governing provincial elections.
ISBN 0409816019

PLEDGES (LAW) - SOUTH AFRICA

—Wille's law of mortgage and pledge in South Africa / T. J. Scott, Susan Scott. – 3rd ed. – Cape Town : Juta, 1987.
lvi,283p.
Previous ed. published in 1961 as: The law of mortgage and pledge in South Africa. Bibliography: pp.xxi-xxii. - Includes index. .
ISBN 0702118966

PLURALISM (SOCIAL SCIENCES)

—Spheres of justice : a defence of pluralism and equality / Michael Walzer. – Oxford : Robertson, 1983.
xviii,345p; 24cm.
Introduction for students to abstract discussions of justice. Includes case studies.
ISBN 0855206837 £15.00

POISONS - AUSTRALIA - SOUTH AUSTRALIA

—Report ... relating to claims for injuries from toxic substances and radiation effects / Law Reform Committee of South Australia. – Adelaide : Government Printer, 1985.
96p. – (87th report).

POISONS - GREAT BRITAIN

—Dilemma of Toxic Substance Regulation / London : MIT Press, 1988.
ISBN 0262132303 Hbk £31.50

—Law on poisons, medicines and related substances / P.F.C. Bayliss. – Beckenham : Ravenswood Publications, 1980.
xviii,103p; 22cm.
Bibliography: p.93. - Includes index.
ISBN 0901812358 £12.25
ISBN 090181234X

POISONS - INDIA

—Medical Jurisprudence and Toxicology / 5th ed. – Allahabad : Law Book Company, 1987.
800p.

POLICE

—Civilian review of complaints against the police : a survey of the United States literature / David C. Brown. – London : Home Office, 1983.
v,39p.
Bibliography: p.29-32.
ISBN 0862521041

—Islington crime survey : crime, victimization and policing in inner-city London / Trevor Jones, Brian MacLean and Jock Young. – Aldershot : Gower, 1986.
xiv, 265p; 23cm.
ISBN 0566052644

—Police and public order in Europe / edited by John Roach and Jurgen Thomaneck. – London : Croom Helm, 1985.
293p; 23cm.
Includes bibliographies and index.
ISBN 0709922426 £18.95

—Views of the Government of the Federation on the report of the Police Prison Vehicle (Death of Suspects) Tribunal of Inquiry / Nigeria. – Apapa : Federal Government Press, 1980.
8p.
At head of title: Federal Republic of Nigeria.

POLICE - AUSTRALIA

—Australia's External Territory Police Forces / Canberra : Australian Institute of Criminology.

—Nature and Scope of Police and Police Related Research / Canberra : Australian Institute of Criminology.

—Police Institutions and Issues : American and Australian Perspectives / Canberra : Australian Institute of Criminology.

—Police Source Book / Canberra : Australian Institute of Criminology.

—Police Training in Australia / Canberra : Australian Institute of Criminology.

—Policing a Democracy / Canberra : Australian Institute of Criminology.

POLICE - AUSTRALIA - NEW SOUTH WALES

—NSW Police Law Handbook / Sydney : Butterworths, 1988.
176p.
This handbook contains sections devoted to interrogation, arrest, and search and seizure. Included are chapters on detention and questioning, powers of arrest, searches, and search warrants. The intended audience is law enforcement officers.

POLICE - AUSTRALIA - WESTERN AUSTRALIA

—Police Offences In Western Australia / Sydney : Butterworths, 1981.
243p.

POLICE - CANADA

—Certain R.C.M.P. activities and the question of governmental knowledge : third report / Commission of Inquiry Concerning Certain Activities of the Royal Canadian Mounted Police. – Ottawa : Canadian Government Publishing Centre, 1981.
xv,527p; 25cm.
Chairman: D.C. McDonald.
ISBN 0660109530

—Community based preventive policing : a review 1984-90 / David K. Wasson, John D. Crawford & Company Ltd. – Ottawa : Ministry of the Solicitor General, 1984.
iii,198p. – (User report).
Bibliography: p.197-198.

—Community policing in the 1980's : recent advances in police programs / edited by Donald J. Loree and Chris Murphy. – Ottawa : Ministry of the Solicitor General, 1986.
v,154p.
'This conference was jointly sponsored by the Canadian Police College ... and by the Secretariat of the Ministry of the Solicitor General of Canada'. - T.p.. Held in Ottawa, March 17-19, 1986.
ISBN 0662158075

—Complete Guide to Police Writing / Agincourt : Carswell, 1984.
190p.
This work for law enforcement students offers an examination of the areas of written communication that are most problematic to police officers. On-the-job police writing and academic essay writing are discussed in the work.

—Freedom and security under the law : second report / Commission of Inquiry Concerning Certain Activities of the Royal Canadian Mounted Police. – 2. – Ottawa : Canadian Government Publishing Centre, 1981.
xxii,1257p; 25cm.
Bibliography: p.1117-1144. Chairman: D.C. McDonald.
ISBN 0660109506 v.2
ISBN 0660109522

—Invasion of Privacy : Police and Electric Surveillance in Canada / Agincourt : Carswell, 1983.
250p.
This book analyzes the legal and ethical dimensions of police surveillance in Canada and discusses the question of the extent of police surveillance powers.

—Legal status of the police : a study paper prepared for the Law Reform Commission of Canada / by Philip C. Stenning. - Ottawa : Law Reform Commission of Canada, 1982.
169p; 25cm. - (Study paper).
ISBN 0662119967

—Ministerial responsibility for national security as it relates to the Offices of Prime Minister, Attorney General, and Solicitor General of Canada / by J.Ll.J. Edwards. - Ottawa : Commission of Inquiry Concerning Certain Activities of the Royal Canadian Mounted Police, 1980.
x, 146 p.; 25 cm.
Includes bibliographical references.
ISBN 0660105012 pbk. £5.25 (£6.30 other countries)

—Parliament and security matters / C.E.S. Franks. - Hull, Quebec : Minister of Supply and Services, 1980.
88p.
Includes bibliographical references. A study prepared for the Commission of Inquiry concerning Certain Activities of the Royal Canadian Mounted Police.
ISBN 0660104997

—The Police Manual of Arrest, Seizure and Interrogation / 4th ed. - Agincourt : Carswell, 1988.
182p.
This work is an updated handbook relected recent Canadian Criminal Code revisions and recent case law affecting police powers of arrest, seizure, and interrogation.

—Police Officers' Manual : 1988 / 11th ed. - Agincourt : Carswell.

—Police Powers and Individual Rights / Montreal : McGill Campus Legal Aid Clinic, 1986.
117p.

—Police, Race and Ethnicity : A Guide For Law Enforcement Officers / Chris Toole. - Toronto : Butterworths, 1986.
256p.
Guidelines for 'on the street' level of policing and providing police officers with administrative considerations. Also considers the structure and practice of relevant criminal law and the function of the Ontario Human Rights Commission in enforcing the Ontario Human Rights Code. The mechanism of the Ontario Human Rights Commission.
ISBN 0409805017 Pbk £18.25

—RCMP and the Management of National Security / Andre Beliveau. - Montreal : Institute for Research on Public Policy.
xiii, 79p.
ISBN 0920380182 Hbk

—Report of the proceedings: Workshop on Police Productivity and Performance, May 25 and 26 1978 / Workshop on Police Productivity and Performance, May 25 and 26, 1978 : edited by Peter Engstad and Michele Lioy. - Ottawa : Communication Division, Solicitor General of Canada, 1980.
xi, 326 p.
On cover: Solicitor General Canada, Research Division. Includes bibliographies.
ISBN 0662108329

POLICE - ENGLAND

—Civil actions against the police / by Richard Clayton and Hugh Tomlinson. - London : Sweet & Maxwell, 1987.
250p; 25cm.
Examines the rights and remedies of the individual against police misconduct. Covers traditional tort actions, assault, false imprisonment, trespass, interference with goods, and malicious prosecution. Emphasis on recent developments, and focuses on the circumstances that may lead to claims. Also contains discussion on civil liability under the Police and Criminal Evidence Act 1984.
ISBN 0421344202 £30.00

—Community constables : a Study of a policing initiative / David Brown, Susan Iles. - London : Home Office, 1985.
v,51p.
Bibliography: p.42-43.

—Conflict and order : the police and labour disputes in England and Wales, 1900-1939 / Jane Morgan. - Oxford : Clarendon, 1987.
325p,4p of plates; 22cm.
Includes bibliography and index.
ISBN 0198201281 £30.00

—Criminal justice revolution : the third Sir Gwilym Morris memorial lecture delivered on 24th October 1986 / by Graham Zellick. - Cardiff? : University of Wales Institute of Science and Technology, 1986.
24p.
Includes bibliographical references.

—English Village Constable 1580-1642 / Oxford : Oxford University Press, 1986.
ISBN 0198229135 Hbk £27.50

—Ethnic minorities and complaints against the police / Philip Stevens and Carole Willis with the assistance of Clare Oxby. - London : Home Office, 1981.
v,40p. - (Research and Planning Unit paper).
Bibliography: p.33-34.
ISBN 0862520266

—Governance of police / Laurence Lustgarten. - London : Sweet & Maxwell, 1986.
xv,197p; 23cm. - (Modern legal studies).
Bibliography: p183-190. - Includes index.
ISBN 0421319003 Hbk £17.00
ISBN 0421319100 Pbk £9.95

—Government reply to the fourth report from the Home Affairs Committee, session 1981-82 HC 98-1 : police complaints procedures / presented to Parliament by the Secretary of State for the Home Department. - London : H.M.S.O., 1982.
19p.
ISBN 0101868103

—McNee's law / Sir David McNee. - London : Collins, 1983.
256p,8p of plates; 23cm.
Includes index.
ISBN 0002170078 £9.95

—Measures of police effectiveness and efficiency / Ian Sinclair, Clive Miller. - London : Home Office, 1984.
v,38p.
Bibliography: p.38.
ISBN 0862521599

—Moriarty's police law : an arrangement of law and regulations for the use of police officers / James Fryer, Walter Stansfield. - 24th ed. - London : Butterworths, 1981.
xviii,767p; 19cm.
Previous ed.: 1976. Includes index.
ISBN 0406846081 Pbk Unpriced

—Police and complaints / Eric Edwards. - London : G.L.C., 1983.
12p. - (Research documents guide).
ISBN 0716813661

—Police and people in London / David J. Smith, Jeremy Gray. - London : Policy Studies Institute, 1983.
354p. - (PSI).
ISBN 085374226X

vol.2 : A group of young black people : Stephen Small 1983.
169p. - (PSI).
ISBN 0853742243

vol.3 : A survey of police officers : David J. Smith 1983.
197p. - (PSI).
ISBN 0853742251

—Police and the community / Eric Edwards. - London : G.L.C., 1983.
20p. - (Research documents guide).
ISBN 0716813688

—Police complaints and discipline procedures / presented to Parliament by the Secretary of State for the Home Department... - London : H.M.S.O., 1983.
ii,23p.
ISBN 0101907206

—Police complaints procedure : a survey of complainants' views / by David Brown. - London : H.M.S.O., 1987.
v,91p; 25cm.
Survey of complainants' views, carried out shortly before the Police and Criminal Evidence Act 1984. Explores tensions involved in the complaints procedure and assesses its effectiveness.
ISBN 0113408536

—Police : powers, procedures and proprieties / edited by John Benyon and Colin Bourn : with a foreword by Lord Scarman. - Oxford : Pergamon, 1986.
xxiv,334p; 24cm.
Bibliography: p299-312. - Includes index.
ISBN 0080326978 Hbk £17.00
ISBN 008032696X Pbk £6.90

—Policing by multi-racial consent : the Handsworth experience / John Brown. - London : Bedford Square Press, 1982.
xv,174p.
Bibligraphy: p173-174.

—Public order review : civil disturbances 1981-1985 / Metropolitan Police Force. - London : Metropolitan Police, 1986.
iv,43p.

—Race and the police / Eric Edwards. - London : G.L.C., 1983.
21p. - (Research documents guide).
ISBN 071681367X

—Triennial review report ... / Police Complaints Board. - 3. - London : HMSO, 1980-.

—Uncovering crime : the police role / David Steer. - London : H.M.S.O., 1980.
vii,136p; 25cm. - (Research studies).
Bibliography: p127-129. At head of title: Royal Commission on Criminal Procedure.
ISBN 0117301264 Pbk £5.00

POLICE - GREAT BRITAIN

—101 Plus Uses Of A Police Helmet / Police Review, 1985.
ISBN 0851640192 Pbk £1.95

—Annual report of the Police Complaints Authority / Police Complaints Authority. - London : H.M.S.O., 1986-.
Continues: Report of the Police Complaints Board.

—Beat Officer's Companion / 2nd ed. - Police Review, 1986.
ISBN 0851640249 Pbk £4.25

—Brixton disorders 10-12 April 1981 : report of an enquiry / by Lord Scarman. - London : H.M.S.O., 1981.
viii,168p; 25cm.
Report of inquiry by Lord Scarman. Discusses causes of the riots and lessons for the future about riot control and prevention.
ISBN 0101842708 Pbk £8.00

—Careers in the Police Force / 2nd ed. - London : Kogan Page, 1986.
96p.
ISBN 18500911703 Hbk £2.95

—Changing policing : a conference based on the Scarman Report, 1 May 1982 : proceedings / edited by David Armstrong. - London : University of London Department of Extra-Mural Studies, 1982.
70p.
'Proceedings of a conference held at the University of London, 1 May 1982'.

—Conduct Unbecoming : The Social Construction of Police Deviance and Control / London : Tavistock Publications, 1985.
300p.
ISBN 0422792101 Pbk £7.95

—Contacts between police and public : findings from the British crime survey / by Peter Southgate and Paul Ekblom. - London : H.M.S.O., 1984.
v,37p; 25cm.
A Home Office Research and Planning Unit report.
ISBN 0113407718

—Conversation Handbook for Policemen / 2nd ed. - Plymouth : Macdonald & Evans, 1984.
128p.
ISBN 0712156259 Pbk £6.00

—Cop World / London : Macmillan, 1984.
352p.
ISBN 0333306880 Hbk £12.95

—Crime and police effectiveness / by Ronald V. Clarke and Mike Hough. - London : H.M.S.O., 1984.
iv,28p; 28cm. - (A Home Office Research and Planning Unit report).
ISBN 0113407734

—Crime control and the police : a review of research / by Pauline Morris and Kevin Heal. - London : H.M.S.O., 1981.
v,67p.
Bibliography: p56-67. A Home Office Research Unit report.
ISBN 0113407076

—Crime, protest, community and police in nineteenth-century Britain / David Jones. - London : Routledge & Kegan Paul, 1982.
xi, 247p.
Includes index. Includes bibliography.
ISBN 0710090080

—Criminal Evidence and Procedure, No. 2 / Wilkie. - 7th ed. - London : Butterworths, 1981. - (Police Promotion Handbooks Ser.).
This work for United Kingdom police officers covers the basic rules of criminal evidence and procedure from the perspective of the officer working in the field.*Police officers*
ISBN 0406841314 Pbk

—Criminal Law, No. 1 / Wilkie. - 6th ed. - London : Butterworths, 1980.
- (Police Promotion Handbooks Ser.).
This work for United Kingdom police officers presents the changes in criminal law brought about by the Theft Act of 1978 and the Criminal Evidence Act of 1979.
Police officers
ISBN 0406841217 Pbk

—Effectiveness of policing / edited by R.V.G. Clarke and J.M. Hough. - Farnborough, Hants. : Gower, 1980.
xiv,169p.
Bibliographies.
ISBN 0566002973

—Establishment of an independent element in the investigation of complaints against the police : report of a working party appointed by the Home Secretary / Home Office. – London : H.M.S.O., 1981.
ii,12p; 25cm.
ISBN 0101819307 unbound £1.70

—Further particulars / Oxford : OUP, 1987.
240. – (Oxford letters and memoirs).
Second volume of C.H. Rolph's memoirs, taking up the story from 'London Particulars' at the end of the First World War. He describes his 25 years with the City Police, rising to the rank of Chief Inspector, his work as a freelance journalist for the New Statesman and at the BBC.*Legal historians, criminologists*
ISBN 0192117904 Hbk £12.50
ISBN 0192821431 Pbk £4.95

—Future of Policing / Cambridge : Institute of Criminology, 1983.
– (Cropwood Papers Ser.).

—Future of policing : papers presented to the 15th Cropwood Round-Table Conference, December 1982 / edited by Trevor Bennett. – Cambridge : University of Cambridge Institute of Criminology, 1983.
iii,173p.
Includes bibliographical references.

—General Police Duties / Wilkie. – 7th ed. – London : Butterworths, 1983.
– (Police Promotion Handbook Ser.: No. 3).
This work for United Kingdom police officers discusses the many changes in the law including: the Highways Act of 1980, the Child Care Act, and the Licensed Premises (Exclusion of Certain Persons) Act of 1980; and the effects on the duties of officers.
ISBN 040684142X Pbk

—General Police Duties P.P.H. 3 / Wilkie. – 7th ed. – London : Butterworths, 1983.
ISBN 040684142X Pbk £4.95

—Guide to the Police and Criminal Evidence Act 1984 / Vaughan T. Bevan and Ken W. Lidstone. – London : Butterworths, 1985.
xv,554.
This text gives a comprehensive dissertation on every aspect of the Act. The book includes a full text of the United Kingdom's Police and Criminal Evidence Act of 1984.
ISBN 0406014302 Pbk

—Inside the British police : a force at work / Simon Holdaway. – Oxford : Basil Blackwell, 1983.
vi,186p; 23cm.
Bibliography: p176-177. - Includes index.
ISBN 0631131124 £14.95

—Law and disorder / John Alderson. – London : Hamilton, 1984.
vii,247p; 23cm.
Includes index.
ISBN 0241112591 £8.95

—Nickers : A Gentleman's Guide to Police Duty / London : Police Review Publishing, 1982.
Illus.
ISBN 085164175X Pbk £2.50

—Notes taken at the time / London : Police Review, 1983.
ISBN 0851640552 Pbk £2.50

—Notes Taken at the Time / London : Sweet & Maxwell, 1983.
Illus.
ISBN 0851640044 Pbk £2.50

—Origins of the vigilante state : the London Metropolitan Police Special Branch before the First World War / Bernard Porter. – London : Weidenfeld and Nicolson, 1987.
xvi,256p,8p of plates; 24cm.
Bibliography: p239-243. - Includes index.
ISBN 0297790676 £15.95

—Plodding / Police Review, 1986.
ISBN 0851640257 Pbk £1.95

—Points to prove / 2nd ed. – Police Review, 1987.
ISBN 085164032X Pbk £5.25

—Police and Criminal Evidence Act 1984 : Guide / Pickover. – Police Review, 1986.
ISBN 0851640214 Pbk £4.95

—Police and Criminal Evidence Bill 1982 : briefings / National Council for Civil Liberties. – 1. – London : The Council, 1983.
various pagings.
Contents: Clause 1: Stop and search of persons and vehicles - Clauses 9 and 10: Police powers to search private premises for evidence - Clauses 9 and 10: Opinion / by Ben Hytner - Part 3. Police powers of arrest - Part 4. Detention of suspects - Part 5. Questioning and treatment of persons by police - Part 6. Codes of practice - Clause 60: 'Confession' statements and the right to silence.

—Police and Law Enforcement / London : Eurospan, 1988.
ISBN 0404112080 Hbk £47.25

—Police and people in London / David J. Smith. – London : Policy Studies Institute, 1983.
350p. – (PSI).
ISBN 0853742235

—Police and the Criminal Evidence Act 1984 / Magrath. – London : Longman Professional, 1985.
ISBN 0851207669 Pbk £19.95

—Police : autonomy and consent / Michael Brogden. – London : Academic Press, 1982.
xv,265p; 24cm.
Bibliography: p251-259. - Includes index.
ISBN 0121351807 £21.00

—Police, Government and Accountability / Qual. – Oxford : Oxford University Press, 1987.
ISBN 0333432266 Pbk £8.95

—Police Law Primer / 2nd ed. – London : Butterworths, 1980.
This one volume work for United Kingdom police officers covers the law relating to everyday police work.
ISBN 0406846510 Pbk

—Police Officer in Court : A Guide to Presenting Evidence / London : Police Review Publishing, 1983.
ISBN 0851640060 Pbk

—Police : Organisation and Command / Plymouth : Macdonald & Evans, 1984.
400p : Illus.. – – (Police Studies Ser.).
ISBN 0712116710 Hbk £7.50

—Police powers and politics / Richard Kinsey. – London : Quartet, 1982.
1v.
ISBN 0704323338 Hbk £9.95
ISBN 0704334127 Pbk £3.95

—Police Promotion Handbooks / London : Butterworths.

—Police response to calls from the public / Paul Ekblom and Kevin Heal. – London : Home Office, 1982.
v,95p; 30cm.
Bibliography: p85-88.
ISBN 0862520657 Pbk Unpriced

—Police, the Constitution and the Community / Koffman. – Abingdon : Professional Books, 1985.
ISBN 0862051053 Hbk £19.75
ISBN 0862051061 Pbk £10.95

—Police - where now? : a public lecture / delivered by John C. Alderson on ... 18th March 1982. – London : Inns of Court School of Law, 1982.
12p; 23cm.

—Policeman's Lot / Repr. of 1979 ed. – London : Police Review Publishing, 1983.
ISBN 0851649939 Pbk £1.95

—Policeman's lot / Police Review, 1983.
ISBN 0851649939 Pbk £1.95

—Policewoman and Equality (1988) / London : Macmillan, 1988.
ISBN 0333424417 Pbk £8.95

—Policing and Social Policy : Proceedings of the Cranfield-Wolfson Colloquium / London : Police Review Publishing, 1984.

—Policing by coercion / Pluto Press, 1983.
ISBN 071681336X Pbk £1.50

—Policing industrial disputes: 1893 to 1985 / Roger Geary. – Cambridge : Cambridge University Press, 1985.
vii,171p; 24cm.
Includes index.
ISBN 052130315X £19.50

—Policing liberal society / Steve Uglow. – Oxford : Oxford University Press, 1988.
viii, 165 p.; 23 cm. – (An OPUS book).
Examines the role of the police force in late twentieth-century Britain; how it has changed, and prospects for the future. Questions whether the police are crime-fighters, social workers, guardians of the law, or maintainers of public order. Suggests that the constitutional role of the police should be re-examined.
ISBN 0192192221 Hbk £19.50

—Policing revolution : police technology, democracy and liberty in Britain / Sarah Manwaring-White. – Brighton : Harvester, 1983.
vii,231p; 23cm.
ISBN 0710805551 Hbk £18.95
ISBN 0710806159 Pbk Unpriced

—Policing the miners' strike / edited by Bob Fine and Robert Millar. – London : Lawrence and Wishart, 1985.
xii,243p.
ISBN 0853156336

—Policing today / edited by Kevin Heal, Roger Tarling and John Burrows, Home Office Research and Planning Unit. – London : H.M.S.O., 1985.
v,176p.
12 studies from the Home Office Research and Planning Unit. Discusses management, efficiency and economy, and police/public relations.
ISBN 0113408005

—Principles of policing / London : Macmillan, 1985.
ISBN 0333382447 Hbk £22.50
ISBN 0333382455 Pbk £7.95

—Public liberty and the police role / Philip Knights. – S.l. : University of Wales. Institute of Science and Technology, 1985.
23p.
Bibliography: p22-23.

—Register of policing research. No. 2 / London : Police Foundation, 1989.
220; 21.
Covers topics in a register of 200 police research projects - includes police management, organisation, policy making, operations, relations with voluntary and statutory agencies, and the history of policing and crime prevention.
ISBN 0947692126 Pbk £9.95

—Report of the Commissioner of Police of the Metropolis for the Year 1983 / London : HMSO, 1984.
ISBN 0101926804 Hbk £9.45

—Report of the Commissioner of Police of the Metropolis for the Year 1985 / London : HMSO, 1986.
ISBN 0101979002 Hbk £11.30

—Report of the Ministry of Defence Police Review Committee : presented to Parliament by the Secretary of State for Defence ... / Ministry of Defence Police Review Committee. – London : H.M.S.O., 1986.
50p.
ISBN 0101985304

—Report of the Police Complaints Board / 8 v. – London : H.M.S.O., 1978-85.
Continued by: Annual report of the Police Complaints Authority.

—Spare a Copper / London : Police Review Publishing, 1982.
ISBN 0851640001 Pbk £1.95

—Spare a copper / Police Review, 1982.
ISBN 0851640001 Pbk £1.95

—Spending on law and order : the police service in England and Wales / M. A. S. Joyce. – London : National Institute of Economic and Social Research, 1985.
64p. – (Discussion paper).

—Taking statements / 2nd ed. – Police Review, 1987.
ISBN 0851640338 Pbk £3.75

—Traffic officer's companion / 3rd ed. – Police Review, 1987.
ISBN 0851640273 Pbk £4.25

—Undercover investigation / London : Butterworths, 1983.
ISBN 0409950769 Hbk £25.00

—Uprising! : the police, the people and the riots in Britain's cities / Martin Kettle and Lucy Hodges. – London : Pan Books, 1982.
271p; 18cm.
ISBN 0330268457

—What is to be done about law and order? / John Lea and Jock Young. – Harmondsworth : Penguin Books in association with the Socialist Society, 1984.
284p.
Includes index. Bibliography: p275-284.
ISBN 0140065938

—White law : racism in the police courts and prisons / Paul Gordon. – London : Pluto Press, 1983.
159p; 20cm.
ISBN 0861047060 Pbk £3.95

—Yankee One and George / Police Review, 1984.
ISBN 0851640133 Pbk £2.50

POLICE – INDIA

—Delhi Police Law : Containing Commentaries on Delhi Police Act, 1978 with Up-to-date Rules and Regulations / Delhi : Allied Book Co., 1987.
303p.

—Police Acts. With 1985 supplement / 5th ed. – Allahabad : Law Book Company, 1983.

—Police Diaries, Statements, Reports, Investigations / 9th ed. 2 Vols. – Allahabad : Law Publishers, 1986.

—Police Handbook / Allahabad : Law Publishers, 1982.

POLICE - IRELAND
—Garda Siochana Guide / 5th ed. – Dublin : Incorporated Law Society of Ireland, 1981.
ISBN 0902027204 Hbk £42.20

POLICE - MALAYSIA
—Police Act, 1967 (Act No. 41 of 1967) / Kuala Lumpur : International Law Books Services.

POLICE - NIGERIA
—Report of the Police Prison Vehicle (Death of Suspects) Tribunal of Inquiry / A. G. O. Agbaje. – Apapa : Federal Government Press, 1980.
23p.
By A.G.O. Agbaje. At head of title: Federal Republic of Nigeria.

POLICE - SCOTLAND
—Policing Scotland / Paul Gordon. – Glasgow : Scottish Council for Civil Liberties, 1980.
133p; 20cm.
Bibliography: p130-133.
ISBN 0906502039 Hbk £5.95
ISBN 0906502020 Pbk £2.25

POLICE - SEYCHELLES
—Annual report of the Police Division, Republic of Seychelles / Seychelles. – v. – Maye : Government Press, 1977.
Continues: Annual report of the Seychelles Police Force. Lacking 1978.

POLICE - SOUTH AFRICA
—Annual report of the Commissioner of South African Police / Pretoria : Government Printer, 1945.

POLICE - UNITED STATES
—Police community relations and the administration of justice / Pamela D. Mayhall. – 3rd ed. – New York : Wiley, 1984.
ix,438p; 25cm.
Previous ed.: published as: Community relations and the administration of justice. 1979. Includes bibliographies and index.
ISBN 0471060445 £27.95

—Police Institutions and Issues : American and Australian Perspectives / Canberra : Australian Institute of Criminology.

POLICE ADMINISTRATION - CANADA
—Organizational police deviance : its structure and control / Clifford D. Shearing. – Toronto : Butterworths, 1981.
ix,208p.
Includes bibliographical references.
ISBN 0409848808

—Study of police management information systems / study team: Ted M. Zaharchuk (project director), Robert M. Atcheson ...et al. – Ottawa : Communication Division, Ministry of the Solicitor General of Canada, 1981.
vii,58p.
Bibliography: p.24-58. 'Prepared by Decision Dynamics Corporation under contract with the Research Division, Ministry of the Solicitor General of Canada' - verso t.p..
ISBN 0662116437

POLICE ADMINISTRATION - GREAT BRITAIN
—Policies for the Police Service / Association of Metropolitan Authorities. – London : The Association, 1982.
8p.

—Policing the Police /. – London : Calder (John), 1980.
ISBN 0714537950 Pbk £8.95

—Uniformed police work and management technology / J.M. Hough. – London : Home Office, 1980.
v,56p. – (Research Unit paper).
Bibliography: p.48-51.

POLICE ADMINISTRATION - UNITED STATES
—Two cultures of policing : street cops and management cops / Elizabeth Reuss-Ianni. – New Brunswick, N.J. : Transaction Books, 1983.
145p; 24cm.
Bibliography: p137-142. - Includes index.
ISBN 0878554696 Unpriced

POLICE CHARGES - ENGLAND
—Cautioning by the police : a consultative document / Home Office. – London : Home Office, 1984.
47p.
Bibliography: p.47.
ISBN 0862521513

—Precedents for police use / by Brian G. Coase. – Chichester : Rose, 1980.
xxxvi,87p; 26cm.
Includes index.
ISBN 0859921530 £12.00

POLICE CORRUPTION - CANADA
—Organizational police deviance : its structure and control / Clifford D. Shearing. – Toronto : Butterworths, 1981.
ix,208p.
Includes bibliographical references.
ISBN 0409848808

POLICE CORRUPTION - GREAT BRITAIN
—Police misconduct : legal remedies / John Harrison. – London : Legal Action Group, 1987.
xxix,218p.
Guide to the remedies and procedures available in this area. Covers police complaints, civil actions against the police, the European Convention on Human Rights, police discipline, judicial review, wrongful convictions, criminal proceedings, and legal aid. Appendices include levels of damages and useful names and addresses.
ISBN 0905099168

—Remedies for police misconduct (LAG) / London : Sweet & Maxwell, 1987.
ISBN 0905099168 Pbk £12.00

POLICE CORRUPTION - HONG KONG
—Hard graft in Hong Kong : scandal; corruption; the ICAC / H. J. Lethbridge. – Hong Kong : Oxford University Press, 1985.
viii,247p.
Bibliography: p232-243.
ISBN 0195838963

POLICE MAGISTRATES - AUSTRALIA - NEW SOUTH WALES
—Magistracy : interim report : first appointments as magistrates under the Local Courts Act, 1982 / New South Wales Law Reform Commission. – Sydney : The Commission, 1983.
xiii,87p. – (L.R.C. 38).

POLICE MAGISTRATES - ENGLAND
—ABC guide to the practice of the magistrates' courts / by Emlyn Williams. – London : Sweet & Maxwell, 1986.
viii,187p; 22cm.
ISBN 0421344903 Pbk £14.50

—Crime and the new magistrate / by Ronald Bartle. – Chichester : Rose, 1985.
vi,65p; 22cm.
Includes index.
ISBN 0859923312 Pbk £6.00

—Criminal justice system model : magistrates' courts sub-model / Susan Rice. – London : Home Office, 1984.
vi,66p.
Bibliography: p.59.
ISBN 0862521254

—Evidence and procedure in the Magistrates' Court / P.J. Rowe, S.J. Knapp. – London : Oyez Longman, 1982.
xxx,220p; 22cm.
Includes index.
ISBN 0851206697 Pbk Unpriced

—Framework of criminal justice / Michael King. – London : Croom Helm, 1981.
159p; 23cm.
Bibliography: p153-156. - Includes index.
ISBN 0709904304 Hbk £10.95
ISBN 0709915004 Pbk £6.50

—Magistrates' court : an index of common penalties and formalities in cases before justices (excluding the juvenile court) / by Ian McLean and Peter Morrish. – 6th ed. – Chichester : Rose, 1984.
205p; 22cm.
Previous ed.: 1980. Includes index.
ISBN 0859922170 £19.50
ISBN 085992369X

—Magistrates' domestic courts : new perspectives / edited by Tony F. Marshall. – London : Home Office, 1984.
v,49p.
Conference papers.
ISBN 0862521696

—Matrimonial jurisdiction of magistrates' courts / by M.D.A. Freeman and Christina M. Lyon. – Chichester : Rose, 1980.
xxv,222p; 21cm.
Includes index.
ISBN 0859921999 Pbk £10.80

—Pre-trial justice : a study of case settlement in magistrates' courts / John Baldwin. – Oxford : Blackwell, 1985.
vi,190p.
Observational research into case settlement in Magistrates' Courts.
ISBN 0631140646 £19.50

—Reciprocal enforcement : a practical guide to magistrates' courts' jurisdiction & procedure in international domestic proceedings / Desmond A.G. James : with a foreword by Dewi E. Davies. – Chichester : Rose, 1984.
133p; 22cm.
Includes index.
ISBN 0859923320 £17.75

POLICE MAGISTRATES - GREAT BRITAIN
—Criminal jurisdiction of magistrates / by Brian Harris. – 11th ed. – Chichester? : Barry Rose, 1988.
lxxxi,848p.
Previous ed.: 1986. Includes index.
ISBN 1870080513

—Criminal jurisdiction of magistrates / by Brian Harris. – 9th ed. – Chichester : Rose, 1984.
lix,707p; 25cm.
Previous ed.: 1983. Includes index.
ISBN 0859923940 Hbk £58.00
ISBN 0859923363 Pbk £47.00

POLICE MAGISTRATES - TRINIDAD & TOBAGO
—Report of the proceedings and papers of the second Magistrates' Workshop / compiled and edited by Roland Crawford on behalf of the Magistrates' Association of the Republic of Trinidad and Tobago. – Port-of-Spain : The Association, 1982.
158p.
'Held on the 13th and 14th September, 1980, Chaguaramas Convention Centre'. At head of title: Republic of Trinidad and Tobago, the Magistrates' Association of the Republic of Trinidad and Tobago.

POLICE PATROL - CANADA
—Reproducing order : a study of police patrol work / Richard V. Ericson. – Toronto : Published in association with the Centre of Criminology, University of Toronto, by University of Toronto Press, 1982.
xii,243p; 24cm. – (Canadian studies in criminology).
Bibliography: p225-236. - Includes index.
ISBN 0802055699 Hbk Unpriced
ISBN 0802064752 Pbk £9.90

POLICE PATROL - ENGLAND
—Police-public encounters / by Peter Southgate with the assistance of Paul Ekblom. – London : H.M.S.O., 1986.
vi,143p; 25cm.
Report from the Research and Planning Unit. Describes a study of everyday contact between the public and uniformed police in London, Birmingham and Bristol. Examines problems during such encounters.
ISBN 011340834X

—Use, effectiveness and impact of police stop and search powers / Carole F. Willis. – London : Home Office, 1983.
v,40p.
Bibliography: p.32-33.
ISBN 0862520983

POLICE POWER
—Report on offences under the Dublin Police Acts and related offences / the Law Reform Commission. – Dublin, 1985.
v,90p. – (LRC).

POLICE POWER - AUSTRALIA - NEW SOUTH WALES
—Criminal procedure : police powers of arrest and detention : discussion paper / Sydney : Law Reform Commission of New South Wales, 1987.
xx,148p. – (D.P.).
Bibliography: p141-144.
ISBN 0730544567

POLICE POWER - CANADA
—Police powers - search and seizure in criminal law enforcement / Law Reform Commission of Canada. – Ottawa : The Commission, 1983.
356,403p; 25cm. – (Working paper).
Added t.p. in French: Les pouvoirs de la police : les fouilles, les perquisitions et les saisies en droit penal. Pages numbered in opposite directions. In English and French.
ISBN 066252277X

POLICE POWER - ENGLAND
—Briefing memorandum on the Police and Criminal Evidence Bill / the Law Society. – London : Law Society, 1982.
5 leaves.

—Governance of police / Laurence Lustgarten. – London : Sweet & Maxwell, 1986.
xv,197p; 23cm. – (Modern legal studies).
Bibliography: p183-190. - Includes index.
ISBN 0421319003 Hbk £17.00
ISBN 0421319100 Pbk £9.95

—Observations on the Police and Criminal Evidence Bill / the Justices' Clerks' Society. – Bristol : The Society, 1983.
34p.

—Police and Criminal Evidence Act 1984 / by Michael Zander : foreword by Leon Brittan. – London : Sweet & Maxwell, 1985.
xxi,315p; 25cm.
Includes index.
ISBN 0421326905 Pbk £12.50

—Police and Criminal Evidence Act 1984 / with annotations by M.D.A. Freeman. – London : Sweet & Maxwell, 1985.
x,185,44,8p; 24cm.
ISBN 0421329009

—Police and Criminal Evidence Bill 1982 : briefings / National Council for Civil Liberties. – 1. – London : The Council, 1983.
various pagings.
Contents: Clause 1: Stop and search of persons and vehicles - Clauses 9 and 10: Police powers to search private premises for evidence - Clauses 9 and 10: Opinion / by Ben Hytner - Part 3. Police powers of arrest - Part 4. Detention of suspects - Part 5. Questioning and treatment of persons by police - Part 6. Codes of practice - Clause 60: 'Confession' statements and the right to silence.

—Police and criminal evidence bill : briefing guide / London : Home Office, 1983.
67p.
ISBN 0862521211

—Police and Criminal Evidence Bill : draft code of practice for the exercise of powers of stop and search / London : Home Office, 1984.
9p.
ISBN 0862521556

—Police and the law / Charles Wegg-Prosser. – 3rd ed. – London : Longman Professional, 1986.
xiv,287p; 20cm. – (It's your law series).
Previous ed.: London : Oyez, 1979. Bibliography: p273-279. - Includes index.
ISBN 0851207588 Pbk £6.95

—Police powers and the individual / St. John A. Robilliard and Jenny McEwan. – Oxford : Basil Blackwell, 1986.
viii,260p; 23cm.
Compares actual police practice with their legal powers. Discusses constraints on and remedies for police misbehaviour.
ISBN 0631139958 Hbk £27.50
ISBN 0631139966 Pbk £9.95

—Police powers in England and Wales / L.H. Leigh. – 2nd ed. – London : Butterworth, 1985.
330p; 22cm.
Previous ed.: 1975. Includes index.
ISBN 0406845417 Hbk £20.00
ISBN 0406845425 Pbk £14.95

—Police powers in England and Wales / 2nd ed. – London : Butterworths, 1985.
ISBN 0406845417 Hbk £19.50
ISBN 0406845425 Pbk £17.50

—Police, the law and the people / Nick Blake. – New ed. – London : Haldane Society of Socialist Lawyers, 1982.
55p.
Includes bibliographical references.
ISBN 0907412025

—Use, effectiveness and impact of police stop and search powers / Carole F. Willis. – London : Home Office, 1983.
v,40p.
Bibliography: p.32-33.
ISBN 0862520983

POLICE POWER – GREAT BRITAIN

—Constable's Pocket Guide to Powers of Arrest and Charges / Lewis Heavens. – 7th ed. – London : Butterworths, 1982.
This work for practitioner and police officer gives a ready reference to the law on arrest and the formulation of charges. The work includes all new laws and the amendments of the old ones relevant to powers of arrest and charges.*Police officers*
ISBN 0406842043 Pbk

—Handbook of Cautions, Oaths and Recognizances, Etc. / 10th ed. – London : Shaw & Sons, 1981.
ISBN 0721904734 Hbk £4.50

—Police and Criminal Evidence Act 1984 (s.66) : codes of practice / Great Britain. – London : H.M.S.O., 1985.
97p.
Provisions supersede some existing rules including the Judges' Rules. Codes cover police powers of stop and search; searching of premises and seizure of property; detention, treatment and questioning by police and identification procedures.
ISBN 011340624X

—Police, Government and Accountability / Qual. – Oxford : Oxford University Press, 1987.
ISBN 0333432266 Pbk £8.95

—Police interrogation: the effects of the Police and Criminal Evidence Act 1984 / Ian McKenzie. – London : Policy Studies Institute, 1989.
250; 21.
A comparison of research data from 1979 with new research data from 1986 in one police station in Brighton.
ISBN 0947692118 Hbk £18.95

—Police law / Card. – 2nd ed. – London : Butterworths, 1988.
ISBN 0406840008 Pbk £15.95

—Police powers and accountability / Oxford : Croom Helm, 1986.
ISBN 0709916604 Hbk £16.95

—Police powers and duties / Nottridge. – London : Fourmat, 1985.
ISBN 0906840821 Pbk £9.95

—Police Powers and the Rights of the Individual / Karen E. Fletcher-Rogers. – London : Waterlow, 1988.
136p.
ISBN 0080330843 Pbk £15.00

—Police, the Constitution and the community : a collection of original essays on issues raised by the Police and Criminal Evidence Act 1984 / edited by John Baxter and Laurence Koffman. – Abingdon : Professional Books, 1985.
274p.
ISBN 0862051053

—Policing by coercion / Louise Christian. – London : GLC Police Committee Support Unit, 1983.
vi,224p. – (Discussion paper).
At head of title page 'The Police and Criminal Evidence Bill'. Includes index.
ISBN 071681336X

—Policing the police / Peter Hain, Martin Kettle, Duncan Campbell, Joanna Rollo. – London : John Calder, 1980.
viii,213p. – (Platform Books).
ISBN 0714537950

POLICE POWER – NEW ZEALAND

—Police powers and the rights of suspects / by Tim McBride. – Auckland : Legal Research Foundation, 1982.
23,8,5p.
'Paper presented at Auckland Law Faculty seminar series 1982 at University of Auckland'.
ISBN 0908581246

POLICE POWER – NIGERIA

—Police and the law in Nigeria / S.G. Ehindero. – Lagos : Times Press, 1986.
xxv,158p.
Bibliography: p.155. - Includes index.
ISBN 9783023608

POLICE POWER – WALES

—Police powers in England and Wales / 2nd ed. – London : Butterworths, 1985.
ISBN 0406845417 Hbk £19.50
ISBN 0406845425 Pbk £17.50

POLICE QUESTIONING – CANADA

—Questioning suspects / Law Reform Commission of Canada. – Ottawa : Canadian Law Reform Commission, 1984.
104,112p; 25cm. – (Working paper).
Cover title: Criminal law - questioning suspects. Added t.p. in French : L'interrogatoire des suspects. Pages numbered in opposite directions. In English and French.
ISBN 0662529162

—Questioning suspects / Law Reform Commission of Canada. – Ottawa : The Commission, 1984.
25,28p. – (Report).
Added t.p. in French: L'interrogatoire des suspects. Pages numbered in opposite directions. Text in English and French.
ISBN 0662533208

POLICE QUESTIONING – ENGLAND

—Cautioning by the police : a consultative document / Home Office. – London : Home Office, 1984.
47p.
Bibliography: p.47.
ISBN 0862521513

—Draft codes of practice for the detention, treatment, questioning and identification of persons by the police; for the searching of premises and seizure of property; and for the exercise of powers of stop and search / London : Home Office, 1985.
iii,80p.
Previous ed.: 1984.

—Draft codes of practice for the detention, treatment, questioning and identification of persons by the police and for the searching of premises and seizure of property / London : Home Office, 1983.
66p.
Revised edition of: Draft codes of practice for the treatment, questioning and identification of persons suspected of crime.
ISBN 086252122X

—Draft codes of practice for the detention, treatment, questioning and identification of persons by the police and for the searching of premises and seizure of property / Rev. ed. – London : Home Office, 1984.
iii,66p.
Previous ed.: 1983.
ISBN 0862521424

—Draft codes of practice for the treatment, questioning and identification of persons suspected of crime / Home Office. – London : Home Office, 1982.
44p.

—Draft codes of practice for the treatment, questioning and identification of persons suspected of crime / Home Office. – Revised draft. – London : Home Office, 1983.
51p.
ISBN 0862520975

—Police interrogation / Barrie Irving, Barrie Irving. – London : H.M.S.O., 1980.
vii,153p; 25cm. – (Research studies).
Bibliography: p66-74. Contents: The psychological approach / Barrie Irving and Linden Hilgendorf - A case study of current practice / Barrie Irving with the assistance of Linden Hilgendorf. At head of title: Royal Commission on Criminal Procedure.
ISBN 0117301221 Pbk £5.70

—Police interrogation : tape recording / J.A. Barnes and N. Webster for the Royal Commission on Criminal Procedure. – London : H.M.S.O., 1980.
x,106p; 25cm. – (Research studies).
Bibliography: p49.
ISBN 0117301272 Pbk £4.75

—Tape recording of police interviews with suspects : field trials : procedural guidance / London : Home Office, 1983.
27p.
ISBN 0862521181

POLICE QUESTIONING – GREAT BRITAIN

—Art of Taking Statements / London : Police Review Publishing, 1984.
ISBN 0851640079 Pbk

—Police interrogation / Police Review, 1987.
ISBN 0851640311 Pbk £5.95

—Police interrogation : an observational study in four police stations / by Paul Softley, with the assistance of David Brown and others. – London : H.M.S.O., 1980.
vii,63p.
Bibliography - p63.
ISBN 0113407017

—Police interrogation : review of literature / Pauline Morris ; and an observational study in four police stations : Paul Softley, with the assistance of David Brown and others. – London : H.M.S.O., 1980.
v,99p. – (Research studies).
Bibliographies.
ISBN 011730123X

—Police interrogation: the effects of the Police and Criminal Evidence Act 1984 / Ian McKenzie. – London : Policy Studies Institute, 1989.
250; 21.
A comparison of research data from 1979 with new research data from 1986 in one police station in Brighton.
ISBN 0947692118 Hbk £18.95

—Taking statements / 2nd ed. – Police Review, 1987.
ISBN 0851640338 Pbk £3.75

—Tape-recording of police interviews with suspects : an interim report / Carole F. Willis. – London : H.M.S.O., 1984.
v,39p.
Outlines background to field trials of tape recording police interviews. Reviews literature describing research methodologies used in trials. Discusses preliminary results of the research.
ISBN 0113407769

POLICE QUESTIONING – NEW ZEALAND

—Police powers and the rights of suspects / by Tim McBride. – Auckland : Legal Research Foundation, 1982.
23,8,5p.
'Paper presented at Auckland Law Faculty seminar series 1982 at University of Auckland'.
ISBN 0908581246

POLICE QUESTIONING – SCOTLAND

—Tape-recording of police interviews with suspected persons in Scotland / report by the Working Group appointed by the Secretary of State for Scotland. – Edinburgh : Scottish Home & Health Department, 1985.
24p.
Title from cover. Accompanied by Appendices 1-2, Research report by Edward C.M. Wozniak (viii,189p) and Technical details (iv,13p).

POLICE REGULATIONS – AUSTRALIA – VICTORIA

—Thirteenth report to Parliament on subordinate legislation concerning : Police Gaols Regulations 1988 (SR No. 292/1988) / Legal and Constitutional Committee. – Melbourne : Government Printer, 1988.
vii,24p.
Includes the texts of the Regulations.

POLICE REGULATIONS – CANADA

—Police Officers' Manual : 1988 / 11th ed. – Agincourt : Carswell.

POLICE REGULATIONS – CANADA – NOVA SCOTIA

—Report of the Commission to Review the Police Act & Regulations / Nathan Green. – Halifax : Queen's Printer, 1981.
96,26,36p.
Commissioner: Nathan Green.

POLICE REGULATIONS – GREAT BRITAIN
—Beat Officer's Companion / London : Police Review Publishing, 1983.
ISBN 0851640036 Pbk £3.25

—Beat Officer's Companion / 2nd ed. – Police Review, 1986.
ISBN 0851640249 Pbk £4.25

POLICE REGULATIONS – INDIA
—Uttar Pradesh Police Regulations / 3rd ed. – Lucknow : Eastern Book Company, 1985.

POLICE REGULATIONS – SCOTLAND
—Scottish Criminal Law : Police Duties and Procedure / Grampian Police. – Aberdeen : Aberdeen University Press.
1590p.
ISBN 0900015454 Hbk

POLICE TRAINING
—Human rights and the police / by J. Alderson. – Strasbourg : Council of Europe, Directorate of Human Rights, 1984.
207p.
Illustrates how awareness of concepts of human rights defined by the European Convention should affect the way police carry out duties. Training guidelines and case law examples are considered.
ISBN 9287103666 PBK £10.90

POLICE TRAINING – CANADA
—Crisis intervention training for police / Don Dutton and Bruce Levens under the auspices of United Way of the Lower Mainland. – Ottawa : Ministry of the Solicitor General, 1985.
66p. – (User report).
Bibliography: p.51.

POLICE TRAINING – ENGLAND
—Police probationer training in race relations / Peter Southgate. – London : Home Office, 1982.
iv,38p.
Bibliography: p.31.
ISBN 0862520630

—Racism awareness training for the police : report of a pilot study for the Home Office / Peter Southgate. – London : Home Office, 1984.
v,17p.
Bibliography: p.17.
ISBN 0862521726

POLICE TRAINING – GREAT BRITAIN
—Police law primer / 3rd ed. – London : Butterworths, 1987.
ISBN 0406846529 Pbk £8.95

—Police training manual / Houghton. – 5th ed. – Maidenhead : McGraw-Hill, 1986.
ISBN 0070847975 Pbk £12.95

POLICY SCIENCES – CANADA
—Policy implementation, compliance and administrative law / Law Reform Commission of Canada. – Ottawa : Law Reform Commission of Canada, 1986.
105,115p; 25cm. – (Working paper).
Cover title: Administrative law - policy implementation, compliance and administrative law. Added t.p. in French: Droit, objectifs publics et observation des normes. Pages numbered in opposite directions. Text in English and French.
ISBN 0662540832

POLICY SCIENCES – CASE STUDIES
—Social research and Royal Commissions / edited by Martin Bulmer. – London : Allen & Unwin, 1980.
xv,198p; 23cm.
Bibliography: p189-192. - Includes index.
ISBN 0043510558 No price

POLITICAL CRIMES AND OFFENCES
—Political offence exception to extradition : the delicate problem of balancing the rights of the individual and the international public order / Christine van den Wijngaert. – Deventer, the Netherlands : Kluwer, 1980.
xxi,263p.
Bibliography: p231-248. Translation from Dutch. Based on the author's thesis, Free University of Brussels, 1979.
ISBN 9026811853

POLITICAL CRIMES AND OFFENCES – CANADA
—Crimes against the state / Law Reform Commission of Canada. – Ottawa : The Commission, 1986.
72,76p. – (Working paper).
Includes bibliographies. Added t.p. in French: Les crimes contre l'etat. Pages numbered in opposite directions. Text in English and French.

POLITICAL CRIMES AND OFFENCES – GREAT BRITAIN
—What is to be done about law and order? / John Lea and Jock Young. – Harmondsworth : Penguin Books in association with the Socialist Society, 1984.
284p.
Includes index. Bibliography: p275-284.
ISBN 0140065938

POLITICAL CRIMES AND OFFENCES – PERU
—Peru : Amnesty International briefing / Amnesty International. – London : Amnesty International, 1985.
15p.
List of the 'disappeared' of Peru (November 1984) in pocket.
ISBN 0862100801

POLITICAL CRIMES AND OFFENCES – WALES
—Political policing in Wales / John Davies, Lord Gifford, Tony Richards. – Cardiff : Welsh Campaign for Civil & Political Liberties, 1984.
111p; 19cm.
ISBN 0947740007 Pbk £1.50

POLITICAL ETHICS
—Manual of Political Ethics / Repr. of 1838 ed. – Aalen Wuertt : Scientia.

POLITICAL PARTICIPATION – GREAT BRITAIN
—Government and the governed : BBC Reith Lectures 1983 / Douglas Wass. – London : Routledge and Kegan Paul, 1984.
viii,120p.
ISBN 0710203128

POLITICAL PARTIES – GREAT BRITAIN
—British interparty conferences : a study of the procedure of conciliation in British politics, 1867-1921 / John D. Fair. – Oxford : Clarendon Press, 1980.
x,354p; 22cm.
Bibliography: p335-342. - Includes index.
ISBN 0198226012 £25.00

—Paying for politics / the report of the Commission upon the financing of political parties. – London : Hansard Society, 1981.
49 p.

POLITICAL PLANNING – SOUTH AFRICA
—Report / Department of Constitutional Development and Planning. – 3. – Pretoria : Government Printer, 1983.
Text in Afrikaans and English.

POLITICAL PRISONERS – AFGHANISTAN
—Afghanistan : torture of political prisoners / Amnesty International. – London : Amnesty International, 1986.
i,51p.
ISBN 0862101077

POLITICAL PRISONERS – ALBANIA
—Albania : political imprisonment and the law / Amnesty International. – London : Amnesty International Publications, 1984.
58p.
ISBN 086210078X

POLITICAL PRISONERS – CHILE
—Where is William Beausire? : disappearance in Chile / Amnesty International. – London : Amnesty International, 1981.
57p.

POLITICAL PRISONERS – EAST TIMOR
—East Timor : violations of human rights : extrajudicial executions, 'disappearances', torture and political imprisonment, 1975-1984 / Amnesty International. – London : Amnesty International Publications, 1985.
vii,92p.
ISBN 0862100852

POLITICAL PRISONERS – GREECE
—Greek case before the Commission of Human Rights of the Council of Europe / Greece. – Athens : R. Ministry of Foreign Affairs, 1970.
v.; 27 cm.
Contents: v. 1. The report of the Commission of Human Rights: unfounded conclusions based on an illegal procedure.

POLITICAL PRISONERS – GUATEMALA
—Guatemala : a government program of political murder / Amnesty International. – London : Amnesty International, 1981.
32p; 30cm.
Cover title.
ISBN 0862100267 Pbk Unpriced

POLITICAL PRISONERS – IRAQ
—Iraq : evidence of torture : an Amnesty International report / London : Amnesty International Publications, 1981.
44p; 30cm.
ISBN 0862100321 unbound Unpriced

POLITICAL PRISONERS – NICARAGUA
—Nicaragua : the human rights record / Amnesty International. – London : Amnesty International, 1986.
36p; 27cm.
ISBN 0862100941 Pbk No price

POLITICAL PRISONERS – PAKISTAN
—Pakistan : the trial and treatment of political prisoners convicted by special military courts / Amnesty Internatiinal. – London : Amnesty International, 1985.
56p.

POLITICAL PRISONERS – PERU
—Peru : 'disappearances', torture and summary executions by government forces after the prison revolts of June 1986 / Amnesty International. – London : Amnesty International, 1987.
ii,71p.
ISBN 0862101166

POLITICAL PRISONERS – PHILIPPINE ISLANDS
—Report of an Amnesty International mission to the Republic of the Philippines 11-28 November 1981 / Amnesty International. – London : Amnesty International Publications, 1982.
ii,127p.
Includes bibliographical references.
ISBN 086210050X

POLITICAL PRISONERS – ROMANIA
—Romania / Amnesty International. – London : Amnesty International, 1980.
19p.

POLITICAL PRISONERS – SRI LANKA
—Report of an Amnesty International mission to Sri Lanka, 31 January-9 February 1982 / Amnesty International. – London : Amnesty International, 1983.
2,iii,72p; 30cm.
ISBN 0862100542 Pbk Unpriced

POLITICAL PRISONERS – TURKEY
—Turkey : testimony on torture / Amnesty International. – London : Amnesty International Publications, 1985.
76p.
ISBN 0862100887

POLITICAL PRISONERS – UGANDA
—Uganda : six years after Amin : torture, killings, disappearances / Amnesty International. – London : Amnesty International, 1985.
40p.

POLITICAL PRISONERS – VIETNAM
—Report of an Amnesty International mission to the Socialist Republic of Viet Nam, 10-21 December 1979 : including memoranda exchanged between the government and Amnesty International / Amnesty International. – London : Amnesty International, 1981.
ii,42p.
ISBN 086210033X

POLITICAL PRISONERS – YUGOSLAVIA
—Yugoslavia : prisoners of conscience / Amnesty International. – New ed. – London : Amnesty International Publications, 1985.
95p.
ISBN 0862100844

—Yugoslavia : prisoners of conscience : an Amnesty International report / Amnesty International. – London : Amnesty International, 1982.
50p.
ISBN 0862100437

POLITICAL PRISONERS – ZAIRE
—Zaire : reports of torture and killings committed by the armed forces in Shaba region / Amnesty International. – London : Amnesty International, 1986.
24p.
ISBN 0862100968

POLITICAL QUESTIONS AND JUDICIAL POWER
—European Parliament and Article 173 of the EEC Treaty / by John Barnard. – Florence : European University Institute, 1987.
59p.

POLITICAL QUESTIONS AND JUDICIAL POWER – ENGLAND
—Politics of the judiciary / J. A. G. Griffith. – 3rd ed. – London : Fontana, 1985.
255p.
ISBN 0006860206

POLITICAL QUESTIONS AND JUDICIAL POWER – GREAT BRITAIN
—Immigration and the judiciary : law and politics in Britain and America / Stephen H. Legomsky. – Oxford : Clarendon, 1987.
xxxix,345p; 24cm.
Bibliography: p327-345.
ISBN 0198255616 £35.00

—Policy arguments in judicial decisions / by John Bell. – Oxford : Clarendon, 1983.
xiv,283p; 23cm.
Bibliography: p271-276. - Includes index.
ISBN 0198253974 Unpriced

POLITICAL QUESTIONS AND JUDICIAL POWER – UNITED STATES
—Immigration and the judiciary : law and politics in Britain and America / Stephen H. Legomsky. – Oxford : Clarendon, 1987.
xxxix,345p; 24cm.
Bibliography: p327-345.
ISBN 0198255616 £35.00

POLITICAL RIGHTS - EUROPEAN COMMUNITY

—Political rights for European citizens / Guido van den Berghe. - Aldershot : Gower, 1982.
xii,245p; 23cm.
Bibliography: p218-235. - Includes index.
ISBN 0566005247 Unpriced

POLITICAL SCIENCE

—Religion, law, and the growth of constitutional thought 1150-1650 / Brian Tierney. - Cambridge : Cambridge University Press, 1982.
xi,114p; 23cm.
Bibliography: p109-114.
ISBN 0521234956 £12.50

—Utilitarianism / On liberty : John Stuart Mill : edited with an introduction by Mary Warnock. - 17th impression. - Glasgow : Fontana, 1985.
352p.
This selection originally published: 1962. Bibliography: p.343-4. - Includes index.

POLITICAL SCIENCE - ENGLAND

—Ancient constitution and the feudal law : a study of English historical thought in the seventeenth century / J.G.A. Pocock. - Reissue with a retrospect i.e. 2nd ed. - Cambridge : Cambridge University Press, 1987.
xv,402p; 24cm.
Second edition to a work examining seventeenth-century English ideas of constitutionalism as a set of beliefs based on the common law. The Retrospect considers how arguments in the original book may be improved in the light of recent work.
ISBN 0521303524 Hbk £27.50
ISBN 052131643X Pbk £8.95

POLITICAL SCIENCE - GREAT BRITAIN

—That noble science of politics : a study in nineteenth-century intellectual history / Stefan Collini, Donald Winch, John Burrow. - Cambridge : Cambridge University Press, 1983.
x,385p; 24cm.
Includes index.
ISBN 052125762X Hbk £25.00
ISBN 0521277701 Pbk £9.95

—Virtue, commerce, and history : essays on political thought and history, chiefly in the eighteenth century / J.G.A. Pocock. - Cambridge : Cambridge University Press, 1985.
x,321p; 24cm.
Includes index.
ISBN 0521257018 Hbk £25.00
ISBN 0521276608 Pbk No price

POLL TAX - GREAT BRITAIN

—Tax on all the people : poll tax / Oxford : Bookspeed, 1988.
ISBN 0946744068 Pbk £1.95

POLL TAX - SCOTLAND

—Butterworths guide to the community charge in Scotland / London : Butterworths, 1989.
Full text of the Abolition of Domestic Rates, Etc (Scot.) Act 1987, with all subordinate legislation to 31 March 1989. With an introduction to the background to the legislation, and a comentary on the statutory provisions. Published by Butterworths on behalf of the Law Society of Scotland.
ISBN 0406147108 SOFTBACK £15.00

—Scottish community charge / Neil Walker. - Edinburgh : W Green & Son, 1989.
Provides full commentary on every section of the Abolition of Domestic Rates Etc. (Scot) Act 1987 and an analysis of subsequent developments with the full set of regulations.
ISBN 0414008634 SOFTBACK

POLLUTION

—Availability of Civil Remedies to Protect Persons and Property from Transfrontier Pollution Injury / Hamburg : I.I.A., 1981.
ix, 163p.

—Cadmium in the environment and its significance to man : an inter- departmental report / Department of Environment : Central Directorate on Environmental Pollution. - London : H.M.S.O., 1980.
- (Pollution paper).
ISBN 0117514756

—Eighth report : oil pollution of the sea / Royal Commission on Environmental Pollution : chairman: Sir Hans Kornberg. - London : HMSO, 1981.
ISBN 0101835809

—International Comparisons in Implementing Pollution Laws / Kenneth Hanf. - Dordrecht : Kluwer, 1983.
352p.
ISBN 089838110X Hbk £78.00

—Law and practice relating to pollution control in the United Kingdom / M. J. Forster. - 2nd ed. - London : Graham & Trotman for the Commission of the European Communities, 1982.
200p.
Previous ed: 1976. Includes index.
ISBN 0860103064 Hbk £18.00
ISBN 0860104400 Pbk £9.00

—Oil pollution from ships : international, United Kingdom and United States law and practice / Richard L. Jarashow, David W. Abecassis. - 2nd ed. - London : Stevens, 1985.
l,619p; 26cm.
Deals with the international law and practice relating to oil pollution from ships, and includes new chapters dealing with United States law and selected aspects of United Kingdom law. There are also chapters on salvage in oil pollution cases and rights and obligations in customary international law. The Civil Jurisdiction and Judgements Act 1982, and Law of the Sea Convention 1982 are included.
ISBN 042047000X £75.00

—Oil pollution of the sea : the government response to the eighth report of the Royal Commission on Environmental Pollution / Great Britain. - London : H.M.S.O., 1983.
ISBN 0117516856

—Pollution of outer space, in particular of the geostationary orbit / W. de Graaff. - Dordrecht : Martinus Nijhoff, 1989.
188. - (Utrecht studies in air and space law).
Survey of the status of the pollution of outer space, dealing with both the scientific and legal aspects. Shows that the emerging international regulations are few, scanty, and in urgent need of elaboration.
ISBN 9024737508 Hbk £39

—Regulation of Toxic and Oxidant Air Pollution in North America / North Ryde : C.C.H. Australia, 1986.
272p.
ISBN 088796351X Pbk £27.95

—Total environment control : the economics of cross-media pollution transfers / by Julian Lowe, David Lewis and Martin Atkins. - Oxford : Pergamon, 1982.
viii,126p; 23cm.
Includes index.
ISBN 0080262767 Pbk £10.95

—Transfrontier Pollution and International Law : Pollution Transfrontiere et le Droit International / Academie de droit international de La Haye, Centre d'etude et de recherche de droit international et de relations internationales Transfrontier pollution ad international law / Hague Academy of International Law, Centre for Studies and Research in International Law and International Relations. - Dordrecht : Martinus Nijhoff, 1986.
133p.
English and French.
ISBN 9024733944 Pbk £50.00

POLLUTION - BELGIUM

—Law and practice relating to pollution control in Belgium and Luxembourg / Dirk Soetemans. - 2nd ed. - London : Graham & Trotman for the Commission of the European Communities, 1982.
200p.
Previous ed: /by J.M. Didier and Associates for Environmental Resources Limited. 1976. Includes index.
ISBN 0860103102 £18.00

POLLUTION - CANADA

—Cross-Border Litigation : Environmental Rights in the Great Lakes Ecosystem / Agincourt : Carswell, 1986.
445p.
This book analyzes the pollution control legislation of the American states and Canadian provinces bordering the Great Lakes and discusses the procedural difficulties confronting potential individual litigants.

POLLUTION - DENMARK

—Law and practice relating to pollution control in Denmark / prepared by C.H. Jensen for Environmental Resources Limited. - 2nd ed. - London : Graham & Trotman for the Commission of the European Communities, 1982.
200p.
Previous ed: 1976. Includes index.
ISBN 0860103129 £18.00

POLLUTION - ENGLAND

—Policing pollution : a study of regulation and enforcement / Genevra Richardson with Anthony Ogus and Paul Burrows. - Oxford : Clarendon Press, 1982.
ix,204p; 23cm.
Includes index.
ISBN 0198275102 Hbk £15.00
ISBN 0198275129 Pbk Unpriced

POLLUTION - EUROPEAN COMMUNITY

—Law and practice relating to pollution control in the member states of the European communities : a comparative survey / M. J. Forster. - 2nd ed. - London : Graham & Trotman for the Commission of the European Communities, 1982.
545p.
Previous ed: 1976.
ISBN 0860103153 £18.00

—Law and practice relating to pollution control in the member states of the European Communities : recent developments / prepared by Environmental Resources Limited. - London : Graham & Trotman for the Commission of the European Communities, 1986.
144p; 22cm.
ISBN 0860108066 £21.00

—State of the environment in the European Community, 1986 / Commission of the European Communities, Directorate-General Environment, Consumer Protection and Nuclear Safety. - Luxembourg : Commission of the European Communities, 1987.
xvi,370p.
ISBN 928256973X

POLLUTION - FRANCE

—Law and practice relating to pollution control in France / William Coulet, Claude Albert Colliard. - 2nd ed. - London : Graham & Trotman for the Commission of the European Communities, 1982.
xxvii,150p; 23cm.
Previous ed.: / by Claude-Albert Colliard. 1976. Bibliography: p141-144. - Includes index.
ISBN 0860103072 £21.00

POLLUTION - GREAT BRITAIN

—Agriculture and pollution : the government response to the seventh report of the Royal Commission on Environmental Pollution / Great Britain. - London : H.M.S.O., 1983.
ISBN 0117500216

—Control of pollution encyclopaedia / editor J.F. Garner : assistant editor D.J. Harris. - n v. - London : Butterworth, 1977-.
26cm.
Tab indexed. Includes index.
ISBN 0406205086 £33.00

—Controlling pollution : principles and prospects : the government's response to the tenth report of the Royal Commission on Environmental Pollution / Great Britain. - London : H.M.S.O., 1984.
vii,35p.
ISBN 0117517585

—Lead in the environment : the government response to the ninth report of the Royal Commission on Environmental Pollution / Great Britain. - London : H.M.S.O., 1983.
v,19p.
ISBN 0117517143

—Managing waste : the duty of care : the Government's response to the eleventh report of the Royal Commission on Environmental Pollution / Central Directorate of Environmental Protection, Department of the Environment. - London : H.M.S.O., 1986.
ISBN 0117518999

—Ninth report : lead in the environment / Royal Commission on Environmental Pollution : Chairman T.R.E. Southwood. - London : H.M.S.O., 1983.
x,183p; 25cm.
Includes index.
ISBN 0101885202 Pbk £9.20

—Tenth report : tackling pollution : experience and prospects / Royal Commission on Environmental Pollution : Chairman: Sir Richard Southwood. - London : H.M.S.O., 1984.
ISBN 0101914903

POLLUTION - GREECE

—Law and practice relating to pollution control in Greece / prepared by J. Timagenis, B Pavlopoulos for Environmental Resources Limited. - 2nd ed. - London : Graham & Trotman for the Commission of the European Communities, 1982.
200p.
Previous ed.: 1976. Bibliography: p139-140. - Includes index.
ISBN 0860103145 £18.00

POLLUTION - INDIA

—Handbook on Pollution Laws / Allahabad : Law Publishers, 1983.

—Water (Prevention and Control of Pollution) Act, 1974 / 1982 repr. - Lucknow : Eastern Book Company, 1984.
147p.

POLLUTION - IRELAND

—Law and practice relating to pollution control in Ireland / prepared by Yvonne Scannell for Environmental Resources Limited. - 2nd ed. - London : Graham & Trotman for the Commission of the European Communities, 1982.
xxix,215p; 22cm.
Previous ed. : 1976. Includes index.
ISBN 0860103137 £18.00

—Law relating to transport of dangerous wastes : Ireland / Shankill, Co. Dublin : European Foundation for the Improvement of Living and Working Conditions, 1987.
vii,58p. - (Research report).
ISBN 9282567605

POLLUTION - ITALY

—Law and practice relating to pollution control in Italy / U. Ruffolo, P. Dell'Anno. - 2nd ed. - London : Published by Graham & Trotman for the Commission of the European Communities, 1982.
200p.
Previous ed: / by P. Dell'Anno. 1976. Bibliography: p197-201. - Includes index.
ISBN 0860103099 £18.00

POLLUTION - LUXEMBOURG

—Law and practice relating to pollution control in Belgium and Luxembourg / Dirk Soetemans. - 2nd ed. - London : Graham & Trotman for the Commission of the European Communities, 1982.
200p.
Previous ed: /by J.M. Didier and Associates for Environmental Resources Limited. 1976. Includes index.
ISBN 0860103102 £18.00

POLLUTION - NETHERLANDS

—Law and practice relating to pollution control in the Netherlands / J. J. de Graeff. - 2nd ed. - London : Graham & Trotman for the Commission of the European Communities, 1982.
200p.
Previous ed: / by J.J. de Graeff and J.M. Polack i.e. Polak for Environmental Resources Limited. 1976. Includes index.
ISBN 0860103110 £18.00

POLLUTION - SCOTLAND

—Air, noise, water and waste : a summary of the law in Scotland / by Francil Lyall. - Glasgow : Planning Exchange, 1982.
vii,195p; 21cm.
Includes index.
ISBN 0905011198 Pbk Unpriced

POLLUTION - WEST GERMANY

—Law and practice relating to pollution control in the Federal Republic of Germany / Heinhard Steiger. - 2nd ed. - London : Graham & Trotman for the Commission of the European Communities, 1982.
xxvii,308p; 23cm.
Previous ed.: 1976 / by Heinhard Steiger and Otto Kimminich. Bibliography: p301-302. Includes index.
ISBN 0860103080 £21.00

POLYGAMY

—Private international law : polygamous marriages : capacity to contract a polygamous marriage and related issues / the Law Commission and Scottish Law Commission. - London : H.M.S.O., 1985.
v,65p.
ISBN 0101959508

POLYGAMY - GREAT BRITAIN

—Polygamous marriages : capacity to contract a polygamous marriage and the concept of the potentially polygamous marriage / The Law Commission and The Scottish Law Commission. - London : H.M.S.O., 1982.
vii,126p; 21cm. - (Consultative memorandum).
ISBN 0117301639

POOR - ENGLAND

—Old Poor Law, 1795-1834 / prepared for the Economic History Society by J.D. Marshall. - 2nd ed. - Basingstoke : Macmillan, 1985.
57p; 22cm.
Previous ed.: 1968. Bibliography: p51-54. - Includes index.
ISBN 0333398807 Pbk £3.95

POOR - GREAT BRITAIN

—Government and urban poverty : inside the policy-making process / Joan Higgins ... et al. - Oxford : Blackwell, 1983.
vi,215p; 22cm.
Bibliography: p202-206. - Includes index.
ISBN 0631129375 Hbk Unpriced
ISBN 063113252X Pbk £5.95

POPISH PLOT, 1678

—Killing of Justice Godfrey : an investigation into England's most remarkable unsolved murder / Stephen Knight. - London : Granada, 1984.
280p,8p of plates; 24cm.
Bibliography: p259-270. - Includes index.
ISBN 0246123516 £10.95

POPULAR ACTIONS - AUSTRALIA

—Standing in public interest litigation / Law Reform Commission. - Canberra : Australian Government Publishing Service, 1985.
xxx,273p. - (Report).
Bibliography: p.259-263 - Includes index.
ISBN 0644013109

POPULATION

—Partial Revision of the Indigenous and Tribal Populations Convention, 1957 (No. 107) / Geneva : International Labour Office, 1988.
iv, 127p.
ISBN 9221060225 Hbk £20.00

POPULATION - INDIA

—Population and Law in India / New Delhi : S. Chand and Company.

POPULATION - LESOTHO

—Law and population growth in Lesotho / Sebastian Poulter...et al. - Roma, Lesotho : Law and Population Project, Faculty of Law, National University of Lesotho, 1981.
96p.

POPULATION - PACIFIC ISLANDS

—Family Law and Population in the Pacific Islands / Suva : University of the South Pacific, Institute of Pacific Studies.

POSSESSION - ENGLAND

—Claims to the possession of land : the law and practice / by Philip Walter and James Harris. - London : Fourmat, 1987.
xlvii,616p; 26cm.
ISBN 1851900004

POSSESSION - GREAT BRITAIN

—Defending Possession Proceedings (LA) / Madge. - London : Sweet & Maxwell, 1987.
ISBN 090509915X Pbk £14.00

—Law of Interdict / London : Butterworths, 1987.
ISBN 040610445X Pbk £17.00

POSTAL SERVICE - CANADA

—Postal Security and Mail Opening : a Review of the Law / Toronto : University of Toronto, Centre of Criminology, 1981.
vi, 233p.
ISBN 0919584527 Pbk £8.00

—Report of the Commission of Inquiry Relating to the Security and Investigation Services Branch Within the Post Office Department / Rene Marin. - Hull, Quebec : Canadian Government Publishing Centre, 1981.
iv,338p.
Commissioner: Rene J. Marin.
ISBN 0660108585

POSTAL SERVICE - GREAT BRITAIN

—Interception of communications in Great Britain / Home Office. - London : H.M.S.O., 1980.
8p.

—Interception of communications in Great Britain : report / by Lord Diplock. - London : H.M.S.O., 1981.
7p; 25cm.
ISBN 0101819102 unbound £1.10

POVERTY

—Creation of world poverty / Teresa Hayter. - London : Pluto Press, 1981.
128p.
Bibliography: p.124-127.
ISBN 0861043391

POVERTY - CANADA

—Economics of Poverty and Income Distribution / Toronto : Butterworths.
192p.
ISBN 0409834750 Hbk

POVERTY - EUROPEAN COMMUNITY

—Anti-Poverty Policy in the European Community / London : Policy Studies Institute, 1984.
271p. - (Conference Papers).

POVERTY - GREAT BRITAIN

—Credit Debt and Poverty / London : Policy Studies Institute, 1988.
ISBN 0853743479 Pbk £8.95

—Dwelling on the threshold / London : Sweet & Maxwell, 1988.
ISBN 0459305611 Hbk £32.00

—Education and Poverty in the United Kingdom : A Background Paper / London : Policy Studies Institute, 1981.

—Low Pay and Poverty in the United Kingdom / London : Policy Studies Institute, 1981.

—Poverty and Policy in the United Kingdom : A Classified Bibliography / London : Policy Studies Institute, 1980.

—Rural Poverty in the United Kingdom / London : Policy Studies Institute, 1981.

POWER OF ATTORNEY - AUSTRALIA

—Community law reform for the Australian Capital Territory : enduring powers of attorney / The Law Reform Commission. - Sydney : The Commission, 1987.
i,13p. - (Discussion paper).

POWER OF ATTORNEY - AUSTRALIA - SOUTH AUSTRALIA

—Report ... relating to powers of attorney / Law Reform Committee of South Australia. - Adelaide : Government Printer, 1981.
17p. - (47th report).

POWER OF ATTORNEY - AUSTRALIA - TASMANIA

—Report on powers of attorney / Law Reform Commission of Tasmania. - Hobart : Government Printer, 1984.
21p. - (Report v no 39).

POWER OF ATTORNEY - CANADA

—Working paper on powers of attorney / Newfoundland Law Reform Commission. - St. John's : The Commission, 1987.
iv,64p.
Includes bibliographical references.

POWER OF ATTORNEY - GREAT BRITAIN

—Incapacitated principal : report on a reference under section 3(1)(e) of the Law Commissions Act 1965 / the Law Commission. - London : H.M.S.O., 1983.
v,104p; 25cm.
ISBN 0101897707

—Powers of Attorney / 5th ed. - London : Oyez Longman, 1981.
- (Oyez Longman Practice Note Ser.: No. 7).
ISBN 0851205798 Hbk £8.95

—Powers of Attorney (LPPN 7) / 6th ed. - London : Longman Professional, 1986.
ISBN 0851210457 Pbk £19.95

POWER OF ATTORNEY - INDIA

—Powers-of-Attorney Act / 2nd ed. - Allahabad : Law Book Company, 1988.
94p.

POWER OF ATTORNEY - MALAYSIA

—Powers of Attorney Ordinance, 1949 (No. 64/1949) and Wills Ordinance, 1959 (No. 38/1959) / Kuala Lumpur : International Law Books Services.

POWER (SOCIAL SCIENCES)

—Authority and power : studies on medieval law and government presented to Walter Ullmann on his seventieth birthday / edited by Brian Tierney and Peter Linehan. - Cambridge : Cambridge University Press, 1980.
x,274p,1leaf of plates; 24cm.
Bibliography: p255-274.
ISBN 0521222753 £25.00

—Misuse of power : the Richard Dimbleby lecture, November 1980 / Lord Denning. - London : British Broadcasting Corporation, 1980.
19p; 21cm. - (The Richard Dimbleby lectures).
ISBN 0563178949 Pbk £1.50

POWERS (LAW) - NEW ZEALAND

—Second report on trustee's powers of investment : miscellaneous powers / Wellington? : the Committee?, 1984.
10,14,2,4p.

PRACTICE AND PROCEDURE

—Cases and Materials on Code of Civil Procedure / B. Nath. - 3rd rev. ed. - Lucknow : Eastern Book Company, 1981.
1,717p.

—Civil Procedure Simplified / R.A. Meagher. - Butterworths, 1983.
336p.
Outline of civil procedure rules and practice. Covers originating and interlocutory applications in chambers, the conduct of actions during the retainer, pleading, discovery, application and trial stages, the subsequent appeal and enforcement of the judgement, and the drafting of court forms. Also looks at the status of more than 13 types of person subject to examination for discovery.
ISBN 0409848786 Hbk £50.00

—Rules of the Supreme Court (Northern Ireland) 1980 / Northern Ireland. - Belfast : HMSO, 1980.
looseleaf.

PRACTICE AND PROCEDURE - AUSTRALIA

—Australian civil procedure / Bernard C. Cairns. - 2nd ed. - Sydney : Law Book Company, 1985.
lxvi,584p.
ISBN 0455206260

—Litigation : Evidence and Procedure / 4th ed. - Butterworths, 1988.
1,108p.
ISBN 0409495077 Hbk £60.00

—Queensland Supreme Court Practice / Butterworths, 1984.
ISBN 0409493015 Hbk £235.00

—Supreme Court Civil Procedure / Butterworths, 1987.
442p.
ISBN 0409492183 Hbk £59.00
ISBN 0409492078 Pbk £39.00

PRACTICE AND PROCEDURE – AUSTRALIA – NEW SOUTH WALES

—Criminal procedure report : the jury in a criminal trial / New South Wales Law Reform Commission. – Sydney : The Commission, 1986.
xxxi,203p. – (L.R.C. 48).
Includes bibliographical references.
ISBN 073051546X Hbk

—Criminal procedure research report : the jury in a criminal trial : empirical studies / Sydney : Law Reform Commission of New South Wales, 1986.
xii,ii,164p. – (RR).
ISBN 0730524477

PRACTICE AND PROCEDURE – AUSTRALIA – QUEENSLAND

—Law and Practice of the District Courts of Queensland / 2nd ed. – Butterworths, 1983.
608p.
ISBN 040949240X Hbk £102.00

—Report of the Law Reform Commission on a bill to consolidate, amend and reform the Supreme Court Acts and ancillary acts regulating civil proceedings in the Supreme Court / Brisbane? : the Commission?, 1982.
159p. – (Q.L.R.C.).

—Working paper on a bill to consolidate, amend and reform the Supreme Court acts and ancillary acts regulating civil proceedings in the Supreme Court / Queensland Law Reform Commission. – Brisbane : The Commission, 1982.
142p. – (Q.L.R.C.W.P.).

PRACTICE AND PROCEDURE – AUSTRALIA – SOUTH AUSTRALIA

—Civil Procedure, South Australia / Butterworths, 1987.
ISBN 0409492396 loose £235.00

—Report ... on the inherited imperial statute law with regard to proceedings in summary jurisdiction / Law Reform Committee of South Australia. – Adelaide : Government Printer, 1981.
16p. – (58th report).

PRACTICE AND PROCEDURE – AUSTRALIA – VICTORIA

—Civil Procedure, Victoria / Butterworths.

—Supreme court rules : guide to time limits, civil proceedings / Melbourne : Law Institute of Victoria, 1983.
31p.
'Supplement to August 1983 Law Institute journal'.

—Victoria Civil Procedure / North Ryde : C.C.H. Australia, 1987.
1,200p.
ISBN 0869039326 Hbk

PRACTICE AND PROCEDURE – CANADA

—Advocacy : views from the bench / Robert F. Reid and Richard E. Holland. – Aurora, Ont. : Canada Law Book, 1984.
xii,164p.
Includes index.
ISBN 0888040245

—Canadian Civil Procedure : Cases and Materials / 3rd ed. – Toronto : Edmond-Montgomery, 1988.
925p.
ISBN 0920722245 Hbk £94.00

—Cases and materials on civil procedure / by James A. Woods. – Toronto : Carswell, 1987.
xviii,838p.
ISBN 0459306618

—Criminal Law Evidence, Practice and Procedure / Agincourt : Carswell, 1988.
606p.

—Federal Court Practice 1988 / Agincourt : Carswell, 1987.
858p.

—Federal Court Practice : 1988 / Agincourt : Carswell, 1987.
800p.
This is a comprehensive guide to the Federal Court Act, Federal Court Rules, Forms, Tariffs and related statutes. Also included is a guide to difficult jurisdictional issues such as the choice between Federal and provincial courts for commencing proceedings and locus standi.

—Fraser and Horn : Conduct of Civil Litigation in British Columbia, 3 vols / Peter Horn. – Toronto : Butterworths.

—Practice and Advocacy in the Supreme Court of Canada / Vancouver : British Columbia Continuing Legal Education Society, 1983.
463p.
ISBN 0865041180 Hbk £65.00

—Practice and Procedure in the Federal Court of Canada / Vancouver : British Columbia Continuing Legal Education Society, 1984.
493p.
ISBN 0865041725 Hbk £75.00

—Practice and Procedure in the Federal Court of Canada / Vancouver : Continuing Legal Education Society of British Columbia, 1984.
493p.
ISBN 0865041784 Hbk £75.00

—Practice Before the Register - 1984 / Vancouver : British Columbia Continuing Legal Education Society, 1984.
203p.
ISBN 0865041725 Hbk £55.00

—Psycholinguistic Principles Applicable to the Formulation of Jury Instructions : an Annotated Bibliography / Ottawa : Canadian Law Information Council, 1985.
60p.
ISBN 0920358853 Pbk £5.00

—Small Claims Court Practice and Procedure / Vancouver : Continuing Legal Education Society of British Columbia, 1988.
434p.
ISBN 0865049718 Hbk £85.00

—Supreme Court of Canada Practice and Advocacy / Vancouver : Continuing Legal Education Society of British Columbia, 1987.
297p.
ISBN 0865043310 Hbk £85.00

—Trial Practice / Vancouver : Continuing Legal Education Society of British Columbia, 1987.
180p.
ISBN 0865043205 Hbk £65.00

PRACTICE AND PROCEDURE – CANADA – BRITISH COLUMBIA

—British Columbia Annual Practice 1988 / Gordon Turriff. – Aurora : Canada Law Book Co.

—Fraser and Horn : Conduct of Civil Litigation in British Columbia, 3 Vols. / John Horn. – Butterworths.

—McLachlin and Taylor : British Columbia Practice, 3 vols / James P. Taylor. – 2nd ed. – Toronto : Butterworths.

—Practice and Procedure in the Supreme Court of British Columbia / Vancouver : British Columbia Continuing Legal Education Society, 1982.
167p.
ISBN 0865040559 Hbk £17.50

—Practice Before the Registrar in British Columbia / Vancouver : British Columbia Continuing Legal Education Society, 1982.
199p.
ISBN 0865040427 Hbk £40.00

PRACTICE AND PROCEDURE – CANADA – NOVA SCOTIA

—Nova Scotia Annotated Rules of Practice / Agincourt : Carswell.
This single volume looseleaf is arranged in eight sections and is published in cooperation with the Law Foundation of Nova Scotia. It consists of a Table of Contents, Judicature Act, Rules of Practice, Forms, Practice Memoranda, Index to Rules, and Index to Forms.

—Nova Scotia civil procedure rules and related rules / made by the Judges of the Supreme Court of Nova Scotia on 2nd December 1971. To come into force on 1st March 1972. – 1. – Halifax, Nova Scotia : Queen's Printer, 1971.
looseleaf.
Includes index.

PRACTICE AND PROCEDURE – CANADA – ONTARIO

—Ontario Annual Practice (O.A.P) / W. A. Derry Miller. – Aurora : Canada Law Book Co, 1985.
This 1987-88 edition of Ontario Annual Practice provides a revised publication up-to-date on the Rules of Practice as well as all significant cases on the Rules of the past 30 years.

—Ontario Civil Procedure, 3 Vols. / Agincourt : Carswell.
This two volume set provides complete textual analysis on practice and procedure topics arising under the Ontario, Canada Rules of Civil Procedure and Courts of Justice Act. Annotated cases relevant to the Ontario Rules and comparisons to rules in other provinces are included in the work.

—Ontario Judicature Act and Rules of Practice, 4 Vols. / G. A. Gale. – Agincourt ; Carswell, 1980.

—Ontario Legal Practice Manual, 2 Vols. / Adeline Y. Harrison. – Toronto : DeBoo.
This manual of practice and procedure for practitioners, law secretaries, law clerks, and students covers such areas as family law, federal and provincial corporate law, and Provincial Court (Civil Division). Six updates per year are provided, as well as a newsletter which analyzes recent civil procedure case law.
ISBN 0888201974 loose £300.00

—Ontario Supreme and District Court Practice 1988 / M. McGowan. – Agincourt : Carswell, 1987.
1106p.

—Ontario Supreme and District Court Practice 1989 / Michael M. McGowan. – Agincourt : Carswell, 1988.
1,192p.

—Ontario Supreme and District Court Practice 1989 / Michael McGowan. – Agincourt : Carswell, 1988.
1,188p.

PRACTICE AND PROCEDURE – COMMONWEALTH

—Civil procedure including courts and evidence / J. M. Jacob. – 1. – London : Butterworths, 1966.
various pagings.
Photocopies of articles from Annual survey of Commonwealth Law 1965-1977 bound together in one volume. Includes bibliographical references. 1972 article onwards by I.H. Jacob and J.M. Jacob. 1976 and 1977 articles entitled: Civil procedure including courts.

PRACTICE AND PROCEDURE – ENGLAND

—Advocacy at the Bar : a beginner's guide / written and illustrated by Keith Evans. – London : Financial Training, 1983.
ix,201p.
ISBN 0906322235

—Chitty and Jacob's Queen's Bench forms / Jack I. H. Jacob. – 21st ed. – London : Sweet & Maxwell, 1986.
xlv,1709p; 26cm.
Includes the appropriate forms other than pleadings, which may be used at any stage in the course of litigation undertaken in the Queen's Bench Division. Each chapter begins with a general note describing the relevant procedures in their operational context. Cross-referenced to 'The Supreme Court Practice'.
ISBN 0421206004 £98.00

—Civil actions against the police / by Richard Clayton and Hugh Tomlinson. – London : Sweet & Maxwell, 1987.
250p; 25cm.
Examines the rights and remedies of the individual against police misconduct. Covers traditional tort actions, assault, false imprisonment, trespass, interference with goods, and malicious prosecution. Emphasis on recent developments, and focuses on the circumstances that may lead to claims. Also contains discussion on civil liability under the Police and Criminal Evidence Act 1984.
ISBN 0421344202 £30.00

—Civil justice quarterly / London : Sweet & Maxwell in association with the Institute of Judicial Administration at the University of Birmingham, 1982-.
25cm.

—Civil justice review / Lord Chancellor's Department. – London : The Department, 1987.
109 leaves.

—Civil justice review / report of the Review Body on Civil Justice. – London : H.M.S.O., 1988.
x,181p.
Presented to Parliament by the Lord High Chancellor by Command of Her Majesty, June 1988.
ISBN 0101039425

—Civil justice review : consultation paper no. 6 : general issues / response by JUSTICE. – London : JUSTICE, 1987.
19p.

—Civil litigation / John O'Hare, Robert N. Hill. – 4th ed. – London : Longman, 1986.
xxvi,507p; 24cm.
Previous ed.: Oyez Longman, 1985. Includes index.
ISBN 0851212220 Pbk £15.95

—Civil litigation / John O'Hare, Robert N. Hill. – 2nd ed. – London : Oyez Longman, 1983.
xxii,429p.
ISBN 0851206883

—Civil procedure / L. D. J. Henderson. – 3rd ed. – London : Sweet & Maxwell, 1983.
xlvii,448p; 23cm.
Previous ed.: 1976. Includes index.
ISBN 0421289104 Hbk Unpriced
ISBN 0421289201 Pbk £9.45

—County Courts Districts (England and Wales) Index of Place Names / 12th ed. – London : HMSO, 1983.
ISBN 0113906315 Hbk £20.00

—Fabric of English civil justice / by Sir Jack I.H. Jacob. – London : Stevens, 1987.
100p; 18cm.
Includes index.
ISBN 0420475303 Hbk £14.50
ISBN 0420475400 Pbk £8.00

—Modern developments in the law of civic procedure / by D.B. Casson and I.H. Dennis. – London : Sweet & Maxwell, 1982.
xxv,112p; 22cm.
Includes index.
ISBN 0421290005 Pbk £4.95

—Odgers' principles of pleading and practice in civil actions in the High Court of Justice / D. B. Casson, I. H. Dennis. – 22nd ed. – London : Stevens, 1981.
lix,565p; 22cm.
Previous ed.: 1975. Includes index.
ISBN 0420457100 Pbk £13.50

—Outline of English civil procedure / by Sir Jack Jacob. – s.l. : Jack Jacob, 1984.
44p in various pagings.
'Prepared for lectures for delivery at the Faculty of Law of the Universities of Florence, Sienna, Milan, Pavia, Rome and Macerata, April 1984.'.

—Practice of the Court of King's Bench and Common Pleas in Personal Actions and Ejectments, 2 Vols. / 6th ed. Repr. of 1824 ed. - Abingdon : Professional Books.
279p.

—Reform of civil procedural law and other procedure / Sir Jack I.H. Jacob. - London : Sweet & Maxwell, 1982.
xii,359p; 26cm.
ISBN 0421301104 £18.50

—Report / Lord Justice Watkins's Working Party on the Criminal Trial. - London : Lord Chancellor's Department, 1982.
23p.

—Report of the Review Body on the Chancery Division of the High Court / presented to Parliament by the Lord High Chancellor. - London : H.M.S.O., 1981.
v,115p; 25cm.
Chairman: Lord Justice Oliver.
ISBN 010182050X

—Supreme Court practice / v. - London : Sweet & Maxwell, 1966-.
Continues: The annual practice. Includes index. Kept up to date by supplements.

PRACTICE AND PROCEDURE - EUROPE

—Manual of European Practice / A. Layton. - London : Sweet & Maxwell, 1986.
Explains English procedure and practice as they apply to cross-border litigation in the light of the 1982 Civil Jurisdiction and Judgements Act. Gives a comparative description of the legal systems of Belgium, Denmark, France, Germany, Ireland, Italy, Luxembourg, the Netherlands, England and Wales, Scotland and Northern Ireland.
ISBN 0421262907 Hbk

Vol. 2
ISBN 0421263008 Hbk

—Manual of European Practice / Layton. - London : Sweet & Maxwell, 1988.
ISBN 0421262907 Hbk

PRACTICE AND PROCEDURE - GREAT BRITAIN

—Atkin's encyclopaedia of court forms in civil proceedings : a user's guide / James Richard Atkin Atkin. - 2nd ed. - London : Butterworths, 1983.
24p; 25cm.

—Butterworth's County Court Precedents and Pleadings / A. V. B. Bartlett. - London : Butterworths.

—Chancery practice handbook / Robert Blackford in collaboration with Colin Jaque : additional material by Richard Archdale. - London : Oyez Longman, 1983.
xx,252p; 24cm.
Includes bibliographies and index.
ISBN 0851207456 £16.50

—County Court Practice : 1984 / London : Butterworths, 1984.

—County Court Practice / Butterworths. - London : Butterworths, 1988.
ISBN 0406163243 Hbk £80.00

—County Court Practice / Butterworth Staff. - London : Butterworths, 1983.
ISBN 0406163162 Hbk £172.50

—County Court Practice and Procedure / 3rd ed. - London : Fourmat, 1984.
ISBN 0906840805 Pbk £10.95

—County Court Practice and Procedure / 3rd ed. - London : Fourmat, 1984.
160p.
ISBN 0906840805 Pbk £10.95

—County Court Practice Handbook / Price. - 8th ed. - London : Longman Professional, 1987.
ISBN 085121147X Pbk £17.95

—Court of Protection Practice / Massey. - 11th ed. - London : Sweet & Maxwell, 1985.
ISBN 0420469206 Hbk £80.00

—Emergency Applications to Magistrates / Whale. - London : Fourmat, 1986.
ISBN 1851900012 Pbk £12.95

—Emergency Applications to Magistrates / London : Fourmat, 1986.
ISBN 1851900012 Pbk £13.00

—Emergency Procedures Handbook / London : Legal Action Group, 1986.
ISBN 0905099109 Pbk

—Evidence and Procedure in Magistrates Courts / Knapp. - 2nd ed. - London : Longman Professional, 1985.
ISBN 0851208681 Pbk £19.95

—Evidence and Procedure in Magistrates' Courts / Stephen Knapp. - London : Oyez Longman, 1982.
- (Oyez Longman Practitioner Ser.).
ISBN 0851202926 Hbk £12.95

—Law and Procedure / Alan Willis. - London : Butterworths, 1987.
ISBN 0406104816 Pbk

—Law as Process : An Anthropological Approach / London : Sweet & Maxwell, 1983.
ISBN 0710200218 Pbk £6.95

—Litigation - Evidence and Procedure / Reaburn. - 3rd ed. - London : Butterworths, 1982.
ISBN 0409307947 Pbk £40.00

—Notes on County Court Practice and Procedure / David Price. - 6th ed. - London : Oyez Longman, 1982.
- (Oyez Longman Practitioner Ser.).
ISBN 0851206301 Hbk £9.95

—Oke's Magisterial Formulist / London : Shaw & Sons.
This looseleaf service provides immediate access to all prescribed forms rel of completed forms and draft leare included.
ISBN 0406326118 Hbk

—Petition procedure in the Court of Session / Norman Dowrie. - 2nd. - Edinburgh : W Green & Son, 1988.
Enlarged version of the first edition, substantially rewritten In the light of the considerable changes in Court of Session practice, particularly in the areas of family law, insolvency and judicial review. Provides a step by step approach to all the types of petition encountered in practice with descriptions of the miscellaneous procedures including appeals. New chapters deal with adoptions, children and applications under the Matrimonial Homes Act.
ISBN 0414008316

—Practice and Procedure in Magistrates' Courts / London : Fourmat, 1982.
186p.
ISBN 0906840503 Pbk £8.95

—Practice and procedure in Magistrates' Courts / 2nd ed. - London : Fourmat, 1986.
ISBN 1851900136 Pbk £12.95

—Practice and Procedure of the Supreme Court, Court of Appeal and High Courts of Nigeria / London : Sweet & Maxwell, 1980.
- (Nigerian Practice Library).
ISBN 0421255706 Hbk £95.00

—Practice of the Superior Courts of Common Law / Repr. of 1850 ed. - Abingdon : Professional Books.

—Practice, Procedure and Sentencing in the Magistrates' Courts / Chichester : Barry Rose, 1986.
543p.
ISBN 0859923606 Hbk £65.00

—Principles of pleading and practice in civil actions / Casson. - 22nd ed. - London : Sweet & Maxwell, 1981.
ISBN 0420457100 Pbk £17.50

—Recovery of interest, practice and precedents / London : Butterworths, 1985.
ISBN 0406261407 Pbk £27.95

—Recovery of Interest : Practice and Precedents / London : Butterworths, 1985.

—Sheriff Court practice / Edinburgh : W Green & Son, 1988.
Explains modern statutory rules of proceedure and the principles and practices which regulate the conduct of civil litigation in the Sheriff Court. Covers drafting and amendment of written pleadings, interim orders, debates, proofs and appeals. Covers the practice and procedure in summary causes and the legislation conferring powers and duties on the Sheriff Court.
ISBN 0414008251 Hbk

—Supreme Court Practice and Procedure / 4th ed. - London : Fourmat, 1987.
ISBN 1851900365 Pbk £12.95

—Supreme Court Practice and Procedure / 3rd ed. - London : Fourmat, 1984.
142p.
ISBN 0906840775 Pbk £8.95

—Technique of advocacy / by John H. Munkman. - London : Sweet & Maxwell, 1986.
xiv,173p.
Originally published: London: Stevens, 1951. Includes bibliographical references.
ISBN 0421361700

—White Books, 2 Vols. / London : Sweet & Maxwell, 1984.
ISBN 0421302801 Hbk £150.00

PRACTICE AND PROCEDURE - INDIA

—Civil Courts Practice and Procedure / Delhi : Vinod Prakashan, 1986.

—Civil Procedure / Lucknow : Eastern Book Company, 1983.
570p.

—Civil Procedure Code / 2nd ed. - Allahabad : Law Publishers, 1982.

—Code of Civil Procedure / 3rd ed. - Calcutta : Eastern Law House, 1986.

—Code of Civil Procedure in 3 Vols / 5th ed. - Allahabad : Law Book Company, 1982-84.

—Supreme Court Practice and Procedure / 4th ed. - Lucknow : Eastern Book Company, 1985.
550p.

PRACTICE AND PROCEDURE - MALAYSIA

—Civil Court Practice / 3rd ed. - Allahabad : Law Book Company, 1986.
1,100p.

—Introduction to civil procedure in Malaysia and Singapore / by Grace Chang. - Singapore : Malayan Law Journal Pte., 1986.
iii,165p.
Includes index.
ISBN 997170045X

—Rules of the High Court 1980 / Kuala Lumpur : Government Printer, 1980.
453p. - (P.U. (A)).

PRACTICE AND PROCEDURE - NEW ZEALAND

—County Court Practice 1983 / D. E. Peck. - Wellington : Butterworths, 1983.
ISBN 0406163162 Hbk

—District Court Practice / J. S. Crutchley. - 8th ed. - Wellington : Butterworths, 1981.
ISBN 0409600466 Hbk

—Practice and Procedure of the High Court and Court of Appeal in New Zealand / 12th ed. - Butterworths.
ISBN 0409667617 loose £264.00

—Practice and procedure of the High Court in New Zealand / Cain. - London : Butterworths, 1981.
ISBN 0409667617 loose £125.00

PRACTICE AND PROCEDURE - NIGERIA

—Civil proceedings by and against the State in Nigeria / by F. Olisa Awogu. - Onitsha : Pacific College Press, 1981.
x,167p.
Includes index.

—Essays on civil proceedings / by A. Obi-Okoye. - Enugu, Nigeria : Fourth Dimension Publishing, 1980.
83p.
ISBN 978156119X Hbk

Vol. 4 / by A. Obi-Okoye. - 1980.
155p.
ISBN 9781561203 Hbk

—Practice and procedure of the High Courts, Nigeria / Sweet & Maxwell, 1980.
ISBN 0421255706 Hbk £99.00

PRACTICE AND PROCEDURE - NORTHERN IRELAND

—Access to justice and civil litigation in Northern Ireland : report of a conference organised by SLS Legal Publications (NI) and the Northern Ireland Consumer Council held in the Queen's University of Belfast on 29 March 1985 / Belfast : SLS Legal Publications, 1985.
ii,76p.

—Civil proceedings in a beleaguered society : a public lecture / delivered by Lord Lowry on ... 17th March 1987. - London : Inns of Court School of Law, 1987.
23p.

—County Court Rules (Northern Ireland) / Consolidated ed. - Belfast : HMSO, 1987-.
looseleaf.
First published 1981.

—Revised Notes on Procedure by Originating Summons and In Actions By Mortgages / Belfast : Queen's University of Belfast.
35p.

PRACTICE AND PROCEDURE - SCOTLAND

—Evidence : report on corroboration, hearsay and related matters in civil proceedings / Scottish Law Commission. - Edinburgh : H.M.S.O., 1986.
vi,63p.
Includes bibliographical references.
ISBN 010237886X

—Introduction to ordinary civil procedure in the sheriff court / Brian Kearney. - Edinburgh : Law Society of Scotland, 1982.
xvi,233,1p.
Bibliography: p.233-234.
ISBN 0902023071

—Petition procedure in the Court of Session / by William W. McBryde and Norman J. Dowie. - Edinburgh : W. Green, 1980.
xvii,94p; 22cm.
Includes index.
ISBN 0414006631 Pbk £7.00

—Practice and procedure in Sheriff Court / London : Fourmat, 1988.
ISBN 1851900373 Pbk £12.95

PRACTICE AND PROCEDURE - SINGAPORE

—Introduction to civil procedure in Malaysia and Singapore / by Grace Chang. – Singapore : Malayan Law Journal Pte., 1986.
iii,165p.
Includes index.
ISBN 997170045X

—Mallal's Supreme Court Practice, Vol 1 / Min Tat Chang. – 2nd ed. – Singapore : Malayan Law Journal, 1983.
1,368p.
ISBN 9971700344 Hbk £500.00

Supplement Vol. 1 1986.
52p.
ISBN 9971700441 Pbk £15.00

PRACTICE AND PROCEDURE - SOUTH AFRICA

—Technique in litigation / Eric Morris. – 3rd ed. – Cape Town : Juta, 1985.
xxxiii, 373 p.; 26 cm.
Includes bibliographical references and index.
ISBN 0702115525 pbk.

PRACTICE AND PROCEDURE - UNITED STATES

—Reconstructing reality in the courtroom / W. Lance Bennett and Martha S. Feldman. – London : Tavistock Publications, 1981.
x, 203p.

PRACTICE AND PROCEDURE - WALES

—County Courts Districts (England and Wales) Index of Place Names / 12th ed. – London : HMSO, 1983.
ISBN 0113906315 Hbk £20.00

—Welsh language in the courts / by J.A. Andrews and L.G. Henshaw. – Aberystwyth : University College of Wales, 1984.
ix,116p.
Includes index. With Welsh version of the oaths.

PRACTICE OF LAW

—Art of the advocate / Richard Du Cann. – 1st ed. reprinted with revisions. – Harmondsworth : Penguin, 1980.
186p; 18cm. – (A pelican original).
Originally published : 1964. .
ISBN 0140206655 Pbk £1.50

—Challenges to the legal profession : law and investment in developing countries : addresses, committee papers and reports of the 19th biennial conference of the International Bar Association at New Delhi / International Bar Association. – Lucknow : Eastern Book Co. in co-ordination with the International Bar Association and the Bar Association of India, 1984.
xx,787p.

—Cross examination in criminal trials / Marcus Stone. – London : Butterworths, 1988.
xix,224p.
Includes index.
ISBN 0406105057 No price (Oct.)

—Journal of professional legal education / Sydney, 1983-.
Index published every two years.

—Practice development for professional firms / Aubrey Wilson. – London : McGraw-Hill, 1984.
xvi,232p; 26cm.
Bibliography: p221-223. - Includes index.
ISBN 0070847614 £15.95

—Technique of persuasion / David Napley : with a foreword by Melford Stevenson. – 3rd ed. – London : Sweet & Maxwell, 1983.
xvi,187p; 18cm.
Follows the same pattern as previous editions, but includes a new section on the strategy and tactics of advocacy. Also considers topics such as preparation for trial, the ethics of advocacy, and presentation in court.
ISBN 0421252804 Hbk £14.00
ISBN 0421252901 Pbk £5.85

—Transnational legal practice : a survey of selected countries / edited by Dennis Campbell. – Deventer, The Netherlands : Kluwer, 1981.
Includes index.
ISBN 9065440186 v. 2

PRACTICE OF LAW - CANADA - ALBERTA

—McLachlin and Taylor : British Columbia Practice, 3 Vols. / James P. Taylor. – 2nd ed. – Butterworths.

PRACTICE OF LAW - COMMONWEALTH

—Admission of Commonwealth lawyers : a technical survey for Commonwealth Law Ministers and the Commonwealth Lawyers' Association / Campbell Alan McLachlan. – London : Commonwealth Secretariat, 1985.
x, 168p.

PRACTICE OF LAW - GREAT BRITAIN

—Code of conduct for the Bar of England and Wales : effective from 1st January 1981 / Senate of the Inns of Court and the Bar. – 2nd ed. Incorporating all amendments up to 31st December 1982. – London : The Senate, 1983.
76p.
Previous ed.: 1981. Includes index.

—Code of conduct for the Bar of England and Wales : effective from 1st January 1981 / Senate of the Inns of Court and the Bar. – 3rd ed. (incorporating all amendments up to 31st December 1984). – London : The Senate, 1985.
74p.
Includes index.

—Multidisciplinary partnerships and allied topics / The Law Society. – London : The Society, 1987.
11p.
Supplement to the Law Society's Gazette, (29 April 1987).

PRACTICE OF LAW - SOUTH AFRICA

—South African Attorneys handbook / Randell and Bax. – 3rd ed. – Durban : Butterworths, 1983.
xxv,345p.
Bibliography: p.xxv. - Includes index. Addendum (Appendix 9) as loose insert.
ISBN 0409050113

PRACTICE (PHILOSOPHY)

—Journal of applied philosophy : journal of the Society for Applied Philosophy / Abingdon : Carfax, 1984.

PRE-SENTENCE INVESTIGATION REPORTS - ENGLAND

—Who uses social inquiry reports? : a study of the use of social inquiry reports outside the courts and their influence upon decisions / Roger Shaw. – Cambridge : Institute of Criminology, 1981.
53p. – (Institute of Criminology occasional papers).
Includes bibliographical references.

PRE-TRIAL INTERVENTION

—Diversion of traffic offenders / by J.K. Canagarayar : with a foreword by J.W. Mohr. – Singapore : Malayan Law Journal, 1981.
xi,229p; 22cm.
Analyses the role of diversion, the directions it should take, its limitations, and whether there is a need to develop identifiable uniform principles and guidelines during the different stages of diversion. Contains examples of various experiments and pilot projects.
ISBN 9971700158 £12.50

PRE-TRIAL INTERVENTION - CANADA

—Pretrial diversion : an overview / by Sharon Moyer. – Ottawa : Solicitor General, Programs Branch, 1982.
12p.
ISBN 0662119177

PRE-TRIAL PROCEDURE - CANADA

—Fitness Interview Test : a Method for Examining Fitness to Stand Trial / Toronto : University of Toronto, Centre of Criminology, 1984.

—Mental disorder and the criminal trial process / Scarborough, Ontario : Butterworths (Canada), 1978.
368.
Focuses on legal problems and procedures peculiar to the use of psychiatric expertise at the pre-trial and trial stages. Fitness to stand trial, 'psychiatric defences', and the consequences of a determination of abnormality are discussed.
ISBN 0409865605 Hbk

PRE-TRIAL PROCEDURE - ENGLAND

—Remands in the absence of the accused / Chris May. – London : Home Office, 1985.
vii,31p.
ISBN 0862522153

PRE-TRIAL PROCEDURE - INDIA

—Law of Pre-Trial Statements, Depositions and Police Diaries / Y.R. Rao. – 2nd ed. – Nagpur : Wadhura & Co, 1987.
763p.

PRECEDENCE - ENGLAND

—Precedence in England and Wales / G.D. Squibb. – Oxford : Clarendon Press, 1981.
xviii,139p; 23cm.
Bibliography: p126-130. - Includes index.
ISBN 0198253893 £12.50

PRECEDENCE - WALES

—Precedence in England and Wales / G.D. Squibb. – Oxford : Clarendon Press, 1981.
xviii,139p; 23cm.
Bibliography: p126-130. - Includes index.
ISBN 0198253893 £12.50

PRELIMINARY EXAMINATIONS (CRIMINAL PROCEDURE) - CANADA

—Preliminary Inquiry / Vancouver : British Columbia Continuing Legal Education Society, 1983.
82p.
ISBN 0865041199 Hbk £50.00

PRELIMINARY EXAMINATIONS (CRIMINAL PROCEDURE) - ENGLAND

—Pre-trial justice : a study of case settlement in magistrates' courts / John Baldwin. – Oxford : Blackwell, 1985.
vi,190p.
Observational research into case settlement in Magistrates' Courts.
ISBN 0631140646 £19.50

PREMISES LIABILITY - AUSTRALIA - AUSTRALIAN CAPITAL TERRITORY

—Occupiers' liability / Law Reform Commission. – Canberra : Australian Government Publishing Service, 1988.
xi,54p. – (Report).
Bibliography: pp. 53-54. Includes draft legislation.
ISBN 0644068965

PREMISES LIABILITY - AUSTRALIA - TASMANIA

—Occupiers' liability / Law Reform Commission of Tasmania. – Hobart : Government Printer, 1988.
6p. – (Report).

PRESS - CANADA

—Journalist's Legal Guide / Agincourt : Carswell, 1986.
266p.

—Law and the media in Canada / Clare F. Beckton. – Toronto, Canada : Carswell, 1982.
xvi, 161 p.; 24 cm.
Includes index. Bibliography: p. xi-xvi.
ISBN 0459344501 pbk.

—Media, the Courts and the Charter / Philip Anisman. – Agincourt : Carswell, 1986.
567p.
This work is a collection of essays on the importance and societal function of the press and other media and the protection afforded to the media in Canada and the U.S. The importance of protecting the news media from governmental interference in Canada is discussed in the book.

—Royal Commission on Newspapers / Tom Kent. – Hull, Quebec : Canadian Government Publishing Centre, 1981.
xiii,296p; 25cm.
Includes index. Chairman: Tom Kent.
ISBN 0660109549

PRESS - ENGLAND

—Essex County Newspapers Limited : a report by the Director General of Fair Trading on an investigation under Section 3 of the Competition Act 1980 / Office of Fair Trading. – London : Office of Fair Trading, 1983.
41p; 30cm.

PRESS - GREAT BRITAIN

—Media law - the rights of journalists and broadcasters / Geoffrey Robertson and Andrew Nicol. – 2nd ed. – London : Longman Professional (UK), 1989.
An updated second edition which covers recent developments including the Copyright and Patents Act 1988. Also covered are the use of government powers over television, the Video Recordings Act, the Cable Act, recent decisions of the European Court of Human Rights, and European Court, and the right of the media to appeal against 'gag' orders.
ISBN 0851215522 Hbk £55

PRESS - INDIA

—Publish and perish / Joseph Minattur. – New Delhi : VIVA, 1982.
80p.

PRESS - SOUTH AFRICA

—Newspaperman's guide to the law / by Kelsey William Stuart. – 3rd ed. – Durban : Butterworth, 1982.
xxx,410p.
Bibliography: p.376-377. - Includes index.
ISBN 0409057657 HBK R85
ISBN 0409057665 PBK R59

PRESS LAW

—Press Laws of the World / New Delhi : Allied Publishers.

PRESS LAW - AUSTRALIA

—Contempt and the media / Australian Law Reform Commission. – Sydney : The Commission, 1986.
182p. – (Discussion paper).
Cover title. Bibliography: p.178-182.

—Media law in Australia / Mark Armstrong, Michael Blakeney, Ray Watterson. – Melbourne : Oxford University Press, 1983.
x,274p; 21cm.
Bibliography: p242-267. - Includes index.
ISBN 0195544447 Hbk Unpriced
ISBN 0195544439 Pbk £13.00

—Media Law : Journalism v. the Law / Melbourne : Law Institute of Victoria, 1986.

—Media Law Seminars 1985 : Centre for Commercial and Applied Legal Research / Monash University, Faculty of Law. – Clayton : Monash University Press, 1985.
ISBN 0867463856 Hbk £40.00

—Reference on contempt of court, tribunals and commissions / Australian Law Reform Commission. – Sydney : The Commission, 1986.
v,134p.
Bibliography: p.130-134.

—Unfair Publication : Defamation and Privacy / Kingston : Australian Government Publishing Service.
273p.

PRESS LAW - CANADA

—The Journalist's Legal Guide / Agincourt : Carswell, 1986.
266p.
This legal manual for working journalists in Canada addresses a variety of relevant legal subjects, including: access to information, contempt, defamation, police powers, court structure, and procedure. A glossary of legal terms is included in the text.

—Libel and Contempt : The Law and the Media / Vancouver : British Columbia Continuing Legal Education Society, 1982.
414p.
ISBN 0865040834 Hbk £65.00

—Media Law Handbook : a Guide for Canadian Journalists, Broadcasters, Photographers and Writers / 2nd ed. – North Vancouver : International Self-Counsel Press, 1983.
146p.
ISBN 0889085749 Hbk £6.50

—Public and media access to the criminal process / Law Reform Commission of Canada. – Ottawa : The Commission, 1987.
106,120p. – (Working paper).
Includes bibliographical references. Added t.p. in French: L'acces du public et des medias au processus penal. Pages numbered in opposite directions. Text in English and French.
ISBN 0662551168

—Public Rights and the Private Press / Toronto : Butterworths, 1981.
224p.
Examines the various points at which the law intersects with journalism, and looks into the complications arising from the increased tendency of the mass media to acquire a monopolistic status in society. Concludes with a speculative enquiry into what the future of media law will be like.
ISBN 0409812951 Hbk £19.95

PRESS LAW - ENGLAND

—Media law : the rights of journalists and broadcasters / Geoffrey Robertson, Andrew G.L. Nicol. – 1st ed. – London : Oyez, 1984.
xxxvi,403p.
Includes bibliographical references and index.
ISBN 0851206506

—People against the press : an enquiry into the Press Council / Geoffrey Robertson. – London : Quartet, 1983.
182p; 23cm.
Includes index.
ISBN 0704323842 £7.95

—Sunday Times case / 1 videocassette. – London : Sweet & Maxwell, 1984.
– (Sweet & Maxwell's lawfilms).

PRESS LAW - FINLAND

—Finnish Press Laws / Helsinki : Suomen valtio, 1984.
45p.
ISBN 951468320X £12.00

PRESS LAW - GREAT BRITAIN

—Essential Law for Journalists / 9th ed. – London : Butterworths, 1985.
ISBN 0406772819 Pbk £8.95

—McNae's Essential Law for Journalists / 9th ed. – London : Butterworths, 1985.
This book for working journalists offers information on the ways in which the law effects their professional activities. The work discusses the changes brought about by the Contempt of Court Act of 1981 and recent case in defamation.
ISBN 0406772819 Pbk £17.75

—Media Law / Nicol. – London : Longman Professional, 1984.
ISBN 0803997264 Pbk £8.50
ISBN 0851206506 Hbk £40.00

—Regulating the media (MLS) / London : Sweet & Maxwell, 1988.
ISBN 0421374500 Hbk
ISBN 0421374608 Pbk

—Sheffield Newspapers Limited : a report by the Director General of Fair Trading on an investigation under section 3 of the Competition Act 1980 / London : Office of Fair Trading, 1981.
72p; 30cm.

—Third report from the Defence Committee, session 1979-80 : the D Notice system : together with the minutes of proceedings of the Committee ... / London : H.M.S.O., 1980.
xxiii,150p; 25cm. – (HC).
Bound with: Observations presented by the Secretary of State for Defence (Cmnd. 8129).
ISBN 010027739X

—Third report from the Defence Committee : the D notice system : House of Commons paper 773 session 1979-80 : observations presented by the Secretary of State for Defence / London : H.M.S.O., 1981.
2p; 25cm.
Bound with: Third report from the Defence Committee.
ISBN 0101812906

—Voluntary Organisations and the Media : An NCVO Practical Guide / London : Bedford Square Press, 1984.
ISBN 0719911206 Hbk £3.50

PRESS LAW - INDIA

—Only the Good News : on the Law of the Press in India / New Delhi, 1987.
514p.

PRESS LAW - MALAYSIA

—Printing Presses and Publications Act, 1984 (Act 301) / Kuala Lumpur : International Law Books Services.

PRESS LAW - NEW ZEALAND

—News media law in New Zealand / by J.F. Burrows. – 2nd ed. – Wellington : Newspaper Publishers' Association of N.Z, 1980.
xxxxv,448p.
Includes bibliographical references and index.
ISBN 0457014601

—Newspaperman's guide to the law / 4th ed. – Wellington : Butterworths (New Zealand), 1986.
ISBN 040903457 Hbk £33.00
ISBN 040905764 Pbk £23.00

PRESS LAW - NIGERIA

—Judicial attitudes to freedom of speech and the press with particular reference to contempt of court / by Isabella E. Adi. – Lagos : Nigerian Institute of Advanced Legal Studies, 1983.
23p.
Seminar paper presented at the Institute on Wednesday, April 20, 1983.

PRESS LAW - SCOTLAND

—Scots law for journalists / Bruce McKain. – 5th. – Edinburgh : W Green & Son, 1988.
The standard text book on media law in Scotland, revised to include new judicial interpretation of the journalistic privilege in quoting from documents not read out in court, the publishing of leaked information, the effects of the Data Protection Act, public right of access to local authority meetings and the way divorces under the reformed procedures may be safely reported. With coverage of the European Courts of Justice and Human Rights, and the new procedure for judicial review.
ISBN 0414008146

—Scottish and Universal Newspapers Limited : a report by the Director General of Fair Trading on an investigation under section 3 of the Competition Act, 1980 / Office of Fair Trading. – London : H.M.S.O., 1983.
45p; 30cm.

PRESS LAW - WEST INDIES

—Trial by jury : social and psychological dynamics / Ramesh Deosaran. – St. Augustine, Trinidad, West Indies : Institute of Social and Economic Research, University of the West Indies, 1985.
324 p.; 23 cm.
Includes indexes. Bibliography: p. 283-297.
ISBN 9766180008 pbk.

PRESSURE GROUPS

—Environmental groups in politics / Philip Lowe & Jane Goyder with additional contributions from Richard Bate, Sarah Buchanan and John McBride. – London : Allen & Unwin, 1983.
xii,208p; 24cm.
Bibliography: p186-197. - Includes index.
ISBN 0043290434 Hbk Unpriced
ISBN 0043290442 Pbk

—Pressure politics in industrial societies : a comparative introduction / Alan R. Ball and Frances Millard. – Basingstoke : Macmillan Education, 1986.
xi,308; 23cm.
Bibliography: p290-302. - Includes index.
ISBN 0333347579 Hbk £25.00
ISBN 0333347587 Pbk £6.95

PRESSURE GROUPS - GREAT BRITAIN

—Government & Pressure Groups in Britain / Richardson. – Oxford : Oxford University Press, 1987.
ISBN 0198761678 Hbk £30.00

—Pressure groups and government in Great Britain / Geoffrey Alderman. – Harlow : Longman, 1984.
vii,164p; 20cm.
Bibliography: p151-157. - Includes index.
ISBN 0582296269 Pbk £3.75

PRESUMPTION OF INNOCENCE - CANADA

—Presumption of innocence / by James C. Morton and Scott C. Hutchinson. – Toronto : Carswell, 1987.
154p.
Bibliography: pp.150-152. - Includes index.
ISBN 0459305816

PRESUMPTIONS (LAW) - AUSTRALIA - SOUTH AUSTRALIA

—Report ... relating to problems of proof of survivorship as between two or more persons dying at about the same time in one accident / Law Reform Committee of South Australia. – Adelaide : Government Printer, 1985.
37p. – (88th report).
Bibliography: p.29.

PRESUMPTIONS (LAW) - CANADA - ALBERTA

—Survivorship / Institute of Law Research and Reform, Edmonton, Alberta. – Edmonton : The Institute, 1986.
65p. – (Report).

PRESUMPTIONS (LAW) - CANADA - BRITISH COLUMBIA

—Report on presumptions of survivorship / Law Reform Commission of British Columbia. – Victoria : Queen's Printer, 1982.
29p.
ISBN 0771883382

PRESUMPTIONS (LAW) - CANADA - MANITOBA

—Report on 'The Survivorship Act' / Law Reform Commission. – Winnipeg : Queen's Printer, 1982.
ii,44p. – (Report).

PREVENTIVE DETENTION - AUSTRALIA

—Remand in Victoria : A Review of the Nature and Size of Facilities Needed / Canberra : Australian Institute of Criminology.

PRICES - GREAT BRITAIN

—Review of legislation on false and misleading price information : report of the inter-departmental working party / Department of Trade and Industry. – London : The Department, 1984.
67p.

PRICES - MALAYSIA

—Price Control Act, 1946 (Act 121) and Control of Supplies Act, 1961 (Act 122) / Kuala Lumpur : International Law Books Services.

PRIMITIVE LAW

—People's law and state law : the Bellagio papers / Antony Allott and Gordon R. Woodman (eds.). – Dordrecht : Foris Publications, 1985.
354p.
Papers presented at the first conference of the Commission on Folk Law and Legal Pluralism at Bellagio, Como, Italy from 21st to 25th September 1981.
ISBN 9067651001

PRIORITIES OF CLAIMS AND LIENS - AUSTRALIA - VICTORIA

—Priorities / Law Reform Commission of Victoria. – Melbourne : The Commission, 1988.
iv,19p. – (Discussion paper).
ISBN 0724167129

PRIORITIES OF CLAIMS AND LIENS - CANADA

—Competing rights to mingled property tracing and the rule in Clayton's case / Law Reform Commission of British Columbia. – Vancouver : Law Reform Commission of British Columbia, 1982.
iv,122p. – (Working paper).
Includes bibliographical references and index.

—Crown priority in insolvency / Anne E. Hardy. – Toronto : Carswell, 1986.
xxxii, 195 p.; 24 cm.
Includes index. Bibliography: p. 179-181.
ISBN 0459391402

—Report on foreign money liabilities / Law Reform Commission of British Columbia. – Vancouver : The Commission, 1983.
64p.
Includes bibliographical references.
ISBN 0771883919

PRIORITIES OF CLAIMS AND LIENS - CANADA - BRITISH COLUMBIA

—Crown as creditor : priorities and privileges / Law Reform Commission of British Columbia. – Vancouver : Law Reform Commission of British Columbia, 1981.
v,179p. – (Working paper).

—Mortgages of land : the priority of further advances / Law Reform Commission of British Columbia. – Vancouver : The Commission, 1985.
iv,76p. – (Working paper).
Includes bibliographical references.

—Report on mortgages of land : the priority of further advances / Law Reform Commission of British Columbia. – Vancouver : The Commission, 1986.
60p.
Includes bibliographical references.
ISBN 0771885067

—Report on the Crown as creditor : priorities and privileges / Law Reform Commission of British Columbia. – Victoria : Queen's Printer, 1982.
99p.
ISBN 0771883404

PRIORITIES OF CLAIMS AND LIENS - GREAT BRITAIN

—Retention of title on the sale of goods / John Parris. - London : Granada, 1982.
186p; 24cm.
Includes index.
ISBN 0246116129 Unpriced

PRIORITIES OF CLAIMS AND LIENS - SCOTLAND

—Equalisation of diligences / Scottish Law Commission. - Edinburgh : The Commission, 1988.
vii,146p. - (Discussion paper).

PRIORITIES OF CLAIMS AND LIENS - SOUTH AFRICA

—Review of preferent claims in insolvency / South African Law Commission. - Pretoria : The Commission, 1984.
viii,75p. - (Report).
Bibliography: p.vii-viii.

PRISON RIOTS - CANADA - QUEBEC

—Report on allegations of ill-treatment of prisoners at Archambault Institution, Quebec, Canada, including a memorandum to the Government of Canada following a mission from 10 to 15 April 1983 / Amnesty International. - London : Amnesty International, 1983.
ii,44p.
ISBN 0862100623

PRISONERS

—Commonwealth Prisoners Act / Law Reform Commission. - Canberra : Australian Government Publishing Service, 1988.
xv,57p. - (Report (interim)).
Bibliography: p.57. Includes text of draft legislation.
ISBN 0644069007

—Conditions of detention and the European Convention on Human Rights and Fundamental Freedoms / Strasbourg : Council of Europe, 1981.
37,ip.

—Human rights in prisons / by A. Reynaud. - Strasbourg : Council of Europe, Directorate of Human Rights, 1986.
218p.
Describes human rights problems prison establishments may encounter. Outlines the relevant international human rights law, in particular the European Convention on Human Rights and its case law.
ISBN 9287108811

—Justice in prison : a report / by Justice. - London : Justice, 1983.
v,96p.
Chairman of committee: Sir Brian MacKenna.
ISBN 0907247032

—Right to Liberty and the Rights of Persons Deprived of Their Liberty as Guaranteed by Article 5 of the European Convention of Human Rights / Strasbourg : Council of Europe, 1981.

—Treatment of prisoners under international law / Nigel S. Rodley. - Paris : Unesco, 1987.
xxii,374; 25cm.
Includes index.
ISBN 0198255519 Hbk £40.00
ISBN 0198255632 Pbk £15.00

PRISONERS - AUSTRALIA

—Australian Prisoners, 1982 / David Biles. - Canberra : Australian Institute of Criminology.

—Groote Eylandt Prisoners : A Research Report / Canberra : Australian Institute of Criminology.

—Prisoners' rights : a study of human rights and Commonwealth prisoners / by Gordon Hawkins. - Canberra : Australian Government Publishing Service, 1986.
vii,102p. - (Occasional paper).
Bibliography: p.95-102.
ISBN 0644054603

—Profile of Federal Prisoners / Canberra : Australian Institute of Criminology.

—Rights and Obligations in a Prison / Canberra : Australian Institute of Criminology.

PRISONERS - AUSTRALIA - NEW SOUTH WALES

—Prison struggle : changing Australia's penal system / George Zdenkowski and David Brown. - Ringwood, Vic., Australia : Penguin Books, 1982.
xxi, 440 p., 8 p. of plates; 21 cm.
Includes bibliographical references and index.
ISBN 014022324X pbk. £14.95

PRISONERS - AUSTRALIA - SOUTH AUSTRALIA

—Report ... relating to locus standi : prisoners' rights / Law Reform Committee of South Australia. - Adelaide : Government Printer, 1982.
6p. - (70th report).

PRISONERS - AUSTRALIA - VICTORIA

—Thirteenth report to Parliament on subordinate legislation concerning : Police Gaols Regulations 1988 (SR No. 292/1988) / Legal and Constitutional Committee. - Melbourne : Government Printer, 1988.
vii,24p.
Includes the texts of the Regulations.

PRISONERS - CANADA

—Psychiatry behind bars : a legal perspective / by Marc E. Schiffer. - Toronto : Butterworths, 1982.
xxiv,509p.
Covers the psychiatric interrogation of accused persons, the myth of confidentiality, forms of treatment, psychiatric treatment and offenders' rights, and the psychiatrist as jailer.
ISBN 0409865613

PRISONERS - CANADA - QUEBEC

—Report on allegations of ill-treatment of prisoners at Archambault Institution, Quebec, Canada, including a memorandum to the Government of Canada following a mission from 10 to 15 April 1983 / Amnesty International. - London : Amnesty International, 1983.
ii,44p.
ISBN 0862100623

PRISONERS - COMMONWEALTH

—Scheme for the transfer of convicted offenders within the Commonwealth : explanatory documentation prepared for Commonwealth jurisidictions / by A.M.F. Webb. - London : Commonwealth Secretariat, 1987.
iii,92p.

PRISONERS - EAST TIMOR

—East Timor : violations of human rights : extrajudicial executions, 'disappearances', torture and political imprisonment, 1975-1984 / Amnesty International. - London : Amnesty International Publications, 1985.
vii,92p.
ISBN 0862100852

PRISONERS - ENGLAND

—NACRO briefing / v. - London : NACRO, 1982-.

PRISONERS - GREAT BRITAIN

—Adult prisons and prisoners in England and Wales 1970-1982 : a review of the findings of social research / Joy Mott. - London : H.M.S.O., 1985.
vi,68p.
Reviews social research results. Compares them with developments in the USA. Concludes that research in the UK has been inadequate, concentrating on prisoners and neglecting the prisons.
ISBN 0113408013

—Communications in Prison (A Short Guide) 1981 / London : Home Office.
ISBN 0862520193 Hbk £5.00

—Imprisonment: the legal status and rights of prisoners / London : Sweet & Maxwell, 1989.
Describes the history and structure of the prison system, focusing on the various categories of prisons and prisoners within it. Analyses the body of case law, including issues such as disciplinary hearings, prisoners' correspondence, visits, and access to the courts. Summarises the law on remission and parole. Contains the European Prison Rules as an appendix.
ISBN 0421322306 Pbk £25.00

PRISONERS - INDIA

—Constitutional Rights of Prisoners / Delhi : Mittal Publications, 1986.

PRISONERS - IRELAND

—Prisoners' rights : a study in Irish prison law / by Raymond Byrne, Gerard W. Hogan, Paul McDermott. - Dublin : Co-op Books, 1981.
xvi,145p.
ISBN 0905441400

PRISONERS - YUGOSLAVIA

—Yugoslavia : prisoners of conscience : an Amnesty International report / Amnesty International. - London : Amnesty International, 1982.
50p.
ISBN 0862100437

PRISONS

—Abolitionism : towards a non-repressive approach to crime : proceedings of the Second International Conference on Prison Abolition, Amsterdam, 1985 / edited by Herman Bianchi, Rene van Swaaningen. - Amsterdam : Free University Press, 1986.
247p.
ISBN 9062561799

—Accountability and prisons : opening up a closed world / edited by Mike Maguire, Jon Vagg, Rod Morgan. - London : Tavistock, 1985.
x,300p; 22cm.
Includes bibliography and index.
ISBN 042279600X Hbk £16.00
ISBN 0422796107 Pbk £7.95

—Alternative measures to imprisonment / by W. Rentzmann and J.P. Robert. - Strasbourg : Council of Europe, 1986.
35p. - (CDAP (85) 6).
A paper presented to the seventh Conference of Directors of Prison Administrations.

—Computers in correctional administration and links with criminal justice : proceedings of the fourth Colloquy on the Use of Computers in the Administration of Justice, Stockholm, 3-5 September 1984 : reports presented at the colloquy / Strasbourg : Council of Europe, 1985.
261p.
At head of cover title: Legal Affairs.
ISBN 9287103917

—Dangerousness and criminal justice / Jean Floud and Warren Young. - London : Heinemann, 1981.
xvii,228p; 23cm.
Bibliography: p203-221. - Includes index. At head of title : Howard League for Penal Reform.
ISBN 0435823078 £14.50

—European prison rules : recommendation no. R (87)3 adopted by the Committee of Ministers of the Council of Europe on 12 February 1987 and Explanatory memorandum / Council of Europe. - Strasbourg : Council of Europe, 1987.
92p.
At head of cover title : Council of Europe, Legal Affairs.
ISBN 9287110352

—Hell-Hole, Robben Island : Reminiscences of a Political Prisoner / London : Spokesman Books, 1984.
192p.
ISBN 0851244076 Hbk £13.50
ISBN 0851244017 Pbk £4.95

—Legitimate grievance : a report on the role of the ombudsman in the prison system / Geoffrey Wener. - London : Prison Reform Trust, 1983.
23p.
Bibliography: p20.
ISBN 0946209030

—Opportunities for progress in systems, organisation and technology in prison administrations, especially with regard to automation and computer technology / by Luigi Daga. - Stasbourg : Council of Europe, 1986.
29p. - (CDAP (85) 5 rev).
A paper presented to the seventh conference of Directors of Prison Administrations. Bibliography: p.27-28.

—Prison information bulletin / Strasbourg : Council of Europe, 1983.

—Prison regimes / study prepared by the Select Committee of Experts on Prison Regimes and Prison Leave. - Strasbourg : Council of Europe, 1986.
33p. - (CDPC (84) 8 rev. addendum VI).

—Prisons and the process of justice / Andrew Rutherford. - Oxford : Oxford University Press, 1986.
xii,217p; 20cm. - (Oxford paperbacks).
Originally published: London : Heinemann, 1984. Bibliography: p193-205. - Includes index.
ISBN 0192819321 Pbk £3.95

—Psychological survival : the experience of long-term imprisonment / Stanley Cohen and Laurie Taylor. - 2nd ed. - Harmondsworth : Penguin, 1981.
239p; 19cm. - (Pelican books).
Previous ed.: 1972. Bibliography: p230-239.
ISBN 014021657X Pbk £2.25

—Recommendations of the Committee of Ministers being of particular interest to prison administrations / Council of Europe. - Strasbourg : Council of Europe, 1981.
various pagings; 30cm.
Introduction by Directorate of Legal Affairs (Division of Crime Problems). At head of title: Legal Affairs.

PRISONS - AUSTRALIA

—Cost of Imprisonment in Australia / Canberra : Australian Institute of Criminology.

—Minimum Standard Guidelines for Australian Prisons / Canberra : Australian Institute of Criminology.

—Sentencing : prisons / The Law Reform Commission. - Sydney : The Commission, 1987.
vii,64p. - (Discussion paper).
Bibliography: pp.63-64.

PRISONS - CANADA

—Canadian Prison Law, 3 vols / Toronto : Butterworths.

—Canadian Prison Law, 3 Vols. / Butterworths.

—Descriptive study of incarerated dangerous offenders / J. Jakimiec ... et al. - Ottawa : Ministry of the Solicitor General, 1986.
23p. - (User report).
Bibliography: p.24.

—Management of Correctional Institutions / Jayewardene. – Toronto : Butterworths, 1981.
208p.
Analyses the aims and objectives of a correctional institution, the context in which it must operate, and the material and human resources available for it to operate, using the framework of extant sociological and physiological theory. Illustrates how from this analysis an efficient program of activity could be derived, using the framework of managerial theory.
ISBN 0409840513 Pbk £21.95

PRISONS - ENGLAND

—Future of the prison system / Roy D. King, Rod Morgan with J.P. Martin, J.E. Thomas. – Farnborough, Hants. : Gower, 1980.
x,229p; 23cm.
Bibliography: p211-217. - Includes index.
ISBN 0566003481 £11.50

—Grievance procedures in prisons : a study of prisoners' applications and petitions / by John Ditchfield and Claire Austin. – London : H.M.S.O., 1986.
vi,71p; 25cm.
Study of prisoners' applications and petitions. Examines the operation of grievance procedures in six prisons for adult male offenders to identify differences in practice between prisons and assess the confidence which inmates and staff have in them.
ISBN 0113408390

—History of English prison administration / Sean McConville. – London : Routledge & Kegan Paul, 1981.
xvii,534p; 23cm.
Bibliography: p483-505. - Includes index.
ISBN 0710006942 £25.00

—Imprisonment in England and Wales : a concise history / Christopher Harding ... et al. – London : Croom Helm, 1985.
xiii,308p,8p of plates; 23cm.
Includes index.
ISBN 0709912943 £25.00

—Prison disciplinary system in England and Wales : presented to Parliament by the Secretary of State for the Home Department / London : H.M.S.O., 1986.
34p; 25cm.
ISBN 0101992009

—Punishment practice by prison Boards of Visitors / Susan Iles ... et al. – London : Home Office, 1984.
iv,41p.
Bibliography: p.40.
ISBN 086252167X

—Reducing the prison population : an exploratory study in Hampshire / David Smith ... et al. – London : Home Office, 1984.
v,65p. – (Research and Planning Unit Paper).
Bibliography: p.56-58.
ISBN 0862521246

—Remands in the absence of the accused / Chris May. – London : Home Office, 1985.
vii,31p.
ISBN 0862522153

—Report of Her Majesty's Chief Inspector of Prisons / v. – London : H.M.S.O., 1982-.

—Report of the Committee on the Prison Disciplinary System / Chairman, Peter J. Prior. – 2 v. – London : H.M.S.O., 1985.
Contents: v.1. Report - v.2. Appendices.
ISBN 0101964102

—Return to an order of the Honourable House of Commons dated 16 July 1987 for report of an inquiry by Her Majesty's Chief Inspector of Prisons for England and Wales into the disturbances in prison service establishments in England between 29 April-2 May 1986 / London : H.M.S.O., 1987.
viii,127p; 30cm.
Spine title: Report of an inquiry by Her Majesty's Chief Inspector of Prisons for England and Wales into the disturbances in prison service establishments in England between 29 April-2 May 1986.
ISBN 0117013366 Pbk £10.00

—Submission to the Home Office on Intermittent custody, Cmnd 9281 / from the National Association for the Care and Resettlement of Offenders. – London : NACRO, 1984.
14p.

—Suspended sentence after ten years : a review and reassessment / A.E. Bottoms. – Leeds : University of Leeds Centre for Social Work and Applied Social Studies, 1980.
i,56p. – (Occasional paper).
Includes bibliographical references.

PRISONS - GREAT BRITAIN

—Adult prisons and prisoners in England and Wales 1970-1982 : a review of the findings of social research / Joy Mott. – London : H.M.S.O., 1985.
vi,68p.
Reviews social research results. Compares them with developments in the USA. Concludes that research in the UK has been inadequate, concentrating on prisoners and neglecting the prisons.
ISBN 0113408013

—Board of visitor adjudications / David Smith, Claire Austin and John Ditchfield. – London : Home Office, 1981.
v,45p. – (Research Unit paper).
Bibliography: p40.
ISBN 0862520045 Unpriced

—Bricks of shame : Britain's prisons / Vivien Stern. – Harmondsworth : Penguin, 1987.
309p; 20cm. – (Penguin special).
ISBN 0140523839

—British prisons / Mike Fitzgerald and Joe Sim. – 2nd ed. – Oxford : Basil Blackwell, 1982.
182p; 23cm.
Previous ed.: 1979. Bibliography: p167-170. - Includes index. Previous control number ISBN 0-631-12606-6.
ISBN 0631125299 Hbk Unpriced
ISBN 0631126066 Pbk Unpriced

—Coming penal crisis : a criminological and theological exploration / edited by A.E. Bottoms and R.H. Preston. – Edinburgh : Scottish Academic Press, 1980.
xii,242p.
Includes bibliographies.
ISBN 070730265X

—Fourth report from the Home Affairs Committee, session 1980-81 : the prison service / Great Britain. – London : H.M.S.O., 1981.
lxiiip. – (HC).
ISBN 0100082912

Vol. 2 : Evidence and appendices 1981.
vii,282p. – (HC).
ISBN 010008091X

—Government reply to the fourth report from the Home Affairs Committee, session 1980-1981 HC 412 : the prison service / presented to Parliament by the Secretary of State for the Home Department. – London : H.M.S.O., 1981.
20p.
ISBN 0101844603

—Government reply to the third report from the Home Affairs Committee, session 1986-87 HC 35-1 : sate and the use of prisons / presented to Parliament by the Secretary of State for the Home Department by Command of Her Majesty, December 1987. – London : HMSO, 1987.
10p.
ISBN 0101026323

—Her Majesty's Chief Insepctor of Prisons Reports : Her Majesty's Detention Centre Eastwood Park / London : Home Office, 1982.

—Her Majesty's Chief Inspector of Prisons Reports : Her Majesty's Prison Cookham Wood / London : Home Office, 1981.
ISBN 0862520118 Hbk

—Her Majesty's Chief Inspector of Prisons Reports : Her Majesty's Prison Erlestoke House / London : Home Office, 1982.
ISBN 0862520096 Hbk

—Her Majesty's Chief Inspector of Prisons Reports : Her Majesty's Prison Featherstone / London : Home Office, 1981.
ISBN 086252010X Hbk

—Her Majesty's Chief Inspector of Prisons Reports : Her Majesty's Prison Gartree / London : Home Office, 1982.
ISBN 0862520290 Hbk

—Her Majesty's Chief Inspector of Prisons Reports : Her Majesty's Prison Glouchester / London : Home Office, 1981.
ISBN 086252024X Hbk

—Her Majesty's Chief Inspector of Prisons Reports : Her Majesty's Prison High Point / London : Home Office, 1981.
ISBN 0862520363 Hbk

—Her Majesty's Chief Inspector of Prisons Reports : Her Majesty's Prison Leeds / London : Home Office, 1981.
ISBN 0862520282 Hbk

—Her Majesty's Chief Inspector of Prisons Reports : Her Majesty's Prison Leyhill / London : Home Office, 1981.
ISBN 0862520355 Hbk

—Her Majesty's Chief Inspector of Prisons Reports : Her Majesty's Prison Raidstone / London : Home Office, 1981.
ISBN 0862520215 Hbk

—Her Majesty's Chief Inspector of Prisons Reports : Her Majesty's Prison Weymouth / London : Home Office, 1981.
ISBN 086252038X Hbk

—HM Prison Brixton : Report / Great Britain Inspectorate of Prisons. – London : Home Office, 1982.
ii, 32p.
ISBN 0862520614 Hbk £1.10

—HM Prison Manchester : Report / London : Home Office, 1982.
ii, 32p.
ISBN 0862520681 Hbk £1.10

—Management Structure in Prison Department Establishments : A Cumulative Document / London : Home Office, 1983.
iii, 26p.

—Managing the long-term prison system : the report of the...Committee / A. J. Langdon. – London : H.M.S.O., 1984.
102p.
Presents the findings of the Control Review Committee for the prison system; including implications for physical security with particular reference to the dispersal system. Recommends central control of long-term allocations and specialised units for prisoners whose behaviour does not respond to the incentives of a better structured system.
ISBN 0113407971

—May report : proceedings of a conference held at Central Hall Westminster, on 30 November 1979 / London : NACRO, 1980.
29p.

—NACRO news digest / London : NACRO, 1979-.

—Prison and the Factory / Massimo Pavarini. – London : Macmillan, 1981.
256p. – (Critical Criminology, General Ser.).
ISBN 0333266676 Hbk £18.00
ISBN 0333266684 Pbk £6.95

—Prison system for the 80s and beyond / NACRO. – London : Nacro, 1983.
vi,73p.
By Andrew Ashworth et al..
ISBN 0850690293

—Prisons and the process of justice : the reductionist challenge / Andrew Rutherford. - London : Heinemann, 1984.
x,214p.
Includes index. Bibliography: p191-203.
ISBN 0434917702

—Race relations in prisons / Elaine Player. – Oxford : Clarendon Press, 1989.
200.
Based on a detailed research project undertaken at the request of the Home Office. Examines three institutions and their staff and inmates, and relates their experiences in detail. Demonstrates difficulties arising from trying to isolate race problems, and identifies problems in trying to enforce policies to eradicate discriminating behaviour.
ISBN 0198256175 Hbk £20

—Reduction of pressure on the prison system, observations on the fifteenth report from the Expenditure Committee / Home Office ... et al. .. – London : H.M.S.O., 1980.
2,33p; 25cm.
ISBN 0101794800 sd £2.00

—Regulating custodial interviews / Police Foundation, 1988.
ISBN 0947692088 Pbk £6.95

—Taking offenders out of circulation / by Stephen Brody and Roger Tarling. – London : H.M.S.O., 1980.
v,42p.
Bibliography: p 38-42. A Home Office Research Unit report.
ISBN 0113407041

—Third report from the Home Affairs Committee, session 1986-87 : state and use of prisons / 2 pt. – London : H.M.S.O., 1987.
30cm. – (H.C.).

PRISONS - NETHERLANDS

—Studies on the Dutch prison system / edited by M.J.M. Brand-Koolen. – Amstelveen Netherlands : Kugler Publications BV, 1987.
viii, 189 p.; 23 cm.
Includes bibliographies.
ISBN 9062990355 pbk.

PRISONS - NIGERIA

—Annual report / Nigeria Prisons Service. – Lagos : Federal Government Press, 1981.
50p.

PRISONS - SCOTLAND

—Prisons and punishment in Scotland : from the Middle Ages to the present / Joy Cameron. – Edinburgh : Canongate, 1983.
x,274p,16p of plates; 23cm.
Bibliography: p237-239. - Includes index.
ISBN 0862410312 £12.95

—Report of Her Majesty's Chief Inspector of Prisons for Scotland ... / v. – Edinburgh : H.M.S.O., 1982-.

PRIVACY

—Business Guide to Privacy and Data 1970 : Protection Legislation / Paris : International Chamber of Commerce.
310p.

—Convention for the Protection of Individuals with Regard to Automatic Processing of Personal Data / Strasbourg : Council of Europe, 1981.
ISBN 9287100225 Hbk £1.00

—Explanatory Report on the European Convention for the Protection of Individuals with Regard to Automatic Processing of Personal Data / Strasbourg : Council of Europe, 1981.

—Guidelines on the protection of privacy and transborder flows of personal data / Organisation for Economic Co-operation and Development. – Paris : Organisation for Economic Co-operation and Development, 1980.
41p.
ISBN 9264121552

—Protecting privacy in two-way electronic services / by David H. Flaherty : foreword by Ronald L. Plasser. – London : Mansell, 1985.
viii,172p; 24cm.
Bibliography: p165-166. - Includes index.
ISBN 0720117445 £23.50

—Right to respect for private and family life, home and correspondence as guaranteed by Article 8 of the European Convention on Human Rights / by Andrew Drzemczewski. – Strasbourg : Council of Europe, Directorate of Human Rights, 1984.
29p.
ISBN 9287103526

PRIVACY – AUSTRALIA

—Action for breach of confidence in Australia / by James Kearney. – Sydney : Legal Books, 1985.
xiv,97p.
Bibliography: p.91-93. - Includes index.
ISBN 0949553204

—Privacy : Proposals / Law Reform Commission. – Canberra : Australian Government Publishing Service, 1983.
xvi, 443p. – (ALRC Report Ser.: No. 22).
ISBN 0644012501 Hbk £10.40

—Privacy : Summary of Report / Law Reform Commission. – Canberra : Australian Government Publishing Service, 1983.
v, 50p. – (ALRC Report Ser.).
ISBN 0644012544 Hbk £2.90

—Unfair Publication : Defamation and Privacy / Kingston : Australian Government Publishing Service.
273p.

PRIVACY – AUSTRALIA – WESTERN AUSTRALIA

—Working paper and survey : privacy and statutory powers of intrusion / Law Reform Commission of Western Australia. – Perth : Law Reform Commission of Western Australia, 1981.
25,ii,112p. – (Project v no 26 part 2).

PRIVACY – CANADA

—Access and privacy : the steps ahead / Canada. – Ottawa : Government of Canada, 1987.
x,57,63,xip.
French title on added t.p.: Acces et renseignements personnels. Pages numbered in opposite directions. Text in English and French.
ISBN 0662554728

—Aspects of Privacy Law : Essays in Honour of Sir Rupert Cross / Butterworths, 1980.
464p.
ISBN 0409833401 Hbk £70.00

—Interim policy guide : Access to Information Act and the Privacy Act / Treasury Board of Canada Secretariat. – 1. – Ottawa : Minister of Supply and Services, 1983.
loose-leaf.
English and French text.
ISBN 0660522551

—Invasion of Privacy : Police and Electric Surveillance in Canada / Agincourt : Carswell, 1983.
250p.
This book analyzes the legal and ethical dimensions of police surveillance in Canada and discusses the question of the extent of police surveillance powers.

—Open and Shut : Enhancing the Right to Know and the Right to Privacy / Ottawa : Canadian Government Publishing Centre, 1987.
130p.

—Practice and Procedure Under the Access to Information and Privacy Acts / Toronto : Butterworths, 1986.
128p.
ISBN 0409811645 Hbk

—Report of the Commission of Inquiry Relating to the Security and Investigation Services Branch Within the Post Office Department / Rene Marin. – Hull, Quebec : Canadian Government Publishing Centre, 1981.
iv,338p.
Commissioner: Rene J. Marin.
ISBN 0660108585

PRIVACY – CANADA – ONTARIO

—Privacy and personal data protection : a report on personal record-keeping by the ministries and agencies of the Ontario government / by Michael Brown, Brenda Billingsley and Rebecca Shamai. – Toronto : Commission on Freedom of Information and Individual Privacy, 1980.
xviii,645p. – (Research publication).

PRIVACY – ENGLAND

—Breach of confidence : comments on Law Commission report on breach of confidence (Law Com. no. 110) : memorandum / by the Council's Law Reform Committee. – London : Law Society, 1982.
5p.

—Breach of confidence : report on a reference under section 3 (1) (e) of the Law Commissions Act 1965 / the Law Commission. – London : H.M.S.O., 1981.
ix,239p; 25cm.
ISBN 0101838808

—Protection of privacy / by Raymond Wacks. – London : Sweet & Maxwell, 1980.
xx,185p; 19cm.
Includes index.
ISBN 0421268409 Hbk £11.50
ISBN 0421268506 Pbk £6.50

PRIVACY – EUROPEAN COMMUNITY

—Protection of Privacy, Automatic Data Processing and Progress in Statistical Documentation / Luxembourg : Office for Official Publications of the European Communities, 1986.
348p.

PRIVACY – GREAT BRITAIN

—Anglo-American privacy law : an economic analysis / Charles J. Hartmann and Stephen M. Renas. – s.l. : s.n., 1985.
36,12p.
Includes bibliographical references.

—Data Protection Act 1984 / with commentary and annotations by Bryan Niblett. – London : Oyez Longman, 1984.
x,155p; 24cm.
ISBN 0851207766 Pbk £16.50

—Data protection : perspectives on information privacy : contributions made to a conference on 11 May 1983 at the University of Leicester / edited by Colin Bourn and John Benyon. – Leicester : University of Leicester, Continuing Education Unit, 1983.
101p; 21cm.
ISBN 090150727X Pbk £5.00

—Guide to the Data Protection Act : its implications for business / Nigel Savage & Chris Edwards. – London : Financial Training, 1984.
ISBN 0906322537

—Interception of communications in Great Britain : report / by Lord Diplock. – London : H.M.S.O., 1981.
7p; 25cm.
ISBN 0101819102 unbound £1.10

—Personal information: privacy and the law / Oxford : Clarendon Press, 1989.
320.
Argues that at the core of the privacy problem is a concern for the use and misuse of personal information. Identifies four main areas of privacy, and suggests that by finding the centre of the problem, it may more easily be solved.
ISBN 0198256116 Hbk £30

—Secrecy of Correspondence is Guaranteed by Law / London : Spokesman Books, 1983.
196p.
ISBN 085124128X Pbk £1.95

PRIVACY – NORWAY

—Decade of computers and law / edited by Jon Bing, Knut S. Selmer. – Oslo : Universitetsforlaget, 1980.
475 p.; 22 cm.
Includes bibliographical references.
ISBN 8200053768

PRIVACY – SOUTH AFRICA

—Professional secrecy in South Africa : a symposium / edited by G. C. Oosthuizen, H. A. Shapiro, S. A. Strauss. – Cape Town : Oxford University Press, 1983.
178p.
ISBN 0195703200

PRIVACY – UNITED STATES

—Anglo-American privacy law : an economic analysis / Charles J. Hartmann and Stephen M. Renas. – s.l. : s.n., 1985.
36,12p.
Includes bibliographical references.

PRIVACY, RIGHT OF – AUSTRALIA

—Privacy / Law Reform Commission. – 3 v. – Canberra : Australian Government Publishing Service, 1983.
– (Report).

PRIVATE COMPANIES – AUSTRIA

—Austrian law on companies with limited liability : as of January 1, 1984 with excerpted provisions of other relevant laws and annotations / editor Julie Goldberg. – Deventer : Kluwer Law and Taxation Publishers, 1985.
124p; 23 cm.
English and German. Includes index. Bibliography: p. 122.
ISBN 9065442294 Hbk £75.00

PRIVATE COMPANIES – CANADA

—Taxation of private corporations and their shareholders / Howard J. Kellough, Peter E. McQuillan. – Toronto : Canadian Tax Foundation, 1983.
ix,825p.
ISBN 0888080174

PRIVATE COMPANIES – ENGLAND

—Buying and selling private companies and businesses / Humphrey Wine. – 3rd ed. – London : Butterworths, 1986.
260p; 23cm.
Previous ed.: 1983. Includes index.
ISBN 0406424187 Pbk £22.50

PRIVATE COMPANIES – GREAT BRITAIN

—Acquisition of private companies / W.J.L. Knight. – 3rd ed. – London : Oyez Longman, 1982.
xviii,228p.
Includes index.
ISBN 0851206212

—Acquisition of private companies / 5th. – London : Longman Professional (UK), 1989.
New edition covers Financial Services Act 1986, the Finance Act 1986, the Income and Corporatin Taxes Act 1988, and the implications of the 1989 Budget. New section on merger control and competition, and includes precedents of agreements for sale both for individual and corporate vendors.
ISBN 085121438X Hbk £35.00

—Acquisition Of Private Companies The / 4th ed. – London : Longman Professional, 1985.
ISBN 0851208843 Hbk £28.00

—Buying and Selling Private Companies / 3rd ed. – London : Butterworths, 1986.
ISBN 0406424187 Pbk £18.50

—Liquidation of Insolvent Private Companies / London : Butterworths, 1988.
ISBN 0406267006 Pbk

—Tolley's Focus on the Purchase and Sale of a Private Company's Shares / 2nd ed. – Croydon : Tolley.
152p.
ISBN 0854591850 Hbk £6.95

—Unquoted companies / London : Macmillan, 1988.
ISBN 03334371995 Hbk £105.00

PRIVATE COMPANIES – SOUTH AFRICA

—Working Guide to the Administration of Private Companies / Durban : Butterworths, 1981.
ISBN 0409029254 Pbk

PRIVATE COMPANIES – WEST GERMANY

—Private company in Germany : a translation and commentary / M.C. Oliver, M.A. Barrister. – 2nd ed. – Deventer, Netherlands : Kluwer Law and Taxation Publishers, 1986.
92p.
Includes English and German text of Gesetz betreffend die Gesellschaften mit beschrankter Haftung.
ISBN 9065442448 Pbk £72.00

PRIVATE MEMBER'S BILLS

—Private Members' Bills / Read. – Cambridge : Cambridge University Press, 1988.
ISBN 0521330513 Hbk £22.50

PRIVATE POLICE – AUSTRALIA

—Policing and Private Security / Canberra : Australian Institute of Criminology.

PRIVATE POLICE – CANADA

—Canadian Private Security Manual / Robert J. Prouse. – Agincourt : Carswell, 1987.
352p.
This work for Canadian private security officers discusses the question of security for emergency situations, investigational procedures, and surveillance in depth.

PRIVATE POLICE – CANADA – ONTARIO

—Contract security in Ontario / Clifford D. Shearing, Margaret B. Farnell, Philip C. Stenning. – Toronto : Centre of Criminology, University of Toronto, 1980.
xii,332p; 25cm.
Bibliography: p.322-331.
ISBN 0919584497

PRIVATE PROSECUTORS - AUSTRALIA

—Standing in public interest litigation / Law Reform Commission. – Canberra : Australian Government Publishing Service, 1985.
xxx,273p. – (Report).
Bibliography: p.259-263 - Includes index.
ISBN 0644013109

PRIVATE PROSECUTORS - CANADA

—Private prosecutions / Law Reform Commission of Canada. – Ottawa : Law Reform Commission of Canada, 1986.
51,59p; 25cm. – (Working paper).
Cover title: Criminal law - private prosecutions. Added t.p. in French: Les poursuites privees. Pages numbered in opposite directions. Text in English and French.
ISBN 0662544595

PRIVATE PROSECUTORS - GREAT BRITAIN

—Private Prosecutions / London : Shaw & Sons, 1988.
ISBN 0721910904 Pbk £9.95

—Private prosecutions / London : Shaw & Sons, 1988.
ISBN 0712910904 Pbk £9.95

PRIVATISATION

—Joint enterprise : roles and relationships of the public and private sectors in the provision of library and information services / report of Library and Information Services Council and British Library Research and Development Department Working Party. – London : H.M.S.O., 1987.
vii, 49p.
On cover: Office of Arts and Libraries.
ISBN 011430016X

PRIVATISATION - GREAT BRITAIN

—British Airways : Civil Aviation Policy and the Privatisation of British Airways / P. J. Forsyth. – London : Institute for Fiscal Studies.
– (Report Ser.).

—Fighting Privatisation : The Victory in Gloucester / London : Spokesman Books, 1984.
– (IWC Pamphlet: No. 87).
ISBN 0901740861 Pbk £0.90

—Privatisation and regulation / Oxford : Oxford University Press, 1986.
ISBN 019877253X Pbk £9.95
ISBN 0198772548 Hbk £25.00

—Privatisation of the Water Authorities in England and Wales / presented to Parliament by the Secretary of State for the Environment ... et al. ... – London : H.M.S.O., 1986.
iv,27p.
ISBN 0101973403

—Privatising London's Airports / D. Thompson. – London : Institute for Fiscal Studies.
– (Report Ser.).

—Selling the state : privatisation in Britain / Cento Veljanovski. – London : Weidenfeld and Nicolson, 1987.
xiv, 239p.
Bibliography: p.213-217.
ISBN 0297790803

PRIVILEGES AND IMMUNITIES - CANADA

—Crown priority in insolvency / Anne E. Hardy. – Toronto : Carswell, 1986.
xxxii, 195 p.; 24 cm.
Includes index. Bibliography: p. 179-181.
ISBN 0459391402

PRIVILEGES AND IMMUNITIES - CANADA - BRITISH COLUMBIA

—Report on the Crown as creditor : priorities and privileges / Law Reform Commission of British Columbia. – Victoria : Queen's Printer, 1982.
99p.
ISBN 0771883404

PRIZE LAW - AUSTRALIA

—Reference on admiralty jurisdiction / Australian Law Reform Commission. – Sydney : The Commission, 1984.
iii,70 leaves.
Bibliography: p.68-70.

PRIZE LAW - SOUTH AFRICA

—Review of the law of prize / South African Law Commission. – Pretoria : The Commission, 1984.
iv,17p. – (Project).

PRIZE-COURTS - AUSTRALIA

—Reference on admiralty jurisdiction / Australian Law Reform Commission. – Sydney : The Commission, 1984.
iii,70 leaves.
Bibliography: p.68-70.

PROBABILITIES

—Evidence, proof and probability / Sir Richard Eggleston. – 2nd ed. – London : Weidenfeld and Nicolson, 1983.
xiv,274p; 22cm.
Previous ed.: 1978. Bibliography: p262-266. - Includes index.
ISBN 0297782622 Hbk £16.50
ISBN 0297782630 Pbk £7.95

PROBATE

—Canadian law of wills / Thomas G. Feeney. – 2nd ed. 2 v. – Toronto : Butterworths, 1982.
Revision of two separate works by the same author: The Canadian law of wills: probate, 1976; and The Canadian law of wills: construction, 1978. Includes bibliographical references and index. Vol. 1: Probate. - Vol 2: Construction.
ISBN 0409829749

—Right Way to Prove a Will / Ibadan : African Universities Press.

PROBATE - AUSTRALIA

—Wills, Probate and the Administration of the Estates of Deceased Persons in Victoria / 2nd ed. – Butterworths, 1988.
272p.
ISBN 0409494747 Hbk £54.00
ISBN 0409338613 Pbk £35.00

PROBATE - AUSTRALIA - NEW SOUTH WALES

—Wills Probate and Administration Service, New South Wales / L.G. Handler. – Butterworths, 1985.
ISBN 0409491314 Hbk

PROBATE - AUSTRALIA - SOUTH AUSTRALIA

—Report ... relating to the reform of the law on wills and intestacies / Law Reform Committee of South Australia. – Adelaide : Government Printer, 1983.
7p. – (72nd report).

PROBATE - AUSTRALIA - VICTORIA

—Griffith's Probate law and practice in Victoria / Ross A. Sundberg. – 3rd ed. – Sydney : Law Book Company, 1983.
xxv,338p.
Includes index.
ISBN 0455204942

PROBATE - AUSTRALIA - WESTERN AUSTRALIA

—Report on recognition of interstate and foreign grants of probate and administration / the Law Reform Commission of Western Australia. – Perth : The Commission, 1984.
128p. – (Project).
Includes bibliographical references.

PROBATE - CANADA

—Annual Report 1979 : Limitation Periods in Actions Against Estates / Victoria : Government of British Columbia, 1980.

—Canadian law of wills / Thomas G. Feeney. – 3rd ed. – Toronto : Butterworths, 1987.
Volume 1 focuses on probate, containing new material on the support of dependants, the administration of settled estates, holograph wills and intestate succession. Volume 2 considers the rules affecting construction in relation to recent probate changes.
ISBN 0409810002 Hbk

—Estate Litigation / Vancouver : British Columbia Continuing Legal Education Society, 1984.
ISBN 0865041520 Hbk £45.00

—Probate Practice Manual - 1984 / Vancouver : British Columbia Continuing Legal Education Society, 1984.
369p.
ISBN 0865041601 Hbk £75.00

—Probate Practice Manual, 1984 / Vancouver : British Columbia Continuing Legal Education Society, 1984.
369p.
ISBN 0865041601 Hbk £70.00

—Probate Practice Manual 1984 / Vancouver : Continuing Legal Education Society of British Columbia, 1984.
369p.
ISBN 0865041601 Hbk £75.00

—Wills/Probate Procedure for Manitoba and Saskatchewan / Jane Gordon. – 3rd ed. – North Vancouver : International Self-Counsel Press, 1985.
81p.
ISBN 088908503X Hbk £5.95

PROBATE - CANADA - ALBERTA

—Probate Guide for Alberta : a Step-by-Step Guide to Probating an Estate / 2nd ed. – North Vancouver : International Self-Counsel Press, 1983.
76p.
ISBN 088908226X Hbk £10.95

PROBATE - CANADA - BRITISH COLUMBIA

—Probate Guide for British Columbia : a Step-by-Step Guide to Probating an Estate / 8th ed. – North Vancouver : International Self-Counsel Press, 1986.
96p.
ISBN 0889081794 Hbk £12.95

PROBATE - CANADA - ONTARIO

—Ontario Estate Practice / J.R. Wilson. – 2nd ed. – Don Mills : CCH Canadian Ltd, 1986.
604p.
ISBN 0887962998 Pbk £39.95

—Probate Guide for Ontario : a Step-by-Step Guide to Probating an Estate / 4th ed. – North Vancouver : International Self-Counsel Press, 1986.
86p.
ISBN 088908355X Hbk £11.95

—Probate Practice : MacDonell, Sheard and Hull / Maurice Cullity. – 3rd ed. – Agincourt : Carswell, 1981.
774p.
This is a comprehensive volume for estate law practitioners in Ontario, Canada. The text covers valid wills, the recognition of holographic wills, survivorship, ancillary letters probate, conflict of laws relating to wills and estates, and numerous other probate topics.

PROBATE - ENGLAND

—Tristram and Coote's probate practice / Henry Charles Coote, R. B. Rowe. – 26th ed. – London : Butterworths, 1983.
lxii, 1178p.
ISBN 0406403163

PROBATE - GREAT BRITAIN

—Current Practice Directions : Family and Probate / London : Family Law, 1988.
ISBN 0853081085 loose £35.00

—Executors, Administration and Probate / Mortimer. – 16th ed. – London : Sweet & Maxwell, 1982.
ISBN 0420455000 Hbk £120.00

—Holloway's Probate Handbook / 6th ed. – London : Oyez Longman, 1982.
– (Oyez Longman Practitioner Ser.).
ISBN 0851206484 Hbk £15.00

—Probate / 11th ed. – London : Fourmat, 1987.
– (LCFS 3).
ISBN 1851900314 Pbk £2.45

—Probate handbook / 8th ed. – London : Longman Professional, 1987.
ISBN 0851212603 Hbk £32.00

—The Probate Manual / 23rd ed. – London : Waterlow, 1988.
382p.
ISBN 0080331092 Hbk £53.95

—Probate manual / Plumb. – 22nd ed. – London : Waterlow, 1985.
ISBN 0080392423 Hbk £19.95

—Probate Practice / Wellington : Butterworths.
This work is a comprehensive treatment of the subject of probate for United Kingdom practitioners in the field. The book provides an up to date reference for contentious and non-contentious probate matters.
ISBN 0406403228 Pbk

—Probate practice / Coote. – 27th ed. – London : Butterworths, 1988.
ISBN 0406403414 Hbk

—Probate Practice and Procedure / A. P. Rogers. – 2nd ed. – London : Fourmat, 1985.
240p.
ISBN 0906840856 Hbk £12.95

—Probate practice and procedure / Rogers. – 3rd ed. – London : Fourmat, 1988.
ISBN 1851900403 Pbk £19.95

—Williams, Mortimer and Sunnucks on executors, administrators and probate / by J.H.G. Sunnucks, J.G. Ross Martyn, K.M. Garnett. – London : Stevens & Sons, 1982.
clxxxviii,1157p; 26cm.
Concerned with probate practice and the work of executors and administrators, discussions of changes in the law of family provision, capital transfer tax and social security. Includes appendices which set out the relevant statutes, rules of court and statutory instruments.
ISBN 0420455000 £75.00

PROBATE - MALAYSIA

—Probate and Administration Act, 1959 (Act 97) / Kuala Lumpur : International Law Books Services.

PROBATE - NEW ZEALAND

—Probate and Administration Practice in New Zealand / J.B.K. Curran. – 4th ed. – Butterworths, 1986.
Includes material from various statutes, regulations, the new High Court Rules, Court decisions, and textbooks. Covers the developments in probate and administration law in New Zealand. Cross-referenced to Garrow and Alston's Law of Wills and Administration 5th edition 1984.
ISBN 0409621412 Hbk £91.30

—Probate Practice / Wellington : Butterworths.
This work is a comprehensive treatment of the subject of probate for United Kingdom practitioners in the field. The book provides an up to date reference for contentious and non-contentious probate matters.
ISBN 0406403228 Pbk

PROBATION – AUSTRALIA

—Legal Basis of Probation / Canberra : Australian Institute of Criminology.

—Probation and Parole : Interstate Supervision and Enforcement / Mary W. Daunton-Fear. – Canberra : Australian Institute of Criminology.

—Probation : Current Positions and New Directions / Canberra : Australian Institute of Criminology.

PROBATION – ENGLAND

—Day centres and probation / S. Fairhead with the the assistance of J. Wilkinson-Grey. – London : Home Office, 1981.
v,39p. – (Research Unit paper).
Bibliography: p.34.
ISBN 0862520185

—East Anglia and East Midlands probation hostels : a descriptive study / E.W. Mendelsohn. – Cambridge : Institute of Criminology, 1984.
95p. – (Occasional papers).
Includes bibliographical references.

—Manchester and Wiltshire multifacility schemes : a research report / Iain Crow, Ken Pease, Margy Hillary. – London? : NACRO, 1980.
iii,40p.
Includes bibliographical references.
ISBN 0850690188

—Probation officers' views of probation : a survey in West Yorkshire / R.I. Mawby. – Leeds : University of Leeds, Centre for Social Work and Applied Social Studies, 1981.
39p. – (Occasional paper).
Bibliography: p.35-39.

—Probation service in England and Wales : statement of national objectives and priorities / Great Britain. – London : Home Office, 1984.
6p.

—Public relations and criminal justice policy / Peter Nokes. – Leeds : Centre for Social Work and Applied Social Studies, 1982.
43p. – (Occasional paper).
'Occasioned by the seminar on Alternatives to Imprisonment ... held October 1980 - October 1981 under the auspices of the Centre for Applied Social Studies'. Bibliography: p.42-43.

—Special requirements in probation or supervision orders : a local case study / W.F. Bullock, W.M.S. Tildesley. – Cambridge : Institute of Criminology, 1984.
iii,131p. – (Occasional paper).
Bibliography: p.129-131.

PROBATION – GREAT BRITAIN

—Alternatives to custody / edited by John Pointing. – 1. – Oxford : Blackwell, 1986.
22cm.
Discusses diversity of options available within the probation services including: autocrime and driver retraining, intermediate treatment for offenders threatened with incarceration, options for problem drinkers, daytime training centres and community work programs.
ISBN 0631147012 Pbk Hbk £17.50
ISBN 0631147020 Pbk £6.95

—Index of Probation Service Research and Experimental Projects / 4th ed. – London : Home Office, 1980.
ISBN 0903727994 Pbk £0.50

—Probation and the community : a practice and policy reader / edited by John Harding. – London : Tavistock, 1987.
vii,248p; 22cm.
Includes bibliographies and index.
ISBN 0422795801 Hbk £16.95
ISBN 0422795909 Pbk £7.95

—Probation journal / London : National Association of Probation Officers, 1974-.
Continues: Probation.

—Probation Officer's Manual / 3rd ed. – London : Butterworths, 1980.
ISBN 0406256047 Pbk

Nineteen Eighty-Three supplement only
This work is a guide to the legal and administrative framework within which the probation officer works in the United Kingdom. The book covers all aspects of probation work from rules, duties, and procedures to the details of penal and training centres and rehabilitation programs.
ISBN 0406256063 Pbk

—Probation officer's manual / 4th ed. – London : Butterworths, 1987.
ISBN 040625608X Pbk £14.95

—Psychiatric Probation Orders : Roles and Expectations of Probation Officers and Psychiatrists / Cambridge : Institute of Criminology, 1980.

PROBATION – INDIA

—Commentaries on Probation of Offenders Act / 4th ed. – Allahabad : Law Publishers, 1983.

—Probation of Offenders Act and Rules : Central and States / 6th ed. – Allahabad : Law Book Company, 1988.

PROCEDURE (LAW)

—Case for the conversational analysis of courtroom interaction : some interactional dimensions of legal procedures / by Philip Wilkinson. – Oxford : Centre for Socio-Legal Studies, 1981.
24p. – (Working paper).
Includes bibliographical references.

—English legal system / by R.J. Walker. – 5th ed. – London : Butterworths, 1980.
xlvi,679p.

ISBN 0406677581

—International adjudication : procedural aspects / V.S. Mani. – The Hague : Martinus Nijhoff, 1980.
xx,456p.
Bibliography: p421-448.
ISBN 9024723671

—Trials on trial : the pure theory of legal procedure / Gordon Tullock. – New York : Columbia University Press, 1980.
xv,255p; 24cm.
Includes index.
ISBN 0231049528 £11.10

PROCEDURE (LAW) – AUSTRALIA

—Practice and procedure of the High Court and the Federal Court of Australia / editor, B.J. Camilleri. – Sydney : Butterworths, 1978.
looseleaf.
ISBN 0409373508

PROCEDURE (LAW) – CANADA

—Carswell's practice cases / Agincourt, Ont. : Carswell, 1977-.
24cm.
First series: vols. 1-50 (1977-85). - Second series: vol. 1, part 1 (Sept. 3, 1985)-. Cumulative index published at intervals.

PROCEDURE (LAW) – ENGLAND

—ABC guide to the practice of the magistrates' courts / by Emlyn Williams. – London : Sweet & Maxwell, 1986.
viii,187p; 22cm.
ISBN 0421344903 Pbk £14.50

—Civil and criminal procedure in a nutshell / Elizabeth Stevens. – London : Sweet & Maxwell, 1981.
vii,86p; 18cm. – (New nutshells).
Includes index.
ISBN 0421280409 Pbk £1.75

—Evidence and procedure in the Magistrates' Court / P.J. Rowe, S.J. Knapp. – London : Oyez Longman, 1982.
xxx,220p; 22cm.
Includes index.
ISBN 0851206697 Pbk Unpriced

—Humphrey's Notes on district registry practice and procedure / Steven A. Frieze. – 23rd ed. – London : Oyez Longman, 1983.
x,200p.
Includes index..
ISBN 0851207316

—Industrial tribunal : a practical guide to employment law and tribunal procedure / by John Mulhern and Ian McLean. – Chichester : Rose, 1982.
280p; 23cm.
Includes index.
ISBN 0859922243 £19.50

—Industrial tribunals : practice and procedure / by Donald B. Williams and D.J. Walker. – London : Butterworth, 1980.
xxii,258p; 25cm.
Includes index. Includes the text of relevant legislation.
ISBN 0406421056 £15.50

—Litigation for the Law Society finals / by Craig Osborne. – London : Sweet & Maxwell, 1987.
xiii,434p; 24cm.
Includes index.
ISBN 0421369205 Pbk £15.95

—Magistrates' courts bill : report on the consolidation of certain enactments relating to the jurisdiction of, and the practice and procedure before, magistrates' courts... / the Law Commission. – London : H.M.S.O., 1980.
7p.
ISBN 0101788703

PROCEDURE (LAW) – GREAT BRITAIN

—Discretionary Powers / Oxford : Oxford University Press, 1986.
ISBN 0198254989 Hbk £30.00

—English legal process / Terence Ingman. – London : Financial Training, 1983.
xxxiv,267p.
ISBN 0906322243

—Industrial tribunals : practice and procedure / by Michael J. Goodman. – 4th ed. – London : Sweet & Maxwell, 1987.
xxv,120p; 22cm.
Overview of the tribunals' principle jurisdictions, and analysis of practice and procedure before industrial tribunals. Covers the changes made by the Wages Act 1986. Contains model forms for application and response to an industrial tribunal, and the text of the Industrial Tribunals (Rules of Procedure) Regulations 1985.
ISBN 0421391200 Pbk No price

—Introduction to criminal and civil litigation / Brian Raymond. – London : Oyez, 1981.
170p; 24cm.
ISBN 0851205569 Pbk Unpriced

PROCEDURE (LAW) – MALAYSIA

—Rules of the Federal Court 1980 / Kuala Lumpur : Government Printer, 1980.
46p. – (P.U. (A)).

—Subordinate courts practice 1981 / by K.S. Dass and Abdul Hamid Bin Haji Mohamed : with a foreword by Tun Mohamed Suffian Bin Hashim : and an introduction by Raja Tan Sri Dr. Azlan Shah. – Johor : Asian Book, 1981.
lix,945p.
Includes index.

PROCEDURE (LAW) – NIGERIA

—Outline of customary court procedure / by R.A.I. Ogbobine. – Benin City, Nigeria : Ruf-Bine, 1985.
vi,46p.
ISBN 9783004514

—Supreme Court Rules 1985 / Nigeria. – Lagos : Federal Government Press, 1985.
98p.

PROCEDURE (LAW) – SOUTH AFRICA

—Civil practice of all courts for blacks in Southern Africa / J.A.M. Khumalo. – 3rd ed. – Cape Town : Juta, 1984.
xli,300p.
Previous ed. (1975) has title: Civil practice and procedure in all Bantu courts in Southern Africa. Bibliography: p.xix. - Includes index.
ISBN 0702114677

PROCEDURE (LAW) – SRI LANKA

—Report of the Sri Lanka Law's Delays and Legal Culture Committee / appointed by Hon. Dr. Nissanka Wijeyeratne, Minister of Justice. – Colombo : Ministry of Justice, 1985.
v,69p.
Chairman: R.S. Wanasundera.

PROCEDURE (LAW) – SWEDEN

—Swedish code of judicial procedure : the translation is that of the wording of the code of judicial procedure as at January 1, 1985 / National Council for Crime Prevention Sweden. – Stockholm : The Council, 1985.
230 p.; 25 cm. – (Report).
ISBN 9138088452 pbk.

PROCESS

—Practical handbook on the operation of the Hague Convention of 15 November 1965 on the service abroad of judicial and extrajudicial documents in civil or commercial matters / Antwerpen : Maarten Kluwer's Internationale Uitgeversonderneming, 1983.
vii,150p.
Bibliography: p148-150.
ISBN 906215073X

PROCESS – AUSTRALIA

—Process of Law in Australia : Intercultural Perspectives / Butterworths, 1988.
454p.
ISBN 0409494488 Pbk £39.00

—Reference on service and execution of process / Australian Law Reform Commission. – Sydney : The Commission, 1984.
v,175p.
Bibliography: p.175.

Research paper no. 3 : Tribunals / Australian Law Reform Commission. – 1984.
vii,87p.
Bibliography: p.86-87.

Research paper no. 5 : Service of other process / Australian Law Reform Commision. – 1984.
iv,64p.
Bibliography: p.64.

Reserach paper no. 7 : Discussion of reference : Draft Interstate Procedure Bill and regulations / Australian Law Reform Commission. – 1986.
iii,80p.
Includes text of draft bill.

—Reference on service and execution of warrants and writs of attachment / Australian Law Reform Commission. – Sydney : The Commission, 1984.
v,109,6p.
Bibliography: p.109.

—Service and execution of process / Law Reform Commission. – Canberra : Australian Government Publishing Service, 1987.
lix,539p. – (Report).
Bibliography: pp.527-531. - Includes index. Includes draft legislation.
ISBN 0644013796

—Statement of preliminary views / Constitutional Commission. Australian Judicial System Advisory Committee. – Canberra : The Commission, 1986.
40p.

PROCESS - AUSTRALIA - NEW SOUTH WALES
—Community law reform program / New South Wales Law Reform Commission. – Sydney : The Commission, 1983.
61p. – (L.R.C. 37).

PROCESS - AUSTRALIA - SOUTH AUSTRALIA
—Report ... relating to maintenance, champerty, embracery and barratry, malicious prosecution and abuse of process / Law Reform Committee of South Australia. – Adelaide : Government Printer, 1987.
86,3p. – (101st report).
Includes text of the Abolition of Obsolete Offences Act (1969).

PROCESS - COMMONWEALTH
—Recognition and enforcement of judgments and orders and the service of process within the Commonwealth : a report of a working meeting held in Nairobi, Kenya, 9-14 January 1980 / London : Commonwealth Secretariat, 1980.
xii,160p.

PROCESS - GREAT BRITAIN
—Commencement of actions in the High Court : new forms and procedure / by Sir Jack I. H. Jacob. – London : Butterworth, 1980.
vii,65p.
ISBN 0406395500

—Due Process of Law / London : Butterworths, 1980.
ISBN 0406176086 Pbk £8.95

—Frankfurter and Due Process / London : Eurospan, 1988.
ISBN 0819156159 Hbk £26.25
ISBN 0819156167 Pbk £15.50

PROCESSUS JUDICIAIRE
—Equality and judicial neutrality / Sheilah L. Martin and Kathleen E. Mahoney, editors. – Toronto : Carswell, 1986.
xxvii, 430 p.; 24 cm.
Papers presented at a conference held in Banff, Alta., May 22-24, 1986. Includes bibliographical references.
ISBN 0459308319

PRODUCT COUNTERFEITING
—Counterfeiting and national laws : counterfeiting and the Paris Convention / memorandum of the Director General. – Geneva : World Intellectual Property Organization, 1986.
46,4p. – (PAC/CE/I/2).
Prepared for an intergovernmental group of experts called Committee of Experts on the Protection Against Counterfeiting and scheduled to meet at W.I.P.O. Headquarters Geneva from May 5 to 7 1986'.

PRODUCT LIABILITY
—Comparative product liability / edited by C. J. Miller. – London : British Institute of International and Comparative Law, 1986.
xv,198p.
Based on revised papers and contributions originally submitted to a colloquium held by the United Kingdom National Committee for Comparative Law at the University of Edinburgh.
ISBN 0903067285

—Hague-Zagreb Essays / Dordrecht : Kluwer, 1978.
xiii, 255p.
ISBN 9028604782 Hbk £62.00

—International product liability : a study of comparative and international legal aspects of product liability / Harry Duintjer Tebbens. – Alphen aan den Kijn : Sijthoff and Noordhoff, 1980.
xix,433p.
Bibliography: p403-420.

—Product Liability Manual / Bern : European Office for Quality Control.

—Products Liability : Conference Papers / Woolloomooloo : International Business Communications, 1986.
ISBN 0949072052 Hbk £55.00

—Professional liability insurance : a one-day conference organised by Lloyd's of London Press Ltd., the London Press Centre, October 3, 1980 / London : Lloyds of London Press, 1981.
58 leaves in various pagings; 31cm.
ISBN 090409393X Hbk £20.00

PRODUCT LIABILITY.- AUSTRALIA
—Product liability / the Law Reform Commission. – Sydney : The Commission, 1988.
xii,86p. – (Discussion paper).
Bibliography: p.85-86.

—Product liability in Australia / Phegan. – North Ryde : Butterworths (Australia), 1983.
ISBN 0409491012 Hbk £30.00

—Product liability in Australia / S.W. Cavanagh and C.S. Phegan. – Sydney : Butterworths, 1983.
xxxvi, 267 p.; 25 cm.
Includes bibliographical references and index.
ISBN 0409491012

PRODUCT LIABILITY - CANADA
—Consumer product warranty reform : regulation in search of rationality / E.P. Belobaba. – Ottawa : Policy research, Analysis and Liasion Directorate, Consumer and Corporate Affairs, 1983.
157p.
Vol. 1 published as: Products liability and personal injury compensation in Canada. Bibliography: p.151-157.
ISBN 0662124162

—Interprovincial product liability litigation / Robert J. Sharpe. – Toronto : Butterworths, 1982.
xxi,145p.
Includes bibliographical references and index.
ISBN 0409866423

—Products Liability : 111 / Vancouver : British Columbia Continuing Legal Education Society, 1984.
ISBN 0865041512 Hbk £45.00

—Products Liability : 1982 / Vancouver : British Columbia Continuing Legal Education Society, 1982.
114p.
ISBN 0865040494 Hbk £45.00

—Products liability / by S.M. Waddams. – 2nd ed. – Toronto : Carswell, 1980.
xxix,282p; 24cm.
Includes index.
ISBN 0459330209

—Products liability and personal injury compensation in Canada : towards integration and rationalization / E.P. Belobaba. – Canada : Policy Research, Analysis and Liaison Directorate, Consumer and Corporate Affairs, 1983.
168p.
Bibliography: p.144-168.
ISBN 0662124154

PRODUCT LIABILITY - EUROPEAN COMMUNITY
—Implementation of EC directive on product liability : an explanatory and consultative note / Department of Trade and Industry. – London : The Department, 1985.
18,xivp.

PRODUCT LIABILITY - GREAT BRITAIN
—Agenda For Implementing New Law Product Liability / Deddington : Pandora Press, 1987.
ISBN 1870317858 £84.00

—Avoiding liability for defective products : a guide to the law on disclaimer of liability clauses in contracts for the sale of goods / Derrick Owles. – London : Product Liability International, 1987.
ix,52p.
ISBN 1850441200

—Defects in Components and Ingredients / Product Liability Briefing, 1988.
ISBN 1870317602 Pbk £4.95

—Defects through Storage and Transport / Product Liability Briefing, 1988.
ISBN 187031770X Pbk £4.95

—Design Defects / Product Liability Briefing, 1988.
ISBN 1870317505 Pbk £6.50

—Design Liability in the Construction Industry / 2nd ed. – Oxford : Blackwell Scientific, 1985.
ISBN 0003830209 Hbk £19.95

—Development of UK Product Safety Law / Product Liability Briefing, 1988.
ISBN 1870317807 Hbk £24.00

—Developments in Aviation Products Liability / London : LLoyd's of London Press, 1985.
ISBN 1850440352 Hbk

—Developments in the law of product liability : being the presidential address of Lord Griffiths, president of the Holdsworth Club of the Faculty of Laws in the Univeristy of Birmingham, 1986-1987 / birmingham : The Holdsworth Club of the University of Birmingham, 1987.
17p. – (The Holdsworth Club).
ISBN 0704409259

—Implementation of EC directive on product liability : an explanatory and consultative note / Department of Trade and Industry. – London : The Department, 1985.
18,xivp.

—Manufacturers' Liability for Defective Goods / Oxford : Blackwell Scientific, 1987.
ISBN 0003833623 Hbk £20.00

—Outline of the law of product liability and consumer protection / by Ronald Irving. – Chichester : Barry Rose, 1980.
312p.
Includes index. Includes texts of the Sale of Goods Act 1979 and the Unfair Contract Terms Act 1977.
ISBN 0859921662

—Product Liability Briefing : Executive Guide / Deddington : Pandora Press, 1987.
ISBN 187031705X Pbk £71.80

—Product liability casebook / London : Lloyd's of London Press, 1984.
ISBN 1850440158 Pbk £32.50

PRODUCT LIABILITY - UNITED STATES
—Motor vehicle safety standards and product liability in the USA / by John Lambert. – London : Economist Intelligence Unit, 1982.
131p.

—Products liability / by S.M. Waddams. – 2nd ed. – Toronto : Carswell, 1980.
xxix,282p; 24cm.
Includes index.
ISBN 0459330209

PROFESSIONAL ETHICS
—Professional responsibility / Paul Finn. – Auckland : Legal Research Foundation, 1987.
254p.
Includes bibliographical references. At head of t.p.: Legal Research Foundation Inc. seminar. 'University of Auckland, 28/29 May, 1987'. - Cover.

Part 2 : paper presented by Mr. Justice Rogers : and commentaries on papers published in part one presented by John C. Hagen ... et al 1987.
p.255-382.
At head of t.p.: Legal Research Foundation Inc. seminar. 'University of Auckland, 28/29 May, 1987'. - Cover.

PROFESSIONAL ETHICS - CANADA
—Professional Responsibility in Civil Law and Common Law / Toronto : DeBoo, 1984.
369p.
ISBN 0888201966 Hbk £75.00

PROFESSIONAL ETHICS - GREAT BRITAIN
—Professional negligence : a journal of liability, ethics and discipline / London : Cass, 1985-.

PROFESSIONAL NEGLIGENCE - GREAT BRITAIN
—Casebook on Profesional Negligence / Oxford : Blackwell Scientific, 1988.
ISBN 0003834182 Hbk £30.00

—Guide to Insurance Professional Negligence Risks / London : Butterworths, 1982.
ISBN 0406257108 Pbk £21.95

—Guide to the Insurance of Professional Negligence Risks / Wellington : Butterworths, 1982.
This book discusses in detail the coverage provided by the 'basic' United Kingdom professional indemnity policy and some of the more popular extensions in common practice. The work provides a general explanation of the law of professional negligence and insurance law.
ISBN 0406257108 Pbk £35.00

—Medical negligence / edited by Michael J. Powers and Nigel H. Harris; consulting editor: Andrew Lockhart-Miriams. – London : Butterworths, 1990.
900; 24cm.
Deals with all aspects of medical negligence claims. The book explains the relevant rules of law, identifies the practical difficulties in bringing an action for damages in respect of negligent medical treatment, and shows how to prepare the medical evidence on liability, how to complete the medical report on quantum, and how to present the experts evidence at court.
ISBN 0406130019 Hbk £120

—Medical Negligence : a Plaintiff's Guide / Agincourt : Cass, 1988.
ISBN 0714633399 Hbk £20.00
ISBN 0714640611 Pbk £12.00

—Professional indemnity claims / London : Architectural Press, 1984.
ISBN 0851397484 Hbk £14.50

—Professional Liability / 2nd ed. – London : Architectural Press, 1986.
ISBN 0851399525 Hbk £19.95

—Professional Negligence / K. M. Stanton. – 2nd ed. – Wellington : Butterworths, 1986.
This book presents a comprehensive review of the law of professional negligence in the United Kingdom. Breach of trust, conversion and fraud, and vicarious liability for conduct of a professional's employees are covered in the work, in addition to professional liability in contract or tort.
ISBN 0406179115 Hbk

—Professional negligence / Mannix. – 3rd ed. – London : Butterworths, 1982.
ISBN 0409309338 Pbk £14.00

—Professional negligence / Stanton. – 2nd ed. – London : Butterworths, 1988.
ISBN 0406179115 Hbk

PROFESSIONAL NEGLIGENCE - NORTHERN IRELAND
—Professional Negligence Today / Ethne Harkness. – Belfast : Queen's University of Belfast.
61p.

PROFESSIONS
—Sociology of the professions : lawyers, doctors and others / edited by Robert Dingwall and Philip Lewis. – London : Macmillan, 1983.
ix,314p; 23cm.
Bibliography: p286-306. - Includes index.
ISBN 0333309618 Hbk £15.00

PROFESSIONS - CANADA - ONTARIO
—Report of the Professional Organizations Committee / H. Allan Leal. – Toronto : Queen's Printer, 1980.
xvi,291p; 23cm.
Chairman: H. Allan Leal.
ISBN 0774348437

PROFESSIONS - EUROPEAN COMMUNITY
—Professions and services in the European Economic Community / by D. Lasok. – Deventer, The Netherlands : Kluwer Law and Taxation Publishers, 1986.
ISBN 9065442537 Hbk

—Professions in the European Community : towards freedom of movement and mutual recognition of qualifications / J.-P. de Crayencour. – Luxembourg : Office for Official Publications of the European Communities, 1981.
137p.
ISBN 9282527913

PROFESSIONS - GREAT BRITAIN
—Promotion for the Professions : A Guide to Practice Development / London : Kogan Page, 1985.
134p.
ISBN 0850389968 Hbk £12.95

PROFIT
—Unlawful gain and legitimate profit in Islamic law : riba, gharar and Islamic banking / Nabil A. Saleh. – Cambridge : Cambridge University Press, 1986.
xii,130p; 24cm. – (Cambridge studies in Islamic civilization).
Examines ban on taking interest and rejection of aleatory contracts in Islamic law. Considers consequent conflict with world banking system. Studies these rules in the four Sunni schools of law and the Ibadi.
ISBN 0521322987 £19.50

PROFIT - ENGLAND
—Profits of crime and their recovery / report of a committee chaired by Sir Derek Hodgson. – London : Heinemann, 1984.
viii,165p; 23cm.
Includes index.
ISBN 0435826506 No price

PROFIT-SHARING - GREAT BRITAIN
—Profit-sharing and share incentive / London : Fitzwilliam, 1988.
ISBN 187055504X Hbk £25.00

PROMISES
—Promises, morals, and law / by P.S. Atiyah. – Oxford : Clarendon Press, 1981.
218p; 23cm.
Includes index.
ISBN 019825377X £14.00

PROMISSORY NOTES - SOUTH AFRICA
—Bills of exchange, cheques and promissory notes in South African law / by F.R. Malan : assisted by C. R. de Beer. – Durban : Butterworths, 1983.
xii,441p.
Bibliography: p.377-391. - Includes index.
ISBN 0409040738

PROPERTY
—New family and the new property / Mary Ann Glendon. – Toronto : Butterworths, 1981.
xvii,269p; 23cm.
ISBN 0409834106

—Principles of Scottish private law / by David M. Walker. – 3rd ed. – Oxford : Clarendon, 1983.
lxxvii,608p; 24cm.
Previous ed. published in 2v.: 1975. Bibliography: plxxiii-lxxvii. - Includes index.
ISBN 0198761341 £30.00

—Property / Andrew Reeve. – London : Macmillan, 1986.
208p; 22cm.
Includes bibliography.
ISBN 0333367960 Hbk £20.00 :
ISBN 0333367979 Pbk £6.95

—Property and political theory / Alan Ryan. – Oxford : Blackwell, 1984.
198p; 24cm.
Includes index.
ISBN 0631136916 £15.00

—Student's Property Statutes / Repr. of 1927 ed. – Aalen Wuertt : Scientia.
xv, 244p.

—Taxes on immovable property : report by the Committee on Fiscal Affairs and the ad hoc Group on Urban Problems / Organisation for Economic Co-operation and Development. – Paris : O.E.C.D., 1983.
201p.
ISBN 9264124756

PROPERTY - AUSTRALIA
—Australian family property law / by I. J. Hardingham and M. A. Neave. – Sydney : Law Book Company, 1984.
liii,647p.
ISBN 0455205132

—Community of Property : Discussion Paper / National Women's Advisory Council. – Canberra : Australian Government Publishing Service, 1982.
34p.
ISBN 0644021802 Hbk £2.00

—Introduction to Property Law / B. Dwyer. – Butterworths, 1988.
223p.
ISBN 0409493082 Pbk £29.00

—Introduction to Property Law / B. M. Dwyer. – Sydney : Butterworths, 1988.
240p.
This volume, intended for student use, describes concepts of property, tenure and estates, registration, the Torrens system, gifts, leases, covenants, mortgages, and other topics.

—Property law : cases and materials / by Ronald Sackville and M.A. Neave. – 3rd ed. – Sydney : Butterworths, 1981.
lxxi,936p.
Includes index.
ISBN 0409300411 Pbk
ISBN 040930042X

—Property Law : Cases and Materials / M. Neave. – 4th ed. – Butterworths, 1988.
1,008p.
ISBN 0409492876 Hbk £79.00
ISBN 0409492884 Pbk £65.00

—Property Offences / M.S. Weinberg. – 2nd ed. – North Ryde : Law Book Co, 1986.
xl, 445p.
ISBN 0455206325 Hbk £65.00
ISBN 0455206333 Pbk £45.00

—Sackville and Neave Property Law : Cases and Materials / C. Rossiter. – 4th ed. – Sydney : Butterworths, 1988.
992p.
The fourth edition of this casebook contains revised materials on the Trade Practices Act, leases, and mortgages.

PROPERTY - AUSTRALIA - NEW SOUTH WALES
—Protected Persons and Their Property in N.S.W. / Mark Robinson. – North Ryde : Law Book Co, 1987.
xiv, 176p.
ISBN 0455207194 Pbk £27.50

PROPERTY - AUSTRALIA - QUEENSLAND
—Working paper on a bill to amend the Property Law Act 1974-1985 / Queensland Law Reform Commission. – Brisbane : The Commission, 1986.
53p. – (Q.L.R.C.W.P.).
Includes the text of the proposed bill.

PROPERTY - AUSTRALIA - SOUTH AUSTRALIA
—Report ... on the inherited imperial statute law in this state relating to the topics of property, trusts, uses, equity and wills / Law Reform Committee of South Australia. – Adelaide : Government Printer, 1980.
16p. – (54th report).

PROPERTY - AUSTRALIA - TASMANIA
—Report on contracts and the disposition of property by minors / Law Reform Commission of Tasmania. – Hobart : Acting Government Printer, 1987.
14p. – (Report).
Includes text of the Infants' Relief Act 1875.

—Working paper on the law relating to contracts and the disposition of property by minors / by D.R.C. Chalmers. – Hobart? : Government Printer?, 1985.
49,iip.
Cover title.

PROPERTY - AUSTRALIA - WESTERN AUSTRALIA
—Alteration of ground levels / the Law Reform Commission of Western Australia. – Perth the Commission, 1984.
89p. – (Discussion paper).

—Report on alteration of ground levels / the Law Reform Commission of Western Australia. – Perth : The Commission, 1986.
94p. – (Project).
Includes bibliographical references.

PROPERTY - CANADA
—Buying and Selling Commercial Property / Vancouver : Continuing Legal Education Society of British Columbia, 1985.
433p.
ISBN 086504189X Hbk £70.00

—Competing Rights to Mingled Property : in Clayton's Case / Victoria : Government of British Columbia, 1983.

—New Law of Expropriation / Stephen F. Waque. – Toronto : DeBoo, 1984.
This text provides analyses of reform legislation in Alberta, Manitoba, New Brunswick, Nova Scotia and Canada. Provincial statutes contain section-by-section commentaries. The main topics discussed are compensation where no land is taken, ways to prove expropriation claims, and types of claims successfully made.
ISBN 0888201532 Hbk £135.00

—Property Law : Cases, Text and Materials / Richard J. Balfour. – Aurora : Canada Law Book Co, 1982.
1400p. – (Case books).
Property Law provides edited versions of the leading real property and personal property cases, statutory references to the Canadian Common Law jurisdictions and textual material and commentary. The historical perspective of the work is complemented by a description and analysis of many recent proposals for reform in this area.

—Property law : cases, text and materials / Balfour. – Aurora : Canada Law Book, 1982.

—Property law : cases, texts, and materials / Derek Mendes da Costa, Richard J. Balfour. – Toronto : Emond-Montgomery, 1982.
xliii,1363p.
Includes index.
ISBN 0920722059

—Property Purchase Tax Act / Vancouver : Continuing Legal Education Society of British Columbia, 1987.
135p.
ISBN 086504323X Hbk £65.00

—Solicitor's Guide to Estate Practice in Ontario / Butterworths, 1986.
280p.
Practical guide covering retainer, application for Probate and Letters of Administration, asset administration, interpretation of wills finding beneficiaries, estate litigation, distribution of estate, preparation and passing off of accounts, and tax returns.
ISBN 0409810266 Hbk £50.00

—Workbook on Estates and Future Interests / Agincourt : Carswell, 1987.
130p.
Discussions include a review of the common law in its present form as it relates to property law, a survey of the rules set in textual format, and a quick review of the subject matter from the advanced reader. This text has been written from use with a first year property text.

PROPERTY - ENGLAND
—Butterworths property law handbook / consulting editor Ernest H. Scamell. – London : Butterworths, 1984.
This work contains all the statutory law of the United Kingdom relevant to property law. The law of trusts, law of succession, law of family assets, and conveyancing are presented in their legislative form.
ISBN 0406258171 PBK £14.95

—Family home / by W.T. Murphy and Hilary Clark. – London : Sweet & Maxwell, 1983.
229p; 19cm. – (Modern legal studies).
Includes index.
ISBN 0421287403 Hbk Unpriced
ISBN 0421287500 Pbk £6.95

—Family property and financial provision / by J.G. Miller. – 2nd ed. – London : Sweet & Maxwell, 1983.
xlvi,517p; 26cm.
Previous ed.: 1974. Includes index.
ISBN 0421282401 £36.00

—Law of property / Bernard Rudden, F. H. Lawson. – 2nd ed. – Oxford : Clarendon, 1982.
ix,247p; 23cm. – (Clarendon law series).
Previous ed.: published as Introduction to the law of property. 1958. Includes index.
ISBN 0198761287 Hbk £14.00
ISBN 0198761295 Pbk £6.95

—Stephen's commentaries on the laws of England / L. Crispin Warmington. – 21st ed. – London : Butterworths, 1950.
xviii,663p.
Index included in Vol. 4. .

—Sweet & Maxwell's property statutes / Nigel Gravell. – 5th ed. – London : Sweet & Maxwell, 1988.
550p; 24cm.
Includes index.
ISBN 0421352701 Pbk £13.00

PROPERTY - GREAT BRITAIN
—Administration of Property / ICSA. – Cambridge : Woodhead-Faulkner, 1986.
ISBN 0902197371 updat £45.00

—Co-ownership / London : Sweet & Maxwell, 1988.
ISBN 0421375000 Hbk £19.50

—Criminal Law : The Protection of Property / A. J. Smith. – London : Sweet & Maxwell, 1986.
ISBN 0420470409 Hbk

—Expropriation in Canada : a Practitioner's Guide / Aurora : Canada Law Book, 1988.

—Fundamentals of Property Management / London : Butterworths, 1988.
ISBN 0409787787 Pbk

—Introduction to Property / London : Butterworths, 1988.
ISBN 0406581002 Hbk
ISBN 0406581010 Pbk

—Introduction to Property Valuation / 2nd ed. – London : Estates Gazette, 1982.
ISBN 0728200589 Pbk £6.50

—Law of Property / Schoeman. – 2nd ed. – London : Butterworths, 1983.
ISBN 0409053120 Hbk £49.50
ISBN 0409053139 Pbk £35.40

—Law of Property / Rudden. – 2nd ed. – Oxford : Oxford University Press, 1982.
ISBN 0198761295 Pbk £8.50

—Property development / Austin-Crowe. – 2nd ed. – Spon (E & FN), 1983.
ISBN 0419128204 Pbk £9.50

—Property Development Library, 4 Vols. / London : Sweet & Maxwell, 1984.

—Property law handbook / London : Butterworths, 1984.
ISBN 0406258171 Pbk £17.50

—Property Valuation Handbook / Reading : College of Estate Management.
ISBN 090213289X Hbk £38.00

—Statistics for property people / London : Estates Gazette, 1986.
ISBN 0728200929 Pbk £14.00

—Survey of Documentary Sources for Property-Holding in London Before the Great Fire / V. A. Harding. – London : London Record Society, 1985.
ISBN 0900952229 Hbk £12.00

—Understanding property law / Roberts. – London : Fontana, 1987.
ISBN 0006860737 Pbk £4.95

—Valuation of property investments / 3rd ed. – London : Estates Gazette, 1984.
ISBN 0728200732 Pbk £10.00

—Wives and property : reform of the married women's property law in nineteenth-century England / Lee Holcombe. – Oxford : Martin Robertson, 1983.
viii,311p; 24cm.
Bibliography: p275-292. - Includes index.
ISBN 0855206071 £15.00

PROPERTY – INDIA

—Hindu Women's Right to Property in India / New Delhi : Deep and Deep Publications, 1986.
528p.

—Indian Stamp Act : With State Amendments / 6th ed. – Allahabad : Law Book Ccompany, 1986.
800p.

—Lahiri's Transfer of Property Act / 11th ed. – Calcutta : Eastern Law House, 1986.
1,047p.

—Stridhana or Woman's Property in Indian Law : An Appraisal of its Concept and Contents / Hoshiarpur : Vishveshvaranand Institute.

—Transfer of Property Act, 2 Vols. / 5th ed. – Allahabad : Law Book Company, 1988.
3,000p.

PROPERTY – NEW ZEALAND

—Economic Approach to Property Value / Auckland : Legal Research Foundation, 1981.
35p.

—New Zealand Conveyancing and Property Reports / Butterworths, 1983.
ISBN 0409701416 Hbk £71.50

—Property Investment / 2nd ed. – Butterworths, 1980.
ISBN 0409600814 Pbk £33.00

PROPERTY – NIGERIA

—Nigerian law of property / by Martin Chukwuka Okany. – Enugu, Nigeria : Fourth Dimension, 1986.
lxii,762p.
Bibliography: p.757-762. - Includes index.
ISBN 9781562153

PROPERTY – SCOTLAND

—Principles of Scottish private law / by David M. Walker. – 4th ed. – Oxford : Clarendon, 1988.
cxi,595p.
Previous ed: 1983. Includes index.
ISBN 0198762178 £40.00

PROPERTY – SINGAPORE

—Property Tax in Singapore / Butterworths, 1985.
256p.
ISBN 040999510X Pbk £50.00

PROPERTY – SOUTH AFRICA

—Family, things and succession / Lee and Honore. – 2nd ed. – Durban : Butterworths, 1983.
xvii,615p.
Bibliography: p.vii-xiv. - Includes index.
ISBN 0409040533

—Law of property / Silberberg and Schoeman. – 2nd ed. – Durban : Butterworth, 1983.
xvi,575p.
Previous ed.: 1975. Bibliography: p.521-3. - Includes index.
ISBN 0409053120 Hbk R98

—Law of property / A.J. Oosthuizen. – Cape Town : Juta, 1981.
xiii,105p.
Bibliography: p.v.
ISBN 0702111937

—Power of a Testator to Dispose of the Property of Another : a Study of the South African Law of Massing and Election, with a Comparative Look at English, Dutch and German Law / Pijnacker : Dutch Efficiency Bureau.
ISBN 9062310273 Hbk £30.80

PROPERTY – SRI LANKA

—Law of Property in Sri Lanka, Vol 1 / Colombo : Lake House Investments.

PROPERTY – USSR

—Soviet law of property : the right to control property and the construction of communism / by George M. Armstrong, Jr. – The Hague : M. Nijhoff Publishers, 1983.
vii,167p.
Includes index. Bibliography: p155-163. Based on the author's thesis (Ph. D.–Princeton).
ISBN 9024728649 Hbk £80.00

PROSECUTION

—How to Frame a Charge / 1981 repr. – Lucknow : Eastern Book Company, 1985.
174p.

PROSECUTION – AUSTRALIA

—Prosecution policy of the Commonwealth : guidelines for the making of decisions in the prosecution process and the considerations upon which these decisions are made / Attorney-General's Department. – Canberra : Australian Government Publishing Service, 1983.
20p.
Originally published: 1982.
ISBN 0644022779

—Prosecution without Trial / Butterworths, 1989.
ca 336p.
ISBN 040949478X Hbk £55.00

—Special Prosecutors Office : Report to the Attorney-General / Canberra : Australian Government Publishing Service, 1983.
15p.
ISBN 0644012528 Hbk £1.70

PROSECUTION – CANADA

—Private prosecutions / Law Reform Commission of Canada. – Ottawa : Law Reform Commission of Canada, 1986.
51,59p; 25cm. – (Working paper).
Cover title: Criminal law - private prosecutions. Added t.p. in French: Les poursuites privees. Pages numbered in opposite directions. Text in English and French.
ISBN 0662544595

PROSECUTION – CYPRUS

—Modern trends concerning the reduction of prosecutions / by Criton G. Tornaritis. – Nicosia : s.l., 1984.
13 leaves.

PROSECUTION – ENGLAND

—Courts, prosecution, and conviction / by Michael McConville and John Baldwin. – Oxford : Clarendon, 1981.
232p; 23cm.
Bibliography: p213-226. - Includes index.
ISBN 0198253559 £12.00

—Independent prosecution service for England and Wales / presented to Parliament by the Secretary of State for the Home Department and the Attorney General... – London : H.M.S.O., 1983.
32p.
ISBN 0101907400

—Investigation and prosecution of criminal offences in England and Wales : the law and procedure / the Royal Commission on Criminal Procedure : Chairman: Sir Cyril Philips. – London : H.M.S.O., 1981.
vii,229p; 25cm.
ISBN 0101809212 Pbk £7.50

—Organisation of an independent prosecution service : a discussion paper / Working Party on Prosecution Arrangements. – London : Home Office, 1982.
11 leaves.

—Prosecutor's handbook / by J.V. Bates. – London : Oyez, 1980.
xxvi,121p; 22cm.
Includes index.
ISBN 0851205100 Pbk £8.95

—Report / the Royal Commission on Criminal Procedure : chairman: Sir Cyril Philips. – London : H.M.S.O., 1981.
xiii,240p; 25cm.
Includes index.
ISBN 0101809204 Pbk £10.00

—Staff resource implications of an independent prosecution system / Peter R. Jones. – London : Home Office, 1983.
v,39p.
Bibliography: p.32.
ISBN 086252119X

—Triable-either-way cases : Crown Court or Magistrates' Court? / by David Riley and Julie Vennard. – London : H.M.S.O., 1988.
52 p.
Discusses whether the balance of either-way business could be redistributed in favour of the Magistrates' Court by encouraging them to accept jurisdiction more often in such cases.
ISBN 0113408900

—Who prosecutes? : the future of the prosecuting service / Association of County Councils. – London : The Association, 1983.
5p.

PROSECUTION – GREAT BRITAIN

—Annual report for the period April ... to March ... from the Director of Public Prosecutions to the Attorney General / Crown Prosecution Service. – London : H.M.S.O., 1987-.
v.
Presented to Parliament in pursuance of Section 9 of the Prosecution of Offences Act 1985, Ch. 23.

—Contested trials in magistrates' courts : the case for the prosecution / Julie Vennard with the assistance of Karen Williams. – London : H.M.S.O., 1980.
vi,26p. – (Research studies).
Bibliography: p 26.
ISBN 0117301256

—Prosecution system : survey of prosecuting solicitors' departments / Mollie Weatheritt in collaboration with Joan MacNaughton; and organisational implications of change : David R. Kaye with the assistance of R.L. Redman and G.J. Brennand. – London : H.M.S.O., 1980.
v,104p. – (Research studies).
ISBN 0117301302

—Prosecutions by private individuals and non-police agencies / K.W. Lidstone, Russell Hogg and Frank Sutcliffe, in collaboration with A.E. Bottoms and Monica A. Walker. – London : H.M.S.O., 1980.
xi,236p. – (Research studies).
Bibliography: p201-203.
ISBN 0117301299

—Role of the Prosecutor / London : LSEPS, 1987.
ISBN 0566057239 Hbk £22.50

PROSECUTION – INDIA

—Police Investigations and Prosecutions / 5th ed. 1986 repr. 1987. – Allahabad : Law Book Company, 1987.
900p.

PROSECUTION – SCOTLAND

—Prosecuting sexual assault / G. Chambers, A. Millar. – Edinburgh : H.M.S.O., 1986.
ix,144p.
Research by the Central Research Unit of the Scottish Office. Reports on police investigation of sexual assault cases and on prosecution and trial methods.
ISBN 0114933715

—Prosecution in the public interest / Susan R. Moody and Jacqueline Tombs. – Edinburgh : Scottish Academic Press, 1982.
xii, 167p.
Examines the decision-making process of the Procurator Fiscal as to whether to prosecute, on what, and by what procedure to prosecute. Bibliography: p.160-163.
ISBN 0707303214 Hbk

PROSTITUTION

—Meeting of Experts on the Exploitation of the Child, November 12-13, 1984, Singapore and the Conference on Child Labour and Child Prostitution, February 21-23, 1986, Kuala Lumpur / convened by the LAWASIA Human Rights Standing Committee : editor, Patricia Hyndman. – Sydney : LAWASIA, 1986.
513p.
Includes bibliographical references.

PROSTITUTION – CANADA

—Pornography and prostitution in Canada : report of the Special Committee on Pornography and Prostitution / Canada. – 2 v. – Ottawa : Canadian Government Publishing Centre, 1985.
ISBN 0660118092

—Pornography and prostitution in Canada : report of the Special Committee on Pornography and Prostitution : summary / Canada. – Ottawa : Department of Justice, 1985.
65,71p.
With French t.p.: La pornographie et la prostitution au Canada. Pages numbered in opposite directions. English and French text.
ISBN 066253686X

—Pornography and prostitution : issues paper : this is a discussion paper / prepared by the Special Committee on Pornography and Prostitution appointed by the Minister of Justice for Canada. – Ottawa, Canada : Dept. of Justice, Communications and Public Affairs, 1983.
ii, 78, 100 p.; 28 cm.
English and French. Title on added t.p.: Pornographie et prostitution.
ISBN 0662527682 pbk.

PROSTITUTION – GREAT BRITAIN

—Report / Criminal Law Revision Committee. – London : H.M.S.O., 1985.
31 p.
ISBN 0101968809

—Reports / London : H.M.S.O., 1984.
ISBN 0101932901 PBK £4.00

—Working paper on offences relating to prostitution and allied offences / London : H.M.S.O., 1982.
vi,57p.
ISBN 011340784X

PROVISIONAL REMEDIES

—Non-appearance before the International Court of Justice : functional and comparative analysis / Jerome B. Elkind. – Dordrecht : Martinus Nijhoff, 1984.
xiv,233p.
Bibliography: 207-213.
ISBN 9024729211 Hbk £110.00

PROXIMATE CAUSE (LAW)

—Causation in the law / by H.L.A. Hart and Tony Honore. – 2nd ed. – Oxford : Clarendon, 1985.
lxxxi,516p; 23cm.
Previous ed.: 1959. Bibliography: p498-507. - Includes index.
ISBN 019825475X Hbk £25.00
ISBN 0198254741 Pbk £14.50

PSYCHIATRIC ETHICS LECTURES

—Psychiatry, law, and ethics / edited by A. Carmi : with contributions by G. Ammon ... et al. – Berlin : Springer-Verlag, 1984.
ISBN 0387157425

PSYCHIATRIC HOSPITALS – ENGLAND

—Compulsory admissions to mental hospitals / Philip Bean. – Chichester : Wiley, 1980.
xii,278p; 24cm.
Bibliography: p267-273. - Includes index.
ISBN 0471277584 £16.70

—Representing the mentally ill and handicapped : a guide to Mental Health Review Tribunals / Larry Gostin and Elaine Rassaby : with a foreword by Tom Harper. – Sunbury : Quartermine House Ltd for National Association for Mental Health and the Legal Action Group, 1980.
xix,215p; 21cm.
Bibliography: p.209. - Includes index.

PSYCHIATRIC SOCIAL WORK – GREAT BRITAIN

—Draft guidelines for approval of social workers under the proposed Mental Health (Amendment) Act : Working Party draft for consultation / Department of Health and Social Security. – London : The Department, 1981.
11p.

PSYCHIATRISTS – UNITED STATES

—Law and psychological practice / Robert L. Schwitzgebel, R. Kirkland Schwitzgebel. – New York : Wiley, 1980.
xv,416p; 24cm.
Includes index.
ISBN 0471766941 £9.00

PSYCHIATRY

—Criminal law and psychiatry / by D.J. Power : co-author D.H.D. Selwood. – S.l. : Barry Rose, 1987.
xviii,265p.
ISBN 1870080254

—Law of Psychiatry and Morality / Cambridge : Cambridge University Press, 1986.
ISBN 0521339545 Pbk £12.95

—Psychiatry and the criminal process / edited by Ronnie Mackay and Ken Russell. – Leicester : Leicester Polytechnic Law School, 1986.
48p. – (Leicester Polytechnic Law School monographs).
Includes bibliographical references.
ISBN 0948997281

—Psychiatry, Human Rights and the Law / Bluglass. – Cambridge : Cambridge University Press, 1985.
ISBN 0521261945 Hbk £30.00

PSYCHIATRY – CANADA

—Psychiatric Issues in Criminal Law / Vancouver : British Columbia Continuing Legal Education Society, 1982.
ISBN 0865040826 Hbk £45.00

PSYCHOANALYSIS

—Thou shalt not be aware : society's betrayal of the child / by Alice Miller : translated from the German by Hildegard and Hunter Hannum. – London : Pluto, 1985.
viii, 331p.
Originally published: Frankfurt am Main: Surkamp Verlag, 1981. Bibliography: p.327-331. Translation of: Du sollst nicht merken.
ISBN 0745300499

PSYCHOLOGICAL TESTS – UNITED STATES

—Evaluating competencies : forensic assessments and instruments / Thomas Grisso. – New York : Plenum, 1986.
x,404p; 24cm.
Bibliography: p365-383. - Includes index.
ISBN 0306421267 No price

PSYCHOLOGY

—Case for the conversational analysis of courtroom interaction : some interactional dimensions of legal procedures / by Philip Wilkinson. – Oxford : Centre for Socio-Legal Studies, 1981.
24p. – (Working paper).
Includes bibliographical references.

—Law and psychology : papers presented at SSRC Law and Psychology Conferences 1979-1980 / edited by Sally LLoyd-Bostock. – Oxford : SSRC Centre for Socio-Legal Studies, 1981.
x,165p; 21cm. – (Conference papers).
Includes bibliographical references. 'The papers in this collection were originally presented at two meetings of the SSRC Law and Psychology Seminar Group, held in Oxford during 1979-1980'.
ISBN 0862260752

—Proof of fact in criminal trials / Marcus Stone. – Edinburgh : W. Green, 1984.
xxiii,390p; 22cm.
ISBN 0414007379

—Psychology and law : topics from an internatinal conference / edited by Dave J. Muller, Derek E. Blackman and Antony Chapman. – Chichester : Wiley, 1984.
xxii,472p; 24cm.
Conference papers. Includes bibliographies and index.
ISBN 0471903361 £29.75

—Psychology in legal contexts : applications and limitations / edited by Sally M.A. Lloyd-Bostock. – London : Macmillan, 1981.
xix,246p. – (Oxford socio-legal studies).

PSYCHOLOGY – AUSTRALIA

—Psychologist in Criminal Justice : An Australian Perspective / Canberra : Australian Institute of Criminology.

—Role of Psychologists in the Criminal Justice System / Canberra : Australian Institute of Criminology.

PSYCHOLOGY – UNITED STATES

—Law and psychological practice / Robert L. Schwitzgebel, R. Kirkland Schwitzgebel. – New York : Wiley, 1980.
xv,416p; 24cm.
Includes index.
ISBN 0471766941 £9.00

PSYCHOPATHIC PERSONALITY – ENGLAND

—Offenders suffering from psychopathic disorder / joint DHSS-Home Office consultation document. – London : Department of Health and Social Security, 1986.
13p.

PUBLIC CONTRACTS – AUSTRALIA

—Public torts and contracts / by Mark Aronson and Harry Whitmore. – Sydney : Law Book Co., 1982.
xviii, 296 p.; 25 cm.
Includes bibliographical references and indexes.
ISBN 0455204411 pbk.

PUBLIC DEFENDERS – CANADA – BRITISH COLUMBIA

—Burnaby, British Columbia experimental public defender project : an evaluation / Patricia Brantingham et al. – 7 v. – Ottawa : Department of Justice, 1981.
Contents: Report 1. Summary - Report 2. Effectiveness analysis - Report 3. Cost analysis - Report 4. Client satisfaction analysis - Report 5. Tariff analysis - Report 6. Relationships analysis - Report 7. Distribution impact analysis. 'Undertaken under contract for the Department of Justice, Canada with the assistance of the British Columbia Legal Services Society'. Report 1 has added t.-p. in French. English and French text of report 1.

PUBLIC DEFENDERS – GREAT BRITAIN

—Public defender : a report / by JUSTICE : chairman of committee James Morton. – London : JUSTICE, 1987.
51p.
ISBN 0907247091

PUBLIC DEFENDERS – UNITED STATES

—Juveniles' waiver of rights : legal and psychological competence / Thomas Grisso. – New York : Plenum, 1981.
xiii,295p; 24cm.
Bibliography: p279-286. - Includes index.
ISBN 0306405261 Unpriced

PUBLIC FINANCE

—Managing Public Money / University Press Of America, 1988.
ISBN 0819165050 Hbk £22.95
ISBN 0819165069 Pbk £11.50

—Public finance in developing countries / A. R. Prest. – 3rd ed. – London : Weidenfeld and Nicolson, 1985.
xiii,236p.
Bibliography: p226-228.
ISBN 0297785788

PUBLIC FINANCE – CANADA

—Local government finance in Canada / Harry M. Kitchen. – Toronto : Canadian Tax Foundation, 1984.
xvii,495p.
Includes bibliographical references and index.
ISBN 0888080204

—Recovery of Unauthorized Disbursements of Public Funds / Victoria : Government of British Columbia, 1980.

PUBLIC FINANCE – GREAT BRITAIN

—Public finance in theory and practice / A.R. Prest, N.A. Barr. – 7th ed. – London : Weidenfeld and Nicolson, 1985.
xvi, 553p.
Includes bibliographical references.

PUBLIC FINANCE – UNITED STATES

—Public finance in theory and practice / Richard A. Musgrave, Peggy B. Musgrave. – 4th ed. – New York : McGraw-Hill, 1984.
xvi,824p; 25cm.
Previous ed: 1980. Includes bibliographies and index.
ISBN 007044126X £26.95

PUBLIC HOUSING

—Crime and public housing : proceedings of a workshop held in September 1980 / edited by Mike Hough and Pat Mayhew. – London : Home Office, 1982.
v,77p. – (Research and Planning Unit paper).
Includes bibliographies.
ISBN 0862520347

PUBLIC HOUSING – ENGLAND

—Council houses and the Housing Act 1980 / by Peter Liell. – London : Butterworths, 1981.
xxxi,457p.
Includes the text of the Act.
ISBN 0406270309

—Council housing / by David C. Hoath. – 2nd ed. – London : Sweet & Maxwell, 1982.
xxvii,223p; 18cm.
Previous ed.: 1978. Includes index.
ISBN 042127610X Hbk Unpriced
ISBN 0421276207 Pbk £6.95

—Housing improvement and repair / Christopher J. Wright. – London : Sweet & Maxwell, 1986.
xiv,130p; 26cm.
Bibliography: p125. - Includes index.
ISBN 0421358203 £16.50

—Preventing rent arrears / Sue Duncan, Keith Kirby. – London : H.M.S.O., 1983.
144p; 21cm.
At head of title: Department of the Environment.
ISBN 0117517100 Pbk £4.00

—Public sector housing law / by D.J. Hughes. – London : Butterworths, 1981.
xxxiv,359p; 22cm.
Includes bibliographies and index.
ISBN 0406600619 Hbk Unpriced
ISBN 0406600600 Pbk Unpriced

—Public sector housing law / D.J. Hughes. – 2nd ed. – London : Butterworths, 1987.
xxxix,329p.
Previous ed.: 1981. Includes bibliographies and index.
ISBN 0406600627 Pbk £14.95

—Race and council housing in Hackney / report of a formal investigation conducted by the Commission for Racial Equality into the allocation of housing in the London Borough of Hackney. – London : The Commission, 1984.
145p; 30cm.
ISBN 0907920411 Pbk Unpriced

PUBLIC HOUSING – GREAT BRITAIN

—Allocation of council housing / Paul Spicker. – London : Shelter, 1983.
43p; 21cm.
ISBN 0901242683 Pbk £1.50

—Homes for the future : statement to Annual Comnference 1985 / by the Labour Party National Executive Committee. – London : Labour Party, 1985.
47p.
ISBN 0861171233

—New tenancy agreements : a model for landlords and tenants based on the Housing Act 1980 / National Consumer Council. – London : The Council, 1981.
22p.
ISBN 0905653378

—Problems of public housing / Policy Studies Institute, 1988.
ISBN 0853743509 Pbk £6.95

—Public sector housing law / 2nd ed. – London : Butterworths, 1987.
ISBN 0406600627 Pbk £16.95

PUBLIC HOUSING – SCOTLAND

—Public sector housing law in Scotland / by Chris Himsworth. – Glasgow : Planning Exchange, 1982.
vii,126p; 22cm.
Includes index.
ISBN 090501118X Pbk Unpriced

PUBLIC LENDING RIGHTS (OF AUTHORS)

—Public lending right : reports of an ALAI symposium and additional materials / edited by H. Cohen Jehoram. – Deventer (Netherlands) : Kluwer Law and Taxation Publishers, 1983.
vi, 198p.
Reports of the 1977 ALAI Antwerp symposium, organised by the Belgian Copyright Association, and additional contributions from Australia - New Zealand, Iceland, Norway, the USA and the UK.
ISBN 9065441344

PUBLIC MEETINGS

—The right of peaceful assembly : its evolution and limits in a democratic society : a conference jointly organised by the British Institute of Human Rights and the United Kingdom Association for European Law in the Old Hall, Lincoln's Inn, on 30th April, 1982 / report prepared by Anthony McNulty. – London : British Institute of Human Rights, 1982.
ii,94p.
ISBN 0950835706

PUBLIC OPINION

—Legal databases in Europe : user attitudes and supplier strategies / Michael Lloyd. – Amsterdam : North-Holland, 1986.
xiii, 218 p.; 24 cm.
At head of title: Commission of the European Communities. 'Report no. EUR 10439 of the Commission of the European Communities'–T.p. verso. Bibliography: p.205.
ISBN 044470048X

PUBLIC OPINION – CANADA

—Law in a Cynical Society : Law and Public Opinion in the 1980's / Dale Gibson. – Agincourt : Carswell, 1985.
484p.

PUBLIC OPINION – GREAT BRITAIN

—People's justice : a major poll of public attitudes on crime and punishment / Stephen Shaw. – London : Prison Reform Trust, 1982.
29p; 30cm.
Cover title.
ISBN 0946209006 Pbk £1.00

PUBLIC OPINION – INDIA

—Law and Public Opinion in India / New Delhi : Deep and Deep Publications, 1985.
311p.

PUBLIC ORDER

—Human rights in internal strife : their international protection / by Theodor Meron. – Cambridge : Grotius, 1987.
xiii,172p.
An examination of the problem of protecting human rights in internal strife and of developing adequate safeguards in areas beyond the scope of the Geneva Conventions.
ISBN 0949009040

—Studies in World Public Order / Myres S. McDougal and Associates. – Dordrecht : Kluwer, 1987.
1,080p.
ISBN 08938389003 Hbk £350.00

PUBLIC ORDER – ENGLAND

—Criminal law : offences relating to public order / the Law Commission. – London : H.M.S.O., 1983.
vii,135p.
ISBN 0102085846

—Public order : a guide to the 1986 Public Order Act / by John Marston. – London : Fourmat Publishing, 1987.
189p.
ISBN 1851900241

—Public order review : civil disturbances 1981-1985 / Metropolitan Police Force. – London : Metropolitan Police, 1986.
iv,43p.

—Scarman and after : essays reflecting on Lord Scarman's report, the riots and their aftermath / edited by John Benyon : with an epilogue by Lord Scarman. – Oxford : Pergamon, 1984.
xiv,292p; 24cm.
Conference papers. Bibliography: p263-274. - Includes index.
ISBN 0080302173 Hbk Unpriced
ISBN 0080302181 Pbk £7.50

—Scarman Report : the Brixton disorders, 10-12 April 1981 : report of an inquiry / by Lord Scarman. – Reprint, with preface. – Harmondsworth : Penguin, 1986.
xx,255p. – (Pelican books).
Previous ed.: 1982.
ISBN 014022744X

—To ride the storm : the 1980 Bristol 'riot' and the state / Harris Joshua, Tina Wallace and Heather Booth. – London : Heinemann, 1983.
vii,221p.
Bibliography: p211-216.
ISBN 0435824813

PUBLIC ORDER – EUROPE

—Political Violence and Civil Disobedience in Western Europe / London : Institute for the Study of Conflict, 1982.
– (Conflict Studies Ser.: No. 145).

PUBLIC ORDER – GREAT BRITAIN

—As I was saying / Police Review, 1985.
ISBN 0851640168 Pbk £6.95

—Broadwater Farm Inquiry / London : CEMT, 1986.
ISBN 094691897 Pbk £4.95

—Civil disorder and civil liberties : evidence to the Scarman inquiry / London : National Council for Civil Liberties, 1981.
46p; 21cm.
ISBN 0901108960

—Conflict and Order / Oxford : Oxford University Press, 1987.
ISBN 0198201281 Hbk £30.00

—Law of Public Order and National Security / Supperstone. – 2nd ed. – London : Butterworths, 1981.
ISBN 0406137013 Hbk £49.00

—Neighbourhood watch : policing the people / London : CENT, 1986.
ISBN 0951119508 Pbk £1.50

—Public disorder : a review of research and a study in one inner city area / by Simon Field and Peter Southgate. – London : H.M.S.O., 1982.
v, 73p.
Bibliographies. Contents: Urban disorders in Britain and America: a review of research/Simon Field - The disturbances of July 1981 in Handsworth, Birmingham: a survey of the views and experiences of male residents/Peter Southgate. A Home Office Research and Planning Unit report.
ISBN 011340767X

—Public Order Act : Elizabeth II, 1986. Chapter 64 / Peter Thornton. – London : Financial Training Publications, 1987.
xxi, 226p.
Bibliography: p.219-220. Includes the text of the Public Order Act 1986.
ISBN 1851850406

—Public order - the new law / London : Butterworths, 1987.
ISBN 0406504407 Pbk £12.50

—Uprising! : the police, the people and the riots in Britain's cities / Martin Kettle and Lucy Hodges. – London : Pan Books, 1982.
271p; 18cm.
ISBN 0330268457

—Urban riots and public order : a select bibliography, 1975-1985 / compiled by: E. Edwards, R. Golland & S. Leach for the GLC Intelligence Unit. – Letchworth : Technical Communications, 1986.
iii,159p; 30cm.
ISBN 0946655103 Hbk

PUBLIC ORDER – SCOTLAND

—Mobbing and rioting / Scottish Law Commission. – Edinburgh : Scottish Law Commission, 1984.
102p. – (Consultative memorandum).

PUBLIC ORDER OFFENCES – AUSTRALIA

—Public order and the law / by Andrew Hiller : with a foreword by Judge Gibney. – Sydney : Law Book Co., 1983.
xx,230p.
Bibliography: p.xix-xx. - Includes index.
ISBN 0455202761
ISBN 0455204101 £26.00

PUBLIC ORDER OFFENCES – ENGLAND

—Government's reply to the third report from the Home Affairs Committee, session 1980-1981 HC271, Vagrancy offences / presented to Parliament by the Secretary of State for the Home Department. – London : H.M.S.O., 1981.
3p; 25cm.
ISBN 0101831102 unbound £0.70

—Offences against public order / the Law Commission. – London : H.M.S.O., 1982.
viii,194p. – (Working paper).
ISBN 0117301620

—Scarman and after : essays reflecting on Lord Scarman's report, the riots and their aftermath / edited by John Benyon : with an epilogue by Lord Scarman. – Oxford : Pergamon, 1984.
xiv,292p; 24cm.
Conference papers. Bibliography: p263-274. - Includes index.
ISBN 0080302173 Hbk Unpriced
ISBN 0080302181 Pbk £7.50

PUBLIC ORDER OFFENCES – GREAT BRITAIN

—Brixton disorders 10-12 April 1981 : report of an enquiry / by Lord Scarman. – London : H.M.S.O., 1981.
viii,168p; 25cm.
Report of inquiry by Lord Scarman. Discusses causes of the riots and lessons for the future about riot control and prevention.
ISBN 0101842708 Pbk £8.00

—Law and order and British politics / edited by Philip Norton. – Aldershot : Gower, 1984.
viii,224p; 23cm.
Bibliography: p215-217. - Includes index.
ISBN 056600688X £16.45

—Offences against public order : including the Public Order Act 1986 / by A.T.H. Smith. – London : Sweet and Maxwell, 1987.
xlvii,326p; 25cm.
Analysis of the Public Order Act 1986, explaining provisions and their practical applications. Also deals with features of existing law not affected by the act, such as obstructing the highway, obstructing a police officer in the execution of his duty, and the possession of offensive weapons.
ISBN 0421365803 Pbk £10.00

—Public order - the new law / Richard Card. – London : Butterworths, 1987.
170p; 25cm.
Includes index.
ISBN 0406504407 Pbk £10.00

—Review of the Public Order Act 1936 and related legislation / presented to Parliament by the Secretary of State for the Home Department and the Secretary of State for Scotland .. – London : H.M.S.O., 1980.
vi,36p; 25cm.
ISBN 0101789106 sd £2.50

—Third report from the Home Affairs Committee, session 1980-81 : vagrancy offences : together with proceedings of the Committee, the minutes of evidence and appendices / London : H.M.S.O., 1981.
xxiv,70p; 25cm. – (HC).
Bound with: The Government's reply.
ISBN 010227181X

—We protest : the public order debate / Peter Thornton. – London : National Council for Civil Liberties, 1985.
96p; 20cm.
ISBN 0946088217 Pbk £2.95

PUBLIC ORDER OFFENCES – IRELAND

—Report on vagrancy and related offences / the Law Reform Commission. – Dublin : The Commission, 1985.
v,129p. – (LRC).
Includes bibliographical references.

PUBLIC POLICY

—Brownlie's Law of public order and national security / edited by Michael Supperstone. – 2nd ed. – London : Butterworths, 1981.
lvii,415p.
Previous ed. entitled: The law relating to public order. Includes index.
ISBN 0406137013

—Comparative arbitration practice and public policy in arbitration / general editor, Pieter Sanders with the cooperation of the T.M.C. Asser Institute for International Law. – Deventer : Kluwer Law and Taxation Publishers, 1987.
x, 402 p.; 25 cm.
At head of title: International Council for Commercial Arbitration. 'VIIIth International Arbitration Congress, New York, 6-9 May 1986'–Series t.p. Includes bibliographical references.
ISBN 9065442960 Pbk £135.00

—Criminal law : offences relating to public order / the Law Commission. – London : H.M.S.O., 1983.
vii,135p.
ISBN 0102085846

—Ethics and mental retardation / edited by Loretta Kopelman and John C. Moskop. – Dordrecht : D. Reidel, 1984.
xvi, 258p.
Includes index.
ISBN 9027716307

—Police and public order in Europe / edited by John Roach and Jurgen Thomaneck. – London : Croom Helm, 1985.
293p; 23cm.
Includes bibliographies and index.
ISBN 0709922426 £18.95

—Review of public order law / presented to Parliament by the Secretary of State for the Home Department and the Secretary of State for Scotland. – London : H.M.S.O., 1985.
iii,53p; 25cm.
ISBN 0101951000

PUBLIC POLICY – AUSTRALIA

—Law, government and public policy / Victoria : Oxford University Press, 1988.
308.
This book examines the relationship between law and public policy in Australia, including a study of legislation. The courts are covered; also how social issues have to be cast in legal terms to be litigated; the impact of decisions on society.
ISBN 0195548485 Hbk £22.50
ISBN 0195548507 Pbk £12.50

PUBLIC POLICY – FRANCE

—French Politics and Public Policy / Martin A. Schain. – London : Pinter Publishers Ltd, 1980.
324p.
ISBN 0903804441 Hbk £18.50

—Socialism, The State, and Public Policy in France / Martin A. Schain. – London : Pinter Publishers Ltd, 1984.
220p.
ISBN 086187384X Hbk £21.00

PUBLIC POLICY – GREAT BRITAIN

—Annual members' conference held in the Lord Chief Justice's Court on Saturday 22nd March 1986 : subject, public order / Chairman His Hon. Judge Hawser. – London : Justice, 1986.
38 leaves.

—Housing Economics and Public Policy / London : Macmillan.
176p. – (Studies in Planning Ser.).
ISBN 0333211073 Pbk £4.95

—Industrial Innovation and Public Policy : Preparing for the 1980's and the 1990's / Walter Zegveld. – London : Pinter Publishers Ltd, 1981.
251p.
ISBN 0903804921 Hbk £17.50
ISBN 0861872509 Pbk £7.75

—Military intervention in democratic societies / edited by Peter J. Rowe & Christopher J. Whelan. – London : Croom Helm, 1985.
312p; 23cm.
Includes bibliographies and index.
ISBN 0709922418 £18.95

—Public disorder : a review of research and a study in one inner city area / by Simon Field and Peter Southgate. – London : H.M.S.O., 1982.
v, 73p.
Bibliographies. Contents: Urban disorders in Britain and America: a review of research/Simon Field - The disturbances of July 1981 in Handsworth, Birmingham: a survey of the views and experiences of male residents/Peter Southgate. A Home Office Research and Planning Unit report.
ISBN 011340767X

—Public Policy and the Use of Torture / London : Quaker Peace & Service, 1980.
32p.
ISBN 0901689114 Pbk £0.50

—Urban riots and public order : a select bibliography, 1975-1985 / compiled by: E. Edwards, R. Golland & S. Leach for the GLC Intelligence Unit. – Letchworth : Technical Communications, 1986.
iii,159p; 30cm.
ISBN 0946655103 Hbk

PUBLIC POLICY – UNITED STATES

—Military intervention in democratic societies / edited by Peter J. Rowe & Christopher J. Whelan. – London : Croom Helm, 1985.
312p; 23cm.
Includes bibliographies and index.
ISBN 0709922418 £18.95

PUBLIC PROSECUTORS – ENGLAND

—Independent prosecution service for England and Wales / presented to Parliament by the Secretary of State for the Home Department and the Attorney General... – London : H.M.S.O., 1983.
32p.
ISBN 0101907400

—Organisation of an independent prosecution service / observations on the Discussion Paper circulated on behalf of the Home Office Working Party on Prosecution Arrangements. – s.l. : the Society, 1983.
19p.

—Public prosecutor : the memoirs of Sir Norman Skelhorn, Director of Public Prosecutions, 1964-1977 / Sir Norman Skelhorn. – London : Harrap, 1981.
8,207p.
ISBN 0245537635

PUBLIC PROSECUTORS – GREAT BRITAIN

—Role of the Prosecutor / London : LSEPS, 1987.
ISBN 0566057239 Hbk £22.50

PUBLIC PROSECUTORS – UNITED STATES

—American prosecutor : a search for identity / Joan E. Jacoby. – Lexington, Mass. : Heath, 1980.
xxvi,305p; 24cm.
'Lexington books'. Includes index.
ISBN 0669032913 £17.50

PUBLIC RECORDS

—Public access to government-held information : a comparative symposium / general editor, Norman S. Marsh ... et al. – London : Stevens, 1987.
xxi, 342 p.; 22 cm.
Includes bibliographical references and index.
ISBN 0420476105 pbk.

PUBLIC RECORDS – GREAT BRITAIN

—Modern public records : selection and access : report of a committee appointed by the Lord Chancellor / Chairman Sir Duncan Wilson : presented to Parliament by the Lord High Chancellor. – London : H.M.S.O., 1981.
xiii,256p,1leaf of plates; 25cm.
ISBN 0101820402 Pbk £8.10

—Modern public records : the government response to the report of the Wilson Committee / presented to Parliament by the Lord High Chancellor ... March 1982. – London : H.M.S.O., 1982.
ii,29p; 25cm.
Response to: Modern public records: selection and access (Cmnd.; 8204).
ISBN 0101853106

—Public Records : 21st Annual Report of the Keeper of Public Records on the Work of the Public Record Office and the 21st Report of the Advisory Council on Public Records, 1979 / London : HMSO, 1981.
ISBN 0100280196 Hbk £3.20

PUBLIC RELATIONS

—Public relations for librarians / K.C. Harrison. – 2nd rev. ed. – Aldershot : Gower, 1982.
xiii,124p; 23cm. – (A Grafton book).
Previous ed.: London : Deutsch, 1973. Bibliography: p120-121. - Includes index.
ISBN 0566034549 Unpriced

PUBLIC RELATIONS – CANADA

—Community based preventive policing : a review 1984-90 / David K. Wasson, John D. Crawford & Company Ltd. – Ottawa : Ministry of the Solicitor General, 1984.
iii,198p. – (User report).
Bibliography: p.197-198.

—Community policing in the 1980's : recent advances in police programs / edited by Donald J. Loree and Chris Murphy. – Ottawa : Ministry of the Solicitor General, 1986.
v,154p.
'This conference was jointly sponsored by the Canadian Police College ... and by the Secretariat of the Ministry of the Solicitor General of Canada'. - T.p.. Held in Ottawa, March 17-19, 1986.
ISBN 0662158075

PUBLIC RELATIONS – ENGLAND

—Ethnic minorities, crime and policing : a survey of the experiences of West Indians and whites / by Mary Tuck and Peter Southgate. – London : H.M.S.O., 1981.
iv,50p.
Bibliography: p50. A Home Office Research and Planning Unit report.
ISBN 0113407653

—Police-public encounters / by Peter Southgate with the assistance of Paul Ekblom. – London : H.M.S.O., 1986.
vi,143p; 25cm.
Report from the Research and Planning Unit. Describes a study of everyday contact between the public and uniformed police in London, Birmingham and Bristol. Examines problems during such encounters.
ISBN 011340834X

—Scarman and after : essays reflecting on Lord Scarman's report, the riots and their aftermath / edited by John Benyon : with an epilogue by Lord Scarman. – Oxford : Pergamon, 1984.
xiv,292p; 24cm.
Conference papers. Bibliography: p263-274. - Includes index.
ISBN 0080302173 Hbk Unpriced
ISBN 0080302181 Pbk £7.50

—Scarman Report : the Brixton disorders, 10-12 April 1981 : report of an inquiry / by Lord Scarman. – Reprint, with preface. – Harmondsworth : Penguin, 1986.
xx,255p. – (Pelican books).
Previous ed.: 1982.
ISBN 014022744X

PUBLIC RELATIONS – GREAT BRITAIN

—Contacts between police and public : findings from the British crime survey / by Peter Southgate and Paul Ekblom. – London : H.M.S.O., 1984.
v,37p; 25cm.
A Home Office Research and Planning Unit report.
ISBN 0113407718

PUBLIC SERVICE EMPLOYMENT – GREAT BRITAIN

—Judicial review of public duties / Oxford : Clarendon Press, 1989.
300.
Examines the principles and remedies which have been applied in public duty cases such as postal strikes and licence applications. Argues that public duties should be taken more seriously by the courts.
ISBN 0198256078 Hbk £30

PUBLIC SERVICE EMPLOYMENT – NIGERIA

—Public servant and the law / by Akintunde Emiola. – Ile-Ife : University of Ife Press, 1985.
xxii,225p.
Includes bibliographical references and index.
ISBN 9781360658

PUBLIC UTILITIES – CANADA

—Pricing and Related Policies of Publicly Owned Electrical Utilities / Halifax : Dalhousie University, Institute of Public Affairs.
ISBN 0889260265 Hbk

PUBLIC UTILITIES – GREAT BRITAIN

—London Electricity Board : a report by the Director General of Fair Trading on an investigation under Section 3 of the Competition Act 1980 / Office of Fair Trading. – London : Office of Fair Trading, 1982.
78p; 30cm.

PUBLIC WELFARE

—Evolution of the British welfare state : a history of social policy since the Industrial Revolution / Derek Fraser. – 2nd ed. – London : Macmillan, 1984.
xxxii,326p; 22cm.
Previous ed.: 1973. Bibliography: p303-322.
ISBN 0333359992

—Social welfare law / general editor David Pollard. – 2. – London : Oyez, 1977.
loose-leaf; 26cm.
ISBN 0851204694 v.2
ISBN 0851204686

—Socio-legal studies and social welfare / Martin Partington : a report for the Government and Law Committee of the Economic and Social Research Council. – London : Economic and Social Research Council, 1986.
78p.
Bibliography: p59-78.
ISBN 0862261872

—Welfare and justice / Maria Los. – Sheffield : Centre for Criminological and Socio-Legal Studies, 1982.
136p.
Bibliography: p.130-136.

PUBLIC WELFARE – AUSTRALIA

—Australian social security law, policy and administration / Terry Carney & Peter Hanks. – Melbourne : Oxford University Press, 1986.
xxv,334p.
Bibliography: p311-326.
ISBN 0195547543

PUBLIC WELFARE - CANADA

—Family law and social welfare legislation in Canada / Ivan Bernier and Andree Lajoie, research coordinators. – Toronto : University of Toronto Press, 1986.
xv, 133 p.; 23 cm.
'Published by the University of Toronto Press in cooperation with the Royal Commission on the Economic Union and Development Prospects for Canada and the Canadian Government Publishing Centre, Supply and Services Canada.'. Includes bibliographies. Contents: Family law in Canada and the financial consequences of marriage breakdown and divorce / Julien D. Payne – Family law and social welfare in Canada / Mary Jane Mossman – Development and trends in Canadian social law, 1940-1984 / Robert D. Bureau, Katherine Lippel, and Lucie Lamarche.
ISBN 0802072941 pbk.

PUBLIC WELFARE - ENGLAND

—Directory of projects (England & Wales) ... for adult offenders, alcoholics, drug takers, homeless single people and people with histories of mental illness / co-produced by FARE ... et al. – Chichester : Rose, 1980.
xiii,257p.
ISBN 0859921883 Unpriced

—Old Poor Law, 1795-1834 / prepared for the Economic History Society by J.D. Marshall. – 2nd ed. – Basingstoke : Macmillan, 1985.
57p; 22cm.
Previous ed.: 1968. Bibliography: p51-54. - Includes index.
ISBN 0333398807 Pbk £3.95

—Relief of poverty, 1834-1914 / prepared for the Economic History Society by Michael E. Rose. – 2nd ed. – Basingstoke : Macmillan, 1986.
92p; 22cm.
Previous ed.: 1972. Includes bibliography and index.
ISBN 0333424158 Pbk £3.95

—Social workers, their clients and the law / Michael Zander. – 3rd ed. – London : Sweet & Maxwell, 1981.
xiv,180p; 22cm.
Previous ed.: 1977. Includes index.
ISBN 0421279303 Pbk £5.75

—Sweet & Maxwell's social work statutes / edited by Richard M. Jones. – 2nd ed. – London : Sweet & Maxwell, 1985.
150p.
Previous ed.: 1980. Includes index.
ISBN 0421348305 Pbk £9.00

PUBLIC WELFARE - GREAT BRITAIN

—Adviser : a bi-monthly guide on social security, housing, money advice and employment / London : National Association of Citizens Advice Bureaux and Shelter, 1986-.
Continues: Rights Workers Bulletin, Housing Aid and In the Black. Supplement: Computanews.

—Encyclopedia of social services law and practice / 2. – London : Sweet & Maxwell, 1985.
loose-leaf.
Includes indexes. Updated by loose-leaf supplements.

—Government and urban poverty : inside the policy-making process / Joan Higgins ... et al. – Oxford : Blackwell, 1983.
vi,215p; 22cm.
Bibliography: p202-206. - Includes index.
ISBN 0631129375 Hbk Unpriced
ISBN 063113252X Pbk £5.95

—Legal foundations of the Welfare State / London : Weidenfeld & Nicolson, 1984.
400p.
ISBN 0297784870 Hbk £16.00
ISBN 0297785346 Pbk £9.00

—Report of the Social Security Advisory Committee ... / London : HMSO, 1981-.

—Social services law / by John Williams. – London : Fourmat, 1981.
xxii,338p; 22cm.
Includes index.
ISBN 185190039X Pbk £18.95

—Test cases for the poor : legal techniques in the politics of social welfare / Tony Prosser. – London : Child Poverty Action Group, 1983.
v,102p.
ISBN 090396371X

—Welfare benefits / by Ruth Lister. – London : Sweet and Maxwell, 1981.
xxvi,284p; 22cm.
Bibliography: p251. - Includes index.
ISBN 0421249609 Pbk £8.00

PUBLIC WELFARE - IRELAND

—Social welfare law in Ireland : a guide to its sources / Gerry Whyte. – Dublin : Round Hall Press, 1987.
86p; 23cm.
Includes index.
ISBN 0947686258 Pbk £9.95 (Mar.)

PUBLIC WELFARE - LIBERIA

—Appendix 14-1 to Decree no. 14 by the People's Redemption Council of the Armed Forces of Liberia : repealing Chapter 89 of the Executive Law entitled an Act to Establish the National Social Security and Welfare Corporation of the Republic of Liberia and creating instead a new Chapter 89 establishing the National Social Security and Welfare Corporation of Liberia, the National Pension Fund, the Employment Injury Fund and the Welfare Fund / Monrovia : Bureau of Printing, Ministry of Foreign Affairs, 1980.
46p.

PUBLIC WELFARE - NORWAY

—Norwegian social law / Asbjrn Kjnstad. – Oslo : Norwegian University Press, 1987.
303p; 23cm.
Presents Norwegian social law as an example of the Nordic model. Discusses social security legislation, its history and administration, financing of social security measures, disablement, and some health and welfare issues.
ISBN 8200059030 £30.00

PUBLISHERS AND PUBLISHING - CANADA

—Impact of reprography on the copyright system / S.J. Liebowitz. – Ottawa : Research and International Affairs Branch, Bureau of Corporate Affairs, Consumer and Corporate Affairs Canada, 1981.
82 p.; 28 cm.
Bibliography: p. 81-82.
ISBN 0662113969 pbk.

PUBLISHERS AND PUBLISHING - GREAT BRITAIN

—Mumbys publishing & bookselling in the twentieth century / Ian Norrie, F. A. Mumby. – 6th ed. – London : Bell & Hyman, 1982.
253p; 24cm.
Previous ed.: published as Publishing and bookselling. London : Cape, 1974. Bibliography: p229-232.
ISBN 0713513411 £12.95

PUBLISHING

—Use of paperbacks in public libraries in the United Kingdom : a review of research / edited by Marilyn Hart. – Loughborough : Centre for Library and Information Management, Department of Library and Information Studies, Loughborough University, 1983.
iii,103p. – (Report).
Includes bibliographical references.
ISBN 0904924483

PUBLISHING - CANADA

—Authors and Publishers : Agreements and Legal Aspects of Publishing / 2nd ed. – Butterworths, 1987.
232p.
Examines the obligations of parties to publishing agreements. Covers all aspects of the law and business practice relating to author-publisher contracts and includes a clause-by-clause analysis of the fundamental provisions of agreements currently used. Revised to include the new copyright legislation and software agreements.
ISBN 0409806285 Hbk £50.00

—Authors and Publishers : Agreements and Legal Aspects of Publishing / Toronto : Butterworths.
184p.
ISBN 0409865214 Pbk £29.95

—Preparing Information on the Law : Guidelines for Writing, Editing and Design / Gayla Reid. – Ottawa : Canadian Law Information Council, 1985.
84p.
ISBN 0920358810 Pbk £10.00

PUBLISHING - GREAT BRITAIN

—Publishing agreements : a book of precedents / edited by Charles Clark. – 2nd ed. – London : Allen & Unwin, 1984.
xvi,230p; 23cm.
Previous ed.: 1980. Includes index.
ISBN 004655016X £15.00

—Sources of funding for research and publication / Helen Peden and Philip Hills. – Leicester : Primary Communications Research Centre, University of Leicester, 1983.
46p; 20x21cm.
Bibliography: p46. - Includes index.
ISBN 0906083249 Pbk Unpriced

PUNISHMENT

—Abolitionism : towards a non-repressive approach to crime : proceedings of the Second International Conference on Prison Abolition, Amsterdam, 1985 / edited by Herman Bianchi, Rene van Swaaningen. – Amsterdam : Free University Press, 1986.
247p.
ISBN 9062561799

—Alternative measures to imprisonment / by W. Rentzmann and J.P. Robert. – Strasbourg : Council of Europe, 1986.
35p. – (CDAP (85) 6).
A paper presented to the seventh Conference of Directors of Prison Administrations.

—Behaviour alteration and the criminal law / Law Reform Commission of Canada. – Ottawa : The Commission, 1985.
48,56p. – (Working paper).
Bibliography: p.44-48. Added t.p. in French: Les techniques de modification du comportement et de droit penal. Cover title: Protection of life : behaviour alteration and the criminal law. Pages numbered in opposite directions. Text in English and French.
ISBN 0662538579

—Consumerist criminology / Leslie T. Wilkins. – London : Heinemann, 1984.
viii,184p; 23cm.
Includes index.
ISBN 0435825283 Pbk £16.00
ISBN 0389204102

—Crime and criminology : a critical introduction / Nigel Walker. – Oxford : Oxford University Press, 1987.
xv,219p; 23cm.
Bibliography: p210-212. - Includes index.
ISBN 0192192124 Hbk £12.95
ISBN 0192891936 Pbk £4.95

—Crime, guilt, and punishment : a philosophical introduction / C.L. Ten. – Oxford : Clarendon, 1987.
176p; 22cm.
Includes bibliography and index.
ISBN 019875082X Hbk £19.50
ISBN 0198750811 Pbk £8.95

—Crime, justice and underdevelopment / edited by Colin Sumner. – London : Heinemann, 1982.
xvi,345p; 23cm.
Bibliography: p312-331. - Includes index.
ISBN 0435828886 £19.50

—Crime, proof and punishment : essays in memory of Sir Rupert Cross / Rupert Cross, Colin Tapper. – London : Butterworths, 1981.
xxvi,336p; 26cm.
Bibliography of works by Sir Rupert Cross: p.323-327. - Includes index. Edited by Colin Tapper.
ISBN 0406569991

—Howard journal : a review of modern methods for the prevention and treatment of crime and juvenile delinquency / London : Howard League for Penal Reform, 1921.
Continued by: The Howard journal of penology and crime prevention. Subtitle varies.

—Is retributivism analytic? / Igor Primorac. – s.l. : s.n., 1981.
9 leaves.
Photo-copy of an article in Philosophy, vol. 56 (1981), p.203-211. Includes bibliographical references.

—Philosophy and the criminal law : Association for Legal and Social Philosophy Tenth Annual Conference at the University of Manchester, 8-10th April 1983 / edited by Antony Duff and Nigel Simmonds. – Wiesbaden West Germany : Franz Steiner, 1984.
120p.
Bibliography: p.117-120.
ISBN 3515041699

—Plato on punishment / Mary Margaret Mackenzie. – Berkeley Calif. : University of California Press, 1981.
vii,278p; 25cm.
Bibliography: p251-259. - Includes index.
ISBN 0520041690 £17.25

—Power to punish : contemporary penality and social analysis / edited by David Garland and Peter Young. – London : Heinemann Educational, 1983.
x,238p; 23cm.
Bibliography: p217-230. - Includes index.
ISBN 0435823256 Hbk £14.50
ISBN 0391029010 : Pbk Unpriced

—Punishment : a philosophical and criminological inquiry / Philip Bean. – Oxford : Robertson, 1981.
viii,215p; 23cm.
Bibliography: p202-210. - Includes index.
ISBN 0855203919 £12.50

—Punishment, danger and stigma : the morality of criminal justice / Nigel Walker. – Oxford : Blackwell, 1980.
200p.
ISBN 0631125426 £8.00

—Punishment : the supposed justifications / Ted Honderich. – Rev.ed. – Harmondsworth : Pelican Books, 1984.
248p.
Revised edition issued in Peregrine Books 1976. ·
ISBN 0140213120

—Standard minimum rulesfor the implementation of non-custodial sanction and measures involving restriction of liberty / Edited by J J J Tulkens for the International Penal and Penitentiary Foundation. – Kluwer Law and Taxation, 1989. 84.
Collection of contributions regarding standard minimum rules, prepared for the meeting ofthe International Penal and Penitentiary Foundation. Covers operational aspects of control, supervision, and the recording and use of information about the offender, and individual obligations to persons subject to enforcment and organizational requirements.
ISBN 9065444173 Pbk £17.50/Dfl 55

—State punishment : political principles and community values / Nicola Lacey. – London : Routledge, 1988.
xiii, 222 p.; 23 cm.
Includes index. Bibliography: p. 202-218.
ISBN 0415001714 CIP rev.

—Trials and punishments / R.A. Duff. – Cambridge : Cambridge University Press, 1986.
336p; 22cm. – (Cambridge studies in philosophy).
Includes bibliography and index.
ISBN 0521308186 £22.50

PUNISHMENT – AUSTRALIA
—Alternatives to Imprisonment / Canberra : Australian Institute of Criminology.

PUNISHMENT – AUSTRALIA – WESTERN AUSTRALIA
—Problem of old convictions / the Law Reform Commission of Western Australia. – Perth : Law Reform Commission of Western Australia, 1984.
97,vip. – (Discussion paper).

—Report on the problem of old convictions / the Law Reform Commission of Western Australia. – Perth : Law Reform Commission of Western Australia, 1986.
267p. – (Project).

PUNISHMENT – CANADA
—From Crime to Punishment / David C. Perrier. – Agincourt : Carswell, 1988.
ca 330p.

PUNISHMENT – ENGLAND
—Crime and the criminal law : reflections of a magistrate and social scientist / by Barbara Wootton. – 2nd ed. – London : Stevens, 1981.
xii,119p; 19cm.
Previous ed.: 1963.
ISBN 0420461701 Hbk Unpriced
ISBN 0420461809 Pbk £5.00

—Criminal and victim : crime and society in early nineteenth-century England / George Rude. – Oxford : Clarendon, 1985.
ix,160p; 22cm.
Includes bibliography and index.
ISBN 0198226462 £17.50

PUNISHMENT – EUROPE
—Spectacle of suffering : executions and the evolution of repression - from a preindustrial metropolis to the European experience / Cambridge : Cambridge University Press, 1984.
286.
Examines the decline of public, physical punishment in the penal system of Western Europe.
ISBN 0521261864 Hbk £30.00

PUNISHMENT – GREAT BRITAIN
—Crime and penal policy / David Smith and A.J. Fowles. – York : Longman, 1986.
24p; 30cm.
Bibliography: p23-24.
ISBN 0582172551 Pbk No price

—Crime and Punishment in Britain : An Analysis of the Penal System in Theory, Law, and Practice / Amsterdam : University Press.

—Crime Guilt and Punishment / Oxford : Oxford University Press, 1987.
ISBN 0198750811 Pbk £8.95
ISBN 019875082X Hbk £19.50

—Crime, Proof and Punishment / London : Butterworths, 1981.
ISBN 0406569991 Hbk £21.50

—Making good : prisons, punishment and beyond / Martin Wright : foreword by Barbara Wootton. – London : Burnett, 1982.
316p; 23cm.
Bibliography: p271-292. - Includes index.
ISBN 0091472202 Hbk Unpriced
ISBN 0091472210 Pbk £5.95

—People's justice : a major poll of public attitudes on crime and punishment / Stephen Shaw. – London : Prison Reform Trust, 1982.
29p; 30cm.
Cover title.
ISBN 0946209006 Pbk £1.00

—Punishment / Oxford : Blackwell, 1981.
ISBN 0855204788 Pbk £6.95

—Punishment and welfare : a history of penal strategies / David Garland. – Aldershot : Gower, 1985.
x,297p; 23cm.
Bibliography: p280-290. - Includes index. Previous control number ISBN 0-435-82327-2.
ISBN 0566008556 £21.45

PUNISHMENT – INDIA
—Law of Culpable Homicide, Murder and Punishment in India / New Delhi : Deep and Deep Publications, 1988.
464p.

PUNISHMENT – PAKISTAN
—Charge-Sheet, Enquiry and Punishment / Karachi : Bureau of Labour Publications, 1983.
36p.

PUNISHMENT – SCOTLAND
—Prisons and punishment in Scotland : from the Middle Ages to the present / Joy Cameron. – Edinburgh : Canongate, 1983.
x,274p,16p of plates; 23cm.
Bibliography: p237-239. - Includes index.
ISBN 0862410312 £12.95

PUNISHMENT – SOCIAL ASPECTS – CANADA
—Cannabis criminals : the social effects of punishment on drug users / by Patricia G. Erickson. – Toronto : Addiction Research Foundation of Ontario, 1980.
179p; 23cm. – (ARF books).
Bibliography: p.159-170. - Includes index.
ISBN 0888680465

PUNISHMENT – SOUTH AFRICA
—Punishment : an introduction to principles / M.A. Rabie, S.A. Strauss. – 3rd ed. – Johannesburg : Lex Patria, 1981.
365p.
Previous ed.: 1979. First published 1977 as: Theories of punishment. Bibliographies: p.333-348. - Includes index.
ISBN 0628018495

PUNISHMENT – UNITED KINGDOM
—Magistrates' Court : An Index of Common Penalties and Formalities in Cases Before Justices / Peter Morrish. – 7th ed. – Chichester : Barry Rose.
262p.

QUALITY CONTROL
—Effect of international consumer protection laws in Europe : third European Seminar on Product Liability, October 15th and 16th 1980 at the Mount Royal Hotel, Marble Arch, London / organised by the Institute of Quality Assurance. – London : European Organisation for Quality Control, 1980.
253p.
'Sponsored by the National Council for Quality & Reliability'. At head of title: European Organisation for Quality Control.

QUALITY CONTROL – CANADA
—Regulation of quality / Scarborough, Ontario : Butterworths (Canada), 1983.
368.
Considers the subjects' ethical, political and legal framework, looking at the rationale for government regulation of quality, regulating quality in product markets, regulating enviromental quality, the administration of the Hazardous Products Acts, regulating occupational health and safety, markets for insurance, regulating the quality of psychotherapeutic services and the control of diesel exhaust pollution.
ISBN 040982495X Hbk

—Regulation of Quality : Products, Service, Workplaces / Toronto : Butterworths, 1983.
368p.

QUALITY CONTROL – EUROPE
—Product Quality, Standardization and the Law : 4th European Seminar on Product Liability / Bern : European Office for Quality Control, 1981.

QUALITY OF LIFE
—Well-being : its meaning, measurement, and moral importance / James Griffin. – Oxford : Clarendon Press, 1988.
xii,412p.
Bibliography: pp.391- 402. - Includes index.
ISBN 0198249039

QUANGOS – AUSTRALIA
—Quangos : The Australian Experience / C. A. Saunders. – Neutral Bay : Hale & Iremonger, 1984.
ISBN 0868060860 Hbk £24.95
ISBN 0868060879 Pbk £11.95

QUEBEC (PROVINCE)
—Canada and the constitution, 1979-1982 : patriation and the charter of rights / Edward McWhinney. – Toronto : University of Toronto Press, 1982.
xii,227p.
Includes bibliographical references and index.
ISBN 0802065015 pbk.

QUOTATIONS
—Dictionary of legal quotations / compiled and edited by Simon James and Chantal Stebbings. – London : Croom Helm, 1987.
250p; 24cm.
Includes indexes.
ISBN 0709914032 £15.00

RACE RELATIONS – ENGLAND
—Police probationer training in race relations / Peter Southgate. – London : Home Office, 1982.
iv,38p.
Bibliography: p.31.
ISBN 0862520630

RACE RELATIONS – GREAT BRITAIN
—Black communities and the legal profession / summary of Nottingham Regional Conference, October 1986. – s.l. : Standing Committee on the Black Communities and the Legal Profession, 1986.
11p.
Includes bibliographical references.

—Code of practice : race relations / Great Britain. – London : The Commission, 1983.
30p.
Cover title: Race relations code of practice for the elimination of racial discrimination and the promotion of equality of opportunity in employment.
ISBN 0907920292

—Race relations in prisons / Elaine Player. – Oxford : Clarendon Press, 1989.
200.
Based on a detailed research project undertaken at the request of the Home Office. Examines three institutions and their staff and inmates, and relates their experiences in detail. Demonstrates difficulties arising from trying to isolate race problems, and identifies problems in trying to enforce policies to eradicate discriminating behaviour.
ISBN 0198256175 Hbk £20

—Teaching about prejudice / by Michael Banton ... et al. : edited by Ben Whitaker. – London : Minority Rights Group, 1983.
24p. – (Report).
Bibliography: p.23-24.
ISBN 0946690006

RACE RELATIONS – NEW ZEALAND
—Report of Advisory Committee on Youth and Law in our Multicultural Society / E. Te R. Tauroa. – Wellington : The Committee, 1983.
284p.

RACE RELATIONS – SOUTH AFRICA
—Some aspects of international law considered in relation to apartheid, racism and racial discrimination / by T.O. Elias. – Lagos : Nigerian Institute of Advanced Legal Studies, 1986.
27p. – (Occasional paper).
ISBN 9782353043

—South Africa and the consociational option : a constitutional analysis / by L.J. Boulle. – Cape Town : Juta, 1984.
xii, 270 p.; 25 cm.
Includes indexes. Bibliography: p. 227-229.
ISBN 0702114340 pbk.

RACIAL DISCRIMINATION
—Incitement to racial hatred : issues and analysis / Canberra : Australian Government Publishing Service, 1982.
31,2p. – (Occasional paper).
ISBN 0644021926

—Incitement to racial hatred : the international experience / Canberra : Australian Government Publishing Service, 1982.
65p. – (Occasional paper).
ISBN 0644022221

—Jews of Africa and Asia : contemporary anti-semitism and other pressures / Tudor Parfitt. – London : Minority Rights Group, 1987.
15p. – (Report).
Bibliography: p.15.
ISBN 0946690561

—U.N. Convention on the Elimination of all Forms of Racial Discrimination / by Natan Lerner. – 2nd ed. – Alphen aan den Rijn : Sijthoff & Noordhoff, 1980.
xvii,259p.
Bibliography: p249-251.

—World minorities / edited by Georgina Ashworth. – Sunbury : Quartermaine House, 1980.
xvii,174p.
Includes bibliography.
ISBN 0905898117

RACIAL DISCRIMINATION – AUSTRALIA
—Conciliation under the Racial Discrimination Act 1975 : a study in theory and practice / by Patrick Pentony. – Canberra : Australian Government Publishing Service, 1986.
xi,206p. – (Occasional paper).
Bibliography: p203-205.
ISBN 064405672X

—Race Problems in ESCAP / Canberra : Australian Institute of Criminology.

RACIAL DISCRIMINATION - BURUNDI

—Burundi since the genocide / by Reginald Kay. – London : Minority Rights Group, 1987.
12p. – (Report).
'This report was first published under the title Selective genocide in Burundi by Professor Rene Lemarchand and David Martin in July 1974'. - Front cover verso.
ISBN 0946690472

RACIAL DISCRIMINATION - CANADA

—Police, Race and Ethnicity : A Guide For Law Enforcement Officers / Chris Toole. – Toronto : Butterworths, 1986.
256p.
Guidelines for 'on the street' level of policing and providing police officers with administrative considerations. Also considers the structure and practice of relevant criminal law and the function of the Ontario Human Rights Commission in enforcing the Ontario Human Rights Code. The mechanism of the Ontario Human Rights Commission.
ISBN 0409805017 Pbk £18.25

RACIAL DISCRIMINATION - ENGLAND

—Race and the police / Eric Edwards. – London : G.L.C., 1983.
21p. – (Research documents guide).
ISBN 071681367X

—Racism awareness training for the police : report of a pilot study for the Home Office / Peter Southgate. – London : Home Office, 1984.
v,17p.
Bibliography: p.17.
ISBN 0862521726

—To ride the storm : the 1980 Bristol 'riot' and the state / Harris Joshua, Tina Wallace and Heather Booth. – London : Heinemann, 1983.
vii,221p.
Bibliography: p211-216.
ISBN 0435824813

RACIAL DISCRIMINATION - GREAT BRITAIN

—Abstracts of race relations research / edited by George Mair and Philip Stevens. – London : Home Office, 1982.
vii,86p.
Includes index.
ISBN 0862520436

—Black communities and the legal profession / summary of Nottingham Regional Conference, October 1986. – s.l. : Standing Committee on the Black Communities and the Legal Profession, 1986.
11p.
Includes bibliographical references.

—Black people and the criminal justice system : report of the NACRO Race Issues Advisory Committee / Clement Richards. – London : NACRO, 1986.
48p.
Includes bibliographical references. Chairman: Clement Richards. Accompanied by 'Summary of the report of the NACRO Race Issues Advisory Committee'.
ISBN 0850690404

—Brixton disorders 10-12 April 1981 : report of an enquiry / by Lord Scarman. – London : H.M.S.O., 1981.
viii,168p; 25cm.
Report of inquiry by Lord Scarman. Discusses causes of the riots and lessons for the future about riot control and prevention.
ISBN 0101842708 Pbk £8.00

—English law and ethnic minority customs / Sebastian Poulter. – London : Butterworth, 1986.
xxviii,300p; 25cm.
ISBN 0406180008 Pbk £22.00

—Ethnic minorities in Britain : a study of trends in their position since 1961 / by Simon Field ... et al. – London : H.M.S.O., 1981.
v,44p.
Bibliography: p42-44. A Home Office Research Unit report.
ISBN 0113407084

—Legal control of racial discrimination / Laurence Lustgarten. – London : Macmillan, 1980.
xxv,263p; 25cm.
Includes index.
ISBN 0333243870 Hbk £25.00
ISBN 0333243889 Pbk £12.00

—Practical guide to discrimination law / London : Grant McIntyre Ltd, 1980.
300p.
ISBN 086216009X £14.95

—Race Relations Act 1976 : time for a change? / Commission for Racial Equality. – London : C.R.E., 1983.
43p; 30cm.
ISBN 0907920306

—Racial discrimination / Ross Anderson, 1984.
ISBN 0863600042 Pbk £2.95

—Racism and equal opportunity policy in the 1980's / Solomos. – Cambridge : Cambridge University Press, 1987.
ISBN 0521330130 Hbk £25.00

—Sex and race discrimination in employment / Poulton. – London : Sweet & Maxwell, 1987.
ISBN 0905099176 Pbk £14.00

—Teaching about prejudice / by Michael Banton ... et al. : edited by Ben Whitaker. – London : Minority Rights Group, 1983.
24p. – (Report).
Bibliography: p.23-24.
ISBN 0946690006

RACIAL DISCRIMINATION - GREAT BRITAIN - GREAT BRITAIN

—Policing immigration : Britain's internal controls / Paul Gordon. – London : Pluto, 1985.
v,160p.
Includes index.
ISBN 0861046234 Pbk £4.95

—Proposed nationality law : Commission for Racial Equality's comments on the government's White Paper on British nationality law : submitted to the Home Office in October 1980 / Great Britain. – London : The Commission, 1980.
4p.
Bound with: Proposed British nationality law: summary of White Paper.

—White law : racism in the police courts and prisons / Paul Gordon. – London : Pluto Press, 1983.
159p; 20cm.
ISBN 0861047060 Pbk £3.95

RACIAL DISCRIMINATION - GUYANA

—Crime, race and culture : a study in a developing country / Howard Jones. – Chichester : Wiley, 1981.
xv,184p; 24cm.
Bibliography: p175-179. - Index.
ISBN 047127996X £12.75

RACIAL DISCRIMINATION - SRI LANKA

—Democracy in peril : Sri Lanka : a country in crisis : report to the LAWASIA Human Rights Standing Committee / by Patricia Hyndman. – Sydney : LAWASIA, 1985.
xi,483p.

RADIATION - AUSTRALIA - SOUTH AUSTRALIA

—Report ... relating to claims for injuries from toxic substances and radiation effects / Law Reform Committee of South Australia. – Adelaide : Government Printer, 1985.
96p. – (87th report).

RADIOACTIVE POLLUTION

—Chernobyl : law and communication : transboundary nuclear air pollution : the legal materials / Philippe Sands. – Cambridge : Grotius, 1988.
xxxiii,312p.
Reproduces texts including multilateral and bilateral treaties, non-binding acts of international organisations and private associations of scholars, and national legislation. Covers the development of the law up to and including the 1986 IAEA Conventions on Early Notification and assistance, and the 1987 Resolution of the Institut de Droit International on Transboundary Air Pollution.
ISBN 0949009229 £38.00

—Convention on Early Notification of a Nuclear Accident and Convention on Assistance in the Case of a Nuclear Accident or Radiological Emergency / Vienna : International Atomic Energy Agency, 1987.
126p. – (Legal series).
ISBN 9201760876

RADIOACTIVE WASTE

—Convention on the physical protection of nuclear material / Vienna : International Atomic Energy Agency, 1982.
– (Legal series).
ISBN 9201760825

RADIOACTIVE WASTE DISPOSAL - EUROPEAN COMMUNITY

—Regulatory framework for storage and disposal of radioactive waste in the member states of the European Community / G.D. Burholt and A. Martin. – London, UK : Published by Graham & Trotman for the Commission of the European Communities, 1988.
ix, 121 p.; 25 cm.
Includes bibliographies.
ISBN 1853331090

RADIOACTIVE WASTE DISPOSAL - PALAU (CAROLINE ISLANDS)

—Micronesia : the problem of Palau / prepared by Roger Clark and Sue Rabitt Roff. – Rev ed. – London : Minority Rights Group, 1987.
22p. – (Report).
Includes bibliographical references.
ISBN 0946690146

RAILWAY MAIL SERVICE - GREAT BRITAIN

—British Railways Board : allocation of facilities on Motorail : a report by the Director General of Fair Trading on an investigation under Section 3 of the Competition Act,1980 / London : Office of Fair Trading, 1983.
33p; 30cm.

RAILWAYS - AUSTRALIA

—General Bylaw : Boards of Appeal Bylaw / Australian National Railways Commission. – Canberra : Australian Government Publishing Service, 1984.
11p.
ISBN 0644031697 Hbk £1.00

RAILWAYS - ENGLAND

—Law of the railway / Leslie James. – London : Barry Rose, 1980.
xlii,479p; 25cm.
Includes index.
ISBN 0859921581 Pbk £12.00

RAILWAYS - GREAT BRITAIN

—British Railways Board : allocation of facilities on Motorail : a report by the Director General of Fair Trading on an investigation under Section 3 of the Competition Act,1980 / London : Office of Fair Trading, 1983.
33p; 30cm.

—Rail Unions in Britain and West Germany : A Study of their Structure and Policies / Wolfgang Steeck. – London : Policy Studies Institute, 1982.
109p.

—Railway and Canal Traffic Cases : 1835-1950, 36 Vols. / Abingdon : Professional Books.

RAILWAYS - INDIA

—Indian Railways Act, 2 Vols. / 3rd ed. – Allahabad : Law Publishers, 1980.

—Indian Railways Act / 6th ed. – Allahabad : Law Book Company, 1980.
lxxii, 1045p.
With 1986 supplement.

—Law of Railway Servants / 2nd ed. – Allahabad : Law Book Company, 1984.
With 1987 supplement.

—Railway Property (Unlawful Possession) Act 1966 / Lucknow : Eastern Book Company, 1983.
471p.

RAILWAYS - WEST GERMANY

—Rail Unions in Britain and West Germany : A Study of their Structure and Policies / Wolfgang Steeck. – London : Policy Studies Institute, 1982.
109p.

RAPE

—Dignity and honour of women as basic and fundamental human rights / by Yougindra Khushalani. – The Hague : Martinus Nijhoff Publishers, 1982.
153p.
Includes index.
ISBN 9024725852 Hbk £105.00

—Women against violence against women / edited by dusty rhodes and Sandra McNeill. – London : Onlywomen Press, 1985.
280p.
ISBN 0906500168

RAPE - AUSTRALIA

—Factors Affecting Sentencing Decisions In Rape Cases / Canberra : Australian Institute of Criminology.

—Inquiry into the substantive law of rape / by Ngaire Naffin. – Adelaide : Women's Adviser's Office, Department of the Premier and Cabinet, 1984.
iii,80p.
Includes bibliographical references.

—Rape Law Reform / Canberra : Australian Institute of Criminology.

—Rape law reform : a collection of conference papers / edited by Jocelynne A. Scutt. – Canberra : Australian Institute of Criminology, 1980.
xxvii,304p.
Bibliography: p.297-304.
ISBN 0642899916

RAPE - AUSTRALIA - SOUTH AUSTRALIA

—Rape law reform in South Australia : a study of the background to the reforms of 1975 and 1976 and of their subsequent impact / P.A. Sallmann and Duncan Chappell. – Adelaide : Adelaide Law Review Association, 1982.
x,110p.
ISBN 0908448023

RAPE - AUSTRALIA - TASMANIA

—Report and recommendations on rape and sexual offences / Law Reform Commission of Tasmania. – Hobart : Government Printer, 1982.
44p. – (Report).

RAPE – AUSTRALIA – VICTORIA
—Rape and allied offences : procedure and evidence / Law Reform Commission of Victoria. – Melbourne : The Commission, 1988.
v,62p. – (Report no 13).
ISBN 0724166351 Hbk

—Rape and allied offences : victims with impaired mental functioning / Law Reform Commission of Victoria. – Melbourne : The Commission, 1987.
39p. – (Discussion paper).
Includes bibliographical references.
ISBN 0724167064

—Rape and alllied offences : substantive aspects / Law Reform Commission of Victoria. – Melbourne : The Commission, 1987.
viii,40p. – (Report no 7).
Includes bibliographical references.

RAPE – CANADA
—...after sexual assault... : your guide to the criminal justice system / Department of Justice Canada. – Ottawa : The Department, 1986.
109p.
ISBN 0662147529

RAPE – COMMONWEALTH
—Report on the Expert Group Meeting of Law Teachers to Develop Curriculum Materials on Violence against Women : London, 11-15 May 1987 / London : Commonwealth Secretariat, 1987.
19p.

RAPE – ENGLAND
—Female sexuality and the law : a study of constructs of female sexuality as they inform statute and legal procedure / Susan S.M. Edwards. – Oxford : Robertson, 1981.
195p; 23cm.
Bibliography: p183-190. - Includes index.
ISBN 085520382X Hbk £12.50
ISBN 0855203854 Pbk £4.95

—Rape and the legal process / by Jennifer Temkin. – London : Sweet & Maxwell, 1987.
220p; 23cm.
Includes index.
ISBN 0421338407 Hbk £16.00
ISBN 0421338504 Pbk £10.00

—Rape on trial / Zsuzsanna Adler. – London : Routledge & Kegan Paul, 1987.
viii,195p; 23cm.
Bibliography: p188-192. - Includes index.
ISBN 0710208049 £15.00

RAPE – GREAT BRITAIN
—Investigating Rape : New approaches for the Police / Oxford : Croom Helm, 1985.
ISBN 0709920989 Hbk £14.95

—Rape controversy / Melissa Benn, Anna Coote, Tess Gill. – 3rd rev. and updated ed. – London : NCCL Rights for Women Unit, 1986.
32p; 20cm.
Rev. ed. - Previous ed. i.e. 2nd ed.: 1983. Bibliography: p32.
ISBN 0946088233 Pbk £1.50

—Rape : the ultimate violation / Pluto Press, 1986.
ISBN 0745300928 Pbk £4.95

—Violence against women : report of an ad-hoc working group / Women's National Commission. – London : Cabinet Office, .
59, 28p.
Includes bibliographical references.

RAPE – INDIA
—Rape and allied offences : some questions of substantive law, procedure and evidence / Law Commission of India. – New Delhi : Govt. of India Press, 1980.
iii,42p. – (84th report).
Includes bibliographical references.

RAPE – IRELAND
—Rape / the Law Reform Commission. – Dublin : The Commission, 1987.
ix,101p. – (Consultation paper).

—Rape : allied offences / the Law Reform Commission. – Dublin : The Commission, 1988.
vii,38p. – (LRC).

RAPE – NEW ZEALAND
—Rape study : a study directed by Mel Smith and Warren Young and undertaken by the Department of Justice and the Institute of Criminology / Mel Smith, Warren Young. – Wellington, N.Z : Dept. of Justice and Institute of Criminology at Victoria University of Wellington, 1983.
2 v.; 30 cm.
Includes bibliographical references. Contents: v. 1. A discussion of law and practice / by Warren Young – v. 2. Research reports.

—Sexual violence : a case for law reform : papers presented at seminar, University of Auckland, 27 August 1982 / by Margaret A. Wilson, J.K. McLay, Lannes Johnson. – Auckland : Legal Research Foundation Inc., 1982.
40p.
ISBN 0908581262

RAPE – SCOTLAND
—Evidence : report on evidence in cases of rape and other sexual offences / Scottish Law Commission. – Edinburgh : H.M.S.O., 1983.
vi,33p.
Includes bibliographical references. Includes Draft Evidence in Sexual Offences (Scotland) Bill.
ISBN 0102028842

RAPE – SOUTH AFRICA
—Women and sexual offences in South Africa / South African Law Commission. – Pretoria : The Commission, 1985.
xvi.,200p. – (Report).
Bibliography: p.vii-xvi.
ISBN 0621096091 Hbk

RAPE – UNITED STATES
—Victim of rape : institutional reactions / Lynda Lytle Holmstrom, Ann Wolbert Burgess. – New ed. – New Brunswick : Transaction, 1983.
xl,293p; 23cm.
Previous ed.: New York : Chichester : Wiley, 1978.
ISBN 0878559329 Pbk Unpriced

RAS TAFARI MOVEMENT
—Rastafarians / E. E. Cashmore. – London : Minority Rights Group, 1984.
11p. – (Report).
Bibliography: p11.

RATES – GREAT BRITAIN
—Rate capping and the law / 2nd ed. – London : Sweet & Maxwell, 1986.
ISBN 0902052063 Pbk £9.25

—Rating valuation and practice guide / London : Longman Professional, 1987.
ISBN 0851213200 Pbk £15.95

RATES – WALES
—Welsh Office Local Government Finance Wales : The Welsh Rate Support Grant Supplementary No. 3 Report 1981-82 / London : HMSO, 1983.

—Welsh Office Local Government Finance Wales : The Welsh Rate Support Grant Supplementary Report 1983-84 / London : HMSO, 1983.

RATING
—Encyclopaedia Rating Law and Practice / Sweet & Maxwell, 1988.
ISBN 0421263105 Hbk £95.00

RATING – GREAT BRITAIN
—Bean and Lockwood's Rating Valuation Practice / Lockwood. – 7th ed. – Sweet & Maxwell, 1987.
ISBN 042047420X Hbk £64.00

—Principle and Practice of Rating Valuation / 4th ed. – London : Estates Gazette, 1984.
ISBN 0728200694 Pbk £22.00

—Ryde on Rating / Wellington : Butterworths.
This text covers the basis of liability, rateable property, exemptions and reliefs, the measure of liability, the valuation list, and the rate of its recovery on land in the United Kingdom. All the important case decisions of the Superior Court and Lands Tribunal are included along with statutes, rules, orders and instruments.
ISBN 0406363153 Pbk

RATIONALISM
—Rationality and relativism / edited by Martin Hollis and Steven Lukes. – Oxford : Basil Blackwell, 1982.
viii,312p; 23cm.
Bibliography: p306-310. - Includes index.
ISBN 0631127739 Hbk Unpriced
ISBN 0631131264 Pbk Unpriced

RAW MATERIALS
—Law and policy of producers' associations / D.E. Pollard. – Oxford : Clarendon, 1984.
xii,372p; 23cm.
Includes index.
ISBN 0198254806 £30.00

RAW MATERIALS – GREAT BRITAIN
—Defects in Natural Commodities and Raw Materials / Product Liability Briefing, 1988.
ISBN 1870317556 Pbk £4.95

REAL ESTATE AGENTS – AUSTRALIA – WESTERN AUSTRALIA
—Estate agents and auctioneers / Law Reform Commission of Victoria. – Melbourne : Government Printer, 1988.
x,46p. – (Report).
At head of cover title: Regulation Review Unit.
ISBN 0724167145

REAL ESTATE AGENTS – CANADA
—Real estate agency law / William F. Foster. – Toronto : Carswell, 1984.
xliii,272p.
Includes bibliographical references and index.
ISBN 0459370502

REAL ESTATE BUSINESS – CANADA
—Defensive Practice of Real Estate / Vancouver : British Columbia Continuing Legal Education Society, 1982.
124p.
ISBN 0865040486 Hbk £12.50

—Real estate law / Barry J. Reiter, R.C.B. Risk, Bradley N. McLellan. – 2nd ed. – Toronto : Emond-Montgomery, 1982.
xcii,1194p.
Includes index.
ISBN 0920722091

REAL ESTATE BUSINESS – ENGLAND
—Law of estate agency and auctions / by J.R. Murdoch. – 2nd ed. – London : Estates Gazette, 1984.
xlii,576p.
Includes bibliographical references and index.

REAL ESTATE BUSINESS – GREAT BRITAIN
—Urban land economics / Paul N. Balchin and Jeffrey L. Kieve. – 3rd ed. – London : Macmillan, 1985.
xvi,302p; 22cm. – (Macmillan building and surveying series).
Previous ed.: 1977. Bibliography: p282-283. - Includes index.
ISBN 0333397843 Pbk £7.95

REAL ESTATE BUSINESS – MALAYSIA
—Sale and purchase of real property in Malaysia / Visu Sinnadurai. – Singapore : Butterworths, 1984.
xliv,511p.
Covers sales and purchase of land in Malaysia, formation of a contract for sale of land, parties to a contract sale, fraud, misrepresentation and illegality, rights of parties pending registration, statutory protection of the purchaser's interest, and rescission and recovery of advance payments.
ISBN 0406181187 Hbk £110

REAL ESTATE BUSINESS – SINGAPORE
—Real Property Financing in Singapore / Singapore : Butterworths, 1988.
390p.

REAL ESTATE DEVELOPMENT
—Land and the law : report of the proceedings of the International Bar Association Section on General Practice seminar in Rome , May 1983 / London : IBA, 1984.
150p.
ISBN 0950587680

—Report of Commission of Inquiry into the North Creek Development Project 1986-87 / submitted to the Governor, Turks and Caicos Islands, by the Commissioner, Mr. Louis Blom-Cooper : presented to parliament by the Secretary of State for Foreign and Commonwealth Affairs by command of Her Majesty, July 1987. – London : H.M.S.O., 1987.
x,148p.
ISBN 0101019521

REAL ESTATE DEVELOPMENT – CANADA
—Real Estate Development / Vancouver : Continuing Legal Education Society of British Columbia, 1988.
242p.
ISBN 0865049769 Hbk £75.00

REAL ESTATE DEVELOPMENT – GREAT BRITAIN
—Land development and the infrastructure Lottery / J. Rowan-Robinson, M.G. Lloyd. – Edinburgh : T. & T. Clark, 1988.
xvi,160p; 22cm.
Includes index. Examines the relationship between local authorities and the private sector in the provision of supporting services and 'infrastructure' for private development. Looks at the discretionary powers of local authorities, at the legislation conferring this discretion and at how this is exercised.
ISBN 0567291499 Pbk £12.50

—Local needs policies and development control strategies : an examination of the role of occupancy restrictions in development control / Martin Loughlin. – Bristol : University of Bristol, School for Advanced Urban Studies, 1984.
107p; 30cm. – (WP).
ISBN 0862921554

—Planning control : philosophies, prospects and practice / edited by M.L. Harrison and R. Mordey. – London : Croom Helm, 1986.
234p; 23cm. – (Croom Helm series in geography and environment).
Bibliography: p227-232. - Includes index.
ISBN 0709937903 £25.00

REAL ESTATE INVESTMENT
—Land and the law : report of the proceedings of the International Bar Association Section on General Practice seminar in Rome , May 1983 / London : IBA, 1984.
150p.
ISBN 0950587680

REAL ESTATE INVESTMENT - UNITED STATES

—Investment in US Real Estate / London : Oyez Longman, 1984.
- (Oyez Longman Intelligence Report Ser.).
ISBN 0851208495 Hbk

REAL ESTATE MANAGEMENT - GREAT BRITAIN

—Maintenance of commercial tenanted proerty / a consultative document by a working party of the Building Surveyors Division of the Royal Institution of Chartered Surveyors, January 1987. - London : The Institution, 1987.
9,12p.

—Property Development Library / Reading : College of Estate Management, 1983.
- (College of Estate Management Handbooks Ser.).

Vol. 2, 4 titles

REAL ESTATE SALES TAX - MALAYSIA

—Introduction to real property gains taxation in Malaysia / by Arjunan Subramaniam. - Kuala Lumpur : Malayan Law Journal, 1982.
x,121p.
Bibliography: p.x. - Includes index.

REAL PROPERTY

—Cheshire and Burn's Modern law of real property / E. H. Burn. - 14th ed. - London : Butterworths, 1988.
1012p; 25cm.
Previous ed.: 1982. Includes index.
ISBN 0406565473 Hbk £32.00
ISBN 0406565481 Pbk £21.95

—Defending possession proceedings / Jan Luba, Nic Madge, and Derek McConnell. - London : Legal Action Group, 1987.
xlvi,229p.
ISBN 090509915X

—Introduction to land law / J.G. Riddall. - 3rd ed. - London : Butterworth, 1983.
xxxii,487p; 26cm.
Previous ed.: 1979. Includes index.
ISBN 0406648344 Hbk Unpriced
ISBN 0406648395 Pbk unpriced

—Legal aspects of alien acquisition of real property / edited by Dennis Campbell. - Deventer : Kluwer, 1980.
206p; 25cm.
Includes index.
ISBN 9026811691 Hbk £104.00

—Megarry's manual of the law of real property / David J. Hayton. - 6th ed. - London : Stevens, 1982.
lvii,615p; 24cm.
Previous ed.: 1975. Bibliography: pli-lii. - Includes index.
ISBN 0420463305 Hbk £19.50
ISBN 0420463402 Pbk £11.50

REAL PROPERTY - AUSTRALIA

—Cases and materials on real property / by P.J. Butt ... et al. - Sydney : Law Book Co., 1980.
xlvi,657p.
Bibliography on leaseholds: p.656-657. - Includes index.
ISBN 0455200440 Pbk
ISBN 0455200696

—Cases and Materials on Real Property / 2nd ed. - North Ryde : Law Book Co, 1985.
xliii, 582p.
ISBN 0455203954 Hbk £63.00
ISBN 0455203962 Pbk £49.50

—Law affecting the valuation of land in Australia / by Alan A. Hyam : with a foreword by R. Else-Mitchell. - North Ryde, N.S.W. : Law Book Co., 1983.
xxxii,246p.
Includes index.
ISBN 0455202079

—Law of securities : an account of the law pertaining to securities over real and personal property under the laws of the Australian States / Edward I.Sykes. - 4th edition. - Sydney : Law Book Company, 1986.
xcv,1043p.
ISBN 0455206287

—Sale of Real Property and Law of Agency in NSW / 4th ed. - Sydney : Butterworths, 1983.
176p.
This book is a working guide for those involved in conveyancing transactions. The fourth edition has been revised and updated to include new materials on the contract of sale of land, strata titles, agents' commissions, registration of titles, valuation of land, and other topics.

REAL PROPERTY - AUSTRALIA - NEW SOUTH WALES

—Law of Real Property in New South Wales / North Ryde : Law Book Co.
xli, 372p.
ISBN 0455202397 Hbk £38.00

—New South Wales Real Property Legislation / North Ryde : C.C.H. Australia, 1987.
360p.
ISBN 0869038885 Hbk

—Real Estate Agency in Victoria / A.H. Goldberg. - 2nd ed. - Butterworths, 1975.
386p.
ISBN 0409420700 Hbk £74.00

—Sale of Real Property and Law of Agency in New South Wales / R. Sorenson. - 4th ed. - Butterworths, 1983.
176p.
ISBN 0409494119 Pbk £26.00

REAL PROPERTY - AUSTRALIA - QUEENSLAND

—Queensland Real Property Legislation / North Ryde : C.C.H. Australia, 1986.
200p.
ISBN 0869038966 Hbk

—Sale of Real Property and Law of Agency in Queensland / W.B. Hutchinson. - Butterworths, 1986.
160p.
This is a working guide for students and those involved with conveyancing transactions. Included are materials on contracts for sale of land, strata titles, registration of titles, agents, commissions, unjust contracts, valuations of land, land subdivisions, and local authority requirements for land development.
ISBN 0409491179 Pbk £26.00

—Working paper on a bill to amend the real property acts with respect to those provisions relating to writs of execution, bills of encumbrance and bills of mortgage, and caveats / Brisbane : The Commission, 1982.
28p. - (Q.L.R.C.W.P.).

REAL PROPERTY - AUSTRALIA - VICTORIA

—Guidebook to Victorian Real Estate Law and Practice / North Ryde : C.C.H. Australia, 1986.
557p.
ISBN 0869035118 Hbk

—Victorian Law of Real Estate / Woolloomooloo : International Business Communications, 1986.
ISBN 094955328X Hbk £19.50

—Victorian Real Property Legislation / North Ryde : C.C.H. Australia, 1986.
288p.
ISBN 086903880X Hbk

REAL PROPERTY - AUSTRALIA - WESTERN AUSTRALIA

—Report on the Strata Titles Act / the Law Reform Commission of Western Australia. - Perth : Law Reform Commission of Western Australia, 1982.
387p. - (Project).

REAL PROPERTY - CANADA

—Anger and Honsberger: law of real property / Harry D. Anger, John D. Honsberger, A. H. Oosterhoff, W. B. Rayner. - 2nd ed. 2 v. - Aurora, Ont. : Canada Law Book Inc., 1985.
cccvi,2099p.
First ed. had title: Canadian law of real property.
Bibliography: p.xxvii-xxviii. - Includes index.
ISBN 0888040261 Hbk

—Anger and Honsberger : the Law of Real Property / Rayner. - 2nd ed. - Aurora : Canada Law Book, 1985.

—Canadian Commercial Real Estate Manual, 3 Vols. / Bernard Gershman. - 0888202415. - Toronto : DeBoo.
Among the main topics discussed in this three looseleaf binder service are financing, taxation and investment analysis, development and conveyancing, agreements, precedents, and checklists. Six updates per year are provided, as well as a complimentary newsletter.

—Estate management practice / 2nd ed. - London : Estates Gazette, 1986.
ISBN 0728200945 Pbk £14.50

—Foundations of Real Estate Financing : The Mathematical Basis / David Baxter. - Toronto : Butterworths, 1983.
353p.

—Introduction to Real Property Law / 2nd ed. - Toronto : Butterworths, 1982.
112p.
ISBN 0409867519 Hbk £23.95

—Introduction to Real Property Law / 3rd ed. - Butterworths, 1987.
120p.
Covers the doctrine of the estate in land, concurrent ownership, a prologue to modern law, and the statutes of uses and modern law. Takes into account recent changes in this area, including family law, easements, and water rights.
ISBN 0409808849 Hbk £23.95

—New Law of Expropriation / Stephen F. Waque. - Toronto : DeBoo, 1984.
This text provides analyses of reform legislation in Alberta, Manitoba, New Brunswick, Nova Scotia and Canada. Provincial statutes contain section-by-section commentaries. The main topics discussed are compensation where no land is taken, ways to prove expropriation claims, and types of claims successfully made.
ISBN 0888201532 Hbk £135.00

—Professional Responsibility in Real Property Transactions for Legal Assistants / Vancouver : British Columbia Continuing Legal Education Society, 1980.
89p.
ISBN 086504001X Hbk £25.00

—Real Estate : Advanced Update for Legal Assistants / Vancouver : Continuing Legal Education Society of British Columbia, 1988.
272p.
ISBN 0865043906 Hbk £75.00

—Real Estate and Landlord and Tenant / 2nd ed. - Agincourt : Carswell, 1986.
853p. - (Bar Admission Course Materials).
This work for the law student is a practical guide to the handling of most real estate transactions under Canadian law. The Planning Act of 1983 and the Land Registration Reform Act of 1984 are reviewed in the text.

—Real Estate Law / 3rd ed. - Toronto : Edmond-Montgomery, 1986.
1,475p.
ISBN 0920722199 Hbk £99.50

—Real estate law / Risk. - 3rd ed. - Aurora : Canada Law Book, 1986.

—Real estate law / Barry J. Reiter, R.C.B. Risk, Bradley N. McLellan. - 2nd ed. - Toronto : Emond-Montgomery, 1982.
xcii,1194p.
Includes index.
ISBN 0920722091

—Real Estate Law / R. C. B. Risk. - 3rd ed. - Aurora : Canada Law Book Co, 1986.
1300p. - (Text Books-Civil).
The third edition of this text has undergone significant changes to make it an even more useful and relevant sourcebook for Canadian Real Estate practitioners. This new edition includes up-to-date forms and materials used in routine real estate transactions reflecting the changes brought about by the Land Registration Reform Act.

—Real Estate Litigation 1987 / Vancouver : Continuing Legal Education Society of British Columbia, 1987.
132p.
ISBN 086504306X Hbk £65.00

—Real Property : 11 / Vancouver : British Columbia Continuing Legal Education Society, 1984.
494p.
ISBN 0865041105 Hbk £65.00

—Real Property 1986 / Vancouver : Continuing Legal Education Society of British Columbia, 1986.
642p.
ISBN 0865042624 Hbk £75.00

—Real Property Assessment : 11 / Vancouver : British Columbia Continuing Legal Education Society, 1983.
69p.
ISBN 0865041210 Hbk £45.00

—Real Property Assessment 1988 / Vancouver : Continuing Legal Education Society of British Columbia, 1988.
126p.
ISBN 0865043825 Hbk £70.00

—Real Property Assessment / Vancouver : British Columbia Continuing Legal Education Society, 1982.
200p.
ISBN 0865040729 Hbk £45.00

—Real Property Assessment and Taxation / Vancouver : Continuing Legal Education Society of British Columbia, 1985.
165p.
ISBN 086504192X Hbk £60.00

—Real Property Assessment II / Vancouver : British Columbia Continuing Legal Education Society, 1983.
69p.
ISBN 0865041210 Hbk £50.00

—Real property reports / Agincourt, Ont. : Carswell, 1977-.
24cm.

—Real Property Reports : With Consolidated and Cumulative Index / Agincourt : Carswell.

—Tentative proposals for changes in limitations legislation / Law Reform Commission of Saskatchewan. - Saskatoon : Law Reform Commission of Saskatchewan, 1981.
27p.

REAL PROPERTY - CANADA - BRITISH COLUMBIA

—Land (Settled Estate) Act / Law Reform Commission of British Columbia. - Vancouver : The Commission, 1988.
iii,38p. - (Working paper).
ISBN 077188625X

REAL PROPERTY - CANADA - NOVA SCOTIA

—Nova Scotia Real Property Practice Manual / Toronto : Butterworths.
ISBN 0409855103 Hbk

REAL PROPERTY - CANADA - ONTARIO

—Real Estate Practice in Ontario / Peter D. Quinn. – 3rd ed. – Toronto : Butterworths, 1982.
304p.
Explains judicial decisions and statutory changes since the second edition. Covers the Foreign Investment Review Act, Ontario New Home Warranties Act, Road Access Act, and the Family Law Reform Act, along with a reorganised chapter on the Planning Act. New chapters on real estate agents, and mortgage default proceeding.
ISBN 0409830046 Hbk £55.00

REAL PROPERTY - CANADA - QUEBEC

—Law of Real Property : Quebec / Repr. of 1932 ed. – Agincourt : Carswell, 1986.
686p.
This work originally published in 1932, is a detailed English language reference guide to the law of 'unmovable property' under the Quebec Civil Code. The book offers a basic understanding of the Quebec law of real property.

REAL PROPERTY - ENGLAND

—Bean and Lockwood's Rating valuation practice / Arthur Lockwood, John C. Bassett, David MacKmin, William Thomas. – 7th ed. – London : Sweet & Maxwell, 1987.
xxxiv,483p; 26cm.
New edition with an enlarged chapter dealing with appeals to the Local Valuation Court and Lands Tribunal, and the role of the valuer appearing before them. The valuation of properties, including retail, office and industrial property, and licensed premises is covered.
ISBN 042047420X £40.00

—Butterworths property law handbook / consulting editor Ernest H. Scamell. – London : Butterworths, 1984.
This work contains all the statutory law of the United Kingdom relevant to property law. The law of trusts, law of succession, law of family assets, and conveyancing are presented in their legislative form.
ISBN 0406258171 PBK £14.95

—Cases and statutes on land law / by E.L.G. Tyler. – 2nd ed. – London : Sweet & Maxwell, 1986.
334p; 22cm.
Previous ed.: 1974. Includes index.
ISBN 0421343508 Pbk £10.00

—Commonhold : freehold flats and freehold ownership of other interdependent buildings : report of a working group / chairman: T.M. Aldridge. – London : H.M.S.O., 1987.
v,101p; 30cm.
ISBN 0101017928

—Elements of land law / Kevin Gray. – London : Butterworths, 1987.
lxxi,1094p; 25cm.
Includes index.
ISBN 0406501602 Hbk £29.00
ISBN 0406501610 Pbk £19.95

—Family home / by W.T. Murphy and Hilary Clark. – London : Sweet & Maxwell, 1983.
229p; 19cm. – (Modern legal studies).
Includes index.
ISBN 0421287403 Hbk Unpriced
ISBN 0421287500 Pbk £6.95

—Green and Henderson: land law / N. Henderson, E. Swinfen Green. – 5th ed. – London : Sweet & Maxwell, 1988.
xvi,217p. – (Concise college texts).
Previous ed.: published as Land law. 1980. Includes index.
ISBN 0421384409 £9.95

—Introduction to land law / J.G. Riddall. – 4th ed. – London : Butterworths, 1988.
547p; 25cm.
Previous ed.: 1983. Includes index.
ISBN 0406648441 Hbk £24.00 :
ISBN 040664845X Pbk £16.00

—Land law / by E. Swinfen Green. – 4th ed. – London : Sweet & Maxwell, 1980.
xiv,188p; 22cm. – (Concise college texts).
Previous ed.: 1975. Includes index.
ISBN 0421254602 Hbk £9.00
ISBN 042125470X Pbk £7.25

—Land law / Patrick J. Dalton. – 3rd ed. – London : Pitman, 1983.
xliii,377p; 22cm.
Previous ed.: London : Oyez, 1975. Includes index.
ISBN 0273018582 Pbk £9.95

—Land law : cases and materials / by R.H. Maudsley and E.H. Burn. – 4th ed. – London : Butterworths, 1980.
lxxx,881p; 26cm.
Previous ed.: 1975. .
ISBN 0406623066 Hbk £24.00
ISBN 0406623074 Pbk £15.95

—Land law in a nutshell / William Howarth. – London : Sweet & Maxwell, 1987.
117p; 22cm.
Includes index.
ISBN 0421368306 Pbk £3.95

—Law of property / Bernard Rudden, F. H. Lawson. – 2nd ed. – Oxford : Clarendon, 1982.
ix,247p; 23cm. – (Clarendon law series).
Previous ed.: published as Introduction to the law of property. 1958. Includes index.
ISBN 0198761287 Hbk £14.00
ISBN 0198761295 Pbk £6.95

—Law of real property / Sir Robert Megarry and H.W.R. Wade. – 5th ed. – London : Stevens, 1984.
cxxviii,123p; 24cm.
Previous ed.: 1975. Includes index.
ISBN 0420467106 Hbk No price
ISBN 0420470301 Pbk £19.75

—Maudsley and Burn's land law : cases and materials / R. H. Maudsley. – 5th ed. – London : Butterworths, 1986.
850p; 26cm.
Previous ed.: published as Land law / by R.H. Maudsley and E.H. Burns. 1980. Includes index.
ISBN 0406623082 Hbk £33.00
ISBN 0406623090 Pbk £22.50

—Modern English land law / by Michael Harwood. – 2nd ed. – London : Sweet & Maxwell, 1982.
xliii,597p; 23cm.
Previous ed.: published as English land law. 1975. Includes index.
ISBN 0421278900 Hbk Unpriced
ISBN 0421279001 Pbk £12.95

—Preston and Newsom's restrictive covenants affecting freehold land / G. H. Newsom, G. L. Newsom. – 7th ed. – London : Sweet & Maxwell, 1982.
xl,387p; 23cm.
Previous ed.: 1976. Includes index.
ISBN 0421284900 £30.00

—Property and politics 1870-1914 : landownership, law, ideology and urban development in England / Avner Offer. – Cambridge : Cambridge University Press, 1981.
xviii,445p; 24cm.
Bibliography: p407-428. - Includes index.
ISBN 0521224144 £27.50

—Property law : the implications of William & Glyn's Bank Ltd. v. Boland : report on a reference under section 3(1)(e) of the Law Commission Act 1965 / the Law Commission. – London : H.M.S.O., 1982.
v,56p.
ISBN 0101863608

—Real property and real people : principles of land law / K.J. Gray, P.D. Symes. – London : Butterworths, 1981.
xxxi,655p; 26cm.
Includes index.
ISBN 0406591105 Hbk Unpriced
ISBN 0406591113 Pbk Unpriced

REAL PROPERTY - GREAT BRITAIN

—British nationality and the right of abode 1945-1983 / by K.J. Gray : by C.C. Turpin. – Deventer : Kluwer, 1986.
vii,269p.
Includes bibliographical references.
ISBN 9065442510

—Common Recoveries : Their Nature and Use / 2nd ed. Repr. of 1770 ed. – Abingdon : Professional Books.
490p.

—Compleate Copyholder : Wherein is Contained a Learned Discourse of the Antiquity and Nature of Manors and Copy-Holds, with the Forme of Keeping a Copy-Hold Court and Court Baron / Repr. of 1673 ed. – Abingdon : Professional Books.
399p.

—Current problems in property law / under the auspices of the Senate of the Inns of Court and the Bat and the Royal Institution of Chartered Surveyors. – London : Senate of the Inns of Court and the Bar, 1986.
217p.
A collection of five papers.

—Essay on the Learning of Contingent Remainers and Executory Devises / 2nd ed. Repr. of 1773 ed. – Abingdon : Professional Books.
491p.

—History of the land law / A.W.B. Simpson. – 2nd ed. – Oxford : Clarendon, 1986.
316p; 22cm.
Previous ed.: published as An introduction to the history of land law. Oxford : Oxford University Press, 1961. Bibliography: p292-295. - Includes index.
ISBN 0198255373 Hbk £25.00
ISBN 0198255365 Pbk £10.50

—Land law lecture notes / Angela Sydenham. – London : Polytechnic of North London Students' Union, 1981.
224p; 21cm.
Bibliography: p221-222. Cover title.
ISBN 0906513014 Pbk £3.00

—Law of Real Property / Wade. – 5th ed. – London : Sweet & Maxwell, 1984.
ISBN 0420470301 Pbk £26.00

—Manual of the law of real property / Hayton. – 6th ed. – London : Sweet & Maxwell, 1982.
ISBN 0420463305 Hbk £26.00
ISBN 0420463402 Pbk £16.50

—Modern law of real property / Burn. – 14th ed. – London : Butterworths, 1988.
ISBN 0406565465 Pbk £19.95
ISBN 0406565481 Hbk £23.95

—Property, divorce and retirement pension rights / by K.J. Gray : by C.C. Turpin. – Deventer : Kluwer, 1986.
vii,269p.
Includes bibliographical references.
ISBN 9065442510

—Property law : rights of reverter : report on a reference under section 3 (1) (e) of the Law Commissions Act 1965 / the Law Commission. – London : H.M.S.O., 1981.
vi,52p; 25cm.
ISBN 0101841000

—Real Property Statutes : Based on Shelford's Real Property Statutes / 2nd ed. – Abingdon : Professional Books, 1984.

—Taxation of land transactions / by Anthony R. Mellows. – 3rd ed. – London : Butterworths, 1982.
xxxiv,483p; 25cm.
Previous ed.: 1978.
ISBN 0406623929

REAL PROPERTY - HONG KONG

—Land compensation and valuation law in Hong Kong / Gordon N. Cruden. – Singapore : Butterworths, 1986.
xxxii,476p.
Collation and analysis of relevant statutory and case law. References are made to Hong Kong cases, as well as English, Scottish, Australian, Canadian, and New Zealand cases.
ISBN 0409995258 Hbk £137.5

REAL PROPERTY - IRELAND

—Land law / by Robert A. Pearce. – London : Sweet & Maxwell, 1985.
200p; 22cm.
Includes index.
ISBN 0421312009 Pbk £17.25

REAL PROPERTY - MALAYSIA

—Sale and purchase of real property in Malaysia / London : Butterworths, 1984.
ISBN 0406181187 Hbk £45.00

—Sale and purchase of real property in Malaysia / Visu Sinnadurai. – Singapore : Butterworths, 1984.
xliv,511p.
Covers sales and purchase of land in Malaysia, formation of a contract for sale of land, parties to a contract sale, fraud, misrepresentation and illegality, rights of parties pending registration, statutory protection of the purchaser's interest, and rescission and recovery of advance payments.
ISBN 0406181187 Hbk £110

—Strata Titles in Malaysia : Law and Practice / Butterworths, 1987.
164p.
Deals with the current law and practice relating to the strata title system in Penninsular Malaysia, Sarawak, and Sabah. Covers the basic features of the Malaysian strata title system, and the rules governing the management corporation and its members, and third parties such as chargees, occupiers and insurers.
ISBN 040999538X Hbk £65.00

REAL PROPERTY - NEW ZEALAND

—Industrial real estate market in New Zealand, 1970-1979 / New Zealand. – Wellington : Government Printer, 1980.
75p. – (Research paper).

REAL PROPERTY - NIGERIA

—Journal of private & property law / v. – Lagos : Department of Private & Property Law, University of Lagos, 1984-.

REAL PROPERTY - NORTHERN IRELAND

—Conveyancing and miscellaneous matters / Great Britain. – Belfast : H.M.S.O., 1983.
vii,153p. – (Discussion document).
At head of title-page: Department of Finance and Personnel for Northern Ireland, Office of Law Reform.
ISBN 033723406X

—Estates and interests and family dealings in land / Land Law Working Group. – Belfast : H.M.S.O., 1981.
v,60p; 21cm. – (Discussion document).
ISBN 0337233438 Pbk £3.50

REAL PROPERTY – SCOTLAND

—Matrimonial Homes (Family Protection) (Scotland) Act 1981 / by D.I. Nichols and M.C. Meston. – Edinburgh : Green, 1982.
vii,68p.
Includes index.
ISBN 0414006879 £15.75

—Rating appeals and the 1985 revaluation : proceedings of a Planning Exchange conference / edited by Clive Martlew. – Glasgow : Planning Exchange, 1985.
29 leaves. – (Occasional paper).

REAL PROPERTY – SINGAPORE

—Real property financing in Singapore / Singapore : Malayan Law Journal, 1988.
390.
Examines the law and practice of the security and documentation involved in real property financial transactions in Singapore. Covers the security and financing devices adopted by financiers to protect their interest, a list of financing institutions, both public and private, and the various financing schemes available. Provides a number of forms and precedents of loans documents.
ISBN 997170062X Hbk

REAL PROPERTY – SOUTH AFRICA

—Property valuation in South Africa / Cape Town : Juta, 1984.
x,181p.
ISBN 0702114855

—Real Estate in South Africa / 2nd ed. – Cape Town : Legal and Financial Publishing Co.

REAL PROPERTY – UNITED STATES

—Structuring foreign investment in US real estate / W D Knight, R L Doernberg. – Kluwer Law and Taxation, 1989.
780.
Explores the considerations of concern to foreign individuals and organisations making US real property investments. Covers US income, estate, and gift tax aspects of foreign investment. Also techniques that may be employed to reduce or eliminate US tax liability. Includes the Foreign Investment in Real Property Act 1980.
ISBN 9065449752 Llf £112/Dfl 350

Supplement 1989.
ISBN 90T275002X Llf £80.75/Dfl 250

REAL PROPERTY – WEST GERMANY

—Real Property in Germany / D. Weber. – 2nd ed. – Plymouth : Macdonald & Evans, 1983.
200p.
ISBN 0712154760 Hbk £18.00

REAL PROPERTY AND TAXATION

—Tax policy towards the national heritage : proceedings of a seminar held in Venice, 1983, during the 37th Congress of the International Fiscal Association / organised by the International Fiscal Association. – Deventer, Netherlands : Kluwer Law and Taxation Publishers, 1984.
ISBN 9065441786

REAL PROPERTY AND TAXATION – CANADA

—Income tax aspects of real estate transactions / Corporate Management Tax Conference 1983. – Toronto : Canadian Tax Foundation, 1983.
xv,450p.

REAL PROPERTY AND TAXATION – GREAT BRITAIN

—Taxation of land transactions / by Anthony R. Mellows. – 3rd ed. – London : Butterworths, 1982.
xxxiv,483p; 25cm.
Previous ed.: 1978.
ISBN 0406623929

REAL PROPERTY TAX

—Rating and income tax / 53 v. – London : Solicitors' Law Stationery Society, 1924.
Continued by: Rating and valuation reporter.

—Rating and valuation reporter / v. – London : Solicitor's Law Stationery Department, 1961-.
Continues: Rating and income tax reporter. Published: London: Rating Publishers, 1965-.
ISBN 00486817

—Taxes on immovable property : report by the Committee on Fiscal Affairs and the ad hoc Group on Urban Problems / Organisation for Economic Co-operation and Development. – Paris : O.E.C.D., 1983.
201p.
ISBN 9264124756

REAL PROPERTY TAX – CANADA

—Real Estate Taxation in Canada / Toronto : DeBoo, 1986.
This book examines the tax aspects of real estate acquired for investment purposes, including relevant law and examples. Among the topics discussed are holding periods, real estate as a tax shelter, and taxation of real estate owned in Canada by non-residents and in a foreign country by Canadians. Annual supplements are planned.
ISBN 088820230X Hbk £135.00

REAL PROPERTY TAX – ENGLAND

—Rates : proposals for rate limitation and reform of the rating system / presented to Parliament by the Secretary of State for the Environment and the Secretary of State for Wales ... – London : H.M.S.O., 1983.
24p.
ISBN 0101900805

REAL PROPERTY TAX – GREAT BRITAIN

—Land taxation / by Malcolm Gammie : general editor, Malcolm Gammie : contributing editor, Jeffrey Bailey. – London : Sweet & Maxwell, 1986-.
Includes index.
ISBN 0421275405 Llf

REAL PROPERTY TAX – MALAYSIA

—Introduction to real property gains taxation in Malaysia / Singapore : Malayan Law Journal, 1982.
121.
Outlines the provisions of the Real Property Gains Tax Act 1976, giving the background and general principles of the tax computation, and examine specific cases. Discusses the administration involved in the returns and assessments, recovery and collection, the offence, and penalties indicated. Appendix reproduces the Real Property Gains Tax Act 1976, and other Acts.

—Introduction to real property gains taxation in Malaysia / by Arjunan Subramaniam. – Kuala Lumpur : Malayan Law Journal, 1982.
x,121p.
Bibliography: p.x. - Includes index.

—Real Property Gains Tax Act 1976 (Act 169) / Kuala Lumpur : International Law Books Services.

REAL PROPERTY TAX – NEW ZEALAND

—Taxation of property transactions / by John Prebble. – Wellington, N.Z. : Butterworths, 1986.
xxxii,237p.
Includes index.
ISBN 040978740X

REAL PROPERTY TAX – SCOTLAND

—Valuation and rating in Scotland: proposals for reform / presented to Parliament by the Secretary of State for Scotland. – London : H.M.S.O., 1983.
10p.
ISBN 0101901801

REAL PROPERTY TAX – SINGAPORE

—Singapore Property Tax Cases [1959-1986] / Singapore : Malayan Law Journal, 1987.
xxii,413.
Collection of cases that was determined by the Judicial Committee of the Privy Council, the Court of Appeal, the High Court, and the Valuation Review Board of Singapore.
ISBN 9971700573 Hbk

REASONING

—Analogical Reasoning in Islamic Jurisprudence / Islamabad : Islamic Research Institute, 1986.
viii, 489p.
ISBN 9694080649 Hbk £20.00

—Reason in Law : Proceedings of the Conference Held in Bologna, 12-15 December 1984 / Milan : Giuffre, 1987.
viii, 384p.

Vol. 2 1988.
viii, 381p.

Vol. 3 1988.
viii, 440p.

REASONING – CANADA

—Reasons for Judgment / Toronto : Butterworths, 1980.
112p.
ISBN 0409843644 Hbk £40.00

RECEIPTS (ACKNOWLEDGMENTS) – INDIA

—Report on documents of title to goods 1978 / Banking Laws Committee (Government of India). – New Delhi : Controller of Publications, 1980.
xx,294p.
Includes index. Chairman: P.V. Rajamannar.

RECOGNITION (INTERNATIONAL LAW)

—Recognition and the United Nationsby John Dugard / Cambridge : Grotius, 1987.
xiv,192p.
An analysis of the impact on the law of recognition of recent developments in the practice of the United Nations on the admission of new members, and of the practical relevance of the modern concepts of peremptory norms of international law and jus cogens.
ISBN 0949009008

—United Nations, international law, and the Rhodesian independence crisis / Jericho Nkala. – Oxford : Clarendon Press, 1985.
xii,288p.
Bibliography: p.275-283. - Includes index.

RECORDS

—Decade of computers and law / edited by Jon Bing,· Knut S. Selmer. – Oslo : Universitetsforlaget, 1980.
475 p.; 22 cm.
Includes bibliographical references.
ISBN 8200053768

RECORDS – CANADA

—Communicating Court Information : Towards a Canadian Records Handling System / Ottawa : Canadian Law Information Council, 1984.
103p.
ISBN 0920358640 Pbk £15.00

RECREATION – GREAT BRITAIN

—Law of public leisure services / by Michael Scott : foreword by Charles Cross. – London : Sweet & Maxwell, 1985.
lvii,352p; 26cm.
Draws together the spectrum of legal rights and duties arising out of the public leisure services, from the taking on of staff, to licensing activities and safety procedures. Includes sections on employment law, duties in tort, commons, open spaces, National Parks, and libraries and museums.
ISBN 0421326808 £25.00

—Planning for leisure in the countryside : papers from a conference held at Oxford September 1982 / organised by the Bar Council, the Law Society and the Royal Institution of Chartered Surveyors. – London : Sweet & Maxwell, 1984.
vi,107p; 25cm.
Conference papers.
ISBN 0421326700 Pbk £18.00

—Recreation and the law / Spon (E & FN), 1984.
ISBN 0419121900 Hbk £18.50
ISBN 0419122001 Pbk £8.95

—Recreation and the Law / London : Sweet & Maxwell, 1984.

RECRUITMENT OF EMPLOYEES – GREAT BRITAIN

—Fair and efficient selection : guidance on equal opportunities policies in recruitment and selection procedures / Great Britain. – London : H.M.S.O., 1986.
50p.
ISBN 0117013013

—Understanding recruitment law / David Newell. – London : Waterlow, 1984.
xi,189p; 21cm. – (Waterlow's business library).
Includes index.
ISBN 0080391559 Pbk £9.75

—Understanding recruitment law / London : Waterlow, 1984.
ISBN 0080391559 Pbk £9.75

REDUNDANCY

—Law of redundancy / 3rd. – London : Sweet & Maxwell, 1989.
Covers compulsory consultation with recognised unions, dismissal, lay-off and start-time and the offer of new employment, redundancy payments, employers' rebates, guaranteed payments and unfair dismissal for redundancy.
ISBN 0421339004

REDUNDANCY – GREAT BRITAIN

—Dismissal and Redundancy Procedures / Mulgan. – London : Butterworths, 1984.
ISBN 040970136X Pbk £30.00

—Guide to Redundancy Law / London : Macmillan, 1985.
256p.
ISBN 0333388526 Hbk £25.00

—Guide to Redundancy Law / London : Macmillan, 1985.
ISBN 0333388526 Hbk £25.00

—Redundancy law and practice / London : Butterworths, 1983.
ISBN 0406258147 Pbk £26.00

REDUNDANCY – NEW ZEALAND

—Dismissal and Redundancy Procedures / Margaret A. Mulgan. – Butterworths, 1985.
Outline of the different procedures which may be taken by the dismissed employee after the termination of the employment contract. Unjustified and 'victimisation' dismissals are examined in detail with the appropriate remedial procedures. Analyses judicial decisions, and deals with the problems of redundancy dismissals and payment of compensation.
ISBN 040970136X Hbk £57.20

REFEREES – ENGLAND

—Official referees' business / by Edgar Fay : Foreword by Sir John Stephenson. – 2nd ed. – London : Sweet & Maxwell, 1988.
xviii,170p; 25cm.
Looks at the developments in the Official Referees' Courts since 1983. Chapters cover the trying of cases outside London, the use of expert witnesses, and Scott Schedules. Contains a new chapter on the position of the Users' Committee, and how to make use of it, and one on construction litigation procedures.
ISBN 0421396903 £29.00

—Report of the Official Referees' Users' Committee ... / Official Referees' Users' Committee. – London : The Committee, 1983.
1st report covers 1983 to 1986.

REFERENDUM - CANADA

—Lawmaking by the People : Referendums and Plebiscites in Canada / Butterworths, 1982.
336p.
Examines the constitutional and philosophical basis for referendums and plebiscites in Canada. Includes a concise framework for voting procedures, the advantages and disadvantages of referendums and plebiscites, direct democracy theory and methods, and the right to vote on certain issues.
ISBN 0409816027 Hbk £95.00

—Lawmaking by the people : referendums and plebiscites in Canada / J. Patrick Boyer. – Toronto : Butterworths, 1982.
xxxii,304p.
Outlines the laws which make possible the existence of political rights in Canada by exploring constitutional conventions such as responsible government, parliamentary democracy, and the role of political parties. It examines municipal and provincial laws regarding signs, posters and parades, as well as federal broadcasting laws governing provincial elections.
ISBN 0409816019

REFERENDUM - GREAT BRITAIN

—Referendum : The End of an Era / Cardiff : University of Wales, 1981.
14p.
ISBN 0708308082 Pbk £0.95

REFORMATORIES FOR WOMEN - ENGLAND

—Dynamics of aggression in women's prisons in England / Alexandra Mandaraka-Sheppard. – Aldershot : Gower, 1986.
xiii,272p; 23cm.
Bibliography: p241-260. - Includes index.
ISBN 0566008637 £17.50

REFRIGERATOR INDUSTRY - GREAT BRITAIN

—Petter Refrigeration Limited : a report by the Director General of Fair Trading on an investigation under section 3 of the Competition Act 1980 / London : Office of Fair Trading, 1981.
56p.

REFUGEES

—Explanatory Report on the European Agreement on Transfer of Responsibility for Refugees / Strasbourg : Council of Europe, 1980.

—Explanatory report on the European Agreement on Transfer of Responsibility for Refugees / Strasbourg : Council of Europe, 1980.
26p; 21cm.
Includes the text of the agreement.

—Legal aspects of the problem of refugees in Cyprus / by Criton G. Tornaritis. – Nicosia : s.n., 1975.
25 leaves.

—Problems raised by certain aspects of the present situation of refugees from the standpoint of the European Convention on Human Rights / by Richard Plender. – Strasbourg : Council of Europe, Directorate of Human Rights, 1984.
38p.
ISBN 9287103550

—Protection of persons satisfying the criteria in the Geneva Convention who are not formally recognised as refugees : recommendation no.R (84)1 adopted by the Committee of Ministers of the Council of Europe on 25 January 1984, and Explanatory memorandum / Council of Europe. – Strasbourg : Council of Europe, 1984.
10p; 21cm.
'... prepared by the ad hoc Committee of Experts on Legal Aspects of Territorial Asylum and Refugees' - preface.
ISBN 9287103275

—Refugee dilemma / by Frances D'Souza and Jeff Crisp : additional research by Stevanne Hill : with a foreword by Prince Sadruddin Aga Khan. – New ed. – London : Minority Rights Group, 1985.
20p. – (Report).
Previous ed.: 1981. Bibliography: p.19.
ISBN 0946690235

—Refugee in international law / Oxford : Oxford University Press, 1983.
ISBN 0198255187 Pbk £9.50

—Refugee in international law / Guy S. Goodwin-Gill. – Oxford Oxfordshire : Clarendon Press, 1983.
xxvii,318p.
Includes index. Bibliography: p306-311.
ISBN 0198253729

—Status of refugees in international law / Foreword by Felix Schnyder. – Leyden : A. W. Sijthoff, 1966.
v.; 25 cm.
Bibliography: v. 1, p. 441-458. Contents: v. 1. Refugee character.

—Territorial asylum / by Atle Grahl-Madsen. – Stockholm : Almqvist & Wiksell International, 1980.
– (Studies in international law).
'Published under the auspices of Svenska institutet for internationell ratt, Uppsala, 1979.'. Includes index.

REFUGEES - AFRICA

—Recommendations from the Arusha Conference on African Refugee Problem : Recommendations de la Conference D'Arusha sur le Probleme des Refugies / Stockholm : Almqvist & Wiksell, 1981.
46p.
ISBN 9171061843 Hbk £25.00

REFUGEES - ASIA

—Report of the Working Group on Current Problems in the International Protection of Refugees and Displaced Persons in Asia, International Institute of Humanitarian Law, San Remo (Italy), 19-22 January 1981 / Working Group on Current Problems in the International Protection of Refugees and Displaced Persons in Asia. – Geneva : under the auspices of the Office of the United Nations High Commissioner for Refugees, 1981.
17p.

REFUGEES - CANADA

—Refugee determination in Canada : proposals for a new system : a report to the Honourable Flora MacDonald, Minister of Employment and Immigration / by W. Gunther Plaut. – Ottawa : Minister of Supply and Services Canada, 1985.
221,286p.
With French t.p.: Reconnaissance au Canada du statut de refugie. Pages numbered in opposite directions. English and French text.
ISBN 0662538234

REFUGEES - GREAT BRITAIN

—Resettling refugees : the lessons of research / by Simon Field. – London : H.M.S.O., 1985.
vi,60p; 25cm.
Bibliographical references: p55-60. A Home Office Research and Planning Unit report.
ISBN 0113408153 Hbk

—Selling for a future : proposals for a British policy on refugees / British Refugee Council. – London : The Council, 1987.
25p.

—Vietnamese refugees : a study of their reception and resettlement in the United Kingdom / London : Home Office, 1982.
iv,63p.
Bibliography: p.56.
ISBN 0862520789

REFUGEES - HAITI

—Haitian refugees in the U.S. / by Alex Stepick : with the assistance of Dale Frederick Swartz. – Updated ed. – London : Minority Rights Group, 1986.
20p. – (Report).
Bibliography: p.18-19.
ISBN 0946690464

REGIONAL ECONOMIC DISPARITIES

—Development of maritime islands as extreme examples of peripheral regions / report prepared by the Committee of Experts on Social and Economic Activities of the Steering Committee for Regional and Municipal Matters, with the assistance of Italo Ferrari. – Strasbourg : Council of Europe, 1986.
26p.

REGIONAL PLANNING

—Planning and the environment in the modern world / Gordon E. Cherry. – London : Mansell Publishing, 1980.
xii,259p; 24cm.
In 3 vols. Includes index.
ISBN 0720109035 £14.75

—Planning law in Western Europe / edited by J.F. Garner and N.P. Gravells. – 2nd. rev. ed. – Amsterdam : North-Holland, 1986.
Bibliography.
ISBN 044487996X

—Proceedings of the seminar on planning law for industry : March 29th-April 2nd 1981, Churchill College, Cambridge, England / organised by the Committee on Environmental Law (Committee F), Section on Business Law, International Bar Association : edited with discussion summaries by John Salter and Patricia Thomas. – 2. – London : International Bar Association in cooperation with Sweet and Maxwell, 1981.
21cm.
ISBN 0950587621 Pbk Unpriced

—Regional development agencies and peripheral regions : report / prepared under the guidance of the Committee of Experts on Social and Economic Activities of the Steering Committee for Regional and Municipal Matters by Jacques Robert. – Strasbourg : Council of Europe, 1985.
23p.

—Scottish planning law and procedure / by Eric Young and Jeremy Rowan-Robinson : with a contribution by C.M.G. Himsworth. – Glasgow : William Hodge, 1985.
xliv,564p.
Supersedes Eric Youngs The law of planning in Scotland. Includes index. Provides a guide through the legislative and regulatory system of Scottish planning law and procedure and sets the subject matter in the context of administrative law. Considerable attention is given to control of development.
ISBN 0852791224

REGIONAL PLANNING - AUSTRALIA - NEW SOUTH WALES

—Environmental planning and development law (NSW) / by A.J. Nott. – Sydney : Penman, 1982.
xlix,417p.
Includes index.
ISBN 0959431608

REGIONAL PLANNING - ENGLAND

—Blundell and Dobry's planning appeals and inquiries / George Dobry, Robert Carnwath. – 3rd ed. – London : Sweet & Maxwell, 1982.
xxi,146p; 25cm.
Reviews planning inquiry and appeals procedure at all levels. Deals with evidence, enforcement notices, refusals, determination of rights, and presentation of appeals before inspectors and the High Court. Includes referrals to the Secretary of State.
ISBN 0421253509 Pbk £9.75

—Guide to development and planning / by R.N.D. Hamilton. – 7th ed. – London : Oyez, 1981.
lxiv,510p; 23cm.
Previous ed.: 1975. Includes index.
ISBN 0851205496 Unpriced

—Ideologies of planning law / Patrick McAuslan. – Oxford : Pergamon, 1980.
xiii,282p; 26cm. – (Pergamon international library).
Includes index.
ISBN 0080236960 £17.00
ISBN 0080251986

—Outline of planning law / Sir Desmond Heap. – 9th ed. – London : Sweet & Maxwell, 1987.
350p; 22cm.
Previous ed.: 1982. Includes index.
ISBN 0421354402 Hbk £20.00
ISBN 042135450X Pbk £12.50

—Planning decisions digest / Michael Purdue and Vincent Fraser. – London : Sweet & Maxwell, 1986.
300p; 24cm.
Covers judicial decisions back to 1948, and selected ministerial decisions since 1974. Brief summaries of each decision are included, and referenced. Material is arranged under subject headings following the structure of the Town and Country Planning Act 1971.
ISBN 0421325704 Pbk £19.00

—Planning inquiries / Gordon Hyde. – London : Sweet & Maxwell, 1983.
75p.
Conference papers.
ISBN 0421318600 Pbk £12.00

—Planning law and procedure / A.E. Telling. – 6th ed. – London : Butterworths, 1982.
xxix,321p.
Previous ed.: 1977. Includes index.
ISBN 0406665095

—Planning law casebook / London : Laureate-Thomson, 1984.
288p.
ISBN 0907392091 Pbk £17.50

—Planning law handbook / by Malcolm Grant. – London : Sweet & Maxwell, 1981.
xxx,488p; 25cm.
ISBN 0421285702 Pbk £12.50

REGIONAL PLANNING - GREAT BRITAIN

—Challenging decision : papers from a conference held at Oxford, September 1985 / organised by the Bar Council, the Law Society and the Royal Institution of Chartered Surveyors. – London : Sweet & Maxwell, 1986.
vi,101p; 25cm.
Conference paper.
ISBN 0421361301 Pbk £22.00

—Contemporary planning policies : papers from a conference entitled Making the Planning System Work held at Oxford, September 1983 / organised by the Bar Council, the Law Society, and the Royal Institution of Chartered Surveyors. – London : Sweet & Maxwell, 1984.
vi,72p; 25cm.
Conference papers.
ISBN 0421326603 Pbk £18.00

—Environmental planning, 1939-1969 / J. B. Cullingworth. – London : HMSO, 1980.
xv,582p,1p. of plates (folded).

—Introduction to town and country planning / John Ratcliffe. – 2nd ed. – London : Hutchinson, 1981.
506p; 22cm.
Previous ed.: 1974. Bibliography: p483-487. - Includes index.
ISBN 0091440203 Hbk £15.00
ISBN 0091440211 Pbk £6.95

—Local plans in British land use planning / by Patsy Healey. – Oxford : Pergamon, 1983.
xv,324p; 24cm.
Bibliography: p303-318. - Includes index.
ISBN 0080252427 £16.50

—Metropolitan problem : papers from a conference held at Oxford, September 1984, organised by the Bar Council, the Law Society, and the Royal Institution of Chartered Surveyors / Gordon V. Hyde. – London : Sweet & Maxwell, 1985.
vi,102p; 25cm. – (Journal of planning and environmental law occasional papers).
ISBN 0421341505 Pbk £19.00

—Planning control : philosophies, prospects and practice / edited by M.L. Harrison and R. Mordey. – London : Croom Helm, 1986.
234p; 23cm. – (Croom Helm series in geography and environment).
Bibliography: p227-232. - Includes index.
ISBN 0709937903 £25.00

—Planning for growth and decline : papers from a conference held at Oxford, September 1986, organised by the Bar Council, the Law Society and the Royal Institution of Chartered Surveyors / London : Sweet & Maxwell, 1987.
vi,70p; 25cm.
Conference proceedings.
ISBN 0421382600 Pbk £20.00

—Planning law and procedure / A.E. Telling. – 7th ed. – London : Butterworth, 1986.
xxxii,351p; 23cm.
Previous ed.: 1982. Includes index.
ISBN 0406665214 Hbk £18.00
ISBN 0406665222 Pbk £11.95

—Town and country planning in Britain / J.B. Cullingworth. – 8th ed. – London : Allen & Unwin, 1982.
369p; 23cm.
Previous ed.: 1979. Bibliography: p349-360. - Includes index.
ISBN 0047110104 Hbk Unpriced
ISBN 0047110112 Pbk Unpriced

—Town and country planning in Britain / J.B. Cullingworth. – 9th ed. – London : Allen & Unwin, 1985.
430p; 22cm.
Previous ed.: 1982. Includes bibliography and index.
ISBN 0047110139 Pbk £8.95

REGIONAL PLANNING - IRELAND

—Guide to planning legislation in the Republic of Ireland / by Kevin Ingram Nowlan. – Dublin : Incorporated Law Society of Ireland, 1988.
xxiii,375p; 26cm.
Includes index.
ISBN 0902027301 No price

REGIONAL PLANNING - NEW ZEALAND

—Planning and development law in New Zealand / by Kenneth A. Palmer : with a foreword by Sir Robin Cooke. – 2nd ed. 2. – Sydney : Law Book Co., 1984.
lviii,1023p.
ISBN 0455203725

REGIONALISM - AFRICA

—Future of regionalism in Africa / edited by Ralph I. Onwuka and Amadu Sesay. – London : Macmillan, 1985.
xiii,272p; 22cm. – (Macmillan international college editions).
Bibliography: p259-264.
ISBN 0333345304

REGIONALISM - ENGLAND

—Regional government in England / edited by Brian W. Hogwood, Michael Keating. – Oxford : Clarendon Press, 1982.
x,277p; 23cm.
Includes index.
ISBN 0198274343 £18.50

REGISTRATION OF BIRTHS, MARRIAGES AND DEATHS - AUSTRALIA - NEW SOUTH WALES

—Registration and certification of births and deaths : discussion paper / New South Wales Law Reform Commission. – Sydney : Government Printer, 1987.
vii,33p. – (D.P. v 17.).
ISBN 0730546276 Hbk

REGISTRATION OF BIRTHS, MARRIAGES AND DEATHS - GREAT BRITAIN

—District Registry Practice / Frieze. – 23rd ed. – London : Longman Professional, 1983.
ISBN 0851210333 Pbk £17.95

REHABILITATION

—Community Alternatives for Young Offenders (CAYO) : interim report / NACRO. – London : National Association for Care and Resettlement of Offenders, 1980.
7p.

—Justice for children / Allison Morris ... et al. – London : Macmillan, 1980.
vii,146p; 22cm.
Bibliography: p.141-146.
ISBN 0333274865 Unpriced
ISBN 0333274873

—Vocational Rehabilitation Services for Disabled Persons : Legislative Provisions / Geneva : International Labour Office, 1982.
ii, 120p.
ISBN 9221030156 Hbk £17.50

REHABILITATION - AUSTRALIA

—Spent convictions / Law Reform Commission. – Canberra : Australian Government Publishing Service, 1987.
viii,126p. – (Report).
Bibliography: p.123-126.
ISBN 0644013702

REHABILITATION - FINLAND

—Dealing with child offenders in Finland : the Scandinavian child welfare system in operation / Matti Joutsen. – Helsinki : Research Institute of Legal Policy, 1980.
121p.
Bibliography: p.95-100.
ISBN 9517040652

REHABILITATION - GREAT BRITAIN

—Community alternatives for juvenile offenders : development kit / NACRO. – London : NACRO, 1983.
47p.
ISBN 0850690277

—Introduction to NACRO's work in education / NACRO. – London : NACRO, 1980.
6p. – (Education).

—Multi-facility induction : the first six months : a report by the Lifeline Project, Manchester, on its induction programme for drug users who wish to reconstruct their lives without recourse to drugs / Lifeline Project. – Manchester : The Project, 1980.
10p.

—NACRO news digest / London : NACRO, 1979-.

REHABILITATION - NEW ZEALAND

—Living down a criminal record : problems and proposals : a discussion paper / Law Reform Division, Department of Justice. – Wellington : The Department, 1985.
31p.
ISBN 0477072151

REHABILITATION CENTRES - ENGLAND

—Day centres and probation / S. Fairhead with the the assistance of J. Wilkinson-Grey. – London : Home Office, 1981.
v,39p. – (Research Unit paper).
Bibliography: p.34.
ISBN 0862520185

REINSTATEMENT - GREAT BRITAIN

—Aftermath of tribunal reinstatement and re-engagement / by Kevin Williams and David Lewis. – London : Department of Employment, 1981.
46p. – (Research paper).
Bibliography: p.45-46.

RELATIVITY

—Rationality and relativism / edited by Martin Hollis and Steven Lukes. – Oxford : Basil Blackwell, 1982.
viii,312p; 23cm.
Bibliography: p306-310. - Includes index.
ISBN 0631127739 Hbk Unpriced
ISBN 0631131264 Pbk Unpriced

RELIGION AND LAW

—Law and religion : the Jewish experience / Ze'ev W. Falk. – Jerusalem : Mesharim, 1981.
238p.
Bibliography: p.237-238.

RELIGION AND LAW - CANADA

—Institute for Christian Studies Act, 1983, Bill Pr021 : An Act Respecting the Institute for Christian Studies / Ontario : Ontario Government Publications Service, 1983.
12p.

RELIGION AND LAW - INDIA

—Interpersonal conflict of laws in India, Pakistan and Bangladesh / David Pearl. – London : Stevens, 1981.
xxviii,176p; 25cm.
Bibliography: p.165-69. Includes index.
ISBN 0420457704

RELIGION AND LAW - PAKISTAN

—Interpersonal conflict of laws in India, Pakistan and Bangladesh / David Pearl. – London : Stevens, 1981.
xxviii,176p; 25cm.
Bibliography: p.165-69. Includes index.
ISBN 0420457704

RELIGION AND LAW - USSR

—Religious minorities in the Soviet Union : a report / prepared for the Minority Rights Group by Michael Bourdeaux and two associates, Kathleen Matchett and Cornelia Gerstenmaier. – Rev. 4th ed. – London : Minority Rights Group, 1984.
24p. – (Report).
Bibliography: p.23.
ISBN 0946690154

RELIGION AND STATE

—Law, religion and the Jewish community / by Graham Zellick. – London : Jews' College, 1987.
Delivered at Jews' College on April 2 1986. Revised February 1987.

RELIGION AND STATE - INDIA

—Religion-State Relationship and Constitutional Rights in India / New Delhi : Deep and Deep Publications, 1987.
468p.
ISBN 8171000096 Hbk £325.00

RELOCATION - GREAT BRITAIN

—Transfer of undertakings : the legal pitfalls : a specially commissioned report / by Patrick Elias and John Bowers. – London : Longman Professional, 1985.
54 leaves.
ISBN 0851208061

REMAINDERS (ESTATES) - ENGLAND

—Essay on the learning of contingent remainders and executory devises / by Charles Fearne. – 9th ed. – London : Saunders and Benning, 1831.
lvi,730p.
Includes index.

REMAINDERS (ESTATES) - GREAT BRITAIN

—Essay on the Learning of Contingent Remainers and Executory Devises / 2nd ed. Repr. of 1773 ed. – Abingdon : Professional Books.
491p.

REMEDIES

—Judicial remedies in international law / Christine D. Gray. – Oxford : Clarendon Press, 1987.
300p; 24cm. – (Oxford monographs in international law).
Includes bibliography and index.
ISBN 0198255713 £30.00

—Legal Remedies / Avtar Singh. – 5th rev. ed. – Lucknow : Eastern Book Company, 1986.
380p.

—Remedial Law Compendium / Manila : National Book Store.

Vol. 1 1984.
424p.
ISBN 9710800477 £25.00

Vol. 2
ISBN 9710805258 £30.00

—Remedies for breach of contract : a comparative account / G.H. Treitel. – Oxford : Clarendon Press, 1988.
xliii,422p.
Includes index. Discusses remedies for a breach of contract from a comparative perspective. Contrasts civil and common law solutions, and differences between English and American common law, and French and German civil law. The aim is to identify types of solutions and consider how far differences in theoretical approaches are reflected in practical results.
ISBN 0198255004 Hbk £45/$60

REMEDIES - AUSTRALIA

—Civil Remedies / Butterworths, 1988.
ca 550p.

—Civil Remedies / Sydney : Butterworths, 1988.
550p.
This work discusses the nature and interrelation of civil remedies. Included are materials on damages, restitution, statutory remedies, injuries to rights in tangible property, personal injuries, and other topics.

—Remedies / by Bruce Kercher and Michael Noone. – Sydney : Law Book Co., 1983.
xxxvi,408p.
Includes index.
ISBN 0455204454 Hbk £62

REMEDIES - AUSTRALIA - SOUTH AUSTRALIA

—Report ... relating to administrative appeals / Law Reform Committee of South Australia. – Adelaide : Government Printer, 1984.
67p. – (82nd report).
Bibliography: p.65-68.

REMEDIES - CANADA

—Cases and Materials on Remedies / Toronto : Edmond-Montgomery, 1988.
ca 1,000p.

—Cases and Materials on Remedies / Cassels. – Aurora : Canada Law Book, 1988.

—Cases and Materials on Remedies / Jamie L. Cassels. – Aurora : Canada Law Book Co, 1988.
1000p.

—Creditors' Remedies : 1985 Supplement / Vancouver : Continuing Legal Education Society of British Columbia, 1986.
19p.
ISBN 0865043779 Hbk £15.00

—New developments in the law of remedies / Don Mills, Ont. : Richard de Boo, 1981.
574p.
Includes index.
ISBN 088820101X

—Remedies : 1983 / Vancouver : British Columbia Continuing Legal Education Society.

—Remedies - 1986 / Vancouver : British Columbia Continuing Legal Education Society, 1986.
313p.
ISBN 0865042578 Hbk £65.00

—Remedies 1986 / Vancouver : Continuing Legal Education Society of British Columbia, 1986.
313p.
ISBN 0865040389 Hbk £65.00

—Remedies : Cases and Materials / Toronto : Edmond-Montgomery, 1988.
ca 1,000p.
ISBN 0920722229 Hbk £100.00

—Remedies for Trademark Infringement / Agincourt : Carswell, 1988.
ca 192p.

—Remedies for Trademark Infringement / Agincourt : Carswell, 1988.
192p.
This book provides a comprehensive discussion of the remedies available for trademark infringement. Topics include the ramifications of injunctive relief, ancillary relief, and monetary remedies. The text also discusses how these various remedies interact with each other.

—Remedies in Tort, 4 Vols. / A. Linden. – Agincourt : Carswell, 1987.
This multi-volume set of looseleaf books provides an in-depth coverage of the area of torts. There are 23 chapters. Discussions include related proceedings, elements the plaintiff must establish to succeed in an action, available defenses, remedies, necessary and proper parties to an action, and practice issues pertaining to tort law. Special features include a legal research guide and sample statements of claims.

—Remedies in Tort, 4 Vols. / Agincourt : Carswell, 1987.
550p.

REMEDIES - CANADA - ALBERTA

—Remedies of unsecured creditors / Institute of Law Research and Reform. – Edmonton : The Institute, 1986.
xiv,370p. – (Report for discussion).
Includes bibliographical references.

REMEDIES - ENGLAND

—Quiet enjoyment : remedies for harassment and illegal eviction / by Andrew Arden and Martin Partington. Edited by S. Carrott and C. Hunter. – 3rd. – London : Legal Action Group, 1990.
127.
Includes index.
ISBN 0905099265 Pbk £11

—Remedies in contract and tort / Donald Harris. – London : Weidenfeld & Nicolson, 1988.
xxxvii,411p.
Includes index.
ISBN 0297793551

—Remedies of English law / by F.H. Lawson, with the assistance of Harvey Teff. – 2nd ed. – London : Butterworths, 1980.
xxii,309p.
This work for students of English law describes the various forms of redress available in England today and the procedures by which they may be obtained. The book covers judicial and non-judicial remedies.
ISBN 0406617201 £11.95

REMEDIES - EUROPEAN COMMUNITY

—Judicial protection in the European Communities / Denis Waelbroeck. – 4th ed. – Deventer : Kluwer Law and Taxation Publishers, 1987.
xviii,510p; 25cm.
Previous ed.: 1983. Includes index. At head of title: Europa Instituut, University of Leiden.
ISBN 9065443274 Pbk No price

—Reports of the ninth Congress, 25-27 September 1980 / Federation Internationale pour le Droit Eruopeen. – 3. – S.l. : FIDE, 1980.
21cm.
Includes papers in French and German.
ISBN 0421278501 Pbk £25.00

REMEDIES - GREAT BRITAIN

—Anton Piller Orders and Mareva Injunctions: a Practitioner's Guide / London : Butterworths, 1987.
ISBN 0406102902 Pbk £28.95

—Equity Doctrines and Remedies / Gummow. – 2nd ed. – London : Butterworths, 1984.
ISBN 040949142X Hbk £52.10
ISBN 0409491527 Pbk £39.30

—Remedies for torts and breach of contract / London : Butterworths, 1987.
ISBN 0406501505 Hbk £24.00

—Remedies for victims of crime / Tucker. – London : Legal Action Group, 1984.
ISBN 0905099060 Pbk £5.00

—Remedies of English Law / 2nd ed. – London : Butterworths, 1980.
ISBN 0406617201 Pbk £12.95

—Remedies under the contract, CS No 3 / Cain. – London : Sweet & Maxwell, 1988.
ISBN 0421381108 Hbk £22.00

REMEDIES - IRAN

—Remedies for breach of contract in Islamic and Iranian law / Glasgow : Royston, 1984.
250p.
ISBN 0946706212 £45.95

REMEDIES - UNITED STATES

—Suing government : citizen remedies for official wrongs / Peter H. Schuck. – New Haven : Yale University Press, 1983.
xxi,262p; 22cm.
Includes index.
ISBN 0300029578 Hbk

RENT - AUSTRALIA

—Commercial Rent Reviews / North Ryde : Law Book Co, 1986.
ISBN 0455206414 Pbk £15.00

RENT - CANADA

—Distress for Rent / Victoria : Government of British Columbia, 1981.

RENT - ENGLAND

—Handbook of rent review / Ronald Bernstein and Kirk Reynolds : consultant editor on valuation and arbitration practice J.C. Hill. – 1. – London : Sweet & Maxwell in collaboration with the Royal Institution of Chartered Surveyors, 1981.
loose-leaf; 32cm.
Includes index.
ISBN 042127980X Unpriced

—Rent control and leasehold enfranchisement / Trevor M. Aldridge. – 8th ed. – London : Oyez, 1980.
205p; 22cm.
Previous ed.: 1977. Includes index.
ISBN 0851205461 Pbk £9.50

RENT - GREAT BRITAIN

—Advisory Committee on Rent Rebates and Rent Allowances / London : HMSO, 1983.
– (Report No. 3 (Final Report)).
ISBN 0117517119 Hbk £4.15

—Casebook on Rent Review and Lease Renewal / Pawlowski. – Oxford : Blackwell Scientific, 1986.
ISBN 0003831957 Hbk £40.00

—Casebook on Rent Review and Lease Renewal / Mark Pawlowski. – London : Collins, 1986.
600p.
ISBN 0003831957 Hbk £35.00

—Fair Rents / 3rd ed. – London : Shaw & Sons, 1985.
ISBN 0721907024 Pbk £7.50

—Fair rents : a practical guide to the law relating to the rents of residential tenancies including the work of rent officers, rent assessment committees and rent tribunals / by John Prophet. – 3rd ed. – London : Shaw and Sons, 1985.
xxxi,243p.
ISBN 0721907024

—Housing Benefit review : report of the review team / Great Britain. – London : H.M.S.O., 1985.
43 p.
ISBN 0101952007

—Rent control and leasehold enfranchisement / 9th. – London : Longman Professional (UK), 1989.
– (Practitioner series).
Guide to rent restriction rules governing the varius types of residential tenancies and the qualifications and procedure for enfranchisement. New edition revised to take account of the Landlord and Tenant Acts 1985, and 1987, and the Housing Act 1988, including details of assured tenancies.
ISBN 0851213871 Hbk £32.50

—Rent Reviews / London : Collins, 1986.
300p.
ISBN 000383106X Hbk £17.50

—Rent reviews / Oxford : Blackwell Scientific, 1987.
ISBN 000383106X Hbk £19.50

—Rent reviews and variable rents / J E Adams. – 2nd ed. – London : Longman Professional, 1984.
– (Longman Practitioner Series).
ISBN 0851212581 Hbk £37.00

—Rent reviews and variable rents / J Adams. – 3rd. – London : Longman Professional (UK), 1989.
– (Practitioner series).
Examines rent review clauses and other methods. Analysis of some 100 cases decided since 1984, and model forms published by the Law Society, the Royal institute of Chartered Surveyors, and the ISVA.
ISBN 0851213863 Hbk £37.50

RENT - MALAYSIA

—Control of Rent Act, 1966 (No. 56 of 1966) / Kuala Lumpur : International Law Books Services.

—Rent Control Legislation in Malaysia / Butterworths, 1986.
292p.
Covers tenancy and licence, premises, parties, rent, rent tribunals, recovery of possession of premises, subtenancies, penal provisions, the repeal provisions, redevelopment, decontrol, and notice to quit.
ISBN 0409995231 Hbk £85.00

—Rent control legislation in Malaysia / London : Butterworths, 1986.
ISBN 0409995231 Hbk £41.00

RENT - NORTHERN IRELAND

—Ground rents and other periodic payments / Land Law Working Group. – Belfast : HMSO, 1980.
iv,42p. – (Discussion document).
At head of cover title: Department of Finance for Northern Ireland, Office of Law Reform.
ISBN 0337233349

RENT - SCOTLAND

—Rent (Scotland) Act 1984 / J Hope. – Edinburgh : W Green & Son, 1986.
Annotated text of the Act reprinted from Scottish Current Law Statutes, along with the rent regulations passed under the earlier legislation, supplemented with a table of cases and index.
ISBN 0414007522

RENTAL HOUSING - LAW AND LEGISLATION - NORTHERN IRELAND

—Ejectment for non-payment of rent / by J. A. Dowling : with a supplement for the Republic of Ireland by G. McCormack. – Belfast : Faculty of Law, the Queen's University of Belfast, 1986.
xvii,84p.
ISBN 0853892695

REPATRIATION

—Revision of the Repatriation of Seamen Convention, 1926 (No. 23) and of the Repatriation (Ship Masters and Apprentices) Recommendation, 1926 (No. 27) / Geneva : International Labour Office, 1987.
ISBN 9221057925 Hbk £15.00

REPATRIATION - AUSTRALIA

—Review of pensions decisions under repatriation legislation : report to the Attorney-General / Administrative Review Council. – Canberra : Australian Government Publishing Service, 1983.
vi,60p. – (Parliamentary paper).
ISBN 0644028920

REPATRIATION - COMMONWEALTH

—Scheme for the transfer of convicted offenders within the Commonwealth : explanatory documentation prepared for Commonwealth jurisidictions / by A.M.F. Webb. – London : Commonwealth Secretariat, 1987.
iii,92p.

REPORTERS AND REPORTING

—Manufacture of news : social problems, deviance and the mass media / Stanley Cohen and Jock Young (editors). – rev. ed. – London : Constable, 1981.
506p.
ISBN 0094637806

REPOSSESSION - AUSTRALIA

—Mortgagee's Power of Sale / Butterworths, 1980.
207p.
ISBN 0409448508 Hbk £48.00

REPOSSESSION - GREAT BRITAIN

—Residential possession proceedings / R Davidson. – 3rd. – London : Longman Professional (UK), 1990.
– (Practitioner series).
Contains legal and procedural instructions as to how to effect or prevent the recovery of possession of residential premises. Explains the relevant law, procedure to adopt, evidence required, and orders the court may make. Over 100 specimen forms.

—Residential possession proceedings / Davidson. – 2nd ed. – London : Longman Professional, 1984.
– (Longman Practitioner Series).
Contains legal and procedural instruction as to how to effect or prevent the recovery of possession of residential premises. Includes over forty specimen forms.
ISBN 0851212751 Pbk £22.00

REPOSSESSION - SCOTLAND
—Recovery of possession of heritable property / Scottish Law Commission. - Edinburgh : The Commission, 1984.
iii,122p. - (Consultative memorandum no 59).
Includes bibliographical references.

REPRESENTATIVE GOVERNMENT AND REPRESENTATION - GREAT BRITAIN
—Representation and Urban Community / London : Macmillan, 1981.
200p.
ISBN 0333288785 Hbk £20.00

REPRESENTATIVE GOVERNMENT AND REPRESENTATION - SOUTH AFRICA
—South Africa and the consociational option : a constitutional analysis / by L.J. Boulle. - Cape Town : Juta, 1984.
xii, 270 p.; 25 cm.
Includes indexes. Bibliography: p. 227-229.
ISBN 0702114340 pbk.

REPRISALS
—Legality of non-forcible counter-measures in international law / Omer Yousif Elagab. - Oxford Oxfordshire : Clarendon Press, 1988.
Includes index. Bibliography: p.
ISBN 019825590X

REPRODUCTION (HUMAN)
—IVF and the status of children / report by the Senate Standing Committee on Constitutional and Legal Affairs on National Uniformity in Laws Relating to the Status of Children Born through the Use of In Vitro Fertilisation. - Canberra : Australian Government Publishing Service, 1985.
xvi,84p. - (Parliamentary paper).
Includes bibliographical references. Chairman: Senator Michael Tate.
ISBN 0644046104

REPRODUCTION (HUMAN) - AUSTRALIA
—Artificial conception : surrogate motherhood : Australian public opinion / New South Wales Law Reform Commission. - Sydney : The Commission, 1987.
xxiii,85p. - (Research report).
Bibliography: p.85. Spine title: Surrogacy survey.
ISBN 0730537986

REPRODUCTION (HUMAN) - AUSTRALIA - NEW SOUTH WALES
—Artificial conception : in vitro fertilization : discussion paper / New South Wales Law Reform Commission. - Sydney : Government Printer, 1987.
xxxiii,189p. - (D.P.).
Bibliography: p.165-183.
ISBN 0730544419

—Artificial conception : report 2 : in vitro fertilization / New South Wales Law Reform Commission. - Sydney : The Commission, 1988.
xxi,175p. - (L.R.C).
Bibliography: p.147-172.. Spine title: In vitro fertilization.
ISBN 0730555712

—Surrogate motherhood / New South Wales Law Reform Commission. - Sydney : Government Printer, 1988.
xviii,143p. - (D.P v 18).
Bibliography: pp.133-141.
ISBN 0730555399 Hbk

REPRODUCTION (HUMAN) - GREAT BRITAIN
—New reproductive techniques : a legal perspective / Douglas J. Cusine. - Aldershot, Hants. : Gower, 1988.
x,261p.
Bibliography: pp238-254. - Includes index.
ISBN 0566054108

—Report of the Committee of Inquiry into Human Fertilisation and Embryology / Chairman: Mary Warnock. - London : H.M.S.O., 1984.
At head of title: Department of Health and Social Security.
ISBN 0101931409

—Reproduction revolution / Wells. - Oxford : Oxford University Press, 1984.
ISBN 0192177362 Hbk £15.00
ISBN 0192860445 Pbk £3.95

—Reproductive technology / Oxford : Blackwell, 1987.
ISBN 0745602096 Pbk £7.95

RESEARCH
—Exchange of Information on Research in European Law / Directorate of Legal Affairs. - London : HMSO, 1983.
112p.
Provides information on research projects in law currently underway in various European and non-European states. Gives publication dates and information on how to obtain copies of final reports.
ISBN 0119836300 Pbk £1.25

RESEARCH - CANADA
—Research and development in Canada: a practical guide to financing, protecting and exploiting new technology / Bereskin, Parr. - Scarborough, Ontario : Butterworths (Canada), 1987.
288.
Gives details on how to manage proprietary information, legally protect new technology, cash in on the many federal and provincial government research and development assistance programmes, pursue private venture captial funding, benefit from tax incentivs available to Canadian research and development, license technology, and how publicly funded institutions can profit from the exploitation of technology.
ISBN 0409805670 Hbk

RESEARCH - ENGLAND
—Future research programme : 1980- / SSRC Centre for Socio- Legal Studies, Wolfson College, Oxford. - Oxford : Centre for Socio-legal Studies, 1980.
115p.
Includes bibliographies.

RESEARCH - EUROPE
—Exchange of Information on Research in European Law / Directorate of Legal Affairs. - London : HMSO, 1983.
112p.
Provides information on research projects in law currently underway in various European and non-European states. Gives publication dates and information on how to obtain copies of final reports.
ISBN 0119836300 Pbk £1.25

RESEARCH AND DEVELOPMENT CONTRACTS
—Research Contracts : Civil-Law Means Promotion Scientific Technical Progress / Dordrecht : Kluwer, 1977.
235p.
ISBN 9028603174 Hbk £59.00

RESEARCH AND DEVELOPMENT CONTRACTS - CANADA
—Research and Development in Canada : A Practical Guide to Financing, Protecting and Exploiting New Technology / Daniel R. Bereskin. - Toronto : Butterworths, 1987.
288p.

RESEARCH AND DEVELOPMENT CONTRACTS - EUROPEAN COMMUNITY
—Organization and management of community research and development : study / Economic and Social Committee of the European Communities. - Brussels : General Secretariat of the Economic and Social Committee, 1980.
vi,159p.

RESEARCH GRANTS - GREAT BRITAIN
—Sources of funding for research and publication / Helen Peden and Philip Hills. - Leicester : Primary Communications Research Centre, University of Leicester, 1983.
46p; 20x21cm.
Bibliography: p46. - Includes index.
ISBN 0906083249 Pbk Unpriced

RESTITUTION
—Benefits conferred under a mistake of law / Law Reform commission of British Columbia. - Vancouver : Law Reform Commission of British Columbia, 1980.
v,161p. - (Working paper).

RESTITUTION - AUSTRALIA - NEW SOUTH WALES
—Community law reform program / New South Wales Law Reform Commission. - Sydney : Government Printer, 1987.
xiii,95p. - (L.R.C).
Bibliography: pp.79-81. Includes text of draft bill.
ISBN 073054429X

RESTITUTION - AUSTRALIA - SOUTH AUSTRALIA
—Report ... relating to the irrecoverability of benefits obtained by reason of mistake of law / Law Reform Committee of South Australia. - Adelaide : Government Printer, 1984.
40p. - (84th report).

RESTITUTION - CANADA
—Restitution / by G.H.L. Fridman, and James G. McLeod. - Toronto, Canada : Carswell Co., 1982.
lxviii, 649 p.; 26 cm.
Includes bibliographical references and index.

—Restitution / James G. McLeod. - Agincourt : Carswell, 1982.
717p.

RESTITUTION - GREAT BRITAIN
—Introduction to the law of restitution / Peter Birks. - Oxford : Clarendon, 1985.
530p; 24cm.
Includes index.
ISBN 0198760744 £35.00

—Introduction to the Law of Restitution / Oxford : Oxford University Press, 1985.
ISBN 0198760744 Hbk £45.00

—Restitution / P. Birks. - London : Sweet & Maxwell, 1986.
ISBN 0420472908 Hbk

RESTITUTION - NEW ZEALAND
—Restitution imposed on property offenders in New Zealand courts : a study of orders and compliance / Burt Galaway, Walton Walker. - Wellington : Department of Justice, 1985.
v,27p. - (Study series).
Bibliography: p.26.

RESTRAINT OF TRADE
—Common law of restraint of trade : a legal and economic analysis / by Michael J. Trebilcock. - Toronto : Carswell, 1986.
xxvi,419p.
ISBN 0459396404

—Law of Monopolies, Restrictive and Unfair Trade Practices / Lucknow : Eastern Book Company, 1984.
134p.

RESTRAINT OF TRADE - AUSTRALIA
—Australian trade practices reporter / by CCH editorial staff : consultant editors R. Baxt, R.G. Blunt, A.I. Tonking. - 2. - North Ryde, N.S.W. : CCH Australia, 1972-.
loose-leaf; 26cm.
Includes current issues of: Australian trade practices reports. Loose-leaf issues accompanied by a summary report. Pre-current 'Commission decisions : authorizations and notifications' filed in transfer binders.
ISBN 0869030264 v.2
ISBN 0869030280 Hbk

—Australian trade practices reports / North Ryde, N.S.W. : CCH Australia, 1978-.
23cm.
Issued as bound volumes, with current issues forming part of the service to the loose-leaf publication: Australian trade practices reporter.

—Developments in Section 52 of the Trade Practices Act 1984-1985 : Centre for Commercial Law and Applied Legal Research / Monash University. - Clayton : Monash University Press.
ISBN 086746397X Hbk £15.00

—Guide to amendments to the Trade Practices Act / Trade Practices Commission. - Canberra : Trade Practices Commission, 1986.
13 leaves.

—Impact of Prosecutions Under the Trade Practices Act / Canberra : Australian Institute of Criminology.

—Mal practice : the administration of the Murphy trade practices act : antitrust as a australian poshlost / V.G. Venturini. - Sydney : Non Mollare, 1980.
ix, 465 p.; 23 cm.
Includes bibliographical references and index.
ISBN 0959462902 pbk.

—Practical uses of Section 52 of the Trade Practices Act / Monash University Staff. - Clayton : Monash University Press, 1984.
ISBN 086746352X Hbk £14.00

—Restrictive trade practices : judgments, materials and policy / Alan A. Ransom and Warren Pengilley. - Sydney : Legal Books Pty, 1985.
xlix,1193p.
Includes index.
ISBN 0949553158

—Sackville and Neave Property Law : Cases and Materials / C. Rossiter. - 4th ed. - Sydney : Butterworths, 1988.
992p.
The fourth edition of this casebook contains revised materials on the Trade Practices Act, leases, and mortgages.

—Trade associations, fairness and competition / by Warren Pengilley. - Sydney : Law Book Company, 1981.
xxvii,247p.
Includes index. Includes text of Trade Practices Act 1974.
ISBN 0455200866

—Trade practices and consumer protection : a commentary on the Trade Practices Act 1974 / by G.Q. Taperell, R.B. Vermeesch, D.J. Harland. - 3rd ed. - Sydney : Butterworths, 1983.
liii,922p.
Previous ed.: 1978. Includes bibliographies and index. Legislation set against the economic and commercial background in which it operates.
ISBN 0409491217 Pbk

RESTRAINT OF TRADE - CANADA

—Annual report for the year ended 31 March ... / Restrictive Trade Practices Commission. - v. - Ottawa : The Commission, 1981.
Text in English and French, 1982 onwards. Added t.p. in French, 1982 onwards: Rapport annuel pour l'exercise clos le 31 mars ... / Commission sur les pratiques restrictives du commerce.
ISBN 07115458

—Competition law amendments : a schematic presentation of Bill C-91 and the present act / Ottawa : Consumer and Corporate Affairs Canada, 1986.
98, 99 p.; 28 cm.
English and French. Title on added t.p.: Reforme de la legislation sur la concurrence. Includes complete text of the Competition Tribunal Act and the Competition Act, including the provisions of the current act that are replaced or changed by Bill C-91.
ISBN 0662542282 pbk.

—Covenants in Restraint of Trade / Victoria : Government of British Columbia, 1984.

RESTRAINT OF TRADE - CANADA - BRITISH COLUMBIA

—Covenants in restraint of trade / Law Reform Commission of British Columbia. - Vancouver : The Commission, 1983.
iii,69p. - (Working paper).
Includes bibliographical references.

—Report on covenants in restraint of trade / Law Reform Commission of British Columbia. - Victoria : Queen's Printer, 1984.
76p.
Includes bibliographical references.
ISBN 077188429X

RESTRAINT OF TRADE - ENGLAND

—Restraint of trade and business secrets : law and practice / Simon Mehigan and David Griffiths. - 1st ed. - London : Longman Professional (UK), 1987.
xxiv,247p; 24cm. - (Longman commercial series).
Coverage includes employment contracts, business sale, partnerships and joint ventures, breach of contract, commercial contracts including licensing, distribution agreements, trade associations, evaluation agreements and performing contracts. List of cases classified according to business type.
ISBN 0851211747 Hbk £42.00

RESTRAINT OF TRADE - EUROPEAN COMMUNITY

—Competition law of Britain and the Common Market / by Valentine Korah. - 3rd ed. - The Hague : Martinus Nijhoff, 1982.
xxvii,352p.
Bibliography: p321-326. Includes index.
ISBN 9024726158 Hbk £140.00

—EEC competition law / D.G. Goyder. - Oxford : Clarendon Press, 1988.
xxxi,447p.
Account of the substantive law, and an assessment of the historical development and overall effectiveness of the competition policy. Suggests ways of improving co-ordination and implementation of competition policy. Examines the foundations of the last thirty years, and how they can be built upon.
ISBN 0198254032 pbk. £18.95
ISBN 0198255357 Hbk £45

—International trade law and practice of the European Community : EEC anti-dumping and other trade protection laws / Ivo van Bael, Jean-Francois Bellis. - Bicester : CCH, 1985.
viii,438p.
Discusses the Community's four main methods of trade protection; anti-dumping rules, anti-subsidy rules, safe-guard measures, and the 'New Commercial Policy Instrument', and comments on the EEC and ECSC Anti-dumping Regulations. Contains tables and annexes.
ISBN 0863250602

—Introductory guide to EEC Competition law and practice / Valentine Korah. - 3rd ed. - Oxford : ESC Publishing, 1986.
xxi,177p; 21cm.
Includes bibliographies and index. Cover title: EEC competition law and practice.
ISBN 0906214394

—Merger control in the EEC : a survey of European competition laws / prepared by the Brussels offices at Avenue de la Joyeuse Entree 1, Blijde Inkomstlaan 1 of : Advokaterne Bredgade 3 ... et al. - Deventer : Kluwer Law and Taxation Publishers, 1988.
xii,306p.
ISBN 9065443541

—Patent licensing and EEC competition rules : Regulation 2349/84 / Valentine Korah. - Oxford : ESC Publishing, 1985.
xiv,126p. - (European competition law monographs).
Includes bibliographies.
ISBN 090621436X

—R & D and the EEC competition rules : Regulation 418/85 / Valentine Korah. - Oxford : ESC Publishing, 1986.
xxi,114p. - (European competition law monographs).
Bibliography: p.xxi.
ISBN 0906214459

—Recent developments in EEC competition law : seminar documentation : Monday 8th December 1986, Cavendish Conference Centre, London W1 / Valentine Korah. - 1. - London : Legal Studies & Services, 1986.
various pagings.
Includes bibliographical references. Chairman: Valentine Korah.

RESTRAINT OF TRADE - GREAT BRITAIN

—Abolishing the Diplock Courts / White. - London : CENT, 1986.
ISBN 0900137274 Pbk £5.95

—Arthur Sanderson & Sons Limited : a report by the Director General of Fair Trading on an investigation under section 3 of the Competition Act 1980 / London : Office of Fair Trading, 1981.
53p.

—Becton Dickinson UK Limited : the supply of hypodermic syringes and hypodermic needles / a report by the Director General of Fair Trading on an investigation under section 3 of the Competition Act 1980. - London : Office of Fair Trading, 1988.
39p.

—Common law of restraint of trade / London : Sweet & Maxwell, 1987.
ISBN 0459396404 Hbk £35.00

—Competition law of Britain and the Common Market / by Valentine Korah. - 3rd ed. - The Hague : Martinus Nijhoff, 1982.
xxvii,352p.
Bibliography: p321-326. Includes index.
ISBN 9024726158 Hbk £140.00

—Consultation paper : safeguards against monopolistic and anti-competitive behaviour / Civil Aviation Authority. - s.l. : s.n., 1987.
9p.

—Petter Refrigeration Limited : a report by the Director General of Fair Trading on an investigation under section 3 of the Competition Act 1980 / London : Office of Fair Trading, 1981.
56p.

—Restrictions on the kind of organisation through which members of professions may offer their services / a report by the Director General of Fair Trading. - London : Office of Fair Trading, 1986.
86p,36p.

—Securities and Investments Board / a report by the Director General of Fair Trading to the Secretary of State for Trade and Industry. - London : Office of Fair Trading, 1987.
77p.

—Sheffield Newspapers Limited : a report by the Director General of Fair Trading on an investigation under section 3 of the Competition Act 1980 / London : Office of Fair Trading, 1981.
72p; 30cm.

—TI Raleigh Industries Limited and Raleigh Limited : a report by the Director General of Fair Trading on an investigation under Section 3 of the Competition Act, 1980 / London : Office of Fair Trading, 1981.
40p.

—Unichem Limited : allocation of shares by co-operative upon reconverting to a public limited company / a report by the Director General of Fair Trading on an investigation under section 3 of the Competition Act 1980. - London : Office of Fair Trading, 1988.
49p.

—W. M. Still & Sons Limited, W. M. Still Service Limited : a report by the Director General of Fair Trading on an investigation under section 3 of the Competition Act 1980 / Office of Fair Trading. - London : Office of Fair Trading, 1982.
39p; 30cm.

—World's Fair Limited and Marcus Publishing PLC : refusal to publish advertisements which contain certain price information : a report by the Director General of Fair Trading on two investigations under section 3 of the Competition Act 1980 / Office of Fair Trading. - London : Office of Fair Trading, 1987.
30p.

RESTRAINT OF TRADE - INDIA

—Guide to Monopolies and Restrictive Trade Practices Act / 2nd ed. - Nagpur : Wadhura & Co, 1982.

—Law and Practice of Restrictive Trade Practices in India / New Delhi : Deep and Deep Publications, 1988.
360p.

—Law of monopolies and restrictive trade practices in India / H.M. Jhala. - 2nd ed. - Bombay : N M Tripathi, 1984.
xxxvii,456p.
Includes index.

RESTRAINT OF TRADE - JAPAN

—Antimonopoly legislation of Japan / edited by Masanao Nakagawa. - Tokyo : Kosei Torihiki Kyokai, 1984.
ix,361p.
Includes index. English-Japanese and Japanese-English indexes.
ISBN 4876220018

RESTRAINT OF TRADE - NEW ZEALAND

—Law of Restrictive Trade Practices in New Zealand / 2nd. ed. - Butterworths, 1982.
ISBN 040960125X Hbk £33.10

—Law of Restrictive Trade Practices in NZ / 2nd ed. - London : Butterworths, 1983.
ISBN 040960125X Hbk £58.00

RESTRAINT OF TRADE - WEST GERMANY

—German antitrust law : an introduction to the German antitrust law with German text and synoptic English translation of the Act against Restraints of Competition / Martin H. Heidenhain, Hannes Schneider. - 2nd rev. ed. - Frankfurt am Main : Fritz Knapp, 1981.
291p.
Previous ed., 1973, published as: The German law against restraints of competition. Added t.p. in German: Das Recht gegen Wettbewerbsbeschrankungen.
ISBN 3781928306

RESTRICTIVE COVENANTS - AUSTRALIA

—Easements and restrictive covenants in Australia / Adrian J. Bradbrook and Marcia A. Neave. - Sydney : Butterworths, 1981.
xlv,422p.
Includes index.
ISBN 0409300489 Hbk £65

—Easements and Restrictive Covenants in Australia / Neave. - London : Butterworths, 1981.
ISBN 0409300489 Hbk £34.00

RESTRICTIVE COVENANTS - ENGLAND

—Land law & landscape / Philip Britton and Ian Thompson. - 1 videocassette. - London : Sweet & Maxwell in association with the University of Warwick, 1986.
- (Sweet & Maxwell's lawfilms).

—Preston and Newsom's restrictive covenants affecting freehold land / G. H. Newsom, G. L. Newsom. - 7th ed. - London : Sweet & Maxwell, 1982.
xl,387p; 23cm.
Previous ed.: 1976. Includes index.
ISBN 0421284900 £30.00

—What should we do about old restrictive covenants? : a consultation paper / Conveyancing Standing Committee. - London : The Committee, 1986.
12p.

RESTRICTIVE COVENANTS - GREAT BRITAIN

—Landlord and tenant : privity of contract and estate : duration of liability of parties to leases / the Law Commission. - London : HMSO, 1986.
iv,101p. - (Working paper).
Includes bibliographical references.
ISBN 0117301760

—Transfer of land, the law of positive and restrictive covenants ... / the Law Commission. - London : H.M.S.O., 1984.
x,331p; 25cm. - (H.C.1983-84).
ISBN 0102201846

RESTRICTIVE COVENANTS - NEW ZEALAND

—Positive covenants affecting land / report of the Property Law and Equity Reform Committee. - Wellington : The Committee, 1985.
85p.

RETAIL TRADE - GREAT BRITAIN

—Law for retailers / Jennifer Brave. - London : Sweet & Maxwell, 1983.
xii,207p; 23cm.
Bibliography: p195-197. - Includes index.
ISBN 0421298103 Hbk Unpriced
ISBN 0421298200 Pbk £7.50

—Retailers, dealers, wholesalers and distributors / Product Liability Briefing, 1988.
ISBN 1870317300 Pbk £6.50

RETIREMENT INCOME
—Living and Retiring Abroad / 2nd ed. – London : Kogan Page, 1988.
ISBN 1850914222 Pbk £6.95

RETIREMENT INCOME - CANADA
—Better pensions for Canadians / Canada. – Ottawa, Ont. : Government of Canada, 1982.
vi, 61, 68, vi p.; 28 cm.
English and French. Title on added t.p.: De meilleures pensions pour les Canadiens.
ISBN 0662520513 pbk.

—Better pensions for Canadians : focus on women / Ottawa : Minister of Supply and Services, 1982.
18,19p.
With French t.p.: De meilleures pensions pour les Canadiens: la part des femmes. English and French text.
ISBN 066252053X

RETIREMENT INCOME - GREAT BRITAIN
—Retirement planning guide / Allied Dunbar. – 2nd ed. – London : Longman Professional (UK), 1988.
ISBN 0851212115 £13.50

—Retirement relief - New CGT Rules / London : CCH, 1986.
ISBN 0863250815 Pbk £7.50

REVOCATION - CANADA - SASKATCHEWAN
—Proposals relating to ademption by equitable conversion / Law Reform Commission of Saskatchewan. – Saskatoon : The Commission, 1984.
12p.
Includes bibliographical references.

RIGHT OF PROPERTY
—Right to private property / Jeremy Waldron. – Oxford : Clarendon Press, 1988.
viii,470p.
Bibliography: pp.446-463. - Includes index..
ISBN 0198249594

RIGHT OF PROPERTY - CANADA
—Competing rights to mingled property tracing and the rule in Clayton's case / Law Reform Commission of British Columbia. – Vancouver : Law Reform Commission of British Columbia, 1982.
iv,122p. – (Working paper).
Includes bibliographical references and index.

RIGHT OF PROPERTY - SOUTH AFRICA
—Anton Piller-type orders / South African Law Commission. – Pretoria : The Commission, 1986.
iii,23 leaves. – (Poject).

RIGHT OF WAY - ENGLAND
—Highways Act 1980 / with annotations by Charles Cross and Stephen Sauvain. – London : Sweet & Maxwell, 1981.
xxix,532p; 25cm.
Includes index.
ISBN 0421281308 £15.00

—Rights of access to neighbouring land : Law Commission Working paper no. 78 : memorandum / by the Council's Law Reform Committee. London : Law Society, 1981.
9p; 30cm.

—Rights of way : a guide to law and practice / by Paul Clayden and John Trevelyan. – Henley-on-Thames : Open Spaces Society, 1983.
viii,359p; 21cm.
Includes index.
ISBN 0946574006 Pbk £4.00
ISBN 0900613491 Ramblers' Association

—Rights of way and access to the countryside / J.F. Garner. – 4th ed. – London : Oyez Longman, 1982.
xi,122p. – (Oyez Longman practice notes).
Title supersedes: Freeman's rights of way. Includes index.
ISBN 085120466X

RIGHT OF WAY - GREAT BRITAIN
—Garner's rights of way / 5th. – London : Longman Professional (UK), 1989.
– (Practitioner series).
Explains how rights of way are created, who is then responsible for them, where to record them and how to get them revoked. New section on the discovery of private rights of way.
ISBN 0851215386 Hbk £17.95

RIGHT TO LIFE (INTERNATIONAL LAW)
—Right to life in international law / edited by B.G. Ramcharan. – Dordrecht : Martinus Nijhoff, 1985.
xii,371p; 25cm. – (International studies in human rights).
ISBN 9024730740 Hbk £175.00

RIGHT TO LIFE (INTERNATIONAL LAW) - INDIA
—Right to Life and Personal Liberty in India / New Delhi : Deep and Deep Publications, 1987.
296p.

RIGHTS (PHILOSOPHY)
—Evolution of rights in liberal theory / Ian Shapiro. – Cambridge : Cambridge University Press, 1986.
x,326p; 24cm.
Bibliography: p307-320. - Includes index.
ISBN 0521320437 Hbk £27.50
ISBN 0521338530 Pbk £8.95

—Rights / by Alan R. White. – Oxford : Clarendon, 1984.
viii,186p; 23cm.
Bibliography: p177-184. - Includes index.
ISBN 0198247168 £12.50

—Theories of rights / edited by Jeremy Waldron. – Oxford : Oxford University Press, 1984.
209p; 21cm. – (Oxford reading in philosophy).
Bibliography: p202-205. - Includes index.
ISBN 0198750633 Pbk £4.95

RISK
—Country risk analysis / John Calverley. – London : Butterworths, 1985.
ix,181p; 23cm.
Includes index.
ISBN 0406005508 No price

RISK - GREAT BRITAIN
—Risk management / Comer. – Maidenhead : McGraw-Hill, 1986.
ISBN 0070849269 Hbk £19.95

RISK ASSESSMENT
—Country risk analysis / John Calverley. – London : Butterworths, 1985.
ix,181p; 23cm.
Includes index.
ISBN 0406005508 No price

RIVERS
—Legal Regime of International Rivers and Lakes / Lucius Caflisch. – Dordrecht : Kluwer, 1981.
442p.
ISBN 9024725658 Hbk £170.00

RIVERS - NEW ZEALAND
—Law relating to water courses : interim report / Property Law and Equity Reform Committee. – Wellington : The Committee, 1983.
15,9,2,8p.

ROAD TRAFFIC
—Encyclopedia of road traffic law and practice / R Hosking, M Brealey. – 4 looseleaf volumes. – London : Sweet & Maxwell, 1989.
Contains annotated versions of the relevant statutes and statutory instruments, a revised EEC section and a section on general procedure in Britain. Includes tables of Statutes, SLs and cases, and an index. Three updating issues per year and 'stop press' bulletins.
ISBN 0421007605 Llf £210.00

ROAD TRAFFIC - AUSTRALIA
—Road Safety and Crime / J. Marjoram. – Canberra : Australian Institute of Criminology.

ROAD TRAFFIC - GREAT BRITAIN
—Encyclopaedia of Road Traffic Law and Practice / London : Sweet & Maxwell, 1988.
ISBN 0421007605 Hbk £210.00

—Mahaffy and Dodson : Road Traffic / 3rd ed. – London : Butterworths.

—Road Traffic Reports : 1986 / N. P. Metcalf. – London : Mason Publications Ltd, 1987.
416p. – (Road Traffic Reports Ser.).
ISBN 0859373398 Hbk £20.00

ROAD TRAFFIC - SCOTLAND
—Road traffic law in Scotland / London : Butterworths, 1989.
Concentrates of those areas of law which arise most frquently in practice. Covers reckless and careless driving, road side breath tests, defences to drink driving cases, construction and use regulations, public service vehicles and carriage of goods by road. Includes relevant EEC legislation and schedules with penalties and the DVLC codes.
ISBN 0406112258

ROAD TRAFFIC ACCIDENTS - AUSTRALIA
—Impact of Advertising Standards on Road Safety : Report, November 1983 / House of Representatives Standing Committee on Road Safety. – Canberra : Australian Government Publishing Service, 1983.
58p.
ISBN 0644029706 Hbk £3.30

ROAD TRAFFIC ACCIDENTS - AUSTRALIA - NEW SOUTH WALES
—Accident compensation / New South Wales Law Reform Commission. – Sydney : The Commission, 1983.
xix,231p. – (Working paper 22).
Includes bibliographical references.

Final report 1 : Report on a transport accidents scheme for New South Wales / New South Wales Law Reform Commission. – 1984.
– (L.R.C. 43).
Includes bibliographies and indexes. Accompanied by: Outline of report on a transport accidents scheme for New South Wales.

—Case study booklet / New South Wales. Law Reform Commission. – Sydney : Law Reform Commission of New South Wales, 1984.
x,66p.

—Traffic accident case studies / New South Wales, Law Reform Commission. – Sydney : New South Wales. Law Reform Commission, 1984.
77p.

ROAD TRAFFIC ACCIDENTS - CANADA
—Motor Vehicle Accident Claims : 1983 / Vancouver : British Columbia Continuing Legal Education Society.

ROAD TRAFFIC ACCIDENTS - GREAT BRITAIN
—Manual of Road Accident Investigation / Watts. – Pitman, 1980.
ISBN 0273013254 Hbk £6.50
Vol. 2 1981.
ISBN 0273016008 Hbk £6.50

ROAD TRAFFIC ENGINEERING - GREAT BRITAIN
—Road Traffic (Jersey) Law, 1956 (as amended up to 3rd February, 1981) / Jersey. – 1. – Jersey : States Greffe, 1981.
loose-leaf.
Subsequently amended up to 25th October, 1983. Cover title.

ROAD TRAFFIC OFFENCES
—Diversion of traffic offenders / by J.K. Canagarayar : with a foreword by J.W. Mohr. – Singapore : Malayan Law Journal, 1981.
xi,229p; 22cm.
Analyses the role of diversion, the directions it should take, its limitations, and whether there is a need to develop identifiable uniform principles and guidelines during the different stages of diversion. Contains examples of various experiments and pilot projects.
ISBN 9971700158 £12.50

—Road traffic offenders and crime policy / by Laszlo Viski. – Budapest : Akademiai Kiado, 1982.
205p.
Bibliographies: p.175-201. - Includes index. Translation of: Kozlekedesi buntetojog. - Tr. by: J. Decsenyi.
ISBN 963052841X

ROAD TRAFFIC OFFENCES - AUSTRALIA
—Alcohol, drugs and road safety : report of the House of Representatives Standing Committee on Road Safety / Canberra : Australian Government Publishing Service, 1980.
xix,166p.
Includes bibliographical references.
ISBN 0642048738

—Australian Road Traffic Offences / London : Butterworths, 1983.
ISBN 040949109X Hbk £28.80

—Traffic Offences / 2nd ed. – Butterworths, 1988.
ca 304p.
ISBN 0409495174 Hbk £49.00

—Traffic offences : an examination of the principles of law governing offences committed by motorists on the roads in Australia / Douglas Brown. – Sydney : Butterworths, 1983.
lx,323p.
Includes index.
ISBN 040949190X

ROAD TRAFFIC OFFENCES - CANADA
—Criminal Code Driving Offences : a Companion Text for Breathalyzer Law in Canada, 3 Vols. / Agincourt : Carswell, 1988.

—Criminal Code Driving Offences : Breathalyzer Law in Canada, 3 Vols. / Agincourt : Carswell, 1988.
This three volume set of looseleaf books provides a comprehensive treatment of the Criminal Code offenses. Offenses include criminal negligence, dangerous driving, failing to remain and driving while disqualified. The elements of each offense and caselaw analyzing such is discussed. Orders of prohibition and the Charter of Rights and Bill of Rights are discussed.

—Impaired Driving 1987 / Vancouver : Continuing Legal Education Society of British Columbia, 1987.
109p.
ISBN 0865043353 Hbk £65.00

—Impaired Driving / Vancouver : British Columbia Continuing Legal Education Society, 1984.
ISBN 0865041253 Hbk £45.00

—Impaired Driving and Breathalyzer Law : Recent Case Law, 1 volume / Toronto : Butterworths.

—Impaired driving and breathalyzer law: recent case law / 1 vol. – Scarborough, Ontario : Butterworths (Canada).
Joint publication with the Legal Service Society of British Columbia. The most litigated sections - 234, 235 and 236 - of the Criminal Code are broken into their component aspects and the appropriate case law relating to each aspect is set out in digest form. Contains a table of cases, and covers impaired driving, failing to provide breath samples, driving with more than 80mg of alcohol in blood, and sentencing.
ISBN 0409806471 Loose leaf

—Law on Speeding and Radar / Paul Douglas Haines. – Toronto : Macmillan of Canada, 1988.
120p.
ISBN 077159531X Pbk £6.95

—Law on Speeding and Radar / Paul D. Haines. – Butterworths, 1985.
136p.
States the law relating to speeding and examines all relevant authorities on speeding and the use of radar in speeding. Examines the identification of speeding as an absolute liability offence and presents a comprehensive picture of how the law has evolved.
ISBN 0409811793 Hbk £36.95

—Report on investigative tests - alcohol, drugs and driving offences / Law Reform Commission of Canada. – Ottawa : Law Reform Commission of Canada, 1983.
33,34p; 25cm. – (Report).
English and French texts back to back. French title: L'alcool, la drogue et la conduit des vehicules.
ISBN 0662527259

ROAD TRAFFIC OFFENCES – ENGLAND

—Offences Relating to Motor Vehicles, England and Wales 1980 : Supplementary Tables / London : Home Office, 1981.
ISBN 0862520231 Pbk £4.00

—Police action on motoring offences / David Riley. – London : Home Office, 1983.
iv,17p.
Bibliography: p.10.
ISBN 0862521130

—Road traffic / Patrick Halnan. – Chichester : Rose for the Magistrates' Association, 1981.
50p; 21cm.
ISBN 0859922073 Pbk £2.50

ROAD TRAFFIC OFFENCES – GREAT BRITAIN

—Drink, drugs and driving / by H.J. Walls and Alistair R. Brownlie. – 2nd ed. – London : Sweet & Maxwell, 1985.
xxix,281p; 22cm.
Previous ed.: 1970. Bibliography: p247-268. - Includes index.
ISBN 0421296003 Pbk £19.50

—Drinking and Driving : A Pocket Guide / London : Police Review Publishing, 1984.
ISBN 0851640109 Pbk

—Drinking and Driving - The Decided Cases / Police Review, 1987.
ISBN 0851640281 Pbk £5.25

—Drinking Driver and the Law / 3rd ed. – London : Shaw & Sons, 1983.
ISBN 0721905226 Pbk £16.00

—Drinking Driver and the Law / 3rd ed. – London : Shaw & Sons, 1983.
ISBN 0721905226 Pbk £16.00

—Drunk-Driving : The New Law / London : Oyez Longman, 1984.
– (Oyez Longman Practice Note Ser.: No. 65).
ISBN 0851208657

—Endorsement of Driving Licence and Disqualification from Driving / Cooper. – 3rd ed. – Chichester : Barry Rose, 1984.
ISBN 0859923428 Pbk £7.50

—Hit and run and uninsured drivers / 5th ed. – Chichester : Barry Rose, 1987.
ISBN 0870080653 Pbk

—Motoring Offences : Incl. the Rules on Drink/Drive and Penalty Points / 2nd ed. – London : Law Society, 1985.
124p.

—New fixed penalty system : and disqualification, endorsement and penalty points : including a detailed guide to part III of the Transport Act 1982 and associated provisions / by Adrain John Turner and Malcolm Marsh. – Chichester : Barry Rose, 1986.
x,170p.
Includes index.

—Penalties for road traffic offences : Schedule 4 to the Road Traffic Act 1972 as amended with editorial notes and additions / compiled by Paul H. Niekirk. – London : Oyez Longman, 1983.
46p; 21cm.
ISBN 0851207413 Pbk £4.25

—Road traffic / London : Longman Professional (UK), 1988.
– (Longman practice notes).
Contains a table of principle offences, notes on common offences, a chapter on evidence, flow charts, checklists, tables showing the rates of elimination of alcohol for the purposes of back-calculation.
ISBN 0851214134 Pbk £9.95

—Road traffic offences / Halnan. – 13th ed. 2 vols. – London : Longman Professional, 1988.
Takes into account recent changes in the law including: Pelican Crossing Regulations and Directions 1987; Motor Vehicle Driving Licences Regulations 1987 and 'Cracknell v Willis'.
ISBN 0851214231 Hbk £186.00

—Suggestions for traffic offence penalties / Magistrates' Association. – 8th ed. – London : The Association, 1983.
4p.

—Traffic officer's companion / 3rd ed. – Police Review, 1987.
ISBN 0851640273 Pbk £4.25

—Wilkinson's road traffic offences / Patrick Halnan, John Spencer. – 12th ed. – London : Longman Professional, 1985.
cxxviii,843p.
ISBN 0851209807

Vol.2 : Sources : prepared by Paul H. Niekirk / Patrick Halnan, John Spencer. – 1985.
xx,718p.
ISBN 0851211011 Hbk

—Wilkinson's road traffic offences / Eleventh edition by Patrick Halnan, John Spencer. – 11th ed. – London : Oyez Longman, 1982.
cx,1318p.
ISBN 0851206689

—Wilkinson's road traffic offences / Patrick Halnan. – 13th ed. 2. – London : Longman, 1987.
24cm.
Previous ed.: 1984. Includes index.
ISBN 0851212891 v.2 £168.00
ISBN 0851213294

—Wilkinson's road traffic offences / Peter Wallis, Halnan. – 14th. 2 vols. – London : Longman Professional (UK), 1989.
New edition revised to take account of the Road Traffic Act 1988; the Road Traffic Offenders Act 1988; the Road Traffic (Consequential Provisions) Act 1988; the Criminal Justice Act 1988.
ISBN 085121159X Hbk £195.00

—Wilkinson's road traffic offences / Patrick Halnan, John Spencer. – 10th ed. – London : Oyez, 1980.
cii,1093p; 24cm.
ISBN 0851204791 £42.50

ROAD TRAFFIC OFFENCES – IRELAND

—Drunken driving and the law / Marc de Blacam. – Dublin : Round Hall, 1986.
111p; 22cm.
Includes index.
ISBN 0947686134 Hbk £15.00
ISBN 0947686126 Pbk £8.95

ROAD TRAFFIC OFFENCES – SOUTH AFRICA

—Motor law / by W.E. Cooper : specialist contributor T.G. Schwar. – Cape Town : Juta, 1982.
cxxvi,740p.
Replaces: South African motor law / by W.E. Cooper and B.R. Bamford. Bibliography: p.xv. - Includes index.
ISBN 0702112534

Vol. 2 : Principles of liability for patrimonial loss / by W.E. Cooper. – 1987.
li,507p.
Replaces: South African motor law / by W.E. Cooper and B.R. Bamford. Bibliography: p.xi-xiii. - Includes index.
ISBN 0702119067 Hbk

ROAD TRAFFIC OFFENCES – SWEDEN

—Studies in the causation and prevention of traffic crime / Thor Norstrom. – Stockholm : Almqvist & Wiksell, 1981.
106p.
Bibliography: p.99-104.
ISBN 9122004211

ROAD TRAFFIC OFFENCES – WALES

—Offences Relating to Motor Vehicles, England and Wales 1980 : Supplementary Tables / London : Home Office, 1981.
ISBN 0862520231 Pbk £4.00

ROAD TRAFFIC REGULATIONS – ENGLAND

—Report of the Inter-Departmental Working Party on Road Traffic Law / London : H.M.S.O., 1981.
vii,66p; 25cm.
ISBN 0115505490 Pbk £4.20

—Road traffic law review : memorandum to the Department of the Environment / Justice. – London : Justice, 1986.
7 leaves.

ROAD TRAFFIC REGULATIONS – GREAT BRITAIN

—Consultation document / Road Traffic Law Review. – London : The Review, 1985.
96,15p.
Chairman: P.M. North.

—Consultation paper : removal, impounding and wheelclamping of vehicles / Road Traffic Law Review. – London : Road Traffic Law Review, 1986.
12,12p.
Chairman: P.M. North.

—Kitchin's road transport law : a summary of the legislation affecting the construction, equipment and use of motor vehicles / James Duckworth. – 26th ed. – London : Butterworths, 1988.
400p; 22cm.
Previous ed.: 1985. Includes index.
ISBN 0406106738 Pbk £20.00

—Law Relating to Traffic / London : Police Review Publishing, 1982.
ISBN 0851649920 Pbk £3.50

—Professional Driver's Guide : A Reference Handbook / 8th rev. ed. – New Malden : Croner Publications, 1986.
ISBN 0900319453 Hbk £6.00

—Road Traffic Bill : Road Traffic Offenders Bill : Road Traffic (Consequential Provisions) Bill : report on the consolidation of certain enactments relating to road traffic / the Law Commission and the Scottish Law Commission. – London : H.M.S.O., 1988.
7p.
ISBN 0101039026

—Road traffic law / McVeagh. – London : Butterworths, 1981.
ISBN 0409798185 loose £127.00

—Road Traffic Law / Publication Department of Grampian Police. – Aberdeen : Aberdeen University Press.
1532p.
ISBN 090001511X Hbk

—Road Traffic, No. 5 / Wilkie. – 7th ed. – London : Butterworths, 1980.
– (Police Promotion Handbooks Ser.).
This work for United Kingdom police officers is a reference book on the subject of road traffic control and law enforcement.*Police officers*
ISBN 0406841624 Pbk

—Road Traffic P.P.H. 5 / Wilkie. – 7th ed. – London : Butterworths, 1980.
Student police
ISBN 0406841624 Pbk £5.95

—Road traffic regulation bill : report on the consolidation of the Road Traffic Regulation Act 1967 and certain related enactments / The Law Commission and The Scottish Law Commission. – London : H.M.S.O., 1984.
17p; 25cm.
ISBN 0101916205

—Test Yourself on the 1987 Highway Code / London : Shaw & Sons, 1987.
ISBN 0721906923 Pbk £1.75

—Traffic Officer's Companion / London : Police Review Publishing, 1982.
ISBN 0851649955 Pbk £2.75

ROAD TRAFFIC REGULATIONS – MALAYSIA

—Road Traffic Ordinance, 1958 (No. 49 of 1958) / Kuala Lumpur : International Law Books Services.

—Statutory Rules Made Under the Road Traffic Ordinance 1958 / Kuala Lumpur : International Law Books Services.

ROAD TRANSPORT

—Hague-Zagreb Essays / Dordrecht : Kluwer, 1978.
xiii, 255p.
ISBN 9028604782 Hbk £62.00

—International carriage of goods by road (CMR) / general editor Jan Theunis. – London : Published under the auspices of the International Road Transport Union by Lloyd's of London, 1987.
353p; 24cm.
Conference proceedings.
ISBN 1850441456 £48.00

—Manager's Guide to International Road Freighting / London : Kogan Page, 1986.
320p.
ISBN 1850911495 Hbk £12.95

ROAD TRANSPORT – ENGLAND

—Butterworths Consolidated Legislation Service /. – Professional Publ.
85p.
ISBN 040901429X £30.00

ROAD TRANSPORT – EUROPE
—Principal Actions of ECMT in the Field of Road Safety / European Conference of Ministers of Transport. – Paris : European Conference of Ministers of Transport, 1986.
443p.

ROAD TRANSPORT – FRANCE
—UK-France road freighting-legal guide / London : Kogan Page, 1988.
ISBN 185091320X Pbk £28.00

ROAD TRANSPORT – GREAT BRITAIN
—Croner's Coach and Bus Operations / New Malden : Croner Publications.

—Goods Operator Licensing / Airey. – London : Kogan Page, 1988.
ISBN 1850914796 Hbk

—Review of Road Freight Regulation in Britain / Bureau of Transport Economics. – Canberra : Australian Government Publishing Service, 1981.
78p. – (BTE Occasional Paper: No. 43).
ISBN 0642067953 Hbk £3.80

—Road transport law / 26th ed. – London : Butterworths, 1988.
ISBN 0406106738 Pbk £19.95

ROAD TRANSPORT – UNITED KINGDOM
—UK-France road freighting-legal guide / London : Kogan Page, 1988.
ISBN 185091320X Pbk £28.00

ROADBLOCKS (POLICE METHODS) – ENGLAND
—No way in Wapping : the effect of the policing of the News International dispute on Wapping residents / a report by the National Council for Civil Liberties. – London : National Council for Civil Liberties, 1986.
41p.
ISBN 0946088276

ROADS
—Encyclopaedia of highway law and practice / Sweet & Maxwell, 1988.
ISBN 0421044500 Hbk £195.00

ROADS – AUSTRALIA – SOUTH AUSTRALIA
—Report ... relating to the review and reappraisal of the twenty-fifth report of this committe sic on the subject of misfeasance and non-feasance / Law Reform Committee of South Australia. – Adelaide : Government Printer, 1986.
48p. – (51st report).
Bibliography: p.39-40.

ROADS – AUSTRALIA – WESTERN AUSTRALIA
—Report on the liability of highway authorities for non-feasance / Law Reform Commission of Western Australia. – Perth : Law Reform Commission of Western Australia, 1981.
116p. – (Project v no 62).

ROADS – ENGLAND
—Highways Act 1980 / with annotations by Charles Cross and Stephen Sauvain. – London : Sweet & Maxwell, 1981.
xxix,532p; 25cm.
Includes index.
ISBN 0421281308 £15.00

ROADS – GREAT BRITAIN
—Highway law / by Stephen J. Sauvain. – London : Sweet and Maxwell, 1989.
lxxiv,404p.
Sets out the common law and statutes in their operative context, with the text numbered in paragraphs. Covers civil liability of highway authorities, inquiries, compensation with particular emphasis on areas such as stopping up, and diversion of highways.
ISBN 0421311908 Hbk £36.00

—Highway law and practice / London : Sweet & Maxwell, 1988.
ISBN 0421311908 Hbk

—Highways Bill : report on the consolidation of the Highways Act 1959 to 1971 and related enactments / chairman: Michael Kerr. – London : H.M.S.O., 1980.
16p.

—Modern Law of Highways / London : Butterworths, 1981.
This book presents detailed coverage of the common law of highways and the Highways Act of 1980 for the practitioner in the United Kingdom. The full text of the Act, along with other relevant legislation, is included in the work along with extensive annotations.
ISBN 0406220808 Hbk

ROBBERY – ENGLAND
—Investigating robbery / Michael Banton. – Aldershot : Gower, 1985.
vii,126p; 22cm.
Bibliography: p109-110. - Includes index.
ISBN 0566051141 £16.50

ROMAN LAW
—Elements of Roman Law / London : Sweet & Maxwell, 1986.
ISBN 0421017805 Pbk £13.50

—Elements of Roman Law / 4th ed. – London : Sweet & Maxwell, Reprint 1986.
ISBN 042107805 Pbk £15.50

—Emperors and lawyers / Tony Honore. – London : Duckworth, 1981.
xv,190p; 26cm.
Bibliography: p183-187. - Includes index.
ISBN 0715614495 Unpriced

—History and Principles of Roman Private Law / Durban : Professional Publisher, 1983.
This book presents a systematic approach to the basic principles of Roman law and its history for students of the subject.
ISBN 0409060631 Pbk £72.00

—History and principles of Roman Private law / London : Butterworths, 1984.
ISBN 0409060631 Pbk £28.50

—Iniuria Types in Roman Law / Budapest : Akademiai Kiado, 1986.
226p.
ISBN 9630544598 Hbk £24.00

—Introduction to Roman law / by Ph. J. Thomas. – Deventer Netherlands : Kluwer Law and Taxation Publishers, 1986.
xv, 168 p.; 25 cm.
Bibliography: p. 168.
ISBN 9065442456 pbk.

—Law of Interdict / London : Butterworths, 1987.
ISBN 040610445X Pbk

—Manual of Roman Law / London : Butterworths, 1986.
ISBN 040905755X Pbk £14.00

—Negotiorum Gestio in South African Law / Durban : Butterworths, 1985.
ISBN 0409060704 Pbk

—Roman Constitutional History / Rotterdam : A.A. Balkema, 1948.
195p.

—Roman Law / Repr. of 1966 ed. – Plymouth : Macdonald & Evans, 1984.
240p. – (M and E Handbook Ser.).
ISBN 0712118535 Pbk £4.95

—Roman, provincial and Islamic law : the origins of the Islamic patronate / Patricia Crone. – Cambridge : Cambridge University Press, 1987.
178p; 23cm. – (Cambridge studies in Islamic civilization).
Examines cultural origins of Islamic Law. Studies hypothesis that a substantial source was Roman law with reference to patronate. Concludes Roman law contributed only through being part of the law of Near Eastern provinces.
ISBN 0521322537 £25.00

—Studies in Justinian's Institute / London : Sweet & Maxwell, 1983.
ISBN 0421303204 Hbk £32.00

—Studies in Justinian's Institutes in memory of J.A.C. Thomas / edited by P.G. Stein and A.D.E Lewis. – London : Sweet & Maxwell, 1983.
xii,209p; 26cm.
Bibliography: p189-197. - Includes index. Includes quotations from the Latin, and 2 papers in German.
ISBN 0421303204 £25.00

—Studies in Roman law in memory of A. Arthur Schiller / edited by Roger S. Bagnall and William V. Harris. – Leiden : Brill, 1986.
xviii,168p; 25cm.
Eleven papers in English; 1 each in German and Italian.
ISBN 9004075682

—Ulpian / Tony Honore. – Oxford : Clarendon Press, 1982.
ix,303p; 24cm.
Bibliography: p285-294. - Includes index.
ISBN 0198253583 Unpriced

ROMAN LAW – SOUTH AFRICA
—Roman Private Law / 4th rev. ed. – Pretoria : University of South Africa, 1984.
455p.
ISBN 0869813161 Pbk £18.50

ROMAN–DUTCH LAW
—Journal of Contemporary Roman-Dutch law / Durban : Butterworths.
– (Eng. and Afrikaans).

ROMAN–DUTCH LAW – SOUTH AFRICA
—Index to the opinions of Roman-Dutch lawyers and the decisions of the courts of the Netherlands which have been digested in the Algemeen Beredeneerd Register of Nassau La Leck (1741-1795) / by the late Alfred Adrian Roberts : edited byt S.I.E. van Tonder. – 8. – Pretoria : Government Printer on behalf of the South African Law Commission, 1985.
– (Research series).

ROMAN–DUTCH LAW – SRI LANKA
—Roman Dutch law in Sri Lanka / by Marleen H.J. .van den Horst. – Amsterdam : Free University Press, 1985.
154 p.; 24 cm.
Rev. translation of: Het Rooms Hollandse recht in Sri Lanka. : Originally presented as the author's thesis (M.A.–Free University, Amsterdam) in 1984. Includes index. Bibliography: p. 138-144.
ISBN 9062562361 pbk.

ROYAL COMMISSIONS – GREAT BRITAIN
—Reflections on the Royal Commission on Legal Services : a public lecture / delivered by Lord Benson. – London : Inns of Court School of Law, 1981.
10p; 23cm.

RULE OF LAW
—Democracy and the rule of law : liberal ideas and marxist critiques / Bob Fine. – London : Pluto, 1984.
viii,231p; 20cm.
Bibliography: p221-228. - Includes index.
ISBN 0861047842 Pbk £7.95

—Development and the Rule of Law, Prevention Versus Cure as a Human Rights Strategy / Geneva : International Commission of Jurists, 1981.
125p.

—Development, Human Rights and the Rule of Law : 1981 Hague Conference / Geneva : International Commission of Jurists, 1981.
237p.

—Marxism and law / Hugh Collins. – Oxford Oxfordshire : Clarendon Press, 1982.
viii,159p.
Bibliography: p150-155. .
ISBN 0198760930 Oxford University Press

—Rule of Law : Foundation of Constitutional Democracy / Carlton : Melbourne University Press, 1988.
504p.
ISBN 0522843476 Hbk £62.95

—Rule of Law : Ideal or Ideology / Monahan. – Agincourt : Carswell, 1987.
ISBN 0459395408 Hbk £20.50

—Rule of Law : Ideal or Ideology / Patrick J. Monahan. – Agincourt : Carswell, 1987.
224p.

—The Rule of Law : Ideal or Ideology / Patrick J. Monahan. – Agincourt : Carswell, 1987.
224p.
This work contains a series of essays responding to recent attacks on the concept of 'Rule of Law'. These essays evaluate the present predicament of the 'Rule of Law' and offer prognosis for the future prospects of the ideal in modern society.

—Trial of Beyers Naude : Christian Witness and the Rule of Law / Geneva : International Commission of Jurists, 1975.
188p.

—West Bank and the Rule of Law / Geneva : International Commission of Jurists, 1980.
128p.

RULE OF LAW – EUROPEAN COMMUNITY
—Rule of Law within the European Communities / Brussels : Editions de l'Universite de Bruxelles.
34p.
ISBN 2800402644 Hbk £50.00

RULE OF LAW – GREAT BRITAIN
—Freedom, State Security and the Rule of Law / London : Sweet & Maxwell, 1988.
ISBN 0421396407 Hbk £36.00

—Rule of law in Britain today / Gillian Peele. – London : Constitutional Reform Centre in cooperation with the Hughenden Foundation, 1987.
18p.
ISBN 0948419075

RULE OF LAW – INDIA
—Rule of Law in a Free Society (1959, Delhi) / Geneva : International Commission of Jurists.

RULE OF LAW – INDONESIA
—Indonesia and the rule of law: twenty years of 'New Order' government / Hans Thoolen. – Pinter, 1987.
224.
Sets out the constitutional provisions and legislation relating to human rights and assesses their practical application.
ISBN 0861879198 Hbk £29.50

RULE OF LAW – NIGERIA
—Demise of the Rule of Law in Nigeria Under the Military : Two Points of View / Olusegun Obasanjo. – Ibadan : University of Ibadan, Institute of African Studies, 1980.
55p.

RULE OF LAW - SOUTH AFRICA

—Freedom, state security and the rule of law : dilemmas of the apartheid society / Anthony S. Mathews. - Cape Town : Juta, 1986.
xxv,312p.
Bibliography: p.xi-xiv. - Includes index.
ISBN 0702118125

RURAL CRIMES - GREAT BRITAIN

—Crime, protest, community and police in nineteenth-century Britain / David Jones. - London : Routledge & Kegan Paul, 1982.
xi, 247p.
Includes index. Includes bibliography.
ISBN 0710090080

RURAL DEVELOPMENT

—Methods to stop rural depopulation and to involve citizens in the development of these regions / report prepared, under the guidance of the members of the Committee of Experts on Social and Economic Activities of the Steering Committee for Regional and Municipal Matters, by Trevor Nuttall. - Strasbourg : Council of Europe, 1980.
i,37p.

RURAL DEVELOPMENT - ASIA

—Rural Development and Human Rights in South Asia / Geneva : International Commission of Jurists, 1983.

RURAL DEVELOPMENT - SOUTHEAST ASIA

—Rural development and human rights in South East Asia : report of a seminar in Penang, December 1981 / organized by the International Commission of Jurists and Consumers' Association of Penang. - Geneva : International Commission of Jurists, 1982.
254p.
ISBN 9290370173

RURAL-URBAN MIGRATION

—Methods to stop rural depopulation and to involve citizens in the development of these regions / report prepared, under the guidance of the members of the Committee of Experts on Social and Economic Activities of the Steering Committee for Regional and Municipal Matters, by Trevor Nuttall. - Strasbourg : Council of Europe, 1980.
i,37p.

RURAL-URBAN MIGRATION - GREAT BRITAIN

—Rural Poverty in the United Kingdom / London : Policy Studies Institute, 1981.

SAFE-DEPOSIT BOXES

—Measures against the transfer and the safekeeping of funds of criminal origin : recommendation no. R(80)10 adopted by the Committee of Ministers of the Council of Europe on 27 June 1980 and explanatory memorandum / Council of Europe. - Strasbourg : Council of Europe, 1981.
12p.
'Prepared by a select committee of experts under the authority of the European Committee on Crime Problems' - verso t.p.. At head of cover title: Council of Europe, Legal Affairs.

SALE OF GOODS

—Chalmers' Sale of Goods Act 1979 : including the Factors Acts 1889 & 1890 / Michael Mark, Jonathan Mance. - 18th ed. - London : Butterworths, 1981.
xcv,405p; 23cm.
This work contains detailed explanations of the recent statutory developments in the United Kingdom in this area of law. A full exposition of the Sale of Goods Act of 1979 is included along with extensive annotations and commentary. Consumer protection issues and legislation are addressed as well.
ISBN 0406564485 Hbk Unpriced
ISBN 0406564493 Pbk Unpriced

—On the road to unification of the law of sales / John Honnold. - Deventer : Kluwer Law and Taxation Publishers, 1983.
31p.
ISBN 9065441662

SALE OF GOODS - AUSTRALIA

—Sale of Goods and Consumer Law /. - North Ryde : Law Book Co, 1986.
x, 102p. - (Nutshells).
ISBN 0455206783

—Sales and consumer law in Australia and New Zealand / by K.C.T. Sutton. - Being 3rd ed. of The law of sale of goods in Australia and New Zealand. - Sydney : Law Book Co., 1983.
lxx,658p.
Includes bibliographical references and index.
ISBN 0455204675

—Time in the performance of contracts : especially for the sale of land / K.E. Lindgren. - 2nd ed. - Sydney : Butterworths, 1982.
xxv,201p.
Previous ed.: 1976. Includes bibliographical references and index.
ISBN 0409303909 Hbk £49

—Vendor and Purchaser : Commentary and Materials / North Ryde : Law book Co, 1985.
xxviii, 436p.
ISBN 0455206066 Hbk £57.50
ISBN 0455206074 Pbk £38.50

SALE OF GOODS - AUSTRALIA - NEW SOUTH WALES

—Community law reform program / New South Wales Law Reform Commission. - Sydney : The Commission, 1984.
84p. - (L.R.C. 40).
Bibliography: p.83-84.

—Sale of goods : second report / New South Wales Law Reform Commission. - Sydney : Government Printer, 1987.
xvii,60p. - (L.R.C.).
Includes bibliographical references. Includes text of draft bill.
ISBN 0730530698

SALE OF GOODS - CANADA

—Bulk Sales Legislation / Victoria : Government of British Columbia, 1983.

—Consumer product warranty reform : regulation in search of rationality / E.P. Belobaba. - Ottawa : Policy research, Analysis and Liasion Directorate, Consumer and Corporate Affairs, 1983.
157p.
Vol. 1 published as: Products liability and personal injury compensation in Canada. Bibliography: p.151-157.
ISBN 0662124162

—Report on the Uniform Sale of Goods Act / Manitoba Law Reform Commission. - Winnipeg : The Commission, 1983.
70p. - (Report).
Includes text of Act.

—Sale of Goods / Butterworths, 1988.
1,024p.
Incorporates detailed references to modern Canadian consumer and personal property security legislation, and recent legislative and case law developments in the area, and includes material on equitable proprietary principles and on relief against forfeiture.
ISBN 0409816264 Hbk £125.00

—Sale of Goods in Canada / 3rd ed. - Agincourt : Carswell, 1986.
603p.

—Sale of Goods in Canada / 3rd ed. - Agincourt : Carswell, 1986.
603p.
This treatise given on the law of sale of goods in Canada has been updated to discuss the recommendations of the Ontario Law Reform Commission's Report on the Sale of Goods, provisions of the International Convention on the Sale of Goods, consumer protection legislation, and related materials on sale of goods.

—Sales and sales financing in Canada : cases and materials / by M.G. Bridge, F.H. Buckley, with the assistance of L.R. Ganong. - Toronto : Carswell, 1981.
xlix,694p.
Includes bibliographical references.
ISBN 0459337505

—Sales of Goods / Agincourt : Carswell, 1986.
200p.
This textbook sets out the basic principles of the law of sale of goods in Canada's four western provinces in legislation and case law. Each paragraph of the text is accompanied by extensive footnotes which summarize relevant case law from Canada, England, and the Commonwealth.

SALE OF GOODS - CANADA - ALBERTA

—Uniform Sale of Goods Act / Institute of Law Research and reform. - Edmonton : The Institute, 1982.
iii,323p. - (Report).

SALE OF GOODS - CANADA - BRITISH COLUMBIA

—Report on personal liability under a mortgage or agreement for sale / Law Reform Commission of British Columbia. - Victoria : Queen's Printer, 1986.
37p.
Date on front cover: 1985. Includes bibliographical references.
ISBN 0771884982

—Report on the buyer's lien : a new consumer remedy / Law Reform Commission of British Columbia. - Vancouver : The Commission, 1987.
iv,62p.
Includes bibliographical references.
ISBN 0771885954

SALE OF GOODS - ENGLAND

—Casebook on sale of goods / by E.R. Hardy Ivamy. - 4th ed. - London : Lloyds of London Press, 1980.
xx,200p.
ISBN 0904093832

—Cases and materials on sale of goods / John Adams. - London : Croom Helm, 1982.
174p; 21cm. - (Croom Helm study guides to commercial law).
Includes index.
ISBN 0709905092 Pbk £6.95

—Proprietary rights and insolvency in sales transactions / by R.M. Goode. - London : Sweet & Maxwell, 1985.
xv,137p; 22cm.
Includes index.
ISBN 0421351403 Pbk £13.00

—Reservation of title : draft Council of Europe Convention (CDCJ(82)15) / memorandum by a Working Party of the Senate of the Inns of Court and the Bar and the Law Society. - London? : the Working Party?, 1983.
4p.
Bound with 'Draft proposal for a Council Directive on the legal consequences of agreements creating simple reservation of title (III/872/79-EN)'.

—Sale of flats / by Edward F. George and Arthur George. - 5th ed. - London : Sweet & Maxwell, 1984.
xxvii,447p; 23cm.
Expanded section on the treatment of remedies. Covers the 1980 Housing Act, and schedule 19 to the 1980 Act on services and service charges is examined in detail. New chapter on leases demanded by secure tenants from local authorities. Contains precedents, including articles of association of a management company.
ISBN 0421305509 £25.00

—Sale of goods / P.S. Atiyah. - 7th ed. - London : Pitman, 1985.
xxxvi,448p; 22cm.
Previous ed.: 1980. Includes index.
ISBN 0273022067 Pbk £9.95

—Sale of goods and consumer credit / A.P. Dobson. - 3rd ed. - London : Sweet & Maxwell, 1984.
xxvii,369p; 22cm.
Previous ed.: 1979. Includes index.
ISBN 0421292105 Hbk £14.50
ISBN 0421292202 Pbk £9.50

—Sale of goods and consumer credit in a nutshell / Alan Bond. - London : Sweet and Maxwell, 1980.
vii,88p; 18cm.
Includes index.
ISBN 0421265809 Pbk £1.50

—Warranties and indemnities on share sales / Neil Sinclair. - London : Oyez Longman, 1984.
xxiv,331p.
Includes index.
ISBN 0851208703

SALE OF GOODS - GREAT BRITAIN

—Benjamin's sale of goods / general editor, A.G. Guest. - 3rd ed. - London : Sweet & Maxwell, 1987.
xvi,1400p.
Contains chapters on the nature and formation of contracts, property and risk, performance, defective goods, consumer protection and remedies. Consideration of international sales, detailing the types of overseas sales, their financing and choice of rules. New edition includes over 100 new cases, and expanded discussion of bills of lading and their nature, c.i.f. contracts, f.o.b. contracts, and international carriage of goods by rail and container transport.
ISBN 0421346701 Hbk £110

—Casebook on sale of goods / E.R. Hardy Ivamy. - 5th ed. - London : Lloyd's of London, 1987.
ix,200p; 22cm.
Previous ed.: 1980. Includes index.
ISBN 1850441170 Pbk No price

—Croner's Buying and Selling Law / Croner Publications. - New Malden : Croner Publications, 1986.

Annual renewal updates

—Farm Gate Sales to the Public / London : Shaw & Sons.
1987p.
ISBN 0721910807 Pbk £7.95

—Goods and services - the new law / by Geoffrey F. Woodroffe. - London : Sweet & Maxwell, 1982.
xviii,164p; 22cm.
Includes index.
ISBN 0421302003 Pbk £9.85

—Guide to Contracting for Sale of Goods / Routledge, 1984.
ISBN 0710200056 Pbk £9.95

—Guide to Contracting for the Sale of Goods / London : Sweet & Maxwell, 1984.

—Guide to Law Society's Conditions of Sale / London : Longman Professional, 1984.
ISBN 0851209521 Pbk £7.90

—Guide to National Conditions of Sale / 20th ed. - London : Oyez Longman, 1981.
ISBN 0851206204 Hbk £2.95

—Guide to National Conditions of Sale / 20th ed. - London : Longman Professional, 1981.
ISBN 0851206204 Pbk £6.95

—Guide to the Law Society's Conditions of Sale / London : Oyez Longman, 1981.
ISBN 0851205542 Hbk £2.95

—Hiring and Leasing : Practice and Precedents / Prichard-Jones. – London : Butterworths, 1988.
ISBN 0406101140 Pbk

—Law of markets and fairs / Croydon : Tolley, 1984.
ISBN 0853143188 Hbk £45.00

—Pease and Chitty's Law of Markets and Fairs / Robert Anthony. – 3rd ed. – Tonbridge : Ernest Benn, 1984.
414p. – (Knights Looseleaf Library).
ISBN 0853143188 Hbk £45.00

—Retention of title on the sale of goods / John Parris. – London : Granada, 1982.
186p; 24cm.
Includes index.
ISBN 0246116129 Unpriced

—Review of the Price Marking (Bargain Offers) Orders 1979 : a report / by the Director General of Fair Trading. – London : Office of Fair Trading, 1981.
57p.

—Right to buy : legislative proposals / Great Britain. – London : Department of the Environment, 1987.
3p.

—Sale and supply of goods / The Law Commission, The Scottish Law Commission. – London : H.M.S.O., 1983.
viii,134p; 21cm. – (Consultative memorandum).
ISBN 0117301655

—Sale and supply of goods / Oxford : Blackwell Scientific, 1987.
ISBN 0003832430 Hbk £20.00

—Sale and Supply of Goods / London : Collins, 1986.
200p.
ISBN 0003832430 Hbk £20.00

—Sale and supply of goods : report on a reference under section 3(1)(e) of the Law Commissions Act 1965 / The Law Commission and the Scottish Law Commission. – London : H.M.S.O., 1987.
vi,125p.
ISBN 0101013728

—Sale of goods / Michael Mark, Jonathan Mance. – 18th ed. – London : Butterworths, 1981.
Sets out the Sale of Goods Act 1979 with annotations and commentaries. Other legislation covered includes: Unfair Contract Terms 1977, Consumer Safety Act 1978, Consumer Transaction (Restriction on Statements) 1976 to 1978, and the Price Markings (Bargain Offers) Order 1979.
ISBN 0406564485 Hbk £28.00
ISBN 0406564493 Pbk £18.00

—Sale of Goods / 4th ed. – Plymouth : Macdonald & Evans, 1980.
176p. – (M and E Handbook Ser.).
ISBN 0712119663 Hbk £3.75

—Sale of goods / 7th ed. – London : Pitman Publishing, 1985.
ISBN 0273022067 Pbk £11.95

—Sale of goods / by P.S. Atiyah. – 6th ed. – London : Pitman, 1980.
xxxvii,423p; 22cm.
Includes index.
ISBN 0273016121 Hbk £52.00

—Sale of goods / 4th ed. – Plymouth : Macdonald & Evans, 1980.
ISBN 0712119663 Pbk £3.95

—Sale of Goods Act 1979 / with annotations by W.H. Thomas. – London : Sweet & Maxwell, 1980.
52p various pagings.
ISBN 0421271604

—Sale of Goods Act 1979 / by Michael C. Blair. – London : Butterworths, 1980.
xx,126p.
Contains text of the Act, p.43-119.

—Sale of goods (CLL) / Guest. – 3rd ed. – London : Sweet & Maxwell, 1987.
ISBN 0421346701 Hbk £110.00

—Sale of Goods Litigation / Richard Spearman. – London : Oyez Longman, 1983.
– (Oyez Longman Practitioner Ser.).
ISBN 0851207391 Hbk £9.95

—Sale of Goods Litigation / Spearman. – London : Longman Professional (UK), 1983.
ISBN 0851206905 Pbk £19.95

—Sales promotion law / Oxford : Blackwell Scientific, 1987.
ISBN 0003833941 Hbk £25.00

—Ship sale and purchase : law and technique / by Iain S. Goldrein. – London : Lloyd's of London, 1985.
345p; 25cm.
Includes index.
ISBN 1850440522 No price (Sept.)

—Supply of Goods and Services Act 1982 / London : Longman Professional, 1982.
ISBN 0851206727 Pbk £16.50

—Supply of Goods and Services Act 1982 : a practical guide / R.G. Lawson. – London : Oyez Longman, 1982.
xix,136p; 22cm.
Includes index.
ISBN 0851206727 Pbk £9.95

—Trade Description Act 1970 / London : Wildy & Sons.

SALE OF GOODS - INDIA

—Sale of Goods Act / 3rd ed. – Allahabad : Universal Book Agency, 1987.

—Sale of Goods Act / 3rd ed. – Allahabad : Law Book Company, 1985.

—Sale of Goods and Hire-Purchase / 3rd ed. – Lucknow : Eastern Book Company, 1985.
189p.

SALE OF GOODS - IRELAND

—Sale of goods and supply of services : a guide to the legislation / Vincent Grogan, Thelma King and Edward J. Donelan. – Dublin : Incorporated Law Society of Ireland, 1983.
xxii,133p.
Includes index.
ISBN 0902027239

SALE OF GOODS - NEW ZEALAND

—Sales and consumer law in Australia and New Zealand / by K.C.T. Sutton. – Being 3rd ed. of The law of sale of goods in Australia and New Zealand. – Sydney : Law Book Co., 1983.
lxx,658p.
Includes bibliographical references and index.
ISBN 0455204675

SALE OF GOODS - SOUTH AFRICA

—Mackeurtan's sale of goods in South Africa / by G. R. J. Hackwill. – 5th ed. – Cape Town : Juta, 1984.
xli,304p.
ISBN 0702114138

SALE OF LAND - AUSTRALIA

—Cumulative Supplement to the Standard Contract for Sale of Land in N.S.W. / North Ryde : Law Book Co, 1987.
146p.

—Sale of Land : Commentary and Cases / Diane Skapinker. – Woolloomooloo : International Business Communications, 1986.
488p.
ISBN 0949553220 Pbk £39.95

—Sale of Real Property and Law of Agency in NSW / 4th ed. – Sydney : Butterworths, 1983.
176p.
This book is a working guide for those involved in conveyancing transactions. The fourth edition has been revised and updated to include new materials on the contract of sale of land, strata titles, agents' commissions, registration of titles, valuation of land, and other topics.

SALE OF LAND - AUSTRALIA - NEW SOUTH WALES

—Contract for the Sale of Land in New South Wales / E.A. Francis. – 3rd ed. – Butterworths, 1986.
136p.
This book is a guide to land transactions in NSW. The third edition contains the standard form of the new 1986 contract in full and includes detailed commentary on each clause by relevant authorities.
ISBN 0409491659 Pbk £22.00

—Standard Contract for Sale of Land in New South Wales with Supplement / North Ryde : Law Book Co, 1985.
lxxiv, 948p.
ISBN 045520697X Hbk £115.50

SALE OF LAND - CANADA

—Remedies and the Sale of Land / Butterworths, 1988.
352p.
Chapters develop the theme of finding ways to enforce, or conversely, to escape the agreement of sale. Examines over 100 ways to get out of or enforce contracts for the sale of land, analyses the operation of the standard sale contract, discusses the classic remedies of damages, and describes possible claims against third parties.
ISBN 0409805343 Hbk £55.00

SALE OF LAND - GREAT BRITAIN

—Sale of land : commentary and cases / Skapinker. – London : Legal Books, 1986.
ISBN 0949553220 Hbk £20.00

—Standard Conditions of Sale of Land / 3rd ed. – London : Oyez Longman, 1982.
– (Oyez Longman Practitioner Ser.).
ISBN 0851206468 Hbk £15.95

SALE OF LAND - SOUTH AFRICA

—Formalities in Respect of Contracts of Sale of Land Act 71 of 1969 / Durban : Butterworths, 1980.
ISBN 0409064068

SALES

—Hague-Zagreb Essays / edited by C.C.A. Voskuil and J.A. Wade. – Dordrecht : M. Nijhoff, 1985.
193p.
At head of title: TMC Asser Instituut. Reports and discussions of the fifth session of the Hague-Zagreb Colloquium, Isle of Krk, Yugoslavia, 1983. Includes bibliographies.
ISBN 9024731704 Hbk £135.00

—Proceedings of Seminar : Protection of Sellers in Transnational Sales - Beyond Letters of Credit, at the Cafe Royal, London, 2- 3 June 1982 / 1. – London : International Bar Association, Section on Business Law, 1982.
various pagings.

SALES - AUSTRALIA

—Australian consumer sales and credit law reporter / North Ryde, N.S.W. : CCH Australia, 1977.
looseleaf.
Looseleaf issues accompanied by a summary report. - Uniform credit law proposals 1978; Trade Practices Commission guidelines 1974-1982; and 1980- cases filed in transfer binders. 'Uniform credit law proposals 1978' filed in transfer binder.
ISBN 0869030760 v.3
ISBN 0869033077

SALES - SOUTH AFRICA

—Law of sale and lease / by A.J. Kerr. – Durban, South Africa : Butterworth Publishers, 1984.
xxxii, 352 p.; 25 cm.
Includes indexes.
ISBN 0409037508 pbk.

SALES PROMOTION

—British code of sales promotion practice / Code of Advertising Practice Committee. – 4th ed. – London : Code of Advertising Practice Committee, 1984.
28p.
Includes index. '... under the general supervision of the Advertising Standards Authority ...'. - p.2.

SALES TAX - AUSTRALIA

—Australian Sales Tax Legislation / 5th ed. – North Ryde : C.C.H. Australia, 1987.
800p.
ISBN 0869039733 Hbk £24.00

SALES TAX - CANADA

—Retail sales tax in Canada / A.J. Robinson. – Toronto : Canadian Tax Foundation, 1986.
165p. – (Canadian Tax Papers: No. 77).
Bibliography: p.152-161. - Includes index.
ISBN 0888080255 Hbk £12.50

SALES TAX - INDIA

—Central Sales Tax Act / New Delhi : Bharat Law House, 1985.

—Central Sales Tax Laws / P. Kothary. – 6th ed. 2 vols. – Nagpur : Wadhura & Co, 1987.

—Delhi and Central Sales Tax / H.P.S. Kohli. – New Delhi : S. Chand and Company.

—Delhi Sales Tax and Central Sales Tax Act / D.B. Narang. – New Delhi : Kalyani Publishers.

—Digest of Supreme Court Sales Tax Cases 1950-1987 / Allahabad : Modern Law Publications, 1987.

—Guide to Sales Tax Laws in Maharashtra / 4th ed. – Nagpur : Wadhura & Co, 1987.

—Law of Central Sales Tax / 4th ed. – Lucknow : Eastern Book Company, 1985.
859p.

—Law of Sales Tax in Uttar Pradesh, 2 Vols. / G.C. Mathur. – 5th ed. – Lucknow : Eastern Book Company, 1986.

—Nabhi's All India Sales Tax Manual, 2 Vols. / New Delhi : Nabhi Publications, 1987.
1,830p.

—Principles of Sales Tax Laws, 2 Vols. / P. Kothary. – 5th ed. – Nagpur : Wadhura & Co, 1987.

—Supreme Court Sales Tax Judgements, 1974-1985 / Allahabad : Law Publishers, 1986.
1,100p.

—Uttar Pradesh Sales Tax Act, 1948 : Together with Rules and Notifications as Amended up to U.P. Act No. 22 of 1984 / 6th ed. – Lucknow : Eastern Book Company, 1985.
220p.

SALES TAX - NEW ZEALAND

—New Zealand goods and services tax guide / Auckland : Commerce Clearing House (New Zealand), 1985-.
Title history: New Zealand duties and sales tax guide (1983-1985);New Zealand sales, goods and services taxes guide (1983-1987). Includes index.

SALES TAX - NIGERIA

—Financing the states : the constitutionality of sales tax laws / by Oluwole Akanle. – Lagos : Nigerian Institute of Advanced Legal Studies, 1983.
21p.
Text of a paper presented at the Nigerian Institute of Advanced Legal Studies Staff Seminar Series on Wednesday, June 15, 1983. Includes bibliographical references.

SALES TAX – SOUTH AFRICA

—Guide to General Sales Tax / Cape Town : Legal & Financial Publishing, 1983.
ISBN 0869940333 Hbk £10.50

—Sales Tax Act / Durban : Butterworths.
– (Eng. and Afrikaans).
ISBN 040905187X Pbk

—Sales Tax Register / Cape Town : Legal & Financial Publishing, 1983.
– (Merlen Ser. of Registers).

—Sales Tax Strategy / Durban : Butterworths.

SALVAGE

—International Regulation of Salvage at Sea / London : LLoyd's of London Press, 1987.
ISBN 1850441502 Hbk

SALVAGE – ENGLAND

—Kennedy's law of salvage / F. D. Rose, David Steel, William Rann Kennedy. – 5th ed. – London : Stevens, 1985.
lxii,833p; 26cm.
Deals with the practical and legal developments that have taken place in the last thirty years. Discusses the widespread acceptance and use of the terms of Lloyd's standard form of salvage agreement (no cure no pay), the preparation in Montreal of a new draft International Convention on salvage, and the effect of legislative activity in the area of oil pollution.
ISBN 0420434305 £70.00

—Maritime law of salvage / by Geoffrey Brice. – London : Stevens, 1983.
xxxvi,539p; 26cm.
Focuses on established principles and topics in which particular developments have been proposed, including the threat to the environment posed by the large laden tanker; the assessment of salvaged value; the liability of salvors for negligence and the limitation and exclusion of the liability. Appendices contain extracts from relevant statutes and statutory instruments.
ISBN 0420462406 £45.00

SALVAGE – GREAT BRITAIN

—Law of Salvage (BSL) / 5th ed. – London : Sweet & Maxwell, 1985.
ISBN 0420434305 Hbk £98.00

—Maritime Law of Salvage / London : Sweet & Maxwell, 1983.
ISBN 0420462406 Hbk £60.00

—Maritime Law of Salvage / London : Sweet & Maxwell, 1983.
ISBN 0420462406 Hbk £72.00

SANCTIONS

—Legality of non-forcible counter-measures in international law / Omer Yousif Elagab. – Oxford Oxfordshire : Clarendon Press, 1988.
Includes index. Bibliography: p.
ISBN 019825590X

SANCTIONS – SOUTH AFRICA

—Some aspects of international law considered in relation to apartheid, racism and racial discrimination / by T.O. Elias. – Lagos : Nigerian Institute of Advanced Legal Studies, 1986.
27p. – (Occasional paper).
ISBN 9782353043

SANCTIONS (INTERNATIONAL LAW)

—Economic sanctions and international enforcement / Margaret P. Doxey. – 2nd ed. – London : Macmillan for the Royal Institute of International Affairs, 1980.
vii,161p; 23cm.
Previous ed.: London : Oxford University Press, 1971. Bibliography: p.145-153. - Includes index.
ISBN 0333257073 £15.00

—International sanctions in contemporary perspective / Margaret P. Doxey. – Basingstoke : Macmillan, 1987.
xi,175p; 23cm.
Includes index.
ISBN 033338945X Hbk £27.50
ISBN 0333389468 Pbk £9.50

—Utility of international economic sanctions / edited by David Leyton-Brown. – London : Croom Helm, 1987.
320p; 23cm.
Includes index.
ISBN 070991699X £25.00

SATELLITES

—Aerospace law : telecommunications satellites / Nicolas Mateesco Matte. – Montreal : Butterworths, 1982.
xxi,354p.
Bibliography: p.347-349. Published in conjunction with the Institute and Centre of Air and Space law, McGill University, Montreal. Focuses on the legal issues raised by the rapid development of satellite systems, including the novel problem of 'signal poaching', and international political issues (including the opportunities afforded the Third World countries by the new technology). Covers INTELSTAT and the commercial use of satellites.
ISBN 0409848654

—Aerospace Law : Telecommunications Satellites / London : Butterworths, 1982.
ISBN 0409848654 Hbk £67.00

—Satellite and Cable : International Protection / Stephen de B. Bate. – London : Oyez Longman, 1984.
– (Oyez Longman Intelligence Report Ser.).
ISBN 0851208614 Hbk

—Satellite and cable television : international protection : a specially commissioned report / by S. Alexander Mosteshar, and Stephen de B. Bate. – London : Longman Professional, 1986.
xiv,134p; 30cm. – (Longman professional intelligence reports).
Originally published: London : Oyez Longman, 1984. Includes index.
ISBN 0851212042 spiral £95.00

—Space, earth and communication / Edward W. Ploman. – London : Pinter, 1984.
xi,237p; 22cm.
Bibliography: p225-229. - Includes index.
ISBN 0861873610 £15.50

—State responsibility and the direct broadcast satellite / Marika Natasha Taishoff. – London : Pinter, 1987.
xii,203p; 24cm.
Bibliography: p183-197. - Includes index. 'A publication of the Graduate Institute of International Studies'.
ISBN 0861877004 Hbk £25

—To see the world / Dordrecht : Martinus Nijhoff, 1989.
600. – (Utrecht studies in air and space law).
Analyses the principles governing the use of artificial earth satellites for international direct television broadcasting, adopted by the United Nations General Assembly in 1982. Proposes revisions to the principles. Includes Appendixes containing United Nations documentation on the subject.
ISBN 9024737443 Hbk £87.50

SATELLITES – EUROPE

—Copyright Problems of Satellite and Cable Television in Europe / Dordrecht : Kluwer, 1987.
208p.
ISBN 0860109526 Hbk Gld125.00

SAVING AND INVESTMENT

—Dependent accumulation and underdevelopment / Andre Gunder Frank. – 1st ed. reprinted. – London : Macmillan, 1982.
xx,226p.
Bibliography: p.202-219. - Includes index.
ISBN 0333239512

SAVING AND INVESTMENT – GREAT BRITAIN

—Savings and Fiscal Privilege / 2nd ed. – London : Institute for Fiscal Studies.
– (Report Ser.).

SAVINGS–BANKS – GREAT BRITAIN

—Trustee savings banks bill : report on the consolidation of the Trustee Savings Banks Acts 1969 to 1978 / the Law Commission and the Scottish Law Commission. – London : H.M.S.O., 1981.
11p; 25cm.
ISBN 0101825706

SCANDINAVIAN COOPERATION

—Cooperation in the Nordic countries : achievements and obstacles / by Frantz Wendt. – Stockholm : Almqvist & Wiksell for the Nordic Council, 1981.
408p.
Bibliography: p.395-400. - Includes index. Translation by Geoffrey Dodd.
ISBN 9122004653

SCHOLARSHIPS – COMMONWEALTH

—Twenty-eighth annual report of the Commonwealth Scholarship Commission in the United Kingdom : for the year ending 30 September 1987 to the Minister for Overseas Development / Commonwealth Scholarship Commission in the United Kingdom. – London : The Commission, 1987.
110p.

SCHOLARSHIPS – GREAT BRITAIN

—Twenty-eighth annual report of the Commonwealth Scholarship Commission in the United Kingdom : for the year ending 30 September 1987 to the Minister for Overseas Development / Commonwealth Scholarship Commission in the United Kingdom. – London : The Commission, 1987.
110p.

SCHOOL CHILDREN – SCOTLAND

—Legal capacity and responsibility of minors and pupils / Scottish Law Commission. – Edinburgh : The Commission, 1985.
280p. – (Consultative memorandum).
Includes bibliographical references.

SCHOOL VIOLENCE – ENGLAND

—Schools, disruptive behaviour and delinquency : a review of research / by John Graham. – London : H.M.S.O., 1988.
v,69p.
Reviews research on effects of schooling on young people. Concludes that schools can by promoting pro-social and stable patterns of behaviour, help protect children from embarking on criminal careers.
ISBN 0113408870

SCHOOLS – CANADA

—Municipal and School Tax Credit Assistance Lien Discharge Act, 1983, Bill 121 : An Act to Provide for the Discharge of Liens Registered Under the Municipal and School Tax Credit Assistance Act / Ontario : Ontario Government Publications Service, 1983.
2p.

—School Law / Vancouver : Continuing Legal Education Society of British Columbia, 1987.
160p.
ISBN 0865043558 Hbk £70.00

—Schools and students : legal aspects of administration / W.H. Giles. – Toronto : Carswell, 1988.
xxix, 206 p.; 24 cm.
Includes index.
ISBN 0459312014

—Schools and Students : Legal Aspects of Administration / Agincourt : Carswell, 1988.
236p.

SCHOOLS – ENGLAND

—Implementing crime prevention measures / by Tim Hope. – London : H.M.S.O., 1985.
vi,75p; 25cm.
Examines practicality of crime prevention methods. Considers situational measures aimed at dealing with specifically defined offences and community involvement in prevention of crime. Illustrates difficulties by case histories.
ISBN 0113408129

SCHOOLS – GREAT BRITAIN

—Essential Law for Teachers / Bloy. – London : Longman Professional, 1980.
ISBN 0851204937 Pbk £12.50

—Independent schools and the European Convention on Human Rights : a joint opinion / by Anthony Lester and David Pannick. – London : ISIS, 1982.
16p.
Published on behalf of The Association of Governing Bodies of Public Schools and The Association of Governing Bodies of Girls' Public Schools.

—Teachers and the Law / J. Partington. – 6th ed. – London : Sweet & Maxwell, 1985.
ISBN 0416421709 Hbk £22.50
ISBN 0416395309 Pbk £12.95

SCIENCE

—Law & science : a selected bibliography / compiled by Morris L. Cohen, Naomi Ronen and Jan Stepan : edited by Vivien B. Shelanski and Marcel C. La Follette. – 2nd ed. reprinted. – Cambridge, Mass. : M.I.T. Press, 1980.
xix,155p; 24cm.
This ed. originally published: 1978. Includes index.
ISBN 026203073X £9.30

SCIENCE – EUROPEAN COMMUNITY

—COST Projects : Collected Agreements Concluded within the Framework of European Cooperation in the Field of Scientific and Technical Research / Luxembourg : Office for Official Publications of the European Communities, 1986.
280p.
ISBN 9282402843 Pbk £1,000.00

SCIENCE AND INDUSTRY

—Exploitation of science and technology : a world force / by Sir Henry Chilver. – Southampton : University of Southampton, 1985.
At head of title page: The Fawley Foundation.

SCIENCE AND LAW

—Juridical law and physical law : towards a realist foundation for human law / by Thomas F. Torrance. – Edinburgh : Scottish Academic Press, 1982.
xii,70p.
ISBN 0707303141

—Records of the Diplomatic Conference for the Conclusion of a Treaty on the International Recording of Scientific Discoveries / Geneva : World Intellectual Property Organization.
216p.

SCIENTISTS

—World of science and the rule of law : a study of the observance and violations of the human rights of scientists in the participating states of the Helsinki Accord / by John Ziman, Paul Sieghart, John Humphrey. – Oxford : Oxford University Press, 1986.
viii,343p; 23cm.
Includes index.
ISBN 0198255160 £19.50

SCOTLAND
—Register of research / Scottish Office. Central Research Unit. – Edinburgh : Scottish Office, 1985.
ii,31p.

SEALS (LAW) – BRITISH COLUMBIA
—Deeds and seals / Law Reform Commission of British Columbia. – Victoria : Government of British Columbia, 1987.
ii,39p. – (Working paper).
Includes bibliographical references.
ISBN 0771886020

SEARCHES AND SEIZURES – AUSTRALIA – WESTERN AUSTRALIA
—Working paper and survey : privacy and statutory powers of intrusion / Law Reform Commission of Western Australia. – Perth : Law Reform Commission of Western Australia, 1981.
25,ii,112p. – (Project v no 26 part 2).

SEARCHES AND SEIZURES – CANADA
—Law of Search and Seizure in Canada / 2nd ed. – Butterworths, 1984.
358p.
Analyses the various processes of issuing and executing search warrants, as well as the different kinds of searches and seizures possible under the Criminal Code and other federal and provincial statutes. Also looks at the effects of the Charter of Rights.
ISBN 0409830283 Hbk £80.00

—Police powers - search and seizure in criminal law enforcement / Law Reform Commission of Canada. – Ottawa : The Commission, 1983.
356,403p; 25cm. – (Working paper).
Added t.p. in French: Les pouvoirs de la police : les fouilles, les perquisitions et les saisies en droit penal. Pages numbered in opposite directions. In English and French.
ISBN 066252277X

—Post-seizure procedures / Law Reform Commission of Canada. – Ottawa : Canadian Law Reform Commission, 1985.
77,84p. – (Working paper).
Includes bibliographical references. Added t.p. in French: Les procedures posterieures a la saisie. Cover title: Criminal law: post-seizure procedures. Pages numbered in opposite directions. Text in English and French.
ISBN 0662534603

—Report on disposition of seized property : post-seizure procedures / Law Reform Commission of Canada. – Ottawa : The Commission, 1986.
76,83p. – (Report).
Includes bibliographical references. Added t.p. in French : La facon de disposer des choses saisies. Pages numbered in opposite directions. Text in English and French.
ISBN 0662540816

—Report on obtaining forensic evidence : investigative procedures in respect of the person / Law Reform Commission of Canada. – Ottawa : The Commission, 1985.
45,48p; 25cm. – (Report).
Added t.p. in French: Rapport sur les techniques d'investigation policiere et les droits de la personne. Cover title: Obtaining forensic evidence. Pages numbered in opposite directions. In English and French.
ISBN 0662537351

—Report on search and seizure / Law Reform Commission of Canada. – Ottawa : The Commission, 1984.
78,86p; 25cm. – (Report).
Added t.p. in French: Rapport sur les fouilles, les perquisitions et les saises. Cover title: Searches and seizures. Pages numbered in opposite directions. Text in English and French.
ISBN 0662532872

—Report on writs of assistance and telewarrants / Law Reform Commission of Canada. – Ottawa : The Commission, 1983.
110,124p; 25cm. – (Report).
Cover-title: Writs of assistance and telewarrants. Added t.p. in French: Rapport sur le mandat de main-forte et le telemandat. Pages numbered in opposite directions. In English and French.
ISBN 0662525159

SEARCHES AND SEIZURES – CANADA – ONTARIO
—Report on powers of entry / Ontario Law Reform Commission. – Toronto : Ministry of the Attorney General, 1983.
v,87p.
Includes text of draft bill.
ISBN 0774381051

SEARCHES AND SEIZURES – ENGLAND
—Draft codes of practice for the detention, treatment, questioning and identification of persons by the police; for the searching of premises and seizure of property; and for the exercise of powers of stop and search / London : Home Office, 1985.
iii,80p.
Previous ed.: 1984.

—Draft codes of practice for the detention, treatment, questioning and identification of persons by the police and for the searching of premises and seizure of property / London : Home Office, 1983.
66p.
Revised edition of: Draft codes of practice for the treatment, questioning and identification of persons suspected of crime.
ISBN 086252122X

—Draft codes of practice for the detention, treatment, questioning and identification of persons by the police and for the searching of premises and seizure of property / Rev. ed. – London : Home Office, 1984.
iii,66p.
Previous ed.: 1983.
ISBN 0862521424

SEARCHES AND SEIZURES – GREAT BRITAIN
—Entry Search and Seizure / London : Butterworths, 1986.
ISBN 0406199108 Pbk £33.00

—Entry, search and seizure / Richard Stone. – London : Sweet & Maxwell, 1985.
lii,326p; 26cm.
Takes into account changes enacted by the Drug Trafficking Offences Act 1986, with a discussion of the application of the Police and Criminal Evidence Act 1985. Considers case law for Anton Piller orders, and Mareva injunctions. Defines the categories of persons and authorities who may lawfully exercise entry powers.
ISBN 0421298901 £35.00

—Law relating to entry, search and seizure / David Feldman. – London : Butterworths, 1986.
500p; 26cm.
Includes index.
ISBN 0406199108 Pbk £27.50

SEARCHES AND SEIZURES – INDIA
—Law of Arrest, Bail, Search and Seizure / 2nd ed. – Lucknow : Eastern Book Company, 1985.

—Search and Seizure under Taxation Laws / Allahabad : Law Publishers, 1982.

SEARCHES AND SEIZURES – NEW ZEALAND
—Statutory powers of entry : seventeenth report of the Public and Administrative Law Reform Committee / Wellington : the Committee?, 1983.
18,42vp.

SEARCHES AND SEIZURES – UNITED STATES
—Search & seizure : constitutional and common law / Polyvios G. Polyviou. – London : Duckworth, 1982.
viii,391p; 26cm.
Includes index.
ISBN 0715615920 £35.00

SECRECY
—Legal implications of disclosure in the public interest : an analysis of prohibitions and protections with particular reference to employers and employees / Yvonne Cripps. – Oxford : ESC, 1986.
xx,299p; 24cm.
Bibliography: p289-296. - Includes index.
ISBN 0906214408 Pbk £32.50

—Secrets : on the ethics of concealment and revelation / Sissela Bok. – Oxford : Oxford University Press, 1984.
xviii,332p; 23cm.
Originally published: New York : Pantheon, 1983. Includes index.
ISBN 0192177338 Pbk £12.95

SECRECY – SOUTH AFRICA
—Professional secrecy in South Africa : a symposium / edited by G. C. Oosthuizen, H. A. Shapiro, S. A. Strauss. – Cape Town : Oxford University Press, 1983.
178p.
ISBN 0195703200

SECURITIES
—Australian national companies and securites legislation with state variations ... / Australia. – 5th ed. 2. – North Ryde, N.S.W. : CCH Australia, 1986.
ISBN 0869037013

—Butterworth's Companies and Securities Codes /. – Sydney : Butterworths.
ISBN 0409492361 pap £16.50

—Comparative Survey of Securities Laws : a Review of the Securities and Related Laws of Fourteen Nations / Dordrecht : Kluwer, 1980.
248p.
ISBN 9026811640 Hbk Gld104.00

—Current developments in international securities commodities and financial futures markets / edited by Koh Kheng Lian ... et al. – Singapore : Butterworths on behalf of the Faculty of Law, National University of Singapore, 1987.
xxxvi,380p.
ISBN 0409995452

—Eurobonds / by F.G. Fisher, III. – London : Euromoney, 1988.
v,231p.
A 'revised work'. - Preface. Previous ed. entitled: International bonds. Bibliography: p.227. - Includes index.
ISBN 1870031512

—Euronotes and euro-commercial paper / Gareth Bullock. – London : Butterworths, 1987.
vii,136p; 23cm.
Includes index.
ISBN 0406104107 £32.00

—Euronotes : RUFs, TRUFs, NIFs, SNIFs and BONUSes / edited by Lloyd Bankson and Michael Lee. – London : Euromoney, 1985.
viii,183p.
ISBN 0903121743

—History of the Eurobond market : the first 21 years / by Ian M. Kerr. – London : Euromoney, 1984.
166p.
ISBN 0903121689

—Hybrid corporate securities : international legal aspects / editors Roger McCormick, Harriet Creamer. – London : Sweet & Maxwell, 1987.
xxi,218p; 22cm.
Analysis of hybrid securities arising from a conference of the International Bar Association. Covers the law applicable to the UK, Canada, the USA, Switzerland, the Netherlands, the Federal Republic of Germany, Austria and France. Looks at the practical and technical aspects of taxation, issuance, and stock exchange regulation in each of these jurisdictions.
ISBN 0421379405 Pbk £17.50

—International bonds / by Frederick G. Fisher, III. – London : Euromoney Publications, 1981.
199p; 30cm.
Bibliography: p195. - Includes index.
ISBN 0903121220 Pbk Unpriced

—International securities : Law and practice / edited by J. Michael Robinson. – London : Euromoney, 1985.
xx,303p.
ISBN 0903121751

—International trade in service : securities / Paris : OECD, 1987.
125p.

—Raising international capital : international bond markets and the European institutions / Charles R. Geisst. – Farnborough : Saxon House, 1980.
xiv,165p.
Bibliography- p 157-158.
ISBN 0566002825 £20.00

—Review of investor protection : a discussion document / by L.C.B. Gower. – London : H.M.S.O., 1982.
iii,142p.
'Commissioned by the Secretary of State for Trade' - introd..
ISBN 0115135405

—Review of investor protection : report / L. C. B. Gower. – London : H.M.S.O., 1985.
vii,64p.
Part 1 published as Command Paper 9125 in Parliamentary Papers 1983-84.
ISBN 0115138234

—Review of investor protection : report : part 1 / by L.C.B. Gower : presented to Parliament by the Secretary of State for Trade and Industry ... – London : H.M.S.O., 1984.
x,212p.
Includes bibliographical references.
ISBN 0101912501

—Role of Parliament in relation to the national companies scheme / report by Senate Standing Committee on Constitutional and Legal Affairs. – Canberra : Australian Government Publishing Service, 1987.
vii,106p. – (Parliamentary paper).
ISBN 0644051175

—Trends in corporate governance and investor protection / by Louis Loss. – Lagos : Lagos University Press, 1981.
64p.
Includes bibliographies.
ISBN 9782264261

—Wardley guide to world money and securities markets / by Lynette J. Kemp. – London : Euromoney Publications, 1984.
xvii,472p.
ISBN 0903121662

SECURITIES - AUSTRALIA

—Annual report and financial statements / National Companies and Securities Commission. – v. – Canberra : Australian Government Publishing Service, 1981.
Second and subsequent report years run 1st July to 30th June.

—Australian national companies and securities legislation : up to date to 1 October 1987 / Australia. – 7th ed. 2. – North Ryde, N.S.W. : CCH Australia, 1987.
Index to legislation in vol. 1.
ISBN 1862640068

—Australian securities law cases / North Ryde, N.S.W. : CCH Australia, 1980.
24cm.
Issued as transfer binders, with current issues forming part of the service to the loose-leaf publication: Australian securities law reporter.

—Australian securities law reporter / 1. – North Ryde, N.S.W. : CCH Australia, 1972-.
looseleaf; 25cm.
Includes current issues of: Australian securities law cases. Loose-leaf issues accompanied by a summary report.
ISBN 0909720274 Hbk

—Butterworth's Companies and Securities Codes / 1987 ed. – Sydney : Butterworths.
ISBN 040949237X Pbk £32.00

Vol. I
ISBN 0409492353 Pbk £24.00

—Butterworths Companies and Securities Code, 2 Vols. / Butterworths, 1988.
ca 1090p 710p.
ISBN 0409493384 Pbk

Vol. 1
ISBN 0409493368 £29.00

Vol. 2
ISBN 0409493376 £9.50

—Butterworths Company and Securities Codes, 1988 : And Related Legislation / Combined ed. – Sydney : Butterworths, 1988.
1600p.

—CCH Australian companies and securities legislation / by the CCH company law editors. – 3. – North Ryde, N.S.W. : CCH Australia, 1987.
looseleaf.
'Publication originally issued in one volume in July 1982 (vol. 2 in November 1983) titled Australian companies legislation' - t.p. verso. Spine title: Australian companies and securities legislation.
ISBN 1862640270

—Companies and securities law journal / v. – Sydney : Law Book Co., 1982-.

—Guidebook to New Zealand Companies and Securities Law / 3rd ed. – North Ryde : C.C.H. Australia, 1987.
400p.
ISBN 0864750188 Hbk

—Introduction to the Securities Industry Codes / C.M. Maxwell. – Sydney : Butterworths, 1988.
256p.

—Introduction to the securities industry codes / by R. Baxt...et al. : assisted by an advisory panel from the Securities Institute of Australia. – 2nd ed. – Sydney : Butterworths, 1982.
xxvi,316p.
Previous ed.: published as 'An introduction to securities industry acts', 1977. Includes bibliographical references and index.
ISBN 0409303402

—New Zealand business : entering the Australian market : Legal Research Foundation Inc. Seminar, 19 November 1985 / Barry J. McWilliams. – Auckland : Legal Research Foundation, 1985.
122p.
Papers presented by Barry J. McWilliams and others.
ISBN 0908581408

—Outline of Companies and Securities Law / Butterworths, 1987.
221p.
ISBN 040949285X Pbk £19.95

—Outline of Companies and Securities Law / Sydney : Butterworths, 1988.
222p.

—Securities Law Seminar Insider Training 1985 : Centre for Commercial Law and Applied Legal Research / Monash University, Faculty of Law. – Clayton : Monash University Press.
ISBN 0867463856 Hbk £17.00

—Small Security Appeals / Administrative Review Council. – Canberra : Australian Government Publishing Service, 1981.
144p.
ISBN 0642066663 Hbk £4.80

—Stock Markets and the Securities Industry : Law and Practice / 3rd ed. – Butterworths, 1988.
340p.
ISBN 0409494674 Pbk £45.00

SECURITIES - CANADA

—Canadian Corporation Precedents / 3rd ed. – Agincourt : Carswell.
440p.
This third edition text provides corporation and securities law precedents. Sample forms utilized from incorporation to dissolution are included. Information pertaining to both private and public corporations are included. Additionally, selected forms and precedents have commentaries analyzing the legal history.

—Canadian Securities Regulation / Butterworths, 1977.
528p.
ISBN 0409841226 Hbk £95.00

Supplement-1983
80p.
ISBN 0409841218 £15.00

—Ontario Securities Act / 16th ed. – Toronto : DeBoo, 1983.
ISBN 0888201567 Hbk £24.95

—Private Placements in Canada / William K. Orr. – Agincourt : Carswell, 1985.
224p.
This book discusses essential statutory concepts, private placement exemptions, offering memoranda, rules governing secondary trading, stock exchange requirements, and other issues pertaining to private placements under Canadian securities law.

—Securities Practice and Procedure / Vancouver : British Columbia Continuing Legal Education Society, 1983.
481p.
ISBN 0865041393 Hbk £65.00

—Securities Practice for Legal Assistants / Vancouver : Continuing Legal Education Society of British Columbia, 1987.
278p.
ISBN 0865043426 Hbk £75.00

—Securities regulation of take-over bids in Canada / by John T. D. Courtright. – Calgary, Alta. : Carswell Legal Publications, Western Division, 1985.
xxii, 122 p.; 24 cm.
Includes index.
ISBN 0459373404 pbk.

SECURITIES - CANADA - BRITISH COLUMBIA

—British Columbia Securities Act Forms / Vancouver : Continuing Legal Education Society of British Columbia, 1987.
323p.
ISBN 0865043167 Hbk £60.00

—British Columbia Securities Act, Regulations, and Policy Statements / Vancouver : Continuing Legal Education Society of British Columbia, 1987.
563p.
ISBN 0865043183 Hbk £75.00

—Securities Act (B.C.) and Regulations : 1988 Update / Vancouver : Continuing Legal Education Society of British Columbia, 1988.
213p.
ISBN 0865049947 Hbk £75.00

—Securities Act (B.C.) and Regulations / Vancouver : Continuing Legal Education Society of British Columbia, 1987.
473p.
ISBN 0865042497 Hbk £85.00

SECURITIES - CANADA - ONTARIO

—Ontario Securities Act and Regulation / 16th ed. – Toronto : DeBoo, 1987.
832p.
This book contains the full text of the Securities Act and Regulation as amended to July, 1987, and policy statements current to the July 1st, 1987 issue of the O.S.C. Bulletin. Also included are the Blanket Rulings and Orders of the Ontario Securities Commission.
ISBN 0888202695 Pbk £24.95

—Ontario Securities Legislation / 14th ed. – North Ryde : C.C.H. Australia, 1988.
508p.
ISBN 0887964486 Pbk £15.95

—Report on political activity, public comment and disclosure by crown employees / Ontario Law Reform Commission. – Toronto : Ministry of the Attorney General, 1986.
xi,381p.
Includes bibliographical references.
ISBN 0772917728

—Securities Law and Practice, 4 Vols. / 2nd ed. – Agincourt : Carswell, 1984.
1570p.
This multi-volume work is a comprehensive guide to securities law in Canada. The Securities Act of Ontario, regulations, blanket rulings, policy statements, and practice notes of the Ontario Securities Commission are included in the work.

SECURITIES - EUROPEAN COMMUNITY

—Supervision of securities markets in the member states of the European Economic Community / Luxembourg : Office for Official Publications of the European Communities, 1981.
255p. – (Studies collection).
At head of title: 'Commission of the European Communities'.
ISBN 9282515222 Hbk

—Supervision of the securities markets in the member states of the European Community : reports on the national systems of control / report on a comparative law study submitted by E. Wymeersch. – Luxembourg : Office for Official Publications of the European Communities, 1981.
219p.
At head of title: Commission of the European Communities.
ISBN 9282522903 Hbk

SECURITIES - GREAT BRITAIN

—Bulletin / the Securities Association. – London : The Association, 1988.
Alternative title: TSA bulletin.

—Companies Act, 1980 : pre-emption rights of shareholders / Council for the Securities Industry. – London : The Council, 1981.
2p.

—Draft rules and regulations for licensed dealers in securities / Council for the Securities Industry. – London : The Council, 1982.
9p. – (Press statement).

—Emerging Securities Markets / London : Euromoney, 1984.
ISBN 090312162X Pbk £75.00

—Expert Systems in Banking and Securities / Jeffcoate. – Ovum, 1988.
ISBN 090396936X Hbk £465.00

—Guidelines for personal dealings by fund managers / Council for the Securities Industry. – Rev. ed. – London : The Council, 1982.
8p. – (CSI).

—Investment in Shares and Securities and Financial Aspects / London : Butterworths, 1987.
ISBN 0406504504 Pbk

—Issues and offers of company securities : the new regimes / by John L. Powell : with a foreword by Clive M. Schmitthoff. – London : Sweet & Maxwell, 1988.
xxvii,154p; 26cm.
Based on: Palmer's company law. 24th ed., ch.23 and 27. Includes index.
ISBN 042139630X £25.00

—Professor Gower's review of investor protection : views of the Council for the Securities Industry / Council for the Securities Industry. – London : The Council, 1982.
9p.

—Revision of the licensed dealers' rules / Council for the Securities Industry. – London : The Council, 1982.
8p. – (Press statement).
Caption title.

—Revision of the licensed dealers' rules : memorandum / by the Department of Trade. – London : Department of Trade, Companies Division, 1982.
16 leaves.

—Rules / The Securities Association. – 3rd ed. 1. – London : The Association, 1988.
looseleaf.
Popular title: TSA rule book.

—Securities regulation in the UK / London : IFR Publishing, 1987.
268p.
Includes schedules 1 & 5 of the Financial Services Act, 1986.
ISBN 0946559368

—Stock exchange listing : the new requirements / Robert R. Pennington. – London : Butterworths, 1985.
ix,199p; 26cm.
Includes the text of The Stock Exchange (Listing) Regulations 1984.
ISBN 0406337004 No price

—Unichem Limited : allocation of shares by co-operative upon reconverting to a public limited company / a report by the Director General of Fair Trading on an investigation under section 3 of the Competition Act 1980. – London : Office of Fair Trading, 1988.
49p.

SECURITIES – JAPAN

—Japanese Banking, Securities and Anti-Monopoly Law / Geoffrey Grice. – Butterworths, 1988.
ca 223p.
ISBN 0406106851 Hbk £125.00

—Japanese banking, securities and anti-monopoly law / edited by Hiroshi Oda, R. Geoffrey Grice. – London : Butterworths, 1988.
174p.
Includes index. '...a selection of papers delivered at the first Japanese Law Conference held at the Faculty of Law, University College London in September 1987'. - Preface.
ISBN 0406106851 £45.00

—Securities market in Japan 1986 / Japan Securities Research Institute. – 7th ed. – Tokyo : Japan Securities Research Institute, 1986.
xiii,215p.
Previous edition: 1985.
ISBN 4890328068

SECURITIES – MALAYSIA

—Companies and Securities H/B Singapore and Malaysia / London : Butterworths, 1984.
ISBN 040999507X Pbk £19.00

—Companies and Securities Handbook Singapore and Malaysia / Butterworths.
ISBN 0409181209 Pbk £195.00

1985 Supplement alone
ISBN 040999507X Pbk £35.00

—Companies and Securities Handbook : Singapore and Malaysia / London : Butterworths, 1984.

—Company Law and Securities Regulation in Malaysia / London : Butterworths, 1987.
ISBN 0409995517 Pbk £28.00

—Securities Industry Act, 1983 (Act 280) and Regulations, 1976 / Kuala Lumpur : International Law Books Services.

SECURITIES – NETHERLANDS

—Netherlands Securities Trading Act and Securities Trading Decree : with supplementary regulations and official commentary / a translation by H.C.S. Warendorf and R.L. Thomas : with the assistance of the Amsterdam Stock Exchange, and with an introduction by F.G.B. Graaf. – Deventer Netherlands : Kluwer Law and Taxation Publishers, 1986.
152p.
ISBN 9065442774 Pbk £50.00

SECURITIES – NEW ZEALAND

—Commercial Securities in New Zealand : an introduction to the Law / S.C. Calderwood. – 2nd ed. – North Ryde : Law Book Co, 1986.
xxxi, 214p.
ISBN 0455207070 Pbk £27.00

—Company Law and Securities Regulation in New Zealand / Mark W. Russell. – Butterworths, 1985.
Treatment of the law using economic history to explain the development of law, and using economic theories and empirical data about companies to explain law and practice. Introductory chapters in various sections identify underlying issues.
ISBN 0409701688 Pbk £71.50

—Company Law and Securities Regulation in New Zealand / Russell. – London : Butterworths, 1984.
ISBN 0409701688 Pbk £38.00

—Company takeovers : a review of the law and practice / Wellington : the Commission, 1983.
130p.

—Company takeovers : a review of the law and practice in New Zealand / Wellington : the Commission, 1983.
119p.

—Corporate Debt Securities : Priority Rules / Auckland : Legal Research Foundation, 1986.

—Guidebook to New Zealand Companies and Securities Law / 3rd ed. – North Ryde : C.C.H. Australia, 1987.
400p.
ISBN 0864750188 Hbk

—New Zealand Companies and Securities Legislation / C.C.H., 1987.
1,000p.
ISBN 086475082X Hbk £34.00

—Proposals for the enactment of regulations under the Securities Act 1978 / Wellington : Securities Commission, 1980.
iii,189p.
Cover title: Proposed recommendations for securities regulations.

—Proposals under the Securities Act 1978 for regulations relating to contributory mortgages / Securities Commission. – Wellington : The Commission, 1981.
50,48p.

—Proposed recommendations for securities regulations / Securities Commission. – Wellington : The Commission, 1981.
xiii,89,2p.

—Report of the Securities Commission for the year ended 31 March ... / New Zealand. – v. – Wellington : Government Printer, 1980-.

—Securities law in New Zealand / Clarke. – London : Butterworths, 1983.
ISBN 0409600490 Pbk £23.50

—Securities Law in New Zealand / R. Clarke. – Butterworths, 1983.
Sets out the Securities Act 1978 with its amendments, the Regulations, and the Exemption Notices issues by the Commission, with useful comments and background information.
ISBN 0409600490 Pbk £54.45

SECURITIES – SINGAPORE

—Companies and Securities H/B Singapore and Malaysia / London : Butterworths, 1984.
ISBN 040999507X Pbk £19.00

—Companies and Securities Handbook Singapore and Malaysia / Butterworths.
ISBN 0409181209 Pbk £195.00

1985 Supplement alone
ISBN 040999507X Pbk £35.00

—Companies and Securities Handbook : Singapore and Malaysia / London : Butterworths, 1984.

—Company Law and Securities Regulation in Singapore / Butterworths, 1987.
ca 170p.
Examines corporate and securities regulation, with reference to Singapore legislation, regulations, non-statutory guidelines, case law and administrative practice.
ISBN 0409995495 Pbk £55.00

SECURITIES – SOUTH AFRICA

—Collective securities depositories and the transfer of securities / by F.R. Malan. – Johannesburg : Rand Afrikaans University, 1983.
iv,257p.
Bibliography: p.240-252. - Includes index.
ISBN 0869702491

—Protection of a purchaser of securities / South African Law Commission. – Pretoria : The Commission, 1987.
ii,47p. – (Project).

—Protection of a purchaser of securities / South African Law Commission. – Pretoria : The Commission, 1987.
xiv,116p. – (Project 62).
Bibliography: pp.ix-xi. Includes draft legislation.
ISBN 0797014608

SECURITIES – UNITED STATES

—Securities and commodities enforcement : criminal prosecutions and civil injunctions / Howard M. Friedman. – Lexington, Mass. : Lexington Books, 1981.
xiii,238p; 24cm.
Includes index.
ISBN 066903617X £21.50

SECURITY (LAW)

—Legal problems of credit and security / by R.M. Goode. – London : Sweet & Maxwell, 1982.
xviii,133p; 22cm.
Includes index.
ISBN 0421302704 Pbk £10.00

SECURITY (LAW) – AUSTRALIA

—Law of securities : an account of the law pertaining to securities over real and personal property under the laws of the Australian States / Edward I.Sykes. – 4th edition. – Sydney : Law Book Company, 1986.
xcv,1043p.
ISBN 0455206287

SECURITY (LAW) – CANADA

—Handbook on the Saskatchewan Personal Property Security Act / by Ronald C.C. Cuming and Roderick J. Wood. – Saskatoon? : Law Reform Commission of Saskatchewan, 1987.
xxx,386p.
'Funded by the Law Foundation of Saskatchewan.' - T.p..
ISBN 0921923007

—Law of guarantee : a treatise on guarantee, indemnity and the standby letter of credit / by Kevin Patrick McGuinness. – Toronto : Carswell, 1986.
lxv,456p.
Bibliography: p.lxii-lxv. - Includes index.
ISBN 0459383906

SECURITY (LAW) – EUROPEAN COMMUNITY

—Security on movable property and receivables in Europe : the principal forms of security in the European Community (except Greece) and Switzerland / edited by Michael G. Dickson ... et al. – Oxford : ESC Publishing, 1988.
227p.
ISBN 0906214491

SECURITY (LAW) – GREAT BRITAIN

—Law and practice of banking / J. Milnes Holden. – 6th ed. – London : Pitman Publishing, 1980.
xliii,459p.
Previous ed.: 1971. Includes index.
ISBN 0273014226

—Legal problems of credit and security / by R.M. Goode. – 2nd ed. – London : Sweet & Maxwell, 1988.
xxxv,218p; 23cm.
Contains chapters on the nature and forms of consensual security and concepts of attachments and perfection. Section on treatment of negative pledges has been expanded. Analysis of the legal nature of subparticipation in loan assessments, and examination of twelve typical priority conflicts and their resolution, and an enlarged chapter on equitable, statutory and contractual set-off and set-off on insolvency.
ISBN 0421384301 Pbk £14.00

—Security over property other than land : consultation document / by A.L. Diamond. – London : Department of Trade and Industry, 1986.
67p.

—Statement on the recommendations of the Security Commission / London : H.M.S.O., 1982.
14p; 25cm.
ISBN 0101854005 unbound £1.90

SECURITY (LAW) – SCOTLAND

—Financing and security in Scots law / by Ian B. Inglis. – Dundee : University of Dundee Centre for Petroleum and Mineral Law Studies, 1980.
47p; 30cm. – (Occasional paper).
An expanded version of a paper given at a conference organised by the Centre on Scots law and the oil industry at Hamilton Hall, St. Andrews, 4-7 April 1979.
ISBN 090634302X Pbk Unpriced

SECURITY (LAW) – SWITZERLAND

—Security on movable property and receivables in Europe : the principal forms of security in the European Community (except Greece) and Switzerland / edited by Michael G. Dickson ... et al. – Oxford : ESC Publishing, 1988.
227p.
ISBN 0906214491

SELF-DEFENCE (INTERNATIONAL LAW)

—War, aggression and self-defence / Yoram Dinstein. – Cambridge : Grotius, 1988.
xxx,292p.
Re-examines the topics of war, aggression and self-defence, as well as related issues such as collective security, and the use of force short of war. The first part deals with such questions as what war is, whilst the second looks at the contemporary prohibition of the use of force and its standing as jus cogens. The third section deals with the concept of self-defence.
ISBN 0949009156 £46.00

SELF-DETERMINATION

—Self-determination in law and practice : the new doctrine in the United Nations / by Michla Pomerance. – The Hague : M. Nijhoff, 1982.
xi,154p.
Includes index. Bibliography: p130-138.
ISBN 9024725941

SELF-DETERMINATION – PALAU (CAROLINE ISLANDS)

—Micronesia : the problem of Palau / prepared by Roger Clark and Sue Rabitt Roff. – Rev ed. – London : Minority Rights Group, 1987.
22p. – (Report).
Includes bibliographical references.
ISBN 0946690146

SELF-EMPLOYMENT – GREAT BRITAIN

—Croner's Reference Book for the Self-Employed and Smaller Business / Croner Publications. – New Malden : Croner Publications.
Annual renewal updates

—Tax for the self-employed / London : Longman Professional, 1988.
– (Allied Dunbar Money Guide).
ISBN 08512113855 Hbk

—Tax for the Self-Employed / 2nd ed. – London : Oyez Longman, 1983.
ISBN 085120712X Hbk £3.50

SELF-EMPLOYMENT – NORTHERN IRELAND

—Recent Developments in Individual Employment Law / Belfast : Queen's University of Belfast, 1982.
31p.

SELF-INCRIMINATION – AUSTRALIA

—Non Curial Privilege Against Self-Incrimination / Clayton : Monash University Press, 1985.
ISBN 0867462841 Hbk £9.50

SELF-INCRIMINATION – NEW ZEALAND

—Privilege against Self Incrimination / Auckland : Legal Research Foundation, 1985.

—Privilege against self-incrimination and reform of the practice of police interrogation / by C.B. Cato. – Auckland : Legal Research Foundation, 1985.
65,11p.
At head of title: Legal Research Foundation Inc. Seminar.
ISBN 0908581394

SEMANTICS (LAW)

—Legal discourse : studies in linguistics, rhetoric and legal analysis / Peter Goodrich. – London : Macmillan, 1987.
x,266p; 23cm. – (Language, discourse, society series).
Bibliography: p247-258. - Includes index.
ISBN 0333419499 £29.50

—Semiotics and legal theory / Bernard S. Jackson. – London : Routledge and Kegan Paul, 1985.
xii,373p; 22cm.
Bibliography: p.349-373.
ISBN 0710097190

SEMIOTICS

—Semiotics and legal theory / Bernard S. Jackson. – London : Routledge and Kegan Paul, 1985.
xii,373p; 22cm.
Bibliography: p.349-373.
ISBN 0710097190

—Semiotics, law and social science / edited by Domenico Carzo and Bernard S. Jackson. – Roma : Gangemi, 1985.
227p.
'Based largely upon papers prepared for a colloquium on legal semiotics organised by Professor Roque Carrion-Wam in March 1985'. Includes bibliographies. At head of title: Congress volume for Aix Colloquium.

SENTENCES

—Dangerousness and criminal justice / Jean Floud and Warren Young. – London : Heinemann, 1981.
xvii,228p; 23cm.
Bibliography: p203-221. - Includes index. At head of title : Howard League for Penal Reform.
ISBN 0435823078 £14.50

SENTENCES (CRIMINAL PROCEDURE)

—Crown Court pattern of sentencing : offenders aged 14 and over : being extracts from the Criminal statisties for England and Wales 1971-1978 / by Ian McLean. – Chichester : Barry Rose, 1981.
254p.
ISBN 085992209X

—Future of sentencing / University of Cambridge Institute of Criminology. – Cambridge : Institute of Criminology, 1982.
i,82p. – (Occasional papers).
Papers delivered at a workshop at Cambridge Criminology Conference, July 1979.

—Past or future crimes : deservedness and dangerousness in the sentencing of criminals / Andrew von Hirsch. – Manchester : Manchester University Press, 1986.
xii,220p; 24cm.
Originally published: New Brunswick, N.J. : Rutgers University Press, 1985. Bibliography: p201-212. - Includes index.
ISBN 0719017122 £21.00
ISBN 0813511151

SENTENCES (CRIMINAL PROCEDURE) – AUSTRALIA

—Drug offences in Australia / by Fiori Rinaldi. – Sydney : Law Book Co., 1986.
xxv,247p.
Includes index.
ISBN 045520649X

—Sentencing / Law Reform Commission. – Canberra : Australian Government Publishing Service, 1988.
lv,203p. – (Report).
Bibliography: p.197-203. Includes draft legislation.
ISBN 0644069104

—Sentencing of federal offenders / The Law Reform Commission. – Canberra : Australian Government Publishing Service, 1980.
34p. – (Discussion paper).

—Sentencing : penalties / the Law Reform Commission. – Sydney : The Commission, 1987.
234p. – (Discussion paper).
Bibliography: p.223-234..

—Sentencing : procedure / The Law Reform Commission. – Sydney : The Commission, 1987.
xii,114p. – (Discussion paper).
Bibliography: pp.111-114.

SENTENCES (CRIMINAL PROCEDURE) – AUSTRALIA – VICTORIA

—Law of homicide in Victoria : the sentence for murder / Law Reform Commission of Victoria. – Melbourne : The Commission, 1985.
viii,27p. – (Report v no 1).
Bibliography: p.25-27.

—Sentencing : state and federal law in Victoria / Richard G. Fox, Arie Freiberg. – Melbourne : Oxford University Press, 1985.
lxxv,615p.
ISBN 0195546563

SENTENCES (CRIMINAL PROCEDURE) – CANADA

—New directions in sentencing / edited by Brian A. Grosman. – Toronto : Butterworths, 1980.
xii, 308 p.; 23 cm.
Papers presented at a conference held in Saskatoon, May, 1979. Includes bibliographical references.
ISBN 0409834602 pbk.

—Sentencing in Canada / by R. Paul Nadin-Davis. – Toronto : Carswell, 1982.
lxxii, 609 p.; 24 cm.
Includes bibliographical references and index.
ISBN 0459348507

—Sentencing in environmental cases : a study paper / prepared for the Law Reform Commission of Canada by John Swaigan and Gail Bunt. – Ottawa : The Commission, 1985.
81p. – (Study paper).
ISBN 0662138295

—Sentencing reform : a Canadian approach / report of the Canadian Sentencing Commission. – Ottawa : Minister of Supply and Services, 1986.
xl,592p.
Bibliography: pp.575-592. Chairman: J. R. Omer Archambault.
ISBN 0660122456

—Sentencing reform : a Canadian approach : summary / report of the Canadian Sentencicng Commission. – Ottawa : Minister of Supply and Services, 1987.
34,37p.
French title on added t.p.: Reformer la sentence. Pages numbered in opposite directions. Text in English and French.
ISBN 0662550757

SENTENCES (CRIMINAL PROCEDURE) – ENGLAND

—Current sentencing practice / David Thomas. – 1. – London : Sweet & Maxwell, 1982.
25cm.
Includes index.
ISBN 0421257407 Llf £120

—English sentencing system / Andrew Ashworth. – 3rd ed. – London : Butterworths, 1981.
xvii,244p; 23cm.
Previous ed.: 1975. Bibliography: p235-236. - Includes index.
ISBN 0406570140 Hbk Unpriced
ISBN 0406570159 Pbk Unpriced

—Judicial discretion in sentencing by judges and magistrates / by Vivian Gerald Hines. – 1. – Chichester : Rose, 1982.
27cm.
Includes index.
ISBN 0859923169 £42.50

—Justice annual members' conference held in the Lord Chief Justice's Court on Saturday 24th March 1984 : subject time and crime / chairman Sir George Waller. – London : Justice, 1984.
58 leaves.

—Juvenile sentencing : is there a tariff? / David Moxon, Peter Jones and Roger Tarling. – London : Home Office, 1985.
v,19p.
Bibliography: p.19.
ISBN 0862521874

—Magistrates' court : an index of common penalties and formalities in cases before justices (excluding the juvenile court) / by Ian McLean and Peter Morrish. – 6th ed. – Chichester : Rose, 1984.
205p; 22cm.
Previous ed.: 1980. Includes index.
ISBN 0859922170 £19.50
ISBN 085992369X

—Observations on the Criminal Justice Bill / the Justices' Clerks' Society. – Bristol b The Society, 1982.
21 leaves.

—Psychology of judicial sentencing / Catherine Fitzmaurice and Ken Pease. – Manchester : Manchester University Press, 1986.
vii,174p; 22cm.
Bibliography: p159-171. - Includes index.
ISBN 0719018196 £19.95

—Psychology of sentencing : approaches to consistency and disparity / edited by Donald C. Pennington and Sally Lloyd-Bostock. – Oxford : Centre for Social-Legal Studies, 1987.
xvi,240p; 24cm.
Includes bibliographies and index.
ISBN 0948774002 Pbk No price

—Public relations and criminal justice policy / Peter Nokes. – Leeds : Centre for Social Work and Applied Social Studies, 1982.
43p. – (Occasional paper).
'Occasioned by the seminar on Alternatives to Imprisonment ... held October 1980 - October 1981 under the auspices of the Centre for Applied Social Studies'. Bibliography: p.42-43.

—Reflections on the English sentencing system : a public lecture / delivered by Sir Rupert Cross on Thursday 28 February, 1980. – London : Inns of Court School of Law, 1980.
15p; 23cm.
Given in the Inns of Court School of Law.

—Sentencing / Eric Stockdale and Keith Devlin. – London : Waterlow, 1987.
xxviii,297p; 24cm.
Bibliography: p285-291. - Includes index.
ISBN 0080392482 £30.00

—Sentencing and penal policy / Andrew Ashworth. – London : Weidenfeld and Nicolson, 1983.
xx,500p; 22cm.
Bibliography: p487-495. - Includes index.
ISBN 0297782363 Hbk Unpriced

—Sentencing and the penal system : text and materials / by Christopher Harding and Laurence Koffman. – London : Sweet & Maxwell, 1988.
xxvii,401p; 25cm.
Bibliography: p385-396. - Includes index.
ISBN 0421357703 Pbk £13.50

—Sentencing approach / Clifford E.M. Chatterton. – Chichester : Rose, 1984.
43p; 22cm.
ISBN 0859923576 Pbk £7.50

—Sentencing by English magistrates as a human process / by Andreas Kapardis. – Nicosia : Asselia, 1985.
xi,288p.
Bibliography: p.270-286. - Includes index.
ISBN 9963750079

—Sentencing law and practice / by C.K. Boyle and M.J. Allen. – London : Sweet & Maxwell, 1985.
xxxvi,338p.
Includes index.
ISBN 0421344008 Pbk £15.00

—Sentencing practice in the Crown Court / by David Moxon. – London : HMSO, 1988.
v,89p.
'A Home Office Research and Planning Unit report'.- T.p..
ISBN 0113409028

—Sentencing : theory, law and practice / Nigel Walker. – London : Butterworth, 1985.
xlix,510p; 26cm.
Bibliography: pxxxiii-xlv. - Includes index.
ISBN 0406252637 Hbk No price
ISBN 0406252815 Pbk No price

—Sentencing young people : what went wrong with the Criminal Justice Act 1982 / Elizabeth Burney. – Aldershot : Gower, 1985.
120p; 22cm.
ISBN 0566051273 £14.50

—Supplementary information on sexual offences and sentencing / Roy Walmsley and Karen White. – London : Home Office, 1980.
iv,72p. – (Research Unit paper).
Information in this paper supplementary to that given in: Sexual offences, consent and sentencing. - H.M.S.O., 1979. - (Home Office research study ; no. 54).

SENTENCES (CRIMINAL PROCEDURE) – GREAT BRITAIN

—Between conviction and sentence : the process of mitigation / Joanna Shapland. – London : Routledge & Kegan Paul, 1981.
vi,167p.
Bibliography: p.165.
ISBN 0710009453

—Practical approach to sentencing / Christopher J. Emmins. – London : Financial Training, 1985.
xxvii,350p; 23cm.
ISBN 0906322669 Pbk
ISBN 0906322715

—Sentence of the court : a handbook for courts on the treatment of offenders / Home Office. – 4th ed. – London : H.M.S.O., 1986.
109p; 21cm.
ISBN 0113408072

—Sentencing reform : guidance or guidelines? / edited by Martin Wasik and Ken Pease. – Manchester : Manchester University Press, 1987.
viii,208p; 23cm.
Includes bibliographies and index.
ISBN 0719018900 £27.50

SENTENCES (CRIMINAL PROCEDURE) – NORTHERN IRELAND

—Sentencing law and practice in Northern Ireland / by C.K. Boyle and M.J. Allen. – Belfast : SLS Legal, 1983.
xxxix,256p; 23cm.
Includes index.
ISBN 0853892245 No price

SENTENCES (CRIMINAL PROCEDURE) – SCOTLAND

—Law and practice of sentencing in Scotland / C.G.B. Nicholson. – Edinburgh : W. Green, 1981.
xxxi,274p; 22cm.
Includes index.
ISBN 0414006844 Pbk Unpriced

SENTENCES (CRIMINAL PROCEDURE) – SOUTH AFRICA

—Punishment : an introduction to principles / M.A. Rabie, S.A. Strauss. – 3rd ed. – Johannesburg : Lex Patria, 1981.
365p.
Previous ed.: 1979. First published 1977 as: Theories of punishment. Bibliographies: p.333-348. - Includes index.
ISBN 0628018495

SENTENCES (CRIMINAL PROCEDURE) – UNITED STATES

—New directions in sentencing / edited by Brian A. Grosman. – Toronto : Butterworths, 1980.
xii, 308 p.; 23 cm.
Papers presented at a conference held in Saskatoon, May, 1979. Includes bibliographical references.
ISBN 0409834602 pbk.

—Reform and punishment : essays on criminal sentencing / Michael Tonry and Franklin E. Zimring, editors. – Chicago : University of Chicago Press, 1983.
viii,210p; 24cm.
Includes bibliographies and index.
ISBN 0226808165 Unpriced

—Sentencing / edited by Hyman Gross, Andrew von Hirsch. – New York : Oxford University Press, 1981.
ix,397p; 25cm.
ISBN 0195027639 Pbk £12.75
ISBN 0195027647 £6.50

—Sentencing reform : guidance or guidelines? / edited by Martin Wasik and Ken Pease. – Manchester : Manchester University Press, 1987.
viii,208p; 23cm.
Includes bibliographies and index.
ISBN 0719018900 £27.50

SENTENCING

—Sentencing by Computer : an Experiment / Norwegian University Press, 1982.
246p.
ISBN 8200064360 Hbk £133.00

SENTENCING – AUSTRALIA

—Australian Sentencing Digest / North Ryde : Law Book Co, 1985.
li, 929p.
Supplement 1985
xvii, 194p.
ISBN 0455206112

—Factors Affecting Sentencing Decisions In Rape Cases / Canberra : Australian Institute of Criminology.

—New Sentencing Options : Penalties and Sentences Act / Melbourne : Law Institute of Victoria, 1986.

—Sentencing Sex Offenders in New South Wales : An Interim Report / Canberra : Australian Institute of Criminology.

—Sentencing the Federal Drug Offender / John Walker. – Canberra : Australian Institute of Criminology.

SENTENCING – AUSTRALIA – NEW SOUTH WALES

—Sentencing Drug Offenders in New South Wales / Canberra : Australian Institute of Criminology.

SENTENCING – CANADA

—Canadian Sentencing Digest : Quantam Service, 2 Vols. / Clarey B. Sproule. – Agincourt : Carswell, 1981.
This looseleaf service digest all Canadian cases an quantum of sentence from 1970 to the present. The work is organized by statute and section.

—Sentencing / 3rd ed. – Butterworths, 1987.
712p.
Coverage of general principles of sentencing, finding an appropriate sentence, procedure, criminal record, psychiatric aspect of sentencing, factors affecting sentence, matters that are not taken into consideration on sentencing, parole and the role of prerogative mercy, suspended sentence and probation, corporate crime, and imprisonment.
ISBN 0409864226 Hbk £95.00

—Sentencing / 2nd ed. – Toronto : Butterworths, 1980.
608p. – (Canadian Legal Text Ser.).
ISBN 0409864218 Hbk £90.00

—Sentencing and Post-Conviction Representation / Vancouver : Continuing Legal Education Society of British Columbia, 1986.
236p.
ISBN 0865042853 Hbk £60.00

SENTENCING – ENGLAND

—English Sentencing System / Ashworth. – 3rd ed. – London : Butterworths, 1981.
ISBN 0406570140 Hbk £14.95
ISBN 0406570159 Pbk £10.95

SENTENCING – GREAT BRITAIN

—Criminal Appeal Reports (Sentencing) / London : Sweet & Maxwell.
Bound Vol.
Indiv. parts

—Current Sentencing Practice, 1 Vol. / London : Sweet & Maxwell, 1982.
ISBN 0421257407 loose £86.00
Service only

—Current Sentencing Practice / London : Sweet & Maxwell, 1988.
ISBN 0421257407 Hbk £120.00

—Practice, Procedure and Sentencing in the Magistrates' Courts / Chichester : Barry Rose, 1986.
543p.
ISBN 0859923606 Hbk £65.00

—Sentencing Handbook : A Guide to Sentencing in the Magistrates' Courts / London : Oyez Longman, 1980.
ISBN 0851204554 Hbk £7.95

—Sentencing reform / Wasik. – Manchester : Manchester University Press, 1987.
ISBN 0719018900 Hbk £29.95

—Sentencing : Theory, Law and Practice / London : Butterworths, 1985.

—Sentencing theory, law and practice / London : Butterworths, 1985.
ISBN 0406252615 Pbk £21.95
ISBN 0406252637 Hbk £33.00

SENTENCING – NEW ZEALAND

—Sentencing in New Zealand / Butterworths.

SENTENCING – UNITED KINGDOM

—Magistrate's Companion : Guide for Magistrates in Announcing Sentence and Other Orders of the Court / 3rd ed. – Chichester : Barry Rose, 1985.
88p.
ISBN 0859922332 Hbk £3.75

—Magistrates' Summary Jurisdiction : Guide to Sentencing Powers / 6th ed. – Chichester : Barry Rose, 1983.
ISBN 0859923681 Hbk £4.50

SENTENCING – ZIMBABWE

—Habitual criminals and the indeterminate sentence / Advisory Committee on Law Reform. – Causeway : The Committee, 1981.
50p. – (Report).

—Habitual criminals and the indeterminate sentence / Advisory Committee on Law Reform. – Causeway : The Committee, 1981.
52 leaves. – (Working paper).

SEPARATE MAINTENANCE

—Quest for security : employees, tenants, wives / by Tony Honore. – London : Stevens, 1982.
xiv,128p; 19cm.
Includes index.
ISBN 0420464107 Hbk £12.00
ISBN 0420464204 Pbk £5.80

SEPARATE MAINTENANCE – ENGLAND

—Maintenance after divorce / John Eekelaar and Mavis Maclean. – Oxford : Clarendon, 1985.
x,171p; 22cm.
Bibliography: p161-168. - Includes index.
ISBN 0198255306 Pbk £19.50
ISBN 0198255292 £8.95

SEPARATE MAINTENANCE – GREAT BRITAIN

—Some tax implications of marriage breakdown / David Moore. – Belfast : SLS Legal Publications, 1987.
35p.
Includes bibliographical references.

SEPARATE MAINTENANCE – SCOTLAND

—Family law, report on aliment and financial provision / Scottish Law Commission. – Edinburgh : H.M.S.O., 1981.
x,239p; 25cm. – (H.C.).
ISBN 0102002827 Pbk £8.40

SEPARATE PROPERTY

—Distribution of matrimonial assets on divorce / Michael L. Rakusen, D. Peter Hunt. – 2nd ed. – London : Butterworths, 1982.
xxii,375p.
Latest supplement held: 1986.
ISBN 0406351015

SEPARATE PROPERTY – ENGLAND

—Family law, orders for sale of property under the Matrimonial Causes Act 1973 / the Law Commission. – London : H.M.S.O., 1980.
iii,18p; 25cm. – (1979-80 H.C. 369).
ISBN 0102369801 sd £1.75

SEPARATE PROPERTY – SCOTLAND

—Family law : report on matrimonial property / Scottish Law Commission. – Edinburgh : H.M.S.O., 1984.
v,35p.
Includes draft Bill.
ISBN 0102467846

SEPARATION – GREAT BRITAIN

—Judicial Separation : A Research Study / Oxford : Social Science Research Council, 1983.
102p.
ISBN 0862260574 Pbk £2.50

—On separation / London : Shaw & Sons, 1981.
ISBN 0721908403 Pbk £11.00

SEPARATION – NORTHERN IRELAND

—Separation and Divorce in Northern Ireland / Belfast : Queen's University of Belfast, 1986.
125p.

SEPARATION OF POWERS – AFRICA

—Contribution of the courts to government : a West African view / A.N.E. Amissah. – Oxford : Clarendon, 1981.
x,382p; 22cm.
Includes index.
ISBN 0198253567 £25.00

SEPARATION OF POWERS – AUSTRALIA

—Parliament, the executive, and the governor-general : a constitutional analysis / George Winterton. – Carlton, Vic. : Melbourne University Press, 1983.
viii, 376 p.; 23 cm.
Includes index. Bibliography: p. 329-346.
ISBN 0522842429

SEPARATION OF POWERS – INDIA

—Judiciary today : a plea for a collegium / Ramakrishna Hedge. – Bangalore : Governmnet of Karnataka, .
80p.

—Judiuciary today : disturbing trends and suggestion for reforms / Ramakrishna Hedge. – s.l. : Government of Karnataka, 1986.
15p.
'Address by Sir Ramakrishna Hedge, Chief Minister of Karnataka, delivered on 27th June, 1986 at the Bar Association of India Conference 1986 held at Bangalore'. - t.p. verso.

SEPARATION OF POWERS – IRELAND

—Constitutional law of Ireland : the law of the executive, legislature, and judicature / David Gwynn Morgan. – Blackrock, County Dublin, Ireland : Round Hall Press in association with Irish Academic Press, 1985.
271 p.; 22 cm.
Includes index. Bibliography: p. 215-253.
ISBN 0950872598 pbk.

SEPARATION OF POWERS – NIGERIA

—Justiciability of constitutional adjudication / a paper presented by Owolabi Kolawole at the Seminar on the Constitutional Adjudication in a Presidential System of Government, a comparative American and Nigerian experience, held at the Nigerian Institute of Advanced Legal Studies, University of Lagos, on Wednesday September 2, 1981. – Lagos : Nigerian Institute of Advanced Legal Studies, 1981.
20p.

SEPARATION OF POWERS – SRI LANKA

—Doctrines of Sovereignty and the Separation of Powers in the Laws of Ceylon / Colombo : Lake House Investments.

—Sri Lanka's hybrid presidential parliamentary system & the separation of powers doctrine / H.M. Zafrullah. – Kuala Lumpur : University of Malaya Press, 1981.
xxii,140p.
Bibliography: p. 133-137. - Includes index.

SERFDOM – ENGLAND

—Kings, lords and peasants in Medieval England : the Common Law of villeinage in the twelfth and thirteenth centuries / by Paul R. Hyams. – Oxford : Clarendon Press, 1980.
xxii,295p; 23cm. – (Oxford historical monographs).
Bibliography: p273-286. - Includes index.
ISBN 019821880X £17.50

SERIAL PUBLICATIONS

—Information chain : proceedings of the UK Serials Group conference, held at Christ Church College Canterbury, 29 March - 1 April 1982 / edited by John A. Urquhart. – London : UK Serials Group, 1983.

SERIAL PUBLICATIONS – GREAT BRITAIN

—Serials : the journal of the United Kingdom Serials Group / Abingdon, Oxon. : The Group, 1988.
ISBN 09530460

SERIALS CONTROL SYSTEMS

—News from ISDS / v. – Paris : ISDS International Centre, 1984.
ISBN 02570009

—Serials '86 : proceedings of the UK Serials Group Conference held at the University of Exeter 24-27 March 1986 / edited by Rodney M. Burton. – S.l. : UK Serials Group, 1986.
vii,188p; 21cm. – (Serials monograph).
ISBN 0906148081

SERIALS CONTROL SYSTEMS - GREAT BRITAIN

—Automation and serials : proceedings of the UK Serials Group Conference held at South Glamorgan Institute of Higher Education, Cardiff 31 March-3 April 1980 / edited by Margaret E. Graham. – Newcastle upon Tyne? : UK Serials Group, 1981.
120p; 21cm. – (Serials monograph).
ISBN 0906148022 Pbk Unpriced

—Serials '83 : proceedings of the UK Serials Group Conference held at the University of Durham, 21-24 March 1983 / edited by Rodney M. Burton. – S.l. : The Group, 1984.
144 p. – (Serials monograph).
ISBN 0906148057

—Serials '84 : proceedings of the UK Serials Group Conference held at the University of Surrey, Guildford, England 26-29 March 1984 / edited by Brian Cox. – Heddington : The Group, 1985.
vii, 168p.
ISBN 0906148065

SERIALS SUBSCRIPTION AGENTS - GREAT BRITAIN

—Role of subscription agents / by Alan Singleton : with a supplementary report on U.K. libraries, trade with agents by Alan Cooper. – Leicester : Primary Communications Research Centre, University of Leicester, 1981.
68p; 21cm. – (Occasional papers).
ISBN 0906083176 Pbk Unpriced

SERVICE INDUSTRIES - EUROPEAN COMMUNITY

—Professions and services in the European Economic Community / by D. Lasok. – Deventer, The Netherlands : Kluwer Law and Taxation Publishers, 1986.
ISBN 9065442537 Hbk

SERVICE INDUSTRIES - GREAT BRITAIN

—Service please : services and the law : a consumer view / prepared for the National Consumer Council by Barbara Lantin and Geoffrey Woodroffe. – London : National Consumer Council, 1981.
35p; 30cm.
ISBN 0905653386 Pbk Unpriced

SERVICE MARKS - GREAT BRITAIN

—Service marks / by Amanda Michaels. – London : Common Law Institute of Intellectual Property, 1983.
19p.
Study commissioned by the Institute of Advanced Legal Studies, London.

—Service marks : a guide to the new law : Trade Marks Act 1938 as amended by the Trade Marks (Amendment) Act 1984 and the Patents, Designs and Marks Act 1986 / Christopher Morcom. – Oxford : ESC Publishing, 1987.
vi,165p.
Includes texts from the Acts.
ISBN 0906214483

SERVITUDES - AUSTRALIA

—Easements and restrictive covenants in Australia / Adrian J. Bradbrook and Marcia A. Neave. – Sydney : Butterworths, 1981.
xlv,422p.
Includes index.
ISBN 0409300489 Hbk £65

SERVITUDES - AUSTRALIA - TASMANIA

—Report on private rights of access to neighbouring land / Law Reform Commission of Tasmania. – Hobart : Government Printer, 1985.
23p. – (Report v no 42).

SERVITUDES - ENGLAND

—Gale on easements / Spencer G. Maurice. – 15th ed. – London : Sweet & Maxwell, 1986.
li,491p; 26cm.
Deals with recent developments in equitable easements, the acquisition and character of easement generally, prescription, registered land, and the extinguishment, release, and disturbance of easements. Includes coverage of the London Building Acts, with annotations in an appendix.
ISBN 0421334606 £55.00

—Rights of access to neighbouring land / the Law Commission. – London : H.M.S.O., 1985.
v,85p.
ISBN 0101969201

—Rights of access to neighbouring land / the Law Commission. – London : H.M.S.O., 1980.
v,70p; 21cm. – (Working paper).
ISBN 0117301582 Pbk £3.90

SERVITUDES - SRI LANKA

—Servitude and Partition / Colombo : Lake House Investments.

SET-OFF - AUSTRALIA - SOUTH AUSTRALIA

—Report relating to the reform of the law of set-off / Law Reform Committee of South Australia. – Adelaide : Government Printer, 1983.
11p. – (75th report).
Includes draft Act.

SET-OFF - CANADA - BRITISH COLUMBIA

—Set-off / Law Reform Commission of British Columbia. – Vancouver : The Commission, 1987.
iv,81p. – (Working paper).
Includes bibliographical references.

SET-OFF - ENGLAND

—Lord Chancellor's review of civil justice in England and Wales : personal injury litigation : a consumer response / National Consumer Council. – London : National Consumer Council, 1986.
38p.
At head to t.p.: Personal injury litigation.

—Set-off / S. Rory Derham. – Oxford : Clarendon, 1987.
320p; 22cm.
Includes bibliography and index.
ISBN 019825556X £30.00

SET-OFF - GREAT BRITAIN

—Law of Set-Off / London : Sweet & Maxwell, 1988.
ISBN 0421324503 Pbk

—Law of Set-Off / London : Sweet & Maxwell, 1986.
ISBN 0421348607 Hbk

—Set-off in insolvencies / Oxford : Oxford University Press, 1988.
ISBN 019825556X Hbk £40.00

SET-OFF - NEW ZEALAND

—Working paper on contribution in civil cases / Contracts and Commercial Law Reform Committee. – Wellington : Contracts and Commercial Law Reform Committee, 1983.
ii,49 leaves.
Bibliography: 1.37. Includes extracts from the Law Reform Act 1936 and the Contributory Negligence Act 1947 and the text of the Civil Liability (Contribution) Act 1978 (U.K.).

SETTLEMENTS (LAW) - CANADA

—Structured Settlements / Agincourt : Carswell, 1984.
250p.

SETTLEMENTS (LAW) - CANADA - BRITISH COLUMBIA

—Settlement offers / Law Reform Commission of British Columbia. – Vancouver : The Commission, 1984.
iii,92p. – (Working paper).
Includes bibliographical references.

SETTLEMENTS (LAW) - ENGLAND

—Jackson's matrimonial finance and taxation / D. T. A. Davies. – 4th ed. 1. – London : Butterworths, 1986.
Previous ed.: 1980. Includes index.
ISBN 0406254478 £45.00

SEX

—Sexual desire : a philosophical investigation / Roger Scruton. – London : Weidenfeld and Nicolson, 1986.
x,428p; 24cm.
Includes index.
ISBN 029778479X Hbk £18.95
ISBN 0297788779 Pbk £8.95

SEX AND LAW - ENGLAND

—Report on the age of consent in relation to sexual offences / Policy Advisory Committee on Sexual Offences : presented to Parliament by the Secretary of State for the Home Department. – London : H.M.S.O., 1981.
v,32p; 25cm.
ISBN 0101821603 unbound £2.70

—Sex and the law / by Fenton Bresler. – London : Century, 1988.
192p; 22cm.
Includes bibliography and index.
ISBN 0091736838 £12.95

SEX AND LAW - GREAT BRITAIN

—Gender, Sex and the Law / Oxford : Croom Helm, 1985.
ISBN 0709939675 Pbk £7.95

SEX AND LAW - NEW ZEALAND

—Sexual Violence : a Case for Law Reform / Auckland : Legal Research Foundation, 1982.

SEX DISCRIMINATION

—Convention on the Elimination of All Forms of Discrimination Against Women : explanatory documentation prepared for Commonwealth jurisdictions / Commonwealth Secretariat. – 4 pamphlets in folder. – London : Commonwealth Secretariat, .
Contents: The Convention on the Elimination of All Forms of Discrimination Against Women text. - Developments towards the elimination of discrimination against women in the Commonwealth. - The Convention on the Elimination of All Forms of Discrimination Against Women: a commentary on the Convention. - Directory of Commonwealth National Machinery.

—Legal protection against sex discrimination : recommendation No. R(85)2 adopted by the Committee of Ministers of the Council of Europe on 5 February 1985 and explanatory memorandum / Council of Europe. – Strasbourg : Council of Europe, 1985.
33p.
'Prepared by a committee of experts set up under the authority of the European Committee on Legal Co-operation (CDCJ)'. At head of cover title: Legal Affairs.
ISBN 9287103895

—Women's work, men's work : the ambivalence of equality / Virginia Novarra. – London : Marion Boyars, 1980.
8,152p; 21cm.
Bibliography : p.146-152.
ISBN 0714526800 £5.95
ISBN 0714526819

SEX DISCRIMINATION - AUSTRALIA

—Sex discrimination legislation in Australia / Constance Larmour. – Canberra : Legislative Research Service, Department of the Parliamentary Library, 1985.
29p. – (Basic paper).

—Superannuation and Insurance and the Sex Discrimination Act 1984 / Kingston : Australian Government Publishing Service, 1986.
127p.
ISBN 0644054964 Hbk £7.95

SEX DISCRIMINATION - ENGLAND

—Job evaluation schemes free of sex bias / Equal Opportunities Commission. – Manchester : The Commission, 1981.
ISBN 0905829395

SEX DISCRIMINATION - EUROPEAN COMMUNITY

—Protective legislation for women in the member states of the European Community / communication by the Commission. – Luxembourg : Office for Official Publications of the European Communities, 1987.
29p. – (COM(87) 105 final).
Includes bibliographical references.
ISBN 9277228741

—Rights of working women in the European Community / by Eve C. Landau. – Luxembourg : Office for Official Publications of the European Communities, 1985.
244p.
At head of title: Commission of the European Communities.
ISBN 9282553418 Hbk £3.00

SEX DISCRIMINATION - GREAT BRITAIN

—Amending the equality laws / Catherine Scorer and Ann Sedley. – London : NCCL Rights for Women Unit, 1983.
38p; 21cm.
ISBN 0946088047 Pbk £0.95

—Amendment of the Equal Pay Act 1970 / Department of Employment. – London : The Department, 1983.
11p. – (Press notice).
Includes text of draft order, Sex discrimination: The Equal Pay (Amendment) Regulations 1983. - With Department of Employment press notice, Equal Pay Act - Amendment.

—Equal pay and opportunities : a study of the implementation and effects of the Equal Pay and Sex Discrimination Acts in 26 organizations / by M.W. Snell, P. Glucklich and M. Povall. – London : Department of Employment, 1981.
7,110p. – (Research paper).
Bibliography: p108-110.

—Equal treatment for men and women / Great Britain. – Equal Opportunities Commission, 1988.
26p.
ISBN 1870358015 Pbk No price

—Equality and sex discrimination law / Katherine O'Donovan and Erika Szyszczak. – Oxford : Blackwell, 1988.
xiv,254p.
Includes bibliographical references and index.
ISBN 0631155988 pbk.

—Equality now! : a magazine of the Equal Opportunities Commission / Manchester : Equal Opportunities Commission, 1983-.
Continues: EOC news.

—Fair and efficient selection : guidance on equal opportunities policies in recruitment and selection procedures / Great Britain. – London : H.M.S.O., 1986.
50p.
ISBN 0117013013

—Gender, sex and the law / edited by Susan Edwards. – London : Croom Helm, 1985.
240p.
Includes index.
ISBN 0709909381 £16.95

—Judging inequality : the effectiveness of the tribunal system in sex discrimination and equal pay cases / Alice M. Leonard. – London : Cobden Trust, 1987.
160p; 20cm.
Includes bibliography.
ISBN 0900137282 Pbk £7.95

—Legal relevance of gender : some aspects of sex-based discrimination / edited by Sheila McLean, Noreen Burrows. – Basingstoke : Macmillan, 1988.
x,287p.
Includes bibliographical references and index.
ISBN 0333407717 Pbk £25.00
ISBN 0333407725 £8.95

—Legislating for change? : review of the sex discrimination legislation : a consultative document / Equal Opportunities Commission. – London : Equal Opportunities Commission, 1986.
47p.

—Men's jobs? women's jobs? : practical guidance on why many jobs are done only by men or only by women, and how this pattern 'job segregation' can and should be changed / London : HMSO, 1986.
vii,34p; 21cm.
At head of title: Equal Opportunities Commission.
ISBN 0117012998 Pbk £2.20

—Part-time employment and sex discrimination legislation in Great Britain : a study of the demand for part-time labour and of sex discrimination in selected organizations and establishments / by Olive Robinson and John Wallace. – London : H.M.S.O., 1984.
53p. – (Research paper).

—Practical guide to discrimination law / London : Grant McIntyre Ltd, 1980.
300p.
ISBN 086216009X £14.95

—Pyrrhic victories : winning sex discrimination and equal pay cases in the industrial tribunals, 1980-84 / Alice M. Leonard. – London : H.M.S.O., 1987.
55p; 30cm. – (Research series).
ISBN 0117013285

—Sex and race discrimination in employment / Poulton. – London : Sweet & Maxwell, 1987.
ISBN 0905099176 Pbk £14.00

—Sex discrimination / Ross Anderson, 1983.
ISBN 0863600050 Pbk £2.95

—Sex Discrimination Act 1986 / Department of Employment. – London : The Department, 1986.
2 leaves. – (Press notice).
Bound with two other press notices.

—Sex Discrimination Act 1986 : summary of provisions / Department of Employment. – London : The Department, 1986.
7 leaves. – (Press notice).
Bound with two other press notices.

—Sex Discrimination Act and advertising : guidance notes / Equal Opportunities Commission. – Manchester : The Commission, 1980.
15p; 21cm.
ISBN 090582931X Pbk Unpriced

—Sex discrimination and retirement / Department of Employment. – London : The Department, 1986.
2,4 leaves. – (Press notice).

—Sex discrimination law / David Pannick. – Oxford : Clarendon, 1985.
xiii,288p; 22cm.
Includes index.
ISBN 0198254814 £30.00

—Sex discrimination law / Oxford : Oxford University Press, 1985.
ISBN 0198254814 Hbk £30.00

—Wage Discrimination : The Sex Discrimination Issue of the 1980's / London : Pinter Publishers Ltd, 1984.
200p.
ISBN 0861872487 Hbk £15.00

—Women on trial : a study of the female suspect, defendant and offender in the criminal law and criminal justice system / Susan S.M. Edwards. – Manchester : Manchester University Press, 1984.
1v.
Bibliography: p227-236. - Includes index.
ISBN 0719009952 £14.50

SEX DISCRIMINATION – INDIA

—Women and the law : constitutional rights and continuing inequalities / Joseph Minattur. – New Delhi : Manohar, 1980.
p.165-178.
Offprint from: Women in contemporary India and South Asia / edited by Alfred de Souza. - 2nd rev. ed. - New Delhi : Manohar, 1980.

SEX DISCRIMINATION – UNITED STATES

—Legal relevance of gender : some aspects of sex-based discrimination / edited by Sheila McLean, Noreen Burrows. – Basingstoke : Macmillan, 1988.
x,287p.
Includes bibliographical references and index.
ISBN 0333407717 Pbk £25.00
ISBN 0333407725 £8.95

SEXUAL HARASSMENT

—Women against violence against women / edited by dusty rhodes and Sandra McNeill. – London : Onlywomen Press, 1985.
280p.
ISBN 0906500168

SEXUAL HARASSMENT – CANADA

—Sexual assault / Agincourt : Carswell, 1984.
ISBN 045936720 Hbk £18.70

—Sexual Harassment in the Workplace / Butterworths, 1987.
256p.
Intends to clarify the meaning and concept of 'sexual harassment'. Identifies its social, economic and legal implications for victims, harassers and employers, and discusses its impact on the working environment. Refers to relevant Canadian case law, and highlights the procedure and criteria developed and adopted by human rights tribunals in Canada.
ISBN 0409805351 Hbk £39.95

—Unwanted sexual attention and sexual harassment : results of a survey of Canadians / S.l. : Canadian Human Rights Commission, Research and Special Studies Branch, 1983.
26, 28 p.; 28 cm.
English and French. Added t.p. in French: Attentions sexuelles non sollicitees et harcelement sexuel.
ISBN 0662523725 pbk.

SEXUAL HARASSMENT – GREAT BRITAIN

—Women and harassment at work / Pluto Press, 1983.
ISBN 086104729X Pbk £3.95

SEXUAL OFFENCES

—Age Of Sex Crime / Women's Press, 1988.
ISBN 0704341166 Pbk £5.95

—Incest : a family pattern / Jean Renvoize. – London : Routledge & Kegan Paul, 1982.
viii,224p; 23cm.
Bibliography : p217-220. - Includes index.
ISBN 0710090730 £7.95

—Lust to kill : a feminist investigation of sexual murder / Deborah Cameron and Elizabeth Frazer. – Cambridge : Polity in association with Basil Blackwell, 1987.
xv,207p; 22cm.
Bibliography: p195-203. - Includes index.
ISBN 0745603351 Hbk £25.00
ISBN 074560336X Pbk £7.95

—Sexual crimes and confrontations : a study of victims and offenders / D.J. West. – Aldershot : Gower, 1987.
x,319p; 22cm.
Bibliography: p285-306. - Includes index.
ISBN 0566053802 £18.50

—Thou shalt not be aware : society's betrayal of the child / by Alice Miller : translated from the German by Hildegard and Hunter Hannum. – London : Pluto, 1985.
viii, 331p.
Originally published: Frankfurt am Main: Surkamp Verlag, 1981. Bibliography: p.327-331. Translation of: Du sollst nicht merken.
ISBN 0745300499

—Women against violence against women / edited by dusty rhodes and Sandra McNeill. – London : Onlywomen Press, 1985.
280p.
ISBN 0906500168

SEXUAL OFFENCES – AUSTRALIA

—Sentencing Sex Offenders in New South Wales : An Interim Report / Canberra : Australian Institute of Criminology.

SEXUAL OFFENCES – AUSTRALIA – TASMANIA

—Report and recommendations on rape and sexual offences / Law Reform Commission of Tasmania. – Hobart : Government Printer, 1982.
44p. – (Report).

SEXUAL OFFENCES – AUSTRALIA – VICTORIA

—Rape and allied offences : procedure and evidence / Law Reform Commission of Victoria. – Melbourne : The Commission, 1987.
iii,31p. – (Discussion paper).
Calatogued from cover. Includes bibliographical references.
ISBN 072414319X

—Rape and allied offences : substantive aspects / Law Reform Commission of Victoria. – Melbourne : The Commission, 1986.
iv,55p. – (Discussion paper).
Includes bibliographical references.

—Rape and allied offences : victims with impaired mental functioning / Law Reform Commission of Victoria. – Melbourne : The Commission, 1987.
39p. – (Discussion paper).
Includes bibliographical references.
ISBN 0724167064

—Sexual offences against people with impaired mental functioning / Law Reform Commission of Victoria. – Melbourne : The Commission, 1988.
ii,52p. – (Report no 15).
ISBN 0724167153 Hbk

SEXUAL OFFENCES – CANADA

—Sexual Abuse Allegations in Custody Litigation / Vancouver : Continuing Legal Education Society of British Columbia, 1987.
484p.

—Sexual Assault / Agincourt : Carswell, 1984.
200p.
This book is a critical analysis of the Canadian Criminal Code provisions governing the offense of sexual assault. Statutory rape and incest, offenses against children, and many other issues are discussed in the work.

—Sexual assault / Agincourt : Carswell, 1984.
ISBN 045936720 Hbk £18.70

—Sexual Assault of Children / Aurora : Canada Law Book Co.
This text provides a practitioner's manual for the handling of cases involving sexual assault of children. Although the primary focus is prosecution, this manual will also include articles and case references outlining procedural steps from complaint through interviewing of witnesses, conduct of trial and admissability of evidence.

—Sexual offences against children in Canada : summary of the report of the Committee on Sexual Offences Against Children and Youths appointed by the Minister of Justice and Attorney General of Canada, the Minister of National Health and Welfare, Government of Canada 1984 / Canada. – Ottawa : Supply and Services Canada, 1984.
viii,80p.
ISBN 0660116987

—Sexual offences against children : report of the committee on Sexual Offences Against Children and Youths appointed by the Minister of Justice and Attorney General of Canada, the Minister of National Health and Welfare / Canada. – 2. – Ottawa : Supply and Services Canada, 1984.
Includes bibliographical references.
ISBN 0660116391

—Sexual offences against the person and the protection of young persons : information paper / Infractions sexuelles contre la personne et protection des jeunes : Jean Chretien, Minister of Justice. – Rev. ed. – Ottawa : Minister of Justice, 1980.
43p.
Parallel English and French text.

—Sexual Offences, Bill C-127 / Vancouver : Continuing Legal Education Society of British Columbia, 1983.
155p.
ISBN 0865041032 Hbk £55.00

—Sexual Offences - Bill C-127 / Vancouver : British Columbia Continuing Legal Education Society, 1983.
155p.
ISBN 0865041032 Hbk £55.00

—Sexual Offences : Bill C-127 / Vancouver : British Columbia Continuing Legal Education Society, 1983.
155p.
ISBN 0865041032 Hbk £45.00

SEXUAL OFFENCES – ENGLAND

—Reform of the law of sexual offences / J.C. Smith : with comments by Antony Grey. – Leeds : University of Leeds, Centre for Social Work and Applied Social Studies, 1981.
ii,17p. – (Occasional paper).

—Sex offenders in the criminal justice system : papers presented to the 12th Cropwood Round Table Conference, December 1979 / edited by D.J. West. – Cambridge : University of Cambridge Institute of Criminology, 1980.
ii,221p.

—Sexual offences : fifteenth report / Criminal Law Revision Committee. - London : H.M.S.O., 1984.
ix,105p; 25cm.
ISBN 0101921306 Pbk £6.40

—Supplementary information on sexual offences and sentencing / Roy Walmsley and Karen White. - London : Home Office, 1980.
iv,72p. - (Research Unit paper).
Information in this paper supplementary to that given in: Sexual offences, consent and sentencing. - H.M.S.O., 1979. - (Home Office research study ; no. 54).

—Unlawful sex : offences, victims and offenders in the criminal justice system of England and Wales / the report of a Howard League working party. - London : Waterlow, 1985.
xvi,264p. - (Waterlow's legal and social policy library).
Includes bibliography and index.
ISBN 0080392202 Pbk £9.95

SEXUAL OFFENCES - GREAT BRITAIN

—Sex Offenders in the Criminal Justice System / Cambridge : Institute of Criminology, 1980.

—Unlawful sex / Howard League. - London : Waterlow, 1985.
ISBN 0080392202 Pbk £9.95

—Working paper on sexual offences / London : H.M.S.O., 1980.
iv,63p.
ISBN 0113407343

SEXUAL OFFENCES - INDIA

—Commentary on Sexual Offences / Allahabad : Ashoka Law House, 1987.
1,000p.

—Immoral Traffic (Prevention) Act / 4th ed. - Allahabad : Law Book Company, 1988.
600p.

—Law of Kidnapping and Sexual Offences / Singh. - Allahabad : Law Book Company, 1988.
500p.

—Rape and allied offences : some questions of substantive law, procedure and evidence / Law Commission of India. - New Delhi : Govt. of India Press, 1980.
iii,42p. - (84th report).
Includes bibliographical references.

SEXUAL OFFENCES - SCOTLAND

—Evidence : report on evidence in cases of rape and other sexual offences / Scottish Law Commission. - Edinburgh : H.M.S.O., 1983.
vi,33p.
Includes bibliographical references. Includes Draft Evidence in Sexual Offences (Scotland) Bill.
ISBN 0102028842

—Investigating sexual assault / Gerry Chambers, Ann Millar. - Edinburgh : H.M.S.O., 1983.
viii,142p. - (A Scottish Office social research study).
Bibliography: p.141-142.
ISBN 0114923272

—Law of incest in Scotland / Scottish Law Commission. - Edinburgh : The Commission, 1980.
iii, 82 p.; 29 cm. - (Memorandum).
Cover title. Includes bibliographical footnotes.

—Law of incest in Scotland : report of a reference under Section 3(1)(e) of the Law Commissions Act 1965 / Scottish Law Commission. - Edinburgh : H.M.S.O., 1981.
vii,74p; 25cm.
ISBN 0101842201 Pbk £4.80

SEXUAL OFFENCES - SOUTH AFRICA

—Women and sexual offences in South Africa / South African Law Commission. - Pretoria : The Commission, 1985.
xvi.,200p. - (Report).
Bibliography: p.vii-xvi.
ISBN 0621096091 Hbk

SHATT AL-ARAB (IRAQ AND IRAN)

—Shatt-al-Arab Boundary question : a legal reappraisal / Kaiyan Homi Kaikobad. - Oxford : Clarendon, 1988.
160p; 24cm. - (Oxford monographs in international law).
Includes bibliography and index.
ISBN 0198255918 £20.00

—Shatt-Al-Arab questions / Oxford : Oxford University Press, 1988.
ISBN 0198255918 Hbk

SHIP MORTGAGES

—Handbook on maritime law / edited by Lennart Hagberg : written by members of the Committee on Maritime and Transport Law of the Section on Business Law of the International Bar Association. - Deventer : Kluwer, 1983.
xxvii,401p.
ISBN 9065440577

Pakistan-Yugoslavia / edited by Lennart Hagberg : written by Members of the Committee on Maritme and Transport Law of the Section on Business Law of the International Bar Association. - 1983.
xxvii,296p.
ISBN 9065440585 Hbk

SHIP PURCHASE - GREAT BRITAIN

—Ship sale and purchase : law and technique / by Iain S. Goldrein. - London : Lloyd's of London, 1985.
345p; 25cm.
Includes index.
ISBN 1850440522 No price

SHIP REGISTRATION

—Handbook on maritime law / edited by Lennart Hagberg : written by members of the Committee on Maritime and Transport Law of the Section on Business Law of the International Bar Association. - Deventer : Kluwer, 1983.
xxvii,401p.
ISBN 9065440577

Pakistan-Yugoslavia / edited by Lennart Hagberg : written by Members of the Committee on Maritme and Transport Law of the Section on Business Law of the International Bar Association. - 1983.
xxvii,296p.
ISBN 9065440585 Hbk

SHIP REGISTRATION - PANAMA

—Panama / by Enrique de Alba. - London : Lloyd's of London, 1987.
128p; 22cm.
Includes index.
ISBN 1850441421 £25.50

SHIP VALUATION

—Ship's value / by Kaj Pineus. - 2nd ed. - London : Lloyd's of London, 1986.
135p; 22cm.
Previous ed.: Gothenburg : Gothenburg Maritime Law Association, 1975. Includes bibliography and index.
ISBN 185044062X £35.00

SHIP-BUILDING

—International Code for the Construction and Equipment of Ships Carrying Dangerous Chemicals in Bulk (IBC, Vol. 2) / International Maritime Organization. - London : International Maritime Organization.
ISBN 9280111620 Hbk £3.75

French
ISBN 9280121294 Hbk £3.75

Russian
ISBN 9280140442 Hbk £3.75

Spanish
ISBN 9280130870 Hbk £3.75

Chinese

—International Code for the Construction and Equipment of Ships Carrying Liquified Gases in Bulk (IGC) / International Maritime Organization. - London : International Maritime Organization.
ISBN 9280111639 Hbk £4.50

French
ISBN 9280121308 Hbk £4.50

Russian
ISBN 9280140450 Hbk £4.50

Spanish
ISBN 9280130889 Hbk £4.50

Chinese

—Shipbuilding contracts / edited by Malcolm A. Clarke. - London : Lloyd's, 1982.
xx,228p.
Includes index. At head of title: Comite Maritime International.
ISBN 0907432255

SHIPBROKERS

—Shipbroking and chartering practice / by Lars Gorton, Rolf Ihre, Arne Sandevarn. - 2nd ed. - London : Lloyd's of London Press, 1984.
xv,298p; 26cm.
Bibliography: p.247. - Includes index.
ISBN 0907432638

SHIPBROKERS - GREAT BRITAIN

—Shipbroking and chartering practice / Gordon. - 2nd ed. - London : Lloyd's of London Press, 1984.
ISBN 0907432638 Hbk £39.00

SHIPPING

—Arrest of ships 4 : People's Republic of China, Nigeria, Oman, Scotland / by Kaw Vun-Ping ... et al. - London : Lloyd's of London Press, 1987.
112p; 22cm.
ISBN 1850441014 £25.00 (July)

—Arrest of ships / by Christopher Hill ... et al. - London : Lloyd's of London Press, 1985.
vi,112p; 22cm.
Includes index.
ISBN 1850440255 £22.50

—Coastal state requirements for foreign fishing / by Gerald K. Moore. - Rev. ed. - Rome : Food and Agriculture Organization of the United Nations, 1983.
iv,242p. - (Legislative study).
Previous ed. published as: Legislation on coastal state requirements for foreign fishing.
ISBN 9251015031

—Code of Safety for Nuclear Merchant Ships / International Maritime Organization. - London : International Maritime Organization, 1982.

French Edition

Spanish Edition

—Dedicated Clean Ballast Tanks / International Maritime Organization. - London : International Maritime Organization, 1982.

—Deepsea mining and the law of the sea / Alexandra Merle Post. - The Hague : M. Nijhoff Publishers, 1983.
xxiii,358p.
Bibliography: p329-358.
ISBN 902473049X

—Development of the law of the sea with special reference to the exclusive economic zone / S.l. : s.n., 1982.
p.297-307.

—Dictionary of Shipping and International Trade Terms / 2nd ed. - Witherby, 1983.
ISBN 0900886706 Pbk £7.50

—Dictionary of shipping and shipbroking terms : French-English and English-French / Dictionnaire du transport et de l'affretement maritime : by Peter R. Brodie. - London : Lloyd's of London Press, 1980.
xvii,195p.
ISBN 0904093824

—Dictionary of shipping terms / by Peter R. Brodie. - London : Lloyd's of London, 1985.
155p; 22cm.
ISBN 1850440697 Pbk £15.00

—Economics of shipping practice and management / Alan E. Branch. - London : Chapman and Hall, 1982.
xii,242p.
ISBN 0412163500 pbk.

—Elements of shipping / Alan E. Branch. - 5th ed. - London : Chapman and Hall, 1981.
xiii,391p; 23cm.
Previous ed.: 1977. Includes index.
ISBN 0412237008 Hbk £12.50
ISBN 0412237105 Pbk Unpriced

—Exclusive economic zone : proceedings of the 7th International Ocean Symposium October 21-22, 1982, the Japan Shipping Club, Tokyo / Tokyo : Ocean Association of Japan, 1983.
82p.
Edited by the Ocean Association of Japan. Title also in Japanese.

—Frontier of the seas : the problems of delimitation : proceedings of the 5th International Ocean Symposium November 26-27, 1980, the Japan Shipping Club, Tokyo / Tokyo : Ocean Association of Japan, 1981.
80p; 26cm.
Edited by the Ocean Association of Japan. Title also in Japanese.

—Hamburg Rules : an appreciation of the cause and effect of the amendments to the Hague Rules and the Hague-Visby Rules / W.E. Astle. - London : Fairplay, 1981.
xii,163p; 25cm.
ISBN 0905045319 Pbk No price

—IMCO news : the magazine of the Inter-Governmental Maritime Consultative Organization / London : IMCO, 1979 - 1982.
n v.
Continued by: IMO news.

—IMO news : the magazine of the International Maritime Organization / London : IMO, 1982.
Continues: IMCO news.

—Inert Gas Systems for Ships Carrying Petroleum Products in Bulk / International Maritime Organization. - London : International Maritime Organization, 1982.

French Edition

—International cooperation in marine science and technology in the Pacific region : proceedings of the 6th International Ocean Symposium November 5-6, 1981, the Japan Shipping Club, Tokyo, Japan / Tokyo : Ocean Association of Japan, 1982.
69p.
Edited by the Ocean Association of Japan. Title also in Japanese.

—International maritime fraud / by Eric Ellen, and Donald Campbell. – London : Sweet & Maxwell, 1981.
viii,174p; 22cm.
Bibliography: p160. - Includes index.
ISBN 0421271507 Pbk £8.00

—International rules of law relating to bills of lading / compiled by W.E. Astle. – London : Fairplay, 1982.
72p; 25cm.
ISBN 0905045343 Pbk No price

—International shipping / London : Lloyds of London Press, 1988.
Examines the framework that shipping operates in, including the institutions and bodies of both governments and the shipping industry. Includes the Liner conference system, and freedom and cooperation versus protectionism and confrontation. The historical background of sea law is also covered.
ISBN 1850441510 Hbk

—Introduction of P & I / Bill Robertson, Steven J. Hazelwood. – London : Lloyds of London Press, 1988.
A practical rather than academic text, covering the origins of P and I clubs, the scope of cover, specialist clubs, and claims and claims handling.
ISBN 1850441634 Hbk

—Law of international sea piracy / Barry Hart Dubner. – The Hague : M. Nijhoff, 1980.
xiii,176p.
Bibliography - p167-173.

—Law of the sea / R.R. Churchill and A.V. Lowe. – Manchester : Manchester University Press, 1983.
xxxiii,321p; 24cm.
Includes bibliographies and index.
ISBN 0719009367 £19.50

—Law of the sea and maritime boundary delimitation in South-East Asia / Kriangsak Kittichaisaree. – Singapore : Oxford University Press, 1987.
xv, 209 p.; 23 cm.
Discusses maritime boundary delimination in international law. Concentrates on South-East Asia, but legal analyses are examined in a global context, using South-East Asian practice as concrete instances to elaborate particular legal problems.
ISBN 0195888626 Hbk £20.00

—Law of the sea : Caracas and beyond / edited by Ram Prakash Anand. – The Hague : Martinus Nijhoff, 1980.
xi,399p.
Contains revised versions of papers presented at the Semimar held in December 1976 in the International Legal Studies Division of the school of International Studies, Jawaharlal Nehru University, New Delhi.

—Legal developments in maritime commerce : matters of general interest and importance arising out of selected legal issues / W.E. Astle. – London : Fairplay, 1983.
viii,125p; 25cm.
ISBN 0905045432 Pbk No price

—Legislation on coastal state requirements for foreign fishing / by Gerald Moore. – Rome : Food and Agriculture Organization of the United Nations, 1981.
viii, 411 p.; 28 cm. – (Legislative study / Food and Agriculture Organization of the United Nations).
ISBN 9251010382 pbk.

—Limitation of liability for maritime claims / by Patrick Griggs and Richard Williams. – London : Lloyd's, 1986.
122p; 22cm.
ISBN 1850440832 £24.00

—Lloyd's Maritime Atlas / 15th ed. – London : LLoyd's of London Press.
ISBN 1850440220 Hbk £30.00

—Lloyd's nautical year book 1988 / London : Lloyd's of London Press, 1987.
488p.
ISBN 1850441340

—Mareva Injunction and associated orders / by David G. Powles. – Abingdon : Professional Books, 1986.
xxiii,160p.
ISBN 0862050693 Pbk
ISBN 0862052033

—Marine environment and the Caracas Convention on the Law of the Sea : a study of the Third United Nations Conference on the Law of the Sea and other Related Marine Environmental Activities / by Ted L. McDorman...et al. – Halifax, Nova Scotia : Dalhousie Ocean Studies Programme, 1981.
ix,127p.
ISBN 0770300790

—Maritime affairs : a world handbook : a reference guide to maritime organizations, conventions and disputes and to the international politics of the sea / compiled and written by Henry W. Degenhard : editorial consultant, Brian Meredith : general editor, Alan J. Day. – Harlow : Longman, 1985.
viii,412p; 26cm. – (A Keesing's reference publication).
Bibliography: p385-390. - Includes index.
ISBN 0582902630 £50.00
ISBN 0810320517

—Maritime boundary / S.P. Jagota. – Dordrecht : M. Nijhoff, 1985.
388p.
Bibliography.
ISBN 902473133X Hbk £175.00

—Maritime laws of the Arabian Gulf Cooperation Council States / written and edited by Richard Price with chapters by Andreas Haberbeck. – London : Graham & Trotman, 1986.
267p; 25cm.
Includes index.
ISBN 086010821X £70.00

Vol.2 / Richard Price : with translations by James Whelan. – 1986.
ix,830p; 25cm.
ISBN 0860108309 Hbk £285.00

—Mobile Offshore Units : Regulations Laid Down by Norwegian Official Control Institutions / New complete. – Oslo : Fabritius og Sonners.
ISBN 8207009225 Hbk £1.452

—Modern liner contracts : an in depth study of current contracts of carriage in liner shipping / London : Lloyd's of London Press, 1984.
90 leaves.
ISBN 1850440328

—New directions in maritime law 1980 : proceedings of an international conference co-sponsored by the Maritime Law Section of the Canadian Bar Association... et al., held at the Faculty of Law, Dalhousie University...1980 / edited by Edgar Gold and Norman G. Letalik. – Halifax, Nova Scotia : Faculty of Law, Dalhousie University, 1980.
ii,324p.
Includes bibliographical references.
ISBN 0770301967

—New directions in the law of the sea : new series / compiled and edited by Kenneth R. Simmonds : with the collaboration of specialist consulting editors. – v. – London : Oceana, 1983.
looseleaf.
ISBN 0379165503

—New law of the sea : selected and edited papers of the Athens colloquium on the law of the sea, September 1982 / edited by Christos L. Rozakis and Constantine A. Stephanou. – Amsterdam : North-Holland, published in collaboration with the Pantios School of Political Science, Athens, 1983.
xiv,354p; 23cm.
Includes index.
ISBN 0444868046 Unpriced

—New trends in maritime navigation : the future of law of the sea and the economy : proceedings of the 4th International Ocean Symposium November 20-22, 1979, the Japan Shipping Club, Tokyo, Japan / Tokyo : Ocean Association of Japan, 1980.
viii,101p; 28cm.
Edited by the Ocean Association of Japan. Title also in Japanese.

—Nigerian shipping laws / by Louis Nnamdi Mbanefo : foreword by Sir Darnley Alexander. – Abingdon : Professional Books, 1983.
xciv,1055p.
ISBN 0862050464

—Noise Levels on Board Ships / International Maritime Organization. – London : International Maritime Organization, 1982.

French Edition

Spanish Edition

—P & I Clubs: law and practice / London : Lloyds of London Press, 1989.
Discusses the constitution, workings and practice of shipowners' mutual protection and in indemnity associations. Covers the historical development and legal structure of clubs. Issues including the Court of Appeal ruling in the cases of the FANTI and PADRE ISLAND are contained, as is the clubs' method for their own reinsurance.
ISBN 1850442304 Hbk

—Procedures for the Control of Ships / International Maritime Organization. – English Edition. – London : International Maritime Organization, 1982.

—Protectionism and the future of international shipping : the nature, development, and role of flag discriminations and preferences, cargo reservations and cabotage restrictions, state intervention and maritime subsidies / Dr. Ademuni-Odeke. – Dordrecht : M. Nijhoff, 1984.
xxviii,446p.
Includes bibliographies and index.
ISBN 9024729181 Hbk £235.00

—Readings in international law from the Naval War College review, 1947-1977 / edited by Richard B. Lillich and John Norton Moore. – Newport, R.I. : Naval War CollegePress, 1980.
2 v.; 24 cm. – (U.S. Naval War College international law studies).
Includes bibliographical references and index. Contents: v. 1. Role of international law and an evolving ocean law.–v. 2. The use of force, human rights, and general international legal issues.

—Resolutions and Other Decisions of the Assembly : 12th Session 1981 (Res. 463-512) / International Maritime Organization. – London : International Maritime Organization, 1982.
ISBN 9280111477 Hbk £12.00

French
ISBN 9280121189 Hbk £12.00

Russian
ISBN 9280140426 Hbk £12.00

Spanish
ISBN 9280130854 Hbk £12.00

Chinese

—Safety Recommendations on the Use of Ports by Nuclear Merchant Ships / International Maritime Organization. – London : International Maritime Organization, 1980.

French Edition

—Seerecht : Testausgabe Law of the sea / Renate Platzoder, Wolfgang Graf Vitzthum. – 1. Aufl. – Baden-Baden : Nomos, 1984.
500 p.; 18 cm.
Contains conventions adopted by the United Nations conferences on the law of the sea, and related legislation of various countries. English and German.
ISBN 3789009318

—Shipping, energy, and environment : Southeast Asian perspectives for the eighties : proceedings of a Workshop held in Honolulu, Hawaii, 10-12 December 1980 / edited by Mark J. Valencia ... et al. – Halifax, N.S. : Dalhousie Ocean Studies Programme, 1982.
xi,333p.
Held at the Environment and Policy Institute of the East-West Center at the University of Hawaii.
ISBN 0770302769

—Systematic index of international water resources treaties, declarations, acts and cases by basin / Repertoire systematique par bassin de traites, declarations, textes legislatifs et jurisprudence concernant les ressources en eau internationales. – Rome : Food and Agriculture Organization of the United Nations, 1984.
xxxiii,332p. – (Legislative study).
Explanatory text in English, French and Spanish.
ISBN 9250021895

—Third United Nations Conference on the Law of the Sea : documents / compiled and edited by Renate Platzoder. – London : Oceana Publications, 1982.
v. 1; 27 cm.
ISBN 0379207249 v. 1 £100

—United Nations Convention on the Law of the Sea, 1982 : a commentary / Myron H. Nordquist. – Dordrecht : Martinus Nijhoff, 1985.
512p.
At head of title: Center for Oceans Law and Policy, University of Virginia.
ISBN 9024731453 Hbk £265.00

—USSR, Eastern Europe and the development of the law of the sea / compiled, translated and edited by William E. Butler. – New ed. 2 v. – London : Oceana, 1983.
looseleaf.
Previously published as: The Eastern European states and the development of the law of the sea / by Viktor Sebek. 1979. Bibliography: Vol. 2.
ISBN 0379208512

SHIPPING - AUSTRALIA

—Admiralty jurisdiction / Sydney : Law Reform Commission, 1984.
20p. – (Discussion paper).

—Civil admiralty jurisdiction / the Law Reform Commission. – Canberra : Australian Government Publishing Service, 1986.
xxi,393p. – (Report).
Bibliography: p.381-387. - Includes index.
ISBN 0644013540

—Reference on admiralty jurisdiction / Australian Law Reform Commission. – Sydney : The Commission, 1984.
xvii,296p.
Bibliography: p.291-296.

Research paper no. 2 : Admiralty jurisdiction in Australia : the courts exercising original and appellate jurisdiction / Australian Law Reform Commission. – 1984.
v,77p.
Bibliography: p.75-77.

Research paper no.3 : Draft legislation : admiralty procedure and rules / Australian Law Reform Commission. – 1985.
iv,136p.
Includes bibliographical references.

SHIPPING - CANADA

—Mortgages of Ships : Marine Security in Canada / Butterworths, 1986.
264p.
ISBN 0409988316 Hbk £95.00

—New directions in maritime law 1984 / editors David J. Sharpe and W. Wylie Spicer. – London : Carswell, 1984.
vi,254p.
Papers given at the New Directions in Maritime Law Conference, Halifax, N.S., May 1984. Includes bibliographical references.
ISBN 0459372106 Hbk £35

SHIPPING - ENGLAND

—Maritime law / Christopher Hill. – 2nd ed. – London : Lloyds of London, 1985.
400p; 24cm.
Previous ed.: London : Pitman, 1981. Includes index.
ISBN 185044045X No price

SHIPPING - GREAT BRITAIN

—Casebook on shipping law / E.R. Hardy Ivamy. – 4th ed. – London : Lloyd's of London Press, 1987.
210p; 22cm.
Previous ed.: 1982. Includes index.
ISBN 1850441308 Pbk £14.50

—Civil jurisdiction and judgements : maritime claims / by D.C. Jackson. – London : Lloyds of London Press, 1987.
386p; 22cm.
Includes index.
ISBN 1850441448 £17.50

—Double Taxation Relief for Shipping / London : LLoyd's of London Press, 1988.
ISBN 1850441650 Hbk

—Farwell's Rule of Nautical Road / 6th ed. – Spon (E & FN), 1983.
ISBN 0870212559 Hbk £14.95

—Futures and Options for Shipping / London, 1987.
ISBN 1850441367 Lloyd's of London Press £28.00

—Lloyd's maritime and commercial law quarterly / v. – London : Lloyd's of London Press, 1974-.
Index in each vol. - Cumulative indexes, 1974-78, 1979-83.

—Merchant Shipping (Linear Conferences) Act 1982 / annotated by E.R. Hardy Ivamy. – London : Lloyd's of London, 1987.
xx,92p; 22cm.
Includes index.
ISBN 1850441030 Pbk £16.50

—Ship and Aircraft Mortgages / London : LLoyd's of London Press, 1988.
ISBN 1850441049 Hbk

—Shipping Finance : Loans, Ship Mortgages and Other Securities / Abingdon : Professional Books, 1984.
ISBN 0862050618 Hbk £63.00
ISBN 0862050669 Pbk

—Tramp ship agency practice / London : Lloyd's of London Press, 1987.
ISBN 1850441480 Hbk £23.50

—Tramp Ship Agency Practice / London : LLoyd's of London Press, 1987.
ISBN 1850441480 Hbk

SHIPPING - SAUDI ARABIA

—Maritime regulations of Saudi Arabia / Hussein M. El-Sayed. – London : Graham & Trotman, 1987.
250p; 24cm.
Includes bibliography and index.
ISBN 0860107361 £70.00

SHIPPING - SINGAPORE

—Ship financing in Singapore / Singapore : Malayan Law Journal, 1983.
xxi,305.
An examination of ship financing in Singapore on two levels; the individual in the commercial world, and the national on the international scene.
ISBN 9971700301 Hbk

SHIPPING - SOUTH AFRICA

—Admiralty jurisdiction and practice in South Africa / by D. J. Shaw. – Cape Town : Juta, 1987.
xxvii,264p.
Bibliography: p. xi. - Includes index.
ISBN 0702118168

—Report on the review of the law of admiralty / South African Law Commission. – S.l. : s.n., 1984.
47p. – (Report).
Photocopy.

SHIPPING - UNITED STATES

—New directions in maritime law 1984 / editors David J. Sharpe and W. Wylie Spicer. – London : Carswell, 1984.
vi,254p.
Papers given at the New Directions in Maritime Law Conference, Halifax, N.S., May 1984. Includes bibliographical references.
ISBN 0459372106 Hbk £35

—U.S. Shipping Act of 1984 / by John McConnell. – London : Lloyd's of London, 1985.
345p; 25cm.
ISBN 1850440360 £38.00

SHIPPING - USSR

—Soviet commercial and maritime arbitration / compiled and edited by William E. Butler. – London : Oceana Publications, 1980.
l v.; 28 cm. – (A Transnational service).
Includes arbitration awards selected from the English language edition of Arbitrazhnaia praktika, issued by the USSR Foreign Trade Arbitration Commission. Loose-leaf for updating.
ISBN 0379206994 £75.00

SHIPPING CONFERENCES

—Carriage of goods by sea / edited by Peter Koh Soon Kwang. – Singapore : Butterworths, 1986.
xviii,198p.
Collection of papers which analyse the legal principles governing carriage of goods by sea, and the Hague/Visby rules. Includes coverage of maritime arbitration, shipowners' limitation of liability, unclean bill of lading, time charterparties, and proposed changes in Malaysian shipping law.
ISBN 0409995150

—Shipping conferences / London : Lloyd's of London, 1983.
viii,255p.
Bibliography: p.253-255. Bibliography: p253-255. Includes text of the Convention on a Code of conduct for liner conferences (1974).
ISBN 9065440895 Hbk £116.00

SHIPPING LAW

—Amendments to the International Convention for the Safety of Life at Sea : 1974 / International Maritime Organization. – London : International Maritime Organization, 1982.

French Edition

Russian Edition

Spanish Edition

—Arrest of ships 2 / Jan Th. F. Theunis ... et al. – 1. – London : Lloyd's, 1986.
22cm.
ISBN 1850440913 £25.00

—Arrest of ships 3 : Malta, Panama, Sweden, United Arab Emirates / by Max Ganado ... et al. – London : Lloyd's of London, 1987.
xx,110p; 22cm.
ISBN 1850441006 £24.00

—Arrest of ships 5 : Bangladesh, Finland, Saudi Arabia, South Africa / by M. Hafizullah ... et al. – London : Lloyd's of London, 1987.
xvi,95p.
ISBN 1850441022

—Arrest of ships 6 : Denmark, Greece, Hong Kong, Kuwait, Qatar / by Allan Philip ... et al. – London : Lloyd's, 1987.
xviii,89p.
ISBN 1850441529

—Basic documents / International Maritime Organization. – London : I.M.O., 1983.
107p.
ISBN 9280111531

—Carriage of dangerous goods by sea : the role of the International Maritime Organisation in international legislation / by Cleopatra Henry. – London : Pinter, 1985.
iii,184; 23cm.
Includes index. Clarifies the work of the IMO revealing its methods and mandate for enacting maritime controls on the transportation of controversial toxins.
ISBN 0861875699 Hbk £25

—Carriage of goods by sea / edited by Peter Koh Soon Kwang. – Singapore : Butterworths, 1986.
xviii,198p.
Collection of papers which analyse the legal principles governing carriage of goods by sea, and the Hague/Visby rules. Includes coverage of maritime arbitration, shipowners' limitation of liability, unclean bill of lading, time charterparties, and proposed changes in Malaysian shipping law.
ISBN 0409995150

—Control of marine pollution in international law / Ramanlal Soni. – Cape Town : Juta, 1985.
301p.
Bibliography: p277-293.
ISBN 0702116602

—Convention on the law of the sea / Drafting Committee. – Geneva : The Conference, 1982.
xvii,221p. – (Working paper).
Text adopted on 30 April 1982 at the eleventh session of the Conference. - Supersedes: Draft convention on the law of the sea (August, 1981). 'This working paper has been prepared for the use of the Drafting Committee at the intersessional meeting to be held from 12 July to 13 or 20 August 1982'.

—Court appointed experts in maritime cases : a comparative law study / by Arthur M. Boal and David R. Owen. – Antwerp : International Maritime Committee, 1981.
ii,83p.
Contents: questionnaire answers, compiled by Arthur M. Boal and David R. Owen.

—Dictionary of Shipping Law / London : Butterworths, 1984.
ISBN 0406623996 Hbk £15.00
ISBN 0406624003 Pbk £10.95

—Draft convention on the law of the sea / United Nations Third Conference on the Law of the Sea, resumed tenth session, Geneva, 3-28 August 1981. – Geneva : United Nations, 1981.
xix,175p; 28cm. – (Document).
Supersedes: Draft convention on the law of the sea: informal text.

—Draft convention on the law of the sea : informal text / United Nations Third Conference on the Law of the Sea, resumed ninth session, Geneva, 28 July to 29 August 1980. – Geneva : United Nations, 1980.
xix,180p; 30cm. – (Document).
Supersedes: Informal composite negotiating text.
Superseded by: Draft convention on the law of the sea.

—Elements of Shipping / 5th ed. – London : Sweet & Maxwell, 1981.

—Exclusive economic zone in international law / David Joseph Attard. – Oxford : Clarendon, 1987.
256p; 24cm. – (Oxford monographs in international law).
Includes index.
ISBN 0198255411 £27.50

—Guide to the Collision Avoidance Rules / J. Lameijer. – London : Stanford Maritime Ltd.
224p.

—IMCO news : the magazine of the Inter-Governmental Maritime Consultative Organization / London : IMCO, 1979 - 1982.
n v.
Continued by: IMO news.

—IMO news : the magazine of the International Maritime Organization / London : IMO, 1982.
Continues: IMCO news.

—Index of multilateral treaties on the law of the sea / edited by P. De Cesari ... et al. – Milano : Giuffre, 1985.
371 p.; 25 cm.
ISBN 8814005532 L26000

—International and legal problems of the gulf / S.H. Amin. – London : Middle East and North African Studies Press, 1981.
235p.
Bibls..
ISBN 0906559057

—International law of the ocean development : basic documents / by Shigeru Oda. – 2nd ed. 2. – Leiden : Sijthoff, 1977.
looseleaf.

—International law of the sea / D. P. O'Connell, I. A. Shearer. – Oxford : Clarendon Press, 1982.
xxxiii,633p; 24cm.
Bibliography: p582-607. - Includes index.
ISBN 019825346X Unpriced

Vol.2 : by D.P. O'Connell : edited by I.A. Shearer 1984.
xxvi,p.636-1201; 24cm.
Bibliography: p1159-1170. - Includes index.
ISBN 0198254695 £40.00

—International Maritime Arbitration / Vancouver : Continuing Legal Education Society of British Columbia, 1988.
338p.
ISBN 0865043663 Hbk £100.00

—International Maritime Law Conv (BSL) 4 vols. / London : Sweet & Maxwell, 1983.
ISBN 042066002 Hbk £310.00

—International maritime law conventions / compiled by Mahararj Nagendra Singh. – Updated ed. 4. – London : Stevens, 1983.
xxvii,,3305p; 26cm.
Previous ed.: published in 1v. as International conventions of maritime shipping. 1973. Includes index.
ISBN 0420466002 £24.00

—International Maritime Organisation / Samir Mankabady. – 2nd ed. – London : Croom Helm, 1987.
xxvii,452p; 23cm.
Previous ed.: published in 1 vol. 1984. Includes index.
ISBN 0709946406 Hbk £50.00

—International Maritime Organization / Samir Mankkabady. – 2nd ed. – London : Croom Helm, 1986.
xxi,450p; 23cm.
Previous ed.: published in 1 vol. 1984. Includes index.
ISBN 0709935919 £45.00

—International Ship Arrest : A Practical Guide / London : LLoyd's of London Press, 1988.
ISBN 1850441901 Hbk

—Law for the world ocean / by Gerard J. Mangone. – London : Stevens, 1981.
ii,313p; 19cm.
Bibliography: p292-300. - Includes index.
ISBN 0421284803 £12.00

—Law, force and diplomacy at sea / Ken Booth. – London : Allen & Unwin, 1985.
xiii,231p,1p folded leaf of plates; 24cm.
ISBN 0043410278 Hbk £18.00
ISBN 0043410286 Pbk £7.95

—Law of maritime delimitation - reflections / Cambridge : Grotius, 1989.
343.
Assesses the scope and meaning of the solutions already reached to the problem of maritime delimitation and submits them to critical analysis. Also intends to identify the directions in which the evolution of the law is heading and to advance some suggestions as to desirable developments.
ISBN 0949009407 Hbk £55.00

—Law of the sea : unilateralism or multilateralism? / by Adeoye Akinsanya. – Lagos : University of Lagos Press, 1980.
52p. – (Monograph series).
Includes bibliographical references.
ISBN 9782264059

—Legal requirements for arrest and enforced sale of vessels : a comparative study / Malcolm H. Pace. – S.l. : s.n., 1983.
xxvi,144 leaves.
Thesis (LL.D.) - University of Malta 1983. Bibliography: p.142-144.

—Mareva injunctions / edited by Marion Hetherington. – Sydney : Law Book Co., 1983.
xv,122p.
Includes index.
ISBN 0455204934

—Marine Encyclopaedic Dictionary / 2nd ed. – London : Lloyd's of London Press, 1988.
ISBN 1850441278 Hbk £37.50

—Marine policy : the international journal for economics, planning and politics of ocean exploitation / v. – Guildford : IPC Science and Technology Press, 1977.
Subtitle varies: from v. 4, no. 3 subtitled: the international journal of ocean affairs.
ISBN 0308597X

—Maritime boundaries and ocean resources / edited by Gerald Blake : International Geographical Union Study Group on the World Political Map. – London : Croom Helm, 1987.
284p; 23cm.
Bibliography: p257-271. - Includes index.
ISBN 0709939744 £27.50

—Maritime dimension / edited by R.P. Barston and Patricia Birnie. – London : Allen & Unwin, 1980.
194p; 23cm.
Includes index.
ISBN 0043410154 Hbk £11.95
ISBN 0043410162 Pbk £5.50

—Maritime Law / Dordrecht : Kluwer, 1976.
108p.
ISBN 9026808941 Hbk £45.00

Vol. 2: Enforced Sales of Vessels 1977.
114p.
ISBN 9026809395 Hbk £57.00

Vol. 3: Mortgage on Vessels and Registration of Vessels, 2 pts. 1983.
324p.
ISBN 9065441298 Hbk £207.00

—Maritime Law Handbook / Hans Christian Albrecht. – Dordrecht : Kluwer, 1987.
350p.

—Maritime Law : Third International Conference / Vancouver : Continuing Legal Education Society of British Columbia, 1986.
566p.
ISBN 0865042721 Hbk £100.00

—Maritime liens and claims / William Tetley with assistance from Brian G. McDonough. – London : Business Law Communications, 1985.
lxiv,686p.
Includes bibliographical references and index.
ISBN 0948406003

—New bearings in the law of the sea : inaugural lecture delivered at the University of Queensland, 29 April 1981 / R.D. Lumb. – St. Lucia, Queensland : University of Queensland Press, 1982.
ISBN 0702216798 pbk.

—Nigerian shipping laws / by Louis Nnamdi Mbanefo : foreword by Sir Darnley Alexander. – Abingdon : Professional Books, 1983.
xciv,1055p.
ISBN 0862050464

—Origin and development of the law of the sea : history of international law revisited / R.P. Anand. – The Hague : Nijhoff, 1983.
xvi,249p; 25cm.
Includes index.
ISBN 9024726174 Hbk £115.00

—Panama / by Enrique de Alba. – London : LLP, 1987.
204p; 22cm.
ISBN 1850441413 £25.50

—Problems of development and ocean management in the eastern Caribbean : economic, legal, environmental and planning aspects : proceedings of an international seminar held in Kingstown, St. Vincent & the Grenadines, West Indies, May 11-13, 1981 / edited by Edgar Gold, Norman G. Letalik, Carlyle L. Mitchell. – 2nd printing. – Halifax, N.S. : Dalhousie Ocean Studies Programme, 1982.
xviii,184p.
'Held under the auspices of the West Indies (Associated States) Council of Ministers and sponsored by the Dalhousie Ocean Studies Programme in cooperation with the Foundation Reshaping the International Order (RIO) '.

—Prospects for a new Law of the Sea : papers read at a seminar conducted by the International Law Association in Sydney on 19 June 1982 / edited by Ivan Shearer. – Sydney, N.S.W. : International Law Association (Australian Branch), 1983.
v, 97, 93 p.; 30 cm.
ISBN 0949685011 pbk. £7.00 (£6.00 to members)

—Resolutions and other decisions / Assembly, International Maritime Organization. – London : The Organization, 1981.
Continues: Resolutions and other decisions / Assembly, Inter- governmental Maritime Consultative Organization.

—Shipping Law / O.C. Giles. – New Delhi : Arnold-Heinemann, 1980.
430p.

—State responsibility and the marine environment : the rules of decision / Brian D. Smith. – Oxford : Clarendon, 1988.
xviii,281p; 24cm. – (Oxford monographs in international law).
Bibliography: p257-276. - Includes index.
ISBN 0198255810 £30.00

—Supplement relating to the annex to the Convention on Facilitation of International Maritime Traffic, 1965 / London : International Maritime Organization, 1982.
63p; 25cm.
ISBN 9280111493 Pbk Unpriced

—Transfer of marine technology to developing nations in international law / Boleslaw A. Boczek. – Honolulu : Law of the Sea Institute, University of Hawaii, 1982.
vi,79p. – (Occasional paper).
Includes bibliographical references.

—United Nations Convention on the law of the sea / Geneva : The Conference, 1982.
xxiv,194p.
Text dated 7 October 1982. - Supersedes: Convention on the law of the sea (April, 1982).

SHIPPING LAW – AFRICA

—Africa and the international law of the sea : a study of the contribution of the African States to the Third United Nations Conference on the Law of the Sea / Nasila S. Rembe. – Alphen aan den Rijn, The Netherlands : Sijthoff & Noordhoff, 1980.
xix, 251 p.; 25 cm. – (Sijthoff publications on ocean development ; v. 6).
Includes bibliographical references and indexes.
ISBN 9028606394 Hbk £98.00

SHIPPING LAW – AUSTRALIA

—MLAANZ journal / the Maritime Law Association of Australia and New Zealand. – v. – Sydney : The Association, 1983.
Supersedes the MLAANZ newsletter. Masthead title: Journal of the MLAANZ.
ISBN 08114293

SHIPPING LAW – CANADA

—Annotated Canada Shipping Act / Christopher Burke. – Butterworths, 1988.
464p.
Deals with Canadian judicial decisions and Canadian legal literature. Includes recent amendments to the legislation itself and to the regulations. Shows how Canada deals with this form of international commerce.
ISBN 0409811459 Hbk

—Canada and the new international law of the sea / Douglas M. Johnston. – Toronto : University of Toronto Press in cooperation with the Royal Commission on the Economic Union and Development Prospects for Canada and the Canadian Government Publishing Centre, 1985.
xviii,124p. – (Collected research studies).
Includes bibliographical references.
ISBN 0802073018

—Canadian Maritime Law and the Offshore : a Primer / Calgary : Canadian Institute of Resources Law.
65p.

—Canadian Regulation of Offshore Installations / Calgary : Canadian Institute of Resources Law.
116p.
ISBN 0919269184 Hbk £17.00

—Current Problems in Maritime Law : Canada, U.S., International / Toronto : DeBoo, 1987.
430p.
ISBN 0888202598 Hbk £79.00

SHIPPING LAW – COMMONWEALTH

—UN Convention on the Law of the Sea 1982 : a guide for national policy making legislation and administration / prepared by E.D. Brown in association with the Commonwealth Secretariat. – London : The Secretariat, 1987.
viii,132p.

SHIPPING LAW – CYPRUS

—Note on the law of Cyprus relating to offshore operations, shipping operations and shipping companies, foreign investments in Cyprus and transit trade / by Criton G. Tornaritis. – Nicosia : s.n., 1984.
52 leaves.

SHIPPING LAW – ENGLAND

—Kennedy's law of salvage / F. D. Rose, David Steel, William Rann Kennedy. – 5th ed. – London : Stevens, 1985.
lxii,833p; 26cm.
Deals with the practical and legal developments that have taken place in the last thirty years. Discusses the widespread acceptance and use of the terms of Lloyd's standard form of salvage agreement (no cure no pay), the preparation in Montreal of a new draft International Convention on salvage, and the effect of legislative activity in the area of oil pollution.
ISBN 0420434305 £70.00

—Maritime law of salvage / by Geoffrey Brice. – London : Stevens, 1983.
xxxvi,539p; 26cm.
Focuses on established principles and topics in which particular developments have been proposed, including the threat to the environment posed by the large laden tanker; the assessment of salvaged value; the liability of salvors for negligence and the limitation and exclusion of the liability. Appendices contain extracts from relevant statutes and statutory instruments.
ISBN 0420462406 £45.00

—Maritime liens / by D.R. Thomas. – London : Stevens, 1980.
xlix,397p.

—Merchant shipping - legislative proposals / presented to Parliament by the Secretary of State for Transport .. – London : H.M.S.O., 1987.
ii,13p; 30cm.
ISBN 0101023928

SHIPPING LAW – GREAT BRITAIN

—Arrest of Ships / London : Lloyd's of London Press, 1985.
ISBN 1850440255 Hbk £25.50

Vol 2 1986.
ISBN 1850440913 Hbk £25.50

Vol 3 1987.
ISBN 1850441006 Hbk £25.50

Vol 4 1987.
ISBN 1850441014 Hbk £25.50

—Aspinall's Reports of Maritime Cases : 1870-1940, 20 Vols. / Professional Books Staff. – Abingdon : Professional Books, 1984.

—Black Book of the Admiralty : with an appendix / edited by Sir Travers Twiss. – 4. – Abingdon, Oxon, : Professional Books, 1985.
A reprint of the original published in 1871?. Includes indexes.

—Carver's carriage by sea / Raoul Colinvaux. – 13th ed. – London : Stevens, 1982.
2v.
Previous ed.:1971.
ISBN 0420451102 £12.00

—Casebook on carriage by sea / by E.R. Hardy Ivamy. – 6th ed. – London : Lloyd's of London, 1985.
256p; 25cm.
Previous ed.: 1982. Includes index.
ISBN 1850440549 Pbk No price

—Cases and materials on the carriage of goods by sea / Martin Dockray. – Abingdon : Professional Books, 1987.
xxvi,804p.
ISBN 0862052599

—Chorley and Giles' shipping law / by O.C. Giles. – 7th ed. – London : Pitman, 1980.
xxix,457.

ISBN 027301319X

—Chorley and Giles' shipping law / O. C. Giles, N. J. J. Gaskell, C. Debattista, Richard J. Swatton. – 8th ed. – London : Pitman, 1987.
lxiii,704p; 23cm.
Previous ed.: 1980. Bibliography: plxii-lxiii. - Includes index.
ISBN 027302194X Pbk £14.95

—Coastal Law / London : Lloyd's of London Press, 1988.
ISBN 1850441642 Hbk

—Collisions at Sea / 12th ed. – London : Sweet & Maxwell, 1987.
– (British Shipping Law Ser.).

—Commencement of Laytime / London : Lloyd's of London Press, 1987.
ISBN 1850441413 Hbk £24.50

—Dictionary of shipping law / by E.R. Hardy Ivamy. – London : Butterworths, 1984.
179p; 23cm. – (Butterworths professional dictionaries series).
ISBN 0406623996 Hbk No price
ISBN 0406624003 Pbk No price

—Dictionary of Shipping Spanish/English / London : Lloyd's of London Press, 1988.
ISBN 1850444537 Pbk

—Elements of Shipping / 5th ed. – London : Chapman & Hall, 1981.
ISBN 0412237008 Hbk £20.00
ISBN 0412237105 Pbk £9.95

—Employment of merchant seamen / Jonathan S. Kitchen. – London : Croom Helm, 1980.
658p; 23cm.
Includes index.
ISBN 0856645273 £60.00

—Encyclopedia of Shipping Law Sources UK / London : LLoyd's of London Press, 1988.
ISBN 1850440115 Hbk £175.00

—Enforcement of maritime claims / by D.C. Jackson. – London : Lloyd's of London Press, 1985.
lxi,483p; 26cm.
ISBN 1850440018

—Friends in conflict : the Anglo-Icelandic cod wars and the law of the sea / Hannes Jonsson. – London : C.Hurst, 1982.
xi,240p.
Bibliography: p225-233.

—Introduction to General Average / Witherby, 1986.
ISBN 0948691107 Pbk £6.00

—Law and Practice of Marine Insurance and Average / London : Sweet & Maxwell, 1988.
ISBN 0420476504 Hbk £145.00

—Law of Marine Insurance and Average / London : Sweet & Maxwell, 1988.
ISBN 0420445005 Hbk £150.00

—Law of Marine Insurance and Average (BSL) / 16th ed. 2 vols. – London : Sweet & Maxwell, 1981.
ISBN 0420445005 Hbk £170.00

—Law of Maritime Liens / Reprint of 1940 edition. – Abingdon : Professional Books.

—Law of Tug, Tow and Pilotage / 2nd ed. – London : Chapman & Hall, 1982.
ISBN 0412250209 Hbk £60.00

—Laytime / 4th ed. – London : Sweet & Maxwell, 1988.
ISBN 042079708 Hbk

—Limitation of Shipowners' Liability / London : Sweet & Maxwell, 1986.
ISBN 042134890 Hbk £38.00

—London Maritime Arbitration / London : LLoyd's of London Press, 1989.
ISBN 1850442045 Hbk

—Maritime law / Christopher Hill. – London : Pitman, 1981.
xxi,394p; 24cm.
Includes index.
ISBN 0273015931

—Maritime Liens / London : Sweet & Maxwell, 1980.
– (British Shipping Laws Ser.).
Analysis of the law of maritime liens and the nature of the right enjoyed by a maritime lienee. Examines the principle liens recognised by the English Admiralty Court; damage; salvage; seamen' wages; and Bottomry bonds. Also looks at the rights in rem enjoyed against the Crown and foreign sovereigns.
ISBN 0420460500 Hbk £58.00

—Maritime Liens (BSL) / London : Sweet & Maxwell, 1980.
ISBN 0421460500 Hbk £65.00

—Merchant Shipping Act : 1970 / London : LLoyd's of London Press, 1987.
ISBN 1850441103 Pbk

—Merchant Shipping Act : 1979 / London : LLoyd's of London Press, 1987.
ISBN 1850441405 Hbk

—Merchant Shipping (Linear Conference) Act 1982 / London : Lloyd's of London Press, 1987.
ISBN 1850441030 Pbk £16.00

—Merchant Shipping (Safety Officials) Regulations 1982 : guidance notes for shipowners, crew employers, ship masters, safety officers, safety representatives and safety committees / issued by Marine Division, Department of Trade. – London : The Division, 1982.
78p.

—Modern Bills of Lading / Oxford : Blackwell Scientific, 1987.
ISBN 0003833224 Hbk £19.95

—New directions in maritime law / Spicer. – London : Sweet & Maxwell, 1985.
ISBN 0459372106 Hbk £35.00

—Payne and Ivamy's Carriage of goods by sea / E. R. Hardy Ivamy. – 12th ed. – London : Butterworths, 1985.
xlix,366p; 22cm.
This textbook is a straightforward discussion of the field of carriage of goods by sea under the laws of the United Kingdom for students of the subject.
ISBN 0406640602 HBK £18.00
ISBN 0406640610 Pbk £14.95

—Pilotage Act 1987 / London : Lloyd's of London Press, 1987.
ISBN 1850441391 Pbk £18.75

—Sea lawyer grade for yachtsmen / 2nd ed. – Oxford : Collins, 1986.
ISBN 0229117627 Pbk £6.95

—Shipbroking and chartering practice / Gordon. – 2nd ed. – London : Lloyd's of London Press, 1984.
ISBN 0907432638 Hbk £39.00

—Shipping and the law / London : Fairplay Publication, 1980.
ISBN 0905045173 Pbk £12.00

—Shipping law / Giles. – 8th ed. – London : Pitman Publishing, 1987.
ISBN 027302194X Pbk £19.95

—Shipping practice / Butterfield. – 11th ed. – London : Pitman Publishing, 1981.
ISBN 0273016164 Pbk £9.95

—Shipping practice : with consideration of the relevant law / C. S. J. Butterfield. – 11th ed. – London : Pitman, 1981.
xi,173p; 22cm.
Previous ed.: 1978. Includes index.
ISBN 0273016164 Pbk Unpriced

SHIPPING LAW – GREECE
—Greek Code of Private Maritime Law / Theodoros B. Karatzas and Nigel P. Ready. – The Hague : Nijhoff, 1982.
viii,98p; 25cm.
Includes index.
ISBN 9024725860 Hbk £75.00/$32.50

SHIPPING LAW – ICELAND
—Friends in conflict : the Anglo-Icelandic cod wars and the law of the sea / Hannes Jonsson. – London : C.Hurst, 1982.
xi,240p.
Bibliography: p225-233.

SHIPPING LAW – NIGERIA
—Nigerian Shipping Cases / Abingdon : Professional Books, 1987.
ISBN 0862052416 Hbk £75.00

—Nigerian Shipping Laws / Abingdon : Professional Books, 1983.
ISBN 0862050464 Hbk £126.50

SHIPPING LAW – NORWAY
—Maritime Law of Norway, Dated July 10th 1893. Laws, Statutes, etc. Norway / Oslo : Fabritius og Sonners, 1896.
1148p.
ISBN 8207009187 Hbk £358.00

SHIPPING LAW – SCOTLAND
—Commentaries on the Law of Scotland in Relation to Mercantile and Maritime Laws, Movable and Heritable Rights and Bankruptcy, 2 Vols. / 3rd ed. Repr. of 1819 ed. – Abingdon : Professional Books.

SHIPPING LAW – SINGAPORE
—Law in Singapore on carriage of goods by sea / by Tan Lee Meng. – Singapore : Malayan Law Journal Pte., 1986.
lv,509p.
Deals with voyage charterparties, time charterparties, demise charterparties, bills of lading, the Carriage of Goods by Sea Act 1872, exclusion of liability, limitation of liability, and limitation of action, loading, proceeding on the voyage, discharge and delivery, laytime and demurrage, salvage and wreck, and remedies for breach of contract.
ISBN 9971700492

SHIPPING LAW – SOUTH AFRICA
—Law of shipping and carriage in South Africa / by B.R. Bamford. – 3rd ed. – Cape Town : Juta, 1983.
xlvi,389p.
Previous ed.: 1973. Includes index.
ISBN 070211376X

—South African Maritime Law and Marine Insurance : Selected Topics / Durban : Professional Publishers, 1983.
ISBN 0409023779 Pbk £55.00

SHIPPING LAW – SPAIN
—Dictionary of Shipping Spanish/English / London : Lloyd's of London Press, 1988.
ISBN 1850444537 Pbk

SHIPPING LAW – UNITED STATES
—Current Problems in Maritime Law : Canada, U.S., International / Toronto : DeBoo, 1987.
430p.
ISBN 0888202598 Hbk £79.00

—U.S. Shipping Act of 1984 / by John McConnell. – London : Lloyd's of London, 1985.
345p; 25cm.
ISBN 1850440360 £38.00

SHIPS
—FAO-ILO-IMO Voluntary Guidelines for the Design, Construction and Equipment of Fishing Vessels / International Maritime Organization. – London : International Maritime Organization, 1980.
French Edition

—Guidelines for the Design and Construction of Offshore Supply Vessels / International Maritime Organization. – London : International Maritime Organization, 1982.

SHIPS – CANADA
—Report of formal investigation into the fire aboard and abandonment of the Canadian tanker Hudson Transport in the St. Lawrence River on December 25, 1981 / Commissioner James K. Hugessen : assessors, J. Augustin Dionne, John J. DeLuca. – Ottawa : Canadian Government Publishing Centre, Supply and Services Canada, 1982.
iii,140p. – (Report of formal investigation).
Bound with French ed.: Rapport de l'investigation formelle sur l'incendie a bord du petrolier canadien Hudson Transport et son abandon dans le fleuve Saint-Laurent le 25 decembre 1981. At head of title: Canada Shipping Act. - Cover title: Hudson Transport.
ISBN 0660519720

SHIPS – GREAT BRITAIN
—Mortgages of Ships / London : Lloyd's of London Press, 1988.
ISBN 1850441049 Hbk

—Shipbuilding credit / Cardiff : University of Wales Press, 1983.
ISBN 07080308430 Pbk £12.00

SHOPLIFTING – ENGLAND
—Customers and thieves : an ethnography of shoplifting / Daniel J.I. Murphy. – Aldershot : Gower, 1986.
xi,266; 23cm.
Bibliography: p246-256. - Includes index.
ISBN 0566008823 £15.00

SHOPLIFTING – GREAT BRITAIN
—Shoplifting, and thefts by shop staff : a review / by the Home Office Standing Committee on Crime Prevention 1983. – London : H.M.S.O., 1983.
23p.
ISBN 0113407890

SHOPS AND OFFICES – CANADA
—Report : The Shops Act : Late-night and Sunday Opening / Committee of Inquiry into Proposals to Amend the Shops Act. – London : HMSO, 1984.
ISBN 0101937601 Hbk £9.15

SHOPS AND OFFICES - GREAT BRITAIN

—Automated Office / Burgess. - Oxford : Blackwell Scientific, 1985.
ISBN 000383008X Pbk £7.95

—Law for Commercial Retailers / London : Sweet & Maxwell.
ISBN 0421347902 Hbk

SHOPS AND OFFICES - INDIA

—Uttar Pradesh Shop and Commercial Establishments Act, 1962 / 3rd ed. - Lucknow : Eastern Book Company, 1984.
410p.

SHOPS AND OFFICES - PAKISTAN

—Law of Shops and Establishments / 12th ed. - Karachi : Bureau of Labour Publications, 1987.
20p.

SHROPSHIRE

—Roll of the Shropshire eyre of 1256 / edited for the Selden Society by Alan Harding. - London : Selden Society, 1981.
1xxiv,403p.

SICKNESS BENEFIT - GREAT BRITAIN

—Extension of the Statutory Sick Pay Scheme in April 1986 / London : Engineering Employers Federation, 1985.

—Guide to Statutory Sick Pay / 3rd ed. - Croydon : Tolley.
120p.
Describes recent changes in the statutory sick pay scheme. Chapter included on maternity.
ISBN 0854593365 Hbk £9.95

—Guide to Statutory Sick Pay / 2nd ed. - Tolley Publishing, 1986.
ISBN 0854592431 Pbk £6.95

—Sick Pay : A Negotiators Guide / London : Labour Research Department, 1985.

—Statutory Sick Pay : A Practical Guide / London : Oyez Longman, 1983.
ISBN 0851207421 Hbk £5.95

—Statutory Sick Pay Guide / London : Engineering Employers Federation.

—Statutory Sick Pay - Practical Guide / 2nd ed. - London : Longman Professional, 1986.
ISBN 0851212336 Pbk £11.95

SIGNALS AND SIGNALLING

—International code of signals / London : IMO, 1985.
vii,175p; 31cm.
Includes index.
ISBN 9280111841 £14.00

SLAVERY

—Slave laws in the Americas / University of Georgia, 1990.
224; 22.
ISBN 0820311790 Hbk £21.50

SLAVERY (ROMAN LAW)

—Selected texts and cases on the Roman law of things : with an excursus on the Roman law of slavery / J.E. Schiller. - Cape Town : Juta, 1982.
xiii,127p; 25cm.
ISBN 0702112941

SMALL BUSINESSES

—Role of local authorities in promoting the creation or operation of small or medium-sized firms within a general policy of endogenous development / report prepared under the guidance of the Committee of Experts on Social and Economic Activities of the Steering Committee for Regional and Municipal Matters by T. Nuttal. - Strasbourg : Council of Europe, 1986.
31p.
Bibliography: p.28-29.

SMALL BUSINESSES - CANADA

—Small Business Venture Capital Act / Vancouver : Continuing Legal Education Society of British Columbia, 1986.
347p.
ISBN 086504290X Hbk £75.00

SMALL BUSINESSES - EUROPE

—Small business in Europe / Dewhurst. - London : Macmillan, 1986.
ISBN 0333384067 Pbk £12.95

SMALL BUSINESSES - GREAT BRITAIN

—Consumer Law for the Small Business / London : Kogan Page, 1983.
160p.
ISBN 0850386187 Hbk £11.95
ISBN 0850386489 Pbk £5.95

—Croner's Reference Book for the Self-Employed and Smaller Business / Croner Publications. - New Malden : Croner Publications.

Annual renewal updates

—Guardian Guide to running a Small Business / London : Kogan Page, 1986.
ISBN 1850910952 Pbk £6.95

—Importing for the Small Business / London : Kogan Page, 1985.
128p.
ISBN 0850388694 Pbk £6.95

—Law for the Small Business / 5th ed. - London : Kogan Page, 1987.
ISBN 0850912157 Pbk £7.50

—Law for the Small Business : 'The Daily Telegraph' Guide / 4th ed. - London : Kogan Page, 1985.
264p.
ISBN 0850388937 Hbk £11.95
ISBN 0850388945 Pbk £6.95

—Lending Packages for Small and Medium-Sized Companies / Oxford : Croom Helm, 1983.
ISBN 070992254X Pbk £8.95

—Passing down the family business: solving the tax problems / 4th. - London : Longman Professional (UK), 1988.
- (Longman Intelligence Report).
Information and advice on reducing the tax burden and maximising the prosperity of the business when transferring control to another member of the family. Outlines tax planning strategies, and how to use tax reliefs to their full advantage.
ISBN 0851212719 Hbk £95.00

—Small Business and the Law / Department of Industry & Commerce. - Repr. of 1981 ed. - Canberra : Australian Government Publishing Service, 1983.
40p. - (Managing the Small Business Ser.).
ISBN 0642069085 Hbk £2.30

—Tax and financial planning for family business / George J Bell. - London : Butterworths, 1984.
ISBN 0406557306 Pbk £16.00

—Tax and Financial Planning for Family Businesses / George J. Bell. - London : Butterworths, 1984.
This book addresses the tax problems faced by owners of small and medium sized family business in the United Kingdom. The work examines the benefits to be gained from allowances, reliefs, exemptions, and Revenue concessions.
ISBN 0406557306 Pbk

SMALL CLAIMS COURTS

—Small claims courts / Oxford : Clarendon Press, 1989.
250; 21.5.
Compares and contrasts some of the principles which have been applied in informal methods of adjudicating small claims, and some of the solutins which have been adopted in eight countries. Analyses the dilemmas which alternative options pose for justice.
ISBN 0198256272 Hbk £25.00

SMALL CLAIMS COURTS - AUSTRALIA - TASMANIA

—Report and recommendations relating to consumer claims and small debts / Law Reform Commission of Tasmania. - Hobart : Government Printer, 1982.
55p. - (Report).

SMALL CLAIMS COURTS - CANADA

—Small Claims Court Materials : Can They Be Read? Can They Be Understood? / Marilyn Hiebert. - Ottawa : Canadian Law Information Council, 1985.
184p.
ISBN 0920358837 Pbk

—Small Claims Court Practice and Procedure / Vancouver : Continuing Legal Education Society of British Columbia, 1988.
434p.
ISBN 0865049718 Hbk £85.00

—Small Claims Litigation / Butterworths, 1988.
160p.
Guide to the conduct of small claims court actions. Takes the reader step by step from the initial client interview and preliminary issues such as limitations, parties and forums, to drafting effective pleadings. Shows how to handle interlocutory proceedings and how to effectively negotiate settlement. Contains annotated Court Rules, and a set of sample forms.
ISBN 0409806528 Pbk £24.95

SMALL CLAIMS COURTS - CANADA - ALBERTA

—Small Claims Court Guide for Alberta : How to Win Your Case / 4th ed. - North Vancouver : International Self-Counsel Press, 1985.
122p.
ISBN 0889082286 Hbk £7.50

SMALL CLAIMS COURTS - CANADA - BRITISH COLUMBIA

—Small Claims Court Guide for British Columbia : How to Win Your Case! / 18th ed. - North Vancouver : International Self-Counsel Press, 1986.
138p.
ISBN 0889081859 Hbk £7.95

SMALL CLAIMS COURTS - CANADA - MANITOBA

—Report on the structure of the courts / Law Reform Commission. - Winnipeg : Queen's Printer Office, 1983.
iii,56p. - (Report).

SMALL CLAIMS COURTS - CANADA - ONTARIO

—Small Claims Court Guide for Ontario : How to Win Your Case! / 6th ed. - North Vancouver : International Self-Counsel Press, 1986.
144p.
ISBN 0889083568 Hbk £7.50

—Small Claims Court Practice in the Ontario Provincial Court (Civil Division)-1987 / Agincourt : Carswell, 1987.
ca 300p.

—Small Claims in Ontario / Community Legal Education Ontario. - Toronto : Community Legal Education Ontario, 1982.
70p.
ISBN 0889030588 Pbk £6.50

SMALL CLAIMS COURTS - ENGLAND

—Civil justice review / Lord Chancellor's Department. - London : The Department, 1986.
50 leaves.
Cover title: Small claims in the County Court.

—Model code of procedure for small claims divisions of county courts / London : National Consumer Council, 1980.
72p.

—Response to 'Small claims in the County Court' / JUSTICE. - London : JUSTICE, 1987.
20p.

SMALL CLAIMS COURTS - NORTHERN IRELAND

—Small claims in Northern Ireland : a 'step-by-step' guide / by D.S. Greer. - 3rd ed. - Belfast : SLS Publications, 1987.
63p. - (The law in action).

—Small claims in Northern Ireland : a 'step-by-step' guide / by D.S. Greer. - 2nd ed. - Belfast : SLS Legal Publications, Faculty of Law, Queen's University, 1982.
49p.
Previous ed.: published as 'Small claims: the new procedure in Northern Ireland', 1979. Includes bibliographical references.
ISBN 0853892172

SMALL CLAIMS COURTS - SCOTLAND

—Small claims procedure in the Sheriff court : detailed proposals : consultation paper / Scottish Courts Administration. - Edinburgh : Scottish Courts Administration, 1987.
94p in various pagings.
Includes example of forms. Issued on behalf of the Lord Advocate and the Sheriff Court Rules Council.

SMALL CLAIMS COURTS - SOUTH AFRICA

—Small Claims Court / Durban : Butterworths.

—You in the small claims court : a practical guide / S.A. Strauss. - Cape Town : Juta, 1985.
xv,126p.
Includes index.
ISBN 0702116637

SMOKING

—Legislative action to combat the world smoking epidemic / by Ruth Roemer : with a foreword by Sir George Godber. - Geneva : World Health Organization, 1982.
131p.
Bibliography: p.121-122.
ISBN 9241560746

SMUGGLING - INDIA

—Conservation of Foreign Exchange and Prevention of Smuggling Act, 1987 / 1987. - Allahabad : Law Book Company.
250p.

—Conservation of Foreign Exchange and Prevention of Smuggling Activities Act / Allahabad : Law Book Company, 1987.
250p.

SOCCER

—Papers from the European Conference on Football Violence : held at the Tickled Trout Hotel, Salmesbury, Preston, Lancashire, 10-13 April 1987 / edited by Tim O'Brien. - Preston? : Lancashire Polytechnic, 1987.
81p.
Bibliographies.
ISBN 090669406X

SOCCER - ENGLAND

—Hooligans abroad : the behaviour and control of English fans in Continental Europe / John Williams, Eric Dunning and Patrick Murphy. - London : Routledge & Kegan Paul, 1984.
xiv,230p,12p of plates; 22cm.
Includes index.
ISBN 0710201435 Pbk £8.95

SOCIAL CONFLICT
—Disputes and settlements : law and human relations in the West / edited by John Bossy. – Cambridge : Cambridge University Press, 1983.
ix,296p; 23cm.
Essays by British, American and French scholars to outline a social history of the West using records of the law in Western Europe from the fall of Rome to the Nineteenth Century.
ISBN 0521252830 £25.00

—Disputes and the law / edited by Maureen Cain and Kalman Kulcsar for the European Coordination Centre for Research and Documentation in Social Sciences. – Budapest : Akademiai Kiado, 1983.
Contains a collection of papers given at a seminar held in Dubrovnik at the Inter-University Centre of Postgraduate Studies in September 1979.
ISBN 9630533790

SOCIAL CONTRACT
—Justice, law, and culture / James K. Feibleman. – Dordrecht : Nijhoff, 1985.
xiii, 208p.
ISBN 9024731054

—Social contract / Michael Lessnoff. – London : Macmillan, 1986.
x,178p; 23cm.
Bibliography: p169-173. - Includes index.
ISBN 0333367901 Hbk £18.00
ISBN 033336791X Pbk £6.95

SOCIAL CONTROL
—Disputes and the law / edited by Maureen Cain and Kalman Kulcsar for the European Coordination Centre for Research and Documentation in Social Sciences. – Budapest : Akademiai Kiado, 1983.
Contains a collection of papers given at a seminar held in Dubrovnik at the Inter-University Centre of Postgraduate Studies in September 1979.
ISBN 9630533790

—Legal System and Social Systems / Etal. – Oxford : Croom Helm, 1985.
ISBN 0709936125 Hbk £18.95

—Private justice / Stuart Henry. – London : Routledge & Kegan Paul, 1983.
ix,245p.
Includes index. Bibliography: p229-235.
ISBN 0710097034 pbk.

—Social democracy and the rule of law / Otto Kirchheimer and Franz Neumann : edited by Keith Tribe : translated by Leena Tanner and Keith Tribe. – London : Allen & Unwin, 1987.
224p; 22cm.
Includes bibliography and index. Translated from the German.
ISBN 0043013007 £25.00

—Transcarceration : essays in the sociology of social control / edited by John Lowman, Robert J. Menzies, T.S. Palys. – Aldershot : Gower, 1987.
x,370p; 22cm.
Includes bibliography and index.
ISBN 0566051060 £19.50

—Visions of social control : crime, punishment and classification / Stanley Cohen. – Cambridge : Polity, 1984.
300p.
ISBN 0745600204 Hbk £19.50
ISBN 0745600212 Pbk £7.95

SOCIAL CONTROL – AUSTRALIA
—Policing a Democracy / Canberra : Australian Institute of Criminology.

SOCIAL CONTROL – GREAT BRITAIN
—Permissiveness and Control : The Fate of the Sixties Legislation / National Deviancy Conference. – London : Macmillan.
224p. – (Critical Criminology Ser.).
ISBN 0333266803 Hbk £12.00
ISBN 0333266811 Pbk £4.95

—Protest, Policing and the Law / P. Leopold. – London : Institute for the Study of Conflict, 1985.
– (Conflict Studies Ser.: No. 175).

SOCIAL CONTROL – TANZANIA
—Law, State and Working Class in Tanzania / London : Dent (J M) & Sons, 1986.
ISBN 085255303X Pbk £9.95

SOCIAL ETHICS
—Injustice, inequality and ethics : a philosophical introduction to moral problems / Robin Barrow. – Brighton, Sussex : Wheatsheaf, 1982.
xii,204p.
Includes index. Bibliography: p199-202.
ISBN 038920269X Barnes & Noble

SOCIAL HISTORY
—Case studies on human rights and fundamental freedoms : a world survey / ed.-in-chief, Willem A. Veenhoven, assistant to the ed.-in-chief, Winifred Crum Ewing, associate editors, Clemens Amelunxen ... et al. – The Hague : Nijhoff, 1975.
5 v; 25 cm.
2 v. Includes bibliographical references.

SOCIAL INDICATORS – CANADA
—North American social report : a comparative study of the quality of life in Canada and the USA from 1964 to 1974 / by Alex C. Michalos. – Dordrecht : Reidel, 1980.
xv,252p; 23cm.
ISBN 9027710856

SOCIAL INDICATORS – UNITED STATES
—North American social report : a comparative study of the quality of life in Canada and the USA from 1964 to 1974 / by Alex C. Michalos. – Dordrecht : Reidel, 1980.
xv,252p; 23cm.
ISBN 9027710856

SOCIAL INSURANCE – GREAT BRITAIN
—Decisions of the Commissioner : National Insurance Acts 1965-1974 and Social Security Act 1975 Invalidity Benefit / London : HMSO.

—Decisions of the Commissioners : National Insurance Acts 1965-1974 and Social Security 1975 Invalidity Benefit / London : HMSO, 1980.
ISBN 0117607088 Hbk £1.90

—DHSS Official Contributions Guides / London : Oyez Longman, 1984.
ISBN 0851207391 Hbk £55.00

—Housing Benefit review : report of the review team / Great Britain. – London : H.M.S.O., 1985.
43 p.
ISBN 0101952007

—National Insurance contributions / London : Butterworths, 1988.
ISBN 0406504601 Pbk

—National Insurance Contributions / Croydon : Tolley, 1988-89.
400p.
ISBN 0854593594 Hbk £18.95

—National Insurance Contributions : Principles and Planning / London : Butterworths, 1986.
ISBN 0406504601 Pbk

SOCIAL INSURANCE – INDIA
—Commentaries on Employees' State Insurance Act, 1948 / 3rd ed. – Lucknow : Eastern Book Company, 1986.
928p.

—Employees' State Insurance Act / 2nd ed. – Calcutta : Eastern Law House, 1984.

—Law of Employees State Insurance / Dwivedi. – 2nd ed. – Allahabad : Law Book Company.
700p.
With 1987 supplement.

SOCIAL INTERACTION
—Social relations and human attributes / Paul Hirst and Penny Woolley. – London : Tavistock, 1982.
xi,297p; 24cm.
Bibliography: p274-286. - Includes index.
ISBN 0422772208 Hbk £12.00
ISBN 0422772305 Pbk £4.95

SOCIAL JUSTICE
—Giving desert its due : social justice and legal theory / Wojciech Sadurski. – Dordrecht : D. Reidel, 1985.
xii, 329p.
Includes index. Bibliography: p 309-318.
ISBN 9027719411 Hbk £47.00

—Social justice and individual responsibility in the welfare state / edited by Jan M. Broekman, Kazimierz Opaek, Djangir A.A. Kerimov : preface by Carl Wellman Soziale Gerechtigkeit und individuelle Verantwortlichkeit im Wohlfahrtsstaat / herausgegeben von Jan M. Broekman, Kazimierz Opaek, Djangir A.A. Kerimov ; vorwort von Carl Wellman. – Stuttgart : F. Steiner Verlag Wiesbaden, 1985.
299 p.; 24 cm. – (Archives for philosophy of law and social philosophy).
English, French, and German. 'Eleventh World Congress of the IVR convened in Helsinki 15-20 August 1983'–P. 5. Includes bibliographical references and index.
ISBN 3515044590 pbk. DM35.00

—Social justice in the liberal state / Bruce A. Ackerman. – New Haven : Yale University Press, 1980.
xii,392p; 24cm.
Includes index.
ISBN 0300024398 £11.00

—Welfare and justice / Maria Los. – Sheffield : Centre for Criminological and Socio-Legal Studies, 1982.
136p.
Bibliography: p.130-136.

SOCIAL JUSTICE – GREAT BRITAIN
—Crime and Social Justice / Paul Takagi. – London : Macmillan, 1981.
232p. – (Critical Criminology Ser.).
ISBN 0333282604 Hbk £18.00
ISBN 0333282612 Pbk £6.95

SOCIAL LEGISLATION
—Dilemmas of law in the welfare state / edited by Gunther Teubner. – Berlin : W. de Gruyter, 1986.
viii,341p. – (Series A, Law).
Includes bibliographies and index.
ISBN 0899251080

—Norwegian Social Law / Oxford : Oxford University Press, 1988.
ISBN 8200059030 Hbk £30.00

—Social policy harmonisation in the European Community / John Holloway. – Farnborough, Hants. : Gower, 1981.
vi,318p; 23cm.
Bibliography: p305-318.
ISBN 0566001969 £10.50

SOCIAL LEGISLATION – AUSTRALIA
—Diary of social legislation and policy / v. – Parkville, Vic. : Institute of Applied Economic and Social Research, University of Melbourne, 1981.
ISBN 07252455

SOCIAL LEGISLATION – CANADA
—Family Day Care Services Act, 1983, Bill Pr019 : An Act Respecting Family Day Care Services / Ontario : Ontario Government Publications Service, 1983.

SOCIAL LEGISLATION – EUROPEAN COMMUNITY
—Future of Community social legislation / Ivor Richard. – Exeter : University of Exeter, 1984.
11p.

SOCIAL LEGISLATION – GREAT BRITAIN
—Introduction to Social Administration in Britain / 6th ed. – London : Hutchinson, 1985.
– (Politics Ser.).
ISBN 0091599717 Hbk £7.95

—Legal context of social work / by J.D. McClean. – 2nd ed. – London : Butterworths, 1980.
xxi,229p.
ISBN 0406621233

—Test cases for the poor : legal techniques in the politics of social welfare / Tony Prosser. – London : Child Poverty Action Group, 1983.
v,102p.
ISBN 090396371X

SOCIAL LEGISLATION – INDIA
—Labour Welfare and Social Security Legislation in India / New Delhi : Deep and Deep Publications, 1984.
302p.

—Licensing Power in India : a Government Action for Social Welfare / New Delhi : S. Chand and Company.

SOCIAL POLICY
—Annotated bibliography public opinion and social policy / by Donald J. Bourgeois. – Ottawa : Ministry of the Solicitor General, 1985.
56p. – (Usier report).

—Social policy harmonisation in the European Community / John Holloway. – Farnborough, Hants. : Gower, 1981.
vi,318p; 23cm.
Bibliography: p305-318.
ISBN 0566001969 £10.50

SOCIAL POLICY – AUSTRALIA
—Diary of social legislation and policy / v. – Parkville, Vic. : Institute of Applied Economic and Social Research, University of Melbourne, 1981.
ISBN 07252455

SOCIAL POLICY – EUROPEAN COMMUNITY
—Leading cases and materials on the social policy of the EEC / Dordrecht : Kluwer, 1989.
556.
Guide to the scope of community law, using basic sources, such as treaty provisions and directives. Examines the problem of the direct effect on, and the relationship between, national and community law.
ISBN 9065443126 Pbk £39/Dfl 125

SOCIAL POLICY – GREAT BRITAIN
—Conversations on Policy / London : Policy Studies Institute, 1984.
88p. – (PSI's Discussion Papers).

—Mental health, social policy and the law / London : Macmillan, 1985.
ISBN 0333373014 Hbk £25.00

—Policing and Social Policy : Proceedings of the Cranfield-Wolfson Colloquium / London : Police Review Publishing, 1984.

SOCIAL POLICY – IRELAND
—Law and social policy : some current problems in Irish law / edited by William Duncan. – Dublin : Dublin University Law Journal, 1987.
133p.
Includes bibliographical references.
ISBN 0951226908

SOCIAL PROBLEMS

—Injustice, inequality and ethics : a philosophical introduction to moral problems / Robin Barrow. - Brighton, Sussex : Wheatsheaf, 1982.
xii,204p.
Includes index. Bibliography: p199-202.
ISBN 038920269X Barnes & Noble

—Manufacture of news : social problems, deviance and the mass media / Stanley Cohen and Jock Young (editors). - rev. ed. - London : Constable, 1981.
506p.
ISBN 0094637806

SOCIAL PROBLEMS - GREAT BRITAIN

—Homeless young offenders : an action programme : the Report of a NACRO Group / NACRO. - London : NACRO, 1981.
69p.
Bibliography: p.67-69.
ISBN 0850690242

SOCIAL ROLE

—Public and private in social life / edited by S.I. Benn and G.F. Gaus. - London : Croom Helm, 1983.
viii,412p; 23cm.
Includes indexes.
ISBN 0709906684 £19.95
ISBN 0312653573

SOCIAL SCIENCE RESEARCH - GREAT BRITAIN

—Social research and Royal Commissions / edited by Martin Bulmer. - London : Allen & Unwin, 1980.
xv,198p; 23cm.
Bibliography: p189-192. - Includes index.
ISBN 0043510558 No price

SOCIAL SCIENCES

—Card catalog of the Peace Palace at the Hague; classification scheme of the systematic catalog / Peace Palace. - 1. - New York : Clearwater, 1980.
various pagings.
With introduction by Warren F. Kuehl. With second copy of classification scheme.

—ESRC newsletter / v. - London : Economic and Social Research Council, 1984-.
Continues SSRC newsletter.

—Social theory as science / Russell Keat and John Urry. - 2nd ed. - London : Routledge & K. Paul, 1982.
xi,301p.
Includes index. Bibliography: p278-295.
ISBN 0710094310

SOCIAL SECURITY

—Balance Development of Long-Term Benefits : Proceedings of the European Institute for Social Security / European Institute for Social Security. - Dordrecht : Kluwer, 1987.
392p.
ISBN 9065442898 Hbk £85.00

—C.P.A.G's supplementary benefit and family income supplement : the legislation / annotations by John Mesher. - 2nd ed. - London : Sweet & Maxwell, 1985.
400p.
Previous ed: published as CPAG's supplementary benefit legislation annotated. 1983. Includes index. Includes the text of the 1976 Supplementary Benefits Act, and the 1970 Family Income Supplements Act.
ISBN 0421342102 Pbk No price

—C.P.A.G's supplementary benefit and family income supplement : the legislation / commentary by John Mesher. - 3rd ed. - London : Sweet & Maxwell, 1985.
xxviii,465p; 24cm.
Previous ed.: 1985. Includes index.
ISBN 0421353805 Pbk £15.00

—Fifty Years of Labour Law and Social Security / Dordrecht : Kluwer, 1986.
166p.
ISBN 9031203653 Pbk £90.00

—Law of social security / A. I. Ogus, E. M. Barendt. - 2nd ed. - London : Butterworths, 1982.
lxxvi,664p.
Previous ed.: 1978.
ISBN 0406633622

—Maintenance of Rights in Social Security / Geneva : International Labour Office, 1983.
101p.
ISBN 9221031314 Hbk £17.50

—Socio-legal studies and social welfare / Martin Partington : a report for the Government and Law Committee of the Economic and Social Research Council. - London : Economic and Social Research Council, 1986.
78p.
Bibliography: p59-78.
ISBN 0862261872

—Supplementary Benefits Appeal Tribunals : a guide to procedure / Department of Health and Social Security. - Rev. ed. - London : H.M.S.O., 1982.
vi,60p; 21cm.
Previous ed.: 1977.
ISBN 0117608440 Pbk £2.00

—Treatment of disabled persons in social security and taxation law / Canberra : Australian Government Publishing Service, 1986.
viii,149p. - (Occasional paper).
Bibliography: p134-149.
ISBN 0644048123

—Yearbook of the European Institute for Social Security / 1978-1980 /. - Dordrecht : Kluwer, 1980.
ISBN 9031201332 Hbk Gld114.00

Part 1: Retirement Age in Europe 1980.
224p.
ISBN 9031201340 Hbk Gld52.00

Part 2: Social Security Reforms in Europe 1980.
288p.
ISBN 9031201359 Hbk Gld65.00

—Yearbook of the European Institute for Social Security / 1980-1981 /. - Dordrecht : Kluwer, 1982.
ISBN 9031201685 Hbk Gld123.00

Part 1: Social Security Reforms in Europe 2 1982.
285p.
ISBN 9031201669 Hbk Gld72.00

Part 2: Social Security and the Economic Crisis 1982.
146p.
ISBN 9031201677 Hbk Gld60.00

—Yearbook of the European Institute for Social Security / 1982-1983 /. - Dordrecht : Kluwer.

SOCIAL SECURITY - AUSTRALIA

—Australian social security law, policy and administration / Terry Carney & Peter Hanks. - Melbourne : Oxford University Press, 1986.
xxv,334p.
Bibliography: p311-326.
ISBN 0195547543

—Australian Social Security Legislation / 2nd ed. - North Ryde : C.C.H. Australia, 1986.
250p.
ISBN 0869036300 Hbk £24.00

—Social Security Law and Policy / North Ryde : Law Book Co, 1986.
xxvi, 272p.
ISBN 0455206155 Pbk £29.50

—Social security reporter / Clayton, Vic. : Legal Service Bulletin Co-operative, 1981.
Indexes: Nos 1-22 in no 22 (Dec 1984); annually in Dec. issue except for 1983.
ISBN 08173524

SOCIAL SECURITY - BELGIUM

—Guide Concerning the Rights and Obligations with Regard to Social Security of Persons Going to Work in Belgium / Luxembourg : Office for Official Publications of the European Communities, 1985.
30p.
ISBN 9282546233 Pbk

SOCIAL SECURITY - CANADA

—Welfare Rights and GAIN / Marjorie Martin. - 3rd ed. - Vancouver : Vancouver People's Law School.
Illus.. - - (Public Legal Education Series).
ISBN 0888470223 Hbk £0.60

SOCIAL SECURITY - EUROPEAN COMMUNITY

—Comparative tables of the social security schemes in the member states of the European Communities : General scheme (employees in industry and commerce) / 12th ed. - Luxembourg : Office for Official Publications of the European Communities, 1982.
119p.
ISBN 9282535207

—Social security law of the European Communities / Philippa Watson. - London : Mansell Information Publishing, 1980.
xiii,277p; 24cm.
Bibliography: p.269-272. - Includes index.
ISBN 0720109264 £17.50

SOCIAL SECURITY - FRANCE

—Guide Concerning the Rights and Obligations with Regard to Social Security of Persons Going to Work in France / Luxembourg : Office for Official Publications of the European Communities, 1985.
43p.
ISBN 9282546373 Hbk

SOCIAL SECURITY - GIBRALTAR

—Guide Concerning the Rights and Obligations with Regard to Social Security of Persons Going to Work in the United Kingdom of Great Britain and Northern Ireland Including Gibraltar / Luxembourg : Office for Official Publications of the European Communities, 1986.
32p.
ISBN 9282546799 Pbk

SOCIAL SECURITY - GREAT BRITAIN

—Adjudication officers' guide / Chief Adjudication Officer. - London : HMSO, 1988.
looseleaf.
Index in each vol.. At head of t.p. : Department of Health and Social Security.

—C.P.A.G.'s income support, the social fund and family credit : the legislation / commentary John Mesher. - 1988 ed. - London : Sweet & Maxwell, 1988.
xxx,381p; 24cm.
Previous ed.: 1987. Includes index.
ISBN 0421402709 Pbk £19.50

—C.P.A.G.'s supplementary benefit and family income supplement : the legislation / commentary by John Mesher. - 4th ed. - London : Sweet & Maxwell, 1987.
500p; 23cm.
Previous ed.: 1985. Kept up to date by supplements.
ISBN 0421382007 Pbk £17.50

—Commissioners' Decisions : Social Security and Child Benefit Acts / London : HMSO, 1985.
ISBN 0117609218 Hbk

Vol. IX, 1983-84
ISBN 0117607851 Hbk £25.00

—DHSS Official Contributions Guides / London : Oyez Longman, 1984.
ISBN 0851207391 Hbk £55.00

—Disabled people on supplementary benefit : interim report / Richard Stowell. - Oxford : Centre for Socio-Legal Studies, 1980.
145p; 21cm. - (Research study).
ISBN 0862260655

—Enforcement of the law relating to social security / report of a NACRO working party. - London : NACRO, 1986.
114p.
Chairman: Sir Norman Price.
ISBN 0850690412

—How to claim state benefits / 2nd ed. - Northcote House, 1988.
ISBN 0746305311 Pbk £5.95

—Law of social security / A.I. Ogus ... et al. - 3rd ed. - London : Butterworths, 1988.
lxxii,634p.
Includes index. At head of cover title: Ogus & Barendt.
ISBN 040663372X

—Law of supplementary benefits / M. S. Rowell, A. M. Wilton. - London : Butterworths, 1982.
xxxi,239p; 22cm.
ISBN 0406649103

—Law Relating to Social Security and Child Benefit, 4 Vols. / London : HMSO.
Sets out the current legislation, both statutes and regulations with footnotes and sidenotes giving the origin of amendments.
ISBN 0117609102 Pbk £95.00

—Law relating to social security : the statutes, regulations and orders as now in force / London : HMSO, 1988.
looseleaf.
Supersedes : The law relating to social security and child benefit (the Brown Books); and The law relating to supplementary benefits and family income supplements (the Yellow Books). At head of title : Department of Health and Social Security. Popular title : the Blue Volumes.

—Law Relating to Supplementary Benefit and Family Income Supplement / London : HMSO, 1984.
Sets out current legislation, both statutes and regulations with footnotes and sidenotes giving the origin of amendments.
ISBN 0117609242 Pbk £41.00

—Law relating to supplementary benefits and family income supplements : the statutes, regulations and orders as now in force / H. V. Roberts. - 3rd ed. 2. - London : HMSO, 1980-.
looseleaf.
Superseded by: The law relating to social security (the Blue volumes). Popular title: the Yellow Books. With supplements of amendments.

—National Insurance and Family Allowances Acts, 4 Vols. / London : HMSO.
ISBN 0117600016 Hbk £1.50

Vol. VI
ISBN 0117605166 Hbk £2.00

Vol. VII
ISBN 0117605166 Hbk £7.00

Vol. VIII
ISBN 011760643X Hbk £15.00

—National Insurance contributions / London : Butterworths, 1988.
ISBN 0406504601 Pbk

—National welfare benefits handbook / London : Child Poverty Action Group, 1987.
288p; 21cm.
Includes index.
ISBN 0946744009 Pbk £4.50

—Non-means tested benefits : the legislation / commentary by David Bonner ... et al. – London : Sweet & Maxwell, 1988.
xliii,546p; 24cm.
Previous ed.: 1987. Includes index.
ISBN 0421402601 Pbk £19.50

—Non-means tested benefits : the legislation / London : Sweet & Maxwell, 1988.
ISBN 0421402601 Pbk £19.50

—Non-means-tested social security benefits / Rowland. – 9th ed. – London : CENT, 1986.
ISBN 0903963965 Pbk £4.00

—Poor law : the mass arrest of homeless claimants in Oxford / by Ros Franey : illustrated by Jim Stanes and Nina Carroll. – London : CHAR, 1983.
93p; 21cm. – (Poverty pamphlet).
ISBN 0906951046 Pbk £1.95

—Reform of social security / presented to Parliament by the Secretary of State for Social Services. – London : HMSO, 1985.
48p.
ISBN 0101951701

v.2 : Programme for change / presented to Parliament by the Secretary of State for Social Services. – 1985.
iii,62p.
ISBN 0101951809 Hbk

v.3 : Background papers / presented to Parliament by the Secretary of State for Social Services. – 1985.
138p.
ISBN 0101951906 Hbk

Technical annex 1985.
51p.
Technical annex to White Paper Cmnd 9691. Contents: 1. Illustrations of individuals' future pensions expectations. 2. Illustrative effects of reforming the structure of income-related benefits.
ISBN 0113210183 Hbk

—Reform of social security / A.W.Dilnot, J.A.Kay and C.N. Morris. – Oxford : Clarendon, 1984.
viii,166; 23cm.
Bibliography: p158-160. - Includes index.
ISBN 0198772262 Pbk £10.00
ISBN 0198772254 £3.95

—Reform of social security : programme for action / presented to Parliament by the Secretary of State for Social Services. – London : H.M.S.O, 1985.
53p.
Includes bibliographical references.
ISBN 0101969104

—Reported decisions of the Commissioner under the Social Security and Child Benefit Acts / Department of Health and Social Security. – v. – London : H.M.S.O., 1980-.
Continues: Reported decisions of the Commissioner under the Social Security, National Insurance and Family Allowances Acts.

—Reported decisons of the Commissioner under the Social Security Act (1975) / Department of Health and Social Security. – v. – London : H.M.S.O., 1982-.
Continues: Reported decisions of the Commissioner under the Social Security and National Insurance (Industrial Injuries) Acts.

—Rights guide to non means tested benefits / Rowlands. – London : Central Books, 1988/89.
ISBN 0946744092 Pbk £4.50

—Seventh report from the Social Services Committee, session 1984-85 : the government's green paper 'Reform of social security', together with the proceedings of the Committee, the minutes of evidence and appendices / London : H.M.S.O., 1985.
liv,100p. – (H.C.).

—Sixth report form the Home Affairs Committee, session 1984-85 : Immigration and Nationality Department of the Home Office, together with the proceedings of the Committee, minutes of evidence and appendices / London : H.M.S.O., 1985.
xxviii,119p. – (H.C.).
ISBN 0102277850

—Social security - abolition of independent appeals under the social fund : special report / by the Council on Tribunals. – London : H.M.S.O., 1986.
6p; 25cm.
ISBN 0101972202

—Social Security and State Benefit / Croydon : Tolley, 1988-89.
530p.
Includes social security reforms on income support, family credit and the revised housing benefit and the social fund.
ISBN 0854593608 Hbk £19.95

—Social security contributions / Neil D. Booth. – London : Butterworths, 1982.
xxviii,204p; 25cm.
Includes index.
ISBN 0406128995 Pbk £8.00

—Social security law in Britain and Ireland : a bibliography / Paul O'Higgins and Martin Partington with the assistance of Sally Hughes. – London : Mansell, 1986.
424p; 24cm.
Includes index.
ISBN 0720117941 £36.00

—Social security taxation : a guide to contributions and contributory conditions under the social security acts / by David W. Williams. – London : Sweet & Maxwell, 1982.
xxxiii,536p; 26cm.
Includes index.
ISBN 0421262303 £40.00

—Social welfare law / David Pearl and Kevin Gray. – London : Croom Helm, 1981.
308p; 23cm.
Bibliography: p265. - Includes index.
ISBN 085664644X Hbk £14.95
ISBN 0709920040 Pbk £8.95

—State Benefits 1986 / London : Labour Research Department.
ISBN 090050885X Hbk £0.90

—Third special report from the Social Services Committee, session 1985-86 : reform of social security : observations by the government on the first report from the Committee, session 1985-86 / London : H.M.S.O., 1986.
vii p. – (H.C. 1985-86).
ISBN 0102484864

—Tolley's Social security and state benefits 1983/84 / by Jim Matthewman and Nigel A.D. Lambert. – Croydon : Tolley, 1984.
xii,496p; 23cm.
Includes index.
ISBN 0854591354 Pbk £10.95

—Tolley's social security and state benefits 1985 / by Jim Matthewman and Nigel A.D. Lambert. – Croydon : Tolley, 1985.
x,485p.
Includes index.
ISBN 0854591737

—'We don't give clothing grants any more' : the 1980 supplementary benefit scheme / Janet Allbeson and Roger Smith. – London : Child Poverty Action Group, 1984.
113p.
Includes bibliographical references.
ISBN 0903963736

—Women won't benefit : the impact of the Social Security Bill on women's rights / Hilary Land and Sue Ward. – London : National Council for Civil Liberties. Rights for Women Unit, 1986.
48p.
ISBN 0946088268

SOCIAL SECURITY – INDIA

—Social Security Legislation for Labour in India / New Delhi : Deep and Deep Publications, 1986.
382p.

SOCIAL SECURITY – IRELAND

—Guide Concerning the Rights and Obligations with Regard to Social Security of Persons Going to Work in Ireland / Luxembourg : Office for Official Publications of the European Communities, 1985.
28p.
ISBN 9282546519 Pbk

—Social security law in Britain and Ireland : a bibliography / Paul O'Higgins and Martin Partington with the assistance of Sally Hughes. – London : Mansell, 1986.
424p; 24cm.
Includes index.
ISBN 0720117941 £36.00

SOCIAL SECURITY – LUXEMBOURG

—Guide Concerning the Rights and Obligations with Regard to Social Security of Persons Going to Work in Luxembourg / Luxembourg : Office for Official Publications of the European Communities, 1985.
34p.
ISBN 9282546659 Pbk

SOCIAL SECURITY – MALAYSIA

—Employees' Social Security Act, 1969 (Act 4) / Kuala Lumpur : International Law Books Services.

SOCIAL SECURITY – NETHERLANDS

—Guide Concerning the Rights and Obligations with Regard to Social Security of Persons Going to Work in the Netherlands / Luxembourg : Office for Official Publications of the European Communities, 1985.
24p.
ISBN 9282546721 Pbk

SOCIAL SECURITY – PHILIPPINES

—Answers to Bar Examination Questions /. – Quezon City : University of the Philippines, Law Center, 1982.
104p.

—First Asian Congress of Labour Law and Social Security / Quezon City : University of the Philippines, Law Center, 1982.
608p.

SOCIAL SECURITY – UNITED KINGDOM

—Guide Concerning the Rights and Obligations with Regard to Social Security of Persons Going to Work in the United Kingdom of Great Britain and Northern Ireland Including Gibraltar / Luxembourg : Office for Official Publications of the European Communities, 1986.
32p.
ISBN 9282546799 Pbk

SOCIAL SECURITY – WEST GERMANY

—Guide Concerning the Rights and Obligations with Regard to Social Security of Persons Going to Work in the FR of Germany / Luxembourg : Office for Official Publications of the European Communities, 1985.
32p.
ISBN 9282546160 Pbk

SOCIAL SECURITY APPEAL TRIBUNALS – GREAT BRITAIN

—Research Study on Supplementary Benefit Appeal Tribunals : Review of Main Findings; Conclusions; Recommendations / London : HMSO.
55p.
ISBN 011760335X Hbk

SOCIAL SECURITY APPEAL TRIBUNALS – NORTHERN IRELAND

—Guide to Social Security Tribunals / Belfast : Queen's University of Belfast, 1986.
200p.

SOCIAL SECURITY COURTS??? – GREAT BRITAIN

—Tribunal representation : the role of advice and advocacy services / Roger Lawrence. – London : Published in association with the National Association of Citizens Advice Bureaux by the Bedford Square Press of the National Council for Voluntary Organisations, 1980.
vii,98p; 30cm.
ISBN 0719910447 Pbk £3.95

SOCIAL SERVICE – GREAT BRITAIN

—Encyclopaedia of Social Services Law / London : Sweet & Maxwell, 1988.
ISBN 0421254505 Hbk £195.00

SOCIAL SERVICE – NORTHERN IRELAND

—Access to personal social services records : Data Protection Act 1984, Section 29(2) Order : social work records, Northern Ireland / Northern Ireland. – Belfast : Department of Health and Social Services, 1985.
8 leaves.

SOCIAL WORK

—Social work with young offenders / Stephen Collins, David Behan. – London : Butterworths, 1981.
xii,148p; 22cm.
The book emphasizes the practical aspects of working with young offenders within the court system of the United Kingdom. Assessment, the family, working with individual offenders, and working with groups are explored in depth in the text.
ISBN 0406556903 Pbk £4.95

SOCIAL WORK – AUSTRALIA

—Law for Youth Workers / North Sydney : Allen & Unwin, 1983.
124p.
ISBN 0868610305 Pbk £12.95

SOCIAL WORK – CANADA

—Guide to Law for Social Workers / Mary Satterfield. – Agincourt : Carswell.
This second edition text reviews the structure of the Canadian legal system. Discussions include the rights of persons living in common law relationships, criteria for awarding support, possible courses of legal action for situations of family violence, basic grounds and procedure for obtaining divorce, custody and access, child protection proceedings, adoption and children that break the law. Also included in the new edition is divorce, custody, support, family property, and young offenders.

SOCIAL WORK - ENGLAND

—Helping the homeless : a report on the work of the LANCE Project for Single Homeless People in Manchester and Stockport / NACRO. – London : NACRO, 1980.
11p. – (Housing and residential services).

—Receiving juvenile justice : adolescents and state care and control / Howard Parker, Maggie Casburn, David Turnbull. – Oxford : Basil Blackwell, 1981.
259p; 23cm.
Criticises official discretion, deviation and diversity in the selection and sentencing process.
ISBN 0631127275 Hbk £12.00
ISBN 0631127453 Pbk £5.50

—Social work decisions in child care : recent research findings and their implications / appraisal by the Research on Child Care Working Party of Child Care Practitioners; report written by Jane Rowe. – London : H.M.S.O., 1985.
73p.
Includes summaries of the reports discussed. At head of title-page: Department of Health and Social Security. 7 sheets of charts in end pocket.
ISBN 0113210469

SOCIAL WORK - GREAT BRITAIN

—Discretion and welfare / edited by Michael Adler and Stewart Asquith. – London : Heinemann Educational, 1981.
vii,296p; 23cm. – (Studies in social policy and welfare).
Conference papers. Bibliography: p273-287. - Index.
ISBN 0435820095 £15.00

—Essential Law for Social Workers / 2nd ed. – London : Oyez Longman, 1981.
ISBN 0851205143 Hbk £9.95

—Introduction to the Social Services / 4th ed. – London : Macmillan, 1983.
208p.
ISBN 0333335430 Pbk £4.95

—Legal Context of Social Work / 2nd ed. – London : Butterworths, 1980.
ISBN 0406621233 Hbk £12.50
ISBN 0406621241 Pbk £7.95

—Social work and child abuse / Ball. – London : Macmillan, 1987.
ISBN 033363973 Hbk £15.00
ISBN 0333363981 Pbk £5.95

—Social work, justice and control / Oxford : Blackwell, 1985.
ISBN 0631137327 Pbk £8.50

—Social work statutes / 2nd ed. – London : Sweet & Maxwell, 1985.
ISBN 0421348305 Pbk £11.00

—Social work with young offenders / Behan. – London : Butterworths, 1981.
ISBN 0406556903 Pbk £7.50

SOCIAL WORK - SCOTLAND

—Social work and criminal law in Scotland / by George Moore and Chris Wood. – Aberdeen : Aberdeen University Press, 1981.
xii,208p; 26cm.
Provides information and guidance about those aspects of the judicial and penal systems and measures relating to child offenders which affect social workers. Chapters cover prosecution, social worker at court, social enquiry reports, non-custodial measures, probation, community service and unpaid work, and custodial measures. Includes bibliography and index.
ISBN 0080257313 Hbk No price

—Social Work (Scotland) Act / Rosemary Gray. – 2nd. – Edinburgh : W Green & Son, 1984.
Full text of the Act as amended and in force, along with prospective amendments as at 25 May 1984. Also with an appendix tabulating legislation, as amended and prospectively amended to the same date, relating to elderly and handicapped persons, welfare rights, children and young persons, mentally ill people and adult offenders.
ISBN 0414007417

SOCIAL WORKERS - CANADA

—Guide to Law for Social Workers / Mary Satterfield. – Agincourt : Carswell.
This second edition text reviews the structure of the Canadian legal system. Discussions include the rights of persons living in common law relationships, criteria for awarding support, possible courses of legal action for situations of family violence, basic grounds and procedure for obtaining divorce, custody and access, child protection proceedings, adoption and children that break the law. Also included in the new edition is divorce, custody, support, family property, and young offenders.

—Law for social workers : a Canadian guide / by Elaine J. Vayda, Mary T. Satterfield. – Toronto, Canada : Carswell, 1984.
xxi, 292 p.; 24 cm.
Includes bibliographies and index.
ISBN 0459366602 pbk.

SOCIAL WORKERS - ENGLAND

—Welfare law and order : a critical introduction to law for social workers / Pete Alcock and Phil Harris. – London : Macmillan, 1982.
xvi,219p. – (Critical texts in social work and the welfare state).
Includes index. Bibliography: p207-213.
ISBN 0333294904

SOCIAL WORKERS - GREAT BRITAIN

—Essential Law for Social Workers / 2nd ed. – London : Oyez Longman, 1981.
ISBN 0851205143 Hbk £9.95

—Legal context of social work / by J.D. McClean. – 2nd ed. – London : Butterworths, 1980.
xxi,229p.
ISBN 0406621233

SOCIALISM

—Law, socialism and democracy / Paul Q. Hirst. – London : Allen & Unwin, 1986.
200p; 22cm.
Includes bibliography and index.
ISBN 0043012531 Hbk £15.00
ISBN 004301254X Pbk £6.95

—On the Legal Institutions of Socialist Democracy / London : Spokesman Books, 1983.
50p.

SOCIALISM - FRANCE

—Socialism, The State, and Public Policy in France / Martin A. Schain. – London : Pinter Publishers Ltd, 1984.
220p.
ISBN 086187384X Hbk £21.00

SOCIALISM - GREAT BRITAIN

—Unequal struggle? : British socialism and the capitalist enterprise / Jim Tomlinson. – London : Methuen, 1982.
160p; 23cm.
Bibliography: p149-157. - Includes index.
ISBN 0416331505 Hbk Unpriced
ISBN 0416331602 Pbk Unpriced

SOCIALIST LAW

—Concept of Socialist law / Oxford : Clarendon Press.
21.5.
Intends to remedy the contempt for law prominent in Socialist writings. Argues that legal institutions would be necessary to adjudicate fairly conflict between private and public interest. Covers the rule of law, natural and legal rights, obligations, and the sources of law.
ISBN 0198252463 Hbk £25.00224

SOCIALIST PROPERTY - USSR

—Soviet law of property : the right to control property and the construction of communism / by George M. Armstrong, Jr. – The Hague : M. Nijhoff Publishers, 1983.
vii,167p.
Includes index. Bibliography: p155-163. Based on the author's thesis (Ph. D.–Princeton).
ISBN 9024728649 Hbk £80.00

SOCIETIES, PERIODICALS, ETC. - GREAT BRITAIN

—Centenary guide to the publications of the Selden Society / Selden Society. – London : The Society, 1987.
242 p. – (Publications).
Supersedes: General guide to the Society's publications (1960).

SOCIOBIOLOGY

—Expanding circle : ethics and sociobiology / Peter Singer. – Oxford : Clarendon Press, 1981.
xii,190p; 22cm.
Includes index.
ISBN 0198246463 £6.95

SOCIOLINGUISTICS

—Linguistic evidence : language, power, and strategy in the courtroom / William M. O'Barr. – New York : Academic Press, 1982.
xv,192p; 24cm.
Bibliography: p182-187. - Includes index.
ISBN 0125235208 £15.60

SOCIOLOGICAL JURISPRUDENCE

—Autopoietic law : a new approach to law and society / edited by Gunther Teubner. – Berlin : W. de Gruyter, 1987.
Includes index and bibliography.

—Case for the conversational analysis of courtroom interaction : some interactional dimensions of legal procedures / by Philip Wilkinson. – Oxford : Centre for Socio-Legal Studies, 1981.
24p. – (Working paper).
Includes bibliographical references.

—Connecting law and society : an introduction to research and theory / Robert L. Kidder. – Englewood Cliffs, N.J. : Prentice-Hall, 1983.
xv,286p; 24cm.
Includes bibliographies and index.
ISBN 0131678094 Unpriced

—Consumer protection, environmental law, and corporate power / Ivan Bernier and Andree Lajoie, research coordinators. – Toronto : University of Toronto Press, 1985.
xv, 220 p.; 23 cm.
'Published ... in cooperation with the Royal Commission on the Economic Union and Development Prospects for Canada and the Canadian Government Publishing Centre, Supply and Services Canada.'. Includes bibliographies.
ISBN 0802072968 pbk.

—Critical legal studies / edited by Peter Fitzpatrick and Alan Hunt. – Oxford : Basil Blackwell, 1987.
197p.
Originally issued as Journal of Law a philosophy, v.14,no.1.
ISBN 0631157182

—Dilemmas of law in the welfare state / edited by Gunther Teubner. – Berlin : W. de Gruyter, 1986.
viii,341p. – (Series A, Law).
Includes bibliographies and index.
ISBN 0899251080

—Disputes and the law / edited by Maureen Cain and Kalman Kulcsar for the European Coordination Centre for Research and Documentation in Social Sciences. – Budapest : Akademiai Kiado, 1983.
Contains a collection of papers given at a seminar held in Dubrovnik at the Inter-University Centre of Postgraduate Studies in September 1979.
ISBN 9630533790

—End of law? / Timothy O'Hagan. – Oxford : Blackwell, 1984.
vii,183p; 23cm.
ISBN 0855205962

—Environment and enforcement : regulation and the social definition of pollution / Keith Hawkins. – Oxford : Clarendon Press, 1983.
xvi,253p.
Includes index. Bibliography: p235-247.
ISBN 0198275145 pbk.

—Essays in law and society / edited by Zenon Bankowski and Geoff Mungham. – London : Routledge & Kegan Paul, 1980.
vii,207p; 24cm.
Includes bibliographies and index.
ISBN 0710004893 Pbk £6.50

—Female sexuality and the law : a study of constructs of female sexuality as they inform statute and legal procedure / Susan S.M. Edwards. – Oxford : Robertson, 1981.
195p; 23cm.
Bibliography: p183-190. - Includes index.
ISBN 085520382X Hbk £12.50
ISBN 0855203854 Pbk £4.95

—In search of law : sociological approaches to law / Vilhelm Aubert. – Oxford : Martin Robertson, 1983.
180p; 22cm.
Bibliography: p174-175. - Includes index.
ISBN 0855204915 Unpriced

—Institutional function and evolution in the criminal process / Richard P. Adelstein. – Oxford : Centre for Socio-Legal Studies, 1980.
126,43p; 21cm. – (Research study).
ISBN 0862260205

—Juridification of social spheres : a comparative analysis in the areas of labor, corporate, antitrust, and social welfare law / edited by Gunther Teubner. – Berlin : De Gruyter, 1987.
viii, 446 p.; 24 cm.
Includes bibliographies and index.
ISBN 0899252729

—Law and social conflict / by Hans-Martin Pawlowski. – Florence : European University Institute, 1983.
19p.
At head of title page: European University Institute, Florence, Department of Political and Social Sciences.

—Law and social control / edited by Eugene Kamenka and Alice Erh-Soon Tay. – London : Edward Arnold, 1980.
ix,198p; 23cm.
Includes index.
ISBN 0713161752 Hbk £8.95
ISBN 0713161760 Pbk £4.95

—Law and society east and west / dharma, li and nomos : by Reinhard May. – Wiesbaden : Franz Steiner, 1985.
251p,9p.
Revised version of the London Doctoral Theses 'An enquiry in comparative jurisprudene. Similarity and disparity between dharma, li, and nomos.'. Bibliography p.227-250. - Includes index.
ISBN 3515045376

—Law drafting and sociology : a seminar report / edited by Antti Kivivuori. – Helsinki : Ministry of Justice, Law Drafting Dept., 1985.
122 p.; 25 cm. – (Publication series / Ministry of Justice, Law Drafting Department).
Includes bibliographical references.
ISBN 9514686764 pbk.

—Law, society, and the economy / Ivan Bernier and Andree Lajoie, research coordinators. – Toronto : University of Toronto Press, 1986.
xv, 230 p.; 23 cm.
Includes bibliographies.
ISBN 0802072917 pbk.

—Law, state and society / edited by Bob Fryer ... et al. – London : Croom Helm, 1981.
234p; 23cm.
Conference papers. Includes bibliographies and index.
ISBN 0709910045 £14.95

—Legal evolution : the story of an idea / Peter Stein. – Cambridge : Cambridge University Press, 1980.
xi,131p; 23cm.
ISBN 0521227836 £9.50

—Legal systems & social systems / edited by Adam Padgorecki, Christopher J. Whelan & Dinesh Khosla. – London : Croom Helm, 1985.
xvii,262p; 23cm.
Includes bibliographies and index.
ISBN 070992075X £18.95

—Legality, ideology and the state / edited by David Sugarman. – London : Academic Press, 1983.
xiv,304p; 24cm.
Includes bibliographies and index.
ISBN 0126760802 Unpriced

—Lon L. Fuller / London : Edward Arnold, 1984.
192p.
ISBN 0713164093 Pbk £9.95

—Modernization and law : theses and thoughts / Kalman Kulcsar. – Budapest : Institute of Sociology, Hungarian Academy of Sciences, 1987.
198p.
Bibliography: pp.181-198..
ISBN 9638301686

—Political economy of law : a third world reader / edited by Yash Ghai, Robin Luckham, Francis Snyder. – Delhi : Oxford University Press, 1987.
xvi,821p.
A view of Indian legal systems as they operate nationally and internationally. Law is analysed in terms of its relationships to economy, the state, political conflict, class, and international relations.
ISBN 0195619919

—Private justice / Stuart Henry. – London : Routledge & Kegan Paul, 1983.
ix,245p.
Includes index. Bibliography: p229-235.
ISBN 0710097034 pbk.

—Rape on trial / Zsuzsanna Adler. – London : Routledge & Kegan Paul, 1987.
viii,195p; 23cm.
Bibliography: p188-192. - Includes index.
ISBN 0710208049 £15.00

—Social justice and individual responsibility in the welfare state / edited by Jan M. Broekman, Kazimierz Opaek, Djangir A.A. Kerimov : preface by Carl Wellman Soziale Gerechtigkeit und individuelle Verantwortlichkeit im Wohlfahrtsstaat / herausgegeben von Jan M. Broekman, Kazimierz Opaek, Djangir A.A. Kerimov ; vorwort von Carl Wellman. – Stuttgart : F. Steiner Verlag Wiesbaden, 1985.
299 p.; 24 cm. – (Archives for philosophy of law and social philosophy).
English, French, and German. 'Eleventh World Congress of the IVR convened in Helsinki 15-20 August 1983'–P. 5. Includes bibliographical references and index.
ISBN 3515044590 pbk. DM35.00

—Socio-legal research in Germany : an account of work in the socio-legal field in the Federal Republic / Geoffrey Wilson : a report to the Social Science Research Council Committee on Social Sciences and the Law. – London : Social Science Research Council, 1980.
115,(21)p.
Bibliography.
ISBN 0862260027

—Socio-legal studies and social welfare / Martin Partington : a report for the Government and Law Committee of the Economic and Social Research Council. – London : Economic and Social Research Council, 1986.
78p.
Bibliography: p59-78.
ISBN 0862261872

—Sociological approaches to law / edited by Adam Podgorecki and Christopher J. Whelan. – London : Croom Helm, 1981.
251p; 23cm.
Includes bibliographies and index.
ISBN 0709927010 £12.95

—Sociology of law / Roman Tomasic. – London : Sage, 1985.
288p.
Includes bibliography and index.
ISBN 0803997167 Pbk £10.00

—Sociology of law : an introduction / Roger Cotterrell. – London : Butterworths, 1984.
xiii,409p; 23cm.
Bibliography: p368-392. - Includes index.
ISBN 0406010684 Hbk No price
ISBN 0406010722 Pbk No price

—Sociology of law and legal anthropology in the Dutch speaking countries / J. van Houtte, editor. – Dordrecht : M. Nijhoff Publishers, 1985.
Bibliography of 'The sociology of law in Dutch-speaking countries': p67-102. Bibliography of 'Current legal anthropology in the Netherlands': p149-162.
ISBN 9024731755

—Solicitors and the wider community / David Podmore. – London : Heinemann, 1980.
xvii,212p.
Includes bibliographies.
ISBN 0435826964

—Substantive and reflexive elements in modern law / by Gunther Teubner. – Florence : European University Institute, 1982.
94p.

—Ungovernable people : the English and their law in the seventeenth and eighteenth centuries / edited by John Brewer and John Styles. – London : Hutchinson, 1983.
400p,4p of plates; 22cm.
Includes index.
ISBN 0091382017 Pbk £6.95

—Verrechtlichung : Begriffe, Merkmale, Grenzen, Auswege / by Gunther Teubner. – Florence : European University Institute, 1984.
104p.
At head of title: European University Institute, Florence, Law Department.

SOCIOLOGICAL JURISPRUDENCE – AUSTRALIA

—Australian journal of law and society / v. – North Ryde : Macquarie University, School of Law, 1982.
ISBN 07293356

—Legislation and society in Australia / edited by Roman Tomasic. – Sydney : The Law Foundation of New South Wales, 1980.
420p.
ISBN 0868610577 Pbk
ISBN 0868610658

SOCIOLOGICAL JURISPRUDENCE – ENGLAND

—Future research programme : 1980- / SSRC Centre for Socio- Legal Studies, Wolfson College, Oxford. – Oxford : Centre for Socio-legal Studies, 1980.
115p.
Includes bibliographies.

—Law and society in England / Bob Roshier and Harvey Teff. – London : Tavistock Publications, 1980.
258p; 23cm.
Bibliography: p226-242. - Includes index.
ISBN 0422767204 Hbk £15.50
ISBN 0422767301 Pbk £7.95

SOCIOLOGICAL JURISPRUDENCE – GREAT BRITAIN

—Annual Report / Centre for Socio-Legal Studies. – v. – Oxford : The Centre, 1984.
Continues: Report of the S.S.R.C. Centre for Socio-Legal Studies.

—Journal of law and society / Oxford : Basil Blackwell, 1974-.
Continues: British journal of law and society.

—Social history and law reform / by O.R. McGregor. – London : Stevens, 1981.
x,66p; 19cm.
Includes index.
ISBN 0420459200 Hbk £9.50
ISBN 0420459308 Pbk £4.25

SOCIOLOGICAL JURISPRUDENCE – PAPUA NEW GUINEA

—Law and social change in Papua New Guinea / editors David Weisbrot, Abdul Paliwala, Akilagpa Sawyerr. – Sydney : Butterworths, 1982.
xxiv, 319p.
'A successor to Fashion of law in New Guinea, edited for Butterworths by B.J. Brown in 1969' - Pref..
Bibliography: p291-301 - Includes index.
ISBN 0409309184

SOCIOLOGICAL JURISPRUDENCE – USSR

—Managing change in the USSR : the politico-legal role of the Soviet jurist / John N. Hazard. – Cambridge : Cambridge University Press, 1983.
ix,182p; 23cm.
'The Goodhart lectures 1982'. Bibliography: p175-177. - Includes index.
ISBN 0521253160 £17.50

SOCIOLOGY

—Development of ethnography in Britain : paper prepared for presentation at the BSA Annual Conference, Lancaster, 1980 / Robert Dingwall, Geoff Payne, Judy Payne. – Oxford : Centre for Socio-Legal Studies, 1980.
19,2p.
Bibliography: p.20-21.

—Power, property and corporatism : the political sociology of planning / James Simmie. – London : Macmillan Press, 1981.
ix,351p.
Bibliography: p.321-345.
ISBN 0333243455

—Rules of sociological method and selected texts on sociology and its method / Emile Durkheim : edited with an introduction by Steven Lukes : translated by W. D. Halls. – London : Macmillan, 1982.
vi,264p.
ISBN 0333280717

—Socio-Legal Problems and Developing Society / New Delhi : Deep and Deep Publications, 1986.
331p.

—Sociolegal Status of Women in India / Delhi : Mittal Publications, 1987.
208p.

SOCIOLOGY – AUSTRALIA

—Law, Capitalism and Democracy : a Sociology of Australian Legal Order / North Sydney : Allen & Unwin, 1983.
180p.
ISBN 0868613819 Pbk £16.95

—Youth and Social Control / Canberra : Australian Institute of Criminology.

SOCIOLOGY – CANADA

—Decade of Adjustment : Legal Perspectives on Contemporary Social Issues / Toronto : Butterworths, 1980.
240p.
ISBN 0409849154 Hbk £31.95

SOCIOLOGY – FRANCE

—Durkheim and modern sociology / Steve Fenton with Robert Reiner and Ian Hamnet. – Cambridge : Cambridge University Press, 1984.
vi,276p; 24cm.
Bibliography: p260-273. - Includes index.
ISBN 0521259231 Hbk £20.00
ISBN 0521277639 Pbk No price

SOCIOLOGY – GREAT BRITAIN

—Child Care and Adult Crime / Ashcraft. – Manchester : Manchester University Press, 1988.
ISBN 0719024692 Hbk £29.50

—Class Power and Urban Policy : Corporations and Labour Unions in City Politics / London : Macmillan, 1982.
256p. – (Sociology, Politics and Cities, Ser.).
ISBN 0333260759 Hbk £12.50
ISBN 0333260767 Pbk £4.95

—Remaking cities : contradictions of the recent urban environment / Alison Ravetz. – London : Croom Helm, 1980.
375p; 23cm.
Bibliography: p349-370. - Includes index.
ISBN 0856642932 £14.95

SOCIOLOGY OF LAW

—Impact of sociology of law on government action: proceedings of a conference on sociology of law, Saarbrucken, Federal Republic of Germany, September 5th-8th, 1977 / Bern : Peter Lang, 1981.
448p.
ISBN 3820461736 Pbk £57.00

—Sociology of law / London : Butterworths, 1984.
ISBN 0406010684 Hbk £17.00
ISBN 0406010722 Pbk £16.95

SOCIOLOGY OF LAW – EUROPE

—European Yearbook in the Sociology of Law 1988 see under 306 / Luxembourg : Office for Official Publications of the European Communities.

SOCIOLOGY OF LAW – GREAT BRITAIN

—Essays in Law and Society / Geoff Mungham. – London : Sweet & Maxwell, 1986.

—Law and Social Change / H. G. Beale. – London : Royal Historical Society, 1984.
– (Studies in History (London) Ser.: Vol. 40).
ISBN 0901050946 Hbk £17.50

SOCIOLOGY OF LAW – PAPUA NEW GUINEA

—Law and Social Change in Papua New Guinea / Paliwala. – London : Butterworths, 1982.
ISBN 0409309184 Pbk £26.00

SOLICITORS - AUSTRALIA - NEW SOUTH WALES

—Fourth report on the legal profession : solicitors' trust accounts / New South Wales Law Reform Commission. - Sydney : The Commission, 1984.
viii,228p. - (L.R.C. 44).
Bibliography: p.212-214. Includes indexes.

—History of Solicitors in New South Wales / Woolloomooloo : International Business Communications, 1984.
ISBN 094955314X Hbk £39.95

SOLICITORS - ENGLAND

—Solicitors and local authorities / by R.J.B. Morris. - Chichester : Rose, 1983.
ciii,349p; 23cm.
Includes index.
ISBN 0859923304 Unpriced

SOLICITORS - GREAT BRITAIN

—PACEA 1984 : Guide for Duty Solicitors / London : Fourmat, 1986.
ISBN 1851900195 Pbk £4.95

—Practical partnership for solicitors / C. Harmer and P. Camp. - 2nd ed. - London : Longman Professional (UK), 1990.
Examines drafting a partnership agreement, taxation, finance, accounts, and matters of professional conduct. Covers the Practice Rules, Publicity Code 1988 and the Introductions and Referrals Code 1988. Includes material on practising abroad, the Overseas Practice Rules 1987, and the effect of the European element and 1992 on the profession. Also deals with Solicitors Incorporated Practice Rules 1988.
ISBN 0851215513 Hbk £29.50

—Practical skills of the solicitor / 2nd ed. - London : Longman Professional, 1985.
- (Practice Today Series).
ISBN 0851209947 Pbk £12.50

—Which firm of solicitors? / 2nd ed. - London : Legalease, 1988.
ISBN 1870854101 Hbk £6.90

SOURCES

—Sources of law, legal change, and ambiguity / Alan Watson. - Edinburgh : T. & T. Clark, 1985.
xviii,164p; 23cm.
Previously published: Philadelphia : University of Pennsylvania Press, 1984.
ISBN 0567093603

SOURCES - ENGLAND

—Law-making process / Michael Zander. - London : Weidenfeld and Nicolson, 1980.
xxvi,309p.
ISBN 0297777505

—Sources of English legal history : law, history and society in England and Wales 1750-1950 / A.H. Manchester. - London : Butterworths, 1984.
xiv,443p; 26cm.
Includes bibliographies and index.
ISBN 0406516596 Unpriced

SOURCES - GREAT BRITAIN

—Select cases of trespass from the King's courts, 1307-1399 / Morris S. Arnold. - London : Selden Society, 1987.
504 p. - (Publications).

SOUTH AFRICA

—Annual report / Department of Development Planning : Constitutional Development Services. - Pretoria : Government Printer, 1987.
Annual reports of two bodies published together. Text in Afikaans and English.

—Beggar your neighbours : apartheid power in Southern Africa / Joseph Hanlon. - London : Catholic Institute for International Relations in collaboration with Currey, 1986.
xi,352p; 24cm.
Includes index.
ISBN 0852553072 Hbk £25.00
ISBN 0946848270 CIIR (pbk) £8.95

—Chronological and subject analysis of South Africa's multilateral and bilateral treaties, 1806-1979 / Jaqueline Audrey Kalley. - Johannesburg : s.n., 1985.
xvi,677 leaves.
Thesis (M.A.) - University of Witwatersrand 1985. Bibliography: p.659-677. - Includes index.

—Mission to South Africa : the Commonwealth report / Malcolm Fraser, Olusegun Obasanjo. - Harmondsworth : Penguin Books for the Commonwealth Secretariat, 1986.
176p.
Co-chairmen: Malcolm Fraser and Olusegun Obasanjo.
ISBN 0140523847

—Natal University law and society review / Durban : University of Natal, 1985.
Continues: Natal University law review.

—United Nations versus South Africa : a legal assessment of United Nations and United Nations related activities in respect of South Africa / Jan C. Heunis. - 1st ed. - Johannesburg : Lex Patria, 1986.
593 p., 1 folded leaf of plates; 25 cm.
: Originally presented as the author's thesis (doctoral–Rand Afrikaans University, 1984). Includes index. Bibliography: p. 583-593.
ISBN 0628030363

SOUTH AFRICA - SOUTH AFRICA

—South Africa in the American mind / Alan Pifer. - Braamfontein : South African Institute of International Affairs, 1981.
17p. - (Commemoration Day Lecture).
ISBN 0909239932

SOVEREIGNTY - GREAT BRITAIN

—Sovereignty / Cambridge : Cambridge University Press, 1986.
ISBN 052133988X Pbk £8.95

SOVEREIGNTY - GRENADA

—Conquest of Grenada : sovereignty in the periphery / M. Shahabuddeen. - Georgetown : University of Guyana, 1986.
xiv,266p.
Includes bibliographical references. Includes the text of the Treaty Establishing the Orgainisation of Eastern Caribbean States.

SOVEREIGNTY - SRI LANKA

—Doctrines of Sovereignty and the Separation of Powers in the Laws of Ceylon / Colombo : Lake House Investments.

SOVIET UNION

—Calendar of Soviet treaties, 1958-1973 / by George Ginsburgs and Robert M. Slusser. - Alphen aan den Rijn : Sijthoff & Noordhoff, 1981.
xx,908p.

—Constitutional development in the USSR : a guide to the soviet constitutions / Aryeh L. Unger. - London : Methuen, 1981.
viii,310p; 22cm.
Bibliography: p297-298. - Includes index. Includes English text of the RSFSR constitution of 1918, and the USSR constitutions of 1924, 1936 and 1977.
ISBN 0416716806 Pbk £13.50
ISBN 0416716903 £7.50

—Soviet law / London : Butterworths, 1983.
ISBN 0406562601 Hbk £19.50

—Soviet Union : The Internal Situation and its Implications for the West / Enstone : Ditchley Foundation, 1982.
- (The Ditchley Conference Reports).

SPACE

—Air and outer space law / Thessaloniki : Institute of International Public Law and International Relations of Thessaloniki, 1981.
xvi,842p.
Includes bibliographies. Includes chapters in French and German.

—Annals of Air and Space Law /. - Montreal : Centre for Research of Air and Space Law, 1980.

Vol. 6 1981.

Vol. 7 1982.

Vol. 8 1983.
570p.

Vol. 9 1984.
583p.

Vol. 10 1985.
609p.

Vol. 11 1986.
484p.

Vol. 12 1987.

—Aspects of space law / E.R.C. van Bogaert. - Deventer : Kluwer, 1985.
ix, 307p.
Includes index. Bibliography: p.287-303.
ISBN 9065440488 Hbk £225.00

—Communications : (includes telecommunications) / Thessaloniki, Greece : Institute of International Public Law and International Relations of Thessaloniki, 1987.
530p.
Includes bibliographical references. Text in English and French.

—Earth-oriented space activities and their legal implications : proceedings of the symposium held on October 15-16, 1981, Centre for Research of Air & Space Law / Les activites spatiales effectuees au service de la terre et leurs implications juridiques. - Montreal : McGill University, 1982.
xii,366p.
English or French texts, English and French preliminaries and closing address.

—International space policy / McIntyre. - Quorum Press, 1988.
ISBN 0899302157 Hbk £39.25

—Law and policy in the space stations' era / Dordrecht : Martinus Nijhoff, 1989.
352. - (Utrecht studies in air and space law 2).
Addresses the policy implications for all current participants in the Space Stations Era. Deals with a constitutional perspective of the treaty-making process in the space field, the optimum framework for management of the US/International Space Station based on a review of the most significant cooperative agreements, and a presentation of commercial issues involved.
ISBN 9024737222 Hbk £52

—Legal definition of outer space / Andrzej Gorbiel. - Lodz : Instytutu Nauk Politycznych, Uniwersytetu Lodzkiego, 1980.
76p. - (Prace miedzyuczelnianego).

—Legality of space militarization / Bruce A. Hurwitz. - Amsterdam : North-Holland, 1986.
xii,252p; 25cm.
Bibliography: p243-252.
ISBN 0444700412 £48.83

—Modern international law of outer space / Pergamon, 1984.
ISBN 0080293670 Hbk £71.40

—Orbit of Space Law / London : Sweet & Maxwell, 1984.
ISBN 0420470107 Hbk £16.00

—Orbit of space law / Damodar Wadegaonkar : foreword by Y.V. Chandrachud. - London : Stevens, 1984.
xii,172p.
Includes index.
ISBN 0420470107

—Outer space and legal liability / by Morris D. Forkosch. - The Hague : Nijhoff, 1982.
xvi,290p.
Includes index. Bibliography: p267-270.
ISBN 9024725828 Hbk £100.00/$43.50

—Outer Space and Military Supremacy : Jurisdiction in International Law / New Delhi : Deep and Deep Publications, 1985.
180p.

—Outer space : new challenges to law and policy / J.E.S. Fawcett. - Oxford : Clarendon, 1984.
vi,169p; 22cm.
Bibliography: p161. - Includes index.
ISBN 0198253982 £16.00

—Pollution of outer space, in particular of the geostationary orbit / W. de Graaff. - Dordrecht : Martinus Nijhoff, 1989.
188. - (Utrecht studies in air and space law).
Survey of the status of the pollution of outer space, dealing with both the scientific and legal aspects. Shows that the emerging international regulations are few, scanty, and in urgent need of elaboration.
ISBN 9024737508 Hbk £39

—Settlement of space law disputes : the present state of the law and perspectives of further development : proceedings of an internat. colloquium, Munich, September 13 and 14, 1979 / organized by the Inst. of Air and Space Law, Univ. of Cologne : ed. by Karl-Heinz Bockstiegel : in cooperation with the Space Law Committee of the Internat. Law Assoc. ... et al. - Koln : Heymann, 1980.
ix, 415 p.; 23 cm.
Includes legislation in English, French and German. Bibliography: p. 201-205.
ISBN 3452187942 pbk. DM148.00

—Soviet military strategy in space / Nicholas L. Johnson. - London : Jane's, 1987.
287p.
ISBN 0710604491

—Space Activities and Emerging International Law / Montreal : Centre for Research of Air and Space Law, 1984.
627p.

—Space activities and emerging international law / edited by Nicolas Mateesco Matte. - Montreal : Centre for Research of Air & Space Law, 1984.
xvii,627p.
Bibliography: p.591-619. - Includes index.
ISBN 0421345802 Hbk £58

—Space Activities and Emerging International Law / Montreal : Centre for Research of Air and Space Law.
627p.

—Space activities and implications : where from and where to at the threshold of the 80's : proceedings of the symposium held on October 16-17, 1980 / Centre for Research of Air & Space Law : d'ou vient-on et ou va-t-on a l'aube des annees 80 : Centre de recherche en droit aerien et spatial. - Montreal : ICASL, McGill University, 1981.
xvi,367p; 24cm.
ISBN 0771700393

—Space debris: legal and policy implications / Dordrecht : Martinus Nijhoff, 1989.
192. – (Utrecht studies in air and space law 6).
Describes the legally relevant aspects of the space debris issue, and analyses the legal and policy implications derived from these facts. Includes discussion of the source of space debris, the risk posed by debris to space activities, and locations of space debris.
ISBN 0792301668 Hbk £43

—Space Law Changes and Expectations at the Turn to Commercial Space Law Activities / Dordrecht : Kluwer, 1987.
32p.
ISBN 9065442561 Pbk £29.50

—Space Policy and Programmes Today and Tomorrow : The Vanishing Duopole / Agincourt : Carswell, 1980.
183p.

—Space policy and programmes today and tomorrow : the vanishing duopole / Nicolas Mateesco Matte. – Montreal : Distributed by ICASL, McGill University, 1980.
xiii, 183 p.; 24 cm.
Bibliography: p. 175-183.
ISBN 0771700148

—United Nations Treaties on Outer Space / Geneva : United Nations Publications.
ISBN 9211002389 Hbk £2.00

—Utilization of outer space and international law / Gijsbertha C.M. Reijnen. – Amsterdam : Elsevier Scientific, 1981.
xvi,179p; 25cm.
Bibliography: p169-171. - Includes index.
ISBN 0444419659 Unpriced

—Utilization of Outer Space and International Law / Amsterdam : Elsevier Science Publishers, 1981.
xvi, 180p.
ISBN 0444419659 Hbk £160.00

—Worldwide Space Law Bibliography / Montreal : De Daro Publishing.
Yearly Update 1988
ISBN 0969270313 Hbk £20.00
Vol. 1: 1900-1976
ISBN 0969270321 Hbk £65.00
Vol. 2: 1976-1986
ISBN 096927033X Hbk £75.00

SPACE - CANADA

—Annals of Air and Space Law-Annales de Droit Aerien et Spatial /. – Agincourt : Carswell.
Vol. 5
Vol. 6
Vol. 7
Vol. 8
Vol. 9
Tenth Anniversary Deluxe Edition
Vol. 11
Vol. 12
This work is an annual collection of leading articles examining problems of present and future interest in the air and space law field.

SPACE WARFARE - USSR

—Soviet military strategy in space / Nicholas L. Johnson. – London : Jane's, 1987.
287p.
ISBN 0710604491

SPACE WEAPONS (INTERNATIONAL LAW)

—Arms Control and Disarmament in Outer Space / Montreal : Centre for Research of Air and Space Law, 1987.
282p.

—Arms control and disarmament in outer space : lecture-seminars given at the Centre for Research of Air and Space Law / edited by Nicolas Mateesco Matte. – Montreal, Canada : Centre for Research of Air and Space Law, McGill University, 1985.
viii, 203 p.; 23 cm.
Includes bibliographical references.
ISBN 0771701233 pbk.

—Space weapons and US strategy / Oxford : Croom Helm, 1985.
ISBN 0709923694 Hbk £25.00

SPECIAL LIBRARIES

—Creating an information service / Sylvia P. Webb : illustrated by Patricia Calderhead. – London : Aslib, 1983.
v,101p; 24cm.
ISBN 0851421865

SPECIFIC PERFORMANCE

—Injunctions and specific performance / by Robert J. Sharpe. – Torontó : Canada Law Book Ltd., 1983.
lxxiv,450p.
ISBN 0888040172

SPECIFIC PERFORMANCE - CANADA

—Injunctions and specific performance / Phil. – Aurora : Canada Law Book, 1983.

SPECIFIC PERFORMANCE - GREAT BRITAIN

—Specific performance / William Goodhart. – London : Butterworths, 1986.
ISBN 0406258090 Hbk £40.00

—Specific performance / Gareth Jones, William Goodhart. – London : Butterworths, 1986.
lxvi,274p; 25cm.
Bibliography: plxv-lxvi. - Includes index.
ISBN 0406258090 £35.00

—Specific Performance of Contracts : Including Those of Public Companies / 5th ed. Repr. of 1911 ed. – Abingdon : Professional Books.
131p.

SPECIFIC PERFORMANCE - NEW ZEALAND

—Rule in White and Carter (Councils) Limited v. McGregor / a report by the Contracts and Commercial Law Reform Committee. – Wellington : Government Printer, 1983.
15p.

SPECULATION

—Futures markets : modelling, managing and monitoring futures trading / edited by Manfred E. Streit. – Oxford : Blackwell, in cooperation with the European University Institute, Florence, 1983.
viii,324p; 24cm.
Includes bibliographies and index.
ISBN 0631132945 Unpriced

SPORT - AUSTRALIA

—Sport and the Law 1985 : Centre for Commercial Law and Applied Legal Research / Monash University, Faculty of Law. – Clayton : Monash University Press.

—Sport and the Law / North Ryde : Law Book Co, 1987.
350p.
ISBN 0455207127 Pbk

SPORT - CANADA

—Sport and Recreation Law in Canada / North Vancouver : International Self-Counsel Press.

—Sport Physical Activity and the Law / Ottawa : Canadian Association for Health, Physical Education and Recreation.

—Sports and Entertainment Law / Vancouver : Continuing Legal Education Society of British Columbia, 1986.
284p.
ISBN 0865042705 Hbk £65.00

—Sports and the Law in Canada / Toronto : Butterworths, 1983.
400p.
ISBN 0409812919 Pbk £40.00

—Sports and the Law in Canada / 2nd ed. – Butterworths, 1988.
416p.
Covers criminal prosecution for hockey violence, collective agreements and labour relations, agents and contract negotiations, government policies in support of sport, discrimination on the basis of sex and nationality, antitrust law aspects of professional league organisation, players' service contracts, public regulation of different sports, tort liability and compensation for sports injuries.
ISBN 0409811815 Pbk £70.00

SPORT - GREAT BRITAIN

—Football Spectator Violence : Report on an Official Working Group / London : HMSO, 1984.
61p.
Report of an official working group. Examines measures available to deal with football-related violence. Stresses the need for co-operation between football and public authorities such as police and central government.
ISBN 0117517496 Hbk £3.80

—Sponsorship / London : Longman Professional (UK), 1987.
– (Longman Intelligence Report).
Looks at the increase in sponsorship expenditure and range of applications, providing guidance to enable companies to realise full marketing potential. Considers aspects of evaluation, setting-up and monitoring of the sponsorship deal.
ISBN 0851213324 Hbk £85.00

—Sponsorship of sport, arts, and leisure : law, tax and business relationships / by Stephen Townley and Edward Grayson : with forewords by Lord Goodman, Dick Jeeps and Sir William Rees-Mogg. – London : Sweet & Maxwell, 1984.
xliii,333p; 23cm.
Guide to the law and tax considerations involved in the business of sponsorship. The legal status of sponsorship rights and licences is interpreted with reference to statute and case law. Intellectual property law, competition law, copyright and the remedies for its infringement, trade-marks, and passing-off are examined.
ISBN 0421304103 £19.75

—Sport and the law / London : Butterworths, 1988.
ISBN 0406253005 Pbk £16.95

—Sport and the law / by Edward Grayson : with forewords by Lord Havers, Denis Howell. – London : Butterworths, 1988.
xviii,376p; 22cm.
Includes index.
ISBN 0406253005 Pbk No price

SPORT AND SAFETY

—Hooligans abroad : the behaviour and control of English fans in Continental Europe / John Williams, Eric Dunning and Patrick Murphy. – London : Routledge & Kegan Paul, 1984.
xiv,230p,12p of plates; 22cm.
Includes index.
ISBN 0710201435 Pbk £8.95

—Skiing and the law / Edinburgh : W Green & Son, 1987.
Covers problems arising from liability for accidents likely to occur in connection with skiing, with reference to past cases incolving skiing and other sports from Scotland, England, France and North America, as well as to the provisions of the Consumer Protection Act.
ISBN 0414008332

SPORT AND SAFETY - GREAT BRITAIN

—Final report / Committee of Inquiry into Crowd Safety and Control at Sports Grounds : Chairman, Mr Justice Popplewell. – London : H.M.S.O., 1984.
85p.
At head of title: Home Office.
ISBN 0101971001

—Guide to safety at sports grounds / London : H.M.S.O., 1986.
75p.
First published 1973.
ISBN 0113408404

—Interim report / Home Office Committee of Inquiry into Crowd Safety and Control at Sports Grounds : Chairman Mr Justice Popplewell. – London : H.M.S.O., 1985.
92p.
Popplewell Inquiry following the Bradford fire, May 1985. Recommends improved police involvement, stricter safety measures, membership-only games and making missile-throwing an offence at sports grounds.
ISBN 0101958501

SQUATTING

—Land, the central human settlement issue / H. Peter Oberlander. – Vancouver : University of British Columbia Press, 1985.
x, 103 p., 4 p. of plates; 24 cm.
Bibliography: p. 93-101.
ISBN 0774802359

SQUATTING - ENGLAND

—Squatting / by A.M. Prichard. – London : Sweet & Maxwell, 1981.
xvi,177p; 19cm.
Includes index.
ISBN 0421267402 Hbk £9.50
ISBN 042126750X Pbk £5.75

SRI LANKA

—Mechanics of constitutional change : the Sri Lankan style / by D.C. Jayasuriya. – Nawala, Sri Lanka : Asian Pathfinder Publishers, 1982.
130p.
Bibliography: p.103-125. - Includes index.

SRI LANKA - SRI LANKA

—Changing the language of the law : the Sri Lanka experience / L. J. Mark Cooray. – Quebec : Presses de l'Universite Laval, 1985.
183p.
ISBN 2763770800

—Sri Lanka : a mounting tragedy of errors: report of a mission to Sri Lanka in January 1984 on behalf of the International Commission of Jurists and its British Section, Justice / Paul Sieghart. – London : International Commission oof Jurists and Justice, 1984.
95p.
Bibliography: p93-94.
ISBN 0907247040

STAMP-DUTY - AUSTRALIA

—Stamp Duty Aspects of Trusts, Settlements and Gifts in Australia / F.P. Zipfinger. – Butterworths, 1984.
367p.
ISBN 0409494216 Hbk £56.00

STAMP-DUTY - ENGLAND

—Butterworths Consolidated Legislation Service /. – Professional Publ.
116p.
ISBN 0409014354 £35.00

STAMP-DUTY - GREAT BRITAIN

—Guide to Stamp Duties / London : CCH, 1987.
ISBN 0863251153 Pbk

—Monroe and Nock The law of stamp duties / R. S. Nock, J. G. Monroe. – 6th ed. – London : Sweet & Maxwell, 1986.
xli,371p; 25cm.
Previous ed.: published as The law of stamp duties. 1976.
Includes index.
ISBN 0421310502 £47.50

—Planning for Stamp Duty Reserve Tax / London : Butterworths, 1987.

—Planning for Stamp Duty Reserve Tax / Ball. – London : Butterworths, 1987.
ISBN 0406051033 Hbk £26.00

—Scope for reforming stamp duties : an Inland Revenue consultative document / Board of Inland Revenue. – London : The Board, 1983.
63p.

—Sergeant and Sims on stamp duties / 9th ed. – London : Butterworths, 1988.
ISBN 0406370435 Hbk £125.00

—Sergeant and Sims on stamp duties and capital duty / B. J. Sims, E. M. E. Sims, R. D. Fulton. – 8th ed. – London : Butterworths, 1982.
li,681p; 26cm. – (Butterworths modern text books).
Previous ed.: 1977. Includes index.
ISBN 0406370354 Unpriced

—Sergeant and Sims on stamp duties and capital duty and stamp duty reserve tax / B. J. Sims, J. F. W. Hinson, E. M. E. Sims, R. D. Fulton. – 9th ed. – London : Butterworths, 1988.
lviii,739p.
Previous ed.: 1982. Includes index. Kept up to date by supplements.
ISBN 0406370435 £110.00 (Jan.)

—Stamp Duties / 3rd ed. – Croydon : Tolley.
240p.
ISBN 0854593683 Hbk £9.95

—Stamp duties and capital duty / B J Sims, J F W Hinson. – London : Butterworths, 1982.
ISBN 0406370354 Hbk £94.00

Supplement-1980 only
ISBN 0406370346 Pbk £75.00

—Stamp duties for conveyancers / Farrand. – 4th ed. – London : Longman Professional, 1986. – (Longman Practice Note. No.48).
ISBN 0851211739 Pbk £15.95

—Stamp Duty Guide / London : Butterworths, 1986.
This practical work for practitioners in the United Kingdom presents a transaction-based analysis of stamp duties. The book explains the administrative procedures involved and discusses how to avoid or minimize the duty wherever possible.
ISBN 0406260303 Pbk

STAMP-DUTY - HONG KONG

—Hong Kong stamp duties / Richards. – London : Longman Professional, 1984.
ISBN 0851208983 Pbk £17.50

STANDARDIZED TERMS OF CONTRACT - SCOTLAND

—Contract law : exchange of standard term forms in contract formation : law reform proposals / Scottish Law Commission. – 2 v. – Edinburgh : The Commission, 1982.
– (Consultation paper).

STATE BANKRUPTCY

—Default and rescheduling : corporate and sovereign borrowers / edited by David Suratgar. – London : Euromoney, in association with International Law Institute, Washington D.C., 1984.
viii,163p.
'Two international conferences, one in London in late 1981 and the other in New York in 1982, provided the basis for this book' - Editor's preface.
ISBN 0903121530

STATE GOVERNMENTS

—Fiscal tiers : the economics of multi-level government / David N. King. – London : Allen & Unwin in association with the Centre for Research on Federal Finance Relations, the Australian National University, 1984.
v,326p; 24cm.
Bibliography: p305-316. - Includes index.
ISBN 0043360815 Hbk Unpriced
ISBN 004336084X Pbk £8.95

STATE GOVERNMENTS - INDIA

—State Autonomy in Indian Federation / New Delhi : Deep and Deep Publications, 1984.
318p.

STATE SECURITY - CANADA

—Freedom and security under the law : second report / Commission of Inquiry Concerning Certain Activities of the Royal Canadian Mounted Police. – 2. – Ottawa : Canadian Government Publishing Centre, 1981.
xxii,1257p; 25cm.
Bibliography: p.1117-1144. Chairman: D.C. McDonald.
ISBN 0660109506 v.2
ISBN 0660109522

—Ministerial responsibility for national security as it relates to the Offices of Prime Minister, Attorney General, and Solicitor General of Canada / by J.Ll.J. Edwards. – Ottawa : Commission of Inquiry Concerning Certain Activities of the Royal Canadian Mounted Police, 1980.
x, 146 p.; 25 cm.
Includes bibliographical references.
ISBN 0660105012 pbk. £5.25 (£6.30 other countries)

—Parliament and security matters / C.E.S. Franks. – Hull, Quebec : Minister of Supply and Services, 1980.
88p.
Includes bibliographical references. A study prepared for the Commission of Inquiry concerning Certain Activities of the Royal Canadian Mounted Police.
ISBN 0660104997

—RCMP and the Management of National Security / Andre Beliveau. – Montreal : Institute for Research on Public Policy.
xiii, 79p.
ISBN 0920380182 Hbk

STATE SECURITY - GREAT BRITAIN

—Brownlie's Law of public order and national security / edited by Michael Supperstone. – 2nd ed. – London : Butterworths, 1981.
lvii,415p.
Previous ed. entitled: The law relating to public order. Includes index.
ISBN 0406137013

—Freedom, State Security and the Rule of Law / London : Sweet & Maxwell, 1988.
ISBN 0421396407 Hbk £36.00

—Law of Public Order and National Security / Supperstone. – 2nd ed. – London : Butterworths, 1981.
ISBN 0406137013 Hbk £49.00

STATE SECURITY - NORWAY

—Norway's Security and European Foreign Policy in the 1980's / Oslo : University of Forlag.
80p.
ISBN 8200057100 Pbk £81.00

—Soviet Union in Artic waters : security implications for the northern flank of NATO / by Willy Ostreng : translated by Eric Hansen from the original Norwegian text. – Honolulu : Law of the Sea Institute, 1987.
ix,77p. – (Occasional paper).
Includes bibliographical references. Translation of: Soviet i nordlige farvann, published by Gylendal Norsk, Oslo, 1982.
ISBN 0911189157

STATE SECURITY - SOUTH AFRICA

—Freedom, state security and the rule of law : dilemmas of the apartheid society / Anthony S. Mathews. – Cape Town : Juta, 1986.
xxv,312p.
Bibliography: p.xi-xiv. - Includes index.
ISBN 0702118125

STATE SUCCESSION

—International law and the new states of Africa : a study of the international legal problems of state succession in the newly independent states of Eastern Africa / by Yilma Makonnen : with a foreword by T.O. Elias. – Addis Ababa : Ethiopian National Agency for UNESCO, 1983.
xxvi, 575 p.; 23 cm.
'Published with the assistance of UNESCO under the Regional Participation Programme for Africa.'. Includes index. Bibliography: p. 541-564.
ISBN 0961193409 pbk. CIP rev.

STATE, THE

—Authority of the state / Leslie Green. – Oxford : Clarendon Press, 1988.
x,273p.
: Revision of thesis (D. Phil.)–University of Oxford, 1984. Includes bibliographic references and index.
ISBN 0198249268

—Bentham and bureaucracy / L.J. Hume. – Cambridge : Cambridge University Press, 1981.
xii,320p; 23cm. – (Cambridge studies in the history and theory of politics).
Bibliography: p303-309. - Includes index.
ISBN 0521235421 £22.50

—Legality, ideology and the state / edited by David Sugarman. – London : Academic Press, 1983.
xiv,304p; 24cm.
Includes bibliographies and index.
ISBN 0126760802 Unpriced

—Rationalism and the modern state / by Patrick Nerhot. – Florence : European University Institute, 1983.
73p.
At head of title: European University Institute, Florence, Law Department.

—Reading Nozick : essays on Anarchy, state and utopia / edited with an introduction by Jeffrey Paul. – Oxford : Basil Blackwell, 1982.
xi,418p; 22cm.
Originally published: Totowa : Rowman & Littlefield, 1981. Bibliography: p412-416.
ISBN 0631129774 Hbk Unpriced
ISBN 0631129782 Pbk Unpriced

—Social contract / Michael Lessnoff. – London : Macmillan, 1986.
x,178p; 23cm.
Bibliography: p169-173. - Includes index.
ISBN 0333367901 Hbk £18.00
ISBN 033336791X Pbk £6.95

—State as defendant : governmental accountability and the redress of individual grievances / Leon Hurwitz. – London : Aldwych Press, 1981.
xv,211p.
Bibliography: p.197-203.
ISBN 0861720172

—State : authority and autonomy / Bill Jordan. – Oxford : Blackwell, 1985.
vi,352p.
Includes bibliography and index.
ISBN 0631142738 £19.50

—States and societies / edited by David Held ... et al. – Oxford : Robertson in association with the Open University, 1983.
x,629p; 23cm. – (An Open University set book).
Includes bibliographies and index.
ISBN 0855206586 Hbk £19.50
ISBN 0855206594 Pbk £5.95

STATE-LOCAL RELATIONS

—Problems of regional and local authorities involved in planning policies : report / prepared under the guidance of the Committee of Experts on Social and Economic Activities of the Steering Committee for Regional and Municipal Matters by Jacques Robert. – Strasbourg : Council of Europe, 1985.
36p.

STATES - NIGERIA

—Legal implications of the creation of more states in Nigeria : being a paper presented at the National Conference on Creation of States in Nigeria / by T. Akinola Aguda. – Ile Ife : Nigerian Institute of Advanced Legal Studies, 1981.
20p; 25cm.

STATES - UNITED STATES

—Subject compilations of state laws 1979-1983 : research guide and annotated bibliography / Cheryl Nyberg and Carol Boast. – Westport : Greenwood, 1984.
x,556p; 24cm.
Includes index.
ISBN 0313233357 No price

STATES, SMALL

—Legal literature in small jurisdictions : a report of a conference held at Osgoode Hall Law School, York University, Downsview, Ontario on 3-5 November 1978 / edited by William Twining and Jenny Uglow for the Canadian Law Information Council, Canada and the Commonwealth Legal Education Association, London. – London : Commonwealth Secretariat, 1981.
188p; 30cm.
Bibliography: p.171-172. - Includes index.
ISBN 085092197X

—Small is dangerous : micro states in a macro world: report of a Study Group of the David Davies Memorial Institute of International Studies / edited by Sheila Harden. – London : Frances Pinter, 1985.
ix,212p.

—Vulnerability : small states in the global society / report of a Commonwealth Consultative Group. – London : Commonwealth Secretariat, 1985.
xii,126p.
Chairman: P. T. Georges.
ISBN 0850922801

STATISTICS

—Crown Court pattern of sentencing : offenders aged 14 and over : being extracts from the Criminal statistics for England and Wales 1971-1978 / by Ian McLean. – Chichester : Barry Rose, 1981.
254p.
ISBN 085992209X

—Women and men in Britain : a research profile / Equal Opportunities Commission. – London : HMSO, 1988.
79p.
Bibliography: pp.74-76. - Includes index.
ISBN 0117013897

STATISTICS - CANADA

—Impact / Ottawa : Ministry of the Solicitor General, 1982-.
Contents: 'a periodical which presents research and statistics about crime and criminal justice'.

—Selected trends in Canadian criminal justice / Research and Statistics Group. – Ottawa : Minister of Supply and Services, 1984.
vi,84p.
ISBN 0660117126

STATISTICS - ENGLAND

—Criminal Statistics England and Wales 1984 / London : HMSO, 1985.
ISBN 010196210X Hbk £12.70

STATISTICS – EUROPE
—European trade unions in figures / Kluwer Law and Taxation, 1989.
Presents a comparative set of data and sources on union membership in ten European countries - Austria, Denmark, France, West Germany, Italy, the Netherlands, Norway, Sweden, Switzerland and the UK. Gives emphasis to comparative definitions of union membership and union density, that is, the ratio of actual to potential memberships.
ISBN 9065444092 Pbk £24.50/Dfl 79

STATISTICS – EUROPEAN COMMUNITY
—Protection of privacy, automatic data processing and progress in statistical documentation / Luxembourg : Office for Official Publications of the European Communities, 1986.
348p. – (Series C).
Eurostat News special edition. 'The papers reproduced in this volume were first presented at an international seminar held under the auspices of the Statistical Office of the European Communities (EUROSTAT) at Luxembourg in December 1984'. - Preface.

STATISTICS – GREAT BRITAIN
—Crime / by Monica A. Walker. – Oxford : Published for the Royal Statistical Society and the Social Science Research Council by Pergamon, 1981.
xii,406p; 26cm.
Bibliography: p281-284. - Includes index. Originally titled: Reviews of United Kingdom statistical sources.
ISBN 0080261043 £18.25

—Criminal Statistics, England and Wales : Supplementary Tables 1980, 4 Vols. / London : Home Office.
ISBN 0862520134 Hbk £18.75

Vol. 2-Proceedings in the Crown Court
ISBN 0862520142 Hbk £12.75

Vol. 3-Tables by Police Force and Some Court Areas
ISBN 0862520142 Hbk £18.75

Vol. 4-Convictions Cautions, D.P.P. Prosecutions, Mentally Disordered Offenders, Appeals Preogative of Mercy, Legal Aid
ISBN 0862520169 Hbk £9.75

—Government statistics : a brief guide to sources / Government Statistical Service. – 1983 ed. – London : Press and Information Service, Central Statistical Office, 1983.
20p.

—Judicial Statistics Annual Report 1983 / Lord Chancellor's Department. – London : HMSO, 1984.
ISBN 0101937008 Hbk £9.10

—Statistics for property people / London : Estates Gazette, 1986.
ISBN 0728200929 Pbk £14.00

—Understanding crime rates : police and public roles in the production of official statistics / Keith Bottomley, Clive Coleman. – Farnborough : Gower, 1981.
ix,170p; 23cm.
Bibliography: p155-160. - Includes index.
ISBN 0566003090 £11.50

—Women and men in Britain : a statistical profile / London : H.M.S.O., 1986.
45p.
ISBN 0117012955

STATISTICS – NIGERIA
—Crime and justice statistics 1985 / Ministry of Finance and Economic Planning, Statistics Division. – Yola, Gongola State : The Ministry, 1986.
vii,85p.
'This issue of the Digest of crime and justice statistics is the first in this series'. - p.i.

STATISTICS – NORTHERN IRELAND
—Commentary on Northern Ireland crime statistics ... / Belfast : HMSO, 1985.

STATISTICS – SCOTLAND
—Civil Judicial Statistics Scotland 1982 / London : HMSO, 1984.
ISBN 0101923503 Hbk £6.35

—Statistical bulletin / Scottish Home and Health Department : prepared by the Government Statistical Service. – v. – Edinburgh : The Department, 1983.
ISBN 02641178

STATISTICS – USSR
—Soviet system of Justice : figures and policy / by Ger P. van den Berg. – The Hague : M. Nijhoff Publishers, 1984.
Includes bibliographical references and index.
ISBN 9024730864

STATISTICS – WALES
—Criminal Statistics England and Wales 1984 / London : HMSO, 1985.
ISBN 010196210X Hbk £12.70

STATUTE OF FRAUDS – CANADA – ALBERTA
—Statute of Frauds and related legislation / Institute of Law Research and Reform. – Edmonton : The Institute, 1985.
iv,88p. – (Report).

STATUTES
—Revised statutes of the Yukon, 1986 : a revision and consolidation fo the statutes of the legislature of the Yukon Territory : proclaimed and published under authority of the Revised Statutes Act / Yukon. – 2. – Whitehorse : Cawley, Queen's Printer, 1986.
Includes index.

—Student's Property Statutes / Repr. of 1927 ed. – Aalen Wuertt : Scientia.
xv, 244p.

STATUTES – AUSTRALIA
—How to Understand An Act of Parliament / 6th ed. – North Ryde : Law Book Co, 1987.
xxxi, 605p.

—Statutes : Rules and Examples / Thomas M. Smith. – 2nd ed. – Butterworths, 1989.
ca 288p.
ISBN 040949397X Pbk £39.00

—Statutes : Rules and Examples / Thomas Smith. – Sydney : Butterworths, 1985.
275p.
This book is designed to teach students how to read and understand statutes and how to apply them to specific sets of circumstances. It describes specific principles and illustrates them with extracts from appropriate cases.
ISBN 0409494232 Pbk

STATUTES – AUSTRALIA – NEW SOUTH WALES
—New South Wales Statutes Annotations, December 1987 / Butterworths, 1988.
1,159p.
ISBN 0409494585 Hbk £150.00

STATUTES – AUSTRALIA – VICTORIA
—Report on the Statute Law Revision Bill / Legal and Constitutional Committee. – Melbourne : Parliament of Victoria, 1983.
iii,12p.

—Report on the Statute Law Revision (Repeals) Bill / Legal and Constitutional Committee. – Melbourne : Parliament of Victoria, 1982.
iii,3p.

—Report to Parliament on a proposal for a Statute Law (Miscellaneous Provisions) Bill / Legal and Constitutional Committee. – Melbourne : Parliament of Victoria, 1985.
xii,189p.

STATUTES – CANADA
—Alphabetical List of Titles of Federal Acts / 4th ed. – Ottawa : Canadian Government Publishing Centre, 1986.
122p.
ISBN 0660531356 Pbk £7.50

—Annual Statutes of Canada (1980-1983), 4 Vols. / Aurora : Canada Law Book Co, Official ed.. – (Statute Services).

—Annual Statutes of Canada : 1984, 2 Vols. / Canada Law Book Publisher. – Aurora : Canada Law Book Co.

—Canada Revised Statutes : 1985, 11 Vols. / Agincourt : Carswell, 1988.

—Canada Statute Annotations (1941-1971) R.S.C. / 1970 Ed. – Aurora : Canada Law Book Co. 523p. – (Statute Services).

—Canada Statute Annotations (R.S.C. 1970) 1941-71, 1 Vol. / Aurora : Canada Law Book Co.
523p.

—Construction of statutes / Elmer A. Driedger. – 2nd ed. – Toronto : Butterworths, 1983.
xvi,385p. – (Canadian legal manual series).
Contains a new chapter on bilingual statutes, and expanded discussion of departure from the ordinary meaning for the professed reason of 'absurdity', and a refinement of the author's commentary on the presumption against retrospective operation.
ISBN 0409828033

—Municipal Act Amendments / Vancouver : British Columbia Continuing Legal Education Society, 1986.
ISBN 0865042586 Hbk £55.00

—Nova Scotia Statute Citator / Agincourt : Carswell.

—Prince Edward Island Annual Bound Statutes, 1975-1980, 1982, 1985-1987 / Agincourt : Carswell.

—Revised Statutes of Canada 1985 / Ottawa : Canadian Government Publishing Centre.

Individual Statutes

—Revised Statutes of Canada, 1985 / Canada Law Book Publisher. – Aurora : Canada Law Book Co.

—Revised Statutes of Canada 1985 / Agincourt : Carswell.

—Saskatchewan Annual Bound Statutes, 1977-1982, 1984-1988 / Agincourt : Carswell.

—Statutes of Saskatchewan Judicially Considered / Agincourt : Carswell.

—Yukon Ordinances, 1972-1982 Annuals : 2nd Session / Agincourt : Carswell.

STATUTES – CANADA – ALBERTA
—Alberta Annual Bound Statutes : 1981-1987 / Agincourt : Carswell.

Subject Index

—Alberta Revised Statutes, 8 Vols. / Agincourt : Carswell, 1980.

—Alberta Revised Statutes Sectional Tables of Concordance : 1970-1980 / Carswell Legal Publications. – Agincourt : Carswell, 1982.
207p.
This book contains the sources of the R.S.A. 1980 s and the disposition of the R.S.A. 1970 s. This book also affords you the opportunity to check and verify updated references with those which have been deleted or superseded from R.S.A. 1980 back to R.S.A. 1970 or from R.S.A. 1970 ahead to R.S.A. 1980.

—Alberta Revised Statutes Sectional Tables of Concordance 1980-1970, 1970-1980 / Agincourt : Carswell, 1982.
207p.

—Alberta Statutes Judicially Considered : Case Annotations, 1980 to Date / Carswell Legal Publications. – Agincourt : Carswell, 1980.

STATUTES – CANADA – BRITISH COLUMBIA
—British Columbia Annual Bound Statutes, 1979-1985 / Agincourt : Carswell.

—British Columbia Revised Statutes : 1979-Up-to-Date, 8 vols. / Agincourt : Carswell, 1985.

—British Columbia Statues Judicially Considered : Case Annotates /. – Agincourt : Carswell.

—British Columbia Statute Citator (1979-Present) / Aurora : Canada Law Book Co. – (Statute Services).

—Sectional Table of Concordance for the Revised Statutes of British Columbia : 1979 / British Columbia Continuing Legal Education Society. – Vancouver : British Columbia Continuing Legal Education Society, 1980.
131p.

—Statutes of British Columbia Judicially Considered / Agincourt : Carswell.

1979-1980

1980 to Date

—Statutes of British Columbia Judicially Considered : Case Annotations, 1 Vol. / Carswell Legal Publications. – Agincourt : Carswell, 1980 to date.
This text contains annotations of the decisions interpreting British Columbia statute law. Included are the Rules of Court, the Acts contained in the Revised Statutes of 1979 and the public statutes enacted since 1979 with cites to all amendments, repeals and new legislation.

STATUTES – CANADA – MANITOBA
—Statutes of Manitoba Judicially Considered / Agincourt : Carswell.
This looseleaf volume includes statutory provisions referred to in a case. It covers the Rules of the Court, the Acts contained in the Revised Statutes of Manitoba 1970, and the public general statutes enacted during the session of 1971 and subsequent sessions.

STATUTES – CANADA – NEW BRUNSWICK
—New Brunswick Statute Citator / Agincourt : Carswell, 1987.
ca 1,250p.

STATUTES – CANADA – NOVA SCOTIA
—Nova Scotia Annual Bound Statutes : 1967-1987 / Agincourt : Carswell.

—Nova Scotia Statute Citator / Agincourt : Carswell, 1985.
610p.
This work focuses on the Revised Statutes of Nova Scotia 1967. It contains the amendments, repeals and consolidation of all public statutes of Nova Scotia since 1967. The statutes are annotated. Brief digests of the interpreting caselaw are included.

STATUTES – CANADA – ONTARIO
—Ontario Annual Bound Statutes 1981-1987 / Agincourt : Carswell.

—Ontario Revised Statutes : 1980, Vols. 1-11 / Agincourt : Carswell.

—Ontario Revised Statutes : Sectional Tables of Concordance 1980-1970, 1970-1980 / Agincourt : Carswell, 1983.
576p.

—Ontario Statute Annotations / R.S.O. 1980 ed. – Aurora : Canada Law Book Co.
1000p. – (Statute Services).

—Ontario Statute Annotations (R.S.O. 1980 Edition) 1930-80 / Aurora : Canada Law Book Co.
1000p.

—Ontario Statute Citator Current Bills Service / Canada Law Book Publisher. – Aurora : Canada Law Book Co.

—Social Work : Annotated Ontario Mental Health Statutes / Agincourt : Carswell, 1988.
358p.

STATUTES - ENGLAND

—Exact Abridgment of All Statutes : Magna Carta, 1641-1666 / 3rd ed. – Abingdon : Professional Books.
566p.

—Halsbury's Statutes of England, 47 Vols. / 2nd ed. – Abingdon : Professional Books.

—Halsbury's statutes of England / Great Britain. – 3rd ed. 53. – London : Butterworths, 1968.
Superseded in part by 4th ed.
ISBN 0406042004

—Statutory interpretation / by the late Sir Rupert Cross. – 2nd ed. – London : Butterworths, 1987.
xviii,206p; 22cm.
Previous ed.: 1976. Includes index.
ISBN 0406570175 Pbk £12.95

STATUTES - GREAT BRITAIN

—Abridgement of the Public Statutes in Force From Magna Carta : In Ninth Year of Henry III to Eleventh Year of George II Inclusive, Continued to First Year of George II inclusive, 2 Vols. / 2nd ed. Repr. of 1762 ed. – Abingdon : Professional Books.
567p.

—Acts of David II 1329-71 / Edinburgh : Edinburgh University Press.
550p. – (Regesta Regum Scottorum Ser.: Vol. 6).
ISBN 0852243952 Hbk £35.00

—Acts of Malcolm IV 1153-1165 / Edinburgh : Edinburgh University Press.
358p. – (Regesta Regum Scottorum Vol. 1).
ISBN 0852241410 Hbk £20.00

—Acts of William I, 1165-1214 / Edinburgh : Edinburgh University Press.
570p. – (Regesta Regum Scottorum Vol. 2).
ISBN 0852241429 Hbk £20.00

—Annual Statutes (Chitty's) 1864-1948, 42 Vols. / Abingdon : Professional Books.

—Butterworth's Annotated Legislation Service : 1939-1981, 280 Vols. / Abingdon : Professional Books.

—Butterworth's Annotated Legislation Service / London : Butterworths.
This service for practitioners provides a working guide to the text of new statutes in the United Kingdom.
ISBN 040654834X Pbk

—Butterworth's Emergency Legislation Service, 158 Vols. / Abingdon : Professional Books, 1984.

—Chronological Table of the Statutes, 2 Vols. / London : HMSO, 1982.
ISBN 0118402323 Hbk £77.00

—Chronological Table of the Statutes, 2 Vols. / London : HMSO, 1983.
ISBN 0118402439 Hbk £84.00
ISBN 0118402552 Hbk £95.00

—Collection of Acts and Records of Parliament : With Reports of Cases in Courts of Law and Equity (1224-1800) Respecting Tithes, 4 Vols. / Repr. of 1801 ed. – Abingdon : Professional Books.
192p.

—Collection of Statutes Connected With the General Administration of Law, 8 Vols. / Repr. of 1817 ed. – Abingdon : Professional Books.
116p.

—Complete Guide for Justices of the Peace : Containing the Common and Statute Laws and Most Authentic Precedents Which Concern the Same / Repr. of 1687 ed. – Abingdon : Professional Books.

—Current Law Back Volumes : Current Law Statutes Annotated 1981, 2 Vols. / London : Sweet & Maxwell, 1982.
ISBN 0421301406 Hbk £36.00

—Current Law Statutes / London : Sweet & Maxwell, 1984.
ISBN 0999000132 Hbk £42.00

1983.
ISBN 0999000131 Hbk £30.00

1987.
ISBN 0999000135 Hbk

1981.
ISBN 0999000129 Hbk £36.00

1985.
ISBN 0999000133 Hbk £45.00

1986.
ISBN 0999000134 Hbk £50.00

1980.
ISBN 0999000128 Hbk £36.00

1982.
ISBN 0999000130 Hbk £30.00

—Current Law Statutes Annotated 1979, 2 Vols. / London : Sweet & Maxwell, 1980.
ISBN 0421269006 Hbk £30.00

—Current Law Statutes Annotated : 1982 / London : Sweet & Maxwell, 1983.
ISBN 0421314702 Hbk £30.00

—Current Law Statutes Annotated 1983 / London : Sweet & Maxwell, 1984.
ISBN 0421325402 Hbk £30.00

—Current Law Statutes Annotated 1984, 4 Vols. / London : Sweet & Maxwell, 1985.
ISBN 0421337907 Hbk £42.00

—Current Law Statutes Annotated Nineteen Eighty, 2 Vols. / London : Sweet & Maxwell, 1981.
ISBN 042128420X Hbk £36.00

—Halsbury's statutes of England and Wales / managing editor Paul Brown. – 4th ed. 50 v. – London : Butterworths, 1985.
With Users guide and Alphabetical list of statutes. Updating service.
ISBN 0406214093

—Index to statutes in force / London : Sweet & Maxwell, 1988.
ISBN 0421317809 Hbk

—Lawes and Acts of Parliament Made by King James the First and His Successours Kinges of Scotland : 1424-1597 / Repr. of 1597 ed. – Abingdon : Professional Books.
116p.

—Laws and Acts Made in the First Parliament of Queen Anne / Repr. of 1702 ed. – Abingdon : Professional Books.
115p.

—Laws and Acts of Parliament : James VII-Anne (1685-1707) / Repr. of 1731 ed. – Abingdon : Professional Books.
117p.

—Laws and Acts of Parliament Made by James I-Charles II : 1424-1681 / Repr. of 1681 ed. – Abingdon : Professional Books.
116p.

—Laws and Acts of Parliament Made by King James I and Royal Successors : 1424-1621 / Repr. of 1682 ed. – Abingdon : Professional Books.
116p.

—Observations on the Acts of Parliament / Repr. of 1686 ed. – Abingdon : Professional Books.
74p.

—Public General Acts and Measure 1983, 3 Vols. / London : HMSO.
ISBN 011840234X Hbk £127.00

Tables and Index 1983
ISBN 0118402358 Pbk £20.00

—Public General Statutes : 1831-1979 / Abingdon : Professional Books.

—Real Property Statutes : Based on Shelford's Real Property Statutes / 2nd ed. – Abingdon : Professional Books, 1984.

—Statute law / 3rd. – London : Longman Professional (UK), 1990.
Investigation of the processes involved in creating statute law, with analysis of the problems resulting. New edition revised to take account of new European Community law, the Law Commission's report on the codification of criminal law, and amendments to the Interpretation Act 1978.

—Statute law / F.A.R. Bennion. – London : Oyez, 1980.
xxii,276p; 22cm.
Bibliography: p265-267. - Includes index.
ISBN 0851205445 £10.00

—Statute law / F. A. R. Bennion. – 2nd ed. – London : Oyez Longman, 1983.
xxvi,339p; 21cm.
Previous ed.: 1980.
ISBN 0851208029

—Statute Law Review / London : Sweet & Maxwell.

Bound Vol.

Back Vols. avail.

—Statutes for the Law Society Finals / London : Sweet & Maxwell, 1985.
ISBN 0421325208 Pbk £16.95

—Statutes in Force, 90 Vols. / London : HMSO.

Back Vols. avail. Index to the Statutes
ISBN 0118402374 Hbk £133.00

—Statutes in Force : Index / London : Sweet & Maxwell.
ISBN 0421317809 Hbk

—Statutory variations / Routledge, 1983.
ISBN 0710093489 Hbk £17.95

—Sweet & Maxwell's Statutes for the Law Society finals / advisory editors, Alasdair Benzie, Christine Elgey, Alastair Murdie : edited by Sweet & Maxwell's legal editorial staff and Robert Spicer. – London : Sweet & Maxwell, 1985.
620p; 24cm.
Includes index.
ISBN 0421325208 Pbk £16.95

STATUTES - INDIA

—Intepretation of Statutes / 7th ed. – Allahabad : Law Book Company, 1984.
400p.

STATUTES - IRELAND

—Acts and Statutes Made in a Parliament Began at Dublin 1769 / Repr. of 1770 ed. – Abingdon : Professional Books.

—Irish Current Law Statutes Annotated / London : Sweet & Maxwell, 1984.
ISBN 0421327405 Hbk £250.00

STATUTES - NEW ZEALAND

—New Zealand Statutes / Butterworths.

—New Zealand Statutes : Current Reprint / Wellington : Butterworths.

—New Zealand Statutes : Current Reprint / Butterworths.

—Public Acts of New Zealand : 1908-date / Professional Books Staff. – Abingdon : Professional Books, 1984.

STATUTES - NEWFOUNDLAND

—Newfoundland Annual Bound Statutes 1971-1986 / Agincourt : Carswell.

STATUTES - NIGERIA

—Nigeria-Federal Statutes in Force 1982 : An Index of the Laws of Nigeria Which Are Still in Force As At the 31st December 1984 / Abingdon : Professional Books, 1984.
ISBN 0862050731 Hbk £24.00

—Nigeria Index to Federal Statutes in Force 1984 / Abingdon : Professional Books, 1985.
ISBN 0862050731 Hbk £19.25
ISBN 0862052009 Pbk £11.00

—Nigerian Current Law Statutes Annotated 1958-1983 / Aba : Law & Educational Publishers.
ISBN 9782436011 Hbk

STATUTES - SCOTLAND

—Elucidations Respecting the Common and Statute Law of Scotland / Repr. of 1800 ed. – Abingdon : Professional Books.
56p.

—Fourth programme of consolidation and statute law revision / Scottish Law Commission. – Edinburgh : H.M.S.O., 1982.
10p.
ISBN 0102516820

—Scots Conveyancing Statutes 1984 / Edinburgh : W Green.
ISBN 0414007484 Hbk £9.75

—Scots Court Statutes 1983 : Reprinted from the Parliament House Book / Edinburgh : W Green, 1983.
ISBN 0414007212 Hbk £21.50

—Scots Courts Statutes Civil 1985 / Edinburgh : W Green.
– (Reprint from Parliament House Book).
ISBN 0414007719 Hbk £19.50

—Scots Courts Statutes Criminal 1985 / Edinburgh : W Green.
– (Reprint from Parliament House Book).
ISBN 0414007727 Hbk £8.50

—Scots Mercantile Law Statutes 1984 / Edinburgh : W Green.
ISBN 0414007441 Hbk £29.25

—Scots Mercantile Law Statutes 1984 / Edinburgh : W Green.
– (Reprint from Parliament House Book).
ISBN 0414007689 Hbk £18.00

—Scots Statutes 1983 : Family Law; Succession, Trusts, Liferents and Judicial Factors / Edinburgh : W Green, 1983.
ISBN 0414007255 Hbk £6.50

—Scots Statutes 1984 : Family Law; Succession, Trusts, Liferents and Judicial Factors / Edinburgh : W Green.
ISBN 041400745X Hbk £14.75

—Statute Law of Scotland : Abridged with Historical Notes / Repr. of 1757 ed. – Abingdon : Professional Books.
57p.

STATUTES - SOUTH AFRICA

—Acta Juridica / W. H. B. Dean. – Kenwyn : Juta & Co, 1986.

Back issues avail. since 1958

—Interpretation of Statutes / Durban : Butterworths.

—Statutes of the Republic of South Africa / I. Isaacs. – Durban : Butterworths.

STATUTES - SWEDEN

—Swedish Statutes, 3 Vols. / Anders Victorin. – Abingdon : Professional Books, 1984. – (Law and the Weaker Party : An Anglo-Swedish Comparative Study Ser.).
ISBN 0862050456 Hbk £21.00

STATUTES - UNITED STATES

—Common law for the age of statutes / Guido Calabresi. – Cambridge, Mass. : Harvard University Press, 1982.
319p; 24cm.
Bibliography: p300-309. - Includes index.
ISBN 0674146042 Unpriced

STATUTORY INTERPRETATION - AUSTRALIA

—Another Look at Statutory Interpretation / Attorney-General's Department. – Canberra : Australian Government Publishing Service, 1982.
32p.
ISBN 0642068895 Hbk £2.00

—Statutory Interpretation in Australia / 3rd ed. – Butterworths, 1988.
288p.
ISBN 0409495255 Hbk £49.00
ISBN 0409308102 Pbk £42.00

STATUTORY INTERPRETATION - GREAT BRITAIN

—Statutory interpretation / 2nd ed. – London : Butterworths, 1987.
ISBN 0406570175 Hbk £11.95

—Statutory interpretation / London : Butterworths, 1984.
ISBN 0406259208 Hbk £95.00

STATUTORY INTERPRETATION - INDIA

—Principles of Statutory Interpretation / 3rd ed. repr. 1984. – New Delhi : Bharat Law House.
lxxx, 664p.

STATUTORY INTERPRETATION - NEW ZEALAND

—Statutory interpretation : problems in communication / Auckland : Oxford University Press (NZ), 1989.
256.
An introduction to statutory interpretation, dealing with common problems in the application of statutes to particular cases and with the common law method of statutory interpretation.
ISBN 019558189X Pbk £20.00

STERILITY

—Legislation on human infertility services and embryo research : a consultation paper / Department of Health and Social Security. – London : H.M.S.O., 1987.
15p.
ISBN 0101004621

STERILITY - GREAT BRITAIN

—Human fertilisation and embryology : a framework for legislation / presented to Parliament by the Secretary of State for Social Services ...et al. by Command of Her Majesty November 1987. – London : H.M.S.O., 1987.
20p.
ISBN 0101025920

STOCK COMPANIES

—Acts and orders relating to joint stock companies / by George R. Harding. – Brisbane : Watson, Ferguson, 1887.
xxviii,239p.
Includes index.

STOCK COMPANIES - GREAT BRITAIN

—Companies Acts : table A 1856-1981 / edited by R.W. Ramage. – London : Butterworths, 1982.
xviii,160p; 23cm.
'Contains the full text of each version of Table A preceded by all relevant extracts from the Act or instrument containing or ... amending it' - Introd..
ISBN 0406351236

STOCK EXCHANGE

—New financial instruments / by Ian Cooper ... et al. – London : Chartered Isntitute of Bankers, 1987.
x,89p.
Includes bibliographical references.
ISBN 0852971907

—Rules and regulations of the Stock Exchange / Stock Exchange. – 1. – London : Council of the Stock Exchange, 1973.
Published by authority of the Council of the Stock Exchange.

STOCK EXCHANGE - AUSTRALIA

—Introduction to the securities industry codes / by R. Baxt...et al. : assisted by an advisory panel from the Securities Institute of Australia. – 2nd ed. – Sydney : Butterworths, 1982.
xxvi,316p.
Previous ed.: published as 'An introduction to securities industry acts', 1977. Includes bibliographical references and index.
ISBN 0409303402

STOCK EXCHANGE - CANADA

—Toronto Stock Exchange : a Procedural Guide for Companies and Their Professional Advisers / Butterworths, 1986.
576p.
ISBN 0409805998 Hbk £95.00

—Vancouver Stock Exchange : Listings, Rules and Policies / Elizabeth Watkins. – Toronto : Butterworths, 1988.
230p.
ISBN 0409809497 Hbk

STOCK EXCHANGE - CANADA - BRITISH COLUMBIA

—Vancouver Stock Exchange : 1988 Update: Timely Material Corporate Disclosure / Vancouver : Continuing Legal Education Society of British Columbia, 1988.
91p.
ISBN 086504998X Hbk £70.00

—Vancouver Stock Exchange Practice for Legal Assistants / Vancouver : Continuing Legal Education Society of British Columbia, 1986.
429p.
ISBN 0865042764 Hbk £65.00

STOCK EXCHANGE - EUROPEAN COMMUNITY

—Legal harmonization and the business enterprise : corporate and capital market law, harmonization policy in Europe and the U.S.A. / by Richard M. Buxbaum and Klaus J. Hopt. – Berlin : De Gruyter, 1988. – (Series A–Law).
Includes index. Bibliography.
ISBN 0899251277 Hbk £96.00

STOCK EXCHANGE - GREAT BRITAIN

—Admission of securities to listing / Stock Exchange. – New loose-leaf ed. Nov. 1984. – London : Council of the Stock Exchange, 1984.
1 v. (loose-leaf).
Includes index.
ISBN 0900872195

—Beginners' Guide To The Stock Market / Penguin, 1986.
ISBN 0140093931 Pbk £3.95

—Big Bang / by Ian M. Kerr. – London : Euromoney Publications, 1986.
180p.
ISBN 187003130X

—Big Bang / Ritchie. – Northcote House, 1988.
ISBN 0746305494 Pbk £4.95

—Bigger Bang / Waterlow, 1987.
ISBN 0080331009 Pbk £5.50

—Company Flotations - Tax and Planning / Cane. – London : Butterworths, 1985.
ISBN 0406259704 Pbk £20.00

—Conflicts of interest in the changing financial world / edited by R.M. Goode. – 1. – London : Institute of Bankers, 1986.
22cm.
Conference proceedings. Includes index.
ISBN 0852971672 £22.75

—Crash and The Coming Crisis / Northcote House, 1988.
ISBN 0746305435 Pbk £4.95

—Crash of 87 / Oxford : Bloomsbury, 1988.
ISBN 0747502137 Hbk £13.95

—Inside the new gilt-edged market / 2nd ed. – Cambridge : Woodhead-Faulkner, 1987.
ISBN 0859413462 Hbk £25.00

—Regulating the city / Open University Press, 1986.
ISBN 0335153828 Pbk £7.95

—Regulations of the International Stock Exchange, 31st May 1988 / International Stock Exchange of the United Kingdom and Republic of Ireland. – London : International Stock Exchange, 1988.
ca. 175p.
Supersedes The Sock Exchange regulations.

—Rules of the International Stock Exchange, 31st May 1988 / International Stock Exchange of the United Kingdom and Republic of Ireland. – London : International Stock Exchange, 1988.
ca. 100p.
Supersedes the Stock Exchange rules.

—Securitisation / Scott. – Cambridge : Woodhead-Faulkner, 1988.
ISBN 0859414167 Hbk £40.00

—Stock Exchange Listing : new requirements / London : Butterworths, 1985.
ISBN 0406337004 Hbk £28.00

—Stock exchange listing : the new requirements / Robert R. Pennington. – London : Butterworths, 1985.
ix,199p; 26cm.
Includes the text of The Stock Exchange (Listing) Regulations 1984.
ISBN 0406337004 No price

—Stock Exchange regulations / Stock Exchange. – London : Council of the Stock Exchange, 1985.
looseleaves in binder; 23cm.
Superseded by Regulations of the International Stock Exchange.

—Stock Exchange rules / Stock Exchange. – London : Council of the Stock Exchange, 1984.
1 v. (loose-leaf).
Superseded by Rules of the International Stock Exchange. Includes index. Published by authority of the Council of the Stock Exchange.

—Stockbroking tomorrow / London : Macmillan, 1985.
ISBN 0333219945 Hbk £27.50

—Trading in currency options / Cambridge : Woodhead-Faulkner, 1987.
ISBN 0859413233 Hbk £45.00

—Trading in gold futures / Cambridge : Woodhead-Faulkner, 1985.
ISBN 0859412687 Hbk £25.00

—Trading in options / 2nd ed. – Cambridge : Woodhead-Faulkner, 1982.
ISBN 0859412180 Hbk £16.95

—Trading in soft commodity futures / Cambridge : Woodhead-Faulkner, 1985.
ISBN 0859412393 Hbk £25.00

STOCK EXCHANGE - HONG KONG

—Investor Prot., Corp. Disclosure and Insider Dealing in HK / London : Butterworths, 1988.
ISBN 0409995460 Hbk

STOCK EXCHANGE - IRELAND

—Regulations of the International Stock Exchange, 31st May 1988 / International Stock Exchange of the United Kingdom and Republic of Ireland. – London : International Stock Exchange, 1988.
ca. 175p.
Supersedes The Sock Exchange regulations.

—Rules of the International Stock Exchange, 31st May 1988 / International Stock Exchange of the United Kingdom and Republic of Ireland. – London : International Stock Exchange, 1988.
ca. 100p.
Supersedes the Stock Exchange rules.

STOCK EXCHANGE - NETHERLANDS

—Netherlands Securities Trading Act and Securities Trading Decree : with supplementary regulations and official commentary / a translation by H.C.S. Warendorf and R.L. Thomas : with the assistance of the Amsterdam Stock Exchange, and with an introduction by F.G.B. Graaf. – Deventer Netherlands : Kluwer Law and Taxation Publishers, 1986.
152p.
ISBN 9065442774 Pbk £50.00

STOCK EXCHANGE - UNITED STATES

—Legal harmonization and the business enterprise : corporate and capital market law, harmonization policy in Europe and the U.S.A. / by Richard M. Buxbaum and Klaus J. Hopt. – Berlin : De Gruyter, 1988. – (Series A–Law).
Includes index. Bibliography.
ISBN 0899251277 Hbk £96.00

STOCK OWNERSHIP - CANADA

—Legal Problems Relating to Shareholders' Agreements / Vancouver : British Columbia Continuing Legal Education Society, 1982.
106p.
ISBN 0865040613 Hbk £12.50

STOCK OWNERSHIP - GREAT BRITAIN

—Consolidated Gold Fields Limited : investigation under section 172 of the Companies Act 1948 : report / by Bryan James Welch and Michael Charles Anthony Osborne for the Department of Trade. – London : H.M.S.O., 1980.
1v.(various pagings).
ISBN 0115129987

—Rules governing substantial acquisition of shares : restrictions of market raids / Council for the Securities Industry. – Rev. ed. – London : The Council, 1982.
15p. – (CSI).

—Shareholders' agreements / Graham Stedman, Janet Jones. – London : Longman, 1986.
xvii,396p; 24cm. – (Longman commercial series).
Includes index.
ISBN 0851210252 £42.50

STOCK OWNERSHIP - SOUTH AFRICA

—Company Share Register / Cape Town : Legal & Financial Publishing, 1983. – (Merlen Ser. of Registers).

STOCK PURCHASE AGREEMENTS (CLOSE CORPORATIONS) - CANADA

—Stock purchase agreements / by Alain John Gaucher. – Toronto, Canada : Carswell, 1984.
xxvii, 286 p.; 24 cm.
Includes index. Bibliography: p. 275-280.
ISBN 045935910X

STOCK TRANSFER - ENGLAND

—Warranties and indemnities on share sales / Neil Sinclair. - London : Oyez Longman, 1984.
xxiv,331p.
Includes index.
ISBN 0851208703

STOCK TRANSFER - GREAT BRITAIN

—Company's purchase of own shares : Section 53 and Schedule 9 Finance Act 1982 / Inland Revenue. - London : Inland Revenue, 1982. - (Statement of practice).

STOCK TRANSFER - MALAYSIA

—Share (Land Based Company) Transfer Tax Act, 1984 (Act 310) / Kuala Lumpur : International Law Books Services.

STOCKHOLDERS - CANADA

—Legal Problems Relating to Shareholders' Agreements / Vancouver : British Columbia Continuing Legal Education Society, 1982.
106p.
ISBN 0865040613 Hbk £12.50

—So You Want a Fight! : Shareholder Rights and Remedies in Canada / North Ryde : C.C.H. Australia, 1986.
195p.
ISBN 0887963668 Pbk £16.95

STOCKS AND SHARES

—International Buffer Stocks : Theory and Practice / Bern : Peter Lang, 1983.
xxix, 342p.
ISBN 3261033185 Pbk £66.00

—Taxation of corporations and shareholders / Martin Norr. - Deventer, Netherlands : Kluwer Law and Taxation Publishers, 1982.
xii, 214 p.; 25 cm.
On page opposite t.p.: International Tax Program, Harvard Law School. Bibliography: p. 199-214.
ISBN 9065440151

STOCKS AND SHARES - AUSTRALIA

—Insider Trading Legislation for Australia : an Outline on the Issues and Alternatives / Kingston : Australian Government Publishing Service.

—Securities Law Seminar Insider Training 1985 : Centre for Commercial Law and Applied Legal Research / Monash University, Faculty of Law. - Clayton : Monash University Press.
ISBN 0867463856 Hbk £17.00

STOCKS AND SHARES - CANADA

—Private Placements in Canada / William K. Orr. - Agincourt : Carswell, 1985.
224p.
This book discusses essential statutory concepts, private placement exemptions, offering memoranda, rules governing secondary trading, stock exchange requirements, and other issues pertaining to private placements under Canadian securities law.

—So You Want a Fight! : Shareholder Rights and Remedies in Canada / North Ryde : C.C.H. Australia, 1986.
195p.
ISBN 0887963668 Pbk £16.95

STOCKS AND SHARES - ENGLAND

—Butterworths Consolidated Legislation Service /. - Professional Publ.
40p.
ISBN 0409014680 £25.00

STOCKS AND SHARES - GREAT BRITAIN

—Beginners' Guide To The Stock Market / Penguin, 1986.
ISBN 0140093931 Pbk £3.95

—Company acquisition of own shares / Michael Wyatt. - London : Oyez Longman, 1983.
xviii,138p; 22cm.
Includes index.
ISBN 0851207189 Pbk Unpriced

—Company acquisition of own shares / Michael Wyatt. - London : Longman, 1986.
180p; 22cm.
New ed.: Previous ed.: 1983. Includes index.
ISBN 0851212506 Pbk £19.95

—Company Purchase of Own Shares / London : Oyez Longman, 1983.

—Company Securities (Insider Dealing) Act 1985 / London : HMSO.
16p.
ISBN 0105408859 Pbk £2.25

—Convertibles and Warrants / London : Euromoney, 1987.
ISBN 1870031202 Pbk £75.00

—Director's duties and insider dealing / Philip L.R. Mitchell. - London : Butterworths, 1982.
xxiv,268p; 22cm.
Includes index.
ISBN 0406295808 Pbk Unpriced

—Directors' Duties and Insider dealing / London : Butterworths, 1982.
ISBN 0406295808 Pbk £14.50

—Disclosure of interests in shares : a consultative document / Department of Trade. - London : The Department, 1980.
20p.

—Focus on Purchase & Sale of Private Co's Shares / 2nd ed. - Croydon : Tolley, 1985.
ISBN 0854591850 Pbk £8.95

—Guide to perks from shares / Franks. - London : Kogan Page, 1988.
ISBN 185095237 Pbk

—Index-Linked Gilts / Cambridge : Woodhead-Faulkner, 1985.
ISBN 085941289X Hbk £30.00

—Inside the new gilt-edged market / 2nd ed. - Cambridge : Woodhead-Faulkner, 1987.
ISBN 0859413462 Hbk £25.00

—Inside the over-the-counter market / Cambridge : Woodhead-Faulkner, 1985.
ISBN 08593413095 Hbk £25.00

—Insider dealing / London : Butterworths, 1988.
ISBN 1862052573 Hbk

—Insider dealing : guidance for members following the Companies Act 1980 / London : Institute of Directors, 1981.
21p; 22cm.

—Investment in Shares and Securities / London : Butterworths, 1988.
ISBN 0406504504 Pbk £40.00

—Investment in Shares and Securities and Financial Aspects / London : Butterworths, 1987.
ISBN 0406504504 Pbk

—Options / London : Euromoney, 1987.
ISBN 1870031563 Pbk £75.00

—Options / Cambridge : Woodhead-Faulkner, 1988.
ISBN 0859414418 Hbk £35.00

—Perks from shares / 2nd ed. - London : Kogan Page, 1985.
ISBN 0850389461 Hbk £8.95
ISBN 085038947X Pbk £4.95

—Personal Equity Plans / Telegraph Publications, 1988.
ISBN 0863672299 Pbk £5.95

—Personal Equity Plans / Cambridge : Woodhead-Faulkner, 1987.
ISBN 0859414191 Pbk £4.95

—Practical Share Valuation / Harry Booth. - London : Butterworths, 1983.
This book provides a practical guide to valuation questions for purposes of tax assessment for practitioners in the United Kingdom. Share valuation, whether that of a private or a public company, often requires negotiation with the Inland Revenue and this manual explores the many issues raised by such negotiations.
ISBN 0406190143 Hbk

—Practical Share Valuation / 2nd ed. - London : Butterworths, 1987.
ISBN 0406190151 Hbk

—Practical share valuation / Booth. - 2nd ed. - London : Butterworths, 1987.
ISBN 0406190143 Hbk £26.00

—Purchase by a Company of its Own Shares / Deloitte Haskins and Sells Staff. - London : Butterworths, 1983.
ISBN 0406252688 Pbk £16.25

—Purchase by a company of its own shares : a consultative document / presented to Parliament by the Secretary of State for Trade .. - London : H.M.S.O., 1980.
iii,42p; 25cm.
ISBN 0101794401 sd £2.25

—Rights of shareholders / 1st. - Oxford : Blackwell Scientific, 1990.
275. - (Blackwell Law Library).
Discusses the exercise of power and control over companies and explains the principles and structure of shareholders rights. Reference is made to European Community proposals for the harmonisation of company law. Considers in some detail self-regulatory codes such as the Stock Exchange 'Yellow Book' and the City Code on Take-Overs and Mergers.*Practitioners, Financial advisers*
ISBN 0632012489 Hbk £35

—Securitisation / Scott. - Cambridge : Woodhead-Faulkner, 1988.
ISBN 0859414167 Hbk £40.00

—Share Capital : Company Law and Taxation / David Bellringer. - London : Butterworths, 1984.
ISBN 0406258163 Hbk

—Share capital : company law and taxation / David Bellringer. - London : Butterworths, 1984.
ISBN 0406258163 Hbk £19.50

—Share options and incentives for directors and employees / Tolley Publishing, 1986.
ISBN 085459180X Pbk £7.95

—Share schemes for directors and employees / London : Butterworths, 1985.
ISBN 0406501203 Pbk £29.95

—Share Valuation Cases / Harry Booth. - London : Butterworths, 1985.
This work is a compendium of extracts from judgements in cases which deal with principles of share valuation in the United Kingdom. The case extracts are presented in alphabetical order.
ISBN 0406009805 Hbk

—Share valuation cases / Harry Booth. - London : Butterworths, 1985.
ISBN 0406009805 Hbk £67.50

—Share valuation handbook / London : Fourmat, 1986.
ISBN 0906840988 Pbk £12.95

—Statement on insider dealing / Council for the Securities Industry. - London : The Council, 1981.
7p. - (CSI).

—Stock Relief / David Williams. - London : Oyez Longman, 1981.
- (Oyez Longman Practical Tax Ser.).
ISBN 0851205852 Hbk £9.95

—Stockbroking tomorrow / London : Macmillan, 1985.
ISBN 0333219945 Hbk £27.50

—Tolley's Focus on the Purchase and Sale of a Private Company's Shares / 2nd ed. - Croydon : Tolley.
152p.
ISBN 0854591850 Hbk £6.95

—Trading financial options / London : Butterworths, 1986.
ISBN 0406100470 Hbk £27.50

—Trading in commodities / 4th ed. - Cambridge : Woodhead-Faulkner, 1983.
ISBN 0859411788 Pbk £10.95
ISBN 0859411796 Hbk £19.95

—Trading in options / 2nd ed. - Cambridge : Woodhead-Faulkner, 1982.
ISBN 0859412180 Hbk £16.95

—Unit trusts / 3rd ed. - Cambridge : Woodhead-Faulkner, 1982.
ISBN 0859412083 Pbk £9.95
ISBN 0959412091 Hbk £17.95

—Warranties and indemnities on share sales / London : Longman Professional, 1984.
ISBN 0851208703 Hbk £29.00

STOCKS AND SHARES - HONG KONG

—Investor Prot., Corp. Disclosure and Insider Dealing in HK / London : Butterworths, 1988.
ISBN 0409995460 Hbk

STOCKS AND SHARES - NEW ZEALAND

—Capital dividends / report of the Property Law and Equity Reform Committee. - Wellington? : the Committee?, 1984.
8,13p,1 leaf,2p.

STOCKS AND SHARES - SOUTH AFRICA

—Company Share Register / Cape Town : Legal & Financial Publishing, 1983.
- (Merlen Ser. of Registers).

STRAIT OF HORMUZ

—International and legal problems of the gulf / S.H. Amin. - London : Middle East and North African Studies Press, 1981.
235p.
Bibls..
ISBN 0906559057

STRAITS

—Baltic Straits / by Gunnar Alexandersson. - The Hague : Nijhoff, 1982.
152p.
Includes index.
ISBN 902472595X Hbk £75.00

—International Straits of the World / Scott C. Traver. - Alphen aan den Rijn : Sijthoff and Noordhoff, 1980.
xiii,272p.
Bibliographies.
ISBN 9028607099 Hbk Gld92.00

—Strait of Dover / by Luc Cuyvers. - Dordrecht : Martinus Nijhoff, 1986.
xvi, 150p. - (International straits of the world).
ISBN 9024732522 Hbk £115.00

STRATEGIC PLANNING

—Strategic management in multinational companies / by Yves Doz. - Oxford : Pergamon, 1985.
250p; 25cm.
ISBN 0080318088 Hbk £19.25
ISBN 008031807X Pbk £10.75

STRATOSPHERIC OZONE - GREAT BRITAIN

—Stratospheric ozone : report ... / United Kingdom Stratospheric Ozone Review Group. - London : HMSO, 1987.
'The Stratospheric Ozone Review Group was set up jointly by the Department of the Environment and the Meteorological Office in November 1985'. - Annex A.

STRIKEBREAKERS - GREAT BRITAIN
—Troops in strikes : military intervention in industrial disputes / Steve Peak. - London : Cobden Trust, 1984.
177p.
Bibliography: p172-174.
ISBN 0900137223

STRIKES
—International labour standards : the case of freedom to strike / by Ruth Ben-Israel. - Deventer : Kluwer Law and Taxation Publishers, 1988.
vii,133p.
'A study prepared for the International Labour Office.' - T.p.. Includes index.
ISBN 9065443177

—Strike / Milan : Giuffre, 1987.
xvi, 554p.

STRIKES - AUSTRALIA
—Strike law in Australia / by Edward I. Sykes. - 2nd ed. - Sydney : Law Book Co., 1982.
xxiii, 369 p.; 25 cm.
Includes bibliographical references and index.
ISBN 0455200890

STRIKES - CANADA
—Strikes and lockouts in Canada 1981 : labour data / Greves et lock-out au Canada 1981. - Ottawa : Canadian Government Publishing Centre, Supply and Services Canada, 1982.
83p.
Parallel English and French text.

STRIKES - EUROPEAN COMMUNITY
—Right to strike in Community law : the incorporation of fundamental rights in the legal order of the European Communities / by Lammy Betten. - Amsterdam : North-Holland, 1985.
xviii, 319p.
At head of title: T.M.C. Asser Instituut, The Hague. Includes index. Bibliography: p.291-306.
ISBN 0444878459

STRIKES - GREAT BRITAIN
—Modern law of strikes / Duggan. - London : Financial Training, 1987.
ISBN 185185066X Pbk £12.95

—Policing the miners' strike / edited by Bob Fine and Robert Millar. - London : Lawrence and Wishart, 1985.
xii,243p.
ISBN 0853156336

—Right to Strike? / London : Institute of Economic Affairs, 1986.
ISBN 0255361904 Pbk £2.50

—Right to strike in Britain/ the English floating charge / K D Ewing, R M Goode. - Kluwer Law and Taxation, 1989.
72. - (Lectures on the common law).
Covers the position under the common law, protection of the trade unions from the common law, legislation and the individual striker, the foundation of security, the priority of security interests, and the second creditors rights over the assets given in security.
ISBN 9065444114 Pbk £15/Dfl 48

—States of emergency : British governments and strikebreaking since 1919 / Keith Jeffery and Peter Hennessy. - London : Routledge & K. Paul, 1983.
312p.
Includes index. Bibliography: p300-304.
ISBN 0710094647

—Strike-free procedures : are they what they seem? / Roy Lewis. - Coventry : University of Warwick. School of Industrial and Business Studies. Industrial Relations Research Unit, 1988.
14 leaves.
Bibliography: p14.

—Strikes in essential services / Gillian S. Morris. - London : Mansell, 1986.
x,221p; 24cm.
Bibliography: p209-215. - Includes index.
ISBN 0720117917 Hbk £25.00
ISBN 0720118697 Pbk £15.00

—Striking a Bargain? / London : Sweet & Maxwell, 1985.
- (Sweet and Maxwell's Law Files Ser.: No. 7).
ISBN 0421340401 loose £29.50

STRUCTURED SETTLEMENTS - CANADA - MANITOBA
—Report on periodic payment of damages for personal injury and death / Manitoba Law Reform Commission. - Winnipeg : The Commission, 1987.
iv,128p. - (Report).
Includes bibliographical references.
ISBN 0771108346

STUDENTS - CANADA
—Schools and Students : Legal Aspects of Administration / Agincourt : Carswell, 1988.
236p.

—Schools and students : legal aspects of administration / W.H. Giles. - Toronto : Carswell, 1988.
xxix, 206 p.; 24 cm.
Includes index.
ISBN 0459312014

STUDY AND TEACHING
—Newsletter / Commonwealth Legal Education Association / Commonwealth Legal Education Association. - v. - London : Commonwealth Legal Education Association, 1974.

—Proceedings of the Conference of Institutions Responsible for Teaching the Subject 'Computers and Law', Rome, 9-11 October 1985 : reports presented at the Conference / Strasbourg : Council of Europe, 1987.
357p; 29cm.
At head of cover title: Legal affairs.
ISBN 9287110603

—Reading the law : a critical introduction to legal method and techniques / Peter Goodrich. - Oxford : Basil Blackwell, 1986.
ix,229p; 23cm.
Introduction to the study of law. Illustrates how lawyers and students read legal texts.
ISBN 0631146296 Hbk £27.50
ISBN 0631146318 Pbk £9.95

—Teacher in international law : (teachings and teachers) / Manfred Lachs. - The Hague : Nijhoff, 1982.
236p; 25cm.
Bibliography: p211-225. - Includes index.
ISBN 9024725666 Unpriced

—Teacher in international law : teachings and teaching / Manfred Lachs. - Rev. 2nd ed. - Dordrecht : M. Nijhoff, 1986.
Includes index. Bibliography.
ISBN 9024733138 pbk.

—Teaching, Research and Training in the Field of Computers and Law / Strasbourg : Council of Europe, 1981.

—Teaching, research and training in the field of 'computers and the law' : recommendation no. R (80)3 adopted by the Committee of Ministers of the Council of Europe on 30 April 1980 and explanatory memorandum / Council of Europe. - Strasbourg : Council of Europe, 1981.
12p.
'Prepared by the Committee of Experts on Legal Data Processing' - verso t.p.. At head of cover title: Council of Europe, Legal Affairs.

—World directory of criminological institutes / compiled and edited by Carla Masotti Santoro. - 4th ed. - Rome : UNSDRI, 1986.
xxvi,582p. - (Publication).
ISBN 9290780029

STUDY AND TEACHING - AUSTRALIA
—Community legal education : preventive legal aid : proceedings of the Commonwealth Legal Aid Commission Seminar / edited by Ben Boer. - Canberra : Commonwealth Legal Aid Commission, 1980.
339p; 25cm.
Includes bibliographical references. Includes index.
ISBN 0642897344

—Continuing legal education in the 1980's : papers and proceedings of the Conference on Continuing Legal Education in the 1980's, conducted by the Law Society of New South Wales and the Law Foundation of New South Wales at the College of Law, Sydney, 13-15 November 1980 / edited by Jan Bowen and Clem Mitchelmore. - Sydney : Law Foundation of New South Wales, 1981.
xii,214,vip.
ISBN 090913619X

—Introduction to Legal Studies / 4th ed. - Butterworths, 1984.
456p.
ISBN 0409494038 Pbk £22.50

STUDY AND TEACHING - AUSTRALIA - NEW SOUTH WALES
—Legal Studies for New South Wales Years 11 and 12 / Butterworths, 1989.
ca 432p.
ISBN 0409494682 Pbk £22.50

STUDY AND TEACHING - AUSTRALIA - SOUTH AUSTRALIA
—Legal Studies for South Australia / Butterworths, 1988.
ca 288p.
ISBN 0409494712 Pbk £ 22.50

STUDY AND TEACHING - CANADA
—Essays on legal education / Centre for Studies in Canadian Legal Education : Neil Gold, editor. - Toronto : Butterworths, 1982.
xi,143p.
Includes bibliographical references.
ISBN 0409822248

—Law and learning : report to the Social Science and Humanities Research Council of Canada / by the Consultative Group on Research and Education in Law. - Ottawa : The Council, 1983.
ix, 186, 212, x p.; 23 cm.
English and French. Title on added t.p.: Le droit et le savoir. Includes bibliographies.
ISBN 0662524365 pbk.

—Law and the citizen : looking to the '80s : a Colloquium on Public Legal Education held on April 29 and 30, 1977 / edited, updated and with present conclusions and recommendations by Frederick B. Sussmann and Bradford W. Morse. - Ottawa, Ont. : University of Ottawa Press, 1981.
ix, 135 p.; 23 cm.
Includes index.
ISBN 2760322297 pbk.

—Legal education for Canadian youth : proceedings of a conference held at the College of Law, University of Saskatchewan, May 22-24, 1980 / edited by Edward R. Myers. - Ottawa : Canadian Law Information Council, 1981.
v,98p. - (Occasional paper).
Bibliography: p.47.
ISBN 0920358144

—Legal education for youth in Canada / Ottawa : Canadian Law Information Council for the Department of Justice, 1980.
iii,76p.
Bibliography: p.42-43.

—Professional competence and the law / editor, Leon E. Trakman : assistant editor, Douglas Watters : sponsored by Dalhousie Law School, the Law Foundation of Nova Scotia, the CLE Society of Nova Scotia, the Canadian Bar Association. - Halifax, Nova Scotia : Dalhousie University Faculty of Law, 1981.
iv,245p. - (Dalhousie Continuing Legal Education Ser.: No. 21).
Includes bibliographical references.
ISBN 0770301274 Hbk £20.00

STUDY AND TEACHING - COMMONWEALTH
—Commonwealth directory of post-graduate law programmes, 1986-87 : a guide to taught Masters programmes in law at Commonwealth universities, seminars and courses conducted by international organisations and sources of scholarship information / London : Legal Division, Commonwealth Secretariat, 1987.
ix,112p.
ISBN 085092314X

—Report on the Expert Group Meeting of Law Teachers to Develop Curriculum Materials on Violence against Women : London, 11-15 May 1987 / London : Commonwealth Secretariat, 1987.
19p.

STUDY AND TEACHING - ENGLAND
—Law and teachers today / Neil Adams. - London : Hutchinson, 1983.
285p; 24cm.
Includes index.
ISBN 0091516102 Unpriced

STUDY AND TEACHING - GREAT BRITAIN
—Black communities and the legal profession / summary of Nottingham Regional Conference, October 1986. - s.l. : Standing Committee on the Black Communities and the Legal Profession, 1986.
11p.
Includes bibliographical references.

—Handbook 1980 / Assocation of Law Teachers. - Coalville : Association of Law Teachers, 1980.
75p.

—Handbook / The Association of Law Teachers. - Sheffield? : Association of Law Teachers, 1986.
80p.

—How to study law / Anthony Bradney ... et al. - London : Sweet & Maxwell, 1986.
237p; 22cm.
ISBN 042134380X Pbk
ISBN 0421343907

—Intermediate examination in laws / University of London. External System. - London : University of London, 1986.
46p.
ISBN 0718707516

Criminal law : subject guide 1986 / University of London. External System. - 1986.
60p.
ISBN 0718707524

English legal system : subject guide 1987 / University of London External system. – 1987.
33p.
ISBN 0718707761

—Law as an academic discipline : a response to the Leverhulme Report and the UGC letter on a strategy for Higher Education into the 1990's / the Committee of Heads of University Law Schools. – S.l. : The Committee, 1984.
iii,20 leaves.

—Law in higher education : into the 1980s / editor: Michael Slade. – Sheffield : Association of Law Teachers, 1980.
176p.
'Proceedings of a special Association of Law Teachers conference held at Bristol Polytechnic 8-10 February 1980' - cover.

—Learning the law / by Glanville Williams. – 11th ed. – London : Stevens, 1982.
viii,241p; 19cm.
Previous ed.: 1978. Includes index. .
ISBN 0420462902 Hbk Unpriced
ISBN 0420463003 Pbk £3.55

—Newsletter / Law Technology Centre & BILETA. – Warwick : LTC, School of Law, University of Warwick, 1987-.

—Studying law / Phillip H. Kenny. – London : Butterworths, 1985.
viii,170p; 23cm.
Bibliography: p162-163. - Includes index.
ISBN 0406016089 Hbk £9.00
ISBN 0406016097 Pbk £4.95

STUDY AND TEACHING – NIGERIA

—Quarter century of legal education in Nigeria : an appraisal / by E.I. Nwogugu. – Lagos : Nigerian Institute of Advanced Legal Studies, 1985.
28p. – (Occasional poaper).
Includes bibliographical references.

STUDY AND TEACHING – NORTHERN IRELAND

—Report of the Committee on Professional Legal Education in Northern Ireland / Belfast : HMSO, 1985.
ix,48p; 25cm.
ISBN 0337041504 Pbk £4.20

STUDY AND TEACHING – TANZANIA

—Limits of legal radicalism : reflections on teaching law at the University of Dar es Salaam / edited by Issa G. Shivji. – Dar es Salaam, Tanzania : Faculty of Law, University of Dar es Salaam, 1986.
135p.
'1961-1986, 25th anniversary volume, Faculty of Law, University of Dar es Salaam'. - T.p.. Includes bibliographical references.

STUDY AND TEACHING – UNITED STATES

—American studies collections in the University of London : a / London : University of London Institute of United States, 1981.
30p.
Based on 'Materials for the study of the United States in libraries of the University of London'.

—Legal education and lawyer competency : curricula for change / Fernand N. Dutile, editor. – Notre Dame : University of Notre Dame Press, 1981.
viii,155p; 21cm.
Conference proceedings.
ISBN 0268012644 £10.50

—Power and policy in quest of the law : essays in honor of Eugene Victor Rostow / edited by Myres S. McDougal, W. Michael Reisman. – The Hague : M. Nijhoff Publishers, 1984.
640p.
Bibliography: p441-447. Includes index.
ISBN 9024729114 Hbk £235.00

STUDY AND TEACHING (CONTINUING EDUCATION)

—Journal of professional legal education / Sydney, 1983-.
Index published every two years.

SUBCONTRACTING – GREAT BRITAIN

—Default by sub-contractors and suppliers / John Parris. – London : Collins, 1985.
320p.
Includes index.
ISBN 0003830470 £17.50

SUBJECT HEADINGS

—Legal thesaurus / compiled by Nigel Smith and Christine Miskin. – Hebden Bridge : Legal Information Resources, 1987.
204p.
ISBN 1870369009

SUBMERGED LANDS – GREAT BRITAIN

—Marginal seabed : United Kingdom legal practice / Geoffrey Marston. – Oxford : Clarendon Press, 1981.
xiii,316p; 22cm.
Bibliography: p299-302. - Includes index.
ISBN 0198253699 £18.50

SUBROGATION

—Subrogation in insurance law / by S.R. Derham. – North Ryde, N.S.W. : Law Book Co. Ltd., 1985.
xxxiii,164p.
Bibliography: p.xxix-xxxiii. - Includes index.
ISBN 0455205922

SUBSIDIES – EUROPEAN COMMUNITY

—State and community aids for European industry : their control and grant / Philip Bentley. – 1 v. – London : European Business Publications, 1983.
looseleaf.
ISBN 0946262012

SUBVERSIVE ACTIVITIES – CANADA

—Crimes against the state / Law Reform Commission of Canada. – Ottawa : The Commission, 1986.
72,76p. – (Working paper).
Includes bibliographies. Added t.p. in French: Les crimes contre l'etat. Pages numbered in opposite directions. Text in English and French.

SUBWAYS – ENGLAND

—Crime on the London Underground / report of a study by the Department of Transport in conjunction with London Underground ... et al. – London : H.M.S.O., 1986.
118p.
Describes a study by the Department of Transport – suggests crime on the Underground is relatively rare – 15300 offences (1600 violent) in 725 million journeys during 1985. Recognises that cost of crime to the system could be 10 million per year and shows that the public are afraid of violence and theft.
ISBN 0115508058

SUCCESSION

—Family, Things and Succession / H.J. Erasmus. – 2nd ed. – Durban : Professional Publishers, 1983.
ISBN 0409040525 Pbk £79.00

—International conventions in the field of succession : explanatory documentation / prepared for Commonwealth jurisdictions by Keith Patchett in association with the Commonwealth Secretariat. – London : Commonwealth Secretariat, 1980.
85p.

—Intestate succession and legal rights / Scottish Law Commission. – Edinburgh : The Commission, 1986.
v,241p. – (Consultative memorandum).
Includes bibliographical references. Catalogued from cover.

—Parry and Clark: the law of succession / 9th. – London : Sweet & Maxwell.
Includes the Family Law Reform Act 1987, and the Inheritance Tax Act of 1984. Also covers the Non-Contentious Probate Rules, and the Insolvency Act 1986. New cases are referred to throughout the text, in particular where they illustrate the exercise of the courts' power to order financial provision for the family of the deceased.
ISBN 0421359803 Hbk £34

SUCCESSION – AUSTRALIA

—Cases and Materials on Succession / R.A. Woodman. – 3rd ed. – North Ryde : Law Book Co, 1984.
xxxix, 794p.
ISBN 0455202826 Hbk £73.00
ISBN 0455202834 Pbk £60.00

—Wills and intestacy in Australia and New Zealand : being a revised and consolidated version of Hardingham, Neave and Ford's The Law of Wills and Hardingham's The Law of Intestate Succession in Australia and New Zealand / by I.J. Hardingham, M.A. Neave, H.A.J. Ford. – Sydney : Law Book Co., 1983.
xliv,518p.
Includes bibliographical references and index.
ISBN 0455204152

SUCCESSION – AUSTRALIA – QUEENSLAND

—Manual of Queensland succession law / by W. A. Lee. – 2nd ed. – Sydney : Law Book Company, 1985.
xlix,268p.
ISBN 0455205620

SUCCESSION – AUSTRALIA – TASMANIA

—Report on succession rights on intestacy / Law Reform Commission of Tasmania. – Hobart : Government Printer, 1985.
21p. – (Report v no 43).

SUCCESSION – AUSTRALIA – WESTERN AUSTRALIA

—Report on recognition of interstate and foreign grants of probate and administration / the Law Reform Commission of Western Australia. – Perth : The Commission, 1984.
128p. – (Project).
Includes bibliographical references.

SUCCESSION – CANADA

—Estates & trusts reports / Agincourt, Ont. : Carswell, 1978-.
24cm.
Cumulative indexes published at intervals.

—Presumptions of Survivorship / Victoria : Government of British Columbia, 1982.

—Statutory Succession Rights / Victoria : Government of British Columbia, 1983.

SUCCESSION – CANADA – BRITISH COLUMBIA

—Report on presumptions of survivorship / Law Reform Commission of British Columbia. – Victoria : Queen's Printer, 1982.
29p.
ISBN 0771883382

—Report on statutory succession rights / Law Reform Commission of British Columbia. – Vancouver : The Commission, 1983.
209p.
Date on title page 1983.
ISBN 0771884087

—Statutory succession rights / Law Reform Commission of British Columbia. – Vancouver : The Commission, 1982.
vii,401p. – (Working paper).

SUCCESSION – CANADA – MANITOBA

—Report on intestate succession / Manitoba Law Reform Commission. – Winnipeg : The Commission, 1985.
iii,66p. – (Report).
Includes bibliographical references.

—Report on 'The Testators Family Maintenance Act' / Manitoba Law Reform Commission. – Winnipeg : The Commission, 1985.
iii,125p. – (Report).
Includes bibliographical references.
ISBN 0771101201

SUCCESSION – ENGLAND

—Distribution on intestacy / the Law Commission. – London : HMSO, 1988.
vii,54p. – (Working paper).
ISBN 0117301906

—Law and practice of intestate succession / by C.H. Sherrin, R.C. Bonehill. – London : Sweet & Maxwell, 1987.
xliii,515p; 25cm.
Areas such as social security benefits, private pension entitlements, bank accounts, small estates and the tax position and law relating to marital homes are covered. Reference has been made within the text to the usually more modern Commonwealth codes, where a contrast can elucidate the English law.
ISBN 0421326301 £39.00

—Law of succession / Anthony R. Mellows. – 4th ed. – London : Butterworths, 1983.
lv,619p; 26cm.
Previous ed.: 1977. Includes index.
ISBN 0406623775 Hbk Unpriced
ISBN 0406623783 Pbk Unpriced

—Parry & Clark on the law of succession / J. B. Clark. – 8th ed. – London : Sweet & Maxwell, 1983.
lxxix,492p; 24cm.
Previous ed.: 1977. Includes index.
ISBN 0421283408 Hbk No price
ISBN 0421283505 Pbk £15.00

—Succession : cases and materials / Cherry E. Wright. – London : Butterworths, 1986.
xxv,436p; 25cm.
Includes index.
ISBN 0406563101 Hbk £20.00
ISBN 040656311X Pbk £15.00

—Transfer of land : title on death / the Law Commission. – London : HMSO, 1987.
viii,106p. – (Working paper).
ISBN 0117301876

—Wills, administration and taxation : a practical guide / by J.S. Barlow, L.C. King, A.G. King. – 2nd ed. – London : Sweet & Maxwell, 1986.
460p.
Previous ed.: 1983. Includes index.
ISBN 0421350806 Pbk £15.00

SUCCESSION – GREAT BRITAIN

—Distribution on Intestacy / London : Oyez Longman, 1981.
ISBN 085120478X Hbk £2.95

—Distribution on Intestacy / London : Longman Professional, 1988.
ISBN 0851214010 Pbk £2.95

—Law of Succession / 4th ed. – London : Butterworths, 1983.
ISBN 0406623783 Pbk £23.95

—Law's Disposal of a Person's Estate Who Dies Without Will or Testament : The Disposal of Estates of Will, Form of Wills, and Directions for Executors etc. / 10th ed. Repr. of 1809 ed. – Abingdon : Professional Books.
492p.

—Passing Down the Family Farm / Robert Venables. – London : Oyez Longman, 1983. – (Oyez Longman Intelligence Report Ser.).
ISBN 0851207367 Hbk £45.00

—Succession : cases and materials / London : Butterworths, 1986.
ISBN 0406563101 Hbk £34.00
ISBN 040656311X Pbk £20.50

—Succinct View of the Rule of Shelley's Case / Repr. of 1794 ed. – Abingdon : Professional Books.
486p.

—Williams, Mortimer and Sunnucks on executors, administrators and probate / by J.H.G. Sunnucks, J.G. Ross Martyn, K.M. Garnett. – London : Stevens & Sons, 1982.
clxxxviii,1157p; 26cm.
Concerned with probate practice and the work of executors and administrators, discussions of changes in the law of family provision, capital transfer tax and social security. Includes appendices which set out the relevant statutes, rules of court and statutory instruments.
ISBN 0420455000 £75.00

SUCCESSION - INDIA
—Indian Succession Act / 5th ed. – Allahabad : Law Book Company, 1985.

—Law of Succession Certificate / 6th ed. – Allahabad : Law Book Company, 1987.

—Sastri's Law of Succession Certificate / 6th ed. – Allahabad : Law Publishers, 1987.

—Vivadaratnakara of Candesvara Thakkura : Law of Partition and Inheritance / Digambar Chattopadhyaya. – Delhi : Gian Publishing House, 1986.
ii, liii, 94, 61, xvp.
ISBN 8121200121 Hbk £140.00

SUCCESSION - NEW ZEALAND
—Wills and intestacy in Australia and New Zealand : being a revised and consolidated version of Hardingham, Neave and Ford's The Law of Wills and Hardingham's The Law of Intestate Succession in Australia and New Zealand / by I.J. Hardingham, M.A. Neave, H.A.J. Ford. – Sydney : Law Book Co., 1983.
xliv,518p.
Includes bibliographical references and index.
ISBN 0455204152

SUCCESSION - NIGERIA
—Casebook on Nigerian Family Law and Succession / Abingdon : Professional Books, 1986.
800p.
ISBN 0862051150 Hbk £42.00

SUCCESSION - SCOTLAND
—Inheritance : who should have a claim to a persons property on death? : is the present law fair? / Scottish Law Commission. – Edinburgh : The Commission, 1986.
35p.

—Scots Statutes 1983 : Family Law; Succession, Trusts, Liferents and Judicial Factors / Edinburgh : W Green, 1983.
ISBN 0414007255 Hbk £6.50

—Scots Statutes 1984 : Family Law; Succession, Trusts, Liferents and Judicial Factors / Edinburgh : W Green.
ISBN 041400745X Hbk £14.75

—Scots Statutes 1985 : Family Law - Succession, Trusts, Liferent andJudicial Factors / Edinburgh : W Green.
– (Reprint from the Parliament House Book).
ISBN 0414007662 Hbk £10.00

—Some miscellaneous topics in the law of succession / Scottish Law Commission. – Edinburgh : The Commission, 1986.
155p. – (Consultative memorandum).

—Succession (Scotland) Act 1964 / by Michael C. Meston. – 3rd ed. – Edinburgh : Green, 1982.
xv,136p; 24cm.
Includes text of the Act. Previous ed.: 1969. Includes index.
ISBN 0414007050 Pbk Unpriced

SUCCESSION - SOUTH AFRICA
—Family, things and succession / Lee and Honore. – 2nd ed. – Durban : Butterworths, 1983.
xvii,615p.
Bibliography: p.vii-xiv. - Includes index.
ISBN 0409040533

—Law of succession / A.J. Oosthuizen. – Cape Town : Juta, 1982.
xiv,96p.
Bibliography: p.v. Includes the text of the Wills Act 7 of 1953.
ISBN 0702112879

—Law of succession in South Africa / by M.M. Corbett, H.R. Hahlo, Gys Hofmeyr : with an appendix on the conflict of laws by Ellison Kahn ; general ed., H. R. Hahlo. – Cape Town : Juta, 1980.
lvi, 739 p.; 25 cm.
Table of statutes: p. xiii-xviii. Table of cases: p. xix-lvi. Includes bibliographical references and index. Latest supplement held: 1985.
ISBN 0702110965 R57.50

—Law of succession : intestate succession / South African Law Commission. – Pretoria : South African Law Commission, 1983.
vii,49p. – (Working paper).
Project 22. Bibliography: pv-vi.

—Review of the law of succession / South African Law Commission. – Pretoria : The Commission, 1986.
ix,34 leaves. – (Project).
Bibliogrpahy: p.iv-viii.

—Review of the law of succession : disqualification from inheriting, substitution, succession rights of adopted children / South African Law Commission. – Pretoria : The Commission, 1987.
ix,99p. – (Project).
Photocopy of original. Includes bibliographical references.
ISBN 0797014020

—Review of the law of succession : intestate succession / South African Law Commission. – Pretoria : The Commission, 1985.
vii,37p. – (Report).
Bibliography: p.vi-vii.
ISBN 0621096113

SUCCESSION - SWEDEN
—New Swedish family legislation : the Marriage Code : the Cohabitees (Joint Homes) Act : the Homosexual Cohabitees Act : the Inheritance Code, chapters 1-3 and 7 / Stockholm : Ministry of Justice, 1988.
37p.
'... translations of ... Swedish legislation published in the Swedish Code of Statutes (SFS)'. - p.1.

SUCCESSION - UNITED KINGDOM
—Law of Succession / 2nd ed. – Plymouth : Macdonald & Evans, 1981.
272p. – (M and E Handbook Ser.).
ISBN 0712112561 Hbk £4.95

SUCCESSION (HINDU LAW)
—Hindu Law of Inheritance : As in the Viramitrodaya of Mitramisa / Delhi : Gian Publishing House, 1986.
xv, 286p.
ISBN 8121200164 Hbk £180.00

—Hindu Succession Act / 2nd ed. – Allahabad : Law Publishers, 1982.

—Hindu Succession Act / Gopalakrishnan. – 5th ed. – Allahabad : Law Book Company, 1981.

—Hindu Succession Act / Allahabad : Law Book Company, 1981.

SUCCESSION (ISLAMIC LAW)
—Islamic law of bequest / Abdulaziz Mohammed Zaid. – London : Scorpion Publishing, 1986.
296p.
Bibliography: p.291-294. - Includes index.
ISBN 090590642X

SUCCESSION (ISLAMIC LAW) - ISLAMIC COUNTRIES
—Islamic law of inheritance : a comparative study with emphasis on contemporary problems / by Hamid Khan. – Lahore : The author, 1980.
vii,195p.
Bibliography: p.190-192. - Includes index.

SUCCESSION (ISLAMIC LAW) - MALAYSIA
—The distribution of estates according to Shafii law / Singapore : Malayan Law Journal, 1976.
vi,72.
Guide to the Islamic law of inheritance as it is practised in Malaysia and Singapore. Gives a summary of the law, and includes distribution of estates according to Shafii law, the Quranic heirs, the Agnatic heirs, the Bair-ul-mal, MINHAJ ET TALIBIN, a table of Quranic heirs, Quranic verses, and Hadith on the law of inheritance.

SUCCESSION (ISLAMIC LAW) - SINGAPORE
—The distribution of estates according to Shafii law / Singapore : Malayan Law Journal, 1976.
vi,72.
Guide to the Islamic law of inheritance as it is practised in Malaysia and Singapore. Gives a summary of the law, and includes distribution of estates according to Shafii law, the Quranic heirs, the Agnatic heirs, the Bair-ul-mal, MINHAJ ET TALIBIN, a table of Quranic heirs, Quranic verses, and Hadith on the law of inheritance.

SUGAR GROWING - GUYANA
—From plantocracy to nationalisation : a profile of sugar in Guyana / M. Shahabuddeen. – Georgetown? : University of Guyana, 1983.
xiii,440p.
Bibliography: p411-440.

SUGAR GROWING - INDIA
—Law Relating to the Sugar Industries in Uttar Pradesh, with Case-Law and Comments as Amended Up-to-Date / Gyan Prakash. – 3rd ed. – Allahabad : Hind Publishing House, 1982.
iv, 340p.

SUMMARY OFFENCES - AUSTRALIA - NEW SOUTH WALES
—Justices Act and Summary Offences, New South Wales / R.N. Howie. – Butterworths, 1980.
ISBN 0409417408 loose £190.00

SUMMARY PROCEEDINGS
—Contested trials in magistrates' courts / by Julie Vennard. – London : H.M.S.O., 1982.
v,32p; 25cm.
Bibliography: p.26-27. 'A Home Office Research and Planning Unit report.'.
ISBN 0113407661

SUMMARY PROCEEDINGS - CANADA - ONTARIO
—Ontario provincial offences procedure / by W. Douglas Drinkwalter, J. Douglas Ewart. – Toronto : Carswell, 1980.
lxiii, 701 p.; 24 cm.
Includes texts of the Provincial offences act, 1979 and the Provincial courts amendment act, 1979. Includes bibliographical references and indexes.
ISBN 0459330306

SUMMARY PROCEEDINGS - ENGLAND
—Case for summary trial : proposals for a redistribution of criminal business / the Justices' Clerks' Society. – Bristol : The Society, 1982.
26p.

—Triable-either-way cases : Crown Court or Magistrates' Court? / by David Riley and Julie Vennard. – London : H.M.S.O., 1988.
52 p.
Discusses whether the balance of either-way business could be redistributed in favour of the Magistrates' Court by encouraging them to accept jurisdiction more often in such cases.
ISBN 0113408900

SUMMARY PROCEEDINGS - NEW ZEALAND
—Summary Proceedings and Police Court Practice / Wellington : Butterworths, 1985.

—Summary Proceedings and Police Court Practice / Butterworths, 1985.
Covers changes in procedure such as increases in jurisdiction of District Court Judges, the removal of a defendant's right to make an unsworn statement from the dock, the liberalization of procedures relating to the prosecution of young persons, the rights of an accused to remain present throughout the hearing, and the power of a Judge to clear a court.
ISBN 0409600474 Hbk £93.90

SUMMONS - GREAT BRITAIN
—Summonses and Charges / R. Houghton. – 3rd rev. ed. – London : Police Review Publishing, 1980.
ISBN 0851649947 Pbk £3.75

—Summonses and Charges / R. Houghton. – 4th rev. ed. – London : Police Review Publishing, 1983.
ISBN 085164001X Pbk £4.25

SUMMONS - NORTHERN IRELAND
—Notes on procedure by originating summons and in actions by mortgagees / by Master Hunter. – 2nd ed. – Belfast : SLS Legal Publications, 1985.
37p.
Cover title: Revised notes on procedure by originating summons and in actions by mortgagees.

SUNDAY LEGISLATION - AUSTRALIA - SOUTH AUSTRALIA
—Report ... relating to the inherited imperial observance of Lord's Day Acts / Law Reform Committee of South Australia. – Adelaide : Government Printer, 1987.
40p. – (92nd report).
Bibliography: p.40.

SUNDAY LEGISLATION - CANADA
—Report : The Shops Act : Late-night and Sunday Opening / Committee of Inquiry into Proposals to Amend the Shops Act. – London : HMSO, 1984.
ISBN 0101937601 Hbk £9.15

SUPPLEMENTAL SECURITY INCOME PROGRAM - GREAT BRITAIN
—Guide to supplementary benefit law / by Jenny Levin. – 3rd ed. – London : Legal Action Group, 1981.
136p.

—Law relating to supplementary benefits and family income supplements : the statutes, regulations and orders as now in force / H. V. Roberts. – 3rd ed. 2. – London : HMSO, 1980-. looseleaf.
Superseded by: The law relating to social security (the Blue volumes). Popular title: the Yellow Books. With supplements of amendments.

—'We don't give clothing grants any more' : the 1980 supplementary benefit scheme / Janet Allbeson and Roger Smith. – London : Child Poverty Action Group, 1984.
113p.
Includes bibliographical references.
ISBN 0903963736

SUPPLEMENTARY BENEFIT - GREAT BRITAIN

—Decisions of the Courts Relating to Supplementary Benefits and Family Income Supplements Legislation 1980 / London : HMSO.
ISBN 0117606758 loose £12.50

Supplement No. 1

Supplement No. 2

—Law Relating to Supplementary Benefit and Family Income Supplement / London : HMSO, 1984.
Sets out current legislation, both statutes and regulations with footnotes and sidenotes giving the origin of amendments.
ISBN 0117609242 Pbk £41.00

—Supplementary Benefits Handbook : A Guide to Claimants' Rights / 10th ed. – London : HMSO, 1984.
162p.
Explains who is entitled to benefits and how to claim them. Describes special rules applying to people in particular situations.
ISBN 0117612189 Pbk £2.50

SUPREME COURT - ENGLAND AND WALES

—ABC guide to the practice of the Supreme Court 1986-87 / by Emlyn Williams. – 44th ed. – London : Sweet & Maxwell, 1987.
200p.; 22cm.
Previous ed.: 1985.
ISBN 0421371803 Pbk £12.50 (May)

—Butterworths Consolidated Legislation Service /. – Professional Publ.
278p.
ISBN 0409014389 £45.00

—Modern developments in the law of civic procedure / by D.B. Casson and I.H. Dennis. – London : Sweet & Maxwell, 1982.
xxv,112p; 22cm.
Includes index.
ISBN 0421290005 Pbk £4.95

—Supreme Court Act 1981 / with annotations by Robin White. – London : Sweet & Maxwell, 1981.
ca.150p; 25cm.
ISBN 0421294108 Pbk £6.85

SUPREME COURT - JAPAN

—Outline of the Japanese Supreme Court / Hideo Wada. – Tokyo : Institute of Social Sciences, Meiji University, 1980.
10p.
Reprint from: Bulletin of the Institute of Social Sciences Meiji University, Vol. 4, no. 1 (1980).

SURETY OF THE PEACE - GREAT BRITAIN

—Criminal law : binding over - the issues / The Law Commission. – London : H.M.S.O., 1987.
vi,113p; 21cm. – (Working paper).
ISBN 011730185X

SURETYSHIP

—Modern contract of guarantee / by James O'Donovan and John C. Phillips. – Sydney : Law Book Company, 1985.
xcv,675p.
ISBN 0455203490

SURETYSHIP - AUSTRALIA - TASMANIA

—Report on suretyship and guarantee / Law Reform Commission of Tasmania. – Hobart : Government Printer, 1987.
30p. – (Report v no 50).

SURETYSHIP - CANADA

—Law of Guarantee : A Treatise on Guarantee, Indemnity and Standby Letter of Credit / Agincourt : Carswell, 1986.
456p.
This text on the Canadian law pertaining to various secondary obligations used to secure debt and other contract loss gives a detailed survey of the modern law as it has developed in the courts of both Canada and England.

—Law of guarantee : a treatise on guarantee, indemnity and the standby letter of credit / by Kevin Patrick McGuinness. – Toronto : Carswell, 1986.
lxv,456p.
Bibliography: p.lxii-lxv. - Includes index.
ISBN 0459383906

SURETYSHIP - ENGLAND

—Rowlatt on the law of principal and surety / David G. M. Marks, Gabriel S. Moss, Sidney Arthur Taylor Rowlatt. – 4th ed. – London : Sweet & Maxwell, 1982.
liv,289p; 26cm.
Covers the construction and effect of guarantees, rights of a surety, loss of securities, bankruptcy, winding up, negotiable instruments, building contracts, and consumer credit. Draws on Commonwealth and United States authorities where appropriate.
ISBN 0421262400 £24.00

SURETYSHIP - GREAT BRITAIN

—Law of Guarantee / London : Sweet & Maxwell, 1986.
ISBN 0459383906 Hbk £45.00

—Law of guarentees / Thomas Putnam and Julienne Walker. – 2nd ed. – London : Longman Professional (UK), 1989.
– (Commercial Series).
Discusses the law relating to contracts where one party agrees to be answerable for the debts or obligations of another to a third party. Deals with guarentees in loans, consumer credit, hire purchase, landlord and tenant (to guarentee payment of rent), building contracts, and commercial contracts. Contains specimen pleadings.
ISBN 0851215395 Hbk £40

—Suretyship / London : Oyez Longman, 1981.
– (Oyez Longman Practice Note Ser.: No. 70).

SURETYSHIP - SOUTH AFRICA

—Caney's the law of suretyship in Africa / C. F. Forsyth. – 3rd ed. – Cape Town : Juta, 1982.
xxi,206p.
Previous ed.: 1970. Bibliography: p.xi-xii. - Includes index.
ISBN 0702113417

SURVEYORS - ENGLAND

—Negligence in surveying and building / Malcolm Ross. – London : Estates Gazette, 1986.
xxii,247p.
Bibliography: p.238-239. - Includes index.
ISBN 0728200953

SURVEYORS - GREAT BRITAIN

—Lloyd's Survey Handbook / 4th ed. – London : LLoyd's of London Press.
ISBN 185044031X Hbk £27.50

—Practice and Procedure for the Quantity Surveyor / Christopher J. Willis. – 8th ed. – London : Collins, 1980.
272p.
ISBN 0003831515 Pbk £9.95

—Surveyor in Court / London : Estates Gazette, 1985.
ISBN 0728200910 Pbk £25.00

SYNDICATES (FINANCE)

—International syndicated loans / by Robert P. McDonald. – London : Euromoney, 1982.
ix,264p.
Bibliography: p.261-262. - Includes index.
ISBN 0903121441

—Legal aspects of syndicated loans / Peter Gabriel. – London : Butterworths, 1986.
xxxvi,276p; 26cm.
Bibliography: p265-267. - Includes index.
ISBN 0406102104 £45.00

SYNDICATES (FINANCE) - GREAT BRITAIN

—Legal Aspects of Syndicated Loans / London : Butterworths, 1986.
ISBN 0406102104 Hbk £50.00

TAKEOVERS AND MERGERS

—International law of take-overs and mergers : southern Europe, Africa, and the Middle East / H. Leigh Ffrench. – 1. – Westport, Conn. : Quorum, 1987.
23cm.
Includes index.
ISBN 0899302068 £48.50

—International law of take-overs and mergers : the EEC, Northern Europe and Scandinavia / H. Leigh Ffrench. – New York : Quorum, 1987.
416p; 22cm.
Includes bibliography and index.
ISBN 0899300774 £51.75

—International mergers and acquisitions / Peter Earl and Frederick G. Fisher, III. – London : Euromoney, 1986.
vii,129p.
ISBN 090312193X

—Tax aspects of acquisitions and mergers / edited by Philip Cooke, Jan M. van der Beek. – 2nd ed. – Deventer : Kluwer, 1983.
150p.
ISBN 9065441514

TAKEOVERS AND MERGERS - AUSTRALIA

—Annotated Takeovers Code / North Ryde : Law Book Co, 1987.
ca 250p.

—Australian Takeovers Practice and Precedents Manual / North Ryde : C.C.H. Australia, 1983.
200p.
ISBN 0869036807 Hbk £63.00

—Control of the acquisition of shares : the new national take-overs code / F.J.O. Ryan. – Sydney : Butterworths, 1981.
ix, 134 p.; 24 cm.
Includes indexes.
ISBN 040930025X pbk.

—Takeovers, Trading Trusts and More, 1984 / Monash University Staff. – Clayton : Monash University Press, 1984.
ISBN 0867463546 Hbk £28.00

TAKEOVERS AND MERGERS - AUSTRALIA - SOUTH AUSTRALIA

—Report ... relating to the consideration of the proposed bill regulating company takeovers / Law Reform Committee of South Australia. – Adelaide : Government Printer, 1980.
7p. – (49th report).

TAKEOVERS AND MERGERS - CANADA

—Recent Developments in Business and Litigation / Vancouver : Continuing Legal Education Society of British Columbia.

TAKEOVERS AND MERGERS - ENGLAND

—Corporate acquisitions and mergers : a practical guide to the legal, financial and administrative implications / London : Graham & Trotman, 1984.
280p.
ISBN 0860105369 £19.50

—Corporate acquisitions and mergers : a practical guide to the legal, financial and administrative implications / P.F.C. Begg : foreword by Lord Hanson. – 2nd ed. – London : Graham & Trotman, 1986.
320p; 22cm.
Previous ed.: 1985. Includes index.
ISBN 0860108139 Hbk £40.00
ISBN 0860108090 Pbk £20.00

TAKEOVERS AND MERGERS - EUROPE

—Mergers and joint ventures in Europe: the law and policy of the EEC / London : Graham & Trotman, 1989.
220; 240mm.
Explores how articles 85 and 86 of the Treaty of Rome would operate in the context of mergers and production joint ventures, and to non EEC firms seeking to acquire firms in the EEC. Analyses the Draft Regulation for the Control of Mergers, and includes its text in the Annexes.
ISBN 185333314X Hbk £50

TAKEOVERS AND MERGERS - EUROPEAN COMMUNITY

—Merger control in the EEC : a survey of European competition laws / prepared by the Brussels offices at Avenue de la Joyeuse Entree 1, Blijde Inkomstlaan 1 of : Advokaterne Bredgade 3 ... et al. – Deventer : Kluwer Law and Taxation Publishers, 1988.
xii,306p.
ISBN 9065443541

—Opinion on the proposal for a tenth Council directive based on Article 54(3)(g) of the Treaty concerning cross-border mergers of public limited companies / (COM(84)727 final) : European Communities. Economic and Social Committee. – Luxembourg : Office for Official Publications of the European Communities, 1985.
9 leaves. – (CES(85) 780).
ISBN 9277085061

TAKEOVERS AND MERGERS - GREAT BRITAIN

—Accountant's Reports on Takeovers, Mergers, Acquisitions and Realisations / Deloitte, Haskins and Sells Staff. – London : Butterworths, 1985.
ISBN 0406500207 Pbk £20.00

—City code on take-overs and mergers / Rev. – London : Issuing Houses Association, 1981.
81p; 22cm.
Previous ed.: / City Working Party. 1976. Pamphlets 'Practice note no.17', 'Principal amendments to the City code' in pocket.

—City code on take-overs and the rules governing substantial acquisitions of shares / April 1985 ed. 1. – London : The Panel on Take-overs and Mergers, 1985.
loose-leaf.
Previous ed.: 1981.
ISBN 0950046663

—City take-over code / by Sir Alexander Johnston. – Oxford : Oxford University Press, 1980.
viii,312p; 22cm.
Includes index.
ISBN 0198284241 No price

—Mergers and acquisitions / Oxford : Blackwell, 1986.
ISBN 0631147470 Hbk £35.00

—Mergers and Acquisitions : Law and Practice / London : Butterworths, 1987.
ISBN 0406103704 Hbk

—Mergers and Acquisitions : Law and Practice / London : Butterworths, 1988.
ISBN 0406103704 Hbk

—Mergers policy : a Department of Trade and Industry paper on the policy and procedures of merger control / London : HMSO, 1988.
iii,40p.
ISBN 0115139990

—Pescod : Takeover Bids / London : Butterworths, 1987.
ISBN 0406103690 Hbk

—Statements / Panel on Take-Overs and Mergers. - v. - London : The Panel, 1968.

—Takeover bids / London : Butterworths, 1988.
Company executives
ISBN 0406103690 Hbk

TAKEOVERS AND MERGERS - INDIA

—S.C. Sen's Mergers, Amalgamations, and Take-Overs : the Law, the Procedure, and the Valuation of Shares / 2nd ed. - Calcutta : Eastern Law House, 1981.
310p.

TAKEOVERS AND MERGERS - MALAYSIA

—Companies Regulations, Rules and Guide Lines on Mergers and Take-Overs / Kuala Lumpur : International Law Books Services.

—Law of Company Purchase and Compensation-Singapore and Malaysia / London : Butterworths, 1984.
ISBN 0406181225 Pbk £22.50

TAKEOVERS AND MERGERS - NEW ZEALAND

—Mergers and takeovers : legal and financial issues : written proceedings of a seminar, 29 August 1985 / Victoria University of Wellington. Department of Accountancy. - Wellington : The University, 1985.
Various pagings.
Includes bibliographical references. Chairman: Whatarangi Winiata.

TAKEOVERS AND MERGERS - SINGAPORE

—Law of Company Purchase and Compensation-Singapore and Malaysia / London : Butterworths, 1984.
ISBN 0406181225 Pbk £22.50

TANKERS - GREAT BRITAIN

—Tanker voyage charter parties / by F. M. Ventris. - S.l. : Kluwer Law Publishers, 1986.
xvi,411p.
ISBN 0903393972

TAPE RECORDINGS - EUROPEAN COMMUNITY

—Piracy of phonograms : a study prepared for the Commission of the European Communities, Directorate-General for Research, Science and Education / Gillian Davies. - Oxford : Published for the Commission of the European Communities, Cultural Sector by ESC Publishing, 1981.
xii,150p; 22cm.
ISBN 0906214076 Pbk Unpriced

TARIFF PREFERENCES

—Generalised system of preferences : review of the first decade: report by the secretary-general / Organisation for Economic Co-operation and Development. - Paris : Organisation for Economic Co-operation and Development, 1983.
98p.

—Legal aspects of trade preferences for developing states : a study in the influence of development needs on the evolution of international law / by Abdulqawi Yusuf. - The Hague : Nijhoff, 1982.
xx,185p; 25cm.
Bibliography: p169-181. - Includes index.
ISBN 9024725836 Unpriced

—Role of tariff quotas in commercial policy / by Michael Rom : with an introduction by Gerard Curzon. - London : Macmillan for the Trade Policy Research Centre, 1978.
272p.
ISBN 0333176383 £12.00

TAX ACCOUNTING - CANADA

—Current developments in measuring business income for tax purposes / Corporate Management Tax Conference, 1981. - Toronto, Canada : Canadian Tax Foundation, 1982.
xi, 326 p.; 23 cm.
Includes bibliographical references.
ISBN 0888080085 pbk. £25.00

TAX ADMINISTRATION AND PROCEDURE - GREAT BRITAIN

—Official Tax Forms Manual / 2nd ed. - London : Oyez Longman, 1982.
ISBN 0851206433 Hbk £12.50

Third edition
ISBN 0851207537 Hbk

—Report / Committee on Enforcement Powers of the Revenue Departments : chairman, Lord Keith of Kinkel. - London : H.M.S.O., 1983.
xiv,334p; 25cm.

Vol.2 : Chapters 16-28 and notes / Committee on Enforcement Powers of the Revenue Departments : chairman, Lord Keith of Kinkel. - 1983.
336-804p; 25cm.

Vol.3 : Chapters 29-33 and notes : Development land tax, petroleum revenue tax, capital transfer tax and stamp duties / Committee on Enforcement Powers of the Revenue Departments : chairman, Lord Keith of Kinkel. - 1984.
iv,251p; 25cm.

TAX ADMINISTRATION AND PROCEDURE - UNITED STATES

—Challenge of tax administration until the end of the 20th century : technical papers and reports of the 15th General Assembly of the Inter-American Center of Tax Administrators (CIAT), Mexico D.F., Mexico, 29 June - 3 July 1981 / Amsterdam : International Bureau of Fiscal Dopcumentation, 1984.
222p.
Bibliography: p.164-166.
ISBN 9070125242

—Fiscal policy and tax legislation and administration : technical papers and reports of the 15th General Assembly of the Inter-American Center of Tax Administrators (CIAT), Caracas, Venezuela, 25-27 February 1981 / Inter-American Center of Tax Administrators. - Amsterdam : International Bureau of Fiscal Documentation, 1983.
200p.
'Sponsored by the Government of Venezuela, the German Society for Technical Cooperation (GTZ) and the Inter-American Center of Tax Administrators (CIAT)
ISBN 9070125226

—Measures for improving the level of voluntary compliance with tax obligations : technical papers and reports of the 18th General Assembly of the Inter-American Center of Tax Administrators (CIAT) Cartagena, Colombia, 21-25 May 1984 / Inter-American Center of Tax Administrators. - Amsterdam : International Bureau of Fiscal Documentation, 1985.
168 p.; 25 cm. - (Publications of the International Bureau of Fiscal Documentation).
Includes bibliographical references.
ISBN 9070125277 pbk.

—Taxpayer control and the effectiveness of the tax administration : technical papers and reports of the 13th General Assembly of the Inter-American Center of Tax Administrators (CIAT), Quito, Ecuador, May 26-June 1, 1979 / Inter-American Center of Tax Administrators. - Amsterdam : International Bureau of Fiscal Documentation, 1980.
164 p.; 25 cm.
ISBN 9070125161 pbk.

TAX AUDITING - UNITED STATES

—Fundamental tax audit considerations : technical papers and reports of the 14th General Assembly of the Inter-American Center of Tax Administrators (CIAT) / Inter-American Center of Tax Administrators. - Amsterdam : International Bureau of Fiscal Documentation, 1981.
198p.
ISBN 9070125188

TAX COLLECTION - UNITED STATES

—Measures for improving the level of voluntary compliance with tax obligations : technical papers and reports of the 18th General Assembly of the Inter-American Center of Tax Administrators (CIAT) Cartagena, Colombia, 21-25 May 1984 / Inter-American Center of Tax Administrators. - Amsterdam : International Bureau of Fiscal Documentation, 1985.
168 p.; 25 cm. - (Publications of the International Bureau of Fiscal Documentation).
Includes bibliographical references.
ISBN 9070125277 pbk.

TAX EVASION

—Colloquy on International Tax Avoidance and Evasion / Strasbourg : Council of Europe, 1980.

—International tax avoidance and evasion : colloquy of 5-7 March 1980 (Strasbourg), compendium of documents / Amsterdam : International Bureau of Fiscal Documentation, 1981.
184p.
ISBN 9070125196

—Recent International Developments to Counter Tax Avoidance and Evasion / International Fiscal Association. - Toronto : DeBoo, 1982. - (IFA Seminars Ser.).
ISBN 0888201168 Hbk £35.00

—Tax avoidance, tax evasion : a survey of the treatment of tax aviodance and tax evasion in the main industrialised countries of the world / compiled in 1982 for Committee N of the Section on Business Law of the International Bar Association by a team of international rapporteurs and updated and revised for this edition. - 2nd ed. - London : International Bar Association in co-operation with Sweet & Maxwell, 1987.
viii,160p.
Includes bibliographical references.
ISBN 0948711124

—Tax avoidance, tax evasion : a survey of the treatment of tax avoidance and tax evasion in the main industrialized countries of the world / compiled for Committee N of the Section on Business Law of the International Bar Association by a team of international rapporteurs. - London : International Bar Association in co-operation with Sweet & Maxwell, 1982.
viii,104p; 22cm.
ISBN 0950587672 Pbk £8.50

—Tax Offences, Black Money and the Law / New Delhi : Deep and Deep Publications, 1987.
416p.

TAX EVASION - CANADA

—Income Tax Administration, Avoidance and Evasion / Robert J. Reid. - Butterworths, 1981.
192p.
ISBN 0409917028 Hbk £28.95

—Tax evasion in Canada / William I. Innes. - Toronto : Carswell, 1987.
xxvi,326p.
Includes index.
ISBN 0459305719

TAX EVASION - GREAT BRITAIN

—Britain's shadow economy / Stephen Smith. - Oxford : Clarendon, 1986.
192p; 22cm.
Includes bibliography and index.
ISBN 0198285698 £16.95

—Report / Committee on Enforcement Powers of the Revenue Departments : chairman, Lord Keith of Kinkel. - London : H.M.S.O., 1983.
xiv,334p; 25cm.

Vol.2 : Chapters 16-28 and notes / Committee on Enforcement Powers of the Revenue Departments : chairman, Lord Keith of Kinkel. - 1983.
336-804p; 25cm.

Vol.3 : Chapters 29-33 and notes : Development land tax, petroleum revenue tax, capital transfer tax and stamp duties / Committee on Enforcement Powers of the Revenue Departments : chairman, Lord Keith of Kinkel. - 1984.
iv,251p; 25cm.

—Tax avoidance and tax evasion / 2nd ed. - London : Sweet & Maxwell, 1987.
ISBN 0948711124 Pbk £15.00

—Tax Avoision / London : Institute of Economic Affairs.

TAX EVASION (INTERNATIONAL LAW)

—Economics of international tax avoidance : political power versus economic law / by Barry Bracewell-Milnes. - Deventer : Kluwer, 1980.
137p.
Includes bibliography.

—International tax avoidance and evasion : four related studies / Paris : O.E.C.D., 1987.
112p.
ISBN 9264129251

TAX EXEMPTION

—Tax policy towards the national heritage : proceedings of a seminar held in Venice, 1983, during the 37th Congress of the International Fiscal Association / organised by the International Fiscal Association. - Deventer, Netherlands : Kluwer Law and Taxation Publishers, 1984.
ISBN 9065441786

TAX EXPENDITURES

—International aspects of tax expenditures : a comparative study / Paul R. McDaniel, Stanley S. Surrey, editors. - Deventer, the Netherlands : Kluwer Law and Taxation, 1984.
ISBN 9065441638

—Tax expenditures : a review of the issues and country practices / report by the Committee on Fiscal Affairs. - Paris : Organisation for Economic Co-operation and Development, 1984.
88p.
Examines how governments account for tax expenditures which favour particular types of taxpayers.
ISBN 9264125892 Hbk £30.00

TAX HAVENS

—Grundy's Tax havens : a world survey / 5th ed. - London : Sweet & Maxwell, 1987.
xxiv,100p; 22cm.
Previous ed.: 1983. Includes index.
ISBN 0421379006 Pbk £26.00

—Recourse to tax havens : use and abuse : proceedings of a seminar held in Paris during the 34th Congress of the International Fiscal Association... / organised by the International Fiscal Association. - Deventer : Kluwer on behalf of the IFA, 1981.
147p; 21cm. - (IFA congress seminar series).
Bibliography: p.141-148.
ISBN 9065440054

—Tax havens and offshore finance : a study of transnational economic development / Richard Anthony Johns. - London : Frances Pinter, 1983.
xiv,259p.
Bibliography: p248-255.

—Tax havens encyclopaedia / edited by Barry Spitz. - 1. - London : Butterworths, 1975.
loose-leaf.
Tab indexed. Includes bibliographies.
ISBN 0406382263 £40.00

—Taxation of domestic shareholders on undistributed income of foreign corporate affiliates : objectives, techniques, and consequences : proceedings of a seminar held in New York in 1986 during the 40th Congress of the International Fiscal Association / edited by Brian J. Arnold. - Deventer, Netherlands : Kluwer Law and Taxation Publishers, 1987.
Includes bibliography.
ISBN 9065443347

TAX HAVENS - CANADA

—Taxation of controlled foreign corporations : an international comparison / Brian J. Arnold. - Toronto, Ont. : Canadian Tax Foundation, 1986.
xxiii, 816; 23 cm. - (Canadian tax paper).
Includes index. Bibliography: p. 797-811.
ISBN 0888080239 pbk. £75.00

TAX HAVENS - GREAT BRITAIN

—International tax avoidance / Board of Inland Revenue. - London : Board of Inland Revenue, 1981.
66 leaves.

—Isle of Man : a low-tax area / by Mark Solly. - Croydon : Tolley, 1984.
ix,458p.
Includes index.
ISBN 0854591397

—Tax Havens and Their Uses / new ed. - London : Economist Intelligence Unit, 1981.
Illus, updated to March 1983. - - (QER Special: No. 105).
ISBN 0900351403 Hbk £60.00

—Taxation of international business / London : Board of Inland Revenue, 1982.
125 leaves.
Revised draft proposals on international tax avoidance.

TAX INCENTIVES - CANADA

—Canadian R & D incentives : their adequacy and impact / Donald G. McFetridge, Jacek P. Warda. - Toronto, Canada : Canadian Tax Foundation, 1983.
vii, 100 p.; 23 cm.
Includes index. Bibliography: p. 93-97.
ISBN 0888080131 pbk. £10.00

TAX PLANNING

—International tax avoidance and evasion : colloquy of 5-7 March 1980 (Strasbourg), compendium of documents / Amsterdam : International Bureau of Fiscal Documentation, 1981.
184p.
ISBN 9070125196

—International tax avoidance and evasion : four related studies / Paris : O.E.C.D., 1987.
112p.
ISBN 9264129251

—International tax planner's manual / Horwath & Horwath International. - Rev. impression. - North Ryde, N.S.W. : CCH Australia, 1985.
xvi,547p.
Includes index.
ISBN 0869038273

—International tax planning / 2nd ed. - London : Butterworths, 1983.
ISBN 0406382379 Hbk £18.00

—International tax planning / Barry Spitz. - 2nd ed. - London : Butterworths, 1983.
xxiii,178p.
This book for the tax planner dealing with international tax issues analyzes the methods of international tax planning and explains the basic techniques. Statutes and treaties in conjunction with case law are used to illustrate the analysis.
ISBN 0406382379 Hbk £18.00

—International tax planning manual / by Horwath & Horwath International. - 2. - North Ryde, N.S.W. : CCH Australia, 1986.
looseleaf.
Includes index.
ISBN 0869037595

—International Tax Systems and Planning Techniques / London : Oyez Longman, 1984.
ISBN 085120760X loose £75.00

—Tax avoidance, tax evasion : a survey of the treatment of tax aviodance and tax evasion in the main industrialised countries of the world / compiled in 1982 for Committee N of the Section on Business Law of the International Bar Association by a team of international rapporteurs and updated and revised for this edition. - 2nd ed. - London : International Bar Association in co-operation with Sweet & Maxwell, 1987.
viii,160p.
Includes bibliographical references.
ISBN 0948711124

—Tax avoidance, tax evasion : a survey of the treatment of tax avoidance and tax evasion in the main industrialized countries of the world / compiled for Committee N of the Section on Business Law of the International Bar Association by a team of international rapporteurs. - London : International Bar Association in co-operation with Sweet & Maxwell, 1982.
viii,104p; 22cm.
ISBN 0950587672 Pbk £8.50

—Tax minimisation techniques : a specially commissioned report / by R.W. Maas. - London : Oyez Longman, 1984.
xi,102leaves; 30cm. - (Oyez Longman intelligence reports).
Previous ed.: 1982.
ISBN 0851209300 spiral £45.00

—World of international tax planning / Milton Grundy. - Cambridge : Cambridge University Press, 1984.
x,143p; 23cm.
Includes index.
ISBN 052125955X £19.50

TAX PLANNING - AUSTRALIA

—Family Taxation Planning / Monash University Staff. - Clayton : Monash University Press, 1984.
ISBN 0867463422 Hbk £18.00

—Tax avoidance 1981 : the new law : being a commentary on part IVA of the Income Tax Assessment Act 1936 together with the text of the legislation / by E.F. Mannix. - Sydney : Butterworths, 1981.
ix,41p.
Includes index.
ISBN 0409357782

TAX PLANNING - CANADA

—Canada Estate Planning Service / Toronto : DeBoo.
Looseleaf service.
ISBN 0888201125 loose £260.00

—Canada Tax Planning Service, 4 Vols. / Toronto : DeBoo.
ISBN 0888202008 loose £425.00

—Estate Planning / Vancouver : British Columbia Continuing Legal Education Society, 1983.
77p.
ISBN 0865040915 Hbk £45.00

—Estate Planning and Administration / Agincourt : Carswell, 1986.
ISBN 045938050 Hbk £30.00

—Estate Planning and Administration / Agincourt : Carswell, 1985-1986.
406p. - (Bar Admission Course Material Ser.).
This text discusses will planning and drafting, administration of an estate and how to advise the executor on applications for probate or distribution of the estate.

—Estate Planning and Administration : Bar Admission Course Material / Agincourt : Carswell, 1987.
406p.

—Estate Planning Handbook / Agincourt : Carswell, 1985.
176p.
This practitioner's handbook of Canadian estate planning law presents numerous precedents and discussions of relevant law. Planning mechanisms to deal with incapacity, terminal illness, and the owner-managed business are addressed in depth.

—Guide to Canadian Personal Tax Planning / Toronto : DeBoo, 1987.
224p.
ISBN 0888202512 Pbk £8.95

—Income Tax Administration, Avoidance and Evasion / Robert J. Reid. - Butterworths, 1981.
192p.
ISBN 0409917028 Hbk £28.95

—Personal Tax Planning / Vancouver : British Columbia Continuing Legal Education Society, 1984.
ISBN 0865041466 Hbk £50.00

—Recent Developments in Estate Planning and Administration / Law Society of Upper Canada. - Toronto : DeBoo, 1980.
- (Special Lectures Ser.).
ISBN 0888200862 Hbk £37.95

—Solicitor's Guide to Corporate Tax Planning / Vancouver : British Columbia Continuing Legal Education Society, 1983.
112p.
ISBN 0865040974 Hbk £45.00

—Tax Planned Will Precedents, 2 Vols. /. - Agincourt : Carswell.
ISBN 0459314300 Hbk £75.75

Vol. 2
This looseleaf service is a guide to tax savings in estate planning in Canada. Annotated precedents, master will form, will instruction checklist, alternative clauses, relevant legislation, coverage of trust, and other relevant materials are included in the two volumes.
ISBN 0459326007 Hbk £50.50

—Tax Planning for Executive and Employee Compensation and Retirement / Toronto : Canadian Tax Foundation, 1985.
- (Conference Reports).

—Taxation and Estate Planning / 3rd ed. - Agincourt : Carswell.

—Taxation and estate planning / by Maurice C. Cullity and Catherine A. Brown. - 2nd ed. - Toronto, Canada : Carswell Co., 1984.
xxvi, 764 p.; 24 cm.
At head of title: Cullity, Forbes, Brown. Includes bibliographical references and index.
ISBN 0459362305 pbk.

—Ward's Tax Law and Planning, 6 Vols. / Beck. - Agincourt : Carswell, 1983.
This multi-volume looseleaf service is a comprehensive treatise on Canadian tax law. Analysis of the statutory language of the Canadian Income Tax Act is the main focus of the work.

—Ward's Tax Law and Planning, 8 Vols. / Agincourt : Carswell, 1988.

TAX PLANNING - CARIBBEAN

—Tax Planning Uses of the Caribbean / London : Oyez Longman, 1984.
- (Oyez Longman Intelligence Report Ser.).
ISBN 0851208533 Hbk

TAX PLANNING - ENGLAND

—Taxation for executors and trustees / by Anthony R. Mellows. - 5th ed. - London : Butterworths, 1981.
xxxiv,428p; 23cm.
Previous ed.: 1976. Includes index.
ISBN 0406623953 £15.00

TAX PLANNING - EUROPE

—Tax Planning for Businesses in Europe / 2nd ed. - London : Butterworths, 1984.
ISBN 0406535515 Hbk

TAX PLANNING - GREAT BRITAIN

—Anti-avoidance legislation / R.K. Ashton. - London : Butterworths, 1981.
xvii,255p; 22cm.
Includes index.
ISBN 0406111405 Pbk Unpriced

—Capital Taxes and Estate Planning Guide / 3rd ed. - London : Longman Professional, 1986.
ISBN 0851212131 Hbk £12.50

—Company Flotations : Tax and Tax Planning / Leon Cane. - London : Butterworths, 1985.
This book is an overall guide to the tax considerations for United Kingdom companies both before and during a public sale. Tax planning for major shareholders and officers is treated in detail in the work. A timetable for flotation is included in the appendix.
ISBN 0406259704 Pbk

—Company Reorganisations : Tax and Tax Planning / Noble. - London : Butterworths, 1986.
ISBN 0406501904 Hbk £35.00

—Coopers and Lybrand: tax and financial planning through pensions / Paul G Meins. - London : Butterworths, 1987.
ISBN 0406500800 Pbk £16.00

—Estate Planning / Croydon : Tolley, 1987.
ISBN 0854592725 Pbk £17.95

—Estate Planning / Croydon : Tolley.
300p.
ISBN 0854592725 Hbk £17.95

—Estate Tax Planning : Including Will Drafting / London : Law Society.
- (Nineteen Eighty-Five Crash Course Transcripts).

—Hambro Capital Taxes and Estate Planning Guide / P. D. Silke. - London : Oyez Longman, 1982.
ISBN 085120662X Hbk £9.95

—Inheritance tax planning / Thornhill. - 2nd ed. - London : Longman Professional, 1988.
ISBN 0851213669 Hbk £85.00

—International tax avoidance / Board of Inland Revenue. – London : Board of Inland Revenue, 1981.
66 leaves.

—Land and Tax Planning / London : Oyez Longman, 1982.
300p. – (Oyez Longman Practical Tax Ser.).
ISBN 0851206077 Hbk £15.00

—Land and Tax Planning / 2nd ed. – London : Longman Professional, 1984.
ISBN 0851208800 Pbk £22.00

—Non-Resident Trusts : The Tax Planning Opportunities / London : Oyez Longman, 1984. – (Oyez Longman Intelligence Report Ser.).
ISBN 0851208169 Hbk

—Offshore tax planning / Oliver Stanley, Giles Clarke. – London : Butterworth, 1986.
180p.
Includes index.
ISBN 0406502102 £30.00

—Offshore tax planning / Vlarke. – London : Butterworths, 1986.
ISBN 0406502102 Hbk £32.00

—Passing down the family business: solving the tax problems / 4th. – London : Longman Professional (UK), 1988.
– (Longman Intelligence Report).
Information and advice on reducing the tax burden and maximising the prosperity of the business when transferring control to another member of the family. Outlines tax planning strategies, and how to use tax reliefs to their full advantage.
ISBN 0851212719 Hbk £95.00

—Potter and Monroe's tax planning with precedents / H. H. Monroe, A. R. Thornhill, K. Prosser, G. Goodfellow. – 10th ed. – London : Sweet & Maxwell, 1987.
xviii,500p; 26cm.
Previous ed.: 1982. Includes index. Kept up to date by supplements.
ISBN 0421334207 £50.00

—Practical tax planning and precedents / London : Longman Professional, 1987.
ISBN 0851213103 loose £110.00

—Practical Tax Saving / Nicholas Noble. – 4th ed. – London : Butterworths, 1984.
ISBN 0406536333 Pbk

—Property tax planning manual / London : Butterworths, 1987.
ISBN 0406137390 Pbk £18.95

—Remuneration planning manual / London : Butterworths, 1986.
ISBN 040650430X Pbk £19.95

—Report of the Working Party on Company Residence, Tax Havens, and Upstream Loans / Edmund Dell. – London : Institute for Fiscal Studies, 1982.
35p; 22cm.
ISBN 0902992309 Pbk Unpriced

—Sumption and Clarke's tax and tax planning / Giles Clarke, Philip Lawton. – 10th ed. – London : Oyez Longman, 1982.
xxvii,265p; 22cm.
Previous ed.: published as Sumption and Lawton's tax and tax planning / by Anthony Sumption and Philip Lawton, 1981. Includes index.
ISBN 0851206921 Pbk Unpriced

—Tax and financial planning for family business / George J Bell. – London : Butterworths, 1984.
ISBN 0406557306 Pbk £16.00

—Tax and financial planning for Lloyd's members / London : Longman Professional, 1988.
– (A Longman Intelligence Report).
ISBN 0851213421 Hbk £85.00

—Tax and financial planning for professional partnerships / Brian Gilligan. – 2nd ed. – London : Butterworths, 1986.
ISBN 0406501807 Pbk £18.50

—Tax and Financial Planning for Professional Partnerships / Brian Gilligan. – 2nd ed. – London : Butterworths, 1986.
This work explains how the tax liability of United Kingdom professional partnerships can be minimized by effective tax planning. The effects of the Finance Act of 1985 on professional partnerships is discussed in detail.
ISBN 0406501807 Pbk

—Tax and financial planning for sportsmen and entertainers / Richard Harvey. – London : Butterworths, 1987.
ISBN 040650220X Pbk £18.50

—Tax avoidance and tax evasion / 2nd ed. – London : Sweet & Maxwell, 1987.
ISBN 0948711124 Pbk £15.00

—Tax Avoision / London : Institute of Economic Affairs.

—Tax efficient personal investments / 2nd ed. – Croydon : Tolley, 1987.
ISBN 0854593152 Pbk £12.95

—Tax Planning for Family Business / London : Butterworths, 1984.
ISBN 0406556806 Pbk

—Tax Planning for Groups of Companies / London : Butterworths, 1985.
This book examines the various aspects of taxation of groups or consortia in the United Kingdom and considers commercial factors to determine the most appropriate group structure. Pro forma tax elections and sample agreements for the surrender of tax advantages between group companies are included.
ISBN 0406075808 Hbk

—Tax planning for groups of companies / London : Butterworths, 1985.
ISBN 0406075808 Hbk £29.95

—Tax planning for medical practitioners / Stephen Burwood. – 2nd ed. – London : Butterworths, 1987.
ISBN 04066190054 Pbk £18.50

—Tax Planning for New Business / 2nd ed. – Croydon : Tolley.
152p.

—Tax planning for new businesses / 2nd ed. – Croydon : Tolley, 1987.
ISBN 0854592032 Pbk £9.95

—Tax Planning for the Family / 2nd ed. – London : Oyez Longman, 1982.
– (Oyez Longman Practical Tax Ser.).
ISBN 0851206891 Hbk £9.50

—Tax planning for the family / 3rd ed. – London : Longman Professional, 1986.
ISBN 0851209203 Pbk £22.00

—Tax Planning on Marriage Breakdown / 2nd ed. – London : Oyez Longman, 1981.
– (Oyez Longman Practical Tax Ser.).
ISBN 0851206182 Hbk £11.50

—Tax planning on marriage breakdown / 4th ed. – London : Longman Professional, 1986.
ISBN 0851210740 Pbk £26.50

—Tax Planning Through Inheritance Trusts / London : Oyez Longman, 1983.
– (Oyez Longman Intelligence Report Ser.).
ISBN 0851208193 Hbk £45.00

—Tax planning through trusts / Robert Venables. – London : Butterworths, 1983.
xxxiv,371p; 24cm.
Includes index.
ISBN 0406406014

—Tax Planning with Precedents / H. H. Monroe. – London : Sweet & Maxwell, 1987.

—Tax strategy for companies / 4th ed. – London : Longman Professional, 1986.
xxviii,511p; 22cm.
Previous ed.: 1983. Includes index.
ISBN 0851209211 Pbk £30.00

—Tax Strategy for Conveyancing and Land Transactions / London : Oyez Longman, 1984.
ISBN 0851208797 Hbk

—Tax strategy for directors, executives and employers / 2nd ed. – London : Longman Professional, 1985.
– (Tax Strategy Series).
ISBN 0851210767 Pbk £30.00

—Taxation and trusts / by Geraint W. Thomas. – London : Sweet & Maxwell, 1981.
xxiv,205p; 19cm.
Includes index.
ISBN 0421277203 Hbk Unpriced
ISBN 0421277300 Pbk £6.95

—Taxation of international business / London : Board of Inland Revenue, 1982.
125 leaves.
Revised draft proposals on international tax avoidance.

—Taxation of Leasing Transactions / London : Butterworths, 1984.
The tax advantages to be gained through leasing transactions in the United Kingdom have led to a series of anti-avoidance measures. This work reviews the incidence of the major taxes levied as they relate to the practice of leasing and shows how through careful tax planning many of the benefits of leasing can be maintained. Incl. Finance Act 1984 Supplement.
ISBN 0406538026 Pbk

—Tolley's tax planning 1982-83 / edited by A. L. Chapman. – Truro : TLPC and Tolley Publishing, 1982.
xxxviii, 806p.
ISBN 0854590897

—Tolley's tax planning 1986 / edited by Glyn Saunders ... et al. – Croydon : Tolley Publishing, 1985.
xiv,890p.
ISBN 0854592032

—Tolley's tax planning 1987 / edited by Glyn Saunders ... et al. – Croydon : Tolley Publishing, 1986.
xv,863p.
Includes index.
ISBN 0854592466

—Tolley's tax planning 1988 / edited by Glyn Saunders, Robert Wareham and Deborah Hicks. – 2 v. – Croydon : Tolley Publishing, 1987.
ISBN 0854593020

—Tolleys tax planning 1985 / edited by Glyn Saunders ... et al. – Croydon : Tolley, 1985.
xiv,911p.
Includes index.
ISBN 0854591435

—Tolleys tax planning supplement / edited by A.L. Chapman. – Croyden : Tolley, 1984.
xxii,170p.
Supplements: Tolleys tax planning. 1982/83 ed.. Includes index.
ISBN 0854591729

—Trusts and tax planning / 3rd ed. – London : Longman Professional, 1987.
ISBN 0851208762 Pbk £35.88

—UK Companies Operating Overseas : Tax and Financial Strategies / M. J. Packman. – 2nd ed. – London : Oyez Longman, 1984.
– (Oyez Longman Intelligence Report Ser.).
ISBN 0851208770 Hbk £45.00

—Utilising company tax losses and reliefs / by Nigel A. Eastaway and Edward P. Magrin. – 2nd ed. – London : Institute of Chartered Accountants in England and Wales, 1982.
xxxiv,321p; 21cm.
Previous ed.: 1979. Includes index.
ISBN 0852913133 Pbk Unpriced

—VAT planning / Croydon : Tolley, 1988.
ISBN 0854592989 Pbk £16.95

—Year End and Accounting Period Tax Planning / G. J. Bell. – 2nd ed. – London : Oyez Longman, 1984.
– (Oyez Longman Practical Tax Ser.).
ISBN 0851208398 Hbk £10.50

TAX PLANNING – HONG KONG

—Hong Kong in International Tax Planning / London : Oyez Longman, 1983.
– (Oyez Longman Intelligence Report Ser.).
ISBN 085120810X Hbk £55.00

TAX PLANNING – IRELAND

—Carroll's tax planning in Ireland / by Michael F. O'Reilly : consultant author Brian A. Carroll. – London : Sweet & Maxwell, 1986.
xxi,467p; 25cm.
Includes index.
ISBN 0421367504 £40.00

TAX PLANNING – SOUTH AFRICA

—How to Re-Organise Your Affairs so as to Pay the Least Amount of Tax / Cape Town : Legal & Financial Publishing, 1983.
ISBN 0869940139 Hbk £13.50

TAX PLANNING – SOUTHEAST ASIA

—Tax Planning Strategies for Companies in South East Asia / London : Oyez Longman, 1984.
– (Oyez Longman Intelligence Report Ser.).
ISBN 0851208126 Hbk

TAX PLANNING – UNITED KINGDOM

—UK-US Tax Planning Under the Treaty / London : Oyez Longman, 1981.
– (Oyez Longman Intelligence Report Ser.).
ISBN 0851205399 Hbk £35.00

TAX PLANNING – UNITED STATES

—Estate Planning Law Locator 1988 / New York : Bowker, 1988.
ISBN 0835223507 Hbk £30.00

—UK-US Tax Planning Under the Treaty / London : Oyez Longman, 1981.
– (Oyez Longman Intelligence Report Ser.).
ISBN 0851205399 Hbk £35.00

TAX PROTESTS AND APPEALS

—Arbitration in taxation / Gustaf Lindencrona, Nils Mattsson. – Deventer, The Netherlands : Kluwer, 1981.
92 p.; 22 cm.
Includes bibliographical references.
ISBN 9065440003 pbk.

TAX PROTESTS AND APPEALS – CANADA

—Need for and the feasibility of an appeals process in regard to municipal grants-in-lieu of taxes : a report prepared for the Minister of Public Works Canada / I.C. Pollack, R. Gaulin, G. Simpson. – Ottawa : Minister of Supply and Services Canada, 1983.
324 p. in various pagings; 28 cm.
English and French. Added t.p.: La necessite et la faisabilite d'une procedure d'appel dans le regime de subventions aux municipalites en compensation d'imp$ots.
ISBN 0662524039

TAX PROTESTS AND APPEALS – GREAT BRITAIN

—Tax appeals handbook / London : Butterworths, 1983.
ISBN 0406535221 Pbk £13.00

TAX PROTESTS AND APPEALS - NORTHERN IRELAND

—Tax appeals : system of General Commissioners of Income Tax for Northern Ireland : a consultative document / London : Board of Inland Revenue, 1987.
6p.

TAXATION

—Adjustments for tax purposes in highly inflationary economics : proceedings of a seminar held in Buenos Aires in 1984 during the 38th Congress of the International Fiscal Association / Deventer, The Netherlands : Kluwer Law and Taxation Publishers, 1985.
ISBN 9065442162

—Comparative tax studies : essays in honor of Richard Goode / edited by Sijbren Cnossen. - Amsterdam : North-Holland Pub. Co., 1983.
xiii, 444 p.; 23 cm.
'Bibliography: works of Richard Goode': p. 431-435. Includes bibliographies.
ISBN 0444864210

—Corporate Tax Procedures : International Bureau of Fiscal Documentation / KPMG International Tax Centre Staff. - Amsterdam : International Bureau of Fiscal Documentation, 1988.
137p.
ISBN 9070125331 Hbk £65.00

—Disregard of a legal entity fortax purposes / Kluwer Law and Taxation, 1989.
560. - (Cahiers de droit fiscal internatinal LXXIVa).
Collections of writings by twenty tax experts in the systems in their own countries, presenting a comparison of the subject.
ISBN 9065444130 Pbk £48/Dfl 150

—Estate Duty Act / E.B.C. - Lucknow : Eastern Book Company, 1984.

—Imputation systems : objectives and consequences : proceedings of a seminar held in Montreal 1982 during the 36th Congress of the International Fiscal Association / organized by the International Fiscal Association. - Deventer : Kluwer, 1983.
129p. - (IFA congress seminar series).
ISBN 9065441212

—Inland Revenue press release / v. - London : Inland Revenue Press Office, 1943.

—International aspects of tax expenditures : a comparative study / Paul R. McDaniel, Stanley S. Surrey, editors. - Deventer, the Netherlands : Kluwer Law and Taxation, 1984.
ISBN 9065441638

—International employment tax handbook / Reading. - Cambridge : Woodhead-Faulkner, 1982.
ISBN 0859411915 Hbk £115.00

—International Tax Agreements : Supplement No. 40 / United Nations. - London : HMSO, 1985.
ISBN 0119083663 Hbk £5.70

—International tax glossary / W. G Kuiper. - Amsterdam : International Bureau of Fiscal Documentation, 1988.
xii, 322 p.; 19 cm.
'Prepared by a working group ... headed by Mr. W.G. Kuiper'–P. iv. 'The first volume of a new series of books, entitled 'International tax manuals''–P. vi.
ISBN 9070125366

—International taxation encyclopaedia / London : Butterworths, 1988.
Service.

—Jurisdiction to tax in international law: theory and practice of legislative fiscal jurisdiction / Kluwer Law and Taxation, 1989.
238. - (Series on International Taxation 9).
Deals with the bases and the limits of the right of states under international lw to create tax obligations on persons within and outside their territory. Describes the practice of states on matters of taxation in terms of the doctrine of jurisdiction in international law. Examines topics such as the taxation of mining activities on the continental shelf.
ISBN 9065444165 Hbk £51/Dfl 160

—Manual of International Taxation / London : Butterworths.

—Multilateral Convention for the Avoidance of Double Taxation of Copyright Royalties : Original Text of the Convention Adopted by the Madrid Conference (1979) / rep. 1987. - Geneva : World Intellectual Property Organization.
41p.

—Nondiscrimination in International Tax Law / Dordrecht : Kluwer, 1986.
304p.
ISBN 9065442669 Hbk Gld135.00

—Practical approach to revenue law / Stephen W. Mayson. - 2nd ed. - London : Financial Training, 1981.
xxxiii,411p.
Includes index.
ISBN 090632209X

—Practical approach to revenue law / Stephen W. Mayson. - 6th ed. - London : Financial Training, 1985.
xliii,559p.
Previous ed.: 1984.
ISBN 090632288X

—Practical approach to revenue law / Stephen W. Mayson. - 3rd ed. - London : Financial Training, 1982.
xl,484p; 23cm.
ISBN 0906322200

—Principles of international double tax relief / London : Butterworths, 1985.
ISBN 0421317507 Hbk £45.00

—Protection of the individual with reagard sic to the acts of the tax and customs administrations : proceedings of the colloquy organised by the Council of Europe in co-operation with the International Centre of Sociological and Penitentiary Research and Studies in Messina 25-27 March 1986 / Strasbourg : Council of Europe, 1986.
39p.
ISBN 9287108749

—Public Trusts and Taxation / Lucknow : Eastern Book Company, 1987.

—Public Trusts and Taxation / Lucknow : Eastern Book Company, 1987.
418p.

—Recent Developments in Tax Treaties and International Taxation / Toronto : DeBoo, 1985.
48p.
ISBN 0888202288 Pbk £25.00

—Recent tax problems / edited by Jacqueline Dyson. - London : Stevens, 1985.
xiv,108p; 22cm.
Includes index.
ISBN 0420474102 Pbk £15.00

—Revenue law : comprising income tax, surtax, capital gains tax, corporation tax, estate duty tax, stamp duties, tax and estate planning / by Barry Pinson. - 5th ed. - London : Sweet & Maxwell, 1971.
lxvi,641p.
Previous ed.: 1970. Includes index.
ISBN 0421163607 Pbk
ISBN 0421163704

—Tax aspects of acquisitions and mergers / edited by Philip Cooke, Jan M. van der Beek. - 2nd ed. - Deventer : Kluwer, 1983.
150p.
ISBN 9065441514

—Tax Laws / New Delhi : Sultan Chand and Sons.

—Tax Locator 1988 / New York : Bowker, 1988.
ISBN 0835223493 Hbk £30.00

—Tax minimisation techniques : a specially commissioned report / by R.W. Maas. - London : Oyez Longman, 1984.
xi,102leaves; 30cm. - (Oyez Longman intelligence reports).
Previous ed.: 1982.
ISBN 0851209300 spiral £45.00

—Tax Reforms and Asset Markets / Stockholm : Industriens Utredningsinstitut, 1985.
181p.

—Tax Treatment of Exchange Gains and Losses / KPMG International Tax Centre and International Bureau of Fiscal Documentation. - Amsterdam : International Bureau of Fiscal Documentation, 1988.
137p.
ISBN 907012534X Hbk £80.00

—The Tax Treatment of Transfer Pricing / International Bureau of Fiscal Documentation. - Amsterdam : International Bureau of Fiscal Documentation, 1988.
ISBN 9070125293 loose £1400.00

Renewal

—Taxation and human rights : proceedings of a seminar held in Brussels in 1987 during the 41st Congress of the International Fiscal Association / Marc Baltus, chairman of the seminar. - Deventer, Netherlands : Kluwer Law and Taxation, 1988.
vii,83p.
ISBN 9065443843

—Taxation in developed countries : an international symposium / organised by the French Ministry of Finance in association with the Committee on Fiscal Affairs of the OECD, Paris, 12th and 13th January 1987. - Paris : O.E.C.D., 1987.
99p.
ISBN 9264129294

—Taxation in European socialist countries / J. van Hoorn and T. Nagy, managing editors : W.G. Kuiper, co-ordinating editor, T.G. Brierley, editor. - 2. - Amsterdam : International Bureau of Fiscal Documentation, 1984.
loose-leaf.
Updated by loose-leaf supplements.

—Taxation international / Croydon, Surrey : Tolley, 1988.
Published as a supplement to Taxation.
ISBN 09547053

—Taxation of international business : dual resident companies : consultative document / London : Inland Revenue, 1984.
7p.

—Taxation of international income / London : Butterworths, 1988.
ISBN 0409788015 Pbk

—Taxation of the income arising from the international seabed : proceedings of a seminar held in Berlin in 1981 during the 35th Congress of the International Fiscal Association / organised by the International Fiscal Association. - Deventer : Kluwer, 1982.
159p. - (IFA congress seminar series).
ISBN 9065440593

—Taxes in France / Francis Lefebvre : adapted by Lionel Halpern. - 3rd ed. - London : Butterworth, 1980.
xiv,233p; 23cm.
This ed. translation and adaptation of: 'Les impots en France'. 11.ed. Paris : Editions Francis Lefebvre, 1979. -.
ISBN 0406520844 £17.50

—Tolley's taxation in the Republic of Ireland 1987-88 / by John Newth and Glyn Saunders : from an original text by Eric L. Harvey. - Croydon : Tolley, 1987.
vii,293p.
Includes index.
ISBN 0854592946

—UK Companies Operating Overseas : Tax and Financial Strategies / M. J. Packman. - London : Oyez Longman, 1981.
- (Oyez Longman Intelligence Report Ser.).
ISBN 0851205321 Hbk £45.00

—UK Companies Operating Overseas : Tax and Financial Strategies / M. J. Packman. - 2nd ed. - London : Oyez Longman, 1984.
- (Oyez Longman Intelligence Report Ser.).
ISBN 0851208770 Hbk £45.00

—United Nations Model Convention for Tax Treaties Between Developed and Developing Countries : a description and analysis / Stanley S. Surrey : with a preface by Helmut F. Debatin. - Amsterdam : International Bureau of Fiscal Documentation, 1980.
x,113p.
Includes bibliographical references.
ISBN 907012517X

—Whillan's Tax Tables, 1984-1985 / London : Butterworths, 1984.
ISBN 0406543194 Hbk

—Wills administration and taxation: a practical guide / Lesley King, Anthony King. - 3rd. - London : Sweet & Maxwell.
Covers substantive law, tax considerations, will drafting. The chapter dealing with inheritance tax has been updated to include the new rules introduced in the Finance Act 1986. Also covers the new provisions of the Insolvency Act 1986. The text is illustrated with worked examples.
ISBN 0421382708 Pbk £17.50

TAXATION - ASIA

—Taxes and Investment in Asia and the Pacific / Amsterdam : International Bureau of Fiscal Documentation, 1988.

Fl looseleaf 1989 suppl. renewal

TAXATION - AUSTRALIA

—1985 Australian master tax guide / North Ryde, N.S.W. : CCH Australia, 1985.
1099p.
'This edition ... incorporates changes that have taken place up to 25 January 1985'. Includes index.
ISBN 0869036602

—Australian Federal Taxation Penalties and Offences / North Ryde : C.C.H. Australia, 1985.
395p.
ISBN 0869038427 Hbk

—Australian Tax Office Practice / Woolloomooloo : International Business Communications, 1986.
ISBN 0949072036 loose £195.00

—Australian Tax Reports Vols. 1-17 (1969-1986) and Australian and New Zealand Income Tax Reports Vols. 1-10 (1936-1968) Consolidated Index and Tables / Butterworths. - Butterworths, 1989.
292p.
ISBN 0409300977 Hbk £110.00
ISBN £79.00 to subscribers

—Australian Tax : Tax Reports : 1969 to Present / Wellington : Butterworths.

Back Vols. avail.

—Australian Taxation Law / C. Coleman. - Sydney : Butterworths, 1988.
900p.

—Bound Australian Tax Cases / North Ryde : C.C.H. Australia.

—Bound Australian Tax Decisions, 6 Vols. / North Ryde : C.C.H. Australia.

—Butterworths Australian Tax Handbook 1989 / Butterworths, 1989.
1,504p.
ISBN 0409302414 Pbk £39.00

—Butterworths Australian Tax Legislation 1989 / Butterworths, 1989.
Vol. 1A
ISBN 0409301523
Vol. 1B
ISBN 0409301531
Vol. 2
ISBN 040930154X

—Butterworths Student Companions /. – Butterworths, 1987.
117p.
ISBN 0409492469

—Butterworths Tax Guide, 3 Vols. / 1st ed. – Butterworths, 1989.
ca 1,650p.
Concise Tax subscribers
ISBN 0409303410 £260.00
With Legislation

—Cases and Materials on Taxation / 2nd ed. – Butterworths, 1984.
790p.
ISBN 0409491624 Hbk £75.00 incl. suppl.
ISBN 0409491721 Pbk £62.50 incl. suppl.
Cumulative Supplement-1986
ISBN 0409491152 £3.00

—Company Tax Recoupment Law / S.W. Gibb. – North Ryde : C.C.H. Australia, 1983.
215p.
ISBN 0869036327 Hbk £40.00

—Institutional Renewal in the Australia Tax Systems / Clayton : Monash University Press, 1985.
ISBN 0867462752 Hbk £9.50

—International transactions and Australian income tax : being a commentary on Division 13 of the Income Tax Assessment Act 1936 together with the text of the Legislation / by E. F. Mannix. – Sydney : Butterworths, 1982.
x,46p.
Includes index.
ISBN 0409493554

—Leading Cases on Australian Income Tax / Mannix. – 5th ed. – North Ryde : Butterworths (Australia), 1984.
ISBN 0409493929 Pbk £31.30

—New Tax Penalties 1984 / Monash University Staff. – Clayton : Monash University Press, 1984.
ISBN 0867463538 Hbk £21.00

—Petroleum Taxation Law / Glenside : Australian Mineral Foundation, 1985.

—Taxation, Inflation and the Role of Government / Turramura : Centre for Independent Studies.
56p.
ISBN 0949769002 Hbk £3.50

—Taxation issues of the 1980s : papers presented at a conference organised by the Centre of Policy Studies, Monash University / John G. Head, editor. – Sydney : Australian Tax Research Foundation, 1983.
xii,438p.
Includes bibliographies and index.
ISBN 0949482005

—Taxation Law and Practice : Revision Exercises / Randwick : New South Wales University Press, 1983.
80p.

—Taxation Law in Australia / Cynthia Coleman. – Butterworths, 1989.
ca 960p.
ISBN 0409301388 Hbk £85.00
ISBN 0409494704 Pbk £75.00

—Taxation of Dividends : The Imputation and Foreign Tax Credit Systems / R. H. Doherty. – Sydney : Butterworths, 1987.
300p.

TAXATION - CANADA

—Allocation of taxing power under the Canadian constitution / G.V. La Forest. – 2nd ed. – Toronto : Canadian Tax Foundation, 1981.
viii,219p.

—Atlantic Provinces Taxation Service / Toronto : DeBoo, 1984.
ISBN 0888201850 Hbk £1750.00

—Background of current fiscal problems / J. Harvey Perry. – Toronto : Canadian Tax Foundation, 1982.
v,159p.
Includes index.
ISBN 0888080107

—Canada From Abroad : Legal, Business and Tax Aspects / North Ryde : C.C.H. Australia.
210p.
ISBN 0887963129 Pbk £16.95

—Canada Tax Cases / Toronto : DeBoo.
This service, updated twice monthly, reports all judgments concerning federal taxation decided by the Supreme Court of Canada, the Federal Court. the Tax Court, and the upper courts of the provinces. Included are headnotes, editorial notes on important decisions, topical and statutory indices, and tables of appeals. Bound volumes of all reported cases are issued semi-annually.
ISBN 0888201672 loose £325.00

—Canada Tax Cases Index and Citator : Consolidated from 1972 / Toronto : DeBoo, 1983.
ISBN 0888201486 Hbk £95.00

—Canada Tax Letter / Toronto : DeBoo.
This series of studies, intended for the tax specialist, contains analyses and opinions of important legislation and jurisprudence. Approximately six issues per year are planned.
ISBN 0888201664 Hbk £140.00

—Canada Tax Manual / Toronto : DeBoo.
This two volume looseleaf sourcebook covers the Canadian Income Tax Act and includes discussion of individual taxation; corporate taxation; business, property, and employment income; taxation of non-residents; and tax appeals cases.
ISBN 0888201362 loose £225.00

—Canada Tax Service / Toronto : DeBoo.
This multi-volume looseleaf service provides a seate taxation; business, property, and employment income; taxation of non-residents; and tax appeals cases.
ISBN 0888201656 loose £725.00

—Canada Tax Words, Phrases and Rules / Toronto : DeBoo, 1986.
ISBN 0888202504 Hbk £160.00
Supplements
This work identifies words, phrases, and rules judicially considered in income tax cases from 1917 to the present. The alphabetical arrangement allows the reader to compare all definitions of a particular word or phrase. Cross-references and annotations are also included. Annual supplements are planned.

—Canada - U.S. Tax Treaty / Vancouver : British Columbia Continuing Legal Education Society, 1985.
73p.
ISBN 0865041857 Hbk £55.00

—Canada's Tax Treaties, 2 Vols. / Butterworths.

—Canadian Current Tax, 1 Vol. / Butterworths.

—Canadian current tax / 5. – Toronto : Butterworths, 1981.
Volumes numbered from 1984 onwards.

—Canadian Tax News / Agincourt : Carswell, 1987.

—Canadian tax policy / Robin W. Boadway, Harry M. Kitchen. – 2nd ed. – Toronto : Canadian Tax Foundation, 1984.
xvi,390p.
Includes bibliographical references and index.
ISBN 0888080212

—Canadian Tax Treaties, 2 vols / Toronto : Butterworths.

—Canadian Taxation / Toronto : DeBoo, 1981.
ISBN 0888201001 Hbk £39.95

—Canadian Taxation of Charities and Donations / Toronto : DeBoo, 1987.
ISBN 088820258X Hbk £135.00
Supplements
This book deals with registered charities and their income tax obligations, fund raisers and donations, and non-profit organizations. Among the materials included are regulations, bulletins, circulars, and an appendix of statutes.

—Canadian Taxpayer / Toronto : DeBoo, 1984.
ISBN 0888201680 Hbk 210.00

—Conference Reports / Toronto : Canadian Tax Foundation, 1984.

—Corporate Taxation / Aurora : Canada Law Book Co, 1984.
585p. – (Text Books-Civil).

—DeBoo Commodity Tax Reports / Toronto : DeBoo.
These monthly reports, dealing with developments in the reform of Canadian commodity tax law, identify actual and potential areas of concern, with emphasis on tax planning and compliance. Also included are relevant discussion papers, draft legislation, and government policy statements.
ISBN 0888202768 loose £150.00

—Family Home and Income Tax / Agincourt : Carswell, 1986.
245p.
This work is a guide to the tax consequences of home ownership in Canada for tax practitioners. The book treats the subject of capital gains exemptions, home improvements, mixed use properties, recreational dwellings, and other tax issues.

—Foreign Tax Credits and Foreign Affiliates / Toronto : Butterworths, 1984.
176p.

—Income Tax and Family Law Handbook, 1 Vol. / Mary Lou Benotto. – Butterworths.
ISBN 0409806471 loose £100.00

—Indians and Taxation in Canada, Second Edition / 2nd ed. – Saskatoon : University of Saskatchewan, Native Law Centre, 1987.
88p.
ISBN 0888801823 Hbk £25.00

—International issues in taxation : the Canadian perspective / Donald J.S. Brean. – Toronto : Canadian Tax Foundation, 1984.
xiii,180p.
Bibliography: p.166-176. - Includes index.
ISBN 0888080190

—International Tax Developments : A Canadian Perspective / Toronto : DeBoo, 1983.
66p.
ISBN 0888202261 Pbk £16.00

—Issues in International Transfer Pricing / Toronto : DeBoo, 1986.
96p.
This review emphasizes practices in Canada and the U.S., with secondary emphasis on practices in Europe and Japan. Also discussed is Revenue Canada's approach to transfer pricing, including Information Circular IC-87-2.
ISBN 0888202636 Pbk £15.00

—Manitoba and Saskatchewan Taxation Service / Toronto : DeBoo, 1984.
ISBN 0888201869 Hbk £175.00

—Municipal and School Tax Credit Assistance Lien Discharge Act, 1983, Bill 121 : An Act to Provide for the Discharge of Liens Registered Under the Municipal and School Tax Credit Assistance Act / Ontario : Ontario Government Publications Service, 1983.
2p.

—Municipal Tax Sales Act, 1983, Bill 138 : An Act Respecting the Sale of Lands for Arrears of Municipal Taxes / Ontario : Ontario Government Publications Service, 1983.
16p.

—New Canada-U.S. Tax Treaty : Impact on Corporations and Individuals / Don Mills : CCH Canadian Ltd, 1985.
ISBN 0887962904 Pbk £12.00

—New Canada-U.S. Tax Treaty with Technical Explanation / Don Mills : CCH Canadian Ltd, 1984.
ISBN 0887962890 Pbk £8.00

—Nineteen Eighty-Five Tax Developments / Toronto : Canadian Tax Foundation, 1985. – (Tax Memo: No. 70).

—Property Purchase Tax Act / Vancouver : Continuing Legal Education Society of British Columbia, 1987.
135p.
ISBN 086504323X Hbk £65.00

—Quest for Reform : The Royal Commission on Taxation Twenty Years Later / Agincourt : Carswell, 1987.
475p.
This work analyzes the history of tax reform in Canada up to and including up-to-date proposals. The author outlines the process and substance of tax reform while comparing it to the Carter Report.

—Real Property Assessment and Taxation / Vancouver : Continuing Legal Education Society of British Columbia, 1985.
165p.
ISBN 086504192X Hbk £60.00

—Structured Settlements / Agincourt : Carswell, 1984.
xx, 250p.
This book for the Canadian practitioner examines the procedure for arriving at a fair settlement figure, the negotiation process, and how to proceed with insurers and Revenue Canada. Actual correspondence relating to a structured award is included in the appendix.

—Tax Administration Reports, 2 Vols. / Goodman. – Toronto : DeBoo.
This service provides an analysis of every new or revised Interpretation Bulletin and Advance Tax Ruling since November 1985. Analyses contain summaries of bulletin contents, a listing of Income Tax Act and Regulations references, cross-references to other relevant bulletins, and evaluations of Revenue Canada's positions. Semi-monthly updates and a complimentary newsletter are also included.
ISBN 0888202237 loose £275.00

—Tax Aspects of General Practice / Vancouver : British Columbia Continuing Legal Education Society, 1985.
646p.
ISBN 0865042233 Hbk £75.00

—Tax Aspects of Incorporation / Toronto : Butterworths, 1983.
128p.

—Tax Aspects of Litigation / Vancouver : British Columbia Continuing Legal Education Society, 1982.
138p.
ISBN 086504077X Hbk £40.00

—Tax Facts 4 : The Canadian Consumer Tax Index and You, No. 4 / Vancouver : Fraser Institute.
ISBN 0889750726 Hbk £4.95

—Tax planning for the Canadian businessman : cradle to grave : papers presented at the 1980 British Columbia Tax Conference / jointly sponsored by the Canadian Tax Foundation in co-operation with the Faculty of Law at the University of British Columbia. – Toronto : Canadian Tax Foundation, 1980.
330p; 28cm.

—Tax policy options in the 1980s / edited by Wayne R. Thirsk, John Whalley. – Toronto : Canadian Tax Foundation, 1982.
vi,452p.
Includes bibliographical notes and index. Papers from Canadian Tax Foundation conference 'Tax policy options in the 1980s' held in Toronto, March 1981.
ISBN 0888080077

—Tax Regulations Reports, 2 Vols. / Toronto : DeBoo.
This service reproduces all Regulations, Schedules, and Draft Regulations pertaining to the Income Tax Act, accompanied by commentaries and analyses. Also contained are discussions of relevant case law, numerical examples, and capital cost allowance classes. Twelve updates per year are planned.
ISBN 0888202814 loose £255.00

—Taxation and Estate Planning / 3rd ed. – Agincourt : Carswell.

—Taxation in Canada / J. Harvey Perry. – 4th ed. – Toronto : Canadian Tax Foundation, 1984.
xii,248p.
Bibliography: p.234-240. - Includes index.

—Taxation of Canadian Oil and Gas Income / R. H. Bowhay. – Toronto : DeBoo, 1986.
This text discusses non-deductibility of payments to the Crown, investment tax credits, successor corporation rules, joint exploration corporations, and the National Energy Program. Annual consolidated supplements are planned.
ISBN 0888202474 Hbk £135.00

—Taxation of Corporations and Shareholders : Cases and Materials / D. Keith McNair. – Agincourt : Carswell, 1986.
616p.
This text contains both cases and materials pertaining to corporate tax. The bulk of the text is explanatory in nature. These explanations are supplemented with short cases extracts to further illustrate a point.

—Taxation of Farmers and Fishermen / Toronto : DeBoo, 1980.
ISBN 0888200803 Hbk £135.00

—Taxation of Lawyers' Accounts / Vancouver : Continuing Legal Education Society of British Columbia, 1986.
130p.
ISBN 086504256X Hbk £55.00

—Taxation of Partnerships in Canada / Carl F. Steiss. – Butterworths, 1983.
104p.
ISBN 0409859761 Hbk £29.95

—Taxation of Party-Party Costs / Vancouver : Continuing Legal Education Society of British Columbia, 1987.
107p.
ISBN 0865042926 Hbk £60.00

—Taxation of private corporations and their shareholders / Howard J. Kellough, Peter E. McQuillan. – Toronto : Canadian Tax Foundation, 1983.
ix,825p.
ISBN 0888080174

—Taxation of Resource Industries / Agincourt : Carswell, 1987.
ca 370p.

—Taxation of Resource Industries / Agincourt : Carswell, 1987.
392p.
This text discusses the relevant sections of the Income Tax Act. Also included are discussions on depletion, successor corporation rules and resource allowances. Special coverage includes sample calculations and tables listing the order of deductions for different types of enterprises.

—Taxes on capital income in Canada : analysis and policy / Robin W. Boadway, Neil Bruce, Jack M. Mintz. – Toronto : Canadian Tax Foundation, 1987.
xi,176p.
Includes index.
ISBN 088808028X Hbk

—U.S. Taxation of Canadian Business Investments / Toronto : DeBoo, 1984.
178p.
ISBN 088820227X Pbk £35.00

—Ward's Tax Law and Planning, 6 Vols. / Beck. – Agincourt : Carswell, 1983.
This multi-volume looseleaf service is a comprehensive treatise on Canadian tax law. Analysis of the statutory language of the Canadian Income Tax Act is the main focus of the work.

—Ward's Tax Law and Planning, 8 Vols. / Agincourt : Carswell, 1988.

TAXATION - CANADA - ALBERTA

—Alberta Corporate Income Tax / Toronto : Butterworths.
– (Alberta Annotated Legislation).

—Alberta Taxation Service / Toronto : DeBoo.
Looseleaf service.
ISBN 0888201389 loose £195.00

TAXATION - CANADA - BRITISH COLUMBIA

—British Columbia Taxation Service / Toronto : DeBoo.
Looseleaf service.
ISBN 0888201133 loose £195.00

TAXATION - CANADA - MANITOBA

—Manitoba and Saskatchewan Taxation Service / Toronto : DeBoo, 1984.
ISBN 0888201869 Hbk £175.00

TAXATION - CANADA - ONTARIO

—Ontario Taxation Service / Toronto : DeBoo.
ISBN 0888201400 Hbk £195.00

—Provincial Land Tax Act : Revised Statutes of Ontario, 1980 / Office of the Legislative Assembly (Ontario). – Ontario : Ontario Government Publications Service, 1983.
42p.

TAXATION - CANADA - QUEBEC

—Quebec Taxation Service / Toronto : DeBoo.
ISBN 0888201419 loose £195.00

TAXATION - CANADA - SASKATCHEWAN

—Manitoba and Saskatchewan Taxation Service / Toronto : DeBoo, 1984.
ISBN 0888201869 Hbk £175.00

TAXATION - CHINA

—Business and Tax Laws of the People's Republic of China / Fred Blaser. – North Ryde : C.C.H. Australia, 1986.
96p.
ISBN 0887963978 Pbk £14.95

—China Tax Guide / Zee. – Oxford : Oxford University Press, 1988.
ISBN 0195840593 Hbk £25.00

—China's foreign economic legislation Chung-kuo tui wai ching chi fa kuei hui pien / 1st ed. – Bejing, China : Foreign Languages Press, 1982.
v. 1; 19 cm.
ISBN 0835109836 pbk.

—Taxation of foreign investment in the People's Republic of China / A J Easson, L Jinyan. – Kluwer Law and Taxation, 1989.
260.
Describes China's tax laws as they relate to foreign business and investment within the context of current economic reforms and the overall policy towards economic relations, including investment incentives and the impact of China's tax treaties. Reference is made to other Chinese legislation. Covers the situation at February 1988.
ISBN 9065443835 Hbk £56.25/Dfl 174

TAXATION - COMMONWEALTH

—Commonwealth Taxation Board of Review Decisions : Consolidated Index and Tables 1925-1986 / Butterworths. – 1st ed. – Butterworths, 1988.
290p.

—Commonwealth Taxation Board of Review Decisions : Old and New Series / Butterworths.
ISBN 0409426008 Hbk

TAXATION - ENGLAND

—Butterworths Concise Tax Service / Butterworths, 1980.
ISBN 0409480592 loose £395.00

—Butterworths Consolidated Legislation Service /. – Professional Publ.
85p.
ISBN 0409014117 £35.00

Transfer Duty Act 40 of 1949
52p.
ISBN 0409014419 £25.00

—Intolerable inquisition? : reflections on the law of tax / by Hubert Monroe. – London : Stevens published under the auspices of Hamlyn Trust, 1981.
xiii,84p; 19cm.
ISBN 0420461906 Hbk £11.25
ISBN 0420462007 4.60

—Taxation for executors and trustees / by Anthony R. Mellows. – 5th ed. – London : Butterworths, 1981.
xxxiv,428p; 23cm.
Previous ed.: 1976. Includes index.
ISBN 0406623953 £15.00

—Taxation of the family / O.P. Wylie. – London : Butterworths, 1983.
xxv,229p; 22cm.
ISBN 0406580200

TAXATION - EUROPE

—Supplementary Service to European Taxation, 13 Vols. / Amsterdam : International Bureau of Fiscal Documentation, 1988.
1989 renewal

—Taxation in Europe : 1983 / Deloitte Haskins and Sells. – London : Oyez Longman, 1983.
ISBN 0906052068 Hbk £10.95

—Taxation of Companies in Europe / International Bureau of Fiscal Documentation. – Amsterdam : International Bureau of Fiscal Documentation, 1988.
– (Guides to European Taxation Ser.: Vol. 2).
Supplements-1989 renewal

—Taxation of Patent Royalties, Dividends, and Interest in Europe / International Bureau of Fiscal Documentation. – Amsterdam : International Bureau of Fiscal Documentation, 1988.
– (Guides to European Taxation Ser.: Vol. 1).
Fl looseleaf 1989 suppl. renewal

TAXATION - EUROPEAN COMMUNITY

—Business law in Europe : legal, tax and labour aspects of business operations in the ten European Community countries and Switzerland / edited by Maarten J. Ellis and Paul M. Storm : Prepared under the auspices of the Association europeenne d'etudes juridiques et fiscales. – Deventer : Kluwer, 1982.
xvi,606p.
Includes bibliographies.
ISBN 9065440402

—Relief from Taxes Granted to Imports Made by Private Persons / Commission of the European Communities. – Kirchberg : Commission of the European Communities, 1984.
71p.
ISBN 9282512991

—Tax law and policy in the EEC / A. J. Easson. – London : Sweet & Maxwell, 1980.
xxi,284p; 26cm.
Bibliography: p270-276. - Includes index.
ISBN 0421270209 £20.00

TAXATION - FRANCE

—Taxes in France / 4th ed. – London : Butterworths, 1986.
This work is a comprehensive look at French taxation law covering income tax, company tax, value added tax, and stamp and registration duties. The major reforms enacted by the Socialist government in France are included in the text.
ISBN 0406520860 Pbk

TAXATION - GIBRALTAR

—Tolley's taxation in Gibraltar 1981-82 / by James Levy and Simon Caplan : with an introduction by Sir Joshua Hassan. – 2nd ed. – Croydon : Tolley, 1982.
vii,152p.
Includes index.
ISBN 0854590447

TAXATION - GREAT BRITAIN

—Accounts, Audit and Taxation of Clubs / London : Butterworths, 1983.

—Advanced taxation / general editors Emile Woolf, Suresh Tanna, Karam Singh. – Plymouth : Macdonald & Evans, 1985.
xx,720p. – (M & E professional studies).
Includes index.
ISBN 0712104887 Pbk £18.50

—Allied Hambro Expatriate Tax and Investment Guide / London : Oyez Longman, 1984.
ISBN 0851208355 Hbk £9.95

—Annotated Tax Cases : 1922-1975, 54 Vols. / Abingdon : Professional Books.

—Bramwell : Taxation of Companies and Company Reconstructions / Guy Brannan. – 3rd ed. – London : Sweet & Maxwell, 1985.
ISBN 1421325003 Hbk £42.00

—British master tax guide : 1986-87 / 5th subscriber ed. – Bicester : CCH, 1986.
viii,744p.
Includes index.
ISBN 0863251137

—British master tax guide 1987-88 / Bicester : CCH Editions, 1987.
vi,801p.
ISBN 0863251323

—British tax cases / v. – Bicester, Oxon. : CCH Editions, 1986.
Kept up to date by looseleaf service.

—British tax encyclopaedia / edited by G.S.A. Wheatcroft and T.M. Wedderburn. – v. – London : Sweet & Maxwell, 1953-.
loose-leaf.
Supplementary pages issued at intervals.

—British tax legislation / 3. – Bicester : CCH Editions, 1982.
Includes index.
ISBN 0863250017 Unpriced

—British tax reporter : a set of volumes detailing British company tax, income tax, capital transfer tax, capital gains tax and development land tax / 6. – Bicester : CCH, 1984.
loose-leaf.
ISBN 0863250270

—British tax system / by J.A. Kay, M.A. King. – 3rd ed. – Oxford : Oxford University Press, 1983.
xvi,270p; 23cm.
Previous ed.: 1980. Bibliography: p248-260. - Includes index.
ISBN 0198772076 Hbk £15.00
ISBN 0198772068 Pbk £5.50

—British Tax System / King. – 4th ed. – Oxford : Oxford University Press, 1986.
ISBN 0198772629 Pbk £6.50
ISBN 0198772637 Hbk £17.50

—British tax system / J.A. Kay, M.A. King. – 4th ed. – Oxford : Oxford University Press, 1986.
viii,261p; 23cm.
Previous ed.: 1983. Bibliography: p241-250. - Includes index.
ISBN 0198772637 Hbk £17.50
ISBN 0198772629 Pbk £6.95

—British value added tax cases / Bicester, Oxon. : CCH Editions, 1985-.
Includes index.

—Budget Tax Tables 1986 / Butterworths. – London : Butterworths, 1986.
ISBN 0406508410 Pbk £2.80

—Business tax handbook / editors Hugh Mainprice, Malcolm J. Finney, Colin P. Cretton. – 2. – London : Kluwer, 1983.
loose-leaf.
Includes index.
ISBN 0903393433

—Butterworth's Budget Tax Tables, 1984 / Butterworth and Co. (Publishers) Ltd. – London : Butterworths, 1984.
ISBN 0406508178 Pbk £6.00

—Butterworth's Budget Tax Tables / Butterworth Staff. – London : Butterworths, 1983.
ISBN 0406508186 Pbk £5.95

—Butterworth's Orange Tax Handbook, 1983-4 / Butterworth Staff. – London : Butterworths, 1984.
ISBN 0406508291 Hbk £45.00

—Butterworth's Orange Tax Handbook 1986-87 / London : Butterworths, 1986.
This annual handbook contains the up to date text of all United Kingdom enactments relating to capital transfer tax, national insurance contributions, stamp duty, and value added tax. The material is arranged chronologically.
ISBN 0406508321 Pbk £35.75

—Butterworth's Orange Tax Handbook / Butterworth Staff. – London : Butterworths, 1983.
ISBN 0406508283 Pbk £38.50

—Butterworth's Tax Tables / Parrington. – London : Butterworths, 1988-89.
ISBN 0406543232 Pbk £2.70

—Butterworth's Tax Treaties / London : Butterworths.
This looseleaf service contains the up to date texts of all the double tax agreements between the United Kingdom and other countries. Agreements relating to income tax, corporation tax, capital gains, and capital transfer tax are covered in this service.

—Butterworth's U.K. Tax Guide 1986-87 / Butterworth Editorial Staff. – London : Butterworths, 1986.
This work contains a detailed discussion of the workings and policy considerations underlying all the principal United Kingdom taxes, including stamp duty. The book includes numerous worked examples, tax tables, and a summary of the Finance Act of 1986.
ISBN 0406504954 Hbk £26.50

—Butterworth's Yellow Tax Handbook, 1983-4 / Butterworth Staff. – London : Butterworths, 1984.
ISBN 0406509999 Hbk £48.00

—Butterworth's Yellow Tax Handbook 1986-87 / London : Butterworths, 1986.
This work provides the text of all legislation in the United Kingdom relating to income tax, capital gains tax, and corporation tax for tax practitioners. The book is extensively cross-referenced and indexed.
ISBN 0406510032 Pbk £42.00

—Butterworth's Yellow Tax Handbook / Butterworth Staff. – London : Butterworths, 1983.
ISBN 0406509980 Pbk £44.00

—Butterworths UK tax guide / London : Butterworths, 1982.

—Capital Allowances / London : Oyez Longman, 1980. Includes December 1982 supplement.
ISBN 0851204864 Hbk £25.00

—Capital taxes : a quarterly commentary / v. – London : Sweet & Maxwell, 1984.
Index in each vol.
ISBN 02659514

—Capital Taxes and Estate Planning Guide / 3rd ed. – London : Longman Professional, 1986.
ISBN 0851212131 Hbk £12.50

—Collection of Decrees by the Court of Exchequer (1650-1798) in Tithe Causes, 4 Vols. / Repr. of 1799 ed. – Abingdon : Professional Books.
197p.

—Companies operating overseas: UK tax, law and practice / John Dixon. – London : Longman Professional (UK), 1986.
– (Commercial series).
Examination of the UK tax implications for any company which trades abroad and is concerned with reducing the risks involved. Looks at problems such as the treatment of double taxation agreements, legislation on controlled foreign companies, and the international VAT implications.
ISBN 0851218770 Pbk £17.50

—Company Flotations - Tax and Planning / Cane. – London : Butterworths, 1985.
ISBN 0406259704 Pbk £20.00

—Company Reorganisations : Tax and Tax Planning / Noble. – London : Butterworths, 1986.
ISBN 0406501904 Hbk £35.00

—Comprehensive Aspects of Taxation / London : Cassell, 1988.
ISBN 0304314250 Pbk £17.95

—Coopers and Lybrand: tax and financial planning through pensions / Paul G Meins. – London : Butterworths, 1987.
ISBN 0406500800 Pbk £16.00

—Covenants : Practical Guide To Tax Advantages / TUAR, 1982.
ISBN 0907164080 Pbk £3.95

—Death and Taxes / Soares. – London : Longman Professional, 1986.
ISBN 0851209309 Pbk £19.95

—Development Land Tax 1976-1980 / London : HMSO, 1980.
– (Taxes Act Ser.).
ISBN 0116412313 Pbk £9.95

Supplement 1982
ISBN 0116413670 Hbk £0.95

Supplement 1983
ISBN 0116413697 Hbk £0.40

—Dictionary of taxation / by Gerry Hart : consultant B.E.V. Sabine. – London : Butterworths, 1981.
v,236p; 23cm. – (Butterworths professional dictionaries series).
ISBN 040652159X Hbk £14.00
ISBN 0406521603 Pbk

—Double Taxation Relief for Shipping / London : LLoyd's of London Press, 1988.
ISBN 1850441650 Hbk

—Expatriate Tax Manual / London : Butterworths, 1985.
ISBN 0406259968 Pbk £15.00

—Expatriates Guide / 2nd ed. – London : Longman Professional, 1986.
ISBN 0851212107 Hbk £13.50

—Finance Bill / memorandum by the Society's Standing Committee on Revenue Law. – London : Law Society, 1982.
53p.

—Focus on Construction Industry Tax Deduction Scheme / Croydon : Tolley, 1983.
ISBN 0854591206 Pbk £6.95

—Focus on Controlled Foreign Companies / Croydon : Tolley, 1984.
ISBN 0854591745 Pbk £11.95

—Focus on the Administration of Taxes / Croydon : Tolley, 1983.
ISBN 0854591311 Pbk £5.95

—Guide to the new Inheritance Tax / Tolley Publishing, 1986.
ISBN 0854592563 Pbk £4.95

—HAC Guide to Taxation of Bloodstock Industry / Stoy Hayward, 1987.
ISBN 0870382005 Hbk £20.00

—Hambro Tax Guide / W. I. Sinclair. – London : Oyez Longman, 1982.
ISBN 0851206700 Hbk £8.95

September 1983 Edition
ISBN 0851207464 Hbk £9.95

—Harrison's Inland Revenue index to tax cases : a judicial dictionary of tax law / prepared on the instructions of the Board of Inland Revenue. – 7th ed. 2 vols. – London : Oyez Longman, 1982.
Loose-leaf.
ISBN 0851206492

—Hiring and Leasing : Practice and Precedents / K. V. Prichard Jones. – London : Butterworths, 1986.
A practical guide to the issues of leasing for the business attorney in the United Kingdom. An extensive appendix of caselaw and commentary is provided.
ISBN 0406101140 Pbk

—How to pay less income tax / London : Pitman Publishing, 1986.
ISBN 0712108254 Pbk £2.95

—Index to Reports of Tax Cases : 1875-1981, 52 Vols. / Abingdon : Professional Books, 1984.
ISBN 0862050707 Hbk £63.00

—Information on LEXIS Prepared Specifically for Tax Specialist / London : Butterworths.

—Inheritance tax / London : Longman Professional, 1988.
ISBN 0851213812 Hbk

—Inheritance tax / London : Pitman Publishing, 1986.
ISBN 0712106928 Pbk £7.95

—Inheritance tax / 3rd ed. – London : Sweet & Maxwell, 1988.
ISBN 042139790X Pbk £110.00

—Inheritance tax / 7th ed. – London : Longman Professional, 1987.
ISBN 085121326X Hbk £48.00
ISBN 0851214673 Pbk

—Inheritance tax guide / Butterworths. – London : Butterworths, 1986.
ISBN 0406500347 Pbk £16.50

—Inheritance tax on lifetime gifts / Ivory. – London : Sweet & Maxwell, 1987.
ISBN 04212379103 Hbk £24.50

—Inheritance tax planning / Thornhill. – 2nd ed. – London : Longman Professional, 1988.
ISBN 0851213669 Hbk £85.00

—Inland Revenue and the taxpayer : proposals in response to the recommendations of the Keith Committee on income tax, capital gains tax and corporation tax : a consultative document / Board of Inland Revenue. – London : H.M.S.O., 1986.
170p.
ISBN 0116413646

—Inland Revenue Clearances / Michael Wyatt. – London : Oyez Longman, 1984.
ISBN 0851207499 Hbk £50.00

—Inland Revenue Official Tax Guides / Oyez Longman Editorial Staff. – London : Oyez Longman, 1983.
ISBN 0851206174 loose £45.00

—Inland Revenue Practices and Concessions / London : Oyez Longman, 1983.
ISBN 0851204988 loose £45.00

—Insolvency : law and taxation / Timothy J. Lyons. – 1st ed. – London : Longman Professional (UK), 1988.
– (Law and Taxation).
Examines legal aspects and tax implications of both company and partnership insolvency. Chapters deal with the enforcement powers of the Inland Revenue and tax planning opportunities prior to and during an insolvency. Contains worked examples, precedents, forms and non-statutory material.
ISBN 0851214193 Hbk £35

—Intellectual property law and taxation / Eastaway. – 3rd ed. – London : Longman Professional, 1988.
ISBN 0851213227 Pbk

—Intellectual property law and taxation / by Richard J. Gallafent, Nigel A. Eastaway and Victor A.F. Dauppe. – London : Oyez, 1981.
xxvi,321p; 24cm. – (Law and tax series).
ISBN 0851205925

—Intellectual property law and taxation / by Richard J. Gallafent, Nigel A. Eastaway, and Victor A. F. Dauppe. – 2nd ed. – London : Oyez Longman, 1984.
xxvi,338p.
ISBN 0851208746

—Introduction to revenue law / F.R. Davies. – 2nd ed. – London : Sweet & Maxwell, 1985.
xxii,416p; 22cm.
Previous ed. by F.R. Davies. 1980. Includes index.
ISBN 0421334304 Hbk £18.00
ISBN 0421334401 Pbk £13.95

—Isle of Man : a low-tax area / by Mark Solly. – Croydon : Tolley, 1984.
ix,458p.
Includes index.
ISBN 0854591397

—Jersey : a low tax area / by Mark Solly. – Croydon : Tolley, 1982.
iv,323p; 24cm.
Includes index.
ISBN 0854590536 Hbk Unpriced
ISBN 0854590544 Pbk £15.00

—Law and Tax for Professional Partnerships / London : Longman Professional, 1984.
ISBN 0851206948 Pbk £24.00

—Law and tax for professional partnerships / Peter White. – London : Oyez, 1984.
xx,182p.
Includes index.
ISBN 0851206948

—Manual of Employee Taxation / London : Butterworths, 1981.

—Matrimonial Finance and Taxation / Davies. – 4th ed. – London : Butterworths, 1986.
ISBN 0406254478 Hbk £52.00

—Moores & Rowland's orange tax guide / London : Butterworths, 1987.
Continues in part: Moores & Rowland's tax guide.

—Moores & Rowland's yellow tax guide / London : Butterworths, 1987.
Continues in part: Moores & Rowland's tax guide.

—Multilingual Glossary of Tax, Financial and Commercial Terms / London : Oyez Longman, 1983.
ISBN 0851207618 Hbk £9.95

—National Taxation : A Practical Handbook / Reading : College of Estate Management.
94p.

—North Sea taxation for the 1990s / Stephen Bond, Michael Devereux and Michael Saunders. – London : Institute for Fiscal Studies, 1987.
113p; 22cm.
Bibliography: p112-113.
ISBN 0902992651 Pbk No price

—Official Tax Forms Manual / 2nd ed. – London : Oyez Longman, 1982.
ISBN 0851206433 Hbk £12.50
Third edition
ISBN 0851207537 Hbk

—Offshore tax planning / Vlarke. – London : Butterworths, 1986.
ISBN 0406502102 Hbk £32.00

—Offshore tax planning / Oliver Stanley, Giles Clarke. – London : Butterworth, 1986.
180p.
Includes index.
ISBN 0406502102 £30.00

—Oil Taxation Acts 1975-1983 / London : HMSO, 1984.
– (Taxes Act Ser.).
ISBN 0116413506 Pbk £11.95

—The Oil Taxation Acts / London : HMSO, 1985.
ISBN 0116413514 Pbk £12.50

—Opportunity lost : a response to the Green Paper on the Reform of Personal Taxation from the Child Poverty Action Group / Ruth Lister and Fran Bennett. – London : Child Poverty Action Group, 1986.
34p.

—Partnership Taxation / 3rd ed. – London : Butterworths, 1987.
ISBN 0406678200 Pbk £25.00

—Passing Down the Family Business : Solving the Tax Problems / Robert Venables. – 2nd ed. – London : Oyez Longman, 1982.
– (Oyez Longman Intelligence Report Ser.).
ISBN 0851207405 Hbk £45.00

—Personal tax losses / London : Butterworths, 1984.
ISBN 0406263604 Pbk £16.50

—Personal Tax Losses / London : Butterworths, 1984.
This practical book shows tax advisers how to maximize tax relief for clients through use of tax losses under the tax laws of the United Kingdom. The work presents a variety of realistic tax planning options in tax loss situations.
ISBN 0406263604 Pbk

—Pinson on revenue law : comprising income tax; capital gains tax; development land tax; corporation tax; inheritance tax; value added tax; stamp duties; tax planning / Roger Thomas. – 17th ed. – London : Sweet & Maxwell, 1986.
lxxx,780p; 25cm.
Previous ed.: 1985. Includes index. Kept up to date by supplements.
ISBN 0421370009 £55.00

—Planning for Stamp Duty Reserve Tax / Ball. – London : Butterworths, 1987.
ISBN 0406051033 Hbk £26.00

—Planning for Stamp Duty Reserve Tax / London : Butterworths, 1987.

—Practical approach to revenue law / Stephen S. Mayson and Susan Blake. – 8th ed. – London : Financial Training, 1987.
xlix,659p.
ISBN 1851850791

—Practical approach to revenue law / Stephen W. Mayson. – 7th ed. – London : Financial Training, 1986.
xlix,640p.
ISBN 1851850414

—Practical inheritance tax / London : Butterworths, 1988.
ISBN 040600710 Pbk

—Practical tax saving / 4th ed. – London : Butterworths, 1984.
ISBN 0406536333 Pbk £22.00

—Principles and Law of Tithing / Repr. of 1806 ed. – Abingdon : Professional Books.
282p.

—Property and construction tax handbook / Spon (E & FN), 1986.
ISBN 0419140506 Hbk £17.50

—Property companies : accounting, audit and tax / London : Butterworths, 1988.
ISBN 0406005249 Pbk

—Property taxes / Croydon : Tolley, 1986.
ISBN 0854592237 Pbk £15.95

—Recent tax problems / London : Sweet & Maxwell, 1986.
ISBN 0420474102 Pbk £16.50

—Reform of personal taxation : presented to Parliament by the Chancellor of the Exchequer by Command of her Majesty March 1986 / London : H.M.S.O., 1986.
82p; 30cm.
Green paper. Proposals for reform of personal taxation. Introduction of new personal tax allowances to all persons to replace married man's allowance. Closer integration between tax and benefits system.
ISBN 0101975600 PBK £8.00

—Reform of revenue law : memorandum / by the Council of the Law Society. – London : Law Society, 1981.
45p; 30cm.

—Reform of revenue law : memorandum / by the Council of the Law Society. – London : Law Society, 1982.
39p.

—Reform of revenue law : memorandum / by the Law Society. – London : Law Society, 1983.
38p.

—Remuneration planning manual / London : Butterworths, 1986.
ISBN 040650430X Pbk £19.95

—Report / Committee on Enforcement Powers of the Revenue Departments : chairman, Lord Keith of Kinkel. – London : H.M.S.O., 1983.
xiv,334p; 25cm.

Vol.2 : Chapters 16-28 and notes / Committee on Enforcement Powers of the Revenue Departments : chairman, Lord Keith of Kinkel. – 1983.
336-804p; 25cm.

Vol.3 : Chapters 29-33 and notes : Development land tax, petroleum revenue tax, capital transfer tax and stamp duties / Committee on Enforcement Powers of the Revenue Departments : chairman, Lord Keith of Kinkel. – 1984.
iv,251p; 25cm.

—Report of the Committee on Enforcement Powers of the Revenue Departments, 3 Vols. / London : HMSO, 1983.
ISBN 0101882203 Hbk £24.50

Vol. 3, 1984
ISBN 0101912005 Hbk £9.95

—Reports of Tax Cases : 1875-1982, 53 Vols. / Professional Books Staff. – Abingdon : Professional Books, 1984.

—Residence, domicile and UK taxation / London : Butterworths, 1986.
ISBN 0406580103 Pbk £32.00

—Retirement relief - New CGT Rules / London : CCH, 1986.
ISBN 0863250815 Pbk £7.50

—Retirement relief; the capital gains tax rules explained / 2nd. – Bicester : CCH Editions Ltd, 1988.
Examines the changes introduced by the 1987 and 1988 Finance Acts. Includes two new chapters on two-tier relief and the Inland Revenue concession on date of disposal. Also covers how retirement relief works, the date of disposal, unincorporated businesses, partners, directors, trustees, full-time employees, furnished holiday lettings, husband and wife, interactions with tax, and a legislation finding list.
ISBN 0863251668 Hbk £15.50

—Revenue investigations manual / Sabine. – London : Butterworths, 1987.
ISBN 0406500703 Pbk £19.50

—Revenue law / London : Financial Training, 1987.
– (SWOT).
ISBN 090632291X Pbk £8.95

—Revenue law / Stuart-Buttle. – 4th ed. – London : Butterworths, 1986.
ISBN 040600532X Pbk £20.95

—Revenue law / John Tiley. – 3rd ed. – London : Butterworths, 1981.
lvi,873,28p; 26cm.
Bibliography: p.xv-xvi. - Includes index. Kept up to date by supplements.
ISBN 0406665958 Pbk
ISBN 0406665966

—Revenue law in Scotland / Simon Mackintosh. – London : Butterworths, 1986.
Starts with an introduction to the Scottish legal system and a discussion of applying UK revenue law in Scotland. Chapters on taxation of persons, property, charities and partnership with longer chapters on trusts and succession. Styles for discretionary and accumulation and maintenance trusts provided.
ISBN 040650170X

—Revenue Law : Principles and Practice / Chris Whitehouse and Elizabeth Stuart-Buttle. – 4th ed. – London : Butterworths, 1986.
600.
This textbook is an introduction to the law of income tax, capital gains tax, corporation tax, and capital transfer tax for students in the United Kingdom.
ISBN 040600532X PBK £19.95

—Revenue law : principles and practice / Chris Whitehouse, Elizabeth Stuart-Buttle. – 5th ed. – London : Butterworths, 1987.
xxxi,671p; 25cm.
Previous ed.: 1986. Includes index.
ISBN 0406005338 Pbk £20.95

—Revenue law : principles and practice / Chris Whitehouse, Elizabeth Stuart-Buttle. – 6th ed. – London : Butterworths, 1988.
xxxi,690p.
Previous ed.: 1987.
ISBN 0406502692

—Roll over relief - New CGT tax rules explained / London : CCH, 1987.
ISBN 0863251196 Pbk £7.00

—Rowland's Tax Guide : 1981-82 / 2nd ed. – London : Butterworths, 1981.
ISBN 0406359164 Pbk £50.00

—Rowland's Tax Guide, 1984-1985 / David Trill. – London : Butterworths, 1984.
ISBN 0406359199 Pbk

—Rowland's Tax Guide / London : Butterworths, 1983.
ISBN 0406359172 Pbk £63.00

—Sage companion / Paradigm, 1988.
ISBN 0948825669 Pbk £5.95

—Share capital : company law and taxation / David Bellringer. – London : Butterworths, 1984.
ISBN 0406258163 Hbk £19.50

—Share Capital : Company Law and Taxation / David Bellringer. – London : Butterworths, 1984.
ISBN 0406258163 Hbk

—Share valuation cases / Harry Booth. – London : Butterworths, 1985.
ISBN 0406009805 Hbk £67.50

—Share valuation handbook / London : Fourmat, 1986.
ISBN 0906840988 Pbk £12.95

—Short history of taxation / B.E.V. Sabine. – London : Butterworths, 1980.
147p; 23cm.
ISBN 0406535205 £7.95

—Short history of taxation / London : Butterworths, 1980.
ISBN 0406535205 Hbk £12.00

—Simon's tax cases / – London : Butterworths, 1974.
Kept up to date by supplement, Simon's weekly tax service. Index in each vol. - Cumulative tables and index, 1973-1985. 1986.

—Simon's tax intelligence / . – London : Butterworths, 1983.

—Simon's taxes : income tax, corporation tax, capital gains tax / John Allsebrook Simon Simon. – rev. 3rd ed. n v, loose leaves in folder. – London : Butterworths, 1983.
26cm.
Updated periodically by supplements.
ISBN 0406072493

B : Schedule D - Capital allowances 1983.
26cm.
Updated periodically by supplements.
ISBN 0406072418

C : Capital gains trusts 1985.
looseleaf.
Previous ed.: 3rd ed. 1970. 'Originally published under the editorship of the Right Hon. Viscount Simon'.
ISBN 0406072426

D : Companies 1983.
26cm.
Updated periodically by supplements.
ISBN 0406072434

E : Individuals 1985.
looseleaf.
Previous ed.: 3rd ed. 1970. 'Originally published under the editorship of the Right Hon. Viscount Simon'.
ISBN 0406072442

F : Double tax relief, agreements 1983.
loose-leaf; 26cm.
Updated periodically by supplements.

H : Statutes - 2, concessions, practice 1982.
26cm.
Updated periodically by supplements.
ISBN 0406072477

I : Tables of statutes and cases, master index 1985.
looseleaf.
Previous ed.: 3rd ed. 1976. 'Originally published under the editorship of the Right Hon. Viscount Simon'.

Tax Acts before 1988 1988.
looseleaf.
Contents: pages discarded from vols. G and H on filing issue 132. Binder title: Former legislation: Taxes Act 1970, Finance Acts etc, 1970-87.

G : Statutes-1 1983.
26cm.
ISBN 0406072469 Hbk

—Simon's Weekly Tax Service / London : Butterworths, 1984.

Cumulative Index, 1973-1982
ISBN 0406070768 Pbk £18.00

—Simon's Weekly Tax Service : Simon's Tax Cases / London : Butterworths.

Cases Only for 1973, 1974, 1975, 1976, 1977, 1978, 1979, 1980 and 1981

Cumulative Index (1973-81)
ISBN 0406069964 Hbk £16.50 each

—Simon's Weekly Tax Service : Simon's Tax Intelligence / Butterworth and Co. (Publishers) Ltd. – London : Butterworths.
This weekly publication provides complete information on developments in the fields of income tax, capital gains tax, corporation tax, capital transfer tax, stamp duty, and value added tax in the United Kingdom.

—Smith's taxation 1985-86 / London : Longman Professional, 1985.
ISBN 0900370637 Pbk £12.75

—Solicitors and VAT / Gizzi. – London : Butterworths, 1986.
ISBN 0406503605 Pbk £8.75

—Some Tax Implications of Marriage Breakdown / Belfast : Queen's University of Belfast, 1981.
26p.

—Stamp Duties / R. S. Nock. – 6th ed. – London : Sweet & Maxwell, 1986.

—Stamp duties and capital duty / B J Sims, J F W Hinson. – London : Butterworths, 1982.
ISBN 0406370354 Hbk £94.00

Supplement-1980 only
ISBN 0406370346 Pbk £75.00

—Stamp Duty for Conveyancers / Roger Gregory. – 3rd ed. – London : Oyez Longman, 1983. – (Oyez Longman Practice Note Ser.: No. 48).
ISBN 0851206352 Hbk £7.95

—Stamp Duty Guide / London : Butterworths, 1986.
This practical work for practitioners in the United Kingdom presents a transaction-based analysis of stamp duties. The book explains the administrative procedures involved and discusses how to avoid or minimize the duty wherever possible.
ISBN 0406260303 Pbk

—Sumption and Clarke's tax and tax planning / Giles Clarke, Philip Lawton. – 10th ed. – London : Oyez Longman, 1982.
xxvii,265p; 22cm.
Previous ed.: published as Sumption and Lawton's tax and tax planning / by Anthony Sumption and Philip Lawton, 1981. Includes index.
ISBN 0851206921 Pbk Unpriced

—Supreme Court Taxing Office : Practice Notes on Taxation of Costs / London : HMSO.
40p.
ISBN 0113906269 Hbk

—Sweet & Maxwell's tax computations and tables 1984/85 / by Clifford S. Perkins : computations on double taxation relief contributed by Richard Briffett. – 2nd ed. – London : Sweet & Maxwell, 1984.
395p; 25cm.
ISBN 042133200X

—Sweet & Maxwell's tax statutes 1984/85 / edited by Sweet & Maxwell's legal editorial staff : advisory editors Julian Farrand, Geoffrey Morse, David Williams. – 3rd ed. – London : Sweet & Maxwell, 1984.
vii,457p.
Previous ed.: 1983. Includes index.
ISBN 0421330902

—Tax and financial planning for family business / George J Bell. – London : Butterworths, 1984.
ISBN 0406557306 Pbk £16.00

—Tax and Financial Planning for Family Businesses / George J. Bell. – London : Butterworths, 1984.
This book addresses the tax problems faced by owners of small and medium sized family business in the United Kingdom. The work examines the benefits to be gained from allowances, reliefs, exemptions, and Revenue concessions.
ISBN 0406557306 Pbk

—Tax and financial planning for Lloyd's members / London : Longman Professional, 1988. – (A Longman Intelligence Report).
ISBN 0851213421 Hbk £85.00

—Tax and Financial Planning for Medical Practitioners / 2nd ed. – London : Butterworths, 1987.
ISBN 0406190054 Pbk

—Tax and Financial Planning for Professional Partnerships / Brian Gilligan. – 2nd ed. – London : Butterworths, 1986.
This work explains how the tax liability of United Kingdom professional partnerships can be minimized by effective tax planning. The effects of the Finance Act of 1985 on professional partnerships is discussed in detail.
ISBN 0406501807 Pbk

—Tax and financial planning for professional partnerships / Brian Gilligan. – 2nd ed. – London : Butterworths, 1986.
ISBN 0406501807 Pbk £18.50

—Tax and financial planning for sportsmen and entertainers / Richard Harvey. – London : Butterworths, 1987.
ISBN 040650220X Pbk £18.50

—Tax and interest tables / Nuttall. – London : Fourmat, 1988.
ISBN 1851900470 Pbk £4.95

—Tax and the Farmer / London : Shaw & Sons, 1988.
ISBN 0721911609 Pbk £9.95

—Tax and the farmer / NFU. – London : Shaw & Sons, 1988.
ISBN 0721911609 Pbk

—Tax appeals handbook / London : Butterworths, 1983.
ISBN 0406535221 Pbk £13.00

—Tax Appeals Handbook / London : Butterworths, 1983.
This work provides the United Kingdom practitioner with a working knowledge of the procedures at appeal, the personalities involved, and the underlying statutes and case law. The legal framework of the tax appeal system is reviewed in depth.
ISBN 0406535221 Pbk

—Tax Aspects of Home Ownership / Butterworth Staff. – London : Butterworths, 1983.
ISBN 0406254311 Pbk £20.00

—Tax Benefits and Family Finance / T. Lyon. – London : Sweet & Maxwell, 1985.
ISBN 0421324600 Hbk

—Tax cards / Croydon : Tolley, 1987/88.
ISBN 0854592660 Pbk £11.95

—Tax Case Leaflets April 1985-March 1986 / London : HMSO.

—Tax Cases : 1875-1982, 53 Vols. / Abingdon : Professional Books.

Individual vols.

Index Vol. 1-52

—Tax efficient personal investments / 2nd ed. – Croydon : Tolley, 1987.
ISBN 0854593152 Pbk £12.95

—Tax for the Self-Employed / 2nd ed. – London : Oyez Longman, 1983.
ISBN 085120712X Hbk £3.50

—Tax for the self-employed / London : Longman Professional, 1988. – (Allied Dunbar Money Guide).
ISBN 08512113855 Hbk

—Tax Investigation Handbook / London : Butterworths, 1981.
ISBN 0406254109 Pbk £25.00

—Tax investigations / Croydon : Tolley, 1988.
ISBN 0854593187 Hbk £14.95

—Tax Law / London : Sweet & Maxwell. – (Irish Law Texts Ser.).
ISBN 0421299304 Hbk

—Tax law and childcare : the case for reform / by Catherine Itzin. – London : National Council for One Parent Families, 1980.
19p.
A collection of essays edited by Catherine Itzin.

—Tax law in the melting pot / a study by the Revenue Law Committee of the Law Society of the 'Ramsay' doctrine after 'Furniss v. Dawson', with proposals. – London : Law Society, 1985.
iii,119p.
Bibliography: p.119.

—Tax on all the people : poll tax / Oxford : Bookspeed, 1988.
ISBN 0946744068 Pbk £1.95

—Tax on Maintenance Payments : 1982-1983 / Joel Newman. – London : Oyez Longman, 1982. – (Oyez Longman Practical Tax Ser.).
ISBN 0851206581 Hbk £45.00

—Tax planning for groups of companies / London : Butterworths, 1985.
ISBN 0406075808 Hbk £29.95

—Tax planning for medical practitioners / Stephen Burwood. – 2nd ed. – London : Butterworths, 1987.
ISBN 04066190054 Pbk £18.50

—Tax planning for new businesses / 2nd ed. – Croydon : Tolley, 1987.
ISBN 0854592032 Pbk £9.95

—Tax planning for the family / 3rd ed. – London : Longman Professional, 1986.
ISBN 0851209203 Pbk £22.00

—Tax planning on marriage breakdown / 4th ed. – London : Longman Professional, 1986.
ISBN 0851210740 Pbk £26.50

—Tax practice manual / Touche Ross & Co. – 2nd ed. – London : Butterworths, 1985.
ISBN 0406402205 Pbk £18.50

—Tax Practice Manual / London : Butterworths, 1982.
This work sets out office procedures and gives numerous examples of sample letters and forms required for a United Kingdom tax practitioner. The book provides separate coverage of procedures and forms for corporate and personal tax work.
ISBN 0406402205 Pbk £35.00

—Tax Practitioner's Diary, 1984-1985 / London : Butterworths, 1984.
ISBN 0406539642 Pbk

—Tax practitioner's diary 1986-1987 / Butterworths. – London : Butterworths, 1986.
ISBN 0406539669 Pbk £8.50

—Tax Practitioner's Diary / Butterworth Staff. – London : Butterworths, 1984.
ISBN 0406539634 Pbk £17.00

—Tax raiders / London : Financial Training, 1985.
ISBN 0906322766 Hbk £10.95

—Tax reform : options for the third term / edited by Bill Robinson : with contributions from Michael Devereux ... et al. – London : IFS, 1987.
65leaves; 30cm.
Bibliography: leaves 64-65.
ISBN 0902992643 Pbk No price

—Tax Strategies for Directors, Executives and Employees / London : Oyez Longman, 1983.
ISBN 0851206735 Hbk £15.00

—Tax Strategy for Companies / 3rd ed. – London : Oyez Longman, 1982.
ISBN 085120693X Hbk £12.50

—Tax strategy for directors, executives and employers / 2nd ed. – London : Longman Professional, 1985. – (Tax Strategy Series).
ISBN 0851210767 Pbk £30.00

—Tax warranties and indemnities / John Clark. – London : Butterworths, 1983.
ISBN 0406395403 Hbk £18.00

—Tax Warranties and Indemnities / John Clark. – London : Butterworths, 1983.
This book reviews and analyzes draft warranties and indemnities typically presented by a purchaser to a vendor of a company in the United Kingdom. The work includes a set of precedents which were developed to accompany the analysis.
ISBN 0406395403 Hbk

—Taxation / general editors Emile Woolf, Suresh Tanna, Karam Singh. – Plymouth : Macdonald & Evans, 1985.
792p. – (M & E professional studies).
Includes index.
ISBN 0712104879 Pbk £14.95

—Taxation / 7th ed. – London : Pitman Publishing, 1986.
ISBN 0712120378 Pbk £7.95

—Taxation - A Handbook for Insurance and Estate Planners / 1986 Edition. – Don Mills : Life Underwriters Association of Canada.
ISBN 0921219032 Hbk £22.50

—Taxation Aspects of Banking Operations / P. F. Swaine. – London : Butterworths, 1985.
This book describes the tax consequences of all significant banking operations and how the effect of various taxes on banks differs from other corporations. An in-depth look at the taxation of banks in the United Kingdom.
ISBN 0406010692 Hbk

—Taxation aspects of banking operations / P F Swaine. – London : Butterworths, 1985.
ISBN 0406010692 Hbk £35.00

—Taxation for Executors and Trustees / 6th ed. – London : Butterworths, 1984.
ISBN 0406623961 Hbk
ISBN 040662397X Pbk

—Taxation of accumulation and discretionary trusts / Tolley Publishing, 1987.
ISBN 0854592709 Pbk £14.95

—Taxation of clubs and voluntary associations / Croydon : Tolley, 1988.
ISBN 0854593179 Hbk £11.95

—Taxation of directors / Sargent. – London : CCH, 1986.
ISBN 0863251129 Pbk £5.00

—Taxation of Farmers and Landowners / 2nd ed. – London : Butterworths, 1984.
This work treats each of the major United Kingdom taxes from the standpoint of estate management and personal tax concerns of farmers and landowners. The book also covers the procedure surrounding tax compliance work. Tax considerations which arise in the maintenance and disposal of land are provided in the appendices.
ISBN 040638391X Hbk

—Taxation of farmers and landowners / 3rd. – London : Butterworths, 1987.
ISBN 040638391X Hbk £20.00

—Taxation of fringe benefits / Sargent. – London : CCH, 1988.
ISBN 0863251455 Pbk £8.50

—Taxation of husband and wife / London : H.M.S.O., 1980.
73p; 25cm.
ISBN 0101809301 Pbk £4.20

—Taxation of insolvent companies / Croydon : Tolley, 1986.
ISBN 0854592326 Pbk £9.95

—Taxation of insurance business / A R Levitt. – London : Butterworths, 1985.
ISBN 0406501009 Hbk £30.00

—Taxation of land transactions / 4th ed. – London : Butterworths, 1988.
ISBN 0406624100 Pbk

—Taxation of Leasing Transactions / London : Butterworths, 1984.
The tax advantages to be gained through leasing transactions in the United Kingdom have led to a series of anti-avoidance measures. This work reviews the incidence of the major taxes levied as they relate to the practice of leasing and shows how through careful tax planning many of the benefits of leasing can be maintained. Incl. Finance Act 1984 Supplement.
ISBN 0406538026 Pbk

—Taxation of leasing transactions / London : Butterworths, 1984.
ISBN 0406538026 Pbk £15.00

—Taxation of legal costs / London : LEST, 1986.
ISBN 0907822657 Pbk £19.50

—Taxation of Lloyd's Underwriters / P H Wolstenholme. – 2nd ed. – London : Butterworths, 1985.
ISBN 0406678804 Pbk £15.00

—Taxation of Lloyd's Underwriters / Croydon : Tolley, 1984.
ISBN 085459129X Pbk £17.50

—Taxation of Lloyds Underwriters / 2nd ed. – Croydon : Tolley.
300p.
ISBN 0854593063 Hbk £29.95

—Taxation of marriage and marriage breakdown / Croydon : Tolley, 1988.
ISBN 0854593233 Hbk

—Taxation of non-resident entertainers and sportsmen / Croydon : Tolley, 1987.
ISBN 0854593128 Hbk £35.00

—Taxation of North Sea Oil / London : Institute for Fiscal Studies, 1981.
24p.

—Taxation of property transactions / London : Butterworths, 1986.
ISBN 040978740X Pbk £30.00

—Taxation of Transactions in Intellectual Property / W. G. Massey. – London : Sweet & Maxwell.
ISBN 042129390X Hbk

—Taxation of Transactions in Intellectual Property / W. G. S. Massey. – London : Sweet & Maxwell, 1982.

—Taxation on divorce and separation / J. Gray. – Bicester : CCH Editions, 1987.
xi,103p; 23cm.
Includes index.
ISBN 0863251072 Pbk No price

—Taxation : the leading authority on the law, practice and administration of taxation / v. – London : Taxation Publishing Co., 1927.
ISBN 00400149

—Taxation Treatment of Interest / London : Butterworths, 1984.
This book brings together all the legislation, case law, and extrastatutory concessions relevant to taxation of interest in the United Kingdom.
ISBN 0406258155 Pbk

—Taxing Currency Fluctuations? / J. R. King. – London : Institute for Fiscal Studies.
– (Report Ser.).

—Taxing Pensions : The Taxation of Occupational Pension Schemes in the United Kingdom / E. M. Hammond. – London : Institute for Fiscal Studies.
– (Report Ser.).

—Teachers and the law / Partington. – 6th ed. – Methuen, 1985.
ISBN 0416395309 Pbk £10.95
ISBN 0416421709 Hbk £18.95

—Time Limits for Tax Claims, Elections and Reliefs / London : Butterworths, 1984.
ISBN 0406535108 Pbk

—Tolley's Accounting Problems of the Companies Acts : Practical Guidance on Recent Legislation / Sells. – Croydon : Tolley, 1984.
136p.
ISBN 0854591478 Hbk £7.95

—Tolley's Anti-Avoidance Provisions / Croydon : Tolley, 1984.
344p.
ISBN 0854591516 Hbk £17.50

—Tolley's Double Taxation Relief / Sells. – Croydon : Tolley.
175p.
ISBN 0510493874 Hbk £8.95

—Tolley's tax bumph 1983-84 / edited by Robert Wareham. – Croydon : Tolley, 1983.
viii,536p.
Includes index.
ISBN 0854591389

—Tolley's tax cases 1988 / by Victor Grout. – 8th ed. – Croydon : Tolley, 1988.
xxvi,516p.
Includes index.
ISBN 0854591508

—Tolley's Tax Cases 1988 / Tolley Publishing, 1988.
ISBN 0854592997 Pbk £17.95

—Tolley's Tax Guide 1988-89 / Rita Burrows. – Croydon : Tolley.
464p.
ISBN 0854593535 Hbk £15.95

—Tolley's taxation of marriage and marriage breakdown / by David Brodie. – Croydon : Tolley, 1988.
xxiii,184p; 23cm.
Includes index.
ISBN 0854593233 Pbk £14.95

—Trust taxation manual / London : Butterworths, 1986.
ISBN 0406503303 Pbk £18.50

—Trusts and Tax Planning / 2nd ed. – London : Oyez Longman, 1982.
– (Oyez Longman Practical Tax Ser.).

—Trusts : Maximising the Tax Advantages / London : Oyez Longman, 1983.
– (Oyez Longman Intelligence Report Ser.).
ISBN 0851207375 Hbk £45.00

—UK oil taxation / 2nd. – London : Longman Professional, 1988.
ISBN 0851214207 Pbk £50

—Understanding Business Taxation / London : Waterlow, 1984.
192p.
ISBN 0080391362 Pbk £7.95

—US/UK double tax treaty / Croydon : Tolley, 1980.
ISBN 0510494218 Pbk £11.50

—Whillan's Tax Tables : 1986-87 / Sheila Parrington. – London : Butterworths, 1986.
These tables cover income tax, capital transfer tax, capital gains tax, corporation tax, and value added tax in the United Kingdom for tax practitioners.
ISBN 0406543216 Pbk £5.50

—Whillan's Tax Tables / 3rd ed. – London : Butterworths, 1983.
ISBN 0406543178 Pbk £6.45

—Wills, administration and taxation : a practical guide / King. – London : Sweet & Maxwell, 1988.
ISBN 0421382708 Pbk £17.50

TAXATION - HONG KONG

—Guidebook to Taxation and Investment Law in Hong Kong / 2nd ed. – North Ryde : C.C.H. Australia, 1985.
276p.
ISBN 0869037811

—Handbook of Hong Kong tax statutes : profits tax, salaries tax, property tax, interest tax, estate duty, stamp duty, Board of Review decisions / by Patrick B. Paul, Leonard van Hien. – Singapore : Butterworths, 1986.
931p.
Includes texts of legislation relating to income tax, salaries tax, profits tax, property tax, estate duty, and stamp duty. Sets out Inland Revenue Departmental Interpretation and Practice Notes, and all published Inland Revenue Board of Review decisions, cross-referenced to the legislation.
ISBN 0409995274 Hbk £163.75

—Hong Kong revenue law / Matthew Bender, 1981.
ISBN 0000999046 Hbk £140.00

—Hong Kong stamp duties / Richards. – London : Longman Professional, 1984.
ISBN 0851208983 Pbk £17.50

—Hong Kong tax cases / Hong Kong : Government Printer, 1983.
looseleaf.
Kept up to date by supplements.

—Hong Kong taxation : law and practice / David Flux. – Rev. ed. – Hong Kong : Chinese University Press, 1982.
xxviii,387p(4 folded); 24cm.
Previous ed.: 1981. Includes index.
ISBN 0421309105 £17.00

—Hong Kong Taxation : Law and Practice / Sha Tin : Chinese University of Hong Kong Press, 1983-84.
xxviii, 403p.
ISBN 9622013066 Hbk £30.50

TAXATION - INDIA

—Burden of Tax in Punjab / New Delhi : Concept Publishing Company, 1983.
xiv, 223p.

—Digest of Wealth Tax Cases 1957 to 1986 / Allahabad : Modern Law Publications, 1986.

—Donogh's Commentaries on the Indian Stamp Act / 9th rev. ed. – Allahabad : Law Publishers, 1986.

—Estate Duty Law / 2nd ed. – Nagpur : Wadhura & Co, 1983.

—Guide to Revenue Law in U.P., 3 Vols. / 4th ed. – Lucknow : Eastern Book Company, 1977.
986p.

1901-1982 1983.
1,406p.

1976-1982 1983.
420p.

—Indian Direct Taxes Law and Practice / Nagpur : Wadhura & Co, 1983.

—Indian Stamp Act : With State Amendments / 6th ed. – Allahabad : Law Book Ccompany, 1986.
800p.

—Interpretation of Taxing Statutes / Allahabad : Law Publishing House, 1984.

—Law and Practice of Wealth Tax and Gift Tax : with Rules and Forms / 4th ed. – New Delhi : Bharat Law House, 1983.

—Law and Practice of Wealth Tax, Gift Tax / 9th ed. – Nagpur : Wadhura & Co, 1982.
ca 425p.

—Law and Tax for the Layman / Bombay : India Book House.

—Law of Partnership : with Tax-Planing at a Glance / Allahabad : Modern Law Publications, 1987.

—Non-Residents : Taxation and Investment in India / G.S. Pikale. – Bombay : Jaico Publishing House.

—Power of Taxation Under the Constitution / Lucknow : Eastern Book Company, 1987.

—Release of Manual of Central Acts and Important Rules : Criminal, Taxation and Labour, 15 Vols. / Allahabad : Law Publishers, 1986.

—Search and Seizure under Taxation Laws / Allahabad : Law Publishers, 1982.

—Stamp Law and Practice / Allahabad : Universal Book Agency.

—Supreme Court on Direct Taxes 1950 to 1986 / Allahabad : Modern Law Publications, 1986.

—Supreme Court on Direct Taxes / New Delhi : Bharat Law House, 1986.

—Supreme Court Sales Tax Judgements, 1974-1985 / Allahabad : Law Publishers, 1986.
1,100p.

—Taxation of Companies : a Handbook / Calcutta : Eastern Law House, 1969.
260p.

—Taxation of Income and Tax Laws / New Delhi : Deep and Deep Publications.
240p.

—Wealth Tax Act with Rules / 2nd ed. – Allahabad : Law Publishers, 1982.

—Wealth Taxation in India / Allahabad : Vohra, 1987.
195p.
ISBN 8185072094 Hbk £150.00

TAXATION - IRELAND

—Tolley's taxation in the Republic of Ireland 1981-82 / by Glyn Saunders and Eric L. Harvey. - Croydon : Tolley, 1981.
x,193p.
Includes index.
ISBN 0854590439

TAXATION - JAPAN

—Japanese international taxation / Miyatake. - Matthew Bender, 1983.
ISBN 0000999083 Hbk £50.00

TAXATION - LAW AND LEGISLATION - AFRICA

—African tax systems / Robert C. Hammond, Marc J. van den Abeelen. - 2. - Amsterdam : International Bureau of Fiscal Documentation, 1983.
loose-leaf.
Includes bibliography. 'Prepared at the request of the United Nations Economic Commission for Africa.' - Editors: Robert C. Hammond and Marc J. van den Abeelen.

TAXATION - LIECHTENSTEIN

—Companies and Taxes in Liechtenstein / Goup. - Vaduz, 1983.
99p.

TAXATION - MALAYSIA

—Malaysian Taxation / London : Butterworths, 1988.
ISBN 0409995622 Pbk

—Revenue law in Singapore and Malaysia / London : Butterworths, 1986.
ISBN 0409995266 Pbk £38.00

—Share (Land Based Company) Transfer Tax Act, 1984 (Act 310) / Kuala Lumpur : International Law Books Services.

—Stamp Ordinance, 1949 (F.M. Ord. No. 59 of 1949) / Kuala Lumpur : International Law Books Services.

TAXATION - NETHERLANDS

—Taxation in the Netherlands / by Gerrit te Spenke. - Deventer : Kluwer, 1985.
xvii,135p; 25cm.
Includes index.
ISBN 9065440836 No price

TAXATION - NEW ZEALAND

—Advance rulings on tax liability / by John Prebble. - Wellington, N.Z. : Victoria University Press, 1986.
191p.
Bibliograpy: p.156-157. - Includes index. Published for the Institute of Policy Studies.
ISBN 0864730586

—Australian Tax Reports Vols. 1-17 (1969-1986) and Australian and New Zealand Income Tax Reports Vols. 1-10 (1936-1968) Consolidated Index and Tables / Butterworths. - Butterworths, 1989.
292p.
ISBN 0409300977 Hbk £110.00
ISBN £79.00 to subscribers

—Butterworth's Tax Brief / Wellington : Butterworths.

—Butterworths Taxation Library, 3 Vols. / Butterworths.
ISBN 0409661287 loose £770.00

Includes subscr. to New Zealand Current Taxation

—Concise Tax Service / Wellington : Butterworths, 1980.

—Essays on Taxation / J. Prebble. - Wellington : Victoria University of Wellington, 1982.
ISBN 0705508307 Hbk £20.00

—Goods and Services Tax Act 1985 : the Application of the Act / Wayne Mapp. - Butterworths, 1986.
ISBN 0409787663 Pbk £36.30

—Introduction to Taxation in New Zealand / Butterworths, 1988.
470p.
ISBN 0409788570 Pbk £45.00

—New Zealand Current Taxation / Butterworths.

—New Zealand Current Taxation / Wellington : Butterworths.

—New Zealand duties guide / Auckland : Commerce Clearing House (New Zealand), 1985-.
Title history; New Zealand duties and sales tax guide (1983-1985). Includes index. Loose-leaf issues accompanied by a summary report.

—New Zealand Duties Legislation / North Ryde : C.C.H. Australia, 1987.
300p.
ISBN 0864750870 Hbk

—New Zealand goods and services tax guide / Auckland : Commerce Clearing House (New Zealand), 1985-.
Title history: New Zealand duties and sales tax guide (1983-1985);New Zealand sales, goods and services taxes guide (1983-1987). Includes index.

—New Zealand Goods and Services Tax Legislation / 2nd ed. - North Ryde : C.C.H. Australia, 1986.
100p.
ISBN 0864750579 Hbk

—Primary Sector Taxation / Butterworths, 1987.

—Rent Control : Cost and Consequences / Turramura : Centre for Independent Studies.
256p.
ISBN 0959648577 Hbk £9.95

—Report of the Task Force on Tax Reform / P.M. McCaw (Chairman). - Wellington : Govt. Printer, 1982.
xiii,274p.

—Simon's Taxes, 9 Vols. / J. F. Avery Jones. - 3rd ed. - Wellington : Butterworths.

—Simon's Weekly Tax Service : Simon's Tax Intelligence / Butterworth and Co. (Publishers) Ltd. - London : Butterworths.
This weekly publication provides complete information on developments in the fields of income tax, capital gains tax, corporation tax, capital transfer tax, stamp duty, and value added tax in the United Kingdom.

—Simon's Weekly Tax Service : Simon's Tax Intelligence and Simon's Tax Cases / Rengan Krishnan. - Wellington : Butterworths, 1986.

—Tax Practitioner 1989 / Butterworths. - Butterworths, 1989.
712p.
ISBN 0409788775 Pbk £55.00

—Tax Reports (New Zealand), 10 Vols. / Wellington : Butterworths, 1986.

Back Vols. avail.

—Tax Reports New Zealand / Butterworths.

—Taxation of Companies and Corporate Investors / Butterworths, 1984.
ISBN 0409701424 Pbk £33.55

—Taxation of Companies and Corporate Investors / Wellington : Butterworths, 1984.
ISBN 0409701424 Pbk

TAXATION - NIGERIA

—Nigerian Tax Handbook / Tolley Publishing, 1987.
ISBN 0854592318 Pbk £11.50

—Nigerian Tax Law / Abingdon : Professional Books, 1986.
350p.
ISBN 0862051169 Hbk

TAXATION - PACIFIC AREA

—Taxation in the Asian-Pacific region : a country by country survey / compiled by Jap Kim Siong and Ahmad Khan. - 2nd rev. ed. - Singapore : Asian-Pacific Tax and Investment Research Centre, 1985.
vi,218p.
Based on the 8-volume loose-leaf work 'Taxes and Investment in Asia and the Pacific' published by the International Bureau of Fiscal Documentation.

TAXATION - PACIFIC ISLANDS

—Taxes and Investment in Asia and the Pacific / Amsterdam : International Bureau of Fiscal Documentation, 1988.

Fl looseleaf 1989 suppl. renewal

TAXATION - PHILIPPINES

—Answers to Bar Examination Questions /. - Quezon City : University of the Philippines, Law Center, 1982.
312p.

—Casebook on Taxation, Fourth Edition / Quezon City : University of the Philippines, Law Center, 1981.
239p.

—Philippine Agrarian Reform and The New Taxation / A.O. Yoingco. - Quezon City : Katha Publishing Co., 1983.

TAXATION - SCOTLAND

—Revenue law in Scotland / Mackintosh. - London : Butterworths, 1986.
ISBN 040650170X Pbk £18.50

—Revenue Law in Scotland / London : Butterworths, 1984.
ISBN 0406258201 Pbk

TAXATION - SINGAPORE

—Handbook of Singapore Tax Statutes, 1985-86 Edition / Laurence Chan. - Butterworths, 1986.
933p.
Contains the texts of important tax legislation, together with amendments and excerpts from the 1986/87 Budget Statement. Covers income tax, double tax treaties, estate duty, payroll tax, property tax surcharge and stamp duty.
ISBN 0409995207 Pbk £99.00

—Property Tax in Singapore / Singapore : Butterworths, 1985.
This book acts as a guide to the working of the property tax system in Singapore. The author discusses the chargeability of properties, the property tax surcharge and exemptions, concessions and refunds available, and the rights and obligations of the property owner. Relevant legislation is reproduced in full in the appendices.

—Property tax in Singapore / London : Butterworths, 1985.
ISBN 040999510X Pbk £19.00

—Property Tax in Singapore / Butterworths, 1985.
256p.
ISBN 040999510X Pbk £50.00

—Revenue law in Singapore and Malaysia / London : Butterworths, 1986.
ISBN 0409995266 Pbk £38.00

—Singapore Property Tax Cases [1959-1986] / Singapore : Malayan Law Journal, 1987.
xxii,413.
Collection of cases that was determined by the Judicial Committee of the Privy Council, the Court of Appeal, the High Court, and the Valuation Review Board of Singapore.
ISBN 9971700573 Hbk

—Singapore Taxation / Damian C.F. Hong. - Butterworths, 1985.
636p.
ISBN 0409995053 Pbk £90.00

TAXATION - SOUTH AFRICA

—Company Law and Company Taxation in South Africa / Keeton. - Cape Town : Legal & Financial Publishing, 1983.
ISBN 0869940171 Hbk £32.50

—South African Tax Journal / H. R. Levin. - Durban : Butterworths, 1985.

—Tax Strategy / 2nd ed. - Durban : Butterworths, 1983.
ISBN 0409013595 Pbk

—Taxation of Co-operative Societies in South Africa / Cape Town : Legal & Financial Publishing, 1983.
ISBN 0869940317 Hbk £13.50

TAXATION - SOUTH KOREA

—Business laws in Korea : investment, taxation, and industrial property / Chan-jin Kim, editor. - Seoul, Korea : Panmun Book Co., 1982.
xii, 799 p.; 24 cm.
Includes bibliographical references.

TAXATION - SOUTHEAST ASIA

—Taxation in the Asian-Pacific region : a country by country survey / compiled by Jap Kim Siong and Ahmad Khan. - 2nd rev. ed. - Singapore : Asian-Pacific Tax and Investment Research Centre, 1985.
vi,218p.
Based on the 8-volume loose-leaf work 'Taxes and Investment in Asia and the Pacific' published by the International Bureau of Fiscal Documentation.

TAXATION - UNITED KINGDOM

—Taxation of woodlands in the UK / Edinburgh : W Green & Son, 1989.
Traces the history and development of the special tax system for woodlands including changes in the income tax provision since April 1988. Covers transitional provision for income tax to 5 April 1993 with relevant statutory provisions and case law on the definition of what constitutes the management of commercial woodlands relative to income tax questions.
ISBN 0414008952 Hbk

TAXATION - UNITED STATES

—Canada - U.S. Tax Treaty / Vancouver : British Columbia Continuing Legal Education Society, 1985.
73p.
ISBN 0865041857 Hbk £55.00

—Fiscal policy and tax legislation and administration : technical papers and reports of the 15th General Assembly of the Inter-American Center of Tax Administrators (CIAT), Caracas, Venezuela, 25-27 February 1981 / Inter-American Center of Tax Administrators. - Amsterdam : International Bureau of Fiscal Documentation, 1983.
200p.
'Sponsored by the Government of Venezuela, the German Society for Technical Cooperation (GTZ) and the Inter-American Center of Tax Administrators (CIAT)'.
ISBN 9070125226

—Handbook on the U.S. - German Tax Convention / International Bureau of Fiscal Documentation. - Amsterdam : International Bureau of Fiscal Documentation, 1988.

Supplements-1989 renewal

—Introduction to United States international taxation / by Paul R. McDaniel, Hugh J. Ault. - 2nd rev. ed. - Deventer : Kluwer, 1981.
209p; 25cm.
Previous ed.: 1977. Includes index.
ISBN 9065440046 Unpriced

—Issues in International Transfer Pricing / Toronto : DeBoo, 1986.
96p.
This review emphasizes practices in Canada and the U.S., with secondary emphasis on practices in Europe and Japan. Also discussed is Revenue Canada's approach to transfer pricing, including Information Circular IC-87-2.
ISBN 0888202636 Pbk £15.00

—New Canada-U.S. Tax Treaty : Impact on Corporations and Individuals / Don Mills : CCH Canadian Ltd, 1985.
ISBN 0887962904 Pbk £12.00

—New Canada-U.S. Tax Treaty with Technical Explanation / Don Mills : CCH Canadian Ltd, 1984.
ISBN 0887962890 Pbk £8.00

—New U.S. Residency Rules for Canadians : Tax Considerations / North Ryde : C.C.H. Australia, 1986.
98p.
ISBN 0887963250 Pbk £12.00

—Rich, the poor and the taxes they pay / by Joseph A. Pechman. – Brighton : Wheatsheaf, 1986.
xvi,317p; 25cm.
Includes index.
ISBN 0745000983 £28.50

—Structuring foreign investment in US real estate / W D Knight, R L Doernberg. – Kluwer Law and Taxation, 1989.
780.
Explores the considerations of concern to foreign individuals and organisations making US real property investments. Covers US income, estate, and gift tax aspects of foreign investment. Also techniques that may be employed to reduce or eliminate US tax liability. Includes the Foreign Investment in Real Property Act 1980.
ISBN 9065449752 Llf £112/Dfl 350

Supplement 1989.
ISBN 90T275002X Llf £80.75/Dfl 250

—Taxation of Direct Investment in the United States / L. Halpern. – London : Butterworths, 1980.
ISBN 0406539588 Pbk £47.50

—Taxpayer control and the effectiveness of the tax administration : technical papers and reports of the 13th General Assembly of the Inter-American Center of Tax Administrators (CIAT), Quito, Ecuador, May 26-June 1, 1979 / Inter-American Center of Tax Administrators. – Amsterdam : International Bureau of Fiscal Documentation, 1980.
164 p.; 25 cm.
ISBN 9070125161 pbk.

—U.S. Taxation of Canadian Business Investments / Toronto : DeBoo, 1984.
178p.
ISBN 088820227X Pbk £35.00

—US/UK double tax treaty / Croydon : Tolley, 1980.
ISBN 0510494218 Pbk £11.50

TAXATION – WEST GERMANY

—Analysis of the German tax system : general principles, taxation of income and capital, unilateral measures for the avoidance of double taxation / Helmut Debatin. – Updated ed. – Amsterdam, Netherlands : International Bureau of Fiscal Documentation, 1981.
1 v. (various pagings); 22 cm.
'Reprinted from Handbook on the United States-German tax convention.'.
ISBN 9070125218 pbk.

—German Turnover Tax Law, 1980 / F. G. Miller. – 1st ed. – Plymouth : Macdonald & Evans, 1980.
176p.
ISBN 0712154825 Pbk £14.50

—Handbook on the U.S. - German Tax Convention / International Bureau of Fiscal Documentation. – Amsterdam : International Bureau of Fiscal Documentation, 1988.

Supplements-1989 renewal

TAXATION AND GOVERNMENT PROPERTY – CANADA

—Need for and the feasibility of an appeals process in regard to municipal grants-in-lieu of taxes : a report prepared for the Minister of Public Works Canada / I.C. Pollack, R. Gaulin, G. Simpson. – Ottawa : Minister of Supply and Services Canada, 1983.
324 p. in various pagings; 28 cm.
English and French. Added t.p.: La necessite et la faisabilite d'une procedure d'appel dans le regime de subventions aux municipalites en compensation d'imp$ots.
ISBN 0662524039

TAXATION (ISLAMIC LAW)

—Islamic law and finance / edited by Chibli Mallat. – London : Graham & Trotman, 1988.
xiv,196p.
Includes bibliographical references and index.
ISBN 185333121X

TAXATION OF ALIENS

—International tax planning / Barry Spitz. – 2nd ed. – London : Butterworths, 1983.
xxiii,178p.
This book for the tax planner dealing with international tax issues analyzes the methods of international tax planning and explains the basic techniques. Statutes and treaties in conjunction with case law are used to illustrate the analysis.
ISBN 0406382379 Hbk £18.00

TAXATION OF ALIENS – UNITED STATES

—Introduction to United States international taxation / by Paul R. McDaniel, Hugh J. Ault. – 2nd rev. ed. – Deventer : Kluwer, 1981.
209p; 25cm.
Previous ed.: 1977. Includes index.
ISBN 9065440046 Unpriced

TAXATION OF BONDS AND SECURITIES – CANADA

—Taxation of Corporations and Shareholders : Cases and Materials / D. Keith McNair. – Agincourt : Carswell, 1986.
616p.
This text contains both cases and materials pertaining to corporate tax. The bulk of the text is explanatory in nature. These explanations are supplemented with short cases extracts to further illustrate a point.

TAXATION OF BONDS AND SECURITIES – GREAT BRITAIN

—Companies purchasing their own shares : memorandum / by the Society's Standing Committee on Revenue Law. – London : Law Society, 1981.
9p; 30cm.
Submitted in reply to the Inland Revenue's consultative document: Companies purchasing their own shares.

TAXATION OF BONDS AND SECURITIES – NEW ZEALAND

—Taxation of Companies and Corporate Investors / Wellington : Butterworths, 1984.
ISBN 0409701424 Pbk

TAXICABS – AUSTRALIA

—On Buying a Job : The Regulation of Taxicabs in Canberra / Turramura : Centre for Independent Studies.
20p.
ISBN 0959648550 Hbk £2.00

TAXICABS – ENGLAND

—British Railways Board : admission of hackney carriages to Brighton Central Railway Station to ply for hire : a report by the Director General of Fair Trading on an investigation under Section 3 of the Competition Act 1980 / Office of Fair Trading. – London : Office of Fair Trading, 1982.
53p; 30cm.

TAXPAYER COMPLIANCE – UNITED STATES

—Measures for improving the level of voluntary compliance with tax obligations : technical papers and reports of the 18th General Assembly of the Inter-American Center of Tax Administrators (CIAT) Cartagena, Colombia, 21-25 May 1984 / Inter-American Center of Tax Administrators. – Amsterdam : International Bureau of Fiscal Documentation, 1985.
168 p.; 25 cm. – (Publications of the International Bureau of Fiscal Documentation).
Includes bibliographical references.
ISBN 9070125277 pbk.

TECHNICAL ASSISTANCE

—Development technology / H.J. Duller. – London : Routledge & K. Paul, 1982.
192p.
Includes index. Bibliography: p173-190.
ISBN 0710009909

TECHNOLOGICAL INNOVATIONS

—Can knowledge survive? / Sir Harry Hookway. – London : British Library, 1986.
8p; 30cm. – (The Fourth British Library Annual Research Lecture).
ISBN 0712330747 Pbk Free

—Shipping, energy, and environment : Southeast Asian perspectives for the eighties : proceedings of a Workshop held in Honolulu, Hawaii, 10-12 December 1980 / edited by Mark J. Valencia ... et al. – Halifax, N.S. : Dalhousie Ocean Studies Programme, 1982.
xi,333p.
Held at the Environment and Policy Institute of the East-West Center at the University of Hawaii.
ISBN 0770302769

—Technological change, rationalisation and industrial relations / edited by Otto Jacobi ... et al. – London : Croom Helm, 1986.
283p; 23cm.
Includes bibliography and index.
ISBN 0709914482 £19.95

TECHNOLOGICAL INNOVATIONS – GREAT BRITAIN

—Making a business of information : a survey of new opportunities / London : H.M.S.O., 1983.
53p; 21cm.
Bibliography: p48. At head of title: Cabinet Office, Information Technology Advisory Panel.
ISBN 0116308249 Pbk £4.20

TECHNOLOGY

—Coming information society / London : British Library, 1984.
1v.
ISBN 0712330364 Pbk

—Transfer of Technology for Development / Paris : International Chamber of Commerce.
42p.

TECHNOLOGY – CANADA

—Technology Agreements / Vancouver : British Columbia Continuing Legal Education Society, 1985.
260p.
ISBN 0865042314 Hbk £65.00

TECHNOLOGY AND INTERNATIONAL AFFAIRS

—Exploitation of science and technology : a world force / by Sir Henry Chilver. – Southampton : University of Southampton, 1985.
At head of title page: The Fawley Foundation.

TECHNOLOGY AND LAW

—State Responsibility for Technological Damage in International Law / Berlin : Duncker and Humblot, 1987.
xxviii, 326p.
ISBN 3428062388 Hbk £136.00

TECHNOLOGY AND LAW – GREAT BRITAIN

—Year Book of law, computers and technology / London : Butterworths, 1990.
25.
ISBN 0406187037 Hbk £24.95

TECHNOLOGY TRANSFER

—Antitrust and direct regulation of international transfer of technology transactions : a comparison and evaluation / Guillermo Cabanellas. – Munich : Verlag Chemie for the Max Planck Institute for Foreign and International Patent Copyright and Competition Law, 1984.
175p.
ISBN 3527260013

—Compilation of legal material dealing with transfer and development of technology / prepared by UNCTAD secretariat. – Geneva : UNCTAD, 1982.
245p. – (TD/B/C.6/81).

—Credit and Guarantee Financing, Transfer of Technology / edited by C.C.A. Voskuil, Z. Parac. J.A. Wade. – Dordrecht : M. Nijhoff, 1987.
xvii,372p.
Includes bibliographical references.
ISBN 9024735297 Hbk £165.00

—Draft International Code of Conduct on the Transfer of Technology : a study in third world development / Wolfgang Fikentscher : assisted by Hans Peter Kunz-Hallstein ... et al. – Weinheim : Verlag Chemie for the Max Planck Institute for Foreign and International Patent, Copyright, and Competition Law, Munich, 1980.
xvi,195p; 24cm.
Bibliography: p.189-191. - Includes index. Includes the text of the Draft Code.
ISBN 3527256989

—Further elaboration and implementation of a strategy for the technological transformation of developing countries : comparative tables of proposals made by regional groups at the first special session of the Committee on Transfer of Technology / prepared by the UNCTAD secretariat. – s.l. : United Nations Conference on Trade and Development, 1984.
43p. – (TD/B/C.6/108).
Item 3 of the provisional agenda for the fifth session of the Committee on Transfer of Technology, Geneva, 22 October 1984.

—International technology licensing : compensation, costs, and negotiation / Farok J. Contractor. – Lexington : Lexington Books, 1981.
xiv,193p; 24cm.
Bibliography: p185-189. - Includes index.
ISBN 0669043591 £22.50

—New, other activities and intiatives : (a) interregional linkages and co-operative arrangements : interregional linkages and co-operative arrangements among developing countries for their technological transformation / report by the UNCTAD secretariat. – s.l. : United Nations Conference on Trade and Development, 1984.
ii, 21p, 3 leaves. – (TD/B/C.6/118).
Item 6 (a) of the provisional agenda for the fifth session of the Committee on Transfer of Technology, Geneva, 22 October 1984.

—Regional Seminar on Licensing and Other Technology Transfer Arrangements / Geneva : World Intellectual Property Organization, 1987.
263p.

—Role of patent information in the transfer of technology : proceedings of the International Conference held at Varna, Bulgaria, May 27-30, 1980 / organised by the World International i.e. Intellectual Property Organization : edited by F.A. Sviridov. – McLean, Va. : Pergamon International Information, 1981.
viii,265p; 23cm.
ISBN 0080275559 Pbk £6.00

—Technology transfer : a case study / Mingsam Santikam. – Singapore : Singapore University Press, 1981.
xiv,270p.
Bibliography: p257-264.

TECHNOLOGY TRANSFER – CHINA

—Intellectual property law in the People's Republic of China : a guide to patents, trade marks and technology transfer / Michael D.Pendleton. – Singapore : Butterworths, 1986.
xvii,138p.
ISBN 0409995193

—Technology transfer in the Peoples' Republic of China : law and practice / Richard J. Goossen. – Dordrecht : M. Nijhoff, 1987.
Bibliography.
ISBN 9024734428

TECHNOLOGY TRANSFER – EUROPEAN COMMUNITY

—Technology transfer within the E.E.C. : a summary of papers and discussion of a seminar held in the house of the Royal Society of Arts on Thursday 31 January 1985 / Foundation for Science and Technology. – London : London Science Centre, 1985.
23p.

TELECOMMUNICATION – LAW AND LEGISLATION – GREAT BRITAIN

—Telecommunications development : draft development control policy note / Department of the Environment. – London : Department of the Environment, 1986.
24p.

TELECOMMUNICATIONS

—Aerospace Law : Telecommunications Satellites / London : Butterworths, 1982.
ISBN 0409848654 Hbk £67.00

—Communications : (includes telecommunications) / Thessaloniki, Greece : Institute of International Public Law and International Relations of Thessaloniki, 1987.
530p.
Includes bibliographical references. Text in English and French.

—Encyclopaedia of International Telecommunications Law / London : Butterworths, 1987.

—Final Acts of the World Administrative Telegraph and Telephone Conference (Geneva, 1973) Telegraph Regulations, Telephone Regulations / Geneva : International Telecommunications Union.

—From Telecommunications to Electronic Services : A Global Spectrum of Definitions, Boundary Lines and Structures / Jeffrey Cunard. – London : Butterworths, 1986.
ISBN 0880631031 Pbk £40.00

—General Tariff Principles : Charging and Accounting in International Telecommunications Services - Series D Recommendations / Geneva : International Telecommunications Union.
ISBN 9261019919 Hbk £38.00

—IFRB Handbook on Radio Regulatory Procedures / Geneva : International Telecommunications Union.
ISBN 9261018327 Hbk £395.00

English
ISBN 9261018319 Hbk £395.00

Spanish
ISBN 9261018335 Hbk £395.00

—Information computer communication policy / Organisation for Economic Co-operation and Development. – Paris : O.E.C.D., 1983.
136p; 24cm.
Discusses the development of computer and communications technologies with relation to the existing legal regulations.
ISBN 9264125272 Pbk £7.00

—International Implications of New Telecommunications Technology / Enstone : Ditchley Foundation.
– (Ditchley Conference Reports).

—International regulation of data services: the debate over the trade and development issues / London : Pinter, 1990.
250.
Bibliography and index included.
ISBN 0861878531 Hbk £30

—International Telecommunication Convention : Final Protocol, Additional Protocols, Compulsory Settlement of Disputes - Nairobi 1982 / Geneva : International Telecommunications Union.
ISBN 9261016529 Hbk £27.00

English
ISBN 9261016510 Hbk £27.00

Spanish
ISBN 9261016537 Hbk £27.00

—Issues in Computing, Telecommunications and Information Policy / Paris : International Chamber of Commerce.
24p.

—Law and economics of transborder telecommunications : a symposium / edited by Ernst-Joachim Mestmacker. – Baden-Baden : Nomos, 1987.
450p.
Includes bibliographical references.
ISBN 3789013684

—Protecting privacy in two-way electronic services / by David H. Flaherty : foreword by Ronald L. Plasser. – London : Mansell, 1985.
viii,172p; 24cm.
Bibliography: p165-166. - Includes index.
ISBN 0720117445 £23.50

—Satellite and Cable : International Protection / Stephen de B. Bate. – London : Oyez Longman, 1984.
– (Oyez Longman Intelligence Report Ser.).
ISBN 0851208614 Hbk

—Telecommunications : pressures and policies for change / Organisation for Economic Co-operation and Development. – Paris : Organisation for Economic Co-operation and Development, 1983.
142p.
ISBN 9264124284

—Teleforum - 1983 : Part III : Legal Aspects of International Telecommunications / Geneva : International Telecommunications Union.

—Telephone tapping and the recording of telecommunications in some Council of Europe member states / Council of Europe Directorate of Legal Affairs. – Strasbourg : Council of Europe, 1982.
12p; 30cm. – (Legislative dossier).
ISBN 9287100551

TELECOMMUNICATIONS – AUSTRALIA

—Communications law and policy in Australia : adapted from Mark Armstrong's Broadcasting law and policy in Australia / Mark Armstrong. – Sydney : Butterworths, 1987.
ISBN 0409493759 LLF A$275

—New media : law & policy / edited by Mark Armstrong. – Kensington, NSW : Faculty of Law, University of New South Wales, 1981.
vii, 237 p.; 25 cm.
Includes bibliographical references.
ISBN 0858238950 pbk.

TELECOMMUNICATIONS – CANADA

—Canadian Telecommunications Regulation Bibliography / Ottawa : Canadian Law Information Council.
ISBN 0921481063 £25.00

—Law of international telecommunications in Canada / Nicolas Mateesco Matte, Ram S. Jakhu. – Baden-Baden : Nomos, 1987.
131p.
Includes bibliographical references.
ISBN 3789013099

—Wiretaps and Conspiracy / Vancouver : British Columbia Continuing Legal Education Society, 1981.
127p.
ISBN 0865040370 Hbk £40.00

TELECOMMUNICATIONS – EUROPEAN COMMUNITY

—Towards a dynamic European economy : green paper on the development of the Common Market for telecommunications services and equipment / communication by the Commission. – Luxembourg : Commission of the European Communities, 987.
192p. – (Document).
ISBN 9277257415

TELECOMMUNICATIONS – GREAT BRITAIN

—British Telecommunications : (pricing policy for the placing of advertisements in yellow pages directories) : a report / by the Director General of Fair Trading .. – London : Office of Fair Trading, 1984.
54p; 30cm.

—Code of practice for consumers / British Telecom. – London : British Telecom, 1984.
24p.

—Communications : a guide to the electronic office for practising lawyers / compiled by the Communications Committee of the Society for Computers and Law. – Milton, Oxon. : The Society, 1983.
39 leaves.
Bibliography: p.39.

—Communications : a guide to the electronic office for practising lawyers / compiled by the Communications Committee of the Society for Computers and Law. – 2nd fully rev ed. – Didcot : The Society, 1985.
iii,67 leaves.
ISBN 0906122198

—Development of UK communications systems : discussion document / Department of Trade and Industry. – London : The Department, 1987.
14 leaves.

—From Telecommunications to Electronic Services / Butterworths. – London : Butterworths, 1986.
ISBN 0880631031 Hbk £27.00

—Interception of communications in Great Britain / Home Office. – London : H.M.S.O., 1980.
8p.

—Report on cable systems / Information Technology Advisory Panel. – London : H.M.S.O., 1982.
54p; 20cm.
At head of title: Cabinet Office. Information Technology Advisory Panel.
ISBN 0116308214 Pbk £3.60

—Telecommunications law and practice / Sweet & Maxwell, 1988.
ISBN 0421377801 Hbk £29.00

TELECOMMUNICATIONS – INDIA

—Law of international telecommunications in India / K.D. Gaur. – Baden-Baden : Nomos, 1988.
219p.
ISBN 3789013102

TELECOMMUNICATIONS – UNITED STATES

—Law of international telecommunications in the United States / Stephen R. Barnett, Michael Botein, Eli M. Noam. – Baden-Baden : Nomos, 1988.
271p.
ISBN 3789013080

TELEVISION ADVERTISING – LONDON

—Thames Television Limited : a report by the Director General of Fair Trading on an investigation under section 3 of the Competition Act 1980 / Office of Fair Trading. – London : Office of Fair Trading, 1984.
87p; 30cm.

TERMS AND PHRASES

—Thesaurus of provincial statutory terminology / compiled and edited by Mary K. McLean, with assistance from Lorna K. Rees-Potter. – 1st ed. – Ottawa : Canadian Law Information Council, 1986.
ix, 179 p.; 28 cm.
ISBN 0920358896 £40.00

TERMS AND PHRASES – CANADA

—Handbook of Canadian legal terminology : revised and updated / William J. Flynn. – Toronto : Stoddart, 1986.
117p.
ISBN 0773751076

TERMS AND PHRASES – SCOTLAND

—Scots law terms and expressions / John Angus Beaton. – Edinburgh : Green, 1982.
116p.
ISBN 0414006917

—Student's glossary of Scottish legal terms / by Andrew Dewar Gibb. – 2nd ed. – Edinburgh : Green, 1982.
100p.
Previous ed.: published as 'Dictionary of words and phrases' by A.W. Dalrymple and Andrew Dewar Gibb, 1946.
ISBN 0414006968

TERRITORIAL WATERS

—Baltic Straits / by Gunnar Alexandersson. – The Hague : Nijhoff, 1982.
152p.
Includes index.
ISBN 902472595X Hbk £75.00

—A Guide to Maritime Boundary Delimitation / Adam J. Kerr. – Agincourt : Carswell, 1986.
136p.
This work addresses the technical aspects of maritime boundaries under international law. The book provides commentary on relevant cases which have been refered to the International Court of Justice.

—Law of the sea and maritime boundary delimitation in South-East Asia / Kriangsak Kittichaisaree. – Singapore : Oxford University Press, 1987.
xv, 209 p.; 23 cm.
Discusses maritime boundary delimination in international law. Concentrates on South-East Asia, but legal analyses are examined in a global context, using South-East Asian practice as concrete instances to elaborate particular legal problems.
ISBN 0195888626 Hbk £20.00

—Law of the sea : unilateralism or multilateralism? / by Adeoye Akinsanya. – Lagos : University of Lagos Press, 1980.
52p. – (Monograph series).
Includes bibliographical references.
ISBN 9782264059

—Law of the Territorial Sea : Evolution and Development / Calcutta : Naya Prokash, 1988.
280p.
ISBN 8185109699 Hbk £200.00

—Maritime boundaries and ocean resources / edited by Gerald Blake : International Geographical Union Study Group on the World Political Map. – London : Croom Helm, 1987.
284p; 23cm.
Bibliography: p257-271. - Includes index.
ISBN 0709939744 £27.50

—Maritime boundary / S.P. Jagota. – Dordrecht : M. Nijhoff, 1985.
388p.
Bibliography.
ISBN 902473133X Hbk £175.00

—Maritime boundary delimitation : an annotated bibliography / Ted L. McDorman, Kenneth P. Beauchamp, Douglas M. Johnston. – Lexington, Mass. : Lexington Books, 1983.
xiii,207p; 24cm.
Includes index.
ISBN 0669061468 Unpriced

—Maritime political boundaries of the world / J.R.V. Prescott. – London : Methuen, 1985.
xv,377p; 24cm.
Bibliography: 355-360. - Includes index.
ISBN 0416417507 £30.00

—Ocean Boundary Making / Saunders. – Oxford : Croom Helm, 1988.
ISBN 0709914954 Hbk £35.00

—Strait of Dover / by Luc Cuyvers. – Dordrecht : Martinus Nijhoff, 1986.
xvi, 150p. – (International straits of the world).
ISBN 9024732522 Hbk £115.00

—Systematic index of international water resources treaties, declarations, acts and cases by basin / Repertoire systematique par bassin de traites, declarations, textes legislatifs et jurisprudence concernant les ressources en eau internationales. – Rome : Food and Agriculture Organization of the United Nations, 1984.
xxxiii,332p. – (Legislative study).
Explanatory text in English, French and Spanish.
ISBN 9250021895

TERRITORIAL WATERS – GREAT BRITAIN

—Waters around the British Isles / London : Sweet & Maxwell, 1987.
ISBN 0198284926 Hbk

—Waters around the British Isles : their conflicting uses : report of a study group of the David Davies Memorial Institute of International Studies / R.B. Clark. – Oxford : Clarendon, 1987.
xvi,386p; 24cm.
Includes index.
ISBN 0198284926 £32.50

TERRORISM

—1987 annual on terrorism / edited by Yonah Alexander, with contributing editors Abraham H. Foxman and Eugene Mastrangelo. – Dordrecht : Martinus Nijhoff, 1989.
528. – (Annual on Terrorism).
Focuses on national, regional and global developments in the field of terrorism. This volume includes the analysis of domestic and international terrorism, selected papers written during 1987, a statistical synopsis and selected documents, reports and addresses.
ISBN 9024738016 Hbk Gld250.00

—British perspectives on terrorism / edited by Paul Wilkinson. – London : Allen & Unwin, 1981.
193p; 23cm.
Originally published: in Terrorism, v.5, no.1 and 2. Includes index.
ISBN 0043270646 Hbk Unpriced
ISBN 0043270654 Pbk Unpriced

—Conference on the Defence of Democracy against Terrorism in Europe - Tasks and Problems, Strasbourg, 12-14 November 1980 : compendium of documents / 1. – Strasbourg : Council of Europe, 1981.
various pagings.
Includes bibliographies. Conferences organised by the Political Affairs Committee of the Parliamentary Assembly of the Council of Europe. Some documents in English and French.

—Extortions under terrorist threats / Council of Europe. – Strasbourg : Council of Europe, 1986.
14p; 21cm. – (Legal affairs).
'... prepared by a select committee of experts under the authority of the European Committee on Crime Problems ... The committee of Ministers of the Council of Europe authorised its publication' - p.3.
ISBN 9287108412

—Legislative responses to terrorism / edited by Yonah Alexander, Allan S. Nanes. – Dordrecht Holland : M. Nijhoff, 1986.
xi, 327p.
ISBN 9024732131

—Living with terrorism : the problem of air piracy / Frank Brenchley. – London : Institute for the Study of Conflict, 1986.
iv,17p.

—New terrorism / edited by William Gutteridge for the Institute for the Study of Conflict. – London : Mansell, 1986.
192p; 24cm.
Includes index.
ISBN 0720118123 £20.00

—Political terrorism : theory, tactics, and counter-measures / Grant Wardlaw. – Cambridge : Cambridge University Press, 1982.
xiii,218p; 24cm.
Bibliography: p204-212. - Includes index.
ISBN 0521250323 Hbk Unpriced
ISBN 0521271479 Pbk

—Review of the operation of the Northern Ireland (Emergency Provisions) Act 1978 / by Sir George Baker : presented to Parliament by the Secretary of State for Northern Ireland. – London : H.M.S.O., 1984.
171p.
ISBN 0101922205

—Review of the operation of the Prevention of Terrorism (Temporary Provisions) Act 1976 / by Earl Jellicoe. – London : H.M.S.O., 1983.
v,144p; 25cm.
At head of title: Home Office.
ISBN 0101880308 Pbk £8.30

—Terrorism and the liberal state / 2nd ed. – London : Macmillan, 1986.
ISBN 0333394917 Pbk £7.95

TERRORISM – GREAT BRITAIN

—Prevention of Terrorism Act : the case for repeal / Catherine Scorer and Patricia Hewitt. – London : National Council for Civil Liberties, 1981.
68p; 20cm.
ISBN 0901108944 Pbk £1.75

—Prevention of terrorism in British Law / Manchester : Manchester University Press, 1986-1988.
ISBN 0719022037 Pbk £9.95

—Prevention of terrorism in British law / Clive Walker. – Manchester : Manchester University Press, 1986.
xi,272p; 25cm.
Bibliography: p236-239. - Includes index.
ISBN 0719017823 £27.50

—Review of the Operation of the Prevention of Terrorism (Temporary Provisions) Act 1984 / by the Viscount Colville of Culross : presented to Parliament by the Secretary of State for the Home Department ... – London : HMSO, 1987.
v,70p.
ISBN 0101026420

TERRORISM – NORTHERN IRELAND

—Use and abuse of emergency legislation in Northern Ireland / Dermot P. J. Walsh. – London? : Cobden Trust, 1983.
138p.
ISBN 0900137207

TERRORISM – SOUTH AFRICA

—Security, terrorism, and torture : detainees' rights in South Africa and Israel : a comparative study / by Harold Rudolph. – Cape Town : Juta, 1984.
xviii, 270 p.; 22 cm.
Includes indexes. Bibliography: p. 253-259.
ISBN 0702115088 pbk. R38.00

TEXT-BOOKS – ENGLAND

—Vickery's law and accounts of executors administrators and trustees / 21st. – London : Cassell plc.
Textbook for people taking examinations for the Institute of Chartered Accountants in England and Wales. Relates developments in the subject, including inheritance tax, since 1980.
ISBN 0304313890

TEXT-BOOKS – GREAT BRITAIN

—Legal environment : business law / 2nd. – London : Cassell plc.
Introductory text-book on business law.
ISBN 0039106020

TEXTILE FABRICS – GREAT BRITAIN

—Arthur Sanderson & Sons Limited : a report by the Director General of Fair Trading on an investigation under section 3 of the Competition Act 1980 / London : Office of Fair Trading, 1981.
53p.

THEFT

—Theft Acts 1968 and 1978 / by Edward Griew. – 5th ed. – London : Sweet & Maxwell, 1986.
xxxiii,269p; 26cm.
For the first time, this edition covers the following major cases; Ghosh, on dishonesty; Morris, on appropriation; Bloxham, on handling; and Wilson, on alternative verdicts. Includes other decisions on theft, taking a conveyance, obtaining property by deception, and the 1978 Act.
ISBN 0421353007 Hbk £21.00
ISBN 0421353104 Pbk £13.95

THEFT – AUSTRALIA

—Car Stealing In Australia : Facts and Figures / Canberra : Australian Institute of Criminology.

THEFT – CANADA

—Criminal intrusion / Law Reform Commission of Canada. – Ottawa : The Commission, 1986.
25,30p. – (Working paper).
Includes bibliographical references. Added t.p. in French: L'intrusion criminelle. Pages numbered in opposite directions. Text in English and French.
ISBN 0662542061

THEFT – ENGLAND

—Burglary in a dwelling : the offence, the offender and the victim / Mike Maguire in collaboration with Trevor Bennett. – London : Heinemann, 1982.
ix,204p; 23cm. – (Heinemann library of criminology and penal reform).
Bibliography: p194-199. - Includes index.
ISBN 0435825674 £13.50

—Burglary in schools : the prospects for prevention / Tim Hope. – London : Home Office, 1982.
iv,47p.
Bibliography: p.38-41.
ISBN 0862520703

—Burglary : police actions and victims views / John Burrows. – London : Home Office, 1986.
v,97p.
Bibliography: p.95-97.
ISBN 0862522331

—Cases and materials on the Thefts Acts / Janet M. Dine. – London : Financial Training, 1985.
xvii,223p.
Includes the text of the Theft Acts, 1968 and 1978.
ISBN 0906322804

—Investigating burglary : the measurement of police performance / by John Burrows. – London : H.M.S.O., 1986.
v,30p; 25cm.
Examines differences in clear-up rates in areas with similar problems. Finds that clear-up rates are not necessarily a reflection of success in arresting burglars, but involve questioning about previous offences.
ISBN 0113408242

—Law of theft / J.C. Smith. – 5th ed. – London : Butterworths, 1984.
xxxii,257p; 26cm.
Previous ed.: 1979. Includes index.
ISBN 0406379084 Hbk Unpriced
ISBN 0406379092 Pbk Unpriced

—Theft Act 1978 / Janet M. Dine. – London : Financial Training, 1985.
xvii,223p.
Includes the text of the Theft Acts, 1968 and 1978.
ISBN 0906322804

—Theft Acts 1968 and 1978 / by Edward Griew. – 4th ed. – London : Sweet & Maxwell, 1982.
xxix,240p; 25cm.
Previous ed.: 1978. Includes index. Includes the texts of The Theft Act 1968 and The Theft Act 1978.
ISBN 0421286407 Hbk Unpriced
ISBN 0421286504 Pbk £9.50

THEFT – GAMBIA

—Memoranda and draft : bills re : christian marriage, matrimonial causes, offences relating to property and lands (Banjul and Kombo St. Mary) / Law Reform Commission of the Gambia. – Banjul : The Commission?, 1985.
xv,112p.
Includes the text of draft legislation.

THEFT – GREAT BRITAIN

—Casebook on the Theft Act / 3rd ed. – London : Police Review Publishing, 1984.
ISBN 0851640117 Pbk

—Casebook On The Theft Acts 1968-78 / 3rd ed. – Police Review, 1984.
ISBN 0851640117 Pbk £4.00

—Casebook on Theft Acts 1968-78 / 3rd ed. - London : Sweet & Maxwell, 1984.
ISBN 0851640117 Pbk £4.50

—Criminal Law, No. 1 / Wilkie. - 6th ed. - London : Butterworths, 1980.
- (Police Promotion Handbooks Ser.).
This work for United Kingdom police officers presents the changes in criminal law brought about by the Theft Act of 1978 and the Criminal Evidence Act of 1979.
Police officers
ISBN 0406841217 Pbk

—Law of Theft / 5th ed. - London : Butterworths, 1984.
ISBN 0406379092 Pbk £13.95

—Residential burglary : the limits of prevention / by Stuart Winchester and Hilary Jackson. - London : H.M.S.O., 1982.
v,42p; 25cm.
Bibliography: p40-42. 'A Home Office Research and Planning Unit report'.
ISBN 0113407696

—Shoplifting, and thefts by shop staff : a review / by the Home Office Standing Committee on Crime Prevention 1983. - London : H.M.S.O., 1983.
23p.
ISBN 0113407890

THEFT - IRELAND

—Receiving stolen property / the Law Reform Commission. - Dublin : The Commission, 1987.
x,130p. - (LRC).

THEORY OF KNOWLEDGE

—Understanding Locke : an introduction to philosophy through John Locke's Essay / John J. Jenkins. - Edinburgh : Edinburgh University Press, 1983.
xviii,256p; 21cm.
Bibliography: p241-252. - Includes index.
ISBN 0852244428 Hbk £15.00
ISBN 0852244495 Pbk Unpriced

THESAURI

—Eurovoc : annex to the index of the Official journal of the European Communities / 2nd ed. 2. - Luxembourg : Office for Official Publications of the European Communities, 1987.
Previous ed.: 1984. Contents: v.1 Alphabetical thesaurus - v.2 Subject-oriented thesaurus. Also published in eight other languages.
ISBN 9277258314

—FAMILY thesaurus : Australian family studies indexing terms / prepared by the Australian Institute of Family Studies : edited by Deborah Whithear. - 2nd ed. - Melbourne : Australian Institute of Family Studies, 1987.
98p.
ISBN 0642118515

—Thesaurus of provincial statutory terminology / compiled and edited by Mary K. McLean, with assistance from Lorna K. Rees-Potter. - 1st ed. - Ottawa : Canadian Law Information Council, 1986.
ix, 179 p.; 28 cm.
ISBN 0920358896 £40.00

THINGS (ROMAN LAW)

—Selected texts and cases on the Roman law of things : with an excursus on the Roman law of slavery / J.E. Schiller. - Cape Town : Juta, 1982.
xiii,127p; 25cm.
ISBN 0702112941

TIME (LAW)

—Time bars in maritime matters : a study / by Kaj Pineus. - London : Lloyd's of London Press, 1982.
168p.
ISBN 0907432425

TIME (LAW) - AUSTRALIA

—Time in the performance of contracts : especially for the sale of land / K.E. Lindgren. - 2nd ed. - Sydney : Butterworths, 1982.
xxv,201p.
Previous ed.: 1976. Includes bibliographical references and index.
ISBN 0409303909 Hbk £49

TIME (LAW) - ENGLAND

—Time restrictions on presentation of divorce and nullity petitions / the Law Commission. - London : H.M.S.O., 1980.
v,83p; 21cm. - (Working paper).
ISBN 0117301566 Pbk £3.50

TIME (LAW) - SCOTLAND

—Report on the Scottish term and quarter days / presented to Parliament by the Lord Advocate by Command of Her Majesty, October 1987. - Edinburgh : HMSO, 1987.
vi,29p.
ISBN 0101020821

—Expense of Time / Law Society (United Kingdom). - 4th ed. - London : Law Society, 1986.
ISBN 0901064734 Hbk £3.00

TIMESHARING

—International timesharing / 2nd ed. - London : Sweet & Maxwell, 1986.
ISBN 095041767X Pbk £24.50

—International timesharing / by James Edmonds. - 1st ed. - London : Services To Lawyers, 1984.
374p.
Bibliography: p.363-365. - Includes index. Includes precedents. Subtitle on cover: a review of United Kingdom law and that of other relevant jurisdictions in relation to timeshare schemes and purchases, including extensive precedents for use in the United Kingdom.
ISBN 0950417653

—International timesharing / 2nd ed. - London : Services to Lawyers, 1986.
xix,591p.
Previous ed.: 1984. Bibliography: p.579-581. - Includes index. Includes precedents. Subtitle on cover: a review of United Kingdom law and that of other relevant jurisdictions in relation to timeshare schemes and purchases, including extensive precedents.
ISBN 095041767X

—Practical timesharing : UK and overseas / London : Butterworths, 1988.
ISBN 0406100500 Pbk

TIMESHARING - GREAT BRITAIN

—Practical Timeshare and Group Ownership / London : Butterworths, 1987.
ISBN 0406103283 Pbk

—Practical timeshare and group ownership / London : Butterworths, 1987.
ISBN 0406103283 Pbk £26.95

TIMESHARING - SOUTH AFRICA

—Sectional titles, share blocks and time-sharing / by C.G. van der Merwe and D.W. Butler. - Durban : Butterworths, 1985.
xiii,573p.
Bibliography: p. xv-xxi. - Includes indexes.
ISBN 0409059293 Hbk R105

TITLE - AFRICA

—Title to territory in Africa : international legal issues / Malcolm Shaw. - Oxford : Clarendon, 1985.
xii,428p; 22cm.
Includes bibliography and index.
ISBN 0198253796 £35.00

TITLE - AUSTRALIA - SOUTH AUSTRALIA

—Jessup's Forms and practice of the Lands Titles Office of South Australia / J. G. Maher. - 6th ed. - Sydney : Law Book Co., 1982.
xii,444p.
Includes index.
ISBN 0455205345

—Report ... relating to reform of the law of delivery of deeds / Law Reform Committee of South Australia. - Adelaide : Government Printer, 1987.
42p. - (77th report).
Includes Bill for an act to amend the Law of Property Act, 1936.

TITLE - AUSTRALIA - VICTORIA

—Delivery of deeds / Law Reform Commissioner, Victoria. - Melbourne : The Commission, 1980.
14p. - (Report no 10).
Includes bibliographical references.

—Priorities / Law Reform Commission of Victoria. - Melbourne : The Commission, 1988.
iv,19p. - (Discussion paper).
ISBN 0724167129

—Sale of land / Law Reform Commission of Victoria. - Melbourne : The Commission, 1988.
iv,40p. - (Discussion paper).
Includes bibliographical references.
ISBN 0724166947

TITLE - CANADA

—Aboriginal Title and Mining Legislation in the Northwest Territories / Saskatoon : University of Saskatchewan, Native Law Centre, 1982.
32p.
ISBN 0888801149 Hbk £8.00

—Indian Title in Canada / Agincourt : Carswell, 1987.
154p.

—Registration of Title to Land, 2 Vols. / Agincourt : Carswell, 1987.
950p.

—Registration of Title to Land / Agincourt : Carswell, 1987.
950p.
This work is a comparitive analysis of the Canadian Torrens Acts with the representative body of Australian, New Zealand, and Tasmanian Acts. The book examines the application of the Torrens system in the context of transfer, leases, mortgages, lis pendens, restrictive covenants, and other dealings in all the jurisdictions.

—Tentative proposals for changes in limitations legislation / Law Reform Commission of Saskatchewan. - Saskatoon : Law Reform Commission of Saskatchewan, 1981.
27p.

TITLE - CANADA - BRITISH COLUMBIA

—Report on deeds and seals / Law Reform Commission of British Columbia. - Vancouver : The Commission, 1988.
ii,47p.
Includes bibliographical references.
ISBN 0771886799

—Report on the Land (Settled Estate) Act / Law Reform Commission of British Columbia. - Vancouver : The Commission, 1988.
41p.
Includes text of the Land (Settled Estate) Act and Trust Variation Act.
ISBN 0771887248

TITLE - CANADA - ONTARIO

—Ontario Land Titles Procedural Guide / Don Mills : CCH Canadian Ltd, 1986.
196p.
ISBN 0887962823 Pbk £8.00

—Title Searching in Ontario / 2nd ed. - Butterworths, 1982.
200p.
Explains the procedure required for a 40-year search of title with a copy of an abstract page and sketches relating to land descriptions, the procedure required under the Land Titles Act, the procedure required under the Condominium Act, under the Registry Act, the Certification of Titles Act, and the provisions allowed under section 29 of the Planning Act.
ISBN 0409834165 Hbk £29.95

TITLE - ENGLAND

—Butterworths Consolidated Legislation Service /. - Professional Publ.
195p.
ISBN 0409014095 £40.00

Sectional Titles Act 94 of 1986
158p.
ISBN 0409014710 £40.00

—Concise land registration practice / Christopher West. - 3rd ed. - London : Sweet & Maxwell, 1982.
xvii,313p; 23cm.
Previous ed.: / by Theodore B.F. Ruoff. 1967. Includes index.
ISBN 0421287705 £19.50

—Deeds and escrows / the Law Commission. - London : H.M.S.O., 1987.
29p. - (1987/88 HC1).
ISBN 010200188X

—Emmet on title : Emmet's notes on perusing titles and on practical conveyancing / J. T. Farrand. - 18th ed. - London : Oyez Longman, 1983.
clxxxviii,1262p.
Previous ed.: 1978. Includes index.
ISBN 0851207332

—Emmet on title : Emmet's notes on perusing titles and on practical conveyancing / J.T. Farrand : assisted by Jane M. Milward. - 19th ed. 2 v. - London : Longman Professional, 1986.
looseleaf.
Includes index.
ISBN 0851211488

—Land registration forms / Christopher West. - 3rd ed. - London : Sweet & Maxwell, 1983.
xv,261p; 23cm.
Previous ed.: 1973. Includes index.
ISBN 0421287608 £19.50

—Memorandum on Law Commission working paper no. 92: Formalities for contracts for sale of land and Law Commission working paper no. 93: Formalities for deeds and esrows / Justice. - London : Justice, .
9 leaves.

—Property law : fourth report on land registration / the Law Commission. - London : HMSO, 1988.
iii,147p. - (H.C. 1987-88).
ISBN 0102680884

—Property law : second report on land registration : inspection of the register / the Law Commission. - London : H.M.S.O., 1985.
iii,43p.
ISBN 0102551855

—Property law : the implications of William & Glyn's Bank Ltd. v. Boland : report on a reference under section 3(1)(e) of the Law Commission Act 1965 / the Law Commission. - London : H.M.S.O., 1982.
v,56p.
ISBN 0101863608

—Property law : third report on land registration, A. overriding interests, B. rectification and indemnity, C. minor interests / the Law Commission. - London : H.M.S.O., 1987.
v,107p.
ISBN 0102269874

—Transfer of land : implied covenants for title / the Law Commission. - London : HMSO, 1988.
v,57,11p. - (Working paper).
Includes excerpts from relevant acts.
ISBN 0117301892

—Transfer of land : the rule in Bain v. Fothergill / the Law Commission. – London : H.M.S.O., 1987.
iv,28p.
ISBN 010101922X

—Transfer of land : the rule in Bain v. Fothergill / The Law Commission. – London : H.M.S.O., 1986.
iv,49p; 21cm. – (Working paper).
Includes bibliographical references.
ISBN 0117301795

—Transfer of land : title on death / the Law Commission. – London : HMSO, 1987.
viii,106p. – (Working paper).
ISBN 0117301876

TITLE - GREAT BRITAIN

—Effective Retention of Title Clauses / Oxford : Blackwell Scientific, 1986.
ISBN 0003830748 Hbk £19.95

—Registered land / by David J. Hayton. – 3rd ed. – London : Sweet & Maxwell, 1981.
xxiii,222p; 20cm.
Previous ed.: 1977. Includes index.
ISBN 042128160X Hbk £10.00
ISBN 0421281707 Pbk £6.50

—Ruoff & Roper on the law and practice of registered conveyancing / Robert B. Roper. – 5th ed. – London : Sweet & Maxwell, 1986.
lxxiv,1233p; 26cm.
Previous ed.: 1979. Includes index.
ISBN 0420469109 £82.00

—Transfer of land : formalities for contracts for sale etc of land / London : H.M.S.O., 1985.
iv,79p. – (Working paper).
ISBN 0117301736

—Transfer of land : formalities for contracts for sale etc. of land / the Law Commission. – London : H.M.S.O., 1987.
37p. – (1987/88 HC2).
ISBN 0102002886

—Transfer of land : formalities for deeds and escrows / London : H.M.S.O., 1985.
iv,44p. – (Working paper).
ISBN 0117301744

—Transfer of land, the law of positive and restrictive covenants ... / the Law Commission. – London : H.M.S.O., 1984.
x,331p; 25cm. – (H.C.1983-84).
ISBN 0102201846

—Williams on Title /. – London : Butterworths.
This text is a comprehensive treatment of the law of title in the United Kingdom. The work provides a thorough discussion of the subject from contract to completion. Extensive quotations from case law and analysis of principles of law are given throughout the text.
ISBN 0406421498 Pbk £33.50

TITLE - MALAYSIA

—National Land Code : a commentary / by Judith E. Sihombing : with a foreword by Tun Dr. Mohamed Suffian. – Kuala Lumpur, Singapore : Malayan Law Journal, 1981.
xxxix,905p.
Includes index.
ISBN 9971700174

—Private caveats : entry, extension, removal and appeals / by Wong Kim Fatt : with a foreword by Mohamed Suffian. – Singapore : Malayan Law Journal, 1980.
xvi,141p.
Contains a table of cases, judicial pronouncements on caveats, applications for entry, extension of private caveats, removal under section 326, 327, appeal under section 418, caveating a portion of land, and taxation of costs.
ISBN 9971700107 Hbk £20.00

TITLE - NEW ZEALAND

—Effect of a caveat on a mortgagee's power of sale : report of the Property Law and Equity Reform Committee / New Zealand. – Wellington : Government Printer, 1981.
7,2p.

—Land Titles Reform / A.G. Lang. – Auckland : Legal Research Foundation, 1983.

TITLE - NORTHERN IRELAND

—Land registry practice in Northern Ireland / by Herbert Wallace. – Belfast : SLS Publications, 1981.
xxiiii,142p.
Includes index. Latest supplement held: 1st, 1982.
ISBN 085389194X

—Land registry practice in Northern Ireland / by Herbert Wallace : assisted by James Derek Reade. – 2nd ed. – Belfast : SLS Legal Publications, 1987.
xxviii,167p.
Previous ed.: 1981. Includes index.
ISBN 0853892938

—Occupiers' rights and constructive notice : the text of a lecture delivered to the Belfast Solicitors' Association on 2 December 1982 / by Hebert Wallace. – Belfast : SLS Legal Publications, 1982.
35p.
Includes bibliographical references.

TITLE - SOUTH AFRICA

—Shrand on Sectional Titles Act / Cape Town : Legal and Financial Publishing Co.
ISBN Hbk £22.50
ISBN supplement 5.50

TITLE EXAMINATIONS - ENGLAND

—Local authority enquiries : how can we eliminate delays? / a consultation paper from the Conveyancing Standing Committee. – London : The Committee, 1987.
20,7p.

TITLES OF HONOUR AND NOBILITY

—Titles and forms of address : a guide to correct use / 18th ed. – London : Black, 1985.
224p.
Previous ed.: 1980. Includes index.
ISBN 0713626941 Pbk £5.95

TORRENS SYSTEM - AUSTRALIA

—Torrens system in Australia / by Douglas J. Whalan. – Sydney : Law Book Co., 1982.
lxvii,410p.
Includes bibliographical references and index.
ISBN 0455203571 Pbk
ISBN 045520358X

TORRENS SYSTEM - AUSTRALIA - VICTORIA

—Torrens register book / Law Reform Commision of Victoria. – Melbourne : The Commission, 1986.
iv,19p. – (Discussion paper).
Includes bibliographical references.

TORRENS SYSTEM - CANADA

—Registration of Title to Land / Agincourt : Carswell, 1987.
950p.
This work is a comparitive analysis of the Canadian Torrens Acts with the representative body of Australian, New Zealand, and Tasmanian Acts. The book examines the application of the Torrens system in the context of transfer, leases, mortgages, lis pendens, restrictive covenants, and other dealings in all the jurisdictions.

TORTS

—Beyond Lex Loci Delicti : Conflicts Methodology and Multistate Torts in American Case Law / Dordrecht : Kluwer, 1987.
550p.
ISBN 9065442766 Pbk £95.00

—Cases Illustrating the Principles of the Laws of Torts / John Charles Miles. – Repr. of 1904 ed. – Aalen Wuertt : Scientia.
xx, 628p.

—Justice, rights and tort law / edited by Michael D. Bayles and Bruce Chapman. – Dordrecht : Reidel, 1983.
vii,272p; 23cm.
Reprinted from Law and Philosophy; v.1, no.3 and v.2, no.1.
ISBN 9027716390 Hbk £90.00

—Law of torts / Harry Street. – 7th ed. – London : Butterworths, 1983.
lvii,506p.
Previous ed.: 1976. Includes index. Cover title: Street on torts.
ISBN 0406662088

—Law Unit : Torts / Lucas. – Stockholm : Anderson Keenan, 1981.
ISBN 0906501245 Pbk £3.70

—Principles of the Law of Tort / 8th ed. – Lucknow : Eastern Book Company, 1986.

—Private international law : choice of law in tort and delict / Great Britain. – London : H.M.S.O., 1984.
xiv,293p. – (Consultative memorandum).
Includes bibliographical references. Prepared by a Joint Working Party of the Law Commission and the Scottish Law Commission.
ISBN 011730168X

TORTS - AUSTRALIA

—Butterworths Student Companions /. – Butterworths, 1984.
128p.
ISBN 0409494127

—Cases on torts / W.L. Morison ... et al. – 5th ed. – Sydney : Law Book Co., 1981.
xxxiv,1011p.
Includes bibliographical notes and index.
ISBN 0455202516 Pbk
ISBN 0455202524

—Introduction to Torts / North Ryde : Law Book Co, 1985.
xxxiv, 307p.
ISBN 0455205574 Hbk £41.50
ISBN 0455205582 Pbk £23.50

—Law of torts / by John G. Fleming. – 6th ed. – Sydney : Law book Company, 1983.
lii,702p; 24cm.
Previous ed.: 1977. Includes bibliographical references and index.
ISBN 0455205477 Hbk £30.00
ISBN 0455205485 Pbk £23.00

—Law of torts / by John G. Fleming. – 7th ed. – Sydney : Law Book Company, 1987.
lxix,706p; 25cm.
Previous ed.: 1983. Includes index.
ISBN 0455207534 Hbk No price
ISBN 0455207542 Pbk No price

—Law of torts in Australia / F.A. Trindade, Peter Cane. – Melbourne : Oxford University Press, 1985.
lxv, 763 p.; 24 cm.
Includes indexes.
ISBN 0195544633 Pbk £39.00
ISBN 0195544641 Hbk £55.00

—Negligence and economic torts : selected aspects : papers presented at seminars conducted by the New South Wales Bar Association / edited by T. Simos. – Sydney : Published by the Law Book Co. for the New South Wales Bar Association, 1980.
vii,159p.
Includes bibliographical references.
ISBN 0455202486

—Public torts and contracts / by Mark Aronson and Harry Whitmore. – Sydney : Law Book Co., 1982.
xviii, 296 p.; 25 cm.
Includes bibliographical references and indexes.
ISBN 0455204411 pbk.

—Torts /. – North Ryde : Law Book Co, 1984.
xii, 108p. – (Nutshells).
ISBN 0455203474

—Torts : Cases and Commentary / D. Hambly. – 2nd ed. – Butterworths, 1985.
1,158p.
ISBN 0409491845 Hbk £87.00
ISBN 040949125X Pbk £63.00

Supplement-1986
75p.
ISBN 0409491187 £4.00

—Torts : cases and commentary / by Harold Luntz,David Hambly and Robert Hayes. – Sydney : Butterworths, 1980.
xxxii,1158p; 1980.
ISBN 0409443514

TORTS - CANADA

—Canadian Cases on the Law of Torts / Agincourt : Carswell.
Vol. 44 1987.

—Canadian Tort Law / Allen M. Linden. – 8th ed. – Butterworths, 1985.
1,072p.
Contains two new chapters on liability for negligent statements, and tort liability of public officials and bodies. The chapter on occupier's liability has been expanded, and the text also includes excerpts from law journals, treaties, and government documents, and review questions.
ISBN 0409845612 Pbk £75.00

—Canadian tort law / Allen M. Linden. – 4th. – Toronto : Butterworths, 1988.
840.
Includes bibliographical references and index. Earlier eds. published as Canadian negligence law. Examines the theoretical foundation of tort law, together with its practical application in the Canadian litigation arena. Contains a new chapter on statute and negligence, a discussion and new material on liability for economic losses, an analysis of the new judicial approach to limitations periods and torts, and a commentary on new privileges developing in the area of libel law.
ISBN 0409801917 Hbk

—Cases and Materials on the Law of Torts / Bruce P. Feldthusen. – 2nd ed. – Agincourt : Carswell, 1986.

—Interspousal Immunity in Tort / Victoria : Government of British Columbia, 1983.

—Introduction to the law of torts / Scarborough, Ontario : Butterworths (Canada), 1978.
312.
Covers the scope of tortious liability, fundamentals of liability, limitations on liability, personal injuries, negligence, injuries to personality, injuries to property, economic loss, injurious abuse of legal process, remedies, and procedural matters.
ISBN 0409830364 Pbk

—Issues in Tort Law / Sanda Rodgers-Magnet. – Agincourt : Carswell, 1983.
388p.
This book is a collection of papers on key issues in Canadian tort law by leading scholars in the field.

—Occupiers' Liability in Canada / Agincourt : Carswell, 1981.
328p.
The book analyzes the common law rules of occupiers liability and comments on legislation in Ontario, Alberta and British Columbia.

—Remedies in Tort, 4 Vols. / A. Linden. – Agincourt : Carswell, 1987.
This multi-volume set of looseleaf books provides an in-depth coverage of the area of torts. There are 23 chapters. Discussions include related proceedings, elements the plaintiff must establish to succeed in an action, available defenses, remedies, necessary and proper parties to an action, and practice issues pertaining to tort law. Special features include a legal research guide and sample statements of claims.

—Remedies in Tort, 4 Vols. / Agincourt : Carswell, 1987.
550p.

—Tort Law / Daniel J. Baum. – Toronto : IPI Publishing, 1982.
84p. – (You and the Law Ser.).
ISBN 0458957003 Pbk £7.95

—Torts in the 80s / Don Mills : R. De Boo, 1983.
504p.
Includes bibliographical references and index.
ISBN 0888201508

TORTS - CANADA - BRITISH COLUMBIA

—Interspousal immunity in tort / Law Reform Commission of British Columbia. – Vancouver : The Commission, 1982.
iii,42p. – (Working paper).
Includes bibliographical references.

—Report on interspousal immunity in tort / Law Reform Commission of British Columbia. – Victoria : Queen's Printer, 983.
21p.

TORTS - CANADA - ONTARIO

—Apportionment of fault in tort / David Cheifetz. – Ontario : Canada Law Book, 1981.
xlii,355p.
ISBN 0888040091

TORTS - ENGLAND

—Accidents, compensation and the law / P.S. Atiyah. – 3rd ed. – London : Weidenfeld and Nicolson, 1980.
xxiv,695p.

ISBN 0297777548

—Cases and statutes on tort / by Paul L. Bradbury. – 3rd ed. – London : Sweet & Maxwell, 1984.
xviii,195p; 22cm.
Previous ed.: 1978. Includes index.
ISBN 0421322004 Pbk £7.85

—Clerk & Lindsell on torts / William Henry Barber Lindsell, R. W. M. Dias. – 15th ed. – London : Sweet & Maxwell, 1982.
cclxiv,1417p; 26cm.
Previous ed.: / general editors Sir Arthur L. Armitage and R.W.M. Dias. 1975. Includes index. Kept up to date by supplements.
ISBN 0421262508 £65.00

—Foundations of the law of tort / Glanville Williams, B.A. Hepple. – 2nd ed. – London : Butterworths, 1984.
xxiv,230p; 23cm.
This text for students in the United Kingdom provides an examination of the underlying principles of tort law and liability in the modern context. The function of tort law and its history, the concepts of damage and fault, the effects of insurance and social security, and possibilities for reform are covered.
ISBN 0406683867 HBK £14.00
ISBN 0406683875 Pbk £10.95

—Introduction to the law of torts / by John G. Fleming. – 2nd ed. – Oxford : Clarendon, 1985.
viii,236p; 23cm. – (Clarendon law series).
Previous ed.: 1967. Includes index.
ISBN 0198761546 Hbk £17.50
ISBN 0198761554 Pbk £8.95

—Law of torts / Margaret Brazier. – 8th ed. – London : Butterworths, 1988.
lix,562p.
Previous ed.: / by Harry Street. 1983. Includes index.
ISBN 0406662118 Pbk £28.00
ISBN 0406662126 £17.95

—Remedies for torts and breach of contract / A.S. Burrows. – London : Butterworths, 1987.
lviii,435p; 22cm.
Includes index.
ISBN 0406501505 Hbk £18.00
ISBN 0406501513 Pbk £12.95

—Remedies in contract and tort / Donald Harris. – London : Weidenfeld & Nicolson, 1988.
xxxvii,411p.
Includes index.
ISBN 0297793551

—Salmond and Heuston on the law of torts / R. F. V. Heuston, R. A. Buckley, John Salmond. – 19th ed. – London : Sweet & Maxwell, 1987.
700p; 25cm.
Previous ed.: 1981. Includes index.
ISBN 0421343001 Hbk £30.00 :
ISBN 0421343109 Pbk £24.00

—Stephen's commentaries on the laws of England / L. Crispin Warmington. – 21st ed. – London : Butterworths, 1950.
xiv,604p.
Index included in Vol. 4. .

—Tort / by C.D. Baker. – 4th ed. – London : Sweet & Maxwell, 1986.
xxxii,398p; 23cm.
Previous ed.: 1981. Includes index.
ISBN 0421349409 Hbk £15.00
ISBN 0421349506 Pbk £8.95

—Tort : cases and materials / compiled by B.A. Hepple, M.H. Matthews. – 3rd ed. – London : Butterworths, 1985.
750p; 25cm.
Previous ed.: 1980. Includes index.
ISBN 0406594848 Hbk £25.00 :
ISBN 0406594902 Pbk £16.95

—Tort in a nutshell / by Ralph Tiernan. – London : Sweet & Maxwell, 1987.
120p; 22cm.
Includes index.
ISBN 0421368403 Pbk £3.95

—Tort law / by R.W.M. Dias and B.S. Markesinis. – Oxford : Clarendon, 1984.
xxxiv,526p; 23cm.
Includes bibliographies and index.
ISBN 0198761503 Hbk £22.50
ISBN 0198761511 Pbk £15.00

—Winfield and Jolowicz on tort / John Anthony Jolowicz, W. V. H. Rogers. – 12th ed. – London : Sweet & Maxwell, 1984.
lxiii,767p; 26cm.
Previous ed.: 1979. Includes index.
ISBN 0421325801 Hbk £28.00
ISBN 0421325909 Pbk £17.50

TORTS - GREAT BRITAIN

—Bradbury : Cases and Statutes on Tort / Brenda Barrett. – 3rd ed. – London : Sweet & Maxwell, 1984.
190p.
ISBN 1421322004 Pbk £8.50

—Breach of statutory duty in tort / by K.M. Stanton. – London : Sweet & Maxwell, 1986.
xvii,155p; 23cm.
Includes index.
ISBN 0421331402 Hbk £12.50
ISBN 042133150X Pbk £9.50

—Casebook on tort / by Tony Weir. – 5th ed. – London : Sweet & Maxwell, 1983.
xxvi,572p; 24cm.
Previous ed.: 1979. Includes index.
ISBN 0421316306 Hbk £24.00
ISBN 0421316403 Pbk £14.50

—Cases in Tort / G. H. Samuel. – Repr. of 1977 ed. – Plymouth : Macdonald & Evans, 1984.
352p. – (M and E Handbook Ser.).
ISBN 0712103562 Pbk £4.25

—Cracknell LSC Torts / 6th ed. – London : Butterworths, 1983.
ISBN 040656714X Pbk £11.95

—Cracknell's Law Students' Companions : Torts / 6th ed. – London : Butterworths, 1983.
This book for law students in the United Kingdom is intended to be used along with textbooks and lecture notes. The work includes case summaries arranged alphabetically by case and relevant statutory materials.
ISBN 040656714X Pbk £22.00

—Foundations of Law of Tort / Hepople. – 2nd ed. – London : Butterworths, 1984.
ISBN 0406683867 Hbk £14.95
ISBN 0406683875 Pbk £10.95

—Introduction to the Law of Torts / 2nd ed. – Oxford : Oxford University Press, 1986.
ISBN 0198761546 Hbk £17.50
ISBN 0198761554 Pbk £8.95

—Law of Tort / London : Duckworth (Gerald), 1986.
ISBN 0715620126 Hbk £29.95

—Law of Torts / 4th ed. – Plymouth : Macdonald & Evans, 1982.
ISBN 0712127046 Pbk £6.50

Supplement-1987
ISBN 0421378409

—Law of Torts / 8th ed. – London : Butterworths, 1988.
ISBN 0406662118 Hbk £34.00
ISBN 0406662126 Pbk £19.95

—Law of Torts / 4th ed. – Plymouth : Macdonald & Evans, 1982.
– (M and E Handbook Ser.).
ISBN 0712127046 Hbk £5.95

—Law of Torts / Stephenson. – London : Financial Training, 1985.
– (SWOT).
ISBN 0906322731 Pbk £7.50

—Remedies for torts and breach of contract / London : Butterworths, 1987.
ISBN 0406501505 Hbk £24.00

—Sweet & Maxwell Law / London : Sweet & Maxwell, 1984.
ISBN 0421321601 Pbk £29.50

File 6, Torts liability of an industrialist 1985.
ISBN 0421340304 Pbk £29.50

—Textbook on torts / London : Financial Training, 1986.
ISBN 1851850260 Pbk £13.95

—Tort : cases and materials / M H Matthews. – 3rd ed. – London : Butterworths, 1985.
ISBN 0406594848 Hbk £32.00
ISBN 0406594902 Pbk £21.95

—Tort law / Markesinis. – Oxford : Oxford University Press, 1984.
ISBN 0198761503 Hbk £22.50
ISBN 0198761511 Pbk £15.00

—Understanding tort law / Powell. – London : Sweet & Maxwell, 1987.

TORTS - INDIA

—Law of Tort / Lucknow : Eastern Book Company, 1987.

—Law of Torts / Dhirajlal. – 21st ed. – Nagpur : Wadhura & Co, 1987.

—Law of Torts / 5th ed. – Allahabad : Law Book Company, 1985.
lxxx, 103p.

—Law of Torts / 4th ed. 1976 repr. – Lucknow : Eastern Book Company, 1981.
528p.

—Torts Made Easy / Allahabad : Kitab Mahal.

TORTS - IRELAND

—Casebook on the Irish law of torts / by Bryan M.E. McMahon and William Binchy : with a foreword by Brian Walsh. – Abingdon, Oxon. : Professional Books, 1983.
xxxix,652p.
Includes bibliographical references and index.
ISBN 0862050502

—Casebook on the Irish Law of Torts / Binchy. – London : Butterworths, 1983.
ISBN 0862050502 Hbk £35.00
ISBN 0862050561 Pbk £25.00

—Irish law of torts / by Bryan M.E. McMahon and William Binchy. – Abingdon, Oxon. : Professional Books, 1981.
lxxvi,620p; 24cm.
Bibliography: p.lxiii. - Includes index.
ISBN 0862050405

—Irish Law of Torts / Binchy. – London : Butterworths, 1982.
ISBN 0862050405 Hbk £36.00

—Report on civil liability for animals / the Law Reform Commission. – Dublin : The Commission, 1982.
v,26p. – (LRC).

TORTS - MALAYSIA

—Practical approach to assessment of liability and damages in tort / by R.K. Nathan. – Singapore : Malayan Law Journal Pte., 1986.
xliv,312p.
Includes bibliographical references and index.
ISBN 9971700514

TORTS - NIGERIA

—Nigerian Law of Tort / London : Sweet & Maxwell.
– (Nigerian Practice Library Ser.).
ISBN 0421312505 Hbk

—Nigerian law of torts / E. Mara-Brown. – London : Sweet & Maxwell, 1987.
v,76p.
Includes index.
ISBN 0421361506

—Nigerian Law of Torts / London : Sweet & Maxwell, 1982.
ISBN 0421291508 Pbk £15.00

TORTS - SCOTLAND

—Introduction to the Scots law of delict / Edinburgh : W Green & Son, 1989.
An introduction to the most important principles and rules, with coverage of negligence, defamation, occupiers' liability, employers' liability and other forms of liability. Case summaries and statutory extracts provided along with references to other sources such as journal articles.
ISBN 0414008901

—Law of delict in Scotland / by David M. Walker. – 2nd ed., rev. – Edinburgh : Published under the auspices of the Scottish Universities Law Institute by W. Green, 1981.
cxli,1111p; 26cm.
Previous ed.: 1966. Includes index.
ISBN 0414006690 Unpriced

TORTS - SOUTH AFRICA

—Law of delict / by P.Q.R. Boberg. – Cape Town : Juta, 1984.
v. 1; 26 cm.
Includes indexes. Bibliography: v. 1, p. xvii-xx. Contents: v. 1. Aquilian liability.
ISBN 070211426X

TORTS - UNITED STATES

—American tort process / John G. Fleming. – Oxford England : Clarendon Press, 1988.
viii, 271 p.; 23 cm.
Includes bibliographical references and index.
ISBN 0198255977

TORTS - WEST GERMANY

—Comparative introduction to the German law of tort / B.S. Markesinis. – Oxford : Clarendon, 1986.
xxix,610p; 24cm.
Includes bibliographies and index. Spine title: The German law of torts.
ISBN 0198255314 £55.00

—German Law of Torts / Oxford : Oxford University Press, 1986.
ISBN 0198255314 Hbk £55.00

TORTS (ROMAN LAW)

—Tortious liability for unintentional harm in the common law and the civil law / by F.H. Lawson, B.S. Markesinis. – 2. – Cambridge : Cambridge University Press, 1982.
Includes index.
ISBN 0521235863 v. 2

TORTURE

—How to Make the Convention against Torture Effective / Geneva : International Commission of Jurists, 1980.
60p.

—Torture / Oxford : Blackwell, 1985.
ISBN 0631137238 Pbk £5.95

—Torture in the eighties / Amnesty International. – Oxford : Robertson, 1984.
250p.
ISBN 0855207809 Hbk £15.00
ISBN 0855207817 Pbk £4.95

TORTURE - AFGHANISTAN

—Afghanistan : torture of political prisoners / Amnesty International. – London : Amnesty International, 1986.
i,51p.
ISBN 0862101077

TORTURE - CHILE

—Chile : evidence of torture / Amnesty International. – London : Amnesty International Publications, 1983.
75p.
ISBN 0862100534

TORTURE - EAST TIMOR

—East Timor : violations of human rights : extrajudicial executions, 'disappearances', torture and political imprisonment, 1975-1984 / Amnesty International. – London : Amnesty International Publications, 1985.
vii,92p.
ISBN 0862100852

TORTURE - GREAT BRITAIN

—Public Policy and the Use of Torture / London : Quaker Peace & Service, 1980.
32p.
ISBN 0901689114 Pbk £0.50

TORTURE - GUATEMALA

—Guatemala : a government program of political murder / Amnesty International. – London : Amnesty International, 1981.
32p; 30cm.
Cover title.
ISBN 0862100267 Pbk Unpriced

TORTURE - IRAQ

—Iraq : evidence of torture : an Amnesty International report / London : Amnesty International Publications, 1981.
44p; 30cm.
ISBN 0862100321 unbound Unpriced

TORTURE - NICARAGUA

—Nicaragua : the human rights record / Amnesty International. – London : Amnesty International, 1986.
36p; 27cm.
ISBN 0862100941 Pbk No price

TORTURE - SOUTH AFRICA

—Detention and Torture in South Africa / DENT, 1987.
ISBN 0852553188 Pbk £7.95

TORTURE - SPAIN

—Spain : the question of torture : documents exchanged by Amnesty International & the Government of Spain / Amnesty International. – London : Amnesty International Publications, 1985.
60p.
Translated from the Spanish.
ISBN 0862100860

TORTURE - TURKEY

—Turkey : testimony on torture / Amnesty International. – London : Amnesty International Publications, 1985.
76p.
ISBN 0862100887

TORTURE - UGANDA

—Uganda : six years after Amin : torture, killings, disappearances / Amnesty International. – London : Amnesty International, 1985.
40p.

TORTURE - ZAIRE

—Zaire : reports of torture and killings committed by the armed forces in Shaba region / Amnesty International. – London : Amnesty International, 1986.
24p.
ISBN 0862100968

TOURIST TRADE - AUSTRALIA

—Australian Travel and Tourism Law Handbook / Butterworths, 1988.
285p.
ISBN 0409493848 Pbk £22.50

TOURIST TRADE - GREAT BRITAIN

—Tourism law / Jim Corke. – Huntingdon, Cams. : Elm, 1988.
xxvi,288p.
Includes bibliography and index.
ISBN 0946139954 tutor's pack £10.95
ISBN 0946139962 £39.00

TOWAGE - GREAT BRITAIN

—Law of Tug, Tow and Pilotage / 2nd ed. – London : Sweet & Maxwell, 1982.
ISBN 0412250209 Hbk £60.00

—Law of Tug, Tow and Pilotage / 2nd ed. – London : Chapman & Hall, 1982.
ISBN 0412250209 Hbk £60.00

TOWING - ENGLAND

—Law of tugs and towage / L. J. Kovats. – Chichester : Barry Rose, 1980.
xxxiv,344p.
ISBN 0859921816

TOWNS - CANADA

—Barrie-Vespra Annexation Act, 1983, Bill 142 : An Act Respecting the City of Barrie and the Township of Vespra / Ontario : Ontario Government Publications Service, 1983.
6p.

—District Municipality of Muskoka Amendment Act, 1983, Bill 106 : An Act to Amend the District Municipality of Muskoka Act / Ontario : Ontario Government Publications Service, 1983.
2p.

—Municipal Private Acts Repeal Act, 1983, Bill 120 : An Act to Repeal Certain Private Acts Related to Municipalities / Ontario : Ontario Government Publications Service, 1983.
9p.

—Smyth Town Plot Land Act, 1983, Bill Pr033 : An Act Respecting Certain Land in the Town of Smyth, in the District of Nipissing / Ontario : Ontario Government Publications Service, 1983.
3p.

—Township of Mattice-Val Cote Act, 1983, Bill Pr039 : An Act to Continue the Corporation of the Union of Townships of Elber and Devitt Under the Name of The Corporation of the Township of Mattice-Val Cote / Ontario : Ontario Government Publications Service, 1983.
1p.

TOWNS - CANADA - ONTARIO

—Town of Harrow Act, 1983, Bill Pr050 : An Act Respecting the Town of Harrow / Ontario : Ontario Government Publications Service, 1983.
2p.

TRADE - AUSTRALIA

—Annotated Trade Practices Act / 8th ed. – North Ryde : Law Book Co, 1987.
xxxv, 413p.
ISBN 0455207399 Pbk £32.00

—Powers of Investigation in Revenue, Companies and Trade Practices Law / R.H. Woellner. – Butterworths, 1983.
486p.
ISBN 0409493813 Pbk £65.00

—Trade Practices Law. Supplement / North Ryde : Law Book Co, 1982.
ISBN 0455205337 £26.00

—Trade Practices Legislation and Materials 1986 / Kingston : Australian Government Publishing Service.

TRADE - CANADA

—Canada-U.S. Free Trade Agreement : Commentary and Related Documents / Richard G. Dearden. – North Ryde : C.C.H. Australia.
138p.
ISBN 0887964583 Pbk £14.95

—Canada-U.S. Free Trade Agreement : Final Text and Analysis / Richard G. Dearden. – North Ryde : C.C.H. Australia.
420p.
ISBN 0887964621 Pbk £22.95

—Splintered Market : Barriers to Interprovincial Trade in Canadian Agriculture / David R. Hughes. – Toronto : Lorimer & Co, 1981.
ISBN 0888625170 Hbk £16.95
ISBN 0888625162 Pbk £7.95

—Trade Law Topics / Steven Cass. – Toronto : Butterworths.
ISBN 0409811890 Hbk £165.00

TRADE - HONG KONG

—Commercial, Business and Trade Laws : Hong Kong 2 volumes / Dobbs Ferry : Oceana, 1982.
ISBN 0379231050 loose £190.00

TRADE - UNITED STATES

—Canada-U.S. Free Trade Agreement : Commentary and Related Documents / Richard G. Dearden. – North Ryde : C.C.H. Australia.
138p.
ISBN 0887964583 Pbk £14.95

—Canada-U.S. Free Trade Agreement : Final Text and Analysis / Richard G. Dearden. – North Ryde : C.C.H. Australia.
420p.
ISBN 0887964621 Pbk £22.95

TRADE AND PROFESSIONAL ASSOCIATIONS - AUSTRALIA

—Trade associations, fairness and competition / by Warren Pengilley. – Sydney : Law Book Company, 1981.
xxvii,247p.
Includes index. Includes text of Trade Practices Act 1974.
ISBN 0455200866

—Trade Practices Legislation and Materials 1986 / Kingston : Australian Government Publishing Service.

TRADE AND PROFESSIONAL ASSOCIATIONS - GREAT BRITAIN

—Restrictions on the kind of organisation through which members of professions may offer their services / a report by the Director General of Fair Trading. – London : Office of Fair Trading, 1986.
86p,36p.

TRADE MARKS

—Cancellation and nullity of trademarks in Colombia / German Cavelier. – Bogota, Colombia : Cavelier Abogados, 1986.
xii,235p.

—Guide to the International Registration of Marks (Madrid Union) / rep. 1984. – Geneva : World Intellectual Property Organization.
167p.

—Importation of products with the same trademark / by German Cavelier. – Bogota, Colombia : Cavelier Abogados, 1985.
9 leaves.

—International Classification of Goods and Services for the Purposes of the Registration of Marks / 5th ed. – Geneva : World Intellectual Property Organization, 1986.

Part 1: Alphabetical List of Goods and Services

—Introduction to trade mark law in the Benelux / W. Mak, H. Molijn : translated by M.V. Snoxall, M.O. Snoxall. – Deventer, The Netherlands : Kluwer, 1982.
Includes index. Bibliography. Translation of: Merkenbescherming in de Benelux.
ISBN 9065440216

—Introduction to Trademark Law and Practice : the Basic Concepts / Geneva : World Intellectual Property Organizations, 1987.
99p.

—Legal Training Course on Trademarks / Geneva : World Intellectual Property Organization, 1982.
ca 600p.

—Part 2: List of Goods and Services in Class Order / Geneva : World Intellectual Property Organization.

Records of the Nairobi Diplomatic Conference for the Adoption of a Treaty on the Protection of the Olympic Symbol (September 24 to 26, 1981)
194p.

—Practical guide to trade marks / Amanda Michaels. – Oxford : ESC Publishing Ltd, 1982.
xxii,226p.
ISBN 0906214122 Hbk £21.50
ISBN 0906214092 Pbk £15.50

—Trademark Registration Treaty (TRT) Original Text of the Treaty and Regulations Adopted by the Vienna Conference (1973) / Geneva : World Intellectual Property Organization.
131p.

—Use and Usefulness of Trademarks in Developing Countries : Collection of Lectures Given at the Asian and Pacific Symposium (1982, Colombo, Sri Lanka) / Geneva : World Intellectual Property Organization.
205p.

—Use of trademarks in Colombia / Bogota, Colombia : Cavelier Abogados, 1985.
22 leaves.

—World trademark law and practice / 2nd ed. – Matthew Bender, 1985.
ISBN 0000999080 Hbk £141.00

TRADE MARKS – AUSTRALIA

—Australian Trade Mark Law / London : Law Book Co, 1982.
ISBN 0455201196 Hbk £35.00

—Australian trade mark law and practice / by D.R. Shanahan. – Sydney : The Law Book Company Ltd, 1982.
lv,522p.
ISBN 0455201196

—Business Names Guide / 3rd ed. – North Ryde : C.C.H. Australia, 1985.
154p.
ISBN 0869034413 Hbk £28.00

—Guidebook to Australian Trade Marks Law and Practice / 2nd ed. – North Ryde : C.C.H. Australia, 1985.
364p.
ISBN 0869035657

—Passing off trade deception trade marks / Charles Joseph Bannon. – Sydney : Butterworths, 1985.
xxv,172p.
ISBN 0409492442 A$59

TRADE MARKS – CANADA

—Canadian Trademarks Act Annotated / Toronto : DeBoo, 1984.
This volume covers the practice, procedure, and legislation of Canadian trade mark law. Practice notes from the Trade Marks Journal, references to the Trade Marks Examination Manual, and a list of 'confusing' and 'non-confusing' trademarks are included in the work.
ISBN 0888201583 Hbk £135.00

—Copyright and Trade Mark Litigation 1988 / Vancouver : Continuing Legal Education Society of British Columbia, 1988.
372p.
ISBN 0865049807 Hbk £85.00

—Framework for evaluating Canada's Trade Marks Act / by Steven Globerman with Mitchell P. Rothman. – Canada : Policy Research, Analysis and Liaison Directorate, Consumer and Corporate Affairs, 1983.
86p.
ISBN 0662124189

—Hughes on Trade Marks, 1 Vol. / Butterworths.

—Hughes on Trade Marks / Toronto : Butterworths.

—Hughes on trade marks / 1 vol. – Scarborough, Ontario : Butterworths (Canada).
Looks at registability, the procedures for registering, amending, assigning and licensing marks, infringement, trade names and passing off actions at common law and under statute.

—Remedies for Trademark Infringement / Agincourt : Carswell, 1988.
ca 192p.

—Remedies for Trademark Infringement / Agincourt : Carswell, 1988.
192p.
This book provides a comprehensive discussion of the remedies available for trademark infringement. Topics include the ramifications of injunctive relief, ancillary relief, and monetary remedies. The text also discusses how these various remedies interact with each other.

—Trade marks and industrial designs / by Immanuel Goldsmith. – Toronto : Carswell, 1982.
ix,344p.
Reprinted from the Canadian Encyclopedic Digest 3rd ed.
ISBN 0459349805

—Trademarks and Unfair Competition / Vancouver : British Columbia Continuing Legal Education Society, 1982.
352p.
ISBN 0865040591 Hbk £55.00

TRADE MARKS – CHINA

—Intellectual property law in the People's Republic of China : a guide to patents, trade marks and technology transfer / Michael D.Pendleton. – Singapore : Butterworths, 1986.
xvii,138p.
ISBN 0409995193

—Patent and Trademark Law of the People's Republic of China (1985) / Geneva : World Intellectual Property Organization, 1984.
66p.

TRADE MARKS – EUROPEAN COMMUNITY

—Memorandum by the Joint Working Party on Intellectual Property : on proposals by the European Commission for a first Council directive to approximate the laws of the member states relating to trade marks and for a Council regulation on Community trade marks : Com (80) 635 Final/2 (published (1981) XXX Common Market Law Reports 357 & 365) / Joint Working Party on Intellectual Property. – London : Senate of the Inns of Court and the Bar, 1981.
13,4,3p; 30cm.
At head of title: The Senate of the Inns of Court and the Bar, The Law Society.

TRADE MARKS – GREAT BRITAIN

—Business Names Act 1985 / London : HMSO.
12p.
ISBN 0105407852 Pbk £1.75

—Concise trade mark law and practice / Peter Meinhardt and Keith R. Havelock. – Aldershot : Gower, 1983.
xv,206p; 24cm.
Bibliography: p187-189. - Includes index.
ISBN 0566023695 Unpriced

—Guide to the Trademarks Act 1938 / CIPA. – London : Sweet & Maxwell, 1988.
ISBN 0421381205 Hbk

—Intellectual property case books / edited by W.R. Cornish. – Oxford : ESC, 1985.
185p.
ISBN 0906214351

—Kerly's law of trade marks and trade names / Robin Jacob. – 12th ed. – London : Sweet & Maxwell, 1986.
830p.
Incorporates developments through legislation and case law, including the provisions of the Trademarks (Amendment) Act 1984, and the Patents, Designs and Marks Act 1986.
ISBN 0421350601 £65.00

—Manager's Guide to Patents, Trade Marks and Copyright / London : Kogan Page, 1986.
ISBN 0850389704 Hbk £12.95

—Manager's Guide to Patents, Trade Marks and Copyright / London : Kogan Page, 1986.
150p.
ISBN 1850912033 Hbk £13.95
ISBN 1850912041 Pbk £6.95

—Passing off / London : Longman Professional, 1988.
ISBN 0851213928 Pbk

—Passing off : law and practice / Silverleaf. – London : Butterworths, 1986.
ISBN 0406253404 Hbk £34.50

—Practical introduction to trade marks / Brian C. Reid. – London : Waterlow, 1984.
viii,184p; 22cm.
Includes index.
ISBN 0080391702 Pbk £14.50
ISBN 0080391621 £7.50

—Practical introduction to trade marks / London : Waterlow, 1984.
ISBN 0080391702 Hbk £14.95

—Service marks / by Amanda Michaels. – London : Common Law Institute of Intellectual Property, 1983.
19p.
Study commissioned by the Institute of Advanced Legal Studies, London.

—Service marks : a guide to the new law : Trade Marks Act 1938 as amended by the Trade Marks (Amendment) Act 1984 and the Patents, Designs and Marks Act 1986 / Christopher Morcom. – Oxford : ESC Publishing, 1987.
vi,165p.
Includes texts from the Acts.
ISBN 0906214483

—Trade Mark Cases and Passing Off Cases, 2 Vols. / London : Sweet & Maxwell, 1986.
ISBN 0421344601 Hbk £98.00

—Trade mark cases and passing off cases / 2 vols. – Sweet & Maxwell, 1986.
ISBN 0421344601 Hbk £110.00

—Trade marks and names / Oxford : ESC, 1985. – (Casebook).
ISBN 0906214351 Pbk £9.00

TRADE MARKS – INDIA

—Trade Mark Cases, 2 Vols. / Calcutta : Eastern Law House, 1985.

—Trade Marks and Passing off / 3rd ed. – Calcutta : Eastern Law House, 1981.

TRADE MARKS – IRELAND

—Irish Trade Marks Law and Practice : Introduction by Mr Justice Declan Costello / Dublin : Gill and Macmillan, 1987.
ISBN 0717114406 Hbk £30.00

TRADE MARKS – MALAYSIA

—Trade Marks Act, 1976 / Kuala Lumpur : International Law Books Services.

TRADE MARKS – SOUTH AFRICA

—South African Law of Trade Marks / Page. – 3rd ed. – Durban : Butterworths.

TRADE MARKS – UNITED STATES

—Guide to United States patent and trademark literature / Brenda M. Rimmer. – London : British Library, Science Reference Library, 1980.
3,24p; 25cm.
Includes index.
ISBN 0902914529 sd £2.50

TRADE MARKS (INTERNATIONAL LAW)

—Counterfeiting and national laws : counterfeiting and the Paris Convention / memorandum of the Director General. – Geneva : World Intellectual Property Organization, 1986.
46,4p. – (PAC/CE/I/2).
Prepared for an intergovernmental group of experts called Committee of Experts on the Protection Against Counterfeiting and scheduled to meet at W.I.P.O. Headquarters Geneva from May 5 to 7 1986'.

—Importation of products with the same trademark / by German Cavelier. – Bogota, Colombia : Cavelier Abogados, 1985.
9 leaves.

TRADE REGULATION

—Judges, law, and businessmen / A.H. Hermann. – Deventer, Netherlands : Kluwer Law and Taxation Publishers, 1983.
ISBN 9065440828

—Legal aspects of doing business in Asia and the Pacific / edited by Dennis Campbell. – Deventer, Netherlands : Kluwer Law and Taxation Publishers, 1984.
– (International business series).
Includes index. Kept up to date by supplements.
ISBN 9065449825

—Legal aspects of doing business in Latin America / edited by Dennis Campbell. – Deventer, The Netherlands : Kluwer Law and Taxation Publishers, 1984.
vii, 351 p.; 25 cm. – (International business series).
Includes index.
ISBN 9065441026

TRADE REGULATION – AFRICA

—Legal aspects of doing business in Africa / edited by Dennis Campbell. – Deventer, The Netherlands : Kluwer Law and Taxation Publishers, 1986.
– (International business series).
Includes index.
ISBN 9065442685

TRADE REGULATION – AUSTRALIA

—Annotated Trade Practices Act / by Russell V. Miller. – 4th ed. – Sydney : Law Book Co., 1983.
339p.
Reproduced from: The Trade Practices Reporting Service. Includes index.

—Australian trade practices reporter / by CCH editorial staff : consultant editors R. Baxt, R.G. Blunt, A.I. Tonking. – 2. – North Ryde, N.S.W. : CCH Australia, 1972-.
loose-leaf; 26cm.
Includes current issues of: Australian trade practices reports. Loose-leaf issues accompanied by a summary report. Pre-current 'Commission decisions : authorizations and notifications' filed in transfer binders.
ISBN 0869030264 v.2
ISBN 0869030280 Hbk

—Australian trade practices reports / North Ryde, N.S.W. : CCH Australia, 1978-.
23cm.
Issued as bound volumes, with current issues forming part of the service to the loose-leaf publication: Australian trade practices reporter.

TRADE REGULATION – AUSTRALIA – NEW SOUTH WALES

—Deregulation : a plan of action to rationalise South Australian legislation : a report to the South Australian Government / by Dianne Gayler. – Adelaide : Government Printer, 1980.
v,85p. – (P.P.).
Includes bibliographical references.

TRADE REGULATION – CYPRUS

—Note on the law of Cyprus relating to offshore operations, shipping operations and shipping companies, foreign investments in Cyprus and transit trade / by Criton G. Tornaritis. – Nicosia : s.n., 1984.
52 leaves.

TRADE REGULATION – EUROPEAN COMMUNITY

—Prohibiting restrictions on trade within the EEC : the theory and application of Articles 30-36 of the EEC Treaty / by Laurence W. Gormley. – Amsterdam : North-Holland, 1985.
xxv,458p.
Bibliography: p.429-443. - Includes index. At head of title: T.M.C. Asser Instituut - The Hague.
ISBN 0444868488

—Submission by the Joint Working Party on Competition Law to the House of Lords Select Committee on the European Communities on procedures for administering EEC competition policy / Joint Working Party on Competition Law. – London : Senate of the Inns of Court and the Bar, 1981.
10p; 30cm.
At head of title: The Senate of the Inns of Court and Bar, The Law Society.

—Suitability of concentration measures for EEC competition policy / Walter Piesch, Ingo Schmidt. – Luxembourg : Office for Official Publications of the European Communities, 1983.
101 p.; 25 cm.
ISBN 9282531783 pbk. £5.50 (U.S.)

TRADE REGULATION - EUROPEAN ECONOMIC COMMUNITY COUNTRIES

—Trading law / Chichester : Barry Rose, 1981-.
From v.2 Trading law reports published as pullout insert in each issue.

TRADE REGULATION - EUROPEAN ECONOMIC COMMUNITY COUNTRIES - CASES

—Trading law reports / v. – Chichester : Barry Rose, 1983.
Published as pullout insert in Trading law.

TRADE REGULATION - GREAT BRITAIN

—How Protection Taxes Exporters / Larry A. Sjaastad. – London : Trade Policy Research Centre, 1985.
87p.

—Law of consumer protection and fair trading / Brian W. Harvey. – 2nd ed. – London : Butterworths, 1982.
xxviii,424p.
Previous ed.: 1978. Bibliography: p.391-397. - Includes index.
ISBN 0406222606 Pbk
ISBN 0406222614

—Trading law / Chichester : Barry Rose, 1981-.
From v.2 Trading law reports published as pullout insert in each issue.

—Trading law reports / . – Chichester : Barry Rose, 1983.
Published as pullout insert in Trading law.

TRADE REGULATION - UNITED STATES

—Regulation and its reform / Stephen Breyer. – Cambridge, Mass. : Harvard University Press, 1982.
xii,472p; 25cm.
Bibliography: p382-385. - Includes index.
ISBN 0674753755 Unpriced

TRADE REGULATION - USSR

—Soviet law and economy / Olimpiad S. Ioffe and Mark W. Janis, editors. – Dordrecht Holland : M. Nijhoff, 1986.
300p. – (Law in Eastern Europe).
Includes index.
ISBN 9024732654 Hbk £165.00

TRADE SECRETS

—Protection of trade secrets : a general guide / W.R. McComas, Mark R. Davison, David M. Gonski. – Sydney : Butterworths, 1981.
xiv,98p.
ISBN 0409300284 Hbk £48

TRADE SECRETS - CANADA

—Protection of trade secrets / Institute of Law Research and Reform. – Edmonton : The Institute, 1984.
159p. – (Report for discussion).
Includes bibliographical references.

—Trade Secrets / Vancouver : Continuing Legal Education Society of British Columbia, 1986.
163p.
ISBN 0865042896 Hbk £65.00

TRADE SECRETS - CANADA - ALBERTA

—Trade secrets / Institute of Law Research and Reform, Edmonton, Alberta and a Federal Provincial Working Party. – Edmonton : The Institute, 1986.
284p. – (Report).
Includes bibliographical references.

TRADE SECRETS - GREAT BRITAIN

—Intellectual property case books / edited by W.R. Cornish. – Oxford : ESC, 1985.
212p.
ISBN 0906214335

TRADE SECRETS - SOUTH AFRICA

—Professional secrecy in South Africa : a symposium / edited by G. C. Oosthuizen, H. A. Shapiro, S. A. Strauss. – Cape Town : Oxford University Press, 1983.
178p.
ISBN 0195703200

TRADE UNIONS

—Freedom of association : digest of decisions and principles of the Freedom of Association Committee of the governing body of the ILO / International Labour Office. – 3rd ed. – Geneva : International Labour Office, 1985.
xii, 140 i.e. 262 p.; 24 cm.
ISBN 9221050734 pbk. £30.00

—General survey on the application of the conventions on freedom of association, the right to organise and collective bargaining and the convention and recommendation concerning rural workers' organisations : third item on the agenda / International Labour Office. – Geneva : International Labour Office, 1983.
157p.
Cover title: Freedom of association and collective bargaining. Report III (Part 4B).
ISBN 9221031284

—Has the Trade Union Movement a Place in Europe? / Exeter : European Atlantic Movement, 1982.

—Inviolability of Trade Union Premises and Communications / Geneva : International Labour Office, 1980.
vi, 43p.
ISBN 9221021785 Hbk £10.00

—Theories of trade unionism : a sociology of industrial relations / Michael Poole. – London : Routledge and Kegan Paul, 1981.
xi,265p; 23cm.
Bibliography: p221-242. - Includes index.
ISBN 0710006950 £12.50

TRADE UNIONS - AUSTRALIA

—Framework of consensus : government, business and trade unions / W. J. Byrt. – Melbourne : Law Book Company Ltd., 1985.
ix,220p.
Bibliography: p211-218.
ISBN 0455205779

—Strike law in Australia / by Edward I. Sykes. – 2nd ed. – Sydney : Law Book Co., 1982.
xxiii, 369 p.; 25 cm.
Includes bibliographical references and index.
ISBN 0455200890

—Trade Practices Legislation and Materials 1986 / Kingston : Australian Government Publishing Service.

—Trade Union Law in Australia : the Legal Status of Australian Trade Unions / Donald W. Rawson. – 2nd ed. – Butterworths, 1985.
224p.
ISBN 0409492736 Hbk £49.00

TRADE UNIONS - AUSTRALIA - NEW SOUTH WALES

—New South Wales Industrial Arbitration Act 1940 : including Regulations and Trade Union Legislation / 4th ed. – North Ryde : C.C.H. Australia, 1986.
328p.
ISBN 0869035983 Hbk

TRADE UNIONS - EUROPE

—European trade unions in figures / Kluwer Law and Taxation, 1989.
Presents a comparative set of data and sources on union membership in ten European countries - Austria, Denmark, France, West Germany, Italy, the Netherlands, Norway, Sweden, Switzerland and the UK. Gives emphasis to comparative definitions of union membership and union density, that is, the ratio of actual to potential memberships.
ISBN 9065444092 Pbk £24.50/Dfl 79

—Has the Trade Union Movement a Place in Europe? / Exeter : European Atlantic Movement, 1982.

TRADE UNIONS - GREAT BRITAIN

—Clearing banks and the trade unions / by L. D. Cowan. – London : Institute of Bankers, 1984.
64p.
'Delivered under the auspices of King's College, London'.
ISBN 0852971168

—Closed shop agreements and arrangements : code of practice / Great Britain. – London : The Department, 1983.
24p.

—Democracy in trade unions / presented to Parliament by the Secretary of State for Employment. – London : H.M.S.O., 1983.
ii,37p.
ISBN 0101877803

—Disclosure to unions : how the law is working : a study of the implementation of ss.17-21 of the Employment Protection Act 1975 / by Arthur Marsh and Roger Hussey. – London : Touche Ross and St Edmunds Hall Industrial Relations Annexe, 1980.
94p; 21cm.

—Employers Guide to the Trade Union Act 1984 / London : Engineering Employers Federation, 1984.
16p.

—Employing Union Members / Income Data Services Staff. – London : Incomes Data Services, 1980.
191p. – (IDS Handbook Ser.: No. 18).

—Governments and trade unions : the British experience, 1964-79 / Denis Barnes and Eileen Reid. – London : Heinemann Educational Books, 1980.
xiii,242p.
ISBN 0435830457

—Governments and Trade Unions : The British Experience, 1964-79 / Eileen Reid. – London : Policy Studies Institute, 1980.

—Hands up for democracy / Trades Union Congress. – London : Trades Union Congress, 1983.
40p.
ISBN 0900878983

—History of British trade unionism / by Henry Pelling. – 4th ed. – London : Macmillan, 1987.
336p; 22cm.
Previous ed.: 1976. Includes bibliography and index.
ISBN 0333442857 £27.50

—Liberties and liabilities : the case for trade union reform / a report of the Trade Union Reform Committee, Chairman Sir Leonard Neal. – London : Centre for Policy Studies, 1980.
viii,57p.
ISBN 0905880323

—Origins of trade union power / by Henry Phelps Brown. – Oxford : Clarendon, 1983.
vi,320p; 25cm.
Includes index.
ISBN 0198771150 £15.00

—Our unions, our democracy : LRD's response to the Tory green paper / Labour Research Department. – London : LRD Publications, 1983.
24p.

—Purging of the Civil Service / National Council for Civil Liberties. – London : National Council for Civil Liberties, 1985.
20p.
ISBN 0946088179

—Rail Unions in Britain and West Germany : A Study of their Structure and Policies / Wolfgang Steeck. – London : Policy Studies Institute, 1982.
109p.

—Re-establishment of Free Trade Unionism : a bill to repeal the Employment, Employment and Training, Trade Union and Wages Acts 1980 to 1988, to re-enact previous legislation repealed by those Acts, and for purposes connected therewith / presented by Tony Benn ... et al. – London : HMSO, 1988.
2p. – (H.C. Bill 1987-88).
ISBN 0103199888

—Some legal issues arising out of the miners' strike 1984/5 / Dawn Oliver. – London : Faculty of Laws, University College London, 1985.
26p. – (Working papers).
Includes bibliographical references. Edited by Dawn Oliver. Caption title.

—Staff associations / Certification Office for Trade Unions and Employers' Associations. – London : Certification Office for Trade Union and Employers' Associations, 1981.
iii,52p.
Supplement to: Annual report of the Certification Officer 1979.

—Striking out strikes : changing employment relations in the British labour market / Charles G. Hanson and Graham Mather. – London : Institute of Economic Affairs, 1988.
94p; 22cm.
ISBN 0255362080

—Trade union acts / London : Sweet & Maxwell, 1985.
ISBN 0421338008 Pbk £17.50

—Trade Union Acts / London : Sweet & Maxwell, 1985.
ISBN 0421338008 Pbk £16.50

—Trade union democracy, members' rights and the law / Patrick Elias and Keith Ewing. – London : Mansell, 1987.
300p; 24cm.
Includes bibliography and index.
ISBN 0720107296 Hbk £30.00 :
ISBN 0720118719 Pbk £16.00

—Trade union immunities / London : H.M.S.O., 1981.
ISBN 0101812809

—Trade union law / London : Butterworths, 1985.
ISBN 0406258309 Hbk £26.50
ISBN 0406258317 Pbk £17.95

—Trade union law / Bryn Perrins. – London : Butterworths, 1985.
350p.
Includes index.
ISBN 0406258309 Hbk £18.00 :
ISBN 0406258317 Pbk £12.00

—Trade union law / Richard Kidner. – 2nd ed. – London : Stevens, 1983.
xl,290p; 25cm.
Previous ed.: London : Sweet & Maxwell, 1979. Includes index.
ISBN 0420465502 £25.00

—Trade union law and the pursuit of prosperity - the next step : submission to the Secretary of State for Employment in response to the green paper on trade union immunities / prepared by Roderick Thomas. – London : Director Publications, 1981.
66p; 30cm.
At head of title: Institute of Directors.

—Trade union powers and the anti-nuclear campaign / London : Lawyers Versus the Bomb, 1982.
19p; 21cm. – (Pamphlet).

—Trade Union Representatives Handbook / London : Industrial Society.

—Trade unionists and the law / Jennifer Horne. – London : Shaw, 1983.
xii,84p; 21cm.
ISBN 072190940X Pbk Unpriced

—Trade Unions and Change in the British Car Industry / Patricia Wallace. – London : Policy Studies Institute, 1984.
72p. – (PSI Research Papers).

—Trade unions and the individual / by Alan Campbell and John Bowyer with assistance from Michael Soole : foreword by Lord Wilberforce. – Oxford : ESC Publishing, 1980.
xliv,491p; 23cm.
Includes index.
ISBN 090621405X Unpriced

—Trade unions and their members / presented to Parliament by the Secretary of State for Employment and the Paymaster General .. – London : H.M.S.O., 1987.
iii,33p; 30cm.
ISBN 0101009526

—Trade unions : selected readings / edited by W.E.J. McCarthy. – 2nd ed. – Harmondsworth : Penguin, 1985.
562p. – (Penguin books).
Previous ed.: 1972.
ISBN 0140226419

—Trade unions, the Labour Party and the law : a study of the Trade Union Act 1913 / K. D. Ewing. – Edinburgh : Edinburgh University Press, 1982.
x,249p; 22cm.
ISBN 0852244533

TRADE UNIONS - INDIA
—Law Relating to Trade Unions in India / 2nd ed. – Lucknow : Eastern Book Company, 1982.
831p.

—Trade Unions Act, 1926 / Lucknow : Eastern Book Company, 1980.
131p.

TRADE UNIONS - IRAN
—Labour unions, law and conditions in Iran (1900-1941) / by Willem Floor. – Durham City : Centre for Middle Eastern and Islamic Studies, University of Durham, 1985.
124p; 21cm. – (Occasional paper series).
Bibliography: p119-124.

TRADE UNIONS - IRELAND
—Irish trade union law / Whyte. – London : Butterworths, 1985.
ISBN 0862050510 Hbk £31.50
ISBN 0862050936 Pbk £22.50

—Irish trade union law / Tony Kerr and Gerry Whyte. – Abingdon : Professional Books, 1985.
lxiv,383p.
ISBN 0862050510

TRADE UNIONS - MALAYSIA
—Trade Unions Act, 1969 (Act 262) and Regulations 1969 (P.U.(A) 390/1982) / Kuala Lumpur : International Law Books Services.

TRADE UNIONS - UNITED STATES
—State and the unions : labour relations, law and the organized labour movement in America, 1880-1960 / Cambridge : Cambridge University Press, 1985.
364.
Examines the impact of the National Labour Relations Act on American trade unions.
ISBN 0521258405 Hbk £35.00
ISBN 0521314526 Pbk £12.50

TRADE UNIONS - WEST GERMANY
—Rail Unions in Britain and West Germany : A Study of their Structure and Policies / Wolfgang Steeck. – London : Policy Studies Institute, 1982.
109p.

TRADE-UNIONS - FRANCE
—Unions, change and crisis : French and Italian union strategy and the political economy, 1945-1980 / Peter Lange, George Ross, Maurizio Vannicelli. – London : Allen & Unwin, 1982.
viii,295p; 25cm.
Includes index.
ISBN 0043310885 Unpriced

TRADE-UNIONS - GREAT BRITAIN
—Ballots and trade union democracy / Roger Undy and Roderick Martin with the assistance of R. Blackwell and J. Hulton. – Oxford : Blackwell, 1984.
viii,240p; 24cm.
ISBN 0631135391 £19.50

TRADE-UNIONS - GREAT BRITAIN - VOTING
—Ballots and trade union democracy / Roger Undy and Roderick Martin with the assistance of R. Blackwell and J. Hulton. – Oxford : Blackwell, 1984.
viii,240p; 24cm.
ISBN 0631135391 £19.50

TRADE-UNIONS - ITALY
—Unions, change and crisis : French and Italian union strategy and the political economy, 1945-1980 / Peter Lange, George Ross, Maurizio Vannicelli. – London : Allen & Unwin, 1982.
viii,295p; 25cm.
Includes index.
ISBN 0043310885 Unpriced

TRADING LAW
—Insider trading / Barry A. K. Rider. – Bristol : Jordan and Sons, 1983.
xix, 338p.
ISBN 0853080755

TRADING LAW - AUSTRALIA
—Australian Trade Practices Legislation / 8th ed. – North Ryde : C.C.H. Australia, 1986.
344p.
ISBN 0869035754 Hbk £24.00

—Guidebook to Australian Trade Practices Law / 5th ed. – North Ryde : C.C.H. Australia, 1987.
450p.
ISBN 0869039717 Pbk £38.00

TRADING LAW - CHINA
—China Trade Law / B. Dewit. – Dordrecht : Kluwer, 1983.
478p.
ISBN 9065441131 Hbk £175.00

TRADING LAW - GREAT BRITAIN
—Butterworth's Trading Law Cases / London : Butterworths.
This comprehensive looseleaf service covers cases dealing with such topics as trade descriptions, weights and measures, food and advertising, consumer credit, hallmarking, prices, and product safety in the United Kingdom.

—Consumer and Trading Law - Cases and Materials / Harvey. – London : Butterworths, 1985.
ISBN 0406012601 Hbk £36.00
ISBN 040601261X Pbk £23.95

—Directive on doorstep selling / Great Britain. – London : Department of Trade and Industry, 1986.
18 leaves.
Proposals for legislation implementing the European Community Council of Ministers Directive of 20 December 1985 (85/577/EEC).

TRADING LAW - NEW ZEALAND
—Competitive Trading in New Zealand : the Commerce Act 1986 / Mark Jones. – Butterworths.
Format of annotated statute; each section of the Act is commented on, with commentary fully integrated with legislation. Appendices cover forms of application for authorisation of prices for controlled goods or services, for authorisation of a restrictive trade practice, form of notification for clearance or authorisation of a merger of takeover proposal, and the Commerce Act (Fees) Regulations 1986.
ISBN 0409787728 Pbk £71.50

—Fair Trading in New Zealand : the Fair Trading Act 1986 / Jones. – Butterworths, 1989.
198p.
ISBN 040978771X Pbk £65.00

—Trade Practices and Consumer Protection / R. B. Vermeesch. – 3rd ed. – Wellington : Butterworths.

TRAFFIC ACCIDENTS - AUSTRALIA - TASMANIA - LAW AND LEGISLATION
—Compensation for victims of motor vehicle accidents / Law Reform Commission of Tasmania. – Hobart : Acting Government Printer, 1987.
76p. – (Report).

TRAFFIC REGULATIONS - GREAT BRITAIN
—Encyclopedia of road traffic law and practice / 4. – London : Sweet & Maxwell, 1960.
loose-leaf.
Includes indexes.

TRANSACTION COSTS
—Markets and false hierarchies : some problems in transaction cost economics / Neil Kay. – San Domenico, Florence : European University Institute, 1987.
52p.
Bibliography: pp.50-52..

TRANSACTIONAL ANALYSIS
—Staying OK / Amy Bjork Harris and Thomas A. Harris. – London : Pan, 1986.
xv,297p; 18cm.
Originally published: London : Cape, 1985. Includes index.
ISBN 033029136X Pbk £2.95

TRANSFER - AUSTRALIA - TASMANIA
—Report and recommendations on the law and procedure relating to the sale of land by instalments / Law Reform Commission of Tasmania. – Hobart : Government Printer, 1983.
25p. – (Report).

TRANSFER - GREAT BRITAIN
—Business transfers and employment law: a practical guide / London : Sweet & Maxwell, 1989.
Outlines the development of the Transfer of Undertakings Regulations, including the loopholes and starting blocks facing the employer involved in a business transfer. Practical consideration of aspects of the law such as 'living down', the effect of regulations on both individual and collective employment law. Appendix of statutory instruments.
ISBN 0421405309 Hbk £27.50

TRANSFER (LAW) - GREAT BRITAIN
—Family law : transfer of money between spouses : the Married Women's Property Act 1964 / the Law Commission. – London : H.M.S.O., 1985.
iii,29p; 21cm. – (Working paper).
ISBN 011730171X

—Transfer of undertakings : the legal pitfalls : a specially commissioned report / by Patrick Elias and John Bowers. – London : Longman Professional, 1985.
54 leaves.
ISBN 0851208061

TRANSFER (LAW) - NORTHERN IRELAND
—Reservation of title clauses / Brice Dickson. – Belfast : SLS Legal Publications, 1987.
ii,96p.
Bibliography: pp.93-94..

TRANSFER (LAW) - SOUTH AFRICA
—Alienation of land : being a supplement to The law of credit agreements and hire-purchase by Diemont and Aronstam / P.J. Aronstam. – Cape Town : Juta, 1985.
xxviii, 186 p.; 25 cm.
Includes indexes. Bibliography: p. 8.
ISBN 070211586X pbk.

TRANSFER PRICING
—Multinational Transfer Pricing / Toronto : Butterworths, 1981.
224p.

—Multinationals beyond the market : intra-firm trade and the control of transfer pricing / edited by Robin Murray. – Brighton : Harvester, 1981.
335p; 24cm. – (Harvester studies in development).
Includes bibliographies and index.
ISBN 0855272031 £22.50

—The Tax Treatment of Transfer Pricing / International Bureau of Fiscal Documentation. – Amsterdam : International Bureau of Fiscal Documentation, 1988.
ISBN 9070125293 loose £1400.00

Renewal

—Transfer pricing and multinational enterprises : three taxation issues : reports of the OECD Committee on Fiscal Affairs, 1984 / Paris : O.E.C.D., 1984.
91p.
ISBN 9264126260

TRANSPORT
—CMR : contracts for the international carriage of goods by road / by D.J. Hill and A.D. Messent. – London : Lloyd's of London Press, 1984.
xliii,288p; 26cm.
Contains the text of the Carriage of Goods by Road Act 1965 and the French (i.e., definitive) text of the CMR.
ISBN 0907432557

—International carriage of goods : some legal problems and possible solutions / edited by C.M. Schmitthoff, R.M. Goode. – London : Centre for Commercial Law Studies, 1988.
xxvii,135p.
Includes index. Includes the text of the Uniform Rules of Conduct for Interchange of Trade Data by Teletransmission (UNCID) and of the United Nations Convention on International Multimodal Transport of Goods.
ISBN 0951066455

—Transport Acts 1981 and 1982 / 2nd ed. – London : Fourmat, 1985.
ISBN 0906840929 Pbk £8.95

—Transport : International Transport Treaties / M.H. Claringbould. – Dordrecht : Kluwer.

TRANSPORT – CANADA

—Canadian Transport Cases (1966-1977), 7 Vols. / Aurora : Canada Law Book Co. – (Law Reports).

—Canadian Transport Cases : 1966-77, 7 Vols. / Aurora : Canada Law Book Co. – (Earlier Series Entitled Canadian Railway and Transport Cases).

Index (Vols. 50-85) of the Earlier Series

—Motor vehicle reports : annotated / Toronto : Carswell, 1988-.

TRANSPORT – GREAT BRITAIN

—Croner's Coach and Bus Operations / New Malden : Croner Publications.

—Transport Acts 1981 and 1982 : Penalty Points, Drinking and Driving, Fixed Penalties / 2nd ed. – London : Fourmat, 1985.
115p.
ISBN 0906840929 Pbk £8.95

—Transport and the environment / Department of Transport. – London : The Department, 1987.
32p.

—Transport and the Farmer / London : Shaw & Sons, 1988.
ISBN 0721911501 Pbk £9.95

TRANSPORT – NEW ZEALAND

—Commercial Transport for New Zealanders / Wellington : Butterworths.
ISBN 0409627119 Pbk

—Legal and practical effects of the Transport Licensing Act (No. 2) 1983 : papers presented by R.J. Craddock ... et al., University of Auckland, 23 February 1984 / R. J. Craddock. – Auckland : Legal Research Foundation, 1984.
46p.
At head of title: Legal Research Foundation Inc. seminar.
ISBN 0908581335

TRAVEL COSTS – AUSTRALIA – VICTORIA

—Fourth report to Parliament on the operation of section 32 of the Interpretation of Legislation Act 1984 concerning : Place Names Committee (Members' Fees and Travelling Allowances) Regulations 1988 (SR No. 251/1988) / Legal and Constitutional Committee. – Melbourne : Government Printer, 1988.
v,6p.
Includes the text of the Regulations.

TREASON – CANADA

—Crimes against the state / Law Reform Commission of Canada. – Ottawa : The Commission, 1986.
72,76p. – (Working paper).
Includes bibliographies. Added t.p. in French: Les crimes contre l'etat. Pages numbered in opposite directions. Text in English and French.

TREASON – GREAT BRITAIN

—Treason in Tudor England : Politics and Paranoia / London : Jonathan Cape.
352p.
ISBN 0224028057 Hbk £16.00

TREASON – MALAYSIA

—Sedition Act, 1948 (Act 15) / Kuala Lumpur : International Law Books Services.

TREASURE TROVE – GREAT BRITAIN

—Treasure trove : law reform issues / The Law Commission. – London : The Commission, 1987.
7 leaves.

TREATIES

—Antarctic Treaty regime : law, environment and resources / edited by Gillian D. Triggs under the general editorship of the British Institute of International and Comparative Law. – Cambridge : Cambridge University Press, 1987.
xxi,237p; 23cm.
Conference papers. Bibliography: p234-235.
ISBN 0521327660 £30.00

—Basic documents in international law / edited by Ian Brownlie. – 3rd ed. – Oxford : Clarendon, 1983.
xi,406p; 21cm.
Previous ed.: 1972. Includes index.
ISBN 0198761589 Hbk £15.00
ISBN 0198761597 Pbk £8.95

—Breach of treaty / by Shabtai Rosenne. – Cambridge : Grotius Publications, 1981.
xii,142p; 24cm.
At head of title: University of Cambridge Research Centre for International Law.
ISBN 0906496365

—Chronological and subject analysis of South Africa's multilateral and bilateral treaties, 1806-1979 / Jaqueline Audrey Kalley. – Johannesburg : s.n., 1985.
xvi,677 leaves.
Thesis (M.A.) - University of Witwatersrand 1985. Bibliography: p.659-677. - Includes index.

—Component units of federal states and international agreements / Luigi Di Marzo. – Aalphen aan den Rijn : Sijthoff & Noordhoff, 1980.
xxvi,242p.
Bibliography: p.229-235.
ISBN 9028603301

—Consultation clauses as means of providing for treaty obedience : a study in the law of treaties / by Judo Umarto Kusumowidagdo. – Stockholm : Almqvist & Wiksell, 1981.
321p; 25cm.
Bibliography: p.311-321.
ISBN 9122004629 Pbk
ISBN 9122004602

—Current International Treaties / Oxford : Croom Helm, 1984.
ISBN 0709917589 Hbk £30.00

—Customary international law and treaties : a study of their interactions and interrelations, with special consideration of the 1969 Vienna Convention on the Law of Treaties / Mark E. Villiger. – Dordrecht : Nijhoff, 1985.
xxxiii, 432p. – (Developments in international law).
Originally presented as the author's Habilitationsschrift (University of Zurich). Includes index. Bibliography: p.409-420.
ISBN 9024729807 Hbk £225.00

—Decisions of international institutions before domestic courts / Christoph Schreuer. – London : Oceana, 1981.
xiii,407p; 25cm.
Revised and updated version of 1977 German original.
ISBN 0379207095

—Draft agreement between the government of the United Kingdom of Great Britain and Northern Ireland and the government of the People's Republic of China on the future of Hong Kong / China. – Hong Kong : Government Printer, 1984.
46p.
'This White Paper reproduces the text of the White Paper published by Her Majesty's Government in London on 26 September 1984.'.

—Effect of treaties in domestic law / the United Kingdom National Committee of Comparative Law : edited by Francis G. Jacobs. – London : Sweet & Maxwell, 1987.
250p; 22cm.
Survey of the effects of treaties in the domestic law of Belgium, Denmark, France, Germany, Italy, the Netherlands, the United Kingdom and the United States. Examines the problem of a states individual treaty responsibilities in conflict with its collective responsibility within the framework of an international organisation. Covers the Hague Convention on Private International Law.
ISBN 0421378700 No price

—Expression of consent by states to be bound by a treaty / Council of Europe Directorate of Legal Affairs. – Strasbourg : Council of Europe, 1987.
122p.
ISBN 9287110441

—Handbook on the United States-German Tax Convention / authors Helmut Debatin, Otto L. Walter : in cooperation with Ernst Weber and Eric Osterweil : general editors Piroska Soos and Eugen Jehle. – 4. – Amsterdam : International Bureau of Fiscal Documentation, 1966.
loose-leaf.
Includes texts of Convention and Protocol. With added title-page in German. Final loose-leaf supplement no. 50 (Dec. 1983). Parallel German and English texts.

—Index of Multilateral Treaties on the Law of the Sea / Milan : Giuffre, 1985.
viii, 376p.

—International conference on liability and compensation for damage in connexion with the carriage of certain substances by sea, 1984 : final act of the conference with resolutions : Protocol of 1984 to amend the International Convention on Civil Liability for Oil Pollution Damage, 1969 : Protocol of 1984 to amend the International Convention on the Establishment of an International Fund for Compensation for Oil Pollution Damage, 1971 ... / London : International Maritime Organization, 1985.
iv,90p.
Includes the text of the International Convention on Civil Liability for Oil Pollution Damage, 1984 and of the International Convention on the Establishment of an International Fund for Compensation for Oil Pollution Damage, 1984.

—International organization and integration : annotated basic documents and descriptive directory of international organizations and arrangements / board of editors, P.J.G. Kapteyn ... et al. : with a foreword by Louis B. Sohn. – 2nd, completely rev. ed. n v. – The Hague : Martinus Nijhoff Publishers, 1981.
25cm.
Tables inserted in each volume. Includes indexes. Contents: v.1A: The United Nations Organization - v.2A: European Communities - v.2B-2K.
ISBN 9024725798

—International organization and integration : annotated basic doucments of international organizations and arrangements / selected by Louis B. Sohn. – Student ed. – Dordrecht Netherlands : Martinus Nijhoff, 1986.
xxviii, 1082 p.; 24 cm.
Includes index. Based on the five-volume set International organization and integration.
ISBN 0898389151 pbk.

—International Treaties and Conventions 1983, Vol. 2 / Kingston : Australian Government Publishing Service, 1986.
360p.
ISBN 0644047143 Hbk £18.70

—International Treaties and Conventions 1984 / Kingston : Australian Government Publishing Service, 1986.
ISBN 0644047402 Hbk £2.20

—Laws of armed conflicts : a collection of conventions, resolutions and other documents / edited by Dietrich Schindler and Jiri Toman. – 3rd rev. ed. – Dordrecht : Nijhoff, 1986.
xxxix,1033p.
Includes index.
ISBN 9024733065

—Multilateral Treaties Between ASEAN Countries / Butterworths, 1986.
235p.
ISBN 0409995185 Hbk £60.00

—Multilateral Treaties : Current Status and Index / Harris. – London : Butterworths, 1984.
ISBN 0406252785 Hbk £110.00

Nineteen Eighty-Six supplement only
ISBN 0406252920 Pbk

—Multilateral Treaties Deposited with the Secretary-General : Status as at 31 December 1986 / Geneva : United Nations Publications.
ISBN 921332931 Hbk £60.00

—Multilateral treaties : index and current status / compiled and annotated within the University of Nottingham Treaty Centre by M.J. Bowman and D.J. Harris. – London : Butterworths, 1984.
xii,516p; 26cm.
Includes index. Kept up to date by supplements.
ISBN 0406252777 Hbk £85.00

—Principles of the Law of Treaties / London : Pinter, 1989.
250.
Translated from the French and updated in the light of the 1986 Convention on the Law of Treaties between States and International Organizations.
ISBN 0861879546 Hbk £30

—Reservations and Interpretative Declarations to Multilateral Treaties / Amsterdam : Elsevier Science Publishers, 1988.
xxviii, 514p.
ISBN 0444703985 Hbk £250.00

—Selected Multilateral Treaties in the Field of the Environment / Geneva : United Nations Publications.
525p.

—Termination of treaties in international law / Oxford : Oxford University Press, 1985.
ISBN 0198761791 Hbk £35.00

—Termination of treaties in international law : the doctrines of Rebus Sic Stantibus and Desuetude / Athanassios Vamvoukos. – Oxford : Clarendon, 1985.
xxiii,325p; 22cm.
Bibliography: p304-315. - Includes index.
ISBN 0198761791 £35.00

—Treaties and alliances of the world / compiled and written by Henry W. Degenhardt. – 3rd ed. – Harlow : Longman, 1981.
ix,409p; 26cm. – (A Keesing's reference publication).
Previous ed.: 1974. Includes index.
ISBN 0582902509 £27.00

—UK/US double tax treaties guide / Jerrold Cohen, Roy R. Greenfield. – London : Oyez Publishing, 1980.
xii,217p; 21cm.
Includes index. Contains text of the 1975 Income Convention with notes by Jerrold Cohen and the text of the 1979 Estates Convention, with notes by Roy R. Greenfield.
ISBN 0851204759 Pbk £10.00

—United Nations Treaties on Outer Space / Geneva : United Nations Publications.
ISBN 9211002389 Hbk £2.00

—Vienna convention on the law of treaties / Ian Sinclair. – 2nd ed. – Manchester : Manchester University Press, 1984.
x,270p; 25cm.
Previous ed.: 1973. Includes index.
ISBN 0719014808 Unpriced

TREATIES – ASIA

—Multilateral treaties between Asian countries / London : Butterworths, 1986.
ISBN 0409995185 Hbk £24.00

TREATIES - CANADA
—Canada's Tax Treaties, 2 Vols. / Butterworths.

TREATIES - CHINA
—Chinese Treaties / Dordrecht : Kluwer, 1975.
328p.
ISBN 9028602259 Hbk £78.00

TREATIES - EUROPEAN COMMUNITY
—Documents concerning the accessions to the European Communities : of the Kingdom of Denmark, Ireland and the United Kingdom of Great Britain and Northern Ireland, the Hellenic Republic, the Kingdom of Spain and the Portuguese Republic / Luxembourg : Office for Official Publications of the European Communites, 1987.
693p.
Vol. 1 entitled: Treaties establishing the European Communities. Also published in the other official languages of the Communities.
ISBN 9277193042

—European Treaties Vocabulary / Luxembourg : Office for Official Publications of the European Communities, 1984.
311p.
ISBN 9282540456 Pbk £800.00

—European Treaties Vocabulary, Part 1 / Luxembourg : Office for Official Publications of the European Communities, 1985.
683p.
ISBN 9282546950 Pbk £1,000.00

—Sweet & Maxwell's European Community treaties : including the European Communities Act 1972 / edited by Sweet & Maxwell's legal editorial staff : advisory editor K.R. Simmonds. – 4th ed. – London : Sweet & Maxwell, 1980.
xvi,410p; 25cm.
Previous ed.: 1977.
ISBN 0421272104 Hbk £11.50
ISBN 0421272201 Pbk £8.50

—Treaties establishing the European Communities : treaties amending these treaties : Single European Act : resolutions, declarations / Luxembourg : Office for Official Publications of the European Communities, 1987.
1118p.
Also published in Spanish, Danish, German, Greek, English, French, Irish, Italian, Dutch and Portuguese. ' ... up to date as at 1 July 1987 ...'. - p.3.
ISBN 9277192259

TREATIES - GREAT BRITAIN
—Treaty series / v. – London : H.M.S.O., 1893-.
Chronological and classified indexes.

TREATIES - UNITED STATES
—United States treaties, executive agreements & guide to participation in international organizations / Gaithersburg : Marketing Internationals Washington Group, 1985.
x,364p; 28cm.
Bibliography: p357-364.
ISBN 0406658609 No price
ISBN 0912257024

TREATIES - USSR
—Calendar of Soviet treaties, 1958-1973 / by George Ginsburgs and Robert M. Slusser. – Alphen aan den Rijn : Sijthoff & Noordhoff, 1981.
xx,908p.

—Calendar of Soviet treaties, 1974-1980 / George Ginsburgs. – Dordrecht : Martinus Nijhoff Publishers, 1987.
ISBN 9024736285 Hbk

TRESPASS - AUSTRALIA
—Occupiers' liability / The Law Reform Commission. – Sydney : The Commission, 1987.
13p. – (Discussion paper).
Bibliography: p.13.

TRESPASS - AUSTRALIA - SOUTH AUSTRALIA
—Report ... relating to owners or occupiers of land and trespassers on that land / Law Reform Committee of South Australia. – Adelaide : Government Printer, 1985.
13p. – (48th report).

—Report ... relating to the law of detinue, conversion and trespass to goods / Law Reform Committee of South Australia. – Adelaide : Government Printer, 1987.
100p. – (95th report).
Bibliography: p.99-100.

TRESPASS - ENGLAND
—Occupiers' liability and access to the countryside / memorandum by the Council's Law Reform Committee. – London : Law Society, 1982.
7p.

—Select cases of trespass from the King's Courts, 1307-1399 / Morris S. Arnold. – London : Selden Society, 1985.
lxxxv,179,179p; 26cm.
Opposite pages of main sequence bear duplicate numbering. Parallel Latin text and English translation.

—Trespass on residential premises : a consultation paper / Home Office. – London : Home Office, 1983.
26p.

TRESPASS - GREAT BRITAIN
—Law of Trespass / Birts. – London : Butterworths, 1987.
ISBN 040614816 Pbk £15.95

—Select cases of trespass from the King's courts, 1307-1399 / Morris S. Arnold. – London : Selden Society, 1987.
504 p. – (Publications).

—Stonehenge : a report into the civil liberties implications of the events relating to the convoys of summer 1985 and 1986 / National Council for Civil Liberties. – London : National Council for Civil Liberties, 1986.
43p.
ISBN 0946088284

TRESPASS - INDIA
—Cattle Trespass Act, 1871 / Vijay Malik. – 2nd ed. – Lucknow : Eastern Book Company, 1982.
138p.

TRIALS
—British Law and Arctic Men : the Celebrated Murder Trials of Sinnisiak and Uluksuk, First Inuit Tried Under White Man's law / Saskatoon : Western Producer Prairie Books.
125p.
ISBN 0888330251 Pbk £8.95

—By Reason of Doubt : the Belshaw Case / Richmond Hill : Irwin Publishing Inc..
208p.
ISBN 0887801250 Pbk £4.95
ISBN 077201390X Pbk £9.95

—Celebrated Trials and Remarkable Cases of Criminal Jurisprudence : From the Earliest Records to the Year 1825, 6 Vols. / Repr. of 1825 ed. – Abingdon : Professional Books.
36p.

—Easing the passing : the trial of Dr John Bodkin Adams / Patrick Devlin. – London : Bodley Head, 1985.
256p; 23cm.
ISBN 0370306279 £9.95

—Famous Trials sound recording / South Yarra : Louis Braille Productions Ltd..

—Fraud trials : a report / by JUSTICE : chairman of committee Beryl Cooper. – London : JUSTICE, 1984.
vii,47p; 22cm.
ISBN 0907247059

—History of the Most Remarkable Trials in Great Britain and Ireland in Capital Cases, 2 Vols. / Repr. of 1715 ed. – Abingdon : Professional Books.
370p.

—Howell's State Trials : 1163-1820, 34 Vols. / T. J. Howell. – Repr. – Abingdon : Professional Books.

—Lindberg case / Rutgers University Press, 1988.
ISBN 0813512336 Hbk £20.50

—Loss of the 'City of Boston' : Inman v. Jenkins : an action for libel, tried at the Liverpool Assizes, before Mr. Justice Lush amd a special jury, on Tuesday and Wednesday, August 30th and 31st, 1870 / Benjamin George Jenkins. – Liverpool : Reported and printed by Lee and Nightingale, 1870.
85p.

—Morocco, Trial in Rabat Arising out of Disturbances on 20 and 21 June, 1981 : Trial in Rabat Arising Out of Disturbances on 20 and 21 June 1981 / Geneva : International Commission of Jurists.
25p.

—Mrs. Harris : the death of the Scarsdale diet doctor / Diana Trilling. – London : Abacus, 1983.
341p.
Originally published: New York : Harcourt Brace Jovanovich, 1981. Previously published: London : Hamilton, 1982.
ISBN 0349133948

—Ordinary Man : The Alexander McLeod-Lindsay Case / Neutral Bay : Hale & Iremonger, 1984.
ISBN 0868060763 Hbk £24.95, 015
ISBN 0868060771 Pbk £10.95, 015

—Report to Parliament on overseas court delays and remedies / Legal and Constitutional Committee. – Melbourne : Parliament of Victoria, 1984.
xxiii,310p.
Bibliography: p.299-310.

—Spycatcher Trial / Richmond : Heinemann, 1988.
208p.
ISBN 0855612398 Hbk £29.95

—State Trials, New Series : 1820-1858 / Abingdon : Professional Books.

—Trial of Beyers Naude : Christian Witness and the Rule of Law / Geneva : International Commission of Jurists, 1975.
188p.

—Trial of Paulin Croos / Colombo : Gunasena and Co..

—Verdict in Peking : the trial of the Gang of Four / David Bonavia. – London : Burnett, 1984.
225p; 24cm.
Includes index.
ISBN 0091562007 £9.95

—Wallace : the final verdict / Roger Wilkes. – London : Bodley Head, 1984.
269p,16p of plates; 22cm.
Bibliography: p261-263. - Includes index.
ISBN 037030571X £8.95

TRIALS - AUSTRALIA
—Royal Commission of Inquiry into Chamberlain Convictions / report of the Commissisoner T.R. Morling. – Canberra : Government Printer, 1987.
379p. – (Parliamentary paper).
At head of cover title: Parliament of the Commonwealth of Australia.
ISBN 0724512985

TRIALS - AUSTRALIA - NEW SOUTH WALES
—Criminal procedure : the jury in a criminal trial : discussion paper / New South Wales Law Reform Commission. – Sydney : Government Printer, 1985.
xxx,285p. – (D.P.).
ISBN 0730514323

TRIALS - CANADA
—Jury Trials / Vancouver : British Columbia Continuing Legal Education Society, 1981.
202p.
ISBN 0865040419 Hbk £11.50

—Scales of Justice : Seven Famous Criminal Cases Recreated / Toronto : Canadian Broadcasting Corporation Enterprises, 1984.
256p.
ISBN 0887941206 Pbk £10.95
ISBN 0887941249 Hbk £16.95

TRIALS - ENGLAND
—Criminal trials : the search for truth / Tom Sargant, Peter Hill. – London : Fabian Society, 1986.
33p.
ISBN 0716313480

—Fraud Trials Committee report / chairman, Lord Roskill. – London : H.M.S.O., 1986.
xi,245p; 25cm.
Examines methods of combating serious commercial fraud. Discusses whether lay juries are capable of understanding evidence in complex fraud trials. Proposes replacement of jury be a Fraud Trials Tribunal in complex cases.
ISBN 0113800088 PBK £9.00

—Improving the presentation of information to juries in fraud trials : a report of four research studies / by the MRC Applied Psychology Unit, Cambridge. – London : H.M.S.O., 1986.
vii,63p; 25cm.
Presents the results of research by the Roskill Fraud Trials Committee on the presentation of evidence to juries.
ISBN 0113800096

TRIALS - GREAT BRITAIN
—Contested trials in magistrates' courts : the case for the prosecution / Julie Vennard with the assistance of Karen Williams. – London : H.M.S.O., 1980.
vi,26p. – (Research studies).
Bibliography: p 26.
ISBN 0117301256

—Famous trials / edited by Harry Hodge and James H. Hodge : selected and introduced by John Mortimer. – Harmondsworth : Viking, 1984.
375p; 23cm.
ISBN 0670803200 £8.95

TRIALS - NIGERIA
—Development and Judicial Trial in Nigeria / Onitsha : Africana-FEP.

TRIALS - NORTHERN IRELAND
—Diplock courts in Northern Ireland : a fair trial? : an analysis of the law, based on a study commissioned by Amnesty International / by Douwe Korff. – Utrecht : Studie-en Informatiecentrum Mensenrechten, 1984.
115p.

TRIALS - SCOTLAND
—Celebrated Criminal Trials in Scotland : 1536-1784 / Repr. of 1784 ed. – Abingdon : Professional Books.

—A guide to the children's hearings / Edinburgh : W Green & Son, 1989.
Explains the complex legal and administrative provisions and procedures of those involved: panel members, parents, reporters, social workers and the children themselves.
ISBN 0414009045

—Prosecuting sexual assault / G. Chambers, A. Millar. - Edinburgh : H.M.S.O., 1986.
ix,144p.
Research by the Central Research Unit of the Scottish Office. Reports on police investigation of sexual assault cases and on prosecution and trial methods.
ISBN 0114933715

TRIALS - SOUTH AFRICA

—Technique in litigation / Eric Morris. - 3rd ed. - Cape Town : Juta, 1985.
xxxiii, 373 p.; 26 cm.
Includes bibliographical references and index.
ISBN 0702115525 pbk.

TRIALS - SRI LANKA

—Famous Criminal Cases of Sri Lanka, Vol. 4 / Colombo : Colombo Apothecaries Company, 1981.

TRIALS - UNITED STATES

—Airman and the carpenter : the Lindbergh kidnapping / Ludovic Kennedy. - London : Collins, 1985.
x,438p,32p ofplates; 24cm.
Bibliography: p425-428. - Includes index.
ISBN 0002170604 £12.95

TRIBAL LAW - INDIA

—Tribal Law and Justice : a Report on the Santal / New Delhi : Concept Publishing Company, 1984.
xxxvi, 741p.

TRIBAL LAW - UNITED STATES

—Indian Tribal Courts in the United States : a Model for Canada? / Saskatoon : University of Saskatchewan, Native Law Centre, 1980.
41p.
ISBN 0888800983 Hbk £5.50

TRIBUNALS

—Courts and Tribunals : a Comparative Study / Budapest : Akademiai Kiado, 1980.
246p.
ISBN 963051799X Hbk £19.00

—Documents on international administrative tribunals / Oxford : Clarendon Press, 1989.
274.
A volume of documents, each of which sets out the interests, purposes, structureand powers of the tribunal to which it relates. Gives an account of the role and responsibility of each tribunal.
ISBN 0198256361 Hbk £27.50

TRIBUNALS - CANADA

—Administrative Tribunals Litigation / Vancouver : Continuing Legal Education Society of British Columbia, 1987.
354p.
ISBN 0865043566 Hbk £85.00

—Handbook of administrative tribunals / Sara Blake. - Scarborough, Ontario : Butterworths (Canada), 1988.
256.
Examination of how tribunals should conduct themselves in order to minimize the risks of judicial review. Cover compliance with prescribed rules, Ontario and Alberta Codes of Procedure, specific procedural rules, parties, notice, disclosure of the case to be met, adjournments, effective participation, the in-camers hearing, evidence, witnesses and the right to make submissions.
ISBN 0409806650 Hbk

—Handbook on the Conduct of Administrative Tribunals / Sara Blake. - Butterworths, 1988.
ca 256p.

—Regulations, Crown Corporations, and Adminstrative Tribunals / Andree Lajoie. - Toronto : University of Toronto Press, 1986.
224p.
ISBN 0802072933 Hbk £16.95

TRIBUNALS - GREAT BRITAIN

—Handbook on the Conduct of Administrative Tribunals / Sara Blake. - Toronto : Butterworths.
256p.

—Industrial tribunal / Mclean. - Chichester : Barry Rose, 1982.
ISBN 0859922243 Hbk £20.00

—Industrial tribunal practice / Walker. - 2nd ed. - Stewart (Henry), 1985.
ISBN 0946700184 Pbk £24.00

—Industrial tribunal practice / London : Longman Professional (UK), 1988.
- (Practitioner series).
Analysis of the expanding case law on procedure with practical hints. Takes account of the procedures ofr equal value claims, with worked examples, precedents and statutory materials.
ISBN 0851213766 Pbk £16.95

—Industrial tribunals / Tolley Publishing, 1984.
ISBN 0854591540 Pbk £14.95

—Industrial tribunals / Pluto Press, 1983.
ISBN 0861043685 Pbk £6.95

—Practice and procedure in industrial tribunals / London : Legal Action Group, 1986.
ISBN 0905099141 Pbk £7.50

—Procedure in Industrial Tribunals / London : Engineering Employers Federation, 1985.

—Tribunal practice and procedures / London : Law Society, 1988.
ISBN 0948736011 Pbk £19.50

TRIBUNALS - INDIA

—Administrative Law and Tribunals / 2nd ed. - Allahabad : Law Book Company, 1988.
700p.

—Administrative Tribunals Act, 1985 / Lucknow : Eastern Book Company, 1986.
932p.

—Commentaries on Administrative Tribunals Act, 1986 / Lucknow : Eastern Book Company, 1987.

—Commentaries on Uttar Pradesh Public Services (Tribunals) Act, 1976 / B.N. Upadhyaya. - 2nd ed. - Lucknow : Eastern Book Company, 1980.
277p.

—Law Relating to Execution of Decrees : Along with Executability of the Orders of Tribunals / Allahabad : Hind Publishing House, 1986.

TRIBUNALS - NEW ZEALAND

—Administrative Tribunals Handbook / Wellington District Law Society. - Butterworths, 1989.
76p.
ISBN 0409702277 Pbk £27.00

TRIBUNALS - NORTHERN IRELAND

—Industrial Tribunals in Northern Ireland / John McKee. - 2nd ed. - Belfast : Queen's University of Belfast, 1986.
125p.

TROVER AND CONVERSION - AUSTRALIA - SOUTH AUSTRALIA

—Report ... relating to the law of detinue, conversion and trespass to goods / Law Reform Committee of South Australia. - Adelaide : Government Printer, 1987.
100p. - (95th report).
Bibliography: p.99-100.

TRUST AND TRUSTEES - AUSTRALIA - TASMANIA

—Report on the variation of private trusts / Law Reform Commission of Tasmania. - Hobart : Acting Government Printer, 1987.
28p. - (Report).
Includes text of Model Bill.

TRUST COMPANIES - NEW ZEALAND

—Trustee companies' internal trading relationships : report of the Property Law and Equity Reform Committee / Wellington : Property Law and Equity Reform Committee, 1982.
6p.

TRUSTS AND TRUSTEES

—Common law trust in the modern world / D.W.M. Waters. - Deventer : Kluwer, 1984.
24p; 25cm.
ISBN 9065442111

—Equity, trusts, specific relief / Durga Das Basu. - 5th ed. - New Delhi : Prentice-Hall, 1983.
xxiv,336p.
Includes index.
ISBN 0876922329

—International tax treatment of common law trusts : proceedings of a seminar held in New York in 1986 during the 40th Congress of the International Fiscal Association / Deventer Netherlands : Kluwer Law and Taxation Publishers, 1987.
ISBN 9065443460

—Jersey law of trusts / by Paul Matthews and Terry Sowden : foreword by Justice Hoffmann. - London : Key Haven, 1988.
102p; 30cm.
Includes index. English text with statutory material in French.
ISBN 1870070070 spiral No price

—Law of trusts in the 80's / by D.W.M. Waters. - Calgary? : University of Calgary, 1980.
37p; 23cm.
Includes bibliographical references. Sponsored by the Faculty of Law, University of Calgary.
ISBN 0459334204

—Law relating to trusts and trustees / Underhill and Hayton. - 14th ed. - London : Butterworths, 1987.
cxxxv,858p; 26cm.
Previous ed.: published as Underhill's law relating to trusts and trustees. 1979. Includes index.
ISBN 040640593X No price

—Report on trusts and analogous institutions / Rapport sur les trusts et institutions analogues : Adair Dyer, Hans van Loon. - Provisional ed. - La Haye : Bureau Permanent de la Conference de la Haye de droit international prive, 1982.
127p.
At head of title: Conference de La Haye de droit international prive Hague Conference on Private International Law. English and French tables of contents as inserts. Parallel English and French text.

—Trusts and trust-like devices / edited by W.A. Wilson. - S.l. : United Kingdom National Committee of Comparative Law, 1981.
244p; 25cm.
'Based on revised papers and contributions originally submitted to a colloquium held by the United Kingdom National Committee for Comparative Law at the University of Exeter'. Includes bibliographical references.

TRUSTS AND TRUSTEES - AUSTRALIA

—Cases and Materials on Equity and Trusts / R.P. Austin. - 3rd ed. - Butterworths, 1989.
1024p.
ISBN 0409495239 Hbk £89.00
ISBN 0409495247 Pbk £69.00

—Cases and materials on equity and trusts / by J.D. Heydon, W.M.C. Gummow, R.P. Austin. - 2nd ed. - Sydney : Butterworths, 1982.
xxxvi,934p.
This book introduces the main principles and remedies of Anglo-Australasian equity. A range of questions have been provided for undergraduate law students.
ISBN 0409309389

—Cases on Trusts / 5th ed. - North Ryde : Law Book Co, 1984.
xxxiii, 925p.
ISBN 0455205116 Hbk £73.00
ISBN 0455205124 Pbk £58.50

—Discretionary Trusts : with 1978 Supplement / R. Baxt. - 2nd ed. - Butterworths, 1984.
235p.
ISBN 040949383X Hbk £55.00

Supplement
ISBN 0409312118 Pbk £10.00

—Jacobs law of trusts in Australia / Roderick Pitt Meagher, W. M. C. Gummow. - 5th ed. - Sydney : Butterworths, 1986.
lxxxiv,1106p.
Previous ed.: 1977. Includes index. Includes texts of Acts.
ISBN 0409490768 Hbk A$94.00
ISBN 0409490792 Pbk A$72.00

—Outline of Equity and Trust / Sydney : Butterworths, 1988.
352p.
This introductory text covers such areas as the nature of eqity, equity assignments, fiduciary obligations, marshalling, contribution, subrogation, discretionary trusts, charitable trusts, and the rights of beneficiaries.

—Outline of Equity and Trusts / Butterworths, 1988.
xlii, 365p.
ISBN 0409493767 Hbk £45.00
ISBN 0409493546 Pbk £35.00

—Principles of the law of trusts / by H.A.J. Ford and W.A. Lee. - Sydney : Law Book Co., 1983.
cxvii,1055p.
Includes bibliographical references and index.
ISBN 045520375X

—Stamp Duty Aspects of Trusts, Settlements and Gifts in Australia / F.P. Zipfinger. - Butterworths, 1984.
367p.
ISBN 0409494216 Hbk £56.00

—Trusts /. - North Ryde : Law Book Co, 1985.
ix, 102p. - (Nutshells).
ISBN 0455206317

—Trusts / Butterworths, 1989.
ca 98p.
ISBN 040949481X Pbk £10.95

—Winding Up Trusts / North Ryde : C.C.H. Australia, 1984.
225p.
ISBN 0869034677 Hbk £50.00

TRUSTS AND TRUSTEES - AUSTRALIA - SOUTH AUSTRALIA

—Report ... on the inherited imperial statute law in this state relating to the topics of property, trusts, uses, equity and wills / Law Reform Committee of South Australia. - Adelaide : Government Printer, 1980.
16p. - (54th report).

TRUSTS AND TRUSTEES - AUSTRALIA - TASMANIA

—Research paper on the variation of private trusts / by E.L.G. Tyler. - Hobart? : Government Printer?, 1985.
54p.

TRUSTS AND TRUSTEES - AUSTRALIA - WESTERN AUSTRALIA

—Report on trustees' powers of investment / Law Reform Commission of Western Australia. - Perth : Government Printer, 1984.
141p. - (Project v no 34 part 5).
Includes bibliographical references.

TRUSTS AND TRUSTEES - CANADA

—Central Trust Company Act, 1983, Bill 097 : An Act Respecting Central Trust Company and Crown Trust Company / Ontario : Ontario Government Publications Service, 1983.
5p.

—Estate and Trusts Reports / Agincourt : Carswell.
These volumes contain the key decisions in estates and trust law from Canadian jurisdictions. Topics include wills, estate administration, devolution of estate, dependents relief, and tax matters relating to trusts. Wills are covered in depth.

—Estates and Trusts Quarterly (E. & T.Q.) 1974-Present / Aurora : Canada Law Book Co.

Current subscription-Outside Canada

Back Vols.

—Law of fiduciaries / by J.C. Shepard. – Toronto, Canada : Carswell, 1981.
xxix, 386 p.; 24 cm.
Includes bibliographical references and index.
ISBN 0459343009 Hbk £33

—Law of Trusts in Canada / Agincourt : Carswell, 1984.
ISBN 045936200 Hbk £41.80

—Text, commentary and cases on law of trusts / 3rd ed. – Agincourt : Carswell, 1987.
ISBN 0459397400 Pbk £22.00

—Text, Commentary and Cases on Trusts / E.E. Gillese. – 3rd ed. – Agincourt : Carswell, 1987.
1,046p.

—Trusts / Vancouver : Continuing Legal Education Society of British Columbia, 1985.
233p.
ISBN 0865042373 Hbk £60.00

TRUSTS AND TRUSTEES - CANADA - BRITISH COLUMBIA

—Report on the Land (Settled Estate) Act / Law Reform Commission of British Columbia. – Vancouver : The Commission, 1988.
41p.
Includes text of the Land (Settled Estate) Act and Trust Variation Act.
ISBN 0771887248

TRUSTS AND TRUSTEES - CANADA - MANITOBA

—Report on investment provisions under 'The Trustee Act' / Law Reform Commission. – Winnipeg : Queen's Printer, 1982.
i,38p. – (Report).

TRUSTS AND TRUSTEES - CANADA - ONTARIO

—Report on the law of trusts / Ontario Law Reform Commission. – 2. – Toronto : Ministry of the Attorney General, 1984.
ISBN 0774389141

TRUSTS AND TRUSTEES - COMMONWEALTH

—Comparative Law of Trusts in the Commonwealth and the Irish Republic / Chichester : Barry Rose.
ISBN 0859921751 Hbk £8.50

TRUSTS AND TRUSTEES - ENGLAND

—Cases and commentary on the law of trusts / Hayton and Marshall. – 8th ed. – London : Stevens, 1986.
796p; 25cm.
Previous ed.: / Nathan and Marshall. 1980. Includes index.
ISBN 042047370X Hbk £32.50 :
ISBN 0420473807 Pbk £21.00

—Cases and commentary on the law of trusts / Nathan and Marshall. – 7th ed. – London : Stevens, 1980.
xxxix,736p; 25cm.
Previous ed.: 1975. Includes index. entitled: Equity through the cases (1st-4th) and A casebook on trusts (5th).
ISBN 0420459901 £28.00
ISBN 0420460004

—Constructive trusts / by A.J. Oakley. – 2nd ed. – London : Sweet & Maxwell, 1987.
200p; 22cm.
Previous ed.: 1978. Includes index.
ISBN 0421347406 Hbk £11.00 :
ISBN 0421347503 Pbk £7.85

—Law of trusts / George W. Keeton. – 11th ed. – Chichester : Rose, 1983.
lxiv,578p; 26cm.
Previous ed.: 1974. Includes index.
ISBN 085992369X £45.00

—Law of trusts / J.G. Riddall. – 3rd ed. – London : Butterworths, 1987.
420p; 24cm.
Previous ed.: 1982. Includes index.
ISBN 0406648425 Pbk £23.00 :
ISBN 0406648433 £14.95

—Maudsley and Burn's Trusts and trustees : cases and materials / E. H. Burn, R. H. Maudsley. – 3rd ed. – London : Butterworths, 1984.
lxvii,828p; 26cm.
This work for students of the law of trusts in the United Kingdom draws its materials from a wide range of sources. The book provides many footnotes and references to non-case literature on the subject.
ISBN 0406623244 HBK £31.00
ISBN 0406623252 Pbk £21.95

—Modern law of trusts / by David B. Parker and Anthony R. Mellows. – 5th ed. – London : Sweet & Maxwell, 1983.
xlviii,492p; 24cm.
Previous ed.: London : Sweet & Maxwell, 1979. Includes index.
ISBN 0421309709 Hbk No price
ISBN 0421309806 Pbk £12.00

—Trusts in a nutshell / Angela Sydenham. – London : Sweet & Maxwell, 1987.
116p; 22cm.
Includes index.
ISBN 0421368500 Pbk £3.95

—Trusts of land / the Law Commission. – London : H.M.S.O., 1985.
iv,76p. – (Working paper).
ISBN 0117301752

—Trusts of Land : overreaching / the Law Commission. – London : H.M.S.O., 1988.
iv,42,20p. – (Working paper).
ISBN 0117301884

TRUSTS AND TRUSTEES - GREAT BRITAIN

—Capital transfer tax : discretionary trusts : memorandum by the Society's Standing Committee on Revenue Law commenting on draft clauses published by the Inland Revenue / Law Society. – London : Law Society, 1982.
9p; 30cm.

—Cases and Commentary On Trusts / Marshall. – 8th ed. – Sweet & Maxwell, 1986.
ISBN 042047370X Hbk £36.00
ISBN 0420473807 Pbk £27.00

—Equity and the Law of Trusts / 5th ed. – London : Butterworths, 1984.
ISBN 0406641676 Hbk £25.00
ISBN 0406641684 Pbk £21.95

—Equity and Trusts / Plymouth : Macdonald & Evans, 1985.
304p. – (M and E Handbook Ser.).
ISBN 0712106685 Hbk £5.50

—Equity and Trusts / London : Financial Training, 1986.
– (SWOT).
ISBN 1851850457 Pbk £7.95

—Equity and Trusts / Plymouth : Macdonald & Evans, 1985.
ISBN 0712106685 Pbk £7.95

—Executorship and Trust Law and Accounts / Suresh Tanna. – Plymouth : Macdonald & Evans, 1985.
360p. – (M and E Professional Studies Ser.).
ISBN 0712104585 Hbk £13.95

—Executorship/Trust Law and Accounts / 2nd ed. – London : Pitman Publishing, 1986.
ISBN 0712107517 Pbk £14.95

—Introduction to Law of Trusts / London : Financial Training, 1986.
ISBN 185185021X Pbk £9.95

—Law of Trusts / Hodkinson. – London : CCH, 1984.
ISBN 086325019X Pbk £20.00

—Law of Trusts / J. Mowbray. – 18th ed. – London : Sweet & Maxwell.
– (Property and Conveyancing Library).
ISBN 0421233907 Hbk

—Law of trusts / J.G. Riddall. – 2nd ed. – London : Butterworths, 1982.
xxxi, 371p.
This textbook for United Kingdom students of trusts deals with the creation of trusts; the appointment, powers, and duties of trustees; and beneficiaries. Hypothetical examples, tables, and diagrams are included in the book.
ISBN 0406648379

—Law of Trusts / 17th ed. – London : Sweet & Maxwell, 1988.
ISBN 0421233907 Hbk

—Law of Trusts / 3rd ed. – London : Butterworths, 1987.
ISBN 0406648425 Hbk £27.00
ISBN 0406648433 Pbk £17.95

—Law Relating to Trusts and Trustees / Wellington : Butterworths.
This book for practitioners in the United Kingdom covers express or declared trusts, trusts implied by law, the administration of a trust, and the consequences of a breach of trust.
ISBN 0406405891 Pbk

—Law Relating to Trusts and Trustees / Hayton. – 14th ed. – London : Butterworths, 1987.
ISBN 040640593X Hbk £110.00

—Maudsley and Burn: trusts and trustees - cases and materials / E H Burn. – 3rd ed. – London : Butterworths, 1984.
ISBN 0406623244 Hbk £35.00
ISBN 0406623252 Pbk £23.95

—Maudsley and Burn's Trusts and trustees - cases and materials / London : Butterworths, 1990.
904; 24cm.
Part one deals with trusts - their nature, requirements and constitutions, trusts and creditors, resulting trusts, constructive trusts and non-charitable purpose trusts; part two covers charities - charitable trusts, Cy-pres, and the administration of charities; part three is trusts and taxes - income tax, capital gains tax and capital transfer tax; and part four deals with trustees - general principles, duties and powers of trustees, variations of trusts, and breach of trust.
ISBN 040659211X PBK £25.95

—Powers and duties of trustees : presented to parliament ... October 1982 / Law Reform Committee. – London : H.M.S.O., 1982.
iv,71p; 25cm. – (Report).
ISBN 0101873301 Hbk £5.25

—Practical trust administration / 2nd ed. – London : Europa Publications, 1984.
ISBN 0905118944 Hbk £17.50

—Practical trust precedents / London : Longman Professional, 1986.
ISBN 0851211836 updat £95.00

—Principles of the law of trusts / by H.A.J. Ford and W.A. Lee. – Sydney : Law Book Co., 1983.
cxvii,1055p.
Includes bibliographical references and index.
ISBN 045520375X

—Raising money from trusts / TUAR, 1981.
ISBN 0907164048 Pbk £2.95

—Revival of the Discretionary Trust : 1983 / Andrew R. Thornhill. – London : Law Society, 1983.
– (Oxford Weekend Courses).

—Sweet & Maxwell Law / London : Sweet & Maxwell, 1984.
ISBN 0421321504 Pbk £29.50

File 5, Trusts : Trustees Fitzkenton Estate 1985.
ISBN 0421340207 Pbk £29.50

—Tax planning through trusts / Robert Venables. – London : Butterworths, 1983.
xxxiv,371p; 24cm.
Includes index.
ISBN 0406406014

—Taxation and trusts / by Geraint W. Thomas. – London : Sweet & Maxwell, 1981.
xxiv,205p; 19cm.
Includes index.
ISBN 0421277203 Hbk Unpriced
ISBN 0421277300 Pbk £6.95

—Taxation for Executors and Trustees / 6th ed. – London : Butterworths, 1984.
ISBN 0406623961 Hbk
ISBN 040662397X Pbk

—Taxation of accumulation and discretionary trusts / Tolley Publishing, 1987.
ISBN 0854592709 Pbk £14.95

—Trust law & practice : pension funds, commercial trusts and charities / London : Cass, 1986-.

—Trust Practice Manual / Deloitte, Haskins and Sells Staff. – London : Butterworths, 1985.
This book provides the basis for setting up standard procedures for the organization and operation of a trust department in a law office in the United Kingdom. Practical issues of management and procedures are addressed in the work.
ISBN 040650010X Pbk

—Trust practice manual / Haskins. – London : Butterworths, 1985.
ISBN 040650010X Pbk £16.50

—Trust taxation manual / London : Butterworths, 1986.
ISBN 0406503303 Pbk £18.50

—Trustees of the Fitzkenton Estate / London : Sweet & Maxwell, 1985.
– (Sweet and Maxwell's Law Files Ser.: No. 5).
ISBN 0421340207 loose £29.50

—Trusts and tax planning / 3rd ed. – London : Longman Professional, 1987.
ISBN 0851208762 Pbk £35.88

—Trusts and Tax Planning / 2nd ed. – London : Oyez Longman, 1982.
– (Oyez Longman Practical Tax Ser.).

—Trusts for Accountants / London : Butterworths, 1987.
ISBN 0406500908 Pbk

—Trusts for accountants / London : Butterworths, 1987.
ISBN 0406500908 Pbk £10.95

—Trusts : Maximising the Tax Advantages / London : Oyez Longman, 1983.
– (Oyez Longman Intelligence Report Ser.).
ISBN 0851207375 Hbk £45.00

TRUSTS AND TRUSTEES - INDIA

—Indian Trusts Act : With Special Reference to Taxation Laws / 3rd ed. – Allahabad : Law Book Company, 1987.
ca 900p.

TRUSTS AND TRUSTEES - IRELAND

—Casebook on Equity and Trusts in Ireland / Abingdon : Professional Books, 1985.
700p.
ISBN 0862051126 Hbk £44.00
ISBN 0862051142 Pbk £34.00

—Casebook on Equity and Trusts in Ireland / London : Butterworths, 1985.
ISBN 0862051126 Hbk £32.50
ISBN 0862051142 Pbk £25.00

—Comparative Law of Trusts in the Commonwealth and the Irish Republic / Chichester : Barry Rose.
ISBN 0859921751 Hbk £8.50

—Equity and the law of trusts in the Republic of Ireland / Ronan Keane. – London : Butterworths, 1988.
liii,387p.
Includes index.
ISBN 0406102708 Hbk £27.50

TRUSTS AND TRUSTEES - LIECHTENSTEIN

—Trust in Liechtenstein law / Watford : Alvescot Press, 1983.
512p.
Translation of: Die Treuhanderschaft des liechtensteinischen Rechts.
ISBN 0950583413 £45.00

TRUSTS AND TRUSTEES - MALAYSIA

—Trustee Act, 1949 (Act 206) and Trustees (Incorporation) Act, 1962 (Act 258) / Kuala Lumpur : International Law Books Services.

TRUSTS AND TRUSTEES - NEW ZEALAND

—Brief Outline of the Law Relating to Trusts, Wills, Executors, and Administrators / 2nd ed. – Wellington : Butterworths, 1982.
ISBN 0409627127 Hbk

—Brief Outline of the Law Relating to Trusts, Wills, Executors, and Administrators / 2nd ed. – Butterworths, 1982.
ISBN 04094267127 Pbk £25.85

—Distributions from share premium accounts : report of the Property Law and Equity Reform Committee / New Zealand. – Wellington? : Government Printer?, 1982.
8,2p.
Cover title.

—Garrow and Kelly's law of trusts and trustees / the original text by J.M.E. Garrow. – 5th ed. – Wellington : Butterworths, 1982.
lxiii,616p.
Contains a new chapter on the investment of trust funds since the Trustee Amendment Act 1974. Passages from previous editions have been rewritten, and there is comment on the case of Bartlett v Barclays Bank.
ISBN 0409600717

—Law of Trusts and Trustees in New Zealand / Kelly. – 5th ed. – London : Butterworths, 1981.
ISBN 0409600717 Hbk £44.50

—Law Relating to Trusts and Trustees / Wellington : Butterworths.
This book for practitioners in the United Kingdom covers express or declared trusts, trusts implied by law, the administration of a trust, and the consequences of a breach of trust.
ISBN 0406405891 Pbk

—Nevill's Law of Trusts, Wills and Administration in New Zealand / 8th ed. – Butterworths, 1985.
Guide to the law of trusts, wills and administration in New Zealand. Includes new chapters on unincorporated associations and construction of wills.
ISBN 040970170X Hbk £76.45
ISBN 0409701858 Pbk £50.05

—Nevill's Law of Trusts, Wills and Administrators in New Zealand / 8th ed. – London : Butterworths, 1985.
ISBN 0409701858 Pbk £26.00

—Second report on trustee's powers of investment : miscellaneous powers / Wellington? : the Committee?, 1984.
10,14,2,4p.

—Second rise and fall of fundamental breach / Brian Coote : G.C. Thorpe : D.W. McMorland. – Auckland : Legal Research Foundation, 1980.
127p.
Includes bibliographical references.
ISBN 0908581084

TRUSTS AND TRUSTEES - NIGERIA

—Equity and trusts in Nigeria / by J.O. Fabunmi. – Ile-Ife : University of Ife Press, 1986.
lii,301p.
Includes bibliographical references and index.
ISBN 9781360453

TRUSTS AND TRUSTEES - SCOTLAND

—Scots Statutes 1983 : Family Law; Succession, Trusts, Liferents and Judicial Factors / Edinburgh : W Green, 1983.
ISBN 0414007255 Hbk £6.50

—Scots Statutes 1984 : Family Law; Succession, Trusts, Liferents and Judicial Factors / Edinburgh : W Green.
ISBN 041400745X Hbk £14.75

—Scots Statutes 1985 : Family Law - Succession, Trusts, Liferent andJudicial Factors / Edinburgh : W Green.
– (Reprint from the Parliament House Book).
ISBN 0414007662 Hbk £10.00

TRUSTS AND TRUSTEES - SOUTH AFRICA

—Law of trusts / South African Law Commission. – Pretoria : South African Law Commission, 1983.
vi,63p. – (Working paper).
Project 9. Bibliography: pv-vi.

—Review of the law of trusts / South African Law Commission. – Pretoria : The Commission, 1987.
viii,135p. – (Report).
Bibliography: p. vii-viii. Includes text of bill.

—South African law of trusts / by Tony Honore. – Cape Town : Juta, 1985.
lxvi,551p.
Previous ed.: 1976. Includes bibliographical references and index.
ISBN 0702115320

—Trusts in South Africa with Up-to-Date Addendum / Cape Town : Legal and Financial Publishing Co.

TRUSTS AND TRUSTEES - UNITED KINGDOM

—Law of Trusts / 2nd ed. Repr. of 1980 ed. – Plymouth : Macdonald & Evans, 1982.
352p. – (M and E Handbook Ser.).
ISBN 0712112553 Hbk £4.95

TRUSTS AND TRUSTEES - UNITED STATES

—Decedents' estates, wills, and trusts in the U.S.A. / by Frank G. Opton. – Deventer, The Netherlands : Kluwer Law and Taxation Publishers, 1986.
Includes index.
ISBN 9065442715 Hbk

TRUSTS AND TRUSTEES (ROMAN LAW)

—Roman law of trusts / David Johnston. – Oxford : Clarendon Press, 1988.
xiii,306p.
Discusses the Roman equivalent of a trust, a fideicommissum, which affected the strategies of succession open to testators. Provides an illustration of the emperor's involvement in building private law. Relates Roman law to social history and uses the development of the trust as a case study in legal evolution.
ISBN 0198252161 Hbk £37.50

TSWANA (BANTU TRIBE) - AFRICA

—Rules and processes : the cultural logic of dispute in an African context / John L. Comaroff, Simon Roberts. – Chicago : University of Chicago, 1981.
ix,293p; 23cm.
Bibliography: p277-288. - Includes index.
ISBN 0226114244 £19.25

TSWANA LAW - AFRICA

—Rules and processes : the cultural logic of dispute in an African context / John L. Comaroff, Simon Roberts. – Chicago : University of Chicago, 1981.
ix,293p; 23cm.
Bibliography: p277-288. - Includes index.
ISBN 0226114244 £19.25

TURKS - BULGARIA

—Bulgaria : imprisonment of ethnic Turks : human rights abuses during the forced assimilation of the ethnic Turkish minority / Amnesty International. – London : Amnesty International, 1986.
40p.
ISBN 0862100976

UNBORN CHILDREN

—Abortion and protection of the human fetus : legal problems in a cross-cultural perspective / edited by Stanislaw J. Frankowski, George F. Cole. – Dordrecht Netherlands : M. Nijhoff, 1988.
xv, 334 p.; 25 cm.
'Under the auspices of the Institute of International and Comparative Law, the University of Santa Clara.' Includes bibliographies.
ISBN 0898389224 Hbk £175.00

UNDERDEVELOPED AREAS

—Aluminium industry and the Third World : multinational corporations and underdevelopment / Ronald Graham. – London : Zed, 1982.
xii,278p; 22cm.
Bibliography: p263-270. - Includes index.
ISBN 0862320577 Pbk

—Dependent accumulation and underdevelopment / Andre Gunder Frank. – 1st ed. reprinted. – London : Macmillan, 1982.
xx,226p.
Bibliography: p.202-219. - Includes index.
ISBN 0333239512

—Development, human rights and the rule of law : report of a conference held in The Hague on 27 April-1 May 1981 / convened by the International Commission of Jurists. – Oxford : Pergamon, 1981.
vi,237p; 23cm.
ISBN 0080289215 Hbk Unpriced
ISBN 0080289517 Pbk £3.75

—Industrialization and developing countries / Alan B. Mountjoy. – 5th ed. – London : Hutchinson, 1982.
256p; 22cm. – (Hutchinson university library).
Previous ed.: 1975. Bibliography: p243-246. - Includes index.
ISBN 0091468019 Pbk £4.95

—International monetary system and the less developed countries / Graham Bird. – 2nd ed. – London : Macmillan, 1982.
xi,352p.
Bibliography: p331-350.
ISBN 0333330021

—Law and state in Papua New Guinea / Peter Fitzpatrick. – London : Academic Press, 1980.
xi,290p; 24cm.
Bibliography: p256-284. - Includes index.
ISBN 0122578805 £12.60

—Mining ventures in developing countries / Erich Schanze. – Deventer : Kluwer, 1981.
281p.
First published: Frankfurt am Main, Metzner; Deventer, Kluwer; 1977- , as 'Rohstofferschliessungsvorhaben in Entwicklungslandern'. Translated from German into English.
ISBN 9065440380

—Some key issues for the world periphery : selected essays / by Miguel S. Wionczek. – Oxford : Pergamon, 1982.
xiv,432p; 24cm.
Includes bibliographies and index.
ISBN 0080257836 £37.50

—Urban planning practice in developing countries / editors, John L. Taylor and David G. Williams. – Oxford : Pergamon, 1982.
x,357p; 24cm. – (Pergamon international library).
Includes bibliographies.
ISBN 0080222250 £19.50

UNDERDEVELOPED AREAS - NIGERIA

—Land law and development : an inaugural lecture delivered at the University of Lagos on Thursday, 17th January, 1980 / by M.I. Jegede. – Lagos : University of Lagos Press, 1981.
39p. – (Inaugural lecture series).
Includes bibliographical references.
ISBN 978226413X

—Transnational investment law and national development / by Samuel K.B. Asante. – Lagos : Published for the Faculty of Law, University of Lagos by the Lagos University Press, 1981.
111p.
ISBN 9782264148

UNDERTAKERS AND UNDERTAKING - AUSTRALIA

—Community law reform for the Australian Capital Territory / Law Reform Commission. – Canberra : Australian Government Publishing Service, 1985.
ix,44p. – (Report).
Bibliography: p.41-42 - Includes index.
ISBN 0644013257

UNDERWATER ARCHAEOLOGY

—Protection of the underwater heritage / Paris : Unesco, 1981.
200p.
Includes bibliographies.
ISBN 9231018639

UNEMPLOYMENT

—Development technology / H.J. Duller. – London : Routledge & K. Paul, 1982.
192p.
Includes index. Bibliography: p173-190.
ISBN 0710009909

—Unemployment and labour market flexibility : the United Kingdom / Guy Standing. – Geneva : International Labour Office, 1986.
xi, 147 p.; 24 cm.
Includes bibliographies.
ISBN 9221052915 pbk. £30.00

UNEMPLOYMENT - CANADA
—Unemployment and Your Rights / Montreal : McGill Campus Legal Aid Clinic, 1983.
36p.

UNEMPLOYMENT - GREAT BRITAIN
—Alternatives to unemployment : special employment measures in Britain / David Metcalf. – London : Policy Studies Institute, 1982.
66p. – (Policy Studies Institute).

UNEMPLOYMENT AND CRIME - GREAT BRITAIN
—Unemployment and magistrates' courts / Iain Crow and Frances Simon. – London : NACRO, 1987.
52p.
ISBN 0850690579

UNEMPLOYMENT INSURANCE - CANADA
—Annotated Unemployment Insurance Act / Agincourt : Carswell, 1988.
420p.

—Annotated Unemployment Insurance Act / 1st ed. – Agincourt : Carswell, 1988.
420p.
This book contains the full text of the Unemployment Insurance Act and Regulations. Also included are the annotated cases which are pertinent to particular sections. There is a complete table of cases and an index.

—Financing Canadian unemployment insurance / Jonathan R. Kesselman. – Toronto : Canadian Tax Foundation, 1983.
xiii,187p.
Bibliography: p.177-183. - Includes index.
ISBN 0888080166

—Unemployment Insurance / Vancouver : British Columbia Continuing Legal Education Society, 1983.
266p.
ISBN 0865041067 Hbk £55.00

—Unemployment Insurance / Bob Ludlow. – Vancouver : Vancouver People's Law School.
Illus.

—Unemployment insurance / by Clare E. Choate. – Toronto : Carswell Co., 1982.
xii, 386 p.; 26 cm.
'Reprinted from the Canadian encyclopedic digest, third edition.'. Includes index.

—Unemployment Insurance / 2nd ed. – Agincourt : Carswell, 1985.
418p.

UNEQUAL TREATIES
—Unequal treaty, 1898-1997 : China, Great Britain, and Hong Kong's new territories / Peter Wesley-Smith. – Hong Kong : Oxford University Press, 1983.
xix, 270 p., 8 p. of plates; 21 cm.
Includes index. Bibliography: p. 242-256.
ISBN 0195837274 pbk.

UNFAIR DISMISSAL - CANADA
—Butterworth's Wrongful Dismissal Practice Manual, 2 vols / Toronto : Butterworths.

—Executive Firing Line : Wrongful Dismissal and the Law / Agincourt : Carswell, 1982.
240p.

—Law of Dismissal in Canada / Aurora : Canada Law Book, 1985.

—Wrongful Dismissal : 1986 / Vancouver : Continuing Legal Education Society of British Columbia, 1986.
150p.
ISBN 0865042667 Hbk £55.00

—Wrongful Dismissal : 1988 Update / Vancouver : Continuing Legal Education Society of British Columbia, 1988.
238p.
ISBN 0865049882 Hbk £70.00

—Wrongful Dismissal / Toronto : DeBoo, 1984.
ISBN 0888201524 Hbk £135.00
Ann. supplement

—Wrongful Dismissal / Toronto : DeBoo, 1984.
This treatise presents the Canadian law of wrongful dismissal. Awards for mental distress, constructive dismissal, punitive damages, just cause for dismissal, special status of Crown employees, and other related issues are discussed in depth in the work.
ISBN 0888201613 Hbk £85.00

—Wrongful Dismissal : Practical Perspectives / Vancouver : Continuing Legal Education Society of British Columbia, 1987.
174p.
ISBN 0865043299 Hbk £65.00

UNFAIR DISMISSAL - GREAT BRITAIN
—Butterworth's Wrongful Dismissal Practice Manual / Toronto : Butterworths.

—Compensation for dismissal / Croydon : Tolley, 1987.
ISBN 0854592733 Pbk £13.95

—Compensation for Dismissal / Croydon : Tolley.
225p.
ISBN 0854592733 Hbk £13.95

—Croner's Guide to Fair Dismissal / New Malden : Croner Publications.

—Law of Unfair Dismissal / John H. Angel. – 2nd ed. – Wellington : Butterworths, 1985.
xlv,444; 22cm.
This book provides a detailed discussion of the law of unfair dismissal in the United Kingdom. The work includes references to the changes brought about by recent legislation, such as, the Employment Protection (Consolidation) Act of 1978 and the Employment Acts of 1980 and 1982.
ISBN 0406107076 Pbk

—Law of Unfair Dismissal / 2nd ed. – London : Butterworths, 1985.
ISBN 0406107076 Pbk £21.95

—Unfair dismissal handbook / 3rd ed. – London : Longman Professional, 1988.
ISBN 0851212522 Pbk

UNFAIR DISMISSAL - NEW ZEALAND
—Law of Unfair Dismissal / John H. Angel. – 2nd ed. – Wellington : Butterworths, 1985.
xlv,444; 22cm.
This book provides a detailed discussion of the law of unfair dismissal in the United Kingdom. The work includes references to the changes brought about by recent legislation, such as, the Employment Protection (Consolidation) Act of 1978 and the Employment Acts of 1980 and 1982.
ISBN 0406107076 Pbk

UNFAIR LABOUR PRACTICES - SOUTH AFRICA
—Principles of unfair labour practice / Theodorus Poolman. – Cape Town : Juta, 1985.
xxx,243p.
Bibliography: p.xi-xxi. - Includes index.
ISBN 0702115657

UNINCORPORATED ASSOCIATIONS
—Handbook of charities, 1987-1988 ... / edited by Erroll Christie and Anne Frazer Simpson. – London : Charities Data Services, 1987.
128 p.
'... a guide for those involved in the educational field, community service and the selection and search for organisations in need of support'.
ISBN 1870914007

UNINCORPORATED ASSOCIATIONS - AUSTRALIA
—Law of domestic or private tribunals / by J.R.S. Forbes. – Sydney : Law Book, 1982.
xxviii, 247 p.; 22 cm.
Includes index.
ISBN 0455204551 pbk.

UNINCORPORATED ASSOCIATIONS - GREAT BRITAIN
—Clients' Rights : Report of a Working Party Established by the National Council for Voluntary Organisations / London : Bedford Square Press, 1985.

—Councils, committees & boards : a handbook of advisory, consultative, executive & similar bodies in British public life / edited by Lindsay Sellar. – a 6th ed. – Beckenham, Kent : CBD Research, 1984.
xiv,430p; 30cm. – (A CBD research publication).
ISBN 090024643X

—Directory of British associations & associations in Ireland / editors: G.P.Henderson & S.P.A.Henderson. – Edition 8. – Beckenham : CBD Research, 1985.
ISBN 0900246456

—Employing People in Voluntary Organisations : An NCVO Practical Guide / London : Bedford Square Press, 1984.
ISBN 0719911095 Hbk £2.95

—Legal environment of the business world / R.B. Buchanan. – Cheltenham : Stanley Thornes, 1982.
xix,230p; 22cm.
Includes index.
ISBN 0859503054 Pbk £3.75

—Legal Structures for Voluntary Organisations / Bates. – London : Bedford Square Press, 1984.
ISBN 0719911168 Pbk £1.95

—Lotteries and Gaming - Voluntary Organisations and the Law / NCVO. – London : Bedford Square Press, 1981.
ISBN 0719910706 Pbk £1.95

UNINCORPORATED SOCIETIES
—Report on incorporation of associations / New South Wales Law Reform Commission. – Sydney, 1982.
136p. – (L.R.C.).
Includes index.

UNINCORPORATED SOCIETIES - ENGLAND
—Unincorporated associations : law and practice / by Jean Warburton. – London : Sweet & Maxwell, 1986.
100p; 22cm.
Guide to the law in respect of sports clubs, political parties, self-help groups, and community associations. Covers funding, the holding of property, rates and taxes, and the rights and liabilities of members. Contains several precedents for the formation of an association and the establishment of rules and objects.
ISBN 0421345403 Pbk £14.00

UNINCORPORATED SOCIETIES - SOUTH AFRICA
—Bamford on the law of partnership and voluntary association in South Africa / by Brian Bamford. – 3rd ed. – Cape Town : Juta, 1982.
xlvii,274p.
Previous ed.: 1971. Includes index.
ISBN 0702112526

UNITED NATIONS
—Agreement between the United Nations and the World Intellectual Property Organization / Geneva : World Intellectual Property Organization.
55p.

—Expanding jurisdiction of the United Nations / M.S. Rajan. – Bombay : Tripathi, 1981.
xii,252p.
ISBN 0379207273 £30.00

—Human rights law-making in the United Nations / Oxford : Oxford University Press, 1986.
ISBN 0198255497 Hbk £35.00

—Juridical Yearbook 1981 / London : HMSO, 1985.
Contains legal documents concerning the United Nations including legislative texts, treaty provisions and a review of the United Nations' legal activities.
ISBN 0119086506 Hbk £25.00

—Legal Restraints on the Use of Force 40 Years after the UN Charter / Dordrecht : Kluwer, 1986.
546p.
ISBN 9024732476 Hbk £215.00

—Procedure of the UN Security Council / Sydney D. Bailey. – 2nd ed. – Oxford : Clarendon press, 1988.
xii,499p.
Bibliography: pp.449-452. - Includes index. A revised and updated edition, taking in new developments, including a new chapter on voting and veto. All aspects of the Security Council's prcedure are covered.
ISBN 0198275668 Hbk £45/$60

—Repertory of Practice of United Nations Organs, Supplement No 5, Vol. 5 : Articles 92-111 of the Charter / Geneva : United Nations Publications.
ISBN 9211332834 Hbk £19.00

—Resolutions of the United Nations Security Council / Dordrecht : Martinus Nijhoff, 1989.
179. – (Legal aspects of international organisation 8).
Presents a picture of the legal questions concerning Security Council resolutions and their place in the international legal order. Makes a comparison of Charter provisions with the Security Council's practice. The last chapter of the book examines the question of whether a Security Council resolution is binding.
ISBN 902473567X Hbk Gld120.00

—Roots and reaches of United Nations actions and decisions / by Moses Moskowitz. – Alphen aan den Rijh : Sijthoff and Noordhoff, 1980.
x,210p.
Includes bibliography.

—System for Settlement of Disputes under the United Nations Convention on the Law of the Sea : a Drafting History and a Commentary / Dordrecht : Kluwer, 1987.
302p.
ISBN 9024733243 Hbk £165.00

—UNCITRAL : the United Nations Commission on International Law / Geneva : United Nations Publications.
ISBN 9211332842 Hbk £15.00

—United Nations and international law / Cambridge : Cambridge University Press, 1986.
ISBN 0521338743 Pbk £2.95

—United Nations and the control of international violence : a legal and political analysis / John F. Murphy. – Manchester : Manchester University Press, 1983.
xii,212p; 24cm.
Includes index.
ISBN 0719009421 £22.50
ISBN 0865980799

—United Nations decision making / by Johan Kaufmann. – Alphen aan den Rijn, Netherlands : Sijthoff & Noordhoff, 1980.
xiv, 283 p.; 25 cm.
Third fully rev. ed.: How United Nations decisions are made / by John G. Hadwen and Johan Kaufmann. 2nd. rev. ed. 1962, c1961. Includes bibliographical references and index.
ISBN 9028604103

—United Nations versus South Africa : a legal assessment of United Nations and United Nations related activities in respect of South Africa / Jan C. Heunis. – 1st ed. – Johannesburg : Lex Patria, 1986.
593 p., 1 folded leaf of plates; 25 cm.
: Originally presented as the author's thesis (doctoral–Rand Afrikaans University, 1984). Includes index. Bibliography: p. 583-593.
ISBN 0628030363

UNITED NATIONS AND NON-MEMBER NATIONS

—Status of observers in the United Nations / R.G. Sybesma- Knol. – Brussels : Vrije Universiteit Brussel, Centrum voor de Studie van het Recht van de Verenigde Naties en de Gespecialiseerde Organisaties, 1981.
xi,484p.
Bibliography: p.456-484. - Includes index.
ISBN 9063210825

UNITED NATIONS RESOLUTIONS

—Legal effect of resolutions and codes of conduct of the United Nations / Deventer : Kluwer, 1986.
16p.
Includes bibliographical references.
ISBN 9065442421

UNITED STATES OF AMERICA

—American studies collections in the University of London : a / London : University of London Institute of United States, 1981.
30p.
Based on 'Materials for the study of the United States in libraries of the University of London'.

—Australian-United States' relations : the extraterritorial application of United States laws / the Parliament of the Commonwealth of Australia Joint Committee on Foreign Affairs and Defence. – Canberra : Australian Government Publishing Service, 1983.
xiii,84p. – (Parliamentary paper).
Includes bibliographical references.

—Grenada : a study in politics and the limits of international law / Scott Davidson. – Aldershot : Avebury, 1987.
xii,196p; 22cm.
Bibliography: p184-190. - Includes index.
ISBN 0566050528 £18.50

—North American social report : a comparative study of the quality of life in Canada and the USA from 1964 to 1974 / by Alex C. Michalos. – Dordrecht : Reidel, 1980.
xv,252p; 23cm.
ISBN 9027710856

UNITED STATES OF AMERICA - UNITED STATES

—Papers of Daniel Webster / Alfred S. Konefsky, Andrew J. King. – Hanover, N.H. : Published for Dartmouth College by the University Press of New England, 1982.
xxxix,571p; 25cm.
Includes index.
ISBN 0874512328 Unpriced

—South Africa in the American mind / Alan Pifer. – Braamfontein : South African Institute of International Affairs, 1981.
17p. – (Commemoration Day Lecture).
ISBN 0909239932

UNITS

—International standards : units of measurement to be used in air and ground operations : annex 5 to the Convention on International Civil Aviation / International Civil Aviation Organization. – 4th ed. - July 1979. 1. – Montreal : International Civil Aviation Organization, 1979 -.
loose-leaf.
Kept up to date by amendments and supplements.

UNIVERSITIES AND COLLEGES

—International handbook of universities and other institutions of higher education / editor, D.J. Aitken : assistant editor, Ann C.M. Taylor. – 9th ed. – London : Macmillan for the International Association of Universities, 1983.
ix, 1131p.
ISBN 0333274466

—Management of a student research project / Keith Howard & John A. Sharp. – Aldershot : Gower, 1983.
xiii,238p; 23cm.
Bibliography: p219-232. - Includes index.
ISBN 0566004623 Hbk Unpriced
ISBN 0566006138 Pbk Unpriced

UNIVERSITIES AND COLLEGES - COMMONWEALTH

—Research opportunities in Commonwealth developing countries : universities, non-university research institutions : a register prepared by the Association of Commonwealth Universities in association with the Commonwealth Secretariat / Association of Commonwealth Universities. – New ed. – London : The Association, 1984.
235p.
Previous ed. published as: Research strengths of universities in the developing countries of the Commonwealth. London, 1978. Includes index.

UNIVERSITIES AND COLLEGES - INDIA

—Commentary on the University Laws in India / Madhya Pradesh, 1986.
220p.

—Misconduct of students : a legal and disciplinary study / Arun Bhattacharjee. – New Delhi : Deep & Deep, 1981.
440p.
Bibliography: p.425-427. - Includes index.

—Uttar Pradesh State Universities Act, 1973 : as Amended Up-to-Date with Exhaustive Comments and Allied Laws / S.N. Srivastava. – Allahabad : Hind Publishing House, 1981.
ii, 146p.

UNIVERSITIES AND COLLEGES - UNITED STATES

—Affirmative action and preferential admissions in higher education : an annotated bibliography / by Kathryn Swanson. – Metuchen : Scarecrow, 1981.
viii,336p; 23cm.
Includes index.
ISBN 0810814110 £12.25

—Beyond the ivory tower : social responsibilities of the modern university / Derek Bok. – Cambridge, Mass. : Harvard University Press, 1982.
318p; 25cm.
Includes index.
ISBN 0674068998 £11.20

UNIVERSITY AND COLLEGE LIBRARIES

—Information for academic library decision making : the case for organizational information management / Charles R. McClure. – London : Aldwych Press, 1980.
xvi,227p; 22cm.
Bibliography: p211-219. - Includes index.
ISBN 0861720113 £19.50

UNIVERSITY AND COLLEGE LIBRARIES - ENGLAND

—Information technology and polytechnic libraries : discussion papers / Council of Polytechnic Librarians. – S.l. : COPOL, 1984.
28p.
ISBN 0907130062

UNIVERSITY AND COLLEGE LIBRARIES - GREAT BRITAIN

—Living with books / Joseph W. Scott. – London : University of London Library Resources Co-ordinating Committee, 1987.
8 p. – (Publication).
ISBN 0718708032

—SCONUL statistical database part 2 : library operations ... / London : Standing Conference of National & University Libraries, 1986.
ISBN 0951936X

—UC & R newsletter / University, College and Research Section of the Library Association. – v. – London : The Section, 1980.
ISBN 0144056X

UNJUST ENRICHMENT

—Benefits conferred under a mistake of law / Law Reform commission of British Columbia. – Vancouver : Law Reform Commission of British Columbia, 1980.
v,161p. – (Working paper).

UNJUST ENRICHMENT - AUSTRALIA - SOUTH AUSTRALIA

—Report ... relating to the irrecoverability of benefits obtained by reason of mistake of law / Law Reform Committee of South Australia. – Adelaide : Government Printer, 1984.
40p. – (84th report).

UNJUST ENRICHMENT - CANADA

—Unjust enrichment / George B. Klippert. – Toronto : Butterworths, 1983.
xlix,389p.
Explains how Canadian restitution law has developed its own independent and unique voice: increasingly relying less on English authority and more on American jurisprudence. Recognises that the Supreme Court of Canada, in the process of affirming the concept of restitution as a distinct head of civil liability, has also carved a way to an independent interpretation of unjust enrichment.
ISBN 0409842931

UNJUST ENRICHMENT - SRI LANKA

—Some Aspects of the Law of Unjust Enrichment / Colombo : Lake House Investments.

UNLAWFUL ENTRY - GREAT BRITAIN

—Entry, search and seizure / Richard Stone. – London : Sweet & Maxwell, 1985.
lii,326p; 26cm.
Takes into account changes enacted by the Drug Trafficking Offences Act 1986, with a discussion of the application of the Police and Criminal Evidence Act 1985. Considers case law for Anton Piller orders, and Mareva injunctions. Defines the categories of persons and authorities who may lawfully exercise entry powers.
ISBN 0421298901 £35.00

—Law relating to entry, search and seizure / David Feldman. – London : Butterworths, 1986.
500p; 26cm.
Includes index.
ISBN 0406199108 Pbk £27.50

UNMARRIED COUPLES - AUSTRALIA

—Living together : young couples in de facto relationships : a report using Australian Family Formation Project Data / prepared for the Australian Institute of Family Studies. – Melbourne : Australian Institute of Family Stuides, 1986.
ii,50p. – (Working paper).
ISBN 0859244466

UNMARRIED COUPLES - AUSTRALIA - STATISTICS

—Living together : young couples in de facto relationships : a report using Australian Family Formation Project Data / prepared for the Australian Institute of Family Studies. – Melbourne : Australian Institute of Family Stuides, 1986.
ii,50p. – (Working paper).
ISBN 0859244466

UNMARRIED COUPLES - LEGAL STATUS, LAWS, ETC - ENGLAND

—Cohabitees / Stephen Parker. – Chichester : Barry Rose, 1981.
xxii,230p.
Bibliography: p224-225.
ISBN 0859922103

UNTOUCHABLES

—Competing equalities : law and the backward classes in India / Marc Galanter. – Berkeley : University of California Press, 1984.
xxii,625p; 24cm.
Bibliography: p575-611. - Includes index.
ISBN 0520042891 Pbk £38.25

URBAN POLICY

—Cities in the developing world : policies for their equitable and efficient growth / Johannes F. Linn. – Oxford : Published for the World Bank by Oxford University Press, 1983.
xxi,230p; 24cm.
Bibliography: p213-223. - Includes index.
ISBN 0195203828 Hbk Unpriced
ISBN 0195203836 Pbk Unpriced

—Inside Third World cities / Stella Lowder. – London : Routledge, 1988.
xii,292p.
Originally published: London : Croom Helm, 1986. Bibliography: pp.270-286. - Includes index.
ISBN 0415027756 No price

—Urban land policy : issues and opportunities / Harold B. Dunkerley, cordinating editor : with the assistance of Christine M.E. Whitehead. – New York : Oxford University Press for the World Bank, 1983.
viii,214p; 25cm.
Bibliography: p199-206. - Includes index.
ISBN 0195204034 £15.00

URBAN POLICY - GREAT BRITAIN

—Government and urban poverty : inside the policy-making process / Joan Higgins ... et al. – Oxford : Blackwell, 1983.
vi,215p; 22cm.
Bibliography: p202-206. - Includes index.
ISBN 0631129375 Hbk Unpriced
ISBN 063113252X Pbk £5.95

URBAN POLICY - SOUTH AFRICA

—Annual report / Department of Development Planning : Constitutional Development Services. – Pretoria : Government Printer, 1987.
Annual reports of two bodies published together. Text in Afikaans and English.

URBAN RENEWAL - GREAT BRITAIN

—Introduction to urban renewal / Michael S. Gibson, Michael J. Langstaff. – London : Hutchinson, 1982.
384p; 24cm.
ISBN 0091475007

URBANIZATION

—Third World city / David Drakakis-Smith. – London : Methuen, 1987.
vi,116p; 21cm. – (Methuen introductions to development).
Includes bibliography and index.
ISBN 041691960X Pbk No price
ISBN 0416919707 correct

—Urbanisation and planning in the 3rd World : spatial perceptions and public participation / Robert B. Potter. – London : Croom Helm, 1985.
284p; 23cm. – (Croom Helm series in geography and environment).
Bibliography: p254-275. - Includes index.
ISBN 0709920555 £19.95

URBANIZATION – LATIN AMERICA

—Latin American urbanization / Douglas Butterworth, John K. Chance. – Cambridge : Cambridge University Press, 1981.
xi,243p; 24cm.
Bibliography: p216-237. - Includes index.
ISBN 0521237130 Hbk £15.00
ISBN 052128175X Pbk £5.50

URBANIZATION – SOUTH AFRICA

—Commission of Inquiry into Township Establishment and Related Matters / Pretoria : Government Printer, 1984.
2 v.; 30 cm.
Title on added t.p.: Kommissie van Ondersoek na Dorpstigting en Verwante Aangeleenthede. First and second reports of the commission.
ISBN 0621084395 pbk. : v. 2 R3.50 (R4.00 other countries)

USSR

—Soviet Codes of Law / Dordrecht : Kluwer, 1980.
1,288p.
ISBN 9028608109 Hbk £495.00

UTILITARIANISM

—Utilitarianism and co-operation / Donald Regan. – Oxford : Clarendon Press, 1980.
315p.
ISBN 0198246099 £12.50
ISBN 0198246366

UTILITARIANISM – GREAT BRITAIN

—English Utilitarians : by Leslie Stephen / 1. – s.l. : Micro-Offset Books, 1900.
Various pagings.
Complete in 3 vols.. Reproduction of 1950 reprint (New York: Peter Smith) of 1900 original published by Duckworth and Co., London. Includes bibliographical references and index. 3 vols. in one.

UTOPIAS

—Reading Nozick : essays on Anarchy, state and utopia / edited with an introduction by Jeffrey Paul. – Oxford : Basil Blackwell, 1982.
xi,418p; 22cm.
Originally published: Totowa : Rowman & Littlefield, 1981. Bibliography: p412-416.
ISBN 0631129774 Hbk Unpriced
ISBN 0631129782 Pbk Unpriced

VALUATION

—Theory and Practice of Valuation / 2nd ed. – Calcutta : Eastern Law House, 1986.

VALUATION – CANADA

—Canada Valuation Service / Toronto : DeBoo.
ISBN 0888201370 loose £275.00

—Valuation 85 : a Conceptual Outline / Fiona Abbott. – 1st ed. – North Ryde : C.C.H. Australia, 1984.
56p.
ISBN 0887962882 Pbk £5.00

VALUATION – GREAT BRITAIN

—Introduction to Valuation / 2nd ed. – London : Macmillan, 1985.
ISBN 0333384377 Pbk £5.95

—Modern methods of valuation / Davies. – 2nd ed. – London : Estates Gazette, 1981.
ISBN 072820049X Hbk £10.00

—Share Valuation Cases / Harry Booth. – London : Butterworths, 1985.
This work is a compendium of extracts from judgements in cases which deal with principles of share valuation in the United Kingdom. The case extracts are presented in alphabetical order.
ISBN 0406009805 Hbk

—Valuation and development appraisal / London : Estates Gazette, 1982.
ISBN 0728201097 Pbk £16.50

—Valuation and investment appraisal / London : Estates Gazette, 1983.
ISBN 0728200686 Pbk £18.00

—Valuation and selection of convertible bonds / Praeger, 1988.
ISBN 0275924661 Hbk £27.50

—Valuation of property investments / 3rd ed. – London : Estates Gazette, 1984.
ISBN 0728200732 Pbk £10.00

—Valuation : principles into practice / 2nd ed. – London : Estates Gazette, 1984.
ISBN 0728201070 Pbk £22.00

VALUATION – HONG KONG

—Land compensation and valuation law in Hong Kong / Gordon N. Cruden. – Singapore : Butterworths, 1986.
xxxii,476p.
Collation and analysis of relevant statutory and case law. References are made to Hong Kong cases, as well as English, Scottish, Australian, Canadian, and New Zealand cases.
ISBN 0409995258 Hbk £137.5

VALUES

—Journal of applied philosophy : journal of the Society for Applied Philosophy / Abingdon : Carfax, 1984.

VANDALISM

—Implementing crime prevention measures / by Tim Hope. – London : H.M.S.O., 1985.
vi,75p; 25cm.
Examines practicality of crime prevention methods. Considers situational measures aimed at dealing with specifically defined offences and community involvement in prevention of crime. Illustrates difficulties by case histories.
ISBN 0113408129

—Vandalism : a bibliography / Jane Pethick and Catherine J. Matthews : prepared for the Task Force on Vandalism (Ontario), chairman L.A. Beaulieu. – Toronto : Centre of Criminology, University of Toronto, 1980.
x,79p; 28cm.
ISBN 0919584462

VANDALISM – CANADA

—Damage to property - vandalism / Law Reform Commission of Canada. – Ottawa : Canadian Law Reform Commission, 1984.
65,77p; 25cm. – (Working paper).
Cover title: Criminal law - damage to property - vandalism. Added t.p. in French: Les dommages aux biens - le vandalisme. Pages numbered in opposite directions. In English and French.
ISBN 0662528956

VANDALISM – GREAT BRITAIN

—Co-ordinating crime prevention efforts : a Home Office Crime Policy Planning Unit report / by F.J. Gladstone. – London : H.M.S.O., 1980.
v,73p; 25cm. – (Home Office research study).
Bibliography: p69-70. A Home Office Crime Policy Planning Unit report.
ISBN 0113407025 Pbk £3.95

VAT – EUROPE

—Guide to V.A.T. in Europe / Price Waterhouse. – London : Graham & Trotman, 1989.
144; 216mm.
A guide to VAT systems in operation in Western Europe, including the EC member states. Emphasis is placed on registration requirements, and there is an explanation of how to reclaim input tax incurred in each state under the EC 8th and 13th VAT directive procedure. The law is as stated in 1988.
ISBN 1853333069 Hbk £25

—Value Added Taxation in Europe / International Bureau of Fiscal Documentation. – Amsterdam : International Bureau of Fiscal Documentation, 1988.
– (Guides to European Taxation Ser.: Vol. 4).

Supplements-1989 renewal

—VAT : Experience of Some European Countries / Dordrecht : Kluwer, 1982.
ISBN 9065440240 Hbk £155.00

VAT – GREAT BRITAIN

—Butterworth's Handbook on the Value Added Tax Act 1983 / London : Butterworths, 1983.
This book includes the text of the Value Added Tax Act of 1983 and provides useful explanatory notes together with examples and cross-references to relevant tax cases. A destination table and comprehensive index is provided.
ISBN 0406075700 Pbk £21.00

—Butterworth's Handbook on the Value Added Tax Act 1983 / London : Butterworths, 1984.
This handbook contains the full text of the Capital Transfer Tax Act of 1984 for the United Kingdom practitioner. A table of cases, comprehensive index, and a destination table is included in the work.
ISBN 0406505349 Pbk

—Collection of Value Added Tax / London : HMSO, 1984.
ISBN 011260501X Hbk £3.95

—Community Law and United Kingdom Value Added Tax / London : Deloitte Haskins & Sells, 1988.
ISBN 0863491235 Hbk £45.00

—Encyclopaedia of Value Added Tax / London : Sweet & Maxwell, 1988.
ISBN 0421178604 loose £190.00

—Encyclopedia of value added tax / consulting editor: G.S.A. Wheatcroft : general editor: J.F. Avery Jones. – v. – London : Sweet & Maxwell, 1973-.
loose-leaf.
Includes index.

—Grout's value added tax cases 1983 / by Victor Grout : with a foreword by Lord Grantchester : consultant Hugh Mainprice. – 2nd ed. – Croydon : Tolley, 1984.
xv,372p.
Includes index.
ISBN 0854591400

—Guide to New VAT Exemption Rules / Tolley Publishing, 1987.
ISBN 0854593071 Hbk £9.95

—Guide to VAT in Business / London : CCH, 1988.
ISBN 0863251366 Pbk

—HM Customs and Excise Official VAT Guides / Oyez Longman Editorial Staff. – London : Oyez Longman, 1983.
ISBN 0851206832 loose £50.00

—How to live with VAT / Daily Mail. – Maidenhead : McGraw-Hill, 1987.
ISBN 0670849439 Pbk £6.75

—Solicitors and VAT / Gizzi. – London : Butterworths, 1986.
ISBN 0406503605 Pbk £8.75

—Taxation of land transactions / 4th ed. – London : Butterworths, 1988.
ISBN 0406624100 Pbk

—Tolley's value added tax 1986-87 / by Robert Wareham and Patrick Noakes. – Croydon : Tolley, 1986.
vii,488p.
Includes index.
ISBN 0854592423

—Tolley's value added tax 1987-88 / by Robert Wareham and Patrick Noakes. – Croydon : Tolley, 1987.
vii,502p.
Includes index.
ISBN 085459292X

—Tolley's value added tax 1988-89 / by Robert Wareham and Nicholas Bowen. – Croydon : Tolley, 1988.
vii,512p.
Includes index.
ISBN 0854593500

—Tolley's Value Added Tax Cases : 1983 / 3rd ed. – Croydon : Tolley.
530p.
ISBN 0854592970 Hbk £29.95

—Touche Ross VAT : a business by business guide / London : Butterworths, 1988.
ISBN 0406501440 Pbk £23.95

—Value Added Tax Tribunal Reports : 1973-82, 10 Vols. / Professional Books Staff. – Abingdon : Professional Books, 1984.

—Value Added Tax Tribunals Report 1984, 4 parts / London : HMSO.
ISBN 0112604986 Hbk £4.55

Part 2
ISBN 0112604994 Hbk £4.15

Part 3
ISBN 0112605028 Hbk £4.55

Part 4
ISBN 0112605095 Hbk £4.15

—VAT / London : Butterworths, 1984.
ISBN 0406514747 loose £210.00

—VAT and the City / London : CCH, 1987.
ISBN 086325120X Pbk £19.50

—VAT and the New Business / London : CCH, 1987.
ISBN 0863251056 Pbk £12.50

—VAT disputes and how to avoid them / London : CCH, 1986.
ISBN 0863251005 Pbk £12.50

—VAT enforcement and appeals manual / London : Butterworths, 1986.
ISBN 0406504202 Pbk £17.95

—VAT Guide and Casebook / Christopher A. L. Preston. – London : Oyez Longman, 1983.
ISBN 0851206611 loose £50.00

—VAT - Imports and exports / London : CCH, 1987.
ISBN 0863251048 Pbk £15.00

—VAT investigations / Croydon : Tolley, 1988.
ISBN 0854593195 Hbk £13.95

—VAT on construction and development work / Oxford : Blackwell Scientific, 1984.
ISBN 0246122501 Hbk £17.95

—VAT on construction and development work / Philip S.D. King. – London : Granada, 1984.
194p; 24cm.
Includes index.
ISBN 0246122501 Hbk £17.95

—VAT planning / Croydon : Tolley, 1988.
ISBN 0854592989 Pbk £16.95

VAT - UNITED KINGDOM

—Croner's Reference Book for V.A.T. (Value Added Tax) / New Malden : Croner Publications, 1986.

VICTIMS OF CRIME

—From crime policy to victim policy : reorienting the justice system / edited by Ezzat A. Fattah. - Basingstoke : Macmillan, 1986.
300p; 22cm.
Conference papers. Includes index.
ISBN 0333399943 £27.50

VICTIMS OF CRIME - AUSTRALIA

—Women as Victims of Crimes / Canberra : Australian Institute of Criminology.

VICTIMS OF CRIME - AUSTRALIA - VICTORIA

—Report to Parliament upon support services for victims of crime / Legal and Constitutional Committee. - Melbourne : Government Printer, 1987.
xxxii,125p.

VICTIMS OF CRIME - CANADA

—Canadian Federal-Provincial Task Force on Justice for Victims of Crime report : highlights / Canada. - Ottawa : Solicitor General Canada, 1983.
35,29p.
With French t.p.: Rapport du Groupe d'Etude Federal-Provincial Canadien sur la Justice pour les Victimes d'Actes Criminels: points saillants. English and French text.
ISBN 0662526007

—Overview and annotated bibliography of the needs of crime victims / Colin Meredith. - Ottawa : Ministry of the Solicitor General, 1984.
138p. - (User report).

—Report / Canadian Federal-Provincial Task Force on Justice for Victims of Crime. - Ottawa : Canadian Government Publishing Centre, 1983.
viii,202p.
ISBN 0660114135

—Services to victims and witnesses of crime in Canada / by Geoff Norquay, Richard Weiler. - Ottawa : Communication Division, Solicitor General Canada, 1981.
163 p.; 28 cm.
'A research report prepared by the Canadian Council on Social Development under contract with the Research Division, Ministry of the Solicitor General of Canada'-Verso t.p.
ISBN 0662117735 pbk.

—Victims and witnesses of crime in Canada / by Dick Weiler and Jean-Guy Desgagne of the Canadian Council on Social Development. - Ottawa : Ministry of Supply and Services, Canada, 1984.
98p,111p.
With French t.p.: Victimes et temoins d'infractions penales au Canada. French and English text.
ISBN 0662530136

—Victims Before the Law / Toronto : Butterworths, 1983.
320p.

—View from the shadows : the Ministry of the Solicitor General of Canada and the making of the justice for victims of crime initiative / Paul Rock. - Oxford : Clarendon, 1986.
xix,396p; 22cm. - (Oxford socio-legal studies).
An empirical study of the evolution of the Canadian Solicitor General's Justice for Victims of Crime Initiative. Focuses on the complexity of policies for victims, and also the more general problems of the policy-making process in a federal government.
ISBN 0198255233 Hbk £35

VICTIMS OF CRIME - GREAT BRITAIN

—Crime victims : needs, services and the voluntary sector / R.I. Mawby, M.L. Gill. - London : Tavistock, 1987.
ix,261p; 22cm.
Bibliography: p241-254. - Includes index.
ISBN 0422614505 Pbk No price

—Effects of crime and the work of victims support schemes / Mike Maguire and Claire Corbett. - Aldershot : Gower, 1987.
xiii,276p; 23cm.
Bibliography: p263-276.
ISBN 0566054124 £17.50

—Remedies for victims of crime / Tucker. - London : Legal Action Group, 1984.
ISBN 0905099060 Pbk £5.00

—Victims in the criminal justice system / Joanna Shapland, Jon Willmore, Peter Duff. - Aldershot : Gower, 1985.
vi,203p; 23cm.
Bibliography: p195-201. - Includes index.
ISBN 0566008947 Hbk £20.45
ISBN 0566008777 Pbk £8.95

—Victims of crime : the dimensions of risk / by Michael R. Gottfredson. - London : H.M.S.O., 1984.
iv,54p; 25cm.
Results of a survey of groups most at risk from crime in England and Wales. Examines lifestyles related to high risks of crime. Provides information for planners of crime-prevention policy.
ISBN 0113407750

VICTIMS OF CRIME - UNITED STATES

—Overview and annotated bibliography of the needs of crime victims / Colin Meredith. - Ottawa : Ministry of the Solicitor General, 1984.
138p. - (User report).

VILLAGES - ENGLAND

—Law of commons and village greens / by Ian Campbell and Paul Clayden. - 3rd ed. - Henley-on-Thames : Commons, Open Spaces and Footpaths Preservation Society, 1980.
80p.
Includes index.

VIOLENCE

—Dangerousness : problems of assessment and prediction / edited by John W. Hinton. - London : Allen & Unwin, 1983.
x,177p; 25cm.
Bibliography: p158-171. - Includes index.
ISBN 0043640214

—Predicting violent behavior : an assessment of clinical techniques / John Monahan : introduction by Stanley L. Brodsky : foreword by Saleem A. Shah. - Beverly Hills : Sage, 1981.
183p; 23cm. - (Sage library of social research 114).
Bibliography: p171-181.
ISBN 0803913133 Hbk Unpriced
ISBN 0803913141 Pbk Unpriced

—Problems in the concepts and definitions of aggression, violence, and some related terms / J.M.G. van der Dennen. - Groningen, Netherlands : Rijksuniversiteit Groningen, Polemologisch Instituut, 1980.
154p. - (Interne publicaties).
Bibliography: pp.129-154.

—United Nations and the control of international violence : a legal and political analysis / John F. Murphy. - Manchester : Manchester University Press, 1983.
xii,212p; 24cm.
Includes index.
ISBN 0719009421 £22.50
ISBN 0865980799

VIOLENCE - GREAT BRITAIN

—Aggression and Crimes of Violence / 2nd ed. - Oxford : Oxford University Press, 1986.
ISBN 0195039440 Pbk £9.00

VIOLENCE IN SPORTS

—Papers from the European Conference on Football Violence : held at the Tickled Trout Hotel, Salmesbury, Preston, Lancashire, 10-13 April 1987 / edited by Tim O'Brien. - Preston? : Lancashire Polytechnic, 1987.
81p.
Bibliographies.
ISBN 090669406X

VIS MAJOR (CIVIL LAW)

—Comparative report on force majeure in Western Europe / edited by Matti Kurkela. - Jyvaskylassa : Union of the Finnish Lawyers Publishing Co., 1982.
134p.
ISBN 951640152X

VOCATIONAL GUIDANCE - ENGLAND

—Career in law / by Brian Hogan. - London : Sweet & Maxwell, 1981.
vii,98p; 18cm.
Bibliography: p92-95. - Includes index.
ISBN 0421280506 Pbk £1.95

VOLUNTEERS - GREAT BRITAIN

—Recruiting volunteers / Hilary Jackson. - London : Home Office, 1985.
iv,50p.
Bibliography: p.49-50.
ISBN 0862521769

—Voluntary but not amateur / London : London Voluntary, 1988.
ISBN 0901171662 Pbk £6.00

WAGES

—Impact of residual disability from illness and injury on the distribution of household income : a lognormal approach / by Yvonne Brittan and Ioannis G. Vlachonikolis. - Oxford : SSRC-Social Science Research Council, 1981.
23p. - (Working paper).

—Revision of the Convention Concerning Statistics of Wages and Hours of Work, 1983 (No. 63) / Geneva : International Labour Office, 1985.

—Revision of the Convention Concerning Statistics of Wages and Hours of Work / Geneva : International Labour Office, 1984.

WAGES - AUSTRALIA

—Wage indexation and its aftermath / by the CCH industrial law editors. - North Ryde, N.S.W. : CCH Australia, 1981.
18p.
Forms part of the service to CCH Australian labour law reporter.
ISBN 0869033476

WAGES - CANADA

—Canadian Payroll Manual / Toronto : DeBoo.
ISBN 088820261X loose £250.00
French edition
This manual covers legislation from the federal government and from all the provinces. Among the topics discussed are labor standards and year-end reporting. Regular updates, a complimentary newsletter, and a client hotline are provided.
ISBN 0888202628 loose £250.00

—Wage Controls in Canada, 1975-78 : a Study of Public Decision Making / Gene R. Swimmer. - Ottawa : Institute for Research on Public Policy, 1980.
xxxiv, 186p.
ISBN 0920380506 Hbk £11.95

WAGES - FRINGE BENEFITS - GREAT BRITAIN

—Fringe benefits : a specially commissioned report / by Robert Maas. - 3rd ed. - London : Oyez Longman, 1984.
xvii,111 leaves; 30cm. - (Oyez Longman intelligence reports).
ISBN 0851209262 spiral No price

—Share options and incentives for directors and employees / Tolley Publishing, 1986.
ISBN 085459180X Pbk £7.95

—Share schemes for directors and employees / London : Butterworths, 1985.
ISBN 0406501203 Pbk £29.95

—Survey of company car schemes / 7th ed. - Tolley Publishing, 1987.
ISBN 0854593144 Hbk £29.50

WAGES - GREAT BRITAIN

—Case for a national minimum wage / Chris Pond and Steve Winyard. - London : Low Pay Unit, 1983.
64p. - (Pamphlet).
Bibliography: p61-63.

—Consultative paper on wages councils / London : Department of Employment, 1985.
13p.

—Equal pay and the industrial tribunals / London : Sweet & Maxwell, 1984.
80p.
ISBN 0421328002 Pbk £7.15

—Guide to the Wages Act 1986 / Fraser P. Davidson. - London : Financial Training, 1986.
136p; 22cm.
Includes index. Includes the text of the Wages Act 1986.
ISBN 1851850473 Pbk £8.50

—Income during initial sickness : a new strategy ... / Department of Health and Social Security. - London : H.M.S.O, 1980.
iii,26p; 25cm. - (Cmnd. 7864).
ISBN 0101786409 sd £2.00

—Labour market structure, industrial organisation and low pay / DAE Labour Studies Group : Christine Craig ... et al. - Cambridge : Cambridge University Press, 1982.
xi,165p; 24cm. - (Occasional paper).
Bibliography: p160-165.
ISBN 0521245796 Unpriced

—Low Pay and Poverty in the United Kingdom / London : Policy Studies Institute, 1981.

—Low pay check : reforming the Truck Acts / Dominic Byrne. - London : Low Pay Unit, 1983.
24p.

—Low Pay or No Pay? A Review of the Theory and Practice of Minimum-Wage Laws / S. R. Dennison. - London : Institute of Economic Affairs, 1984.
ISBN 0255361750 Pbk £2.50

—Low Wages, Family Circumstances and Minimum Wage Legislation / London : Policy Studies Institute, 1985.
97p. - (Family Income Support Part 10).

—PAYE Audits / London : Butterworths, 1988.
ISBN 0406263000 Pbk

—Payment Systems and Productivity / Thorpe. - London : Macmillan, 1986.
ISBN 333394828 Hbk £29.50

—Payroll Handbook / 2nd ed. - Croydon : Tolley.
336p.
Relates legal, financial and adminstrative problems of payroll managers and departments. Includes provisions of Finance Act 1988.
ISBN 0854593632 Hbk £21.00

—Payroll Handbook / Tolley Publishing, 1987.
ISBN 0854592601 Pbk £16.95

—Policies Against Low Pay : An International Perspective / London : Policy Studies Institute, 1984.
208p. – (PSI Research Papers).

—Taxation of fringe benefits / Sargent. – London : CCH, 1988.
ISBN 0863251455 Pbk £8.50

—Wage Discrimination : The Sex Discrimination Issue of the 1980's / London : Pinter Publishers Ltd, 1984.
200p.
ISBN 0861872487 Hbk £15.00

—Wages and the law / London : Shaw & Sons, 1988.
ISBN 0721911102 Pbk

—Who needs the wages councils? / Low Pay Unit. – London : Low Pay Unit, 1983.
56p. – (Low pay unit publication).
Bibliography: p54.

WAGES – INDIA

—Commentaries on Payment of Wages Act, 1936 / 3rd ed. – Lucknow : Eastern Book Company, 1983.
814p.

—Minimum Wages Act : With Central and U.P. Rules and Notifications Fixing Minimum Wages in Various Industries and Establishments / 5th ed. – Lucknow : Eastern Book Company, 1985.

—Payment of Wages Act (Act 4 of 1936) : with Central State Rules / 3rd ed. – Allahabad : Law Book Company, 1987.
915p.

WALES

—Welsh Development Agency Act 1974 / London : HMSO, 1983.
ISBN 0118027255 Hbk £1.25

—Welsh Veto : The Wales Act 1978 and the Referendum / J. Barry Jones. – Cardiff : University of Wales, 1983.
238p.
ISBN 0708308317 Hbk £11.95

WAR

—Basic Rules of the Geneva Conventions and Their Additional Protocols / Geneva : Comite International de la Croix-Rouge, 1983.
63p.

—Causes of wars : and other essays / Michael Howard. – London : Temple Smith, 1983.
190p.
ISBN 0851172229 £10.00

—Commentary on the Additional Protocols of 8 June 1977 to the Geneva Conventions of 12 August 1949 / Geneva : Comite International de la Croix-Rouge, 1987.
xxxv, 1,625p.

—Constraints of the Waging of War / Geneva : Comite International de la Croix-Rouge, 1987.
175p.

—Constraints on the Waging of War / Dordrecht : Kluwer, 1987.
175p.
ISBN 0898389240 Pbk Gld85.00

—Cultural norms, war and the environment / edited by Arthur H. Westing. – Oxford : Oxford University Press, 1988.
xiv,177p.
On t.p.: Sipri, Stockholm International Peace Research Institute; UNEP, United Nations Environment Programme. Includes bibliographical references and index.
ISBN 0198291256 Hbk £42.00

—Documents on the Laws of War / Guelff. – Oxford : Oxford University Press, 1982.
ISBN 0198761171 Hbk £20.00
ISBN 019876118X Pbk £12.95

—Documents on the Laws of War / Richard Guelff. – Geneva : Comite International de la Croix-Rouge, 1982.
498p.

—Geneva Conventions of August 12, 1949 / repr. 1986. – Geneva : Comite International de la Croix-Rouge.
245p.

—Handbook on the Law of War for Armed Forces / Geneva : Comite International de la Croix-Rouge, 1987.
254p.

—How wars end : the United Nations and the termination of armed conflicts, 1946-1964 / Oxford : Clarendon Press, 1982.
400p.
ISBN 0198274246 £35.00

Vol.2 1982.
720p.
ISBN 0198274629 £45.00

—Humanity in warfare : International law conflicts / Methuen, 1983.
ISBN 0416348106 Pbk £7.50

—Justice in Wartime / London : Spokesman Books, 1983.
232p.
ISBN 0851240895 Hbk £6.00

—Law of War and the Armed Forces / 2nd ed. – Geneva : Comite International de la Croix-Rouge, 1981.
44p.

—Laws of Armed Conflicts : a Collection of Conventions, Resolutions and Other Documents / J. Toman. – 3rd rev. ed. – Dordrecht : Kluwer.
958p.
ISBN 9028633065 Hbk £375.00

—New Zealand in Vietnam : a Study of the Use of Force in International Law / Palmerston North : Dunmore Press Ltd., 1987.
ISBN 0864690584 Pbk £16.45

—Science of peace / by J.G. Starke. – 2nd ed. – Sydney : Law Books, 1986.
xvi,193p.
Previous ed. published by A.W. Sijthoff, 1968. Bibliography: p.180-183. Includes index.
ISBN 0949553298

—State of emergency and permissible measures of derogation / A. M. Singhvi. – Bombay : Lawasia-Bar Association of India, 1986.
45p.
Working paper of the Joint Regional Conference (Asia) of the International Bar Association, Law Asia and Bar Association of India (Bombay, Feb.22-23, 1986) on Topic 2 'International support for protection of human rights'. Includes references, p30-41.

—Waging war : a philosophical introduction / Ian Clark. – Oxford : Clarendon Press, 1988.
154 p.; 23 cm.
Bibliography: p. 143-147. Includes index.
ISBN 0198273258

—War and conscience in the nuclear age / Sydney D. Bailey. – Basingstoke : Macmillan, 1987.
xviii,210p; 23cm.
Bibliography: p200-202. - Includes index.
ISBN 0333436857 Hbk £25.00
ISBN 0333443845 Pbk £12.95

—War in international society : a study in international sociology / Evan Luard. – London : Tauris, 1986.
468p.
Includes bibliographical references and index.
ISBN 1850430128 £24.50

—War, law and labour / Oxford : Oxford University Press, 1987.
ISBN 0198255381 Hbk £27.50

WAR – AUSTRALIA

—Emergency powers / by H. P. Lee. – Sydney : Law Book Company, 1984.
xl,334p.
Includes index. Bibliography: pxxxiii-xl.
ISBN 0455202729

WAR – ENGLAND

—Trial and error : the Maguires, the Guildford pub bombings and British justice / Robert Kee. – London : Hamish Hamilton, 1986.
284p; 22cm.
Includes index.
ISBN 0241119588 £10.95

WAR – GREAT BRITAIN

—Emergency powers in peacetime / by David Bonner. – London : Sweet & Maxwell, 1985.
220p; 22cm.
Includes index.
ISBN 0421310707 Hbk £14.00
ISBN 0421310804 Pbk £8.00

WAR – NORTHERN IRELAND

—Use and abuse of emergency legislation in Northern Ireland / Dermot P. J. Walsh. – London? : Cobden Trust, 1983.
138p.
ISBN 0900137207

WAR CRIMES

—Commission of Inquiry on War Criminals Report / Ottawa : Canadian Government Publishing Centre, 1986.
966p.
ISBN 0660121727 Pbk £39.95

—Nuremberg and after : the continuing history of war crimes and crimes against humanity / by Geoffrey Best. – Reading : University of Reading, 1984.
29p.
ISBN 0704902141

—Prevent the Crime of Silence : The Report of the Vietnam War Crimes Tribunal / Peter Limqueco. – London : Spokesman Books, 1983.
384p.
ISBN 0713901802 Hbk £10.00

—War Crimes in Vietnam / Vladimir Dedijer. – London : Spokesman Books.
40p.

—Witness of war crimes in Lebanon / testimony given to the Nordic Commission, Oslo, October 1982. – London : EAFORD, 1983.
xviii,146p; 22cm.
ISBN 0863720056 Pbk £4.50

WAR (INTERNATIONAL LAW)

—Arab-Israeli conflict : a politico-legal analysis / J.R. Gainsborough. – Aldershot : Gower, 1987.
xxxv,345p; 23cm.
Bibliography: p319-334. - Includes index.
ISBN 0566008181 £25.00

—Commentary on the additional protocols of 8 June 1977 to the Geneva Conventions of 12 August 1949 / Claude Pilloud ... et al : editors, Yves Sandoz, Christophe Swinarski, Bruno Zimmerman. – Geneva : International Committee of the Red Cross, 1987.
xxxv,1625p.
Bibliography: pp.1581-1596. - Includes index.
ISBN 9024734606 Hbk £250.00

—Conference on the application of international humanitarian law : March 12th, 1986, London SW1 / report on the proceedings by Michael A. Meyer. – s.l. : s.n., 1986.
23,vp.
'Organised by the British Red Cross Society'. - Front cover.

—Current legal regulation of the use of force / edited by A. Cassese. – Dordrecht : Martinus Nijhoff, 1986.
xiv,536p.
Includes bibliographical references.

—Documents on the laws of war / edited by Adam Roberts and Richard Guelff. – Oxford : Clarendon Press, 1981.
xiii,498p.
Bibliography: p483-488.
ISBN 019876118X pbk.

—Humanity in warfare : the modern history of the international law of armed conflicts / Geoffrey Best. – London : Weidenfeld and Nicolson, 1980.
xi,400p; 23cm.
Bibliography: p.376-387. - Includes index.
ISBN 0297777378

—International law and the use of force by national liberation movements / Heather A. Wilson. – Oxford : Clarendon, 1988.
208p; 24cm.
Includes bibliography and index.
ISBN 0198255705 £22.50

—Law of war / Ingrid Detter de Lupis. – Cambridge : Cambridge University Press, 1987.
xx,411p; 23cm.
Bibliography: p367-406. - Includes index.
ISBN 0521343372 Hbk £40.00
ISBN 0521348382 Pbk £15.00

—Laws of armed conflicts : a collection of conventions, resolutions and other documents / edited by Dietrich Schindler and Jiri Toman. – 2nd rev. ed. – Alphen aan den Rijn : Sitjhoff & Noordhoft, 1981.
xxxiv,933p.
ISBN 9028601996

—Laws of armed conflicts : a collection of conventions, resolutions and other documents / edited by Dietrich Schindler and Jiri Toman. – 3rd rev. ed. – Dordrecht : Nijhoff, 1986.
xxxix,1033p.
Includes index.
ISBN 9024733065

—Protocol additional to the Geneva conventions for the protection of victims of international armed conflicts and the United Nations Convention on the Law of the Sea : repercussions on the law of naval warfare : report to the Committee for the Protection of Human Life in Armed Conflict of the International Society for Military Law and Law of War / by Elmar Rauch. – Berlin : Duncker & Humblot, 1984.
165p; 24cm.
ISBN 3428057031

—Sir William Scott, Lord Stowell / Cambridge : Cambridge University Press.
Analyses Sir William Scott's work as a judge of the admiralty court during the Revolutionary and Napoleonic wars. Illustrates his contribution to the development of the international law of war, especially concerning neutral and belligerent rights at sea.
ISBN 0521340764

—War and conscience in the nuclear age / Sydney D. Bailey. – Basingstoke : Macmillan, 1987.
xviii,210p; 23cm.
Bibliography: p200-202. - Includes index.
ISBN 0333436857 Hbk £25.00
ISBN 0333443845 Pbk £12.95

—War crimes and laws of war / Donald A. Wells. – Lanham : University Press of America, 1984.
x,137p; 24cm.
Bibliography: p123-132. - Includes index.
ISBN 081913841X Hbk No price
ISBN 0819138428 Pbk £8.25

WAR VICTIMS

—Application of humanitarian law : selective bibliography prepared by the Peace Palace Library / Center for Studies and Research of the Hague Academy of International Law : bibliographie selective preparee par la Bibliotheque du Palais de la Paix : Centre d'Etude et de Recherche de l'Academie du droit Internationale de la Haye. – The Hague : Center for Studies and Research of the Hague Academy of International Law, 1986.
80p.
Preliminary material in English and French.

—Assisting the victims of armed conflict and other disasters / Dordrecht : Martinus Nijhoff, 1989.
264.
Contains papers given at the conference, with brief summaries, and annexes giving the text of treaty provisions and other documents. Goes beyond armed conflict, and looks at other disasters as well, including problems of offering humanitarian assistance in such situations.
ISBN 0792301633 Hbk £47.50

—Conference on the application of international humanitarian law : March 12th, 1986, London SW1 / report on the proceedings by Michael A. Meyer. – s.l. : s.n., 1986.
23,vp.
'Organised by the British Red Cross Society'. - Front cover.

—Development and principles of international humanitarian law : course given in July 1982 at the University of Strasbourg as part of the courses organized by the International Institute of Human Rights / by Jean Pictet. – Dordrecht Netherlands : M. Nijhoff, 1985.
108p.
Bibliography. Translation of: Developpement et principes du droit international humanitaire.
ISBN 9024731992 Pbk £49.50

—Development of international humanitarian law / by Geza Herczegh. – Budapest : Akademiai Kiado, 1984.
239p.
Bibliography: p231-235.
ISBN 9630534487

—Enforcement of human rights in peace and war and the future of humanity / Nagendra Singh. – Dordrecht : Nijhoff, 1986.
ISBN 9024733022 Hbk

—Etudes et essais sur le droit international humanitaire et sur les principes de la Croix-Rouge en l'honneur de Jean Pictet : Studies and essays on international humanitarian law and Red Cross principles in honour of Jean Pictet / Christophe Swinarski, redacteur. – The Hague : Martinus Nijhoff, 1984.
English and French. Bibliography.
ISBN 9024730791 Pbk £150.00

—International humanitarian assistance : disaster relief actions in international law and organization / Peter Macalister-Smith. – Hague : M. Nijhoff Publishers, 1985.
260p.
ISBN 9024729939 Hbk £130.00

—Law of non-international armed conflict : Protocol II to the 1949 Geneva conventions / edited by Howard S. Levie. – Dordrecht : M. Nijhoff, 1987.
xiii, 635 p.; 25 cm.
'A record of certain of the proceedings of the 1974-1977 Geneva Diplomatic Conference on the Reaffirmation and Development of International Humanitarian Law Applicable in Armed Conflicts which drafted the 1977 Protocol additional to the Geneva conventions of 12 August 1949, and relating to the protection of victims of non-international armed conflicts (Protocol II)'–T.p. verso. Includes indexes.
ISBN 9024734916 Hbk £275.00

—New Rules for Victims of Armed Conflicts : Commentary on the Two 1977 Protocols Additional to the Geneva Convention of 1949 / Karl J. Partsch. – Dordrecht : Kluwer, 1981.
1,100p.
ISBN 9024725372 Hbk Gld340.00

—New rules for victims of armed conflicts : commentary on the two 1977 protocols additional to the Geneva Conventions of 1949 / by Michael Bothe, Karl Josef Partsch, Waldemar A. Solf, with the collaboration of Martin Eaton. – The Hague : Martinus Nijhoff Publishers, 1982.
xxi,746p.
Bibliography: p. 707-716.
ISBN 9024725372

WARDSHIP - GREAT BRITAIN

—Wardship Proceedings / 2nd ed. – London : Oyez Longman, 1982.
– (Oyez Longman Practice Note Ser.: No. 21).
ISBN 0851206360 Hbk £7.95

WARRANTS (LAW) - AUSTRALIA

—Reference on service and execution of warrants and writs of attachment / Australian Law Reform Commission. – Sydney : The Commission, 1984.
v,109,6p.
Bibliography: p.109.

WARRANTS (LAW) - CANADA

—Issuance of search warrants : a manual / prepared for the Law Reform Commission of Canada by Lee Paikin. – Ottawa : The Commission, 1980.
iv,119p. – (Study paper).
ISBN 0662109635

WARRANTS (LAW) - CANADA - CANADA

—Report on writs of assistance and telewarrants / Law Reform Commission of Canada. – Ottawa : The Commission, 1983.
110,124p; 25cm. – (Report).
Cover-title: Writs of assistance and telewarrants. Added t.p. in French: Rapport sur le mandat de main-forte et le telemandat. Pages numbered in opposite directions. In English and French.
ISBN 0662525159

WASTE DISPOSAL

—Industrial hazardous waste management / Paris : United Nations Environment Programme, 1983.
79p.
Includes bibliogrpahical references.

—Inter-Governmental Conference on the Convention on the Dumping of Wastes at Sea /. – London : International Maritime Organization.

Russian Edition

Spanish Edition

—Legal regime of the protection of the Mediterranean against pollution from land-based sources / Dublin : Tycooly International, 1984.
256p.
ISBN 0907567827 Hbk £19.50
ISBN 0907567835 Pbk £11.50

—Settlement of international water law disputes in international drainage basins / by B.R. Chauhan. – Berlin : Schmidt, 1981.
480p; 21cm.
ISBN 3503019294

WASTE DISPOSAL - AUSTRALIA - VICTORIA

—Fourteenth report to Parliament on subordinate legislation concerning : M.M.B.W. By-law no. 250: Trade Waste / Legal and Constitutional Committee. – Melbourne : Government Printer, 1988.
v,5p.
Includes the text of the By-law.

WASTE DISPOSAL - CANADA - ONTARIO

—Drainage Cases : Ontario 1898-1903, 2 Vols. / Scully. – Agincourt : Carswell, 1983.

WASTE DISPOSAL - ENGLAND

—Law of sewers and drains under the Public Health Acts / by J.F. Garner. – 6th ed. – London : Shaw & Sons, 1981.
xxxviii,206p; 22cm.
Previous ed.: 1975. Includes index. .
ISBN 0721905811 Pbk Unpriced

WASTE DISPOSAL - GREAT BRITAIN

—Disposal of Abandoned Vehicles and Other Refuse / London : Shaw & Sons, 1981.
– (Shaway Guide: No. 4).
ISBN 0721908756 Pbk £2.50

—Eleventh report : managing waste : the duty of care / Richard Southwood. – London : HMSO, 1986.
Chairman: Sir Richard Southwood.
ISBN 0101967500

—Landfilling wastes / London : HMSO, 1986.
ISBN 0117518913

—Managing waste : the duty of care : the Government's response to the eleventh report of the Royal Commission on Environmental Pollution / Central Directorate of Environmental Protection, Department of the Environment. – London : H.M.S.O., 1986.
ISBN 0117518999

—Water and sewerage law : consultation paper / Department of the Environment, Welsh Office. – London : Department of the Environment, 1986.
44p.

WASTE DISPOSAL - NETHERLANDS

—Law Relating to Transport of Dangerous Wastes, Netherlands / V. di Martino. – Luxembourg : Office for Official Publications of the European Communities, 1987.
132p.
ISBN 9282567575 Pbk £450.00

WASTE DISPOSAL - UNITED KINGDOM

—Law Relating to Transport of Dangerous Wastes, United Kingdom / V. di Martino. – Luxembourg : Office for Official Publications of the European Communities, 1987.
104p.
ISBN 9282567524 Pbk £350.00

WASTE (LAW) - CANADA - MANITOBA

—Report on small projects / Manitoba Law Reform Commission. – Winnipeg : The Commission, 1985.
iv,48p. – (Report).
Includes bibliographical references.
ISBN 0771101074

WASTE PRODUCTS - GREAT BRITAIN

—Landfilling wastes / London : HMSO, 1986.
ISBN 0117518913

WASTE RECYCLING - GREAT BRITAIN

—Eleventh report : managing waste : the duty of care / Richard Southwood. – London : HMSO, 1986.
Chairman: Sir Richard Southwood.
ISBN 0101967500

—Resource recovery : a report for the Royal Commission on Environmental Pollution / prepared by Environmental Resources Limited. – 1. – London : HMSO, 1986.
various pagings.
ISBN 0117301329

WATER

—International groundwater resources law / by Julio A. Barberis for the Legislation Branch, FAO Legal Office. – Rome : Food and Agriculture Organization of the United Nations, 1986.
vii,67p. – (Legislative study).
ISBN 925102507X

—Law of international water resources : some general conventions, declarations, and resolutions adopted by governments, international legal institutions, and international organizations, on the management of international water resources / compiled by Dante A. Caponera. – Rome : Food and Agriculture Organization of the United Nations, 1980.
xi, 324 p.; 28 cm.
Includes bibliographical references.
ISBN 9251010366 pbk.

—Settlement of international water law disputes in international drainage basins / by B.R. Chauhan. – Berlin : Schmidt, 1981.
480p; 21cm.
ISBN 3503019294

—Water law in selected European Countries : (Cyprus, Finland, the Netherlands, Union of Soviet Socialist Republics, Yugoslavia) / Food and Agriculture Organization. – Rome : Food and Agriculture Organization of the United Nations, 1983.
ISBN 9251014906

WATER - AFRICA

—Africa's shared water resources : legal and institutional aspects of the Nile, Niger and Senegal river systems / by Bonaya Godana. – London : Pinter, 1985.
220p; 23cm.
Includes bibliography and index.
ISBN 086187563X £17.50

WATER - AUSTRALIA - VICTORIA

—Managing the water industry : the accounting, reporting and auditing dimension : a report to the Public Bodies Review Committee / from E. McL. Holmes. – Melbourne : Public Bodies Review Committee, 1982.
xi,237p.

WATER - CANADA

—Interjurisdictional Issues in Canadian Water Management / Calgary : Canadian Institute of Resources Law.
127p.
ISBN 0919269273 Hbk £22.00

WATER - CANADA - ONTARIO

—Ontario Water Resources Act : Revised Regulations of Ontario, 1980 / Office of the Legislative Assembly (Ontario). – Ontario : Ontario Government Publications Service, 1983.
199p.

WATER - CARIBBEAN

—Water Resources Legislation and Administration in Selected Caribbean Countries / Geneva : United Nations Publications.
ISBN 9211231051 Hbk £16.50

WATER - ENGLAND

—Aspects of water law / by A.S. Wisdom. – Chichester : Barry Rose, 1981.
xxi,102p; 21cm.
Includes index.
ISBN 0859921549 Pbk £12.50

—Water law : principles and practice / Richard Macrory. – London : Longman Professional, 1985.
xiii,167p; 22cm.
ISBN 0851209556

WATER - GREAT BRITAIN

—Law and Management of Water Resources and Supply / Skeet. – London : Shaw & Sons, 1981.
ISBN 0721909108 Pbk £16.00

—Law and Management of Water Resources and Supply / L. Skeet. – London : Shaw & Sons, 1981.
ISBN 0721909108 Pbk £16.00

—Privatisation of the Water Authorities in England and Wales / presented to Parliament by the Secretary of State for the Environment ... et al. ... - London : H.M.S.O., 1986.
iv,27p.
ISBN 0101973403

—Water and sewerage law : consultation paper / Department of the Environment, Welsh Office. - London : Department of the Environment, 1986.
44p.

—Water law / 2nd ed. - London : Longman Professional, 1985.
ISBN 0851209556 Pbk £19.95

WATER - INDIA
—Water (Prevention and Control of Pollution) Act, 1974 / 1982 repr. - Lucknow : Eastern Book Company, 1984.
147p.

WATER - ISLAMIC COUNTRIES
—Water Laws in Moslem Countries, Vol. 2 / Rome : FAO, Food and Agricultural Organization of the United Nations, 1978.
314p.
ISBN 9251005362 Hbk £19.50

WATER - MALAYSIA
—Explanatory Handbook on the Water Supply Rules / Kuala Lumpur : International Law Books Services.

WATER POLLUTION
—Environment and enforcement : regulation and the social definition of pollution / Keith Hawkins. - Oxford : Clarendon Press, 1983.
xvi,253p.
Includes index. Bibliography: p235-247.
ISBN 0198275145 pbk.

—Nitrate in water : a report of the Nitrate Coordination Group / Central Directorate of Environmental Protection, Department of the Environment. - London : H.M.S.O., 1986.
ISBN 0117518662

—Pollution of international watercourses : search for substantive rules and principles of law / by J.G. Lammers. - The Hague : M. Nijhoff, 1984.
xxvi, 724 p.; 25 cm.
Includes indexes. Bibliography: p. 663-703.
ISBN 9024729556 Hbk £275.00

WATER POLLUTION - ASIA
—Water management and environmental protection in Asia and the Pacific / edited by Ichiro Kato ... et al. - Tokyo : University of Tokyo Press, 1983.
x, 202 p.; 24 cm.
Includes bibliographies and index.
ISBN 0860083357 Y5000

WATER POLLUTION - GHANA
—Ghana, water supply and control : a record and analysis of legislation / by A.J. Adamson ... et al. - London : Commonwealth Secretariat, 1985.
xv, 133 p.; 30 cm.
Bibliography: p. 113-122. Includes indexes.
ISBN 085092278X pbk. £10.00

WATER POLLUTION - GREAT BRITAIN
—Water and the environment : the implementation of Part II of the Control of Pollution Act 1974 : joint circular / from the Department of the Environment and Welsh Office. - London : H.M.S.O., 1984.
- (Circular).
ISBN 0117517437

—Water environment : the next steps : the Government's proposals for environmental protection under a privatised water industry / Department of the Environment, Welsh Office. - London? : The Department, 1986.
44p.

—Water pollution law / by William Howarth. - London : Shaw, 1988.
xxxvii,608p.
Bibliography: p.580-594. - Includes index.
ISBN 0721911005 £19.95

—Water pollution law / London : Shaw & Sons, 1988.
ISBN 0721911005 Hbk £19.95

WATER POLLUTION - JAPAN
—Water management and environmental protection in Asia and the Pacific / edited by Ichiro Kato ... et al. - Tokyo : University of Tokyo Press, 1983.
x, 202 p.; 24 cm.
Includes bibliographies and index.
ISBN 0860083357 Y5000

WATER POLLUTION - UNITED STATES
—Water management and environmental protection in Asia and the Pacific / edited by Ichiro Kato ... et al. - Tokyo : University of Tokyo Press, 1983.
x, 202 p.; 24 cm.
Includes bibliographies and index.
ISBN 0860083357 Y5000

WATER-RIGHTS - CANADA
—Aboriginal Water Rights in Canada : a Study of Aboriginal Title to Water and Indian Water Rights / Calgary : Canadian Institute of Resources Law.
231p.
ISBN 0919269230 Hbk £30.00

—Framework of Water Rights Legislation in Canada / Calgary : Canadian Institute of Resources Law.
103p.
ISBN 0919269214 Hbk £20.00

WATER-RIGHTS - NEW ZEALAND
—Law relating to water courses : interim report / Property Law and Equity Reform Committee. - Wellington : The Committee, 1983.
15,9,2,8p.

WATER-RIGHTS (INTERNATIONAL LAW)
—Law of international water resources : some general conventions, declarations, and resolutions adopted by governments, international legal institutions, and international organizations, on the management of international water resources / compiled by Dante A. Caponera. - Rome : Food and Agriculture Organization of the United Nations, 1980.
xi, 324 p.; 28 cm.
Includes bibliographical references.
ISBN 9251010366 pbk.

—Settlement of international water law disputes in international drainage basins / by B.R. Chauhan. - Berlin : Schmidt, 1981.
480p; 21cm.
ISBN 3503019294

—Systematic index of international water resources treaties, declarations, acts and cases by basin / Repertoire systematique par bassin de traites, declarations, textes legislatifs et jurisprudence concernant les ressources en eau internationales. - Rome : Food and Agriculture Organization of the United Nations, 1984.
xxxiii,332p. - (Legislative study).
Explanatory text in English, French and Spanish.
ISBN 9250021895

WELFARE LAW - CANADA
—Annotated Child Welfare Act / Hartrick and Lazor. - Agincourt : Carswell, 1983.
460p.

—Social Service Tax Act, 1984 / Vancouver : British Columbia Continuing Legal Education Society, 1984.
ISBN 0865041474 Hbk £55.00

WELFARE LAW - GREAT BRITAIN
—Journal of Social Welfare Law / Christina M. Lyon. - London : Sweet & Maxwell.
Bound Vol.
Single copy
Back Vols. avail.

WELFARE LAW - INDIA
—Labour Welfare and Social Security Legislation in India / New Delhi : Deep and Deep Publications, 1984.
302p.

—Labour Welfare Laws and Employment Conditions in India / New Delhi : Deep and Deep Publications, 1985.
235p.

—Licensing Power in India : a Government Action for Social Welfare / New Delhi : S. Chand and Company.

—Social Security Legislation for Labour in India / New Delhi : Deep and Deep Publications, 1986.
382p.

WELFARE LAW - PAKISTAN
—Workers Welfare Fund Ordinance / Karachi : Bureau of Labour Publications, 1986.

WELFARE STATE
—Evolution of the British welfare state : a history of social policy since the Industrial Revolution / Derek Fraser. - 2nd ed. - London : Macmillan, 1984.
xxxii,326p; 22cm.
Previous ed.: 1973. Bibliography: p303-322.
ISBN 0333359992

WELFARE STATE - GREAT BRITAIN
—Holes in the Welfare Net / London : Bedford Square Press.
ISBN 0719909392 Hbk £6.95
ISBN 0719909406 Pbk £3.95

—Immigrants and the Welfare State / NACAB. - London : CENT, 1983.
ISBN 0906072069 Pbk £4.80

—Legal Foundations of the Welfare State (LIC) / Weidenfeld & Nicolson, 1985.
ISBN 0297784870 Hbk £18.95
ISBN 0297785346 Pbk £12.95

—National welfare benefits / Read. - London : Central Books, 1988/89.
ISBN 0946744084 Pbk £5.50

—National welfare benefits handbook / Lakhani. - 16th ed. - London : CENT, 1986.
ISBN 0906963957 Pbk £4.00

—Over-ruled on Welfare / Arthur Seldon. - London : Institute of Economic Affairs.

—Paying for Welfare / Oxford : Blackwell, 1985.
ISBN 0631139729 Pbk £7.95

—State Benefits 1986 / London : Labour Research Department.
ISBN 090050885X Hbk £0.90

WELFARE STATE - INDIA
—Welfare State and Supreme Court in India / New Delhi : Deep and Deep Publications, 1986.
140p.

WELSH LANGUAGE
—Welsh language in the courts / by J.A. Andrews and L.G. Henshaw. - Aberystwyth : University College of Wales, 1984.
ix,116p.
Includes index. With Welsh version of the oaths.

WHITE COLLAR CRIMES
—Cheats at work : an anthropology of workplace crime / Gerald Mars. - London : Unwin Paperbacks, 1983.
xii,242p; 20cm.
Originally published: London : Allen and Unwin, 1982. Bibliography: p229-234. - Includes index.
ISBN 0043011667 Pbk £2.95

—Economic crime in Europe / edited by L.H. Leigh. - London : Macmillan for the London School of Economics and Political Science, 1980.
xii,211p; 23cm.
Conference papers. Includes bibliographies and index.
ISBN 0333248406 £20.00

—Regulating fraud : white-collar crime and the criminal process / Michael Levi. - London : Tavistock, 1987.
416p; 24cm.
Includes bibliography and index.
ISBN 0422611603 £35.00

WHITE COLLAR CRIMES - CANADA
—Reserach on white collar crime : exploring the issues / S.E. Varette ... et al. - Ottawa : Ministry of the Solicitor General, 1985.
84,36p. - (User report).
Biliography: 4 pages.

WHITE COLLAR CRIMES - UNITED STATES
—National strategy for containing white-collar crime / edited by Herbert Edelhertz, Charles Rogovin. - Lexington : Lexington, 1980.
xii,138p; 24cm.
Conference papers.
ISBN 0669031666 £10.50

—White collar crime / Edwin H. Sutherland : with an introduction by Gilbert Geis and Colin Goff. - Uncut version. - New Haven : Yale University Press, 1983.
xxxiii,291p; 24cm.
Previous ed.: New York : Dryden, 1949. Includes index.
ISBN 0300029217 Hbk

WIDOW'S SHARE - CANADA - MANITOBA
—Report on an examination of 'the Dower Act' / Manitoba Law Reform Commission. - Winnipeg : Manitoba Law Reform Commission, 1984.
v,283p. - (Report).

WIDOW'S SHARE - SOUTH AFRICA
—Review of the law of succession : the introduction of a legitimate portion or the granting of a right to maintenance to the surviving spouse / South African Law Commission. - Pretoria : The Commission, 1987.
x,46p. - (Report).
Bibliography: pp.v-ix. Includes draft legislation.
ISBN 0621113603

WIDOWS - SOUTH AFRICA
—Review of the law of succession : the introduction of a legitimate portion or the granting of a right to maintenance to the surviving spouse / South African Law Commission. - Pretoria : The Commission, 1987.
x,46p. - (Report).
Bibliography: pp.v-ix. Includes draft legislation.
ISBN 0621113603

WILDLIFE CONSERVATION
—Convention on International Trade in Endangered Species of Wild Fauna and Flora. E.C. Annual Report / Luxembourg : Office for Official Publications of the European Communities, 1986.
426p.
ISBN 9282564983 Pbk £1,400.00

—International trade in endangered species / Dordrecht : Martinus Nijhoff, 1989.
424.
Discusses each article of the Convention on International Trade in Endangered Species, each with a separate chapter. Gives background information on the drafting of the treaty, problems of implementation and economic consequences of world trade in wildlife and plants.
ISBN 0792301145 Hbk £75

—International wildlife law : an analysis of international treaties concerned with the conservation of wildlife / by Simon Lyster. – Cambridge : Grotius Publications, 1985.
xxiii,470p.
Covers the international conventions on whaling, wetlands, protection of cultural and natural heritage, international trade in endangered species, and Antarctic marine living resources.
ISBN 0906496225

—Legislation on wildlife, hunting, and protected areas in some European countries / by Christian du Saussay for the Legislation Branch, Legal Office. – Rome : Food and Agriculture Organization of the United Nations, 1980.
vi, 49 p.; 28 cm. – (Legislative study).
Includes bibliographies references.
ISBN 9251008787 pbk.

WILDLIFE CONSERVATION - AFRICA

—Legislation on wildlife and protected areas in Africa / by Christian du Saussay for Legislation Branch, Legal Office, FAO. – Rome : Food and Agriculture Organization of the United Nations, 1984.
vii,158p. – (Legislative study).
Includes bibliographical references.
ISBN 9251011710

WILDLIFE CONSERVATION - UNITED STATES

—American wildlife law / Thomas A. Lund. – Berkeley : University of California Press, 1980.
ix,177p; 24cm.
Includes index.
ISBN 0520038835 £7.75

WILLS

—Canadian law of wills / Thomas G. Feeney. – 2nd ed. 2 v. – Toronto : Butterworths, 1982.
Revision of two separate works by the same author: The Canadian law of wills: probate, 1976; and The Canadian law of wills: construction, 1978. Includes bibliographical references and index. Vol. 1: Probate. - Vol 2: Construction.
ISBN 0409829749

—Right Way to Prove a Will / Ibadan : African Universities Press.

—Second-best bed : a diversion on wills / Fenton Bresler : illustrations by Michael Heath. – London : Weidenfeld and Nicolson, 1983.
158p; 23cm.
ISBN 0297782134 £7.50

—Wills administration and taxation: a practical guide / Lesley King, Anthony King. – 3rd. – London : Sweet & Maxwell.
Covers substantive law, tax considerations, will drafting. The chapter dealing with inheritance tax has been updated to include the new rules introduced in the Finance Act 1986. Also covers the new provisions of the Insolvency Act 1986. The text is illustrated with worked examples.
ISBN 0421382708 Pbk £17.50

—Write Your Own Will / Ibadan : African Universities Press.

—Writing a living will : using a durable power of attorney / Praeger, 1988.
ISBN 0275928012 Hbk £24.95
ISBN 0275929396 Pbk £10.75

WILLS - AUSTRALIA

—Australian Wills Precedents / 3rd ed. – London : Butterworths, 1980.
ISBN 0409370533 Hbk £25.60

—Hutley's Australian Wills Precedents / Gary Tamsitt. – 4th ed. – 1989.
ca 240p.
ISBN 0409494887 Hbk £49.00

—Hutley's Wills Precedents / 4th ed. – Sydney : Butterworths, 1988.
256p.
This text, intended for both student and practitioners, includes materials on wills and trusts and examples of complete wills. The fourth edition changes the form of the precedents to the legislative drafting style.

—Will Making and the Administration of Estates : a Short Guide / Butterworths, 1984.
223p.
This book aims at assisting the practitioner in the drafting of a will which accurately effects and carries out the wishes of the testator and then the efficient administration of the estate after death.
ISBN 0409492329 Hbk £36.00

—Wills and intestacy in Australia and New Zealand : being a revised and consolidated version of Hardingham, Neave and Ford's The Law of Wills and Hardingham's The Law of Intestate Succession in Australia and New Zealand / by I.J. Hardingham, M.A. Neave, H.A.J. Ford. – Sydney : Law Book Co., 1983.
xliv,518p.
Includes bibliographical references and index.
ISBN 0455204152

—Wills, Probate and the Administration of the Estates of Deceased Persons in Victoria / 2nd ed. – Butterworths, 1988.
272p.
ISBN 0409494747 Hbk £54.00
ISBN 0409338613 Pbk £35.00

WILLS - AUSTRALIA - NEW SOUTH WALES

—Community law reform program / New South Wales Law Reform Commission. – Sydney : The Commission, 1986.
175p. – (L.R.C. 47).
Includes bibliographical references.
ISBN 0730514943 Hbk

—Wills Probate and Administration Service, New South Wales / L.G. Handler. – Butterworths, 1985.
ISBN 0409491314 Hbk

WILLS - AUSTRALIA - SOUTH AUSTRALIA

—Report ... relating to the reform of the law on wills and intestacies / Law Reform Committee of South Australia. – Adelaide : Government Printer, 1983.
7p. – (72nd report).

WILLS - AUSTRALIA - TASMANIA

—Report on reform in the law of wills / Law Reform Commission of Tasmania. – Hobart : Government Printer, 1983.
17p. – (Report v no 35).

WILLS - AUSTRALIA - VICTORIA

—Wills Precedents (Victoria) / N.B. Dowdle. – North Ryde : Law Book Co, 1986.
xvii, 144p.
ISBN 0455203067 Hbk £35.00

WILLS - AUSTRALIA - WESTERN AUSTRALIA

—Report on wills : substantial compliance / Law Reform Commission of Western Australia. – Perth : The Commission, 1985.
60p. – (Project).
Includes bibliographical references.

—Wills : substantial compliance / the Law Reform Commission of Western Australia. – Perth : Law Reform Commission of Western Australia, 1984.
37p. – (Discussion paper).

WILLS - CANADA

—Canadian forms of wills / Rodney Hull, Michael M. K. Fitzpatrick. – 4th ed. – Toronto : Carswell, 1982.
lxix,333p.
Previous ed.: 1970. Bibliography: p.293. - Includes index.
ISBN 0459347004

—Canadian Law of Wills, 2 vols / 3rd ed. – Toronto : Butterworths, 1986.
864p.

—Canadian law of wills / Thomas G. Feeney. – 3rd ed. – Toronto : Butterworths, 1987.
Volume 1 focuses on probate, containing new material on the support of dependants, the administration of settled estates, holograph wills and intestate succession. Volume 2 considers the rules affecting construction in relation to recent probate changes.
ISBN 0409810002 Hbk

—Current Wills and Estates Practice / Vancouver : British Columbia Continuing Legal Education Society, 1982.
59p.
ISBN 086504046X Hbk £25.00

—Estate and Trusts Reports / Agincourt : Carswell.
These volumes contain the key decisions in estates and trust law from Canadian jurisdictions. Topics include wills, estate administration, devolution of estate, dependents relief, and tax matters relating to trusts. Wills are covered in depth.

—Estate Planning and Administration / Agincourt : Carswell, 1985-1986.
406p. – (Bar Admission Course Material Ser.).
This text discusses will planning and drafting, administration of an estate and how to advise the executor on applications for probate or distribution of the estate.

—Estates & trusts reports / Agincourt, Ont. : Carswell, 1978-.
24cm.
Cumulative indexes published at intervals.

—Interpretation of Wills / Victoria : Government of British Columbia, 1982.

—Making a Will / Community Legal Education Ontario. – 4th rev. ed. – Toronto : Community Legal Education Ontario, 1982.
30p.
ISBN 0889030561 Pbk £6.50

—Making and Revocation of Wills / Victoria : Government of British Columbia, 1981.

—O'Brien's Encyclopedia of Forms : Division Five-Wills and Trusts / Aurora : Canada Law Book Co.
– (Abridgments and Encyclopedias).
Supplement

—Tax Planned Will Precedents, 2 Vols. /. – Agincourt : Carswell.
ISBN 0459314300 Hbk £75.75

Vol. 2
This looseleaf service is a guide to tax savings in estate planning in Canada. Annotated precedents, master will form, will instruction checklist, alternative clauses, relevant legislation, coverage of trust, and other relevant materials are included in the two volumes.
ISBN 0459326007 Hbk £50.50

—Wills and Estates / 3rd ed. rev. ed. – Vancouver : Vancouver People's Law School.
39p : Illus.. – (Public Legal Education Series).
ISBN 0888470304 Hbk £0.60

—Wills Drafting 1983 / Vancouver : Continuing Legal Education Society of British Columbia, 1983.
204p.
ISBN 0865041288 Hbk £60.00

—Wills Drafting / Vancouver : British Columbia Continuing Legal Education Society, 1980.
404p.

—Wills Practice / Vancouver : Continuing Legal Education Society of British Columbia, 1986.
176p.
ISBN 0865042969 Hbk £65.00

—Wills/Probate Procedure for Manitoba and Saskatchewan / Jane Gordon. – 3rd ed. – North Vancouver : International Self-Counsel Press, 1985.
81p.
ISBN 088908503X Hbk £5.95

WILLS - CANADA - ALBERTA

—Wills for Alberta : How to Make Your Own Will / 6th ed. – North Vancouver : International Self-Counsel Press, 1985.
108p.
ISBN 0889082294 Hbk £6.50

WILLS - CANADA - BRITISH COLUMBIA

—Interpretation of wills / Law Reform Commission of British Columbia. – Vancouver : Law Reform Commission of British Columbia, 1981.
iv,164p. – (Working paper).

—Report on interpretation of wills / Law Reform Commission of British Columbia. – Victoria : Queen's Printer, 1982.
58p.
ISBN 0771883455

—Report on statutory succession rights / Law Reform Commission of British Columbia. – Vancouver : The Commission, 1983.
209p.
Date on title page 1983.
ISBN 0771884087

—Statutory succession rights / Law Reform Commission of British Columbia. – Vancouver : The Commission, 1982.
vii,401p. – (Working paper).

—Testamentary intent and unexpected circumstances / Law Reform Commission of British Columbia. – Vancover : The Commission, 1987.
iv,77p. – (Working paper).
Includes bibliographical references.
ISBN 0771886047

—Wills for British Columbia : How to Make Your Own Will / 13th ed. – North Vancouver : International Self-Counsel Press, 1988.
ISBN 0889084327 Hbk

WILLS - CANADA - MANITOBA

—Report on sections 33 and 34 of 'The Wills Act' / Manitoba Law Reform Commission. – Winnipeg : The Commission, 1986.
ii,34p. – (Report).
Includes bibliographical references.

—Report on small projects / Manitoba Law Reform Commission. – Winnipeg : The Commission, 1985.
iv,48p. – (Report).
Includes bibliographical references.
ISBN 0771101074

WILLS - CANADA - ONTARIO

—Probate Practice : MacDonell, Sheard and Hull / Maurice Cullity. – 3rd ed. – Agincourt : Carswell, 1981.
774p.
This is a comprehensive volume for estate law practitioners in Ontario, Canada. The text covers valid wills, the recognition of holographic wills, survivorship, ancillary letters probate, conflict of laws relating to wills and estates, and numerous other probate topics.

—Wills for Ontario : How to Make Your Own Will / 8th ed. – North Vancouver : International Self-Counsel Press, 1986.
112p.
ISBN 0889083584 Hbk £5.95

WILLS - CANADA - SASKATCHEWAN

—Proposals relating to ademption by equitable conversion / Law Reform Commission of Saskatchewan. - Saskatoon : The Commission, 1984.
12p.
Includes bibliographical references.

WILLS - ENGLAND

—Brighouse's precedents of wills and life transfers / Edward F. George, Arthur George, Henry Brighouse. - 11th ed. - London : Sweet & Maxwell, 1986.
176p; 25cm.
Covers taxation, including the provisions of the Finance Act 1986, settled property, divorce, children and issues, agricultural and business property, unquoted shares, and transfers of value inter vivos and the exemptions. Contains 50 precedents, and 63 common form clauses.
ISBN 0421330708 £22.00

—Theobald on wills / J. B. Clark. - 14th ed. - London : Stevens, 1982.
cxcviii,842p; 26cm.
Previous ed.: 1971. Bibliography: pcxcvii-cxcviii. - Includes index. Latest supplement held: 1st, 1983.
ISBN 0420452508 £78.00

—Will precedents and capital transfer tax / D.T. Davies. - 2nd ed. - London : Butterworths, 1983.
xxi,231p; 26cm.
ISBN 040617511X

—Will precedents and inheritance tax / D.T. Davies. - 3rd ed. - London : Butterworth, 1988.
xxiii,283p.
Previous ed.: published as Will precedents and capital transfer tax. 1983. Includes index.
ISBN 0406175128 £25.00

—Williams' law relating to wills / C. H. Sherrin, R. F. D. Barlow, R. A. Wallington. - 6th ed. 2 vols. - London : Butterworths, 1987.
25cm.
This work is presented in two volumes containing narrative and precedents on wills in the United Kingdom. The book has been updated in the light of the Administration of Justice Act of 1982 and changes to the capital transfer tax.
ISBN 0406421978 £166
ISBN 0406421994

WILLS - GREAT BRITAIN

—Estate Tax Planning : Including Will Drafting / London : Law Society.
- (Nineteen Eighty-Five Crash Course Transcripts).

—Jarman on Wills / Repr. of 1951 ed. - London : Sweet & Maxwell, 1986.
- (Sweet and Maxwell Library Reprints).
ISBN 0421355301 Hbk £150.00

—Law of Wills /. - London : Sweet & Maxwell.
ISBN 0420469400 Pbk

—Law of Wills and Administration / Alston. - London : Butterworths, 1984.
ISBN 0409601306 Hbk £40.00

—Law's Disposal of a Person's Estate Who Dies Without Will or Testament : The Disposal of Estates of Will, Form of Wills, and Directions for Executors etc. / 10th ed. Repr. of 1809 ed. - Abingdon : Professional Books.
492p.

—Leaving Money to Charity / TUAR, 1983.
ISBN 0907164129 Pbk £1.95

—Modern wills precedents / 2nd ed. - London : Butterworths, 1987.
ISBN 0406334617 Hbk £24.00

—Office and Duty of Executors : Treatise of Wills and Executors Directed to Testators in the Choice of Their Executors and Contrivance of Their Wills / Repr. of 1774 ed. - Abingdon : Professional Books.
494p.

—Succinct View of the Rule of Shelley's Case / Repr. of 1794 ed. - Abingdon : Professional Books.
486p.

—Will Draftsman's Handbook / 2nd ed. - London : Oyez Longman, 1982.
ISBN 0851206115 Hbk £11.95

—Will Draftsman's Handbook / 3rd ed. - London : Oyez Longman, 1983.
ISBN 0851208037 Hbk £13.50

—Will draftsman's handbook / 5th ed. - London : Longman Professional, 1987.
ISBN 0851212743 Pbk £18.95

—Will precedents and Capital Transfer Tax / 2nd ed. - London : Butterworths, 1983.
ISBN 040617511X Hbk £21.00

—Williams on wills / R F D Barlow, R A Wallington. - 6th ed. 2 vols. - London : Butterworths, 1987.
ISBN 0406421978 Hbk £175.00

—Wills / Edited by Clive Brand. - London : Longman Professional, 1988.
- (Longman Practice Notes Series).
ISBN 085121410X Pbk

—Wills, administration and taxation : a practical guide / King. - London : Sweet & Maxwell, 1988.
ISBN 0421382708 Pbk £17.50

WILLS - INDIA

—Law of Wills along with Model Forms / 3rd ed. - Allahabad : Law Publishers, 1982.

WILLS - MALAYSIA

—Powers of Attorney Ordinance, 1949 (No. 64/1949) and Wills Ordinance, 1959 (No. 38/1959) / Kuala Lumpur : International Law Books Services.

WILLS - NEW ZEALAND

—Brief Outline of the Law Relating to Trusts, Wills, Executors, and Administrators / 2nd ed. - Wellington : Butterworths, 1982.
ISBN 0409627127 Hbk

—Brief Outline of the Law Relating to Trusts, Wills, Executors, and Administrators / 2nd ed. - Butterworths, 1982.
ISBN 04094267127 Pbk £25.85

—Family Protection and Testamentary Promises in New Zealand / Butterworths, 1985.
Discusses the principles behind the statutory provisions, and the cases in support of the Law of Family Protection and the Law of Testamentary Promises. Considers the amendments to the text if the statutory provisions dealing with Family Protection, particularly those which have given rights to new classes of claimants such as grandchildren.
ISBN 0409701432 Hbk £69.30

—Law of Wills and Administration / 5th ed. - Butterworths, 1984.
Takes into account the significant developments made by the Wills Amendment Act 1977, and amendments to the Administration Act 1969, and the Status of Children Act 1969.
ISBN 0409601306 Hbk £90.75

—Nevill's Law of Trusts, Wills and Administration in New Zealand / 8th ed. - Butterworths, 1985.
Guide to the law of trusts, wills and administration in New Zealand. Includes new chapters on unincorporated associations and construction of wills.
ISBN 040970170X Hbk £76.45
ISBN 0409701858 Pbk £50.05

—Nevill's Law of Trusts, Wills and Administrators in New Zealand / 8th ed. - London : Butterworths, 1985.
ISBN 0409701858 Pbk £26.00

—Nevill's Will Drafting Handbook / 4th ed. - Butterworths, 1988.
149p.
ISBN 0409702226 Hbk £54.00

—Will-Draftsman's Handbook / 4th ed. - Butterworths, 1987.
ISBN 0409652415 Hbk

—Wills and intestacy in Australia and New Zealand : being a revised and consolidated version of Hardingham, Neave and Ford's The Law of Wills and Hardingham's The Law of Intestate Succession in Australia and New Zealand / by I.J. Hardingham, M.A. Neave, H.A.J. Ford. - Sydney : Law Book Co., 1983.
xliv,518p.
Includes bibliographical references and index.
ISBN 0455204152

WILLS - SCOTLAND

—Making and revocation of wills / Scottish Law Commission. - Edinburgh : The Commission, 1986.
ii,84p. - (Consultative memorandum).

WILLS - SOUTH AFRICA

—Power of a Testator to Dispose of the Property of Another : a Study of the South African Law of Massing and Election, with a Comparative Look at English, Dutch and German Law / Pijnacker : Dutch Efficiency Bureau.
ISBN 9062310273 Hbk £30.80

—Review of the law of succession : alteration and revocation of wills / South African Law Commission. - Pretoria : The Commission, 1987.
vii,86 leaves. - (Project).
Bibliography: leaves vi-viii.

—Review of the law of succession : formalitites of a will / South African Law Commission. - Pretoria : South African Law Commission, 1986.
xiii,139 leaves. - (Project).
Bibliography: p.viii-xiii.

WINDING UP - GREAT BRITAIN

—Compulsory Winding Up Procedure / 2nd ed. - London : Longman Professional, 1987.
ISBN 0851211798 Pbk £3.95

—Winding-up and bankruptcy procedures / Shaws Linton Publications, 1988.
ISBN 0906653142 Hbk £12.95

WINDING UP - INDIA

—Companies Winding-up / 2nd ed. - Allahabad : Law Book Company, 1988.
700p.

WINDING UP - MALAYSIA

—Companies (Winding-up) Rules, (P.U.(A) 289/1972) / Kuala Lumpur : International Law Books Services.

WIRE-TAPPING

—Letters rogatory for the interception of telecommunications : Recommendation no.R (85) 10 adopted by the Committee of Ministers of the Council of Europe on 28 June 1985 and Explanatory memorandum / Council of Europe. - Strasbourg : Council of Europe, 1986.
15p; 21cm. - (Legal affairs).
'... prepared by a select committee of experts under the authority of the European Committee on Crime Problems' - p.3.
ISBN 9287108390

—Telephone tapping and the recording of telecommunications in some Council of Europe member states / Council of Europe Directorate of Legal Affairs. - Strasbourg : Council of Europe, 1982.
12p; 30cm. - (Legislative dossier).
ISBN 9287100551

WIRE-TAPPING - GREAT BRITAIN

—Interception of communications in Great Britain : report / by Lord Diplock. - London : H.M.S.O., 1981.
7p; 25cm.
ISBN 0101819102 unbound £1.10

WITNESSES

—Child Witness : Do the Courts Abuse Children / Drinkwater. - New York : British Psychological Society, 1988.
ISBN 0901715891 Pbk £5.00

—Evaluating witness evidence : recent psychological research and new perspectives / edited by Sally M.A. Lloyd-Bostock and Brian R. Clifford. - Chichester : Wiley, 1983.
x,305p; 24cm.
Includes bibliographies and index.
ISBN 0471104639 Hbk

—Eyewitness identification : a system handbook / Gary L. Wells. - Toronto : Carswell, 1988.
xiv,142p. - (The Carswell law enforcement series).
Bibliography: pp.105-115. - Includes index.
ISBN 0459311611

WITNESSES - AUSTRALIA

—Evidence reference / Australian Law Reform Commission. - Sydney : The Commission, 1982.
vii,141p.
Includes bibliographical references.

WITNESSES - AUSTRALIA - TASMANIA

—Child witnesses in sexual assault / Kate Warner. - Hobart : Law Reform Commission of Tasmania, 1987.
123p. - (Discussion paper).
Includes bibliographical references.

WITNESSES - AUSTRALIA - WESTERN AUSTRALIA - FEES

—Payment of witnesses in civil proceedings / the Law Reform Commission of Western Australia. - Perth : Law Reform Commission of Western Australia, 1988.
iii,11 leaves. - (Discussion paper).

WITNESSES - CANADA

—Examination of Witnesses 2 / Vancouver : Continuing Legal Education Society of British Columbia, 1986.
202p.
ISBN 0865043000 Hbk £55.00

—Examination of Witnesses / Vancouver : Continuing Legal Education Society of British Columbia, 1985.
241p.
ISBN 0865042438 Hbk £45.00

—Services to victims and witnesses of crime in Canada / by Geoff Norquay, Richard Weiler. - Ottawa : Communication Division, Solicitor General Canada, 1981.
163 p.; 28 cm.
'A research report prepared by the Canadian Council on Social Development under contract with the Research Division, Ministry of the Solicitor General of Canada'-Verso t.p.
ISBN 0662117735 pbk.

—So, You Have to Go to Court : a Child's Guide to Testifying as a Witness in Child Abuse Cases / Anne Watson-Russell. - Butterworths, 1986.
48p.
ISBN 040980519X Pbk £7.95

—Victims and witnesses of crime in Canada / by Dick Weiler and Jean-Guy Desgagne of the Canadian Council on Social Development. – Ottawa : Ministry of Supply and Services, Canada, 1984.
98p,111p.
With French t.p.: Victimes et temoins d'infractions penales au Canada. French and English text.
ISBN 0662530136

WITNESSES - GREAT BRITAIN
—Child's Voice in Court of Law / London : Butterworths, 1982.
ISBN 0409870544 Hbk £30.00

—Eyewitness Testimony / Loftus. – Cambridge : Cambridge University Press, 1984.
ISBN 0521255643 Hbk £30.00

—Witnesses in the criminal courts : a report / by Justice : chairman of committee Peter Crawford. – London : Justice, 1986.
25p.
ISBN 0907247067

WITNESSES - HONG KONG
—Report on competence and compellability of spouses in criminal proceedings / the Law Reform Commission of Hong Kong. – Hong Kong : The Commission, 1988.
viii,181p. – (Topic).
Bibliography:pp. 180-181.

WITNESSES - IRELAND
—Report on competence and compellability of spouses as witnesses / the Law Reform Commission. – Dublin : The Commission, 1985.
v,86p. – (LRC).
Includes general scheme of a bill to reform the law relating to the evidence of spouses in criminal cases.

WITNESSES - SCOTLAND
—Evidence of children and other potentially vulnerable witnesses / Scottish Law Commission. – Edinburgh : The Commission, 1988.
iv,160p. – (Discussion paper).

WOMEN
—Convention on the Elimination of All Forms of Discrimination Against Women : explanatory documentation prepared for Commonwealth jurisdictions / Commonwealth Secretariat. – 4 pamphlets in folder. – London : Commonwealth Secretariat, .
Contents: The Convention on the Elimination of All Forms of Discrimination Against Women text. - Developments towards the elimination of discrimination against women in the Commonwealth. - The Convention on the Elimination of All Forms of Discrimination Against Women: a commentary on the Convention. - Directory of Commonwealth National Machinery.

—Female Criminality / Lucknow : Eastern Book Company, 1985.

—Latin American Women / edited by Olivia Harris. – London : Minority Rights Group, 1982.
22p. – (Report).
Bibliography: p.21. - List of films: p.22.

—Position of Women in Hindu Law / 1913 repr. – New Delhi : Inter-India Publications, 1984.
vi, ii, xxxii, xix, 707p.
ISBN 8121001641 Hbk £380.00

—Woman's role in economic development / Ester Boserup. – Aldershot : Gower, 1986.
283p.
Originally published: George Allen & Unwin, 1970. Bibliography: pp.263-275. - Includes index. Published in association with the London School of Economics and Political Science.
ISBN 0566051397

—Women and Crime / L. Gelsthorpe. – Cambridge : Institute of Criminology.
1981p.

—Women and men in Britain : a research profile / Equal Opportunities Commission. – London : HMSO, 1988.
79p.
Bibliography: pp.74-76. - Includes index.
ISBN 0117013897

—Women, crime and justice / edited by Susan K. Datesman, Frank R. Scarpitti. – New York : Oxford University Press, 1980.
viii,376p; 21cm.
Includes bibliographies.
ISBN 0195026764 Pbk £3.95

—Women employment and European law / Oxford : Eclipse, 1988.
ISBN 1870771001 Hbk £25.00

—Women-in-law : explorations in law, family and sexuality / edited by Julia Brophy and Carol Smart. – London : Routledge & Kegan Paul, 1985.
x,219p.
ISBN 0710202598

—Women, power and political systems / edited by Margherita Rendel with the assistance of Georgina Ashworth. – London : Croom Helm, 1981.
262p; 23cm.
Includes bibliographies and index.
ISBN 0709922043 £12.95

—Women's Law : an introduction to feminist jurisprudence / Tove Stang Dahl : translated by Ronald L. Craig. – Oslo : Norwegian University Press, 1987.
195p; 23cm.
A theoretical introduction, and a discussion of three areas within women's law; the legal situation affecting housewives, paid workers, and women as recipients of social security benefits.
ISBN 8200184900 £20.00

—Women's rights : a practical guide / Anna Coote and Tess Gill : drawings by Posy Simmonds. – 3rd ed. – Harmondsworth : Penguin, 1981.
555p; 20cm.
Previous ed.: 1977. Includes index.
ISBN 0140465324 Pbk £3.95

WOMEN - AFRICA
—Female circumcision, excision and infibulation : the facts and proposals for change / edited by Scilla McLean and Stella Efua Graham : with contributions from Marie Assaad ... et al. – 2nd rev. ed. – London : Minority Rights Group, 1985.
21p. – (Report).
Bibliography: p.11.

—Women in sub-Saharan Africa / Edda Ivan-Smith, Nidhi Tandon and Jane Connors. – London : Minority Rights Group, 1988.
18p. – (Report).
Includes bibliographical references.
ISBN 094669057X

WOMEN - ASIA
—Women in Asia / edited by Rounaq Jahan. – Rev. ed. – London : Minority Rights Group, 1982.
24p. – (Report).
Previous ed.: 1980. Includes bibliographical notes.

WOMEN - AUSTRALIA
—Women as Participants In the Criminal Justice System / Canberra : Australian Institute of Criminology.

—Women as Victims of Crimes / Canberra : Australian Institute of Criminology.

WOMEN - CANADA
—Taking of 28 : Women Challenge the Constitution / Toronto.
124p.
ISBN 0889610835 Pbk £6.95

—Tentative proposals for an equality of status of married persons act / Law Reform Commission of Saskatchewan. – Saskatoon : Law Reform Commission of Saskatchewan, 1981.
68p.
Includes bibliographical references.

—Women and the constitution in Canada / edited by Audrey Doerr and Micheline Carrier. – Ottawa : Canadian Advisory Council on the Status of Women, 1981.
x,223p.
Includes bibliographical notes. Contains papers prepared for Canadian Advisory Council on the Status of Women conference scheduled for September 1980.
ISBN 0660108720

—Women and Work : Inequality in the Labour Market / Erin Phillips. – Toronto : Lorimer & Co, 1983.
– (Canadian Issues Ser.).
ISBN 0888626088 Hbk £15.95
ISBN 088862607X Pbk £6.95

—Women in Canadian Law / Markham : Fitzhenry and Whiteside.
96p.
ISBN 0889023778 Pbk £4.95

—Women, the Law and the Economy / Toronto : Butterworths, 1985.
414p.
ISBN 0409988650 Pbk £31.95

WOMEN - CANADA - MANITOBA
—Report on 'The Married Women's Property Act' and related matters / Manitoba Law Reform Commission. – Winnipeg : The Commission, 1985.
i,76p. – (Report).
Includes bibliographical references.
ISBN 0771101163

WOMEN - CARIBBEAN
—Women and the law / Norma Monica Forde. – Cave Hill, Barbados : Institute of Social and Economic Research, University of the West Indies, 1981.
x,125p.
Includes bibliographies.

WOMEN - COMMONWEALTH
—Decade of Women and the Law in the Commonwealth / London : Commonwealth Secretariat, 1985.

—Decade of women and the law in the Commonwealth / prepared by Margaret Rogers for the Hubert Humphrey Institute of Public Affairs in association with the Commonwealth Secretariat. – London : Legal Division, Commonwealth Secretariat, 1985.
xvii,342p.
ISBN 0850922720

WOMEN - ENGLAND
—Women and the law / Susan Atkins and Brenda Hoggett. – Oxford : Basil Blackwell, 1984.
234p; 24cm.
Includes index.
ISBN 0855201819 Hbk £17.50
ISBN 0855201800 Pbk No price

WOMEN - EUROPEAN COMMUNITY
—Protective legislation for women in the member states of the European Community / communication by the Commission. – Luxembourg : Office for Official Publications of the European Communities, 1987.
29p. – (COM(87) 105 final).
Includes bibliographical references.
ISBN 9277228741

WOMEN - GAMBIA
—Women and legal affairs / a paper jointly prepared by Mariam Denton, Amie Bensouda, Fola Mendy Allen. – Banjul, the Gambia? : s.n., 1985.
10p.
At head of cover title: The Gambia National Women's Council and Bureau. Cover title: End of Women's Decade Conference on Women in Development, 24th-26th April 1985.

WOMEN - GREAT BRITAIN
—Criminal Women / Oxford : Blackwell, 1985.
ISBN 0745600883 Pbk £5.95

—Gender Crime and Justice / Open University Press, 1988.
ISBN 0335155057 Hbk £25.00

—Sexual divisions in law / Katherine O'Donovan. – London : Weidenfeld and Nicolson, 1985.
xii,242p; 23cm.
Bibliography: p226-233. - Includes index.
ISBN 0297786644 Hbk £16.95
ISBN 0297786652 Pbk £8.95

—Welsh law of women : studies presented to Professor Daniel A. Binchy on his eightieth birthday, 3 June 1980 / edited by Dafydd Jenkins and Morfydd E. Owen. – Cardiff : Published on behalf of the Board of Celtic Studies by University of Wales Press, 1980.
x,253P; 22cm.
Includes index.
ISBN 070830771X £12.95

—Wives and property : reform of the married women's property law in nineteenth-century England / Lee Holcombe. – Oxford : Martin Robertson, 1983.
viii,311p; 24cm.
Bibliography: p275-292. - Includes index.
ISBN 0855206071 £15.00

—Women and harassment at work / Pluto Press, 1983.
ISBN 086104729X Pbk £3.95

—Women and men in Britain : a statistical profile / London : H.M.S.O., 1986.
45p.
ISBN 0117012955

—Women in law / Smart. – Routledge, 1985.
ISBN 0710202598 Pbk £7.50
ISBN 0710206070 Hbk £19.95

—Women won't benefit : the impact of the Social Security Bill on women's rights / Hilary Land and Sue Ward. – London : National Council for Civil Liberties. Rights for Women Unit, 1986.
48p.
ISBN 0946088268

WOMEN - INDIA
—Hindu Women's Right to Property in India / New Delhi : Deep and Deep Publications, 1986.
528p.

—Indian Women and the Law in Canada / Citizens Minus. – Ottawa : Canadian Government Publishing Centre, 1980.
108p.
ISBN 0662018540 Pbk £2.98

—Protection of Women under the Law : an Annotated Bibliography / Badar Anwar. – New Delhi : Deep and Deep Publications, 1982.
200p.

—Sociolegal Status of Women in India / Delhi : Mittal Publications, 1987.
208p.

—Stridhana or Woman's Property in Indian Law : An Appraisal of its Concept and Contents / Hoshiarpur : Vishveshvaranand Institute.

—Woman and the Law / New Delhi : Intellectual Book Corner, 1985.
xii, 228p.

—Women and the law : constitutional rights and continuing inequalities / Joseph Minattur. - New Delhi : Manohar, 1980.
p.165-178.
Offprint from: Women in contemporary India and South Asia / edited by Alfred de Souza. - 2nd rev. ed. - New Delhi : Manohar, 1980.

WOMEN - ISLAMIC COUNTRIES
—Arab women / edited by Ann Dearden. - 2nd rev. and updated ed. - London : Minority Rights Group, 1983.
16p. - (Report).
Bibliography: p.15.
ISBN 0903114887

WOMEN - SINGAPORE
—Legal Status of Singapore Women / Singapore Association of Women Lawyers. - Singapore : Asiapac Books and Educational Aids.
ISBN 9971985128 Hbk £1.40

WOMEN - SRI LANKA
—Legal Status of the Female in the Sri Lanka Law on Family Relations / Colombo : Gunasena and Co..

WOMEN - SWAZILAND
—Law and the other sex : the legal position of women in Swaziland / by Alice Kavanagh Armstrong and Ronald Thandabantu Nhlapo. - Mbabane : Webster, 1985.
150p.
Bibliography: p148-150.

WOMEN - TRINIDAD & TOBAGO
—Developing legal status of women in Trinidad and Tobago / by Stephanie Daly. - Port-of-Spain : National Commission on the Status of Women, 1982.
136p.
Includes bibliographical references and index.

WOMEN - WALES
—Welsh Law of Women / Morfydd Owen. - Cardiff : University of Wales, 1980.
253p.
ISBN 070830771X Hbk £12.95

WOMEN - ZIMBABWE
—Zimbabwean women in colonial and customary law / by Joan May. - Gweru : Mambu Press, 1983.
vii,128p.
Bibliography: p.123-128. Cover title: Zimbabwean women in customary and colonial law.
ISBN 0869222406

WOMEN (INTERNATIONAL LAW)
—Dignity and honour of women as basic and fundamental human rights / by Yougindra Khushalani. - The Hague : Martinus Nijhoff Publishers, 1982.
153p.
Includes index.
ISBN 9024725852 Hbk £105.00

WOMEN LAWYERS - GREAT BRITAIN
—Women and the law / edited by Sue McLaughlin. - London : Faculty of Laws, University College London, 1987.
75p. - (Working papers).
Includes bibliographical references.

WOMEN PRISONERS - AUSTRALIA
—Women Prisoners In Victoria : A Review of the Nature and Size of Facilities Needed / Canberra : Australian Institute of Criminology.

WOMEN PRISONERS - ENGLAND
—Dynamics of aggression in women's prisons in England / Alexandra Mandaraka-Sheppard. - Aldershot : Gower, 1986.
xiii,272p; 23cm.
Bibliography: p241-260. - Includes index.
ISBN 0566008637 £17.50

WOMEN PRISONERS - GREAT BRITAIN
—Imprisonment of women / Oxford : Blackwell, 1986.
ISBN 063114319X Pbk £7.95

WOMEN PRISONERS - NORTHERN IRELAND
—Strip searching : an inquiry into the strip searching of women remand prisoners at Armagh Prison between 1982 and 1985 / London : National Council for Civil Liberties, 1986.
36p; 20cm.
ISBN 0946088209 Pbk £1.95

WOMEN PRISONERS - SCOTLAND
—Women's imprisonment : a study in social control / Pat Carlen. - London : Routledge & K. Paul, 1983.
viii,248p.
Includes index. Bibliography: p240-245.
ISBN 0710094418

WOMEN'S RIGHTS
—Industrialisation and reproductive rights / by Paulin sic Jackson. - Florence : European University Institute, 1986.
ii,24p.
Bibliography: p.22-24.

—Women's rights : a practical guide / Anna Coote and Tess Gill : drawings by Posy Simmonds. - 3rd ed. - Harmondsworth : Penguin, 1981.
555p; 20cm.
Previous ed.: 1977. Includes index.
ISBN 0140465324 Pbk £3.95

WOMEN'S RIGHTS - CANADA
—Women and the constitution in Canada / edited by Audrey Doerr and Micheline Carrier. - Ottawa : Canadian Advisory Council on the Status of Women, 1981.
x,223p.
Includes bibliographical notes. Contains papers prepared for Canadian Advisory Council on the Status of Women conference scheduled for September 1980.
ISBN 0660108720

—Women's Economic Equality Act, 1983, Bill 108 : An Act to Provide for Affirmative Action and Equal Pay for Work of Equal Value / Ontario : Ontario Government Publications Service, 1983.
11p.

—Womens Rights in Ireland / Dublin, 1983.
223p.
ISBN 0907085687 Pbk £4.95

WOMEN'S RIGHTS - EUROPEAN COMMUNITY
—Rights of working women in the European Community / by Eve C. Landau. - Luxembourg : Office for Official Publications of the European Communities, 1985.
244p.
At head of title: Commission of the European Communities.
ISBN 9282553418 Hbk £3.00

WOMEN'S RIGHTS - GREECE
—Economic Rights of Women in Ancient Greece / Edinburgh : Edinburgh University Press.
180p.
ISBN 0852244231 Pbk £7.50

WOMEN'S RIGHTS - SWAZILAND
—Law and the other sex : the legal position of women in Swaziland / by Alice Kavanagh Armstrong and Ronald Thandabantu Nhlapo. - Mbabane : Webster, 1985.
150p.
Bibliography: p148-150.

WORK - CANADA
—Non-Unionized Workers Protection Act, 1983, Bill 115 : An Act Respecting the Rights of Non-Unionized Workers / Ontario : Ontario Government Publications Service, 1983.
3p.

WORK - GREAT BRITAIN
—Worker-controlled businesses and the law / Spokesman Books, 1988.
ISBN 0851244521 Hbk £25.00
ISBN 0851244629 Pbk £8.95

WORK ENVIRONMENT - CANADA
—Workplace pollution / Law Reform Commission of Canada. - Ottawa : The Commission, 1986.
94,106p. - (Working paper).
Includes bibliographical references. Added t.p. in French: La pollution en milieu de travail. Pages numbered in opposite directions. Text in English and French.
ISBN 0662545702

WORKERS' COMPENSATION
—Report to the House of Assembly of the Select Committee on Workers' Compensation / Nova Scotia. - Halifax : Queen's Printer, 1981.
65p.
Includes bibliographical references.

WORKERS' COMPENSATION - AUSTRALIA
—Accident compensation in Australia : no-fault schemes / by Mark A. Robinson. - Sydney : Legal Books Pty., 1987.
xiv,94p.
Bibliography: pp.86-89. - Includes index.
ISBN 094955331X

—Australian workers compensation guide / 3. - North Ryde, N.S.W. : CCH Australia, 1984.
looseleaf.
Originally published: as part of Australian labour law reporter, 1977-. Includes index. Loose-leaf issues accompanied by a summary report.
ISBN 0869034839

—Guidebook to Workers Compensation in Australia / 5th ed. - North Ryde : C.C.H. Australia, 1986.
624p.
ISBN 086903846X Pbk £38.00

—Workers' compensation legislation in Australia 1980 / Department of Social Security. - Canberra : Australian Government Publishing Service, 1981.
ix,100p.
Previously published as: 'Conspectus of workers' compensation legislation in Australia as at 1 January 19–'.

WORKERS' COMPENSATION - AUSTRALIA - NEW SOUTH WALES
—Accident compensation / New South Wales Law Reform Commission. - Sydney : The Commission, 1983.
viii,62p. - (L.R.C. 41).

—New South Wales Workers' Compensation Act 1926 / 3rd ed. - North Ryde : C.C.H. Australia, 1985.
424p.
ISBN 0869035983 Hbk £24.00

—Workers Compensation, New South Wales / Butterworths, 1987.
ISBN 0409492868 Hbk £210.00

—Workers' Compensation Law and Practice in New South Wales / North Ryde : C.C.H. Australia, 1983.
309p.
ISBN 0869033484 Hbk

WORKERS' COMPENSATION - AUSTRALIA - TASMANIA
—Report on section 9(7), (8) and (9) of the Worker's Compensation Act 1927 / Law Reform Commission of Tasmania. - Hobart? : Goverment Printer?, 1985.
17p. - (Report).

WORKERS' COMPENSATION - AUSTRALIA - VICTORIA
—Accident compensation Victoria / by L.R. Boyes and M. O'Loghlen. - 1. - Sydney : Butterworths, 1987.
looseleaf.
Supersedes: Workers compensation, Victoria, by Anderson and Rendit. Includes: Accident and workers compensation reports.
ISBN 0409492795

—Principles of the law of workers' compensation, particularly in Victoria / by E. F. Hill and J. B. Bingeman. - Sydney : Law Book Company Limited, 1981.
xxiv,276p.
ISBN 0455200882

—Workers compensation, Victoria / Anderson & Rendit. - 3rd ed. 1. - Sydney : Butterworths, 1980.
looseleaf.
Superseded by: Accident compensation, Victoria, by Boyes and O'Loghlen. Final looseleaf insertion dated August 1987.
ISBN 0409320609

WORKERS' COMPENSATION - CANADA
—Worker's Compensation in Canada / Butterworths, 1983.
208p.

—Workers' Compensation / Vancouver : Continuing Legal Education Society of British Columbia, 1988.
474p.
ISBN 0865049939 Hbk £85.00

—Workers' compensation in Canada / by Terence G. Ison. - Toronto : Butterworths, 1983.
xxvii,179p.
Includes index.
ISBN 040984005X

—Workers' Compensation Practice and Procedure / Vancouver : British Columbia Continuing Legal Education Society, 1982.
265p.
ISBN 086504063X Hbk £50.00

WORKERS' COMPENSATION - CANADA - ONTARIO

—Workers' Compensation in Ontario / Butterworths, 1987.
256p.
Guide to matters falling within the jurisdiction of the Ontario Workers' Compensation Board. Deals with practice and procedure of the Board as they currently exist, and makes reference to various published documents of the WCB on issues of policy and procedure. Section examines the availability of civil actions.
ISBN 0409804908 Hbk £80.00

WORKERS' COMPENSATION - GREAT BRITAIN
—Butterworth's Workmen's Compensation Cases : 1908-1950, 41 Vols. / Professional Books Staff. - Abingdon : Professional Books, 1984.

—Compensation for industrial injury : a guide to the revised scheme of benefits for work accidents and diseases / by Richard Lewis. - Abingdon : Professional Books, 1987.
359p; 25cm.
ISBN 0862052149

—Effect of ex post compensation on absence from work / by Paul Fenn. - Oxford : Centre for Socio-Legal Studies, 1980.
23p. - (Working paper).
Bibliography: p.23.

—Industrial injuries benefits scheme / Mark Rowland. – London : Legal Action Group, 1983.
xxvii,122p.
Includes index.
ISBN 0905099052

—Social Security Act 1975 : reform of the industrial injuries scheme / presented to Parliament by the Secretary of State for Social Services .. – London : H.M.S.O., 1981.
iv,30p; 25cm.
At head of title: Department of Health and Social Security.
ISBN 0101840209 unbound £3.05

—Workmen's compensation in twentieth century Britain : law, history and social policy / P.W.J. Bartrip. – Aldershot : Gower, 1987.
262p; 22cm.
Includes index.
ISBN 056605485X £17.50

—Wounded soldiers of industry : industrial compensation policy 1833-1897 / P.W.J. Bartrip and S.B. Burman. – Oxford : Clarendon, 1983.
xi,253p; 23cm. – (Oxford socio-legal studies).
Includes index.
ISBN 0198275099 £15.00

WORKERS' COMPENSATION – INDIA

—Commentaries on Workmen's Compensation Act, 1923 / 4th ed. – Lucknow : Eastern Book Company, 1987.

—Commentaries on Workmen's Compensation Act, 1923 / G. Saran. – 4th rev. ed. – Lucknow : Eastern Book Company, 1984.
692p.

—Workmen's Compensation Act, 1923 : Commentary and Case-Law / Delhi : Metropolitan Book Co, 1987.
296p.
ISBN 8120002601 Hbk £150.00

—Workmen's Compensation Act / 3rd ed. – Allahabad : Law Book Company, 1986.
1,050p.

WORKERS' COMPENSATION – LAW AND LEGISLATION – NEW ZEALAND

—Accident compensation coverage : the administration of the Accident compensation act 1972 / J.L. Fahy. – 4th ed. – Wellington : Accident Compensation Commission, 1980.
55 p.; 21 cm.
ISBN 0477063705 Hbk

WORKERS' COMPENSATION – MALAYSIA

—Workmen's Compensation Act, 1952 (Act 273) and Regulations 1953 (P.U.(A) 329/1983) / Kuala Lumpur : International Law Books Services.

WORKING CONDITIONS – EUROPE

—Long Suffering British Workers : Working Time in Europe / London : Labour Research Department.
24p.
ISBN 0900508434 Hbk £0.60

WORKING CONDITIONS – GREAT BRITAIN

—Long Suffering British Workers : Working Time in Europe / London : Labour Research Department.
24p.
ISBN 0900508434 Hbk £0.60

WORKS COUNCILS

—Cooperation between management and labor : a survey of co-determination mechanisms in European corporations / Walter Kolvenbach. – Deventer, Netherlands : Kluwer Law and Taxation Publishers, 1982.
89 p.; 25 cm.
ISBN 9065440666 pbk.

WORKS COUNCILS – YUGOSLAVIA

—Workers' management in Yugoslavia : recent developments and trends / edited by Najdan Pasic, Stanislav Grozdanic, Milorad Radevic. – Geneva : International Labour Office, 1982.
viii, 198 p.; 24 cm.
ISBN 9221030342 hard £25.00

WORLD BAND

—IMF and the World Bank in Africa : conditionality, impact, and alternatives / edited by Kjell J. Havnevik. – Uppsala : Scandinavian Institute of African Studies, 1987.
177 p.; 23 cm.
Includes bibliographies.
ISBN 9171062645

WORLD POLITICS

—Conflict and compromise : international law and world order in a revolutionary age / Edward McWhinney. – Alphen aan den Rijn : Sijthoff and Noordhoff, 1981.
160p.
Bibliography: p156-158.
ISBN 0887940900

—Development and the environmental crisis : red or green alternatives? / Michael Redclift. – London : Methuen, 1984.
149p; 23cm.
Bibliography: p131-146. - Includes index.
ISBN 0416321305 Hbk Unpriced
ISBN 0416321402 Pbk Unpriced

—Politics of international economic relations / Joan Edelman Spero. – 3rd. ed. – London : Allen & Unwin, 1985.
viii,447p.
Bibliography: p405-431.
ISBN 0043820441

—Stitches in time : the Commonwealth in world politics / Arnold Smith with Clyde Sanger. – London : Deutsch, 1981.
xix,322p.

WORLD WAR, 1914–1918

—War, law and labour : the Munitions Acts, state regulation and the unions, 1915-1921 / Gerry R. Rubin. – Oxford : Clarendon Press, 1987.
288p; 22cm.
Includes index.
ISBN 0198255381 £25.00

WRECKS

—Protection of the underwater heritage / Paris : Unesco, 1981.
200p.
Includes bibliographies.
ISBN 9231018639

WRIT OF DEBT – AUSTRALIA

—Reference on service and execution of warrants and writs of attachment / Australian Law Reform Commission. – Sydney : The Commission, 1984.
v,109,6p.
Bibliography: p.109.

WRITS – GREAT BRITAIN

—Style writs for a Sheriff Court Ordinary Cause / Edinburgh : W Green & Son, 1989.
Provides styles of written pleading in a range of writs for a variety of ordinary action commonly encountered in a Sheriff Court practice.
ISBN 0414008456 Hbk

WRITS – INDIA

—Law of Writs / 3rd ed. – Lucknow : Eastern Book Company, 1983.
1,070p.

WRITS – NIGERIA

—Prerogative writs and orders under Nigerian law and constitution / by S.I.O. Aguolu. – Enugu : Star Printing and Publishing Company, 1981.
xxii,167p.
Includes index.

YEAR BOOKS

—Year Books, 11 Vols. / Abingdon : Professional Books.

Individual vols.

Unbound

YORUBA LAW

—Administration of justice in the customary courts of Yorubaland / J.O. Ajibola. – Ibadan : University Press, 1982.
ix,89p.
ISBN 019575753X

ZIMBABWE

—United Nations, international law, and the Rhodesian independence crisis / Jericho Nkala. – Oxford : Clarendon Press, 1985.
xii,288p.
Bibliography: p.275-283. - Includes index.

ZONING LAW – ENGLAND

—Guide to development and planning / by R.N.D. Hamilton. – 7th ed. – London : Oyez, 1981.
lxiv,510p; 23cm.
Previous ed.: 1975. Includes index.
ISBN 0851205496 Unpriced

—Planning decisions digest / Michael Purdue and Vincent Fraser. – London : Sweet & Maxwell, 1986.
300p; 24cm.
Covers judicial decisions back to 1948, and selected ministerial decisions since 1974. Brief summaries of each decision are included, and referenced. Material is arranged under subject headings following the structure of the Town and Country Planning Act 1971.
ISBN 0421325704 Pbk £19.00

—Planning law and procedure / A.E. Telling. – 6th ed. – London : Butterworths, 1982.
xxix,321p.
Previous ed.: 1977. Includes index.
ISBN 0406665095

—Planning law casebook / London : Laureate-Thomson, 1984.
288p.
ISBN 0907392091 Pbk £17.50

PUBLISHERS

A-Tieto Oy
Aleksanterinkatu 29 B 29, SF-33100, Tampere, Finland

A-Z Publications
Nicosia, Cyprus

Aarhus Universitetsforlag
Aarhus Universitet, 8000 Aarhus C, Denmark
Phone: (06) 197033

Abacus →Sphere Books Ltd

ABC Enterprises
GPO Box 4444, Crows Nest, NSW 2065, Australia

ABC Publishers Ltd
4 Presidential Road, P O Box 2975, Enugu, Nigeria

Aberdeen University Press
Farmers Hall, Aberdeen, AB9 2XT, Scotland
Phone: 0224 630724
Fax: 0224 643286

Abhinav Publications
E - 37 Hauz Khas, New Delhi 110 016, India
Phone: 666387

Abhishek Publications
3625 Sector 23 - D, Chandigark 160 023, India

Aboriginal Law Research Unit →University of New South Wales, Aboriginal Law Research Unit

Academic & University Publishers Group
1 Gower Street, London WC1, England
Phone: 01-580 3994

Academic Books Ltd
National House, Apollo Bunder, Bombay 400 001, India
P O BOX 567, Harare, India
Phone: 706729

Academic Press →Harcourt Brace Jovanovich

ACAS
Clifton House, Euston Road, London, NW1, England
Phone: 01-388 5100

Accademia Nazionale dei Lincei
Via della Lungara 10, I-00165 Roma, Italy
Phone: 06 650831

Accident Compensation Commission → Government Departments

Acco Amersfoort
Postbus 395, 3800 AJ Amersfoort, Netherlands

Acco Uitgevery
Tiensestraat 134-136, 3000 Leuven, Belgium
Phone: 0932 16 233520

Action for the Victims of Medical Accidents
135 Stockwell Road, London, SW9 9TN, England
Phone: 01-737 2434

Adam Smith Institute →ASI Research Ltd

Addiction Research Foundation of Ontario
33 Russell Street, Toronto, ON M5S 2S1, Canada

Addison-Wesley Publishers Ltd
Finchampstead Road, Wokingham, Berkshire, RG11 2NZ, England
Phone: 0734 794035

Adelaide Law Review Association
University of Adelaide, GPO Box 498, Adelaide, S.A. 5001, Australia
Phone: (08) 2234333

Advisory Service for Squatters
2 St. Pauls Road, London, N1, England
Phone: 01-359 8814

African Law Reports
Trinity College, Oxford, OX1 3BH, England
Phone: 0865 271476

African Universities Press
New Oluyole Ind. Estate, Phase 2, PMB 5617, Ibadan, Lagos Expressway, Nigeria

Afro World
31 Grenfell Tower, Lancaster Road, London, W11 1TG, England
Phone: 01-727 3181

Age Concern
60 Pitcairn Road, Mitcham, Surrey CR4 3LL, England
Phone: 01-640 5431

Age Concern Scotland
33 Castle Street, Edinburgh, EH2 3DN, Scotland
Phone: 031-225 5000

Ahmadu Bello University Press Ltd
PMB 1094, Zaria, Kaduna State, Nigeria

Ainsworth (Keith) Pty Ltd
Unit 4, 66a Abel Street, Penrith, NSW 2750, Australia

AIR
PO Box 48688, Sta. Bental, Vancouver, BC 7X 1A6, Canada

Aitchison Fund
3rd floor, 40 Portland Place, London, W1N 4BA, England
Phone: 01-637 2507

Ajanta Books International
1 - UB Jawahar Nagar, Bunglow Road, Delhi 110 007, India
Phone: 2917375,2926182

Ajanta Publications (India)
1-U.B. Jawahar Nagar, Bungalow Road, Delhi 110007, India

Ajaya Publishing House
Sethji Ki Kothi, Bharatpur, Rajasthan, India

Akademiai Kiado
Pb 24, U, Alkotmany U.21, 1363 Budapest, Hungary
Phone: 01 111010

Akademiforlaget →Esselte studium/ Akademiforlaget

Al Shaybani Society of International Law
4 Diagoras Street, Kermia Building, P O Box 1938, Nicosia, Cyprus
P O Box 4247, Nicosia, Cyprus

Albatross Books Pty Ltd
PO Box 320, Sutherland, NSW 2232, Australia

Aldwych Press
3 Henrietta Street, London, WC2E 8LU, England
Phone: 01-240 0856
Fax: 01-379 0609

Alemar-Phoenix Publishing House In
927 Quezon Avenue, Quezon City 3008, Philippines

Alexander Turnbull Library
Molesworth Street, PO Box 12349, Wellington North, Wellington 1, New Zealand
Phone: (4) 722101

All Africa Conference of Churches
Information Department, POB 20301, Nairobi Westlands, Kenya

All India Congress Committee
Publications Department, 5 Dr. Rajendra Prasad Road, New Delhi 110 001, India

All India Institute of Local Self Government
11 Horniman Circle, Fort, Bombay 400 001, India

All India Reporter Ltd
Medows House, Nagindas Master Road, Fort, Bombay 400 023, India
Phone: 274204
Congress Nagar, Nagpur 440012, India
Phone: 23321

Allahabad Law Agency
19 University Road, Allahabad 2, Uttar Pradesh, India

Allan (Philip) Publishers Ltd
Market Place, Deddington, Oxford OX5 4SE, England
Phone: 0869 38652
Fax: 0865 726753

Allan Wingate
44 Hill Street, London, W1X 8LB, England
Phone: 01-493 6777

Allen & Unwin
15-17 Broadwick Street, London W1V 1FP
Phone: 01-439 3126
Fax: 01-734 3884

Allen & Unwin Australia Pty Ltd
11th floor, NCR House, 8 Napier Street, PO Box 764, North Sydney, NSW, Australia
Phone: 02 9226399
Fax: 02 9224317

Allen & Unwin New Zealand Ltd
60 Cambridge Terrace, Wellington, New Zealand

Allen Lane →Penguin Books Ltd

Allen (W. H.) & Co plc
44 Hill Street, London W1X 8LB, England
Phone: 01-968 7554
Allison & Busby

Allied Publishers Pvt Ltd
13/14 Asaf Ali Road, POB 155, New Delhi 110 002, India
Phone: 275001, 270366
Fax: TX; 315153

Allison & Busby →Allen (W. H.) & Co plc

Allyn & Bacon →Simon & Schuster International Group

Almqvist & Wiksell Foerlag AB
Brunnsgraend 4, Box 2120, 10313 Stockholm, Sweden
Box 2052, 103 12 Stockholm, Sweden
Phone: 08 7893000

Almqvist & Wiksell International
Drottninggt 108, Box 45150, S-104 30 Stockholm, Sweden
Gamla Brogatan 26, P O Box 638, 101 28 Stockholm, Sweden
Phone: 010 468 237990
Fax: TX: 12430
Iustus forlag, Norstedt & Soners forlag

Alternative Publishing Co-operative Ltd
40 Levey Street, P O Box 146, Chippendale, NSW 2008, Australia
Phone: 02 6984249

Alumni Publisher
J I Geusanulun 17, POB 272, Bandung, Indonesia

Alvescot Press
PO Box 280, London, WC1R 4AG, England

Amar Prakashan
A-One-139 B, Lawrence Road, New Delhi 110 035, India
Phone: 713182

Ambassade de France
Service de Presse at d'Information, 58 Knightsbridge, London SW1, England

American Enterprise Institute for Public Policy Research
1150 17th Street NW, Washington DC 20036, USA
Phone: 202 862 5800
Fax: 202 862 7178

American Library Association
50 East Huron Street, Chicago, IL 60611, USA
Phone: 312 944 6780
Fax: 312 440 9374

Amnesty International Publications
1 Easton Street, London, WC1X 8DJ, England
Phone: 01-833 1771
Fax: 01-833 5100

Andrew (Peter) Publishing Co
4 Charlecot Road, Droitwich, Worcestershire WR9 7RP, England
Phone: 0905 778543

Angus & Robertson
PO Box 290, North Ryde, NSW 2113, Australia
Phone: 02 8884111

Angus & Robertson (UK) Ltd
16 Golden Square, London, W1R 4BN, England
Phone: 01-437 9602
Fax: 01-434 2080

Antalfy (Michael L.)
9 Theodore St, Bendigo, Victoria 3550, Australia

Antilles Publications
PO Box 815E, Eagle Hall, St. Michael, Barbados

Applied Science → Elsevier Applied Science Publishers Ltd

Arabian Information → Graham & Trotman Ltd

Arbetarskyddsfonden & Arbetslivscentrum
Box 1122, 111 81, Stockholm, Sweden

Architectural Press → Butterworth & Co (Publishers) Ltd

Archive Editions
The Broadway, Farnham Common, Slough SL2 3PQ, England
Phone: 028 14 6633
Fax: 028 14 6746

Arlington
130 Arlington Road, Camden Town, London NW1 7HP, England
Phone: 01-482 4581

Armstrong (Alan) Ltd
2 Arkwright Road, Reading RG2 0SQ, England
Phone: 0734 751855
Fax: 0734 755164

Army Educational Stores
A 22/1, Naraina Industrial, Phase 1, New Delhi 110 028, India
Nicholson Road, Ambala, Haryana, India

Arno Spitz → Berlin Verlag Arno Spitz

Arnold-Heinman Publishers (India) Put Ltd
AB/9, 1st Floor, Safdarjang Enclave, New Delhi 110 029, India

Arthur Young Management Services
Moor House, London Wall, London EC4 5HP, England

Article 19 Research and Information Centre on Censorship
90 Borough High Street, London, SE1 1LL, England
Phone: 01-403 4822

Ashford Press Publishing
1 Church Road, Shedfield, Southampton, Hampshire, SO3 2HW, England
Phone: 0329 834265
Fax: 01-935 1991

Ashish Publishing House
8/81 Punjabi Bagh, New Delhi, 110 026, India
Phone: 500581,5410924

Ashok Publishing House
Gaulati 781 000, Assam, India

ASI Research Ltd
P O Box 316, London, SW1P 3DJ, England
Phone: 01-222 4995
Adam Smith Institute

Asia Publishing House
18-20 K. Dubash Marg, Bombay, India

Asian Book Company
8A Jalan Sulaiman, 83000 Batu Pahat, Johor, India

Asian Research Services
Eastern Commercial Centre, 2/F Room 201, 397 Hennessy Road, Hong Kong
Phone: 5-733641

Aslib
Information House, 26/27 Boswell Street, London, WC1N 3JZ, England

Asselia Publishing Company
PO Box 4198, Nicosia, Cyprus

Associated Business Press
76 Shoe Lane, London, EC4A 3JB, England
Phone: 01-583 8888

Associated Magazines Ltd (Publications)
New Carmelite House, Carmelite Street, London, EC4Y 0JA, England
Phone: 01-353 6000
Fax: 01-353 1866

Association for Canadian Studies in Australia & New Zealand
C/O School of Earth Sciences, Macguarie University, North Ryde, NSW 2113, Australia

Association for Curriculum Development
PO Box 563, London N16 8XD, England
Phone: 01-254 9323

Association of Indian Universities
Deendayal Upadhya Marg, New Delhi 110 002, India

Association of Law Societies of the Republic of South Africa → South African Publishers, State Library

Association of Law Teachers
c/o Department of Public Sector Administration and Law, Sheffield City Polytechnic, Pond Street, Sheffield S1 1WB, England

Association of Metropolitan Authorities
35 Great Smith Street, Westminster, London SW1P 3BJ, England

Assuranseforeningen Gard
G Jensidige, Postboks 1563 Myrene, Arendal, Norway

ATC (Publications) Ltd
Eynsham Hall, North Leigh, Witney, Oxon, OX8 6PW, England
Phone: 0993 882553

Ateneo de Manila University Press
Layola Heights, Quezon City, POB 154, Manila, Philippines

Athlone Press
44 Bedford Row, London, WC1R 4LY, England
Phone: 01-405 9836

Atma Ram & Sons
Kashmere Gate, POB 1429, Delhi 110 006, India
Phone: 223092

Attorney General's Chambers [Isle of Man]
c/o Central Government Offices, Bucks Road, Douglas, Isle of Man
Phone: 0624 26262

Attorney General's Chambers [Sudan]
P O Box 302, Khartoum, Sudan

Auckland University Press
Auckland University, Private Bag, Auckland, New Zealand

Australasian Political Studies Association
Flinders University, Bedford Park, S.A. 5042, Australia
Phone: (08) 2752398

Australia & New Zealand Book Co Pty Ltd
PO Box 459, Brookvale, NSW 2100, Australia
P O Box 33406, Auckland 9, New Zealand
Phone: 444 5346; 444 6102
Fax: TX; 60184

Australian Academy of the Humanities
GPO Box 93, Canberra, ACT 2601, Australia

Australian Civil Liberties Union
Box 137, Carlton, Victoria 3053, Australia

Australian Copyright Council
24 Alfred Street, Milsons Point, NSW 2061, Australia

Australian Database Development Association
PO Box 53, Hawthorn, Victoria 3122, Australia

Australian Film & Television School
Box 126, North Ryde, NSW 2113, Australia

Australian Government Publishing Service
GPO Box 84, Canberra, ACT 2601, Australia
Fax: (062) 954 455
Wentworth Avenue, Kingston, ACT 2604, Australia

Australian Institute of Aboriginal Studies
PO Box 553, Canberra City, ACT 2601, Australia

Australian Institute of Criminology
PO Box 126, Wooden, ACT 2606, Australia

Australian Institute of Family Studies
300 Queen Street, Melbourne, Victoria 3000, Australia

Australian Institute of International Affairs
PO Box E181, Canberra, ACT 2600, Australia
Phone: 062 492169

Australian Law Librarians Group
W A Branch, c/o The Librarian, Deputy Crown Solicitor's Office, GPOB U1994, Perth, W A 6001, Australia
Phone: 09 4257130

Australian Law Reform Commission
99 Elizabeth Street, Sydney, NSW 2000, Australia

Australian Mineral Foundation
Conyngham Street, Private Bag 97, Glenside, SA 5065, Australia
Phone: 08-797821

Australian Mining & Petroleum Law Association Ltd
8th Floor, 160 Queen Street, Melbourne, Victoria 3000, Australia
P O Box 363, Dickson, ACT 2602, Australia
Phone: 062-498955

Australian National University Press
c/o Pergamon Press (Australia) Pty Ltd, 19a Boundary St, Rushcutters Bay, NSW 2011, Australia
PO Box 544, Potts Point, NSW 2011, Australia

Australian National University, Research School of Social Services, Dept of Law
PO Box 4, Canberra, ACT 2601, Australia
Phone: 062-492184
Research School of Social Sciences, Dept of Law, Australian National University

Australian Society of Authors
PO Box 450, Milsons Point, NSW 2061, Australia

Australian Studies Centre
27 Russell Square, London, WC1, England
Phone: 01-580 5876

Australian Tax Research Foundation
7th level, 64 Castlereagh St, Sydney, NSW 2000, Australia
19th Level, CAGA Centre, 8 Bent Street, Sydney, NSW 2001, Australia

Avebury Publishing Co Ltd
C/o Gower Publishing Co Ltd, Gower House, Croft Road, Aldershot, Hants, England
Phone: 0252-331551
Fax: 0252-344405

Avero Publications Ltd
20 Great North Road, Newcastle-upon-Tyne, NE24 4PS, England
Phone: 091 261 5790

Bagchi (K. P.) & Co
286 B B Ganguli St, Calcutta 700 012, India

Bailey Bros & Swinfen Ltd
Warner House, Bowles Well Gardens, Folkestone, Kent CT19 6Ph, England
Phone: 0303 850501
Fax: 0303 850162
Scarecrow Press

Balkema (A. A.)
Vijerweg 8, NL-3062 GP Rotterdam, (Postbus 1675, NL-3000 BR Rotterdam), Netherlands
Phone: 010 4145119

Bangladesh Institute of Development Studies
Adamjee Court, Motijheel Commercial Area, Dhaka 2, Bangladesh

Bank of England
Threadneedle Street, London, EC2R 8AH, England
Phone: 01-601 4444

Bankers Books Ltd
10 Lombard Street, London EC3V 9AS, England
Phone: 01-623 3531
Fax: 01-929 4301

Bankers Publishing Concern
26 South Patel Nagar, New Delhi, India

Barker (Arthur)
91 Clapham High Street, London, SW4 9TA, England
Phone: 01-622 9933
Fax: 01-627 3361

Barmarick Publications
Enholmes Hall, Patrington, Hull, HU12 0PR, England
Phone: 0964 630033

Basset Publications
60 North Hill, Plymouth, PL4 8HF, England
Phone: 0752-771463

Batsford (B. T.) Ltd
4 Fitzhardinge Street, London W1H 0AH, England
Phone: 01-486 8484
Fax: 01-487 4296

Battenburg (Ernst) →Verlag Ernst Battenburg Verlags-und Vertriebs GMBH

Bay Books Pty Ltd
61-69 Anzac Parade, Kensington, NSW 2033, Australia

BBC
35 Lime Grove, London, W12 8EE, England
Phone: 01-743 2122

Beattie (Derek) Publishing
PO Box 29, Twickenham TW1 3BN, England
Phone: 01-891 3513

Beckschec, H Verlagsbuchhandlung Oscar Beck
Wikelmstrasse 9, 8000 Munich, West Germany
Beckshec

Beckshec →Beckschec, H Verlagsbuchhandlung Oscar Beck

Bedford Square Press →National Council for Voluntary Organisations

Belhaven Press
25 Floral Street, London, WC2E 9DS, England
Phone: 01-240 9233
Fax: 01-379 5553

Bell & Hyman
Warner House, Bowles Well Gardens, Folkestone, Kent, CT19 6PH, England
Phone: 0303 850501
Fax: 0303 850162
15-17 Broadwick Street, London, W1V 1FP, England
Phone: 01-439 3126
Fax: 01-734 3884

Bender (Matthew) & Co Inc
17 Clifton Road, London N3 2AS, England
Phone: 01-346 2776
11 Penn Plaza, New York, NY 10001, USA
Phone: 212 967 7707
Fax: 212 244 3188

Benjamins (John) Publishing Co
Amsteldijk 44, NL-1007 HA Amsterdam, Netherlands
Phone: 020 738156
Postbus 52519, NL-1007, HA Amersterdam, Netherlands

Benn (Ernest) →Black (A. & C.)

Bennett (James), Library Services
4 Collaroy St, Collaroy, NSW 2097, Australia

Berg Publishers Ltd
77 Morrell Avenue, Oxford, OX4 1NQ, England
Phone: 0865 245104
Fax: 0865 791165

Berlin Verlag Arno Spitz
Pacelli Alle 5, Ehrenbergstrasse 29, Berlin 33 1000, West Germany
Phone: 030-8326232
Arno Spitz

Bestseller Publications Ltd
Princess House, 50 Eastcastle Street, London W1N 7AP, England
Phone: 01-631 5070
Fax: 01-631 0169
Bracken Books

Bharat Law House
J-10/13 Rajouri Gardens, New Delhi 110 027, India
Phone: 5438066

Bharatiya Publishing House
42-43 UB Jawaharragar, Delhi 110 007, India

BI Publications
359 Dadabhai Road, Flora Fountain, Bombay 400 001, India
35 Mount Road, Madras, India

Biblios Publishers Distribution Services Ltd
Star Road, Partridge Green, Horsham, West Sussex RH13 8LD, England
Phone: 0403 710971
Fax: 0403 711143

Bibliotech
E block, Childers St, Acton, ACT 2601, Australia

Bischoff (A. G.)
58 Allcroft Road, Reading, Berkshire, RG1 5HN, England
Phone: 0734 863891

Bishen Singh Mahendra Pal Singh
23-A Connaught PL, POB 137, Dehradun 248 001, India
Phone: 24048

Black (A. & C.)
35 Bedford Row, London, WC1R 4JH, England
Phone: 01-242 0946
Fax: 01-831 8478
Benn (Ernest),

Black Community Programmes South Africa
1 Cambridge Terrace, London, NW1 4LJ, England

Black Rose Books
3981 Blud. St Laurent, 416 Floor, Montreal, PQ H2W 1Y5, Canada
Phone: 514-8444076

Blackstone Press
PO Box 51, Fairfield, Victoria 3078, Australia

Blackstone Press Ltd
Aldine Place, London W12 8AA, England
Phone: 01-740 1173
Fax: 01-740 1184

Blackwell (Basil) Ltd
108 Cowley Road, Oxford, OX4 1JF, England
Phone: 0865 791100
Fax: 0865 791347

Blackwell Scientific Publications (Australia) Pty Ltd
107 Barry Street, Carlton, Vic. 3053, Australia
Phone: 03 347 0300, 03 347 5001

Blackwell Scientific Publications Ltd
Osney Mead, Oxford, OX2 0EL, England
Phone: 0865 240201
Fax: 0865 721205

Blake's →Diplomatic & Consular Publishing Services

Bloomsbury Publishing Ltd
2 Soho Square, London W1V 5DE, England
Phone: 0622 882000
Fax: 0622 78036

Board of Inland Revenue
Somerset House, Strand, London WC2R 1LB, England

Bodleian Law Library
Manor Road, Oxford OX1 3BG, England
Phone: 0865 271463

Bodley Head
31 Bedford Square, London WC1B 3SG, England
Phone: 01-255 2393
Fax: 01-255 1620

Body Corporate Publications
PO Box 579, Elsternwick, Victoria 3185, Australia.

Book Centre (Textbook Sales Ltd)
Colonial Mutual Buildings, Gordon Avenue, PO Box 3799, Harare, Zimbabwe
Phone: (10) 790691

Book Collectors Society of Australia
PO Box 442, Hawthorn, Vic, 3122, Australia
C/O The Treasurer, 64 Young Street, Cremorne, NSW 2090, Australia

Bookland Ltd
1 Sarkar Ghosh Lane, Calcutta 700 006, India
Pan Bazara, Gauhati, Assam, India

Boolarong Publications
PO Box 1130, Fortitude Valley, Queensland 4006, Australia

Boole Press Ltd
51 Sandycove Road, PO Box 5, Dun Laoghaire, Co Dublin, Ireland
Phone: 0001-808025
Fax: 0001-805990

Bowker-Saur Ltd
c/o Butterworth (Publishers) Ltd, Borough Green, Sevenoaks, Kent TN15 8PH, England
Phone: 0732 884567
Fax: 0732 884079
R R Bowker, K.G. Saur, Stirling University Press

Boyars (Marion) Publishers Ltd
24 Lacy Road, London SW15 1NL, England
Phone: 01-788 9522

BPP Publishing Ltd
BPP House, Aldine Place, London W12 8AA, England
Phone: 01-740 1111
Fax: 01-740 1184
DP Publications

BR Gruner BV Publishing Co
Niewe Heiengracht 31, NL-1011 RM Amsterdam, Netherlands
Gruner

BR Publishing Corp
29/9 Nargia Park, Shashtri Nagar, Delhi 110 007, India

Bracken Books →Bestseller Publications Ltd

Bridgefoot
18 Merrion Square, Dublin 2, Eire

Brill (E. J.)
Plantijnstraat 2, NL-2321 JC Leiden, Netherlands
Phone: 071 312624
Postbus 9000, NL-2300 PA Leiden, Netherlands

British Agencies for Adoption & Fostering
11 Southwark Street, London SE1 1RQ, England
Phone: 01-407 8800

British Association for Canadian Studies
c/o Royal Commonwealth Society Library, Northumberland Avenue, London WC2N 5BJ, England
Phone: 01-930 6733

British Columbia Continuing Legal Education Society ion
203, 1148 Hornby Street, Vancouver, BC V62 2C3, Canada

British Copyright Council
29-33 Berners Street, London W1P 4AA, England
Phone: 01-580 5544

British Institute of Human Rights
17 Russell Square, London WC1B 5DR, England
Phone: 01-637 0420

British Institute of International & Comparative Law
Charles Clore House, 17 Russell Square, London, WC1, England
Phone: 01-636 5802

British Library Research & Development Group
2 Sheraton Street, London, W1V 4BH, England
Phone: 01-323 7054
Fax: 01-323 7251

British Media Publications
Windsor Court, East Grinstead House, East Grinstead, West Sussex RH19 1XA, England
Phone: 0342 26972
Fax: 0342 315130

British Medical Association
BMA House, Tavistock Square, London, WC1H 9JP, England
Phone: 01-387 4499
Fax: 01-388 2544

British Medical Journal
BMA House, Tavistock Square, London, WC1H 9JP, England
Phone: 01-387 4499
Fax: 01-383 6402

British North Americal Research Organisation
Grosvenor Gardens House, Grosvenor Gardens, London, SW1, England
Phone: 01-828 6644

British Overseas Trade Board
1 Victoria Street, London SW1, England
Phone: 01-215 7877

British Parliamentary Group for World Government
St Stephens House, Victoria Embankment, London, SW1, England
Phone: 01-930 0034

British Property Federation
35 Catherine Place, London, SW1E 6DY, England
Phone: 01-828 0111

British Psychological Society
St Andrews House, 48 Princess Road East, Leicester LE1 7DR, England
Phone: 0533 549568
Fax: 0533 544248

British Society for the History of Science
31 High Street, Stanford-in-the vale, Faringdon, Oxon, SN7 8LH, England

Broadview Press Ltd
PO Box 1243, Peterborough, Ontario K9J 7H5., Canada
Phone: 705-743 8990

Brooker & Friend
21-23 College Street, Wellington 1, (PO Box 43), New Zealand
P O Box 43, New Zealand

Brown Legal Publications
CP 180, Cowansville, P. Quebec, J2K 3H6, Canada

Bruylant (Emile)
Rue de la Regence 67, B-1000 Bruxelles, Belgium
Phone: 02 5129845
Fax: 02 5117202

BSP Professional
Osney Mead, Oxford, OX2 0EL, England
Phone: 0865-240201
Fax: 0865-721205

Building Publishers
POB 229, 0127 Silvertown, South Africa

Building Societies Association
3 Savile Row, London W1X 1AF, England
Phone: 01-734 0655
Fax: 01-734 6416

Bulzoni Editore srl
Via dei Liburni 14, I-00185 Roma, Italy
Phone: 06-4455207

Bureau of Labour Publications
Business Centre, Dunolly Road, POB 5833, Karachi 2, Pakistan

Burnett & Company
21 Tower Street, London, WC2H 9NS, England
Phone: 01-836 0606

Burns & Maceachern Ltd
62 Railside Road, Suite 3, Don Mills, Ontario M3A 7A6, Canada

Burroughs & Co Ltd
517-7th Avenue, S.W. Calgary, Alta T2P 0Y4, Canada

Business Books Ltd
Brookmount House, 62-65 Chandos Place, London WC2N 4NW, England
Phone: 01-240 3411

Business Council of Australia
GPO Box 387 D, Melbourne, Victoria 3001, Australia

Business Education Publishers Ltd
Leighton House, 17 Vine Place, Sunderland SR1 3NA, England
Phone: 091-567 4963
Fax: 091-510 9442

Business Law Communications Ltd
53 Fleet Street, London, EC4Y 1BY, England
Phone: 01-353 8154
Grays Farm Production Village, Grays Farm Road, Orpington, Kent, England

Business Law Education Centre
140 William Road, Melbourne, Victoria 3000, Australia
Phone: 03 675383

Butterworth & Co Asia Pte Ltd
30 Robinson Road, No 12-01, Tuang Sing Towers, Singapore
Butterworths (Asia)

Butterworth & Co (Publishers) Ltd
Borough Green, Sevenoaks, Kent TN15 8PH, England
Phone: 0732 884567
Fax: 0432 884079
Butterworths, Architectural Press

Butterworths → Butterworth & Co (Publishers) Ltd

Butterworths (Asia) → Butterworth & Co Asia Pte Ltd

Butterworths (Canada)
2265 Midland Avenue, Scarborough, Ontario, M1P 4S1, Canada
Phone: 416-292 1421
Fax: 416 292 6970

Butterworths of New Zealand Ltd
205-207 Victoria Street, Wellington, New Zealand

Butterworths Pty Ltd
271-273 Lane Cove Road, North Ryde, NSW 2113, Australia
Phone: 887 3444
Fax: 887 4555

CAA → Civil Aviation Authority

Cabay Libraire-Editeur
Agora 11, 1348 Louvain-la-Neuve, Belgium

Cabinet Office
Whitehall, London SW1A 2AZ, England
Phone: 01-273 3000

Calder (John) Publishers Ltd
18 Brewer Street, London W1R 4AS, England
Phone: 01-734 3786

Caledonian Books
Slains House, Collieston, Ellon, Aberdeenshire AB4 9RT, Scotland
Phone: 035 887 275/288

Cambray
Kent House, P-33 Mission Row Extension, Calcutta 700013, India

Cambridge University Library → University of Cambridge, Library

Cambridge University Press
The Edinburgh Building, Shaftesbury Road, Cambridge CB2 2RU, England
Phone: 0223 312393
Fax: 0223 31502

Cambridge University Press [Australia]
PO Box 85, Oakleigh, Victoria 3166, Australia

Campaign for Comprehensive Education
17 Grand Avenue, London SW15 6HH, England

Campaign for Justice in Divorce
PO Box 9, Hereford HR1 3UT, England

Canada Law Book Co
240 Edward Street, Aurora, Ontario L4G 3S9, Canada
Phone: 416 773 6300

Canadian Advisory Council on the Status of Women
110 O'Connor Street, Ottawa, Ontario, K1P 5R5, Canada
Phone: 613 992 4975

Canadian Arbitration, Conciliation and Amicable Composition Centre → International Federation of Commercial Arbitration Institutions

Canadian Arctic Resources Committee
Room 11, 46 Elgin Street, Ottawa, Ontario, K1P 5K6, Canada
Phone: 613-236 7379

Canadian Association for Health, Physical Education & Recreation, Inc.
333 River Road, 12th Floor, Ottawa, Ontario, K1L 8H9, Canada
Phone: 613-7485622

Canadian Broadcasting Corporation Enterprises,
Mutual Street, POB 500, Station A, Toronto, Ontario, M5W 1E6, Canada
P O Box 4039, Station A, Toronto, Ont. M5W 2P6
Phone: 416-925 3311

Canadian Council on Social Development
55 Parkdale Avenue, POB 3505, Station C, Parkdale Avenue, Ottawa, Ontario K1Y 4G1, Canada
Phone: 613 728 1865

Canadian Criminal Justice Association
55 Parkland Avenue, Ottawa, Ontario, K1Y 1E5, Canada
Phone: 613-725 3715

Canadian Economic Policy Unit
Montreal, Canada

Canadian Government Publishing Centre
Supply and Services Canada, Ottawa, K1A 0S9, Canada
Phone: 819 997 2560
Fax: TX; 0534296

Canadian Human Rights Foundation
1980 Sherbrooke St W., Suite 340, Montreal, Quebec H3H 1E8, Canada
Phone: 514 932 7826

Canadian Institute for the Administration of Justice
Faculte de Droit, Universite de Montreal, CP 6128, Canada

Canadian Institute of International Affairs
15 Kings College Circle, Toronto, Ontario, M5S 2V9, Canada
Phone: 416 979 1851

Canadian Institute of Mining & Metallurgy
Suite 400, 1130 West Sherbrooke Street, Montreal, PQ H3A 2M8, Canada
Phone: 514 842 3461
Fax: TX; 5562344

Canadian Institute of Resources Law
2500 University Drive NW, Calgary, Alta, T2N 1N4, Canada
Phone: 403 220-3200
Fax: TX; 3821545

Canadian Law Information Council
161 Laurier Avenue, West, 5th Floor, Ottawa, Ontario, K1P 5J2, Canada

Canadian Library Association
200 Elgin Street, Ottawa, Ontario, K2P 1L5, Canada
Phone: 613 232 9625

Canadian Tax Foundation
100 University Avenue, Toronto, Ontario, M5J 1V6, Canada.
Publications Dept, 130 Adelaide St. W., Suite 1900, Toronto, Ontario M5H 3P5, Canada
Phone: 416 863 9784
Fax: 416 863 9585

Canberra College of Advanced Education Libary
PO Box 1, Belconnen, ACT 2616, Australia
Phone: 062 522051

Cape (Jonathan)
32 Bedford Square, London WC1B 3SG, England
Phone: 01-225 2393
Fax: 01-255 1620

Careers & Occupational Information Centre
Room W1103, Moonfoot, Sheffield S1 4PQ, England
Phone: 0742 704563
Fax: 0742 752035

CARFAC
36 Elgin Street, Ottawa, Ontario K1P 5K5, Canada

Carfax Publishing Company
PO Box 25, Abingdon, Oxon OX14 1RW, England

Carleton University
Colonel By Drive, Ottawa, Ontario K15 5B6, Canada

Carswell Co Ltd
2330 Midland Avenue, Agincourt, Ontario, M1S 1P7, Canada
Phone: 416-291 8421

Casdec Ltd
Broadwood View, Chester le Street, Co Durham DH3 3NJ, England
Phone: 091-388 0421

Cass (Frank) & Co Ltd
Gainsborough House, 11 Gainsborough Road, London E11 1RS, England
Phone: 01-530 4226
Fax: 01-530 7795

Cassell plc
Artillery House, Artillery Row, London SW1P 1RT, England
Phone: 01-222 7676
Fax: 01-799 1514
Distribution, Cassell plc, Stanley House, 3 Fleets Lane, Poole, Dorset BH15 3AJ, England
Phone: 0202 670581
Chapman (Geoffrey), Tycooly

Castle Books
3 Blackdown, Leamington Spa, Warks CV32 6RA, England
Phone: 0926 28370

Castlevale Publishers Ltd
William House, 14 Worple Road, London SW19 4DD, England
Phone: 01-879 1973

Catholic Audio Visual Centre
50 Abbotsford Road, Homebush, NSW 2140, Australia

Catholic Truth Society
38-40 Eccleston Square, London SW1V 1PD, England
Phone: 01-834 4392
CTS

Cave (H. W.) & Co Ltd
81 Sir Baron Jayatilaka Mawatha, POB 25 Colombo 01, Sri Lanka

Caxton Street Legal Service
PO Box 320, Paddington, Queensland 4064, Australia

CBD Research Ltd
15 Wickham Road, Beckenham, Kent BR3 2JS, England
Phone: 01-650 7745

CBI →Confederation of British Industry

CCH Australia
PO Box 230, North Ryde, NSW 2113, Australia
Phone: 02-8882555

CCH Canadian Ltd
6 Garamond Court, Don Mills, Ontario, M3C 1Z5, Canada.
Phone: 416 441 2992
Fax: 416 441 3418

CCH Editions Ltd
Telford Road, Bicester, Oxfordshire OX6 0XD, England
Phone: 0869 253300
Fax: 0869 245814

CCH (NZ)
17 Kahika Road, Beachhaven, Auckland, New Zealand
P O Box 2378, New Zealand

CD Howe Institute
125 Adelaide St. East, Toronto, Ontario, M5C 1L7, Canada
Howe Institute

CEDAR Press
George Street, POB 616, Bridgetown, Barbados
Phone: 427 2681
Fax: TX; 2335

CEMT
2 rue Andre-Pascal, 75775 Paris cedex 16, France
Phone: 4524 8200
Fax: 4524 8500

Central Books Ltd
14 The Leathermarket, London SE1 3ER, England
Phone: 01-407 5447
Fax: 01-378 1811

Central Law Agency
11 University Road, Allahabad 211-002, India

Central Office of Information
Hercules Road, London SE1, England
Phone: 01-928 2345
COI

Central Services Unit for University & Polytechnic Careers Advisory Services
Crawford House, Precinct Centre, Manchester M13 9EP, England
Phone: 061-273 4233
Fax: 061-273 6657

Centre d'Edition du Gouvernement du Canada Approvisionement et SCGPC,
270 rue Albert Street, Ottawa, Ontario, Canada, K1A OS9

Centre for Criminological and Socio-Legal Studies →University of Sheffield, Centre for Criminological & Socio-Legal Studies

Centre for Environmental Management and Planning →University of Aberdeen, Centre for Environmental Management & Planning

Centre for Independent Studies
PO Box 92, St Leonards, NSW 2065, Australia
PO Box 32, Turramura, NSW 2074, Australia

Centre for Industrial Relations, University of Toronto →University of Toronto, Center for Industrial Relations

Centre for Legal & Business Information
Rectory Road, Great Waldingfiled, Sudbury, Suffolk CO10 0TL, England
Phone: 0787 78607

Centre for Professional Development
PO Box 459, South Melbourne, Victoria 3205, Australia

Centre for Research of Air & Space Law,
Mc Gill University, 3690 Peel Street, Montreal Quebec, H3A 1W9, Canada

Centre for Socio-Legal Studies, Social Science Research Council
Wolfson College, Oxford OX2 6UD, England
SSRC-Social Science Research Council

Centre of Advanced Study in Ancient Indian History & Culture →University of Calcutta

Centre of Criminology, University of Toronto →University of Toronto, Centre of Criminology

Century Hutchinson (Australia) Pty Ltd
PO Box 496, Hawthorn, Victoria 3122, Australia

Certification Office for Trade Unions & Employers' Associations
PO Box 244, 29 Lincolns Inn Fields, London WC2, England
Phone: 01-242 6855

Chadwyck-Healey Ltd
Cambridge Place, Cambridge CB2 1NR, England
Phone: 0223 311479

Chaitanya Publishing House
5-A University Road, Allahabad 211 002, India

Chand (S.) & Co Pvt Ltd
POB 5733, Ram Nagar, New Delhi 110 055, India

Chapman & Hall →Routledge, Chapman & Hall

Chapman (Geoffrey) →Cassell plc

Chapman (Paul) Publishing Ltd
144 Liverpool Road, London N1 1LA, England
Phone: 01-609 5315

Chartered Institute of Public Finance & Accountancy
3 Robert Street,, London WC2N 6BH, England
Phone: 01 930 3456

Chatterjee Publishers
49/A Banerjee Para Road, Calcutta 700 041, India

Chatto & Windus Ltd
30 Bedford Square, London WC1B 3SG, England
Phone: 01-255 2393
Fax: 01-255 1620
Hogarth Press

Checkmate/Arnold →Edward Arnold (Publishers) Ltd

Chetara Publications
E 180 Greater Kailash Part II, New Delhi 110 048, India

Child Poverty Action Group
1 Bath Street, London EC1, England
Phone: 01-253 3406

Children Need Fathers
18 Green Lane, Grendon, Atherstone, Warwickshire CV9 2PL, England
Phone: 0827 72427

Children's Legal Centre
20 Compton Terrace, London N1 2UN, England
Phone: 01-359 6251/2

Chinese University Press
Chinese University of Hong Kong, Sha Tin, New Territories, Hong Kong
Phone: 0-612211 EXT. 661

Chugh Publications
P O Box 101, 2 Strachey Road, Civil Lines, Allahabad 380 001, India

Churchill Livingstone
Robert Stevenson House, 1-3 Baxters Place, Leith Walk, Edinburgh EH1 3AF, Scotland
Phone: 031-556 2424
Fax: 031-558 1278

Cisalpino-la Goliardica
Via Rezia, 4-20135 Milano, Italy
Phone: 02-5452154

Citizens Rights Office
1 Macklin Street, Drury Lane, London WC2B 5NH, England
Phone: 01-405 5942

City of Coventry Libraries Arts & Museums Department, Librariess Division
Council House, Earl Street, Coventry, England

Civil Aviation Authority
45 Kingsway, London WC2, England
Phone: 01-359 7311
CAA

Clarendon Press →Oxford University Press

Clark (T. & T.) Ltd
59 George Street, Edinburgh EH2 2LQ, Scotland
Phone: 031-225 4703
Fax: 031-622 4282

Clarke (James) & Co
PO Box 60, Cambridge CB1 2NT, England
Phone: 0223 350865
Fax: 0223 66951

Classical Publishing Co
28 Shopping Centre, Karampura, New Delhi 100 015, India
Phone: 563689

Clearing House on Migration Issues
Ecumenical Migration Centre, 133 Church St, Richmond, Victoria 3121, Australia

Clement (Publishers) Ltd
Chequers, Sharrington, Melton Constable, Norfolk NR24 2PG, England
Phone: 0263 860308

Clio Distribution Services
55 St Thomas Street, Oxford OX1 1JG, England
Phone: 0865 250333
Fax: 0865 790358

Cobden Trust
21 Tabard Street, London SE1, England
Phone: 01-403 3888

Code of Advertising Practice Committee
Brook House, 2-16 Torrington Place, London WC1E 7HN, England
Phone: 01-580 5555
Fax: 01-631 3051

Coghill Publishing
PO Box 94, Malvern, Victoria 3144, Australia

COI →Central Office of Information

College of Estate Management
Whiteknights, Reading, Berkshire RG6 2AW, England

College of Management
Dunchurch, Rugby, Warwickshire CV22 6QW, England

Collets
Denington Estate, Wellingborough, Northants NN8 2QT, England
Phone: 0933 224351

Collins (William) Sons & Co Ltd
8 Grafton Street, London W1X 3LA, England
Phone: 01-493 7070
Fax: 01-493 3061
Fontana

Colombo Apothecaries Co Ltd
POB 31, Colombo, Sri Lanka

Columba Press
The Rise, Mount Merrion, Blackrock, Co Dublin, Eire
Phone: 0001 832954

Columbia University Press
c/o Wolfgang Wingerter, 15a Epsom Road, Guildford, Surrey GU1 3JT, England

Comite International de la Croix-Rouge
17 Av de la Paix, CH-1211 Geneve 11, Switzerland

Commercial Economic Advisory Service of Australia
PO Box 104, St Leonards, NSW 2065, Australia

Commission for Racial Equality
Elliot House, 10-12 Allington Street, London SE1E 5EH, England
Phone: 01-828 7022
CRE

Commission of the European Communities
rue Alcide de Gasper, Kirchberg, 3423/3446 COMMER LU, Luxembourg
200 Rue de la Loi, 1040 Brussels, Belgiuum
Phone: 02-2351111
Fax: TX; 21877

Commonwealth Secretariat (Legal Division)
Marlborough House, Pall Mall, London SW1Y 5HX, England
Phone: 01-839 3411

Communist Party of Great Britain
16 St. John Street, London EC1, England
Phone: 01-251 4406

Community Legal Education Ontario
62 Noole Street, Torento, Ontario, M6K 2C9, Canada
Phone: 416-530 1800

Company Law Institute of India Pvt Ltd
88 Thayagaraya Road, Madras 600 017, India

Concept Publishing Co
H-13 Bali Nagar, POB 6274, New Delhi 110 015, India
Phone: 503967

Conch Magazine Ltd
113 Douglas Road, POB 573, Owerri, Imo State, Nigeria

Confederation of British Industry
Centre Point, New Oxford Street, London WC1A 1DV, England
Phone: 01-379 7400
CBI

Conservative Political Centre
32 Smith Square, Westminster, London SW1P 3HH, England
Phone: 01-222 9000
Fax: 01-222 1135

Constable & Co Ltd
10 Orange Street, London WC2H 7EG, England
Phone: 01-930 0801

Construction Group
Longman House, Burnt Hill, Harlow, Essex CM20

Construction Publications
PO Box 1341, Crows Nest, NSW 2065, Australia

Consumer Credit Legal Service
174 Victoria Parade, East Melbourne, Victoria 3002, Australia

Consumers' Association
2 Marylebone Road, London NW1 4DX, England
Phone: 01-486 5544

Context Legal Services Ltd
Unit 5, Grove Park, Waltham Road, White Waltham, Maidenhead, England
Phone: 0628 8826655

Continuing Legal Education Society of British Columbia,
Suite 200, 1148 Hornby Street, Vancouver, BC V6Z 2C3, Canada

Contracts and Commercial Law Reform Committee

New Zealand Law Commission, Box 2590, Wellington, New Zealand

Cooryco Media
GPO Box 2498V, Melbourne, Victoria 3001, Australia

Copp Clark Publishing Co
517 Wellington Street West, Toronto, Ontario, M5V 1G1, Canada
Phone: 416 238 6074
Fax: 416 238 6075

Cork University Press
University College, Cork, Eire
Phone: 010 35321276871

Coronet Books
311 Bainbridge Street, Philadelphia, PA 19147, USA
Phone: 215 925 2762
1 Elizabeth Place, Mairangi Bay, Auckland 10, New Zealand
Phone: 9 478 2134

Corpus Information Services
1450 Don Mills Road, Don Mills, Ontario, M35 2X7, Canada
Phone: 416 445 6641
Fax: 416 442 2077

Council for Scientific & Industrial Research
POB 395, 0001 Pretoria, South Africa

Council of Europe
Av. de l'Europe, BP 431 R6, F-67006 Strasbourg Cedax, France, 1558, 1559
Phone: 886 14961
Directorate of Human Rights, Directorate of Press & Information

Craftsman Publishing
Private Bag 260, Burwood, Victoria 3125, Australia

CRE → Commission for Racial Equality

Criminal Law Reform Committee
c/o New Zealand Law Commission, PO Box 2590, Wellington, New Zealand

Croner Publications
46-50 Coombe Road, New Malden, Surrey KT3 4QL, England

Croom Helm Australia
c/o Methuen Australia Pty Ltd, 44 Waterloo Road, North Ryde, NSW 2133, Australia

Croom Helm Ltd
Provident House, Burrell Row, Beckenham, Kent BR3 1AT, England

Crown Prosecution
Home Office, Queen Anne's Gate, London SW1, England
Phone: 01-273 3000
Prosecuting Solicitors Society of England and Wales

CTS → Catholic Truth Society

Cujas SA, Editions
4-8 Rue de la Maison Blanche, F-75013 Paris, France

Current Book House
Maruti Lane, Raghunath Dadaji 57, POB 10071, Bombay 400 001

Current Events
15 Rajpur Road, Dehra Dun, Uttar Pradesh, India

Dag Hammarskjold Foundation
Dag Hammarskjold Centre, Oure Slottsgatan 2, S-752 20 Uppsala, Sweden

Daily Mail
New Carmelite House, Carmelite Street, London EC4, England
Phone: 01-606 1234

Dalhousie University
Halifax, NS, B3H 4H8, Canada
Phone: 902 424 2526

Dalton Publishing
GPO Box 549, Canberra City, ACT 2601, Australia

David & Charles Ltd
Brunel House, Newton Abbot, Devon TQ12 4PU, England
Phone: 0626 61121
Fax: 0626 64463

Dawson Microfiche
Cannon House, Parkfarm Road, Folkestone, Kent CT19 5EE, England

De Daro Publishing
2075 University Street, Suite 900, Montreal, PQ H3A 2L1, Canada
6537 Mountain Sights Avenue, Montreal, P Q H3W 2Z5, Canada

De Gruyter (Walter) & Co
Genthiner Strasse 13, D-1000 Berlin 30, West Germany
Phone: 030 26005-0
Fax: 030 26005251
Postfach 110240, D-1000 Berlin 11, West Germany

De Tempel
Uitgeverij BVBA, Tempelhof 41, B-8000 Brugge, Belgium

Deakin University Press
Deakin University, Geelong, Victoria 3217, Australia
Phone: 052 471 156
Fax: 052 442 777

Deboo (Richard) Ltd
51 Wellington Street, Toronto, Ontario, M5T 1H2, Canada

Deckers (R.) Verlag
IM Weifer 10, Postfach 102640, Heidelberg 6900, West Germany
Phone: 06221 489250

Deep & Deep Publications
D-1/24 Rajouri Gardens, New Delhi 110 027, India
Phone: 504498

Deloitte Haskins & Sells
Melrose House, 42 Dingwall Road, Croydon, Surrey CR0 2NE, England
Phone: 01-681 5242
Fax: 01-760 0897

Dent (J. M.) & Sons Ltd
91 Clapham High Street, London SW4 7TA, England
Phone: 01-622 9933
Fax: 01-672 3361

Dent (J. M.) Pty Ltd
112 Lewis Road, Knoxfield, Victoria 3180, Australia
Phone: 03-221 7333
Fax: 03-221 9885

Department of Education & Science
Elizabeth House, York Road, London SE1 7PH, England

Department of Employment
97 Tottenham Court Road, London W1, England
Phone: 01-636 8616
Caxton House, Tothill Street, London SW1H 9NF, England
Phone: 01-273 3000

Department of History, University of New Brunswick → University of New Brunswick

Department of Labour Library
Publications Bureau, POB 575, Colombo 01, Sri Lanka

Department of Management Studies, University of Waikato → University of Waikato

Department of Political Science, University of Tasmania → University of Tasmania, Dept of Political Science

Department of the Environment
2 Marsham Street, London SW1, England
Phone: 01-276 3000

Department of Trade and Industry
1 Victoria Street, London SW1H 0ET, England
Phone: 01-215 7877

Design Council Books
28 Haymarket, London SW1Y 4SU, England
Phone: 01-839 8000
Fax: 01-925 2130

Detselig Enterprises Ltd
Suite 205, 17 14th Street NW, Canada
POB 399, Calgary, Alta, T3A 2G3, Canada
Phone: 403 283 0900

Deutsch (Andre)
105 Great Russell Street, London WC1B 3LJ, England
Phone: 01-850 2746
Fax: 01-631 3253
c§o David and Charles Inc, PO Box 257, North Pomfret, USA

Development Academy of the Philippines
San Miguel Avenue, Ortigas Pasig, POB 5160 MCC, Makati Metro Manila, Philippines

Devon & Cornwall Record Society
7 The Close, Exeter EX1 1EZ, England

Dewan dan Pustaka
Jalan Wisma Putra, POB 10803, 50926 Kuala Lumpur, Malaysia

Dhanpat Rai & Sons
1682 Nai Sarak, Delhi 110 006, India

Diplomatic & Consular Publishing Services
Thirlestane Works, Colney Hatch Lane, London N10, England
Blake's

Directorate of Human Rights →Council of Europe

Directorate of Press & Information →Council of Europe

Ditchley Foundation
Ditchley Park, Enstone, Oxford OX7 4ER, England
Phone: 060 872 346

Divine Word University of Tacloban
Tacloban City 7101, Philippines

DK Publications
29/9 Nargia Park, Shakti Nagar, Delhi 110 007, India

Dominican Publications
69 Upper O'Connell Street, Dublin 1, Eire
42 Parnell Street, Dublin 1, Eire
Phone: 0001 721611

Douglas & McIntyre Ltd
1615 Venables Street, Vancouver, BC, V5L 2H1, Canada
Phone: 604 254 7191
Fax: 604 254 9099

Dow Jones-Irwin Inc
1818 Ridge Road, Homewood, IL 60430, USA
Phone: 312 798 6000
Fax: 312 798 7296

DP Publications →BPP Publishing Ltd

DP Publications Ltd
8 Warehouse, Grand Union Industrial Estate, Unit 6, Abbey Road, London, NW10 7UL
Phone: 01-965 8898

Droz SA
Librarie, 11 rue Massot, CP 389, CH-1211 Geneve, Switzerland
Phone: 022 466666
Fax: 022 472391

Dryden Press
One Salt Creek Lane, Hinsdale, IL 60521, USA
Phone: 312 920 2450

Duckworth (Gerald) & Co Ltd
The Old Piano Factory, 43 Gloucester Crescent, London NW1 7DY, England
Phone: 01-485 3484

Duncker & Humblot
Dietrich-Schafer-Weg 9, Postfach 410329, D-1000, Berlin 41, GFR
Phone: 030 790006-0

Dunmore Press
109 Napier Road, POB 5115, Palmerston North, New Zealand

Dunrod Press
8 Brown's Road, Newtownabbey, Co. Antrim BT36 8RN, Northern Ireland
Phone: 023-13 2362

Dutch Efficiency Bureau
Krammer 7, NL-2641 TZ, Pijnacker, Netherlands
Phone: 01736 4431
Postbus 90, NL-2640, Pijnacker, Netherlands

East African Literature Bureau →University of Dar es Salaam

East African Publishing House
Lusaka Close, PO Box 30571, Nairobi, Kenya

East and West Publishing Co
22 Corner Chambers, Chundrigar Road, Karachi 0102, Pakistan

Eastern Book Agency
4 Wood Street, Calcutta 700 016, India

Eastern Book Co
34 Lalbagh, Lucknow 226 001, India
Phone: 43171, 44328, 46517

Eastern Law House Pvt Ltd
54 Ganesh Chunder Avenue, Calcutta 700 013, India
Phone: 244999

Eastern Pubishers
8-C Ramarath Majundar Street, Calcutta 9, West Bengal, India

Economic & Social Research Institute
4 Burlington Road, Dublin 4, Eire
Phone: 0001 760115

Economist Intelligence Unit
Spencer House, 27 St. James's Place, London SW1 1NT, England

Economist Publications Ltd
40 Duke Street, London W1A 1DW, England
Phone: 01-493 6711
Fax: 01-499 9767

Edinburgh University Press
22 George Square, Edinburgh EH8 9LT, Scotland
Phone: 031 667 1011
Fax: 031 667 7938

Editions de l'Universite de Bruxelles
av Paul Heger 26, B-1050 Bruxelles, Belgium

Editions Rodopi b.v.
Keizersgracht 302-304, NL 1016 Ex Amsterdam, Netherlands

Editoriale Scientifica
via Chiatamone 606, I-80212 Napoli, Italy

Editrice Pontificia Universita Gregoriana
Piazza della Pilotta 4, I-00187 Roma, Italy

Edmond Montgomery
The Esplanade, Suite 309, Toronto, Ontario, M5E 1A7, Canada.

Edsall (B.) & Co Ltd
124 Belgrave Road, London SW1V 2BL, England

Edward Arnold (Australia)
PO Box 234, Caulfield East, Victoria 3145, Australia

Edward Arnold (Publishers) Ltd
41 Bedford Square, London, WC1B 3DQ, England
Phone: 01-637 7161
Fax: 01-436 5776
Checkmate/Arnold

Election Archives
CA/33 Delhi, 100 027, India

Electronica Books →IEEE Computer Society Press

Ell (David) Press
PO Box 168, Chippendale, NSW 2008, Australia

Elliot Right Way Books
Kingswood Buildings, Brighton Road, Lower Kingswood, Tadworth, Surrey KY20 6TD, England

Elm Publications
Seaton House, Kings Ripton, Huntingdon, Cambs PE17 2NJ, England
Phone: 04873 238

Elsevier Applied Science Publishers Ltd
Crown House, Linton Road, Barking, Essex IG11 8JU, England
Phone: 01-594 7272
Fax: 01-594 5942
Applied Science

Elsevier Science Publishers BV
Molenwerf 1, Postbus 211, NL-1000 AE Amsterdam, Netherlands
Phone: 020 5159222
Postbus 2400, 1000 CK Amsterdam, Netherlands
Phone: (020) 5862911
North Holland

Employer's Federation of India
Army & Navy Building, 148 Mahatma Gandhi Road, Fort, Bombay 400 001, India

Engel (Norbert Paul)
Elbinger Strasse 3, Postfach 1670, D-7640 Kehl am Rhein, West Germany
Phone: 07851 2463

Engineering Employers Federation
61 Broadway House, Tothill Street, London SW1H 9NQ, England
Phone: 222 7777
Fax: 222 2782

Engineering Industry Training Board
54 Clarendon Road, Watford, Hertfordshire, WD1 1LB
Phone: 0923 38441
Fax: 0923 43025

Engineering Law Publications of India
308 Rajerdra Nagar, Lucknow 226 004, India

Environmental Council
Grand Annex Building, 84 Boulcott Street, Wellington, New Zealand
PO Box 10382, New Zealand

Environmental Meditation International Inc
171 Nepean Street, Suite 200, Ottawa, Ontario, K2P OB4, Canada

Equal Opportunities Commission
Overseas House, Quay Street, Manchester M3 3HN, England
Phone: 061-833 9244

Equation →Thorsons Publishing Group Ltd

Erma di Bretschneider
Via Cassiodora 19, POB 6192, I-00193 Roma, Italy
Phone: 06 6874127
L'Erma di Bretschneider

ESC Publishing Ltd
Mill Street, Oxford OX2 0JU, England
Phone: 0865 249248
Fax: 0865 792301

Ess Ess Publications
4835/24 Ansari Road, New Delhi 110 002, India
Phone: 269667

Esselte Studium
Scheelegatan 24, Stockholm 11285, Sweden
Sundbybergsvagen, 1, 171 76 Solna, Sweden
Phone: 08-734 3000

Esselte studium/ Akademiforlaget
Karl Gustavsgatan 13, Box 3075, 400 10 Goteburg, Sweden
Phone: (031) 179600
Akademiforlaget

Estates Gazette
151 Wardour Street, London W1V 4BN, England
Phone: 01-437 0141
Fax: 01-437 2432

Ethiope Publishing Corp
Murtala Mohammed Street, PMB 1192, Benin City, Nigeria

Eurasia Publishing House Pvt Ltd
Ram Nagar, New Delhi 100 055, India

Euromoney plc
Nestor House, Playhouse Yard, London EC4V 5EX, England
Phone: 01-236 3288

Europa Publications Ltd
18 Bedford Square, London WC1B 3JN, England
Phone: 01-580 8236

European Atlantic Movement
7 Cathedral Close, Exeter, EX1 1EZ

European Book Service - PBD Ltd
St Leonards House, West Malling, Kent ME19 6PE, England
Phone: 0732 841149

European Business Publications
Chequers, Sharrington, Melton Constable, Norfolk NR24 2PG, England
Phone: 0263 860308

European Conference of Ministers of Transport
33 rue de Franqueville, 75006 Paris, France
Phone: 1-452 48200

European Law Centre Ltd
7 Swallow Place, London, W1
Phone: 409 3322
Fax: 629 0373

European Office for Quality Control
Postfach 2613, CH-3001 Bern, Switzerland

European Parliament
Kirchberg, Luxembourg

European Space Agency
DTI, Ashdown House, Room 123, Victoria Street, London SW1E 6RB, England
Phone: 01-212 5638

European Study Conferences Ltd
Douglas House, Queens Square, Corby, Northamptonshire NN17 1PL, England
Phone: 0536 204224
Fax: 0536 204218

Eurospan Ltd
3 Henrietta Street, London WC2E 8LU, England
Phone: 01-240 0856
John Hopkins University, Foreign Policy Institute, University of Georgia

Eurostudy Publishing Co Ltd
Ludgate House, 107 Fleet Street, London EC4A 2AB, England
Phone: 01-583 1025
Fax: 01-583 1895

Evidence Law Reform Committee
Wellington, New Zealand

Faber & Faber Ltd
3 Queen Square, London WC1N 3AU, England
Phone: 01-278 6881
Fax: 01-278 3817

Fabian Society
11 Dartmouth Street, London SW1H 9BN, England
Phone: 01-222 8877

Fabritius Og Sonners
Brobekkun 80, Oslo 5, Norway
Phone: 02 640888

Facts on File
Collins Street, Oxford OX4 1XJ, England
Phone: 0865 728399
Fax: 0865 726753

Faculty of Commerce & Business, University of British Columbia → University of British Columbia, Faculty of Commerce & Business

Faculty of Environmental Studies, York University → University of York

Faculty of Law Library, University of the West Indies → University of the West Indies, Faculty of Law Library

Fairplay Publications Ltd
20 Ullswater Crescent, Coulsdon, Surrey CR3 2HR, England
Phone: 01-660 2811
Fax: 01-660 2824

Family Law
c/o Jordan & Sons Ltd, 21 St Thomas Street, Bristol BS1 6JS, England
Phone: 0272 230600
Fax: 0272 230063

Family Rights Group
6-9 Manor Gardens, Holloway Road, London N7 6LA, England
Phone: 01 272 7308/4231

Farming Press Books
4 Friars Courtyard, 30-32 Princes Street, Ipswich, Suffolk IP1 1RJ, England
Phone: 0473 43011
Fax: 0473 240501

Faul (Denis)
St.Patrick's Academy, Dungannon, Co Tyrone, Ulster

Federal Publications (S) Pte Ltd
Times Jurong, 2 Jurong Port Road, Singapore 2261, Singapore

Federal Trust For Education & Research
Europe House, 1A Whitehall Place, London SW1A 2HA, England
Phone: 839 6625/930 4551

Ferguson (John) Pty Ltd
133 Macguarie Street, Sydney, NSW 2000, Australia
Kippax Street, Surrey Hills, NSW 2010
Phone: 02 2122766

Financial Times Business Information
50-64 Broadway, London SW1H 0DB, England
Phone: 01-799 2002
Fax: 01 799 2259

Financial Times Limited
50-64 Broadway, London SW1H 0DB, England
Phone: 01-799 2002
Fax: 01-799 2259

Financial Training Publications
131 Holland Park Avenue, London W11, England
Phone: 01 603 4688

Finska Vetenskaps-Societeten
Snellmaninkatu 9-11, SF-00170 Helsinki, Finland

Firma KLM Pvt Ltd
257 B B B Garguly Street, Calcutta 700 012, India
Phone: 274391

Fitzhenry & Whiteside
195 Allstate, Markham P, Ontario, Canada

Fitzroy Legal Service
PO Box 297, Fitzroy, Vic. 3065, Australia

Fitzwilliam Publishing
Fitzwilliam House, 32 Trumpington Street, Cambridge CB2 1QY, England
Phone: 0223 66733

Flecbon Corp
POB 6123, Karachi 2, Pakistan

Fontana → Collins (William) Sons & Co Ltd

Food & Agriculture Organization of the United Nations
Via delle Terme di Caracalla, 1-00100 Rome, Italy
Phone: 06 57971

Foreign & Commonwealth Office
Kings Street, London SW1, England
Phone: 01-233 3000

Foreign Service Institute
Room 701, Ermita Center Building, 1350 Roxas Blvd Cor. Sta. Monica Street, Ermita, Manila, Philippines

Forum of Free Enterprise
Sohrab House, 235 Dr Dadabhai Naoroji Road, Bombay 400 001, India

Four Courts Press
Kill Lane, Blackrock, Dublin, Eire
Phone: 01 541688

Fourmat Publishing
27-28 St Albans Place, Islington Green, London N1 0NX, England
Phone: 01-226 7497
Fax: 01-359 3031
White Lodge Publishing

Fourth Dimension Publishing Co Ltd
Plot 64A City Layout, PMB 01164, Enugu, Anambra State, Nigeria

Fraser Institute
626 Bute Street, Vancouver, BC, V6E 3M1
Phone: 604 688 0221
Fax: 604 688 8539

Freeman (A. R.)
PO Box 649, Belconnen, ACT 2617, Australia

Freeman (W H) & Co Ltd
20 Beaumont Street, Oxford OX1 2NQ, England
Phone: 0865 726975

Futura → Macdonald & Co (Publishers) Ltd

G Allan Roeher Institute → Roeher (G. Allan) Institute

Gabbay (E. & J.)
251 Leigham Court Road, London SW16 2SB, England

Gantheaume Press
1185 Hay Street, West Perth 6005, PO Box 296, Australia

Garcia (R. M.) Publishing House Inc
903 Quezon Avenue, Quezon City, POB 1860, Manila, Philippines

Garland Publishing Inc
136 Madison Avenue, New York, NY 10016, USA
Phone: 212 686 7492

Garnstone Press Ltd
c/o George Philip & Son Ltd, 12-14 Long Acre, London WC2 9LP, England
Phone: 079 87 370
Burlington Farm House, Barlinton, Nr. Petworth, W. Sussex, England

Gee & Co → Professional Publishing Ltd

Genrock Publications
65 The Terrace, Wellington, New Zealand
PO Box 491, New Zealand

Geological Survey of Zambia
POB RW 135, Ridgeway, Lusaka, Zambia

Ghana Publishing Corporation
OH Barnes Road, POB 4348, Accra, Ghana
Private Post Bag, Tema, Ghana

Ghana Universities Press
POB 4219, Accra, Ghana

Ghosh (P.) & Co
College Street Market, Calcutta 700 012, India
5 Dhakuriakalbari Lane, Calcutta 700 060, India

Gian Publishing House
29/6 Shakti Nagar, Delhi 110 007, India
Phone: 503468,7125269

Gill & Macmillan
Goldenbridge, Inchicore, Dublin 8, Eire
Phone: 0001 531005
15-17 Eden Quay, Dublin 1, Eire

Gingerbread
32 Wellington Street, London WC2E 7BN, England
Phone: 01-240 0953

Giuffre
via Statuto 2, Milan 20121, Italy
via Busto Arsizio, 40, 20151, Milano
Phone: 02 3010106

Glasgow (Mary) Publications Ltd
Avenue House, 131-133 Holland Park Avenue, London W11 4UT, England
Phone: 01-603 4688
Fax: 01-602 5197

GLC Publishers Ltd
115 Nugget Avenue,, Agincourt, Ontario, M1S 3B1, Canada
Phone: 416 291 2926
Fax: 416 291 0241

Gokhale Institute of Public Affairs
N R Colony, Bull Temple Road, Bangalore 560 019, India

Gollancz
14 Henrietta Street, Covent Garden, London WC2E 8QJ, England
Phone: 01-836 2006
Fax: 01-379 0934

Gondwanaland Press
24 Glasgow Street, Kelburn, Wellington 5, New Zealand

Government Departments
Mulgrece Street, Private Bag, Wellington 1, New Zealand
Phone: (4) 737320
Accident Compensation Commission

Government of British Columbia
878 Viewfield Road, Victoria Road, Victoria, BC, V8 V 1X4, Canada
Law Reform Commission of British Columbia

Government of Ontario
Toronto, 180 Bloor Street West, Toronto, Ontario M5S 2V6, Canada

Government of the Isle of Man
Bucks Road, Douglas, Isle of Man
Phone: 0624 26262
Isle of Man Government

Government of West Bengal Press
Publication Branch, 38 Gopal Nagar Road, Calcutta 700 027, India

Government Printer [Sierra Leone]
c/o Government Printing Dept, Freetown, Sierra Leone

Government Printer [South Africa]
Private Bag X85, 0001 Pretoria, South Africa
Phone: 012 32-39731

Government Printing & Stationery
Charni Road, Bombay 400 004, India

Government Printing Press
P O Box 469, Kano, Nigeria

Govi-Verlag
Beethovenplatz 1-3, 6000 Frankfurt am Main, West Germany
Phone: 069-75441
Fax: 061 96 70160

Gower Publishing Co Ltd
Gower House, Croft Road, Aldershot, Hampshire GU11 3HR., England
Phone: 0252 331551
Fax: 0252 344405
Maurice Temple Smith

Grafton Books
8 Grafton Street, London W1X 3LA, England
Phone: 01-493 7070
Fax: 01-493 3061

Graham & Trotman Ltd
Sterling House, 66 Wilton Road, London SW1V 1DE, England
Phone: 821 1123
Fax: 630 5229
Arabian Information

Granada Publishing Ltd
8 Grafton Stret, London W1X 3LA, England
Phone: 493 7070
Fax: 493 3061

Grant MacIntyre Ltd
c/o JM Dent & Sons Ltd, 100 Scarsdale Road, Don Mills, Ontario, M3B 2R8, Canada

Green (W.) & Son Ltd
2-10 St Giles Street, Edinburgh EH1 1PU, Scotland
Phone: 031-225 4879
Fax: 031-225 2104
Scottish Universities Law Institute

Greenlight Publishing Co
3 Monica Street, Doncaster East, Victoria 3109, Australia

Greenpeace
30-31 Islington Green, London N1, England
Phone: 01-354 5100
Fax: 01-359 4062
5 Caledonian Road, London N1, England
Phone: 01-837 7557

Greenwood Press Inc
88 Post Road W, Box 5007, Westport, CT 06881, USA
Phone: 203 226 3571
Fax: 203 222 1502
47 Pokfulam Road, G/F, Hong Kong
Phone: 5 468212

Greer (Ian) Associates
6 Buckingham Place, London SW1E 6HR, England
Phone: 01-630 5651

Gregarian Publications
1402 D'Aguilar Place, No 7 D'Aguilar Street, Central, Hong Kong
Phone: 5-266073

Grigg (Kenneth N.)
54 Wattle Valley Road, Canterbury, Victoria 3126, Australia

Grotius Publishing Ltd
PO Box 115, Cambridge CB3 9BP, England
Phone: 0223 323410
Fax: 0223 313545

Gruner →BR Gruner BV Publishing Co

Gunasena (M. D.) & Co Ltd
217 Olcott Mawatha, PO Box 248, Colombo 11, Sri Lanka

Gwelfryn Publications
Gwelfryn, Llandidnoes Road, Newtown, Powys SY16 4HX, Wales

H & H Scientific Consultants Ltd
PO Box MT27, Leeds LS17 8QP, England
Phone: 0532 687189

Hakkert (Adolf M.)
Herman de Marlaan 8, Uithoorn, Netherlands
Calle Alfambra 26, 35010 Las Palmas de Gran Canaria, Spain
Phone: 28277350

Haldane Society
2 Garden Court, Temple, London, EC4
Phone: 01-353 1633

Hale & Iremonger Pty Ltd
Box W, 64 Hayes Street, Neutral Bay, NSW 2089, Australia
GPO Box 2552, Sydney, NSW 2001
Phone: 02 5604758

Hale (Robert) Ltd
Clerkenwell House, Clerkenwell Green, London EC1R 0HT, England
Phone: 01-251 2661
Fax: 01-251 0584

Hambledon Press
102 Gloucester Avenue, London NW1 8HX, England
Phone: 01-586 0817

Hamish Hamilton Ltd
27 Wright Lane, London W8 5TZ, England
Phone: 01-938 3388
Fax: 01-937 8704

Hammonia Verlag GmbH
Tangstedter Landstrasse 83, Postfach 620228, 2000 Hamburg 62, W Germany
Phone: 040 52010310

Hansib Publishing Ltd
3rd Floor, Tower House, 139-149 Fonthill Road, London N4 3HF, England
Phone: 01-281 1191
Jubo

Hansischer Gildenverlag
Joachim Heitmann & Co, Theodorstrasse 41C, 2000 Hamburg 50, West Germany

Harcourt Brace Jovanovich
24-28 Oval Road, London NW1 7DX, England
Phone: 01-267 4466
Fax: 01-482 2293
Academic Press

Harcourt Brace Jovanovich Group [Australia]
Locked Bag 16, Marrickville, NSW 2204, Australia

Harcourt Brace Jovanovich [NZ]
10 Moa Street, Otahuhu, Auckland 6, PO Box 22-245, New Zealand

Harmsworth Publications Ltd
New Carmelite House, Carmelite Street, London EC4Y 0JA, England
Phone: 01-353 6000

Harper & Row Ltd
Middleton House, 34-42 Cleveland Street, London W1P 5FB, England
Phone: 01-636 8300
Fax: 01-631 3594

Harrap Ltd
19-23 Ludgate Hill, London EC4M 7PD, England
Phone: 01-248 6444
Fax: 01-248 3357

Harrassowitz (Otto)
Tanustrasse 8, Postfach 2929, Wiesloaden 6200, West Germany
Phone: 061 21 521046
Fax: 061 21 537321

Harrison-Ede Book Publishing Co
PO Box 346, Nunawading, Victoria 3131, Australia

Harvard University Press
126 Buckingham Palace Road, London SW1, England
Phone: 730 9208

Harvester Press Microfilm Publications Ltd
16 Ship Street, Brighton, Sussex BN1 1AD, England
Phone: 0273 28320

Hawthorns Publishing Ltd
23 Warham Road, Otford, Sevenoaks, Kent TN14 5PF, England
Phone: 095-92 2325

Hayward Publications
23 Mount Vernon Place, Nelson, New Zealand

Headline Book Publishing plc
Headline House, 79 Great Titchfield Street, London W1P 7FN, England
Phone: 01-631 1687
Fax: 01-631 1958

Heinemann
Michelin House, 81 Fulham Road, London SW3 6RB, England
Phone: 01-581 9393
Fax: 01-589 8419

Heinemann Educational Books (East Africa) Ltd
PO Box 45314, Nairobi, Kenya

Heinemann Educational Books (Nigeria) Ltd
Ighodaro Road, Jericho, PMB 5205, Ibadan, Oyo State, Nigeria

Heinemann Publishers (NZ)
Cnr College Road and Kilham Avenue, Northcote, Auckland 9, New Zealand
P O Box 36064, New Zealand

Helm (Christopher) Ltd
Imperial House, 21-25 North Street, Bromley, Kent BR1 1SD, England
Phone: 01-466 6622
Fax: 01-290 0281

Hemstall Press Ltd
27 Ingham Road, London NW6 1DG, England
Phone: 01-435 8987

Heriot-Watt University
Riccarton, Edinburgh EH14 4AS, Scotland
Phone: 031 449 5111

Heritage Books
10-14 Calcutta Crescent, POB 610, Agaga, Lagos State, Nigeria

Heymanns (Carl) Verlag KG
Luxemburger Strasse 449, D-5000 Koln, West Germany
Phone: 0221 460100
Fax: 4601069

Hill of Content Publishing Co Pty Ltd
86 Bourke Street, Melbourne, Victoria 3000, Australia
Phone: (03) 654 3144
Fax: (03) 662 2527

Himalayan Books
17/L Connaught Circus, POB 328, New Delhi 110 001, India
Phone: 352126, 351731

Hind Publishing House
629 University Road, Allahabad 211 002, India

Hindustan Law Book Co
Krishnapara, Meerut, Uttar Pradesh, India

HLT Group ltd
200 Greyhound Road, London W14 9RY, England
Phone: 01-385 3377

HMSO Books
St Crispins, Duke Street, Norwich NR3 1PD, England
Phone: 0603 622211
Fax: 0603 7582

Hobsons Publishing plc
Bateman Street, Cambridge CB2 1LZ, England
Phone: 0223 354551
Fax: 0223 323154

Hodder & Stoughton (Australia) Pty Ltd
Rydalmere Business Park, 10-16 South Stret, Rydalmere, NSW 2116, Australia
Phone: 02 638 5299
Fax: 02 684 4942

Hodder & Stoughton Ltd
Mill Road, Dunton Green, Sevenoaks, Kent TN13 2YA, England
Phone: 0732 450111
Fax: 0732 460134
Sceptre

Hodder & Stoughton [NZ]
46 View Road, Glenfield, Auckland 10, New Zealand
PO Box 3858, New Zealand

Hogarth Press →Chatto & Windus Ltd

Holdsworth Club, University of Birmingham → University of Birmingham, Holdsworth Club

Home Office Research Unit
50 Queen Anne's Gate, London SW1H 9AT, England
Phone: 01-273 3000

Horwitz Grahame Pty Ltd
PO Box 306, Cammeray, NSW 2062, Australia

House Information Services Ltd
178-202 Gt Portland Street, London W1N 6HN, England
Phone: 01-637 2400

House of Anansi Press
35 Britain Street, Torento, Ontario, M5A 1R7, Canada

Housing Corporation
149 Tottenham Court Road, London W1P 0EN, England
Phone: 01-387 9446

Housing Corporation of New Zealand
NZ Government Printing Office, Private Bag, Wellington, New Zealand

Howard League For Penal Reform
320/332 Kennington Park Road, London SE11 4PP, England
Phone: 01-735 3317

Howe Institute →CD Howe Institute

Huang →University of the West Indies

Hulton Educational →Thornes (Stanley) & Hulton (Publishers) Ltd

Human Sciences Research Council
Private Bag X41, 0001 Pretoria, South Africa

Hurst (C.) & Co (Publishers) Ltd
38 King Street, London WC2E 8JT, England
Phone: 01-240 2666

Hutchinson Education Ltd
Brookmount House, 62-65 Chandos Place, London WC2N 4NW, England
Phone: 01-836 3411
Fax: 01-836 1409

Hydatum
PO Box 4, Ross-on-Wye, Herefordshire HR9 6EB, England
Phone: 0600 890599

Hyland House Publishing Pty Ltd
23 Bray Street, South Yarra, Victoria 3000, Australia
Phone: 03-2416336

IBC Financial Books
12-13 Little Newport Street, London WC2H 7PP, England
Phone: 01-437 4343

IBC Technical Services Ltd
IBC House, Canada Road, Byfleet, Weybridge, Surrey KT14 7JL, England
Lest

ICSA
Fitzwilliam House, 32 Trumpington Street, Cambridge CB2 1QY, England
Phone: 0223 66733
Fax: 0223 461428

IEEE Computer Society Press
345 E. 46th Street, New York, NY 10017-2394, USA
Phone: 212-705-7900
Fax: 202-728-9614
Electronica Books

IIR Pty Ltd
Suite 1503, 275 Alfred Street North, North Sydney, NSW 2060, Australia

Immel Publishing Ltd
Ely House, 37 Dover Street, London W1X 3RB, England
Phone: 01-409 1799
Fax: 01-409 1525

Incomes Data Services
193 St John Street, London EC1V 4LS, England
Phone: 01-250 3434

Incorporated Law Society of Ireland
Solicitors Buildings, Four Courts, Dublin 7, Eire

India Book House Pvt Ltd
Mahalaxmi Chamber, 5th floor, 22 Bhulabhai Desai Marg, Bombay 400 026, India

Indian Bibliographies Bureau
2153/2 Fountain Chan Indara, Delhi 110 006, India

Indian Institute of Advanced Study
Rashtrapati Nivas, Summer Hill, Simla 171 005, India

Indian Institute of Public Administration
Indrapastha Estate, Ring Road, New Delhi 110 002, India

Indian Investment Centre
Jeevan Vihar Bldg, Parliament Street, New Delhi 110 001, India

Indian Law Institute
Bhagwandas Road, New Delhi 110-001, India

Indian Press (Publications) Pvt Ltd
36 Pannalal Road, Allahabad 211 002, India
Phone: 53190

Indian Research Institute
78 Serpentine Lane, Calcutta 700 001, India

Industrial Law Publishers
1741 Near Kradia Police Gate, Ahmedabad 380 001, India

Industrial Relations Centre, Queen's University →Queen's University, Industrial Relations Centre

Industrial Society
3 Carlton House Terrace, London SW1Y 5DG, England
Phone: 01-839 4300
Fax: 01-930 7558

Industrieforbundet →Industriforbundets forlag

Industriens Utredningsinstitut
Greogatan 34, 5tr, S-114.53, Stockholm, Sweden
Phone: 02602 2442

Industriforbundets forlag
Storgatan 19, Box 5501, 11485 Stockholm, Sweden
Industrieforbundet

Information Australia
45 Flinders Lane, Melbourne, Victoria 3000, Australia

Infoscan Ltd
32 Elmdale Avenue,, Ottawa,, Ontario, K1M 1A2, Canada

Institut fur Asienkunde
Rothenbaumchaussee 32, D-2000 Hamburg 13, West Germany
Phone: 040 443001-03

Institut fur Internationale Angelenheiten, Universitat Hamburg →Universitat Hamburg

Institute du Transport Aerien
4 rue Solferino, Paris 75007, France

Institute for Development Studies, University of Nairobi →University of Nairobi

Institute for Fiscal Studies
180-182 Tottenham Court Road, London W1P 9LE, England
Phone: 01-636 3784

Institute for Research on Public Policy [Canada]
PO Box 3670, Halifax South, NS, B3J 3KS, Canada
2149 rue Mackay, Suite 102, Montreal, PQ H3G 2J2, Canada

Institute for Research on Public Policy [UK]
12-12A Golden Square, London W1R 3AF, England

Institute for the Study of Conflict
12-12A Golden Square, London W1R 3AF, England
Phone: 01-439 7381

Institute for the Study of Drugs Dependence
18 Hatton Place, Hatton Garden, London EC1, England
Phone: 01-430 1991

Institute of Advanced Legal Studies →University of London, Institute of Advanced Legal Studies

Institute of African Studies, University of Ibadan →University of Ibadan

Institute of Applied Social & Economic Research
PO Box 5854, Boroko, Papua New Guinea

Institute of Bankers
10 Lombard Street, London EC4, England
Phone: 01-623 3531

Institute of Banking & Finance
10 Ansom Road, Suite 812-813, 8th floor, International Plaza, Singapore 0207, Singapore

Institute of Building
Englemere, Kings Ride, Ascot, Berks SL5 8BL, England

Institute of Chartered Accountants in England & Wales
Gloucester House, 399 Silbury Boulevard, Central Milton Keynes, MK9 2HL, England
Phone: 0908 668833

Institute of Criminology, Cambridge University →University of Cambridge, Institute of Criminology

Institute of Directors in Australia
16 O'Connell Street, Sydney, NSW 2000, Australia

Institute of Economic Affairs
2 Lord North Street, London SW1P 3LB, England
Phone: 01-799 3745

Institute of Housing
9 White Lion Street, London N1 9XJ, England
Phone: 01-837 4280
Fax: 01-278 2705

Institute of Intergovernmental Relations, Queen's University →Queen's University, Institute of Intergovernmental Relations

Institute of Judicial Administration, University of Birmingham →University of Birmingham, Institute of Judicial Administration

Institute of Labour Studies, National University of Lesotho →National University of Lesotho

Institute of Latin American Studies, University of Glasgow →University of Glasgow, Institute of Latin American Studies

Institute of Law Research and Reform
Edmonton, Alberta

Institute of Organization & Industrial Sociology
Howitzvej 60, DK-2000 Kobenhagen F, Denmark

Institute of Pacific Studies, University of the South Pacific →University of the South Pacific

Institute of Personnel Management
IPM House, Camp Street, Wimbledon, London SW19 4UW, England
Phone: 01-946 9100
Fax: 01-879 1565

Institute of Public Administration
Vergemount Hall, Clonskeah, Dublin 4, Eire
57-61 Lansdowne Road, Ballsbridge, Dublin, Eire

Institute of Social & Economic Research, University of the West Indies →University of the West Indies, Institute of Social & Economic Research

Institute of Southeast Asian Studies
Heng Mui Keng Terrace, Pasir, Panjang, Singapore 0511

Institute of Trading Standard Administration
Metropolitan House, 37 Victoria Avenue, Southend-on-Sea, SS2 6DA
Phone: 0702 338313

Institution of Surveyors, Australia, New South Wales Division
363 Pitt Street, Sydney NSW 2000, Australia
Phone: 02 2122934

Intellectual Book Corner
23 Darya Garj, Partap Gali, Ansari Road, New Delhi 110 002, India
Phone: 279911

Inter Documentation Co AG
Industriestrasse 7, CH-6300 Zug, Switzerland

Inter-India Publications
D-17 Raja Garden Extension, New Delhi 110 055, India

InterChange Books
InterChange Studios, 15 Wilkin Street, London NW5 3NG, England
Phone: 01-267 9421

Internationaal Belasting Documentatie Bureau
Sarphatistraat 124, 1018BZ Amsterdam, Netherlands
Phone: 020 267726
International Bureau of Fiscal Documentation

International Books Distributors
66 Wood Lane End, Hemel Hempstead, Hertfordshire HP2 4RG, England

International Bureau of Fiscal Documentation →Internationaal Belasting Documentatie Bureau

International Business Communications Pty Ltd
16 Riley Street, Woolloomoolou, NSW 2011, Australia
Phone: (02) 231 6547
Fax: (02) 332 1448

International Chamber of Commerce
38 Cours Albert, F - 75008, Paris, France
Phone: 1-45623456

International Commission of Jurists
109 Route de Chere, BP 120, CH - 1224 Chene Bougeries, Geneve, Switzerland
Phone: 022 493544/5

International Defense & Aid Fund for Southern Africa
Canon Collins House, 64 Essex Road, London N1 8LR, England
Phone: 01-359 9181

International Federation of Commercial Arbitration Institutions
c/o Institute for International Cooperation, University of Ottawa, Ottawa, Ontario K1N 6N5, Canada
Phone: 613 232 1476
Canadian Arbitration, Conciliation and Amicable Composition Centre

International Institute for Strategic Studies
23 Tavistock Street, London WC2E 7NP, England
Phone: 01-379 7676

International Labour Office
ILO Publications, 4 Rte des Morillons, CH - 1211 Geneve 22, Switzerland
Phone: 022 997952

International Law Book Co
1562 Church Road, Kashmere Gate, GPOB 1792, Delhi 110 006, India

International Law Books Service
No 14, (1st floor), Lorong Bunus Enam, Off Jalan Masijd India, 50100 Kualar Lumpur, Malaysia

International Maritime Organisation
4 Albert Embankment, London SE1 7SR, England
Phone: 01-735 7611

International Public Relations Pty Ltd
PO Box 1072, Canberra City, ACT 2601, Australia
Phone: 062 497266

International Self-Counsel Press Ltd
1481 Charlotte Road, North Vancouver, BC, V7J 1H1, Canada

International Telecommunications Union
Place des Nations, Geneva 20 1211, Switzerland.
Phone: 022 995111
Fax: 022 337256

International Union for Conservation of Nature & Natural Resources.
CH - 1196 Gland, Switzerland

Interstate Corporate Affairs Commission
Level 27, Australia Square, Sydney, NWS 2000, Australia
Phone: 02 275789

Intertrade Publications (India) Pvt Ltd
55 Gariahat Road, Ballygunge, POB 10210, Calcutta 700 019, India

Investment & Tax Planning Services
7 Regal Street, London NW1 7TH, England
Phone: 01-267 0133

IPC Building & Contract Journals Ltd
Unit 1, 2 Barkside Industrial Estate, Hopton Street, London SE1, England
Phone: 01-928 3567

IPC Science and Technology Press Ltd
c/o Butterworths, PO Box 63, Westbury House, Bury Street, Guildford, Surry GU2 5BH, England
Phone: 0342 326972

IPI, Canada
44 Charles Street West, Apt. 4410, Toronto, Ontario, M4I 1R8, Canada

Irish Academic Press Ltd
Kill Lane, Blackrock, Dublin, Eire
Phone: 0001 892922

Irish Association of Law Teachers
c/o Faculty of Law, University College Galway, Eire

Irish Manuscripts Commission
73 Merrion Square, Dublin 2, Eire
Phone: 0001 761610

Iroqrafts Ltd, R.R.
2 Ohsweken, Ontario, NOA 1MO, Canada

Irwin Publishing Inc
1800 Steeles Avenue, W Concord, Ontario, L4K 2P3, Canada

Islamic Foundation Bangladesh
67 Purana Palton, Dhaka 2, Bangladesh
Phone: 251395

Islamic Research Institute
POB 1035, Islamabad, Pakistan

Isle of Man Government →Government of the Isle of Man

Issuing Houses Association
Granite House, 101 Cannon Street, London EC4N 5BA, England
Phone: 01-283 7334

Ithaca Press
PO Box 362, Oxford, OX2 6ET, England

Iustus forlag →Almqvist & Wiksell International

Ivanhoe Press Ltd
17 Standingford House, Cave Street, Oxford OX4 1BA, England
Phone: 0865 791006

Jacaranda Wiley
65 Park Road, Milton, Queensland 4604, Australia
GPO Box 859, Brisbane, 4001, Australia

Jai Press Inc
55 Old Post Road, No 2 PO Box 1678, Greenwich, CT 06836, USA
Phone: 203 661 7602

Jaico Publishing House
127 Mahatma Gandhi Road, Bombay 400 023, India
Phone: 022 270621

Jain Brothers
Vidya Vihar, Pilani, Rajasthan, India
256 Bapu Bazar, Udaipur, Rasjastjan, India
Phone: 20779

Jain Law Agency
Shop-cum-flat 8, Sector 22-D, Chandigarh, India

James Cook University Publications
University Bookshop, James Cook University of North Queensland, Townsville PO Box 999, Queensland 4811, Australia
Phone: 077 793711

Jameson Publishing
90 Princes Street, Edinburgh EH2 2ER, Scotland
Phone: 031-225 5408

Japan Securities Research Institute
c/o Tokyo Syoken Kaikan, 1-5-8 Nihonbashi-Kayaba-Cho Chuo Ku, Tokyo 103, Japan
Phone: 03-669-0737

Jay Books
30 The Boundary, Langton Green, Tunbridge Wells, Kent TN3 0YB, England
Phone: 0892 45198

JMC Press
388 Quezon Avenue, Quezon City, Philippines
Katka

Jofleur Publications
Acacia House, Shirburn Street, Watlington, Oxford, England
Phone: 049 161 2513

John Fairfax Direct Marketing
PO Box 803, Marrickville, NSW 2204, Australia

John Hopkins University, Foreign Policy Institute →Eurospan Ltd

Johnston & Bacon
P O BOX 1, Stirling, Scotland
Phone: 0786 841867

Joint Council for the Welfar of Immigrants
44 Theobalds Road, London WC1X 8SP, England
Phone: 01-405 5527

Jordan & Sons Ltd
21 St Thomas Street, Bristol BS1 6JS, England

Joseph (Michael)
27 Wrights Lane, London W8 5TZ, England
Phone: 01-937 7255
Fax: 01-937 8704

Jossey-Bass Publishers Ltd
28 Banner Street, London EC1Y 8QE, England
Phone: 01-253 1516
Fax: 01-253 5206

Jubo →Hansib Publishing Ltd

Justice for Children
35 Wellington Street, London WC2E 7BN, England
Phone: 01-836 5917

Justices's Clerks' Society
Nelson Street, Bristol, England
Phone: 0272 297841

Juta & Co Ltd
PO Box 30, Cape Town, 8000, S. Africa
Fax: (021) 715 010
PO Box 123, 7790 Kenwyn, S. Africa

K.G. Saur →Bowker-Saur Ltd

Kalyani Publishers
4863/2B Bharat Ram Road, 24 Daryaganj, New Delhi 110 002, India

Karnatak University
Dharwar 580 003, India

Katka →JMC Press

Kazi Publications
121 Zalqarnain, Ganpat Road, POB 1845, Lahore, Pakistan

Kegan Paul International Ltd
11 New Fetter Lane, London, EC4P 4EE
Phone: 01-583 9855
Fax: 01 583 0701
Routledge & Kegan Paul

Kent County Council Education Department
County Education Officer, Springfield, Maidstone, Kent ME14 2LJ, England
Phone: 0622 671411
Fax: 0622 690897

Kent State University Press
101 Franklin Hall, Kent, OH 4442, USA
Phone: 216 672 7913

Kenya Literature Bureau
Community Building, Ngong Road, PO Box 30022, Nairobi, Kenya

Key Haven Publications
61 Harrington Gardens, London SW7 4DZ, England
Phone: 01 244 8503

Key Porter Books Ltd
70 The Esplanade, Toronto, Ontario, M5E 1R2, Canada
Phone: 416 862 7779
Fax: 416 862 2304

Khosla (N. M.) & Co
24 Deepak Peddar Road, Bombay 400 026, India
Phone: 350218

Kimber (William) →Thorsons Publishing Group Ltd

King's Fund Institute
126 Albert Street, London NW1 7NF, England
Phone: 01 485 9589

Kirby (A. A.)
25 Orana Avenue, Kirrawee, NSW 2232, Australia

Kitab Mahal
22 Sarojini Naidu Marg, Allahabad 211 001, India

Kluwer Group Academic Publishers
Kamerlingh Onnesweg 7 - 11, Postbus 322, NL - 3300 AH Dordrecht, Netherlands
Phone: 078 334933

Kluwer Law
Africa House, Kingsway, London WC2, England
Phone: 01-831 0391

Knapp, Fritz GmbH Verlag
Neue Mainzer Strasse 60, 6000 Frankfurt-am-Main 1, West Germany
Phone: 069 280151
Postfach 11151, D - 6000 Frankfurt 11, GFR

Knight (Charles) & Co Ltd
Tolley House, Scarbrook Road, Croydon, Surrey, England
Phone: 01 688 4163

Kogan Page Ltd
120 Pentonville Road, London N1 9NJ, England
Phone: 01-278 0433
Fax: 01-837 6348

Kothari Book Depot
Acharya Donde Marg, Parel, Bombay 400 012, India

L'Erma di Bretschneider →Erma di Bretschneider

La Trobe University
Borchardt Library, Bundoora, Victoria 3083, Australia

Labour Law Publications
873 Sultan Bazar, Hyderabad, Andhra Pradesh, India

Labour Research Dept
78 Blackfriars Road, London SE1 8HF, England
Phone: 01-928 3649
Fax: 01-928 0621

Lake House Investments Ltd
41 WAD Ramanayake Mawatha, POB 1453, Colombo 07, Sri Lanka

Lakimiesliiton Kustannus Oy
Uudermaankatu 4 - 6 F, SF - 00120 Helsinki, Finland

Lancer International
POB 3802, New Delhi 110 049, India

Lang (Herbert) et Compagnie AG
Berne, Switzerland

Lang (Peter) →Verlag Peter Lang AG

Laureate-Thomson Press
7 Swallow Place, London W1R 8AB, England
Phone: 01 629 0373

Lavis Marketing
The Old Malthouse, 19A Paradise Street, Oxford, OX1 1LD, England
Phone: 0865 249838

Law Academy
1-9-322 Vidyarager, Hyderabad 500 045, India

Law & Education Publishers Ltd
Plot 61 Aba/Owerri Road, GRA POB 588, Aba, Imo State, Nigeria

Law and Management House
Bhatia Building, G T Road, Glaziabad, Uttar Pradesh, India

Law Book Co
18-B Sardar Patel Marg, POB 1-004, Allahabad 211 001, India
Phone: 4178, 4305

Law Book Co Ltd
44-50 Waterloo Road, North Ryde, NSW 2113, Australia
Phone: 01 887 0177
31 Market Street, Sydney, NSW 2000, Australia

Law Book House
543/2 Sadashiv Peth, Laxmi Road, Poona 2, Maharashtra, India

Law Book Mart
Aminuddaula Park, Lucknow, Uttar Pradesh, India

Law Centres Federation
Duchess House, 18 Warren Street, London W1, England
Phone: 01 387 8570

Law Commission
37/38 John Street, London WC1N 2BQ, England
Phone: 01-242 0861
Fax: 01-242 1885

Law Foundation of New South Wales
PO Box 1027, North Sydney, NSW 2060, Australia
Phone: 02 2212800

Law Institute of Victoria
465 Little Bourke Street, Victoria 3000, Australia
GPO Box 263C, Melbourne, Victoria 3001, Australia
Phone: 03 6023922

Law Journal Publications
Jayendraganj, Gwalior 474009, India

Law Notes Lending Library
25-26 Chancery Lane, London WC2A 1NB, England
Phone: 01 405 0780/6151

Law Publishers
Sardar Patel Marg, POB 1077, Allahabad 211 001, India
Phone: 094, 2835, 3716,2298

Law Reform Commission
Ardilaun Centre, 111 St Stephen's Green, Dublin 2, Eire
Phone: 0001 715699

Law Reform Commission of British Columbia
→Government of British Columbia

Law Reform Commission of New South Wales
Goodsell Building, Sydney, NSW 2000, Australia
Phone: 02-228-7215

Law Reform Commission of Papua New Guinea
PO Worlds Strip, Waigani, N.C.D., Papua New Guinea

Law Reports International
Trinity College, Oxford, OX1 3BH, England
Phone: 0865 279883/279893

Law Society
113 Chancery Lane, London WC2A 1PL, England
Phone: 01-242 1222
Fax: 01-405 9522

Law Society of Scotland
P O Box 75, 26 Drumsheugh Gardens, Edinburgh EH3 7YR, Scotland

Law Society of Upper Canada
Osgoode Hall, 13 Queen Street West, Toronto, Ontario, M5H 2N6, Canada

Lawyer's Home
Opp Old High Court Building, Indore 3, Madhya Pradesh, India

Legal Action Group
1st Floor, 242-244 Pentonville Road, London N1 9UN, England
Phone: 01-833 2931

Legal & Financial Publishing Co
Suite 641 - 644, Grand Parade Centre, Adderley St, 8001 Cape Town, S. Africa
POB 3461, 8000 Cape Town, S.A

Legal Books
34-49 Martin Place, Sydney, NSW 2000, Australia
Phone: 231 6547
Fax: 332 1448

Legal Information Resources
Rodmer Clough, Blackshawhead, Hebden Bridge, W. Yorkshire, HX7 7PJ, England
Phone: 0422 843433
Fax: 0422 843332

Legal Management Consultancy Services
15 Palmer Lane, Darlinghurst, PO Box 183, Sydney 2001, Australia
Phone: 02 334626

Legal Research Foundation
University of Auckland, Private Bag, Auckland 1, New Zealand

Legalease
3 Clifton Road, London W9 1SZ, England

Leicester University Press
Fielding Johnson Building, University of Leicester, Iniversity Road, Leicester, LE1 7RH, England
Phone: 0533 523333
Fax: 0523 522200

Leksand Press
10/44 Morton Street, Wollstonecraft, NSW 2065, Australia
Phone: 02 432909

Leo Cussen Institute for Continuing Legal Education
408 La Trobe Street, Melbourne, Victoria 3000, Australia
Phone: 03 329 0633

Lest →IBC Technical Services Ltd

Lester & Orpen Denny Publishers
78 Sullivan Street, Toronto, Ontario, M5T 1C1, Canada

Letts (Charles) & Co Ltd
Diary House, Borough Road, London SE1 1DW, England
Phone: 01-407 8891
Fax: 01-403 6729

Liber AB
Slottsgatan 24, S - 205 10 Malmo, Sweden, 040 258600
Box 3071, 103 61 Stockholm, Sweden
Phone: 08-7399000

Liberfoerlag
Sortergatan 23 Fack, 16289 Vaellinby, Sweden

Library Association
7 Ridgmount Street, London WC2E 7AE, England
Phone: 01-636 7543

Liechtenstein Verlag AG
Schwefel Strass 33, Postfach 133, FL - 9490 Vaduz, Liechtenstein
Phone: 075 2241423925

Life Underwriters Association of Canada
41 Lesmill Road, Don Mills, Ontario, M3B 2T3, Canada

Lillas (Michael Francis & Christine Anne)
PO Box 538, Burnie, Tasmania 7320, Australia

Lippincot (J.B.)
E. Washington Square, Philadelphia, PA 19105, USA
Phone: 215 238 4200
Fax: 215 238 4227

Lloyd (Chris) Sales & Management Services
463 Ashley Road, Parkstone, Poole, Dorset BH14 0AX, England
Phone: 0202 715349
Fax: 0202 736191
Translegal AG

Lloyds of London Press Ltd
1 Singer Street, London EC2A 4LQ, England
Phone: 01-250 1500
Sales Office, Sheepen Place, Colchester CO3 3LP, England
Phone: 0206 772277
Fax: 0206 46273

Lofthouse Publishing
29 Ropergate, Pontefract, W Yorkshire WF8 1LG, England
Phone: 0977 701315
Fax: 0977 790783

Lok Sabha Secretariat
Publication Department, 40 Parliament House, New Delhi 110 001, India

London Housing Aid Centre →SHAC

London Record Society
University of London, Institute of Historical Research, Senate House, Malet Street, London WC1E 7HU, England
Phone: 01-636 7950

London Voluntary Service Council
68 Chalton Street, London NW1 1JR, England
Phone: 01 388 0241

Longman Cheshire Pty Ltd
95 Coventry Street, South Melbourne, Victoria 3205, Australia
Phone: 03 697 0666
Fax: 03 699 2041

Longman Group UK Ltd, Professional & Business Communications Division
21-27 Lamb's Conduit Street, London WC1 3NJ, England
Phone: 01-242 2548
Fax: 01-831 8119

Longman Professional Publishing Pty Ltd
c/o Longman Cheshire, 95 Coventry Street, South Melbourne, Victoria, Australia

Lord Chancellor's Department
S E Circuit Office, Thanet House, 232 The Strand, London WC2R 1DA, England
Phone: 01-353 8060

Lorimer (James) & Co
35 Britain Street, Toronto, Ontario, M5A 3V8, Canada

Louisiana State University Press
Highland Road, Baton Rouge, LA 70893, USA
Phone: 504 388 6666

Low Pay Unit
9 Upper Berkeley Street, London W1H 8BY, England
Phone: 01-262 7278

LSEPS
Houghton Street, London WC2

Lucas Publications
264-272 Derby Road, Bootle, Merseyside, L20 8QL, England
Phone: 051 922 1642

M/S Aziz Publishers
c/o Aziz Book Depot, Urdu Bazar, Lahore, Pakistan

MC Enterprises
PO Box 31-046, Christchurch, New Zealand

MCB University Press Ltd
62 Toller Lane, Bradford, West Yorkshire BD8 9BY, England
Phone: 0274 499821
Fax: 0274 547143
MCB University Press, Shaws Linton Publications

MacCorquodale & Co Ltd
Newton Le Willows, Bedale, N Yorkshire, England

Macdonald & Co (Publishers) Ltd
Third Floor, Greater London House, Hampstead Road, London NW1 7QX, England
Phone: 01-377 4600
Fax: 01-377 4749
Futura

Macdonald & Evans Ltd
128 Long Acre, London WC2E 9AN, England
Phone: 01-379 7383
Fax: 01-240 5771

MacGregor (J. M.) Pty Ltd
PO Box 40, Double Bay, NSW 2028, Australia
Phone: 02 351923

Maclean-Hunter Ltd
481 University Avenue, Toronto, Ontario, M5G 1Y3, Canada.

Macmillan Company of Australia
107 Moray Street, South Melbourne, Victoria 3205, Australia

Macmillan Education Ltd
4 Little Essex Street, London WC2, England
Phone: 01 836 6633

Macmillan India Ltd
2/10 Ansari Road, New Delhi 110 002, India
Phone: 272993

Macmillan Press Ltd
Stockton House, 1 Melbourne Place, London WC2B 4LF, England
Phone: 01 836 6633
Fax: 01 379 4980

Macquarie Library
PO Box 228, Willoughby, NSW 2068, Australia

Madras Book Agency
337 Thambu Chetty Street, Madras 600 001, India

Maharashtra Legislature Secretariat
Council Hall, Bombay 400 001, India

Maitland Publications
88 Brighton Street, Petersham, NSW 2049, Australia

Malaya Law Review
c/o Faculty of Law, National University of Singapore, Kent Ridge, Singapore 0511, Singapore

Malayan Law Journal Pte Ltd
3 Shenton Way 14 - 03, Shenton House, Singapore 0106

Malaysian Law Publications
Sdn Bhd, No 18 Lorong Bunus Enam, off Jalan Masjid India, Kuala Lumpur, Malaysia

Mallinson Rendel Publishers
5A Grass Street, Wellington 1, New Zealand
PO Box 9409, New Zealand

MAM
PO Box 1722, Nicosia, Cyprus
Phone: (021) 72744

Mambo Press
Senga Road, POB 779, Gweru, Zimbabwe

Manchester University Press
Oxford Road, Manchester M13 9PL, England
Phone: 061 273 5539
Fax: 061 274 5539

Mann (George) Books
PO Box 22, Maidstone, Kent ME14 1AH, England

Manohar Publications
Daryagari, 1 Ansari Road, Panna Chawan, New Delhi 110 002, India
Phone: 275162

Mansell Publishing Ltd
Artillery House, Artillery Row, London SW1P 1RT, England
Phone: 01-222 7676
Fax: 01-799 1514

Mansoor Book House
2 Kutelery Road, Lahore, Pakistan

Marga Institute
Sri Lanka Centre for Development Studies, 61 Issipathana Mawatha, POB 601, Colombo 05, Sri Lanka
Sri Lanka Centre for Development Studies

Mason (Kenneth) Publications Ltd
Aldine House, 33 Welbek Street, London W1M 8LX, England

Massey University Publications
Private Bag, Palmerston North, New Zealand

Maurice Temple Smith →Gower Publishing Co Ltd

McClelland & Stewart Ltd
481 University Avenue, Toronto, Ontario, M5G 2E9, Canada
Phone: 416 598 1114
Fax: 416 598 7764

McGill-Queen's University Press
855 Sherbrooke Street West, Montreal, P.Q., H3A 2T5, Canada
Phone: 514 398 3750

McGraw-Hill Book Co NZ
5 Joval Place, Wiri, Manukau City, Auckland, New Zealand

McGraw-Hill Book Co (UK) Ltd
Shoppenhangers Road, Maidenhead, Berks, SL6 2QL

McLaren Micropublishing
PO Box 972, Station F, Toronto, Ontario, M4Y 2N9, Canada

Meckler Ltd
Grosvenor Gardens House, Grosvenor Gardens, London SW1W 0BS, England
Phone: 01 931 9985
Fax: 01 931 8908

Medical Defence Union
3 Devonshire Place, London W1N 2EA, England

Melanie Publications
28 Elphenstone Road, Hobart, Tasmania 7000, Australia

Melbourne University Press
268 Drummond Street, Carlton, Victoria 3053, Australia
Phone: 03 341 6212
Fax: 03 344 6214

Mercier Press Ltd
4 Bridge Street, Cork, Eire
Phone: 010 3532 504022

Merehurst Ltd
5 Great James Street, London WC1N 3DA, England
Phone: 01-242 5969
Fax: 01-405 1129

Merrill Publishing Co
Holywell House, Osney Mead, Oxford OX2 0ES, England
Phone: 0865 791497
Fax: 0865 727830

Methodist Publishing House
Wellington Road, Wimbledon, London SW19 8EV, England

Methuen Publications
150 Laird Drive, Toronto, Ontario M4G 3V7, Canada

Metropolitan Book Co Pvt Ltd
1 Netaji Subhash Marg, Delhi 110-001, India

Metzner (A.) Verlag
Zeppelinallee 43, D - 6000 Frankfurt 1, GFR
Phone: 069 793009
Fax: 793009-48
Postfach 970148, D - 6000 Frankfurt 97, GFR

Micromedia Ltd
158 Pearl Street, Toronto, Ontario, M5H 1L3, Canada
Phone: 416 593 5211

Middle East Technical University
Public Relations & Publications Office, Ismet Inonu Bulvari, Ankara, Turkey

Milan Law Publishers
15-2 Navijivan, POB 4591, Bombay 400 008, India

Ministry for the Environment
Grand Annexe Building, 82 Boulcott Street, Wellington, New Zealand
PO Box 10-241, New Zealand

Ministry of Agriculture
Swetterham Road, Kuala Lumpur, Malaysia

Ministry of Education Cultural Service
Nicosia, Cyprus

Ministry of Lands, Housing & Urban Development
POB 20671, Dar es Salaam, Tanzania

Ministry of Law and Justice
Legislative Department, ILI Building, Bhagwan Dass Road, New Delhi 110 001, India

Ministry of Works and Housing
Dept of Publication, Civil Lines, Delhi 110 054, India

MIT Press Ltd
126 Buckingham Palace Road, London SW1W 9SD, England
Phone: 01 730 9208

Mitchell Search
Mitchell College of Advanced Education, Bathurst, NSW 2795, Australia
Private Bag 31, Bathurst 2795, Australia

Modern Law House
45 Vivekanand Marg, Vasudeva Market, Allahabad 3, Uttar Pradesh, India,
Vasudeva Market, Allahabad 3, Uttar Pradesh, India

Modern Law Publications
8 Hastings Road, Allahabad 1, India
Phone: 2778 54495

Mohr (J. C. B.) (Paul Siebeck)
Wilhelmstrasse 18, Postfach 2040, D - 7400 Tubingen, West Germany
Phone: 07071-26064

Monash Law Book Co-Operative Ltd
Clayton, Victoria 3168, Australia

Monash University, Department of Environmental Science
Clayton, Victoria 3168, Australia

Monitor Press
Rectory Road, Great Waldingfield, Sudbury, Suffolk CO10 0Tl, England
Phone: 0787 78607

Morija Sesuto Book Depot
PO Box 4, Morija 190, Lesotho

Mosby (C.V.)
11830 Westline Industrial Drive, Saint Louis, MO 63146, USA
Phone: 314 872 8370
Fax: 314 432 1380

Moth Iotha Teoranta
31 Elgin Heights, Bray, Co. Wicklow, Eire

Motilal Banarsidaas
41 U A Bungalow Road, Jawahar Nagar, Delhi 110 007, India
Phone: 2911985,2918335

Mount Allison University
Sackville, New Brunswick, E0A 3C0, Canada

Mukherjee (A.) & Co Pvt Ltd
2 Bankim Chatterjee Street, Calcutta 700 073, India

Muller (C. F.)
Im Weiher 10, Postfach 102640, 6900 Heidelberg 1, Germany
Phone: 06221-489250
Fax: TX:461727

Munshiram Manoharlal Publishers Pvt Ltd
54 Rani Jhansi Road, POB 5715, New Delhi 110 055, India
Phone: 513841

Murray (John) Publishers Ltd
50 Albermarle Street, London W1X 4BD, England

Museums Association of Australia
PO Box K346, Haymarket, NSW 2000, Australia

Nabhi Publications
N-67 (1st floor), Munshi Ram Building, Connaught Circus, POB 37, New Delhi 110 001, India
Phone: 3310451

NACAB →National Association of Citizens Advice Bureaux

Nad Nominees
GPO Box 1655, Sydney, NSW 2001, Australia

Nalanda Press
159 Bidhan Sarani, Calcutta 6, West Bengal, India

Napier Press
Step Rock House, St. Andrews, Fife, KY16 9AT, Scotland

National Academy
9 Ansari Market, Daryaganj, Delhi 6, India

National Association of Citizens Advice Bureaux
115 Pentonville Road, London N1, England
Phone: 01 833 2181
NACAB

National Book Store Inc
701 Rizal Avenue, Sta Cruz, PO Box 1934, Manila, Philippines

National Council For Civil Liberties
21 Tabard Street, London SE1 4LA, England
Phone: 01 403 3888
NCCL

National Council For One Parent Families
255 Kentish Town Road, London NW5 2LX, England
Phone: 01 267 1361

National Council for Voluntary Organisations
26 Bedford Square, London WC1B 3HU, England
Phone: 01-636 4066
Bedford Square Press

National Economic Development Authority
Amber Avenue, Pasig, Metro Manila, POB 419, Greenhills, Manila, Philippines

National Education Co of Zambia Ltd
Chishango Road, PO Box 2664, Lusaka, Zambia

National Foster Care Association
Francis House, Francis Street, London SW1P 1DE, England
Phone: 01 828 6266

National Fund for Research into Crippling Diseases
Vincent House, North Parade, Horsham, West Sussex RH12 2PB, England
Phone: 0403 210406
Fax: 0403 210541

National Housing Authority
Quezon Memorial Circle, Elliptical Road, Diliman, Quezon City, Philippines

National Institute of Public Administration
Dhaka University Campus, Nilkhet, Dhaka 2, Bangladesh
University Road, Karachi 12, Pakistan

National Library of Australia
Caberra, ACT 2600, Australia
Phone: 062 621111
Fax: 062 571703

National Productivity Council
5-6 Institutional Area, Lodi Road, New Delhi 110 003, India

National Turfgrass Council
3 Ferrands Park Way, Harden, Bingley, W. Yorkshire, BD16 1HZ, England
Phone: 0274 565131

National University of Lesotho
Institute of Labour Studies, Private Bag, Maseru 100, Lesotho
Institute of Labour Studies, National University of Lesotho

National Youth Bureau
17-23 Albion Street, Leicester LE1 6GD, England
Phone: 0533 471200

Natraj Publishers
17 Rajpur Road, Dehradun, U P 248 001, India
Phone: 3382

Natural Resources Board of Zimbabwe
POB 8070, Causeway, Harare, Zimbabwe

Natural Resources Institute
177 Dysart Road, Winnipeg, Man. R3T 2N2, Canada

Navman Prakashan
Madar Gate, Sarai Ratan Lal, Aligarh, Uttar Pradesh, India

Navrang
RB-7 Inderpuri, New Delhi 110 012, India

Naya Prokash
206 Bidhan Sarani, Calcutta 700 006, India
Phone: 349556

NCCL →National Council For Civil Liberties

Nelson Canada
1120 Birchmount Road, Scarborough, Ontario, M1K 5G4, Canada
Phone: 416 752 9100
Fax: 416 752 9646

Nelson (Thomas) & Sons [UK]
Nelson House, Mayfield Road, Walton-on-Thames, Surrey, KT12 5PL, England
Phone: 0932 246133

Nelson (Thomas) Ltd [Australia]
480 La Trobe Street, Melbourne, Victoria 3000, Australia
Thomas Nelson

Neville Spearman (Jersey) Ltd
PO Box 75, Normandy House, St Helier, Jersey, Channel Islands, UK

Nevis Institute
91 George Street, Edinburgh EH2 3ES, Scotland
Phone: 031 225 2003

New Age Publishers Pvt Ltd
12 Bankim Chatterjee Street, Calcutta 700 012, India

New Book Stall
Pan Bazar, Gauhati 1, Assam, India
Ghandi Market, G T Road, Asansol, Burdwan, West Bengal, India

New Commercial Publishing Co
4 St John's Terrace, London, W10 4RB, England

New Day Publishers
11 Lands Street, Project 6, POB 167, Quezon City 3008, Philippines

New Education Press
27A Old Gloucester Street, London WC1N 3XX, England

New Gujarat Law House
Bava Latif Street, Three Gates, Almedabad, Gujarat, India

New Literature Publishing Co
181 Dr. Dadabhoy Naoroji Road, Fort, Bombay 400 001, India

New South Wales Legislative Council
Parliament House, Sydney, NSW 2000, Australia

New South Wales University Press
Box 1, PO Kensington, NSW 2033, Australia
Phone: 02 697 3403
Tafe Educational

New Ulster Movement Ltd
34 Ailesbury Cresent, Belfast BT7 1EZ, N. Ireland

New York University Press
70 Washington Square S., New York, NY 10012, USA
Phone: 212 998 2575
Fax: 212 674 7858

New Zealand Government Printing Office
Mulgreve Street, Private Bag, Wellington 1, New Zealand

New Zealand Institute of International Affairs
6 Waiteata Road, Wellington, New Zealand

New Zealand Institute of Surveyors
7th floor, Barclays House, 36 Customhouse Quay, Wellington 2, New Zealand

New Zealand Library Association
20 Brandon Street, Wellington 1, New Zealand

Newspaper Publishers Association
2nd floor, Newspaper House, 93 Boulcott Street, Wellington, New Zealand

Nigerian Institute of Advanced Legal Studies
University of Lagos, Lagos, Nigeria

Nigerian Institute of International Affairs
Kofo Abayomi Road, Victoria Island, GPOB 1727, Lagos, Nigeria

Nigerian Law Publications
28 Sabiu-Ajose Crescent, PO BOX 1114, Surulere, Lagos State, Nigeria

Nijhoff (Martinus)
Spuiblvd 50, NL-3311 AD, Dordrecht, Netherlands
Phone: 078 334922
c/o Brill E.J. (USA) Inc., 24 Hudson Street, Kinderhook, NY 12106, USA
Phone: 518 758 1411
Fax: 518 758 1959

Nimbus Publishing Ltd
6371 Lady Hammond Road, POB 9301, Station A, Halifax, N.S. B3K 5N5, Canada
Phone: 902 455 4286
Fax: 902 455 3652

Nomos Verlags GmbH & Co KG
Waldseestrasse 3 - 5, Postfach 610, D - 7570 Baden - Baden, West Germany
Phone: 07221 2104-0

Norstedt & Soners forlag →Almqvist & Wiksell International

North Holland →Elsevier Science Publishers BV

Northcote House Publishers Ltd
Harper & Row House, Estover Road, Plymouth, Devon PL6 7PZ, England
Phone: 0752 705251
Fax: 0752 777603

Northern Ireland Legal Quarterly →Queens University of Belfast

Northwick Publishers
14 Bevere Close, Bevere, Worcester, WR3 7QH, England
Phone: 0905 56876

Northwood Publications
100 Avenue Road, London NW3 3TP, England

Norton (W. W.) & Co Ltd
37 Great Russell Street, London WC1B 3NU, England
Phone: 01-323 1579

Norwegian University Press
Kolstadg 110-12, Postboks 2959 Toyen, N-0608 Oslo 6, Norway

November House
1004 Hamilton Street, Vancouver, BC, V6B 2R9, Canada
PO Box 49298, Vancouver, B C V7X 1L3, Canada

Novosti Press Agency
3 Rosary Gardens, London, SW7 4NW
Phone: 373 7350

Nwamife Publishers Ltd
10 Ibiam Street, Uwani POB 430, Enugu, Anambra State, Nigeria

Nyt fra Samfundsvidenskaberne
Blagardsgade 23 B/4, DK - 2200 Kobenhavn N,, Denmark

Oceana Publications Inc
58 Carey Street, London WC2, England
Phone: 01 405 5464

Odense University Press
Pjentedamsg 36, DK - 5000, Odense C, Denmark

Oelgeschlager, Gunn & Hain Inc
131 Clarendon Street, Boston, MA 02116, USA
Phone: 617 647 3609

OFA-Edition →Office Arabe de Presse et de Documentation

Office Arabe de Presse et de Documentation
67 Place Chabandar, BP 3550, Damaxcus, Syria
OFA-Edition

Office for Official Publications of the European Communities
2 Rue Mercier, BP 1003, Luxembourg

Office of Fair Trading
Field House, 15-25 Bream's Buildings, London EC4A 1PR, England
Phone: 01-242 2858

Oliver & Boyd
Robert Stevenson House, 1-3 Baxter's Place, Leith Walk, Edinburgh EH1 3BB, Scotland
Phone: 031-556 2424
Fax: 031-558 1278

Om Prakash Jitendra Kumar
Chawri Bazar, Delhi 110 001, India

Online Publications
Blenheim House, Ash Hill Drive, Pinner, Middx HA5 2AE, England
Phone: 01-868 4466
Fax: 01-868 9933

Ontario Economic Council
1141 Clarkson Road, Mississauga, Ontario, L5J 2W1, Canada

Ontario Institute for Studies in Education
252 Bloor Street, Toronto, Ontario, M5S 1V6, Canada

Ontario Ministry of Government Service
Publications Service, Ferguson Block, 9th Floor, Queen's Park, Toronto, Ontario, M7A 1N8, Canada

Open Spaces Society
25A Bell Street, Henley-on-Thames, OXON, RG9 2BA
Phone: 0491 573535

Open University Press
Celtic Court, Buckingham, MK18 1XW, England
Phone: 0280 822211
Fax: 0280 823233

Oregon Health Sciences University
Department of Psychiatry, 114 Gaines Hall, 840 S. W. Gaines Road, Portland, Oregon OR 97201, USA

Organisation for Economic Co-operation & Development (OECD)
2 Rue Andre Pascal, 75016 Paris, France
Phone: (1) 45248200

Orient Longman Ltd
5-9-41/1 Bashir Bagh, Hyderabad 500 029, India
Phone: 220343,236111

Oryx Press
2214 N. Central Avenue, Phoenix, AZ 85004-1483, USA
Phone: 602 254 6156
Fax: 602 253 2741

Oughtershaw Press
38 Wangalla Road, Lane Cove, NSW 2066, Australia
POB 733, Chatswood, NSW 2067, Australia

OUP →Oxford University Press

OUP/Institute of Psychiatry →Oxford University Press

Overseas Development Administration
Eland House, Stag Place, London SW1, England
Phone: 01 213 3000
Library Room, 175 Abercrombie House, Eaglesham Road, East Kilbride, Glasgow, G75 8EB
Phone: 035 52 41199

Ovum
7 Rathbone Street, London W1P 1AF, England
Phone: 01 637 4661

Oxford & IBH Publishing Co
66 Janpath, 2nd floor, New Delhi 110 001, India
Phone: 321035

Oxford Microform Publications Ltd
Headington Hill Hall, Oxford OX3 0BW, England

Oxford Polytechnic Press
Headington, Oxford, OX3 0BP, England
Phone: 0865 64777

Oxford University Press
Walton Street, Oxford OX2 6DP, England
Phone: 0865 56767
Fax: 0865 56646
OUP, Clarendon Press, OUP/Institute of Psychiatry

Oxford University Press [Australia]
253 Normanby Road, South Melbourne Road, Victoria 3205, Australia
Phone: 03 646 4200
Fax: 03 646 3251

Oxford University Press [Hong Kong]
18/F Warwick House, Tong Chong Street, Quarry Bay, Hong Kong

Oxford University Press [India]
2/11 Ansari Road, Daryaganj, POB 7035, New Delhi 110 002, India
Phone: 202 1029, 202198

Oxford University Press [NZ]
1A Matai Road, Green Lane, Auckland, New Zealand
PO Box 11-149, Ellerslie, New Zealand

Oxford University Press [Singapore]
Unit 221, Ubi Av 4,, Singapore 1440, Singapore

Oxfordshire County Record Office
County Hall, Oxford OX1 1ND, England
Phone: 0865 815203

Oyez Longman Publishing Ltd
21-27 Lamb's Conduit Street, London WC1N 3NJ, England
Phone: 01-242 2548

Padma Publications Ltd
53/55 Laxmi Buildings, Sir P M Road, Bombay 400 001, India

Pahuja Bros
Kadam Kuan, Patna 3, Bihar, India

Pakistan Institute of Development Economics
POB 1091, Islamabad, Pakistan

Pakistan Law Times Publications
Kabir Street, Urdu Bazar, Lahore, Pakistan

Pan Books Ltd
Cavaye Place, London SW10 9PG, England
Sales, Accounts, Hamilton Close, Houndmills, Basingstoke, Hants, RG21 2YT
Phone: 0256 464481
Fax: 0256 464481 X242

Panchayat Publications
Nr High Court Building, Hyderabad 500 002, India

Pandora Press →Unwin Hyman Ltd

Paradigm Publishing
Avenue House, 131-133 Holland Park Avenue, London W11 4UT, England
Phone: 01 603 4688
Fax: 01 602 5197

Parimal Prakashan
Parimal Khadeshwar, Aurangabad 431 001, India
194 Sohbatia Bagh, Allahabad 6, India

Park Place Publishing (Dundee) Ltd
11 Whitehall Street, Dundee DD1 4AE, Scotland

Pathfinder Press Ltd
215A Thomas Street, Haymarket, NSW 2000, Australia
Phone: 02 2112332

Peace Plans
c/o JM Zube, Oxley Street, Berima, NSW 2577, Australia

Peguis Publishers Ltd
462 Hargrave Street, Winnipeg, Man. R3A OX5, Canada

Pelican →Penguin Books Ltd

Penguin Books Australia Ltd
487 Maroondah Hury, POB 257, Ringwood, Vic 3134, Australia
Phone: 03 8712400
Fax: 03 8709618

Penguin Books Ltd
27 Wrights Lane, London W8, England
Phone: 01 938 2200
Fax: 01 937 8704
Allen Lane, Pelican, Viking

Penguin Books (NZ)
182-190 Wairau Road, Takapuna, Auckland, New Zealand

Penman Press
6 Woniora Avenue, Wahroonga, NSW 2076, Australia
PO Box 4143, Sydney 2001, Australia

People's Publishing House Pvt Ltd
5E Rhani Jansi Road, New Delhi 110 055, India
Phone: 529365

Pepar Publications Ltd
50 Knightlow Road, Birmingham B17 8QB, England
Phone: 021-642 3453

Pergamon Infoline
12 Vandy Street, London EC2A 2DE, England
Phone: 01-377 4650

Petroleum News Southeast Asia Ltd
6/F, 146 Prince Edward Road, West, Kowloon, Hong Kong
Phone: 3-805294-5

Petty Publishing Co Pty Ltd
13 Calder Road, Rydalmere, NSW 2116, Australia
Phone: 02 6387490

Phillimore & Co Ltd
Shopwyke Hall, Chichester, West Sussex PO20 6BQ, England
Phone: 0243 787636

Phoenix Publishing House Inc
927 Quezon Avenue, Quezon City, Philippines

Piatkus Books
5 Windmill Street, London W1P 1HF, England
Phone: 01-631 0710
Fax: 01-436 7137

Pinter (F.) Publishers Ltd
25 Floral Street, London WC2E 9DS, England
Phone: 01-240 9233
Fax: 01-379 5553

Pioneer Publications
87 Netaji Road, Pollachi, Tamil Nadu, India

Pitman (Isaac) Pty Ltd
158-164 Bouverie Street, Carleton, Victoria 3053, Australia
Phone: 03-3473055

Pitman Publishing
128 Long Acre, London WC2E 9AN, England
Phone: 01-379 7383
Fax: 01-240 5771

Pitman Publishing (NZ)
c/o Paul Longman, 182-190 Wairu Road, Takapuna, Auckland 9, New Zealand

Planning Exchange
186 Bath Street, Glasgow G2 4HG, Scotland
Phone: 041 332 8541

Pluto Press
Swallow House, 11-21 Northdown Street, London N1 9BN, England
Phone: 01-837 3322
Fax: 01-278 1677

Pluto Press Australia
PO Box 199, Leichhardt, NSW 2040, Australia
Phone: 02 519 3676

Police Foundation
314-316 Vauxhall Bridge Road, London, SW1V 1AA, England
Phone: 01-828 1438

Police Review Publishing Co Ltd
14 St Cross Street, Hatton Garden, London EC1N 8FE, England

Policy Journals
Old Vicarage, Hermitage, Newbury, Berks RG16 9SU, England
Phone: 0635 200466

Policy Studies Institute
1-2 Castle Lane, London SW1E 6DR, England
100 Park Village East, London, NW1 3SR
Phone: 387 2171
Fax: 388 0914

Polity Press
Dales Brewery, Gwydir Street, Cambridge CB1 2LJ, England
Phone: 0223 324315
Fax: 0223 461385

Polynesian Press
Samoa House, 283 Karangahope Road, Auckland, New Zealand

Polytech Publishers
36 Hatburn Road, Offerton, Stockport, Cheshire, SK2 5DB, England

Pontifical Institute of Mediaeval Studies
Dept. of Publications, 59 Queens Park Crescent, Toronto, Ontario, M5S 2C4, Canada
Phone: 416 926 7144

Poolbeg Press Ltd
Knocksedan House, Forrest Great, Sword, Co Dublin, Eire
Phone: 0001 401133

Popular Education Publishers
Raja Ram Mehta Nagar, Madras 29, Tamil Nadu, India

Popular Prakashan Pvt Ltd
35-C Pandit Madar Mohan, Malavija Marg Tadeo, Bombay 400 034, India

Potoroo Press
21 Rockley Road, South Yarra, Victoria 3141, Australia

Praeger Publishers
c/o Eurospan Ltd, 3 Henrietta Street, London WC2E 8LU, England
Phone: 01-240 0856
Fax: 01-379 0609

Pragati Prakashan
Lajput Rai Market, Begum Pul, POB 62, Meerut 250 001, India
Phone: 73022

Prakashan Kendra
Sitapur Road, Near Railway Crossing, Lucknow 226 007, India

Precambrian Research Unit, University of Cape Town → University of Cape Town, Precambrian Reseach Unit

Premier Book House
Room 2, Shahir Market, Anarkali, PO Box 1888, Lahore 2, Pakistan

Premier Publishers (India)
F-117 Sudershan Park, New Delhi 110 015, India

Prentice Hall of Australia
7 Grosvenor Place, Brookvale, NSW 2100, Australia

Prentice-Hall of India Pvt Ltd
M-97 Connaught Circus, New Delhi 110 001, India
Phone: 352590

Prestel
Telephone House, Temple Avenue, London EC4, England
Phone: 01 822 1122

Primary Education Publications
5 Dakara Place, Frenchs Forest, NSW 2086, Australia

Primavera
24 Allen Street, Leichart, NSW 2040, Australia

Princeton University Press
c/o Wolfgang Wingester, 15a Epsom Road, Guildford, Surrey, GU1 3JT, England
Phone: 0483 68364
41 William Street, Princeton, NJ 08540, USA
Phone: 609 452 4900
Fax: 609 895 1081

Printwell Publishers
C-123 Mangal Marg, Bapau Nagar, Jaipur 302015, India

Prism Press
2 South Street, Bridport, Dorset, DT6 3NQ, England
Phone: 0308 27022
Fax: 0308 27376
c/o George Philip Services Ltd, PO Box 1, Littlehampton, West Sussex, BN17 7EN, England
Phone: 0903 717453/5

Prison Reform Trust
59 Caledonian Road, London N1 9BU, England
Phone: 01 278 9815

Product Liability Briefing
Index House, 29 Hatherly Road, London E17 6SE, England
Phone: 01-509 2196

Professional Books Ltd
46 Milton Trading Estate, Milton, Abingdon, Oxfordshire OX14 4SY, England
Phone: 0235 861234
Fax: 0235 861601

Professional Publishers (Pty) Ltd
8 Walters Place, Waterval Park, Mayville, Durban 4000, South Africa
Phone: 010 2731 294247
Fax: 010 2731 283255

Professional Publishing Ltd
7 Swallow Place, London W1, England
Phone: 01 409 3322
Fax: 01 629 0373
Gee & Co

Profex
Trafalgar House, Greville Place, London NW7 3SA, England
Phone: 01-959 3611

Progressive Corporation Pvt Ltd
51 Mahatma Ghandi Road, Bombay 400 002, India

Property Law and Equity Reform Committee
c§o New Zealand Law Commission, PO Box 2590, Wellington, New Zealand
Phone: 733 453
Fax: 710 959

Wellington, New Zealand

Property Lawyer
Dunsley South, Park Road, Forest Row, E. Sussex RH18 5BX, England
Phone: 034 282 3094
Fax: 034 282 3688

PROPO (National Prisoners Movement)
BM PROP, London WC1N 3XX, England
Phone: 01 542 3744
97 Caledonian Road, London N1
Phone: 01 278 3328

Prosecuting Solicitors Society of England and Wales → Crown Prosecution

Prospect Publishing
16 Riley Street, Woolloomooloo 2011, Australia

Publications Department, University of Poona → University of Poona

Punjab University
Publication Bureau, c/o Hazara Singh, Patiala 147 002, India

QL Systems Ltd
112 Kent Street, Tower B, Ste 1210, Ottawa, ON K1P 5P2, Canada

Quadri Publishers
255 Sarwar Shaheed Road, Karachi 1, Pakistan

Quaid-i-Azam Academy
297 M A Jinnah Road, Karachi 5, Pakistan

Quaker Peace & Service
Friends House, Euston Road, London NW1 2BJ, England
Phone: 01 387 3601

Quartet Books Ltd
27 Goodge Street, London W1P 1FD, England
Phone: 01 636 3992/0968
Fax: 01 439 6489

Queen Elizabeth II Arts Council of N.Z.
3rd Floor, 110-116 Courtenay Place, POB 6040, Wellington, New Zealand

Queen's University, Industrial Relations Centre
Kingston, Ontario K7L 3N6, Canada
Industrial Relations Centre, Queen's University

Queen's University, Institute of Intergovernmental Relations
Institute of Intergovernmental Relations, Kingston, Ontario K7L 3N6, Canada
Institute of Intergovernmental Relations, Queen's University

Queens Printer
10255 104th Street, Edmonton, Alberta, Canada

Queens University of Belfast
Faculty of Law, University Road, Belfast BT7 1NN, Northern Ireland
Northern Ireland Legal Quarterly

Quins Pte Ltd
621 Aljunied Road, No 06 - 01 Lipo Building, Singapore 1438, Singapore

Quorum Press → Saint Andrew Press

R R Bowker → Bowker-Saur Ltd

Radiant Publishers
State Bank of India Building, E-155 Kalkaji, New Delhi 110-019, India
Phone: 635477

Ram Narain Lal Beni Prasad
4 Katra Road, Allahabad 211 002, India
Oila Road, Rohtak 124001, India

Rangnath Publications
23 Tandon House, Daryaganj, Delhi 100 002, India

Ravenswood Publications Ltd
PO Box 24, Beckenham, Kent BR3 3AL, England
Phone: 0293 32846

Reader's Digest Association
25 Berkeley Square, London W1X 6AB, England
Phone: 01 629 8144
Fax: 01 449 9751

Reader's Digest Association (Canada)
215 Redfern Avenue, Westmount, Montreal, PQ H32, Canada
Phone: 514 934 0751
Fax: 514 932 3637

Redfern Legal Centre Publishing
18 George Street, Redfern 2016, Australia

Reed (A. H. & A. W.) Ltd
Private Bag, Wellington, New Zealand

Reed Methuen Publishers
39 Rawene Road, Birkenhead, Auckland 10, New Zealand

Release
1 Elgin Avenue, London W9 3PR, England
Phone: 01 289 1123

Reliance Publishing House
3026/7-H Ranjit Nagar, New Delhi 110 008, India

Research School of Social Sciences, Dept of Law, Australian National University → Australian National University, Research School of Social Services, Dept of Law

Reserve Bank of New Zealand
2 The Terrace, Wellington, New Zealand

Reuter Simkin Ltd
26-28 Bedford Row, London WC1R 4HE, England
Phone: 01-405 6852
Fax: 01-405 3677

Rex Bookstore
84 P Florentino Avenue, Quezon City, Philippines

Rhodes University Library
PO Box 184, 6140 Grahamstown, S. Africa

RIBA Publications Ltd
Finsbury Mission, Moreland Street, London EC1V 8BB, England
Phone: 01-251 0791
Fax: 01-253 1085

Rights of Women
374 Grays Inn Road, London WC1X 8BB, England
Phone: 01 278 6349

Robinson Publishing
11 Shepherd House, 5 Shepherd Street, London W1Y 7LD, England
Phone: 01-493 1064
Fax: 01-629 0316

Roeher (G. Allan) Institute
Kinsmen Building, 4700 Keele Street, York University Campus, Downsview, Ontario, M3J 1P3, Canada
G Allan Roeher Institute

Rose (Barry) UK
Little London, Chichester, West Sussex, PO19 1PG, England

Ross Anderson Publications Ltd
Larkhill House, 160 St Georges Road, Bolton BL1 2PJ, England
Phone: 0204 31289

Rosters Ltd
60 Welbeck Street, London W1M 7HS, England
Phone: 01-935 4550
Fax: 01-486 9037

Rota
Dept of History & Archeology, Amory Building, University of Exeter, Bennes Drive, Exeter, EX4 4RJ, England

Round Hall Press
Kill Lane, Blackrock, Dublin, Eire
Phone: 0001 892922

Routledge & Kegan Paul →Kegan Paul International Ltd

Routledge, Chapman & Hall
11 New Fetter Lane, London EC4P 4EE, England
Phone: 01-583 9855
Fax: 01-583 0701
Tavistock Publications, Chapman & Hall, Spon (E. & F.) Ltd

Royal Book Company
402 Rehmar Center, Zaibunisa Street, PO Box 7737, Karachi 3, Pakistan

Royal Historical Society
University College London, Gower Street, London WC1E 6BT, England
Phone: 01 387 7532

Royal Institute of Chartered Surveyors
12 Great George Street, London SW1P 3AD, England
Phone: 01-222 7000
Fax: 01-222 9430

Royal Institute of Public Administration
3 Birdcage Walk, London SW1H 9JH, England
Phone: 01-222 2248

Royston Ltd
10 Crown Road North, Glasgow G12 9DH, Scotland
Phone: 041-339 1867

Rubin (Ken)
68 Second Avenue, Ottawa, Ontario, K1S 2H5, Canada
212 Third Avenue, Ottawa K15 2K3, Canada

Rutgers University Press
109 Church Street, New Brunswick, NJ 08901, USA
Phone: 201 932 7764
Fax: 201 932 7039

Sage Publications
28 Banner Street, London EC1, England
Phone: 01-253 1516
Fax: 01-253 5206

Saint Andrew Press
121 George Street, Edinburgh EH2 4YN, Scotland
Phone: 031-225 5722
Quorum Press

Saint Anthony's Press
Peaseholme Green, York YO1 2PW, England
Phone: 0904 59861, 1263

Saltire Society
9 Fountain Close, High Street, Edinburgh, EH1 1TF, Scotland
Phone: 031 556 1836

Sangam Books Ltd
Sangam Books Ltd, 57 London Fruit Exchange, London E1 6EP, England
Phone: 01 377 6399

Sarkar (B.) & Sons
6/1B Madan Mitra Lane, Calcutta 700 006, India

Sarkar (M. C.) & Sons
14 Bankim Chatterjee Street, Calcutta 700 012, India

Satvahan Publications
119 Masijd Moth, New Delhi 110 049, India

Saunders (W. B.)
24-28 Oval Road, London NW1 7DX, England
Phone: 01-267 4466
Fax: 01-482 2293

Scandinavian Institute of African Studies
Dragarbrunnsgt 24, Box 1703, S - 751 47 Uppsala, Sweden

Scarecrow Press →Bailey Bros & Swinfen Ltd

SCCA Publishing
40 Tyndalls Park Road, Bristol BS8 1PL, England
Phone: 0272 738261

Sceptre →Hodder & Stoughton Ltd

Schmidt (Erich) Verlag
Genthiner Strasse 30, 1000 Berlin 30, West Germany
Phone: 030 250085

Schmidt (Otto), KG Verlag
Ulmenalle 96 - 98, 5000 Koln 51, West Germany
Phone: 0221 373025
Fax: 0221 373751

School of Applied Studies, University of Bristol →University of Bristol, School of Applied Studies

School of Criminology and Forensic Studies → University of Edinburgh, School of Criminology and Forensic Studies

School of Criminology and Forensic Studies, University of Edinburgh →University of Edinburgh, School of Criminology and Forensic Studies

School of Education, University of Newcastle-upon-Tyne →University of Newcastle upon Tyne, School of Education

Scientia Verlag und Antiquariat
Adlerstrasse 65, 7080 Aalen Wuertt 1, West Germany
Phone: 07361 41700

Scolar Press
Gower House, Croft Road, Aldershot, Surrey GU11 3HR, England
Phone: 0252 331551

Scoop Publications
c/o V J Nurcombe, 8 Kingfisher Drive, Over, Winsford, Cheshire CW7 1PF, England
Phone: 0606 558242

Scorpion Publishing Ltd
Victoria House, Victoria Road, Buckhurst Hill, Essex IG9 5ES, England
Phone: 01-506 0606

Scottish Academic Press Ltd
33 Montgomery Street, Edinburgh, EH7 5JX, Scotland
Phone: 031 556 2796
Fax: 031 313 2773

Scottish Association of Citizens Advice Bureaux
26 George Square, Edinburgh, EH8 9EW, Scotland
Phone: 031 667 0156

Scottish Council for Voluntary Organisations
18-19 Claremont Crescent, Edinburgh EH7 4QD, Scotland
Phone: 031-556 3882

Scottish Courts Administration
PO Box 37, 28 North Bridge, Edinburgh, EH1 1RA
Phone: 031 226 5911 X66

Scottish Law Commission
140 Causewayside, Edinburgh EH9, Scotland
Phone: 031 668 2131

Scottish Office
New St Andrew's House, St James Centre, Edinburgh EH1 3TG, Scotland
Phone: 031-556 8400

Scottish Universities Law Institute →Green (W.) & Son Ltd

Seatrade Publications
Fairfax House, Causon Road, Colchester, Essex CO1 1RJ, England
Phone: 0206 45121

Secker & Warburg Ltd
Michelin House, 81 Fulham Road, London SW3 6RB, England
Phone: 01-581 9393
Fax: 01 589 8419

Securities Commission
PO Box 1179, Wellington, New Zealand
Phone: 729 830
Fax: 728 076

New Zealand

Self-Counsel Press Ltd
1481 Charlotte Road, North Vancouver, BC, V7J 1H1, Canada
Phone: 604 986 3366
Fax: 604 986 3947

Serendip Publications
POB 333, Wamberal, NSW 2260, Australia

Services to Lawyers Ltd
Sardinia House, 52 Lincoln's Inn Fields, London WC2A 3LZ, England
Unit 1, Robin Road, Knaphill, Woking, Surrey, GU21 2LY, England
Phone: 04867 88686

Severn House Publishers Ltd
40-42 William IV Street, London WC2N 4DF, England
Phone: 01-240 9683
Fax: 01-379 6489

Seychelles National Printing Co
POB 205, Victoria Mafe, Seychelles

SHAC
189a Old Brompton Road, London SW5, England
Phone: 01 373 7841
London Housing Aid Centre

Shaikh Muhammad Ashref
7 Aibak Road, New Anarkali, Lahore 7, Pakistan

Sharpe (M. E.) Inc
80 Business Park Drive, Armonk, NY 10504, USA
Phone: 914-273-1800
Fax: 914-273-2106

Shaw & Sons Ltd
Shaway House, Bell Green Lane, Lower Sydenham, London SE26 5AE, England
Phone: 01 778 5131
Fax: 01 676 0174

Shaws Linton Publications →MCB University Press Ltd

Shelter
157 Waterloo Road, London SE1 8UW, England
Phone: 01 633 9377
88 Old Street, London EC1V 9HU, England
Phone: 01 253 0202

Shennan (M. R.)
4 Albany Court, Noble Park, Victoria 3174, Australia

Shuter & Shooter Pty Ltd
PO Box 109, Pietermaritzburg 3200, S Africa

Sijthoff & Noordhoff International Publishers
1600 Research Boulevard, Rockville, USA
Phone: 301 251 0950

Simon & Schuster International Group
66 Wood Lane End, Hemel Hempstead, Herts HP2 4RG, England
Phone: 0442 231555
Fax: 0442 212485
Allyn & Bacon

Sinclair Browne Ltd
92 Muswell Hill Road, London N10 3JR, England

Singapore Insurance Training Centre
Wing on Life Bldg, 150 Cecil St, 05 - 010, Singapore 0106, Singapore

Singapore University Press
University of Singapore, Kent Ridge Campus, Singapore 0511

Sitaraman (C.) & Co
33 Royapettah High Road, Madras 600 014, India

Skinner (Thomas) Directories Ltd
Windsor Court, East Grinstead House, East Grinstead, West Sussex RH19 1XA, England
Phone: 0342 26972

Social Science Press
157 Blaxland Road, Wentworth Falls, NSW 2782, Australia

Socialantropologiska Institutionen
Fiskartorpsvaegen 160 D, Fact 10405, Stockholm 50, Sweden

Society for Computers and Law
1st floor, 12 Station Road, Didcot, OXON, OX11 7LW, England
Phone: 0235 811303

Society of Local Authority Chief Executives
Pelham House, St.Andrew's Lane, Lewes, E. Sussex, England
County Hall, Northampton, NN1 1DN

Society of Management Accountants of Canada
154 E. Main Street, Hamilton, Ontario, L8N 3C3, Canada

Sociological Association of Ireland
Dept of Social Studies, Queens University of Belfast, Belfast BT7 1NN, N Ireland
Phone: 0232 245133

Somaiya Publications Pvt Ltd
F-6 Bank Bank of Baroda Bldg, Parliament Street, New Delhi 110 001, India

Sono Nis Press
1745 Blanshard Street, Victoria, BC V8W 2J8, Canada

South African Institute of International Affairs
PO Box 31596, Braamfontein 2017, S. Africa

South African Institute of Race Relations
68 de Korte Street, PO Box 97, 2000 Johannesburg, S. Africa

South African Library
Queen Victoria Street, POB 496, 8000 Cape Town, S. Africa

South African Publishers, State Library
PO Box 397, 0001 Pretoria, South Africa
Phone: (012) 218931
Association of Law Societies of the Republic of South Africa

Souvenir Press Ltd
43 Great Russell Street, London WC1B 3PA, England
Phone: 01-580 9307

Sphere Books Ltd
27 Wright's Lane, London, W8 5TZ, England
Phone: 01-937 8070
Fax: 01-937 8704
Abacus

Spokesman Books
Bertrand Russell House, Gamble Street, Nottingham, NG7 4ET, England
Phone: 0602 708318

Spon (E. & F.) Ltd →Routledge, Chapman & Hall

Springer-Verlag GmbH & Co KG
Heidelberger Pl 3, D - 1000 Berlin 33, Germany
Phone: 030 82070-0,8214092
Fax: 030 8214091
Postfach 3113400, D - 1000 Berlin 31, GFR

Springwood Books Ltd
Springwood House, The Avenue, Ascot, Berks SL5 7LY, England
Phone: 0990 24053

Sri Lanka Centre for Development Studies → Marga Institute

SSRC-Social Science Research Council →Centre for Socio-Legal Studies, Social Science Research Council

Staatsdrukkery en Uitgeversbedryt
Chr. Plantynstraat 1- 9, The Hague, Netherlands

Stanford Maritime
14 Long Acre, London WC2E 9LP, England
59 Grosvenor Street, London W1X 9DA, England
Phone: 01 493 5841

Star Books
4/5-B Asaf Ali Road, New Delhi 110002, India
Phone: 268651

State Information Service
Talaat Harb Street, Cairo, Egypt

Statens Invandrarverk
Vikboplan 5-7, Box 6113, 60006 Norrkoeping, Sweden
Phone: 011 156000

Stationery Office Dublin
Ballsbridge, Dublin 4, Eire
St Martin's House, Waterloo Road, Dublin 4, Eire

Steiner (Franz) Verlag GmbH
Friedrichstrasse 24, Postfach 5529, Wiesbaden 6200, West Germany
Birkenwaldstra 44, 7000 Stuttgart 1, W Germany
Phone: 0711 25820
Fax: 0711 291450

Sterling Publishers Pvt Ltd
L-10 Green Park Extension, New Delhi 110 016, India

Stevens & Son Ltd
11 New Fetter Lane, London EC4P 4EE, England
Phone: 01 583 9855

Stevens Samuel Hakkert & Co
125 Bermondsey Road, Toronto, Ontario, M4A 1X3, Canada

Stewart (Henry) Publications
88 Baker St, London, W1M 1DL, England
Phone: 01-935 2382

Stirling University Press →Bowker-Saur Ltd

Stock Exchange Press
London & International Publishers Ltd, 49 St James's Street, London SW1A 1JT, England
Phone: 01-499 5042

Stockwell (Arthur H.) Ltd
Elms Court, Torrs Park, Ilfracombe, Devon EX34 8BA, England
Phone: 0271 62557

Stone & Cox Ltd
100 Simcoe Street, Toronto, Ont M5H 3G2, Canada

Stoy Hayward
8 Baker Street, London W1M 1DA, England
Phone: 01-486 5888
Fax: 01-935 5465

Struik (C.) Publishers
Oswald Pirow St, Foreshore, POB 1144, 8000 Cape Town, S. Africa

Study Panorama Publishing Co
Suite 2, Level 2, 383 George Street, Sydney, NSW 2000, Australia
PO Box 4, Gladesville, NSW 2111, Australia

Sudetendeutscher Rat e. V.
Hochstrasse 6 - 8, D-8000 Munchen 80, Germany, GFR

Suffolk Record Office
County Hall, Ipswich IP4 2JS, England
Phone: 0473 230000

Sultan Chand & Sons
23 Daryaganj, New Delhi 110 002, India

Suomalainen Lakimiesyhdistys RY
Annankatu 16B, 00120 Helsinki 12, Finland

Suomen filosofinen yhdistus ry - Filosojian
Laitos, Unioninkata 40B, SF - 00170 Helsinki, Finland

Suomen Valtio
c/o Valtion Painatuskeskus, P1 516, SF-00101 Helsinki, Finland

Sussex European Research Centre, University of Sussex →University of Sussex, Sussex European Research Centre

Sweet & Maxwell Ltd
11 New Fetter Lane, London EC4P 4EE, England
Phone: 01 583 9855
Fax: 01 583 0701

Swets & Zeitlinger BV
Heereweg 3476, Postbus 800, NL - 2161 CA Lisse, Netherlands
Phone: 02521 19113

Swift Publishing Ltd
1-7 Albion Place, Britton Street, London EC1M 5RE, England
Phone: 01 251 2535

Swinburne College of Technology
John Street, Hawthorn, Victoria 3122, Australia
Phone: 03 8190111

Ta-Ha Publishers Ltd
1 Wynne Road, London SW9 0BB, England
Phone: 01-737 7266
Fax: 01-675 4156

Tafe Educational →New South Wales University Press

Tampere Peace Research Institute
c/o Helena Rytovvori, Tampere Yliopisto, Politukan Tutkimuslaitos, SF - 33101 Tampere, Finland

Tancred Press
PO Box 2254, Rotorua, New Zealand

Tasmania Government Publications
2 Salamanda Place, Hibart, Tasmania 7000, Australia

Tata Institute of Social Sciences
Sion-Trombay Road, Deonar, Bombay 400 008, India

Tauris (I. B.) & Co Ltd
3 Henrietta Street, London WC2E 8PW, England
Phone: 01-836 5814

Tavistock Publications →Routledge, Chapman & Hall

Taxation Publications
P O Box 365, Cremorne, NSW 2090, Australia

Taxation Publishing Co
3 Daryaganj, Delhi 110 006, India

Taxbriefs Ltd
193 St John Street, London EC1V 4QA, England
Phone: 01-250 0967
Fax: 01-251 8867

Taylor & Francis Ltd
4 John Street, London WC1N 2ET, England
Phone: 01-405 2237
Fax: 01-831 2035

Technical Communications
100 High Avenue, Letchworth, Hertfordshire, SG6 3RR, England
Phone: 04626 79987

Telegraph Publications
Peterborough Court, South Quay, 181 Marsh Wall, London E14 9SR, England
Phone: 01-538 5000

Telesystemes-Questel
83-85 blvd. Vincent Auriol, Paris 75013, France

Telford (Thomas) Ltd
Thomas Telford House, 1 Heron Quay, London E14 9XF, England
Phone: 01-987 6999
Fax: 01-538 5746

Telles Langdon Publications
29 Park Street, Croydon, Surrey CR0 1YD, England

Tennison (Patrick) Enterprises
375 High Street, Ashburton, Victoria 3147, Australia

Thacker & Co Ltd
18-20 Kaikushroo Dubash Marg, POB 190, Bombay 400 001, India

Thames Publishers
Halley Court, Jordan Hill, Oxford OX2 8EJ, England

Third World Publications Ltd
151 Stratford Court, Birmingham B11 1RD, England
Phone: 021-773 6572

Thomas Nelson →Nelson (Thomas) Ltd [Australia]

Thomson Press Pvt (India) Ltd
Publications Division, K Block, Connaught Circus, New Delhi 110 001, India

Thornes (Stanley) & Hulton (Publishers) Ltd
Old Station Drive, Leckhampton, Cheltenham, Glos GL53 0DN, England
Phone: 0242 584429
Fax: 0242 221914
Hulton Educational

Thorsons Publishing Group Ltd
Denington Estate, Wellingborough, Northants NN8 2RQ, England
Phone: 0933 440033
Fax: 0933 440512
Equation, Kimber (William)

THR Book Centre
31 Curzon Street, London W1Y 7AE, England
Capacity House, 2-6 Rothsay House, Tower Bridge Road, London SE1 4UD, England

Tiedeakatemia
Suomalainen Tiedeakatemia, Mariankatu 5, SF - 00170 Helsinki, Finland

Times Books International Pte Ltd
Times Centre, 1 New Industrial Road, Singapore 1953, Singapore

Timmins (H.)
c/o Robert Hale, Clerkenwell House, Clerkenwell Green, London EC1 0HT, England
Phone: 01-251 2661
Fax: 01-251 0584

Tisara Prakashakayo Ltd
129 Dutugemunu St, Kohuwala, Dehiwala, Sri Lanka

Tolley Publishing Co Ltd
Tolley House, 2 Addiscombe Road, Croydon, Surrey CR9 5AF, England
Phone: 01 686 9141
Fax: 01 686 3155

Topaz Publications
64 Upper Georges Street, Dun Laoghaire, Co Dublin, Eire

Trade Policy Research Centre
1 Gough Square, London EC4A 3DE, England
Phone: 01 353 6371

Trade Practices Commission
Benjamin Offices, Chan Street, Belconnen, ACT 2617, Australia
Phone: (062) 641166
Fax: (062) 642803

Trans-Canada
70 The Esplande, 2nd floor, Toronto, Ontario H5E 1R2, Canada

Translegal AG →Lloyd (Chris) Sales & Management Services

Travancore Law House
Mahatma Gandhi Road, Ernakulam, 682011, Kerala, India

Treharne Publishers
PO Box 30055, Wainoni, Christchurch, New Zealand

Tripathi (N. M.) Pvt Ltd
164 Samaldas Ghandi Marg, Bombay 400 002, India

Turnaround Press
384 Everett Avenue, Palo Alto, CA 94301, USA
Phone: 415 325 9348

TVNZ Publishing
PO Box 3819, Auckland, New Zealand

Tycooly →Cassell plc

Ueberreuter, Carl Druck und Verlag
M. Salzer, Alser Strasse 24, Postfach 60, 1095 Vienna, Austria
Phone: 481538

UGA Editions S.A.
Styn Streuvelslaan, 73, B - 8710 Kortrijk - Heule, Belgium
Phone: 0932 56355881

UNESCO
7 Pl de Fontenoy, F - 75700 Paris, France

Uni Druck Novotny & Soellner
Amalienstrasse 83, 8000 Muenchen 40, West Germany
Phone: 089 282022

United Kingdom National Committee of Comparative Law
Charles Clore House, 17 Russell Square, London WC1B 5DP, England

United Law Publishers
87 Itwaria Bazar, Indore 452 002, India

United Nations Institute for Namibia
POB 33811, Lusaka, Zambia

United Nations Publications
Palais des Nations, Postf, 1211 Geneve 10, Switzerland
Phone: 022 346011

Universal Book Traders
80 Gokhale Market, Opp. New Courts, POB 1321, Delhi 110 054, India

Universitat Hamburg
Institute fur International Angelegenheiten, Rothenbaumchaussee 21 - 23, D-2000 Hamburg 13, W. Germany
Institut fur Internationale Angelenheiten, Universitat Hamburg

Universitatsverlag Freiburg
42 Perolles, CH - 1700 Freibourg, Switzerland
Phone: 037 246812

Universitetsforlaget
Postbox 2977, Toyen 0608, Oslo 6, Norway

Universities Federation for Animal Welfare (UFAW)
8 Hamilton Close, South Mimms, Potters Bar, Herts EN6 3QD, England
Phone: 0707 58202

University Book Agency
15-B Elgin Road, POB 63, Allahabad 211 001, India

University of Aberdeen, Centre for Environmental Management & Planning
48 College Bounds, Aberdeen, Scotland
Phone: 0224 272480
Centre for Environmental Management and Planning

University of Alberta Press
141 Athabasca Hall, Edmonton, Alta. T6G 2E8, Canada, Canada

University of Birmingham, Holdsworth Club
P O Box 363, Birmingham B15 2TT, England
Holdsworth Club, University of Birmingham

University of Birmingham, Institute of Judicial Administration
PO Box 363, Birmingham B15 2TT, England
Institute of Judicial Administration, University of Birmingham

University of Bombay
Publications Dept, University Road, Fort, Bombay 400 032, India

University of Bristol, School of Applied Studies
Bristol BS8 1TH, England
Phone: 0272 24161
School of Applied Studies, University of Bristol

University of British Columbia, Faculty of Commerce & Business
Vancouver, BC, V6T 1W5, Canada
Faculty of Commerce & Business, University of British Columbia

University of British Columbia Press
303-6344 Memorial Road, Vancouver, BC, V6 1W5, Canada

University of British Columbia, Westwater Research Center
2053 Main Hall, Vancouver, B.C. V6T 1Y8, Canada, V6T 1W5, Canada
Westwater Research Center, University of British Columbia

University of Calcutta
Centre of Advanced Study in Ancient Indian History & Culture, 51-2 Hazra Road, Calcutta, India
Centre of Advanced Study in Ancient Indian History & Culture

University of Calgary Press
2500 University Drive, N W Calgary, Alberta T2N 1N4, Canada

University of California Press Ltd
C/O Wolfgang Wingerter, 15a Epsom Road, Guildford, Surrey GU1 3JJ, England

University of Cambridge, African Studies Centre
Free School Lane, Cambridge CB2 3RQ, England
Phone: 0223 334396
Fax: 0223 334748

University of Cambridge, Institute of Criminology
7 West Road, Cambridge CB3 9DT, England
Institute of Criminology, Cambridge University

University of Cambridge, Library
West Road, Cambridge CB3 9DR, England
Phone: 0223 61441
Cambridge University Library, Cambridge University Library

University of Cape Town
7700 Rondebosch, S. Africa

University of Cape Town, Precambrian Reseach Unit
Department of Geology, Private Bag, 7700 Rondesboch, S. Africa
Precambrian Research Unit, University of Cape Town

University of Chicago Press Ltd
5801 Ellis Avenue, 4th Floor, Chicago, IL 60637, USA
Phone: 312 702 7700
Fax: 312 702 9756

University of Dar es Salaam
SLP 35091, Dar es Salaam, Tanzania
East African Literature Bureau

University of East Anglia
Norwich NR4 7TJ, England
Phone: 0603 56161

University of Edinburgh, School of Criminology and Forensic Studies
Old College, South Bridge, Edinburgh EH8 9YL, Scotland

School of Criminology and Forensic Studies, University of Edinburgh

University of Exeter
Publications Office, Reed Hall, Streatham Drive, Exeter EX4 4QR, England
Phone: 0392 263066

University of Georgia →Eurospan Ltd

University of Glasgow, Institute of Latin American Studies
Glasgow G12 8QG, Scotland
Phone: 041 339 8855X546
Institute of Latin American Studies, University of Glasgow

University of Hong Kong Press
Bethanie, 139 Pokfulam Road, Hong Kong

University of Ibadan
Inst. of African Studies, Ibadan, Oyo State, Nigeria
Institute of African Studies, University of Ibadan

University of Ife Press
Ile-Ife, Oyo State, Nigeria

University of Keele
Keele, Newcastle, Staffordshire, ST5 5BG, England

University of Kent Press
University Centre, Avebury Avenue, Tunbridge, Kent TN9 1TG, England

University of Lagos
PO Box 12003, Lagos, Nigeria

University of Lagos Library
Akoka, Lagos State, Nigeria

University of Lagos Press
Center for Cultural Studies, University of Lagos, Yaba, Nigeria

University of London, Institute of Advanced Legal Studies
Charles Clore House, 17 Russell Square, London WC1B 5DR, England
Phone: 01-637 1731
Institute of Advanced Legal Studies, Institute of Advanced Legal Studies

University of London Press
Mill Road, Dunton Green, Sevenoaks, Kent TN13 2YA, England

University of London, Queen Mary College, Centre for Commercial Law Studies
339 Mile End Road, London E1 4NS, England

University of Nairobi
Institute for Development Studies, PO Box 30197, Nairobi, Kenya
Institute for Development Studies, University of Nairobi

University of Nebraska Press
901 N 17th Street, Lincoln, NE 68588-0520, USA
Phone: 402 472 3581
Fax: 402 472 2410

University of New Brunswick
Department of History, c/o Acadiensis Press, POB 4400, Fredericton, N.B, E3B 5A3, Canada
Department of History, University of New Brunswick

University of New England
Publications Office, Armidale, NSW 2351, Australia
Phone: 067 732757

University of New South Wales, Aboriginal Law Research Unit
P O Box 1, Kensington, NSW 2033, Australia
Aboriginal Law Research Unit

University of New South Wales, Faculty of Law
PO Box 1, Kensington, NSW 2033, Australia

University of Newcastle
Rankin Drive, Shortland, NSW 2308, Australia

University of Newcastle upon Tyne, School of Education
St Thomas Street, Newcastle-upon-Tyne, NE1 7RU, England
Phone: 091 232 8511
School of Education, University of Newcastle-upon-Tyne

University of Nottingham, Department of Adult Education
C-Block, Cherry Tree Buildings, University Park, Nottingham NG7 2RD, England
Phone: 0602 484848

University of Otago Press
PO Box 56, Dunedin, New Zealand

University of Ottawa Press
603 Cumberland, Ottawa, Ontario, K1N 6N5, Canada

University of Papua New Guinea
POB 4820, University Post Office, Port Moresby, NCD, Papua New Guinea

University of Poona
Publications Department, Ganeshkind, Poona 411 007, India
Publications Department, University of Poona

University of Port Elizabeth
Publications Dept, The Library, Private Bag X6058, 6000 Port Elizabeth, South Africa

University of Queensland Press
PO Box 42, St. Lucia, Queensland 4067, Australia
Phone: 07 377 2127
Fax: 07 870 8719

University of Sheffield, Centre for Criminological & Socio-Legal Studies
Western Bank, Sheffield S10, England
Phone: 0742 768555
Centre for Criminological and Socio-Legal Studies

University of South Africa
PO Box 392, 0001, Pretoria, S. Africa

University of Stellenbosch
7600 Stellenbosch, S. Africa

University of Sussex, Sussex European Research Centre
Falmer, Brighton BN1 9RF, England
Sussex European Research Centre, University of Sussex

University of Tasmania, Centre for Environmental Studies
GPO Box 252C, Hobart, Tasmania 7001, Australia

University of Tasmania, Dept of Political Science
GPO Box 252 c, Holbart, Tasmania 7001, Australia
Phone: 002 20201
Department of Political Science, University of Tasmania

University of the Philippines
Law Centre, Bocobo Hall, Diliman, Quezon City 3004, Philippines

University of the South Pacific
Institute of Pacific Studies, GPOB 1168, Suva, Fiji
Institute of Pacific Studies, University of the South Pacific

University of the West Indies
Institute of Social & Economic Research, Cave Hill, Barbados, West Indies, Canada
Phone: 225 1310
Huang

University of the West Indies, Faculty of Law Library
Cave Hill, Barbados
Faculty of Law Library, University of the West Indies

University of the West Indies, Institute of Social & Economic Research
Cave Hill, Barbados
Phone: 225 1310
Institute of Social & Economic Research, University of the West Indies

University of Toronto
84 Queens Park, Toronto, M5S 2B5, Canada

University of Toronto, Center for Industrial Relations
St George Campus, Toronto, Ontario M5S 1A1, Canada
Phone: 416 978 2239
Centre for Industrial Relations, University of Toronto

University of Toronto, Centre of Criminology
Room 8001, 130 St George Street, Toronto, Ontario, M5S 1A1, Canada
Phone: 416 978 2239
Centre of Criminology, University of Toronto

University of Toronto Press
Front Campus, University of Toronto, Ontario, M5S 1A6, Canada

University of Waikato
Dept of Management Studies, Private Bag, Hamilton, New Zealand
Department of Management Studies, University of Waikato

University of Wales Press
6 Gwynneth Street, Cathays, Cardiff CF2 4YD, Wales
Phone: 0222 231919
Fax: 0222 369040

University of Waterloo, Waterloo Public Interest Research Groups
Room 217A, Campus Centre, University of Waterloo, Waterloo, Ontario, N2L 3G1, Canada
General Services Complex, Room 123, University of Waterloo, Ontario N2L 3G1, Canada
Waterloo Public Interest Research Group, Waterloo University

University of Western Australia Press
Tuart House, Mounts Bay Road & Crawley Avenue, Nedsland, Perth, WA 6009, Australia
Phone: 09 380 3182
Fax: 09 389 1053

University of Windsor Press
Windsor, Ontario, N9B 3P4, Canada

University of York
Faculty of Environmental Studies, 4700 Keele Street, 550A Scott Library, Downsview, Ontario, M3J 2R2, Canada
Faculty of Environmental Studies, York University

University of Zambia
Publications Office, POB 32379, Lusaka, Zambia

University of Zimbabwe
Publications Office, POB MP 45, Mount Pleasant, Harare, Zimbabwe

University Press Ltd [Nigeria]
Three Crowns Building, Jericho, PMB 5095, Ibadan, Oyo State, Nigeria

University Press [Netherlands]
Postbox 1850, Amsterdam, Netherlands

University Press of America
4720 Boston Way, Lanham, MD 20706, USA
Phone: 301 459 3366

Unwin Hyman Ltd
15-17 Broadwick Street, London W1V 1FP, England
Phone: 01-439 3126
Fax: 01-734 3884
Pandora Press

Unwin Paperbacks
15-17 Broadwick Street, London W1V 1FP, England
Phone: 01-439 3126
Fax: 01-734 3884

Uppal Publishing House
3 Ansari Road, Daryaganj, New Delhi 110 002, India

Uppsala universitetsbibliotek
Dag Hammarskjolds vag 1, Box 510, 5-751 20 Uppsala, Sweden
Phone: 018 183900

Vakils, Feffer & Simons Ltd
Hague Building, 9 Spott Road, Bombay 400 038, India

Van Duren Publishers Ltd
P O Box 1, Gerrards Cross, Bucks SL9 7AE, England
Phone: 0753 886575

Van Gorcum & Co BV
Industrieweg 38, NL - 9403, AB Assen
Postbus 43, NL - 9400, AA Assen, Netherlands

Van Schaik (Edms) Bpk (pty) Ltd
Libri Bldg, Church St, POB 724, 0001 Pretoria, S Africa

Vancouver Peoples Law School
2110 - C, West 12th Avenue, Vancouver, BC, V6K 3N2, Canada

Vanier Institute of the Family
120 Holland, 3rd Floor, Ottawa, Ontario, K1Y OX6, Canada

Vann Press
18305 20th Avenue N, Plymouth, MN 55447, USA
Phone: 612 473 0714

Variorum
20 Pembridge Mews, London W11 3EQ, England
32 Connaught Street, Northampton, NN1 3BP

VCH Verlagsgesellscaft GmbH
Pappelallee 3, Postfach 1260, 1280 D - 6940 Weinheim, W. Germany

VDI - Verlag GmbH
Heinrichstrasse 24, Postfach 8228, D - 4000 Dusseldorf 1, Germany, GFR

Venus Book Stall
Poona 411 002, India

Veritas International Publishing
120 Fifth Avenue, Calgary, AB, T2G OE2, Canada

Veritas Publications
Veritas House, 7-8 Lower Abbey Street, Dublin 1, Eire
Phone: 0001 788177
Fax: 0001 744913

Veriag Ernst Battenburg Verlags-und Vertriebs GMBH
Prinzregentenstrasse 79, Postfach 800349, D-8000 Muenchen 80, West Germany, GFR
Battenburg (Ernst)

Verlag Peter Lang AG
Jupiterstrasse 15, Postfach 277, CH - 3000 Bern 15, Switzerland
Lang (Peter)

Victoria University of Wellington
P O Box 196, Wellington, New Zealand

Victoria University Press
14 Kelburn Parade, Wellington, New Zealand

Victorian Commercial Teachers Association
33-37 Hotham Street, Collingwood, Vic. 3066, Australia
P O Box 361, Abbotsford, Vic. 3067, Australia

Victorian Council of Social Service
290 Wellington Street, Collingwood, Victoria 3066, Australia

Vikas Publishing House Pvt Ltd
5 Ansari Road, Daryaganj, New Delhi 110 002, India

Viking → Penguin Books Ltd

Vinod Prakashan
45 Daryaganj, Delhi 110 006, India

Virago Press
20-23 Mandela Street, London NW1 0HQ, England
Phone: 01-383 5150
Fax: 01-255 1620

Vittorio Klostermann GmbH
Frauenlobstrasse 22, Postfach 900601, D-6000 Frankfurt 90, W. Germany
Phone: 069 774011

Vohra Publishers & Distributors
36 M G Marg, (Behind Plaza), Civil Lines, Allahabad 211 001, India

Voluntary Euthanasia Society of Victoria
PO Box 23, Glen Iris, Vic. 3146, Australia

Vora & Company Publishers Pvt Ltd
3 Round Building, Kalbadevi Road, Bombay 400 002, India

Wadhwa & Co
Abyankar Lane, Nagpur 440 012, India

Wakefield Press
282 Richmond Road, Netley, S. Australia 5037, Australia
PO Box 588, Cowardilla 5033, Australia

Ward Lock Ltd
8 Clifford Street, London W1X 1RB, England
Phone: 01-439 3100
Fax: 01-439 1582

Ward River Press Ltd
Knocksedan House, Forrest Great, Swords, Co Dublin, Eire
Phone: 0001 401133

Waterloo Public Interest Research Group, Waterloo University → University of Waterloo, Waterloo Public Interest Research Groups

Waterlow Ltd
Holywell House, Worship Street, London EC2A 2EN, England
Oyez House, PO Box 55, 27 Crimscott Street, London, SE1 5TS
Phone: 232 1123
Fax: 231 1825

Waterville Publishing House
POB 195, Accra, Ghana
Phone: 663124,662415

WatPat
421 King Street. North, Waterloo, Ontario, N2J 4E4, Canada
PO Box 697, Waterloo, Ontario N2J 3B8, Canada

Watts & Partners
10 Independents Road, Blackheath, London SE3 9LF, England
Phone: 01-318 7700
Fax: 01-318 6943

Wayland (Publishers) Ltd
c/o Bailey Bros & Swinfen, Warner House, Bowles Well Gardens, Wear Bay Road, Folkestone, Kent CT19 6PH, England
Phone: 0303 850501
Fax: 0303 850162
61 Western Road, Hove, E Sussex, BN3 1JD
Phone: 0273 722561
Fax: 0273 29314

Webster (R. M.)
15 Grosvenor Crescent, Edinburgh EH12 5EL, Scotland
Phone: 031 337 6291

Wedge Publishing Foundation
POB 1000, Jordan Station, Ontario, LOR 150, Canada

Weekly Notes Printings Works Pvt Ltd
34 Ballygunge Circular Road, Calcutta 700 019, India

Weidenfeld (George) & Nicolson Ltd
91 Clapham High Street, London SW4 7TA, England
Phone: 01-622 9933

Wells (Owen) Publishing Co
23 Eaton Road, Ilkley, W Yorkshire LS29 9PU, England
Phone: 0943 602270

Weltforum VerlagsgesellschaftmbH fur Politik und ans Landskunde
Jintorettostrasse 1, 8000 Muenchen 19, West Germany

Western Producer Prairie Books
2310 Millar Avenue, POB 2500, Saskatoon, Sask., S7K 2C4, Canada

Westport Publications Ltd
3 Henrietta Street, London WC2E 8LT, England
Phone: 01-240 1003

Westview Press
5500 Central Avenue, Boulder, CO 80301, USA
Phone: 303 444 3541
Fax: 303 449 3356

Westwater Research Center, University of British Columbia → University of British Columbia, Westwater Research Center

Whau Publications
P O Box 8055, Kensington, Whangarei, New Zealand

Wheatsheaf Books Ltd
66 Wood Lane End, Hemel Hempstead, Herts HP2 4RG, England
Phone: 0442 231555
Fax: 0442 212485

Wheeler (A. H.) & Co Pvt Ltd
23 L B Shashtri Marg, Allahabad 211 001, India

Whitcoulls
P O Box 5844, Christchurch, New Zealand

White Lodge Publishing → Fourmat Publishing

Whitlock (A.)
541 St Kilda Road, Melbourne, Victoria 3004, Australia

Wilco Publishing House
33 Ropewalk Lane, Rampart Row, Fort, Bombay 400 001, India

Wild & Wooley
16 Darghan Street, Glebe, NSW 2037, Australia

Wildgrass Books
POB 318, Fitzroy, Victoria 3065, Australia
1 Elsie Street, Boronia, Vic. 3155, Australia

Wildwood House Ltd
Prince of Wales Passage, 117 Hampstead Road, London NW1 3EF, England
Gower House, Croft Road, Aldershot, Hants GU11 3HR, England
Phone: 0252 331551

Wildy & Sons Ltd
Lincoln's Inn Archway, Carey Street, London WC2A 2JD, England
Phone: 01 242 5778

Wiley (John) & Sons Ltd
Baffins Lane, Chichester, West Sussex PO19 1UD, England
Phone: 0243 779777
Fax: 0243 775878

Wilson et Lafleur
39 rue la Notre-Dame ouest, Montreal, PQ, H2Y 1S5, Canada

Wissenschaftlicher Verlag
Dr. Ulrich Schulz Kirchrer, Erfurter Strasse 2, Postfach 9, D-6270 Idstein 2, West Germany

Witherby & Co Ltd
32-36 Aylesbury Street, London EC1R 0ET, England
Phone: 01-251 5341
Fax: 01-251 1296

Witherby (H. F. & G.) Ltd
14 Henrietta Street, London WC2E 8QJ, England
Phone: 01-836 2006

Witwatersrand University Press
1 Jan Smuts Avenue, 2001 Johannesburg, South Africa

Wolfhound Press Ltd
68 Mountjoy Square, Dublin 1, Eire
Phone: 0001 740354

Women's Press
229 College No. 20, Toronto, Ontario M5T 1R4, Canada

Wood (R. D.)
34 Murray Avenue, Bromley, Kent, BR1 3DQ, England

Woodhead-Faulkner (Publishers) Ltd
Fitzwilliam House, 32 Trumpington Street, Cambridge CB2 1QY, England
Phone: 0223 66733
Fax: 0223 68539

World Health Organisation
27 Av. Appia, CH - 1211, Geneve 27, Switzerland
Phone: 022 912111

World Intellectual Property Organisation
34 Chemin des Colombettes, CH - 1211 Geneve 20, Switzerland
Phone: 022 999111

World Jnana Sadhak Society
Babupara-Mishradlodge, Jalpaiguri 735 101, India

World Microfilm Publications Ltd
62 Queen's Grove, London NW8 6ER, England
Phone: 01-586 3092

World University Service (UK)
20/21 Compton Terrace, London N1 2UN, England
Phone: 01-226 6747

Yale University Press Ltd
13 Bedford Square, London WC1B 3JF, England
Phone: 01-580 2693
Fax: 01-631 3913
302 Temple Street, New Haven, CT 06520, USA
Phone: 203 432 0960
Fax: 203 432 0948

Young Man & Co
888 Nai Sarak, Delhi 6, India

Zaklad Narodowy im Ossolinskich
Ul Rynek 9, POB 911, PL- 50-106 Wrocfaw, Poland
Phone: 38625

Zalums & Stafford (Australia)
12 Keith Road, Blackpool, SA 5051, Australia
The Library, Flinders, University of S Australia, Bedford Park, S. Australia 5042

Zwan
11-21 Northdown Street, London N1 9BN, England
Phone: 01-837 3322
Fax: 01-278 1677